Learn about literature online

Visit LITWEB at
http://www.wwnorton.com/introlit

LITWEB is an online companion to
The Norton Introduction to Literature

Edited by Ann Woodlief
Virginia Commonwealth University

User ID: LITWEB
Password: WWNLIT7

Highlights

- **In-depth workshops on 19 authors and works**, including biographies, annotated weblinks, and questions/topics for further exploration.
- **Hypertext glossary and "Writing about Literature" sections**, including a guide to MLA citation.
- Forums and resource pages for students and instructors.

Featured Authors and Works

W. H. Auden, "Musée des Beaux Arts" • James Baldwin, "Sonny's Blues" • William Blake, "London" • Anne Bradstreet, "To My Dear and Loving Husband" • Gwendolyn Brooks, "To the Diaspora" • Kate Chopin, "The Story of an Hour" • Emily Dickinson, "[Because I could not stop for Death--]" • John Donne, "A Valediction: Forbidding Mourning" • William Faulkner, "A Rose for Emily" • Charlotte Perkins Gilman, "The Yellow Wallpaper" • Lorraine Hansberry, *A Raisin in the Sun* • Nathaniel Hawthorne, "Young Goodman Brown • Li-Young Lee, "Persimmons" • Edna St. Vincent Millay, "[I, being born a woman and distressed]" • Flannery O'Connor, "A Good Man is Hard to Find" • Adrienne Rich, "Diving into the Wreck" • William Shakespeare, *Hamlet* • Sophocles, *Antigone* • Walt Whitman, "[I celebrate myself and sing myself]"

The Norton Introduction to Literature

SHORTER SEVENTH EDITION

The Norton Introduction to

Literature

SHORTER SEVENTH EDITION

Jerome Beaty

J. Paul Hunter

W. W. NORTON & COMPANY

NEW YORK • LONDON

The text of this book is composed in Optima and Stone Serif, with the display set in Optima
and Stone Serif. Composition by Maple-Vail. Manufacturing by Quebecorp. Book design by Joan
Greenfield.

Editor: Peter Simon
Developmental Editor: Carol Flechner
Associate Managing Editor: Marian Johnson
Production Manager: Diane O'Connor
Project editor: Kate Lovelady
Editorial Assistants: Kristin Sheerin, Elizabeth Suhay, Katharine Nicholson Ings
Text Design: Joan Greenfield
Cover Design: Debra Morton-Hoyt
Art Research: Neil Ryder Hoos

Library of Congress Cataloging-in-Publication Data
The Norton introduction to literature / [edited by] Jerome Beaty,
  J. Paul Hunter, Carl E. Bain. — Shorter 7th ed.
      p. cm.
    Includes bibliographical references and index.

   ISBN 0-393-97222-4 (pbk.)

    1. Literature—Collections. I. Beaty, Jerome, 1924– .
II. Hunter, J. Paul, 1934– . III. Bain, Carl E.
PN6014.N67 1998a
808—dc21   97-24451
                                                       CIP

W. W. Norton & Company, Inc., 500 Fifth Avenue, New York, NY 10110
http://www.wwnorton.com
W. W. Norton & Company Ltd., 10 Coptic Street, London WC1A 1PU

2 3 4 5 6 7 8 9 0

Contents

Exploring Contexts 301

Evaluating Fiction 477

Reading More Fiction 527

Poetry

Poetry: Reading, Responding, Writing 596

Understanding the Text 620

18 INTERNAL STRUCTURE 758

19 EXTERNAL FORM 782

THE SONNET 785

Exploring Contexts 824

Evaluating Poetry 929

Reading More Poetry 941

Drama

Drama: Reading, Responding, Writing 992

Understanding the Text 1019

Exploring Contexts 1317

Evaluating Drama 1578

Appendices

Writing about Literature A3

Foreword to the Shorter Seventh Edition

Reading is action. Even though it is often done quietly and alone, reading is a profoundly social activity, and a vigorous and demanding one. There is nothing passive about reading; it requires attention, energy, an act of will. Texts have the potential for meaning, implication, response, and result; but the reader must activate them, give them life, and turn them from quiet print into a lively interplay of ideas and feelings. Reading makes things happen, usually in the mind and imagination, but sometimes in the larger world as well, for the process of reading involves not just the consciousness of the self but an awareness of the other—what is beyond the self. Reading doesn't just happen to you; you have to **do** it, and doing it involves decision, reaching out, discovery, awareness. Reading is an act of power, and learning how to get the most out of its possibilities can be an invigorating activity. For all its association with quietness, solitude, and the sedentary life, reading involves—at its deepest level—action and interaction.

Through seven editions, *The Norton Introduction to Literature* has been committed to helping students learn to read and enjoy literature. This edition, like those before it, offers many different ways of building and reinforcing the skills of reading; in addition to studying literature in terms of its elements, our book emphasizes reading works in different contexts—authorial, historical, cultural and critical. We have strengthened our offering of texts in contextual groups in this edition with the addition of three new chapters, one per genre, entitled "Critical Contexts: A Casebook." Each "Critical Contexts" chapter includes a primary work (in fiction, William Faulkner's "A Rose for Emily;" in poetry, Sylvia Plath's "Daddy," and in drama, Sophocles's *Antigone*) and several critical responses to that work. In addition, the fiction casebook contains two examples of student writing—the first, a personal response, and the second, a research paper in MLA style. As in previous editions, we have provided many new selections.

The Seventh Edition, like its predecessors, offers in a single volume a complete course in reading and writing about literature. It is both an anthology and a textbook—a teaching anthology—for the indispensable course in which college student and college teacher begin to read literature, and to write about it, seriously together.

The works are arranged in order to introduce a reader to the study of literature. Each genre is approached in three logical steps. Fiction, for example, is introduced by *Fiction: Reading, Responding, Writing* which treats the purpose and nature of fiction, the reading experience, and the first steps one takes to begin writing about fiction. This is followed by the seven-chapter section called *Understanding the Text*, in which stories are analyzed by questions of craft, the so-called elements of fiction; this section ends with a chapter entitled "The Whole Text," which makes use of all or most of the analytical aids offered in the previous chapters, putting them together to see the work as a whole. The third section, *Exploring Contexts*, suggests some ways of seeing a work of literature interacting with its temporal and cultural contexts and reaching out beyond the page.

The sections on reading, analyzing, and placing the work in context are followed, in each genre, by guidance in taking that final and extremely difficult step—evaluation. *Evaluating Poetry,* for example, discusses how one would go about assessing the merits of two poems, not to offer definitive judgments, a litmus test, or even a checklist or formula, but to show how one goes about bringing to consciousness, defining, modifying, articulating, and negotiating one's judgments about a work of literature.

Ending each genre, *Reading More* _____ is a reservoir of additional examples, for independent study or a different approach. The book's arrangement seeks to facilitate the reader's movement from narrower to broader questions, mirroring the way people read—wanting to learn more as they experience more.

We offer a full section on *Writing about Literature.* In it we deal both with the writing process as applied to literary works—choosing a topic, gathering evidence, developing an argument, and so forth—and with the varieties of a reader's written responses, from copying and paraphrasing to analysis and interpretation: we explore not merely the hows, but the whats and whys as well.

In this section we also offer a discussion of critical approaches, designed to provide the student with a basic overview of contemporary critical theory, as well as an introduction to its terminology.

New to the Seventh Edition is a section on using and citing secondary sources. This section, when coupled with the new student research paper on page 472, provides a brief but useful first reference for writers of literary research papers.

The Seventh Edition includes 42 stories, 8 of which are new; 302 poems, 75 of which are new; and 13 plays, 3 of which are new.

In fiction, we have added new stories by Timothy Findley, Ernest Hemingway, James Joyce, Margaret Laurence, D. H. Lawrence, Katherine Mansfield, Flannery O'Connor, Paul Ruffin, Audre Thomas, and Edith Wharton.

The poetry section has been similarly infused with selections familiar and fresh, with newly included works by Elizabeth Alexander, W. H. Auden, Aphra Behn, Earle Birney, Elizabeth Bishop, Louise Bogan, Amy Clampitt, Sarah N. Cleghorn, Frances Cornford, Countee Cullen, Chitra Banerjee Divakaruni, Hilda Doolittle, Paul Lawrence Dunbar, James Emanuel, Anne Finch, Allen Ginsberg, Seamus Heaney, Anthony Hecht, Leigh Hunt, Mary Karr, D. H. Lawrence, Emma Lazarus, Denise Levertov, Dorothy Livesay, Richard Lovelace, James Masao Mitsui, Pat Mora, Oswald Mbuyiseni Mtshali, Ogden Nash, Dwight Okita, Sharon Olds, Mary Oliver, Simon J. Ortiz, Wilfred Owen, Adrienne Rich, Liz Rosenberg, D.G. Rosetti, Yvonne Sapia, William Shakespeare, Mary Ellen Solt, Cathy Song, Chidioch Tichbourne, Diane Wakoski, Alice Walker, Richard Wilbur, and Miller Williams.

New to the drama section are David Ives's very funny one-act, *Sure Thing,* Lorraine Hansberry's *A Raisin in the Sun,* and Arthur Miller's classic *Death of a Salesman.*

Certain editorial procedures that proved their usefulness in earlier editions have been retained. First of all, the works are annotated, as is customary in Norton anthologies; the notes are informational and not interpretative, for the aim is to help readers understand and appreciate the work, not to dictate a meaning or a response. In order to avoid giving the impression that all literature was written at the same time, we have noted at the right margin after each selection the date of first book publication (or, when preceded by a *p,* first periodical publication or, when the date appears at the left margin, the year of composition).

One editorial feature has changed, however. The glossaries that used to appear at the end of each chapter have been replaced by a single, comprehensive glossary in the back of the book. This change was requested by most adopters of the Sixth Edition, and should prove more useful to students.

One exciting new feature of *The Norton Introduction to Literature* isn't bound into the book itself. *The Norton Introduction to Literature Web Site,* prepared by Annette Woodlief of Virginia Commonwealth University, provides students and teachers with in-depth reading prompts and exercises designed to inspire creative reading and writing about literature, as well as links to useful literary resources.

Visit http://www.wwnorton.com/introlit to view a demonstration of this unique ancillary.

In all our work on this edition we have been guided by teachers in other English departments and in our own, by students who wrote us as the authors of the textbook they were using, and by those who were able to approach us after class as their teachers: we hope that with such help we have been able to offer you a solid and stimulating introduction to the experience of literature.

Acknowledgments   We would like to thank our teachers, for their example in the love of literature and in the art of sharing that love; our students, for their patience as we are learning from them to be better teachers of literature; our wives and children, for their understanding when the work of preparing this text made us seem less than perfectly loving husbands and fathers.

We would also like to thank our colleagues, many of whom have taught our book and evaluated our efforts, for their constant encouragement and enlightenment. Of our colleagues at Emory University and the University of Chicago, we would like especially to thank Jim Boyle, John Bugge, Louis Corrigan, William B. Dillingham, Larry Eby, Mark Sanders, Ron Schuchard, Deborah Sitter, John Sitter, Sally Wolff King and Emily Wright (Emory) and Jonathan Martin, Robert von Hallberg, Michelle Hawley, Anne Elizabeth Murdy, Janel Mueller, Vicky Olwell, Richard Strier, and John Wright (Chicago). For their help in selecting papers by student writers, we would like to thank Geneva Ballard, Theresa Budniakiewicz, Rebecca S. Ries, and Avantika Rohatgi, of Indiana University—Purdue University at Indianapolis, and Thomas Miller, Tilly Warnock, Lisa-Anne Culp, Loren Goodman, Brendan McBryde, and Ruthe Thompson, at the University of Arizona. We also thank the students whose papers we include: Daniel Bronson, Geoffrey Clement, Teri Garrity, Meaghan E. Parker, Sara Rosen, Sherry Schnake, Kimberly Smith, Thaddeus Smith, Jeanette Sperhac, Caryl Zook and Willow Crystal. For their work on the *Instructor's Guide,* we thank Kelly Mays, New Mexico State University, and Gayla McGlamery and Bryan Crockett, Loyola College in Baltimore.

We would like to thank the many teachers whose comments on the Sixth Edition have helped us plan the Seventh: Professor Frank Acuna, Mt. San Antonio College; Professor Connie Adair, Marshalltown Community College; Professor Howard C. Adams, Frostburg State University; Professor Sandra Adickes, Winona State University; Professor Jan Agard, Muskegon Community College; Professor Alan Ainsworth, Houston Community College; Professor Ken Allen, Modesto Junior College; Professor Mary Ann Ardoline, Northhampton County Community College; Professor Valerie Arms, Drexel University; Professor Herman Asarnow, University of Portland; Professor Earl Bader, Villanova University; Professor Cindy Baer, San Jose State University; Professor Elizabeth Balfour-Boehm, Lakehead University; Professor Mary Baron, University of North Florida; Professor Joseph Bartolomeo, University of Massachusetts, Amherst; Professor John Batty-Sylvan, City College of San Francisco; Professor R. D. Becker, Standing Rock College; Professor Michael Beehler, Montana State University; Professor Franz Blatta, University of Nebraska; Professor John Boening, University of Toledo; Professor Elizabeth Bouchard, Wilbur Wright Junior College; Professor Bridget Boulton, Truckee Meadows Community College; Professor Debra Boyd, Winthrop University; Professor Lawrence Bright, Bakersfield College; Professor Ludiger Brinker, Macomb Community College;

Professor Robert Brophy, California State University; Professor V. Brown, Laredo Community College; Professor Jeffrey Brunner, University of Minnesota; Professor David Burton, University of Tennessee–Memphis; Professor Pauline Buss, William Rainey Harper College; Professor Marilyn Button, Lincoln University; Professor Kathleen Carlson, Franklin College; Professor Marilyn A. Carlson, Augustana College; Professor Thomas Carper, University of Southern Maine; Professor Olivia Carr Edenfield, Georgia Southern University; Professor Basil Clark, Saginaw Valley State University; Professor John Cleman, California State University at Los Angeles; Professor Evelyn Cobley, University of Victoria; Professor Thomas F. Connolly, Suffolk University; Professor C. Gordon Craig, University of Alberta; Professor Bryan Crockett, Loyola College; Professor Kathleen Cronin, Montana State University of Technology; Professor Toni Culjack, LaSalle University; Professor Jackie Cumby, Mercer University; Professor Elizabeth Curtin, Salisbury State University; Professor C. Custer, Plymouth State College; Professor Elizabeth Daeumer, Eastern Michigan University; Professor Frances Davidson, Mercer County College; Professor Frank Day, Clemson University; Professor Nancy Dayton, Taylor University; Professor Isabella Dibari, Diablo Valley College; Professor Wilfred O. Dietrich, Blinn College; Professor Sandy Dimon, Georgia College; Professor Raymond Dolle, Indiana State University; Professor Diana Doswell, Community College at Calvert; Professor Dixie Durham, Chapman University; Professor William Dynes, University of Indianapolis; Professor J. P. Earls, St. John's University; Professor Isaac Elimimian, California Polytechnic–San Luis Obispo; Professor Mary Etter, Davenport College; Dr. LaMona Evans, University of Central Oklahoma; Professor Don Fay, Kennesaw State College; Professor Chris Ferns, Mount Saint Vincent University; Professor James Fetler, Foothill College; Professor Bonnie Flaig, Kalamazoo Valley Community College; Professor Kate Flood, Onondaga Community College; Professor Douglas Fossek, Santa Barbara City College; Professor Craig Foster, Santa Rosa Junior College; Professor Michael Friedlander, Sacramento City College; Professor David Galef, University of Mississippi; Professor Marc Garcia, San Diego State University; Professor Jill Geare, Pasadena City College; Professor Marshall Bruce Gentry, University of Indianapolis; Professor Patricia Genz, Charles County Community College; Professor Jacqueline George, Erie Community College; Professor Karen Gleeman, Normandale Community College; Professor Brad Gooch, William Paterson College; Professor Marcia Goodman, Diablo Valley College; Professor Susan Grady, Greenville Technical College; Professor George L. Grant, San Jose State University; Professor Louis Greiff, Alfred University; Professor Joan Grumman, Santa Barbara City College; Professor Paul Guess, Diablo Valley College; Professor Ellen Haggar, The College of Charleston; Professor Robert Hagstrom, Jamestown Community College; Professor Joan Hall, University of Mississippi; Professor Edward Hancock, Truckee Meadows Community College; Professor F. J. Hartland, St. Francis College; Professor Peter Hawkes, East Stroudsburg University; Professor Margaret Hawks, Glendale College; Professor Tace Hedrick, Penn State at Harrisburg; Professor Lynne Hefferson, University of Vermont; Professor Donna Henrickson, Ball State University; Professor Anne Herzog, West Chester University; Professor Edwin Hetfield, Onondaga Community College; Professor John Hillman, Essex Community College; Professor Eric F. Hoem, Mt. Hood Community College; Professor Peter Hogue, California State University; Professor Elsie Holmes, Trinity Western University; Professor R. C. Hoover, Wenatchee Valley College; Professor Roger Horn, Charles County Community College; Professor Jean Horton, Concordia College; Professor Karen Houck, Bellevue Community College; Professor Douglas Howard, St. John Fisher College; Professor John Hussey, Fairmont State University; Professor Paula Huston, California Polytechnic, San Luis Obispo; Professor Nancy Hynes, College of St. Benedict; Professor Carol Jagielnak, University of Wisconsin, Parkside; Professor Mary Ann Janda, Utica College; Professor Dolores Johnson, Seattle University; Professor Ulrike Kalt, Odessa College; Professor Sukeshi Kamra, Okanagan University College; Dr. M. E. Karim, Rockford College; Professor John Kijinski, Idaho State University; Professor Thomas Kinsella, Richard Stockton College; Professor Lincoln Konkle, Trenton State College; Professor Philip Kowalski, North Shore Community College; Professor Carl Kremer, William Woods University; Professor Jayne Kribbs-Drake, Temple University; Professor Ellen Kruse, Diablo Valley College; Professor Harold Kugelmass, Onondaga Community College; Professor Paul LaChanc, Frostburg State University; Professor Jane Lasky, Middlesex Community College; Professor David J. Leigh, SJ, Seattle University; Professor Daniel Lowe, Community College of Allegheny County; Professor Mary Anne Lutz, Frostburg State University; Professor Thomas Mack, University of South Carolina at Aiken; Professor Barbara McCarthy, Worcester Polytechnic Institute; Professor Barbara McClain, Contra Costa College; Professor Ken McKay, Brock University; Professor Therese Mackey, West Georgia College; Professor Thomas Madden, Eastern Oregon State College; Professor Rick Madigan, East Stroudsburg University; Professor Nancy Malone, Diablo Valley College; Professor Fort Manno, William Paterson College; Professor Aug Martinez, De Anza College; Professor Charlotte Martinez-Cappellini, Jamestown Community College; Professor J. M. Massi, Washington State University; Professor Tom Miller, University of Arizona; Professor Dorothy Minor, Tulsa Junior College; Professor Susan R. Mondschein, State University of New York at Buffalo; Professor Betty Montgomery, Ittawamba Community College; Professor Renate Muendel, West Chester University; Professor Roxanne Munch, Joliet Junior College; Professor Paul Munn, Saginaw Valley State University; Professor Anne Myles, Richard Stockton College; Professor Joseph Nassar, Rochester Institute of Technology; Professor James Nicosia, Montclair State University; Professor Ervin Nieves, Rutgers University at Newark; Professor Elizabeth Nollen, West Chester University; Professor James Nye, Southwestern Oklahoma State University; Professor Brennan O'Donnell, Loyola College; Professor Maureen O'Leary, Diablo Valley College; Professor Michael O'Neill, Oklahoma State University; Professor Glenn Omans, Temple University; Professor Kofi Owasu, Carleton College; Professor Len Palosaari, Augsberg College; Professor Sharon Papworth, Ricks College; Professor Barbara Patrick, Rowan College; Professor Barbara Pell, Trinity Western University; Professor John Pennington, St. Norbert College; Professor Katrina Perez, Santa Barbara City College; Professor Daniel Peterson, Southern University; Professor Donald Peterson, California State University; Professor Renee Pigeon, California State University, San Bernadino; Professor Gerald Pike, Santa Barbara City College; Professor Linda Plutynski, West Valley College–Saratoga; Professor Fran J. Polek, Gonzaga University; Professor Norman Prinsky, Augusta College; Professor Zelda Provenzano, University of Pennsylvania; Professor Renee Ramsey, Indiana State University; Professor Lyn P. Relph, California State University; Professor Paul Rice, Coastal Carolina University; Professor Michael Riherd, Pasadena City College; Professor Sharon Robinson, Russell Sage College; Professor Allen Rubin, Pace University; Professor John Rudin, Sacramento City College; Professor Helen Ruggieri, Jamestown Community College; Professor Don Russ, Kennesaw State College; Professor Anne Salvatore, Rider University; Professor Peggy Samuels, Drew University; Professor James Saunders, University of Toledo; Professor Nancy Shankle, Abilene Christian University; Professor Marilyn Shapiro, Lawrence Technological University; Professor Michael Sheldon, Indiana State University; Professor Leonard Slade, State University of New York at Albany; Professor Nelson Smith, University of Victoria; Professor Don Smith, Community College of Southern Nevada; Professor Guy Smith, Santa Barbara City College; Professor Betty Solomon, Diablo Valley College; Professor Randy Southard, Moraine Valley Community College; Professor Anne Spurlock, Mississippi State University; Professor Nadine St. Louis, University of Wisconsin–Eau Claire; Professor Rusty Standridge, Greenville Technical College; Professor Stan Stanko, Brescia College; Professor Emily Stauffer, Franklin College; Professor M. H. Strelow, Williamette University; Professor David Strong, Gonzaga University; Professor Jenny Sullivan, Northern Virginia Community College; Professor Phil Sullivan, University of Utah; Professor Timothy Thompson, Pacific University; Professor Dorothy Thompson, Winthrop University; Professor Lee Tobin, Seton Hill College; Professor Michael Treschow, Okanagan University College; Professor Edna Troiano, Charles County Community College; Professor Jean Troy-Smith, State University of New York at Oswego; Professor John Vacca, University of Wisconsin–Platteville; Professor Kenneth Van Dorn, Lincoln University; Professor John Venne, Ball State University; Professor T. Mike Walker, Cabrillo College; Professor Donna Walsh, Memorial University of Newfoundland; Professor Mason Wang, Saginaw Valley State University; Professor Ruth Warkentin, California State University, Dominguez Hills; Professor Donald Watt, State University of New York, Geneseo; Professor Elizabeth Weber, University of Indianapolis; Professor David Weekes, Eastern Washington University; Professor William West, Onondaga Community College; Professor Terry Whalen, Saint Mary's University; Professor Martha Widmayer, Millersville University of Pennsylvania; Professor Catherine Wilcoxsen, Rowan College; Professor Dale M. Wilkie, University of Alberta; Professor Jack Williams, California State University; Professor Jack Wills, Fairmont State College; Professor Sarah Witte, Eastern Oregon State College; Professor Eric Wolfe, University of Mississippi; Professor Peter Wood, Trenton State College; Professor Regenia Woodberry, University of Central Oklahoma; Professor Kathleen Wright, Westmoreland County Community College; Professor William Yarrow, Joliet Junior College; and Professor Ursula Yates, West Chester University.

And we thank also those who helped us with previous editions: Elizabeth Alkagond, Columbia College; M. Allen, Bakersfield College; Marjorie Allen, LaSalle University; Preston Allen, Miami-Dade Community College; Sally Allen, North Georgia College; Bruce Anawalt, Washington State University; Anne Andrews, Mississippi State University; Charles Angel, Bridgewater State College; Booker Anthony, Fayetteville State University; Robert Arledge, Southern University at New Orleans; Michael Atkinson, University of Cincinnati; Janet Auten, American University; Sylvia Baer, Gloucester County College; Raymond Bailey, Bishop State Community College; Lee Baker, High Point College; Harold Bakst, Minneapolis Community College; Nancy Barendse, Christopher Newport College; Chris Barkley, Palomar College; Linda Barlow, Fayetteville State University; William Barnette, Prestonsburg Community College; Dr. Barney, Citrus College; E. Barnton, California State University, Bakersfield; Harry E. Batty, University of Maine; Shawn Beaty, Hokkaido University; Nancy Beers, Temple University; Linda Bensel-Meyers, University of Tennessee, Knoxville; Lawrence Berkoben, California State University; Tracey Besmark, Ashland Community College; Barbara Bird, St. Petersburg Community College; Lillian Bisson, Marymount College; Clark Blaise, University of Iowa; T. E. Blom, University of British Columbia; Roy L. Bond, University of Texas at Dallas; Steven Bouler, Tuskegee University; Veleda Boyd, Tarleton State University; Helen Bridge, Chabot College; Sandra Brim, North Georgia College; Loretta Brister, Tarleton State University; Patrick Broderick, Santa Rosa Junior College; Robert Brophy, California State University, Long Beach; Theresa Brown, Tufts University; William Brown, Philadelphia College of Textiles and Science; Virginia Brumbach, Eastfield College; C. Bryant, Colby College; Edward Burns, William Paterson College of New Jersey; Daniel Cahill, University of Northern Iowa; Martha Campbell, St. Petersburg Community College at Tarpon Springs; William Campbell, Monroe Community College; D.

Cano, Santa Monica Community College; Nathan Carb, Rowan College of New Jersey; Roger Carlstrom, Yakima Valley Community College; Martha Carpentier, Seton Hall University; Anne Carr, Southeast Community College; Conrad Carroll, Northern Kentucky University; Gisela Casines, Florida International University; Ahwadhesh Chaudhary, Texas College; Dr. Clark, Citrus College; John Clower, Indiana University–Purdue University at Indianapolis; Steven Cole, Temple University; Cindy Collins, Fullerton College; Kathleen Collins, Creighton University; Marianne Conroy, McGill University; Pat Conner, Memphis State University; Martha Cook, Longwood College; Holly Cordova, Contra Costa College; Susan Cornett, St. Petersburg Community College at Tarpon Springs; Brian Corrigan, North Georgia College; Betty Corum, Owensboro Community College; Beverly Cotton, Cerritos College; Delmar Crisp, Wesleyan College; Virginia Critchlow, Monroe Community College; Carol Cunningham-Ruiz, Bakersfield College; Lennett Daigle, North Georgia College; Christopher Dark, Tarleton State University; Vivian Davis, Eastfield College; Hugh Dawson, University of San Francisco; Martha Day, Richard Bland College; George Diamond, Moravian College; Helen DiBona, North Carolina Central University; Sister Mary Colleen Dillon, Thomas More College; Marvin Diogenes, University of Arizona; Frank Dobson, Indiana University–Purdue University at Indianapolis; Minna Doskow, Rowan College of New Jersey; Donald Dowdey, Virginia Wesleyan College; Bonnie Duncan, Upper Iowa University; Timothy Dykstal, Auburn University; Wayne Eason, University of North Carolina at Charlotte; Paula Eckard, University of North Carolina at Charlotte; Mary Eiser, Kauai Community College; Marianne Eismann, Wake Forest University; Joyce Ellis, North Carolina Central University; Reed Ellis, St. John's Community College; Peggy Endel, Florida International University; James Erickson, Wichita State University; Dessagene Ewing, Delaware County Community College; Jim Ewing, North Georgia College; Sasha Feinstein, Indiana University; Charles Feldstein, Florida Community College at Jacksonville; Norman Feltes, York University; Jean Fields, Lindenwood College; Mildred Flynn, South Dakota University; Eileen Foley, University of Maine; Dolores Formicella, Delaware County Community College; Elsa Ann Gaines, North Georgia College; Dennis Gaitner, Frostburg State University; Reloy Garcia, Creighton University; Joseph Glaser, Western Kentucky University; Andrea Glebe, University of Nevada; Karen Gleeman, Normandale Community College; C. Golliher, Victor Valley College; Douglas Gordon, Christopher Newport College; Donna Gormly, Eastfield College; Kathryn Graham, Virginia Polytechnic Institute and State University; Pat Gregory, Community College of Philadelphia; Ann Grigsby, University of New Mexico; Alan Grob, Rice University; Lynda Haas, Hillsborough Community College; Florence Halle, Memphis State University; Jerry Harris, Western Oregon State College; Sydney Harrison, Manatee Community College; Joan Hartman, William Patterson College; Charles Hatten, Bellarmine College; Bruce Henderson, Fullerton College; Nancy Henry, SUNY at Binghamton; David Hernandez, Eastfield College; Robert Herzog, Monroe Community College; Laura Higgs, Clemson University; David Hill, SUNY College at Oswego; Robert Hipkiss, California State University; David Hoegberg, Indiana University–Purdue University at Indianapolis; Eartha Holley, Delaware State University; R. C. Hoover, Wenatchee Valley College; Roger Horn, Charles County Community College; L. C. Howard, Skyline College; Erlene Hubly, University of Northern Iowa; William Hudson, Radford University; David Hufford, Iowa Western Community College; Deirdre Hughes, Fullerton College; Dr. Humphrey, Citrus College; Kathryn Montgomery Hunter, Northwestern University School of Medicine; Lisa Hunter, University of Wisconsin Medical School; P. Hunter, Los Angeles Valley College; Edelina Huntley, Appalachian State University; Robert Huntley, Washington and Lee University; Sharon Irvin, Florida Institute of Technology; Sylvia Iskander, University of Southwestern

Louisiana; Eleanor James, Montgomery County Community College; Anne Johnson, Jacksonville State University; Christopher Johnson, Missouri Valley College; Craig Johnson, Hillsborough Community College; Darryl Johnson, St. Cloud State University; Dolores Johnson, Seattle University; Karen Johnson, Indiana University–Purdue University at Indianapolis; Dr. Jones, Citrus College; Grace Jones, Owensboro Community College; Walter Kalaidjian, St. Cloud State University; Frank Kastor, Wichita State University; E. Kenney, Colby College; Don King, Central Washington University; Andrew Kirk, University of California, Davis; John Klijinski, Idaho State University; William Klink, Charles County Community College; Michael Krasny, San Francisco State University; Anne Krause, Yakima Valley Community College; Harold Kuglemass, Onondaga Community College; Stuart Kurland, Muhlenberg College; Donald Lawler, East Carolina University; Lynn Lewis, Memphis State University; Vincent J. Liesenfeld, University of Oklahoma; Jun Liu, California State University, Los Angeles; Travis Livingston, Tarleton State University; Lillian Liwag-Sutcliffe, Old Dominion University; Mary Lowe-Evans, University of West Florida; Michael Lund, Longwood College; Kathleen Lyons, Bellarmine College; Thomas Mack, University of South Carolina; Patricia MacVaugh, Lehigh County Community College; Emory Maiden, Appalachian State University; Christina Malcolmson, Bates College; Dexter Marks, Jersey City State College; William Martin, Tarleton State University; Frank Mason, University of South Florida; Pam Mathis, North Arkansas Community College; Laura May, St. Petersburg Community College; Katherine Maynard, Rider College; R. McAllister, Victor Valley College; Kathleen McCloy, Shoreline Community College; Betty J. McCommas, Ouachita Baptist University; Clare McDonnell, Neumann College; Frank McLaughlin, Ramapo College; Thomas McLaughlin, Appalachian State University; William McMahon, Western Kentucky University; Terrence McNally, Northern Kentucky University; Alan McNarie, University of Hawaii; Nyan McNeill, Foothill College; Jay Meek, University of North Dakota; Ivan Melada, University of New Mexico; Donna Melancon, Xavier University; Linda Merions, LaSalle University; Darlene Mettler, Wesleyan College; R. Metzger, Los Angeles Valley College; Brian Michaels, Diane Middlebrook (Stanford University) St. John's Community College; Daniel Miller, Northern Kentucky University; George Miller, University of Delaware; Ron Miller, University of West Florida; Leslie Mittelman, California State University, Long Beach; Rosa Mizerski, West Valley College; Rosemary Moffett, Elizabethtown Community College; Warren Moore, Loyola College; Mike Moran, University of Georgia; Dean Morgan, Olympic College; William Morgan, Illinois State University; William Morris, University of South Florida; Sharon Morrow, University of Southern Indiana; Renate Muendel, West Chester University; Gordon Mundell, University of Nebraska; David Murdoch, Rochester Institute of Technology; Carol Murphy, Roanoke College; Thomas Murray, Trenton State College; Joseph Nacca, Community College of Finger Lakes; Joseph Nasser, Rochester Institute of Technology; Mary Neil, Eastfield College; Kay Nelson, St. Cloud University; Dorothy Newman, Southern University; Lee Nicholson, Modesto Junior College; Mimi Nicholson, University of Southern Indiana; Elizabeth Nollen, West Chester University; Dale Norris, Des Moines Community College; Robert Ochsner, University of Maryland at Baltimore; Sarah Oglesby, Madisonville Community College; Francis Olley, Saint Joseph's University; Ann Olson, Central Washington University; Regina Oost, Wesleyan College; Mildred Orenstein, Drexel University; Kathleen O'Shea, Monroe Community College; Thornton Penfield, Southern University; Christopher Penna, University of Delaware; Rita Perkins, Camden County College; Donald Peterson, City College of San Francisco; Steven Phelan, Rollins College; Randall Popken, Tarleton State University; Robert Post, University of Washington; Pamela Postma, University of North Carolina at Greensboro; Linda Ray Pratt, University of Nebraska;

Ross Primm, Columbia College; Richard Quaintance, Rutgers University; James Randall, Coe College; Rosemary Raynal, Davidson College; Mary Rea, Indiana University–Purdue University at Indianapolis; Thomas Redshaw, University of St. Thomas; Ron Reed, Hazard Community College; Donna Reiss, Tidewater Community College; Alan Richardson, Boston College; Ann Richey, Virginia Polytechnic Institute and State University; Joan Richmond, Tarleton State University; Harold Ridley, LeMoyne College; Leonard Roberts, Northampton Area Community College; Douglas Robinson, University of Mississippi; J. Robinson, Victor Valley College; Beate Rodewald, Palm Beach Atlantic College; Ruben Rodriguez, Tarleton State University; Owen Rogal, St. Ambrose University; Eva Rosenn, Wesleyan College; William Rossiter, Flathead Valley College; Connie Rothwell, University of North Carolina; Don Rud, Texas Tech University; Don Russ, Kennesaw State College; Charles J. Rzepka, Boston University; Christina Savage, Long Beach City College; Vicki Scannell, Pierce College; Paul Schacht, SUNY College at Geneseo; Steven Scherwatzky, Merrimack College; Marie Schiebold, Skyline College; Ronald Schleifer, University of Oklahoma; Linda Schmidt, Iowa Western Community College; Roger Schmidt, Idaho State College; Michael Schoenecke, Texas Tech University; Jane Schultz, Indiana University–Purdue University at Indianapolis; Lucille Schultz, University of Cincinnati; Carolyn Segal, Lehigh University; JoAnn Seiple, University of North Carolina; Bill Senior, Broward Community College; Pat Shalter, Reading Area Community College; Lewis Sheffler, Missouri Valley College; Richard Siciliano, Charles County Community College; Odette Sims, Modesto Junior College; Judy Jo Small, North Carolina State University; Louise Smith, University of Massachusetts; Peter Smith, Wesleyan College; Stephen Smith, LaSalle University; Thomas Sonith, Widener University; B. Spears, Victor Valley College; Dr. Spencer, California State University, Bakersfield; Rich Sprouse, North Georgia College; Ann Spurlock, Mississippi State University; David Stacey, Missouri Valley College; Nancy Stahl, Indiana University–Purdue University at Indianapolis; Jamie Steckelberg, University of North Dakota; James Stick, Des Moines Community College; Bruce Stillians, University of Hawaii; McKay Sundwall, East Carolina University; Kathryn Swanson, Augsburg College; John Taylor, College of Marin; Judith Taylor, Northern Kentucky University; David Thibodaux, University of Southwestern Louisiana; Victor Thompson, Thomas Nelson Community College; Charles Thornbury, College of St. Benedict; Mike Thro, Tidewater Community College; Kathleen Tickner, Brevard Community College; Edna Troiano, Charles County Community College; Gail Tubbs, Washington College; Richard Turner, Indiana University–Purdue University at Indianapolis; Teresa Tweet, Augustana College; D. Unrue, University of Nevada; Margaret Vail, Xavier University; Diana Valdina, Cayuga County Community College; Kenneth Vandover, Lincoln University; Eleanor Vassal, St. Petersburg Community College; Tim Viator, North Georgia College; Richard Victor, Saddleback College; Jeanne Walker, University of Delaware; Cynthia Wall, University of Virginia; Leslie Wallace, De Anza College; W. Wallis, Los Angeles Valley College; R. Warkentin, California State University, Dominguez Hills; David Weekes, Eastern Washington University; Edwin Weihe, Seattle University; Ronald Wendling, Saint Joseph's University; Agnes Whitsel, Mercer University; Keith Wicker, Henderson Community College; Inga Wiehl, Yakima Valley College; Waller Wigginton, Idaho State University; Arthur Williams, Louisiana School for Mathematics, Science and the Arts; Jack Williams, California State University; James Wilson, University of Southwestern Louisiana; Sharon Wilson, Fort Hays State University; Sandra Witt, University of Northern Iowa; Susan Wolstenholme, Cayuga County Community College; Strohn Woodward, University of Maine; James Wyatt, Lindsey Wilson College; Linda Yakle, St. Petersburg Community College; and Dr. Zounes, Los Angeles Valley College.

Finally, we would like to thank our friends at W. W. Norton & Company: Allen Clawson, Carol Flechner, Roberta Flechner, Lauren Graessle, Steve Hoge, Neil Hoos, Katharine Nicholson Ings, Marian Johnson, Anna Karvellas, Kate Lovelady, Kirsten Miller, Debra Morton-Hoyt, Diane O'Connor, Kristin Sheerin, Peter Simon, and Elizabeth Suhay.

The Norton Introduction to Literature

SHORTER SEVENTH EDITION

Fiction

Fiction: Reading, Responding, Writing

Fiction

SPENCER HOLST

The Zebra Storyteller

Once upon a time there was a Siamese cat who pretended to be a lion and spoke inappropriate Zebraic.

That language is whinnied by the race of striped horses in Africa.

Here now: An innocent zebra is walking in a jungle and approaching from another direction is the little cat; they meet.

"Hello there!" says the Siamese cat in perfectly pronounced Zebraic. "It certainly is a pleasant day, isn't it? The sun is shining, the birds are singing, isn't the world a lovely place to live today!"

5 The zebra is so astonished at hearing a Siamese cat speaking like a zebra, why—he's just fit to be tied.

So the little cat quickly ties him up, kills him, and drags the better parts of the carcass back to his den.

The cat successfully hunted zebras many months in this manner, dining on filet mignon of zebra every night, and from the better hides he made bow neckties and wide belts after the fashion of the decadent princes of the Old Siamese court.

He began boasting to his friends he was a lion, and he gave them as proof the fact that he hunted zebras.

The delicate noses of the zebras told them there was really no lion in the neighborhood. The zebra deaths caused many to avoid the region. Superstitious, they decided the woods were haunted by the ghost of a lion.

10 One day the storyteller of the zebras was ambling, and through his mind ran plots for stories to amuse the other zebras, when suddenly his eyes brightened, and he said, "That's it! I'll tell a story about a Siamese cat who learns to speak our language! What an idea! That'll make 'em laugh!"

Just then the Siamese cat appeared before him, and said, "Hello there! Pleasant day today, isn't it!"

The zebra storyteller wasn't fit to be tied at hearing a cat speaking his language, because he'd been thinking about that very thing.

He took a good look at the cat, and he didn't know why, but there was something about his looks he didn't like, so he kicked him with a hoof and killed him. That is the function of the storyteller.

1971

The Zebra Storyteller" suggests that the purpose of stories is to prepare us for the unexpected. Though the storyteller thinks he is just spinning stories out of his own imagination in order to amuse, his stories prove to be practical. When the extraordinary occurs—like a Siamese cat speaking Zebraic—the storyteller is prepared because he has already imagined it, and he alone is able to protect his tribe against the unheard-of.

Other storytellers make the function of fiction less extraordinary. According to them, fiction enables readers to avoid projecting false hopes and fears (such as the zebras' superstitious belief that they are being preyed on by the ghost of a lion) and shows them what they can actually expect in their everyday lives, so that they can prepare themselves. In George Eliot's novel *Adam Bede*, Hetty Sorrel is being paid admiring attention by the young squire, and she dreams of elopement, marriage, all sorts of vague pleasures. She does not dream that she will be seduced, made pregnant, abandoned. Her imagination has not been trained to project any "narrative" other than her dreams: "Hetty had never read a novel," George Eliot tells us, "[so] how could she find a shape for her expectations?"

We are all storytellers, then, of one stripe or another. Whenever we plan the future or ponder a decision, we are telling stories—projecting expectations through narrative. Whether we tell stories or read them, we are educating our imaginations, either extending our mental experience in the actual, as Hetty might have done by reading novels, or preparing ourselves for the extraordinary and unexpected, like the zebra storyteller.

The actual and the extraordinary suggest two different uses readers make of fiction. Sometimes we want to read about people like ourselves, or about places, experiences, and ideas that are familiar and agreeable. Most of us initially prefer American literature and twentieth-century literature to literature remote in time or place. Indeed, stories must somehow be related to our own lives before we can find them intellectually or emotionally meaningful. No matter what our literary experience and taste, most of us relate in a special way to stories about people like us, experiences like our own, and especially to a story that mentions our hometown or neighborhood or the name of the street that we used to walk along on our way to school. No one would deny that one of the many things that fiction may be "for" is learning about ourselves and the world around us.

But occasionally the last thing we want is a story about people like ourselves, experiences like those of our everyday lives, and places and times like here and now. On such occasions we want (or are accused of wanting) to escape. If fiction must be relevant enough to relate meaningfully to us, it must also be "irrelevant," different, strange—as strange, perhaps, as a Siamese cat speaking Zebraic. It must take us out of ourselves, out of the confining vision of our own eyes, which is conditioned by our own background and experience, and show us that there are ways of looking at the world other than our own. So, in addition to many stories about approximately our own time and place, this collection includes a sprinkling of stories written in the last century, a few written in vastly different cultures, and a few written about worlds that have not existed or do not (yet) exist.

What a story shows us or teaches us we may call its **message**—an objective, universal truth that we were unaware of before reading the story. We gradually learn, however, that stories tell us not so much what life means as what it's like. Rather than abstract or "objective" truths, stories deal with perceptions. These perceptions may be translated into messages, but we soon discover that the messages boil down to things like "There's good and there's bad in everybody," "Hurting people is wrong," and "Everything is not what it seems"—messages we do not need Western Union, much less Western litera-ture, to deliver. Indeed, we do not have to agree with what a story says or shows so long as we are convinced that if we had *those* eyes and were *there*, this is what we might see.

Whenever we can say yes, we are convinced, then we have been able to go beyond the limitations of our own vision, our own past and conditions. We are able to see a new world, or the same old world in a new way. And by recognizing that we can see things differently, we realize that things we used to think were fixed, objective entities "out there," were fixed only in our perceptions. Or, as is too often the case, we realize that we have been accepting things at face value; we have been perceiving what habit and convention have told us is "really there." Stories, then, may awaken us to look at things for ourselves. For example, we "know" that most ordinary tabletops are rectangu-lar, but in a story we may be told that such a tabletop is diamond-shaped. We under-stand that if we were to look at the tabletop from a certain angle it would appear diamond-shaped. But doesn't that mean that the tabletop is rectangular only when we look at it from a certain angle? How often do we look at a tabletop from that angle? We look again, and we recognize that though we've always "known" such a tabletop is rectangular, we may have never actually *seen* it as one. The story has not only allowed us to see reality from another angle, but it has helped us to sharpen our own vision, our own experience.

In reading a story, you are also telling a story or many stories, projecting the possible futures of the events and the characters' lives much as you project your own future actions in the "story" of your own life. Your projection of the story's future—what is going to happen next—is conditioned by the details, including the specific words, of the story. But it is also conditioned by your life experience—your sense of what life is like—and by your reading experience—your sense of what stories are like. When, as the story unfolds, your **expectations** are modified or the unexpected occurs, fiction and your reality interact: you may simply reject the story's version of what life or the world is like—it's only fiction, after all—or you may reexamine your own views, adding possi-bilities or at least tentatively questioning what you formerly took for granted (do I really see a rectangle when I look at the tabletop?).

Ordinarily when we read, however, we may be only vaguely conscious—if we are conscious at all—of projecting the course and outcome of the story and, therefore, only vaguely aware—if at all—of how the story affirms or modifies our total experience. We may be able to learn to heighten our awareness, and thus the impact of the story upon us and the pleasure we derive from it, by artificially stopping our reading at certain points and asking ourselves what we expect to happen or expect to be revealed next. In reading the story that follows, "Kill Day on the Government Wharf," we might pause, for example, at the end of paragraph 24 and articulate—perhaps even briefly write down—what we expect to happen as this story develops, substantiating our expecta-tions by indicating how details within the story (Robert's night fears, for example?) con-tribute to those expectations. We might stop again after another twenty-four paragraphs (after paragraph 48) and check on how our earlier expectations have been reinforced, modified, added to, or replaced by new ones generated by new details and developments in the story. These stopping points are only examples: you may pause at any point and ask yourself what it is that you are anticipating.

Something like this taking in of detail, remembering past detail, and projecting forward is, going on at some level of consciousness in any involved reading of a story. It's what reading narrative is about. Though stop-and-go reading may seem artificial and awkward for a time—as touch typing does to someone who used to hunt and peck—keeping track of your thoughts while reading will increase your understanding of and your pleasure in reading. The purpose of such increased awareness, then, is not so much to improve your chances of guessing correctly how a story will develop and come out, but to make you aware of the possibilities that the text as well as your experience suggest about life. In other words, when you read with heightened consciousness, you enrich your responses and your experience of reading narrative.

AUDREY THOMAS

Kill Day on the Government Wharf

"I only wish," she said, refilling his coffee mug, "that it was all a little more primitive."

The man, intent on his fried bread and tomato, did not hear or chose to ignore the wistfulness in her voice. Mouth full, he chuckled, and then, swallowing, "All what?"

"All *this*," she said impatiently, gesturing toward the inside of the little cabin. They were sitting by the window, having breakfast. It was nine o'clock on a Sunday morning and the sky outside bulged and sagged with heavy bundles of dirty-looking clouds. He wanted to get back out on the water before it rained.

"I thought you liked it here," he said, challenging her with a smile. She was playing games again.

"I do. I love it. I really don't ever want to go back. But," she said, looking at him over the rim of her mug, "seeing that the old man died only a few months later, don't you think it was rather unkind of Fate to have suggested plumbing and electricity to him? I mean," she added with a smile, "also seeing as how we were going to be the reluctant beneficiaries of all that expense."

"You may be reluctant," he said, wiping his mouth, "I'm not. I think we were damned lucky myself."

She shrugged and stood up to clear the table, rubbing the small of her back unconsciously. She had acquired a slight tan in the ten days she'd been away and he thought how well she looked. There was a sprinkling of pale greeny-coppery freckles across her nose and along her arms. She looked strong and self-reliant and almost pretty as she stood by the window with the stacked plates in her hand. It was not myth, he thought, or a white lie to make them feel better. Women really do look lovely when they're pregnant. Sometimes she would say to him, quite seriously,

"Tom, do you think I'm pretty?" or

"Tom, what would you say about me if you saw me across the room?"

Her questions made him impatient and embarrassed and he usually ended up by returning some smart remark because he was both a shy and a truthful man. He wished she would ask him now, but he did not volunteer his vision. Instead he got up and said,

"Where's Robert?"

"Right on the porch. I can see him. He has a dish full of oysters and clams and a hermit crab in a whelk shell. He's been fascinated by it for two days now. I didn't know," she added, "that barnacles were little creatures. They've got little hand-like things that come out and scoop the water looking for food."

"Yes, I believe those are actually their feet," he said. "My grandfather told me that years ago. They stand on their heads, once they become fixed, and kick the food into their mouths for the rest of their lives. Now *that's* primitive for you." He drew on his pullover again. "How would you feel if I had another little fish-around before it rains? Then I'll take Robert for a walk and let you have some peace."

"Oh he's all right, except sometimes when he wants to crawl all over me. He's actually better here than at home. Everything excites him. He could live here forever as well."

"You must go back soon," he reminded her gently, "whether you like it or not."

"I don't want to. I hate the city. And I like it better here now," she said, "than later on, when all the summer people come."

"You don't get lonely?"

"No, not at all." She was embarrassed to admit it and irritated he had asked. "I walk and sit and look and read my books at night or listen to the radio. And there's Robert of course. He's become afraid of the dark, though," she said thoughtfully, "I wonder why. He wakes me up at night."

"Weren't you?" he challenged. "I was."

She turned, surprised. She had been of course, but she was a very nervous, sickly child.

"Yes." She stood at the sink, soapy hands held out of the water, poised over a plate, remembering. "I used to lie very still because I was absolutely sure there was someone in the room. If he knew I was awake, or if I should call out, he would strangle me or slit my throat."

"Footsteps on stairs," he said, rolling a cigarette.

"Faces outside windowpanes," she countered.

"And don't forget," he added, "the boy may actually have seen something. A deer, or even the Hoopers' dog. I've seen him stand up and pull that curtain back after his nap. Leave the light on." He put the tobacco tin back on the window sill and got up. "Leave the bathroom light on. It won't break us."

"Won't that make him weak?" she cried, "Isn't that giving in to his fears?"

"Not really. He'll outgrow it. I think maybe that kind of strength comes from reassurance." He kissed the back of her hair. "See you later on."

"Bring us back a fish," she said, reminding him of his role as provider, knowing in her heart it was all one to him whether he landed a fish or not. She was jealous of his relationship with the little boat, the oars, the sea. He would come back with a look of almost sensual pleasure on his face.

He went out, banging the door, and she could hear him teasing the little boy, explaining something. She left the dishes to dry and poured herself another cup of coffee. The baby kicked and she patted her abdomen as if to reassure it. Boy or girl, dark or light, she wondered idly but not very earnestly. It was out of her hands, like the weather and the tides. But would she really like to have it out here, maybe alone, with Robert crying from the prison of his crib or huddled at the foot of her bed, marked and possibly scarred forever by the groaning and the blood? Robert had been quick, amazingly and blessedly quick for a first child; the doctor had told her this indicated a rapid labour for the second. In her own way she was shy, particularly about physical things. Could she really go along to old Mrs. Hooper's and ask for help, or accept the possibility of being taken off the Island by one of the local fishing boats, observed by the taciturn, sun-baked faces of the men to whom she would be, if known at all, simply another of the summer folk.

It was easier in the old days, she felt, when there were no choices. She smiled at herself, for Tom, if he had been listening, would have added "and childbed fever, and babies dying, and women worn out before they'd hardly begun." He called her a romantic and accused her of never thinking things through. *He* was the one who could really have survived here without complaint, in the old days. He was the one who had the strength to drag up driftwood from the little rocky beach, and saw it up by hand, and the knowledge that enabled him to mend things or to start a perfect fire every time. He hauled his rowboat down to the wharf below their place on a triangular carrier he'd made from old wheels off a discarded pram, pulled it down the narrow ramp, which could be very steep when the tide was out, lowered it over the side, stepped in carefully and rowed away. When he was around she was jealous of his strength and his knowledge— he had grown up in the country and by the sea. She was a city girl and forever yearning after the names of things. She dreamed; he did. Her hands were clumsy, except when loving her husband or her son, and she often regretted that she had never learned to knit or weave or even to play an instrument. She liked to read and to walk and to talk and felt herself to be shallow and impractical.

Yet since they had found the cabin she had experienced a certain degree of content and growing self-respect. She had learned to bake good, heavy bread in the little two-burner hotplate/oven which she hoped to replace, eventually, with an old, iron, wood- or oil-burning stove; she had learned about ammonia for wasp stings and how to recognize the edible mushrooms that grew in profusion near the abandoned schoolhouse. She could even light a fire now, almost every time.

She had bought a booklet on edible plants and was secretly learning something about the sustaining nature of the various weeds and plants that grew so profusely around her. She had started an herb garden in an old bureau drawer and already had visions of bunches of herbs drying from the kitchen ceiling, jars of rose-hip and blackberry jam, mushrooms keeping in brine in heavy earthen-

30

ware crocks. Things could be learned from books and by experiment. She got a pencil and jotted down on a piece of drawing paper a list:

cod	thistles	pick salal
salmon	stinging nettles	?maybe sell some of our apples
oysters	blackberries	?my bread
mussels	apples	
	mushrooms	
	dandelions	

plant a garden, make beer, ?a goat and chickens for Robert and the baby.

Then she laughed and crumpled up the paper and threw it in the potbelly stove (her pride and joy and a present discovered for her by Tom) which heated the little kitchen. The fire was nearly out. She would set some bread and then take Robert down on the dock until Tom returned.

"Robbie," she called, knocking on the window, "d'you want to help me make bread?" From his expression she could tell he hadn't heard so she went to the other side of the room—Tom had knocked most of the wall out to make one big room out of two—and opened the front door. It was chilly and she shivered. "Hey, d'you want to help me make some bread?"

He nodded, sturdy and solemn like his father, but with her light skin and hair. She undid his jacket and kissed him. His cheeks were very red.

35 "Your ears are cold," she laughed, holding his head, like a ball between her hands. "And you smell like the sea. Where did you put your cap?"

"I dunno, I want some juice." He wriggled away from her and she thought with a stab of regret, "So soon?" and tried to fix him as he was at just that moment, red-cheeked and fat, with his bird-bright eyes and cool, sea-smelling skin, to remember him like that forever.

"Come on," he said, tugging at her skirt, "juice and cookies."

"Who said anything about cookies?" she asked in mock severity.

"Juice," he repeated, quite sure of himself. "And two cookies. I'm allowed two cookies."

40 "Says who?"

"Juice and two cookies," he said, climbing onto a chair by the kitchen table.

Afterward, after they had smelled the yeast and kneaded the dough and made a tiny loaf for Robert in a muffin tin, she covered the bread and left it near the still-warm stove and took the child down to the wharf to watch the fishermen. There were three boats in: the *Trincomali*, the *Sutil* and the *Mary T* and they jostled one another in the slightly choppy water. She looked out toward the other islands for Tom, but couldn't see him. Then carefully she and the little boy went down the ramp to the lower dock, where most of the activity was taking place. A few of the Indians she knew by sight, had seen them along the road or in the little store which served that end of the Island; but most of the ten or so people on the dock or sitting on the decks of boats were strangers to her and she felt suddenly rather presumptuous about coming down at all, like some sightseer—which was, of course, exactly what she was.

"Do you mind if we come down?" she called above the noise of the hysterical gulls and a radio which was blaring in one of the cabins. Two young men in identical red-plaid lumberjackets were drinking beer and taking a break on the deck of the *Mary T.* They looked up at her as she spoke, looked without curiosity, she felt, but simply recognizing her as a fact, like the gulls or the flapping fish, of their Sunday morning.

"Suit yourself, Missus," said an older man who seemed to be in charge. "But mind you don't slip on them boards."

She looked down. He was right, of course. The main part of the lower dock was, by now, viscous and treacherous with blood and the remains of fish gut. The men in their gumboots stepped carefully. The kill had been going on for at least an hour and the smell of fish and the cry of gulls hung thick in the heavy air. There was an almost palpable curtain of smell and sound and that, with the sight of the gasping fish, made her dizzy for a moment, turned the wharf into an old-fashioned wood-planked roundabout such as she had clung to, in parks, as a child, while she, the little boy, the Indians, the gulls, the small-eyed, gasping fish, the grey and swollen sky spun round and round in a cacophony of sound and smell and pure sensation. She willed herself to stop, but felt slightly sick—as she often had on the actual roundabouts of her childhood—and buried her face in the sweet-smelling hair of her child, as if he were a posy. She breathed deeply, sat up, and smiled. No-one had seen—except perhaps the two young Indians. Everyone else was busy. She smiled and began to enjoy and register what she was seeing.

Everywhere there were fish in various stages of life or death. Live cod swam beneath the decks of the little boats, round and round, bumping into one another as though they were part of some mad children's game, seeking desperately for a way out to the open sea. Then one of the men, with a net, would scoop up a fish, fling it onto the wharf where it would be clubbed by another man and disembowelled swiftly by a third, the guts flung overboard to the raucous gulls. Often the fish were not dead when they were gutted. She could see that, and it should have mattered. The whole thing should have mattered: the clubbing, the disembowelment, the sad stupid faces of the cod with their receding chins and silly Chinamen's beards. Yet instead of bothering, it thrilled her, this strange Sunday morning ritual of death and survival.

The fish were piled haphazardly in garbage cans, crammed in, tails any old way, and carried up the ramp by two of the men to be weighed on the scales at the top. The sole woman, also Indian and quite young, her hair done up in curlers under a pale pink chiffon scarf, carefully wrote down the weights as they were called out. "Ninety-nine." "Seventy-eight." Hundreds of pounds of cod to be packed in ice until the truck came and took them to the city on the evening ferry boat. And at how much a pound, she wondered. Fish was expensive in the city— too expensive, she thought—and wondered how much, in fact, went to these hard-working fishermen. But she dared not ask. Their faces, if not hostile, were closed to her, intent upon the task at hand. There was almost a rhythm to it, and although they did not sing, she felt the instinctual lift and drop and slice of the three who were actually responsible for the kill. If she had been a composer she could have written it down. One question from her and it might all be ruined.

For a moment the sun slipped out, and she turned her face upward, feeling very happy and alive just to be there, on this particular morning, watching the hands of these fishermen, hands that glittered with scales, like mica, in the sunlight, listening to the thud of the fish, the creaking and wheeling of the gulls. A year ago, she felt, the whole scene would have sickened her—now, in a strange way, she understood and was part of it. Crab-like, she could feel a new self forming underneath the old, brittle, shell—could feel herself expanding, breaking free. The child kicked, as if in recognition—a crab within a crab. If only Tom—but the living child tugged at her arm.

"I'm hungry."

"Ah, Robert. Wait a while." She was resentful. Sulky. He knew how to beat her.

"I want to pee. I want to pee *and* poop," he added defiantly.

She sighed. "Okay you win. Let's go." She got up stiffly, from sitting in one position for so long. A cod's heart beat by itself just below the ramp. Carefully she avoided it, walking in a heavy dream up the now steeper ramp (the tide was going out already) and up the path to her cabin.

Still in a dream she cared for the child and wiped his bottom and punched the bread, turning the little oven on to heat. After the child had been given a sandwich she put him down for a nap and sat at the kitchen table, dreaming. The first few drops of rain began to fall but these she did not see. She saw Tom and a fishing boat and living out their lives together here away from the noise and terror of the city. Fish—and apples—and bread. Making love in the early morning, rising to love with the sun, the two of them—and Robert—and the baby. She put the bread in the oven, wishing now that Tom would come back so she could talk to him.

"You only like the island," he had said, "because you know you can get off. Any time. You're playing at being a primitive. Like a still life of dead ducks or partridges or peonies with just one ant. Just let it be."

"What's wrong with wanting to be simple and uncluttered?" she had cried.

"Nothing," he had replied, "if that's what you really are."

She began a pie, suddenly restless, when there was a knock on the door. It startled her and the baby kicked again.

"Hello," she said, too conscious of her rolled-up sleeves and floury hands. "Can I help you?"

It was one of the young Indians.

"The fellows say you have a telephone Missus. Could I use it? My brother-in-law wuz supposed to pick us up and he ain't come."

"Of course. It's right there." She retreated to the kitchen and sliced apples, trying not to listen. But of course there was no wall. Short of covering her ears there was little she could do.

"Hey. Thelma. Is that you Thelma? Well where the hell is Joe? Yeah. All morning. Naw. I'm calling from the house up above. Oh yeah? Well tell him to get the hell up here quick. Yeah. Okay. Be seeing you."

She heard the phone replaced and then he came around the big fireplace, which, with the potbelly stove, divided the one large room partially into two.

"Say," he said, "I got blood all over your phone. Have you got a rag?"

She looked at his hands, which were all scored with shallow cuts, she could see, and the blood still bright orange-red and seeping.

"You're hurt."

"Naw," he said proudly, standing with his weight on one leg, "it's always like that when we do the cod. The knives is too sharp. *You* know," he added with a smile, as if she really did. Little drops of blood fell as he spoke, spattering on the linoleum floor.

"Don't you want some Band-aids, at least?"

"Wouldn't last two minutes in that wet," he said, "but give me a rag to clean up the phone."

"I'll do it," she said, bending awkwardly to one of the bottom cupboards to get a floor cloth. She preceded him into the living-room. He was right: the receiver was bright with blood, and some spots of blood decorated an air-letter, like notary's seals, which she had left open on the desk. Snow White in her pale-ness. He became Rose Red. "What am I thinking of?" she blushed.

"I sure am sorry," he said, looking at her with his dark bright eyes. "I didn't mean to mess up your things." She stood before him, the cloth bright with his blood, accepting his youth, his maleness, his arrogance. Her own pale blood drummed loudly in her ears.

"If you're positive you're all right," she managed.

"Yeah. Can't be helped. It'll heal over by next Sunday." He held his hands out to her and she could see, along with the seeping blood, the thin white wire-like lines of a hundred former scars. Slowly she reached out and dipped two fingers in the blood, then raised them and drew them across her forehead and down across each cheek.

"Christ," he said softly, then took the clean end of the rag and spit on it and gently wiped her face. She was very conscious of her bigness and leaned slightly forward so he would not have to brush against her belly. What would *their* children have been like?

Then the spell broke and he laughed self-consciously and looked around.

"Sure is a nice place you've got here," but she was aware he didn't mean it. What would his ideal be? He was very handsome with his coarse dark hair and red plaid lumberjacket.

"Well," she said, with her face too open, too revealing.

"Well," he answered, eager now to go. "Yeah. See you around. Thanks for the use of your phone."

She nodded and he was gone.

When Tom returned the little house was rich with the smells of bread and rhu-barb pie and coffee.

"Any luck?"

"Yes," he said, "and no. I didn't catch anything—but you did."

"I did?" she said, puzzled.

"Yeah. One of the fishermen gave me this for you. He said you let him use the phone. It was very nice of him, I must say."

And there, cleaned and filleted, presumably with the knife that had cut him so, was a beautiful bit of cod. She took it in her hands, felt the cool rasping texture of it, and wondered for an alien moment if his tongue would feel like that—cool, rough as a cat's tongue, tasting of fish.

85   "What did he say?" she asked, her back to the man.

"He said 'give this to the Missus.' Why?"

"Nothing. I thought he was kind of cheeky. He made me feel old."

Later that night on their couch before the fire, she startled him by the violence of her lovemaking. He felt somehow she was trying to possess him, devour him, maybe even exorcise him. And why hadn't she cooked the cod for supper? She had said that all of a sudden she didn't feel like fish. He stared at her, asleep, her full mouth slightly open, and felt the sad and immeasurable gulf between them, then sat up for a moment and pulled the curtain back, looking vainly for the reassurance of the moon behind the beaded curtain of the rain. The man shook his head. There were no answers, only questions. One could only live and accept. He turned away from his wife and dove effortlessly into a deep, cool, dreamless sleep. The rain fell on the little cabin, and on the trees and on the government wharf below, where, with persistence, it washed away all traces of the cod and the kill, except for two beer bottles, which lolled against the pilings as the two young Indians had lolled earlier that day. The rain fell; the baby kicked. The woman moaned a little in her sleep and moved closer to the reassuring back of the puzzle who was her husband. And still the rain fell on, and Sunday night— eventually—turned into Monday morning.

1981

One of the pleasures of reading and one of the ways of penetrating the meaning and effectiveness of stories is through our emotional responses, which often begin with our rooting for, identifying with, admiring, or despising one character or the other, wishing for one outcome or another. Our wishes and fears, our expectations and emotions, and the kind of world we imagine that the characters inhabit make up the major register of our emotional responses to fiction. And one of the first moves from reading to writing about fiction may well involve this "partisanship."

"Kill Day on the Government Wharf" begins with an utterance by the woman that is difficult to evaluate: " 'I only wish . . . that it was all a little more primitive.' " And during the first scene—at least until her husband, Tom, leaves—we may be uncertain whether we are "supposed to" agree with her yearning for the primitive and the natural or with Tom's practical but perhaps unimaginative appreciation of plumbing and electricity, and his belief that she is unrealistic, a "romantic" (paragraph 29). Until he leaves we are as close to him and his thoughts—"He wanted . . ." (paragraph 3); "he thought . . ." (paragraph 7); etc.—as we are to her. From that point on, however, we are almost exclusively looking through the eyes of the woman in the story, seeing what she sees and even sharing her thoughts. It is natural, then, that we should be on "her side," approve of her and her attitudes and wish her well. So the discussion of the fear of darkness, her being alone, the ugly or frightening details of the clubbing and disembowelling of the fish, the abrupt appearance of the Indian, and the ominous title of the story may lead us to expect, or fear, violence, may make us fear for her safety, putting us more fully on her side, perhaps to the point of identifying with her. Whether that emotional identification persists when she tries to imagine what the young Indian's tongue would feel like (paragraph 84) or when she tells her husband that the Indian was "cheeky" (paragraph 87) may depend in part on our gender, our moral attitudes, and our experience. But we must also pay close attention to the details and words of the story.

Try writing down your view of a story like this in essay form before discussing it with others. You will then have a record of your uninfluenced, unchallenged view. Later, you may be surprised to find that some of your classmates do not agree with you. But in discussing or arguing for your views you may discover not only that there are reasonable differences of opinion, but that what one believes about the future beyond the story reveals something about that person. A second paper may be either an argument with someone else's position or a composite or new view based on your discussion and exchange with classmates. And you may want to look at what you learned about yourself from your arguments about the story.

These ideas for papers are meant to be more than suggested writing assignments. They also suggest one *way* of writing about literature and are meant to show that writing about a story is not some special or arcane art but just a somewhat more formal, responsible, committed way of talking about what you have read. Think of the last time you saw a movie with a friend and left the theater discussing the film. If you were to put such responses down on paper, look at them carefully, think about them a bit, and try to make your views or responses convincing, you would be taking the first step toward writing about literature. You could even call it literary criticism.

Writing about the characters and events in stories as if they were real people and real happenings, and writing about your responses to and opinions about them, is only one kind of writing about literature. You can only write such a paper *after* you have read the whole story and formed an opinion, and your "argument" will involve going back to the story seeking out details to support your position, and, perhaps, situating where you are coming from in terms of personal experience, moral or religious views, and so on. But reading a story is not just something to argue or even think about after you have read it. It is first of all an experience—made up of thoughts and feelings—that happens *while you are in the very act of reading.*

One of the things most of us do when we are actively engaged in reading a story is to anticipate or interpret: what will happen next? what kind of person is a given character? how is the world of the story related to the world as I know it? what kind of a story is it? will it end happily or not? You will notice two aspects to such anticipation. One involves our experience, direct or indirect, in the world, and may be thought of as referential or representational; that is, we take the nouns to refer to real things—the word *table* calls up a more or less concrete image of a table—and from the words describing characters we imagine more or less real people and their actions and choices as potentially if not actually real. We have discussed "Kill Day on the Government Wharf" as if the woman and her husband were real people living in the real world. The other aspect is literary. We pay attention to the words themselves, to their sounds, their connotations, their relation to other words that look or sound like them, and not just to what they denote—tables or fish or jewels. Stories can even play with these referential and literary aspects of words, surprising us by shifting from one aspect to another. The zebra who did not tell stories was astonished, and the words say "he's just fit to be tied." This is a common figure of speech, and we do not expect to take the words "seriously" or referentially. We are surprised, then, when the story does: "So the little cat quickly ties him up. . . ."

We are aware that a story is a story and that telling a story involves certain conventions—for example, stories are generally written in the past tense, though we like to imagine them as happening in a kind of present, with the end not yet known. Different kinds of stories, too, have their own conventions: fairy tales and sometimes other fantasies, like "The Zebra Storyteller," begin with "Once upon a time"; in ghost stories and certain other scary stories there is almost always a beautiful young woman threatened by danger; these stories, adventure stories, and comic stories almost always end happily; and so on.

Anticipation begins at the beginning—or even earlier. As soon as we read the title of the story that follows, "The Jewelry," we start: will it be lost? stolen? inherited? Our anticipation is channeled by first- or secondhand life experience—how we think jewelry functions in "the real world." Notice that this anticipation is triggered by the title. Life experiences do not come with titles to guide us, but our reading experience tells us that titles are significant, worth paying attention to if we are to anticipate and understand. Perhaps not as early as our reading of the title, but soon, we begin to anticipate a shape or configuration of the entire story. Based on our own real experiences and what we've read, we project a vague shape early on, frequently adjusting it as we proceed through the story, but always connected to it as we read on. With the first sentence of "The Jewelry"—"Having met the girl one evening, at the house of the office-superintendent, M. Lantin became enveloped in love as in a net"—we begin casting our own net. The story will involve love. What do we know or believe about love? about different kinds of love? about the possible outcomes of falling in love? What is the connection between love and jewelry? We are not yet prepared to define that connection, but we may have tentative expectations about it. Though the first sentence may be summarized in "real" or experiential terms as "M. Lantin has fallen (deeply) in love," the precise *words* in the sentence that describe falling in love are "became enveloped in love as in a net." Does this merely emphasize how deeply he has fallen in love, or is there something uncomfortable, painful, even ominous about the words—note, about the *words*—"enveloped as in a net"? How we anticipate and interpret what the story "means" or "says about life" will be conditioned throughout by our life experience, by such literary "devices" as the title, by the precise words of the story, and by our experience with kinds of stories and what usually happens and eventuates in such stories. We must remain tentative in our expectations, however, and alert to changes and modifications, as this story will show, for example, when the fourth paragraph of this story concludes with "and [he] married her," we must abandon the love-and-courtship story we anticipated and imagine an entirely new set of possibilities.

GUY DE MAUPASSANT

The Jewelry[1]

Having met the girl one evening, at the house of the office-superintendent, M. Lantin became enveloped in love as in a net.

She was the daughter of a country-tutor, who had been dead for several years.

1. Translated by Lafcadio Hearn.

Afterward she had come to Paris with her mother, who made regular visits to several bourgeois families of the neighborhood, in hopes of being able to get her daughter married. They were poor and respectable, quiet and gentle. The young girl seemed to be the very ideal of that pure good woman to whom every young man dreams of entrusting his future. Her modest beauty had a charm of angelic shyness; and the slight smile that always dwelt about her lips seemed a reflection of her heart.

Everybody sang her praises; all who knew her kept saying: "The man who gets her will be lucky. No one could find a nicer girl than that."

M. Lantin, who was then chief clerk in the office of the Minister of the Interior, with a salary of 3,500 francs a year,[2] demanded her hand, and married her.

He was unutterably happy with her. She ruled his home with an economy so   5
adroit that they really seemed to live in luxury. It would be impossible to conceive of any attentions, tendernesses, playful caresses which she did not lavish upon her husband; and such was the charm of her person that, six years after he married her, he loved her even more than he did the first day.

There were only two points upon which he ever found fault with her—her love of the theater, and her passion for false jewelry.

Her lady-friends (she was acquainted with the wives of several small office holders) were always bringing her tickets for the theaters; whenever there was a performance that made a sensation, she always had her *loge* secured, even for first performances; and she would drag her husband with her to all these entertainments, which used to tire him horribly after his day's work. So at last he begged her to go to the theater with some lady-acquaintances who would consent to see her home afterward. She refused for quite a while—thinking it would not look very well to go out thus unaccompanied by her husband. But finally she yielded, just to please him; and he felt infinitely grateful to her therefor.

Now this passion for the theater at last evoked in her the desire of dress. It was true that her toilette remained simple, always in good taste, but modest; and her sweet grace, her irresistible grace, ever smiling and shy, seemed to take fresh charm from the simplicity of her robes. But she got into the habit of suspending in her pretty ears two big cut pebbles, fashioned in imitation of diamonds; and she wore necklaces of false pearls, bracelets of false gold, and haircombs studded with paste-imitations of precious stones.

Her husband, who felt shocked by this love of tinsel and show, would often say—"My dear, when one has not the means to afford real jewelry, one should appear adorned with one's natural beauty and grace only—and these gifts are the rarest of jewels."

But she would smile sweetly and answer: "What does it matter? I like those   10
things—that is my little whim. I know you are right; but one can't make oneself over again. I've always loved jewelry so much!"

And then she would roll the pearls of the necklaces between her fingers, and make the facets of the cut crystals flash in the light, repeating: "Now look at them—see how well the work is done. You would swear it was real jewelry."

2. A midlevel bureaucratic wage, perhaps about $25,000 to $30,000 today.

He would then smile in his turn, and declare to her: "You have the tastes of a regular Gypsy."

Sometimes, in the evening, when they were having a chat by the fire, she would rise and fetch the morocco box in which she kept her "stock" (as M. Lantin called it)—would put it on the tea-table, and begin to examine the false jewelry with passionate delight, as if she experienced some secret and mysterious sensations of pleasure in their contemplation; and she would insist on putting one of the necklaces round her husband's neck, and laugh till she couldn't laugh any more, crying out: "Oh! how funny you look!" Then she would rush into his arms, and kiss him furiously.

One winter's night, after she had been to the Opera, she came home chilled through, and trembling. Next day she had a bad cough. Eight days after that, she died of pneumonia.

Lantin was very nearly following her into the tomb. His despair was so frightful that in one single month his hair turned white. He wept from morning till night, feeling his heart torn by inexpressible suffering—ever haunted by the memory of her, by the smile, by the voice, by all the charm of the dead woman.

Time did not assuage his grief. Often during office hours his fellow-clerks went off to a corner to chat about this or that topic of the day—his cheeks might have been seen to swell up all of a sudden, his nose wrinkle, his eyes fill with water—he would pull a frightful face, and begin to sob.

He had kept his dead companion's room just in the order she had left it, and he used to lock himself up in it every evening to think about her—all the furniture, and even all her dresses, remained in the same place they had been on the last day of her life.

But life became hard for him. His salary, which, in his wife's hands, had amply sufficed for all household needs, now proved scarcely sufficient to supply his own few wants. And he asked himself in astonishment how she had managed always to furnish him with excellent wines and with delicate eating which he could not now afford at all with his scanty means.

He got a little into debt, like men obliged to live by their wits. At last one morning that he happened to find himself without a cent in his pocket, and a whole week to wait before he could draw his monthly salary, he thought of selling something; and almost immediately it occurred to him to sell his wife's "stock"—for he had always borne a secret grudge against the flash-jewelry that used to annoy him so much in former days. The mere sight of it, day after day, somewhat spoiled the sad pleasure of thinking of his darling.

He tried a long time to make a choice among the heap of trinkets she had left behind her—for up to the very last day of her life she had kept obstinately buying them, bringing home some new thing almost every night—and finally he resolved to take the big pearl necklace which she used to like the best of all, and which he thought ought certainly to be worth six or eight francs, as it was really very nicely mounted for an imitation necklace.

He put it in his pocket, and walked toward the office, following the boulevards, and looking for some jewelry-store on the way, where he could enter with confidence.

Finally he saw a place and went in; feeling a little ashamed of thus exposing his misery, and of trying to sell such a trifling object.

"Sir," he said to the jeweler, "please tell me what this is worth."

The jeweler took the necklace, examined it, weighed it, took up a magnifying glass, called his clerk, talked to him in whispers, put down the necklace on the counter, and drew back a little bit to judge of its effect at a distance.

M. Lantin, feeling very much embarrassed by all these ceremonies, opened his mouth and began to declare—"Oh! I know it can't be worth much" . . . when the jeweler interrupted him saying:

"Well, sir, that is worth between twelve and fifteen thousand francs; but I cannot buy it unless you can let me know exactly how you came by it."

The widower's eyes opened enormously, and he stood gaping—unable to understand. Then after a while he stammered out: "You said? . . . Are you sure?" The jeweler, misconstruing the cause of this astonishment, replied in a dry tone—"Go elsewhere if you like, and see if you can get any more for it. The very most I would give for it is fifteen thousand. Come back and see me again, if you can't do better."

M. Lantin, feeling perfectly idiotic, took his necklace and departed; obeying a confused desire to find himself alone and to get a chance to think.

But the moment he found himself in the street again, he began to laugh, and he muttered to himself: "The fool!—oh! what a fool; If I had only taken him at his word. Well, well!—a jeweler who can't tell paste from real jewelry!"

And he entered another jewelry-store, at the corner of the Rue de la Paix. The moment the jeweler set eyes on the necklace, he examined—"Hello! I know that necklace well—it was sold here!"

M. Lantin, very nervous, asked:

"What's it worth?"

"Sir, I sold it for twenty-five thousand francs. I am willing to buy it back again for eighteen thousand—if you can prove to me satisfactorily, according to legal presciptions, how you came into possession of it"—This time, M. Lantin was simply paralyzed with astonishment. He said: "Well . . . but please look at it again, sir. I always thought until now that it was . . . was false."

The jeweler said:

"Will you give me your name, sir?"

"Certainly. My name is Lantin; I am employed at the office of the Minister of the Interior. I live at No. 16, Rue des Martyrs."

The merchant opened the register, looked, and said: "Yes; this necklace was sent to the address of Madame Lantin, 16 Rue des Martyrs, on July 20th, 1876."

And the two men looked into each other's eyes—the clerk wild with surprise; the jeweler suspecting he had a thief before him.

The jeweler resumed:

"Will you be kind enough to leave this article here for twenty-four hours only—I'll give you a receipt."

M. Lantin stuttered: "Yes-ah! certainly." And he went out folding up the receipt, which he put in his pocket.

Then he crossed the street, went the wrong way, found out his mistake,

25

30

35

40

returned by way of the Tuileries, crossed the Seine, found out he had taken the wrong road again, and went back to the Champs-Elysées without being able to get one clear idea into his head. He tried to reason, to understand. His wife could never have bought so valuable an object as that. Certainly not. But then, it must have been a present! . . . A present from whom? What for?

He stopped and stood stock-still in the middle of the avenue.

A horrible suspicion swept across his mind. . . . She? . . . But then all those other pieces of jewelry must have been presents also! . . . Then it seemed to him that the ground was heaving under his feet; that a tree, right in front of him, was falling toward him; he thrust out his arms instinctively, and fell senseless.

45   He recovered his consciousness again in a drug-store to which some bystanders had carried him. He had them lead him home, and he locked himself into his room.

Until nightfall he cried without stopping, biting his handkerchief to keep himself from screaming out. Then, completely worn out with grief and fatigue, he went to bed, and slept a leaden sleep.

A ray of sunshine awakened him, and he rose and dressed himself slowly to go to the office. It was hard to have to work after such a shock. Then he reflected that he might be able to excuse himself to the superintendent, and he wrote to him. Then he remembered he would have to go back to the jeweler's; and shame made his face purple. He remained thinking a long time. Still he could not leave the necklace there; he put on his coat and went out.

It was a fine day; the sky extended all blue over the city, and seemed to make it smile. Strollers were walking aimlessly about, with their hands in their pockets.

Lantin thought as he watched them passing: "How lucky the men are who have fortunes! With money a man can even shake off grief—you can go where you please—travel—amuse yourself! Oh! if I were only rich!"

50   He suddenly discovered he was hungry—not having eaten anything since the evening before. But his pockets were empty; and he remembered the necklace. Eighteen thousand francs! Eighteen thousand francs!—that was a sum—that was!

He made his way to the Rue de la Paix and began to walk backward and forward on the sidewalk in front of the store. Eighteen thousand francs! Twenty times he started to go in; but shame always kept him back.

Still he was hungry—very hungry—and had not a cent. He made one brusque resolve, and crossed the street almost at a run, so as not to let himself have time to think over the matter; and he rushed into the jeweler's.

As soon as he saw him, the merchant hurried forward, and offered him a chair with smiling politeness. Even the clerks came forward to stare at Lantin, with gaiety in their eyes and smiles about their lips.

The jeweler said: "Sir, I made inquiries; and if you are still so disposed, I am ready to pay you down the price I offered you."

55   The clerk stammered: "Why, yes—sir, certainly."

The jeweler took from a drawer eighteen big bills,[3] counted them, and held

---

3. French paper money varies in size; the larger the bill, the larger the denomination.

them out to Lantin, who signed a little receipt, and thrust the money feverishly into his pocket.

Then, as he was on the point of leaving, he turned to the ever-smiling merchant, and said, lowering his eyes: "I have some—I have some other jewelry, which came to me in the same—from the same inheritance. Would you purchase them also from me?"

The merchant bowed, and answered: "Why, certainly, sir—certainly. . . ." One of the clerks rushed out to laugh at his ease; another kept blowing his nose as hard as he could.

Lantin, impassive, flushed and serious, said: "I will bring them to you."

And he hired a cab to get the jewelry.   60

When he returned to the store, an hour later, he had not yet breakfasted. They examined the jewelry—piece by piece—putting a value on each. Nearly all had been purchased from that very house.

Lantin, now, disputed estimates made, got angry, insisted on seeing the books, and talked louder and louder the higher the estimates grew.

The big diamond earrings were worth 20,000 francs; the bracelets, 35,000; the brooches, rings and medallions, 16,000; a set of emeralds and sapphires, 14,000; solitaire, suspended to a gold neckchain, 40,000; the total value being estimated at 196,000 francs.

The merchant observed with mischievous good nature: "The person who owned these must have put all her savings into jewelry."

Lantin answered with gravity: "Perhaps that is as good a way of saving money   65
as any other." And he went off, after having agreed with the merchant that an expert should make a counter-estimate for him the next day.

When he found himself in the street again, he looked at the Column Vendôme[4] with the desire to climb it, as if it were a May pole. He felt jolly enough to play leapfrog over the Emperor's head—up there in the blue sky.

He breakfasted at Voisin's[5] restaurant, and ordered wine at 20 francs a bottle.

Then he hired a cab and drove out to the Bois.[6] He looked at the carriages passing with a sort of contempt, and a wild desire to yell out to the passers-by: "I am rich, too—I am! I have 200,000 francs!"

The recollection of the office suddenly came back to him. He drove there, walked right into the superintendent's private room, and said: "Sir, I come to give you my resignation. I have just come into a fortune of *three* hundred thousand francs." Then he shook hands all round with his fellow-clerks; and told them all about his plans for a new career. Then he went to dinner at the Café Anglais.

Finding himself seated at the same table with a man who seemed to him quite   70
genteel, he could not resist the itching desire to tell him, with a certain air of coquetry, that he had just inherited a fortune of *four* hundred thousand francs.

For the first time in his life he went to the theater without feeling bored by the performance; and he passed the night in revelry and debauch.

---

4. Famous column with a statue of Napoleon at the top.   5. Like the Café Anglais below, a well-known and high-priced restaurant.   6. Large Parisian park where the rich took their outings.

Six months after he married again. His second wife was the most upright of spouses, but had a terrible temper. She made his life very miserable.

1883

Stories are not always written. Ballads and even epics were sung, plays are still acted out on the stage, and most cultures have or had oral storytellers. Writing, however, makes a difference. Oral or dramatic "readings" or performances are communal, the responses tend to be uniform (though there's always the person in the audience who laughs at the wrong time), and the purpose of the performances is more overtly to move or persuade the group or community. They have a closer relation to classical rhetoric, political speeches, or concerts than written narrative does. We read, usually, alone, most of the time silently, and if there are—and there usually are—emotions, they are deeply personal, not shared. There is a tendency, then, in literary criticism, and in reading for and discussing literature in class, to stress interpretation, the "ideas" in literary texts, or the formal structures, and to slight somewhat the emotional or affective aspect of our essentially solitary literary experience. But though it may be difficult to develop the vocabulary needed to talk about literature (we have to get beyond "I liked it" and "I didn't like it"), we must never forget the deeply stirring response that literature engenders and the differences in kinds and depths of response that different works stimulate.

QUESTIONS

1. What specific words or phrases in the first two paragraphs of "The Jewelry" alert you to the possibility that all may not be as it seems? How are these expectations or fears allayed in the next few paragraphs? What new fears or expectations are aroused very soon thereafter?
2. Since the story is called "The Jewelry" and life does not come wrapped in such convenient titles, you may come to suspect the truth before M. Lantin does. How does your attitude toward him change?

WRITING SUGGESTIONS

1. Stop "The Zebra Storyteller" after paragraph 5 (". . . fit to be tied"), and in five to ten paragraphs write your own ending.
2. Rewrite the scene between the Indian and the wife in "Kill Day on the Government Wharf," giving the Indian's perception of the woman and his thoughts.
3. Write a new two- or three-page ending to "Kill Day on the Government Wharf" that shows or suggests a different outcome.
4. Write an "off-stage" scene that shows how Lantin's first wife got one or more pieces of the jewelry.

Understanding the Text

PLOT

In "The Zebra Storyteller" you can see the skeleton of the typical short story **plot** or **plot structure.** *Plot* simply means the arrangement of the **action,** an imagined event or a series of such events.

Action usually involves **conflict,** a struggle between opposing forces, and it often falls into something like the same five parts that we find in a play: exposition, rising action, turning point (or climax), falling action, conclusion. The conflict in this little tale is between the Siamese cat and the zebras, especially the zebra storyteller. The first part of the action, called the **exposition,** introduces the characters, situation, and, usually, time and place. The exposition here is achieved in three sentences: the time is "once upon a," the place Africa, the characters a Siamese cat who speaks Zebraic and an innocent zebra, and the situation their meeting. We then enter the second part of the plot, the **rising action:** events that complicate the situation and intensify or complicate the conflict or introduce new ones. The first event here is the meeting between an innocent zebra and the Zebraic-speaking cat. That initial conflict of zebra and cat is over in a hurry—the zebra who is "fit to be tied" is tied up and eaten. Complications build with the cat's continuing success in killing zebras, and the zebras' growing fears and consequent superstitious belief that the ghost of a lion haunts the region preying on zebras. The **turning point** or **climax** of the action is the third part of the story, the appearance of the zebra storyteller: until now the cat has had it all his way, but his luck is about to change. From this point on the complications that grew in the first part of the story are untangled—the zebra storyteller, for example, is not surprised when he meets a Siamese cat speaking Zebraic "because he'd been thinking about that very thing"; this is the fourth part of the story, the reverse movement or **falling action.** The story ends at the fifth part, the **conclusion:** the point at which the situation that was destabilized at the beginning of the story (when the Zebraic-speaking cat appeared) becomes stable once more: Africa is again free of cats speaking the language of zebras.

This typical arrangement of the action of a story is not just a formula for composing a narrative or for critical analysis; it also has its emotional and intellectual effect on your responses as reader. The exposition invites you to begin immediately building images of the time and place of the action, the people, the situation, and the issues involved, and even to identify with or root for one or more of the participants. You choose to be on the side of the zebras or the Siamese cat (though your choice is guided by the language and details of the story: the cat speaks "inappropriate" Zebraic; the zebra is introduced as "innocent"). As the situation becomes more complicated during the rising action, you are led to be increasingly concerned with how "your" zebras, the "good guys," are going to get out of this worsening situation (the cat eating more and more zebras), or, if the complications of the rising action are positive (as in the marriage and prosperity and happiness of M. Lantin in "The Jewelry"), you become more and more concerned about what is going to happen to turn things around (for even if you do not know about turning points in narrative, you know that sometimes things in stories and even in real life—knock on wood—seem too good to be true or too good to last). Consciously or unconsciously you become involved in the story, trying to anticipate how the complications will unravel, how everything will come out.

Another aspect of structure that affects you, the reader, is the order in which the events are told. In life, actions occur one after the other, sequentially. Not all stories, however, describe events chronologically. It is then, when historical order is disturbed, that a plot is created. "The king died and then the queen died," to use one critic's example, is not a plot, for it has not been "tampered with." "The queen died after the king died" includes the same historical events, but the order in which they are reported has been changed. The reader of the first sentence focuses on the king first; the reader of the second sentence focuses on the queen. While essentially the same thing has been said, the difference in focus and emphasis changes the effect and, in the broadest sense, the meaning as well. The **history** has been structured into plot.

The ordering of events, then, provides stories with structure and plot, and has its consequences in effect and meaning. The first opportunity for **structuring** a story is at the beginning, and beginnings are consequently particularly sensitive and important. Why does a story begin where it does? No event (at least since the Big Bang) is a true beginning; your own life story begins before you were born and even before you were conceived. So to begin a story the author has to make a **selection,** to indicate that for the purposes of this story the beginning is a given point rather than any other. "Having met the girl one evening, at the house of the office-superintendent, M. Lantin became enveloped in love as in a net." That first sentence of "The Jewelry" seems a perfectly natural and "innocent" way to begin a story that will involve Lantin and his wife. But why not begin with a slightly modified paragraph 5: "M. Lantin was perfectly happy in his marriage"? or with paragraph 9, inserting a new first sentence: "M. Lantin was perfectly happy with his wife and smiled at her two little faults: her love of the theater, and her passion for false jewelry. He felt shocked by . . ."? After all, this last sentence would immediately introduce the jewelry that gives the story its title. Or the story could begin with the death of the girl's father, her move with her mother to Paris, and so on. These are the earliest events mentioned in the exposition, and so in the unstructured history they would come first. In searching for a reason for Maupassant's beginning, we might look at what we learn and what is emphasized in the beginning as it now stands: the class of Lantin and his income; the girl's beauty, modesty, respectability, poverty, and her mother's search for a husband for her; Lantin's falling in love as if into a "net." It might be useful to consider on your own or in an assigned essay how the details in these first eight paragraphs affect your reading, responding, and understanding of the people, events, and "meaning" of the story. Or you might want to explain why John Cheever's "The Country Husband," in this chapter, begins, "To begin at the beginning, the airplane from Minneapolis in which Francis Weed was traveling East ran into heavy weather," rather than with, say, paragraph 11, when the Weeds are preparing to go out on the evening on which Francis meets the baby-sitter; or even, with a few adjustments, with paragraph 15, when the baby-sitter opens the door and Francis sees her for the first time, for it is with their encounter that the story seems truly to begin.

   The point at which a story ends is also a sensitive and meaningful aspect of its structure. A typical beginning—first sentence (Lantin meets the girl) or first **discriminated occasion** (the first encounter of a zebra with the Zebraic-speaking cat)—destabilizes the history: something happens that changes the ordinary life of one or more characters and sets off a new course of events, which constitute the story. A typical ending either reestablishes the old order (no more cats eating zebras) or establishes a new one (Lantin remarried). Endings, like beginnings, affect the reader and suggest meaning. And like beginnings, they are arbitrary structures that interrupt history, for all stories (or more precisely, histories) about individuals end the same way, as Margaret Atwood somewhat cynically suggests in "Happy Endings": *"John and Mary die. John and Mary die. John and Mary die."* That is only true, of course, if you equate the story with the history, for the history not only extends backward as far as you can see but also forward to the end of the lives of those in the story. (And why not the lives of their children, grandchildren, and so on?) Not all stories end with the deaths of the characters who interest us; in fact, of the stories in this and the introductory chapters only Atwood's ends with the deaths of both its major characters, while "The Zebra Storyteller" ends with the death of the Zebraic-speaking cat. Where a story ends goes a long way to determining how it affects us and what we make of it. "The Zebra Storyteller" ends with the triumph of the zebra over the Siamese cat, leaving us with the feeling that good guys win, and with a moral that leads us to the "point" or meaning of the story. "Kill Day on the Government Wharf" leaves us without an answer and pushes us back into our own experiences and beliefs to choose between the romantic views of the wife or the practical views of the husband.

   All questions about the effect or meaning of beginnings and endings follow from an assumption that we must now recognize: there are reasons for the structures of the narrative. Indeed, in a short story, in part because of its brevity, every detail, every arrangement or ordering must "count." One writer has said that if there is a gun on the wall at the beginning of a story, it must be fired by the end. The relevance of events or details is not limited, however, merely to future action—events in the plot—for most seem to have relevance in other ways. In paragraph 9 of "The Country Husband," for example, Francis Weed listens to "the evening sounds of Shady Hill." These include a door slamming, the sound of someone cutting grass—which do not lead to events but may establish the nature of the suburban setting—and the sound of someone playing (badly) Beethoven's "Moonlight Sonata," which may on the one hand reinforce Weed's thoughtful or dreamy mood or introduce "romance" into the story, and on the other hand, because of the petulant and self-pitying performance, show why Weed is dissatisfied with the shallowness of his suburban neighbors and perhaps suburban life. Notice the "may" and the "perhaps" in the previous sentence. The relevancy of a detail to a story is not always as simple and incontrovertible as the inevitable shooting of the gun. Though you ought to be alert as to how the details function in affecting you or contributing to your visualization or understanding of the people, incidents, and issues of the story, there is not necessarily a precise answer to the question of how a detail functions. In Cheever's story, why does Mr. Nixon shout "Varmints! Rascals! . . . Avaunt and quit my sight!" at the squirrels? What does it add? What would be lost

> *"The king died and then the queen died," is a story. "The king died, and then the queen died of grief" is a plot.*
>
> —E. M. FORSTER

without it? You may see the effects and implications differently from your classmates; indeed you may not have chosen this detail to interrogate at all. These differences of selection and explanation may shed light on why readers respond to, understand, and judge stories differently.

Structuring a story is not just a matter of choosing where to begin or end it, or of choosing or inventing affective and meaningful details, but also of ordering all the events in between. Sometimes, as Atwood says, the plot is "just one thing after another, a what and a what and a what." Even when that is the case, sometimes the reader is forced to think back to prior events. In a detective story, for example, the crime has usually been committed before the story begins, in the history and not in the plot. At the end, when the detective explains "who done it," you must think back not only to the crime, but to all the hints or clues that you have been given, including false clues or "red herrings" that make you look in the wrong direction. In such a story we expect the ending to explain what happened earlier. Sometimes, however, a story moves back; that is, instead of making you think of earlier events, it actually breaks into its own order, reaches back into the history, and presents or dramatizes a scene that happened before the fictional present. In James Baldwin's "Sonny's Blues," for example, there is such a replay or **flashback** (or rather a series of flashbacks). There is a very brief scene from the past triggered by the word "safe" (paragraph 79), the narrator recalling his father's words, which then leads to a specific dramatized scene—the last time the narrator talked to his mother. This is followed by another scene—the narrator's conversation with Sonny after their mother's funeral. This scene of course follows the previous one but in terms of where the story began (the fictional present) it is in the past and, therefore, is in fact a flashback. Nor does the story return to the fictional present for some time—"I read about Sonny's trouble in the spring. Little Grace died in the fall . . ." (paragraph 177)—when Sonny has been living with the narrator for two weeks, and it proceeds from that point to the end.

One reason for structuring the history into plot is to engage the reader's attention, to make the reader read on. This can be done not only by arousing the reader's expectations of what will happen next but also by generating **curiosity**—the desire to know what is happening or has happened. It is the sheer power of curiosity, for example, that keeps us reading intensely when we know as little as Watson or Sherlock Holmes himself at the beginning of a story or "case." But it is not only the detective story that plays upon our curiosity. "Sonny's Blues" begins, "I read about it in the paper . . . ," and that "it" without antecedent is repeated seven times in the first paragraph and first two sentences of the second paragraph. Read those first two paragraphs and stop. If you try at this point to examine what is going on in your mind, you more than likely will find that you are asking yourself what "it" might refer to, and you will probably have framed for yourself several possible answers. It may be in part for this reason that Baldwin begins how and where he does, getting you engaged in the story, so that you will read on. Even a title, such as "The Zebra Storyteller," "A Very Old Man with Enormous Wings," or "The Secret Sharer," can make us curious enough to pick up a story; after that, it's up to the story to keep us engaged.

Perhaps stronger than curiosity is **suspense**—that particular kind of expectation involving anticipation of and doubt about what is going to happen next (as differentiated from expectations about what a character is like, what the theme is or how it will develop, and so on). Even in reading a little fable like "The Zebra Storyteller" our minds are—or should be—at work: a cat speaking Zebraic is killing zebras; the zebra storyteller thinking of plots comes up with the idea of a story about a cat that learns to speak Zebraic: "What an idea! That'll make 'em laugh!" he tells himself. Then he meets the cat—what will happen next? How many possibilities did you or can you anticipate? Even though you now know the ending, you could go back to this point in the story and, recalling your expectations, reconstruct or reinvent the rest of the story.

Sometimes the suspense is generated and defined not so much by what happens within the story as it is by what we expect from stories. In "The Jewelry," for example, when Lantin's wife dies so early in the story, we know this is not the end; something is going to happen or be revealed because there are several pages left and stories do not go on unless something is going to happen. But what? Lantin grieves so intensely, locks himself in her room . . . will her ghost return? He is going bankrupt, he looks over his wife's jewelry, and when he goes to sell a piece he finds it is not mere costume jewelry, but real. How much sooner than Lantin himself do you realize the source of the jewelry? There is a certain satisfaction in seeing the truth before he does. But *then* what do you expect to happen next? Do you anticipate his debauching? How did you expect the story to end?

If you were to pause just before reading the final paragraph of the Maupassant story and consciously explore your expectations, you would see that these are based on both fictional and actual conventions—indeed, most of us would probably assume the story could have ended with the word "debauch," without the final brief paragraph, and that the story would end with the irony of Lantin's getting pleasure out of his having been betrayed. We can accept this even within our conventional moral terms—he may get bitter pleasures for a time, but he will soon tire of such pleasures or be undone by them.

The final paragraph, however, if it does not contradict, deepens the irony: now he has a truly "upright" wife—and he is miserable. Our conventional expectations that morality brings happiness, that infidelity and debauchery lead to various kinds of ruin, are wrenched into question. He has tired of debauchery, but is he better off leading a moral life? Is the world amoral—or even immoral? Do good guys finish last? We do not have to believe this, but to read the story fully we need to call our perhaps more optimistic and conventional views into question.

In order to keep you engaged and alert, a story must make you ask questions about what will happen or what will be revealed next. To respond fully to a story you must be alert to the signals and guess along with the author. One way of seeing whether and how your mind is engaged in your reading is to pause at crucial points in the story and consciously explore what you think is coming. At least in one aspect, fiction is a guessing game.

Like all guessing games, from quiz shows to philosophy, the plot game in fiction has certain guidelines. A well-structured plot will play fair with you, offering at appropriate points all the necessary indications or clues to what will happen next, not just springing new and essential information on you at the last minute ("Meanwhile, unknown to our hero, the Marines were just on the other side of the hill . . ."). It is this playing fair that makes the ending of a well-structured story satisfying or, when you look back on it, inevitable. Most stories also offer a number of reasonable but false signals (red herrings) to get you off the scent, so that in a well-structured story the ending, though inevitable, is also surprising. And though there is usually an overarching action from beginning to end, in many stories there are layers of expectation or suspense, so that as soon as one question is answered another comes forth to replace it, keeping you in doubt as to the final outcome.

Unlike most guessing games, however, the reward is not for the right guess—anticipating the outcome before the final paragraph—but for the number of guesses, right *and* wrong, that you make, the number of signals you respond to. If you are misled by none of the false signals in the early pages of a story—by Sonny's friend saying, " 'Listen. They'll let him out and then it'll just start all over again' " (paragraph 36), for example— you may be closer to being "right," but you have missed many of the implications of the story. But, more important, you have missed the pleasure of *learning* the "truth" a story has to offer, and you know how much less meaningful it is to be told something than to learn for yourself, through your own experience. Fiction is a way of transmitting not just perception but experience.

Though plot is the structuring of events, an event can be an outcome or consequence as well as a happening, and the expectation, surprise, and perception surrounding plot structure can involve meaning as well as action, as we have seen in the worldview suggested by the ending of "The Jewelry." Maupassant's ending upsets our conventional thinking about human conduct and morality. Though expectations based on social, moral, or literary conventions that support the ordinary are not so consciously aroused as are those aroused by action and adventure—the kind of expectation described by the term *suspense*—their fulfillment, modification, or contradiction is a significant aim and effect of many stories. Fiction is in part a guessing game, but it is not merely a game. Many stories seek to give new insights into human perception, experience, meaning, or at least to challenge our more or less unconsciously held beliefs. They strive to tell truths—new, subjective truths, but truths—even though they "lie" about the actuality of the people and events represented. But first they have to get your attention, and one way is by arousing your curiosity and exciting your anticipation. That is one of the primary functions of plot. Alertness to signals, anticipating what is to come next, and remembering what has been said and signaled earlier are essential to fully appreciating and understanding stories and their structures. That is how you should function as a reader of plot.

MARGARET ATWOOD

Happy Endings

John and Mary meet.
What happens next?
If you want a happy ending, try A.

A.   John and Mary fall in love and get married. They both have worthwhile and remunerative jobs which they find stimulating and challenging. They buy a charming house. Real estate values go up. Eventually, when they can afford live-in help, they have two children, to whom they are devoted. The children turn out well. John and Mary have a stimulating and challenging sex life and worthwhile friends. They go on fun vacations together. They retire. They both have hobbies which they find stimulating and challenging. Eventually they die. This is the end of the story.

5   B.   Mary falls in love with John but John doesn't fall in love with Mary. He merely uses her body for selfish pleasure and ego gratification of a tepid kind. He comes to her apartment twice a week and she cooks him dinner, you'll notice that he doesn't even consider her worth the price of a dinner out, and after he's eaten the dinner he fucks her and after that he falls asleep, while

she does the dishes so he won't think she's untidy, having all those dirty dishes lying around, and puts on fresh lipstick so she'll look good when he wakes up, but when he wakes up he doesn't even notice, he puts on his socks and his shorts and his pants and his shirt and his tie and his shoes, the reverse order from the one in which he took them off. He doesn't take off Mary's clothes, she takes them off herself, she acts as if she's dying for it every time, not because she likes sex exactly, she doesn't, but she wants John to think she does because if they do it often enough surely he'll get used to her, he'll come to depend on her and they will get married, but John goes out the door with hardly so much as a good-night and three days later he turns up at six o'clock and they do the whole thing over again.

Mary gets run-down. Crying is bad for your face, everyone knows that and so does Mary but she can't stop. People at work notice. Her friends tell her John is a rat, a pig, a dog, he isn't good enough for her, but she can't believe it. Inside John, she thinks, is another John, who is much nicer. This other John will emerge like a butterfly from a cocoon, a Jack from a box, a pit from a prune, if the first John is only squeezed enough.

One evening John complains about the food. He has never complained about the food before. Mary is hurt.

Her friends tell her they've seen him in a restaurant with another woman, whose name is Madge. It's not even Madge that finally gets to Mary: it's the restaurant. John has never taken Mary to a restaurant. Mary collects all the sleeping pills and aspirins she can find, and takes them and a half a bottle of sherry. You can see what kind of a woman she is by the fact that it's not even whiskey. She leaves a note for John. She hopes he'll discover her and get her to the hospital in time and repent and then they can get married, but this fails to happen and she dies.

John marries Madge and everything continues as in A.

C. John, who is an older man, falls in love with Mary, and Mary, who is only 10 twenty-two, feels sorry for him because he's worried about his hair falling out. She sleeps with him even though she's not in love with him. She met him at work. She's in love with someone called James, who is twenty-two also and not yet ready to settle down.

John on the contrary settled down long ago: this is what is bothering him. John has a steady, respectable job and is getting ahead in his field, but Mary isn't impressed by him, she's impressed by James, who has a motorcycle and a fabulous record collection. But James is often away on his motorcycle, being free. Freedom isn't the same for girls, so in the meantime Mary spends Thursday evenings with John. Thursdays are the only days John can get away.

John is married to a woman called Madge and they have two children, a charming house which they bought just before the real estate values went up, and hobbies which they find stimulating and challenging, when they have the time. John tells Mary how important she is to him, but of course he can't leave his wife because a commitment is a commitment. He goes on about this more than is necessary and Mary finds it boring, but older men can keep it up longer so on the whole she has a fairly good time.

One day James breezes in on his motorcycle with some top-grade California hybrid and James and Mary get higher than you'd believe possible and they climb into bed. Everything becomes very underwater, but along comes John, who has a key to Mary's apartment. He finds them stoned and entwined. He's hardly in any position to be jealous, considering Madge, but nevertheless he's overcome with despair. Finally he's middle-aged, in two years he'll be bald as an egg and he can't stand it. He purchases a handgun, saying he needs it for target practice—this is the thin part of the plot, but it can be dealt with later—and shoots the two of them and himself.

Madge, after a suitable period of mourning, marries an understanding man called Fred and everything continues as in A, but under different names.

15   D. Fred and Madge have no problems. They get along exceptionally well and are good at working out any little difficulties that may arise. But their charming house is by the seashore and one day a giant tidal wave approaches. Real estate values go down. The rest of the story is about what caused the tidal wave and how they escape from it. They do, though thousands drown, but Fred and Madge are virtuous and lucky. Finally on high ground they clasp each other, wet and dripping and grateful, and continue as in A.

E. Yes, but Fred has a bad heart. The rest of the story is about how kind and understanding they both are until Fred dies. Then Madge devotes herself to charity work until the end of A. If you like, it can be "Madge," "cancer," "guilty and confused," and "bird watching."

F. If you think this is all too bourgeois, make John a revolutionary and Mary a counterespionage agent and see how far that gets you. Remember, this is Canada. You'll still end up with A, though in between you may get a lustful brawling saga of passionate involvement, a chronicle of our times, sort of.

You'll have to face it, the endings are the same however you slice it. Don't be deluded by any other endings, they're all fake, either deliberately fake, with malicious intent to deceive, or just motivated by excessive optimism if not by downright sentimentality.

The only authentic ending is the one provided here:

20   *John and Mary die. John and Mary die. John and Mary die.*

So much for endings. Beginnings are always more fun. True connoisseurs, however, are known to favor the stretch in between, since it's the hardest to do anything with.

That's about all that can be said for plots, which anyway are just one thing after another, a what and a what and a what.

Now try How and Why.

1983

JOHN CHEEVER

The Country Husband

To begin at the beginning, the airplane from Minneapolis in which Francis Weed was traveling East ran into heavy weather. The sky had been a hazy blue, with the clouds below the plane lying so close together that nothing could be seen of the earth. The mist began to form outside the windows, and they flew into a white cloud of such density that it reflected the exhaust fires. The color of the cloud darkened to gray, and the plane began to rock. Francis had been in heavy weather before, but he had never been shaken up so much. The man in the seat beside him pulled a flask out of his pocket and took a drink. Francis smiled at his neighbor, but the man looked away; he wasn't sharing his pain killer with anyone. The plane began to drop and flounder wildly. A child was crying. The air in the cabin was overheated and stale, and Francis' left foot went to sleep. He read a little from a paper book that he had bought at the airport, but the violence of the storm divided his attention. It was black outside the ports. The exhaust fires blazed and shed sparks in the dark, and, inside, the shaded lights, the stuffiness, and the window curtains gave the cabin an atmosphere of intense and misplaced domesticity. Then the light flickered and went out. "You know what I've always wanted to do?" the man beside Francis said suddenly. "I've always wanted to buy a farm in New Hampshire and raise beef cattle." The stewardess announced that they were going to make an emergency landing. All but the children saw in their minds the spreading wings of the Angel of Death. The pilot could be heard singing faintly, "I've got sixpence, jolly, jolly sixpence. I've got sixpence to last me all my life . . ."[1] There was no other sound.

The loud groaning of the hydraulic valves swallowed up the pilot's song, and there was a shrieking high in the air, like automobile brakes, and the plane hit flat on its belly in a cornfield and shook them so violently that an old man up forward howled, "Me kidneys! Me kidneys!" The stewardess flung open the door, and someone opened an emergency door at the back, letting in the sweet noise of their continuing mortality—the idle splash and smell of a heavy rain. Anxious for their lives, they filed out of the doors and scattered over the cornfield in all directions, praying that the thread would hold. It did. Nothing happened. When it was clear that the plane would not burn or explode, the crew and the stewardess gathered the passengers together and led them to the shelter of a barn. They were not far from Philadelphia, and in a little while a string of taxis took them into the city. "It's just like the Marne,"[2] someone said, but there was surprisingly little relaxation of that suspiciousness with which many Americans regard their fellow travelers.

In Philadelphia, Francis Weed got a train to New York. At the end of that journey, he crossed the city and caught just as it was about to pull out the com-

---

1. Song popular with Allied troops in World War II.   2. On September 8, 1914, over 1,000 Paris taxicabs were requisitioned to move troops to the Marne River to halt the encircling Germans.

muting train that he took five nights a week to his home in Shady Hill.

He sat with Trace Bearden. "You know, I was in that plane that just crashed outside Philadelphia," he said. "We came down in a field . . ." He had traveled faster than the newspapers or the rain, and the weather in New York was sunny and mild. It was a day in late September, as fragrant and shapely as an apple. Trace listened to the story, but how could he get excited? Francis had no powers that would let him re-create a brush with death—particularly in the atmosphere of a commuting train, journeying through a sunny countryside where already, in the slum gardens, there were signs of harvest. Trace picked up his newspaper, and Francis was left alone with his thoughts. He said good night to Trace on the platform at Shady Hill and drove in his secondhand Volkswagen up to the Blenhollow neighborhood, where he lived.

5   The Weeds' Dutch Colonial house was larger than it appeared to be from the driveway. The living room was spacious and divided like Gaul,[3] into three parts. Around an ell to the left as one entered from the vestibule was the long table, laid for six, with candles and a bowl of fruit in the center. The sounds and smells that came from the open kitchen door were appetizing, for Julia Weed was a good cook. The largest part of the living room centered on a fireplace. On the right were some bookshelves and a piano. The room was polished and tranquil, and from the windows that opened to the west there was some late-summer sunlight, brilliant and as clear as water. Nothing here was neglected; nothing had not been burnished. It was not the kind of household where, after prying open a stuck cigarette box, you would find an old shirt button and a tarnished nickel. The hearth was swept, the roses on the piano were reflected in the polish of the broad top, and there was an album of Schubert waltzes on the rack. Louisa Weed, a pretty girl of nine, was looking out the western windows. Her young brother Henry was standing beside her. Her still younger brother, Toby, was studying the figures of some tonsured monks drinking beer on the polished brass of the woodbox. Francis, taking off his hat and putting down his paper, was not consciously pleased with the scene; he was not that reflective. It was his element, his creation, and he returned to it with that sense of lightness and strength with which any creature returns to his home. "Hi, everybody," he said. "The plane from Minneapolis . . ."

Nine times out of ten, Francis would be greeted with affection, but tonight the children are absorbed in their own antagonisms. Francis had not finished his sentence about the plane crash before Henry plants a kick in Louisa's behind. Louisa swings around, saying, *"Damn you!"* Francis makes the mistake of scolding Louisa for bad language before he punishes Henry. Now Louisa turns on her father and accuses him of favoritism. Henry is always right; she is persecuted and lonely; her lot is hopeless. Francis turns to his son, but the son has justification for the kick—she hit him first; she hit him on the ear, which is dangerous. Louisa agrees with this passionately. She hit him on the ear, and she *meant* to hit him on the ear, because he messed up her china collection. Henry says that this is a lie. Little Toby turns away from the woodbox to throw in some evidence for

3. Ancient France (Gaul) is so described by Julius Caesar in *The Gallic War*.

Louisa. Henry claps his hand over little Toby's mouth. Francis separates the two boys but accidentally pushes Toby into the woodbox. Toby begins to cry. Louisa is already crying. Just then, Julia Weed comes into that part of the room where the table is laid. She is a pretty, intelligent woman, and the white in her hair is premature. She does not seem to notice the fracas. "Hello, darling," she says serenely to Francis. "Wash your hands, everyone. Dinner is ready." She strikes a match and lights the six candles in this vale of tears.[4]

This simple announcement, like the war cries of the Scottish chieftains, only refreshes the ferocity of the combatants. Louisa gives Henry a blow on the shoulder. Henry, although he seldom cries, has pitched nine innings and is tired. He bursts into tears. Little Toby discovers a splinter in his hand and begins to howl. Francis says loudly that he has been in a plane crash and that he is tired. Julia appears again from the kitchen and, still ignoring the chaos, asks Francis to go upstairs and tell Helen that everything is ready. Francis is happy to go; it is like getting back to headquarters company.[5] He is planning to tell his oldest daughter about the airplane crash, but Helen is lying on her bed reading a *True Romance* magazine, and the first thing Francis does is to take the magazine from her hand and remind Helen that he has forbidden her to buy it. She did not buy it, Helen replies. It was given to her by her best friend, Bessie Black. Everybody reads *True Romance*. Bessie Black's father reads *True Romance*. There isn't a girl in Helen's class who doesn't read *True Romance*. Francis expresses his detestation of the magazine and then tells her that dinner is ready—although from the sounds downstairs it doesn't seem so. Helen follows him down the stairs. Julia has seated herself in the candlelight and spread a napkin over her lap. Neither Louisa nor Henry has come to the table. Little Toby is still howling, lying face down on the floor. Francis speaks to him gently: "Daddy was in a plane crash this afternoon, Toby. Don't you want to hear about it?" Toby goes on crying. "If you don't come to the table now, Toby," Francis says, "I'll have to send you to bed without any supper." The little boy rises, gives him a cutting look, flies up the stairs to his bedroom, and slams the door. "Oh, dear," Julia says, and starts to go after him. Francis says that she will spoil him. Julia says that Toby is ten pounds underweight and has to be encouraged to eat. Winter is coming, and he will spend the cold months in bed unless he has his dinner. Julia goes upstairs. Francis sits down at the table with Helen. Helen is suffering from the dismal feeling of having read too intently on a fine day, and she gives her father and the room a jaded look. She doesn't understand about the plane crash, because there wasn't a drop of rain in Shady Hill.

Julia returns with Toby, and they all sit down and are served. "Do I have to look at that big, fat slob?" Henry says, of Louisa. Everybody but Toby enters into this skirmish, and it rages up and down the table for five minutes. Toward the end, Henry puts his napkin over his head and, trying to eat that way, spills spinach all over his shirt. Francis asks Julia if the children couldn't have their dinner earlier. Julia's guns are loaded for this. She can't cook two dinners and lay two

4. Common figurative reference to earthly life (vale is valley), though here the tears are literal.
5. That is, like escaping from combat to relative safety behind the lines.

tables. She paints with lightning strokes that panorama of drudgery in which her youth, her beauty, and her wit have been lost. Francis says that he must be understood; he was nearly killed in an airplane crash, and he doesn't like to come home every night to a battlefield. Now Julia is deeply concerned. Her voice trembles. He doesn't come home every night to a battlefield. The accusation is stupid and mean. Everything was tranquil until he arrived. She stops speaking, puts down her knife and fork, and looks into her plate as if it is a gulf. She begins to cry. "Poor Mummy!" Toby says, and when Julia gets up from the table, drying her tears with a napkin, Toby goes to her side. "Poor Mummy," he says. "Poor Mummy!" And they climb the stairs together. The other children drift away from the battlefield, and Francis goes into the back garden for a cigarette and some air.

It was a pleasant garden, with walks and flower beds and places to sit. The sunset had nearly burned out, but there was still plenty of light. Put into a thoughtful mood by the crash and the battle, Francis listened to the evening sounds of Shady Hill. "Varmints! Rascals!" old Mr. Nixon shouted to the squirrels in his bird-feeding station. "Avaunt and quit my sight!" A door slammed. Someone was cutting grass. Then Donald Goslin, who lived at the corner, began to play the "Moonlight Sonata."[6] He did this nearly every night. He threw the tempo out the window and played it *rubato*[7] from beginning to end, like an outpouring of tearful petulance, lonesomeness, and self-pity—of everything it was Beethoven's greatness not to know. The music rang up and down the street beneath the trees like an appeal for love, for tenderness, aimed at some lovely housemaid—some fresh-faced, homesick girl from Galway, looking at old snapshots in her third-floor room. "Here, Jupiter, here, Jupiter," Francis called to the Mercers' retriever. Jupiter crashed through the tomato vines with the remains of a felt hat in his mouth.

10   Jupiter was an anomaly. His retrieving instincts and his high spirits were out of place in Shady Hill. He was as black as coal, with a long, alert, intelligent, rakehell face. His eyes gleamed with mischief, and he held his head high. It was the fierce, heavily collared dog's head that appears in heraldry, in tapestry, and that used to appear on umbrella handles and walking sticks. Jupiter went where he pleased, ransacking wastebaskets, clotheslines, garbage pails, and shoe bags. He broke up garden parties and tennis matches, and got mixed up in the processional at Christ Church on Sunday, barking at the men in red dresses.[8] He crashed through old Mr. Nixon's rose garden two or three times a day, cutting a wide swath through the Condesa de Sastagos,[9] and as soon as Donald Goslin lighted his barbecue fire on Thursday nights, Jupiter would get the scent. Nothing the Goslins did could drive him away. Sticks and stones and rude commands only moved him to the edge of the terrace, where he remained, with his gallant and heraldic muzzle, waiting for Donald Goslin to turn his back and reach for the salt. Then he would spring onto the terrace, lift the steak lightly off the fire,

6. Beethoven's Sonata no. 14, a famous and frequently sentimentalized piano composition.   7. With intentional deviations from strict tempo.   8. Probably the choir.   9. Uncommon yellow and red roses, difficult to grow.

and run away with the Goslins' dinner. Jupiter's days were numbered. The Wrightsons' German gardener or the Farquarsons' cook would soon poison him. Even old Mr. Nixon might put some arsenic in the garbage that Jupiter loved. "Here, Jupiter, Jupiter!" Francis called, but the dog pranced off, shaking the hat in his white teeth. Looking at the windows of his house, Francis saw that Julia had come down and was blowing out the candles.

Julia and Francis Weed went out a great deal. Julia was well liked and gregarious, and her love of parties sprang from a most natural dread of chaos and loneliness. She went through the morning mail with real anxiety, looking for invitations, and she usually found some, but she was insatiable, and if she had gone out seven nights a week, it would not have cured her of a reflective look—the look of someone who hears distant music—for she would always suppose that there was a more brilliant party somewhere else. Francis limited her to two week-night parties, putting a flexible interpretation on Friday, and rode through the weekend like a dory in a gale. The day after the airplane crash, the Weeds were to have dinner with the Farquarsons.

Francis got home late from town, and Julia got the sitter while he dressed, and then hurried him out of the house. The party was small and pleasant, and Francis settled down to enjoy himself. A new maid passed the drinks. Her hair was dark, and her face was round and pale and seemed familiar to Francis. He had not developed his memory as a sentimental faculty. Wood smoke, lilac, and other such perfumes did not stir him, and his memory was something like his appendix—a vestigial repository. It was not his limitation at all to be unable to escape the past; it was perhaps his limitation that he had escaped it so successfully. He might have seen the maid at other parties, he might have seen her taking a walk on Sunday afternoons, but in either case he would not be searching his memory now. Her face was, in a wonderful way, a moon face—Norman or Irish—but it was not beautiful enough to account for his feeling that he had seen her before, in circumstances that he ought to be able to remember. He asked Nellie Farquarson who she was. Nellie said that the maid had come through an agency, and that her home was Trénon, in Normandy—a small place with a church and a restaurant that Nellie had once visited. While Nellie talked on about her travels abroad, Francis realized where he had seen the woman before. It had been at the end of the war. He had left a replacement depot with some other men and taken a three-day pass in Trénon. On their second day, they had walked out to a crossroads to see the public chastisement of a young woman who had lived with the German commandant during the Occupation.

It was a cool morning in the fall. The sky was overcast, and poured down onto the dirt crossroads a very discouraging light. They were on high land and could see how like one another the shapes of the clouds and the hills were as they stretched off toward the sea. The prisoner arrived sitting on a three-legged stool in a farm cart. She stood by the cart while the Mayor read the accusation and the sentence. Her head was bent and her face was set in that empty half smile behind which the whipped soul is suspended. When the Mayor was finished, she undid her hair and let it fall across her back. A little man with a gray mustache cut off her hair with shears and dropped it on the ground. Then, with a bowl of soapy water and a straight razor, he shaved her skull clean. A woman approached and began to undo the fastenings of her clothes, but the prisoner pushed her aside and undressed herself. When she pulled her chemise over her head and threw it on the ground, she was naked. The women jeered; the men were still. There was no change in the falseness or the plaintiveness of the prisoner's smile. The cold wind made her white skin rough and hardened the nipples of her breasts. The jeering ended gradually, put down by the recognition of their common humanity. One woman spat on her, but some inviolable grandeur in her nakedness lasted through the ordeal. When the crowd was quiet, she turned—she had begun to cry—and, with nothing on but a pair of worn black shoes and stockings, walked down the dirt road alone away from the village. The round white face had aged a little, but there was no question but that the maid who passed his cocktails and later served Francis his dinner was the woman who had been punished at the crossroads.

The war seemed now so distant and that world where the cost of partisanship had been death or torture so long ago. Francis had lost track of the men who had been with him in Vésey. He could not count on Julia's discretion. He could not tell anyone. And if he had told the story now, at the dinner table, it would have been a social as well as a human error. The people in the Farquarsons' living room seemed united in their tacit claim that there had been no past, no war— that there was no danger or trouble in the world. In the recorded history of human arrangements, this extraordinary meeting would have fallen into place, but the atmosphere of Shady Hill made the memory unseemly and impolite. The prisoner withdrew after passing the coffee, but the encounter left Francis feeling languid; it had opened his memory and his senses, and left them dilated. Julia went into the house. Francis stayed in the car to take the sitter home.

15   Expecting to see Mrs. Henlein, the old lady who usually stayed with the children, he was surprised when a young girl opened the door and came out onto the lighted stoop. She stayed in the light to count her textbooks. She was frowning and beautiful. Now, the world is full of beautiful young girls, but Francis saw here the difference between beauty and perfection. All those endearing flaws, moles, birthmarks, and healed wounds were missing, and he experienced in his consciousness that moment when music breaks glass, and felt a pang of recognition as strange, deep and wonderful as anything in his life. It hung from her frown, from an impalpable darkness in her face—a look that impressed him as a direct appeal for love. When she had counted her books, she came down the steps and opened the car door. In the light, he saw that her cheeks were wet. She got in and shut the door.

"You're new," Francis said.

"Yes. Mrs. Henlein is sick. I'm Anne Murchison."

"Did the children give you any trouble?"

"Oh, no, no." She turned and smiled at him unhappily in the dim dashboard light. Her light hair caught on the collar of her jacket, and she shook her head to set it loose.

20   "You've been crying."

"Yes."

"I hope it was nothing that happened in our house."

"No, no, it was nothing that happened in your house." Her voice was bleak. "It's no secret. Everybody in the village knows. Daddy's an alcoholic, and he just called me from some saloon and gave me a piece of his mind. He thinks I'm immoral. He called just before Mrs. Weed came back."

"I'm sorry."

"Oh, *Lord!*" She gasped and began to cry. She turned toward Francis, and he took her in his arms and let her cry on his shoulder. She shook in his embrace, and this movement accentuated his sense of the fineness of her flesh and bone. The layers of their clothing felt thin, and when her shuddering began to diminish, it was so much like a paroxysm of love that Francis lost his head and pulled her roughly against him. She drew away. "I live on Belleview Avenue," she said. "You go down Lansing Street to the railroad bridge."

"All right." He started the car.

"You turn left at that traffic light. . . . Now you turn right here and go straight on toward the tracks."

The road Francis took brought him out of his own neighborhood, across the tracks, and toward the river, to a street where the near-poor lived, in houses whose peaked gables and trimmings of wooden lace conveyed the purest feelings of pride and romance, although the houses themselves could not have offered much privacy or comfort, they were all so small. The street was dark, and, stirred by the grace and beauty of the troubled girl, he seemed, in turning into it, to have come into the deepest part of some submerged memory. In the distance, he saw a porch light burning. It was the only one, and she said that the house with the light was where she lived. When he stopped the car, he could see beyond the porch light into a dimly lighted hallway with an old-fashioned clothes tree. "Well, here we are," he said, conscious that a young man would have said something different.

She did not move her hands from the books, where they were folded, and she turned and faced him. There were tears of lust in his eyes. Determinedly—not sadly—he opened the door on his side and walked around to open hers. He took her free hand, letting his fingers in between hers, climbed at her side the two concrete steps, and went up a narrow walk through a front garden where dahlias, marigolds, and roses—things that had withstood the light frosts—still bloomed, and made a bittersweet smell in the night air. At the steps, she freed her hand and then turned and kissed him swiftly. Then she crossed the porch and shut the door. The porch light went out, then the light in the hall. A second later, a light went on upstairs at the side of the house, shining into a tree that was still covered with leaves. It took her only a few minutes to undress and get into bed, and then the house was dark.

Julia was asleep when Francis got home. He opened a second window and got into bed to shut his eyes on that night, but as soon as they were shut—as soon as he had dropped off to sleep—the girl entered his mind, moving with perfect freedom through its shut doors and filling chamber after chamber with her light, her perfume, and the music of her voice. He was crossing the Atlantic with her on the old *Mauretania*[1] and, later, living with her in Paris. When he woke from his dream, he got up and smoked a cigarette at the open window. Getting back into bed, he cast around in his mind for something he desired to do that would injure no one, and he thought of skiing. Up through the dimness in his mind rose the image of a mountain deep in snow. It was late in the day. Wherever his eyes looked, he saw broad and heartening things. Over his shoulder, there was a snow-filled valley, rising into wooded hills where the trees dimmed the whiteness like a sparse coat of hair. The cold deadened all sound but the loud, iron clanking of the lift machinery. The light on the trails was blue, and it was harder than it had been a minute or two earlier to pick the turns, harder to judge—now that the snow was all deep blue—the crust, the ice, the bare spots, and the deep piles of dry powder. Down the mountain he swung, matching his speed against the contours of a slope that had been formed in the first ice age, seeking with ardor some simplicity of feeling and circumstance. Night fell then, and he drank a Martini with some old friend in a dirty country bar.

In the morning, Francis' snow-covered mountain was gone, and he was left with his vivid memories of Paris and the *Mauretania*. He had been bitten gravely. He washed his body, shaved his jaws, drank his coffee, and missed the seventy-thirty-one. The train pulled out just as he brought his car to the station, and the longing he felt for the coaches as they drew stubbornly away from him reminded him of the humors of love. He waited for the eight-two, on what was now an empty platform. It was a clear morning; the morning seemed thrown like a gleaming bridge of light over his mixed affairs. His spirits were feverish and high. The image of the girl seemed to put him into a relationship to the world that was mysterious and enthralling. Cars were beginning to fill up the parking lot, and he noticed that those that had driven down from the high land above Shady Hill were white with hoarfrost. This first clear sign of autumn thrilled him. An express train—a night train from Buffalo or Albany—came down the tracks between the platforms, and he saw that the roofs of the foremost cars were covered with a skin of ice. Struck by the miraculous physicalness of everything, he smiled at the passengers in the dining car, who could be seen eating eggs and wiping their mouths with napkins as they traveled. The sleeping-car compartments, with their soiled bed linen, trailed through the fresh morning like a string of rooming-house windows. Then he saw an extraordinary thing; at one of the bedroom windows sat an unclothed woman of exceptional beauty, combing her golden hair. She passed like an apparition through Shady Hill, combing and combing her hair, and Francis followed her with his eyes until she was out of sight. Then old Mrs. Wrightson joined him on the platform and began to talk.

"Well, I guess you must be surprised to see me here the third morning in a row," she said, "but because of my window curtains I'm becoming a regular commuter. The curtains I bought on Monday I returned on Tuesday, and the curtains I bought Tuesday I'm returning today. On Monday, I got exactly what I

1. The original *Mauretania* (1907–1935), sister ship of the *Lusitania,* which was sunk by the Germans in 1915, was the most famous transatlantic liner of its day.

wanted—it's a wool tapestry with roses and birds—but when I got them home, I found they were the wrong length. Well, I exchanged them yesterday, and when I got them home, I found they were still the wrong length. Now I'm praying to high heaven that the decorator will have them in the right length, because you know my house, you *know* my living-room windows, and you can imagine what a problem they present. I don't know what to do with them."

"I know what to do with them," Francis said.

"What?"

"Paint them black on the inside, and shut up." 35

There was a gasp from Mrs. Wrightson, and Francis looked down at her to be sure that she knew he meant to be rude. She turned and walked away from him, so damaged in spirit that she limped. A wonderful feeling enveloped him, as if light were being shaken about him, and he thought again of Venus combing and combing her hair as she drifted through the Bronx. The realization of how many years had passed since he had enjoyed being deliberately impolite sobered him. Among his friends and neighbors, there were brilliant and gifted people—he saw that—but many of them, also, were bores and fools, and he had made the mistake of listening to them all with equal attention. He had confused a lack of discrimination with Christian love, and the confusion seemed general and destructive. He was grateful to the girl for this bracing sensation of independence. Birds were singing—cardinals and the last of the robins. The sky shone like enamel. Even the smell of ink from his morning paper honed his appetite for life, and the world that was spread out around him was plainly a paradise.

If Francis had believed in some hierarchy of love—in spirits armed with hunting bows, in the capriciousness of Venus and Eros[2]—or even in magical potions, philters, and stews, in scapulae and quarters of the moon,[3] it might have explained his susceptibility and his feverish high spirits. The autumnal loves of middle age are well publicized, and he guessed that he was face to face with one of these, but there was not a trace of autumn in what he felt. He wanted to sport in the green woods, scratch where he itched, and drink from the same cup.

His secretary, Miss Rainey, was late that morning—she went to a psychiatrist three mornings a week—and when she came in, Francis wondered what advice a psychiatrist would have for him. But the girl promised to bring back into his life something like the sound of music. The realization that this music might lead him straight to a trial for statutory rape at the country courthouse collapsed his happiness. The photograph of his four children laughing into the camera on the beach at Gay Head reproached him. On the letterhead of his firm there was a drawing of the Laocoön,[4] and the figure of the priest and his sons in the coils of the snake appeared to him to have the deepest meaning.

He had lunch with Pinky Trabert. At a conversational level, the mores of his

2. Roman name for the goddess of love (Greek: *Aphrodite*) and Greek name for her son (Roman: *Cupid*).
3. Love-inducing and predictive magic. *Scapulae:* shoulderblades or bones of the back.   4. Famous Greek statue, described here, now in the Vatican museum; the "meaning" for Weed seems to reside in the physical struggle, not in the legend (in which the priest and his sons were punished for warning the Trojans about the wooden horse).

friends were robust and elastic, but he knew that the moral card house would come down on them all—on Julia and the children as well—if he got caught taking advantage of a baby-sitter. Looking back over the recent history of Shady Hill for some precedent, he found there was none. There was no turpitude; there had not been a divorce since he lived there; there had not even been a breath of scandal. Things seemed arranged with more propriety even than in the Kingdom of Heaven. After leaving Pinky, Francis went to a jeweler's and bought the girl a bracelet. How happy this clandestine purchase made him, how stuffy and comical the jeweler's clerks seemed, how sweet the women who passed at his back smelled! On Fifth Avenue, passing Atlas with his shoulders bent under the weight of the world,[5] Francis thought of the strenuousness of containing his physicalness within the patterns he had chosen.

He did not know when he would see the girl next. He had the bracelet in his inside pocket when he got home. Opening the door of his house, he found her in the hall. Her back was to him, and she turned when she heard the door close. Her smile was open and loving. Her perfection stunned him like a fine day—a day after a thunderstorm. He seized her and covered her lips with his, and she struggled but she did not have to struggle for long, because just then little Gertrude Flannery appeared from somewhere and said, "Oh, Mr. Weed . . ."

Gertrude was a stray. She had been born with a taste for exploration, and she did not have it in her to center her life with her affectionate parents. People who did not know the Flannerys concluded from Gertrude's behavior that she was the child of a bitterly divided family, where drunken quarrels were the rule. This was not true. The fact that little Gertrude's clothing was ragged and thin was her own triumph over her mother's struggle to dress her warmly and neatly. Garrulous, skinny, and unwashed, she drifted from house to house around the Blenhollow neighborhood, forming and breaking alliances based on an attachment to babies, animals, children her own age, adolescents, and sometimes adults. Opening your front door in the morning, you would find Gertrude sitting on your stoop. Going into the bathroom to shave, you would find Gertrude using the toilet. Looking into your son's crib, you would find it empty, and, looking further, you would find that Gertrude had pushed him in his baby carriage into the next village. She was helpful, pervasive, honest, hungry, and loyal. She never went home of her own choice. When the time to go arrived, she was indifferent to all its signs. "Go home, Gertrude," people could be heard saying in one house or another, night after night. "Go home, Gertrude. It's time for you to go home now, Gertrude." "You had better go home and get your supper, Gertrude." "I told you to go home twenty minutes ago, Gertrude." "Your mother will be worrying about you, Gertrude." "Go home, Gertrude, go home."

There are times when the lines around the human eye seem like shelves of eroded stone and when the staring eye itself strikes us with such a wilderness of animal feeling that we are at a loss. The look Francis gave the little girl was ugly and queer, and it frightened her. He reached into his pockets—his hands were

5. In Greek legend the Titan Atlas supported the heavens on his shoulders but has come to be depicted as bearing the globe; the statue is at Rockefeller Center.

shaking—and took out a quarter. "Go home, Gertrude, go home, and don't tell anyone, Gertrude. Don't—" He choked and ran into the living room as Julia called down to him from upstairs to hurry and dress.

The thought that he would drive Anne Murchison home later that night ran like a golden thread through the events of the party that Francis and Julia went to, and he laughed uproariously at dull jokes, dried a tear when Mabel Mercer told him about the death of her kitten, and stretched, yawned, sighed, and grunted like any other man with a rendezvous at the back of his mind. The bracelet was in his pocket. As he sat talking, the smell of grass was in his nose, and he was wondering where he would park the car. Nobody lived in the old Parker mansion, and the driveway was used as a lovers' lane. Townsend Street was a dead end, and he could park there, beyond the last house. The old lane that used to connect Elm Street to the riverbanks was overgrown, but he had walked there with his children, and he could drive his car deep enough into the brushwoods to be concealed.

The Weeds were the last to leave the party, and their host and hostess spoke of their own married happiness while they all four stood in the hallway saying good night. "She's my girl," their host said, squeezing his wife. "She's my blue sky. After sixteen years, I still bite her shoulders. She makes me feel like Hannibal crossing the Alps."[6]

The Weeds drove home in silence. Francis brought the car up the driveway   45
and sat still, with the motor running. "You can put the car in the garage," Julia said as she got out. "I told the Murchison girl she could leave at eleven. Someone drove her home." She shut the door, and Francis sat in the dark. He would be spared nothing then, it seemed, that a fool was not spared: ravening lewdness, jealousy, this hurt to his feelings that put tears in his eyes, even scorn—for he could see clearly the image he now presented, his arms spread over the steering wheel and his head buried in them for love.

Francis had been a dedicated Boy Scout when he was young, and, remembering the precepts of his youth, he left his office early the next afternoon and played some round-robin squash, but, with his body toned up by exercise and a shower, he realized that he might better have stayed at his desk. It was a frosty night when he got home. The air smelled sharply of change. When he stepped into the house, he sensed an unusual stir. The children were in their best clothes, and when Julia came down, she was wearing a lavender dress and her diamond sunburst. She explained the stir: Mr. Hubber was coming at seven to take their photograph for the Christmas card. She had put out Francis' blue suit and a tie with some color in it, because the picture was going to be in color this year. Julia was lighthearted at the thought of being photographed for Christmas. It was the kind of ceremony she enjoyed.

Francis went upstairs to change his clothes. He was tired from the day's work and tired with longing, and sitting on the edge of the bed had the effect of deep-

6. The Carthaginian general (274–183 B.C.) attacked the Romans from the rear by crossing the Alps, considered impregnable, with the use of elephants.

ening his weariness. He thought of Anne Murchison, and the physical need to express himself, instead of being restrained by the pink lamps of Julia's dressing table, engulfed him. He went to Julia's desk, took a piece of writing paper, and began to write on it. "Dear Anne, I love you, I love you, I love you . . ." No one would see the letter, and he used no restraint. He used phrases like "heavenly bliss," and "love nest." He salivated, sighed, and trembled. When Julia called him to come down, the abyss between his fantasy and the practical world opened so wide that he felt it affected the muscles of his heart.

Julia and the children were on the stoop, and the photographer and his assistant had set up a double battery of floodlights to show the family and the architectural beauty of the entrance to their house. People who had come home on a late train slowed their cars to see the Weeds being photographed for their Christmas card. A few waved and called to the family. It took half an hour of smiling and wetting their lips before Mr. Hubber was satisfied. The heat of the lights made an unfresh smell in the frosty air, and when they were turned off, they lingered on the retina of Francis' eyes.

Later that night, while Francis and Julia were drinking their coffee in the living room, the doorbell rang. Julia answered the door and let in Clayton Thomas. He had come to pay for some theatre tickets that she had given his mother some time ago, and that Helen Thomas had scrupulously insisted on paying for, though Julia had asked her not to. Julia invited him in to have a cup of coffee. "I won't have any coffee," Clayton said, "but I will come in for a minute." He followed her into the living room, said good evening to Francis, and sat awkwardly in a chair.

50   Clayton's father had been killed in the war, and the young man's fatherlessness surrounded him like an element. This may have been conspicuous in Shady Hill because the Thomases were the only family that lacked a piece; all the other marriages were intact and productive. Clayton was in his second or third year of college, and he and his mother lived alone in a large house, which she hoped to sell. Clayton had once made some trouble. Years ago, he had stolen some money and run away; he had got to California before they caught up with him. He was tall and homely, wore hornrimmed glasses, and spoke in a deep voice.

"When do you go back to college, Clayton?" Francis asked.

"I'm not going back," Clayton said. "Mother doesn't have the money, and there's no sense in all this pretense. I'm going to get a job, and if we sell the house, we'll take an apartment in New York."

"Won't you miss Shady Hill?" Julia asked.

"No," Clayton said. "I don't like it."

55   "Why not?" Francis asked.

"Well, there's a lot here I don't approve of," Clayton said gravely. "Things like the club dances. Last Saturday night, I looked in toward the end and saw Mr. Granner trying to put Mrs. Minot into the trophy case. They were both drunk. I disapprove of so much drinking."

"It was Saturday night," Francis said.

"And all the dovecotes are phony," Clayton said. "And the way people clutter up their lives. I've thought about it a lot, and what seems to me to be really wrong with Shady Hill is that it doesn't have any future. So much energy is spent in perpetuating the place—in keeping out undesirables, and so forth—that the only idea of the future anyone has is just more and more commuting trains and more parties. I don't think that's healthy. I think people ought to be able to dream big dreams about the future. I think people ought to be able to dream great dreams."

"It's too bad you couldn't continue with college," Julia said.

"I want to go to divinity school," Clayton said.   60

"What's your church?" Francis asked.

"Unitarian, Theosophist, Transcendentalist, Humanist,"[7] Clayton said.

"Wasn't Emerson a transcendentalist?" Julia asked.

"I mean the English transcendentalists," Clayton said. "All the American transcendentalists were goops."

"What kind of job do you expect to get?" Francis asked.   65

"Well, I'd like to work for a publisher," Clayton said, "but everyone tells me there's nothing doing. But it's the kind of thing I'm interested in. I'm writing a long verse play about good and evil. Uncle Charlie might get me into a bank, and that would be good for me. I need the discipline. I have a long way to go in forming my character. I have some terrible habits. I talk too much. I think I ought to take vows of silence. I ought to try not to speak for a week, and discipline myself. I've thought of making a retreat at one of the Episcopalian monasteries, but I don't like Trinitarianism."

"Do you have any girl friends?" Francis asked.

"I'm engaged to be married," Clayton said. "Of course, I'm not old enough or rich enough to have my engagement observed or respected or anything, but I bought a simulated emerald for Anne Murchison with the money I made cutting lawns this summer. We're going to be married as soon as she finishes school."

Francis recoiled at the mention of the girl's name. Then a dingy light seemed to emanate from his spirit, showing everything—Julia, the boy, the chairs—in their true colorlessness. It was like a bitter turn of the weather.

"We're going to have a large family," Clayton said. "Her father's a terrible   70
rummy, and I've had my hard times, and we want to have lots of children. Oh, she's wonderful, Mr. and Mrs. Weed, and we have so much in common. We like all the same things. We sent out the same Christmas card last year without planning it, and we both have an allergy to tomatoes, and our eyebrows grow together in the middle. Well, goodnight."

Julia went to the door with him. When she returned, Francis said that Clayton was lazy, irresponsible, affected, and smelly. Julia said that Francis seemed to be getting intolerant; the Thomas boy was young and should be given a chance.

---

7. All are deviations from orthodox Christianity and tend to be more man- than God-oriented, though their differences hardly seem reconcilable; the American transcendentalists (see below) tended to change the emphasis from the study of thought to belief in "intuition."

Julia had noticed other cases where Francis had been short-tempered. "Mrs. Wrightson has asked everyone in Shady Hill to her anniversary party but us," she said.

"I'm sorry, Julia."

"Do you know why they didn't ask us?"

"Why?"

75   "Because you insulted Mrs. Wrightson."

"Then you know about it?"

"June Masterson told me. She was standing behind you."

Julia walked in front of the sofa with a small step that expressed, Francis knew, a feeling of anger.

"I did insult Mrs. Wrightson, Julia, and I meant to. I've never liked her parties, and I'm glad she's dropped us."

80   "What about Helen?"

"How does Helen come into this?"

"Mrs. Wrightson's the one who decides who goes to the assemblies."

"You mean she can keep Helen from going to the dances?"

"Yes."

85   "I hadn't thought of that."

"Oh. I knew you hadn't thought of it," Julia cried, thrusting hiltdeep into this chink of his armor. "And it makes me furious to see this kind of stupid thoughtlessness wreck everyone's happiness."

"I don't think I've wrecked anyone's happiness."

"Mrs. Wrightson runs Shady Hill and has run it for the last forty years. I don't know what makes you think that in a community like this you can indulge every impulse you have to be insulting, vulgar, and offensive."

"I have very good manners," Francis said, trying to give the evening a turn toward the light.

90   "Damn you, Francis Weed!" Julia cried, and the spit of her words struck him in the face. "I've worked hard for the social position we enjoy in this place, and I won't stand by and see you wreck it. You must have understood when you settled here that you couldn't expect to live like a bear in a cave."

"I've got to express my likes and dislikes."

"You can conceal your dislikes. You don't have to meet everything head on, like a child. Unless you're anxious to be a social leper. It's no accident that we get asked out a great deal! It's no accident that Helen has so many friends. How would you like to spend your Saturday nights at the movies? How would you like to spend your Sunday raking up dead leaves? How would you like it if your daughter spent the assembly nights sitting at her window, listening to the music from the club? How would you like it—" He did something then that was, after all, not so unaccountable, since her words seemed to raise up between them a wall so deadening that he gagged. He struck her full in the face. She staggered and then, a moment later, seemed composed. She went up the stairs to their room. She didn't slam the door. When Francis followed, a few minutes later, he found her packing a suitcase.

"Julia, I'm very sorry."

"It doesn't matter," she said. She was crying.

"Where do you think you're going?"   95

"I don't know. I just looked at a timetable. There's an eleven-sixteen into New York. I'll take that."

"You can't go, Julia."

"I can't stay. I know that."

"I'm sorry about Mrs. Wrightson, Julia, and I'm—"

"It doesn't matter about Mrs. Wrightson. That isn't the trouble."   100

"What is the trouble?"

"You don't love me."

"I do love you, Julia."

"No, you don't."

"Julia, I do love you, and I would like to be as we were—sweet and bawdy and   105
dark—but now there are so many people."

"You hate me."

"I don't hate you, Julia."

"You have no idea of how much you hate me. I think it's subconscious. You don't realize the cruel things you've done."

"What cruel things, Julia?"

"The cruel acts your subconscious drives you to in order to express your hatred   110
of me."

"What, Julia?"

"I've never complained."

"Tell me."

"You don't know what you're doing."

"Tell me."   115

"Your clothes."

"What do you mean?"

"I mean the way you leave your dirty clothes around in order to express your subconscious hatred of me."

"I don't understand."

"I mean your dirty socks and your dirty pajamas and your dirty underwear   120
and your dirty shirts!" She rose from kneeling by the suitcase and faced him, her eyes blazing and her voice ringing with emotion. "I'm talking about the fact that you've never learned to hang up anything. You just leave your clothes all over the floor where they drop, in order to humiliate me. You do it on purpose!" She fell on the bed, sobbing.

"Julia, darling!" he said, but when she felt his hand on her shoulder she got up.

"Leave me alone," she said. "I have to go." She brushed past him to the closet and came back with a dress. "I'm not taking any of the things you've given me," she said. "I'm leaving my pearls and the fur jacket."

"Oh, Julia!" Her figure, so helpless in its self-deceptions, bent over the suitcase made him nearly sick with pity. She did not understand how desolate her life would be without him. She didn't understand the hours that working women have to keep. She didn't understand that most of her friendships existed within the framework of their marriage, and that without this she would find herself alone. She didn't understand about travel, about hotels, about money. "Julia, I can't let you go! What you don't understand, Julia, is that you've come to be dependent on me."

She tossed her head back and covered her face with her hands. "Did you say that *I* was dependent on *you?*" she asked. "Is that what you said? And who is it that tells you what time to get up in the morning and when to go to bed at night? Who is it that prepares your meals and picks up your dirty clothes and invites your friends to dinner? If it weren't for me, your neckties would be greasy and your clothing would be full of moth holes. You were alone when I met you, Francis Weed, and you'll be alone when I leave. When Mother asked you for a list to send out invitations to our wedding, how many names did you have to give her? Fourteen!"

125   "Cleveland wasn't my home, Julia."

"And how many of your friends came to the church? Two!"

"Cleveland wasn't my home, Julia."

"Since I'm not taking the fur jacket," she said quietly, "you'd better put it back into storage. There's an insurance policy on the pearls that comes due in January. The name of the laundry and maid's telephone number—all those things are in my desk. I hope you won't drink too much, Francis. I hope that nothing bad will happen to you. If you do get into serious trouble, you can call me."

"Oh, my darling, I can't let you go!" Francis said. "I can't let you go, Julia!" He took her in his arms.

130   "I guess I'd better stay and take care of you for a little while longer," she said.

Riding to work in the morning, Francis saw the girl walk down the aisle of the coach. He was surprised; he hadn't realized that the school she went to was in the city, but she was carrying books, she seemed to be going to school. His surprise delayed his reaction, but then he got up clumsily and stepped into the aisle. Several people had come between them, but he could see her ahead of him, waiting for someone to open the car door, and then, as the train swerved, putting out her hand to support herself as she crossed the platform into the next car. He followed her through that car and halfway through another before calling her name—"Anne! Anne!"—but she didn't turn. He followed her into still another car, and she sat down in an aisle seat. Coming up to her, all his feelings warm and bent in her direction, he put his hand on the back of her seat—even this touch warmed him—and leaning down to speak to her, he saw that it was not Anne. It was an older woman wearing glasses. He went on deliberately into another car, his face red with embarrassment and the much deeper feeling of having his good sense challenged; for if he couldn't tell one person from another, what evidence was there that his life with Julia and the children had as much reality as his dreams of iniquity in Paris or the litter, the grass smell, and the cave-shaped trees in Lovers' Lane.

Late that afternoon, Julia called to remind Francis that they were going out for dinner. A few minutes later, Trace Bearden called. "Look, fellar," Trace said. "I'm calling for Mrs. Thomas. You know? Clayton, that boy of hers, doesn't seem able to get a job, and I wondered if you could help. If you'd call Charlie Bell—I know he's indebted to you—and say a good word for the kid, I think Charlie would—"

"Trace, I hate to say this," Francis said, "but I don't feel that I can do anything for that boy. The kid's worthless. I know it's a harsh thing to say, but it's a fact. Any kindness done for him would backfire in everybody's face. He's just a worthless kid, Trace, and there's nothing else to be done about it. Even if we got him a job, he wouldn't be able to keep it for a week. I know that to be a fact. It's an awful thing, Trace, and I know it is, but instead of recommending that kid, I'd feel obligated to warn people against him—people who knew his father and would naturally want to step in and do something. I'd feel obliged to warn them. He's a thief . . ."

The moment this conversation was finished, Miss Rainey came in and stood by his desk. "I'm not going to be able to work for you any more, Mr. Weed," she said. "I can stay until the seventeenth if you need me, but I've been offered a whirlwind of a job, and I'd like to leave as soon as possible."

She went out, leaving him to face alone the wickedness of what he had done to the Thomas boy. His children in their photograph laughed and laughed, glazed with all the bright colors of summer, and he remembered that they had met a bagpiper on the beach that day and he had paid the piper a dollar to play them a battle song of the Black Watch.[8] The girl would be at the house when he got home. He would spend another evening among his kind neighbors, picking and choosing dead-end streets, cart tracks, and the driveways of abandoned houses. There was nothing to mitigate his feeling—nothing that laughter or a game of softball with the children would change—and, thinking back over the plane crash, the Farquarsons' new maid, and Anne Murchison's difficulties with her drunken father, he wondered how he could have avoided arriving at just where he was. He was in trouble. He had been lost once in his life, coming back from a trout stream in the north woods, and he had now the same bleak realization that no amount of cheerfulness or hopefulness or valor or perseverance could help him find, in the gathering dark, the path that he'd lost. He smelled the forest. The feeling of bleakness was intolerable, and he saw clearly that he had reached the point where he would have to make a choice.

He could go to a psychiatrist, like Miss Rainey; he could go to church and confess his lusts; he could go to a Danish-massage parlor[9] in the West Seventies that had been recommended by a salesman; he could rape the girl or trust that he would somehow be prevented from doing this; or he could get drunk. It was his life, his boat, and, like every other man, he was made to be the father of thousands, and what harm could there be in a tryst that would make them both feel more kindly toward the world? This was the wrong train of thought, and he came back to the first, the psychiatrist. He had the telephone number of Miss Rainey's doctor, and he called and asked for an immediate appointment. He was insistent with the doctor's secretary—it was his manner in business—and when she said that the doctor's schedule was full for the next few weeks, Francis

8. Originally a British Highland regiment that became a line regiment and distinguished itself in battle.
9. Sometimes fronts for houses of prostitution.

demanded an appointment that day and was told to come at five.

The psychiatrist's office was in a building that was used mostly by doctors and dentists, and the hallways were filled with the candy smell of mouthwash and memories of pain. Francis' character had been formed upon a series of private resolves—resolves about cleanliness, about going off the high diving board or repeating any other feat that challenged his courage, about punctuality, honesty, and virtue. To abdicate the perfect loneliness in which he had made his most vital decisions shattered his concept of character and left him now in a condition that felt like shock. He was stupefied. The scene for his *miserere mei Deus*[1] was, like the waiting room of so many doctor's offices, a crude token gesture toward the sweets of domestic bliss: a place arranged with antiques, coffee tables, potted plants, and etchings of snow-covered bridges and geese in flight, although there were no children, no marriage bed, no stove, even, in this travesty of a house, where no one had ever spent the night and where the curtained windows looked straight onto a dark air shaft. Francis gave his name and address to a secretary and then saw, at the side of the room, a policeman moving toward him. "Hold it, hold it," the policeman said. "Don't move. Keep your hands where they are."

"I think it's all right, Officer," the secretary began. "I think it will be—"

"Let's make sure," the policeman said, and he began to slap Francis' clothes, looking for what—pistols, knives, an icepick? Finding nothing, he went off and the secretary began a nervous apology: "When you called on the telephone, Mr. Weed, you seemed very excited, and one of the doctor's patients has been threatening his life, and we have to be careful. If you want to go in now?" Francis pushed open a door connected to an electrical chime, and in the doctor's lair sat down heavily, blew his nose into a handkerchief, searched in his pockets for cigarettes, for matches, for something, and said hoarsely, with tears in his eyes, "I'm in love, Dr. Herzog."

140   It is a week or ten days later in Shady Hill. The seven-fourteen has come and gone, and here and there dinner is finished and the dishes are in the dish-washing machine. The village hangs, morally and economically, from a thread; but it hangs by its thread in the evening light. Donald Goslin has begun to worry the "Moonlight Sonata" again. *Marcato ma sempre pianissimo!*[2] He seems to be wringing out a wet bath towel, but the housemaid does not heed him. She is writing a letter to Arthur Godfrey.[3] In the cellar of his house, Francis Weed is building a coffee table. Dr. Herzog recommends woodwork as a therapy, and Francis finds some true consolation in the simple arithmetic involved and in the holy smell of new wood. Francis is happy. Upstairs, little Toby is crying, because he is tired. He puts off his cowboy hat, gloves, and fringed jacket, unbuckles the belt studded with gold and rubies, the silver bullets and holsters, slips off his suspenders, his checked shirt, and Levi's, and sits on the edge of his bed to pull off his high boots. Leaving this equipment in a heap, he goes to the closet and takes his space suit off a nail. It is a struggle for him to get into the long tights, but he succeeds.

---

1. "Have mercy upon me, O God"; first words of Psalm 51.   2. Stressed but always very softly.
3. At the time of the story, host of a daytime radio program especially popular with housewives.

He loops the magic cape over his shoulders and, climbing onto the footboard of his bed, he spreads his arms and flies the short distance to the floor, landing with a thump that is audible to everyone in the house but himself.

"Go home, Gertrude, go home," Mrs. Masterson says. "I told you to go home an hour ago, Gertrude. It's way past your suppertime, and your mother will be worried. Go home!" A door on the Babcocks' terrace flies open, and out comes Mrs. Babcock without any clothes on, pursued by a naked husband. (Their children are away at boarding school, and their terrace is screened by a hedge.) Over the terrace they go and in at the kitchen door, as passionate and handsome a nymph and satyr as you will find on any wall in Venice. Cutting the last of the roses in her garden, Julia hears old Mr. Nixon shouting at the squirrels in his bird-feeding station. "Rapscallions! Varmints! Avaunt and quit my sight!" A miserable cat wanders into the garden, sunk in spiritual and physical discomfort. Tied to its head is a small straw hat—a doll's hat—and it is securely buttoned into a doll's dress, from the skirts of which protrudes its long, hairy tail. As it walks, it shakes its feet, as if it had fallen into water.

"Here, pussy, pussy, pussy!" Julia calls.

"Here, pussy, here, poor pussy!" But the cat gives her a skeptical look and stumbles away in its skirts. The last to come is Jupiter. He prances through the tomato vines, holding in his generous mouth the remains of an evening slipper. Then it is dark; it is a night where kings in golden suits ride elephants over the mountains.[4]

1958

JAMES BALDWIN

Sonny's Blues

I read about it in the paper, in the subway, on my way to work. I read it, and I couldn't believe it, and I read it again. Then perhaps I just stared at it, at the newsprint spelling out his name, spelling out the story. I stared at it in the swinging lights of the subway car, and in the faces and bodies of the people, and in my own face, trapped in the darkness which roared outside.

It was not to be believed and I kept telling myself that, as I walked from the subway station to the high school. And at the same time I couldn't doubt it. I was scared, scared for Sonny. He became real to me again. A great block of ice got settled in my belly and kept melting there slowly all day long, while I taught my classes algebra. It was a special kind of ice. It kept melting, sending trickles of ice water all up and down my veins, but it never got less. Sometimes it hardened and

---

4. See Sinclair Lewis, *Main Street* (1920), in which the protagonist finds the small town of Gopher Prairie stifling and leaves with her son for Washington, D.C., where, she tells him, " 'We're going to find elephants with golden howdahs from which peep young maharanees with necklaces of rubies. . . .' "

seemed to expand until I felt my guts were going to come spilling out or that I was going to choke or scream. This would always be at a moment when I was remembering some specific thing Sonny had once said or done.

When he was about as old as the boys in my classes his face had been bright and open, there was a lot of copper in it; and he'd had wonderfully direct brown eyes, and great gentleness and privacy. I wondered what he looked like now. He had been picked up, the evening before, in a raid on an apartment downtown, for peddling and using heroin.

I couldn't believe it: but what I mean by that is that I couldn't find any room for it anywhere inside me. I had kept it outside me for a long time. I hadn't wanted to know. I had had suspicions, but I didn't name them, I kept putting them away. I told myself that Sonny was wild, but he wasn't crazy. And he'd always been a good boy, he hadn't ever turned hard or evil or disrespectful, the way kids can, so quick, so quick, especially in Harlem. I didn't want to believe that I'd ever see my brother going down, coming to nothing, all that light in his face gone out, in the condition I'd already seen so many others. Yet it had happened and here I was, talking about algebra to a lot of boys who might, every one of them for all I knew, be popping off needles every time they went to the head.[1] Maybe it did more for them than algebra could.

5   I was sure that the first time Sonny had ever had horse,[2] he couldn't have been much older than these boys were now. These boys, now, were living as we'd been living then, they were growing up with a rush and their heads bumped abruptly against the low ceiling of their actual possibilities. They were filled with rage. All they really knew were two darknesses, the darkness of their lives, which was now closing in on them, and the darkness of the movies, which had blinded them to that other darkness, and in which they now, vindictively, dreamed, at once more together than they were at any other time, and more alone.

When the last bell rang, the last class ended, I let out my breath. It seemed I'd been holding it for all that time. My clothes were wet—I may have looked as though I'd been sitting in a steam bath, all dressed up, all afternoon. I sat alone in the classroom a long time. I listened to the boys outside, downstairs, shouting and cursing and laughing. Their laughter struck me for perhaps the first time. It was not the joyous laughter which—God knows why—one associates with children. It was mocking and insular, its intent was to denigrate. It was disenchanted, and in this, also, lay the authority of their curses. Perhaps I was listening to them because I was thinking about my brother and in them I heard my brother. And myself.

One boy was whistling a tune, at once very complicated and very simple, it seemed to be pouring out of him as though he were a bird, and it sounded very cool and moving through all that harsh, bright air, only just holding its own through all those other sounds.

I stood up and walked over to the window and looked down into the courtyard. It was the beginning of the spring and the sap was rising in the boys. A teacher passed through them every now and again, quickly, as though he or she

---

1. Lavatory.   2. Heroin.

couldn't wait to get out of that courtyard, to get those boys out of their sight and off their minds. I started collecting my stuff. I thought I'd better get home and talk to Isabel.

The courtyard was almost deserted by the time I got downstairs. I saw this boy standing in the shadow of a doorway, looking just like Sonny. I almost called his name. Then I saw that it wasn't Sonny, but somebody we used to know, a boy from around our block. He'd been Sonny's friend. He'd never been mine, having been too young for me, and, anyway, I'd never liked him. And now, even though he was a grown-up man, he still hung around that block, still spent hours on the street corners, was always high and raggy. I used to run into him from time to time and he'd often work around to asking me for a quarter or fifty cents. He always had some real good excuse, too, and I always gave it to him. I don't know why.

But now, abruptly, I hated him. I couldn't stand the way he looked at me, partly like a dog, partly like a cunning child. I wanted to ask him what the hell he was doing in the school courtyard. 10

He sort of shuffled over to me, and he said, "I see you got the papers. So you already know about it."

"You mean about Sonny? Yes, I already know about it. How come they didn't get you?"

He grinned. It made him repulsive and it also brought to mind what he'd looked like as a kid. "I wasn't there. I stay away from them people."

"Good for you." I offered him a cigarette and I watched him through the smoke. "You come all the way down here just to tell me about Sonny?"

"That's right." He was sort of shaking his head and his eyes looked strange, as though they were about to cross. The bright sun deadened his damp dark brown skin and it made his eyes look yellow and showed up the dirt in his kinked hair. He smelled funky. I moved a little away from him and I said, "Well, thanks. But I already know about it and I got to get home." 15

"I'll walk you a little ways," he said. We started walking. There were a couple of kids still loitering in the courtyard and one of them said goodnight to me and looked strangely at the boy beside me.

"What're you going to do?" he asked me. "I mean, about Sonny?"

"Look. I haven't seen Sonny for over a year, I'm not sure I'm going to do anything. Anyway, what the hell *can* I do?"

"That's right," he said quickly, "ain't nothing you can do. Can't much help old Sonny no more, I guess."

It was what I was thinking and so it seemed to me he had no right to say it. 20

"I'm surprised at Sonny, though," he went on—he had a funny way of talking, he looked straight ahead as though he were talking to himself—"I thought Sonny was a smart boy, I thought he was too smart to get hung."

"I guess he thought so too," I said sharply, "and that's how he got hung. And how about you? You're pretty goddamn smart, I bet."

Then he looked directly at me, just for a minute. "I ain't smart," he said. "If I was smart, I'd have reached for a pistol a long time ago."

"Look. Don't tell *me* your sad story, if it was up to me, I'd give you one." Then

I felt guilty—guilty, probably, for never having supposed that the poor bastard *had* a story of his own, much less a sad one, and I asked, quickly, "What's going to happen to him now?"

25   He didn't answer this. He was off by himself some place.

"Funny thing," he said, and from his tone we might have been discussing the quickest way to get to Brooklyn, "when I saw the papers this morning, the first thing I asked myself was if I had anything to do with it. I felt sort of responsible."

I began to listen more carefully. The subway station was on the corner, just before us, and I stopped. He stopped, too. We were in front of a bar and he ducked slightly, peering in, but whoever he was looking for didn't seem to be there. The juke box was blasting away with something black and bouncy and I half watched the barmaid as she danced her way from the juke box to her place behind the bar. And I watched her face as she laughingly responded to something someone said to her, still keeping time to the music. When she smiled one saw the little girl, one sensed the doomed, still-struggling woman beneath the battered face of the semi-whore.

"I never *give* Sonny nothing," the boy said finally, "but a long time ago I come to school high and Sonny asked me how it felt." He paused, I couldn't bear to watch him, I watched the barmaid, and I listened to the music which seemed to be causing the pavement to shake. "I told him it felt great." The music stopped, the barmaid paused and watched the juke box until the music began again. "It did."

All this was carrying me some place I didn't want to go. I certainly didn't want to know how it felt. It filled everything, the people, the houses, the music, the dark, quicksilver barmaid, with menace; and this menace was their reality.

30   "What's going to happen to him now?" I asked again.

"They'll send him away some place and they'll try to cure him." He shook his head. "Maybe he'll even think he's kicked the habit. Then they'll let him loose"— he gestured, throwing his cigarette into the gutter. "That's all."

"What do you mean, that's *all?*"

But I knew what he meant.

"I *mean*, that's all." He turned his head and looked at me, pulling down the corners of his mouth. "Don't you know what I mean?" he asked, softly.

35   "How the hell *would* I know what you mean?" I almost whispered it, I don't know why.

"That's right," he said to the air, "how would *he* know what I mean?" He turned toward me again, patient and calm, and yet I somehow felt him shaking, shaking as though he were going to fall apart. I felt that ice in my guts again, the dread I'd felt all afternoon; and again I watched the barmaid, moving about the bar, washing glasses, and singing. "Listen. They'll let him out and then it'll just start all over again. That's what I mean."

"You mean—they'll let him out. And then he'll just start working his way back in again. You mean he'll never kick the habit. Is that what you mean?"

"That's right," he said, cheerfully. "*You* see what I mean."

"Tell me," I said at last, "why does he want to die? He must want to die, he's killing himself, why does he want to die?"

He looked at me in surprise. He licked his lips. "He don't want to die. He wants   40
to live. Don't nobody want to die, ever."

Then I wanted to ask him—too many things. He could not have answered, or
if he had, I could not have borne the answers. I started walking. "Well, I guess
it's none of my business."

"It's going to be rough on old Sonny," he said. We reached the subway station.
"This is your station?" he asked. I nodded. I took one step down. "Damn!" he
said, suddenly. I looked up at him. He grinned again. "Damn it if I didn't leave
all my money home. You ain't got a dollar on you, have you? Just for a couple of
days, is all."

All at once something inside gave and threatened to come pouring out of me.
I didn't hate him any more. I felt that in another moment I'd start crying like a
child.

"Sure," I said. "Don't sweat." I looked in my wallet and didn't have a dollar, I
only had a five. "Here," I said. "That hold you?"

He didn't look at it—he didn't want to look at it. A terrible, closed look came   45
over his face, as though he were keeping the number on the bill a secret from
him and me. "Thanks," he said, and now he was dying to see me go. "Don't
worry about Sonny. Maybe I'll write him or something."

"Sure," I said. "You do that. So long."

"Be seeing you," he said. I went on down the steps.

And I didn't write Sonny or send him anything for a long time. When I finally
did, it was just after my little girl died, and he wrote me back a letter which made
me feel like a bastard.

Here's what he said:

Dear brother,   50
    You don't know how much I needed to hear from you. I wanted to write you
many a time but I dug how much I must have hurt you and so I didn't write. But
now I feel like a man who's been trying to climb up out of some deep, real deep
and funky hole and just saw the sun up there, outside. I got to get outside.
    I can't tell you much about how I got here. I mean I don't know how to tell
you. I guess I was afraid of something or I was trying to escape from something
and you know I have never been very strong in the head (smile). I'm glad Mama
and Daddy are dead and can't see what's happened to their son and I swear if I'd
known what I was doing I would never have hurt you so, you and a lot of other
fine people who were nice to me and who believed in me.
    I don't want you to think it had anything to do with me being a musician. It's
more than that. Or maybe less than that. I can't get anything straight in my head
down here and I try not to think about what's going to happen to me when I get
outside again. Sometime I think I'm going to flip and *never* get outside and sometime I think I'll come straight back. I tell you one thing, though, I'd rather blow
my brains out than go through this again. But that's what they all say, so they tell
me. If I tell you when I'm coming to New York and if you could meet me, I sure
would appreciate it. Give my love to Isabel and the kids and I was sure sorry to
hear about little Gracie. I wish I could be like Mama and say the Lord's will be
done, but I don't know it seems to me that trouble is the one thing that never does

get stopped and I don't know what good it does to blame it on the Lord. But maybe it does some good if you believe it.

Your brother,
Sonny

Then I kept in constant touch with him and I sent him whatever I could and I went to meet him when he came back to New York. When I saw him many things I thought I had forgotten came flooding back to me. This was because I had begun, finally, to wonder about Sonny, about the life that Sonny lived inside. This life, whatever it was, had made him older and thinner and it had deepened the distant stillness in which he had always moved. He looked very unlike my baby brother. Yet, when he smiled, when we shook hands, the baby brother I'd never known looked out from the depths of his private life, like an animal waiting to be coaxed into the light.

"How you been keeping?" he asked me.

55   "All right. And you?"

"Just fine." He was smiling all over his face. "It's good to see you again."

"It's good to see you."

The seven years' difference in our ages lay between us like a chasm: I wondered if these years would ever operate between us as a bridge. I was remembering, and it made it hard to catch my breath, that I had been there when he was born; and I had heard the first words he had ever spoken. When he started to walk, he walked from our mother straight to me. I caught him just before he fell when he took the first steps he ever took in this world.

"How's Isabel?"

60   "Just fine. She's dying to see you."

"And the boys?"

"They're fine, too. They're anxious to see their uncle."

"Oh, come on. You know they don't remember me."

"Are you kidding? Of course they remember you."

65   He grinned again. We got into a taxi. We had a lot to say to each other, far too much to know how to begin.

As the taxi began to move, I asked, "You still want to go to India?"

He laughed. "You still remember that. Hell, no. This place is Indian enough for me."

"It used to belong to them," I said.

And he laughed again. "They damn sure knew what they were doing when they got rid of it."

70   Years ago, when he was around fourteen, he'd been all hipped on the idea of going to India. He read books about people sitting on rocks, naked, in all kinds of weather, but mostly bad, naturally, and walking barefoot through hot coals and arriving at wisdom. I used to say that it sounded to me as though they were getting away from wisdom as fast as they could. I think he sort of looked down on me for that.

"Do you mind," he asked, "if we have the driver drive alongside the park? On the west side—I haven't seen the city in so long."

"Of course not," I said. I was afraid that I might sound as though I were humoring him, but I hoped he wouldn't take it that way.

So we drove along, between the green of the park and the stony, lifeless elegance of hotels and apartment buildings, toward the vivid, killing streets of our childhood. These streets hadn't changed, though housing projects jutted up out of them now like rocks in the middle of a boiling sea. Most of the houses in which we had grown up had vanished, as had the stores from which we had stolen, the basements in which we had first tried sex, the rooftops from which we had hurled tin cans and bricks. But houses exactly like the houses of our past yet dominated the landscape, boys exactly like the boys we once had been found themselves smothering in these houses, came down into the streets for light and air and found themselves encircled by disaster. Some escaped the trap, most didn't. Those who got out always left something of themselves behind, as some animals amputate a leg and leave it in the trap. It might be said, perhaps, that I had escaped, after all, I was a school teacher; or that Sonny had, he hadn't lived in Harlem for years. Yet, as the cab moved uptown through streets which seemed, with a rush, to darken with dark people, and as I covertly studied Sonny's face, it came to me that what we both were seeking through our separate cab windows was that part of ourselves which had been left behind. It's always at the hour of trouble and confrontation that the missing member aches.

We hit 110th Street and started rolling up Lenox Avenue. And I'd known this avenue all my life, but it seemed to me again, as it had seemed on the day I'd first heard about Sonny's trouble, filled with a hidden menace which was its very breath of life.

"We almost there," said Sonny.

"Almost." We were both too nervous to say anything more.

We live in a housing project. It hasn't been up long. A few days after it was up it seemed uninhabitably new, now, of course, it's already rundown. It looks like a parody of the good, clean, faceless life—God knows the people who live in it do their best to make it a parody. The beat-looking grass lying around isn't enough to make their lives green, the hedges will never hold out the streets, and they know it. The big windows fool no one, they aren't big enough to make space out of no space. They don't bother with the windows, they watch the TV screen instead. The playground is most popular with the children who don't play at jacks, or skip rope, or roller skate, or swing, and they can be found in it after dark. We moved in partly because it's not too far from where I teach, and partly for the kids; but it's really just like the houses in which Sonny and I grew up. The same things happen, they'll have the same things to remember. The moment Sonny and I started into the house I had the feeling that I was simply bringing him back into the danger he had almost died trying to escape.

Sonny has never been talkative. So I don't know why I was sure he'd be dying to talk to me when supper was over the first night. Everything went fine, the oldest boy remembered him, and the youngest boy liked him, and Sonny had remembered to bring something for each of them; and Isabel, who is really much nicer than I am, more open and giving, had gone to a lot of trouble about dinner and was genuinely glad to see him. And she's always been able to tease Sonny in

75

a way that I haven't. It was nice to see her face so vivid again and to hear her laugh and watch her make Sonny laugh. She wasn't, or, anyway, she didn't seem to be, at all uneasy or embarrassed. She chatted as though there were no subject which had to be avoided and she got Sonny past his first, faint stiffness. And thank God she was there, for I was filled with that icy dread again. Everything I did seemed awkward to me, and everything I said sounded freighted with hidden meaning. I was trying to remember everything I'd heard about dope addiction and I couldn't help watching Sonny for signs. I wasn't doing it out of malice. I was trying to find out something about my brother. I was dying to hear him tell me he was safe.

"Safe!" my father grunted, whenever Mama suggested trying to move to a neighborhood which might be safer for children. "Safe, hell! Ain't no place safe for kids, nor nobody."

80   He always went on like this, but he wasn't, ever, really as bad as he sounded, not even on weekends, when he got drunk. As a matter of fact, he was always on the lookout for "something a little better," but he died before he found it. He died suddenly, during a drunken weekend in the middle of the war, when Sonny was fifteen. He and Sonny hadn't ever got on too well. And this was partly because Sonny was the apple of his father's eye. It was because he loved Sonny so much and was frightened for him, that he was always fighting with him. It doesn't do any good to fight with Sonny. Sonny just moves back, inside himself, where he can't be reached. But the principal reason that they never hit it off is that they were so much alike. Daddy was big and rough and loud-talking, just the opposite of Sonny, but they both had—that same privacy.

Mama tried to tell me something about this, just after Daddy died. I was home on leave from the army.

This was the last time I ever saw my mother alive. Just the same, this picture gets all mixed up in my mind with pictures I had of her when she was younger. The way I always see her is the way she used to be on a Sunday afternoon, say, when the old folks were talking after the big Sunday dinner. I always see her wearing pale blue. She'd be sitting on the sofa. And my father would be sitting in the easy chair, not far from her. And the living room would be full of church folks and relatives. There they sit, in chairs all around the living room, and the night is creeping up outside, but nobody knows it yet. You can see the darkness growing against the windowpanes and you hear the street noises every now and again, or maybe the jangling beat of a tambourine from one of the churches close by, but it's real quiet in the room. For a moment nobody's talking, but every face looks darkening, like the sky outside. And my mother rocks a little from the waist, and my father's eyes are closed. Everyone is looking at something a child can't see. For a minute they've forgotten the children. Maybe a kid is lying on the rug, half asleep. Maybe somebody's got a kid in his lap and is absent-mindedly stroking the kid's head. Maybe there's a kid, quiet and big-eyed, curled up in a big chair in the corner. The silence, the darkness coming, and the darkness in the faces frighten the child obscurely. He hopes that the hand which strokes his forehead will never stop—will never die. He hopes that there will never come a time when the old folks won't be sitting around the living room, talking about where they've come from, and what they've seen, and what's happened to them and their kinfolk.

But something deep and watchful in the child knows that this is bound to end, is already ending. In a moment someone will get up and turn on the light. Then the old folks will remember the children and they won't talk any more that day. And when light fills the room, the child is filled with darkness. He knows that every time this happens he's moved just a little closer to that darkness outside. The darkness outside is what the old folks have been talking about. It's what they've come from. It's what they endure. The child knows that they won't talk any more because if he knows too much about what's happened to *them*, he'll know too much too soon, about what's going to happen to *him*.

The last time I talked to my mother, I remember I was restless. I wanted to get out and see Isabel. We weren't married then and we had a lot to straighten out between us.

There Mama sat, in black, by the window. She was humming an old church song, *Lord, you brought me from a long ways off.* Sonny was out somewhere. Mama kept watching the streets. 85

"I don't know," she said, "if I'll ever see you again, after you go off from here. But I hope you'll remember the things I tried to teach you."

"Don't talk like that," I said, and smiled. "You'll be here a long time yet."

She smiled, too, but she said nothing. She was quiet for a long time. And I said, "Mama, don't you worry about nothing. I'll be writing all the time, and you be getting the checks. . . ."

"I want to talk to you about your brother," she said, suddenly. "If anything happens to me he ain't going to have nobody to look out for him."

"Mama," I said, "ain't nothing going to happen to you *or* Sonny. Sonny's all right. He's a good boy and he's got good sense." 90

"It ain't a question of his being a good boy," Mama said, "nor of his having good sense. It ain't only the bad ones, nor yet the dumb ones that gets sucked under." She stopped, looking at me. "Your Daddy once had a brother," she said, and she smiled in a way that made me feel she was in pain. "You didn't never know that, did you?"

"No," I said, "I never knew that," and I watched her face.

"Oh, yes," she said, "your Daddy had a brother." She looked out of the window again. "I know you never saw your Daddy cry. But *I* did—many a time, through all these years."

I asked her, "What happened to his brother? How come nobody's ever talked about him?"

This was the first time I ever saw my mother look old. 95

"His brother got killed," she said, "when he was just a little younger than you are now. I knew him. He was a fine boy. He was maybe a little full of the devil, but he didn't mean nobody no harm."

Then she stopped and the room was silent, exactly as it had sometimes been on those Sunday afternoons. Mama kept looking out into the streets.

"He used to have a job in the mill," she said, "and, like all young folks, he just liked to perform on Saturday nights. Saturday nights, him and your father would drift around to different places, go to dances and things like that, or just sit around with people they knew, and your father's brother would sing, he had a fine voice, and play along with himself on his guitar. Well, this particular Saturday night, him and your father was coming home from some place, and they were both a little drunk and there was a moon that night, it was bright like day. Your father's brother was feeling kind of good, and he was whistling to himself, and he had his guitar slung over his shoulder. They was coming down a hill and beneath them was a road that turned off from the highway. Well, your father's brother, being always kind of frisky, decided to run down this hill, and he did, with that guitar banging and clanging behind him, and he ran across the road, and he was making water behind a tree. And your father was sort of amused at him and he was still coming down the hill, kind of slow. Then he heard a car motor and that same minute his brother stepped from behind the tree, into the road, in the moonlight. And he started to cross the road. And your father started to run down the hill, he says he don't know why. This car was full of white men. They was all drunk, and when they seen your father's brother they let out a great whoop and holler and they aimed the car straight at him. They was having fun, they just wanted to scare him, the way they do sometimes, you know. But they was drunk. And I guess the boy, being drunk, too, and scared, kind of lost his head. By the time he jumped it was too late. Your father says he heard his brother scream when the car rolled over him, and he heard the wood of that guitar when it give, and he heard them strings go flying, and he heard them white men shouting, and the car kept on a-going and it ain't stopped till this day. And, time your father got down the hill, his brother weren't nothing but blood and pulp."

Tears were gleaming on my mother's face. There wasn't anything I could say.

100   "He never mentioned it," she said, "because I never let him mention it before you children. Your Daddy was like a crazy man that night and for many a night thereafter. He says he never in his life seen anything as dark as that road after the lights of that car had gone away. Weren't nothing, weren't nobody on that road, just your Daddy and his brother and that busted guitar. Oh, yes. Your Daddy never did really get right again. Till the day he died he weren't sure but that every white man he saw was the man that killed his brother."

She stopped and took out her handkerchief and dried her eyes and looked at me.

"I ain't telling you all this," she said, "to make you scared or bitter or to make you hate nobody. I'm telling you this because you got a brother. And the world ain't changed."

I guess I didn't want to believe this. I guess she saw this in my face. She turned away from me, toward the window again, searching those streets.

"But I praise my Redeemer," she said at last, "that He called your Daddy home before me. I ain't saying it to throw no flowers at myself, but, I declare, it keeps me from feeling too cast down to know I helped your father get safely through this world. Your father always acted like he was the roughest, strongest man on earth. And everybody took him to be like that. But if he hadn't had me there— to see his tears!"

She was crying again. Still, I couldn't move. I said, "Lord, Lord, Mama, I didn't   105
know it was like that."

"Oh, honey," she said, "there's a lot that you don't know. But you are going
to find out." She stood up from the window and came over to me. "You got to
hold on to your brother," she said, "and don't let him fall, no matter what it
looks like is happening to him and no matter how evil you gets with him. You
going to be evil with him many a time. But don't you forget what I told you, you
hear?"

"I won't forget," I said. "Don't you worry, I won't forget. I won't let nothing
happen to Sonny."

My mother smiled as though she was amused at something she saw in my
face. Then, "You may not be able to stop nothing from happening. But you got
to let him know you's *there*."

Two days later I was married, and then I was gone. And I had a lot of things
on my mind and I pretty well forgot my promise to Mama until I got shipped
home on a special furlough for her funeral.

And, after the funeral, with just Sonny and me alone in the empty kitchen, I   110
tried to find out something about him.

"What do you want to do?" I asked him.

"I'm going to be a musician," he said.

For he had graduated, in the time I had been away, from dancing to the juke
box to finding out who was playing what, and what they were doing with it, and
he had bought himself a set of drums.

"You mean, you want to be a drummer?" I somehow had the feeling that
being a drummer might be all right for other people but not for my brother
Sonny.

"I don't think," he said, looking at me very gravely, "that I'll ever be a good   115
drummer. But I think I can play a piano."

I frowned. I'd never played the role of the oldest brother quite so seriously
before, had scarcely ever, in fact, *asked* Sonny a damn thing. I sensed myself in
the presence of something I didn't really know how to handle, didn't understand. So I made my frown a little deeper as I asked: "What kind of musician do
you want to be?"

He grinned. "How many kinds do you think there are?"

"Be *serious*," I said.

He laughed, throwing his head back, and then looked at me. "I *am* serious."

"Well, then, for Christ's sake, stop kidding around and answer a serious ques-   120
tion. I mean, do you want to be a concert pianist, you want to play classical
music and all that, or—or what?" Long before I finished he was laughing again.
"For Christ's *sake*, Sonny!"

He sobered, but with difficulty. "I'm sorry. But you sound so—*scared!*" and he
was off again.

"Well, you may think it's funny now, baby, but it's not going to be so funny
when you have to make your living at it, let me tell you *that*." I was furious
because I knew he was laughing at me and I didn't know why.

"No," he said, very sober now, and afraid, perhaps, that he'd hurt me, "I don't want to be a classical pianist. That isn't what interests me. I mean"—he paused, looking hard at me, as though his eyes would help me to understand, and then gestured helplessly, as though perhaps his hand would help—"I mean, I'll have a lot of studying to do, and I'll have to study *everything*, but, I mean, I want to play *with*—jazz musicians." He stopped. "I want to play jazz," he said.

Well, the word had never before sounded as heavy, as real, as it sounded that afternoon in Sonny's mouth. I just looked at him and I was probably frowning a real frown by this time. I simply couldn't see why on earth he'd want to spend his time hanging around nightclubs, clowning around on bandstands, while people pushed each other around a dance floor. It seemed—beneath him, somehow. I had never thought about it before, had never been forced to, but I suppose I had always put jazz musicians in a class with what Daddy called "good-time people."

125   "Are you *serious*?"

"Hell, *yes*, I'm serious."

He looked more helpless than ever, and annoyed, and deeply hurt.

I suggested, helpfully: "You mean—like Louis Armstrong?"

His face closed as though I'd struck him. "No. I'm not talking about none of that old-time, down home crap."

130   "Well, look, Sonny, I'm sorry, don't get mad. I just don't altogether get it, that's all. Name somebody—you know, a jazz musician you admire."

"Bird."

"Who?"

"Bird! Charlie Parker![3] Don't they teach you nothing in the goddamn army?"

I lit a cigarette. I was surprised and then a little amused to discover that I was trembling. "I've been out of touch," I said. "You'll have to be patient with me. Now. Who's this Parker character?"

135   "He's just one of the greatest jazz musicians alive," said Sonny, sullenly, his hands in his pockets, his back to me. "Maybe *the* greatest," he added, bitterly, "that's probably why *you* never heard of him."

"All right," I said, "I'm ignorant. I'm sorry. I'll go out and buy all the cat's records right away, all right?"

"It don't," said Sonny, with dignity, "make any difference to me. I don't care what you listen to. Don't do me no favors."

I was beginning to realize that I'd never seen him so upset before. With another part of my mind I was thinking that this would probably turn out to be one of those things kids go through and that I shouldn't make it seem important by pushing it too hard. Still, I didn't think it would do any harm to ask: "Doesn't all this take a lot of time? Can you make a living at it?"

He turned back to me and half leaned, half sat, on the kitchen table. "Everything takes time," he said, "and—well, yes, sure, I can make a living at it. But what I don't seem to be able to make you understand is that it's the only thing I want to do."

---

3. Charlie ("Bird") Parker (1920–1955), brilliant saxophonist and innovator of jazz; working in New York in the mid-1940s, he developed, with Dizzy Gillespie and others, the style of jazz called "bebop." He was a narcotics addict.

"Well, Sonny," I said gently, "you know people can't always do exactly what   140
they *want* to do—"

"*No,* I don't know that," said Sonny, surprising me. "I think people *ought* to
do what they want to do, what else are they alive for?"

"You getting to be a big boy," I said desperately, "it's time you started thinking
about your future."

"I'm thinking about my future," said Sonny, grimly. "I think about it all the
time."

I gave up. I decided, if he didn't change his mind, that we could always talk
about it later. "In the meantime," I said, "you got to finish school." We had
already decided that he'd have to move in with Isabel and her folks. I knew this
wasn't the ideal arrangement because Isabel's folks are inclined to be dicty[4] and
they hadn't especially wanted Isabel to marry me. But I didn't know what else to
do. "And we have to get you fixed up at Isabel's."

There was a long silence. He moved from the kitchen table to the window.   145
"That's a terrible idea. You know it yourself."

"Do you have a *better* idea?"

He just walked up and down the kitchen for a minute. He was as tall as I was.
He had started to shave. I suddenly had the feeling that I didn't know him at all.

He stopped at the kitchen table and picked up my cigarettes. Looking at me
with a kind of mocking, amused defiance, he put one between his lips. "You
mind?"

"You smoking already?"

He lit the cigarette and nodded, watching me through the smoke. "I just   150
wanted to see if I'd have the courage to smoke in front of you." He grinned and
blew a great cloud of smoke to the ceiling. "It was easy." He looked at my face.
"Come on, now. I bet you was smoking at my age, tell the truth."

I didn't say anything but the truth was on my face, and he laughed. But now
there was something very strained in his laugh. "Sure. And I bet that ain't all you
was doing."

He was frightening me a little. "Cut the crap," I said. "We already decided that
you was going to go and live at Isabel's. Now what's got into you all of a sudden?"

"*You* decided it," he pointed out. "*I* didn't decide nothing." He stopped in
front of me, leaning against the stove, arms loosely folded. "Look, brother. I
don't want to stay in Harlem no more, I really don't." He was very earnest. He
looked at me, then over toward the kitchen window. There was something in his
eyes I'd never seen before, some thoughtfulness, some worry all his own. He
rubbed the muscle of one arm. "It's time I was getting out of here."

"Where do you want to *go,* Sonny?"

"I want to join the army. Or the navy, I don't care. If I say I'm old enough,   155
they'll believe me."

Then I got mad. It was because I was so scared. "You must be crazy. You goddamn fool, what the hell do you want to go and join the *army* for?"

"I just told you. To get out of Harlem."

4. Snobbish, bossy.

"Sonny, you haven't even finished *school*. And if you really want to be a musician, how do you expect to study if you're in the *army?*"

He looked at me, trapped, and in anguish. "There's ways. I might be able to work out some kind of deal. Anyway, I'll have the G.I. Bill when I come out."

160 "*If* you come out." We stared at each other. "Sonny, please. Be reasonable. I know the setup is far from perfect. But we got to do the best we can."

"I ain't learning nothing in school," he said. "Even when I go." He turned away from me and opened the window and threw his cigarette out into the narrow alley. I watched his back. "At least, I ain't learning nothing you'd want me to learn." He slammed the window so hard I thought the glass would fly out, and turned back to me. "And I'm sick of the stink of these garbage cans!"

"Sonny," I said, "I know how you feel. But if you don't finish school now, you're going to be sorry later that you didn't." I grabbed him by the shoulders. "And you only got another year. It ain't so bad. And I'll come back and I swear I'll help you do *whatever* you want to do. Just try to put up with it till I come back. Will you please do that? For me?"

He didn't answer and he wouldn't look at me.

"Sonny. You hear me?"

165 He pulled away. "I hear you. But you never hear anything *I* say."

I didn't know what to say to that. He looked out of the window and then back at me. "OK," he said, and sighed. "I'll try."

Then I said, trying to cheer him up a little, "They got a piano at Isabel's. You can practice on it."

And as a matter of fact, it did cheer him up for a minute. "That's right," he said to himself. "I forgot that." His face relaxed a little. But the worry, the thoughtfulness, played on it still, the way shadows play on a face which is staring into the fire.

But I thought I'd never hear the end of that piano. At first, Isabel would write me, saying how nice it was that Sonny was so serious about his music and how, as soon as he came in from school, or wherever he had been when he was supposed to be at school, he went straight to that piano and stayed there until suppertime. And, after supper, he went back to that piano and stayed there until everybody went to bed. He was at the piano all day Saturday and all day Sunday. Then he bought a record player and started playing records. He'd play one record over and over again, all day long sometimes, and he'd improvise along with it on the piano. Or he'd play one section of the record, one chord, one change, one progression, then he'd do it on the piano. Then back to the record. Then back to the piano.

170 Well, I really don't know how they stood it. Isabel finally confessed that it wasn't like living with a person at all, it was like living with sound. And the sound didn't make any sense to her, didn't make any sense to any of them—naturally. They began, in a way, to be afflicted by this presence that was living in their home. It was as though Sonny were some sort of god, or monster. He moved in an atmosphere which wasn't like theirs at all. They fed him and he ate, he washed himself, he walked in and out of their door; he certainly wasn't nasty or

unpleasant or rude, Sonny isn't any of those things; but it was as though he were all wrapped up in some cloud, some fire, some vision all his own; and there wasn't any way to reach him.

At the same time, he wasn't really a man yet, he was still a child, and they had to watch out for him in all kinds of ways. They certainly couldn't throw him out. Neither did they dare to make a great scene about that piano because even they dimly sensed, as I sensed, from so many thousands of miles away, that Sonny was at that piano playing for his life.

But he hadn't been going to school. One day a letter came from the school board and Isabel's mother got it—there had, apparently, been other letters but Sonny had torn them up. This day, when Sonny came in, Isabel's mother showed him the letter and asked where he'd been spending his time. And she finally got it out of him that he'd been down in Greenwich Village, with musicians and other characters, in a white girl's apartment. And this scared her and she started to scream at him and what came up, once she began—though she denies it to this day—was what sacrifices they were making to give Sonny a decent home and how little he appreciated it.

Sonny didn't play the piano that day. By evening, Isabel's mother had calmed down but then there was the old man to deal with, and Isabel herself. Isabel says she did her best to be calm but she broke down and started crying. She says she just watched Sonny's face. She could tell, by watching him, what was happening with him. And what was happening was that they penetrated his cloud, they had reached him. Even if their fingers had been a thousand times more gentle than human fingers ever are, he could hardly help feeling that they had stripped him naked and were spitting on that nakedness. For he also had to see that his presence, that music, which was life or death to him, had been torture for them and that they had endured it, not at all for his sake, but only for mine. And Sonny couldn't take that. He can take it a little better today than he could then but he's still not very good at it and, frankly, I don't know anybody who is.

The silence of the next few days must have been louder than the sound of all the music ever played since time began. One morning, before she went to work, Isabel was in his room for something and she suddenly realized that all of his records were gone. And she knew for certain that he was gone. And he was. He went as far as the navy would carry him. He finally sent me a postcard from some place in Greece and that was the first I knew that Sonny was still alive. I didn't see him any more until we were both back in New York and the war had long been over.

He was a man by then, of course, but I wasn't willing to see it. He came by the house from time to time, but we fought almost every time we met. I didn't like the way he carried himself, loose and dreamlike all the time, and I didn't like his friends, and his music seemed to be merely an excuse for the life he led. It sounded just that weird and disordered.

Then we had a fight, a pretty awful fight, and I didn't see him for months. By and by I looked him up, where he was living, in a furnished room in the Village, and I tried to make it up. But there were lots of other people in the room and Sonny just lay on his bed, and he wouldn't come downstairs with me, and he treated these other people as though they were his family and I weren't. So I got mad and then he got mad, and then I told him that he might just as well be dead as live the way he was living. Then he stood up and he told me not to worry about him any more in life, that he *was* dead as far as I was concerned. Then he pushed me to the door and the other people looked on as though nothing were happening, and he slammed the door behind me. I stood in the hallway, staring at the door. I heard somebody laugh in the room and then the tears came to my eyes. I started down the steps, whistling to keep from crying, I kept whistling to myself, *You going to need me, baby, one of these cold, rainy days.*

I read about Sonny's trouble in the spring. Little Grace died in the fall. She was a beautiful little girl. But she only lived a little over two years. She died of polio and she suffered. She had a slight fever for a couple of days, but it didn't seem like anything and we just kept her in bed. And we would certainly have called the doctor, but the fever dropped, she seemed to be all right. So we thought it had just been a cold. Then, one day, she was up, playing, Isabel was in the kitchen fixing lunch for the two boys when they'd come in from school, and she heard Grace fall down in the living room. When you have a lot of children you don't always start running when one of them falls, unless they start screaming or something. And, this time, Gracie was quiet. Yet, Isabel says that when she heard that *thump* and then that silence, something happened to her to make her afraid. And she ran to the living room and there was little Grace on the floor, all twisted up, and the reason she hadn't screamed was that she couldn't get her breath. And when she did scream, it was the worst sound, Isabel says, that she'd ever heard in all her life, and she still hears it sometimes in her dreams. Isabel will sometimes wake me up with a low, moaning, strangling sound and I have to be quick to awaken her and hold her to me and where Isabel is weeping against me seems a mortal wound.

I think I may have written Sonny the very day that little Grace was buried. I was sitting in the living room in the dark, by myself, and I suddenly thought of Sonny. My trouble made his real.

One Saturday afternoon, when Sonny had been living with us, or anyway, been in our house, for nearly two weeks, I found myself wandering aimlessly about the living room, drinking from a can of beer, and trying to work up courage to search Sonny's room. He was out, he was usually out whenever I was home, and Isabel had taken the children to see their grandparents. Suddenly I was standing still in front of the living room window, watching Seventh Avenue. The idea of searching Sonny's room made me still. I scarcely dared to admit to myself what I'd be searching for. I didn't know what I'd do if I found it. Or if I didn't.

180On the sidewalk across from me, near the entrance to a barbecue joint, some people were holding an old-fashioned revival meeting. The barbecue cook, wearing a dirty white apron, his conked[5] hair reddish and metallic in the pale sun, and a cigarette between his lips, stood in the doorway, watching them. Kids and older people paused in their errands and stood there, along with some older men

5. Processed: straightened and greased.

and a couple of very tough-looking women who watched everything that happened on the avenue, as though they owned it, or were maybe owned by it. Well, they were watching this, too. The revival was being carried on by three sisters in black, and a brother. All they had were their voices and their Bibles and a tambourine. The brother was testifying[6] and while he testified two of the sisters stood together, seeming to say, amen, and the third sister walked around with the tambourine outstretched and a couple of people dropped coins into it. Then the brother's testimony ended and the sister who had been taking up the collection dumped the coins into her palm and transferred them to the pocket of her long black robe. Then she raised both hands, striking the tambourine against the air, and then against one hand, and she started to sing. And the two other sisters and the brother joined in.

It was strange, suddenly, to watch, though I had been seeing these meetings all my life. So, of course, had everybody else down there. Yet, they paused and watched and listened and I stood still at the window. " 'Tis the old ship of Zion," they sang, and the sister with the tambourine kept a steady, jangling beat, "it has rescued many a thousand!" Not a soul under the sound of their voices was hearing this song for the first time, not one of them had been rescued. Nor had they seen much in the way of rescue work being done around them. Neither did they especially believe in the holiness of the three sisters and the brother, they knew too much about them, knew where they lived, and how. The woman with the tambourine, whose voice dominated the air, whose face was bright with joy, was divided by very little from the woman who stood watching her, a cigarette between her heavy, chapped lips, her hair a cuckoo's nest, her face scarred and swollen from many beatings, and her black eyes glittering like coal. Perhaps they both knew this, which was why, when, as rarely, they addressed each other, they addressed each other as Sister. As the singing filled the air the watching, listening faces underwent a change, the eyes focusing on something within; the music seemed to soothe a poison out of them; and time seemed, nearly, to fall away from the sullen, belligerent, battered faces, as though they were fleeing back to their first condition, while dreaming of their last. The barbecue cook half shook his head and smiled, and dropped his cigarette and disappeared into his joint. A man fumbled in his pockets for change and stood holding it in his hand impatiently, as though he had just remembered a pressing appointment further up the avenue. He looked furious. Then I saw Sonny, standing on the edge of the crowd. He was carrying a wide, flat notebook with a green cover, and it made him look, from where I was standing, almost like a schoolboy. The coppery sun brought out the copper in his skin, he was very faintly smiling, standing very still. Then the singing stopped, the tambourine turned into a collection plate again. The furious man dropped in his coins and vanished, so did a couple of the women, and Sonny dropped some change in the plate, looking directly at the woman with a little smile. He started across the avenue, toward the house. He has a slow, loping walk, something like the way Harlem hipsters walk, only he's imposed on this his own half-beat. I had never really noticed it before.

6. Publicly professing belief.

I stayed at the window, both relieved and apprehensive. As Sonny disappeared from my sight, they began singing again. And they were still singing when his key turned in the lock.

"Hey," he said.

"Hey, yourself. You want some beer?"

185   "No. Well, maybe." But he came up to the window and stood beside me, looking out. "What a warm voice," he said.

They were singing *If I could only hear my mother pray again!*

"Yes," I said, "and she can sure beat that tambourine."

"But what a terrible song," he said, and laughed. He dropped his notebook on the sofa and disappeared into the kitchen. "Where's Isabel and the kids?"

"I think they went to see their grandparents. You hungry?"

190   "No." He came back into the living room with his can of beer. "You want to come some place with me tonight?"

I sensed, I don't know how, that I couldn't possibly say no. "Sure. Where?"

He sat down on the sofa and picked up his notebook and started leafing through it. "I'm going to sit in with some fellows in a joint in the Village."

"You mean, you're going to play, tonight?"

"That's right." He took a swallow of his beer and moved back to the window. He gave me a sidelong look. "If you can stand it."

195   "I'll try," I said.

He smiled to himself and we both watched as the meeting across the way broke up. The three sisters and the brother, heads bowed, were singing *God be with you till we meet again.* The faces around them were very quiet. Then the song ended. The small crowd dispersed. We watched the three women and the lone man walk slowly up the avenue.

"When she was singing before," said Sonny, abruptly, "her voice reminded me for a minute of what heroin feels like sometimes—when it's in your veins. It makes you feel sort of warm and cool at the same time. And distant. And—and sure." He sipped his beer, very deliberately not looking at me. I watched his face. "It makes you feel—in control. Sometimes you've got to have that feeling."

"Do you?" I sat down slowly in the easy chair.

"Sometimes." He went to the sofa and picked up his notebook again. "Some people do."

200   "In order," I asked, "to play?" And my voice was very ugly, full of contempt and anger.

"Well"—he looked at me with great, troubled eyes, as though, in fact, he hoped his eyes would tell me things he could never otherwise say—"they *think* so. And *if* they think so—!"

"And what do *you* think?" I asked.

He sat on the sofa and put his can of beer on the floor. "I don't know," he said, and I couldn't be sure if he were answering my question or pursuing his thoughts. His face didn't tell me. "It's not so much to *play*. It's to *stand* it, to be able to make it at all. On any level." He frowned and smiled: "In order to keep from shaking to pieces."

"But these friends of yours," I said, "they seem to shake themselves to pieces pretty goddamn fast."

"Maybe." He played with the notebook. And something told me that I should curb my tongue, that Sonny was doing his best to talk, that I should listen. "But of course you only know the ones that've gone to pieces. Some don't—or at least they haven't *yet* and that's just about all *any* of us can say." He paused. "And then there are some who just live, really, in hell, and they know it and they see what's happening and they go right on. I don't know." He sighed, dropped the notebook, folded his arms. "Some guys, you can tell from the way they play, they on something *all* the time. And you can see that, well, it makes something real for them. But of course," he picked up his beer from the floor and sipped it and put the can down again, "they *want* to, too, you've got to see that. Even some of them that say they don't—*some,* not all."

"And what about you?" I asked—I couldn't help it. "What about you? Do *you* want to?"

He stood up and walked to the window and I remained silent for a long time. Then he sighed. "Me," he said. Then: "While I was downstairs before, on my way here, listening to that woman sing, it struck me all of a sudden how much suffering she must have had to go through—to sing like that. It's *repulsive* to think you have to suffer that much."

I said: "But there's no way not to suffer—is there, Sonny?"

"I believe not," he said and smiled, "but that's never stopped anyone from trying." He looked at me. "Has it?" I realized, with this mocking look, that there stood between us, forever, beyond the power of time or forgiveness, the fact that I had held silence—so long!—when he had needed human speech to help him. He turned back to the window. "No, there's no way not to suffer. But you try all kinds of ways to keep from drowning in it, to keep on top of it, and to make it seem—well, like *you.* Like you did something, all right, and now you're suffering for it. You know?" I said nothing. "Well you know," he said, impatiently, "why *do* people suffer? Maybe it's better to do something to give it a reason, *any* reason."

"But we just agreed," I said, "that there's no way not to suffer. Isn't it better, then, just to—take it?"

"But nobody just takes it," Sonny cried, "that's what I'm telling you! *Everybody* tries not to. You're just hung up on the *way* some people try—it's not *your* way!"

The hair on my face began to itch, my face felt wet. "That's not true," I said, "that's not true. I don't give a damn what other people do, I don't even care how they suffer. I just care how *you* suffer." And he looked at me. "Please believe me," I said, "I don't want to see you—die—trying not to suffer."

"I won't," he said flatly, "die trying not to suffer. At least, not any faster than anybody else."

"But there's no need," I said, trying to laugh, "is there? in killing yourself."

I wanted to say more, but I couldn't. I wanted to talk about will power and how life could be—well, beautiful. I wanted to say that it was all within; but was it? or, rather, wasn't that exactly the trouble? And I wanted to promise that I

205

210

215

would never fail him again. But it would all have sounded—empty words and lies.

So I made the promise to myself and prayed that I would keep it.

"It's terrible sometimes, inside," he said, "that's what's the trouble. You walk these streets, black and funky and cold, and there's not really a living ass to talk to, and there's nothing shaking, and there's no way of getting it out—that storm inside. You can't talk it and you can't make love with it, and when you finally try to get with it and play it, you realize *nobody's* listening. So *you've* got to listen. You got to find a way to listen."

And then he walked away from the window and sat on the sofa again, as though all the wind had suddenly been knocked out of him. "Sometimes you'll do *anything* to play, even cut your mother's throat." He laughed and looked at me. "Or your brother's." Then he sobered. "Or your own." Then: "Don't worry. I'm all right now and I think I'll *be* all right. But I can't forget—where I've been. I don't mean just the physical place I've been, I mean where I've *been*. And *what* I've been."

"What have you been, Sonny?" I asked.

220   He smiled—but sat sideways on the sofa, his elbow resting on the back, his fingers playing with his mouth and chin, not looking at me. "I've been something I didn't recognize, didn't know I could be. Didn't know anybody could be." He stopped, looking inward, looking helplessly young, looking old. "I'm not talking about it now because I feel *guilty* or anything like that—maybe it would be better if I did, I don't know. Anyway, I can't really talk about it. Not to you, not to anybody," and now he turned and faced me. "Sometimes, you know, and it was actually when I was most *out* of the world, I felt that I was in it, that I was *with* it, really, and I could play or I didn't really have to *play*, it just came out of me, it was there. And I don't know how I played, thinking about it now, but I know I did awful things, those times, sometimes, to people. Or it wasn't that I *did* anything to them—it was that they weren't real." He picked up the beer can; it was empty; he rolled it between his palms: "And other times—well, I needed a fix, I needed to find a place to lean, I needed to clear a space to *listen*—and I couldn't find it, and I—went crazy, I did terrible things to *me*, I was terrible *for* me." He began pressing the beer can between his hands, I watched the metal begin to give. It glittered, as he played with it like a knife, and I was afraid he would cut himself, but I said nothing. "Oh well. I can never tell you. I was all by myself at the bottom of something, stinking and sweating and crying and shaking, and I smelled it, you know? *my* stink, and I thought I'd die if I couldn't get away from it and yet, all the same, I knew that everything I was doing was just locking me in with it. And I didn't know," he paused, still flattening the beer can, "I didn't know, I still *don't* know, something kept telling me that maybe it was good to smell your own stink, but I didn't think that *that* was what I'd been trying to do—and—who can stand it?" and he abruptly dropped the ruined beer can, looking at me with a small, still smile, and then rose, walking to the window as though it were the lodestone rock. I watched his face, he watched the avenue. "I couldn't tell you when Mama died—but the reason I wanted to leave Harlem so bad was to get away from drugs. And then, when I ran away, that's what I was

running from—really. When I came back, nothing had changed, *I* hadn't changed, I was just—older." And he stopped, drumming with his fingers on the windowpane. The sun had vanished, soon darkness would fall. I watched his face. "It can come again," he said, almost as though speaking to himself. Then he turned to me. "It can come again," he repeated. "I just want you to know that."

"All right," I said, at last. "So it can come again. All right."

He smiled, but the smile was sorrowful. "I had to try to tell you," he said.

"Yes," I said. "I understand that."

"You're my brother," he said, looking straight at me, and not smiling at all.

"Yes," I repeated, "yes. I understand that."   225

He turned back to the window, looking out. "All that hatred down there," he said, "all that hatred and misery and love. It's a wonder it doesn't blow the avenue apart."

We went to the only nightclub on a short, dark street, downtown. We squeezed through the narrow, chattering, jampacked bar to the entrance of the big room, where the bandstand was. And we stood there for a moment, for the lights were very dim in this room and we couldn't see. Then, "Hello, boy," said the voice and an enormous black man, much older than Sonny or myself, erupted out of all that atmospheric lighting and put an arm around Sonny's shoulder. "I been sitting right here," he said, "waiting for you."

He had a big voice, too, and heads in the darkness turned toward us.

Sonny grinned and pulled a little away, and said, "Creole, this is my brother. I told you about him."

Creole shook my hand. "I'm glad to meet you, son," he said, and it was clear   230
that he was glad to meet me *there,* for Sonny's sake. And he smiled, "You got a real musician in *your* family," and he took his arm from Sonny's shoulder and slapped him, lightly, affectionately, with the back of his hand.

"Well. Now I've heard it all," said a voice behind us. This was another musician, and a friend of Sonny's, a coal-black, cheerful-looking man, built close to the ground. He immediately began confiding to me, at the top of his lungs, the most terrible things about Sonny, his teeth gleaming like a lighthouse and his laugh coming up out of him like the beginning of an earthquake. And it turned out that everyone at the bar knew Sonny, or almost everyone; some were musicians, working there, or nearby, or not working, some were simply hangers-on, and some were there to hear Sonny play. I was introduced to all of them and they were all very polite to me. Yet, it was clear that, for them, I was only Sonny's brother. Here, I was in Sonny's world. Or, rather: his kingdom. Here, it was not even a question that his veins bore royal blood.

They were going to play soon and Creole installed me, by myself, at a table in a dark corner. Then I watched them, Creole, and the little black man, and Sonny, and the others, while they horsed around, standing just below the bandstand. The light from the bandstand spilled just a little short of them and, watching them laughing and gesturing and moving about, I had the feeling that they, nevertheless, were being most careful not to step into that circle of light too suddenly; that if they moved into the light too suddenly, without thinking, they would perish in flame. Then, while I watched, one of them, the small black man, moved into the light and crossed the bandstand and started fooling around with his drums. Then—being funny and being, also, extremely ceremonious—Creole took Sonny by the arm and led him to the piano. A woman's voice called Sonny's name and a few hands started clapping. And Sonny, also being funny and being ceremonious, and so touched, I think, that he could have cried, but neither hiding it nor showing it, riding it like a man, grinned, and put both hands to his heart and bowed from the waist.

Creole then went to the bass fiddle and a lean, very bright-skinned brown man jumped up on the bandstand and picked up his horn. So there they were, and the atmosphere on the bandstand and in the room began to change and tighten. Someone stepped up to the microphone and announced them. Then there were all kinds of murmurs. Some people at the bar shushed others. The waitress ran around, frantically getting in the last orders, guys and chicks got closer to each other, and the lights on the bandstand, on the quartet, turned to a kind of indigo. Then they all looked different there. Creole looked about him for the last time, as though he were making certain that all his chickens were in the coop, and then he—jumped and struck the fiddle. And there they were.

All I know about music is that not many people ever really hear it. And even then, on the rare occasions when something opens within, and the music enters, what we mainly hear, or hear corroborated, are personal, private, vanishing evocations. But the man who creates the music is hearing something else, is dealing with the roar rising from the void and imposing order on it as it hits the air. What is evoked in him, then, is of another order, more terrible because it has no words, and triumphant, too, for that same reason. And his triumph, when he triumphs, is ours. I just watched Sonny's face. His face was troubled, he was working hard, but he wasn't with it. And I had the feeling that, in a way, everyone on the bandstand was waiting for him, both waiting for him and pushing him along. But as I began to watch Creole, I realized that it was Creole who held them all back. He had them on a short rein. Up there, keeping the beat with his whole body, wailing on the fiddle, with his eyes half closed, he was listening to everything, but he was listening to Sonny. He was having a dialogue with Sonny. He wanted Sonny to leave the shoreline and strike out for the deep water. He was Sonny's witness that deep water and drowning were not the same thing—he had been there, and he knew. And he wanted Sonny to know. He was waiting for Sonny to do the things on the keys which would let Creole know that Sonny was in the water.

235   And, while Creole listened, Sonny moved, deep within, exactly like someone in torment. I had never before thought of how awful the relationship must be between the musician and his instrument. He has to fill it, this instrument, with the breath of life, his own. He has to make it do what he wants it to do. And a piano is just a piano. It's made out of so much wood and wires and little hammers and big ones, and ivory. While there's only so much you can do with it, the only way to find this out is to try; to try and make it do everything.

And Sonny hadn't been near a piano for over a year. And he wasn't on much better terms with his life, not the life that stretched before him now. He and the piano stammered, started one way, got scared, stopped; started another way, panicked, marked time, started again; then seemed to have found a direction, panicked again, got stuck. And the face I saw on Sonny I'd never seen before. Everything had been burned out of it, and, at the same time, things usually hidden were being burned in, by the fire and fury of the battle which was occurring in him up there.

Yet, watching Creole's face as they neared the end of the first set, I had the feeling that something had happened, something I hadn't heard. Then they finished, there was scattered applause, and then, without an instant's warning, Creole started into something else, it was almost sardonic, it was *Am I Blue*.[7] And, as though he commanded, Sonny began to play. Something began to happen. And Creole let out the reins. The dry, low, black man said something awful on the drums, Creole answered, and the drums talked back. Then the horn insisted, sweet and high, slightly detached perhaps, and Creole listened, commenting now and then, dry, and driving, beautiful and calm and old. Then they all came together again, and Sonny was part of the family again. I could tell this from his face. He seemed to have found, right there beneath his fingers, a damn brand-new piano. It seemed that he couldn't get over it. Then, for a while, just being happy with Sonny, they seemed to be agreeing with him that brand-new pianos certainly were a gas.

Then Creole stepped forward to remind them that what they were playing was the blues. He hit something in all of them, he hit something in me, myself, and the music tightened and deepened, apprehension began to beat the air. Creole began to tell us what the blues were all about. They were not about anything very new. He and his boys up there were keeping it new, at the risk of ruin, destruction, madness, and death, in order to find new ways to make us listen. For, while the tale of how we suffer, and how we are delighted, and how we may triumph is never new, it always must be heard. There isn't any other tale to tell, it's the only light we've got in all this darkness.

And this tale, according to that face, that body, those strong hands on those strings, has another aspect in every country, and a new depth in every generation. Listen, Creole seemed to be saying, listen. Now these are Sonny's blues. He made the little black man on the drums know it, and the bright, brown man on the horn. Creole wasn't trying any longer to get Sonny in the water. He was wishing him Godspeed. Then he stepped back, very slowly, filling the air with the immense suggestion that Sonny speak for himself.

Then they all gathered around Sonny and Sonny played. Every now and again one of them seemed to say, amen. Sonny's fingers filled the air with life, his life. But that life contained so many others. And Sonny went all the way back, he really began with the spare, flat statement of the opening phrase of the song. Then he began to make it his. It was very beautiful because it wasn't hurried and

240

---

7. A favorite jazz standard, brilliantly recorded by Billie Holiday.

it was no longer a lament. I seemed to hear with what burning he had made it his, and what burning we had yet to make it ours, how we could cease lamenting. Freedom lurked around us and I understood, at last, that he could help us to be free if we would listen, that he would never be free until we did. Yet, there was no battle in his face now, I heard what he had gone through, and would continue to go through until he came to rest in earth. He had made it his: that long line, of which we knew only Mama and Daddy. And he was giving it back, as everything must be given back, so that, passing through death, it can live forever. I saw my mother's face again, and felt, for the first time, how the stones of the road she had walked on must have bruised her feet. I saw the moonlit road where my father's brother died. And it brought something else back to me, and carried me past it, I saw my little girl again and felt Isabel's tears again, and I felt my own tears begin to rise. And I was yet aware that this was only a moment, that the world waited outside, as hungry as a tiger, and that trouble stretched above us, longer than the sky.

Then it was over. Creole and Sonny let out their breath, both soaking wet, and grinning. There was a lot of applause and some of it was real. In the dark, the girl came by and I asked her to take drinks to the bandstand. There was a long pause, while they talked up there in the indigo light and after awhile I saw the girl put a Scotch and milk on top of the piano for Sonny. He didn't seem to notice it, but just before they started playing again, he sipped from it and looked toward me, and nodded. Then he put it back on top of the piano. For me, then, as they began to play again, it glowed and shook above my brother's head like the very cup of trembling.[8]

1957

QUESTIONS

1. We are advised by Margaret Atwood that if we want a happy ending, to try her sketch A. Does it have a happy ending? What does she claim is the only authentic ending for a story? What is the difference between the way Atwood uses the word "plot" and the way it is used in the introduction to this chapter?
2. Rearrange the incidents in "The Country Husband" in chronological order. The structured story begins, "To begin at the beginning . . ." and tells about the near-crash of Francis's plane. Why is that the beginning? What is it the beginning of?
3. Describe the location, appearance, and socioeconomic makeup of Shady Hill in "The Country Husband." Why is the dog Jupiter "an anomaly" (paragraph 10)? Why do Clayton Thomas and Anne also not "belong"? Who wins the struggle between Francis Weed and Shady Hill?
4. The opening scene of "Sonny's Blues" is not the first incident in Sonny and his brother's relationship. Why does the story begin here? Does this story have a "happy ending"? According to Atwood, Baldwin should, in all honesty, carry on with the story until both Sonny and his brother die. Why does Baldwin's story end here?

8. See Isaiah 51:17, 22–23: "Awake, awake, stand up, O Jerusalem, which hast drunk at the hand of the Lord the cup of his fury; thou hast drunken the dregs of the cup of trembling, and wrung them out. . . . Behold, I have taken out of thine hand the cup of trembling, even the dregs of the cup of my fury; thou shalt no more drink it again: But I will put it into the hand of them that afflict thee; . . ."

5. In "Sonny's Blues," how is the first-person narrator, the person telling the story, identified or characterized in the first sentence? in the first paragraph? in the first couple pages? in the story as a whole?

WRITING SUGGESTIONS

1. Choose one of Atwood's "stories" (or conflate two or three) and write a scene or two illustrating the "How" or the "Why."
2. Compare the treatment of marital infidelity in Cheever's "The Country Husband" and Maupassant's "The Jewelry," or one or more of the sketches in Atwood's "Happy Endings."
3. Write a story or a sketch or outline of a story centering on the same situation in "The Country Husband" but set in the 1990s and in a place you know.
4. Rearrange the episodes in "Sonny's Blues" as they would appear in the hypothetical history—that is, in chronological order. Pick the three or four changes that seem to you most important. Describe the difference in effect and significance that Baldwin has achieved with his structuring or rearrangement.

2

POINT OF VIEW

Structuring involves more than plot and the ordering of events; selection involves more than the choosing or inventing of incidents. What would "Sonny's Blues" be like seen through the eyes of Sonny? What incidents might he choose to tell? In what order might he arrange them?

Who is telling us the story—whose words are we reading? Where does this person stand in relation to what is going on in the story? In drama, events appear before us directly. Narrative, unlike drama, is always mediated. In narrative, someone is always *between* us and the events—a viewer, a speaker, or both. The way a story is mediated is a key element in fictional structure. This mediation involves both the angle of vision—the point from which the people, events, and other details are viewed—and also the words in which the story is embodied. The viewing aspect is called the **focus,** and the verbal aspect the **voice.** Both are generally lumped together in the term **point of view.**

Focus acts much as a camera does, choosing what we can look at and the angle at which we can view it, framing, proportioning, emphasizing—even distorting. Plot is a structure that places us in a time relationship to the history; focus places us in a spatial relationship.

We must pay careful attention to the focus at any given point in a story. Is it fixed or mobile? Does it stay at more or less the same angle to, and at the same distance from, the characters and action, or does it move around or in and out? In the first three and a half paragraphs of Ambrose Bierce's "An Occurrence at Owl Creek Bridge," for example, we seem to be seeing through the lens of a camera that can swing left or right, up or down, but that stays pretty much at the same angle and distance from the bridge. By the middle of the fourth paragraph, however, we're inside the mind of the man who's about to be hanged: "The arrangement commended itself to his judgment. . . . He looked a moment. . . . A piece of dancing driftwood caught his attention. . . . How slowly it appeared to move!" From now on we are inside the condemned man's head. The focus is more limited in scope—for almost all the rest of the story we can see and hear only what he sees and hears. But because the focus is internal as well as limited, we can also know what he thinks. This limited, internal focus is usually called the **centered** or **central consciousness.**

The centered consciousness has been perhaps the most popular focus in fiction for the past hundred years—through most of the history of the modern short story, in fact—and its tightly controlled range and concentration on a single individual seem particularly suited for the short form. During much of this period, fiction, both long and short, has been in one sense realistic—that is, treating the everyday and the natural. It has become increasingly clear, however, that the apparently real is not necessarily what "is" but what is *perceived by* the senses and mind of the individual. (This is sometimes called **psychological realism.**) The centered consciousness, in which things, people, and events are narrated as if perceived through the filter of an individual character's consciousness, has, therefore, seemed the more realistic way to tell a story. It is a comfortable focus for readers, too. On the one hand, we can identify with someone whose thoughts and perception we share, even if the character is fallible, like Lantin in "The Jewelry." We can identify with point of view in a story told in the first person ("I"), too, but we are too close at times. We cannot escape. The camera cannot pull back as it can in a third-person story.

First-person stories, like Edgar Allan Poe's "The Cask of Amontillado," are always limited, too, and almost always get inside the speaker's mind, though Montresor hides his plans from us. While the speaker cannot withdraw spatially from the narrator, he or she almost always is withdrawn temporally; that is, the "I" telling the story is older than the "I" experiencing the events. The narrator of Poe's story, for example, is telling what happened fifty years earlier.

The psychological realism gained by having a limited narrator exacts a price from the reader. If we don't hold the author (or the story) responsible for the absolute truth, validity, accuracy, and opinions of the focal character—if he or she is just telling us what he or she thinks, feels, sees—we must accept the possibility that the narrator's vision may be **unreliable.** At a significant point in "An Occurrence at Owl Creek Bridge," for example, you will find that the camera pulls back from Peyton Farquhar and you are made to recognize to what extent his consciousness is a reliable witness to what has been going on. The history here is only an occurrence; the limited point of view structures the mere occurrence into a story.

When the point of view is **limited,** whether to a first-person narrator or to a centered consciousness, it is tied to that individual. When he or she leaves the room, the camera must go, too, and if we are to know what happens in the room when the focal character is gone, some means of bringing the information to that character must be devised, such as a letter or a report by another character. The camera may pull back out of the character's mind or even, as in "An Occurrence at Owl Creek Bridge," above and away from the character, but it does not generally jump around. An unlimited point of view permits such freedom. In "The Zebra Storyteller" we are with the first zebra (who is killed) when he meets a cat speaking Zebraic and are told he is "astonished." We learn that the zebras can smell no lion and so "decided the woods were haunted by the ghost of a lion," and we get inside the mind of the storyteller and "hear" him speaking to himself. Throughout, the story seems free to see matter from one focus or another and even to dip inside a character's mind.

There are no laws governing point of view in fiction, but there is a general feeling that once a point of view is chosen it ought to be consistent. The movement of the focus at the beginning of "An Occurrence at Owl Creek Bridge" is not a jump but a narrowing down: the panorama at the beginning of the story, apparently from the point of view and in the voice of a distant observer, is adjusted and then we settle in, which is not an uncommon device (note how many movies used to begin with a panoramic shot of a town and gradually focused on a house or room). When toward the end of the story the "camera" moves back and away from Peyton Farquhar, we find there has been another reason for the panoramic shot at the beginning. There has been no jumping around and the narrowing and widening seem to be justifiable and meaningful. There are stories in this anthology—

"The Most Dangerous Game," "Barn Burning," and "The Lame Shall Enter First," for example—in which the point of view does shift—or jump—from a previously established centered consciousness. Whether these are "flaws" must be judged in each case in terms of function: is the shift merely a narrative convenience or manipulation, or is it consistent with or does it contribute to the significance or vision of the story?

Focus and voice often coincide; that is why they are commonly lumped together as point of view. There is no discrepancy that I can see (or hear) between the viewing and the telling in "The Cask of Amontillado," for example. But sometimes there is a discrepancy. Like the focus, the voice in "An Occurrence at Owl Creek Bridge" at the beginning of the story is not centered in Peyton Farquhar. But even when the focus narrows on him, the voice telling the story is not his; note, for example, "As these thoughts, *which have here to be set down in words,* were flashed into the doomed man's brain" (paragraph 7—emphasis added). The discrepancy may prepare a careful reader for later developments in the story.

I have used the common term **narrator** in the usual way—to mean the person who tells the story. You will have noticed that often the narrator really is a person in the story, like Montresor, the narrator in "The Cask of Amontillado." But how about the narrator in "An Occurrence at Owl Creek Bridge"? Who is it who sets down Farquhar's words and can say things that Farquhar is not thinking, such as "Death is a dignitary who, when he comes announced, is to be received with formal manifestations of respect, even by those most familiar with him. In the code of military etiquette silence and fixity are forms of deference" (paragraph 2). Where is the speaker standing? What kind of person is this narrator?

Is Ambrose Bierce the narrator? Where the narrator plays some role in the story we are less likely to identify him or her with the author; where the narrator is an unidentified voice we often tend to do so. To say that Bierce is the narrator of "An Occurrence at Owl Creek Bridge" is not necessarily wrong, but it can be misleading. We can dig up a few facts about the author's life and read them into the story, or, worse, read the character or detail of the story into the author's life. It is more prudent, therefore, especially on the basis of a single story, not to speak of the author but of the author's **persona,** the voice or figure of the author who tells and structures the story, who may or may not resemble in nature or values the actual person of the author. Mary Anne Evans wrote novels under the name of George Eliot; her first-person narrator speaks of "himself." That male narrator may be a good example of the persona or representative that most authors construct to "write" their stories.

We say *write* the stories. The narrator of "An Occurrence at Owl Creek Bridge" has to "set down in words" what Farquhar is thinking. But just as poets write of singing their songs (poems), so we often speak of telling a story, and we speak of a narrator, which means a teller. There are stories, usually with first-person narrators, that make much of the convention of oral storytelling—Louise Erdrich's "Love Medicine" for example. "The Cask of Amontillado" is more subtly "oral." It even has an **auditor,** someone other than the reader—that is, a character or characters within the fiction—to whom the "speech" is addressed. The "You" in the second sentence is no more you the reader than the "I" is Poe. He is a silent character within the fiction, here one whose identity or role can, with some thought, be identified.

We are used to thinking of a story in terms of its plot, so that to summarize a story usually means giving a plot summary. But if you shift focus and voice, you will often find that though the history has not changed, the story has. You might want to test this out by rewriting "The Cask of Amontillado" in the voice and focus of the auditor, or

"The Country Husband" in the voice and focus of Anne, the baby-sitter, or Francis Weed's wife.

It would be difficult to rewrite "Dreams" using a different focus. The point of view or, more precisely, the focus in "Dreams" is **unlimited**—that is, it shifts from one character's view and mind to another. Here, indeed, the focus is not even limited by the consciousness, for we are party to some of the character's dreams; nor, indeed, is it limited to "characters" in the usual sense since we are given even the dog Thurber's dreams and thoughts (see, for example, paragraphs 6, 54, 167). If Margaret Atwood's "Happy Endings" is about plot structure, "Dreams," in its way, is about focus. The focus of the narrative is unlimited because the very concept of the limited focus or perspective of the individual mind is made doubtful. We not only may be able to dream each other's dreams, our very minds or consciousness may be someone else's dream!

Point of view has been discussed here largely as a matter of structure, as having a role in creating the story and making it this story and no other. This structuring also engenders meaning and effect. What is the effect, for example, of having such a scoundrel as Montresor tell the story of "The Cask of Amontillado" in the first person? How do we feel about him during the story? Whose side are we on? Do we admire his cleverness or wit? Would we if the story were told from some other point of view? We can talk about how without the shift of the focus to Farquhar Bierce would not have a story, but what is the effect of the surprise ending of that story? How surprising is it? Do we feel cheated? Do we admire the cleverness of the telling? The shifting, unlimited focus of "Dreams" challenges and unsettles the reader's own sense of a verifiable reality and of having a completely and unquestionably autonomous self. "Sonny's Blues" should be the brother's story, for the outward action, the incidents, chiefly involve him, but the point of view is Sonny's and the meaning for us is the meaning for him. By sharing the experience with him, we must ask whether he/we has/have done the right thing. What do we learn? What do we feel? Much of what a story means, much of its effect upon us, depends on the eyes through which it is seen and on the voice that tells it to us.

EDGAR ALLAN POE

The Cask of Amontillado

The thousand injuries of Fortunato I had borne as I best could, but when he ventured upon insult I vowed revenge. You, who so well know the nature of my soul, will not suppose, however, that I gave utterance to a threat. *At length* I would be avenged; this was a point definitively settled—but the very definitiveness with which it was resolved precluded the idea of risk. I must not only punish but punish with impunity. A wrong is unredressed when retribution overtakes its redresser. It is equally unredressed when the avenger fails to make himself felt as such to him who has done the wrong.

It must be understood that neither by word nor deed had I given Fortunato cause to doubt my good will. I continued, as was my wont, to smile in his face, and he did not perceive that my smile *now* was at the thought of his immolation.

He had a weak point—this Fortunato—although in other regards he was a man to be respected and even feared. He prided himself upon his connoisseurship in wine. Few Italians have the true virtuoso spirit. For the most part their enthusiasm is adopted to suit the time and opportunity, to practice imposture upon the British and Austrian *millionaires*. In painting and gemmary, Fortunato, like his countrymen, was a quack, but in the matter of old wines he was sincere. In this respect I did not differ from him materially;—I was skilful in the Italian vintages myself, and bought largely whenever I could.

It was about dusk, one evening during the supreme madness of the carnival season, that I encountered my friend. He accosted me with excessive warmth, for he had been drinking much. The man wore motley. He had on a tight-fitting parti-striped dress, and his head was surmounted by the conical cap and bells. I was so pleased to see him that I should never have done wringing his hand.

5   I said to him—"My dear Fortunato, you are luckily met. How remarkably well you are looking to-day. But I have received a pipe[1] of what passes for Amontillado, and I have my doubts."

"How?" said he. "Amontillado? A pipe? Impossible! And in the middle of the carnival!"

"I have my doubts," I replied; "and I was silly enough to pay the full Amontillado price without consulting you in the matter. You were not to be found, and I was fearful of losing a bargain."

"Amontillado!"

"I have my doubts."

10   "Amontillado!"

"And I must satisfy them."

"Amontillado!"

"As you are engaged, I am on my way to Luchresi. If any one has a critical turn it is he. He will tell me——"

"Luchresi cannot tell Amontillado from Sherry."

15   "And yet some fools will have it that his taste is a match for your own."

"Come, let us go."

"Whither?"

"To your vaults."

"My friend, no; I will not impose upon your good nature. I perceive you have an engagement. Luchresi——"

20   "I have no engagement;—come."

"My friend, no. It is not the engagement, but the severe cold with which I perceive you are afflicted. The vaults are insufferably damp. They are encrusted with nitre."

"Let us go, nevertheless. The cold is merely nothing. Amontillado! You have been imposed upon. And as for Luchresi, he cannot distinguish Sherry from Amontillado."

Thus speaking, Fortunato possessed himself of my arm; and putting on a mask

1. A cask holding 126 gallons.

of black silk and drawing a *roquelaire*[2] closely about my person, I suffered him to hurry me to my palazzo.

There were no attendants at home; they had absconded to make merry in honour of the time. I had told them that I should not return until the morning, and had given them explicit orders not to stir from the house. These orders were sufficient, I well knew, to insure their immediate disappearance, one and all, as soon as my back was turned.

I took from their sconces two flambeaux, and giving one to Fortunato, bowed him through several suites of rooms to the archway that led into the vaults. I passed down a long and winding staircase, requesting him to be cautious as he followed. We came at length to the foot of the descent, and stood together upon the damp ground of the catacombs of the Montresors.

The gait of my friend was unsteady, and the bells upon his cap jingled as he strode.

"The pipe," said he.

"It is farther on," said I; "but observe the white web-work which gleams from these cavern walls."

He turned towards me, and looked into my eyes with two filmy orbs that distilled the rheum of intoxication.

"Nitre?" he asked, at length.

"Nitre," I replied. "How long have you had that cough?"

"Ugh! ugh! ugh!—ugh! ugh! ugh!—ugh! ugh! ugh!—ugh! ugh! ugh!—ugh! ugh! ugh!"

My poor friend found it impossible to reply for many minutes.

"It is nothing," he said, at last.

"Come," I said, with decision, "we will go back; your health is precious. You are rich, respected, admired, beloved; you are happy, as once I was. You are a man to be missed. For me it is no matter. We will go back; you will be ill, and I cannot be responsible. Besides, there is Luchresi——"

"Enough," he said; "the cough is a mere nothing; it will not kill me. I shall not die of a cough."

"True—true," I replied; "and, indeed, I had no intention of alarming you unneccessarily—but you should use all proper caution. A draught of this Medoc[3] will defend us from the damps."

Here I knocked off the neck of a bottle which I drew from a long row of its fellows that lay upon the mould.

"Drink," I said, presenting him the wine.

He raised it to his lips with a leer. He paused and nodded to me familiarly, while his bells jingled.

"I drink," he said, "to the buried that repose around us."

"And I to your long life."

He again took my arm, and we proceeded.

"These vaults," he said, "are extensive."

"The Montresors," I replied, "were a great and numerous family."

2. Roquelaure: man's heavy, knee-length cloak.   3. Like De Grâve (below), a French wine.

"I forget your arms."

"A huge human foot d'or,[4] in a field azure; the foot crushes a serpent rampant whose fangs are imbedded in the heel."

"And the motto?"

"Nemo me impune lacessit."[5]

"Good!" he said.

The wine sparkled in his eyes and the bells jingled. My own fancy grew warm with the Medoc. We had passed through long walls of piled skeletons, with casks and puncheons intermingling, into the inmost recesses of the catacombs. I paused again, and this time I made bold to seize Fortunato by an arm above the elbow.

"The nitre!" I said; "see, it increases. It hangs like moss upon the vaults. We are below the river's bed. The drops of moisture trickle among the bones. Come, we will go back ere it is too late. Your cough——"

"It is nothing," he said; "let us go on. But first, another draught of the Medoc."

I broke and reached him a flaçon of De Grâve. He emptied it at a breath. His eyes flashed with a fierce light. He laughed and threw the bottle upwards with a gesticulation I did not understand.

I looked at him in surprise. He repeated the movement—a grotesque one.

"You do not comprehend?" he said.

"Not I," I replied.

"Then you are not of the brotherhood."

"How?"

"You are not of the masons."[6]

"Yes, yes," I said; "yes, yes."

"You? Impossible! A mason?"

"A mason," I replied.

"A sign," he said, "a sign."

"It is this," I answered producing from beneath the folds of my *roquelaire* a trowel.

"You jest," he exclaimed, recoiling a few paces. "But let us proceed to the Amontillado."

"Be it so," I said, replacing the tool beneath the cloak and again offering him my arm. He leaned upon it heavily. We continued our route in search of the Amontillado. We passed through a range of low arches, descended, passed on, and descending again, arrived at a deep crypt, in which the foulness of the air caused our flambeaux rather to glow than flame.

At the most remote end of the crypt there appeared another less spacious. Its walls had been lined with human remains, piled to the vault overhead, in the fashion of the great catacombs of Paris. Three sides of this interior crypt were still ornamented in this manner. From the fourth side the bones had been thrown down, and lay promiscuously upon the earth, forming at one point a mound of some size. Within the wall thus exposed by the displacing of the bones, we per-

---

4. Of gold.   5. "No one provokes me with impunity."   6. Masons or Freemasons, an international secret society condemned by the Catholic Church. Montresor means by mason one who builds with stone, brick, etc.

ceived a still interior crypt or recess, in depth about four feet, in width three, in height six or seven. It seemed to have been constructed for no especial use within itself, but formed merely the interval between two of the colossal supports of the roof of the catacombs, and was backed by one of their circumscribing walls of solid granite.

It was in vain that Fortunato, uplifting his dull torch, endeavoured to pry into the depth of the recess. Its termination the feeble light did not enable us to see.

"Proceed," I said; "herein is the Amontillado. As for Luchresi——" 70

"He is an ignoramus," interrupted my friend, as he stepped unsteadily forward, while I followed immediately at his heels. In an instant he had reached the extremity of the niche, and finding his progress arrested by the rock, stood stupidly bewildered. A moment more and I had fettered him to the granite. In its surface were two iron staples, distant from each other about two feet, horizontally. From one of these depended a short chain, from the other a padlock. Throwing the links about his waist, it was but the work of a few seconds to secure it. He was too much astounded to resist. Withdrawing the key I stepped back from the recess.

"Pass your hand," I said, "over the wall; you cannot help feeling the nitre. Indeed, it is *very* damp. Once more let me *implore* you to return. No? Then I must positively leave you. But I will first render you all the little attentions in my power."

"The Amontillado!" ejaculated my friend, not yet recovered from his astonishment.

"True," I replied; "the Amontillado."

As I said these words I busied myself among the pile of bones of which I have 75 before spoken. Throwing them aside, I soon uncovered a quantity of building stone and mortar. With these materials and with the aid of my trowel, I began vigorously to wall up the entrance of the niche.

I had scarcely laid the first tier of the masonry when I discovered that the intoxication of Fortunato had in great measure worn off. The earliest indication I had of this was a low moaning cry from the depth of the recess. It was *not* the cry of a drunken man. There was then a long and obstinate silence. I laid the second tier, and the third, and the fourth; and then I heard the furious vibration of the chain. The noise lasted for several minutes, during which, that I might hearken to it with the more satisfaction, I ceased my labours and sat down upon the bones. When at last the clanking subsided, I resumed the trowel, and finished without interruption the fifth, the sixth, and the seventh tier. The wall was now nearly upon a level with my breast. I again paused, and holding the flambeaux over the mason-work, threw a few feeble rays upon the figure within.

A succession of loud and shrill screams, bursting suddenly from the throat of the chained form, seemed to thrust me violently back. For a brief moment I hesitated, I trembled. Unsheathing my rapier, I began to grope with it about the recess; but the thought of an instant reassured me. I placed my hand upon the solid fabric of the catacombs and felt satisfied. I reapproached the wall. I replied to the yells of him who clamoured. I re-echoed, I aided, I surpassed them in volume and in strength. I did this, and the clamourer grew still.

It was now midnight, and my task was drawing to a close. I had completed the eighth, the ninth and the tenth tier. I had finished a portion of the last and the eleventh; there remained but a single stone to be fitted and plastered in. I struggled with its weight; I placed it partially in its destined position. But now there came from out the niche a low laugh that erected the hairs upon my head. It was succeeded by a sad voice, which I had difficulty in recognizing as that of the noble Fortunato. The voice said—

"Ha! ha! ha!—he! he! he!—a very good joke, indeed—an excellent jest. We will have many a rich laugh about it at the palazzo—he! he! he!—over our wine—he! he! he!"

80   "The Amontillado!" I said.

"He! he! he!—he! he! he!—yes, the Amontillado. But is it not getting late? Will not they be awaiting us at the palazzo—the Lady Fortunato and the rest? Let us be gone."

"Yes," I said, "let us be gone."

"For the love of God, Montresor!"

"Yes," I said, "for the love of God!"

85   But to these words I hearkened in vain for a reply. I grew impatient. I called aloud—

"Fortunato!"

No answer. I called again—

"Fortunato!"

No answer still. I thrust a torch through the remaining aperture and let it fall within. There came forth in return only a jingling of the bells. My heart grew sick; it was the dampness of the catacombs that made it so. I hastened to make an end of my labour. I forced the last stone into its position; I plastered it up. Against the new masonry I re-erected the old rampart of bones. For the half of a century no mortal has disturbed them. *In pace requiescat!*[7]

1846

AMBROSE BIERCE

An Occurrence at Owl Creek Bridge

I

A man stood upon a railroad bridge in Northern Alabama, looking down into the swift waters twenty feet below. The man's hands were behind his back, the wrists bound with a cord. A rope loosely encircled his neck. It was attached to a stout cross-timber above his head, and the slack fell to the level of his knees. Some loose boards laid upon the sleepers supporting the metals of the railway supplied a footing for him and his executioners—two private soldiers of the Federal army,

---

7. May he rest in peace!

directed by a sergeant, who in civil life may have been a deputy sheriff. At a short remove upon the same temporary platform was an officer in the uniform of his rank, armed. He was a captain. A sentinel at each end of the bridge stood with his rifle in the position known as "support," that is to say, vertical in front of the left shoulder, the hammer resting on the forearm thrown straight across the chest—a formal and unnatural position, enforcing an erect carriage of the body. It did not appear to be the duty of these two men to know what was occurring at the centre of the bridge; they merely blockaded the two ends of the foot plank which traversed it.

Beyond one of the sentinels nobody was in sight; the railroad ran straight away into a forest for a hundred yards, then, curving, was lost to view. Doubtless there was an outpost further along. The other bank of the stream was open ground—a gentle acclivity crowned with a stockade of vertical tree trunks, loop-holed for rifles, with a single embrasure through which protruded the muzzle of a brass cannon commanding the bridge. Midway of the slope between bridge and fort were the spectators—a single company of infantry in line, at "parade rest," the butts of the rifles on the ground, the barrels inclining slightly backward against the right shoulder, the hands crossed upon the stock. A lieutenant stood at the right of the line, the point of his sword upon the ground, his left hand resting upon his right. Excepting the group of four at the centre of the bridge not a man moved. The company faced the bridge, staring stonily, motionless. The sentinels, facing the banks of the stream, might have been statues to adorn the bridge. The captain stood with folded arms, silent, observing the work of his subordinates but making no sign. Death is a dignitary who, when he comes announced, is to be received with formal manifestations of respect, even by those most familiar with him. In the code of military etiquette silence and fixity are forms of deference.

The man who was engaged in being hanged was apparently about thirty-five years of age. He was a civilian, if one might judge from his dress, which was that of a planter. His features were good—a straight nose, firm mouth, broad forehead, from which his long, dark hair was combed straight back, falling behind his ears to the collar of his well-fitting frock coat. He wore a moustache and pointed beard, but no whiskers; his eyes were large and dark grey and had a kindly expression which one would hardly have expected in one whose neck was in the hemp. Evidently this was no vulgar assassin. The liberal military code makes provision for hanging many kinds of people, and gentlemen are not excluded.

The preparations being complete, the two private soldiers stepped aside and each drew away the plank upon which he had been standing. The sergeant turned to the captain, saluted and placed himself immediately behind that officer, who in turn moved apart one pace. These movements left the condemned man and the sergeant standing on the two ends of the same plank, which spanned three of the cross-ties of the bridge. The end upon which the civilian stood almost, but not quite, reached a fourth. This plank had been held in place by the weight of the captain; it was now held by that of the sergeant. At a signal from the former, the latter would step aside, the plank would tilt and the con-demned man go down between two ties. The arrangement commended itself to his judgment as simple and effective. His face had not been covered nor his eyes bandaged. He looked a moment at his "unsteadfast footing," then let his gaze wander to the swirling water of the stream racing madly beneath his feet. A piece of dancing driftwood caught his attention and his eyes followed it down the current. How slowly it appeared to move! What a sluggish stream!

5   He closed his eyes in order to fix his last thoughts upon his wife and children. The water, touched to gold by the early sun, the brooding mists under the banks at some distance down the stream, the fort, the soldiers, the piece of drift—all had distracted him. And now he became conscious of a new disturbance. Striking through the thought of his dear ones was a sound which he could neither ignore nor understand, a sharp, distinct, metallic percussion like the stroke of a black-smith's hammer upon the anvil; it had the same ringing quality. He wondered what it was, and whether immeasurably distant or near by—it seemed both. Its recurrence was regular, but as slow as the tolling of a death knell. He awaited each stroke with impatience and—he knew not why—apprehension. The intervals of silence grew progressively longer, the delays became maddening. With their greater infrequency the sounds increased in strength and sharpness. They hurt his ear like the thrust of a knife; he feared he would shriek. What he heard was the ticking of his watch.

He unclosed his eyes and saw again the water below him. "If I could free my hands," he thought, "I might throw off the noose and spring into the stream. By diving I could evade the bullets, and, swimming vigorously, reach the bank, take to the woods, and get away home. My home, thank God, is as yet outside their lines; my wife and little ones are still beyond the invader's farthest advance."

As these thoughts, which have here to be set down in words, were flashed into the doomed man's brain rather than evolved from it, the captain nodded to the sergeant. The sergeant stepped aside.

II

Peyton Farquhar was a well-to-do planter, of an old and highly-respected Ala-bama family. Being a slave owner, and, like other slave owners, a politician, he was naturally an original secessionist and ardently devoted to the Southern cause. Circumstances of an imperious nature which it is unnecessary to relate here, had prevented him from taking service with the gallant army which had fought the disastrous campaigns ending with the fall of Corinth,[1] and he chafed under the inglorious restraint, longing for the release of his energies, the larger life of the soldier, the opportunity for distinction. That opportunity, he felt, would come, as it comes to all in war time. Meanwhile he did what he could. No service was too humble for him to perform in aid of the South, no adventure too perilous for him to undertake if consistent with the character of a civilian who was at heart a soldier, and who in good faith and without too much qualification assented to at least a part of the frankly villainous dictum that all is fair in love and war.

---

1. Corinth, Mississippi, captured by General Ulysses S. Grant in April 1862.

One evening while Farquhar and his wife were sitting on a rustic bench near the entrance to his grounds, a grey-clad soldier rode up to the gate and asked for a drink of water. Mrs. Farquhar was only too happy to serve him with her own white hands. While she was gone to fetch the water, her husband approached the dusty horseman and inquired eagerly for news from the front.

"The Yanks are repairing the railroads," said the man, "and are getting ready for another advance. They have reached the Owl Creek bridge, put it in order, and built a stockade on the other bank. The commandant has issued an order, which is posted everywhere, declaring that any civilian caught interfering with the railroad, its bridges, tunnels, or trains, will be summarily hanged. I saw the order."

"How far is it to the Owl Creek bridge?" Farquhar asked.

"About thirty miles."

"Is there no force on this side the creek?"

"Only a picket post half a mile out, on the railroad, and a single sentinel at this end of the bridge."

"Suppose a man—a civilian and student of hanging—should elude the picket post and perhaps get the better of the sentinel," said Farquhar, smiling, "what could he accomplish?"

The soldier reflected. "I was there a month ago," he replied. "I observed that the flood of last winter had lodged a great quantity of driftwood against the wooden pier at this end of the bridge. It is now dry and would burn like tow."

The lady had now brought the water, which the soldier drank. He thanked her ceremoniously, bowed to her husband, and rode away. An hour later, after nightfall, he repassed the plantation, going northward in the direction from which he had come. He was a Federal scout.

III

As Peyton Farquhar fell straight downward through the bridge, he lost consciousness and was as one already dead. From this state he was awakened—ages later, it seemed to him—by the pain of a sharp pressure upon his throat, followed by a sense of suffocation. Keen, poignant agonies seemed to shoot from his neck downward through every fibre of his body and limbs. These pains appeared to flash along well-defined lines of ramification, and to beat with an inconceivably rapid periodicity. They seemed like streams of pulsating fire heating him to an intolerable temperature. As to his head, he was conscious of nothing but a feeling of fullness—of congestion. These sensations were unaccompanied by thought. The intellectual part of his nature was already effaced; he had power only to feel, and feeling was torment. He was conscious of motion. Encompassed in a luminous cloud, of which he was now merely the fiery heart, without material substance, he swung through unthinkable arcs of oscillation, like a vast pendulum. Then all at once, with terrible suddenness, the light about him shot upward with the noise of a loud plash; a frightful roaring was in his ears, and all was cold and dark. The power of thought was restored; he knew that the rope had broken and he had fallen into the stream. There was no additional strangulation; the noose about his neck was already suffocating him, and kept the water from his lungs. To die of hanging at the bottom of a river!—the idea seemed to him ludicrous. He opened his eyes in the blackness and saw above him a gleam of light, but how distant, how inaccessible! He was still sinking, for the light became fainter and fainter until it was a mere glimmer. Then it began to grow and brighten, and he knew that he was rising toward the surface—knew it with reluctance, for he was now very comfortable. "To be hanged and drowned," he thought, "that is not so bad; but I do not wish to be shot. No; I will not be shot; that is not fair."

He was not conscious of an effort, but a sharp pain in his wrist apprised him that he was trying to free his hands. He gave the struggle his attention, as an idler might observe the feat of a juggler, without interest in the outcome. What splendid effort!—what magnificent, what superhuman strength! Ah, that was a fine endeavour! Bravo! The cord fell away; his arms parted and floated upward, the hands dimly seen on each side in the growing light. He watched them with a new interest as first one and then the other pounced upon the noose at his neck. They tore it away and thrust it fiercely aside, its undulations resembling those of a water-snake. "Put it back, put it back!" He thought he shouted these words to his hands, for the undoing of the noose had been succeeded by the direst pang which he had yet experienced. His neck ached horribly; his brain was on fire; his heart, which had been fluttering faintly, gave a great leap, trying to force itself out at his mouth. His whole body was racked and wrenched with an insupportable anguish! But his disobedient hands gave no heed to the command. They beat the water vigorously with quick, downward strokes, forcing him to the surface. He felt his head emerge; his eyes were blinded by the sunlight; his chest expanded convulsively, and with a supreme and crowning agony his lungs engulfed a great draught of air, which instantly he expelled in a shriek!

20   He was now in full possession of his physical senses. They were, indeed, preternaturally keen and alert. Something in the awful disturbance of his organic system had so exalted and refined them that they made record of things never before perceived. He felt the ripples upon his face and heard their separate sounds as they struck. He looked at the forest on the bank of the stream, saw the individual trees, the leaves and the veining of each leaf—the very insects upon them, the locusts, the brilliant-bodied flies, the grey spiders stretching their webs from twig to twig. He noted the prismatic colors in all the dewdrops upon a million blades of grass. The humming of the gnats that danced above the eddies of the stream, the beating of the dragon flies' wings, the strokes of the water spiders' legs, like oars which had lifted their boat—all these made audible music. A fish slid along beneath his eyes and he heard the rush of its body parting the water.

He had come to the surface facing down the stream; in a moment the visible world seemed to wheel slowly round, himself the pivotal point, and he saw the bridge, the fort, the soldiers upon the bridge, the captain, the sergeant, the two privates, his executioners. They were in silhouette against the blue sky. They shouted and gesticulated, pointing at him; the captain had drawn his pistol, but did not fire; the others were unarmed. Their movements were grotesque and horrible, their forms gigantic.

Suddenly he heard a sharp report and something struck the water smartly within a few inches of his head, spattering his face with spray. He heard a second report, and saw one of the sentinels with his rifle at his shoulder, a light cloud of blue smoke rising from the muzzle. The man in the water saw the eye of the man on the bridge gazing into his own through the sights of the rifle. He observed that it was a grey eye, and remembered having read that grey eyes were keenest and that all famous marksmen had them. Nevertheless, this one had missed.

A counter swirl had caught Farquhar and turned him half round; he was again looking into the forest on the bank opposite the fort. The sound of a clear, high voice in a monotonous singsong now rang out behind him and came across the water with a distinctness that pierced and subdued all other sounds, even the beating of the ripples in his ears. Although no soldier, he had frequented camps enough to know the dread significance of that deliberate, drawling, aspirated chant; the lieutenant on shore was taking a part in the morning's work. How coldly and pitilessly—with what an even, calm intonation, presaging and enforcing tranquillity in the men—with what accurately-measured intervals fell those cruel words:

"Attention, company. . . . Shoulder arms. . . . Ready. . . . Aim. . . . Fire."

Farquhar dived—dived as deeply as he could. The water roared in his ears like the voice of Niagara, yet he heard the dulled thunder of the volley, and rising again toward the surface, met shining bits of metal, singularly flattened, oscillating slowly downward. Some of them touched him on the face and hands, then fell away, continuing their descent. One lodged between his collar and neck; it was uncomfortably warm, and he snatched it out.

As he rose to the surface, gasping for breath, he saw that he had been a long time under water; he was perceptibly farther down stream—nearer to safety. The soldiers had almost finished reloading; the metal ramrods flashed all at once in the sunshine as they were drawn from the barrels, turned in the air, and thrust into their sockets. The two sentinels fired again, independently and ineffectually.

The hunted man saw all this over his shoulder; he was now swimming vigorously with the current. His brain was as energetic as his arms and legs; he thought with the rapidity of lightning.

"The officer," he reasoned, "will not make that martinet's error a second time. It is as easy to dodge a volley as a single shot. He has probably already given the command to fire at will. God help me, I cannot dodge them all!"

An appalling plash within two yards of him, followed by a loud rushing sound, *diminuendo*, which seemed to travel back through the air to the fort and died in an explosion which stirred the very river to its deeps! A rising sheet of water, which curved over him, fell down upon him, blinded him, strangled him! The cannon had taken a hand in the game. As he shook his head free from the commotion of the smitten water, he heard the deflected shot humming through the air ahead, and in an instant it was cracking and smashing the branches in the forest beyond.

"They will not do that again," he thought; "the next time they will use a charge of grape. I must keep my eye upon the gun; the smoke will apprise me— the report arrives too late; it lags behind the missile. It is a good gun."

Suddenly he felt himself whirled round and round—spinning like a top. The water, the banks, the forest, the now distant bridge, fort and men—all were com-mingled and blurred. Objects were represented by their colors only; circular hori-zontal streaks of color—that was all he saw. He had been caught in a vortex and was being whirled on with a velocity of advance and gyration which made him giddy and sick. In a few moments he was flung upon the gravel at the foot of the left bank of the stream—the southern bank—and behind a projecting point which concealed him from his enemies. The sudden arrest of his motion, the abrasion of one of his hands on the gravel, restored him and he wept with delight. He dug his fingers into the sand, threw it over himself in handfuls and audibly blessed it. It looked like gold, like diamonds, rubies, emeralds; he could think of nothing beautiful which it did not resemble. The trees upon the bank were giant garden plants; he noted a definite order in their arrangement, inhaled the fragrance of their blooms. A strange, roseate light shone through the spaces among their trunks, and the wind made in their branches the music of æolian harps. He had no wish to perfect his escape, was content to remain in that enchanting spot until retaken.

A whizz and rattle of grapeshot among the branches high above his head roused him from his dream. The baffled cannoneer had fired him a random fare-well. He sprang to his feet, rushed up the sloping bank, and plunged into the forest.

All that day he travelled, laying his course by the rounding sun. The forest seemed interminable; nowhere did he discover a break in it, not even a wood-man's road. He had not known that he lived in so wild a region. There was some-thing uncanny in the revelation.

By nightfall he was fatigued, footsore, famishing. The thought of his wife and children urged him on. At last he found a road which led him in what he knew to be the right direction. It was as wide and straight as a city street, yet it seemed untravelled. No fields bordered it, no dwelling anywhere. Not so much as the barking of a dog suggested human habitation. The black bodies of the great trees formed a straight wall on both sides, terminating on the horizon in a point, like a diagram in a lesson in perspective. Overhead, as he looked up through this rift in the wood, shone great golden stars looking unfamiliar and grouped in strange constellations. He was sure they were arranged in some order which had a secret and malign significance. The wood on either side was full of singular noises, among which—once, twice, and again—he distinctly heard whispers in an unknown tongue.

His neck was in pain, and, lifting his hand to it, he found it horribly swollen. He knew that it had a circle of black where the rope had bruised it. His eyes felt congested; he could no longer close them. His tongue was swollen with thirst; he relieved its fever by thrusting it forward from between his teeth into the cool air. How softly the turf had carpeted the untravelled avenue! He could no longer feel the roadway beneath his feet!

Doubtless, despite his suffering, he fell asleep while walking, for now he sees another scene—perhaps he has merely recovered from a delirium. He stands at the gate of his own home. All is as he left it, and all bright and beautiful in the morning sunshine. He must have travelled the entire night. As he pushes open the gate and passes up the wide white walk, he sees a flutter of female garments; his wife, looking fresh and cool and sweet, steps down from the verandah to meet him. At the bottom of the steps she stands waiting, with a smile of ineffable joy, an attitude of matchless grace and dignity. Ah, how beautiful she is! He springs forward with extended arms. As he is about to clasp her, he feels a stunning blow upon the back of the neck; a blinding white light blazes all about him, with a sound like the shock of a cannon—then all is darkness and silence!

Peyton Farquhar was dead; his body, with a broken neck, swung gently from side to side beneath the timbers of the Owl Creek bridge.

1891

TIMOTHY FINDLEY

Dreams

For R. E. Turner

Doctor Menlo was having a problem: he could not sleep and his wife—the other Doctor Menlo—was secretly staying awake in order to keep an eye on him. The trouble was that, in spite of her concern and in spite of all her efforts, Doctor Menlo—whose name was Mimi—was always nodding off because of her exhaustion.

She had tried drinking coffee, but this had no effect. She detested coffee and her system had a built-in rejection mechanism. She also prescribed herself a week's worth of Dexedrine to see if that would do the trick. *Five mg*[1] *at bedtime*— all to no avail. And even though she put the plastic bottle of small orange hearts beneath her pillow and kept augmenting her intake, she would wake half an hour later with a dreadful start to discover the night was moving on to morning.

Everett Menlo had not yet declared the source of his problem. His restless condition had begun about ten days ago and had barely raised his interest. Soon, however, the time spent lying awake had increased from one to several hours and then, on Monday last, to all-night sessions. Now he lay in a state of rigid apprehension—eyes wide open, arms above his head, his hands in fists—like a man in pain unable to shut it out. His neck, his back and his shoulders constantly harried him with cramps and spasms. Everett Menlo had become a full-blown insomniac.

Clearly, Mimi Menlo concluded, her husband was refusing to sleep because he believed something dreadful was going to happen the moment he closed his eyes. She had encountered this sort of fear in one or two of her patients. Everett, on the other hand, would not discuss the subject. If the problem had been hers, he would have said *such things cannot occur if you have gained control of yourself.*

---

1. Milligrams.

Mimi began to watch for the dawn. She would calculate its approach by listening for the increase of traffic down below the bedroom window. The Menlos'
home was across the road from The Manulife Centre—corner of Bloor and Bay
streets. Mimi's first sight of daylight always revealed the high, white shape of its
terraced storeys. Their own apartment building was of a modest height and colour—twenty floors of smoky glass and polished brick. The shadow of the Manulife would crawl across the bedroom floor and climb the wall behind her, grey
with fatigue and cold.

The Menlo beds were an arm's length apart, and lying like a rug between them
was the shape of a large, black dog of unknown breed. All night long, in the dark
of his well, the dog would dream and he would tell the content of his dreams the
way that victims in a trance will tell of being pursued by posses of their nameless
fears. He whimpered, he cried and sometimes he howled. His legs and his paws
would jerk and flail and his claws would scrabble desperately against the parquet
floor. Mimi—who loved this dog—would lay her hand against his side and let
her fingers dabble in his coat in vain attempts to soothe him. Sometimes, she
had to call his name in order to rouse him from his dreams because his heart
would be racing. Other times, she smiled and thought: *at least there's one of us
getting some sleep.* The dog's name was Thurber and he dreamed in beige and
white.

Everett and Mimi Menlo were both psychiatrists. His field was schizophrenia;
hers was autistic children. Mimi's venue was the Parkin Institute at the University
of Toronto; Everett's was the Queen Street Mental Health Centre. Early in their
marriage they had decided never to work as a team and not—unless it was a
matter of financial life and death—to accept employment in the same institution. Both had always worked with the kind of physical intensity that kills, and
yet they gave the impression this was the only tolerable way in which to function. It meant there was always a sense of peril in what they did, but the peril—
according to Everett—made their lives worth living. This, at least, had been his
theory twenty years ago when they were young.

Now, for whatever unnamed reason, peril had become his enemy and Everett
Menlo had begun to look and behave and lose his sleep like a haunted man. But
he refused to comment when Mimi asked him what was wrong. Instead, he gave
the worst of all possible answers a psychiatrist can hear who seeks an explanation
of a patient's silence: he said there was *absolutely nothing wrong.*

"You're sure you're not coming down with something?"

"Yes."

"And you wouldn't like a massage?"

"I've already told you: no."

"Can I get you anything?"

"No."

"And you don't want to talk?"

"That's right."

"Okay, Everett . . ."

"Okay, what?"

"Okay, nothing. I only hope you get some sleep tonight."

Everett stood up. "Have you been spying on me, Mimi?"   20

"What do you mean by *spying?*"

"Watching me all night long."

"Well, Everett, I don't see how I can fail to be aware you aren't asleep when we share this bedroom. I mean—I can hear you grinding your teeth. I can see you lying there wide awake."

"When?"

"All the time. You're staring at the ceiling."   25

"I've never stared at the ceiling in my whole life. I sleep on my stomach."

"You sleep on your stomach *if* you sleep. But you have not been sleeping. Period. No argument."

Everett Menlo went to his dresser and got out a pair of clean pyjamas. Turning his back on Mimi, he put them on.

Somewhat amused at the coyness of this gesture, Mimi asked what he was hiding.

"Nothing!" he shouted at her.   30

Mimi's mouth fell open. Everett never yelled. His anger wasn't like that; it manifested itself in other ways, in silence and withdrawal, never shouts.

Everett was staring at her defiantly. He had slammed the bottom drawer of his dresser. Now he was fumbling with the wrapper of a pack of cigarettes.

Mimi's stomach tied a knot.

Everett hadn't touched a cigarette for weeks.

"Please don't smoke those," she said. "You'll only be sorry if you do." 35

"And you," he said, "will be sorry if I don't."

"But, dear . . ." said Mimi.

"Leave me for Christ's sake alone!" Everett yelled.

Mimi gave up and sighed and then she said: "all right. Thurber and I will go and sleep in the living-room. Good-night."

Everett sat on the edge of his bed. His hands were shaking.   40

"Please," he said—apparently addressing the floor. "Don't leave me here alone. I couldn't bear that."

This was perhaps the most chilling thing he could have said to her. Mimi was alarmed; her husband was genuinely terrified of something and he would not say what it was. If she had not been who she was—if she had not known what she knew—if her years of training had not prepared her to watch for signs like this, she might have been better off. As it was, she had to face the possibility the strongest, most sensible man on earth was having a nervous breakdown of major proportions. Lots of people have breakdowns, of course; but not, she had thought, the gods of reason.

"All right," she said—her voice maintaining the kind of calm she knew a child afraid of the dark would appreciate. "In a minute I'll get us something to drink. But first, I'll go and change. . . ."

Mimi went into the sanctum of the bathroom, where her nightgown waited for her—a portable hiding-place hanging on the back of the door. "You stay there," she said to Thurber, who had padded after her. "Mama will be out in just a moment."

45   Even in the dark, she could gauge Everett's tension. His shadow—all she could see of him—twitched from time to time and the twitching took on a kind of lurching rhythm, something like the broken clock in their living-room.

Mimi lay on her side and tried to close her eyes. But her eyes were tied to a will of their own and would not obey her. Now she, too, was caught in the same irreversible tide of sleeplessness that bore her husband backward through the night. Four or five times she watched him lighting cigarettes—blowing out the matches, courting disaster in the bedclothes—conjuring the worst of deaths for the three of them: a flaming pyre on the twentieth floor.

All this behaviour was utterly unlike him; foreign to his code of disciplines and ethics; alien to everything he said and believed. *Openness, directness, sharing of ideas, encouraging imaginative response to every problem. Never hide troubles. Never allow despair* . . . These were his directives in everything he did. Now, he had thrown them over.

One thing was certain. She was not the cause of his sleeplessness. She didn't have affairs and neither did he. He might be ill—but whenever he'd been ill before, there had been no trauma; never a trauma like this one, at any rate. Perhaps it was something about a patient—one of his tougher cases; a wall in the patient's condition they could not break through; some circumstance of someone's lack of progress—a sudden veering towards a catatonic state, for instance—something that Everett had not foreseen that had stymied him and was slowly . . . what? Destroying his sense of professional control? His self-esteem? His scientific certainty? If only he would speak.

Mimi thought about her own worst case: a child whose obstinate refusal to communicate was currently breaking her heart and, thus, her ability to help. If ever she had needed Everett to talk to, it was now. All her fellow doctors were locked in a battle over this child; they wanted to take him away from her. Mimi refused to give him up; he might as well have been her own flesh and blood. Everything had been done—from gentle holding sessions to violent bouts of manufactured anger—in her attempt to make the child react. She was staying with him every day from the moment he was roused to the moment he was induced to sleep with drugs.

50   His name was Brian Bassett and he was eight years old. He sat on the floor in the furthest corner he could achieve in one of the observation-isolation rooms where all the autistic children were placed when nothing else in their treatment—nothing of love or expertise—had managed to break their silence. Mostly, this was a signal they were coming to the end of life.

There in his four-square, glass-box room, surrounded by all that can tempt a child if a child can be tempted—toys and food and story-book companions—Brian Bassett was in the process, now, of fading away. His eyes were never closed and his arms were restrained. He was attached to three machines that nurtured him with all that science can offer. But of course, the spirit and the will to live cannot be fed by force to those who do not want to feed.

Now, in the light of Brian Bassett's utter lack of willing contact with the world around him—his utter refusal to communicate—Mimi watched her husband through the night. Everett stared at the ceiling, lit by the Manulife building's distant lamps, borne on his back further and further out to sea. She had lost him, she was certain.

When, at last, he saw that Mimi had drifted into her own and welcome sleep, Everett rose from his bed and went out into the hall, past the simulated jungle of the solarium, until he reached the dining-room. There, all the way till dawn, he amused himself with two decks of cards and endless games of Dead Man's Solitaire.

Thurber rose and shuffled after him. The dining-room was one of Thurber's favourite places in all his confined but privileged world, for it was here—as in the kitchen—that from time to time a hand descended filled with the miracle of food. But whatever it was that his master was doing up there above him on the table-top, it wasn't anything to do with feeding or with being fed. The playing cards had an old and dusty dryness to their scent and they held no appeal for the dog. So he once again lay down and he took up his dreams, which at least gave his paws some exercise. This way, he failed to hear the advent of a new dimension to his master's problem. This occurred precisely at 5:45 A.M. when the telephone rang and Everett Menlo, having rushed to answer it, waited breathless for a minute while he listened and then said: "yes" in a curious, strangulated fashion. Thurber—had he been awake—would have recognized in his master's voice the signal for disaster.

For weeks now, Everett had been working with a patient who was severely and uniquely schizophrenic. This patient's name was Kenneth Albright, and while he was deeply suspicious, he was also oddly caring. Kenneth Albright loved the detritus of life, such as bits of woolly dust and wads of discarded paper. He loved all dried-up leaves that had drifted from their parent trees and he loved the dead bees that had curled up to die along the window-sills of his ward. He also loved the spiderwebs seen high up in the corners of the rooms where he sat on plastic chairs and ate with plastic spoons.

Kenneth Albright talked a lot about his dreams. But his dreams had become, of late, a major stumbling block in the process of his recovery. Back in the days when Kenneth had first become Doctor Menlo's patient, the dreams had been overburdened with detail: "over-cast," as he would say, "with characters" and over-produced, again in Kenneth's phrase, "as if I were dreaming the dreams of Cecil B. de Mille."[2]

Then he had said: "but a person can't really dream someone else's dreams. Or can they, Doctor Menlo?"

2. Cecil Blount De Mille (1881–1959), motion-picture producer and director best known for his lavishly spectacular films on Biblical subjects.

"No" had been Everett's answer—definite and certain.

Everett Menlo had been delighted, at first, with Kenneth Albright's dreams. They had been immensely entertaining—complex and filled with intriguing detail. Kenneth himself was at a loss to explain the meaning of these dreams, but as Everett had said, it wasn't Kenneth's job to explain. That was Everett's job. His job and his pleasure. For quite a long while, during these early sessions, Everett had written out the dreams, taken them home and recounted them to Mimi.

60   Kenneth Albright was a paranoid schizophrenic. Four times now, he had attempted suicide. He was a fiercely angry man at times—and at other times as gentle and as pleasant as a docile child. He had suffered so greatly, in the very worst moments of his disease, that he could no longer work. His job—it was almost an incidental detail in his life and had no importance for him, so it seemed—was returning reference books, in the Metro Library, to their places in the stacks. Sometimes—mostly late of an afternoon—he might begin a psychotic episode of such profound dimensions that he would attempt his suicide right behind the counter and even once, in the full view of everyone, while riding in the glass-walled elevator. It was after this last occasion that he was brought, in restraints, to be a resident patient at the Queen Street Mental Health Centre. He had slashed his wrists with a razor—but not before he had also slashed and destroyed an antique copy of *Don Quixote,* the pages of which he pasted to the walls with blood.

For a week thereafter, Kenneth Albright—just like Brian Bassett—had refused to speak or to move. Everett had him kept in an isolation cell, force-fed and drugged. Slowly, by dint of patience, encouragement and caring even Kenneth could recognize as genuine, Everett Menlo had broken through the barrier. Kenneth was removed from isolation, pampered with food and cigarettes, and he began relating his dreams.

At first there seemed to be only the dreams and nothing else in Kenneth's memory. Broken pencils, discarded toys and the telephone directory all had roles to play in these dreams but there were never any people. All the weather was bleak and all the landscapes were empty. Houses, motor cars and office buildings never made an appearance. Sounds and smells had some importance; the wind would blow, the scent of unseen fires was often described. Stairwells were plentiful, leading nowhere, all of them rising from a subterranean world that Kenneth either did not dare to visit or would not describe.

The dreams had little variation, one from another. The themes had mostly to do with loss and with being lost. The broken pencils were all given names and the discarded toys were given to one another as companions. The telephone books were the sources of recitations—hours and hours of repeated names and numbers, some of which—Everett had noted with surprise—were absolutely accurate.

All of this held fast until an incident occurred one morning that changed the face of Kenneth Albright's schizophrenia forever; an incident that stemmed—so it seemed—from something he had dreamed the night before.

65   Bearing in mind his previous attempts at suicide, it will be obvious that Kenneth Albright was never far from sight at the Queen Street Mental Health Centre.

He was, in fact, under constant observation; constant, that is, as human beings and modern technology can manage. In the ward to which he was ultimately consigned, for instance, the toilet cabinets had no doors and the shower-rooms had no locks. Therefore, a person could not ever be alone with water, glass or shaving utensils. (All the razors were cordless automatics.) Scissors and knives were banned, as were pieces of string and rubber bands. A person could not even kill his feet and hands by binding up his wrists or ankles. Nothing poisonous was anywhere available. All the windows were barred. All the double doors between this ward and the corridors beyond were doors with triple locks and a guard was always near at hand.

Still, if people want to die, they will find a way. Mimi Menlo would discover this to her everlasting sorrow with Brian Bassett. Everett Menlo would discover this to his everlasting horror with Kenneth Albright.

On the morning of April 19th, a Tuesday, Everett Menlo, in the best of health, had welcomed a brand-new patient into his office. This was Anne Marie Wilson, a young and brilliant pianist whose promising career had been halted mid-flight by a schizophrenic incident involving her ambition. She was, it seemed, no longer able to play and all her dreams were shattered. The cause was simple, to all appearances: Anne Marie had a sense of how, precisely, the music should be and she had not been able to master it accordingly. "Everything I attempt is terrible," she had said—in spite of all her critical accolades and all her professional success. Other doctors had tried and failed to break the barriers in Anne Marie, whose hands had taken on a life of their own, refusing altogether to work for her. Now it was Menlo's turn and hope was high.

Everett had been looking forward to his session with this prodigy. He loved all music and had thought to find some means within its discipline to reach her. She seemed so fragile, sitting there in the sunlight, and he had just begun to take his first notes when the door flew open and Louise, his secretary, had said: "I'm sorry, Doctor Menlo. There's a problem. Can you come with me at once?"

Everett excused himself.

Anne Marie was left in the sunlight to bide her time. Her fingers were moving around in her lap and she put them in her mouth to make them quiet.   70

Even as he'd heard his secretary speak, Everett had known the problem would be Kenneth Albright. Something in Kenneth's eyes had warned him there was trouble on the way: a certain wariness that indicated all was not as placid as it should have been, given his regimen of drugs. He had stayed long hours in one position, moving his fingers over his thighs as if to dry them on his trousers; watching his fellow patients come and go with abnormal interest—never, however, rising from his chair. An incident was on the horizon and Everett had been waiting for it, hoping it would not come.

Louise had said that Doctor Menlo was to go at once to Kenneth Albright's ward. Everett had run the whole way. Only after the attendant had let him in past the double doors, did he slow his pace to a hurried walk and wipe his brow. He didn't want Kenneth to know how alarmed he had been.

Coming to the appointed place, he paused before he entered, closing his eyes, preparing himself for whatever he might have to see. *Other people have killed themselves: I've seen it often enough,* he was thinking. *I simply won't let it affect me.* Then he went in.

The room was small and white—a dining-room—and Kenneth was sitting down in a corner, his back pressed out against the walls on either side of him. His head was bowed and his legs drawn up and he was obviously trying to hide without much success. An intern was standing above him and a nurse was kneeling down beside him. Several pieces of bandaging with blood on them were scattered near Kenneth's feet and there was a white enamel basin filled with pinkish water on the floor beside the nurse.

75   "Morowetz," Everett said to the intern. "Tell me what has happened here." He said this just the way he posed such questions when he took the interns through the wards at examination time, quizzing them on symptoms and prognoses.

But Morowetz the intern had no answer. He was puzzled. What had happened had no sane explanation.

Everett turned to Charterhouse, the nurse.

"On the morning of April 19th, at roughly ten-fifteen, I found Kenneth Albright covered with blood," Ms Charterhouse was to write in her report. "His hands, his arms, his face and his neck were stained. I would say the blood was fresh and the patient's clothing—mostly his shirt—was wet with it. Some—a very small amount of it—had dried on his forehead. The rest was uniformly the kind of blood you expect to find free-flowing from a wound. I called for assistance and meanwhile attempted to ascertain where Mister Albright might have been injured. I performed this examination without success. I could find no source of bleeding anywhere on Mister Albright's body."

Morowetz concurred.

80   The blood was someone else's.

"Was there a weapon of any kind?" Doctor Menlo had wanted to know.

"No, sir. Nothing," said Charterhouse.

"And was he alone when you found him?"

"Yes, sir. Just like this in the corner."

85   "And the others?"

"All the patients in the ward were examined," Morowetz told him.

"And?"

"Not one of them was bleeding."

Everett said: "I see."

90   He looked down at Kenneth.

"This is Doctor Menlo, Kenneth. Have you anything to tell me?"

Kenneth did not reply.

Everett said: "When you've got him back in his room and tranquillized, will you call me, please?"

Morowetz nodded.

95   The call never came. Kenneth had fallen asleep. Either the drugs he was given had knocked him out cold, or he had opted for silence. Either way, he was incommunicado.

No one was discovered bleeding. Nothing was found to indicate an accident, a violent attack, an epileptic seizure. A weapon was not located. Kenneth Albright had not a single scratch on his flesh from stem, as Everett put it, to gudgeon. The blood, it seemed, had fallen like the rain from heaven: unexplained and inexplicable.

Later, as the day was ending, Everett Menlo left the Queen Street Mental Health Centre. He made his way home on the Queen streetcar and the Bay bus. When he reached the apartment, Thurber was waiting for him. Mimi was at a goddamned meeting.

That was the night Everett Menlo suffered the first of his failures to sleep. It was occasioned by the fact that, when he wakened sometime after three, he had just been dreaming. This, of course, was not unusual—but the dream itself was perturbing. There was someone lying there, in the bright white landscape of a hospital dining-room. Whether it was a man or a woman could not be told, it was just a human body, lying down in a pool of blood.

Kenneth Albright was kneeling beside this body, pulling it open the way a child will pull a Christmas present open—yanking at its strings and ribbons, wanting only to see the contents. Everett saw this scene from several angles, never speaking, never being spoken to. In all the time he watched—the usual dream eternity—the silence was broken only by the sound of water dripping from an unseen tap. Then, Kenneth Albright rose and was covered with blood, the way he had been that morning. He stared at Doctor Menlo, looked right through him and departed. Nothing remained in the dining-room but plastic tables and plastic chairs and the bright red thing on the floor that once had been a person. Everett Menlo did not know and could not guess who this person might have been. He only knew that Kenneth Albright had left this person's body in Everett Menlo's dream.

Three nights running, the corpse remained in its place and every time that Everett entered the dining-room in the nightmare he was certain he would find out who it was. On the fourth night, fully expecting to discover he himself was the victim, he beheld the face and saw it was a stranger.

But there are no strangers in dreams; he knew that now after twenty years of practice. *There are no strangers; there are only people in disguise.*

Mimi made one final attempt in Brian Bassett's behalf to turn away the fate to which his other doctors—both medical and psychiatric—had consigned him. Not that, as a group, they had failed to expend the full weight of all they knew and all they could do to save him. One of his medical doctors—a woman whose name was Juliet Bateman—had moved a cot into his isolation room and stayed with him twenty-four hours a day for over a week. But her health had been undermined by this and when she succumbed to the Shanghai flu she removed herself for fear of infecting Brian Bassett.

The parents had come and gone on a daily basis for months in a killing routine of visits. But parents, their presence and their loving, are not the answer when a child has fallen into an autistic state. They might as well have been strangers. And so they had been advised to stay away.

Brian Bassett was eight years old—*unlucky eight,* as one of his therapists had said—and in every other way, in terms of physical development and mental capability, he had always been a perfectly normal child. Now, in the final moments of his life, he weighed a scant thirty pounds, when he should have weighed twice that much.

105   Brian had not been heard to speak a single word in over a year of constant observation. Earlier—long ago as seven months—a few expressions would visit his face from time to time. Never a smile—but often a kind of sneer, a passing of judgment, terrifying in its intensity. Other times, a pinched expression would appear—a signal of the shyness peculiar to autistic children, who think of light as being unfriendly.

Mimi's militant efforts in behalf of Brian had been exemplary. Her fellow doctors thought of her as *Bassett's crazy guardian angel.* They begged her to remove herself in order to preserve her health. Being wise, being practical, they saw that all her efforts would not save him. But Mimi's version of being a guardian angel was more like being a surrogate warrior: a hired gun or a samurai. Her cool determination to thwart the enemies of silence, stillness and starvation gave her strengths that even she had been unaware were hers to command.

Brian Bassett, seated in his corner on the floor, maintained a solemn composure that lent his features a kind of unearthly beauty. His back was straight, his hands were poised, his hair was so fine he looked the very picture of a spirit waiting to enter a newborn creature. Sometimes Mimi wondered if this creature Brian Bassett waited to inhabit could be human. She thought of all the animals she had ever seen in all her travels and she fell upon the image of a newborn fawn as being the most tranquil and the most in need of stillness in order to survive. If only all the natural energy and curiosity of a newborn beast could have entered into Brian Bassett, surely, they would have transformed the boy in the corner into a vibrant, joyous human being. But it was not to be.

On the 29th of April—one week and three days after Everett had entered into his crisis of insomnia—Mimi sat on the floor in Brian Bassett's isolation room, gently massaging his arms and legs as she held him in her lap.

His weight, by now, was shocking—and his skin had become translucent. His eyes had not been closed for days—for weeks—and their expression might have been carved in stone.

110   "Speak to me. Speak," she whispered to him as she cradled his head beneath her chin. "Please at least speak before you die."

Nothing happened. Only silence.

Juliet Bateman—wrapped in a blanket—was watching through the observation glass as Mimi lifted up Brian Bassett and placed him in his cot. The cot had metal sides—and the sides were raised. Juliet Bateman could see Brian Bassett's eyes and his hands as Mimi stepped away.

Mimi looked at Juliet and shook her head. Juliet closed her eyes and pulled her blanket tighter like a skin that might protect her from the next five minutes.

Mimi went around the cot to the other side and dragged the IV stand in closer to the head. She fumbled for a moment with the long plastic lifelines—anti-dehydrants, nutrients—and she adjusted the needles and brought them down inside the nest of the cot where Brian Bassett lay and she lifted up his arm in order to insert the tubes and bind them into place with tape.

This was when it happened—just as Mimi Menlo was preparing to insert the second tube.

Brian Bassett looked at her and spoke.

"No," he said. "Don't."

Don't meant death.

Mimi paused—considered—and set the tube aside. Then she withdrew the tube already in place and she hung them both on the IV stand.

All right, she said to Brian Bassett in her mind, *you win.*

She looked down then with her arm along the side of the cot—and one hand trailing down so Brian Bassett could touch it if he wanted to. She smiled at him and said to him: "not to worry. Not to worry. None of us is ever going to trouble you again." He watched her carefully. "Goodbye, Brian," she said. "I love you."

Juliet Bateman saw Mimi Menlo say all this and was fairly sure she had read the words on Mimi's lips just as they had been spoken.

Mimi started out the room. She was determined now there was no turning back and that Brian Bassett was free to go his way. But just as she was turning the handle and pressing her weight against the door—she heard Brian Bassett speak again.

"Goodbye," he said.

And died.

Mimi went back and Juliet Bateman, too, and they stayed with him another hour before they turned out his lights. "Someone else can cover his face," said Mimi. "I'm not going to do it." Juliet agreed and they came back out to tell the nurse on duty that their ward had died and their work with him was over.

On the 30th of April—a Saturday—Mimi stayed home and made her notes and she wondered if and when she would weep for Brian Bassett. Her hand, as she wrote, was steady and her throat was not constricted and her eyes had no sensation beyond the burning itch of fatigue. She wondered what she looked like in the mirror, but resisted that discovery. Some things could wait. Outside it rained. Thurber dreamed in the corner. Bay Street rumbled in the basement.

Everett, in the meantime, had reached his own crisis and because of his desperate straits a part of Mimi Menlo's mind was on her husband. Now he had not slept for almost ten days. *We really ought to consign ourselves to hospital beds,* she thought. Somehow, the idea held no persuasion. It occurred to her that laughter might do a better job, if only they could find it. The brain, when over-extended, gives us the most surprisingly simple propositions, she concluded. *Stop,* it says to us. *Lie down and sleep.*

Five minutes later, Mimi found herself still sitting at the desk, with her fountain pen capped and her fingers raised to her lips in an attitude of gentle prayer. It required some effort to re-adjust her gaze and re-establish her focus on the surface of the window glass beyond which her mind had wandered. Sitting up, she had been asleep.

Thurber muttered something and stretched his legs and yawned, still asleep.

Mimi glanced in his direction. *We've both been dreaming*, she thought, *but his dream continues.*

Somewhere behind her, the broken clock was attempting to strike the hour of three. Its voice was dull and rusty, needing oil.

Looking down, she saw the words *BRIAN BASSETT* written on the page before her and it occurred to her that, without his person, the words were nothing more than extrapolations from the alphabet—something fanciful we call a "name" in the hope that, one day, it will take on meaning.

She thought of Brian Bassett with his building blocks—pushing the letters around on the floor and coming up with more acceptable arrangements: *TINA STERABBS . . . IAN BRETT BASS . . . BEST STAB the RAIN:* a sentence. He had known all along, of course, that *BRIAN BASSETT* wasn't what he wanted because it wasn't what he was. He had come here against his will, was held here against his better judgment, fought against his captors and finally escaped.

But where was here to Ian Brett Bass? Where was here to Tina Sterabbs? Like Brian Bassett, they had all been here in someone else's dreams, and had to wait for someone else to wake before they could make their getaway.

135   Slowly, Mimi uncapped her fountain pen and drew a firm, black line through Brian Bassett's name. *We dreamed him,* she wrote, *that's all. And then we let him go.*

Seeing Everett standing in the doorway, knowing he had just returned from another Kenneth Albright crisis, she had no sense of apprehension. All this was only as it should be. Given the way that everything was going, it stood to reason Kenneth Albright's crisis had to come in this moment. If he managed, at last, to kill himself then at least her husband might begin to sleep again.

Far in the back of her mind a carping, critical voice remarked that any such thoughts were *deeply unfeeling and verging on the barbaric.* But Mimi dismissed this voice and another part of her brain stepped forward in her defence. *I will weep for Kenneth Albright,* she thought, *when I can weep for Brian Bassett. Now, all that matters is that Everett and I survive.*

Then she strode forward and put out her hand for Everett's briefcase, set the briefcase down and helped him out of his topcoat. She was playing wife. It seemed to be the thing to do.

For the next twenty minutes Everett had nothing to say, and after he had poured himself a drink and after Mimi had done the same, they sat in their chairs and waited for Everett to catch his breath.

140   The first thing he said when he finally spoke was: "finish your notes?"

"Just about," Mimi told him. "I've written everything I can for now." She did not elaborate. "You're home early," she said, hoping to goad him into saying something new about Kenneth Albright.

"Yes," he said. "I am." But that was all.

Then he stood up—threw back the last of his drink and poured another. He lighted a cigarette and Mimi didn't even wince. He had been smoking now three days. The atmosphere between them had been, since then, enlivened with a magnetic kind of tension. But it was a moribund tension, slowly beginning to dissipate.

Mimi watched her husband's silent torment now with a kind of clinical detachment. This was the result, she liked to tell herself, of her training and her discipline. The lover in her could regard Everett warmly and with concern, but the psychiatrist in her could also watch him as someone suffering a nervous breakdown, someone who could not be helped until the symptoms had multiplied and declared themselves more openly.

Everett went into the darkest corner of the room and sat down hard in one of   145
Mimi's straight-backed chairs: the ones inherited from her mother. He sat, prim, like a patient in a doctor's office, totally unrelaxed and nervy; expressionless. Either he had come to receive a deadly diagnosis, or he would get a clean bill of health.

Mimi glided over to the sofa in the window, plush and red and deeply comfortable; a place to recuperate. The view—if she chose to turn only slightly sideways—was one of the gentle rain that was falling onto Bay Street. Sopping-wet pigeons huddled on the window-sill; people across the street in the Manulife building were turning on their lights.

A renegade robin, nesting in their eaves, began to sing.

Everett Menlo began to talk.

"Please don't interrupt," he said at first.

"You know I won't," said Mimi. It was a rule that neither one should interrupt   150
the telling of a case until they had been invited to do so.

Mimi put her fingers into her glass so the ice-cubes wouldn't click. She waited.

Everett spoke—but he spoke as if in someone else's voice, perhaps the voice of Kenneth Albright. This was not entirely unusual. Often, both Mimi and Everett Menlo spoke in the voices of their parents. What was unusual, this time, was that, speaking in Kenneth's voice, Everett began to sweat profusely—so profusely that Mimi was able to watch his shirt front darkening with perspiration.

"As you know," he said, "I have not been sleeping."

This was the understatement of the year. Mimi was silent.

"I have not been sleeping because—to put it in a nutshell—I have been afraid   155
to dream."

Mimi was somewhat startled by this. Not by the fact that Everett was afraid to dream, but only because she had just been thinking of dreams herself.

"I have been afraid to dream, because in all my dreams there have been bodies. Corpses. Murder victims."

Mimi—not really listening—idly wondered if she had been one of them.

"In all my dreams, there have been corpses," Everett repeated. "But I am not the murderer. Kenneth Albright is the murderer, and, up to this moment, he has left behind him fifteen bodies: none of them people I recognize."

Mimi nodded. The ice-cubes in her drink were beginning to freeze her fingers.   160
Any minute now, she prayed, they would surely melt.

"I gave up dreaming almost a week ago," said Everett, "thinking that if I did, the killing pattern might be altered; broken." Then he said tersely; "it was not. The killings have continued. . . ."

"How do you know the killings have continued, Everett, if you've given up your dreaming? Wouldn't this mean he had no place to hide the bodies?"

In spite of the fact she had disobeyed their rule about not speaking, Everett answered her.

"I know they are being continued because I have seen the blood."

165   "Ah, yes. I see."

"No, Mimi. No. You do not see. The blood is not a figment of my imagination. The blood, in fact, is the only thing not dreamed." He explained the stains on Kenneth Albright's hands and arms and clothes and he said: "It happens every day. We have searched his person for signs of cuts and gashes—even for internal and rectal bleeding. Nothing. We have searched his quarters and all the other quarters in his ward. His ward is locked. His ward is isolated in the extreme. None of his fellow patients was ever found bleeding—never had cause to bleed. There were no injuries—no self-inflicted wounds. We thought of animals. Perhaps a mouse—a rat. But nothing. Nothing. Nothing . . . We also went so far as to strip-search all the members of the staff who entered that ward and I, too, offered myself for this experiment. Still nothing. Nothing. No one had bled."

Everett was now beginning to perspire so heavily he removed his jacket and threw it on the floor. Thurber woke and stared at it, startled. At first, it appeared to be the beast that had just pursued him through the woods and down the road. But, then, it sighed and settled and was just a coat; a rumpled jacket lying down on the rug.

Everett said: "We had taken samples of the blood on the patient's hands—on Kenneth Albright's hands and on his clothing and we had these samples analysed. No. It was not his own blood. No, it was not the blood of an animal. No, it was not the blood of a fellow patient. No, it was not the blood of any members of the staff. . . ."

Everett's voice had risen.

170   "Whose blood was it?" he almost cried. "Whose the hell was it?"

Mimi waited.

Everett Menlo lighted another cigarette. He took a great gulp of his drink.

"Well . . ." He was calmer now; calmer of necessity. He had to marshall the evidence. He had to put it all in order—bring it into line with reason. "Did this mean that—somehow—the patient had managed to leave the premises—do some bloody deed and return without our knowledge of it? That is, after all, the only possible explanation. Isn't it?"

Mimi waited.

175   "Isn't it?" he repeated.

"Yes," she said. "It's the only possible explanation."

"Except there is no way out of that place. There is absolutely no way out."

Now, there was a pause.

"But one," he added—his voice, again, a whisper.

180   Mimi was silent. Fearful—watching his twisted face.

"Tell me," Everett Menlo said—the perfect innocent, almost the perfect child in quest of forbidden knowledge. "Answer me this—be honest: is there blood in dreams?"

Mimi could not respond. She felt herself go pale. Her husband—after all, the sanest man alive—had just suggested something so completely mad he might as well have handed over his reason in a paper bag and said to her, *burn this.*

"The only place that Kenneth Albright goes, I tell you, is into dreams," Everett said. "That is the only place beyond the ward into which the patient can or does escape."

Another—briefer—pause.

"It is real blood, Mimi. Real. And he gets it all from dreams. *My dreams.*"   185

They waited for this to settle.

Everett said: "I'm tired. I'm tired. I cannot bear this any more. I'm tired. . . ."

Mimi thought, *good. No matter what else happens, he will sleep tonight.*

He did. And so, at last, did she.

Mimi's dreams were rarely of the kind that engender fear. She dreamt more gen-   190
tle scenes with open spaces that did not intimidate. She would dream quite often of water and of animals. Always, she was nothing more than an observer; roles were not assigned her; often, this was sad. Somehow, she seemed at times locked out, unable to participate. These were the dreams she endured when Brian Bassett died: field trips to see him in some desert setting; underwater excursions to watch him floating amongst the seaweed. He never spoke, and, indeed, he never appeared to be aware of her presence.

That night, when Everett fell into his bed exhausted and she did likewise, Mimi's dream of Brian Bassett was the last she would ever have of him and some-how, in the dream, she knew this. What she saw was what, in magical terms, would be called a disappearing act. Brian Bassett vanished. Gone.

Sometime after midnight on May Day morning, Mimi Menlo awoke from her dream of Brian to the sound of Thurber thumping the floor in a dream of his own.

Everett was not in his bed and Mimi cursed. She put on her wrapper and her slippers and went beyond the bedroom into the hall.

No lights were shining but the street lamps far below and the windows gave no sign of stars.

Mimi made her way past the jungle, searching for Everett in the living-room.   195
He was not there. She would dream of this one day; it was a certainty.

"Everett?"

He did not reply.

Mimi turned and went back through the bedroom.

"Everett?"

She heard him. He was in the bathroom and she went in through the door.   200
"Oh," she said, when she saw him. "Oh, my God."

Everett Menlo was standing in the bathtub, removing his pyjamas. They were soaking wet, but not with perspiration. They were soaking wet with blood.

For a moment, holding his jacket, letting its arms hang down across his belly and his groin, Everett stared at Mimi, blank-eyed from his nightmare.

Mimi raised her hands to her mouth. She felt as one must feel, if helpless, watching someone burn alive.

205   Everett threw the jacket down and started to remove his trousers. His pyjamas, made of cotton, had been green. His eyes were blinded now with blood and his hands reached out to find the shower taps.

"Please don't look at me," he said. "I . . . Please go away."

Mimi said: "no." She sat on the toilet seat. "I'm waiting here," she told him, "until we both wake up."

1988

QUESTIONS

1. Who is the auditor, the "You," addressed in the first paragraph of "The Cask of Amontillado"? (You may want to wait until you have finished the last sentence of the story before answering.) When is the story being told? Why? How does your knowledge of the auditor and the occasion influence the story's effect?

2. Looking back over "An Occurrence at Owl Creek Bridge," how many of Peyton Farquhar's sensory perceptions can you reinterpret now that you know what must have been really happening?

3. What does the last sentence in "Dreams"—" 'I'm waiting here,' she told him, 'until we both wake up' "—mean or suggest? (This question does not imply that there is only one meaning or implication.) How are the meanings related to point of view? For example, if the entire story is a dream of Mimi's, then hers is the only center of consciousness (or unconsciousness). Other meanings also seem to require a specific point of view.

4. How many dreamers are there in "Dreams" (give at least one specific paragraph reference for each)? Which of the dreamers' dreams are connected to or shared with another dreamer?

5. In paragraph 133, Mimi makes other names and phrases out of the letters of Brian Bassett's name, then adds, "He had known all along, of course, that *BRIAN BASSETT* wasn't what he wanted because it wasn't what he was. He had come here against his will, was held here against his better judgment, fought against his captors and finally escaped." In the next paragraph, she adds that he had "been here in someone else's dreams, and had to wait for someone else to wake before [he] could make [his] getaway." She also assumes that there was a "here" for the others—Ian Brett Bass, Tina Sterabbs—who are just names made from the letters of his. What is Mimi saying here? What seems to be her sense of reality? Of the relation of body and spirit? (Paragraph 107 might also be helpful in trying to answer these questions.)

WRITING SUGGESTIONS

1. Write a parody of "The Cask of Amontillado" set in modern times, perhaps on a college campus ("A Barrel of Bud"?).

2. Write a "pre-text" narrating the "thousand injuries" and the insult that triggered Montresor's revenge, or sketch several possibilities for such a pre-text narrated from various points of view.

3. Compare the effect of the endings of "Dreams" and "An Occurrence at Owl Creek Bridge," and how that effect is achieved by the use of focus and voice.

4. Using question 5, above, as a guide, write an essay on "Body, Spirit, and Reality in Thomas Findley's 'Dreams.'"

3

CHARACTERIZATION

In a good many stories the narrator is a disembodied offstage voice, without an identity or a personal history, without influence on the action, without qualities other than those that a voice and style may suggest. So it is in some of the earlier stories in this volume—"The Zebra Storyteller," "The Jewelry," "An Occurrence at Owl Creek Bridge." Poe's narrator, however, not only tells us the story but has a part in the action as well; without him we not only would not know the story, but neither would there be a story. He looks back into his past; he is there in the story, speaking, listening, reacting. In addition to being the narrator, he is a **character:** someone who acts, appears, or is referred to as playing a part in a work.

> The foundation of good fiction
> is character-creation and
> nothing else. . . . Style counts;
> plot counts; originality of
> outlook counts. But none of
> these counts anything like so
> much as the convincingness of
> the characters.
>
> —ARNOLD BENNETT

The most common term for the character with the leading male role is **hero,** the "good guy," who opposes the **villain,** or "bad guy." The leading female character is the **heroine.** Heroes and heroines are usually larger than life, stronger or better than most human beings, almost godlike (and there's even a brand of heroes nowadays so close to being godlike that they are called superheroes). In most modern fiction, however, the leading character is much more ordinary, more like the rest of us. Such a character is called the **antihero,** not because he opposes the hero but because he is not like a hero in stature or perfection. An older and more neutral term than hero for the leading character, a term that does not imply either the presence or absence of outstanding virtue (and with the added advantage of referring equally to male and female), is **protagonist,** whose opponent is the **antagonist.** You might get into long and pointless arguments by calling Lantin or Montresor a hero, but both are their story's protagonist.

The **major characters** are those we see more of over a longer period of time; we learn more about them, and we think of them as more complex and, therefore, frequently more "realistic" than the **minor characters,** the figures who fill out the story. These major characters can grow and change, as Lantin does and as Judith does in Doris Lessing's "Our Friend Judith"; by the end of these stories both protagonists have acted unpredictably based on what we learned earlier in the story about them and their past actions. Characters who can thus "surprise convincingly," an influential critic says, are **round characters.** Because Poe's characters are not very complex and do not change in surprising ways, they are called **flat.** But we must be careful not to let terms like *flat* and *round* turn into value judgments. Because flat characters are less complex than round ones it is easy to assume they are artistically inferior; we need only to think of the characters of Charles Dickens, almost all of whom are flat, to realize that this is not always true.

The terms *flat* and *round,* like the terms *hero* and *antihero,* are not absolute or precise. They designate extremes or tendencies, not pigeonholes. Is Poe's Montresor entirely flat? Is Shakespeare's Falstaff? Charlie Chaplin's Little Tramp? Little Orphan Annie? Are all these characters equally flat? We will probably agree that Baldwin's Sonny is a round character, but what about Findley's Mimi or Everett Menlo? Cheever's Francis Weed? Are they all equally round? Our answers are less important than our looking carefully at these characters to see what we know about each of them, to what degree they can be summed up in a phrase or a sentence; to discover how we learned what we know about them and how our judgment has been controlled by the story; to think about and perhaps judge the assumptions about human motivation, behavior, and nature that underlie the character and his or her characterization. Flat and round are useful as categories but are even more useful as tools of investigation, as ways of focusing our attention and sharpening our perception.

Though most of Dickens's flat characters are highly individualized, not to say unique, some, like Fagin, the avaricious Jewish moneylender, are **stereotypes:** characters based on conscious or unconscious cultural assumptions that sex, age, ethnic or national identification, occupation, marital status, and so on are predictably accompanied by certain character traits, actions, even values.

The stereotype may be very useful in creating a round character, one who can surprise convincingly: Judith, according to a Canadian woman, is "one of your typical English spinsters." Judith, however, acts in ways that deny the limitations of the stereotype. A stereotype is, after all, only a quick—and superficial—form of classification, and classification is a common first step in definitions. One of the chief ways we have of describing or defining is by placing the thing to be defined in a category or class and then distinguishing it from the other members of that class. A good deal of **characterization**—the art, craft, method of presentation, or creation of fictional personages—involves a similar process. Characters are almost inevitably identified by category—by sex, age, nationality, occupation, and so on. We learn, for example, that Major Monarch, in Henry James's "The Real Thing," is a middle-aged English gentleman.

Paradoxically, the more groups a character is placed in, the more individual he or she becomes. Fenstad's mother, for example, is an old woman, a protective and critical mother, two separate but closely related stereotypes that categorize her, but she is also a social, political, and intellectual radical, which significantly individualizes her within the various categories into which she fits.

Not all generalizations involve cultural stereotypes, of course. Some may involve generalized character traits that the story or narrator defines for us (and that we must accept unless events in the story prove otherwise). Physical characteristics also serve as categories. As with stereotypes, when physical characteristics are multiplied, the result is more and more particularizing or individualizing. The detailed physical description of Judith makes it possible to visualize her rather fully, almost to recognize her as an individual:

Judith is tall, small-breasted, slender. Her light brown hair is parted in the centre and cut straight around her neck. A high straight forehead, straight nose, and full grave mouth are setting for her eyes, which are green, large and prominent. Her lids are very white, fringed with gold, and moulded close over the eyeball. . . . (paragraph 7)

There are many other ways in which a character is characterized and individualized besides stereotyping and "destereotyping," and besides classifying and particularizing by physical description. In most cases we see what characters do and hear what they say; we sometimes learn what they think, and what other people think or say about them; we often know what kind of clothes they wear, what and how much they own, treasure, or covet; we may be told about their childhood, parents, or some parts of their past.

Though characterization is gradual, taking place sequentially through the story, it is not, as it may seem natural to assume, entirely cumulative. We do not begin with an empty space called Judith or Francis Weed or Sonny and fill it in gradually by adding physical traits, habitual actions, ways of speaking, and so on. Our imagination does not work that way. Rather, just as at each point in the action we project some sort of configuration of how the story will come out or what the world of the story will be like or mean, so we project a more or less complete image of each character at the point at which the he or she is first mentioned or appears. This image is based on the initial reference in the text, our reading, and life experiences and associations (Don't you have an image of a Herb? a Maude? a spinster?). The next time the character is mentioned, or when he or she speaks or acts, we do not so much "adjust" our first impression as we project a new image (just as in the plot we project a new series of developments and a new outcome). There may be some carryover, but we do not in the course of the story put the character together like a Mr. Potato Head. Instead, we overlay one image on the other, and though the final image may be the most enduring, the early images do not all disappear: our view of the character is multidimensional, flickering, like a time-lapse photograph. Perhaps that is why it is rare that any actor in a film based on a novel or story matches the way we imagined that character if we have read the book or story first—our imagination has not one image but rather a sequence of images associated with that character. It is also why some of us feel that seeing the film before reading the book hobbles the imagination. A particular character's physical attributes, for example, may not be described in a novel until after that character has been involved in some incident; the reader may then need to adjust his earlier vision of that character, which is not an option for the viewer of a film. It is thus the reader, rather than a casting director, who finalizes a character in his or her own imagination.

For no matter how many methods of characterization are employed, at some point the definition of the individual stops. No matter how individualized the character may be, he or she remains a member of a number of groups, and we make certain assumptions about that character based on our fixed or stereotyped notions of those groups. To destroy a stereotype, a story must introduce a stereotype to destroy. And somehow the destereotyped character, no matter how particularized, remains to some degree representative. If Judith turns out to be not as prudish and prissy as the stereotype of the English spinster has led us to believe, we may well conclude that the stereotype is false and that Judith is more representative of the real English spinster than the stereotype is. Indeed, this tendency to generalize from the particulars of a story extends beyond cultural groups, sometimes to human character at large: if Sonny can change his ways after years of habitual conduct, then human character, the story might seem to say, is not permanently fixed at birth, in infancy, childhood, ever.

One of the reasons it is so difficult to discuss character is precisely that the principles of definition and evaluation of fictional characters (not of their characterizations, the way they are presented) are the same as those we use for real people, an area of violent controversy and confusion. The very term *character,* when it refers not to a fictional personage but to a combination of qualities in a human being, is somewhat ambiguous. It usually has moral overtones, often favorable (a man of character); it is sometimes neutral but evaluative (character reference). Judgment about character (not characterization, remember) usually involves moral terms like *good* and *bad* and *strong* and *weak.* **Personality** usually implies that which distinguishes or individualizes a person, and the judgment called for is not so much moral as social—*pleasing* or *displeasing.* An older term, **nature** (it is in one's nature to be so or do such), usually implies something inherent or inborn, something fixed and thus predictable. The **existential character** implies the opposite; that is, whatever our past, our conditioning, our pattern or previous behavior, we can, by choice, by free will, change all that right this minute, as Sonny does.

> *A man, woman or child, cannot buy a morsel of pickled salmon, look at his shoe, or bring in a mug of ale; a solitary object cannot pass on the other side of the way; a boy cannot take a bite at a turnip or hold a horse; a by-stander cannot answer the simplest question; a dog cannot fall into a doze; a bird cannot whet his bill; a pony cannot have a peculiar nose, nor a pig one ear, but out peeps the first germ of "character."*
>
> —R. H. HORNE

Fictional characters thus frequently seem to be part of the history that lies behind the story or beyond the story as part of our own world, to exist in a reality that is detachable from the words and events of the story in which they appear. We feel we might recognize Tom Jones, Jane Eyre, or Sherlock Holmes on the street, and we might be able to anticipate what they would say or do in *our* world, outside the story. Fictional characters are neither real nor detachable, of course, and they exist only in the words of the works in which they are presented. We must not forget the distinction between the character and the characterization, the method by which he or she is presented; so we must be careful to distinguish the *good character,* meaning someone whom, if real, we would consider virtuous, and the *good characterization,* meaning a fictional person who, no matter what his or her morality or behavior, is well presented.

We must recognize that characters are not finally detachable—that they have roles, functions, limitations, and their very existence in the context of the story; we must not confuse fictional characters with real people, or character with characterization. This is not to say, however, that we may not learn about real people from characters in fiction or learn to understand fictional characters in part from what we know about real people. For real people, too, exist in a context of other people and other elements, their history and geography and their "narrator," the one who is representing them—that is, *you.* Indeed, it may be worth paying particular attention to how stories create the images of people and what those images assume about human character precisely because this process and these assumptions are so similar to the way we get to know and understand real people. For we are all artists representing reality to ourselves. If we study the art of characterization we may become better artists, able to enrich both our reading and our lives.

HENRY JAMES

The Real Thing

I

When the porter's wife, who used to answer the house-bell, announced "A gen-tleman and a lady, sir" I had, as I often had in those days—the wish being father to the thought—an immediate vision of sitters. Sitters my visitors in this case proved to be; but not in the sense I should have preferred. There was nothing at first however to indicate that they mightn't have come for a portrait. The gentle-man, a man of fifty, very high and very straight, with a moustache slightly griz-zled and a dark grey walking-coat admirably fitted, both of which I noted professionally—I don't mean as a barber or yet as a tailor—would have struck me as a celebrity if celebrities often were striking. It was a truth of which I had for some time been conscious that a figure with a good deal of frontage was, as one might say, almost never a public institution. A glance at the lady helped to remind me of this paradoxical law: she also looked too distinguished to be a "personality." Moreover one would scarcely come across two variations together.

Neither of the pair immediately spoke—they only prolonged the preliminary gaze suggesting that each wished to give the other a chance. They were visibly shy; they stood there letting me take them in—which, as I afterwards perceived, was the most practical thing they could have done. In this way their embar-rassment served their cause. I had seen people painfully reluctant to mention that they desired anything so gross as to be represented on canvas; but the scru-ples of my new friends appeared almost insurmountable. Yet the gentleman might have said "I should like a portrait of my wife," and the lady might have said "I should like a portrait of my husband." Perhaps they weren't husband and wife—this naturally would make the matter more delicate. Perhaps they wished to be done together—in which case they ought to have brought a third person to break the news.

"We come from Mr. Rivet," the lady finally said with a dim smile that had the effect of a moist sponge passed over a "sunk"[1] piece of painting, as well as of a vague allusion to vanished beauty. She was as tall and straight, in her degree, as her companion, and with ten years less to carry. She looked as sad as a woman could look whose face was not charged with expression; that is her tinted oval mask showed waste as an exposed surface shows friction. The hand of time had played over her freely, but to an effect of elimination. She was slim and stiff, and so well-dressed, in dark blue cloth, with lappets and pockets and buttons, that it was clear she employed the same tailor as her husband. The couple had an inde-finable air of prosperous thrift—they evidently got a good deal of luxury for their money. If I was to be one of their luxuries it would behove me to consider my terms.

"Ah, Claude Rivet recommended me?" I echoed; and I added that it was very

---

1. When colors lose their brilliance after they have dried on the canvas, they have "sunk in."

kind of him, though I could reflect that, as he only painted landscape, this wasn't a sacrifice.

The lady looked very hard at the gentleman, and the gentleman looked round the room. Then staring at the floor a moment and stroking his moustache, he rested his pleasant eyes on me with the remark: "He said you were the right one."

"I try to be, when people want to sit."

"Yes, we should like to," said the lady anxiously.

"Do you mean together?"

My visitors exchanged a glance. "If you could do anything with *me* I suppose it would be double," the gentleman stammered.

"Oh yes, there's naturally a higher charge for two figures than for one."

"We should like to make it pay," the husband confessed.

"That's very good of you," I returned, appreciating so unwonted a sympathy—for I supposed he meant pay the artist.

A sense of strangeness seemed to draw on the lady.

"We mean for the illustrations—Mr. Rivet said you might put one in."

"Put in—an illustration?" I was equally confused.

"Sketch her off, you know," said the gentleman, colouring.

It was only then that I understood the service Claude Rivet had rendered me; he had told them how I worked in black-and-white, for magazines, for story-books, for sketches of contemporary life, and consequently had copious employ-ment for models. These things were true, but it was not less true—I may confess it now; whether because the aspiration was to lead to everything or to nothing I leave the reader to guess—that I couldn't get the honours, to say nothing of the emoluments, of a great painter of portraits out of my head. My "illustrations" were my pot-boilers; I looked to a different branch of art—far and away the most interesting it had always seemed to me—to perpetuate my fame. There was no shame in looking to it also to make my fortune; but that fortune was by so much further from being made from the moment my visitors wished to be "done" for nothing. I was disappointed; for in the pictorial sense I had immediately *seen* them. I had seized their type—I had already settled what I would do with it. Something that wouldn't absolutely have pleased them, I afterwards reflected.

"Ah you're—you're—a—?" I began as soon as I had mastered my surprise. I couldn't bring out the dingy word "models": it seemed so little to fit the case.

"We haven't had much practice," said the lady.

"We've got to *do* something, and we've thought that an artist in your line might perhaps make something of us," her husband threw off. He further men-tioned that they didn't know many artists and that they had gone first, on the off-chance—he painted views of course, but sometimes put in figures; perhaps I remembered—to Mr. Rivet, whom they had met a few years before at a place in Norfolk where he was sketching.

"We used to sketch a little ourselves," the lady hinted.

"It's very awkward, but we absolutely *must* do something," her husband went on.

"Of course we're not so *very* young," she admitted with a wan smile.

With the remark that I might as well know something more about them the husband had handed me a card extracted from a neat new pocket-book—their appurtenances were all of the freshest—and inscribed with the words "Major Monarch." Impressive as these words were they didn't carry my knowledge much further; but my visitor presently added: "I've left the army and we've had the misfortune to lose our money. In fact our means are dreadfully small."

"It's awfully trying—a regular strain," said Mrs. Monarch.   25

They evidently wished to be discreet—to take care not to swagger because they were gentlefolk. I felt them willing to recognise this as something of a drawback, at the same time that I guessed at an underlying sense—their consolation in adversity—that they *had* their points. They certainly had; but these advantages struck me as preponderantly social; such for instance as would help to make a drawing-room look well. However, a drawing-room was always, or ought to be, a picture.

In consequence of his wife's allusion to their age Major Monarch observed: "Naturally it's more for the figure that we thought of going in. We can still hold ourselves up." On the instant I saw that the figure was indeed their strong point. His "naturally" didn't sound vain, but it lighted up the question. "*She* has the best one," he continued, nodding at his wife with a pleasant after-dinner absence of circumlocution. I could only reply, as if we were in fact sitting over our wine, that this didn't prevent his own from being very good; which led him in turn to make answer: "We thought that if you ever have to do people like us we might be something like it. *She* particularly—for a lady in a book, you know."

I was so amused by them that, to get more of it, I did my best to take their point of view; and though it was an embarrassment to find myself appraising physically, as if they were animals on hire or useful blacks, a pair whom I should have expected to meet only in one of the relations in which criticism is tacit, I looked at Mrs. Monarch judicially enough to be able to exclaim after a moment with conviction: "Oh yes, a lady in a book!" She was singularly like a bad illustration.

"We'll stand up, if you like," said the Major; and he raised himself before me with a really grand air.

I could take his measure at a glance—he was six feet two and a perfect gentle-   30
man. It would have paid any club in process of formation and in want of a stamp to engage him at a salary to stand in the principal window. What struck me at once was that in coming to me they had rather missed their vocation; they could surely have been turned to better account for advertising purposes. I couldn't of course see the thing in detail, but I could see them make somebody's fortune—I don't mean their own. There was something in them for a waistcoat-maker, an hotel-keeper or a soap-vendor. I could imagine "We always use it" pinned on their bosoms with the greatest effect; I had a vision of the brilliancy with which they would launch a table d'hôte.

Mrs. Monarch sat still, not from pride but from shyness, and presently her husband said to her; "Get up, my dear, and show how smart you are." She obeyed, but she had no need to get up to show it. She walked to the end of the studio and then came back blushing, her fluttered eyes on the partner of her appeal. I was reminded of an incident I had accidentally had a glimpse of in Paris being with a friend there, a dramatist about to produce a play, when an actress came to him to ask to be entrusted with a part. She went through her paces before him, walked up and down as Mrs. Monarch was doing. Mrs. Monarch did it quite as well, but I abstained from applauding. It was very odd to see such people apply for such poor pay. She looked as if she had ten thousand a year. Her husband had used the word that described her: she was in the London current jargon essentially and typically "smart." Her figure was, in the same order of ideas, conspicuously and irreproachably "good." For a woman of her age her waist was surprisingly small; her elbow moreover had the orthodox crook. She held her head at the conventional angle, but why did she come to *me?* She ought to have tried on jackets at a big shop. I feared my visitors were not only destitute but "artistic"—which would be a great complication. When she sat down again I thanked her, observing that what a draughtsman most valued in his model was the faculty of keeping quiet.

"Oh *she* can keep quiet," said Major Monarch. Then he added jocosely: "I've always kept her quiet."

"I'm not a nasty fidget, am I?" It was going to wring tears from me, I felt, the way she hid her head, ostrich-like, in the other's broad bosom.

The owner of this expanse addressed his answer to me. "Perhaps it isn't out of place to mention—because we ought to be quite business-like, oughtn't we?— that when I married her she was known as the Beautiful Statue."

35   "Oh dear!" said Mrs. Monarch ruefully.

"Of course I should want a certain amount of expression," I rejoined.

"Of *course!*"—and I had never heard such unanimity.

"And then I suppose you know that you'll get awfully tired."

"Oh we *never* get tired!" they eagerly cried.

40   "Have you had any kind of practice?"

They hesitated—they looked at each other. "We've been photographed— *immensely,*" said Mrs. Monarch.

"She means the fellows have asked us themselves," added the Major.

"I see—because you're so good-looking."

"I don't know what they thought, but they were always after us."

45   "We always got our photographs for nothing," smiled Mrs. Monarch.

"We might have brought some, my dear," her husband remarked.

"I'm not sure we have any left. We've given quantities away," she explained to me.

"With our autographs and that sort of thing," said the Major.

"Are they to be got in the shops?" I enquired as a harmless pleasantry.

50   "Oh yes, *hers*—they used to be."

"Not now," said Mrs. Monarch with her eyes on the floor.

II

I could fancy the "sort of thing" they put on the presentation copies of their photographs, and I was sure they wrote a beautiful hand. It was odd how quickly I was sure of everything that concerned them. If they were now so poor as to have to earn shillings and pence they could never have had much of a margin. Their good looks had been their capital, and they had good-humouredly made the most of the career that this resource marked out for them. It was in their faces, the blankness, the deep intellectual repose of the twenty years of country-house visiting that had given them pleasant intonations. I could see the sunny drawing-rooms, sprinkled with periodicals she didn't read, in which Mrs. Monarch had continuously sat; I could see the wet shrubberies in which she had walked, equipped to admiration for either exercise. I could see the rich covers[2] the Major had helped to shoot and the wonderful garments in which, late at night, he repaired to the smoking-room to talk about them. I could imagine their leggings and waterproofs, their knowing tweeds and rugs, their rolls of sticks and cases of tackle and neat umbrellas; and I could evoke the exact appearance of their servants and the compact variety of their luggage on the platforms of country stations.

They gave small tips, but they were liked; they didn't do anything themselves, but they were welcome. They looked so well everywhere; they gratified the general relish for stature, complexion and "form." They knew it without fatuity or vulgarity, and they respected themselves in consequence. They weren't superficial; they were thorough and kept themselves up—it had been their line. People with such a taste for activity had to have some line. I could feel how even in a dull house they could have been counted on for the joy of life. At present something had happened—it didn't matter what, their little income had grown less, it had grown least—and they had to do something for pocket-money. Their friends could like them, I made out, without liking to support them. There was something about them that represented credit—their clothes, their manners, their type; but if credit is a large empty pocket in which an occasional chink reverberates, the chink at least must be audible. What they wanted of me was to help to make it so. Fortunately they had no children—I soon divined that. They would also perhaps wish our relations to be kept secret: this was why it was "for the figure"—the reproduction of the face would betray them.

I liked them—I felt, quite as their friends must have done—they were so simple; and I had no objection to them if they would suit. But somehow with all their perfections I didn't easily believe in them. After all they were amateurs, and the ruling passion of my life was the detestation of the amateur. Combined with this was another perversity—an innate preference for the represented subject over the real one: the defect of the real one was so apt to be a lack of representation. I liked things that appeared; then one was sure. Whether they *were* or not was a subordinate and almost always a profitless question. There were other considerations, the first of which was that I already had two or three recruits in use, notably a young person with big feet, in alpaca, from Kilburn, who for a couple of years had come to me regularly for my illustrations and with whom I was still—perhaps ignobly—satisfied. I frankly explained to my visitors how the case stood, but they had taken more precautions than I supposed. They had reasoned out their opportunity, for Claude Rivet had told them of the projected *édition de*

2. Flocks of game birds.

luxe of one of the writers of our day—the rarest of the novelists—who, long neglected by the multitudinous vulgar and dearly prized by the attentive (need I mention Philip Vincent?) had had the happy fortune of seeing, late in life, the dawn and then the full light of a higher criticism; an estimate in which on the part of the public there was something really of expiation. The edition preparing, planned by a publisher of taste, was practically an act of high reparation; the wood-cuts with which it was to be enriched were the homage of English art to one of the most independent representatives of English letters. Major and Mrs. Monarch confessed to me they had hoped I might be able to work *them* into my branch of the enterprise. They knew I was to do the first of the books, "Rutland Ramsay," but I had to make clear to them that my participation in the rest of the affair—this first book was to be a test—must depend on the satisfaction I should give. If this should be limited my employers would drop me with scarce common forms. It was therefore a crisis for me, and naturally I was making special preparations, looking about for new people, should they be necessary, and securing the best types. I admitted however that I should like to settle down to two or three good models who would do for everything.

55   "Should we have often to—a—put on special clothes?" Mrs. Monarch timidly demanded.

"Dear yes—that's half the business."

"And should we be expected to supply our own costumes?"

"Oh no; I've got a lot of things. A painter's models put on—or put off—anything he likes."

"And you mean—a—the same?"

60   "The same?"

Mrs. Monarch looked at her husband again.

"Oh she was just wondering," he explained, "if the costumes are in *general* use." I had to confess that they were, and I mentioned further that some of them—I had a lot of genuine greasy last-century things—had served their time, a hundred years ago, on living world-stained men and women; on figures not perhaps so far removed, in that vanished world, from *their* type, the Monarchs', *quoi!*[3] of a breeched and bewigged age. "We'll put on anything that *fits*," said the Major.

"Oh I arrange that—they fit in the pictures."

"I'm afraid I should do better for the modern books. I'd come as you like," said Mrs. Monarch.

65   "She has got a lot of clothes at home: they might do for contemporary life," her husband continued.

"Oh I can fancy scenes in which you'd be quite natural." And indeed I could see the slipshod rearrangements of stale properties—the stories I tried to produce pictures for without the exasperation of reading them—whose sandy tracts the good lady might help to people. But I had to return to the fact that for this sort of work—the daily mechanical grind—I was already equipped: the people I was working with were fully adequate.

---

3. Whatever.

"We only thought we might be more like *some* characters," said Mrs. Monarch mildly, getting up.

Her husband also rose; he stood looking at me with a dim wistfulness that was touching in so fine a man.

"Wouldn't it be rather a pull sometimes to have—a—to have—?" He hung fire; he wanted me to help him by phrasing what he meant. But I couldn't—I didn't know. So he brought it out awkwardly: "The *real* thing; a gentleman, you know, or a lady." I was quite ready to give a general assent—I admitted that there was a great deal in that. This encouraged Major Monarch to say, following up his appeal with an unacted gulp: "It's awfully hard—we've tried everything." The gulp was communicative; it proved too much for his wife. Before I knew it Mrs. Monarch had dropped again upon a divan and burst into tears. Her husband sat down beside her, holding one of her hands; whereupon she quickly dried her eyes with the other, while I felt embarrassed as she looked up at me. "There isn't a confounded job I haven't applied for—waited for—prayed for. You can fancy we'd be pretty bad first. Secretaryships and that sort of thing? You might as well ask for a peerage. I'd be *anything*—I'm strong; a messenger or a coalheaver. I'd put on a gold-laced cap and open carriage-doors in front of the haberdasher's; I'd hang about a station to carry portmanteaux; I'd be a postman. But they won't *look* at you; there are thousands as good as yourself already on the ground. *Gentlemen,* poor beggars, who've drunk their wine, who've kept their hunters!"

I was as reassuring as I knew how to be, and my visitors were presently on their feet again while, for the experiment, we agreed on an hour. We were discussing it when the door opened and Miss Churm came in with a wet umbrella. Miss Churm had to take the omnibus to Maida Vale and then walk half a mile. She looked a trifle blowsy and slightly splashed. I scarcely ever saw her come in without thinking fresh how odd it was that, being so little in herself, she should yet be so much in others. She was a meagre little Miss Churm, but was such an ample heroine of romance. She was only a freckled cockney, but she could represent everything, from a fine lady to a shepherdess; she had the faculty as she might have had a fine voice or long hair. She couldn't spell and she loved beer, but she had two or three "points," and practice, and a knack, and mother-wit, and a whimsical sensibility, and a love of the theatre, and seven sisters, and not an ounce of respect, especially for the h.[4] The first thing my visitors saw was that her umbrella was wet, and in their spotless perfection they visibly winced at it. The rain had come on since their arrival.

"I'm all in a soak; there *was* a mess of people in the 'bus. I wish you lived near a stytion," said Miss Churm. I requested her to get ready as quickly as possible, and she passed into the room in which she always changed her dress. But before going out she asked me what she was to get into this time.

"It's the Russian princess, don't you know?" I answered; "the one with the 'golden eyes,' in black velvet, for the long thing in the *Cheapside*."

"Golden eyes? I *say*!" cried Miss Churm, while my companions watched her with intensity as she withdrew. She always arranged herself, when she was late,

70

---

4. Working-class Londoners, especially in the East End (cockneys), drop *h*'s 'orribly.

before I could turn around; and I kept my visitors a little on purpose, so that they might get an idea, from seeing her, what would be expected of themselves. I mentioned that she was quite my notion of an excellent model—she was really very clever.

"Do you think she looks like a Russian princess?" Major Monarch asked with lurking alarm.

75 "When I make her, yes."

"Oh if you have to *make* her—!" he reasoned, not without point.

"That's the most you can ask. There are so many who are not makeable."

"Well now, *here's* a lady"—and with a persuasive smile he passed his arm into his wife's—"who's already made!"

"Oh I'm not a Russian princess," Mrs. Monarch protested a little coldly. I could see she had known some and didn't like them. There at once was a complication of a kind I never had to fear with Miss Churm.

80 This young lady came back in black velvet—the gown was rather rusty and very low on her lean shoulders—and with a Japanese fan in her red hands. I reminded her that in the scene I was doing she had to look over some one's head. "I forget whose it is; but it doesn't matter. Just look over a head."

"I'd rather look over a stove," said Miss Churm; and she took her station near the fire. She fell into position, settled herself into a tall attitude, gave a certain backward inclination to her head and a certain forward droop to her fan, and looked, at least to my prejudiced sense, distinguished and charming, foreign and dangerous. We left her looking so while I went downstairs with Major and Mrs. Monarch.

"I believe I could come about as near it as that," said Mrs. Monarch.

"Oh, you think she's shabby, but you must allow for the alchemy of art."

However, they went off with an evident increase of comfort founded on their demonstrable advantage in being the real thing. I could fancy them shuddering over Miss Churm. She was very droll about them when I went back, for I told her what they wanted.

85 "Well, if *she* can sit I'll tyke to bookkeeping," said my model.

"She's very ladylike," I replied as an innocent form of aggravation.

"So much the worse for *you*. That means she can't turn round."

"She'll do for the fashionable novels."

"Oh yes, she'll *do* for them!" my model humorously declared. "Ain't they bad enough without her?" I had often sociably denounced them to Miss Churm.

III

90 It was for the elucidation of a mystery in one of these works that I first tried Mrs. Monarch. Her husband came with her, to be useful if necessary—it was sufficiently clear that as a general thing he would prefer to come with her. At first I wondered if this were for "propriety's" sake—if he were going to be jealous and meddling. The idea was too tiresome, and if it had been confirmed it would speedily have brought our acquaintance to a close. But I soon saw there was nothing in it and that if he accompanied Mrs. Monarch it was—in addition to

the chance of being wanted—simply because he had nothing else to do. When they were separate his occupation was gone and they never *had* been separate. I judged rightly that in their awkward situation their close union was their main comfort and that this union had no weak spot. It was a real marriage, an encouragement to the hesitating, a nut for pessimists to crack. Their address was humble—I remember afterwards thinking it had been the only thing about them that was really professional—and I could fancy the lamentable lodgings in which the Major would have been left alone. He could sit there more or less grimly with his wife—he couldn't sit there anyhow without her.

He had too much tact to try and make himself agreeable when he couldn't be useful; so when I was too absorbed in my work to talk he simply sat and waited. But I liked to hear him talk—it made my work, when not interrupting it, less mechanical, less special. To listen to him was to combine the excitement of going out with the economy of staying at home. There was only one hindrance—that I seemed not to know any of the people this brilliant couple had known. I think he wondered extremely, during the term of our intercourse, whom the deuce I *did* know. He hadn't a stray sixpence of an idea to fumble for, so we didn't spin it very fine; we confined ourselves to questions of leather and even of liquor— saddlers and breeches-makers and how to get excellent claret cheap—and matters like "good trains" and the habits of small game. His lore on these last subjects was astonishing—he managed to interweave the station-master with the ornithologist. When he couldn't talk about greater things he could talk cheerfully about smaller, and since I couldn't accompany him into reminiscences of the fashionable world he could lower the conversation without a visible effort to my level.

So earnest a desire to please was touching in a man who could so easily have knocked one down. He looked after the fire and had an opinion on the draught of the stove without my asking him, and I could see that he thought many of my arrangements not half knowing. I remember telling him that if I were only rich I'd offer him a salary to come and teach me how to live. Sometimes he gave a random sigh of which the essence might have been: "Give me even such a bare old barrack as *this*, and I'd do something with it!" When I wanted to use him he came alone; which was an illustration of the superior courage of women. His wife could bear her solitary second floor, and she was in general more discreet; showing by various small reserves that she was alive to the propriety of keeping our relations markedly professional—not letting them slide into sociability. She wished it to remain clear that she and the Major were employed, not cultivated, and if she approved of me as a superior, who could be kept in his place, she never thought me quite good enough for an equal.

She sat with great intensity, giving the whole of her mind to it, and was capable of remaining for an hour almost as motionless as before a photographer's lens. I could see she had been photographed often, but somehow the very habit that made her good for that purpose unfitted her for mine. At first I was extremely pleased with her ladylike air, and it was a satisfaction, on coming to follow her lines, to see how good they were and how far they could lead the pencil. But after a little skirmishing I began to find her too insurmountably stiff;

do what I would with it my drawing looked like a photograph or a copy of a photograph. Her figure had no variety of expression—she herself had no sense of variety. You may say that this was my business and was only a question of placing her. Yet I placed her in every conceivable position and she managed to obliterate their differences. She was always a lady certainly, and into the bargain was always the same lady. She was the real thing, but always the same thing. There were moments when I rather writhed under the serenity of her confidence that she *was* the real thing. All her dealings with me and all her husband's were an implication that this was lucky for *me*. Meanwhile I found myself trying to invent types that approached her own, instead of making her own transform itself—in the clever way that was not impossible for instance to poor Miss Churm. Arrange as I would and take the precautions I would, she always came out, in my pictures, too tall—landing me in the dilemma of having represented a fascinating woman as seven feet high, which (out of respect perhaps to my own very much scantier inches) was far from my idea of such personage.

The case was worse with the Major—nothing I could do would keep *him* down, so that he became useful only for representation of brawny giants. I adored variety and range, I cherished human accidents, the illustrative note; I wanted to characterise closely, and the thing in the world I most hated was the danger of being ridden by a type. I had quarrelled with some of my friends about it; I had parted company with them for maintaining that one *had* to be, and that if the type was beautiful—witness Raphael and Leonardo[5]—the servitude was only a gain. I was neither Leonardo nor Raphael—I might only be a presumptuous young modern searcher; but I held that everything was to be sacrificed sooner than character. When they claimed that the obsessional form could easily *be* character I retorted, perhaps superficially, "Whose?" It couldn't be everybody's— it might end in being nobody's.

95   After I had drawn Mrs. Monarch a dozen times I felt surer even than before that the value of such a model as Miss Churm resided precisely in the fact that she had no positive stamp, combined of course with the other fact that what she did have was a curious and inexplicable talent for imitation. Her usual appearance was like a curtain which she could draw up at request for a capital performance. This performance was simply suggestive; but it was a word to the wise— it was vivid and pretty. Sometimes even I thought it, though she was plain herself, too insipidly pretty; I made it a reproach to her that the figures drawn from her were monotonously (*bêtement*,[6] as we used to say) graceful. Nothing made her more angry: it was so much of her pride to feel she could sit for characters that had nothing in common with each other. She would accuse me at such moments of taking away her "reputytion."

It suffered a certain shrinkage, this queer quantity, from the repeated visits of my new friends. Miss Churm was greatly in demand, never in want of employment, so I had no scruple in putting her off occasionally, to try them more at my

5. Raffaello Sanzio (1483–1520), Leonardo da Vinci (1452–1519), famous Italian Renaissance painters. Leonardo was also an inventor, military engineer, architect, sculptor, anatomist, and so forth.
6. Foolishly.

ease. It was certainly amusing at first to do the real thing—it was amusing to do Major Monarch's trousers. They *were* the real thing, even if he did come out colossal. It was amusing to do his wife's back hair—it was so mathematically neat—and the particular "smart" tension of her tight stays. She lent herself especially to positions in which the face was somewhat averted or blurred; she abounded in ladylike back views and *profils perdus.*[7] When she stood erect she took naturally one of the attitudes in which court-painters represent queens and princesses; so that I found myself wondering whether, to draw out this accomplishment, I couldn't get the editor of the *Cheapside* to publish a really royal romance, "A Tale of Buckingham Palace." Sometimes however the real thing and the make-believe came into contact; by which I mean that Miss Churm, keeping an appointment or coming to make one on days when I had much work in hand, encountered her invidious rivals. The encounter was not on their part, for they noticed her no more than if she had been the housemaid; not from intentional loftiness, but simply because as yet, professionally, they didn't know how to fraternise, as I could imagine they would have liked—or at least that the Major would. They couldn't talk about the omnibus—they always walked; and they didn't know what else to try—she wasn't interested in good trains or cheap claret. Besides, they must have felt—in the air—that she was amused at them, secretly derisive of their ever knowing how. She wasn't a person to conceal the limits of her faith if she had had a chance to show them. On the other hand Mrs. Monarch didn't think her tidy; for why else did she take pains to say to me—it was going out of the way, for Mrs. Monarch—that she didn't like dirty women?

One day when my young lady happened to be present with my other sitters—she even dropped in, when it was convenient, for a chat—I asked her to be so good as to lend a hand in getting tea, a service with which she was familiar and which was one of a class that, living as I did in a small way, with slender domestic resources, I often appealed to my models to render. They liked to lay hands on my property, to break the sitting, and sometimes the china—it made them feel Bohemian. The next time I saw Miss Churm after this incident she surprised me greatly by making a scene about it—she accused me of having wished to humiliate her. She hadn't resented the outrage at the time, but had seemed obliging and amused, enjoying the comedy of asking Mrs. Monarch, who sat vague and silent, whether she would have cream and sugar, and putting an exaggerated simper into the question. She had tried intonations—as if she too wished to pass for the real thing—till I was afraid my other visitors would take offence.

Oh they were determined not to do this, and their touching patience was the measure of their great need. They would sit by the hour, uncomplaining, till I was ready to use them; they would come back on the chance of being wanted and would walk away cheerfully if it failed. I used to go to the door with them to see in what magnificent order they retreated. I tried to find other employment for them—I introduced them to several artists. But they didn't "take," for reasons I could appreciate, and I became rather anxiously aware that after such disappointments they fell back upon me with a heavier weight. They did me the honor

7. Incomplete profile, showing more of the back of the head and less of the face.

to think me most *their* form. They weren't romantic enough for the painters, and in those days there were few serious workers in black-and-white. Besides, they had an eye to the great job I had mentioned to them—they had secretly set their hearts on supplying the right essence for my pictorial vindication of our fine novelist. They knew that for this undertaking I should want no costume-effects, none of the frippery of past ages—that it was a case in which everything would be contemporary and satirical and presumably genteel. If I could work them into it their future would be assured, for the labour would of course be long and the occupation steady.

One day Mrs. Monarch came without her husband—she explained his absence by his having had to go to the City.[8] While she sat there in her usual relaxed majesty there came at the door a knock which I immediately recognised as the subdued appeal of a model out of work. It was followed by the entrance of a young man whom I at once saw to be a foreigner and who proved in fact an Italian acquainted with no English word but my name, which he uttered in a way that made it seem to include all others. I hadn't then visited his country, nor was I proficient in his tongue; but as he was not so meanly constituted— what Italian is?—as to depend only on that member for expression he conveyed to me, in familiar but graceful mimicry, that he was in search of exactly the employment in which the lady before me was engaged. I was not struck with him at first, and while I continued to draw I dropped few signs of interest or encouragement. He stood his ground however—not importunately, but with a dumb dog-like fidelity in his eyes that amounted to innocent impudence, the manner of a devoted servant—he might have been in the house for years— unjustly suspected. Suddenly it struck me that this very attitude and expression made a picture; whereupon I told him to sit down and wait till I should be free. There was another picture in the way he obeyed me, and I observed as I worked that there were others still in the way he looked wonderingly, with his head thrown back, about the high studio. He might have been crossing himself in Saint Peter's. Before I finished I said to myself "The fellow's a bankrupt orange-monger, but a treasure."

When Mrs. Monarch withdrew he passed across the room like a flash to open the door for her, standing there with the rapt pure gaze of the young Dante spellbound by the young Beatrice.[9] As I never insisted, in such situations, on the blankness of the British domestic, I reflected that he had the making of a ser-vant—and I needed one, but couldn't pay him to be only that—as well as of a model; in short I resolved to adopt my bright adventurer if he would agree to officiate in the double capacity. He jumped at my offer, and in the event my rashness—for I had really known nothing about him—wasn't brought home to me. He proved a sympathetic though a desultory ministrant, and had in a won-derful degree the *sentiment de la pose*.[1] It was uncultivated, instinctive, a part of the happy instinct that had guided him to my door and helped him to spell out

8. Financial and legal center of London.   9. Dante Alighieri (1265–1321), Italian poet, author of *The Divine Comedy*, was inspired for life poetically and spiritually by Beatrice Portinari, whom he first saw when they were children and saw only infrequently thereafter.   1. Instinct for striking poses.

my name on the card nailed to it. He had had no other introduction to me than a guess, from the shape of my high north window, seen outside, that my place was a studio and that as a studio it would contain an artist. He had wandered to England in search of fortune, like other itinerants, and had embarked, with a partner and a small green hand-cart, on the sale of penny ices. The ices had melted away and the partner had dissolved in their train. My young man wore tight yellow trousers with reddish stripes and his name was Oronte. He was sallow but fair, and when I put him into some old clothes of my own he looked like an Englishman. He was as good as Miss Churm, who could look, when requested, like an Italian.

IV

I thought Mrs. Monarch's face slightly convulsed when, on her coming back with her husband, she found Oronte installed. It was strange to have to recognise in a scrap of a lazzarone[2] a competitor to her magnificent Major. It was she who scented danger first, for the Major was anecdotically unconscious. But Oronte gave us tea, with a hundred eager confusions—he had never been concerned in so queer a process—and I think she thought better of me for having at last an "establishment." They saw a couple of drawings that I had made of the establishment, and Mrs. Monarch hinted that it never would have struck her he had sat for them. "Now the drawings you make from *us,* they look exactly like us," she reminded me, smiling in triumph; and I recognized that this was indeed just their defect. When I drew the Monarchs I couldn't anyhow get away from them—get into the character I wanted to represent; and I hadn't the least desire my model should be discoverable in my picture. Miss Churm never was, and Mrs. Monarch thought I hid her, very properly, because she was vulgar; whereas if she was lost it was only as the dead who go to heaven are lost—in the gain of an angel the more.

By this time I had got a certain start with "Rutland Ramsay," the first novel in the great projected series; that is I had produced a dozen drawings, several with the help of the Major and his wife, and I had sent them in for approval. My understanding with the publishers, as I have already hinted, had been that I was to be left to do my work, in this particular case, as I liked, with the whole book committed to me; but my connexion with the rest of the series was only contingent. There were moments when, frankly, it *was* a comfort to have the real thing under one's hand; for there were characters in "Rutland Ramsay" that were very much like it. There were people presumably as erect as the Major and women of as good a fashion as Mrs. Monarch. There was a great deal of country-house life—treated, it is true, in a fine fanciful ironical generalised way—and there was a considerable implication of knickerbockers and kilts. There were certain things I had to settle at the outset; such things for instance as the exact appearance of the hero and the particular bloom and figure of the heroine. The author of course gave me a lead, but there was a margin for interpretation. I took the Monarchs

2. Street person.

into my confidence, I told them frankly what I was about, I mentioned my embarrassments and alternatives. "Oh take *him!*" Mrs. Monarch murmured sweetly, looking at her husband; and "What could you want better than my wife?" the Major enquired with the comfortable candour that now prevailed between us.

I wasn't obliged to answer these remarks—I was only obliged to place my sitters. I wasn't easy in mind, and I postponed a little timidly perhaps the solving of my question. The book was a large canvas, the other figures were numerous, and I worked off at first some of the episodes in which the hero and the heroine were not concerned. When once I had set *them* up I should have to stick to them—I couldn't make my young man seven feet high in one place and five feet nine in another. I inclined on the whole to the latter measurement, though the Major more than once reminded me that *he* looked about as young as any one. It was indeed quite possible to arrange him, for the figure, so that it would have been difficult to detect his age. After the spontaneous Oronte had been with me a month, and after I had given him to understand several times over that his native exuberance would presently constitute an insurmountable barrier to our further intercourse, I waked to a sense of his heroic capacity. He was only five feet seven, but the remaining inches were latent. I tried him almost secretly at first, for I was really rather afraid of the judgment my other models would pass on such a choice. If they regarded Miss Churm as little better than a snare what would they think of the representation by a person so little the real thing as an Italian street-vendor of a protagonist formed by a public school?

If I went a little in fear of them it wasn't because they bullied me, because they had got an oppressive foothold, but because in their really pathetic decorum and mysteriously permanent newness they counted on me so intensely. I was therefore very glad when Jack Hawley came home: he was always of such good counsel. He painted badly himself, but there was no one like him for putting his finger on the place. He had been absent from England for a year; he had been somewhere—I don't remember where—to get a fresh eye. I was in a good deal of dread of any such organ, but we were old friends; he had been away for months and a sense of emptiness was creeping into my life. I hadn't dodged a missile for a year.

105   He came back with a fresh eye, but with the same old black velvet blouse, and the first evening he spent in my studio we smoked cigarettes till the small hours. He had done no work himself, he had only got the eye; so the field was clear for the production of my little things. He wanted to see what I had produced for the *Cheapside,* but he was disappointed in the exhibition. That at least seemed the meaning of two or three comprehensive groans which, as he lounged on my big divan, his leg folded under him, looking at my latest drawings, issued from his lips with the smoke of the cigarette.

"What's the matter with you?" I asked.

"What's the matter with *you?*"

"Nothing save that I'm mystified."

"You are indeed. You're quite off the hinge. What's the meaning of this new fad?" And he tossed me, with visible irreverence, a drawing in which I happened to have depicted both my elegant models. I asked if he didn't think it good, and he replied that it struck him as execrable, given the sort of thing I had always represented myself to him as wishing to arrive at; but I let that pass—I was so anxious to see exactly what he meant. The two figures in the picture looked colossal, but I supposed this was *not* what he meant, inasmuch as, for aught he knew the contrary, I might have been trying for some such effect. I maintained that I was working exactly in the same way as when he last had done me the honour to tell me I might do something some day. "Well, there's a screw loose somewhere," he answered; "wait a bit and I'll discover it." I depended upon him to do so: where else was the fresh eye? But he produced at last nothing more luminous than "I don't know—I don't like your types." This was lame for a critic who had never consented to discuss with me anything but the question of execution, the direction of strokes and the mystery of values.

"In the drawings you've been looking at I think my types are very handsome."   110
"Oh they won't do!"
"I've been working with new models."
"I see you have. *They* won't do."
"Are you very sure of that?"
"Absolutely—they're stupid."   115
"You mean *I* am—for I ought to get round that."
"You *can't*—with such people. Who are they?"
I told him, so far as was necessary, and he concluded heartlessly: "Ce sont des gens qu'il faut mettre à la porte."[3]
"You've never seen them; they're awfully good"—I flew to their defence.
"Not seen them? Why all this recent work of yours drops to pieces with them.   120
It's all I want to see of them."
"No one else has said anything against it—the *Cheapside* people are pleased."
"Everyone else is an ass, and the *Cheapside* people the biggest asses of all. Come, don't pretend at this time of day to have pretty illusions about the public, especially about publishers and editors. It's not for *such* animals you work—it's for those who know, *coloro che sanno*;[4] so keep straight for *me* if you can't keep straight for yourself. There was a certain sort of thing you used to try for—and a very good thing it was. But this twaddle isn't *in* it." When I talked with Hawley later about "Rutland Ramsay" and its possible successors he declared that I must get back into my boat again or I should go to the bottom. His voice in short was the voice of warning.

I noted the warning, but I didn't turn my friends out of doors. They bored me a good deal; but the very fact that they bored me admonished me not to sacrifice them—if there was anything to be done with them—simply to irritation. As I look back at this phase they seem to me to have pervaded my life not a little. I have a vision of them as most of the time in my studio, seated against the wall on an old velvet bench to be out of the way, and resembling the while a pair of patient courtiers in a royal ante-chamber. I'm convinced that during the coldest weeks of the winter they held their ground because it saved them fire. Their newness was losing its gloss, and it was impossible not to feel them objects of charity. Whenever Miss Churm arrived they went away, and after I was fairly launched

3. "That kind of person should be shown the door."   4. Dante, *The Divine Comedy*, "The Inferno," 4:131: actually, *color che sanno*—"those who know."

in "Rutland Ramsay" Miss Churm arrived pretty often. They managed to express to me tacitly that they supposed I wanted her for the low life of the book, and I let them suppose it, since they had attempted to study the work—it was lying about the studio—without discovering that it dealt only with the highest circles. They had dipped into the most brilliant of our novelists without deciphering many passages. I still took an hour from them, now and again, in spite of Jack Hawley's warning: it would be time enough to dismiss them, if dismissal should be necessary, when the rigour of the season was over. Hawley had made their acquaintance—he had met them at my fireside—and thought them a ridiculous pair. Learning that he was a painter they tried to approach him, to show him too that they were the real thing; but he looked at them, across the big room, as if they were miles away: they were a compendium of everything he most objected to in the social system of his country. Such people as that, all convention and patent-leather, with ejaculations that stopped conversation, had no business in a studio. A studio was a place to learn to see, and how could you see through a pair of feather-beds?

The main inconvenience I suffered at their hands was that at first I was shy of letting it break upon them that my artful little servant had begun to sit to me for "Rutland Ramsay." They knew I had been odd enough—they were prepared by this time to allow oddity to artists—to pick a foreign vagabond out of the streets when I might have had a person with whiskers and credentials, but it was some time before they learned how high I rated his accomplishments. They found him in an attitude more than once, but they never doubted I was doing him as an organ-grinder.There were several things they never guessed, and one of them was that for a striking scene in the novel, in which a footman briefly figured, it occurred to me to make use of Major Monarch as the menial. I kept putting this off, I didn't like to ask him to don the livery—besides the difficulty of finding a livery to fit him. At last, one day late in the winter, when I was at work on the despised Oronte, who caught one's idea on the wing, and was in the glow of feeling myself go very straight, they came in, the Major and his wife, with their society laugh about nothing (there was less and less to laugh at); came on like country-callers—they always reminded me of that—who have walked across the park after church and are presently persuaded to stay to luncheon. Luncheon was over, but they could stay to tea—I knew they wanted it. The fit was on me, however, and I couldn't let my ardour cool and my work wait, with the fading daylight, while my model prepared it. So I asked Mrs. Monarch if she would mind laying it out—a request which for an instant brought all the blood to her face. Her eyes were on her husband's for a second, and some mute telegraphy passed between them. Their folly was over the next instant; his cheerful shrewdness put an end to it. So far from pitying their wounded pride, I must add, I was moved to give it as complete a lesson as I could. They bustled about together and got out the cups and saucers and made the kettle boil. I know they felt as if they were waiting on my servant, and when the tea was prepared I said: "He'll have a cup, please—he's tired." Mrs. Monarch brought him one where he stood, and he took it from her, as if he had been a gentleman at a party squeezing a crush-hat with an elbow.

Then it came over me that she had made a great effort for me—made it with a kind of nobleness—and that I owed her a compensation. Each time I saw her after this I wondered what the compensation could be. I couldn't go on doing the wrong thing to oblige them. Oh it *was* the wrong thing, the stamp of the work for which they sat—Hawley was not the only person to say it now. I sent in a large number of the drawings I had made for "Rutland Ramsay," and I received a warning that was more to the point than Hawley's. The artistic adviser of the house for which I was working was of opinion that many of my illustrations were not what had been looked for. Most of these illustrations were the subjects in which the Monarchs had figured. Without going into the question of what *had* been looked for, I had to face the fact that at this rate I shouldn't get the other books to do. I hurled myself in despair on Miss Churm—I put her through all her paces. I not only adopted Oronte publicly as my hero, but one morning when the Major looked in to see if I didn't require him to finish a *Cheapside* figure for which he had begun to sit the week before, I told him I had changed my mind— I'd do the drawing from my man. At this my visitor turned pale and stood looking at me. "Is *he* your idea of an English gentleman?" he asked.

I was disappointed, I was nervous, I wanted to get on with my work; so I replied with irritation: "Oh my dear Major—I can't be ruined for *you!*" . . .

It was a horrid speech, but he stood another moment—after which, without a word, he quitted the studio. I drew a long breath, for I said to myself that I shouldn't see him again. I hadn't told him definitely that I was in danger of having my work rejected, but I was vexed at his not having felt the catastrophe in the air, read with me the moral of our fruitless collaboration, the lesson that in the deceptive atmosphere of art even the highest respectability may fail of being plastic.

I didn't owe my friends money, but I did see them again. They reappeared together three days later, and, given all the other facts, there was something tragic in that one. It was a clear proof they could find nothing else in life to do. They had threshed the matter out in a dismal conference—they had digested the bad news that they were not in for the series. If they weren't useful to me even for the *Cheapside* their function seemed difficult to determine, and I could only judge at first that they had come, forgivingly, decorously, to take a last leave. This made me rejoice in secret that I had little leisure for a scene; for I had placed both my other models in position together and I was pegging away at a drawing from which I hoped to derive glory. It had been suggested by the passage in which Rutland Ramsay, drawing up a chair to Artemisia's piano-stool, says extraordinary things to her while she ostensibly fingers out a difficult piece of music. I had done Miss Churm at the piano before—it was an attitude in which she knew how to take on an absolutely poetic grace. I wished the two figures to "compose" together with intensity, and my little Italian had entered perfectly into my conception. The pair were vividly before me, the piano had been pulled out; it was a charming show of blended youth and murmured love, which I had only to catch and keep. My visitors stood and looked at it, and I was friendly to them over my shoulder.

They made no response, but I was used to silent company and went on with my work, only a little disconcerted—even though exhilarated by the sense that *this* was at least the ideal thing—at not having got rid of them after all. Presently I heard Mrs. Monarch's sweet voice beside or rather above me: "I wish her hair were a little better done." I looked up and she was staring with a strange fixedness at Miss Churm, whose back was turned to her. "Do you mind my just touching it?" she went on—a question which made me spring up for an instant as with the instinctive fear that she might do the young lady a harm. But she quieted me with a glance I shall never forget—I confess I should like to have been able to paint *that*—and went for a moment to my model. She spoke to her softly, laying a hand on her shoulder and bending over her; and as the girl, understanding, gratefully assented, she disposed her rough curls, with a few quick passes, in such a way as to make Miss Churm's head twice as charming. It was one of the most heroic personal services I've ever seen rendered. Then Mrs. Monarch turned away with a low sigh and, looking about her as if for something to do, stooped to the floor with a noble humility and picked up a dirty rag that had dropped out of my paint-box.

130   The Major meanwhile had also been looking for something to do, and, wandering to the other end of the studio, saw before him my breakfast-things neglected, unremoved. "I say, can't I be useful *here?*" he called out to me with an irrepressible quaver. I assented with a laugh that I fear was awkward, and for the next ten minutes, while I worked, I heard the light clatter of china and the tinkle of spoons and glass. Mrs. Monarch assisted her husband—they washed up my crockery, they put it away. They wandered off into my little scullery, and I afterwards found that they had cleaned my knives and that my slender stock of plate had an unprecedented surface. When it came over me, the latent eloquence of what they were doing, I confess that my drawing was blurred for a moment—the picture swam. They had accepted their failure, but they couldn't accept their fate. They had bowed their heads in bewilderment to the perverse and cruel law in virtue of which the real thing could be so much less precious than the unreal; but they didn't want to starve. If my servants were my models; then my models might be my servants. They would reverse the parts—the others would sit for the ladies and gentlemen and *they* would do the work. They would still be in the studio—it was an intense dumb appeal to me not to turn them out. "Take us on," they wanted to say—"we'll do *anything*."

My pencil dropped from my hand; my sitting was spoiled and I got rid of my sitters, who were also evidently rather mystified and awestruck. Then, alone with the Major and his wife I had a most uncomfortable moment. He put their prayer into a single sentence: "I say, you know—just let *us* do for you, can't you?" I couldn't—it was dreadful to see them emptying my slops; but I pretended I could, to oblige them, for about a week. Then I gave them a sum of money to go away, and I never saw them again. I obtained the remaining books, but my friend Hawley repeats that Major and Mrs. Monarch did me a permanent harm, got me into false ways. If it be true I'm content to have paid the price—for the memory.

1892, 1909

CHARLES BAXTER

Fenstad's Mother

On Sunday morning after communion Fenstad drove across town to visit his mother. Behind the wheel, he exhaled with his hand flat in front of his mouth to determine if the wine on his breath could be detected. He didn't think so. Fenstad's mother was a lifelong social progressive who was amused by her son's churchgoing, and, wine or no wine, she could guess where he had been. She had spent her life in the company of rebels and deviationists, and she recognized all their styles.

Passing a frozen pond in the city park, Fenstad slowed down to watch the skaters, many of whom he knew by name and skating style. From a distance they were dots of color ready for flight, frictionless. To express grief on skates seemed almost impossible, and Fenstad liked that. He parked his car on a residential block and took out his skates from the back seat, where he kept them all winter. With his fingertips he touched the wooden blade guards, thinking of the time. He checked his watch; he had fifteen minutes.

Out on the ice, still wearing his churchy Sunday-morning suit, tie, and overcoat, but now circling the outside edge of the pond with his bare hands in his overcoat pockets, Fenstad admired the overcast sky and luxuriated in the brittle cold. He was active and alert in winter but felt sleepy throughout the summer. He passed a little girl in a pink jacket, pushing a tiny chair over the ice. He waved to his friend Ann, an off-duty cop, practicing her twirls. He waved to other friends. Without exception they waved back. As usual, he was impressed by the way skates improved human character.

Twenty minutes later, in the doorway of her apartment, his mother said, "Your cheeks are red." She glanced down at his trousers, damp with melted snow. "You've been skating." She kissed him on the cheek and turned to walk into her living room. "Skating after church? Isn't that some sort of doctrinal error?"

"It's just happiness," Fenstad said. Quickly he checked her apartment for any signs of memory loss or depression. He found none and immediately felt relief. The apartment smelled of soap and Lysol, the signs of an old woman who wouldn't tolerate nonsense. Out on her coffee table, as usual, were the letters she was writing to her congressman and to political dictators around the globe. Fenstad's mother pleaded for enlightened behavior and berated the dictators for their bad political habits.

She grasped the arm of the sofa and let herself down slowly. Only then did she smile. "How's your soul, Harry?" she asked. "What's the news?"

He smiled back and smoothed his hair. Martin Luther King's eyes locked into his from the framed picture on the wall opposite him. In the picture King was shaking hands with Fenstad's mother, the two of them surrounded by smiling faces. "My soul's okay, Ma," he said. "It's a hard project. I'm always working on it." He reached down for a chocolate-chunk cookie from a box on top of the television. "Who brought you these?"

"Your daughter Sharon. She came to see me on Friday." Fenstad's mother tilted her head at him. "You *want* to be a good person, but she's the real article. Goodness comes to her without any effort at all. She says you have a new girlfriend. A pharmacist this time. Susan, is it?" Fenstad nodded. "Harry, why does your generation always have to find the right person? Why can't you learn to live with the wrong person? Sooner or later everyone's wrong. Love isn't the most important thing, Harry, far from it. Why can't you see that? I still don't comprehend why you couldn't live with Eleanor." Eleanor was Fenstad's ex-wife. They had been divorced for a decade, but Fenstad's mother hoped for a reconciliation.

"Come on, Ma," Fenstad said. "Over and done with, gone and gone." He took another cookie.

10 "You live with somebody so that you're living with *somebody*, and then you go out and do the work of the world. I don't understand all this pickiness about lovers. In a pinch anybody'll do, Harry, believe me."

On the side table was a picture of her late husband, Fenstad's mild, middle-of-the-road father. Fenstad glanced at the picture and let the silence hang between them before asking, "How are you, Ma?"

"I'm all right." She leaned back in the sofa, whose springs made a strange, almost human groan. "I want to get out. I spend too much time in this place in January. You should expand my horizons. Take me somewhere."

"Come to my composition class," Fenstad said. "I'll pick you up at dinnertime on Tuesday. Eat early."

"They'll notice me," she said, squinting. "I'm too old."

15 "I'll introduce you," her son said. "You'll fit right in."

Fenstad wrote brochures in the publicity department of a computer company during the day, and taught an extension English-composition class at the downtown campus of the state university two nights a week. He didn't need the money; he taught the class because he liked teaching strangers and because he enjoyed the sense of hope that classrooms held for him. This hopefulness and didacticism he had picked up from his mother.

On Tuesday night she was standing at the door of the retirement apartment building, dressed in a dark blue overcoat—her best. Her stylishness was belied slightly by a pair of old fuzzy red earmuffs. Inside the car Fenstad noticed that she had put on perfume, unusual for her. Leaning back, she gazed out contentedly at the nighttime lights.

"Who's in this group of students?" she asked. "Working-class people, I hope. Those are the ones you should be teaching. Anything else is just a career."

"Oh, they work, all right." He looked at his mother and saw, as they passed under a streetlight, a combination of sadness and delicacy in her face. Her usual mask of tough optimism seemed to be deserting her. He braked at a red light and said, "I have a hairdresser and a garage mechanic and a housewife, a Mrs. Nelson, and three guys who're sanitation workers. Plenty of others. One guy you'll really like is a young black man with glasses who sits in the back row and reads *Workers' Vanguard* and Bakunin[1] during class. He's brilliant. I don't know why

---

1. *Workers' Vanguard* was an anarchist magazine published from 1932 to 1939 in New York. Its founders set out to "Americanize" the doctrines of Mikhail Bakunin (1814–1876), an anarchist and Russian revolutionary whose quarrel with Karl Marx split the European revolutionary movement apart, and to reform American society on the basis of industrial syndicates and decentralized communes.

he didn't test out of this class. His name's York Follette, and he's—"

"I want to meet him," she said quickly. She scowled at the moonlit snow. "A   20
man with ideas. People like that have gone out of my life." She looked over at
her son. "What I hate about being my age is how *nice* everyone tries to be. I
was never nice, but now everybody is pelting me with sugar cubes." She opened
her window an inch and let the cold air blow over her, ruffling her stiff gray
hair.

When they arrived at the school, snow had started to fall, and at the other end
of the parking lot a police car's flashing light beamed long crimson rays through
the dense flakes. Fenstad's mother walked deliberately toward the door, shaking
her head mistrustfully at the building and the police. Approaching the steps, she
took her son's hand. "I liked the columns on the old buildings," she said, "the
old university buildings, I mean. I liked Greek Revival better than this Modernist-
bunker stuff." Inside, she blinked in the light at the smooth, waxed linoleum
floors and cement-block walls. She held up her hand to shade her eyes. Fenstad
took her elbow to guide her over the snow melting in puddles in the entryway.
"I never asked you what you're teaching tonight."

"Logic," Fenstad said.

"Ah." She smiled and nodded. "Dialectics!"

"Not quite. Just logic."

She shrugged. She was looking at the clumps of students standing in the glare   25
of the hallway, drinking coffee from paper cups and smoking cigarettes in the
general conversational din. She wasn't used to such noise: she stopped in the
middle of the corridor underneath a wall clock and stared happily in no particular direction. With her eyes shut she breathed in the close air, smelling of wet
overcoats and smoke, and Fenstad remembered how much his mother had
always liked smoke-filled rooms, where ideas fought each other, and where some
of those ideas died.

"Come on," he said, taking her hand again. Inside Fenstad's classroom six
people sat in the angular postures of pre-boredom. York Follette was already in
the back row, his copy of *Workers' Vanguard* shielding his face. Fenstad's mother
headed straight for him and sat down in the desk next to his. Fenstad saw them
shake hands, and in two minutes they were talking in low, rushed murmurs. He
saw York Follette laugh quietly and nod. What was it that blacks saw and appreciated in his mother? They had always liked her—written to her, called her,
checked up on her—and Fenstad wondered if they recognized something in his
mother that he himself had never been able to see.

At seven thirty-five most of the students had arrived and were talking to each
other vigorously, as if they didn't want Fenstad to start and thought they could
delay him. He stared at them, and when they wouldn't quiet down, he made
himself rigid and said, "Good evening. We have a guest tonight." Immediately
the class grew silent. He held his arm out straight, indicating with a flick of his
hand the old woman in the back row. "My mother," he said. "Clara Fenstad."
For the first time all semester his students appeared to be paying attention: they
turned around collectively and looked at Fenstad's mother, who smiled and
waved. A few of the students began to applaud; others joined in. The applause

was quiet but apparently genuine. Fenstad's mother brought herself slowly to her feet and made a suggestion of a bow. Two of the students sitting in front of her turned around and began to talk to her. At the front of the class Fenstad started his lecture on logic, but his mother wouldn't quiet down. This was a class for adults. They were free to do as they liked.

Lowering his head and facing the blackboard, Fenstad reviewed problems in logic, following point by point the outline set down by the textbook: *post hoc* fallacies, false authorities, begging the question, circular reasoning, *ad hominem* arguments, all the rest. Explaining these problems, his back turned, he heard sighs of boredom, boldly expressed. Occasionally he glanced at the back of the room. His mother was watching him carefully, and her face was expressing all the complexity of dismay. Dismay radiated from her. Her disappointment wasn't personal, because his mother didn't think that people as individuals were at fault for what they did. As usual, her disappointed hope was located in history and in the way people agreed with already existing histories.

She was angry with him for collaborating with grammar. She would call it unconsciously installed authority. Then she would find other names for it.

30 "All right," he said loudly, trying to make eye contact with someone in the room besides his mother, "let's try some examples. Can anyone tell me what, if anything, is wrong with the following sentence? 'I, like most people, have a unique problem.' "

The three sanitation workers, in the third row, began to laugh. Fenstad caught himself glowering and singled out the middle one.

"Yes, it is funny, isn't it?"

The man in the middle smirked and looked at the floor. "I was just thinking of my unique problem."

"Right," Fenstad said. "But what's wrong with saying, 'I, like most people, have a unique problem'?"

35 "Solving it?" This was Mrs. Nelson, who sat by the window so that she could gaze at the tree outside, lit by a streetlight. All through class she looked at the tree as if it were a lover.

"Solving what?"

"Solving the problem you have. What is the problem?"

"That's actually not what I'm getting at," Fenstad said. "Although it's a good *related* point. I'm asking what might be wrong logically with that sentence."

"It depends," Harold Ronson said. He worked in a service station and sometimes came to class wearing his work shirt with his name tag, HAROLD, stitched into it. "It depends on what your problem is. You haven't told us your problem."

40 "No," Fenstad said, "my problem is *not* the problem." He thought of Alice in Wonderland and felt, physically, as if he himself were getting small. "Let's try this again. What might be wrong with saying that most people have a unique problem?"

"You shouldn't be so critical," Timothy Melville said. "You should look on the bright side, if possible."

"What?"

"He's right," Mrs. Nelson said. "Most people have unique problems, but many people do their best to help themselves, such as taking night classes or working at meditation."

"No doubt that's true," Fenstad said. "But why can't most people have a unique problem?"

"Oh, I disagree," Mrs. Nelson said, still looking at her tree. Fenstad glanced at it and saw that it was crested with snow. It *was* beautiful. No wonder she looked at it. "I believe that most people do have unique problems. They just shouldn't talk about them all the time."

"Can anyone," Fenstad asked, looking at the back wall and hoping to see something there that was not wall, "can anyone give me an example of a unique problem?"

"Divorce," Barb Kjellerud said. She sat near the door and knitted during class. She answered questions without looking up. "Divorce is unique."

"No, it isn't!" Fenstad said, failing in the crucial moment to control his voice. He and his mother exchanged glances. In his mother's face for a split second was the history of her compassionate, ambivalent attention to him. "Divorce is not unique." He waited to calm himself. "It's everywhere. Now try again. Give me a unique problem."

Silence. "This is a trick question," Arlene Hubbly said. "I'm sure it's a trick question."

"Not necessarily. Does anyone know what *unique* means?"

"One of a kind," York Follette said, gazing at Fenstad with dry amusement. Sometimes he took pity on Fenstad and helped him out of jams. Fenstad's mother smiled and nodded.

"Right," Fenstad crowed, racing toward the blackboard as if he were about to write something. "So let's try again. Give me a unique problem."

"You give *us* a unique problem," one of the sanitation workers said. Fenstad didn't know whether he'd been given a statement or a command. He decided to treat it as a command.

"All right," he said. He stopped and looked down at his shoes. Maybe it *was* a trick question. He thought for ten seconds. Problem after problem presented itself to him. He thought of poverty, of the assaults on the earth, of the awful complexities of love. "I can't think of one," Fenstad said. His hands went into his pockets.

"That's because problems aren't personal," Fenstad's mother said from the back of the room. "They're collective." She waited while several students in the class sat up and nodded. "And people must work together on their solutions." She talked for another two minutes, taking the subject out of logic and putting it neatly in politics, where she knew it belonged.

The snow had stopped by the time the class was over. Fenstad took his mother's arm and escorted her to the car. After letting her down on the passenger side and starting the engine, he began to clear the front windshield. He didn't have a scraper and had forgotten his gloves, so he was using his bare hands. When he brushed the snow away on his mother's side, she looked out at him, surprised, a terribly aged Sleeping Beauty awakened against her will.

Once the car had warmed up, she was in a gruff mood and repositioned herself under the seat belt while making quiet but aggressive remarks. The sight of the new snow didn't seem to calm her. "Logic," she said at last. "That wasn't logic. Those are just rhetorical tactics. It's filler and drudgery."

"I don't want to discuss it now."

"All right. I'm sorry. Let's talk about something more pleasant."

60   They rode together in silence. Then she began to shake her head. "Don't take me home," she said. "I want to have a spot of tea somewhere before I go back. A nice place where they serve tea, all right?"

He parked outside an all-night restaurant with huge front plate-glass windows; it was called Country Bob's. He held his mother's elbow from the car to the door. At the door, looking back to make sure that he had turned off his headlights, he saw his tracks and his mother's in the snow. His were separate footprints, but hers formed two long lines.

Inside, at the table, she sipped her tea and gazed at her son for a long time. "Thanks for the adventure, Harry. I do appreciate it. What're you doing in class next week? Oh, I remember. How-to papers. That should be interesting."

"Want to come?"

"Very much. I'll keep quiet next time, if you want me to."

Fenstad shook his head. "It's okay. It's fun having you along. You can say whatever you want. The students loved you. I knew you'd be a sensation, and you were. They'd probably rather have you teaching the class than me."

65   He noticed that his mother was watching something going on behind him, and Fenstad turned around in the booth so that he could see what it was. At first all he saw was a woman, a young woman with long hair wet from snow and hanging in clumps, talking in the aisle to two young men, both of whom were nodding at her. Then she moved on to the next table. She spoke softly. Fenstad couldn't hear her words, but he saw the solitary customer to whom she was speaking shake his head once, keeping his eyes down. Then the woman saw Fenstad and his mother. In a moment she was standing in front of them.

She wore two green plaid flannel shirts and a thin torn jacket. Like Fenstad, she wore no gloves. Her jeans were patched, and she gave off a strong smell, something like hay, Fenstad thought, mixed with tar and sweat. He looked down at her feet and saw that she was wearing penny loafers with no socks. Coins, old pennies, were in both shoes; the leather was wet and cracked. He looked in the woman's face. Under a hat that seemed to collapse on either side of her head, the woman's face was thin and chalk-white except for the fatigue lines under her eyes. The eyes themselves were bright blue, beautiful, and crazy. To Fenstad, she looked desperate, percolating slightly with insanity, and he was about to say so to his mother when the woman bent down toward him and said, "Mister, can you spare any money?"

Involuntarily, Fenstad looked toward the kitchen, hoping that the manager would spot this person and take her away. When he looked back again, his mother was taking her blue coat off, wriggling in the booth to free her arms from the sleeves. Stopping and starting again, she appeared to be stuck inside the coat; then she lifted herself up, trying to stand, and with a quick, quiet groan slipped the coat off. She reached down and folded the coat over and held it toward the woman. "Here," she said. "Here's my coat. Take it before my son stops me."

"Mother, you can't." Fenstad reached forward to grab the coat, but his mother pulled it away from him.

When Fenstad looked back at the woman, her mouth was open, showing several gray teeth. Her hands were outstretched, and he understood, after a moment, that this was a posture of refusal, a gesture saying no, and that the woman wasn't used to it and did it awkwardly. Fenstad's mother was standing and trying to push the coat toward the woman, not toward her hands but lower, at waist level, and she was saying, "Here, here, here, here." The sound, like a human birdcall, frightened Fenstad, and he stood up quickly, reached for his wallet, and removed the first two bills he could find, two twenties. He grabbed the woman's chapped, ungloved left hand.

"Take these," he said, putting the two bills in her icy palm, "for the love of   70 God, and please go."

He was close to her face. Tonight he would pray for her. For a moment the woman's expression was vacant. His mother was still pushing the coat at her, and the woman was unsteadily bracing herself. The woman's mouth was open, and her stagnant-water breath washed over him. "I know you," she said. "You're my little baby cousin."

"Go away, please," Fenstad said. He pushed at her. She turned, clutching his money. He reached around to put his hands on his mother's shoulders. "Ma," he said, "she's gone now. Mother, sit down. I gave her money for a coat." His mother fell down on her side of the booth, and her blue coat rolled over on the bench beside her, showing the label and the shiny inner lining. When he looked up, the woman who had been begging had disappeared, though he could still smell her odor, an essence of wretchedness.

"Excuse me, Harry," his mother said. "I have to go to the bathroom."

She rose and walked toward the front of the restaurant, turned a corner, and was out of sight. Fenstad sat and tried to collect himself. When the waiter came, a boy with an earring and red hair in a flattop, Fenstad just shook his head and said, "More tea." He realized that his mother hadn't taken off her earmuffs, and the image of his mother in the ladies' room with her earmuffs on gave him a fit of uneasiness. After getting up from the booth and following the path that his mother had taken, he stood outside the ladies'-room door and, when no one came in or out, he knocked. He waited for a decent interval. Still hearing no answer, he opened the door.

His mother was standing with her arms down on either side of the first sink.   75 She was holding herself there, her eyes following the hot water as it poured from the tap around the bright porcelain sink down into the drain, and she looked furious. Fenstad touched her and she snapped toward him.

"Your logic!" she said.

He opened the door for her and helped her back to the booth. The second cup of tea had been served, and Fenstad's mother sipped it in silence. They did not converse. When she had finished, she said, "All right. I do feel better now. Let's go."

At the curb in front of her apartment building he leaned forward and kissed her on the cheek. "Pick me up next Tuesday," she said. "I want to go back to that class." He nodded. He watched as she made her way past the security guard at the front desk; then he put his car into drive and started home.

That night he skated in the dark for an hour with his friend, Susan, the pharmacist. She was an excellent skater; they had met on the ice. She kept late hours and, like Fenstad, enjoyed skating at night. She listened attentively to his story about his mother and the woman in the restaurant. To his great relief she recommended no course of action. She listened. She didn't believe in giving advice, even when asked.

80   The following Tuesday, Fenstad's mother was again in the back row next to York Follette. One of the fluorescent lights overhead was flickering, which gave the room, Fenstad thought, a sinister quality, like a debtors' prison or a refuge for the homeless. He'd been thinking about such people for the entire week. For seven days now he had caught whiffs of the woman's breath in the air, and one morning, Friday, he thought he caught a touch of the rotten-celery smell on his own breath, after a particularly difficult sales meeting.

Tonight was how-to night. The students were expected to stand at the front of the class and read their papers, instructing their peers and answering questions if necessary. Starting off, and reading her paper in a frightened monotone, Mrs. Nelson told the class how to bake a cheese soufflé. Arlene Hubbly's paper was about mushroom hunting. Fenstad was put off by the introduction. "The advantage to mushrooms," Arlene Hubbly read, "is that they are delicious. The disadvantage to mushrooms is that they can make you sick, even die." But then she explained how to recognize the common shaggymane by its cylindrical cap and dark tufts; she drew a model on the board. She warned the class against the *Clitocybe illudens,* the Jack-o'-Lantern. "Never eat a mushroom like this one or *any* mushroom that glows in the dark. Take heed!" she said, fixing her gaze on the class. Fenstad saw his mother taking rapid notes. Harold Ronson, the mechanic, reading his own prose painfully and slowly, told the class how to get rust spots out of their automobiles. Again Fenstad noticed his mother taking notes. York Follette told the class about the proper procedures for laying down attic insulation and how to know when enough was enough, so that a homeowner wouldn't be robbed blind, as he put it, by the salesmen, in whose ranks he had once counted himself.

Barb Kjellerud had brought along a cassette player, and told the class that her hobby was ballroom dancing; she would instruct them in the basic waltz. She pushed the play button on the tape machine, and "Tales from the Vienna Woods" came booming out. To the accompaniment of the music she read her paper, illustrating, as she went, how the steps were to be performed. She danced alone in front of them, doing so with flair. Her blond hair swayed as she danced, Fenstad noticed. She looked a bit like a contestant in a beauty contest who had too much personality to win. She explained to the men the necessity of leading. Someone had to lead, she said, and tradition had given this responsibility to the male. Fenstad heard his mother snicker.

When Barb Kjellerud asked for volunteers, Fenstad's mother raised her hand. She said she knew how to waltz and would help out. At the front of the class she made a counterclockwise motion with her hand, and for the next minute, sitting at the back of the room, Fenstad watched his mother and one of the sanitation workers waltzing under the flickering fluorescent lights.

"What a wonderful class," Fenstad's mother said on the way home. "I hope you're paying attention to what they tell you."

Fenstad nodded. "Tea?" he asked.   85

She shook her head. "Where're you going after you drop me off?"

"Skating," he said. "I usually go skating. I have a date."

"With the pharmacist? In the dark?"

"We both like it, Ma." As he drove, he made an all-purpose gesture. "The moon and the stars," he said simply.

When he left her off, he felt unsettled. He considered, as a point of courtesy,   90
staying with her a few minutes, but by the time he had this idea he was already away from the building and was headed down the street.

He and Susan were out on the ice together, skating in large circles, when Susan pointed to a solitary figure sitting on a park bench near the lake's edge. The sky had cleared; the moon gave everything a cold, fine-edged clarity. When Fenstad followed the line of Susan's finger, he saw at once that the figure on the bench was his mother. He realized it simply because of the way she sat there, drawn into herself, attentive even in the winter dark. He skated through the uncleared snow over the ice until he was standing close enough to speak to her. "Mother," he said, "what are you doing here?"

She was bundled up, a thick woolen cap drawn over her head, and two scarves covering much of her face. He could see little other than the two lenses of her glasses facing him in the dark. "I wanted to see you two," she told him. "I thought you'd look happy, and you did. I like to watch happiness. I always have."

"How can you see us? We're so far away."

"That's how I saw you."

This made no sense to him, so he asked, "How'd you get here?"   95

"I took a cab. That part was easy."

"Aren't you freezing?"

"I don't know. I don't know if I'm freezing or not."

He and Susan took her back to her apartment as soon as they could get their boots on. In the car Mrs. Fenstad insisted on asking Susan what kind of safety procedures were used to ensure that drugs weren't smuggled out of pharmacies and sold illegally, but she didn't appear to listen to the answer, and by the time they reached her building, she seemed to be falling asleep. They helped her up to her apartment. Susan thought that they should give her a warm bath before putting her into bed, and, together, they did. She did not protest. She didn't even seem to notice them as they guided her in and out of the bathtub.

Fenstad feared that his mother would catch some lung infection, and it turned   100
out to be bronchitis, which kept her in her apartment for the first three weeks of

February, until her cough went down. Fenstad came by every other day to see how she was, and one Tuesday, after work, he went up to her floor and heard piano music: an old recording, which sounded much-played, of the brightest and fastest jazz piano he had ever heard—music of superhuman brilliance. He swung open the door to her apartment and saw York Follette sitting near his mother's bed. On the bedside table was a small tape player, from which the music poured into the room.

Fenstad's mother was leaning back against the pillow, smiling, her eyes closed.

Follette turned toward Fenstad. He had been talking softly. He motioned toward the tape machine and said, "Art Tatum.[2] It's a cut called 'Battery Bounce.' Your mother's never heard it."

"Jazz, Harry," Fenstad's mother said, her eyes still closed, not needing to see her son. "York is explaining to me about Art Tatum and jazz. Next week he's going to try something more progressive on me." Now his mother opened her eyes. "Have you ever heard such music before, Harry?"

They were both looking at him. "No," he said, "I never heard anything like it."

105   "This is my unique problem, Harry." Fenstad's mother coughed and then waited to recover her breath. "I never heard enough jazz." She smiled. "What glimpses!" she said at last.

After she recovered, he often found her listening to the tape machine that York Follette had given her. She liked to hear the Oscar Peterson[3] Trio as the sun set and the lights of evening came on. She now often mentioned glimpses. Back at home, every night, Fenstad spoke about his mother in his prayers of remembrance and thanksgiving, even though he knew she would disapprove.

1990

<hr />

DORIS LESSING

Our Friend Judith

I stopped inviting Judith to meet people when a Canadian woman remarked, with the satisfied fervour of one who has at last pinned a label on a rare specimen: "She is, of course, one of your typical English spinsters."

This was a few weeks after an American sociologist, having elicited from Judith the facts that she was fortyish, unmarried, and living alone, had enquired of me: "I suppose she has given up?" "Given up what?" I asked; and the subsequent discussion was unrewarding.

Judith did not easily come to parties. She would come after pressure, not so much—one felt—to do one a favour, but in order to correct what she believed to be a defect in her character. "I really ought to enjoy meeting new people more

<hr />

2. Art Tatum (1910–1956), jazz pianist renowned for his harmonic imagination and extravagant virtuosity.   3. Oscar Peterson (b. 1925), jazz pianist and composer, greatly influenced by Tatum.

than I do," she said once. We reverted to an earlier pattern of our friendship: odd evenings together, an occasional visit to the cinema, or she would telephone to say: "I'm on my way past you to the British Museum. Would you care for a cup of coffee with me? I have twenty minutes to spare."

It is characteristic of Judith that the word "spinster," used of her, provoked fascinated speculation about other people. There are my aunts, for instance: aged seventy-odd, both unmarried, one an ex-missionary from China, one a retired matron of a famous London hospital. These two old ladies live together under the shadow of the cathedral in a country town. They devote much time to the Church, to good causes, to letter writing with friends all over the world, to the grandchildren and the great-grandchildren of relatives. It would be a mistake, however, on entering a house in which nothing has been moved for fifty years, to diagnose a condition of fossilised late-Victorian integrity. They read every book review in the *Observer* or the *Times*,[1] so that I recently got a letter from Aunt Rose enquiring whether I did not think that the author of *On the Road*[2] was not— perhaps?—exaggerating his difficulties. They know a good deal about music, and write letters of encouragement to young composers they feel are being neglected—"You must understand that anything new and original takes time to be understood." Well-informed and critical Tories, they are as likely to dispatch telegrams of protest to the Home Secretary[3] as letters of support. These ladies, my aunts Emily and Rose, are surely what is meant by the phrase "English spinster." And yet, once the connection has been pointed out, there is no doubt that Judith and they are spiritual cousins, if not sisters. Therefore it follows that one's pitying admiration for women who have supported manless and uncomforted lives needs a certain modification?

One will, of course, never know; and I feel now that it is entirely my fault that I shall never know. I had been Judith's friend for upward of five years before the incident occurred which I involuntarily thought of—stupidly enough—as the first time Judith's mask slipped.

A mutual friend, Betty, had been given a cast-off Dior[4] dress. She was too short for it. Also she said: "It's not a dress for a married woman with three children and a talent for cooking. I don't know why not, but it isn't." Judith was the right build. Therefore one evening the three of us met by appointment in Judith's bedroom, with the dress. Neither Betty nor I was surprised at the renewed discovery that Judith was beautiful. We had both often caught each other, and ourselves, in moments of envy when Judith's calm and severe face, her undemonstratively perfect body, succeeded in making everyone else in a room or a street look cheap.

Judith is tall, small-breasted, slender. Her light brown hair is parted in the centre and cut straight around her neck. A high straight forehead, straight nose,

1. Prestigious London newspapers representing roughly the younger, more liberal establishment and the Establishment proper, respectively.   2. Jack Kerouac (1922–1969), a leading writer of the Beat Generation, 1950s forerunners of the hippies. Kerouac heroes felt themselves completely cut off from and victimized by American society.   3. Head of the British government department responsible for domestic matters.   4. Famous French designer of high fashions.

a full grave mouth are setting for her eyes, which are green, large and prominent. Her lids are very white, fringed with gold, and moulded close over the eyeball, so that in profile she has the look of a staring gilded mask. The dress was of dark green glistening stuff, cut straight, with a sort of loose tunic. It opened simply at the throat. In it Judith could of course evoke nothing but classical images. Diana, perhaps, back from the hunt, in a relaxed moment? A rather intellectual wood nymph who had opted for an afternoon in the British Museum Reading Room? Something like that. Neither Betty nor I said a word, since Judith was examining herself in a long mirror, and must know she looked magnificent.

Slowly she drew off the dress and laid it aside. Slowly she put on the old cord skirt and woollen blouse she had taken off. She must have surprised a resigned glance between us, for she then remarked, with the smallest of mocking smiles: "One surely ought to stay in character, wouldn't you say?" She added, reading the words out of some invisible book, written not by her, since it was a very vulgar book, but perhaps by one of us: "It does everything *for* me, I must admit."

"After seeing you in it," Betty cried out, defying her, "I can't bear for anyone else to have it. I shall simply put it away." Judith shrugged, rather irritated. In the shapeless skirt and blouse, and without makeup, she stood smiling at us, a woman at whom forty-nine out of fifty people would not look twice.

10   A second revelatory incident occurred soon after. Betty telephoned me to say that Judith had a kitten. Did I know that Judith adored cats? "No, but of course she would," I said.

Betty lived in the same street as Judith and saw more of her than I did. I was kept posted about the growth and habits of the cat and its effect on Judith's life. She remarked for instance that she felt it was good for her to have a tie and some responsibility. But no sooner was the cat out of kittenhood than all the neighbours complained. It was a tomcat, ungelded, and making every night hideous. Finally the landlord said that either the cat or Judith must go, unless she was prepared to have the cat "fixed."[5] Judith wore herself out trying to find some person, anywhere in Britain, who would be prepared to take the cat. This person would, however, have to sign a written statement not to have the cat "fixed." When Judith took the cat to the vet to be killed, Betty told me she cried for twenty-four hours.

"She didn't think of compromising? After all, perhaps the cat might have preferred to live, if given the choice?"

"Is it likely I'd have the nerve to say anything so sloppy to Judith? It's the nature of a male cat to rampage lustfully about, and therefore it would be morally wrong for Judith to have the cat fixed, simply to suit her own convenience."

"She said that?"

15   "She wouldn't have to *say* it, surely?"

A third incident was when she allowed a visiting young American, living in Paris, the friend of a friend and scarcely known to her, to use her flat while she visited her parents over Christmas. The young man and his friends lived it up for ten days of alcohol and sex and marijuana, and when Judith came back it took a

5. Gelded, castrated.

week to get the place clean again and the furniture mended. She telephoned twice to Paris, the first time to say that he was a disgusting young thug and if he knew what was good for him he would keep out of her way in the future; the second time to apologise for losing her temper. "I had a choice either to let someone use my flat, or to leave it empty. But having chosen that you should have it, it was clearly an unwarrantable infringement of your liberty to make any conditions at all. I do most sincerely ask your pardon." The moral aspects of the matter having been made clear, she was irritated rather than not to receive letters of apology from him—fulsome, embarrassed, but above all, baffled.

It was the note of curiosity in the letters—he even suggested coming over to get to know her better—that irritated her most. "What do you suppose he means?" she said to me. "He lived in my flat for ten days. One would have thought that should be enough, wouldn't you?"

The facts about Judith, then, are all in the open, unconcealed, and plain to anyone who cares to study them; or, as it became plain she feels, to anyone with the intelligence to interpret them.

She has lived for the last twenty years in a small two-roomed flat high over a busy West London street. The flat is shabby and badly heated. The furniture is old, was never anything but ugly, is now frankly rickety and fraying. She has an income of two hundred pounds[6] a year from a dead uncle. She lives on this and what she earns from her poetry, and from lecturing on poetry to night classes and extramural university classes.

She does not smoke or drink, and eats very little, from preference, not self-discipline.

She studied poetry and biology at Oxford, with distinction.

She is a Castlewell. That is, she is a member of one of the academic upper-middleclass families, which have been producing for centuries a steady supply of brilliant but sound men and women who are the backbone of the arts and sciences in Britain. She is on cool good terms with her family, who respect her and leave her alone.

She goes on long walking tours, by herself, in such places as Exmoor or West Scotland.

Every three or four years she publishes a volume of poems.

The walls of her flat are completely lined with books. They are scientific, classical and historical; there is a great deal of poetry and some drama. There is not one novel. When Judith says: "Of course I don't read novels," this does not mean that novels have no place, or a small place, in literature; or that people should not read novels; but that it must be obvious she can't be expected to read novels.

I had been visiting her flat for years before I noticed two long shelves of books, under a window, each shelf filled with the works of a single writer. The two writers are not, to put it at the mildest, the kind one would associate with Judith. They are mild, reminiscent, vague and whimsical. Typical English *belles-lettres,* in fact, and by definition abhorrent to her. Not one of the books in the two shelves has been read; some of the pages are still uncut. Yet each book is inscribed or

6. About one-third or even one-half of a subsistence income.

dedicated to her: gratefully, admiringly, sentimentally and, more than once, amorously. In short, it is open to anyone who cares to examine these two shelves, and to work out dates, to conclude that Judith from the age of fifteen to twenty-five had been the beloved young companion of one elderly literary gentleman, and from twenty-five to thirty-five the inspiration of another.

During all that time she had produced her own poetry, and the sort of poetry, it is quite safe to deduce, not at all likely to be admired by her two admirers. Her poems are always cool and intellectual; that is their form, which is contradicted or supported by a gravely sensuous texture. They are poems to read often; one has to, to understand them.

I did not ask Judith a direct question about these two eminent but rather fusty lovers. Not because she would not have answered, or because she would have found the question impertinent, but because such questions are clearly unnecessary. Having those two shelves of books where they are, and books she could not conceivably care for, for their own sake, is publicly giving credit where credit is due. I can imagine her thinking the thing over, and deciding it was only fair, or perhaps honest, to place the books there; and this despite the fact that she would not care at all for the same attention be paid to her. There is something almost contemptuous in it. For she certainly despises people who feel they need attention.

For instance, more than once a new emerging wave of "modern" young poets have discovered her as the only "modern" poet among their despised and well-credited elders. This is because, since she began writing at fifteen, her poems have been full of scientific, mechanical and chemical imagery. This is how she thinks, or feels.

30   More than once has a young poet hastened to her flat, to claim her as an ally, only to find her totally and by instinct unmoved by words like "modern," "new," "contemporary." He has been outraged and wounded by her principle, so deeply rooted as to be unconscious, and to need no expression but a contemptuous shrug of the shoulders, that publicity seeking or to want critical attention is despicable. It goes without saying that there is perhaps one critic in the world she has any time for. He has sulked off, leaving her on her shelf, which she takes it for granted is her proper place, to be read by an appreciative minority.

Meanwhile she gives her lectures, walks alone through London, writes her poems, and is seen sometimes at a concert or a play with a middleaged professor of Greek, who has a wife and two children.

Betty and I had speculated about this professor, with such remarks as: Surely she must sometimes be lonely? Hasn't she ever wanted to marry? What about that awful moment when one comes in from somewhere at night to an empty flat?

It happened recently that Betty's husband was on a business trip, her children visiting, and she was unable to stand the empty house. She asked Judith for a refuge until her own home filled again.

Afterwards Betty rang me up to report: "Four of the five nights Professor Adams came in about ten or so."

35   "Was Judith embarrassed?"

"Would you expect her to be?"

"Well, if not embarrassed, at least conscious there was a situation?"

"No, not at all. But I must say I don't think he's good enough for her. He can't possibly understand her. He calls her Judy."

"Good God."

"Yes. But I was wondering. Suppose the other two called her Judy—'little Judy'—imagine it! Isn't it awful? But it does rather throw a light on Judith?"

"It's rather touching."

"I suppose it's touching. But *I* was embarrassed—oh, not because of the situation. Because of how she was, with him. 'Judy, is there another cup of tea in that pot?' And she, rather daughterly and demure, pouring him one."

"Well yes, I can see how you felt."

"Three of the nights he went to her bedroom with her—very casual about it, because she was being. But he was not there in the mornings. So I asked her. You know how it is when you ask her a question. As if you've been having long conversations on that very subject for years and years, and she is merely continuing where you left off last. So when she says something surprising, one feels such a fool to be surprised?"

"Yes. And then?"

"I asked her if she was sorry not to have children. She said yes, but one couldn't have everything."

"One can't have everything, she said?"

"Quite clearly feeling she *has* nearly everything. She said she thought it was a pity, because she would have brought up children very well."

"When you come to think of it, she would, too."

"I asked about marriage, but she said on the whole the role of a mistress suited her better."

"She used the word 'mistress'?"

"You must admit it's the accurate word."

"I suppose so."

"And then she said that while she liked intimacy and sex and everything, she enjoyed waking up in the morning alone and *her own person.*"

"Yes, *of course.*"

"Of course. But now she's bothered because the professor would like to marry her. Or he feels he ought. At least, he's getting all guilty and obsessive about it. She says she doesn't see the point of divorce, and anyway, surely it would be very hard on his poor old wife after all these years, particularly after bringing up two children so satisfactorily. She talks about his wife as if she's a kind of nice old charwoman, and it wouldn't be *fair* to sack her, you know. Anyway. What with one thing and another. Judith's going off to Italy soon in order *to collect herself.*"

"But how's she going to pay for it?"

"Luckily the Third Programme's[7] commissioning her to do some arty programmes. They offered her a choice of The Cid—El Thid[8] you know—and the Borgias. Well, the Borghese, then. And Judith settled for the Borgias."

---

7. British Broadcasting Corporation public radio service (and now also television channel) specializing in classical music, literature and plays, lectures, etc.   8. Castilian, standard Spanish, pronunciation of El Cid (rhymes with *steed*), the title of an eleventh-century soldier-hero and hero of many works of literature.

"The Borgias," I said, *"Judith?"*

"Yes, quite. I said that too, in that tone of voice. She saw my point. She says the epic is right up her street, whereas the Renaissance has never been on her wave length. Obviously it couldn't be, all the magnificence and cruelty and *dirt*. But of course chivalry and a high moral code and all those idiotically noble goings-on are right on her wave length."

"Is the money the same?"

"Yes. But is it likely Judith would let money decide? No, she said that one should always choose something new, that isn't up one's street. Well, because it's better for her character, and so on, to get herself unsettled by the Renaissance. She didn't say *that*, of course."

"Of course not."

Judith went to Florence; and for some months postcards informed us tersely of her doings. Then Betty decided she must go by herself for a holiday. She had been appalled by the discovery that if her husband was away for a night she couldn't sleep; and when he went to Australia for three weeks, she stopped living until he came back. She had discussed this with him, and he had agreed that if she really felt the situation to be serious, he would despatch her by air, to Italy, in order to recover her self-respect. As she put it.

I got this letter from her: "It's no use, I'm coming home. I might have known. Better face it, once you're really married you're not fit for man nor beast. And if you remember what I used to be like! *Well!* I moped around Milan. I sunbathed in Venice, then I thought my tan was surely worth something, so I was on the point of starting an affair with another lonely soul, but I lost heart, and went to Florence to see Judith. She wasn't there. She'd gone to the Italian Riviera. I had nothing better to do, so I followed her. When I saw the place I wanted to laugh, it's so much not Judith, you know, all those palms and umbrellas and gaiety at all costs and ever such an ornamental blue sea. Judith is in an enormous stone room up on the hillside above the sea, with grape vines all over the place. You should see her, she's got beautiful. It seems for the last fifteen years she's been going to Soho[9] every Saturday morning to buy food at an Italian shop. I must have looked surprised, because she explained she liked Soho. I suppose because all that dreary vice and nudes and prostitutes and everything prove how right she is to be as she is? She told the people in the shop she was going to Italy, and the *signora*[1] said, what a coincidence, she was going back to Italy too, and she did hope an old friend like Miss Castlewell would visit her there. Judith said to me: 'I felt lacking, when she used the word friend. Our relations have always been formal. Can you understand it?' she said to me. 'For fifteen years,' I said to her. She said: 'I think I must feel it's a kind of imposition, don't you know, expecting people to feel friendship for one.' *Well*. I said: 'You ought to understand it, because you're like that yourself.' 'Am I?' she said. 'Well, think about it,' I said. But I could see she didn't want to think about it. Anyway, she's here, and

9. A section of London roughly equivalent to Greenwich Village in New York—foreign restaurants and groceries, haunt of writers, painters, and so forth—but in recent years increasingly known for prostitutes and pornography.   1. Proprietress.

I've spent a week with her. The widow Maria Rineiri inherited her mother's house, so she came home, from Soho. On the ground floor is a tatty little *rosticceria*[2] patronised by the neighbours. They are all working people. This isn't tourist country, up on the hill. The widow lives above the shop with her little boy, a nasty little brat of about ten. Say what you like, the English are the only people who know how to bring up children, I don't care if that's insular. Judith's room is at the back, with a balcony. Underneath her room is the barber's shop, and the barber is Luigi Rineiri, the widow's younger brother. Yes, I was keeping him until the last. He is about forty, tall dark handsome, a great *bull,* but rather a sweet fatherly bull. He has cut Judith's hair and made it lighter. Now it looks like a sort of gold helmet. Judith is all brown. The widow Rineiri has made her a white dress and a green dress. They fit, for a change. When Judith walks down the street to the lower town, all the Italian males take one look at the golden girl and melt in their own oil like ice cream. Judith takes all this in her stride. She sort of acknowledges the homage. Then she strolls into the sea and vanishes into the foam. She swims five miles every day. *Naturally.* I haven't asked Judith whether she has collected herself, because you can see she hasn't. The widow Rineiri is matchmaking. When I noticed this I wanted to laugh, but luckily I didn't because Judith asked me, really wanting to know: 'Can you see me married to an Italian barber?' (Not being snobbish, but stating the position, so to speak.) 'Well yes,' I said, 'you're the only women I know who I can see married to an Italian barber.' Because it wouldn't matter who she married, she'd always be her *own person.* 'At any rate, for a time,' I said. At which she said, asperously,[3] 'You can use phrases like for a time in England but not in Italy.' Did you ever see England, at least London, as the home of licence, liberty and free love? No, neither did I, but of course she's right. Married to Luigi it would be the family, the neighbours, the church and the *bambini.*[4] All the same she's thinking about it, believe it or not. Here she's quite different, all relaxed and free. She's melting in the attention she gets. The widow mothers her and makes her coffee all the time, and listens to a lot of good advice about how to bring up that nasty brat of hers. Unluckily she doesn't take it. Luigi is crazy for her. At mealtimes she goes to the *trattoria*[5] in the upper square and all the workmen treat her like a goddess. Well, a film star then. I said to her, you're mad to come home. For one thing her rent is ten bob[6] a week, and you eat *pasta* and drink red wine till you bust for about one and six-pence. No, she said, it would be nothing but self-indulgence to stay. Why? I said. She said, she's got nothing to stay for. (Ho ho.) And besides, she's done her research on the Borghese, though so far she can't see her way to an honest pre-sentation of the facts. What made these people tick? she wants to know. And so she's only staying because of the cat. I forgot to mention the cat. This is a town of cats. The Italians here love their cats. I wanted to feed a stray cat at the table, but the waiter said no; and after lunch, all the waiters came with trays crammed with leftover food and stray cats came from everywhere to eat. And at dark when the tourists go in to feed and the beach is empty—you know how empty and

---

2. Grill.   3. Sharply, harshly.   4. Children.   5. Inexpensive restaurant.   6. Shillings. There were 20 shillings to the pound; *one and sixpence,* below, is one and a half shillings.

forlorn a beach is at dusk?—well cats appear from everywhere. The beach seems to move, then you see it's cats. They go stalking along the thin inch of grey water at the edge of the sea, shaking their paws crossly at each step, snatching at the dead little fish, and throwing them with their mouths up on to the dry stand. Then they scamper after them. You've never seen such a snarling and fighting. At dawn when the fishing boats come in to the empty beach, the cats are there in dozens. The fisherman throw them bits of fish. The cats snarl and fight over it. Judith gets up early and goes down to watch. Sometimes Luigi goes too, being tolerant. Because what he really likes is to join the evening promenade with Judith on his arm around and around the square of the upper town. Showing her off. Can you *see* Judith? But she does it. Being tolerant. But she smiles and enjoys the attention she gets, there's no doubt about it.

"She has a cat in her room. It's a kitten really, but it's pregnant. Judith says she can't leave until the kittens are born. The cat is too young to have kittens. Imagine Judith. She sits on her bed in that great stone room, with her bare feet on the stone floor, and watches the cat, and tries to work out why a healthy uninhibited Italian cat always fed on the best from the *rosticceria* should be neurotic. Because it is. When it sees Judith watching it gets nervous and starts licking at the roots of its tail. But Judith goes on watching, and says about Italy that the reason why the English love the Italians is because the Italians make the English feel superior. They have no discipline. And that's a despicable reason for one nation to love another. Then she talks about Luigi and says he has no sense of guilt, but a sense of sin; whereas she has no sense of sin but she has guilt. I haven't asked her if this has been an insuperable barrier, because judging from how she looks, it hasn't. She says she would rather have a sense of sin, because sin can be atoned for, and if she understood sin, perhaps she would be more at home with the Renaissance. Luigi is very healthy, she says, and not neurotic. He is a Catholic of course. He doesn't mind that she's an atheist. His mother has explained to him that the English are all pagans, but good people at heart. I suppose he thinks a few smart sessions with the local priest would set Judith on the right path for good and all. Meanwhile the cat walks nervously around the room, stopping to lick, and when it can't stand Judith watching it another second, it rolls over on the floor, with its paws tucked up, and rolls up its eyes, and Judith scratches its lumpy pregnant stomach and tells it to relax. It makes *me* nervous to see her, it's not like her, I don't know why. Then Luigi shouts up from the barber's shop, then he comes up and stands at the door laughing, and Judith laughs, and the widow says: Children, enjoy yourselves. And off they go, walking down to the town eating ice cream. The cat follows them. It won't let Judith out of its sight, like a dog. When she swims miles out to sea, the cat hides under a beach hut until she comes back. Then she carries it back up the hill, because that nasty little boy chases it. *Well.* I'm coming home tomorrow thank God, to my dear old Billy, I was mad ever to leave him. There is something about Judith and Italy that has upset me, I don't know what. The point is, what on earth can Judith and Luigi *talk* about? Nothing. How can they? And of course it doesn't matter. So I turn out to be a prude as well. See you next week."

It was my turn for a dose of the sun, so I didn't see Betty. On my way back from Rome I stopped off in Judith's resort and walked up through narrow streets to the upper town, where, in the square with the vine-covered *trattoria* at the corner, was a house with Rosticceria written in black paint on a cracked wooden board over a low door. There was a door curtain of red beads, and flies settled on the beads. I opened the beads with my hands and looked into a small dark room with a stone counter. Loops of salami hung from metal hooks. A glass bell covered some plates of cooked meats. There were flies on the salami and on the glass bell. A few tins on the wooden shelves, a couple of pale loaves, some wine casks and an open case of sticky pale green grapes covered with fruit flies seemed to be the only stock. A single wooden table with two chairs stood in a corner, and two workmen sat there, eating lumps of sausage and bread. Through another bead curtain at the back came a short, smoothly fat, slender-limbed woman with greying hair. I asked for Miss Castlewell, and her face changed. She said in an offended, offhand way: "Miss Castlewell left last week." She took a white cloth from under the counter, and flicked at the flies on the glass bell. "I'm a friend of hers," I said, and she said: *Si,*[7] and put her hands palm down on the counter and looked at me, expressionless. The workmen got up, gulped down the last of their wine, nodded and went. She *ciao'*d[8] them; and looked back at me. Then, since I didn't go, she called: "Luigi!" A shout came from the back room, there was a rattle of beads, and in came first a wiry sharp-faced boy, and then Luigi. He was tall, heavy-shouldered, and his black rough hair was like a cap, pulled low over his brows. He looked good-natured, but at the moment uneasy. His sister said something, and he stood beside her, an ally, and confirmed: "Miss Castlewell went away." I was on the point of giving up, when through the bead curtain that screened off a dazzling light eased a thin tabby cat. It was ugly and it walked uncomfortably, with its back quarters bunched up. The child suddenly let out a "Sssss" through his teeth, and the cat froze. Luigi said something sharp to the child, and something encouraging to the cat, which sat down, looked straight in front of it, then began frantically licking at its flanks. "Miss Castlewell was offended with us," said Mrs. Rineiri suddenly, and with dignity. "She left early one morning. We did not expect her to go." I said: "Perhaps she had to go home and finish some work."

Mrs. Rineiri shrugged, then sighed. Then she exchanged a hard look with her brother. Clearly the subject had been discussed, and closed forever.

"I've known Judith a long time," I said, trying to find the right note. "She's a remarkable woman. She's a poet." But there was no response to this at all. Meanwhile the child, with a fixed bared-teeth grin, was staring at the cat, narrowing his eyes. Suddenly he let out another "Sssssss" and added a short high yelp. The cat shot backwards, hit the wall, tried desperately to claw its way up the wall, came to its senses and again sat down and began its urgent, undirected licking at its fur. This time Luigi cuffed the child, who yelped in earnest, and then ran out into the street past the cat. Now that the way was clear the cat shot across the floor, up onto the counter, and bounded past Luigi's shoulder and straight through the bead curtain into the barber's shop, where it landed with a thud.

7. "Yes."   8. Said good-bye to.

70 "Judith was sorry when she left us," said Mrs. Rineiri uncertainly. "She was crying."

"I'm sure she was."

"And so," said Mrs. Rineiri, with finality, laying her hands down again, and looking past me at the bead curtain. That was the end. Luigi nodded brusquely at me, and went into the back. I said goodbye to Mrs. Rineiri and walked back to the lower town. In the square I saw the child, sitting on the running board of a lorry[9] parked outside the *trattoria,* drawing in the dust with his bare toes, and directing in front of him a blank, unhappy stare.

I had to go through Florence, so I went to the address Judith had been at. No, Miss Castlewell had not been back. Her papers and books were still here. Would I take them back with me to England? I made a great parcel and brought them back to England.

I telephoned Judith and she said she had already written for the papers to be sent, but it was kind of me to bring them. There had seemed to be no point, she said, in returning to Florence.

75 "Shall I bring them over?"

"I would be very grateful, of course."

Judith's flat was chilly, and she wore a bunchy sage-green woollen dress. Her hair was still a soft gold helmet, but she looked pale and rather pinched. She stood with her back to a single bar of electric fire—lit because I demanded it— with her legs apart and her arms folded. She contemplated me.

"I went to the Rineiris' house."

"Oh. Did you?"

80 "They seemed to miss you."

She said nothing.

"I saw the cat too."

"Oh. Oh, I suppose you and Betty discussed it?" This was with a small unfriendly smile.

"Well, Judith, you must see we were likely to?"

85 She gave this her consideration and said: "I don't understand why people discuss other people. Oh—I'm not criticising you. But I don't see why you are so interested. I don't understand human behaviour and I'm not particularly interested."

"I think you should write to the Rineiris."

"I wrote and thanked them, of course."

"I don't mean that."

"You and Betty have worked it out?"

90 "Yes, we talked about it. We thought we should talk to you, so you should write to the Rineiris."

"Why?"

"For one thing, they are both very fond of you."

"Fond," she said smiling.

"Judith, I've never in my life felt such an atmosphere of being let down."

9. Truck.

Judith considered this. "When something happens that shows one there is 95
really a complete gulf in understanding, what is there to say?"

"It could scarcely have been a complete gulf in understanding. I suppose you
are going to say we are being interfering?"

Judith showed distaste. "That is a very stupid word. And it's a stupid idea. No
one can interfere with me if I don't let them. No, it's that I don't understand
people. I don't understand why you or Betty should care. Or why the Rineiris
should, for that matter," she added with the small tight smile.

"Judith!"

"If you've behaved stupidly, there's no point in going on. You put an end
to it."

"What happened? Was it the cat?"   100

"Yes, I suppose so. But it's not important." She looked at me, saw my ironical
face, and said: "The cat was too young to have kittens. That is all there was to it."

"Have it your way. But that is obviously not all there is to it."

"What upsets me is that I don't understand at all why I was so upset then."

"What happened? Or don't you want to talk about it?"

"I don't give a damn whether I talk about it or not. You really do say the most 105
extraordinary things, you and Betty. If you want to know, I'll tell you. What does
it matter?"

"I would like to know, of course."

"*Of course!*" she said. "In your place I wouldn't care. Well, I think the essence
of the thing was that I must have had the wrong attitude to that cat. Cats are
supposed to be independent. They are supposed to go off by themselves to have
their kittens. This one didn't. It was climbing up on to my bed all one night and
crying for attention. I don't like cats on my bed. In the morning I saw she was in
pain. I stayed with her all that day. Then Luigi—he's the brother, you know."

"Yes."

"Did Betty mention him? Luigi came up to say it was time I went for a swim.
He said the cat should look after itself. I blame myself very much. That's what
happens when you submerge yourself in somebody else."

Her look at me was now defiant; and her body showed both defensiveness and 110
aggression. "Yes. It's true. I've always been afraid of it. And in the last few weeks
I've behaved badly. It's because I let it happen."

"Well, go on."

"I left the cat and swam. It was late, so it was only for a few minutes. When I
came out of the sea the cat had followed me and had had a kitten on the beach.
That little beast Michele—the son, you know?—well, he always teased the poor
thing, and now he had frightened her off the kitten. It was dead, though. He
held it up by the tail and waved it at me as I came out of the sea. I told him to
bury it. He scooped two inches of sand away and pushed the kitten in—on the
beach, where people are all day. So I buried it properly. He had run off. He was
chasing the poor cat. She was terrified and running up the town. I ran too. I
caught Michele and I was so angry I hit him. I don't believe in hitting children.
I've been feeling beastly about it ever since."

"You were angry."

"It's no excuse. I would never have believed myself capable of hitting a child. I hit him very hard. He went off, crying. The poor cat had got under a big lorry parked in the square. Then she screamed. And then a most remarkable thing happened. She screamed just once, and all at once cats just materialised. One minute there was just one cat, lying under a lorry, and the next, dozens of cats. They sat in a big circle around the lorry, all quite still, and watched my poor cat."

"Rather moving," I said.

"Why?"

"There is no evidence one way or the other," I said in inverted commas, "that the cats were there out of concern for a friend in trouble."

"No," she said energetically. "There isn't. It might have been curiosity. Or anything. How do we know? However, I crawled under the lorry. There were two paws sticking out of the cat's back end. The kitten was the wrong way round. It was stuck. I held the cat down with one hand and I pulled the kitten out with the other." She held out her long white hands. They were still covered with fading scars and scratches. "She bit and yelled, but the kitten was alive. She left the kitten and crawled across the square into the house. Then all the cats got up and walked away. It was the most extraordinary thing I've ever seen. They vanished again. One minute they were all there, and then they had vanished. I went after the cat, with the kitten. Poor little thing, it was covered with dust—being wet, don't you know. The cat was on my bed. There was another kitten coming, but it got stuck too. So when she screamed and screamed I just pulled it out. The kittens began to suck. One kitten was very big. It was a nice fat black kitten. It must have hurt her. But she suddenly bit out—snapped, don't you know, like a reflex action, at the back of the kitten's head. It died, just like that. Extraordinary, isn't it?" she said, blinking hard, her lips quivering. "She was its mother, but she killed it. Then she ran off the bed and went downstairs into the shop under the counter. I called to Luigi. You know, he's Mrs. Rineiri's brother."

"Yes, I know."

"He said she was too young, and she was badly frightened and very hurt. He took the alive kitten to her but she got up and walked away. She didn't want it. Then Luigi told me not to look. But I followed him. He held the kitten by the tail and he banged it against the wall twice. Then he dropped it into the rubbish heap. He moved aside some rubbish with his toe, and put the kitten there and pushed rubbish over it. Then Luigi said the cat should be destroyed. He said she was badly hurt and it would always hurt her to have kittens."

"He hasn't destroyed her. She's still alive. But it looks to me as if he were right."

"Yes, I expect he was."

"What upset you—that he killed the kitten?"

"Oh no, I expect the cat would if he hadn't. But that isn't the point, is it?"

"What is the point?"

"I don't think I really know." She had been speaking breathlessly, and fast. Now she said slowly: "It's not a question of right or wrong, is it? Why should it be? It's a question of what one is. That night Luigi wanted to go promenading with me. For him, that was *that*. Something had to be done, and he'd done it.

₁₁₅

₁₂₀

₁₂₅

But I felt ill. He was very nice to me. He's a very good person," she said, defiantly.

"Yes, he looks it."

"That night I couldn't sleep. I was blaming myself. I should never have left the cat to go swimming. Well, and then I decided to leave the next day. And I did. And that's all. The whole thing was a mistake, from start to finish."

"Going to Italy at all?"

"Oh, to go for a holiday would have been all right."   130

"You've done all that work for nothing? You mean you aren't going to make use of all that research?"

"No. It was a mistake."

"Why don't you leave it a few weeks and see how things are then?"

"Why?"

"You might feel differently about it."   135

"What an extraordinary thing to say. Why should I? Oh, you mean, time passing, healing wounds—that sort of thing? What an extraordinary idea. It's always seemed to me an extraordinary idea. No, right from the beginning I've felt ill at ease with the whole business, not myself at all."

"Rather irrationally, I should have said."

Judith considered this, very seriously. She frowned while she thought it over. Then she said: "But if one cannot rely on what one feels, what can one rely on?"

"On what one thinks, I should have expected you to say."

"Should you? Why? Really, you people are all very strange. I don't understand   140
you." She turned off the electric fire, and her face closed up. She smiled, friendly and distant, and said: "I don't really see any point at all in discussing it."

1963

QUESTIONS

1. At the end of "The Real Thing," the narrator says that though it may have done his art some harm, he is glad of his experience with the Monarchs "for the memory." What is so valuable about the memory? Did it not seem a rather painful experience?

2. How would you describe the relationship between Harry Fenstad and his mother? What signs are there that he loves her? What evidence is there that he is concerned about her aging? How would you describe her attitude toward him? What signs are there of affection, admiration? There are, in the course of the story, two specific differences of opinion between Fenstad and his mother—her views of love, marriage, and his relationship to his first wife (paragraphs 8–11), and the scene with the homeless woman (paragraphs 66–73)—as well as differences that might be described broadly as political (paragraphs 55 and 58). What is the effect on these differences on your view of their characters? Whose side are you on? To what extent do your own political beliefs influence your judgment of the characters? To what extent may it be said that Fenstad's mother's viewing everything politically and his viewing everything in personal or "liberal humanistic" terms (find examples of both) suggest a difference in their questions?

3. Because we are told the story of "Our Friend Judith" by a friend, we never get to know Judith from the inside and are never very close to the action. This seems to have the effect of lessening the suspense and perhaps even our interest in or feelings for Judith. What is gained by this focus and voice? How does it change the meaning of the story? The friend says she blundered and lost her opportunity to find out what Judith and her life were

really like. How did she lose the opportunity? Was it really a blunder? Could she have found out what she wanted to know if she had not "blundered"? What is the friend "really" like?

WRITING SUGGESTIONS

1. Do you agree with Henry James that "real people" do not look like the popular stereotypes of their class, occupation, status, and so on? Write a personal essay describing your own experience of meeting someone who did or did not look like the stereotype: a president, member of congress, mayor; an author, a poet; a woman lawyer; a major league baseball/football/basketball player; an actor.

2. Trace your views of the character of Fenstad's mother from the first paragraph to the final scene, following both changes and consistencies.

3. Write an analysis of the character of the narrator of "Our Friend Judith." Base your interpretation solidly on specific passages, incidents, and attitudes in the story.

4. Write for or against one of these two interpretations of Judith's character. Or show why neither is satisfactory:

   a. Judith seems to be cool, intellectual, and respectable, but she's really fiery and passionate; she's hypocritical, since she lives one kind of life in the open and another in secret.

   b. Judith is her own woman. She does not need a man to lean on or depend on, but has her own full life, her profession, and does her own thing in her own way, the way men are praised for doing but women often condemned for doing.

4

SETTING

All stories, like all individuals, are embedded in a context or **setting**—a time and place. The time can be contemporary ("Fenstad's Mother") or historical ("The Cask of Amontillado") or even mythically vague ("The Zebra Storyteller"). It can be very limited, only a few minutes elapsing ("An Occurrence at Owl Creek Bridge") or some years ("Sonny's Blues"). The place can be rather fixed and interior ("The Yellow Wallpaper") or varied ("Our Friend Judith"). It can be foreign ("The Cask of Amontillado") or American ("The Country Husband") or tied to a region ("Sánchez" and the San Joaquin Valley) or a locale ("Sonny's Blues" and Harlem). Just as character and plot are so closely interrelated as to be ultimately indistinguishable (see Chapter 3), so too are character, plot, and setting. Paradoxically, to see this interpenetration, we must think of them first as separable elements. The individuals in the stories are embedded in the specific context, and the more we know of the setting, and of the relationship of the character to the setting, the more likely we are to understand the character and the story.

Even in a story like "Fenstad's Mother," where the setting seems ordinary and unobtrusive, it interacts with plot and character. The snow, for example, gives Fenstad and us the opportunity to see that his strong-minded, spunky mother is nonetheless old and weak and drags her feet—"his tracks and his mother's. . . . His were separate footprints, but hers formed two long lines" (paragraph 61)—and makes her attempt to offer her coat to the homeless woman a beautiful but rather extreme act of charity, and her braving the cold to watch him and Susan skate a sign of her love for him. At times, details of the setting, such as clothing, furniture, and other items of choice, also can characterize: Fenstad's mother's apartment "smelled of soap and Lysol, the signs of an old woman who wouldn't tolerate nonsense" (paragraph 5). The classroom also offers Fenstad and his mother a setting in which to display their different views of knowledge and different ways of relating to others.

Place or setting is seldom insignificant or unrelated to a larger historical context. "The Jewelry" is set in Paris in the late 1870s. Naturally, you might say, since it was written by a Frenchman in the early 1880s; he's just writing about his own time and place. True enough, but the cynicism, the somewhat bitter irony of the story set among the bourgeoisie and the bureaucracy, owes a good deal of its tone to the recent (1870–1871) defeat of France and the siege and occupation of Paris by the Prussian Bismarck. (France paid Germany a billion dollars in reparations, an unheard-of amount in those days, and did so, to the world's astonishment, in just three years. Might this have something to do with the emphasis on money in the story?) The interaction of tone and times, setting and situation, are fused in this story in a way that would scarcely be possible in another context. Money, adultery, and high living are not unknown in our society, but it would be difficult to rewrite this story by setting it in New York in the 1990s.

John Cheever's "The Country Husband" is set in the early to middle 1950s, close enough to our time so that we know the important things about the period—Elvis, Marilyn, all that. World War II seems distant, but not too distant: a man in midlife crisis served in the army during that time. It is set in suburban New York, not too remote or exotic a setting, since it has many of the qualities of the suburbs of any medium-sized to large city in the 1990s. Yet the story is still somewhat of a period piece. The myth of the calm, comfortable good life—peace and plenty in the suburbs after the decades of Depression and war, the milieu of "Leave It to Beaver" and "Father Knows Best"—still prevailed. Airplane accidents and alcoholic fathers and memories of war were banned. And it seemed, at certain times, boring, almost unbearably so. All the excitement, all the romance of life, was gone, kept away by rows of white picket fences. Yes, we have suburbs like Shady Hill, but not many of the wives stay at home like Julia Weed and we no longer believe they are fenced off from the problems and promises of the Big City. The setting of this 1958 story makes of Francis a "weed," and though there are still crabgrass and dandelions in some of our finest neighborhoods, he and history would be difficult to transplant.

"The Country Husband" is, despite its relative modernity, a historical story. Its time, place, and historical setting interact with its narrative. Some stories are more overtly historical, and their milieu—or the stereotypes associated with it—are more obviously significant than those in Cheever's tale. The protagonist and the plot of "The Cask of Amontillado" are Machiavellian (characterized by subtle or unscrupulous cunning; after the Italian Renaissance politician and writer Niccolò Machiavelli, 1469–1527), and the story is set in Italy during the Renaissance. The Puritan goodman Brown lives in the reign of King William (1689–1702) in Salem, Massachusetts, where in 1692 the famous witch trials were held—what better place and time for a story whose subject is a witches' meeting and whose theme has to do with man's natural depravity? An *English* "spinster" seems (or seemed) much more prudish and virginal than just any old spinster, Italian lovers more sensual than Anglo-Saxon ones, and in "Our Friend Judith" testing those conventions is, virtually, the story.

In some stories setting, even when appropriate and natural, can symbolize whole ways of life or value systems. In "The Lady with the Dog," Yalta with its fruit, seashore, and semitropical climate exemplifies a more passionate, pleasurable, exciting life than the cold and cloudy, bureaucratic, intellectually rarefied air and routine of Moscow. Mexico, the California Sierra Nevada mountains, and Stockton, as presented in Richard Dokey's "Sánchez," offer three very different ways of life and sets of values. Sánchez's son, Jesús, for example, is proud of his job at the cannery in Stockton and of his room, though his father sees only the soiled bed and walls, the bare light bulbs; Jesús is proud of the "entertainment," a shabby pool hall and a movie house, that leaves his father "beyond disappointment." The plot—both the ending and the subtle mystery at the center of the action—cannot be entirely understood in isolation from the setting and the characters' relation to the setting.

Jing-Mei Woo, the narrator of "A Pair of Tickets," explores the relation of place, heritage, and ethnic identity. Living in San Francisco she had, at fifteen, "vigorously denied that I had any Chinese whatsoever below my skin" (paragraph 2), but at thirty-six, as she crosses the border from Hong Kong into China, she finds that she is "becoming Chinese." In Guangzhou, however, she discovers that within the vast change of place and cultures, in the modern world, at least among the privileged, there is a homogeneity: though men and women are working without safety belts or helmets on a scaffold made of bamboo held together with plastic strips, the hotel she is taken to "looks like a grander version of the Hyatt Regency." There are "shopping arcades and restaurants all encased in granite and glass," and in the rooms color television, a wet bar, Coke Classic, M & M's, Johnnie Walker Red, and so on. Her father's family circumvents her plan to have a Chinese feast, and they dine on hamburgers, french fries, apple pie à la mode, delivered by room service. In the modern city of Shanghai, meeting her twin half-sisters for the first time, she finds she is Chinese not because of place or face, but because of "blood." But within this story is another story, her mother's story, with another setting in time and conditions. Fleeing from Kweilin and the advance of the Japanese army in 1944, Jing-Mei's mother was forced by overwhelming circumstances to abandon her twin babies. Jing-Mei can now explain a good deal about her own past, about her mother and their relationship, from the story of her actions and the historical circumstances of the war.

If one of the functions of literature is to help us understand others and the way they see the world, setting—the time and place in which the fictional characters and action are embedded—is an essential element.

RICHARD DOKEY

Sánchez

That summer the son of Juan Sánchez went to work for the Flotill Cannery in Stockton. Juan drove with him to the valley in the old Ford.

While they drove, the boy, whose name was Jesús, told him of the greatness of the cannery, of the great aluminum buildings, the marvelous machines, and the belts of cans that never stopped running. He told him of the building on one side of the road where the cans were made and how the cans ran in a metal tube across the road to the cannery. He described the food machines, the sanitary precautions. He laughed when he spoke of the labeling. His voice was serious about the money.

When they got to Stockton, Jesús directed him to the central district of town, the skid row where the boy was to live while he worked for the Flotill. It was a cheap hotel on Center Street. The room smelled. There was a table with one chair. The floor was stained like the floor of a public urinal and the bed was soiled, as were the walls. There were no drapes on the windows. A pall spread out from the single light bulb overhead that was worked with a length of grimy string.

"I will not stay much in the room," Jesús said, seeing his father's face. "It is only for sleep. I will be working overtime, too. There is also the entertainment."

Jesús led him from the room and they went out into the street. Next to the hotel there was a vacant lot where a building had stood. The hole which was left had that recent, peculiar look of uprootedness. There were the remains of the foundation, the broken flooring, and the cracked bricks of tired red to which the gray blotches of mortar clung like dried phlegm. But the ground had not yet taken on the opaqueness of wear that the air and sun give it. It gleamed dully in the light and held to itself where it had been torn, as earth does behind a plow. Juan studied the hole for a time; then they walked up Center Street to Main, passing other empty lots, and then moved east toward Hunter Street. At the corner of Hunter and Main a wrecking crew was at work. An iron ball was suspended from the end of a cable and a tall machine swung the ball up and back and then whipped it forward against the building. The ball was very thick-looking, and when it struck the wall the building trembled, spurted dust, and seemed to cringe inward. The vertical lines of the building had gone awry. Juan shook each time the iron struck the wall.

"They are tearing down the old buildings," Jesús explained. "Redevelopment," he pronounced. "Even my building is to go someday."

Juan looked at his son. "And what of the men?" he asked. "Where do the men go when there are no buildings?"

Jesús, who was a head taller than his father, looked down at him and then shrugged in that Mexican way, the head descending and cocking while the shoulders rise as though on puppet strings. "¿Quien sabe?"[1]

"And the large building there?" Juan said, looking across the rows of parked cars in Hunter Square. "The one whose roof rubs the sky. Of what significance?"

10   "That is the new courthouse," Jesús said.

"There are no curtains on the windows."

"They do not put curtains on such windows," Jesús explained.

"No," sighed Juan, "that is true."

They walked north on Hunter past the new Bank of America and entered an old building. They stood to one side of the entrance. Jesús smiled proudly and inhaled the stale air.

15   "This is the entertainment," he said.

Juan looked about. A bar was at his immediate left, and a bald man in a soiled apron stood behind it. Beyond the bar there were many thick-wooded tables covered with green material. Men crouched over them and cone-shaped lights hung low from the ceiling casting broad cones of light downward upon the men and tables. Smoke drifted and rolled in the light and pursued the men when they moved quickly. There was the breaking noise of balls striking together, the hard wooden rattle of the cues in the racks upon the wall, the humming slither of the scoring disks along the loose wires overhead, the explosive cursing of the men. The room was warm and dirty. Juan shook his head.

"I have become proficient at the game," Jesús said.

"This is the entertainment," Juan said, still moving his head.

Jesús turned and walked outside. Juan followed. The boy pointed across the parked cars past the courthouse to a marquee on Main Street. "There are also motion pictures," Jesús said.

20   Juan had seen a movie as a young man working in the fields near Fresno. He had understood no English then. He sat with his friends in the leather seats that

---

1. "Who knows?"

had gum under the arms and watched the images move upon the white canvas. The images were dressed in expensive clothes. There was laughing and dancing. One of the men did kissing with two very beautiful women, taking turns with each when the other was absent. This had embarrassed Juan, the embracing and unhesitating submission of the women with so many unfamiliar people to watch. Juan loved his wife, was very tender and gentle with her before she died. He never went to another motion picture, even after he had learned English, and this kept him from the Spanish films as well.

"We will go to the cannery now," Jesús said, taking his father's arm. "I will show you the machines."

Juan permitted himself to be led away, and they moved back past the bank to where the men were destroying the building. A ragged hole, like a wound, had been opened in the wall. Juan stopped and watched. The iron ball came forward tearing at the hole, enlarging it, exposing the empty interior space that had once been a room. The floor of the room teetered at a precarious angle. The wood was splintered and very dry in the noon light.

"I do not think I will go to the cannery," Juan said.

The boy looked at his father like a child who has made a toy out of string and bottle caps only to have it ignored.

"But it is honorable work," Jesús said, suspecting his father. "And it pays well." 25

"Honor," Juan said. "Honor is a serious matter. It is not a question of honor. You are a man now. All that is needed is a room and a job at the Flotill. Your father is tired, that is all."

"You are disappointed," Jesús said, hanging his head.

"No," Juan said. "I am beyond disappointment. You are my son. Now you have a place in the world. You have the Flotill."

Nothing more was said, and they walked to the car. Juan got in behind the wheel. Jesús stood beside the door, his arms at his sides, the fingers spread. Juan looked up at him. The boy's eyes were big.

"You are my son," Juan said, "and I love you. Do not have disappointment. I 30 am not of the Flotill. Seeing the machines would make it worse. You understand, niño?"[2]

"Sí, Papa," Jesús said. He put a hand on his father's shoulder.

"It is a strange world, niñito," Juan said.

"I will earn money. I will buy a red car and visit you. All in Twin Pines will be envious of the son of Sánchez, and they will say that Juan Sánchez has a son of purpose."

"Of course, Jesús mío," Juan said. He bent and placed his lips against the boy's hand. "I will look for the bright car. I will write regardless." He smiled, showing yellowed teeth. "Goodbye, querido," he said. He started the car, raced the engine once too high, and drove off up the street.

When Juan Sánchez returned to Twin Pines, he drove the old Ford to the top 35 of Bear Mountain and pushed it over. He then proceeded systematically to burn all that was of importance to him, all that was of nostalgic value, and all else that

2. Son. *Niñito:* dear son. *Querido:* dear one.

meant nothing in itself, like the extra chest of drawers he had kept after his wife's death, the small table in the bedroom, and the faded mahogany stand in which he kept his pipe and tobacco and which sat next to the stuffed chair in the front room. He broke all the dishes, cups, plates, discarded all the cooking and eating utensils in the same way. The fire rose in the blue wind carrying dust wafers of ash in quick, breathless spirals and then released them in a panoply of diluted smoke, from which they drifted and spun and fell like burnt snow. The forks, knives, and spoons became very black with a flaky crust of oxidized metal. Then Juan burned his clothing, all that was unnecessary, and the smoke dampened and took on a thick smell. Finally he threw his wife's rosary into the flames. It was a cheap one, made of wood, and disappeared immediately. He went into his room then and lay down on the bed. He went to sleep.

When he woke, it was dark and cool. He stepped outside, urinated, and then returned, shutting the door. The darkness was like a mammoth held breath, and he felt very awake listening to the beating of his heart. He would not be able to sleep now, and so he lay awake thinking.

He thought of his village in Mexico, the baked white clay of the small houses spread like little forts against the stillness of the bare mountains, the men with their great wide hats, their wide, white pants, and their naked, brown-skinned feet, splayed against the fine dust of the road. He saw the village cistern and the women all so big and slow, always with child, enervated by the earth and the unbearable sun, the enervation passing into their very wombs like the acceptance, slow, silent blood. The men walked bent as though carrying the air or sky, slept against the buildings in the shade like old dogs, ate dry, hot food that dried them inside and seemed to bake the moisture from the flesh, so that the men and women while still young had faces like eroded fields and fingers like stringy, empty stream beds. It was a hard land. It took the life of his father and mother before he was twelve and the life of his aunt, with whom he then lived, before he was sixteen.

When he was seventeen he went to Mexicali because he had heard much of America and the money to be obtained there. They took him in a truck with other men to work in the fields around Bakersfield, then in the fields near Fresno. On his return to Mexicali he met La Belleza, as he came to call her: loveliness. He married her when he was nineteen and she only fifteen. The following year she had a baby girl. It was stillborn and the birth almost killed her, for the doctor said the passage was oversmall. The doctor cautioned him (warned him, really) La Belleza could not have children and live, and he went outside into the moonlight and wept.

He had heard much of the liveliness of the Sierra Nevada above what was called the Mother Lode, and because he feared the land, believed almost that it possessed the power to kill him—as it had killed his mother and father, his aunt, was, in fact, slow killing so many of his people—he wanted to run away from it to the high white cold of the California mountains, where he believed his heart would grow, his blood run and, perhaps, the passage of La Belleza might open. Two years later he was taken in the trucks to Stockton in the San Joaquin Valley to pick tomatoes, and he saw the Sierra Nevada above the Mother Lode.

It was from a distance, of course, and in the summer, so that there was no   40
snow. But when he returned he told La Belleza about the blueness of the mountains in the warm, still dawn, the extension of them, the aristocracy of their
unmoving height, and that they were only fifty miles away from where he had
stood.

He worked very hard now and saved his money. He took La Belleza back to
his village, where he owned the white clay house of his father. It was cheaper to
live there while he waited, fearing the sun, the dust, and the dry, airless silence,
for the money to accumulate. That fall La Belleza became pregnant again by an
accident of passion and the pregnancy was very difficult. In the fifth month the
doctor—who was an atheist—said that the baby would have to be taken or else
the mother would die. The village priest, a very loud, dramatic man—an educated man who took pleasure in striking a pose—proclaimed the wrath of God in
the face of such sacrilege. It was the child who must live, the priest cried. The
pregnancy must go on. There was the immortal soul of the child to consider. But
Juan decided for the atheist doctor, who did take the child. La Belleza lost much
blood. At one point her heart had stopped beating. When the child was torn
from its mother and Juan saw that it was a boy, he ran out of the clay house of
his father and up the dusty road straight into a hideous red moon. He cursed the
earth, the sky. He cursed his village, himself, the soulless indifference of the
burnt mountains. He cursed God.

Juan was very afraid now, and though it cost more money, he had himself
tied by the atheist doctor so that he could never again put the life of La Belleza
in danger, for the next time, he knew with certainty, would kill her.

The following summer he went again on the trucks to the San Joaquin Valley.
The mountains were still there, high and blue in the quiet dawn, turned to a
milky pastel by the heat swirls and haze of midday. Sometimes at night he
stepped outside the shacks in which the men were housed and faced the darkness. It was tragic to be so close to what you wanted, he would think, and be
unable to possess it. So strong was the feeling in him, particularly during the hot,
windless evenings, that he sometimes went with the other men into Stockton,
where he stood on the street corners of skid row and talked, though he did not
get drunk on cheap wine or go to the whores, as did the other men. Nor did he
fight.

They rode in old tilted trucks covered with canvas and sat on rude benches
staring out over the slats of the tail gate. The white glare of headlights crawled
up and lay upon them, waiting to pass. They stared over the whiteness. When
the lights swept out and by, the glass of the side windows shone. Behind the
windows sometimes there would be the ghost flash of an upturned face, before
the darkness clamped shut. Also, if one of the men had a relative who lived in
the area, there was the opportunity to ride in a car.

He had done so once. He had watched the headlights of the car pale, then   45
whiten the back of one of the trucks. He saw the faces of the men turned outward
and the looks on the faces that seemed to float upon the whiteness of the light.
The men sat forward, arms on knees, and looked over the glare into the darkness.
After that he always rode in the trucks.

When he returned to his village after that season's harvest, he knew they could wait no longer. He purchased a dress of silk for La Belleza and in a second-hand store bought an American suit for himself. He had worked hard, sold his father's house, saved all his money, and on a bright day in early September they crossed the border at Mexicali and caught the Greyhound for Fresno.

Juan got up from his bed to go outside. He stood looking up at the stars. The stars were pinned to the darkness, uttering little flickering cries of light, and as always he was moved by the nearness and profusion of their agony. His mother had told him the stars were a kind of purgatory in which souls burned in cold, silent repentance. He had wondered after her death if the earth too were not a star burning in loneliness, and he could never look at them later without thinking this and believing that the earth must be the brightest of all stars. He walked over to the remains of the fire. A dull heat came from the ashes and a column of limp smoke rose and then bent against the night wind. He studied the ashes for a time and then looked over the tall pine shapes to the southern sky. It was there all right. He could feel the dry char of its heat, that deeper, dryer burning. He imagined it, of course. But it was there nevertheless. He went back into the cabin and lay down, but now his thoughts were only of La Belleza and the beautiful Sierra Nevada.

From Fresno all the way up the long valley to Stockton they had been full with pride and expectation. They had purchased oranges and chocolate bars and they ate them laughing. The other people on the bus looked at them, shook their heads, and slept or read magazines. He and La Belleza gazed out the window at the land.

In Stockton they were helped by a man named Eugenio Mendez. Juan had met him while picking tomatoes in the delta. Eugenio had eight children and a very fat but very kind and tolerant wife named Anilla. He had helped them find a cheap room off Center Street, where they stayed while determining their next course of action. Eugenio had access to a car, and it was he who drove them finally to the mountains.

50   It was a day like no other day in his life: to be sitting in the car with La Belleza, to be in this moving car with his Belleza heading straight toward the high, lovely mountains. The car traveled from the flatness of the valley into the rolling brown swells of the foothills, where hundreds of deciduous and evergreen oaks grew, their puffball shapes like still pictures of exploding holiday rockets, only green, but spreading up and out and then around and down in nearly perfect canopies. At Jackson the road turned and began an immediate, constant climb upward.

It was as though his dream about it had materialized. He had never seen so many trees, great with dignity: pines that had gray bark twisted and stringy like hemp; others whose bark resembled dry, flat ginger cookies fastened with black glue about a drum, and others whose bark pulled easily away; and those called redwoods, standing stiff and tall, amber-hued with straight rolls of bark as thick as his fist, flinging out high above great arms of green. And the earth, rich red, as though the blood of scores of Indians had just flowed there and dried. Dark patches of shadow stunned with light, blue flowers, orange flowers, birds, even deer. They saw them all on that first day.

"¿A dónde vamos?" Eugenio had asked. "Where are we going?"

"*Bellísima,*" Juan replied. "Into much loveliness."

They did not reach Twin Pines that day. But on their return a week later they inquired in Jackson about the opportunity of buying land or a house in the mountains. The man, though surprised, told them of the sawmill town of Twin Pines, where there were houses for sale.

Their continued luck on that day precipitated the feeling in Juan that it was indeed the materialization of a dream. He had been able in all those years to save two thousand dollars, and a man had a small shack for sale at the far edge of town. He looked carefully at Juan, at La Belleza and Eugenio and said "One thousand dollars," believing they could never begin to possess such a sum. When Juan handed him the money, the man was so struck that he made out a bill of sale. Juan Sanchez and his wife had their home in the Sierra.

When Juan saw the cabin close up, he knew the man had stolen their money. It was small, the roof slanted to one side, the door would not close evenly. The cabin was gradually falling downhill. But it was theirs and he could, with work, repair it. Hurriedly they drove back to Jackson, rented a truck, bought some cheap furniture and hauled it back to the cabin. When they had moved in, Juan brought forth a bottle of whiskey and for the first time in his life proceeded to get truly drunk.

Juan was very happy with La Belleza. She accepted his philosophy completely, understood his need, made it her own. In spite of the people of the town, they created a peculiar kind of joy. And anyway Juan had knowledge about the people.

Twin Pines had been founded, he learned, by one Benjamin Carter, who lived with his daughter in a magnificent house on the hill overlooking town. This Benjamin Carter was a very wealthy man. He had come to the mountains thirty years before to save his marriage, for he had been poor once and loved when he was poor, but then he grew very rich because of oil discovered on his father's Ohio farm and he went away to the city and became incapable of love in the pursuit of money and power. When he at last married the woman whom he had loved, a barrier had grown between them, for Ben Carter had changed but the woman had not. Then the woman became ill and Ben Carter promised her he would take her West, all the way West away from the city so that it could be as it had been in the beginning of their love. But the woman was with child. And so Ben Carter rushed to the California mountains, bought a thousand acres of land, and hurried to build his house before the rain and snows came. He hired many men and the house was completed, except for the interior work and the furnishings. All that winter men he had hired worked in the snow to finish the house while Ben Carter waited with his wife in the city. When it was early spring they set out for California, Ben Carter, his wife, and the doctor, who strongly advised against the rough train trip and the still rougher climb by horse and wagon from Jackson to the house. But the woman wanted the child born properly, so they went. The baby came the evening of their arrival at the house, and the woman died all night having it. It was this Ben Carter who lived with that daughter now in the great house on the hill, possessing her to the point, it was said about his madness, that he had murdered a young man who had shown interest in her.

Juan learned all this from a Mexican servant who had worked at the great house from the beginning, and when he told the story to La Belleza she wept because of its sadness. It was a tragedy of love, she explained, and Juan—soaring to the heights of his imagination—believed that the town, all one hundred souls, had somehow been infected with the tragedy, as they were touched by the shadow of the house itself, which crept directly up the highway each night when the sun set. This was why they left dead chickens and fish on the porch of the cabin or dumped garbage into the yard. He believed he understood something profound and so did nothing about these incidents, which, after all, might have been the pranks of boys. He did not want the infection to touch him, nor the deeper infection of their prejudice because he was Mexican. He was not indifferent. He was simply too much in love with La Belleza and the Sierra Nevada. Finally the incidents stopped.

60   Now the life of Juan Sánchez entered its most beautiful time. When the first snows fell he became delirious, running through the pines, shouting, rolling on the ground, catching the flakes in his open mouth, bringing them in his cupped hands to rub in the hair of La Belleza, who stood in the doorway of their cabin laughing at him. He danced, made up a song about snowflakes falling on a desert and then a prayer which he addressed to the Virgin of Snowflakes. That night while the snow fluttered like wings against the bedroom window, he celebrated the coming of the whiteness with La Belleza.

He understood that first year in the mountains that love was an enlargement of himself, that it enabled him to be somehow more than he had ever been before, as though certain pores of his senses had only just been opened. Whereas before he had desired the Sierra Nevada for its beauty and contrast to his harsh fatherland, now he came to acquire a love for it, and he loved it as he loved La Belleza; he loved it as a woman. Also in that year he came to realize that there was a fear or dread about such love. It was more a feeling than anything else, something which reached thought now and then, particularly in those last moments before sleep. It was an absolutely minor thing. The primary knowledge was of the manner in which this love seemed to assimilate everything, rejecting all that would not yield. This love was a kind of blindness.

That summer Juan left La Belleza at times to pick the crops of the San Joaquin Valley. He had become good friends with the servant of the big house and this man had access to the owner's car, which he always drove down the mountain in a reckless but confident manner. After that summer Juan planned also to buy a car, not out of material desire, but simply because he believed this man would one day kill himself, and also because he did not wish to be dependent.

He worked in the walnuts near the town of Linden and again in the tomatoes of the rich delta. He wanted very much to have La Belleza with him, but that would have meant more money and a hotel room in the skid row, and that was impossible because of the pimps and whores, the drunks and criminals and the general despair, which the police always tapped at periodic intervals, as one does a vat of fermenting wine. The skid row was a place his love could not assimilate, but he could not ignore it because so many of his people were lost there. He stayed in the labor camps, which were also bad because of what the men did with themselves, but they were tolerable. He worked hard and as often as he could and gazed at the mountains, which he could always see clearly in the morning light. When tomato season was over he returned to La Belleza.

Though the town would never accept them as equals, it came that summer to tolerate their presence. La Belleza made straw baskets which she sold to the townspeople and which were desired for their beauty and intricacy of design. Juan carved animals, a skill he had acquired from his father, and these were also sold. The activity succeeded so well that Juan took a box of these things to Jackson, where they were readily purchased. The following spring he was able to buy the Ford.

Juan acquired another understanding that second year in the mountains. It was, he believed, that love, his love, was the single greatness of which he was capable, the thing which ennobled him and gave him honor. Love, he became convinced, was his only ability, the one success he had accomplished in a world of insignificance. It was a simple thing, after all, made so painfully simple each time he went to the valley to work with his face toward the ground, every time he saw the men in the fields and listened to their talk and watched them drive off to the skid row at night. After he had acquired this knowledge, the nights he had to spend away from La Belleza were occupied by a new kind of loneliness, as though a part of his body had been separated from the whole. He began also to understand something more of the fear or dread that seemed to trail behind love.

It happened late in the sixth year of their marriage. It was impossible, of course, and he spent many hours at the fire in their cabin telling La Belleza of the impossibility, for the doctor had assured him that all had been well tied. He had conducted himself on the basis of that assumption. But doctors can be wrong. Doctors can make mistakes. La Belleza was with child.

For the first five months the pregnancy was not difficult, and he came almost to believe that indeed the passage of La Belleza would open. He prayed to God. He prayed to the earth and sky. He prayed to the soul of his mother. But after the fifth month the true sickness began and he discarded prayer completely in favor of blasphemy. There was no God and never could be God in the face of such sickness, such unbelievable human sickness. Even when he had her removed to the hospital in Stockton, the doctors could not stop it, but it continued so terribly that he believed that La Belleza carried sickness itself in her womb.

After seven months the doctors decided to take the child. They brought La Belleza into a room with lights and instruments. They worked on her for a long time and she died there under the lights with the doctors cursing and perspiring above the large wound of her pain. They did not tell him of the child, which they had cleaned and placed in an incubator, until the next day. That night he sat in the Ford and tried to see it all, but he could only remember the eyes of La Belleza in the vortex of pain. They were of an almost eerie calmness. They had possessed calmness, as one possesses the truth. Toward morning he slumped sideways on the seat and went to sleep.

So he put her body away in the red earth of the town cemetery beyond the cabin. The pines came together overhead and in the heat of midday a shadow sprinkled with spires of light lay upon the ground so that the earth was cool and clean to smell. He did not even think of taking her back to Mexico, since, from the very beginning she had always been part of that dream he had dreamed. Now she would be always in the Sierra Nevada, with the orange and blue flowers, the quiet, deep whiteness of winter, and all that he ever was or could be was with her.

70   But he did not think these last thoughts then, as he did now. He had simply performed them out of instinct for their necessity, as he had performed the years of labor while waiting for the infant Jesús to grow to manhood. Jesús. Why had he named the boy Jesús? That, perhaps, had been instinct too. He had stayed after La Belleza's death for the boy, to be with him until manhood, to show him the loveliness of the Sierra Nevada, to instruct him toward true manhood. But Jesús. Ah, Jesús. Jesús the American. Jesús of the Flotill. Jesús understood nothing. Jesús, he believed, was forever lost to knowledge. That day with Jesús had been his own liberation.

For a truth had come upon him after the years of waiting, the ultimate truth that he understood only because La Belleza had passed through his life. Love was beauty, La Belleza and the Sierra Nevada, a kind of created or made thing. But there was another kind of love, a very profound, embracing love that he had felt of late blowing across the mountains from the south and that, he knew now, had always been there from the beginning of his life, disguised in the sun and wind. In this love there was blood and earth and, yes, even God, some kind of god, at least the power of a god. This love wanted him for its own. He understood it, that it had permitted him to have La Belleza and that without it there could have been no Belleza.

Juan placed an arm over his eyes and turned to face the wall. The old bed sighed. An image went off in his head and he remembered vividly the lovely body of La Belleza. In that instant the sound that loving had produced with the bed was alive in him like a forgotten melody, and his body seemed to swell and press against the ceiling. It was particularly cruel because it was so sudden, so intense, and came from so deep within him that he knew it must all still be alive somewhere, and that was the cruelest part of all. He wept softly and held the arm across his eyes.

In the dark morning the people of the town were awakened by the blaze of fire that was the house of Juan Sánchez. Believing that he had perished in the flames, several of the townspeople placed a marker next to the grave of his wife with his name on it. But, of course, on that score they were mistaken. Juan Sánchez had simply gone home.

1981

AMY TAN

A Pair of Tickets

The minute our train leaves the Hong Kong border and enters Shenzhen, China, I feel different. I can feel the skin on my forehead tingling, my blood rushing through a new course, my bones aching with a familiar old pain. And I think, My mother was right. I am becoming Chinese.

"Cannot be helped," my mother said when I was fifteen and had vigorously denied that I had any Chinese whatsoever below my skin. I was a sophomore at Galileo High in San Francisco, and all my Caucasian friends agreed: I was about as Chinese as they were. But my mother had studied at a famous nursing school in Shanghai, and she said she knew all about genetics. So there was no doubt in her mind, whether I agreed or not: Once you are born Chinese, you cannot help but feel and think Chinese.

"Someday you will see," said my mother. "It's in your blood, waiting to be let go."

And when she said this, I saw myself transforming like a werewolf, a mutant tag of DNA suddenly triggered, replicating itself insidiously into a *syndrome,* a cluster of telltale Chinese behaviors, all those things my mother did to embarrass me—haggling with store owners, pecking her mouth with a toothpick in public, being color-blind to the fact that lemon yellow and pale pink are not good combinations for winter clothes.

But today I realize I've never really known what it means to be Chinese. I am thirty-six years old. My mother is dead and I am on a train, carrying with me her dreams of coming home. I am going to China.

We are going to Guangzhou, my seventy-two-year-old father, Canning Woo, and I, where we will visit his aunt, whom he has not seen since he was ten years old. And I don't know whether it's the prospect of seeing his aunt or if it's because he's back in China, but now he looks like he's a young boy, so innocent and happy I want to button his sweater and pat his head. We are sitting across from each other, separated by a little table with two cold cups of tea. For the first time I can ever remember, my father has tears in his eyes, and all he is seeing out the train window is a sectioned field of yellow, green, and brown, a narrow canal flanking the tracks, low rising hills, and three people in blue jackets riding an ox-driven cart on this early October morning. And I can't help myself. I also have misty eyes, as if I had seen this a long, long time ago, and had almost forgotten.

In less than three hours, we will be in Guangzhou, which my guidebook tells me is how one properly refers to Canton these days. It seems all the cities I have heard of, except Shanghai, have changed their spellings. I think they are saying China has changed in other ways as well. Chungking is Chongqing. And Kweilin is Guilin. I have looked these names up, because after we see my father's aunt in Guangzhou, we will catch a plane to Shanghai, where I will meet my two half-sisters for the first time.

They are my mother's twin daughters from her first marriage, little babies she was forced to abandon on a road as she was fleeing Kweilin for Chungking in 1944. That was all my mother had told me about these daughters, so they had remained babies in my mind, all these years, sitting on the side of a road, listening to bombs whistling in the distance while sucking their patient red thumbs.

And it was only this year that someone found them and wrote with this joyful news. A letter came from Shanghai, addressed to my mother. When I first heard about this, that they were alive, I imagined my identical sisters transforming from little babies into six-year-old girls. In my mind, they were seated next to each other at a table, taking turns with the fountain pen. One would write a neat row of characters: *Dearest Mama. We are alive.* She would brush back her wispy bangs and hand the other sister the pen, and she would write: *Come get us. Please hurry.*

10   Of course they could not know that my mother had died three months before, suddenly, when a blood vessel in her brain burst. One minute she was talking to my father, complaining about the tenants upstairs, scheming how to evict them under the pretense that relatives from China were moving in. The next minute she was holding her head, her eyes squeezed shut, groping for the sofa, and then crumpling softly to the floor with fluttering hands.

So my father had been the first one to open the letter, a long letter it turned out. And they did call her Mama. They said they always revered her as their true mother. They kept a framed picture of her. They told her about their life, from the time my mother last saw them on the road leaving Kweilin to when they were finally found.

And the letter had broken my father's heart so much—these daughters calling my mother from another life he never knew—that he gave the letter to my mother's old friend Auntie Lindo and asked her to write back and tell my sisters, in the gentlest way possible, that my mother was dead.

But instead Auntie Lindo took the letter to the Joy Luck Club and discussed with Auntie Ying and Auntie An-mei what should be done, because they had known for many years about my mother's search for her twin daughters, her endless hope. Auntie Lindo and the others cried over this double tragedy, of losing my mother three months before, and now again. And so they couldn't help but think of some miracle, some possible way of reviving her from the dead, so my mother could fulfill her dream.

So this is what they wrote to my sisters in Shanghai: "Dearest Daughters, I too have never forgotten you in my memory or in my heart. I never gave up hope that we would see each other again in a joyous reunion. I am only sorry it has been too long. I want to tell you everything about my life since I last saw you. I want to tell you this when our family comes to see you in China. . . ." They signed it with my mother's name.

15   It wasn't until all this had been done that they first told me about my sisters, the letter they received, the one they wrote back.

"They'll think she's coming, then," I murmured. And I had imagined my sisters now being ten or eleven, jumping up and down, holding hands, their pigtails bouncing, excited that their mother—*their* mother—was coming, whereas my mother was dead.

"How can you say she is not coming in a letter?" said Auntie Lindo. "She is their mother. She is your mother. You must be the one to tell them. All these years, they have been dreaming of her." And I thought she was right.

But then I started dreaming, too, of my mother and my sisters and how it would be if I arrived in Shanghai. All these years, while they waited to be found, I had lived with my mother and then had lost her. I imagined seeing my sisters at the airport. They would be standing on their tiptoes, looking anxiously, scanning from one dark head to another as we got off the plane. And I would recognize them instantly, their faces with the identical worried look.

"*Jyejye, Jyejye*. Sister, Sister. We are here," I saw myself saying in my poor version of Chinese.

"Where is Mama?" they would say, and look around, still smiling, two flushed and eager faces. "Is she hiding?" And this would have been like my mother, to stand behind just a bit, to tease a little and make people's patience pull a little on their hearts. I would shake my head and tell my sisters she was not hiding.

"Oh, that must be Mama, no?" one of my sisters would whisper excitedly, pointing to another small woman completely engulfed in a tower of presents. And that, too, would have been like my mother, to bring mountains of gifts, food, and toys for children—all bought on sale—shunning thanks, saying the gifts were nothing, and later turning the labels over to show my sisters, "Calvin Klein, 100% wool."

I imagined myself starting to say, "Sisters, I am sorry, I have come alone . . ." and before I could tell them—they could see it in my face—they were wailing, pulling their hair, their lips twisted in pain, as they ran away from me. And then I saw myself getting back on the plane and coming home.

After I had dreamed this scene many times—watching their despair turn from horror into anger—I begged Auntie Lindo to write another letter. And at first she refused.

"How can I say she is dead? I cannot write this," said Auntie Lindo with a stubborn look.

"But it's cruel to have them believe she's coming on the plane," I said. "When they see it's just me, they'll hate me."

"Hate you? Cannot be." She was scowling. "You are their own sister, their only family."

"You don't understand," I protested.

"What I don't understand?" she said.

And I whispered, "They'll think I'm responsible, that she died because I didn't appreciate her."

And Auntie Lindo looked satisfied and sad at the same time, as if this were true and I had finally realized it. She sat down for an hour, and when she stood up she handed me a two-page letter. She had tears in her eyes. I realized that the very thing I had feared, she had done. So even if she had written the news of my mother's death in English, I wouldn't have had the heart to read it.

"Thank you," I whispered.

The landscape has become gray, filled with low flat cement buildings, old factories, and then tracks and more tracks filled with trains like ours passing by in the opposite direction. I see platforms crowded with people wearing drab Western clothes, with spots of bright colors: little children wearing pink and yellow, red and peach. And there are soldiers in olive green and red, and old ladies in gray tops and pants that stop mid-calf. We are in Guangzhou.

Before the train even comes to a stop, people are bringing down their belongings from above their seats. For a moment there is a dangerous shower of heavy suitcases laden with gifts to relatives, half-broken boxes wrapped in miles of string to keep the contents from spilling out, plastic bags filled with yarn and vegetables and packages of dried mushrooms, and camera cases. And then we are caught in a stream of people rushing, shoving, pushing us along, until we find ourselves in one of a dozen lines waiting to go through customs. I feel as if I were getting on a number 30 Stockton bus in San Francisco. I am in China, I remind myself. And somehow the crowds don't bother me. It feels right. I start pushing too.

I take out the declaration forms and my passport. "Woo," it says at the top, and below that, "June May," who was born in "California, U.S.A.," in 1951. I wonder if the customs people will question whether I'm the same person as in the passport photo. In this picture, my chin-length hair is swept back and artfully styled. I am wearing false eyelashes, eye shadow, and lip liner. My cheeks are hollowed out by bronze blusher. But I had not expected the heat in October. And now my hair hangs limp with the humidity. I wear no makeup; in Hong Kong my mascara had melted into dark circles and everything else had felt like layers of grease. So today my face is plain, unadorned except for a thin mist of shiny sweat on my forehead and nose.

35   Even without makeup, I could never pass for true Chinese. I stand five-foot-six, and my head pokes above the crowd so that I am eye level only with other tourists. My mother once told me my height came from my grandfather, who was a northerner, and may have even had some Mongol blood. "This is what your grandmother once told me," explained my mother. "But now it is too late to ask her. They are all dead, your grandparents, your uncles, and their wives and children, all killed in the war, when a bomb fell on our house. So many generations in one instant."

She had said this so matter-of-factly that I thought she had long since gotten over any grief she had. And then I wondered how she knew they were all dead.

"Maybe they left the house before the bomb fell," I suggested.

"No," said my mother. "Our whole family is gone. It is just you and I."

"But how do you know? Some of them could have escaped."

40   "Cannot be," said my mother, this time almost angrily. And then her frown was washed over by a puzzled blank look, and she began to talk as if she were trying to remember where she had misplaced something. "I went back to that house. I kept looking up to where the house used to be. And it wasn't a house, just the sky. And below, underneath my feet, were four stories of burnt bricks and wood, all the life of our house. Then off to the side I saw things blown into the yard, nothing valuable. There was a bed someone used to sleep in, really just a metal frame twisted up at one corner. And a book, I don't know what kind, because every page had turned black. And I saw a teacup which was unbroken but filled with ashes. And then I found my doll, with her hands and legs broken, her hair burned off. . . . When I was a little girl, I had cried for that doll, seeing it all alone in the store window, and my mother had bought it for me. It was an American doll with yellow hair. It could turn its legs and arms. The eyes moved up and down. And when I married and left my family home, I gave the doll to my youngest niece, because she was like me. She cried if that doll was not with her always. Do you see? If she was in the house with that doll, her parents were

there, and so everybody was there, waiting together, because that's how our family was."

The woman in the customs booth stares at my documents, then glances at me briefly, and with two quick movements stamps everything and sternly nods me along. And soon my father and I find ourselves in a large area filled with thousands of people and suitcases. I feel lost and my father looks helpless.

"Excuse me," I say to a man who looks like an American. "Can you tell me where I can get a taxi?" He mumbles something that sounds Swedish or Dutch.

"Syau Yen! Syau Yen!" I hear a piercing voice shout from behind me. An old woman in a yellow knit beret is holding up a pink plastic bag filled with wrapped trinkets. I guess she is trying to sell us something. But my father is staring down at this tiny sparrow of a woman, squinting into her eyes. And then his eyes widen, his face opens up and he smiles like a pleased little boy.

"*Aiyi! Aiyi!*"—Auntie Auntie!—he says softly.

"Syau Yen!" coos my great-aunt. I think it's funny she has just called my father   45 "Little Wild Goose." It must be his baby milk name, the name used to discourage ghosts from stealing children.

They clasp each other's hands—they do not hug—and hold on like this, taking turns saying, "Look at you! You are so old. Look how old you've become!" They are both crying openly, laughing at the same time, and I bite my lip, trying not to cry. I'm afraid to feel their joy. Because I am thinking how different our arrival in Shanghai will be tomorrow, how awkward it will feel.

Now Aiyi beams and points to a Polaroid picture of my father. My father had wisely sent pictures when he wrote and said we were coming. See how smart she was, she seems to intone as she compares the picture to my father. In the letter, my father had said we would call her from the hotel once we arrived, so this is a surprise, that they've come to meet us. I wonder if my sisters will be at the airport.

It is only then that I remember the camera. I had meant to take a picture of my father and his aunt the moment they met. It's not too late.

"Here, stand together over here," I say, holding up the Polaroid. The camera flashes and I hand them the snapshot. Aiyi and my father still stand close together, each of them holding a corner of the picture, watching as their images begin to form. They are almost reverentially quiet. Aiyi is only five years older than my father, which makes her around seventy-seven. But she looks ancient, shrunken, a mummified relic. Her thin hair is pure white, her teeth are brown with decay. So much for stories of Chinese women looking young forever, I think to myself.

Now Aiyi is crooning to me: "*Jandale.*" So big already. She looks up at me, at   50 my full height, and then peers into her pink plastic bag—her gifts to us, I have figured out—as if she is wondering what she will give to me, now that I am so old and big. And then she grabs my elbow with her sharp pincerlike grasp and turns me around. A man and a woman in their fifties are shaking hands with my father, everybody smiling and saying, "Ah! Ah!" They are Aiyi's oldest son and his wife, and standing next to them are four other people, around my age, and a little girl who's around ten. The introductions go by so fast, all I know is that one of them is Aiyi's grandson, with his wife, and the other is her granddaughter, with her husband. And the little girl is Lili, Aiyi's great-granddaughter.

Aiyi and my father speak the Mandarin dialect from their childhood, but the rest of the family speaks only the Cantonese of their village. I understand only Mandarin but can't speak it that well. So Aiyi and my father gossip unrestrained in Mandarin, exchanging news about people from their old village. And they stop only occasionally to talk to the rest of us, sometimes in Cantonese, sometimes in English.

"Oh, it is as I suspected," says my father, turning to me. "He died last summer." And I already understood this. I just don't know who this person, Li Gong, is. I feel as if I were in the United Nations and the translators had run amok.

"Hello," I say to the little girl. "My name is Jing-mei." But the little girl squirms to look away, causing her parents to laugh with embarrassment. I try to think of Cantonese words I can say to her, stuff I learned from friends in Chinatown, but all I can think of are swear words, terms for bodily functions, and short phrases like "tastes good," "tastes like garbage," and "she's really ugly." And then I have another plan: I hold up the Polaroid camera, beckoning Lili with my finger. She immediately jumps forward, places one hand on her hip in the manner of a fashion model, juts out her chest, and flashes me a toothy smile. As soon as I take the picture she is standing next to me, jumping and giggling every few seconds as she watches herself appear on the greenish film.

By the time we hail taxis for the ride to the hotel, Lili is holding tight onto my hand, pulling me along.

55   In the taxi, Aiyi talks nonstop, so I have no chance to ask her about the different sights we are passing by.

"You wrote and said you would come only for one day," says Aiyi to my father in an agitated tone. "One day! How can you see your family in one day! Toishan is many hours' drive from Guangzhou. And this idea to call us when you arrive. This is nonsense. We have no telephone."

My heart races a little. I wonder if Auntie Lindo told my sisters we would call from the hotel in Shanghai?

Aiyi continues to scold my father. "I was so beside myself, ask my son, almost turned heaven and earth upside down trying to think of a way! So we decided the best was for us to take the bus from Toishan and come into Guangzhou—meet you right from the start."

And now I am holding my breath as the taxi driver dodges between trucks and buses, honking his horn constantly. We seem to be on some sort of long freeway overpass, like a bridge above the city. I can see row after row of apartments, each floor cluttered with laundry hanging out to dry on the balcony. We pass a public bus, with people jammed in so tight their faces are nearly wedged against the window. Then I see the skyline of what must be downtown Guangzhou. From a distance, it looks like a major American city, with highrises and construction going on everywhere. As we slow down in the more congested part of the city, I see scores of little shops, dark inside, lined with counters and shelves. And then there is a building, its front laced with scaffolding made of bamboo poles held together with plastic strips. Men and women are standing on narrow platforms, scraping the sides, working without safety straps or helmets. Oh, would OSHA[1] have a field day here, I think.

Aiyi's shrill voice rises up again: "So it is a shame you can't see our village, our house. My sons have been quite successful, selling our vegetables in the free market. We had enough these last few years to build a big house, three stories, all of new brick, big enough for our whole family and then some. And every year, the money is even better. You Americans aren't the only ones who know how to get rich!"

The taxi stops and I assume we've arrived, but then I peer out at what looks like a grander version of the Hyatt Regency. "This is communist China?" I wonder out loud. And then I shake my head toward my father. "This must be the wrong hotel." I quickly pull out our itinerary, travel tickets, and reservations. I had explicitly instructed my travel agent to choose something inexpensive, in the thirty-to-forty-dollar range. I'm sure of this. And there it says on our itinerary: Garden Hotel, Huanshi Dong Lu. Well, our travel agent had better be prepared to eat the extra, that's all I have to say.

The hotel is magnificent. A bellboy complete with uniform and sharp-creased cap jumps forward and begins to carry our bags into the lobby. Inside, the hotel looks like an orgy of shopping arcades and restaurants all encased in granite and glass. And rather than be impressed, I am worried about the expense, as well as the appearance it must give Aiyi, that we rich Americans cannot be without our luxuries even for one night.

But when I step up to the reservation desk, ready to haggle over this booking mistake, it is confirmed. Our rooms are prepaid, thirty-four dollars each. I feel sheepish, and Aiyi and the others seem delighted by our temporary surroundings. Lili is looking wide-eyed at an arcade filled with video games.

Our whole family crowds into one elevator, and the bellboy waves, saying he will meet us on the eighteenth floor. As soon as the elevator door shuts, everybody becomes very quiet, and when the door finally opens again, everybody talks at once in what sounds like relieved voices. I have the feeling Aiyi and the others have never been on such a long elevator ride.

Our rooms are next to each other and are identical. The rugs, drapes, bedspreads are all in shades of taupe. There's a color television with remote-control panels built into the lamp table between the two twin beds. The bathroom has marble walls and floors. I find a built-in wet bar with a small refrigerator stocked with Heineken beer, Coke Classic, and Seven-Up, mini-bottles of Johnnie Walker Red, Bacardi rum, and Smirnoff vodka, and packets of M & M's, honey-roasted cashews, and Cadbury chocolate bars. And again I say out loud, "This is communist China?"

My father comes into my room. "They decided we should just stay here and visit," he says, shrugging his shoulders. "They say, Less trouble that way. More time to talk."

1. Occupational Safety and Health Administration.

"What about dinner?" I ask. I have been envisioning my first real Chinese feast for many days already, a big banquet with one of those soups steaming out of a carved winter melon, chicken wrapped in clay, Peking duck, the works.

My father walks over and picks up a room service book next to a *Travel & Leisure* magazine. He flips through the pages quickly and then points to the menu. "This is what they want," says my father.

So it's decided. We are going to dine tonight in our rooms, with our family, sharing hamburgers, french fries, and apple pie à la mode.

70   Aiyi and her family are browsing the shops while we clean up. After a hot ride on the train, I'm eager for a shower and cooler clothes.

The hotel has provided little packets of shampoo which, upon opening, I discover is the consistency and color of hoisin sauce.[2] This is more like it, I think. This is China. And I rub some in my damp hair.

Standing in the shower, I realize this is the first time I've been by myself in what seems like days. But instead of feeling relieved, I feel forlorn. I think about what my mother said, about activating my genes and becoming Chinese. And I wonder what she meant.

Right after my mother died, I asked myself a lot of things, things that couldn't be answered, to force myself to grieve more. It seemed as if I wanted to sustain my grief, to assure myself that I had cared deeply enough.

But now I ask the questions mostly because I want to know the answers. What was that pork stuff she used to make that had the texture of sawdust? What were the names of the uncles who died in Shanghai? What had she dreamt all these years about her other daughters? All the times when she got mad at me, was she really thinking about them? Did she wish I were they? Did she regret that I wasn't?

---

75   At one o'clock in the morning, I awake to tapping sounds on the window. I must have dozed off and now I feel my body uncramping itself. I'm sitting on the floor, leaning against one of the twin beds. Lili is lying next to me. The others are asleep, too, sprawled out on the beds and floor. Aiyi is seated at a little table, looking very sleepy. And my father is staring out the window, tapping his fingers on the glass. The last time I listened my father was telling Aiyi about his life since he last saw her. How he had gone to Yenching University, later got a post with a newspaper in Chungking, met my mother there, a young widow. How they later fled together to Shanghai to try to find my mother's family house, but there was nothing there. And then they traveled eventually to Canton and then to Hong Kong, then Haiphong and finally to San Francisco. . . .

"Suyuan didn't tell me she was trying all these years to find her daughters," he is now saying in a quiet voice. "Naturally, I did not discuss her daughters with her. I thought she was ashamed she had left them behind."

"Where did she leave them?" asks Aiyi. "How were they found?"

---

2. Sweet brownish-red sauce made from soybeans, sugar, water, spices, garlic, and chili.

I am wide awake now. Although I have heard parts of this story from my mother's friends.

"It happened when the Japanese took over Kweilin," says my father.

"Japanese in Kweilin?" says Aiyi. "That was never the case. Couldn't be. The Japanese never came to Kweilin." 80

"Yes, that is what the newspapers reported. I know this because I was working for the news bureau at the time. The Kuomintang[3] often told us what we could say and could not say. But we knew the Japanese had come into Kwangsi Province. We had sources who told us how they had captured the Wuchang-Canton railway. How they were coming overland, making very fast progress, marching toward the provincial capital."

Aiyi looks astonished. "If people did not know this, how could Suyuan know the Japanese were coming?"

"An officer of the Kuomintang secretly warned her," explains my father. "Suyuan's husband also was an officer and everybody knew that officers and their families would be the first to be killed. So she gathered a few possessions and, in the middle of the night, she picked up her daughters and fled on foot. The babies were not even one year old."

"How could she give up those babies!" sighs Aiyi. "Twin girls. We have never had such luck in our family." And then she yawns again.

"What were they named?" she asks. I listen carefully. I had been planning on 85 using just the familiar "Sister" to address them both. But now I want to know how to pronounce their names.

"They have their father's surname, Wang," says my father. "And their given names are Chwun Yu and Chwun Hwa."

"What do the names mean?" I ask.

"Ah." My father draws imaginary characters on the window. "One means 'Spring Rain,' the other 'Spring Flower,' " he explains in English, "because they born in the spring, and of course rain come before flower, same order these girls are born. Your mother like a poet, don't you think?"

I nod my head. I see Aiyi nod her head forward, too. But it falls forward and stays there. She is breathing deeply, noisily. She is asleep.

"And what does Ma's name mean?" I whisper. 90

" 'Suyuan,' " he says, writing more invisible characters on the glass. "The way she write it in Chinese, it mean 'Long-Cherished Wish.' Quite a fancy name, not so ordinary like flower name. See this first character, it mean something like 'Forever Never Forgotten.' But there is another way to write 'Suyuan.' Sound exactly the same, but the meaning is opposite." His finger creates the brushstrokes of another character. "The first part look the same: 'Never Forgotten.' But the last part add to first part make the whole word mean 'Long-Held Grudge.' Your mother get angry with me, I tell her her name should be Grudge."

My father is looking at me, moist-eyed. "See, I pretty clever, too, hah?"

I nod, wishing I could find some way to comfort him. "And what about my name," I ask, "what does 'Jing-mei' mean?"

---

3. National People's Party, led by Generalissimo Chiang Kai-shek (1887–1975).

"Your name also special," he says. I wonder if any name in Chinese is not something special. " 'Jing' like excellent *jing*. Not just good, it's something pure, essential, the best quality. *Jing* is good leftover stuff when you take impurities out of something like gold, or rice, or salt. So what is left—just pure essence. And 'Mei,' this is common *mei*, as in *meimei*, 'younger sister.' "

95

I think about this. My mother's long-cherished wish. Me, the younger sister who was supposed to be the essence of the others. I feed myself with the old grief, wondering how disappointed my mother must have been. Tiny Aiyi stirs suddenly, her head rolls and then falls back, her mouth opens as if to answer my question. She grunts in her sleep, tucking her body more closely into the chair.

"So why did she abandon those babies on the road?" I need to know, because now I feel abandoned too.

"Long time I wondered this myself," says my father. "But then I read that letter from her daughters in Shanghai now, and I talk to Auntie Lindo, all the others. And then I knew. No shame in what she done. None."

"What happened?"

"Your mother running away—" begins my father.

100

"No, tell me in Chinese," I interrupt. "Really, I can understand."

He begins to talk, still standing at the window, looking into the night.

After fleeing Kweilin, your mother walked for several days trying to find a main road. Her thought was to catch a ride on a truck or wagon, to catch enough rides until she reached Chungking, where her husband was stationed.

She had sewn money and jewelry into the lining of her dress, enough, she thought, to barter rides all the way. If I am lucky, she thought, I will not have to trade the heavy gold bracelet and jade ring. These were things from her mother, your grandmother.

By the third day, she had traded nothing. The roads were filled with people, everybody running and begging for rides from passing trucks. The trucks rushed by, afraid to stop. So your mother found no rides, only the start of dysentery pains in her stomach.

105

Her shoulders ached from the two babies swinging from scarf slings. Blisters grew on the palms from holding two leather suitcases. And then the blisters burst and began to bleed. After a while, she left the suitcases behind, keeping only the food and a few clothes. And later she also dropped the bags of wheat flour and rice and kept walking like this for many miles, singing songs to her little girls, until she was delirious with pain and fever.

Finally, there was not one more step left in her body. She didn't have the strength to carry those babies any farther. She slumped to the ground. She knew she would die of her sickness, or perhaps from thirst, from starvation, or from the Japanese, who she was sure were marching right behind her.

She took the babies out of the slings and sat them on the side of the road, then lay down next to them. You babies are so good, she said, so quiet. They smiled back, reaching their chubby hands for her, wanting to be picked up again. And then she knew she could not bear to watch her babies die with her.

She saw a family with three young children in a cart going by. "Take my babies, I beg you," she cried to them. But they stared back with empty eyes and never stopped.

She saw another person pass and called out again. This time a man turned around, and he had such a terrible expression—your mother said it looked like death itself—she shivered and looked away.

When the road grew quiet, she tore open the lining of her dress, and stuffed jewelry under the shirt of one baby and money under the other. She reached into her pocket and drew out the photos of her family, the picture of her father and mother, the picture of herself and her husband on their wedding day. And she wrote on the back of each the names of the babies and this same message: "Please care for these babies with the money and valuables provided. When it is safe to come, if you bring them to Shanghai, 9 Weichang Lu, the Li family will be glad to give you a generous reward. Li Suyuan and Wang Fuchi."

And then she touched each baby's cheek and told her not to cry. She would go down the road to find them some food and would be back. And without looking back, she walked down the road, stumbling and crying, thinking only of this one last hope, that her daughters would be found by a kindhearted person who would care for them. She would not allow herself to imagine anything else.

She did not remember how far she walked, which direction she went, when she fainted, or how she was found. When she awoke, she was in the back of a bouncing truck with several other sick people, all moaning. And she began to scream, thinking she was now on a journey to Buddhist hell. But the face of an American missionary lady bent over her and smiled, talking to her in a soothing language she did not understand. And yet she could somehow understand. She had been saved for no good reason, and it was now too late to go back and save her babies.

When she arrived in Chungking, she learned her husband had died two weeks before. She told me later she laughed when the officers told her this news, she was so delirious with madness and disease. To come so far, to lose so much and to find nothing.

I met her in a hospital. She was lying on a cot, hardly able to move, her dysentery had drained her so thin. I had come in for my foot, my missing toe, which was cut off by a piece of falling rubble. She was talking to herself, mumbling.

"Look at these clothes," she said, and I saw she had on a rather unusual dress for wartime. It was silk satin, quite dirty, but there was no doubt it was a beautiful dress.

"Look at this face," she said, and I saw her dusty face and hollow cheeks, her eyes shining black. "Do you see my foolish hope?"

"I thought I had lost everything, except these two things," she murmured. "And I wondered which I would lose next. Clothes or hope? Hope or clothes?"

"But now, see here, look what is happening," she said, laughing, as if all her prayers had been answered. And she was pulling hair out of her head as easily as one lifts new wheat from wet soil.

It was an old peasant woman who found them. "How could I resist?" the peasant woman later told your sisters when they were older. They were still sitting obediently near where your mother had left them, looking like little fairy queens waiting for their sedan to arrive.

120   The woman, Mei Ching, and her husband, Mei Han, lived in a stone cave. There were thousands of hidden caves like that in and around Kweilin so secret that the people remained hidden even after the war ended. The Meis would come out of their cave every few days and forage for food supplies left on the road, and sometimes they would see something that they both agreed was a tragedy to leave behind. So one day they took back to their cave a delicately painted set of rice bowls, another day a little footstool with a velvet cushion and two new wedding blankets. And once, it was your sisters.

They were pious people, Muslims, who believed the twin babies were a sign of double luck, and they were sure of this when, later in the evening, they discovered how valuable the babies were. She and her husband had never seen rings and bracelets like those. And while they admired the pictures, knowing the babies came from a good family, neither of them could read or write. It was not until many months later that Mei Ching found someone who could read the writing on the back. By then, she loved these baby girls like her own.

In 1952 Mei Han, the husband, died. The twins were already eight years old, and Mei Ching now decided it was time to find your sisters' true family.

She showed the girls the picture of their mother and told them they had been born into a great family and she would take them back to see their true mother and grandparents. Mei Ching told them about the reward, but she swore she would refuse it. She loved these girls so much, she only wanted them to have what they were entitled to—a better life, a fine house, educated ways. Maybe the family would let her stay on as the girls' amah. Yes, she was certain they would insist.

Of course, when she found the place at 9 Weichang Lu, in the old French Concession, it was something completely different. It was the site of a factory building, recently constructed, and none of the workers knew what had become of the family whose house had burned down on that spot.

125   Mei Ching could not have known, of course, that your mother and I, her new husband, had already returned to that same place in 1945 in hopes of finding both her family and her daughters.

Your mother and I stayed in China until 1947. We went to many different cities—back to Kweilin, to Changsha, as far south as Kunming. She was always looking out of one corner of her eye for twin babies, then little girls. Later we went to Hong Kong, and when we finally left in 1949 for the United States, I think she was even looking for them on the boat. But when we arrived, she no longer talked about them. I thought, At last, they have died in her heart.

When letters could be openly exchanged between China and the United States, she wrote immediately to old friends in Shanghai and Kweilin. I did not know she did this. Auntie Lindo told me. But of course, by then, all the street names had changed. Some people had died, others had moved away. So it took many years to find a contact. And when she did find an old schoolmate's address and wrote asking her to look for her daughters, her friend wrote back and said this was impossible, like looking for a needle on the bottom of the ocean. How did she know her daughters were in Shanghai and not somewhere else in China? The friend, of course, did not ask, How do you know your daughters are still alive?

So her schoolmate did not look. Finding babies lost during the war was a matter of foolish imagination, and she had no time for that.

But every year, your mother wrote to different people. And this last year, I think she got a big idea in her head, to go to China and find them herself. I remember she told me, "Canning, we should go, before it is too late, before we are too old." And I told her we were already too old, it was already too late.

I just thought she wanted to be a tourist! I didn't know she wanted to go and look for her daughters. So when I said it was too late, that must have put a terrible thought in her head that her daughters might be dead. And I think this possibility grew bigger and bigger in her head, until it killed her.

Maybe it was your mother's dead spirit who guided her Shanghai schoolmate to find her daughters. Because after your mother died, the schoolmate saw your sisters, by chance, while shopping for shoes at the Number One Department Store on Nanjing Dong Road. She said it was like a dream, seeing these two women who looked so much alike, moving down the stairs together. There was something about their facial expressions that reminded the schoolmate of your mother.

She quickly walked over to them and called their names, which of course, they did not recognize at first, because Mei Ching had changed their names. But your mother's friend was so sure, she persisted. "Are you not Wang Chwun Yu and Wang Chwun Hwa?" she asked them. And then these double-image women became very excited, because they remembered the names written on the back of an old photo, a photo of a young man and woman they still honored, as their much-loved first parents, who had died and become spirit ghosts still roaming the earth looking for them.

———————————

At the airport, I am exhausted. I could not sleep last night. Aiyi had followed me into my room at three in the morning, and she instantly fell asleep on one of the twin beds, snoring with the might of a lumberjack. I lay awake thinking about my mother's story, realizing how much I have never known about her, grieving that my sisters and I had both lost her.

And now at the airport, after shaking hands with everybody, waving good-bye, I think about all the different ways we leave people in this world. Cheerily waving good-bye to some at airports, knowing we'll never see each other again. Leaving others on the side of the road, hoping that we will. Finding my mother in my father's story and saying good-bye before I have a chance to know her better.

Aiyi smiles at me as we wait for our gate to be called. She is so old. I put one arm around her and one arm around Lili. They are the same size, it seems. And then it's time. As we wave good-bye one more time and enter the waiting area, I get the sense I am going from one funeral to another. In my hand I'm clutching a pair of tickets to Shanghai. In two hours we'll be there.

The plane takes off. I close my eyes. How can I describe to them in my broken Chinese about our mother's life? Where should I begin?

"Wake up, we're here," says my father. And I awake with my heart pounding in my throat. I look out the window and we're already on the runway. It's gray outside.

And now I'm walking down the steps of the plane, onto the tarmac and toward the building. If only, I think, if only my mother had lived long enough to be the one walking toward them. I am so nervous I cannot even feel my feet. I am just moving somehow.

Somebody shouts, "She's arrived!" And then I see her. Her short hair. Her small body. And that same look on her face. She has the back of her hand pressed hard against her mouth. She is crying as though she had gone through a terrible ordeal and were happy it is over.

140 And I know it's not my mother, yet it is the same look she had when I was five and had disappeared all afternoon, for such a long time, that she was convinced I was dead. And when I miraculously appeared, sleepy-eyed, crawling from underneath my bed, she wept and laughed, biting the back of her hand to make sure it was true.

And now I see her again, two of her, waving, and in one hand there is a photo, the Polaroid I sent them. As soon as I get beyond the gate, we run toward each other, all three of us embracing, all hesitations and expectations forgotten.

"Mama, Mama," we all murmur, as if she is among us.

My sisters look at me, proudly. *"Meimei jandale,"* says one sister proudly to the other. "Little Sister has grown up." I look at their faces again and I see no trace of my mother in them. Yet they still look familiar. And now I also see what part of me is Chinese. It is so obvious. It is my family. It is in our blood. After all these years, it can finally be let go.

My sisters and I stand, arms around each other, laughing and wiping the tears from each other's eyes. The flash of the Polaroid goes off and my father hands me the snapshot. My sisters and I watch quietly together, eager to see what develops.

145 The gray-green surface changes to the bright colors of our three images, sharpening and deepening all at once. And although we don't speak, I know we all see it: Together we look like our mother. Her same eyes, her same mouth, open in surprise to see, at last, her long-cherished wish.

1989

ANTON CHEKHOV

The Lady with the Dog[1]

I

It was said that a new person had appeared on the sea-front: a lady with a little dog. Dmitri Dmitritch Gurov, who had by then been a fortnight at Yalta,[2] and so was fairly at home there, had begun to take an interest in new arrivals. Sitting in Verney's pavilion, he saw, walking on the sea-front, a fair-haired young lady of medium height, wearing a *béret*; a white Pomeranian dog was running behind her.

And afterwards he met her in the public gardens and in the square several times a day. She was walking alone, always wearing the same *béret,* and always with the same white dog; no one knew who she was, and every one called her simply "the lady with the dog."

"If she is here alone without a husband or friends, it wouldn't be amiss to make her acquaintance," Gurov reflected.

He was under forty, but he had a daughter already twelve years old, and two sons at school. He had been married young, when he was a student in his second year, and by now his wife seemed half as old again as he. She was a tall, erect woman with dark eyebrows, staid and dignified, and, as she said of herself, intellectual. She read a great deal, used phonetic spelling, called her husband, not Dmitri, but Dimitri, and he secretly considered her unintelligent, narrow, inelegant, was afraid of her, and did not like to be at home. He had begun being unfaithful to her long ago—had been unfaithful to her often, and, probably on that account, almost always spoke ill of women, and when they were talked about in his presence, used to call them "the lower race."

It seemed to him that he had been so schooled by bitter experience that he might call them what he liked, and yet he could not get on for two days together without "the lower race." In the society of men he was bored and not himself, with them he was cold and uncommunicative; but when he was in the company of women he felt free, and knew what to say to them and how to behave; and he was at ease with them even when he was silent. In his appearance, in his character, in his whole nature, there was something attractive and elusive which allured women and disposed them in his favour; he knew that, and some force seemed to draw him, too, to them.

Experience often repeated, truly bitter experience, had taught him long ago that with decent people, especially Moscow people—always slow to move and irresolute—every intimacy, which at first so agreeably diversifies life and appears a light and charming adventure, inevitably grows into a regular problem of extreme intricacy, and in the long run the situation becomes unbearable. But at every fresh meeting with an interesting woman this experience seemed to slip

---

1. Translated by Constance Garnett.   2. Russian city on the Black Sea; a resort for southern vacations.

out of his memory, and he was eager for life, and everything seemed simple and amusing.

One evening he was dining in the gardens, and the lady in the *béret* came up slowly to take the next table. Her expression, her gait, her dress, and the way she did her hair told him that she was a lady, that she was married, that she was in Yalta for the first time and alone, and that she was dull there. . . . The stories told of the immorality in such places as Yalta are to a great extent untrue; he despised them, and knew that such stories were for the most part made up by persons who would themselves have been glad to sin if they had been able; but when the lady sat down at the next table three paces from him, he remembered these tales of easy conquests, of trips to the mountains, and the tempting thought of a swift, fleeting love affair, a romance with an unknown woman, whose name he did not know, suddenly took possession of him.

He beckoned coaxingly to the Pomeranian, and when the dog came up to him he shook his finger at it. The Pomeranian growled: Gurov shook his finger at it again.

The lady looked at him and at once dropped her eyes.

"He doesn't bite," she said, and blushed.

"May I give him a bone?" he asked; and when she nodded he asked courteously, "Have you been long in Yalta?"

"Five days."

"And I have already dragged out a fortnight here."

There was a brief silence.

"Time goes fast, and yet it is so dull here!" she said, not looking at him.

"That's only the fashion to say it is dull here. A provincial will live in Belyov or Zhidra and not be dull, and when he comes here it's 'Oh, the dulness! Oh, the dust!' One would think he came from Grenada."[3]

She laughed. Then both continued eating in silence, like strangers, but after dinner they walked side by side; and there sprang up between them the light jesting conversation of people who are free and satisfied, to whom it does not matter where they go or what they talk about. They walked and talked of the strange light on the sea: the water was of a soft warm lilac hue, and there was a golden streak from the moon upon it. They talked of how sultry it was after a hot day. Gurov told her that he came from Moscow, that he had taken his degree in Arts, but had a post in a bank; that he had trained as an opera-singer, but had given it up, that he owned two houses in Moscow. . . . And from her he learnt that she had grown up in Petersburg, but had lived in S—— since her marriage two years before, that she was staying another month in Yalta, and that her husband, who needed a holiday too, might perhaps come and fetch her. She was not sure whether her husband had a post in a Crown Department[4] or under the Provincial Council—and was amused by her own ignorance. And Gurov learnt, too, that she was called Anna Sergeyevna.

Afterwards he thought about her in his room at the hotel—thought she would

---

3. Romantic city in southern Spain.   4. Department appointed by the czar or an elective local council (*zemstvo*).

certainly meet him next day; it would be sure to happen. As he got into bed he thought how lately she had been a girl at school, doing lessons like his own daughter; he recalled the diffidence, the angularity, that was still manifest in her laugh and her manner of talking with a stranger. This must have been the first time in her life she had been alone in surroundings in which she was followed, looked at, and spoken to merely from a secret motive which she could hardly fail to guess. He recalled her slender, delicate neck, her lovely grey eyes.

"There's something pathetic about her, anyway," he thought, and fell asleep.

        II

A week had passed since they had made acquaintance. It was a holiday. It was sultry indoors, while in the street the wind whirled the dust round and round, and blew people's hats off. It was a thirsty day, and Gurov often went into the pavilion, and pressed Anna Sergeyevna to have syrup and water or an ice. One did not know what to do with oneself.

In the evening when the wind had dropped a little, they went out on the groyne to see the steamer come in. There were a great many people walking about the harbour; they had gathered to welcome some one, bringing bouquets. And two peculiarities of a well-dressed Yalta crowd were very conspicuous: the elderly ladies were dressed like young ones, and there were great numbers of generals.

Owing to the roughness of the sea, the steamer arrived late, after the sun had set, and it was a long time turning about before it reached the groyne. Anna Sergeyevna looked through her lorgnette at the steamer and the passengers as though looking for acquaintances, and when she turned to Gurov her eyes were shining. She talked a great deal and asked disconnected questions, forgetting next moment what she had asked; then she dropped her lorgnette in the crush.

The festive crowd began to disperse; it was too dark to see people's faces. The wind had completely dropped, but Gurov and Anna Sergeyevna still stood as though waiting to see some one else come from the steamer. Anna Sergeyevna was silent now, and sniffed the flowers without looking at Gurov.

"The weather is better this evening," he said. "Where shall we go now? Shall we drive somewhere?"

She made no answer.

Then he looked at her intently, and all at once put his arm round her and kissed her on the lips, and breathed in the moisture and the fragrance of the flowers; and he immediately looked round him, anxiously wondering whether any one had seen them.

"Let us go to your hotel," he said softly. And both walked quickly.

The room was close and smelt of the scent she had bought at the Japanese shop. Gurov looked at her and thought: "What different people one meets in the world!" From the past he preserved memories of careless, good-natured women, who loved cheerfully and were grateful to him for the happiness he gave them, however brief it might be; and of women like his wife who loved without any genuine feeling, with superfluous phrases, affectedly, hysterically, with an expression that suggested that it was not love nor passion, but something more significant; and of two or three others, very beautiful, cold women, on whose faces he had caught a glimpse of a rapacious expression—an obstinate desire to snatch from life more than it could give, and these were capricious, unreflecting, domineering, unintelligent women not in their first youth, and when Gurov grew cold to them their beauty excited his hatred, and the lace on their linen seemed to him like scales.

But in this case there was still the diffidence, the angularity of inexperienced youth, an awkward feeling; and there was a sense of consternation as though some one had suddenly knocked at the door. The attitude of Anna Sergeyevna— "the lady with the dog"—to what had happened was somehow peculiar, very grave, as though it were her fall—so it seemed, and it was strange and inappropriate. Her face dropped and faded, and on both sides of it her long hair hung down mournfully; she mused in a dejected attitude like "the woman who was a sinner" in an old-fashioned picture.

30 "It's wrong," she said. "You will be the first to despise me now."

There was a water-melon on the table. Gurov cut himself a slice and began eating it without haste. There followed at least half an hour of silence.

Anna Sergeyevna was touching; there was about her the purity of a good, simple woman who had seen little of life. The solitary candle burning on the table threw a faint light on her face, yet it was clear that she was very unhappy.

"How could I despise you?" asked Gurov. "You don't know what you are saying."

"God forgive me," she said, and her eyes filled with tears. "It's awful."

35 "You seem to feel you need to be forgiven."

"Forgiven? No. I am a bad, low woman; I despise myself and don't attempt to justify myself. It's not my husband but myself I have deceived. And not only just now; I have been deceiving myself for a long time. My husband may be a good, honest man, but he is a flunkey! I don't know what he does there, what his work is, but I know he is a flunkey! I was twenty when I was married to him. I have been tormented by curiosity; I wanted something better. 'There must be a different sort of life,' I said to myself. I wanted to live! To live, to live! . . . I was fired by curiosity . . . you don't understand it, but, I swear to God, I could not control myself; something happened to me: I could not be restrained. I told my husband I was ill, and came here. . . . And here I have been walking about as though I were dazed, like a mad creature; . . . and now I have become a vulgar, contemptible woman whom any one may despise."

Gurov felt bored already, listening to her. He was irritated by the naïve tone, by this remorse, so unexpected and inopportune; but for the tears in her eyes, he might have thought she was jesting or playing a part.

"I don't understand," he said softly. "What is it you want?"

She hid her face on his breast and pressed close to him.

40 "Believe me, believe me, I beseech you . . ." she said. "I love a pure, honest life, and sin is loathsome to me. I don't know what I am doing. Simple people say: 'The Evil One has beguiled me.' And I may say of myself now that the Evil One has beguiled me."

"Hush, hush! . . ." he muttered.

He looked at her fixed, scared eyes, kissed her, talked softly and affectionately, and by degrees she was comforted, and her gaiety returned; they both began laughing.

Afterwards when they went out there was not a soul on the sea-front. The town with its cypresses had quite a deathlike air, but the sea still broke noisily on the shore; a single barge was rocking on the waves, and a lantern was blinking sleepily on it.

They found a cab and drove to Oreanda.

"I found out your surname in the hall just now: it was written on the board— Von Diderits," said Gurov. "Is your husband a German?"   45

"No; I believe his grandfather was a German, but he is an Orthodox Russian himself."

At Oreanda they sat on a seat not far from the church, looked down at the sea, and were silent. Yalta was hardly visible through the morning mist; white clouds stood motionless on the mountain-tops. The leaves did not stir on the trees, grasshoppers chirruped, and the monotonous hollow sound of the sea rising up from below, spoke of the peace, of the eternal sleep awaiting us. So it must have sounded when there was no Yalta, no Oreanda here; so it sounds now, and it will sound as indifferently and monotonously when we are all no more. And in this constancy, in this complete indifference to the life and death of each of us, there lies hid, perhaps, a pledge of our eternal salvation, of the unceasing movement of life upon earth, of unceasing progress towards perfection. Sitting beside a young woman who in the dawn seemed so lovely, soothed and spellbound in these magical surroundings—the sea, mountains, clouds, the open sky—Gurov thought how in reality everything is beautiful in this world when one reflects: everything except what we think or do ourselves when we forget our human dignity and the higher aims of our existence.

A man walked up to them—probably a keeper—looked at them and walked away. And this detail seemed mysterious and beautiful, too. They saw a steamer come from Theodosia, with its lights out in the glow of dawn.

"There is dew on the grass," said Anna Sergeyevna, after a silence.

"Yes. It's time to go home."   50

They went back to the town.

Then they met every day at twelve o'clock on the sea-front, lunched and dined together, went for walks, admired the sea. She complained that she slept badly, that her heart throbbed violently; asked the same questions, troubled now by jealousy and now by the fear that he did not respect her sufficiently. And often in the square or gardens, when there was no one near them, he suddenly drew her to him and kissed her passionately. Complete idleness, these kisses in broad daylight while he looked round in dread of some one's seeing them, the heat, the smell of the sea, and the continual passing to and fro before him of idle, well-dressed, well-fed people, made a new man of him; he told Anna Sergeyevna how beautiful she was, how fascinating. He was impatiently passionate, he would not move a step away from her, while she was often pensive and continually urged him to confess that he did not respect her, did not love her in the least, and thought of her as nothing but a common woman. Rather late almost every evening they drove somewhere out of town, to Oreanda or to the waterfall; and the expedition was always a success, the scenery invariably impressed them as grand and beautiful.

They were expecting her husband to come, but a letter came from him, saying that there was something wrong with his eyes, and he entreated his wife to come home as quickly as possible. Anna Sergeyevna made haste to go.

"It's a good thing I am going away," she said to Gurov. "It's the finger of destiny!"

55   She went by coach and he went with her. They were driving the whole day. When she had got into a compartment of the express, and when the second bell had rung, she said:

"Let me look at you once more . . . look at you once again. That's right."

She did not shed tears, but was so sad that she seemed ill, and her face was quivering.

"I shall remember you . . . think of you," she said. "God be with you; be happy. Don't remember evil against me. We are parting forever—it must be so, for we ought never to have met. Well, God be with you."

The train moved off rapidly, its lights soon vanished from sight, and a minute later there was no sound of it, as though everything had conspired together to end as quickly as possible that sweet delirium, that madness. Left alone on the platform, and gazing into the dark distance, Gurov listened to the chirrup of the grasshoppers and the hum of the telegraph wires, feeling as though he had only just waked up. And he thought, musing, that there had been another episode or adventure in his life, and it, too, was at an end, and nothing was left of it but a memory. . . . He was moved, sad, and conscious of a slight remorse. This young woman whom he would never meet again had not been happy with him; he was genuinely warm and affectionate with her, but yet in his manner, his tone, and his caresses there had been a shade of light irony, the coarse condescension of a happy man who was, besides, almost twice her age. All the time she had called him kind, exceptional, lofty; obviously he had seemed to her different from what he really was, so he had unintentionally deceived her. . . .

60   Here at the station was already a scent of autumn; it was a cold evening.

"It's time for me to go north," thought Gurov as he left the platform. "High time!"

III

At home in Moscow everything was in its winter routine; the stoves were heated, and in the morning it was still dark when the children were having breakfast and getting ready for school, and the nurse would light the lamp for a short time. The frosts had begun already. When the first snow has fallen, on the first day of sledge-driving it is pleasant to see the white earth, the white roofs, to draw soft, delicious breath, and the season brings back the days of one's youth. The old limes and birches, white with hoar-frost, have a good-natured expression; they are nearer to one's heart than cypresses and palms, and near them one doesn't want to be thinking of the sea and the mountains.

Gurov was Moscow born; he arrived in Moscow on a fine frosty day, and when he put on his fur coat and warm gloves, and walked along Petrovka, and when on Saturday evening he heard the ringing of the bells, his recent trip and the places he had seen lost all charm for him. Little by little he became absorbed in Moscow life, greedily read three newspapers a day, and declared he did not read the Moscow papers on principle! He already felt a longing to go to restaurants, clubs, dinner-parties, anniversary celebrations, and he felt flattered at entertaining distinguished lawyers and artists, and at playing cards with a professor at the doctors' club. He could already eat a whole plateful of salt fish and cabbage. . . .

In another month, he fancied, the image of Anna Sergeyevna would be shrouded in a mist in his memory, and only from time to time would visit him in his dreams with a touching smile as others did. But more than a month passed, real winter had come, and everything was still clear in his memory as though he had parted with Anna Sergeyevna only the day before. And his memories glowed more and more vividly. When in the evening stillness he heard from his study the voices of his children, preparing their lessons, or when he listened to a song or the organ at the restaurant, or the storm howled in the chimney, suddenly everything would rise up in his memory: what had happened on the groyne, and the early morning with the mist on the mountains, and the steamer coming from Theodosia, and the kisses. He would pace a long time about his room, remembering it all and smiling; then his memories passed into dreams, and in his fancy the past was mingled with what was to come. Anna Sergeyevna did not visit him in dreams, but followed him about everywhere like a shadow and haunted him. When he shut his eyes he saw her as though she were living before him, and she seemed to him lovelier, younger, tenderer than she was; and he imagined himself finer than he had been in Yalta. In the evenings she peeped out at him from the bookcase, from the fireplace, from the corner—he heard her breathing, the caressing rustle of her dress. In the street he watched the women, looking for some one like her.

He was tormented by an intense desire to confide his memories to some one. But in his home it was impossible to talk of his love, and he had no one outside; he could not talk to his tenants nor to any one at the bank. And what had he to talk of? Had he been in love, then? Had there been anything beautiful, poetical, or edifying or simply interesting in his relations with Anna Sergeyevna? And there was nothing for him but to talk vaguely of love, of woman, and no one guessed what it meant; only his wife twitched her black eyebrows, and said: "The part of a lady-killer does not suit you at all, Dimitri."

One evening, coming out of the doctors' club with an official with whom he had been playing cards, he could not resist saying:

"If only you knew what a fascinating woman I made the acquaintance of in Yalta!"

The official got into his sledge and was driving away, but turned suddenly and shouted:

"Dmitri Dmitritch!"

"What?"

"You were right this evening: the sturgeon was a bit too strong!"

These words, so ordinary, for some reason moved Gurov to indignation, and struck him as degrading and unclean. What savage manners, what people! What senseless nights, what uninteresting, uneventful days! The rage for card-playing, the gluttony, the drunkenness, the continual talk always about the same thing. Useless pursuits and conversations always about the same things absorb the better part of one's time, the better part of one's strength, and in the end there is left a life grovelling and curtailed, worthless and trivial, and there is no escaping or getting away from it—just as though one were in a madhouse or a prison.

Gurov did not sleep all night, and was filled with indignation. And he had a headache all next day. And the next night he slept badly; he sat up in bed, thinking, or paced up and down his room. He was sick of his children, sick of the bank; he had no desire to go anywhere or to talk of anything.

In the holidays in December he prepared for a journey, and told his wife he was going to Petersburg to do something in the interests of a young friend—and he set off for S——. What for? He did not very well know himself. He wanted to see Anna Sergeyevna and to talk with her—to arrange a meeting, if possible.

75   He reached S—— in the morning, and took the best room at the hotel, in which the floor was covered with grey army cloth, and on the table was an inkstand, grey with dust and adorned with a figure on horseback, with its hat in its hand and its head broken off. The hotel porter gave him the necessary information; Von Diderits lived in a house of his own in Old Gontcharny Street—it was not far from the hotel: he was rich and lived in good style, and had his own horses; every one in the town knew him. The porter pronounced the name "Dridirits."

Gurov went without haste to Old Gontcharny Street and found the house. Just opposite the house stretched a long grey fence adorned with nails.

"One would run away from a fence like that," thought Gurov, looking from the fence to the windows of the house and back again.

He considered: to-day was a holiday, and the husband would probably be at home. And in any case it would be tactless to go into the house and upset her. If he were to send her a note it might fall into her husband's hands, and then it might ruin everything. The best thing was to trust to chance. And he kept walking up and down the street by the fence, waiting for the chance. He saw a beggar go in at the gate and dogs fly at him; then an hour later he heard a piano, and the sounds were faint and indistinct. Probably it was Anna Sergeyevna playing. The front door suddenly opened, and an old woman came out, followed by the familiar white Pomeranian. Gurov was on the point of calling to the dog, but his heart began beating violently, and in his excitement he could not remember the dog's name.

He walked up and down, and loathed the grey fence more and more, and by now he thought irritably that Anna Sergeyevna had forgotten him, and was perhaps already amusing herself with some one else, and that that was very natural in a young woman who had nothing to look at from morning till night but that confounded fence. He went back to his hotel room and sat for a long while on the sofa, not knowing what to do, then he had dinner and a long nap.

80   "How stupid and worrying it is!" he thought when he woke and looked at the dark windows: it was already evening. "Here I've had a good sleep for some reason. What shall I do in the night?"

He sat on the bed, which was covered by a cheap grey blanket, such as one sees in hospitals, and he taunted himself in his vexation:

"So much for the lady with the dog . . . so much for the adventure. . . . You're in a nice fix. . . ."

That morning at the station a poster in large letters had caught his eye. "The Geisha"[5] was to be performed for the first time. He thought of this and went to the theatre.

"It's quite possible she may go to the first performance," he thought.

The theatre was full. As in all provincial theatres, there was a fog above the chandelier, the gallery was noisy and restless; in the front row the local dandies were standing up before the beginning of the performance, with their hands behind them; in the Governor's box the Governor's daughter, wearing a boa, was sitting in the front seat, while the Governor himself lurked modestly behind the curtain with only his hands visible; the orchestra was a long time tuning up; the stage curtain swayed. All the time the audience were coming in and taking their seats Gurov looked at them eagerly.

Anna Sergeyevna, too, came in. She sat down in the third row, and when Gurov looked at her his heart contracted, and he understood clearly that for him there was in the whole world no creature so near, so precious, and so important to him; she, this little woman, in no way remarkable, lost in a provincial crowd, with a vulgar lorgnette in her hand, filled his whole life now, was his sorrow and his joy, the one happiness that he now desired for himself, and to the sounds of the inferior orchestra, of the wretched provincial violins, he thought how lovely she was. He thought and dreamed.

A young man with small side-whiskers, tall and stooping, came in with Anna Sergeyevna and sat down beside her; he bent his head at every step and seemed to be continually bowing. Most likely this was the husband whom at Yalta, in a rush of bitter feeling, she had called a flunkey. And there really was in his long figure, his side-whiskers, and the small bald patch on his head, something of the flunkey's obsequiousness; his smile was sugary, and in his buttonhole there was some badge of distinction like the number on a waiter.

During the first interval the husband went away to smoke; she remained alone in her stall. Gurov, who was sitting in the stalls, too, went up to her and said in a trembling voice, with a forced smile:

"Good-evening."

She glanced at him and turned pale, then glanced again with horror, unable to believe her eyes, and tightly gripped the fan and the lorgnette in her hands, evidently struggling with herself not to faint. Both were silent. She was sitting, he was standing, frightened by her confusion and not venturing to sit down beside her. The violins and the flute began tuning up. He felt suddenly frightened; it seemed as though all the people in the boxes were looking at them. She got up and went quickly to the door; he followed her, and both walked senselessly along passages, and up and down stairs, and figures in legal, scholastic, and civil service uniforms, all wearing badges, flitted before their eyes. They caught glimpses of ladies, of fur coats hanging on pegs; the draughts blew on them,

85

90

5. Operetta by Sidney Jones (1861–1946) that toured eastern Europe in 1898–1899.

bringing a smell of stale tobacco. And Gurov, whose heart was beating violently, thought:

"Oh, heavens! Why are these people here and this orchestra! . . ."

And at that instant he recalled how when he had seen Anna Sergeyevna off at the station he had thought that everything was over and they would never meet again. But how far they were still from the end!

On the narrow, gloomy staircase over which was written "To the Amphitheatre," she stopped.

"How you have frightened me!" she said, breathing hard, still pale and overwhelmed. "Oh, how you have frightened me! I am half dead. Why have you come? Why?"

"But do understand, Anna, do understand . . ." he said hastily in a low voice. "I entreat you to understand. . . ."

She looked at him with dread, with entreaty, with love; she looked at him intently, to keep his features more distinctly in her memory.

"I am so unhappy," she went on, not heeding him. "I have thought of nothing but you all the time; I live only in the thought of you. And I wanted to forget, to forget you; but why, oh, why, have you come?"

On the landing above them two schoolboys were smoking and looking down, but that was nothing to Gurov; he drew Anna Sergeyevna to him, and began kissing her face, her cheeks, and her hands.

"What are you doing, what are you doing!" she cried in horror, pushing him away. "We are mad. Go away to-day; go away at once. . . . I beseech you by all that is sacred, I implore you. . . . There are people coming this way!"

Some one was coming up the stairs.

"You must go away," Anna Sergeyevna went on in a whisper. "Do you hear, Dmitri Dmitritch? I will come and see you in Moscow. I have never been happy; I am miserable now, and I never, never shall be happy, never! Don't make me suffer still more! I swear I'll come to Moscow. But now let us part. My precious, good, dear one, we must part!"

She pressed his hand and began rapidly going downstairs, looking round at him, and from her eyes he could see that she really was unhappy. Gurov stood for a little while, listened, then, when all sound had died away, he found his coat and left the theatre.

IV

And Anna Sergeyevna began coming to see him in Moscow. Once in two or three months she left S——, telling her husband that she was going to consult a doctor about an internal complaint—and her husband believed her, and did not believe her. In Moscow she stayed at the Slaviansky Bazaar hotel, and at once sent a man in a red cap to Gurov. Gurov went to see her, and no one in Moscow knew of it.

Once he was going to see her in this way on a winter morning (the messenger had come the evening before when he was out). With him walked his daughter, whom he wanted to take to school: it was on the way. Snow was falling in big wet flakes.

"It's three degrees above freezing-point, and yet it is snowing," said Gurov to his daughter. "The thaw is only on the surface of the earth; there is quite a different temperature at a greater height in the atmosphere."

"And why are there no thunderstorms in the winter, father?"

He explained that, too. He talked, thinking all the while that he was going to see *her*, and no living soul knew of it, and probably never would know. He had two lives: one, open, seen and known by all who cared to know, full of relative truth and of relative falsehood, exactly like the lives of his friends and acquaintances; and another life running its course in secret. And through some strange, perhaps accidental, conjunction of circumstances, everything that was essential, of interest and of value to him, everything in which he was sincere and did not deceive himself, everything that made the kernel of his life, was hidden from other people; and all that was false in him, the sheath in which he hid himself to conceal the truth—such, for instance, as his work in the bank, his discussions at the club, his "lower race," his presence with his wife at anniversary festivities—all that was open. And he judged of others by himself, not believing in what he saw, and always believing that every man had his real, most interesting life under the cover of secrecy and under the cover of night. All personal life rested on secrecy, and possibly it was partly on that account that civilised man was so nervously anxious that personal privacy should be respected.

After leaving his daughter at school, Gurov went on to the Slaviansky Bazaar. He took off his fur coat below, went upstairs, and softly knocked at the door. Anna Sergeyevna, wearing his favourite grey dress, exhausted by the journey and the suspense, had been expecting him since the evening before. She was pale; she looked at him, and did not smile, and he had hardly come in when she fell on his breast. Their kiss was slow and prolonged, as though they had not met for two years.

"Well, how are you getting on there?" he asked. "What news?"

"Wait; I'll tell you directly. . . . I can't talk."   110

She could not speak; she was crying. She turned away from him, and pressed her handkerchief to her eyes.

"Let her have her cry out. I'll sit down and wait," he thought, and he sat down in an arm-chair.

Then he rang and asked for tea to be brought him, and while he drank his tea she remained standing at the window with her back to him. She was crying from emotion, from the miserable consciousness that their life was so hard for them; they could only meet in secret, hiding themselves from people, like thieves! Was not their life shattered?

"Come, do stop!" he said.

It was evident to him that this love of theirs would not soon be over, that he   115 could not see the end of it. Anna Sergeyevna grew more and more attached to him. She adored him, and it was unthinkable to say to her that it was bound to have an end some day; besides, she would not have believed it!

He went up to her and took her by the shoulders to say something affectionate and cheering, and at that moment he saw himself in the looking-glass.

His hair was already beginning to turn grey. And it seemed strange to him that he had grown so much older, so much plainer during the last few years. The shoulders on which his hands rested were warm and quivering. He felt compassion for this life, still so warm and lovely, but probably already not far from beginning to fade and wither like his own. Why did she love him so much? He always seemed to women different from what he was, and they loved in him not himself, but the man created by their imagination, whom they had been eagerly seeking all their lives; and afterwards, when they noticed their mistake, they loved him all the same. And not one of them had been happy with him. Time passed, he had made their acquaintance, got on with them, parted, but he had never once loved; it was anything you like, but not love.

And only now when his head was grey he had fallen properly, really in love—for the first time in his life.

Anna Sergeyevna and he loved each other like people very close and akin, like husband and wife, like tender friends; it seemed to them that fate itself had meant them for one another, and they could not understand why he had a wife and she a husband; and it was as though they were a pair of birds of passage, caught and forced to live in different cages. They forgave each other for what they were ashamed of in their past, they forgave everything in the present, and felt that this love of theirs had changed them both.

120   In moments of depression in the past he had comforted himself with any arguments that came into his mind, but now he no longer cared for arguments; he felt profound compassion, he wanted to be sincere and tender. . . .

"Don't cry, my darling," he said. "You've had your cry; that's enough. . . . Let us talk now, let us think of some plan."

Then they spent a long while taking counsel together, talked of how to avoid the necessity for secrecy, for deception, for living in different towns and not seeing each other for long at a time. How could they be free from this intolerable bondage?

"How? How?" he asked, clutching his head. "How?"

And it seemed as though in a little while the solution would be found, and then a new and splendid life would begin; and it was clear to both of them that they had still a long, long road before them, and that the most complicated and difficult part of it was only just beginning.

1899

QUESTIONS

1. In "Sánchez," why did Juan Sánchez want to leave his native village in Mexico? Why did he choose the Sierra Nevada above Stockton as his new home? How does the central district of Stockton appear to Juan? to Jesús? to you?

2. The mother of Jing-mei Woo, in "A Pair of Tickets," told her that being Chinese is a matter of genetics and Jing-mei finds that that is true. What is the role of place and time (history), then, in this story?

3. Yalta, where "The Lady with the Dog" opens, is a resort on the Black Sea; Moscow, where Gurov lives, is described at the beginning of section III. To what extent do the settings relate to the events and emotions of the story? How do other details—such as the watermelon in section II (Yalta) and the slightly "off" sturgeon in section III (Moscow)—relate to the settings and the attitudes and feelings associated with the places? Which are conventionally assumed to be more real, the feelings we have on holiday or those in our everyday lives? How is this convention related to our expectations about the outcome of the story? to the meaning of the story?

WRITING SUGGESTIONS

1. Using specific textual passages to support your position, write an essay on "Sánchez" about Jésus' parentage, the implication of his name and the relation to setting and character; or write about whether Juan going "home" means (a) he went back to Mexico, or (b) he committed suicide.
2. Compare the use of episodes from World War II in "The Country Husband" and "A Pair of Tickets."
3. Write a personal narrative about a visit to a place important in your family history that you had never visited before and how you felt about your relation to that place; or about an episode that made you recognize or affirm your ethnic identity or heritage.
4. Write a fifth section of "The Lady with the Dog."

5

SYMBOLS

One of the chief devices for bridging the gap between the writer's vision and the reader's is the **symbol,** commonly defined as something that stands for something else: a flower, for example, may be seen as a symbol of a particular state. Symbols are generally **figurative;** that is, they compare or put together two *unlike* things. A senator, on the other hand, represents a state *literally:* the state is a governmental unit, and the senator is a member of the government. But the flower has nothing to do with government and so represents the state only figuratively.

But why speak of anything in terms of something else? Why should snakes commonly be symbolic of evil? Sure, some snakes are poisonous, but for some people so are bees, and a lot of snakes are not only harmless but actually helpful ecologically. (In Kipling's *The Jungle Book* the python Ka, while frightening, is on the side of law and order.) Through repeated use over the centuries, the snake has become a traditional symbol of evil—not just danger, sneakiness, and repulsiveness, but theological, absolute evil. Had Peyton Farquhar, in "An Occurrence at Owl Creek Bridge," been confronted by a snake when he was thrown ashore, we would not necessarily have said, "Aha—snake, symbol of Evil," though that potential meaning might have hovered around the incident and sent us looking backward and forward in the story for supporting evidence that this snake was being used symbolically. However, when we discover that the stranger in "Young Goodman Brown" has a walking stick upon which is carved the image of a snake, we are much more likely to find it such a symbol because of other, related potential symbols or meanings in the context: the term *goodman,* used throughout the story, suggests the distinct possibility that Brown (how common a name) stands for more than a "mere" individual young man. Brown's bride is named Faith—a common name among the early Puritans, but together with *goodman,* suggesting symbolic possibilities. Then, just before the stranger with the walking stick appears, Brown says, "What if the devil himself should be at my very elbow!"

A single item, even something as traditionally fraught with meaning as a snake or a rose, becomes a symbol only when its potentially symbolic meaning is confirmed by something else in the story, just as a point needs a second point to define a line. Multiple symbols, potential symbols, direct and indirect hints such as Brown's mention of the devil: these are among the ways in which details may be identified as symbols (for interpreting symbols is relatively easy once you know what is and what probably is not a symbol).

One form of what may be called an indirect hint is repetition. That an "old maid" like Judith should have a cat seems so ordinary it borders on the trite. But when she chooses to have her male cat put to death rather than neutered, it is likely to make some of us sit up and take notice. This choice may suggest something about the unconventional in her character, but we probably don't think of the cat as itself representing anything. What happens, though, when there appears another cat, a female this time, whose sex life calls forth strange behavior on Judith's part? And when the killing of a kitten interrupts Judith's affair with Luigi? It is difficult to say when or if the literal cats shade off into symbols, for they remain so solidly cats in the story. All we can say for sure is that cats become more important in reading and understanding Lessing's story than, say, the cask of Amontillado does in Poe's story. The cask remains a thing pure and simple. Repetition, then, calls attention to details and may alert us to potential symbolic overtones, but it does not necessarily turn a thing into a symbol; as long as we get the suggestions of significance, however, agreeing on exactly what—or when— something may be called a symbol is not important.

Direct hints may take the form of explicit statements. (Authors are not so anxious to hide their meanings as some readers are prone to believe.) We also may be alerted to the fact that something is standing for something else when it does not by itself seem to make literal sense. It does not take us long to realize that "Young Goodman Brown" is not entirely as realistic a story as "Sonny's Blues" or "The Lady with the Dog." When things do not seem explicable in terms of everyday reality, we often look beyond them for some meaning.

We must remember, however, that symbols do not exist solely for the transmission of a meaning we can paraphrase; they do not disappear from the story, our memory, or our response once their "meaning" has been sucked out of them. Faith's pink ribbons and Judith's cats are objects in their stories, whatever meanings or suggestions of meanings they give rise to.

Few symbols can be exhausted or neatly translated into an abstract phrase or equivalent: the "something else" that the "something" stands for is ultimately elusive. After you have read Ann Beattie's "Janus," try to paraphrase just what the bowl stands for. Or explain with certainty what Faith's pink ribbon symbolizes in "Young Goodman Brown." It is not that the bowl and the ribbon mean nothing, but that they mean so many things that no single equivalence will do; even an abstract statement seems to reduce rather than fully explain the significance to the reader.

When a figure is expressed as an explicit comparison, often signaled by *like* or *as,* it is called a **simile:** "eyes as blue as the sky"; "the baby brother I'd never known looked out from the depths of his private life, like an animal waiting to be coaxed into the light" ("Sonny's Blues"). An implicit comparison or identification of one thing with another unlike itself, without a verbal signal but just seeming to say "A *is* B," is called a **metaphor:** "What I hate about being my age is how *nice* everyone tries to be. . . . everybody is pelting me with sugar cubes" ("Fenstad's Mother"). Sometimes all figures are loosely referred to as metaphors.

You can't give a great symbol a "meaning," anymore than you can give a cat a "meaning." Symbols are organic units of consciousness with a life of their own, and you can never explain them away. . . . An allegorical image has a meaning . . . ; symbols . . . don't "mean something." They stand for units of human feeling, human experience. A complex of emotional experience is a symbol.

—D. H. LAWRENCE

An **allegory** is like a metaphor in that one thing (usually nonrational, abstract, religious) is implicitly spoken of in terms of something that is concrete and usually sensuous (perceptible by the senses), but the comparison in allegory is extended to include a whole work or a large portion of a work. *The Pilgrim's Progress* is probably the most famous prose allegory in English; its central character is named Christian; he was born in the City of Destruction and sets out for the Celestial City, passes through the Slough of Despond and Vanity Fair, meets men named Pliable and Obstinate, and so on.

When an entire story, like "Young Goodman Brown," is symbolic, it is sometimes called a **myth.** *Myth* originally meant a story of communal origin that provided an explanation or religious interpretation of man, nature, the universe, and the relation between them. When used by one culture to describe the stories of another culture, the word usually implies that the stories are false: we speak of classical myths, but Christians do not speak of Christian myth. We also apply the term *myth* now to stories by individuals, sophisticated authors, but often there is still the implication that the mythic story relates to a communal or group experience, whereas a symbolic story may be more personal or private. It is hard to draw the line firmly: "Young Goodman Brown" appears to have clearly national, American, and thus mythic, implications while "Janus" seems primarily personal and thus symbolic. A plot or character element that recurs in cultural or cross-cultural myths, such as images of the devil as in "Young Goodman Brown," is now widely called an **archetype.**

A symbol can be as brief and local as a metaphor or as extended as an allegory. Like an allegory, it usually speaks in concrete terms of the non- or superrational, the abstract, that which is not immediately perceived by the senses. Though some allegories can be complex, with paraphrasable equivalences, allegory usually implies one-to-one relationships (as do the names from *The Pilgrim's Progress*), and literary symbols usually have highly complex or even inexpressible equivalences, as in "Janus." "Janus" is complexly symbolic in that there are areas of meaning or implication that cannot be rendered in other terms or conveniently separated from the particulars of the story. The ultimate unparaphrasable nature of most symbolic images or stories is not vagueness but richness, not disorder but complexity.

NATHANIEL HAWTHORNE

Young Goodman Brown

Young goodman Brown came forth, at sunset, into the street of Salem village,[1] but put his head back, after crossing the threshold, to exchange a parting kiss with his young wife. And Faith, as the wife was aptly named, thrust her own pretty head into the street, letting the wind play with the pink ribbons of her cap, while she called to goodman Brown.

"Dearest heart," whispered she, softly and rather sadly, when her lips were close to his ear, "pr'y thee, put off your journey until sunrise, and sleep in your own bed to-night. A lone woman is troubled with such dreams and such thoughts, that she's afeard of herself, sometimes. Pray, tarry with me this night, dear husband, of all nights in the year!"

"My love and my Faith," replied young goodman Brown, "of all nights in the

---

1. Salem, Massachusetts, Hawthorne's birthplace (1804), was the scene of the famous witch trials of 1692; *goodman:* husband, master of household.

year, this one night must I tarry away from thee. My journey, as thou callest it, forth and back again, must needs be done 'twixt now and sunrise. What, my sweet, pretty wife, dost thou doubt me already, and we but three months married!"

"Then, God bless you!" said Faith, with the pink ribbons, "and may you find all well, when you come back."

"Amen!" cried goodman Brown. "Say thy prayers, dear Faith, and go to bed at   5 dusk, and no harm will come to thee."

So they parted; and the young man pursued his way, until, being about to turn the corner by the meeting-house, he looked back, and saw the head of Faith still peeping after him, with a melancholy air, in spite of her pink ribbons.

"Poor little Faith!" thought he, for his heart smote him. "What a wretch am I, to leave her on such an errand! She talks of dreams, too. Methought, as she spoke, there was trouble in her face, as if a dream had warned her what work is to be done to-night. But, no, no! 't would kill her to think it. Well; she's a blessed angel on earth; and after this one night, I'll cling to her skirts and follow her to Heaven."

With this excellent resolve for the future, goodman Brown felt himself justified in making more haste on his present evil purpose. He had taken a dreary road, darkened by all the gloomiest trees of the forest, which barely stood aside to let the narrow path creep through, and closed immediately behind. It was all as lonely as could be; and there is this peculiarity in such a solitude, that the traveler knows not who may be concealed by the innumerable trunks and the thick boughs overhead; so that, with lonely footsteps, he may yet be passing through an unseen multitude.

"There may be a devilish Indian behind every tree," said goodman Brown, to himself; and he glanced fearfully behind him, as he added, "What if the devil himself should be at my very elbow!"

His head being turned back, he passed a crook of the road, and looking for-   10 ward again, beheld the figure of a man, in grave and decent attire, seated at the foot of an old tree. He arose, at goodman Brown's approach, and walked onward, side by side with him.

"You are late, goodman Brown," said he. "The clock of the Old South was striking as I came through Boston; and that is full fifteen minutes agone."

"Faith kept me back awhile," replied the young man, with a tremor in his voice, caused by the sudden appearance of his companion, though not wholly unexpected.

It was now deep dusk in the forest, and deepest in that part of it where these two were journeying. As nearly as could be discerned, the second traveler was about fifty years old, apparently in the same rank of life as goodman Brown, and bearing a considerable resemblance to him, though perhaps more in expression than features. Still, they might have been taken for father and son. And yet, though the elder person was as simply clad as the younger, and as simple in manner too, he had an indescribable air of one who knew the world, and would not have felt abashed at the governor's dinner-table, or in king William's[2] court,

2. William III (1650–1702), ruler of England from 1689 to 1702, until 1694 jointly with his wife, Mary II.

were it possible that his affairs should call him thither. But the only thing about him, that could be fixed upon as remarkable, was his staff, which bore the likeness of a great black snake, so curiously wrought, that it might almost be seen to twist and wriggle itself, like a living serpent. This, of course, must have been an ocular deception, assisted by the uncertain light.

"Come, goodman Brown!" cried his fellow-traveler, "this is a dull pace for the beginning of a journey. Take my staff, if you are so soon weary."

"Friend," said the other, exchanging his slow pace for a full stop, "having kept covenant by meeting thee here, it is my purpose now to return whence I came. I have scruples, touching the matter thou wot'st of."

"Sayest thou so?" replied he of the serpent, smiling apart. "Let us walk on, nevertheless, reasoning as we go, and if I convince thee not, thou shalt turn back. We are but a little way in the forest, yet."

"Too far, too far!" exclaimed the goodman, unconsciously resuming his walk. "My father never went into the woods on such an errand, nor his father before him. We have been a race of honest men and good Christians, since the days of the martyrs. And shall I be the first of the name of Brown, that ever took this path, and kept"—

"Such company, thou wouldst say," observed the elder person, interpreting his pause. "Good, goodman Brown! I have been as well acquainted with your family as with ever a one among the Puritans; and that's no trifle to say. I helped your grandfather, the constable, when he lashed the Quaker woman so smartly through the streets of Salem. And it was I that brought your father a pitch-pine knot, kindled at my own hearth, to set fire to an Indian village, in king Philip's[3] war. They were my good friends, both; and many a pleasant walk have we had along this path, and returned merrily after midnight. I would fain be friends with you, for their sake."

"If it be as thou sayest," replied goodman Brown, "I marvel they never spoke of these matters. Or, verily, I marvel not, seeing that the least rumor of the sort would have driven them from New-England. We are a people of prayer, and good works, to boot, and abide no such wickedness."

"Wickedness or not," said the traveler with the twisted staff, "I have a very general acquaintance here in New-England. The deacons of many a church have drunk the communion wine with me; the selectmen, of divers towns, make me their chairman; and a majority of the Great and General Court are firm supporters of my interest. The governor and I, too—but these are state-secrets."

"Can this be so!" cried goodman Brown, with a stare of amazement at his undisturbed companion. "Howbeit, I have nothing to do with the governor and council; they have their own ways, and are no rule for a simple husbandman, like me. But, were I to go on with thee, how should I meet the eye of that good old man, our minister, at Salem village? Oh, his voice would make me tremble, both Sabbath-day and lecture-day!"[4]

Thus far, the elder traveler had listened with due gravity, but now burst into

---

3. Metacom or Metacomet, chief of the Wampanoag Indians, known as King Philip, led a war against the New England colonists in 1675–1676 that devastated many frontier communities.   4. The day— in the New England colonies usually a Thursday—for an informal sermon.

a fit of irrepressible mirth, shaking himself so violently, that his snake-like staff actually seemed to wriggle in sympathy.

"Ha! ha! ha!" shouted he, again and again; then composing himself, "Well, go on, goodman Brown, go on; but, pr'y thee, don't kill me with laughing!"

"Well, then, to end the matter at once," said goodman Brown, considerably nettled, "there is my wife, Faith. It would break her dear little heart; and I'd rather break my own!"

"Nay, if that be the case," answered the other, "e'en[5] go thy ways, goodman Brown. I would not, for twenty old women like the one hobbling before us, that Faith should come to any harm."

As he spoke, he pointed his staff at a female figure on the path, in whom goodman Brown recognized a very pious and exemplary dame, who had taught him his catechism, in youth, and was still his moral and spiritual adviser, jointly with the minister and deacon Gookin.

"A marvel, truly, that goody[6] Cloyse should be so far in the wilderness, at night-fall!" said he. "But, with your leave, friend, I shall take a cut through the woods, until we have left this Christian woman behind. Being a stranger to you, she might ask whom I was consorting with, and whither I was going."

"Be it so," said his fellow-traveler. "Betake you to the woods, and let me keep the path."

Accordingly, the young man turned aside, but took care to watch his companion, who advanced softly along the road, until he had come within a staff's length of the old dame. She, meanwhile, was making the best of her way, with singular speed for so aged a woman, and mumbling some indistinct words, a prayer, doubtless, as she went. The traveler put forth his staff, and touched her withered neck with what seemed the serpent's tail.

"The devil!" screamed the pious old lady.

"Then goody Cloyse knows her old friend?" observed the traveler, confronting her, and leaning on his writhing stick.

"Ah, forsooth, and is it your worship, indeed?" cried the good dame. "Yea, truly is it, and in the very image of my old gossip, goodman Brown, the grandfather of the silly fellow that now is. But, would your worship believe it? my broomstick hath strangely disappeared, stolen, as I suspect, by that unhanged witch, goody Cory, and that, too, when I was all anointed with the juice of smallage and cinque-foil and wolf's-bane"[7]—

"Mingled with fine wheat and the fat of a new-born babe," said the shape of old goodman Brown.

"Ah, your worship knows the receipt," cried the old lady, cackling aloud. "So, as I was saying, being all ready for the meeting, and no horse to ride on, I made up my mind to foot it; for they tell me, there is a nice young man to be taken into communion to-night. But now your good worship will lend me your arm, and we shall be there in a twinkling."

"That can hardly be," answered her friend. "I may not spare you my arm, goody Cloyse, but here is my staff, if you will."

So saying, he threw it down at her feet, where, perhaps, it assumed life, being

___

5. Just.   6. Short for "goodwife" or housewife.   7. Plants traditionally associated with witchcraft.

one of the rods which its owner had formerly lent to the Egyptian Magi.[8] Of this fact, however, goodman Brown could not take cognizance. He had cast up his eyes in astonishment, and looking down again, beheld neither goody Cloyse nor the serpentine staff, but his fellow-traveler alone, who waited for him as calmly as if nothing had happened.

"That old woman taught me my catechism!" said the young man; and there was a world of meaning in this simple comment.

They continued to walk onward, while the elder traveler exhorted his companion to make good speed and persevere in the path, discoursing so aptly, that his arguments seemed rather to spring up in the bosom of his auditor, than to be suggested by himself. As they went, he plucked a branch of maple, to serve for a walking-stick, and began to strip it of the twigs and little boughs, which were wet with evening dew. The moment his fingers touched them, they became strangely withered and dried up, as with a week's sunshine. Thus the pair proceeded, at a good free pace, until suddenly, in a gloomy hollow of the road, goodman Brown sat himself down on the stump of a tree, and refused to go any farther.

"Friend," said he, stubbornly, "my mind is made up. Not another step will I budge on this errand. What if a wretched old woman do choose to go to the devil, when I thought she was going to Heaven! Is that any reason why I should quit my dear Faith, and go after her?"

40   "You will think better of this, by-and-by," said his acquaintance, composedly. "Sit here and rest yourself awhile; and when you feel like moving again, there is my staff to help you along."

Without more words, he threw his companion the maple stick, and was as speedily out of sight, as if he had vanished into the deepening gloom. The young man sat a few moments, by the roadside, applauding himself greatly, and thinking with how clear a conscience he should meet the minister, in his morning-walk, nor shrink from the eye of good old deacon Gookin. And what calm sleep would be his, that very night, which was to have been spent so wickedly, but purely and sweetly now, in the arms of Faith! Amidst these pleasant and praise-worthy meditations, goodman Brown heard the tramp of horses along the road, and deemed it advisable to conceal himself within the verge of the forest, conscious of the guilty purpose that had brought him thither, though now so happily turned from it.

On came the hoof-tramps and the voices of the riders, two grave old voices, conversing soberly as they drew near. These mingled sounds appeared to pass along the road, within a few yards of the young man's hiding-place; but owing, doubtless, to the depth of the gloom, at that particular spot, neither the travelers nor their steeds were visible. Though their figures brushed the small boughs by the way-side, it could not be seen that they intercepted, even for a moment, the faint gleam from the strip of bright sky, athwart which they must have passed. Goodman Brown alternately crouched and stood on tip-toe, pulling aside the

8. Exodus 7:8–12. The Lord instructs Moses to have his brother Aaron, high priest of the Hebrews, throw down his rod before the pharaoh, whereupon it will be turned into a serpent. The pharaoh has his magicians (magi) do likewise, "but Aaron's rod swallowed up their rods."

branches, and thrusting forth his head as far as he durst, without discerning so much as a shadow. It vexed him the more, because he could have sworn, were such a thing possible, that he recognized the voices of the minister and deacon Gookin, jogging along quietly, as they were wont to do, when bound to some ordination or ecclesiastical council. While yet within hearing, one of the riders stopped to pluck a switch.

"Of the two, reverend Sir," said the voice like the deacon's, "I had rather miss an ordination-dinner than to-night's meeting. They tell me that some of our community are to be here from Falmouth[9] and beyond, and others from Connecticut and Rhode-Island; besides several of the Indian powows, who, after their fashion, know almost as much deviltry as the best of us. Moreover, there is a goodly young woman to be taken into communion."

"Mighty well, deacon Gookin!" replied the solemn old tones of the minister. "Spur up, or we shall be late. Nothing can be done, you know, until I get on the ground."

The hoofs clattered again, and the voices, talking so strangely in the empty air, passed on through the forest, where no church had ever been gathered, nor solitary Christian prayed. Whither, then, could these holy men be journeying, so deep into the heathen wilderness? Young goodman Brown caught hold of a tree, for support, being ready to sink down on the ground, faint and overburthened with the heavy sickness of his heart. He looked up to the sky, doubting whether there really was a Heaven above him. Yet, there was the blue arch, and the stars brightening in it.

"With Heaven above, and Faith below, I will yet stand firm against the devil!" cried goodman Brown.

While he still gazed upward, into the deep arch of the firmament, and had lifted his hands to pray, a cloud, though no wind was stirring, hurried across the zenith, and hid the brightening stars. The blue sky was still visible, except directly overhead, where this black mass of cloud was sweeping swiftly northward. Aloft in the air, as if from the depths of the cloud, came a confused and doubtful sound of voices. Once, the listener fancied that he could distinguish the accents of town's-people of his own, men and women, both pious and ungodly, many of whom he had met at the communion-table, and had seen others rioting at the tavern. The next moment, so indistinct were the sounds, he doubted whether he had heard aught but the murmur of the old forest, whispering without a wind. Then came a stronger swell of those familiar tones, heard daily in the sunshine, at Salem village, but never, until now, from a cloud of night. There was one voice, of a young woman, uttering lamentations, yet with an uncertain sorrow, and entreating for some favor, which, perhaps, it would grieve her to obtain. And all the unseen multitude, both saints and sinners, seemed to encourage her onward.

"Faith!" shouted goodman Brown, in a voice of agony and desperation; and the echoes of the forest mocked him, crying—"Faith! Faith!" as if bewildered wretches were seeking her, all through the wilderness.

9. A port in extreme southern Massachusetts; Salem is in northern Massachusetts.

The cry of grief, rage, and terror, was yet piercing the night, when the unhappy husband held his breath for a response. There was a scream, drowned immediately in a louder murmur of voices, fading into far-off laughter, as the dark cloud swept away, leaving the clear and silent sky above goodman Brown. But something fluttered lightly down through the air, and caught on the branch of a tree. The young man seized it, and beheld a pink ribbon.

50   "My Faith is gone!" cried he, after one stupefied moment. "There is no good on earth; and sin is but a name. Come, devil! for to thee is this world given."

And maddened with despair, so that he laughed loud and long, did goodman Brown grasp his staff and set forth again, at such a rate, that he seemed to fly along the forest-path, rather than to walk or run. The road grew wilder and drearier, and more faintly traced, and vanished at length, leaving him in the heart of the dark wilderness, still rushing onward, with the instinct that guides mortal man to evil. The whole forest was peopled with frightful sounds; the creaking of the trees, the howling of wild beasts, and the yell of Indians; while, sometimes, the wind tolled like a distant church-bell, and sometimes gave a broad roar around the traveler, as if all Nature were laughing him to scorn. But he was himself the chief horror of the scene, and shrank not from its other horrors.

"Ha! ha! ha!" roared goodman Brown, when the wind laughed at him. "Let us hear which will laugh loudest! Think not to frighten me with your deviltry! Come witch, come wizard, come Indian powow, come devil himself! and here come goodman Brown. You may as well fear him as he fear you!"

In truth, all through the haunted forest, there could be nothing more frightful than the figure of goodman Brown. On he flew, among the black pines, brandishing his staff with frenzied gestures, now giving vent to an inspiration of horrid blasphemy, and now shouting forth such laughter, as set all the echoes of the forest laughing like demons around him. The fiend in his own shape is less hideous, than when he rages in the breast of man. Thus sped the demoniac on his course, until, quivering among the trees, he saw a red light before him, as when the felled trunks and branches of a clearing have been set on fire, and throw up their lurid blaze against the sky, at the hour of midnight. He paused, in a lull of the tempest that had driven him onward, and heard the swell of what seemed a hymn, rolling solemnly from a distance, with the weight of many voices. He knew the tune; it was a familiar one in the choir of the village meeting-house. The verse died heavily away, and was lengthened by a chorus, not of human voices, but of all the sounds of the benighted wilderness, pealing in awful harmony together. Goodman Brown cried out; and his cry was lost to his own ear, by its unison with the cry of the desert.

In the interval of silence, he stole forward, until the light glared full upon his eyes. At one extremity of an open space, hemmed in by the dark wall of the forest, arose a rock, bearing some rude, natural resemblance either to an altar or a pulpit, and surrounded by four blazing pines, their tops a flame, their stems untouched, like candles at an evening meeting. The mass of foliage, that had overgrown the summit of the rock, was all on fire, blazing high into the night, and fitfully illuminating the whole field. Each pendent twig and leafy festoon was in a blaze. As the red light arose and fell, a numerous congregation alternately shone forth, then disappeared in shadow, and again grew, as it were, out of the darkness, peopling the heart of the solitary woods at once.

"A grave and dark-clad company!" quoth goodman Brown. 55

In truth, they were such. Among them, quivering to-and-fro, between gloom and splendor, appeared faces that would be seen, next day, at the council-board of the province, and others which, Sabbath after Sabbath, looked devoutly heavenward, and benignantly over the crowded pews, from the holiest pulpits in the land. Some affirm, that the lady of the governor was there. At least, there were high dames well known to her, and wives of honored husbands, and widows, a great multitude, and ancient maidens, all of excellent repute, and fair young girls, who trembled, lest their mothers should espy them. Either the sudden gleams of light, flashing over the obscure field, bedazzled goodman Brown, or he recognized a score of the church-members of Salem village, famous for their especial sanctity. Good old deacon Gookin had arrived, and waited at the skirts of that venerable saint, his revered pastor. But, irreverently consorting with these grave, reputable, and pious people, these elders of the church, these chaste dames and dewy virgins, there were men of dissolute lives and women of spotted fame, wretches given over to all mean and filthy vice, and suspected even of horrid crimes. It was strange to see, that the good shrank not from the wicked, nor were the sinners abashed by the saints. Scattered, also, among their pale-faced enemies, were the Indian priests, or powows, who had often scared their native forest with more hideous incantations than any known to English witchcraft.

"But, where is Faith?" thought goodman Brown; and, as hope came into his heart, he trembled.

Another verse of the hymn arose, a slow and solemn strain, such as the pious love, but joined to words which expressed all that our nature can conceive of sin, and darkly hinted at far more. Unfathomable to mere mortals is the lore of fiends. Verse after verse was sung, and still the chorus of the desert swelled between, like the deepest tone of a mighty organ. And, with the final peal of that dreadful anthem, there came a sound, as if the roaring wind, the rushing streams, the howling beasts, and every other voice of the unconverted wilderness, were mingling and according with the voice of guilty man, in homage to the prince of all. The four blazing pines threw up a loftier flame, and obscurely discovered shapes and visages of horror on the smoke-wreaths, above the impious assembly. At the same moment, the fire on the rock shot redly forth, and formed a glowing arch above its base, where now appeared a figure. With reverence be it spoken, the apparition bore no slight similitude, both in garb and manner, to some grave divine of the New-England churches.

"Bring forth the converts!" cried a voice, that echoed through the field and rolled into the forest.

At the word, goodman Brown stept forth from the shadow of the trees, and 60
approached the congregation, with whom he felt a loathful brotherhood, by the sympathy of all that was wicked in his heart. He could have well nigh sworn, that the shape of his own dead father beckoned him to advance, looking downward from a smoke-wreath, while a woman, with dim features of despair, threw out her hand to warn him back. Was it his mother? But he had no power to

retreat one step, nor to resist, even in thought, when the minister and good old deacon Gookin, seized his arms, and led him to the blazing rock. Thither came also the slender form of a veiled female, led between goody Cloyse, that pious teacher of the catechism, and Martha Carrier, who had received the devil's promise to be queen of hell. A rampant hag was she! And there stood the proselytes, beneath the canopy of fire.

"Welcome, my children," said the dark figure, "to the communion of your race! Ye have found, thus young, your nature and your destiny. My children, look behind you!"

They turned; and flashing forth, as it were, in a sheet of flame, the fiend-worshippers were seen; the smile of welcome gleamed darkly on every visage.

"There," resumed the sable form, "are all whom ye have reverenced from youth. Ye deemed them holier than yourselves, and shrank from your own sin, contrasting it with their lives of righteousness, and prayerful aspirations heavenward. Yet, here are they all, in my worshipping assembly! This night it shall be granted you to know their secret deeds; how hoary-bearded elders of the church have whispered wanton words to the young maids of their households; how many a woman, eager for widow's weeds, has given her husband a drink at bedtime, and let him sleep his last sleep in her bosom; how beardless youths have made haste to inherit their fathers' wealth; and how fair damsels—blush not, sweet ones!—have dug little graves in the garden, and bidden me, the sole guest, to an infant's funeral. By the sympathy of your human hearts for sin, ye shall scent out all the places—whether in church, bed-chamber, street, field, or forest—where crime has been committed, and shall exult to behold the whole earth one stain of guilt, one mighty blood-spot. Far more than this! It shall be yours to penetrate, in every bosom, the deep mystery of sin, the fountain of all wicked arts, and which, inexhaustibly supplies more evil impulses than human power—than my power, at its utmost!—can make manifest in deeds. And now, my children, look upon each other."

They did so; and, by the blaze of the hell-kindled torches, the wretched man beheld his Faith, and the wife her husband, trembling before that unhallowed altar.

"Lo! there ye stand, my children," said the figure, in a deep and solemn tone, almost sad, with its despairing awfulness, as if his once angelic nature could yet mourn for our miserable race. "Depending upon one another's hearts, ye had still hoped, that virtue were not all a dream. Now are ye undeceived! Evil is the nature of mankind. Evil must be your only happiness. Welcome, again, my children, to the communion of your race!"

"Welcome!" repeated the fiend-worshippers, in one cry of despair and triumph.

And there they stood, the only pair, as it seemed, who were yet hesitating on the verge of wickedness, in this dark world. A basin was hollowed, naturally, in the rock. Did it contain water, reddened by the lurid light? or was it blood? or, perchance, a liquid flame? Herein did the Shape of Evil dip his hand, and prepare to lay the mark of baptism upon their foreheads, that they might be partakers of the mystery of sin, more conscious of the secret guilt of others, both in deed and thought, than they could now be of their own. The husband cast one look at his pale wife, and Faith at him. What polluted wretches would the next glance shew them to each other, shuddering alike at what they disclosed and what they saw!

"Faith! Faith!" cried the husband. "Look up to Heaven, and resist the Wicked One!"

Whether Faith obeyed, he knew not. Hardly had he spoken, when he found himself amid calm night and solitude, listening to a roar of the wind, which died heavily away through the forest. He staggered against the rock and felt it chill and damp, while a hanging twig, that had been all on fire, besprinkled his cheek with the coldest dew.

The next morning, young goodman Brown came slowly into the street of Salem village, staring around him like a bewildered man. The good old minister was taking a walk along the graveyard, to get an appetite for breakfast and meditate his sermon, and bestowed a blessing, as he passed, on goodman Brown. He shrank from the venerable saint, as if to avoid an anathema. Old deacon Gookin was at domestic worship, and the holy words of his prayer were heard through the open window. "What God doth the wizard pray to?" quoth goodman Brown. Goody Cloyse, that excellent old Christian, stood in the early sunshine, at her own lattice, catechising a little girl, who had brought her a pint of morning's milk. Goodman Brown snatched away the child, as from the grasp of the fiend himself. Turning the corner by the meeting-house, he spied the head of Faith, with the pink ribbons, gazing anxiously forth, and bursting into such joy at sight of him, that she skipt along the street, and almost kissed her husband before the whole village. But, goodman Brown looked sternly and sadly into her face, and passed on without a greeting.

Had goodman Brown fallen asleep in the forest, and only dreamed a wild dream of a witch-meeting?

Be it so, if you will. But, alas! it was a dream of evil omen for young goodman Brown. A stern, a sad, a darkly meditative, a distrustful, if not a desperate man, did he become, from the night of that fearful dream. On the Sabbath-day, when the congregation were singing a holy psalm, he could not listen, because an anthem of sin rushed loudly upon his ear, and drowned all the blessed strain. When the minister spoke from the pulpit, with power and fervid eloquence, and, with his hand on the open bible, of the sacred truths of our religion, and of saint-like lives and triumphant deaths, and of future bliss or misery unutterable, then did goodman Brown turn pale, dreading, lest the roof should thunder down upon the gray blasphemer and his hearers. Often, awakening suddenly at midnight, he shrank from the bosom of Faith, and at morning or eventide, when the family knelt down at prayer, he scowled, and muttered to himself, and gazed sternly at his wife, and turned away. And when he had lived long, and was borne to his grave, a hoary corpse, followed by Faith, an aged woman, and children and grandchildren, a goodly procession, besides neighbors, not a few, they carved no hopeful verse upon his tomb-stone; for his dying hour was gloom.

1835

ANN BEATTIE

Janus

The bowl was perfect. Perhaps it was not what you'd select if you faced a shelf of bowls, and not the sort of thing that would inevitably attract a lot of attention at a crafts fair, yet it had real presence. It was as predictably admired as a mutt who has no reason to suspect he might be funny. Just such a dog, in fact, was often brought out (and in) along with the bowl.

Andrea was a real estate agent, and when she thought that some prospective buyers might be dog lovers, she would drop off her dog at the same time she placed the bowl in the house that was up for sale. She would put a dish of water in the kitchen for Mondo, take his squeaking plastic frog out of her purse and drop it on the floor. He would pounce delightedly, just as he did every day at home, batting around his favorite toy. The bowl usually sat on a coffee table, though recently she had displayed it on top of a pine blanket chest and on a lacquered table. It was once placed on a cherry table beneath a Bonnard[1] still life, where it held its own.

Everyone who has purchased a house or who has wanted to sell a house must be familiar with some of the tricks used to convince a buyer that the house is quite special: a fire in the fireplace in early evening; jonquils in a pitcher on the kitchen counter, where no one ordinarily has space to put flowers; perhaps the slight aroma of spring, made by a single drop of scent vaporizing from a lamp bulb.

The wonderful thing about the bowl, Andrea thought, was that it was both subtle and noticeable—a paradox of a bowl. Its glaze was the color of cream and seemed to glow no matter what light it was placed in. There were a few bits of color in it—tiny geometric flashes—and some of these were tinged with flecks of silver. They were as mysterious as cells seen under a microscope; it was difficult not to study them, because they shimmered, flashing for a split second, and then resumed their shape. Something about the colors and their random placement suggested motion. People who liked country furniture always commented on the bowl, but then it turned out that people who felt comfortable with Biedermeier[2] loved it just as much. But the bowl was not at all ostentatious, or even so noticeable that anyone would suspect that it had been put in place deliberately. They might notice the height of the ceiling on first entering a room, and only when their eye moved down from that, or away from the refraction of sunlight on a pale wall, would they see the bowl. Then they would go immediately to it and comment. Yet they always faltered when they tried to say something. Perhaps it was because they were in the house for a serious reason, not to notice some object.

5   Once, Andrea got a call from a woman who had not put in an offer on a house she had shown her. That bowl, she said—would it be possible to find out where

1. Pierre Bonnard (1867–1947), French painter.   2. Unpretentious Central European furniture made primarily between 1820 and 1840.

the owners had bought that beautiful bowl? Andrea pretended that she did not know what the woman was referring to. A bowl, somewhere in the house? Oh, on a table under the window. Yes, she would ask, of course. She let a couple of days pass, then called back to say that the bowl had been a present and the people did not know where it had been purchased.

When the bowl was not being taken from house to house, it sat on Andrea's coffee table at home. She didn't keep it carefully wrapped (although she transported it that way, in a box); she kept it on the table, because she liked to see it. It was large enough so that it didn't seem fragile, or particularly vulnerable if anyone sideswiped the table or Mondo blundered into it at play. She had asked her husband to please not drop his house key in it. It was meant to be empty.

When her husband first noticed the bowl, he had peered into it and smiled briefly. He always urged her to buy things she liked. In recent years, both of them had acquired many things to make up for all the lean years when they were graduate students, but now that they had been comfortable for quite a while, the pleasure of new possessions dwindled. Her husband had pronounced the bowl "pretty," and he had turned away without picking it up to examine it. He had no more interest in the bowl than she had in his new Leica.[3]

She was sure that the bowl brought her luck. Bids were often put in on houses where she had displayed the bowl. Sometimes the owners, who were always asked to be away or to step outside when the house was being shown, didn't even know that the bowl had been in their house. Once—she could not imagine how—she left it behind, and then she was so afraid that something might have happened to it that she rushed back to the house and sighed with relief when the woman owner opened the door. The bowl, Andrea explained—she had purchased a bowl and set it on the chest for safekeeping while she toured the house with the prospective buyers, and she . . . She felt like rushing past the frowning woman and seizing her bowl. The owner stepped aside, and it was only when Andrea ran to the chest that the lady glanced at her a little strangely. In the few seconds before Andrea picked up the bowl, she realized that the owner must have just seen that it had been perfectly placed, that the sunlight struck the bluer part of it. Her pitcher had been moved to the far side of the chest, and the bowl predominated. All the way home, Andrea wondered how she could have left the bowl behind. It was like leaving a friend at an outing—just walking off. Sometimes there were stories in the paper about families forgetting a child somewhere and driving to the next city. Andrea had only gone a mile down the road before she remembered.

In time, she dreamed of the bowl. Twice, in a waking dream—early in the morning, between sleep and a last nap before rising—she had a clear vision of it. It came into sharp focus and startled her for a moment—the same bowl she looked at every day.

She had a very profitable year selling real estate. Word spread, and she had more 10 clients than she felt comfortable with. She had the foolish thought that if only

3. An expensive German camera.

the bowl were an animate object she could thank it. There were times when she wanted to talk to her husband about the bowl. He was a stockbroker, and sometimes told people that he was fortunate to be married to a woman who had such a fine aesthetic sense and yet could also function in the real world. They were a lot alike, really—they had agreed on that. They were both quiet people—reflective, slow to make value judgments, but almost intractable once they had come to a conclusion. They both liked details, but while ironies attracted her, he was more impatient and dismissive when matters became many sided or unclear. But they both knew this; it was the kind of thing they could talk about when they were alone in the car together, coming home from a party or after a weekend with friends. But she never talked to him about the bowl. When they were at dinner, exchanging their news of the day, or while they lay in bed at night listening to the stereo and murmuring sleepy disconnections, she was often tempted to come right out and say that she thought that the bowl in the living room, the cream-colored bowl, was responsible for her success. But she didn't say it. She couldn't begin to explain it. Sometimes in the morning, she would look at him and feel guilty that she had such a constant secret.

Could it be that she had some deeper connection with the bowl—a relationship of some kind? She corrected her thinking: how could she imagine such a thing, when she was a human being and it was a bowl? It was ridiculous. Just think of how people lived together and loved each other . . . But was that always so clear, always a relationship? She was confused by these thoughts, but they remained in her mind. There was something within her now, something real, that she never talked about.

The bowl was a mystery, even to her. It was frustrating, because her involvement with the bowl contained a steady sense of unrequited good fortune; it would have been easier to respond if some sort of demand were made in return. But that only happened in fairy tales. The bowl was just a bowl. She did not believe that for one second. What she believed was that it was something she loved.

In the past, she had sometimes talked to her husband about a new property she was about to buy or sell—confiding some clever strategy she had devised to persuade owners who seemed ready to sell. Now she stopped doing that, for all her strategies involved the bowl. She became more deliberate with the bowl, and more possessive. She put it in houses only when no one was there, and removed it when she left the house. Instead of just moving a pitcher or a dish, she would remove all the other objects from a table. She had to force herself to handle them carefully, because she didn't really care about them. She just wanted them out of sight.

She wondered how the situation would end. As with a lover, there was no exact scenario of how matters would come to a close. Anxiety became the operative force. It would be irrelevant if the lover rushed into someone else's arms, or wrote her a note and departed to another city. The horror was the possibility of the disappearance. That was what mattered.

15   She would get up at night and look at the bowl. It never occurred to her that she might break it. She washed and dried it without anxiety, and she moved it

often, from coffee table to mahogany corner table or wherever, without fearing an accident. It was clear that she would not be the one who would do anything to the bowl. The bowl was only handled by her, set safely on one surface or another; it was not very likely that anyone would break it. A bowl was a poor conductor of electricity: it would not be hit by lightning. Yet the idea of damage persisted. She did not think beyond that—to what her life would be without the bowl. She only continued to fear that some accident would happen. Why not, in a world where people set plants where they did not belong, so that visitors touring a house would be fooled into thinking that dark corners got sunlight—a world full of tricks?

She had first seen the bowl several years earlier, at a crafts fair she had visited half in secret, with her lover. He had urged her to buy the bowl. She didn't *need* any more things, she told him. But she had been drawn to the bowl, and they had lingered near it. Then she went on to the next booth, and he came up behind her, tapping the rim against her shoulder as she ran her fingers over a wood carving. "You're still insisting that I buy that?" she said. "No," he said. "I bought it for you." He had bought her other things before this—things she liked more, at first—the child's ebony-and-turquoise ring that fitted her little finger; the wooden box, long and thin, beautifully dovetailed, that she used to hold paper clips; the soft gray sweater with a pouch pocket. It was his idea that when he could not be there to hold her hand she could hold her own—clasp her hands inside the lone pocket that stretched across the front. But in time she became more attached to the bowl than to any of his other presents. She tried to talk herself out of it. She owned other things that were more striking or valuable. It wasn't an object whose beauty jumped out at you; a lot of people must have passed it by before the two of them saw it that day.

Her lover had said that she was always too slow to know what she really loved. Why continue with her life the way it was? Why be two-faced, he asked her. He had made the first move toward her. When she would not decide in his favor, would not change her life and come to him, he asked her what made her think she could have it both ways. And then he made the last move and left. It was a decision meant to break her will, to shatter her intransigent ideas about honoring previous commitments.

Time passed. Alone in the living room at night, she often looked at the bowl sitting on the table, still and safe, unilluminated. In its way, it was perfect: the world cut in half, deep and smoothly empty. Near the rim, even in dim light, the eye moved toward one small flash of blue, a vanishing point on the horizon.

1986

QUESTIONS

1. Why does goodman Brown go to a witches' meeting?
2. Why does Faith Brown, his wife, wear pink ribbons?
3. In reading "Janus," what impression do you get of Andrea—and her attachment to the bowl—in the first half of the story? What expectations—if any—are aroused by that first

half? What does it mean to you that Andrea thought the bowl was meant to be empty (paragraph 6)? What other qualities of the bowl seem to suggest something about Andrea or her life? In paragraph 14, Andrea wonders how the situation would end. This probably makes some readers, perhaps most, think about how this story is going to end. How does it? Where did Andrea get the bowl? How significant is that? Why is the story called "Janus"?

WRITING SUGGESTIONS

1. Write a parody of "Young Goodman Brown" or an imitation, perhaps in the style of Stephen King or Anne Rice.
2. Write an analysis of the symbolism used in one of the stories in "Fiction: Reading, Responding, Writing" or in one of the stories in the first three chapters of this textbook.
3. Paraphrase several possible meanings of the bowl in "Janus." Argue for one or explain how the symbol of the bowl may be both meaningful and yet elude any possible paraphrase of its meaning.

STUDENT WRITING

Geoffrey Clement's essay on "Sonny's Blues" (from Chapter 1) responds to the second writing suggestion above. In it, he deftly traces the symbolism and the thematic and evaluative force of images of water in its solid (ice), liquid, and gaseous (steam, boiling) states in the story.

The Struggle to Surface in the Water of "Sonny's Blues"

Geoffrey Clement

In "Sonny's Blues," James Baldwin employs water as a symbol that enables him to concentrate more clearly on the lack of and the crucial need for a real sense of communication among members of society. As Baldwin captures the intensity of Sonny's and his brother's struggles to understand their situation, he vividly depicts a society that seeks to swallow up the souls of its inhabitants and gradually to drown them spiritually. Thus, Baldwin illustrates quite clearly his sense of the hopelessness in man's plight. In portraying the struggle of street life in Harlem, he uses water in its opposite forms--frozen water and boiling water--and toward the end of the story, as Sonny's and his brother's revelations help to resolve the conflict, the water becomes calm.

Initially, and as a result of Sonny's arrest, Sonny's brother gradually realizes that he has not fulfilled his promise and that his feelings of love for his brother have certainly gone unexpressed, if indeed they exist. As a result, he feels physically the coldness that has permeated his emotional life: "It was a special kind of ice. It kept melting, sending trickles of ice water all up and down my veins, but it never got less. Sometimes it hardened and seemed to expand . . ." (par. 2). So the ice represents his guilt and his fears, both of which will lessen little. Although he learns to adapt to these feelings, they occasionally resurface. Upon Sonny's return from prison, for example, his brother thinks, "and thank God she [his wife] was there, for I was filled with that icy dread again. Everything I did seemed awkward to me, and everything I said sounded freighted with hidden meaning. . . . I was dying to hear him tell me he was safe" (par. 78). In addition to this guilt, Sonny's brother experiences much of the same emotional turmoil that Sonny has endured. In this passage in particular, he is seeking reassurance that there is a way to survive their imprisonment without having to feel the pain Sonny felt. Baldwin not only uses ice to show the brother's disappointment in his failures as a brother but also to point to the brother's own struggle for security, identity, and communication.

As Sonny's brother begins to realize that within him there has grown a heart hardened and haunted by the cold darkness of Harlem's streets, he also begins to recognize many of the realities that his brother has faced and that he too must eventually face. Sonny's brother is spiritually walking through "the vivid, killing streets of our childhood. These streets hadn't changed, though housing projects jutted up out of them now like rocks in the middle of a boiling sea" (par. 73). Here, Baldwin paints an almost hellish picture of pain and suffering, of emotional torment and fears, and of spiritual drowning and isolation, all of which slowly become real in the mind of Sonny's brother. He begins to feel for the first time in his life the depth of his denial of his brother. Tragically, he finds that when he is ready to reach out to help Sonny, he cannot, for he is even more lost and confused than Sonny himself. Sonny's brother wants desperately to save Sonny from the inevitable struggle, yet he learns from Sonny that "the storm inside" (par. 217) will pass over only with the constant expression of love. Clearly, the process of revelation is a very dramatic one, since Sonny's brother comes to understand Sonny's need for a giving, communicating, responsible relationship, a commitment

filled with careful listening, compassion, and understanding. Sonny does
not believe he can make his brother understand his experiences with
drugs: "I can never tell you. I was all by myself at the bottom of
something . . . and I thought I'd die if I couldn't get away from it
and yet, all the same, I knew that everything I was doing was just
locking me in with it" (par. 220). Once his brother grasps the
importance of listening with love and understanding, however, Sonny is
finally able to reach out.

Toward the end of the story, the ice and the boiling sea come
together, and there is peace; Sonny is able to reach out, and he starts
to swim in the calmer water. Now, he finds freedom in expressing his
struggles through his music, while at the same time alerting his
audience to the lessons he has learned. Creole "wanted Sonny to leave
the shoreline and strike out for the deep water. He was Sonny's witness
that deep water and drowning were not the same thing" (par. 234). As
Sonny ventures further and further into his own understanding of life's
struggles, he tries, his brother tells us, "to find new ways to make us
listen. For, while the tale of how we suffer, and how we are delighted,
and how we may triumph is never new, it always must be heard . . .
it's the only light we've got in all this darkness" (par. 238). In a
powerful way, Sonny taught the audience to listen: "Freedom lurked
around us and I understood, at last, that he could help us be free if
we would listen, that we would never be free until we did" (par. 240).
The boiling rage of the streets and the coldness within his heart are
reconciled as the brother finally witnesses "Sonny's world" (par. 231).
Finally, he recognizes that Sonny has found the strength of knowing
that he has discovered in music the outlet through which he can express
himself and warn others of his mistakes. He sends up to the bandstand
not water, not ice, but Scotch and milk. Sonny sips it in a sort of
communion and puts it back on top of the piano, where "it glowed and
shook above [his] head like the very cup of trembling" (par. 241).

Thoughout his story, Baldwin stresses the lack of companionship to
try to manipulate the reader's emotions. Playing on the contrasts
between forms of water, he draws parallels to the theme of emotional
conflict within the minds of Sonny and his brother. While the sea is
calmer toward the end, there is still a sense of rage, because only in

the expression of his struggle is Sonny able to find meaning,
satisfaction, and forgiveness for his brother. The streets, society's
common ground, still try to isolate its members as each person
individually struggles to reach the surface. But if the struggler can
find a listening helper, which Sonny finds in his brother, then he will
reach the surface and breathe the fulfilling breath of love. The cup of
trembling will be taken out of the struggler's hand, the Bible tells
us, and will be put "into the hand of them that afflict thee" (p. 70n.).
Light gracefully touches and penetrates the surface of the water, and
the cup of trembling is still.

6

THEME

If you ask what a story is "about," an author is likely to answer by telling you the **subject.** Indeed, many authors tell you the subject in their titles: "An Occurrence at Owl Creek Bridge," "Her First Ball." Though a subject is always concrete, it may be stated at greater length than the few words of a title: "a man's thoughts as he faces execution for spying during the Civil War" ("An Occurrence at Owl Creek Bridge"); "a young girl's excitement at her first grown-up dance and an incident that temporarily depresses her" ("Her First Ball").

A friend might be more likely to tell you what a story is about by giving you a summary of the action: During World War II, a Chinese woman who is fleeing the Japanese has to abandon her twin daughters. Having escaped, she searches for them but cannot find them. She moves to America and there has another daughter. The mother dies, and not long after, a letter from China reveals that the twins have been found, alive and grown up. The "American" daughter—who does not identify herself as "Chinese-American" but just American—goes to China, finds her sisters, and sees the resemblance to her and her mother in their faces. She knows now that she "is Chinese." (We sometimes call this a **plot summary,** but you will notice that this summary describes the history, the events, in more or less chronological order, while the plot arranges or structures the history differently. In "A Pair of Tickets," remember, Jing-Mei Woo does not know the story of her mother's wartime experience or about the survival of her sisters until the latter part of the story.)

> To Generalize is to be an Idiot.
> To Particularize is the Alone
> Distinction of Merit. General
> Knowledges are those
> Knowledges that Idiots
> possess.
>
> —WILLIAM BLAKE

Your teacher may well explain a story by summarizing its **theme.** Some refer to the central idea, the thesis, or even the message of the story, and that is roughly what we mean by theme: a generalization or abstraction from the story. Thus, the subject of "Young Goodman Brown" may be said to be a coven (witches' meeting) or, more fully, "a young colonial New England husband is driven mad by finding everyone he thought good and pure attending a witches' meeting." The theme may be "everyone partakes of evil" or, more succinctly, "the Fall." There are, as you can see, degrees of generalization and abstraction; subject (a young man finds that everyone is evil) shades off into theme, which itself can be more or less general and abstract.

Discussions of literature in or out of class sometimes seem to suggest that stories exist for their themes, that we read only to get the "point" or message. But most themes, you must admit, are somewhat less than earth-shattering. That all men and women are evil may be debatable, but it certainly isn't news. That not all unmarried women (even English women) of a certain age are prudish, dried up, and repressed—an apparent theme of "Our Friend Judith"—is rather widely recognized, something we scarcely need a dozen or so pages of fiction to find out. No wonder, then, that some skeptics contend that stories are only elaborate ways of "saying something simple," that literature is a game in which authors hide their meanings under shells of words. Of course, reading a dozen or so pages of a story like "Our Friend Judith" can be enjoyable. Could it be that we really read fiction for fun, and all our talk about themes is just hiding from our Puritan natures the fact that we are goofing off? But articulating the theme of a story is neither the purpose of nor the excuse for reading fiction, nor do authors hide their meanings like Easter eggs. In order to relate his or her unique vision of reality to an absent and unknown reader, a writer must find a way of communicating—some common ground on which to meet the various unique individuals who will read the story.

Common experiences, common assumptions, common language, and common-places offer such ground. Readers reach out from their own subjective worlds toward that new and different vision of the author with the help of the common elements (the general), and especially through the commonplaces of theme, bringing back the particulars and generalizations of the story to their own reading and living experience. In "Janus," the reader sees a successful suburban real estate agent who is married to a stockbroker but who has lost her lover, a man she truly loved, because she could not or would not decide to leave her husband; a woman whose world is "perfect," but cut in half and empty, like the beloved bowl her lover picked out for her and gave her. Generalizing, the reader may conclude that what the story says (its theme) is that life, or a full or happy life, is more than convention and material success, that love is more important than comfort and "perfection." Though the reader's own situation and choices may be considerably different from those of the protagonist in Beattie's story, he or she may be led by the story to ponder what is truly important and valuable in life, what "the perfect life" consists of, thereby coming to a greater understanding of the story—and, whether he or she agrees with the conclusions of the story or not, to a fuller understanding of the issues and theme of the story.

> Every description in words . . . is a generalization. That is the nature of words. There are no individuals conveyed in words but only more or less specific generalizations. . . .
>
> —WILLIAM WIMSATT

The significance of any story is modified to some extent by the reader's experience of books and life. You should not reduce every story to the dimensions of what you already know and feel, but you should reach out to the story and bring it back to you as an addition to and modification of your own experience. To make a story yours, to make it more than a yarn about a woman who sells real estate and has been unfaithful to her stockbroker husband and was left by her lover because she would not get a divorce, requires translating it somehow into terms that, while not necessarily psychological or moral precepts, alter or broaden to some degree your own vision of yourself, others, life in general.

In Chapter 5 we saw that even though a symbol suggests the meaning beyond the particulars of the fiction, it remains a detail in the fictional world—the snakelike staff of the stranger in "Young Goodman Brown" remains a staff, Judith's cats remain cats. Some critics would say that this is true also of theme and that theme is related to the story as integrally as symbolic meaning is to detail; that is, rather than "Young Goodman Brown" telling us something we did not know before, its theme and its story modify each other. The theme as stated relates to spiritual evil, the kind of evil suggested by the snake and Satan figures. But this theme is not entirely portable: it cannot be taken out of the story and used as a substitute for what the story "means"; nor can it, without qualification, be used to explain all the significant details in the story. The facts that Brown is a newlywed, that Faith wears pink (coquettish?) ribbons, and that she, whom Brown thought so pure and innocent, shows up at the meeting of witches and sinners, suggest a more specific kind of evil than the spiritual or theological evil suggested by the snake and Satan: moral or, even more specifically, sexual evil. This means we must modify our definition of the theme. But how? What does the story imply about the relationship of sex and evil? Is all sex evil? Is Original Sin sexual? Some details—the snake, the Satanic guide—suggest a theme; other details modify it; still others—Brown's behavior after the night of the witches' meeting—may modify it further, so that the theme, though an approximate version of it may be abstracted from the story, remains embedded in it, ultimately inseparable from the details of plot, character, setting, and symbol.

A statement that can do justice to all the complexity and all the particulars of the story is not likely to take the simple form of a message. Indeed, it is the complex particularity of literature, its ultimate irreducibility, that makes critics and teachers reject message (which suggests a simple packaged statement) as a suitable term even for the paraphrasable thematic content of a story.

"Young Goodman Brown" is an allegorical story whose details do function as symbols with paraphrasable meanings, yet even its theme refuses to be reduced to a simple statement. "Her First Ball" is neither an allegory nor a **parable,** a short fiction that illustrates an explicit moral lesson. Though realistic, however, it is a short, rather simple story that seems to have a simple theme overtly enunciated by one of the characters, Leila's elderly partner. But the scene with the elderly partner is not the end of the story. Leila goes on to dance with a young partner and seems to forget the man's "message." What is the story "saying"? Is her forgetting "bad"? "sad"? "good"? The specifics of the story modify and enrich all the generalizations we can abstract from it, while these themes and questions, if we recognize them, modify and enrich our reading, our experience of the story.

To some readers, inferring themes seems like pulling rabbits out of hats. Not too much conjuring is needed, however, to infer the theme of "Young Goodman Brown": we can derive the theme of theological evil from the symbols (the snake-staff, Satan figure, names) and test physical details—like pink ribbons and the narrative situation (the three-month marriage)—that have sexual implications against the theme to see if we must modify our paraphrase. The title of "Counterparts" clearly suggests why Farrington so cruelly beats his son Tom and suggests, too, what the story sees as one of the major roots of domestic violence and thus the theme. In "Her First Ball" a character raises a general issue that is tested by subsequent events in the story and modified by them.

There are, of course, other ways that details suggest generalizations or meaning, and other ways to abstract meaning from detail. Aided by footnotes, perhaps, you likely noticed the **allusions**—references to history, the Bible, sometimes literature, paintings, and so on—in "Young Goodman Brown." The scene is Salem in the time of King

William—that is, about the time of the Salem witch trials—and the stranger's serpentine staff is related to those of the pharaoh's Egyptian magi, which turn to snakes. So allusion as well as symbols, plot, focus and voice, and character are elements that contribute to and must be accounted for in paraphrasing a theme. That is why theme is important and why it comes last in a discussion of the elements of fiction.

But remember, the theme is an inadequate abstraction from the story; the story and its details do not disappear or lose significance once distilled into theme, nor could you reconstruct a story merely from its paraphrased theme. Indeed, theme and story, history and structure, do not so much interact, are not so much interrelated, as they are fused, inseparable.

KATHERINE MANSFIELD

Her First Ball

Exactly when the ball began Leila would have found it hard to say. Perhaps her first real partner was the cab. It did not matter that she shared the cab with the Sheridan girls and their brother. She sat back in her own little corner of it, and the bolster on which her hand rested felt like the sleeve of an unknown young man's dress suit; and away they bowled, past waltzing lampposts and houses and fences and trees.

"Have you really never been to a ball before, Leila? But, my child, how too weird—" cried the Sheridan girls.

"Our nearest neighbor was fifteen miles," said Leila softly, gently opening and shutting her fan.

Oh, dear, how hard it was to be indifferent like the others! She tried not to smile too much; she tried not to care. But every single thing was so new and exciting . . . Meg's tuberoses, Jose's long loop of amber, Laura's little dark head, pushing above her white fur like a flower through snow. She would remember for ever. It even gave her a pang to see her cousin Laurie throw away the wisps of tissue paper he pulled from the fastening of his new gloves. She would like to have kept those wisps as a keepsake, as a remembrance. Laurie leaned forward and put his hand on Laura's knee.

5   "Look here, darling," he said. "The third and the ninth as usual, Twig?"

Oh, how marvellous to have a brother! In her excitement Leila felt that if there had been time, if it hadn't been impossible, she couldn't have helped crying because she was an only child, and no brother had ever said "Twig?" to her; no sister would ever say, as Meg said to Jose that moment, "I've never known your hair go up more successfully than it has tonight!"

But, of course, there was no time. They were at the drill hall already; there were cabs in front of them and cabs behind. The road was bright on either side with moving fan-like lights, and on the pavement gay couples seemed to float through the air; little satin shoes chased each other like birds.

"Hold on to me, Leila; you'll get lost," said Laura.

"Come on, girls, let's make a dash for it," said Laurie.

Leila put two fingers on Laura's pink velvet cloak, and they were somehow   10
lifted past the big gold lantern, carried along the passage, and pushed into the
little room marked "Ladies." Here the crowd was so great there was hardly space
to take off their things; the noise was deafening. Two benches on either side were
stacked high with wraps. Two old women in white aprons ran up and down
tossing fresh armfuls. And everybody was pressing forward trying to get at the
little dressing table and mirror at the far end.

A great quivering jet of gas lighted the ladies' room. It couldn't wait; it was
dancing already. When the door opened again and there came a burst of tuning
from the drill hall, it leaped almost to the ceiling.

Dark girls, fair girls were patting their hair, tying ribbons again, tucking handkerchiefs down the front of their bodices, smoothing marble-white gloves. And
because they were all laughing it seemed to Leila that they were all lovely.

"Aren't there any invisible hairpins?" cried a voice. "How most extraordinary!
I can't see a single invisible hairpin."

"Powder my back, there's a darling," cried some one else.

"But I must have a needle and cotton. I've torn simply miles and miles of the   15
frill," wailed a third.

Then, "Pass them along, pass them along!" The straw basket of programs was
tossed from arm to arm. Darling little pink-and-silver programs, with pink pencils and fluffy tassels. Leila's fingers shook as she took one out of the basket. She
wanted to ask someone, "Am I meant to have one too?" but she had just time to
read: "Waltz 3. *Two, Two in a Canoe.* Polka 4. *Making the Feathers Fly,*" when Meg
cried, "Ready, Leila?" and they pressed their way through the crush in the passage towards the big double doors of the drill hall.

Dancing had not begun yet, but the band had stopped tuning, and the noise
was so great it seemed that when it did begin to play it would never be heard.
Leila, pressing close to Meg, looking over Meg's shoulder, felt that even the little
quivering colored flags strung across the ceiling were talking. She quite forgot to
be shy; she forgot how in the middle of dressing she had sat down on the bed
with one shoe off and one shoe on and begged her mother to ring up her cousins
and say she couldn't go after all. And the rush of longing she had had to be
sitting on the veranda of their forsaken upcountry home, listening to the baby
owls crying "More pork" in the moonlight, was changed to a rush of joy so sweet
that it was hard to bear alone. She clutched her fan, and, gazing at the gleaming,
golden floor, the azaleas, the lanterns, the stage at one end with its red carpet
and gilt chairs and the band in a corner, she thought breathlessly, "How heavenly; how simply heavenly!"

All the girls stood grouped together at one side of the doors, the men at the
other, and the chaperones in dark dresses, smiling rather foolishly, walked with
little careful steps over the polished floor towards the stage.

"This is my little country cousin Leila. Be nice to her. Find her partners; she's
under my wing," said Meg, going up to one girl after another.

Strange faces smiled at Leila—sweetly, vaguely. Strange voices answered, "Of   20 course, my dear." But Leila felt the girls didn't really see her. They were looking towards the men. Why didn't the men begin? What were they waiting for? There they stood, smoothing their gloves, patting their glossy hair and smiling among themselves. Then, quite suddenly, as if they had only just made up their minds that that was what they had to do, the men came gliding over the parquet. There was a joyful flutter among the girls. A tall, fair man flew up to Meg, seized her program, scribbled something; Meg passed him on to Leila. "May I have the pleasure?" He ducked and smiled. There came a dark man wearing an eyeglass, then cousin Laurie with a friend, and Laura with a little freckled fellow whose tie was crooked. Then quite an old man—fat, with a big bald patch on his head—took her program and murmured, "Let me see, let me see!" And he was a long time comparing his program, which looked black with names, with hers. It seemed to give him so much trouble that Leila was ashamed. "Oh, please don't bother," she said eagerly. But instead of replying the fat man wrote something, glanced at her again. "Do I remember this bright little face?" he said softly. "Is it known to me of yore?" At that moment the band began playing; the fat man disappeared. He was tossed away on a great wave of music that came flying over the gleaming floor, breaking the groups up into couples, scattering them, sending them spinning. . . .

Leila had learned to dance at boarding school. Every Saturday afternoon the boarders were hurried off to a little corrugated iron mission hall where Miss Eccles (of London) held her "select" classes. But the difference between that dusty-smelling hall—with calico texts on the walls, the poor terrified little woman in a brown velvet toque with rabbit's ears thumping the cold piano, Miss Eccles poking the girls' feet with her long white wand—and this was so tremendous that Leila was sure if her partner didn't come and she had to listen to that marvelous music and to watch the others sliding, gliding over the golden floor, she would die at least, or faint, or lift her arms and fly out of one of those dark windows that showed the stars.

"Ours, I think—" Some one bowed, smiled, and offered her his arm; she hadn't to die after all. Some one's hand pressed her waist, and she floated away like a flower that is tossed into a pool.

"Quite a good floor, isn't it?" drawled a faint voice close to her ear.

"I think it's most beautifully slippery," said Leila.

"Pardon!" The faint voice sounded surprised. Leila said it again. And there was a tiny pause before the voice echoed. "Oh, quite!" and she was swung round again.

He steered so beautifully. That was the great difference between dancing with girls and men, Leila decided. Girls banged into each other, and stamped on each other's feet; the girl who was gentleman always clutched you so.

The azaleas were separate flowers no longer; they were pink and white flags streaming by.

"Were you at the Bells' last week?" the voice came again. It sounded tired. Leila wondered whether she ought to ask him if he would like to stop.

"No, this is my first dance," said she.

Her partner gave a little gasping laugh. "Oh, I say," he protested.

"Yes, it is really the first dance I've ever been to." Leila was most fervent. It was such a relief to be able to tell somebody. "You see, I've lived in the country all my life up until now. . . ."

At that moment the music stopped, and they went to sit on two chairs against the wall. Leila tucked her pink satin feet under and fanned herself, while she blissfully watched the other couples passing and disappearing through the swing doors.

"Enjoying yourself, Leila?" asked Jose, nodding her golden head.

Laura passed and gave her the faintest little wink; it made Leila wonder for a moment whether she was quite grown up after all. Certainly her partner did not say very much. He coughed, tucked his handkerchief away, pulled down his waistcoat, took a minute thread off his sleeve. But it didn't matter. Almost immediately the band started, and her second partner seemed to spring from the ceiling.

"Floor's not bad," said the new voice. Did one always begin with the floor? And then, "Were you at the Neaves' on Tuesday?" And again Leila explained. Perhaps it was a little strange that her partners were not more interested. For it was thrilling. Her first ball! she was only at the beginning of everything. It seemed to her that she had never known what the night was like before. Up till now it had been dark, silent, beautiful very often—oh, yes—but mournful somehow. Solemn. And now it would never be like that again—it had opened dazzling bright.

"Care for an ice?" said her partner. And they went through the swing doors, down the passage, to the supper room. Her cheeks burned, she was fearfully thirsty. How sweet the ices looked on little glass plates, and how cold the frosted spoon was, iced too! And when they came back to the hall there was the fat man waiting for her by the door. It gave her quite a shock again to see how old he was; he ought to have been on the stage with the fathers and mothers. And when Leila compared him with her other partners he looked shabby. His waistcoat was creased, there was a button off his glove, his coat looked as if it was dusty with French chalk.

"Come along, little lady," said the fat man. He scarcely troubled to clasp her, and they moved away so gently, it was more like walking than dancing. But he said not a word about the floor. "Your first dance, isn't it?" he murmured.

"How *did* you know?"

"Ah," said the fat man, "that's what it is to be old!" He wheezed faintly as he steered her past an awkward couple. "You see, I've been doing this kind of thing for the last thirty years."

"Thirty years?" cried Leila. Twelve years before she was born!

"It hardly bears thinking about, does it?" said the fat man gloomily. Leila looked at his bald head, and she felt quite sorry for him.

"I think it's marvelous to be still going on," she said kindly.

"Kind little lady," said the fat man, and he pressed her a little closer, and hummed a bar of the waltz. "Of course," he said, "you can't hope to last anything like as long as that. No-o," said the fat man, "long before that you'll be sitting up there on the stage, looking on, in your nice black velvet. And these pretty arms will have turned into little short fat ones, and you'll beat time with such a differ-ent kind of fan—a black bony one." The fat man seemed to shudder. "And you'll smile away like the poor old dears up there, and point to your daughter, and tell the elderly lady next to you how some dreadful man tried to kiss her at the club ball. And your heart will ache, ache"—the fat man squeezed her closer still, as if he really was sorry for that poor heart—"because no one wants to kiss you now. And you'll say how unpleasant these polished floors are to walk on, how danger-ous they are. Eh, Mademoiselle Twinkletoes?" said the fat man softly.

Leila gave a light little laugh, but she did not feel like laughing. Was it—could it all be true? It sounded terribly true. Was this first ball only the beginning of her last ball after all? At that the music seemed to change; it sounded sad, sad it rose upon a great sigh. Oh, how quickly things changed! Why didn't happiness last for ever? For ever wasn't a bit too long.

45   "I want to stop," she said in a breathless voice. The fat man led her to the door.

"No," she said. "I won't go outside. I won't sit down. I'll just stand here, thank you." She leaned against the wall, tapping with her foot, pulling up her gloves and trying to smile. But deep inside her a little girl threw her pinafore over her head and sobbed. Why had he spoiled it all?

"I say, you know," said the fat man, "you mustn't take me seriously, little lady."

"As if I should!" said Leila, tossing her small dark head and sucking her underlip. . . .

Again the couples paraded. The swing doors opened and shut. Now new music was given out by the bandmaster. But Leila didn't want to dance any more. She wanted to be home, or sitting on the veranda listening to those baby owls. When she looked through the dark windows at the stars, they had long beams like wings. . . .

50   But presently a soft, melting, ravishing tune began, and a young man with curly hair bowed before her. She would have to dance, out of politeness, until she could find Meg. Very stiffly she walked into the middle; very haughtily she put her hand on his sleeve. But in one minute, in one turn, her feet glided, glided. The lights, the azaleas, the dresses, the pink faces, the velvet chairs, all became one beautiful flying wheel. And when her next partner bumped her into the fat man and he said, "Par*don*," she smiled at him more radiantly than ever. She didn't even recognize him again.

                                                                                    1922

JAMES JOYCE

Counterparts

The bell rang furiously and, when Miss Parker went to the tube, a furious voice called out in a piercing North of Ireland accent:

—Send Farrington here!

Miss Parker returned to her machine, saying to a man who was writing at a desk:

—Mr Alleyne wants you upstairs.

The man muttered *Blast him!* under his breath and pushed back his chair to 5 stand up. When he stood up he was tall and of great bulk. He had a hanging face, dark wine-coloured, with fair eyebrows and moustache: his eyes bulged forward slightly and the whites of them were dirty. He lifted up the counter and, passing by the clients, went out of the office with a heavy step.

He went heavily upstairs until he came to the second landing, where a door bore a brass plate with the inscription *Mr Alleyne*. Here he halted, puffing with labour and vexation, and knocked. The shrill voice cried:

—Come in!

The man entered Mr Alleyne's room. Simultaneously Mr Alleyne, a little man wearing gold-rimmed glasses on a cleanshaven face, shot his head up over a pile of documents. The head itself was so pink and hairless that it seemed like a large egg reposing on the papers. Mr Alleyne did not lose a moment:

—Farrington? What is the meaning of this? Why have I always to complain of you? May I ask you why you haven't made a copy of that contract between Bodley and Kirwan? I told you it must be ready by four o'clock.

—But Mr Shelley said, sir— 10

—*Mr Shelley said, sir.* . . . Kindly attend to what I say and not to what *Mr Shelley says, sir.* You have always some excuse or another for shirking work. Let me tell you that if the contract is not copied before this evening I'll lay the matter before Mr Crosbie. . . . Do you hear me now?

—Yes, sir.

—Do you hear me now? . . . Ay and another little matter! I might as well be talking to the wall as talking to you. Understand once for all that you get a half an hour for your lunch and not an hour and a half. How many courses do you want, I'd like to know. . . . Do you mind me, now?

—Yes, sir.

Mr Alleyne bent his head again upon his pile of papers. The man stared fixedly 15 at the polished skull which directed the affairs of Crosbie & Alleyne, gauging its fragility. A spasm of rage gripped his throat for a few moments and then passed, leaving after it a sharp sensation of thirst. The man recognised the sensation and felt that he must have a good night's drinking. The middle of the month was passed and, if he could get the copy done in time, Mr Alleyne might give him an order on the cashier. He stood still, gazing fixedly at the head upon the pile of papers. Suddenly Mr Alleyne began to upset all the papers, searching for something. Then, as if he had been unaware of the man's presence till that moment, he shot up his head again, saying:

—Eh? Are you going to stand there all day? Upon my word, Farrington, you take things easy!

—I was waiting to see . . .

—Very good, you needn't wait to see. Go downstairs and do your work.

The man walked heavily towards the door and, as he went out of the room, he heard Mr Alleyne cry after him that if the contract was not copied by evening Mr Crosbie would hear of the matter.

20   He returned to his desk in the lower office and counted the sheets which remained to be copied. He took up his pen and dipped it in the ink but he continued to stare stupidly at the last words he had written: *In no case shall the said Bernard Bodley be* . . . The evening was falling and in a few minutes they would be lighting the gas: then he could write. He felt that he must slake the thirst in his throat. He stood up from his desk and, lifting the counter as before, passed out of the office. As he was passing out the chief clerk looked at him inquiringly.

—It's all right, Mr Shelley, said the man, pointing with his finger to indicate the objective of his journey.

The chief clerk glanced at the hat-rack but, seeing the row complete, offered no remark. As soon as he was on the landing the man pulled a shepherd's plaid cap out of his pocket, put it on his head and ran quickly down the rickety stairs. From the street door he walked on furtively on the inner side of the path towards the corner and all at once dived into a doorway. He was now safe in the dark snug of O'Neill's shop, and, filling up the little window that looked into the bar with his inflamed face, the colour of dark wine or dark meat, he called out:

—Here, Pat, give us a g.p., like a good fellow.

The curate brought him a glass of plain porter. The man drank it at a gulp and asked for a caraway seed. He put his penny on the counter and, leaving the curate to grope for it in the gloom, retreated out of the snug as furtively as he had entered it.

25   Darkness, accompanied by a thick fog, was gaining upon the dusk of February and the lamps in Eustace Street had been lit. The man went up by the houses until he reached the door of the office, wondering whether he could finish his copy in time. On the stairs a moist pungent odour of perfumes saluted his nose: evidently Miss Delacour had come while he was out in O'Neill's. He crammed his cap back again into his pocket and re-entered the office, assuming an air of absent-mindedness.

—Mr Alleyne has been calling for you, said the chief clerk severely. Where were you?

The man glanced at the two clients who were standing at the counter as if to intimate that their presence prevented him from answering. As the clients were both male the chief clerk allowed himself a laugh.

—I know that game, he said. Five times in one day is a little bit. . . . Well, you better look sharp and get a copy of our correspondence in the Delacour case for Mr Alleyne.

This address in the presence of the public, his run upstairs and the porter he had gulped down so hastily confused the man and, as he sat down at his desk to get what was required, he realised how hopeless was the task of finishing his copy of the contract before half past five. The dark damp night was coming and he longed to spend it in the bars, drinking with his friends amid the glare of gas and the clatter of glasses. He got out the Delacour correspondence and passed out of the office. He hoped Mr Alleyne would not discover that the last two letters were missing.

The moist pungent perfume lay all the way up to Mr Alleyne's room. Miss Delacour was a middle-aged woman of Jewish appearance. Mr Alleyne was said to be sweet on her or on her money. She came to the office often and stayed a long time when she came. She was sitting beside his desk now in an aroma of perfumes, smoothing the handle of her umbrella and nodding the great black feather in her hat. Mr Alleyne had swivelled his chair round to face her and thrown his right foot jauntily upon his left knee. The man put the correspondence on the desk and bowed respectfully but neither Mr Alleyne nor Miss Delacour took any notice of his bow. Mr Alleyne tapped a finger on the correspondence and then flicked it towards him as if to say: *That's all right: you can go.*

The man returned to the lower office and sat down again at his desk. He stared intently at the incomplete phrase: *In no case shall the said Bernard Bodley be . . .* and thought how strange it was that the last three words began with the same letter. The chief clerk began to hurry Miss Parker, saying she would never have the letters typed in time for post. The man listened to the clicking of the machine for a few minutes and then set to work to finish his copy. But his head was not clear and his mind wandered away to the glare and rattle of the public-house. It was a night for hot punches. He struggled on with his copy, but when the clock struck five he had still fourteen pages to write. Blast it! He couldn't finish it in time. He longed to execrate aloud, to bring his fist down on something violently. He was so enraged that he wrote *Bernard Bernard* instead of *Bernard Bodley* and had to begin again on a clean sheet.

He felt strong enough to clear out the whole office singlehanded. His body ached to do something, to rush out and revel in violence. All the indignities of his life enraged him. . . . Could he ask the cashier privately for an advance? No, the cashier was no good, no damn good: he wouldn't give an advance. . . . He knew where he would meet the boys: Leonard and O'Halloran and Nosey Flynn. The barometer of his emotional nature was set for a spell of riot.

His imagination had so abstracted him that his name was called twice before he answered. Mr Alleyne and Miss Delacour were standing outside the counter and all the clerks had turned round in anticipation of something. The man got up from his desk. Mr Alleyne began a tirade of abuse, saying that two letters were missing. The man answered that he knew nothing about them, that he had made a faithful copy. The tirade continued: it was so bitter and violent that the man

30

could hardly restrain his fist from descending upon the head of the manikin before him.

—I know nothing about any other two letters, he said stupidly.

35   —*You—know—nothing*. Of course you know nothing, said Mr Alleyne. Tell me, he added, glancing first for approval to the lady beside him, do you take me for a fool? Do you think me an utter fool?

The man glanced from the lady's face to the little egg-shaped head and back again; and, almost before he was aware of it, his tongue had found a felicitous moment:

—I don't think, sir, he said, that that's a fair question to put to me.

There was a pause in the very breathing of the clerks. Everyone was astounded (the author of the witticism no less than his neighbours) and Miss Delacour, who was a stout amiable person, began to smile broadly. Mr Alleyne flushed to the hue of a wild rose and his mouth twitched with a dwarf's passion. He shook his fist in the man's face till it seemed to vibrate like the knob of some electric machine:

—You impertinent ruffian! You impertinent ruffian! I'll make short work of you! Wait till you see! You'll apologise to me for your impertinence or you'll quit the office instanter! You'll quit this, I'm telling you, or you'll apologise to me!

40   He stood in a doorway opposite the office watching to see if the cashier would come out alone. All the clerks passed out and finally the cashier came out with the chief clerk. It was no use trying to say a word to him when he was with the chief clerk. The man felt that his position was bad enough. He had been obliged to offer an abject apology to Mr Alleyne for his impertinence but he knew what a hornet's nest the office would be for him. He could remember the way in which Mr Alleyne had hounded little Peake out of the office in order to make room for his own nephew. He felt savage and thirsty and revengeful, annoyed with himself and with everyone else. Mr Alleyne would never give him an hour's rest; his life would be a hell to him. He had made a proper fool of himself this time. Could he not keep his tongue in his cheek? But they had never pulled together from the first, he and Mr Alleyne, ever since the day Mr Alleyne had overheard him mimicking his North of Ireland accent to amuse Higgins and Miss Parker: that had been the beginning of it. He might have tried Higgins for the money, but sure Higgins never had anything for himself. A man with two establishments to keep up, of course he couldn't. . . .

He felt his great body again aching for the comfort of the public-house. The fog had begun to chill him and he wondered could he touch Pat in O'Neill's. He could not touch him for more than a bob[1]—and a bob was no use. Yet he must get money somewhere or other: he had spent his last penny for the g.p. and soon it would be too late for getting money anywhere. Suddenly, as he was fingering

1. A shilling. There were 20 shillings to the pound. Though the American equivalent of the pound was $5, this does not indicate present-day buying power. Notice that a glass of porter (beer) was 1 penny; since there were 12 pence to the shilling, the beer was just over 2 cents a glass.

his watch-chain, he thought of Terry Kelly's pawn-office in Fleet Street. That was the dart![2] Why didn't he think of it sooner?

He went through the narrow alley of Temple Bar quickly, muttering to himself that they could all go to hell because he was going to have a good night of it. The clerk in Terry Kelly's said *A crown!*[3] but the consignor held out for six shillings; and in the end the six shillings was allowed him literally. He came out of the pawn-office joyfully, making a little cylinder of the coins between his thumb and fingers. In Westmoreland Street the footpaths were crowded with young men and women returning from business and ragged urchins ran here and there yelling out the names of the evening editions. The man passed through the crowd, looking on the spectacle generally with proud satisfaction and staring masterfully at the office-girls. His head was full of the noises of tram-gongs and swishing trolleys and his nose already sniffed the curling fumes of punch. As he walked on he preconsidered the terms in which he would narrate the incident to the boys:

—So, I just looked at him—coolly, you know, and looked at her. Then I looked back at him again—taking my time, you know. *I don't think that that's a fair question to put to me,* says I.

Nosey Flynn was sitting up in his usual corner of Davy Byrne's and, when he heard the story, he stood Farrington a half-one, saying it was as smart a thing as ever he heard. Farrington stood a drink in his turn. After a while O'Halloran and Paddy Leonard came in and the story was repeated to them. O'Halloran stood tailors of malt,[4] hot, all round and told the story of the retort he had made to the chief clerk when he was in Callan's of Fownes's Street; but, as the retort was after the manner of the liberal shepherds[5] in the eclogues, he had to admit that it was not so clever as Farrington's retort. At this Farrington told the boys to polish off that and have another.

Just as they were naming their poisons who should come in but Higgins! Of course he had to join in with the others. The men asked him to give his version of it, and he did so with great vivacity for the sight of five small hot whiskies was very exhilarating. Everyone roared laughing when he showed the way in which Mr Alleyne shook his fist in Farrington's face. Then he imitated Farrington, saying, *And here was my nabs,*[6] *as cool as you please,* while Farrington looked at the company out of his heavy dirty eyes, smiling and at times drawing forth stray drops of liquor from his moustache with the aid of his lower lip.

When that round was over there was a pause. O'Halloran had money but neither of the other two seemed to have any; so the whole party left the shop somewhat regretfully. At the corner of Duke Street Higgins and Nosey Flynn bevelled off to the left while the other three turned back towards the city. Rain was drizzling down on the cold streets and, when they reached the Ballast Office, Farrington suggested the Scotch House. The bar was full of men and loud with the noise of tongues and glasses. The three men pushed past the whining match-sellers at

45

---

2. [Right] plan, idea.   3. Five shillings.   4. Measures of unblended whiskey.   5. Gertrude, in *Hamlet* IV.vii.168–70, says the "long purples" (flowers) that "cold maids" call "dead men's fingers" are called by "liberal shepherds" by another, "grosser" (clearly phallic) name.   6. Gentleman.

the door and formed a little party at the corner of the counter. They began to exchange stories. Leonard introduced them to a young fellow named Weathers who was performing at the Tivoli as an acrobat and knockabout *artiste*. Farrington stood a drink all round. Weathers said he would take a small Irish and Apollinaris.[7] Farrington, who had definite notions of what was what, asked the boys would they have an Apollinaris too; but the boys told Tim to make theirs hot. The talk became theatrical. O'Halloran stood a round and then Farrington stood another round, Weathers protesting that the hospitality was too Irish. He promised to get them in behind the scenes and introduce them to some nice girls. O'Halloran said that he and Leonard would go but that Farrington wouldn't go because he was a married man; and Farrington's heavy dirty eyes leered at the company in token that he understood he was being chaffed. Weathers made them all have just one little tincture at his expense and promised to meet them later on at Mulligan's in Poolbeg Street.

When the Scotch House closed they went round to Mulligan's. They went into the parlour at the back and O'Halloran ordered small hot specials all round. They were all beginning to feel mellow. Farrington was just standing another round when Weathers came back. Much to Farrington's relief he drank a glass of bitter[8] this time. Funds were running low but they had enough to keep them going. Presently two young women with big hats and a young man in a check suit came in and sat at a table close by. Weathers saluted them and told the company that they were out of the Tivoli. Farrington's eyes wandered at every moment in the direction of one of the young women. There was something striking in her appearance. An immense scarf of peacock-blue muslin was wound round her hat and knotted in a great bow under her chin; and she wore bright yellow gloves, reaching to the elbow. Farrington gazed admiringly at the plump arm which she moved very often and with much grace; and when, after a little time, she answered his gaze he admired still more her large dark brown eyes. The oblique staring expression in them fascinated him. She glanced at him once or twice and, when the party was leaving the room, she brushed against his chair and said *O, pardon!* in a London accent. He watched her leave the room in the hope that she would look back at him, but he was disappointed. He cursed his want of money and cursed all the rounds he had stood, particularly all the whiskies and Apollinaris which he had stood to Weathers. If there was one thing that he hated it was a sponge. He was so angry that he lost count of the conversation of his friends.

When Paddy Leonard called him he found that they were talking about feats of strength. Weathers was showing his biceps muscle to the company and boasting so much that the other two had called on Farrington to uphold the national honour. Farrington pulled up his sleeve accordingly and showed his biceps muscle to the company. The two arms were examined and compared and finally it was agreed to have a trial of strength. The table was cleared and the two men rested their elbows on it, clasping hands. When Paddy Leonard said *Go!* each was

---

7. Irish whiskey and mineral water.   8. Beer; cheaper than Irish whiskey or hot drinks.

to try to bring down the other's hand on to the table. Farrington looked very serious and determined.

The trial began. After about thirty seconds Weathers brought his opponent's hand slowly down on to the table. Farrington's dark wine-coloured face flushed darker still with anger and humiliation at having been defeated by such a stripling.

—You're not to put the weight of your body behind it. Play fair, he said.   50

—Who's not playing fair? said the other.

—Come on again. The two best out of three.

The trial began again. The veins stood out on Farrington's forehead, and the pallor of Weathers' complexion changed to peony. Their hands and arms trembled under the stress. After a long struggle Weathers again brought his opponent's hand slowly on to the table. There was a murmur of applause from the spectators. The curate, who was standing beside the table, nodded his red head towards the victor and said with loutish familiarity:

—Ah! that's the knack!

—What the hell do you know about it? said Farrington fiercely, turning on   55
the man. What do you put in your gab for?

—Sh, sh! said O'Halloran, observing the violent expression of Farrington's face. Pony up, boys. We'll have just one little smahan[9] more and then we'll be off.

A very sullen-faced man stood at the corner of O'Connell Bridge waiting for the little Sandymount tram to take him home. He was full of smouldering anger and revengefulness. He felt humiliated and discontented; he did not even feel drunk; and he had only twopence in his pocket. He cursed everything. He had done for himself in the office, pawned his watch, spent all his money; and he had not even got drunk. He began to feel thirsty again and he longed to be back again in the hot reeking public-house. He had lost his reputation as a strong man, having been defeated twice by a mere boy. His heart swelled with fury and, when he thought of the woman in the big hat who had brushed against him and said *Pardon!* his fury nearly choked him.

His tram let him down at Shelbourne Road and he steered his great body along in the shadow of the wall of the barracks. He loathed returning to his home. When he went in by the side-door he found the kitchen empty and the kitchen fire nearly out. He bawled upstairs:

—Ada! Ada!

His wife was a little sharp-faced woman who bullied her husband when he   60
was sober and was bullied by him when he was drunk. They had five children. A little boy came running down the stairs.

—Who is that? said the man, peering through the darkness.

—Me, pa.

—Who are you? Charlie?

—No, pa. Tom.

9. Bit, smidgen.

65 —Where's your mother?

—She's out at the chapel.

—That's right. . . . Did she think of leaving any dinner for me?

—Yes, pa. I—

—Light the lamp. What do you mean by having the place in darkness? Are the other children in bed?

70 The man sat down heavily on one of the chairs while the little boy lit the lamp. He began to mimic his son's flat accent, saying half to himself: *At the chapel. At the chapel, if you please!* When the lamp was lit he banged his fist on the table and shouted:

—What's for my dinner?

—I'm going . . . to cook it, pa, said the little boy.

The man jumped up furiously and pointed to the fire.

—On that fire! You let the fire out! By God, I'll teach you to do that again!

75 He took a step to the door and seized the walking-stick which was standing behind it.

—I'll teach you to let the fire out! he said, rolling up his sleeve in order to give his arm free play.

The little boy cried *O, pa!* and ran whimpering round the table, but the man followed him and caught him by the coat. The little boy looked about him wildly but, seeing no way of escape fell upon his knees.

—Now, you'll let the fire out the next time! said the man, striking at him viciously with the stick. Take that, you little whelp!

The boy uttered a squeal of pain as the stick cut his thigh. He clasped his hands together in the air and his voice shook with fright.

80 —O, pa! he cried. Don't beat me, pa! And I'll . . . I'll say a *Hail Mary* for you. . . . I'll say a *Hail Mary* for you, pa, if you don't beat me. . . . I'll say a *Hail Mary*. . . .

1914

QUESTIONS

1. Leila, in "Her First Ball," soon shakes off the gloomy thoughts offered her by her older partner. Is she an empty-headed girl too shallow to think of serious things, or is she just young and healthy, enjoying life?
2. Note the physical descriptions of Farrington and Mr Alleyne in "Counterparts": how are they related to Farrington's frustration? to the final scene? How many occasions are there in the story that attribute to Farrington's mood? How many are his fault? How do you feel about Farrington in his first encounter with Mr Alleyne? in his final smart remark to Alleyne? Whose side are you on in the arm-wrestling match?

WRITING SUGGESTIONS

1. Rewrite "Her First Ball," using another focus and voice.
2. Write a descriptive essay tracing your response to (feelings about) Farrington and his situation(s) from the beginning to the end of the story.

3. Compare Farrington and Francis Weed (in Cheever's "The Country Husband") as men frustrated with their lives, touching on their character, circumstances (including the settings of the stories), their behavior, and how they relate to their situations at the end of the stories.

7

THE WHOLE TEXT

Plot, point of view, character, setting, symbol, and theme are useful concepts. But they do not really exist as discrete parts or constituents of a finished work. Analyzing a story

Discussing story-writing in terms of plot, character, and theme is like trying to describe the expression on a face by saying where the eyes, nose, and mouth are.

—FLANNERY O'CONNOR

means breaking it down into pieces we can handle. Analyzing may require talking or writing about a story in terms of its "elements," but we must remain aware of the arbitrariness of those distinctions and of the inextricable, organic integrity of the story itself. As you read the stories that follow in this chapter, apply all that you have learned about the history, the structure, and the elements of fiction, but be especially alert as to how the elements interact. Notice how, after taking it apart in order to analyze it, we can put the story back together.

JOSEPH CONRAD

The Secret Sharer

I

On my right hand there were lines of fishing-stakes resembling a mysterious system of half-submerged bamboo fences, incomprehensible in its division of the domain of tropical fishes, and crazy[1] of aspect as if abandoned for ever by some nomad tribe of fishermen now gone to the other end of the ocean; for there was no sign of human habitation as far as the eye could reach. To the left a group of barren islets, suggesting ruins of stone walls, towers, and blockhouses, had its

---

1. Irregular, rickety.

foundations set in a blue sea that itself looked solid, so still and stable did it lie below my feet; even the track of light from the westering sun shone smoothly, without that animated glitter which tells of an imperceptible ripple. And when I turned my head to take a parting glance at the tug which had just left us anchored outside the bar, I saw the straight line of the flat shore joined to the stable sea, edge to edge, with a perfect and unmarked closeness, in one leveled floor half brown, half blue under the enormous dome of the sky. Corresponding in their insignificance to the islets of the sea, two small clumps of trees, one on each side of the only fault in the impeccable joint, marked the mouth of the river Meinam[2] we had just left on the first preparatory stage of our homeward journey; and, far back on the inland level, a larger and loftier mass, the grove surrounding the great Paknam pagoda, was the only thing on which the eye could rest from the vain task of exploring the monotonous sweep of the horizon. Here and there gleams as of a few scattered pieces of silver marked the windings of the great river; and on the nearest of them, just within the bar, the tug steaming right into the land became lost to my sight, hull and funnel and masts, as though the impassive earth had swallowed her up without an effort, without a tremor. My eye followed the light cloud of her smoke, now here, now there, above the plain, according to the devious curves of the stream, but always fainter and farther away, till I lost it at last behind the mitre-shaped hill of the great pagoda. And then I was left alone with my ship, anchored at the head of the Gulf of Siam.

She floated at the starting-point of a long journey, very still in an immense stillness, the shadows of her spars flung far to the eastward by the setting sun. At that moment I was alone on her decks. There was not a sound in her—and around us nothing moved, nothing lived, not a canoe on the water, not a bird in the air, not a cloud in the sky. In this breathless pause at the threshold of a long passage we seemed to be measuring our fitness for a long and arduous enterprise, the appointed task of both our existences to be carried out, far from all human eyes, with only sky and sea for spectators and for judges.

There must have been some glare in the air to interfere with one's sight, because it was only just before the sun left us that my roaming eyes made out beyond the highest ridge of the principal islet of the group something which did away with the solemnity of perfect solitude. The tide of darkness flowed on swiftly; and with tropical suddenness a swarm of stars came out above the shadowy earth, while I lingered yet, my hand resting lightly on my ship's rail as if on the shoulder of a trusted friend. But, with all that multitude of celestial bodies staring down at one, the comfort of quiet communion with her was gone for good. And there were also disturbing sounds by this time—voices, footsteps forward; the steward flitted along the main deck, a busily ministering spirit; a hand-bell tinkled urgently under the poop deck. . . .

I found my two officers waiting for me near the supper table, in the lighted

2. The Menan (Chao Phraya) runs through Bangkok, Thailand, into the Gulf of Siam. The Paknam Pagoda stands at the mouth of the river.

cuddy. We sat down at once, and as I helped the chief mate, I said:

5   "Are you aware that there is a ship anchored inside the islands? I saw her mast-heads above the ridge as the sun went down."

He raised sharply his simple face, overcharged by a terrible growth of whisker, and emitted his usual ejaculations, "Bless my soul, sir! You don't say so!"

My second mate was a round-cheeked, silent young man, grave beyond his years, I thought; but as our eyes happened to meet I detected a slight quiver on his lips. I looked down at once. It was not my part to encourage sneering on board my ship. It must be said, too, that I knew very little of my officers. In consequence of certain events of no particular significance, except to myself, I had been appointed to the command only a fortnight before. Neither did I know much of the hands forward. All these people had been together for eighteen months or so, and my position was that of the only stranger on board. I mention this because it has some bearing on what is to follow. But what I felt most was my being a stranger to the ship; and if all the truth must be told, I was somewhat of a stranger to myself. The youngest man on board (barring the second mate), and untried as yet by a position of the fullest responsibility, I was willing to take the adequacy of the others for granted. They had simply to be equal to their tasks; but I wondered how far I should turn out faithful to that ideal conception of one's own personality every man sets up for himself secretly.

Meantime the chief mate, with an almost visible effect of collaboration on the part of his round eyes and frightful whiskers, was trying to evolve a theory of the anchored ship. His dominant trait was to take all things into earnest consideration. He was of a painstaking turn of mind. As he used to say, he "liked to account to himself" for practically everything that came in his way, down to a miserable scorpion he had found in his cabin a week before. The why and the wherefore of that scorpion—how it got on board and came to select his room rather than the pantry (which was a dark place and more what a scorpion would be partial to), and how on earth it managed to drown itself in the inkwell of his writing-desk—had exercised him infinitely. The ship within the islands was much more easily accounted for; and just as we were about to rise from table he made his pronouncement. She was, he doubted not, a ship from home lately arrived. Probably she drew too much water to cross the bar except at the top of spring tides. Therefore she went into that natural harbor to wait for a few days in preference to remaining in an open roadstead.

"That's so," confirmed the second mate suddenly, in his slightly hoarse voice. "She draws over twenty feet. She's the Liverpool ship *Sephora* with a cargo of coal. Hundred and twenty-three days from Cardiff."

10   We looked at him in surprise.

"The tugboat skipper told me when he come on board for your letters, sir," explained the young man. "He expects to take her up the river the day after tomorrow."

After thus overwhelming us with the extent of his information he slipped out of the cabin. The mate observed regretfully that he "could not account for that young fellow's whims." What prevented him telling us all about it at once, he wanted to know.

I detained him as he was making a move. For the last two days the crew had had plenty of hard work, and the night before they had very little sleep. I felt painfully that I—a stranger—was doing something unusual when I directed him to let all hands turn in without setting an anchor-watch.[3] I proposed to keep on deck myself till one o'clock or thereabouts. I would get the second mate to relieve me at that hour.

"He will turn out the cook and the steward at four," I concluded, "and then give you a call. Of course at the slightest sign of any sort of wind we'll have the hands up and make a start at once."

He concealed his astonishment. "Very well, sir." Outside the cuddy he put his head in the second mate's door to inform him of my unheard-of caprice to take a five hours' anchor-watch on myself. I heard the other raise his voice incredulously—"What? The captain himself?" Then a few more murmurs, a door closed, then another. A few moments later I went on deck.

My strangeness, which had made me sleepless, had prompted that unconventional arrangement, as if I had expected in those solitary hours of the night to get on terms with the ship of which I knew nothing, manned by men of whom I knew very little more. Fast alongside a wharf, littered like any ship in port with a tangle of unrelated things, invaded by unrelated shore people, I had hardly seen her yet properly. Now, as she lay cleared for sea, the stretch of her main deck seemed to me very fine under the stars. Very fine, very roomy for her size, and very inviting. I descended the poop and paced the waist, my mind picturing to myself the coming passage through the Malay Archipelago, down the Indian Ocean, and up the Atlantic. All its phases were familiar enough to me, every characteristic, all the alternatives which were likely to face me on the high seas— everything! . . . except the novel responsibility of command. But I took heart from the reasonable thought that the ship was like other ships, the men like other men, and that the sea was not likely to keep any special surprises expressly for my discomfiture.

Arrived at that comforting conclusion, I bethought myself of a cigar and went below to get it. All was still down there. Everybody at the after end of the ship was sleeping profoundly. I came out again on the quarter-deck, agreeably at ease in my sleeping suit on that warm, breathless night, barefooted, a glowing cigar in my teeth, and, going forward, I was met by the profound silence of the fore end of the ship. Only as I passed the door of the forecastle I heard a deep, quiet, trustful sigh of some sleeper inside. And suddenly I rejoiced in the great security of the sea as compared with the unrest of the land, in my choice of that untempted life presenting no disquieting problems, invested with an elementary moral beauty by the absolute straightforwardness of its appeal and by the singleness of its purpose.

The riding-light[4] in the fore-rigging burned with a clear, untroubled, as if symbolic, flame, confident and bright in the mysterious shades of the night. Passing on my way aft along the other side of the ship, I observed that the rope side-

15

3. A detachment of seamen kept on deck while the ship lies at anchor.   4. Special light displayed by a ship while ("riding") at anchor.

ladder, put over, no doubt, for the master of the tug when he came to fetch away our letters, had not been hauled in as it should have been. I became annoyed at this, for exactitude in small matters is the very soul of discipline. Then I reflected that I had myself peremptorily dismissed my officers from duty, and by my own act had prevented the anchor-watch being formally set and things properly attended to. I asked myself whether it was wise ever to interfere with the established routine of duties even from the kindest of motives. My action might have made me appear eccentric. Goodness only knew how that absurdly whiskered mate would "account" for my conduct, and what the whole ship thought of that informality of their new captain. I was vexed with myself.

Not from compunction certainly, but, as it were mechanically, I proceeded to get the ladder in myself. Now a side-ladder of that sort is a light affair and comes in easily, yet my vigorous tug, which should have brought it flying on board, merely recoiled upon my body in a totally unexpected jerk. What the devil! . . . I was so astounded by the immovableness of that ladder that I remained stockstill, trying to account for it to myself like that imbecile mate of mine. In the end, of course, I put my head over the rail.

20   The side of the ship made an opaque belt of shadow on the darkling glassy shimmer of the sea. But I saw at once something elongated and pale floating very close to the ladder. Before I could form a guess a faint flash of phosphorescent light, which seemed to issue suddenly from the naked body of a man, flickered in the sleeping water with the elusive, silent play of summer lightning in a night sky. With a gasp I saw revealed to my stare a pair of feet, the long legs, a broad livid back immersed right up to the neck in a greenish cadaverous glow. One hand, awash, clutched the bottom rung of the ladder. He was complete but for the head. A headless corpse! The cigar dropped out of my gaping mouth with a tiny plop and a short hiss quite audible in the absolute stillness of all things under heaven. At that I suppose he raised up his face, a dimly pale oval in the shadow of the ship's side. But even then I could only barely make out down there the shape of his black-haired head. However, it was enough for the horrid, frost-bound sensation which had gripped me about the chest to pass off. The moment of vain exclamations was past too. I only climbed on the spare spar and leaned over the rail as far as I could, to bring my eyes nearer to that mystery floating alongside.

As he hung by the ladder, like a resting swimmer, the sea-lightning played about his limbs at every stir; and he appeared in it ghastly, silvery, fish-like. He remained as mute as a fish, too. He made no motion to get out of the water, either. It was inconceivable that he should not attempt to come on board, and strangely troubling to suspect that perhaps he did not want to. And my first words were prompted by just that troubled incertitude.

"What's the matter?" I asked in my ordinary tone, speaking down to the face upturned exactly under mine.

"Cramp," it answered, no louder. Then slightly anxious, "I say, no need to call any one."

25   "I was not going to," I said.

"Are you alone on deck?"

"Yes."

I had somehow the impression that he was on the point of letting go the ladder to swim away beyond my ken—mysterious as he came. But, for the moment, this being appearing as if he had risen from the bottom of the sea (it was certainly the nearest land to the ship) wanted only to know the time. I told him. And he, down there, tentatively:

"I suppose your captain's turned in?"

"I am sure he isn't," I said.

He seemed to struggle with himself, for I heard something like the low, bitter murmur of doubt. "What's the good?" His next words came out with a hesitating effort.

"Look here, my man. Could you call him out quietly?"

I thought the time had come to declare myself.

"*I* am the captain."

I heard a "By Jove!" whispered at the level of the water. The phosphorescence flashed in the swirl of the water all about his limbs, his other hand seized the ladder.

"My name's Leggatt."

The voice was calm and resolute. A good voice. The self-possession of that man had somehow induced a corresponding state in myself. It was very quietly that I remarked:

"You must be a good swimmer."

"Yes. I've been in the water practically since nine o'clock. The question for me now is whether I am to let go this ladder and go on swimming till I sink from exhaustion or—to come on board here."

I felt this was no mere formula of desperate speech, but a real alternative in the view of a strong soul. I should have gathered from this that he was young; indeed, it is only the young who are ever confronted by such clear issues. But at the time it was pure intuition on my part. A mysterious communication was established already between us two—in the face of that silent, darkened tropical sea. I was young, too; young enough to make no comment. The man in the water began suddenly to climb up the ladder, and I hastened away from the rail to fetch some clothes.

Before entering the cabin I stood still, listening in the lobby at the foot of the stairs. A faint snore came through the closed door of the chief mate's room. The second mate's door was on the hook, but the darkness in there was absolutely soundless. He, too, was young and could sleep like a stone. Remained the steward, but he was not likely to wake up before he was called. I got a sleeping suit out of my room, and, coming back on deck, saw the naked man from the sea sitting on the main-hatch, glimmering white in the darkness, his elbows on his knees and his head in his hands. In a moment he had concealed his damp body in a sleeping suit of the same gray-stripe pattern as the one I was wearing, and followed me like my double on the poop. Together we moved right aft, barefooted, silent.

30

35

40

"What is it?" I asked in a deadened voice, taking the lighted lamp out of the binnacle, and raising it to his face.

"An ugly business."

He had rather regular features; a good mouth; light eyes under somewhat heavy, dark eyebrows; a smooth, square forehead; no growth on his cheeks; a small, brown mustache, and a well-shaped, round chin. His expression was concentrated, meditative, under the inspecting light of the lamp I held up to his face; such as a man thinking hard in solitude might wear. My sleeping suit was just right for his size. A well-knit young fellow of twenty-five at most. He caught his lower lip with the edge of white, even teeth.

45 "Yes," I said, replacing the lamp in the binnacle. The warm, heavy tropical night closed upon his head again.

"There's a ship over there," he murmured.

"Yes, I know. The *Sephora*. Did you know of us?"

"Hadn't the slightest idea. I am the mate of her—" He paused and corrected himself. "I should say I *was*."

"Aha! Something wrong?"

50 "Yes. Very wrong indeed. I've killed a man."

"What do you mean? Just now?"

"No, on the passage. Weeks ago. Thirty-nine south. When I say a man—"

"Fit of temper," I suggested confidently.

The shadowy, dark head, like mine, seemed to nod imperceptibly above the ghostly gray of my sleeping suit. It was, in the night, as though I had been faced by my own reflection in the depths of a sombre and immense mirror.

55 "A pretty thing to have to own up to for a Conway[5] boy," murmured my double distinctly.

"You're a Conway boy?"

"I am," he said, as if startled. Then, slowly . . . "Perhaps you too . . ."

It was so; but being a couple of years older I had left before he joined. After a quick interchange of dates a silence fell; and I thought suddenly of my absurd mate with his terrific whiskers and the "Bless my soul—you don't say so" type of intellect. My double gave me an inkling of his thoughts by saying:

"My father's a parson in Norfolk. Do you see me before a judge and jury on that charge? For myself I can't see the necessity. There are fellows that an angel from heaven—And I am not that. He was one of those creatures that are just simmering all the time with a silly sort of wickedness. Miserable devils that have no business to live at all. He wouldn't do his duty and wouldn't let anybody else do theirs. But what's the good of talking! You know well enough the sort of ill-conditioned snarling cur . . ."

60 He appealed to me as if our experiences had been as identical as our clothes. And I knew well enough the pestiferous danger of such a character where there are no means of legal repression. And I knew well enough also that my double

5. The wooden battleship *Conway* was used to train young officers for the Royal Navy and merchant service.

there was no homicidal ruffian. I did not think of asking him for details, and he told me the story roughly in brusque, disconnected sentences. I needed no more. I saw it all going on as though I were myself inside that other sleeping suit.

"It happened while we were setting a reefed foresail, at dusk. Reefed foresail! You understand the sort of weather. The only sail we had left to keep the ship running; so you may guess what it had been like for days. Anxious sort of job, that. He gave me some of his cursed insolence at the sheet.[6] I tell you I was overdone with this terrific weather that seemed to have no end to it. Terrific, I tell you—and a deep ship. I believe the fellow himself was half crazed with funk. It was no time for gentlemanly reproof, so I turned round and felled him like an ox. He up and at me. We closed just as an awful sea made for the ship. All hands saw it coming and took to the rigging, but I had him by the throat, and went on shaking him like a rat, the men above us yelling. 'Look out! Look out!' Then a crash as if the sky had fallen on my head. They say that for over ten minutes hardly anything was to be seen of the ship—just the three masts and a bit of the forecastle head and of the poop all awash driving along in a smother of foam. It was a miracle that they found us, jammed together behind the forebits. It's clear that I meant business, because I was holding him by the throat still when they picked us up. He was black in the face. It was too much for them. It seems they rushed us aft together, gripped as we were, screaming 'Murder!' like a lot of lunatics, and broke into the cuddy. And the ship running for her life, touch and go all the time, any minute her last in a sea fit to turn your hair gray only a-looking at it. I understand that the skipper, too, started raving like the rest of them. The man had been deprived of sleep for more than a week, and to have this spring on him at the height of a furious gale nearly drove him out of his mind. I wonder they didn't fling me overboard after getting the carcass of their precious shipmate out of my fingers. They had rather a job to separate us, I've been told. A sufficiently fierce story to make an old judge and a respectable jury sit up a bit. The first thing I heard when I came to myself was the maddening howling of that endless gale, and on that the voice of the old man. He was hanging on to my bunk, staring into my face out of his sou'wester.

" 'Mr. Leggatt, you have killed a man. You can act no longer as chief mate of this ship.' "

His care to subdue his voice made it sound monotonous. He rested a hand on the end of the skylight to steady himself with, and all that time did not stir a limb, so far as I could see. "Nice little tale for a quiet tea party," he concluded in the same tone.

One of my hands, too, rested on the end of the skylight; neither did I stir a limb, so far as I knew. We stood less than a foot from each other. It occurred to me that if old "Bless my soul—you don't say so" were to put his head up the companion and catch sight of us, he would think he was seeing double, or imagine himself come upon a scene of weird witchcraft: the strange captain having a

6. Rope or chain attached to the lower corner of a sail used for shortening or slackening it.

quiet confabulation by the wheel with his own gray ghost. I became very much concerned to prevent anything of the sort. I heard the other's soothing undertone:

65   "My father's a parson in Norfolk," it said. Evidently he had forgotten he had told me this important fact before. Truly a nice little tale.

"You had better slip down into my stateroom now," I said, moving off stealthily. My double followed my movements; our bare feet made no sound; I let him in, closed the door with care, and, after giving a call to the second mate, returned on deck for my relief.

"Not much sign of any wind yet," I remarked when he approached.

"No, sir. Not much," he assented sleepily in his hoarse voice, with just enough deference, no more, and barely suppressing a yawn.

"Well, that's all you have to look out for. You have got your orders."

70   "Yes, sir."

I paced a turn or two on the poop and saw him take up his position face forward with his elbow in the ratlines of the mizzen-rigging before I went below. The mate's faint snoring was still going on peacefully. The cuddy lamp was burning over the table on which stood a vase with flowers, a polite attention from the ship's provision merchant—the last flowers we should see for the next three months at the very least. Two bunches of bananas hung from the beam symmetrically, one on each side of the rudder-casing. Everything was as before in the ship—except that two of her captain's sleeping suits were simultaneously in use, one motionless in the cuddy, the other keeping very still in the captain's stateroom.

It must be explained here that my cabin had the form of the capital letter L, the door being within the angle and opening into the short part of the letter. A couch was to the left, the bedplace to the right; my writing-desk and the chronometers' table faced the door. But any one opening it, unless he stepped right inside, had no view of what I call the long (or vertical) part of the letter. It contained some lockers surmounted by a bookcase; and a few clothes, a thick jacket or two, caps, oilskin coat, and such-like, hung on hooks. There was at the bottom of that part a door opening into my bathroom, which could be entered also directly from the saloon. But that way was never used.

The mysterious arrival had discovered the advantage of this particular shape. Entering my room, lighted strongly by a big bulkhead lamp swung on gimbals above my writing-desk, I did not see him anywhere till he stepped out quietly from behind the coats hung in the recessed part.

"I heard somebody moving about, and went in there at once," he whispered.

75   I, too, spoke under my breath.

"Nobody is likely to come in here without knocking and getting permission."

He nodded. His face was thin and the sunburn faded, as though he had been ill. And no wonder. He had been, I heard presently, kept under arrest in his cabin for nearly nine weeks. But there was nothing sickly in his eyes or in his expression. He was not a bit like me, really; yet, as we stood leaning over my bedplace, whispering side by side, with our dark heads together and our backs to the door, anybody bold enough to open it stealthily would have been treated to the uncanny sight of a double captain busy talking in whispers with his other self.

"But all this doesn't tell me how you came to hang on to our side-ladder," I inquired, in the hardly audible murmurs we used, after he had told me something more of the proceedings on board the *Sephora* once the bad weather was over.

"When we sighted Java Head[7] I had had time to think all those matters out several times over. I had six weeks of doing nothing else, and with only an hour or so every evening for a tramp on the quarterdeck."

He whispered, his arms folded on the side of my bedplace, staring through the open port. And I could imagine perfectly the manner of this thinking out—a stubborn if not a steadfast operation; something of which I should have been perfectly incapable.

"I reckoned it would be dark before we closed with the land," he continued, so low that I had to strain my hearing, near as we were to each other, shoulder touching shoulder almost. "So I asked to speak to the old man. He always seemed very sick when he came to see me—as if he could not look me in the face. You know, that foresail saved the ship. She was too deep to have run long under bare poles. And it was I that managed to set it for him. Anyway, he came. When I had him in my cabin—he stood by the door looking at me as if I had the halter round my neck already—I asked him right away to leave my cabin door unlocked at night while the ship was going through Sunda Straits. There would be the Java coast within two or three miles, off Anjer Point. I wanted nothing more. I've had a prize for swimming my second year in the Conway."

"I can believe it," I breathed out.

"God only knows why they locked me in every night. To see some of their faces you'd have thought they were afraid I'd go about at night strangling people. Am I a murdering brute? Do I look it? By Jove! if I had been he wouldn't have trusted himself like that into my room. You'll say I might have chucked him aside and bolted out, there and then—it was dark already. Well, no. And for the same reason I wouldn't think of trying to smash the door. There would have been a rush to stop me at the noise, and I did not mean to get into a confounded scrimmage. Somebody else might have got killed—for I would not have broken out only to get chucked back, and I did not want any more of that work. He refused, looking more sick than ever. He was afraid of the men, and also of that old second mate of his who had been sailing with him for years—a gray-headed old humbug; and his steward, too, had been with him devil knows how long— seventeen years or more—a dogmatic sort of loafer who hated me like poison, just because I was the chief mate. No chief mate ever made more than one voyage in the *Sephora*, you know. Those two old chaps ran the ship. Devil only knows what the skipper wasn't afraid of (all his nerve went to pieces altogether in that

80

7. A famous landmark for clipper ships engaged in the China trade on the western end of Java, the southern entrance to the Sunda Straits mentioned below; the killing thus took place some 1,500 miles south of the present scene.

hellish spell of bad weather we had)—of what the law would do to him—of his wife, perhaps. Oh yes! she's on board. Though I don't think she would have meddled. She would have been only too glad to have me out of the ship in any way. The 'brand of Cain'[8] business, don't you see? That's all right. I was ready enough to go off wandering on the face of the earth—and that was price enough to pay for an Abel of that sort. Anyhow, he wouldn't listen to me. 'This thing must take its course. I represent the law here.' He was shaking like a leaf. 'So you won't?' 'No!' 'Then I hope you will be able to sleep on that," I said, and turned my back on him. 'I wonder that *you* can,' cries he, and locks the door.

"Well, after that, I couldn't. Not very well. That was three weeks ago. We have had a slow passage through the Java Sea; drifted about Carimata[9] for ten days. When we anchored here they thought, I suppose, it was all right. The nearest land (and that's five miles) is the ship's destination; the consul would soon set about catching me; and there would have been no object in bolting to these islets there. I don't suppose there's a drop of water on them. I don't know how it was, but tonight that steward, after bringing me my supper, went out to let me eat it, and left the door unlocked. And I ate it—all there was, too. After I had finished I strolled out on the quarterdeck. I don't know that I meant to do anything. A breath of fresh air was all I wanted, I believe. Then a sudden temptation came over me. I kicked off my slippers and was in the water before I had made up my mind fairly. Somebody heard the splash and they raised an awful hullabaloo. "He's gone! Lower the boats! He's committed suicide! No, he's swimming.' Certainly I was swimming. It's not easy for a swimmer like me to commit suicide by drowning. I landed on the nearest islet before the boat left the ship's side. I heard them pulling about in the dark, hailing, and so on, but after a bit they gave up. Everything quieted down and the anchorage became as still as death. I sat down on a stone and began to think. I felt certain they would start searching for me at daylight. There was no place to hide on those stony things—and if there had been, what would have been the good? But now I was clear of that ship I was not going back. So after a while I took off all my clothes, tied them up in a bundle with a stone inside, and dropped them in the deep water on the outer side of that islet. That was suicide enough for me. Let them think what they liked, but I didn't mean to drown myself. I meant to swim till I sank—but that's not the same thing. I struck out for another of these little islands, and it was from that one that I first saw your riding-light. Something to swim for. I went on easily, and on the way I came upon a flat rock a foot or two above water. In the daytime, I dare say, you might make it out with a glass from your poop. I scrambled up on it and rested myself for a bit. Then I made another start. That last spell must have been over a mile."

His whisper was getting fainter and fainter, and all the time he stared straight out through the porthole, in which there was not even a star to be seen. I had not interrupted him. There was something that made comment impossible, in

8. Genesis 4:15.   9. The Karimata Islands in the straits between Borneo and Sumatra, some 300 miles northeast of the Sunda Straits.

his narrative, or perhaps in himself; a sort of feeling, a quality, which I can't find a name for. And when he ceased, all I found was a futile whisper, "So you swam for our light?"

"Yes—straight for it. It was something to swim for. I couldn't see any stars low down because the coast was in the way, and I couldn't see the land, either. The water was like glass. One might have been swimming in a confounded thousand feet deep cistern with no place for scrambling out anywhere; but what I didn't like was the notion of swimming round and round like a crazed bullock before I gave out; and as I didn't mean to go back . . . No. Do you see me being hauled back, stark naked, off one of these little islands by the scruff of the neck and fighting like a wild beast? Somebody would have got killed for certain, and I did not want any of that. So I went on. Then your ladder—"

"Why didn't you hail the ship?" I asked, a little louder.

He touched my shoulder lightly. Lazy footsteps came right over our heads and stopped. The second mate had crossed from the other side of the poop and might have been hanging over the rail, for all we knew.

"He couldn't hear us talking—could he?" My double breathed into my very ear anxiously.

His anxiety was an answer, a sufficient answer, to the question I had put to him. An answer containing all the difficulty of that situation. I closed the port-hole quietly, to make sure. A louder word might have been overheard.

"Who's that?" he whispered then.

"My second mate. But I don't know much more of the fellow than you do."

And I told him a little about myself. I had been appointed to take charge while I least expected anything of the sort, not quite a fortnight ago. I didn't know either the ship or the people. Hadn't had the time in port to look about me or size anybody up. And as to the crew, all they knew was that I was appointed to take the ship home. For the rest, I was almost as much of a stranger on board as himself, I said. And at the moment I felt it most acutely. I felt that it would take very little to make me a suspect person in the eyes of the ship's company.

He had turned about meantime; and we, the two strangers in the ship, faced each other in identical attitudes.

"Your ladder—" he murmured, after a silence. "Who'd have thought of finding a ladder hanging over at night in a ship anchored out here! I felt just then a very unpleasant faintness. After the life I've been leading for nine weeks, anybody would have got out of condition. I wasn't capable of swimming round as far as your rudder-chains. And, lo and behold! there was a ladder to get hold of. After I gripped it I said to myself, 'What's the good?' When I saw a man's head looking over I thought I would swim away presently and leave him shouting—in whatever language it was. I didn't mind being looked at. I—I liked it. And then you speaking to me so quietly—as if you had expected me—made me hold on a little longer. It had been a confounded lonely time—I don't mean while swimming. I was glad to talk a little to somebody that didn't belong to the *Sephora*. As to asking for the captain, that was a mere impulse. It could have been no use, with all the ship knowing about me and the other people pretty certain to be

90

95

round here in the morning. I don't know—I wanted to be seen, to talk with somebody, before I went on. I don't know what I would have said. . . . 'Fine night, isn't it?' or something of the sort."

"Do you think they will be round here presently?" I asked, with some incredulity.

"Quite likely," he said faintly.

He looked extremely haggard all of a sudden. His head rolled on his shoulders.

"H'm. We shall see then. Meantime get into that bed," I whispered. "Want help? There."

100   It was a rather high bedplace with a set of drawers underneath. This amazing swimmer really needed the lift I gave him by seizing his leg. He tumbled in, rolled over on his back, and flung one arm across his eyes. And then, with his face nearly hidden, he must have looked exactly as I used to look in that bed. I gazed upon my other self for a while before drawing across carefully the two green serge curtains which ran on a brass rod. I thought for a moment of pinning them together for greater safety, but I sat down on the couch, and once there I felt unwilling to rise and hunt for a pin. I would do it in a moment. I was extremely tired, in a peculiarly intimate way, by the strain of stealthiness, by the effort of whispering, and the general secrecy of this excitement. It was three o'clock by now, and I had been on my feet since nine, but I was not sleepy; I could not have gone to sleep. I sat there, fagged out, looking at the curtains, trying to clear my mind of the confused sensation of being in two places at once, and greatly bothered by an exasperating knocking in my head. It was a relief to discover suddenly that it was not in my head at all, but on the outside of the door. Before I could collect myself, the words "Come in" were out of my mouth, and the steward entered with a tray, bringing in my morning coffee. I had slept, after all, and I was so frightened that I shouted, "This way! I am here, steward," as though he had been miles away. He put down the tray on the table next the couch and only then said, very quietly, "I can see you are here, sir." I felt him give me a keen look, but I dared not meet his eyes just then. He must have wondered why I had drawn the curtains of my bed before going to sleep on the couch. He went out, hooking the door open as usual.

I heard the crew washing decks above me. I knew I would have been told at once if there had been any wind. Calm, I thought, and I was doubly vexed. Indeed, I felt dual more than ever. The steward reappeared suddenly in the doorway. I jumped up from the couch so quickly that he gave a start.

"What do you want here?"

"Close your port, sir—they are washing decks."

"It is closed," I said, reddening.

105   "Very well, sir." But he did not move from the doorway and returned my stare in an extraordinary, equivocal manner for a time. Then his eyes, wavered, all his expression changed, and in a voice unusually gentle, almost coaxingly.

"May I come in to take the empty cup away, sir?"

"Of course!" I turned my back on him while he popped in and out. Then I unhooked and closed the door and even pushed the bolt. This sort of thing could not go on very long. The cabin was as hot as an oven, too. I took a peep at my double, and discovered that he had not moved; his arm was still over his eyes; but his chest heaved, his hair was wet, his chin glistened with perspiration. I reached over him and opened the port.

"I must show myself on deck," I reflected.

Of course, theoretically, I could do what I liked, with no one to say nay to me within the whole circle of the horizon; but to lock my cabin door and take the key away I did not dare. Directly I put my head out of the companion I saw the group of my two officers, the second mate barefooted, the chief mate in long india-rubber boots, near the break of the poop, and the steward half-way down the poop ladder talking to them eagerly. He happened to catch sight of me and dived, the second ran down on the main deck shouting some order or other, and the chief mate came to meet me, touching his cap.

There was a sort of curiosity in his eye that I did not like. I don't know whether the steward had told them that I was "queer" only, or downright drunk, but I know the man meant to have a good look at me. I watched him coming with a smile which, as he got into point-blank range, took effect and froze his very whiskers. I did not give him time to open his lips. 110

"Square the yards by lifts and braces before the hands go to breakfast."

It was the first particular order I had given on board that ship; and I stayed on deck to see it executed too. I had felt the need of asserting myself without loss of time. That sneering young cub got taken down a peg or two on that occasion, and I also seized the opportunity of having a good look at the face of every fore-mast man as they filed past me to go to the after braces. At breakfast time, eating nothing myself, I presided with such frigid dignity that the two mates were only too glad to escape from the cabin as soon as decency permitted; and all the time the dual working of my mind distracted me almost to the point of insanity. I was constantly watching myself, my secret self, as dependent on my actions as my own personality, sleeping in that bed, behind that door which faced me as I sat at the head of the table. It was very much like being mad, only it was worse, because one was aware of it.

I had to shake him for a solid minute, but when at last he opened his eyes it was in the full possession of his senses, with an inquiring look.

"All's well so far," I whispered. "Now you must vanish into the bathroom."

He did so, as noiseless as a ghost, and I then rang for the steward, and facing 115 him boldly, directed him to tidy up my stateroom while I was having my bath— "and be quick about it." As my tone admitted of no excuses, he said, "Yes, sir," and ran off to fetch his dustpan and brushes. I took a bath and did most of my dressing, splashing, and whistling softly for the steward's edification, while the secret sharer of my life stood drawn bolt upright in that little space, his face looking very sunken in daylight, his eyelids lowered under the stern, dark line of his eyebrows drawn together by a slight frown.

When I left him there to go back to my room the steward was finishing dusting. I sent for the mate and engaged him in some insignificant conversation. It was, as it were, trifling with the terrific character of his whiskers; but my object was to give him an opportunity for a good look at my cabin. And then I could at last shut, with a clear conscience, the door of my stateroom and get my double back into the recessed part. There was nothing else for it. He had to sit still on a small folding stool, half smothered by the heavy coats hanging there. We listened to the steward going into the bathroom out of the saloon, filling the water-bottles there, scrubbing the bath, setting things to rights, whisk, bang, clatter—out again into the saloon—turn the key—click. Such was my scheme for keeping my second self invisible. Nothing better could be contrived under the circumstances. And there we sat: I at my writing-desk ready to appear busy with some papers, he behind me, out of sight of the door. It would not have been prudent to talk in daytime; and I could not have stood the excitement of that queer sense of whispering to myself. Now and then, glancing over my shoulder, I saw him far back there, sitting rigidly on the low stool, his bare feet close together, his arms folded, his head hanging on his breast—and perfectly still. Anybody would have taken him for me.

I was fascinated by it myself. Every moment I had to glance over my shoulder. I was looking at him when a voice outside the door said:

"Beg pardon, sir."

"Well!" . . . I kept my eyes on him, and so when the voice outside the door announced, "There's a ship's boat coming our way, sir," I saw him give a start—the first movement he had made for hours. But he did not raise his bowed head.

120   "All right. Get the ladder over."

I hesitated. Should I whisper something to him? But what? His immobility seemed to have been never disturbed. What could I tell him he did not know already? . . . Finally I went on deck.

II

The skipper of the *Sephora* had a thin, red whisker all round his face, and the sort of complexion that goes with hair of that color; also the particular, rather smeary shade of blue in the eyes. He was not exactly a showy figure; his shoulders were high, his stature but middling—one leg slightly more bandy than the other. He shook hands, looking vaguely around. A spiritless tenacity was his main characteristic, I judged. I behaved with a politeness which seemed to disconcert him. Perhaps he was shy. He mumbled to me as if he were ashamed of what he was saying; gave his name (it was something like Archbold—but at this distance of years I hardly am sure), his ship's name, and a few other particulars of that sort, in the manner of a criminal making a reluctant and doleful confession. He had had terrible weather on the passage out—terrible—terrible—wife aboard, too.

By this time we were seated in the cabin and the steward brought in a tray with a bottle and glasses. "Thanks! No." Never took liquor. Would have some water, though. He drank two tumblerfuls. Terrible thirsty work. Ever since daylight had been exploring the islands round his ship.

"What was that for—fun?" I asked with an appearance of polite interest.

125   "No!" He sighed. "Painful duty."

As he persisted in his mumbling and I wanted my double to hear every word, I hit upon the notion of informing him that I regretted to say I was hard of hearing.

"Such a young man too!" he nodded, keeping his smeary, blue, unintelligent eyes fastened upon me. "What was the cause of it—some disease?" he inquired, without the least sympathy and as if he thought that, if so, I'd got no more than I deserved.

"Yes; disease," I admitted in a cheerful tone which seemed to shock him. But my point was gained, because he had to raise his voice to give me his tale. It is not worth while to record that version. It was just over two months since all this had happened, and he had thought so much about it that he seemed completely muddled as to its bearings, but still immensely impressed.

"What would you think of such a thing happening on board your own ship? I've had the *Sephora* for these fifteen years. I am a well-known shipmaster."

He was densely distressed—and perhaps I should have sympathized with him if I had been able to detach my mental vision from the unsuspected sharer of my cabin as though he were my second self. There he was on the other side of the bulkhead, four or five feet from us, no more, as we sat in the saloon. I looked politely at Captain Archbold (if that was his name), but it was the other I saw, in a gray sleeping suit, seated on a low stool, his bare feet close together, his arms folded, and every word said between us falling into the ears of his dark head bowed on his chest. 130

"I have been at sea now, man and boy, for seven and thirty years, and I've never heard of such a thing happening in an English ship. And that it should be my ship. Wife on board, too."

I was hardly listening to him.

"Don't you think," I said, "that the heavy sea which, you told me, came aboard just then might have killed the man? I have seen the sheer weight of a sea kill a man very neatly, by simply breaking his neck."

"Good God!" he uttered impressively, fixing his smeary blue eyes on me. "The sea! No man killed by the sea ever looked like that." He seemed positively scandalized at my suggestion. And as I gazed at him, certainly not prepared for anything original on his part, he advanced his head close to mine and thrust his tongue out at me so suddenly that I couldn't help starting back.

After scoring over my calmness in this graphic way he nodded wisely. If I had seen the sight, he assured me, I would never forget it as long as I lived. The weather was too bad to give the corpse a proper sea burial. So next day at dawn they took it up on the poop, covering its face with a bit of bunting; he read a short prayer, and then, just as it was, in its oilskins and long boots, they launched it amongst those mountainous seas that seemed ready every moment to swallow up the ship herself and the terrified lives on board of her. 135

"That reefed foresail saved you," I threw in.

"Under God—it did," he exclaimed fervently. "It was by a special mercy, I firmly believe, that it stood some of those hurricane squalls."

"It was the setting of that sail which—" I began.

"God's own hand in it," he interrupted me. "Nothing less could have done it. I don't mind telling you that I hardly dared give the order. It seemed impossible that we could touch anything without losing it, and then our last hope would have been gone."

140   The terror of that gale was on him yet. I let him go on for a bit, then said casually—as if returning to a minor subject:

"You were very anxious to give up your mate to the shore people, I believe?"

He was. To the law. His obscure tenacity on that point had in it something incomprehensible and a little awful; something, as it were, mystical, quite apart from his anxiety that he should not be suspected of "countenancing any doings of that sort." Seven and thirty virtuous years at sea, of which over twenty of immaculate command, and the last fifteen in the *Sephora*, seemed to have laid him under some pitiless obligation.

"And you know," he went on, groping shamefacedly amongst his feelings, "I did not engage that young fellow. His people had some interest with my owners. I was in a way forced to take him on. He looked very smart, very gentlemanly, and all that. But do you know—I never liked him, somehow. I am a plain man. You see, he wasn't exactly the sort for the chief mate of a ship like the *Sephora*."

I had become so connected in thoughts and impressions with the secret sharer of my cabin that I felt as if I, personally, were being given to understand that I, too, was not the sort that would have done for the chief mate of a ship like the *Sephora*. I had no doubt of it in my mind.

145   "Not at all the style of man. You understand," he insisted superfluously, looking hard at me.

I smiled urbanely. He seemed at a loss for a while.

"I suppose I must report a suicide."

"Beg pardon?"

"Sui-cide! That's what I'll have to write to my owners directly I get in."

150   "Unless you manage to recover him before tomorrow," I assented dispassionately. . . . "I mean, alive."

He mumbled something which I really did not catch, and I turned my ear to him in a puzzled manner. He fairly bawled:

"The land—I say, the mainland is at least seven miles off my anchorage."

"About that."

My lack of excitement, of curiosity, of surprise, of any sort of pronounced interest, began to arouse his distrust. But except for the felicitous pretense of deafness I had not tried to pretend anything. I had felt utterly incapable of playing the part of ignorance properly, and therefore was afraid to try. It is also certain that he had brought some ready-made suspicions with him, and that he viewed my politeness as a strange and unnatural phenomenon. And yet how else could I have received him? Not heartily! That was impossible for psychological reasons, which I need not state here. My only object was to keep off his inquiries. Surlily? Yes, but surliness might have provoked a point-blank question. From its novelty to him and from its nature, punctilious courtesy was the manner best calculated to restrain the man. But there was the danger of his breaking through my defense bluntly. I could not, I think, have met him by a direct lie, also for psychological (not moral) reasons. If he had only known how afraid I was of his putting my feeling of identity with the other to the test! But, strangely enough (I thought of it only afterward), I believe that he was not a little disconcerted by the reverse side of that weird situation, by something in me that reminded him of the man he was seeking—suggested a mysterious similitude to the young fellow he had distrusted and disliked from the first.

However that might have been the silence was not very prolonged. He took 155
another oblique step.

"I reckon I had no more than a two-mile pull to your ship. Not a bit more."

"And quite enough, too, in this awful heat," I said.

Another pause full of mistrust followed. Necessity, they say, is mother of invention, but fear, too, is not barren of ingenious suggestions. And I was afraid he would ask me point-blank for news of my other self.

"Nice little saloon, isn't it?" I remarked, as if noticing for the first time the way his eyes roamed from one closed door to the other. "And very well fitted out, too. Here, for instance," I continued, reaching over the back of my seat negligently and flinging the door open, "is my bathroom."

He made an eager movement, but hardly gave it a glance. I got up, shut the 160
door of the bathroom, and invited him to have a look round, as if I were very proud of my accommodation. He had to rise and be shown round, but he went through the business without any raptures whatever.

"And now we'll have a look at my stateroom," I declared, in a voice as loud as I dared to make it, crossing the cabin to the starboard side with purposely heavy steps.

He followed me in and gazed around. My intelligent double had vanished. I played my part.

"Very convenient—isn't it?"

"Very nice. Very comf . . ." He didn't finish, and went out brusquely as if to escape from some unrighteous wiles of mine. But it was not to be. I had been too frightened not to feel vengeful; I felt I had him on the run, and I meant to keep him on the run. My polite insistence must have had something menacing in it, because he gave in suddenly. And I did not let him off a single item: mates' rooms, pantry, storerooms, the very sail-locker, which was also under the poop—he had to look into them all. When at last I showed him out on the quarter-deck he drew a long, spiritless sigh, and mumbled dismally that he must really be going back to his ship now. I desired my mate, who had joined us, to see to the captain's boat.

The man of whiskers gave a blast on the whistle which he used to wear hang- 165
ing round his neck, and yelled, "*Sephora*'s away!" My double down there in my cabin must have heard, and certainly could not feel more relieved than I. Four fellows came running out from somewhere forward and went over the side, while my own men, appearing on deck too, lined the rail. I escorted my visitor to the gangway ceremoniously, and nearly overdid it. He was a tenacious beast. On the very ladder he lingered, and in that unique, guiltily conscientious manner of sticking to the point:

"I say . . . you . . . you don't think that—"

I covered his voice loudly.

"Certainly not. . . . I am delighted. Goodbye."

I had an idea of what he meant to say, and just saved myself by the privilege of defective hearing. He was too shaken generally to insist, but my mate, close witness of that parting, looked mystified and his face took on a thoughtful cast. As I did not want to appear as if I wished to avoid all communication with my officers, he had the opportunity to address me.

170   "Seems a very nice man. His boat's crew told our chaps a very extraordinary story, if what I am told by the steward is true. I suppose you had it from the captain, sir?"

"Yes. I had a story from the captain."

"A very horrible affair—isn't it, sir?"

"It is."

"Beats all these tales we hear about murders in Yankee ships."

175   "I don't think it beats them. I don't think it resembles them in the least."

"Bless my soul—you don't say so! But of course I've no acquaintance whatever with American ships, not I, so I couldn't go against your knowledge. It's horrible enough for me. . . . But the queerest part is that those fellows seemed to have some idea the man was hidden aboard here. They had really. Did you ever hear of such a thing?"

"Preposterous—isn't it?"

We were walking to and fro athwart the quarter-deck. No one of the crew forward could be seen (the day was Sunday), and the mate pursued:

"There was some little dispute about it. Our chaps took offense. 'As if we would harbor a thing like that,' they said. 'Wouldn't you like to look for him in our coal-hole?' Quite a tiff. But they made it up in the end. I suppose he did drown himself. Don't you, sir?"

180   "I don't suppose anything."

"You have no doubt in the matter, sir?"

"None whatever."

I left him suddenly. I felt I was producing a bad impression, but with my double down there it was most trying to be on deck. And it was almost as trying to be below. Altogether a nerve-trying situation. But on the whole I felt less torn in two when I was with him. There was no one in the whole ship whom I dared take into my confidence. Since the hands had got to know his story, it would have been impossible to pass him off for any one else, and an accidental discovery was to be dreaded now more than ever. . . .

The steward being engaged in laying the table for dinner, we could talk only with our eyes when I first went down. Later in the afternoon we had a cautious try at whispering. The Sunday quietness of the ship was against us; the stillness of air and water around her was against us; the elements, the men were against us—everything was against us in our secret partnership; time itself—for this could not go on for ever. The very trust in Providence was, I supposed, denied to his guilt. Shall I confess that this thought cast me down very much? And as to the chapter of accidents which counts for so much in the book of success, I could only hope that it was closed. For what favorable accident could be expected?

185   "Did you hear everything?" were my first words as soon as we took up our position side by side, leaning over my bedplace.

He had. And the proof of it was his earnest whisper, "The man told you he hardly dared to give the order."

I understood the reference to be to that saving foresail.

"Yes. He was afraid of it being lost in the setting."

"I assure you he never gave the order. He may think he did, but he never gave it. He stood there with me on the break of the poop after the maintopsail blew away, and whimpered about our last hope—positively whimpered about it and nothing else—and the night coming on! To hear one's skipper go on like that in such weather was enough to drive any fellow out of his mind. It worked me up into a sort of desperation. I just took it into my own hands and went away from him, boiling, and—But what's the use telling you? *You* know! . . . Do you think that if I had not been pretty fierce with them I should have got the men to do anything? Not it! The boss'en[1] perhaps? Perhaps! It wasn't a heavy sea—it was a sea gone mad! I suppose the end of the world will be something like that; and a man may have the heart to see it coming once and be done with it—but to have to face it day after day . . . I don't blame anybody. I was precious little better than the rest. Only—I was an officer of that old coal-wagon, anyhow. . . ."

"I quite understand," I conveyed that sincere assurance into his ear. He was out of breath with whispering; I could hear him pant slightly. It was all very simple. The same strung-up force which had given twenty-four men a chance, at least, for their lives had, in a sort of recoil, crushed an unworthy mutinous existence.   190

But I had no leisure to weigh the merits of the matter—footsteps in the saloon, a heavy knock. "There's enough wind to get under way with, sir." Here was the call of a new claim upon my thoughts and even upon my feelings.

"Turn the hands up," I cried through the door. "I'll be on deck directly."

I was going out to make the acquaintance of my ship. Before I left the cabin our eyes met—the eyes of the only two strangers on board. I pointed to the recessed part where the little camp-stool awaited him and laid my finger on my lips. He made a gesture—somewhat vague—a little mysterious, accompanied by a faint smile, as if of regret.

This is not the place to enlarge upon the sensations of a man who feels for the first time a ship move under his feet to his own independent word. In my case they were not unalloyed. I was not wholly alone with my command; for there was that stranger in my cabin. Or, rather, I was not completely and wholly with her. Part of me was absent. That mental feeling of being in two places at once affected me physically as if the mood of secrecy had penetrated my very soul. Before an hour had elapsed since the ship had begun to move, having occasion to ask the mate (he stood by my side) to take a compass bearing of the Pagoda, I caught myself reaching up to his ear in whispers. I say I caught myself, but enough had escaped to startle the man. I can't describe it otherwise than by saying that he shied. A grave, preoccupied manner, as though he were in possession of some perplexing intelligence, did not leave him henceforth. A little later I moved away from the rail to look at the compass with such a stealthy gait that the helmsman noticed it—and I could not help noticing the unusual roundness of his eyes. These are trifling instances, though it's to no commander's advantage

---

1. *Bosun* or *boatswain:* a petty officer in charge of the deck crew and of the rigging.

to be suspected of ludicrous eccentricities. But I was also more seriously affected. There are to a seaman certain words, gestures, that should in given conditions come as naturally, as instinctively, as the winking of a menaced eye. A certain order should spring on to his lips without thinking; a certain sign should get itself made, so to speak, without reflection. But all unconscious alertness had abandoned me. I had to make an effort of will to recall myself back (from the cabin) to the conditions of the moment. I felt that I was appearing an irresolute commander to those people who were watching me more or less critically.

195   And, besides, there were the scares. On the second day out, for instance, coming off the deck in the afternoon (I had straw slippers on my bare feet) I stopped at the open pantry door and spoke to the steward. He was doing something there with his back to me. At the sound of my voice he nearly jumped out of his skin, as the saying is, and incidentally broke a cup.

"What on earth's the matter with you?" I asked, astonished.

He was extremely confused. "Beg your pardon, sir. I made sure you were in your cabin."

"You see I wasn't."

"No, sir. I could have sworn I had heard you moving in there not a moment ago. It's most extraordinary . . . very sorry, sir."

200   I passed on with an inward shudder. I was so identified with my secret double that I did not even mention the fact in those scanty, fearful whispers we exchanged. I suppose he had made some slight noise of some kind or other. It would have been miraculous if he hadn't at one time or another. And yet, haggard as he appeared, he looked always perfectly self-controlled, more than calm—almost invulnerable. On my suggestion he remained almost entirely in the bathroom, which, upon the whole, was the safest place. There could be really no shadow of an excuse for any one ever wanting to go in there, once the steward had done with it. It was a very tiny place. Sometimes he reclined on the floor, his legs bent, his head sustained on one elbow. At others I would find him on the camp-stool, sitting in his gray sleeping suit and with his cropped dark hair like a patient, unmoved convict. At night I would smuggle him into my bedplace, and we would whisper together, with the regular footfalls of the officer of the watch passing and repassing over our heads. It was an infinitely miserable time. It was lucky that some tins of fine preserves were stowed in a locker in my stateroom; hard bread I could always get hold of; and so he lived on stewed chicken, pâté de foie gras, asparagus, cooked oysters, sardines—on all sorts of abominable sham-delicacies out of tins. My early morning coffee he always drank; and it was all I dared do for him in that respect.

Every day there was the horrible maneuvering to go through so that my room and then the bathroom should be done in the usual way. I came to hate the sight of the steward, to abhor the voice of that harmless man. I felt that it was he who would bring on the disaster of discovery. It hung like a sword over our heads.

The fourth day out, I think (we were then working down the east side of the Gulf of Siam, tack for tack,[2] in light winds and smooth water)—the fourth day, I

---

2. By a series of shiftings back and forth of sails.

say, of this miserable juggling with the unavoidable, as we sat at our evening meal, that man, whose slightest movement I dreaded, after putting down the dishes ran up on deck busily. This could not be dangerous. Presently he came down again; and then it appeared that he had remembered a coat of mine which I had thrown over a rail to dry after having been wetted in a shower which had passed over the ship in the afternoon. Sitting stolidly at the head of the table I became terrified at the sight of the garment on his arm. Of course he made for my door. There was no time to lose.

"Steward!" I thundered. My nerves were so shaken that I could not govern my voice and conceal my agitation. This was the sort of thing that made my terrifically whiskered mate tap his forehead with his forefinger. I had detected him using that gesture while talking on deck with a confidential air to the carpenter. It was too far to hear a word, but I had no doubt that this pantomime could only refer to the strange new captain.

"Yes, sir," the pale-faced steward turned resignedly to me. It was this maddening course of being shouted at, checked without rhyme or reason, arbitrarily chased out of my cabin, suddenly called into it, sent flying out of his pantry on incomprehensible errands, that accounted for the growing wretchedness of his expression.

"Where are you going with that coat?"   205

"To your room, sir."

"Is there another shower coming?"

"I'm sure I don't know, sir. Shall I go up again and see, sir?"

"No! never mind."

My object was attained, as of course my other self in there would have heard   210
everything that passed. During this interlude my two officers never raised their eyes off their respective plates; but the lip of that confounded cub, the second mate, quivered visibly.

I expected the steward to hook my coat on and come out at once. He was very slow about it; but I dominated my nervousness sufficiently not to shout after him. Suddenly I became aware (it could be heard plainly enough) that the fellow for some reason or other was opening the door of the bathroom. It was the end. The place was literally not big enough to swing a cat in. My voice died in my throat and I went stony all over. I expected to hear a yell of surprise and terror, and made a movement, but had not the strength to get on my legs. Everything remained still. Had my second self taken the poor wretch by the throat? I don't know what I could have done next moment if I had not seen the steward come out of my room, close the door, and then stand quietly by the sideboard.

"Saved," I thought. "But, no! Lost! Gone! He was gone!"

I laid my knife and fork down and leaned back in my chair. My head swam. After a while, when sufficiently recovered to speak in a steady voice, I instructed my mate to put the ship round at eight o'clock himself.

"I won't come on deck," I went on. "I think I'll turn in, and unless the wind shifts I don't want to be disturbed before midnight. I feel a bit seedy."

"You did look middling bad a little while ago," the chief mate remarked with-   215
out showing any great concern.

They both went out, and I stared at the steward clearing the table. There was nothing to be read on that wretched man's face. But why did he avoid my eyes? I asked myself. Then I thought I should like to hear the sound of his voice.

"Steward!"

"Sir!" Startled as usual.

"Where did you hang up that coat?"

220   "In the bathroom, sir." The usual anxious tone. "It's not quite dry yet, sir."

For some time longer I sat in the cuddy. Had my double vanished as he had come? But of his coming there was an explanation, whereas his disappearance would be inexplicable. . . . I went slowly into my dark room, shut the door, lighted the lamp, and for a time dared not turn round. When at last I did I saw him standing bolt upright in the narrow recessed part. It would not be true to say I had a shock, but an irresistible doubt of his bodily existence flitted through my mind. Can it be, I asked myself, that he is not visible to other eyes than mine? It was like being haunted. Motionless, with a grave face, he raised his hands slightly at me in a gesture which meant clearly, "Heavens! what a narrow escape!" Narrow indeed. I think I had come creeping quietly as near insanity as any man who has not actually gone over the border. That gesture restrained me, so to speak.

The mate with the terrific whiskers was now putting the ship on the other tack. In the moment of profound silence which follows upon the hands going to their stations I heard on the poop his raised voice: "Hard alee!"[3] and the distant shout of the order repeated on the main deck. The sails, in that light breeze, made but a faint fluttering noise. It ceased. The ship was coming round slowly; I held my breath in the renewed stillness of expectation; one wouldn't have thought that there was a single living soul on her decks. A sudden brisk shout, "Mainsail haul!" broke the spell, and in the noisy cries and rush overhead of the men running away with the main brace we two, down in my cabin, came together in our usual position by the bedplace.

He did not wait for my question. "I heard him fumbling here and just managed to squat myself down in the bath," he whispered to me. "The fellow only opened the door and put his arm in to hang the coat up. All the same. . . ."

"I never thought of that," I whispered back, even more appalled than before at the closeness of the shave, and marveling at that something unyielding in his character which was carrying him through so finely. There was no agitation in his whisper. Whoever was being driven distracted, it was not he. He was sane. And the proof of his sanity was continued when he took up the whispering again.

225   "It would never do for me to come to life again."

It was something that a ghost might have said. But what he was alluding to was his old captain's reluctant admission of the theory of suicide. It would obviously serve his turn—if I had understood at all the view which seemed to govern the unalterable purpose of his action.

"You must maroon me as soon as ever you can get amongst these islands off the Cambodje[4] shore," he went on.

___

3. That is, put the helm all the way over to the side away from the wind.   4. Cambodian.

"Maroon you! We are not living in a boy's adventure tale," I protested. His scornful whispering took me up.

"We aren't indeed! There's nothing of a boy's tale in this. But there's nothing else for it. I want no more. You don't suppose I am afraid of what can be done to me? Prison or gallows or whatever they may please. But you don't see me coming back to explain such things to an old fellow in a wig and twelve respectable tradesmen, do you? What can they know whether I am guilty or not—or of *what* I am guilty, either? That's my affair. What does the Bible say? 'Driven off the face of the earth.'⁵ Very well. I am off the face of the earth now. As I came at night so I shall go."

"Impossible!" I murmured. "You can't."

"Can't? .... Not naked like a soul on the Day of Judgment. I shall freeze on to this sleeping suit. The Last Day is not yet—and . . . you have understood thoroughly. Didn't you?"

I felt suddenly ashamed of myself. I may say truly that I understood—and my hesitation in letting that man swim away from my ship's side had been a mere sham sentiment, a sort of cowardice.

"It can't be done now till next night," I breathed out. "The ship is on the offshore tack and the wind may fail us."

"As long as I know that you understand," he whispered. "But of course you do. It's a great satisfaction to have got somebody to understand. You seem to have been there on purpose." And in the same whisper, as if we two whenever we talked had to say things to each other which were not fit for the world to hear, he added, "It's very wonderful."

We remained side by side talking in our secret way—but sometimes silent or just exchanging a whispered word or two at long intervals. And as usual he stared through the port. A breath of wind came now and again into our faces. The ship might have been moored in dock, so gently and on an even keel she slipped through the water, that did not murmur even at our passage, shadowy and silent like a phantom sea.

At midnight I went on deck, and to my mate's great surprise put the ship round on the other tack. His terrible whiskers flitted round me in silent criticism. I certainly should not have done it if it had been only a question of getting out of that sleepy gulf as quickly as possible. I believe he told the second mate, who relieved him, that it was a great want of judgment. The other only yawned. That intolerable cub shuffled about so sleepily and lolled against the rails in such a slack, improper fashion that I came down on him sharply.

"Aren't you properly awake yet?"

"Yes, sir! I am awake."

"Well, then, be good enough to hold yourself as if you were. And keep a look out. If there's any current we'll be closing with some islands long before daylight."

The east side of the gulf is fringed with islands, some solitary, others in groups. On the blue background of the high coast they seem to float on silvery patches

230

235

240

5. Genesis 4:14.

of calm water, arid and gray, or dark green and rounded like clumps of evergreen bushes, with the larger ones, a mile or two long, showing the outlines of ridges, ribs of gray rock under the dank mantle of matted leafage. Unknown to trade, to travel, almost to geography, the manner of life they harbor is an unsolved secret. There must be villages—settlements of fishermen at least—on the largest of them, and some communication with the world is probably kept up by native craft. But all that forenoon, as we headed for them, fanned along by the faintest of breezes, I saw no sign of man or canoe in the field of the telescope I kept on pointing at the scattered group.

At noon I gave no orders for a change of course, and the mate's whiskers became much concerned and seemed to be offering themselves unduly to my notice. At last I said:

"I am going to stand right in. Quite in—as far as I can take her."

The stare of extreme surprise imparted an air of ferocity also to his eyes, and he looked truly terrific for a moment.

"We're not doing well in the middle of the gulf," I continued casually. "I am going to look for the land breezes tonight."

"Bless my soul! Do you mean, sir, in the dark amongst the lot of all them islands and reefs and shoals?"

"Well, if there are any regular land breezes at all on this coast one must get close inshore to find them—mustn't one?"

"Bless my soul!" he exclaimed again under his breath. All that afternoon he wore a dreamy, comtemplative appearance which in him was a mark of perplexity. After dinner I went into my stateroom as if I meant to take some rest. There we two bent our dark heads over a half-unrolled chart lying on my bed.

"There," I said. "It's got to be Koh-ring.[6] I've been looking at it ever since sunrise. It has got two hills and a low point. It must be inhabited. And on the coast opposite there is what looks like the mouth of a biggish river—with some town, no doubt, not far up. It's the best chance for you that I can see."

"Anything. Koh-ring let it be."

He looked thoughtfully at the chart as if surveying chances and distances from a lofty height—and following with his eyes his own figure wandering on the blank land of Cochin-China, and then passing off that piece of paper clean out of sight into uncharted regions. And it was as if the ship had two captains to plan her course for her. I had been so worried and restless running up and down that I had not had the patience to dress that day. I had remained in my sleeping suit, with straw slippers and a soft floppy hat. The closeness of the heat in the gulf had been most oppressive, and the crew were used to see me wandering in that airy attire.

"She will clear the south point as she heads now," I whispered into his ear. "Goodness only knows when, though—but certainly after dark. I'll edge her in to half a mile, as far as I may be able to judge in the dark . . ."

"Be careful," he murmured warningly—and I realized suddenly that all my

6. *Koh* or *Ko* means *island;* there are a large number of islands with that prefix at the head of the Gulf of Siam, but not, apparently, a Koh-ring.

future, the only future for which I was fit, would perhaps go irretrievably to pieces in any mishap to my first command.

I could not stop a moment longer in the room. I motioned him to get out of sight and made my way on the poop. That unplayful cub had the watch. I walked up and down for a while thinking things out, then beckoned him over.

"Send a couple of hands to open the two quarter-deck ports," I said mildly.

He actually had the impudence, or else so forgot himself in his wonder at such an incomprehensible order, as to repeat:

"Open the quarter-deck ports! What for, sir?"

"The only reason you need concern yourself about is because I tell you to do so. Have them opened wide and fastened properly."

He reddened and went off, but I believe made some jeering remark to the carpenter as to the sensible practice of ventilating a ship's quarter-deck. I know he popped into the mate's cabin to impart the fact to him, because the whiskers came on deck, as it were by chance, and stole glances at me from below—for signs of lunacy or drunkenness, I suppose.

A little before supper, feeling more restless than ever, I rejoined, for a moment, my second self. And to find him sitting so quietly was surprising, like something against nature, inhuman.

I developed my plan in a hurried whisper.

"I shall stand in as close as I dare and then put her round. I shall presently find means to smuggle you out of here into the sail-locker, which communicates with the lobby. But there is an opening, a sort of square for hauling the sails out, which gives straight on the quarterdeck and which is never closed in fine weather, so as to give air to the sails. When the ship's way is deadened in stays[7] and all the hands are aft at the main braces you shall have a clear road to slip out and get overboard through the open quarter-deck port. I've had them both fastened up. Use a rope's end to lower yourself into the water so as to avoid a splash—you know. It could be heard and cause some beastly complication."

He kept silent for a while, then whispered, "I understand."

"I won't be there to see you go," I began with an effort. "The rest . . . I only hope I have understood too."

"You have. From first to last"—and for the first time there seemed to be a faltering, something strained in his whisper. He caught hold of my arm, but the ringing of the supper bell made me start. He didn't though; he only released his grip.

After supper I didn't come below again till well past eight o'clock. The faint, steady breeze was loaded with dew; and the wet, darkened sails held all there was of propelling power in it. The night, clear and starry, sparkled darkly, and the opaque, lightless patches shifting slowly amongst the low stars were the drifting islets. On the port bow there was a big one more distant and shadowily imposing by the great space of sky it eclipsed.

On opening the door I had a back view of my very own self looking at a chart.

7. When the ship's forward motion is slowed or stopped while its head is being turned toward the wind for the purpose of shifting the sail.

He had come out of the recess and was standing near the table.

"Quite dark enough," I whispered.

He stepped back and leaned against my bed with a level, quiet glance. I sat on the couch. We had nothing to say to each other. Over our heads the officer of the watch moved here and there. Then I heard him move quickly. I knew what that meant. He was making for the companion; and presently his voice was outside my door.

"We are drawing in pretty fast, sir. Land looks rather close."

270 "Very well," I answered. "I am coming on deck directly."

I waited till he was gone out of the cuddy, then rose. My double moved too. The time had come to exchange our last whispers, for neither of us was ever to hear each other's natural voice.

"Look here!" I opened a drawer and took out three sovereigns. "Take this, anyhow. I've got six and I'd give you the lot, only I must keep a little money to buy some fruit and vegetables for the crew from native boats as we go through Sunda Straits."

He shook his head.

"Take it," I urged him, whispering desperately. "No one can tell what . . ."

275 He smiled and slapped meaningly the only pocket of the sleeping jacket. It was not safe, certainly. But I produced a large old silk handkerchief of mine, and tying the three pieces of gold in a corner, pressed it on him. He was touched, I suppose, because he took it at last and tied it quickly round his waist under the jacket, on his bare skin.

Our eyes met; several seconds elapsed, till, our glances still mingled, I extended my hand and turned the lamp out. Then I passed through the cuddy, leaving the door of my room wide open. . . . "Steward!"

He was still lingering in the pantry in the greatness of his zeal, giving a rub-up to a plated cruet stand the last thing before going to bed. Being careful not to wake up the mate, whose room was opposite, I spoke in an undertone.

He looked round anxiously. "Sir!"

"Can you get me a little hot water from the galley?"

280 "I am afraid, sir, the galley fire's been out for some time now."

"Go and see."

He fled up the stairs.

"Now," I whispered loudly into the saloon—too loudly, perhaps, but I was afraid I couldn't make a sound. He was by my side in an instant—the double captain slipped past the stairs—through a tiny dark passage . . . a sliding door. We were in the sail-locker, scrambling on our knees over the sails. A sudden thought struck me. I saw myself wandering barefooted, bareheaded, the sun beating on my dark poll. I snatched off my floppy hat and tried hurriedly in the dark to ram it on my other self. He dodged and fended off silently. I wonder what he thought had come to me before he understood and suddenly desisted. Our hands met gropingly, lingered united in a steady, motionless clasp for a second. . . . No word was breathed by either of us when they separated.

I was standing quietly by the pantry door when the steward returned.

285 "Sorry, sir. Kettle barely warm. Shall I light the spirit-lamp?"

"Never mind."

I came out on deck slowly. It was now a matter of conscience to shave the land as close as possible—for now he must go overboard whenever the ship was put in stays. Must! There could be no going back for him. After a moment I walked over to leeward and my heart flew into my mouth at the nearness of the land on the bow. Under any other circumstances I would not have held on a minute longer. The second mate had followed me anxiously.

I looked on till I felt I could command my voice.

"She will weather," I said then in a quiet tone.

"Are you going to try that, sir?" he stammered out incredulously.   290

I took no notice of him and raised my tone just enough to be heard by the helmsman.

"Keep her good full."[8]

"Good full, sir."

The wind fanned my cheek, the sails slept, the world was silent. The strain of watching the dark loom of the land grow bigger and denser was too much for me. I had to shut my eyes—because the ship must go closer. She must! The stillness was intolerable. Were we standing still?

When I opened my eyes the second view started my heart with a thump. The   295 black southern hill of Koh-ring seemed to hang right over the ship like a towering fragment of the everlasting night. On that enormous mass of blackness there was not a gleam to be seen, not a sound to be heard. It was gliding irresistibly towards us and yet seemed already within reach of the hand. I saw the vague figures of the watch grouped in the waist, gazing in awed silence.

"Are you going on, sir?" inquired an unsteady voice at my elbow.

I ignored it. I had to go on.

"Keep her full. Don't check her way. That won't do now," I said warningly.

"I can't see the sails very well," the helmsman answered me, in strange, quavering tones.

Was she close enough? Already she was, I won't say in the shadow of the land,   300 but in the very blackness of it, already swallowed up as it were, gone too close to be recalled, gone from me altogether.

"Give the mate a call," I said to the young man who stood at my elbow as still as death. "And turn all hands up."

My tone had a borrowed loudness reverberated from the height of the land. Several voices cried out together, "We are all on deck, sir."

Then stillness again, with the great shadow gliding closer, towering higher, without a light, without a sound. Such a hush had fallen on the ship that she might have been a bark of the dead floating in slowly under the very gate of Erebus.

"My God! Where are we?"

It was the mate moaning at my elbow. He was thunderstruck, and as it were   305 deprived of the moral support of his whiskers. He clapped his hands and absolutely cried out, "Lost!"

---

8. That is, keep the ship's sails filled with wind.

"Be quiet," I said sternly.

He lowered his tone, but I saw the shadowy gesture of his despair. "What are we doing here?"

"Looking for the land wind."

He made as if to tear his hair, and addressed me recklessly.

310   "She will never get out. You have done it, sir. I knew it'd end in something like this. She will never weather, and you are too close now to stay. She'll drift ashore before she's round. O my God!"

I caught his arm as he was raising it to batter his poor devoted head, and shook it violently.

"She's ashore already," he wailed, trying to tear himself away.

"Is she? . . . Keep good full there!"

"Good full, sir," cried the helmsman in a frightened, thin, childlike voice.

315   I hadn't let go the mate's arm and went on shaking it. "Ready about,[9] do you hear? You go forward"—shake—"and stop there"—shake—"and hold your noise"—shake—"and see these head-sheets properly overhauled"—shake, shake—shake.

And all the time I dared not look towards the land lest my heart should fail me. I released my grip at last and he ran forward as if fleeing for dear life.

I wondered what my double there in the sail-locker thought of this commotion. He was able to hear everything—and perhaps he was able to understand why, on my conscience, it had to be thus close—no less. My first order "Hard alee!" re-echoed ominously under the towering shadow of Koh-ring as if I had shouted in a mountain gorge. And then I watched the land intently. In that smooth water and light wind it was impossible to feel the ship coming-to.[1] No! I could not feel her. And my second self was making now ready to slip out and lower himself overboard. Perhaps he was gone already. . . ?

The great black mass brooding over our very mast-heads began to pivot away from the ship's side silently. And now I forgot the secret stranger ready to depart, and remembered only that I was a total stranger to the ship. I did not know her. Would she do it? How was she to be handled?

I swung the mainyard and waited helplessly. She was perhaps stopped, and her very fate hung in the balance, with the black mass of Koh-ring like the gate of the everlasting night towering over her taffrail. What would she do now? Had she way on her[2] yet? I stepped to the side swiftly, and on the shadowy water I could see nothing except a faint phosphorescent flash revealing the glassy smoothness of the sleeping surface. It was impossible to tell—and I had not learned yet the feel of my ship. Was she moving? What I needed was something easily seen, a piece of paper, which I could throw overboard and watch. I had nothing on me. To run down for it I didn't dare. There was no time. All at once my strained, yearning stare distinguished a white object floating within a yard of the ship's side—white, on the black water. A phosphorescent flash passed under

9. That is, be ready to shift the sails (tack). The head-sheets, below, are the lines attached to the sails of the forward mast, and to overhaul is to slacken a rope by pulling it in the opposite direction to that used in hoisting a sail and thus loosening the blocks.   1. Coming to a standstill.   2. Was she moving?

it. What was that thing? . . . I recognized my own floppy hat. It must have fallen off his head . . . and he didn't bother. Now I had what I wanted—the saving mark for my eyes. But I hardly thought of my other self, now gone from the ship, to be hidden for ever from all friendly faces, to be a fugitive and a vagabond on the earth, with no brand of the curse on his sane forehead to stay a slaying hand . . . too proud to explain.

And I watched the hat—the expression of my sudden pity for his mere flesh.   320
It had been meant to save his homeless head from the dangers of the sun. And now—behold—it was saving the ship, by serving me for a mark to help out the ignorance of my strangeness. Ha! It was drifting forward, warning me just in time that the ship had gathered sternway.

"Shift the helm," I said in a low voice to the seaman standing still like a statue.

The man's eyes glistened wildly in the binnacle light as he jumped round to the other side and spun round the wheel.

I walked to the break of the poop. On the overshadowed deck all hands stood by the forebraces waiting for my order. The stars ahead seemed to be gliding from right to left. And all was so still in the world that I heard the quiet remark, "She's round," passed in a tone of intense relief between two seamen.

"Let go and haul."

The foreyards ran round with a great noise, amidst cheery cries. And now the   325
frightful whiskers made themselves heard giving various orders. Already the ship was drawing ahead. And I was alone with her. Nothing! no one in the world should stand now between us, throwing a shadow on the way of silent knowledge and mute affection; the perfect communion of a seaman with his first command.

Walking to the taffrail, I was in time to make out, on the very edge of a darkness thrown by a towering black mass like the very gateway of Erebus—yes, I was in time to catch an evanescent glimpse of my white hat left behind to mark the spot where the secret sharer of my cabin and of my thoughts, as though he were my second self, had lowered himself into the water to take his punishment: a free man, a proud swimmer striking out for a new destiny.

1912

The first paragraph of the story clearly functions as exposition, especially in describing the **setting**—the place and time of day. Its last sentence suggests something of the situation: the speaker is alone with *his* ship. It also establishes the focus and voice. In the description of the scene in the Gulf of Siam, there are some words that, though appropriate, are not necessarily inevitable. These are words that might not be used by just any narrator or in just any circumstances and so may characterize the speaker or his situation. In the first sentence alone you may notice "mysterious," "incomprehensible," even "crazy," which, though it deals with the physical irregularity of the fences, also suggests the irrational. These words arouse suspense and so further the plot, but they may also suggest something of the theme. And, since another speaker would be likely to see things somewhat differently and use different words, his choices may also characterize the speaker. Some of the details of the paragraph may also be symbolic.

QUESTIONS AND WRITING SUGGESTIONS

1. How does the second paragraph further advance the description of setting, of situation, of theme? Are any of the details here symbolic or potentially symbolic? The last sentence of this paragraph seems to relate directly to theme, though it may also help characterize the narrator. There are many such sentences in the story—an example might be "And suddenly I rejoiced in the great security of the sea . . ." (paragraph 17). Collect five or six such sentences and see how they relate not only to theme but to other elements.
2. How does paragraph 7 characterize the second mate, explain the narrator's situation, and further arouse suspense and define the theme?
3. How does the description of the episode with the scorpion (paragraph 8) characterize the chief mate and, when looked back upon later, further the plot and suspense? How does the chief mate's propensity for logical explanations relate to the theme?
4. How does the "unconventional arrangement" of the narrator-captain's standing the first anchor-watch relate to his character? to the plot? to the theme(s)?
5. When the narrator notices that the rope side-ladder has not been hauled in, he blames himself for having disturbed the ship's routine and conjectures about how he will look in the eyes of the officers and crew and how his conduct will be "accounted" for by the chief mate. All this relates to the characters of the two men, the plot or suspense, and the theme. It is just then that "the secret sharer" appears at the very end of that same ladder. Is he, then, in some way symbolic? If so, how? In the light of all that follows, is it good or bad to break the rules? Does following or breaking rules seem to have anything to do with being a captain? Explain.
6. What is the effect of paragraph 20, in which "something elongated and pale" appears at the bottom of the ladder? How many elements are involved in that description (including the first sentence of the next paragraph)?
7. When Leggatt is aboard and dressed in the captain's sleeping suit, he is described as looking like the captain's "double." That, plus Leggatt's arriving from the sea naked, looking like a fish, being phosphorescent and oblong, together with the title of the story and the narrator's seeing his first command as a test, has led a substantial number of critics and other readers to view these details as Freudian symbols and to attribute to this story a Freudian, or at least a psychological, theme. Make out the best case you can for such a reading of the story. What happens to the specifics of the situation, the characters, the plot? Which details are symbolic in your version, and which are not? Now make out the best case *against* such a reading. If you are so committed to one position or the other that you cannot see how there can be another side, pair yourself off with someone else in the class who has made the best counterargument.
8. When Leggatt tells his story, there is a shift in the focus and voice. How does this story within a story function in the plot of "The Secret Sharer"? How does it help define the character of Leggatt? How does it relate to the theme of "the double" in the larger story?
9. Why does the captain hide Leggatt rather than turn him in? How do all the elements of the story contribute to your answering this question?
10. The captain of the *Sephora* tells his version of Leggatt's crime, but the narrator says, "It is not worth while to record that version. It was just over two months since all this had happened, and . . . he seemed completely muddled . . ." (paragraph 128). Yet the narrator is telling his and Leggatt's story at a "distance of years," and there is a bit of Archbold's story in the paragraphs that follow. Write a fuller (two- or three-page) version of how the *Sephora* captain would tell the story. How does this shift in focus and voice affect the plot? the characterization of the captain of the *Sephora*? of Leggatt? of the narrator of "The Secret Sharer"? the theme?
11. Archbold believes Leggatt was too gentlemanly to be chief mate of the *Sephora*, and the narrator, so identified now with Leggatt, thinks Archbold would not consider the narrator himself a suitable chief mate (much less captain). How would you analyze this notion in terms of focus? character? symbol? theme?
12. There seems to be a turn in the story after Archbold leaves: ironically, Leggatt seems

more of a burden to the narrator, who now seems to see himself in his role as captain: "I was not wholly alone with my command; for there was that stranger in my cabin. . . . Part of me was absent" (paragraph 194). What is the effect of this feeling of split identity on the plot? How does it relate to focus? The whole story can be read as the initiation of the narrator into leadership or captaincy. How does Leggatt figure in that initiation theme? How does his character relate to it? Is he a symbol? If you think he is, of what is he a symbol? How do the final episode and final two paragraphs of the story relate to this portion of the plot, this view of Leggatt, this theme? Can you imagine this story—the story of a new captain taking over command of a strange ship, with mates not of his own choosing and not of his own "kind," of the strained relations between the new captain and the other officers, of his routine and unroutine orders, of his emotional state, and of his first daring act of seamanship, of all this—without any mention of, or presence of, or story of, a Leggatt, a secret sharer? Write a brief synopsis of such a story. Is there some way in which you might still call it "The Secret Sharer"? Who has the secret and with whom does he share it?

13. How does the captain's giving Leggatt his hat figure in the plot? What does it suggest about the narrator's character and feelings? Of what, if anything, might it be a symbol?

14. Write a sequel to "The Secret Sharer" about what happens to Leggatt after he leaves the ship, using as much evidence as you can from the elements and details of Conrad's story but with a new focus and voice.

The story that follows is funnier than, but just as meaningful as, "The Secret Sharer." It is the title story, or chapter, of a work that calls itself a novel but can also be seen as a collection of related but separable stories (indeed, many of the chapters were first published separately as stories, and a new edition of *Love Medicine* adds four new stories or chapters and rearranges the original sequence). Reading the whole novel or collection may enrich your understanding and enjoyment of the parts, but this story is, as you will see, quite wonderful, enjoyable, and understandable by itself. It is a somewhat unfamiliar world you will be entering; though nearer to us in time and space, it is perhaps even stranger than the world of "The Secret Sharer." Stop reading after paragraph 18, look at the first of the Questions and Writing Suggestions on page 273, and get your bearings.

LOUISE ERDRICH

Love Medicine

I never really done much with my life, I suppose. I never had a television. Grandma Kashpaw had one inside her apartment at the Senior Citizens, so I used to go there and watch my favorite shows. For a while she used to call me the biggest waste on the reservation and hark back to how she saved me from my own mother, who wanted to tie me in a potato sack and throw me in a slough. Sure, I was grateful to Grandma Kashpaw for saving me like that, for raising me, but gratitude gets old. After a while, stale. I had to stop thanking her. One day I told her I had paid her back in full by staying at her beck and call. I'd do anything for Grandma. She knew that. Besides, I took care of Grandpa like nobody else could, on account of what a handful he'd gotten to be.

But that was nothing. I know the tricks of mind and body inside out without ever having trained for it, because I got the touch. It's a thing you got to be born with. I got secrets in my hands that nobody ever knew to ask. Take Grandma Kashpaw with her tired veins all knotted up in her legs like clumps of blue snails. I take my fingers and I snap them on the knots. The medicine flows out of me. The touch. I run my fingers up the maps of those rivers of veins or I knock very gentle above their hearts or I make a circling motion on their stomachs, and it helps them. They feel much better. Some women pay me five dollars.

I couldn't do the touch for Grandpa, though. He was a hard nut. You know, some people fall right through the hole in their lives. It's invisible, but they come to it after time, never knowing where. There is this woman here, Lulu Lamartine, who always had a thing for Grandpa. She loved him since she was a girl and always said he was a genius. Now she says that his mind got so full it exploded.

How can I doubt that? I know the feeling when your mental power builds up too far. I always used to say that's why the Indians got drunk. Even statistically we're the smartest people on the earth. Anyhow with Grandpa I couldn't hardly believe it, because all my youth he stood out as a hero to me. When he started getting toward second childhood he went through different moods. He would stand in the woods and cry at the top of his shirt. It scared me, scared everyone, Grandma worst of all.

5   Yet he was so smart—do you believe it?—that he *knew* he was getting foolish.

He said so. He told me that December I failed school and come back on the train to Hoopdance. I didn't have nowhere else to go. He picked me up there and he said it straight out: "I'm getting into my second childhood." And then he said something else I still remember: "I been chosen for it. I couldn't say no." So I figure that a man so smart all his life—tribal chairman and the star of movies and even pictured in the statehouse and on cans of snuff—would know what he's doing by saying yes. I think he was called to second childhood like anybody else gets a call for the priesthood or the army or whatever. So I really did not listen too hard when the doctor said this was some kind of disease old people got eating too much sugar. You just can't tell me that a man who went to Washington and gave them bureaucrats what for could lose his mind from eating too much Milky Way. No, he put second childhood on himself.

Behind those songs he sings out in the middle of Mass, and back of those stories that everybody knows by heart, Grandpa is thinking hard about life. I know the feeling. Sometimes I'll throw up a smokescreen to think behind. I'll hitch up to Winnipeg and play the Space Invaders for six hours, but all the time there and back I will be thinking some fairly deep thoughts that surprise even me, and I'm used to it. As for him, if it was just the thoughts there wouldn't be no problem. Smokescreen is what irritates the social structure, see, and Grandpa has done things that just distract people to the point they want to throw him in the cookie jar where they keep the mentally insane. He's far from that, I know for sure, but even Grandma had trouble keeping her patience once he started sneaking off to Lamartine's place. He's not supposed to have his candy, and Lulu feeds it to him. That's *one* of the reasons why he goes.

Grandma tried to get me to put the touch on Grandpa soon after he began stepping out. I didn't want to, but before Grandma started telling me again what a bad state my bare behind was in when she first took me home, I thought I should at least pretend.

I put my hands on either side of Grandpa's head. You wouldn't look at him and say he was crazy. He's a fine figure of a man, as Lamartine would say, with all his hair and half his teeth, a beak like a hawk, and cheeks like the blades of a hatchet. They put his picture on all the tourist guides to North Dakota and even copied his face for artistic paintings. I guess you could call him a monument all of himself. He started grinning when I put my hands on his templates, and I knew right then he knew how come I touched him. I knew the smokescreen was going to fall.

And I was right: just for a moment it fell.   10

"Let's pitch whoopee," he said across my shoulder to Grandma.

They don't use that expression much around here anymore, but for damn sure it must have meant something. It got her goat right quick.

She threw my hands off his head herself and stood in front of him, overmatching him pound for pound, and taller too, for she had a growth spurt in middle age while he had shrunk, so now the length and breadth of her surpassed him. She glared and spoke her piece into his face about how he was off at all hours tomcatting and chasing Lamartine again and making a damn old fool of himself.

"And you got no more whoopee to pitch anymore anyhow!" she yelled at last, surprising me so my jaw just dropped, for us kids all had pretended for so long that those rustling sounds we heard from their side of the room at night never happened. She sure had pretended it, up till now, anyway. I saw that tears were in her eyes. And that's when I saw how much grief and love she felt for him. And it gave me a real shock to the system. You see I thought love got easier over the years so it didn't hurt so bad when it hurt, or feel so good when it felt good. I thought it smoothed out and old people hardly noticed it. I thought it curled up and died, I guess. Now I saw it rear up like a whip and lash.

She loved him. She was jealous. She mourned him like the dead.   15

And he just smiled into the air, trapped in the seams of his mind.

So I didn't know what to do. I was in a laundry then. They was like parents to me, the way they had took me home and reared me. I could see her point for wanting to get him back the way he was so at least she could argue with him, sleep with him, not be shamed out by Lamartine. She'd always love him. That hit me like a ton of bricks. For one whole day I felt this odd feeling that cramped my hands. When you have the touch, that's where longing gets you. I never loved like that. It made me feel all inspired to see them fight, and I wanted to go out and find a woman who I would love until one of us died or went crazy. But I'm not like that really. From time to time I heal a person all up good inside, however when it comes to the long shot I doubt that I got staying power.

And you need that, staying power, going out to love somebody. I knew this quality was not going to jump on me with no effort. So I turned my thoughts back to Grandma and Grandpa. I felt her side of it with my hands and my tangled guts, and I felt his side of it within the stretch of my mentality. He had gone out to lunch one day and never came back. He was fishing in the middle of

Matchimanito. And there was big thoughts on his line, and he kept throwing them back for even bigger ones that would explain to him, say, the meaning of how we got here and why we have to leave so soon. All in all, I could not see myself treating Grandpa with the touch, bringing him back, when the real part of him had chose to be off thinking somewhere. It was only the rest of him that stayed around causing trouble, after all, and we could handle most of it without any problem.

Besides, it was hard to argue with his reasons for doing some things. Take Holy Mass. I used to go there just every so often, when I got frustrated mostly, because even though I know the Higher Power dwells everyplace, there's something very calming about the cool greenish inside of our mission. Or so I thought, anyway. Grandpa was the one who stripped off my delusions in this matter, for it was he who busted right through what Father calls the sacred serenity of the place.

20 We filed in that time. Me and Grandpa. We sat down in our pews. Then the rosary got started up pre-Mass and that's when Grandpa filled up his chest and opened his mouth and belted out them words.

HAIL MARIE FULL OF GRACE.

He had a powerful set of lungs.

And he kept on like that. He did not let up. He hollered and he yelled them prayers, and I guess people was used to him by now, because they only muttered theirs and did not quit and gawk like I did. I was getting red-faced, I admit. I give him the elbow once or twice, but that wasn't nothing to him. He kept on. He shrieked to heaven and he pleaded like a movie actor and he pounded his chest like Tarzan in the Lord I Am Not Worthies. I thought he might hurt himself. Then after a while I guess I got used to it, and that's when I wondered: how come?

So afterwards I out and asked him. "How come? How come you yelled?"

25 "God don't hear me otherwise," said Grandpa Kashpaw.

I sweat. I broke right into a little cold sweat at my hairline because I knew this was perfectly right and for years not one damn other person had noticed it. God's been going deaf. Since the Old Testament, God's been deafening up on us. I read, see. Besides the dictionary, which I'm constantly in use of, I had this Bible once. I read it. I found there was discrepancies between then and now. It struck me. Here God used to raineth bread from clouds, smite the Phillipines, sling fire down on red-light districts where people got stabbed. He even appeared in person every once in a while. God used to pay attention, is what I'm saying.

Now there's your God in the Old Testament and there is Chippewa Gods as well. Indian Gods, good and bad, like tricky Nanabozho or the water monster, Missepeshu, who lives over in Matchimanito. That water monster was the last God I ever heard to appear. It had a weakness for young girls and grabbed one of the Pillagers off her rowboat. She got to shore all right, but only after this monster had its way with her. She's an old lady now. Old Lady Pillager. She still doesn't like to see her family fish that lake.

Our Gods aren't perfect, is what I'm saying, but at least they come around. They'll do a favor if you ask them right. You don't have to yell. But you do have to know, like I said, how to ask in the right way. That makes problems, because to ask proper was an art that was lost to the Chippewas once the Catholics gained ground. Even now, I have to wonder if Higher Power turned it back, if we got to yell, or if we just don't speak its language.

I looked around me. How else could I explain what all I had seen in my short life—King smashing his fist in things, Gordie drinking himself down to the Bismarck hospitals, or Aunt June left by a white man to wander off in the snow. How else to explain the times my touch don't work, and farther back, to the oldtime Indians who was swept away in the outright germ warfare and dirty-dog killing of the whites. In those times, us Indians was so much kindlier than now.

We took them in.   30

Oh yes, I'm bitter as an old cutworm just thinking of how they done to us and doing still.

So Grandpa Kashpaw just opened my eyes a little there. Was there any sense relying on a God whose ears was stopped? Just like the government? I says then, right off, maybe we got nothing but ourselves. And that's not much, just personally speaking. I know I don't got the cold hard potatoes it takes to understand everything. Still, there's things I'd like to do. For instance, I'd like to help some people like my Grandpa and Grandma Kashpaw get back some happiness within the tail ends of their lives.

I told you once before I couldn't see my way clear to putting the direct touch on Grandpa's mind, and I kept my moral there, but something soon happened to make me think a little bit of mental adjustment wouldn't do him and the rest of us no harm.

It was after we saw him one afternoon in the sunshine courtyard of the Senior Citizens with Lulu Lamartine. Grandpa used to like to dig there. He had his little dandelion fork out, and he was prying up them dandelions right and left while Lamartine watched him.

"He's scratching up the dirt, all right," said Grandma, watching Lamartine   35 watch Grandpa out the window.

Now Lamartine was about half the considerable size of Grandma, but you would never think of sizes anyway. They were different in an even more noticeable way. It was the difference between a house fixed up with paint and picky fence, and a house left to weather away into the soft earth, is what I'm saying. Lamartine was jacked up, latticed, shuttered, and vinyl sided, while Grandma sagged and bulged on her slipped foundations and let her hair go the silver gray of rain-dried lumber. Right now, she eyed the Lamartine's pert flowery dress with such a look it despaired me. I knew what this could lead to with Grandma. Alternating tongue storms and rock-hard silences was hard on a man, even one who didn't notice, like Grandpa. So I went fetching him.

But he was gone when I popped through the little screen door that led out on the courtyard. There was nobody out there either, to point which way they went. Just the dandelion fork quibbling upright in the ground. That gave me an idea. I snookered over to the Lamartine's door and I listened in first, then knocked. But nobody. So I went walking through the lounges and around the card tables. Still nobody. Finally it was my touch that led me to the laundry room. I cracked the door. I went in. There they were. And he was really loving her up good, boy, and she was going hell for leather. Sheets was flapping on the lines above, and washcloths, pillowcases, shirts was also flying through the air, for they was trying to clear out a place for themselves in a high-heaped but shallow laundry cart. The washers and dryers was all on, chock-full of quarters, shaking and moaning. I couldn't hear what Grandpa and the Lamartine was billing and cooing, and they couldn't hear me.

I didn't know what to do, so I went inside and shut the door.

The Lamartine wore a big curly light-brown wig. Looked like one of them squeaky little white-people dogs. Poodles they call them. Anyway, that wig is what saved us from the worse. For I could hardly shout and tell them I was in there, no more could I try and grab him. I was trapped where I was. There was nothing I could really do but hold the door shut. I was scared of somebody else upsetting in and really getting an eyeful. Turned out though, in the heat of the clinch, as I was trying to avert my eyes you see, the Lamartine's curly wig jumped off her head. And if you ever been in the midst of something and had a big change like that occur in the someone, you can't help know how it devastates your basic urges. Not only that, but her wig was almost with a life of its own. Grandpa's eyes were bugging at the change already, and swear to God if the thing didn't rear up and pop him in the face like it was going to start something. He scrambled up, Grandpa did, and the Lamartine jumped up after him all addled looking. They just stared at each other, huffing and puffing, with quizzical expression. The surprise seemed to drive all sense completely out of Grandpa's mind.

40   "The letter was what started the fire," he said. "I never would have done it."

"What letter?" said the Lamartine. She was stiff-necked now, and elegant, even bald, like some alien queen. I gave her back the wig. The Lamartine replaced it on her head, and whenever I saw her after that, I couldn't help thinking of her bald, with special powers, as if from another planet.

"That was a close call," I said to Grandpa after she had left.

But I think he had already forgot the incident. He just stood there all quiet and thoughtful. You really wouldn't think he was crazy. He looked like he was just about to say something important, explaining himself. He said something, all right, but it didn't have nothing to do with anything that made sense.

He wondered where the heck he put his dandelion fork. That's when I decided about the mental adjustment.

45   Now what was mostly our problem was not so much that he was not all there, but that what was there of him often hankered after Lamartine. If we could put a stop to that, I thought, we might be getting someplace. But here, see, my touch was of no use. For what could I snap my fingers at to make him faithful to Grandma? Like the quality of staying power, this faithfulness was invisible. I know it's something that you got to acquire, but I never known where from. Maybe there's no rhyme or reason to it, like my getting the touch, and then again maybe it's a kind of magic.

It was Grandma Kashpaw who thought of it in the end. She knows things. Although she will not admit she has a scrap of Indian blood in her, there's no doubt in my mind she's got some Chippewa. How else would you explain the way she'll be sitting there, in front of her TV story, rocking in her armchair and suddenly she turns on me, her brown eyes hard as lake-bed flint.

"Lipsha Morrissey," she'll say, "you went out last night and got drunk."

How did she know that? I'll hardly remember it myself. Then she'll say she just had a feeling or ache in the scar of her hand or a creak in her shoulder. She is constantly being told things by little aggravations in her joints or by her household appliances. One time she told Gordie never to ride with a crazy Lamartine boy. She had seen something in the polished-up tin of her bread toaster. So he didn't. Sure enough, the time came we heard how Lyman and Henry went out of control in their car, ending up in the river. Lyman swam to the top, but Henry never made it.

Thanks to Grandma's toaster, Gordie was probably spared.

Someplace in the blood Grandma Kashpaw knows things. She also remembers things, I found. She keeps things filed away. She's got a memory like them video games that don't forget your score. One reason she remembers so many details about the trouble I gave her in early life is so she can flash back her total when she needs to.

Like now. Take the love medicine. I don't know where she remembered that from. It came tumbling from her mind like an asteroid off the corner of the screen.

Of course she starts out by mentioning the time I had this accident in church and did she leave me there with wet overhalls? No she didn't. And ain't I glad? Yes I am. Now what you want now, Grandma?

But when she mentions them love medicines, I feel my back prickle at the danger. These love medicines is something of an old Chippewa specialty. No other tribe has got them down so well. But love medicines is not for the layman to handle. You don't just go out and get one without paying for it. Before you get one, even, you should go through one hell of a lot of mental condensation. You got to think it over. Choose the right one. You could really mess up your life grinding up the wrong little thing.

So anyhow, I said to Grandma I'd give this love medicine some thought. I knew the best thing was to go ask a specialist like Old Lady Pillager, who lives up in a tangle of bush and never shows herself. But the truth is I was afraid of her, like everyone else. She was known for putting the twisted mouth on people, seizing up their hearts. Old Lady Pillager was serious business, and I have always thought it best to steer clear of that whenever I could. That's why I took the powers in my own hands. That's why I did what I could.

I put my whole mentality to it, nothing held back. After a while I started to remember things I'd heard gossiped over.

I heard of this person once who carried a charm of seeds that looked like baby pearls. They was attracted to a metal knife, which made them powerful. But I didn't know where them seeds grew. Another love charm I heard about I couldn't go along with, because how was I suppose to catch frogs in the act, which it required. Them little creatures is slippery and fast. And then the powerfullest of all, the most extreme, involved nail clips and such. I wasn't anywhere near asking

Grandma to provide me all the little body bits that this last love recipe called for. I went walking around for days just trying to think up something that would work.

Well I got it. If it hadn't been the early fall of the year, I never would have got it. But I was sitting underneath a tree one day down near the school just watching people's feet go by when something tells me, look up! Look up! So I look up, and I see two honkers, Canada geese, the kind with little masks on their faces, a bird what mates for life. I see them flying right over my head naturally preparing to land in some slough on the reservation, which they certainly won't get off of alive.

It hits me, anyway. Them geese, they mate for life. And I think to myself, just what if I went out and got a pair? And just what if I fed some part—say the goose heart—of the female to Grandma and Grandpa ate the other heart? Wouldn't that work? Maybe it's all invisible, and then maybe again it's magic. Love is a stony road. We know that for sure. If it's true that the higher feelings of devotion get lodged in the heart like people say, then we'd be home free. If not, eating goose heart couldn't harm nobody anyway. I thought it was worth my effort, and Grandma Kashpaw thought so, too. She had always known a good idea when she heard one. She borrowed me Grandpa's gun.

So I went out to this particular slough, maybe the exact same slough I never got thrown in by my mother, thanks to Grandma Kashpaw, and I hunched down in a good comfortable pile of rushes. I got my gun loaded up. I ate a few of these soft baloney sandwiches Grandma made me for lunch. And then I waited. The cattails blown back and forth above my head. Them stringy blue herons was spearing up their prey. The thing I know how to do best in this world, the thing I been training for all my life, is to wait. Sitting there and sitting there was no hardship on me. I got to thinking about some funny things that happened. There was this one time that Lulu Lamartine's little blue tweety bird, a paraclete, I guess you'd call it, flown up inside her dress and got lost within there. I recalled her running out into the hallway trying to yell something, shaking. She was doing a right good jig there, cutting the rug for sure, and the thing is it *never* flown out. To this day people speculate where it went. They fear she might perhaps of crushed it in her corsets. It sure hasn't ever yet been seen alive. I thought of funny things for a while, but then I used them up, and strange things that happened started weaseling their way into my mind.

60   I got to thinking quite naturally of the Lamartine's cousin named Wristwatch. I never knew what his real name was. They called him Wristwatch because he got his father's broken wristwatch as a young boy when his father passed on. Never in his whole life did Wristwatch take his father's watch off. He didn't care if it worked, although after a while he got sensitive when people asked what time it was, teasing him. He often put it to his ear like he was listening to the tick. But it was broken for good and forever, people said so, at least that's what they thought.

Well I saw Wristwatch smoking in his pickup one afternoon and by nine that evening he was dead.

He died sitting at the Lamartine's table, too. As she told it, Wristwatch had just eaten himself a good-size dinner and she said would he take seconds on the hot dish when he fell over to the floor. They turnt him over. He was gone. But here's the strange thing: when the Senior Citizen's orderly took the pulse he noticed that the wristwatch Wristwatch wore was now working. The moment he died the wristwatch started keeping perfect time. They buried him with the watch still ticking on his arm.

I got to thinking. What if some gravediggers dug up Wristwatch's casket in two hundred years and that watch was still going? I thought what question they would ask and it was this: Whose hand wound it?

I started shaking like a piece of grass at just the thought.

Not to get off the subject or nothing. I was still hunkered in the slough. It was passing late into the afternoon and still no honkers had touched down. Now I don't need to tell you that the waiting did not get to me, it was the chill. The rushes was very soft, but damp. I was getting cold and debating to leave, when they landed. Two geese swimming here and there as big as life, looking deep into each other's little pinhole eyes. Just the ones I was looking for. So I lifted Grandpa's gun to my shoulder and I aimed perfectly, and *blam! Blam!* I delivered two accurate shots. But the thing is, them shots missed. I couldn't hardly believe it. Whether it was that the stock had warped or the barrel got bent someways, I don't quite know, but anyway them geese flown off into the dim sky, and Lipsha Morrissey was left there in the rushes with evening fallen and his two cold hands empty. He had before him just the prospect of another day of bone-cracking chill in them rushes, and the thought of it got him depressed.

Now it isn't my style, in no way, to get depressed.

So I said to myself, Lipsha Morrissey, you're a happy S.O.B. who could be covered up with weeds by now down at the bottom of this slough, but instead you're alive to tell the tale. You might have problems in life, but you still got the touch. You got the power, Lipsha Morrissey. Can't argue that. So put your mind to it and figure out how not to be depressed.

I took my advice. I put my mind to it. But I never saw at the time how my thoughts led me astray toward a tragic outcome none could have known. I ignored all the danger, all the limits, for I was tired of sitting in the slough and my feet were numb. My face was aching. I was chilled, so I played with fire. I told myself love medicine was simple. I told myself the old superstitions was just that—strange beliefs. I told myself to take the ten dollars Mary MacDonald had paid me for putting the touch on her arthritis joint, and the other five I hadn't spent yet from winning bingo last Thursday. I told myself to go down to the Red Owl store.

And here is what I did that made the medicine backfire. I took an evil shortcut. I looked at birds that was dead and froze.

All right. So now I guess you will say, "Slap a malpractice suit on Lipsha Morrissey."

I heard of those suits. I used to think it was a color clothing quack doctors had to wear so you could tell them from the good ones. Now I know better that it's law.

As I walked back from the Red Owl with the rock-hard, heavy turkeys, I argued to myself about malpractice. I thought of faith. I thought to myself that faith could be called belief against the odds and whether or not there's any proof. How does that sound? I thought how we might have to yell to be heard by Higher Power, but that's not saying it's not *there*. And that is faith for you. It's belief even when the goods don't deliver. Higher Power makes promises we all know they can't back up, but anybody ever go and slap an old malpractice suit on God? Or the U.S. government? No they don't. Faith might be stupid, but it gets us through. So what I'm heading at is this. I finally convinced myself that the real actual power to the love medicine was not the goose heart itself but the faith in the cure.

I didn't believe it, I knew it was wrong, but by then I had waded so far into my lie I was stuck there. And then I went one step further.

The next day, I cleaned the hearts away from the paper packages of gizzards inside the turkeys. Then I wrapped them hearts with a clean hankie and brung them both to get blessed up at the mission. I wanted to get official blessings from the priest, but when Father answered the door to the rectory, wiping his hands on a little towel, I could tell he was a busy man.

75   "Booshoo,[1] Father," I said. "I got a slight request to make of you this afternoon."

"What is it?" he said.

"Would you bless this package?" I held out the hankie with the hearts tied inside it.

He looked at the package, questioning it.

"It's turkey hearts," I honestly had to reply.

80   A look of annoyance crossed his face.

"Why don't you bring this matter over to Sister Martin," he said. "I have duties."

And so, although the blessing wouldn't be as powerful, I went over to the Sisters with the package.

I rung the bell, and they brought Sister Martin to the door. I had her as a music teacher, but I was always so shy then. I never talked out loud. Now, I had grown taller than Sister Martin. Looking down, I saw that she was not feeling up to snuff. Brown circles hung under her eyes.

"What's the matter?" she said, not noticing who I was.

85   "Remember me, Sister?"

She squinted up at me.

"Oh yes," she said after a moment. "I'm sorry, you're the youngest of the Kashpaws. Gordie's brother."

Her face warmed up.

"Lipsha," I said, "that's my name."

90   "Well, Lipsha," she said, smiling broad at me now, "what can I do for you?"

They always said she was the kindest-hearted of the Sisters up the hill, and she was. She brought me back into their own kitchen and made me take a big yellow wedge of cake and a glass of milk.

---

1. *Bonjour,* French for "good day."

"Now tell me," she said, nodding at my package. "What have you got wrapped up so carefully in those handkerchiefs?"

Like before, I answered honestly.

"Ah," said Sister Martin. "Turkey hearts." She waited.

"I hoped you could bless them." 95

She waited some more, smiling with her eyes. Kindhearted though she was, I began to sweat. A person could not pull the wool down over Sister Martin. I stumbled through my mind for an explanation, quick, that wouldn't scare her off.

"They're a present," I said, "for Saint Kateri's statue."

"She's not a saint yet."

"I know," I stuttered on. "In the hopes they will crown her."

"Lipsha," she said, "I never heard of such a thing." 100

So I told her. "Well the truth is," I said, "it's a kind of medicine."

"For what?"

"Love."

"Oh Lipsha," she said after a moment, "you don't need any medicine. I'm sure any girl would like you exactly the way you are."

I just sat there. I felt miserable, caught in my pack of lies. 105

"Tell you what," she said, seeing how bad I felt, "my blessing won't make any difference anyway. But there is something you can do."

I looked up at her, hopeless.

"Just be yourself."

I looked down at my plate. I knew I wasn't much to brag about right then, and I shortly became even less. For as I walked out the door I stuck my fingers in the cup of holy water that was sacred from their touches. I put my fingers in and blessed the hearts, quick, with my own hand.

I went back to Grandma and sat down in her little kitchen at the Senior Citizens. 110 I unwrapped them hearts on the table, and her hard agate eyes went soft. She said she wasn't even going to cook those hearts up but eat them raw so their power would go down strong as possible.

I couldn't hardly watch when she munched hers. Now that's true love. I was worried about how she would get Grandpa to eat his, but she told me she'd think of something and don't worry. So I did not. I was supposed to hide off in her bedroom while she put dinner on a plate for Grandpa and fixed up the heart so he'd eat it. I caught a glint of the plate she was making for him. She put that heart smack on a piece of lettuce like in a restaurant and then attached to it a little heap of boiled peas.

He sat down. I was listening in the next room.

She said, "Why don't you have some mash potato?" So he had some mash potato. Then she gave him a little piece of boiled meat. He ate that. Then she said, "Why you didn't never touch your salad yet. See that heart? I'm feeding you it because the doctor said your blood needs building up."

I couldn't help it, at that point I peeked through a crack in the door.

I saw Grandpa picking at that heart on his plate with a certain look. He didn't 115 look appetized at all, is what I'm saying. I doubted our plan was going to work.

Grandma was getting worried, too. She told him one more time, loudly, that he had to eat that heart.

"Swallow it down," she said. "You'll hardly notice it."

He just looked at her straight on. The way he looked at her made me think I was going to see the smokescreen drop a second time, and sure enough it happened.

"What you want me to eat this for so bad?" he asked her uncannily.

Now Grandma knew the jig was up. She knew that he knew she was working medicine. He put his fork down. He rolled the heart around his saucer plate.

120 "I don't want to eat this," he said to Grandma. "It don't look good."

"Why it's fresh grade-A," she told him. "One hundred percent."

He didn't ask percent what, but his eyes took on an even more warier look.

"Just go on and try it," she said, taking the salt shaker up in her hand. She was getting annoyed. "Not tasty enough? You want me to salt it for you?" She waved the shaker over his plate.

"All right, skinny white girl!" She had got Grandpa mad. Oopsy-daisy, he popped the heart into his mouth. I was about to yawn loudly and come out of the bedroom. I was about ready for this crash of wills to be over, when I saw he was still up to his old tricks. First he rolled it into one side of his cheek. "Mmmmm," he said. Then he rolled it into the other side of his cheek. "Mmmmmmmm," again. Then he stuck his tongue out with the heart on it and put it back, and there was no time to react. He had pulled Grandma's leg once too far. Her goat was got. She was so mad she hopped up quick as a wink and slugged him between the shoulderblades to make him swallow.

125 Only thing is, he choked.

He choked real bad. A person can choke to death. You ever sit down at a restaurant table and up above you there is a list of instructions what to do if something slides down the wrong pipe? It sure makes you chew slow, that's for damn sure. When Grandpa fell off his chair better believe me that little graphic illustrated poster fled into my mind. I jumped out the bedroom. I done everything within my power that I could do to unlodge what was choking him. I squeezed underneath his rib cage. I socked him in the back. I was desperate. But here's the factor of decision: he wasn't choking on the heart alone. There was more to it than that. It was other things that choked him as well. It didn't seem like he wanted to struggle or fight. Death came and tapped his chest, so he went just like that. I'm sorry all through my body at what I done to him with that heart, and there's those who will say Lipsha Morrissey is just excusing himself off the hook by giving song and dance about how Grandpa gave up.

Maybe I can't admit what I did. My touch had gone worthless, that is true. But here is what I seen while he lay in my arms.

You hear a person's life will flash before their eyes when they're in danger. It was him in danger, not me, but it was *his* life come over me. I saw him dying, and it was like someone pulled the shade down in a room. His eyes clouded over and squeezed shut, but just before that I looked in. He was still fishing in the middle of Matchimanito. Big thoughts was on his line and he had half a case of beer in the boat. He waved at me, grinned, and then the bobber went under.

Grandma had gone out of the room crying for help. I bunched my force up in my hands and I held him. I was so wound up I couldn't even breathe. All the moments he had spent with me, all the times he had hoisted me on his shoulders or pointed into the leaves was concentrated in that moment. Time was flashing back and forth like a pinball machine. Lights blinked and balls hopped and rubber bands chirped, until suddenly I realized the last ball had gone down the drain and there was nothing. I felt his force leaving him, flowing out of Grandpa never to return. I felt his mind weakening. The bobber going under in the lake. And I felt the touch retreat back into the darkness inside my body, from where it came.

One time, long ago, both of us were fishing together. We caught a big old   130
snapper what started towing us around like it was a motor. "This here fishline is pretty damn good," Grandpa said. "Let's keep this turtle on and see where he takes us." So we rode along behind that turtle, watching as from time to time it surfaced. The thing was just about the size of a washtub. It took us all around the lake twice, and as it was traveling, Grandpa said something as a joke. "Lipsha," he said, "we are glad your mother didn't want you because we was always looking for a boy like you who would tow us around the lake."

"I ain't no snapper. Snappers is so stupid they stay alive when their head's chopped off," I said.

"That ain't stupidity," said Grandpa. "Their brain's just in their heart, like yours is."

When I looked up, I knew the fuse had blown between my heart and my mind and that a terrible understanding was to be given.

Grandma got back into the room and I saw her stumble. And then she went down too. It was like a house you can't hardly believe has stood so long, through years of record weather, suddenly goes down in the worst yet. It makes sense, is what I'm saying, but you still can't hardly believe it. You think a person you know has got through death and illness and being broke and living on commodity rice will get through anything. Then they fold and you see how fragile were the stones that underpinned them. You see how instantly the ground can shift you thought was solid. You see the stop signs and the yellow dividing markers of roads you traveled and all the instructions you had played according to vanish. You see how all the everyday things you counted on was just a dream you had been having by which you run your whole life. She had been over me, like a sheer overhang of rock dividing Lipsha Morrissey from outer space. And now she went underneath. It was as though the banks gave way on the shores of Matchimanito, and where Grandpa's passing was just the bobber swallowed under by his biggest thought, her fall was the house and the rock under it sliding after, sending half the lake splashing up to the clouds.

Where there was nothing.   135

You play them games never knowing what you see. When I fell into the dream alongside of both of them I saw that the dominions I had defended myself from anciently was but delusions of the screen. Blips of light. And I was scot-free now, whistling through space.

I don't know how I come back. I don't know from where. They was slapping my face when I arrived back at Senior Citizens and they was oxygenating her. I saw her chest move, almost unwilling. She sighed the way she would when somebody bothered her in the middle of a row of beads she was counting. I think it irritated her to no end that they brought her back. I knew from the way she looked after they took the mask off, she was not going to forgive them disturbing her restful peace. Nor was she forgiving Lipsha Morrissey. She had been stepping out onto the road of death, she told the children later at the funeral. I asked was there any stop signs or dividing markers on that road, but she clamped her lips in a vise the way she always done when she was mad.

Which didn't bother me. I knew when things had cleared out she wouldn't have no choice. I was not going to speculate where the blame was put for Grandpa's death. We was in it together. She had slugged him between the shoulders. My touch had failed him, never to return.

All the blood children and the took-ins, like me, came home from Minneapolis and Chicago, where they had relocated years ago. They stayed with friends on the reservation or with Aurelia or slept on Grandma's floor. They were struck down with grief and bereavement to be sure, every one of them. At the funeral I sat down in the back of the church with Albertine. She had gotten all skinny and ragged haired from cramming all her years of study into two or three. She had decided that to be a nurse was not enough for her so she was going to be a doctor. But the way she was straining her mind didn't look too hopeful. Her eyes were bloodshot from driving and crying. She took my hand. From the back we watched all the children and the mourners as they hunched over their prayers, their hands stuffed full of Kleenex. It was someplace in that long sad service that my vision shifted. I began to see things different, more clear. The family kneeling down turned to rocks in a field. It struck me how strong and reliable grief was, and death. Until the end of time, death would be our rock.

140   So I had perspective on it all, for death gives you that. All the Kashpaw children had done various things to me in their lives—shared their folks with me, loaned me cash, beat me up in secret—and I decided, because of death, then and there I'd call it quits. If I ever saw King again, I'd shake his hand. Forgiving somebody else made the whole thing easier to bear.

Everybody saw Grandpa off into the next world. And then the Kashpaws had to get back to their jobs, which was numerous and impressive. I had a few beers with them and I went back to Grandma, who had sort of got lost in the shuffle of everybody being sad about Grandpa and glad to see one another.

Zelda had sat beside her the whole time and was sitting with her now. I wanted to talk to Grandma, say how sorry I was, that it wasn't her fault, but only mine. I would have, but Zelda gave me one of her looks of strict warning as if to say, "I'll take care of Grandma. Don't horn in on the women."

If only Zelda knew, I thought, the sad realities would change her. But of course I couldn't tell the dark truth.

It was evening, late. Grandma's light was on underneath a crack in the door. About a week had passed since we buried Grandpa. I knocked first but there wasn't no answer, so I went right in. The door was unlocked. She was there but she didn't notice me at first. Her hands were tied up in her rosary, and her gaze was fully absorbed in the easy chair opposite her, the one that had always been

Grandpa's favorite. I stood there, staring with her, at the little green nubs in the cloth and plastic armrest covers and the sad little hair-tonic stain he had made on the white doily where he laid his head. For the life of me I couldn't figure what she was staring at. Thin space. Then she turned.

"He ain't gone yet," she said.

Remember that chill I luckily didn't get from waiting in the slough? I got it now. I felt it start from the very center of me, where fear hides, waiting to attack. It spiraled outward so that in minutes my fingers and teeth were shaking and clattering. I knew she told the truth. She seen Grandpa. Whether or not he had been there is not the point. She had *seen* him, and that meant anybody else could see him, too. Not only that but, as is usually the case with these here ghosts, he had a certain uneasy reason to come back. And of course Grandma Kashpaw had scanned it out.

I sat down. We sat together on the couch watching his chair out of the corner of our eyes. She had found him sitting in his chair when she walked in the door.

"It's the love medicine, my Lipsha," she said. "It was stronger than we thought. He came back even after death to claim me to his side."

I was afraid. "We shouldn't have tampered with it," I said. She agreed. For a while we sat still. I don't know what she thought, but my head felt screwed on backward. I couldn't accurately consider the situation, so I told Grandma to go to bed. I would sleep on the couch keeping my eye on Grandpa's chair. Maybe he would come back and maybe he wouldn't. I guess I feared the one as much as the other, but I got to thinking, see, as I lay there in darkness, that perhaps even through my terrible mistakes some good might come. If Grandpa did come back, I thought he'd return in his right mind. I could talk with him. I could tell him it was all my fault for playing with power I did not understand. Maybe he'd forgive me and rest in peace. I hoped this. I calmed myself and waited for him all night.

He fooled me though. He knew what I was waiting for, and it wasn't what he was looking to hear. Come dawn I heard a blood-splitting cry from the bedroom and I rushed in there. Grandma turnt the lights on. She was sitting on the edge of the bed and her face looked harsh, pinched-up, gray.

"He was here," she said. "He came and laid down next to me in bed. And he touched me."

Her heart broke down. She cried. His touch was so cold. She laid back in bed after a while, as it was morning, and I went to the couch. As I lay there, falling asleep, I suddenly felt Grandpa's presence and the barrier between us like a swollen river. I felt how I had wronged him. How awful was the place where I had sent him. Behind the wall of death, he'd watched the living eat and cry and get drunk. He was lonesome, but I understood he meant no harm.

"Go back," I said to the dark, afraid and yet full of pity. "You got to be with your own kind now," I said. I felt him retreating, like a sigh, growing less. I felt his spirit as it shrunk back through the walls, the blinds, the brick courtyard of Senior Citizens. "Look up Aunt June," I whispered as he left.

I slept late the next morning, a good hard sleep allowing the sun to rise and warm the earth. It was past noon when I awoke. There is nothing, to my mind, like a long sleep to make those hard decisions that you neglect under stress of wakefulness. Soon as I woke up that morning, I saw exactly what I'd say to Grandma. I had gotten humble in the past week, not just losing the touch but getting jolted into the understanding that would prey on me from here on out. Your life feels different on you, once you greet death and understand your heart's position. You wear your life like a garment from the mission bundle sale ever after—lightly because you realize you never paid nothing for it, cherishing because you know you won't ever come by such a bargain again. Also you have the feeling someone wore it before you and someone will after. I can't explain that, not yet, but I'm putting my mind to it.

155   "Grandma," I said, "I got to be honest about the love medicine."

She listened. I knew from then on she would be listening to me the way I had listened to her before. I told her about the turkey hearts and how I had them blessed. I told her what I used as love medicine was purely a fake, and then I said to her what my understanding brought me.

"Love medicine ain't what brings him back to you, Grandma. No, it's something else. He loved you over time and distance, but he went off so quick he never got the chance to tell you how he loves you, how he doesn't blame you, how he understands. It's true feeling, not no magic. No supermarket heart could have brung him back."

She looked at me. She was seeing the years and days I had no way of knowing, and she didn't believe me. I could tell this. Yet a look came on her face. It was like the look of mothers drinking sweetness from their children's eyes. It was tenderness.

"Lipsha," she said, "you was always my favorite."

160   She took the beads off the bedpost, where she kept them to say at night, and she told me to put out my hand. When I did this, she shut the beads inside of my fist and held them there a long minute, tight, so my hand hurt. I almost cried when she did this. I don't really know why. Tears shot up behind my eyelids, and yet it was nothing. I didn't understand, except her hand was so strong, squeezing mine.

The earth was full of life and there were dandelions growing out the window, thick as thieves, already seeded, fat as big yellow plungers. She let my hand go. I got up. "I'll go out and dig a few dandelions," I told her.

Outside, the sun was hot and heavy as a hand on my back. I felt it flow down my arms, out my fingers, arrowing through the ends of the fork into the earth. With every root I prized up there was return, as if I was kin to its secret lesson. The touch got stronger as I worked through the grassy afternoon. Uncurling from me like a seed out of the blackness where I was lost, the touch spread. The spiked leaves full of bitter mother's milk. A buried root. A nuisance people dig up and throw in the sun to wither. A globe of frail seeds that's indestructible.

1982

QUESTIONS AND WRITING SUGGESTIONS

1. In the first dramatized scene, Lipsha, the narrator, at Grandma Kashpaw's request, tries to "put the touch" on Grandpa. By this time, some seventeen or eighteen paragraphs into the story, focus and voice and the setting and situation have been established; you should be getting a good idea of Lipsha's character, you should be forming some fairly definite expectations about the plot, and, with the help of the title, you should have some glimmers about the developing theme. Write down what you have observed of the structure and elements of the story and what you expect to happen. As you read on, note how your expectations are fulfilled or modified: in what ways are these surprises or changes in expectations related to plot? character? theme? and how do they define the world of the fiction? differ from your prior view of the world? To what extent are they convincing?

2. Voice is a dominant element in this story, and it is in large measure through Lipsha's voice that we infer his character. His language is ungrammatical—the story opens with "I never really *done* much . . ." and is full of phrases like "I don't got"—and his malapropisms (ludicrous misuse of words)—"templates" for "temples," "laundry" for "quandary," and "Phillipines" for "Philistines"—tend to undercut his apparent confidence in his literary skills ("Besides the dictionary, which I'm constantly in use of, I had this Bible once. I read it." [paragraph 26]). His limitations, skillfully indicated, extend to his somewhat naive view of reality—or causality: for example, his version of why Grandpa has symptoms of senility, his "thoughtful" acceptance of Grandpa's illuminating insight that God is going deaf. These errors, attitudes, and views, however, are endearing and often quite funny. Some of them will turn out, in strange ways, to seem almost wise. His kindness and good nature show through the errors and naivete, and he is capable of insights that, though naive and tender, are not ludicrous: "I thought love got easier over the years so it didn't hurt so bad when it hurt, or feel so good when it felt good" (paragraph 14); "From time to time I heal a person all up good inside, however when it comes to the long shot I doubt I got staying power. / And you need that, staying power, going out to love somebody" (paragraphs 17 and 18). His voice reveals character and theme, and his character is instrumental in this plot. A challenging topic for a paper might be to show not only how the theme is presented in this story through a character who is not well educated or intellectually profound, but how the character's very limitations contribute meaning and force to that theme.

3. How is "love medicine" related to the plot? to Grandma's and Lipsha's characters? to theme? In what way(s) may it be considered a symbol?

4. Lipsha tells the stories of Lulu's "tweety bird" that disappeared up her dress and of Wristwatch, whose broken watch started keeping time after its owner dropped dead. He then says, "Not to get off the subject or nothing" (paragraph 65). Are these stories off the subject? How do they arouse expectations? How do they function in the plot? What do they tell you of Lipsha's character? of the nature of the people on the reservation? Are they related to the theme? if so, how? When he thinks of Wristwatch's grave being dug up in two hundred years, the watch still running, and the diggers asking, "Whose hand wound it?" he says he "started shaking like a piece of grass at just the thought" (paragraph 64). Is it with awe and fear or with laughter? Do you find it awesome or funny? If there is a difference between how you feel and how you believe Lipsha feels, what is the effect? What is the relationship of this difference to plot, character, voice, and the other elements of the story? How is this episode related to the "subject" he does not mean to be getting off of when the story continues: for example, he says he fires two "accurate" shots at the geese but the shots miss; how does this affect your view of his "reliability" and thus your reading of character? plot? theme? How does it affect your reading of his glance forward, "I never saw at the time how my thoughts led me astray toward a tragic outcome none could have known" (paragraph 68)? There is a death involved. Is it "tragic"? How do you respond to it? He says he took "an evil shortcut" in practicing love medicine: does that mean that he has discovered that the old beliefs are not "superstitions" or "strange" as he thought at the time?

5. Toward the end of the story, Lipsha tells Grandma that it was not "love medicine" that brought Grandpa's ghost back to her but love itself, not magic but feeling. Grandma looks at him tenderly and says, " 'Lipsha, . . . you was always my favorite' " (paragraph 159). Explain this passage in terms of the plot (but be sure to remember Lulu); in terms of Lipsha's character; in terms of Grandma's; in terms of theme (and you might even want to think of "love medicine" as symbol).

Like "Love Medicine," "The Watcher" is also told in the first person and is funny and serious. Charlie is only eleven when the incidents occur, but the voice is that of an older Charlie. His language, like Lipsha's, is the chief source of the humor, but his is not ungrammatical or sprinkled with malapropisms; rather, it is sophisticated, wry, and a bit sardonic. It fits the serious aspects of the story, which is not, as in "Love Medicine," about love. Just as you did in reading "Love Medicine," you might stop at an early point in the story (paragraph 27 is a possibility) and take stock of your responses thus far, your attitude toward the narrator, and what, if anything, you are anticipating.

GUY VANDERHAEGHE

The Watcher

I suppose it was having a bad chest that turned me into an observer, a watcher, at an early age.

"Charlie has my chest," my mother often informed friends. "A real weakness there," she would add significantly, thumping her own wishbone soundly.

I suppose I had. Family lore had me narrowly escaping death from pneumonia at the age of four. It seems I spent an entire Sunday in delirium, soaking the sheets. Dr. Carlyle was off at the reservoir rowing in his little skiff and couldn't be reached—something for which my mother illogically refused to forgive him. She was a woman who nursed and tenaciously held dark grudges. Forever after that incident the doctor was slightlingly and coldly dismissed in conversation as a "man who betrayed the public's trust."

Following that spell of pneumonia, I regularly suffered from bouts of bronchitis, which often landed me in hospital in Fortune, forty miles away. Compared with the oxygen tent and the whacking great needles that were buried in my skinny rump there, being invalided at home was a piece of cake. Coughing and hacking, I would leaf through catalogues and read comic books until my head swam with print-fatigue. My diet was largely of my own whimsical choosing— hot chocolate and graham wafers were supplemented by sticky sweet cough-drops, which I downed one after the another until my stomach could take no more, revolted, and tossed up the whole mess.

5   With the first signs of improvement in my condition my mother moved her baby to the living-room chesterfield, where she and the radio could keep me company. The electric kettle followed me and was soon burbling in the corner, jetting steam into the air to keep my lungs moist and pliable. Because I was nei-

ther quite sick nor quite well, these were the best days of my illnesses. My stay at home hadn't yet made me bored and restless, my chest no longer hurt when I breathed, and that loose pocket of rattling phlegm meant I didn't have to worry about going back to school just yet. So I luxuriated in this steamy equatorial climate, tended by a doting mother as if I were a rare tropical orchid.

My parents didn't own a television and so my curiosity and attention were focused on my surroundings during my illnesses. I tried to squeeze every bit of juice out of them. Sooner than most children I learned that if you kept quiet and still and didn't insist on drawing attention to yourself as many kids did, adults were inclined to regard you as being one with the furniture, as significant and sentient as a hassock. By keeping mum I was treated to illuminating glances into an adult world of conventional miseries and scandals.

I wasn't sure at the age of six what a miscarriage was, but I knew that Ida Thompson had had one and that now her plumbing was buggered. And watching old lady Kuznetzky hang her washing, through a living-room window trickling with condensed kettle steam, I was able to confirm for myself the rumour that the old girl eschewed panties. As she bent over to rummage in her laundry basket I caught a brief glimpse of huge, white buttocks that shimmered in the pale spring sunshine.

I also soon knew (how I don't remember exactly) that Norma Ruggs had business with the Liquor Board Store when she shuffled by our window every day at exactly 10:50 a.m. She was always at the store door at 11:00 when they unlocked and opened up for business. At 11:15 she trudged home again, a pint of ice cream in one hand, a brown paper bag disguising a bottle of fortified wine in the other, and her blotchy complexion painted a high colour of shame.

"Poor old girl," my mother would say whenever she caught sight of Norma passing by in her shabby coat and sloppy man's overshoes. They had been in high school together, and Norma had been class brain and valedictorian. She had been an obliging, dutiful girl and still was. For the wine wasn't Norma's—the ice cream was her only vice. The booze was her husband's, a vet who had come back from the war badly crippled.

All this careful study of adults may have made me old before my time. In any case it seemed to mark me in some recognizable way as being "different" or "queer for a kid." When I went to live with my grandmother in July of 1959 she spotted it right away. Of course, she was only stating the obvious when she declared me skinny and delicate, but she also noted in her vinegary voice that my eyes had a bad habit of never letting her go, and that I was the worst case of little pitchers having big ears that she had ever come across.

I ended up at my grandmother's because in May of that year my mother's bad chest finally caught up with her, much to her and everyone else's surprise. It had been pretty generally agreed by all her acquaintances that Mabel Bradley's defects in that regard were largely imagined. Not so. A government-sponsored X-ray programme discovered tuberculosis, and she was packed off, pale and drawn with worry, for a stay in the sanatorium at Fort Qu'Appelle.

For roughly a month, until the school year ended, my father took charge of me and the house. He was a desolate, lanky, drooping weed of a man who had married late in life but nevertheless had been easily domesticated. I didn't like him much.

My father was badly wrenched by my mother's sickness and absence. He scrawled her long, untidy letters with a stub of gnawed pencil, and once he got shut of me, visited her every weekend. He was a soft and sentimental man whose eyes ran to water at the drop of a hat, or more accurately, death of a cat. Unlike his mother, my Grandma Bradley, he hadn't a scrap of flint or hard-headed common sense in him.

But then neither had any of his many brothers and sisters. It was as if the old girl had unflinchingly withheld the genetic code for responsibility and practicality from her pin-headed offspring. Life for her children was a series of thundering defeats, whirlwind calamities, or, at best, hurried strategic retreats. Businesses crashed and marriages failed, for they had—my father excepted—a taste for the unstable in partners marital and fiscal.

15   My mother saw no redeeming qualities in any of them. By and large they drank too much, talked too loudly, and raised ill-mannered children—monsters of depravity whose rudeness provided my mother with endless illustrations of what she feared I might become. "You're eating just like a pig," she would say, "exactly like your cousin Elvin." Or to my father, "You're neglecting the belt. He's starting to get as lippy as that little snot Muriel."

And in the midst, in the very eye of this familial cyclone of mishap and discontent, stood Grandma Bradley, as firm as a rock. Troubles of all kinds were laid on her doorstep. When my cousin Criselda suddenly turned big-tummied at sixteen and it proved difficult to ascertain with any exactitude the father, or even point a finger of general blame in the direction of a putative sire, she was shipped off to Grandma Bradley until she delivered. Uncle Ernie dried out on Grandma's farm and Uncle Ed hid there from several people he had sold prefab, assemble-yourself, crop-duster airplanes to.

So it was only family tradition that I should be deposited there. When domestic duties finally overwhelmed him, and I complained too loudly about fried-egg sandwiches for dinner *again,* my father left the bacon rinds hardening and curling grotesquely on unwashed plates, the slut's wool eddying along the floor in the currents of a draft, and drove the one hundred and fifty miles to the farm, *right then and there.*

My father, a dangerous man behind the wheel, took any extended trip seriously, believing the highways to be narrow, unnavigable ribbons of carnage. This trip loomed so dangerously in his mind that, rather than tear a hand from the wheel, or an eye from the road, he had me, *chronic sufferer of lung disorders,* light his cigarettes and place them carefully in his dry lips. My mother would have killed him.

"You'll love it at Grandma's," he kept saying unconvincingly, "you'll have a real boy's summer on the farm. It'll build you up, the chores and all that. And good fun too. You don't know it now, but you are living the best days of your life right now. What I wouldn't give to be a kid again. You'll love it there. There's chickens and *everything.*"

It wasn't exactly a lie. There were chickens. But the *everything*—as broad and over-   20
whelming and suggestive of possibilities as my father tried to make it sound—
didn't cover much. It certainly didn't comprehend a pony or a dog as I had
hoped, chickens being the only livestock on the place.

It turned out that my grandmother, although she had spent most of her life
on that particular piece of ground and eventually died there, didn't care much
for the farm and was entirely out of sympathy with most varieties of animal life.
She did keep chickens for the eggs, although she admitted that her spirits lifted
considerably in the fall when it came time to butcher the hens.

Her flock was a garrulous, scraggly crew that spent their days having dust
baths in the front yard, hiding their eggs, and, fleet and ferocious as hunting
cheetahs, running down scuttling lizards which they trampled and pecked to
death while their shiny, expressionless eyes shifted dizzily in their stupid heads.
The only one of these birds I felt any compassion for was Stanley the rooster, a
bedraggled male who spent his days tethered to a stake by a piece of bailer twine
looped around his leg. Poor Stanley crowed heart-rendingly in his captivity: his
comb drooped pathetically, and he was utterly crestfallen as he lecherously eyed
his bantam beauties daintily scavenging. Grandma kept him in this unnatural
bondage to prevent him fertilizing the eggs and producing blood spots in the
yolks. Being a finicky eater I approved this policy, but nevertheless felt some guilt
over Stanley.

No, the old Bradley homestead, all that encompassed by my father's *everything*, wasn't very impressive. The two-storey house, though big and solid,
needed paint and shingles. A track had been worn in the kitchen linoleum clean
through to the floorboards and a long rent in the screen door had been stitched
shut with waxed thread. The yard was little more than a tangle of thigh-high
ragweed and sowthistle to which the chickens repaired for shade. A windbreak
of spruce on the north side of the house was dying from lack of water and the
competition from Scotch thistle. The evergreens were no longer green; their sere
needles fell away from the branches at the touch of a hand.

The abandoned barn out back was flanked by two mountainous rotted piles
of manure which I remember sprouting button mushrooms after every warm
soaker of a rain. That pile of shit was the only useful thing in a yard full of junk:
wrecked cars, old wagon wheels, collapsing sheds. The barn itself was mightily
decayed. The paint had been stripped from its planks by rain, hail, and dry, blis-
tering winds, and the roof sagged like a tired nag's back. For a small boy it was
an ominous place on a summer day. The air was still and dark and heavy with
heat. At the sound of footsteps rats squeaked and scrabbled in the empty man-
gers, and the sparrows which had spattered the rafters white with their dung
whirred about and fluted ghostly cries.

In 1959 Grandma Bradley would have been sixty-nine, which made her a   25
child of the gay nineties—although the supposed gaiety of that age didn't seem
to have made much impress upon the development of her character. Physically
she was an imposing woman. Easily six feet tall, she carried a hundred and eighty
pounds on her generous frame without prompting speculation as to what she

had against girdles. She could touch the floor effortlessly with the flat of her palms and pack an eighty-pound sack of chicken feed on her shoulder. She dyed her hair auburn in defiance of local mores, and never went to town to play bridge, whist, or canasta without wearing a hat and getting dressed to the teeth. Grandma loved card games of all varieties and considered anyone who didn't a mental defective.

A cigarette always smouldered in her trap. She smoked sixty a day and rolled them as thin as knitting needles in an effort at economy. These cigarettes were so wispy and delicate they tended to get lost between her swollen fingers.

And above all she believed in plain speaking. She let me know that as my father's maroon Meteor pulled out of the yard while we stood waving goodbye on the front steps.

"Let's get things straight from the beginning," she said without taking her eyes off the car as it bumped toward the grid road. "I don't chew my words twice. If you're like any of the rest of them I've had here, you've been raised as wild as a goddamn Indian. Not one of my grandchildren have been brought up to mind. Well, you'll mind around here. I don't jaw and blow hot air to jaw and blow hot air. I belted your father when he needed it, and make no mistake I'll belt you. Is that understood?"

"Yes," I said with a sinking feeling as I watched my father's car disappear down the road, swaying from side to side as its suspension was buffeted by potholes.

30   "These bloody bugs are eating me alive," she said, slapping her arm. "I'm going in."

I trailed after her as she slopped back into the house in a pair of badly mauled, laceless sneakers. The house was filled with a half-light that changed its texture with every room. The venetian blinds were drawn in the parlour and some flies carved Immelmanns in the dark air that smelled of cellar damp. Others battered their bullet bodies *tip-tap, tip-tap* against the window-panes.

In the kitchen my grandmother put the kettle on the stove to boil for tea. After she had lit one of her matchstick smokes, she inquired through a blue haze if I was hungry.

"People aren't supposed to smoke around me," I informed her. "Because of my chest. Dad can't even smoke in our house."

"That so?" she said genially. Her cheeks collapsed as she drew on her butt. I had a hint there, if I'd only known it, of how she'd look in her coffin. "You won't like it here then," she said. "I smoke all the time."

35   I tried a few unconvincing coughs. I was ignored. She didn't respond to the same signals as my mother.

"My mother has a bad chest, too," I said. "She's in a TB sanatorium."

"So I heard," my grandmother said, getting up to fetch the whistling kettle. "Oh, I suspect she'll be as right as rain in no time with a little rest. TB isn't what it used to be. Not with all these new drugs." She considered. "That's not to say though that your father'll ever hear the end of it. Mabel was always a silly little shit that way."

I almost fell off my chair. I had never thought I'd live to hear the day my mother was called a silly little shit.

"Drink tea?" asked Grandma Bradley, pouring boiling water into a brown teapot.

I shook my head. 40

"How old are you anyway?" she asked.

"Eleven."

"You're old enough then," she said, taking down a cup from the shelf. "Tea gets the kidneys moving and carries off the poisons in the blood. That's why all the Chinese live to be so old. They all live to be a hundred."

"I don't know if my mother would like it," I said. "Me drinking tea."

"You worry a lot for a kid," she said, "don't you?" 45

I didn't know how to answer that. It wasn't a question I had ever considered. I tried to shift the conversation.

"What's there for a kid to do around here?" I said in an unnaturally inquisitive voice.

"Well, we could play cribbage."

"I don't know how to play cribbage."

She was genuinely shocked. "What!" she exclaimed. "Why, you're eleven 50 years old! Your father could count a cribbage hand when he was five. I taught all my kids to."

"I never learned how," I said. "We don't even have a deck of cards at our house. My father hates cards. Says he had too much of them as a boy."

At this my grandmother arched her eyebrows. "Is that a fact? Well, hoity-toity."

"So, since I don't play cards," I continued in a strained manner I imagined was polite, "what could I do—I mean, for fun?"

"Make your own fun," she said. "I never considered fun such a problem. Use your imagination. Take a broomstick and make like Nimrod."

"Who's Nimrod?" I asked. 55

"Pig ignorant," she said under her breath, and then louder, directly to me, "Ask me no questions and I'll tell you no lies. Drink your tea."

And that, for the time being, was that.

It's all very well to tell someone to make their own fun. It's the making of it that is the problem. In a short time I was a very bored kid. There was no one to play with, no horses to ride, no gun to shoot gophers, no dog for company. There was nothing to read except the *Country Guide* and *Western Producer*. There was nothing or nobody interesting to watch. I went through my grandmother's drawers but found nothing as surprising there as I had discovered in my parents'.

Most days it was so hot that the very idea of fun boiled out of me and evaporated. I moped and dragged myself listlessly around the house in the loose-jointed, water-boned way kids have when they can't stand anything, not even their precious selves.

On my better days I tried to take up with Stanley the rooster. Scant chance of 60 that. Tremors of panic ran through his body at my approach. He tugged desperately on the twine until he jerked his free leg out from under himself and collapsed in the dust, his heart bumping the tiny crimson scallops of his breast feathers, the black pellets of his eyes glistening, all the while shitting copiously. Finally, in the last extremes of chicken terror, he would allow me to stroke his yellow beak and finger his comb.

I felt sorry for the captive Stanley and several times tried to take him for a walk, to give him a chance to take the air and broaden his limited horizons. But this prospect alarmed him so much that I was always forced to return him to his stake in disgust while he fluttered, squawked and flopped.

So fun was a commodity in short supply. That is, until something interesting turned up during the first week of August. Grandma Bradley was dredging little watering canals with a hoe among the corn stalks on a bright blue Monday morning, and I was shelling peas into a colander on the front stoop, when a black car nosed diffidently up the road and into the yard. Then it stopped a good twenty yards short of the house as if its occupants weren't sure of their welcome. After some time, the doors opened and a man and woman got carefully out.

The woman wore turquoise-blue pedal-pushers, a sloppy black turtleneck sweater, and a gash of scarlet lipstick swiped across her white, vivid face. This was my father's youngest sister, Aunt Evelyn.

The man took her gently and courteously by the elbow and balanced her as she edged up the front yard in her high heels, careful to avoid turning an ankle on a loose stone, or in an old tyre track.

65   The thing which immediately struck me about the man was his beard—the first I had ever seen. Beards weren't popular in 1959—not in our part of the world. His was a randy, jutting, little goat's-beard that would have looked wicked on any other face but his. He was very tall and his considerable height was accented by a lack of corresponding breadth to his body. He appeared to have been racked and stretched against his will into an exceptional and unnatural anatomy. As he walked and talked animatedly, his free hand fluttered in front of my aunt. It sailed, twirled and gambolled on the air. Like a butterfly enticing a child, it seemed to lead her hypnotized across a yard fraught with perils for city-shod feet.

My grandmother laid down her hoe and called sharply to her daughter.

"Evvie!" she called. "Over here, Evvie!"

At the sound of her mother's voice my aunt's head snapped around and she began to wave jerkily and stiffly, striving to maintain a tottering balance on her high-heeled shoes. It wasn't hard to see that there was something not quite right with her. By the time my grandmother and I reached the pair, Aunt Evelyn was in tears, sobbing hollowly and jamming the heel of her palm into her front teeth.

The man was speaking calmly to her. "Control. Control. Deep, steady breaths. Think sea. Control. Control. Control. Think sea, Evelyn. Deep. Deep. Deep," he muttered.

70   "What the hell is the matter, Evelyn?" my grandmother asked sharply. "And who is *he?*"

"Evelyn is a little upset," the man said, keeping his attention focused on my aunt. "She's having one of her anxiety attacks. If you'd just give us a moment we'll clear this up. She's got to learn to handle stressful situations." He inclined his head in a priestly manner and said, "Be with the sea, Evelyn. Deep. Deep. Sink in the sea."

"It's her damn nerves again," said my grandmother.

"Yes," the man said benignly, with a smile of blinding condescension. "Sort of."

"She's been as nervous as a cut cat all her life," said my grandmother, mostly to herself.

"Momma," said Evelyn, weeping. "Momma."   75

"Slide beneath the waves, Evelyn. Down, down, down to the beautiful pearls," the man chanted softly. This was really something.

My grandmother took Aunt Evelyn by her free elbow, shook it, and said sharply, "Evelyn, shut up!" Then she began to drag her briskly toward the house. For a moment the man looked as if he had it in mind to protest, but in the end he meekly acted as a flanking escort for Aunt Evelyn as she was marched into the house. When I tried to follow, my grandmother gave me one of her looks and said definitely, "You find something to do out here."

I did. I waited a few minutes and then duck-walked my way under the parlour window. There I squatted with my knobby shoulder blades pressed against the siding and the sun beating into my face.

My grandmother obviously hadn't wasted any time with the social niceties. They were fairly into it.

"Lovers?" said my grandmother. "Is that what it's called now? Shack-up, you   80 mean."

"Oh, Momma," said Evelyn, and she was crying, "it's all right. We're going to get married."

"You believe that?" said my grandmother. "You believe that geek is going to marry you?"

"Thompson," said the geek, "my name is Thompson, Robert Thompson, and we'll marry as soon as I get my divorce. Although Lord only knows when that'll be."

"That's right," said my grandmother, "Lord only knows." Then to her daughter, "You got another one. A real prize off the midway, didn't you? Evelyn, you're a certifiable lunatic."

"I didn't expect this," said Thompson. "We came here because Evelyn has   85 had a bad time of it recently. She hasn't been eating or sleeping properly and consequently she's got herself run down. She finds it difficult to control her emotions, don't you, darling?"

I thought I heard a mild yes.

"So," said Thompson, continuing, "we decided Evelyn needs some peace and quiet before I go back to school in September."

"School," said my grandmother. "Don't tell me you're some kind of teacher?" She seemed stunned by the very idea.

"No," said Aunt Evelyn, and there was a tremor of pride in her voice that testified to her amazement that she had been capable of landing such a rare and remarkable fish. "Not a teacher. Robert's a graduate student of American Literature at the University of British Columbia."

"Hoity-toity," said Grandmother. "A graduate student. A graduate student of   90 American Literature."

"Doctoral programme," said Robert.

"And did you ever ask yourself, Evelyn, what the hell this genius is doing with you? Or is it just the same old problem with you—elevator panties? Some guy comes along and pushes the button. Up, down. Up, down."

The image this created in my mind made me squeeze my knees together deliciously and stifle a giggle.

"Mother," said Evelyn, continuing to bawl.

95 "Guys like this don't marry barmaids," said my grandmother.

"Cocktail hostess," corrected Evelyn. "I'm a cocktail hostess."

"You don't have to make any excuses, dear," said Thompson pompously. "Remember what I told you. You're past the age of being judged."

"What the hell is that supposed to mean?" said my grandmother. "And by the way, don't start handing out orders in my house. You won't be around long enough to make them stick."

"That remains to be seen," said Thompson.

100 "Let's go, Robert," said Evelyn nervously.

"Go on upstairs, Evelyn. I want to talk to your mother."

"You don't have to go anywhere," said my grandmother. "You can stay put."

"Evelyn, go upstairs." There was a pause and then I heard the sound of a chair creaking, then footsteps.

"Well," said my grandmother at last, "round one. Now for round two—get the hell out of my house."

105 "Can't do that."

"Why the hell not?"

"It's very difficult to explain," he said.

"Try."

"As you can see for yourself, Evelyn isn't well. She is very highly strung at the moment. I believe she is on the verge of a profound personality adjustment, a breakthrough." He paused dramatically. "Or breakdown."

110 "It's times like this that I wished I had a dog on the place to run off undesirables."

"The way I read it," said Thompson, unperturbed, "is that at the moment two people bulk very large in Evelyn's life. You and me. She needs the support and love of us both. You're not doing your share."

"I ought to slap your face."

"She has come home to try to get a hold of herself. We have to bury our dislikes for the moment. She needs to be handled very carefully."

"You make her sound like a trained bear. *Handled.* What that girl needs is a good talking to, and I am perfectly capable of giving her that."

115 "No, Mrs. Bradley," Thompson said firmly in that maddeningly self-assured tone of his. "If you don't mind me saying so, I think that's part of her problem. It's important now for you to just let Evelyn *be.*"

"Get out of my house," said my grandmother, at the end of her tether.

"I know it's difficult for you to understand," he said smoothly, "but if you understood the psychology of this you would see it's impossible for me to go; or for that matter, for Evelyn to go. If I leave she'll feel *I've* abandoned her. It can't be done. We're faced with a real psychological balancing act here."

"Now I've heard everything," said my grandmother. "Are you telling me you'd have the gall to move into a house where you're not wanted and just . . . just *stay there?*"

"Yes," said Thompson. "And I think you'll find me quite stubborn on this particular point."

"My God," said my grandmother. I could tell by her tone of voice that she had never come across anyone like Mr. Thompson before. At a loss for a suitable reply, she simply reiterated, "My God."

"I'm going upstairs now," said Thompson. "Maybe you could get the boy to bring in our bags while I see how Evelyn is doing. The car isn't locked." The second time he spoke his voice came from further away; I imagined him paused in the doorway. "Mrs. Bradley, please let's make this stay pleasant for Evelyn's sake."

She didn't bother answering him.

When I barged into the house some time later with conspicuous noisiness, I found my grandmother standing at the bottom of the stairs staring up the steps. "Well, I'll be damned," she said under her breath. "I've never seen anything like that. Goddamn freak." She even repeated it several times under her breath. "Goddamn freak. Goddamn freak."

Who could blame me if, after a boring summer, I felt my chest tighten with anticipation. Adults could be immensely interesting and entertaining if you knew what to watch for.

At first things were disappointingly quiet. Aunt Evelyn seldom set forth outside the door of the room she and her man inhabited by squatters' right. There was an argument, short and sharp, between Thompson and Grandmother over this. The professor claimed no one had any business prying into what Evelyn did up there. She was an adult and had the right to her privacy and her own thoughts. My grandmother claimed *she* had a right to know what was going on up there, even if nobody else thought she did.

I could have satisfied her curiosity on that point. Not much was going on up there. Several squints through the keyhole had revealed Aunt Evelyn lolling about the bedspread in a blue housecoat, eating soda crackers and sardines, and reading a stack of movie magazines she had me lug out of the trunk of the car.

Food, you see, was beginning to become something of a problem for our young lovers. Grandma rather pointedly set only three places for meals, and Evelyn, out of loyalty to her boyfriend, couldn't very well sit down and break bread with us. Not that Thompson didn't take such things in his stride. He sauntered casually and conspicuously about the house as if he owned it, even going so far as to poke his head in the fridge and rummage in it like some pale, hairless bear. At times like that my grandmother was capable of looking through him as if he didn't exist.

On the second day of his stay Thompson took up with me, which was all right as far as I was concerned. I had no objection. Why he decided to do this I'm not sure exactly. Perhaps he was looking for some kind of an ally, no matter how weak. Most likely he wanted to get under the old lady's skin. Or maybe he just couldn't bear not having anyone to tell how wonderful he was. Thompson was that kind of a guy.

I was certainly let in on the secret. He was a remarkable fellow. He dwelt at great length on those things which made him such an extraordinary human being. I may have gotten the order of precedence all wrong, but if I remember correctly there were three things which made Thompson very special and different from all the other people I would ever meet, no matter how long or hard I lived.

130   First, he was going to write a book about a poet called Allen Ginsberg[1] which was going to knock the socks off everybody who counted. It turned out he had actually met this Ginsberg the summer before in San Francisco and asked him if he could write a book about him and Ginsberg had said, Sure, why the hell not? The way Thompson described what it would be like when he published this book left me with the impression that he was going to spend most of the rest of his life riding around on people's shoulders and being cheered by a multitude of admirers.

Second, he confessed to knowing a tremendous amount about what made other people tick and how to adjust their mainsprings when they went kaflooey. He knew all this because at one time his own mainspring had gotten a little out of sorts. But now he was a fully integrated personality with a highly creative mind and a strong intuitive sense. That's why he was so much help to Aunt Evelyn in her time of troubles.

Third, he was a Buddhist.

The only one of these things which impressed me at the time was the bit about being a Buddhist. However, I was confused, because in the *Picture Book of the World's Great Religions* which we had at home, all the Buddhists were bald, and Thompson had a hell of a lot of hair, more than I had ever seen on a man. But even though he wasn't bald, he had an idol. A little bronze statue with the whimsical smile and slightly crossed eyes which he identified as Padma-sam-bhava.[2] He told me that it was a Tibetan antique he had bought in San Francisco as an object of veneration and an aid to his meditations. I asked him what a meditation was and he offered to teach me one. So I learned to recite with great seriousness and flexible intonation one of his Tibetan meditations, while my grandmother glared across her quintessentially Western parlour with unbelieving eyes.

I could soon deliver. "A king must go when his time has come. His wealth, his friends and his relatives cannot go with him. Wherever men go, wherever they stay, the effect of their past acts follows them like a shadow. Those who are in the grip of desire, the grip of existence, the grip of ignorance, move helplessly round through the spheres of life, as men or gods or as wretches in the lower regions."

135   Not that an eleven-year-old could make much of any of *that*.

---

1. American poet (1926–1997) whose epic poem *Howl* (1956) is a significant product of the Beat movement.   2. Legendary Buddhist mystic who introduced Tantric Buddhism to Tibet. His followers emphasize Tantric ritual, worship, and yoga.

Which is not to say that even an eleven-year-old could be fooled by Robert Thompson. In his stubbornness, egoism and blindness he was transparently un-Buddhalike. To watch him and my grandmother snarl and snap their teeth over that poor, dry bone, Evelyn, was evidence enough of how firmly bound we all are to the wretched wheel of life and its stumbling desires.

No, even his most effective weapon, his cool benevolence, that patina of patience and forbearance which Thompson displayed to Grandmother, could crack.

One windy day when he had coaxed Aunt Evelyn out for a walk I followed them at a distance. They passed the windbreak of spruce, and at the sagging barbed-wire fence he gallantly manipulated the wires while my aunt floundered over them in an impractical dress and crinoline. It was the kind of dippy thing she would decide to wear on a hike.

Thompson strode along through the rippling grass like a wading heron, his baggy pant-legs flapping and billowing in the wind. My aunt moved along gingerly behind him, one hand modestly pinning down her wind-teased dress in the front, the other hand plastering the back of it to her behind.

It was only when they stopped and faced each other that I realized that all the time they had been traversing the field they had been arguing. A certain vaguely communicated agitation in the attitude of her figure, the way his arm stabbed at the featureless wash of sky, implied a dispute. She turned toward the house and he caught her by the arm and jerked it. In a fifties calendar fantasy her dress lifted in the wind, exposing her panties. I sank in the grass until their seed tassels trembled against my chin. I wasn't going to miss watching this for the world.

She snapped and twisted on the end of his arm like a fish on a line. Her head was flung back in an exaggerated, antique display of despair; her head rolled grotesquely from side to side as if her neck were broken.

Suddenly Thompson began striking awkwardly at her exposed buttocks and thighs with the flat of his hand. The long, gangly arm slashed like a flail as she scampered around him, the radius of her escape limited by the distance of their linked arms.

From where I knelt in the grass I could hear nothing. I was too far off. As far as I was concerned there were no cries and no pleading. The whole scene, as I remember it, was shorn of any of the personal idiosyncrasies which manifest themselves in violence. It appeared a simple case of retribution.

That night, for the first time, my aunt came down to supper and claimed her place at the table with queenly graciousness. She wore shorts, too, for the first time, and gave a fine display of mottled, discoloured thighs which reminded me of bruised fruit. She made sure, almost as if by accident, that my grandmother had a good hard look at them.

Right out of the blue my grandmother said, "I don't want you hanging around that man any more. You stay away from him."

"Why?" I asked rather sulkily. He was the only company I had. Since my aunt's arrival Grandmother had paid no attention to me whatsoever.

It was late afternoon and we were sitting on the porch watching Evelyn squeal as she swung in the tyre swing Thompson had rigged up for me in the barn. He had thrown a length of stray rope over the runner for the sliding door and hung a tyre from it. I hadn't the heart to tell him I was too old for tyre swings.

Aunt Evelyn seemed to be enjoying it though. She was screaming and girlishly kicking up her legs. Thompson couldn't be seen. He was deep in the settled darkness of the barn, pushing her back and forth. She disappeared and reappeared according to the arc which she travelled through. Into the barn, out in the sun. Light, darkness. Light, darkness.

Grandma ignored my question. "Goddamn freak," she said, scratching a match on the porch rail and lighting one of her rollies. "Wait and see, he'll get his wagon fixed."

150   "Aunt Evelyn likes him," I noted pleasantly, just to stir things up a bit.

"Your Aunt Evelyn's screws are loose," she said sourly. "And he's the son of a bitch who owns the screwdriver that loosened them."

"He must be an awful smart fellow to be studying to be a professor at a university," I commented. It was the last dig I could chance.

"One thing I know for sure," snapped my grandmother. "He isn't smart enough to lift the toilet seat when he pees. There's evidence enough for that."

After hearing that, I took to leaving a few conspicuous droplets of my own as a matter of course on each visit. Every little bit might help things along.

155   I stood in his doorway and watched Thompson meditate. And don't think that, drenched in *satori*[3] as he was, he didn't know it. He put on quite a performance sitting on the floor in his underpants. When he came out of his trance he pretended to be surprised to see me. While he dressed we struck up a conversation.

"You know, Charlie," he said while he put on his sandals (I'd never seen a grown man wear sandals in my entire life), "you remind me of my little Padma-sambhava," he said, nodding to the idol squatting on his dresser. "For a while, you know, I thought it was the smile, but it isn't. It's the eyes."

"Its eyes are crossed," I said, none too flattered at the comparison.

"No they're not," he said good-naturedly. He tucked his shirt-tail into his pants. "The artist, the maker of that image, set them fairly close together to suggest—aesthetically speaking—the intensity of inner vision, its concentration." He picked up the idol and, looking at it, said, "These are very watchful eyes, very knowing eyes. Your eyes are something like that. From your eyes I could tell you're an intelligent boy." He paused, set Padma-sambhava back on the dresser, and asked. "Are you?"

I shrugged.

160   "Don't be afraid to say if you are," he said. "False modesty can be as corrupting as vanity. It took me twenty-five years to learn that."

"I usually get all A's on my report card," I volunteered.

"Well, that's something," he said, looking around the room for his belt. He

---

3. A state of enlightenment in Buddhism, achieved by intensive meditation.

picked a sweater off a chair and peered under it. "Then you see what's going on around here, don't you?" he asked. "You see what your grandmother is mistakenly trying to do?"

I nodded.

"That's right," he said. "You're a smart boy." He sat down on the bed. "Come here."

I went over to him. He took hold of me by the arms and looked into my eyes with all the sincerity he could muster. "You know, being intelligent means responsibilities. It means doing something worth while with your life. For instance, have you given any thought as to what you would like to be when you grow up?"

"A spy," I said.

The silly bugger laughed.

It was the persistent, rhythmic thud that first woke me, and once wakened, I picked up the undercurrent of muted clamour, of stifled struggle. The noise seeped through the beaverboard wall of the adjoining bedroom into my own, a storm of hectic urgency and violence. The floorboards of the old house squeaked; I heard what sounded like a strangled curse and moan, then a fleshy, meaty concussion which I took to be a slap. Was he killing her at last? Choking her with the silent, poisonous care necessary to escape detection?

I remembered Thompson's arm flashing frenziedly in the sunlight. My aunt's discoloured thighs. My heart creaked in my chest with fear. And after killing her? Would the madman stop? Or would he do us all in, one by one?

I got out of bed on unsteady legs. The muffled commotion was growing louder, more distinct. I padded into the hallway. The door to their bedroom was partially open, and a light showed. Terror made me feel hollow; the pit of my stomach ached.

They were both naked, something which I hadn't expected, and which came as quite a shock. What was perhaps even more shocking was the fact that they seemed not only oblivious of me, but of each other as well. She was slung around so that her head was propped on a pillow resting on the footboard of the bed. One smooth leg was draped over the edge of the bed and her heel was beating time on the floorboards (the thud which woke me) as accompaniment to Thompson's plunging body and the soft, liquid grunts of expelled air which he made with every lunge. One of her hands gripped the footboard and her knuckles were white with strain.

I watched until the critical moment, right through the growing frenzy and ardour. They groaned and panted and heaved and shuddered and didn't know themselves. At the very last he lifted his bony, hatchet face with the jutting beard to the ceiling and closed his eyes; for a moment I thought he was praying as his lips moved soundlessly. But then he began to whimper and his mouth fell open and he looked stupider and weaker than any human being I had ever seen before in my life.

"Like pigs at the trough," my grandmother said at breakfast. "With the boy up there too."

My aunt turned a deep red, and then flushed again so violently that her thin lips appeared to turn blue.

175   I kept my head down and went on shovelling porridge. Thompson still wasn't invited to the table. He was leaning against the kitchen counter, his bony legs crossed at the ankles, eating an apple he had helped himself to.

"He didn't hear anything," my aunt said uncertainly. She whispered conspiratorially across the table to Grandmother. "Not at that hour. He'd been asleep for hours."

I thought it wise, even though it meant drawing attention to myself, to establish my ignorance. "Hear what?" I inquired innocently.

"It wouldn't do any harm if he had," said Thompson, calmly biting and chewing the temptress's fruit.

"You wouldn't see it, would you?" said Grandma Bradley. "It wouldn't matter to you what he heard? You'd think that was manly."

180   "Manly has nothing to do with it. Doesn't enter into it," said Thompson in that cool way he had. "It's a fact of life, something he'll have to find out about sooner or later."

Aunt Evelyn began to cry. "Nobody is ever pleased with me," she spluttered. "I'm going crazy trying to please you both. I can't do it." She began to pull nervously at her hair. "He made me," she said finally in a confessional, humble tone to her mother.

"Evelyn," said my grandmother, "you have a place here. I would never send you away. I want you here. But he has to go. I want him to go. If he is going to rub my nose in it that way he has to go. I won't have that man under my roof."

"Evelyn isn't apologizing for anything," Thompson said. "And she isn't running away either. You can't force her to choose. It isn't healthy or fair."

"There have been other ones before you," said Grandma. "This isn't anything new for Evelyn."

185   "Momma!"

"I'm aware of that," he said stiffly, and his face vibrated with the effort to smile. "Provincial mores have never held much water with me. I like to think I'm above all that."

Suddenly my grandmother spotted me. "What are you gawking at!" she shouted. "Get on out of here!"

I didn't budge an inch.

"Leave him alone," said Thompson.

190   "You'll be out of here within a week," said Grandmother. "I swear."

"No," he said smiling. "When I'm ready."

"You'll go home and go with your tail between your legs. Last night was the last straw," she said. And by God you could tell she meant it.

Thompson gave her his beatific Buddha-grin and shook his head from side to side, very, very slowly.

A thunderstorm was brewing. The sky was a stew of dark, swollen clouds and a strange apple-green light. The temperature stood in the mid-nineties, not a breath of breeze stirred, my skin crawled and my head pounded above my eyes and through the bridge of my nose. There wasn't a thing to do except sit on the bottom step of the porch, keep from picking up a sliver in your ass, and scratch the dirt with a stick. My grandmother had put her hat on and driven into town on some unexplained business. Thompson and my aunt were upstairs in their bedroom, sunk in a stuporous, sweaty afternoon's sleep.

Like my aunt and Thompson, all the chickens had gone to roost to wait for   195
rain. The desertion of his harem had thrown the rooster into a flap. Stanley trotted neurotically around his tethering post, stopping every few circuits to beat his bedraggled pinions and crow lustily in masculine outrage. I watched him for a bit without much curiosity, and then climbed off the step and walked toward him, listlessly dragging my stick in my trail.

"Here Stanley, Stanley," I called, not entirely sure how to summon a rooster, or instil in him confidence and friendliness.

I did neither. My approach only further unhinged Stanley. His stride lengthened, the tempo of his pace increased, and his head began to dart abruptly from side to side in furtive despair. Finally, in a last desperate attempt to escape, Stanley upset himself trying to fly. He landed in a heap of disarranged, stiff, glistening feathers. I put my foot on his string and pinned him to the ground.

"Nice pretty, pretty Stanley," I said coaxingly, adopting the tone that a neighbour used with her budgie, since I wasn't sure how one talked to a bird. I slowly extended my thumb to stroke his bright-red neck feathers. Darting angrily, he struck the ball of my thumb with a snappish peck and simultaneously hit my wrist with his heel spur. He didn't hurt me, but he did startle me badly. So badly I gave a little yelp. Which made me feel foolish and more than a little cowardly.

"You son of a bitch," I said, reaching down slowly and staring into one unblinking glassy eye in which I could see my face looming larger and larger. I caught the rooster's legs and held them firmly together. Stanley crowed defiantly and showed me his wicked little tongue.

"Now, Stanley," I said, "relax, I'm just going to stroke you. I'm just going to   200
stroke you. I'm just going to pet Stanley."

No deal. He struck furiously again with a snake-like agility, and bounded in my hand, wings beating his poultry smell into my face. A real fighting cock at last. Maybe it was the weather. Perhaps his rooster pride and patience would suffer no more indignities.

The heat, the sultry menace of the gathering storm, made me feel prickly, edgy. I flicked my middle finger smartly against his tiny chicken skull, hard enough to rattle his pea-sized brain. "You like that, buster?" I asked him, and snapped him another one for good measure. He struck back again, his comb red, crested, and rubbery with fury.

I was angry myself. I turned him upside down and left him dangling, his wings drumming against the legs of my jeans. Then I righted him abruptly; he looked dishevelled, seedy and dazed.

"OK, Stanley," I said, feeling the intoxication of power. "I'm boss here, and you behave." There was a gleeful edge to my voice, which surprised me a little. I realized I was hoping this confrontation would escalate. Wishing that he would provoke me into something.

205   Strange images came into my head: the bruises on my aunt's legs; Thompson's face drained of life, lifted like an empty receptacle toward the ceiling, waiting to be filled, the tendons of his neck stark and rigid with anticipation.

I was filled with anxiety, the heat seemed to stretch me, to tug at my nerves and my skin. Two drops of sweat, as large and perfectly formed as tears, rolled out of my hairline and splashed on to the rubber toes of my runners.

"Easy, Stanley," I breathed to him, "easy," and my hand crept deliberately towards him. This time he pecked me in such a way, directly on the knuckle, that it actually hurt. I took up my stick and rapped him on the beak curtly, the prim admonishment of a schoolmarm. I didn't hit him very hard, but it was hard enough to split the length of his beak with a narrow crack. The beak fissured like the nib of a fountain pen. Stanley squawked, opened and closed his beak spasmodically, bewildered by the pain. A bright jewel of blood bubbled out of the split and gathered to a trembling bead.

"There," I said excitedly, "now you've done it. How are you going to eat with a broken beak? You can't eat anything with a broken beak. You'll starve, you stupid goddamn chicken."

A wind that smelled of rain had sprung up. It ruffled his feathers until they moved with a barely discernible crackle.

210   "Poor Stanley," I said, and at last, numbed by the pain, he allowed me to stroke the gloss of his lacquer feathers.

I wasn't strong enough or practised enough to do a clean and efficient job of wringing his neck, but I succeeded in finishing him off after two clumsy attempts. Then because I wanted to leave the impression that a skunk had made off with him, I punched a couple of holes in his breast with my jack knife and tried to dribble some blood on the ground. Poor Stanley produced only a few meagre spots; this corpse refused to bleed in the presence of its murderer. I scattered a handful of his feathers on the ground and buried him in the larger of the two manure piles beside the barn.

"I don't think any skunk got that rooster," my grandmother said suspiciously, nudging at a feather with the toe of her boot until, finally disturbed, it was wafted away by the breeze.

Something squeezed my heart. How did she know?

"Skunks hunt at night," she said. "Must have been somebody's barn cat."

215   "You come along with me," my grandmother said. She was standing in front of the full-length hall mirror, settling on her hat, a deadly-looking hat pin poised above her skull. "We'll go into town and you can buy a comic book at the drugstore."

It was Friday and Friday was shopping day. But Grandma didn't wheel her battered De Soto to the kerb in front of the Brite Spot Grocery, she parked it in front of Maynard & Pritchard, Barristers and Solicitors.

"What are we doing here?" I asked.

Grandma was fumbling nervously with her purse. Small-town people don't like to be seen going to the lawyer's. "Come along with me. Hurry up."

"Why do I have to come?"

"Because I don't want you making a spectacle of yourself for the half-wits and   220
loungers to gawk at," she said. "Let's not give them too much to wonder about."

Maynard & Pritchard, Barristers and Solicitors, smelled of wax and varnish and probity. My grandmother was shown into an office with a frosted pane of glass in the door and neat gilt lettering that announced it was occupied by D. F. Maynard, QC. I was ordered to occupy a hard chair, which I did, battering my heels on the rungs briskly enough to annoy the secretary into telling me to stop it.

My grandmother wasn't closeted long with her Queen's Counsel before the door opened and he glided after her into the passageway. Lawyer Maynard was the neatest man I had ever seen in my life. His suit fit him like a glove.

"The best I can do," he said, "is send him a registered letter telling him to remove himself from the premises, but it all comes to the same thing. If that doesn't scare him off, you'll have to have recourse to the police. That's all there is to it. I told you that yesterday and you haven't told me anything new today, Edith, that would make me change my mind. Just let him know you won't put up with him any more."

"No police," she said. "I don't want the police digging in my family's business and Evelyn giving one of her grand performances for some baby-skinned consta-ble straight out of the depot. All I need is to get her away from him for a little while, then I could tune her in. I could get through to her in no time at all."

"Well," said Maynard, shrugging, "we could try the letter, but I don't think it   225
would do any good. He has the status of a guest in your home; just tell him to go."

My grandmother was showing signs of exasperation. "But he *doesn't* go. That's the point. I've told him and told him. But he *won't*."

"Mrs. Bradley," said the lawyer emphatically, "Edith, as a friend, don't waste your time. The police."

"I'm through wasting my time," she said.

Pulling away from the lawyer's office, my grandmother began a spirited con-versation with herself. A wisp of hair had escaped from under her hat, and the dye winked a metallic red light as it jiggled up and down in the hot sunshine.

"I've told him and told him. But he won't listen. The goddamn freak thinks   230
we're involved in a christly debating society. He thinks I don't mean business. But I mean business. I do. There's more than one way to skin a cat or scratch a dog's ass. We'll take the wheels off his little red wagon and see how she pulls."

"What about my comic book?" I said, as we drove past the Rexall.

"Shut up."

Grandma drove the De Soto to the edge of town and stopped it at the Ogdens' place. It was a service station, or rather had been until the BA company had taken out their pumps and yanked the franchise, or whatever you call it, on the two brothers. Since then everything had gone steadily downhill. Cracks in the window-panes had been taped with masking tape, and the roof had been patched with flattened tin cans and old licence plates. The building itself was surrounded by an acre of wrecks, sulking hulks rotten with rust, the guts of their upholstery spilled and gnawed by rats and mice.

But the Ogden brothers still carried on a business after a fashion. They stripped their wrecks for parts and were reputed to be decent enough mechanics whenever they were sober enough to turn a wrench or thread a bolt. People brought work to them whenever they couldn't avoid it, and the rest of the year gave them a wide berth.

235   The Ogdens were famous for two things: their meanness and their profligacy as breeders. The place was always aswarm with kids who never seemed to wear pants except in the most severe weather, and tottered about the premises, their legs smeared with grease, shit, or various combinations of both.

"Wait here," my grandmother said, slamming the car door loudly enough to bring the two brothers out of their shop. Through the open door I saw a motor suspended on an intricate system of chains and pulleys.

The Ogdens stood with their hands in the pockets of their bib overalls while my grandmother talked to them. They were quite a sight. They didn't have a dozen teeth in their heads between them, even though the oldest brother couldn't have been more than forty. They just stood there, one sucking on a cigarette, the other on a Coke. Neither one moved or changed his expression, except once, when a tow-headed youngster piddled too close to Grandma. He was lazily and casually slapped on the side of the head by the nearest brother and ran away screaming, his stream cavorting wildly in front of him.

At last, their business concluded, the boys walked my grandmother back to the car.

"You'll get to that soon?" she said, sliding behind the wheel.

240   "Tomorrow all right?" said one. His words sounded all slack and chewed, issuing from his shrunken, old man's mouth.

"The sooner the better. I want that seen to, Bert."

"What seen to?" I asked.

"Bert and his brother Elwood are going to fix that rattle that's been plaguing me."

"Sure thing," said Elwood. "Nothing but clear sailing."

245   "What rattle?" I said.

"What rattle? What rattle? The one in the glove compartment," she said, banging it with the heel of her hand. "That rattle. You hear it?"

Thompson could get very edgy some days. "I should be working on my dissertation," he said, coiled in the big chair. "I shouldn't be wasting my time in this shit-hole. I should be working!"

"So why aren't you?" said Evelyn. She was spool knitting. That and reading movie magazines were the only things she ever did.

"How the christ do I work without a library? You see a goddamn library within a hundred miles of this place?"

250   "Why do you need a library?" she said calmly. "Can't you write?"

"Write?" he said, looking at the ceiling. "Write, she says. What the hell do you know about it? What the hell do *you* know about it?"

"I can't see why you can't write."

"Before you write, you research. That's what you do, you *research.*"

"So bite my head off. It wasn't my idea to come here."

"It wasn't me that lost my goddamn job. How the hell were we supposed to pay the rent?"

"You could have got a job."

"I'm a student. Anyway, I told you, if I get a job my wife gets her hooks into me for support. I'll starve to death before I support that bitch."

"We could go back."

"How many times does it have to be explained to you? I don't get my scholarship cheque until the first of September. We happen to be broke. Absolutely. In fact, you're going to have to hit the old lady up for gas and eating money to get back to the coast. We're stuck here. Get that into your empty fucking head. The Lord Buddha might have been able to subsist on a single bean a day; I can't."

My grandmother came into the room. The conversation stopped.

"Do you think," she said to Thompson, "I could ask you to do me a favour?"

"Why, Mrs. Bradley," he said, smiling, "whatever do you mean?"

"I was wondering whether you could take my car into town to Ogdens' to get it fixed."

"Oh," said Thompson. "I don't know where it is. I don't think I'm your man."

"Ask anyone where it is. They can tell you. It isn't hard to find."

"Why would you ask me to do you a favour, Mrs. Bradley?" inquired Thompson complacently. Hearing his voice was like listening to someone drag their nails down a blackboard.

"Well, you can be goddamn sure I wouldn't," said Grandma, trying to keep a hold of herself, "except that I'm right in the middle of doing my pickling and canning. I thought you might be willing to move your lazy carcass to do something around here. Every time I turn around I seem to be falling over those legs of yours." She looked at the limbs in question as if she would like to dock them somewhere in the vicinity of the knee.

"No, I don't think I can," said Thompson easily, stroking his goat beard. "And why the hell can't you?"

"Oh, let's just say I don't trust you, Mrs. Bradley. I don't like to leave you alone with Evelyn. Lord knows what ideas you might put in her head."

"Or take out."

"That's right. Or take out," said Thompson with satisfaction. "You can't imagine the trouble it took me to get them in there." He turned to Evelyn. "She can't imagine the trouble, can she, dear?"

Evelyn threw her spool knitting on the floor and walked out of the room.

"Evelyn's mad and I'm glad," shouted Thompson at her back. "And I know how to tease her!"

"Charlie, come here," said Grandma. I went over to her. She took me firmly by the shoulder. "From now on," said my grandma, "my family is off limits to you. I don't want to see you talking to Charlie here, or to come within sniffing distance of Evelyn."

"What do you think of that idea, Charlie?" said Thompson. "Are you still my friend or what?"

I gave him a wink my grandma couldn't see. He thought that was great; he laughed like a madman. "Superb," he said. "Superb. There's no flies on Charlie. What a diplomat."

"What the hell is the matter with you, Mr. Beatnik?"[4] asked Grandma, annoyed beyond bearing. "What's so goddamn funny?"

"Ha, ha!" roared Thompson. "What a charming notion! Me a beatnik!"

280 Grandma Bradley held the mouthpiece of the phone very close to her lips as she spoke into it. "No, it can't be brought in. You'll have to come out here to do the job."

She listened with an intent expression on her face. Spotting me pretending to look in the fridge, she waved me out of the kitchen with her hand. I dragged myself out and stood quietly in the hallway.

"This is a party line," she said, "remember that."

Another pause while she listened.

"OK," she said and hung up.

285 I spent some of my happiest hours squatting in the corn patch. I was completely hidden in there; even when I stood, the maturing stalks reached a foot or more above my head. It was a good place. On the hottest days it was relatively cool in that thicket of green where the shade was dark and deep and the leaves rustled and scraped and sawed drily overhead.

Nobody ever thought to look for me there. They could bellow their bloody lungs out for me and I could just sit and watch them getting uglier and uglier about it all. There was some satisfaction in that. I'd just reach up and pluck myself a cob. I loved raw corn. The newly formed kernels were tiny, pale pearls of sweetness that gushed juice. I'd munch and munch and smile and smile and think, why don't you drop dead?

It was my secret place, my sanctuary, where I couldn't be found or touched by them. But all the same, if I didn't let them intrude on me—that didn't mean I didn't want to keep tabs on things.

At the time I was watching Thompson stealing peas at the other end of the garden. He was like some primitive man who lived in a gathering culture. My grandma kept him so hungry he was constantly prowling for food: digging in cupboards, rifling the refrigerator, scrounging in the garden.

Clad only in Bermuda shorts he was a sorry sight. His bones threatened to rupture his skin and jut out every which way. He sported a scrub-board chest with two old pennies for nipples, and a wispy garland of hair decorated his

4. A derisive term for adherents to the 1950s Beat movement, a social and literary rebellion against "square" conventions.

sunken breastbone. His legs looked particularly rackety; all gristle, knobs and sinew.

We both heard the truck at the same time. It came bucking up the approach, spurting gravel behind it. Thompson turned around, shaded his eyes and peered at it. He wasn't much interested. He couldn't get very curious about the natives.

The truck stopped and a man stepped out on to the runningboard of the '51 IHC. He gazed around him, obviously looking for something or someone. This character had a blue handkerchief sprinkled with white polka dots tied in a triangle over his face. Exactly like an outlaw in an Audie Murphy[5] Western. A genuine goddamn Jesse James.

He soon spotted Thompson standing half-naked in the garden, staring stupidly at this strange sight, his mouth bulging with peas. The outlaw ducked his head back into the cab of the truck, said something to the driver, and pointed. The driver then stepped out on to his runningboard and, standing on tippy-toe, peered over the roof of the cab at Thompson. He too wore a handkerchief tied over his mug, but his was red.

Then they both got down from the truck and began to walk very quickly toward Thompson with long, menacing strides.

"Fellows?" said Thompson.

At the sound of his voice the two men broke into a stiff-legged trot, and the one with the red handkerchief, while still moving, stooped down smoothly and snatched up the hoe that lay at the edge of the garden

"What the hell is going on here, boys?" said Thompson, his voice pitched high with concern.

The man with the blue mask reached Thompson first. One long arm, a dirty clutch of fingers on its end, snaked out and caught him by the hair and jerked his head down. Then he kicked him in the pit of the stomach with his work boots.

"OK, fucker," he shouted, "too fucking smart to take a fucking hint?" and he punched him on the side of the face with several short, snapping blows that actually tore Thompson's head out of his grip. Thompson toppled over clumsily and fell in the dirt. "Get fucking lost," Blue Mask said more quietly.

"Evelyn!" yelled Thompson to the house. "Jesus Christ, Evelyn!"

I crouched lower in the corn patch and began to tremble. I was certain they were going to kill him.

"Shut up," said the man with the hoe. He glanced at the blade for a second, considered, then rotated the handle in his hands and hit Thompson a quick chop on the head with the blunt side. "Shut your fucking yap," he repeated.

"Evelyn! Evelyn! Oh God!" hollered Thompson, "I'm being murdered! For God's sake, somebody help me!" The side of his face was slick with blood.

"I told you shut up, cock sucker," said Red Mask, and kicked him in the ribs several times. Thompson groaned and hugged himself in the dust.

5. World War II's most decorated GI, Murphy (1924–1971) went on to star in low-budget Western films as a baby-faced hero.

"Now you get lost, fucker," said the one with the hoe, "because if you don't stop bothering nice people we'll drive a spike in your skull."

"Somebody help me!" Thompson yelled at the house.

"Nobody there is going to help you," Blue Mask said. "You're all on your own, smart arse."

"You bastards," said Thompson, and spat ineffectually in their direction.

For his defiance he got struck a couple of chopping blows with the hoe. The last one skittered off his collar-bone with a sickening crunch.

"That's enough," said Red Mask, catching the handle of the hoe. "Come on."

The two sauntered back toward the truck, laughing. They weren't in any hurry to get out of there. Thompson lay on his side staring at their retreating backs. His face was wet with tears and blood.

The man with the red mask looked back over his shoulder and wiggled his ass at Thompson in an implausible imitation of effeminacy. "Was it worth it, tiger?" he shouted. "Getting your ashes hauled don't come cheap, do it?"

This set them off again. Passing me they pulled off their masks and stuffed them in their pockets. They didn't have to worry about Thompson when they had their backs to him; he couldn't see their faces. But I could. No surprise. They were the Ogden boys.

When the truck pulled out of the yard, its gears grinding, I burst out of my hiding place and ran to Thompson, who had got to his knees and was trying to stop the flow of blood from his scalp with his fingers. He was crying. Another first for Thompson. He was the first man I'd seen cry. It made me uncomfortable.

"The sons of bitches broke my ribs," he said, panting with shallow breaths. "God, I hope they didn't puncture a lung."

"Can you walk?" I asked.

"Don't think I don't know who's behind this," he said, getting carefully to his feet. His face was white. "You saw them," he said. "You saw their faces from the corn patch. We got the bastards."

He leaned a little on me as we made our way to the house. The front door was locked. We knocked. No answer. "Let me in, you old bitch!" shouted Thompson.

"Evelyn, open the goddamn door!" Silence. I couldn't hear a thing move in the house. It was as if they were all dead in there. It frightened me.

He started to kick the door. A panel splintered. "Open this door! Let me in, you old slut, or I'll kill you!"

Nothing.

"You better go," I said nervously. I didn't like this one little bit. "Those guys might come back and kill you."

"Evelyn!" he bellowed. "Evelyn!"

He kept it up for a good five minutes, alternately hammering and kicking the door, pleading with and threatening the occupants. By the end of that time he was sweating with exertion and pain. He went slowly down the steps, sobbing, beaten. "You saw them," he said, "we have the bastards dead to rights."

He winced when he eased his bare flesh on to the hot seat-covers of the car.

"I'll be back," he said, starting the motor of the car. "This isn't the end of this."

When Grandma was sure he had gone, the front door was unlocked and I was let in. I noticed my grandmother's hands trembled a touch when she lit her cigarette.

"You can't stay away from him, can you?" she said testily.

"You didn't have to do that," I said. "He was hurt. You ought to have let him in."

"I ought to have poisoned him a week ago. And don't talk about things you don't know anything about."

"Sometimes," I said, "all of you get on my nerves." 330

"Kids don't have nerves. Adults have nerves. They're the only ones entitled to them. And don't think I care a plugged nickel what does, or doesn't, get on your nerves."

"Where's Aunt Evelyn?"

"Your Aunt Evelyn is taken care of," she replied.

"Why wouldn't she come to the door?"

"She had her own road to Damascus.[6] She has seen the light. Everything has 335
been straightened out," she said. "Everything is back to normal."

He looked foolish huddled in the back of the police car later that evening. When the sun began to dip, the temperature dropped rapidly, and he was obviously cold dressed only in his Bermuda shorts. Thompson sat all hunched up to relieve the strain on his ribs, his hands pressed between his knees, shivering.

My grandmother and the constable spoke quietly by the car for some time; occasionally Thompson poked his head out the car window and said something. By the look on the constable's face when he spoke to Thompson, it was obvious he didn't care for him too much. Thompson had that kind of effect on people. Several times during the course of the discussion the constable glanced my way.

I edged a little closer so I could hear what they were saying.

"He's mad as a hatter," said my grandmother. "I don't know anything about two men. If you ask me, all this had something to do with drugs. My daughter says that this man takes drugs. He's some kind of beatnik."

"Christ," said Thompson, drawing his knees up as if to scrunch himself into a 340
smaller, less noticeable package, "the woman is insane."

"One thing at a time, Mrs. Bradley," said the RCMP constable.

"My daughter is finished with him," she said. "He beats her, you know. I want him kept off my property."

"I want to speak to Evelyn," Thompson said. He looked bedraggled and frightened. "Evelyn and I will leave this minute if this woman wants. But I've got to talk to Evelyn."

"My daughter doesn't want to see you, mister. She's finished with you," said Grandma Bradley, shifting her weight from side to side. She turned her attention

6. According to biblical legend, Saul (later Paul) was on his way to Damascus to subdue the Christians there when he was stopped by a vision of Jesus. He was temporarily blinded, and his conversion was immediate.

to the constable. "He beats her," she said, "bruises all over her. Can you imagine?"

345   "The boy knows," said Thompson desperately. "He saw them. How many times do I have to tell you?" He piped his voice to me. "Didn't you, Charlie? You saw them, didn't you?"

"Charlie?" said my grandmother. This was news to her.

I stood very still.

"Come here, son," said the constable.

I walked slowly over to them.

350   "Did you see the faces of the men?" the constable asked, putting a hand on my shoulder. "Do you know the men? Are they from around here?"

"How would he know?" said my grandmother. "He's a stranger."

"He knows them. At least he saw them," said Thompson. "My little Padmasambhava never misses a trick," he said, trying to jolly me. "You see everything, don't you, Charlie? You remember everything, don't you?"

I looked at my grandmother, who stood so calmly and commandingly, waiting.

"Hey, don't look to her for the answers," said Thompson nervously. "Don't be afraid of her. You remember everything, don't you?"

355   He had no business begging me. I had watched their game from the sidelines long enough to know the rules. At one time he had imagined himself a winner. And now he was asking me to save him, to take a risk, when I was more completely in her clutches than he would ever be. He forgot I was a child. I depended on her.

Thompson, I saw, was powerless. He couldn't protect me. God, I remembered more than he dreamed. I remembered how his lips had moved soundlessly, his face pleading with the ceiling, his face blotted of everything but abject urgency. Praying to a simpering, cross-eyed idol. His arm flashing as he struck my aunt's bare legs. Crawling in the dirt, covered with blood.

He had taught me that "Those who are in the grip of desire, the grip of existence, the grip of ignorance, move helplessly round through the spheres of life, as men or gods or as wretches in the lower regions." Well, he was helpless now. But he insisted on fighting back and hurting the rest of us. The weak ones like Evelyn and me.

I thought of Stanley the rooster and how it had felt when the tendons separated, the gristle parted and the bones crunched under my twisting hands.

"I don't know what he's talking about," I said to the constable softly. "I didn't see anybody."

360   "Clear out," said my grandmother triumphantly. "Beat it."

"You dirty little son of a bitch," he said to me. "You mean little bugger."

He didn't understand much. He had forced me into the game, and now that I was a player and no longer a watcher he didn't like it. The thing was that I was good at the game. But he, being a loser, couldn't appreciate that.

Then suddenly he said, "Evelyn." He pointed to the upstairs window of the house and tried to get out of the back seat of the police car. But of course he couldn't. They take the handles off the back doors. Nobody can get out unless they are let out.

"Goddamn it!" he shouted. "Let me out! She's waving to me! She wants me!"

I admit that the figure was hard to make out at that distance. But any damn fool could see she was only waving goodbye.   365

1982

QUESTIONS

1. What is the focus of the narration? the voice? What expectations of plot, theme, character are aroused by the first fifteen or eighteen paragraphs? What are your early interpretations of the title? Trace "watching" through the story and its relation to character, plot, and theme.
2. For some time the narrator summarizes his childhood and gives brief character sketches of members of his family. How would you describe the narrator's characterizations—are they jovial? sympathetic? loving? critical? sardonic? nasty? What do you think of the narrator during these early (twenty to thirty) paragraphs? Does your view of him change in the course of the story? If so, how many times, in what ways, and when? How does the narrator's character relate to the incidents of the story (plot) and theme?
3. Though there is a brief scene with the father in paragraphs 18 and 19, the first lengthy, fully discriminated scene takes place in paragraphs 28 to 57. How does the scene contribute to the picture of the setting? characterization? theme?
4. It is not until paragraph 62 that "something interesting turned up"—the arrival of Aunt Evelyn and Robert Thompson. Did the first sixty-plus paragraphs hold your interest despite the absence of incident? If so, how? What expectations, if any, did those first paragraphs engender? What expectations or curiosity is aroused by the new arrivals? How does it contribute to the characterization of the narrator (Charlie)? Grandma Bradley? What are your first responses to and opinions of Aunt Evelyn? Thompson? What is the tone of the scene? What conflict is building? Whose side are you on in the ensuing argument? Why? Whose side is the narrator on? How do you know?
5. How does the narrator know what Evelyn does during the day? How does he know that Thompson beats her? What resemblance does Thompson see between Charlie and Padma-sambhava? Why does Charlie think Thompson a "silly bugger" when he laughs at what Charlie tells him he wants to be when he grows up (paragraph 167)? How is this related to Thompson's character? Charlie's situation? the theme?
6. On the evening of the day Thompson whipped Evelyn, why does she come down to dinner in shorts (paragraph 144)? What does that tell you about her character? about Thompson? What expectations are aroused? In paragraphs 190 and 191, Grandma says Thompson will be out of the house in a week, but he says he won't. Who do you think will prove to be right? Why? What did you expect Grandma to do to get rid of Thompson? How was your expectation related to the characters? to plot? to theme?
7. How does paragraph 194 contribute to setting? expectations? characterization? How is the scene between Charlie and Stanley that follows related to details earlier in the story? What is the effect of the scene on the characterization of Charlie? on the theme? Is Stanley a symbol? Explain, by indicating what you mean by "symbol" and, if you think he is a symbol, what it is he symbolizes.
8. How is paragraph 355 related to plot? Charlie's character? theme?
9. How many previous scenes and details are echoed or brought to bear on the final scene (paragraphs 336 to the end of story)? How does that scene derive from and impinge upon the characterization of Charlie? How does it bring out, reinforce, or define the theme?

WRITING SUGGESTIONS

See pages 256–57 and 273–74 for additional writing suggestions.

1. Show how the discussion of "The Country Husband" or "Sonny's Blues" in the chapter on plot would be modified and expanded by writing a essay on the whole text of the story.
2. Write a brief analytical essay on "The Secret Sharer" in terms of symbol or "Love Medicine" in terms of theme.
3. Write an essay on the whole text of "The Real Thing" or "The Yellow Wallpaper" (in "Reading More Fiction").

Exploring Contexts

8

THE AUTHOR'S WORK AS CONTEXT: FLANNERY O'CONNOR

Even if it were desirable to read a story as a thing in itself, separate from every-thing else we had ever read or seen and from everything else the author had written, this is in practice impossible. We can read Faulkner or Atwood or Poe for the first time only once. After we read a second and then a third story by an author, we begin to recognize the voice and have a sense of familiarity, as we would with a growing acquaintance. Each story is part of the author's entire body of work—the **canon**—which, taken together, forms something like a huge single entity, a vision, a world, a "super-work."

The author's voice and vision soon create in us certain expectations—of action, structure, characterization, world view, language. We come to expect short sentences from Hemingway, long ones from Faulkner, a certain amount of violence from both. We are not surprised if a Conrad story is set in Africa or Asia or aboard ship, but we are surprised if a Faulkner story takes place outside Mississippi (his portion of which, we soon learn, he calls Yoknapatawpha).

When we find an author's vision attractive or challenging, we naturally want to find out more about it, reading not only the literary works in the canon but the author's nonfictional prose—essays, letters, anything we can find that promises a fuller or clearer view of that unique way of looking at the world. Such knowledge is helpful—within limits. D. H. Lawrence warned us to trust the tale and not the teller. A statement of beliefs or of intentions is not necessarily the same as what a given work may show or achieve; and, on the other hand, writers often embody in their art what they cannot articulate, what indeed may not be expressible, in discursive prose.

In this chapter we will look briefly but closely at the work of Flannery O'Connor. We will look both at the differences and the similarities among three of her works.

The short stories and brief selections from O'Connor's letters and essays in this chap-ter are meant to make you feel more at home (and interested) in O'Connor's world and to raise questions about the relationship of the individual work to an author's work as a whole.

In this chapter we offer three of Flannery O'Connor's stories, including the title sto-ries of her first volume of short stories, *A Good Man Is Hard to Find* (1955), and her last, *Everything That Rises Must Converge* (published posthumously in 1965). Her career was short, its latter stages hampered by the periodic and intensifying painful and debilitating bouts of lupus, but her accomplishments were considerable: she died at thirty-nine, having published some thirty-one stories, two novels, essays, and reviews.

O'Connor's fiction is set most often in the American South, rural or urban, and her characters are most often Southerners, white or black. Consequently, her subject is often racism. O'Connor has a keen eye for realistic detail and for her characters' self-deception and the truth that lies beneath the surface of language and self-image. Her means of releasing this inner truth is often violence, which shocks the reader into looking beyond the surface and the conventional to discover a truth, often an uncomfortable truth, that lies within. Though O'Connor is a deeply religious and serious writer, her stories are replete with irony and wit, and are sometimes downright funny. Indeed, as you will see, she is not above mixing comedy and horror or using comic pratfalls seriously.

The central, sometimes obsessive concerns and assumptions that permeate an author's work not only relate the individual stories to each other, mutually illuminating and enriching them, but they also serve as the author's trademark. It is not difficult to recognize or even parody a story by O'Connor.

Embodying these larger concerns and underlying such larger structures as plot, focus, and voice are the basic characteristics of the author's language, such as **diction,** the choice and use of words; sentence structure; **rhetorical tropes,** figures of thought and speech; **imagery;** and **rhythm**—in other words, the author's **style.**

Flannery O'Connor

Perhaps because of the uniqueness of style, the vocabulary for discussing stylistic elements is not precise or accessible. We can broadly characterize diction as **formal** ("The Cask of Amontillado") or **informal** (most of the stories in this collection), and within the broad term *informal* we can identify a level of language that approximates the speech of ordinary people and call it **colloquial** ("A Good Man Is Hard to Find"). But to characterize precisely an author's diction so that it adequately describes his or her work and marks it off from the work of contemporaries is a difficult task indeed. We can note Faulkner's long sentences, but it is hard to get much definition in the stylistic fingerprint of an author merely by measuring the lengths of sentences or tabulating connectives (though these qualities no doubt do subliminally contribute to the effect of the works on readers and do help to identify the author).

Diction and sentence structure contribute to the **tone** of a work, or the implied attitude or stance of the author toward the characters and events, an aspect somewhat analogous to tone of voice. When what is being said and the tone are consistent, it is difficult to separate one from the other; when there seems to be a discrepancy, we have some words that are useful to describe the difference. If the language seems exaggerated, we call it **overstatement** or **hyperbole.** Sometimes it will be the narrator, sometimes a character, who uses language so intensive or exaggerated that we must read it at a discount, as it were, and judge the speaker's accuracy or honesty in the process. When Julian's mother, in "Everything That Rises Must Converge," says, " 'I've always had a great respect for my colored friends. . . . I'd do anything in the world for them . . .' " (paragraph 32), we know she protests too much, that she is exaggerating, and we see her racism through or underneath her language. When, in "A Good Man Is Hard to Find," The Misfit approaches Bailey's car that she has rolled over into a ditch, he says, "I see you all had you a little spill" (paragraph 74), a bit of obvious **understatement** or **litotes.** When a word or expression carries not only its literal meaning, but a different meaning for the speaker as well, we have an example of **verbal irony.** When Fortunato says, "I shall not die of a cough," Montresor's "True—true" may seem reassuring, but we learn later in the story why it is both accurate and ominous. There are also nonverbal forms of irony, the most common of which is **dramatic irony,** in which a character holds a position or has an expectation that is reversed or fulfilled in an unexpected way. Knowing her husband's habit of drinking himself into unconsciousness, Elizabeth Bates (in D. H. Lawrence's "Odour of Chrysanthemums") expects him to be brought home like a log. How is her expectation fulfilled? She had also said bitterly, "But he needn't come rolling in here in his pit-dirt, for *I* won't wash him," and yet she does. Why is her determination altered? As you read through (in "Reading More Fiction") "Odour of Chrysanthemums," watch for other reversed or unexpectedly fulfilled expectations. Close to dramatic irony but not involving outcome, close to verbal irony but not entirely embedded in words, is a kind created by the gap between the character's and the narrator's (and reader's) interpretation or values. In "A Good Man Is Hard to Find," the grandmother's careful attention to her dress, she believes, assures respect: "In case of an accident, anyone seeing her dead on the highway would know at once that she was a lady" (paragraph 12). She takes this seriously; most readers find it ludicrous or pathetic. This gap is frequently present in O'Connor's stories. It is not demeaning to her characters, but testimony both to her keen realistic observation and to her knowledge of her characters from the inside.

Another, highly emphasized element of style is **imagery.** In its broadest sense imagery includes any sensory detail or evocation in a work. Note how much more imagery in that sense we find in "Fenstad's Mother" than in, say, "The Zebra Storyteller." Imagery in this broad sense, however, is so prevalent in literature that it would take exhaustive statistics to differentiate styles by counting the number of sensory elements per hundred or thousand words, categorizing the images as primarily visual, tactile, and so forth. In a more restricted sense, imagery refers to figurative language (see Chapter 5 on symbols), particularly that which defines an abstraction or any emotional or psychological state with a sensory comparison. The opening paragraph of "Odour of Chrysanthemums" illustrates the broader definition of imagery, and this passage from later in the same story may represent the figurative sense: "Life with its smoky burning gone from him, had left him apart. . . . In her womb was ice of fear. . . ."

We might say that if an author's vision gives us his or her profile, the style gives us a fingerprint—though the fingerprint is unique and definitive, it is also harder to come by than a glimpse of a profile. Ultimately, however, vision and style are less distinguishable from each other than the profile-fingerprint image suggests. For vision and style, just like history and structure, do more than interact: they are inextricably fused or compounded.

A Good Man Is Hard to Find

The grandmother didn't want to go to Florida. She wanted to visit some of her connections in east Tennessee and she was seizing at every chance to change Bailey's mind. Bailey was the son she lived with, her only boy. He was sitting on the edge of his chair at the table, bent over the orange sports section of the *Journal*. "Now look here, Bailey," she said, "see here, read this," and she stood with one hand on her thin hip and the other rattling the newspaper at his bald head. "Here this fellow that calls himself The Misfit is aloose from the Federal Pen and headed toward Florida and you read here what it says he did to these people. Just you read it. I wouldn't take my children in any direction with a criminal like that aloose in it. I couldn't answer to my conscience if I did."

Bailey didn't look up from his reading so she wheeled around then and faced the children's mother, a young woman in slacks, whose face was as broad and innocent as a cabbage and was tied around with a green head-kerchief that had two points on the top like a rabbit's ears. She was sitting on the sofa, feeding the baby his apricots out of a jar. "The children have been to Florida before," the old lady said. "You all ought to take them somewhere else for a change so they would see different parts of the world and be broad. They never have been to east Tennessee."

The children's mother didn't seem to hear her but the eight-year-old boy, John Wesley, a stocky child with glasses, said, "If you don't want to go to Florida, why dontcha stay at home?" He and the little girl, June Star, were reading the funny papers on the floor.

"She wouldn't stay at home to be queen for a day," June Star said without raising her yellow head.

5　"Yes and what would you do if this fellow, The Misfit, caught you?" the grandmother asked.

"I'd smack his face," John Wesley said.

"She wouldn't stay at home for a million bucks," June Star said. "Afraid she'd miss something. She has to go everywhere we go."

"All right, Miss," the grandmother said. "Just remember that the next time you want me to curl your hair."

June Star said her hair was naturally curly.

The next morning the grandmother was the first one in the car, ready to go. She had her big black valise that looked like the head of a hippopotamus in one corner, and underneath it she was hiding a basket with Pitty Sing,[1] the cat, in it. She didn't intend for the cat to be left alone in the house for three days because he would miss her too much and she was afraid he might brush against one of the gas burners and accidentally asphyxiate himself. Her son, Bailey, didn't like to arrive at a motel with a cat.

She sat in the middle of the back seat with John Wesley and June Star on either side of her. Bailey and the children's mother and the baby sat in front and they left Atlanta at eight forty-five with the mileage on the car at 55890. The grandmother wrote this down because she thought it would be interesting to say how many miles they had been when they got back. It took them twenty minutes to reach the outskirts of the city.

The old lady settled herself comfortably, removing her white cotton gloves and putting them up with her purse on the shelf in front of the back window. The children's mother still had on slacks and still had her head tied up in a green kerchief, but the grandmother had on a navy blue straw sailor hat with a bunch of white violets on the brim and a navy blue dress with a small white dot in the print. Her collars and cuffs were white organdy trimmed with lace and at her neckline she had pinned a purple spray of cloth violets containing a sachet. In case of an accident, anyone seeing her dead on the highway would know at once that she was a lady.

She said she thought it was going to be a good day for driving, neither too hot nor too cold, and she cautioned Bailey that the speed limit was fifty-five miles an hour and that the patrolmen hid themselves behind billboards and small clumps of trees and sped out after you before you had a chance to slow down. She pointed out interesting details of the scenery: Stone Mountain; the blue granite that in some places came up to both sides of the highway; the brilliant red clay banks slightly streaked with purple; and the various crops that made rows of green lace-work on the ground. The trees were full of silver-white sunlight and the meanest of them sparkled. The children were reading comic magazines and their mother had gone back to sleep.

"Let's go through Georgia fast so we won't have to look at it much," John Wesley said.

"If I were a little boy," said the grandmother, "I wouldn't talk about my native state that way. Tennessee has the mountains and Georgia has the hills."

"Tennessee is just a hillbilly dumping ground," John Wesley said, "and Georgia is a lousy state too."

"You said it," June Star said.

"In my time," said the grandmother, folding her thin veined fingers, "children

1. Named after Pitti-Sing, one of the "three little maids from school" in Gilbert and Sullivan's operetta *The Mikado* (1885).

were more respectful of their native states and their parents and everything else. People did right then. Oh look at the cute little pickaninny!" she said and pointed to a Negro child standing in the door of a shack. "Wouldn't that make a picture, now?" she asked and they all turned and looked at the little Negro out of the back window. He waved.

"He didn't have any britches on," June Star said.

20   "He probably didn't have any," the grandmother explained. "Little niggers in the country don't have things like we do. If I could paint, I'd paint that picture," she said.

The children exchanged comic books.

The grandmother offered to hold the baby and the children's mother passed him over the front seat to her. She set him on her knee and bounced him and told him about the things they were passing. She rolled her eyes and screwed up her mouth and stuck her leathery thin face into his smooth bland one. Occasionally he gave her a faraway smile. They passed a large cotton field with five or six graves fenced in the middle of it, like a small island. "Look at the graveyard!" the grandmother said, pointing it out. "That was the old family burying ground. That belonged to the plantation."

"Where's the plantation?" John Wesley asked.

"Gone With the Wind," said the grandmother. "Ha. Ha."

25   When the children finished all the comic books they had brought, they opened the lunch and ate it. The grandmother ate a peanut butter sandwich and an olive and would not let the children throw the box and the paper napkins out the window. When there was nothing else to do they played a game by choosing a cloud and making the other two guess what shape it suggested. John Wesley took one the shape of a cow and June Star guessed a cow and John Wesley said, no, an automobile, and June Star said he didn't play fair, and they began to slap each other over the grandmother.

The grandmother said she would tell them a story if they would keep quiet. When she told a story, she rolled her eyes and waved her head and was very dramatic. She said once when she was a maiden lady she had been courted by a Mr. Edgar Atkins Teagarden from Jasper, Georgia. She said he was a very good-looking man and a gentleman and that he brought her a watermelon every Saturday afternoon with his initials cut in it, E. A. T. Well, one Saturday, she said, Mr. Teagarden brought the watermelon and there was nobody at home and he left it on the front porch and returned in his buggy to Jasper, but she never got the watermelon, she said, because a nigger boy ate it when he saw the initials, E. A. T.! This story tickled John Wesley's funny bone and he giggled and giggled but June Star didn't think it was any good. She said she wouldn't marry a man that just brought her a watermelon on Saturday. The grandmother said she would have done well to marry Mr. Teagarden because he was a gentleman and had bought Coca-Cola stock when it first came out and that he had died only a few years ago, a very wealthy man.

They stopped at The Tower for barbecued sandwiches. The Tower was a part stucco and part wood filling station and dance hall set in a clearing outside of Timothy. A fat man named Red Sammy Butts ran it and there were signs stuck here and there on the building and for miles up and down the highway saying, TRY RED SAMMY'S FAMOUS BARBECUE. NONE LIKE FAMOUS RED SAMMY'S! RED SAM! THE FAT BOY WITH THE HAPPY LAUGH! A VETERAN! RED SAMMY'S YOUR MAN!

Red Sammy was lying on the bare ground outside The Tower with his head under a truck while a gray monkey about a foot high, chained to a small chinaberry tree, chattered nearby. The monkey sprang back into the tree and got on the highest limb as soon as he saw the children jump out of the car and run toward him.

Inside, The Tower was a long dark room with a counter at one end and tables at the other and dancing space in the middle. They all sat down at a board table next to the nickelodeon[2] and Red Sam's wife, a tall burnt-brown woman with hair and eyes lighter than her skin, came and took their order. The children's mother put a dime in the machine and played "The Tennessee Waltz," and the grandmother said that tune always made her want to dance. She asked Bailey if he would like to dance but he only glared at her. He didn't have a naturally sunny disposition like she did and trips made him nervous. The grandmother's brown eyes were very bright. She swayed her head from side to side and pretended she was dancing in her chair. June Star said play something she could tap to so the children's mother put in another dime and played a fast number and June Star stepped out onto the dance floor and did her tap routine.

"Ain't she cute?" Red Sam's wife said, leaning over the counter. "Would you   30
like to come be my little girl?"

"No I certainly wouldn't," June Star said. "I wouldn't live in a broken-down place like this for a million bucks!" and she ran back to the table.

"Ain't she cute?" the woman repeated, stretching her mouth politely.

"Aren't you ashamed?" hissed the grandmother.

Red Sam came in and told his wife to quit lounging on the counter and hurry up with these people's order. His khaki trousers reached just to his hip bones and his stomach hung over them like a sack of meal swaying under his shirt. He came over and sat at a table nearby and let out a combination sigh and yodel. "You can't win," he said. "You can't win," and he wiped his sweating red face off with a gray handkerchief. "These days you don't know who to trust," he said. "Ain't that the truth?"

"People are certainly not nice like they used to be," said the grandmother.   35

"Two fellers come in here last week," Red Sammy said, "driving a Chrysler. It was a old beat-up car but it was a good one and these boys looked all right to me. Said they worked at the mill and you know I let them fellers charge the gas they bought? Now why did I do that?"

"Because you're a good man!" the grandmother said at once.

"Yes'm, I suppose so," Red Sam said as if he were struck with this answer.

His wife brought the orders, carrying the five plates all at once without a tray, two in each hand and one balanced on her arm. "It isn't a soul in this green

2. Jukebox.

world of God's that you can trust," she said. "And I don't count nobody out of that, not nobody," she repeated, looking at Red Sammy.

40   "Did you read about that criminal, The Misfit, that's escaped?" asked the grandmother.

"I wouldn't be a bit surprised if he didn't attact this place right here," said the woman. "If he hears about it being here, I wouldn't be none surprised to see him. If he hears it's two cent in the cash register, I wouldn't be a tall surprised if he . . ."

"That'll do," Red Sam said. "Go bring these people their Co'-Colas," and the woman went off to get the rest of the order.

"A good man is hard to find," Red Sammy said. "Everything is getting terrible. I remember the day you could go off and leave your screen door unlatched. Not no more."

He and the grandmother discussed better times. The old lady said that in her opinion Europe was entirely to blame for the way things were now. She said the way Europe acted you would think we were made of money and Red Sam said it was no use talking about it, she was exactly right. The children ran outside into the white sunlight and looked at the monkey in the lacy chinaberry tree. He was busy catching fleas on himself and biting each one carefully between his teeth as if it were a delicacy.

45   They drove off again into the hot afternoon. The grandmother took cat naps and woke up every few minutes with her own snoring. Outside of Toombsboro she woke up and recalled an old plantation that she had visited in this neighborhood once when she was a young lady. She said the house had six white columns across the front and that there was an avenue of oaks leading up to it and two little wooden trellis arbors on either side in front where you sat down with your suitor after a stroll in the garden. She recalled exactly which road to turn off to get to it. She knew that Bailey would not be willing to lose any time looking at an old house, but the more she talked about it, the more she wanted to see it once again and find out if the little twin arbors were still standing. "There was a secret panel in this house," she said craftily, not telling the truth but wishing that she were, "and the story went that all the family silver was hidden in it when Sherman came through but it was never found . . ."

"Hey!" John Wesley said. "Let's go see it! We'll find it! We'll poke all the woodwork and find it! Who lives there? Where do you turn off at? Hey Pop, can't we turn off there?"

"We never have seen a house with a secret panel!" June Star shrieked. "Let's go to the house with the secret panel! Hey Pop, can't we go see the house with the secret panel!"

"It's not far from here, I know," the grandmother said. "It wouldn't take over twenty minutes."

Bailey was looking straight ahead. His jaw was as rigid as a horseshoe. "No," he said.

50   The children began to yell and scream that they wanted to see the house with the secret panel. John Wesley kicked the back of the front seat and June Star hung over her mother's shoulder and whined desperately into her ear that they never had any fun even on their vacation, that they could never do what THEY

wanted to do. The baby began to scream and John Wesley kicked the back of the seat so hard that his father could feel the blows in his kidney.

"All right!" he shouted and drew the car to a stop at the side of the road. "Will you all shut up? Will you all just shut up for one second? If you don't shut up, we won't go anywhere."

"It would be very educational for them," the grandmother murmured.

"All right," Bailey said, "but get this: this is the only time we're going to stop for anything like this. This is the one and only time."

"The dirt road that you have to turn down is about a mile back," the grandmother directed. "I marked it when we passed."

"A dirt road," Bailey groaned.   55

After they had turned around and were headed toward the dirt road, the grandmother recalled other points about the house, the beautiful glass over the front doorway and the candle-lamp in the hall. John Wesley said that the secret panel was probably in the fireplace.

"You can't go inside this house," Bailey said. "You don't know who lives there."

"While you all talk to the people in front, I'll run around behind and get in a window," John Wesley suggested.

"We'll all stay in the car," his mother said.

They turned onto the dirt road and the car raced roughly along in a swirl of   60
pink dust. The grandmother recalled the times when there were no paved roads and thirty miles was a day's journey. The dirt road was hilly and there were sudden washes in it and sharp curves on dangerous embankments. All at once they would be on a hill, looking down over the blue tops of trees for miles around, then the next minute, they would be in a red depression with the dust-coated trees looking down on them.

"This place had better turn up in a minute," Bailey said, "or I'm going to turn around."

The road looked as if no one had traveled on it in months.

"It's not much farther," the grandmother said and just as she said it, a horrible thought came to her. The thought was so embarrassing that she turned red in the face and her eyes dilated and her feet jumped up, upsetting her valise in the corner. The instant the valise moved, the newspaper top she had over the basket under it rose with a snarl and Pitty Sing, the cat, sprang onto Bailey's shoulder.

The children were thrown to the floor and their mother, clutching the baby, out the door onto the ground; the old lady was thrown into the front seat. The car turned over once and landed right-side-up in a gulch off the side of the road. Bailey remained in the driver's seat with the cat—gray-striped with a broad white face and an orange nose—clinging to his neck like a caterpillar.

As soon as the children saw they could move their arms and legs, they scram-   65
bled out of the car, shouting, "We've had an ACCIDENT!" The grandmother was curled up under the dashboard, hoping she was injured so that Bailey's wrath would not come down on her all at once. The horrible thought she had had before the accident was that the house she had remembered so vividly was not in Georgia but in Tennessee.

Bailey removed the cat from his neck with both hands and flung it out the window against the side of a pine tree. Then he got out of the car and started looking for the children's mother. She was sitting against the side of the red gutted ditch, holding the screaming baby, but she only had a cut down her face and a broken shoulder. "We've had an ACCIDENT!" the children screamed in a frenzy of delight.

"But nobody's killed," June Star said with disappointment as the grandmother limped out of the car, her hat still pinned to her head but the broken front brim standing up at a jaunty angle and the violet spray hanging off the side. They all sat down in the ditch, except the children, to recover from the shock. They were all shaking.

"Maybe a car will come along," said the children's mother hoarsely.

"I believe I have injured an organ," said the grandmother, pressing her side, but no one answered her. Bailey's teeth were clattering. He had on a yellow sport shirt with bright blue parrots designed in it and his face was as yellow as the shirt. The grandmother decided that she would not mention that the house was in Tennessee.

70   The road was about ten feet above and they could see only the tops of the trees on the other side of it. Behind the ditch they were sitting in there were more woods, tall and dark and deep. In a few minutes they saw a car some distance away on top of a hill, coming slowly as if the occupants were watching them. The grandmother stood up and waved both arms dramatically to attract their attention. The car continued to come on slowly, disappeared around a bend and appeared again, moving even slower, on top of the hill they had gone over. It was a big black battered hearselike automobile. There were three men in it.

It came to a stop just over them and for some minutes, the driver looked down with a steady expressionless gaze to where they were sitting, and didn't speak. Then he turned his head and muttered something to the other two and they got out. One was a fat boy in black trousers and a red sweat shirt with a silver stallion embossed on the front of it. He moved around on the right side of them and stood staring, his mouth partly open in a kind of loose grin. The other had on khaki pants and a blue striped coat and a gray hat pulled down very low, hiding most of his face. He came around slowly on the left side. Neither spoke.

The driver got out of the car and stood by the side of it, looking down at them. He was an older man than the other two. His hair was just beginning to gray and he wore silver-rimmed spectacles that gave him a scholarly look. He had a long creased face and didn't have on any shirt or undershirt. He had on blue jeans that were too tight for him and was holding a black hat and a gun. The two boys also had guns.

"We've had an ACCIDENT!" the children screamed.

The grandmother had the peculiar feeling that the bespectacled man was someone she knew. His face was as familiar to her as if she had known him all her life but she could not recall who he was. He moved away from the car and began to come down the embankment, placing his feet carefully so that he wouldn't slip. He had on tan and white shoes and no socks, and his ankles were red and thin. "Good afternoon," he said. "I see you all had you a little spill."

"We turned over twice!" said the grandmother.   75

"Oncet," he corrected. "We seen it happen. Try their car and see will it run, Hiram," he said quietly to the boy with the gray hat.

"What you got that gun for?" John Wesley asked. "Whatcha gonna do with that gun?"

"Lady," the man said to the children's mother, "would you mind calling them children to sit down by you? Children make me nervous. I want all you all to sit down right together there where you're at."

"What are you telling US what to do for?" June Star asked.

Behind them the line of woods gaped like a dark open mouth. "Come here,"   80
said their mother.

"Look here now," Bailey began suddenly, "we're in a predicament! We're in . . ."

The grandmother shrieked. She scrambled to her feet and stood staring. "You're The Misfit!" she said. "I recognized you at once!"

"Yes'm," the man said, smiling slightly as if he were pleased in spite of himself to be known, "but it would have been better for all of you, lady, if you hadn't of reckernized me."

Bailey turned his head sharply and said something to his mother that shocked even the children. The old lady began to cry and The Misfit reddened.

"Lady," he said, "don't you get upset. Sometimes a man says things he don't   85
mean. I don't reckon he meant to talk to you thataway."

"You wouldn't shoot a lady, would you?" the grandmother said and removed a clean handkerchief from her cuff and began to slap at her eyes with it.

The Misfit pointed the toe of his shoe into the ground and made a little hole and then covered it up again. "I would hate to have to," he said.

"Listen," the grandmother almost screamed, "I know you're a good man. You don't look a bit like you have common blood. I know you must come from nice people!"

"Yes mam," he said, "finest people in the world." When he smiled he showed a row of strong white teeth. "God never made a finer woman than my mother and my daddy's heart was pure gold," he said. The boy with the red sweat shirt had come around behind them and was standing with his gun at his hip. The Misfit squatted down on the ground. "Watch them children, Bobby Lee," he said. "You know they make me nervous." He looked at the six of them huddled together in front of him and he seemed to be embarrassed as if he couldn't think of anything to say. "Ain't a cloud in the sky," he remarked, looking up at it. "Don't see no sun but don't see no cloud neither."

"Yes, it's a beautiful day," said the grandmother. "Listen," she said, "you   90
shouldn't call yourself The Misfit because I know you're a good man at heart. I can just look at you and tell."

"Hush!" Bailey yelled. "Hush! Everybody shut up and let me handle this!" He was squatting in the position of a runner about to sprint forward but he didn't move.

"I pre-chate that, lady," The Misfit said and drew a little circle in the ground with the butt of his gun.

"It'll take a half a hour to fix this here car," Hiram called, looking over the raised hood of it.

"Well, first you and Bobby Lee get him and that little boy to step over yonder with you," The Misfit said, pointing to Bailey and John Wesley. "The boys want to ast you something," he said to Bailey. "Would you mind stepping back in them woods there with them?"

95   "Listen," Bailey began, "we're in a terrible predicament! Nobody realizes what this is," and his voice cracked. His eyes were as blue and intense as the parrots in his shirt and he remained perfectly still.

The grandmother reached up to adjust her hat brim as if she were going to the woods with him but it came off in her hand. She stood staring at it and after a second she let it fall on the ground. Hiram pulled Bailey up by the arm as if he were assisting an old man. John Wesley caught hold of his father's hand and Bobby Lee followed. They went off toward the woods and just as they reached the dark edge, Bailey turned and supporting himself against a gray naked pine trunk, he shouted, "I'll be back in a minute, Mamma, wait on me!"

"Come back this instant!" his mother shrilled but they all disappeared into the woods.

"Bailey Boy!" the grandmother called in a tragic voice but she found she was looking at The Misfit squatting on the ground in front of her. "I just know you're a good man," she said desperately. "You're not a bit common!"

"Nome, I ain't a good man," The Misfit said after a second as if he had considered her statement carefully, "but I ain't the worst in the world neither. My daddy said I was a different breed of dog from my brothers and sisters. 'You know,' Daddy said, 'it's some that can live their whole life out without asking about it and it's others has to know why it is, and this boy is one of the latters. He's going to be into everything!' " He put on his black hat and looked up suddenly and then away deep into the woods as if he were embarrassed again. "I'm sorry I don't have on a shirt before you ladies," he said, hunching his shoulders slightly. "We buried our clothes that we had on when we escaped and we're just making do until we can get better. We borrowed these from some folks we met," he explained.

100   "That's perfectly all right," the grandmother said. "Maybe Bailey has an extra shirt in his suitcase."

"I'll look and see terrectly," The Misfit said.

"Where are they taking him?" the children's mother screamed.

"Daddy was a card himself," The Misfit said. "You couldn't put anything over on him. He never got in trouble with the Authorities though. Just had the knack of handling them."

"You could be honest too if you'd only try," said the grandmother. "Think how wonderful it would be to settle down and live a comfortable life and not have to think about somebody chasing you all the time."

105   The Misfit kept scratching in the ground with the butt of his gun as if he were thinking about it. "Yes'm, somebody is always after you," he murmured.

The grandmother noticed how thin his shoulder blades were just behind his hat because she was standing up looking down on him. "Do you ever pray?" she asked.

He shook his head. All she saw was the black hat wiggle between his shoulder blades. "Nome," he said.

There was a pistol shot from the woods, followed closely by another. Then silence. The old lady's head jerked around. She could hear the wind move through the tree tops like a long satisfied insuck of breath. "Bailey Boy!" she called.

"I was a gospel singer for a while," The Misfit said. "I been most everything. Been in the arm service, both land and sea, at home and abroad, been twict married, been an undertaker, been with the railroads, plowed Mother Earth, been in a tornado, seen a man burnt alive oncet," and looked up at the children's mother and the little girl who were sitting close together, their faces white and their eyes glassy; "I even seen a woman flogged," he said.

"Pray, pray," the grandmother began, "pray, pray . . ." 110

"I never was a bad boy that I remember of," The Misfit said in an almost dreamy voice, "but somewheres along the line I done something wrong and got sent to the penitentiary. I was buried alive," and he looked up and held her attention to him by a steady stare.

"That's when you should have started to pray," she said. "What did you do to get sent to the penitentiary that first time?"

"Turn to the right, it was a wall," The Misfit said, looking up again at the cloudless sky. "Turn to the left, it was a wall. Look up it was a ceiling, look down it was a floor. I forgot what I done, lady. I set there and set there, trying to remember what it was I done and I ain't recalled it to this day. Oncet in a while, I would think it was coming to me, but it never come."

"Maybe they put you in by mistake," the old lady said vaguely.

"Nome," he said. "It wasn't no mistake. They had the papers on me." 115

"You must have stolen something," she said.

The Misfit sneered slightly. "Nobody had nothing I wanted," he said. "It was a head-doctor at the penitentiary said what I had done was kill my daddy but I known that for a lie. My daddy died in nineteen ought nineteen of the epidemic flu and I never had a thing to do with it. He was buried in the Mount Hopewell Baptist churchyard and you can go there and see for yourself."

"If you would pray," the old lady said, "Jesus would help you."

"That's right," The Misfit said.

"Well then, why don't you pray?" she asked trembling with delight suddenly. 120

"I don't want no hep," he said. "I'm doing all right by myself."

Bobby Lee and Hiram came ambling back from the woods. Bobby Lee was dragging a yellow shirt with bright blue parrots in it.

"Thow me that shirt, Bobby Lee," The Misfit said. The shirt came flying at him and landed on his shoulder and he put it on. The grandmother couldn't name what the shirt reminded her of. "No, lady," The Misfit said while he was buttoning it up, "I found out the crime don't matter. You can do one thing or you can do another, kill a man or take a tire off his car, because sooner or later you're going to forget what it was you done and just be punished for it."

The children's mother had begun to make heaving noises as if she couldn't get her breath. "Lady," he asked, "would you and that little girl like to step off yonder with Bobby Lee and Hiram and join your husband?"

125   "Yes, thank you," the mother said faintly. Her left arm dangled helplessly and she was holding the baby, who had gone to sleep, in the other. "Hep that lady up, Hiram," The Misfit said as she struggled to climb out of the ditch, "and Bobby Lee, you hold onto that little girl's hand."

"I don't want to hold hands with him," June Star said. "He reminds me of a pig."

The fat boy blushed and laughed and caught her by the arm and pulled her off into the woods after Hiram and her mother.

Alone with The Misfit, the grandmother found that she had lost her voice. There was not a cloud in the sky nor any sun. There was nothing around her but woods. She wanted to tell him that he must pray. She opened and closed her mouth several times before anything came out. Finally she found herself saying, "Jesus, Jesus," meaning, Jesus will help you, but the way she was saying it, it sounded as if she might be cursing.

"Yes'm," The Misfit said as if he agreed. "Jesus thown everything off balance. It was the same case with Him as with me except He hadn't committed any crime and they could prove I had committed one because they had the papers on me. Of course," he said, "they never shown me my papers. That's why I sign myself now. I said long ago, you get you a signature and sign everything you do and keep a copy of it. Then you'll know what you done and you can hold up the crime to the punishment and see do they match and in the end you'll have something to prove you ain't been treated right. I call myself The Misfit," he said, "because I can't make what all I done wrong fit what all I gone through in punishment."

130   There was a piercing scream from the woods, followed closely by a pistol report. "Does it seem right to you, lady, that one is punished a heap and another ain't punished at all?"

"Jesus!" the old lady cried. "You've got good blood! I know you wouldn't shoot a lady! I know you come from nice people! Pray! Jesus, you ought not to shoot a lady. I'll give you all the money I've got!"

"Lady," The Misfit said, looking beyond her far into the woods, "there never was a body that give the undertaker a tip."

There were two more pistol reports and the grandmother raised her head like a parched old turkey hen crying for water and called, "Bailey Boy, Bailey Boy!" as if her heart would break.

"Jesus was the only One that ever raised the dead." The Misfit continued, "and He shouldn't have done it. He thrown everything off balance. If He did what He said, then it's nothing for you to do but throw away everything and follow Him, and if He didn't, then it's nothing for you to do but enjoy the few minutes you got left the best way you can—by killing somebody or burning down his house or doing some other meanness to him. No pleasure but meanness," he said and his voice had become almost a snarl.

"Maybe He didn't raise the dead," the old lady mumbled, not knowing what   135
she was saying and feeling so dizzy that she sank down in the ditch with her legs
twisted under her.

"I wasn't there so I can't say He didn't," The Misfit said. "I wisht I had of been
there," he said, hitting the ground with his fist. "It ain't right I wasn't there
because if I had of been there I would of known. Listen lady," he said in a high
voice, "if I had of been there I would of known and I wouldn't be like I am
now." His voice seemed about to crack and the grandmother's head cleared for
an instant. She saw the man's face twisted close to her own as if he were going to
cry and she murmured, "Why you're one of my babies. You're one of my own
children!" She reached out and touched him on the shoulder. The Misfit sprang
back as if a snake had bitten him and shot her three times through the chest.
Then he put his gun down on the ground and took off his glasses and began to
clean them.

Hiram and Bobby Lee returned from the woods and stood over the ditch, looking down at the grandmother who half sat and half lay in a puddle of blood with
her legs crossed under her like a child's and her face smiling up at the cloudless
sky.

Without his glasses, The Misfit's eyes were red-rimmed and pale and defense-
less-looking. "Take her off and throw her where you thrown the others," he said,
picking up the cat that was rubbing itself against his leg.

"She was a talker, wasn't she?" Bobby Lee said, sliding down the ditch with a
yodel.

"She would of been a good woman," The Misfit said, "if it had been somebody   140
there to shoot her every minute of her life."

"Some fun!" Bobby Lee said.

"Shut up, Bobby Lee," The Misfit said. "It's no real pleasure in life."

1955

The Lame Shall Enter First

Sheppard sat on a stool at the bar that divided the kitchen in half, eating his
cereal out of the individual pasteboard box it came in. He ate mechanically, his
eyes on the child, who was wandering from cabinet to cabinet in the panelled
kitchen, collecting the ingredients for his breakfast. He was a stocky blond boy
of ten. Sheppard kept his intense blue eyes fixed on him. The boy's future was
written in his face. He would be a banker. No, worse. He would operate a small
loan company. All he wanted for the child was that he be good and unselfish and
neither seemed likely. Sheppard was a young man whose hair was already white.
It stood up like a narrow brush halo over his pink sensitive face.

The boy approached the bar with the jar of peanut butter under his arm, a
plate with a quarter of a small chocolate cake on it in one hand and the ketchup
bottle in the other. He did not appear to notice his father. He climbed up on the
stool and began to spread peanut butter on the cake. He had very large round

ears that leaned away from his head and seemed to pull his eyes slightly too far apart. His shirt was green but so faded that the cowboy charging across the front of it was only a shadow.

"Norton," Sheppard said, "I saw Rufus Johnson yesterday. Do you know what he was doing?"

The child looked at him with a kind of half attention, his eyes forward but not yet engaged. They were a paler blue than his father's as if they might have faded like the shirt; one of them listed, almost imperceptibly, toward the outer rim.

5   "He was in an alley," Sheppard said, "and he had his hand in a garbage can. He was trying to get something to eat out of it." He paused to let this soak in. "He was hungry," he finished, and tried to pierce the child's conscience with his gaze.

The boy picked up the piece of chocolate cake and began to gnaw it from one corner.

"Norton," Sheppard said, "do you have any idea what it means to share?"

A flicker of attention. "Some of it's yours," Norton said.

"Some of it's *his*," Sheppard said heavily. It was hopeless. Almost any fault would have been preferable to selfishness—a violent temper, even a tendency to lie.

10   The child turned the bottle of ketchup upside down and began thumping ketchup onto the cake.

Sheppard's look of pain increased. "You are ten and Rufus Johnson is fourteen," he said. "Yet I'm sure your shirts would fit Rufus." Rufus Johnson was a boy he had been trying to help at the reformatory for the past year. He had been released two months ago. "When he was in the reformatory, he looked pretty good, but when I saw him yesterday, he was skin and bones. He hasn't been eating cake with peanut butter on it for breakfast."

The child paused. "It's stale," he said. "That's why I have to put stuff on it."

Sheppard turned his face to the window at the end of the bar. The side lawn, green and even, sloped fifty feet or so down to a small suburban wood. When his wife was living, they had often eaten outside, even breakfast, on the grass. He had never noticed then that the child was selfish. "Listen to me," he said, turning back to him, "look at me and listen."

The boy looked at him. At least his eyes were forward.

15   "I gave Rufus a key to this house when he left the reformatory—to show my confidence in him and so he would have a place he could come to and feel welcome any time. He didn't use it, but I think he'll use it now because he's seen me and he's hungry. And if he doesn't use it, I'm going out and find him and bring him here. I can't see a child eating out of garbage cans."

The boy frowned. It was dawning upon him that something of his was threatened.

Sheppard's mouth stretched in disgust. "Rufus's father died before he was born," he said. "His mother is in the state penitentiary. He was raised by his grandfather in a shack without water or electricity and the old man beat him every day. How would you like to belong to a family like that?"

"I don't know," the child said lamely.

"Well, you might think about it sometime," Sheppard said.

Sheppard was City Recreational Director. On Saturdays he worked at the refor-   20
matory as a counselor, receiving nothing for it but the satisfaction of knowing
he was helping boys no one else cared about. Johnson was the most intelligent
boy he had worked with and the most deprived.

Norton turned what was left of the cake over as if he no longer wanted it.

"Maybe he won't come," the child said and his eyes brightened slightly.

"Think of everything you have that he doesn't!" Sheppard said. "Suppose you
had to root in garbage cans for food? Suppose you had a huge swollen foot and
one side of you dropped lower than the other when you walked?"

The boy looked blank, obviously unable to imagine such a thing.

"You have a healthy body," Sheppard said, "a good home. You've never been   25
taught anything but the truth. Your daddy gives you everything you need and
want. You don't have a grandfather who beats you. And your mother is not in
the state penitentiary."

The child pushed his plate away. Sheppard groaned aloud.

A knot of flesh appeared below the boy's suddenly distorted mouth. His face
became a mass of lumps with slits for eyes. "If she was in the penitentiary," he
began in a kind of racking bellow, "I could go to seeeeee her." Tears rolled down
his face and the ketchup dribbled on his chin. He looked as if he had been hit in
the mouth. He abandoned himself and howled.

Sheppard sat helpless and miserable, like a man lashed by some elemental
force of nature. This was not a normal grief. It was all part of his selfishness. She
had been dead for over a year and a child's grief should not last so long. "You're
going on eleven years old," he said reproachfully.

The child began an agonizing high-pitched heaving noise.

"If you stop thinking about yourself and think what you can do for somebody   30
else," Sheppard said, "then you'll stop missing your mother."

The boy was silent but his shoulders continued to shake. Then his face collapsed and he began to howl again.

"Don't you think I'm lonely without her too?" Sheppard said. "Don't you
think I miss her at all? I do, but I'm not sitting around moping. I'm busy helping
other people. When do you see me just sitting around thinking about my troubles?"

The boy slumped as if he were exhausted but fresh tears streaked his face.

"What are you going to do today?" Sheppard asked, to get his mind on something else.

The child ran his arm across his eyes. "Sell seeds," he mumbled.   35

Always selling something. He had four quart jars full of nickels and dimes he
had saved and he took them out of his closet every few days and counted them.
"What are you selling seeds for?"

"To win a prize."

"What's the prize?"

"A thousand dollars."

"And what would you do if you had a thousand dollars?"   40

"Keep it," the child said and wiped his nose on his shoulder.

"I feel sure you would," Sheppard said. "Listen," he said and lowered his voice to an almost pleading tone, "suppose by some chance you did win a thousand dollars. Wouldn't you like to spend it on children less fortunate than yourself? Wouldn't you like to give some swings and trapezes to the orphanage? Wouldn't you like to buy poor Rufus Johnson a new shoe?"

The boy began to back away from the bar. Then suddenly he leaned forward and hung with his mouth open over his plate. Sheppard groaned again. Everything came up, the cake, the peanut butter, the ketchup—a limp sweet batter. He hung over it gagging, more came, and he waited with his mouth open over the plate as if he expected his heart to come up next.

"It's all right," Sheppard said, "it's all right. You couldn't help it. Wipe your mouth and go lie down."

45   The child hung there a moment longer. Then he raised his face and looked blindly at his father.

"Go on," Sheppard said. "Go on and lie down."

The boy pulled up the end of his t-shirt and smeared his mouth with it. Then he climbed down off the stool and wandered out of the kitchen.

Sheppard sat there staring at the puddle of half-digested food. The sour odor reached him and he drew back. His gorge rose. He got up and carried the plate to the sink and turned the water on it and watched grimly as the mess ran down the drain. Johnson's sad thin hand rooted in garbage cans for food while his own child, selfish, unresponsive, greedy, had so much that he threw it up. He cut off the faucet with a thrust of his fist. Johnson had a capacity for real response and had been deprived of everything from birth; Norton was average or below and had had every advantage.

He went back to the bar to finish his breakfast. The cereal was soggy in the cardboard box but he paid no attention to what he was eating. Johnson was worth any amount of effort because he had the potential. He had seen it from the time the boy had limped in for his first interview.

50   Sheppard's office at the reformatory was a narrow closet with one window and a small table and two chairs in it. He had never been inside a confessional but he thought it must be the same kind of operation he had here, except that he explained, he did not absolve. His credentials were less dubious than a priest's; he had been trained for what he was doing.

When Johnson came in for his first interview, he had been reading over the boy's record—senseless destruction, windows smashed, city trash boxes set afire, tires slashed—the kind of thing he found where boys had been transplanted abruptly from the country to the city as this one had. He came to Johnson's I. Q. score. It was 140. He raised his eyes eagerly.

The boy sat slumped on the edge of his chair, his arms hanging between his thighs. The light from the window fell on his face. His eyes, steel-colored and very still, were trained narrowly forward. His thin dark hair hung in a flat forelock across the side of his forehead, not carelessly like a boy's, but fiercely like an old man's. A kind of fanatic intelligence was palpable in his face.

Sheppard smiled to diminish the distance between them.

The boy's expression did not soften. He leaned back in his chair and lifted a monstrous club foot to his knee. The foot was in a heavy black battered shoe with a sole four or five inches thick. The leather parted from it in one place and the end of an empty sock protruded like a gray tongue from a severed head. The case was clear to Sheppard instantly. His mischief was compensation for the foot.

"Well Rufus," he said, "I see by the record here that you don't have but a year to serve. What do you plan to do when you get out?"

"I don't make no plans," the boy said. His eyes shifted indifferently to something outside the window behind Sheppard in the far distance.

"Maybe you ought to," Sheppard said and smiled.

Johnson continued to gaze beyond him.

"I want to see you make the most of your intelligence," Sheppard said. "What's most important to you? Let's talk about what's important to *you*." His eyes dropped involuntarily to the foot.

"Study it and git your fill," the boy drawled.

Sheppard reddened. The black deformed mass swelled before his eyes. He ignored the remark and the leer the boy was giving him. "Rufus," he said, "you've got into a lot of senseless trouble but I think when you understand why you do these things, you'll be less inclined to do them." He smiled. They had so few friends, saw so few pleasant faces, that half his effectiveness came from nothing more than smiling at them. "There are a lot of things about yourself that I think I can explain to you," he said.

Johnson looked at him stonily. "I ain't asked for no explanation," he said. "I already know why I do what I do."

"Well good!" Sheppard said. "Suppose you tell me what's made you do the things you've done?"

A black sheen appeared in the boy's eyes. "Satan," he said. "He has me in his power."

Sheppard looked at him steadily. There was no indication on the boy's face that he had said this to be funny. The line of his thin mouth was set with pride. Sheppard's eyes hardened. He felt a momentary dull despair as if he were faced with some elemental warping of nature that had happened too long ago to be corrected now. This boy's questions about life had been answered by signs nailed on the pine trees: DOES SATAN HAVE YOU IN HIS POWER? REPENT OR BURN IN HELL. JESUS SAVES. He would know the Bible with or without reading it. His despair gave way to outrage. "Rubbish!" he snorted. "We're living in the space age! You're too smart to give me an answer like that."

Johnson's mouth twisted slightly. His look was contemptuous but amused. There was a glint of challenge in his eyes.

Sheppard scrutinized his face. Where there was intelligence anything was possible. He smiled again, a smile that was like an invitation to the boy to come into a school room with all its windows thrown open to the light. "Rufus," he said, "I'm going to arrange for you to have a conference with me once a week. Maybe there's an explanation for your explanation. Maybe I can explain your devil to you."

After that he had talked to Johnson every Saturday for the rest of the year. He talked at random, the kind of talk the boy would never have heard before. He talked a little above him to give him something to reach for. He roamed from simple psychology and the dodges of the human mind to astronomy and the space capsules that were whirling around the earth faster than the speed of sound and would soon encircle the stars. Instinctively he concentrated on the stars. He wanted to give the boy something to reach for besides his neighbor's goods. He wanted to stretch his horizons. He wanted him to *see* the universe, to see that the darkest parts of it could be penetrated. He would have given anything to be able to put a telescope in Johnson's hands.

Johnson said little and what he did say, for the sake of his pride, was in dissent or senseless contradiction, with the clubfoot raised always to his knee like a weapon ready for use, but Sheppard was not deceived. He watched his eyes and every week he saw something in them crumble. From the boy's face, hard but shocked, braced against the light that was ravaging him, he could see that he was hitting dead center.

70   Johnson was free now to live out of garbage cans and rediscover his old ignorance. The injustice of it was infuriating. He had been sent back to the grandfather; the old man's imbecility could only be imagined. Perhaps the boy had by now run away from him. The idea of getting custody of Johnson had occurred to Sheppard before, but the fact of the grandfather had stood in the way. Nothing excited him so much as thinking what he could do for such a boy. First he would have him fitted for a new orthopedic shoe. His back was thrown out of line every time he took a step. Then he would encourage him in some particular intellectual interest. He thought of the telescope. He could buy a second-hand one and they could set it up in the attic window. He sat for almost ten minutes thinking what he could do if he had Johnson here with him. What was wasted on Norton would cause Johnson to flourish. Yesterday when he had seen him with his hand in the garbage can, he had waved and started forward. Johnson had seen him, paused a split-second, then vanished with the swiftness of a rat, but not before Sheppard had seen his expression change. Something had kindled in the boy's eyes, he was sure of it, some memory of the lost light.

He got up and threw the cereal box in the garbage. Before he left the house, he looked into Norton's room to be sure he was not still sick. The child was sitting cross-legged on his bed. He had emptied the quart jars of change into one large pile in front of him, and was sorting it out by nickels and dimes and quarters.

That afternoon Norton was alone in the house, squatting on the floor of his room arranging packages of flower seeds in rows around himself. Rain slashed against the window panes and rattled in the gutters. The room had grown dark but every few minutes it was lit by silent lightning and the seed packages showed up gaily on the floor. He squatted motionless like a large pale frog in the midst of this potential garden. All at once his eyes became alert. Without warning the rain had stopped. The silence was heavy as if the downpour had been hushed by violence. He remained motionless, only his eyes turning.

Into the silence came the distinct click of a key turning in the front door lock. The sound was a very deliberate one. It drew attention to itself and held it as if it were controlled more by a mind than by a hand. The child leapt up and got into the closet.

The footsteps began to move in the hall. They were deliberate and irregular, a light and then a heavy one, then a silence as if the visitor had paused to listen himself or to examine something. In a minute the kitchen door screeked. The footsteps crossed the kitchen to the refrigerator. The closet wall and the kitchen wall were the same. Norton stood with his ear pressed against it. The refrigerator door opened. There was a prolonged silence.

He took off his shoes and then tiptoed out of the closet and stepped over the seed packages. In the middle of the room, he stopped and remained where he was, rigid. A thin bony-face boy in a wet black suit stood in his door, blocking his escape. His hair was flattened to his skull by the rain. He stood there like an irate drenched crow. His look went through the child like a pin and paralyzed him. Then his eyes began to move over everything in the room—the unmade bed, the dirty curtains on the one large window, a photograph of a wide-faced young woman that stood up in the clutter on top of the dresser.

The child's tongue suddenly went wild. "He's been expecting you, he's going to give you a new shoe because you have to eat out of garbage cans!" he said in a kind of mouse-like shriek.

"I eat out of garbage cans," the boy said slowly with a beady stare, "because I like to eat out of garbage cans. See?"

The child nodded.

"And I got ways of getting my own shoe. See?"

The child nodded, mesmerized.

The boy limped in and sat down on the bed. He arranged a pillow behind him and stretched his short leg out so that the big black shoe rested conspicuously on a fold of the sheet.

Norton's gaze settled on it and remained immobile. The sole was as thick as a brick.

Johnson wiggled it slightly and smiled. "If I kick somebody *once* with this," he said, "it learns them not to mess with me."

The child nodded.

"Go in the kitchen," Johnson said, "and make me a sandwich with some of that rye bread and ham and bring me a glass of milk."

Norton went off like a mechanical toy, pushed in the right direction. He made a large greasy sandwich with ham hanging out the sides of it and poured out a glass of milk. Then he returned to the room with the glass of milk in one hand and the sandwich in the other.

Johnson was leaning back regally against the pillow. "Thanks, waiter," he said and took the sandwich.

Norton stood by the side of the bed, holding the glass.

The boy tore into the sandwich and ate steadily until he finished it. Then he took the glass of milk. He held it with both hands like a child and when he lowered it for breath, there was a rim of milk around his mouth. He handed Norton the empty glass. "Go get me one of them oranges in there, waiter," he said hoarsely.

90   Norton went to the kitchen and returned with the orange. Johnson peeled it with his fingers and let the peeling drop in the bed. He ate it slowly, spitting the seeds out in front of him. When he finished, he wiped his hands on the sheet and gave Norton a long appraising stare. He appeared to have been softened by the service. "You're his kid all right," he said. "You got the same stupid face."

The child stood there stolidly as if he had not heard.

"He don't know his left hand from his right," Johnson said with a hoarse pleasure in his voice.

The child cast his eyes a little to the side of the boy's face and looked fixedly at the wall.

"Yaketty yaketty yak," Johnson said, "and never says a thing."

95   The child's upper lip lifted slightly but he didn't say anything.

"Gas," Johnson said. "Gas."

The child's face began to have a wary look of belligerence. He backed away slightly as if he were prepared to retreat instantly. "He's good," he mumbled. "He helps people."

"Good!" Johnson said savagely. He thrust his head forward. "Listen here," he hissed, "I don't care if he's good or not. He ain't *right!*"

Norton looked stunned.

100   The screen door in the kitchen banged and someone entered. Johnson sat forward instantly. "Is that him?" he said.

"It's the cook," Norton said. "She comes in the afternoon."

Johnson got up and limped into the hall and stood in the kitchen door and Norton followed him.

The colored girl was at the closet taking off a bright red raincoat. She was a tall light-yellow girl with a mouth like a large rose that had darkened and wilted. Her hair was dressed in tiers on top of her head and leaned to the side like the Tower of Pisa.

Johnson made a noise through his teeth. "Well look at Aunt Jemima," he said.

105   The girl paused and trained an insolent gaze on them. They might have been dust on the floor.

"Come on," Johnson said, "let's see what all you got besides a nigger." He opened the first door to his right in the hall and looked into a pink-tiled bathroom. "A pink can!" he murmured.

He turned a comical face to the child. "Does he sit on that?"

"It's for company," Norton said, "but he sits on it sometimes."

"He ought to empty his head in it," Johnson said.

110   The door was open to the next room. It was the room Sheppard had slept in since his wife died. An ascetic-looking iron bed stood on the bare floor. A heap of Little League baseball uniforms was piled in one corner. Papers were scattered over a large roll-top desk and held down in various places by his pipes. Johnson stood looking into the room silently. He wrinkled his nose. "Guess who?" he said.

The door to the next room was closed but Johnson opened it and thrust his head into the semi-darkness within. The shades were down and the air was close with a faint scent of perfume in it. There was a wide antique bed and a mammoth dresser whose mirror glinted in the half light. Johnson snapped the light switch by the door and crossed the room to the mirror and peered into it. A silver comb and brush lay on the linen runner. He picked up the comb and began to run it through his hair. He combed it straight down on his forehead. Then he swept it to the side, Hitler fashion.

"Leave her comb alone!" the child said. He stood in the door, pale and breathing heavily as if he were watching sacrilege in a holy place.

Johnson put the comb down and picked up the brush and gave his hair a swipe with it.

"She's dead," the child said.

"I ain't afraid of dead people's things," Johnson said. He opened the top   115
drawer and slid his hand in.

"Take your big fat dirty hands off my mother's clothes!" the child said in a high suffocated voice.

"Keep your shirt on, sweetheart," Johnson murmured. He pulled up a wrinkled red polka dot blouse and dropped it back. Then he pulled out a green silk kerchief and whirled it over his head and let it float to the floor. His hand continued to plow deep into the drawer. After a moment it came up gripping a faded corset with four dangling metal supporters. "Thisyer must be her saddle," he observed.

He lifted it gingerly and shook it. Then he fastened it around his waist and jumped up and down, making the metal supporters dance. He began to snap his fingers and turn his hips from side to side. "Gonter rock, rattle and roll," he sang. "Gonter rock, rattle and roll. Can't please that woman, to save my doggone soul." He began to move around, stamping the good foot down and slinging the heavy one to the side. He danced out the door, past the stricken child and down the hall toward the kitchen.

A half hour later Sheppard came home. He dropped his raincoat on a chair in the hall and came as far as the parlor door and stopped. His face was suddenly transformed. It shone with pleasure. Johnson sat, a dark figure, in a high-backed pink upholstered chair. The wall behind him was lined with books from floor to ceiling. He was reading one. Sheppard's eyes narrowed. It was a volume of the Encyclopedia Britannica. He was so engrossed in it that he did not look up. Sheppard held his breath. This was the perfect setting for the boy. He had to keep him here. He had to manage it somehow.

"Rufus!" he said, "it's good to see you boy!" and he bounded forward with his   120
arm outstretched.

Johnson looked up, his face blank. "Oh hello," he said. He ignored the hand as long as he was able but when Sheppard did not withdraw it, he grudgingly shook it.

Sheppard was prepared for this kind of reaction. It was part of Johnson's make-up never to show enthusiasm.

"How are things?" he said. "How's your grandfather treating you?" He sat down on the edge of the sofa.

"He dropped dead," the boy said indifferently.

125 "You don't mean it!" Sheppard cried. He got up and sat down on the coffee table nearer the boy.

"Naw," Johnson said, "he ain't dropped dead. I wisht he had."

"Well where is he?" Sheppard muttered.

"He's gone with a remnant to the hills," Johnson said. "Him and some others. They're going to bury some Bibles in a cave and take two of different kinds of animals and all like that. Like Noah. Only this time it's going to be fire, not flood."

Sheppard's mouth stretched wryly. "I see," he said. Then he said, "In other words the old fool has abandoned you?"

130 "He ain't no fool," the boy said in an indignant tone.

"Has he abandoned you or not?" Sheppard asked impatiently.

The boy shrugged.

"Where's your probation officer?"

"I ain't supposed to keep up with him," Johnson said. "He's supposed to keep up with me."

135 Sheppard laughed. "Wait a minute," he said. He got up and went into the hall and got his raincoat off the chair and took it to the hall closet to hang it up. He had to give himself time to think, to decide how he could ask the boy so that he would stay. He couldn't force him to stay. It would have to be voluntary. Johnson pretended not to like him. That was only to uphold his pride, but he would have to ask him in such a way that his pride could still be upheld. He opened the closet door and took out a hanger. An old gray winter coat of his wife's still hung there. He pushed it aside but it didn't move. He pulled it open roughly and winced as if he had seen the larva inside a cocoon. Norton stood in it, his face swollen and pale, with a drugged look of misery on it. Sheppard stared at him. Suddenly he was confronted with a possibility. "Get out of there," he said. He caught him by the shoulder and propelled him firmly into the parlor and over to the pink chair where Johnson was sitting with the encyclopedia in his lap. He was going to risk everything in one blow.

"Rufus," he said, "I've got a problem. I need your help."

Johnson looked up suspiciously.

"Listen," Sheppard said, "we need another boy in the house." There was a genuine desperation in his voice. "Norton here has never had to divide anything in his life. He doesn't know what it means to share. And I need somebody to teach him. How about helping me out? Stay here for a while with us, Rufus. I need your help." The excitement in his voice made it thin.

The child suddenly came to life. His face swelled with fury. "He went in her room and used her comb!" he screamed, yanking Sheppard's arm. "He put on her corset and danced with Leola, he . . ."

140 "Stop this!" Sheppard said sharply. "Is tattling all you're capable of? I'm not asking you for a report on Rufus's conduct. I'm asking you to make him welcome here. Do you understand?

"You see how it is?" he asked, turning to Johnson.

Norton kicked the leg of the pink chair viciously, just missing Johnson's swollen foot. Sheppard yanked him back.

"He said you weren't nothing but gas!" the child shrieked.

A sly look of pleasure crossed Johnson's face.

Sheppard was not put back. These insults were part of the boy's defensive mechanism. "What about it, Rufus?" he said. "Will you stay with us for a while?"

Johnson looked straight in front of him and said nothing. He smiled slightly and appeared to gaze upon some vision of the future that pleased him.

"I don't care," he said and turned a page of the encyclopedia. "I can stand anywhere."

"Wonderful." Sheppard said. "Wonderful."

"He said," the child said in a throaty whisper, "you didn't know your left hand from your right."

There was a silence.

Johnson wet his finger and turned another page of the encyclopedia.

"I have something to say to both of you," Sheppard said in a voice without inflection. His eyes moved from one to the other of them and he spoke slowly as if what he was saying he would say only once and it behooved them to listen. "If it made any difference to me what Rufus thinks of me," he said, "then I wouldn't be asking him here. Rufus is going to help me out and I'm going to help him out and we're both going to help you out. I'd simply be selfish if I let what Rufus thinks of me interfere with what I can do for Rufus. If I can help a person, all I want is to do it. I'm above and beyond simple pettiness."

Neither of them made a sound. Norton stared at the chair cushion. Johnson peered closer at some fine print in the encyclopedia. Sheppard was looking at the tops of their heads. He smiled. After all, he had won. The boy was staying. He reached out and ruffled Norton's hair and slapped Johnson on the shoulder. "Now you fellows sit here and get acquainted," he said gaily and started toward the door. "I'm going to see what Leola left us for supper."

When he was gone, Johnson raised his head and looked at Norton. The child looked back at him bleakly. "God, kid," Johnson said in a cracked voice, "how do you stand it?" His face was stiff with outrage. "He thinks he's Jesus Christ!"

II

Sheppard's attic was a large unfinished room with exposed beams and no electric light. They had set the telescope up on a tripod in one of the dormer windows. It pointed now toward the dark sky where a sliver of moon, as fragile as an egg shell, had just emerged from behind a cloud with a brilliant silver edge. Inside, a kerosene lantern set on a trunk cast their shadows upward and tangled them, wavering slightly, in the joints overhead. Sheppard was sitting on a packing box, looking through the telescope, and Johnson was at his elbow, waiting to get at it. Sheppard had bought it for fifteen dollars two days before at a pawn shop.

"Quit hoggin it," Johnson said.

Sheppard got up and Johnson slid onto the box and put his eye to the instrument.

Sheppard sat down on a straight chair a few feet away. His face was flushed with pleasure. This much of his dream was a reality. Within a week he had made it possible for this boy's vision to pass through a slender channel to the stars. He looked at Johnson's bent back with complete satisfaction. The boy had on one of Norton's plaid shirts and some new khaki trousers he had bought him. The shoe would be ready next week. He had taken him to the brace shop the day after he came and had him fitted for a new shoe. Johnson was as touchy about the foot as if it were a sacred object. His face had been glum while the clerk, a young man with a bright pink bald head, measured the foot with his profane hands. The shoe was going to make the greatest difference in the boy's attitude. Even a child with normal feet was in love with the world after he had got a new pair of shoes. When Norton got a new pair, he walked around for days with his eyes on his feet.

Sheppard glanced across the room at the child. He was sitting on the floor against a trunk, trussed up in a rope he had found and wound around his legs from his ankles to his knees. He appeared so far away that Sheppard might have been looking at him through the wrong end of the telescope. He had had to whip him only once since Johnson had been with them—the first night when Norton had realized that Johnson was going to sleep in his mother's bed. He did not believe in whipping children, particularly in anger. In this case, he had done both and with good results. He had had no more trouble with Norton.

160   The child hadn't shown any positive generosity toward Johnson but what he couldn't help, he appeared to be resigned to. In the mornings Sheppard sent the two of them to the Y swimming pool, gave them money to get their lunch at the cafeteria and instructed them to meet him in the park in the afternoon to watch his Little League baseball practice. Every afternoon they had arrived at the park, shambling, silent, their faces closed each on his own thoughts as if neither were aware of the other's existence. At least he could be thankful there were no fights.

Norton showed no interest in the telescope. "Don't you want to get up and look through the telescope, Norton?" he said. It irritated him that the child showed no intellectual curiosity whatsoever. "Rufus is going to be way ahead of you."

Norton leaned forward absently and looked at Johnson's back.

Johnson turned around from the instrument. His face had begun to fill out again. The look of outrage had retreated from his hollow cheeks and was shored up now in the caves of his eyes, like a fugitive from Sheppard's kindness. "Don't waste your valuable time, kid," he said. "You seen the moon once, you seen it."

Sheppard was amused by these sudden turns of perversity. The boy resisted whatever he suspected was meant for his improvement and contrived when he was vitally interested in something to leave the impression he was bored. Sheppard was not deceived. Secretly Johnson was learning what he wanted him to learn—that his benefactor was impervious to insult and that there were no cracks in his armor of kindness and patience where a successful shaft could be driven. "Some day you may go to the moon," he said. "In ten years men will probably be making round trips there on schedule. Why you boys may be spacemen. Astronauts!"

"Astro-nuts," Johnson said.

165   "Nuts or nauts," Sheppard said, "it's perfectly possible that you, Rufus Johnson, will go to the moon."

Something in the depths of Johnson's eyes stirred. All day his humor had been glum. "I ain't going to the moon and get there alive," he said, "and when I die I'm going to hell."

"It's at least possible to get to the moon," Sheppard said dryly. The best way to handle this kind of thing was with gentle ridicule. "We can see it. We know it's there. Nobody has given any reliable evidence there's a hell."

"The Bible has give the evidence," Johnson said darkly, "and if you die and go there you burn forever."

The child leaned forward.   170

"Whoever says it ain't a hell," Johnson said, "is contradicting Jesus. The dead are judged and the wicked are damned. They weep and gnash their teeth while they burn," he continued, "and it's everlasting darkness."

The child's mouth opened. His eyes appeared to grow hollow.

"Satan runs it," Johnson said.

Norton lurched up and took a hobbled step toward Sheppard. "Is she there?" he said in a loud voice. "Is she there burning up?" He kicked the rope off his feet. "Is she on fire?"

"Oh my God," Sheppard muttered. "No no," he said, "of course she isn't.   175
Rufus is mistaken. Your mother isn't anywhere. She's not unhappy. She just isn't." His lot would have been easier if when his wife died he had told Norton she had gone to heaven and that some day he would see her again, but he could not allow himself to bring him up on a lie.

Norton's face began to twist. A knot formed in his chin.

"Listen," Sheppard said quickly and pulled the child to him, "your mother's spirit lives on in other people and it'll live on in you if you're good and generous like she was."

The child's pale eyes hardened in disbelief.

Sheppard's pity turned to revulsion. The boy would rather she be in hell than nowhere. "Do you understand?" he said. "She doesn't exist." He put his hand on the child's shoulder. "That's all I have to give you," he said in a softer, exasperated tone, "the truth."

Instead of howling, the boy wrenched himself away and caught Johnson by   180
the sleeve. "Is she there, Rufus?" he said. "Is she there, burning up?"

Johnson's eyes glittered. "Well," he said, "she is if she was evil. Was she a whore?"

"Your mother was not a whore," Sheppard said sharply. He had the sensation of driving a car without brakes. "Now let's have no more of this foolishness. We were talking about the moon."

"Did she believe in Jesus?" Johnson asked.

Norton looked blank. After a second he said, "Yes," as if he saw that this was necessary. "She did," he said. "All the time."

"She did not," Sheppard muttered.   185

"She did all the time," Norton said. "I heard her say she did all the time."

"She's saved," Johnson said.

The child still looked puzzled. "Where?" he said. "Where is she at?"

"On high," Johnson said.

"Where's that?" Norton gasped.   190

"It's in the sky somewhere," Johnson said, "but you got to be dead to get there. You can't go in no space ship." There was a narrow gleam in his eyes now like a beam holding steady on its target.

"Man's going to the moon," Sheppard said grimly, "is very much like the first fish crawling out of the water onto land billions and billions of years ago. He didn't have an earth suit. He had to grow his adjustments inside. He developed lungs."

"When I'm dead will I go to hell or where she is?" Norton asked.

"Right now you'd go where she is," Johnson said, "but if you live long enough, you'll go to hell."

195 Sheppard rose abruptly and picked up the lantern. "Close the window, Rufus," he said. "It's time we went to bed."

On the way down the attic stairs he heard Johnson say in a loud whisper behind him, "I'll tell you all about it tomorrow, kid, when Himself has cleared out."

The next day when the boys came to the ball park, he watched them as they came from behind the bleachers and around the edge of the field. Johnson's hand was on Norton's shoulder, his head bent toward the younger boy's ear, and on the child's face there was a look of complete confidence, of dawning light. Sheppard's grimace hardened. This would be Johnson's way of trying to annoy him. But he would not be annoyed. Norton was not bright enough to be damaged much. He gazed at the child's dull absorbed little face. Why try to make him superior? Heaven and hell were for the mediocre, and he was that if he was anything.

The two boys came into the bleachers and sat down about ten feet away, facing him, but neither gave him any sign of recognition. He cast a glance behind him where the Little Leaguers were spread out in the field. Then he started for the bleachers. The hiss of Johnson's voice stopped as he approached.

"What have you fellows been doing today?" he asked genially.

200 "He's been telling me . . ." Norton started.

Johnson pushed the child in the ribs with his elbow. "We ain't been doing nothing," he said. His face appeared to be covered with a blank glaze but through it a look of complicity was blazoned forth insolently.

Sheppard felt his face grow warm, but he said nothing. A child in a Little League uniform had followed him and was nudging him in the back of the leg with a bat. He turned and put his arm around the boy's neck and went with him back to the game.

That night when he went to the attic to join the boys at the telescope, he found Norton there alone. He was sitting on the packing box, hunched over, looking intently through the instrument. Johnson was not there.

"Where's Rufus?" Sheppard asked.

205 "I said where's Rufus?" he said louder.

"Gone somewhere," the child said without turning around.

"Gone where?" Sheppard asked.

"He just said he was going somewhere. He said he was fed up looking at stars."

"I see," Sheppard said glumly. He turned and went back down the stairs. He searched the house without finding Johnson. Then he went to the living room and sat down. Yesterday he had been convinced of his success with the boy. Today he faced the possibility that he was failing with him. He had been over-lenient, too concerned to have Johnson like him. He felt a twinge of guilt. What difference did it make if Johnson liked him or not? What was that to him? When the boy came in, they would have a few things understood. As long as you stay here there'll be no going out at night by yourself, do you understand?

I don't have to stay here. It ain't nothing to me staying here.   210

Oh my God, he thought. He could not bring it to that. He would have to be firm but not make an issue of it. He picked up the evening paper. Kindness and patience were always called for but he had not been firm enough. He sat holding the paper but not reading it. The boy would not respect him unless he showed firmness. The doorbell rang and he went to answer it. He opened it and stepped back, with a pained disappointed face.

A large dour policeman stood on the stoop, holding Johnson by the elbow. At the curb a patrol car waited. Johnson looked very white. His jaw was thrust for-ward as if to keep from trembling.

"We brought him here first because he raised such a fit," the policeman said, "but now that you've seen him, we're going to take him to the station and ask him a few questions."

"What happened?" Sheppard muttered.

"A house around the corner from here," the policeman said. "A real smash   215 job, dishes broken all over the floor, furniture turned upside down . . ."

"I didn't have a thing to do with it!" Johnson said. "I was walking along mind-ing my own bidnis when this cop came up and grabbed me."

Sheppard looked at the boy grimly. He made no effort to soften his expression.

Johnson flushed. "I was just walking along," he muttered, but with no convic-tion in his voice.

"Come on, bud," the policeman said.

"You ain't going to let him take me, are you?" Johnson said. "You believe me,   220 don't you?" There was an appeal in his voice that Sheppard had not heard there before.

This was crucial. The boy would have to learn that he could not be protected when he was guilty. "You'll have to go with him, Rufus," he said.

"You're going to let him take me and I tell you I ain't done a thing?" Johnson said shrilly.

Sheppard's face became harder as his sense of injury grew. The boy had failed him even before he had had a chance to give him the shoe. They were to have got it tomorrow. All his regret turned suddenly on the shoe; his irritation at the sight of Johnson doubled.

"You made out like you had all this confidence in me," the boy mumbled.

"I did have," Sheppard said. His face was wooden.   225

Johnson turned away with the policeman but before he moved, a gleam of pure hatred flashed toward Sheppard from the pits of his eyes.

Sheppard stood in the door and watched them get into the patrol car and drive away. He summoned his compassion. He would go to the station tomorrow and see what he could do about getting him out of trouble. The night in jail would not hurt him and the experience would teach him that he could not treat with impunity someone who had shown him nothing but kindness. Then they would go get the shoe and perhaps after a night in jail it would mean even more to the boy.

The next morning at eight o'clock the police sergeant called and told him he could come pick Johnson up. "We booked a nigger on that charge," he said. "Your boy didn't have nothing to do with it."

Sheppard was at the station in ten minutes, his face hot with shame. Johnson sat slouched on a bench in a drab outer office, reading a police magazine. There was no one else in the room. Sheppard sat down beside him and put his hand tentatively on his shoulder.

230   The boy glanced up—his lip curled—and back to the magazine.

Sheppard felt physically sick. The ugliness of what he had done bore in upon him with a sudden dull intensity. He had failed him at just the point where he might have turned him once and for all in the right direction. "Rufus," he said, "I apologize. I was wrong and you were right. I misjudged you."

The boy continued to read.

"I'm sorry."

The boy wet his finger and turned a page.

235   Sheppard braced himself. "I was a fool, Rufus," he said.

Johnson's mouth slid slightly to the side. He shrugged without raising his head from the magazine.

"Will you forget it, this time?" Sheppard said. "It won't happen again."

The boy looked up. His eyes were bright and unfriendly. "I'll forget it," he said, "but you better remember it." He got up and stalked toward the door. In the middle of the room he turned and jerked his arm at Sheppard and Sheppard jumped up and followed him as if the boy had yanked an invisible leash.

"Your shoe," he said eagerly, "today is the day to get your shoe!" Thank God for the shoe!

240   But when they went to the brace shop, they found that the shoe had been made two sizes too small and a new one would not be ready for another ten days. Johnson's temper improved at once. The clerk had obviously made a mistake in the measurements but the boy insisted the foot had grown. He left the shop with a pleased expression, as if, in expanding, the foot had acted on some inspiration of its own. Sheppard's face was haggard.

After this he redoubled his efforts. Since Johnson had lost interest in the telescope, he bought a microscope and a box of prepared slides. If he couldn't impress the boy with immensity, he would try the infinitesimal. For two nights Johnson appeared absorbed in the new instrument, then he abruptly lost interest in it, but he seemed content to sit in the living room in the evening and read the encyclopedia. He devoured the encyclopedia as he devoured his dinner, steadily and without dint to his appetite. Each subject appeared to enter his head, be ravaged, and thrown out. Nothing pleased Sheppard more than to see the boy slouched on the sofa, his mouth shut, reading. After they had spent two or three evenings like this, he began to recover his vision. His confidence returned. He knew that some day he would be proud of Johnson.

On Thursday night Sheppard attended a city council meeting. He dropped the boys off at a movie on his way and picked them up on his way back. When they reached home, an automobile with a single red eye above its windshield was waiting in front of the house. Sheppard's lights as he turned into the driveway illuminated two dour faces in the car.

"The cops!" Johnson said. "Some nigger has broke in somewhere and they've come for me again."

"We'll see about that," Sheppard muttered. He stopped the car in the driveway and switched off the lights. "You boys go in the house and go to bed," he said. "I'll handle this."

He got out and strode toward the squad car. He thrust his head in the window. 245 The two policemen were looking at him with silent knowledgeable faces. "A house on the corner of Shelton and Mills," the one in the driver's seat said. "It looks like a train run through it."

"He was in the picture show downtown," Sheppard said. "My boy was with him. He had nothing to do with the other one and he had nothing to do with this one. I'll be responsible."

"If I was you," the one nearest him said, "I wouldn't be responsible for any little bastard like him."

"I said I'd be responsible," Sheppard repeated coldly. "You people made a mistake the last time. Don't make another."

The policemen looked at each other. "It ain't our funeral," the one in the driver's seat said, and turned the key in the ignition.

Sheppard went in the house and sat down in the living room in the dark. He 250 did not suspect Johnson and he did not want the boy to think he did. If Johnson thought he suspected him again, he would lose everything. But he wanted to know if his alibi was airtight. He thought of going to Norton's room and asking him if Johnson had left the movie. But that would be worse. Johnson would know what he was doing and would be incensed. He decided to ask Johnson himself. He would be direct. He went over in his mind what he was going to say and then he got up and went to the boy's door.

It was open as if he had been expected but Johnson was in bed. Just enough light came in from the hall for Sheppard to see his shape under the sheet. He came in and stood at the foot of the bed. "They've gone," he said. "I told them you had nothing to do with it and that I'd be responsible."

There was a muttered "Yeah," from the pillow.

Sheppard hesitated. "Rufus," he said, "you didn't leave the movie for anything at all, did you?"

"You make out like you got all this confidence in me!" a sudden outraged voice cried, "and you ain't got any! You don't trust me no more now than you did then!" The voice, disembodied, seemed to come more surely from the depths of Johnson than when his face was visible. It was a cry of reproach, edged slightly with contempt.

255   "I do have confidence in you," Sheppard said intensely. "I have every confidence in you. I believe in you and I trust you completely."

"You got your eye on me all the time," the voice said sullenly. "When you get through asking me a bunch of questions, you're going across the hall and ask Norton a bunch of them."

"I have no intention of asking Norton anything and never did," Sheppard said gently. "And I don't suspect you at all. You could hardly have got from the picture show downtown and out here to break in a house and back to the picture show in the time you had."

"That's why you believe me!" the boy cried, "—because you think I couldn't have done it."

"No, no!" Sheppard said. "I believe you because I believe you've got the brains and the guts not to get in trouble again. I believe you know yourself well enough now to know that you don't have to do such things. I believe that you can make anything of yourself that you set your mind to."

260   Johnson sat up. A faint light shone on his forehead but the rest of his face was invisible. "And I could have broke in there if I'd wanted to in the time I had," he said.

"But I know you didn't," Sheppard said. "There's not the least trace of doubt in my mind."

There was a silence. Johnson lay back down. Then the voice, low and hoarse, as if it were being forced out with difficulty, said, "You don't want to steal and smash up things when you've got everything you want already."

Sheppard caught his breath. The boy was thanking him! He was thanking him! There was gratitude in his voice. There was appreciation. He stood there, smiling foolishly in the dark, trying to hold the moment in suspension. Involuntarily he took a step toward the pillow and stretched out his hand and touched Johnson's forehead. It was cold and dry like rusty iron.

"I understand. Good night, son," he said and turned quickly and left the room. He closed the door behind him and stood there, overcome with emotion.

265   Across the hall Norton's door was open. The child lay on the bed on his side, looking into the light from the hall.

After this, the road with Johnson would be smooth.

Norton sat up and beckoned to him.

He saw the child but after the first instant, he did not let his eyes focus directly on him. He could not go in and talk to Norton without breaking Johnson's trust. He hesitated, but remained where he was a moment as if he saw nothing. Tomorrow was the day they were to go back for the shoe. It would be a climax to the good feeling between them. He turned quickly and went back into his own room.

The child sat for some time looking at the spot where his father had stood. Finally his gaze became aimless and he lay back down.

270   The next day Johnson was glum and silent as if he were ashamed that he had revealed himself. His eyes had a hooded look. He seemed to have retired within himself and there to be going through some crisis of determination. Sheppard could not get to the brace shop quickly enough. He left Norton at home because

he did not want his attention divided. He wanted to be free to observe Johnson's reaction minutely. The boy did not seem pleased or even interested in the prospect of the shoe, but when it became an actuality, certainly then he would be moved.

The brace shop was a small concrete warehouse lined and stacked with the equipment of affliction. Wheel chairs and walkers covered most of the floor. The walls were hung with every kind of crutch and brace. Artificial limbs were stacked on the shelves, legs and arms and hands, claws and hooks, straps and human harnesses and unidentifiable instruments for unnamed deformities. In a small clearing in the middle of the room there was a row of yellow plastic-cushioned chairs and a shoe-fitting stool. Johnson slouched down in one of the chairs and set his foot up on the stool and sat with his eyes on it moodily. What was roughly the toe had broken open again and he had patched it with a piece of canvas; another place he had patched with what appeared to be the tongue of the original shoe. The two sides were laced with twine.

There was an excited flush on Sheppard's face; his heart was beating unnaturally fast.

The clerk appeared from the back of the shop with the new shoe under his arm. "Got her right this time!" he said. He straddled the shoe-fitting stool and held the shoe up, smiling as if he had produced it by magic.

It was a black slick shapeless object, shining hideously. It looked like a blunt weapon, highly polished.

Johnson gazed at it darkly.   275

"With this shoe," the clerk said, "you won't know you're walking. You'll think you're riding!" He bent his bright pink bald head and began gingerly to unlace the twine. He removed the old shoe as if he were skinning an animal still half alive. His expression was strained. The unsheathed mass of foot in the dirty sock made Sheppard feel queasy. He turned his eyes away until the new shoe was on. The clerk laced it up rapidly. "Now stand up and walk around," he said, "and see if that ain't power glide." He winked at Sheppard. "In that shoe," he said, "he won't know he don't have a normal foot."

Sheppard's face was bright with pleasure.

Johnson stood up and walked a few yards away. He walked stiffly with almost no dip in his short side. He stood for a moment, rigid, with his back to them.

"Wonderful!" Sheppard said. "Wonderful." It was as if he had given the boy a new spine.

Johnson turned around. His mouth was set in a thin icy line. He came back to   280
the seat and removed the shoe. He put his foot in the old one and began lacing it up.

"You want to take it home and see if it suits you first?" the clerk murmured.

"No," Johnson said. "I ain't going to wear it at all."

"What's wrong with it?" Sheppard said, his voice rising.

"I don't need no new shoe," Johnson said. "And when I do, I got ways of getting my own." His face was stony but there was a glint of triumph in his eyes.

"Boy," the clerk said, "is your trouble in your foot or in your head?"   285

"Go soak your skull," Johnson said. "Your brains are on fire."

The clerk rose glumly but with dignity and asked Sheppard what he wanted done with the shoe, which he dangled dispiritedly by the lace.

Sheppard's face was a dark angry red. He was staring straight in front of him at a leather corset with an artificial arm attached.

The clerk asked him again.

290   "Wrap it up," Sheppard muttered. He turned his eyes to Johnson. "He's not mature enough for it yet," he said. "I had thought he was less of a child."

The boy leered. "You been wrong before," he said.

That night they sat in the living room and read as usual. Sheppard kept himself glumly entrenched behind the Sunday New York *Times*. He wanted to recover his good humor, but every time he thought of the rejected shoe, he felt a new charge of irritation. He did not trust himself even to look at Johnson. He realized that the boy had refused the shoe because he was insecure. Johnson had been frightened by his own gratitude. He didn't know what to make of the new self he was becoming conscious of. He understood that something he had been was threatened and he was facing himself and his possibilities for the first time. He was questioning his identity. Grudgingly, Sheppard felt a slight return of sympathy for the boy. In a few minutes, he lowered his paper and looked at him.

Johnson was sitting on the sofa, gazing over the top of the encyclopedia. His expression was trancelike. He might have been listening to something far away. Sheppard watched him intently but the boy continued to listen, and did not turn his head. The poor kid is lost, Sheppard thought. Here he had sat all evening, sullenly reading the paper, and had not said a word to break the tension. "Rufus," he said.

Johnson continued to sit, stock-still, listening.

295   "Rufus," Sheppard said in a slow hypnotic voice, "you can be anything in the world you want to be. You can be a scientist or an architect or an engineer or whatever you set your mind to, and whatever you set your mind to be, you can be the best of its kind." He imagined his voice penetrating to the boy in the black caverns of his psyche. Johnson leaned forward but his eyes did not turn. On the street a car door closed. There was a silence. Then a sudden blast from the door bell.

Sheppard jumped up and went to the door and opened it. The same policeman who had come before stood there. The patrol car waited at the curb.

"Lemme see that boy," he said.

Sheppard scowled and stood aside. "He's been here all evening," he said. "I can vouch for it."

The policeman walked into the living room. Johnson appeared engrossed in his book. After a second he looked up with an annoyed expression, like a great man interrupted at his work.

300   "What was that you were looking at in that kitchen window over on Winter Avenue about a half hour ago, bud?" the policeman asked.

"Stop persecuting this boy!" Sheppard said. "I'll vouch for the fact he was here. I was here with him."

"You heard him," Johnson said. "I been here all the time."

"It ain't everybody makes tracks like you," the policeman said and eyed the clubfoot.

"They couldn't be his tracks," Sheppard growled, infuriated. "He's been here all the time. You're wasting your own time and you're wasting ours." He felt the *ours* seal his solidarity with the boy. "I'm sick of this," he said. "You people are too damn lazy to go out and find whoever is doing these things. You come here automatically."

The policeman ignored this and continued looking through Johnson. His eyes   305
were small and alert in his fleshy face. Finally he turned toward the door. "We'll get him sooner or later," he said, "with his head in a window and his tail out."

Sheppard followed him to the door and slammed it behind him. His spirits were soaring. This was exactly what he had needed. He returned with an expectant face.

Johnson had put the book down and was sitting there, looking at him slyly. "Thanks," he said.

Sheppard stopped. The boy's expression was predatory. He was openly leering.

"You ain't such a bad liar yourself," he said.

"Liar?" Sheppard murmured. Could the boy have left and come back? He felt   310
himself sicken. Then a rush of anger sent him forward. "Did you leave?" he said furiously. "I didn't see you leave."

The boy only smiled.

"You went up in the attic to see Norton," Sheppard said.

"Naw," Johnson said, "that kid is crazy. He don't want to do nothing but look through that stinking telescope."

"I don't want to hear about Norton," Sheppard said harshly. "Where were you?"

"I was sitting on that pink can by my ownself," Johnson said. "There wasn't   315
no witnesses."

Sheppard took out his handkerchief and wiped his forehead. He managed to smile.

Johnson rolled his eyes. "You don't believe in me," he said. His voice was cracked the way it had been in the dark room two nights before. "You make out like you got all this confidence in me but you ain't got any. When things get hot, you'll fade like the rest of them." The crack became exaggerated, comic. The mockery in it was blatant. "You don't believe in me. You ain't got no confidence," he wailed. "And you ain't any smarter than that cop. All that about tracks—that was a trap. There wasn't any tracks. That whole place is concreted in the back and my feet were dry."

Sheppard slowly put the handkerchief back in his pocket. He dropped down on the sofa and gazed at the rug beneath his feet. The boy's clubfoot was set within the circle of his vision. The pieced-together shoe appeared to grin at him with Johnson's own face. He caught hold of the edge of the sofa cushion and his knuckles turned white. A chill of hatred shook him. He hated the shoe, hated the foot, hated the boy. His face paled. Hatred choked him. He was aghast at himself.

He caught the boy's shoulder and gripped it fiercely as if to keep himself from falling. "Listen," he said, "you looked in that window to embarrass me. That was all you wanted—to shake my resolve to help you, but my resolve isn't shaken. I'm stronger than you are. I'm stronger than you are and I'm going to save you. The good will triumph."

320 "Not when it ain't true," the boy said. "Not when it ain't right."

"My resolve isn't shaken," Sheppard repeated. "I'm going to save you."

Johnson's look became sly again. "You ain't going to save me," he said. "You're going to tell me to leave this house. I did those other two jobs too—the first one as well as the one I done when I was supposed to be in the picture show."

"I'm not going to tell you to leave," Sheppard said. His voice was toneless, mechanical. "I'm going to save you."

Johnson thrust his head forward. "Save yourself," he hissed. "Nobody can save me but Jesus."

325 Sheppard laughed curtly. "You don't deceive me," he said. "I flushed that out of your head in the reformatory. I saved you from that, at least."

The muscles in Johnson's face stiffened. A look of such repulsion hardened on his face that Sheppard drew back. The boy's eyes were like distorting mirrors in which he saw himself made hideous and grotesque. "I'll show you," Johnson whispered. He rose abruptly and started headlong for the door as if he could not get out of Sheppard's sight quick enough, but it was the door to the back hall he went through, not the front door. Sheppard turned on the sofa and looked behind him where the boy had disappeared. He heard the door to his room slam. He was not leaving. The intensity had gone out of Sheppard's eyes. They looked flat and lifeless as if the shock of the boy's revelation were only now reaching the center of his consciousness. "If he would only leave," he murmured. "If he would only leave now of his own accord."

The next morning Johnson appeared at the breakfast table in the grandfather's suit he had come in. Sheppard pretended not to notice but one look told him what he already knew, that he was trapped, that there could be nothing now but a battle of nerves and that Johnson would win it. He wished he had never laid eyes on the boy. The failure of his compassion numbed him. He got out of the house as soon as he could and all day he dreaded to go home in the evening. He had a faint hope that the boy might be gone when he returned. The grandfather's suit might have meant he was leaving. The hope grew in the afternoon. When he came home and opened the front door, his heart was pounding.

He stopped in the hall and looked silently into the living room. His expectant expression faded. His face seemed suddenly as old as his white hair. The two boys were sitting close together on the sofa, reading the same book. Norton's cheek rested against the sleeve of Johnson's black suit. Johnson's finger moved under the lines they were reading. The elder brother and the younger. Sheppard looked woodenly at this scene for almost a minute. Then he walked into the room and took off his coat and dropped it on a chair. Neither boy noticed him. He went on to the kitchen.

Leola left the supper on the stove every afternoon before she left and he put it on the table. His head ached and his nerves were taut. He sat down on the kitchen stool and remained there, sunk in his depression. He wondered if he could infuriate Johnson enough to make him leave of his own accord. Last night what had enraged him was the Jesus business. It might enrage Johnson, but it depressed him. Why not simply tell the boy to go? Admit defeat. The thought of facing Johnson again sickened him. The boy looked at him as if he were the guilty one, as if he were a moral leper. He knew without conceit that he was a good man, that he had nothing to reproach himself with. His feelings about Johnson now were involuntary. He would like to feel compassion for him. He would like to be able to help him. He longed for the time when there would be no one but himself and Norton in the house, when the child's simple selfishness would be all he had to contend with, and his own loneliness.

He got up and took three serving dishes off the shelf and took them to the   330
stove. Absently he began pouring the butterbeans and the hash into the dishes. When the food was on the table, he called them in.

They brought the book with them. Norton pushed his place setting around to the same side of the table as Johnson's and moved his chair next to Johnson's chair. They sat down and put the book between them. It was a black book with red edges.

"What's that you're reading?" Sheppard asked, sitting down.

"The Holy Bible," Johnson said.

God give me strength, Sheppard said under his breath.

"We lifted it from a ten cent store," Johnson said.   335

"We?" Sheppard muttered. He turned and glared at Norton. The child's face was bright and there was an excited sheen to his eyes. The change that had come over the boy struck him for the first time. He looked alert. He had on a blue plaid shirt and his eyes were a brighter blue than he had ever seen them before. There was a strange new life in him, the sign of new and more rugged vices. "So now you steal?" he said, glowering. "You haven't learned to be generous but you have learned to steal."

"No he ain't," Johnson said. "I was the one lifted it. He only watched. He can't sully himself. It don't make any difference about me. I'm going to hell anyway."

Sheppard held his tongue.

"Unless," Johnson said, "I repent."

"Repent, Rufus," Norton said in a pleading voice. "Repent, hear? You don't   340
want to go to hell."

"Stop talking this nonsense," Sheppard said, looking sharply at the child.

"If I do repent, I'll be a preacher," Johnson said. "If you're going to do it, it's no sense in doing it halfway."

"What are you going to be, Norton," Sheppard asked in a brittle voice, "a preacher too?"

There was a glitter of wild pleasure in the child's eyes. "A space man!" he shouted.

"Wonderful," Sheppard said bitterly.   345

"Those space ships ain't going to do you any good unless you believe in Jesus,"

Johnson said. He wet his finger and began to leaf through the pages of the Bible. "I'll read you where it says so," he said.

Sheppard leaned forward and said in a low furious voice, "Put that Bible up, Rufus, and eat your dinner."

Johnson continued searching for the passage.

"Put that Bible up!" Sheppard shouted.

350   The boy stopped and looked up. His expression was startled but pleased.

"That book is something for you to hide behind," Sheppard said. "It's for cowards, people who are afraid to stand on their own feet and figure things out for themselves."

Johnson's eyes snapped. He backed his chair a little way from the table. "Satan has you in his power," he said. "Not only me. You too."

Sheppard reached across the table to grab the book but Johnson snatched it and put it in his lap.

Sheppard laughed. "You don't believe in that book and you know you don't believe in it!"

355   "I believe it!" Johnson said. "You don't know what I believe and what I don't."

Sheppard shook his head. "You don't believe it. You're too intelligent."

"I ain't too intelligent," the boy muttered. "You don't know nothing about me. Even if I didn't believe it, it would still be true."

"You don't believe it!" Sheppard said. His face was a taunt.

"I believe it!" Johnson said breathlessly. "I'll show you I believe it!" He opened the book in his lap and tore out a page of it and thrust it into his mouth. He fixed his eyes on Sheppard. His jaws worked furiously and the paper crackled as he chewed it.

360   "Stop this," Sheppard said in a dry, burnt-out voice. "Stop it."

The boy raised the Bible and tore out a page with his teeth and began grinding it in his mouth, his eyes burning.

Sheppard reached across the table and knocked the book out of his hand. "Leave the table," he said coldly.

Johnson swallowed what was in his mouth. His eyes widened as if a vision of splendor were opening up before him. "I've eaten it!" he breathed. "I've eaten it like Ezekiel and it was honey to my mouth!"[1]

"Leave this table," Sheppard said. His hands were clenched beside his plate.

365   "I've eaten it!" the boy cried. Wonder transformed his face. "I've eaten it like Ezekiel and I don't want none of your food after it nor no more ever."

"Go then," Sheppard said softly. "Go. Go."

The boy rose and picked up the Bible and started toward the hall with it. At the door he paused, a small black figure on the threshold of some dark apocalypse. "The devil has you in his power," he said in a jubilant voice and disappeared.

After supper Sheppard sat in the living room alone. Johnson had left the house but he could not believe that the boy had simply gone. The first feeling of re-

---

1. Ezekiel 3:1–3. The Lord in a vision told Ezekiel to eat a roll and go speak to the captive Israelites; when he ate, "it was in my mouth as honey for sweetness."

lease had passed. He felt dull and cold as at the onset of an illness and dread had settled in him like a fog. Just to leave would be too anticlimactic an end for Johnson's taste; he would return and try to prove something. He might come back a week later and set fire to the place. Nothing seemed too outrageous now.

He picked up the paper and tried to read. In a moment he threw it down and got up and went into the hall and listened. He might be hiding in the attic. He went to the attic door and opened it.

The lantern was lit, casting a dim light on the stairs. He didn't hear anything.   370
"Norton," he called, "are you up there?" There was no answer. He mounted the narrow stairs to see.

Amid the strange vine-like shadows cast by the lantern, Norton sat with his eye to the telescope. "Norton," Sheppard said, "do you know where Rufus went?"

The child's back was to him. He was sitting hunched, intent, his large ears directly above his shoulders. Suddenly he waved his hand and crouched closer to the telescope as if he could not get near enough to what he saw.

"Norton!" Sheppard said in a loud voice.

The child didn't move.

"Norton!" Sheppard shouted.   375

Norton started. He turned around. There was an unnatural brightness about his eyes. After a moment he seemed to see that it was Sheppard. "I've found her!" he said breathlessly.

"Found who?" Sheppard said.

"Mamma!"

Sheppard steadied himself in the door way. The jungle of shadows around the child thickened.

"Come and look!" he cried. He wiped his sweaty face on the tail of his plaid   380
shirt and then put his eye back to the telescope. His back became fixed in a rigid intensity. All at once he waved again.

"Norton," Sheppard said, "you don't see anything in the telescope but star clusters. Now you've had enough of that for one night. You'd better go to bed. Do you know where Rufus is?"

"She's there!" he cried, not turning around from the telescope. "She waved at me!"

"I want you in bed in fifteen minutes," Sheppard said. After a moment he said, "Do you hear me, Norton?"

The child began to wave frantically.

"I mean what I say," Sheppard said. "I'm going to call in fifteen minutes and   385
see if you're in bed."

He went down the steps again and returned to the parlor. He went to the front door and cast a cursory glance out. The sky was crowded with the stars he had been fool enough to think Johnson could reach. Somewhere in the small wood behind the house, a bull frog sounded a low hollow note. He went back to his chair and sat a few minutes. He decided to go to bed. He put his hands on the arms of the chair and leaned forward and heard, like the first shrill note of a disaster warning, the siren of a police car, moving slowly into the neighborhood and nearer until it subsided with a moan outside the house.

He felt a cold weight on his shoulders as if an icy cloak had been thrown about him. He went to the door and opened it.

Two policemen were coming up the walk with a dark snarling Johnson between them, handcuffed to each. A reporter jogged alongside and another policeman waited in the patrol car.

"Here's your boy," the dourest of the policemen said. "Didn't I tell you we'd get him?"

390   Johnson jerked his arm down savagely. "I was waitin for you!" he said. "You wouldn't have got me if I hadn't of wanted to get caught. It was my idea." He was addressing the policemen but leering at Sheppard.

Sheppard looked at him coldly.

"Why did you want to get caught?" the reporter asked, running around to get beside Johnson. "Why did you deliberately want to get caught?"

The question and the sight of Sheppard seemed to throw the boy into a fury. "To show up that big tin Jesus!" he hissed and kicked his leg out at Sheppard. "He thinks he's God. I'd rather be in the reformatory than in his house, I'd rather be in the pen! The Devil has him in his power. He don't know his left hand from his right, he don't have as much sense as his crazy kid!" He paused and then swept on to his fantastic conclusion. "He made suggestions to me!"

Sheppard's face blanched. He caught hold of the door facing.

395   "Suggestions?" the reporter said eagerly, "what kind of suggestion?"

"Immor'l suggestions!" Johnson said. "What kind of suggestions do you think? But I ain't having none of it, I'm a Christian, I'm . . ."

Sheppard's face was tight with pain. "He knows that's not true," he said in a shaken voice. "He knows he's lying. I did everything I knew how for him. I did more for him than I did for my own child. I hoped to save him and I failed, but it was an honorable failure. I have nothing to reproach myself with. I made no suggestions to him."

"Do you remember the suggestions?" the reporter asked. "Can you tell us exactly what he said?"

"He's a dirty atheist," Johnson said. "He said there wasn't no hell."

400   "Well, they seen each other now," one of the policemen said with a knowing sigh. "Let's us go."

"Wait," Sheppard said. He came down one step and fixed his eyes on Johnson's eyes in a last desperate effort to save himself. "Tell the truth, Rufus," he said. "You don't want to perpetrate this lie. You're not evil, you're mortally confused. You don't have to make up for that foot, you don't have to . . ."

Johnson hurled himself forward. "Listen at him!" he screamed. "I lie and steal because I'm good at it! My foot don't have a thing to do with it! The lame shall enter first! The halt'll be gathered together. When I get ready to be saved, Jesus'll save me, not that lying stinking atheist, not that . . ."

"That'll be enough out of you," the policeman said and yanked him back. "We just wanted you to see we got him," he said to Sheppard, and the two of them turned around and dragged Johnson away, half turned and screaming back at Sheppard.

"The lame'll carry off the prey!" he screeched, but his voice was muffled inside the car. The reporter scrambled into the front seat with the driver and slammed the door and the siren wailed into the darkness.

Sheppard remained there, bent slightly like a man who has been shot but continues to stand. After a minute he turned and went back in the house and sat down in the chair he had left. He closed his eyes on a picture of Johnson in a circle of reporters at the police station, elaborating his lies. "I have nothing to reproach myself with," he murmured. His every action had been selfless, his one aim had been to save Johnson for some decent kind of service, he had not spared himself, he had sacrificed his reputation, he had done more for Johnson than he had done for his own child. Foulness hung about him like an odor in the air, so close that it seemed to come from his own breath. "I have nothing to reproach myself with," he repeated. His voice sounded dry and harsh. "I did more for him than I did for my own child." He was swept with a sudden panic. He heard the boy's jubilant voice. Satan has you in his power.

"I have nothing to reproach myself with," he began again. "I did more for him than I did for my own child." He heard his voice as if it were the voice of his accuser. He repeated the sentence silently.

Slowly his face drained of color. It became almost gray beneath the white halo of his hair. The sentence echoed in his mind, each syllable like a dull blow. His mouth twisted and he closed his eyes against the revelation. Norton's face rose before him, empty, forlorn, his left eye listing almost imperceptibly toward the outer rim as if it could not bear a full view of grief. His heart constricted with a repulsion for himself so clear and intense that he gasped for breath. He had stuffed his own emptiness with good works like a glutton. He had ignored his own child to feed his vision of himself. He saw the clear-eyed Devil, the sounder of hearts, leering at him from the eyes of Johnson. His image of himself shrivelled until everything was black before him. He sat there paralyzed, aghast.

He saw Norton at the telescope, all back and ears, saw his arm shoot up and wave frantically. A rush of agonizing love for the child rushed over him like a transfusion of life. The little boy's face appeared to him transformed; the image of his salvation; all light. He groaned with joy. He would make everything up to him. He would never let him suffer again. He would be mother and father. He jumped up and ran to his room, to kiss him, to tell him that he loved him, that he would never fail him again.

The light was on in Norton's room but the bed was empty. He turned and dashed up the attic stairs and at the top reeled back like a man on the edge of a pit. The tripod had fallen and the telescope lay on the floor. A few feet over it, the child hung in the jungle of shadows, just below the beam from which he had launched his flight into space.

1965

Everything That Rises Must Converge

Her doctor had told Julian's mother that she must lose twenty pounds on account of her blood pressure, so on Wednesday nights Julian had to take her downtown on the bus for a reducing class at the Y. The reducing class was designed for working girls over fifty, who weighed from 165 to 200 pounds. His mother was one of the slimmer ones, but she said ladies did not tell their age or weight. She would not ride the buses by herself at night since they had been integrated, and because the reducing class was one of her few pleasures, necessary for her health, and *free,* she said Julian could at least put himself out to take her, considering all she did for him. Julian did not like to consider all she did for him, but every Wednesday night he braced himself and took her.

She was almost ready to go, standing before the hall mirror, putting on her hat, while he, his hands behind him, appeared pinned to the door frame, waiting like Saint Sebastian for the arrows to begin piercing him.[1] The hat was new and had cost her seven dollars and a half. She kept saying, "Maybe I shouldn't have paid that for it. No, I shouldn't have. I'll take it off and return it tomorrow. I shouldn't have bought it."

Julian raised his eyes to heaven. "Yes, you should have bought it," he said. "Put it on and let's go." It was a hideous hat. A purple velvet flap came down on one side of it and stood up on the other; the rest of it was green and looked like a cushion with the stuffing out. He decided it was less comical than jaunty and pathetic. Everything that gave her pleasure was small and depressed him.

She lifted the hat one more time and set it down slowly on top of her head. Two wings of gray hair protruded on either side of her florid face, but her eyes, sky-blue, were as innocent and untouched by experience as they must have been when she was ten. Were it not that she was a widow who had struggled fiercely to feed and clothe and put him through school and who was supporting him still, "until he got on his feet," she might have been a little girl that he had to take to town.

5   "It's all right, it's all right," he said. "Let's go." He opened the door himself and started down the walk to get her going. The sky was a dying violet and the houses stood out darkly against it, bulbous liver-colored monstrosities of a uniform ugliness though no two were alike. Since this had been a fashionable neighborhood forty years ago, his mother persisted in thinking they did well to have an apartment in it. Each house had a narrow collar of dirt around it in which sat, usually, a grubby child. Julian walked with his hands in his pockets, his head down and thrust forward and his eyes glazed with the determination to make himself completely numb during the time he would be sacrificed to her pleasure.

The door closed and he turned to find the dumpy figure, surmounted by the

---

1. Discovered to be a Christian, Sebastian, Roman commander in Milan, was tied to a tree, shot with arrows, and left for dead. (He recovered, but when he reasserted his faith he was clubbed to death.)

atrocious hat, coming toward him. "Well," she said, "you only live once and paying a little more for it, I at least won't meet myself coming and going."

"Some day I'll start making money," Julian said gloomily—he knew he never would—"and you can have one of those jokes whenever you take the fit." But first they would move. He visualized a place where the nearest neighbors would be three miles away on either side.

"I think you're doing fine," she said, drawing on her gloves. "You've only been out of school a year. Rome wasn't built in a day."

She was one of the few members of the Y reducing class who arrived in hat and gloves and who had a son who had been to college. "It takes time," she said, "and the world is in such a mess. This hat looked better on me than any of the others, though when she brought it out I said, 'Take that thing back. I wouldn't have it on my head,' and she said, 'Now wait till you see it on,' and when she put it on me, I said, 'We-ull,' and she said, 'If you ask me, that hat does something for you and you do something for the hat, and besides,' she said, 'with that hat, you won't meet yourself coming and going.' "

Julian thought he could have stood his lot better if she had been selfish, if she had been an old hag who drank and screamed at him. He walked along, saturated in depression, as if in the midst of his martyrdom he had lost his faith. Catching sight of his long, hopeless, irritated face, she stopped suddenly with a grief-stricken look, and pulled back on his arm. "Wait on me," she said. "I'm going back to the house and take this thing off and tomorrow I'm going to return it. I was out of my head. I can pay the gas bill with that seven-fifty."

He caught her arm in a vicious grip. "You are not going to take it back," he said. "I like it."

"Well," she said, "I don't think I ought . . ."

"Shut up and enjoy it," he muttered, more depressed than ever.

"With the world in the mess it's in," she said, "it's a wonder we can enjoy anything. I tell you, the bottom rail is on the top."

Julian sighed.

"Of course," she said, "if you know who are you, you can go anywhere." She said this every time he took her to the reducing class. "Most of them in it are not our kind of people," she said, "but I can be gracious to anybody. I know who I am."

"They don't give a damn for your graciousness," Julian said savagely. "Knowing who you are is good for one generation only. You haven't the foggiest idea where you stand now or who you are."

She stopped and allowed her eyes to flash at him. "I most certainly do know who I am," she said, "and if you don't know who you are, I'm ashamed of you."

"Oh hell," Julian said.

"Your great-grandfather was a former governor of this state," she said. "Your grandfather was a prosperous land-owner. Your grandmother was a Godhigh."

"Will you look around you," he said tensely, "and see where you are now?" and he swept his arm jerkily out to indicate the neighborhood, which the growing darkness at least made less dingy.

"You remain what you are," she said. "Your great-grandfather had a plantation and two hundred slaves."

"There are no more slaves," he said irritably.

"They were better off when they were," she said. He groaned to see that she
was off on that topic. She rolled onto it every few days like a train on an open
track. He knew every stop, every junction, every swamp along the way, and knew
the exact point at which her conclusion would roll majestically into the station:
"It's ridiculous. It's simply not realistic. They should rise, yes, but on their own
side of the fence."

25   "Let's skip it," Julian said.

"The ones I feel sorry for," she said, "are the ones that are half white. They're
tragic."

"Will you skip it?"

"Suppose we were half white. We would certainly have mixed feelings."

"I have mixed feelings now," he groaned.

30   "Well let's talk about something pleasant," she said. "I remember going to
Grandpa's when I was a little girl. Then the house had double stairways that went
up to what was really the second floor—all the cooking was done on the first. I
used to like to stay down in the kitchen on account of the way the walls smelled.
I would sit with my nose pressed against the plaster and take deep breaths. Actually the place belonged to the Godhighs but your grandfather Chestny paid the
mortgage and saved it for them. They were in reduced circumstances," she said,
"but reduced or not, they never forgot who they were."

"Doubtless that decayed mansion reminded them," Julian muttered. He never
spoke of it without contempt or thought of it without longing. He had seen it
once when he was a child before it had been sold. The double stairways had
rotted and been torn down. Negroes were living in it. But it remained in his mind
as his mother had known it. It appeared in his dreams regularly. He would stand
on the wide porch, listening to the rustle of oak leaves, then wander through the
high-ceilinged hall into the parlor that opened onto it and gaze at the worn rugs
and faded draperies. It occurred to him that it was he, not she, who could have
appreciated it. He preferred its threadbare elegance to anything he could name
and it was because of it that all the neighborhoods they had lived in had been a
torment to him—whereas she had hardly known the difference. She called her
insensitivity "being adjustable."

"And I remember the old darky who was my nurse, Caroline. There was no
better person in the world. I've always had a great respect for my colored friends,"
she said. "I'd do anything in the world for them and they'd . . ."

"Will you for God's sake get off that subject?" Julian said. When he got on a
bus by himself, he made it a point to sit down beside a Negro, in reparation as it
were for his mother's sins.

"You're mighty touchy tonight," she said. "Do you feel all right?"

35   "Yes I feel all right," he said. "Now lay off."

She pursed her lips. "Well, you certainly are in a vile humor," she observed. "I
just won't speak to you at all."

They had reached the bus stop. There was no bus in sight and Julian, his hands
still jammed in his pockets and his head thrust forward, scowled down the empty

street. The frustration of having to wait on the bus as well as ride on it began to creep up his neck like a hot hand. The presence of his mother was borne in upon him as she gave a pained sigh. He looked at her bleakly. She was holding herself very erect under the preposterous hat, wearing it like a banner of her imaginary dignity. There was in him an evil urge to break her spirit. He suddenly unloosened his tie and pulled it off and put it in his pocket.

She stiffened. "Why must you look like *that* when you take me to town?" she said. "Why must you deliberately embarrass me?"

"If you'll never learn where you are," he said, "you can at least learn where I am."

"You look like a—thug," she said.   40

"Then I must be one," he murmured.

"I'll just go home," she said. "I will not bother you. If you can't do a little thing like that for me . . ."

Rolling his eyes upward, he put his tie back on. "Restored to my class," he muttered. He thrust his face toward her and hissed, "True culture is in the mind, the *mind*," he said, and tapped his head, "the mind."

"It's in the heart," she said, "and in how you do things and how you do things is because of who you *are*."

"Nobody in the damn bus cares who you are."   45

"I care who I am," she said icily.

The lighted bus appeared on top of the next hill and as it approached, they moved out into the street to meet it. He put his hand under her elbow and hoisted her up on the creaking step. She entered with a little smile, as if she were going into a drawing room where everyone had been waiting for her. While he put in the tokens, she sat down on one of the broad front seats for three which faced the aisle. A thin woman with protruding teeth and long yellow hair was sitting on the end of it. His mother moved up beside her and left room for Julian beside herself. He sat down and looked at the floor across the aisle where a pair of thin feet in red and white canvas sandals were planted.

His mother immediately began a general conversation meant to attract anyone who felt like talking. "Can it get any hotter?" she said and removed from her purse a folding fan, black with a Japanese scene on it, which she began to flutter before her.

"I reckon it might could," the woman with the protruding teeth said, "but I know for a fact my apartment couldn't get no hotter."

"It must get the afternoon sun," his mother said. She sat forward and looked   50
up and down the bus. It was half filled. Everybody was white. "I see we have the bus to ourselves," she said. Julian cringed.

"For a change," said the woman across the aisle, the owner of the red and white canvas sandals. "I come on one the other day and they were thick as fleas— up front and all through."

"The world is in a mess everywhere," his mother said. "I don't know how we've let it get in this fix."

"What gets my goat is all those boys from good families stealing automobile tires," the woman with the protruding teeth said. "I told my boy, I said you may not be rich but you been raised right and if I ever catch you in any such mess, they can send you on to the reformatory. Be exactly where you belong."

"Training tells," his mother said. "Is your boy in high school?"

55   "Ninth grade," the woman said.

"My son just finished college last year. He wants to write but he's selling typewriters until he gets started," his mother said.

The woman leaned forward and peered at Julian. He threw her such a malevolent look that she subsided against the seat. On the floor across the aisle there was an abandoned newspaper. He got up and got it and opened it out in front of him. His mother discreetly continued the conversation in a lower tone but the woman across the aisle said in a loud voice, "Well that's nice. Selling typewriters is close to writing. He can go right from one to the other."

"I tell him," his mother said, "that Rome wasn't built in a day."

Behind the newspaper Julian was withdrawing into the inner compartment of his mind where he spent most of his time. This was a kind of mental bubble in which he established himself when he could not bear to be a part of what was going on around him. From it he could see out and judge but in it he was safe from any kind of penetration from without. It was the only place where he felt free of the general idiocy of his fellows. His mother had never entered it but from it he could see her with absolute clarity.

60   The old lady was clever enough and he thought that if she had started from any of the right premises, more might have been expected of her. She lived according to the laws of her own fantasy world, outside of which he had never seen her set foot. The law of it was to sacrifice herself for him after she had first created the necessity to do so by making a mess of things. If he had permitted her sacrifices, it was only because her lack of foresight had made them necessary. All of her life had been a struggle to act like a Chestny without the Chestny goods, and to give him everything she thought a Chestny ought to have; but since, said she, it was fun to struggle, why complain? And when you had won, as she had won, what fun to look back on the hard times! He could not forgive her that she had enjoyed the struggle and that she thought *she* had won.

What she meant when she said she had won was that she had brought him up successfully and had sent him to college and that he had turned out so well—good looking (her teeth had gone unfilled so that his could be straightened), intelligent (he realized he was too intelligent to be a success), and with a future ahead of him (there was of course no future ahead of him). She excused his gloominess on the grounds that he was still growing up and his radical ideas on his lack of practical experience. She said he didn't yet know a thing about "life," that he hadn't even entered the real world—when already he was as disenchanted with it as a man of fifty.

The further irony of all this was that in spite of her, he had turned out so well. In spite of going to only a third-rate college, he had, on his own initiative, come out with a first-rate education; in spite of growing up dominated by a small mind, he had ended up with a large one; in spite of all her foolish views, he was free of prejudice and unafraid to face facts. Most miraculous of all, instead of being blinded by love for her as she was for him, he had cut himself emotionally free of her and could see her with complete objectivity. He was not dominated by his mother.

The bus stopped with a sudden jerk and shook him from his meditation. A woman from the back lurched forward with little steps and barely escaped falling in his newspaper as she righted herself. She got off and a large Negro got on. Julian kept his paper lowered to watch. It gave him a certain satisfaction to see injustice in daily operation. It confirmed his view that with a few exceptions there was no one worth knowing within a radius of three hundred miles. The Negro was well dressed and carried a briefcase. He looked around and then sat down on the other end of the seat where the woman with the red and white canvas sandals was sitting. He immediately unfolded a newspaper and obscured himself behind it. Julian's mother's elbow at once prodded insistently into his ribs. "Now you see why I won't ride on these buses by myself," she whispered.

The woman with the red and white canvas sandals had risen at the same time the Negro sat down and had gone further back in the bus and taken the seat of the woman who had got off. His mother leaned forward and cast her an approving look.

Julian rose, crossed the aisle, and sat down in the place of the woman with   65
the canvas sandals. From this position, he looked serenely across at his mother. Her face had turned an angry red. He stared at her, making his eyes the eyes of a stranger. He felt his tension suddenly lift as if he had openly declared war on her.

He would have liked to get in conversation with the Negro and to talk with him about art or politics or any subject that would be above the comprehension of those around them, but the man remained entrenched behind his paper. He was either ignoring the change of seating or had never noticed it. There was no way for Julian to convey his sympathy.

His mother kept her eyes fixed reproachfully on his face. The woman with the protruding teeth was looking at him avidly as if he were a type of monster new to her.

"Do you have a light?" he asked the Negro.

Without looking away from his paper, the man reached in his pocket and handed him a packet of matches.

"Thanks," Julian said. For a moment he held the matches foolishly. A NO SMOK-   70
ING sign looked down upon him from over the door. This alone would not have deterred him; he had no cigarettes. He had quit smoking some months before because he could not afford it. "Sorry," he muttered and handed back the matches. The Negro lowered the paper and gave him an annoyed look. He took the matches and raised the paper again.

His mother continued to gaze at him but she did not take advantage of his momentary discomfort. Her eyes retained their battered look. Her face seemed to be unnaturally red, as if her blood pressure had risen. Julian allowed no glimmer of sympathy to show on his face. Having got the advantage, he wanted desperately to keep it and carry it through. He would have liked to teach her a lesson that would last her a while, but there seemed no way to continue the point. The Negro refused to come out from behind his paper.

Julian folded his arms and looked stolidly before him, facing her but as if he did not see her, as if he had ceased to recognize her existence. He visualized a scene in which, the bus having reached their stop, he would remain in his seat and when she said, "Aren't you going to get off?" he would look at her as a stranger who had rashly addressed him. The corner they got off on was usually deserted, but it was well lighted and it would not hurt her to walk by herself the four blocks to the Y. He decided to wait until the time came and then decide whether or not he would let her get off by herself. He would have to be at the Y at ten to bring her back, but he could leave her wondering if he was going to show up. There was no reason for her to think she could always depend on him.

He retired again into the high-ceilinged room sparsely settled with large pieces of antique furniture. His soul expanded momentarily but then he became aware of his mother across from him and the vision shriveled. He studied her coldly. Her feet in little pumps dangled like a child's and did not quite reach the floor. She was training on him an exaggerated look of reproach. He felt completely detached from her. At that moment he could with pleasure have slapped her as he would have slapped a particularly obnoxious child in his charge.

He began to imagine various unlikely ways by which he could teach her a lesson. He might make friends with some distinguished Negro professor or lawyer and bring him home to spend the evening. He would be entirely justified but her blood pressure would rise to 300. He could not push her to the extent of making her have a stroke, and moreover, he had never been successful at making any Negro friends. He had tried to strike up an acquaintance on the bus with some of the better types, with ones that looked like professors or ministers or lawyers. One morning he had sat down next to a distinguished-looking dark brown man who had answered his questions with a sonorous solemnity but who had turned out to be an undertaker. Another day he had sat down beside a cigar-smoking Negro with a diamond ring on his finger, but after a few stilted pleasantries, the Negro had rung the buzzer and risen, slipping two lottery tickets into Julian's hand as he climbed over him to leave.

75   He imagined his mother lying desperately ill and his being able to secure only a Negro doctor for her. He toyed with that idea for a few minutes and then dropped it for a momentary vision of himself participating as a sympathizer in a sit-in demonstration. This was possible but he did not linger with it. Instead, he approached the ultimate horror. He brought home a beautiful suspiciously Negroid woman. Prepare yourself, he said. There is nothing you can do about it. This is the woman I've chosen. She's intelligent, dignified, even good, and she's suffered and she hasn't thought it *fun*. Now persecute us, go ahead and persecute us. Drive her out of here, but remember, you're driving me too. His eyes were narrowed and through the indignation he had generated, he saw his mother across the aisle, purple-faced, shrunken to the dwarf-like proportions of her moral nature, sitting like a mummy beneath the ridiculous banner of her hat.

He was tilted out of his fantasy again as the bus stopped. The door opened with a sucking hiss and out of the dark a large, gaily dressed, sullen-looking colored woman got on with a little boy. The child, who might have been four, had on a short plaid suit and a Tyrolean hat with a blue feather in it. Julian hoped that he would sit down beside him and that the woman would push in beside his mother. He could think of no better arrangement.

As she waited for her tokens, the woman was surveying the seating possibilities—he hoped with the idea of sitting where she was least wanted. There was something familiar-looking about her but Julian could not place what it was. She was a giant of a woman. Her face was set not only to meet opposition but to seek it out. The downward tilt of her large lower lip was like a warning sign: DON'T TAMPER WITH ME. Her bulging figure was encased in a green crepe dress and her feet overflowed in red shoes. She had on a hideous hat. A purple velvet flap came down on one side of it and stood up on the other; the rest of it was green and looked like a cushion with the stuffing out. She carried a mammoth red pocket-book that bulged throughout as if it were stuffed with rocks.

To Julian's disappointment, the little boy climbed up on the empty seat beside his mother. His mother lumped all children, black and white, into the common category, "cute," and she thought little Negroes were on the whole cuter than little white children. She smiled at the little boy as he climbed on the seat.

Meanwhile the woman was bearing down upon the empty seat beside Julian. To his annoyance, she squeezed herself into it. He saw his mother's face change as the woman settled herself next to him and he realized with satisfaction that this was more objectionable to her than it was to him. Her face seemed almost gray and there was a look of dull recognition in her eyes, as if suddenly she had sickened at some awful confrontation. Julian saw that it was because she and the woman had, in a sense, swapped sons. Though his mother would not realize the symbolic significance of this, she would feel it. His amusement showed plainly on his face.

The woman next to him muttered something unintelligible to herself. He was conscious of a kind of bristling next to him, a muted growling like that of an angry cat. He could not see anything but the red pocketbook upright on the bulging green thighs. He visualized the woman as she had stood waiting for her tokens—the ponderous figure, rising from the red shoes upward over the solid hips, the mammoth bosom, the haughty face, to the green and purple hat.

His eyes widened.

The vision of the two hats, identical, broke upon him with the radiance of a brilliant sunrise. His face was suddenly lit with joy. He could not believe that Fate had thrust upon his mother such a lesson. He gave a loud chuckle so that she would look at him and see that he saw. She turned her eyes on him slowly. The blue in them seemed to have turned a bruised purple. For a moment he had an uncomfortable sense of her innocence, but it lasted only a second before principle rescued him. Justice entitled him to laugh. His grin hardened until it said to her as plainly as if he were saying aloud: Your punishment exactly fits your pettiness. This should teach you a permanent lesson.

Her eyes shifted to the woman. She seemed unable to bear looking at him and to find the woman preferable. He became conscious again of the bristling presence at his side. The woman was rumbling like a volcano about to become active. His mother's mouth began to twitch slightly at one corner. With a sinking heart, he saw incipient signs of recovery on her face and realized that this was going to strike her suddenly as funny and was going to be no lesson at all. She kept her eyes on the woman and an amused smile came over her face as if the woman were a monkey that had stolen her hat. The little Negro was looking up at her with large fascinated eyes. He had been trying to attract her attention for some time.

"Carver!" the woman said suddenly. "Come heah!"

When he saw that the spotlight was on him at last, Carver drew his feet up and turned himself toward Julian's mother and giggled.

"Carver!" the woman said. "You heah me? Come heah!"

Carver slid down from the seat but remained squatting with his back against the base of it, his head turned slyly around toward Julian's mother, who was smiling at him. The woman reached a hand across the aisle and snatched him to her. He righted himself and hung backwards on her knees, grinning at Julian's mother. "Isn't he cute?" Julian's mother said to the woman with the protruding teeth.

"I reckon he is," the woman said without conviction.

The Negress yanked him upright but he eased out of her grip and shot across the aisle and scrambled, giggling wildly, onto the seat beside his love.

"I think he likes me," Julian's mother said, and smiled at the woman. It was the smile she used when she was being particularly gracious to an inferior. Julian saw everything was lost. The lesson had rolled off her like rain on a roof.

The woman stood up and yanked the little boy off the seat as if she were snatching him from contagion. Julian could feel the rage in her at having no weapon like his mother's smile. She gave the child a sharp slap across his leg. He howled once and then thrust his head into her stomach and kicked his feet against her shins. "Behave," she said vehemently.

The bus stopped and the Negro who had been reading the newspaper got off. The woman moved over and set the little boy down with a thump between herself and Julian. She held him firmly by the knee. In a moment he put his hands in front of his face and peeped at Julian's mother through his fingers.

"I see yoooooooo!" she said and put her hand in front of her face and peeped at him.

The woman slapped his hand down. "Quit yo' foolishness," she said, "before I knock the living Jesus out of you!"

Julian was thankful that the next stop was theirs. He reached up and pulled the cord. The woman reached up and pulled it at the same time. Oh my God, he thought. He had the terrible intuition that when they got off the bus together, his mother would open her purse and give the little boy a nickel. The gesture would be as natural to her as breathing. The bus stopped and the woman got up and lunged to the front, dragging the child, who wished to stay on, after her. Julian and his mother got up and followed. As they neared the door, Julian tried to relieve her of her pocketbook.

"No," she murmured, "I want to give the little boy a nickel."

"No!" Julian hissed. "No!"

She smiled down at the child and opened her bag. The bus door opened and the woman picked him up by the arm and descended with him, hanging at her hip. Once in the street she set him down and shook him.

Julian's mother had to close her purse while she got down the bus step but as soon as her feet were on the ground, she opened it again and began to rummage inside. "I can't find but a penny," she whispered, "but it looks like a new one."

"Don't do it!" Julian said fiercely between his teeth. There was a streetlight on the corner and she hurried to get under it so that she could better see into her pocketbook. The woman was heading off rapidly down the street with the child still hanging backward on her hand.

"Oh little boy!" Julian's mother called and took a few quick steps and caught up with them just beyond the lamppost. "Here's a bright new penny for you," and she held out the coin, which shone bronze in the dim light.

The huge woman turned and for a moment stood, her shoulders lifted and her face frozen with frustrated rage, and stared at Julian's mother. Then all at once she seemed to explode like a piece of machinery that had been given one ounce of pressure too much. Julian saw the black fist swing out with the red pocketbook. He shut his eyes and cringed as he heard the woman shout, "He don't take nobody's pennies!" When he opened his eyes, the woman was disappearing down the street with the little boy staring wide-eyed over her shoulder. Julian's mother was sitting on the sidewalk.

"I told you not to do that," Julian said angrily. "I told you not to do that!"

He stood over her for a minute, gritting his teeth. Her legs were stretched out in front of her and her hat was on her lap. He squatted down and looked her in the face. It was totally expressionless. "You got exactly what you deserved," he said. "Now get up."

He picked up her pocketbook and put what had fallen out back in it. He picked the hat up off her lap. The penny caught his eye on the sidewalk and he picked that up and let it drop before her eyes into the purse. Then he stood up and leaned over and held his hands out to pull her up. She remained immobile. He sighed. Rising above them on either side were black apartment buildings, marked with irregular rectangles of light. At the end of the block a man came out of a door and walked off in the opposite direction. "All right," he said, "suppose somebody happens by and wants to know why you're sitting on the sidewalk?"   105

She took the hand and, breathing hard, pulled heavily up on it and then stood for a moment, swaying slightly as if the spots of light in the darkness were circling around her. Her eyes, shadowed and confused, finally settled on his face. He did not try to conceal his irritation. "I hope this teaches you a lesson," he said. She leaned forward and her eyes raked his face. She seemed trying to determine his identity. Then, as if she found nothing familiar about him, she started off with a headlong movement in the wrong direction.

"Aren't you going on to the Y?" he asked.

"Home," she muttered.

"Well, are we walking?"

For answer she kept going. Julian followed along, his hands behind him. He saw no reason to let the lesson she had had go without backing it up with an explanation of its meaning. She might as well be made to understand what had happened to her. "Don't think that was just an uppity Negro woman," he said. "That was the whole colored race which will no longer take your condescending pennies. That was your black double. She can wear the same hat as you, and to be sure," he added gratuitously (because he thought it was funny), "it looked better on her than it did on you. What all this means," he said, "is that the old world is gone. The old manners are obsolete and your graciousness is not worth a damn." He thought bitterly of the house that had been lost for him. "You aren't who you think you are," he said.   110

She continued to plow ahead, paying no attention to him. Her hair had come undone on one side. She dropped her pocketbook and took no notice. He stooped and picked it up and handed it to her but she did not take it.

"You needn't act as if the world had come to an end," he said, "because it hasn't. From now on you've got to live in a new world and face a few realities for a change. Buck up," he said, "it won't kill you."

She was breathing fast.

"Let's wait on the bus," he said.

115   "Home," she said thickly.

"I hate to see you behave like this," he said. "Just like a child. I should be able to expect more of you." He decided to stop where he was and make her stop and wait for a bus. "I'm not going any farther," he said stopping. "We're going on the bus."

She continued to go on as if she had not heard him. He took a few steps and caught her arm and stopped her. He looked into her face and caught his breath. He was looking into a face he had never seen before. "Tell Grandpa to come get me," she said.

He stared, stricken.

"Tell Caroline to come get me," she said.

120   Stunned, he let her go and she lurched forward again, walking as if one leg were shorter than the other. A tide of darkness seemed to be sweeping her from him. "Mother!" he cried. "Darling, sweetheart, wait!" Crumpling, she fell to the pavement. He dashed forward and fell at her side, crying, "Mamma, Mamma!" He turned her over. Her face was fiercely distorted. One eye, large and staring, moved slightly to the left as if it had become unmoored. The other remained fixed on him, raked his face again, found nothing and closed.

"Wait here, wait here!" he cried and jumped up and began to run for help toward a cluster of lights he saw in the distance ahead of him. "Help, help!" he shouted, but his voice was thin, scarcely a thread of sound. The lights drifted farther away the faster he ran and his feet moved numbly as if they carried him nowhere. The tide of darkness seemed to sweep him back to her, postponing from moment to moment his entry into the world of guilt and sorrow.

1965

Passages from Essays and Letters

from "The Fiction Writer and His Country"

. . . when I look at stories I have written I find that they are, for the most part, about people who are poor, who are afflicted in both mind and body, who have little—or at best a distorted—sense of spiritual purpose, and whose actions do not apparently give the reader a great assurance of the joy of life.

Yet how is this? For I am no disbeliever in spiritual purpose and no vague believer. I see from the standpoint of Christian orthodoxy. This means that for me the meaning of life is centered in our Redemption by Christ and what I see in the world I see in its relation to that.

Some may blame preoccupation with the grotesque on the fact that here we have a Southern writer and that this is just the type of imagination that Southern life fosters. . . . I find it hard to believe that what is observable behavior in one section can be entirely without parallel in another. At least, of late, Southern writers have had the opportunity of pointing out that none of us invented Elvis Presley and that that youth is himself probably less an occasion for concern than his popularity, which is not restricted to the Southern part of the country.

When you can assume that your audience holds the same beliefs you do, you can relax a little and use more normal means of talking to it; when you have to assume that it does not, then you have to make your vision apparent by shock—to the hard of hearing you shout, and for the almost-blind you draw large and startling figures.

from "The Grotesque in Southern Fiction"

All novelists are fundamentally seekers and describers of the real, but the realism of each novelist will depend on his view of the ultimate reaches of reality. . . . If the novelist is in tune with this [modern scientific] spirit, if he believes that actions are predetermined by psychic make-up or the economic situation or some other determinable factor, then he will be concerned above all with an accurate reproduction of the things that most immediately concern man, with the natural forces that he feels control his destiny. . . .

On the other hand, if the writer believes that our life is and will remain essentially mysterious, . . . then what he sees on the surface will be of interest to him only as he can go through it into an experience of mystery itself. . . . [F]or this kind of writer, the meaning of a story does not begin except at a depth where adequate motivation and adequate psychology and the various determinations have been exhausted. Such a writer will be interested in what we don't understand rather than in what we do.

from "The Nature and Aim of Fiction"[1]

. . . The beginning of human knowledge is through the senses, and the fiction writer begins where human perception begins. He appeals through the senses, and you cannot appeal to the senses with abstractions. . . . [F]iction is so very much an incarnational art.

Now the word *symbol* scares a good many people off, just as the word *art* does. They seem to feel that a symbol is some mysterious thing put in arbitrarily by

---

1. These selections and those that follow (from "Writing Short Stories") are composites, edited from O'Connor manuscripts by Sally and Robert Fitzgerald in *Mystery and Manners*.

O'Connor alongside self-portrait with peacock

the writer to frighten the common reader—sort of a literary Masonic grip that is only for the initiated. They seem to think that it is a way of saying something that you aren't actually saying, and so . . . they approach it as if it were a problem in algebra. Find *x*. And when they do find or think they find this abstraction, *x*, then they go off with an elaborate sense of satisfaction and the notion that they have "understood" the story. . . .

I think for the fiction writer himself, symbols are something he uses simply as a matter of course. You might say that these are details that, while having their essential place in the literal level of the story, operate in depth as well as on the surface, increasing the story in every direction.

People have a habit of saying, "What is the theme of your story?" and they expect you to give them a statement. . . . And when they've got a statement . . . , they go off happy and feel it is no longer necessary to read the story. . . . , but for the fiction writer himself the whole story is the meaning, because it is an experience, not an abstraction.

from "Writing Short Stories"

. . . A story is a complete dramatic action—and in good stories, the characters are shown through the action and the action is controlled through the characters, and the result of this is meaning that derives from the whole presented experience.

. . . Nothing essential to the main experience can be left out of a short story. All the action has to be satisfactorily accounted for in terms of motivation, and there has to be a beginning, a middle, and an end, though not necessarily in that order.

. . . I prefer to talk about the meaning in a story rather than the theme of a story. People talk about the theme of a story as if the theme were like the string that a sack of chicken feed is tied with. They think that if you can pick out the theme, the way you pick the right thread in the chicken-feed sack, you can rip the story open and feed the chickens. But this is not the way meaning works in fiction.

When you can state the theme of a story, when you can separate it from the story itself, then you can be sure the story is not a very good one. The meaning of a story has to be embodied in it, has to be made concrete in it. A story is a way to say something that can't be said any other way, and it takes every word in the story to say what the meaning is. You tell a story because a statement would be inadequate.

An idiom characterizes a society, and when you ignore the idiom, you are very likely ignoring the whole social fabric that could make a meaningful character. You can't cut characters off from their society and say much about them as individuals. You can't say anything meaningful about the mystery of a personality unless you put that personality in a believable and significant social context.

from "On Her Own Work"

In most English classes the short story has become a kind of literary specimen to be dissected. Every time a story of mine appears in a Freshman anthology, I have a vision of it, with its little organs laid open, like a frog in a bottle.

I realize that a certain amount of this what-is-the-significance has to go on, but I think something has gone wrong in the process when, for so many students, the story becomes simply a problem to be solved, something which you evaporate to get Instant Enlightenment.

A story isn't any good unless it successfully resists paraphrase, unless it hangs on and expands in the mind. Properly, you analyze to enjoy, but it's equally true that to analyze with any discrimination, you have to have enjoyed already, and I think that the best reason to hear a story read is that it should stimulate that primary enjoyment.

I often ask myself what makes a story work, and what makes it hold up as a story, and I have decided that it is probably some action, some gesture of a character that is unlike any other in the story, one which indicates where the real heart of the story lies. This would have to be an action or a gesture which was both totally right and totally unexpected; it would have to be one that was both in character and beyond character; it would have to suggest both the world and eternity. The action or gesture I'm talking about would have to be on the anagogical level, that is, the level which has to do with the Divine life and our participation in it. It would be a gesture that transcended any neat allegory that might have been intended or any pat moral categories a reader could make. It would be a gesture which somehow made contact with mystery.

. . . in my own stories I have found that violence is strangely capable of returning my characters to reality and preparing them to accept their moment of grace. . . .

We hear many complaints about the prevalence of violence in modern fiction, and it is always assumed that this violence is a bad thing and meant to be an end in itself. With the serious writer, violence is never an end in itself. It is the extreme situation that best reveals what we are essentially. . . .

from "Novelist and Believer"

. . . Great fiction . . . is not simply an imitation of feeling. The good novelist not only finds a symbol for feeling, he finds a symbol and a way of lodging it which tells the intelligent reader whether this feeling is adequate or inadequate, whether it is moral or immoral, whether it is good or evil. And his theology, even in its most remote reaches, will have a direct bearing on this.

. . . The artist penetrates the concrete world in order to find at its depths the image of its source, the image of ultimate reality. This in no way hinders his perception of evil but rather sharpens it, for only when the natural world is seen as good does evil become intelligible as a destructive force and a necessary result of our freedom.

from the Letters

TO A PROFESSOR OF ENGLISH, 28 MARCH 1961

The meaning of a story should go on expanding for the reader the more he thinks about it, but meaning cannot be captured in an interpretation. If teachers are in the habit of approaching a story as if it were a research problem for which any answer is believable so long as it is not obvious, then I think students will never learn to enjoy fiction. Too much interpretation is certainly worse than too little, and where feeling for a story is absent, theory will not supply it.

TO LOUISE AND TOM GOSSETT, 10 APRIL 1961

I have just read a review of my book [The Violent Bear It Away], long and damming [sic], which says it don't give us hope and courage and that all novels should give us hope and courage. I think if the novel is to give us virtue the selection of hope and courage is rather arbitrary—why not charity, peace, patience, joy, benignity, long-suffering and fear of the Lord? Or faith? The fact of the matter is that the modern mind opposes courage to faith. It also demands that the novel provide us with gifts that only religion can give. I don't think the novel can offend against the truth, but I think its truths are more particular than general. But this is a large subject and I ain't no aesthetician.

TO ROSLYN BARNES, 17 JUNE 1961

Can you tell me if the statement: "everything that rises must converge" is a true proposition in physics? I can easily see its moral, historical and evolutionary significance, but I want to know if it is also a correct physical statement.

TO "A," 22 JULY 1961

I had a story that I had written a first draft sort of on and Caroline thought as usual that it wasn't dramatic enough (and she was right) and told me all the things that I tell you when I read one of yours. She did think the structure was good and the situation. All I got to do is write the story. This one is called "The Lame Shall Enter First."

TO "A," 16 SEPTEMBER 1961

The thing I am writing now is surely going to convince Jack [the author John Hawkes] that I am of the Devil's party. It is out of hand right now but I am hoping I can bring it into line. It is a composite of all the eccentricities of my writing and for this reason may not be any good, maybe almost a parody. But what you start, you ought to carry through and if it is no good, I don't have to publish it. I am thinking of changing the title to "The Lame Will Carry Off the Prey."

TO JOHN HAWKES, 28 NOVEMBER 1961

You haven't convinced me that I write with the Devil's will or belong in the romantic tradition and I'm prepared to argue some more with you on this if I can remember where we left off at. I think the reason we can't agree on this is because there is a difference in our two devils. My Devil has a name, a history and a definite plan. His name is Lucifer, he's a fallen angel, his sin is pride, and his aim is the destruction of the Divine plan. Now I judge that your Devil is co-equal to God, not his creature: that pride is his virtue not his sin; and that his aim is not to destroy the Divine plan because there isn't any Divine plan to destroy. My Devil is objective and yours is subjective. You say one becomes "evil" when one leaves the herd. I say that depends entirely on what the herd is doing.

TO "A," 9 DECEMBER 1961

Some friends of mine in Texas wrote me that a friend of theirs went into a bookstore looking for a paperback copy of A *Good Man*. The clerk said, "We don't have that one but we have another by that author, called *The Bear That Ran Away With It*. I foresee the trouble I am going to have with "Everything That Rises Must Converge"—"Every Rabbit That Rises Is a Sage."

TO CECIL DAWKINS, 6 SEPTEMBER 1962

About the story ["The Lame Shall Enter First"] I certainly agree that it don't work and have never felt that it did, but in heaven's name where do you get the idea that Sheppard represents Freud? Freud never entered my mind and looking back over it, I can't make him fit now. The story is about a man who thought he was good and thought he was doing good when he wasn't. Freud was a great one, wasn't he, for bringing home to people the fact that they weren't what they thought they were, so if Freud were in this, which he is not, he would certainly be on the other side of the fence from Shepp. The story doesn't work because I don't know, don't sympathize, don't like Mr. Sheppard in the way that I know and like most of my other characters. This is a story, not a statement. I think you ought to look for simpler explanations of why things don't work and not mess around with philosophical ideas where they haven't been intended or don't apply. There's nothing in the story that could possibly suggest that Sheppard represents Freud. This is some theory of which you are possessed. I am wondering if this kind of theorizing could be what is interfering with your getting going on some writing. Don't mix up thought-knowledge with felt-knowledge. If Sheppard represents anything here, it is, as he realizes at the end of the story, the empty man who fills up his emptiness with good works.

TO "A," 3 NOVEMBER 1962

. . . In that story of mine ["The Lame Shall Enter First"] . . . the little boy wouldn't have been looking for his mother if she hadn't been a good one when she was alive. This of course could be debated, but it's nowhere suggested in the story that she wasn't a good one.

TO MARION MONTGOMERY, 16 JUNE 1963

I never wrote and thanked you for innerducing me at Georgia or for the copy of *The Sermon of Introduction,* but I liked them. They made up for my present lack of popularity with the *Atlanta Journal-Constitution* book page, that alert sheet of Sunday criticism. Did you ever see their mention of "Everything That Rises Must Converge"? Unsigned. I suspect somebody from Atlanta U. did it.

TO "A," 1 SEPTEMBER 1963

The topical is poison. I got away with it in "Everything That Rises" but only because I say a plague on everybody's house as far as the race business goes.

QUESTIONS

1. What does the scene at Red Sam's Barbecue in "A Good Man Is Hard to Find" add to the story? How does it contribute to the characterization of the main characters? help define the society and its values? prepare for what follows?
2. How does Sheppard explain why Norton throws up ("The Lame Shall Enter First," paragraph 48)? Why do you think Norton throws up (other than his putting peanut butter and ketchup on his cake)?
3. What internal evidence is there that "The Lame Shall Enter First," "A Good Man Is Hard to Find," and "Everything That Rises Must Converge" are by the same author?

WRITING SUGGESTIONS

1. Write a character sketch of the grandmother in "A Good Man Is Hard to Find," and indicate how and why your response to the grandmother changes, shifts, or is intensified from the beginning to the end of the story.
2. Briefly retell the story of "Everything That Rises Must Converge" from the point of view, perhaps even in the voice, of the African-American woman who is wearing "*the* hat."
3. Compare the function of money in "The Lame Shall Enter First" and "The Jewelry" or "Counterparts."

9

LITERARY KIND AS CONTEXT: INITIATION STORIES

Themes are useful for grouping stories together for comparison, both to highlight similarities and to reveal differences in history and structure and so to discover the uniqueness of the work. Types of characters—stereotypes—are useful for the same purpose: to show both the common qualities and the unique combination of qualities in a particular character in a story. Though all grouping and classification, used poorly, can blur distinctions and make all members of a group seem the same, when used well they do not blur but bring into focus the individuality of each member or being.

Literary criticism lacks the specific and agreed-on system of classification of biology, so that its terms are not so fixed as *phylum, genus, species*. In general, we use the term **genre** for the largest commonly agreed-on categories: fiction, poetry, drama. We use the term **subgenre** for the divisions of a genre—subgenres of fiction, for example, are novel, novella, short story, and so on. A **kind** is a species or subcategory within a subgenre.

One kind of short story, so common that some maintain it is not a kind but is equivalent to the subgenre short story itself, is the **initiation story,** in which a character—often but not always a child or young person—first learns a significant truth about the universe, reality, society, people, himself or herself. Such a subject tends to dictate the main outlines of the story's action: it begins with the protagonist in a state of innocence or mistaken belief (exposition); it leads up to the moment of illumination or the discovery of the truth (rising action to climax or turning point); and it ends usually with some indication of the result of that discovery (falling action to conclusion). This kind is particularly suitable to a short story because it lends itself to brief treatment: the illumination is more or less sudden—there is no need for lengthy development, for multiple scenes or settings, for much time to pass, for too many complications of action or a large cast of characters—yet it can encapsulate a whole life or important segment of a life and wide-ranging, significant themes.

If you've been reading this anthology from the beginning, you have already run into a number of initiation stories, and you may have some idea of what sorts of truths their protagonists discover. Young goodman Brown discovers the universality of evil in human beings. The captain in "The Secret Sharer" discovers that someone very much like him, virtually his double and therefore probably he himself, is not only capable of murder but may, under certain circumstances and in his capacity as a captain or leader, consciously choose murder as the lesser of evils. Leila ("Her First Ball") comes across the truth that youth is fleeting (you cannot say she really learns it, since by the end of that very short story she has forgotten it). We have also seen that one may retreat from the truth physically or psychologically, as does Brown, or remain unchanged or revert to one's former state, as does Leila.

Since to the young all things seem possible—one can be a doctor, novelist, tennis star, saint, and swinger, serially or simultaneously—many of the truths learned in initiation stories have to do with limitation. The girl in "Boys and Girls" learns that she is "only a girl." Sometimes a child learns the difference between words and reality in the adult world, as Hazel does in "Gorilla, My Love."

Sometimes, the initiation takes place as an unscheduled event, as in "Gorilla, My Love." At other times there is a ritual or **rite of passage,** such as a formal entry into society ("Her First Ball").

By the time you finish this chapter you should have some idea of the variations possible within the initiation story, and, as you look back to such stories as "Sonny's Blues," "The Country Husband," "Her First Ball," and many of the others, you should have a still better idea of the range of stories in this kind. Adults may be initiated as well as children and adolescents; the truths may be bitter or pleasing, cosmic, social, psychological; the initiates may change forever, retreat, shrug off what they have learned. By seeing all these stories as part of the large group of initiation stories you may the more readily notice the differences in the protagonists, the learning experiences, and the results of the initiations on the protagonists, whether they are permanent or temporary, life-denying or life-enhancing. You may, in other words, have gone a long way toward defining the unique vision of the story, its precise and individual illumination of reality. And that's the function of classification in the first place.

TONI CADE BAMBARA

Gorilla, My Love

That was the year Hunca Bubba changed his name. Not a change up, but a change back, since Jefferson Winston Vale was the name in the first place. Which was news to me cause he'd been my Hunca Bubba my whole lifetime, since I couldn't manage Uncle to save my life. So far as I was concerned it was a change completely to somethin soundin very geographical weatherlike to me, like somethin you'd find in a almanac. Or somethin you'd run across when you sittin in the navigator seat with a wet thumb on the map crinkly in your lap, watchin the roads and signs so when Granddaddy Vale say "Which way, Scout," you got sense enough to say take the next exit or take a left or whatever it is. Not that Scout's my name. Just the name Granddaddy call whoever sittin in the navigator seat. Which is usually me cause I don't feature sittin in the back with the pecans. Now, you figure pecans all right to be sittin with. If you thinks so, that's your business. But they dusty sometime and make you cough. And they got a way of slidin around and dippin down sudden, like maybe a rat in the buckets. So if you scary like me, you sleep with the lights on and blame it on Baby Jason and, so as not to waste good electric, you study the maps. And that's how come I'm in the navigator seat most times and get to be called Scout.

So Hunca Bubba in the back with the pecans and Baby Jason, and he in love. And we got to hear all this stuff about this woman he in love with and all. Which really ain't enough to keep the mind alive, though Baby Jason got no better sense than to give his undivided attention and keep grabbin at the photograph which is just a picture of some skinny woman in a countrified dress with her hand shot up to her face like she shame fore cameras. But there's a movie house in the background which I ax about. Cause I am a movie freak from way back, even though it do get me in trouble sometime.

Like when me and Big Brood and Baby Jason was on our own last Easter and couldn't go to the Dorset cause we'd seen all the Three Stooges they was. And the RKO Hamilton was closed readying up for the Easter Pageant that night. And the West End, the Regun and the Sunset was too far, less we had grownups with us which we didn't. So we walk up Amsterdam Avenue to the Washington and *Gorilla, My Love* playin, they say, which suit me just fine, though the "my love" part kinda drag Big Brood some. As for Baby Jason, shoot, like Granddaddy say, he'd follow me into the fiery furnace if I say come on. So we go in and get three bags of Havmore potato chips which not only are the best potato chips but the best bags for blowin up and bustin real loud so the matron come trottin down the aisle with her chunky self, flashin that flashlight dead in your eye so you can give her some lip, and if she answer back and you already finish seein the show anyway, why then you just turn the place out. Which I love to do, no lie. With Baby Jason kickin at the seat in front, egging me on, and Big Brood mumblin bout what fiercesome things we goin do. Which means me. Like when the big boys come up on us talkin bout Lemme a nickel. It's me that hide the money. Or when the bad boys in the park take Big Brood's Spaudeen[1] way from him. It's me that jump on they back and fight awhile. And it's me that turns out the show if the matron get too salty.

So the movie come on and right away it's this churchy music and clearly not about no gorilla. Bout Jesus. And I am ready to kill, not cause I got anything gainst Jesus. Just that when you fixed to watch a gorilla picture you don't wanna get messed around with Sunday School stuff. So I am mad. Besides, we see this raggedy old brown film *King of Kings*[2] every year and enough's enough. Grown-ups figure they can treat you just anyhow. Which burns me up. There I am, my feet up and my Havmore potato chips really salty and crispy and two jawbreakers in my lap and the money safe in my shoe from the big boys, and there comes this Jesus stuff. So we all go wild. Yellin, booin, stompin and carrying on. Really to wake the man in the booth up there who musta went to sleep and put on the wrong reels. But no, cause he holler down to shut up and then he turn the sound up so we really gotta holler like crazy to even hear ourselves good. And the matron ropes off the children section and flashes her light all over the place and

---

1. Probably refers to "Spaldeen," the small pink rubber ball made by the Spalding company and used for stick-ball.   2. Although there is a 1961 version of the film, this probably refers to the silent-movie version made in the 1920s.

we yell some more and some kids slip under the rope and run up and down the aisle just to show it take more than some dusty ole velvet rope to tie us down. And I'm flingin the kid in front of me's popcorn. And Baby Jason kickin seats. And it's really somethin. Then here come the big and bad matron, the one they let out in case of emergency. And she totin that flashlight like she gonna use it on somebody. This here the colored matron Brandy and her friends call Thunderbuns. She do not play. She do not smile. So we shut up and watch the simple ass picture.

5   Which is not so simple as it is stupid. Cause I realized that just about anybody in my family is better than this god they always talkin about. My daddy wouldn't stand for nobody treatin any of us that way. My mama specially. And I can just see it now, Big Brood up there on the cross talkin bout Forgive them Daddy cause they don't know what they doin. And my Mama say Get on down from there you big fool, whatcha think this is, playtime? And my Daddy yellin to Granddaddy to get him a ladder cause Big Brood actin the fool, his mother side of the family showin up. And my mama and her sister Daisy jumpin on them Romans beatin them with they pocketbooks. And Hunca Bubba tellin them folks on they knees they better get out the way and go get some help or they goin to get trampled on. And Granddaddy Vale sayin Leave the boy alone, if that's what he wants to do with his life we ain't got nothin to say about it. Then Aunt Daisy givin him a taste of that pocketbook, fussin bout what a damn fool old man Granddaddy is. Then everybody jumpin in his chest like the time Uncle Clayton went in the army and come back with only one leg and Granddaddy say somethin stupid about that's life. And by this time Big Brood off the cross and in the park playin handball or skully[3] or somethin. And the family in the kitchen throwin dishes at each other, screamin bout if you hadn't done this I wouldn't had to do that. And me in the parlor trying to do my arithmetic yellin Shut it off.

Which is what I was yellin all by myself which make me a sittin target for Thunderbuns. But when I yell We want our money back, that gets everybody in chorus. And the movie windin up with this heavenly cloud music and the smart-ass up there in his hole in the wall turns up the sound again to drown us out. Then there comes Bugs Bunny which we already seen so we know we been had. No gorilla my nuthin. And Big Brood say Awwww sheeet, we goin to see the manager and get our money back. And I know from this we business. So I brush the potato chips out of my hair which is where Baby Jason like to put em, and I march myself up the aisle to deal with the manager who is a crook in the first place for lyin out there sayin *Gorilla, My Love* playin. And I never did like the man cause he oily and pasty at the same time like the bad guy in the serial, the one that got a hideout behind a push-button bookcase and play "Moonlight Sonata"[4] with gloves on. I knock on the door and I am furious. And I am alone, too. Cause Big Brood suddenly got to go so bad even though my mama told us bout goin in them nasty bathrooms. And I hear him sigh like he disgusted when

---

3. A basketball game that tests shooting skill and can be played alone or as a contest between two people.   4. Popular name for Beethoven's Sonata no. 14. The man who plays this song with gloves on refers to the ever-creepy *Phantom of the Opera*.

he get to the door and see only a little kid there. And now I'm really furious cause I get so tired grownups messin over kids cause they little and can't take em to court. What is it, he say to me like I lost my mittens or wet myself or am somebody's retarded child. When in reality I am the smartest kid P.S. 186 ever had in its whole lifetime and you can ax anybody. Even them teachers that don't like me cause I won't sing them Southern songs or back off when they tell me my questions are out of order. And cause my Mama come up there in a minute when them teachers start playin the dozens[5] behind colored folks. She stalks in with her hat pulled down bad and that Persian lamb coat draped back over one hip on account of she got her fist planted there so she can talk that talk which gets us all hypnotized, and teacher be comin undone cause she know this could be her job and her behind cause Mama got pull with the Board and bad by her own self anyhow.

So I kick the door open wider and just walk right by him and sit down and tell the man about himself and that I want my money back and that goes for Baby Jason and Big Brood too. And he still trying to shuffle me out the door even though I'm sittin which shows him for the fool he is. Just like them teachers do fore they realize Mama like a stone on that spot and ain't backin up. So he ain't gettin up off the money. So I was forced to leave, takin the matches from under his ashtray, and set a fire under the candy stand, which closed the raggedy ole Washington down for a week. My Daddy had the suspect it was me cause Big Brood got a big mouth. But I explained right quick what the whole thing was about and I figured it was even-steven. Cause if you say Gorilla, My Love, you supposed to mean it. Just like when you say you goin to give me a party on my birthday, you gotta mean it. And if you say me and Baby Jason can go South pecan haulin with Granddaddy Vale, you better not be comin up with no stuff about the weather look uncertain or did you mop the bathroom or any other trickified business. I mean even gangsters in the movies say My word is my bond. So don't nobody get away with nothin far as I'm concerned. So Daddy put his belt back on. Cause that's the way I was raised. Like my Mama say in one of them situations when I won't back down, Okay Badbird, you right. Your point is well-taken. Not that Badbird my name, just what she say when she tired arguin and know I'm right. And Aunt Jo, who is the hardest head in the family and worse even than Aunt Daisy, she say, You absolutely right Miss Muffin, which also ain't my real name but the name she gave me one time when I got some medicine shot in my behind and wouldn't get up off her pillows for nothin. And even Granddaddy Vale—who got no memory to speak of, so sometime you can just plain lie to him, if you want to be like that—he say, Well if that's what I said, then that's it. But this name business was different they said. It wasn't like Hunca Bubba had gone back on his word or anything. Just that he was thinkin bout gettin married and was usin his real name now. Which ain't the way I saw it at all.

So there I am in the navigator seat. And I turned to him and just plain ole ax

5. Ritualized game or contest in which two participants exchange insults directed against each other's relatives.

him. I mean I come right on out with it. No sense goin all around that barn the old folks talk about. And like my mama say, Hazel—which is my real name and what she remembers to call me when she bein serious—when you got somethin on your mind, speak up and let the chips fall where they may. And if anybody don't like it, tell em to come see your mama. And Daddy look up from the paper and say, You hear your Mama good, Hazel. And tell em to come see me first. Like that. That's how I was raised.

So I turn clear round in the navigator seat and say, "Look here, Hunca Bubba or Jefferson Windsong Vale or whatever your name is, you gonna marry this girl?"

10   "Sure am," he say, all grins.

And I say, "Member that time you was baby-sittin me when we lived at four-o-nine and there was this big snow and Mama and Daddy got held up in the country so you had to stay for two days?"

And he say, "Sure do."

"Well. You remember how you told me I was the cutest thing that ever walked the earth?"

"Oh, you were real cute when you were little," he say, which is supposed to be funny. I am not laughin.

15   "Well. You remember what you said?"

And Granddaddy Vale squintin over the wheel and axin Which way, Scout. But Scout is busy and don't care if we all get lost for days.

"Watcha mean, Peaches?"

"My name is Hazel. And what I mean is you said you were going to marry *me* when I grew up. You were going to wait. That's what I mean, my dear Uncle Jefferson." And he don't say nuthin. Just look at me real strange like he never saw me before in life. Like he lost in some weird town in the middle of night and lookin for directions and there's no one to ask. Like it was me that messed up the maps and turned the road posts round. "Well, you said it, didn't you?" And Baby Jason lookin back and forth like we playin ping-pong. Only I ain't playin. I'm hurtin and I can hear that I am screamin. And Granddaddy Vale mumblin how we never gonna get to where we goin if I don't turn around and take my naviga-tor job serious.

"Well, for cryin out loud, Hazel, you just a little girl. And I was just teasin."

20   " 'And I was just teasin,' " I say back just how he said it so he can hear what a terrible thing it is. Then I don't say nuthin. And he don't say nuthin. And Baby Jason don't say nuthin nohow. Then Granddaddy Vale speak up. "Look here, Precious, it was Hunca Bubba what told you them things. This here, Jefferson Winston Vale." And Hunca Bubba say, "That's right. That was somebody else. I'm a new somebody."

"You a lyin dawg," I say, when I meant to say treacherous dog, but just couldn't get hold of the word. It slipped away from me. And I'm crying and crumplin down in the seat and just don't care. And Granddaddy say to hush and steps on the gas. And I'm losin my bearins and don't even know where to look on the map cause I can't see for cryin. And Baby Jason cryin too. Cause he is my blood brother and understands that we must stick together or be forever lost, what with grown-ups playin change-up and turnin you round every which way so bad. And don't even say they sorry.

1972

ALICE MUNRO

Boys and Girls

My father was a fox farmer. That is, he raised silver foxes, in pens; and in the fall and early winter, when their fur was prime, he killed them and skinned them and sold their pelts to the Hudson's Bay Company or the Montreal Fur Traders. These companies supplied us with heroic calendars to hang, one on each side of the kitchen door. Against a background of cold blue sky and black pine forests and treacherous northern rivers, plumed adventurers planted the flags of England or of France; magnificent savages bent their backs to the portage.

For several weeks before Christmas, my father worked after supper in the cellar of our house. The cellar was white-washed, and lit by a hundred-watt bulb over the worktable. My brother Laird and I sat on the top step and watched. My father removed the pelt inside-out from the body of the fox, which looked surprisingly small, mean and rat-like, deprived of its arrogant weight of fur. The naked, slippery bodies were collected in a sack and buried at the dump. One time the hired man, Henry Bailey, had taken a swipe at me with this sack, saying, "Christmas present!" My mother thought that was not funny. In fact she disliked the whole pelting operation—that was what the killing, skinning, and preparation of the furs was called—and wished it did not have to take place in the house. There was the smell. After the pelt had been stretched inside-out on a long board my father scraped away delicately, removing the little clotted webs of blood vessels, the bubbles of fat; the smell of blood and animal fat, with the strong primitive odour of the fox itself, penetrated all parts of the house. I found it reassuringly seasonal, like the smell of oranges and pine needles.

Henry Bailey suffered from bronchial troubles. He would cough and cough until his narrow face turned scarlet, and his light blue, derisive eyes filled up with tears; then he took the lid off the stove, and, standing well back, shot out a great clot of phlegm—hsss—straight into the heart of the flames. We admired him for this performance and for his ability to make his stomach growl at will, and for his laughter, which was full of high whistlings and gurglings and involved the whole faulty machinery of his chest. It was sometimes hard to tell what he was laughing at, and always possible that it might be us.

After we had been sent to bed we could still smell fox and still hear Henry's laugh, but these things, reminders of the warm, safe, brightly lit downstairs world, seemed lost and diminished, floating on the stale cold air upstairs. We were afraid at night in the winter. We were not afraid of *outside* though this was the time of year when snowdrifts curled around our house like sleeping whales and the wind harassed us all night, coming up from the buried fields, the frozen swamp, with its old bugbear chorus of threats and misery. We were afraid of *inside,* the room where we slept. At this time the upstairs of our house was not finished. A brick chimney went up one wall. In the middle of the floor was a square hole, with a wooden railing around it; that was where the stairs came up. On the other side of the stairwell were the things that nobody had any use for any more—a soldiery roll of linoleum, standing on end, a wicker baby carriage, a fern basket, china jugs and basins with cracks in them, a picture of the Battle of Balaclava,[1] very sad to look at. I had told Laird, as soon as he was old enough to understand such things, that bats and skeletons lived over there; whenever a man escaped from the county jail, twenty miles away, I imagined that he had somehow let himself in the window and was hiding behind the linoleum. But we had rules to keep us safe. When the light was on, we were safe as long as we did not step off the square of worn carpet which defined our bedroom-space; when the light was off no place was safe but the beds themselves. I had to turn out the light kneeling on the end of my bed, and stretching as far as I could to reach the cord.

5   In the dark we lay on our beds, our narrow life rafts, and fixed our eyes on the faint light coming up the stairwell, and sang songs. Laird sang "Jingle Bells," which he would sing any time, whether it was Christmas or not, and I sang "Danny Boy." I loved the sound of my own voice, frail and supplicating, rising in the dark. We could make out the tall frosted shapes of the windows now, gloomy and white. When I came to the part, *When I am dead, as dead I well may be*—a fit of shivering caused not by the cold sheets but by pleasurable emotion almost silenced me. *You'll kneel and say, an Ave there above me*—What was an Ave? Every day I forgot to find out.

Laird went straight from singing to sleep. I could hear his long, satisfied, bubbly breaths. Now for the time that remained to me, the most perfectly private and perhaps the best time of the whole day, I arranged myself tightly under the covers and went on with one of the stories I was telling myself from night to night. These stories were about myself, when I had grown a little older; they took place in a world that was recognizably mine, yet one that presented opportunities for courage, boldness and self-sacrifice, as mine never did. I rescued people from a bombed building (it discouraged me that the real war had gone on so far away from Jubilee). I shot two rabid wolves who were menacing the schoolyard (the teachers cowered terrified at my back). I rode a fine horse spiritedly down the main street of Jubilee, acknowledging the townspeople's gratitude for some yet-to-be-worked-out piece of heroism (nobody ever rode a horse there, except King Billy in the Orangemen's Day[2] parade). There was always riding and shooting in these stories, though I had only been on a horse twice—bareback because we did not own a saddle—and the second time I had slid right around and

---

1. An indecisive Crimean War battle fought on October 25, 1854.   2. The Orange Society is an Irish Protestant group named after William of Orange, who, as King William III of England, defeated the Catholic James II. The society sponsors an annual procession on July 12 to commemorate the victory of William III at the Battle of the Boyne (1690).

dropped under the horse's feet; it had stepped placidly over me. I really was learning to shoot, but I could not hit anything yet, not even tin cans on fence posts.

Alive, the foxes inhabited a world my father made for them. It was surrounded by a high guard fence, like a medieval town, with a gate that was padlocked at night. Along the streets of this town were ranged large, sturdy pens. Each of them had a real door that a man could go through, a wooden ramp along the wire, for the foxes to run up and down on, and a kennel—something like a clothes chest with airholes—where they slept and stayed in winter and had their young. There were feeding and watering dishes attached to the wire in such a way that they could be emptied and cleaned from the outside. The dishes were made of old tin cans, and the ramps and kennels of odds and ends of old lumber. Everything was tidy and ingenious; my father was tirelessly inventive and his favourite book in the world was *Robinson Crusoe*.[3] He had fitted a tin drum on a wheelbarrow, for bringing water down to the pens. This was my job in summer, when the foxes had to have water twice a day. Between nine and ten o'clock in the morning, and again after supper, I filled the drum at the pump and trundled it down through the barnyard to the pens, where I parked it, and filled my watering can and went along the streets. Laird came too, with his little cream and green gardening can, filled too full and knocking against his legs and slopping water on his canvas shoes. I had the real watering can, my father's, though I could only carry it three-quarters full.

The foxes all had names, which were printed on a tin plate and hung beside their doors. They were not named when they were born, but when they survived the first year's pelting and were added to the breeding stock. Those my father had named were called names like Prince, Bob, Wally and Betty. Those I had named were called Star or Turk, or Maureen or Diana. Laird named one Maud after a hired girl we had when he was little, one Harold after a boy at school, and one Mexico, he did not say why.

Naming them did not make pets out of them, or anything like it. Nobody but my father ever went into the pens, and he had twice had blood-poisoning from bites. When I was bringing them their water they prowled up and down on the paths they had made inside their pens, barking seldom—they saved that for nighttime, when they might get up a chorus of community frenzy—but always watching me, their eyes burning, clear gold, in their pointed, malevolent faces. They were beautiful for their delicate legs and heavy, aristocratic tails and the bright fur sprinkled on dark down their backs—which gave them their name—but especially for their faces, drawn exquisitely sharp in pure hostility, and their golden eyes.

Besides carrying water I helped my father when he cut the long grass, and the lamb's quarter and flowering money-musk, that grew between the pens. He cut with the scythe and I raked into piles. Then he took a pitchfork and threw fresh-cut grass all over the top of the pens, to keep the foxes cooler and shade their

10

---

3. Novel (1719) by Daniel Defoe about a man shipwrecked on a desert island; it goes into great detail about his ingenious contraptions.

coats, which were browned by too much sun. My father did not talk to me unless it was about the job we were doing. In this he was quite different from my mother, who, if she was feeling cheerful, would tell me all sorts of things—the name of a dog she had had when she was a little girl, the names of boys she had gone out with later on when she was grown up, and what certain dresses of hers had looked like—she could not imagine now what had become of them. Whatever thoughts and stories my father had were private, and I was shy of him and would never ask him questions. Nevertheless I worked willingly under his eyes, and with a feeling of pride. One time a feed salesman came down into the pens to talk to him and my father said, "Like to have you meet my new hired man." I turned away and raked furiously, red in the face with pleasure.

"Could of fooled me," said the salesman. "I thought it was only a girl."

After the grass was cut, it seemed suddenly much later in the year. I walked on stubble in the earlier evening, aware of the reddening skies, the entering silences, of fall. When I wheeled the tank out of the gate and put the padlock on, it was almost dark. One night at this time I saw my mother and father standing talking on the little rise of ground we called the gangway, in front of the barn. My father had just come from the meathouse; he had his stiff bloody apron on, and a pail of cut-up meat in his hand.

It was an odd thing to see my mother down at the barn. She did not often come out of the house unless it was to do something—hang out the wash or dig potatoes in the garden. She looked out of place, with her bare lumpy legs, not touched by the sun, her apron still on and damp across the stomach from the supper dishes. Her hair was tied up in a kerchief, wisps of it falling out. She would tie her hair up like this in the morning, saying she did not have time to do it properly, and it would stay tied up all day. It was true, too; she really did not have time. These days our back porch was piled with baskets of peaches and grapes and pears, bought in town, and onions and tomatoes and cucumbers grown at home, all waiting to be made into jelly and jam and preserves, pickles and chili sauce. In the kitchen there was a fire in the stove all day, jars clinked in boiling water, sometimes a cheesecloth bag was strung on a pole between two chairs, straining blue-black grape pulp for jelly. I was given jobs to do and I would sit at the table peeling peaches that had been soaked in the hot water, or cutting up onions, my eyes smarting and streaming. As soon as I was done I ran out of the house, trying to get out of earshot before my mother thought of what she wanted me to do next. I hated the hot dark kitchen in summer, the green blinds and the flypapers, the same old oilcloth table and wavy mirror and bumpy linoleum. My mother was too tired and preoccupied to talk to me, she had no heart to tell about the Normal School Graduation Dance; sweat trickled over her face and she was always counting under her breath, pointing at jars, dumping cups of sugar. It seemed to me that work in the house was endless, dreary and peculiarly depressing; work done out of doors, and in my father's service, was ritualistically important.

I wheeled the tank up to the barn, where it was kept, and I heard my mother saying, "Wait till Laird gets a little bigger, then you'll have a real help."

15   What my father said I did not hear. I was pleased by the way he stood lis-

tening, politely as he would to a salesman or a stranger, but with an air of wanting to get on with his real work. I felt my mother had no business down here and I wanted him to feel the same way. What did she mean about Laird? He was no help to anybody. Where was he now? Swinging himself sick on the swing, going around in circles, or trying to catch caterpillars. He never once stayed with me till I was finished.

"And then I can use her more in the house," I heard my mother say. She had a dead-quiet, regretful way of talking about me that always made me uneasy. "I just get my back turned and she runs off. It's not like I had a girl in the family at all."

I went and sat on a feed bag in the corner of the barn, not wanting to appear when this conversation was going on. My mother, I felt, was not to be trusted. She was kinder than my father and more easily fooled, but you could not depend on her, and the real reasons for the things she said and did were not to be known. She loved me, and she sat up late at night making a dress of the difficult style I wanted, for me to wear when school started, but she was also my enemy. She was always plotting. She was plotting now to get me to stay in the house more, although she knew I hated it (*because* she knew I hated it) and keep me from working for my father. It seemed to me she would do this simply out of perversity, and to try her power. It did not occur to me that she could be lonely, or jealous. No grown-up could be; they were too fortunate. I sat and kicked my heels monotonously against a feedbag, raising dust, and did not come out till she was gone.

At any rate, I did not expect my father to pay any attention to what she said. Who could imagine Laird doing my work—Laird remembering the padlock and cleaning out the watering-dishes with a leaf on the end of a stick, or even wheeling the tank without it tumbling over? It showed how little my mother knew about the way things really were.

I have forgotten to say what the foxes were fed. My father's bloody apron reminded me. They were fed horsemeat. At this time most farmers still kept horses, and when a horse got too old to work, or broke a leg or got down and would not get up, as they sometimes did, the owner would call my father, and he and Henry went out to the farm in the truck. Usually they shot and butchered the horse there, paying the farmer from five to twelve dollars. If they had already too much meat on hand, they would bring the horse back alive, and keep it for a few days or weeks in our stable, until the meat was needed. After the war the farmers were buying tractors and gradually getting rid of horses altogether, so it sometimes happened that we got a good healthy horse, that there was just no use for any more. If this happened in the winter we might keep the horse in our stable till spring, for we had plenty of hay and if there was a lot of snow—and the plow did not always get our road cleared—it was convenient to be able to go to town with a horse and cutter.[4]

The winter I was eleven years old we had two horses in the stable. We did not

---

4. A small, light sleigh.

know what names they had had before, so we called them Mack and Flora. Mack was an old black workhorse, sooty and indifferent. Flora was a sorrel mare, a driver. We took them both out in the cutter. Mack was slow and easy to handle. Flora was given to fits of violent alarm, veering at cars and even at other horses, but we loved her speed and high-stepping, her general air of gallantry and abandon. On Saturdays we went down to the stable and as soon as we opened the door on its cosy, animal-smelling darkness Flora threw up her head, rolled her eyes, whinnied despairingly and pulled herself through a crisis of nerves on the spot. It was not safe to go into her stall; she would kick.

This winter also I began to hear a great deal more on the theme my mother had sounded when she had been talking in front of the barn. I no longer felt safe. It seemed that in the minds of the people around me there was a steady undercurrent of thought, not to be deflected, on this one subject. The word *girl* had formerly seemed to me innocent and unburdened, like the world *child;* now it appeared that it was no such thing. A girl was not, as I had supposed, simply what I was; it was what I had to become. It was a definition, always touched with emphasis, with reproach and disappointment. Also it was a joke on me. Once Laird and I were fighting, and for the first time ever I had to use all my strength against him; even so, he caught and pinned my arm for a moment, really hurting me. Henry saw this, and laughed, saying, "Oh, that there Laird's gonna show you, one of these days!" Laird was getting a lot bigger. But I was getting bigger too.

My grandmother came to stay with us for a few weeks and I heard other things. "Girls don't slam doors like that." "Girls keep their knees together when they sit down." And worse still, when I asked some questions, "That's none of girls' business." I continued to slam the doors and sit as awkwardly as possible, thinking that by such measures I kept myself free.

When spring came, the horses were let out in the barnyard. Mack stood against the barn wall trying to scratch his neck and haunches, but Flora trotted up and down and reared at the fences, clattering her hooves against the rails. Snow drifts dwindled quickly, revealing the hard grey and brown earth, the familiar rise and fall of the ground, plain and bare after the fantastic landscape of winter. There was a great feeling of opening-out, of release. We just wore rubbers now, over our shoes; our feet felt ridiculously light. One Saturday we went out to the stable and found all the doors open, letting in the unaccustomed sunlight and fresh air. Henry was there, just idling around looking at his collection of calendars which were tacked up behind the stalls in a part of the stable my mother had probably never seen.

"Come to say goodbye to your old friend Mack?" Henry said. "Here, you give him a taste of oats." He poured some oats into Laird's cupped hands and Laird went to feed Mack. Mack's teeth were in bad shape. He ate very slowly, patiently shifting the oats around in his mouth, trying to find a stump of a molar to grind it on. "Poor old Mack," said Henry mournfully. "When a horse's teeth's gone, he's gone. That's about the way."

25   "Are you going to shoot him today?" I said. Mack and Flora had been in the stable so long I had almost forgotten they were going to be shot.

Henry didn't answer me. Instead he started to sing in a high, trembly, mock-ing-sorrowful voice, *Oh, there's no more work, for poor Uncle Ned, he's gone where the good darkies go.*[5] Mack's thick, blackish tongue worked diligently at Laird's hand. I went out before the song was ended and sat down on the gangway.

I had never seen them shoot a horse, but I knew where it was done. Last sum-mer Laird and I had come upon a horse's entrails before they were buried. We had thought it was a big black snake, coiled up in the sun. That was around in the field that ran up beside the barn. I thought that if we went inside the barn, and found a wide crack or knothole to look through we would be able to see them do it. It was not something I wanted to see; just the same, if a thing really happened, it was better to see it, and know.

My father came down from the house, carrying the gun.

"What are you doing here?" he said.

"Nothing."

"Go on up and play around the house."

He sent Laird out of the stable. I said to Laird, "Do you want to see them shoot Mack?" and without waiting for an answer led him around to the front door of the barn, opened it carefully, and went in. "Be quiet or they'll hear us," I said. We could hear Henry and my father talking in the stable, then the heavy, shuf-fling steps of Mack being backed out of his stall.

In the loft it was cold and dark. Thin, crisscrossed beams of sunlight fell through the cracks. The hay was low. It was a rolling country, hills and hollows, slipping under our feet. About four feet up was a beam going around the walls. We piled hay up in one corner and I boosted Laird up and hoisted myself. The beam was not very wide; we crept along it with our hands flat on the barn walls. There were plenty of knotholes, and I found one that gave me the view I wanted—a corner of the barnyard, the gate, part of the field. Laird did not have a knothole and began to complain.

I showed him a widened crack between two boards. "Be quiet and wait. If they hear you you'll get us in trouble."

My father came in sight carrying the gun. Henry was leading Mack by the halter. He dropped it and took out his cigarette papers and tobacco; he rolled cigarettes for my father and himself. While this was going on Mack nosed around in the old, dead grass along the fence. Then my father opened the gate and they took Mack through. Henry led Mack way from the path to a patch of ground and they talked together, not loud enough for us to hear. Mack again began searching for a mouthful of fresh grass, which was not to be found. My father walked away in a straight line, and stopped short at a distance which seemed to suit him. Henry was walking away from Mack too, but sideways, still negligently holding on to the halter. My father raised the gun and Mack looked up as if he had noticed something and my father shot him.

Mack did not collapse at once but swayed, lurched sideways and fell, first on his side; then he rolled over on his back and, amazingly, kicked his legs for a few seconds in the air. At this Henry laughed, as if Mack had done a trick for him.

30

35

5. Lines from the Stephen Foster song "Old Uncle Ned."

Laird, who had drawn a long, groaning breath of surprise when the shot was fired, said out loud, "He's not dead." And it seemed to me it might be true. But his legs stopped, he rolled on his side again, his muscles quivered and sank. The two men walked over and looked at him in a businesslike way; they bent down and examined his forehead where the bullet had gone in, and now I saw his blood on the brown grass.

"Now they just skin him and cut him up," I said. "Let's go." My legs were a little shaky and I jumped gratefully down into the hay. "Now you've seen how they shoot a horse," I said in a congratulatory way, as if I had seen it many times before. "Let's see if any barn cat's had kittens in the hay." Laird jumped. He seemed young and obedient again. Suddenly I remembered how, when he was little, I had brought him into the barn and told him to climb the ladder to the top beam. That was in the spring, too, when the hay was low. I had done it out of a need for excitement, a desire for something to happen so that I could tell about it. He was wearing a little bulky brown and white checked coat, made down from one of mine. He went all the way up, just as I told him, and sat down on the top beam with the hay far below him on one side, and the barn floor and some old machinery on the other. Then I ran screaming to my father, "Laird's up on the top beam!" My father came, my mother came, my father went up the ladder talking very quietly and brought Laird down under his arm, at which my mother leaned against the ladder and began to cry. They said to me, "Why weren't you watching him?" but nobody ever knew the truth. Laird did not know enough to tell. But whenever I saw the brown and white checked coat hanging in the closet, or at the bottom of the rag bag, which was where it ended up, I felt a weight in my stomach, the sadness of unexorcized guilt.

I looked at Laird who did not even remember this, and I did not like the look on this thin, winter-pale face. His expression was not frightened or upset, but remote, concentrating. "Listen," I said, in an unusually bright and friendly voice, "you aren't going to tell, are you?"

"No," he said absently.

"Promise."

"Promise," he said. I grabbed the hand behind his back to make sure he was not crossing his fingers. Even so, he might have a nightmare; it might come out that way. I decided I had better work hard to get all thoughts of what he had seen out of his mind—which, it seemed to me, could not hold very many things at a time. I got some money I had saved and that afternoon we went into Jubilee and saw a show, with Judy Canova,[6] at which we both laughed a great deal. After that I thought it would be all right.

Two weeks later I knew they were going to shoot Flora. I knew from the night before, when I heard my mother ask if the hay was holding out all right, and my father said, "Well, after to-morrow there'll just be the cow, and we should be able to put her out to grass in another week." So I knew it was Flora's turn in the morning.

This time I didn't think of watching it. That was something to see just one

6. American comedian best known for her yodeling in hillbilly movies of the 1940s.

time. I had not thought about it very often since, but sometimes when I was busy, working at school, or standing in front of the mirror combing my hair and wondering if I would be pretty when I grew up, the whole scene would flash into my mind: I would see the easy, practised way my father raised the gun, and hear Henry laughing when Mack kicked his legs in the air. I did not have any great feeling of horror and opposition, such as a city child might have had; I was too used to seeing the death of animals as a necessity by which we lived. Yet I felt a little ashamed, and there was a new wariness, a sense of holding-off, in my attitude to my father and his work.

It was a fine day, and we were going around the yard picking up tree branches that had been torn off in winter storms. This was something we had been told to do, and also we wanted to use them to make a teepee. We heard Flora whinny, and then my father's voice and Henry's shouting, and we ran down to the barnyard to see what was going on.

The stable door was open. Henry had just brought Flora out, and she had broken away from him. She was running free in the barnyard, from one end to the other. We climbed up on the fence. It was exciting to see her running, whinnying, going up on her hind legs, prancing and threatening like a horse in a Western movie, an unbroken ranch horse, though she was just an old driver, an old sorrel mare. My father and Henry ran after her and tried to grab the dangling halter. They tried to work her into a corner, and they had almost succeeded when she made a run between them, wild-eyed, and disappeared around the corner of the barn. We heard the rails clatter down as she got over the fence, and Henry yelled, "She's into the field now!"

That meant she was in the long L-shaped field that ran up by the house. If she got around the center, heading towards the lane, the gate was open; the truck had been driven into the field this morning. My father shouted to me, because I was on the other side of the fence, nearest the lane, "Go shut the gate!"

I could run very fast. I ran across the garden, past the tree where our swing was hung, and jumped across a ditch into the lane. There was the open gate. She had not got out, I could not see her up on the road; she must have run to the other end of the field. The gate was heavy. I lifted it out of the gravel and carried it across the roadway. I had it half-way across when she came in sight, galloping straight towards me. There was just time to get the chain on. Laird came scrambling through the ditch to help me.

Instead of shutting the gate, I opened it as wide as I could. I did not make any decision to do this, it was just what I did. Flora never slowed down; she galloped straight past me, and Laird jumped up and down, yelling, "Shut it, shut it!" even after it was too late. My father and Henry appeared in the field a moment too late to see what I had done. They only saw Flora heading for the township road. They would think I had not got there in time.

They did not waste any time asking about it. They went back to the barn and got the gun and the knives they used, and put these in the truck; then they turned the truck around and came bouncing up the field toward us. Laird called to them, "Let me go too, let me go too!" and Henry stopped the truck and they took him in. I shut the gate after they were all gone.

50   I supposed Laird would tell. I wondered what would happen to me. I had never disobeyed my father before, and I could not understand why I had done it. Flora would not really get away. They would catch up with her in the truck. Or if they did not catch her this morning somebody would see her and telephone us this afternoon or tomorrow. There was no wild country here for her to run to, only farms. What was more, my father had paid for her, we needed the meat to feed the foxes, we needed the foxes to make our living. All I had done was make more work for my father who worked hard enough already. And when my father found out about it he was not going to trust me any more; he would know that I was not entirely on his side. I was on Flora's side, and that made me no use to anybody, not even to her. Just the same, I did not regret it; when she came running at me and I held the gate open, that was the only thing I could do.

I went back to the house, and my mother said, "What's all the commotion?" I told her that Flora had kicked down the fence and got away. "Your poor father," she said, "now he'll have to go chasing over the countryside. Well, there isn't any use planning dinner before one." She put up the ironing board. I wanted to tell her, but thought better of it and went upstairs and sat on my bed.

Lately I had been trying to make my part of the room fancy, spreading the bed with old lace curtains, and fixing myself a dressing-table with some leftovers of cretonne for a skirt. I planned to put up some kind of barricade between my bed and Laird's, to keep my section separate from his. In the sunlight, the lace curtains were just dusty rags. We did not sing at night any more. One night when I was singing Laird said, "You sound silly," and I went right on but the next night I did not start. There was not so much need to anyway, we were no longer afraid. We knew it was just old furniture over there, old jumble and confusion. We did not keep to the rules. I still stayed awake after Laird was asleep and told myself stories, but even in these stories something different was happening, mysterious alterations took place. A story might start off in the old way, with a spectacular danger, a fire or wild animals, and for a while I might rescue people; then things would change around, and instead, somebody would be rescuing me. It might be a boy from our class at school, or even Mr. Campbell, our teacher, who tickled girls under the arms. And at this point the story concerned itself at great length with what I looked like—how long my hair was, and what kind of dress I had on; by the time I had these details worked out the real excitement of the story was lost.

It was later than one o'clock when the truck came back. The tarpaulin was over the back, which meant there was meat in it. My mother had to heat dinner up all over again. Henry and my father had changed from their bloody overalls into ordinary working overalls in the barn, and they washed their arms and necks and faces at the sink, and splashed water on their hair and combed it. Laird lifted his arm to show off a streak of blood. "We shot old Flora," he said, "and cut her up in fifty pieces."

"Well I don't want to hear about it," my mother said. "And don't come to my table like that."

55   My father made him go and wash the blood off.

We sat down and my father said grace and Henry pasted his chewing-gum on the end of his fork, the way he always did; when he took it off he would have us admire the pattern. We began to pass the bowls of steaming, overcooked vegetables. Laird looked across the table at me and said proudly, distinctly, "Anyway it was her fault Flora got away."

"What?" my father said.

"She could of shut the gate and she didn't. She just open' it up and Flora run out."

"Is that right?" my father said.

Everybody at the table was looking at me. I nodded, swallowing food with great difficulty. To my shame, tears flooded my eyes.   60

My father made a curt sound of disgust. "What did you do that for?"

I did not answer. I put down my fork and waited to be sent from the table, still not looking up.

But this did not happen. For some time nobody said anything, then Laird said matter-of-factly, "She's crying."

"Never mind," my father said. He spoke with resignation, even good humour, the words which absolved and dismissed me for good. "She's only a girl," he said.

I didn't protest that, even in my heart. Maybe it was true.   65

1968

QUESTIONS

1. What is the nature of the initiation in "Boys and Girls"? in "Gorilla, My Love"? How are the two initiation experiences similar? How do they differ?
2. The phrase "only a girl" appears twice in Alice Munro's story. How do the contexts differ? How do the implications of the phrase differ at each appearance (that is, what does it mean or suggest each time)?

WRITING SUGGESTIONS

1. Using "Gorilla, My Love" as a model, write a personal narrative in which you describe an initiation (real or fictional) in your own life.
2. Find a pattern of words or images that recurs throughout one of the stories in this chapter. Relate the pattern to the story's theme, citing evidence from the story.

10

FORM AS CONTEXT: THE SHORT SHORT STORY

The short short story, a story of about 2,000 words or less, though it has been around for a long time, has suddenly become popular. There have been many attempts to explain this phenomenon, explanations ranging from the shrinking attention span "caused" by television, to the hurried, fragmented nature of modern life, to our disenchantment with lengthy explanations of behavior by psychologists, politicians, and novelists. There have also been attempts to define the form generically. Its boundaries have been those of the anecdote, the vignette, the parable, the poem, the short story proper; yet all these borders have been contested.

Length is not just an aspect of form, however; it also contributes significantly to a story's effect and to your consequent response. You rarely read a full-length novel in a single sitting, so not only is there a momentary recapitulation in your mind as you pick up the narrative again—something like the excerpts from the previous episode in a television miniseries—but you have lived another period of your life outside of the narrative. When you sit down to read again you are not exactly the same repository of experiences as when you put the book down, and not only are you at a different point in your life, your mood may have drastically changed as well. The novel has advantages, however, in its duration and in the times of your readings and departures: you are likely to recall the characters, scenes, and incidents, in one order or another, in more or less accurate detail, from time to time during the period you are away from the text. The novel thereby gets a texture, layers of memories and views from different angles, that is rarely obtained by a short story, and never by a short short story. You usually read a short story in a single sitting, and though it has an immediate and concentrated impact and you pause a moment and savor its emotional and intellectual effect, you can rarely recall it in all its detail; yet rarely, too, do you immediately begin at the beginning and read it through once again. The effect of the short short story is stronger; even if the aftereffect is of the same duration (and it often is longer, because its economy has left so much out that you have to supply a great deal yourself), it is stronger compared to the length of time of your reading. You can remember, if not all, at least almost all the details. Yet it is not uncommon for strongly impressed readers to read the story again immediately. So the differences between novels, short stories, and short short stories are not merely their formal length, but the different way we read and respond to them.

Although you may be able to read four or five short short stories in the time it takes to read one short story, you will probably find the experience overwhelming rather than satisfying. The effects of short short stories are so strong and so concentrated that reading several is likely to overcharge your response system. You might try to take a break between each of the stories in this chapter, using the time to rehearse the story in your mind, to recall its details and its words, and to fill in the particulars that the story's conciseness can only imply. And when one of these stories affects you, you may want to write an account of your emotive and intellectual responses, what you recall, and what you force yourself to supply.

The stories in this chapter represent a sampling of short short stories the editors found emotionally or intellectually moving, stories that reverberated in the mind long after the story ended. (And note that there are other stories in the anthology that fit the definition or hover around or just over the border: "The Zebra Storyteller," "Happy Endings," "The Cask of Amontillado," and "Her First Ball.")

They also represent the limits and the variety of the form. Chopin's story shares the ironic reversal that perhaps comes from Maupassant, though Chopin's is, as its title suggests, limited to an hour of fictional time. Hemingway's story spans not much more time while García Márquez's spans years, defying any unity or constricting of time the brevity of the narrative might lead you to expect. Jamaica Kincaid's "Girl" does not seem so much to span time as to compact it: the story is largely the words of mother to daughter (with two brief responses by the daughter). The near-monologue does not take place at one moment, however; rather, we can infer (there are no internal time indica-tors)—in part from the repetition, in part from memories of our own childhood—that its instructions were repeated time and time again over the years the girl was growing up. "A Very Old Man with Enormous Wings" represents the many short short tales that are fantasies—written in a literary mode involving the consciously unreal—about places, societies, or beings that never existed, do not exist, or do not yet exist, or with qualities that are beyond or counter to the ordinary or commonsensical. Often such fantasies tease us with the possibilities of allegory but are more than likely symbolic—untranslat-able into "messages" or ordinary "meaning." They exist on their own terms, representing certain aspects of human experience in fantasy more precisely than might be done in discursive prose, scientific formulas, graphs, charts.

KATE CHOPIN

The Story of an Hour

Knowing that Mrs. Mallard was afflicted with a heart trouble, great care was taken to break to her as gently as possible the news of her husband's death.

It was her sister Josephine who told her, in broken sentences; veiled hints that revealed in half concealing. Her husband's friend Richards was there, too, near her. It was he who had been in the newspaper office when intelligence of the railroad disaster was received, with Brently Mallard's name leading the list of "killed." He had only taken the time to assure himself of its truth by a second telegram, and had hastened to forestall any less careful, less tender friend in bear-ing the sad message.

She did not hear the story as many women have heard the same, with a paralyzed inability to accept its significance. She wept at once, with sudden, wild abandonment, in her sister's arms. When the storm of grief had spent itself she went away to her room alone. She would have no one follow her.

There stood, facing the open window, a comfortable, roomy armchair. Into this she sank, pressed down by a physical exhaustion that haunted her body and seemed to reach into her soul.

5   She could see in the open square before her house the tops of trees that were all aquiver with the new spring life. The delicious breath of rain was in the air. In the street below a peddler was crying his wares. The notes of a distant song which some one was singing reached her faintly, and countless sparrows were twittering in the eaves.

There were patches of blue sky showing here and there through the clouds that had met and piled one above the other in the west facing her window.

She sat with her head thrown back upon the cushion of the chair, quite motionless, except when a sob came up into her throat and shook her, as a child who has cried itself to sleep continues to sob in its dreams.

She was young, with a fair, calm face, whose lines bespoke repression and even a certain strength. But now there was a dull stare in her eyes, whose gaze was fixed away off yonder on one of those patches of blue sky. It was not a glance of reflection, but rather indicated a suspension of intelligent thought.

There was something coming to her and she was waiting for it, fearfully. What was it? She did not know; it was too subtle and elusive to name. But she felt it, creeping out of the sky, reaching toward her through the sounds, the scents, the color that filled the air.

10   Now her bosom rose and fell tumultuously. She was beginning to recognize this thing that was approaching to possess her, and she was striving to beat it back with her will—as powerless as her two white slender hands would have been.

When she abandoned herself a little whispered word escaped her slightly parted lips. She said it over and over under her breath: "free, free, free!" The vacant stare and the look of terror that had followed it went from her eyes. They stayed keen and bright. Her pulses beat fast, and the coursing blood warmed and relaxed every inch of her body.

She did not stop to ask if it were or were not a monstrous joy that held her. A clear and exalted perception enabled her to dismiss the suggestion as trivial.

She knew that she would weep again when she saw the kind, tender hands folded in death; the face that had never looked save with love upon her, fixed and gray and dead. But she saw beyond that bitter moment a long procession of years to come that would belong to her absolutely. And she opened and spread her arms out to them in welcome.

There would be no one to live for her during those coming years; she would live for herself. There would be no powerful will bending hers in that blind persistence with which men and women believe they have a right to impose a private will upon a fellow-creature. A kind intention or a cruel intention made the act seem no less a crime as she looked upon it in that brief moment of illumination.

And yet she had loved him—sometimes. Often she had not. What did it mat- 15
ter! What could love, the unsolved mystery, count for in face of this possession
of self-assertion which she suddenly recognized as the strongest impulse of her
being!

"Free! Body and soul free!" she kept whispering.

Josephine was kneeling before the closed door with her lips to the keyhole,
imploring for admission. "Louise, open the door! I beg; open the door—you will
make yourself ill. What are you doing, Louise? For heaven's sake open the door."

"Go away. I am not making myself ill." No; she was drinking in a very elixir
of life through that open window.

Her fancy was running riot along those days ahead of her. Spring days, and
summer days, and all sorts of days that would be her own. She breathed a quick
prayer that life might be long. It was only yesterday she had thought with a
shudder that life might be long.

She arose at length and opened the door to her sister's importunities. There 20
was a feverish triumph in her eyes, and she carried herself unwittingly like a
goddess of Victory. She clasped her sister's waist, and together they descended
the stairs. Richards stood waiting for them at the bottom.

Some one was opening the front door with a latchkey. It was Brently Mallard
who entered, a little travel-stained, composedly carrying his grip-sack and
umbrella. He had been far from the scene of accident, and did not even know
there had been one. He stood amazed at Josephine's piercing cry; at Richards'
quick motion to screen him from the view of his wife.

But Richards was too late.

When the doctors came they said she had died of heart disease—of joy that
kills.

1891

GABRIEL GARCÍA MÁRQUEZ

A Very Old Man with Enormous Wings[1]

A Tale for Children

On the third day of rain they had killed so many crabs inside the house that
Pelayo had to cross his drenched courtyard and throw them into the sea, because
the newborn child had a temperature all night and they thought it was due to
the stench. The world had been sad since Tuesday. Sea and sky were a single ash-
gray thing and the sands of the beach, which on March nights glimmered like
powdered light, had become a stew of mud and rotten shellfish. The light was so
weak at noon that when Pelayo was coming back to the house after throwing

1. Translated by Gregory Rabassa.

away the crabs, it was hard for him to see what it was that was moving and groaning in the rear of the courtyard. He had to go very close to see that it was an old man, a very old man, lying face down in the mud, who, in spite of his tremendous efforts, couldn't get up, impeded by his enormous wings.

Frightened by that nightmare, Pelayo ran to get Elisenda, his wife, who was putting compresses on the sick child, and he took her to the rear of the courtyard. They both looked at the fallen body with mute stupor. He was dressed like a ragpicker. There were only a few faded hairs left on his bald skull and very few teeth in his mouth, and his pitiful condition of a drenched great-grandfather had taken away any sense of grandeur he might have had. His huge buzzard wings, dirty and half-plucked, were forever entangled in the mud. They looked at him so long and so closely that Pelayo and Elisenda very soon overcame their surprise and in the end found him familiar. Then they dared speak to him, and he answered in an incomprehensible dialect with a strong sailor's voice. That was how they skipped over the inconvenience of the wings and quite intelligently concluded that he was a lonely castaway from some foreign ship wrecked by the storm. And yet, they called in a neighbor woman who knew everything about life and death to see him, and all she needed was one look to show them their mistake.

"He's an angel," she told them. "He must have been coming for the child, but the poor fellow is so old that the rain knocked him down."

On the following day everyone knew that a flesh-and-blood angel was held captive in Pelayo's house. Against the judgment of the wise neighbor woman, for whom angels in those times were the fugitive survivors of a celestial conspiracy, they did not have the heart to club him to death. Pelayo watched over him all afternoon from the kitchen, armed with his bailiff's club, and before going to bed he dragged him out of the mud and locked him up with the hens in the wire chicken coop. In the middle of the night, when the rain stopped, Pelayo and Elisenda were still killing crabs. A short time afterward the child woke up without a fever and with a desire to eat. Then they felt magnanimous and decided to put the angel on a raft with fresh water and provisions for three days and leave him to his fate on the high seas. But when they went out into the courtyard with the first light of dawn, they found the whole neighborhood in front of the chicken coop having fun with the angel, without the slightest reverence, tossing him things to eat through the openings in the wire as if he weren't a supernatural creature but a circus animal.

5   Father Gonzaga arrived before seven o'clock, alarmed at the strange news. By that time onlookers less frivolous than those at dawn had already arrived and they were making all kinds of conjectures concerning the captive's future. The simplest among them thought that he should be named mayor of the world. Others of sterner mind felt that he should be promoted to the rank of five-star general in order to win all wars. Some visionaries hoped that he could be put to stud in order to implant on earth a race of winged wise men who could take charge of the universe. But Father Gonzaga, before becoming a priest, had been a robust woodcutter. Standing by the wire, he reviewed his catechism in an instant and asked them to open the door so that he could take a close look at

that pitiful man who looked more like a huge decrepit hen among the fascinated chickens. He was lying in a corner drying his open wings in the sunlight among the fruit peels and breakfast leftovers that the early risers had thrown him. Alien to the impertinences of the world, he only lifted his antiquarian eyes and murmured something in his dialect when Father Gonzaga went into the chicken coop and said good morning to him in Latin. The parish priest had his first suspicion of an imposter when he saw that he did not understand the language of God or know how to greet His ministers. Then he noticed that seen close up he was much too human: he had an unbearable smell of the outdoors, the back side of his wings was strewn with parasites and his main feathers had been mistreated by terrestrial winds, and nothing about him measured up to the proud dignity of angels. Then he came out of the chicken coop and in a brief sermon warned the curious against the risks of being ingenuous. He reminded them that the devil had the bad habit of making use of carnival tricks in order to confuse the unwary. He argued that if wings were not the essential element in determining the difference between a hawk and an airplane, they were even less so in the recognition of angels. Nevertheless, he promised to write a letter to his bishop so that the latter would write to his primate so that the latter would write to the Supreme Pontiff in order to get the final verdict from the highest courts.

His prudence fell on sterile hearts. The news of the captive angel spread with such rapidity that after a few hours the courtyard had the bustle of a marketplace and they had to call in troops with fixed bayonets to disperse the mob that was about to knock the house down. Elisenda, her spine all twisted from sweeping up so much marketplace trash, then got the idea of fencing in the yard and charging five cents admission to see the angel.

The curious came from far away. A traveling carnival arrived with a flying acrobat who buzzed over the crowd several times, but no one paid any attention to him because his wings were not those of an angel but, rather, those of a sidereal bat. The most unfortunate invalids on earth came in search of health: a poor woman who since childhood had been counting her heartbeats and had run out of numbers; a Portuguese man who couldn't sleep because the noise of the stars disturbed him; a sleepwalker who got up at night to undo the things he had done while awake; and many others with less serious ailments. In the midst of that shipwreck disorder that made the earth tremble, Pelayo and Elisenda were happy with fatigue, for in less than a week they had crammed their rooms with money and the line of pilgrims waiting their turn to enter still reached beyond the horizon.

The angel was the only one who took no part in his own act. He spent his time trying to get comfortable in his borrowed nest, befuddled by the hellish heat of the oil lamps and sacramental candles that had been placed along the wire. At first they tried to make him eat some mothballs, which, according to the wisdom of the wise neighbor woman, were the food prescribed for angels. But he turned them down, just as he turned down the papal lunches[2] that the penitents brought him, and they never found out whether it was because he was an angel

---

2. Choice, extremely expensive meals.

or because he was an old man that in the end he ate nothing but eggplant mush. His only supernatural virtue seemed to be patience. Especially during the first days, when the hens pecked at him, searching for the stellar parasites that proliferated in his wings, and the cripples pulled out feathers to touch their defective parts with, and even the most merciful threw stones at him, trying to get him to rise so they could see him standing. The only time they succeeded in arousing him was when they burned his side with an iron for branding steers, for he had been motionless for so many hours that they thought he was dead. He awoke with a start, ranting in his hermetic language and with tears in his eyes, and he flapped his wings a couple of times, which brought on a whirlwind of chicken dung and lunar dust and a gale of panic that did not seem to be of this world. Although many thought that his reaction had been one not of rage but of pain, from then on they were careful not to annoy him, because the majority understood that his passivity was not that of a hero taking his ease but that of a cataclysm in repose.

Father Gonzaga held back the crowd's frivolity with formulas of maidservant inspiration while awaiting the arrival of a final judgment on the nature of the captive. But the mail from Rome showed no sense of urgency. They spent their time finding out if the prisoner had a navel, if his dialect had any connection with Aramaic, how many times he could fit on the head of a pin, or whether he wasn't just a Norwegian with wings. Those meager letters might have come and gone until the end of time if a providential event had not put an end to the priest's tribulations.

10   It so happened that during those days, among so many other carnival attractions, there arrived in town the traveling show of the woman who had been changed into a spider for having disobeyed her parents. The admission to see her was not only less than the admission to see the angel, but people were permitted to ask her all manner of questions about her absurd state and to examine her up and down so that no one would ever doubt the truth of her horror. She was a frightful tarantula the size of a ram and with the head of a sad maiden. What was most heart-rending, however, was not her outlandish shape but the sincere affliction with which she recounted the details of her misfortune. While still practically a child she had sneaked out of her parents' house to go to a dance, and while she was coming back through the woods after having danced all night without permission, a fearful thunderclap rent the sky in two and through the crack came the lightning bolt of brimstone that changed her into a spider. Her only nourishment came from the meatballs that charitable souls chose to toss into her mouth. A spectacle like that, full of so much human truth and with such a fearful lesson, was bound to defeat without even trying that of a haughty angel who scarcely deigned to look at mortals. Besides, the few miracles attributed to the angel showed a certain mental disorder, like the blind man who didn't recover his sight but grew three new teeth, or the paralytic who didn't get to walk but almost won the lottery, and the leper whose sores sprouted sunflowers. Those consolation miracles, which were more like mocking fun, had already ruined the angel's reputation when the woman who had been changed into a spider finally crushed him completely. That was how Father Gonzaga was cured forever of his

insomnia and Pelayo's courtyard went back to being as empty as during the time it had rained for three days and crabs walked through the bedrooms.

The owners of the house had no reason to lament. With the money they saved they built a two-story mansion with balconies and gardens and high netting so that crabs wouldn't get in during the winter, and with iron bars on the windows so that angels wouldn't get in. Pelayo also set up a rabbit warren close to town and gave up his job as bailiff for good, and Elisenda bought some satin pumps with high heels and many dresses of iridescent silk, the kind worn on Sunday by the most desirable women in those times. The chicken coop was the only thing that didn't receive any attention. If they washed it down with creolin[3] and burned tears of myrrh inside it every so often, it was not in homage to the angel but to drive away the dungheap stench that still hung everywhere like a ghost and was turning the new house into an old one. At first, when the child learned to walk, they were careful that he not get too close to the chicken coop. But then they began to lose their fears and got used to the smell, and before the child got his second teeth he'd gone inside the chicken coop to play, where the wires were falling apart. The angel was no less standoffish with him than with other mortals, but he tolerated the most ingenious infamies with the patience of a dog who had no illusions. They both came down with chicken pox at the same time. The doctor who took care of the child couldn't resist the temptation to listen to the angel's heart, and he found so much whistling in the heart and so many sounds in his kidneys that it seemed impossible for him to be alive. What surprised him most, however, was the logic of his wings. They seemed so natural on that completely human organism that he couldn't understand why other men didn't have them too.

When the child began school it had been some time since the sun and rain had caused the collapse of the chicken coop. The angel went dragging himself about here and there like a stray dying man. They would drive him out of the bedroom with a broom and a moment later find him in the kitchen. He seemed to be in so many places at the same time that they grew to think that he'd been duplicated, that he was reproducing himself all through the house, and the exasperated and unhinged Elisenda shouted that it was awful living in that hell full of angels. He could scarcely eat and his antiquarian eyes had also become so foggy that he went about bumping into posts. All he had left were the bare cannulae of his last feathers. Pelayo threw a blanket over him and extended him the charity of letting him sleep in the shed, and only then did they notice that he had a temperature at night, and was delirious with the tongue twisters of an old Norwegian. That was one of the few times they became alarmed, for they thought he was going to die and not even the wise neighbor woman had been able to tell them what to do with dead angels.

And yet he not only survived his worst winter, but seemed improved with the first sunny days. He remained motionless for several days in the farthest corner of the courtyard, where no one would see him, and at the beginning of December some large, stiff feathers began to grow on his wings, the feathers of a scarecrow,

3. A disinfectant.

which looked more like another misfortune of decrepitude. But he must have known the reason for those changes, for he was quite careful that no one should notice them, that no one should hear the sea chanteys that he sometimes sang under the stars. One morning Elisenda was cutting some bunches of onions for lunch when a wind that seemed to come from the high seas blew into the kitchen. Then she went to the window and caught the angel in his first attempts at flight. They were so clumsy that his fingernails opened a furrow in the vegetable patch and he was on the point of knocking the shed down with the ungainly flapping that slipped on the light and couldn't get a grip on the air. But he did manage to gain altitude. Elisenda let out a sign of relief, for herself and for him, when she saw him pass over the last houses, holding himself up in some way with the risky flapping of a senile vulture. She kept watching him even when she was through cutting the onions and she kept on watching until it was no longer possible for her to see him, because then he was no longer an annoyance in her life but an imaginary dot on the horizon of the sea.

1968

ERNEST HEMINGWAY

A Clean, Well-Lighted Place

It was late and every one had left the café except an old man who sat in the shadow the leaves of the tree made against the electric light. In the day time the street was dusty, but at night the dew settled the dust and the old man liked to sit late because he was deaf and now at night it was quiet and he felt the difference. The two waiters inside the café knew that the old man was a little drunk, and while he was a good client they knew that if he became too drunk he would leave without paying, so they kept watch on him.

"Last week he tried to commit suicide," one waiter said.

"Why?"

"He was in despair."

5   "What about?"

"Nothing."

"How do you know it was nothing?"

"He has plenty of money."

They sat together at a table that was close against the wall near the door of the café and looked at the terrace where the tables were all empty except where the old man sat in the shadow of the leaves of the tree that moved slightly in the wind. A girl and a soldier went by in the street. The street light shone on the brass number on his collar. The girl wore no head covering and hurried beside him.

10   "The guard will pick him up," one waiter said.

"What does it matter if he gets what he's after?"

"He had better get off the street now. The guard will get him. They went by five minutes ago."

The old man sitting in the shadow rapped on his saucer with his glass. The younger waiter went over to him.

"What do you want?"

The old man looked at him. "Another brandy," he said.   15

"You'll be drunk," the waiter said. The old man looked at him. The waiter went away.

"He'll stay all night," he said to his colleague. "I'm sleepy now. I never get into bed before three o'clock. He should have killed himself last week."

The waiter took the brandy bottle and another saucer from the counter inside the café and marched out to the old man's table. He put down the saucer and poured the glass full of brandy.

"You should have killed yourself last week," he said to the deaf man. The old man motioned with his finger. "A little more," he said. The waiter poured on into the glass so that the brandy slopped over and ran down the stem into the top saucer of the pile. "Thank you," the old man said. The waiter took the bottle back inside the café. He sat down at the table with his colleague again.

"He's drunk now," he said.   20

"He's drunk every night."

"What did he want to kill himself for?"

"How should I know."

"How did he do it?"

"He hung himself with a rope."   25

"Who cut him down?"

"His niece."

"Why did they do it?"

"Fear for his soul."

"How much money has he got?"   30

"He's got plenty."

"He must be eighty years old."

"Anyway I should say he was eighty."

"I wish he would go home. I never get to bed before three o'clock. What kind of hour is that to go to bed?"

"He stays up because he likes it."   35

"He's lonely. I'm not lonely. I have a wife waiting in bed for me."

"He had a wife once too."

"A wife would be no good to him now."

"You can't tell. He might be better with a wife."

"His niece looks after him. You said she cut him down."   40

"I know."

"I wouldn't want to be that old. An old man is a nasty thing."

"Not always. This old man is clean. He drinks without spilling. Even now, drunk. Look at him."

"I don't want to look at him. I wish he would go home. He has no regard for those who must work."

45   The old man looked from his glass across the square, then over at the waiters.

"Another brandy," he said, pointing to his glass. The waiter who was in a hurry came over.

"Finished," he said, speaking with that omission of syntax stupid people employ when talking to drunken people or foreigners. "No more tonight. Close now."

"Another," said the old man.

"No. Finished." The waiter wiped the edge of the table with a towel and shook his head.

50   The old man stood up, slowly counted the saucers, took a leather coin purse from his pocket and paid for the drinks, leaving half a peseta tip.

The waiter watched him go down the street, a very old man walking unsteadily but with dignity.

"Why didn't you let him stay and drink?" the unhurried waiter asked. They were putting up the shutters. "It is not half-past two."

"I want to go home to bed."

"What is an hour?"

55   "More to me than to him."

"An hour is the same."

"You talk like an old man yourself. He can buy a bottle and drink at home."

"It's not the same."

"No, it is not," agreed the waiter with a wife. He did not wish to be unjust. He was only in a hurry.

60   "And you? You have no fear of going home before your usual hour?"

"Are you trying to insult me?"

"No, hombre, only to make a joke."

"No," the waiter who was in a hurry said, rising from pulling down the metal shutters. "I have confidence. I am all confidence."

"You have youth, confidence, and a job," the older waiter said. "You have everything."

65   "And what do you lack?"

"Everything but work."

"You have everything I have."

"No. I have never had confidence and I am not young."

"Come on. Stop talking nonsense and lock up."

70   "I am of those who like to stay late at the café," the older waiter said. "With all those who do not want to go to bed. With all those who need a light for the night."

"I want to go home and into bed."

"We are of two different kinds," the older waiter said. He was now dressed to go home. "It is not only a question of youth and confidence although those things are very beautiful. Each night I am reluctant to close up because there may be some one who needs the café."

"Hombre, there are bodegas[1] open all night long."

---

1. Houses of prostitution.

"You do not understand. This is a clean and pleasant café. It is well lighted. The light is very good and also, now, there are shadows of the leaves."

"Good night," said the younger waiter.   75

"Good night," the other said. Turning off the electric light he continued the conversation with himself. It is the light of course but it is necessary that the place be clean and pleasant. You do not want music. Certainly you do not want music. Nor can you stand before a bar with dignity although that is all that is provided for these hours. What did he fear? It was not fear or dread. It was a nothing that he knew too well. It was all a nothing and a man was nothing too. It was only that and light was all it needed and a certain cleanness and order. Some lived in it and never felt it but he knew it all was nada y pues nada[2] y nada y pues nada. Our nada who art in nada, nada be thy name thy kingdom nada thy will be nada in nada as it is in nada. Give us this nada our daily nada and nada us our nada as we nada our nadas and nada us not into nada but deliver us from nada; pues nada. Hail nothing full of nothing, nothing is with thee. He smiled and stood before a bar with a shining steam pressure coffee machine.

"What's yours?" asked the barman.

"Nada."

"Otro loco mas,"[3] said the barman and turned away.

"A little cup," said the waiter.   80

The barman poured it for him.

"The light is very bright and pleasant but the bar is unpolished," the waiter said.

The barman looked at him but did not answer. It was too late at night for conversation.

"You want another copita?"[4] the barman asked.

"No, thank you," said the waiter and went out. He disliked bars and bodegas.   85
A clean, well-lighted café was a very different thing. Now, without thinking further, he would go home to his room. He would lie in the bed and finally, with daylight, he would go to sleep. After all, he said to himself, it is probably only insomnia. Many must have it.

1933

JAMAICA KINCAID

Girl

Wash the white clothes on Monday and put them on the stone heap; wash the color clothes on Tuesday and put them on the clothesline to dry; don't walk barehead in the hot sun; cook pumpkin fritters in very hot sweet oil; soak your little cloths right after you take them off; when buying cotton to make yourself

2. Nothing and then nothing. . . .   3. One more nut.   4. Drink.

a nice blouse, be sure that it doesn't have gum on it, because that way it won't hold up well after a wash; soak salt fish overnight before you cook it; is it true that you sing benna[1] in Sunday school?; always eat your food in such a way that it won't turn someone else's stomach; on Sundays try to walk like a lady and not like the slut you are so bent on becoming; don't sing benna in Sunday school; you mustn't speak to wharf-rat boys, not even to give directions; don't eat fruits on the street—flies will follow you; *but I don't sing benna on Sundays at all and never in Sunday school;* this is how to sew on a button; this is how to make a buttonhole for the button you have just sewed on; this is how to hem a dress when you see the hem coming down and so to prevent yourself from looking like the slut I know you are so bent on becoming; this is how you iron your father's khaki shirt so that it doesn't have a crease; this is how you iron your father's khaki pants so that they don't have a crease; this is how you grow okra— far from the house, because okra tree harbors red ants; when you are growing dasheen, make sure it gets plenty of water or else it makes your throat itch when you are eating it; this is how you sweep a corner; this is how you sweep a whole house; this is how you sweep a yard; this is how you smile to someone you don't like too much; this is how you smile to someone you don't like at all; this is how you smile to someone you like completely; this is how you set a table for tea; this is how you set a table for dinner; this is how you set a table for dinner with an important guest; this is how you set a table for lunch; this is how you set a table for breakfast; this is how to behave in the presence of men who don't know you very well, and this way they won't recognize immediately the slut I have warned you against becoming; be sure to wash every day, even if it is with your own spit; don't squat down to play marbles—you are not a boy, you know; don't pick people's flowers—you might catch something; don't throw stones at blackbirds, because it might not be a blackbird at all; this is how to make a bread pudding; this is how to make doukona;[2] this is how to make pepper pot; this is how to make a good medicine for a cold; this is how to make a good medicine to throw away a child before it even becomes a child; this is how to catch a fish; this is how to throw back a fish you don't like, and that way something bad won't fall on you; this is how to bully a man; this is how a man bullies you; this is how to love a man, and if this doesn't work there are other ways, and if they don't work don't feel too bad about giving up; this is how to spit up in the air if you feel like it, and this is how to move quick so that it doesn't fall on you; this is how to make ends meet; always squeeze bread to make sure it's fresh; *but what if the baker won't let me feel the bread?;* you mean to say that after all you are really going to be the kind of woman who the baker won't let near the bread?

1983

---

1. Popular music, calypso.   2. A spicy pudding, often made from plantains and wrapped in a plantain or banana leaf.

QUESTIONS

1. How do the details in paragraphs 5 through 10 in "The Story of an Hour" prepare for the reversal that comes in paragraph 11? Did you find the turn surprising? convincing?
2. When do you get to distinguish between the two waiters in "A Clean, Well-Lighted Place"? Mark the places and the words or details. Write a brief character sketch of each. Go back to the beginning of the story and identify the speaker of each line of dialogue, and be prepared to defend your decision. Explain the two middle sentences in paragraph 76—"It was all a nothing . . . a certain cleanness and order"—and relate them to the title and theme of the story.
3. What humorous elements do you find in "A Very Old Man with Enormous Wings"? How do they function? Is the old man a symbol? If so, does he "stand for" something you can name or paraphrase? If you cannot say what he stands for, how can he be a symbol? If we do not read this story symbolically, how can we deal with its fantastic elements? take the story seriously as "literature"?
4. What images of the characters of the girl and her mother emerge from your reading of "Girl"? How are those images created?

WRITING SUGGESTIONS

1. Write a personal essay either about grief and its complexities or about another experience in which an initial and expected emotion gave way to something like its opposite.
2. Compare "A Very Old Man with Enormous Wings" and "A Hunger Artist" (in "Reading More Fiction") as "meaningful fantasies."
3. Write a personal essay called "Boy" or "Another Girl" that deals with the oft-repeated and multiple instructions, advice, and commands of a parent (not necessarily a mother).

11

CULTURE AS CONTEXT

Over the past two hundred years, the meaning of the word *culture* has changed from "enabling growth" (as in agri*culture*), to the arts or familiarity with the arts ("high culture," "a cultured person"), to a way of life ("Japanese culture"). In everyday use it sometimes is associated with race, though it is usually distinguished from race in that culture is social rather than biological, learned from other members of the group or from experience rather than inherited through the genes (as *race,* narrowly defined, is). Its current use is transitional and a sort of stopgap response to modern life: while it was used for a time to designate "primitive" groups (tribes) and their way of life, then applied to present-day national groups, it has been complicated by the worldwide spread of knowledge, experience, and interdependence of both material culture—clothing (jeans), tools, appliances, means of travel (cars and jets), and communication (television, computers, "the information highway")—and cultural ideas, like social and political organization (democracy, for example) or economic organization (such as the market economy), or tastes (like "American" popular music).

Often for the individual, the family, or larger groups, there is or seems to be a clash between the traditional culture of the group that has been passed on for generations or centuries and the practical pressures of survival (culture developed as a means of survival) in the modern world. As a result, we have developed the term *multiculturalism,* whose definition and evaluation are intellectual and emotional battlegrounds.

Americans tend to think theirs is the only multicultural society and theirs the only struggle to define what that means or should mean. We have become more and more conscious of how questionable the term "American culture" is or was, more and more aware that it represents not something clear and "natural," but the power structure of the nation. (This is not just a matter of race and gender: for some time "American" meant northeastern, Christian [even Protestant], and at least second-generation.) In our new awareness we have taken what we used to consider "subcultures" into account, often with hyphens—African-American, Asian-American, and so on—though, of course, all residents of North America are immigrants (even Native Americans and Native Canadians apparently came to this continent across the Bering Straits or some earlier bridge from Asia).

Multiculturalism implies rejection of the older idea of assimilation, of America as "melting pot," which meant, in effect, "Reject your group's culture and adopt ours" (that is, the culture of the majority or of those in power). But for some, multiculturalism strongly implies separatism as well, almost an adversarial stance toward other "subcultures," a last-ditch effort to retain the culture of the homeland or place of origin. So there is developing—influenced, interestingly, by forces in Eastern Europe after the breakup of the Soviet Union—what some call "transculturalism," a retention of something of the original, learned culture blended with other cultures and modern experience or "American" culture.

Whatever the outcome, it seems safe to say that our notions of "American" and of "culture" are in flux, even as world culture is in flux. (Notice, for example, that when June May gets to China—in "A Pair of Tickets"—her family takes her to a hotel much like a Hyatt Regency and orders hamburgers, french fries, and apple pie à la mode.) If culture is a means of survival and trans- or multiculturalism is the nature of contemporary culture, for survival's sake we must be aware not only of our own heritage but of that of others and of all our experiences of the here and now.

These two stories offer two different aspects of culture both as a theme and a context. The first of these, Katherine Anne Porter's "Holiday," introduces the narrator and the reader to a German peasant culture that had been "transplanted" to Texas generations ago but remains virtually uninfluenced by the southern "American" culture around it. The narrator is intrigued by the patriarchal, close-knit family and society that seem fully self-contained and unchanging, so turned inward that not only do all the members of the family look alike, but even the suitors of the Müllers's daughter look as if they were her brothers. The community and family are the units, with each individual in a permanent and appropriate role, sharing burdens, sorrow, and pleasures, and the whole devoted almost obsessively to work and to survival of the group. Ironically, what the narrator, the stranger from the wider world, comes to realize is that for all of the differences, human life is the same (see, for example, paragraph 59).

The second story, Margaret Laurence's "The Rain Child," deals with the difference between culture and nationality or race. Though Ruth was born and educated in England, her parents are African, and to Africa she has returned as the story opens. She cannot speak "her own" language, however, and she dislikes African food, insists on European dress, and finds some African practices "savage": she is an "outcast" in her native land. She is shocked to find, however, that to her young English friend she is only "almost" European. She is between two worlds, two cultures, and the story does not suggest any easy resolution.

KATHERINE ANNE PORTER

Holiday

At that time I was too young for some of the troubles I was having, and I had not yet learned what to do with them. It no longer can matter what kind of troubles they were, or what finally became of them. It seemed to me then there was nothing to do but run away from them, though all my tradition, background, and training had taught me unanswerably that no one except a coward ever runs away from anything. What nonsense! They should have taught me the difference between courage and foolhardiness, instead of leaving me to find it out for myself. I learned finally that if I still had the sense I was born with, I would take off like a deer at the first warning of certain dangers. But this story I am about to tell you happened before this great truth impressed itself upon me—that we do not run from the troubles and dangers that are truly ours, and it is better to learn what they are earlier than later, and if we don't run from the others, we are fools.

I confided to my friend Louise, a former schoolmate about my own age, not my troubles but my little problem: I wanted to go somewhere for a spring holiday, by myself, to the country, and it should be very simple and nice and, of course, not expensive, and she was not to tell anyone where I had gone; but if she liked, I would send her word now and then, if anything interesting was happening. She said she loved getting letters but hated answering them; and she knew the very place for me, and she would not tell anybody anything. Louise had then—she has it still—something near to genius for making improbable persons, places, and situations sound attractive. She told amusing stories that did not turn grim on you until a little while later, when by chance you saw and heard for yourself. So with this story. Everything was just as Louise had said, if you like, and everything was, at the same time, quite different.

"I know the very place," said Louise, "a family of real old-fashioned German peasants, in the deep blackland Texas farm country, a household in real patriarchal style—the kind of thing you'd hate to live with but is very nice to visit. Old father, God Almighty himself, with whiskers and all; Old mother, matriarch in men's shoes; endless daughters and sons and sons-in-law and fat babies falling about the place; and fat puppies—my favourite was a darling little black thing named Kuno—cows, calves, and sheep and lambs and goats and turkeys and guineas roaming up and down the shallow green hills, ducks and geese on the ponds. I was there in the summer when the peaches and watermelons were in——"

"This is the end of March," I said, doubtfully.

5   "Spring comes early there," said Louise. "I'll write to the Müllers about you, you just get ready to go."

"Just where is this paradise?"

"Not far from the Louisiana line," said Louise. "I'll ask them to give you my attic—oh, that was a sweet place! It's a big room, with the roof sloping to the floor on each side, and the roof leaks a little when it rains, so the shingles are all stained in beautiful streaks, all black and grey and mossy green, and in one corner there used to be a stack of dime novels, *The Duchess,* Ouida, Mrs. E.D.E.N. Southworth, Ella Wheeler Wilcox's poems—one summer they had a lady boarder who was a great reader, and she went off and left her library. I loved it! And everybody was so healthy and good-hearted, and the weather was perfect. . . . How long do you want to stay?"

I hadn't thought of this, so I said at random, "About a month."

A few days later I found myself tossed off like an express package from a dirty little crawling train onto the sodden platform of a country station, where the stationmaster emerged and locked up the waiting room before the train had got round the bend. As he clumped by me he shifted his wad of tobacco to his cheek and asked, "Where you goin'?"

10   "To the Müller farm," I said, standing beside my small trunk and suitcase with the bitter wind cutting through my thin coat.

"Anybody meet you?" he asked, not pausing.

"They *said* so."

"All right," he said, and got into his little ragged buckboard with a sway-backed horse and drove away.

I turned my trunk on its side and sat on it facing the wind and the desolate mud-colored shapeless scene and began making up my first letter to Louise. First I was going to tell her that unless she was to be a novelist, there was no excuse for her having so much imagination. In daily life, I was going to tell her, there are also such useful things as the plain facts that should be stuck to, through thick and thin. Anything else led to confusion like this. I was beginning to enjoy my letter to Louise when a sturdy boy about twelve years old crossed the platform. As he neared me, he took off his rough cap and bunched it in his thick hand, dirt-stained at the knuckles. His round cheeks, his round nose, his round chin were a cool, healthy red. In the globe of his face, as neatly circular as if drawn in bright crayon, his narrow, long, tip-tilted eyes, clear as pale-blue water, seemed out of place, as if two incompatible strains had collided in making him. They were beautiful eyes, and the rest of the face was not to be taken seriously. A blue woollen blouse buttoned up to his chin ended abruptly at his waist as if he would outgrow it in another half hour, and his blue drill breeches flapped about his ankles. His old clodhopper shoes were several sizes too big for him. Altogether, it was plain he was not the first one to wear his clothes. He was a cheerful, detached, self-possessed apparition against the tumbled brown earth and ragged dark sky, and I smiled at him as well as I could with a face that felt like wet clay.

He smiled back slightly without meeting my eye, motioning for me to take up   15
my suitcase. He swung my trunk to his head and tottered across the uneven platform, down the steps slippery with mud where I expected to see him crushed beneath his burden like an ant under a stone. He heaved the trunk into the back of his wagon with a fine smash, took my suitcase and tossed it after, then climbed up over one front wheel while I scrambled my way up over the other.

The pony, shaggy as a wintering bear, eased himself into a grudging trot, while the boy, bowed over with his cap pulled down over his ears and eyebrows, held the reins slack and fell into a brown study. I studied the harness, a real mystery. It met and clung in all sorts of unexpected places; it parted company in what appeared to be strategic seats of jointure. It was mended sketchily in risky places with bits of hairy rope. Other seemingly unimportant parts were bound together irrevocably with wire. The bridle was too long for the pony's stocky head, so he had shaken the bit out of his mouth at the start, apparently, and went his own way at his own pace.

Our vehicle was an exhausted specimen of something called a spring wagon, who knows why? There were no springs, and the shallow enclosed platform at the back, suitable for carrying various plunder, was worn away until it barely reached midway of the back wheels, one side of it steadily scraping the iron tire. The wheels themselves spun not dully around and around in the way of common wheels, but elliptically, being loosened at the hubs, so that we proceeded with a drunken, hilarious swagger, like the rolling motion of a small boat on a choppy sea.

The soaked brown fields fell away on either side of the lane, all rough with winter-worn stubble ready to sink and become earth again. The scanty leafless woods ran along an edge of the field nearby. There was nothing beautiful in those woods now except the promise of spring, for I detested bleakness, but it gave me pleasure to think that beyond this there might be something else beautiful in its own being, a river shaped and contained by its banks, or a field stripped down to its true meaning, ploughed and ready for the seed. The road turned abruptly and was almost hidden for a moment, and we were going through the woods. Closer sight of the crooked branches assured me that spring was beginning, if sparely, reluctantly: the leaves were budding in tiny cones of watery green besprinkling all the new shoots; a thin sedate rain began again to fall, not so opaque as a fog, but a mist that merely deepened overhead, and lowered, until the clouds became rain in one swathing, delicate grey.

As we emerged from the woods, the boy roused himself and pointed forward, in silence. We were approaching the farm along the skirts of a fine peach orchard, now faintly colored with young bud, but there was nothing to disguise the gaunt and aching ugliness of the farmhouse itself. In this Texas valley, so gently modulated with small crests and shallows, "rolling country" as the farmers say, the house was set on the peak of the barest rise of ground, as if the most infertile spot had been thriftily chosen for building a shelter. It stood there staring and naked, an intruding stranger, strange even beside the barns ranged generously along the back, low-eaved and weathered to the color of stone.

20   The narrow windows and the steeply sloping roof oppressed me; I wished to turn away and go back. I had come a long way to be so disappointed, I thought, and yet I must go on, for there could be nothing here for me more painful than what I had left. But as we drew near the house, now hardly visible except for the yellow lamplight in the back, perhaps in the kitchen, my feelings changed again toward warmth and tenderness, or perhaps just an apprehension that I could feel so, maybe, again.

The wagon drew up before the porch, and I started climbing down. No sooner had my foot touched ground than an enormous black dog of the detestable German shepherd breed leaped silently at me, and as silently I covered my face with my arms and leaped back. "Kuno, down!" shouted the boy, lunging at him. The front door flew open and a young girl with yellow hair ran down the steps and seized the ugly beast by the scruff. "He does not mean anything," she said seriously in English. "He is only a dog."

Just Louise's darling little puppy Kuno, I thought, a year or so older. Kuno whined, apologized by bowing and scraping one front paw on the ground, and the girl holding his scruff said, shyly and proudly, "I teach him that. He has always such bad manners, but I teach him!"

I had arrived, it seemed, at the moment when the evening chores were about to begin. The entire Müller household streamed out of the door, each man and woman going about the affairs of the moment. The young girl walked with me up the porch and said, "This is my brother Hans," and a young man paused to shake hands and passed by. "This is my brother Fritz," she said, and Fritz took my hand and dropped it as he went. "My sister Annetje," said the young girl, and a quiet young woman with a baby draped loosely like a scarf over her shoulder smiled and held out her hand. Hand after hand went by, their palms variously younger or older, broad or small, male or female, but all thick hard decent peasant hands, warm and strong. And in every face I saw again the pale, tilted eyes, on every head that taffy-colored hair, as though they might all be brothers and sisters, though Annetje's husband and still another daughter's husband had gone by after greeting me. In the wide hall with a door at front and back, full of cloudy light and the smell of soap, the old mother, also on her way out, stopped to offer her hand. She was a tall strong-looking woman wearing a three-cornered black wool shawl on her head, her skirts looped up over a brown flannel petticoat. Not from her did the young ones get those water-clear eyes. Hers were black and shrewd and searching, a band of hair showed black streaked with grey, her seamed dry face was brown as seasoned bark, and she walked in her rubber boots with the stride of a man. She shook my hand briefly and said in German English that I was welcome, smiling and showing her blackened teeth.

"This is my girl Hatsy," she told me, "and she will show you to your room." Hatsy took my hand as if I were a child needing a guide. I followed her up a flight of steps steep as a ladder, and there we were, in Louise's attic room, with the sloping roof. Yes, the shingles were stained all the colors she had said. There were the dime novels heaped in the corner. For once, Louise had got it straight, and it was homely and familiar, as if I had seen it before. "My mother says we could give you a better place on the downstairs," said Hatsy, in her soft blurred English, "but *she* said in her letter you would like it so." I told her indeed I did like it so. She went down the steep stairs then, and her brother came up as if he were climbing a tree, with the trunk on his head and the suitcase in his right hand, and I could not see what kept the trunk from crashing back to the bottom, as he used the left hand to climb with. I wished to offer help but feared to insult him, having noted well the tremendous ease and style with which he had hurled the luggage around before, a strong man doing his turn before a weakling audience. He put his burden down and straightened up, wriggling his shoulders and panting only a little. I thanked him and he pushed his cap back and pulled it forward again, which I took for some sort of polite response, and clattered out hugely. Looking out of my window a few minutes later, I saw him setting off across the fields carrying a lighted lantern and a large steel trap.

I began changing my first letter to Louise. "I'm going to like it here. I don't quite know why, but it's going to be all right. Maybe I can tell you later——" 25

The sound of the German speech in the household below was part of the pleasantness, for they were not talking to me and did not expect me to answer. All the German I understood then was contained in five small deadly sentimental songs of Heine's, learned by heart; and this was a very different tongue, Low German corrupted by three generations in a foreign country. A dozen miles away, where Texas and Louisiana melted together in a rotting swamp whose sluggish under-tow of decay nourished the roots of pine and cedar, a colony of French emigrants had lived out two hundred years of exile, not wholly incorruptible, but mystically faithful to the marrow of their bones, obstinately speaking their old French by then as strange to the French as it was to the English. I had known many of these families during a certain long summer happily remembered, and here again, listening to another language nobody could understand except those of this small farming community, I knew that I was again in a house of perpetual exile. These were solid, practical, hard-bitten, land-holding German peasants, who struck their mattocks into the earth deep and held fast wherever they were, because to them life and the land were one indivisible thing; but never in any wise did they confuse nationality with habitation.

I liked the thick warm voices, and it was good not to have to understand what they were saying. I loved that silence which means freedom from the constant pressure of other minds and other opinions and other feelings, that freedom to fold up in quiet and go back to my own center, to find out again, for it is always a rediscovery, what kind of creature it is that rules me finally, makes all the decisions no matter who thinks they make them, even I; who little by little takes everything away except the one thing I cannot live without, and who will one day say, "Now I am all you have left—take me." I paused there a good while listening to this muted unknown language which was silence with music in it; I could be moved and touched but not troubled by it, as by the crying of frogs or the wind in the trees.

The catalpa tree at my window would, I noticed, when it came into leaf, shut off my view of the barns and the fields beyond. When in bloom the branches would almost reach through the window. But now they were a thin screen through which the calves, splotchy red and white, moved prettily against the weathered darkness of the sheds. The brown fields would soon be green again; the sheep washed by the rains and become clean grey. All the beauty of the landscape now was in the harmony of the valley rolling fluently away to the wood's edge. It was an inland country, with the forlorn look of all unloved things; winter in this part of the south is a moribund coma, not the northern death sleep with the sure promise of resurrection. But in my south, my loved and never-forgotten country, after her long sickness, with only a slight stirring, an opening of the eyes between one breath and the next, between night and day, the earth revives and bursts into the plenty of spring with fruit and flowers together, spring and summer at once under the hot shimmering blue sky.

The freshening wind promised another light sedate rain to come at evening. The voices below stairs dispersed, rose again, separately calling from the yards and barns. The old woman strode down the path toward the cow sheds, Hatsy running behind her. The woman wore her wooden yoke, with the milking pails covered and closed with iron hasps, slung easily across her shoulders, but her daughter carried two tin milking pails on her arm. When they pushed back the bars of cedar which opened onto the fields, the cows came through lowing and crowding, and the calves scampered each to his own dam with reaching, opened mouths. Then there was the battle of separating the hungry children from their mothers when they had taken their scanty share. The old woman slapped their little haunches with her open palm, Hatsy dragged at their halters, her feet slipping wide in the mud, the cows bellowed and brandished their horns, the calves bawled like rebellious babies. Hatsy's long yellow braids whisked around her shoulders, her laughter was a shrill streak of gaiety above the angry cow voices and the raucous shouting of the old woman.

From the kitchen porch below came the sound of splashing water, the creaking of the pump handle, and the stamping boots of men. I sat in the window watching the darkness come on slowly, while all the lamps were being lighted. My own small lamp had a handle on the oil bowl, like a cup's. There was also a lantern with a frosted chimney hanging by a nail on the wall. A voice called to me from the foot of my stairs and I looked down into the face of a dark-skinned, flaxen-haired young woman, far advanced in pregnancy, and carrying a prosperous year-old boy on her hip, one arm clutching him to her, the other raised above her head so that her lantern shone upon their heads. "The supper is now ready," she said, and waited for me to come down before turning away.

In the large square room the whole family was gathering at a long table covered with a red checkered cotton cloth, with heaped-up platters of steaming food at either end. A crippled and badly deformed servant girl was setting down pitchers of milk. Her face was so bowed over it was almost hidden, and her whole body was maimed in some painful, mysterious way, probably congenital, I supposed, though she seemed wiry and tough. Her knotted hands shook continually, her wagging head kept pace with her restless elbows. She ran unsteadily around the table scattering plates, dodging whoever stood in her way; no one moved aside for her, or spoke to her, or even glanced after her when she vanished into the kitchen.

The men then moved forward to their chairs. Father Müller took his patriarch's place at the head of the table, Mother Müller looming behind him like a dark boulder. The younger men ranged themselves about on one side, the married ones with their wives standing back of their chairs to serve them, for three generations in this country had not made them self-conscious or disturbed their ancient customs. The two sons-in-law and three sons rolled down their shirt sleeves before beginning to eat. Their faces were polished with recent scrubbing and their open collars were damp.

Mother Müller pointed to me, then waved her hand at her household, telling off their names rapidly. I was a stranger and a guest, so was seated on the men's side of the table, and Hatsy, whose real name turned out to be Huldah, the maiden of the family, was seated on the children's side of the board, attending to them and keeping them in order. These infants ranged from two years to ten, five in number—not counting the one still straddling his mother's hip behind his father's chair—divided between the two married daughters. The children ravened and gorged and reached their hands into the sugar bowl to sprinkle sugar on everything they ate, solemnly elated over their food and paying no attention to Hatsy, who struggled with them only a little less energetically than she did with the calves, and ate almost nothing. She was about seventeen years old, pale-lipped and too thin, and her sleek fine butter-yellow hair, streaked light and dark, real German peasant hair, gave her an air of fragility. But she shared the big-boned structure and the enormous energy and animal force that was like a bodily presence itself in the room; and seeing Father Müller's pale-grey deep-set choleric eyes and high cheekbones, it was easy to trace the family resemblance around the table: it was plain that poor Mother Müller had never had a child of her own—black-eyed, black-haired South Germany people. True, she had borne them, but that was all; they belonged to their father. Even the tawny Gretchen, expecting another baby, obviously the pet of the family, with the sly smiling manner of a spoiled child, who wore the contented air of a lazy, healthy young animal, seeming always about to yawn, had hair like pulled taffy and those slanted clear eyes. She stood now easing the weight of her little boy on her husband's chair back, reaching with her left arm over his shoulder to refill his plate from time to time.

Annetje, the eldest daughter, carried her newly born baby over her shoulder, where he drooled comfortably down her back, while she spooned things from platters and bowls for her husband. Whenever their eyes met, they smiled with a gentle, reserved warmth in their eyes, the smile of long and sure friendship.

35   Father Müller did not in the least believe in his children's marrying and leaving home. Marry, yes, of course; but must that take a son or daughter from him? He always could provide work and a place in the household for his daughters' husbands, and in time he would do the same for his sons' wives. A new room had lately been built on, to the northeast, Annetje explained to me, leaning above her husband's head and talking across the table, for Hatsy to live in when she should be married. Hatsy turned very beautifully pink and ducked her head almost into her plate, then looked up boldly and said, "Jah, jah, I am marrit now soon!" Everybody laughed except Mother Müller, who said in German that girls at home never knew when they were well off—no, they must go bringing in husbands. This remark did not seem to hurt anybody's feelings, and Gretchen said it was nice that I was going to be here for the wedding. This reminded Annetje of something, and she spoke in English to the table at large, saying that the Lutheran pastor had advised her to attend church oftener and put her young ones in Sunday school, so that God would give her a blessing with her fifth child. I counted around again, and sure enough, with Gretchen's unborn, there were eight children at that table under the age of ten; somebody was going to need a blessing in all that crowd, no doubt. Father Müller delivered a short speech to his daughter in German, then turned to me and said, "What I say iss, it iss all craziness to go to church and pay a preacher goot money to talk his nonsense. Say rather that he pay me to come and lissen, then I vill go!" His eyes glared with sudden fierceness above his square speckled grey and yellow beard that sprouted directly out from the high cheekbones. "He thinks, so, that my time maybe costs nothing? That iss goot! Let him pay me!"

Mother Müller snorted and shuffled her feet. "Ach, you talk, you talk. Now you vill make the pastor goot and mad if he hears. Vot ve do, if he vill not chrissen the babies?"

"You give him goot money, he vill chrissen," shouted Father Müller. "You vait und see!"

"Ah sure, dot iss so," agreed Mother Müller. "Only do not let him hear!"

There was a gust of excited talk in German, with much rapping of knife handles on the table. I gave up trying to understand, but watched their faces. It sounded like a pitched battle, but they were agreeing about something. They were united in their tribal scepticisms, as in everything else. I got a powerful impression that they were all, even the sons-in-law, one human being divided into several separate appearances. The crippled servant girl brought in more food and gathered up plates and went away in her limping run, and she seemed to me the only individual in the house. Even I felt divided into many fragments, having left or lost a part of myself in every place I had travelled, in every life mine had touched, above all, in every death of someone near to me that had carried into the grave some part of my living cells. But the servant, she was whole, and belonged nowhere.

I settled easily enough into the marginal life of the household ways and habits. Day began early at the Müllers', and we ate breakfast by yellow lamplight, with the grey damp winds blowing with spring softness through the open windows. The men swallowed their last cups of steaming coffee standing, with their hats on, and went out to harness the horses to the ploughs at sunrise. Annetje, with her fat baby slung over her shoulder, could sweep a room or make a bed with one hand, all finished before the day was well begun; and she spent the rest of the day outdoors, caring for the chickens and the pigs. Now and then she came in with a shallow boxful of newly hatched chickens, abject dabs of wet fluff, and put them on a table in her bedroom where she might tend them carefully on their first day. Mother Müller strode about hugely, giving orders right and left, while Father Müller, smoothing his whiskers and lighting his pipe, drove away to town with Mother Müller calling out after him final directions and instructions about household needs. He never spoke a word to her and appeared not to be listening, but he always returned in a few hours with every commission and errand performed exactly. After I had made my own bed and set my attic in order, there was nothing at all for me to do, and I walked out of this enthusiastic bustle into the lane, feeling extremely useless. But the repose, the almost mystical inertia of their minds in the midst of this muscular life, communicated itself to me little by little, and I absorbed it gratefully in silence and felt all the hidden knotted painful places in my own mind beginning to loosen. It was easier to breathe, and I might even weep, if I pleased. In a very few days I no longer felt like weeping.

One morning I saw Hatsy spading up the kitchen garden plot, and my offer to help, to spread the seeds and cover them, was accepted. We worked at this for several hours each morning, until the warmth of the sun and the stooping posture induced in me a comfortable vertigo. I forgot to count the days, they were one like the other except as the colors of the air changed, deepening and warming to keep step with the advancing season, and the earth grew firmer underfoot with the swelling tangle of crowding roots.

The children, so hungry and noisy at the table, were peaceable little folk who played silent engrossed games in the front yard. They were always kneading mud into loaves and pies and carrying their battered dolls and cotton rag animals through the operations of domestic life. They fed them, put them to bed; they got them up and fed them again, set them to their chores making more mud loaves; or they would harness themselves to their carts and gallop away to a great shady chestnut tree on the opposite side of the house. Here the tree became the *Turnverein*,[1] and they themselves were again human beings, solemnly ambling about in a dance and going through the motions of drinking beer. Miraculously changed once more into horses, they harnessed themselves and galloped home. They came at call to be fed and put to sleep with the docility of their own toys or animal playmates. Their mothers handled them with instinctive, constant gentleness; they never seemed to be troubled by them. They were as devoted and caretaking as a cat with her kittens.

Sometimes I took Annetje's next to youngest child, a baby of two years, in her little wagon, and we would go down through the orchard, where the branches were beginning to sprout in cones of watery green, and into the lane for a short distance. I would turn again into a smaller lane, smoother because less travelled, and we would go slowly between the aisle of mulberry trees where the fruit was beginning to hang and curl like green furry worms. The baby would sit in a compact mound of flannel and calico, her pale-blue eyes tilted and shining under her cap, her two lower teeth showing in a rapt smile. Sometimes several of the other children would follow along quietly. When I turned, they all turned without question, and we would proceed back to the house as sedately as we had set out.

The narrow lane, I discovered, led to the river, and it became my favorite walk. Almost every day I went along the edge of the naked wood, passionately occupied with looking for signs of spring. The changes there were so subtle and gradual I found one day that branches of willows and sprays of blackberry vine alike were covered with fine points of green; the color had changed overnight, or so it seemed, and I knew that tomorrow the whole valley and wood and edge of the river would be quick and feathery with golden green blowing in the winds.

45 And it was so. On that day I did not leave the river until after dark and came home through the marsh with the owls and night jars crying over my head, calling in a strange and broken chorus in the woods until the farthest answering cry was a ghostly echo. When I went through the orchard the trees were all abloom with fireflies. I stopped and looked at it for a long time, then walked slowly, amazed, for I had never seen anything that was more beautiful to me. The trees were freshly budded out with pale bloom, the branches were immobile in the thin darkness, but the flower clusters shivered in a soundless dance of delicately woven light, whirling as airily as leaves in a breeze, as rhythmically as water in a fountain. Every tree was budded out with this living, pulsing fire as fragile and cool as bubbles. When I opened the gate their light shone on my hands like fox fire. When I looked back, the shimmer of golden light was there, it was no dream.

Hatsy was on her knees in the dining room, washing the floor with heavy dark rags. She always did this work at night, so the men with their heavy boots would not be tracking it up again and it would be immaculate in the morning. She turned her young face to me in a stupor of fatigue. "Ottilie! Ottilie!" she called, loudly, and before I could speak, she said, "Ottilie will give you supper. It is

1. Gym, gymnastics club.

waiting, all ready." I tried to tell her that I was not hungry, but she wished to reassure me. "Look, we all must eat. Now or then, it's no trouble." She sat back on her heels, and raising her head, looked over the window sill at the orchard. She smiled and paused for a moment and said happily, "Now it is come spring. Every spring we have that." She bent again over the great pail of water with her mops.

The crippled servant came in, stumbling perilously on the slippery floor, and set a dish before me, lentils with sausage and red chopped cabbage. It was hot and savory and I was truly grateful, for I found I was hungry, after all. I looked at her—so her name was Ottilie?—and said, "Thank you." "She can't talk," said Hatsy, simply stating a fact that need not be emphasized. The blurred, dark face was neither young nor old, but crumpled into criss cross wrinkles, irrelevant either to age or suffering; simply wrinkles, patternless blackened seams as if the perishable flesh had been wrung in a hard cruel fist. Yet in that mutilated face I saw high cheekbones, slanted water-blue eyes, the pupils very large and strained with the anxiety of one peering into a darkness full of danger. She jarred heavily against the table as she turned, her bowed back trembling with the perpetual working of her withered arms, and ran away in aimless, driven haste.

Hatsy sat on her heels again for a moment, tossed her braids back over her shoulder and said, "That is Ottilie. She is not sick now. She is only like that since she was sick when she was a baby. But she can work so well as I can. She cooks. But she cannot talk so you can understand." She went up on her knees, bowed over, and began to scrub again, with new energy. She was really a network of thin taut ligaments and long muscles elastic as woven steel. She would always work too hard, and be tired all her life, and never know that this was anything but perfectly natural; everybody worked all the time, because there was always more work waiting when they had finished what they were doing then. I ate my supper and took my plate to the kitchen and set it on the table. Ottilie was sitting in a kitchen chair with her feet in the open oven, her arms folded and her head waggling a little. She did not see or hear me.

At home, Hatsy wore an old brown corduroy dress and galoshes without stockings. Her skirts were short enough to show her thin legs, slightly crooked below the knees, as if she had walked too early. "Hatsy, she's a good, quick girl," said Mother Müller, to whom praising anybody or anything did not come easily. On Saturdays, Hatsy took a voluminous bath in a big tub in the closet back of the kitchen, where also were stored the extra chamber pots, slop jars, and water jugs. She then unplaited her yellow hair and bound up the crinkled floss with a wreath of pink cotton rosebuds, put on her pale-blue China silk dress, and went to the Turnverein to dance and drink a seidel of dark-brown beer with her suitor, who resembled her brothers enough to be her brother, though I think nobody ever noticed this except myself, and I said nothing because it would have been the remark of a stranger and hopeless outsider. On Sundays, the entire family went to the Turnverein after copious washings, getting into starched dresses and shirts, and getting the baskets of food stored in the wagons. The servant, Ottilie, would rush out to see them off, standing with both shaking arms folded over her forehead, shading her troubled eyes to watch them to the turn of the lane. Her mute-ness seemed nearly absolute; she had no coherent language of signs. Yet three times a day she spread that enormous table with solid food, freshly baked bread, huge platters of vegetables, immoderate roasts of meat, extravagant tarts, stru-dels, pies—enough for twenty people. If neighbors came in for an afternoon on some holiday, Ottilie would stumble into the big north room, the parlor, with its golden oak melodeon, a harsh-green Brussels carpet, Nottingham lace curtains, crocheted lace antimacassars on the chair backs, to serve them coffee with cream and sugar and thick slices of yellow cake.

50   Mother Müller sat but seldom in her parlor, and always with an air of formal unease, her knotted big fingers cramped in a cluster. But Father Müller often sat there in the evenings, where no one ventured to follow him unless commanded; he sometimes played chess with his elder son-in-law, who had learned a good while ago that Father Müller was a good player who abhorred an easy victory, and he dared not do less than put up the best fight he was able, but even so, if Father Müller felt himself winning too often, he would roar, "No, you are not trying! You are not doing your best. Now we stop this nonsense!" and son-in-law would find himself dismissed in temporary disgrace.

Most evenings, however, Father Müller sat by himself and read *Das Kapital*.[2] He would settle deeply into the red plush base rocker and spread the volume upon a low table before him. It was an early edition in blotty black German type, stained and ragged in its leather cover, the pages falling apart, a very bible. He knew whole chapters almost by heart, and added nothing to, took nothing from, the canonical, once-delivered text. I cannot say at that time of my life I had never heard of *Das Kapital*, but I had certainly never known anyone who had read it, though if anyone mentioned it, it was always with profound disapproval. It was not a book one had to read in order to reject it. And here was this respectable old farmer who accepted its dogma as a religion—that is to say, its legendary inapplicable precepts were just, right, proper, one must believe in them, of course, but life, everyday living, was another and unrelated thing. Father Müller was the richest man in his community; almost every neighboring farmer rented land from him, and some of them worked it on the share system. He explained this to me one evening after he had given up trying to teach me chess. He was not surprised that I could not learn, at least not in one lesson, and he was not surprised either that I knew nothing about *Das Kapital*. He explained his own arrangements to me thus: "These men, they cannot buy their land. The land must be bought, for Kapital owns it, and Kapital will not give back to the worker the land that is his. Well, somehow, I can always buy land. Why? I do not know. I only know that with my first land here I made good crops to buy more land, and so I rent it cheap, more than anybody else I rent it cheap, I lend money so my neighbors do not fall into the hands of the bank, and so I am not Kapital. Someday these workers, they can buy land from me, for less than they can get it

---

2. Major work (1867–1894) of Karl Marx (1818–1883), founder of communism. It holds that all aspects of social life are determined by economic needs, that change occurs naturally through conflict of eco-nomic forces outside individual actions.

anywhere else. Well, that is what I can do, that is all." He turned over a page, and his angry grey eyes looked out at me under his shaggy brows. "I buy my land with my hard work, all my life, and I rent it cheap to my neighbors, and then they say they will not elect my son-in-law, my Annetje's husband, to be sheriff because I am atheist. So then I say, all right, but next year you pay more for your land or more shares of your crops. If I am atheist I will act like one. So, my Annetje's husband is sheriff, that is all."

He had put a stubby forefinger on a line to mark his place, and now he sank himself into his book, and I left quietly without saying good night.

The *Turnverein* was an octagonal pavilion set in a cleared space in a patch of woods belonging to Father Müller. The German colony came here to sit about in the cool shade, while a small brass band played cloppity country dances. The girls danced with energy and direction, their starched petticoats rustling like dry leaves. The boys were more awkward, but willing; they clutched their partners' waists and left crumpled sweaty spots where they clutched. Here Mother Müller took her ease after a hard week. Her gaunt limbs would relax, her knees spread squarely apart, and she would gossip over her beer with the women of her own generation. They would cast an occasional caretaking glance at the children playing nearby, allowing the younger mothers freedom to dance or sit in peace with their own friends.

On the other side of the pavilion, Father Müller would sit with the sober grandfathers, their long curved pipes wagging on their chests as they discussed local politics with profound gravity, their hard peasant fatalism tempered only a little by a shrewd worldly distrust of all officeholders not personally known to them, all political plans except their own immediate ones. When Father Müller talked, they listened respectfully, with faith in him as a strong man, head of his own house and his community. They nodded slowly whenever he took his pipe from his mouth and gestured, holding it by the bowl as if it were a stone he was getting ready to throw. On our way back from the *Turnverein* one evening, Mother Müller said to me, "Well, now, by the grace of Gott it is all settled between Hatsy and her man. It is next Sunday by this time they will be marrit."

All the folk who usually went to the *Turnverein* on Sundays came instead to the Müller house for the wedding. They brought useful presents, mostly bed linen, pillow covers, a white counterpane, with a few ornaments for the bridal chamber—a home-braided round rug in many colors, a brass-bottomed lamp with a round pink chimney decorated with red roses, a stone china washbowl and pitcher also covered with red roses; and the bridegroom's gift to the bride was a necklace, a double string of red coral twigs. Just before the short ceremony began, he slipped the necklace over her head with trembling hands. She smiled up at him shakily and helped him disentangle her short veil from the coral, then they joined hands and turned their faces to the pastor, not letting go until time for the exchange of rings—the widest, thickest, reddest gold bands to be found, no doubt—and at that moment they both stopped smiling and turned a little pale. The groom recovered first, and bent over—he was considerably taller than she—and kissed her on the forehead. His eyes were a deep blue, and his hair not really Müller taffy color, but a light chestnut; a good-looking, gentle-tempered boy, I decided, and he looked at Hatsy as if he liked what he saw. They knelt and clasped hands again for the final prayer, then stood together and exchanged the bridal kiss, a very chaste reserved one, still not on the lips. Then everybody came to shake hands and the men all kissed the bride and the women all kissed the groom. Some of the women whispered in Hatsy's ear, and all burst out laughing except Hatsy, who turned red from her forehead to her throat. She whispered in turn to her husband, who nodded in agreement. She then tried to slip away quietly, but the watchful young girls were after her, and shortly we saw her running through the blossoming orchard, holding up her white ruffled skirts, with all the girls in pursuit, shrieking and calling like excited hunters, for the first to overtake and touch her would be the next bride. They returned, breathless, dragging the lucky one with them, and held her against her ecstatic resistance, while all the young boys kissed her.

The guests stayed on for a huge supper, and Ottilie came in, wearing a fresh blue apron, sweat beaded in the wrinkles of her forehead and around her formless mouth, and passed the food around the table. The men ate first and then Hatsy came in with the women for the first time, still wearing her square little veil of white cotton net bound on her hair with peach blossoms shattered in the bride's race. After supper, one of the girls played waltzes and polkas on the melodeon, and everyone danced. The bridegroom drew gallons of beer from a keg set up in the hall, and at midnight everybody went away, warmly emotional and happy. I went down to the kitchen for a pitcher of hot water. The servant was still setting things to rights, hobbling between table and cupboard. Her face was a brown smudge of anxiety, her eyes were wide and dazed. Her uncertain hands rattled among the pans, but nothing could make her seem real, or in any way connected with the life around her. Yet when I set my pitcher on the stove, she lifted the heavy kettle and poured the scalding water into it without spilling a drop.

The clear honey green of the early morning sky was a mirror of the bright earth. At the edge of the woods there had sprung a reticent blooming of small white and pale-colored flowers. The peach trees were now each a separate nosegay of shell rose and white. I left the house, meaning to take the short path across to the lane of mulberries. The women were deep in the house, the men were away to the fields, the animals were turned into the pastures, and only Ottilie was visible, sitting on the steps of the back porch peeling potatoes. She gazed in my direction with eyes that fell short of me, and seemed to focus on a point midway between us, and gave no sign. Then she dropped her knife and rose, her mouth opened and closed several times, she strained toward me, motioning with her right hand. I went to her, her hands came out and clutched my sleeve, and for a moment I feared to hear her voice. There was no sound from her, but she drew me along after her, full of some mysterious purpose of her own. She opened the door of a dingy bitter-smelling room, windowless, which opened off the kitchen, beside the closet where Hatsy took her baths. A lumpy narrow cot and chest of drawers supporting a blistered looking-glass almost filled the space. Ottilie's lips moved, struggling for speech, as she pulled and tumbled over a heap of rubbish in the top drawer. She took out a photograph and put it in my hands. It was in the old style, faded to a dirty yellow, mounted on cardboard elaborately clipped and gilded at the edges.

I saw a girl child about five years old, a pretty smiling German baby, looking curiously like a slightly elder sister of Annetje's two-year-old, wearing a frilled frock and a prodigious curl of blonde hair, called a roach, on the crown of her head. The strong legs, round as sausages, were encased in long white ribbed stockings, and the square firm feet were laced into old-fashioned soft-soled black boots. Ottilie peered over the picture, twisted her neck, and looked up into my face. I saw the slanted water-blue eyes and the high cheekbones of the Müllers again, mutilated, almost destroyed, but unmistakable. This child was what she had been, and she was without doubt the elder sister of Annetje and Gretchen and Hatsy; in urgent pantomime she insisted that this was so—she patted the picture and her own face, and strove terribly to speak. She pointed to the name written carefully on the back, Ottilie, and touched her mouth with her bent knuckles. Her head wagged in her perpetual nod; her shaking hand seemed to flap the photograph at me in a roguish humor. The bit of cardboard connected her at once somehow to the world of human beings I knew; for an instant some filament lighter than cobweb spun itself out between that living center in her and in me, a filament from some center that held us all bound to our unescapable common source, so that her life and mine were kin, even a part of each other, and the painfulness and strangeness of her vanished. She knew well that she had been Ottilie, with those steady legs and watching eyes, and she was Ottilie still within herself. For a moment, being alive, she knew she suffered, for she stood and shook with silent crying, smearing away her tears with the open palm of her hand. Even while her cheeks were wet, her face changed. Her eyes cleared and fixed themselves upon that point in space which seemed for her to contain her unaccountable and terrible troubles. She turned her head as if she had heard a voice and disappeared in her staggering run into the kitchen, leaving the drawer open and the photograph face downward on the chest.

At midday meal she came hurrying and splashing coffee on the white floor, restored to her own secret existence of perpetual amazement, and again I had been a stranger to her like all the rest but she was no stranger to me, and could not be again.

The youngest brother came in, holding up an opossum he had caught in his trap. He swung the furry body from side to side, his eyes fairly narrowed with pride as he showed us the mangled creature. "No, it is cruel, even for the wild animals," said gentle Annetje to me, "but boys love to kill, they love to hurt things. I am always afraid he will trap poor Kuno." I thought privately that Kuno, a wolfish, ungracious beast, might well prove a match for any trap. Annetje was full of silent, tender solicitudes. The kittens, the puppies, the chicks, the lambs and calves were her special care. She was the only one of the women who caressed the weanling calves when she set the pans of milk before them. Her child seemed as much a part of her as if it were not yet born. Still, she seemed to have forgotten that Ottilie was her sister. So had all the others. I remembered how Hatsy had spoken her name but had not said she was her sister. Their silence about her was, I realized, exactly that—simple forgetfulness. She moved among them as invisible to their imaginations as a ghost. Ottilie their sister was something painful that had happened long ago and now was past and done for; they could not live with that memory or its visible reminder—they forgot her in pure self-defense. But I could not forget her. She drifted into my mind like a bit of weed carried in a current and caught there, floating but fixed, refusing to be carried away. I reasoned it out. The Müllers, what else could they have done with Ottilie? By a physical accident in her childhood she had been stripped of everything but her mere existence. It was not a society or a class that pampered its invalids and the unfit. So long as one lived, one did one's share. This was her place, in this family she had been born and must die; did she suffer? No one asked, no one looked to see. Suffering went with life, suffering and labor. While one lived one worked, that was all, and without complaints, for no one had time to listen, and everybody had his own troubles. So, what else could they have done with Ottilie? As for me, I could do nothing but promise myself that I would forget her, too; and to remember her for the rest of my life.

Sitting at the long table, I would watch Ottilie clattering about in her tormented haste, bringing in that endless food that represented all her life's labors. My mind would follow her into the kitchen where I could see her peering into the great simmering kettles, the crowded oven, her whole body a mere machine of torture. Straight up to the surface of my mind the thought would come urgently, clearly, as if driving time toward the desired event: Let it be now, let it be *now*. Not even tomorrow, no, today. Let her sit down quietly in her rickety chair by the stove and fold those arms, and let us find her there like that, with her head fallen forward on her knees. She will rest then. I would wait, hoping she might not come again, ever again, through that door I gazed at with wincing eyes, as if I might see something unendurable enter through it. Then she would come, and it was only Ottilie, after all, in the bosom of her family, and one of its most useful and competent members; and they with a deep right instinct had learned to live with her disaster on its own terms, and hers; they had accepted and then made use of what was for them only one more painful event in a world full of troubles, many of them much worse than this. So, a step at a time, I followed the Müllers as nearly as I could in their acceptance of Ottilie, and the use they made of her life, for in some way that I could not quite explain to myself, I found great virtue and courage in their steadiness and refusal to feel sorry for anybody, least of all for themselves.

Gretchen bore her child, a son, conveniently between the hours of supper and bedtime, one evening of friendly and domestic-sounding rain. The next day brought neighboring women from miles around, and the child was bandied about among them as if he were a new kind of medicine ball. Sedate and shy at dances, emotional at weddings, they were ribald and jocose at births. Over coffee and beer the talk grew broad, the hearty gutturals were swallowed in the belly of laughter; those honest hard-working wives and mothers saw life for a few hours as a hearty low joke, and it did them good. The baby bawled and suckled like a young calf, and the men of the family came in for a look and added their joyful improprieties.

Cloudy weather drove them home earlier than they had meant to go. The whole sky was lined with smoky black and grey vapor hanging in ragged wisps like soot in a chimney. The edges of the woods turned dull purple as the horizon reddened slowly, then faded, and all across the sky ran a deep shuddering mumble of thunder. All the Müllers hurried about getting into rubber boots and oilcloth overalls, shouting to each other, making their plan of action. The youngest boy came over the ridge of the hill with Kuno helping him to drive the sheep down into the fold. Kuno was barking, the sheep were baaing and bleating, the horses freed from the ploughs were excited; they whinnied and trotted at the lengths of their halters, their ears laid back. The cows were bawling in distress and the calves cried back to them. All the men went out among the animals to round them up and quiet them and get them enclosed safely. Even as Mother Müller, her half-dozen petticoats looped about her thighs and tucked into her hip boots, was striding to join them in the barns, the cloud rack was split end to end by a shattering blow of lightning, and the cloudburst struck the house with the impact of a wave against a ship. The wind broke the windowpanes and the floods poured through. The roof beams strained and the walls bent inward, but the house stood to its foundations. The children were huddled into the inner bedroom with Gretchen. "Come and sit on the bed with me now," she told them calmly, "and be still." She sat up with a shawl around her, suckling the baby. Annetje came then and left her baby with Gretchen, too; and standing at the doorsteps with one arm caught over the porch rail, reached down into the furious waters which were rising to the very threshold and dragged in a half-drowned lamb. I followed her. We could not make ourselves heard above the cannonade of thunder, but together we carried the creature into the hall under the stairs, where we rubbed the drowned fleece with rags and pressed his stomach to free him from the water and finally got him sitting up with his feet tucked under him. Annetje was merry with triumph and kept saying in delight, "Alive, alive! look!"

We left him there when we heard the men shouting and beating at the kitchen door and ran to open it for them. They came in, Mother Müller among them, wearing her yoke and milk pails. She stood there with the water pouring from her skirts, the three-cornered piece of black oilcloth on her head dripping, her rubber boots wrinkled down with the weight of her petticoats stuffed into them. She and Father Müller stood near each other, looking like two gnarled lightning-struck old trees, his beard and oilcloth garments streaming, both their faces suddenly dark and old and tired, tired once for all; they would never be rested again in their lives. Father Müller suddenly roared at her, "Go get yourself dry clothes. Do you want to make yourself sick?"

"Ho," she said, taking off her milk yoke and setting the pails on the floor. "Go change yourself. I bring you dry socks." One of the boys told me she had carried a day-old calf on her back up a ladder against the inside wall of the barn and had put it safely in the hayloft behind a barricade of bales. Then she had lined up the cows in the stable, and, sitting on her milking stool in the rising water, she had milked them all. She seemed to think nothing of it.

"Hatsy!" she called, "come help with this milk!" Little pale Hatsy came flying barefoot because she had been called in the midst of taking off her wet shoes, her

65

thick yellow and silver braids thumping on her shoulders as she ran. Her new husband followed her, rather shy of his mother-in-law.

"Let me," he said, wishing to spare his dear bride such heavy work, and started to lift the great pails. "No!" shouted Mother Müller, so the poor young man nearly jumped out of his shirt, "not you. The milk is not business for a man." He fell back and stood there with dark rivulets of mud seeping from his boots, watching Hatsy pour the milk into pans. Mother Müller started to follow her husband to attend him, but said at the door, turning back, "Where is Ottilie?", and no one knew, no one had seen her. "Find her," said Mother Müller, going. "Tell her we want supper now."

Hatsy motioned to her husband, and together they tiptoed to the door of Ottilie's room and opened it silently. The light from the kitchen showed them Ottilie, sitting by herself, folded up on the edge of the bed. Hatsy threw the door wide open for more light and called in a high penetrating voice as if to a deaf person or one at a great distance, "Ottilie! Suppertime. We are hungry!", and the young pair left the kitchen to look under the stairway to see how Annetje's lamb was getting on. Then Annetje, Hatsy, and I got brooms and began sweeping the dirty water and broken glass from the floors of the hall and dining room.

The storm lightened gradually, but the flooding rain continued. At supper there was talk about the loss of animals and their replacement. All the crops must be replanted, the season's labor was for nothing. They were all tired and wet, but they ate heartily and calmly, to strengthen themselves against all the labor of repairing and restoring which must begin early tomorrow morning.

By morning the drumming on the roof had almost ceased; from my window I looked upon a sepia-colored plain of water moving slowly to the valley. The roofs of the barns sagged like the ridge poles of a tent, and a number of drowned animals floated or were caught against the fences. At breakfast Mother Müller sat groaning over her coffee cup. "Ach," she said, "what it is to have such a pain in the head. Here too," she thumped her chest. "All over. Ach, Gott, I'm sick." She got up sighing hoarsely, her cheeks flushed, calling Hatsy and Annetje to help her in the barn.

They all came back very soon, their skirts draggled to the knees, and the two sisters were supporting their mother, who was speechless and could hardly stand. They put her to bed, where she lay without moving, her face scarlet. Everybody was confused, no one knew what to do. They tucked the quilts about her, and she threw them off. They offered her coffee, cold water, beer, but she turned her head away. The sons came in and stood beside her, and joined the cry: "Mutterchen, Mutti, Mutti,[3] what can we do? Tell us, what do you need?" But she could not tell them. It was impossible to ride the twelve miles to town for a doctor; fences and bridges were down, the roads were washed out. The family crowded into the room, unnerved in panic, lost unless the sick woman should come to herself and tell them what to do for her. Father Müller came in and, kneeling beside her, he took hold of her hands and spoke to her most lovingly, and when

_____

3. Endearing terms for *Mother*.

she did not answer him he broke out crying openly in a loud voice, the great tears rolling, "Ach, Gott, Gott. A hundert tousand tollars in the bank"—he glared around at his family and spoke broken English to them, as if he were a stranger to himself and had forgotten his own language—"and tell me, tell, what goot does it do?"

This frightened them, and all at once, together, they screamed and called and implored her in a tumult utterly beyond control. The noise of their grief and terror filled the place. In the midst of this, Mother Müller died.

In the midafternoon the rain passed, and the sun was a disc of brass in a cruelly bright sky. The waters flowed thickly down to the river, leaving the hill bald and brown, with the fences lying in a flattened tangle, the young peach trees stripped of bloom and sagging at the roots. In the woods had occurred a violent eruption of ripe foliage of a jungle thickness, glossy and burning, a massing of hot peacock green with cobalt shadows.

The household was in such silence, I had to listen carefully to know that anyone lived there. Everyone, even the younger children, moved on tiptoe and spoke in whispers. All afternoon the thud of hammers and the whine of a saw went on monotonously in the barn loft. At dark, the men brought in a shiny coffin of new yellow pine with rope handles and set it in the hall. It lay there on the floor for an hour or so, where anyone passing had to step over it. Then Annetje and Hatsy, who had been washing and dressing the body, appeared in the doorway and motioned: "You may bring it in now."

Mother Müller lay in state in the parlor throughout the night, in her black silk dress with a scrap of white lace at the collar and a small lace cap on her hair. Her husband sat in the plush chair near her, looking at her face, which was very contemplative, gentle, and remote. He wept at intervals, silently, wiping his face and head with a big handkerchief. His daughters brought him coffee from time to time. He fell asleep there toward morning.

The light burned in the kitchen nearly all night, too, and the sound of Ottilie's heavy boots thumping about unsteadily was accompanied by the locust whirring of the coffee mill and the smell of baking bread. Hatsy came to my room. "There's coffee and cake," she said, "you'd better have some," and turned away crying, crumbling her slice in her hand. We stood about and ate in silence. Ottilie brought in a fresh pot of coffee, her eyes bleared and fixed, her gait as aimless-looking and hurried as ever, and when she spilled some on her own hand, she did not seem to feel it.

For a day longer they waited; then the youngest boy went to fetch the Lutheran pastor, and a few neighbors came back with them. By noon many more had arrived, spattered with mud, the horses heaving and sweating. At every greeting the family gave way and wept afresh, as naturally and openly as children. Their faces were drenched and soft with their tears; there was a comfortable relaxed look in the muscles of their faces. It was good to let go, to have something to weep for that nobody need excuse or explain. Their tears were at once a luxury and a cure of souls. They wept away the hard core of secret trouble that is in the heart of each separate man, secure in a communal grief; in sharing it, they consoled each other. For a while they would visit the grave and remember, and then life would arrange itself again in another order, yet it would be the same. Already the thoughts of the living were turning to tomorrow, when they would be at the work of rebuilding and replanting and repairing—even now, today, they would hurry back from the burial to milk the cows and feed the chickens, and they might weep again and again for several days, until their tears could heal them at last.

On that day I realized, for the first time, not death, but the terror of dying. When they took the coffin out to the little country hearse and I saw that the procession was about to form, I went to my room and lay down. Staring at the ceiling, I heard and felt the ominous order and purpose in the movements and sounds below—the creaking harness and hoofbeats and grating wheels, the muted grave voices—and it was as if my blood fainted and receded with fright, while my mind stayed wide awake to receive the awful impress. Yet when I knew they were leaving the yard, the terror began to leave me. As the sounds receded, I lay there not thinking, not feeling, in a mere drowse of relief and weariness.

Through my half-sleep I heard the howling of a dog. It seemed to be a dream, and I was troubled to awaken. I dreamed that Kuno was caught in the trap; then I thought he was really caught, it was no dream and I must wake, because there was no one but me to let him out. I came broad awake, the cry rushed upon me like a wind, and it was not the howl of a dog. I ran downstairs and looked into Gretchen's room. She was curled up around her baby, and they were both asleep. I ran to the kitchen.

80   Ottilie was sitting in her broken chair with her feet on the edge of the open oven, where the heat had died away. Her hands hung at her sides, the fingers crooked into the palm; her head lay back on her shoulders, and she howled with a great wrench of her body, an upward reach of the neck, without tears. At sight of me she got up and came over to me and laid her head on my breast, and her hands dangled forward a moment. Shuddering, she babbled and howled and waved her arms in a frenzy through the open window over the stripped branches of the orchard toward the lane where the procession had straightened out into formal order. I took hold of her arms where the unnaturally corded muscles clenched and strained under her coarse sleeves; I led her out to the steps and left her sitting there, her head wagging.

In the barnyard there remained only the broken-down spring wagon and the shaggy pony that had brought me to the farm on the first day. The harness was still a mystery, but somehow I managed to join pony, harness, and wagon not too insecurely, or so I could only hope; and I pushed and hauled and tugged at Ottilie and lifted her until she was in the seat and I had the reins in hand. We careened down the road at a grudging trot, the pony jolting like a churn, the wheels spinning elliptically in a truly broad comedy swagger. I watched the jovial antics of those wheels with attention, hoping for the best. We slithered into round pits of green mud, and jogged perilously into culverts where small bridges had been. Once, in what was left of the main road, I stood up to see if I might overtake the funeral train; yes, there it was, going inchmeal up the road over the little hill, a bumbling train of black beetles crawling helter-skelter over clods.

Ottilie, now silent, was doubled upon herself, slipping loosely on the edge of the seat. I caught hold of her stout belt with my free hand, and my fingers slipped between her clothes and bare flesh, ribbed and gaunt and dry against my knuckles. My sense of her realness, her humanity, this shattered being that was a woman, was so shocking to me that a howl as doglike and despairing as her own rose in me unuttered and died again, to be a perpetual ghost. Ottilie slanted her eyes and peered at me, and I gazed back. The knotted wrinkles of her face were grotesquely changed, she gave a choked little whimper, and suddenly she laughed out, a kind of yelp but unmistakably laughter, and clapped her hands for joy, the grinning mouth and suffering eyes turned to the sky. Her head nodded and wagged with the clownish humor of our trundling lurching progress. The feel of the hot sun on her back, the bright air, the jolly senseless staggering of the wheels, the peacock green of the heavens: something of these had reached her. She was happy and gay, and she gurgled and rocked in her seat, leaning upon me and waving loosely around her as if to show me what wonders she saw.

Drawing the pony to a standstill, I studied her face for a while and pondered my ironical mistake. There was nothing I could do for Ottilie, selfishly as I wished to ease my heart of her; she was beyond my reach as well as any other human reach, and yet, had I not come nearer to her than I had to anyone else in my attempt to deny and bridge the distance between us, or rather, her distance from me? Well, we were both equally the fools of life, equally fellow fugitives from death. We had escaped for one day more at least. We would celebrate our good luck, we would have a little stolen holiday, a breath of spring air and freedom on this lovely, festive afternoon.

Ottilie fidgeted, uneasy at our stopping. I flapped the reins, the pony moved on, we turned across the shallow ditch where the small road divided from the main travelled one. I measured the sun westering gently; there would be time enough to drive to the river down the lane of mulberries and to get back to the house before the mourners returned. There would be plenty of time for Ottilie to have a fine supper ready for them. They need not even know she had been gone.

p. 1960

MARGARET LAURENCE

The Rain Child

I recall the sky that day—overcast, the flat undistinguished grey nearly forgotten by us here during the months of azure which we come to regard as rights rather than privileges. As always when the rain hovers, the air was like syrup, thick and heavily still, over-sweet with flowering vines and the occasional ripe paw-paw that had fallen and now lay yellow and fermented, a winery for ants.

I was annoyed at having to stay in my office so late. Annoyed, too, that I found the oppressive humidity just before the rains a little more trying each year.

I have always believed myself particularly well-suited to this climate. Miss Povey, of course, when I was idiotic enough to complain one day about the heat, hinted that the change of life might be more to blame than the weather.

"Of course, I remember how bothersome you found the heat one season," I parried. "Some years ago, as I recollect."

We work well together and even respect one another. Why must we make such petty stabs? Sitting depressed at my desk, I was at least thankful that when a breeze quickened we would receive it here. Blessings upon the founders of half a century ago who built Eburaso Girls' School at the top of the hill, for at the bottom the villagers would be steaming like crabs in a soup pot.

My leg hurt more than it had in a long time, and I badly wanted a cup of tea. Typical of Miss Povey, I thought, that she should leave yet another parental interview to me. Twenty-seven years here, to my twenty-two, and she still felt acutely uncomfortable with African parents, all of whom in her eyes were equally unenlightened. The fact that one father might be an illiterate cocoa farmer, while the next would possibly be a barrister from the city—such distinctions made no earthly difference to Hilda Povey. She was positive that parents would fail to comprehend the importance of sending their little girls to school with the proper clothing, and she harped upon this subject in a thoroughly tedious manner, as though the essence of education lay in the possession of six pairs of cotton knickers.[1] Malice refreshed me for a moment. Then, as always, it began to chill. Were we still women, in actuality, who could bear only grudges, make venom for milk? I exaggerated for a while in this lamentably oratorical style, dramatizing the trivial for lack of anything great. Hilda, in point of fact, was an excellent headmistress. Like a budgerigar she darted and fussed through her days, but underneath the twittering there was a strong disciplined mind and a heart more pious than mine. Even in giving credit to her, however, I chose words churlishly—why had I not thought "devout" instead of "pious," with its undertones of self-righteousness? What could she possibly have said in my favour if she had been asked? That I taught English competently, even sometimes with love? That my irascibility was mainly reserved for my colleagues? The young ones in Primary did not find me terrifying, once they grew used to the sight of the lady in stout white drill skirt and drab lilac smock faded from purple, her greying hair arranged in what others might call a chignon, but for me could only be termed a bun, a lady of somewhat uncertain gait, clumping heavily into the classroom with her ebony cane. They felt free to laugh, my forest children, reticent and stiff in unaccustomed dresses, as we began the alien speech. "What are we doing, class?" And, as I sat down clumsily on the straight chair, to show them, they made their murmured and mirthful response—"We ah siddeen." The older girls in Middle School also seemed to accept me readily enough. Since Miss Harvey left us to marry that fool of a government geologist, I have had the senior girls for English literature and composition. Once when we were taking *Daffodils,* Kwaale came to class with her arms full of wild orchids for me. How absurd Wordsworth seemed here then. I spoke instead about Akan poetry, and read them the drum prelude *Anyane-*

---

1. Underpants (British).

anyane in their own tongue as well as the translation. Miss Povey, hearing of it, took decided umbrage. Well. Perhaps she would not have found much to say in my favour after all.

I fidgeted and perspired, beginning to wonder if Dr. Quansah would show up that day at all. Then, without my having heard his car or footsteps, he stood there at my office door, his daughter Ruth beside him.

"Miss—" He consulted a letter which he held in his hand. "Miss Violet Nedden?"

"Yes." I limped over to meet him. I was, stupidly, embarrassed that he had spoken my full name. Violet, applied to me, is of course quite ludicrous and I detest it. I felt as well the old need to explain my infirmity, but I refrained for the usual reasons. I do not know why it should matter to me to have people realize I was not always like this, but it does. In the pre-sulpha days when I first came here, I developed a tropical sore which festered badly; this is the result. But if I mention it to Africans, they tend to become faintly apologetic, as though it were somehow their fault that I bear the mark of Africa upon myself in much the same way as any ulcerated beggar of the streets.

Dr. Quansah, perhaps to my relief, did not seem much at ease either. Awkwardly, he transferred Miss Povey's typewritten instructions to his left hand in order to shake hands with me. A man in his middle fifties, I judged him to be. Thickly built, with hands which seemed too immense to be a doctor's. He was well dressed, in a beige linen suit of good cut, and there was about his eyes a certain calm which his voice and gestures lacked.

His daughter resembled him, the same strong coarse features, the same skin   10
shade, rather a lighter brown than is usual here. At fifteen she was more plump and childish in figure than most of our girls her age. Her frock was pretty and expensive, a blue cotton with white daisies on it, but as she was so stocky it looked too old for her.

"I don't know if Miss Povey told you," Dr. Quansah began, "but Ruth has never before attended school in this—in her own country."

I must have shown my surprise, for he hastened on. "She was born in England and has lived all her life there. I went there as a young man, you see, to study medicine, and when I graduated I had the opportunity to stay on and do malaria research. Ultimately my wife joined me in London. She—she died in England. Ruth has been in boarding schools since she was six. I have always meant to return here, of course. I had not really intended to stay away so long, but I was very interested in malaria research, and it was an opportunity that comes only once. Perhaps I have even been able to accomplish a certain amount. Now the government here is financing a research station, and I am to be in charge of it. You may have heard of it—it is only twenty miles from here."

I could see that he had had to tell me so I should not think it odd for an African to live away from his own country for so many years. Like my impulse to explain my leg. We are all so anxious that people should not think us different. See, we say, I am not peculiar—wait until I tell you how it was with me.

"Well," I said slowly, "I do hope Ruth will like it here at Eburaso."

My feeling of apprehension was so marked, I remember, that I attempted exor-   15 cism by finding sensible reasons. It was only the season, I thought, the inevitable tension before the rains, and perhaps the season of regrets in myself as well. But I was not convinced.

"I, too, hope very much she will like it here," Dr. Quansah said. He did not sound overly confident.

"I'm sure I shall," Ruth said suddenly, excitedly, her round face beaming. "I think it's great fun, Miss Nedden, coming to Africa like this."

Her father and I exchanged quick and almost fearful glances. She had spoken, of course, as any English schoolgirl might speak, going abroad.

I do not know how long Ruth Quansah kept her sense of adventure. Possibly it lasted the first day, certainly not longer. I watched her as carefully as I could, but there was not much I could do.

20   I had no difficulty in picking her out from a group of girls, although she wore the same light green uniform. She walked differently, carried herself differently. She had none of their easy languor. She strode along with brisk intensity, and in consequence perspired a great deal. At meals she ate virtually nothing. I asked her if she had no appetite, and she looked at me reproachfully.

"I'm starving," she said flatly. "But I can't eat this food, Miss Nedden. I'm sorry, but I just can't. That awful mashed stuff, sort of greyish yellow, like some funny kind of potatoes—it makes me sick."

"I'm afraid you'll have to get used to cassava," I said, restraining a smile, for she looked so serious and so offended. "African food is served to the girls here, naturally. Personally I'm very fond of it, groundnut stew and such. Soon you won't find it strange."

She gave me such a hostile glance that I wondered uneasily what we would do if she really determined to starve herself. Thank heaven she could afford to lose a few pounds.

Our girls fetched their own washing water in buckets from our wells. The evening trek for water was a time of singing, of shouted gossip, of laughter, just as it was each morning for their mothers in the villages, taking the water vessels to the river. The walk was not an easy one for me, but one evening I stumbled rather irritably and unwillingly down the stony path to the wells.

25   Ruth was there, standing apart from the others. Each of the girls in turn filled a bucket, hoisted it up onto her head, and sauntered off, still chattering and waving, without spilling a drop. Ruth was left alone to fill her bucket. Then, carrying it with both her hands clenched around the handle, she began to struggle back along the path. Perhaps foolishly, I smiled. It was done only in encouragement, but she mistook my meaning.

"I expect it looks very funny," she burst out. "I expect they all think so, too."

Before I could speak she had swung the full bucket and thrown it from her as hard as she could. The water struck at the ground, turning the dust to ochre mud, and the bucket rattled and rolled, dislodging pebbles along its way. The laughter among the feathery *niim* trees further up the path suddenly stopped, as a dozen pairs of hidden eyes peered. Looking bewildered, as though she were surprised and shocked by what she had done, Ruth sat down, her sturdy legs rigid in front of her, her child's soft face creased in tears.

"I didn't know it would be like this, here," she said at last. "I didn't know it at all."

In the evenings the senior girls were allowed to change from their school uniforms to African cloth, and they usually did so, for they were very concerned with their appearance and they rightly believed that the dark-printed lengths of mammy-cloth were more becoming to them than their short school frocks. Twice a week it was my responsibility to hobble over and make the evening rounds of the residence. Ruth, I noticed, changed into one of her English frocks, a different one each time, it appeared. Tact had never been my greatest strength, but I tried to suggest that it might be better if she would wear cloth like the rest.

"Your father would be glad to buy one for you, I'm sure." 30

"I've got one—it was my mother's," Ruth replied. She frowned. "I don't know how to put it on properly. They—they'd only laugh if I asked them. And anyway—"

Her face took on that defiance which is really a betrayal of uncertainty.

"I don't like those cloths," she said clearly. "They look like fancy-dress costumes to me. I'd feel frightfully silly in one. I suppose the people here haven't got anything better to wear."

In class she had no restraint. She was clever, and she knew more about English literature and composition than the other girls, for she had been taught always in English, whereas for the first six years of their schooling they had received most of their instruction in their own language. But she would talk interminably, if allowed, and she rushed to answer my questions before anyone else had a chance. Abenaa, Mary Ansah, Yaa, Kwaale, and all the rest would regard her with eyes which she possibly took to be full of awe for her erudition. I knew something of those bland brown eyes, however, and I believed them to contain only scorn for one who would so blatantly show off. But I was wrong. The afternoon Kwaale came to see me, I learned that in those first few weeks the other girls had believed, quite simply, that Ruth was insane.

The junior teachers live in residence in the main building, but Miss Povey and 35 I have our own bungalows, hers on one side of the grounds, mine on the other. A small grove of bamboo partially shields my house, and although Yindo the garden boy deplores my taste, I keep the great spiny clumps of prickly pear that grow beside my door. Hilda Povey grows zinnia and nasturtiums, and spends hours trying to coax an exiled rosebush into bloom, but I will have no English flowers. My garden burns magnificently with jungle lily and poinsettia, which Yindo gently uproots from the forest and puts in here.

The rains had broken and the air was cool and lightened. The downpour began predictably each evening around dusk, so I was still able to have my tea outside. I was exceedingly fond of my garden chair. I discovered it years ago at Jillaram's Silk Palace, a tatty little Indian shop in the side streets of the city which I seldom visited. The chair was rattan with a high fan-shaped back like a throne or a peacock's tail, enamelled in Chinese red and decorated extravagantly with gilt. I had never seen anything so splendidly garish, so I bought it. The red had since been subdued by sun and the gilt was flaking, but I still sat enthroned in it each afternoon, my ebony sceptre by my side.

I did not hear Kwaale until she greeted me. She was wearing her good cloth, an orange one patterned with small black stars that wavered in their firmament as she moved. Kwaale had never been unaware of her womanhood. Even as a child she walked with that same slow grace. We did not need to hope that she would go on and take teacher training or anything of that sort. She would marry when she left school, and I believed that would be the right thing for her to do. But sometimes it saddened me to think of what life would probably be for her, bearing too many children in too short a span of years, mourning the inevitable deaths of some of them, working bent double at the planting and hoeing until her slim straightness was warped. All at once I felt ashamed in the presence of this young queen, who had only an inheritance of poverty to return to, ashamed of my comfort and my heaviness, ashamed of my decrepit scarlet throne and trivial game.

"Did you want to see me, Kwaale?" I spoke brusquely.

"Yes." She sat down on the stool at my feet. At first they had thought Ruth demented, she said, but now they had changed their minds. They had seen how well she did on her test papers. She was sane, they had decided, but this was so much the worse for her, for now she could be held responsible for what she did.

40 "What does she do, Kwaale?"

"She will not speak with us, nor eat with us. She pretends not to eat at all. But we have seen her. She has money, you know, from her father. The big palm grove—she goes there, and eats chocolate and biscuits. By herself. Not one to anyone else. Such a thing."

Kwaale was genuinely shocked. Where these girls came from, sharing was not done as a matter of moral principle, but as a necessary condition of life.

"If one alone eats the honey," Kwaale said primly in Twi, "it plagues his stomach."

It was, of course, a proverb. Kwaale was full of them. Her father was a village elder in Eburaso, and although he did precious little work, he was a highly respected man. He spoke continuously in proverbs and dispensed his wisdom freely. He was a charming person, but it was his wife, with the cassava and peppers and medicinal herbs she sold in the market, who had made it possible for some of their children to obtain an education.

45 "That is not all," Kwaale went on. "There is much worse. She becomes angry, even at the young ones. Yesterday Ayesha spoke to her, and she hit the child on the face. Ayesha—if it had been one of the others, even—"

Ayesha, my youngest one, who had had to bear so much. Tears of rage must have come to my eyes, for Kwaale glanced at me, then lowered her head with that courtesy of the heart which forbids the observing of another's pain. I struggled with myself to be fair to Ruth. I called to mind the bleakness of her face as she trudged up the path with the water bucket.

"She is lonely, Kwaale, and does not quite know what to do. Try to be patient with her."

Kwaale sighed. "It is not easy—"

Then her resentment gained command. "The stranger is like passing water in the drain," she said fiercely.

50 Another of her father's proverbs. I looked at her in dismay.

"There is a different saying on that subject," I said dryly, at last. "We had it in chapel not so long ago—don't you remember? From Exodus. 'Thou shalt not oppress a stranger, for ye know the heart of a stranger, seeing ye were strangers in the land of Egypt.' "

But Kwaale's eyes remained implacable. She had never been a stranger in the land of Egypt.

When Kwaale had gone, I sat unmoving for a while in my ridiculous rattan throne. Then I saw Ayesha walking along the path, so I called to her. We spoke together in Twi, Ayesha and I. She had begun to learn English, but she found it difficult and I tried not to press her beyond her present limits. She did not even speak her own language very well, if it was actually her own language—no one knew for certain. She was tiny for her age, approximately six. In her school dress she looked like one of those stick figures I used to draw as a child—billowing garments, straight lines for limbs, and the same disproportionately large eyes.

"Come here, Ayesha."

Obediently she came. Then, after the first moment of watchful survey which she still found necessary to observe, she scrambled onto my lap. I was careful— we were all careful here—not to establish bonds of too great affection. As Miss Povey was fond of reminding us, these were not our children. But with Ayesha, the rule was sometimes hard to remember. I touched her face lightly with my hand.

"Did an older girl strike you, little one?"

She nodded wordlessly. She did not look angry or upset. She made no bid for sympathy because she had no sense of having been unfairly treated. A slap was not a very great injury to Ayesha.

"Why?" I asked gently. "Do you know why she did that thing?"

She shook her head. Then she lifted her eyes to mine.

"Where is the monkey today?"

She wanted to ignore the slap, to forget it. Forgetfulness was her protection. Sometimes I wondered, though, how much could be truly forgotten and what happened to it when it was entombed.

"The monkey is in my house," I said. "Do you want to see her?"

"Yes." So we walked inside and brought her out into the garden, my small and regal Ankyeo, who was named, perhaps frivolously, after a great queen mother of this country. I did not know what species of monkey Ankyeo was. She was delicate-boned as a bird, and her fur was silver. She picked with her doll fingers at a pink hibiscus blossom, and Ayesha laughed. I wanted to make Ankyeo per- form all her tricks, in order to hear again that rare laughter. But I knew I must not try to go too fast. After a while Ayesha tired of watching the monkey and sat cross-legged beside my chair, the old look of passivity on her face. We would have to move indoors before the rain started, but for the moment I left her as she was.

Ruth did not approach silently, as Kwaale and Ayesha had done, but with a loud crunching of shoes on the gravel path. When she saw Ayesha she stopped.

"I suppose you know."

"Yes. But it was not Ayesha who told me."

"Who, then?"

Of course I would not tell her. Her face grew sullen.

"Whoever it was, I think it was rotten of her to tell—"

70 "It did not appear that way to the girl in question. She was protecting the others from you, and that is a higher good in her eyes than any individual honour in not tattling."

"Protecting—from me?" There was desolation in her voice, and I relented.

"They will change, Ruth, once they see they can trust you. Why did you hit Ayesha?"

"It was a stupid thing to do," Ruth said in a voice almost inaudible with shame, "and I felt awful about it, and I'm terribly sorry. But she—she kept asking me something, you see, over and over again, in a sort of whining voice, and I—I just couldn't stand it any more."

"What did she ask you?"

75 "How should I know?" Ruth said. "I don't speak Twi."

I stared at her. "Not—any? I thought you might be a little rusty, but I never imagined—my dear child, it's your own language, after all."

"My father has always spoken English to me," she said. "My mother spoke in Twi, I suppose, but she died when I was under a year old."

"Why on earth didn't you tell the girls?"

"I don't know. I don't know why I didn't—"

80 I noticed then how much thinner she had grown and how her expression had altered. She no longer looked like a child. Her eyes were implacable as Kwaale's.

"They don't know anything outside this place," she said. "I don't care if I can't understand what they're saying to each other. I'm not interested, anyway."

Then her glance went to Ayesha once more.

"But why were they so angry—about her? I know it was mean, and I said I was sorry. But the way they all looked—"

"Ayesha was found by the police in Lagos," I said reluctantly. "She was sent back to this country because one of the constables recognized her speech as Twi. We heard about her and offered to have her here. There are many like her, I'm afraid, who are not found or heard about. She must have been stolen, you see, or sold when she was very young. She has not been able to tell us much. But the Nigerian police traced her back to several slave-dealers. When they discovered her she was being used as a child prostitute. She was very injured when she came to us here."

85 Ruth put her head down on her hands. She sat without speaking. Then her shoulders, hunched and still, began to tremble.

"You didn't know," I said. "There's no point in reproaching yourself now."

She looked up at me with a kind of naïve horror, the look of someone who recognizes for the first time the existence of cruelty.

"Things like that really happen here?"

I sighed. "Not just here. Evil does not select one place for its province."

90 But I could see that she did not believe me. The wind was beginning to rise, so we went indoors. Ayesha carried the stool, Ruth lifted my red throne, and I limped after them, feeling exhausted and not at all convinced just then that God

was in His heaven. What a mercy for me that the church in whose mission school I had spent much of my adult life did not possess the means of scrutinizing too precisely the souls of its faithful servants.

We had barely got inside the bungalow when Ayesha missed the monkey. She flew outside to look for it, but no amount of searching revealed Ankyeo. Certain the monkey was gone forever, Ayesha threw herself down on the damp ground. While the wind moaned and screeched, the child, who never wept for herself, wept for a lost monkey and would not be comforted. I did not dare kneel beside her. My leg was too unreliable, and I knew I would not be able to get up again. I stood there, lumpish and helpless, while Ruth in the doorway shivered in her thin and daisied dress.

Then, like a veritable angel of the Lord, Yindo appeared, carrying Ankyeo. Immediately I experienced a resurrection of faith, while at the same time thinking how frail and fickle my belief must be, to be so influenced by a child and a silver-furred monkey.

Yindo grinned and knelt beside Ayesha. He was no more than sixteen, a tall thin-wristed boy, a Dagomba from the northern desert. He had come here when he was twelve, one of the scores of young who were herded down each year to work the cocoa farms because their own arid land had no place for them. He was one of our best garden boys, but he could not speak to anyone around here except in hesitant pidgin English, for no one here knew his language. His speech lack never bothered him with Ayesha. The two communicated in some fashion without words. He put the monkey in her arms and she held Ankyeo closely. Then she made a slight and courtly bow to Yindo. He laughed and shook his head. Drawing from his pocket a small charm, he showed it to her. It was the dried head of a chameleon, with blue glass beads and a puff of unwholesome-looking fur tied around it. Ayesha understood at once that it was this object which had enabled Yindo to find the monkey. She made another and deeper obeisance and from her own pocket drew the only thing she had to offer, a toffee wrapped in silver foil which I had given her at least two weeks ago. Yindo took it, touched it to his talisman, and put both carefully away.

Ruth had not missed the significance of the ritual. Her eyes were dilated with curiosity and contempt.

"He believes in it, doesn't he?" she said. "He actually believes in it." ^{95}

"Don't be so quick to condemn the things you don't comprehend," I said sharply.

"I think it's horrible." She sounded frightened. "He's just a savage, isn't he, just a—"

"Stop it, Ruth. That's quite enough."

"I hate it here!" she cried. "I wish I were back at home."

"Child," I said, "this is your home." ^{100}

She did not reply, but the denial in her face made me marvel at my own hypocrisy.

Each Friday, Dr. Quansah drove over to see Ruth, and usually on these afternoons he would call in at my bungalow for a few minutes to discuss her progress. At first our conversations were completely false, each of us politely telling the other that Ruth was getting on reasonably well. Then one day he dropped the pretence.

"She is very unhappy, isn't she? Please—don't think I am blaming you, Miss Nedden. Myself, rather. It is too different. What should I have done, all those years ago?"

"Don't be offended, Dr. Quansah, but why wasn't she taught her own language?"

He waited a long moment before replying. He studied the clear amber tea in his cup.

"I was brought up in a small village," he said at last. "English came hard to me. When I went to Secondary School I experienced great difficulty at first in understanding even the gist of the lectures. I was determined that the same thing would not happen to Ruth. I suppose I imagined she would pick up her own language easily, once she returned here, as though the knowledge of one's family tongue was inherited. Of course, if her mother had lived—"

He set down the teacup and knotted his huge hands together in an unexpressed anguish that was painful to see.

"Both of them uprooted," he said. "It was my fault, I guess, and yet—"

He fell silent. Finally, his need to speak was greater than his reluctance to reveal himself.

"You see, my wife hated England, always. I knew, although she never spoke of it. Such women don't. She was a quiet woman, gentle, and—obedient. My parents had chosen her and I had married her when I was a very young man, before I first left this country. Our differences were not so great, then, but later in those years in London—she was like a plant, expected to grow where the soil is not suitable for it. My friends and associates—the places I went for dinner— she did not accompany me. I never asked her to entertain those people in our house. I could not—you see that?"

I nodded and he continued in the same low voice with its burden of self-reproach.

"She was illiterate," he said. "She did not know anything of my life, as it became. She did not want to know. She refused to learn. I was—impatient with her. I know that. But—"

He turned away so I would not see his face.

"Have you any idea what it is like," he cried, "to need someone to talk to, and not to have even one person?"

"Yes," I said. "I have a thorough knowledge of that."

He looked at me in surprise, and when he saw that I did know, he seemed oddly relieved, as though, having exchanged vulnerabilities, we were neither of us endangered. My ebony cane slipped to the ground just then, and Dr. Quansah stooped and picked it up; automatically and casually, hardly noticing it, and I was startled at myself, for I had felt no awkwardness in the moment either.

"When she became ill," he went on, "I do not think she really cared whether she lived or not. And now, Ruth—you know, when she was born, my wife called her by an African name which means 'child of the rain.' My wife missed the sun so very much. The rain, too, may have stood for her own tears. She had not wanted to bear the child so far from home."

Unexpectedly, he smiled, the dark features of his face relaxing, becoming less blunt and plain.

"Why did you leave your country and come here, Miss Nedden? For the church? Or for the sake of the Africans?"

I leaned back in my mock throne and rearranged, a shade ironically, the folds   120
of my lilac smock.

"I thought so, once," I replied. "But now I don't know. I think I may have come here mainly for myself, after all, hoping to find a place where my light could shine forth. Not a very palatable admission, perhaps."

"At least you did not take others along on your pilgrimage."

"No. I took no one. No one at all."

We sat without speaking, then, until the tea grew cold and the dusk gathered.

It was through me that Ruth met David Mackie. He was an intent, lemon-haired   125
boy of fifteen. He had been ill and was therefore out from England, staying with his mother while he recuperated. Mrs. Mackie was a widow. Her husband had managed an oil-palm plantation for an African owner, and when he died Clare Mackie had stayed on and managed the place herself. I am sure she made a better job of it than her husband had, for she was one of those frighteningly efficient women under whose piercing eye, one felt, even the oil palms would not dare to slacken their efforts. She was slender and quick, and she contrived to look dashing and yet not unfeminine in her corded jodhpurs and open-necked shirt, which she wore with a silk paisley scarf at the throat. David was more like his father, thoughtful and rather withdrawn, and maybe that is why I had agreed to help him occasionally with his studies, which he was then taking by correspondence.

The Mackies' big whitewashed bungalow, perched on its cement pillars and fringed around with languid casuarina trees, was only a short distance from the school, on the opposite side of the hill to the village. Ruth came to my bungalow one Sunday afternoon, when I had promised to go to the Mackies', and as she appeared bored and despondent, I suggested she come along with me.

After I had finished the lesson, Ruth and David talked together amicably enough while Mrs. Mackie complained about the inadequacies of local labour and I sat fanning myself with a palm leaf and feeling grateful that fate had not made me one of Clare Mackie's employees.

"Would you like to see my animals?" I heard David ask Ruth, his voice still rather formal and yet pleased, too, to have a potential admirer for his treasures.

"Oh yes." She was eager; she understood people who collected animals. "What have you got?"

"A baby crocodile," he said proudly, "and a cutting-grass—that's a bush rat,   130
you know—and several snakes, non-poisonous ones, and a lot of assorted toads. I shan't be able to keep the croc long, of course. They're too tricky to deal with. I had a duiker, too, but it died."

Off they went, and Mrs. Mackie shrugged.

"He's mad about animals. I think they're disgusting. But he's got to have something to occupy his time, poor dear."

When the two returned from their inspection of David's private zoo, we drove back to the school in the Mackies' bone-shaking jeep. I thought no more about the visit until late the next week, when I realized that I had not seen Ruth after classes for some days. I asked her, and she looked at me guilelessly, certain I would be as pleased as she was herself.

"I've been helping David with his animals," she explained enthusiastically. "You know, Miss Nedden, he wants to be an animal collector when he's through school. Not a hobby—he wants to work at it always. To collect live specimens, you see, for places like Whipsnade[2] and Regent's Park Zoo. He's lent me a whole lot of books about it. It's awfully interesting, really it is."

135   I did not know what to say. I could not summon up the sternness to deny her the first friendship she had made here. But of course it was not "here," really. She was drawn to David because he spoke in the ways she knew, and of things which made sense to her. So she continued to see him. She borrowed several of my books to lend to him. They were both fond of poetry. I worried, of course, but not for what might be thought the obvious reasons. Both Ruth and David needed companionship, but neither was ready for anything more. I did not have the fears Miss Povey would have harboured if she had known. I was anxious for another reason. Ruth's friendship with David isolated her more than ever from the other girls. She made even less effort to get along with them now, for David was sufficient company.

Only once was I alarmed about her actual safety, the time when Ruth told me she and David had found an old fishing pirogue and had gone on the river in it.

"The river—" I was appalled. "Ruth, don't you know there are crocodiles there?"

"Of course." She had no awareness of having done anything dangerous. "That's why we went. We hoped to catch another baby croc, you see. But we had no luck."

"You had phenomenal luck," I snapped. "Don't you ever do that again. Not ever."

140   "Well, all right," she said regretfully. "But it was great fun."

The sense of adventure had returned to her, and all at once I realized why. David was showing Africa to her as she wanted to be shown it—from the outside.

I felt I should tell Dr. Quansah, but when I finally did he was so upset that I was sorry I had mentioned it.

"It is not a good thing," he kept saying. "The fact that this is a boy does not concern me half so much, to be frank with you, as the fact that he is a European."

"I would not have expected such illogicalities from you, Dr. Quansah." I was annoyed, and perhaps guilty as well, for I had permitted the situation.

---

2. A town, northwest of London, famous for its zoo in which the animals are kept uncaged; Regent's Park is in London.

Dr. Quansah looked thoughtfully at me.   145

"I do not think it is that. Yes—maybe you are right. I don't know. But I do not want my daughter to be hurt by any—stupidity. I know that."

"David's mother is employed as manager by an African owner."

"Yes," Dr. Quansah said, and his voice contained a bitterness I had not heard in it before, "but what does she say about him, in private?"

I had no reply to that, for what he implied was perfectly true. He saw from my face that he had not been mistaken.

"I have been away a long time, Miss Nedden," he said, "but not long enough   150 to forget some of the things that were said to me by Europeans when I was young."

I should not have blurted out my immediate thought, but I did.

"You have been able to talk to me—"

"Yes." He smiled self-mockingly. "I wonder if you know how much that has surprised me?"

Why should I have found it difficult then, to look at him, at the face whose composure I knew concealed such aloneness? I took refuge, as so often, in the adoption of an abrupt tone.

"Why should it be surprising? You liked people in England. You had friends   155 there."

"I am not consistent, I know. But the English at home are not the same as the English abroad—you must have realized that. You are not typical, Miss Nedden. I still find most Europeans here as difficult to deal with as I ever did. And yet—I seem to have lost touch with my own people, too. The young laboratory technicians at the station—they do not trust me, and I find myself getting so very impatient with them, losing my temper because they have not comprehended what I wanted them to do, and—"

He broke off. "I really should not bother you with all this."

"Oh, but you're not." The words came out with an unthinking swiftness which mortified me later when I recalled it. "I haven't so many people I can talk with, either, you know."

"You told me as much, once," Dr. Quansah said gently. "I had not forgotten."

Pride has so often been my demon, the tempting conviction that one is able to   160 see the straight path and to point it out to others. I was proud of my cleverness when I persuaded Kwaale to begin teaching Ruth Quansah the language of her people. Each afternoon they had lessons, and I assisted only when necessary to clarify some point of grammar. Ruth, once she started, became quite interested. Despite what she had said, she was curious to know what the other girls talked about together. As for Kwaale, it soothed her rancour to be asked to instruct, and it gave her an opportunity to learn something about Ruth, to see her as she was and not as Kwaale's imagination had distorted her. Gradually the two became, if not friends, at least reasonably peaceful acquaintances. Ruth continued to see David, but as her afternoons were absorbed by the language lessons, she no longer went to the Mackies' house quite so often.

Then came the Odwira. Ruth asked if she might go down to the village with

Kwaale, and as most of the girls would be going, I agreed. Miss Povey would have liked to keep the girls away from the local festivals, which she regarded as dangerously heathen, but this quarantine had never proved practicable. At the time of the Odwira the girls simply disappeared, permission or not, like migrating birds.

Late that afternoon I saw the school lorry setting off for Eburaso, so I decided to go along. We swerved perilously down the mountain road, and reached the village just in time to see the end of the procession, as the chief, carried in palanquin under his saffron umbrella, returned from the river after the rituals there. The palm-wine libations had been poured, the souls of the populace cleansed. Now the Eburasahene would offer the new yams to the ancestors, and then the celebrations would begin. Drumming and dancing would go on all night, and the next morning Miss Povey, if she were wise, would not ask too many questions.

The mud and thatch shanties of the village were empty of inhabitants and the one street was full. Shouting, singing, wildly excited, they sweated and thronged. Everyone who owned a good cloth was wearing it, and the women fortunate enough to possess gold earrings or bangles were flaunting them before the covetous eyes of those whose bracelets and beads were only coloured glass. For safety I remained in the parked lorry, fearing my unsteady leg in such a mob.

I spotted Kwaale and Ruth. Kwaale's usual air of tranquillity had vanished. She was all sun-coloured cloth and whirling brown arms. I had never seen anyone with such a violence of beauty as she possessed, like surf or volcano, a spendthrift splendour. Then, out of the street's turbulence of voices I heard the low shout of a young man near her.

165   "Fire a gun at me."

I knew what was about to happen, for the custom was a very old one. Kwaale threw back her head and laughed. Her hands flicked at her cloth and for an instant she stood there naked except for the white beads around her hips, and her *amoanse,* the red cloth between her legs. Still laughing, she knotted her cloth back on again, and the young man put an arm around her shoulders and drew her close to him.

Ruth, tidy and separate in her frock with its pastel flowers, stared as though unable to believe what she had seen. Slowly she turned and it was then that she saw me. She began to force her way through the crowd of villagers. Instantly Kwaale dropped the young man's hand and went after her. Ruth stood beside the lorry, her eyes appealing to me.

"You saw—you saw what she—"

Kwaale's hand was clawing at her shoulder then, spinning her around roughly.

170   "What are you telling her? It is not for you to say!"

Kwaale thought I would be bound to disapprove. I could have explained the custom to Ruth, as it had been explained to me many years ago by Kwaale's father. I could have told her it used to be "Shoot an arrow," for Mother Nyame created the sun with fire, and arrows of the same fire were shot into the veins of mankind and became life-blood. I could have said that the custom was a reminder that women are the source of life. But I did not, for I was by no means sure that either Kwaale or the young man knew the roots of the tradition or that they cared. Something was permitted at festival time—why should they care about anything other than the beat of their own blood?

"Wait, Ruth, you don't understand—"

"I understand what she is," Ruth said distinctly. "She's nothing but a—"

Kwaale turned upon her viciously.

"Talk, you! Talk and talk. What else could you do? No man here would want you as his wife—you're too ugly." 175

Ruth drew away, shocked and uncertain. But Kwaale had not finished.

"Why don't you go? Take all your money and go! Why don't you?"

I should have spoken then, tried to explain one to the other. I think I did, after a paralyzed moment, but it was too late. Ruth, twisting away, struggled around the clusters of people and disappeared among the trees on the path that led back to the mountain-top.

The driver had trouble in moving the lorry through the jammed streets. By the time we got onto the hill road Ruth was not there. When we reached the school I got out and limped over to the Primary girls who were playing outside the main building. I asked if they had seen her, and they twirled and fluttered around me like green and brown leaves, each trying to outdo the others in impressing me with their display of English.

"Miss Neddeen, I seein' she. Wit' my eye I seein' she. She going deah—" 180

The way they pointed was the road to the Mackies' house.

I did not especially want the lorry to go roaring into the Mackies' compound as though the errand were urgent or critical, so when we sighted the casuarina trees I had the driver stop. I walked slowly past David's menagerie, where the cutting-grass scratched in its cage and the snakes lay in bright apathetic coils. Some sense of propriety made me hesitate before I had quite reached the house. Ruth and David were on the verandah, and I could hear their voices. I suppose it was shameful of me to listen, but it would have been worse to appear at that moment.

"If it was up to me—" David's voice was strained and tight with embarrassment. "But you know what she's like."

"What did she say, David? What did she say?" Ruth's voice, desperate with her need to know, her fear of knowing.

"Oh, well—nothing much." 185

"Tell me!"

Then David, faltering, ashamed, tactless.

"Only that African girls mature awfully young, and she somehow got the daft notion that—look here, Ruth, I'm sorry, but when she gets an idea there's nothing anyone can do. I know it's a lot of rot. I know you're not the ordinary kind of African. You're almost—almost like a—like us."

It was his best, I suppose. It was not his fault that it was not good enough. She cried out, then, and although the casuarina boughs hid the two from my sight, I could imagine their faces well enough, and David's astounded look at the hurt in her eyes.

"Almost—" she said. Then, with a fury I would not have believed possible, "No, I'm not! I'm not like you at all. I won't be!" 190

"Listen, Ruth—"

But she had thrust off his hand and had gone. She passed close to the place where I stood but she did not see me. Once again I watched her running. Running and running, into the forest where I could not follow.

I was frantic lest Miss Povey should find out and notify Dr. Quansah before we could find Ruth. I had Ayesha go all through the school and grounds, for she could move more rapidly and unobtrusively than I. I waited, stumping up and down my garden, finally forcing myself to sit down and assume at least the appearance of calm. At last Ayesha returned. Only tiredness showed in her face, and my heart contracted.

"You did not find her, little one?"

195   She shook her head. "She is not here. She is gone."

Gone. Had she remained in the forest, then, with its thorns and strangular vines, its ferned depths that could hide death, its green silences? Or had she run as far as the river, dark and smooth as oil, deceptively smooth, with its saurian kings who fed on whatever flesh they could find? I dared not think.

I did something then that I had never before permitted myself to do. I picked up Ayesha and held the child tightly, not for her consoling but for my own. She reached out and touched a finger to my face.

"You are crying. For her?"

Then Ayesha sighed a little, resignedly.

200   "Come then," she said. "I will show you where she is."

Had I known her so slightly all along, my small Ayesha whose childhood lay beaten and lost somewhere in the shanties and brothels of Takoradi or Kumasi, the airless upper rooms of palm-wine bars in Lagos or Kaduna? Without a word I rose and followed her.

We did not have far to go. The gardeners' quarters were at the back of the school grounds, surrounded by *niim* trees and a few banana palms. In the last hut of the row, Yindo sat cross-legged on the packed-earth floor. Beside him on a dirty and torn grass mat Ruth Quansah lay, face down, her head buried in her arms.

Ayesha pointed. Why had she wanted to conceal it? To this day I do not really know, nor what the hut recalled to her, nor what she felt, for her face bore no more expression than a pencilled stick-child's, and her eyes were as dull as they had been when she first came to us here.

Ruth heard my cane and my dragged foot. I know she did. But she did not stir.

205   "Madam—" Yindo's voice was nearly incoherent with terror. "I beg you. You no give me sack. I Dagomba man, madam. No got bruddah dis place. I beg you, mek I no go lose dis job—"

I tried to calm him with meaningless sounds of reassurance. Then I asked him to tell me. He spoke in a harsh whisper, his face averted.

"She come dis place like she crez'. She say—do so." He gestured unmistakably. "I—I try, but I can no do so for she. I too fear."

He held out his hands then in an appeal both desperate and hopeless. He was a desert man. He expected no mercy here, far from the dwellings of his tribe.

Ruth still had not moved. I do not think she had even heard Yindo's words. At last she lifted her head, but she did not speak. She scanned slowly the mud walls, the tin basin for washing, the upturned box that served as table, the old hurricane lamp, and in a niche the grey and grinning head of the dead chameleon, around it the blue beads like naïve eyes shining and beside it the offering of a toffee wrapped in grimy silver paper.

I stood there in the hut doorway, leaning on my ebony cane to support my cumbersome body, looking at the three of them but finding nothing simple enough to say. What words, after all, could possibly have been given to the outcast children?

I told Dr. Quansah. I did not spare him anything, nor myself either. I imagined he would be angry at my negligence, my blundering, but he was not.

"You should not blame yourself in this way," he said. "I do not want that. It is—really, I think it is a question of time, after all."

"Undoubtedly. But in the meantime?"

"I don't know." He passed a hand across his forehead. "I seem to become tired so much more than I used to. Solutions do not come readily any more. Even for a father like myself, who relies so much on schools, it is still not such an easy thing, to bring up a child without a mother."

I leaned back in my scarlet chair. The old rattan received my head, and my absurdly jagged breath eased.

"No," I said. "I'm sure it can't be easy."

We were silent for a moment. Then with some effort Dr. Quansah began to speak, almost apologetically.

"Coming back to this country after so long away—you know, I think that is the last new thing I shall be able to do in my life. Does that seem wrong? When one grows older, one is aware of so many difficulties. Often they appear to outweigh all else."

My hands fumbled for my cane, the ebony that was grown and carved here. I found and held it, and it both reassured and mocked me.

"Perhaps," I said deliberately. "But Ruth—"

"I am taking her away. She wants to go. What else can I do? There is a school in the town where a cousin of mine lives."

"Yes. I see. You cannot do anything else, of course."

He rose. "Goodbye," he said, "and—"

But he did not finish the sentence. We shook hands, and he left.

———————————

At Eburaso School we go on as before. Miss Povey and I still snipe back and forth, knowing in our hearts that we rely upon our differences and would miss them if they were not there. I still teach my alien speech to the young ones, who continue to impart to it a kind of garbled charm. I grow heavier and I fancy my lameness is more pronounced, although Kwaale assures me this is not the case. In few enough years I will have reached retirement age.

Sitting in my garden and looking at the sun on the prickly pear and the poinsettia, I think of that island of grey rain where I must go as a stranger, when the time comes, while others must remain as strangers here.

1963

QUESTIONS

1. The idea of a holiday occurs at both the beginning and, in a different sense, at the end of "Holiday." How does the first of these relate to the theme of an encounter of cultures and the second to the theme of the central reality of life as work and survival? What does it mean that this German peasant society "never in any wise . . . confuse[d] nationality and habitation" (paragraph 26)? How do you understand the narrator's judgment that only Ottilie "belonged nowhere" (paragraph 39)? that Ottilie's life and the narrator's "were kin" (paragraph 59)? that they were "fools of life" (paragraph 83)?

2. Why is Miss Povey upset at the narrator of "The Rain Child" for reading to the children in "their own tongue" (paragraph 5)? Ruth enjoys David's teaching her about Africa because he shows it to her "from the outside"; why should that please her? Why is Ruth shocked when David says she's "almost . . . like us" (paragraph 188)? Who are the "outcast children" (paragraph 210)? How many are there? Explain the title. Though it initially applies to Ruth, how does the final paragraph suggest that it may also apply to the narrator?

WRITING SUGGESTIONS

1. Rewrite an early portion of "Holiday" from the point of view of one of the Müllers (perhaps the boy who greets the narrator).
2. Compare Ruth and the narrator as "Rain Children."
3. Write a response, parody, or rebuttal of a portion of either of the two stories: a feminist view of the mealtime customs in "Holiday," for example, or a separatist (Nation of Islam?) view of the narrator of or the situation in "The Rain Child."

12

CRITICAL CONTEXTS:
A FICTION CASEBOOK

We have already seen that although stories may be read as if they stand alone, they are enriched by being situated in authorial, literary, or cultural/historical contexts. Once a work has earned a place in the literature, it is also surrounded by a critical context—readers who write about the work and others who engage those readers or critics in dialogue about that work. To write critically about a work is to engage not only the text, but also those who have written about the text. It is always advisable, however, to read the story first, reread it, and read it still more times until you have come to terms with it; that is, settled in your own mind what you think about the story and how you evaluate it. Then—and only then—should you go to other critics, "secondary sources." My own experience is that when I read the criticism before I have made up my own mind, *all* the critics seem "right" (and the most recently read the "most clearly right"), and my own responses are dulled or lost. On the other hand, when I have settled on my own responses to the story, I can read critics and pick up *additional* information or insights that can enrich rather than erase my own response and judgment. Reading criticism should be an enriching experience, not one that robs you of your individual responses.

> *In each [literary work] there is something (an individual intuition—or a concept which can never be expressed in other terms). It is like the square root of two or like π, which cannot be expressed by rational numbers but only as their limit. Criticism of [literature] is like 1.414 . . . or 3.1415. . . . not all it would be, yet all that can be had and very useful.*
>
> —WILLIAM WIMSATT

The story that stands here in the middle of critical discussion is William Faulkner's popular, classic, and controversial "A Rose for Emily." It is followed by a student paper in which the author was asked to come to terms with the story before reading the critical discussions that have surrounded it almost since its first publication more than sixty years ago. There are well over a hundred (perhaps hundreds of) critical essays and commentaries on this story—according to a recent Modern Language Association bibliography, thirty-seven pieces on the story have been published since 1981. It is virtually impossible, then, to fully "report" the history of the critical discussion of this fascinating story. The four critical pieces reprinted here are not necessarily the best (and not necessarily not the best), nor are they fully representative of the spectrum of comment and argument about the story. They are, instead, suggestive of some of the kinds of approaches or the kinds of aspects of a story that have been singled out for analysis, response, judgment.

Lawrence R. Rodgers's "'We all said, "she will kill herself"'": The Narrator/Detective in William Faulkner's 'A Rose for Emily,'" situates Faulkner's story in a literary kind, the detective story, matching details of the story to generally accepted definitions of the ingredients of detective fiction.

The second essay, George L. Dillon's "Styles of Reading," though it first appeared in a highly theoretical "professional" Journal, groups a variety of actual student responses into three categories, and many students who have read this essay agree that it does indeed represent the way they read and the kinds of questions they ask of a text. The essay is abbreviated here (we use asterisks to indicate our deletions): in its original form it demonstrated with long passages from other critics that student approaches were analogous to professional critical readings. Its purpose here is to represent and clarify various ways students or professional critics read this—or any—story, and to make students more conscious of what they are doing and what they might do in reading fiction.

The third piece, Judith Fetterley's "A Rose for 'A Rose for Emily,'" is adapted from her book *The Resisting Reader: A Feminist Approach to American Fiction,* and, as the title of the book suggests, it is because Emily is a woman—indeed, a lady—that the revelation of what she has done seems grotesque. Faulkner, she says, sees Emily as "a woman victimized and betrayed by the system of sexual politics, who nevertheless has discovered, within the structures that victimize her, sources of power for herself." Faulkner has implied this, she says, indicating but not quoting occasional comments of his. There are other passages from Faulkner's conversations, however, that scarcely identify him as a feminist. There are two such passages, for example, in *The Paris Review Interviews: Writers at Work,* first series (Baltimore: Penguin, 1958). The first quotation suggests that "the perfect milieu for the artist to work in" is a brothel. The house is quiet in the mornings, the best time to write, the work is easy, and the pay adequate; the job offers him whatever social life he wants, "gives him a certain standing in his society," and "all the inmates of the house are female and would defer to him and call him 'sir'" (124). The second is more sweeping and perhaps more outrageous: "Success is feminine and like a woman; if you cringe before her, she will override you. So the way to treat her is to show her the back of your hand" (125). This is not to discount Fetterley's feminist reading of the story, but only to make you wary of trusting what an author says about his or her own work—trust the tale and not the teller. We naturally and properly read stories as if they are communications from another human mind and experience that we are trying to understand (reading, as one critic has suggested, as a member of the "authorial audience"). And all readings must begin with this intention. But we also know that even our friends sometimes tell us things about themselves, their attitudes and actions, that they do not know they are revealing, and sometimes claim intentions or accomplishments that we know not to be "true." We must be alert to the possibility that even authors cannot always distinguish between what they meant and what they have said. We must, then, see a work, another critic has said, "as it cannot see itself." It is only proper to acknowledge the profundity and power of an author's vision and art but probably not a good idea to claim to know fully the author's "intention" (even if you've read a quotation by the author that purports to define that intention).

When a work has engaged a number of critics, and especially when there is something in the work that is difficult or controversial, subsequent commentaries need to acknowledge the previous readings and, by contradicting or modifying their conclusions with new evidence or more persuasive argument, justify still another essay on the oft-debated topic. Gene M. Moore's "Of Time and Its Mathematical Progression: Problems of Chronology in Faulkner's 'A Rose for Emily'" is just such an essay. It raises once again perhaps the most frequently discussed aspect of Faulkner's story: the precise dating of the events (including Emily's dates of birth and death). Moore cuts some knots and tightens others, establishing a new chronology, and, while admitting residual inconsistencies, offers an explanation of how these came about. It should serve here as an exemplary critical argument—engaging both the story and its commentators.

A NOTE ON DOCUMENTATION

Alert readers will notice that these commentaries use different forms of documentation. Dillon's essay was published in 1982 and Fetterley's book in 1978. Both give their references in notes at the end of their article—for example, "1. Brooke-Rose, 'The Readerhood of Man,' in *The Reader in the Text,* ed. Susan R. Suleiman and Inge Crosman (Princeton: Princeton University Press, 1980), 120–48" (Dillon); "See *Faulkner in the University: Class Conferences at the University of Virginia 1957–1958,* edited by Frederick L. Gwynn and Joseph L. Blotner (Charlottesville: University of Virginia Press, 1959), 87–88; *Faulkner at Nagano,* edited by Robert A. Jeliffe (Tokyo: Kenkyusha, 1956), 71" (Fetterley)—and neither gives a bibliography or a list of "works cited." The essays of Rodgers and Moore—published in 1995 and 1992, respectively—give such a list and interpolate the references with the page number(s) in the text parenthetically—for example, "(Going 53)," "(Wilson 56)." The suggested standard form for literary essays and books is set by the Modern Language Association; between the publication of the earlier and the later essays, it changed the form it recommended. Not everyone uses the newer form. But it is not only for that reason that the older form has been left here in the older essays: whenever you do literary research in books and articles from earlier decades, you will run into this earlier form, so it is just as well to be familiar with it. You will note that this documentation is standard for *literary* commentary. Critical and scholarly works in other disciplines—psychology, chemistry, and so forth—use other forms. One of the best sources for all the major forms—and for other assistance in research methods and the writing of research papers—is Melissa Walker's *Writing Research Papers,* fourth edition (New York: W. W. Norton, 1997).

WILLIAM FAULKNER

A Rose for Emily

I

When Miss Emily Grierson died, our whole town went to her funeral: the men through a sort of respectful affection for a fallen monument, the women mostly out of curiosity to see the inside of her house, which no one save an old manservant—a combined gardener and cook—had seen in at least ten years.

It was a big, squarish frame house that had once been white, decorated with cupolas and spires and scrolled balconies in the heavily lightsome style of the seventies, set on what had once been our most select street. But garages and cotton gins had encroached and obliterated even the august names of that neighborhood; only Miss Emily's house was left, lifting its stubborn and coquettish decay above the cotton wagons and the gasoline pumps—an eyesore among eyesores. And now Miss Emily had gone to join the representatives of those august names where they lay in the cedar-bemused cemetery among the ranked and anonymous graves of Union and Confederate soldiers who fell at the battle of Jefferson.

Alive, Miss Emily had been a tradition, a duty, and a care; a sort of hereditary obligation upon the town, dating from that day in 1894 when Colonel Sartoris, the mayor—he who fathered the edict that no Negro woman should appear on the streets without an apron—remitted her taxes, the dispensation dating from the death of her father on into perpetuity. Not that Miss Emily would have accepted charity. Colonel Sartoris invented an involved tale to the effect that Miss Emily's father had loaned money to the town, which the town, as a matter of business, preferred this way of repaying. Only a man of Colonel Sartoris' generation and thought could have invented it, and only a woman could have believed it.

When the next generation, with its more modern ideas, became mayors and aldermen, this arrangement created some little dissatisfaction. On the first of the year they mailed her a tax notice. February came, and there was no reply. They wrote her a formal letter, asking her to call at the sheriff's office at her convenience. A week later the mayor wrote her himself, offering to call or to send his car for her, and received in reply a note on paper of an archaic shape, in a thin, flowing calligraphy in faded ink, to the effect that she no longer went out at all. The tax notice was also enclosed, without comment.

5   They called a special meeting of the Board of Aldermen. A deputation waited upon her, knocked at the door through which no visitor had passed since she ceased giving china-painting lessons eight or ten years earlier. They were admitted by the old Negro into a dim hall from which a stairway mounted into still more shadow. It smelled of dust and disuse—a close, dank smell. The Negro led them into the parlor. It was furnished in heavy, leather-covered furniture. When the Negro opened the blinds of one window, a faint dust rose sluggishly about their thighs, spinning with slow motes in the single sun-ray. On a tarnished gilt easel before the fireplace stood a crayon portrait of Miss Emily's father.

They rose when she entered—a small, fat woman in black, with a thin gold chain descending to her waist and vanishing into her belt, leaning on an ebony cane with a tarnished gold head. Her skeleton was small and spare; perhaps that was why what would have been merely plumpness in another was obesity in her. She looked bloated, like a body long submerged in motionless water, and of that pallid hue. Her eyes, lost in the fatty ridges of her face, looked like two small pieces of coal pressed into a lump of dough as they moved from one face to another while the visitors stated their errand.

She did not ask them to sit. She just stood in the door and listened quietly until the spokesman came to a stumbling halt. Then they could hear the invisible watch ticking at the end of the gold chain.

Her voice was dry and cold. "I have no taxes in Jefferson. Colonel Sartoris explained it to me. Perhaps one of you can gain access to the city records and satisfy yourselves."

"But we have. We are the city authorities, Miss Emily. Didn't you get a notice from the sheriff, signed by him?"

"I received a paper, yes," Miss Emily said. "Perhaps he considers himself the sheriff. . . . I have no taxes in Jefferson."

"But there is nothing on the books to show that, you see. We must go by the—"

"See Colonel Sartoris. I have no taxes in Jefferson."

"But, Miss Emily—"

"See Colonel Sartoris." (Colonel Sartoris had been dead almost ten years.) "I have no taxes in Jefferson. Tobe!" The Negro appeared. "Show these gentlemen out."

II

So she vanquished them, horse and foot, just as she had vanquished their fathers thirty years before about the smell. That was two years after her father's death and a short time after her sweetheart—the one we believed would marry her— had deserted her. After her father's death she went out very little; after her sweetheart went away, people hardly saw her at all. A few of the ladies had the temerity to call, but were not received, and the only sign of life about the place was the Negro man—a young man then—going in and out with a market basket.

"Just as if a man—any man—could keep a kitchen properly," the ladies said; so they were not surprised when the smell developed. It was another link between the gross, teeming world and the high and mighty Griersons.

A neighbor, a woman, complained to the mayor, Judge Stevens, eighty years old.

"But what will you have me do about it, madam?" he said.

"Why, send her word to stop it," the woman said. "Isn't there a law?"

"I'm sure that won't be necessary," Judge Stevens said. "It's probably just a snake or a rat that nigger of hers killed in the yard. I'll speak to him about it."

The next day he received two more complaints, one from a man who came in diffident deprecation. "We really must do something about it, Judge. I'd be the last one in the world to bother Miss Emily, but we've got to do something." That night the Board of Aldermen met—three gray-beards and one younger man, a member of the rising generation.

"It's simple enough," he said. "Send her word to have her place cleaned up. Give her a certain time to do it in, and if she don't . . ."

"Dammit, sir," Judge Stevens said, "will you accuse a lady to her face of smelling bad?"

So the next night, after midnight, four men crossed Miss Emily's lawn and slunk about the house like burglars, sniffing along the base of the brickwork and at the cellar openings while one of them performed a regular sowing motion with his hand out of a sack slung from his shoulder. They broke open the cellar door and sprinkled lime there, and in all the outbuildings. As they recrossed the lawn, a window that had been dark was lighted and Miss Emily sat in it, the light behind her, and her upright torso motionless as that of an idol. They crept quietly across the lawn and into the shadow of the locusts that lined the street. After a week or two the smell went away.

25   That was when people had begun to feel really sorry for her. People in our town, remembering how old lady Wyatt, her great-aunt, had gone completely crazy at last, believed that the Griersons held themselves a little too high for what they really were. None of the young men were quite good enough for Miss Emily and such. We had long thought of them as a tableau; Miss Emily a slender figure in white in the background, her father a spraddled silhouette in the foreground, his back to her and clutching a horsewhip, the two of them framed by the back-flung front door. So when she got to be thirty and was still single, we were not pleased exactly, but vindicated; even with insanity in the family she wouldn't have turned down all of her chances if they had really materialized.

When her father died, it got about that the house was all that was left to her; and in a way, people were glad. At last they could pity Miss Emily. Being left alone, and a pauper, she had become humanized. Now she too would know the old thrill and the old despair of a penny more or less.

The day after his death all the ladies prepared to call at the house and offer condolence and aid, as is our custom. Miss Emily met them at the door, dressed as usual and with no trace of grief on her face. She told them that her father was not dead. She did that for three days, with the ministers calling on her, and the doctors, trying to persuade her to let them dispose of the body. Just as they were about to resort to law and force, she broke down, and they buried her father quickly.

We did not say she was crazy then. We believed she had to do that. We remembered all the young men her father had driven away, and we knew that with nothing left, she would have to cling to that which had robbed her, as people will.

III

She was sick for a long time. When we saw her again, her hair was cut short, making her look like a girl, with a vague resemblance to those angels in colored church windows—sort of tragic and serene.

30   The town had just let the contracts for paving the sidewalks, and in the summer after her father's death they began to work. The construction company came with niggers and mules and machinery, and a foreman named Homer Barron, a Yankee—a big, dark, ready man, with a big voice and eyes lighter than his face. The little boys would follow in groups to hear him cuss the niggers, and the niggers singing in time to the rise and fall of picks. Pretty soon he knew everybody in town. Whenever you heard a lot of laughing anywhere about the square, Homer Barron would be in the center of the group. Presently we began to see him and Miss Emily on Sunday afternoons driving in the yellow-wheeled buggy and the matched team of bays from the livery stable.

At first we were glad that Miss Emily would have an interest, because the ladies all said, "Of course a Grierson would not think seriously of a Northerner, a day laborer." But there were still others, older people, who said that even grief could not cause a real lady to forget *noblesse oblige*—without calling it *noblesse oblige*. They just said, "Poor Emily. Her kinsfolk should come to her." She had some kin in Alabama; but years ago her father had fallen out with them over the estate of old lady Wyatt, the crazy woman, and there was no communication between the two families. They had not even been represented at the funeral.

And as soon as the old people said, "Poor Emily," the whispering began. "Do you suppose it's really so?" they said to one another. "Of course it is. What else could . . ." This behind their hands; rustling of craned silk and satin behind jalousies closed upon the sun of Sunday afternoon as the thin, swift clop-clop-clop of the matched team passed: "Poor Emily."

She carried her head high enough—even when we believed that she was fallen. It was as if she demanded more than ever the recognition of her dignity as the last Grierson; as if it had wanted that touch of earthiness to reaffirm her imperviousness. Like when she bought the rat poison, the arsenic. That was over a year after they had begun to say "Poor Emily," and while the two female cousins were visiting her.

"I want some poison," she said to the druggist. She was over thirty then, still a slight woman, though thinner than usual, with cold, haughty black eyes in a face the flesh of which was strained across the temples and about the eyesockets as you imagine a lighthouse-keeper's face ought to look. "I want some poison," she said.

"Yes, Miss Emily. What kind? For rats and such? I'd recom—" 35

"I want the best you have. I don't care what kind."

The druggist named several. "They'll kill anything up to an elephant. But what you want is—"

"Arsenic," Miss Emily said. "Is that a good one?"

"Is . . . arsenic? Yes ma'am. But what you want—"

"I want arsenic." 40

The druggist looked down at her. She looked back at him, erect, her face like a strained flag. "Why, of course," the druggist said. "If that's what you want. But the law requires you to tell what you are going to use it for."

Miss Emily just stared at him, her head tilted back in order to look him eye for eye, until he looked away and went and got the arsenic and wrapped it up. The Negro delivery boy brought her the package; the druggist didn't come back. When she opened the package at home there was written on the box, under the skull and bones: "For rats."

IV

So the next day we all said, "She will kill herself"; and we said it would be the best thing. When she had first begun to be seen with Homer Barron, we had said, "She will marry him." Then we said, "She will persuade him yet," because Homer himself had remarked—he liked men, and it was known that he drank with the younger men in the Elk's Club—that he was not a marrying man. Later we said,

"Poor Emily," behind the jalousies as they passed on Sunday afternoon in the glittering buggy, Miss Emily with her head high and Homer Barron with his hat cocked and a cigar in his teeth, reins and whip in a yellow glove.

Then some of the ladies began to say that it was a disgrace to the town and a bad example to the young people. The men did not want to interfere, but at last the ladies forced the Baptist minister—Miss Emily's people were Episcopal—to call upon her. He would never divulge what happened during that interview, but he refused to go back again. The next Sunday they again drove about the streets, and the following day the minister's wife wrote to Miss Emily's relations in Alabama.

45   So she had blood-kin under her roof again and we sat back to watch developments. At first nothing happened. Then we were sure that they were to be married. We learned that Miss Emily had been to the jeweler's and ordered a man's toilet set in silver, with the letters H. B. on each piece. Two days later we learned that she had bought a complete outfit of men's clothing, including a nightshirt, and we said, "They are married." We were really glad. We were glad because the two female cousins were even more Grierson than Miss Emily had ever been.

So we were not surprised when Homer Barron—the streets had been finished some time since—was gone. We were a little disappointed that there was not a public blowing-off, but we believed that he had gone on to prepare for Miss Emily's coming, or to give her a chance to get rid of the cousins. (By that time it was a cabal, and we were all Miss Emily's allies to help circumvent the cousins.) Sure enough, after another week they departed. And, as we had expected all along, within three days Homer Barron was back in town. A neighbor saw the Negro man admit him at the kitchen door at dusk one evening.

And that was the last we saw of Homer Barron. And of Miss Emily for some time. The Negro man went in and out with the market basket, but the front door remained closed. Now and then we would see her at a window for a moment, as the men did that night when they sprinkled the lime, but for almost six months she did not appear on the streets. Then we knew that this was to be expected too; as if that quality of her father which had thwarted her woman's life so many times had been too virulent and too furious to die.

When we next saw Miss Emily, she had grown fat and her hair was turning gray. During the next few years it grew grayer and grayer until it attained an even pepper-and-salt iron-gray, when it ceased turning. Up to the day of her death at seventy-four it was still that vigorous iron-gray, like the hair of an active man.

From that time on her front door remained closed, save for a period of six or seven years, when she was about forty, during which she gave lessons in china-painting. She fitted up a studio in one of the downstairs rooms, where the daughters and grand-daughters of Colonel Sartoris' contemporaries were sent to her with the same regularity and in the same spirit that they were sent on Sundays with a twenty-five cent piece for the collection plate. Meanwhile her taxes had been remitted.

50   Then the newer generation became the backbone and the spirit of the town, and the painting pupils grew up and fell away and did not send their children to her with boxes of color and tedious brushes and pictures cut from the ladies'

magazines. The front door closed upon the last one and remained closed for good. When the town got free postal delivery Miss Emily alone refused to let them fasten the metal numbers above her door and attach a mailbox to it. She would not listen to them.

Daily, monthly, yearly we watched the Negro grow grayer and more stooped, going in and out with the market basket. Each December we sent her a tax notice, which would be returned by the post office a week later, unclaimed. Now and then we would see her in one of the downstairs windows—she had evidently shut up the top floor of the house—like the carven torso of an idol in a niche, looking or not looking at us, we could never tell which. Thus she passed from generation to generation—dear, inescapable, impervious, tranquil, and perverse.

And so she died. Fell ill in the house filled with dust and shadows, with only a doddering Negro man to wait on her. We did not even know she was sick; we had long since given up trying to get any information from the Negro. He talked to no one, probably not even to her, for his voice had grown harsh and rusty, as if from disuse.

She died in one of the downstairs rooms, in a heavy walnut bed with a curtain, her gray head propped on a pillow yellow and moldy with age and lack of sunlight.

V

The Negro met the first of the ladies at the front door and let them in, with their hushed, sibilant voices and their quick, curious glances, and then he disappeared. He walked right through the house and out the back and was not seen again.

The two female cousins came at once. They held the funeral on the second day, with the town coming to look at Miss Emily beneath a mass of bought flowers, with the crayon face of her father musing profoundly above the bier and the ladies sibilant and macabre; and the very old men—some in their brushed Confederate uniforms—on the porch and the lawn, talking of Miss Emily as if she had been a contemporary of theirs, believing that they had danced with her and courted her perhaps, confusing time with its mathematical progression, as the old do, to whom all the past is not a diminishing road, but, instead, a huge meadow which no winter ever quite touches, divided from them now by the narrow bottleneck of the most recent decade of years.

Already we knew that there was one room in that region above stairs which no one had seen in forty years, and which would have to be forced. They waited until Miss Emily was decently in the ground before they opened it.

The violence of breaking down the door seemed to fill this room with pervading dust. A thin, acrid pall as of the tomb seemed to lie everywhere upon this room decked and furnished as for a bridal: upon the valance curtains of faded rose color, upon the rose-shaded lights, upon the dressing table, upon the delicate array of crystal and the man's toilet things backed with tarnished silver, silver so tarnished that the monogram was obscured. Among them lay a collar and tie, as if they had just been removed, which, lifted, left upon the surface a pale crescent in the dust. Upon a chair hung the suit, carefully folded; beneath it the two mute shoes and the discarded socks.

The man himself lay in the bed.

For a long while we just stood there, looking down at the profound and flesh-less grin. The body had apparently once lain in the attitude of an embrace, but now the long sleep that outlasts love, that conquers even the grimace of love, had cuckolded him. What was left of him, rotted beneath what was left of the nightshirt, had become inextricable from the bed in which he lay; and upon him and upon the pillow beside him lay that even coating of the patient and biding dust.

60   Then we noticed that in the second pillow was the indentation of a head. One of us lifted something from it, and leaning forward, that faint and invisible dust dry and acrid in the nostrils, we saw a long strand of iron-gray hair.

1931

STUDENT WRITING

Daniel Bronson's paper is a direct (unreasearched) response to "A Rose for Emily." In his paper, Daniel traces the theme of resistance to change in the story, which he supports with examples from the text.

"Like the Sand of the Hourglass . . ."

Daniel Bronson

The year 1865 saw the end of the Civil War between the Union and the Confederacy, and saw the beginning of a "New South." With the many changes pressed upon the South, the so-called "Old South" could no longer exist. For example, people could not own slaves as they had in the past, and they couldn't survive anymore simply by belonging to a family with an "august name." These changes didn't happen overnight however; they took many years to occur. In William Faulkner's "A Rose for Emily," we are shown the transition from Old South to New South as it takes place in the little town of Jefferson, and we see how Miss Emily Grierson, survivor of the Old South, resists these changes.

Jefferson was once inhabited by many well-off families who were members of the Old South's aristocratic class. As time, and the Reconstruction, marched on, these families slowly disappeared. Eventually, the last true living legacy of the Old South in Jefferson was Miss Emily Grierson. She had been raised to be a Southern Belle, an upstanding member of society, and she clung to her world of the Old South. She kept a black servant, Tobe, who did everything for her, just as if he were a slave, and she lived in "a big, squarish frame house that had once been white, decorated with cupolas and spires and scrolled balconies in the heavily lightsome style of the seventies, set on what had once been our most select street" (par. 2). With the infiltration of the New South, however, "garages and cotton gins . . . encroached and obliterated even the august names of that neighborhood" (par. 2). Yet the house remained, "lifting its stubborn and coquettish decay above the cotton wagons and the gasoline pumps," just as its willful inhabitant "carried her head high . . . even when we believed that she was fallen" (par. 33).

The house was all that Miss Emily really had left after her father died. When he passed away, Miss Emily spent three days denying his death and not letting the doctors and ministers dispose of the body. Though it is not told first in the story, this was the first time Miss Emily had rejected the truth in order to retain her world of the past: a world in which other members of the Old South, such as Colonel Sartoris, lived on after they too had died.

Colonel Sartoris also represented the Old South, and he protected Emily when her father died. As mayor of Jefferson at the time, he remitted her taxes, and since no aristocratic woman such as Miss Emily could possibly lower herself to accept charity, came up with a story of how her father had loaned money to Jefferson and this was how Miss Emily was to be repaid. "Only a man of Colonel Sartoris' generation and thought could have invented it, and only a woman could have believed it" (par. 3). So when Miss Emily was later approached by members of the generation of city authorities who wanted her taxes, she held onto the past and told them repeatedly to see Colonel Sartoris, even though he had been dead for almost ten years. Furthermore, when city authorities asked her whether or not she received "a notice from the sheriff, signed by him," she remarks, "Perhaps he considers himself the sheriff" (pars. 9, 10). Obviously, Miss Emily didn't accept that whoever was the new sheriff was really the sheriff. As far as she was concerned, the sheriff was still the same person it was several years ago.

We are shown not only the government of the Old South Jefferson, when it sided with Miss Emily, and the government of the New South Jefferson, when it was against Miss Emily, but we also catch a glimpse of Jefferson's government when it was still under transition. About two years after her father's death, a smell developed around Miss Emily's house. The "member of the rising generation" on the Board of Aldermen said that the solution to the problem was "'simple enough. . . . Send her word to have her place cleaned up. Give her acertain time to do it in, and if she don't . . .'" At that point the remaining Old South revealed itself when the eighty-year-old mayor, Judge Stevens, irately asked, "will you accuse a lady to her face of smelling bad?" (pars. 22, 23). It is apparent that though there were some old-timers left, just as Jefferson changed, so did its people.

Members of the Old South were very honorable, graceful and above all, dignified. They had great respect for each other and for each other's feelings, and were quick to help one another whenever possible. Most importantly however, they always retained their dignity, no matter what. Miss Emily preserved her world of the Old South by hanging on to her dignity. It was because her dignity was so essential to her that a major conflict arose when Miss Emily met Homer Barron. Homer was a personification of Reconstruction and was Miss Emily's opposite in every way. He was a Yankee, a solicializer, a member of the vulgar, haphazard post-war generation, and "a day laborer," having been hired to build Jefferson's sidewalks and thereby contribute to the urbanization of the town.

When opposites attracted however, Miss Emily put her dignity on the line and was seen "on Sunday afternoons driving in the yellow-wheeled buggy and the matched team of bays from the livery stable" with Homer (par. 30). The ladies of the town said, "'Of course a Grierson would not think seriously of a Northerner,'" and the "older people," those of the Old South, "said that even grief could not cause a real lady to forget noblesse oblige—without calling it noblesse oblige." (par. 31). As time passed, Homer and Miss Emily were seen again and again, until finally, "some of the ladies began to say that it was a disgrace to the town and a bad example to the young people. The men did not want to interfere, but at last the ladies forced the Baptist minister . . . to call upon her" (par. 44). Then "the minister's wife wrote to Miss Emily's relations in Alabama" (par. 44). When they arrived, Miss Emily realized she had to do something to preserve her dignity and pride that kept her Old South alive.

Her choices were few: marry Homer, or separate from him completely. At first it appeared that Miss Emily and Homer were either married or getting ready to be married, for she "ordered a man's toilet set in silver, with the letters H.B. on each piece" and she "bought a complete outfit of men's clothing, including a nightshirt" (par. 45). Unfortunately, while this may have kept her reputation from being tarnished as far as the New South people were concerned, it was still not enough for Miss Emily's Old South dignity. Itdemanded that she never demean herself to being married to a Northerner. Therefore, in order to keep Homer, but not what he was or what he stood for, Miss Emily killed him, then kept him in a bed where she could be with him when she chose without "compromising her dignity." This violence and necrophilia reflect her wish to hold onto the South's dead past as well as her own and the price she pays to do so.

Miss Emily retained her sense of her dignity and her private version of the world of the Old South for the rest of her life. She was a "monument," "a tradition, a duty, and a care" (pars. 1, 3). Living secluded, she surrounded herself as best as she could by locking herself in her old house with only her memories and her black servant. When she died, she did so in dignity, "in a heavy walnut bed with a curtain, her gray head propped on a pillow" (par. 53). With her death went her Old South world as well, leaving behind only "the very old men--some in their brushed Confederate uniforms" to remind the New South of the past (par. 55) and to offer a rose of remembrance and respect for Emily.

LAWRENCE R. RODGERS

"We all said, 'she will kill herself'": The Narrator/Detective in William Faulkner's "A Rose for Emily"*

William Faulkner's most famous short story, "A Rose for Emily," is a classic expression of American gothicism. Rich in interpretive possibility and long a crit-

*From *Clues: A Journal of Detection* 16 (1995): 117–29.

ical favorite, this 1929 story is a dark parable of the decline of southern sensibility. Its impact relies on a slow accretion of atmospheric detail, with each new detail further illuminating the many mysteries surrounding the life of confederate matriarch Emily Grierson. The story also may be read within the framework of a related popular genre, the classical detective story, whose American origins are traced to Edgar Allen Poe. It is commonly known that Faulkner learned much about genre-writing from his fellow southerner. He capitalized on Poe's legacy in novels such as *Intruder in the Dust* (1948) and *Knight's Gambit* (1949) as well as in "An Error in Chemistry," his 1946 short story published in *Ellery Queen's Mystery Magazine*. Faulkner's ability to expand and rework the devices of the detective story in these later works makes him a worthy successor to Poe.[1] But it is in the earlier, less straightforward story of detection, "A Rose for Emily," that Faulkner's lifelong interest in shaping his fiction around the theme of detection can be observed in its nascent form, and the important presence of the detective figure throughout his fiction can begin to be more fully appreciated.

While it might initially seem surprising that 20th-century America's premier novelist would draw so freely from the conventions of formula fiction, Faulkner was, to his frustration, well-versed with the necessities of writing with mass publication in mind. Any number of his works betray his willingness to annex popular conventions. His sixth novel *Sanctuary* is a case in point.[2] Frustrated by a mounting stack of what he considered brilliant fiction with no press to publish it, he sat down in late January of 1929 and in four months completed the sensational *Sanctuary*, which would remain his bleakest, most unrelentingly ruthless examination of the modern world. As he would later tell an audience, the novel was "basely conceived . . . I thought of the most horrific idea I could think of and wrote it" with the goal of making money (qtd. in Minter 107). Shortly after *Sanctuary's* acceptance, in April 1930, while the near-broke writer was still awaiting royalties, "A Rose for Emily" appeared in *The Forum*. Having already had it rejected by *Scribner's,* Faulkner was thrilled to receive his first short story publication, less for the honor than for the fact that he desperately needed money to pay mounting medical costs and back bills for materials used in restoring his home, Rowen Oak.

Following the example of "A Rose for Emily," the bulk of Faulkner's short fiction was produced in assembly-line spurts of productivity and aimed toward quick publication in national magazines, which, in turn, helped finance the slower pace of his more involved, less marketable novels. Biographer Frederick Karl notes that Faulkner earned more from selling four short stories to *Saturday Evening Post* than from the combined royalties of his first four novels (401). Nonetheless, the shy southerner much preferred to don the guise of the solitary romantic artist laboring purely for the sake of his craft. But in light of his lifelong financial difficulties, such a pose merely placated his ongoing taste for self-invention. However much he scorned the popular marketplace in favor of writing what he viewed as Art with a capital A, he always maintained close contact with a broad-based, "nonliterary" readership.[3]

In his well-known discussion of detective story conventions in *Adventure, Mystery and Romance,* John Cawelti provides a useful, simple litmus test for establishing whether a text follows the classical detective formula. In his scheme, there are three conditions that must be met: 1) the story must have a mystery that needs solving; 2) there must be concealed facts that a detective has to explore; and 3) these facts must become clear in the end (132). "A Rose for Emily" easily satisfies these conditions. Homer Barron, a laborer from the North, comes to work in the tightly knit community of Jefferson, Mississippi. Seen in the company of Emily, the eccentric daughter of one of Jefferson's finest families, Homer's courtship fuels town gossip. Various loosely related details soon mount up to suggest something is seriously amiss. Homer mysteriously disappears, re-appears and then disappears again not long after Miss Emily purchases rat poison. A foul smell emanates from her old home, causing some men from the town to sneak into her yard to sprinkle it with lime. Emily herself goes through profound physical changes, growing fat and grey-headed. Finally, after her death, Homer's disappearance is solved in what Irving Howe has wryly noted makes for a hair-raising conclusion (265). Miss Emily, aware of the town's penchant for judgment, ruled by the codes of etiquette of a once-proud lineage, and unable to fathom the changing conditions of the new South, has indeed poisoned Homer and retreated (with his corpse) into the recesses of her attic, where, liberated from prying eyes, she has been allowed to carry on her illicit love affair in post-mortem privacy. The evidence betraying her necrophilia is a single strand of iron-grey hair lying on a head-shaped indentation next to the corpse, which, much like the values that Emily tried to uphold by removing her affairs from public view, has become a grotesque, rotted perversion of its former self.

In light of all the praise given over to the originality, ambiguity, technical merit, and skillful manipulation of discontinuous, fragmentary narrative time in "A Rose for Emily," it is, within these considerations, an interestingly conventional detective tale. Its pattern of action is ordered around the basic elements of the popular genre: a southern setting circumscribing an eerie, decaying mansion; a curious disappearance; portents of a murder, in this case a poisoning; an unlikely, peculiar suspect, and a mysterious locked room whose assortment of clues turns up a corpse, a murderer and, finally, a solution to a macabre, but oddly plausible crime. What appears to be missing here is the detective, the detached figure whose analytic insight allows him (or, more rarely, her) to solve the crime and thus restore rationality and a sense of order to a world of uncertainty.

However, on examination, we find that Faulkner (who made a career of stretching the boundaries of convention, literary and otherwise, to suit his own needs) provides a kind of detective, but with an inventive twist. Cawelti notes that a detective story need not contain a professional crime solver like a Maigret, Dupin or a Holmes as long as some character "performs the role of successful inquirer" (132).

In "A Rose for Emily" the unnamed narrator that pieces together the fragmented decline of the Grierson lineage plays just such a role. More originally, this narrator/detective is also an unknowing driving force behind Emily's crime. Speaking in the "we" voice, the narrator, an overwhelming presence throughout the narrative, embodies the town's shared sentiments toward Emily. Having spent years not only observing, but also commenting and rendering judgment upon the woman described as "a tradition, a duty, and a care,"[4] this *vox populi* is so persistent in assuming its natural right to intrude on Emily's life, that she—obsessively mindful of the need to honor the town's, and her father's, rigid code of genteel behavior—chooses murder rather than a public flouting of the town's values. The dramatic distance on display here provides an ironic layer to the narrative. As the observers of the conflict between the teller-of-tale's desire to solve the curious mysteries that surround Emily's life—indeed, his complicity in shaping them—and his undetective-like detachment from her crimes, readers occupy the tantalizing position of having insight into unraveling the mystery which the narrator lacks.

A classical detective story, quite simply, begins with an unsolved crime and moves toward its solution. Introduced into an world of ambiguity, mystery, and multiple possibilities, the reader is steadily made aware of key details that eventually allow a series of events to be placed into a comprehendable order. In "A Rose for Emily" the air of mystery commences with the first sentence: "When Miss Emily Grierson died, our whole town went to her funeral: the men through a sort of respectful affection for a fallen monument, the women mostly out of curiosity to see the inside of her house, which no one save an old manservant . . . had seen in at least ten years" (119). Playing off the detective convention of entering a locked room and delaying the revelation of its contents until the story's conclusion, this teasing beginning invites the reader to participate in unraveling the mysteries that have led up to Emily's funeral. However, making order out of Emily's life is a complicated matter, since the narrator recalls the details through a non-linear filter.

Cloaking an additional layer of mystery on Emily's story, the narrator's disjointed, associational recollection of details has led readers and critics to become the surrogate detectives of Faulkner's world. They have tried to "unscramble" the chronology and thus "solve" the structural ambiguities of the story by reconstructing Faulkner's calendar.[5] With evidence sparse and at times contradictory, these attempts, relying on close reading, conjecture, and extra-textual evidence, have yielded several slightly different time-lines. Although these time-lines claim to be pedagogically useful in allowing students to grasp "the elusive, illusive quality of time that lies at the heart of the story" (Going 53), their more immediate appeal is as a kind of armchair detective's game. They offer the challenge of taking the story's one exact reference to time (the remitting of Colonel Sartoris' taxes "in 1894") and combining it with the two dozen or so more approximate references to come up with a set of dates corresponding to the major events of Emily's life. Since the temporal world of Faulkner's Yoknapatawpha County remains relatively consistent (if inexact) throughout his entire corpus, other texts besides "A Rose for Emily," like his 1929 novel *Sartoris,* also help provide clues. Thus the more familiar the detective-critic becomes with the entire Faulkner corpus, the more equipped he or she is to place the events of Emily's life in the context of Yoknapatawpha County's overall pattern of myth.

But beyond offering superficial clarification about the plot, an exact chronology hardly seems to matter. As is invariably the case with Faulkner, appreciating the text's brilliance only begins with comprehending the plot, however ordered. Reduced to its basic situation, "A Rose for Emily" is fairly standard melodrama, probably loosely based on a conflation of actual odd events that occurred around Oxford in the 1920s (cf. Cullen and Watkins 70–71). Faulkner's plots can be brilliantly imagined, but what infuses this particular story with its force is the *manner* in which the plot is related to us by the purportedly innocuous observer of Emily's life. In other words, Faulkner conceives of "A Rose for Emily" quite cunningly by bending the traditional presentation of the detective. The narrative's overwhelming presence is the narrator himself, speaking as a representative voice of Jefferson (or, in using the "we" pronoun throughout, perhaps even as the collective voice of the town). In culling the data of Emily's life, the narrator/detective's favored posture is, in the classic mode of the genre, one of surveillance and, less classically, one of judgment. From the initial sentence, the narrator demands not just to retell the events of Emily's life, but to relish the manner in which the town intrudes upon them. Town members try to collect her taxes, insist on burying her father, attempt to rid her house of its odor, force the Baptist minister and her Alabama relatives into her home, and, after her death, eagerly break into her mysterious upstairs room.

Fully in keeping with the town's invasive aesthetic of observation, the narrator/detective's willingness to pass judgment on all he witnesses so completely overturns the illusion of objectivity that he speaks, if you will, not as the detached soloist of a Greek chorus, but as a prime participant in the tragic drama he relates. The ways of interpreting Emily's decision to murder Homer are numerous, as the many critical pieces on the story bear out. For simple clarification, they can be summarized along two lines. One group finds the murder growing out of Emily's demented attempt to forestall the inevitable passage of time— toward her abandonment by Homer, toward her own death, and toward the steady encroachment of the North and the New South on something loosely defined as the "tradition" of the Old South. Another view sees the murder in more psychological terms. It grows out of Emily's complex relationship to her father, who, by elevating her above all of the eligible men of Jefferson, insured that to yield to what one commentator called the "normal emotions" associated with desire, his daughter had to "retreat into a marginal world, into fantasy" (O'Connor 184).

These lines of interpretation complement more than critique each other, and collectively they offer an interesting range of views on the story. Together, they de-emphasize the element of detection, viewing the murder and its solution not as the central action but as manifestations of the principal element, the decline of the Grierson lineage and all it represents. Recognizing the way in which the story makes use of the detective genre, however, adds another interpretive layer to the story by making the narrator—or more precisely, the collective sensibility the narrator represents—a central player in the pattern of action. Detective stories typically place less emphasis on the crime, the criminal, and the victim than on the detective. Detectives such as Dupin, Holmes, Poirot, Sergeant Cuff, Dr. Gideon Fell, and Nero Wolfe may be detached from the society they observe but they still rest at the center of the author's narrative world. Faulkner bends his narrator/detective in some obvious ways away from these more traditional examples. Strictly speaking, his detective is no nearer Poe's Dupin than Emily is a recreation of Minister D, the master criminal of "The Purloined Letter." But the narrative is an ongoing investigation of Emily's life and the narrator is the principal detective in this investigation.

Much of the story's action is centered around the combination of Emily's desire to remain isolated and the narrator and his fellow townsfolk's refusal to honor that desire. Consider, among many examples, the language of intrusion and judgment implied in the following passages.

> They were not surprised when the smell developed.

> That was when people had begun to feel really sorry for her. People in our town . . . believed that the Griersons held themselves a little too high for what they really were.

> So when she got to be thirty and was still single, we were not pleased exactly, but vindicated.

> When her father died, it got about that the house was all that was left to her; and in a way, people were glad. At last they could pity Miss Emily.

> We did not say she was crazy then. We believed she had to do that.

> As soon as the old people said, "Poor Emily," the whispering began.

> She carried her head high enough—even when we believed that she was fallen.

And finally, the story's most startling and significant statement made shortly after Emily purchases rat poison: "So the next day we all said, 'she will kill herself'; and *we said it would be the best thing*" (my emphasis, 121–26). The town, it is evident, has made Emily its obsession, with every detail of her life subject to discussion, speculation and assessment. Without means by which to carry on her affair in public (and a noticeably diminishing lack of interest on Homer's part, since he "liked men" and was not ready to settle down), Emily insures her isolation in a cunningly ironic and comic verbal reversal on the town's recommendation of suicide; she herself kills Homer Barron, and from the town's point of view, it was the best thing.

"The detective novel features two expulsions of 'bad' or socially unfit characters: the victim and the murderer" (Grella 49). In the context of the genre, as George Grella describes it, Homer is a classic victim because he is guilty of an unpardonable crime against the community. He was born in the North, which in the world of Jefferson, Mississippi, since the days of the Civil War, has been a capital offense. After he disappears, no more attention is paid to him ("that was the last we saw of Homer Barron" [127]). The town's purported lack of interest can be formally explained as a crafty plotting device of Faulkner's to draw suspicion away from the existence of the murder (which is further obscured by the temporal shifts in the narrative). To this end, the narrator casually mentions Homer for the first time in the story as the "sweetheart" who "deserted" Emily. But it is also significant that as a northerner—as well as a common day-laborer— Homer represents the kind of unwelcomed resident and ineligible mate the town wants to repel if it is to preserve its traditional arrangements. His very proximity to Emily is, according to Jefferson's ladies, "a disgrace to the town and a bad example to the young people" (126). Homer is, to echo Grella's apt phrase, "an exceptionally murderable man" (49)—a victim whose disappearance invites a conspiracy of silence.

The very failure of the narrator and the town to "solve" the crime until the murderer herself has died indicates much about the true nature of the society in which the murder occurred. If we assume that the narrator/detective and other townsfolk know about the crime (although the textual evidence for this can only be ambiguously inferred), we also realize that for the town to reveal Emily's crime and indicate what it will do in response is far more complicated than silently ignoring the entire matter. For the people of Jefferson, the illusion of *noblesse oblige* is to be preserved at all costs, whether it means remitting Emily's taxes, inviting her Alabama kinfolk to come to Jefferson and regulate her embarrassing courtship, or ignoring a murder by passing off the foul smell emanating from her house shortly after Homer's disappearance as "probably just a snake or a rat."

This conveniently evasive speculation comes from Judge Stevens (whose son is likely Gavin Stevens, the detective/lawyer/chess aficionado in *Knight's Gambit*). The statement can be read several ways. It emphasizes Emily's status as a Poe-like "least-likely" criminal, a misfit so unsuited for the role of murderer that the town's leading citizen does not suspect her. In this light, the Judge's pronouncement is not a red herring, but its opposite, a statement that has the effect of allowing a very real clue to be introduced before allowing a purportedly disinterested observer to shift the narrative's emphasis away from the crime. However, it can also be suggested that, given the facts at hand (e.g., Emily's resistance to allowing her father to be buried and Steven's reluctance to accuse a "lady" of smelling bad), Stevens' statement is not the naive observation of a casual onlooker but a conveniently calculating means on his part of preserving order, glossing over the rather obvious fact that a well-known citizen has a murder victim rotting inside her house. Where the reader stands in relation to the very tangible clue of the smell depends on his or her willingness to accept the judge's explanation at face value. Like the best detective writers, Faulkner is able to offer pieces of information about the crime, thus putting the careful reader on equal footing with characters in the story, but to do so in such a way as to delay the obvious solution until more substantial proof of the murder comes forth.

That proof comes in the story's final three paragraphs, beginning with the one-sentence paragraph: "The man himself lay in the bed." The crime is both confirmed and solved; the detective pattern is compressed into one climactic scene, which inventively re-imagines a version of Poe's "locked room" mystery, "The Murders in the Rue Morgue." In the classic locked-room story, Dupin unravels the story behind a mother and daughter's murder, which has occurred in an apartment where all the windows and doors are sealed from the inside. In Faulkner's version, a victim's body is similarly discovered inside a mysterious upstairs room, whose door has to be broken down to gain admittance. But since the killer's identity and the mechanism of the murder are readily apparent, the narrator's puzzle is not solved simply by answering "who done it" and "how she done it." The narrator has the more challenging goal of comprehending the gruesome spectacle in the context of the town's obsession with Emily's entire life. This is accomplished with the miniscule clue of a single strand of hair, a temporarily "hidden object" that once detected sets Emily's disturbed mind state into stark relief and provides the town with just the kind of hindsight evidence it needs to justify all of the attention it paid to her over the years.

Finally, in a single sentence, Faulkner skillfully brings the mystery to a close and leaves the reader to reflect upon the narrator/detective's involvement in Emily's deranged decision to murder Homer Barron. As an inventive precursor to Faulkner's own later detective characters, this narrator is an example of how the author, rather than simply mimicking other detective stories, re-worked the classical devices of detection to suit his own ends. "A Rose for Emily" is a notable example of Faulkner's talent for taking the raw materials of his surroundings and working them into original forms—whether this meant drawing from his literary antecedents, re-configuring actual events, or delving into his own considerable imagination. John T. Irwin, in his discussion of *Knight's Gambit,* sets Faulkner next to Poe as a "worthy successor" and a "formidable competitor to the [detective] genre's originator" (173). When viewed as a detective story, "A Rose for Emily" helps buttress this claim and thereby furthers our appreciation of Faulkner's lifelong interest in laying out and then solving the many curious mysteries of what he famously termed his "own little postage stamp of native soil" (qtd. in Minter 76).

NOTES

1. For discussions of Faulkner's debt to Poe, see especially Irwin Cawelti, 134; and Stronks, 11.
2. *Sanctuary* exhibits its own interesting connections to the classical detective story. In his famous 1933 preface to the novel French novelist André Malraux remarked that *Sanctuary* was "a novel with a detective-story atmosphere but without detectives"; qtd. in Sundquist, 47.
3. For a thorough discussion of Faulkner and popular short fiction see Matthews, 3–37.
4. All subsequent quotes from the primary text are from *Collected Stories of William Faulkner,* 119–30, and will be cited internally by page number.
5. In the Merrill Literary Casebook series for "A Rose for Emily," editor M. Thomas Inge reprints four articles that posit slightly different time-lines, all of which focus on the story's chronology: see 34, 50–53, 83, 84–86, 90–92.

WORKS CITED

Cawelti, John G. *Adventure, Mystery, and Romance: Formula Stories as Art and Popular Culture.* Chicago: U of Chicago P, 1976.

Cullen, John B., and Floyd C. Watkins, *Old Times in the Faulkner Country.* Chapel Hill: U of North Carolina P, 1961.

Faulkner, William. *Collected Stories of William Faulkner.* New York: Vintage, 1977.

Going, William T. "Chronology in Teaching 'A Rose for Emily.'" *A Rose for Emily.* Ed. M. Thomas Inge. Columbus: Merrill, 1970. 50–53.

Grella, George. "Murder and Manners: The Formal Detective Novel." *Dimensions of Detective Fiction.* Ed. Larry N. Landrum, Pat Browne, and Ray B. Browne. Bowling Green, OH: Bowling Green State University Popular Press, 1976. 37–57.

Howe, Irving. *William Faulkner: A Critical Study*. New York: Vintage, 1962.

Inge, M. Thomas, ed. *A Rose for Emily*. Columbus: Merrill, 1970.

Irwin, John T. *"Knight's Gambit:* Poe, Faulkner, and the Tradition of the Detective Story." *Faulkner and the Short Story*. Ed. Evans Harrington and Ann J. Abadie. Jackson: U of Mississippi P, 1992. 149–73.

Karl, Frederick R. *William Faulkner: An American Writer*. New York: Weidenfeld and Nicolson, 1989.

Matthews, John T. "Shortened Stories: Faulkner and the Market." *Faulkner and the Short Story*. Ed. Evans Harrington and Ann J. Abadie. Jackson: UP of Mississippi. 3–37.

Minter, David. *William Faulkner: His Life and Work*. Baltimore: Johns Hopkins UP, 1980.

O'Connor, William. "The State of Faulkner Criticism." *Sewanee Review* 60 (1952): 184.

Stronks, James. "A Poe Source for Faulkner? 'To Helen' and 'A Rose for Emily.'" *Poe Newlsletter* I (Apr. 1968): 11.

Sundquist, Eric. *Faulkner: The House Divided*. Baltimore: Johns Hopkins UP, 1983.

GEORGE L. DILLON

Styles of Reading∗

One of the things readers do with stories is to talk about them. These stories have not said it all, and readers derive evident pleasure from completing them, commenting on them, making them their own in various ways. Christine Brooke-Rose has recently called attention to the strategic incompleteness of good stories—spelling everything out treats the reader as stupid—and has suggested a classification of stories according to the tasks they leave to readers, or in which they entangle readers.[1] If we look at actual, published discussions of a story, however, we find no two of them answering the same set of questions, which suggests that we should look for questions (pre)inscribed in the reader as well as the text—the text, it is a matter of fact, has not very narrowly constrained the set of questions the readers have posed. As soon as we raise the matter of the actual performance of readers, however, we encounter a plethora of variables, and it has become something of a fashion in discussions of reading to enumerate them, often, it seems, to frighten scholars back to the study of narrative competence and the ways texts constrain, or should constrain interpretations. ∗ ∗ ∗ If we are concerned with how people actually do read stories, however, these lists outline an area for research. ∗ ∗ ∗ Perhaps there are underlying regularities which *in fact* shape readers' performances; perhaps there are none. In this article, I will examine readings of Faulkner's "A Rose for Emily," and focus initially on one area of variation—the answers readers have given to questions about the chronological

∗From *Poetics Today* 3, no. 2 (1982):77–88. Copyright 1982 by The Porter Institute for Poetics and Semiotics, Tel Aviv University. Reprinted by permission of The Porter Institute for Poetics and Semiotics, Tel Aviv University.

sequence, or "event chain," of the story—to see how wild the variation is and what hope there may be of identifying regularities of performance.

One reason for focusing on event chains is that these have been among the most intensively studied of the many aspects of story comprehension. * * * Readers employ two basic operations in building event chains: connection and inference. No story I know of spells out all of the terms and connections in an event chain (Miss Emily's motive for murdering Homer Barron, for example, is left for the reader to infer, as is the connection of the arsenic to the murder), and a story that did spell them all out would treat the reader as inconceivably stupid. Two distinctions are in order here: event chains are not precisely chronological, though I think they do correspond closely to * * * chronological sequences, that is, a certain sequentiality is implicit in the notions of motive, action, cause, response, and consequence, but not necessarily clock or calendar time, nor do pieces of the overall chain have to be strictly ordered; different sequences may overlap. This point is quite clear in regard to "A Rose for Emily": it seems possible to establish a chronology of the story that orders all of its major incidents, though it is very difficult to do so,[2] and it is not necessary to have worked out such a time scheme in order to get major portions of the event chain straight. Second, event chains are not "plots" * * * [t]hat is, they are shapeless and open-ended; they do not account for any sense of beginning, climax, or conclusion. * * * [E]vent chains are part of the comprehension of all narratives; indeed, of all happenings, not just stories. * * *

When we survey the published criticism of "A Rose for Emily," we find a large and bewildering array of questions about the event chain that have been answered. These include:

1. Why weren't there suitable suitors for Emily?
2. How does Emily respond to being denied suitors?
3. Why does Emily take up with Homer Barron?
4. What happened when he left? Did he abandon her? Why did he come back?
5. Why did she kill him?
6. Why did the smell disappear after only one week?
7. What did Miss Emily think of the men scattering lime around her house?
8. How did the hair come to be on the pillow? How much hair is a *strand?*
9. What was her relationship to Tobe?
10. Did she lie beside the corpse? How often, for what period of years?
11. Why did she not leave the house for the last decade of her life?
12. Did she not know Colonel Sartoris had been dead ten years when she faced down the Aldermen?
13. How crazy was she (unable to distinguish fantasy from reality)?
14. Why does she allow so much dust in her house?

There is also one question that has been asked but not answered, as far as I know: What transpired when the Baptist minister visited her? As the specialists in story comprehension have noted, once we realize that a Story Comprehender must have the power to carry out inferences in order to comprehend even the simplest story and give it that power, the problem becomes one of limiting the inferences drawn to some "relevant" subset of the possible ones. * * * [B]ut it is not clear how to apply this principle [of relevance] to the fourteen questions and answers, since every one of those questions was answered by at least one critic who felt the answer was relevant to the interpretation of the story—relevant to determining her motives, naming her actions, and so on. Of course, some of these event-chain inferences are stimulated by the particular interpretation a critic is putting forth, but there does not seem to be any basis on which to separate those inferences that are made independent of an interpretation from those which are not * * * . People do not agree on the story to then disagree on the interpretation. It is simply not true that, as Wolfgang Iser claims, "On the level of plot, then, there is a high degree of intersubjective consensus," with subjective variation arising at the level of significance.[3] In fact, when we look at the list of questions that have been answered, the construction of event chains seems wildly unconstrained.

If we look at whole readings, however, some system and pattern does emerge. There are two surveys of the criticism of this story, and both find it fairly easy to group the readings into three classes (though the classes are somewhat differently defined).[4] We could group the readings according to what one might call "approaches," suggesting by that term some set of general questions readers taking a particular approach tend to pose of texts they read. This notion can be pushed in two, opposite directions. Taking it one way, we could argue that the variation considered so far does not directly reflect the way readers read but the way critics write about stories when they have an eye toward publication * * * . Taken the other way, these approaches could be viewed as personal styles or preferences in reading that happen to have acquired some public sanction. We generally have some style of reading before we know much about "approaches," after all, though we may learn other questions to ask when we study literature. In any case, one must have learned the approach in order to use it * * * . Some light on the matter is shed, I think, by the very copious transcripts of interviews with undergraduate English majors about "A Rose for Emily" published by Norman Holland in *5 Readers Reading*.

Holland's students also show three distinct approaches, and these approaches match up with the types of approaches in the published criticism[, t]hough * * * they do seem to be giving what they feel are their own responses and to be responding in somewhat original—but consistent—ways to his questions. Also, * * * the criticism they chose to be influenced by as much reflects their cognitive styles as it determines them. Holland's study strongly suggests that there are styles of reading stories, characteristic ways that readers interrogate texts, and that the "approaches" in the criticism are indeed rooted in the critics' own styles of reading and appeal to like-minded readers. I will illustrate this correspondence for three basic styles, which I will call the Character-Action-Moral (CAM) style, the Digger for Secrets style, and the Anthropologist style.

The CAM style differs markedly from the other two in treating the meaning (or significance) as more or less evident in the story: the reader makes the text his own, and makes the reading more apparent, by elaborating the event chain in the direction of the main character's traits, motives, thoughts, responses, and choices. To do this, CAM readers treat the world of the text as an extension or portion of the real world, the characters as real persons, so that we will recognize the experience of characters as being like our own experience; hence it can be understood or explained just as we would understand our own experience. Thus, the inferences they draw are based on commonsense notions of the way the world is, people are, etc. The other two styles appropriate the text not by immersion, but by analytic distance, probing and abstracting behind what is said; they assume that the world of the text is an edited version of our world—a *structure* rather than a glimpse or fragment. The CAM reader works by amalgamating the story into the body of his own beliefs and practical axioms about how life is or should be, the analytic styles by postulating the otherness or strangeness of the text.

The standard CAM reading contains lists of traits that account for the actions of the main character in a straightforward evaluative fashion * * * . The actions are assumed to be pointers toward relatively permanent and pervasive characteristics, and one often finds "it could be otherwise" speculations in CAM readings (e.g., "A Rose for Emily" could have had a happy outcome if Homer Barron had been a marrying man—West;[5] if another man had proposed to Emily after she finished with Homer, she would have declined the offer because she felt herself already married—Sam, in Holland [pp. 138–39]). That is, the notion of character seems to presuppose the freedom of individuals to choose their responses to their situations, and stories like "A Rose for Emily" are treated as collisions between characters and situations—as *tragedies,* in the traditional Butcher/Bradley sense:

> Perhaps the horrible and the admirable aspects of Miss Emily's final deed arise from the same basic fact of her character: she insists on meeting the world on her own terms. She never cringes, she never begs for sympathy, she refuses to shrink into an amiable old maid, she never accepts the community's ordinary judgments or values. This independence of spirit and pride can, and does in her case, twist the individual into a sort of monster, but, at the same time, this refusal to accept the hero values carries with it a dignity and courage.[6] * * *

* * * We can see here the way the common notion of tragedy directs the reading toward character analysis; it also introduces three other questions, namely, those of awareness, tragic flaw, and moral. The evoking or constructing of character seems to lead directly to inference o[f] the character's thoughts. When done naïvely, the results are fairly obtrusive, as when Holland's Sam says Emily has an awareness that "things were moving on, that things were changing, and yet, a similar awareness that she was unable to change along with them" (p. 137). More subtle is a partial merging of reader's and character's points of view. The reader talks about the character in terms the character himself might use: "She lost her honor, and what else could she do but keep him [Homer] forever, make him hers in the only way she possibly could?" (Sam. p. 137). * * *

This construction of an inner logic for the character is essential to the drawing of the moral: once we have realized the character's viewpoint, we can see the fatal flaw, the impulses or tendencies in ourselves that we should not give in to. If this immersion and identification with the character (which is plainly the identification of the character with the reader, in terms of himself) fails, * * * the CAM reader must direct his attention away from the details that suggest Miss Emily is not "like us" (above all, the questions about sleeping next to the corpse).

* * *

In sum, then, the CAM style is not afraid to state the obvious; it does not try to be ingenious or clever, but solid and useful; it does not assume the author is fashioning puzzles for us to solve, or playing tricks on us. The story conceals nothing—it is merely, of necessity, incomplete. For Diggers for Secrets, however, the story enwraps secrets, the narrator hides them[,] * * * and the reader must uncover them. The title of Edward Stone's *A Certain Morbidness* suggests how he will read "A Rose for Emily."[7] Diggers for Secrets expect narrators to screen us from the "reality,"

> But when, during her early spinsterhood, her father dies and she refuses for three days to hand his putrefying body over for burial, we are shocked by this irrational action, even though in keeping with his standpoint of noncommitment Faulkner tries to minimize it ("We remembered all the young men her father had driven away, and we knew that with nothing left, she would have to cling to that which had robbed her, as people will"). (Stone, 96)

and expect the author only to give us clues:

> For Faulkner, so far from withholding all clues to Homer Barron's whereabouts, scatters them with a precise prodigality; since his is a story primarily of character, it is to his purpose to saturate our awareness of Miss Emily's abnormality as he goes, so that the last six shocking words merely put the final touch on that purpose. (p. 65)

Sebastian, who is Holland's Digger, also comments on the evenhandedness of the narrator, whom he describes as switching sides (p. 177), and he too finds the maxim about holding on to that which robbed her a screen rather than an explanation: "Shouldn't have put that in, Bill," he says (p. 186). He even proposes to see through the author: "I wanted to see what unconscious things he would reveal about the South" (p. 186).

When Diggers for Secrets explain the psychology of characters, they employ the categories of depth and abnormal psychology * * * and frequently "diagnose" motives the characters would not be aware of and in terms they might well not accept. Sebastian uses the terms *sexuality, obsession,* and *necrophilia* heavily and confidently, but he still falls short, in eloquence at least, of * * * Edward Stone:

> Her passionate, almost sexual relationship with her dead father forces her to distrust the living body of Homer and to kill him so that he will resemble the dead father she can never forget.
>
> Not only does this obsessed spinster continue for some years to share a marriage bed with the body of the man she poisoned—she evidently derives either erotic gratification or spiritual sustenance (both?) from these ghastly nuptials. She becomes, in short, a necrophile or a veritable saprophytic organism; for we learn that the "slender figure in white" that was the young Miss Emily becomes, as

though with the middle-aged propriety that the marriage customarily brings, fat! (Stone, 96)

* * * In a similar vein, Sebastian draws numerous inferences about the Negro servant Tobe's complicity in Emily's crime, about her "affair" with Homer, about the details of her sleeping with his corpse (how can a woman perform an act of necrophilia on a man?), and so on.

Symbolism being a ready avenue to non-obvious meanings, these readers find symbolic significances and secrets in details that the CAM readers either pass over or handle prosaically: Miss Emily's house for Stone is an isolated fortress, a forbidden, majestic stronghold; * * * for Sebastian, the title is richly ironic, "an unforgiveable irony in one sense: 'A Rose by any other name would not smell half as sweet!' There's not much sweetness about *her* rose. So I think the title refers to the decomposition of living matter, and so I take it ironically" (p. 182). * * * One expects such ironies from an author presumed to conceal.

An interesting feature of "A Rose for Emily" is that it contains not only a literal hidden secret (which Sebastian objects to as a bit too overt) but a "reader" as well (the narrator). That is, people who habitually look for the dirty reality behind appearances are open to the charge of prurience, a charge that would be easy to level at these readers, and one that the story conveniently allows us to displace onto the narrator ("the community") instead. So the taint of corruption spreads to the town, all these readers say, but, of course, not to *us*.[8] Thus in a sense, the abnormal becomes normal, and the story acquires the universality that raises it from case history to literature. The search for the abnormal and perverse finally leads back to the unacknowledged parts of our selves.

* * *

Though the Diggers for Secrets make use of abstractive codes that explain what is going on in the story, their interest in "what's really going on" does, as we have seen, lead to inferences elaborating the event chain. The third group, the Anthropologists, have much less to say about events than either of the first two groups. Their interest, rather, is in identifying the cultural norms and values that explain what characters indisputably do and say. Like Diggers for Secrets, these readers go beneath the surface and state things that are implicit and not said, though what they bring out is not a secret, but the general principles and values which the story illustrates as an example. To some degree, early readings that talk of a conflict in "A Rose for Emily" between the North and the South, or old versus new South, outline this approach, but these readings tended to be brief and schematic, as if critics were not willing to reopen old wounds.[9] And, too, Faulkner was on record as not intending such an interpretation.[10] When a reader is especially engaged in the critique of the norms and values of American society, however, the story takes on interest as an extended exemplum. Thus the two instances of this style of reading, Holland's Shep and Judith Fetterley, are both radicals. For Shep, who is Holland's example of a sixties radical, the characters and events of the story exemplify forces of social struggle—class struggle, racial struggle, and above all the struggle between true and false values. Thus he says Emily's father represents the old code, the dead hand of the past; Homer Barron represents the forces of aimless technology; Emily herself was, he says, "perpetuating the same ethos in which her father lived" (p. 61); "In a way, Miss Emily is a descendant of the culture hero, except that she's a descendant of the culture hero in his waning phase" (p. 166); "They had a very rigid formal code and it was perhaps very much a dead code by the time she got her hands on it, but it represented something which the new people weren't able to offer an adequate substitute for" (p. 161). Proceeding at such a lofty plane, he is fairly indifferent to the detailed goings-on of the event chain, though he does infer Emily's response to the lime-scattering incident—namely, scorn for the men—and he is willing to speculate under Holland's urging. He offers two motives for the murder, first, simple revenge, to keep him from leaving her; but he also evolves a second, mythic explanation, which I quote at some length:

> She can reverse the social decay process by putting her lover, representative of all of them ["the newcomers"] through a physical decay process and coming to relish the sight. This would also give some sort of, quote, explanation, unquote, for her necrophilic hangups. The fact that she wanted her father's body around to . . . preserve it from decay—she was denying the end of the line thing symbolized by putting it underground and letting the earth have it. (p. 171)

* * * So there is a double or triple pattern of explanation here—commonsense psychology (she wanted revenge), operation of social forces, and mythic patterns; these explanations seem somewhat detached from each other and so the reading is not completely totalized.

If Shep is an example of a sixties radical, then Judith Fetterley, in her book *The Resisting Reader*[11] represents a kind of seventies version of the same basic style of reading. Fetterley focuses on stating the social norms and codes that explain the events of the story—there is very little in the way of constructive activity of motives, actions, responses, and consequences, except for a brief discussion of the lime-scattering incident. She also offers two motives for the murder: first, that Emily murdered Homer because she had to have a man (thus illustrating the brainwashing of the code), but she also offers the following symbolic/mythic account:

> Having been consumed by her father, Emily in turn feeds off Homer Barron, becoming, after his death, suspiciously fat. Or, to put it another way, it is as if, after her father's death, she has reversed his act of incorporating her by incorporating and becoming him, metamorphosed from the slender figure in white to the obese figure in black whose hair is "a vigorous iron-gray, like the hair of an active man." She has taken into herself the violence in him which thwarted her and has reenacted it upon Homer Barron. (pp. 42–43)

On first reading, this seems very much like Stone's celebration of Faulkner's "ghoulish evolution" of the gothic, but on closer examination, the passage is really suggesting a crude form of retributive justice, a pointed, if lurid, warning to the upholders of patriarchy. It is striking that the same elementary operations—*connecting* her growing fat to Homer's murder and *inferring* a causal link—result in such different explanations.

Like Shep, Fetterley makes heavy use of symbolic interpretation and the logic of example: Emily's confinement by her father represents confinement of women by patriarchy; the remission of taxes signifies continued dependence of women on men; the men's treatment of her, and her ability to buffalo them and commit murder without punishment, are explained in terms of the code of the "lady" who is assumed to be out of touch with reality, and must be kept so; Emily represents the town itself, and in discovering her nature, they discover their own. The focus of Fetterley's interest is in flushing the codes out of hiding and explaining what happens in terms of them, though it is not a totalizing reading in that she doesn't claim to have explained everything in the story in terms of the codes; this treatment represents the extreme of abstraction away from the events and surface of the story toward allegory and parable. That's what it means to be a Resisting Reader: to refuse to give yourself to the work, to accept any of its givens—and in fact, to bring precisely those axioms into question.

Clearly, then, these three styles or approaches are asking different questions of the text, and constructing what are to various degrees different stories in the course of answering them. * * * Readers predisposed to a certain style of reading[, however] will, when faced with the same text, come up with some very similar stories along with some very similar explanations.

* * * [T]he notion that these styles are, or can become, general patterns of thinking, rather than a learned decorum of literary criticism, seems to derive support from the consideration that we also exhibit differences of styles in thinking about real people and events. We think of ourselves and others as conscious, moral agents shaping our destinies in situations benign and hostile, but also as mysteries to ourselves and others, and/or as enacting typical social roles and attitudes. There is some basis for concluding that we understand literature and life in the same or similar ways, and that some of the ways we read literature will be applied in reading others of life's texts.

NOTES

1. Brooke-Rose, "The Readerhood of Man," in *The Reader in the Text,* ed. Susan R. Suleiman and Inge Crosman (Princeton: Princeton University Press, 1980), 120–48.
2. At least five chronologies have appeared in print, all differing: William T. Going, "Chronology in Teaching 'A Rose for Emily.'" *Exercise Exchange* 5 (1958): 8–11; Robert W. Woodward, "The Chronology of 'A Rose for Emily,'" *Exercise Exchange* 13 (1966): 17–19; Paul D. McGlynn, "The Chronology of 'A Rose for Emily,'" *Studies in Short Fiction* 6 (1969): 461–62; Helen E. Nebeker, "Chronology Revisited," *Studies in Short Fiction* 8 (1971): 471–73; and Menakhem Perry, "Literary Dynamics: How the Order of a Text Creates Its Meaning," *Poetics Today* 1 (1979): 35–63; 311–61.
3. Wolfgang Iser, *The Act of Reading* (Baltimore: Johns Hopkins University Press, 1978), 123. Iser's definition of *significance* as "the reader's absorption of the meaning into his own existence" (p. 151) leaves us in need of an intermediate term between it and *plot* (event chains)—something like *explanation,* which is constructed to account for events (e.g., in terms of character traits, maxims of behavior, mythic patterns, etc.) but which is not necessarily the amalgamation of the

story into the reader's subjectivity. For one thing, explanation need not be evaluative. I am using *interpretation* in a broad sense here to mean the reader's commentary minus any plot summary, though even the latter is usually tailored to fit the commentary.

4. See Norman Holland, *5 Readers Reading* (New Haven: Yale University Press, 1975), 21–24 (cited in the text as Holland, or Holland's Sam); and Perry, "Literary Dynamics," 62–63 et passim.

5. Ray B. West, "Atmosphere and Theme in Faulkner's 'A Rose for Emily,'" in *William Faulkner: Four Decades of Criticism*, ed. Linda W. Wagner (East Lansing: Michigan State University Press, 1973), 192–98. Cited in the text as West.

6. Cleanth Brooks and Robert Penn Warren, *Understanding Fiction* (New York: Crofts, 1948), * * * [413].

7. Stone, *A Certain Morbidness* (Carbondale: Southern Illinois University Press, 1969). Cited in the text as Stone.

8. For Ruth Sullivan, however, the narrator is a prying, probing voyeur, and so are we readers. See "The Narrators in 'A Rose for Emily,'" *Journal of Narrative Technique* 1 (1971): 159–78.

9. Frederick Gwynn and Joseph L. Blotner, *Faulkner in the University* (New York: Vintage Books, 1965), 47–48.

10. There is one style which I find attested only in Holland's interviews (and in some of the papers of David Bleich's students), that we might call the Visualizer style, the style of Holland's Sandra, whose comments * * * are strongly weighted to descriptions of characters' expressions and feelings, decors and other physical details and commentary on the suitability of words, images and tonal effects in the narration. This is perhaps the most surface- or craft-conscious of the styles, and the reason it does not appear in the published readings is that it is more a style of appreciation than explanation, or, to put it another way, it is more concerned with explaining the details of the style and presentation * * * than with the story. * * *

11. Fetterley, *The Resisting Reader* (Bloomington and London: Indiana University Press, 1978).

JUDITH FETTERLEY

A Rose for "A Rose for Emily"*

In "A Rose for Emily" * * * grotesque reality * * * becomes explicit. Justifying Faulkner's use of the grotesque has been a major concern of critics who have written on the story. If, however, one approaches "A Rose for Emily" from a feminist perspective, one notices that the grotesque aspects of the story are a result of its violation of the expectations generated by the conventions of sexual politics. The ending shocks us not simply by its hint of necrophilia; more shock-

*From *The Resisting Reader: A Feminist Approach to American Fiction*, by Judith Fetterley (Bloomington and London: Indiana University Press, 1978). Copyright 1978 by Judith Fetterley. Reprinted by permission.

ing is the fact that it is a woman who provides the hint. It is one thing for Poe to spend his nights in the tomb of Annabel Lee and another thing for Miss Emily Grierson to deposit a strand of iron-gray hair on the pillow beside the rotted corpse of Homer Barron. Further, we do not expect to discover that a woman has murdered a man. * * * To reverse [the] "natural" pattern inevitably produces the grotesque.

Faulkner, however, is not interested in invoking the kind of grotesque which is the consequence of reversing the clichés of sexism for the sake of a cheap thrill. * * * Rather, Faulkner invokes the grotesque in order to illuminate and define the true nature of the conventions on which it depends. "A Rose for Emily" is a story not of a conflict between the South and the North or between the old order and the new; it is a story of the patriarchy North and South, new and old, and of the sexual conflict within it. As Faulkner himself has implied,[1] it is a story of a woman victimized and betrayed by the system of sexual politics, who nevertheless has discovered, within the structures that victimize her, sources of power for herself. * * * "A Rose for Emily" is the story of how to murder your gentleman caller and get away with it. Faulkner's story is an analysis of how men's attitudes toward women turn back upon themselves; it is a demonstration of the thesis that it is impossible to oppress without in turn being oppressed, it is impossible to kill without creating the conditions for your own murder. "A Rose for Emily" is the story of a *lady* and of her revenge for that grotesque identity.

"When Miss Emily Grierson died, our whole town went to her funeral." The public and communal nature of Emily's funeral, a festival that brings the town together, clarifying its social relationships and revitalizing its sense of the past, indicates her central role in Jefferson. Alive, Emily is town property and the subject of shared speculation; dead, she is town history and the subject of legend. It is her value as a symbol, however obscure and however ambivalent, of something that is of central significance to the identity of Jefferson and to the meaning of its history that compels the narrator to assume a communal voice to tell her story. For Emily * * * is a man-made object, a cultural artifact, and what she is reflects and defines the culture that has produced her.

The history the narrator relates to us reveals Jefferson's continuous emotional involvement with Emily. Indeed, though she shuts herself up in a house which she rarely leaves and which no one enters, her furious isolation is in direct proportion to the town's obsession with her: * * * she is the object of incessant attention; her every act is immediately consumed by the town for gossip and seized on to justify their interference in her affairs. Her private life becomes a public document that the town folk feel free to interpret at will, and they are alternately curious, jealous, spiteful, pitying, partisan, proud, disapproving, admiring, and vindicated. Her funeral is not simply a communal ceremony; it is also the climax of their invasion of her private life and the logical extension of their voyeuristic attitude toward her. Despite the narrator's demurral, getting inside Emily's house is the all-consuming desire of the town's population, both male and female; while the men may wait a little longer, their motive is still prurient curiosity: "Already we knew that there was one room in that region above stairs which no one had seen in forty years, and which would have to be forced. They waited until Miss Emily was decently in the ground before they opened it."

In a context in which the overtones of violation and invasion are so palpable, the word "decently" has that ironic ring which gives the game away. When the men finally do break down the door, they find that Emily has satisfied their prurience with a vengeance and in doing so has created for them a mirror image of themselves. The true nature of Emily's relation to Jefferson is contained in the analogies between what those who break open that room see in it and what has brought them there to see it. The perverse, violent, and grotesque aspects of the sight of Homer Barron's rotted corpse in a room decked out for a bridal and now faded and covered in dust reflects back to them the perverseness of their own prurient interest in Emily, the violence implicit in their continued invasions of her life, and the grotesqueness of the symbolic artifact they have made of her—their monument, their idol, their lady. Thus, the figure that Jefferson places at the center of its legendary history does indeed contain the clue to the meaning of that history—a history which began long before Emily's funeral and long before Homer Barron's disappearance or appearance and long before Colonel Sartoris' fathering of edicts and remittances. It is recorded in that emblem which lies at the heart of the town's memory and at the heart of patriarchal culture: "We had long thought of them as a tableau, Miss Emily a slender figure in white in the background, her father a spraddled silhouette in the foreground, his back to her and clutching a horsewhip, the two of them framed by the back-flung front door."

The importance of Emily's father in shaping the quality of her life is insistent throughout the story. Even in her death the force of his presence is felt; above her dead body sits "the crayon face of her father musing profoundly," symbolic of the degree to which he has dominated and shadowed her life, "as if that quality of her father which had thwarted her woman's life so many times had been too virulent and too furious to die." The violence of this consuming relationship is made explicit in the imagery of the tableau. Although the violence is apparently directed outward—the upraised horsewhip against the would-be suitor—the real object of it is the woman-daughter, forced into the background and dominated by the phallic figure of the spraddled father whose back is turned on her and who prevents her from getting out at the same time that he prevents them from getting in. [Emily's] * * * spatial confinement [is] * * * a metaphor for her psychic confinement: her identity is determined by the constructs of her father's mind, and she can no more escape from his creation of her as "a slender figure in white" than she can escape his house.

What is true for Emily in relation to her father is equally true for her in relation to Jefferson: her status as a lady is a cage from which she cannot escape. To them she is always *Miss* Emily; she is never referred to and never thought of as otherwise. In omitting her title from his, Faulkner emphasizes the point that the real violence done to Emily is in making her a "Miss"; the omission is one of his roses for her. Because she is *Miss* Emily *Grierson*, Emily's father dresses her in white, places her in the background, and drives away her suitors. Because she is Miss Emily Grierson, the town invests her with that communal significance which makes her the object of their obsession and the subject of their incessant scrutiny. And because she is a lady, the town is able to impose a particular code of behavior on her ("But there were still others, older people, who said that even grief could not cause a real lady to forget *noblesse oblige*") and to see in her failure to live up to that code an excuse for interfering in her life. As a lady, Emily is venerated, but veneration results in the more telling emotions of envy and spite: "It was another link between the gross, teeming world and the high and mighty Griersons"; "People . . . believed that the Griersons held themselves a little too high for what they really were." The violence implicit in the desire to see the monument fall and reveal itself for clay suggests the violence inherent in the original impulse to venerate.

The violence behind veneration is emphasized through another telling emblem in the story. Emily's position as a hereditary obligation upon the town dates from "that day in 1894 when Colonel Sartoris, the mayor—he who fathered the edict that no Negro woman should appear on the streets without an apron on—remitted her taxes, the dispensation dating from the death of her father on into perpetuity." The conjunction of these two actions in the same syntactic unit is crucial, for it insists on their essential similarity. It indicates that the impulse to exempt is analogous to the desire to restrict, and that what appears to be a kindness or an act of veneration is in fact an insult. Sartoris' remission of Emily's taxes is a public declaration of the fact that a lady is not considered to be, and hence not allowed or enabled to be, economically independent (consider, in this connection, Emily's lessons in china painting; they are a latter-day version of Sartoris' "charity" and a brilliant image of Emily's economic uselessness). His act is a public statement of the fact that a lady, if she is to survive, must have either husband or father, and that, because Emily has neither, the town must assume responsibility for her. The remission of taxes that defines Emily's status dates from the death of her father, and she is handed over from one patron to the next, the town instead of husband taking on the role of father. Indeed, the use of the word "fathered" in describing Sartoris' behavior as mayor underlines the fact that his chivalric attitude toward Emily is simply a subtler and more dishonest version of her father's horsewhip.

The narrator is the last of the patriarchs who take upon themselves the burden of defining Emily's life, and his violence toward her is the most subtle of all. His tone of incantatory reminiscence and nostalgic veneration seems free of the taint of horsewhip and edict. Yet a thoroughgoing contempt for the "ladies" who spy and pry and gossip out of their petty jealousy and curiosity is one of the clearest strands in the narrator's consciousness. Emily is exempted from the general indictment because she is a *real* lady—that is, eccentric, slightly crazy, obsolete, a "stubborn and coquettish decay," absurd but indulged; "dear, inescapable, impervious, tranquil, and perverse"; indeed, anything and everything but human.

Not only does "A Rose for Emily" expose the violence done to a woman by making her a lady; it also explores the particular form of power the victim gains from this position and can use on those who enact this violence. "A Rose for Emily" is concerned with the consequences of violence for both the violated and the violators. One of the most striking aspects of the story is the disparity between Miss Emily Grierson and the Emily to whom Faulkner gives his rose in ironic imitation of the chivalric behavior the story exposes. The form of Faulkner's title establishes a camaraderie between author and protagonist and signals that a distinction must be made between the story Faulkner is telling and the story the narrator is telling. This distinction is of major importance because it suggests, of course, that the narrator, looking through a patriarchal lens, does not see Emily at all but rather a figment of his own imagination created in conjunction with the cumulative imagination of the town: * * * nobody sees *Emily*. And because nobody sees *her,* she can literally get away with murder. Emily is characterized by her ability to understand and utilize the power that accrues to her from the fact that men do not see her but rather their concept of her: "'I have no taxes in Jefferson. Colonel Sartoris explained it to me. . . . Tobe! . . . Show these gentlemen out." Relying on the conventional assumptions about ladies who are expected to be neither reasonable nor in touch with reality, Emily presents an impregnable front that vanquishes the men "horse and foot, just as she had vanquished their fathers thirty years before." In spite of their "modern" ideas, this new generation, when faced with Miss Emily, are as much bound by the code of gentlemanly behavior as their fathers were ("They rose when she entered"). This code gives Emily a power that renders the gentlemen unable to function in a situation in which a lady neither sits down herself nor asks them to. They are brought to a "stumbling halt" and can do nothing when confronted with her refusal to engage in rational discourse. Their only recourse in the face of such eccentricity is to engage in behavior unbecoming to gentlemen, and Emily can count on their continuing to see themselves as gentlemen and her as a lady and on their returning a verdict of helpless noninterference.

It is in relation to Emily's disposal of Homer Barron, however, that Faulkner demonstrates most clearly the power of conventional assumptions about the nature of ladies to blind the town to what is going on and to allow Emily to murder with impunity. When Emily buys the poison, it never occurs to anyone that she intends to use it on Homer, so strong is the presumption that ladies when jilted commit suicide, not murder. And when her house begins to smell, the women blame it on the eccentricity of having a man servant rather than a woman, "as if a man—any man—could keep a kitchen properly." And then they hint that her eccentricity may have shaded over into madness, "remembering how old lady Wyatt, her great aunt, had gone completely crazy at last." The presumption of madness, that preeminently female response to bereavement, can be used to explain away much in the behavior of ladies whose activities seem a bit odd.

But even more pointed is what happens when the men try not to explain but to do something about the smell: "'Dammit, sir,' Judge Stevens said, 'will you accuse a lady to her face of smelling bad?'" But if a lady cannot be told that she smells, then the cause of the smell cannot be discovered and so her crime is "perfect." Clearly, the assumptions behind the Judge's outraged retort go beyond the myth that ladies are out of touch with reality. His outburst insists that it is the responsibility of gentlemen to make them so. Ladies must not be confronted with facts; they must be shielded from all that is unpleasant. Thus Colonel Sartoris remits Emily's taxes with a palpably absurd story, designed to protect her from an awareness of her poverty and her dependence on charity, and to protect him from having to confront her with it. And thus Judge Stevens will not confront Emily with the fact that her house stinks, though she is living in it and can hardly be unaware of the odor. Committed as they are to the myth that ladies and bad smells cannot coexist, these gentlemen insulate themselves from reality. And by defining a lady as a subhuman and hence sublegal entity, they have created a situation their laws can't touch. They have made it possible for Emily to be extra-legal: "'Why, of course,' the druggist said, 'If that's what you want. But the law requires you to tell what you are going to use it for.' Miss Emily just stared at him, her head tilted back in order to look him eye for eye, until he looked away and went and got the arsenic and wrapped it up." And, finally, they have created a situation in which they become the criminals: "So the next night, after midnight, four men crossed Miss Emily's lawn and slunk about the house like burglars." Above them, "her upright torso motionless as that of an idol," sits Emily, observing them act out their charade of chivalry. As they leave, she confronts them with the reality they are trying to protect her from: she turns on the light so that they may see her watching them. One can only wonder at the fact, and regret, that she didn't call the sheriff and have them arrested for trespassing.

Not only is "A Rose for Emily" a supreme analysis of what men do to women by making them ladies; it is also an exposure of how this act in turn defines and recoils upon men. This is the significance of the dynamic that Faulkner establishes between Emily and Jefferson. And it is equally the point of the dynamic implied between the tableau of Emily and her father and the tableau which greets the men who break down the door of that room in the region above the stairs. When the would-be "suitors" finally get into her father's house, they discover the consequences of his oppression of her, for the violence contained in the rotted corpse of Homer Barron is the mirror image of the violence represented in the tableau, the back-flung front door flung back with a vengeance. Having been consumed by her father, Emily in turn feeds off Homer Barron, becoming, after his death, suspiciously fat. Or, to put it another way, it is as if, after her father's death, she has reversed his act of incorporating her by incorporating and becoming him, metamorphosed from the slender figure in white to the obese figure in black whose hair is "a vigorous iron-gray, like the hair of an active man." She has taken into herself the violence in him which thwarted her and has reenacted it upon Homer Barron.

That final encounter, however, is not simply an image of the reciprocity of violence. Its power of definition also derives from its grotesqueness, which makes finally explicit the grotesqueness that has been latent in the description of Emily throughout the story: "Her skeleton was small and spare; perhaps that was why what would have been merely plumpness in another was obesity in her. She looked bloated, like a body long submerged in motionless water, and of that pallid hue. Her eyes, lost in the fatty ridges of her face, looked like two small pieces of coal pressed into a lump of dough." The impact of this description depends on the contrast it establishes between Emily's reality as a fat, bloated figure in black and the conventional image of a lady—expectations that are fostered in the town by its emblematic memory of Emily as a slender figure in white and in us by the narrator's tone of romantic invocation and by the passage itself. Were she not expected to look so different, were her skeleton not small and spare, Emily would not be so grotesque. Thus, the focus is on the grotesqueness that results when stereotypes are imposed upon reality. And the implication of this focus is that the real grotesque is the stereotype itself. If Emily is both lady and grotesque, then the syllogism must be completed thus: the idea of a lady is grotesque. So Emily is metaphor and mirror for the town of Jefferson; and when, at the end, the town folk finally discover who and what she is, they have in fact encountered who and what they are. * * * [T]he efforts to read "A Rose for Emily" as a parable of the relations between North and South, or as a conflict between an old order and a new, or as a story about the human relation to Time, don't work because the attempt to make Emily representative of such concepts stumbles over the fact that woman's condition is not the "human" condition.[2] To understand Emily's experience requires a primary awareness of the fact that she is a woman.

But, more important, Faulkner provides us with an image of retaliation. [Emily] does not simply acquiesce; she prefers to murder rather than to die. In this respect she is a welcome change from the image of woman as willing victim that fills the pages of our literature. * * * Nevertheless, Emily's action is still reaction. "A Rose for Emily" exposes the poverty of a situation in which turnabout is the only possibility and in which one's acts are neither self-generated nor self-determined but are simply a response to and a reflection of forces outside oneself. Though Emily may be proud, strong, and indomitable, her murder of Homer Barron is finally an indication of the severely limited nature of the power women can wrest from the system that oppresses them. * * * Emily's act * * * is possible only because it can be kept secret; and it can be kept secret only at the cost of exploiting her image as a lady. * * *

Patriarchal culture is based to a considerable extent on the argument that men and women are made for each other and on the conviction that "masculinity" and "feminity" are the natural reflection of that divinely ordained complement. Yet, if one reads * * * "A Rose for Emily" as [an] analys[i]s of the consequences of a massive differentiation of everything according to sex, one sees that in reality a sexist culture is one in which men and women are not simply incompatible but murderously so. * * * Emily murders Homer Barron because she must at any cost get a man. The * * * between cultural myth and cultural reality * * * suggest[s] that in this disparity is the ultimate grotesque.

NOTES

1. See *Faulkner in the University: Class Conferences at the University of Virginia 1957–1958,* edited by Frederick L. Gwynn and Joseph I. Blotner (Charlottesville: University of Virginia Press, 1959), 87–88; *Faulkner at Nagamo,* edited by Robert A. Jeliffe (Tokyo: Kenkyusha, 1956), 71.
2. For a sense of some of the difficulties involved in reading the story in these terms, I refer the reader to the collection of criticism edited by M. Thomas Inge, *A Rose for Emily* (Columbus, Ohio: Merrill, 1970).

GENE M. MOORE

Of Time and Its Mathematical Progression: Problems of Chronology in Faulkner's "A Rose for Emily"*

Over the past 30 years, no fewer than *eight* different chronologies have been proposed to account for the events occurring in William Faulkner's celebrated short story "A Rose for Emily."[1] These chronologies cover a span of 14 years (Miss Emily was born between 1850 and 1864, and died between 1924 and 1938), and they make use of many different kinds of evidence: not only internal temporal references and cross-references in the story, but also historical, biographical, canonical, and even forensic evidence. Given the amount of interest generated by this question and the range of evidence employed in the various arguments, it is remarkable that no one seems ever to have regarded the original manuscript as a possible source of chronological information; in fact, evidence from the manuscript makes it possible to solve some of the problems of Miss Emily's chronology by fixing the date of her father's death.

While critics have recognized the importance of time to a proper understanding of the story[,] * * * they have also complained, in strong and vivid language, of the difficulty of establishing a consistent chronology: "Faulkner destroys chronological time in his story" (Magalaner and Volpe, cited in Inge 63); he uses "a complicatedly disjunctive time scheme" (Wilson 56) that "twists chronology almost beyond recognition" (Sullivan 167); his technique is an "abandonment of chronology" (A. M. Wright, cited in Sullivan 167). Yet whether the story of Miss Emily Grierson is to be understood in terms of conflict between the North and the South, between the Old South and the New South, or between the "past" and the "present," for the sake of all these arguments it is vitally important to establish her own chronological place in the historical context of the passing generations. What dates are carved on Miss Emily's tombstone?

The task at hand has never been stated more simply than by William T. Going in the earliest of the chronologies: "By means of internal or external evidence, date the major events of Emily Grierson's life" (8). Yet in practice it is often difficult to distinguish "internal" from "external" evidence. Is evidence from the unrevised manuscript of "A Rose for Emily" internal or external? What about

---

*From *Studies in Short Fiction* 29 (Spring 1992): 195–204.   1. These chronologies were proposed by— in chronological order—Going (1958), Hagopian et al. (1964), Woodward (1966), McGlynn (1969), Nebeker (1970 and 1971), Wilson (1972), Brooks (1978), and Perry (1979). The first four were reprinted in Inge's 1970 casebook. Cleanth Brooks refers to five chronologies in this casebook (382n), but I have only been able to discover four, and my count is confirmed by the list in one of the suggestions for short papers at the end of Inge's volume (127). Helen E. Nebeker has proposed two different chronologies (the first in "Emily's Rose . . . : Thematic Implications" and the second in "Emily's Rose . . . : A Postscript" and "Chronology Revised"). Although different evidence is used, Nebeker's second chronology agrees with that proposed by Hagopian et al.

references to Judge Stevens or Colonel Sartoris in other works by Faulkner? In general, what constitutes legitimate chronological evidence? In cases of conflict, what forms of evidence should take precedence over others? The "internal" chronology of a given work may or may not prove to be consistent, and may or may not be attached (consistently or inconsistently) to a variety of "external" chronologies based on information such as references occurring in other works by the same author (*canonical* evidence), or what we know about the author's life (*biographical* evidence) or the context of history in general (*historical* evidence). In each case, specific chronological references can be either *absolute,* in the form of dates (such as the single reference to 1894 in "A Rose for Emily"); *relative* to other references (e.g., "the summer after her father's death," "thirty years before"); or *contextual,* establishing a measure of time with reference to historical or natural codes of temporality outside the text (e.g., allusions to the Civil War signify 1861–65; the graying of Miss Emily's hair is a gradual process; dead bodies decompose at a certain rate under certain conditions, etc.). The discrepancies among the eight chronologies are largely a result of underlying differences of opinion about the relative weights to be accorded these various kinds of evidence.

The specific difficulty of establishing a chronology for Miss Emily arises largely because the first half of her story is told essentially in reverse chronological order, and the events in it are described not in terms of dates or specific historical references, but most often in terms of her age at the time. Anchoring this "internal" chronology in history requires, in effect, that we find at least one point of attachment between "internal" references to Miss Emily's age or activities, and "external" references to dates or known historical events.

Most of the discussion in the eight chronologies has centered upon two problematic events in her life: the remission of her taxes by Colonel Sartoris in 1894 [paragraph 3], and the period of china-painting lessons "when she was about forty" [paragraph 49]. 1894 is the only date mentioned in the story, but its exact position in Miss Emily's life (i.e., her age at the time) is by no means certain. In the third paragraph of the story, reference is made to "that day in 1894 when Colonel Sartoris, the mayor . . . remitted her taxes, the dispensation dating from the death of her father on into perpetuity." ∗ ∗ ∗ This means, at the least, that her father died no later than 1894. We are told that at the time of her father's death Miss Emily had "got to be thirty and was still single" [paragraph 25]; and when she buys the poison about two years later, the narrator reminds us that "She was over thirty then" [paragraph 34]. The year 1864 is thus a *terminus ad quem* for Miss Emily's birth, and is respected as such by all the chronologists.

Some, however, have taken 1894 as the point of attachment between Emily's life and historical chronology, assuming that her taxes were remitted immediately following her father's death, and that he accordingly died that same year (McGlynn, Wilson). Her age at the time is taken as 30 (McGlynn) or 32 (Wilson), indicating that she was born in 1862 or 1864 and died in 1936 or 1938. However, "A Rose for Emily" was first published in 1930, creating a "glaring discrepancy" that led Helen E. Nebeker to revise her original chronology ("Chronology Revised" 471), and that in Menakhem Perry's opinion leads to "absurd conclusions" (344n26). Nebeker and Perry take 1930, the date of publication, as a *terminus ad quem* for Miss Emily's death, which means that the year 1856 becomes the corresponding *terminus* for her birth.[2]

The remission of Miss Emily's taxes is mentioned twice in the story: first as occurring in 1894, and second in connection with the period of her china-painting lessons "when she was about forty": the narrator ends the paragraph describing these lessons with the remark that "Meanwhile her taxes had been remitted" (128). Some chronologists have taken this "Meanwhile" to mean that Miss Emily must have been "about forty" in 1894, and that she was therefore born in 1854 and died in 1928 (Hagopian et al., Nebeker, "Emily's Rose . . . : A Postscript" and "Chronology Revised"). Brooks's chronology is a numerical compromise between those of Going and Hagopian et al., according to which Miss Emily, born in 1852, would have been 42 in 1894. Perry also takes this "Meanwhile" as indicative of simultaneity: "She was exempted from taxation in the period when she gave china-painting lessons" (344n26). In other words, much of the discrepancy among the various chronologies can be understood as a result of the choice of where to attach the historical "anchor" of the remission of taxes in 1894: to the death of Miss Emily's father when she was "over thirty," or to the china-painting period when she was "about forty"?

Surprisingly, what no one seems to have noticed or taken seriously is that in the original manuscript Faulkner assigned a different date to the remission of Miss Emily's taxes and a specific date to her father's death: the corresponding passage in the manuscript speaks of "that day in 1904 when Colonel Sartoris . . . remitted her taxes dating from the death of her father 16 years back, on into perpetuity" (Inge 8).[3] One can only speculate about why Faulkner found it necessary to shift the date of Colonel Sartoris's gallant action back ten years from 1904 to 1894, and to delete all reference to the "16 years" since the father's death. Perhaps 16 years seemed too long for Miss Emily to remain actively on the minds of city officials? In any event, it is clear that when Faulkner originally committed the story to paper, her taxes were remitted not in 1894 but in 1904, 16 years after the death of her father in 1888. Restoring Faulkner's alterations and deletions may seem to run counter to the editorial principle of respecting the author's final intentions; but keeping the original dates in mind can help untangle the story's chronology.

The altered date and the omission of the reference to "16 years back" in the typescript version need not mean that Faulkner had necessarily changed his mind about the date of Miss Emily's father's death. Had he moved it back the same 10 years, she would have to have been born before 1848 to have been over

2. The provisional futurism of a situation in which Miss Emily dies fictionally some years after the announcement of her death in the "real" world, as posited in half of the published chronologies (those of Woodward, McGlynn, Nebeker ["Emily's Rose . . . : Thematic Implications"], and Wilson), is not without literary precedent. * * * In the case of "A Rose for Emily," the "inconvenience" indeed exists only if one claims to identify the fictional world of Miss Emily with the historical world of William Faulkner; but this claim is at the origin of any attempt to set up a chronology.   3. This oversight is all the more remarkable in view of the fact that a quite legible reproduction of the first manuscript page was printed as an illustration in Inge's 1970 casebook, which all the later critics have cited as a reference.

30 by 1878, and would thus have been of the same generation as the Civil War veterans who attend her funeral. As Brooks noted,

> The "very old men—some in their brushed Confederate uniforms" who, at the funeral, talked "of Miss Emily as if she had been a contemporary of theirs, believing that they had danced with her and courted her" must have been a number of years older than she. (*WF: Toward Yoknapatawpha and Beyond* 383)[4]

However, in the earliest of the chronologies, William T. Going invoked Faulkner's authority to the effect that Miss Emily was born in 1850 and died in 1924, since 1924 was the date assigned to "A Rose for Emily" in Malcolm Cowley's Viking Portable edition of Faulkner's works (1946), in which Cowley noted editorially that dates were assigned "with the author's consent and later with his advice at doubtful points" (cited in Inge 51).[5] Going set the date of her father's death as early as 1882.

Manuscript evidence cannot solve all the chronological problems, since the china-painting period is defined not only in connection with Miss Emily's being "about forty," but also retrospectively, working backward from later events: the death of Colonel Sartoris, the visit of the tax delegation, and her own death. We are told that no one had seen the house's interior for "at least ten years" before she died [paragraph 1], and that the visit of the tax delegation (which may or may not have been the last visit before her death, but is in any case the only visit we are told about) took place "eight or ten years" after she ceased giving china-painting lessons [paragraph 5] and "almost ten years" after the death of Colonel Sartoris [paragraph 14].[6] In other words, she died at least 18 years after the last lessons were given: 18 years before her death at age 74, Miss Emily would have been 56 years old, so that if the lessons lasted for "a period of six or seven years" [paragraph 49], Miss Emily could not have been "about forty" at the time, but would instead have been about 50. Paul D. McGlynn has attempted to disregard this problem by suggesting that "Of course 'about forty' might well be a genteel euphemism for 'about fifty'" (Inge 91; cf. Wilson 59); but this suggestion still does not explain why the narrator would protect Miss Emily's age only at this particular point and not elsewhere. Would anyone wish to read the narrator's two references to her being "over thirty" as genteel euphemisms for "over forty," or the announcement of her "death at seventy-four" as a coded euphemism for 84? In effect, the chronology to be established by tracing the course of Miss Emily's life forward from the time of her father's death fails to square with the chronology to be derived retrospectively from the time of her own death.

Interpreting the reference to "at least ten years" as possibly allowing for as

---

4. On similar historical gounds, one could argue that the Homer Barron episode must be set much later, since the actual streets of Oxford were not paved until the 1920s (Cullen and Watkins 71, cited in Inge 17).   5. Cowley also acknowledged in his Introduction that "As one book leads into another, Faulkner sometimes falls into inconsistencies of detail." He added that "these errors are comparatively few and inconsequential. . . . I should judge that most of them are afterthoughts rather than oversights" (Cowley 7–8).   6. In the place of the reference to the china-painting lessons as having ceased "eight or ten years earlier" (120), the unrevised manuscript reads "6 or 7 years ago" (Faulkner, *Manuscripts* 189).

much as 20 years is also no solution, since the visit of the tax delegation is the peg from which the date of the smell "thirty years before" is hung. Internal references indicate that Homer Barron must have died when Miss Emily was about 33 or 34 years old: at least 40 years before her own death (equal to the "at least ten years" since the last visit plus the 30 years since the smell), and two years after her father's death, which occurred when she was already at least 30. A limit is thereby set to the range of time included in "at least": her last visit had to occur "at least ten years" and at most 12 years before her death, since if it occurred more than 12 years earlier, she would have been under 30 when her father died.

In summary, the chronologies can be divided roughly into two groups: one group—Woodward, McGlynn, Nebeker ("Emily's Rose . . . : Thematic Implications"), and Wilson—connects the tax remission of 1894 with her father's death (Emily is between 30 and 34 in 1894); while the other—Going, Hagopian et al., Nebeker ("Emily's Rose . . . : A Postscript" and "Chronology Revised"), Brooks, and Perry—links the reference to 1894 with the period of china-painting (i.e., Emily is "about forty," or between 39 and 42, in 1894). The first group tends to disregard the narrator's reference to the remission of taxes as being retroactive: "the dispensation dating from the death of her father on into perpetuity" [paragraph 3]. Taxes are collected annually—"On the first of the year they mailed her a tax notice" [paragraph 4]—so that if Miss Emily's taxes were remitted the same year her father died, the narrator's reference to the retroactive nature of the remission would appear to be unnecessary.

This much can be determined on the basis of "internal" references alone; but the references to Colonel Sartoris and to Judge Stevens lead us outside the story to look for external canonical evidence in the form of references to these gentlemen in other works by Faulkner. If Judge Stevens was already 80 years old and mayor at the time of the smell (which the chronologies date variously between 1884 and 1896), then he is probably too old to be Judge Lemuel Stevens, the father of Gavin Stevens, who is mentioned in Faulkner's late works: he would have been between 102 and 114 years old at the time of his death in 1918— perhaps not an altogether impossible age, but one remarkable enough to be worth mentioning. Nevertheless, most of the glossaries and indexes have identified the elderly Judge Stevens of "A Rose for Emily" with Judge Lemuel * * * .

Similar problems arise with the reference to a Colonel Sartoris who was mayor in 1894 and who died "almost ten years" before the visit of the tax delegation (and thus about 20 years before Miss Emily's death, when she was about 54). Once again, there is some doubt about which Colonel Sartoris is meant: Faulkner has described the early history of the Sartoris family more thoroughly than that of the Stevenses, so that it appears correspondingly more difficult to imagine a strange new Colonel Sartoris, unique to "A Rose for Emily" and unmentioned elsewhere, who could have been mayor in 1894. Faulkner's works mention two Colonel Sartorises: Colonel John Sartoris, who dies too early to have been Miss Emily's mayor in 1894, and his son Bayard—"the banker with his courtesy title acquired partly by inheritance and partly by propinquity" (Reivers 74)—who dies too late. * * *

However, the original date of 1904 for the mayoral edict may help to solve this problem as well, since young Bayard Sartoris could well have been mayor at that time. We are told in *The Reivers* of his propensity for passing edicts, although he is not specifically named as mayor; when his matched carriage horses are startled by a home-made automobile, "by the next night there was formally recorded into the archives of Jefferson a city ordinance against the operation of any mechanically propelled vehicle inside the corporate limits" (27–28); additional information in *The Reivers* makes it possible to date this incident as having occurred in 1904. The Colonel's tendency to govern by radical edict is mentioned in "A Rose for Emily" as well, since it was "he who fathered the edict that no Negro woman should appear on the streets without an apron" (par. 3).

In conclusion, the neglected manuscript evidence, by allowing us to fix the date of the death of Miss Emily's father in 1888, makes it possible to establish a chronology that is different from the eight that have been suggested previously (although it differs from that of Perry by only one year). Perhaps when Faulkner decided to move the time of Miss Emily's tax remission back by ten years, he simply failed to consider the consequences of this alteration for the rest of the chronology. Yet whether the year in question is 1894 or 1904, the internal inconsistency of the period of her china-painting remains, together with the canonical inconsistencies concerning the identities of Judge Stevens and Colonel Sartoris. The ancient Civil War veterans who try to remember Miss Emily are not alone in having to cope with the problem of "confusing time with its mathematical progression."

APPENDIX: A CHRONOLOGY FOR MISS EMILY GRIERSON

1856: Miss Emily is born; the narrator never mentions her birth directly, but his reference to "the day of her death at seventy-four" (127–28) defines the parameters of any chronology in terms of a span of 74 years.

1870–1879: The Grierson house is built "in the heavily lightsome style of the seventies" (119), thus presumably during the 1870s.

1888: Her father dies after "she got to be thirty" (123).

1889: She meets Homer Barron "the summer after her father's death" (124).

1890: She buys arsenic from the druggist "over a year after they had begun to say 'Poor Emily'. . . . She was over thirty then" (125). She poisons Homer Barron, who disappears "two years after her father's death"; a smell is noticed "a short time after" (122), which is also "thirty years before" the tax visit (121).

1893–1900: Miss Emily is "about forty"; she gives lessons in china-painting "for a period of six or seven years" (128).

1894: "Meanwhile" (119, 128) Colonel Sartoris, the mayor, remits her taxes.

1920: She is visited by a deputation of the Board of Aldermen "eight or ten years" after she stops giving china-painting lessons (120) and "almost ten years" (121) after the death of Colonel Sartoris.

1930: She dies "at least ten years" (119) since her last visit, presumably from the tax deputation; after her funeral, the room, "which no one had seen in forty years" (129), is opened.

WORKS CITED

Brooks, Cleanth. *William Faulkner: The Yoknapatawpha Country*. New Haven: Yale UP, 1963.

———. *William Faulkner: Toward Yoknapatawpha and Beyond*. New Haven: Yale UP, 1978.

Cowley, Malcolm. Introduction. *The Portable Faulkner*. New York: Viking, 1946. 1–24.

Cullen, John B., and Floyd C. Watkins. "Miss Emily." *Old Times in the Faulkner Country*. Chapel Hill: U of North Carolina P, 1961. 70–71. Rpt. in Inge 17–18.

Faulkner, William. *Collected Stories of William Faulkner*. New York: Random, 1950.

———. *Flags in the Dust*. New York: Random, 1973.

———. *Requiem for a Nun*. New York: Random, 1950.

———. *The Reivers*. New York: Random, 1962.

———. "A Rose for Emily." *Collected Stories* 119–30.

———. *The Unvanquished*. New York: Random, 1938.

———. *William Faulkner Manuscripts: These 13*. Ed. Noel Polk. New York: Garland, 1985. 188–214.

Ford, Margaret Patricia, and Suzanne Kincaid. *Who's Who in Faulkner*. N.p.: Louisiana State UP, 1963.

* * *

Going, William T. "Chronology in Teaching 'A Rose for Emily.'" *Exercise Exchange* 5 (February 1958): 8–11. Rpt. in Inge 50–53.

Hagopian, John V., W. Gordon Cunliffe, and Martin Dolch. "A Rose for Emily," *Insight I: Analyses of American Literature*. Frankfurt: Hirschgraben, 1964. 43–50. Rpt. in Inge 76–83.

Inge, M. Thomas. *William Faulkner: A Rose for Emily*. The Charles E. Merrill Literary Casebook Series. Columbus, OH: Merrill, 1970.

Kirk, Robert W., and Marvin Klotz. *Faulkner's People: A Complete Guide and Index to Characters in the Fiction of William Faulkner*. Berkeley: U of California P, 1963.

McGlynn, Paul D. "The Chronology of 'A Rose for Emily.'" *Studies in Short Fiction* 6 (1969): 461–62. Rpt. in Inge 90–92.

Nebeker, Helen E. "Emily's Rose of Love: Thematic Implications of Point of View in Faulkner's 'A Rose for Emily.'" *Bulletin of the Rocky Mountain Modern Language Association* 24 (1970): 3–13.

———. "Emily's Rose of Love: A Postscript." *Bulletin of the Rocky Mountain Modern Language Association* 24 (1970): 190–91.

———. "Chronology Revised." *Studies in Short Fiction* 8 (1971): 471–73.

Perry, Menakhem. "Literary Dynamics: How the Order of a Text Creates its Meanings [With an Analysis of Faulkner's 'A Rose for Emily']." *Poetics Today* 1:1–2 (Autumn 1979): 35–64, 311–61.

Runyan, Harry. *A Faulkner Glossary*. New York: Citadel, 1964.

Sullivan, Ruth. "The Narrator in 'A Rose for Emily.'" *Journal of Narrative Technique* 1 (1971): 159–78.

Wilson, G. R., Jr. "The Chronology of Faulkner's 'A Rose for Emily' Again." *Notes on Mississippi Writers* 5 (Fall 1972): 56, 44, 58–62.

Woodward, Robert H. "The Chronology of 'A Rose for Emily.'" *Exercise Exchange* 8 (March 1966): 17–19. Rpt. in Inge 84–86.

Willow D. Crystal
Professor Akerley
English 1002
9 May 1998

"One of us . . .": Concepts of the Private and the Public
in William Faulkner's "A Rose for Emily"

Throughout "A Rose for Emily," William Faulkner introduces a
tension between what is private, or belongs to the individual, and what
is public, or the possession of the group. "When Miss Emily Grierson
died," the tale begins,

> our whole town went to her funeral: the men through a sort of
> respectful affection for a fallen monument, the women mostly
> out of curiosity to see the inside of her house. . . . (119)

The men of the small town of Jefferson, Mississippi, are motivated to
attend Miss Emily's funeral for "public" reasons; the women, to see
"the inside of her house," that private realm which has remained
inaccessible for "at least ten years."

This opposition of the private with the public has intrigued
critics of Faulkner's tale since the story was first published.
Distinctions between the private and the public are central to Lawrence
R. Rodgers's argument in his essay "'We all said, "she will kill
herself"': The Narrator / Detective in William Faulkner's 'A Rose for
Emily.'" The very concept of the detective genre demands that there "be
concealed facts . . . [which] must become clear in the end" (Rodgers
119), private actions which become public knowledge. In her feminist
tribute--"A Rose for 'A Rose for Emily'"--Judith Fetterley uses the
private / public dichotomy to demonstrate the "grotesque reality"
(Fetterley 34) of the patriarchal social system in Faulkner's story.
According to Fetterley, Miss Emily's "*private* life becomes a *public*
document that the town folk feel free to interpret at will" (36,
emphasis added). Thus, while critics such as Rodgers and Fetterley
offer convincing--if divergent--interpretations of "A Rose for Emily,"
it is necessary first to understand in Faulkner's eerie and enigmatic
story the relationship between the public and the private, and the
consequences of this relationship within the story and on the reader.

The most explicit illustration of the opposition between the public and the private occurs in the social and economic interactions between the town of Jefferson, represented by the narrator's "we," and the reclusive Miss Emily. "Alive," the narrator explains, "Miss Emily had been a tradition, a duty, and a care; a sort of hereditary obligation upon the town, dating from that day in 1894 when Colonel Sartoris, the mayor, . . . remitted her taxes, the dispensation dating from the death of her father on into perpetuity" (120). Ironically (and this is one of the prime examples of the complexity of the relationship of private and public in the story), the price of privacy for Miss Emily becomes the loss of that very privacy. Despite--or perhaps because of--her refusal to buy into the community, the citizens of Jefferson determine that it is their "duty," their "hereditary obligation," to oversee her activities. When, for example, Miss Emily's house begins to emit an unpleasant smell, the town officials decide to solve the problem by dusting her property with lime. When she refuses to provide a reason why she wants to buy poison, the druggist scrawls "'For rats'" (126) across the package, literally and protectively overwriting her silence.

Arguably, the townspeople's actions serve to protect Miss Emily's privacy--by preserving her perceived gentility--as much as they effectively destroy it with their intrusive zeal. But in this very act of protection they reaffirm the town's proprietary relation to the public "monument" which is Miss Emily and, consequently, reinforce her inability to make decisions for herself.

While the communal narrator and Miss Emily appear to be polar opposites--one standing for the public while the other fiercely defends her privacy--the two are united when an outsider such as Homer Barron appears in their midst. If Miss Emily serves as a representation--an icon, an inactive "tableau," an "idol"--of traditional antebellum southern values, then Homer represents all that is new and different. A "'day laborer'" (124) from the North, Homer comes to Jefferson to pave the sidewalks, a task which itself suggests the modernization of the town.

The secret and destructive union between these two representational figures implies a complex relationship between the private with the public. When Miss Emily kills Homer and confines his remains to a room in her attic, where, according to Lawrence R. Rodgers, "she has been allowed to carry on her illicit love affair in post-mortem privacy" (119), this grotesque act ironically suggests that she has capitulated to the code of gentility that Jefferson imagines her to embody. This code demands the end of a romantic affair which some residents deemed "a disgrace to the town and a bad example to the young people" (126), thus placing traditions and the good of the community above Miss Emily's own wishes. Through its insistence on Miss Emily's symbolic relation to a bygone era, the town--via the narrator-- becomes "an unknowing driving force behind Emily's crime" (Rodgers 120). Her private act is both the result of and a support for public norms and expectations.

At the same time, however, the act of murder also marks Miss Emily's corruption of that very code. By killing Homer in private, Miss Emily deliberately flouts public norms, and by eluding explicit detection until after her own death, she asserts the primacy of the private. The murder of the outsider in their midst thus leads Miss Emily to achieve paradoxically both a more complete privacy--a marriage of sorts without a husband--and a role in the preservation of the community.

Yet the elaborate relationship between Jefferson and Miss Emily is not the only way in which Homer's murder may be understood as a casualty of the tension between the public and the private. When Miss Emily kills Homer, Rodgers contends,

> from the town's point of view, it was the best thing. . . .
> Homer represents the kind of unwelcome resident and
> ineligible mate the town wants to repel if it is to preserve
> its traditional arrangements. (125)

The people of Jefferson and Miss Emily join in a struggle to "repel" the outside and to ensure a private, inner order and tradition. This complicity creates intriguing parallels among the illicit, fatal union of Homer and Miss Emily, the reunion of the North and the South following the Civil War. In this reformulation of the private and the public, Miss Emily becomes, as Fetterley notes, a "metaphor and mirror for the town of Jefferson" (43). Miss Emily's honor is the townspeople's honor, her preservation their preservation.

Finally, the parallels between Miss Emily's secretive habits and the narrator's circuitous presentation of the story lead to a third dimension of the negotiations between the private and the public in "A Rose for Emily," a dimension in which Faulkner as author and the collective "we" as narrator confront their public consumers, the readers. Told by the anonymous narrator as if retrospectively, "A Rose for Emily" skips forward and backward in time, omitting details and deferring revelations to such a degree that many critics have gone to extreme lengths to establish reliable chronologies for the tale.[1] The much-debated "we" remains anonymous and unreachable throughout the tale--maintaining a virtually unbreachable privacy--even as it invites the public (the reader) to participate in the narrator's acts of detection and revelation. "The dramatic distance on display here," Rodgers observes,

> provides an ironic layer to the narrative. As the observers
> of the conflict between the teller-of-tale's desire to solve
> the curious mysteries that surround Emily's life--indeed, his
> [*sic*] complicity in shaping them--and his undetective-like
> detachment from her crimes, readers occupy the tantalizing
> position of having insight into unraveling the mystery which
> the narrator lacks. (120-21)

The reader is thus a member of the communal "we"--party to the narrator's investigation and Jefferson's voyeuristic obsession with Miss Emily--but also apart, removed to a plane from which "insight" into and observation of the narrator's own actions and motives become possible. The reader, just like Miss Emily, Homer, and the town of Jefferson itself, becomes a crucial element in the tension between the public and the private.

Thus, public and private are, in the end, far from exclusive categories. And for all of its literal as well as figurative insistence on opposition and either / or structures, Faulkner's "A Rose for Emily" enacts the provocative idea of being "[o]ne of us" (Faulkner 130), of being both an individual *and* a member of a community, both a private entity *and* a participant in the public sphere.

[1]Gene M. Moore's essay "Of Time and Its Mathematical Progression: Problems of Chronology in Faulkner's 'A Rose for Emily'" documents the proliferation of such chronologies.

Works Cited

Faulkner, William. "A Rose for Emily." *Collected Stories of William Faulkner.* New York: Random, 1950. 119-30.

Fetterley, Judith. "A Rose for 'A Rose for Emily.'" *The Resisting Reader: A Feminist Approach to American Fiction.* Bloomington: Indiana UP, 1978. 34-45.

Moore, Gene M. "Of Time and Its Mathematical Progression: Problems of Chronology in Faulkner's 'A Rose for Emily.'" *Studies in Short Fiction* 29 (Spring 1992): 195-204.

Rodgers, Lawrence R. "'We all said, "she will kill herself"': The Narrator / Detective in William Faulkner's 'A Rose for Emily.'" *Clues: A Journal of Detection* 16 (1995): 117-29.

Evaluating Fiction

To evaluate a work of literature—to determine its worth or quality—is one of the most fundamental, significant, and difficult activities in literary study. It is impossible to dodge such questions as "Is this story good?" "Is it great?" "Is it better than that one? . . . that other one?" "Is it worth reading? studying?" It is equally impossible to answer such questions definitively, for all time and for all readers.

It is, however, usually possible to answer the question "Do you like this story?" and often possible to answer "Do you like this one more than or less than that other?" Whether you like a story or not when you first read it is therefore probably the proper place to *begin.* But it is a dangerous place to *stop* the process of evaluation. If our appreciation and understanding of literature is to grow, and if we are not content simply to accept without question the authority of "those who know best," we must learn to isolate, analyze, and articulate what it is *we* like about a story and to search out in our minds and experience the reasons *we* like it. We must listen to other readers' responses too—those of our classmates, professors, professional critics like those in the previous chapter—responses that may reinforce our own, may show us things to appreciate in the story that we missed, or may challenge the viability of our reasons, if not that of our responses.

The story that follows has aroused considerable controversy. After you read it, and *before* you read the two responses and evaluations that follow, take some time—maybe enough to reread the story—and consider your own response and evaluation, perhaps writing them down. Then go on to what the other readers say.

RICHARD CONNELL

The Most Dangerous Game

"Off there to the right—somewhere—is a large island," said Whitney. "It's rather a mystery—"

"What island is it?" Rainsford asked.

"The old charts call it 'Ship-Trap Island,' " Whitney replied. "A suggestive name, isn't it? Sailors have a curious dread of the place. I don't know why. Some superstition—"

"Can't see it," remarked Rainsford, trying to peer through the dank tropical night that was palpable as it pressed its thick warm blackness in upon the yacht.

"You've good eyes," said Whitney, with a laugh, "and I've seen you pick off a moose moving in the brown fall bush at four hundred yards, but even you can't see four miles or so through a moonless Caribbean night."

"Nor four yards," admitted Rainsford. "Ugh! It's like moist black velvet."

"It will be light in Rio," promised Whitney. "We should make it in a few days. I hope the jaguar guns have come from Purdey's. We should have some good hunting up the Amazon. Great sport, hunting."

"The best sport in the world," agreed Rainsford.

"For the hunter," amended Whitney. "Not for the jaguar."

"Don't talk rot, Whitney," said Rainsford. "You're a big-game hunter, not a philosopher. Who cares how a jaguar feels?"

"Perhaps the jaguar does," observed Whitney.

"Bah! They've no understanding."

"Even so, I rather think they understand one thing—fear. The fear of pain and the fear of death."

"Nonsense," laughed Rainsford. "This hot weather is making you soft, Whitney. Be a realist. The world is made up of two classes—the hunters and the huntees. Luckily, you and I are hunters. Do you think we've passed that island yet?"

"I can't tell in the dark. I hope so."

"Why?" asked Rainsford.

"The place has a reputation—a bad one."

"Cannibals?" suggested Rainsford.

"Hardly. Even cannibals wouldn't live in such a God-forsaken place. But it's gotten into sailor lore, somehow. Didn't you notice that the crew's nerves seemed a bit jumpy today?"

"They were a bit strange, now you mention it. Even Captain Nielsen—"

"Yes, even that tough-minded old Swede, who'd go up to the devil himself and ask him for a light. Those fishy blue eyes held a look I never saw there before. All I could get out of him was: 'This place has an evil name among sea-faring men, sir.' Then he said to me, very gravely: 'Don't you feel anything?'—as if the air about us was actually poisonous. Now, you mustn't laugh when I tell you this—I did feel something like a sudden chill.

"There was no breeze. The sea was as flat as a plate-glass window. We were drawing near the island then. What I felt was a—a mental chill; a sort of sudden dread."

"Pure imagination," said Rainsford. "One superstitious sailor can taint the whole ship's company with his fear."

"Maybe. But sometimes I think sailors have an extra sense that tells them when they are in danger. Sometimes I think evil is a tangible thing—with wave lengths, just as sound and light have. An evil place can, so to speak, broadcast vibrations of evil. Anyhow, I'm glad we're getting out of this zone. Well, I think I'll turn in now, Rainsford."

"I'm not sleepy," said Rainsford. "I'm going to smoke another pipe up on the after deck."

"Good night, then, Rainsford. See you at breakfast."

"Right. Good night, Whitney."

There was no sound in the night as Rainsford sat there, but the muffled throb of the engine that drove the yacht swiftly through the darkness, and the swish and ripple of the wash of the propeller.

Rainsford, reclining in a steamer chair, indolently puffed on his favorite brier. The sensuous drowsiness of the night was on him. "It's so dark," he thought, "that I could sleep without closing my eyes; the night would be my eyelids—"

An abrupt sound startled him. Off to the right he heard it, and his ears, expert in such matters, could not be mistaken. Again he heard the sound, and again. Somewhere, off in the blackness, some one had fired a gun three times.

Rainsford sprang up and moved quickly to the rail, mystified. He strained his eyes in the direction from which the reports had come, but it was like trying to see through a blanket. He leaped upon the rail and balanced himself there, to get greater elevation; his pipe, striking a rope, was knocked from his mouth. He lunged for it; a short, hoarse cry came from his lips as he realized he had reached too far and had lost his balance. The cry was pinched off short as the bloodwarm waters of the Caribbean Sea closed over his head.

He struggled up to the surface and tried to cry out, but the wash from the speeding yacht slapped him in the face and the salt water in his open mouth made him gag and strangle. Desperately he struck out with strong strokes after the receding lights of the yacht, but he stopped before he had swum fifty feet. A certain cool-headedness had come to him; it was not the first time he had been in a tight place. There was a chance that his cries could be heard by some one aboard the yacht, but that chance was slender, and grew more slender as the yacht raced on. He wrestled himself out of his clothes, and shouted with all his power. The lights of the yacht became faint and ever-vanishing fireflies; then they were blotted out entirely by the night.

Rainsford remembered the shots. They had come from the right, and doggedly he swam in that direction, swimming with slow, deliberate strokes, conserving his strength. For a seemingly endless time he fought the sea. He began to count his strokes; he could do possibly a hundred more and then—

Rainsford heard a sound. It came out of the darkness, a high screaming sound, the sound of an animal in an extremity of anguish and terror.

He did not recognize the animal that made the sound; he did not try to; with fresh vitality he swam toward the sound. He heard it again; then it was cut short by another noise, crisp, staccato.

"Pistol shot," muttered Rainsford, swimming on.

Ten minutes of determined effort brought another sound to his ears—the most welcome he had ever heard—the muttering and growling of the sea breaking on a rocky shore. He was almost on the rocks before he saw them; on a night less calm he would have been shattered against them. With his remaining strength he dragged himself from the swirling waters. Jagged crags appeared to jut into the opaqueness; he forced himself upward, hand over hand. Gasping, his hands raw, he reached a flat place at the top. Dense jungle came down to the very edge of the cliffs. What perils that tangle of trees and underbrush might hold for him did not concern Rainsford just then. All he knew was that he was safe from his enemy, the sea, and that utter weariness was on him. He flung himself down at the jungle edge and tumbled headlong into the deepest sleep of his life.

When he opened his eyes he knew from the position of the sun that it was late in the afternoon. Sleep had given him new vigor; a sharp hunger was picking at him. He looked about him, almost cheerfully.

"Where there are pistol shots, there are men. Where there are men, there is food," he thought. But what kind of men, he wondered, in so forbidding a place? An unbroken front of snarled and ragged jungle fringed the shore.

40   He saw no sign of a trail through the closely knit web of weeds and trees; it was easier to go along the shore, and Rainsford floundered along by the water. Not far from where he had landed, he stopped.

Some wounded thing, by the evidence a large animal, had thrashed about in the underbrush; the jungle weeds were crushed down and the moss was lacerated; one patch of weeds was stained crimson. A small, glittering object not far away caught Rainsford's eye and he picked it up. It was an empty cartridge.

"A twenty-two," he remarked. "That's odd. It must have been a fairly large animal too. The hunter had his nerve with him to tackle it with a light gun. It's clear that the brute put up a fight. I suppose the first three shots I heard was when the hunter flushed his quarry and wounded it. The last shot was when he trailed it here and finished it."

He examined the ground closely and found what he had hoped to find—the print of hunting boots. They pointed along the cliff in the direction he had been going. Eagerly, he hurried along, now slipping on a rotten log or a loose stone, but making headway; night was beginning to settle down on the island.

Bleak darkness was blacking out the sea and jungle when Rainsford sighted the lights. He came upon them as he turned a crook in the coast line, and his first thought was that he had come upon a village, for there were many lights. But as he forged along he saw to his great astonishment that all the lights were in one enormous building—a lofty structure with pointed towers plunging upward into the gloom. His eyes made out the shadowy outlines of a palatial château; it was set on a high bluff, and on three sides of it cliffs dived down to where the sea licked greedy lips in the shadows.

45   "Mirage," thought Rainsford. But it was no mirage, he found, when he opened the tall spiked iron gate. The stone steps were real enough; the massive door with a leering gargoyle for a knocker was real enough; yet about it all hung an air of unreality.

He lifted the knocker, and it creaked up stiffly, as if it had never before been used. He let it fall, and it startled him with its booming loudness. He thought he heard steps within; the door remained closed. Again Rainsford lifted the heavy knocker, and let it fall. The door opened then, opened as suddenly as if it were on a spring, and Rainsford stood blinking in the river of glaring gold light that poured out. The first thing Rainsford's eyes discerned was the largest man Rainsford had ever seen—a gigantic creature, solidly made and blackbearded to the waist. In his hand the man held a long-barreled revolver, and he was pointing it straight at Rainsford's heart.

Out of the snarl of beard two small eyes regarded Rainsford.

"Don't be alarmed," said Rainsford, with a smile which he hoped was disarming. "I'm no robber. I fell off a yacht. My name is Sanger Rainsford of New York City."

The menacing look in the eyes did not change. The revolver pointed as rigidly as if the giant were a statue. He gave no sign that he understood Rainsford's words, or that he had even heard them. He was dressed in uniform, a black uniform trimmed with gray astrakhan.

"I'm Sanger Rainsford of New York," Rainsford began again. "I fell off a yacht. 50 I am hungry."

The man's only answer was to raise with his thumb the hammer of his revolver. Then Rainsford saw the man's free hand go to his forehead in a military salute, and he saw him click his heels together and stand at attention. Another man was coming down the broad marble steps, an erect, slender man in evening clothes. He advanced to Rainsford and held out his hand.

In a cultivated voice marked by a slight accent that gave it added precision and deliberateness, he said: "It is a very great pleasure and honor to welcome Mr. Sanger Rainsford, the celebrated hunter, to my home."

Automatically Rainsford shook the man's hand.

"I've read your book about hunting snow leopards in Tibet, you see" explained the man. "I am General Zaroff."

Rainsford's first impression was that the man was singularly handsome; his 55 second was that there was an original, almost bizarre quality about the general's face. He was a tall man past middle age, for his hair was a vivid white; but his thick eyebrows and pointed military mustache were as black as the night from which Rainsford had come. His eyes, too, were black and very bright. He had high cheek bones, a sharp-cut nose, a spare, dark face, the face of a man used to giving orders, the face of an aristocrat. Turning to the giant in uniform, the general made a sign. The giant put away his pistol, saluted, withdrew.

"Ivan is an incredibly strong fellow," remarked the general, "but he has the misfortune to be deaf and dumb. A simple fellow, but, I'm afraid, like all his race, a bit of a savage."

"Is he Russian?"

"He is a Cossack," said the general, and his smile showed red lips and pointed teeth. "So am I."

"Come," he said, "we shouldn't be chatting here. We can talk later. Now you want clothes, food, rest. You shall have them. This is a most restful spot."

Ivan had reappeared, and the general spoke to him with lips that moved but 60 gave forth no sound.

"Follow Ivan, if you please, Mr. Rainsford," said the general. "I was about to have my dinner when you came. I'll wait for you. You'll find that my clothes will fit you, I think."

It was to a huge, beam-ceilinged bedroom with a canopied bed big enough for six men that Rainsford followed the silent giant. Ivan laid out an evening suit, and Rainsford, as he put it on, noticed that it came from a London tailor who ordinarily cut and sewed for none below the rank of duke.

The dining room to which Ivan conducted him was in many ways remarkable. There was a medieval magnificence about it; it suggested a baronial hall of feudal times with its oaken panels, its high ceiling, its vast refectory table where two-score men could sit down to eat. About the hall were the mounted heads of many animals—lions, tigers, elephants, moose, bears; larger or more perfect specimens Rainsford had never seen. At the great table the general was sitting, alone.

"You'll have a cocktail, Mr. Rainsford," he suggested. The cocktail was surpassingly good; and, Rainsford noted, the table appointments were of the finest—the linen, the crystal, the silver, the china.

65   They were eating *borsch,* the rich, red soup with whipped cream so dear to Russian palates. Half apologetically General Zaroff said: "We do our best to preserve the amenities of civilization here. Please forgive any lapses. We are well off the beaten track, you know. Do you think the champagne has suffered from its long ocean trip?"

"Not in the least," declared Rainsford. He was finding the general a most thoughtful and affable host, a true cosmopolite. But there was one small trait of the general's that made Rainsford uncomfortable. Whenever he looked up from his plate he found the general studying him, appraising him narrowly.

"Perhaps," said General Zaroff, "you were surprised that I recognized your name. You see, I read all books on hunting published in English, French, and Russian. I have but one passion in my life, Mr. Rainsford, and it is the hunt."

"You have some wonderful heads here," said Rainsford as he ate a particularly well cooked filet mignon. "That Cape buffalo is the largest I ever saw."

"Oh, that fellow. Yes, he was a monster."

70   "Did he charge you?"

"Hurled me against a tree," said the general. "Fractured my skull. But I got the brute."

"I've always thought," said Rainsford, "that the Cape buffalo is the most dangerous of all big game."

For a moment the general did not reply; he was smiling his curious red-lipped smile. Then he said slowly: "No. You are wrong, sir. The Cape buffalo is not the most dangerous big game." He sipped his wine. "Here in my preserve on this island," he said in the same slow tone, "I hunt more dangerous game."

Rainsford expressed his surprise. "Is there big game on this island?"

75   The general nodded. "The biggest."

"Really?"

"Oh, it isn't here naturally, of course. I have to stock the island."

"What have you imported, general?" Rainsford asked. "Tigers?"

The general smiled. "No," he said. "Hunting tigers ceased to interest me some years ago. I exhausted their possibilities, you see. No thrill left in tigers, no real danger. I live for danger, Mr. Rainsford."

80   The general took from his pocket a gold cigarette case and offered his guest a long black cigarette with a silver tip; it was perfumed and gave off a smell like incense.

"We will have some capital hunting, you and I," said the general. "I shall be most glad to have your society."

"But what game—" began Rainsford.

"I'll tell you," said the general. "You will be amused, I know. I think I may say, in all modesty, that I have done a rare thing. I have invented a new sensation. May I pour you another glass of port, Mr. Rainsford?"

"Thank you, general."

The general filled both glasses, and said: "God makes some men poets. Some He makes kings, some beggars. Me He made a hunter. My hand was made for the trigger, my father said. He was a very rich man with a quarter of a million acres in the Crimea, and he was an ardent sportsman. When I was only five years old he gave me a little gun, specially made in Moscow for me, to shoot sparrows with. When I shot some of his prize turkeys with it, he did not punish me; he complimented me on my marksmanship. I killed my first bear in the Caucasus when I was ten. My whole life has been one prolonged hunt. I went into the army—it was expected of noblemen's sons—and for a time commanded a division of Cossack cavalry, but my real interest was always the hunt. I have hunted every kind of game in every land. It would be impossible for me to tell you how many animals I have killed."

The general puffed at his cigarette.

"After the debacle in Russia[1] I left the country, for it was imprudent for an officer of the Czar to stay there. Many noble Russians lost everything. I, luckily, had invested heavily in American securities, so I shall never have to open a tea room in Monte Carlo or drive a taxi in Paris. Naturally, I continued to hunt—grizzlies in your Rockies, crocodiles in the Ganges, rhinoceroses in East Africa. It was in Africa that the Cape buffalo hit me and laid me up for six months. As soon as I recovered I started for the Amazon to hunt jaguars, for I had heard they were unusually cunning. They weren't." The Cossack sighed. "They were no match at all for a hunter with his wits about him, and a high-powered rifle. I was bitterly disappointed. I was lying in my tent with a splitting headache one night when a terrible thought pushed its way into my mind. Hunting was beginning to bore me! And hunting, remember, had been my life. I have heard that in America business men often go to pieces when they give up the business that has been their life."

"Yes, that's so," said Rainsford.

The general smiled. "I had no wish to go to pieces," he said. "I must do something. Now, mine is an analytical mind, Mr. Rainsford. Doubtless that is why I enjoy the problems of the chase."

"No doubt, General Zaroff."

"So," continued the general, "I asked myself why the hunt no longer fascinated me. You are much younger than I am, Mr. Rainsford, and have not hunted as much, but you perhaps can guess the answer."

"What was it?"

85

90

1. The Revolution of 1917, which overthrew the czar and prepared the way for Communist rule.

"Simply this: hunting had ceased to be what you call 'a sporting proposition.' It had become too easy. I always got my quarry. Always. There is no greater bore than perfection."

The general lit a fresh cigarette.

95   "No animal had a chance with me any more. That is no boast; it is a mathematical certainty. The animal had nothing but his legs and his instinct. Instinct is no match for reason. When I thought of this it was a tragic moment for me, I can tell you."

Rainsford leaned across the table, absorbed in what his host was saying.

"It came to me as an inspiration what I must do," the general went on.

"And that was?"

The general smiled the quiet smile of one who had faced an obstacle and surmounted it with success. "I had to invent a new animal to hunt," he said.

100   "A new animal? You're joking."

"Not at all," said the general. "I never joke about hunting. I needed a new animal. I found one. So I bought this island, built this house, and here I do my hunting. The island is perfect for my purposes—there are jungles with a maze of trails in them, hills, swamps—"

"But the animal, General Zaroff?"

"Oh," said the general, "it supplies me with the most exciting hunting in the world. No other hunting compares with it for an instant. Every day I hunt, and I never grow bored now, for I have a quarry with which I can match my wits."

Rainsford's bewilderment showed in his face.

105   "I wanted the ideal animal to hunt," explained the general. "So I said: 'What are the attributes of an ideal quarry?' And the answer was, of course: 'It must have courage, cunning, and, above all, it must be able to reason.' "

"But no animal can reason," objected Rainsford.

"My dear fellow," said the general, "there is one that can."

"But you can't mean—" gasped Rainsford.

"And why not?"

110   "I can't believe you are serious, General Zaroff. This is a grisly joke."

"Why should I not be serious? I am speaking of hunting."

"Hunting? Good God, General Zaroff, what you speak of is murder."

The general laughed with entire good nature. He regarded Rainsford quizzically. "I refuse to believe that so modern and civilized a young man as you seem to be harbors romantic ideas about the value of human life. Surely your experiences in the war—"

"Did not make me condone cold-blooded murder," finished Rainsford stiffly.

115   Laughter shook the general. "How extraordinarily droll you are!" he said. "One does not expect nowadays to find a young man of the educated class, even in America, with such a naïve, and, if I may say so, mid-Victorian point of view. It's like finding a snuff-box in a limousine. Ah, well, doubtless you had Puritan ancestors. So many Americans appear to have had. I'll wager you'll forget your notions when you go hunting with me. You've a genuine new thrill in store for you, Mr. Rainsford."

"Thank you, I'm a hunter, not a murderer."

"Dear me," said the general, quite unruffled, "again that unpleasant word. But I think I can show you that your scruples are quite ill founded."

"Yes?"

"Life is for the strong, to be lived by the strong, and, if need be, taken by the strong. The weak of the world were put here to give the strong pleasure. I am strong. Why should I not use my gift? If I wish to hunt, why should I not? I hunt the scum of the earth—sailors from tramp ships—lascars, blacks, Chinese, whites, mongrels—a thoroughbred horse or hound is worth more than a score of them."

"But they are men," said Rainsford hotly.   120

"Precisely," said the general. "That is why I use them. It gives me pleasure. They can reason, after a fashion. So they are dangerous."

"But where do you get them?"

The general's left eyelid fluttered down in a wink. "This island is called Ship-Trap," he answered. "Sometimes an angry god of the high seas sends them to me. Sometimes, when Providence is not so kind, I help Providence a bit. Come to the window with me."

Rainsford went to the window and looked out toward the sea.

"Watch! Out there!" exclaimed the general, pointing into the night. Rains-   125
ford's eyes saw only blackness, and then, as the general pressed a button, far out to sea Rainsford saw the flash of lights.

The general chuckled. "They indicate a channel," he said, "where there's none: giant rocks with razor edges crouch like a sea monster with wide-open jaws. They can crush a ship as easily as I crush this nut." He dropped a walnut on the hardwood floor and brought his heel grinding down on it. "Oh, yes," he said, casually, as if in answer to a question, "I have electricity. We try to be civilized here."

"Civilized? And you shoot down men?"

A trace of anger was in the general's black eyes, but it was there for but a second, and he said, in his most pleasant manner: "Dear me, what a righteous young man you are! I assure you I do not do the thing you suggest. That would be barbarous. I treat these visitors with every consideration. They get plenty of good food and exercise. They get into splendid physical condition. You shall see for yourself tomorrow."

"What do you mean?"

"We'll visit my training school," smiled the general. "It's in the cellar. I have   130
about a dozen pupils down there now. They're from the Spanish bark San Lucar that had the bad luck to go on the rocks out there. A very inferior lot, I regret to say. Poor specimens and more accustomed to the deck than to the jungle."

He raised his hand, and Ivan, who served as waiter, brought thick Turkish coffee. Rainsford, with an effort, held his tongue in check.

"It's a game, you see," pursued the general blandly. "I suggest to one of them that we go hunting. I give him a supply of food and an excellent hunting knife. I give him three hours' start. I am to follow, armed only with a pistol of the smallest caliber and range. If my quarry eludes me for three whole days, he wins the game. If I find him"—the general smiled—"he loses."

"Suppose he refuses to be hunted?"

"Oh," said the general, "I give him his option, of course. He need not play that game if he doesn't wish to. If he does not wish to hunt, I turn him over to Ivan. Ivan once had the honor of serving as official knouter to the Great White Czar,[2] and he has his own ideas of sport. Invariably, Mr. Rainsford, invariably they choose the hunt."

135   "And if they win?"

The smile on the general's face widened. "To date I have not lost," he said.

Then he added, hastily: "I don't wish you to think me a braggart, Mr. Rainsford. Many of them afford only the most elementary sort of problem. Occasionally I strike a tartar. One almost did win. I eventually had to use the dogs."

"The dogs?"

"This way, please. I'll show you."

140   The general steered Rainsford to a window. The lights from the windows sent a flickering illumination that made grotesque patterns on the courtyard below, and Rainsford could see moving about there a dozen or so huge black shapes; as they turned toward him, their eyes glittered greenly.

"A rather good lot, I think," observed the general. "They are let out at seven every night. If anyone should try to get into my house—or out of it—something extremely regrettable would occur to him." He hummed a snatch of song from the Folies Bergère.[3]

"And now," said the general, "I want to show you my new collection of heads. Will you come with me to the library?"

"I hope," said Rainsford, "that you will excuse me tonight, General Zaroff. I'm really not feeling at all well."

"Ah, indeed?" the general inquired solicitously. "Well, I suppose that's only natural, after your long swim. You need a good, restful night's sleep. Tomorrow you'll feel like a new man, I'll wager. Then we'll hunt, eh? I've one rather promising prospect—"

145   Rainsford was hurrying from the room.

"Sorry you can't go with me tonight," called the general. "I expect rather fair sport—a big, strong black. He looks resourceful—Well, good night, Mr. Rainsford; I hope you have a good night's rest."

The bed was good, and the pajamas of the softest silk, and he was tired in every fiber of his being, but nevertheless Rainsford could not quiet his brain with the opiate of sleep. He lay, eyes wide open. Once he thought he heard stealthy steps in the corridor outside his room. He sought to throw open the door; it would not open. He went to the window and looked out. His room was high up in one of the towers. The lights of the château were out now; and it was dark and silent, but there was a fragment of sallow moon, and by its wan light he could see, dimly, the courtyard; there, weaving in and out in the pattern of shadow, were black, noiseless forms; the hounds heard him at the window and looked up, expectantly, with their green eyes. Rainsford went back to bed and lay down. By many methods he tried to put himself to sleep. He had achieved a doze when,

2. Probably Nicholas II (1868–1918), who was overthrown by the Revolution and executed; White designates those opposed to the Communists, or Reds.   3. Paris theater and music hall.

just as morning began to come, he heard, far off in the jungle, the faint report of a pistol.

General Zaroff did not appear until luncheon. He was dressed faultlessly in the tweeds of a country squire. He was solicitous about the state of Rainsford's health.

"As for me," sighed the general, "I do not feel so well. I am worried, Mr. Rainsford. Last night I detected traces of my old complaint."

To Rainsford's questioning glance the general said: "Ennui. Boredom."   150

Then, taking a second helping of *crêpes suzette,* the general explained: "The hunting was not good last night. The fellow lost his head. He made a straight trail that offered no problems at all. That's the trouble with these sailors; they have dull brains to begin with, and they do not know how to get about in the woods. They do excessively stupid and obvious things. It's most annoying. Will you have another glass of Chablis, Mr. Rainsford?"

"General," said Rainsford firmly, "I wish to leave this island at once."

The general raised his thickets of eyebrows; he seemed hurt. "But, my dear fellow," the general protested, "you've only just come. You've had no hunting—"

"I wish to go today," said Rainsford. He saw the dead black eyes of the general on him, studying him. General Zaroff's face suddenly brightened.

He filled Rainsford's glass with venerable Chablis from a dusty bottle.   155

"Tonight," said the general, "we will hunt—you and I."

Rainsford shook his head. "No, general," he said, "I will not hunt."

The general shrugged his shoulders and delicately ate a hothouse grape. "As you wish, my friend," he said. "The choice rests entirely with you. But may I not venture to suggest that you will find my idea of sport more diverting than Ivan's?"

He nodded toward the corner to where the giant stood, scowling, his thick arms crossed on his hogshead of a chest.

"You don't mean—" cried Rainsford.   160

"My dear fellow," said the general, "have I not told you I always mean what I say about hunting? This is really an inspiration. I drink to a foeman worthy of my steel—at last."

The general raised his glass, but Rainsford sat staring at him.

"You'll find this game worth playing," the general said enthusiastically. "Your brain against mine. Your woodcraft against mine. Your strength and stamina against mine. Outdoor chess! And the stake is not without value, eh?"

"And if I win—" began Rainsford huskily.

"I'll cheerfully acknowledge myself defeated if I do not find you by midnight   165
of the third day," said General Zaroff. "My sloop will place you on the mainland near a town."

The general read what Rainsford was thinking.

"Oh, you can trust me," said the Cossack. "I will give you my word as a gentleman and a sportsman. Of course you, in turn, must agree to say nothing of your visit here."

"I'll agree to nothing of the kind," said Rainsford.

"Oh," said the general, "in that case—But why discuss that now? Three days hence we can discuss it over a bottle of Veuve Cliquot,[4] unless—"

170 The general sipped his wine.

Then a businesslike air animated him. "Ivan," he said to Rainsford, "will supply you with hunting clothes, food, a knife. I suggest you wear moccasins; they leave a poorer trail. I suggest too that you avoid the big swamp in the southeast corner of the island. We call it Death Swamp. There's quicksand there. One foolish fellow tried it. The deplorable part of it was that Lazarus followed him. You can imagine my feelings, Mr. Rainsford. I loved Lazarus; he was the finest hound in my pack. Well, I must beg you to excuse me now. I always take a siesta after lunch. You'll hardly have time for a nap, I fear. You'll want to start, no doubt. I shall not follow till dusk. Hunting at night is so much more exciting than by day, don't you think? Au revoir, Mr. Rainsford, au revoir."

General Zaroff, with a deep, courtly bow, strolled from the room.

From another door came Ivan. Under one arm he carried khaki hunting clothes, a haversack of food, a leather sheath containing a long-bladed hunting knife; his right hand rested on a cocked revolver thrust in the crimson sash about his waist. . . .

Rainsford had fought his way through the bush for two hours. "I must keep my nerve. I must keep my nerve," he said through tight teeth.

175 He had not been entirely clear-headed when the château gates snapped shut behind him. His whole idea at first was to put distance between himself and General Zaroff, and, to this end, he had plunged along, spurred on by the sharp rowels of something very like panic. Now he had got a grip on himself, had stopped, and was taking stock of himself and the situation.

He saw that straight flight was futile; inevitably it would bring him face to face with the sea. He was in a picture with a frame of water, and his operations, clearly, must take place within that frame.

"I'll give him a trail to follow," muttered Rainsford, and he struck off from the rude paths he had been following into the trackless wilderness. He executed a series of intricate loops; he doubled on his trail again and again, recalling all the lore of the fox hunt, and all the dodges of the fox. Night found him leg-weary, with hands and face lashed by the branches, on a thickly wooded ridge. He knew it would be insane to blunder on through the dark, even if he had the strength. His need for rest was imperative and he thought: "I have played the fox, now I must play the cat of the fable."[5] A big tree with a thick trunk and outspread branches was nearby, and, taking care to leave not the slightest mark, he climbed up into the crotch, and stretching out on one of the broad limbs, after a fashion, rested. Rest brought him new confidence and almost a feeling of security. Even so zealous a hunter as General Zaroff could not trace him there, he told himself; only the devil himself could follow that complicated trail through the jungle after dark. But, perhaps, the general was a devil—

4. A fine champagne; Chablis, above, is a very dry white Burgundy table wine.   5. The fox boasts of his many tricks to elude the hounds; the cat responds he knows only one to climb the nearest tree but that this is worth more than all the fox's tricks.

An apprehensive night crawled slowly by like a wounded snake, and sleep did not visit Rainsford, although the silence of a dead world was on the jungle. Toward morning when a dingy gray was varnishing the sky, the cry of some startled bird focused Rainsford's attention in that direction. Something was coming through the bush, coming slowly, carefully, coming by the same winding way Rainsford had come. He flattened himself down on the limb, and through a screen of leaves almost as thick as tapestry, he watched. The thing that was approaching was a man.

It was General Zaroff. He made his way along with his eyes fixed in utmost concentration on the ground before him. He paused, almost beneath the tree, dropped to his knees and studied the ground. Rainsford's impulse was to hurl himself down like a panther, but he saw that the general's right hand held something metallic—a small automatic pistol.

The hunter shook his head several times, as if he were puzzled. Then he straightened up and took from his case one of his black cigarettes; its pungent incense-like smoke floated up to Rainsford's nostrils.

180

Rainsford held his breath. The general's eyes had left the ground and were traveling inch by inch up the tree. Rainsford froze there, every muscle tensed for a spring. But the sharp eyes of the hunter stopped before they reached the limb where Rainsford lay; a smile spread over his brown face. Very deliberately he blew a smoke ring into the air; then he turned his back on the tree and walked carelessly away, back along the trail he had come. The swish of the underbrush against his hunting boots grew fainter and fainter.

The pent-up air burst hotly from Rainsford's lungs. His first thought made him feel sick and numb. The general could follow a trail through the woods at night; he could follow an extremely difficult trail; he must have uncanny powers; only by the merest chance had the Cossack failed to see his quarry.

Rainsford's second thought was even more terrible. It sent a shudder of cold horror through his whole being. Why had the general smiled? Why had he turned back?

Rainsford did not want to believe what his reason told him was true, but the truth was as evident as the sun that had by now pushed through the morning mists. The general was playing with him! The general was saving him for another day's sport! The Cossack was the cat; he was the mouse.[6] Then it was that Rainsford knew the full meaning of terror.

"I will not lose my nerve. I will not."

185

He slid down the tree, and struck off again into the woods. His face was set and he forced the machinery of his mind to function. Three hundred yards from his hiding place he stopped where a huge dead tree leaned precariously on a smaller, living one. Throwing off his sack of food, Rainsford took his knife from its sheath and began to work with all his energy.

The job was finished at last, and he threw himself down behind a fallen log a hundred feet away. He did not have to wait long. The cat was coming again to play with the mouse.

---

6. A cat, sure of his prey, plays with a mouse before killing him.

Following the trail with the sureness of a bloodhound, came General Zaroff. Nothing escaped those searching black eyes, no crushed blade of grass, no bent twig, no mark, no matter how faint, in the moss. So intent was the Cossack on his stalking that he was upon the thing Rainsford had made before he saw it. His foot touched the protruding bough that was the trigger. Even as he touched it, the general sensed his danger and leaped back with the agility of an ape. But he was not quite quick enough; the dead tree, delicately adjusted to rest on the cut living one, crashed down and struck the general a glancing blow on the shoulder as it fell; but for his alertness, he must have been smashed beneath it. He staggered, but he did not fall; nor did he drop his revolver. He stood there, rubbing his injured shoulder, and Rainsford, with fear again gripping his heart, heard the general's mocking laugh ring through the jungle.

"Rainsford," called the general, "if you are within sound of my voice, as I suppose you are, let me congratulate you. Not many men know how to make a Malay man-catcher. Luckily, for me, I too have hunted in Malacca. You are proving interesting, Mr. Rainsford. I am going now to have my wound dressed; it's only a slight one. But I shall be back. I shall be back."

190   When the general, nursing his bruised shoulder, had gone, Rainsford took up his flight again. It was flight now, a desperate, hopeless flight, that carried him on for some hours. Dusk came, then darkness, and still he pressed on. The ground grew softer under his moccasins; the vegetation grew ranker, denser; insects bit him savagely. Then, as he stepped forward, his foot sank into the ooze. He tried to wrench it back, but the muck sucked viciously at his foot as if it were a giant leech. With a violent effort, he tore his foot loose. He knew where he was now. Death Swamp and its quicksand.

His hands were tight closed as if his nerve were something tangible that someone in the darkness was trying to tear from his grip. The softness of the earth had given him an idea. He stepped back from the quicksand a dozen feet or so and, like some huge prehistoric beaver, he began to dig.

Rainsford had dug himself in in France[7] when a second's delay meant death. That had been a placid pastime compared to his digging now. The pit grew deeper; when it was above his shoulders, he climbed out and from some hard saplings cut stakes and sharpened them to a fine point. These stakes he planted in the bottom of the pit with the points sticking up. With flying fingers he wove a rough carpet of weeds and branches and with it he covered the mouth of the pit. Then, wet with sweat and aching with tiredness, he crouched behind the stump of a lightning-charred tree.

He knew his pursuer was coming; he heard the padding sound of feet on the soft earth, and the night breeze brought him the perfume of the general's cigarette. It seemed to Rainsford that the general was coming with unusual swiftness; he was not feeling his way along, foot by foot. Rainsford, crouching there, could not see the general, nor could he see the pit. He lived a year in a minute. Then he felt an impulse to cry aloud with joy, for he heard the sharp crackle of the

---

7. During World War I he had quickly dug a hole or trench to shelter himself from exploding shells, bullets, and so forth.

breaking branches as the cover of the pit gave way; he heard the sharp scream of pain as the pointed stakes found their mark. He leaped up from his place of concealment. Then he cowered back. Three feet from the pit a man was standing, with an electric torch in his hand.

"You've done well, Rainsford," the voice of the general called. "Your Burmese tiger pit has claimed one of my best dogs. Again you score. I think, Mr. Rainsford, I'll see what you can do against my whole pack. I'm going home for a rest now. Thank you for a most amusing evening."

At daybreak Rainsford, lying near the swamp, was awakened by a sound that   195
made him know that he had new things to learn about fear. It was a distant sound, faint and wavering, but he knew it. It was the baying of a pack of hounds.

Rainsford knew he could do one of two things. He could stay where he was and wait. That was suicide. He could flee. That was postponing the inevitable. For a moment he stood there, thinking. An idea that held a wild chance came to him, and, tightening his belt, he headed away from the swamp.

The baying of the hounds drew nearer, then still nearer, nearer, ever nearer. On a ridge Rainsford climbed a tree. Down a watercourse, not a quarter of a mile away, he could see the bush moving. Straining his eyes, he saw the lean figure of General Zaroff; just ahead of him Rainsford made out another figure whose wide shoulders surged through the tall jungle weeds; it was the giant Ivan, and he seemed pulled forward by some unseen force; Rainsford knew that Ivan must be holding the pack in leash.

They would be on him any minute now. His mind worked frantically. He thought of a native trick he had learned in Uganda. He slid down the tree. He caught hold of a springy young sapling and to it he fastened his hunting knife, with the blade pointing down the trail; with a bit of wild grapevine he tied back the sapling. Then he ran for his life. The hounds raised their voices as they hit the fresh scent. Rainsford knew now how an animal at bay feels.

He had to stop to get his breath. The baying of the hounds stopped abruptly, and Rainsford's heart stopped too. They must have reached the knife.

He shinnied excitedly up a tree and looked back. His pursuers had stopped.   200
But the hope that was in Rainsford's brain when he climbed died, for he saw in the shallow valley that General Zaroff was still on his feet. But Ivan was not. The knife, driven by the recoil of the springing tree, had not wholly failed.

Rainsford had hardly tumbled to the ground when the pack took up the cry again.

"Nerve, nerve, nerve!" he panted, as he dashed along. A blue gap showed between the trees dead ahead. Ever nearer drew the hounds. Rainsford forced himself on toward that gap. He reached it. It was the shore of the sea. Across a cove he could see the gloomy gray stone of the château. Twenty feet below him the sea rumbled and hissed. Rainsford hesitated. He heard the hounds. Then he leaped far out into the sea. . . .

When the general and his pack reached the place by the sea, the Cossack stopped. For some minutes he stood regarding the blue-green expanse of water. He shrugged his shoulders. Then he sat down, took a drink of brandy from a silver flask, lit a perfumed cigarette, and hummed a bit from "Madame Butterfly."[8]

General Zaroff had an exceedingly good dinner in his great paneled dining hall that evening. With it he had a bottle of Pol Roger and half a bottle of Chambertin.[9] Two slight annoyances kept him from perfect enjoyment. One was the thought that it would be difficult to replace Ivan; the other was that his quarry had escaped him; of course the American hadn't played the game—so thought the general as he tasted his after-dinner liqueur. In his library he read, to soothe himself, from the works of Marcus Aurelius.[1] At ten he went up to his bedroom. He was deliciously tired, he said to himself, as he locked himself in. There was a little moonlight so, before turning on his light, he went to the window and looked down at the courtyard. He could see the great hounds, and he called: "Better luck another time," to them. Then he switched on the light.

205   A man, who had been hiding in the curtains of the bed, was standing there.

"Rainsford!" screamed the general. "How in God's name did you get here?"

"Swam," said Rainsford. "I found it quicker than walking through the jungle."

The general sucked in his breath and smiled. "I congratulate you," he said. "You have won the game."

Rainsford did not smile. "I am still a beast at bay," he said, in a low, hoarse voice. "Get ready, General Zaroff."

210   The general made one of his deepest bows. "I see," he said. "Splendid! One of us is to furnish a repast for the hounds. The other will sleep in this very excellent bed. On guard, Rainsford. . . ."

He had never slept in a better bed, Rainsford decided.

1924

A good many readers like "The Most Dangerous Game." In class it is often a favorite, or even *the* favorite. Other readers recommend dropping this story from the anthology because it is "unworthy," not really literature. Is this simply ignorance on the one hand or snobbery on the other?

Here are two brief papers, somewhat like those a student might write in class, the first supporting "The Most Dangerous Game," the second responding to the first.

8. Opera (1904) by Giacomo Puccini (1858–1924).   9. Pol Roger is champagne; Chambertin is a highly esteemed red Burgundy wine.   1. Roman emperor (A.D. 161–180), Stoic philosopher, writer, and humanitarian.

Why "The Most Dangerous Game" Is Good Literature

Thaddeus Smith

"The Most Dangerous Game" by Richard Connell is exciting. Things
happen in it, and you want to read on because you want to find out what
will happen next and how it will come out. Too often the things we need
to read for class are boring, nothing happens, or, if something does
happen, it happens inside somebody's head. But here things happen
outside; I mean, there's real action.

Not only is there action, but that action is important, a real life-
and-death struggle. This story is not just about whether somebody used
the wrong fork or had a good time or didn't have a good time at a
party.

The good guy wins, the story ends happily, and when you finish
reading it, you feel good about things. Sometimes in class I think only
real downers are supposed to be good stories, like life always has to
be full of gloom and doom. Now all of us die sooner or later, of
course, but that's only the end, a minute or a month or something, and
there's all the rest of the time when we're not dead and not really in
the process of dying. That's life, and that's what a good story should
be about.

"The Most Dangerous Game" is fun to read. Sometimes I think that
what are supposed to be the "good" stories are the ones I don't like.
But popular stories can be good: there have been several movies made of
"The Most Dangerous Game" and several stories adapted from it with just
a few things changed. But, I'm told, the world of literature isn't a
democracy--you don't vote for what's Literature. When I say I like
Stephen King--and I'm sure not the only one, because he sells lots and
lots of book--teachers or English majors say wait fifty years and see if
his stuff is still around.

Well, "The Most Dangerous Game" is over seventy years old, older than
at least three-quarters of the stories in this anthology, so it's stood
the test of time, whatever that is.

Why "The Most Dangerous Game" Is Not Good Literature

Sara Rosen

Though "The Most Dangerous Game" may be "a good read," at least the first time through, and I have nothing against someone reading it or even liking it in its way, I don't think it ought to be in *The Norton Introduction to Literature*. Being in the anthology gives it a status it does not deserve. It makes it the subject of serious study by college students, and college students ought to be engaged in more challenging and thought-provoking reading material, even if outside of class they are reading Stephen King and the likes of "The Most Dangerous Game."

Though it's true that a life-and-death struggle is important--for the person involved--it has no relevance for us, no outreach: it does not relate to our experience nor does it really illuminate anything about our experience or the way we look at life. I don't mean that a worthy story must have a "message," necessarily, but it should have a "theme," something that explores a significant area of human experience and understanding.

I admit that there is something like suspense in Connell's story, but that is not enough. There's nothing wrong with suspense in itself-- expectations of one sort or another are part of every good work--but here the suspense is manipulated at the price of consistency. Note how we're seeing things from Rainsford's perspective (not through his eyes and mind exactly, not in the first person, but over his shoulder) until near the end when he leaps into the sea. At that point, when we're supposed to want most to know what happens next, there's the more or less artificial suspense added by three dots and a break on the page, and then we're not with Rainsford but Zaroff, just to make us wonder if Rainsford did indeed die. It's a cheap trick. Besides, don't we know from the beginning that in this kind of story the hero never dies, so isn't the suspense really phony? What's wrong with stories like this is the unrealistic, wish-fulfilling way it looks at reality: it tells us that good guys always finish first; they win because they're good.

While good guys do sometimes finish first, and plenty of good stories end happily, more or less, like "Sonny Blues," and "The Secret Sharer," life is not always like that, and this victory seems a little too easy.

Finally, Rainsford has no "character"; he's just a good guy because he's an American and his life is threatened by a bad guy who's a Russian; and the bad guy is just a bad guy, with no redeeming human qualities--it's all about guys in white hats versus guys in black hats.

These are not polished and conclusive arguments, of course. Had the writer of the first paper read the response, he might have had more to say. About the alleged absence of theme in "The Most Dangerous Game," for example:

There is a theme in Connell's story. It is a very important one, one that you have to think about, and that some people will agree with, though it is not a theme that you necessarily have to agree with in order to appreciate the story. Notice it is set just after the Russian Revolution, and Zaroff (the "son of the czar") is a cruel aristocrat from the czarist regime who believes in power, believes that might-makes-right, and believes some people are better than others and have a right to do what they will with their "inferiors," even kill them for pleasure. Rainsford at the beginning is a hunter/exploiter, never thinking what the "inferior" beast, the hunted, feels like. Having been put in the place of the hunted he will no doubt learn to have more reverence for life, more sympathy for the underdog.

The opponent, hearing this contention that there is a significant theme in the story, might well respond that the theme as described is too pat, and that it is presented through too convenient (as well as unbelievable) a situation, too much of a setup.

This, then, is only one example of the kinds of arguments readers can use to support their judgments. We need to go on from there to consider what we read for ("a good read"? "an illumination of human life and experience"?), and what we mean by "the reader," the one judging the story to be "good."

Let us assume for the moment that "the readers" can be represented roughly by the people in this class—you, those who agree with you about stories, and those who, though they are more or less like you, do not always agree with you. We said earlier that if our appreciation and understanding of literature is to grow, and if we are not merely to accept what those considered "authorities" say is good or great, we must learn to isolate, analyze, and articulate what *we* like (or dislike) in a story. And, we said, we must listen to those with other responses as they articulate their reasons.

Now for the test. The next story is by a Nobel laureate and much revered writer, William Faulkner, and this, like "A Rose for Emily," is one of his most admired stories. It has some of the same attractive qualities as "The Most Dangerous Game"— conflict, action, suspense—but there are those who find it critically flawed. Regardless of which side we are on, we must take seriously both those who have reservations and questions and the author's and the story's established reputation. But first, we must read it.

WILLIAM FAULKNER

Barn Burning

The store in which the Justice of the Peace's court was sitting smelled of cheese. The boy, crouched on his nail keg at the back of the crowded room, knew he smelled cheese, and more: from where he sat he could see the ranked shelves close-packed with the solid, squat, dynamic shapes of tin cans whose labels his stomach read, not from the lettering which meant nothing to his mind but from the scarlet devils and the silver curve of fish—this, the cheese which he knew he smelled and the hermetic meat which his intestines believed he smelled coming in intermittent gusts momentary and brief between the other constant one, the smell and sense just a little of fear because mostly of despair and grief, the old fierce pull of blood. He could not see the table where the Justice sat and before which his father and his father's enemy (*our enemy* he thought in that despair; *ourn! mine and hisn both! He's my father!*) stood, but he could hear them, the two of them that is, because his father had said no word yet:

"But what proof have you, Mr. Harris?"

"I told you. The hog got into my corn. I caught it up and sent it back to him. He had no fence that would hold it. I told him so, warned him. The next time I put the hog in my pen. When he came to get it I gave him enough wire to patch up his pen. The next time I put the hog up and kept it. I rode down to his house and saw the wire I gave him still rolled on to the spool in his yard. I told him he could have the hog when he paid me a dollar pound fee. That evening a nigger came with the dollar and got the hog. He was a strange nigger. He said, 'He say to tell you wood and hay kin burn.' I said, 'What?' 'That whut he say to tell you,' the nigger said. 'Wood and hay kin burn.' That night my barn burned. I got the stock out but I lost the barn."

"Where is the nigger? Have you got him?"

5   "He was a strange nigger, I tell you. I don't know what became of him."

"But that's not proof. Don't you see that's not proof?"

"Get that boy up here. He knows." For a moment the boy thought too that the man meant his older brother until Harris said, "Not him. The little one. The boy," and, crouching, small for his age, small and wiry like his father, in patched and faded jeans even too small for him, with straight, uncombed, brown hair and eyes gray and wild as storm scud, he saw the men between himself and the table part and become a lane of grim faces, at the end of which he saw the Justice, a shabby, collarless, graying man in spectacles, beckoning him. He felt no floor under his bare feet; he seemed to walk beneath the palpable weight of the grim turning faces. His father, stiff in his black Sunday coat donned not for the trial but for the moving, did not even look at him. *He aims for me to lie,* he thought, again with that frantic grief and despair. *And I will have to do hit.*

"What's your name, boy?" the Justice said.

"Colonel Sartoris Snopes," the boy whispered.

"Hey?" the Justice said. "Talk louder. Colonel Sartoris? I reckon anybody named for Colonel Sartoris in this country can't help but tell the truth, can they?" The boy said nothing. *Enemy! Enemy!* he thought; for a moment he could not even see, could not see that the Justice's face was kindly nor discern that his voice was troubled when he spoke to the man named Harris: "Do you want me to question this boy?" But he could hear, and during those subsequent long seconds while there was absolutely no sound in the crowded little room save that of quiet and intent breathing it was as if he had swung outward at the end of a grape vine, over a ravine, and at the top of the swing had been caught in a prolonged instant of mesmerized gravity, weightless in time.

"No!" Harris said violently, explosively. "Damnation! Send him out of here!" Now time, the fluid world, rushed beneath him again, the voices coming to him again through the smell of cheese and sealed meat, the fear and despair and the old grief of blood:

"This case is closed. I can't find against you, Snopes, but I can give you advice. Leave this country and don't come back to it."

His father spoke for the first time, his voice cold and harsh, level, without emphasis: "I aim to. I don't figure to stay in a country among people who . . ." he said something unprintable and vile, addressed to no one.

"That'll do," the Justice said. "Take your wagon and get out of this country before dark. Case dismissed."

His father turned, and he followed the stiff black coat, the wiry figure walking a little stiffly from where a Confederate provost's man's[1] musket ball had taken him in the heel on a stolen horse thirty years ago, followed the two backs now, since his older brother had appeared from somewhere in the crowd, no taller than the father but thicker, chewing tobacco steadily, between the two lines of grim-faced men and out of the store and across the worn gallery and down the sagging steps and among the dogs and half-grown boys in the mild May dust, where as he passed a voice hissed:

"Barn burner!"

Again he could not see, whirling; there was a face in a red haze, moonlike, bigger than the full moon, the owner of it half again his size, he leaping in the red haze toward the face, feeling no blow, feeling no shock when his head struck the earth, scrabbling up and leaping again, feeling no blow this time either and tasting no blood, scrabbling up to see the other boy in full flight and himself already leaping into pursuit as his father's hand jerked him back, the harsh, cold voice speaking above him: "Go get in the wagon."

It stood in a grove of locusts and mulberries across the road. His two hulking

10

15

---

1. Military policeman's.

sisters in their Sunday dresses and his mother and her sister in calico and sunbonnets were already in it, sitting on and among the sorry residue of the dozen and more movings which even the boy could remember—the battered stove, the broken beds and chairs, the clock inlaid with mother-of-pearl, which would not run, stopped at some fourteen minutes past two o'clock of a dead and forgotten day and time, which had been his mother's dowry. She was crying, though when she saw him she drew her sleeve across her face and began to descend from the wagon. "Get back," the father said.

"He's hurt. I got to get some water and wash his . . ."

20   "Get back in the wagon," his father said. He got in too, over the tail-gate. His father mounted to the seat where the older brother already sat and struck the gaunt mules two savage blows with the peeled willow, but without heat. It was not even sadistic; it was exactly that same quality which in later years would cause his descendants to overrun the engine before putting a motor car into motion, striking and reining back in the same movement. The wagon went on, the store with its quiet crowd of grimly watching men dropped behind; a curve in the road hid it. *Forever* he thought. *Maybe he's done satisfied now, now that he has . . .* stopping himself, not to say it aloud even to himself. His mother's hand touched his shoulder.

"Does hit hurt?" she said.

"Naw," he said. "Hit don't hurt. Lemme be."

"Can't you wipe some of the blood off before hit dries?"

"I'll wash to-night," he said. "Lemme be, I tell you."

25   The wagon went on. He did not know where they were going. None of them ever did or ever asked, because it was always somewhere, always a house of sorts waiting for them a day or two days or even three days away. Likely his father had already arranged to make a crop on another farm before he . . . Again he had to stop himself. He (the father) always did. There was something about his wolf-like independence and even courage when the advantage was at least neutral which impressed strangers, as if they got from his latent ravening ferocity not so much a sense of dependability as a feeling that his ferocious conviction in the rightness of his own actions would be of advantage to all whose interest lay with his.

That night they camped, in a grove of oaks and beeches where a spring ran. The nights were still cool and they had a fire against it, of a rail lifted from a nearby fence and cut into lengths—a small fire, neat, niggard almost, a shrewd fire; such fires were his father's habit and custom always, even in freezing weather. Older, the boy might have remarked this and wondered why not a big one; why should not a man who had not only seen the waste and extravagance of war, but who had in his blood an inherent voracious prodigality with material not his own, have burned everything in sight? Then he might have gone a step farther and thought that that was the reason: that niggard blaze was the living fruit of nights passed during those four years in the woods hiding from all men, blue or gray,[2] with his strings of horses (captured horses, he called them). And older still, he might have divined the true reason: that the element of fire spoke to some deep mainspring of his father's being, as the element of steel or of pow-

2. The colors of Union and Confederate Civil War (1861–1865) uniforms, respectively.

der spoke to other men, as the one weapon for the preservation of integrity, else breath were not worth the breathing, and hence to be regarded with respect and used with discretion.

But he did not think this now and he had seen those same niggard blazes all his life. He merely ate his supper beside it and was already half asleep over his iron plate when his father called him, and once more he followed the stiff back, the stiff and ruthless limp, up the slope and on to the starlit road where, turning, he could see his father against the stars but without face or depth—a shape black, flat, and bloodless as though cut from tin in the iron folds of the frockcoat which had not been made for him, the voice harsh like tin and without heat like tin:

"You were fixing to tell them. You would have told him." He didn't answer. His father struck him with the flat of his hand on the side of the head, hard but without heat, exactly as he had struck the two mules at the store, exactly as he would strike either of them with any stick in order to kill a horse fly, his voice still without heat or anger: "You're getting to be a man. You got to learn. You got to learn to stick to your own blood or you ain't going to have any blood to stick to you. Do you think either of them, any man there this morning, would? Don't you know all they wanted was a chance to get at me because they knew I had them beat? Eh?" Later, twenty years later, he was to tell himself, "If I had said they wanted only truth, justice, he would have hit me again." But now he said nothing. He was not crying. He just stood there. "Answer me," his father said.

"Yes," he whispered. His father turned.

"Get on to bed. We'll be there tomorrow."   30

Tomorrow they were there. In the early afternoon the wagon stopped before a paintless two-room house identical almost with the dozen others it had stopped before even in the boy's ten years, and again, as on the other dozen occasions, his mother and aunt got down and began to unload the wagon, although his two sisters and his father and brother had not moved.

"Likely hit ain't fitten for hawgs," one of the sisters said.

"Nevertheless, fit it will and you'll hog it and like it," his father said. "Get out of them chairs and help your Ma unload."

The two sisters got down, big, bovine, in a flutter of cheap ribbons; one of them drew from the jumbled wagon bed a battered lantern, the other a worn broom. His father handed the reins to the older son and began to climb stiffly over the wheel. "When they get unloaded, take the team to the barn and feed them." Then he said, and at first the boy thought he was still speaking to his brother: "Come with me."

"Me?" he said.   35

"Yes," his father said. "You."

"Abner," his mother said. His father paused and looked back—the harsh level stare beneath the shaggy, graying, irascible brows.

"I reckon I'll have a word with the man that aims to begin to-morrow owning me body and soul for the next eight months."

They went back up the road. A week ago—or before last night, that is—he would have asked where they were going, but not now. His father had struck him before last night but never before had he paused afterward to explain why; it was as if the blow and the following calm, outrageous voice still rang, repercussed, divulging nothing to him save the terrible handicap of being young, the light weight of his few years, just heavy enough to prevent his soaring free of the world as it seemed to be ordered but not heavy enough to keep him footed solid in it, to resist it and try to change the course of its events.

40   Presently he could see the grove of oaks and cedars and the other flowering trees and shrubs, where the house would be, though not the house yet. They walked beside a fence massed with honeysuckle and Cherokee roses and came to a gate swinging open between two brick pillars, and now, beyond a sweep of drive, he saw the house for the first time and at that instant he forgot his father and the terror and despair both, and even when he remembered his father again (who had not stopped) the terror and despair did not return. Because, for all the twelve movings, they had sojourned until now in a poor country, a land of small farms and fields and houses, and he had never seen a house like this before. *Hit's big as a courthouse* he thought quietly, with a surge of peace and joy whose reason he could not have thought into words, being too young for that: *They are safe from him. People whose lives are a part of this peace and dignity are beyond his touch, he no more to them than a buzzing wasp: capable of stinging for a little moment but that's all; the spell of this peace and dignity rendering even the barns and stable and cribs which belong to it impervious to the puny flames he might contrive* . . . this, the peace and joy, ebbing for an instant as he looked again at the stiff black back, the stiff and implacable limp of the figure which was not dwarfed by the house, for the reason that it had never looked big anywhere and which now, against the serene columned backdrop, had more than ever that impervious quality of something cut ruthlessly from tin, depthless, as though, sidewise to the sun, it would cast no shadow. Watching him, the boy remarked the absolutely undeviating course which his father held and saw the stiff foot come squarely down in a pile of fresh droppings where a horse had stood in the drive and which his father could have avoided by a simple change of stride. But it ebbed only for a moment, though he could not have thought this into words either, walking on in the spell of the house, which he could even want but without envy, without sorrow, certainly never with that ravening and jealous rage which unknown to him walked in the ironlike black coat before him: *Maybe he will feel it too. Maybe it will even change him now from what maybe he couldn't help but be.*

They crossed the portico. Now he could hear his father's stiff foot as it came down on the boards with clocklike finality, a sound out of all proportion to the displacement of the body it bore and which was not dwarfed either by the white door before it, as though it had attained to a sort of vicious and ravening minimum not to be dwarfed by anything—the flat, wide, black hat, the formal coat of broadcloth which had once been black but which had now that friction-glazed greenish cast of the bodies of old house flies, the lifted sleeve which was too large, the lifted hand like a curled claw. The door opened so promptly that the boy knew the Negro must have been watching them all the time, an old man with neat grizzled hair, in a linen jacket, who stood barring the door with his body, saying, "Wipe yo foots, white man, fo you come in here. Major ain't home nohow."

"Get out of my way, nigger," his father said, without heat too, flinging the door back and the Negro also and entering, his hat still on his head. And now the boy saw the prints of the stiff foot on the doorjamb and saw them appear on the pale rug behind the machinelike deliberation of the foot which seemed to bear (or transmit) twice the weight which the body compassed. The Negro was shouting "Miss Lula! Miss Lula!" somewhere behind them, then the boy, deluged as though by a warm wave by a suave turn of carpeted stair and a pendant glitter of chandeliers and a mute gleam of gold frames, heard the swift feet and saw her too, a lady—perhaps he had never seen her like before either—in a gray, smooth gown with lace at the throat and an apron tied at the waist and the sleeves turned back, wiping cake or biscuit dough from her hands with a towel as she came up the hall, looking not at his father at all but at the tracks on the blond rug with an expression of incredulous amazement.

"I tried," the Negro cried. "I tole him to . . ."

"Will you please go away?" she said in a shaking voice. "Major de Spain is not at home. Will you please go away?"

His father had not spoken again. He did not speak again. He did not even look at her. He just stood stiff in the center of the rug, in his hat, the shaggy iron-gray brows twitching slightly above the pebble-colored eyes as he appeared to examine the house with brief deliberation. Then with the same deliberation he turned; the boy watched him pivot on the good leg and saw the stiff foot drag round the arc of the turning, leaving a final long and fading smear. His father never looked at it, he never once looked down at the rug. The Negro held the door. It closed behind them, upon the hysteric and indistinguishable woman-wail. His father stopped at the top of the steps and scraped his boot clean on the edge of it. At the gate he stopped again. He stood for a moment, planted stiffly on the stiff foot, looking back at the house. "Pretty and white, ain't it?" he said. "That's sweat. Nigger sweat. Maybe it ain't white enough yet to suit him. Maybe he wants to mix some white sweat with it."

Two hours later the boy was chopping wood behind the house within which his mother and aunt and the two sisters (the mother and aunt, not the two girls, he knew that; even at this distance and muffled by walls the flat loud voices of the two girls emanated an incorrigible idle inertia) were setting up the stove to prepare a meal, when he heard the hooves and saw the linen-clad man on a fine sorrel mare, whom he recognized even before he saw the rolled rug in front of the Negro youth following on a fat bay carriage horse—a suffused, angry face vanishing, still at full gallop, beyond the corner of the house where his father and brother were sitting in the two tilted chairs; and a moment later, almost before he could have put the axe down, he heard the hooves again and watched the sorrel mare go back out of the yard, already galloping again. Then his father began to shout one of the sisters' names, who presently emerged backward from the kitchen door dragging the rolled rug along the ground by one end while the other sister walked behind it.

"If you ain't going to tote, go on and set up the wash pot," the first said.

"You, Sarty!" the second shouted. "Set up the wash pot!" His father appeared at the door, framed against that shabbiness, as he had been against that other bland perfection, impervious to either, the mother's anxious face at his shoulder.

"Go on," the father said. "Pick it up." The two sisters stooped, broad, lethargic; stooping, they presented an incredible expanse of pale cloth and a flutter of tawdry ribbons.

50   "If I thought enough of a rug to have to git hit all the way from France I wouldn't keep hit where folks coming in would have to tromp on hit," the first said. They raised the rug.

"Abner," the mother said. "Let me do it."

"You go back and git dinner," his father said. "I'll tend to this."

From the woodpile through the rest of the afternoon the boy watched them, the rug spread flat in the dust beside the bubbling wash-pot, the two sisters stooping over it with that profound and lethargic reluctance, while the father stood over them in turn, implacable and grim, driving them though never raising his voice again. He could smell the harsh homemade lye they were using; he saw his mother come to the door once and look toward them with an expression not anxious now but very like despair; he saw his father turn, and he fell to with the axe and saw from the corner of his eye his father raise from the ground a flattish fragment of field stone and examine it and return to the pot, and this time his mother actually spoke: "Abner. Abner. Please don't. Please, Abner."

Then he was done too. It was dusk; the whippoorwills had already begun. He could smell coffee from the room where they would presently eat the cold food remaining from the mid-afternoon meal, though when he entered the house he realized they were having coffee again probably because there was a fire on the hearth, before which the rug now lay spread over the backs of the two chairs. The tracks of his father's foot were gone. Where they had been were now long, water-cloudy scoriations resembling the sporadic course of a Lilliputian mowing machine.

55   It still hung there while they ate the cold food and then went to bed, scattered without order or claim up and down the two rooms, his mother in one bed, where his father would later lie, the older brother in the other, himself, the aunt, and the two sisters on pallets on the floor. But his father was not in bed yet. The last thing the boy remembered was the depthless, harsh silhouette of the hat and coat bending over the rug and it seemed to him that he had not even closed his eyes when the silhouette was standing over him, the fire almost dead behind it, the stiff foot prodding him awake. "Catch up the mule," his father said.

When he returned with the mule his father was standing in the black door, the rolled rug over his shoulder. "Ain't you going to ride?" he said.

"No. Give me your foot."

He bent his knee into his father's hand, the wiry, surprising power flowed smoothly, rising, he rising with it, on to the mule's bare back (they had owned a saddle once; the boy could remember it though not when or where) and with the same effortlessness his father swung the rug up in front of him. Now in the starlight they retraced the afternoon's path, up the dusty road rife with honeysuckle, through the gate and up the black tunnel of the drive to the lightless house, where he sat on the mule and felt the rough warp of the rug drag across his thighs and vanish.

"Don't you want me to help?" he whispered. His father did not answer and now he heard again that stiff foot striking the hollow portico with that wooden and clocklike deliberation, that outrageous overstatement of the weight it carried. The rug, hunched, not flung (the boy could tell that even in the darkness) from his father's shoulder struck the angle of wall and floor with a sound unbelievably loud, thunderous, then the foot again, unhurried and enormous; a light came on in the house and the boy sat, tense, breathing steadily and quietly and just a little fast, though the foot itself did not increase its beat at all, descending the steps now; now the boy could see him.

"Don't you want to ride now?" he whispered. "We kin both ride now," the 60
light within the house altering now, flaring up and sinking. *He's coming down the stairs now,* he thought. He had already ridden the mule up beside the horse block; presently his father was up behind him and he doubled the reins over and slashed the mule across the neck, but before the animal could begin to trot the hard, thin arm came round him, the hard, knotted hand jerking the mule back to a walk.

In the first red rays of the sun they were in the lot, putting plow gear on the mules. This time the sorrel mare was in the lot before he heard it at all, the rider collarless and even bareheaded, trembling, speaking in a shaking voice as the woman in the house had done, his father merely looking up once before stooping again to the hame he was buckling, so that the man on the mare spoke to his stooping back:

"You must realize you have ruined that rug. Wasn't there anybody here, any of your women . . ." he ceased, shaking, the boy watching him, the older brother leaning now in the stable door, chewing, blinking slowly and steadily at nothing apparently. "It cost a hundred dollars. But you never had a hundred dollars. You never will. So I'm going to charge you twenty bushels of corn against your crop. I'll add it in your contract and when you come to the commissary you can sign it. That won't keep Mrs. de Spain quiet but maybe it will teach you to wipe your feet off before you enter her house again."

Then he was gone. The boy looked at his father, who still had not spoken or even looked up again, who was now adjusting the logger-head in the hame.

"Pap," he said. His father looked at him—the inscrutable face, the shaggy brows beneath which the gray eyes glinted coldly. Suddenly the boy went toward him, fast, stopping as suddenly. "You done the best you could!" he cried. "If he wanted hit done different why didn't he wait and tell you how? He won't git no twenty bushels! He won't git none! We'll gether hit and hide hit! I kin watch . . ."

"Did you put the cutter back in that straight stock like I told you?" 65

"No, sir," he said.

"Then go do it."

That was Wednesday. During the rest of that week he worked steadily, at what was within his scope and some which was beyond it, with an industry that did not need to be driven nor even commanded twice; he had this from his mother, with the difference that some at least of what he did he liked to do, such as splitting wood with the half-size axe which his mother and aunt had earned, or saved money somehow, to present him with at Christmas. In company with the two older women (and on one afternoon, even one of the sisters), he built pens for the shoat and the cow which were a part of his father's contract with the landlord, and one afternoon, his father being absent, gone somewhere on one of the mules, he went to the field.

They were running a middle buster[3] now, his brother holding the plow straight while he handled the reins, and walking beside the straining mule, the rich black soil shearing cool and damp against his bare ankles, he thought *Maybe this is the end of it. Maybe even that twenty bushels that seems hard to have to pay for just a rug will be a cheap price for him to stop forever and always from being what he used to be;* thinking, dreaming now, so that his brother had to speak sharply to him to mind the mule: *Maybe he even won't collect the twenty bushels. Maybe it will all add up and balance and vanish—corn, rug, fire; the terror and grief, the being pulled two ways like between two teams of horses—gone, done with for ever and ever.*

70   Then it was Saturday; he looked up from beneath the mule he was harnessing and saw his father in the black coat and hat. "Not that," his father said. "The wagon gear." And then, two hours later, sitting in the wagon bed behind his father and brother on the seat, the wagon accomplished a final curve, and he saw the weathered paintless store with its tattered tobacco- and patent-medicine posters and the tethered wagons and saddle animals below the gallery. He mounted the gnawed steps behind his father and brother, and there again was the lane of quiet, watching faces for the three of them to walk through. He saw the man in spectacles sitting at the plank table and he did not need to be told this was a Justice of the Peace; he sent one glare of fierce, exultant, partisan defiance at the man in collar and cravat now, whom he had seen but twice before in his life, and that on a galloping horse, who now wore on his face an expression not of rage but of amazed unbelief which the boy could not have known was at the incredible circumstance of being sued by one of his own tenants, and came and stood against his father and cried at the Justice: "He ain't done it! He ain't burnt . . ."

"Go back to the wagon," his father said.

"Burnt?" the Justice said. "Do I understand this rug was burned too?"

"Does anybody here claim it was?" his father said. "Go back to the wagon." But he did not, he merely retreated to the rear of the room, crowded as that other had been, but not to sit down this time, instead, to stand pressing among the motionless bodies, listening to the voices:

"And you claim twenty bushels of corn is too high for the damage you did to the rug?"

75   "He brought the rug to me and said he wanted the tracks washed out of it. I washed the tracks out and took the rug back to him."

"But you didn't carry the rug back to him in the same condition it was in before you made the tracks on it."

His father did not answer, and now for perhaps half a minute there was no sound at all save that of breathing, the faint, steady suspiration of complete and intent listening.

"You decline to answer that, Mr. Snopes?" Again his father did not answer.

---

3. A double moldboard plow that throws a ridge of earth both ways.

"I'm going to find against you, Mr. Snopes. I'm going to find that you were responsible for the injury to Major de Spain's rug and hold you liable for it. But twenty bushels of corn seems a little high for a man in your circumstances to have to pay. Major de Spain claims it cost a hundred dollars. October corn will be worth about fifty cents. I figure that if Major de Spain can stand a ninety-five dollar loss on something he paid cash for, you can stand a five-dollar loss you haven't earned yet. I hold you in damages to Major de Spain to the amount of ten bushels of corn over and above your contract with him, to be paid to him out of your crop at gathering time. Court adjourned."

It had taken no time hardly, the morning was but half begun. He thought they would return home and perhaps back to the field, since they were late, far behind all other farmers. But instead his father passed on behind the wagon, merely indicating with his hand for the older brother to follow with it, and crossed the road toward the blacksmith shop opposite, pressing on after his father, overtaking him, speaking, whispering up at the harsh, calm face beneath the weathered hat: "He won't git no ten bushels neither. He won't git one. We'll . . ." until his father glanced for an instant down at him, the face absolutely calm, the grizzled eyebrows tangled above the cold eyes, the voice almost pleasant, almost gentle:

"You think so? Well, we'll wait till October anyway." 80

The matter of the wagon—the setting of a spoke or two and the tightening of the tires—did not take long either, the business of the tires accomplished by driving the wagon into the spring branch behind the shop and letting it stand there, the mules nuzzling into the water from time to time, and the boy on the seat with the idle reins, looking up the slope and through the sooty tunnel of the shed where the slow hammer rang and where his father sat on an upended cypress bolt, easily, either talking or listening, still sitting there when the boy brought the dripping wagon up out of the branch and halted it before the door.

"Take them on to the shade and hitch," his father said. He did so and returned. His father and the smith and a third man squatting on his heels inside the door were talking, about crops and animals; the boy, squatting too in the ammoniac dust and hoof-parings and scales of rust, heard his father tell a long and unhurried story out of the time before the birth of the older brother even when he had been a professional horsetrader. And then his father came up beside him where he stood before a tattered last year's circus poster on the other side of the store, gazing rapt and quiet at the scarlet horses, the incredible poisings and convolutions of tulle and tights and the painted leers of comedians, and said, "It's time to eat."

But not at home. Squatting beside his brother against the front wall, he watched his father emerge from the store and produce from a paper sack a segment of cheese and divide it carefully and deliberately into three with his pocket knife and produce crackers from the same sack. They all three squatted on the gallery and ate, slowly, without talking; then in the store again, they drank from a tin dipper tepid water smelling of the cedar bucket and of living beech trees. And still they did not go home. It was a horse lot this time, a tall rail fence upon and along which men stood and sat and out of which one by one horses were led, to be walked and trotted and then cantered back and forth along the road while the slow swapping and buying went on and the sun began to slant westward, they—the three of them—watching and listening, the older brother with his muddy eyes and his steady, inevitable tobacco, the father commenting now and then on certain of the animals, to no one in particular.

It was after sundown when they reached home. They ate supper by lamplight, then, sitting on the doorstep, the boy watched the night fully accomplish, listening to the whippoorwills and the frogs, when he heard his mother's voice: "Abner! No! No! Oh, God. Oh, God. Abner!" and he rose, whirled, and saw the altered light through the door where a candle stub now burned in a bottle neck on the table and his father, still in the hat and coat, at once formal and burlesque as though dressed carefully for some shabby and ceremonial violence, emptying the reservoir of the lamp back into the five-gallon kerosene can from which it had been filled, while the mother tugged at his arm until he shifted the lamp to the other hand and flung her back, not savagely or viciously, just hard, into the wall, her hands flung out against the wall for balance, her mouth open and in her face the same quality of hopeless despair as had been in her voice. Then his father saw him standing in the door.

85   "Go to the barn and get that can of oil we were oiling the wagon with," he said. The boy did not move. Then he could speak.

"What . . ." he cried. "What are you . . ."

"Go get that oil," his father said. "Go."

Then he was moving, running, outside the house, toward the stable: this the old habit, the old blood which he had not been permitted to choose for himself, which had been bequeathed him willy nilly and which had run for so long (and who knew where, battening on what of outrage and savagery and lust) before it came to him. *I could keep on,* he thought. *I could run on and on and never look back, never need to see his face again. Only I can't. I can't,* the rusted can in his hand now, the liquid sploshing in it as he ran back to the house and into it, into the sound of his mother's weeping in the next room, and handed the can to his father.

"Ain't you going to even send a nigger?" he cried. "At least you sent a nigger before!"

90   This time his father didn't strike him. The hand came even faster than the blow had, the same hand which had set the can on the table with almost excruciating care flashing from the can toward him too quick for him to follow it, gripping him by the back of his shirt and on to tiptoe before he had seen it quit the can, the face stooping at him in breathless and frozen ferocity, the cold, dead voice speaking over him to the older brother, who leaned against the table, chewing with that steady, curious, sidewise motion of cows:

"Empty the can into the big one and go on. I'll catch up with you."

"Better tie him up to the bedpost," the brother said.

"Do like I told you," the father said. Then the boy was moving, his bunched shirt and the hard, bony hand between his shoulder-blades, his toes just touching the floor, across the room and into the other one, past the sisters sitting with spread heavy thighs in the two chairs over the cold hearth, and to where his mother and aunt sat side by side on the bed, the aunt's arms about his mother's shoulders.

"Hold him," the father said. The aunt made a startled movement. "Not you," the father said. "Lennie. Take hold of him. I want to see you do it." His mother took him by the wrist. "You'll hold him better than that. If he gets loose don't you know what he is going to do? He will go up yonder." He jerked his head toward the road. "Maybe I'd better tie him."

"I'll hold him," his mother whispered.   95

"See you do then." Then his father was gone, the stiff foot heavy and measured upon the boards, ceasing at last.

Then he began to struggle. His mother caught him in both arms, he jerking and wrenching at them. He would be stronger in the end, he knew that. But he had no time to wait for it. "Lemme go!" he cried. "I don't want to have to hit you!"

"Let him go!" the aunt said. "If he don't go, before God, I am going up there myself!"

"Don't you see I can't?" his mother cried. "Sarty! Sarty! No! No! Help me, Lizzie!"

Then he was free. His aunt grasped at him but it was too late. He whirled,   100
running, his mother stumbled forward on to her knees behind him, crying to the nearer sister: "Catch him, Net! Catch him!" But that was too late too, the sister (the sisters were twins, born at the same time, yet either of them now gave the impression of being, encompassing as much living meat and volume and weight as any other two of the family) not yet having begun to rise from the chair, her head, face, alone merely turned, presenting to him in the flying instant an astonishing expanse of young female features untroubled by any surprise even, wearing only an expression of bovine interest. Then he was out of the room, out of the house, in the mild dust of the starlit road and the heavy rifeness of honeysuckle, the pale ribbon unspooling with terrific slowness under his running feet, reaching the gate at last and turning in, running, his heart and lungs drumming, on up the drive toward the lighted house, the lighted door. He did not knock, he burst in, sobbing for breath, incapable for the moment of speech; he saw the astonished face of the Negro in the linen jacket without knowing when the Negro had appeared.

"De Spain!" he cried, panted. "Where's . . ." then he saw the white man too emerging from a white door down the hall. "Barn!" he cried. "Barn!"

"What?" the white man said. "Barn?"

"Yes!" the boy cried. "Barn!"

"Catch him!" the white man shouted.

But it was too late this time too. The Negro grasped his shirt, but the entire   105
sleeve, rotten with washing, carried away, and he was out that door too and in the drive again, and had actually never ceased to run even while he was screaming into the white man's face.

Behind him the white man was shouting, "My horse! Fetch my horse!" and he thought for an instant of cutting across the park and climbing the fence into the road, but he did not know the park nor how high the vine-massed fence might be and he dared not risk it. So he ran on down the drive, blood and breath roaring; presently he was in the road again though he could not see it. He could not hear either: the galloping mare was almost upon him before he heard her, and even then he held his course, as if the very urgency of his wild grief and need must in a moment more find his wings, waiting until the ultimate instant to hurl himself aside and into the weed-choked roadside ditch as the horse thundered past and on, for an instant in furious silhouette against the stars, the tranquil early summer night sky which, even before the shape of the horse and rider vanished, stained abruptly and violently upward: a long, swirling roar incredible and soundless, blotting the stars, and he springing up and into the road again, running again, knowing it was too late yet still running even after he heard the shot and, an instant later, two shots, pausing now without knowing he had ceased to run, crying "Pap! Pap!", running again before he knew he had begun to run, stumbling, tripping over something and scrabbling up again without ceasing to run, looking backward over his shoulder at the glare as he got up, running on among the invisible trees, panting, sobbing, "Father! Father!"

At midnight he was sitting on the crest of a hill. He did not know it was midnight and he did not know how far he had come. But there was no glare behind him now and he sat now, his back toward what he had called home for four days anyhow, his face toward the dark woods which he would enter when breath was strong again, small, shaking steadily in the chill darkness, hugging himself into the remainder of his thin, rotten shirt, the grief and despair now no longer terror and fear but just grief and despair. *Father. My father,* he thought. "He was brave!" he cried suddenly, aloud but not loud, no more than a whisper: "He was! He was in the war! He was in Colonel Sartoris' cav'ry!" not knowing that his father had gone to that war a private in the fine old European sense, wearing no uniform, admitting the authority of and giving fidelity to no man or army or flag, going to war as Malbrouck[4] himself did: for booty—it meant nothing and less than nothing to him if it were enemy booty or his own.

The slow constellations wheeled on. It would be dawn and then sun-up after a while and he would be hungry. But that would be to-morrow and now he was only cold, and walking would cure that. His breathing was easier now and he decided to get up and go on, and then he found that he had been asleep because he knew it was almost dawn, the night almost over. He could tell that from the whippoorwills. They were everywhere now among the dark trees below him, constant and inflectioned and ceaseless, so that, as the instant for giving over to the day birds drew nearer and nearer, there was no interval at all between them. He got up. He was a little stiff, but walking would cure that too as it would the cold, and soon there would be the sun. He went on down the hill, toward the dark woods within which the liquid silver voices of the birds called unceasing—the rapid and urgent beating of the urgent and quiring heart of the late spring night. He did not look back.

1939

The most common reservations about this story can be summarized as three "charges":

---

4. The duke of Marlborough (1650–1722), an English general whose name became distorted as Malbrough and Malbrouch in English and French popular songs celebrating his exploits.

1. Faulkner's style is bad. His sentences are often too long and complicated, vague, unnecessarily wordy, and sometimes hard to read.
2. The structure of the story seems almost haphazard: it wanders off the subject or out of focus.
3. The reasons the story gives—and insists upon—for people acting the way they do are unrealistic and shallow.

Can a story with a dubious style, form, theme, and vision of human actions and motives be good, much less great? Should we, must we, like it, or at least recognize its "literary value"?

Let us see a few examples of what those who find the story flawed might isolate, analyze, and articulate. We can begin with Faulkner's awkward and obscure style and pick out an early sentence—the second sentence of the story—as evidence:

> The boy, crouched on his nail keg at the back of the crowded room, knew he smelled cheese, and more: from where he sat he could see the ranked shelves close-packed with the solid, squat, dynamic shapes of tin cans whose labels his stomach read, not from the lettering which meant nothing to his mind but from the scarlet devils and the silver curve of fish—this, the cheese which he knew he smelled and the hermetic meat which his intestines believed he smelled coming in intermittent gusts momentary and brief between the other constant one, the smell and sense just a little of fear because mostly of despair and grief, the old fierce pull of blood.

Even those who do not mind taking some pains in reading will probably acknowledge that this sentence is not immediately clear. The chief problem is how to relate the final phrase "the old fierce pull of blood" to the rest of the sentence, and so to discover what the sentence as a whole means. After a little work, you may decide that what the sentence says is that there is not only the smell of cheese and the imagined smell of canned meat but also the smell of despair and grief and even some smell of fear; and that despair, grief, and fear are in the boy's "blood," that is, inherited, in his genes. We still cannot be sure whether this implies that acquired traits or experiences are hereditary or whether "blood" means something else, and we still cannot be sure whether the smell of fear is imaginary—like the smell of the meat in the cans—or real—like the smell of the cheese (perhaps the smell of the sweat that comes with fear, or the odor some say fear gives off). But even if we have been successful in our unraveling of the meaning, what is the value of a sentence that has to be worked over so much and whose meaning even then is doubtful?

Now as to the matter of form. One reason "The Most Dangerous Game" is just a slick adventure story, some people say, is that everything in it is manipulated to heighten suspense. But if we criticize Connell for shifting focus for his own purposes, what can we say about the shifting of the focus in "Barn Burning"? One such shift occurs when the narrator is explaining why the man who burns other people's barns lights only a small neat fire when it is for his own use (paragraph 26):

> Older, the boy might have remarked this and wondered why not a big one; why should not a man who had not only seen the waste and extravagance of war, but who had in his blood an inherent voracious prodigality with material not his own, have burned everything in sight? Then he might have gone a step farther and thought that that was the reason: that niggard blaze was the living fruit of nights passed during those four years in the woods hiding from all men, blue or gray, with his strings of horses (captured horses, he called them). And older still, he might have divined the true reason: that the element of fire spoke to some deep mainspring of his father's being, as the element of steel or of powder spoke to other men, as the one weapon for the preservation of integrity, else

breath were not worth the breathing, and hence to be regarded with respect and used with discretion.

Is it okay to shift the focus temporally like this because the purpose of the shift is not "merely" to enhance the suspense but to clarify the meaning, to reveal "the true reason"?

Besides shifting to a time outside the story's present, sometimes the focus moves away from the boy's consciousness, which, like Rainsford's in "The Most Dangerous Game," dominates the rest of the story. When the father climbs aboard the wagon and immediately starts hitting the mules with a willow switch, the narrator comments (paragraph 20),

It was not even sadistic; it was exactly that same quality which in later years would cause his descendants to overrun the engine before putting a motor car into motion, striking and reining back in the same movement.

The time moves backward as well as forward and it always seems to do so in order to clarify or emphasize the meaning or illustrate the concept of "blood"—inborn, inherited habits or feelings. So, when his father tells him to get a can of oil the boy knows will be used to burn still another barn, despite the boy's repugnance at the act, he does it (paragraph 88):

Then he was moving, running, outside the house, toward the stable: this the old habit, the old blood which he had not been permitted to choose for himself, which had been bequeathed him willy nilly and which had run for so long (and who knew where, battening on what of outrage and savagery and lust) before it came to him. *I could keep on,* he thought. *I could run on and on and never look back, never need to see his face again. Only I can't. I can't,* . . .

This passage leads us directly into the third reservation or question, that having to do with the story's vision of the springs of human action. Can we accept that such habits, such capacities or incapacities, are bred into the "blood"? Can we even accept that this is a concept to be taken seriously, even if we cannot accept it? And if it is a serious concept, to what does it lead? to genetic determinism of one kind or another? to justifying "class"? to racism?

And, to go back to the earlier passage about the fire: what does it mean that "the element of fire spoke to some deep mainspring of his father's being, as the element of steel or of powder spoke to other men"? And how is it that fire, swords, guns—violence—can be weapons "for the preservation of integrity," without which life is not worth living? What "integrity" is the father so intent on preserving? And what kind of "discretion" does the father show in his use of fire? What makes whether we accept the meaning of this passage crucial is that it is not embedded in the fiction, as part of the action and thoughts of the characters—the boy, let us say—but it is separated from them by the shift in focus and by the flat statement that we are being given the "true reason"; so it has the authority of the story/author and we either have to believe it or discount the whole vision of the story.

And if we look beneath the surface of these "true reasons" and the "pull of blood" and look at the events of the story itself, we begin to suspect a "hidden agenda," an ideology that determines what the characters are seen to do and why.

Why is it that the boy overcomes or betrays the "pull of blood" only when the "aristocratic" Major de Spain's barn is to be burned? Is the blood of the highborn somehow more valuable than that of the low? (Though a Snopes, the boy's first name is that of the aristocrat Colonel Sartoris.) Is some blood better than others? some loyalties better than others? Or is property a higher good than blood?

The selection of certain key passages or incidents, the analysis and interpretation of the text, can be used to directly confront these critical comments and questions, as well as to explore other, more positive areas of the story and its accomplishment. And the objections themselves can be examined in terms of what unspoken assumptions they make about what makes a story good and what agendas they hide.

The long second sentence of "Barn Burning" does indeed put extraordinary emphasis on "blood." The concept here embodied in the word "blood" can stand such emphasis, even demands it, for "blood" is one of the forces that conflict within the boy. Therefore the sentence, though it may seem difficult, really gives ready access to the meaning of the story by calling attention to one of its key elements. Part of its length, too, consists in magnificent particularizing detail, the kind that convinces you that the author knows what he is talking about, and really "sees" the scene. The density of detail is also necessary in realizing (making real) the boy's sensations. The detail and the focus of the sentence also indicate where the significant action of the story is to take place—that is, inside the boy—and so we are made to understand and perhaps feel with him. Finally, the move from the smell of cheese to the "smell" of canned meat, to that of fear, is crucial: the smell of cheese is real. The smell of meat is inside the can and though it cannot actually be smelled while the can is intact it is real and is there. So what this suggests is that the boy's sensory imagination does not falsify, it just penetrates into things beyond the immediate present sense perceptions. This gives reality to the smell of despair, grief, fear—not necessarily real to the senses, but really there beneath the surface, real to the imagination. What the sentence does, then, is open up our notions of reality to include not just what the senses tell us, but what the imagination can sense. And since it does so through sensory images that gradually shade off into the imaginative, we are not just told that the imaginative is valid but we are made to feel that this is so. Thus the sentence that seemed unnecessarily long, complex, and difficult turns out to be functional. It does what no short sentence or series of sentences would be likely to manage.

Complexity, even obscurity, is not in all cases "bad"—as the criticism of the sentence seemed to assume. The literary value of language and detail does not necessarily follow rules of usage but questions of function—whether they work to create, reveal, intensify, the meaning and effect of the story.

Before going on to address the issue of the structure or theme of "Barn Burning," it may be appropriate to suggest that it is precisely in this merging of the physical and the imaginative, moral or psychological, that one of the strengths of the story—and of Faulkner—lies. The force that opposes blood, we soon learn, is the boy's sense of right and wrong. His father is accused of maliciously burning down Mr. Harris's barn. The boy knows his father is guilty. But when Harris demands the boy be called before the judge, the boy knows that because his ties to his father are those of "blood," he must lie. When the judge asks if Harris really wants the boy questioned, there is a pause. For the boy,

> . . . it was as if he had swung outward at the end of a grape vine, over a ravine, and at the top of the swing had been caught in a prolonged instant of mesmerized gravity, weightless in time. (paragraph 10)

Most readers would acknowledge the appropriateness of the image both to the feeling of suspense and to the experience of the boy, and the intervention of the image suspends the meaning and imitates the boy's suspense. When Harris says the boy does not have to testify, "the smell of cheese and sealed meat, the fear and despair and the old grief of blood" return to the boy's consciousness. The importance and meaning of fear, despair, and grief in the "blood" is now a little clearer.

Faulkner's complexity, "idiosyncrasies" (what some call "flaws"), and difficulty (sometimes called "obscurity") usually come from this interpenetration of imagination and sensory reality or other things that we usually keep separate, like past and present. Each episode, character, detail, is saturated with the full world of his fiction, and its function seems to be primarily to embody that world rather than to further the plot or make a statement. The present is informed by the past and informs the future. Characters (Major de Spain) and names (Colonel Sartoris) that are minor or casual here are central elsewhere in Faulkner's canon, like actors in a repertory theater. The fiction is all one seamless, interconnected, timeless world. The interpenetration of community and generations is essential to the vision.

This gives both a smaller and larger role to the concept of "blood." "Blood" alone—inherited traits, customs, motives—does not determine behavior, but it is one of the multitude of communal and traditional forces that condition behavior. Though "blood" can explain many acts and impulses, its force does not eliminate free will. The boy does, after all, choose to warn the Major of his father's intention, chooses morality over blood. To claim that it was only Major de Spain's class or property that moved the boy to consider betraying his father is to ignore the fact that the story opens with his being on the verge of doing so in the Harris case. The father's crimes went well beyond the destruction of property; indeed it was the primacy of property over principles in his scheme of values that led him to serve neither North nor South but Mammon (by being a nonpartisan horse thief) during the Civil War.

Explaining the function of what may at first have seemed defects does not close the discussion about the merits of a work or the nature and function of literature. The discussion of the value of "Barn Burning" does not necessarily end here.

Until now, we have depersonalized the evaluations, assuming that the pros and cons are intellectual positions that have little or nothing to do with an individual reader, and that the "evidence" is always in the story. But already we have seen that some of the response to Faulkner is ideological, based on social or political values that have little to do with whether the focus shifts or the sentences are too long. We must admit that not all evidence of value is "on the page"; some beauty is in the eyes of the beholder. Let us constantly be aware of our own responses and try at the same time to account for those responses in terms of both the narrative strategies and our own prejudices or predispositions.

BHARATI MUKHERJEE

The Management of Grief

A woman I don't know is boiling tea the Indian way in my kitchen. There are a lot of women I don't know in my kitchen, whispering, and moving tactfully. They open doors, rummage through the pantry, and try not to ask me where things are kept. They remind me of when my sons were small, on Mother's Day or when Vikram and I were tired, and they would make big, sloppy omelets. I would lie in bed pretending I didn't hear them.

Dr. Sharma, the treasurer of the Indo-Canada Society, pulls me into the hallway. He wants to know if I am worried about money. His wife, who has just come up from the basement with a tray of empty cups and glasses, scolds him. "Don't bother Mrs. Bhave with mundane details." She looks so monstrously pregnant her baby must be days overdue. I tell her she shouldn't be carrying heavy things. "Shaila," she says, smiling, "this is the fifth." Then she grabs a teenager by his shirttails. He slips his Walkman off his head. He has to be one of her four children, they have the same domed and dented foreheads. "What's the official word now?" she demands. The boy slips the headphones back on. "They're acting evasive, Ma. They're saying it could be an accident or a terrorist bomb."

All morning, the boys have been muttering, Sikh Bomb, Sikh Bomb. The men, not using the word, bow their heads in agreement. Mrs. Sharma touches her forehead at such a word. At least they've stopped talking about space debris and Russian lasers.

Two radios are going in the dining room. They are tuned to different stations. Someone must have brought the radios down from my boys' bedrooms. I haven't gone into their rooms since Kusum came running across the front lawn in her bathrobe. She looked so funny, I was laughing when I opened the door.

The big TV in the den is being whizzed through American networks and cable channels.

"Damn!" some man swears bitterly. "How can these preachers carry on like nothing's happened?" I want to tell him we're not that important. You look at the audience, and at the preacher in his blue robe with his beautiful white hair, the potted palm trees under a blue sky, and you know they care about nothing.

The phone rings and rings. Dr. Sharma's taken charge. "We're with her," he keeps saying. "Yes, yes, the doctor has given calming pills. Yes, yes, pills are having necessary effect." I wonder if pills alone explain this calm. Not peace, just a deadening quiet. I was always controlled, but never repressed. Sound can reach me, but my body is tensed, ready to scream. I hear their voices all around me. I hear my boys and Vikram cry, "Mommy, Shaila!" and their screams insulate me, like headphones.

The woman boiling water tells her story again and again. "I got the news first. My cousin called from Halifax before six A.M., can you imagine? He'd gotten up for prayers and his son was studying for medical exams and he heard on a rock channel that something had happened to a plane. They said first it had disappeared from the radar, like a giant eraser just reached out. His father called me, so I said to him, what do you mean, 'something bad'? You mean a hijacking? And he said, *behn,*[1] there is no confirmation of anything yet, but check with your neighbors because a lot of them must be on that plane. So I called poor Kusum straightaway. I knew Kusum's husband and daughter were booked to go yesterday."

Kusum lives across the street from me. She and Satish had moved in less than

5

1. "No."

a month ago. They said they needed a bigger place. All these people, the Sharmas and friends from the Indo-Canada Society had been there for the housewarming. Satish and Kusum made homemade tandoori on their big gas grill and even the white neighbors piled their plates high with that luridly red, charred, juicy chicken. Their younger daughter had danced, and even our boys had broken away from the Stanley Cup telecast to put in a reluctant appearance. Everyone took pictures for their albums and for the community newspapers—another of our families had made it big in Toronto—and now I wonder how many of those happy faces are gone. "Why does God give us so much if all along He intends to take it away?" Kusum asks me.

10   I nod. We sit on carpeted stairs, holding hands like children. "I never once told him that I loved him," I say. I was too much the well brought up woman. I was so well brought up I never felt comfortable calling my husband by his first name.

"It's all right," Kusum says. "He knew. My husband knew. They felt it. Modern young girls have to say it because what they feel is fake."

Kusum's daughter, Pam, runs in with an overnight case. Pam's in her McDonald's uniform. "Mummy! You have to get dressed!" Panic makes her cranky. "A reporter's on his way here."

"Why?"

"You want to talk to him in your bathrobe?" She starts to brush her mother's long hair. She's the daughter who's always in trouble. She dates Canadian boys and hangs out in the mall, shopping for tight sweaters. The younger one, the goody-goody one according to Pam, the one with a voice so sweet that when she sang *bhajans*[2] for Ethiopian relief even a frugal man like my husband wrote out a hundred dollar check, *she* was on that plane. *She* was going to spend July and August with grandparents because Pam wouldn't go. Pam said she'd rather waitress at McDonald's. "If it's a choice between Bombay and Wonderland, I'm picking Wonderland," she'd said.

15   "Leave me alone," Kusum yells. "You know what I want to do? If I didn't have to look after you now, I'd hang myself."

Pam's young face goes blotchy with pain. "Thanks," she says, "don't let me stop you."

"Hush," pregnant Mrs. Sharma scolds Pam. "Leave your mother alone. Mr. Sharma will tackle the reporters and fill out the forms. He'll say what has to be said."

Pam stands her ground. "You think I don't know what Mummy's thinking? *Why her?* that's what. That's sick! Mummy wishes my little sister were alive and I were dead."

Kusum's hand in mine is trembly hot. We continue to sit on the stairs.

20   She calls before she arrives, wondering if there's anything I need. Her name is Judith Templeton and she's an appointee of the provincial government. "Multi-

2. Hymns.

culturalism?" I ask, and she says, "partially," but that her mandate is bigger. "I've been told you knew many of the people on the flight," she says. "Perhaps if you'd agree to help us reach the others. . . ?"

She gives me time at least to put on tea water and pick up the mess in the front room. I have a few *samosas*[3] from Kusum's housewarming that I could fry up, but then I think, why prolong this visit?

Judith Templeton is much younger than she sounded. She wears a blue suit with a white blouse and a polka dot tie. Her blond hair is cut short, her only jewelry is pearl drop earrings. Her briefcase is new and expensive looking, a gleaming cordovan leather. She sits with it across her lap. When she looks out the front windows onto the street, her contact lenses seem to float in front of her light blue eyes.

"What sort of help do you want from me?" I ask. She has refused the tea, out of politeness, but I insist, along with some slightly stale biscuits.

"I have no experience," she admits. "That is, I have an MSW and I've worked in liaison with accident victims, but I mean I have no experience with a tragedy of this scale—"

"Who could?" I ask.   25

"—and with the complications of culture, language, and customs. Someone mentioned that Mrs. Bhave is a pillar—because you've taken it more calmly."

At this, perhaps, I frown, for she reaches forward, almost to take my hand. "I hope you understand my meaning, Mrs. Bhave. There are hundreds of people in Metro directly affected, like you, and some of them speak no English. There are some widows who've never handled money or gone on a bus, and there are old parents who still haven't eaten or gone outside their bedrooms. Some houses and apartments have been looted. Some wives are still hysterical. Some husbands are in shock and profound depression. We want to help, but our hands are tied in so many ways. We have to distribute money to some people, and there are legal documents—these things can be done. We have interpreters, but we don't always have the human touch, or maybe the right human touch. We don't want to make mistakes, Mrs. Bhave, and that's why we'd like to ask you to help us."

"More mistakes, you mean," I say.

"Police matters are not in my hands," she answers.

"Nothing I can do will make any difference," I say. "We must all grieve in our   30
own way."

"But you are coping very well. All the people said, Mrs. Bhave is the strongest person of all. Perhaps if the others could see you, talk with you, it would help them."

"By the standards of the people you call hysterical, I am behaving very oddly and very badly, Miss Templeton." I want to say to her, *I wish I could scream, starve, walk into Lake Ontario, jump from a bridge.* "They would not see me as a model. I do not see myself as a model."

---

3. Fried turnovers filled with meat or vegetable mixtures.

I am a freak. No one who has ever known me would think of me reacting this way. This terrible calm will not go away.

She asks me if she may call again, after I get back from a long trip that we all must make. "Of course," I say. "Feel free to call, anytime."

35   Four days later, I find Kusum squatting on a rock overlooking a bay in Ireland. It isn't a big rock, but it juts sharply out over water. This is as close as we'll ever get to them. June breezes balloon out her sari and unpin her knee-length hair. She has the bewildered look of a sea creature whom the tides have stranded.

It's been one hundred hours since Kusum came stumbling and screaming across my lawn. Waiting around the hospital, we've heard many stories. The police, the diplomats, they tell us things thinking that we're strong, that knowledge is helpful to the grieving, and maybe it is. Some, I know, prefer ignorance, or their own versions. The plane broke into two, they say. Unconsciousness was instantaneous. No one suffered. My boys must have just finished their breakfasts. They loved eating on planes, they loved the smallness of plates, knives, and forks. Last year they saved the airline salt and pepper shakers. Half an hour more and they would have made it to Heathrow.

Kusum says that we can't escape our fate. She says that all those people— our husbands, my boys, her girl with the nightingale voice, all those Hindus, Christians, Sikhs, Muslims, Parsis, and atheists on that plane—were fated to die together off this beautiful bay. She learned this from a swami in Toronto.

I have my Valium.

Six of us "relatives"—two widows and four widowers—choose to spend the day today by the waters instead of sitting in a hospital room and scanning photographs of the dead. That's what they call us now: relatives. I've looked through twenty-seven photos in two days. They're very kind to us, the Irish are very understanding. Sometimes understanding means freeing a tourist bus for this trip to the bay, so we can pretend to spy our loved ones through the glassiness of waves or in sunspeckled cloud shapes.

40   I could die here, too, and be content.

"What is that, out there?" She's standing and flapping her hands and for a moment I see a head shape bobbing in the waves. She's standing in the water, I, on the boulder. The tide is low, and a round, black, headsized rock has just risen from the waves. She returns, her sari end dripping and ruined and her face is a twisted remnant of hope, the way mine was a hundred hours ago, still laughing but inwardly knowing that nothing but the ultimate tragedy could bring two women together at six o'clock on a Sunday morning. I watch her face sag into blankness.

"That water felt warm, Shaila," she says at length.

"You can't," I say. "We have to wait for our turn to come."

I haven't eaten in four days, haven't brushed my teeth.

45   "I know," she says. "I tell myself I have no right to grieve. They are in a better place than we are. My swami says I should be thrilled for them. My swami says depression is a sign of our selfishness."

Maybe I'm selfish. Selfishly I break away from Kusum and run, sandals slapping against stones, to the water's edge. What if my boys aren't lying pinned under the debris? What if they aren't stuck a mile below that innocent blue chop? What if, given the strong currents. . . .

Now I've ruined my sari, one of my best. Kusum has joined me, knee-deep in water that feels to me like a swimming pool. I could settle in the water, and my husband would take my hand and the boys would slap water in my face just to see me scream.

"Do you remember what good swimmers my boys were, Kusum?"

"I saw the medals," she says.

One of the widowers, Dr. Ranganathan from Montreal, walks out to us, car-   50
rying his shoes in one hand. He's an electrical engineer. Someone at the hotel mentioned his work is famous around the world, something about the place where physics and electricity come together. He has lost a huge family, something indescribable. "With some luck," Dr. Ranganathan suggests to me, " a good swimmer could make it safely to some island. It is quite possible that there may be many, many microscopic islets scattered around."

"You're not just saying that?" I tell Dr. Ranganathan about Vinod, my elder son. Last year he took diving as well.

"It's a parent's duty to hope," he says. "It is foolish to rule out possibilities that have not been tested. I myself have not surrendered hope."

Kusum is sobbing once again. "Dear lady," he says, laying his free hand on her arm, and she calms down.

"Vinod is how old?" he asks me. He's very careful, as we all are. *Is,* not was.

"Fourteen. Yesterday he was fourteen. His father and uncle were going to take   55
him down to the Taj and give him a big birthday party. I couldn't go with them because I couldn't get two weeks off from my stupid job in June." I process bills for a travel agent. June is a big travel month.

Dr. Ranganathan whips the pockets of his suit jacked inside out. Squashed roses, in darkening shades of pink, float on the water. He tore the roses off creepers in somebody's garden. He didn't ask anyone if he could pluck the roses, but now there's been an article about it in the local papers. When you see an Indian person, it says, please give him or her flowers.

"A strong youth of fourteen," he says, "can very likely pull to safety a younger one."

My sons, though four years apart, were very close. Vinod wouldn't let Mithun drown. *Electrical engineering,* I think, foolishly perhaps: this man knows important secrets of the universe, things closed to me. Relief spins me lightheaded. No wonder my boys' photographs haven't turned up in the gallery of photos of the recovered dead. "Such pretty roses," I say.

"My wife loved pink roses. Every Friday I had to bring a bunch home. I used to say, why? After twenty-odd years of marriage you're still needing proof positive of my love?" He has identified his wife and three of his children. Then others from Montreal, the lucky ones, intact families with no survivors. He chuckles as he wades back to shore. Then he swings around to ask me a question. "Mrs. Bhave, you are wanting to throw in some roses for your loved ones? I have two big ones left."

60   But I have other things to float: Vinod's pocket calculator; a half-painted model B-52 for my Mithun. They'd want them on their island. And for my husband? For him I let fall into the calm, glassy waters a poem I wrote in the hospital yesterday. Finally he'll know my feelings for him.

"Don't tumble, the rocks are slippery," Dr. Ranganathan cautions. He holds out a hand for me to grab.

Then it's time to get back on the bus, time to rush back to our waiting posts on hospital benches.

Kusum is one of the lucky ones. The lucky ones flew here, identified in multiplicate their loved ones, then will fly to India with the bodies for proper ceremonies. Satish is one of the few males who surfaced. The photos of faces we saw on the walls in an office at Heathrow and here in the hospital are mostly of women. Women have more body fat, a nun said to me matter-of-factly. They float better.

Today I was stopped by a young sailor on the street. He had loaded bodies, he'd gone into the water when—he checks my face for signs of strength—when the sharks were first spotted. I don't blush, and he breaks down. "It's all right," I say. "Thank you." I had heard about the sharks from Dr. Ranganathan. In his orderly mind, science brings understanding, it holds no terror. It is the shark's duty. For every deer there is a hunter, for every fish a fisherman.

65   The Irish are not shy; they rush to me and give me hugs and some are crying. I cannot imagine reactions like that on the streets of Toronto. Just strangers, and I am touched. Some carry flowers with them and give them to any Indian they see.

After lunch, a policeman I have gotten to know quite well catches hold of me. He says he thinks he has a match for Vinod. I explain what a good swimmer Vinod is.

"You want me with you when you look at photos?" Dr. Ranganathan walks ahead of me into the picture gallery. In these matters, he is a scientist, and I am grateful. It is a new perspective. "They have performed miracles," he says. "We are indebted to them."

The first day or two the policemen showed us relatives only one picture at a time; now they're in a hurry, they're eager to lay out the possibles, and even the probables.

The face on the photo is of a boy much like Vinod; the same intelligent eyes, the same thick brows dipping into a V. But this boy's features, even his cheeks, are puffier, wider, mushier.

70   "No." My gaze is pulled by other pictures. There are five other boys who look like Vinod.

The nun assigned to console me rubs the first picture with a fingertip. "When they've been in the water for a while, love, they look a little heavier." The bones under the skin are broken, they said on the first day—try to adjust your memories. It's important.

"It's not him. I'm his mother. I'd know."

"I know this one!" Dr. Ranganathan cries out suddenly from the back of the gallery. "And this one!" I think he senses that I don't want to find my boys. "They are the Kutty brothers. They were also from Montreal." I don't mean to be crying. On the contrary, I am ecstatic. My suitcase in the hotel is packed heavy with dry clothes for my boys.

The policeman starts to cry. "I am so sorry, I am so sorry, ma'am. I really thought we had a match."

With the nun ahead of us and the policeman behind, we, the unlucky ones without our children's bodies, file out of the makeshift gallery.   75

From Ireland most of us go on to India. Kusum and I take the same direct flight to Bombay, so I can help her clear customs quickly. But we have to argue with a man in uniform. He has large boils on his face. The boils swell and glow with sweat as we argue with him. He wants Kusum to wait in line and he refuses to take authority because his boss is on a tea break. But Kusum won't let her coffins out of sight, and I shan't desert her though I know that my parents, elderly and diabetic, must be waiting in a stuffy car in a scorching lot.

"You bastard!" I scream at the man with the popping boils. Other passengers press closer. "You think we're smuggling contraband in those coffins!"

Once upon a time we were well brought up women; we were dutiful wives who kept our heads veiled, our voices shy and sweet.

In India, I become, once again, an only child of rich, ailing parents. Old friends of the family come to pay their respects. Some are Sikh, and inwardly, involuntarily, I cringe. My parents are progressive people; they do not blame communities for a few individuals.

In Canada it is a different story now.   80

"Stay longer," my mother pleads. "Canada is a cold place. Why would you want to be all by yourself?" I stay.

Three months pass. Then another.

"Vikram wouldn't have wanted you to give up things!" they protest. They call my husband by the name he was born with. In Toronto he'd changed to Vik so the men he worked with at his office would find his name as easy as Rod or Chris. "You know, the dead aren't cut off from us!"

My grandmother, the spoiled daughter of a rich *zamindar*,[4] shaved her head with rusty razor blades when she was widowed at sixteen. My grandfather died of childhood diabetes when he was nineteen, and she saw herself as the harbinger of bad luck. My mother grew up without parents, raised indifferently by an uncle, while her true mother slept in a hut behind the main estate house and took her food with the servants. She grew up a rationalist. My parents abhor mindless mortification.

The zamindar's daughter kept stubborn faith in Vedic rituals; my parents   85
rebelled. I am trapped between two modes of knowledge. At thirty-six, I am too old to start over and too young to give up. Like my husband's spirit, I flutter between worlds.

Courting aphasia, we travel. We travel with our phalanx of servants and poor relatives. To hill stations and to beach resorts. We play contract bridge in dusty

4. Landowner.

gymkhana clubs. We ride stubby ponies up crumbly mountain trails. At tea dances, we let ourselves be twirled twice round the ballroom. We hit the holy spots we hadn't made time for before. In Varanasi, Kalighat, Rishikesh, Hardwar, astrologers and palmists seek me out and for a fee offer me cosmic consolations.

Already the widowers among us are being shown new bride candidates. They cannot resist the call of custom, the authority of their parents and older brothers. They must marry; it is the duty of a man to look after a wife. The new wives will be young widows with children, destitute but of good family. They will make loving wives, but the men will shun them. I've had calls from the men over crackling Indian telephone lines. "Save me," they say, these substantial, educated, successful men of forty. "My parents are arranging a marriage for me." In a month they will have buried one family and returned to Canada with a new bride and partial family.

I am comparatively lucky. No one here thinks of arranging a husband for an unlucky widow.

Then, on the third day of the sixth month into this odyssey, in an abandoned temple in a tiny Himalayan village, as I make my offering of flowers and sweet-meats to the god of a tribe of animists, my husband descends to me. He is squatting next to a scrawny *sadhu* in moth-eaten robes. Vikram wears the vanilla suit he wore the last time I hugged him. The *sadhu* tosses petals on a butter-fed flame, reciting Sanskrit mantras and sweeps his face of flies. My husband takes my hands in his.

90   *You're beautiful,* he starts. Then, *What are you doing here?*

Shall I stay? I ask. He only smiles, but already the image is fading. *You must finish alone what we started together.* No seaweed wreathes his mouth. He speaks too fast just as he used to when we were an envied family in our pink split-level. He is gone.

In the windowless altar room, smoky with joss sticks and clarified butter lamps, a sweaty hand gropes for my blouse. I do not shriek. The *sadhu* arranges his robe. The lamps hiss and sputter out.

When we come out of the temple, my mother says, "Did you feel something weird in there?"

My mother has no patience with ghosts, prophetic dreams, holy men, and cults.

95   "No," I lie. "Nothing."

But she knows that she's lost me. She knows that in days I shall be leaving.

Kusum's put her house up for sale. She wants to live in an ashram in Hardwar. Moving to Hardwar was her swami's idea. Her swami runs two ashrams, the one in Hardwar and another here in Toronto.

"Don't run away," I tell her.

"I'm not running away," she says. "I'm pursuing inner peace. You think you or that Ranganathan fellow are better off?"

100   Pam's left for California. She wants to do some modelling, she says. She says when she comes into her share of the insurance money she'll open a yoga-cum-aerobics studio in Hollywood. She sends me postcards so naughty I daren't leave them on the coffee table. Her mother has withdrawn from her and the world.

The rest of us don't lose touch, that's the point. Talk is all we have, says Dr. Ranganathan, who has also resisted his relatives and returned to Montreal and to his job, alone. He says, whom better to talk with than other relatives? We've been melted down and recast as a new tribe.

He calls me twice a week from Montreal. Every Wednesday night and every Saturday afternoon. He is changing jobs, going to Ottawa. But Ottawa is over a hundred miles away, and he is forced to drive two hundred and twenty miles a day. He can't bring himself to sell his house. The house is a temple, he says; the king-sized bed in the master bedroom is a shrine. He sleeps on a folding cot. A devotee.

There are still some hysterical relatives. Judith Templeton's list of those needing help and those who've "accepted" is in nearly perfect balance. Acceptance means you speak of your family in the past tense and you make active plans for moving ahead with your life. There are courses at Seneca and Ryerson[5] we could be taking. Her gleaming leather briefcase is full of college catalogues and lists of cultural societies that need our help. She has done impressive work, I tell her.

"In the textbooks on grief management," she replies—I am her confidante, I realize, one of the few whose grief has not sprung bizarre obsessions—"there are stages to pass through: rejection, depression, acceptance, reconstruction." She has compiled a chart and finds that six months after the tragedy, none of us still reject reality, but only a handful are reconstructing. "Depressed Acceptance" is the plateau we've reached. Remarriage is a major step in reconstruction (though she's a little surprised, even shocked, over *how* quickly some of the men have taken on new families). Selling one's house and changing jobs and cities is healthy.

How do I tell Judith Templeton that my family surrounds me, and that like   105
creatures in epics, they've changed shapes? She sees me as calm and accepting but worries that I have no job, no career. My closest friends are worse off than I. I cannot tell her my days, even my nights, are thrilling.

She asks me to help with families she can't reach at all. An elderly couple in Agincourt whose sons were killed just weeks after they had brought their parents over from a village in Punjab. From their names, I know they are Sikh. Judith Templeton and a translator have visited them twice with offers of money for air fare to Ireland, with bank forms, power-of-attorney forms, but they have refused to sign, or to leave their tiny apartment. Their sons' money is frozen in the bank. Their sons' investment apartments have been trashed by tenants, the furnishings sold off. The parents fear that anything they sign or any money they receive will end the company's or the country's obligations to them. They fear they are selling their sons for two airline tickets to a place they've never seen.

The high-rise apartment is a tower of Indians and West Indians, with a sprinkling of Orientals. The nearest bus stop kiosk is lined with women in saris. Boys practice cricket in the parking lot. Inside the building, even I wince a bit from

5. Seneca College of Applied Arts and Technology, in Willowdale; Ryerson Polytechnical Institute, Toronto.

the ferocity of onion fumes, the distinctive and immediate Indianness of frying *ghee*, but Judith Templeton maintains a steady flow of information. These poor old people are in imminent danger of losing their place and all their services.

I say to her, "They are Sikh. They will not open up to a Hindu woman." And what I want to add is, as much as I try not to, I stiffen now at the sight of beards and turbans. I remember a time when we all trusted each other in this new country, it was only the new country we worried about.

The two rooms are dark and stuffy. The lights are off, and an oil lamp sputters on the coffee table. The bent old lady has let us in, and her husband is wrapping a white turban over his oiled, hip-length hair. She immediately goes to the kitchen, and I hear the most familiar sound of an Indian home, tap water hitting and filling a teapot.

110   They have not paid their utility bills, out of fear and the inability to write a check. The telephone is gone; electricity and gas and water are soon to follow. They have told Judith their sons will provide. They are good boys, and they have always earned and looked after their parents.

We converse a bit in Hindi. They do not ask about the crash and I wonder if I should bring it up. If they think I am here merely as a translator, then they may feel insulted. There are thousands of Punjabi-speakers, Sikhs, in Toronto to do a better job. And so I say to the old lady, "I too have lost my sons, and my husband, in the crash."

Her eyes immediately fill with tears. The man mutters a few words which sound like a blessing. "God provides and God takes away," he says.

I want to say, but only men destroy and give back nothing. "My boys and my husband are not coming back," I say. "We have to understand that."

Now the old woman responds. "But who is to say? Man alone does not decide these things." To this her husband adds his agreement.

115   Judith asks about the bank papers, the release forms. With a stroke of the pen, they will have a provincial trustee to pay their bills, invest their money, send them a monthly pension.

"Do you know this woman?" I ask them.

The man raises his hand from the table, turns it over and seems to regard each finger separately before he answers. "This young lady is always coming here, we make tea for her and she leaves papers for us to sign." His eyes scan a pile of papers in the corner of the room. "Soon we will be out of tea, then will she go away?"

The old lady adds, "I have asked my neighbors and no one else gets *angrezi*[6] visitors. What have we done?"

"It's her job," I try to explain. "The government is worried. Soon you will have no place to stay, no lights, no gas, no water."

120   "Government will get its money. Tell her not to worry, we are honorable people."

I try to explain the government wishes to give money, not take. He raises his hand. "Let them take," he says. "We are accustomed to that. That is no problem."

6. English, Anglo.

"We are strong people," says the wife. "Tell her that."

"Who needs all this machinery?" demands the husband. "It is unhealthy, the bright lights, the cold air on a hot day, the cold food, the four gas rings. God will provide, not government."

"When our boys return," the mother says. Her husband sucks his teeth. "Enough talk," he says.

Judith breaks in. "Have you convinced them?" The snaps on her cordovan briefcase go off like firecrackers in that quiet apartment. She lays the sheaf of legal papers on the coffee table. "If they can't write their names, an X will do— I've told them that."

Now the old lady has shuffled to the kitchen and soon emerges with a pot of tea and two cups. "I think my bladder will go first on a job like this," Judith says to me, smiling. "If only there was some way of reaching them. Please thank her for the tea. Tell her she's very kind."

I nod in Judith's direction and tell them in Hindi, "She thanks you for the tea. She thinks you are being very hospitable but she doesn't have the slightest idea what it means."

I want to say, humor her. I want to say, my boys and my husband are with me too, more than ever. I look in the old man's eyes and I can read his stubborn, peasant's message: *I have protected this woman as best I can. She is the only person I have left. Give to me or take from me what you will, but I will not sign for it. I will not pretend that I accept.*

In the car, Judith says, "You see what I'm up against? I'm sure they're lovely people, but their stubbornness and ignorance are driving me crazy. They think signing a paper is signing their sons' death warrants, don't they?"

I am looking out the window. I want to say, *In our culture, it is a parent's duty to hope.*

"Now Shaila, this next woman is a real mess. She cries day and night, and she refuses all medical help. We may have to—"

"—Let me out at the subway," I say.

"I beg your pardon?" I can feel those blue eyes staring at me.

It would not be like her to disobey. She merely disapproves, and slows at a corner to let me out. Her voice is plaintive. "Is there anything I said? Anything I did?"

I could answer her suddenly in a dozen ways, but I choose not to. "Shaila? Let's talk about it," I hear, then slam the door.

A wife and mother begins her new life in a new country, and that life is cut short. Yet her husband tells her: Complete what we have started. We, who stayed out of politics and came halfway around the world to avoid religious and political feuding have been the first in the New World to die from it. I no longer know what we started, nor how to complete it. I write letters to the editors of local papers and to members of Parliament. Now at least they admit it was a bomb. One MP answers back, with sympathy, but with a challenge. You want to make a difference? Work on a campaign. Work on mine. Politicize the Indian voter.

My husband's old lawyer helps me set up a trust. Vikram was a saver and a careful investor. He had saved the boys' boarding school and college fees. I sell the pink house at four times what we paid for it and take a small apartment downtown. I am looking for a charity to support.

We are deep in the Toronto winter, gray skies, icy pavements. I stay indoors, watching television. I have tried to assess my situation, how best to live my life, to complete what we began so many years ago. Kusum has written me from Hardwar that her life is now serene. She has seen Satish and has heard her daughter sing again. Kusum was on a pilgrimage, passing through a village when she heard a young girl's voice, singing one of her daughter's favorite *bhajans*. She followed the music through the squalor of a Himalayan village, to a hut where a young girl, an exact replica of her daughter, was fanning coals under the kitchen fire. When she appeared, the girl cried out, "Ma!" and ran away. What did I think of that?

I think I can only envy her.

140   Pam didn't make it to California, but writes me from Vancouver. She works in a department store, giving make-up hints to Indian and Oriental girls. Dr. Ranganathan has given up his commute, given up his house and job, and accepted an academic position in Texas where no one knows his story and he has vowed not to tell it. He calls me now once a week.

I wait, I listen, and I pray, but Vikram has not returned to me. The voices and the shapes and the nights filled with visions ended abruptly several weeks ago.

I take it as a sign.

One rare, beautiful, sunny day last week, returning from a small errand on Yonge Street, I was walking through the park from the subway to my apartment. I live equidistant from the Ontario Houses of Parliament and the University of Toronto. The day was not cold, but something in the bare trees caught my attention. I looked up from the gravel, into the branches and the clear blue sky beyond. I thought I heard the rustling of larger forms, and I waited a moment for voices. Nothing.

"What?" I asked.

145   Then as I stood in the path looking north to Queen's Park and west to the university, I heard the voices of my family one last time. *Your time has come*, they said. *Go, be brave.*

I do not know where this voyage I have begun will end. I do not know which direction I will take. I dropped the package on a park bench and started walking.

1988

Let us begin a reader-oriented discussion of this story, by thinking of ourselves first as a general reader reading the opening of this story for the first time:

> A woman I don't know is boiling tea the Indian way in my kitchen. There are a lot of women I don't know in my kitchen, whispering, and moving tactfully. They open doors, rummage through the pantry, and try not to ask me where things are kept. They remind me of when my sons were small, on Mother's Day or when Vikram and I were tired, and they would make big, sloppy omelets. I would lie in bed pretending I didn't hear them.

We are plunged immediately into the mind of an "I" whose identity we do not know, in a setting specified only as in or near a kitchen, and in a situation about which we know nothing. There is no exposition, no explanation. The more familiar past tense of most stories is absent; we are thrust into a narrative present without known precedent or purpose. The uncertainty makes us look at every word and detail for clues: "my kitchen" and "my sons . . . on Mother's Day" soon identifies the narrator as a mature female.

At this point, whether we find this indirection and uncertainty annoying or engaging (for making us work to figure out what is going on), we may ask a question or two not about the story but about ourselves. The first two stories in this chapter were not only written by men but were almost entirely about men. (No women appear in "The Most Dangerous Game," and the mother, aunt, and daughter in "Barn Burning" are peripheral.) "The Management of Grief" is not only written by a woman but tells the story through the consciousness of a woman, a strong and intelligent woman. On the other hand, this woman is a mother, somewhat older than most college students. The boy in "Barn Burning," though younger than you, is living through a part of life you have already lived through and so know something about firsthand. How much does the age of the central character have to do not just with your understanding, but with your feelings, your affective response to what you are reading?

The name "Vikram" in the first paragraph for many of us suggests little except foreignness, but "Dr. Sharma, the treasurer of the Indo-Canada Society" (paragraph 2), tells us enough about the cultural setting for the moment. In the ensuing conversation we learn the name of the narrator—Shaila Bhave—and that there has been an accident, perhaps a terrorist bombing, which may explain what seems to be the confusion of the opening scene.

The bomb, the next sentence tells us, may have been a Sikh bomb, and in the eighth paragraph we learn that it was a passenger plane that was, or might have been, bombed. What is a Sikh? Why would a Sikh bomb a plane full of people? Does the average reader in the United States read this story with the same attitudes and emotions as the average Euro-Canadian? Indo-Canadian? Indian? Sikh?

This is not to say that an eighteen-year-old male of Polish descent living in Cleveland cannot read this story with strong emotions and with deep sympathy for and understanding of Shaila Bhave and her tragedy. But would his responses be the same in nature and intensity as those of a middle-aged Indo-Canadian woman living in Toronto or Vancouver? Nor is this to suggest that even a Canadian mother of Indian heritage can feel what Shaila Bhave feels. Indeed, the title and the story suggest that only outsiders can believe that grief can be "managed." The story seems at once to urge empathy and to reveal the chasm between onlookers (like us) and those stricken.

For Indians, Sikhs, and some Canadians (Indian and others), this incident (which is based on an actual disaster) is also likely to be controversial, even though the story itself does not concentrate on assessing blame or the political tensions or causes involved. Whether or not a story takes sides, touching on an issue that readers recognize as controversial inevitably affects how those readers evaluate the story. This does not necessarily mean that all Sikhs or all Indians hold one view. People often disagree with their own government's or community's actions—as many Americans did during the Vietnam war. The point is not that controversial stories are bad or that considering the politics or ideology of a work in evaluating it is bad. But we need to recognize the ideological or political factor in our assessment, to acknowledge who and where we are, where we are coming from, when we say, "This story is good" or "That story is lousy."

Evaluating a story, then, means reading carefully (and widely), learning as much as we can about the elements of fiction, of literary and cultural contexts, and of narrative strategies, and articulating our analyses; being honest about our own responses and feeling responsible for articulating them as clearly and convincingly as possible; taking our opinions seriously but listening with attention and an open mind to the judgments and reasoning of other readers. It requires as well some examination and knowledge of ourselves, of what in ourselves conditions our responses to fiction, and a willingness to look at what underlies our judgments and how we might learn and grow. Assessing the value of a story is difficult and a firm evaluation elusive in part because it means examining more than words on a page: it means examining so many ideas, beliefs, and feelings we take for granted. It means examining and, to a degree, evaluating our outer world and inner selves.

Reading More Fiction

LOUISA MAY ALCOTT

My Contraband[1]

Doctor Franck came in as I sat sewing up the rents in an old shirt, that Tom might go tidily to his grave. New shirts were needed for the living, and there was no wife or mother to "dress him handsome when he went to meet the Lord," as one woman said, describing the fine funeral she had pinched herself to give her son.

"Miss Dane, I'm in a quandary," began the Doctor, with that expression of countenance which says as plainly as words, "I want to ask a favor, but I wish you'd save me the trouble."

"Can I help you out of it?"

"Faith! I don't like to propose it, but you certainly can, if you please."

5   "Then name it, I beg."

"You see a Reb has just been brought in crazy with typhoid; a bad case every way; a drunken, rascally little captain somebody took the trouble to capture, but whom nobody wants to take the trouble to cure. The wards are full, the ladies worked to death, and willing to be for our own boys, but rather slow to risk their lives for a Reb. Now, you've had the fever, you like queer patients, your mate will see to your ward for a while, and I will find you a good attendant. The fellow won't last long, I fancy; but he can't die without some sort of care, you know. I've put him in the fourth story of the west wing, away from the rest. It is airy, quiet, and comfortable there. I'm on that ward, and will do my best for you in every way. Now, then, will you go?"

"Of course I will, out of perversity, if not common charity; for some of these people think that because I'm an abolitionist I am also a heathen, and I should rather like to show them that, though I cannot quite love my enemies, I am willing to take care of them."

"Very good; I thought you'd go; and speaking of abolition reminds me that you can have a contraband for servant, if you like. It is that fine mulatto fellow who was found burying his rebel master after the fight, and, being badly cut

---

1. Union commander General Benjamin Butler called southern slaves who had fled north "contraband"; therefore, they need not be returned to their "owners."

over the head, our boys brought him along. Will you have him?"

"By all means,—for I'll stand to my guns on that point, as on the other; these black boys are far more faithful and handy than some of the white scamps given me to serve, instead of being served by. But is this man well enough?"

"Yes, for that sort of work, and I think you'll like him. He must have been a handsome fellow before he got his face slashed; not much darker than myself; his master's son, I dare say, and the white blood makes him rather high and haughty about some things. He was in a bad way when he came in, but vowed he'd die in the street rather than turn in with the black fellows below; so I put him up in the west wing, to be out of the way, and he's seen to the captain all the morning. When can you go up?"

"As soon as Tom is laid out, Skinner moved, Haywood washed, Marble dressed, Charley rubbed, Downs taken up, Upham laid down, and the whole forty fed."

We both laughed, though the Doctor was on his way to the dead-house and I held a shroud on my lap. But in a hospital one learns that cheerfulness is one's salvation; for, in an atmosphere of suffering and death, heaviness of heart would soon paralyze usefulness of hand, if the blessed gift of smiles had been denied us.

In an hour I took possession of my new charge, finding a dissipated-looking boy of nineteen or twenty raving in the solitary little room, with no one near him but the contraband in the room adjoining. Feeling decidedly more interest in the black man than in the white, yet remembering the Doctor's hint of his being "high and haughty," I glanced furtively at him as I scattered chloride of lime about the room to purify the air, and settled matters to suit myself. I had seen many contrabands, but never one so attractive as this. All colored men are called "boys," even if their heads are white; this boy was five-and-twenty at least, strong-limbed and manly, and had the look of one who never had been cowed by abuse or worn with oppressive labor. He sat on his bed doing nothing; no book, no pipe, no pen or paper anywhere appeared, yet anything less indolent or listless than his attitude and expression I never saw. Erect he sat, with a hand on either knee, and eyes fixed on the bare wall opposite, so rapt in some absorbing thought as to be unconscious of my presence, though the door stood wide open and my movements were by no means noiseless. His face was half averted, but I instantly approved the Doctor's taste, for the profile which I saw possessed all the attributes of comeliness belonging to his mixed race. He was more quadroon than mulatto, with Saxon features, Spanish complexion darkened by exposure, color in lips and cheek, waving hair, and an eye full of the passionate melancholy which in such men always seems to utter a mute protest against the broken law that doomed them at their birth. What could he be thinking of? The sick boy cursed and raved, I rustled to and fro, steps passed the door, bells rang, and the steady rumble of army-wagons came up from the street, still he never stirred. I had seen colored people in what they call "the black sulks," when, for days, they neither smiled nor spoke, and scarcely ate. But this was something more than that; for the man was not dully brooding over some small grievance; he seemed to see an all-absorbing fact or fancy recorded on the wall, which was a blank to me. I wondered if it were some deep wrong or sorrow, kept alive by memory and impotent regret; if he mourned for the dead master to whom he had been faithful to the end; or if the liberty now his were robbed of half its sweetness by the knowledge that some one near and dear to him still languished in the hell from which he had escaped. My heart quite warmed to him at that idea; I wanted to know and comfort him; and, following the impulse of the moment, I went in and touched him on the shoulder.

In an instant the man vanished and the slave appeared. Freedom was too new a boon to have wrought its blessed changes yet; and as he started up, with his hand at his temple, and an obsequious "Yes, Missis," any romance that had gathered round him fled away, leaving the saddest of all sad facts in living guise before me. Not only did the manhood seem to die out of him, but the comeliness that first attracted me; for, as he turned, I saw the ghastly wound that had laid open cheek and forehead. Being partly healed, it was no longer bandaged, but held together with strips of that transparent plaster which I never see without a shiver, and swift recollections of the scenes with which it is associated in my mind. Part of his black hair had been shorn away, and one eye was nearly closed; pain so distorted, and the cruel sabre-cut so marred that portion of his face, that, when I saw it, I felt as if a fine medal had been suddenly reversed, showing me a far more striking type of human suffering and wrong than Michael Angelo's bronze prisoner.[2] By one of those inexplicable processes that often teach us how little we understand ourselves, my purpose was suddenly changed; and, though I went in to offer comfort as a friend, I merely gave an order as a mistress.

"Will you open these windows? this man needs more air."   15

He obeyed at once, and, as he slowly urged up the unruly sash, the handsome profile was again turned toward me, and again I was possessed by my first impression so strongly that I involuntarily said,—

"Thank you."

Perhaps it was fancy, but I thought that in the look of mingled surprise and something like reproach which he gave me, there was also a trace of grateful pleasure. But he said, in that tone of spiritless humility these poor souls learn so soon,—

"I isn't a white man, Missis, I'se a contraband."

"Yes, I know it; but a contraband is a free man, and I heartily congratulate   20 you."

He liked that; his face shone, he squared his shoulders, lifted his head, and looked me full in the eye with a brisk,—

"Thank ye, Missis; anything more to do fer yer?"

"Doctor Franck thought you would help me with this man, as there are many patients and few nurses or attendants. Have you had the fever?"

"No, Missis."

"They should have thought of that when they put him here; wounds and   25 fevers should not be together. I'll try to get you moved."

He laughed a sudden laugh: if he had been a white man, I should have called

2. Probably a reference to Michelangelo's marble sculpture *The Dying Slave* (executed before 1513), commissioned by Pope Julius II for his tomb.

it scornful; as he was a few shades darker than myself, I suppose it must be considered an insolent, or at least an unmannerly one.

"It don't matter, Missis. I'd rather be up here with the fever than down with those niggers; and there isn't no other place fer me."

Poor fellow! that was true. No ward in all the hospital would take him in to lie side by side with the most miserable white wreck there. Like the bat in Æsop's fable,[3] he belonged to neither race; and the pride of one and the helplessness of the other, kept him hovering alone in the twilight a great sin has brought to overshadow the whole land.

"You shall stay, then; for I would far rather have you than my lazy Jack. But are you well and strong enough?"

30   "I guess I'll do, Missis."

He spoke with a passive sort of acquiescence,—as if it did not much matter if he were not able, and no one would particularly rejoice if he were.

"Yes, I think you will. By what name shall I call you?"

"Bob, Missis."

Every woman has her pet whim; one of mine was to teach the men self-respect by treating them respectfully. Tom, Dick, and Harry would pass, when lads rejoiced in those familiar abbreviations; but to address men often old enough to be my father in that style did not suit my old-fashioned ideas of propriety. This "Bob" would never do; I should have found it as easy to call the chaplain "Gus" as my tragical-looking contraband by a title so strongly associated with the tail of a kite.

35   "What is your other name?" I asked. "I like to call my attendants by their last names rather than by their first."

"I'se got no other, Missis; we has our masters' names, or do without. Mine's dead, and I won't have anything of his 'bout me."

"Well, I'll call you Robert, then, and you may fill this pitcher for me, if you will be so kind."

He went; but, through all the tame obedience years of servitude had taught him, I could see that the proud spirit his father gave him was not yet subdued, for the look and gesture with which he repudiated his master's name were a more effective declaration of independence than any Fourth-of-July orator could have prepared.

We spent a curious week together. Robert seldom left his room, except upon my errands; and I was a prisoner all day, often all night, by the bedside of the rebel. The fever burned itself rapidly away, for there seemed little vitality to feed it in the feeble frame of this old young man, whose life had been none of the most righteous, judging from the revelations made by his unconscious lips; since more than once Robert authoritatively silenced him, when my gentler hushings were of no avail, and blasphemous wanderings or ribald camp-songs made my cheeks burn and Robert's face assume an aspect of disgust. The captain was the gentleman in the world's eye, but the contraband was the gentleman in mine;— I was a fanatic, and that accounts for such depravity of taste, I hope. I never asked

---

3. In "The Bat, the Birds, and the Beast," the Bat hesitates to join either the Birds or the Beasts during a battle between them. When the battle has ended, the Bat finds himself unwelcome in both camps.

Robert of himself, feeling that somewhere there was a spot still too sore to bear the lightest touch; but, from his language, manner, and intelligence, I inferred that his color had procured for him the few advantages within the reach of a quick-witted, kindly-treated slave. Silent, grave, and thoughtful, but most serviceable, was my contraband; glad of the books I brought him, faithful in the performance of the duties I assigned to him, grateful for the friendliness I could not but feel and show toward him. Often I longed to ask what purpose was so visibly altering his aspect with such daily deepening gloom. But I never dared, and no one else had either time or desire to pry into the past of this specimen of one branch of the chivalrous "F.F.V.s."[4]

On the seventh night, Dr. Franck suggested that it would be well for some one, besides the general watchman of the ward, to be with the captain, as it might be his last. Although the greater part of the two preceding nights had been spent there, of course I offered to remain,—for there is a strange fascination in these scenes, which renders one careless of fatigue and unconscious of fear until the crisis is past. 40

"Give him water as long as he can drink, and if he drops into a natural sleep, it may save him. I'll look in at midnight, when some change will probably take place. Nothing but sleep or a miracle will keep him now. Good-night."

Away went the Doctor; and, devouring a whole mouthful of grapes, I lowered the lamp, wet the captain's head, and sat down on a hard stool to begin my watch. The captain lay with his hot, haggard face turned toward me, filling the air with his poisonous breath, and feebly muttering, with lips and tongue so parched that the sanest speech would have been difficult to understand. Robert was stretched on his bed in the inner room, the door of which stood ajar, that a fresh draught from his open window might carry the fever-fumes away through mine. I could just see a long, dark figure, with the lighter outline of a face, and, having little else to do just then, I fell to thinking of this curious contraband, who evidently prized his freedom highly, yet seemed in no haste to enjoy it. Dr. Franck had offered to send him on to safer quarters, but he had said, "No, thank yer, sir, not yet," and then had gone away to fall into one of those black moods of his, which began to disturb me, because I had no power to lighten them. As I sat listening to the clocks from the steeples all about us, I amused myself with planning Robert's future, as I often did my own, and had dealt out to him a generous hand of trumps wherewith to play this game of life which hitherto had gone so cruelly against him, when a harsh choked voice called,—

"Lucy!"

It was the captain, and some new terror seemed to have gifted him with momentary strength.

"Yes, here's Lucy," I answered, hoping that by following the fancy I might quiet him,—for his face was damp with the clammy moisture, and his frame shaken with the nervous tremor that so often precedes death. His dull eye fixed upon me, dilating with a bewildered look of incredulity and wrath, till he broke out fiercely,— 45

"That's a lie! she's dead,—and so's Bob, damn him!"

4. Finest Families of Virginia.

Finding speech a failure, I began to sing the quiet tune that had often soothed delirium like this; but hardly had the line,—

"See gentle patience smile on pain,"

passed my lips, when he clutched me by the wrist, whispering like one in mortal fear,—

"Hush! she used to sing that way to Bob, but she never would to me. I swore I'd whip the devil out of her, and I did; but you know before she cut her throat she said she'd haunt me, and there she is!"

He pointed behind me with an aspect of such pale dismay, that I involuntarily glanced over my shoulder and started as if I had seen a veritable ghost; for, peering from the gloom of that inner room, I saw a shadowy face, with dark hair all about it, and a glimpse of scarlet at the throat. An instant showed me that it was only Robert leaning from his bed's foot, wrapped in a gray army-blanket, with his red shirt just visible above it, and his long hair disordered by sleep. But what a strange expression was on his face! The unmarred side was toward me, fixed and motionless as when I first observed it,—less absorbed now, but more intent. His eye glittered, his lips were apart like one who listened with every sense, and his whole aspect reminded me of a hound to which some wind had brought the scent of unsuspected prey.

"Do you know him, Robert? Does he mean you?"

"Laws, no, Missis; they all own half-a-dozen Bobs: but hearin' my name woke me; that's all."

He spoke quite naturally, and lay down again, while I returned to my charge, thinking that this paroxysm was probably his last. But by another hour I perceived a hopeful change; for the tremor had subsided, the cold dew was gone, his breathing was more regular, and Sleep, the healer, had descended to save or take him gently away. Doctor Franck looked in at midnight, bade me keep all cool and quiet, and not fail to administer a certain draught as soon as the captain woke. Very much relieved, I laid my head on my arms, uncomfortably folded on the little table, and fancied I was about to perform one of the feats which practice renders possible,—"sleeping with one eye open," as we say: a half-and-half doze, for all senses sleep but that of hearing; the faintest murmur, sigh, or motion will break it, and give one back one's wits much brightened by the brief permission to "stand at ease." On this night the experiment was a failure, for previous vigils, confinement, and much care had rendered naps a dangerous indulgence. Having roused half-a-dozen times in an hour to find all quiet, I dropped my heavy head on my arms, and, drowsily resolving to look up again in fifteen minutes, fell fast asleep.

The striking of a deep-voiced clock awoke me with a start. "That is one," thought I; but, to my dismay, two more strokes followed, and in remorseful haste I sprang up to see what harm my long oblivion had done. A strong hand put me back into my seat, and held me there. It was Robert. The instant my eye met his my heart began to beat, and all along my nerves tingled that electric flash which foretells a danger that we cannot see. He was very pale, his mouth grim, and both eyes full of sombre fire; for even the wounded one was open now, all the more sinister for the deep scar above and below. But his touch was steady, his voice quiet, as he said,—

"Sit still, Missis; I won't hurt yer, nor scare yer, ef I can help it, but yer waked too soon."

"Let me go, Robert,—the captain is stirring,—I must give him something." 55

"No, Missis, yer can't stir an inch. Look here!"

Holding me with one hand, with the other he took up the glass in which I had left the draught, and showed me it was empty.

"Has he taken it?" I asked, more and more bewildered.

"I flung it out o' winder, Missis; he'll have to do without."

"But why, Robert? why did you do it?" 60

"'Kase I hate him!"

Impossible to doubt the truth of that; his whole face showed it, as he spoke through his set teeth, and launched a fiery glance at the unconscious captain. I could only hold my breath and stare blankly at him, wondering what mad act was coming next. I suppose I shook and turned white, as women have a foolish habit of doing when sudden danger daunts them; for Robert released my arm, sat down upon the bedside just in front of me, and said, with the ominous quietude that made me cold to see and hear,—

"Don't yer be frightened, Missis; don't try to run away, fer the door's locked and the key in my pocket; don't yer cry out, fer yer'd have to scream a long while, with my hand on yer mouth, 'efore yer was heard. Be still, an' I'll tell yer what I'm gwine to do."

"Lord help us! he has taken the fever in some sudden, violent way, and is out of his head. I must humor him till some one comes"; in pursuance of which swift determination, I tried to say, quite composedly,—

"I will be still and hear you; but open the window. Why did you shut it?" 65

"I'm sorry I can't do it, Missis; but yer'd jump out, or call, if I did, an' I'm not ready yet. I shut it to make yer sleep, an' heat would do it quicker'n anything else I could do."

The captain moved, and feebly muttered "Water!" Instinctively I rose to give it to him, but the heavy hand came down upon my shoulder, and in the same decided tone Robert said,—

"The water went with the physic; let him call."

"Do let me go to him! he'll die without care!"

"I mean he shall;— don't yer meddle, if yer please, Missis." 70

In spite of his quiet tone and respectful manner, I saw murder in his eyes, and turned faint with fear; yet the fear excited me, and, hardly knowing what I did, I seized the hands that had seized me, crying,—

"No, no; you shall not kill him! It is base to hurt a helpless man. Why do you hate him? He is not your master."

"He's my brother."

I felt that answer from head to foot, and seemed to fathom what was coming, with a prescience vague, but unmistakable. One appeal was left to me, and I made it.

75   "Robert, tell me what it means? Do not commit a crime and make me accessory to it. There is a better way of righting wrong than by violence;—let me help
you find it."

My voice trembled as I spoke, and I heard the frightened flutter of my heart;
so did he, and if any little act of mine had ever won affection or respect from
him, the memory of it served me then. He looked down, and seemed to put some
question to himself; whatever it was, the answer was in my favor, for when his
eyes rose again, they were gloomy, but not desperate.

"I *will* tell yer, Missis; but mind, this makes no difference; the boy is mine. I'll
give the Lord a chance to take him fust: if He don't, I shall."

"Oh, no! remember he is your brother."

An unwise speech; I felt it as it passed my lips, for a black frown gathered on
Robert's face, and his strong hands closed with an ugly sort of grip. But he did
not touch the poor soul gasping there behind him, and seemed content to let
the slow suffocation of that stifling room end his frail life.

80   "I'm not like to forgit dat, Missis, when I've been thinkin' of it all this week. I
knew him when they fetched him in, an' would 'a' done it long 'fore this, but I
wanted to ask where Lucy was; he knows,—he told to-night,—an' now he's done
for."

"Who is Lucy?" I asked hurriedly, intent on keeping his mind busy with any
thought but murder.

With one of the swift transitions of a mixed temperament like this, at my
question Robert's deep eyes filled, the clenched hands were spread before his
face, and all I heard were the broken words,—

"My wife,—he took her—"

In that instant every thought of fear was swallowed up in burning indignation
for the wrong, and a perfect passion of pity for the desperate man so tempted to
avenge an injury for which there seemed no redress but this. He was no longer
slave or contraband, no drop of black blood marred him in my sight, but an
infinite compassion yearned to save, to help, to comfort him. Words seemed so
powerless I offered none, only put my hand on his poor head, wounded, homeless, bowed down with grief for which I had no cure, and softly smoothed the
long, neglected hair, pitifully wondering the while where was the wife who must
have loved this tender-hearted man so well.

85   The captain moaned again, and faintly whispered, "Air!" but I never stirred.
God forgive me! just then I hated him as only a woman thinking of a sister woman's wrong could hate. Robert looked up; his eyes were dry again, his mouth
grim. I saw that, said, "Tell me more," and he did; for sympathy is a gift the
poorest may give, the proudest stoop to receive.

"Yer see, Missis, his father,—I might say ours, ef I warn't ashamed of both of
'em,—his father died two years ago, an' left us all to Marster Ned,—that's him
here, eighteen then. He always hated me, I looked so like old Marster: he don't,—
only the light skin an' hair. Old Marster was kind to all of us, me 'specially, an'
bought Lucy off the next plantation down there in South Carolina, when he
found I liked her. I married her, all I could; it warn't much, but we was true to
one another till Marster Ned come home a year after an' made hell fer both of

us. He sent my old mother to be used up in his rice-swamp in Georgy; he found me with my pretty Lucy, an' though young Miss cried, an' I prayed to him on my knees, an' Lucy run away, he wouldn't have no mercy; he brought her back, an'—took her."

"Oh, what did you do?" I cried, hot with helpless pain and passion.

How the man's outraged heart sent the blood flaming up into his face and deepened the tones of his impetuous voice, as he stretched his arm across the bed, saying, with a terribly expressive gesture,—

"I half murdered him, an' to-night I'll finish."

"Yes, yes—but go on now; what came next?"   90

He gave me a look that showed no white man could have felt a deeper degradation in remembering and confessing these last acts of brotherly oppression.

"They whipped me till I couldn't stand, an' then they sold me further South. Yer thought I was a white man once,—look here!"

With a sudden wrench he tore the shirt from neck to waist, and on his strong, brown shoulders showed me furrows deeply ploughed, wounds which, though healed, were ghastlier to me than any in that house. I could not speak to him, and, with the pathetic dignity a great grief lends the humblest sufferer, he ended his brief tragedy by simply saying,—

"That's all, Missis. I'se never seen her since, an' now I never shall in this world,—maybe not in t'other."

"But, Robert, why think her dead? The captain was wandering when he said   95
those sad things; perhaps he will retract them when he is sane. Don't despair; don't give up yet."

"No, Missis, I 'spect he's right; she was too proud to bear that long. It's like her to kill herself. I told her to, if there was no other way; an' she always minded me, Lucy did. My poor girl! Oh, it warn't right! No, by God, it warn't!"

As the memory of this bitter wrong, this double bereavement, burned in his sore heart, the devil that lurks in every strong man's blood leaped up; he put his hand upon his brother's throat, and, watching the white face before him, muttered low between his teeth,—

"I'm lettin' him go too easy; there's no pain in this; we a'n't even yet. I wish he knew me. Marster Ned! it's Bob; where's Lucy?"

From the captain's lips there came a long faint sigh, and nothing but a flutter of the eyelids showed that he still lived. A strange stillness filled the room as the elder brother held the younger's life suspended in his hand, while wavering between a dim hope and a deadly hate. In the whirl of thoughts that went on in my brain, only one was clear enough to act upon. I must prevent murder, if I could,—but how? What could I do up there alone, locked in with a dying man and a lunatic?—for any mind yielded utterly to any unrighteous impulse is mad while the impulse rules it. Strength I had not, nor much courage, neither time nor will for stratagem, and chance only could bring me help before it was too late. But one weapon I possessed,—a tongue,—often a woman's best defence; and sympathy, stronger than fear, gave me power to use it. What I said Heaven only knows, but surely Heaven helped me; words burned on my lips, tears streamed from my eyes, and some good angel prompted me to use the one name that had power to arrest my hearer's hand and touch his heart. For at that moment I heartily believed that Lucy lived, and this earnest faith roused in him a like belief. He listened with the lowering look of one in whom brute instinct was sovereign for the time,—a look that makes the noblest countenance base. He was but a man,—a poor, untaught, outcast, outraged man. Life had few joys for him; the world offered him no honors, no success, no home, no love. What future would this crime mar? and why should he deny himself that sweet, yet bitter morsel called revenge? How many white men, with all New England's freedom, culture, Christianity, would not have felt as he felt then? Should I have reproached him for a human anguish, a human longing for redress, all now left him from the ruin of his few poor hopes? Who had taught him that self-control, self-sacrifice, are attributes that make men masters of the earth, and lift them nearer heaven? Should I have urged the beauty of forgiveness, the duty of devout submission? He had no religion, for he was no saintly "Uncle Tom," and Slavery's black shadow seemed to darken all the world to him, and shut out God. Should I have warned him of penalties, of judgments, and the potency of law? What did he know of justice, or the mercy that should temper that stern virtue, when every law, human and divine, had been broken on his hearthstone? Should I have tried to touch him by appeals to filial duty, to brotherly love? How had his appeals been answered? What memories had father and brother stored up in his heart to plead for either now? No,—all these influences, these associations, would have proved worse than useless, had I been calm enough to try them. I was not; but instinct, subtler than reason, showed me the one safe clue by which to lead this troubled soul from the labyrinth in which it groped and nearly fell. When I paused, breathless, Robert turned to me, asking, as if human assurances could strengthen his faith in Divine Omnipotence,—

"Do you believe, if I let Marster Ned live, the Lord will give me back my Lucy?"

"As surely as there is a Lord, you will find her here or in the beautiful hereafter, where there is no black or white, no master and no slave."

He took his hand from his brother's throat, lifted his eyes from my face to the wintry sky beyond, as if searching for that blessed country, happier even than the happy North. Alas, it was the darkest hour before the dawn!—there was no star above, no light below but the pale glimmer of the lamp that showed the brother who had made him desolate. Like a blind man who believes there is a sun, yet cannot see it, he shook his head, let his arms drop nervelessly upon his knees, and sat there dumbly asking that question which many a soul whose faith is firmer fixed than his has asked in hours less dark than this,—"Where is God?" I saw the tide had turned, and strenuously tried to keep this rudderless life-boat from slipping back into the whirlpool wherein it had been so nearly lost.

"I have listened to you, Robert; now hear me, and heed what I say, because my heart is full of pity for you, full of hope for your future, and a desire to help you now. I want you to go away from here, from the temptation of this place, and the sad thoughts that haunt it. You have conquered yourself once, and I honor you for it, because, the harder the battle, the more glorious the victory; but it is safer to put a greater distance between you and this man. I will write you letters, give you money, and send you to good old Massachusetts to begin your new life a freeman,—yes, and a happy man; for when the captain is himself again, I will learn where Lucy is, and move heaven and earth to find and give her back to you. Will you do this, Robert?"

Slowly, very slowly, the answer came; for the purpose of a week, perhaps a year, was hard to relinquish in an hour.   105

"Yes, Missis, I will."

"Good! Now you are the man I thought you, and I'll work for you with all my heart. You need sleep, my poor fellow; go, and try to forget. The captain is alive, and as yet you are spared that sin. No, don't look there; I'll care for him. Come, Robert, for Lucy's sake."

Thank Heaven for the immortality of love! for when all other means of salvation failed, a spark of this vital fire softened the man's iron will, until a woman's hand could bend it. He let me take from him the key, let me draw him gently away, and lead him to the solitude which now was the most healing balm I could bestow. Once in his little room, he fell down on his bed and lay there, as if spent with the sharpest conflict of his life. I slipped the bolt across his door, and unlocked my own, flung up the window, steadied myself with a breath of air, then rushed to Doctor Franck. He came; and till dawn we worked together, saving one brother's life, and taking earnest thought how best to secure the other's liberty. When the sun came up as blithely as if it shone only upon happy homes, the Doctor went to Robert. For an hour I heard the murmur of their voices; once I caught the sound of heavy sobs, and for a time a reverent hush, as if in the silence that good man were ministering to soul as well as body. When he departed he took Robert with him, pausing to tell me he should get him off as soon as possible, but not before we met again.

Nothing more was seen of them all day; another surgeon came to see the captain, and another attendant came to fill the empty place. I tried to rest, but could not, with the thought of poor Lucy tugging at my heart, and was soon back at my post again, anxiously hoping that my contraband had not been too hastily spirited away. Just as night fell there came a tap, and, opening, I saw Robert literally "clothed, and in his right mind." The Doctor had replaced the ragged suit with tidy garments, and no trace of the tempestuous night remained but deeper lines upon the forehead, and the docile look of a repentant child. He did not cross the threshold, did not offer me his hand,—only took off his cap, saying, with a traitorous falter in his voice,—

"God bless yer, Missis! I'm gwine."   110

I put out both my hands, and held his fast.

"Good-by, Robert! Keep up good heart, and when I come home to Massachusetts we'll meet in a happier place than this. Are you quite ready, quite comfortable for your journey?"

"Yes, Missis, yes; the Doctor's fixed everything! I'se gwine with a friend of his; my papers are all right, an' I'm as happy as I can be till I find"—

He stopped there; then went on, with a glance into the room,—

"I'm glad I didn't do it, an' I thank yer, Missis, fer hinderin' me—thank yer hearty; but I'm afraid I hate him jest the same."   115

Of course he did; and so did I; for these faulty hearts of ours cannot turn perfect in a night, but need frost and fire, wind and rain, to ripen and make them ready for the great harvest-home. Wishing to divert his mind, I put my poor mite into his hand, and, remembering the magic of a certain little book, I gave him mine, on whose dark cover whitely shone the Virgin Mother and the Child, the grand history of whose life the book contained. The money went into Robert's pocket with a grateful murmur, the book into his bosom, with a long look and a tremulous—

"I never saw *my* baby, Missis."

I broke down then; and though my eyes were too dim to see, I felt the touch of lips upon my hands, heard the sound of departing feet, and knew my contraband was gone.

When one feels an intense dislike, the less one says about the subject of it the better; therefore I shall merely record that the captain lived,—in time was exchanged; and that, whoever the other party was, I am convinced the Government got the best of the bargain. But long before this occurred, I had fulfilled my promise to Robert; for as soon as my patient recovered strength of memory enough to make his answer trustworthy, I asked, without any circumlocution,—

120   "Captain Fairfax, where is Lucy?"

And too feeble to be angry, surprised, or insincere, he straightway answered,—

"Dead, Miss Dane."

"And she killed herself when you sold Bob?"

"How the devil did you know that?" he muttered, with an expression half-remorseful, half-amazed; but I was satisfied, and said no more.

125   Of course this went to Robert, waiting far away there in a lonely home,—waiting, working, hoping for his Lucy. It almost broke my heart to do it; but delay was weak, deceit was wicked; so I sent the heavy tidings, and very soon the answer came,—only three lines; but I felt that the sustaining power of the man's life was gone.

"I tort I'd never see her any more; I'm glad to know she's out of trouble. I thank yer, Missis; an' if they let us, I'll fight fer yer till I'm killed, which I hope will be 'fore long."

Six months later he had his wish, and kept his word.

Every one knows the story of the attack on Fort Wagner; but we should not tire yet of recalling how our Fifty-Fourth,[5] spent with three sleepless nights, a day's fast, and a march under the July sun, stormed the fort as night fell, facing death in many shapes, following their brave leaders through a fiery rain of shot and shell, fighting valiantly for "God and Governor Andrew,"—how the regiment that went into action seven hundred strong, came out having had nearly half its number captured, killed, or wounded, leaving their young commander to be buried, like a chief of earlier times, with his body-guard around him, faithful to the death. Surely, the insult turns to honor, and the wide grave needs no monument but the heroism that consecrates it in our sight; surely, the hearts that held him nearest, see through their tears a noble victory in the seeming sad

---

5. The Fifty-Fourth was a Massachusetts regiment of African-American soldiers that distinguished itself in the attack on Fort Wagner, South Carolina. It was the subject of the 1989 film *Glory*.

defeat; and surely, God's benediction was bestowed, when this loyal soul answered, as Death called the roll, "Lord, here am I, with the brothers Thou hast given me!"

The future must show how well that fight was fought; for though Fort Wagner once defied us, public prejudice is down; and through the cannon-smoke of that black night, the manhood of the colored race shines before many eyes that would not see, rings in many ears that would not hear, wins many hearts that would not hitherto believe.

When the news came that we were needed, there was none so glad as I to   130
leave teaching contrabands, the new work I had taken up, and go to nurse "our boys," as my dusky flock so proudly called the wounded of the Fifty-Fourth. Feeling more satisfaction, as I assumed my big apron and turned up my cuffs, than if dressing for the President's levee, I fell to work in Hospital No. 10 at Beaufort. The scene was most familiar, and yet strange; for only dark faces looked up at me from the pallets so thickly laid along the floor, and I missed the sharp accent of my Yankee boys in the slower, softer voices calling cheerily to one another, or answering my questions with a stout, "We'll never give it up, Missis, till the last Reb's dead," or, "If our people's free, we can afford to die."

Passing from bed to bed, intent on making one pair of hands do the work of three, at least, I gradually washed, fed, and bandaged my way down the long line of sable heroes, and coming to the very last, found that he was my contraband. So old, so worn, so deathly weak and wan, I never should have known him but for the deep scar on his cheek. That side lay uppermost, and caught my eye at once; but even then I doubted, such an awful change had come upon him, when, turning to the ticket just above his head, I saw the name, "Robert Dane." That both assured and touched me, for, remembering that he had no name, I knew that he had taken mine. I longed for him to speak to me, to tell how he had fared since I lost sight of him, and let me perform some little service for him in return for many he had done for me; but he seemed asleep; and as I stood re-living that strange night again, a bright lad, who lay next him softly waving an old fan across both beds, looked up and said,—

"I guess you know him, Missis?"

"You are right. Do you?"

"As much as any one was able to, Missis."

"Why do you say 'was,' as if the man were dead and gone?"   135

"I s'pose because I know he'll have to go. He's got a bad jab in the breast, an' is bleedin' inside, the Doctor says. He don't suffer any, only gets weaker 'n' weaker every minute. I've been fannin' him this long while, an' he's talked a little; but he don't know me now, so he's most gone, I guess."

There was so much sorrow and affection in the boy's face, that I remembered something, and asked, with redoubled interest,—

"Are you the one that brought him off? I was told about a boy who nearly lost his life in saving that of his mate."

I dare say the young fellow blushed, as any modest lad might have done; I could not see it, but I heard the chuckle of satisfaction that escaped him, as he glanced from his shattered arm and bandaged side to the pale figure opposite.

140 "Lord, Missis, that's nothin'; we boys always stan' by one another, an' I warn't goin' to leave him to be tormented any more by them cussed Rebs. He's been a slave once, though he don't look half so much like it as me, an' I was born in Boston."

He did not; for the speaker was as black as the ace of spades,—being a sturdy specimen, the knave of clubs would perhaps be a fitter representative,—but the dark freeman looked at the white slave with the pitiful, yet puzzled expression I have so often seen on the faces of our wisest men, when this tangled question of Slavery presented itself, asking to be cut or patiently undone.

"Tell me what you know of this man; for, even if he were awake, he is too weak to talk."

"I never saw him till I joined the regiment, an' no one 'peared to have got much out of him. He was a shut-up sort of feller, an' didn't seem to care for anything but gettin' at the Rebs. Some say he was the fust man of us that enlisted; I know he fretted till we were off, an' when we pitched into Old Wagner, he fought like the devil."

"Were you with him when he was wounded? How was it?"

145 "Yes, Missis. There was somethin' queer about it; for he 'peared to know the chap that killed him, an' the chap knew him. I don't dare to ask, but I rather guess one owned the other some time; for, when they clinched, the chap sung out, 'Bob!' an' Dane, 'Marster Ned!'—then they went at it."

I sat down suddenly, for the old anger and compassion struggled in my heart, and I both longed and feared to hear what was to follow.

"You see, when the Colonel,—Lord keep an' send him back to us!—it a'n't certain yet, you know, Missis, though it's two days ago we lost him,—well, when the Colonel shouted, 'Rush on, boys, rush on!' Dane tore away as if he was goin' to take the fort alone; I was next him, an' kept close as we went through the ditch an' up the wall. Hi! warn't that a rusher!" and the boy flung up his well arm with a whoop, as if the mere memory of that stirring moment came over him in a gust of irrepressible excitement.

"Were you afraid?" I said, asking the question women often put, and receiving the answer they seldom fail to get.

"No, Missis!"—emphasis on the "Missis"—"I never thought of anything but the damn' Rebs, that scalp, slash, an' cut our ears off, when they git us. I was bound to let daylight into one of 'em at least, an' I did. Hope he liked it!"

150 "It is evident that you did. Now go on about Robert, for I should be at work."

"He was one of the fust up; I was just behind, an' though the whole thing happened in a minute, I remember how it was, for all I was yellin' an' knockin' round like mad. Just where we were, some sort of an officer was wavin' his sword an' cheerin' on his men; Dane saw him by a big flash that come by; he flung away his gun, give a leap, an' went at that feller as if he was Jeff, Beauregard, an' Lee,[6] all in one. I scrabbled after as quick as I could, but was only up in time to

---

6. Jefferson Davis (1808–1889), president of the Confederate states; Pierre Beauregard (1818–1893), Confederate general whose firing on Fort Sumter began the war and who commanded troops in a Confederate victory at the Battle of Bull Run; Robert E. Lee (1807–1870), commanding general of the Confederate army.

see him git the sword straight through him an' drop into the ditch. You needn't ask what I did next, Missis, for I don't quite know myself; all I'm clear about is, that I managed somehow to pitch that Reb into the fort as dead as Moses, git hold of Dane, an' bring him off. Poor old feller! we said we went in to live or die; he said he went in to die, an' he's done it."

I had been intently watching the excited speaker; but as he regretfully added those last words I turned again, and Robert's eyes met mine,—those melancholy eyes, so full of an intelligence that proved he had heard, remembered, and reflected with that preternatural power which often outlives all other faculties. He knew me, yet gave no greeting; was glad to see a woman's face, yet had no smile wherewith to welcome it; felt that he was dying, yet uttered no farewell. He was too far across the river to return or linger now; departing thought, strength, breath, were spent in one grateful look, one murmur of submission to the last pang he could ever feel. His lips moved, and, bending to them, a whisper chilled my cheek, as it shaped the broken words,—

"I'd 'a' done it,—but it's better so,—I'm satisfied."

Ah! well he might be,—for, as he turned his face from the shadow of the life that was, the sunshine of the life to be touched it with a beautiful content, and in the drawing of a breath my contraband found wife and home, eternal liberty and God.

1869

CHARLOTTE PERKINS GILMAN

The Yellow Wallpaper

It is very seldom that mere ordinary people like John and myself secure ancestral halls for the summer.

A colonial mansion, a hereditary estate, I would say a haunted house, and reach the height of romantic felicity—but that would be asking too much of fate!

Still I will proudly declare that there is something queer about it.

Else, why should it be let so cheaply? And why have stood so long untenanted?

John laughs at me, of course, but one expects that in marriage.   5

John is practical in the extreme. He has no patience with faith, an intense horror of superstition, and he scoffs openly at any talk of things not to be felt and seen and put down in figures.

John is a physician, and *perhaps*—(I would not say it to a living soul, of course, but this is dead paper and a great relief to my mind—) *perhaps* that is one reason I do not get well faster.

You see he does not believe I am sick!

And what can one do?

10   If a physician of high standing, and one's own husband, assures friends and relatives that there is really nothing the matter with one but temporary nervous depression—a slight hysterical tendency—what is one to do?

My brother is also a physician, and also of high standing, and he says the same thing.

So I take phosphates or phosphites—whichever it is, and tonics, and journeys, and air, and exercise, and am absolutely forbidden to "work" until I am well again.

Personally, I disagree with their ideas.

Personally, I believe that congenial work, with excitement and change, would do me good.

15   But what is one to do?

I did write for a while in spite of them; but it *does* exhaust me a good deal—having to be so sly about it, or else meet with heavy opposition.

I sometimes fancy that in my condition if I had less opposition and more society and stimulus—but John says the very worst thing I can do is to think about my condition, and I confess it always makes me feel bad.

So I will let it alone and talk about the house.

The most beautiful place! It is quite alone, standing well back from the road, quite three miles from the village. It makes me think of English places that you read about, for there are hedges and walls and gates that lock, and lots of separate little houses for the gardeners and people.

20   There is a *delicious* garden! I never saw such a garden—large and shady, full of box-bordered paths, and lined with long grape-covered arbors with seats under them.

There were greenhouses, too, but they are all broken now.

There was some legal trouble, I believe, something about the heirs and co-heirs; anyhow, the place has been empty for years.

That spoils my ghostliness, I am afraid, but I don't care—there is something strange about the house—I can feel it.

I even said so to John one moonlight evening, but he said what I felt was a *draught,* and shut the window.

25   I get unreasonably angry with John sometimes. I'm sure I never used to be so sensitive. I think it is due to this nervous condition.

But John says if I feel so, I shall neglect proper self-control; so I take pains to control myself—before him, at least, and that makes me very tired.

I don't like our room a bit. I wanted one downstairs that opened on the piazza and had roses all over the window, and such pretty old-fashioned chintz hangings! but John would not hear of it.

He said there was only one window and not room for two beds, and no near room for him if he took another.

He is very careful and loving, and hardly lets me stir without special direction.

30   I have a schedule prescription for each hour in the day; he takes all care from me, and so I feel basely ungrateful not to value it more.

He said we came here solely on my account, that I was to have perfect rest and all the air I could get. "Your exercise depends on your strength, my dear," said he, "and your food somewhat on your appetite; but air you can absorb all the time." So we took the nursery at the top of the house.

It is a big, airy room, the whole floor nearly, with windows that look all ways, and air and sunshine galore. It was nursery first and then playroom and gymnasium, I should judge; for the windows are barred for little children, and there are rings and things in the walls.

The paint and paper look as if a boys' school had used it. It is stripped off—the paper—in great patches all around the head of my bed, about as far as I can reach, and in a great place on the other side of the room low down. I never saw a worse paper in my life.

One of those sprawling flamboyant patterns committing every artistic sin.

It is dull enough to confuse the eye in following, pronounced enough to constantly irritate and provoke study, and when you follow the lame uncertain curves for a little distance they suddenly commit suicide—plunge off at outrageous angles, destroy themselves in unheard of contradictions.

The color is repellant, almost revolting; a smouldering unclean yellow, strangely faded by the slow-turning sunlight.

It is a dull yet lurid orange in some places, a sickly sulphur tint in others.

No wonder the children hated it! I should hate it myself if I had to live in this room long.

There comes John, and I must put this away,—he hates to have me write a word.

We have been here two weeks, and I haven't felt like writing before, since that first day.

I am sitting by the window now, up in this atrocious nursery, and there is nothing to hinder my writing as much as I please, save lack of strength.

John is away all day, and even some nights when his cases are serious.

I am glad my case is not serious!

But these nervous troubles are dreadfully depressing.

John does not know how much I really suffer. He knows there is no *reason* to suffer, and that satisfies him.

Of course it is only nervousness. It does weigh on me so not to do my duty in any way!

I mean to be such a help to John, such a real rest and comfort, and here I am a comparative burden already!

Nobody would believe what an effort it is to do what little I am able,—to dress and entertain, and order things.

It is fortunate Mary is so good with the baby. Such a dear baby!

And yet I *cannot* be with him, it makes me so nervous.

I suppose John never was nervous in his life. He laughs at me so about this wallpaper!

At first he meant to repaper the room, but afterwards he said that I was letting it get the better of me, and that nothing was worse for a nervous patient than to give way to such fancies.

He said that after the wallpaper was changed it would be the heavy bedstead, and then the barred windows, and then that gate at the head of the stairs, and so on.

"You know the place is doing you good," he said, "and really, dear, I don't care to renovate the house just for a three months' rental."

"Then do let us go downstairs," I said, "there are such pretty rooms there."

Then he took me in his arms and called me a blessed little goose, and said he would go down cellar, if I wished, and have it whitewashed into the bargain.

But he is right enough about the beds and windows and things.

It is an airy and comfortable room as any one need wish, and, of course, I would not be so silly as to make him uncomfortable just for a whim.

I'm really getting quite fond of the big room, all but that horrid paper.

Out of one window I can see the garden, those mysterious deep-shaded arbors, the riotous old-fashioned flowers, and bushes and gnarly trees.

Out of another I get a lovely view of the bay and a little private wharf belonging to the estate. There is a beautiful shaded lane that runs down there from the house. I always fancy I see people walking in these numerous paths and arbors, but John has cautioned me not to give way to fancy in the least. He says that with my imaginative power and habit of story-making, a nervous weakness like mine is sure to lead to all manner of excited fancies, and that I ought to use my will and good sense to check the tendency. So I try.

I think sometimes that if I were only well enough to write a little it would relieve the press of ideas and rest me.

But I find I get pretty tired when I try.

It is so discouraging not to have any advice and companionship about my work. When I get really well, John says we will ask Cousin Henry and Julia down for a long visit; but he says he would as soon put fireworks in my pillow-case as to let me have those stimulating people about now.

I wish I could get well faster.

But I must not think about that. This paper looks to me as if it *knew* what a vicious influence it had!

There is a recurrent spot where the pattern lolls like a broken neck and two bulbous eyes stare at you upside down.

I get positively angry with the impertinence of it and the everlastingness. Up and down and sideways they crawl, and those absurd, unblinking eyes are everywhere. There is one place where two breadths didn't match, and the eyes go all up and down the line, one a little higher than the other.

I never saw so much expression in an inanimate thing before, and we all know how much expression they have! I used to lie awake as a child and get more entertainment and terror out of blank walls and plain furniture than most children could find in a toy-store.

I remember what a kindly wink the knobs of our big, old bureau used to have, and there was one chair that always seemed like a strong friend.

I used to feel that if any of the other things looked too fierce I could always hop into that chair and be safe.

The furniture in this room is no worse than inharmonious, however, for we had to bring it all from downstairs. I suppose when this was used as a playroom they had to take the nursery things out, and no wonder! I never saw such ravages as the children have made here.

The wallpaper, as I said before, is torn off in spots, and it sticketh closer than a brother—they must have had perseverance as well as hatred.

Then the floor is scratched and gouged and splintered, the plaster itself is dug out here and there, and this great heavy bed which is all we found in the room, looks as if it had been through the wars.

But I don't mind it a bit—only the paper.

There comes John's sister. Such a dear girl as she is, and so careful of me! I must not let her find me writing.

She is a perfect and enthusiastic housekeeper, and hopes for no better profession. I verily believe she thinks it is the writing which made me sick!

But I can write when she is out, and see her a long way off from these windows.

There is one that commands the road, a lovely shaded winding road, and one that just looks off over the country. A lovely country, too, full of great elms and velvet meadows.

This wallpaper has a kind of sub-pattern in a different shade, a particularly irritating one, for you can only see it in certain lights, and not clearly then.

But in the places where it isn't faded and where the sun is just so—I can see a strange, provoking, formless sort of figure, that seems to skulk about behind that silly and conspicuous front design.

There's sister on the stairs!

Well, the Fourth of July is over! The people are all gone and I am tired out. John thought it might do me good to see a little company, so we just had mother and Nellie and the children down for a week.

Of course I didn't do a thing. Jennie sees to everything now.

But it tired me all the same.

John says if I don't pick up faster he shall send me to Weir Mitchell[1] in the fall.

But I don't want to go there at all. I had a friend who was in his hands once, and she says he is just like John and my brother, only more so!

Besides, it is such an undertaking to go so far.

I don't feel as if it was worth while to turn my hand over for anything, and I'm getting dreadfully fretful and querulous.

I cry at nothing, and cry most of the time.

Of course I don't when John is here, or anybody else, but when I am alone.

And I am alone a good deal just now. John is kept in town very often by serious cases, and Jennie is good and lets me alone when I want her to.

So I walk a little in the garden or down that lovely lane, sit on the porch under the roses, and lie down up here a good deal.

I'm getting really fond of the room in spite of the wallpaper. Perhaps *because* of the wallpaper.

It dwells in my mind so!

1. Silas Weir Mitchell (1829–1914), American physician, novelist, and specialist in nerve disorders, popularized the rest cure.

I lie here on this great immovable bed—it is nailed down, I believe—and follow that pattern about by the hour. It is as good as gymnastics, I assure you. I start, we'll say, at the bottom, down in the corner over there where it has not been touched, and I determine for the thousandth time that I *will* follow that pointless pattern to some sort of conclusion.

I know a little of the principle of design, and I know this thing was not arranged on any laws of radiation, or alternation, or repetition, or symmetry, or anything else that I ever heard of.

It is repeated, of course, by the breadths, but not otherwise.

Looked at in one way each breadth stands alone, the bloated curves and flourishes—a kind of "debased Romanesque" with *delirium tremens*—go waddling up and down in isolated columns of fatuity.

100 But, on the other hand, they connect diagonally, and the sprawling outlines run off in great slanting waves of optic horror, like a lot of wallowing seaweeds in full chase.

The whole thing goes horizontally, too, at least it seems so, and I exhaust myself in trying to distinguish the order of its going in that direction.

They have used a horizontal breadth for a frieze, and that adds wonderfully to the confusion.

There is one end of the room where it is almost intact, and there, when the crosslights fade and the low sun shines directly upon it, I can almost fancy radiation after all,—the interminable grotesque seem to form around a common center and rush off in headlong plunges of equal distraction.

It makes me tired to follow it. I will take a nap I guess.

105 I don't know why I should write this.

I don't want to.

I don't feel able.

And I know John would think it absurd. But I *must* say what I feel and think in some way—it is such a relief!

But the effort is getting to be greater than the relief.

110 Half the time now I am awfully lazy, and lie down ever so much.

John says I mustn't lose my strength, and has me take cod liver oil and lots of tonics and things, to say nothing of ale and wine and rare meat.

Dear John! He loves me very dearly, and hates to have me sick. I tried to have a real earnest reasonable talk with him the other day, and tell him how I wish he would let me go and make a visit to Cousin Henry and Julia.

But he said I wasn't able to go, nor able to stand it after I got there; and I did not make out a very good case for myself, for I was crying before I had finished.

It is getting to be a great effort for me to think straight. Just this nervous weakness I suppose.

115 And dear John gathered me up in his arms, and just carried me upstairs and laid me on the bed, and sat by me and read to me till it tired my head.

He said I was his darling and his comfort and all he had, and that I must take care of myself for his sake, and keep well.

He says no one but myself can help me out of it, that I must use my will and self-control and not let any silly fancies run away with me.

There's one comfort, the baby is well and happy, and does not have to occupy this nursery with the horrid wallpaper.

If we had not used it, that blessed child would have! What a fortunate escape! Why, I wouldn't have a child of mine, an impressionable little thing, live in such a room for worlds.

I never thought of it before, but it is lucky that John kept me here after all, I can stand it so much easier than a baby, you see.

Of course I never mention it to them any more—I am too wise,—but I keep watch of it all the same.

There are things in that paper that nobody knows but me, or ever will.

Behind that outside pattern the dim shapes get clearer every day.

It is always the same shape, only very numerous.

And it is like a woman stooping down and creeping about behind that pattern. I don't like it a bit. I wonder—I begin to think—I wish John would take me away from here!

It is so hard to talk with John about my case, because he is so wise, and because he loves me so.

But I tried it last night.

It was moonlight. The moon shines in all around just as the sun does.

I hate to see it sometimes, it creeps so slowly, and always comes in by one window or another.

John was asleep and I hated to waken him, so I kept still and watched the moonlight on that undulating wallpaper till I felt creepy.

The faint figure behind seemed to shake the pattern, just as if she wanted to get out.

I got up softly and went to feel and see if the paper *did* move, and when I came back John was awake.

"What is it, little girl?" he said. "Don't go walking about like that—you'll get cold."

I thought it was a good time to talk, so I told him that I really was not gaining here, and that I wished he would take me away.

"Why, darling!" said he, "our lease will be up in three weeks, and I can't see how to leave before.

"The repairs are not done at home, and I cannot possibly leave town just now. Of course if you were in any danger, I could and would, but you really are better, dear, whether you can see it or not. I am a doctor, dear, and I know. You are gaining flesh and color, your appetite is better, I feel really much easier about you."

"I don't weigh a bit more," said I, "nor as much; and my appetite may be better in the evening when you are here, but it is worse in the morning when you are away!"

"Bless her little heart!" said he with a big hug, "she shall be as sick as she pleases! But now let's improve the shining hours by going to sleep, and talk about it in the morning!"

"And you won't go away?" I asked gloomily.

140   "Why, how can I, dear? It is only three weeks more and then we will take a nice little trip of a few days while Jennie is getting the house ready. Really dear you are better!"

"Better in body perhaps—" I began, and stopped short, for he sat up straight and looked at me with such a stern, reproachful look that I could not say another word.

"My darling," said he, "I beg of you, for my sake and for our child's sake, as well as for your own, that you will never for one instant let that idea enter your mind! There is nothing so dangerous, so fascinating, to a temperament like yours. It is a false and foolish fancy. Can you not trust me as a physician when I tell you so?"

So of course I said no more on that score, and we went to sleep before long. He thought I was asleep first, but I wasn't, and lay there for hours trying to decide whether that front pattern and the back pattern really did move together or separately.

On a pattern like this, by daylight, there is a lack of sequence, a defiance of law, that is a constant irritant to a normal mind.

145   The color is hideous enough, and unreliable enough, and infuriating enough, but the pattern is torturing.

You think you have mastered it, but just as you get well underway in following, it turns a back-somersault and there you are. It slaps you in the face, knocks you down, and tramples upon you. It is like a bad dream.

The outside pattern is a florid arabesque, reminding one of a fungus. If you can imagine a toadstool in joints, an interminable string of toadstools, budding and sprouting in endless convolutions—why, that is something like it.

That is, sometimes!

There is one marked peculiarity about this paper, a thing nobody seems to notice but myself, and that is that it changes as the light changes.

150   When the sun shoots in through the east window—I always watch for that first long, straight ray—it changes so quickly that I never can quite believe it.

That is why I watch it always.

By moonlight—the moon shines in all night when there is a moon—I wouldn't know it was the same paper.

At night in any kind of light, in twilight, candlelight, lamplight, and worst of all by moonlight, it becomes bars! The outside pattern I mean, and the woman behind it is as plain as can be.

I didn't realize for a long time what the thing was that showed behind, that dim sub-pattern, but now I am quite sure it is a woman.

155   By daylight she is subdued, quiet. I fancy it is the pattern that keeps her so still. It is so puzzling. It keeps me quiet by the hour.

I lie down ever so much now. John says it is good for me, and to sleep all I can.

Indeed he started the habit by making me lie down for an hour after each meal.

It is a very bad habit I am convinced, for you see I don't sleep.

And that cultivates deceit, for I don't tell them I'm awake—O no!

The fact is I am getting a little afraid of John.   160

He seems very queer sometimes, and even Jennie has an inexplicable look.

It strikes me occasionally, just as a scientific hypothesis,—that perhaps it is the paper!

I have watched John when he did not know I was looking, and come into the room suddenly on the most innocent excuses, and I've caught him several times *looking at the paper!* And Jennie too. I caught Jennie with her hand on it once.

She didn't know I was in the room, and when I asked her in a quiet, a very quiet voice, with the most restrained manner possible, what she was doing with the paper—she turned around as if she had been caught stealing, and looked quite angry—asked me why I should frighten her so!

Then she said that the paper stained everything it touched, that she had found   165
yellow smooches on all my clothes and John's, and she wished we would be more careful!

Did not that sound innocent? But I know she was studying that pattern, and I am determined that nobody shall find it out but myself!

Life is very much more exciting now than it used to be. You see I have something more to expect, to look forward to, to watch. I really do eat better, and am more quiet than I was.

John is so pleased to see me improve! He laughed a little the other day, and said I seemed to be flourishing in spite of my wallpaper.

I turned it off with a laugh. I had no intention of telling him it was *because* of the wallpaper—he would make fun of me. He might even want to take me away.

I don't want to leave now until I have found it out. There is a week more, and   170
I think that will be enough.

I'm feeling ever so much better! I don't sleep much at night, for it is so interesting to watch developments; but I sleep a good deal in the daytime.

In the daytime it is tiresome and perplexing.

There are always new shoots on the fungus, and new shades of yellow all over it. I cannot keep count of them, though I have tried conscientiously.

It is the strangest yellow, that wallpaper! It makes me think of all the yellow things I ever saw—not beautiful ones like buttercups, but old foul, bad yellow things.

But there is something else about that paper—the smell! I noticed it the   175
moment we came into the room, but with so much air and sun it was not bad. Now we have had a week of fog and rain, and whether the windows are open or not, the smell is here.

It creeps all over the house.

I find it hovering in the dining-room, skulking in the parlor, hiding in the hall, lying in wait for me on the stairs.

It gets into my hair.

Even when I go to ride, if I turn my head suddenly and surprise it—there is that smell!

180   Such a peculiar odor, too! I have spent hours in trying to analyze it, to find what it smelled like.

It is not bad—at first, and very gentle, but quite the subtlest, most enduring odor I ever met.

In this damp weather it is awful, I wake up in the night and find it hanging over me.

It used to disturb me at first. I thought seriously of burning the house—to reach the smell.

But now I am used to it. The only thing I can think of that it is like is the *color* of the paper! A yellow smell.

185   There is a very funny mark on this wall, low down, near the mopboard. A streak that runs round the room. It goes behind every piece of furniture, except the bed, a long, straight, even *smooch,* as if it had been rubbed over and over.

I wonder how it was done and who did it, and what they did it for. Round and round and round—round and round and round—it makes me dizzy!

I really have discovered something at last.

Through watching so much at night, when it changes so, I have finally found out.

The front pattern *does* move—and no wonder! The woman behind shakes it!

190   Sometimes I think there are a great many women behind, and sometimes only one, and she crawls around fast, and her crawling shakes it all over.

Then in the very bright spots she keeps still, and in the very shady spots she just takes hold of the bars and shakes them hard.

And she is all the time trying to climb through. But nobody could climb through that pattern—it strangles so; I think that is why it has so many heads.

They get through, and then the pattern strangles them off and turns them upside down, and makes their eyes white!

If those heads were covered or taken off it would not be half so bad.

195   I think that woman gets out in the daytime!

And I'll tell you why—privately—I've seen her!

I can see her out of every one of my windows!

It is the same woman, I know, for she is always creeping, and most women do not creep by daylight.

200   I see her in that long shaded lane, creeping up and down. I see her in those dark grape arbors, creeping all around the garden.

I see her on that long road under the trees, creeping along, and when a carriage comes she hides under the blackberry vines.

I don't blame her a bit. It must be very humiliating to be caught creeping by daylight!

I always lock the door when I creep by daylight. I can't do it at night, for I know John would suspect something at once.

And John is so queer now, that I don't want to irritate him. I wish he would take another room! Besides, I don't want anybody to get that woman out at night but myself.

I often wonder if I could see her out of all the windows at once.

But, turn as fast as I can, I can only see out of one at one time.   205

And though I always see her, she *may* be able to creep faster than I can turn!

I have watched her sometimes away off in the open country, creeping as fast as a cloud shadow in a high wind.

If only that top pattern could be gotten off from the under one! I mean to try it, little by little.

I have found out another funny thing, but I shan't tell it this time! It does not do to trust people too much.

There are only two more days to get this paper off, and I believe John is begin-   210 ning to notice. I don't like the look in his eyes.

And I heard him ask Jennie a lot of professional questions about me. She had a very good report to give.

She said I slept a good deal in the daytime.

John knows I don't sleep very well at night, for all I'm so quiet!

He asked me all sorts of questions, too, and pretended to be very loving and kind.

As if I couldn't see through him!   215

Still, I don't wonder he acts so, sleeping under this paper for three months.

It only interests me, but I feel sure John and Jennie are secretly affected by it.

Hurrah! This is the last day, but it is enough. John to stay in town over night, and won't be out until this evening.

Jennie wanted to sleep with me—the sly thing! but I told her I should undoubtedly rest better for a night all alone.

That was clever, for really I wasn't alone a bit! As soon as it was moonlight   220 and that poor thing began to crawl and shake the pattern, I got up and ran to help her.

I pulled and she shook, I shook and she pulled, and before morning we had peeled off yards of that paper.

A strip about as high as my head and half around the room.

And then when the sun came and that awful pattern began to laugh at me, I declared I would finish it to-day!

We go away to-morrow, and they are moving all my furniture down again to leave things as they were before.

Jennie looked at the wall in amazement, but I told her merrily that I did it out   225 of pure spite at the vicious thing.

She laughed and said she wouldn't mind doing it herself, but I must not get tired.

How she betrayed herself that time!

But I am here, and no person touches this paper but me,—not *alive*!

She tried to get me out of the room—it was too patent! But I said it was so quiet and empty and clean now that I believed I would lie down again and sleep all I could; and not to wake me even for dinner—I would call when I woke.

So now she is gone, and the servants are gone, and the things are gone, and   230

there is nothing left but that great bedstead nailed down, with the canvas mattress we found on it.

We shall sleep downstairs to-night, and take the boat home to-morrow.

I quite enjoy the room, now it is bare again.

How those children did tear about here!

This bedstead is fairly gnawed!

235　But I must get to work.

I have locked the door and thrown the key down into the front path.

I don't want to go out, and I don't want to have anybody come in, till John
comes.

I want to astonish him.

I've got a rope up here that even Jennie did not find. If that woman does get
out, and tries to get away, I can tie her!

240　But I forgot I could not reach far without anything to stand on!

This bed will *not* move!

I tried to lift and push it until I was lame, and then I got so angry I bit off a
little piece at one corner—but it hurt my teeth.

Then I peeled off all the paper I could reach standing on the floor. It sticks
horribly and the pattern just enjoys it! All those strangled heads and bulbous
eyes and waddling fungus growths just shriek with derision!

I am getting angry enough to do something desperate. To jump out of the
window would be admirable exercise, but the bars are too strong even to try.

245　Besides I wouldn't do it. Of course not. I know well enough that a step like
that is improper and might be misconstrued.

I don't like to *look* out of the windows even—there are so many of those creeping women, and they creep so fast.

I wonder if they all come out of that wallpaper as I did?

But I am securely fastened now by my well-hidden rope—you don't get *me*
out in the road there!

I suppose I shall have to get back behind the pattern when it comes night, and
that is hard!

250　It is so pleasant to be out in this great room and creep around as I please!

I don't want to go outside. I won't, even if Jennie asks me to.

For outside you have to creep on the ground, and everything is green instead
of yellow.

But here I can creep smoothly on the floor, and my shoulder just fits in that
long smooch around the wall, so I cannot lose my way.

Why there's John at the door!

255　It is no use, young man, you can't open it!

How he does call and pound!

Now he's crying for an axe.

It would be a shame to break down that beautiful door!

"John dear!" said I in the gentlest voice, "the key is down by the front steps,
under a plantain leaf!"

260　That silenced him for a few moments.

Then he said—very quietly indeed, "Open the door, my darling!"

"I can't," said I. "The key is down by the front door under a plantain leaf!"

And then I said it again, several times, very gently and slowly, and said it so often that he had to go and see, and he got it of course, and came in. He stopped short by the door.

"What is the matter?" he cried. "For God's sake, what are you doing!"

I kept on creeping just the same, but I looked at him over my shoulder.

"I've got out at last," said I, "in spite of you and Jane? And I've pulled off most of the paper, so you can't put me back!"

Now why should that man have fainted? But he did, and right across my path by the wall, so that I had to creep over him every time!

1892

EDITH WHARTON

Souls Belated

Their railway carriage had been full when the train left Bologna; but at the first station beyond Milan their only remaining companion—a courtly person who ate garlic out of a carpetbag—had left his crumb-strewn seat with a bow.

Lydia's eye regretfully followed the shiny broadcloth of his retreating back till it lost itself in the cloud of touts and cab drivers hanging about the station; then she glanced across at Gannett and caught the same regret in his look. They were both sorry to be alone.

"*Par-ten-za!*"[1] shouted the guard. The train vibrated to a sudden slamming of doors; a waiter ran along the platform with a tray of fossilized sandwiches; a belated porter flung a bundle of shawls and bandboxes into a third-class carriage; the guard snapped out a brief *Partenza!* which indicated the purely ornamental nature of his first shout; and the train swung out of the station.

The direction of the road had changed, and a shaft of sunlight struck across the dusty red-velvet seats into Lydia's corner. Gannett did not notice it. He had returned to his *Revue de Paris*,[2] and she had to rise and lower the shade of the farther window. Against the vast horizon of their leisure such incidents stood out sharply.

Having lowered the shade, Lydia sat down, leaving the length of the carriage between herself and Gannett. At length he missed her and looked up.

"I moved out of the sun," she hastily explained.

He looked at her curiously: the sun was beating on her through the shade.

"Very well," he said pleasantly; adding, "You don't mind?" as he drew a cigarette case from his pocket.

It was a refreshing touch, relieving the tension of her spirit with the sugges-

1. "Departing," equivalent of "All aboard."   2. Intellectual literary review revived in 1894.

tion that, after all, if he could *smoke*—! The relief was only momentary. Her experience of smokers was limited (her husband had disapproved of the use of tobacco) but she knew from hearsay that men sometimes smoked to get away from things; that a cigar might be the masculine equivalent of darkened windows and a headache. Gannett, after a puff or two, returned to his review.

10   It was just as she had foreseen; he feared to speak as much as she did. It was one of the misfortunes of their situation that they were never busy enough to necessitate, or even to justify, the postponement of unpleasant discussions. If they avoided a question it was obviously, unconcealably because the question was disagreeable. They had unlimited leisure and an accumulation of mental energy to devote to any subject that presented itself; new topics were in fact at a premium. Lydia sometimes had premonitions of a famine-stricken period when there would be nothing left to talk about, and she had already caught herself doling out piecemeal what, in the first prodigality of their confidences, she would have flung to him in a breath. Their silence therefore might simply mean that they had nothing to say; but it was another disadvantage of their position that it allowed infinite opportunity for the classification of minute differences. Lydia had learned to distinguish between real and factitious silences; and under Gannett's she now detected a hum of speech to which her own thoughts made breathless answer.

How could it be otherwise, with that thing between them? She glanced up at the rack overhead. The *thing* was there, in her dressing bag, symbolically suspended over her head and his. He was thinking of it now, just as she was; they had been thinking of it in unison ever since they had entered the train. While the carriage had held other travelers they had screened her from his thoughts; but now that he and she were alone she knew exactly what was passing through his mind; she could almost hear him asking himself what he should say to her.

The thing had come that morning, brought up to her in an innocent-looking envelope with the rest of their letters, as they were leaving the hotel at Bologna. As she tore it open, she and Gannett were laughing over some ineptitude of the local guidebook—they had been driven, of late, to make the most of such incidental humors of travel. Even when she had unfolded the document she took it for some unimportant business paper sent abroad for her signature, and her eye traveled inattentively over the curly *Whereases* of the preamble until a word arrested her: Divorce. There it stood, an impassable barrier, between her husband's name and hers.

She had been prepared for it, of course, as healthy people are said to be prepared for death, in the sense of knowing it must come without in the least expecting that it will. She had known from the first that Tillotson meant to divorce her—but what did it matter? Nothing mattered, in those first days of supreme deliverance, but the fact that she was free; and not so much (she had begun to be aware) that freedom had released her from Tillotson as that it had given her to Gannett. This discovery had not been agreeable to her self-esteem. She had preferred to think that Tillotson had himself embodied all her reasons for leaving him; and those he represented had seemed cogent enough to stand in no need of reinforcement. Yet she had not left him till she met Gannett. It was her love for Gannett that had made life with Tillotson so poor and incomplete a business. If she had never, from the first, regarded her marriage as a full canceling of her claims upon life, she had at least, for a number of years, accepted it as a provisional compensation,—she had made it "do." Existence in the commodious Tillotson mansion in Fifth Avenue—with Mrs. Tillotson senior commanding the approaches from the second-story front windows—had been reduced to a series of purely automatic acts. The moral atmosphere of the Tillotson interior was as carefully screened and curtained as the house itself: Mrs. Tillotson senior dreaded ideas as much as a draft in her back. Prudent people liked an even temperature; and to do anything unexpected was as foolish as going out in the rain. One of the chief advantages of being rich was that one need not be exposed to unforeseen contingencies: by the use of ordinary firmness and common sense one could make sure of doing exactly the same thing every day at the same hour. These doctrines, reverentially imbibed with his mother's milk, Tillotson (a model son who had never given his parents an hour's anxiety) complacently expounded to his wife, testifying to his sense of their importance by the regularity with which he wore galoshes on damp days, his punctuality at meals, and his elaborate precautions against burglars and contagious diseases. Lydia, coming from a smaller town, and entering New York life through the portals of the Tillotson mansion, had mechanically accepted this point of view as inseparable from having a front pew in church and a parterre[3] box at the opera. All the people who came to the house revolved in the same small circle of prejudices. It was the kind of society in which, after dinner, the ladies compared the exorbitant charges of their children's teachers, and agreed that, even with the new duties on French clothes, it was cheaper in the end to get everything from Worth,[4] while the husbands, over their cigars, lamented municipal corruption, and decided that the men to start a reform were those who had no private interests at stake.

To Lydia this view of life had become a matter of course, just as lumbering about in her mother-in-law's landau had come to seem the only possible means of locomotion, and listening every Sunday to a fashionable Presbyterian divine the inevitable atonement for having thought oneself bored on the other six days of the week. Before she met Gannett her life had seemed merely dull; his coming made it appear like one of those dismal Cruikshank prints[5] in which the people are all ugly and all engaged in occupations that are either vulgar or stupid.

It was natural that Tillotson should be the chief sufferer from this readjustment of focus. Gannett's nearness had made her husband ridiculous, and a part of the ridicule had been reflected on herself. Her tolerance laid her open to a suspicion of obtuseness from which she must, at all costs, clear herself in Gannett's eyes.

She did not understand this until afterwards. At the time she fancied that she

15

---

3. Part of theater beneath balcony at back of main floor; "orchestra circle."   4. Charles F. Worth (1825–1895), Anglo-French dress designer, for years the leading arbiter of women's styles.   5. George Cruikshank (1792–1878), caricaturist, satirist, and book illustrator (including *Oliver Twist* and *Uncle Tom's Cabin*).

had merely reached the limits of endurance. In so large a charter of liberties as the mere act of leaving Tillotson seemed to confer, the small question of divorce or no divorce did not count. It was when she saw that she had left her husband only to be with Gannett that she perceived the significance of anything affecting their relations. Her husband, in casting her off, had virtually flung her at Gannett: it was thus that the world viewed it. The measure of alacrity with which Gannett would receive her would be the subject of curious speculation over afternoon tea tables and in club corners. She knew what would be said—she had heard it so often of others! The recollection bathed her in misery. The men would probably back Gannett to "do the decent thing"; but the ladies' eyebrows would emphasize the worthlessness of such enforced fidelity; and after all, they would be right. She had put herself in a position where Gannett "owed" her something; where, as a gentleman, he was bound to "stand the damage." The idea of accepting such compensation had never crossed her mind; the so-called rehabilitation of such a marriage had always seemed to her the only real disgrace. What she dreaded was the necessity of having to explain herself; of having to combat his arguments; of calculating, in spite of herself, the exact measure of insistence with which he pressed them. She knew not whether she most shrank from his insisting too much or too little. In such a case the nicest sense of proportion might be at fault; and how easily to fall into the error of taking her resistance for a test of his sincerity! Whichever way she turned, an ironical implication confronted her: she had the exasperated sense of having walked into the trap of some stupid practical joke.

Beneath all these preoccupations lurked the dread of what he was thinking. Sooner or later, of course, he would have to speak; but that, in the meantime, he should think, even for a moment, that there was any use in speaking, seemed to her simply unendurable. Her sensitiveness on this point was aggravated by another fear, as yet barely on the level of consciousness; the fear of unwillingly involving Gannett in the trammels[6] of her dependence. To look upon him as the instrument of her liberation; to resist in herself the least tendency to a wifely taking possession of his future, had seemed to Lydia the one way of maintaining the dignity of their relation. Her view had not changed, but she was aware of a growing inability to keep her thoughts fixed on the essential point—the point of parting with Gannett. It was easy to face as long as she kept it sufficiently far off: but what was this act of mental postponement but a gradual encroachment on his future? What was needful was the courage to recognize the moment when, by some word or look, their voluntary fellowship should be transformed into a bondage the more wearing that it was based on none of those common obligations which make the most imperfect marriage in some sort a center of gravity.

When the porter, at the next station, threw the door open, Lydia drew back, making way for the hoped-for intruder; but none came, and the train took up its leisurely progress through the spring wheat fields and budding copses. She now began to hope that Gannett would speak before the next station. She watched him furtively, half-disposed to return to the seat opposite his, but there was an artificiality about his absorption that restrained her. She had never before seen

---

6. Shackles; confining or restricting circumstances.

him read with so conspicuous an air of warding off interruption. What could he be thinking of? Why should he be afraid to speak? Or was it her answer that he dreaded?

The train paused for the passing of an express, and he put down his book and leaned out of the window. Presently he turned to her with a smile.

"There's a jolly old villa out here," he said.

His easy tone relieved her, and she smiled back at him as she crossed over to his corner.

Beyond the embankment, through the opening in a mossy wall, she caught sight of the villa, with its broken balustrades, its stagnant fountains, and the stone satyr closing the perspective of a dusky grass walk.

"How should you like to live there?" he asked as the train moved on.

"There?"

"In some such place, I mean. One might do worse, don't you think so? There must be at least two centuries of solitude under those yew trees. Shouldn't you like it?"

"I—I don't know," she faltered. She knew now that he meant to speak.

He lit another cigarette. "We shall have to live somewhere, you know," he said as he bent above the match.

Lydia tried to speak carelessly. *"Je n'en vois pas la nécessité!*[7] Why not live everywhere, as we have been doing?"

"But we can't travel forever, can we?"

"Oh, forever's a long word," she objected, picking up the review he had thrown aside.

"For the rest of our lives then," he said, moving nearer.

She made a slight gesture which caused his hand to slip from hers.

"Why should we make plans? I thought you agreed with me that it's pleasanter to drift."

He looked at her hesitatingly. "It's been pleasant, certainly; but I suppose I shall have to get at my work again some day. You know I haven't written a line since—all this time," he hastily amended.

She flamed with sympathy and self-reproach. "Oh, if you mean *that*—if you want to write—of course we must settle down. How stupid of me not to have thought of it sooner! Where shall we go? Where do you think you could work best? We oughtn't to lose any more time."

He hesitated again. "I had thought of a villa in these parts. It's quiet; we shouldn't be bothered. Should you like it?"

"Of course I should like it." She paused and looked away. "But I thought—I remember your telling me once that your best work had been done in a crowd—in big cities. Why should you shut yourself up in a desert?"

Gannett, for a moment, made no reply. At length he said, avoiding her eye as carefully as she avoided his: "It might be different now; I can't tell, of course, till I try. A writer ought not to be dependent on his *milieu;* it's a mistake to humor oneself in that way; and I thought that just at first you might prefer to be—"

7. I don't see why.

40   She faced him. "To be what?"

"Well—quiet. I mean—"

"What do you mean by 'at first'?" she interrupted.

He paused again. "I mean after we are married."

She thrust up her chin and turned toward the window. "Thank you!" she tossed back at him.

"Lydia!" he exclaimed blankly; and she felt in every fiber of her averted person that he had made the inconceivable, the unpardonable mistake of anticipating her acquiescence.

45   The train rattled on and he groped for a third cigarette. Lydia remained silent.

"I haven't offended you?" he ventured at length, in the tone of a man who feels his way.

She shook her head with a sigh. "I thought you understood," she moaned. Their eyes met and she moved back to his side.

"Do you want to know how not to offend me? By taking it for granted, once for all, that you've said your say on the odious question and that I've said mine, and that we stand just where we did this morning before that—that hateful paper came to spoil everything between us!"

"To spoil everything between us? What on earth do you mean? Aren't you glad to be free?"

50   "I was free before."

"Not to marry me," he suggested.

"But I don't *want* to marry you!" she cried.

She saw that he turned pale. "I'm obtuse, I suppose," he said slowly. "I confess I don't see what you're driving at. Are you tired of the whole business? Or was I simply a—an excuse for getting away? Perhaps you didn't care to travel alone? Was that it? And now you want to chuck me?" His voice had grown harsh. "You owe me a straight answer, you know; don't be tenderhearted!"

Her eyes swam as she leaned to him. "Don't you see it's because I care—because I care so much? Oh, Ralph! Can't you see how it would humiliate me? Try to feel it as a woman would! Don't you see the misery of being made your wife in this way? If I'd known you as a girl—that would have been a real marriage! But now—this vulgar fraud upon society—and upon a society we despised and laughed at—this sneaking back into a position that we've voluntarily forfeited: don't you see what a cheap compromise it is? We neither of us believe in the abstract 'sacredness' of marriage; we both know that no ceremony is needed to consecrate our love for each other; what object can we have in marrying, except the secret fear of each that the other may escape, or the secret longing to work our way back gradually—oh, very gradually—into the esteem of the people whose conventional morality we have always ridiculed and hated? And the very fact that, after a decent interval, these same people would come and dine with us—the women who talk about the indissolubility of marriage, and who would let me die in a gutter today because I am 'leading a life of sin'—doesn't that disgust you more than their turning their backs on us now? I can stand being cut by them, but I couldn't stand their coming to call and asking what I meant to do about visiting that unfortunate Mrs. So-and-so!"

55   She paused, and Gannett maintained a perplexed silence.

"You judge things too theoretically," he said at length, slowly. "Life is made up of compromises."

"The life we ran away from—yes! If we had been willing to accept them"—she flushed—"we might have gone on meeting each other at Mrs. Tillotson's dinners."

He smiled slightly. "I didn't know that we ran away to found a new system of ethics. I supposed it was because we loved each other."

"Life is complex, of course; isn't it the very recognition of that fact that separates us from the people who see it *tout d'une pièce*?[8] If *they* are right—if marriage is sacred in itself and the individual must always be sacrificed to the family—then there can be no real marriage between us, since our—our being together is a protest against the sacrifice of the individual to the family." She interrupted herself with a laugh. "You'll say now that I'm giving you a lecture on sociology! Of course one acts as one can—as one must, perhaps—pulled by all sorts of invisible threads; but at least one needn't pretend, for social advantages, to subscribe to a creed that ignores the complexity of human motives—that classifies people by arbitrary signs, and puts it in everybody's reach to be on Mrs. Tillotson's visiting list. It may be necessary that the world should be ruled by conventions—but if we believed in them, why did we break through them? And if we don't believe in them, is it honest to take advantage of the protection they afford?"

Gannett hesitated. "One may believe in them or not; but as long as they do rule the world it is only by taking advantage of their protection that one can find a *modus vivendi*."[9]

"Do outlaws need a *modus vivendi*?"

He looked at her hopelessly. Nothing is more perplexing to man than the mental process of a woman who reasons her emotions.

She thought she had scored a point and followed it up passionately. "You do understand, don't you? You see how the very thought of the thing humiliates me! We are together today because we choose to be—don't let us look any farther than that!" She caught his hands. "*Promise* me you'll never speak of it again; promise me you'll never *think* of it even," she implored, with a tearful prodigality of italics.

Through what followed—his protests, his arguments, his final unconvinced submission to her wishes—she had a sense of his but half-discerning all that, for her, had made the moment so tumultuous. They had reached that memorable point in every heart history when, for the first time, the man seems obtuse and the woman irrational. It was the abundance of his intentions that consoled her, on reflection, for what they lacked in quality. After all, it would have been worse, incalculably worse, to have detected any overreadiness to understand her.

2

When the train at nightfall brought them to their journey's end at the edge of one of the lakes, Lydia was glad that they were not, as usual, to pass from one

8. All of a piece.   9. Way of living.

solitude to another. Their wanderings during the year had indeed been like the flight of outlaws: through Sicily, Dalmatia, Transylvania[1] and Southern Italy they had persisted in their tacit avoidance of their kind. Isolation, at first, had deepened the flavor of their happiness, as night intensifies the scent of certain flowers; but in the new phase on which they were entering, Lydia's chief wish was that they should be less abnormally exposed to the action of each other's thoughts.

She shrank, nevertheless, as the brightly-looming bulk of the fashionable Anglo-American hotel on the water's brink began to radiate toward their advancing boat its vivid suggestion of social order, visitors' lists, Church services, and the bland inquisition of the *table d'hôte*.[2] The mere fact that in a moment or two she must take her place on the hotel register as Mrs. Gannett seemed to weaken the springs of her resistance.

They had meant to stay for a night only, on their way to a lofty village among the glaciers of Monte Rosa; but after the first plunge into publicity, when they entered the dining room, Lydia felt the relief of being lost in a crowd, of ceasing for a moment to be the center of Gannett's scrutiny; and in his face she caught the reflection of her feeling. After dinner, when she went upstairs, he strolled into the smoking room, and an hour or two later, sitting in the darkness of her window, she heard his voice below and saw him walking up and down the terrace with a companion cigar at his side. When he came up he told her he had been talking to the hotel chaplain—a very good sort of fellow.

"Queer little microcosms, these hotels! Most of these people live here all summer and then migrate to Italy or the Riviera. The English are the only people who can lead that kind of life with dignity—those soft-voiced old ladies in Shetland shawls somehow carry the British Empire under their caps. *Civis Romanus sum*.[3] It's a curious study—there might be some good things to work up here."

He stood before her with the vivid preoccupied stare of the novelist on the trail of a "subject." With a relief that was half painful she noticed that, for the first time since they had been together, he was hardly aware of her presence.

"Do you think you could write here?"

"Here? I don't know." His stare dropped. "After being out of things so long one's first impressions are bound to be tremendously vivid, you know. I see a dozen threads already that one might follow—"

He broke off with a touch of embarrassment.

"Then follow them. We'll stay," she said with sudden decision.

"Stay here?" he glanced at her in surprise, and then, walking to the window, looked out upon the dusky slumber of the garden.

"Why not?" she said at length, in a tone of veiled irritation.

"The place is full of old cats in caps who gossip with the chaplain. Shall you like—I mean, it would be different if—"

She flamed up.

"Do you suppose I care? It's none of their business."

---

1. Dalmatia, then part of Austria (now Croatia) along the Adriatic coast; Transylvania, then part of Hungary (now of Romania).   2. Table at a hotel where all the guests eat together.   3. "I am a citizen of Rome," that is, a member of the dominant nation.

"Of course not; but you won't get them to think so."

"They may think what they please."   80

He looked at her doubtfully.

"It's for you to decide."

"We'll stay," she repeated.

Gannett, before they met, had made himself known as a successful writer of short stories and of a novel which had achieved the distinction of being widely discussed. The reviewers called him "promising," and Lydia now accused herself of having too long interfered with the fulfillment of his promise. There was a special irony in the fact, since his passionate assurances that only the stimulus of her companionship could bring out his latent faculty had almost given the dignity of a "vocation" to her course: there had been moments when she had felt unable to assume, before posterity, the responsibility of thwarting his career. And, after all, he had not written a line since they had been together: his first desire to write had come from renewed contact with the world! Was it all a mistake then? Must the most intelligent choice work more disastrously than the blundering combinations of chance? Or was there a still more humiliating answer to her perplexities? His sudden impulse of activity so exactly coincided with her own wish to withdraw, for a time, from the range of his observation, that she wondered if he too were not seeking sanctuary from intolerable problems.

"You must begin tomorrow!" she cried, hiding a tremor under the laugh with   85
which she added, "I wonder if there's any ink in the inkstand?"

Whatever else they had at the Hotel Bellosguardo, they had, as Miss Pinsent said, "a certain tone." It was to Lady Susan Condit that they owed this inestimable benefit; an advantage ranking in Miss Pinsent's opinion above even the lawn tennis courts and the resident chaplain. It was the fact of Lady Susan's annual visit that made the hotel what it was. Miss Pinsent was certainly the last to underrate such a privilege: "It's so important, my dear, forming as we do a little family, that there should be someone to give *the tone;* and no one could do it better than Lady Susan—an earl's daughter and a person of such determination. Dear Mrs. Ainger now—who really *ought,* you know, when Lady Susan's away—absolutely refuses to assert herself." Miss Pinsent sniffed derisively. "A bishop's niece!—my dear, I saw her once actually give in to some South Americans—and before us all. She gave up her seat at table to oblige them—such a lack of dignity! Lady Susan spoke to her very plainly about it afterwards."

Miss Pinsent glanced across the lake and adjusted her auburn front.[4]

"But of course I don't deny that the stand Lady Susan takes is not always easy to live up to—for the rest of us, I mean. Monsieur Grossart, our good proprietor, finds it trying at times, I know—he has said as much, privately, to Mrs. Ainger and me. After all, the poor man is not to blame for wanting to fill his hotel, is he? And Lady Susan is so difficult—so very difficult—about new people. One might almost say that she disapproves of them beforehand, on principle. And

4. Band(s) of false hair or set of false curls worn over forehead.

yet she's had warnings—she very nearly made a dreadful mistake once with the Duchess of Levens, who dyed her hair and—well, swore and smoked. One would have thought that might have been a lesson to Lady Susan." Miss Pinsent resumed her knitting with a sigh. "There are exceptions, of course. She took at once to you and Mr. Gannett—it was quite remarkable, really. Oh, I don't mean that either—of course not! It was perfectly natural—we *all* thought you so charming and interesting from the first day—we knew at once that Mr. Gannett was intellectual, by the magazines you took in; but you know what I mean. Lady Susan is so very—well, I won't say prejudiced, as Mrs. Ainger does—but so prepared *not* to like new people, that her taking to you in that way was a surprise to us all, I confess."

Miss Pinsent sent a significant glance down the long laurustinus[5] alley from the other end of which two people—a lady and gentleman—were strolling toward them through the smiling neglect of the garden.

90   "In this case, of course, it's very different; that I'm willing to admit. Their looks are against them; but, as Mrs. Ainger says, one can't exactly tell them so."

"She's very handsome," Lydia ventured, with her eyes on the lady, who showed, under the dome of a vivid sunshade, the hourglass figure and superlative coloring of a Christmas chromo.[6]

"That's the worst of it. She's too handsome."

"Well, after all, she can't help that."

"Other people manage to," said Miss Pinsent skeptically.

95   "But isn't it rather unfair of Lady Susan—considering that nothing is known about them?"

"But, my dear, that's the very thing that's against them. It's infinitely worse than any actual knowledge."

Lydia mentally agreed that, in the case of Mrs. Linton, it possibly might be.

"I wonder why they came here?" she mused.

"That's against them too. It's always a bad sign when loud people come to a quiet place. And they've brought van loads of boxes—her maid told Mrs. Ainger's that they meant to stop indefinitely."

100   "And Lady Susan actually turned her back on her in the salon?"

"My dear, she said it was for our sakes: that makes it so unanswerable! But poor Grossart *is* in a way! The Lintons have taken his most expensive suite, you know—the yellow damask drawing room above the portico—and they have champagne with every meal!"

They were silent as Mr. and Mrs. Linton sauntered by; the lady with tempestuous brows and challenging chin; the gentleman, a blond stripling, trailing after her, head downward, like a reluctant child dragged by his nurse.

"What does your husband think of them, my dear?" Miss Pinsent whispered as they passed out of earshot.

Lydia stooped to pick a violet in the border.

105   "He hasn't told me."

"Of your speaking to them, I mean. Would he approve of that? I know how

---

5. Tall evergreens that grow in the Mediterranean section of Europe.   6. Colored lithograph.

very particular nice Americans are. I think your action might make a difference; it would certainly carry weight with Lady Susan."

"Dear Miss Pinsent, you flatter me!"

Lydia rose and gathered up her book and sunshade.

"Well, if you're asked for an opinion—if Lady Susan asks you for one—I think you ought to be prepared," Miss Pinsent admonished her as she moved away.

3

Lady Susan held her own. She ignored the Lintons, and her little family, as Miss Pinsent phrased it, followed suit. Even Mrs. Ainger agreed that it was obligatory. If Lady Susan owed it to the others not to speak to the Lintons, the others clearly owed it to Lady Susan to back her up. It was generally found expedient, at the Hotel Bellosguardo, to adopt this form of reasoning. 110

Whatever effect this combined action may have had upon the Lintons, it did not at least have that of driving them away. Monsieur Grossart, after a few days of suspense, had the satisfaction of seeing them settle down in his yellow damask *premier*[7] with what looked like a permanent installation of palm trees and silk cushions, and a gratifying continuance in the consumption of champagne. Mrs. Linton trailed her Doucet[8] draperies up and down the garden with the same challenging air, while her husband, smoking innumerable cigarettes, dragged himself dejectedly in her wake; but neither of them, after the first encounter with Lady Susan, made any attempt to extend their acquaintance. They simply ignored their ignorers. As Miss Pinsent resentfully observed, they behaved exactly as though the hotel were empty.

It was therefore a matter of surprise, as well as of displeasure, to Lydia, to find, on glancing up one day from her seat in the garden, that the shadow which had fallen across her book was that of the enigmatic Mrs. Linton.

"I want to speak to you," that lady said, in a rich hard voice that seemed the audible expression of her gown and her complexion.

Lydia started. She certainly did not want to speak to Mrs. Linton.

"Shall I sit down here?" the latter continued, fixing her intensely-shaded eyes on Lydia's face, "or are you afraid of being seen with me?" 115

"Afraid?" Lydia colored. "Sit down, please. What is it that you wish to say?"

Mrs. Linton, with a smile, drew up a garden chair and crossed one openwork[9] ankle above the other.

"I want you to tell me what my husband said to your husband last night."

Lydia turned pale.

"My husband—to yours?" she faltered, staring at the other. 120

"Didn't you know they were closeted together for hours in the smoking room after you went upstairs? My man didn't get to bed until nearly two o'clock and when he did I couldn't get a word out of him. When he wants to be aggravating

---

7. The first floor above the ground floor. 8. Jacques Doucet (1853–1929), French dress designer and manufacturer. 9. Stockings—knit, lace, and so forth—in which the pattern left openings in the material; at one time shocking. The London *Daily News* said in September 1890, "Openwork stockings will be the only wear when the weather gets a bit warmer."

I'll back him against anybody living!" Her teeth and eyes flashed persuasively upon Lydia. "But you'll tell me what they were talking about, won't you? I know I can trust you—you look so awfully kind. And it's for his own good. He's such a precious donkey and I'm so afraid he's got into some beastly scrape or other. If he'd only trust his own old woman! But they're always writing to him and setting him against me. And I've got nobody to turn to." She laid her hand on Lydia's with a rattle of bracelets. "You'll help me, won't you?"

Lydia drew back from the smiling fierceness of her brows.

"I'm sorry—but I don't think I understand. My husband has said nothing to me of—of yours."

The great black crescents above Mrs. Linton's eyes met angrily.

125 "I say—is that true?" she demanded.

Lydia rose from her seat.

"Oh, look here, I didn't mean that, you know—you mustn't take one up so! Can't you see how rattled I am?"

Lydia saw that, in fact, her beautiful mouth was quivering beneath softened eyes.

"I'm beside myself!" the splendid creature wailed, dropping into her seat.

130 "I'm so sorry," Lydia repeated, forcing herself to speak kindly; "but how can I help you?"

Mrs. Linton raised her head sharply.

"By finding out—there's a darling!"

"Finding what out?"

"What Trevenna told him."

135 "Trevenna—?" Lydia echoed in bewilderment.

Mrs. Linton clapped her hand to her mouth.

"Oh, Lord—there, it's out! What a fool I am! But I supposed of course you knew; I supposed everybody knew." She dried her eyes and bridled. "Didn't you know that he's Lord Trevenna? I'm Mrs. Cope."

Lydia recognized the names. They had figured in a flamboyant elopement which had thrilled fashionable London some six months earlier.

"Now you see how it is—you understand, don't you?" Mrs. Cope continued on a note of appeal. "I knew you would—that's the reason I came to you. I suppose *he* felt the same thing about your husband; he's not spoken to another soul in the place." Her face grew anxious again. "He's awfully sensitive, generally—he feels our position, he says—as if it wasn't *my* place to feel that! But when he does get talking there's no knowing what he'll say. I know he's been brooding over something lately, and I *must* find out what it is—it's to his interest that I should. I always tell him that I think only of his interest; if he'd only trust me! But he's been so odd lately—I can't think what he's plotting. You will help me, dear?"

140 Lydia, who had remained standing, looked away uncomfortably.

"If you mean by finding out what Lord Trevenna has told my husband, I'm afraid it's impossible."

"Why impossible?"

"Because I infer that it was told in confidence."

Mrs. Cope stared incredulously.

"Well, what of that? Your husband looks such a dear—anyone can see he's   145
awfully gone on you. What's to prevent your getting it out of him?"

Lydia flushed.

"I'm not a spy!" she exclaimed.

"A spy—a spy? How dare you?" Mrs. Cope flamed out. "Oh, I don't mean that
either! Don't be angry with me—I'm so miserable." She essayed a softer note.
"Do you call that spying—for one woman to help out another? I do need help so
dreadfully! I'm at my wits' end with Trevenna, I am indeed. He's such a boy—a
mere baby, you know; he's only two-and-twenty." She dropped her orbed lids.
"He's younger than me—only fancy, a few months younger. I tell him he ought
to listen to me as if I was his mother; oughtn't he now? But he won't, he won't!
All his people are at him, you see—oh, I know *their* little game! Trying to get him
away from me before I can get my divorce—that's what they're up to. At first he
wouldn't listen to them; he used to toss their letters over to me to read; but now
he reads them himself, and answers 'em too, I fancy; he's always shut up in his
room, writing. If I only knew what his plan is I could stop him fast enough—he's
such a simpleton. But he's dreadfully deep too—at times I can't make him out.
But I know he's told your husband everything—I knew that last night the minute
I laid eyes on him. And I *must* find out—you must help me—I've got no one else
to turn to!"

She caught Lydia's fingers in a stormy pressure.

"Say you'll help me—you and your husband."   150

Lydia tried to free herself.

"What you ask is impossible; you must see that it is. No one could interfere
in—in the way you ask."

Mrs. Cope's clutch tightened.

"You won't, then? You won't?"

"Certainly not. Let me go, please."   155

Mrs. Cope released her with a laugh.

"Oh, go by all means—pray don't let me detain you! Shall you go and tell
Lady Susan Condit that there's a pair of us—or shall I save you the trouble of
enlightening her?"

Lydia stood still in the middle of the path, seeing her antagonist through a
mist of terror. Mrs. Cope was still laughing.

"Oh, I'm not spiteful by nature, my dear; but you're a little more than flesh
and blood can stand! It's impossible, is it? Let you go, indeed! You're too good to
be mixed up in my affairs, are you? Why, you little fool, the first day I laid eyes
on you I saw that you and I were both in the same box—that's the reason I spoke
to you."

She stepped nearer, her smile dilating on Lydia like a lamp through a fog.   160

"You can take your choice, you know; I always play fair. If you'll tell I'll promise not to. Now then, which is it to be?"

Lydia, involuntarily, had begun to move away from the pelting storm of
words; but at this she turned and sat down again.

"You may go," she said simply. "I shall stay here."

4

She stayed there for a long time, in the hypnotized contemplation, not of Mrs. Cope's present, but of her own past. Gannett, early that morning, had gone off on a long walk—he had fallen into the habit of taking these mountain tramps with various fellow lodgers; but even had he been within reach she could not have gone to him just then. She had to deal with herself first. She was surprised to find how, in the last months, she had lost the habit of introspection. Since their coming to the Hotel Bellosguardo she and Gannett had tacitly avoided themselves and each other.

165   She was aroused by the whistle of the three o'clock steamboat as it neared the landing just beyond the hotel gates. Three o'clock! Then Gannett would soon be back—he had told her to expect him before four. She rose hurriedly, her face averted from the inquisitorial façade of the hotel. She could not see him just yet; she could not go indoors. She slipped through one of the overgrown garden alleys and climbed a steep path to the hills.

It was dark when she opened their sitting-room door. Gannett was sitting on the window ledge smoking a cigarette. Cigarettes were now his chief resource: he had not written a line during the two months they had spent at the Hotel Bellosguardo. In that respect, it had turned out not to be the right *milieu* after all.

He started up at Lydia's entrance.

"Where have you been? I was getting anxious."

She sat down in a chair near the door.

170   "Up the mountain," she said wearily.

"Alone?"

"Yes."

Gannett threw away his cigarette: the sound of her voice made him want to see her face.

"Shall we have a little light?" he suggested.

175   She made no answer and he lifted the globe from the lamp and put a match to the wick. Then he looked at her.

"Anything wrong? You look done up."

She sat glancing vaguely about the little room, dimly lit by the pallid-globed lamp, which left in twilight the outlines of the furniture, of his writing table heaped with books and papers, of the tea roses and jasmine drooping on the mantelpiece. How like home it had all grown—how like home!

"Lydia, what is wrong?" he repeated.

She moved away from him, feeling for her hatpins and turning to lay her hat and sunshade on the table.

180   Suddenly she said: "That woman has been talking to me."

Gannett stared.

"That woman? What woman?"

"Mrs. Linton—Mrs. Cope."

He gave a start of annoyance, still as she perceived, not grasping the full import of her words.

185   "The deuce! She told you—?"

"She told me everything."

Gannett looked at her anxiously.

"What impudence! I'm so sorry that you should have been exposed to this, dear."

"Exposed!" Lydia laughed.

Gannett's brow clouded and they looked away from each other.

"Do you know *why* she told me? She had the best of reasons. The first time she laid eyes on me she saw that we were both in the same box."

"Lydia!"

"So it was natural, of course, that she should turn to me in a difficulty."

"What difficulty?"

"It seems she has reason to think that Lord Trevenna's people are trying to get him away from her before she gets her divorce—"

"Well?"

"And she fancied he had been consulting with you last night as to—as to the best way of escaping from her."

Gannett stood up with an angry forehead.

"Well—what concern of yours was all this dirty business? Why should she go to you?"

"Don't you see? It's so simple. I was to wheedle his secret out of you."

"To oblige that woman?"

"Yes; or, if I was unwilling to oblige her, then to protect myself."

"To protect yourself? Against whom?"

"Against her telling everyone in the hotel that she and I are in the same box."

"She threatened that?"

"She left me the choice of telling it myself or of doing it for me."

"The beast!"

There was a long silence. Lydia had seated herself on the sofa, beyond the radius of the lamp, and he leaned against the window. His next question surprised her.

"When did this happen? At what time, I mean?"

She looked at him vaguely.

"I don't know—after luncheon, I think. Yes, I remember; it must have been at about three o'clock."

He stepped into the middle of the room and as he approached the light she saw that his brow had cleared.

"Why do you ask?" she said.

"Because when I came in, at about half-past three, the mail was just being distributed, and Mrs. Cope was waiting as usual to pounce on her letters; you know she was always watching for the postman. She was standing so close to me that I couldn't help seeing a big official-looking envelope that was handed to her. She tore it open, gave one look at the inside, and rushed off upstairs like a whirlwind, with the director shouting after her that she had left all her other letters behind. I don't believe she ever thought of you again after that paper was put into her hand."

"Why?"

"Because she was too busy. I was sitting in the window, watching for you, when the five o'clock boat left, and who should go on board, bag and baggage, valet and maid, dressing bags and poodle, but Mrs. Cope and Trevenna. Just an hour and a half to pack up in! And you should have seen her when they started. She was radiant—shaking hands with everybody—waving her handkerchief from the deck—distributing bows and smiles like an empress. If ever a woman got what she wanted just in the nick of time that woman did. She'll be Lady Trevenna within a week, I'll wager."

"You think she has her divorce?"

"I'm sure of it. And she must have got it just after her talk with you."

Lydia was silent.

220   At length she said, with a kind of reluctance, "She was horribly angry when she left me. It wouldn't have taken long to tell Lady Susan Condit."

"Lady Susan Condit has not been told."

"How do you know?"

"Because when I went downstairs half an hour ago I met Lady Susan on the way—"

He stopped, half smiling.

225   "Well?"

"And she stopped to ask if I thought you would act as patroness to a charity concert she is getting up."

In spite of themselves they both broke into a laugh. Lydia's ended in sobs and she sank down with her face hidden. Gannett bent over her, seeking her hands.

"That vile woman—I ought to have warned you to keep away from her; I can't forgive myself! But he spoke to me in confidence; and I never dreamed—well, it's all over now."

Lydia lifted her head.

230   "Not for me. It's only just beginning."

"What do you mean?"

She put him gently aside and moved in her turn to the window. Then she went on, with her face turned toward the shimmering blackness of the lake, "You see of course that it might happen again at any moment."

"What?"

"This—this risk of being found out. And we could hardly count again on such a lucky combination of chances, could we?"

235   He sat down with a groan.

Still keeping her face toward the darkness, she said, "I want you to go and tell Lady Susan—and the others."

Gannett, who had moved toward her, paused a few feet off.

"Why do you wish me to do this?" he said at length, with less surprise in his voice than she had been prepared for.

"Because I've behaved basely, abominably, since we came here: letting these people believe we were married—lying with every breath I drew—"

240   "Yes, I've felt that too," Gannett exclaimed with sudden energy.

The words shook her like a tempest: all her thoughts seemed to fall about her in ruins.

"You—you've felt so?"

"Of course I have." He spoke with low-voiced vehemence. "Do you suppose I like playing the sneak any better than you do? It's damnable."

He had dropped on the arm of a chair, and they stared at each other like blind people who suddenly see.

"But you have liked it here," she faltered.   245

"Oh, I've liked it—I've liked it." He moved impatiently. "Haven't you?"

"Yes," she burst out; "that's the worst of it—that's what I can't bear. I fancied it was for your sake that I insisted on staying—because you thought you could write here; and perhaps just at first that really was the reason. But afterwards I wanted to stay myself—I loved it." She broke into a laugh. "Oh, do you see the full derision of it? These people—the very prototypes of the bores you took me away from, with the same fenced-in view of life, the same keep-off-the-grass morality, the same little cautious virtues and the same little frightened vices— well, I've clung to them, I've delighted in them, I've done my best to please them. I've toadied Lady Susan, I've gossiped with Miss Pinsent, I've pretended to be shocked with Mrs. Ainger. Respectability! It was the one thing in life that I was sure I didn't care about, and it's grown so precious to me that I've stolen it because I couldn't get it in any other way."

She moved across the room and returned to his side with another laugh.

"I who used to fancy myself unconventional! I must have been born with a cardcase in my hand.[1] You should have seen me with that poor woman in the garden. She came to me for help, poor creature, because she fancied that, having 'sinned,' as they call it, I might feel some pity for others who had been tempted in the same way. Not I! She didn't know me. Lady Susan would have been kinder, because Lady Susan wouldn't have been afraid. I hated the woman—my one thought was not to be seen with her—I could have killed her for guessing my secret. The one thing that mattered to me at that moment was my standing with Lady Susan!"

Gannett did not speak.   250

"And you—you've felt it too!" she broke out accusingly. "You've enjoyed being with these people as much as I have; you've let the chaplain talk to you by the hour about The Reign of Law and Professor Drummond.[2] When they asked you to hand the plate in church I was watching you—*you wanted to accept.*"

She stepped close, laying her hand on his arm.

"Do you know, I begin to see what marriage is for. It's to keep people away from each other. Sometimes I think that two people who love each other can be saved from madness only by the things that come between them—children, duties, visits, bores, relations—the things that protect married people from each other. We've been too close together—that has been our sin. We've seen the nakedness of each other's souls."

She sank again on the sofa, hiding her face in her hands.

Gannett stood above her perplexedly: he felt as though she were being swept   255
away by some implacable current while he stood helpless on its bank.

---

1. That is, a member of that part of society (the upper class) that makes formal social calls and leaves calling cards.   2. Henry Drummond (1851–1897), Scottish clergyman who attempted to reconcile science and religion and published *Natural Law in the Spiritual World* (1893).

At length he said, "Lydia, don't think me a brute—but don't you see yourself that it won't do?"

"Yes, I see it won't do," she said without raising her head.

His face cleared.

"Then we'll go tomorrow."

260   "Go—where?"

"To Paris; to be married."

For a long time she made no answer; then she asked slowly, "Would they have us here if we were married?"

"Have us here?"

"I mean Lady Susan—and the others."

265   "Have us here? Of course they would."

"Not if they knew—at least, not unless they could pretend not to know."

He made an impatient gesture.

"We shouldn't come back here, of course; and other people needn't know—no one need know."

She sighed. "Then it's only another form of deception and a meaner one. Don't you see that?"

270   "I see we're not accountable to any Lady Susans on earth!"

"Then why are you ashamed of what we are doing here?"

"Because I'm sick of pretending that you're my wife when you're not—when you won't be."

She looked at him sadly.

"If I were your wife you'd have to go on pretending. You'd have to pretend that I'd never been—anything else. And our friends would have to pretend that they believed what you pretended."

275   Gannett pulled off the sofa tassel and flung it away.

"You're impossible," he groaned.

"It's not I—it's our being together that's impossible. I only want you to see that marriage won't help it."

"What will help it then?"

She raised her head.

280   "My leaving you."

"Your leaving me?" He sat motionless, staring at the tassel which lay at the other end of the room. At length some impulse of retaliation for the pain she was inflicting made him say deliberately:

"And where would you go if you left me?"

"Oh!" she cried.

He was at her side in an instant.

285   "Lydia—Lydia—you know I didn't mean it; I couldn't mean it! But you've driven me out of my senses; I don't know what I'm saying. Can't you get out of this labyrinth of self-torture? It's destroying us both."

"That's why I must leave you."

"How easily you say it!" He drew her hands down and made her face him. "You're very scrupulous about yourself—and others. But have you thought of me? You have no right to leave me unless you've ceased to care—"

"It's because I care—"

"Then I have a right to be heard. If you love me you can't leave me." Her eyes defied him.   290

"Why not?"

He dropped her hands and rose from her side.

"Can you?" he said sadly.

The hour was late and the lamp flickered and sank. She stood up with a shiver and turned toward the door of her room.

5

At daylight a sound in Lydia's room woke Gannett from a troubled sleep. He sat   295
up and listened. She was moving about softly, as though fearful of disturbing him. He heard her push back one of the creaking shutters; then there was a moment's silence, which seemed to indicate that she was waiting to see if the noise had roused him.

Presently she began to move again. She had spent a sleepless night, probably, and was dressing to go down to the garden for a breath of air. Gannett rose also; but some undefinable instinct made his movements as cautious as hers. He stole to his window and looked out through the slats of the shutter.

It had rained in the night and the dawn was gray and lifeless. The cloud-muffled hills across the lake were reflected in its surface as in a tarnished mirror. In the garden, the birds were beginning to shake the drops from the motionless laurustinus boughs.

An immense pity for Lydia filled Gannett's soul. Her seeming intellectual independence had blinded him for a time to the feminine cast of her mind. He had never thought of her as a woman who wept and clung: there was a lucidity in her intuitions that made them appear to be the result of reasoning. Now he saw the cruelty he had committed in detaching her from the normal conditions of life; he felt, too, the insight with which she had hit upon the real cause of their suffering. Their life was "impossible," as she had said—and its worst penalty was that it had made any other life impossible for them. Even had his love lessened, he was bound to her now by a hundred ties of pity and self-reproach; and she, poor child, must turn back to him as Latude returned to his cell.[3]

A new sound startled him: it was the stealthy closing of Lydia's door. He crept to his own and heard her footsteps passing down the corridor. Then he went back to the window and looked out.

A minute or two later he saw her go down the steps of the porch and enter   300
the garden. From his post of observation her face was invisible, but something about her appearance struck him. She wore a long traveling cloak and under its folds he detected the outline of a bag or bundle. He drew a deep breath and stood watching her.

She walked quickly down the laurustinus alley toward the gate; there she paused a moment, glancing about the little shady square. The stone benches

3. Jean Henry de Latude (1725–1805), an adventurer who kept escaping and getting put back in various French jails over a period of thirty-five years.

under the trees were empty, and she seemed to gather resolution from the solitude about her, for she crossed the square to the steamboat landing, and he saw
her pause before the ticket office at the head of the wharf. Now she was buying
her ticket. Gannet turned his head a moment to look at the clock: the boat was
due in five minutes. He had time to jump into his clothes and overtake her—

He made no attempt to move; an obscure reluctance restrained him. If any
thought emerged from the tumult of his sensations, it was that he must let her
go if she wished it. He had spoken last night of his rights: what were they? At the
last issue, he and she were two separate beings, not made one by the miracle of
common forbearances, duties, abnegations, but bound together in a *noyade*[4] of
passion that left them resisting yet clinging as they went down.

After buying her ticket, Lydia had stood for a moment looking out across the
lake; then he saw her seat herself on one of the benches near the landing. He and
she, at that moment, were both listening for the same sound: the whistle of the
boat as it rounded the nearest promontory. Gannett turned again to glance at
the clock: the boat was due now.

Where would she go? What would her life be when she had left him? She had
no near relations and few friends. There was money enough . . . but she asked so
much of life, in ways so complex and immaterial. He thought of her as walking
barefooted through a stony waste. No one would understand her—no one would
pity her—and he, who did both, was powerless to come to her aid.

305   He saw that she had risen from the bench and walked toward the edge of the
lake. She stood looking in the direction from which the steamboat was to come;
then she turned to the ticket office, doubtless to ask the cause of the delay. After
that she went back to the bench and sat down with bent head. What was she
thinking of?

The whistle sounded; she started up, and Gannett involuntarily made a movement toward the door. But he turned back and continued to watch her. She stood
motionless, her eyes on the trail of smoke that preceded the appearance of the
boat. Then the little craft rounded the point, a dead white object on the leaden
water: a minute later it was puffing and backing at the wharf.

The few passengers who were waiting—two or three peasants and a snuffy
priest—were clustered near the ticket office. Lydia stood apart under the trees.

The boat lay alongside now; the gangplank was run out and the peasants went
on board with their baskets of vegetables, followed by the priest. Still Lydia did
not move. A bell began to ring querulously; there was a shriek of steam, and
someone must have called to her that she would be late, for she started forward,
as though in answer to a summons. She moved waveringly, and at the edge of
the wharf she paused. Gannett saw a sailor beckon to her; the bell rang again and
she stepped upon the gangplank.

Halfway down the short incline to the deck she stopped again; then she
turned and ran back to the land. The gangplank was drawn in, the bell ceased to
ring, and the boat backed out into the lake. Lydia, with slow steps, was walking
toward the garden.

---

4. Flood, drowning.

As she approached the hotel she looked up furtively and Gannett drew back   310
into the room. He sat down beside a table; a Bradshaw⁵ lay at his elbow, and
mechanically, without knowing what he did, he began looking out the trains to
Paris.

1899

FRANZ KAFKA

A Hunger Artist¹

During these last decades the interest in professional fasting has markedly diminished. It used to pay very well to stage such great performances under one's own
management, but today that is quite impossible. We live in a different world
now. At one time the whole town took a lively interest in the hunger artist; from
day to day of his fast the excitement mounted; everybody wanted to see him at
least once a day; there were people who bought season tickets for the last few
days and sat from morning till night in front of his small barred cage; even in
the nighttime there were visiting hours, when the whole effect was heightened
by torch flares; on fine days the cage was set out in the open air, and then it was
the children's special treat to see the hunger artist; for their elders he was often
just a joke that happened to be in fashion, but the children stood open-mouthed,
holding each other's hands for greater security, marveling at him as he sat there
pallid in black tights, with his ribs sticking out so prominently, not even on a
seat but down among straw on the ground, sometimes giving a courteous nod,
answering questions with a constrained smile, or perhaps stretching an arm
through the bars so that one might feel how thin it was, and then again withdrawing deep into himself, paying no attention to anyone or anything, not even
to the all-important striking of the clock that was the only piece of furniture in
his cage, but merely staring into vacancy with half shut eyes, now and then taking a sip from a tiny glass of water to moisten his lips.

Besides casual onlookers there were also relays of permanent watchers selected
by the public, usually butchers, strangely enough, and it was their task to watch
the hunger artist day and night, three of them at a time, in case he should have
some secret recourse to nourishment. This was nothing but a formality, insti-
tuted to reassure the masses, for the initiates knew well enough that during his
fast the artist would never in any circumstances, not even under forcible compulsion, swallow the smallest morsel of food: the honor of his profession forbade it.
Not every watcher, of course, was capable of understanding this, there were often
groups of night watchers who were very lax in carrying out their duties and deliberately huddled together in a retired corner to play cards with great absorption,
obviously intending to give the hunger artist the chance of a little refreshment,
which they supposed he could draw from some private hoard. Nothing annoyed

---

5. *Continental Railway Guide.* George Bradshaw (1801–1853) compiled numerous railroad guides and
timetables.   1. Translated by Edwin and Willa Muir.

the artist more than such watchers; they made him miserable; they made his fast seem unendurable; sometimes he mastered his feebleness sufficiently to sing during their watch for as long as he could keep going, to show them how unjust their suspicions were. But that was of little use; they only wondered at his cleverness in being able to fill his mouth even while singing. Much more to his taste were the watchers who sat close up to the bars, who were not content with the dim night lighting of the hall but focused him in the full glare of the electric pocket torch given them by the impresario. The harsh light did not trouble him at all, in any case he could never sleep properly, and he could always drowse a little, whatever the light, at any hour, even when the hall was thronged with noisy onlookers. He was quite happy at the prospect of spending a sleepless night with such watchers; he was ready to exchange jokes with them, to tell them stories out of his nomadic life, anything at all to keep them awake and demonstrate to them again that he had no eatables in his cage and that he was fasting as not one of them could fast. But his happiest moment was when the morning came and an enormous breakfast was brought them, at his expense, on which they flung themselves with the keen appetite of healthy men after a weary night of wakefulness. Of course there were people who argued that this breakfast was an unfair attempt to bribe the watchers, but that was going rather too far, and when they were invited to take on a night's vigil without a breakfast, merely for the sake of the cause, they made themselves scarce, although they stuck stubbornly to their suspicions.

Such suspicions, anyhow, were a necessary accompaniment to the profession of fasting. No one could possibly watch the hunger artist continuously, day and night, and so no one could produce first-hand evidence that the fast had really been rigorous and continuous; only the artist himself could know that, he was therefore bound to be the sole completely satisfied spectator of his own fast. Yet for other reasons he was never satisfied; it was not perhaps mere fasting that had brought him to such skeleton thinness that many people had regretfully to keep away from his exhibitions, because the sight of him was too much for them, perhaps it was dissatisfaction with himself that had worn him down. For he alone knew, what no other initiate knew, how easy it was to fast. It was the easiest thing in the world. He made no secret of this, yet people did not believe him, at the best they set him down as modest, most of them, however, thought he was out for publicity or else was some kind of cheat who found it easy to fast because he had discovered a way of making it easy, and then had the impudence to admit the fact, more or less. He had to put up with all that, and in the course of time had got used to it, but his inner dissatisfaction always rankled, and never yet, after any term of fasting—this must be granted to his credit—had he left the cage of his own free will. The longest period of fasting was fixed by his impresario at forty days, beyond that term he was not allowed to go, not even in great cities, and there was good reason for it, too. Experience had proved that for about forty days the interest of the public could be stimulated by a steadily increasing pressure of advertisement, but after that the town began to lose interest, sympathetic support began notably to fall off; there were of course local variations as between one town and another or one country and another, but as a general rule forty days marked the limit. So on the fortieth day the flower-bedecked cage was opened, enthusiastic spectators filled the hall, a military band played, two doctors entered the cage to measure the results of the fast, which were announced through a megaphone, and finally two young ladies appeared, blissful at having been selected for the honor, to help the hunger artist down the few steps leading to a small table on which was spread a carefully chosen invalid repast. And at this very moment the artist always turned stubborn. True, he would entrust his bony arms to the outstretched helping hands of the ladies bending over him, but stand up he would not. Why stop fasting at this particular moment, after forty days of it? He had held out for a long time, an illimitably long time; why stop now, when he was in his best fasting form, or rather, not yet quite in his best fasting form? Why should he be cheated of the fame he would get for fasting longer, for being not only the record hunger artist of all time, which presumably he was already, but for beating his own record by a performance beyond human imagination, since he felt that there were no limits to his capacity for fasting? His public pretended to admire him so much, why should it have so little patience with him; if he could endure fasting longer, why shouldn't the public endure it? Besides, he was tired, he was comfortable sitting in the straw, and now he was supposed to lift himself to his full height and go down to a meal the very thought of which gave him a nausea that only the presence of the ladies kept him from betraying, and even that with an effort. And he looked up into the eyes of the ladies who were apparently so friendly and in reality so cruel, and shook his head, which felt too heavy on its strengthless neck. But then there happened yet again what always happened. The impresario came forward, without a word—for the band made speech impossible—lifted his arms in the air above the artist, as if inviting Heaven to look down upon its creature here in the straw, this suffering martyr, which indeed he was, although in quite another sense; grasped him round the emaciated waist, with exaggerated caution, so that the frail condition he was in might be appreciated; and committed him to the care of the blenching ladies, not without secretly giving him a shaking so that his legs and body tottered and swayed. The artist now submitted completely; his head lolled on his breast as if it had landed there by chance; his body was hollowed out; his legs in a spasm of self-preservation clung close to each other at the knees, yet scraped on the ground as if it were not really solid ground, as if they were only trying to find solid ground; and the whole weight of his body, a feather-weight after all, relapsed onto one of the ladies, who, looking round for help and panting a little—this post of honor was not at all what she had expected it to be—first stretched her neck as far as she could to keep her face at least free from contact with the artist, when finding this impossible, and her more fortunate companion not coming to her aid but merely holding extended on her own trembling hand the little bunch of knucklebones that was the artist's, to the great delight of the spectators burst into tears and had to be replaced by an attendant who had long been stationed in readiness. Then came the food, a little of which the impresario managed to get between the artist's lips, while he sat in a kind of half-fainting trance, to the accompaniment of cheerful patter designed to distract the public's attention from the artist's condition; after that, a toast was drunk to the public, supposedly prompted by a whisper from the artist in the impresario's ear; the band confirmed it with a mighty flourish, the spectators melted away, and no one had any cause to be dissatisfied with the proceedings, no one except the hunger artist himself, he only, as always.

So he lived for many years, with small regular intervals of recuperation, in visible glory, honored by the world, yet in spite of that troubled in spirit, and all the more troubled because no one would take his trouble seriously. What comfort could he possibly need? What more could he possibly wish for? And if some good-natured person, feeling sorry for him, tried to console him by pointing out that his melancholy was probably caused by fasting, it could happen, especially when he had been fasting for some time, that he reacted with an outburst of fury and to the general alarm began to shake the bars of his cage like a wild animal. Yet the impresario had a way of punishing these outbreaks which he rather enjoyed putting into operation. He would apologize publicly for the artist's behavior, which was only to be excused, he admitted, because of the irritability caused by fasting; a condition hardly to be understood by well-fed people; then by natural transition he went on to mention the artist's equally incomprehensible boast that he could fast for much longer than he was doing; he praised the high ambition, the good will, the great self-denial undoubtedly implicit in such a statement; and then quite simply countered it by bringing out photographs, which were also on sale to the public, showing the artist on the fortieth day of a fast lying in bed almost dead from exhaustion. This perversion of the truth, familiar to the artist though it was, always unnerved him afresh and proved too much for him. What was a consequence of the premature ending of his fast was here presented as the cause of it! To fight against this lack of understanding, against a whole world of non-understanding, was impossible. Time and again in good faith he stood by the bars listening to the impresario, but as soon as the photographs appeared he always let go and sank with a groan back on to his straw, and the reassured public could once more come close and gaze at him.

5   A few years later when the witnesses of such scenes called them to mind, they often failed to understand themselves at all. For meanwhile the aforementioned change in public interest had set in; it seemed to happen almost overnight; there may have been profound causes for it, but who was going to bother about that; at any rate the pampered hunger artist suddenly found himself deserted one fine day by the amusement seekers, who went streaming past him to other more favored attractions. For the last time the impresario hurried him over half Europe to discover whether the old interest might still survive here and there; all in vain; everywhere, as if by secret agreement, a positive revulsion from professional fasting was in evidence. Of course it could not really have sprung up so suddenly as all that, and many premonitory symptoms which had not been sufficiently remarked or suppressed during the rush and glitter of success now came retrospectively to mind, but it was now too late to take any countermeasures. Fasting would surely come into fashion again at some future date, yet that was no comfort for those living in the present. What, then, was the hunger artist to do? He had been applauded by thousands in his time and could hardly come down to showing himself in a street booth at village fairs, and as for adopting another

profession, he was not only too old for that but too fanatically devoted to fasting. So he took leave of the impresario, his partner in an unparalleled career, and hired himself to a large circus; in order to spare his own feelings he avoided reading the conditions of his contract.

A large circus with its enormous traffic in replacing and recruiting men, animals and apparatus can always find a use for people at any time, even for a hunger artist, provided of course that he does not ask too much, and in this particular case anyhow it was not only the artist who was taken on but his famous and long-known name as well, indeed considering the peculiar nature of his performance, which was not impaired by advancing age, it could not be objected that here was an artist past his prime, no longer at the height of his professional skill, seeking a refuge in some quiet corner of a circus; on the contrary, the hunger artist averred that he could fast as well as ever, which was entirely credible, he even alleged that if he were allowed to fast as he liked, and this was at once promised him without more ado, he could astound the world by establishing a record never yet achieved, a statement which certainly provoked a smile among the other professionals, since it left out of account the change in public opinion, which the hunger artist in his zeal conveniently forgot.

He had not, however, actually lost his sense of the real situation and took it as a matter of course that he and his cage should be stationed, not in the middle of the ring as a main attraction, but outside, near the animal cages, on a site that was after all easily accessible. Large and gaily painted placards made a frame for the cage and announced what was to be seen inside it. When the public came thronging out in the intervals to see the animals, they could hardly avoid passing the hunger artist's cage and stopping there for a moment, perhaps they might even have stayed longer had not those pressing behind them in the narrow gangway, who did not understand why they should be held up on their way toward the excitements of the menagerie, made it impossible for anyone to stand gazing quietly for any length of time. And that was the reason why the hunger artist, who had of course been looking forward to these visiting hours as the main achievement of his life, began instead to shrink from them. At first he could hardly wait for the intervals; it was exhilarating to watch the crowds come streaming his way, until only too soon—not even the most obstinate self-deception, clung to almost consciously, could hold out against the fact—the conviction was borne in upon him that these people, most of them, to judge from their actions, again and again, without exception, were all on their way to the menagerie. And the first sight of them from the distance remained the best. For when they reached his cage he was at once deafened by the storm of shouting and abuse that arose from the two contending factions, which renewed themselves continuously, of those who wanted to stop and stare at him—he soon began to dislike them more than the others—not out of real interest but only out of obstinate self-assertiveness, and those who wanted to go straight on to the animals. When the first great rush was past, the stragglers came along, and these, whom nothing could have prevented from stopping to look at him as long as they had breath, raced past with long strides, hardly even glancing at him, in their haste to get to the menagerie in time. And all too rarely did it happen that he had a stroke of luck, when some father of a family fetched up before him with his children, pointed a finger at the hunger artist and explained at length what the phenomenon meant, telling stories of earlier years when he himself had watched similar but much more thrilling performances, and the children, still rather uncomprehending, since neither inside nor outside school had they been sufficiently prepared for this lesson—what did they care about fasting?—yet showed by the brightness of their intent eyes that new and better times might be coming. Perhaps, said the hunger artist to himself many a time, things would be a little better if his cage were set not quite so near the menagerie. That made it too easy for people to make their choice, to say nothing of what he suffered from the stench of the menagerie, the animals' restlessness by night, the carrying past of raw lumps of flesh for the beasts of prey, the roaring at feeding times, which depressed him continually. But he did not dare to lodge a complaint with the management; after all, he had the animals to thank for the troops of people who passed his cage, among whom there might always be one here and there to take an interest in him, and who could tell where they might seclude him if he called attention to his existence and thereby to the fact that, strictly speaking, he was only an impediment on the way to the menagerie.

A small impediment, to be sure, one that grew steadily less. People grew familiar with the strange idea that they could be expected, in times like these, to take an interest in a hunger artist, and with this familiarity the verdict went out against him. He might fast as much as he could, and he did so; but nothing could save him now, people passed him by. Just try to explain to anyone the art of fasting! Anyone who has no feeling for it cannot be made to understand it. The fine placards grew dirty and illegible, they were torn down; the little notice board telling the number of fast days achieved, which at first was changed carefully every day, had long stayed at the same figure, for after the first few weeks even this small task seemed pointless to the staff; and so the artist simply fasted on and on, as he had once dreamed of doing, and it was no trouble to him, just as he had always foretold, but no one counted the days, no one, not even the artist himself, knew what records he was already breaking, and his heart grew heavy. And when once in a time some leisurely passer-by stopped, made merry over the old figure on the board and spoke of swindling, that was in its way the stupidest lie ever invented by indifference and inborn malice, since it was not the hunger artist who was cheating; he was working honestly, but the world was cheating him of his reward.

Many more days went by, however, and that too came to an end. An overseer's eye fell on the cage one day and he asked the attendants why this perfectly good cage should be left standing there unused with dirty straw inside it; nobody knew, until one man, helped out by the notice board, remembered about the hunger artist. They poked into the straw with sticks and found him in it. "Are you still fasting?" asked the overseer. "When on earth do you mean to stop?" "Forgive me, everybody," whispered the hunger artist; only the overseer, who had his ear to the bars, understood him. "Of course," said the overseer, and tapped his forehead with a finger to let the attendants know what state the man was in, "we forgive you." "I always wanted you to admire my fasting," said the hunger artist. "We do admire it," said the overseer, affably. "But you shouldn't admire it," said the hunger artist. "Well, then we don't admire it," said the overseer, "but why shouldn't we admire it?" "Because I have to fast, I can't help it," said the hunger artist. "What a fellow you are," said the overseer, "and why can't you help it?" "Because," said the hunger artist, lifting his head a little and speaking, with his lips pursed, as if for a kiss, right into the overseer's ear, so that no syllable might be lost, "because I couldn't find the food I liked. If I had found it, believe me, I should have made no fuss and stuffed myself like you or anyone else." These were his last words, but in his dimming eyes remained the firm though no longer proud persuasion that he was still continuing to fast.

"Well, clear this out now!" said the overseer, and they buried the hunger artist, straw and all. Into the cage they put a young panther. Even the most insensitive felt it refreshing to see this wild creature leaping around the cage that had so long been dreary. The panther was all right. The food he liked was brought him without hesitation by the attendants; he seemed not even to miss his freedom; his noble body, furnished almost to the bursting point with all that it needed, seemed to carry freedom around with it too; somewhere in his jaws it seemed to lurk; and the joy of life streamed with such ardent passion from his throat that for the onlookers it was not easy to stand the shock of it. But they braced themselves, crowded round the cage, and did not want ever to move away.

10

1924

D. H. LAWRENCE

Odour of Chrysanthemums

I

The small locomotive engine, Number 4, came clanking, stumbling down from Selston with seven full waggons. It appeared round the corner with loud threats of speed, but the colt that it startled from among the gorse, which still flickered indistinctly in the raw afternoon, outdistanced it at a canter. A woman, walking up the railway line to Underwood, drew back into the hedge, held her basket aside, and watched the footplate of the engine advancing. The trucks thumped heavily past, one by one, with slow inevitable movement, as she stood insignificantly trapped between the jolting black waggons and the hedge; then they curved away towards the coppice where the withered oak leaves dropped noiselessly, while the birds, pulling at the scarlet hips beside the track, made off into the dusk that had already crept into the spinney. In the open, the smoke from the engine sank and cleaved to the rough grass. The fields were dreary and forsaken, and in the marshy strip that led to the whimsey, a reedy pit-pond, the fowls had already abandoned their run among the alders, to roost in the tarred fowl-house. The pit-bank loomed up beyond the pond, flames like red sores licking its ashy sides, in the afternoon's stagnant light. Just beyond rose the tapering chimneys and the clumsy black headstocks of Brinsley Colliery. The two wheels were spinning fast up against the sky, and the winding-engine rapped out its little spasms. The miners were being turned up.

The engine whistled as it came into the wide bay of railway lines beside the colliery, where rows of trucks stood in harbour.

Miners, single, trailing and in groups, passed like shadows diverging home. At the edge of the ribbed level of sidings squat a low cottage, three steps down from the cinder track. A large bony vine clutched at the house, as if to claw down the tiled roof. Round the bricked yard grew a few wintry primroses. Beyond, the long garden sloped down to a bush-covered brook course. There were some twiggy apple trees, winter-crack trees, and ragged cabbages. Beside the path hung dishevelled pink chrysanthemums, like pink cloths hung on bushes. A woman came stooping out of the felt-covered fowl-house, half-way down the garden. She closed and padlocked the door, then drew herself erect, having brushed some bits from her white apron.

She was a tall woman of imperious mien, handsome, with definite black eyebrows. Her smooth black hair was parted exactly. For a few moments she stood steadily watching the miners as they passed along the railway: then she turned towards the brook course. Her face was calm and set, her mouth was closed with disillusionment. After a moment she called:

5   "John!" There was no answer. She waited, and then said distinctly:

"Where are you?"

"Here!" replied a child's sulky voice from among the bushes. The woman looked piercingly through the dusk.

"Are you at that brook?" she asked sternly.

For answer the child showed himself before the raspberry-canes that rose like whips. He was a small, sturdy boy of five. He stood quite still, defiantly.

10   "Oh!" said the mother, conciliated. "I thought you were down at that wet brook—and you remember what I told you—"

The boy did not move or answer.

"Come, come on in," she said more gently, "it's getting dark. There's your grandfather's engine coming down the line!"

The lad advanced slowly, with resentful, taciturn movement. He was dressed in trousers and waistcoat of cloth that was too thick and hard for the size of the garments. They were evidently cut down from a man's clothes.

As they went slowly towards the house he tore at the ragged wisps of chrysanthemums and dropped the petals in handfuls along the path.

15   "Don't do that—it does look nasty," said his mother. He refrained, and she, suddenly pitiful, broke off a twig with three or four wan flowers and held them against her face. When mother and son reached the yard her hand hesitated, and instead of laying the flower aside, she pushed it in her apron-band. The mother and son stood at the foot of the three steps looking across the bay of lines at the passing home of the miners. The trundle of the small train was imminent. Suddenly the engine loomed past the house and came to a stop opposite the gate.

The engine-driver, a short man with round grey beard, leaned out of the cab high above the woman.

"Have you got a cup of tea?" he said in a cheery, hearty fashion.

It was her father. She went in, saying she would mash.[1] Directly, she returned.

"I didn't come to see you on Sunday," began the little grey-bearded man.

"I didn't expect you," said his daughter.   20

The engine-driver winced; then, reassuming his cheery, airy manner, he said: "Oh, have you heard then? Well, and what do you think——?"

"I think it is soon enough," she replied.

At her brief censure the little man made an impatient gesture, and said coaxingly, yet with dangerous coldness:

"Well, what's a man to do? It's no sort of life for a man of my years, to sit at   25 my own hearth like a stranger. And if I'm going to marry again it may as well be soon as late—what does it matter to anybody?"

The woman did not reply, but turned and went into the house. The man in the engine-cab stood assertive, till she returned with a cup of tea and a piece of bread and butter on a plate. She went up the steps and stood near the footplate of the hissing engine.

"You needn't 'a' brought me bread an' butter," said her father. "But a cup of tea"—he sipped appreciatively—"it's very nice." He sipped for a moment or two, then: "I hear as Walter's got another bout on," he said.

"When hasn't he?" said the woman bitterly.

"I heered tell of him in the 'Lord Nelson'[2] braggin' as he was going to spend that b—— afore he went: half a sovereign[3] that was."

"When?" asked the woman.   30

"A' Sat'day night—I know that's true."

"Very likely," she laughed bitterly. "He gives me twenty-three shillings."

"Aye, it's a nice thing, when a man can do nothing with his money but make a beast of himself!" said the grey-whiskered man. The woman turned her head away. Her father swallowed the last of his tea and handed her the cup.

"Aye," he sighed, wiping his mouth. "It's a settler, it is——"

He put his hand on the lever. The little engine strained and groaned, and the   35 train rumbled towards the crossing. The woman again looked across the metals. Darkness was settling over the spaces of the railway and trucks: the miners, in grey sombre groups, were still passing home. The winding-engine pulsed hurriedly, with brief pauses. Elizabeth Bates looked at the dreary flow of men, then she went indoors. Her husband did not come.

The kitchen was small and full of firelight; red coals piled glowing up the chimney mouth. All the life of the room seemed in the white, warm hearth and the steel fender reflecting the red fire. The cloth was laid for tea; cups glinted in the shadows. At the back, where the lowest stairs protruded into the room, the boy sat struggling with a knife and a piece of white wood. He was almost hidden in the shadow. It was half-past four. They had but to await the father's coming

---

1. Prepare (tea).   2. A public house, pub.   3. A sovereign was about half a week's wage; there are 20 shillings (see below) to the pound.

to begin tea. As the mother watched her son's sullen little struggle with the wood, she saw herself in his silence and pertinacity; she saw the father in her child's indifference to all but himself. She seemed to be occupied by her husband. He had probably gone past his home, slunk past his own door, to drink before he came in, while his dinner spoiled and wasted in waiting. She glanced at the clock, then took the potatoes to strain them in the yard. The garden and fields beyond the brook were closed in uncertain darkness. When she rose with the saucepan, leaving the drain steaming into the night behind her, she saw the yellow lamps were lit along the high road that went up the hill away beyond the space of the railway lines and the field.

Then again she watched the men trooping home, fewer now and fewer.

Indoors the fire was sinking and the room was dark red. The woman put her saucepan on the hob, and set a batter pudding near the mouth of the oven. Then she stood unmoving. Directly, gratefully, came quick young steps to the door. Someone hung on the latch a moment, then a little girl entered and began pulling off her outdoor things, dragging a mass of curls, just ripening from gold to brown, over her eyes with her hat.

Her mother chid her for coming late from school, and said she would have to keep her at home the dark winter days.

40   "Why, mother, it's hardly a bit dark yet. The lamp's not lighted, and my father's not home."

"No, he isn't. But it's a quarter to five! Did you see anything of him?"

The child became serious. She looked at her mother with large, wistful blue eyes.

"No, mother, I've never seen him. Why? Has he come up an' gone past, to Old Brinsley? He hasn't, mother, 'cos I never saw him."

"He'd watch that," said the mother bitterly, "he'd take care as you didn't see him. But you may depend upon it, he's seated in the 'Prince o' Wales.' He wouldn't be this late."

45   The girl looked at her mother piteously.

"Let's have our teas, mother, should we?" said she.

The mother called John to table. She opened the door once more and looked out across the darkness of the lines. All was deserted: she could not hear the winding-engines.

"Perhaps," she said to herself, "he's stopped to get some ripping[4] done."

They sat down to tea. John, at the end of the table near the door, was almost lost in the darkness. Their faces were hidden from each other. The girl crouched against the fender slowly moving a thick piece of bread before the fire. The lad, his face a dusky mark on the shadow, sat watching her who was transfigured in the red glow.

50   "I do think it's beautiful to look in the fire," said the child.

"Do you?" said her mother. "Why?"

"It's so red, and full of little caves—and it feels so nice, and you can fair smell it."

---

4. Coal-mining term for taking down the roof of an underground road in order to make it higher.

"It'll want mending directly," replied her mother, "and then if your father comes he'll carry on and say there never is a fire when a man comes home sweating from the pit.—A public-house is always warm enough."

There was silence till the boy said complainingly: "Make haste, our Annie."

"Well, I am doing! I can't make the fire do it no faster, can I?"

"She keeps wafflin'[5] it about so's to make 'er slow," grumbled the boy.

"Don't have such an evil imagination, child," replied the mother.

Soon the room was busy in the darkness with the crisp sound of crunching. The mother ate very little. She drank her tea determinedly, and sat thinking. When she rose her anger was evident in the stern unbending of her head. She looked at the pudding in the fender, and broke out:

"It is a scandalous thing as a man can't even come home to his dinner! If it's crozzled[6] up to a cinder I don't see why I should care. Past his very door he goes to get to a public-house, and here I sit with his dinner waiting for him——"

She went out. As she dropped piece after piece of coal on the red fire, the shadows fell on the walls, till the room was almost in total darkness.

"I canna see," grumbled the invisible John. In spite of herself, the mother laughed.

"You know the way to your mouth," she said. She set the dustpan outside the door. When she came again like a shadow on the hearth, the lad repeated, complaining sulkily:

"I canna see."

"Good gracious!" cried the mother irritably, "you're as bad as your father if it's a bit dusk!"

Nevertheless she took a paper spill from a sheaf on the mantelpiece and proceeded to light the lamp that hung from the ceiling in the middle of the room. As she reached up, her figure displayed itself just rounding with maternity.

"Oh, mother——!" exclaimed the girl.

"What?" said the woman, suspended in the act of putting the lamp-glass over the flame. The copper reflector shone handsomely on her, as she stood with uplifted arm, turning to face her daughter:

"You've got a flower in your apron!" said the child, in a little rapture at this unusual event.

"Goodness me!" exclaimed the woman, relieved. "One would think the house was afire." She replaced the glass and waited a moment before turning up the wick. A pale shadow was seen floating vaguely on the floor.

"Let me smell!" said the child, still rapturously, coming forward and putting her face to her mother's waist.

"Go along, silly!" said the mother, turning up the lamp. The light revealed their suspense so that the woman felt it almost unbearable. Annie was still bending at her waist. Irritably, the mother took the flowers out from her apron-band.

"Oh, mother—don't take them out!" Annie cried, catching her hand and trying to replace the sprig.

5. Waving.   6. Shriveled.

"Such nonsense!" said the mother, turning away. The child put the pale chrysanthemums to her lips, murmuring:

"Don't they smell beautiful!"

75   Her mother gave a short laugh.

"No," she said, "not to me. It was chrysanthemums when I married him, and chrysanthemums when you were born, and the first time they ever brought him home drunk, he'd got brown chrysanthemums in his button-hole."

She looked at the children. Their eyes and their parted lips were wondering. The mother sat rocking in silence for some time. Then she looked at the clock.

"Twenty minutes to six!" In a tone of fine bitter carelessness she continued: "Eh, he'll not come now till they bring him. There he'll stick! But he needn't come rolling in here in his pit-dirt, for *I* won't wash him. He can lie on the floor——Eh, what a fool I've been, what a fool! And this is what I came here for, to this dirty hole, rats and all, for him to slink past his very door. Twice last week—he's begun now——"

She silenced herself, and rose to clear the table.

80   While for an hour or more the children played, subduedly intent, fertile of imagination, united in fear of the mother's wrath, and in dread of their father's home-coming, Mrs. Bates sat in her rocking-chair making a "singlet" of thick cream-coloured flannel, which gave a dull wounded sound as she tore off the grey edge. She worked at her sewing with energy, listening to the children, and her anger wearied itself, lay down to rest, opening its eyes from time to time and steadily watching, its ears raised to listen. Sometimes even her anger quailed and shrank, and the mother suspended her sewing, tracing the footsteps that thudded along the sleepers outside; she would lift her head sharply to bid the children "hush," but she recovered herself in time, and the footsteps went past the gate, and the children were not flung out of their playworld.

But at last Annie sighed, and gave in. She glanced at her waggon of slippers, and loathed the game. She turned plaintively to her mother.

"Mother!"—but she was inarticulate.

John crept out like a frog from under the sofa. His mother glanced up.

"Yes," she said, "just look at those shirtsleeves!"

85   The boy held them out to survey them, saying nothing. Then somebody called in a hoarse voice away down the line, and suspense bristled in the room, till two people had gone by outside, talking.

"It is time for bed," said the mother.

"My father hasn't come," wailed Annie plaintively. But her mother was primed with courage.

"Never mind. They'll bring him when he does come—like a log." She meant there would be no scene. "And he may sleep on the floor till he wakes himself. I know he'll not go to work tomorrow after this!"

The children had their hands and faces wiped with a flannel.[7] They were very

_____
7. Washrag.

quiet. When they had put on their nightdresses, they said their prayers, the boy mumbling. The mother looked down at them, at the brown silken bush of intertwining curls in the nape of the girl's neck, at the little black head of the lad, and her heart burst with anger at their father who caused all three such distress. The children hid their faces in her skirts for comfort.

When Mrs. Bates came down, the room was strangely empty, with a tension of expectancy. She took up her sewing and stitched for some time without raising her head. Meantime her anger was tinged with fear.

90

II

The clock struck eight and she rose suddenly, dropping her sewing on her chair. She went to the stairfoot door, opened it, listening. Then she went out, locking the door behind her.

Something scuffled in the yard, and she started though she knew it was only the rats with which the place was overrun. The night was very dark. In the great bay of railway lines, bulked with trucks, there was no trace of light, only away back she could see a few yellow lamps at the pit-top, and the red smear of the burning pit-bank on the night. She hurried along the edge of the track, then, crossing the converging lines, came to the stile by the white gates, whence she emerged on the road. Then the fear which had led her shrank. People were walking up to New Brinsley; she saw the lights in the houses; twenty yards further on were the broad windows of the "Prince of Wales," very warm and bright, and the loud voices of men could be heard distinctly. What a fool she had been to imagine that anything had happened to him! He was merely drinking over there at the "Prince of Wales." She faltered. She had never yet been to fetch him, and she never would go. So she continued her walk towards the long straggling line of houses, standing blank on the highway. She entered a passage between the dwellings.

"Mr. Rigley?—Yes! Did you want him? No, he's not in at this minute."

The raw-boned woman leaned forward from her dark scullery and peered at the other, upon whom fell a dim light through the blind of the kitchen window.

"Is it Mrs. Bates?" she asked in a tone tinged with respect.

95

"Yes. I wondered if your Master was at home. Mine hasn't come yet."

" 'Asn't 'e! Oh, Jack's been 'ome an 'ad 'is dinner an' gone out. 'E's just gone for 'alf an hour afore bedtime. Did you call at the 'Prince of Wales'?"

"No——"

"No, you didn't like——! It's not very nice." The other woman was indulgent. There was an awkward pause. "Jack never said nothink about—about your Mester," she said.

"No!—I expect he's stuck in there!"

100

Elizabeth Bates said this bitterly, and with recklessness. She knew that the woman across the yard was standing at her door listening, but she did not care. As she turned:

"Stop a minute! I'll just go an' ask Jack if 'e knows anythink," said Mrs. Rigley.

"Oh, no—I wouldn't like to put—!"

"Yes, I will, if you will just step inside an' see as th' childer doesn't come downstairs and set theirselves afire."

105   Elizabeth Bates, murmuring a remonstrance, stepped inside. The other woman apologized for the state of the room.

The kitchen needed apology. There were little frocks and trousers and childish undergarments on the squab[8] and on the floor, and a litter of playthings everywhere. On the black American cloth[9] of the table were pieces of bread and cake, crusts, slops, and a teapot with cold tea.

"Eh, ours is just as bad," said Elizabeth Bates, looking at the woman, not at the house. Mrs. Rigley put a shawl over her head and hurried out, saying:

"I shanna be a minute."

The other sat, noting with faint disapproval the general untidiness of the room. Then she fell to counting the shoes of various sizes scattered over the floor. There were twelve. She sighed and said to herself, "No wonder!"—glancing at the litter. There came the scratching of two pairs of feet on the yard, and the Rigleys entered. Elizabeth Bates rose. Rigley was a big man, with very large bones. His head looked particularly bony. Across his temple was a blue scar, caused by a wound got in the pit, a wound in which the coal-dust remained blue like tattooing.

110   " 'Asna 'e come whoam yit?" asked the man, without any form of greeting, but with deference and sympathy. "I couldna say wheer he is—'e's non ower theer!"—he jerked his head to signify the "Prince of Wales."

" 'E's 'appen[1] gone up to th' 'Yew,' " said Mrs. Rigley.

There was another pause. Rigley had evidently something to get off his mind:

"Ah left 'im finishin' a stint," he began. "Loose-all[2] 'ad bin gone about ten minutes when we com'n away, an' I shouted, 'Are ter comin', Walt?' an' 'e said 'Go on, Ah shanna be but a 'ef a minnit,' so we com'n ter th' bottom, me an' Browers, thinkin' as 'e wor just behint, an' 'ud come up i' th' next bantle[3]——"

He stood perplexed, as if answering a charge of deserting his mate. Elizabeth Bates, now again certain of disaster, hastened to reassure him:

115   "I expect 'e's gone up to th' 'Yew Tree,' as you say. It's not the first time. I've fretted myself into a fever before now. He'll come home when they carry him."

"Ay, isn't it too bad!" deplored the other woman.

"I'll just step up to Dick's an' see if 'e *is* theer," offered the man, afraid of appearing alarmed, afraid of taking liberties.

"Oh, I wouldn't think of bothering you that far," said Elizabeth Bates, with emphasis, but he knew she was glad of his offer.

As they stumbled up the entry, Elizabeth Bates heard Rigley's wife run across the yard and open her neighbour's door. At this, suddenly all the blood in her body seemed to switch away from her heart.

---

8. Sofa.   9. Enameled oilcloth.   1. Perhaps.   2. Signal to quit work and come to the surface.   3. An open seat or car of the lift or elevator that takes the miners to the surface.

"Mind!" warned Rigley. "Ah've said many a time as Ah'd fill up them ruts in 120
this entry, sumb'dy 'll be breakin' their legs yit."

She recovered herself and walked quickly along with the miner.

"I don't like leaving the children in bed, and nobody in the house," she said.

"No, you dunna!" he replied courteously. They were soon at the gate of the
cottage.

"Well, I shanna be many minnits. Dunna you be frettin' now, 'e'll be all
right," said the butty.[4]

"Thank you very much, Mr. Rigley," she replied. 125

"You're welcome!" he stammered, moving away. "I shanna be many minnits."

The house was quiet. Elizabeth Bates took off her hat and shawl, and rolled
back the rug. When she had finished, she sat down. It was a few minutes past nine.
She was startled by the rapid chuff of the winding-engine at the pit, and the sharp
whirr of the brakes on the rope as it descended. Again she felt the painful sweep of
her blood, and she put her hand to her side, saying aloud, "Good gracious!—it's
only the nine o'clock deputy going down," rebuking herself.

She sat still, listening. Half an hour of this, and she was wearied out.

"What am I working up like this for?" she said pitiably to herself, "I s'll only
be doing myself some damage."

She took out her sewing again. 130

At a quarter to ten there were footsteps. One person! She watched for the door
to open. It was an elderly woman, in a black bonnet and a black woollen shawl—
his mother. She was about sixty years old, pale, with blue eyes, and her face all
wrinkled and lamentable. She shut the door and turned to her daughter-in-law
peevishly.

"Eh, Lizzie, whatever shall we do, whatever shall we do!" she cried.

Elizabeth drew back a little, sharply.

"What is it, mother?" she said.

The elder woman seated herself on the sofa. 135

"I don't know, child, I can't tell you!"—she shook her head slowly. Elizabeth
sat watching her, anxious and vexed.

"I don't know," replied the grandmother, sighing very deeply. "There's no end
to my troubles, there isn't. The things I've gone through, I'm sure it's
enough ——!" She wept without wiping her eyes, the tears running.

"But, mother," interrupted Elizabeth, "what do you mean? What is it?"

The grandmother slowly wiped her eyes. The fountains of her tears were
stopped by Elizabeth's directness. She wiped her eyes slowly.

"Poor child! Eh, you poor thing!" she moaned. "I don't know what we're going 140
to do, I don't—and you as you are—it's a thing, it is indeed!"

Elizabeth waited.

"Is he dead?" she asked, and at the words her heart swung violently, though
she felt a slight flush of shame at the ultimate extravagance of the question. Her
words sufficiently frightened the old lady, almost brought her to herself.

4. Buddy, fellow worker.

"Don't say so, Elizabeth! We'll hope it's not as bad as that; no, may the Lord spare us that, Elizabeth. Jack Rigley came just as I was sittin' down to a glass afore going to bed, an' 'e said, ' 'Appen you'll go down th' line, Mrs. Bates. Walt's had an accident. 'Appen you'll go an' sit wi' 'er till we can get him home.' I hadn't time to ask him a word afore he was gone. An' I put my bonnet on an' come straight down, Lizzie. I thought to myself, 'Eh, that poor blessed child, if anybody should come an' tell her of a sudden, there's no knowin'; what'll 'appen to 'er.' You mustn't let it upset you, Lizzie—or you know what to expect. How long is it, six months—or is it five, Lizzie? Ay!"—the old woman shook her head—"time slips on, it slips on! Ay!"

Elizabeth's thoughts were busy elsewhere. If he was killed—would she be able to manage on the little pension and what she could earn?—she counted up rapidly. If he was hurt—they wouldn't take him to the hospital—how tiresome he would be to nurse!—but perhaps she'd be able to get him away from the drink and his hateful ways. She would—while he was ill. The tears offered to come to her eyes at the picture. But what sentimental luxury was this she was beginning?—She turned to consider the children. At any rate she was absolutely necessary for them. They were her business.

145   "Ay!" repeated the old woman, "it seems but a week or two since he brought me his first wages. Ay—he was a good lad, Elizabeth, he was, in his way. I don't know why he got to be such a trouble, I don't. He was a happy lad at home, only full of spirits. But there's no mistake he's been a handful of trouble, he has! I hope the Lord'll spare him to mend his ways. I hope so, I hope so. You've had a sight o' trouble with him, Elizabeth, you have indeed. But he was a jolly enough lad wi' me, he was, I can assure you. I don't know how it is. . . ."

The old woman continued to muse aloud, a monotonous irritating sound, while Elizabeth thought concentratedly, startled once, when she heard the winding-engine chuff quickly, and the brakes skirr with a shriek. Then she heard the engine more slowly, and the brakes made no sound. The old woman did not notice. Elizabeth waited in suspense. The mother-in-law talked, with lapses into silence.

"But he wasn't your son, Lizzie, an' it makes a difference. Whatever he was, I remember him when he was little, an' I learned to understand him and to make allowances. You've got to make allowances for them—"

It was half-past ten, and the old woman was saying: "But it's trouble from beginning to end; you're never too old for trouble, never too old for that——" when the gate banged back, and there were heavy feet on the steps.

"I'll go, Lizzie, let me go," cried the old woman, rising. But Elizabeth was at the door. It was a man in pit-clothes.

150   "They're bringin' 'im, Missis," he said. Elizabeth's heart halted a moment. Then it surged on again, almost suffocating her.

"Is he—is it bad?" she asked.

The man turned away, looking at the darkness:

"The doctor says 'e'd been dead hours. 'E saw 'im i' th' lamp-cabin."

The old woman, who stood just behind Elizabeth, dropped into a chair and folded her hands, crying: "Oh, my boy, my boy!"

"Hush!" said Elizabeth, with a sharp twitch of a frown. "Be still, mother, don't   155
waken th' children: I wouldn't have them down for anything!"

The old woman moaned softly, rocking herself. The man was drawing away.
Elizabeth took a step forward.

"How was it?" she asked.

"Well, I couldn't say for sure," the man replied, very ill at ease. " 'E wor finishin' a stint an' th' butties 'ad gone, an' a lot o' stuff come down atop 'n 'im."

"And crushed him?" cried the widow, with a shudder.

"No," said the man, "it fell at th' back of 'im. 'E wor under th' face, an' it niver   160
touched 'im. It shut 'im in. It seems 'e wor smothered."

Elizabeth shrank back. She heard the old woman behind her cry:

"What?—what did 'e say it was?"

The man replied, more loudly: "'E wor smothered!"

Then the old woman wailed aloud, and this relieved Elizabeth.

"Oh, mother," she said, putting her hands on the old woman, "don't waken   165
th' children, don't waken th' children."

She wept a little, unknowing, while the old mother rocked herself and
moaned. Elizabeth remembered that they were bringing him home, and she
must be ready. "They'll lay him in the parlour," she said to herself, standing a
moment pale and perplexed.

Then she lighted a candle and went into the tiny room. The air was cold and
damp, but she could not make a fire, there was no fireplace. She set down the
candle and looked round. The candlelight glittered on the lustre-glasses,[5] on the
two vases that held some of the pink chrysanthemums, and on the dark mahogany. There was a cold, deathly smell of chrysanthemums in the room. Elizabeth
stood looking at the flowers. She turned away, and calculated whether there
would be room to lay him on the floor, between the couch and the chiffonier.
She pushed the chairs aside. There would be room to lay him down and to step
round him. Then she fetched the old red tablecloth, and another old cloth,
spreading them down to save her bit of carpet. She shivered on leaving the
parlour; so, from the dresser-drawer she took a clean shirt and put it at the
fire to air. All the time her mother-in-law was rocking herself in the chair and
moaning.

"You'll have to move from there, mother," said Elizabeth. "They'll be bringing
him in. Come in the rocker."

The old mother rose mechanically, and seated herself by the fire, continuing
to lament. Elizabeth went into the pantry for another candle, and there, in the
little penthouse[6] under the naked tiles, she heard them coming. She stood still
in the pantry doorway, listening. She heard them pass the end of the house,
and come awkwardly down the three steps, a jumble of shuffling footsteps and
muttering voices. The old woman was silent. The men were in the yard.

Then Elizabeth heard Matthews, the manager of the pit, say: "You go in first,   170
Jim. Mind!"

5. Glass pendants around the edge of an ornamental vase.   6. Structure, usually with a sloping roof,
attached to house.

The door came open, and the two women saw a collier backing into the room, holding one end of a stretcher, on which they could see the nailed pitboots of the dead man. The two carriers halted, the man at the head stooping to the lintel of the door.

"Wheer will you have him?" asked the manager, a short, white-bearded man.

Elizabeth roused herself and came from the pantry carrying the unlighted candle.

"In the parlour," she said.

175   "In there, Jim!" pointed the manager, and the carriers backed round into the tiny room. The coat with which they had covered the body fell off as they awkwardly turned through the two doorways, and the women saw their man, naked to the waist, lying stripped for work. The old woman began to moan in a low voice of horror.

"Lay th' stretcher at th' side," snapped the manager, "an' put 'im on th' cloths. Mind now, mind! Look you now——!"

One of the men had knocked off a vase of chrysanthemums. He stared awkwardly, then they set down the stretcher. Elizabeth did not look at her husband. As soon as she could get in the room, she went and picked up the broken vase and the flowers.

"Wait a minute!" she said.

The three men waited in silence while she mopped up the water with a duster.

180   "Eh, what a job, what a job, to be sure!" the manager was saying, rubbing his brow with trouble and perplexity. "Never knew such a thing in my life, never! He'd no business to ha' been left. I never knew such a thing in my life! Fell over him clean as a whistle, an' shut him in. Not four foot of space, there wasn't—yet it scarce bruised him."

He looked down at the dead man, lying prone, half naked, all grimed with coal-dust.

" ' 'Sphyxiated,' the doctor said. It *is* the most terrible job I've ever known. Seems as if it was done o' purpose. Clean over him, an' shut 'im in, like a mousetrap"—he made a sharp, descending gesture with his hand.

The colliers standing by jerked aside their heads in hopeless comment.

The horror of the thing bristled upon them all.

185   Then they heard the girl's voice upstairs calling shrilly: "Mother, mother—who is it? Mother, who is it?"

Elizabeth hurried to the foot of the stairs and opened the door:

"Go to sleep!" she commanded sharply. "What are you shouting about? Go to sleep at once—there's nothing——"

Then she began to mount the stairs. They could hear her on the boards, and on the plaster floor of the little bedroom. They could hear her distinctly:

"What's the matter now?—what's the matter with you, silly thing?"—her voice was much agitated, with an unreal gentleness.

190   "I thought it was some men come," said the plaintive voice of the child. "Has he come?"

"Yes, they've brought him. There's nothing to make a fuss about. Go to sleep now, like a good child."

They could hear her voice in the bedroom, they waited whilst she covered the children under the bedclothes.

"Is he drunk?" asked the girl, timidly, faintly.

"No! No—he's not! He's—he's asleep."

"Is he asleep downstairs?" 195

"Yes—and don't make a noise."

There was silence for a moment, then the men heard the frightened child again:

"What's that noise?"

"It's nothing, I tell you, what are you bothering for?"

The noise was the grandmother moaning. She was oblivious of everything, 200 sitting on her chair rocking and moaning. The manager put his hand on her arm and bade her "Sh-sh!!"

The old woman opened her eyes and looked at him. She was shocked by this interruption, and seemed to wonder.

"What time is it?"—the plaintive thin voice of the child, sinking back unhappily into sleep, asked this last question.

"Ten o'clock," answered the mother more softly. Then she must have bent down and kissed the children.

Matthews beckoned to the men to come away. They put on their caps, and took up the stretcher. Stepping over the body, they tiptoed out of the house. None of them spoke till they were far from the wakeful children.

When Elizabeth came down she found her mother alone on the parlour floor, 205 leaning over the dead man, the tears dropping on him.

"We must lay him out," the wife said. She put on the kettle, then returning knelt at the feet, and began to unfasten the knotted leather laces. The room was clammy and dim with only one candle, so that she had to bend her face almost to the floor. At last she got off the heavy boots and put them away.

"You must help me now," she whispered to the old woman. Together they stripped the man.

When they arose, saw him lying in the naïve dignity of death, the women stood arrested in fear and respect. For a few moments they remained still, looking down, the old mother whimpering. Elizabeth felt countermanded. She saw him, how utterly inviolable he lay in himself. She had nothing to do with him. She could not accept it. Stooping, she laid her hand on him, in claim. He was still warm, for the mine was hot where he had died. His mother had his face between her hands, and was murmuring incoherently. The old tears fell in succession as drops from wet leaves; the mother was not weeping, merely her tears flowed. Elizabeth embraced the body of her husband, with cheek and lips. She seemed to be listening, inquiring, trying to get some connection. But she could not. She was driven away. He was impregnable.

She rose, went into the kitchen, where she poured warm water into a bowl, brought soap and flannel and a soft towel.

"I must wash him," she said. 210

Then the old mother rose stiffly, and watched Elizabeth as she carefully washed his face, carefully brushing the big blonde moustache from his mouth with the flannel. She was afraid with a bottomless fear, so she ministered to him. The old woman, jealous, said:

"Let me wipe him!"—and she kneeled on the other side drying slowly as Elizabeth washed, her big black bonnet sometimes brushing the dark head of her daughter. They worked thus in silence for a long time. They never forgot it was death, and the touch of the man's dead body gave them strange emotions, different in each of the women; a great dread possessed them both, the mother felt the lie was given to her womb, she was denied; the wife felt the utter isolation of the human soul, the child within her was a weight apart from her.

At last it was finished. He was a man of handsome body, and his face showed no traces of drink. He was blonde, full-fleshed, with fine limbs. But he was dead.

"Bless him," whispered his mother, looking always at his face, and speaking out of sheer terror. "Dear lad—bless him!" She spoke in a faint sibilant ecstasy of fear and mother love.

215   Elizabeth sank down again to the floor, and put her face against his neck, and trembled and shuddered. But she had to draw away again. He was dead, and her living flesh had no place against his. A great dread and weariness held her: she was so unavailing. Her life was gone like this.

"White as milk he is, clear as a twelve-month baby, bless him, the darling!" the old mother murmured to herself. "Not a mark on him, clear and clean and white, beautiful as ever a child was made," she murmured with pride. Elizabeth kept her face hidden.

"He went peaceful, Lizzie—peaceful as sleep. Isn't he beautiful, the lamb? Ay— he must ha' made his peace, Lizzie. 'Appen he made it all right, Lizzie, shut in there. He'd have time. He wouldn't look like this if he hadn't made his peace. The lamb, the dear lamb. Eh, but he had a hearty laugh. I loved to hear it. He had the heartiest laugh, Lizzie, as a lad——"

Elizabeth looked up. The man's mouth was fallen back, slightly open under the cover of the moustache. The eyes, half shut, did not show glazed in the obscurity. Life with its smoky burning gone from him, had left him apart and utterly alien to her. And she knew what a stranger he was to her. In her womb was ice of fear, because of this separate stranger with whom she had been living as one flesh. Was this what it all meant—utter, intact separateness, obscured by heat of living? In dread she turned her face away. The fact was too deadly. There had been nothing between them, and yet they had come together, exchanging their nakedness repeatedly. Each time he had taken her, they had been two isolated beings, far apart as now. He was no more responsible than she. The child was like ice in her womb. For as she looked at the dead man, her mind, cold and detached, said clearly: "Who am I? What have I been doing? I have been fighting a husband who did not exist. *He* existed all the time. What wrong have I done? What was that I have been living with? There lies the reality, this man."—And her soul died in her for fear: she knew she had never seen him, he had never seen her, they had met in the dark and had fought in the dark, not knowing whom they met nor whom they fought. And now she saw, and turned silent in seeing. For she had been wrong. She had said he was something he was not; she had felt familiar with him. Whereas he was apart all the while, living as she never lived, feeling as she never felt.

In fear and shame she looked at his naked body, that she had known falsely. And he was the father of her children. Her soul was torn from her body and stood apart. She looked at his naked body and was ashamed, as if she had denied it. After all, it was itself. It seemed awful to her. She looked at his face, and she turned her own face to the wall. For his look was other than hers, his way was not her way. She had denied him what he was—she saw it now. She had refused him as himself.—And this had been her life, and his life.—She was grateful to death, which restored the truth. And she knew she was not dead.

And all the while her heart was bursting with grief and pity for him. What had he suffered? What stretch of horror for this helpless man! She was rigid with agony. She had not been able to help him. He had been cruelly injured, this naked man, this other being, and she could make no reparation. There were the children—but the children belonged to life. This dead man had nothing to do with them. He and she were only channels through which life had flowed to issue in the children. She was a mother—but how awful she knew it now to have been a wife. And he, dead now, how awful he must have felt it to be a husband. She felt that in her next world he would be a stranger to her. If they met there, in the beyond, they would only be ashamed of what had been before. The children had come, for some mysterious reason, out of both of them. But the children did not unite them. Now he was dead, she knew how eternally he was apart from her, how eternally he had nothing more to do with her. She saw this episode of her life closed. They had denied each other in life. Now he had withdrawn. An anguish came over her. It was finished then: it had become hopeless between them long before he died. Yet he had been her husband. But how little!

"Have you got his shirt, 'Lizabeth?"

Elizabeth turned without answering, though she strove to weep and behave as her mother-in-law expected. But she could not, she was silenced. She went into the kitchen and returned with the garment.

"It is aired," she said, grasping the cotton shirt here and there to try. She was almost ashamed to handle him; what right had she or anyone to lay hands on him; but her touch was humble on his body. It was hard work to clothe him. He was so heavy and inert. A terrible dread gripped her all the while: that he could be so heavy and utterly inert, unresponsive, apart. The horror of the distance between them was almost too much for her—it was so infinite a gap she must look across.

At last it was finished. They covered him with a sheet and left him lying, with his face bound. And she fastened the door of the little parlour, lest the children should see what was lying there. Then, with peace sunk heavy on her heart, she went about making tidy the kitchen. She knew she submitted to life, which was her immediate master. But from death, her ultimate master, she winced with fear and shame.

1914

Poetry

Poetry: Reading, Responding, Writing

If you're already a reader of poetry, you know: poetry reading is not just an intellectual and bookish activity; it is about feeling. Reading poetry well means responding to it: if you respond on a feeling level, you are likely to read more accurately, with deeper understanding, and with greater pleasure. And, conversely, if you read poetry accurately, and with attention to detail, you will almost certainly respond—or learn how to respond—to it on an emotional level. Reading poetry involves conscious articulation through language, and reading and responding come to be, for experienced readers of poetry, very nearly one. But those who teach poetry—and there are a lot of us, almost all enthusiasts about both poetry as a subject and reading as a craft—have discovered something else: writing about poetry helps both the reading and the responding processes. Responding involves remembering and reflecting as well. As you recall your own past and make associations between things in the text and things you already know and feel, you will not only respond more fully to a particular poem, but improve your reading skills more generally. Your knowledge and life experience informs your reading of what is before you, and allows you to connect things within the text—events, images, words, sounds—so that meanings and feelings develop and accumulate. Prior learning creates expectations: of pattern, repetition, association, or causality. Reflecting on the text—and on expectations produced by themes and ideas in the text—re-creates old feelings but directs them in new, often unusual ways. Poems, even when they are about things we have no experience of, connect to things we do know and order our memories, thoughts, and feelings in new and newly challenging ways.

> *Poetry is a way of taking life by the throat.*
>
> —ROBERT FROST

A course in reading poetry can ultimately enrich your life by helping you become more articulate and more sensitive to both ideas and feelings: that's the larger goal. But the more immediate goal—and the route to the larger one—is to make you a better reader of texts and a more precise and careful writer yourself. Close attention to one text makes you appreciate, and understand, textuality and its possibilities more generally. Texts may be complex and even unstable in some ways; they do not affect all readers the same way, and they work through language that has its own volatilities and complexities. But paying attention to how you read—developing specific questions to ask and working on your reading skills systematically—can take a lot of the guesswork out of reading texts and give you a sense of greater satisfaction in your interpretations.

READING

Poems, perhaps even more than other texts, can sharpen your reading skills because they tend to be so compact, so fully dependent on concise expressions of feeling. In poems, ideas and feelings are packed tightly into just a few lines. The experiences of life are very concentrated here, and meanings emerge quickly, word by word. Poems often show us the very process of putting feelings into a language that can be shared with others—to *say* feelings in a communicable way. Poetry can be intellectual too, explaining and exploring ideas, but its focus is more often on how people feel than how they think. Poems work out a shareable language for feeling, and one of poetry's most insistent virtues involves its attempt to express the inexpressible. How can anyone, for example, put into words what it means to be in love or how it feels to lose someone one cares about? Poetry tries, and it often captures a shade of emotion that feels just right to a reader. No single poem can be said to represent all the things that love or death feels like or means, but one of the joys of experiencing poetry occurs when we read a poem and want to say, "Yes, that is just what it is like; I know exactly what that line means but I've never been able to express it so well." Poetry can be the voice of our feelings even when our minds are speechless with grief or joy. Reading is no substitute for living, but it can make living more abundant and more available.

Here are two poems that talk about the sincerity and depth of love between two people. Each is written as if it were spoken by one person to his or her lover, and each is definite and powerful about the intensity and quality of love; but the poems work in quite different ways—the first one asserting the strength and depth of love, the second implying intense feeling by reminiscing about earlier events in the relationship between the two people.

ELIZABETH BARRETT BROWNING

How Do I Love Thee?

How do I love thee? Let me count the ways.
I love thee to the depth and breadth and height
My soul can reach, when feeling out of sight
For the ends of Being and ideal Grace.
I love thee to the level of every day's   5
Most quiet need, by sun and candlelight.
I love thee freely, as men strive for Right;
I love thee purely, as they turn from Praise;
I love thee with the passion put to use
In my old griefs, and with my childhood's faith.   10
I love thee with a love I seemed to lose
With my lost saints—I love thee with the breath,
Smiles, tears, of all my life!—and, if God choose,
I shall but love thee better after death.

                                                       1850

JAROLD RAMSEY

The Tally Stick

Here from the start, from our first of days, look:
I have carved our lives in secret on this stick
of mountain mahogany the length of your arms
outstretched, the wood clear red, so hard and rare.
5   It is time to touch and handle what we know we share.

Near the butt, this intricate notch where the grains
converge and join: it is our wedding.
I can read it through with a thumb and tell you now
who danced, who made up the songs, who meant us joy.
10   These little arrowheads along the grain,
they are the births of our children. See,
they make a kind of design with these heavy crosses,
the deaths of our parents, the loss of friends.

Over it all as it goes, of course, I
15   have chiseled Events, History—random
hashmarks cut against the swirling grain.
See, here is the Year the World Went Wrong,
we thought, and here the days the Great Men fell.
The lengthening runes of our lives run through it all.

20   See, our tally stick is whittled nearly end to end;
delicate as scrimshaw, it would not bear you up.
Regrets have polished it, hand over hand.
Yet let us take it up, and as our fingers
like children leading on a trail cry back
25   our unforgotten wonders, sign after sign,
we will talk softly as of ordinary matters,
and in one another's blameless eyes go blind.   p. 1977

The first poem is direct, but fairly abstract. It lists several ways in which the poet feels love and connects them to some noble ideas of higher obligations—to justice (line 7), for example, and to spiritual aspiration (lines 2–4). It suggests a wide range of things that love can mean and notices a variety of emotions. It is an ardent statement of feeling and asserts a permanence that will extend even beyond death. It contains admirable thoughts and memorable phrases that many lovers would like to hear said to themselves. What it does not do is say very much about what the relationship between the two lovers is like on an everyday basis, what experiences they have had together, what distinguishes their relationship from that of other devoted or ideal lovers. Its appeal is to our general sense of what love is like and how intense feelings can be; it does not offer everyday details. Love may differ from person to person and even from moment to moment, and so can poems about love.

"The Tally Stick" is much more concrete. The whole poem concentrates on a single object that, like "How Do I Love Thee?," "counts" or "tallies" the ways in which this couple love one another. This stick stands for their love and becomes a kind of physical reminder of it: its natural features—the notches and arrowheads and cross marks (lines 6, 10, and 12) along with the marks carved on it (lines 15–16, 20–21)—indicate events in the story of the relationship. (We could say that the stick *symbolizes* their love; later on, we will look at a number of terms like this that can be used to make it easier to talk about some aspects of poems, but for now it is enough to notice that the stick serves the lovers as a reminder and a marker of some specific details of their love.) It is a special kind of reminder to them because its language is "secret" (line 2), something they can share privately (except that we as readers of the poem are sort of looking over their shoulders, not intruding but sharing their secret). The poet interprets the particular features of the stick as standing for particular events—their wedding and the births of their children, for example—and carves marks into it as reminders of other events (lines 15 ff.). The stick itself becomes a very personal object, and in the last stanza of the poem it is as if we watch the lovers touching the stick together and reminiscing over it, gradually dissolving into their emotions and each other as they recall the "unforgotten wonders" (line 25) of their lives together.

Both poems are powerful statements of feelings, each in its own way. Various readers will respond differently to each poem; the effect these poems have on their readers will lead some to prefer one and some the other. Personal preference does not mean that objective standards for poetry cannot be found (some poems are better than others, and later we will look in detail at features that help us to evaluate poems), but we need have no preconceived standard that all poetry must be one thing or another or work in one particular way. Some good poems are quite abstract, others quite specific. Any poem that helps us to articulate and clarify human feelings and ideas has a legitimate claim on us as readers.

Both "How Do I Love Thee?" and "The Tally Stick" are written as if they were addressed to the partner in the love relationship, and both talk directly about the intensity of the love. The poem below talks only indirectly about the quality and intensity of love. It is written as if it were a letter from a woman to her husband who has gone on a long journey on business. It directly expresses how much she misses him and indirectly suggests how much she cares about him.

EZRA POUND

The River-Merchant's Wife: A Letter

(after Rihaku[1])

While my hair was still cut straight across my forehead
I played about the front gate, pulling flowers.
You came by on bamboo stilts, playing horse,
You walked about my seat, playing with blue plums.

---

1. The Japanese name for Li Po, an eighth-century Chinese poet. Pound's poem is a loose paraphrase of Li Po's.

5   And we went on living in the village of Chokan:
Two small people, without dislike or suspicion.

At fourteen I married My Lord you.
I never laughed, being bashful.
Lowering my head, I looked at the wall.
10   Called to, a thousand times, I never looked back.

At fifteen I stopped scowling,
I desired my dust to be mingled with yours
For ever and for ever and for ever.
Why should I climb the look out?

15   At sixteen you departed,
You went into far Ku-to-yen, by the river of swirling eddies,
And you have been gone five months.
The monkeys make sorrowful noise overhead.

You dragged your feet when you went out.
20   By the gate now, the moss is grown, the different mosses,
Too deep to clear them away!

The leaves fall early this autumn, in wind.
The paired butterflies are already yellow with August
Over the grass in the West garden;
25   They hurt me. I grow older.
If you are coming down through the narrows of the river Kiang,
Please let me know beforehand,
And I will come out to meet you
    As far as Cho-fu-Sa.   1915

The "letter" tells us only a few facts about the nameless merchant's wife: that she is about sixteen and a half years old, that she married at fourteen and fell in love with her husband a year later, that she is now very lonely. About their relationship we know only that they were childhood playmates in a small Chinese village, that their marriage originally was not a matter of personal choice, and that the husband unwillingly went away on a long journey five months ago. But the words tell us a great deal about how the young wife feels, and the simplicity of her language suggests her sincere and deep longing. The daily noises she hears seem "sorrowful" (line 18), and she worries about the dangers of the far-away place where her husband is, thinking of it in terms of its perilous "river of swirling eddies" (line 16). She thinks of how moss has grown up over the unused gate, and more time seems to her to have passed than actually has (lines 22–25). Nostalgically she remembers their innocent childhood, when they played together without deeper love or commitment (lines 1–6), and contrasts that with her later satisfaction in their love (lines 11–14) and with her present anxiety, loneliness, and desire. We do not need to know the details of the geography of the river Kiang or how far Cho-fu-Sa is to sense that her wish to see him is very strong, that her desire is powerful enough to make her venture beyond the ordinary geographical bounds of her existence so that their reunion will come sooner. The closest she comes to a direct statement about her love is her statement that she desired that her dust be mingled with his "For ever and for ever and for ever" (lines 12–13). But her single-minded vision of the world, her perception of even the beauty of nature as only a record of her husband's absence and the passage of time, and her plain, apparently uncalculated language about her rejection of other suitors and her shutting out of the rest of the world all show her to be committed, desirous, nearly desperate for his presence. In a different sense, she has also counted the ways that she loves her man.

Here is another poem about marriage that expresses a very different set of attitudes and feelings.

DENISE LEVERTOV

Wedding-Ring

My wedding-ring lies in a basket
as if at the bottom of a well.
Nothing will come to fish it back up
and onto my finger again.
              It lies 5
among keys to abandoned houses,
nails waiting to be needed and hammered
into some wall,
telephone numbers with no names attached,
idle paperclips. 10
              It can't be given away
for fear of bringing ill-luck.
              It can't be sold
for the marriage was good in its own
time, though that time is gone. 15
              Could some artificer
beat into it bright stones, transform it
into a dazzling circlet no one could take
for solemn betrothal or to make promises
living will not let them keep? Change it 20
into a simple gift I could give in friendship?
                                            1978

The artifact—the ring—at the center of this poem is out-of-date and abandoned, standing for a worn-out and terminated marriage. Unlike the eager and committed voice in the previous poem, the voice here is tired, resigned, sad; the poem's speaker seems willing to try for a new and better relationship but is also hesitant, cautious, and perhaps somewhat disillusioned by previous experience. This, too, is a poem about love, but the moment of love has long since passed, and the poem focuses on the feelings of aftermath.

Poems can be about the meaning of a relationship or about disappointment just as easily as about emotional fulfillment, and poets are often very good at suggesting the contradictions and uncertainties in relationships. Like other people, poets often find love quaint or downright funny, too, mainly because it involves human beings who, however serious their intentions and concerns, are often inept, uncertain, and self-contradictory—in short, human. Showing us ourselves as others see us is one of the more useful tasks that poems perform, but the poems that result can be just as entertaining and pleasurable as they are educational. Here is a poem that imagines a very strange scene, a kind of fantasy of what happens when we *think* too much about sex or love, and it is likely to leave us laughing, whether or not we take it seriously as a statement of human anxiety and of the tendency to intellectualize too much.

TOM WAYMAN

Wayman in Love

At last Wayman gets the girl into bed.
He is locked in one of those embraces
so passionate his left arm is asleep
when suddenly he is bumped in the back.
5 "Excuse me," a voice mutters, thick with German.
Wayman and the girl sit up astounded
as a furry gentleman in boots and a frock coat
climbs in under the covers.

"My name is Doktor Marx," the intruder announces
10 settling his neck comfortably on the pillow.
"I'm here to consider for you the cost of a kiss."
He pulls out a notepad. "Let's see now,
we have the price of the mattress, this room must be rented,
your time off work, groceries for two,
15 medical fees in case of accidents . . ."

"Look," Wayman says,
"couldn't we do this later?"
The philosopher sighs, and continues: "You are affected too, Miss.
If you are not working, you are going to resent
20 your dependent position. This will influence
I assure you, your most intimate moments . . ."

"Doctor, please," Wayman says. "All we want
is to be left alone."
But another beard, more nattily dressed,
25 is also getting into the bed.
There is a shifting and heaving of bodies
as everyone wriggles out room for themselves.
"I want you to meet a friend from Vienna,"
Marx says. "This is Doktor Freud."

30 The newcomer straightens his glasses,
peers at Wayman and the girl.
"I can see," he begins,
"that you two have problems . . ."   1973

RESPONDING

The poems we have looked at so far all describe, though in quite different ways, feelings associated with loving or being attached to someone and the expression—either physical or verbal—of those feelings. Watching how poems work out a language for feeling can help us to work out a language for our own feelings, but the process is also reciprocal: being conscious of feelings we already have can lead us into poems more surely and with more satisfaction. Readers with a strong romantic bent—and with strong yearnings or positive memories of desire—will be likely to find "The Tally Stick" and "The River-Merchant's Wife: A Letter" easy to respond to and like, while those more skeptical of human institutions and male habits may find the disillusionment and resignation of "Wedding-Ring" to be more satisfying.

> *If I feel physically as if the top of my head were taken off, I know that is poetry.*
>
> —EMILY DICKINSON

Poems can be about all kinds of experiences, and not all the things we find in them will replicate (or even relate to) experiences we may have individually had. But sharing through language will often enable us to get in touch with feelings—of love or anger, fear or confidence—we did not know we had. The next few poems involve another, far less pleasant set of feelings than those usually generated by love, but even here, where our experience may be limited, we are able to respond, to feel the tug of emotions within us that we may not be fully aware of. In the following poem, a father struggles to understand and control his grief over the death of a seven-year-old son. We don't have to be a father or to have lost a loved one to be aware of—and even share—the speaker's pain because our own experiences will have given us some idea of what such a loss would feel like. And the words and strategies of the poem may activate expectations created by our previous experiences.

BEN JONSON

On My First Son

Farewell, thou child of my right hand,[2] and joy;
My sin was too much hope of thee, loved boy:
Seven years thou wert lent to me, and I thee pay,
Exacted by thy fate, on the just[3] day.
O could I lose all father now! for why   5
Will man lament the state he should envý,
To have so soon 'scaped world's and flesh's rage,
And, if no other misery, yet age?
Rest in soft peace, and asked, say, "Here doth lie
Ben Jonson his[4] best piece of poetry."   10

---

2. A literal translation of the son's name, Benjamin.   3. Exact; the son died on his seventh birthday, in 1603.   4. Ben Jonson's (a common Renaissance form of the possessive).

For whose sake henceforth all his vows be such
As what he loves may never like too much.   1616

This poem's attempts to rationalize the boy's death are quite conventional. Although the father tries to be comforted by pious thoughts, his feelings keep showing through. The poem's beginning—with its formal "farewell" and the rather distant-sounding address to the dead boy ("child of my right hand")—cannot be sustained for long: both of the first two lines end with bursts of emotion. It is as if the father is trying to explain the death to himself and to keep his emotions under control, but cannot quite manage it. Even the punctuation suggests the way his feelings compete with conventional attempts to put the death into some sort of perspective that will soften the grief, and the comma near the end of each of the first two lines marks a pause that cannot quite hold back the overflowing emotion. But finally the only "idea" that the poem supports is that the father wishes he did not feel so intensely; in the fifth line he fairly blurts that he wishes he could lose his fatherly emotions, and in the final lines he resolves never again to "like" so much that he can be this deeply hurt. Philosophy and religion offer their useful counsels in this poem, but they prove far less powerful than feeling. Rather than drawing some kind of moral about what death means, the poem presents the actuality of feeling as inevitable and nearly all-consuming.

The poem that follows similarly tries to suppress the rawness of feelings about the death of a loved one, but here the survivor is haunted by memories of his wife when he sees a physical object—a vacuum cleaner—that he associates with her.

HOWARD NEMEROV

The Vacuum

The house is so quiet now
The vacuum cleaner sulks in the corner closet,
Its bag limp as a stopped lung, its mouth
Grinning into the floor, maybe at my
Slovenly life, my dog-dead youth.

I've lived this way long enough,
But when my old woman died her soul
Went into that vacuum cleaner, and I can't bear
To see the bag swell like a belly, eating the dust
And the woolen mice, and begin to howl

Because there is old filth everywhere
She used to crawl, in the corner and under the stair.
I know now how life is cheap as dirt,
And still the hungry, angry heart
Hangs on and howls, biting at air.   1955

The poem is about a vacuum in the husband's life, but the title refers most obviously to the vacuum cleaner that, like the tally stick we looked at earlier, seems to stand for many of the things that were once important in the life he had together with his wife. The cleaner is a reminder of the dead wife ("my old woman," line 7) because of her devotion to cleanliness. But to the surviving husband buried in the filth of his life it seems as if the machine has become almost human, a kind of ghost of her: it "sulks" (line 2), it has lungs and a mouth (line 3), and it seems to grin, making fun of what has become of him. He "can't bear" (line 8) to see it in action because it then seems too much alive, too much a reminder of her life. The poem records his paralysis, his inability to do more than discover that life is "cheap as dirt" without her ordering and cleansing presence for him. At the end it is *his* angry heart that acts like the haunting machine, howling and biting at air as if he has merged with her spirit and the physical object that memorializes her. This poem puts a strong emphasis on the stillness of death and the way it makes things seem to stop; it captures in words the hurt, the anger, the inability to understand, the vacuum that remains when a loved one dies and leaves a vacant space. But here we do not see the body or hear a direct good-bye to the dead person; rather we encounter the feeling that lingers and won't go away, recalled through memory by an especially significant object, a mere thing but one that has been personalized to the point of becoming nearly human in itself. (The event described here is, by the way, fictional; the poet's wife did not in fact die. Like a dramatist or writer of fiction, the poet may simply *imagine* an event in order to analyze and articulate how such an event might feel in certain circumstances.)

Here is another poem about the death of a loved one:

SHARON OLDS

The Glass

I think of it with wonder now,
the glass of mucus that stood on the table
next to my father all weekend. The cancer
is growing fast in his throat now,
and as it grows it sends out pus like the   5
sun sending out flares, those pouring
tongues. So my father has to gargle, hack,
spit a mouth full of thick stuff
into the glass every ten minutes or so,
scraping the rim up his lower lip to   10
get the last bit off his skin, then he
sets the glass down on the table and it
sits there, like a glass of beer foam,
shiny and faintly golden, he gurgles and
coughs and reaches for it again and   15
gets the heavy sputum out,
full of bubbles and moving around like yeast—
he is like some god producing food from his own mouth.

He himself can eat nothing anymore,
20   just a swallow of milk sometimes,
cut with water, and even then it
can't always get past the tumor,
and the next time the saliva comes up it's
chalkish and ropey, he has to roll it in his
25   throat to form it and get it up and dis-
gorge the elliptical globule into the cup—
and the wonder to me is that it did not disgust me,
that glass of phlegm that stood there all day and
filled slowly with compound globes and I'd
30   empty it and it would fill again and
shimmer there on the table until the
room seemed to turn around it
in an orderly way, a model of the solar system
turning around the gold sun,
35   my father the dark earth that used to
lie at the center of the universe
now turning with the rest of us
around the bright glass of spit
on the table, these last mouthfuls.   1990

Like "The Vacuum," "The Glass" reflects on a loved one through unconventional images, material objects that suggest pain and unpleasantness rather than joy and love. The "glass" of the title is not a mirror that reflects a beautiful face, not a crafted objet d'art, but rather a simple tumbler, and it is full of mucus—not a very appealing object. The loved one, the father of the person who is speaking the poem, is dying of cancer, and the indicators of his condition are painfully detailed. The sights and sounds are disgusting rather than pleasant; the body fluids are pus and spit, and the human sounds are gargling, gurgling, and hacking. It is almost as if the poem tries to create a picture as ugly as possible, for the father's physical struggle just to swallow and spit is chronicled moment by painful moment. "[T]he wonder to me," says the daughter who views the daily struggle and records it for us in the poem, "is that it did not disgust me" (line 27), and the poem transforms the central object of disgust ("that glass of phlegm," line 28) into something that stands for the daughter's love and the father's ability to accept it even in his deteriorating condition. The daughter's act of staying and emptying the glass represents not only fortitude and loyalty but the steadying influence of stability and predictability. She begins to see the glass itself—its regular filling and emptying of life and coming death—as a kind of center around which human activity revolves "in an orderly way" (line 33). The father, once the center of the family's universe, now seems to move with the others "around" (line 38) the fact of death as represented by the glass. It is an awful picture—awful in its details, awful in its implications of loss—but it is also beautiful in its own way. The poem shows that life and love can be portrayed, explained, and imprinted on our memories by even the most unattractive events, objects, and words.

Sometimes poems are a way of confronting feelings. Sometimes they explore feelings in detail and try to intellectualize or rationalize them. At other times, poems generate responses by recalling an experience many years in the past. In the following two poems, for example, memories of childhood provide perspective on two very different kinds of events. In the first, written as if the person speaking the poem were in the fifth grade, a child's sense of death is portrayed through her exploration of a photograph that makes her grandfather's earlier presence vivid to her memory—a memory that lingers primarily through smell and touch. In the second poem, another childhood memory— this time of overshoes—takes an adult almost physically back into childhood. As you read the two poems, keep track of (or perhaps even jot down) your responses. How much of your feeling is due to your own past experiences? In which specific places? What family photographs do you remember most vividly? What feelings did they invoke that make them so memorable? How are your memories different from those expressed in "Fifth Grade Autobiography"? in "The Fury of Overshoes"? Which feelings expressed in each poem are similar to your own? Where do your feelings differ most strongly? How would you articulate your responses to memories differently? In what ways does an awareness of your similar—and different—experiences and feelings make you a better reader of the poem?

RITA DOVE

Fifth Grade Autobiography

I was four in this photograph fishing
with my grandparents at a lake in Michigan.
My brother squats in poison ivy.
His Davy Crockett cap
sits squared on his head so the raccoon tail   5
flounces down the back of his sailor suit.

My grandfather sits to the far right
in a folding chair,
and I know his left hand is on
the tobacco in his pants pocket   10
because I used to wrap it for him
every Christmas. Grandmother's hips
bulge from the brush, she's leaning
into the ice chest, sun through the trees
printing her dress with soft   15
luminous paws.

I am staring jealously at my brother;
the day before he rode his first horse, alone.
I was strapped in a basket
behind my grandfather.   20
He smelled of lemons. He's died—

but I remember his hands.   1989

ANNE SEXTON

The Fury of Overshoes

They sit in a row
outside the kindergarten,
black, red, brown, all
with those brass buckles.
5   Remember when you couldn't
buckle your own
overshoe
or tie your own
shoe
10   or cut your own meat
and the tears
running down like mud
because you fell off your
tricycle?
15   Remember, big fish,
when you couldn't swim
and simply slipped under
like a stone frog?
The world wasn't
20   yours.
It belonged to
the big people.
Under your bed
sat the wolf
25   and he made a shadow
when cars passed by
at night.
They made you give up
your nightlight
30   and your teddy
and your thumb.
Oh overshoes,
don't you
remember me,
35   pushing you up and down
in the winter snow?
Oh thumb,
I want a drink,
it is dark,
40   where are the big people,
when will I get there,
taking giant steps
all day,
each day
45   and thinking
nothing of it?

1974

There is much more going on in the poems that we have glanced at than we have taken time to consider, but even the quickest look at these poems suggests something of the range of feelings that poems can offer—the depth of feeling, the clarity, the experience that may be articulately and precisely shared. Not all poems are as accessible as those we've looked at so far, and even the ones that are accessible usually yield themselves to us more readily and more fully if we approach them systematically by developing specific reading habits and skills—just as someone learning to play tennis systematically learns the rules, the techniques, the things to watch out for that are distinctive to the pleasures and hazards of that skill or craft. It helps if you develop a sense of what to expect, and the chapters that follow will help you to an understanding of the things that poets can do—and thus of what poems can do for you.

But knowing what to expect isn't everything. As a prospective reader of poetry, you should always be open—to new experiences, new feelings, new ideas. Every poem in the world is a potential new experience, and no matter how sophisticated you become, you can still be surprised (and delighted) by new poems—and by rereading old ones. Good poems bear many, many rereadings, and often one discovers something new with every new reading: there is no such thing as "mastering" a poem, and good poems are not exhausted by repeated readings. Be willing to let poems surprise you when you come to them; let them come on their own terms, let them be themselves. If you are open to poetry, you are also open to much more that the world can offer you.

No one can give you a method that will offer you total experience of all poems. But because many characteristics of an individual poem are characteristics that one poem shares with other poems, there are guidelines that can prompt you to ask the right questions. The chapters that follow will help you in detail with a variety of problems, but meanwhile here is a checklist of some things to remember:

1. *Read the syntax literally.* What the words say literally in normal sentences is only a starting point, but it is the place to start. Not all poems use normal prose syntax, but most of them do, and you can save yourself embarrassment by paraphrasing accurately (that is, rephrasing what the poem literally says, in plain prose) and not simply free-associating from an isolated word or phrase.

2. *Articulate for yourself what the title, subject, and situation make you expect.* Poets often use false leads and try to surprise you by doing shocking things, but defining expectation lets you be conscious of where you are when you begin.

3. *Identify the poem's situation.* What is said is often conditioned by where it is said and by whom. Identifying the speaker and his or her place in the situation puts what he or she says in perspective.

4. *Find out what is implied by the traditions behind the poem.* Verse forms, poetic kinds, and metrical patterns all have a frame of reference, traditions of the way they are usually used and for what. For example, the anapest (two unstressed syllables followed by a stressed one, as in the word *Tennessee*) is usually used for comic poems, and when poets use it "straight" they are aware of their "departure" and are probably making a point by doing it.

5. *Bother the reference librarian.* Look up anything you don't understand: an unfamiliar word (or an ordinary word used in an unfamiliar way), a place, a person, a myth, an idea—anything the poem uses. When you can't find what you need or don't know where to look, ask for help.

6. *Remember that poems exist in time, and times change.* Not only the meanings of words, but whole ways of looking at the universe vary in different ages. Consciousness of time works two ways: your knowledge of history provides a context for

reading the poem, and the poem's use of a word or idea may modify your notion of a particular age.

7. *Take a poem on its own terms.* Adjust to the poem; don't make the poem adjust to you. Be prepared to hear things you do not want to hear. Not all poems are about your ideas, nor will they always present emotions you want to feel. But be tolerant and listen to the poem's ideas, not only to your desire to revise them for yourself.

8. *Be willing to be surprised.* Things often happen in poems that turn them around. A poem may seem to suggest one thing at first, then persuade you of its opposite, or at least of a significant qualification or variation.

9. *Assume there is a reason for everything.* Poets do make mistakes, but in poems that show some degree of verbal control it is usually safest to assume that the poet chose each word carefully; if the choice seems peculiar to us, it is often *we* who are missing something. Try to account for everything in a poem and see what kind of sense you can make of it. Poets make choices; try to figure out a coherent pattern that explains the text as it stands.

10. *Argue.* Discussion usually results in clarification and keeps you from being too dependent on personal biases and preoccupations that sometimes mislead even the best readers. Talking a poem over with someone else (especially someone very different) can expand your perspective.

WRITING ABOUT POEMS

If you have been keeping notes on your personal responses to the poems you've read, you have already taken an important step toward writing about them. There are many different ways to write about poems, just as there are many different things to say. (The chapter in the back of the book on "Writing about Literature" suggests many different kinds of topics.) But all writing begins from a clear sense of the poem itself and your responses to it, so the first steps (long before formally sitting down to write) are to read the poem over several times and keep notes on the things that strike you and the questions that remain.

Formulating a clear series of questions will usually help lead you to an appropriate approach to the poem and to a good topic. Learning to ask the right questions can save you a lot of time. Some questions—the kinds of questions implied in the ten guidelines for reading listed above—are basic and more or less apply to all poems. But each poem makes demands of its own, too, because of its distinctive way of going about its business, so you will usually want to make a list of what seem to you the crucial questions for that poem. Here are—just to give you an example—some questions that could be useful in leading you to a paper topic on the first of the poems printed at the end of this chapter.

1. How does the title affect your reading of and response to the poem?
2. What is the poem about?
3. What makes the poem interesting to read?
4. Who is the speaker? What role does the speaker have in the poem?
5. What effect does the poem have on you as a reader? Do you think the poet intended to have such an effect?
6. What is distinctive about the poet's use of language? Which words especially contribute to the poem's effect?

What *is* poetry? Let your definition be cumulative as you read more and more poems. No dictionary definition will cover all that you find, and it is better to discover for yourself poetry's many ingredients, its many effects, its many ways of acting. What can it do for you? Wait and see. Begin to add up its effects after you have read carefully— after you have studied and reread—a hundred or so poems; that will be a beginning, and you will be able to add to that total as long as you continue to read new poems or reread old ones.

PRACTICING READING: SOME POEMS ON LOVE

ANNE BRADSTREET

To My Dear and Loving Husband

If ever two were one, then surely we.
If ever man were loved by wife, then thee;
If ever wife was happy in a man,
Compare with me ye women if you can.
5   I prize thy love more than whole mines of gold,
Or all the riches that the East doth hold.
My love is such that rivers cannot quench,
Nor aught but love from thee give recompense.
Thy love is such I can no way repay;
10   The heavens reward thee manifold, I pray.
Then while we live, in love let's so persever,
That when we live no more we may live ever.   1678

WILLIAM SHAKESPEARE

[Shall I compare thee to a summer's day?]

Shall I compare thee to a summer's day?
Thou art more lovely and more temperate.
Rough winds do shake the darling buds of May,
And summer's lease hath all too short a date.
5   Sometime too hot the eye of heaven shines,
And often is his gold complexion dimmed;
And every fair from fair sometime declines,
By chance or nature's changing course untrimmed.
But thy eternal summer shall not fade,
10   Nor lose possession of that fair thou ow'st,
Nor shall Death brag thou wand'rest in his shade,
When in eternal lines to time thou grow'st.
   So long as men can breathe or eyes can see,
   So long lives this,[5] and this gives life to thee.   1609

5. This poem.

LEIGH HUNT

Rondeau

Jenny kissed me when we met,
    Jumping from the chair she sat in;
Time, you thief, who love to get
    Sweets into your list, put that in:
Say I'm weary, say I'm sad,   5
    Say that health and wealth have missed me,
Say I'm growing old, but add,
    Jenny kissed me.   p. 1838

DENISE LEVERTOV

Love Poem

'We are good for each other.'
                —X

What you give me is

the extraordinary sun
splashing its light
                into astonished trees.

A branch   5
of berries, swaying

under the feet of a bird.

I know
other joys—they taste
bitter, distilled as they are   10
from roots, yet I thirst for them.

But you—
you give me

the flash of golden daylight
in the body's   15
midnight,
warmth of the fall noonday
between the sheets in the dark.   1978

W. H. AUDEN

[Stop all the clocks, cut off the telephone]

Stop all the clocks, cut off the telephone,
Prevent the dog from barking with a juicy bone,
Silence the pianos and with muffled drum
Bring out the coffin, let the mourners come.

5   Let aeroplanes circle moaning overhead
Scribbling on the sky the message He Is Dead,
Put crêpe bows round the white necks of the public doves,
Let the traffic policemen wear black cotton gloves.

He was my North, my South, my East and West,
10   My working week and my Sunday rest,
My noon, my midnight, my talk, my song;
I thought that love would last for ever: I was wrong.

The stars are not wanted now: put out every one;
Pack up the moon and dismantle the sun;
15   Pour away the ocean and sweep up the wood;
For nothing now can ever come to any good.

ca. 1936

MARGE PIERCY

To Have without Holding

Learning to love differently is hard,
love with the hands wide open, love
with the doors banging on their hinges,
the cupboard unlocked, the wind
5   roaring and whimpering in the rooms
rustling the sheets and snapping the blinds
that thwack like rubber bands
in an open palm.

It hurts to love wide open
10   stretching the muscles that feel
as if they are made of wet plaster,
then of blunt knives, then
of sharp knives.

It hurts to thwart the reflexes
15   of grab, of clutch; to love and let

go again and again. It pesters to remember
the lover who is not in the bed,
to hold back what is owed to the work
that gutters like a candle in a cave
without air, to love consciously,   20
conscientiously, concretely, constructively.

I can't do it, you say it's killing
me, but you thrive, you glow
on the street like a neon raspberry,
You float and sail, a helium balloon   25
bright bachelor's button blue and bobbing
on the cold and hot winds of our breath,
as we make and unmake in passionate
diastole and systole the rhythm
of our unbound bonding, to have   30
and not to hold, to love
with minimized malice, hunger
and anger moment by moment balanced.   1980

ELIZABETH BISHOP

Casabianca[6]

Love's the boy stood on the burning deck
trying to recite "The boy stood on
the burning deck." Love's the son
   stood stammering elocution
     while the poor ship in flames went down.   5

Love's the obstinate boy, the ship,
even the swimming sailors, who
would like a schoolroom platform, too,
   or an excuse to stay
     on deck. And love's the burning boy.   10

                               1946

6. The name of a young boy who remained (during the "Battle of the Nile") at his post on a burning
ship because, he believed, his father (an admiral) had not released him from duty. He was celebrated in
a popular poem by Felicia Dorothea Hemans (1793–1835) that began "The boy stood on the burning
deck" (line 2).

JOHN DRYDEN

[Why should a foolish marriage vow][7]

Why should a foolish marriage vow,
   Which long ago was made,
Oblige us to each other now
   When passion is decayed?
5 We loved, and we loved, as long as we could,
   Till our love was loved out in us both;
But our marriage is dead when the pleasure is fled:
   'Twas pleasure first made it an oath.

If I have pleasures for a friend,
10   And farther love in store,
What wrong has he whose joys did end,
   And who could give no more?
'Tis a madness that he should be jealous of me,
   Or that I should bar him of another:
15 For all we can gain is to give ourselves pain,
   When neither can hinder the other.

1671

MARY, LADY CHUDLEIGH

To the Ladies

Wife and servant are the same,
But only differ in the name:
For when that fatal knot is tied,
Which nothing, nothing can divide,
5 When she the word *Obey* has said,
And man by law supreme has made,
Then all that's kind is laid aside,
And nothing left but state and pride.
Fierce as an eastern prince he grows,
10 And all his innate rigor shows:
Then but to look, to laugh, or speak,
Will the nuptial contract break.
Like mutes, she signs alone must make,
And never any freedom take,
15 But still be governed by a nod,
And fear her husband as her god:
Him still must serve, him still obey,
And nothing act, and nothing say,

7. A song, sung by a woman character, in Dryden's play *Marriage à la Mode*.

But what her haughty lord thinks fit,
Who, with the power, has all the wit.
Then shun, oh! shun that wretched state,
And all the fawning flatterers hate.
Value yourselves, and men despise:
You must be proud, if you'll be wise.

20

1703

RICHARD LOVELACE

To Althea, from Prison

When love with unconfinèd wings
  Hovers within my gates,
And my divine Althea brings
  To whisper at the grates;
When I lie tangled in her hair,
  And fettered to her eye,
The gods that wanton in the air
  Know no such liberty.

5

When flowing cups run swiftly round,
  With no allaying Thames,[8]
Our careless heads with roses bound,
  Our hearts with loyal flames;
When thirsty grief in wine we steep,
  When healths and draughts go free,
Fishes that tipple in the deep
  Know no such liberty.

10

15

When, like committed linnets, I
  With shriller throat shall sing
The sweetness, mercy, majesty
  And glories of my king;
When I shall voice aloud how good
  He is, how great should be,
Enlargèd winds that curl the flood
  Know no such liberty.

20

Stone walls do not a prison make,
  Nor iron bars a cage;
Minds innocent and quiet take
  That for an hermitage:
If I have freedom in my love,
  And in my soul am free,
Angels alone that soar above
  Enjoy such liberty.

25

30

1649

8. The river that runs through London.

EDNA ST. VINCENT MILLAY

[What lips my lips have kissed, and where, and why]

What lips my lips have kissed, and where, and why,
I have forgotten, and what arms have lain
Under my head till morning; but the rain
Is full of ghosts tonight, that tap and sigh
Upon the glass and listen for reply,   5
And in my heart there stirs a quiet pain
For unremembered lads that not again
Will turn to me at midnight with a cry.
Thus in the winter stands the lonely tree,
Nor knows what birds have vanished one by one,   10
Yet knows its boughs more silent than before:
I cannot say what loves have come and gone;
I only know that summer sang in me
A little while, that in me sings no more.   1923

WILLIAM SHAKESPEARE

[Let me not to the marriage of true minds]

Let me not to the marriage of true minds
Admit impediments.[9] Love is not love
Which alters when it alteration finds,
Or bends with the remover to remove:
Oh, no! it is an ever-fixéd mark,   5
That looks on tempests and is never shaken;
It is the star to every wandering bark,
Whose worth's unknown, although his height be taken.[1]
Love's not Time's fool, though rosy lips and cheeks
Within his bending sickle's compass come;   10
Love alters not with his brief hours and weeks,
But bears it out even to the edge of doom.
If this be error and upon me proved,
I never writ, nor no man ever loved.   1609

9. The Marriage Service contains this address to the witnesses: "If any of you know cause or just impediments why these persons should not be joined together. . . ."   1. That is, measuring the altitude of stars (for purposes of navigation) is not a measurement of value.

QUESTIONS

1. Which love poem in this chapter seems to you the most effective? the most moving? the most accurate in its representation of human emotions? the most beautiful in its sentiments? Pick out specific things in each poem you have chosen that help to make it work for you. Did you choose the same poem to answer each question? What did you learn about your own tastes and judgments from comparing the answers you gave to each question?
2. In Levertov's "Love Poem," what different "gifts" help to define the quality of affection? Compare the method of summing up ways of loving with that in "How Do I Love Thee?" (Browning) and in "The Tally Stick" (Ramsey).
3. What, exactly, do we know about the person who has just died in Auden's "Stop all the clocks"? What different strategies does the speaker of the poem use to convey the depth of his emotion? In what sense is this a love poem?
4. Did you notice that "To the Ladies" was written in 1703? Were you surprised by your response to it when you read it? If not, does the date of publication modify your response? Why?

WRITING SUGGESTIONS

1. If you were writing a love poem comparing your love to a winter's day, what features of the season would you emphasize? What features of a spring day would you use? Write a paragraph on the virtues of each of these seasons, showing how features associated with them can be made into compliments appropriate to a lover.
2. Of all the love poems in this chapter, which one would you most like to have addressed to you? which least? Write a prose answer to the author of either poem you have chosen, explaining what seemed to you most (or least) complimentary in what the poem said about you.
3. Jot down your responses to all of the marriage poems in this chapter. Which one most accurately expresses your ideal of a good marriage? Why do you think so? What does your choice say about you?

Understanding the Text

13

TONE

Poetry is full of surprises. Poems express anger or outrage just as effectively as love or sadness, and good poems can be written about going to a rock concert or having lunch or cutting the lawn, as well as about making love or smelling flowers or listening to Beethoven. Even poems on "predictable" subjects can surprise us with unpredicted attitudes, unusual events, or a sudden twist. Knowing that a poem is about some particular subject—love, for example, or death—may give us a general idea of what to expect, but it never tells us altogether what we will find in a particular poem. Responding to a poem fully means being open to the poem and its surprises, being willing to let the poem guide us to its own stances, feelings, and ideas—to an explanation of a topic that may be very different from what we expect or what we think. Letting a poem speak to us means being willing to listen to *how* the poem says what it says—hearing the tone of voice implied in the way the words are spoken. *What* a poem says involves its **theme,** a statement about its subject. *How* a poem makes that statement involves its **tone,** the attitude or feelings it expresses about the theme.

The following two poems—one about death and one about love—express different attitudes and feelings from the poems we have read so far.

MARGE PIERCY

Barbie Doll

This girlchild was born as usual
and presented dolls that did pee-pee
and miniature GE stoves and irons
and wee lipsticks the color of cherry candy.
5 Then in the magic of puberty, a classmate said:
You have a great big nose and fat legs.

She was healthy, tested intelligent,
possessed strong arms and back,
abundant sexual drive and manual dexterity.

She went to and fro apologizing.   10
Everyone saw a fat nose on thick legs.

She was advised to play coy,
exhorted to come on hearty,
exercise, diet, smile and wheedle.
Her good nature wore out   15
like a fan belt.
So she cut off her nose and her legs
and offered them up.

In the casket displayed on satin she lay
with the undertaker's cosmetics painted on,   20
a turned-up putty nose,
dressed in a pink and white nightie.
Doesn't she look pretty? everyone said.
Consummation at last.
To every woman a happy ending.   25

1973

W. D. SNODGRASS

Leaving the Motel

Outside, the last kids holler
Near the pool: they'll stay the night.
Pick up the towels; fold your collar
Out of sight.

Check: is the second bed   5
Unrumpled, as agreed?
Landlords have to think ahead
In case of need,

Too. Keep things straight: don't take
The matches, the wrong keyrings—   10
We've nowhere we could keep a keepsake—
Ashtrays, combs, things

That sooner or later others
Would accidentally find.
Check: take nothing of one another's   15
And leave behind

Your license number only,
Which they won't care to trace;
We've paid. Still, should such things get lonely,
Leave in their vase   20

An aspirin to preserve
Our lilacs, the wayside flowers

We've gathered and must leave to serve
A few more hours;

25   That's all. We can't tell when
We'll come back, can't press claims,
We would no doubt have other rooms then,
Or other names.   1968

The first poem, "Barbie Doll," has the strong note of sadness that characterizes many death poems, but its emphasis is not on the girl's death but on the disappointments in her life. The only "scene" in the poem (lines 19–23) portrays the unnamed girl at rest in her casket, but the still body in the casket contrasts not with vitality but with frustration and anxiety: her life since puberty (lines 5–6) had been full of apologies and attempts to change her physical appearance and emotional makeup. The rest she achieves in death is not, however, a triumph, despite what people say (line 23). Although the poem's last two words are "happy ending," this girl without a name has died in embarrassment and without fulfillment, and the final lines are ironic, meaning the opposite of what they say. The cheerful comments at the end lack force and truth because of what we already know; we understand them as ironic because they underline how unhappy the girl was and how false her cosmeticized corpse is to the sad truth of her life.

The poem's concern is to suggest the falsity and destructiveness of those standards of female beauty that have led to the tragedy of the girl's life. In an important sense, the poem is not really *about* death at all in spite of the fact that the girl's death and her repaired corpse are central to it. As the title suggests, the poem dramatizes how standardized, commercialized notions of femininity and prettiness can be painful and destructive to those whose bodies do not precisely fit the conformist models, and the poem attacks vigorously those conventional standards and the widespread, unthinking acceptance of them.

"Leaving the Motel" similarly goes in quite a different direction from many poems on the subject of love. Instead of expressing assurance about how love lasts and endures, or about the sincerity and depth of affection, this poem describes a parting of lovers after a brief, surreptitious sexual encounter. But it does not emphasize sexuality or eroticism in the meeting of the nameless lovers (we see them only as they prepare to leave), nor does it suggest why or how they have found each other, or what either of them is like as a person. Its focus is on how careful they must be not to get caught, how exact and calculating they must be in their planning, how finite and limited their encounter must be, how sealed off this encounter is from the rest of their lives. The poem relates the tiny details the lovers must think of, the agreements they must observe, and the ritual checklist of their duties ("Check . . . Keep things straight . . . Check . . . ," lines 5, 9, 15). Affection and sentiment have their small place in the poem (notice the care for the flowers, lines 19–24, and the thought of "press[ing] claims," line 26), but the emphasis is on temporariness, uncertainty, and limits. The poem is about an illicit, perhaps adulterous, sexual encounter, but there is no sex in the poem, only a kind of archaeological record of lust.

Labeling a poem as a "love poem" or a "death poem" is primarily a matter of convenience; such categories indicate the **subject** of a poem or the event or **topic** it chooses to engage. But as the poems we have been looking at suggest, poems that may be loosely called love poems or death poems may differ widely from one another, express totally different attitudes or ideas, and concentrate on very different aspects of the subject. The main advantages of grouping poems in this way for study is that a reader can become conscious of individual differences: a reading of two poems side by side may suggest how each is distinctive in what it has to say and how it says it.

The theme of a poem may be expressed in several different ways, and poems often have more than one theme. We could say, for example, that the theme of "Leaving the Motel" is that illicit love is secretive, careful, transitory, and short on emotion and sentiment, or that secret sexual encounters tend to be brief, calculated, and characterized by restrained or hesitant feelings. "Barbie Doll" suggests that commercialized standards destroy human values; that rigid and idealized notions of normality cripple those who are different; that people are easily and tragically led to accept evaluations thrust upon them by others; that American consumers tend to be conformists, easily influenced in their outlook by advertising and by commercial products; that children who do not conform to middle-class standards and notions don't have a chance. The poem implies each of these statements, and all are quite central to it. But none of these statements individually nor all of them together would fully express or explain the poem itself. To state the themes in such a brief and abstract way—though it may be helpful in clarifying what the poem does and does not say—does not do justice to the experience of the poem, the way it works on us as readers, the way we respond. Poems affect us in all sorts of ways—emotional and psychological as well as rational—and often a poem's dramatization of a story, an event, or a moment bypasses our rational responses and affects us far more deeply than a clear and logical argument would.

Sometimes poems express feelings directly and quite simply:

LINDA PASTAN

love poem

I want to write you
a love poem as headlong
as our creek
after thaw
when we stand   5
on its dangerous
banks and watch it carry
with it every twig
every dry leaf and branch
in its path   10
every scruple
when we see it
so swollen
with runoff
that even as we watch   15
we must grab
each other

and step back
we must grab each
other or
get our shoes
soaked we must
grab each other   1988

20

   The directness and simplicity of this poem suggest how the art and craft of poems work. The poem expresses the desire to write a love poem even as the love poem itself begins to proceed; the desire and the resultant poem exist side by side, and in reading the poem we seem to watch and hear the poet's creative process at work in developing appropriate metaphors and means of expression. The poem must be "headlong" (line 2), to match the power of a love that needs to be compared to the irresistible forces of nature. The poem should, like the love it expresses and the swollen creek it describes, sweep everything along, and it should represent (and reproduce) the sense of watching that the lovers have when they observe natural processes at work. The poem, like the action it represents, has to suggest to readers the kind of desire that grabbing each other means to the lovers.

   The lovers in this poem seem, at least to themselves, to own the world they observe, but in fact they are controlled by it. The creek on whose banks they stand is "our creek" (line 3), but what they observe as they watch its rising currents requires them ("must," lines 16, 19, 22) to "grab each other" over and over again. It is as if their love is part of nature itself, which subjects them to forces larger than themselves. Everything—twigs, leaves, branches, scruples—is carried along by the powerful currents after the "thaw" (line 4), and the poem replicates the repeated action of the lovers as if to power along observant readers just as the lovers are powered along by what they see. But the poem (and their love) admits dangers, too; it is the fact of danger that propels the lovers to each other. The poem suggests that love provides a kind of haven, but the haven hardly involves passivity or peace; instead, it requires the kind of grabbing that means activity and boldness and deep passion. Love here is no quiet or simple matter even if the expression of it in poems can be direct and based on a simple observation of experience. The "love poem" itself—linked as it is with the headlong currents of the creek from which the lovers are protecting themselves—even represents that which is beyond love and that, therefore, both threatens it and at the same time makes it happen. The power of poetry is thus affirmed at the center of the poem, but what poetry is about (love and life) is suggested to be more important. Poetry makes things happen but is not itself a substitute for life, just a means to make it more energetic and meaningful.

   Poems, then, differ widely from one another even when they share a common subject. And the subjects of poetry also vary widely. It isn't true that there are certain "poetic" subjects and that there are others that aren't appropriate to poetry. Any human activity, thought, or feeling can be the subject of poetry. Poetry often deals with beauty and the softer, more attractive human emotions, but it can deal with ugliness and unattractive human conduct as well, for poetry seeks to represent human beings and human events, showing us ourselves not only as we would like to be but as we are. Good poetry gets written about all kinds of topics, in all kinds of forms, with all kinds of attitudes. Here, for example, is a poem about a prison inmate—and about the conflict between individual and societal values.

ETHERIDGE KNIGHT

Hard Rock Returns to Prison from the Hospital for the Criminal Insane

Hard Rock was "known not to take no shit
From nobody," and he had the scars to prove it:
Split purple lips, lumped ears, welts above
His yellow eyes, and one long scar that cut
Across his temple and plowed through a thick   5
Canopy of kinky hair.

The WORD was that Hard Rock wasn't a mean nigger
Anymore, that the doctors had bored a hole in his head,
Cut out part of his brain, and shot electricity
Through the rest. When they brought Hard Rock back,   10
Handcuffed and chained, he was turned loose,
Like a freshly gelded stallion, to try his new status.
And we all waited and watched, like indians at a corral,
To see if the WORD was true.

As we waited we wrapped ourselves in the cloak   15
Of his exploits: "Man, the last time, it took eight
Screws to put him in the Hole."[1] "Yeah, remember when he
Smacked the captain with his dinner tray?" "He set
The record for time in the Hole—67 straight days!"
"Ol Hard Rock! man, that's one crazy nigger."   20
And then the jewel of a myth that Hard Rock had once bit
A screw on the thumb and poisoned him with syphilitic spit.

The testing came, to see if Hard Rock was really tame.
A hillbilly called him a black son of a bitch
And didn't lose his teeth, a screw who knew Hard Rock   25
From before shook him down and barked in his face.
And Hard Rock did *nothing*. Just grinned and looked silly,
His eyes empty like knot holes in a fence.

And even after we discovered that it took Hard Rock
Exactly 3 minutes to tell you his first name,   30
We told ourselves that he had just wised up,
Was being cool; but we could not fool ourselves for long,
And we turned away, our eyes on the ground. Crushed.
He had been our Destroyer, the doer of things
We dreamed of doing but could not bring ourselves to do,   35
The fears of years, like a biting whip,
Had cut grooves too deeply across our backs.   1968

---

1. Solitary confinement. *Screws:* guards.

The picture of Hard Rock as a kind of hero to other prison inmates is established early in the poem through a retelling of the legends circulated about him; the straightforward chronology of the poem sets up the mystery of how he will react after his "treatment" in the hospital. The poem identifies with those who wait; they are hopeful that Hard Rock's spirit has not been broken by surgery or shock treatments, and the lines crawl almost to a stop with disappointment in stanza 4. The *"nothing"* (line 27) of Hard Rock's response to teasing and taunting and the emptiness of his eyes ("like knot holes in a fence," line 28) reduce the heroic hopes and illusions to despair. The final stanza recounts the observers' attempts to reinterpret, to hang onto hope that their symbol of heroism could stand up against the best efforts to tame him, but the spirit has gone out of the hero-worshipers, too, and the poem records them as beaten, conformed, deprived of their spirit as Hard Rock has been of his. The poem records the despair of the hopeless, and it protests against the cruel exercise of power that can curb even as rebellious a figure as Hard Rock.

The following poem is equally full of anger and disappointment, but it expresses its attitudes in a very different way.

WILLIAM BLAKE

London

I wander through each chartered street,
Near where the chartered Thames does flow,
And mark in every face I meet
Marks of weakness, marks of woe.

5   In every cry of every man,
In every Infant's cry of fear,
In every voice, in every ban,
The mind-forged manacles I hear.

How the Chimney-sweeper's cry
10   Every black'ning Church appalls;
And the hapless Soldier's sigh
Runs in blood down Palace walls.

But most through midnight streets I hear
How the youthful Harlot's curse
15   Blasts the new-born Infant's tear,
And blights with plagues the Marriage hearse.

                                                    1794

The poem gives a strong sense of how London feels to this particular observer; it is cluttered, constricting, oppressive. The wordplay here articulates and connects the strong emotions he associates with London experiences. The repeated words—"every," for example, or "cry"—intensify the sense of total despair in the city and weld connections between things not necessarily related—the cries of street vendors, for example, with the cries for help. The twice-used word "chartered" implies strong feelings, too. The streets, instead of seeming alive with people or bustling with movement, are rigidly, coldly determined, controlled, cramped. Likewise the river seems as if it were planned, programmed, laid out by an oppressor. In actual fact, the course of the Thames through the city had been altered (slightly) by the government before Blake's time, but most important is the word's emotional force, the sense it projects of constriction and artificiality: the person speaking experiences London as if human artifice had totally altered nature. Moreover, according to the poem, people are victimized, "marked" by their confrontations with urbanness and the power of institutions: the "Soldier's sigh" that "runs in blood down Palace walls" vividly suggests, through a metaphor that visually depicts the speaker's feelings, both the powerlessness of the individual and the callousness of power. The "description" of the city has clearly become, by now, a subjective, highly emotional, and vivid expression of how the speaker feels about London and what it represents to him.

> *Poetry makes nothing happen.*
>
> —W. H. AUDEN

Another thing about "London": at first it looks like an account of a personal experience, as if the speaker is describing and interpreting as he goes along: "I wander through each chartered street." But soon it is clear that he is describing many wanderings, putting together impressions from many walks, re-creating a typical walk—which shows him "every" person in the streets, allows him to generalize about the churches being "appalled" (literally, made white) by the cry of the representative Chimney-sweeper, and leads to his conclusions about soldiers, prostitutes, and infants. What we are given is not a personal record of an event, but a representation of it, as it seems in retrospect—not a story, not a narrative or chronological account of events, but a dramatization of self that compresses many experiences into one.

"London" is somber in spite of the poet's playfulness with words. Wordplay may be witty and funny if it calls attention to its own cleverness, but here it involves the discovery of unsuspected (but meaningful) connections between things. The tone of "London" is sad, despairing, and angry; reading "London" aloud, one would try to show in one's voice the strong feelings that the poem expresses, just as one would try to reproduce tenderness and caring and passion in reading aloud "The Tally Stick" or "How Do I Love Thee?"

> *When power leads man toward arrogance, poetry reminds him of his limitations. When power narrows the areas of man's concern, poetry reminds him of the richness and diversity of his existence. When power corrupts, poetry cleanses.*
>
> —JOHN F. KENNEDY

The following two poems are "about" animals, although both of them place their final emphasis on what human beings are like: the animal in each case is only the means to the end of exploring human nature. The poems share a common assumption that animal behavior may appear to reflect human habits and conduct and may reveal much about ourselves, and in each case the character central to the poem is revealed to be surprisingly unlike the way she thinks of herself. But the poems are very different from one another. Read each poem aloud, and try to imagine what each main character is like. What tones of voice do you use to help express the character of the killer in the first poem? What demands on your voice does the second poem make?

MAXINE KUMIN

Woodchucks

Gassing the woodchucks didn't turn out right.
The knockout bomb from the Feed and Grain Exchange
was featured as merciful, quick at the bone
and the case we had against them was airtight,
both exits shoehorned shut with puddingstone,[2]
but they had a sub-sub-basement out of range.

Next morning they turned up again, no worse
for the cyanide than we for our cigarettes
and state-store Scotch, all of us up to scratch.
They brought down the marigolds as a matter of course
and then took over the vegetable patch
nipping the broccoli shoots, beheading the carrots.

The food from our mouths, I said, righteously thrilling
to the feel of the .22, the bullets' neat noses.
I, a lapsed pacifist fallen from grace
puffed with Darwinian pieties for killing,
now drew a bead on the littlest woodchuck's face.
He died down in the everbearing roses.

Ten minutes later I dropped the mother. She
flipflopped in the air and fell, her needle teeth
still hooked in a leaf of early Swiss chard.
Another baby next. O one-two-three
the murderer inside me rose up hard,
the hawkeye killer came on stage forthwith.

There's one chuck left. Old wily fellow, he keeps
me cocked and ready day after day after day.
All night I hunt his humped-up form. I dream
I sight along the barrel in my sleep.
If only they'd all consented to die unseen
gassed underground the quiet Nazi way.   1972

ADRIENNE RICH

Aunt Jennifer's Tigers

Aunt Jennifer's tigers prance across a screen,
Bright topaz denizens of a world of green.

---

2. A mixture of cement, pebbles, and gravel.

They do not fear the men beneath the tree;
They pace in sleek chivalric certainty.

Aunt Jennifer's fingers fluttering through her wool   5
Find even the ivory needle hard to pull.
The massive weight of Uncle's wedding band
Sits heavily upon Aunt Jennifer's hand.

When Aunt is dead, her terrified hands will lie
Still ringed with ordeals she was mastered by.   10
The tigers in the panel that she made
Will go on prancing, proud and unafraid.   1951

If you read "Woodchucks" aloud, how would your tone of voice change from beginning to end? What tone would you use to read the ending? How does the hunter feel
about her increasing attraction to violence? Why does the poem begin by calling the
gassing of the woodchucks "merciful" and end by describing it as "the quiet Nazi way"?
What names does the hunter call herself? How does the name-calling affect your feelings about her? Exactly when does the hunter begin to *enjoy* the feel of the gun and the
idea of killing? How does the poet make that clear?

Why are tigers a particularly appropriate contrast to the quiet and subdued manner
of Aunt Jennifer? What words used to describe the tigers seem particularly significant?
In what ways is the tiger an opposite of Aunt Jennifer? In what ways does it externalize
her secrets? Why are Aunt Jennifer's hands described as "terrified"? What clues does the
poem give about why Aunt Jennifer is so afraid? How does the poem make you feel
about Aunt Jennifer? about her tigers? about her life? How would you describe the tone
of the poem? How does the poet feel about Aunt Jennifer?

Twenty years after writing "Aunt Jennifer's Tigers," Adrienne Rich said this about the
poem:

> In writing this poem, composed and apparently cool as it is, I thought I was creating a
> portrait of an imaginary woman. But this woman suffers from the opposition of her imagi-
> nation, worked out in tapestry, and her life style, "ringed with ordeals she was mastered
> by." It was important to me that Aunt Jennifer was a person as distinct from myself as
> possible—distanced by the formalism of the poem, by its objective, observant tone—even
> by putting the woman in a different generation. In those years formalism was part of the
> strategy—like asbestos gloves, it allowed me to handle materials I couldn't pick up bare-
> handed.[3]

Not often do we have such an explicit comment on a poem by its author, and we
don't actually have to have it to understand and experience the force of the poem
(although such a statement may clarify why the author chose particular modes of presentation and how the poem fits into the author's own patterns of thinking and growing).
Most poems contain within them what we need to know in order to tap the human and
artistic resources they offer us.

Subject, theme, and tone: each of these categories gives us a way to begin considering poems and showing how one poem differs from another. Comparing poems on the

---

3. From "When We Dead Awaken: Writing as Re-Vision," a talk given in December 1971 at the Women's
Forum of the Modern Language Association.

same subject or with a similar theme or tone can lead to a clearer understanding of each individual poem and can refine our responses to the subtleties of individual differences. The title of a poem ("Leaving the Motel," for example) or the way the poem first introduces its subject often can give us a sense of what to expect, but we need to be open to surprise, too. No two poems are going to be exactly alike in their effect on us; the variety of possible poems multiplies when you think of all the possible themes and tones that can be explored within any single subject. Varieties of feeling often coincide with varieties of thinking, and readers open to the pleasures of the unexpected may find themselves learning, growing, becoming more sensitive to ideas and human issues as well as more articulate about feelings and thoughts they already have.

MANY TONES: POEMS ABOUT FAMILY RELATIONSHIPS

SEAMUS HEANEY

Mid-Term Break

I sat all morning in the college sick bay
Counting bells knelling classes to a close.
At two o'clock our neighbors drove me home.

In the porch I met my father crying—
He had always taken funerals in his stride—   5
And Big Jim Evans saying it was a hard blow.

The baby cooed and laughed and rocked the pram
When I came in, and I was embarrassed
By old men standing up to shake my hand

And tell me they were "sorry for my trouble,"   10
Whispers informed strangers I was the eldest,
Away at school, as my mother held my hand

In hers and coughed out angry tearless sighs.
At ten o'clock the ambulance arrived
With the corpse, stanched and bandaged by the nurses.   15

Next morning I went up into the room. Snowdrops
And candles soothed the bedside; I saw him
For the first time in six weeks. Paler now,

Wearing a poppy bruise on his left temple,
He lay in the four foot box as in his cot.   20
No gaudy scars, the bumper knocked him clear.

A four foot box, a foot for every year.   1966

PAT MORA

Elena

My Spanish isn't enough.
I remember how I'd smile
listening to my little ones,
understanding every word they'd say,
their jokes, their songs, their plots.   5
    Vamos a pedirle dulces a mamá. Vamos.[4]

---

4. "Let's go ask mama for sweets. Let's go."

But that was in Mexico.
Now my children go to American high schools.
They speak English. At night they sit around
10 the kitchen table, laugh with one another.
I stand by the stove and feel dumb, alone.
I bought a book to learn English.
My husband frowned, drank more beer.
My oldest said, "*Mamá*, he doesn't want you
15 to be smarter than he is." I'm forty,
embarrassed at mispronouncing words,
embarrassed at the laughter of my children,
the grocer, the mailman. Sometimes I take
my English book and lock myself in the bathroom,
20 say the thick words softly,
for if I stop trying, I will be deaf
when my children need my help.

1985

ALBERTO ALVARO RÍOS

Mi Abuelo[5]

Where my grandfather is is in the ground
where you can hear the future like an
Indian with his ear at the tracks. A
pipe leads down to him so that sometimes
5 he whispers what will happen to a man
in town or how he will meet the best-
dressed woman tomorrow and how the best
man at her wedding will chew the ground
next to her. Mi abuelo is the man
10 who talks through all the mouths in my house. An
echo of me hitting the pipe sometimes
to stop him from saying "my hair is a
sieve" is the only other sound. It is a
phrase that among all others is the best,
15 he says, and "my hair is a sieve" is sometimes
repeated for hours out of the ground
when I let him, but mostly I don't. "An
abuelo should be much more than a man
like you!" He stops then, and speaks: "I am a man
20 who has served ants with the attitude of a
waiter, who has made each smile as only an
ant who is fat can, and they liked me best,
but there is nothing left." Yet, I know he ground
green coffee beans as a child, and sometimes
25 he will talk about his wife, and sometimes
about when he was deaf and a man

5. "My grandfather."

cured him by mail and he heard ground
hogs talking, or about how he walked with a
cane he chewed on when he got hungry. At best,
mi abuelo is a liar. I see an   30
old picture of him at nani's with an
off-white yellow center mustache and sometimes
that's all I know for sure. He talks best
about these hills, slowest waves, and where this man
is going, and I'm convinced his hair is a   35
sieve, that his fever is cool now in the ground.
Mi abuelo is an ordinary man.
I look down the pipe, sometimes, and see a
ripple-topped stream in its best suit, in the ground.   1980

SHARON OLDS

I Go Back to May 1937

I see them standing at the formal gates of their colleges,
I see my father strolling out
under the ochre sandstone arch, the
red tiles glinting like bent
plates of blood behind his head, I   5
see my mother with a few light books at her hip
standing at the pillar made of tiny bricks with the
wrought-iron gate still open behind her, its
sword-tips black in the May air,
they are about to graduate, they are about to get married,   10
they are kids, they are dumb, all they know is they are
innocent, they would never hurt anybody.
I want to go up to them and say Stop,
don't do it—she's the wrong woman,
he's the wrong man, you are going to do things   15
you cannot imagine you would ever do,
you are going to do bad things to children,
you are going to suffer in ways you never heard of,
you are going to want to die. I want to go
up to them there in the late May sunlight and say it,   20
her hungry pretty blank face turning to me,
her pitiful beautiful untouched body,
his arrogant handsome blind face turning to me,
his pitiful beautiful untouched body,
but I don't do it. I want to live. I   25
take them up like the male and female
paper dolls and bang them together
at the hips like chips of flint as if to
strike sparks from them, I say
Do what you are going to do, and I will tell about it.   30
                                                          1987

ELIZABETH ALEXANDER

West Indian Primer

for Clifford L. Alexander, Sr.
1898–1989

"On the road between Spanish Town
and Kingston," my grandfather said,
"I was born." His father a merchant,
Jewish, from Italy or Spain.

5   In the great earthquake the ground split
clean, and great-grandfather fell
in the fault with his goat. I don't know
how I got this tale and do not ask.

His black mother taught my grand-
10   father figures, fixed codfish cakes
and fried plantains, drilled cleanliness,
telling the truth, punctuality.

"There is no man more honest,"
my father says. Years later
15   I read that Jews passed through my
grandfather's birthplace frequently.

I know more about Toussaint[6]
and Hispaniola[7] than my own
Jamaica and my family tales
20   I finger the stories like genie

lamps. I write this West Indian primer.   1990

ROBERT HAYDEN

Those Winter Sundays

Sundays too my father got up early
and put his clothes on in the blueblack cold,
then with cracked hands that ached
from labor in the weekday weather made
5   banked fires blaze. No one ever thanked him.

I'd wake and hear the cold splintering, breaking.
When the rooms were warm, he'd call,

---

6. Self-educated, Haitian black soldier and liberator who lived from 1743 to 1803.   7. The first island claimed by Columbus for Spain in 1492. It houses the modern nations of Haiti and the Dominican Republic.

and slowly I would rise and dress,
fearing the chronic angers of that house,
Speaking indifferently to him,   10
who had driven out the cold
and polished my good shoes as well.
What did I know, what did I know
of love's austere and lonely offices?   1966

JAMES MASAO MITSUI

Because of My Father's Job

Spring hailstones would drive us
into the garage. I'd explain away
the smell of my father's tsukemono[8] crock
with its rock-weight,
saying he needed his cabbage   5
like Popeye's spinach. I'd divert attention
to the moonsnail shell,
carried across the mountains from Puget Sound
by my sister. We'd shake off cobwebs,
listen to the dancing surf.   10

I still use the smell of cabbage,
like kelp & fishbone, as an anchor
although I have no memories of father
scooping butter clams
out of the gravel at Point-of-Arches   15
near Shi Shi Beach. Nothing
to connect him to the wind
on the headland at Strawberry Point,
the breakers unfolding a story
of poetry, edges & days   20
that don't always balance.

I have no memories of father
naming me
after Jimmy Osler of Skykomish,
who worked in the depot   25
and laughed so easily.
Who didn't change his friendship in '41.

I have copied the moustache
we shaved off my father once
when he was drunk. Last December   30

---

8. Japanese self-pickled vegetables.

I sat at a motel kitchen table,
on the Oregon coast,
writing poems by candlelight.
My shadow fluttered on the walls & ceiling
35   as white waves
thundered & slid toward the cabin.
Turning to a mirror
I found his thick biceps
flexing themselves.
40   It doesn't matter now that he drank too much,
embarrassed the moon with his curses & songs.   1986

SIMON J. ORTIZ

My Father's Song

Wanting to say things,
I miss my father tonight.
His voice, the slight catch,
the depth from his thin chest,
5   the tremble of emotion
in something he has just said
to his son, his song:

We planted corn one Spring at Acu—
we planted several times
10   but this one particular time
I remember the soft damp sand
in my hand.

My father had stopped at one point
to show me an overturned furrow;
15   the plowshare had unearthed
the burrow nest of a mouse
in the soft moist sand.

Very gently, he scooped tiny pink animals
into the palm of his hand
20   and told me to touch them.
We took them to the edge
of the field and put them in the shade
of a sand moist clod.

I remember the very softness
25   of cool and warm sand and tiny alive mice
and my father saying things.   1976

ERIN MOURÉ

Thirteen Years

I am in a daydream of my uncle,
his shirt out at his daughter's wedding,
white scoop of the shirt-tail bobbing
on the dance floor & him in it, no,
his drunk friend pawing me, it was *his* shirt dangling,   5
I forgot this
my youngest cousin in his dress pants downing straight whisky,
& me too, tying tin cans to his sister's car.
The sour taste of it. Drink this, he said.

I am wondering how we live at all   10
or if we do.
The puppy we grew up with came from the same uncle's farm.
His shirt-tail beneath his suit jacket, dancing.
The friend of the family touching my new chest.
They told me not to say so.   15
I'll drive you to the motel, he said, his breath close.
No. Be nice to him, they said, & waved me off from the table.
I was so scared.
Everyone had been drinking. Including me. Thirteen years old.
Who the hell did my cousin marry.   20
I tell you.   1988

QUESTIONS

1. Consider carefully how the tone of Hayden's "Those Winter Sundays" is created. What activities of the father inspire the son's admiration? Which words of the son are especially effective in suggesting his attitude toward his father? Why is the phrase "what did I know" repeated in line 13? What are the connotations of the word "austere" in line 14? How old does the son seem to be at the time the poem is written? How can you tell?

2. In Alexander's "West Indian Primer," characterize the speaker's great-grandfather; her great-grandmother. How much specific detail are we given about each? What qualities does the grandfather seem to take from each? How do they fit together? Describe the attitude the poem expresses toward each of these ancestors. Explain the poem's title.

3. In Mora's "Elena," what is the tone of the "smile" in line 2? of the husband's frown and beer drinking in line 13? (That is, what kind of attitude does each express toward its audience?) In what tone of voice would you read the quotation in lines 14–15?

WRITING SUGGESTIONS

1. How did you respond to Mouré's "Thirteen Years"? What is the main thing the speaker is trying to say to us? How does she feel about herself and her relatives as she recounts this adolescent experience? How do her attitudes differ from those of other members of her family? Describe the poem's tone. Write a brief narrative paragraph describing as succinctly as possible exactly what happened at the wedding.

2. Compare the tone of voice used in reading Heaney's "Mid-Term Break" aloud to that in Mitsui's "Because of My Father's Job." Pick out three or four key words from each poem that seem to help control the tone. Then, concentrating on the words you have isolated, write a short essay—no more than 600 words—in which you compare the tone of the two poems.

14

SPEAKER: WHOSE VOICE DO WE HEAR?

Poems are personal. The thoughts and feelings they express belong to a specific person, and however general or universal their sentiments seem to be, poems come to us as the expression of an individual human voice. That voice is often the voice of the poet. But not always. Poets sometimes create a "character" just as writers of fiction or drama do—people who speak for them only indirectly. A character may, in fact, be very different from the poet, just as a character in a play or story is different from the author, and that person, the **speaker** of the poem, may express ideas or feelings very different from the poet's own. In the following poem, *two* individual voices in fact speak, and it is clear that, rather than himself speaking directly to us, the poet, Thomas Hardy, has chosen to create two speakers, both female, each of whom has a distinctive voice, personality, and character.

THOMAS HARDY

The Ruined Maid

"O 'Melia,[1] my dear, this does everything crown!
Who could have supposed I should meet you in Town?
And whence such fair garments, such prosperi-ty?"—
"O didn't you know I'd been ruined?" said she.

—"You left us in tatters, without shoes or socks,   5
Tired of digging potatoes, and spudding up docks;[2]
And now you've gay bracelets and bright feathers three!"—
"Yes: that's how we dress when we're ruined," said she.

—"At home in the barton[3] you said 'thee' and 'thou,'
And 'thik oon,' and 'theäs oon,' and 't'other'; but now   10

---

1. Short for Amelia.   2. Spading up weeds.   3. Farmyard.

Your talking quite fits 'ee for high compa-ny!"—
"Some polish is gained with one's ruin," said she.

—"Your hands were like paws then, your face blue and bleak
But now I'm bewitched by your delicate cheek,
15   And your little gloves fit as on any la-dy!"—
"We never do work when we're ruined," said she.

—"You used to call home-life a hag-ridden dream,
And you'd sigh, and you'd sock;[4] but at present you seem
To know not of megrims[5] or melancho-ly!"—
20   "True. One's pretty lively when ruined," said she.

—"I wish I had feathers, a fine sweeping gown,
And a delicate face, and could strut about Town!"—
"My dear—a raw country girl, such as you be,
Cannot quite expect that. You ain't ruined," said she.

1866

The first voice, that of a young woman who has remained back on the farm, is designated typographically (that is, by the way the poem is printed): there are dashes at the
beginning and end of each but the first of her speeches. She speaks the first part of each
stanza (a stanza is a section of a poem designated by spacing), usually the first three
lines. The second young woman, a companion and coworker on the farm in years gone
by, regularly gets the last line in each stanza (and in the last stanza, two lines), so it is
easy to tell who is talking at every point. Also, the two speakers are just as clearly
distinguished by what they say, how they say it, and what sort of person each proves to
be. The nameless stay-at-home shows little knowledge of the world, and everything
surprises her: seeing her former companion at all, but especially seeing her well
clothed, cheerful, and polished; and as the poem develops she shows increasing envy
of her more worldly friend. She is the "raw country girl" (line 23) that the other speaker
says she is, and she still speaks the country dialect ("fits 'ee," line 11, for example) that
she notices her friend has lost (lines 9–11). The "ruined" young woman ('Melia), on the
other hand, says little except to keep repeating the refrain about having been ruined,
but even the slight variations she plays on that theme suggest her sophistication and
amusement at her farm friend, although she still uses a rural "ain't" at the end. We are
not told the full story of their lives (was the "ruined" young woman thrown out? did she
run away from home or work?), but we know enough (that they've been separated for
some time, that the stay-at-home did not know where the other had gone) to allow the
dialogue to articulate the contrast between them: one is still rural, inexperienced, and
innocent; the other is sophisticated, citified, and "ruined." The style of speech of each
speaker then does the rest.

It is equally obvious that there is a speaker (or, in this case, actually a singer) in
stanzas 2 through 9 of the following poem:

---

4. Deliver angry blows.   5. Migraine headaches.

X. J. KENNEDY

In a Prominent Bar in Secaucus One Day

To the tune of "The Old Orange Flute" or the tune of
"Sweet Betsy from Pike"

In a prominent bar in Secaucus[6] one day
Rose a lady in skunk with a topheavy sway,
Raised a knobby red finger—all turned from their beer—
While with eyes bright as snowcrust she sang high and clear:

"Now who of you'd think from an eyeload of me   5
That I once was a lady as proud as could be?
Oh I'd never sit down by a tumbledown drunk
If it wasn't, my dears, for the high cost of junk.

"All the gents used to swear that the white of my calf
Beat the down of a swan by a length and a half.   10
In the kerchief of linen I caught to my nose
Ah, there never fell snot, but a little gold rose.

"I had seven gold teeth and a toothpick of gold.
My Virginia cheroot was a leaf of it rolled
And I'd light it each time with a thousand in cash—   15
Why the bums used to fight if I flicked them an ash.

"Once the toast of the Biltmore,[7] the belle of the Taft,
I would drink bottle beer at the Drake, never draft,
And dine at the Astor on Salisbury steak
With a clean tablecloth for each bite I did take.   20

"In a car like the Roxy[8] I'd roll to the track,
A steel-guitar trio, a bar in the back,
And the wheels made no noise, they turned over so fast,
Still it took you ten minutes to see me go past.

"When the horses bowed down to me that I might choose,   25
I bet on them all, for I hated to lose.
Now I'm saddled each night for my butter and eggs
And the broken threads race down the backs of my legs.

"Let you hold in mind, girls, that your beauty must pass
Like a lovely white clover that rusts with its grass.   30
Keep your bottoms off barstools and marry you young
Or be left—an old barrel with many a bung.

"For when time takes you out for a spin in his car
You'll be hard-pressed to stop him from going too far

6. A small town on the Hackensack River in New Jersey, a few miles west of Manhattan.   7. Like the
Taft, Drake, and Astor, a once-fashionable New York hotel.   8. A luxurious old New York theater and
movie house, the site of many "world premieres" in the heyday of Hollywood.

35   And be left by the roadside, for all your good deeds,
Two toadstools for tits and a face full of weeds."

All the house raised a cheer, but the man at the bar
Made a phonecall and up pulled a red patrol car
And she blew us a kiss as they copped her away
40   From that prominent bar in Secaucus, N.J.   1961

Again, we learn about the character primarily through her own words, although we don't have to believe everything she tells us about her past. From her introduction in the first stanza we get some general notion of her appearance and condition, but it is she who tells us that she is a junkie (line 8), a prostitute (line 27), and that her face and figure have seen better days (lines 32, 36). That information could make her a sad case, and the poem might lament her state or allow her to lament it, but instead the poem presents her in a light and friendly way. She is anxious to give advice and sound righteous (line 31, for example), but she's also enormously cheerful about herself, and her spirit repeatedly bursts through her song. Her performance gives her a lot of pleasure as she exaggerates outrageously about her former luxury and prominence, and even her departure in a patrol car she chooses to treat as a grand exit, throwing a kiss to her audience. The comedy is bittersweet, perhaps, but she is allowed to present herself, through her own words and attitudes, as a likable character—someone who has survived life's disappointments and retained her dignity and her sense of theatricality. The glorious fiction of her life, narrated with energy and polish in the manner of a practiced and accomplished liar, betrays some rather naive notions of good taste and luxurious living (lines 18–26). But this "lady in skunk" has a picturesque and engaging style, a refreshing sense of humor about herself, and a flair for drama. Like the cheap fur she wears, her experiences in what she considers high life satisfy her sense of style and celebration. The self-portrait accumulates, almost completely through how she talks about herself, and the poet develops our attitude toward her by allowing her to recount her story herself, in her own words—or rather in words chosen for her by the author.

The following poem uses the idea of speaker in a very different way and for quite different tonal purposes:

ADRIENNE RICH

Letters in the Family

I: Catalonia, 1936

Dear Parents:
                I'm the daughter
you didn't bless when she left,
an unmarried woman wearing a khaki knapsack
with a poor mark in Spanish.
                I'm writing now
5   from a plaster-dusted desk in a town
pocked street by street with hand grenades,

some of them, dear ones, thrown by me.
This is a school: the children are at war.
You don't need honors in schoolroom Spanish here
to be of use and my right arm   10
's as strong as anyone's. I sometimes think
all languages are spoken here,
even mine, which you got zero in.
Don't worry. Don't try to write. I'm happy,
if you could know it.   15
                                   Rochelle.

II: Yugoslavia, 1944[9]

Dear Chana,
                         where are you now?
Am sending this pocket-to-pocket
(though we both know pockets we'd hate to lie in).
They showed me that poem you gave Reuven,
about the match: 20
Chana, you know, I never was
for martyrdom. I thought we'd try our best,
ragtag mission that we were,
then clear out if the signals looked too bad.
Something in you drives things ahead for me   25
but if I can I mean to stay alive.
We're none of us giants, you know,
just small, frail, inexperienced romantic people.
But there are things we learn.
You know the sudden suck of empty space   30
between the jump and the ripcord pull?
I hate it. I hate it so,
I've hated you for your dropping
ecstatically in free-fall, in the training,
your look, dragged on the ground, of knowing   35
precisely why you were there.
                              My mother's
still in Palestine. And yours
still there in Hungary. Well, there we are.
When this is over—
                      I'm
      your earthbound friend to the end, still yours—
                                   Esther.   40

9. "See *Hannah Senesh: Her Life and Diary* (New York: Schocken, 1973). Born in Budapest, 1921, Hannah Senesh became a Zionist and emigrated to Palestine at the age of eighteen; her mother and brother remained in Europe. In 1943, she joined an expedition of Jews who trained under the British to parachute behind Nazi lines in Europe and connect with the partisan underground, to rescue Jews in Hungary, Romania, and Czechoslovakia. She was arrested by the Nazis, imprisoned, tortured, and executed in November 1944. Like the other letter-writers, 'Esther' is an imagined person.

   See also Ruth Whitman's long poem, *The Testing of Hannah Senesh* (Detroit: Wayne State University Press, 1986)." (AR)

III: Southern Africa, 1986

Dear children:

           We've been walking nights
a long time over rough terrain,
sometimes through marshes. Days we hide
under what bushes we can find.

45   Our stars steer us. I write
on my knee by a river with a weary hand,
and the weariness will come through
this letter that should tell you
nothing but love. I can't say where we are,

50   what weeds are in bloom, what birds cry at dawn.
The less you know the safer.
But not to know how you are going on—
Matile's earache, Emma's lessons, those tell-tale
eyes and tongues, so quick—are you remembering

55   to be brave and wise and strong?
At the end of this hard road
we'll sit all together at one meal
and I'll tell you everything: the names
of our comrades, how the letters

60   were routed to you, why I left.
And I'll stop and say, "Now you,
grown so big, how was it for you, those times?
Look, I know you in detail, every inch of each
sweet body, haven't I washed and dried you
a thousand times?"

65   And we'll eat and tell our stories
together. That is my reason.

               Ma.   1989

As in Hardy's "The Ruined Maid," this poem uses different voices, and here they are clearly distinguished as different "historical" characters—Rochelle, Esther, and "Ma," women from three separate places and times who in letter form tell their own stories. In each case, the individual story is part of some larger historical moment, and although all three characters are (as the author's footnote points out) fictional, the three stories together present a kind of history of female heroism in difficult cultural moments.

Try reading the poem aloud so you can hear how different in tone the three voices sound; each woman has distinctive expressions and syntax of her own. All are in part defined by their relationships to families left behind, but all are defined even more fully by their own idealistic determination to resist the larger social and political forces in the cultures where they are at the time they write their letters. Telling stories, the pleasure identified by the third speaker as the ultimate purpose of her actions (lines 56–62), is important to all three speakers as a way of defining themselves in relation to their families; to the poem, the telling of separate stories by the different speakers becomes the collective means to exemplify the power of women in history in action.

Some speakers in poems are not, however, nearly so heroic or attractive, and some poems create a speaker who makes us dislike him or her, also because of what the poet makes him or her say, as the following poem does. Here the speaker, as the title implies, is a monk, but he shows himself to be most unspiritual: mean, self-righteous, and despicable.

ROBERT BROWNING

Soliloquy of the Spanish Cloister[1]

Gr-r-r—there go, my heart's abhorrence!
    Water your damned flower-pots, do!
If hate killed men, Brother Lawrence,
    God's blood, would not mine kill you!
What? your myrtle-bush wants trimming?   5
    Oh, that rose has prior claims—
Needs its leaden vase filled brimming?
    Hell dry you up with its flames!

At the meal we sit together:
    Salve tibi![2] I must hear   10
Wish talk of the kind of weather,
    Sort of season, time of year:
Not a plenteous cork-crop: scarcely
    Dare we hope oak-galls,[3] *I doubt:*
What's the Latin name for "parsley"?   15
    What's the Greek name for Swine's Snout?

Whew! We'll have our platter burnished,
    Laid with care on our own shelf!
With a fire-new spoon we're furnished,
    And a goblet for ourself,   20
Rinsed like something sacrificial
    Ere 'tis fit to touch our chaps[4]—
Marked with L. for our initial!
    (He-he! There his lily snaps!)

Saint, forsooth! While brown Dolores   25
    —Squats outside the Convent bank
With Sanchicha, telling stories,
    Steeping tresses in the tank,
Blue-black, lustrous, thick like horsehairs,
    —Can't I see his dead eye glow,   30
Bright as 'twere a Barbary corsair's?[5]
    (That is, if he'd let it show!)

When he finishes refection,[6]
    Knife and fork he never lays

---

1. Monastery.   2. "Hail to thee" (Latin). Italics usually indicate the words of Brother Lawrence.
3. Abnormal growth on oak trees, used for tanning.   4. Jaws.   5. African pirate's.   6. A meal.

35 Cross-wise, to my recollection,
        As do I, in Jesu's praise.
    I the Trinity illustrate,
        Drinking watered orange-pulp—
    In three sips the Arian[7] frustrate;
40   —While he drains his at one gulp.

    Oh, those melons? If he's able
        We're to have a feast! so nice!
    One goes to the Abbot's table,
        All of us get each a slice.
45 How go on your flowers? None double?
        Not one fruit-sort can you spy?
    Strange!—And I, too, at such trouble,
        —Keep them close-nipped on the sly!

    There's a great text in Galatians,
50   Once you trip on it, entails
    Twenty-nine distinct damnations,[8]
        One sure, if another fails:
    If I trip him just a-dying,
        Sure of heaven as sure can be,
55 Spin him round and send him flying
        Off to hell, a Manichee?[9]

    Or, my scrofulous French novel
        On gray paper with blunt type!
    Simply glance at it, you grovel
60   Hand and foot in Belial's gripe:[1]
    If I double down its pages
        At the woeful sixteenth print,
    When he gathers his greengages,
        Ope a sieve and slip it in't?

65 Or, there's Satan!—one might venture
        ledge one's soul to him, yet leave
    Such a flaw in the indenture
        —As he'd miss till, past retrieve,
    Blasted lay that rose-acacia
70   We're so proud of! Hy, Zy, Hine . . .[2]
    'St, there's Vespers! *Plena gratiâ*
        Ave, Virgo.[3] Gr-r-r—you swine!

                                        1842

Not many poems begin with a growl, and this harsh sound turns out to be fair warn-ing that we are about to get to know a real beast, even though he is in the clothing of a

---

7. A heretical sect that denied the Trinity.   8. Galatians 5:15–23 provides a long list of possible offenses, but they do not add up to 29.   9. A heretic. According to the Manichean heresy, the world was divided into the forces of good and evil, equally powerful.   1. In the clutches of Satan.   2. Possibly the beginning of an incantation or curse.   3. The opening words of the *Ave Maria*, here reversed: "Full of grace, Hail, Virgin" (Latin).

religious man. In line 1, he has already shown himself to hold a most uncharitable attitude toward his fellow monk, Brother Lawrence, and by line 4 he has uttered two profanities and admitted his intense feelings of hatred and vengefulness. His ranting and roaring is full of exclamation points (four in the first stanza!), and he reveals his own personality and character when he imagines curses and unflattering nicknames for Brother Lawrence or plots malicious jokes on him. By the end, we have accumulated no knowledge of Brother Lawrence that makes him seem a fit target for such rage (except that he is pious, dutiful, and pleasant—perhaps enough to make this sort of speaker despise him), but we have discovered the speaker to be lecherous (stanza 4), full of false piety (stanza 5), malicious in trivial matters (stanza 6), ready to use his theological learning to sponsor damnation rather than salvation (stanza 7), a closet reader and viewer of pornography within the monastery (stanza 8)—even willing to risk his own soul in order to torment Brother Lawrence (last stanza).

The speaker is made to characterize himself; the details accrue and accumulate into a fairly full portrait, and here we do not have even an opening and closing "objective" description (as in Kennedy's "In a Prominent Bar") or another speaker (as in Hardy's "The Ruined Maid") to give us perspective. Except for the moments when the speaker mimics or parodies Brother Lawrence (usually in italic type), we have only the speaker's own words and thoughts. But that is enough; the poet has controlled them so carefully that we clearly know what he thinks of the speaker he has created—that he is a mean-spirited, vengeful hypocrite, a thoroughly disreputable and unlikable character. The whole poem has been about him and his attitudes; the point of the poem has been to characterize the speaker and develop in us a dislike of him and what he stands for— total hypocrisy.

In reading a poem like this aloud, we would want our voice to suggest all the unlikable features of a hypocrite. We would also need to suggest, through the tone of voice we used, the author's contemptuous mocking of the rage and hypocrisy, and we would want, like an actor, to create strong disapproval in the hearer. The poem's words (the ones the author has given to the speaker) clearly imply those attitudes, and we would want our voice to express them. Usually there is much more to a poem than the identification and characterization of the speaker, but in many cases it is necessary to identify the speaker and determine his or her character before we can appreciate what else goes on in the poem. And sometimes, as here, in looking for the speaker of the poem, we come near to the center of the poem itself.

Sometimes the effect of a poem depends on our recognizing the temporal position of the speaker as well as her or his identity. The following poem, for example, quickly makes plain that a childhood experience is at the center of the action and that the speaker is female:

TESS GALLAGHER

Sudden Journey

Maybe I'm seven in the open field—
the straw-grass so high
only the top of my head makes a curve
of brown in the yellow. Rain then.

5 First a little. A few drops on my
wrist, the right wrist. More rain.
My shoulders, my chin. Until I'm looking up
to let my eyes take the bliss.
I open my face. Let the teeth show. I
10 pull my shirt down past the collar-bones.
I'm still a boy under my breast spots.
I can drink anywhere. The rain. My
skin shattering. Up suddenly, needing
to gulp, turning with my tongue, my arms out
15 running, running in the hard, cold plenitude
of all those who reach earth by falling.

1984

The sense of adventure and wonder here has a lot to do with the childlike sentence structure and choice of words at the beginning of the poem. Sentences are short, observations direct and simple. The rain becomes exciting and blissful and totally absorbing as the child's actions and reactions take over the poem in lines 2–13. But not all of the poem takes place in a child's mind in spite of the precise and impressive re-creation of childish responses and feelings. The opening line makes clear that we are sliding into a supposition of the past; "maybe I'm seven" makes clear that we, as conspiring adults, are pretending ourselves into earlier time. And at the end the word "plenitude"—crucial to interpreting the poem's full effect and meaning—makes clear that we are finding an adult perspective on the incident. Elsewhere, too, the adult world gives the incident meaning. In line 12, for example, the joke about being able to drink anywhere depends on an adult sense of what being a boy might mean. The "journey" of the poem's title is not only the little girl's running in the rain, but also the adult movement into a past re-created and newly understood.

The speaker in the following poem positions herself very differently, but we do not get a full sense of her until the poem is well along. As you read, try to imitate the tone of voice you think this kind of person would use. Exactly when do you begin to feel that you know what she is like?

DOROTHY PARKER

A Certain Lady

Oh, I can smile for you, and tilt my head,
  And drink your rushing words with eager lips,
And paint my mouth for you a fragrant red,
  And trace your brows with tutored finger-tips.
5 When you rehearse your list of loves to me,
  Oh, I can laugh and marvel, rapturous-eyed.
And you laugh back, nor can you ever see
  The thousand little deaths my heart has died.
And you believe, so well I know my part,

That I am gay as morning, light as snow,   10
And all the straining things within my heart
  You'll never know.

Oh, I can laugh and listen, when we meet,
  And you bring tales of fresh adventurings—
Of ladies delicately indiscreet,   15
  Of lingering hands, and gently whispered things.
And you are pleased with me, and strive anew
  To sing me sagas of your late delights.
Thus do you want me—marveling, gay, and true—
  Nor do you see my staring eyes of nights.   20
And when, in search of novelty, you stray,
  Oh, I can kiss you blithely as you go . . .
And what goes on, my love, while you're away,
  You'll never know.   1937

To whom does the speaker seem to be talking? What sort of person is he? How do you feel about him? Which habits and attitudes of his do you like least? How soon can you tell that the speaker is not altogether happy about his conversation and conduct? In what tone of voice would you read the first twenty-two lines aloud? What attitude would you try to express toward the person spoken to? What tone would you use for the last two lines? How would you describe the speaker's personality? What aspects of her behavior are most crucial to the poem's effect?

It is easy to assume that the speaker in a poem is an extension of the poet. Is the speaker in this poem Dorothy Parker? Maybe. A lot of Parker's poems present a similar world-weary posture and a kind of cynicism about romantic love (look, for example, at "One Perfect Rose" on page 735). But the poem is hardly an example of self-revelation, a giving away of personal secrets. If it were, it would be silly, not to say risky, to address her lover in a way that gives damaging facts about a pose she has been so careful to set up.

In poems such as "The Ruined Maid," "In a Prominent Bar," and "Soliloquy of the Spanish Cloister," we are in no danger of mistaking the speaker for the poet, once we have recognized that poets may create speakers who participate in specific situations much as in fiction or drama. When there is a pointed discrepancy between the speaker and what we know of the poet—when the speaker is a woman, for example, and the poet is a man—we know we have a created speaker to contend with and that the point (or at least one point) in the poem is to observe the characterization carefully. In "A Certain Lady" we may be less sure, and in other poems the discrepancy between speaker and poet may be even more uncertain. What are we to make, for example, of the speaker in "Woodchucks" in the previous chapter? Is that speaker the real Maxine Kumin? At best (without knowing something quite specific about the author) we can only say "maybe" to that question. What we can be sure of is the sort of person the speaker is portrayed to be—someone (a man? a woman?) surprised to discover feelings and attitudes that contradict values apparently held confidently. And that is exactly what we need to know for the poem to have its effect.

A similar kind of self-mocking of the speaker is present in the following poem, but here the mockery is put to less revelatory, more comic ends.

A. R. AMMONS

Needs

I want something suited to my special needs
I want chrome hubcaps, pin-on attachments
and year round use year after year
I want a workhorse with smooth uniform cut,
5   dozer blade and snow blade & deluxe steering
wheel
I want something to mow, throw snow, tow
and sow with
I want precision reel blades
10   I want a console styled dashboard
I want an easy spintype recoil starter
I want combination bevel and spur gears, 14
gauge stamped steel housing and
washable foam element air cleaner
15   I want a pivoting front axle and extrawide
turf tires
I want an inch of foam rubber inside a vinyl
covering
and especially if it's not too much, if I
20   can deserve it, even if I can't pay for it
I want to mow while riding.

1970

The poet here may be teasing himself about his desire for comfort and ease—and showing how readily advertisements and catalog descriptions manipulate us. But the speaker doesn't have to be the author for the teasing to work. In fact, the effect is to tease those attitudes no matter who holds them by teasing a speaker who illustrates the attitudes. It doesn't matter to the poem whether the speaker is the poet himself or some totally invented character. If the speaker is a version of the poet himself—perhaps a *side* of his personality that he is exploring—the portrait is still fictional in an important sense. The poem presents not a whole human being (*no* poem could do that) but only a version of him—a mood perhaps, an aspect, an attitude, a part of that person. The poet presents someone with an obsession, in this case a small and not very damaging one, and allows him to spout phrases as if he were reciting from an ad or a sales catalog. The "portrait" is made more comic by a clear sense the poem projects that what we have here is only a part of the person, an interest grown too intense, gone askew, gotten out of proportion, something that happens to most of us from time to time. All we know about the speaker is that he has a one-track mind, that he is obsessed by his own luxurious comfort. He may not even be a "he": there is nothing in the poem that makes us certain that the speaker is male. It is customary to think of the speaker in a poem written by a man as "he" and in a poem written by a woman as "she" (as in Maxine Kumin's "Woodchucks") unless the poem presents contrary evidence; but it is merely a convenience, a habit, nothing more.

Even when poets present themselves as if they were speaking directly to us in their own voices, their poems present only a partial portrait, something considerably less than the full personality and character of the poet. Even when there is not an obviously created character—someone with distinct characteristics that are different from those of the poet—strategies of characterization are used to present the person speaking in one way and not another. Even in a poem like the following one, which contains identifiable auto-biographical details, it is still a good idea to talk of the speaker instead of the poet, although here it is probable that the poet is writing about a personal, actual experience, and it is certain that he is making a character of himself—that is, characterizing himself in a certain way, emphasizing some parts of himself and not others.

WILLIAM WORDSWORTH

She Dwelt among the Untrodden Ways

She dwelt among the untrodden ways
    Beside the springs of Dove,[4]
A Maid whom there were none to praise
    And very few to love:

A violet by a mossy stone   5
    Half hidden from the eye!
—Fair as a star, when only one
    Is shining in the sky.

She lived unknown, and few could know
    When Lucy ceased to be;   10
But she is in her grave, and, oh,
    The difference to me!   1800

It is hard to say whether this poem is more about Lucy or about how the speaker feels about her death. Her simple life, far removed from fame and known only to a few, is said nevertheless to have been beautiful. We know little about her beyond her name and where she lived, in a beautiful but then-isolated section of northern England. We don't know if she was young or old, only that the speaker thinks of her as "fair" and compares her to a "violet by a mossy stone." What we do know is that the speaker is deeply pained by her death, so deeply that he is almost inarticulate with grief, lapsing into simple exclamation ("oh," line 11) and unable to articulate the "difference" that her death makes.

Did Lucy actually live? Was she a friend of the poet? We don't know; the poem doesn't tell us, and even biographers of Wordsworth are unsure. What we do know is that Wordsworth was able to represent grief over the death very powerfully. Whether the speaker is the historical Wordsworth or not, that speaker is a major focus of the poem, and it is his feelings that the poem isolates and expresses. We need to recognize some characteristics of the speaker and be sensitive to his feelings for the poem to work.

The following poem similarly seems to draw upon an actual occurrence and to present a speaker who is the poet herself.

4. A small stream in the Lake District in northern England, near where Wordsworth lived in Dove Cottage at Grasmere.

SHARON OLDS

The Lifting

Suddenly my father lifted up his nightie, I
turned my head away but he cried out
Shar!, my nickname, so I turned and looked.
He was sitting in the high cranked-up hospital bed with the
5   gown up, around his neck,
to show me the weight he had lost. I looked
where his solid ruddy stomach had been
and I saw the skin fallen into loose
soft hairy rippled folds
10   lying in a pool of folds
down at the base of his abdomen,
the gaunt torso of a big man
who will die soon. Right away
I saw how much his hips are like mine,
15   the long, white angles, and then
how much his pelvis is shaped like my daughter's,
a chambered whelk-shell hollowed out,
I saw the folds of skin like something
poured, a thick batter, I saw
20   his rueful smile, the cast-up eyes as he
shows me his old body, he knows
I will be interested, he knows I will find him
appealing. If anyone had told me I would sit
by him and he would pull up his nightie and I would look
25   at him, his naked body, the thick
bud of his glans, his penis in all that
dark hair, look at him
in affection and uneasy wonder
I would not have believed it. But now I can still
30   see the tiny snowflakes, white and
night-blue, on the cotton of the gown as it
rises the way we were promised at death it would rise,
the veils would fall from our eyes, we would know everything.   1990

Other poems by Olds written at about the same time also recount moments in the
approaching death of a father—compare, for example, "The Glass" on page 605; and
the similar situations may suggest that the poet was herself struggling with such an event;
and the nickname in line 3 fits. But even if we were to read enough about the poet's life
to be sure that the poem was based on an actual event, we would still have to be careful
about assuming that the speaker was, only and simply, the poet herself. It may well be
that the "I" in this poem is very close to the historical Sharon Olds in 1990, but we are
still well advised as readers to think of the speaker in the poem as the woman characterized specifically in the text and not necessarily as identical to the poet.

The poems we have looked at in this chapter—and the group that follows at the end of the chapter—all suggest the value of beginning the reading of any poem with simple questions: Who is speaking? What do we know about him or her? What kind of person is she or he? Putting together the evidence that the poem presents in answer to such questions can often take us a long way into the poem. For some poems, such questions won't help a great deal because the speaking voice is too indistinct or the character behind the poem too scantily presented. But asking such questions will often lead you toward the central experience the poem offers. At the very least, the question of speaker helps clarify the tone of voice, and it often provides guidance to the larger situation the poem explores.

FRANCES CORNFORD

The New-Born Baby's Song

When I was twenty inches long,
I could not hear the thrushes' song;
The radiance of morning skies
Was most displeasing to my eyes.

For loving looks, caressing words,   5
I cared no more than sun or birds;
But I could bite my mother's breast,
And that made up for all the rest.   1923

AUDRE LORDE

Hanging Fire

I am fourteen
and my skin has betrayed me
the boy I cannot live without
still sucks his thumb
in secret   5
how come my knees are
always so ashy
what if I die
before morning
and momma's in the bedroom   10
with the door closed.

I have to learn how to dance
in time for the next party
my room is too small for me

15   suppose I die before graduation
      they will sing sad melodies
      but finally
      tell the truth about me
      There is nothing I want to do
20   and too much
      that has to be done
      and momma's in the bedroom
      with the door closed.

      Nobody even stops to think
25   about my side of it
      I should have been on Math Team
      my marks were better than his
      why do I have to be
      the one
30   wearing braces
      I have nothing to wear tomorrow
      will I live long enough
      to grow up
      and momma's in the bedroom
35   with the door closed.   1978

GWENDOLYN BROOKS

We Real Cool

THE POOL PLAYERS,
SEVEN AT THE GOLDEN SHOVEL.

We real cool. We
Left school. We

Lurk late. We
Strike straight. We

5   Sing sin. We
Thin gin. We

Jazz June. We
Die soon.   1950

SIR THOMAS WYATT

They Flee from Me

They flee from me, that sometime did me seek,
With naked foot stalking in my chamber.
I have seen them, gentle, tame, and meek,
That now are wild, and do not remember
That sometime they put themselves in danger   5
To take bread at my hand; and now they range,
Busily seeking with a continual change.

Thankéd be Fortune it hath been otherwise,
Twenty times better; but once in special,
In thin array, after a pleasant guise,   10
When her loose gown from her shoulders did fall,
And she me caught in her arms long and small.[5]
And therewith all sweetly did me kiss
And softly said, "Dear heart, how like you this?"

It was no dream, I lay broad waking.   15
But all is turned, thorough[6] my gentleness,
Into a strange fashion of forsaking;
And I have leave to go, of her goodness,
And she also to use newfangleness.[7]
But since that I so kindely[8] am servéd,   20
I fain[9] would know what she hath deservéd.   1557

WALT WHITMAN

[I celebrate myself, and sing myself]

I celebrate myself, and sing myself,
And what I assume you shall assume,
For every atom belonging to me as good belongs to you.

I loafe and invite my soul,
I lean and loafe at my ease observing a spear of summer grass.   5

My tongue, every atom of my blood, form'd from this soil, this air,
Born here of parents born here from parents the same, and their parents
   the same,
I, now thirty-seven years old in perfect health begin,
Hoping to cease not till death.
Creeds and schools in abeyance,   10

---

5. Slender.   6. Through.   7. Fondness for novelty.   8. That is, in kind.   9. Eagerly.

Retiring back a while sufficed at what they are, but never forgotten,
I harbor for good or bad, I permit to speak at every hazard,
Nature without check with original energy.

1855, 1881

PAT MORA

La Migra

I

Let's play *La Migra*[1]
I'll be the Border Patrol.
You be the Mexican maid.
I get the badge and sunglasses.
5   You can hide and run,
but you can't get away
because I have a jeep.
I can take you wherever
I want, but don't ask
10   questions because
I don't speak Spanish.
I can touch you wherever
I want but don't complain
too much because I've got
15   boots and kick—if I have to,
and I have handcuffs.
Oh, and a gun.
Get ready, get set, run.

II

Let's play *La Migra*
20   You be the Border Patrol.
I'll be the Mexican woman.
Your jeep has a flat,
and you have been spotted
by the sun.
25   All you have is heavy: hat,
glasses, badge, shoes, gun.
I know this desert,
where to rest,
where to drink.
30   Oh, I am not alone.

---

1. Border patrol agents.

You hear us singing
and laughing with the wind,
Agua dulce brota aquí,
aquí, aquí,[2] but since you
can't speak Spanish,
you do not understand.
Get ready.

35

1993

SEAMUS HEANEY

The Outlaw

Kelly's kept an unlicensed bull, well away
From the road: you risked fine but had to pay

The normal fee if cows were serviced there.
Once I dragged a nervous Friesian on a tether

Down a lane of alder, shaggy with catkin,   5
Down to the shed the bull was kept in.

I gave Old Kelly the clammy silver, though why
I could not guess. He grunted a curt 'Go by

Get up on that gate.' And from my lofty station
I watched the business-like conception.   10

The door, unbolted, whacked back against the wall.
The illegal sire fumbled from his stall

Unhurried as an old steam engine shunting,
He circled, snored and nosed. No hectic panting,

Just the unfussy ease of a good tradesman;   15
Then an awkward, unexpected jump, and

His knobbed forelegs straddling her flank,
He slammed life home, impassive as a tank,

Dropping off like a tipped-up load of sand.
'She'll do,' said Kelly and tapped his ash-plant   20

Across her hindquarters. 'If not, bring her back.'
I walked ahead of her, the rope now slack

While Kelly whooped and prodded his outlaw
Who, in his own time, resumed the dark, the straw.   1969

2. "Sweet water springs here, here, here."

MARGARET ATWOOD

Death of a Young Son by Drowning

He, who navigated with success
the dangerous river of his own birth
once more set forth

on a voyage of discovery
into the land I floated on
but could not touch to claim.

His feet slid on the bank,
the currents took him;
he swirled with ice and trees in the swollen water

and plunged into distant regions,
his head a bathysphere;
through his eyes' thin glass bubbles

he looked out, reckless adventurer
on a landscape stranger than Uranus
we have all been to and some remember.

There was an accident; the air locked,
he was hung in the river like a heart.
They retrieved the swamped body,

cairn of my plans and future charts,
with poles and hooks
from among the nudging logs.

It was spring, the sun kept shining, the new grass
leapt to solidity;
my hands glistened with details.

After the long trip I was tired of waves.
My foot hit rock. The dreamed sails
collapsed, ragged.

       I planted him in his country
       like a flag.

1970

QUESTIONS

1. What, precisely, do we know about the speaker in Lorde's "Hanging Fire"? How much self-confidence does she have? How can you tell? How does she feel about herself?

2. Characterize the speaker in Heaney's "The Outlaw." What in particular fascinates him about the breeding operation? What, exactly, does he see? How do the two participants respond to the central event? How do the observers respond? Why does the poem describe the path to Kelly's so fully? Why does the "nervous Friesian" (line 4) have to be dragged? Why is the money paid to Kelly described as "clammy silver" (line 7)? Why does the speaker decide to employ an "unlicensed bull" (line 1)? What or whom does the title of the poem refer to?

3. What kind of journey does the mother make in Atwood's "Death of a Young Son by Drowning"? How are the son's and mother's journeys related? Explain the final image in lines 28–29.

WRITING SUGGESTION

The speakers in Ammons's "Needs" and Heaney's "The Outlaw" both reveal themselves to have desires and needs that they are not themselves fully conscious of. Analyze carefully just what elements in the poem make clear to us the "secret" aspects of their characters. Compare the character of the speaker (and the strategies used to characterize her) in Maxine Kumin's "Woodchucks" (page 628). Choose either "Needs" or "The Outlaw" to compare in detail with "Woodchucks," and write a short (600- to 700-word) essay in which you characterize the speakers in the two poems, making clear what kind of attitude each poem develops toward its speaker.

15

SITUATION AND SETTING: WHAT HAPPENS? WHERE? WHEN?

Questions about the speaker ("Who" questions) in a poem almost always lead to questions of "Where?" "When?" and "Why?" Identifying the speaker usually is, in fact, part of a larger process of defining the entire imagined **situation** in a poem: What is happening? Where is it happening? Who is the speaker speaking to? Who else is present? Why is this event occurring? In order to understand the dialogue in Hardy's "The Ruined Maid," for example, we need to recognize that the friends are meeting after an extended period of separation, and that they meet in a town setting rather than the rural area in which they grew up together. We infer (from the opening lines) that the meeting is accidental, and that no other friends are present for the conversation. The poem's whole "story" depends on their situation: after leading separate lives for some time they have some catching up to do. We don't know what specific town is involved, or what year, season, or time of day because those details are not important to the poem's effect. But crucial to the poem are the where and when questions that define the situation and relationship of the two speakers, and the answer to the why question—that the meeting is by chance—is important, too. In another poem we looked at in the previous chapter, Parker's "A Certain Lady," the specific moment and place are not important, but we do need to notice that the "lady" is talking to (or having an imaginary conversation with) her lover and that they are talking about a relationship of some duration.

It is difficult / to get the news from poems / yet men die miserably every day / for lack / of what is found there.

—WILLIAM CARLOS WILLIAMS

Sometimes a *specific* time and place (**setting**) may be important. The "lady in skunk" sings her life story "in a prominent bar in Secaucus," a smelly and unfashionable town in New Jersey, but on no particular occasion ("one day"). In "Soliloquy of the Spanish Cloister," the setting (a monastery) adds to the irony because of the gross inappropriateness of such sentiments and attitudes in a supposedly holy place.

The title of the following poem suggests that place may be important, and it is, although you may be surprised to discover exactly what exists at this address and what uses the speaker makes of it.

JAMES DICKEY

Cherrylog Road

Off Highway 106
At Cherrylog Road I entered
The '34 Ford without wheels,
Smothered in kudzu,[1]
With a seat pulled out to run   5
Corn whiskey down from the hills,

And then from the other side
Crept into an Essex
With a rumble seat of red leather
And then out again, aboard   10
A blue Chevrolet, releasing
The rust from its other color,

Reared up on three building blocks.
None had the same body heat;
I changed with them inward, toward   15
The weedy heart of the junkyard,
For I knew that Doris Holbrook
Would escape from her father at noon

And would come from the farm
To seek parts owned by the sun   20
Among the abandoned chassis,
Sitting in each in turn
As I did, leaning forward
As in a wild stock-car race

In the parking lot of the dead.   25
Time after time, I climbed in
And out the other side, like
An envoy or movie star
Met at the station by crickets.
A radiator cap raised its head,   30

Become a real toad or a kingsnake
As I neared the hub of the yard,
Passing through many states,
Many lives, to reach
Some grandmother's long Pierce-Arrow   35
Sending platters of blindness forth

From its nickel hubcaps
And spilling its tender upholstery
On sleepy roaches,

---

1. A rapidly growing vine, introduced from Japan to combat erosion but now covering whole fields and groves of trees, especially in the deep South.

40
The glass panel in between
Lady and colored driver
Not all the way broken out,

The back-seat phone
Still on its hook.
45
I got in as though to exclaim,
"Let us go to the orphan asylum,
John; I have some old toys
For children who say their prayers."

I popped with sweat as I thought
50
I heard Doris Holbrook scrape
Like a mouse in the southern-state sun
That was eating the paint in blisters
From a hundred car tops and hoods.
She was tapping like code,

55
Loosening the screws,
Carrying off headlights,
Sparkplugs, bumpers,
Cracked mirrors and gear-knobs,
Getting ready, already,
60
To go back with something to show

Other than her lips' new trembling
I would hold to me soon, soon,
Where I sat in the ripped back seat
Talking over the interphone,
65
Praying for Doris Holbrook
To come from her father's farm

And to get back there
With no trace of me on her face
To be seen by her red-haired father
70
Who would change, in the squalling barn,
Her back's pale skin with a strop,
Then lay for me

In a bootlegger's roasting car
With a string-triggered 12-gauge shotgun
75
To blast the breath from the air.
Not cut by the jagged windshields,
Through the acres of wrecks she came
With a wrench in her hand,

Through dust where the blacksnake dies
80
Of boredom, and the beetle knows
The compost has no more life.
Someone outside would have seen
The oldest car's door inexplicably
Close from within:

85
I held her and held her and held her,
Convoyed at terrific speed

By the stalled, dreaming traffic around us,
So the blacksnake, stiff
With inaction, curved back
Into life, and hunted the mouse   90

With deadly overexcitement,
The beetles reclaimed their field
As we clung, glued together,
With the hooks of the seat springs
Working through to catch us red-handed   95
Amidst the gray breathless batting

That burst from the seat at our backs.
We left by separate doors
Into the changed, other bodies
Of cars, she down Cherrylog Road   100
And I to my motorcycle
Parked like the soul of the junkyard

Restored, a bicycle fleshed   ✓
With power, and tore off
Up Highway 106, continually   105
Drunk on the wind in my mouth,
Wringing the handlebar for speed,
Wild to be wreckage forever.   1964

The *exact* location of the junkyard is not important (there is no Highway 106 near the real Cherrylog Road in North Georgia), but we do need to know that the setting is rural, that the time is summer and that the summer is hot, and that moonshine whiskey is native to the area. Following the story is no problem once we have sorted out these few facts, and we are prepared to meet the cast of characters: Doris Holbrook, her red-haired father, and the speaker. About each we learn just enough to appreciate the sense of vitality, adventure, and power that constitute the major effects of the poem.

The situation of lovemaking in another setting than the junkyard would not produce the same effects, and the exotic sense of a forbidden meeting in this unlikely place helps to re-create the speaker's sense of the episode. For him, it is memorable (notice all the tiny details he remembers), powerful (notice his reaction when he gets back on his motorcycle), dreamlike (notice the sense of time standing still, especially in lines 85–89), and important (notice how the speaker perceives his environment as changed by their lovemaking, lines 88–91 and 98–100). The wealth of details about setting also helps us to raise other, related questions. Why does the speaker fantasize about being shot by the father (lines 72–75)? Why, in a poem so full of details, do we find out so little about what Doris Holbrook looks like? What gives us the sense that this incident is a composite of episodes, an event that was repeated many times? What gives us the impression that the events occurred long ago? What makes the speaker feel so powerful at the end? What does he mean when he talks of himself as being "wild to be wreckage forever"? All of the poem's attention to the speaker's reactions, reflections, and memories is intricately tied up with the particulars of setting. Making love in a junkyard is crucial to the speaker's sense of both power and wreckage, and to him Doris is merely a matter of excitement, adventure, and pale skin, appreciated because she makes the world seem different and because she is willing to take risks and to suffer for meeting him like this. The more we probe the poem with questions about situation, the more likely we are to catch the poem's full effect.

The plot of "Cherrylog Road" is fairly easy to sort out, but its effect is more complex than the simple story suggests. The next poem we will look at is, at first glance, much more difficult to follow. Part of the difficulty is that the poem is from an earlier age and its language and sentence structure may seem a bit unfamiliar, and part is because the action in the poem is so closely connected to what is being said. But its opening lines—addressed to someone who is resisting the speaker's suggestions—disclose the situation, and gradually we can figure out the scene: a man is trying to convince a woman that they should make love. When a flea happens by, the speaker uses it for an unlikely example; it becomes part of his argument. And once we recognize the situation, we can readily follow (and be amused by) the speaker's witty and intricate argument.

JOHN DONNE

The Flea

Mark but this flea, and mark in this[2]
How little that which thou deny'st me is;
It sucked me first, and now sucks thee,
And in this flea our two bloods mingled be;
5   Thou know'st that this cannot be said
A sin, nor shame, nor loss of maidenhead.
    Yet this enjoys before it woo,
    And pampered[3] swells with one blood made of two,
    And this, alas, is more than we would do.[4]

10   Oh stay, three lives in one flea spare,
Where we almost, yea more than, married are.
This flea is you and I, and this
Our marriage bed, and marriage temple is;
Though parents grudge, and you, we're met
15   And cloistered in these living walls of jet.
    Though use[5] make you apt to kill me,
    Let not to that, self-murder added be,
    And sacrilege, three sins in killing three.

    Cruel and sudden, hast thou since
20   Purpled thy nail in blood of innocence?
Wherein could this flea guilty be,
Except in that drop which it sucked from thee?
Yet thou triumph'st, and say'st that thou
Find'st not thyself, nor me, the weaker now;

2. Medieval preachers and rhetoricians asked their hearers to "mark" (look at) an object that illustrated a moral or philosophical lesson they wished to emphasize.   3. Fed luxuriously.   4. According to contemporary medical theory, conception involved the literal mingling of the lovers' blood.
5. Habit.

'Tis true; then learn how false, fears be;   25
Just so much honor, when thou yield'st to me,
Will waste, as this flea's death took life from thee.   1633

The scene in "The Flea" develops almost as it would in the theater. Action occurs even as the poem is being written. Between stanzas 1 and 2, the woman makes a move to kill the flea (as stanza 2 opens, the speaker is trying to stop her), and between stanzas 2 and 3 she has squashed the flea with her fingernail. Once we make sense of what the speaker says, the action is just as clear from the words as if we had stage directions in the margin. All of the speaker's verbal cleverness and all of his specious arguments follow from the situation, and in this poem (as in Browning's "Soliloquy of the Spanish Cloister") we watch as if we were observing a scene in a play. The speaker is, in effect, giving a dramatic monologue for our benefit.

Neither time nor place is important to "The Flea," except that the speaker and his friend must be assumed to be in the same place and to have the leisure for some playfulness. The situation could occur anywhere a man, a woman, and a flea could be together: indoors, outdoors, morning, evening, city, country, in cottage or palace, on a boat or in a bedroom. We do know, from the date of publication of the poem (1633), that the poet, Donne, was writing about people of almost four centuries ago, but the conduct he describes might equally happen in later ages. Only the habits of language (and perhaps the speaker's religious attitudes) date the poem; the situation could just as easily be set in any age or place.

The two poems that follow have simpler plots, but in each case the heart of the poem is in the basic situation:

RITA DOVE

Daystar

She wanted a little room for thinking:
but she saw diapers steaming on the line,
a doll slumped behind the door.

So she lugged a chair behind the garage
to sit out the children's naps.   5

Sometimes there were things to watch—
the pinched armor of a vanished cricket,
a floating maple leaf. Other days
she stared until she was assured
when she closed her eyes   10
she'd see only her own vivid blood.

She had an hour, at best, before Liza appeared
pouting from the top of the stairs.

And just *what* was mother doing
15 out back with the field mice? Why,

building a palace. Later
that night when Thomas rolled over and
lurched into her, she would open her eyes
and think of the place that was hers
20 for an hour—where
she was nothing,
pure nothing, in the middle of the day.   1986

LINDA PASTAN

To a Daughter Leaving Home

When I taught you
at eight to ride
a bicycle, loping along
beside you
5 as you wobbled away
on two round wheels,
my own mouth rounding
in surprise when you pulled
ahead down the curved
10 path of the park,
I kept waiting
for the thud
of your crash as I
sprinted to catch up,
15 while you grew
smaller, more breakable
with distance,
pumping, pumping
for your life, screaming
20 with laughter,
the hair flapping
behind you like a
handkerchief waving
goodbye.   1988

Both these poems involve motherhood, but they take entirely different stances about it and have very different tones. The mother in Dove's "Daystar" is overwhelmed by the demands of young children and needs a room of her own. All she can manage, however, is a brief hour in a chair behind the garage. The situation is virtually the whole story here. Nothing really happens except that daily events (washing diapers, picking up toys, looking at crickets and leaves, explaining the world to children, having sex) crowd her brief private hour and make it precious. Being "nothing" (lines 21 and 22) takes on great value in these circumstances, and the poem makes much of the setting: an isolated chair behind the garage. Setting in poems often means something much more specific about a particular culture or social history, but here time and place are given value by the circumstances of the situation for one frazzled mother.

The particulars of time and place in Pastan's "To a Daughter Leaving Home" are even less specific, but the incident the poem describes happened a long time ago, and it is important to notice that its vividness in the poem is a function of memory. The mother is the speaker here, and we are told very little about her, at least directly. But she is thinking back nostalgically to a moment long ago when her daughter made an earlier (but briefer) departure from home, and the poem implies the occasion for her doing so. The daughter now is old enough to "leave" home in a full sense; the poem does not tell us why or what the present circumstances are, but the title tells us the situation. We may infer quite a bit about the speaker here—her affection for the daughter, the kind of mother she has been, her anxiety at the new departure that seems to reflect the earlier wobbly ride into the distance—but as in "Daystar" the poem is all situation. There are almost no details of present action, and we have no specific information about place or time for either the remembered event or the present one.

> A poem . . . begins as a lump in the throat, a sense of wrong, a homesickness, a lovesickness. . . . It finds the thought and the thought finds the words.
>
> —ROBERT FROST

Some poems, however, depend heavily on historical specifics and a knowledge of actual places and events. The following poem, for example, depends not only on knowing some facts about a particular event but on the parallels between that event and circumstances surrounding the poet and his immediate readers.

JOHN MILTON

On the Late Massacre in Piedmont

Avenge, O Lord, thy slaughtered saints, whose bones
    Lie scattered on the Alpine mountains cold;
    Even them who kept thy truth so pure of old
    When all our fathers worshiped stocks and stones,
Forget not: in thy book record their groans   5
    Who were thy sheep and in their ancient fold
    Slain by the bloody Piemontese that rolled
    Mother with infant down the rocks. Their moans
The vales redoubled to the hills, and they
    To heaven. Their martyred blood and ashes sow   10
    O'er all th' Italian fields, where still doth sway
    The triple tyrant:[6] that from these may grow

6. The Pope's tiara featured three crowns.

>   A hundredfold, who having learnt thy way
>   Early may fly the Babylonian woe.[7]

       1655

The "slaughtered saints" were members of the Waldensians—a heretical sect that had long been settled in southern France and northern Italy (the Piedmont). Though a minority, the Waldensians were allowed freedom of worship until 1655, when their protection under the law was taken away and locals attacked them, killing large numbers. This poem, then, is not a private meditation, but rather a public statement about a well-known "news" event. The reader, to fully understand the poem and respond to it meaningfully, must therefore be acquainted with its historical context, including the massacre itself and the significance it had for Milton and his English audience.

Milton wrote the poem shortly after the Piedmont massacre of 1655 became known in England, and implicit in its "meaning" is a parallel Milton's readers would have felt between the events in the Piedmont and current English politics. Milton signals the analogy early on by calling the dead Piedmontese "saints," the term then regularly used by English Protestants of the Puritan stamp to describe themselves and to thereby assert their belief that every individual Christian—not just those few "special" religious heroes singled out in the Catholic tradition—lived a heroic life. By identifying the Waldensians with the English Puritans—their beliefs were in some ways quite similar, and both were minorities in a larger political and cultural context—Milton was warning his fellow Puritans that, if the Stuart monarchy were reestablished, what had just happened to the Waldensians could happen to them as well. Following the Restoration in 1660, tight restrictions were in fact placed on the Puritan "sects" under the new monarchy. In lines 12 and 14, the poem alludes to dangers of religious rule by dominant groups by invoking standard images of Catholic power and persecution; the heir to the English throne (who succeeded to the throne as Charles II in 1660) was spending his exile in Catholic Europe and was, because of his sympathetic treatment of Catholic associates and friends, thought perhaps to be himself a Catholic. Chauvinistic Englishmen, who promoted rivalries with Catholic powers like France, considered him a traitor.

Many poems, like this one, make use of historical occurrences and situations to create a widely evocative set of angers, sympathies, and conclusions. Sometimes a poet's intention in recording a particular moment or event is to commemorate it or comment upon it. A poem written about a specific occasion is usually called an **occasional poem,** and such a poem is **referential;** that is, it *refers* to a certain historical time or event. Sometimes, it is hard to place ourselves fully enough in another time or place to imagine sympathetically what a particular historical moment would have been like, and even the best poetic efforts do not necessarily transport us there. For such poems we need, at the least, specific historical information—plus a willingness on our part as readers to be transported, by a name, a date, or a dramatic situation.

Time or place may, of course, be used much less specifically and still be important to a poem; frequently a poem's setting draws upon common notions of a particular time or place. Setting a poem in a garden, for example, or writing about apples almost inevitably reminds many readers of the Garden of Eden because it is part of the Western heritage of belief or knowledge. Even people who don't read at all or who lack Judeo-

---

7. In Milton's day, Protestants often likened the Roman Church to Babylonian decadence, called the church "the whore of Babylon," and read Revelation 17 and 18 as an allegory of its coming destruction.

Christian religious commitments are likely to know about Eden, and a poet writing in our culture can count on that. An **allusion** is a reference to something outside the poem that carries a history of meaning and strong emotional associations. For example, gardens may carry suggestions of innocence and order, or temptation and the Fall, or both, depending on how the poem handles the allusion. Well-known places from history or myth may be popularly associated with particular ideas or values or ways of life.

The place involved in a poem is its **spatial setting,** and the time is its **temporal setting.** The temporal setting may involve a specific date or an era, a season of the year or a time of day. We tend, for example, to think of spring as a time of discovery and growth, and poems set in spring are likely to make use of that association; morning usually suggests discovery as well—beginnings, vitality, the world fresh and new—even to those of us who in reality take our waking slow. Temporal or spatial setting is often used to influence our expectation of theme and tone, although the poet may then go on to surprise us by making something very different of our expectation. Setting is often an important factor in creating the mood in poems just as in stories, plays, or films. Often the details of setting have a lot to do with the way we ultimately respond to the poem's subject or theme, as in this poem:

SYLVIA PLATH

Point Shirley

From Water-Tower Hill to the brick prison
The shingle booms, bickering under
The sea's collapse.
Snowcakes break and welter. This year
The gritted wave leaps   5
The seawall and drops onto a bier
Of quahog chips,[8]
Leaving a salty mash of ice to whiten

In my grandmother's sand yard. She is dead,
Whose laundry snapped and froze here, who   10
Kept house against
What the sluttish, rutted sea could do.
Squall waves once danced
Ship timbers in through the cellar window;
A thresh-tailed, lanced   15
Shark littered in the geranium bed—

Such collusion of mulish elements
She wore her broom straws to the nub.
Twenty years out
Of her hand; the house still hugs in each drab   20
Stucco socket
The purple egg-stones: from Great Head's knob

8. Chips from quahog clam shells, common on the New England coast.

To the filled-in Gut
The sea in its cold gizzard ground those rounds.

25   Nobody wintering now behind
The planked-up windows where she set
Her wheat loaves
And apple cakes to cool. What is it
Survives, grieves
30   So, over this battered, obstinate spit
Of gravel? The waves'
Spewed relics clicker masses in the wind,

Gray waves the stub-necked eiders ride.
A labor of love, and that labor lost.
35   Steadily the sea
Eats at Point Shirley. She died blessed,
And I come by
Bones, bones only, pawed and tossed,
A dog-faced sea.
40   The sun sinks under Boston, bloody red.

I would get from these dry-papped stones
The milk your love instilled in them.
The black ducks dive.
And though your graciousness might stream,
45   And I contrive,
Grandmother, stones are nothing of home
To that spumiest dove.
Against both bar and tower the black sea runs.   1960

One does not have to know the New England coast by personal experience to find it vividly re-created in Plath's poem. A reader who knows that coast or another like it may have an advantage in being able to respond more quickly to the poem's precision of description, but the poem does not depend on the reader's having such knowledge. The exact location of Point Shirley, near Boston, is not especially important, but visualization of the setting is. Crucial to the poem's tone and mood is the sense of the sea as aggressor, a force powerful enough to change the contours of the coast and invade the privacy of yards and homes. The energy, relentlessness, and impersonality of the sea met their match, though only temporarily, in the speaker's grandmother, who "[k]ept house against / What the sluttish, rutted sea could do" (lines 11–12). The grandmother *belonged* in this setting, and it seemed hers, but twenty years of her absence (since her death) now begin to show. Still, the marks of her obstinacy and love are there, although ultimately doomed by the sea's more enduring power.

Details—and how they are amassed—are important here rather than historic particulars of time and place. The grays and whites and drab colors of the sea and its leavings provide both a visual sense of the scene and the mood for the poem. The stubbornness that the speaker admired in the grandmother comes to seem a part of that tenacious grayness. Nothing happens rapidly here; things wear down. Even the "bloody red" (line 40) of the sun's setting—an ominous sign that adds a vivid fright to the dullness rather than brightening it—makes promises that seem slow and long-term. The toughness of the boarded-up house is a monument to the grandmother's loving care and becomes a way for the speaker to touch her human spirit, but the poem's final emphasis is on the relentless black sea, which continues to run against the landmarks and fortresses that had been identified with the setting in the very first line.

Queries about situation and setting begin as simple questions of identification but frequently become more complex when we sort out all the implications. Often it takes only a moment to determine a poem's situation, but it may take much longer to discover all of the things that time and place imply, for their meanings may depend upon visual details, or upon actual historical occurrences, or upon habitual ways of thinking about certain times and places—or all three at once. As you read the following poem, notice how the setting—another shore—prepares us for the speaker's moods and ideas, and then watch how the movement of his mind is affected by what he sees.

MATTHEW ARNOLD

Dover Beach[9]

The sea is calm tonight.
The tide is full, the moon lies fair
Upon the straits; on the French coast the light
Gleams and is gone; the cliffs of England stand,
Glimmering and vast, out in the tranquil bay.   5
Come to the window, sweet is the night-air!
Only, from the long line of spray
Where the sea meets the moon-blanched land,
Listen! you hear the grating roar
Of pebbles which the waves draw back, and fling,   10
At their return, up the high strand,
Begin, and cease, and then again begin,
With tremulous cadence slow, and bring
The eternal note of sadness in.

Sophocles long ago   15
Heard it on the Aegean, and it brought
Into his mind the turbid ebb and flow
Of human misery;[1] we
Find also in the sound a thought,
Hearing it by this distant northern sea.   20

The Sea of Faith
Was once, too, at the full, and round earth's shore
Lay like the folds of a bright girdle furled.
But now I only hear
Its melancholy, long, withdrawing roar,   25

9. At the narrowest point on the English Channel. The light on the French coast (lines 3–4) would be about twenty miles away.   1. In *Antigone*, lines 637–46, the chorus compares the fate of the house of Oedipus to the waves of the sea.

Retreating, to the breath
Of the night-wind, down the vast edges drear
And naked shingles[2] of the world.

Ah, love, let us be true
30   To one another! for the world, which seems
To lie before us like a land of dreams,
So various, so beautiful, so new,
Hath really neither joy, nor love, nor light,
Nor certitude, nor peace, nor help for pain;
35   And we are here as on a darkling plain
Swept with confused alarms of struggle and flight,
Where ignorant armies clash by night.

ca. 1851

Exactly what is the dramatic situation in "Dover Beach"? How soon are you aware that someone is being spoken to? How much are we told about the person spoken to? How would you describe the speaker's mood? What does the speaker's mood have to do with time and place? Do any details of present place and time help to account for his tendency to talk repeatedly of the past and the future? How important is it to the poem's total effect that the beach here involves an international border? What particulars of the Dover Beach seem especially important to the poem's themes? to its emotional effects?

Not all poems have an identifiable situation or setting, just as not all poems have a speaker who is entirely distinct from the author. Poems that simply present a series of thoughts and feelings directly, in a contemplative, meditative, or reflective way, may not set up any kind of action, plot, or situation at all, preferring to speak directly without the intermediary of a dramatic device. But most poems depend crucially upon a sense of place, a sense of time, and an understanding of human interaction in scenes that resemble the strategies of drama or film. And questions about these matters will often lead you to define not only the "facts," but also the feelings central to the design a poem has upon us.

---

2. Pebble-strewn beaches.

SITUATIONS

MARGARET ATWOOD

Siren Song

This is the one song everyone
would like to learn: the song
that is irresistible:

the song that forces men
to leap overboard in squadrons   5
even though they see the beached skulls

the song nobody knows
because anyone who has heard it
is dead, and the others can't remember.

Shall I tell you the secret   10
and if I do, will you get me
out of this bird suit?

I don't enjoy it here
squatting on this island
looking picturesque and mythical   15

with these two feathery maniacs,
I don't enjoy singing
this trio, fatal and valuable.

I will tell the secret to you,
to you, only to you.   20
Come closer. This song

is a cry for help: Help me!
Only you, only you can,
you are unique

at last. Alas   25
it is a boring song
but it works every time.   1974

ANDREW MARVELL

To His Coy Mistress

Had we but world enough, and time,
This coyness,[3] lady, were no crime.
We would sit down, and think which way
To walk, and pass our long love's day.
5   Thou by the Indian Ganges' side
Shouldst rubies[4] find: I by the tide
Of Humber[5] would complain. I would
Love you ten years before the Flood,
And you should if you please refuse
10   Till the conversion of the Jews.[6]
My vegetable love[7] should grow
Vaster than empires, and more slow;
An hundred years should go to praise
Thine eyes, and on thy forehead gaze;
15   Two hundred to adore each breast,
But thirty thousand to the rest.
An age at least to every part,
And the last age should show your heart.
For, lady, you deserve this state;[8]
20   Nor would I love at lower rate.
    But at my back I always hear
Time's wingèd chariot hurrying near;
And yonder all before us lie
Deserts of vast eternity.
25   Thy beauty shall no more be found,
Nor, in thy marble vault, shall sound
My echoing song; then worms shall try
That long preserved virginity,
And your quaint honor turn to dust,
30   And into ashes all my lust:
The grave's a fine and private place,
But none, I think, do there embrace.
    Now therefore, while the youthful hue
Sits on thy skin like morning dew,[9]
35   And while thy willing soul transpires[1]
At every pore with instant fires,

---

3. Hesitancy, modesty (not necessarily suggesting calculation).   4. Talismans that are supposed to preserve virginity.   5. A small river that flows through Marvell's hometown of Hull. *Complain:* write love complaints, conventional songs lamenting the cruelty of love.   6. Which, according to popular Christian belief, will occur just before the end of the world.   7. Which is capable only of passive growth, not of consciousness. The "vegetable soul" is lower than the other two divisions of the soul, "animal" and "rational."   8. Dignity.   9. The text reads "glew." "Lew" (warmth) has also been suggested as an emendation.   1. Breathes forth.

Now let us sport us while we may,
And now, like am'rous birds of prey,
Rather at once our time devour
Than languish in his slow-chapped[2] pow'r.   40
Let us roll all our strength and all
Our sweetness up into one ball,
And tear our pleasures with rough strife
Thorough[3] the iron gates of life.
Thus, though we cannot make our sun   45
Stand still,[4] yet we will make him run.[5]   1681

MARY KARR

Hubris

The man in the next office
was born a dwarf.
Mornings, when we wait
for the elevator, he quotes Whitman,
while I shamelessly covet   5
his gray baseball jacket.
Maybe he doesn't mean
to be a figure of courage
with his cane and his corkscrew knee,
this smart man who can't reach   10
some sinks. No doubt he'd like
to take the stairs like me,
two at a pop. Instead,
as the elevator numbers fail
to fall to us fast enough,   15
he waves me on—*It'll come
eventually,* he says with cheer.
He grows ever smaller
in the stairwell. I ascend.   p. 1996

2. Slow-jawed. Chronos (Time), ruler of the world in early Greek myth, devoured all of his children except Zeus, who was hidden. Later, Zeus seized power (see line 46 and note).   3. Through.   4. To lengthen his night of love with Alcmene, Zeus made the sun stand still.   5. Each sex act was believed to shorten life by one day.

HART CRANE

Episode of Hands

The unexpected interest made him flush.
Suddenly he seemed to forget the pain,—
Consented,—and held out
One finger from the others.

5   The gash was bleeding, and a shaft of sun
That glittered in and out among the wheels,
Fell lightly, warmly, down into the wound.

And as the fingers of the factory owner's son,
That knew a grip for books and tennis
10   As well as one for iron and leather,—
As his taut, spare fingers wound the gauze
Around the thick bed of the wound,
His own hands seemed to him
Like wings of butterflies
15   Flickering in sunlight over summer fields.

The knots and notches,—many in the wide
Deep hand that lay in his,—seemed beautiful.
They were like the marks of wild ponies' play,—
Bunches of new green breaking a hard turf.

20   And factory sounds and factory thoughts
Were banished from him by that larger, quieter hand
That lay in his with the sun upon it.
And as the bandage knot was tightened
The two men smiled into each other's eyes.

1920

EMILY BRONTË

The Night-Wind

In summer's mellow midnight,
A cloudless moon shone through
Our open parlor window
And rosetrees wet with dew.

I sat in silent musing,
5   The soft wind waved my hair:
It told me Heaven was glorious,
And sleeping Earth was fair.

I needed not its breathing
To bring such thoughts to me,   10
But still it whispered lowly,
"How dark the woods will be!

"The thick leaves in my murmur
Are rustling like a dream,
And all their myriad voices   15
Instinct[6] with spirit seem."

I said, "Go, gentle singer,
Thy wooing voice is kind,
But do not think its music
Has power to reach my mind.   20

"Play with the scented flower,
The young tree's supple bough,
And leave my human feelings
In their own course to flow."

The wanderer would not leave me;   25
Its kiss grew warmer still—
"O come," it sighed so sweetly,
"I'll win thee 'gainst thy will.

"Have we not been from childhood friends?
Have I not loved thee long?   30
As long as thou hast loved the night
Whose silence wakes my song.

"And when thy heart is laid at rest
Beneath the church-yard stone
I shall have time enough to mourn   35
And thou to be alone."

September 11, 1840

---

6. Infused.

TIMES

WILLIAM SHAKESPEARE

[*Full many a glorious morning have I seen*]

Full many a glorious morning have I seen
Flatter the mountain-tops with sovereign eye,
Kissing with golden face the meadows green,
Gilding pale streams with heavenly alchymy;
5   Anon permit the basest clouds to ride
With ugly rack[7] on his celestial face,
And from the forlorn world his visage hide,
Stealing unseen to west with this disgrace:
Even so my sun one early morn did shine,
10   With all-triumphant splendor on my brow;
But, out! alack! he was but one hour mine,
The region cloud hath mask'd him from me now.
    Yet him for this my love no whit disdaineth;
    Suns of the world may stain when heaven's sun staineth.   1609

SYLVIA PLATH

Morning Song

Love set you going like a fat gold watch.
The midwife slapped your footsoles, and your bald cry
Took its place among the elements.

Our voices echo, magnifying your arrival. New statue.
5   In a drafty museum, your nakedness
Shadows our safety. We stand round blankly as walls.

I'm no more your mother
Than the cloud that distils a mirror to reflect its own slow
Effacement at the wind's hand.

10   All night your moth-breath
Flickers among the flat pink roses. I wake to listen:
A far sea moves in my ear.

---

7 Moss.

One cry, and I stumble from bed, cow-heavy and floral
In my Victorian nightgown.
Your mouth opens clean as a cat's. The window square   15

Whitens and swallows its dull stars. And now you try
Your handful of notes;
The clear vowels rise like balloons.   1961

AMY CLAMPITT
_____

Meridian

First daylight on the bittersweet-hung
sleeping porch at high summer : dew
all over the lawn, sowing diamond-
point-highlighted shadows :
the hired man's shadow revolving   5
along the walk, a flash of milkpails
passing : no threat in sight, no hint
anywhere in the universe, of that

apathy at the meridian, the noon
of absolute boredom : flies   10
crooning black lullabies in the kitchen,
milk-soured crocks, cream separator
still unwashed : what is there to life
but chores and more chores, dishwater,
fatigue, unwanted children : nothing   15
to stir the longueur of afternoon

except possibly thunderheads :
climbing, livid, turreted alabaster
lit up from within by splendor and terror
—forked lightning's   20
                    split-second disaster.   1985

W. H. AUDEN
_____

As I Walked Out One Evening

As I walked out one evening,
    Walking down Bristol Street,
The crowds upon the pavement
    Were fields of harvest wheat.

And down by the brimming river
   I heard a lover sing
Under an arch of the railway:
   'Love has no ending.

'I'll love you, dear, I'll love you
   Till China and Africa meet,
And the river jumps over the mountain
   And the salmon sing in the street,

'I'll love you till the ocean
   Is folded and hung up to dry
And the seven stars go squawking
   Like geese about the sky.

'The years shall run like rabbits,
   For in my arms I hold
The Flower of the Ages,
   And the first love of the world.'

But all the clocks in the city
   Began to whirr and chime:
'O let not Time deceive you,
   You cannot conquer Time.

'In the burrows of the Nightmare
   Where Justice naked is,
Time watches from the shadow
   And coughs when you would kiss.

'In headaches and in worry
   Vaguely life leaks away,
And Time will have his fancy
   To-morrow or to-day.

'Into many a green valley
   Drifts the appalling snow;
Time breaks the threaded dances
   And the diver's brilliant bow.

'O plunge your hands in water,
   Plunge them in up to the wrist;
Stare, stare in the basin
   And wonder what you've missed.

'The glacier knocks in the cupboard,
   The desert sighs in the bed,
And the crack in the tea-cup opens
   A lane to the land of the dead.

'Where the beggars raffle the banknotes
   And the Giant is enchanting to Jack,
And the Lily-white Boy is a Roarer,
   And Jill goes down on her back.

5

10

15

20

25

30

35

40

45

'O look, look in the mirror,
    O look in your distress;
Life remains a blessing   50
    Although you cannot bless.

'O stand, stand at the window
    As the tears scald and start;
You shall love your crooked neighbour   55
    With your crooked heart.'

It was late, late in the evening,
    The lovers they were gone;
The clocks had ceased their chiming,
    And the deep river ran on.   60

November 1937

PLACES

ANTHONY HECHT

A Hill

In Italy, where this sort of thing can occur,
I had a vision once—though you understand
It was nothing at all like Dante's, or the visions of saints,
And perhaps not a vision at all. I was with some friends,
5   Picking my way through a warm sunlit piazza
In the early morning. A clear fretwork of shadows
From huge umbrellas littered the pavement and made
A sort of lucent shallows in which was moored
A small navy of carts. Books, coins, old maps,
10   Cheap landscapes and ugly religious prints
Were all on sale. The colors and noise
Like the flying hands were gestures of exultation,
So that even the bargaining
Rose to the ear like a voluble godliness.
15   And then, when it happened, the noises suddenly stopped,
And it got darker; pushcarts and people dissolved
And even the great Farnese Palace itself
Was gone, for all its marble; in its place
Was a hill, mole-colored and bare. It was very cold,
20   Close to freezing, with a promise of snow.
The trees were like old ironwork gathered for scrap
Outside a factory wall. There was no wind,
And the only sound for a while was the little click
Of ice as it broke in the mud under my feet.
25   I saw a piece of ribbon snagged on a hedge,
But no other sign of life. And then I heard
What seemed the crack of a rifle. A hunter, I guessed;
At least I was not alone. But just after that
Came the soft and papery crash
30   Of a great branch somewhere unseen falling to earth.

And that was all, except for the cold and silence
That promised to last forever, like the hill.

Then prices came through, and fingers, and I was restored
To the sunlight and my friends. But for more than a week
35   I was scared by the plain bitterness of what I had seen.
All this happened about ten years ago,
And it hasn't troubled me since, but at last, today,
I remembered that hill; it lies just to the left
Of the road north of Poughkeepsie; and as a boy
40   I stood before it for hours in wintertime.   1967

SUSAN MUSGRAVE

I Am Not a Conspiracy
Everything Is Not Paranoid
The Drug Enforcement Administration
Is Not Everywhere

Paul comes from Toronto on Sunday
to photograph me here in my
new image. We drive to a cornfield
where I stand looking uncomfortable.
The corn-god has an Irish accent—   5
I can hear him whispering, "Whiskey!"

And the cows. They, too, are in the
corn, entranced like figures in effigy.
Last summer in Mexico I saw purses at the
market made from unborn calfskin—   10
I've been wondering where they came from
ever since, the soft skins I ran my hands
down over, that made me feel like shuddering.

I was wrong. The corn-god is whispering
"Cocaine!" He is not Irish, after all,   15
but D.E.A. wanting to do business. He
demands to know the names of all my friends,
wants me to tell him who's dealing.

I confess I'm growing restless as the
camera goes on clicking, standing naked in the   20
high-heel shoes I bought last summer in Mexico.
"We want names," say the cows, who suddenly
look malevolent. They are tearing the ears
off the innocent corn. They call it an
investigation.   25

Paul calls to them, "Come here, cows!"
though I don't even want them in the picture.
What Paul sees is something different from
me; my skin feels like shuddering when those
cows run their eyes down over me.   30

"But didn't you smuggle this poem into Canada?"
asks the cow with the mirrored sunglasses.
"As far as we can tell, this is not a
Canadian poem. Didn't you write it
in Mexico?"   35

                                                                    1985

THOMAS GRAY

Elegy Written in a Country Churchyard

The curfew tolls the knell of parting day,
   The lowing herd wind slowly o'er the lea,
The plowman homeward plods his weary way,
   And leaves the world to darkness and to me.

5   Now fades the glimmering landscape on the sight,
   And all the air a solemn stillness holds,
Save where the beetle wheels his droning flight,
   And drowsy tinklings lull the distant folds;

Save that from yonder ivy-mantled tower
10   The moping owl does to the moon complain
Of such, as wandering near her secret bower,
   Molest her ancient solitary reign.

Beneath those rugged elms, that yew tree's shade,
   Where heaves the turf in many a moldering heap,
15   Each in his narrow cell forever laid,
   The rude[8] forefathers of the hamlet sleep.

The breezy call of incense-breathing Morn,
   The swallow twittering from the straw-built shed,
The cock's shrill clarion, or the echoing horn.[9]
20   No more shall rouse them from their lowly bed.

For them no more the blazing hearth shall burn,
   Or busy housewife ply her evening care;
No children run to lisp their sire's return,
   Or climb his knees the envied kiss to share.

25   Oft did the harvest to their sickle yield,
   Their furrow oft the stubborn glebe[1] has broke;
How jocund did they drive their team afield!
   How bowed the woods beneath their sturdy stroke!

Let not Ambition mock their useful toil,
30   Their homely joys, and destiny obscure;
Nor Grandeur hear with a disdainful smile
   The short and simple annals of the poor.

The boast of heraldry,[2] the pomp of power,
   And all that beauty, all that wealth e'er gave,
35   Awaits alike the inevitable hour.
   The paths of glory lead but to the grave.

---

8. Unlearned.   9. The hunter's horn.   1. Soil.   2. Noble birth.

Nor you, ye proud, impute to these the fault,
    If Memory o'er their tomb no trophies[3] raise,
Where through the long-drawn aisle and fretted[4] vault
    The pealing anthem swells the note of praise   40

Can storied urn or animated[5] bust
    Back to its mansion call the fleeting breath?
Can Honor's voice provoke the silent dust,
    Or Flattery soothe the dull cold ear of Death?

Perhaps in this neglected spot is laid   45
    Some heart once pregnant with celestial fire;
Hands that the rod of empire might have swayed,
    Or waked to ecstasy the living lyre.

But Knowledge to their eyes her ample page
    Rich with the spoils of time did ne'er unroll;   50
Chill Penury repressed their noble rage,
    And froze the genial current of the soul.

Full many a gem of purest ray serene,
    The dark unfathomed caves of ocean bear:
Full many a flower is born to blush unseen,   55
    And waste its sweetness on the desert air.

Some village Hampden,[6] that with dauntless breast
    The little tyrant of his fields withstood;
Some mute inglorious Milton here may rest,
    Some Cromwell guiltless of his country's blood.   60

The applause of listening senates to command,
    The threats of pain and ruin to despise,
To scatter plenty o'er a smiling land,
    And read their history in a nation's eyes,

Their lot forbade: nor circumscribed alone   65
    Their growing virtues, but their crimes confined;
Forbade to wade through slaughter to a throne,
    And shut the gates of mercy on mankind,

The struggling pangs of conscious truth to hide,
    To quench the blushes of ingenuous shame,   70
Or heap the shrine of Luxury and Pride
    With incense kindled at the Muse's flame.

Far from the madding crowd's ignoble strife,
    Their sober wishes never learned to stray;

3. An ornamental or symbolic group of figures depicting the achievements of the deceased.   4. Decorated with intersecting lines in relief.   5. Lifelike. *Storied urn:* a funeral urn with an epitaph or pictured story inscribed on it.   6. John Hampden (1594–1643), who, both as a private citizen and as a member of Parliament, zealously defended the rights of the people against the autocratic policies of Charles I.

75   Along the cool sequestered vale of life
            They kept the noiseless tenor of their way.

        Yet even these bones from insult to protect
            Some frail memorial still erected nigh,
        With uncouth rhymes and shapeless sculpture decked,[7]
80   Implores the passing tribute of a sigh.

        Their name, their years, spelt by the unlettered Muse,
            The place of fame and elegy supply:
        And many a holy text around she strews,
            That teach the rustic moralist to die.

85   For who to dumb Forgetfulness a prey,
            This pleasing anxious being e'er resigned,
        Left the warm precincts of the cheerful day,
            Nor cast one longing lingering look behind?

        On some fond breast the parting soul relies,
90   Some pious drops the closing eye requires;
        Even from the tomb the voice of Nature cries,
            Even in our ashes live their wonted fires.

        For thee, who mindful of the unhonored dead
            Dost in these lines their artless tale relate;
95   If chance, by lonely contemplation led,
            Some kindred spirit shall inquire thy fate,

        Haply some hoary-headed swain may say,
            "Oft have we seen him at the peep of dawn
        Brushing with hasty steps the dews away
100   To meet the sun upon the upland lawn.

        "There at the foot of yonder nodding beech
            That wreathes its old fantastic roots so high,
        His listless length at noontide would he stretch,
            And pore upon the brook that babbles by.

105   "Hard by yon wood, now smiling as in scorn,
            Muttering his wayward fancies he would rove,
        Now drooping, woeful wan, like one forlorn,
            Or crazed with care, or crossed in hopeless love.

        "One morn I missed him on the customed hill,
110   Along the heath and near his favorite tree;
        Another came; nor yet beside the rill,
            Nor up the lawn, nor at the wood was he;

        "The next with dirges due in sad array
            Slow through the churchway path we saw him borne.
115   Approach and read (for thou canst read) the lay,
            Graved on the stone beneath yon aged thorn."

---

7. Cf. the "storied urn or animated bust" (line 41) dedicated inside the church to the "proud" (line 37).

The Epitaph

Here rests his head upon the lap of Earth
  A youth to Fortune and to Fame unknown.
Fair Science[8] frowned not on his humble birth,
  And Melancholy marked him for her own.   120

Large was his bounty, and his soul sincere,
  Heaven did a recompense as largely send:
He gave to Misery all he had, a tear,
  He gained from Heaven ('twas all he wished) a friend.

No farther seek his merits to disclose,   125
  Or draw his frailties from their dread abode
(There they alike in trembling hope repose),
  The bosom of his Father and his God.   1751

8. Learning.

COMPARING PLACES AND TIMES: THE SENSE OF CULTURAL OTHERNESS

YVONNE SAPIA

Grandmother, a Caribbean Indian, Described by My Father

Nearly a hundred when she died,
mi viejita[9]
was an open boat,
and I had no map
5 to show her the safe places.
There was much to grieve.
Her shoulders were stooped.
Her hands were never young.
They broke jars
10 at the watering holes,
like bones, like hearts.

When she was a girl,
she was given the island
but no wings.
15 She wanted wings,
though she bruised
like a persimmon.
She was not ruined
before her marriage.
20 But after the first baby died,
she disappeared in the middle
of days to worship
her black saint,
after the second,
25 to sleep with a hand towel
across her eyes.

I had to take care
not to exhume
from the mound of memory
30 these myths, these lost ones.
Born sleek as swans
on her river, my brother,
the man you have met
who has one arm,

9. My little old woman or mother. (YS)

and I glided into the sun.   35
Other children poured forth,
and by the time I was sixteen
I lost my place
in her thatched house.

She let me go,   40
and she did not come to the pier
the day the banana boat
pushed away from her shore
towards Nueva York
where I had heard   45
there would be room for me.   1987

AGHA SHAHID ALI

Postcard from Kashmir

(for Pavan Sahgal)

Kashmir shrinks into my mailbox,
my home a neat four by six inches.

I always loved neatness. Now I hold
the half-inch Himalayas in my hand.

This is home. And this the closest   5
I'll ever be to home. When I return,
the colors won't be so brilliant,
the Jhelum's waters[1] so clean,
so ultramarine. My love
so overexposed.   10

And my memory will be a little
out of focus, in it
a giant negative, black
and white, still undeveloped.   1987

CATHY SONG

Heaven

He thinks when we die we'll go to China.
Think of it—a Chinese heaven
where, except for his blond hair,

---

1. The river Jhelum runs through Kashmir and Pakistan.

the part that belongs to his father,
everyone will look like him.
China, that blue flower on the map,
bluer than the sea
his hand must span like a bridge
to reach it.
An octave away.

I've never seen it.
It's as if I can't sing that far.
But look—
on the map, this black dot.
Here is where we live,
on the pancake plains
just east of the Rockies,
on the other side of the clouds.
A mile above the sea,
the air is so thin, you can starve on it.
No bamboo trees
But the alpine equivalent,
reedy aspen with light, fluttering leaves.
Did a boy in Guangzhou[2] dream of this
as his last stop?

I've heard the trains at night
whistling past our yards,
what we've come to own,
the broken fences, the whiny dog, the rattletrap cars.
It's still the wild west,
mean and grubby,
the shootouts and fistfights in the back alley.
With my son the dreamer
and my daughter, who is too young to walk,
I've sat in this spot
and wondered why here?
Why in this short life,
this town, this creek they call a river?

He had never planned to stay,
the boy who helped to build
the railroads for a dollar a day.[3]
He had always meant to go back.
When did he finally know
that each mile of track led him further away,
that he would die in his sleep,
dispossessed,
having seen Gold Mountain,

2. Usually called Canton, a seaport city in southeastern China.   3. The railroads used immigrant day
labor (most of it Chinese) to lay the tracks in the nineteenth century.

the icy wind tunneling through it,
these landlocked, makeshift ghost towns?

It must be in the blood,   50
this notion of returning.
It skipped two generations, lay fallow,
the garden an unmarked grave.
On a spring sweater day
it's as if we remember him.   55
I call to the children.
We can see the mountains
shimmering blue above the air.
If you look really hard
says my son the dreamer,   60
leaning out from the laundry's rigging,
the work shirts fluttering like sails,
you can see all the way to heaven.   1988

CHITRA BANERJEE DIVAKARUNI

Indian Movie, New Jersey

Not like the white filmstars, all rib
and gaunt cheekbone, the Indian sex-goddess
smiles plumply from behind a flowery
branch. Below her brief red skirt, her thighs
are satisfying-solid, redeeming   5
as tree trunks. She swings her hips
and the men-viewers whistle. The lover-hero
dances in to a song, his lip-sync
a little off, but no matter, we
know the words already and sing along.   10
It is safe here, the day
golden and cool so no one sweats,
roses on every bush and the Dal Lake
clean again.
                    The sex-goddess switches   15
to thickened English to emphasize
a joke. We laugh and clap. Here
we need not be embarrassed by words
dropping like lead pellets into foreign ears.
The flickering movie-light   20
wipes from our faces years of America, sons
who want mohawks and refuse to run
the family store, daughters who date
on the sly.
                    When at the end the hero   25
dies for his friend who also

loves the sex-goddess and now can marry her,
we weep, understanding. Even the men
clear their throats to say, "What *qurbani!*[4]
30   What *dosti!*"[5] After, we mill around
unwilling to leave, exchange greetings
and good news: a new gold chain, a trip
to India. We do not speak
of motel raids, canceled permits, stones
35   thrown through glass windows, daughters and sons
raped by Dotbusters.[6]
        In this dim foyer
we can pull around us the faint, comforting smell
of incense and *pakoras,*[7] can arrange
40   our children's marriages with hometown boys and girls,
open a franchise, win a million
in the mail. We can retire
in India, a yellow two-storied house
with wrought-iron gates, our own
45   Ambassador car. Or at least
move to a rich white suburb, Summerfield
or Fort Lee, with neighbors that will
talk to us. Here while the film-songs still echo
in the corridors and restrooms, we can trust
50   in movie truths: sacrifice, success, love and luck,
the America that was supposed to be.   1990

QUESTIONS

1. In Karr's "Hubris," explain exactly how the narrative sequence works. How (and why) does the speaker's perspective on the "dwarf" change? What does the title mean?

2. In Agha Shahid Ali's "Postcard from Kashmir," how far away from "home" does the speaker seem to be when he receives the postcard? Would the poem be more effective if we knew more specifics about place and how long he had been away from Kashmir? Why or why not?

WRITING SUGGESTIONS

1. Choose one of the poems you've read in this chapter, and try to connect it to an experience in your own life that has helped you to appreciate the poem. Write a page or two explaining how the poem speaks to your particular situation.

2. Consult at least three handbooks of literary terms, and compare their definitions of *aubade* and *aube*. Consider the morning poems by Shakespeare and Plath. Choose *one* of these poems, and analyze how closely it relates to the tradition of morning poems described in the handbooks. Write a short essay (no more than two pages long) in which you explain how the poem achieves its effects by employing and modifying or rejecting the standard expectations of how mornings are to be described in poetry.

---

4. Sacrifice.   5. Friendship.   6. Anti-Indian gangs in New Jersey.   7. Fried appetizers.

STUDENT WRITING

Below is an excerpt from one student's first response to Linda Pastan's "To a Daughter Leaving Home." The student's assignment was similar to Writing Suggestion 1. Note how she asks Pastan questions about meaning as a way of articulating her own response to and questions about the poem.

A Letter to an Author

Kimberly Smith

Dear Linda,

I read your poem "To a Daughter Leaving Home" and it really grabbed my attention. I felt as if I were in your head knowing exactly how you felt when you wrote it. It was a feeling that a father, mother or even a child could understand. I also understand that you were born in New York, as I was. After reading the poem and finding out that we were born in the same place, I felt a connection to you. I came to Tucson from New Jersey and it was a very big culture shock. Knowing you are from the east gave me an easy feeling, a feeling of home.

I can remember back when I learned how to ride a bike. My father gave me the incentive that if I could ride to him without falling, then he would take me out for a lobster dinner. So, I did. I was ten and I got on that bike and peddled away until I could catch my balance and my Dad could let me go. I know now that learning to ride my bike meant more than my father watching me ride down the road. It was a symbol of freedom and growing up. It was time for my parents to let go a little more. I saw that same feeling in your poem also. Is that what you meant? Did you intend the bike image to portray a feeling of growing up and moving along in life?

It seemed to me that you wrote the poem to represent stages of a child's life. The first stage is from the beginning to the line "on two round wheels" (line 6). This stage, I believe, is when a baby is learning to walk and he or she wobbles around until getting the hang of it. The second stage is until the line "sprinted to catch up" (line 14). These are the elementary years and maybe junior high, when the child is trying to be on her own and do things for herself. I can remember this stage very well. I thought that I was at an age where I did not need my parents' help anymore. I used to say, "Mom, I am eleven years old and I am old enough to stay alone. I don't need a baby-sitter." The next stage, which I believe is one of the biggest changes in a child's life, ends at the line "with laughter" (line 20). This stage, to me, is very clearly marked high school. The idea about growing more distant I related to very well. That is because I definitely grew up a lot and learned a lot during high school. I got a car and finally felt like an individual, with her own mind. I was able to make my own decisions which was very important to me.

The language you have chosen is very simple, just like the stages of a child's life. Your sentences are short and to the point. I believe that you arranged the poem in the way you did to show a balance. The arrangement of the poem on paper is straight, just like a bike ride and just as parents want their child's life to be. I believe that you chose your words very carefully. For example, "thud" (line 12) has a deep and powerful meaning. It coincides with the last word of the poem, "goodbye" (line 24). Thud is a very final word as if you fell and you heard a big thud. "Goodbye" (line 24) has that same meaning here. You get a feeling of the end instead of just a new beginning. That is what I felt when I read those words. Did you intend to show that same connection between the words "thud" (line 12) and "goodbye" (line 24) that I saw?

There is one impression that I am getting from you in your poem that I do not agree with. I am not sure if you are intending this, but I got the feeling that you have the idea that as children go farther away that they become more fragile. That may be true in some cases, but if children are brought up in an environment that they are held in a glass box all of their life, then, in that case, it is definitely about time that they moved out on their own. Everyone is going to make mistakes but they only mean something if you can fix them yourself. I always tell my father that I appreciate his advice but sometimes I need to figure things out on my own and that making mistakes is all about growing up.

 I learned a lot from your poem. I hope you enjoy my comments and feelings.

Yours truly,

Kimberly Smith

16

LANGUAGE

Fiction and drama depend upon language just as poetry does, but in a poem almost everything comes down to the particular meanings and implications of individual words. In stories and plays, we are likely to keep our attention primarily on character and plot—what is happening in front of us or in the action as we imagine it in our minds—and although words are crucial to how we imagine the characters and how we respond to what happens to them, we are not as likely to pause over any one word as we may need to in a poem. Because poems often are short and use only a few words, a lot depends on every single one. Poetry sometimes feels like prose that is distilled: only the most essential words are there. Just barely enough is said to communicate in the most basic way, using the most elemental signs of meaning and feeling—and each chosen for exactly the right shade of meaning. But elemental does not necessarily mean simple, and these signs may be very rich in their meanings and complex in their effects.

PRECISION AND AMBIGUITY

Let's look first at poems that create some of their most important effects by examining—or playing with—a single word. Often multiple meanings of a word or its shiftiness and uncertainty are at issue. Here, for example, is a short poem that depends almost entirely on the way we think about the word *play.* It was written by a writer traveling through the American South early in the twentieth century when she saw a textile mill, which then employed quite young children, right next to a golf course.

SARAH CLEGHORN

[*The golf links lie so near the mill*]

The golf links lie so near the mill
That almost every day
The laboring children can look out
And see the men at play.

p. 1915

The poem doesn't *say* that we expect men to work and children to play; it just assumes our expectation and builds an effect of **dramatic irony**—an incongruity between what we expect and what actually occurs—out of the observation. Almost all of the poem's devastating effect is saved for the final word, after the situation has been carefully described and the irony set up.

The following two poems depend on the ambiguity of a word used over and over to illustrate its refusal to be pinned down to a single meaning.

ANNE FINCH, COUNTESS OF WINCHELSEA

There's No To-Morrow

A Fable imitated from Sir Roger L'Estrange

Two long had Lov'd, and now the Nymph desir'd,
The Cloak of Wedlock, as the Case requir'd;
Urg'd that, the Day he wrought her to this Sorrow,
He Vow'd, that he wou'd marry her To-Morrow.
Agen he Swears, to shun the present Storm,   5
That he, To-Morrow, will that Vow perform.
The Morrows in their due Successions came;
Impatient still on Each, the pregnant Dame
Urg'd him to keep his Word, and still he swore the same.
When tir'd at length, and meaning no Redress,   10
But yet the Lye not caring to confess,
He for his Oath this Salvo chose to borrow,
That he was Free, since there was no To-Morrow;
For when it comes in Place to be employ'd,
'Tis then To-Day; To-Morrow's ne'er enjoy'd.   15
The Tale's a Jest, the Moral is a Truth;
To-Morrow and To-Morrow, cheat our Youth:
In riper Age, To-Morrow still we cry,
Not thinking, that the present Day we Dye;
Unpractis'd all the Good we had Design'd;   20
There's No To-Morrow to a Willing Mind.   1713

CHARLES BERNSTEIN

Of Time and the Line

George Burns[1] likes to insist that he always
takes the straight lines; the cigar in his mouth

---

1. American comedian (1896–1996), who played straight man to his wife, Gracie Allen.

is a way of leaving space between the
lines for a laugh. He weaves lines together
by means of a picaresque narrative;
not so Hennie Youngman,[2] whose lines are strictly paratactic. My father pushed a
line of ladies' dresses—not down the street
in a pushcart but upstairs in a fact'ry
office. My mother has been more concerned
with her hemline. Chairman Mao[3] put forward
Maoist lines, but that's been abandoned (mostly) for the East-West line of malarkey
so popular in these parts. The prestige
of the iambic line has recently
suffered decline, since it's no longer so
clear who "I" am, much less who *you* are. When
making a line, better be double sure
what you're lining in & what you're lining
out & which side of the line you're on; the
world is made up so (Adam didn't so much
name as delineate). Every poem's got
a prosodic lining, some of which will
unzip for summer wear. The lines of an
imaginary are inscribed on the
social flesh by the knifepoint of history.
Nowadays, you can often spot a work
of poetry by whether it's in lines
or no; if it's in prose, there's a good chance
it's a poem. While there is no lesson in
the line more useful than that of the picket line, the line that has caused the most adversity is the bloodline. In Russia
everyone is worried about long lines;
back in the USA, it's strictly soup-
lines. "Take a chisel to write," but for an
actor a line's got to be cued. Or, as
they say in math, it takes two lines to make
an angle but only one lime to make
a Margarita.   1991

The Finch poem repeatedly explores the shifting sands of the word "to-morrow," first noting how different people may think of its meanings differently, then showing how its ambiguity is anchored in time and the whole process of meaning. The Bernstein poem finds a great variety of completely different meanings of the word "line." How many different meanings can you distinguish in the poem? What does "Time" (in the title) have to do with the poem?

2. American comedian (b. 1906).   3. Mao Zedong (1893–1976), leader of the revolution that established China as a communist nation.

Here is a far more personal and emotional poem that uses a single word, "terminal," to explore the changing relationship between two people—a father (who speaks the poem) and daughter.

YVOR WINTERS

At the San Francisco Airport

to my daughter, 1954

This is the terminal: the light
Gives perfect vision, false and hard;
The metal glitters, deep and bright.
Great planes are waiting in the yard—
They are already in the night.   5

And you are here beside me, small,
Contained and fragile, and intent
On things that I but half recall—
Yet going whither you are bent.
I am the past, and that is all.   10

But you and I in part are one:
The frightened brain, the nervous will,
The knowledge of what must be done,
The passion to acquire the skill
To face that which you dare not shun.   15

The rain of matter upon sense
Destroys me momently. The score:
There comes what will come. The expense
Is what one thought, and something more—
One's being and intelligence.   20

This is the terminal, the break.
Beyond this point, on lines of air,
You take the way that you must take;
And I remain in light and stare—
In light, and nothing else, awake.   25

1954

The key word here is chosen because it can mean more than one thing; in this case, the importance of the word involves its **ambiguity** (an ability to mean more than one thing) rather than its **precision** (exactness).

The several possible meanings of a single word are probed soberly and thoughtfully. What does it *mean* to be in a place called a "terminal"? the poem asks. As the parting of father and daughter is explored carefully, the place of parting and the means of transportation begin to take on meanings larger than their simple referential ones. The poem is full of contrasts—young and old, light and dark, past and present, security and adventure. The father ("I am the past," line 10) remains in the light, among known objects and experience familiar to his many years; the daughter is about to depart into the night, the unknown, the uncertain future. But they both share a sense of the necessity of the parting, of the need for the daughter to mature, gain knowledge, acquire experience. Is she going off to school? to college? to her first job? We don't know, but her plane ride clearly means a new departure and a clean break with childhood, dependency, the past.

So much depends upon the word "terminal." It refers to the airport building, of course, but it also implies a boundary, an extremity, a terminus, something that is limited, a junction, a place where a connection may be broken. Important as well is the unambiguous meaning of certain words, that is, what these other words **denote.** The final stanza is articulated flatly, as if the speaker has recovered from the momentary confusion of stanza 4, when "being and intelligence" are lost in the emotion of the parting itself. The words "break," "point," "way," and "remain" are almost unemotional and colorless; they do not make value judgments or offer personal views, but rather define and describe. The sharp articulation of the last stanza stresses the **denotations** of the words employed. It is as if the speaker is trying to disengage himself from the emotion of the situation and just give the facts.

Words, however, are more than hard blocks of meaning on whose sense everyone agrees. They also have a more personal side, and they carry emotional force and shades of suggestion. The words we use indicate not only what we mean but how we feel about it, and we choose words that we hope will engage others emotionally and persuasively, in conversation and daily usage as well as in poems. A person who holds office is, quite literally (and unemotionally), an "officeholder," a word that clearly denotes what he or she does. But if we want to convince someone that an officeholder is wise, trustworthy, and deserving of political support we may call that person a "civil servant," a "political leader," or an "elected official," whereas if we want to promote distrust or contempt of officeholders we might call them "politicians" or "bureaucrats" or "political hacks." These latter words have clear **connotations**—suggestions of emotional coloration that imply our attitude and invite a similar one on the part of our hearers. What words **connote** can be just as important to a poem as what they denote, although some poems depend primarily on denotation and some more on connotation.

> *A poet is, before anything else, a person who is passionately in love with language.*
>
> —W. H. AUDEN

"At the San Francisco Airport" seems to depend primarily on denotation; the speaker tries to *specify* the meanings and implications of the parting with his daughter, and his tendency to split categories neatly for the two of them at first contributes to the sense of clarity and certainty which the speaker wants to project. He is the past (line 10) and what remains (line 24); he has age and experience, his life is the known quantity, he stands in the light. She, on the other hand, is committed to the adventure of going into the night; she seems small, fragile, and her identity exists in the uncertain future. Yet the connotations of some words carry strong emotional force as well as clear definition: that the daughter seems "small" and "fragile" to the speaker suggests his fear for her, something quite different from her sense of adventure. The neat, clean categories keep breaking down, and the speaker's feelings keep showing through. In stanza 1, the speaker tells us that the light in the terminal gives "perfect vision," but he also notices, indirectly, its artificial quality: it is "false" and "hard," suggesting the limits of the rationalism he tries to maintain. That artificial light shines over most of the poem and honors the speaker's effort, but the whole poem represents his struggle, and in stanza 4 the signals of disturbance are very strong as, despite an insistence on a vocabulary of calculation, his rational facade collapses completely. If we have observed his verbal strategies carefully, we should not be surprised to find him at the end just *staring* in the artificial light, merely awake, although the poem has shown him to be unconsciously awake to much more than he will candidly admit.

"At the San Francisco Airport" is an unusually intricate and complicated poem, and it offers us, if we are willing to examine precisely its carefully crafted fabric, rich insight into how complex it is to be human and to have human feelings and foibles when we think we must be rational machines. But connotations can work more simply. The following epitaph, for example, even though it describes the mixed feelings one person has about another, depends heavily on the common connotations of fairly common words.

WALTER DE LA MARE

Slim Cunning Hands

Slim cunning hands at rest, and cozening eyes—
Under this stone one loved too wildly lies;
How false she was, no granite could declare;
    Nor all earth's flowers, how fair.   1950

What the speaker in "Slim Cunning Hands" remembers about the dead woman—her hands, her eyes—tells part of the story; her physical presence was clearly important to him, and the poem's other nouns—stone, granite, flowers—all remind us of her death and its finality. All these words denote objects having to do with rituals that memorialize a departed life. Granite and stone connote finality as well, and flowers connote fragility and suggest the shortness of life (which is why they have become the symbolic language of funerals). The way the speaker talks about the woman expresses, in just a few words, the complexity of his love for her. She was loved, he says, too "wildly"—by him perhaps, and apparently by others. The excitement she offered is suggested by the word, and also the lack of control. The words "cunning" and "cozening" help us interpret both her wildness and falsity; they suggest her calculation, cleverness, and untrustworthiness as well as her skill, persuasiveness, and ability to please. And the word "fair," a simple yet very inclusive word, suggests how totally attractive the speaker finds her: her beauty is just as incapable of being expressed by flowers as her fickleness is of being expressed in something as permanent as stone. But the word "fair," in the emphatic position as the final word, also implies two other meanings that seem to resonate, ironically with what we have already learned about her from the speaker: "impartial" and "just." "Impartial" she may be in her preferences (as the word "false" suggests), but to the speaker she is hardly "just," and the final defining word speaks both to her appearance and (ironically) to her character. Simple words here tell us perhaps all we need to know of a long story— or at least the speaker's version of it.

Words like "fair" and "cozening" are clearly loaded; they imply more emotionally than they literally mean. They have strong, clear connotations and tell us what to think, what evaluation to make, and they suggest the basis for the evaluation. Both words in the title of the following poem similarly turn out to be key ones in its meaning and effect:

PAT MORA

Gentle Communion

Even the long-dead are willing to move.
Without a word, she came with me from the desert.
Mornings she wanders through my rooms
making beds, folding socks.

5   Since she can't hear me anymore,
Mamande[4] ignores the questions I never knew
to ask, about her younger days, her red
hair, the time she fell and broke her nose
in the snow. I will never know.

10   When I try to make her laugh,
to disprove her sad album face, she leaves
the room, resists me as she resisted
grinning for cameras, make-up, English.

While I write, she sits and prays,
15   feet apart, legs never crossed,
the blue housecoat buttoned high
as her hair dries white, girlish
around her head and shoulders.

She closes her eyes, bows her head,
20   and like a child presses her hands together,
her patient flesh steeple, the skin
worn, like the pages of her prayer book.

Sometimes I sit in her wide-armed
chair as I once sat in her lap.
25   Alone, we played a quiet I Spy.
She peeled grapes I still taste.

She removes the thin skin, places
the luminous coolness on my tongue.
I know not to bite or chew. I wait
30   for the thick melt,
our private green honey.   1991

4. A child's conflation of *mama grande* (Spanish for "grandmother").

Neither of the words in the title appears in the text itself, but both resonate throughout the poem. "Communion" is the more powerful of the words; here, it comes to imply the close ritualized relationship between the speaker and "Mamande." Mamande has long been dead but now returns, recalling to the speaker a host of memories and providing a sense of history and family identity. To the speaker, the reunion has a powerful value, reminding her of rituals, habits, and beliefs that "place" her and affirm her heritage. The past is strong in the speaker's mind and in the poem. Many details are recalled from album photographs—the blue housecoat (line 16), the sad face (line 11), the white hair that was once red (lines 7–8 and 17), the posture at prayer (lines 19–22), the big chair (lines 23–24), the plain old-fashioned style (line 13)—and the speaker's childhood memories fade into them as she recalls a specific intimate moment.

The full effect of the word "communion"—which describes an intimate moment of union and a ritual—comes only in the final lines when the speaker remembers the secret of the grapes and recalls their sensuous feel and taste. The moment brings together the experience of different generations and cultures and represents a sacred sharing: the Spanish grandmother had resisted English, modernity, and show (line 13), and the speaker is a poet, writing (and publishing) in English, but the two have a common "private" (line 31) moment ritually shared and forever memorable. At the end, too, the full sense of "gentle" becomes evident—a word that sums up the softness, quietness, and understatedness of the experience, the personal qualities of "Mamande," and the unpretentious but dignified social level of the family heritage. Throughout the text, other words—ordinary, simple, and precise—are chosen with equal care to suggest the sense of personal dignity, revealed identity, and verbal power that the speaker comes to accept as her own. Look especially at the words "move" (line 1), "steeple" (line 21), and "luminous" (line 28).

In the two poems that follow we can readily see why the specific words are chosen because, although both poems express a male preference for the same sort of feminine appearance, the grounds of appeal are vastly different.

BEN JONSON

Still to Be Neat[5]

Still[6] to be neat, still to be dressed,
As you were going to a feast;
Still to be powdered, still perfumed;
Lady, it is to be presumed,
Though art's hid causes are not found,   5
All is not sweet, all is not sound.

Give me a look, give me a face
That makes simplicity a grace;
Robes loosely flowing, hair as free;
Such sweet neglect more taketh me   10

5. A song from Jonson's play *The Silent Woman* (1609–1610).   6. Continually.

Than all th' adulteries of art.
They strike mine eyes, but not my heart.   1609

ROBERT HERRICK

Delight in Disorder

A sweet disorder in the dress
Kindles in clothes a wantonness.
A lawn[7] about the shoulders thrown
Into a fine distractiön;
5   An erring lace, which here and there
Enthralls the crimson stomacher,[8]
A cuff neglectful, and thereby
Ribbands[9] to flow confusedly;
A winning wave, deserving note,
10   In the tempestuous petticoat;
A careless shoestring, in whose tie
I see a wild civility;
Do more bewitch me than when art
Is too precise[1] in every part.   1648

The poem "Still to Be Neat" begins by describing a woman who looks too neat and orderly; she seems too perfect to be believed, the speaker says, and he has to assume that there is a reason for such overly fastidious grooming, that she is covering up something. He worries that something is wrong underneath—that not all is "sweet" and "sound." "Sweet" could mean several things; its meaning becomes clearer when it is repeated in the next stanza in a more specific context. "Sound" begins to suggest the speaker's moral earnestness: it is a strong word, implying a suspicion that something is deeply wrong.

When "sweet" is repeated in line 10, it has taken on specific attributes from what the speaker has said about things he likes in a less calculated physical appearance. Now it appears to mean easy, attractive, unpremeditated. And when the speaker springs "adulteries" on us in the next line as a description of the woman's cosmeticizing, it is clear what he fears—that the appearance of the too neat, too made-up woman covers moral flaws, that she is trying to appear as someone she is not. "Adulteries" suggests the addition of something foreign, something unlike her own nature, and it is a strong, disapproving word. The "soundness" he had worried about involves her integrity; his objection is certainly moral, probably sexual. He wants a woman to be simple and chaste; he wants women to be just what they seem to be.

---

7. Scarf of fine linen.   8. Ornamental covering for the breasts.   9. Ribbons.   1. In the sixteenth and seventeenth centuries, Puritans were often called Precisians because of their fastidiousness.

The speaker in "Delight in Disorder" wants his women easy and simple too, but for different reasons. He finds disorder "sweet" (line 1), and seems almost to be answering the first speaker, providing a different rationale for artless appearance. His grounds of preference are clear early: his support of "wantonness" (line 2) is close to the opposite in its moral suppositions of the first speaker's disapproval of "adulteries." This speaker wants a careless look because he thinks it's sexy, and many of the words he chooses suggest sensuality and availability: "distraction" (line 4), "erring" (line 5), "tempestuous" (line 10), "wild" (line 12). The speakers in the two poems read informality of dress very differently and have very different expectations of the person who dresses in a particular way. We find out quite a lot about each speaker. Their common subject allows us to see clearly how different they are, and how what one sees is in the eye of the beholder, how values and assumptions are built into the words one chooses even for description. Jonson has created a speaker who wants an informally clad woman who has a natural grace and ease of manner because she is confident of herself, dependable, and chaste. Herrick has created a speaker who finds informality of dress fetching and sexy and indicative of sensuality and availability.

Words are the starting point for all poetry, and almost every word is likely to be significant, either denotatively, connotatively, or both. Poets who know their craft pick each word with care to express exactly what needs to be expressed and to suggest every emotional shade that the poem is calculated to evoke in us. Often individual words qualify and amplify one another—suggestions clarify other suggestions, and meanings grow upon meanings—and thus the way the words are put together can be important, too. Notice, for example, that in "Slim Cunning Hands" the final emphasis is on how *fair* in appearance the woman was; the speaker's last word describes the quality he can't forget in spite of her lack of a different kind of fairness and his distrust of her, the quality that, even though it doesn't justify everything else, mitigates all the disappointment and hurt.

That word does not stand all by itself, however, any more than any other word in a poem can be considered all alone. Every word exists within larger units of meaning— sentences, patterns of comparisons and contrasts, the whole poem—and where the word is and how it is used are often important. The final word or words may be especially emphatic (as in "Slim Cunning Hands"), and words that are repeated take on a special intensity, as "terminal" does in "At the San Francisco Airport" or as "chartered" and "cry" do in "London" (p. 626). Certain words often stand out, because they are used in an unusual way (like "chartered" in "London" or "adulteries" in "Still to Be Neat") or because they are given an artificial prominence—through unusual sentence structure, for example, or because the title calls special attention to them.

Sometimes word choice in poems is less dramatic and less obviously "significant" but equally important. Simple appropriateness is often, in fact, what makes the words in a poem work, and when words do not call special attention to themselves they are sometimes the most effective. Precision of denotation may be just as impressive and productive of specific effects as the resonance or ambiguous suggestiveness of connotation. Often poems achieve their power by a combination of verbal effects, setting off elaborate figures of speech (which we will discuss shortly) or other complicated strategies with simple words chosen to mark exact actions, moments, or states of mind. Notice, for example, how carefully the following poem produces its complex description of emotional patterns by delineating precise stages (which are then elaborated) of feeling.

EMILY DICKINSON

[*After great pain, a formal feeling comes*—]

After great pain, a formal feeling comes—
The Nerves sit ceremonious, like Tombs—
The stiff Heart questions was it He, that bore,
And Yesterday, or Centuries before?

5 The Feet, mechanical, go round—
Of Ground, or Air, or Ought—
A Wooden way
Regardless grown,
A Quartz contentment, like a stone—

10 This is the Hour of Lead—
Remembered, if outlived,
As Freezing Persons recollect the Snow—
First—Chill—then Stupor—then the letting go—

ca. 1862

In the following poem, notice how the title calls upon us to wonder, from the beginning, how playful and how patterned the boy's bedtime romp with his father is. As you read it, try to be conscious of the emotional effects created by the choice of words that seem to be key ones. Which words establish the bond between the two males?

THEODORE ROETHKE

My Papa's Waltz

The whiskey on your breath
Could make a small boy dizzy;
But I hung on like death:
Such waltzing was not easy.

5 We romped until the pans
Slid from the kitchen shelf;
My mother's countenance
Could not unfrown itself.

The hand that held my wrist
10 Was battered on one knuckle;
At every step you missed
My right ear scraped a buckle.

You beat time on my head
With a palm caked hard by dirt,
Then waltzed me off to bed   15
Still clinging to your shirt.   1948

Exactly what is the situation in "My Papa's Waltz"? What are the economic circumstances in the family? How can you tell? What indications are there of the family's social
class? of the father's line of work? How would you characterize the speaker? How does
the poem indicate his pleasure in the bedtime ritual? Which words suggest the boy's
excitement? Which suggest his anxiety? How can you tell how the speaker feels about
his father? What clues are there about what the mother is like? How can you tell that
the experience is remembered at some years' distance? What clues are there in the word
choice that an adult is remembering a childhood experience? How scared was the boy
at the time? How does the grown adult now evaluate his emotions when he was a boy?
In what sense is the poem a tribute to memories of the father? How would you describe
the poem's tone?

The subtlety and force of word choice is sometimes very much affected by **word
order,** the way the sentences are put together. Sometimes poems are driven to unusual
word order because of the demands of rhyme and meter, but ordinarily poets use word
order very much as prose writers do, to create a particular emphasis. When an unusual
word order is used, you can be pretty sure that something there merits special attention.
Notice the odd constructions in the second and third stanzas of "My Papa's Waltz"—
the way the speaker talks about the abrasion of buckle on ear in line 12, for example.
He does not say that the buckle scraped his ear, but rather puts it the other way round—
a big difference in the kind of effect created, for it avoids placing blame and refuses to
specify any unpleasant effect. Had he said that the buckle scraped his ear—the normal
way of putting it—we would have to worry about the fragile ear. The **syntax** (sentence
structure) of the poem channels our feeling and helps to control what we think of the
"waltz."

The most curious part of the poem is the second stanza, for it is there that the silent
mother appears, and the syntax there is peculiar in two places. In lines 5–6, the connection between the romping and the pans falling is stated oddly: "We romped *until* the
pans / Slid from the kitchen shelf." The speaker does not say that they knocked down
the pans or imply that there was awkwardness, but he does suggest energetic activity
and duration. He implies intensity, almost design—as though the romping would not be
complete until the pans fell. And the sentence about the mother—odd but effective—
makes her position clear. She is a silent bystander in this male ritual, and her frown
seems molded on her face. It is not as if she is frightened or angry, but as if she, too, is
performing a ritual, holding a frown on her face as if it is part of her role in the ritual, as
well as perhaps a facet of her stern character. The syntax implies that she *has to* maintain
the frown, and the falling of the pans almost seems to be for her benefit. She disapproves, but she is still their audience.

Sometimes poems create, as well, a powerful sense of the way minds and emotions
work by varying normal syntactical order in special ways. Listen, for example, in the
following poem to the speaker's sudden loss of vocal control in the midst of what seems
to be a calm analysis of her feelings about sexual behavior.

SHARON OLDS

Sex without Love

How do they do it, the ones who make love
without love? Beautiful as dancers,
gliding over each other like ice-skaters
over the ice, fingers hooked
5   inside each other's bodies, faces
red as steak, wine, wet as the
children at birth whose mothers are going to
give them away. How do they come to the
come to the   come to the   God   come to the
10   still waters, and not love
the one who came there with them, light
rising slowly as steam off their joined
skin? These are the true religious,
the purists, the pros, the ones who will not
15   accept a false Messiah, love the
priest instead of the God. They do not
mistake the lover for their own pleasure,
they are like great runners: they know they are alone
with the road surface, the cold, the wind,
20   the fit of their shoes, their over-all cardio-
vascular health—just factors, like the partner
in the bed, and not the truth, which is the
single body alone in the universe
against its own best time.   1984

The poem starts calmly enough, with a simple rhetorical question implying that the speaker just cannot understand sex without love. The second through fourth lines compare such sexual activity with some distant aesthetic, with two carefully delineated examples, and the speaker—although plainly disapproving—seems coolly, almost chillingly, in control of the analysis and evaluation. But by the end of the fourth line, something begins to seem odd: "hooked" seems too ugly and extreme a way to characterize the lovers' fingers, however much the speaker may disapprove, and by line 6, the syntax seems to break down. How does "wine" fit the syntax of the line? Is it parallel with "steak," another example of redness? or is it somehow related to the last part of the sentence, parallel with "faces"? But neither of these possibilities quite works. At best, the punctuation is faulty; at worst the speaker's mind is working too fast for the language it can generate, scrambling its images. We can't yet be quite sure what is going on, but by the ninth line the lack of control is manifest with the compulsive repeating (three times) of "come to the" and the interjected "God."

Such verbal behavior—here concretized by the way the poem orders its words— invites us to reevaluate the speaker's moralism relative to her emotional involvement with the issues and with her representation of sexuality itself. The speaker's values, as well as those who have sex without love, become a subject for evaluation.

Words are the basic building materials of poetry. They are of many kinds and are used in many different ways and in different—sometimes surprising—combinations. Words are seldom simple or transparent, even when we know their meanings and recognize their syntax as ordinary and conventional. The careful examination of them individually and collectively is a crucial part of the process of reading poems, and learning exactly what kinds of questions to ask about the words that poems use and how poems use them is one of the most basic—and rewarding—skills a reader of poetry can develop.

Here is a group of poems illustrating varieties of word usages and word orders. The discussion of language continues later in this chapter with an explanation of figures of speech.

GERARD MANLEY HOPKINS

Pied Beauty[2]

Glory be to God for dappled things—
   For skies of couple-color as a brinded[3] cow;
     For rose-moles all in stipple[4] upon trout that swim;
Fresh-firecoal chestnut-falls;[5] finches' wings;
   Landscape plotted and pieced—fold, fallow, and plow;   5
     And all trades, their gear and tackle and trim.
All things counter, original, spare, strange;
   Whatever is fickle, freckled (who knows how?)
     With swift, slow; sweet, sour; adazzle, dim;
He fathers-forth whose beauty is past change: 10
   Praise him.   1877

MARY OLIVER

Morning

Salt shining behind its glass cylinder.
Milk in a blue bowl. The yellow linoleum.
The cat stretching her black body from the pillow.
The way she makes her curvaceous response to the small, kind gesture.
Then laps the bowl clean.   5
Then wants to go out into the world
where she leaps lightly and for no apparent reason across the lawn,
then sits, perfectly still, in the grass.

2. Particolored beauty: having patches or sections of more than one color.   3. Streaked or spotted.   4. Rose-colored dots or flecks.   5. Fallen chestnuts as red as burning coals.

10

I watch her a little while, thinking:
what more could I do with wild words?
I stand in the cold kitchen, bowing down to her.
I stand in the cold kitchen, everything wonderful around me.   1992

WILLIAM CARLOS WILLIAMS

The Red Wheelbarrow

so much depends
upon

a red wheel
barrow

5

glazed with rain
water

beside the white
chickens.   1923

E. E. CUMMINGS

[in Just-][6]

in Just-
spring   when the world is mud-
luscious the little
lame balloonman

5

whistles   far   and wee

and eddieandbill come
running from marbles and
piracies and it's
spring

10

when the world is puddle-wonderful

the queer
old balloonman whistles
far   and   wee
and bettyandisbel come dancing

15

from hop-scotch and jump-rope and
it's
spring

6. The first poem in the series *Chansons innocentes*.

and
the
goat-footed   20
balloonMan   whistles
far
and
wee[7]   1923

RICHARD ARMOUR

Hiding Place

*A speaker at a meeting of the New York State Frozen Food Locker
Association declared that the best hiding place in event of an
atomic explosion is a frozen-food locker, where "radiation will not
penetrate."[8]*

—NEWS ITEM

Move over, ham
   And quartered cow,
My Geiger says
   The time is now.

Yes, now I lay me   5
   Down to sleep,
And if I die,
   At least I'll keep.   1954

OGDEN NASH

Reflections on Ice-Breaking

Candy
Is dandy
But liquor
Is quicker.[9]   1929

---

7. Pan, whose Greek name means "everything," is traditionally represented with a syrinx (or the pipes of Pan). The upper half of his body is human, the lower half goat, and as the father of Silenus he is associated with the spring rites of Dionysus.   8. Before home freezers became popular, many Americans rented lockers in specially equipped commercial buildings.   9. Nash later is said to have proposed two more lines: "Pot / Is not."

EMILY DICKINSON

[*I dwell in Possibility—*]

I dwell in Possibility—
A fairer House than Prose—
More numerous of Windows—
Superior—for Doors—

5   Of Chambers as the Cedars—
Impregnable of Eye—
And for an Everlasting Roof
The Gambrels[1] of the Sky—

Of Visitors—the fairest—
10   For Occupation—This—
The spreading wide my narrow Hands
To gather Paradise—

ca. 1862

1. Roofs with double slopes.

METAPHOR AND SIMILE

The language of poetry is almost always visual and pictorial. Rather than depending primarily on abstract ideas and elaborate reasoning, poems depend mainly upon concrete and specific words that create images in our minds. Poems thus help us to see things fresh and new, or to feel them suggestively through our other physical senses, such as hearing or touch. But, most often, poetry uses the sense of sight in that it helps us form, in our minds, visual impressions, images that communicate more directly than concepts. We "see" yellow leaves on a branch, a father and son waltzing precariously, or two lovers sitting together on the bank of a stream, so that our response begins from a vivid impression of exactly what is happening. Some people think that those media and arts that challenge the imagination of a hearer or reader—radio drama, for example, or poetry—allow us to respond more fully than those (such as television or theater) that actually show things more fully to our physical senses. Certainly they leave more to our imagination, to our mind's eye.

But being visual does not just mean describing, telling us facts, indicating shapes, colors, and specific details and giving us precise discriminations through exacting verbs, nouns, adverbs, and adjectives. Often the vividness of the picture in our minds depends upon comparisons. What we are trying to imagine is pictured in terms of something else familiar to us, and we are asked to think of one thing as if it were something else. Many such comparisons, or **figures of speech,** in which something is pictured or figured forth in terms of something already familiar to us, are taken for granted in daily life. Things we can't see or that aren't familiar to us are imaged as things we already know; for example, God is said to be like a father, Italy is said to be shaped like a boot, life is compared to a forest, a journey, or a sea. When the comparison is explicit—that is, when one thing is directly compared to something else—the figure is called a **simile.** When the comparison is implicit, with something described as if it were something else, it is called a **metaphor.**

Poems use **figurative language** much of the time. A poem may insist that death is like a sunset or sex like an earthquake or that the way to imagine how it feels to be spiritually secure is to think of the way a shepherd takes care of his sheep. The pictorialness of our imagination may *clarify* things for us—scenes, states of mind, ideas—but at the same time it stimulates us to think of how those pictures make us *feel*. Pictures, even when they are mental pictures or imagined visions, may be both denotative and connotative, just as individual words are: they may clarify and make precise, and they may channel our feelings.

In the poem that follows, the poet helps us to visualize the old age and approaching death of the speaker by making comparisons with familiar things—the coming of winter, the approach of sunset, and the dying embers of a fire.

WILLIAM SHAKESPEARE

[*That time of year thou mayst in me behold*]

That time of year thou mayst in me behold
When yellow leaves, or none, or few, do hang

Upon those boughs which shake against the cold,
Bare ruined choirs, where late the sweet birds sang.
5   In me thou see'st the twilight of such day
As after sunset fadeth in the west;
Which by and by[2] black night doth take away,
Death's second self,[3] that seals up all in rest.
In me thou see'st the glowing of such fire,
10   That on the ashes of his youth doth lie,
As the deathbed whereon it must expire,
Consumed with that which it was nourished by.
This thou perceiv'st, which makes thy love more strong,
To love that well which thou must leave ere long.   1609

The first four lines of "That time of year" evoke images of the late autumn; but notice that the poet does not have the speaker say directly that his physical condition and age make him resemble autumn. He draws the comparison without stating that it is a comparison: you can see, he says, my own state in the coming of winter, when the leaves are almost all off the trees. The speaker portrays himself *indirectly* by talking about the passing of the year. The poem uses metaphor; that is, one thing is pictured *as if* it were something else. "That time of year" goes on to another metaphor in lines 5–8 and still another in lines 9–12, and each of the metaphors contributes to our understanding of the speaker's sense of his old age and approaching death. More important, however, is the way the metaphors give us feelings, an emotional sense of the speaker's age and of his own attitude toward aging. Through the metaphors we come to understand, appreciate, and to some extent share the increasing sense of anxiety and urgency that the poem expresses. Our emotional sense of the poem is largely influenced by the way each metaphor is developed and by the way each metaphor leads, with its own kind of internal logic, to another.

The images of late autumn in the first four lines all suggest loneliness, loss, and nostalgia for earlier times. As in the rest of the poem, our eyes are imagined to be the main vehicle for noticing the speaker's age and condition; the phrase "thou mayst in me behold" (line 1) introduces what we are asked to see, and in both lines 5 and 9 we are similarly told "In me thou see'st. . . ." The picture of the trees shedding their leaves suggests that autumn is nearly over, and we can imagine trees either with yellow leaves, or without leaves, or with just a trace of foliage remaining—the latter perhaps most feelingly suggesting the bleakness and loneliness that characterize the change of seasons, the ending of the life cycle. But other senses are invoked, too. The boughs shaking against the cold represent an appeal to our tactile sense, and the next line appeals to our sense of hearing, although only as a reminder that the birds no longer sing. (Notice how exact the visual representation is of the bare, or nearly bare, limbs, even as the cold and the lack of birds are noted; birds lined up like a choir on risers would have made a striking visual image on the barren limbs one above the other, but now there is only the *reminder* of what used to be. The present is quiet, bleak, trembly, and lonely; it is the absence of color, song, and life that creates the strong visual impression, a reminder of what formerly was.)

2. Shortly.   3. Sleep.

The next four lines are slightly different in tone, and the color changes. From a black-and-white landscape with a few yellow leaves, we come upon a rich and almost warm reminder of a faded sunset. But a somber note does enter the poem in these lines through another figure of speech, **personification,** which involves treating an abstraction, such as death or justice or beauty, as if it were a person. The poem is talking about the coming of night and of sleep, and Sleep is personified and identified as the "second self" of Death (that is, as a kind of "double" for death). The main emphasis is on how night and sleep close in on our sense of twilight, and only secondarily does a reminder of death enter the poem. But it does enter.

The third metaphor—that of the dying embers of a fire—begins in line 9 and continues to color and warm the bleak cold that the poem began with, but it also sharpens the reminder of death. The three main metaphors in the poem work in a way to make our sense of old age and approaching death more familiar, but also more immediate: moving from barren trees, to fading twilight, to dying embers suggests a sensuous increase of color and warmth, but also an increasing urgency. The first metaphor involves a whole season, or at least a segment of one, a matter of days or possibly weeks; the second involves the passing of a single day, reducing the time scale to a matter of minutes, and the third draws our attention to that split second when a glowing ember fades into a gray ash. The final part of the fire metaphor introduces the most explicit sense of death so far, as the metaphor of embers shifts into a direct reminder of death. Embers, which had been a metaphor of the speaker's aging body, now themselves become, metaphorically, a deathbed; the vitality that nourishes youth is used up just as a log in a fire is. The urgency of the reminder of coming death has now peaked. It is friendlier but now seems immediate and inevitable, a natural part of the life process, and the final two lines then make an explicit plea to make good and intense use of the remaining moments of human relationship.

"That time of year" represents an unusually intricate use of images to organize a poem and focus its emotional impact. Not all poems are so skillfully made, and not all depend on such a full and varied use of metaphor. But most poems use metaphors for at least part of their effect, and often a poem is based on a single metaphor that is fully developed as the major way of making the poem's statement and impact, as in the following poem about the role of a mother and wife.

LINDA PASTAN

Marks

My husband gives me an A
for last night's supper,
an incomplete for my ironing,
a B plus in bed.
My son says I am average,   5
an average mother, but if
I put my mind to it
I could improve.
My daughter believes
in Pass / Fail and tells me   10

I pass. Wait 'til they learn
I'm dropping out.   1978

The speaker in "Marks" is obviously not thrilled with the idea of continually being judged, and the metaphor of marks (or grades) as a way of talking about her performance of roles in the family suggests her irritation. The list of the roles implies the many things expected of her, and the three different systems of marking (letter grades, categories to be checked off on a chart, and pass/fail) detail the difficulties of multiple standards. The poem retains the language of schooldays all the way to the end ("learn," line 11; "dropping out," line 12), and the major effect of the poem depends on the irony of the speaker's surrendering to the metaphor the family has thrust upon her; if she is to be judged as if she were a student, she retains the right to leave the system. Ironically, she joins the system (adopts the metaphor for herself) in order to defeat it.

The following poem depends from the beginning—even from its title—on a single metaphor and the values associated with it.

DAVID WAGONER

My Father's Garden

On his way to the open hearth where white-hot steel
Boiled against furnace walls in wait for his lance
To pierce the fireclay and set loose demons
And dragons in molten tons, blazing
5   Down to the huge satanic caldrons,
Each day he would pass the scrapyard, his kind of garden.

In rusty rockeries of stoves and brake drums,
In grottoes of sewing machines and refrigerators,
He would pick flowers for us: small gears and cogwheels
10   With teeth like petals, with holes for anthers,
Long stalks of lead to be poured into toy soldiers,
Ball bearings as big as grapes to knock them down.

He was called a melter. He tried to keep his brain
From melting in those tyger-mouthed mills
15   Where the same steel reappeared over and over
To be reborn in the fire as something better
Or worse: cannons or cars, needles or girders,
Flagpoles, swords, or plowshares.

But it melted. His classical learning ran
20   Down and away from him, not burning bright.
His fingers culled a few cold scraps of Latin
And Greek, *magna sine laude*,[4] for crosswords

---

4. Without great distinction; a reversal of the usual *magna cum laude*.

And brought home lumps of tin and sewer grills
As if they were his ripe prize vegetables.   1987

The poem is a tribute to the speaker's father and the things he understands and values in his ordinary, workingman's life. The father is a "melter" (line 13) in the steel mills (lines 14–15), and what he values are the things made from what he helps to produce. His avocation has developed from his vocation: he collects metal objects from the scrapyard and brings them home just as some other men would pick flowers for their families. The scrapyard is, says the speaker, "his kind of garden" (line 6). The life led by the father has been a hard one, but he shows love for his children in the only way he knows how—by bringing home things that mean something to him and that can be made into toys his children will come to value. Describing these scraps as the products of his garden—"As if they were his ripe prize vegetables" (line 24)—has the effect of making them seem home-grown, carefully tended, nurtured by the father into a useful beauty. Instead of crude and ugly pieces of scrap, they become—through the metaphor of the poem—examples of value and beauty corresponding to the warm feelings the speaker has for a father who did what he could with what he knew and what he had.

Poets often are self-conscious and explicit about the ways they use language metaphorically, and sometimes (as in the following poem) they celebrate the richness of language that makes their art possible:

ROBERT FRANCIS

Hogwash

The tongue that mothered such a metaphor
Only the purest purist could despair of.

Nobody ever called swill sweet but isn't
Hogwash a daisy in a field of daisies?

What beside sports and flowers could you find   5
To praise better than the American language?

Bruised by American foreign policy
What shall I soothe me, what defend me with

But a handful of clean unmistakable words—
Daisies, daisies, in a field of daisies?   10

                                                                             1965

The poet here claims little for his own invention and not much for the art of poetry, insisting that the American language itself is responsible for miraculous conceptions. The poet plays cheerfully here with what words offer—the pun on "purest" and "purist" (line 2), for example, and the taunting (but misleading) similarity of the beginnings of "swill" and "sweet" (line 3)—but insists that poems and poets only articulate things already realized in common speech, where metaphors are "mothered" (line 1). "Hogwash," although never explicitly glossed or discussed in the poem, is the primary example: What *does* "hogwash" mean? How do hogs wash themselves and in what? to what purpose and effect? How did the term get invented as a metaphor, and what are its visual implications? And what is it doing as an example of beauty in a poem about "clean unmistakable words" (line 9)? But then the poem plays even more fully with "daisy" (lines 4 and 10) as metaphor and idiomatic expression. A "daisy" is a great success, a breakthrough, a beaut, a perfect example, and the word "hogwash" is such a daisy, an instance of such a success: a "daisy in a field of daisies," a success of successes, a wonder in a language full of wonders.

Not everything American, according to this poem, is as praiseworthy as its language, and the word "hogwash" ultimately has its context established in the poem's fourth stanza when the speaker finally tells us why the word is so soothing and so pertinent. Poets, the poem says, need words and metaphors that are not always images of beauty because the world is full of things that are not altogether beautiful, and metaphors of ugliness can be "daisies," too.

Not all poets feel as positive as Francis claims to be here about the raw materials they have to work with in language. Ultimately, of course, the modesty of the poet's claims here about his own inventiveness becomes as comic as the metaphor of "hogwash" itself and the poem's characterization of foreign policy, for it is the poem that makes this particular use of the metaphor, no matter where or when it was invented: the wit belongs to the poem, not the language. Poets make use of whatever idioms, expressions, inherited metaphors, and traditions of language come their way, and they turn them to their own uses, sometimes quite surprisingly.

The difficulty of conveying what some experiences are like and how we feel about them sometimes leads poets to startling comparisons and figures of speech that may at first seem far-fetched but that, in one way or another, do in fact suggest the quality of the experience or the feelings associated with it. Sometimes they use a series of metaphors, as if no single act of visualization will serve but several together may suggest the full complexity of the experience or cumulatively define the feeling precisely. Metaphors open up virtually endless possibilities of comparison, giving words a chance to be more than words, offering our mind's eye a challenge to keep up with the fertile and articulate imagination of writers who make it their business to see things that ordinary people miss, noticing the most surprising likenesses and conveying feelings more powerfully than politicians usually do.

Sometimes, in poetry as in prose, comparisons are made explicitly, as in the following poem.

ROBERT BURNS

A Red, Red Rose

O, my luve's like a red, red rose
That's newly sprung in June.
O, my luve is like the melodie
That's sweetly played in tune.

As fair art thou, my bonnie lass,   5
So deep in luve am I;
And I will luve thee still, my dear,
Till a' the seas gang[5] dry.

Till a' the seas gang dry, my dear,
And the rocks melt wi' the sun;   10
And I will luve thee still, my dear,
While the sands o' life shall run.

And fare thee weel, my only luve,
And fare thee weel a while!
And I will come again, my luve,   15
Though it were ten thousand mile.   1796

The first four lines make two explicit comparisons: the speaker says that his love is "like a . . . rose" and "like [a] melodie." Such *explicit* comparison is called a simile, and usually (as here) the comparison involves the words "like" or "as." Similes work much as do metaphors, except that they usually are used more passingly, more incidentally; they make a quick comparison and usually do not elaborate, whereas metaphors often extend over a long section of a poem (in which case they are called **extended metaphors**) or even over the whole poem, as in "Marks" (in which case they are called **controlling metaphors**).

The two similes in "A Red, Red Rose" assume that we already have a favorable opinion of roses and of melodies. Here the poet does not develop the comparison or even remind us of attractive details about roses or tunes. He pays the quick compliment and moves on. Similes sometimes develop more elaborate comparisons than this and occasionally even control long sections of a poem (in which case they are called **analogies**), but usually a simile is briefer and relies more fully on something we already know. The speaker in "My Papa's Waltz" says that he hung on "like death"; he doesn't have to explain or elaborate the comparison: we know the anxiety he refers to.

Like metaphors, similes may imply both meaning and feeling; they may both explain something and invoke feelings about it. All figurative language involves an attempt to clarify something *and* to help readers feel a certain way about it. Saying that one's love is like a rose implies a delicate and fragile beauty and invites our senses into play so that we can share sensuously a response to fragrant appeal and soft touch, just as the shivering boughs and dying embers in "That time of year" explain separation and loss at the same time that they invite us to share the cold sense of loneliness and the warmth of old friendship.

Once you are alerted to look for them, you will find figures of speech in poem after poem; they are among the most common devices through which poets share their vision with us.

The following poem uses a variety of metaphors to describe sexual experiences.

5. Go.

ADRIENNE RICH

Two Songs

1

Sex, as they harshly call it,
I fell into this morning
at ten o'clock, a drizzling hour
of traffic and wet newspapers.
I thought of him who yesterday
clearly didn't
turn me to a hot field
ready for plowing,
and longing for that young man
piercéd me to the roots
bathing every vein, etc.[6]
All day he appears to me
touchingly desirable,
a prize one could wreck one's peace for.
I'd call it love if love
didn't take so many years
but lust too is a jewel
a sweet flower and what
pure happiness to know
all our high-toned questions
breed in a lively animal.

2

That "old last act"!
And yet sometimes
all seems post coitum triste[7]
and I a mere bystander.
Somebody else is going off,
getting shot to the moon.
Or, a moon-race!
Split seconds after
my opposite number lands
I make it—
we lie fainting together
at a crater-edge
heavy as mercury in our moonsuits
till he speaks
in a different language
yet one I've picked up
through cultural exchanges . . .

---

6. See the opening lines of the Prologue to Chaucer's *Canterbury Tales*.   7. Sadness after sexual union.

we murmur the first moonwords:
Spasibo.[8] Thanks. O.K.   40

                                                            1964

The first "song" begins straightforwardly as narration ("Sex . . . I fell into this morning / at ten o'clock"), but the vividness of sex and desire is communicated mostly by
figure. The speaker describes her body as "a hot field / ready for plowing" (lines 7–8)—
quite unlike her resistant body yesterday—and her longing is also described by metaphor, in this case an elaborate one borrowed from another poem. After so sensual and
urgent a beginning, the song turns more thoughtful and philosophical, but even the
intellectual sorting between love and lust comes to depend on figures: lust is a "jewel"
(line 17) and a "flower" (line 18). After the opening pace and excitement, those later
metaphors seem calm and tame, moving the poem from the lust of its beginning to a
contemplative reflection on the value and beauty of momentary physical pleasures.

The second song depends on two closely related metaphors, and here the metaphors
for sex are highly self-conscious and a little comic. The song begins on a plaintive note,
considering the classic melancholic feeling after sex; the speaker pictures herself as
isolated, left out, "a bystander" (line 25), while someone else is having sexual pleasure.
This pleasure of others is described through two colloquial expressions (both metaphors)
for sexual climax: "going off" (line 26) and "getting shot to the moon" (line 27). Suddenly the narrator pretends to take sex as space travel seriously and creates a metaphor
of her own: sexual partners running a "moon-race" (line 28). The rest of the poem enacts
the metaphor in the context of the space race between the United States and Russia in
the early 1960s. The race, not exactly even but close enough, is described in detail, and
the speaker tells her story in a self-conscious, comic way. These are international relations, foreign affairs, and the lovers appropriately say their thank-yous separately in
Russian and English, then communicate an international *"O.K."*

RANDALL JARRELL

The Death of the Ball Turret Gunner[9]

From my mother's sleep I fell into the State,
And I hunched in its belly till my wet fur froze.
Six miles from earth, loosed from its dream of life,
I woke to black flak and the nightmare fighters.
When I died they washed me out of the turret with a hose.   5

                                                            1945

8. Russian for "thanks."   9. "A ball turret was a plexiglass sphere set into the belly of a B-17 or
B-24 and inhabited by two .50 caliber machine-guns and one man, a short, small man. When this
gunner tracked with his machine-guns a fighter attacking his bomber from below, he revolved with
the turret; hunched upside-down in his little sphere, he looked like the foetus in the womb. The
fighters which attacked him were armed with cannon firing explosive shells. The hose was a steam
hose." (RJ)

DOROTHY LIVESAY

Other

1

Men prefer an island
With its beginning ended:
Undertone of waves
Trees overbended.

5   Men prefer a road
Circling, shell-like
Convex and fossiled
Forever winding inward.

Men prefer a woman
10   Limpid in sunlight
Held as a shell
On a sheltering island . . .

Men prefer an island.

2

But I am mainland
15   O I range
From upper country to the inner core:
From sageland, brushland, marshland
To the sea's floor.

Show me an orchard where I have not slept,
20   A hollow where I have not wrapped
The sage about me, and above, the still
Stars clustering
Over the ponderosa pine, the cactus hill.

Tell me a time
25   I have not loved,
A mountain left unclimbed:
A prairie field
Where I have not furrowed my tongue,
Nourished it out of the mind's dark places;
30   Planted with tears unwept
And harvested as friends, as faces.

O find me a dead-end road
I have not trodden
A logging road that leads the heart away
35   Into the secret evergreen of cedar roots
Beyond sun's farthest ray—
Then, in a clearing's sudden dazzle,
There is no road; no end; no puzzle.

But do not show me! For I know
The country I caress:
A place where none shall trespass
None possess:
A mainland mastered
From its inaccess.

————

Men prefer an island.

40
45
1955

EMILY DICKINSON

[*Wild Nights—Wild Nights!*]

Wild Nights—Wild Nights!
Were I with thee
Wild Nights should be
Our luxury!

Futile—the Winds—
To a Heart in port—
Done with the Compass—
Done with the Chart!

Rowing in Eden—
Ah, the Sea!
Might I but moor—Tonight—
In Thee!

5
10

ca. 1861

AGHA SHAHID ALI

The Dacca Gauzes

*. . . for a whole year he sought
to accumulate the most exquisite
Dacca gauzes.*
        —OSCAR WILDE / *The Picture
            of Dorian Gray*

Those transparent Dacca gauzes
known as woven air, running
water, evening dew:

a dead art now, dead over
5   a hundred years. "No one
now knows," my grandmother says,

"what it was to wear
or touch that cloth." She wore
it once, an heirloom sari from

10   her mother's dowry, proved
genuine when it was pulled, all
six yards, through a ring.

Years later when it tore,
many handkerchiefs embroidered
15   with gold-thread paisleys

were distributed among
the nieces and daughters-in-law.
Those too now lost.

In history we learned: the hands
20   of weavers were amputated,
the looms of Bengal silenced,

and the cotton shipped raw
by the British to England.
History of little use to her,

25   my grandmother just says
how the muslins of today
seem so coarse and that only

in autumn, should one wake up
at dawn to pray, can one
30   feel that same texture again.

One morning, she says, the air
was dew-starched: she pulled
it absently through her ring.   1987

JOHN DONNE

[*Batter my heart, three-personed God; for You*][1]

Batter my heart, three-personed God; for You
As yet but knock, breathe, shine, and seek to mend;
That I may rise and stand, o'erthrow me, and bend
Your force, to break, blow, burn, and make me new.
5   I, like an usurped town, to another due,

1. *Holy Sonnets*, 14.

Labor to admit You, but Oh, to no end!
Reason, Your viceroy[2] in me, me should defend,
But is captived, and proves weak or untrue.
Yet dearly I love You, and would be loved fain,[3]
But am betrothed unto Your enemy: 10
Divorce me, untie or break that knot again,
Take me to You, imprison me, for I,
Except You enthrall me, never shall be free,
Nor ever chaste, except You ravish me.   1633

ANONYMOUS[4]

The Twenty-third Psalm

The Lord is my shepherd; I shall not want.
He maketh me to lie down in green pastures: he leadeth me beside
    the still waters.
He restoreth my soul: he leadeth me in the paths of righteousness
    for his name's sake.
Yea, though I walk through the valley of the shadow of death,
    I will fear no evil: for thou art with me;
    thy rod and thy staff they comfort me.
Thou preparest a table before me in the presence of mine enemies:
    thou anointest my head with oil; my cup runneth over.   5
Surely goodness and mercy shall follow me all the days of my life:
    and I will dwell in the house of the Lord for ever.

2. One who rules as the representative of a higher power.   3. Gladly.   4. Traditionally attributed to King David. The English translation printed here is from the King James Version.

SYMBOL

The word *symbol* is often used sloppily and sometimes pretentiously, but properly used the term suggests one of the most basic things about poems—their ability to get beyond what words signify and make larger claims about meanings in the verbal world. All words go beyond themselves. They are not simply a collection of sounds: they signify something beyond their sounds, often things or actions or ideas. Words describe not only a verbal universe but a world in which actions occur, acts have implications, and events mean. Sometimes words not only signify something beyond themselves—a rock or a tree or a cloud—but symbolize something as well—solidity or life or dreams. Words can—when their implications are agreed on by tradition, convention, or habit—stand for things beyond their most immediate meanings or significations and become symbols, and even simple words that have accumulated no special power from previous use may be given special significance in special circumstances—either in poetry or in life itself.

A **symbol** is, put simply, something that stands for something else. The everyday world is full of common examples; a flag, a logo, a trademark, or a skull and crossbones all suggest things beyond themselves, and everyone is likely to understand what their display is meant to indicate, whether or not the viewer shares a commitment to what the object represents. In common usage a prison is a symbol of confinement, constriction, and loss of freedom, and in specialized traditional usage a cross may symbolize oppression, cruelty, suffering, death, resurrection, triumph, or the intersection of two separate things, traditions, or ideas (as in crossroads and crosscurrents, for example). The specific symbolic significance is controlled by the context; a reader may often decide what it is by looking at contiguous details in the poem and by examining the poem's attitude toward a particular tradition or body of beliefs. A star means one kind of thing to a Jewish poet and something else to a Christian poet, still something else to a sailor or actor. In a very literal sense, words themselves are all symbols (they stand for an object, action, or quality, not just for letters or sounds), but symbols in poetry are said to be those words and groups of words that have a range of reference beyond their literal signification or denotation.

Poems sometimes create a symbol out of a thing, action, or event that has no previously agreed upon symbolic significance. In the following poem, for example, a random gesture is given symbolic significance.

SHARON OLDS

Leningrad Cemetery, Winter of 1941[5]

That winter, the dead could not be buried.
The ground was frozen, the gravediggers weak from hunger,
the coffin wood used for fuel. So they were covered with something
and taken on a child's sled to the cemetery
5   in the sub-zero air. They lay on the soil,

---

5. The 900-day siege of Leningrad during World War II began in September 1941.

some of them wrapped in dark cloth
bound with rope like the tree's ball of roots
when it waits to be planted; others wound in sheets,
their pale, gauze, tapered shapes
stiff as cocoons that will split down the center   10
when the new life inside is prepared;
but most lay like corpses, their coverings
coming undone, naked calves
hard as corded wood spilling
from under a cloak, a hand reaching out   15
with no sign of peace, wanting to come back
even to the bread made of glue and sawdust,
even to the icy winter, and the siege.   p. 1979

All of the corpses—frozen, neglected, beginning to be in disarray—vividly stamp upon our minds a sense of the horrors of war, and the detailed picture of the random, uncounted clutter of bodies is likely to stay in our minds long after we have finished reading the poem. Several of the details are striking, and the poem's language heightens our sense of them. The corpses wound in sheets, for example, are described in "their pale, gauze, tapered shapes" (line 9), and they are compared to cocoons that one day will split and emit new life; and the limbs that dangle loose when the coverings come undone are said to be "hard as corded wood spilling" (line 14). But clearly the most memorable sight is the hand dangling from one corpse that is coming unwrapped, for the poet invests that hand with special significance, giving its gesture *meaning*. The hand is described as "reaching out . . . wanting to come back" (lines 15–16): it is as if the dead can still gesture even if they cannot speak, and the gesture seems to signify the desire of the dead to come back at any price. They would be glad to be alive, even under the grim conditions that attend the living in Leningrad during this grim war. Suddenly the grimness that we—living—have been witnessing pales by comparison with what the dead have lost simply by being dead. The hand has been made to *symbolize* the desire of the dead to return, to be alive, to be still among us, anywhere. The hand reaches out in the poem as a gesture that means; the poet has made it a symbol of desire.

The whole array of dead bodies in the poem might be said to be symbolic as well. As a group, they stand for the human waste that the war has produced, and their dramatic visual presence provides the poem with a dramatic visualization of how war and its requirements have no time for decency, not even the decency of burial. The bodies are a symbol in the sense that they stand for what the poem as a whole asserts.

The poem that follows also arises out of a historical moment, but this time the event is a personal one that the poet gives a significance by the interpretation he puts upon it.

JAMES DICKEY

The Leap

The only thing I have of Jane MacNaughton
Is one instant of a dancing-class dance.
She was the fastest runner in the seventh grade,
My scrapbook says, even when boys were beginning
5 To be as big as the girls,
But I do not have her running in my mind,
Though Frances Lane is there, Agnes Fraser,
Fat Betty Lou Black in the boys-against-girls
Relays we ran at recess: she must have run

10 Like the other girls, with her skirts tucked up
So they would be like bloomers,
But I cannot tell; that part of her is gone.
What I do have is when she came,
With the hem of her skirt where it should be
15 For a young lady, into the annual dance
Of the dancing class we all hated, and with a light
Grave leap, jumped up and touched the end
Of one of the paper-ring decorations

To see if she could reach it. She could,
20 And reached me now as well, hanging in my mind
From a brown chain of brittle paper, thin
And muscular, wide-mouthed, eager to prove
Whatever it proves when you leap
In a new dress, a new womanhood, among the boys
25 Whom you easily left in the dust
Of the passionless playground. If I said I saw
In the paper where Jane MacNaughton Hill,

Mother of four, leapt to her death from a window
Of a downtown hotel, and that her body crushed-in
30 The top of a parked taxi, and that I held
Without trembling a picture of her lying cradled
In that papery steel as though lying in the grass,
One shoe idly off, arms folded across her breast,
I would not believe myself. I would say
35 The convenient thing, that it was a bad dream
Of maturity, to see that eternal process

Most obsessively wrong with the world
Come out of her light, earth-spurning feet
Grown heavy: would say that in the dusty heels
40 Of the playground some boy who did not depend
On speed of foot, caught and betrayed her.
Jane, stay where you are in my first mind:
It was odd in that school, at that dance.

I and the other slow-footed yokels sat in corners
Cutting rings out of drawing paper   45

Before you leapt in your new dress
And touched the end of something I began,
Above the couples struggling on the floor,
New men and women clutching at each other
And prancing foolishly as bears: hold on   50
To that ring I made for you, Jane—
My feet are nailed to the ground
By dust I swallowed thirty years ago—
While I examine my hands.   1967

Memory is crucial to "The Leap." The fact that Jane MacNaughton's graceful leap in dancing class has stuck in the speaker's mind for all these years means that this leap was important to him, meant something to him, stood for something in his mind. For the speaker, the leap is an "instant" and the "only thing" he has of Jane. Its grace and ease are what he remembers, and he struggles at several points to articulate its meaning (lines 15–26, 44–50), but even without articulation or explanation it is there in his head as a visual memory, a symbol for him of something beyond himself, something he cannot do, something he wanted to be. What that leap had stood for, or symbolized, was boldness, confidence, accomplishment, maturity, the ability to go beyond her fellow students in dancing class—the transcending of childhood by someone beginning to be a woman. Her feet now seem "earth-spurning" (line 38) in that original leap, and they separate her from everyone else. Jane MacNaughton was beyond the speaker's abilities and any attempt he could make to articulate his hopes, but not beyond his dreams. And even before articulation, she symbolized that dream.

The leap to her death seems cruelly inappropriate and ironic in the context of her earlier leap. In memory she is suspended in air, as if there were no gravity, no coming back to earth, as if life could exist as dream. And so the photograph, re-created in precise detail, is a cruel dashing of the speaker's dream—a detailed record of the ending of a leap, a denial of the suspension in which his memory had held her. His dream is grounded; her mortality is insistent. But what the speaker wants to hang on to (line 42) is still that symbolic moment which, although now confronted in more mature implications, will never be altogether replaced or surrendered.

The leap is ultimately symbolic in the *poem,* too, not just in the speaker's mind. In the poem (and for us as readers) the symbolism of the leap is double: the first leap is aspiration, and the second is the frustration and grounding of high hopes; the two are complementary, one unable to be imagined without the other. The poem is horrifying in some ways, a dramatic reminder that human beings don't ultimately transcend their mortality, their limits, no matter how heroic or unencumbered by gravity they may seem to an observer. But it is not altogether sad and despairing either, partly because it notices and affirms the validity of the original leap and partly because another symbol is created and elaborated in the poem. That symbol is the paper chain.

The chain connects Jane to the speaker both literally and figuratively. It is, in part, *his* paper chain which she had leaped to touch in dancing class (lines 18–19), and he thinks of her first leap as "touch[ing] the end of something I began" (line 47). He and the other "slow-footed," earthbound "yokels" (line 44) were the makers of the chain, and thus they are connected to her original leap, just as a photograph glimpsed in the paper connects the speaker to her second leap. The paper in the chain is "brittle" (line 21), and its creators seem dull artisans compared to the artistic performer that Jane was. They are heavy and "left in the dust" (lines 25, 52–53), and she is "light" (line 16) and able to transcend them but even in transcendence touching their lives and what they are able to do. And so the paper chain becomes the poem's symbol of linkage, connecting lower accomplishment to higher possibility, the artisan to the artist, material substance to the act of imagination. And the speaker at the end examines the hands that made the chain because those hands certify his connection to her and the imaginative leap she had made for him. The chain thus symbolizes not only the lower capabilities of those who cannot leap like the budding Jane could, but (later) the connection with her leap as both transcendence and mortality. Like the leap itself, the chain has been elevated to special meaning, given symbolic significance, by the poet's treatment of it. A leap and a chain have no necessary significance in themselves to most of us—at least no significance that we have all agreed upon together—but they may be given significance in specific circumstances or a specific text.

But some objects and acts do have a significance built in because of past usage in literature, or tradition, or the stories a culture develops to explain itself and its values. Over the years some things have acquired an agreed-upon significance, an accepted value in our minds. They already stand for something before the poet cites them; they are **traditional symbols.** Their uses in poetry have to do with the fact that poets can count on a recognition of their traditional suggestions and meanings outside the poem, and the poem does not have to propose or argue a particular symbolic value. Birds, for example, traditionally symbolize flight, freedom from confinement, detachment from earthbound limits, the ability to soar beyond rationality and transcend mortal limits. Traditionally, birds have also been linked with imagination, especially poetic imagination, and poets often identify with them as pure and ideal singers of songs, as in Keats's "Ode to a Nightingale." One of the most traditional symbols is the rose. It may be a simple and fairly plentiful flower in its season, but it has been allowed to stand for particular qualities for so long that to name it raises predictable expectations. Its beauty, delicacy, fragility, shortness of life, and depth of color have made it a symbol of the transitoriness of beauty, and countless poets have counted on its accepted symbolism—sometimes to compliment a friend (as Burns does in "A Red, Red Rose") or sometimes to make a point about the nature of symbolism. The following poem draws on, in a quite traditional way, the traditional meanings.

JOHN CLARE

Love's Emblem

Go, rose, my Chloe's[6] bosom grace:
   How happy should I prove,
Could I supply that envied place
   With never-fading love.

5   Accept, dear maid, now summer glows,
   This pure, unsullied gem,

---

6. A standard "poetic" name for a woman in traditional love poetry.

Love's emblem in a full-blown rose,
   Just broken from the stem.

Accept it as a favorite flower
   For thy soft breast to wear;   10
'Twill blossom there its transient hour,
   A favorite of the fair.

Upon thy cheek its blossom glows,
   As from a mirror clear,
Making thyself a living rose,   15
   In blossom all the year.

It is a sweet and favorite flower
   To grace a maiden's brow,
Emblem of love without its power—
   A sweeter rose art thou.   20

The rose, like hues of insect wing,
   May perish in an hour;
'Tis but at best a fading thing,
   But thou'rt a living flower.

The roses steeped in morning dews   25
   Would every eye enthrall,
But woman, she alone subdues;
   Her beauty conquers all.   1873

    The speaker in "Love's Emblem" sends the rose to Chloe to decorate her bosom (lines 1, 10) and reflect the blush of her cheek and brow (lines 13, 18), and he goes on to mention some of the standard meanings: the rose is pure (line 6), transitory (line 11), fragrant, beautiful, and always appreciated (line 17). The poet here does not elaborate or argue these things; he counts on the tradition, habits of mind built on familiarity and repetition (though, of course, readers unfamiliar with the tradition will not respond in the same way—that is one reason it is difficult to read with full appreciation texts from another linguistic or cultural tradition). To say that the rose is an emblem of love is to say that it traditionally symbolizes love, and the speaker expects Chloe to accept his gift readily; she will understand it as a compliment, a pledge, and a bond. She will understand, too, that her admirer is being conventional and complimentary in going on to call her (and women in general) a rose (line 20), except that her qualities are said to be more lasting than those of a momentary flower.

    Poems often use traditional symbols to invoke predictable responses—in effect using shortcuts to meaning and power by repeating acts of signification and symbolization sanctioned by time and cultural habit. But often poets examine the tradition even as they employ it, and sometimes they revise or reverse meanings built into the tradition. Some of the poems at the end of this chapter question the usual meanings of roses in poetry and evaluate as they go. Symbols do not necessarily stay the same over time, and poets often turn even the most traditional of symbols to their own original uses. Knowing the traditions of poetry—reading a lot of poems and observing how they tend to use certain words, metaphors, and symbols—can be very useful in reading new poems, but traditions modify and individual poems do highly individual things. Knowing the past never means being able to predict new texts with confidence. Symbolism makes things happen, but individual poets and texts determine what will happen and how.

Sometimes symbols—traditional or not—become so insistent in the world of a poem that the larger referential world is left almost totally behind. In such cases the symbol is everything, and the poem does not just *use* symbols but becomes a **symbolic poem,** usually a highly individualized one dependent on an internal system introduced by the individual poet.

Here is an example of such a poem:

WILLIAM BLAKE

The Sick Rose[7]

O rose, thou art sick.
The invisible worm
That flies in the night
In the howling storm

5 Has found out thy bed
Of crimson joy,
And his dark secret love
Does thy life destroy.

1794

The poem does not seem to be about a rose, but about what the rose represents—not in this case something altogether understandable through the traditional meanings of rose.

We know that the rose is usually associated with beauty and love, often with sex; and here several key terms have sexual connotations: "bed," "worm," and "crimson joy." The violation of the rose by the worm is the poem's main concern; the violation seems to have involved secrecy, deceit, and "dark" motives, and the result is sickness rather than the joy of love. The poem is sad; it involves a sense of hurt and tragedy, nearly of despair. The poem cries out against the misuse of the rose, against its desecration, implying that instead of a healthy joy in sensuality and sexuality, there has been in this case destruction and hurt because of misunderstanding and repression and lack of sensitivity.

But to say so much about this poem I have had to extrapolate from other poems by this poet, and have introduced information from outside the poem. Fully symbolic poems often require that, and thus they ask us to go beyond the formal procedures of reading that we have discussed so far. As presented in this poem, the rose is not part of the normal world that we ordinarily see, and it is symbolic in a special sense. The poet does not simply take an object from that everyday world and give it special significance, making it a symbol in the same sense that the leap or the corpse's hand is a symbol. Here the rose seems to belong to its own world, a world made entirely inside the poem

7. In Renaissance emblem books, the scarab beetle, worm, and rose are closely associated: the beetle feeds on dung, and the smell of the rose is fatal to it.

or the poet's head. The rose is not referential, or not primarily so. The whole poem is symbolic; it is not paraphrasable; it lives in its own world. But what is the rose here a symbol of? In general terms, we can say from what the poem tells us; but we may not be as confident as we can be in the more nearly everyday world of "The Leap" or "Leningrad Cemetery, Winter of 1941," poems that contain actions we recognize from the world of probabilities in which we live. In "The Sick Rose," it seems inappropriate to ask the standard questions: What rose? Where? Which worm? What are the particulars here? In the world of this poem worms can fly and may be invisible. We are altogether in a world of meanings that have been formulated according to a particular system of knowledge and code of belief. We will only feel comfortable and confident in that world if we read many poems written by the poet (in this case William Blake) within the same symbolic system.

Negotiation of meanings in symbolic poems can be very difficult indeed. The skill of reading symbolic poems is an advanced skill that depends on special knowledge of authors and of the special traditions they work from. But usually the symbols you will find in poems *are* referential, and these meanings are readily discoverable from the careful study of the poems themselves, as in poems like "The Leap" and "Love's Emblem."

EDMUND WALLER

Song

> Go, lovely rose!
> Tell her that wastes her time and me
>   That now she knows,
> When I resemble[8] her to thee,
> How sweet and fair she seems to be.   5
>
>   Tell her that's young,
> And shuns to have her graces spied,
>   That hadst thou sprung
> In deserts, where no men abide,
> Thou must have uncommended died.   10
>
>   Small is the worth
> Of beauty from the light retired;
>   Bid her come forth,
> Suffer herself to be desired,
> And not blush so to be admired.   15
>
>   Then die! that she
> The common fate of all things rare
>   May read in thee;
> How small a part of time they share
> That are so wondrous sweet and fair!   20

1645

8. Compare.

EMILY DICKINSON

[Go not too near a House of Rose—]

Go not too near a House of Rose—
The depredation of a Breeze
Or inundation of a Dew
Alarms its walls away—

5   Nor try to tie the Butterfly,
Nor climb the Bars of Ecstasy,
In insecurity to lie
Is Joy's insuring quality.

ca. 1878

ALFRED, LORD TENNYSON

Now Sleeps the Crimson Petal[9]

Now sleeps the crimson petal, now the white;
Nor waves the cypress in the palace walk;
Nor winks the gold fin in the porphyry font;[1]
The firefly wakens; waken thou with me.

5   Now droops the milk-white peacock like a ghost,
And like a ghost she glimmers on to me.

Now lies the Earth all Danaë[2] to the stars,
And all thy heart lies open unto me.

Now slides the silent meteor on, and leaves
10   A shining furrow, as thy thoughts in me.

Now folds the lily all her sweetness up,
And slips into the bosom of the lake;
So fold thyself, my dearest, thou, and slip
Into my bosom and be lost in me.

1847

---

9. A song from *The Princess*.   1. Stone fishbowl. *Porphyry:* a red stone containing fine white crystals.   2. A princess, confined in a tower, seduced by Zeus after he became a shower of gold in order to gain access to her.

DOROTHY PARKER

One Perfect Rose

A single flow'r he sent me, since we met.
  All tenderly his messenger he chose;
Deep-hearted, pure, with scented dew still wet—
  One perfect rose.

I knew the language of the floweret;   5
  "My fragile leaves," it said, "his heart enclose."
Love long has taken for his amulet
  One perfect rose.

Why is it no one ever sent me yet
  One perfect limousine, do you suppose?   10
Ah no, it's always just my luck to get
  One perfect rose.   1937

ROO BORSON

After a Death

Seeing that there's no other way,
I turn his absence into a chair.
I can sit in it,
gaze out through the window.
I can do what I do best   5
and then go out into the world.
And I can return then with my useless love,
to rest,
because the chair is there.   1989

HOWARD NEMEROV

The Town Dump

"The art of our necessities is strange,
That can make vile things precious."[3]

A mile out in the marshes, under a sky
Which seems to be always going away

3. *King Lear* III.ii.70–71.

In a hurry, on that Venetian land threaded
With hidden canals, you will find the city
Which seconds ours (so cemeteries, too,
Reflect a town from hillsides out of town),
Where Being most Becomingly[4] ends up
Becoming some more. From cardboard tenements,
Windowed with cellophane, or simply tenting
In paper bags, the angry mackerel eyes
Glare at you out of stove-in, sunken heads
Far from the sea; the lobster, also, lifts
An empty claw in his most minatory
Of gestures; oyster, crab, and mussel shells
Lie here in heaps, savage as money hurled
Away at the gate of hell. If you want results,
These are results.
                    Objects of value or virtue,
However, are also to be picked up here,
Though rarely, lying with bones and rotten meat,
Eggshells and mouldy bread, banana peels
No one will skid on, apple cores that caused
Neither the fall of man nor a theory
Of gravitation.[5] People do throw out
The family pearls by accident, sometimes,
Not often; I've known dealers in antiques
To prowl this place by night, with flashlights, on
The off-chance of somebody's having left
Derelict chairs which will turn out to be
By Hepplewhite,[6] a perfect set of six
Going to show, I guess, that in any sty
Someone's heaven may open and shower down
Riches responsive to the right dream; though
It is a small chance, certainly, that sends
The ghostly dealer, heavy with fly-netting
Over his head, across these hills in darkness,
Stumbling in cut-glass goblets, lacquered cups,
And other products of his dreamy midden[7]
Penciled with light and guarded by the flies.

For there are flies, of course. A dynamo
Composed, by thousands, of our ancient black
Retainers, hums here day and night, steady
As someone telling[8] beads, the hum becoming

---

4. "Being" and "Becoming" have been, since Heraclitus, the standard antinomies in Western philosophy, standing for (respectively) the eternal and that which changes.   5. According to legend, Sir Isaac Newton's discovery of the principle of gravitation followed his being hit on the head by a falling apple.   6. A late eighteenth-century cabinetmaker and furniture designer, famed for his simplification of neoclassic lines. No pieces known to have been actually made by Hepplewhite survive.   7. Refuse heap. (The term is usually used to describe those primitive refuse heaps that have been untouched for centuries and in which archaeologists dig for shards and artifacts of older cultures.)   8. Counting.

A high whine at any disturbance; then,
Settled again, they shine under the sun
Like oil-drops, or are invisible as night,   45
By night.
          All this continually smoulders,
Crackles, and smokes with mostly invisible fires
Which, working deep, rarely flash out and flare,
And never finish. Nothing finishes;
The flies, feeling the heat, keep on the move.   50
Among the flies, the purefying fires,
The hunters by night, acquainted with the art
Of our necessities, and the new deposits
That each day wastes with treasure, you may say
There should be ratios. You may sum up   55
The results if you want results. But I will add
That wild birds, drawn to the carrion and flies,
Assemble in some numbers here, their wings
Shining with light, their flight enviably free,
Their music marvelous, though sad, and strange.   60

                                              1958

QUESTIONS

1. List all of the neologisms and other unusual words in Hopkins's "Pied Beauty." Find the most precise synonym you can for each. How can you tell exactly what these words contribute to the poem? Explain the effects of the repeated consonant sounds (alliteration) and repeated vowel sounds (assonance) in the poem. What are the advantages of making up original words to describe highly individualized effects? What are the disadvantages?

2. Compare Dickinson's "I dwell in Possibility—" with two of her other poems, "A narrow Fellow in the Grass" (page 755) and "After great pain, a formal feeling comes—." What patterns of word use do you see in the three poems? What kinds of vocabulary do they have in common? what patterns of syntax? what strategies of organization?

3. Characterize as fully as you can the speaker in Donne's "Batter my heart, three-personed God." Explain how the metaphor of invasion and resistance works in the poem. What effect does this central metaphor have on our conception of the speaker? Explain the terms "imprison" (line 12) and "enthrall" (line 13). Explain "chaste" and "ravish" (line 14). How do these two sets of terms relate to the poem's central metaphor?

4. List every term in "The Twenty-third Psalm" that relates to the central metaphor of shepherding. Explain the metaphors of anointing and the overfull cup in line 5. (If you have trouble with this metaphor and do not understand the historical/cultural reference, ask a reference librarian to guide you to biblical commentaries that explain the practices referred to here.) What is the "house of the Lord" (line 6), and how does it relate to the basic metaphor of the psalm? (Again, if you are not sure of the historical/cultural reference, consult biblical commentaries or other historical sources on social and economic structures of the ancient Middle East.)

WRITING SUGGESTIONS

1. Read back through the poems you have read so far in the course, and pick out one in which a single word seems to you crucial to that poem's total effect. Write a short essay in which you work out carefully how the poem's meaning and tone depend upon that one word.

2. With the help of a reference librarian, find several pictures of B-17 bombers, and study carefully the design and appearance of the ball turret. Try to find a picture of the gunner at work in the turret, and note carefully his body position. Explain, in a paragraph, how Jarrell's poem "The Death of the Ball Turret Gunner" uses the visual details of the ball turret to create the fetal and birth metaphors in the poem.
3. With the help of a reference librarian, find at least half a dozen more poems that are about roses. Read them all carefully, and make a list of all the things that the rose seems to stand for in the poems. Write a paragraph about each poem showing how a specific symbolism for rose is established.

17

THE SOUNDS OF POETRY

A lot of what happens in a poem happens in your mind's eye, but some of it happens in your voice. Poems are full of sounds and silences as well as words and sentences that are meaningful. Besides choosing words for their meanings, poets sometimes choose words because words involve certain sounds, and poems use sound effects to create a mood or establish a tone, just as films do. Sometimes the sounds of words are crucial to what is happening in the text of the poem.

The following poem explores the sounds of a particular word, tries them on, and analyzes them in relation to the word itself.

HELEN CHASIN

The Word Plum

The word *plum* is delicious
pout and push, luxury of
self-love, and savoring murmur

full in the mouth and falling
like fruit   5

taut skin
pierced, bitten, provoked into
juice, and tart flesh

question
and reply, lip and tongue   10
of pleasure.   1968

The poem savors the sounds of the word as well as the taste and feel of the fruit itself. It is almost as if the poem is tasting the sounds and rolling them carefully on the tongue. The second and third lines even replicate the *p, l, uh,* and *m* sounds of the word while at the same time imitating the squishy sounds of eating the fruit. Words like "delicious" and "luxury" sound juicy, and other words imitate sounds of satisfaction and pleasure—"murmur," for example. Even the process of eating is in part re-created aurally. The tight,

> *Poetry is a comforting piece of fiction set to more or less lascivious music.*
>
> —H. L. MENCKEN

clipped sounds of "taut skin / pierced" suggest the way teeth sharply break the skin and slice quickly into the solid flesh of a plum, and as the tartness is described, the words ("provoked," "question") force the lips to pucker and the tongue and palate to meet and hold, as if the mouth were savoring a tart fruit. The poet is having fun here re-creating the various sense appeals of a plum, teasing the sounds and meanings out of available words. The words must mean something appropriate and describe something accurately first of all, of course, but when they can also imitate the sounds and feel of the process, they can do double duty. Not many poems manipulate sound as intensely or as fully as "The Word *Plum*," but many poems at least contain passages in which the sounds of life are reproduced by the human voice reading the poem. To get the full effect of this poem—and of many others—reading aloud is essential; that way, you can pay attention to the vocal rhythms and articulate the sounds as the poem calls for them to be reproduced by the human voice.

Almost always a poem's effect will be helped by reading it aloud, using your voice to pronounce the words so that the poem becomes a spoken communication. Historically, poetry began as an oral phenomenon, and often poems that seem very difficult when looked at silently come alive when they are turned into sound. Early bards chanted their verses, and the music of poetry—its cadences and rhythms—developed from this kind of performance. Often performances of primitive poetry (and sometimes in later ages) were accompanied by some kind of musical instrument. The rhythms of any poem become clearer when you say or hear them.

Poetry is almost always a vocal art, dependent on the human voice to become its full self (for some exceptions look at the shaped verse in Chapter 19). In a sense, it begins to exist as a real phenomenon when a reader reads and actualizes it. Poems don't really achieve their full meaning when they merely exist on a page; a poem on a page is more a score or set of stage directions for a poem than a poem itself. Sometimes, in fact, it is hard to experience the poem at all unless you hear it; the actual experience of saying the words aloud or hearing them spoken is very good practice for learning to hear in your mind's ear when you read silently. A good poetry reading might easily convince you of the importance of a good voice sensitive to the poem's requirements, but you can also persuade yourself by reading poems aloud in the privacy of your own room. An audience is even better, however, because then there is someone to share the pleasure in the sounds themselves and consider what they imply. At its oral best, much poetry is communal.

MONA VAN DUYN

What the Motorcycle Said

Br-r-r-am-m-m, rackety-am-m, OM, *Am:*
All—r-r-room, r-r-ram, ala-bas-ter—
Am, the world's my oyster.

I hate plastic, wear it black and slick,
hate hardhats, wear one on my head,   5
that's what the motorcycle said.

Passed phonies in Fords, knocked down billboards, landed
on the other side of The Gap, and Whee,
bypassed history.

When I was born (The Past), baby knew best.   10
They shook when I bawled, took Freud's path,
threw away their wrath.

R-r-rackety-am-m. *Am.* War, rhyme,
soap, meat, marriage, the Phantom Jet
are shit, and like that.   15

Hate pompousness, punishment, patience, am into Love,
hate middle-class moneymakers, live on Dad,
that's what the motorcycle said.

Br-r-r-am-m-m. It's Nowsville, man. Passed Oldies, Uglies,
Straighties, Honkies. I'll never be   20
mean, tired or unsexy.

Passed cigarette suckers, souses, mother-fuckers,
losers, went back to Nature and found
how to get VD, stoned.

Passed a cow, too fast to hear her moo, *"I* rolled   25
our leaves of grass into one ball.
I am the grassy All."

Br-r-r-am-m-m, rackety-am-m, OM, *Am:*
All—gr-r-rin, oooohgah, gl-l-utton—
Am, the world's my smilebutton.   30

                                                    1973

Saying this poem as if you were a motorcycle with the power of speech (sort of) is part of the poem's fun, and the rich, loud sounds of a motorcycle revving up concentrate and intensify the effect and enrich the pleasure. It's a shame not to hear a poem like this aloud; a lot of it is missed if you don't try to imitate the sounds or to pick up the motor's rhythms in the poem. A performance here is clearly worth it: a human being as motorcycle, motorcycle as human being.

And it's a good poem, too. It does something interesting, important, and maybe a bit subversive. The speaking motorcycle seems to take on the values of some of its riders, the noisy and obtrusive ones that readers are most likely to associate with motorcycles. The riders made fun of here are themselves sort of mindless and mechanical; they are the sort who have cult feelings about their group, who travel in packs, and who live no life beyond their machines. The speaking motorcycle, like such riders, grooves on power and speed, lives for the moment, and has little respect for people, the past, institutions, or anything beyond its own small world. It is self-centered, modish, ignorant, and inarticulate; but it is proud as well, mighty proud, and feels important in its own sounds. That's what the motorcycle says.

The following poem uses sound effects efficiently, too.

KENNETH FEARING

Dirge

1-2-3 was the number he played but today the number came 3-2-1;
Bought his Carbide at 30, and it went to 29; had the favorite at Bowie[1]
    but the track was slow—

O executive type, would you like to drive a floating-power, knee-action,
    silk-upholstered six? Wed a Hollywood star? Shoot the course in 58?
    Draw to the ace, king, jack?
O fellow with a will who won't take no, watch out for three cigarettes
    on the same, single match; O democratic voter born in August under
    Mars, beware of liquidated rails—

Denouement to denouement, he took a personal pride in the certain,
5   certain way he lived his own, private life,
But nevertheless, they shut off his gas; nevertheless, the bank foreclosed;
    nevertheless, the landlord called; nevertheless, the radio broke,

And twelve o'clock arrived just once too often,
Just the same he wore one gray tweed suit, bought one straw hat, drank
    one straight Scotch, walked one short step, took one long look, drew
    one deep breath,
Just one too many,

10   And wow he died as wow he lived,
Going whop to the office and blooie home to sleep and biff got married
    and bam had children and oof got fired,
Zowie did he live and zowie did he die,

With who the hell are you at the corner of his casket, and where the
    hell're we going on the right-hand silver knob, and who the hell cares
    walking second from the end with an American Beauty[2] wreath from
    why the hell not,

Very much missed by the circulation staff of the New York Evening Post;
    deeply, deeply mourned by the B.M.T.[3]
Wham, Mr. Roosevelt; pow, Sears Roebuck; awk, big dipper; bop, sum-
15   mer rain; Bong, Mr., bong, Mr., bong, Mr., bong.

                                                      1935

As the title implies, "Dirge" is a kind of musical lament, in this case for a certain sort
of businessman who took a lot of chances and saw his investments and life go down the

---

1. A racetrack in Maryland. *Carbide:* the Union Carbide Corporation.   2. A variety of rose.   3. A
New York City subway line.

drain in the depression of the early 1930s. Reading this poem aloud is a big help partly because it contains expressive cartoon words that echo the action, words like "oof" and "blooie" (which primarily carry their meaning in their sounds, for they have practically no literal or referential meaning). Reading aloud also helps us notice that the poem employs rhythms much as a song would and that it frequently shifts its pace and mood. Notice how carefully the first two lines are balanced, and then how quickly the rhythm shifts as the "executive type" begins to be addressed directly in line 3. (Line 2 is long and dribbles over in the narrow pages of a book like this; a lot of the lines here are especially long, and the irregularity of the line lengths is one aspect of the special sound effects the poem creates.) In the direct address, the poem first picks up a series of advertising features, which it recites in rapid-fire order rather like the advertising phrases in "Needs" (page 650). In stanza 3 here, the rhythm shifts again, but the poem gives us helpful clues about how to read. Line 5 sounds like prose and is long, drawn out, and rather dull (rather like its subject), but line 6 sets up a regular (and monoto-

> *There are only three things . . .*
> *that a poem must reach: the*
> *eye, the ear, and what we may*
> *call the heart or the mind. It is*
> *the most important of all to*
> *reach the heart of the reader.*
> *And the surest way to reach*
> *the heart is through the ear.*
>
> —ROBERT FROST

nous) rhythm with its repeated "nevertheless," which punctuates the rhythm like a drumbeat: "But nevertheless, *tuh-tuh-tuh-tuh-tuh;* nevertheless, *tuh-tuh-tuh-tuh;* nevertheless, *tuh-tuh-tuh-tuh;* nevertheless, *tuh-tuh-tuh-tuh-tuh.*" In the next stanza, the repetitive phrasing comes again, this time guided by the word "one" in cooperation with other words of one syllable: "wore *one* gray tweed suit, bought *one* straw hat, *tuh* one *tuh-tuh, tuh* one *tuh-tuh, tuh* one *tuh-tuh, tuh* one *tuh-tuh.*" And then a new rhythm and a new technique in stanza 5 as the language of comic books is imitated to describe in violent, exaggerated terms the routine of his life. You have to say words like "whop" and "zowie" aloud and in the rhythm of the whole sentence to get the full effect of how boring his life is, no matter how he tries to jazz it up with exciting words. And so it goes—repeated words, shifting rhythms, emphasis on routine and averageness—until the final bell ("Bong . . . bong . . . bong . . . bong") tolls rhythmically for the dead man in the final clanging line.

Sometimes sounds in poems just provide special effects, rather like a musical score behind a film, setting mood and getting us into an appropriate frame of mind. But often sound and meaning go hand in hand, and the poet finds words that in their sounds echo the action. A word that captures or approximates the sound of what it describes, such as "splash" or "squish" or "murmur" is called an **onomatopoeic** word, and the device itself is called **onomatopoeia.** And similar things can be done poetically with pacing and rhythm, sounds and pauses. The punctuation, the length of vowels, and the combination of consonant sounds help to control the way we read so that we can use our voice to imitate what is being described. The poems at the end of this discussion (pages 749–56) suggest several ways that such imitations of pace and pause may occur: by echoing the lapping of waves on a shore, for example ("Like as the waves").

Here is a classic passage in which a skillful poet talks about the virtues of making the sound echo the sense—and shows at the same time how to do it:

ALEXANDER POPE

Sound and Sense[4]

337   But most by numbers[5] judge a poet's song,
   And smooth or rough, with them, is right or wrong;
   In the bright muse though thousand charms conspire,[6]
340   Her voice is all these tuneful fools admire,
   Who haunt Parnassus[7] but to please their ear,
   Not mend their minds; as some to church repair,
   Not for the doctrine, but the music there.
   These, equal syllables[8] alone require,
345   Though oft the ear the open vowels tire,
   While expletives[9] their feeble aid do join,
   And ten low words oft creep in one dull line,
   While they ring round the same unvaried chimes,
   With sure returns of still expected rhymes.
350   Where'er you find "the cooling western breeze,"
   In the next line, it "whispers through the trees";
   If crystal streams "with pleasing murmurs creep,"
   The reader's threatened (not in vain) with "sleep."
   Then, at the last and only couplet fraught
355   With some unmeaning thing they call a thought,
   A needless Alexandrine[1] ends the song,
   That, like a wounded snake, drags its slow length along.
   Leave such to tune their own dull rhymes, and know
   What's roundly smooth, or languishingly slow;
360   And praise the easy vigor of a line,
   Where Denham's strength and Waller's[2] sweetness join.
   True ease in writing comes from art, not chance,
   As those move easiest who have learned to dance.
   'Tis not enough no harshness gives offense,
365   The sound must seem an echo to the sense:
   Soft is the strain when Zephyr[3] gently blows,
   And the smooth stream in smoother numbers flows;
   But when loud surges lash the sounding shore,
   The hoarse, rough verse should like the torrent roar.
370   When Ajax[4] strives, some rock's vast weight to throw,
   The line too labors, and the words move slow;

4. From *An Essay on Criticism,* Pope's poem on the art of poetry and the problems of literary criticism. The passage excerpted here follows a discussion of several common weaknesses of critics—failure to regard an author's intention, for example, or overemphasis on clever metaphors and ornate style. 5. Meter, rhythm, sound. 6. Unite. 7. A mountain in Greece, traditionally associated with the muses and considered the seat of poetry and music. 8. Regular accents. 9. Filler words, such as "do." 1. A six-foot line, sometimes used in pentameter poems to vary the pace mechanically. Line 357 is an alexandrine. 2. Sir John Denham and Edmund Waller, seventeenth-century poets credited with perfecting the heroic couplet. 3. The west wind. 4. A Greek hero of the Trojan War, noted for his strength.

Not so, when swift Camilla[5] scours the plain,
Flies o'er th' unbending corn, and skims along the main.
Hear how Timotheus'[6] varied lays surprise,
And bid alternate passions fall and rise!   375
While, at each change, the son of Libyan Jove[7]
Now burns with glory, and then melts with love;
Now his fierce eyes with sparkling fury glow,
Now sighs steal out, and tears begin to flow:
Persians and Greeks like turns of nature[8] found,   380
And the world's victor stood subdued by sound!
The pow'r of music all our hearts allow,
And what Timotheus was, is DRYDEN now.   1711

A lot of things are going on here simultaneously. The poem uses a number of echoic or onomatopoeic words, and pleasant and unpleasant consonant sounds are used in some lines to underline a particular point or add some mood music. When the poet talks about a particular weakness in poetry, he illustrates it at the same time—by using open vowels (line 345), expletives (line 346), monosyllabic words (line 347), predictable rhymes (lines 350–53), or long, slow lines (line 357). And the good qualities of poetry he talks about and illustrates as well (line 360, for example). But the main effects of the passage come from an interaction of several strategies at once. The effects are fairly simple and easy to spot, but their causes involve a lot of poetic ingenuity. In line 340, for example, a careful cacophonous effect is achieved by the repetition of the $\overline{oo}$ vowel sound and the repetition of the _l_ consonant sound together with the interruption (twice) of the rough _f_ sound in the middle; no one wants to be caught admiring that music when the poet gets through with us, but the careful harmony of the preceding sounds has set us up beautifully. And the pace of lines 347, 357, and 359 is carefully controlled by clashing consonant sounds as well as by the use of long vowels. Line 347 moves incredibly slowly and seems much longer than it is because almost all the one-syllable words end in a consonant that refuses to blend with the beginning of the next word, making the words hard to say without distinct, awkward pauses between them. In lines 357 and 359, long vowels such as those in "wounded," "snake," "slow," "along," "roundly," and "smooth" help to slow down the pace, and the trick of juxtaposing awkward, unpronounceable consonants is again employed. The commas also provide nearly a full stop in the midst of these lines to slow us down still more. Similarly, the harsh lashing of the shore in lines 368–69 is partly accomplished by onomatopoeia, partly by a shift in the pattern of stress, which creates irregular waves in line 368, and partly by the dominance of rough consonants in line 369. (In Pope's time, the English _r_ was still trilled gruffly so that it could be made to sound extremely rrrough and harrrsh.) Almost every line in this passage demonstrates how to make sound echo sense.

As "Sound and Sense" and "Dirge" suggest, sound is most effectively manipulated in poetry when the rhythm of the voice is carefully controlled so that not only are the

---

5. A woman warrior in _The Aeneid._   6. The court musician of Alexander the Great, celebrated in a famous poem by Dryden (see line 383) for the power of his music over Alexander's emotions.   7. In Greek tradition, the chief god of any people was often given the name Zeus (Jove), and the chief god of Libya (the Greek name for all of Africa) was called Zeus Ammon. Alexander visited his oracle and was proclaimed son of the god.   8. Similar alternations of emotion.

proper sounds heard, but they are heard at precisely the right moment. Pace and rhythm are nearly as important to a good poem as they are to a good piece of music. The human voice naturally develops certain rhythms in speech; some syllables and some words receive more stress than others. Just as multisyllabic words put more stress on some syllables than others (dictionaries always indicate which syllables are stressed), words in the context of a sentence receive more or less stress, depending on meaning. One-syllable words are thus sometimes stressed and sometimes not. A careful poet controls the flow of stresses so that, in many poems, a certain basic rhythm (or **meter**) develops almost like a quiet percussion instrument in the background. Not all poems are metered, and not all metered poems follow a single dominant rhythm, but many poems are written in one pervasive pattern, and it is useful to look for patterns of stress.

Here is a poem that names and illustrates many of the meters. If you hear someone reading it aloud and chart the unstressed (˘) and stressed (‾) syllables, you should have a chart similar to that done by the poet himself in the text.

SAMUEL TAYLOR COLERIDGE

Metrical Feet

Lesson for a Boy

Trōchĕe trīps frŏm lōng tŏ shōrt;[9]
From long to long in solemn sort
Slōw Spōndēe stālks; strōng fōōt! yet ill able
Ēvĕr tŏ cōme ŭp wĭth Dāctȳl trĭsȳllăblĕ.
Ĭāmbĭcs mārch frŏm shōrt tŏ lōng—
Wĭth ă lēap ănd ă bōund thĕ swĭft Ānăpĕsts thrōng;
One syllable long, with one short at each side,
Ămphībrăchȳs hāstes wĭth ă stātelȳ stride—
Fīrst ănd lāst bēĭng lōng, mĭddlĕ shōrt, Ămphīmācer
Strīkes hĭs thūndērĭng hōofs līke ă prōud hīgh-brĕd Rācer.
If Derwent[1] be innocent, steady, and wise,
And delight in the things of earth, water, and skies;
Tender warmth at his heart, with these meters to show it,
With sound sense in his brains, may make Derwent a poet—
May crown him with fame, and must win him the love
Of his father on earth and his Father above.
            My dear, dear child!
Could you stand upon Skiddaw,[2] you would not from its whole ridge
See a man who so loves you as your fond s. t. COLERIDGE.

1806

9. The long and short marks over syllables are Coleridge's.   1. Written originally for Coleridge's son Hartley, the poem was later adapted for his younger son, Derwent.   2. A mountain in the lake country of northern England (where Coleridge lived in his early years), near the town of Derwent.

The following poem exemplifies **dactylic** rhythm (‾ ˘ ˘, or a stressed syllable followed by two unstressed ones).

WENDY COPE

Emily Dickinson

Higgledy-piggledy
Emily Dickinson
Liked to use dashes
Instead of full stops.

Nowadays, faced with such   5
Idiosyncrasy,
Critics and editors
Send for the cops.   1986

Limericks rely on **anapestic** meter (˘˘‾, or two unstressed syllables followed by a stressed one), although usually the first two syllables are in iambic meter (see below).

ANONYMOUS

[There was a young lady of Riga]

There was a young lady of Riga
Who went for a ride on a tiger;
  They returned from the ride
  With the lady inside,
And a smile on the face of the tiger.   5

The following poem is composed in the more common **trochaic** meter (‾˘, a stressed syllable followed by an unstressed one).

SIR JOHN SUCKLING

Song

Why so pale and wan, fond Lover?
  Prithee why so pale?

Will, when looking well can't move her,
    Looking ill prevail?
        Prithee why so pale?

Why so dull and mute, young Sinner?
    Prithee why so mute?
Will, when speaking well can't win her,
    Saying nothing do 't?
        Prithee why so mute?

Quit, quit, for shame, this will not move,
    This cannot take her;
If of her self she will not love,
    Nothing can make her,
        The Devil take her.

                                        1646

The basic meter in the following poem, as in "Sound and Sense," is the most common one in English, **iambic** ($\smile$ $-$, an unstressed syllable followed by a stressed one).

JOHN DRYDEN

To the Memory of Mr. Oldham[3]

Farewell, too little, and too lately known,
Whom I began to think and call my own;
For sure our souls were near allied, and thine
Cast in the same poetic mold with mine.
One common note on either lyre did strike,
And knaves and fools we both abhorred alike.
To the same goal did both our studies drive;
The last set out the soonest did arrive.
Thus Nisus fell upon the slippery place,
While his young friend performed and won the race.[4]
O early ripe! to thy abundant store
What could advancing age have added more?
It might (what nature never gives the young)
Have taught the numbers[5] of thy native tongue.
But satire needs not those, and wit will shine
Through the harsh cadence of a rugged line.[6]

3. John Oldham (1653–1683), who like Dryden (see lines 3–6) wrote satiric poetry.   4. In Vergil's *Aeneid* (Book V), Nisus (who is leading the race) falls and then trips the second runner so that his friend Euryalus can win.   5. Rhythms.   6. In Dryden's time, the English *r* was pronounced with a harsh, trilling sound.

A noble error, and but seldom made,
When poets are by too much force betrayed.
Thy generous fruits, though gathered ere their prime,
Still showed a quickness; and maturing time   20
But mellows what we write to the dull sweets of rhyme.
Once more, hail and farewell; farewell, thou young,
But ah too short, Marcellus[7] of our tongue;
Thy brows with ivy, and with laurels bound;
But fate and gloomy night encompass thee around.   25

1684

Once you have figured out the basic meter or rhythm of a poem, you can often find some interesting things by looking carefully at the departures from the pattern. Departures from the basic iambic meter of "To the Memory of Mr. Oldham," for example, suggest some of the imaginative things that poets can do within the apparently very restrictive requirements of traditional meter. Try marking the stressed and unstressed syllables in "To the Memory of Mr. Oldham" and then look carefully at each place that varies from the basic iambic pattern. Which of these variations call special attention to a particular sound or action being talked about in the poem? Which ones specifically mimic or echo the sense? Which variations seem to exist primarily for emphasis? Which ones seem primarily intended to mark structural breaks in the poem?

WILLIAM SHAKESPEARE

[Like as the waves make towards the pebbled shore]

Like as the waves make towards the pebbled shore,
So do our minutes hasten to their end,
Each changing place with that which goes before,
In sequent toil all forwards do contend.[8]
Nativity, once in the main[9] of light,   5
Crawls to maturity, wherewith being crowned,
Crooked[1] eclipses 'gainst his glory fight,
And Time that gave doth now his gift confound.[2]
Time doth transfix[3] the flourish set on youth
And delves the parallels[4] in beauty's brow,   10
Feeds on the rarities of nature's truth,
And nothing stands but for his scythe to mow.

7. The nephew of the Roman emperor Augustus; he died at twenty, and Vergil celebrated him in *The Aeneid*, Book VI.   8. Struggle. *Sequent:* successive.   9. High seas. *Nativity:* newborn life.   1. Perverse.   2. Bring to nothing.   3. Pierce.   4. Lines, wrinkles.

And yet to times in hope[5] my verse shall stand,
Praising thy worth, despite his cruel hand.   1609

JAMES MERRILL

Watching the Dance

1. BALANCHINE'S[6]

Poor savage, doubting that a river flows
But for the myriad eddies made
By unseen powers twirling on their toes,

Here in this darkness it would seem
5   You had already died, and were afraid.
Be still. Observe the powers. Infer the stream.

2. DISCOTHÈQUE

Having survived entirely your own youth,
Last of your generation, purple gloom
Investing you, sit, Jonah,[7] beyond speech,

10   And let towards the brute volume VOOM whale mouth
VAM pounding viscera VAM VOOM
A teenage plankton luminously twitch.   1967

ALFRED, LORD TENNYSON

Break, Break, Break

Break, break, break,
    On thy cold gray stones, O Sea!
And I would that my tongue could utter
    The thoughts that arise in me.

5   O, well for the fisherman's boy,
    That he shouts with his sister at play!
O, well for the sailor lad,
    That he sings in his boat on the bay!

And the stately ships go on
10   To their haven under the hill;

---

5. In the future.   6. George Balanchine, Russian-born (1894) ballet choreographer and teacher.
7. According to Jonah 4, Jonah sat in gloom near Nineveh after its residents repented and God decided
to spare the city from destruction.

But O for the touch of a vanished hand,
    And the sound of a voice that is still!

Break, break, break,
    At the foot of thy crags, O Sea!
But the tender grace of a day that is dead   15
    Will never come back to me.

ca. 1834

STEVIE SMITH

Our Bog Is Dood

Our Bog is dood, our Bog is dood,
They lisped in accents mild,
But when I asked them to explain
They grew a little wild.
How do you know your Bog is dood   5
My darling little child?

We know because we wish it so
That is enough, they cried,
And straight within each infant eye
Stood up the flame of pride,   10
And if you do not think it so
You shall be crucified.

Then tell me, darling little ones,
What's dood, suppose Bog is?
Just what we think, the answer came,   15
Just what we think it is.
They bowed their heads. Our Bog is ours
And we are wholly his.

But when they raised them up again
They had forgotten me   20
Each one upon each other glared
In pride and misery
For what was dood, and what their Bog
They never could agree.

Oh sweet it was to leave them then,   25
And sweeter not to see,
And sweetest of all to walk alone
Beside the encroaching sea,
The sea that soon should drown them all,
That never yet drowned me.   30

1950

EARLE BIRNEY

Irapuato[8]

For reasons any
                    brigadier
                              could tell
this is a favorite nook for
5   massacre

Toltex by Mixtex Mixtex by Aztex
Aztex by Spanishtex Spanishtex by
Mexitex by Mexitex by Mexitex by Texaco
So any farmer can see how the strawberries
10   are the biggest and reddest
       in the whole damn continent

but why
          when arranged under
                                 the market flies

15   do they look like small clotting hearts?

                                                    1962

EDGAR ALLAN POE

The Raven

Once upon a midnight dreary, while I pondered, weak and weary,
Over many a quaint and curious volume of forgotten lore,
While I nodded, nearly napping, suddenly there came a tapping,
As of some one gently rapping, rapping at my chamber door.
5   " 'Tis some visitor," I muttered, "tapping at my chamber door—
                    Only this, and nothing more."

Ah, distinctly I remember it was in the bleak December,
And each separate dying ember wrought its ghost upon the floor.
Eagerly I wished the morrow;—vainly I had sought to borrow
10   From my books surcease of sorrow—sorrow for the lost Lenore—
For the rare and radiant maiden whom the angels name Lenore—
                    Nameless here for evermore.

And the silken sad uncertain rustling of each purple curtain
Thrilled me—filled me with fantastic terrors never felt before;
15   So that now, to still the beating of my heart, I stood repeating

8. A city in central Mexico, northwest of Mexico City.

" 'Tis some visitor entreating entrance at my chamber door;—
Some late visitor entreating entrance at my chamber door;
           This it is, and nothing more."

Presently my soul grew stronger; hesitating then no longer,
"Sir," said I, "or Madam, truly your forgiveness I implore;   20
But the fact is I was napping, and so gently you came rapping,
And so faintly you came tapping, tapping at my chamber door,
That I scarce was sure I heard you"—here I opened wide the door;—
           Darkness there, and nothing more.

Deep into that darkness peering, long I stood there wondering, fearing,   25
Doubting, dreaming dreams no mortal ever dared to dream before;
But the silence was unbroken, and the darkness gave no token,
And the only word there spoken was the whispered word, "Lenore!"
This I whispered, and an echo murmured back the word, "Lenore!"—
           Merely this, and nothing more.   30

Back into the chamber turning, all my soul within me burning,
Soon I heard again a tapping somewhat louder than before.
"Surely," said I, "surely that is something at my window lattice;
Let me see, then, what thereat is, and this mystery explore—
Let my heart be still a moment and this mystery explore;—   35
           'Tis the wind and nothing more!"

Open here I flung the shutter, when, with many a flirt and flutter,
In there stepped a stately raven of the saintly days of yore;
Not the least obeisance made he; not an instant stopped or stayed he;
But, with mien of lord or lady, perched above my chamber door—   40
Perched upon a bust of Pallas[9] just above my chamber door—
           Perched, and sat, and nothing more.

Then this ebony bird beguiling my sad fancy into smiling,
By the grave and stern decorum of the countenance it wore,
"Though thy crest be shorn and shaven, thou," I said, "art sure no
    craven,   45
Ghastly grim and ancient raven wandering from the Nightly shore—
Tell me what thy lordly name is on the Night's Plutonian shore!"
           Quoth the raven, "Nevermore."

Much I marvelled this ungainly fowl to hear discourse so plainly,
Though its answer little meaning—little relevancy bore;   50
For we cannot help agreeing that no living human being
Ever yet was blessed with seeing bird above his chamber door—
Bird or beast upon the sculptured bust above his chamber door,
           With such name as "Nevermore."

But the raven, sitting lonely on the placid bust, spoke only   55
That one word, as if his soul in that one word he did outpour.
Nothing farther then he uttered—not a feather then he fluttered—
Till I scarcely more than muttered "Other friends have flown before—

---

9. Athena, the Greek goddess of wisdom.

On the morrow *he* will leave me, as my hopes have flown before."
60   Then the bird said "Nevermore."

Startled at the stillness broken by reply so aptly spoken,
"Doubtless," said I, "what it utters is its only stock and store
Caught from some unhappy master whom unmerciful Disaster
Followed fast and followed faster till his songs one burden bore—
65   Till the dirges of his Hope that melancholy burden bore
                Of 'Never—nevermore.' "

But the raven still beguiling all my sad soul into smiling,
Straight I wheeled a cushioned seat in front of bird and bust and door;
Then, upon the velvet sinking, I betook myself to linking
70   Fancy unto fancy, thinking what this ominous bird of yore—
What this grim, ungainly, ghastly, gaunt, and ominous bird of yore
                Meant in croaking "Nevermore."

This I sat engaged in guessing, but no syllable expressing
To the fowl whose fiery eyes now burned into my bosom's core;
75   This and more I sat divining, with my head at ease reclining
On the cushion's velvet lining that the lamplight gloated o'er,
But whose velvet violet lining with the lamplight gloating o'er,
                She shall press, ah, nevermore!

Then, methought, the air grew denser, perfumed from an unseen censer
80   Swung by angels whose faint foot-falls tinkled on the tufted floor.
"Wretch," I cried, "thy God hath lent thee—by these angels he hath sent
      thee
Respite—respite and nepenthe[1] from thy memories of Lenore!
Quaff, oh quaff this kind nepenthe and forget this lost Lenore!"
                Quoth the raven, "Nevermore."

85   "Prophet!" said I, "thing of evil!—prophet still, if bird or devil!—
Whether Tempter sent, or whether tempest tossed thee here ashore,
Desolate, yet all undaunted, on this desert land enchanted—
On this home by Horror haunted—tell me truly, I implore—
Is there—*is* there balm in Gilead?[2]—tell me—tell me, I implore!"
90   Quoth the raven, "Nevermore."

"Prophet!" said I, "thing of evil—prophet still, if bird or devil!
by that Heaven that bends above us—by that God we both adore—
Tell this soul with sorrow laden if, within the distant Aidenn,
It shall clasp a sainted maiden whom the angels name Lenore—
95   Clasp a rare and radiant maiden whom the angels name Lenore."
                Quoth the raven, "Nevermore."

"Be that word our sign of parting, bird or fiend!" I shrieked upstarting—
"Get thee back into the tempest and the Night's Plutonian shore!
Leave no black plume as a token of that lie thy soul hath spoken!
100   Leave my loneliness unbroken!—quit the bust above my door!

---

1. A drug reputed by the Greeks to cause forgetfulness or sorrow.   2. Cf. Jeremiah 8:22.

Take thy beak from out my heart, and take thy form from off my door!"
Quoth the raven, "Nevermore."

And the raven, never flitting, still is sitting, still is sitting
On the pallid bust of Pallas just above my chamber door;
And his eyes have all the seeming of a demon's that is dreaming,   105
And the lamp-light o'er him streaming throws his shadow on the floor;
And my soul from out that shadow that lies floating on the floor
Shall be lifted—nevermore!

                                                                                  1844

GERARD MANLEY HOPKINS

Spring and Fall:

to a young child

Márgarét áre you gríeving
Over Goldengrove unleaving?
Leáves, like the things of man, you
With your fresh thoughts care for, can you?
Áh! ás the heart grows older   5
It will come to such sights colder
By and by, nor spare a sigh
Though worlds of wanwood leafmeal[3] lie;
And yet you wíll weep and know why.
Now no matter, child, the name: 10
Sórrow's spríngs áre the same.
Nor mouth had, no nor mind, expressed
What heart heard of, ghost[4] guessed:
It ís the blight man was born for,
It is Margaret you mourn for.   15

1880

EMILY DICKINSON

[A narrow Fellow in the Grass]

A narrow Fellow in the Grass
Occasionally rides—
You may have met Him—did you not
His notice sudden is—

3. Broken up, leaf by leaf (analogous to "piecemeal"). *Wanwood:* pale, gloomy woods.   4. Soul.

The Grass divides as with a Comb—
A spotted shaft is seen—
And then it closes at your feet
And opens further on—

He likes a Boggy Acre
A Floor too cool for Corn—
Yet when a Boy, and Barefoot—
I more than once at Noon

Have passed, I thought, a Whip lash
Unbraiding in the Sun
When stooping to secure it
It wrinkled, and was gone—

Several of Nature's People
I know, and they know me—
I feel for them a transport
Of cordiality—

But never met this Fellow
Attended, or alone
Without a tighter breathing
And Zero at the Bone—

1866

ROBERT HERRICK

To the Virgins, to Make Much of Time

Gather ye rosebuds while ye may,
    Old time is still a-flying;
And this same flower that smiles today
    Tomorrow will be dying.

The glorious lamp of heaven, the sun,
    The higher he's a-getting,
The sooner will his race be run,
    And nearer he's to setting.

That age is best which is the first,
    When youth and blood are warmer;
But being spent, the worse, and worst
    Times still succeed the former.

Then be not coy, but use your time,
    And, while ye may, go marry;
For, having lost but once your prime,
    You may forever tarry.

1648

QUESTIONS

1. Read the following poems aloud: "Break, Break, Break" and "The Raven." As you read each, try to be especially conscious of the way punctuation and spacing guide your pauses and of the pace you develop as you become accustomed to the prevailing rhythms of the poem. What function does repetition have in the reading aloud of each poem?
2. Scan—that is, mark all of the stressed syllables and chart their pattern in—Shakespeare's "Like as the waves make towards the pebbled shore." What variations do you find on the basic iambic pentameter pattern? What functions do the variations perform in each case?
3. Read Herrick's "To the Virgins, to Make Much of Time" aloud. Then have someone else read it aloud to you. Compare the *pace* of the readings. Compare the stress on particular words and syllables. To what extent does the basic metrical pattern in the poem come to control the voice? Do you notice more similarities in the two readings as you and the other reader progress through the poem? why?

WRITING SUGGESTIONS

1. Read Pope's "Sound and Sense" over carefully twice—once silently and once aloud—and then mark the stressed and unstressed syllables. Draw up a chart indicating, line by line, exactly what the patterns of stress are, and then single out all the lines that have major variations from the basic iambic pentameter pattern. Pick out half a dozen lines with variations that seem to you worthy of comment, and write a paragraph on each in which you show how the varied metrical pattern contributes to the specific effects achieved in that line. (You will probably notice that in most of the lines other strategies also contribute to the sound effects, but confine your discussion to the achievement through metrical pattern.)
2. Try your hand at writing limericks in imitation of "There was a young lady of Riga" (study the rhythmic patterns and line lengths carefully, and imitate them exactly in your poem). Begin your limerick with "There once was a ———— from ————" (use a place for which you think you can find a comic rhyme).
3. Scan line by line Suckling's "Song." In an essay of no more than 500 words, show in detail how the varied metrical pattern in the final stanza abruptly changes the tone of the poem and reverses the poem's direction.

18

INTERNAL STRUCTURE

"**P**roper words in proper places": that is the way one great writer of English prose (Jonathan Swift) described good writing. Finding appropriate words is not the easiest of tasks for a poet, and already we have looked at some of the implications for readers of the verbal choices a poet makes. But a poet's decision about where to put those words—how to arrange them for maximum effect—is also difficult, for individual words, metaphors, and symbols not only exist as part of a phrase or sentence or rhythmic pattern but also as part of the larger whole of the poem itself. How are the words to be ordered and the poem organized? What will come first and what last? What will be its "plot"? How will it be conceived as a whole? How is some sort of structure to be created? What principle or idea of organization will inform the poem? How are words, sentences, images, ideas, and feelings to be combined into something that holds together, seems complete, and will have an effect upon us as readers?

Looking at these questions from the point of view of the poet (What shall I plan? Where shall I begin?) can help the reader notice the effect of structural decisions. Every poem is different from every other one, and independent, individual decisions must, therefore, be made about how to organize. But there are also patterns of organization that poems fall into, sometimes because of the subject matter, sometimes because of the effect intended, sometimes for other reasons. Often poets consciously decide on a particular organizational strategy; sometimes they may reach instinctively for one or happen into a structure that suits the needs of the moment, one onto which a creator can hang the words and sentences one by one and group by group.

When there is a story to be told, the organization of a poem may be fairly simple. Here, for example, is a poem that tells a rather simple story, largely in chronological fashion (first . . . and then . . .):

EDWIN ARLINGTON ROBINSON

Mr. Flood's Party

Old Eben Flood, climbing alone one night
Over the hill between the town below

And the forsaken upland hermitage
That held as much as he should ever know
On earth again of home, paused warily.   5
The road was his and not a native near;
And Eben, having leisure, said aloud,
For no man else in Tilbury Town to hear:

"Well, Mr. Flood, we have the harvest moon
Again, and we may not have many more;   10
The bird is on the wing, the poet says,[1]
And you and I have said it here before.
Drink to the bird." He raised up to the light
The jug that he had gone so far to fill,
And answered huskily: "Well, Mr. Flood,   15
Since you propose it, I believe I will."

Alone, as if enduring to the end
A valiant armor of scarred hopes outworn
He stood there in the middle of the road
Like Roland's ghost winding a silent horn.[2]   20
Below him, in the town among the trees,
Where friends of other days had honored him,
A phantom salutation of the dead
Rang thinly till old Eben's eyes were dim

Then, as a mother lays her sleeping child   25
Down tenderly, fearing it may awake
He set the jug down slowly at his feet
With trembling care, knowing that most things break;
And only when assured that on firm earth
It stood, as the uncertain lives of men   30
Assuredly did not, he paced away,
And with his hand extended paused again:

"Well, Mr. Flood, we have not met like this
In a long time; and many a change has come
To both of us, I fear, since last it was   35
We had a drop together. Welcome home!"
Convivially returning with himself,
Again he raised the jug up to the light;
And with an acquiescent quaver said:
"Well, Mr. Flood, if you insist, I might.   40

"Only a very little, Mr. Flood—
For auld lang syne. No more, sir; that will do."
So, for the time, apparently it did,
And Eben evidently thought so too;
For soon amid the silver loneliness   45

1. Edward Fitzgerald, in "The Rubáiyat of Omar Khayyám" (more or less a translation of an Arab original), so describes the "Bird of Time."   2. In French legend Roland's powerful ivory horn was used to warn his allies of impending attack.

Of night he lifted up his voice and sang,
Secure, with only two moons listening,
Until the whole harmonious landscape rang—

"For auld lang syne." The weary throat gave out,
50 The last word wavered, and the song was done.
He raised again the jug regretfully
And shook his head, and was again alone.
There was not much that was ahead of him,
And there was nothing in the town below—
55 Where strangers would have shut the many doors
That many friends had opened long ago.   1921

The fairly simple **narrative structure** here is based on the gradual unfolding of the story. Old Eben is introduced and "placed" in relation to the town and his home, and then the "plot" unfolds: he sits down in the road, reviews his life, reflects on the present, and has a drink. Several drinks, in fact, as he thinks about passing time and growing old; and he sings and considers going "home." Not much happens, really: what we get is a vignette of Mr. Flood between two places and two times, but there *is* action, and the poem's movement—its organization and structure—depends on it: Mr. Flood in motion, in stasis, and then, again, contemplating motion. Here is story, and chronological movement, such as it is. You could say that a narrative of sort takes place (rather like that in Dickey's "Cherrylog Road" [page 661]), though sparely. The poem's organization—its structural principle—involves the passing of time, action moving forward, a larger story being revealed by the few moments depicted here.

"Mr. Flood's Party" presents about as much story as a short poem ever does, but as with most poems the emphasis is not really on the developing action—which all seems fairly predictable once we "get" who Eben is, how old he is, and what "position" he occupies in the communal memory of Tilbury Town and vice versa. Rather, the movement forward in time dictates the shape of the poem, determines the way it presents its images, ideas, themes. There's an easy-to-follow chronology here, and nearly everything takes place within it: you could say that a story is told—with a beginning, middle, and end—and that time structures how the revelation of facts takes place.

But even here, in one of the most simple of narrative structures, there are complications to be noted. One complication is in the use of time itself, for "old" time and "present" time seem posed against each other as a structural principle, too, one in tension with the chronological movement: Eben's past, as contrasted with his present and limited future, focuses the poem's attention, and in some ways the contrast between what was and what is seems even more important than the brief movement through present time that gets the most obvious attention in the poem. Then, too, "character"— Eben's character and that of the townspeople of later generations—gets a lot of the poem's attention, even as the chronology moves forward. More than one structural principle is at work here. We may identify the main movement of the poem as chronological and its principal structure as narrative, but to be fair and full in our discussion we have to note several other competing organizational forces at work—principles of comparison and contrast, for example, and of descriptive elaboration.

Most poems work with this kind of complexity, and identifying a single structure behind any poem involves a sense of what kind of organizational principle makes it work, while at the same time recognizing that other principles repeatedly, perhaps continually, compete for our attention. A poem's *structure* involves its conceptual framework—what principle best explains its organization and movement—and it is often useful to identify one dominating kind of structure, such as narrative structure, that gives the poem its shape. But it is well to recognize from the start that most poems follow paradigmatic models loosely. As with other "elements" of a poem, finding an appropriate label to describe the structure of a particular poem can help in analyzing the poem's other aspects, but there is nothing magic in the label itself.

> *Back of the idea of organic form is the concept that there is a form in all things (and in our experience) which the poet can discover and reveal.*
>
> —DENISE LEVERTOV

Purely narrative poems are often very long, much longer than can be included in a book like this, and often there are many features that are not, strictly speaking, closely connected to the narrative or linked to a strict chronology. Very often a poem moves on from a narrative of an event to some sort of commentary or reflection upon it. Reflection can be included along the way or may be implicit in the way the story is narrated, as in Kumin's "Woodchucks" (page 628), where our major attention is more on the narrator and her responses than on the events in the story as such.

Just as poems sometimes take on a structure like that of a story, they sometimes borrow the structures of plays. The following poem has a **dramatic structure;** it consists of a series of scenes, each of which is presented vividly and in detail:

HOWARD NEMEROV

The Goose Fish

On the long shore, lit by the moon
To show them properly alone,
Two lovers suddenly embraced
So that their shadows were as one.
The ordinary night was graced   5
For them by the swift tide of blood
That silently they took at flood.
And for a little time they prized
    Themselves emparadised.

Then, as if shaken by stage-fright   10
Beneath the hard moon's bony light,
They stood together on the sand
Embarrassed in each other's sight
But still conspiring hand in hand,
Until they saw, there underfoot,   15
As though the world had found them out,
The goose fish turning up, though dead,
    His hugely grinning head.

There in the china light he lay,
20   Most ancient and corrupt and gray.
They hesitated at his smile,
Wondering what it seemed to say
To lovers who a little while
Before had thought to understand,
25   By violence upon the sand,
The only way that could be known
    To make a world their own.

It was a wide and moony grin
Together peaceful and obscene;
30   They knew not what he would express,
So finished a comedian
He might mean failure or success,
But took it for an emblem of
Their sudden, new and guilty love
35   To be observed by, when they kissed,
    That rigid optimist.

So he became their patriarch,
Dreadfully mild in the half-dark.
His throat that the sand seemed to choke,
40   His picket teeth, these left their mark
But never did explain the joke
That so amused him, lying there
While the moon went down to disappear
Along the still and tilted track
45   That bears the zodiac.   1955

The first stanza sets the scene—a sandy shore in moonlight—and presents, in fact, the major action of the poem. The rest of the poem dramatizes the lovers' reactions: their initial embarrassment and feelings of guilt (stanza 2), their attempt to interpret the goose fish's smile (stanza 3), their decision to make him, whatever his meaning, the "emblem" of their love (stanza 4), and their acceptance of the fish's ambiguity and of their own relationship (stanza 5). The five stanzas do not exactly present five different scenes, but they do present separate dramatic moments, even if only a few minutes apart. Almost like a play of five very short acts, the poem traces the drama of the lovers' discovery of themselves, of their coming to terms with the meaning of their action. As in many plays, the central event (their lovemaking) is not the central focus of the drama, although the drama is based upon that event and could not take place without it. Here, that event is depicted only briefly but very vividly through figurative language: "they took at flood" the "swift tide of blood," and the immediate effect is to make them briefly feel "emparadised." But the poem concentrates on their later reactions, not on the act of love itself.

Their sudden discovery of the fish is a rude shock and injects a grotesque, almost macabre, note into the poem. From a vision of paradise, the poem seems for a moment to turn toward gothic horror when the lovers discover that they have, after all, been seen—and by such a ghoulish spectator. The last three stanzas gradually re-create the intruder in their minds, as they are forced to admit that their act of love does not exist in isolation as they had at first hoped, and they begin to see it as part of a continuum, as part of their relationship to the larger world, even (at the end) putting it into the context of the rotating world and its seasons as the moon disappears into its zodiac. In retrospect, we can see that even at the moment of passion they were in touch with larger processes controlled by the presiding mood ("the swift tide of blood"), but neither the lovers nor we had understood their act as such then, and the poem is about their gradual recognition of their "place" in time and space.

Stages of feeling and knowing rather than specific visual scenes are responsible for the poem's progress, and its dramatic structure depends upon internal perceptions and internal states of mind rather than dialogue and events. Visualization and images help to organize the poem, too. Notice in particular how the two most striking visual features of the poem—the fish and the moon—are presented stanza by stanza. In stanza 1, the fish is not yet noticed, and the moon exists plain; it is only mentioned, not described, and its light serves as a stage spotlight to assure not center-stage attention, but rather total privacy: it is a kind of lookout for the lovers. The stage imagery, barely suggested by the light in stanza 1, is articulated in stanza 2, and there the moon is said to be "hard" and its light "bony"; its features have characteristics that seem more appropriate to the fish, which has now become visible. In stanza 3, the moon's light has come to seem fragile ("china") as it is said to expose the fish directly; the role of the moon as lookout and protector seems abandoned, or at least endangered. No moon appears in stanza 4, but the fish's grin is described as "wide and moony," almost as if the two onlookers, one earthly and dead, the other heavenly and eternal, had become merged in the poem, as they nearly had been by the imagery in stanza 2. And by stanza 5, the fish has become a friend—by now he is a comedian, optimist, emblem, and a patriarch of their love—and his new position in collaboration with the lovers is presided over by the moon going about its eternal business. The moon has provided the stage light for the poem and the means by which not only the fish but the meaning of the lovers' act has been discovered. The moon has also helped to organize the poem, partly as a dramatic accessory, partly as imagery.

The following poem is also dramatic, but it seems to represent a composite of several similar experiences (compare Blake's "London" [page 626] and Dickey's "Cherrylog Road" [page 661]) rather than a single event—a fairly common pattern in dramatic poems:

PHILIP LARKIN

Church Going

Once I am sure there's nothing going on
I step inside, letting the door thud shut.
Another church: matting, seats, and stone,
And little books; sprawlings of flowers, cut
For Sunday, brownish now; some brass and stuff
Up at the holy end; the small neat organ;
And a tense, musty, unignorable silence,

5

Brewed God knows how long. Hatless, I take off
My cycle-clips in awkward reverence,

10   Move forward, run my hand around the font.
From where I stand, the roof looks almost new—
Cleaned, or restored? Someone would know: I don't.
Mounting the lectern, I peruse a few
Hectoring large-scale verses, and pronounce
15   "Here endeth" much more loudly than I'd meant.
The echoes snigger briefly. Back at the door
I sign the book, donate an Irish sixpence,
Reflect the place was not worth stopping for.

Yet stop I did: in fact I often do,
20   And always end much at a loss like this,
Wondering what to look for; wondering, too,
When churches fall completely out of use
What we shall turn them into, if we shall keep
A few cathedrals chronically on show,
25   Their parchment, plate and pyx in locked cases,
And let the rest rent-free to rain and sheep.
Shall we avoid them as unlucky places?

Or, after dark, will dubious women come
To make their children touch a particular stone;
30   Pick simples[3] for a cancer; or on some
Advised night see walking a dead one?
Power of some sort or other will go on
In games, in riddles, seemingly at random;
But superstition, like belief, must die,
35   And what remains when disbelief has gone?
Grass, weedy pavement, brambles, buttress, sky,

A shape less recognizable each week,
A purpose more obscure. I wonder who
Will be the last, the very last, to seek
40   This place for what it was; one of the crew
That tap and jot and know what rood-lofts[4] were?
Some ruin-bibber,[5] randy for antique,
Or Christmas-addict, counting on a whiff
Of gown-and-bands and organ-pipes and myrrh?
45   Or will he be my representative,

Bored, uninformed, knowing the ghostly silt
Dispersed, yet tending to this cross of ground
Through suburb scrub because it held unspilt
So long and equably what since is found
50   Only in separation—marriage, and birth,

---

3. Medicinal herbs.   4. Galleries atop the screens (on which crosses are mounted) that divide the naves or main bodies of churches from the choirs or chancels.   5. Literally, ruin-drinker: someone extremely attracted to antiquarian objects.

And death, and thoughts of these—for whom was built
This special shell? For, though I've no idea
What this accoutered frowsty barn is worth,
It pleases me to stand in silence here;

A serious house on serious earth it is,   55
In whose blent air all our compulsions meet,
Are recognized, and robed as destinies.
And that much never can be obsolete,
Since someone will forever be surprising
A hunger in himself to be more serious,   60
And gravitating with it to this ground,
Which, he once heard, was proper to grow wise in,
If only that so many dead lie round.   1955

Ultimately, the poem's emphasis is upon what it means to visit churches, what sort of phenomenon church buildings represent, and what is to be made of the fact that "church going" (in the usual sense of the word) has declined so much. The poem uses a *different* sort of church going (visitation by tourists) to consider larger philosophical questions about the relationship of religion to culture and history. The poem is, finally, a rather philosophical one about the directions of English culture, and through an enumeration of religious objects and rituals it reviews the history of how we got to our present historical circumstance. It tells a kind of story first, through one lengthy dramatized scene, in order to comment later on what the place and the experience may mean, and the larger conclusion derives from the particulars of what the speaker does and touches. The action is really over by the end of stanza 2, and that action, we are told, stands for many such visits to similar churches; after that, all is reflection and discussion, five stanzas' worth.

"Church Going" is a curious poem in many ways. It goes to a lot of trouble to characterize its speaker, who seems a rather odd choice as a commentator on the state of religion. His informal attire (he takes off his cycle-clips at the end of stanza 1) and his not exactly worshipful behavior do not at first make us expect him to be a serious philosopher about what all this means. He is not disrespectful or sacrilegious, and before the end of stanza 1 he has tried to describe the "awkward reverence" he feels; but his overly somber imitation of part of the service stamps him as playful, a little satirical, and as a tourist here, not someone who regularly drops in for prayer or meditation in the usual sense. And yet those early details do give him credentials, in a way; he knows the names of religious objects and has some of the history of churches in his grasp. Clearly he does this sort of church going often ("Yet stop I did: in fact I often do," line 19) because he wonders seriously what it all means—now—in comparison to what it meant to religious worshipers in times past. Ultimately, he takes the church itself seriously and its cultural meaning and function just as seriously (lines 55 ff.), and understands the importance of the church in the history of his culture. In this poem, the drama is, relatively speaking, brief, but it gives a context for the more digressive and rambling free-floating reflections that grow out of the dramatic experience.

Sometimes poems are organized by contrasts, setting one thing up conveniently against another that is quite different. Look, for example, at the two worlds in the following poem, and notice how carefully the contrasts are developed.

PAT MORA

Sonrisas

I live in a doorway
between two rooms, I hear
quiet clicks, cups of black
coffee, *click, click* like facts
5   budgets, tenure, curriculum,
from careful women in crisp beige
suits, quick beige smiles
that seldom sneak into their eyes.

I peek
10   in the other room señoras
in faded dresses stir sweet
milk coffee, laughter whirls
with steam from fresh *tamales*
    sh, sh, mucho ruido,[6]
15   they scold one another,
press their lips, trap smiles
in their dark, Mexican eyes.

                                                1986

    Here different words, habits, and values characterize the different worlds of the two sets of characters, and the poem is largely organized on the basis of the contrasts between them. The meaning of the poem (the difference between the two worlds) is very nearly the same as the structure itself.

    Poems often have **discursive structures,** too; that is, they are sometimes organized like a treatise, an argument, or an essay. "First," they say, "and second . . . and third. . . ." This sort of 1-2-3 structure takes a variety of forms depending on what one is enumerating or arguing. Here, for example, is a poem that is about three people who have died. The poem honors all three, but makes clear and sharp distinctions among them. Most of the differences are, in fact, articulated by the way comparisons and contrasts are suggested by the structure itself: the earth is "sweet," "bright," or "dark," depending on the person about to be described. As you read the poem, try to articulate just what sort of person each of the three is represented to be.

JAMES WRIGHT

Arrangements with Earth for Three Dead Friends

Sweet earth, he ran and changed his shoes to go
Outside with other children through the fields.

6. A lot of noise.

He panted up the hills and swung from trees
Wild as a beast but for the human laughter
That tumbled like a cider down his cheeks.   5
Sweet earth, the summer has been gone for weeks,
And weary fish already sleeping under water
Below the banks where early acorns freeze.
Receive his flesh and keep it cured of colds.
Button his coat and scarf his throat from snow.   10

And now, bright earth, this other is out of place
In what, awake, we speak about as tombs.
He sang in houses when the birds were still
And friends of his were huddled round till dawn
After the many nights to hear him sing.   15
Bright earth, his friends remember how he sang
Voices of night away when wind was one.
Lonely the neighborhood beneath your hill
Where he is waved away through silent rooms.
Listen for music, earth, and human ways.   20

Dark earth, there is another gone away,
But she was not inclined to beg of you
Relief from water falling or the storm.
She was aware of scavengers in holes
Of stone, she knew the loosened stones that fell   25
Indifferently as pebbles plunging down a well
And broke for the sake of nothing human souls.
Earth, hide your face from her where dark is warm.
She does not beg for anything, who knew
The change of tone, the human hope gone gray.   30

1957

Why, in stanza 1, is the earth represented as a parent? What does addressing the earth here as "sweet" seem to mean? How does the address to earth as "bright" fit the dead person described in stanza 2? In what different senses is the person described in stanza 3 "dark"? Why is the earth asked to give attention secretly to this person? Exactly what kind of person was she? How does the poem make you feel about her? Is there any cumulative point in describing three such different people in the same poem? What is accomplished by having the poem's three stanzas addressed to various aspects of earth? Similar discursive structures help to organize poems such as Shelley's "Ode to the West Wind" (page 775), where the wind is shown driving a leaf in Part I, a cloud in Part II, a wave in Part III, and then, after a summary and statement of the speaker's ambitious hope in Part IV, is asked to make the speaker a lyre in Part V.

Poems may borrow their organizational strategies from many places, imitating chronological, visual, or discursive shapes in reality or in other works of art. Sometimes poems strive to be almost purely descriptive of someone or something (using **descriptive structures**), in which case organizational decisions have to be made much as a painter or photographer would make them, deciding first how the whole scene should look, then putting the parts into proper place for the whole. But there are differences demanded by the poetic medium: a poem has to present the details sequentially, not all at once as an actual picture more or less can, so the poet must decide where the description starts (at the left? center? top?) and what sort of movement to use (linear across the scene? clockwise?). But if having words instead of paint or film has some disadvantages, it also has particular assets: figurative language can be a part of description, or an adjunct to it. A poet can insert a comparison at any point without necessarily disturbing the unity of what he or she describes.

Some poems use **imitative structures,** mirroring as exactly as possible the structure of something that already exists as an object and can be seen—another poem perhaps, as in Koch's "Variations on a Theme by William Carlos Williams" (page 853). Or a poem may use **reflective** (or **meditative**) **structures,** pondering a subject, theme, or event, and letting the mind play with it, skipping (sometimes illogically but still usefully) from one sound to another, or to related thoughts or objects as the mind receives them.

Here is a poem that involves several different organizational principles but ultimately takes its structure from an important emotional shift in the speaker's attitude as her mind reviews, ponders, and rethinks events of long ago.

SHARON OLDS

The Victims

When Mother divorced you, we were glad. She took it and
took it, in silence, all those years and then
kicked you out, suddenly, and her
kids loved it. Then you were fired, and we
5   grinned inside, the way people grinned when
Nixon's helicopter lifted off the South
Lawn for the last time.[7] We were tickled
to think of your office taken away,
your secretaries taken away,
10   your lunches with three double bourbons,
your pencils, your reams of paper. Would they take your
suits back, too, those dark
carcasses hung in your closet, and the black
noses of your shoes with their large pores?
15   She had taught us to take it, to hate you and take it
until we pricked with her for your
annihilation, Father. Now I
pass the bums in doorways, the white
slugs of their bodies gleaming through slits in their
20   suits of compressed silt, the stained
flippers of their hands, the underwater
fire of their eyes, ships gone down with the

---

7. When Richard Nixon resigned the U.S. presidency on August 8, 1974, his exit from the White House (by helicopter from the lawn) was televised live.

lanterns lit, and I wonder who took it and
took it from them in silence until they had
given it all away and had nothing   25
left but this.   1984

"The Victims" divides basically into two parts. In the first two-thirds of the poem (from line 1 to the middle of line 17), the speaker evokes her father (the "you" of lines 1, 3, and so forth), who had been guilty of terrible habits and behavior when the speaker was young and was kicked out suddenly and divorced by the speaker's mother (lines 1–3). He was then fired from his job (line 4) and lost his whole way of life (lines 8–12), and the speaker (taught by the mother, lines 15–17) recalls celebrating every defeat and every loss ("we pricked with her for your annihilation," lines 16–17). The mother is regarded as a victim ("She took it and took it, in silence, all those years" [lines 1–2]), and the speaker forms an indivisible unit with her and the other children ("her kids," lines 3–4). They are the "we" of the first part of the poem. They were "glad" (line 1) at the divorce; they "loved it" (line 4) when the mother kicked out the father; they "grinned" (line 5) when the father was fired; they were "tickled" (line 7) when he lost his job, his secretaries, and his daily life. Only at the end of the first section does the speaker (now older but remembering what it was like to be a child) recognize that the mother was responsible for the easy, childish vision of the father's guilt ("She had taught us to take it, to hate you and take it" [line 15]); nevertheless, all sympathy in this part of the poem is with the mother and her children, while all of the imagery is entirely unfavorable to the father. The family reacted to the father's misfortunes the way observers responded to the retreat in disgrace of Richard Nixon from the U.S. presidency. The father seems to have led a luxurious and insensitive life, with lots of support in his office (lines 8–11), fancy clothes (lines 12–14), and decadent lunches (line 10); his artificial identity seemed haunting and daunting (lines 11–14) to the speaker as child.

But in line 17, the poem shifts focus and shifts gears. The "you" in the poem is now, suddenly, "Father." A bit of sympathy begins to surface for "bums in doorways" (line 18), who begin to seem like victims, too; their bodies are "slugs" (line 19), their suits are made of residual waste pressed into regimented usefulness (lines 19–20), and their hands are constricted into mechanical "flippers" (line 21). Their eyes contain fire (line 22), but it is as if they retain only a spark of life in their submerged and dying state. The speaker has not forgotten the cruelty and insensitivity remembered in the first part of the poem, but the blame seems to have shifted somewhat and the father is not the only villain, nor are the mother and children the only victims. Look carefully at how the existence of street people recalls earlier details about the father, how sympathy for his plight is elicited from us, and how the definition of victim shifts.

Imagery, words, attitudes, and narrative are different in the two parts of the poem, and the second half carefully qualifies the first, as if to illustrate the more mature and considered attitudes of the speaker in her older years—a qualification of the easy imitation of the earlier years when the mother's views were thoroughly dominant and seemed sensible and adequate. Change has governed the poem's structure here; differences in age, attitude, and tone are supported by entirely different sets of terms, attitudes, and versions of causality.

The paradigms (or models) for organizing poems are, finally, not all that different from those of prose. It may be easier to organize something short rather than something long, but the question of intensity becomes comparatively more important in shorter works. Basically, the problem of how to organize one's material is, for the writer, first of all a matter of deciding what kind of thing one wants to create, of having its purposes and effects clearly in mind. That means that every poem will differ somewhat from every other, but it also means that patterns of purpose—narrative, dramatic, discursive, descriptive, imitative, or reflective—may help writers organize and formulate their ideas. A consciousness of purpose and effect can help the reader see *how* a poem proceeds toward its goal. Seeing how a poem is organized is, in turn, often a good way of seeing where it is going and what its real concerns and purposes may be. Often a poem's organization helps to make clear the particular effects that the poet wishes to generate. In a good poem, means and end are closely related, and a reader who is a good observer of one will be able to discover the other.

ANONYMOUS

Sir Patrick Spens

The king sits in Dumferling toune,[8]
    Drinking the blude-reid[9] wine:
"O whar will I get guid sailor,
    To sail this ship of mine?"

5   Up and spake an eldern knicht,
        Sat at the king's richt knee:
    "Sir Patrick Spens is the best sailor
        That sails upon the sea."

    The king has written a braid[1] letter
10   And signed it wi' his hand,
    And sent it to Sir Patrick Spens,
        Was walking on the sand.

    The first line that Sir Patrick read,
        A loud lauch[2] lauched he;
15   The next line that Sir Patrick read,
        The tear blinded his ee.[3]

    "O wha is this has done this deed,
        This il deed done to me,
    To send me out this time o' the year,
20   To sail upon the sea?

    "Make haste, make haste, my merry men all,
        Our guid ship sails the morn."
    "O say na sae,[4] my master dear,
        For I fear a deadly storm.

---

8. Town.   9. Blood-red.   1. Broad: explicit.   2. Laugh.   3. Eye.   4. Not so.

"Late, late yestre'en I saw the new moon   25
   Wi' the auld moon in her arm,
And I fear, I fear, my dear mastér,
   That we will come to harm."

O our Scots nobles were richt laith[5]
   To weet their cork-heeled shoon,[6]   30
But lang owre a'[7] the play were played
   Their hats they swam aboon.[8]

O lang, lang, may their ladies sit,
   Wi' their fans into their hand,
Or ere they see Sir Patrick Spens   35
   Come sailing to the land.

O lang, lang, may the ladies stand
   Wi' their gold kems[9] in their hair,
Waiting for their ain[1] dear lords,
   For they'll see them na mair.   40

Half o'er, half o'er to Aberdour
   It's fifty fadom deep,
And there lies guid Sir Patrick Spens
   Wi' the Scots lords at his feet.

probably thirteenth century

T. S. ELIOT

Journey of the Magi[2]

"A cold coming we had of it,
Just the worst time of the year
For a journey, and such a long journey:
The ways deep and the weather sharp,
The very dead of winter."[3]   5
And the camels galled, sore-footed, refractory,
Lying down in the melting snow.
There were times we regretted
The summer palaces on slopes, the terraces,
And the silken girls bringing sherbet.   10
Then the camel men cursing and grumbling
And running away, and wanting their liquor and women,
And the night-fires going out, and the lack of shelters,

5. Right loath: very reluctant.   6. To wet their cork-heeled shoes. Cork was expensive, and, therefore, such shoes were a mark of wealth and status.   7. Before all.   8. Their hats swam above them. 9. Combs.   1. Own.   2. The wise men who followed the star of Bethlehem. See Matthew 2:1–12.   3. An adaptation of a passage from a 1622 sermon by Lancelot Andrewes.

And the cities hostile and the towns unfriendly
15 And the villages dirty and charging high prices:
A hard time we had of it.
At the end we preferred to travel all night,
Sleeping in snatches,
With the voices singing in our ears, saying
20 That this was all folly.

    Then at dawn we came down to a temperate valley,
Wet, below the snow line, smelling of vegetation;
With a running stream and a water-mill beating the darkness,
And three trees on the low sky,[4]
25 And an old white horse galloped away in the meadow.
Then we came to a tavern with vine-leaves over the lintel,
Six hands at an open door dicing for pieces of silver,
And feet kicking the empty wine-skins.
But there was no information, and so we continued
30 And arrived at evening, not a moment too soon
Finding the place; it was (you may say) satisfactory.

    All this was a long time ago, I remember,
And I would do it again, but set down
This set down
35 This: were we led all that way for
Birth or Death? There was a Birth, certainly,
We had evidence and no doubt. I had seen birth and death,
But had thought they were different; this Birth was
Hard and bitter agony for us, like Death, our death.
40 We returned to our places, these Kingdoms,[5]
But no longer at ease here, in the old dispensation,
With an alien people clutching their gods.
I should be glad of another death.   1927

EMILY DICKINSON
_____

[*The Wind begun to knead the Grass—*]

The Wind begun to knead the Grass—
As Women do a Dough—
He flung a Hand full at the Plain—
A Hand full at the Sky—

4. Suggestive of the three crosses of the Crucifixion (Luke 23:32–33). The Magi see several objects that suggest later events in Christ's life: pieces of silver (see Matthew 26:14–16), the dicing (see Matthew 27:35), the white horse (see Revelation 6:2 and 19:11–16), and the empty wine-skins (see Matthew 9:17, possibly relevant also to lines 41–42).   5. The Bible only identifies the wise men as "from the east," and subsequent tradition has made them kings. In Persia, magi were members of an ancient priestly caste.

The Leaves unhooked themselves from Trees—   5
And started all abroad—
The Dust did scoop itself like Hands—
And throw away the Road—
The Wagons quickened on the Street—
The Thunders gossiped low—   10
The Lightning showed a Yellow Head—
And then a livid Toe—
The Birds put up the Bars to Nests—
The Cattle flung to Barns—
Then came one drop of Giant Rain—   15
And then, as if the Hands
That held the Dams—had parted hold—
The Waters Wrecked the Sky—
But overlooked my Father's House—
Just Quartering a Tree—   20

1864

ROO BORSON

Save Us From

Save us from night,
from bleak open highways
without end, and the fluorescent
oases of gas stations,
from the gunning of immortal   5
engines past midnight,
when time has no meaning,
from all-night cafés,
their ghoulish slices of pie,
and the orange ruffle on the   10
apron of the waitress,
the matching plastic chairs,
from orange and brown and
all unearthly colors,
banish them back to the test tube,   15
save us from them,
from those bathrooms with a
moonscape of skin in the mirror,
from fatigue, its merciless brightness,
when each cell of the body stands on end,   20
and the sensation of teeth,
and the mind's eternal sentry,
and the unmapped city
with its cold bed.

25   Save us from insomnia,
         its treadmill,
         its school bells and factory bells,
         from living-rooms like the tomb,
         their plaid chesterfields
30   and galaxies of dust,
         from chairs without arms,
         from any matched set of furniture,
         from floor-length drapes which
         close out the world,
35   from padded bras and rented suits,
         from any object in which horror is concealed.
         Save us from waking after nightmares,
         save us from nightmares,
         from other worlds,
40   from the mute, immobile contours
         of dressers and shoes,
         from another measureless day, save us.   1989

WILLIAM CARLOS WILLIAMS

The Dance

In Brueghel's great picture, The Kermess,[6]
the dancers go round, they go round and
around, the squeal and the blare and the
tweedle of bagpipes, a bugle and fiddles
5   tipping their bellies (round as the thick-
sided glasses whose wash they impound)
their hips and their bellies off balance
to turn them. Kicking and rolling about
the Fair Grounds, swinging their butts, those
10   shanks must be sound to bear up under such
rollicking measures, prance as they dance
in Brueghel's great picture, The Kermess.   1944

---

6. A painting by Pieter Brueghel the Elder (1525?–1569).

PERCY BYSSHE SHELLEY

Ode to the West Wind

I

O wild West Wind, thou breath of Autumn's being,
Thou, from whose unseen presence the leaves dead
Are driven, like ghosts from an enchanter fleeing,

Yellow, and black, and pale, and hectic red,
Pestilence-stricken multitudes: O thou,   5
Who chariotest to their dark wintry bed

The wingéd seeds, where they lie cold and low,
Each like a corpse within its grave, until
Thine azure sister of the Spring shall blow

Her clarion[7] o'er the dreaming earth, and fill   10
(Driving sweet buds like flocks to feed in air)
With living hues and odors plain and hill:

Wild Spirit, which art moving everywhere;
Destroyer and preserver; hear, oh, hear!

II

Thou on whose stream, mid the steep sky's commotion,   15
Loose clouds like earth's decaying leaves are shed,
Shook from the tangled boughs of Heaven and Ocean,

Angels[8] of rain and lightning: there are spread
On the blue surface of thine aëry surge,
Like the bright hair uplifted from the head   20

Of some fierce Maenad,[9] even from the dim verge
Of the horizon to the zenith's height,
The locks of the approaching storm. Thou dirge

Of the dying year, to which this closing night
Will be the dome of a vast sepulcher,   25
Vaulted with all thy congregated might

Of vapors, from whose solid atmosphere
Black rain, and fire, and hail will burst: oh, hear!

III

Thou who didst waken from his summer dreams
The blue Mediterranean, where he lay,   30
Lulled by the coil of his crystálline streams,

---

7. Trumpet call.   8. Messengers.   9. A frenzied female votary of Dionysus, the Greek god of vegetation and fertility who was supposed to die in the fall and rise again each spring.

Beside a pumice isle in Baiae's bay,[1]
And saw in sleep old palaces and towers
Quivering within the wave's intenser day,

35   All overgrown with azure moss and flowers
So sweet, the sense faints picturing them! Thou
For whose path the Atlantic's level powers

Cleave themselves into chasms, while far below
The sea-blooms and the oozy woods which wear
40   The sapless foliage of the ocean, know

Thy voice, and suddenly grow gray with fear,
And tremble and despoil themselves:[2] oh, hear!

IV

If I were a dead leaf thou mightest bear;
If I were a swift cloud to fly with thee;
45   A wave to pant beneath thy power, and share

The impulse of thy strength, only less free
Than thou, O uncontrollable! If even
I were as in my boyhood, and could be

The comrade of thy wanderings over Heaven,
50   As then, when to outstrip thy skyey speed
Scarce seemed a vision; I would ne'er have striven

As thus with thee in prayer in my sore need.
Oh, lift me as a wave, a leaf, a cloud!
I fall upon the thorns of life! I bleed!

55   A heavy weight of hours has chained and bowed
One too like thee: tameless, and swift, and proud.

V

Make me thy lyre, even as the forest is:
What if my leaves are falling like its own!
The tumult of thy mighty harmonies

60   Will take from both a deep, autumnal tone,
Sweet though in sadness. Be thou, Spirit fierce,
My spirit! Be thou me, impetuous one!

Drive my dead thoughts over the universe
Like withered leaves to quicken a new birth!
65   And, by the incantation of this verse,

Scatter, as from an unextinguished hearth
Ashes and sparks, my words among mankind!
Be through my lips to unawakened earth

---

1. Where Roman emperors had erected villas, west of Naples.   2. "The vegetation at the bottom of the sea . . . sympathizes with that of the land in the change of seasons." (PBS)

The trumpet of a prophecy! O Wind,
If Winter comes, can Spring be far behind?   70

                                                          1820

LOUISE BOGAN

Evening in the Sanitarium[3]

The free evening fades, outside the windows fastened with decorative
    iron grilles.
The lamps are lighted; the shades drawn; the nurses are watching a
    little.
It is the hour of the complicated knitting on the safe bone needles; of
    the games of anagrams and bridge;
The deadly game of chess; the book held up like a mask.

The period of the wildest weeping, the fiercest delusion, is over.   5
The women rest their tired half-healed hearts; they are almost well.
Some of them will stay almost well always: the blunt-faced woman
    whose thinking dissolved
Under academic discipline; the manic-depressive girl
Now leveling off; one paranoiac afflicted with jealousy.
Another with persecution. Some alleviation has been possible.   10

O fortunate bride, who never again will become elated after childbirth!
O lucky older wife, who has been cured of feeling unwanted!
To the suburban railway station you will return, return,
To meet forever Jim home on the 5:35.
You will be again as normal and selfish and heartless as anybody else.   15

There is life left: the piano says it with its octave smile.
The soft carpets pad the thump and splinter of the suicide to be.
Everything will be splendid: the grandmother will not drink habitually.
The fruit salad will bloom on the plate like a bouquet
And the garden produce the blue-ribbon aquilegia.   20

The cats will be glad; the fathers feel justified; the mothers relieved.
The sons and husbands will no longer need to pay the bills.
Childhoods will be put away, the obscene nightmare abated.

At the ends of the corridors the baths are running.
Mrs. C. again feels the shadow of the obsessive idea.   25
Miss R. looks at the mantel-piece, which must mean something.

                                                          1941

---

3. "Originally published with the subtitle 'Imitated from Auden'." (LB)

QUESTIONS

1. How many different "scenes" can you identify in "Sir Patrick Spens"? Where does each scene begin and end? How are the transitions made from scene to scene? How is the "fading" effect between scenes accomplished?
2. Why does the last line of Williams's "The Dance" repeat the first line? How do the line breaks early in the poem help to control the poem's rhythm and pace? What differences do you notice in the choice of words early in the poem and then later? How is the poem organized?
3. What words and patterns are repeated in the different stanzas of Shelley's "Ode to the West Wind"? What differences are there from stanza to stanza? What "progress" does the poem make? In what sense is the poem "revolutionary" or "cyclical"? What contribution to the structure of the poem do the sound patterns make? How do the rhymes and repeated stanza patterns contribute to the tone of the poem? to its meaning?
4. Look back over the poems you have read earlier in the course, and pick out one of them that seems to you particularly effective in the way it is put together. Read it over several times and consider carefully how it is organized, that is, what principles of structure it uses. What does the choice of speaker, situation, and setting have to do with its structure? What other artistic decisions seem to you crucial in creating the poem's structure?

WRITING SUGGESTIONS

1. After doing the reading and analysis suggested in question 4 above, write a detailed essay in which you consider fully the structural principles at work in the poem. The length of your essay will depend on the length of the poem you choose—but also on the complexity of its structure.
2. Look back at Dickey's "Cherrylog Road" (page 661) and reread it carefully. Then look for another poem in which memory of a much earlier event plays an important structural function. Compare the poems in detail, noting how (in each case) memory influences the way the event is reconstructed. What details of the event are in each case omitted in the retelling? What parts are lengthened or dwelt upon? What, in each case, is the point of having the event recalled later rather than from an immediate recollection?

    Write a three- or four-page essay comparing the structuring function of memory in the two poems, noting in each case exactly how the structural principles at work in the poem help to create the poem's final tone.

STUDENT WRITING

Below is one student's response to the first Writing Suggestion. The student focuses primarily on the phrases in "The Victims" that involve "taking" as he describes the structure of the poem.

Structure and Language in "The Victims"

by Sharon Olds

In Sharon Olds' poem "The Victims" we hear a son or daughter, already grown, speaking to a father whom he/she lost as a result of divorce. It reads like part accusation and part confession. As the poem progresses attitudes such as bitterness and spite toward the father soften, and at the end the reader is left with the same ambivalent feelings as the speaker herself[1] feels.

The poem is divided into two parts, from line 1 to line 17 and from there to the end. The first portion is in many ways a narration, the story line. The speaker relives the experience. Both the language ("her kids loved it," "we grinned inside," "We were tickled") and symbolism (the comparison of suits to carcasses and shoe tips to noses) used here suggest that this is a child's perspective on the situation. This portion is also spoken in the past tense. In the second portion we hear a more reflective and contemplative adult. It is spoken in the present tense ("Now I . . ." [line 17]), and combines both the speaker's bitterness (which dominates the first portion) as well as her pity and sense of guilt towards her father.

The two portions are framed by similar phrases: "She took it and took it, in silence . . ." (line 1), "She had taught us to take it, to hate you and take it . . ." (line 15), "I wonder who took it and took it from them in silence . . ." (lines 23–24). In the final lines of the poem these words take on a deep meaning and enable the reader to read the poem in a completely different manner.

When we first read the words "took it and took it in silence" we assume the mother took some sort of abuse in silence. She taught her children to take the abuse in silence and to hate their father. The final repetition of that phrase: "I wonder who took it and took it from them in silence until they had given it all away and had nothing left but this" (lines 23–26), reminds us of the meaning of the word "take." "Taking it" can mean taking abuse, but it can also mean taking in the ordinary sense as in taking money or a gift or love. One is active and one is passive. If we adopt the active form, the poem is still meaningful, only this time it is the father who is the victim. He is the one who gave all he had. The mother took and took (money, love, attention) and taught her children to take and to hate. One hint to support this interpretation might be the first line of the poem, which suggests that the mother was something more than a passive victim ("When mother divorced you . . . ," ". . . kicked you out . . ."). Again the ambiguity of the phrase strengthens the sense of ambivalence which a child must feel when her parents divorce. It is never clear who "the Victims" are in the poem, perhaps all of them.

Silence is another strong theme in the poem. Note the following examples: "took it, in silence" (line 2), "we grinned inside . . ." (line 5), "I wonder . . ." (line 23), "took it from them in silence . . ." (line 24). The strongest example of the silence, the lack of communication, and the alienation comes in the last section and the metaphor of the bums in doorways. The speaker compares her father to the drunken bums she sees and describes them in such a way that the image of fish or sunken ships becomes vivid ("white slugs of their bodies," "slits in their suits of compressed silt," "stained flippers," "underwater fire of their eyes"). The father is in some other, "underwater" world where sounds from the outside are inaudible. The only sound we hear in this poem is the speaker's voice. Silence and alienation predominated in her childhood, and now as an adult she is still unable to reach her father.

While on the surface this poem seems to be one of anger and accusation, a closer reading indicates a deeper, more complex view of human experience. Things are seldom as clearly defined and one-sided as they appear to a child.

Note

[1] It is not apparent whether the speaker is male or female. I chose to refer to her as a female simply because the poet is a female. It seems that the experience and feelings related are not exclusive to one sex or the other.

19

EXTERNAL FORM

Most poems of more than a few lines are divided into stanzas, groups of lines divided from other groups by white space on the page. Putting some space between groupings of lines has the effect of sectioning the poem, giving its physical appearance a series of divisions that often mark breaks in thought, changes of scenery or imagery, or other shifts in structure or direction. In Donne's "The Flea" (page 664), for example, the stanza divisions mark distinctive stages in the action: between the first and second stanzas, the speaker stops his companion from killing the flea; between the second and third stanzas, the companion follows through on her intention and kills the flea. In Nemerov's "The Goose Fish" (page 761), the stanzas mark stages in the self-perception of the lovers; each of the stanzas is a more or less distinct scene, and the scenes unfold almost like a series of slides. Not all stanzas are quite so neatly patterned as are the ones in these two poems, but any formal division of a poem into stanzas is important to consider: what appear to be gaps or silences may be structural indicators.

Historically, stanzas have most often been organized by patterns of rhyme, and thus stanza divisions have been a visual indicator of patterns in sound. In most traditional stanza forms, the pattern of rhyme is repeated in stanza after stanza throughout the poem, until voice and ear become familiar with the pattern and come to expect it and, in a sense, to depend on it. The accumulation of pattern allows us to "hear" variations as well, just as we do in music. The rhyme thus becomes an organizational device in the poem—a formal, external determiner of organization, as distinguished from the internal, structural determiners we considered in Chapter 18—and ordinarily the metrical patterns stay constant from stanza to stanza. In Shelley's "Ode to the West Wind," for example, the first and third lines in each stanza rhyme, and the middle line then rhymes with the first and third lines of the next stanza. (In indicating rhyme, a different letter of the alphabet is conventionally used to represent each sound; in the following example, if we begin with "being" as *a* and "dead" as *b*, then "fleeing" is also *a*, and "red" and "bed" are *b*.)

O wild West Wind, thou breath of Autumn's being,	*a*
Thou, from whose unseen presence the leaves dead	*b*
Are driven, like ghosts from an enchanter fleeing,	*a*
Yellow, and black, and pale, and hectic red,	*b*
Pestilence-stricken multitudes: O thou,	*c*
Who chariotest to their dark wintry bed	*b*

The wingéd seeds, where they lie cold and low,	c
Each like a corpse within its grave, until	d
Thine azure sister of the Spring shall blow	c

In this stanza form, known as **terza rima,** the stanzas are linked to each other by a common sound: one rhyme sound from each stanza is picked up in the next stanza, and so on to the end of the poem (though sometimes poems have sections that use varied rhyme schemes). This stanza form was used by Dante in *The Divine Comedy,* written in Italian in the early 1300s. Terza rima is not all that common in English because it is a rhyme-rich stanza form—that is, it requires many rhymes, and thus many different rhyme words—and English is, relatively speaking, a rhyme-poor language (not as rich in rhyme possibilities as Italian or French). One reason for this is that English derives from so many different language families that it has fewer similar word endings than languages that have remained more "pure"—that is, more dependent for vocabulary on the roots and patterns found in a single language family.

Contemporary poets seldom use rhyme, finding it neither necessary nor appealing, but until the twentieth century the music of rhyme was central to both the sound and the formal conception of most poems. Because poetry was originally an oral art (and its texts not always written down) various kinds of **memory devices** (sometimes called **mnemonic devices**) were built into poems to help reciters remember them. Rhyme was one such device, and most people still find it easier to memorize poetry that rhymes. The simple pleasure of hearing familiar sounds repeated at regular intervals may also help to account for the traditional popularity of rhyme, and perhaps plain habit (for both poets and hearers) had a lot to do with why rhyme flourished for so many centuries as a standard expectation. Rhyme also helps to give poetry a special aural quality that distinguishes it from prose, a significant advantage in ages that worry about decorum and propriety and are anxious to preserve a strong sense of poetic tradition. Some ages have been very concerned that poetry should not in any way be mistaken for prose or made to serve prosaic functions, and the literary critics and theorists in those ages made extraordinary efforts to emphasize the distinctions between poetry, which was thought to be artistically superior, and prose, which was thought to be primarily utilitarian. A pride in elitism and a fear that an expanded reading public could ultimately dilute the possibilities of traditional art forms have been powerful cultural forces in Western civilization, and if such forces were not themselves responsible for creating rhyme in poetry, they at least helped to preserve a sense of its necessity. But rhyme and other patterns of repeated sounds are also important, for various historical and cultural reasons, to non-Western languages and poetic traditions as well.

There are at least two other reasons for rhyme. One is complex and hard to state justly without long explanations. It involves traditional ideas about the symmetrical relationship of different aspects of the world and the function of poetry to reflect the universe as human learning has understood it. Many cultures (especially in earlier centuries) have assumed that rhyme was proper to verse, perhaps even essential. Poets in these ages and cultures would have felt themselves eccentric to compose poems any other way. Some English poets (especially in the Renaissance) did experiment—very successfully—with **blank verse** (that is, verse that did not rhyme but that nevertheless had strict metrical requirements), but the cultural pressure for rhyme was almost constant. Why? As noted above, custom or habit may account for part of the assumption that rhyme was necessary, but probably not all of it. Rather, the poets' sense that poetry was an imitation of larger relationships in the universe made it seem natural to use rhyme to represent or re-create a sense of harmony, correspondence, symmetry, and order. The sounds of poetry were thus (they thought) reminders of the harmonious cosmos, of the music of the spheres that animated the planets, the processes of nature, the interrelationship of all created things and beings. Probably poets never said to themselves, "I shall now tunefully emulate the harmony of God's carefully ordered universe," but the tendency to use rhyme and other repetitions or re-echoings of sound (such as **alliteration** or **assonance**) nevertheless stemmed ultimately from basic assumptions about how the universe worked. In a modern world increasingly perceived as fragmented, rambling, and unrelated, there is of course less of a tendency to testify to a sense of harmony and symmetry. It would be too easy and too mechanical to think that rhyme in a poem specifically means that the poet has a firm sense of cosmic order, and that an unrhymed poem testifies to chaos, but cultural assumptions do affect the expectations of both poets and readers, and cultural tendencies create a kind of pressure upon the individual creator. If you take a survey course (or a series of related "period" courses in English or American literature), you will readily notice the diminishing sense of the need for—or relevance of—rhyme. And other linguistic and national traditions similarly vary usages in different times, depending on the philosophical and cultural assumptions of the time and place.

One other reason for using rhyme is that it provides a kind of discipline for the poet, a way of harnessing poetic talents and keeping a rein on the imagination, so that the results are ordered, controlled, put into some kind of meaningful and recognizable form. Robert Frost used to be fond of saying that writing poems without rhyme was like playing tennis without a net. Writing good poetry does require a lot of discipline, and Frost speaks for many (perhaps most) traditional poets in suggesting that rhyme can be a major source of that discipline. But it is not the only possible source, and more recent poets have usually felt they would rather play by new rules or invent their own as they go along; they have, therefore, sought their sources of discipline elsewhere, preferring the sparer tones that unrhymed poetry provides. It is not that contemporary poets cannot think of rhyme words or that they do not care about the sounds of their poetry; rather, recent poets have consciously decided not to work with rhyme and to use instead other aural and metrical devices and other strategies for organizing stanzas, just as they have chosen to work with experimental and variable rhythms instead of writing necessarily in the traditional English meters. Some modern poets, though, have protested the abandonment of rhyme and have continued to write rhymed verse successfully in a more or less traditional way.

> *Concentration is the very*
> *essence of poetry.*
>
> —AMY LOWELL

The amount and density of rhyme vary widely in stanza and verse forms, from elaborate and intricate patterns of rhyme to more casual or spare sound repetitions. The **Spenserian stanza,** for example, is even more rhyme-rich than terza rima, using only three rhyme sounds in nine rhymed lines, as in Keats's *The Eve of St. Agnes:*

Her falt'ring hand upon the balustrade,	a
Old Angela was feeling for the stair,	b
When Madeline, St. Agnes' charméd maid,	a
Rose, like a missioned spirit, unaware:	b
With silver taper's light, and pious care,	b
She turned, and down the agéd gossip led	c
To a safe level matting. Now prepare,	b
Young Porphyro, for gazing on that bed;	c
She comes, she comes again, like ring dove frayed and fled	c

On the other hand, the **ballad stanza** has only one set of rhymes in four lines; lines 1 and 3 in each stanza do not rhyme at all (from "Sir Patrick Spens"):

The king sits in Dumferling toune,	*a*
Drinking the blude-reid wine:	*b*
"O whar will I get guid sailor,	*c*
To sail this ship of mine?"	*b*

Most stanza forms use a metrical pattern as well as a rhyme scheme. Terza rima, for example, involves iambic meter (unstressed and stressed syllables alternating regularly) and each line has five beats (pentameter). Most of the Spenserian stanza (the first eight lines) is also in iambic pentameter, but the ninth line in each stanza has one extra foot (thus, the last line is in iambic hexameter). The ballad stanza, also iambic, as are most English stanza and verse forms, alternates three-beat and four-beat lines; lines 1 and 3 are unrhymed iambic tetrameter (four beats), and lines 2 and 4 are rhymed iambic trimeter (three beats).

THE SONNET

The **sonnet** is one of the most persistent verse forms. From its origins in the Middle Ages as a prominent form in Italian and French poetry, it dominated English poetry in the late sixteenth and early seventeenth centuries and then was revived several times from the early nineteenth century onward. A sonnet, except for some early experiments with length, is always fourteen lines long and is usually written in iambic pentameter. It is most often printed as if it were a *single* stanza, although in reality it has several formal divisions that represent its rhyme schemes and formal breaks. As a popular and traditional verse form in English for more than four centuries, the sonnet has been surprisingly resilient even in ages that largely reject rhyme. It continues to attract a variety of poets, including (curiously) radical and even revolutionary poets who find its formal demands, discipline, and set outcome very appealing. Its uses, although quite varied, can be illustrated fairly precisely. As a verse form, the sonnet is contained, compact, demanding; whatever it does, it must do concisely and quickly. To be effective, it must take advantage of the possibilities inherent in its shortness and its relative rigidity. It is best suited to intensity of feeling and concentration of expression. Not too surprisingly, one subject it frequently discusses is confinement itself.

WILLIAM WORDSWORTH

Nuns Fret Not

Nuns fret not at their convent's narrow room;
And hermits are contented with their cells;
And students with their pensive citadels;
Maids at the wheel, the weaver at his loom,
Sit blithe and happy; bees that soar for bloom,   5

High as the highest Peak of Furness-fells,[1]
Will murmur by the hour in foxglove bells:[2]
In truth the prison, unto which we doom
Ourselves, no prison is: and hence for me,
In sundry moods, 'twas pastime to be bound
Within the sonnet's scanty plot of ground;
Pleased if some souls (for such there needs must be)
Who have felt the weight of too much liberty,
Should find brief solace there, as I have found.   1807

10

Most sonnets are structured according to one of two principles of division. On one principle, the sonnet divides into three units of four lines each and a final unit of two lines, and sometimes the line spacing reflects this division. On the other, the fundamental break is between the first eight lines (called an octave) and the last six (called a sestet). The 4-4-4-2 sonnet is usually called the **English** or **Shakespearean sonnet,** and ordinarily its rhyme scheme reflects the structure: the scheme of *abab cdcd efef gg* is the classic one, but many variations from that pattern still reflect the basic 4-4-4-2 division. The 8-6 sonnet is usually called the **Italian** or **Petrarchan sonnet** (the Italian poet Petrarch was an early master of this structure), and its "typical" rhyme scheme is *abbaabba cdecde,* although it too produces many variations that still reflect the basic division into two parts.

The two kinds of sonnet structures are useful for two different sorts of argument. The 4-4-4-2 structure works very well for constructing a poem that wants to make a three-step argument (with a quick summary at the end), or for setting up brief, cumulative images. "That time of year thou mayst in me behold" (page 713), for example, uses the 4-4-4-2 structure to mark the progressive steps toward death and the parting of friends by using three distinct images, then summarizing. "Let me not to the marriage of true minds" (page 618) works very similarly, following the kind of organization that in Chapter 18 was referred to as the 1-2-3 structure—and doing it compactly and economically.

Here, on the other hand, is a poem that uses the 8-6 pattern:

HENRY CONSTABLE

[*My lady's presence makes the roses red*]

My lady's presence makes the roses red,
Because to see her lips they blush for shame.
The lily's leaves, for envy, pale became,
And her white hands in them this envy bred.
The marigold the leaves abroad doth spread,
Because the sun's and her power is the same.
The violet of purple colour came,
Dyed in the blood she made my heart to shed.

5

---

1. Mountains in England's Lake District, where Wordsworth lived. ⸻ 2. Flowers from which digitalis (a heart medicine) began to be made in 1799.

In brief: all flowers from her their virtue take;
From her sweet breath their sweet smells do proceed;   10
The living heat which her eyebeams doth make
Warmeth the ground and quickeneth the seed.
The rain, wherewith she watereth the flowers,
Falls from mine eyes, which she dissolves in showers.   1594

The first eight lines argue that the lady's presence is responsible for the color of all of nature's flowers, and the final six lines summarize and extend that argument to smells and heat—and finally to the rain that the lady draws from the speaker's eyes. That kind of two-part structure, in which the octave states a proposition or generalization and the sestet provides a particularization or application of it, has a variety of uses. The final lines may, for example, reverse the first eight and achieve a paradox or irony in the poem, or the poem may nearly balance two comparable arguments. Basically, the 8-6 structure lends itself to poems with two points to make, or to those that wish to make one point and then illustrate it.

Sometimes the neat and precise structure is altered—either slightly, as in Words-worth's "Nuns Fret Not," above (where the 8-6 structure is more of an $8^1/_2$-$5^1/_2$ structure), or more radically as particular needs or effects may demand. And the two basic structures certainly do not define all the structural possibilities within a fourteen-line poem, even if they do suggest the most traditional ways of taking advantage of the sonnet's compact and well-kept container.

The sonnets in this chapter by Sidney, Shakespeare, and Constable survive from a golden age of English sonnet writing in the late sixteenth century, an age that set the pattern for expectations in the English tradition of form, subject matter, and tone. The sonnet came to England from Italy via France, and imitations of Petrarch's famous sonnet sequence to Laura became the rage. Thousands upon thousands of sonnets were written in those years, often in sequences of a hundred or more sonnets each; the sequences explored the many moods of love and usually had a light thread of narrative that pur-ported to recount a love affair between the male poet and a female lover who was almost always golden-haired, beautiful, disdainful, and inaccessible. Her beauty was described in a series of exaggerated comparisons: her eyes were like the sun ("When Nature made her chief work, Stella's eyes"), her teeth like pearls, her cheeks like roses, her skin like ivory, and so on, but the adherence to these conventions was always play-ful, and it became a game of wit to play variations upon expectations ("My lady's pres-ence makes the roses red" and "My mistress' eyes are nothing like the sun"). Sometimes the female lover was unreceptive, unavailable, or rejecting, and sometimes male friend-ship or homosexual love rivaled the usual male / female relationship. Almost always teasing and witty, these poems were not necessarily as true to life as they pretended, but they provided historically an expectation of what sonnets were to be.

Many modern sonnets continue to be about love or private life, and many continue to use a personal, apparently open and sincere tone. But poets often find the sonnet's compact form and rigid demands equally useful for many varieties of subject, theme, and tone. Besides love, sonnets often treat other subjects: politics, philosophy, discovery of a new world. And tones vary widely too, from the anger and remorse of "Th' expense of spirit in a waste of shame" (page 932) and righteous outrage of "On the Late Massacre in Piedmont" (page 667) to the tender awe of "How Do I Love Thee?" (page 597). Many poets seem to take the kind of comfort Wordsworth describes in the careful limits of the form, finding in its two basic variations (the English sonnet such as "My mistress' eyes" [page 794] and the Italian sonnet such as "London, 1802" [page 792]) a sufficiency of convenient ways to organize their materials into coherent structures.

JOHN KEATS

On the Sonnet

If by dull rhymes our English must be chained,
And like Andromeda,[3] the sonnet sweet
Fettered, in spite of painéd loveliness,
Let us find, if we must be constrained,
5   Sandals more interwoven and complete
To fit the naked foot of Poesy:[4]
Let us inspect the lyre, and weigh the stress
Of every chord,[5] and see what may be gained
By ear industrious, and attention meet;
10   Misers of sound and syllable, no less
Than Midas[6] of his coinage, let us be
Jealous of dead leaves in the bay-wreath crown;[7]
So, if we may not let the Muse be free,
She will be bound with garlands of her own.

1819

COUNTEE CULLEN

Yet Do I Marvel

I doubt not God is good, well-meaning, kind,
And did He stoop to quibble could tell why
The little buried mole continues blind,
Why flesh that mirrors Him must some day die,
5   Make plain the reason tortured Tantalus[8]

3. Who, according to Greek myth, was chained to a rock so that she would be devoured by a sea monster. She was rescued by Perseus, who married her. When she died she was placed among the stars.   4. In a letter that contained this sonnet, Keats expressed impatience with the traditional Petrarchan and Shakespearean sonnet forms: "I have been endeavoring to discover a better sonnet stanza than we have."   5. Lyre string.   6. The legendary king of Phrygia who asked, and got, the power to turn all he touched to gold.   7. The bay tree was sacred to Apollo, god of poetry, and bay wreaths came to symbolize true poetic achievement. The withering of the bay tree is sometimes considered an omen of death. *Jealous:* suspiciously watchful.   8. In Greek myth he was condemned, for ambiguous reasons, to stand up to his neck in water he couldn't drink and to be within sight of fruit he couldn't reach to eat.

Is baited by the fickle fruit, declare
If merely brute caprice dooms Sisyphus[9]
To struggle up a never-ending stair.
Inscrutable His ways are, and immune
To catechism by a mind too strewn   10
With petty cares to slightly understand
What awful brain compels His awful hand.
Yet do I marvel at this curious thing:
To make a poet black, and bid him sing!   1925

EMMA LAZARUS

The New Colossus

Not like the brazen giant of Greek fame,
With conquering limbs astride from land to land;
Here at our sea-washed, sunset gates shall stand
A mighty woman with a torch, whose flame
Is the imprisoned lightning, and her name   5
Mother of Exiles.[1] From her beacon-hand
Glows world-wide welcome; her mild eyes command
The air-bridged harbor that twin cities frame.
"Keep ancient lands, your storied pomp!" cries she
With silent lips. "Give me your tired, your poor,   10
Your huddled masses yearning to breathe free,
The wretched refuse of your teeming shore.
Send these, the homeless, tempest-tost to me,
I lift my lamp beside the golden door!"

November 1883

HELEN CHASIN

Joy Sonnet in a Random Universe

Sometimes I'm happy: la la la la la la la
la la la la la la la la la la la la la la la la la la
la la la la. Tum tum ti tum. La la la la la la
la la la la la la la la la la la la la la la la la la.
Hey nonny nonny. La la la la la la la la la   5
la la la la la la la la la la la la. Vo do di o do.

9. The king of Corinth who, in Greek myth, was condemned eternally to roll a huge stone
uphill.   1. The Statue of Liberty, in New York harbor.

Poo poo pi doo. La la la la la la la la la la
la la la la la la la la la la la la la la la la la
la la. Whack a doo. La la la la la la la. Sh-
boom, sh-boom. La la la la la la la la la la
la la la la la la la la la la la la la la la la la
la la. Dum di dum. La la la la la la la la la
la la la la la la la la la. Tra la la. Tra la la
la la la la la la la la la la. Yeah yeah yeah.

10

1968

JOHN MILTON

[*When I consider how my light is spent*]

When I consider how my light is spent,
   Ere half my days, in this dark world and wide,
   And that one talent which is death to hide[2]
   Lodged with me useless, though my soul more bent
5 To serve therewith my Maker, and present
   My true account, lest he returning chide;
   "Doth God exact day-labor, light denied?"
   I fondly ask; but Patience to prevent[3]
That murmur, soon replies, "God doth not need
10 Either man's work or his own gifts; who best
   Bear his mild yoke, they serve him best. His state
Is kingly. Thousands at his bidding speed
   And post o'er land and ocean without rest:
   They also serve who only stand and wait."

1652?

HELENE JOHNSON

Sonnet to a Negro in Harlem

You are disdainful and magnificent—
Your perfect body and your pompous gait,
Your dark eyes flashing solemnly with hate,
Small wonder that you are incompetent

---

2. In the parable of the talents (Matthew 25), the servants who earned interest on their master's money (his talents) while he was away were called "good and faithful"; the one who hid the money and simply returned it was condemned and sent away. Usury, a deadly sin under Catholicism, was regarded by Puritans as a metaphor for attaining salvation.   3. Forestall. *Fondly:* foolishly.

To imitate those whom you so despise—   5
Your shoulders towering high above the throng,
Your head thrown back in rich, barbaric song,
Palm trees and mangoes stretched before your eyes.
Let others toil and sweat for labor's sake
And wring from grasping hands their meed of gold.   10
Why urge ahead your supercilious feet?
Scorn will efface each footprint that you make.
I love your laughter arrogant and bold.
You are too splendid for this city street.   p. 1927

PERCY BYSSHE SHELLEY

Ozymandias[4]

I met a traveler from an antique land
Who said: Two vast and trunkless legs of stone
Stand in the desert. . . . Near them, on the sand,
Half sunk, a shattered visage lies, whose frown,
And wrinkled lip, and sneer of cold command,   5
Tell that its sculptor well those passions read
Which yet survive, stamped on these lifeless things,
The hand that mocked them, and the heart that fed:
And on the pedestal these words appear:
"My name is Ozymandias, King of Kings: 10
Look on my works, ye Mighty, and despair!"
Nothing beside remains. Round the decay
Of that colossal wreck, boundless and bare
The lone and level sands stretch far away.   1818

ARCHIBALD LAMPMAN

Winter Evening

To-night the very horses springing by
Toss gold from whitened nostrils. In a dream
The streets that narrow to the westward gleam
Like rows of golden palaces; and high

---

4. The Greek name for Rameses II, thirteenth-century-B.C. pharaoh of Egypt. According to a first-century-B.C. Greek historian, Diodorus Siculus, the largest statue in Egypt was inscribed: "I am Ozymandias, king of kings; if anyone wishes to know what I am and where I lie, let him surpass me in some of my exploits."

5   From all the crowded chimneys tower and die
       A thousand aureoles. Down in the west
       The brimming plains beneath the sunset rest,
       One burning sea of gold. Soon, soon shall fly
       The glorious vision, and the hours shall feel
10   A mightier master; soon from height to height,
       With silence and the sharp unpitying stars,
       Stern creeping frosts, and winds that touch like steel,
       Out of the depth beyond the eastern bars,
       Glittering and still shall come the awful night.   1899

GWENDOLYN BROOKS

First Fight. Then Fiddle.

       First fight. Then fiddle. Ply the slipping string
       With feathery sorcery; muzzle the note
       With hurting love; the music that they wrote
       Bewitch, bewilder. Qualify to sing
5   Threadwise. Devise no salt, no hempen thing
       For the dear instrument to bear. Devote
       The bow to silks and honey. Be remote
       A while from malice and from murdering.
       But first to arms, to armor. Carry hate
10   In front of you and harmony behind.
       Be deaf to music and to beauty blind.
       Win war. Rise bloody, maybe not too late
       For having first to civilize a space
       Wherein to play your violin with grace.   1949

WILLIAM WORDSWORTH

London, 1802

       Milton! thou should'st be living at this hour:
       England hath need of thee: she is a fen
       Of stagnant waters: altar, sword, and pen,
       Fireside, the heroic wealth of hall and bower,
5   Have forfeited their ancient English dower
       Of inward happiness. We are selfish men;
       Oh! raise us up, return to us again;
       And give us manners, virtue, freedom, power.
       Thy soul was like a star, and dwelt apart:

Thou hadst a voice whose sound was like the sea: 10
Pure as the naked heavens, majestic, free,
So didst thou travel on life's common way,
In cheerful godliness; and yet thy heart
The lowliest duties on herself did lay.

1802

CLAUDE McKAY

The White House

Your door is shut against my tightened face,
And I am sharp as steel with discontent;
But I possess the courage and the grace
To bear my anger proudly and unbent.
The pavement slabs burn loose beneath my feet,   5
And passion rends my vitals as I pass,
A chafing savage, down the decent street,
Where boldly shines your shuttered door of glass.
Oh, I must search for wisdom every hour,
Deep in my wrathful bosom sore and raw,   10
And find in it the superhuman power
To hold me to the letter of your law!
Oh, I must keep my heart inviolate
Against the poison of your deadly hate.   1937

SIR PHILIP SIDNEY

[When Nature made her chief work, Stella's eyes][5]

When Nature made her chief work, Stella's eyes,
In color black[6] why wrapped she beams so bright?
Would she in beamy black, like painter wise,
Frame daintiest luster mixed of shades and light?
Or did she else that sober hue devise,   5
In object best to knit and strength our sight,
Lest if no veil those brave gleams did disguise,

---

5. From Sidney's sonnet sequence *Astrophel and Stella,* usually credited with having started the vogue of sonnet sequences in Elizabethan England.   6. Black was frequently used in the Renaissance to mean absence of light, and ugly or foul (see line 10).

They sunlike should more dazzle than delight?
Or would she her miraculous power show,
10   That, whereas black seems Beauty's contrary,
She even in black doth make all beauties flow?
Both so and thus: she, minding[7] Love should be
Placed ever there, gave him this mourning weed
To honor all their deaths who for her bleed.

1582

WILLIAM SHAKESPEARE

[My mistress' eyes are nothing like the sun]

My mistress' eyes are nothing like the sun;
Coral is far more red than her lips' red;
If snow be white, why then her breasts are dun;[8]
If hairs be wires, black wires grow on her head.
5   I have seen roses damasked[9] red and white,
But no such roses see I in her cheeks;
And in some perfumes is there more delight
Than in the breath that from my mistress reeks.
I love to hear her speak, yet well I know
10   That music hath a far more pleasing sound;
I grant I never saw a goddess go;[1]
My mistress, when she walks, treads on the ground.
And yet, by heaven, I think my love as rare
As any she belied with false compare.

1609

DIANE ACKERMAN

Sweep Me through Your Many-Chambered Heart

Sweep me through your many-chambered heart
if you like, or leave me here, flushed
amid the sap-ooze and blossom: one more dish
in the banquet called April, or think me hard-
5   won all your days full of women. Weeks

7. Remembering that.   8. Mouse-colored.   9. Variegated.   1. Walk.

later, till I felt your arms around
me like a shackle, heard all the sundown
wizardries the fired body speaks.
Tell me why, if it was no more than this,
the unmuddled tumble, the renegade kiss,   10
today, rapt in a still life and unaware,
my paintbrush dropped like an amber hawk;
thinking I'd heard your footfall on the stair,
I listened, heartwise, for the knock.   1978

STANZA FORMS

Many stanza forms are represented in this book. Some have names because they have been used over and over by different poets. Others were invented for a particular use in a particular poem and may never be repeated again. Most traditional stanzas are based on rhyme schemes, but some use other kinds of predictable sound patterns; early English poetry, for example, used alliteration to construct a balance between the first and second half of each line. Sometimes, especially when poets interact with each other within a strong community, highly elaborate *verse forms* have been developed that set up stanzas as part of a scheme for the whole poem. The poets of medieval Provence were especially inventive, subtle, and elaborate in their construction of complex verse forms, some of which have been copied by poets ever since. The **sestina,** for example, depends on the measured repetition of words (rather than just sounds) in particular places; see, for example, Bishop's "Sestina" (page 798), and try to decipher the pattern. (There are also double and even triple sestinas, tough tests of a poet's ingenuity.) And the **villanelle,** another Provençal form, depends on the patterned repetition of whole lines (see Dylan Thomas's "Do Not Go Gentle into That Good Night" [page 797]). Different cultures and different languages develop their own patterns and measures—not all poetries are parallel to English poetry—and they vary from age to age as well as nation to nation.

You can probably deduce the principles involved in each of the following stanza or verse forms by looking carefully at a poem that uses it; if you have trouble, look at the definitions in the glossary on page A57.

heroic couplet	"Sound and Sense"	page 744
tetrameter couplet	"To His Coy Mistress"	page 674
limerick	"There was a young lady of Riga"	page 747
free verse	"Dirge"	page 742
blank verse	"Tintern Abbey"	page 980

What are stanza forms good for? What use is it to recognize them? Why do poets bother? Matters discussed in this chapter so far have suggested two reasons: (1) Breaks between stanzas provide convenient pauses for reader and writer, something roughly equivalent to paragraphs in prose. The eye thus picks up the places where some kind of pause or break or change of focus occurs. (2) Poets sometimes use stanza forms, as they do rhyme itself, as a discipline: writing in a certain kind of stanza form imposes a shape on their act of imagination. But visual spaces and unexpected print divisions also mean that poems sometimes *look* unusual and require special visual attention, attention that does not always follow the logic of sound patterns or syntax. After the following poems illustrating some common stanza forms, you will find a section on poems that employ special configurations and shapes to establish their meanings and effects.

DYLAN THOMAS

Do Not Go Gentle into That Good Night[2]

Do not go gentle into that good night,
Old age should burn and rave at close of day;
Rage, rage against the dying of the light.

Though wise men at their end know dark is right,
Because their words had forked no lightning they   5
Do not go gentle into that good night.

Good men, the last wave by, crying how bright
Their frail deeds might have danced in a green bay,
Rage, rage against the dying of the light.

Wild men who caught and sang the sun in flight,   10
And learn, too late, they grieved it on its way,
Do not go gentle into that good night.

Grave men, near death, who see with blinding sight
Blind eyes could blaze like meteors and be gay,
Rage, rage against the dying of the light.   15

And you, my father, there on the sad height,
Curse, bless, me now with your fierce tears, I pray.
Do not go gentle into that good night.
Rage, rage against the dying of the light.   1952

MARIANNE MOORE

Poetry

I, too, dislike it: there are things that are important beyond all this
                                                                      fiddle.
   Reading it, however, with a perfect contempt for it, one discovers in
   it after all, a place for the genuine.
         Hands that can grasp, eyes
            that can dilate, hair that can rise   5
               if it must, these things are important not because a

high-sounding interpretation can be put upon them but because they
                                                                        are
      useful. When they become so derivative as to become unintelligible,
      the same thing may be said for all of us, that we
            do not admire what   10

2. Written during the final illness of the poet's father.

we cannot understand: the bat
    holding on upside down or in quest of something to

eat, elephants pushing, a wild horse taking a roll, a tireless wolf under
a tree, the immovable critic twitching his skin like a horse that feels a
                                        flea, the base-

15   ball fan, the statistician—
        nor is it valid
            to discriminate against "business documents and

school-books"[3]; all these phenomena are important. One must make a
                                    distinction
    however: when dragged into prominence by half poets, the result is
                                  not poetry,

20   nor till the poets among us can be
        "literalists of
        the imagination"[4]—above
            insolence and triviality and can present

for inspection, "imaginary gardens with real toads in them," shall we
                                  have

25   it. In the meantime, if you demand on the one hand,
      the raw material of poetry in
        all its rawness and
        that which is on the other hand
        genuine, you are interested in poetry.   1921

ELIZABETH BISHOP

Sestina

September rain falls on the house.
In the failing light, the old grandmother
sits in the kitchen with the child
beside the Little Marvel Stove,
5   reading the jokes from the almanac,
laughing and talking to hide her tears.

She thinks that her equinoctial tears
and the rain that beats on the roof of the house

3. "*Diary of Tolstoy*, p. 84: 'Where the boundary between prose and poetry lies, I shall never be able to understand. The question is raised in manuals of style, yet the answer to it lies beyond me. Poetry is verse: Prose is not verse. Or else poetry is everything with the exception of business documents and school books.'" (MM)   4. "'Literalists of the imagination.' Yeats, *Ideas of Good and Evil* (A. H. Bullen, 1903), p. 182. 'The limitation of his view was from the very intensity of his vision; he was a too literal realist of imagination, as others are of nature; and because he believed that the figures seen by the mind's eye, when exalted by inspiration, were "eternal existences," symbols of divine essences, he hated every grace of style that might obscure their lineaments.'" (MM)

were both foretold by the almanac,
but only known to a grandmother.   10
The iron kettle sings on the stove.
She cuts some bread and says to the child,

It's time for tea now; but the child
is watching the teakettle's small hard tears
dance like mad on the hot black stove,   15
the way the rain must dance on the house.
Tidying up, the old grandmother
hangs up the clever almanac

on its string. Birdlike, the almanac
hovers half open above the child,   20
hovers above the old grandmother
and her teacup full of dark brown tears.
She shivers and says she thinks the house
feels chilly, and puts more wood in the stove.

It was to be, says the Marvel Stove.   25
I know what I know, says the almanac.
With crayons the child draws a rigid house
and a winding pathway. Then the child
puts in a man with buttons like tears
and shows it proudly to the grandmother.   30

But secretly, while the grandmother
busies herself about the stove,
the little moons fall down like tears
from between the pages of the almanac
into the flower bed the child   35
has carefully placed in the front of the house.

Time to plant tears, says the almanac.
The grandmother sings to the marvellous stove
and the child draws another inscrutable house.   1965

ISHMAEL REED

beware : do not read this poem

tonite   , thriller was
abt an ol woman   , so vain she
surrounded herself w /
   many mirrors

it got so bad that finally she   5
locked herself indoors & her
whole life became the
   mirrors

one day the villagers broke
into her house   ,   but she was too
swift for them   .   she disappeared
    into a mirror

each tenant who bought the house
after that   ,   lost a loved one to
        the ol woman in the mirror :
        first a little girl
        then a young woman
        then the young woman / s husband

the hunger of this poem is legendary
it has taken in many victims
back off from this poem
it has drawn in yr feet
back off from this poem
it has drawn in yr legs

back off from this poem
it is a greedy mirror
you are into this poem   .   from
    the waist down
nobody can hear you can they   ?
this poem has had you up to here
    belch
this poem aint got no manners
you cant call out frm this poem
relax now & go w / this poem
move & roll on to this poem
do not resist this poem
this poem has yr eyes
this poem has his head
this poem has his arms
this poem has his fingers
this poem has his fingertips
this poem is the reader & the
reader this poem

statistic   :   the us bureau of missing persons reports
            that in 1968 over 100,000 people disappeared
            leaving no solid clues
                nor trace   only
        a space   in the lives of their friends   1970

THE WAY A POEM LOOKS

Stanza breaks and other kinds of print spaces are important, primarily to guide the voice and mind to a clearer sense of sound and meaning. But there are exceptions. A few poems are written to be seen rather than heard, and their appearance on the page is crucial to their effect. Cummings's poem "l(a," for example, tries to visualize typographically what the poet asks you to see in your mind's eye. Occasionally, too, poems are composed in a specific shape so that the poem looks like a physical object. The poems that follow in this chapter—some old, some new—illustrate ways in which visual effects may be created. Even though poetry has traditionally been thought of as oral—words to be said, sung, or performed rather than looked at—the idea that poems can also be related to painting and the visual arts is an old one. Theodoric in ancient Greece is credited with inventing **technopaegnia**—that is, the construction of poems with visual appeal. Once, the shaping of words to resemble an object was thought to have mystical power, but more recent attempts at **concrete poetry** or **shaped verse** are usually playful exercises (such as Solt's "Lilac") that attempt to supplement (or replace) verbal meanings with devices from painting and sculpture.

Reading a poem like Herbert's "Easter Wings" aloud wouldn't make much sense. Our eyes are everything for a poem like that. A more frequent poetic device involves asking the eyes to become a guide for the voice. The following poem depends upon recognition of some standard typographical symbols and knowledge of their names. We have to say those names to read the poem.

FRANKLIN P. ADAMS

Composed in the Composing Room

At stated .ic times
I love to sit and—off rhymes
Till ,tose at last I fall
Exclaiming "I don't ∧ all."

Though I'm an * objection   5
By running this in this here §
This ☞ of the Fleeting Hour,
This lofty -ician Tower—

A ¶er's hope dispels
All fear of deadly ‖.   10
You think these [ ] are a pipe?
Well, not on your †eotype.

                                                             1914

We create the right term here when we verbalize, putting the visual signs together with the words or letters printed in the poem, for example making the word "periodic" out of ".ic" or "high Phoenician" out of "-ician." Like "Easter Wings," "Composed in the

Composing Room" uses typography in an extreme way; here the eyes (and mind) are drawn into a punlike game that offers more puzzle-solving pleasure than emotional effect. More often poets give us—by the visual placement of sounds—a guide to reading, inviting us to regulate the pace of our reading, notice pauses or silences, pay attention both to the syntax of the poem and to the rhetoric of the voice, thus providing us a kind of musical score for reading.

E. E. CUMMINGS

[*Buffalo Bill 's*][5]

Buffalo Bill 's
    defunct
            who used to
            ride a watersmooth-silver
                                    stallion
    and break onetwothreefourfive pigeonsjustlikethat
                                                    Jesus

    he was a handsome man
                            and what i want to know is
    how do you like your blueeyed boy
    Mister Death   1923

The unusual spacing of words here, with some run together and others widely separated, provides a guide to reading, regulating both speed and sense, so that the poem can capture aloud some of the excitement and wonder of a boy's enthusiasm for a theatrical act as spectacular as that of Buffalo Bill. A good reader-aloud, with only this typographical guidance, can capture some of the wide-eyed boy's responses, remembered now in retrospect from a later perspective.

In prose, syntax and punctuation are the main guides to the voice of a reader, providing indicators of emphasis, pace, and speed; in poetry as well they are more conventional and more common guides than extreme forms of typography, such as in "Buffalo Bill 's." Reading a poem sensitively is in some ways a lot like reading a piece of prose sensitively: one has to pay close attention to the way the sentences are put together and how they are punctuated. A good reader makes use of appropriate pauses as well as thundering emphasis; silence as well as sound is part of any poem, and reading punctuation is as important as knowing how to say the words.

Beyond punctuation, the placement and spacing of lines on the page may be helpful to a reader even when that placement is not as radical as it is in "Buffalo Bill 's." The fact that poetry looks different from prose is not an accident; decisions to make lines one length instead of another have as much to do with vocal breaks and phrasing as with functions of syntax or meaning. In a good poem, there are few accidents, not even

5. Portraits XXI.

in the way the poem meets the eye, for as readers our eyes are the most direct route to our voices; they are our scanner and director, our prompter and guide.

The eye also may help the ear in poetry in another way—guiding us to notice repeated sounds by repeated visual patterns in letters. The most common rhymes in poems occur at the ends of lines, and the arrangement of lines (the typography of the poem) often calls attention to the pattern of sounds because of the similar appearance of line-ending words, as in sonnets and other traditional verse forms and sometimes in radically unconventional patterns. Not all words that rhyme have similar spellings, of course, but similarities of word appearance seem to imply a relationship of sound, too, and many poems hint at their stanza patterns and verse forms by their spatial arrangement and repeated patterns at ends of lines.

Visual devices are often entertainments to amuse, puzzle, or tease readers of poetry whose chief expectations are about sound, but sometimes poets achieve surprising (and lasting) original effects by manipulations of print space. Stanzas—visual breaks in poems that indicate some kind of unit of meaning or measurement—ultimately are more than visual devices, for they point to structural questions and ultimately frame and formalize the content of poems. But they involve—as do the similar visual patterns of words that rhyme—part of the "score" of poems, and suggest one more way that sight becomes a guide to sound in many poems.

GEORGE HERBERT

Easter Wings

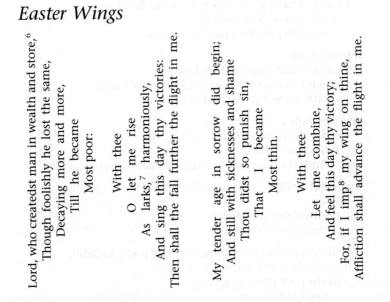

1633

6. In plenty.   7. Which herald the morning.   8. Engraft. In falconry, to engraft feathers in a damaged wing, so as to restore the powers of flight (*OED*).

MARY OLIVER

Goldenrod

On roadsides,
　in fall fields,
　　in rumpy bunches,
　　　saffron and orange and pale gold,

5　in little towers,
　　soft as mash,
　　　sneeze-bringers and seed-bearers,
　　　　full of bees and yellow beads and perfect flowerlets

and orange butterflies.
10　　I don't suppose
　　　much notice comes of it, except for honey,
　　　　and how it heartens the heart with its

blank blaze.
　　I don't suppose anything loves it except, perhaps,
15　　　the rocky voids
　　　　filled by its dumb dazzle.

For myself,
　　I was just passing by, when the wind flared
　　　and the blossoms rustled,
20　　　　and the glittering pandemonium

leaned on me.
　　I was just minding my own business
　　　when I found myself on their straw hillsides,
　　　　citron and butter-colored,

25　and was happy, and why not?
　　Are not the difficult labors of our lives
　　　full of dark hours?
　　　　And what has consciousness come to anyway, so far,

that is better than these light-filled bodies?
30　　All day
　　　on their airy backbones
　　　　they toss in the wind,

they bend as though it was natural and godly to bend,
　　they rise in a stiff sweetness,
35　　　in the pure peace of giving
　　　　one's gold away.
　　　　　　　　　　　　　　　　　　　　　　　　1992

E. E. CUMMINGS

[l(a]

l(a

le
af
fa
ll   5

s)
one
l

iness   1958

MARY ELLEN SOLT

Lilac

1968

QUESTIONS

1. Chart the rhyme scheme of Keats's "On the Sonnet," and then, after a careful reading aloud of the poem, mark the major structural breaks in the poem. At what points do the structural breaks and the breaks in rhyme pattern coincide? At what points do they conflict? Can you account for the variations in terms of the poem's meaning?
2. Describe the structure of Shelley's "Ozymandias." In what sense is it an Italian sonnet? Describe the rhyme scheme of this sonnet, and justify (if you can) its unusual pattern.
3. Is Chasin's "Joy Sonnet in a Random Universe" a sonnet? On what grounds can you justify calling it a sonnet?
4. What conventions of description is Shakespeare's "My mistress' eyes are nothing like the sun" working against? How can you tell? Describe the tone of the poem. What strategies, beyond the basic one of inverting conventions, help to create the poem's special tone?
5. Characterize the "you" in Johnson's "Sonnet to a Negro in Harlem." Describe the speaker's tone toward him. Describe the function of setting in the poem.

WRITING SUGGESTIONS

1. Consider the structure of McKay's "The White House" and the poem's themes of confinement and exclusion. In what specific ways does the poem use the tight restrictions of the sonnet form? Write an essay of about two pages on the way content and form interact in the poem.
2. Consider carefully the structure and sequencing in Brooks's "First Fight. Then Fiddle." Notice how various uses of sound in the poem (rhyme, onomatopoeia, and alliteration, for example) help to enforce its themes and tones. In an essay of about 600 words, show the relationship between "sound and sense" in the poem.

THE WHOLE TEXT

In the previous seven chapters, we have been thinking about one thing at a time—setting, word choice, symbolism, meter, stanza form, and so on—and we have discussed each poem primarily in terms of a single issue. Learning to deal with one problem at a time is good educational practice and in the long run will make you a more careful and more effective reader of poems. Still, the elements of poems do not work individually but in combination, and in considering even the simplest elements (speaker, for example, or setting) we have noticed how categories overlap—how, for example, the question of setting in Dickey's "Cherrylog Road" quickly merges into questions about the speaker, his state of mind, his personality, his distance from the central

> *All good poetry . . . is forged slowly and patiently, and link by link with sweat and blood and tears.*
>
> —LORD ALFRED DOUGLAS

events in the poem. Thinking about a single issue never fully does justice to an individual poem; no poem depends for all its effects on just one device or one element of craft. Poems are complex wholes that demand varieties of attention, and ultimately *all* the questions you have been learning to ask need to be applied to any poem you read. Reading any poem fully and well involves all the questions about craft, form, and tradition that you can think to ask, all the ones we've asked so far, and many others you may learn to ask on the basis of more experience in reading poems. Not all questions are equally relevant to all poems, of course, but moving systematically through your whole list of questions will ultimately enable you to get beyond the fragmentation of particular issues and approach the whole poem and its multiple ways of creating effects. In this chapter we will consider how the various elements of poems work together.

Here is a short poem in which several of the issues we have considered come up almost simultaneously:

ELIZABETH JENNINGS

Delay

The radiance of that star that leans on me
Was shining years ago. The light that now

Glitters up there my eye may never see
And so the time lag teases me with how

5   Love that loves now may not reach me until
Its first desire is spent. The star's impulse
Must wait for eyes to claim it beautiful
And love arrived may find us somewhere else.   1953

In most poems, several issues come up more or less at once, and the analytic practice of separating issues is a convenience rather than an assertion of priority or order. In "Delay," a lot of the basic questions (about speaker, situation, and setting, for example) seem to be put on hold in the beginning, but if we proceed systematically the poem begins to open itself to us. The first line identifies the "I" (or rather, in this case, "me") of the poem as an observer of the bright star that is the main object in the poem and the principal source of its imagery, its "plot," and its analogical argument. But we learn little detail about the speaker. She surfaces again in lines 4 and 5 and with someone else ("us") in line 8, but she is always in the objective case—acted on rather than acting. All that is certain about her is that she has some knowledge of the time it takes light from the stars to reach her and that she contemplates deeply and at length about the meaning and effect of such time lags. We are given even less detail about setting and situation; somewhere the speaker is watching a bright star and meditating on the fact that she is seeing it long, long after its actual light was sent forth. Her location is not specified, and the time, though probably night, could be any night (we do know that the speaker lives in the age of modern astronomy, that is, that the speed of light and the distance of the stars from Earth are understood); the only other explicit clues we have about situation involves the "us" of the final line and the fact that the speaker's concern with time seems oddly personal, something that matters to her emotional life—not merely a matter of stellar knowledge.

The poem's language helps us understand much more about the speaker and her situation, as does the poem's structure and stanza form. The most crucial word in the first stanza is probably the verb "leans" (line 1); certainly it is the most unusual and surprising word. Because a star cannot literally *lean* on its observer, the word seems to suggest the speaker's perception of her relationship to the star. Perhaps she feels that the star impinges on her, that she is somehow *subject* to its influence, though not in the popular, astrological sense. Here the star influences the speaker because she understands something about the way the universe works and can apply her knowledge of light and light years in an analogical way to her own life: it "leans" because it tells her something about how observers are affected by their relationships to what they observe. And it is worth noticing how fully the speaker thinks of herself as object rather than actor. Here, as throughout the poem, she is acted upon; things happen *to* her—the star leans on her, the time lag teases her (line 4), love may not reach her (line 5), and she (along with someone else) is the object sought in the final line.

Other crucial words also help clarify the speaker and her situation. The words "radiance" (line 1) and "[g]litters" (line 3) are fairly standard ones to describe stars, but here their standard meanings are carefully qualified by their position in time. The radiance is from years ago and seems to be unavailable to the speaker, who now sees only glitter, something far less warm and resonant. And the word "impulse" in line 6 invokes technical knowledge about light. Here a star is not impulsive or quickly spent but must "wait" for its reception in the eye of the beholder, where it becomes "beautiful"; in physics, an impulse combines force and duration. Hence, the receiver of light—the beholder, the acted-upon—becomes important, and we begin to see why the speaker always appears as object: she is the receiver and interpreter, and the light is not complete—its duration not established—until she receives and interprets it. The star does, after all, "lean" on (depend on) her in some objective sense as well as the subjective one in which she first seems to report it.

The stanza form suggests that the poem may have stages and that its meaning may emerge in two parts, a suggestion that is in fact confirmed by the poem's form and structure. The first stanza is entirely about stars and star-gazing, but the second stanza establishes the analogy with love that becomes the poem's central metaphor. Now, too, more becomes clear about the speaker and her situation. Her concern is about delay, "time lag" (line 4), and the fact that "Love that loves now may not reach me until / Its first desire is spent" (lines 5–6), a strong indication that her initial observation of the star is driven by feeling and her emotional context. Her attempt to put the remoteness of feeling into a perspective that will enable understanding and patience becomes the "plot" of the poem, and her final calm recognition about "us"—that "love arrived may find us somewhere else"—is, if not comforting, nevertheless a recognition that patience is important and that some things do last. Even the sounds of the poem—in this case the way rhyme is used—help support the meaning of the poem and the tone it achieves. The rhymes in the first part of the poem reflect perfectly the stable sense of ancient stars, while in the second stanza the sounds involve near-rhyme: there is harmony here, but in human life and emotion nothing is quite perfect.

Here is another short poem that deserves similar detailed attention to its several elements:

ANONYMOUS

Western Wind

Western wind, when wilt thou blow,
   The small rain down can rain?
Christ, if my love were in my arms
   And I in my bed again!   fifteenth century

Perhaps the most obvious thing here is the poem's structure: its first two lines seem to have little to do with the last two. How are we to account for these two distinct and apparently unrelated directions, the calm concern with natural processes in the first part and the emotional outburst about loneliness and lovelessness in the second? The best route to the whole poem is still to begin with the most simple of questions—who? when? where? what is happening?—and proceed to more difficult and complex ones.

As in Jennings's "Delay," the speaker here offers little explicit autobiography. In the first two lines, there is no personal information. The question these lines ask could be delivered quite impersonally; they could be part of a philosophical meditation. The abbreviated syntax at the end of line 1 (the question of causality is not fully stated, and we have to supply the "so that" implied at the end of the line) may suggest strong feeling and emotional upset, but it tells us nothing intimate and offers little information except that the time is spring (that's when the western wind blows). No place is indicated, no year, no particulars of situation. But the next two lines, while remaining inexplicit about exact details, make the speaker's situation clear enough: his love is no longer in his arms, and he wishes she were. (We don't really know genders here, and our guess is based on what we think of as typical practice in fifteenth-century England.)

The poem's language is a study in contrast, and it guides us to see the two-part structure clearly. The question asked of the wind in the first two lines involves straightforward, steady language, but the third line bursts with agony and personal despair. The power of the first word of the third line—especially in an age of belief—suggests a speaker ready to state his loss in the strongest possible terms, and the parallel statements of loss in lines 3 and 4 suggest not only the speaker's physical relationship to his love but also his displacement from home: he is deprived of both place and love, human contact and contact with his past. His longing for a world ordered according to his past experience is structured to parallel his longing for the spring wind that brings the world back to life. The two parts of the poem both express a desire for return—to life, to order, to causal relationships within the world. Setting has in fact become a central theme in the poem, and what the poem expresses tonally involves a powerful desire for stability and belonging—an effect that grows out of our sense of the speaker's situation and character. Speaker, setting, language, and structure here intertwine to create the intense focus of the poem.

Here is another short poem in which the several elements noticeably interrelate:

ROBERT HERRICK

Upon Julia's Clothes

Whenas in silks my Julia goes
Then, then, methinks, how sweetly flows
That liquefaction of her clothes.

Next, when I cast mine eyes, and see
5   That brave[1] vibration, each way free,
O, how that glittering taketh me!

1648

The poem is unabashed in its admiration of the way Julia looks, and nearly everything in its six short lines contributes to its celebratory tone. Perhaps the most striking thing about the poem involves its unusual, highly suggestive use of words. "[G]oes" at the end of line 1 may be the first word to call special attention to itself, though we will return in a minute to the very first word of the poem. "Walks" or "moves" would seem to be more obvious choices; "goes" is more neutral and less specific and in most circumstances would seem an inferior choice, but here the point seems to be to describe Julia in a kind of seamless and unspecified motion and from a specific angle, because

---

1. Handsome, showy.

the poem is anxious to record the effect of Julia's movement on the speaker (already a second element becomes crucial) rather than the specifics of Julia herself. Another word that seems especially important is "liquefaction" (line 3), also an unusual and suggestive word about motion. Again it implies no specific kind of motion, just smoothness and seamlessness, and it is applied not to Julia but to her clothes—the kind of indirection that doesn't really fool anybody. Other words that might repay a close look include "vibration" in line 5 (the speaker is finally willing to be a little more direct), "brave" and "free" (also in line 5), and "glittering" and "taketh" in line 6.

Had we begun conventionally by thinking about speaker, situation, and setting, we would have quickly noticed the precise way that the speaker chose to clothe Julia: "in silks," which move almost as one with her body. And we would have noticed that the speaker positions himself almost as voyeur (standing for us as observers, of course, but also for himself as the central figure in the poem). Not much detail about situation or setting is given (and the speaker is characterized only as a viewer and appreciator), but one thing about the scene is crucial. It takes us back to the first word of the poem, "whenas." The slightly quaint quality of the word may at first obscure, to a modern reader, just what it tells us about the situation, that it is a *kind* of scene rather than a single event. "Whenas" is very close to "whenever"; the speaker's claim seems to be that he responds this way *whenever* Julia dons her silks—apparently fairly often, at least in his memory or imagination.

Most of the speaker's language is sensual and rather provocative (he is anxious to share his responses with others so that *everyone* will know just how "taking" Julia is), but there is one rather elaborate (though somewhat disguised) metaphor that suggests his awareness of his own calculation and its consequences. In the beginning of the second stanza he describes how he "cast" his eyes: it is a metaphor from fishing, a frequent one in love poetry about luring, chasing, and catching. Julia is the object. The metaphor continues two lines later, but the angler is himself caught: he is taken by the "glittering" lure. This turning of the tables, drawing as it does on a traditional, common image that is then modified to help characterize the speaker, gives a little depth to the show: whatever the slither and glitter, there is not just showing off and sensuality but a catch in this angling.

Many other elements in the poem are worth comment, especially because they quickly relate to each other. Consider the way the poet uses sounds, first of all in picking words like "liquefaction" that are themselves almost onomatopoeic, but then also using rhyme very cleverly. There are only two rhyme sounds in the poem, one in the first stanza, the other in the second. The long *ee* of the second becomes almost exclamatory, and the three words of the first seem to become linked in a kind of separate grammar of their own, as if "goes," "flows," and "clothes" were all part of a single action—pretty much what the poem claims on a thematic level. A lot is going on in this short and simple poem, and although a reader can get at it step by step by thinking about element after element, the interlocking of the elements is finally what is most impressive. It's easy to see that the plot here reenacts the familiar stances of woman as object and man as gazer, but we need to be flexible enough in our analysis and reading to consider not only all the analytical categories, but also the ways in which they work together.

Going back to poems read earlier in the book—with the methods and approaches you have learned since then—can be useful in seeing how different elements of poems interrelate. Look, for example, at the stanza divisions in Dickey's "Cherrylog Road" (page 661) and consider how the neatly spaced, apparently discrete units work against the sometimes frantic pacing of the poem. Or consider the character of the speaker, or the fundamental metaphor of "wreckage" that sponsors the poem, relative to the idea of the speaker. Go back and read Kumin's "Woodchucks" (page 628) while thinking about structural questions; or consider how the effaced speaker works in Rich's "Aunt Jennifer's Tigers" (page 628); or think about metaphor in Nemerov's "The Vacuum" (page 604).

Here are several new poems to analyze. As you read them, think about the elements discussed in the first seven chapters—but rather than thinking about a single element at a time, try to consider relationships, how the different elements combine to make you respond not to a single device but to a complex set of strategies and effects.

W. H. AUDEN

Musée des Beaux Arts²

About suffering they were never wrong,
The Old Masters: how well they understood
Its human position; how it takes place
While someone else is eating or opening a window or just walking
    dully along;
5   How, when the aged are reverently, passionately waiting
For the miraculous birth, there always must be
Children who did not specially want it to happen, skating
On a pond at the edge of the wood:
They never forgot
10 That even the dreadful martyrdom must run its course
Anyhow in a corner, some untidy spot
Where the dogs go on with their doggy life and the torturer's horse
Scratches its innocent behind on a tree.
In Brueghel's *Icarus*,³ for instance: how everything turns away
15 Quite leisurely from the disaster; the plowman may
Have heard the splash, the forsaken cry,
But for him it was not an important failure; the sun shone
As it had to on the white legs disappearing into the green
Water; and the expensive delicate ship that must have seen
20 Something amazing, a boy falling out of the sky,
Had somewhere to get to and sailed calmly on.

    1938

---

2. The Museum of the Fine Arts, in Brussels.   3. *Landscape with the Fall of Icarus*, by Pieter Brueghel the Elder (1525?–1569), located in the Brussels Museum. According to Greek myth, Daedalus and his son Icarus escaped from imprisonment by using homemade wings of feathers and wax; but Icarus flew too near the sun, the wax melted, and he fell into the sea and drowned. In the Brueghel painting the central figure is a peasant plowing, and several other figures are more immediately noticeable than Icarus, who, disappearing into the sea, is easy to miss in the lower right-hand corner. Equally ignored by the figures is a dead body in the woods.

GEORGE HERBERT

The Collar

I struck the board[4] and cried, "No more;
        I will abroad!
What? shall I ever sigh and pine?
My lines[5] and life are free, free as the road,
    Loose as the wind, as large as store.[6]   5
        Shall I be still in suit?[7]
Have I no harvest but a thorn
To let me blood, and not restore
What I have lost with cordial[8] fruit?
        Sure there was wine   10
Before my sighs did dry it; there was corn
    Before my tears did drown it.
Is the year only lost to me?
    Have I no bays[9] to crown it,
No flowers, no garlands gay? All blasted?   15
        All wasted?
Not so, my heart; but there is fruit,
    And thou hast hands.
Recover all thy sigh-blown age
On double pleasures: leave thy cold dispute   20
Of what is fit, and not. Forsake thy cage,
        Thy rope of sands,[1]
Which petty thoughts have made, and made to thee
Good cable, to enforce and draw,
        And be thy law,   25
While thou didst wink[2] and wouldst not see.
        Away! take heed;
        I will abroad.
Call in thy death's-head[3] there; tie up thy fears.
        He that forbears   30
    To suit and serve his need,
        Deserves his load."
But as I raved and grew more fierce and wild
        At every word,
Methought I heard one calling, *Child!*   35
        And I replied, *My Lord.*   1633

---

4. Table.   5. Lot.   6. A storehouse; that is, in abundance.   7. In service to another.   8. Reviving, restorative.   9. Laurel wreaths of triumph.   1. Moral restrictions.   2. That is, close your eyes to the weaknesses of such restrictions.   3. *Memento mori*, a skull intended to remind people of their mortality.

EMILY DICKINSON

[*My Life had stood—a Loaded Gun—*]

My Life had stood—a Loaded Gun—
In Corners—till a Day
The Owner passed—identified—
And carried Me away—

5 And now We roam in Sovereign Woods—
And now We hunt the Doe—
And every time I speak for Him—
The Mountains straight reply—

And do I smile, such cordial light
10 Upon the Valley glow—
It is as a Vesuvian face
Had let its pleasure through—

And when at Night—Our good Day done—
I guard My Master's Head—
15 'Tis better than the Eider-Duck's
Deep Pillow—to have shared—

To foe of His—I'm deadly foe—
None stir the second time—
On whom I lay a Yellow Eye—
20 Or an emphatic Thumb—

Though I than He—may longer live
He longer must—than I—
For I have but the power to kill,
Without—the power to die—

ca. 1863

ROBERT FROST

Design

I found a dimpled spider, fat and white,
On a white heal-all,[4] holding up a moth
Like a white piece of rigid satin cloth—
Assorted characters of death and blight
5 Mixed ready to begin the morning right,
Like the ingredients of a witches' broth—

4. A plant, also called the "all-heal" and "self-heal," with tightly clustered violet-blue flowers.

A snow-drop spider, a flower like a froth,
And dead wings carried like a paper kite.

What had that flower to do with being white,
The wayside blue and innocent heal-all?   10
What brought the kindred spider to that height,
Then steered the white moth thither in the night?
What but design of darkness to appall?—
If design govern in a thing so small.   1936

_____

D. H. LAWRENCE

Piano

Softly, in the dusk, a woman is singing to me;
Taking me back down the vista of years, till I see
A child sitting under the piano, in the boom of the tingling strings
And pressing the small, poised feet of a mother who smiles as she sings.

In spite of myself, the insidious mastery of song   5
Betrays me back, till the heart of me weeps to belong
To the old Sunday evenings at home, with winter outside
And hymns in the cozy parlor, the tinkling piano our guide.

So now it is vain for the singer to burst into clamor
With the great black piano appassionato. The glamour   10
Of childish days is upon me, my manhood is cast
Down in the flood of remembrance, I weep like a child for the past.
                                                              1918

_____

JONATHAN SWIFT

A Description of a City Shower

   Careful observers may foretell the hour
(By sure prognostics) when to dread a shower:
While rain depends,⁵ the pensive cat gives o'er
Her frolics, and pursues her tail no more
Returning home at night, you'll find the sink⁶   5
Strike your offended sense with double stink.
If you be wise, then go not far to dine;
You'll spend in coach hire more than save in wine.

_____

5. Impends, is imminent.   6. Sewer.

A coming shower your shooting corns presage,
10   Old achés throb, your hollow tooth will rage.
Sauntering in coffeehouse is Dulman[7] seen;
He damns the climate and complains of spleen.
    Meanwhile the South, rising with dabbled wings,
A sable cloud athwart the welkin flings,
15   That swilled more liquor than it could contain,
And, like a drunkard, gives it up again.
Brisk Susan whips her linen from the rope,
While the first drizzling shower is borne aslope:
Such is that sprinkling which some careless quean[8]
20   Flirts on you from her mop, but not so clean:
You fly, invoke the gods; then turning, stop
To rail; she singing, still whirls on her mop.
Not yet the dust had shunned the unequal strife,
But, aided by the wind, fought still for life,
25   And wafted with its foe by violent gust,
'Twas doubtful which was rain and which was dust.
Ah! where must needy poet seek for aid,
When dust and rain at once his coat invade?
Sole coat, where dust cemented by the rain
30   Erects the nap, and leaves a mingled stain.
    Now in contiguous drops the flood comes down,
Threatening with deluge this devoted town.
To shops in crowds the daggled females fly,
Pretend to cheapen[9] goods, but nothing buy.
35   The Templar spruce, while every spout's abroach,[1]
Stays till 'tis fair, yet seems to call a coach.
The tucked-up sempstress walks with hasty strides,
While streams run down her oiled umbrella's sides.
Here various kinds, by various fortunes led,
40   Commence acquaintance underneath a shed.
Triumphant Tories and desponding Whigs
Forget their feuds, and join to save their wigs.
Boxed in a chair the beau impatient sits,
While spouts run clattering o'er the roof by fits,
45   And ever and anon with frightful din
The leather sounds; he trembles from within.
So when Troy chairmen bore the wooden steed,
Pregnant with Greeks impatient to be freed
(Those bully Greeks, who, as the moderns do,
50   Instead of paying chairmen, run them through),[2]
Laocoön struck the outside with his spear,
And each imprisoned hero quaked for fear[3]
    Now from all parts the swelling kennels[4] flow,
And bear their trophies with them as they go:

---

7. A type name (from "dull man").   8. Wench, slut.   9. Bargain for. *Daggled* (line 33): spattered
with mud.   1. Pouring out water. *The Templar:* a young man studying law.   2. Run them through
with swords.   3. *The Aeneid* II.40–53.   4. Open gutters in the middle of the street.

Filth of all hues and odors seem to tell   55
What street they sailed from, by their sight and smell.
They, as each torrent drives with rapid force,
From Smithfield or St. Pulchre's shape their course,
And in huge confluence joined at Snow Hill ridge,
Fall from the conduit prone to Holborn Bridge.[5]   60
Sweepings from butchers' stalls, dung, guts, and blood,
Drowned puppies, stinking sprats[6] all drenched in mud,
Dead cats, and turnip tops, come tumbling down the flood.   1710

SIR WALTER RALEGH

The Author's Epitaph, Made by Himself

Even such is time, which takes in trust
Our youth, our joys, and all we have,
And pays us but with age and dust,
Who in the dark and silent grave
When we have wandered all our ways   5
Shuts up the story of our days,
And from which earth, and grave, and dust
The Lord shall raise me up, I trust.   1628

ANNE SEXTON

With Mercy for the Greedy

for my friend, Ruth, who urges me to make an appointment for
The Sacrament of Confession

Concerning your letter in which you ask
me to call a priest and in which you ask
me to wear The Cross that you enclose;
your own cross,
your dog bitten cross,   5
no larger than a thumb,
small and wooden, no thorns, this rose.

I pray to its shadow,
that gray place
where it lies on your letter . . . deep, deep.   10

5. *Smithfield:* site of cattle and sheep markets at the foot of Snow Hill. *St. Pulchre's:* church of St. Sepulchre. Holborn Conduit drained into a foul-smelling sewer at Holborn Bridge.   6. Small herrings.

I detest my sins and I try to believe
in The Cross. I touch its tender hips, its dark jawed face,
its solid neck, its brown sleep.

15 True. There is
a beautiful Jesus.
He is frozen to his bones like a chunk of beef.
How desperately he wanted to pull his arms in!
How desperately I touch his vertical and horizontal axes!
But I can't. Need is not quite belief.

20 All morning long
I have worn
your cross, hung with package string around my throat.
It tapped me lightly as a child's heart might,
tapping second hand, softly waiting to be born.
25 Ruth, I cherish the letter you wrote.

My friend, my friend, I was born
doing reference work in sin, and born
confessing it. This is what poems are:
with mercy
30 for the greedy;
they are the tongue's wrangle,
the world's pottage, the rat's star.   1962

QUESTIONS

1. Consider the setting of Auden's "Musée des Beaux Arts" both in the sense of the painting and of its location in the museum. In what different ways do the two settings become important? How does the use of setting relate to the way the speaker is conceived? Define the role played by all of the other characters in the poem, including the people on the ship. Whose attitudes (or perhaps words) are being echoed or parodied in line 20? Describe the poem's structure.
2. Consider the elements of speaker and situation simultaneously when you analyze Herbert's "The Collar."
3. Consider the interrelation of the elements of speaker, words and word order, and stanza form in Dickinson's "My Life had stood—a Loaded Gun—."
4. Consider the interrelationships among speaker, structure, stanza form, and tone in Frost's "Design."
5. Consider the question of word choices in connection with the issues of speaker and setting in Lawrence's "Piano."

WRITING SUGGESTION

Find a reproduction of the Brueghel painting on which Auden's poem "Musée des Beaux Arts" is based. "Read" the painting carefully, and notice which details Auden mentions and which he does not. What aspect(s) of the painting does he choose to emphasize? What does he ignore? Write a three-page essay in which you show exactly how Auden *uses* the Brueghel painting in his poem.

STUDENT WRITING

Below is a whole-text analysis of Maxine Kumin's "Woodchucks" (page 628). In it, the student addresses the setting, language, tone, structure, rhythm, and, finally, the meaning of the poem.

Tragedy in Five Stanzas: "Woodchucks"

Meaghan E. Parker

Maxine Kumin's poem, "Woodchucks," is not, as the title might suggest, about cute, furry woodchucks, but instead describes how the speaker changes as she tries to kill them, revealing aspects of human attitudes towards killing. The speaker undergoes an internal conflict as she realizes her capacity for murder during her battle with the woodchucks. She is caught up in the age-old struggle of humans against nature, except that this time, it takes place in the modern, technological world. This battle is presented in five dramatic scenes, marked by six-line stanzas; the poem's structure echoes the format of a classical tragedy in five acts. The poem is subtly organized, each stanza rhyming *abcacb*, and more or less employing a pentameter line, mixing iambs with anapests. Although the rhyme and meter remain mostly constant over the course of this highly structured poem, the tone and pacing change with each stanza, as the speaker's attitudes transform during the struggle with the woodchucks. The poet indicates the development of the speaker's internal conflict by employing word choice to change the tone from slightly humorous and relaxed to indignant martial righteousness and finally to a harsh and primitive hunter's voice, and utilizing pacing and meter to build the action to its climax.

The poem is set in small-town North America, where the speaker grows marigolds, broccoli, carrots, roses and chard in her garden. Although the speaker buys the gas bomb from the "Feed and Grain Exchange," she is not a farmer, since she has only a "vegetable patch" (lines 2 and 11). Therefore, her killing of the woodchucks is not an occupational or economic necessity; the woodchucks were merely a nuisance, and the speaker is sort of dabbling in killing. The first line states that the "gassing . . . didn't turn out right," not that it didn't work, emphasizing with this understatement the dilettantish air of the speaker's activities (line 1). The first stanza employs a playful humor: the gas is called a "knockout bomb," like some comic-book weapon, and the speaker makes a pun on the word "airtight" (lines 2-4). The store "featured" the bomb, as if it were displayed and advertised as a consumer desirable, not as a agent of death (line 3). Line 3 utilizes anapestic feet to add to the humorous tone, and most of the lines of stanza 1 are composed of long clauses, creating an even, calm pacing. The speaker and her compatriots ("we") had a made a "case against them," suggesting that the decision to kill the woodchucks was a calm, rational, legal event, yet the woodchucks evade the law by escaping "out of range" underground (lines 4-6). The escalation of the battle is indicated by the military term "range" and the woodchucks' refusal to play by the rules (line 6).

The second stanza is less light-hearted; even though the irrepressible woodchucks "turned up again" "up to scratch," they are now unmistakably opponents to the "we," who attacked them with "cyanide" (lines 7-9). The weapon seems more sinister now; not just gas from a "merciful" "knockout bomb," but murderous cyanide. The last three lines are a litany of the woodchuck's crimes against nature, each one described as increasing in savagery and wanton destruction. First, they merely "brought down the marigolds," but in a "matter of course," thoughtless way, then they "took over" the vegetables, as if they were marauding bandits conquering the speaker's territory (lines 10-11). The speaker is horrified at the "nipping" and "beheading" of the vegetables; the use of the execution-style word "beheading" to create indignation at the death of a plant is ironic, probably consciously on the part of the speaker, since she had tried to execute the woodchuck (line 12). The litany of crimes is reeled off in quick anapestic feet, subtly hinting at the irony of the speaker's anger at the woodchucks and the ridiculousness of the escalating battle.

The action picks up pace in stanza 3, the center of the poem and the point at which the speaker makes her transformation from silent killer to murderous hunter. She indignantly implies that the woodchucks would steal "the food from our mouths": a cliché that is supposed to indicate what heartless criminals the woodchucks are, even though the poem does not indicate that the speaker is a subsistence farmer who would starve without the vegetables (line 13). Even so, she enjoys the feel of the gun, "righteously thrilling" to have the weapon of her justified revenge in her hands (line 13). The ".22" and the "bullets' neat noses" feel right and good, and while the woodchucks are depersonalized into the enemy, the bullets gain "noses" (line 14). The killer is "righteous," "fallen from grace" and "puffed with Darwinian pieties"; these heavy-handed, Bible-thumping words echo religious and political leaders' sermons against evil enemies. The pace of the first four lines of this stanza is heavy and martial, booming with polysyllabic words and stirring phrases. The meter is the most irregular in this stanza, with the two stressed syllables and similar sounds of "*lapsed*" and "*pacifist*" pounding the contrast home between the speaker's current manifestation as righteous killer and her former beliefs (line 15). Lines 15 and 16 begin with a stress, on "I" and "puffed"; the majority of the other lines in the poem begin with an unstressed syllable, so this pair of exceptions stands out, at the exact center of the poem, and present the turning point of her attitudes towards killing. Now "fallen from grace," she is "puffed" like a self-righteous windbag, and exchanges her pacifism for the maxim of survival of the fittest (lines 15–16). Line 17 begins the switch in tone from martial sloganeering to impersonal, hunting slang, as the speaker "drew a bead" on a woodchuck and kills him. His death is contrasted with the perennialness of the "everbearing roses," for whose sake he dies; this phrase indicates an undercurrent of regret at the killing of the woodchuck (line 18).

The fourth stanza speeds up, using short, harsh clashing words in

short simple clauses, instead of the sermonizing phrases of the last
stanza. The speaker says she "dropped the mother": "drop" is a crude,
impersonal, and unfeeling word for "shot dead," and indicates the
speaker's new callous attitude towards the killing of the woodchucks
(line 19). Similarly, the description of the woodchuck "flipflopp[ing] in
the air" is gratuitous and violent, and the stress on "flip," since the
first syllable of the line should be unstressed, emphasizes the visual
image of the helpless, blown-away woodchuck (line 20). The speaker
immediately moves on: "another baby next" is killed without comment
(line 22). In the same line, she counts down "0 one-two-three" for the
three woodchucks she's killed, and the three strong stresses lead into
the climax of the poem, where she announces what she's become:
"murderer" and "hawkeye killer" (lines 23-24). The killer comes "on
stage forthwith," as the speaker appears fully transformed by her
killing, her capability for murderous action arising from her nature to
triumph over her professed pacifism. The stage metaphor reinforces the
five-act tragic structure that the poem mirrors and line 24 brings the
poem to its climax in the fourth stanza.

Throughout the poem, the poet uses the directions down and up to
contrast life and death. The woodchucks "turn up" alive (line 7), "up
to scratch" (line 9) from their "sub-sub-basement," but then they
"brought down the marigolds" (line 10), so they "died down in the . . .
roses" (line 18), "flipflopped and fell" after being "dropped" (lines 19-
20). The speaker, on the other hand, was "up to scratch" (line 9) but
"[fell] from grace" (line 15), so the "murderer inside [her] rose up
hard," as her former pacifist self died down and was reborn as a killer
(line 23). In the final stanza, the speaker, now living as this new
self, describes her continuing struggle with the woodchuck and the
tolls this battle is taking on her, as she remains "cocked and ready
day after day after day" and her obsession with hunting this elusive
prey keeps her awake at night, dreaming of shooting (lines 26-28). The
pacing slows, as the action falls from the climax, and an unenumerated
amount of time elapses, but still there is not resolution and thus no
victory; the speaker realizes she has lost already to the woodchucks;
the tragedy is that they have already stolen her former innocence of
murder and killing and now she will never have peace. The final two

lines echo the beginning of the poem: "gassing" from line 1 and
"gassed" from line 30 are each stressed syllables beginning a line,
hus neatly bookending the poem. The speaker suggests that if the
woodchucks had died from the gas, she would not have directly
confronted the woodchucks and their deaths and thus undergone this
tragic change into an obsessive hunter. However, this statement
contains a telling historical allusion which suggests that the gassing
wouldn't have been an easy moral way out either: the speaker wishes
they had died "gassed underground the quiet Nazi way" (line 30). The
speaker wished the deaths had been quiet, efficient, clean, non-
confrontational and unwitnessed by her, so she could deny any
complicity to her conscience. However, this indicates an important
contradiction: gassing is still murder, as the Nazis made abundantly
clear, no matter how "merciful." The poet draws a parallel between what
we consider the "mercy killing" of animals and the "murder" of human
beings, and thus the poem describes how delusions of righteousness
cause people to wield unnecessary power over others, and how this
damages and changes their sense of self as they realize and accept the
human capability for acts of murder.

Exploring Contexts

21

THE AUTHOR'S WORK IN CONTEXT: ADRIENNE RICH

The poet featured in this chapter, Adrienne Rich, has had a long and very distinguished career. Many readers and critics regard her as the best poet writing today. And a careful reader of her work will find similarities of interest, strategy, and taste from her earliest poems—published shortly after World War II, in 1951—to her newest ones. There is a distinctive mind and orientation at work in all her poems; one can speak about characteristic features in Rich's poetry just as surely as one does about characteristic features in the work of Keats even though she has already written many more poems over a much longer period of years. Throughout her career of almost fifty years, Rich has, for example, steadfastly remained interested in social and political issues and has often concentrated on themes relating to women's consciousness and the societal roles of women. Furthermore, her poems have always been conceived with a powerful sense of functional structure and cast into lyric modes that reflect sensitively their respective moods and tones. And the voice has always been firm and clear, setting out images vividly and taking a stand in matters of conscience. But over the years the voice has changed quite a lot, too, and Rich's views on a number of issues have modified and developed. Many of the changes in Rich's ideas and attitudes reflect changing concerns among American (and especially women) intellectuals in the second half of the twentieth century, and her poems represent both changed social conditions and sharply altered social, political, and philosophical attitudes. But they also reflect altered personal circumstances and changes in lifestyle and expressions of sexual preference. Rich married in her early twenties and had three children by the time she was thirty; many of her early poems are about heterosexual love, and some of them are quite explicitly about sex (see, for example, "Two Songs," page 720). More recently she has been involved in a long-term lesbian relationship and has written, again quite explicitly, about sex between women. In her poems one can trace not only the contours of her evolving personal and political life and commitments, but (even more important for the study of poetry generally) one can see as well how changes *within* the poet and *in her social and cultural context* alter the themes and directions of her work and even change the formal nature of what she tries to do.

The fear of poetry is an indication that we are cut off from our own reality.

—MURIEL RUKEYSER

One way to study Rich as an "author in context" is to read carefully what she has to say about herself and her poems: she is unusually straightforward, explicit, and articulate, and to read her describing her own development is to be guided carefully through her changing ideas about what is important both to the individual subjective consciousness and to societal attitudes and changing roles. Gathered at the end of this chapter are a series of excerpts from Rich's writing about herself and about poetry more generally, and you can use these self-conscious reflections as a kind of commentary on the poems included here and elsewhere in the book.

Adrienne Rich circa 1970

Here is a chronological list of the poems and prose commentary included elsewhere in this book. You can deal with the issues of an author in context in one of three ways: (1) read the commentary, then the poems; (2) read the poems, then the commentary; or (3) read the poems and commentary intermixed, in chronological order. Each selection is dated, usually (as throughout this volume) by publication date below the poem on the right, but sometimes (when Rich herself has been insistent about it) by the date of composition listed below the poem on the left.

Aunt Jennifer's Tigers	(1951)	p. 628
Two Songs	(1964)	p. 720
Letters in the Family	(1989)	p. 642

An even better way to study Adrienne Rich (or any poet) is to go to the library and read all (or as much as you can find) of her writing and consider in detail how the various texts interact. Most poets, even John Keats, who lived only to age twenty-five, change a lot during their careers, and many of the changes correspond to larger social and cultural changes in their own time and nation. The best way to think about the contexts of a poet's life and career is to read as much as possible of her or his own work along with that of relevant contemporaries. Watching a poet develop within various traditions and contexts can lead to a relatively balanced assessment of a particular career and also to a more exact assessment of what poetry is about in a particular time, era, or culture.

Studying Rich's career in context suggests a number of larger literary, cultural, and historical issues—the kinds of issues that will be explored more fully in the next two chapters. You may well want to think about Adrienne Rich again after you have read the poems in the other chapters—especially the poems in the "Constructing Identity, Exploring Gender" section of Chapter 24.

At a Bach Concert

Coming by evening through the wintry city
We said that art is out of love with life.
Here we approach a love that is not pity.

This antique discipline, tenderly severe,
Renews belief in love yet masters feeling,
Asking of us a grace in what we bear.

Form is the ultimate gift that love can offer—
The vital union of necessity
With all that we desire, all that we suffer.

A too-compassionate art is half an art.
Only such proud restraining purity
Restores the else-betrayed, too-human heart.   1951

Storm Warnings

The glass has been falling all the afternoon,
And knowing better than the instrument
What winds are walking overhead, what zone
Of gray unrest is moving across the land,
I leave the book upon a pillowed chair
And walk from window to closed window, watching
Boughs strain against the sky

And think again, as often when the air
Moves inward toward a silent core of waiting,
How with a single purpose time has traveled
By secret currents of the undiscerned
Into this polar realm. Weather abroad
And weather in the heart alike come on
Regardless of prediction.

Between foreseeing and averting change
Lies all the mastery of elements
Which clocks and weatherglasses cannot alter.
Time in the hand is not control of time,
Nor shattered fragments of an instrument
A proof against the wind; the wind will rise,
We can only close the shutters.

I draw the curtains as the sky goes black
And set a match to candles sheathed in glass
Against the keyhole draught, the insistent whine
Of weather through the unsealed aperture.
This is our sole defense against the season;
These are the things that we have learned to do
Who live in troubled regions.   1951

Living in Sin

She had thought the studio would keep itself;
no dust upon the furniture of love.

Half heresy, to wish the taps less vocal,
the panes relieved of grime. A plate of pears,
a piano with a Persian shawl, a cat   5
stalking the picturesque amusing mouse
had risen at his urging.
Not that at five each separate stair would writhe
under the milkman's tramp; that morning light
so coldly would delineate the scraps   10
of last night's cheese and three sepulchral bottles;
that on the kitchen shelf among the saucers
a pair of beetle-eyes would fix her own—
envoy from some village in the moldings . . .
Meanwhile, he, with a yawn,   15
sounded a dozen notes upon the keyboard,
declared it out of tune, shrugged at the mirror,
rubbed at his beard, went out for cigarettes;
while she, jeered by the minor demons,
pulled back the sheets and made the bed and found   20
a towel to dust the table-top,
and let the coffee-pot boil over on the stove.
By evening she was back in love again,
though not so wholly but throughout the night
she woke sometimes to feel the daylight coming   25
like a relentless milkman up the stairs.   1955

Snapshots of a Daughter-in-Law

1

You, once a belle in Shreveport,
with henna-colored hair, skin like a peachbud,
still have your dresses copied from that time,
and play a Chopin prelude
called by Cortot: *"Delicious recollections*   5
float like perfume through the memory."

Your mind now, mouldering like wedding-cake,
heavy with useless experience, rich
with suspicion, rumor, fantasy,
crumbling to pieces under the knife-edge   10
of mere fact. In the prime of your life.

Nervy, glowering, your daughter
wipes the teaspoons, grows another way.

2

Banging the coffee-pot into the sink
she hears the angels chiding, and looks out   15
past the raked gardens to the sloppy sky.
Only a week since They said: *Have no patience.*

The next time it was: *Be insatiable.*
Then: *Save yourself; others you cannot save.*[1]
Sometimes she's let the tapstream scald her arm,
a match burn to her thumbnail,

or held her hand above the kettle's snout
right in the woolly steam. They are probably angels,
since nothing hurts her any more, except
each morning's grit blowing into her eyes.

3

A thinking woman sleeps with monsters.
The beak that grips her, she becomes. And Nature,
that sprung-lidded, still commodious
steamer-trunk of *tempora* and *mores*[2]
gets stuffed with it all: the mildewed orange-flowers,
the female pills, the terrible breasts
of Boadicea[3] beneath flat foxes' heads and orchids.

Two handsome women, gripped in argument,
each proud, acute, subtle, I hear scream
across the cut glass and majolica
like Furies[4] cornered from their prey:
The argument *ad feminam,*[5] all the old knives
that have rusted in my back, I drive in yours,
ma semblable, ma soeur![6]

4

Knowing themselves too well in one another:
their gifts no pure fruition, but a thorn,
the prick filed sharp against a hint of scorn . . .
Reading while waiting
for the iron to heat,
writing, *My Life had stood—a Loaded Gun—*[7]
in that Amherst pantry while the jellies boil and scum,
or, more often,
iron-eyed and beaked and purposed as a bird,
dusting everything on the whatnot every day of life.

---

1. According to Matthew 27:42, the chief priests, scribes, and elders mocked the crucified Jesus by saying, "He saved others; himself he cannot save."   2. Times and customs.   3. Queen of the ancient Britons. When her husband died, the Romans seized the territory he ruled and scourged Boadicea; she then led a heroic but ultimately unsuccessful revolt.   4. In Roman mythology, the three sisters were the avenging spirits of retributive justice.   5. "To the woman" (Latin). The *argumentum ad hominem* (literally, argument to the man) is (in logic) an argument aimed at a person's individual prejudices or special interests.   6. "My mirror-image [or 'double'], my sister." Baudelaire, in the prefatory poem to *Les Fleurs du Mal,* addresses (and attacks) his "hypocrite reader" as "mon semblable, mon frère" ("my double, my brother").   7. " 'My Life had stood—a Loaded Gun—' [Poem No. 754], Emily Dickinson, *Complete Poems,* ed. T. H. Johnson, 1960, p. 369." (AR)

5

Dulce ridens, dulce loquens,[8]   50
she shaves her legs until they gleam
like petrified mammoth-tusk.

6

When to her lute Corinna sings[9]
neither words nor music are her own;
only the long hair dipping   55
over her cheek, only the song
of silk against her knees
and these
adjusted in reflections of an eye.

Poised, trembling and unsatisfied, before   60
an unlocked door, that cage of cages,
tell us, you bird, you tragical machine—
is this *fertilisante douleur?*[1] Pinned down
by love, for you the only natural action,
are you edged more keen   65
to prise the secrets of the vault? has Nature shown
her household books to you, daughter-in-law,
that her sons never saw?

7

"To have in this uncertain world some stay
which cannot be undermined, is   70
of the utmost consequence."[2]
                          Thus wrote
a woman, partly brave and partly good,
who fought with what she partly understood.
Few men about her would or could do more,
hence she was labeled harpy, shrew and whore.   75

8

"You all die at fifteen," said Diderot,[3]
and turn part legend, part convention.
Still, eyes inaccurately dream

---

8. "Sweet [or 'winsome'] laughter, sweet chatter." The phrase (slightly modified here) concludes Horace's *Ode* 1.22, describing the appeal of a mistress.   9. The opening line of a famous Elizabethan lyric (by Thomas Campion) in which Corinna's music is said to control totally the poet's happiness or despair.   1. "Enriching pain" (French).   2. " '. . . is of the utmost consequence,' from Mary Wollstonecraft, *Thoughts on the Education of Daughters*, London, 1787." (AR)   3. " 'Vous mourez toutes a quinze ans,' from the *Lettres à Sophie Volland*, quoted by Simone de Beauvoir in *Le Deuxième Sexe*, vol. II, pp. 123–4." (AR) Editor of the *Encyclopédie* (the central document of the French Enlightenment), Diderot became disillusioned with the traditional education of women and undertook an experimental education for his own daughter.

behind closed windows blankening with steam.
Deliciously, all that we might have been,
all that we were—fire, tears,
wit, taste, martyred ambition—
stirs like the memory of refused adultery
the drained and flagging bosom of our middle years.

9

Not that it is done well, but
that it is done at all?[4] Yes, think
of the odds! or shrug them off forever.
This luxury of the precocious child,
Time's precious chronic invalid,—
would we, darlings, resign it if we could?
Our blight has been our sinecure:
mere talent was enough for us—
glitter in fragments and rough drafts.

Sigh no more, ladies.
                        Time is male
and in his cups drinks to the fair.
Bemused by gallantry, we hear
our mediocrities over-praised,
indolence read as abnegation,
slattern thought styled intuition,
every lapse forgiven, our crime
only to cast too bold a shadow
or smash the mould straight off.

For that, solitary confinement,
tear gas, attrition shelling.
Few applicants for that honor.

10

                            Well,
she's long about her coming, who must be
more merciless to herself than history.[5]
Her mind full to the wind, I see her plunge
breasted and glancing through the currents,
taking the light upon her
at least as beautiful as any boy
or helicopter,

---

4. Samuel Johnson's comment on women preachers: "Sir, a woman's preaching is like a dog's walking on his hinder legs. It is not done well, but you are surprised to find it done at all." (Boswell's *Life of Johnson*, ed. L. F. Powell and G. B. Hill [Oxford: Clarendon, 1934–64], I, 463.) 5. "Cf. *Le Deuxième Sexe*, vol. II, p. 574: '. . . elle arrive du fond des ages, de Thèbes, de Minos, de Chichen Itza; et elle est aussi le totem planté au coeur de la brousse africaine; c'est un helicoptère et c'est un oiseau; et voilà la plus grande merveille: sous ses cheveux peints le bruissement des feuillages devient une pensée et des paroles s'échappent de ses seins.' " (AR)

　　　　　　　　poised, still coming,
　　　her fine blades making the air wince

　　but her cargo
　　no promise then:　　　　　　　　　　　　　　　　　　　　115
　　delivered
　　palpable
　　ours.

1958–1960

In *When We Dead Awaken,* Rich describes her consciousness during the time she
was writing this poem:

> Over two years I wrote a 10-part poem called "Snapshots of a Daughter-in-Law," in a
> longer, looser mode than I've ever trusted myself with before. It was an extraordinary
> relief to write that poem. It strikes me now as too literary, too dependent on allusion; I
> hadn't found the courage yet to do without authorities, or even to use the pronoun "I"—
> the woman in the poem is always "she." One section of it, #2, concerns a woman who
> thinks she is going mad; she is haunted by voices telling her to resist and rebel, voices
> which she can hear but not obey.

Diving into the Wreck

First having read the book of myths,
and loaded the camera,
and checked the edge of the knife-blade,
I put on
the body-armor of black rubber　　　　　　　　　　　　　　　5
the absurd flippers
the grave and awkward mask.
I am having to do this
not like Cousteau with his
assiduous team　　　　　　　　　　　　　　　　　　　　　10
aboard the sun-flooded schooner
but here alone.

There is a ladder.
The ladder is always there
hanging innocently　　　　　　　　　　　　　　　　　　　15
close to the side of the schooner.
We know what it is for,
we who have used it.
Otherwise
it's a piece of maritime floss　　　　　　　　　　　　　　20
some sundry equipment.

I go down.
Rung after rung and still

the oxygen immerses me
25   the blue light
the clear atoms
of our human air.
I go down.
My flippers cripple me,
30   I crawl like an insect down the ladder
and there is no one
to tell me when the ocean
will begin.

First the air is blue and then
35   it is bluer and then green and then
black I am blacking out and yet
my mask is powerful
it pumps my blood with power
the sea is another story
40   the sea is not a question of power
I have to learn alone
to turn my body without force
in the deep element.

And now: it is easy to forget
45   what I came for
among so many who have always
lived here
swaying their crenellated fans
between the reefs
50   and besides
you breathe differently down here.

I came to explore the wreck.
The words are purposes.
The words are maps.
55   I came to see the damage that was done
and the treasures that prevail.
I stroke the beam of my lamp
slowly along the flank
of something more permanent
60   than fish or weed

the thing I came for:
the wreck and not the story of the wreck
the thing itself and not the myth
the drowned face always staring
65   toward the sun
the evidence of damage
worn by salt and sway into this threadbare beauty
the ribs of the disaster
curving their assertion
70   among the tentative haunters.

This is the place.
And I am here, the mermaid whose dark hair
streams black, the merman in his armored body
We circle silently
about the wreck   75
we dive into the hold.
I am she: I am he

whose drowned face sleeps with open eyes
whose breasts still bear the stress
whose silver, copper, vermeil cargo lies   80
obscurely inside barrels
half-wedged and left to rot
we are the half-destroyed instruments
that once held to a course
the water-eaten log   85
the fouled compass

We are, I am, you are
by cowardice or courage
the one who find our way
back to this scene   90
carrying a knife, a camera
a book of myths
in which
our names do not appear.

1972

Power

Living   in the earth-deposits   of our history

Today a backhoe divulged   out of a crumbling flank of earth
one bottle   amber   perfect   a hundred-year-old
cure for fever   or melancholy   a tonic
for living on this earth   in the winters of this climate   5

Today I was reading about Marie Curie:
she must have known she suffered   from radiation sickness
her body bombarded for years   by the element
she had purified
It seems she denied to the end   10
the source of the cataracts on her eyes
the cracked and suppurating skin   of her finger-ends
till she could no longer hold   a test-tube or a pencil

She died   a famous woman   denying
her wounds   15
denying
her wounds   came   from the same source as her power   1978

Walking Down the Road

On a clear night in Live Oak you can see
the stars glittering low as from the deck
of a frigate.
In Live Oak without pavements you can walk
5   the fronts of old homesteads, past tattered palms,
original rosebushes, thick walnut trees
ghosts of the liveoak groves
the whitemen cleared. On a night like this
the old California thickens and bends
10   the Baja streams out like lava-melt
we are no longer the United States
we're a lost piece of Mexico
maybe dreaming the destruction
of the Indians, reading the headlines,
15   how the gringos marched into Mexico City
forcing California into the hand
of Manifest Destiny, law following greed.
And the pale lies trapped in the flickering boxes
here in Live Oak tonight, they too follow.
20   One thing follows on another, that is time:
Carmel in its death-infested prettiness,
thousands of skeletons stacked in the *campo santo*:[6]
the spring fouled by the pickaxe:
the flag dragged on to the moon:
25   the crystal goblet smashed: grains of the universe
flashing their angry tears, here in Live Oak.   1989

Delta

If you have taken this rubble for my past
raking through it for fragments you could sell
know that I long ago moved on
deeper into the heart of the matter
5   If you think you can grasp me, think again:
my story flows in more than one direction
a delta springing from the riverbed
with its five fingers spread   1989

---

6. Sacred field, cemetery (Spanish).

History⁷

Should I simplify my life for you?
Don't ask how I began to love men.
Don't ask how I began to love women.
Remember the forties songs, the slowdance numbers
the small sex-filled gas-rationed Chevrolet?   5
Remember walking in the snow and who was gay?
Cigarette smoke of the movies, silver-and-gray
profiles, dreaming the dreams of he-and-she
breathing the dissolution of the wisping silver plume?
Dreaming that dream we leaned applying lipstick   10
by the gravestone's mirror when we found ourselves
playing in the cemetery.   In Current Events she said
the war in Europe is over, the Allies
and she wore no lipstick have won the war
and we raced screaming out of Sixth Period.   15

Dreaming that dream
we had to maze our ways through a wood
where lips were knives breasts razors and I hid
in the cage of my mind scribbling
this map stops where it all begins   20
into a red-and-black notebook.
Remember after the war when peace came down
as plenty for some and they said we were saved
in an eternal present and we knew the world could end?
—remember after the war when peace rained down   25
on the winds from Hiroshima Nagasaki Utah Nevada?⁸
and the socialist queer Christian teacher jumps from the hotel window?
and L.G. saying *I want to sleep with you but not for sex*
and the red-and-black enamelled coffee-pot dripped slow through the
    dark grounds
—appetite terror power tenderness   30
the long kiss in the stairwell the switch thrown
on two Jewish Communists⁹ married to each other
the definitive crunch of glass at the end of the wedding?
(When shall we learn, what should be clear as day,
We cannot choose what we are free to love?)   35

1995

---

7. The fourth poem in a series called "Inscriptions."   8. Sites of atomic-bomb explosions, the first two
in Japan near the end of World War II, the last two test sites in the desert.   9. Julius and Ethel Rosenberg, executed by the United States as spies.

INTERVIEWS AND PERSONAL REFLECTIONS

from *Talking with Adrienne Rich*[1]

* * * I think of myself as using poetry as a chief means of self-exploration—one of several means, of which maybe another would be dreams, really thinking about, paying attention to dreams, but the poem, like the dream, does this through images and it is in the images of my poems that I feel I am finding out more about my own experience, my sense of things. But I don't think of myself as having a position or a self-description which I'm then going to present in the poem.

When I started writing poetry I was tremendously conscious of, and very much in need of, a formal structure that could be obtained from outside, into which I could pour whatever I had, whatever I thought I had to express. But I think that was a part of a whole thing that I see, now as a teacher, very much with young writers, of using language more as a kind of façade than as either self-revelation or as a probe into one's own consciousness. I think I would attribute a lot of the change in my poetry simply to the fact of growing older, undergoing certain kinds of experiences, realizing that formal metrics were not going to suffice me in dealing with those experiences, realizing that experience itself is much more fragmentary, much more sort of battering, much ruder than these structures would allow, and it had to find its own form.

I have a very strong sense about the existence of poetry in daily life and poetry being part of the world as it is, and that the attempt to reduce poetry to what is indited on a page just limits you terribly. . . . The poem is the poetry of things lodged in the innate shape of the experience. My saying "The moment of change is the only poem" is the kind of extreme statement you feel the need to make at certain times if only to force someone to say, "But I always thought a poem is something written on a piece of paper," you know, and to say: "But look, how did those words get on that piece of paper." There had to be a mind; there had to be an experience; the mind had to go through certain shocks, certain stresses, certain strains, and if you're going to carry the poem back to its real beginnings it's that moment of change. I feel that we are always writing.

When I was in my twenties * * * I was going through a very sort of female thing—of trying to distinguish between the ego that is capable of writing poems, and then this other kind of being that you're asked to be if you're a woman, who is, in a sense, denying that ego. I had great feelings of split about that for many years actually, and there are a lot of poems I couldn't write even, because I didn't want to confess to having that much aggression, that much ego, that much sense of myself. I had always thought of my first book as being a book of very well-tooled

---

1. A transcript of a conversation recorded March 9, 1971, and printed in the *Ohio Review*, Fall 1971.

poems of a sort of very bright student, which I was at that time, but poems in which the unconscious things never got to the surface. But there's a poem in that book about a woman who sews a tapestry and the tapestry has figures of tigers on it. But the woman is represented as being completely . . . her hand is burdened by the weight of the wedding band, and she's meek, and she's fearful, and the only way in which she can express any other side of her nature is in embroidering these tigers. Well, I thought of that as almost a formal exercise, but when I go back and look at that poem I really think it's saying something about what I was going through. And now that's lessened a great deal for all sorts of reasons . . . that split.

from *An Interview with Adrienne Rich*[2]

I would have said ten or fifteen years ago that I would not even want to identify myself as a woman poet. That term *has* been used pejoratively; I just don't think it can be at this point. You know, for a woman the act of creation is prototypically to produce children, while the act of creating with language—I'm not saying that women writers haven't been accepted; certainly, more have been accepted than women lawyers or doctors. Still, a woman writer feels, she is going against the grain—or there has been this sense until very recently (if there isn't still). Okay, it's all right to be a young thing and write verse. But a friend of mine was telling me about meeting a noted poet at a cocktail party. She'd sent him a manuscript for a contest he was judging. She went up to him and asked him about it, and he looked at her and said, "Young girls *are* poems; they shouldn't write them." This attitude toward women poets manifests itself so strongly that you are made to feel you are becoming the thing you are not.

If a man is writing, he's gone through all the nonsense and said "Okay, I am a poet and I'm still a man. They don't cancel each other out or, if they do, then I'll opt to be a poet." He's not writing for a hostile sex, a breed of critics who by virtue of their sex are going to look at his language and pass judgment on it. That does happen to a woman. I don't know why the woman poet has been slower than the woman novelist in taking risks though I'm very grateful that this is no longer so. I feel that I dare to think further than I would have dared to think ten years ago—and *that* certainly is going to affect my writing. And I now dare to entertain thoughts and speculations that then would have seemed unthinkable.

Many of the male writers whom I very much admire—Galway Kinnell, James Wright, W. S. Merwin—are writing poetry of such great desolation. They come from different backgrounds, write in different ways, and yet all seem to write out of a sense of doom, as if we were fated to carry on these terribly flawed relationships. I think it's expressive of a feeling that "we, the masters, have created a world that's impossible to live in and that probably may not be livable in, in a very literal

2. By David Kalstone, in the *Saturday Review*, April 22, 1972.

sense. What we thought, what we'd been given to think is our privilege, our right, and our sexual prerogative has led to this, to our doom." I guess a lot of women— if not a lot of women poets—are feeling that there has to be some other way, that human life is messed-up but that it doesn't have to be *this* desolate.

Today, much poetry by women is charged with anger and uses voices of rage and anger that I don't think were ever used in poetry before. In poets like Sylvia Plath and Diane Wakoski, say, those voices are so convincing that it is impossible to describe them by using those favorite adjectives of phallic criticism—shrill and hysterical. Well, Sylvia Plath is dead. I always maintained from the first time I read her last poems that her suicide was not necessary, that she could have gone on and written poems that would have given us even more insight into the states of anger and willfulness, even of self-destructiveness, that women experience. She didn't need literally to destroy herself in order to reflect and express those things. Diane Wakoski is a young woman. She's changing a lot and will continue to change. What I admire in her, besides her energy and dynamism and quite a beautiful gift for snatching the image that she wants out of the air, is her honesty. No woman has written before about her face and said she hated it, that it had served her ill, that she wished she could throw acid in it. That's very shocking. But I think all women, even the most beautiful women, at times have felt that in a kind of self-hatred. Because the *face* is supposed to be the *woman*.

A lot of poetry is becoming more oral. Certainly, it's true of women and black poets. Reading black poetry on the printed page gives no sense of the poem, if you're going to look at that poetry the way you look at poems by Richard Wilbur. Yet you can hear these poets read and realize it's the oldest kind of poetry.

I think the energy of language comes somewhat from the pressure and need and unbearableness of what's being done to you. It's not the same energy you find in the blues. The blues are a grief language, a lost language, and a cry of pain, usually in a woman's voice, which is interesting. For a long time you sing the blues, and then you begin to say, "I'm tired of singing the blues. I want something else." And that's what you're hearing now. There seems to be a connection between an oppressed condition and having access to certain kinds of energy, vitality, and subjectivity. For women as well as blacks. Though I don't feel there is a necessary cause-and-effect relationship; what seems to happen is that being on top, being in a powerful position leads to a divorce between one's unruly, chaotic, revolutionary sensitivity and one's reason, sense of order and of maintaining a hold. And, therefore, you have at the bottom of the pile, so to speak, a kind of churning energy that gets lost up there among the administrators.

I don't know how or whether poetry changes anything. But neither do I know how or whether bombing or even community organizing changes anything when we are pitted against a massive patriarchal system armed with supertechnology. I believe in subjectivity—that a lot of male Left leaders have turned into Omnipotent Administrators, because their "masculinity" forced them to deny their subjectivity. I believe in dreams and visions and "the madness of art." And at moments I can conceive of a women's movement that will show the way to humanizing technology and fusing dreams and skills and visions and reason to begin the healing of the human race. But I don't want women to take over the world and run it the way men have, or to take on—yet again!—the burden of carrying the subjectivity of the race. Women are a vanguard now, and I believe will increasingly become so, because we have—Western women, Third World women, all women—known and felt the pain of the human condition most consistently. But in the end it can't be women alone.

from *When We Dead Awaken: Writing as Re-Vision*[3]

Most, if not all, human lives are full of fantasy—passive daydreaming which need not be acted on. But to write poetry or fiction, or even to think well, is not to fantasize, or to put fantasies on paper. For a poem to coalesce, for a character or an action to take shape, there has to be an imaginative transformation of reality which is in no way passive. And a certain freedom of the mind is needed—freedom to press on, to enter the currents of your thought like a glider pilot, knowing that your motion can be sustained, that the buoyancy of your attention will not be suddenly snatched away. Moreover, if the imagination is to transcend and transform experience it has to question, to challenge, to conceive of alternatives, perhaps to the very life you are living at that moment. You have to be free to play around with the notion that day might be night, love might be hate, nothing can be too sacred for the imagination to turn into its opposite or to call experimentally by another name. For writing is re-naming. Now, to be maternally with small children all day in the old way, to be with a man in the old way of marriage, requires a holding-back, a put-

Rich in the classroom circa 1978

ting-aside of that imaginative activity, and demands instead a kind of conservatism. I want to make it clear that I am *not* saying that in order to write well, or think well, it is necessary to become unavailable to others, or to become a devouring ego. This has been the myth of the masculine artist and thinker; and I do not accept it. But to be a female human being trying to fulfill traditional female functions in a traditional way *is* in direct conflict with the subversive function of the imagination. The word traditional is important here. There must be ways, and we will be finding out more and more about them, in which the

---

3. First published in *College English* in 1972; this version, slightly revised, is included in *On Lies, Secrets, and Silence: Selected Prose: 1966–1978* (1979).

energy of creation and the energy of relation can be united. But in those earlier years I always felt the conflict as a failure of love in myself. I had thought I was choosing a full life: the life available to most men, in which sexuality, work, and parenthood could coexist. But I felt, at twenty-nine, guilt toward the people closest to me, and guilty toward my own being.

I wanted, then, more than anything, the one thing of which there was never enough: time to think, time to write. The fifties and early sixties were years of rapid revelations: the sit-ins and marches in the South, the Bay of Pigs, the early antiwar movement, raised large questions—questions for which the masculine world of the academy around me seemed to have expert and fluent answers. But I needed to think for myself—about pacifism and dissent and violence, about poetry and society, and about my own relationship to all these things. For about ten years I was reading in fierce snatches, scribbling in notebooks, writing poetry in fragments; I was looking desperately for clues, because if there were no clues then I thought I might be insane. I wrote in a notebook about this time:

> Paralyzed by the sense that there exists a mesh of relationships—e.g., between my anger at the children, my sensual life, pacifism, sex (I mean sex in its broadest significance, not merely sexual desire)—an interconnectedness which, if I could see it, make it valid, would give me back myself, make it possible to function lucidly and passionately. Yet I grope in and out among these dark webs.

I think I began at this point to feel that politics was not something "out there" but something "in here" and of the essence of my condition.

In the late fifties I was able to write, for the first time, directly about experiencing myself as a woman. The poem was jotted in fragments during children's naps, brief hours in a library, or at 3 A.M. after rising with a wakeful child. I despaired of doing any continuous work at this time. Yet I began to feel that my fragments and scraps had a common consciousness and a common theme, one which I would have been very unwilling to put on paper at an earlier time because I had been taught that poetry should be "universal," which meant, of course, nonfemale. Until then I had tried very much *not* to identify myself as a female poet.

How Does a Poet Put Bread on the Table?[4]

But how does a poet put bread on the table? Rarely, if ever, by poetry alone. Of the four lesbian poets at the Nuyorican Poets Café about whose lives I know something, one directs an underfunded community arts project, two are untenured college teachers, one an assistant dean of students at a state university. Of other poets I know, most teach, often part time, without security but year round; two are on disability; one does clerical work; one cleans houses; one is a paid organizer; one has a paid editing job. Whatever odd money comes in erratically from readings and workshops, grants, permissions fees, royalties, prizes can be very odd money indeed, never to be counted on and almost always small: checks have to be chased down, grants become fewer and more competitive in a worsening political and economic climate. Most poets who teach at universities are

4. From *What Is Found There: Notebooks on Poetry and Politics* (1993).

untenured, without pension plans or group health insurance, or are employed at public and community colleges with heavy teaching loads and low salaries. Many give unpaid readings and workshops as part of their political "tithe."

Inherited wealth accounts for the careers of some poets: to inherit wealth is to inherit time. Most of the poets I know, hearing of a sum of money, translate it not into possessions, but into time—that precious immaterial necessity of our lives. It's true that a poem can be attempted in brief interstitial moments, pulled out of the pocket and worked on while waiting for a bus or riding a train or while children nap or while waiting for a new batch of clerical work or blood samples to come in. But only certain kinds of poems are amenable to these conditions. Sometimes the very knowledge of coming interruption dampens the flicker. And there is a difference between the ordinary "free" moments stolen from exhausting family strains, from alienating labor, from thought chained by material anxiety, and those other moments that sometimes arrive in a life being lived at its height though under extreme tension; perhaps we are waiting to initiate some act we believe will catalyze change but whose outcome is uncertain; perhaps we are facing personal or communal crisis in which everything unimportant seems to fall away and we are left with our naked lives, the brevity of life itself, and words. At such times we may experience a speeding-up of our imaginative powers, images and voices rush together in a kind of inevitability, what was externally fragmented is internally recognized, and the hand can barely keep pace.

But such moments presuppose other times: when we could simply stare into the wood grain of a door, or the trace of bubbles in a glass of water as long as we wanted to, *almost* secure in the knowledge that there would be no interruption—times of slowness, or purposelessness.

Often such time feels like a luxury, guiltily seized when it can be had, fearfully taken because it does not seem like work, this abeyance, but like "wasting time" in a society where personal importance—even job security—can hinge on acting busy, where the phrase "keeping busy" is a common idiom, where there is, for activists, so much to be done.

Most, if not all, of the names we know in North American poetry are the names of people who have had some access to freedom in time—that privilege of some which is actually a necessity for all. The struggle to limit the working day is a sacred struggle for the worker's freedom in time. To feel herself or himself, for a few hours or a weekend, as a free being with choices—to plant vegetables and later sit on the porch with a cold beer, to write poetry or build a fence or fish or play cards, to walk without a purpose, to make love in the daytime. To sleep late. Ordinary human pleasures, the self's re-creation. Yet every working generation has to reclaim that freedom in time, and many are brutally thwarted in the effort. Capitalism is based on the abridgment of that freedom.

Poets in the United States have either had some kind of private means, or help from people with private means, have held full-time, consuming jobs, or have chosen to work in low-paying, part-time sectors of the economy, saving their creative energies for poetry, keeping their material wants simple. Interstitial living, where the art itself is not expected to bring in much money, where the artist may move from a clerical job to part-time, temporary teaching to subsistence living on the land to waitressing or doing construction or translating, typesetting, or ghostwriting. In the 1990s this kind of interstitial living is more difficult, risky, and wearing than it has ever been, and this is a loss to all the arts—as much as the shrinkage of arts funding, the censorship-by-clique, the censorship by the Right, the censorship by distribution.

A Communal Poetry[5]

One day in New York in the late 1980s, I had lunch with a poet I'd known for more than twenty years. Many of his poems were—are—embedded in my life. We had read together at the antiwar events of the Vietnam years. Then, for a long time, we hardly met. As a friend, he had seemed to me withheld, defended in a certain way I defined as masculine and with which I was becoming in general impatient; yet often, in their painful beauty, his poems told another story. On this day, he was as I had remembered him: distant, stiff, shy perhaps. The conversation stumbled along as we talked about our experiences with teaching poetry,

Adrienne Rich today.

which seemed a safe ground. I made some remark about how long it was since last we'd talked. Suddenly, his whole manner changed: *You disappeared! You simply disappeared.* I realized he meant not so much from his life as from a landscape of poetry to which he thought we both belonged and were in some sense loyal.

If anything, those intervening years had made me feel more apparent, more visible—to myself and to others—as a poet. The powerful magnet of the women's liberation movement—and the women's poetry movement it released—had drawn me to coffeehouses where women were reading new kinds of poems; to emerging "journals of liberation" that published women's poems, often in a context of political articles and the beginnings of feminist criticism; to bookstores selling chapbooks and pamphlets from the new women's presses; to a woman poet's workshops with women in prison; to meetings with other women poets in Chinese restaurants, coffee shops, apartments, where we talked not only of poetry, but of the conditions that make it possible or impossible. It had never occurred to me that I was disappearing—rather, that I was, along with other women poets, beginning to appear. In fact, we were taking part in an immense shift in human consciousness.

My old friend had, I believe, not much awareness of any of this. It was, for him, so off-to-the-edge, so out-of-the-way; perhaps so dangerous, it seemed I had sunk, or dived, into a black hole. Only later, in a less constrained and happier meeting, were we able to speak of the different ways we had perceived that time.

He thought there had been a known, defined poetic landscape and that as

5. From *What Is Found There: Notebooks on Poetry and Politics* (1993).

poetic contemporaries we simply shared it. But whatever poetic "generation" I belonged to, in the 1950s I was a mother, under thirty, raising three small children. Notwithstanding the prize and the fellowship to Europe that my first book of poems had won me, there was little or no "appearance" I then felt able to claim as a poet, against that other profound and as yet unworded reality.

CHRONOLOGY

1929	Born in Baltimore, Maryland, May 16. Began writing poetry as a child under the encouragement and supervision of her father, Dr. Arnold Rich, from whose "very Victorian, pre-Raphaelite" library, Rich later recalled, she read Tennyson, Keats, Arnold, Blake, Rossetti, Swinburne, Carlyle, and Pater.
1951	A.B., Radcliffe College. Phi Beta Kappa. *A Change of World* chosen by W. H. Auden for the Young Poets Award and published.
1952–1953	Guggenheim Fellowship; travel in Europe and England. Marriage to Alfred H. Conrad, an economist who taught at Harvard. Residence in Cambridge, Massachusetts, 1953–66.
1955	Birth of David Conrad. Publication of *The Diamond Cutters and Other Poems*, which won the Ridgely Torrence Memorial Award of the Poetry Society of America.
1957	Birth of Paul Conrad.
1959	Birth of Jacob Conrad.
1960	National Institute of Arts and Letters Award for poetry. Phi Beta Kappa poet at William and Mary College.
1961–1962	Guggenheim Fellowship; residence with family in the Netherlands.
1962	Bollingen Foundation grant for translation of Dutch poetry.
1962–1963	Amy Lowell Travelling Fellowship.
1963	*Snapshots of a Daughter-in-Law* published. Bess Hokin Prize of *Poetry* magazine.
1965	Phi Beta Kappa poet at Swarthmore College.
1966	*Necessities of Life* published, nominated for the National Book Award. Phi Beta Kappa poet at Harvard College. Move to New York City, where Alfred Conrad taught at City College of New York. Residence there from 1966 on. Increasingly active politically in protests against the war in Vietnam.
1966–1968	Lecturer at Swarthmore College.
1967–1969	Adjunct Professor of Writing in the Graduate School of the Arts, Columbia University.
1967	*Selected Poems* published in Britain. Litt.D., Wheaton College.
1968	Eunice Tietjens Memorial Prize of *Poetry* magazine. Began teaching in the SEEK and Open Admissions Programs at City College of New York.
1969	*Leaflets* published.
1970	Death of Alfred Conrad.
1971	*The Will to Change* published. Shelley Memorial Award of the Poetry Society of America. Increasingly identifies with the women's movement as a radical feminist.
1972–1973	Fanny Hurst Visiting Professor of Creative Literature at Brandeis University.
1973	*Diving into the Wreck* published.
1973–1974	Ingram Merrill Foundation research grant; began work on a book on the history and myths of motherhood.
1974	National Book Award for *Diving into the Wreck*. Rich rejected the award as an individual, but accepted it, in a statement written with Audre Lorde and Alice Walker, two other nominees, in the name of all women:

> We . . . together accept this award in the name of all the women
> whose voices have gone and still go unheard in a patriarchal world, and in

the name of those who, like us, have been tolerated as token women in this culture, often at great cost and in great pain. . . . We symbolically join here in refusing the terms of patriarchal competition and declaring that we will share this prize among us, to be used as best we can for women. . . . We dedicate this occasion to the struggle for self-determination of all women, of every color, identification or derived class . . . the women who will not understand yet; the silent women whose voices have been denied us, the articulate women who have given us strength to do our work.

Professor of English, City College of New York.

1975   *Poems: Selected and New* published.

1976   Professor of English at Douglass College. *Of Woman Born: Motherhood as Experience and Institution* published. *Twenty-one Love Poems* published.

1978   *The Dream of a Common Language: Poems 1974–1977* published.

1979   *On Lies, Secrets, and Silence: Selected Prose 1966–1978* published. Leaves Douglass College and New York City; moves to Montague, Massachusetts; edits, with Michelle Cliff, the lesbian-feminist journal, *Sinister Wisdom*.

1981   *A Wild Patience Has Taken Me This Far: Poems 1978–1981* published.

1984   *The Fact of a Doorframe: Poems Selected and New 1950–1984* published. Moves to Santa Cruz, California.

1986   *Blood, Bread, and Poetry: Selected Prose 1979–1985* published. Professor of English at Stanford University.

1989   *Time's Power: Poems 1985–1988* published.

1990   Member of the Department of Literature of the American Academy and Institute of Arts and Letters.

1991   *An Atlas of the Difficult World* published.

1992   Wins *Los Angeles Times* Book Prize for *An Atlas of the Difficult World,* the Lenore Marshall/*Nation* Prize for Poetry, and Nicholas Roerich Museum Poet's Prize; is co-winner of the Frost Silver Medal for distinguished lifetime achievement.

1993   *What Is Found There: Notebooks on Poetry and Politics* published.

1994   Awarded MacArthur fellowship.

1996   Awarded the Tanning Prize, given by the Academy of American Poets.

QUESTION

What significant differences do you notice among the poems by Adrienne Rich that appear throughout this volume? Can you tell quickly an early Rich poem from a later one? What are the differences in subject matter? in style? in situation? in strategies of argument? Try to read all the Rich poems in the book at one sitting, working in poems to be found elsewhere in the text in their appropriate chronological place. Characterize, as fully as you can, the voice of the poems written in the 1950s; in the 1960s; 1970s; 1980s; 1990s. In what ways does the voice seem to change? What similarities do you see in her work from beginning to end?

WRITING SUGGESTIONS

1. In what sense is "At a Bach Concert" typical of Rich's early poetry? Compare "Storm Warnings" and "Aunt Jennifer's Tigers" in terms of the comments Rich makes about her early work in the passage quoted from *When We Dead Awaken: Writing as Re-Vision* (pages 839–40). What "typical" features do the poems share? Write a detailed analysis (about 1,500 words) of "At a Bach Concert," showing how it is (or is not) typical of Rich's early work.

2. Carefully considering plot, characterization, and structure, write an essay in which you detail the ways "Diving into the Wreck" is and is not typical of Rich's recent work. (Alternate version: Are there other poems that strike you as more typical of later Rich? If so, choose one and show how it is characteristic of Rich's later ideas and strategies.)

22

LITERARY TRADITION AS CONTEXT

The more poetry you read, the better a reader of poetry you are likely to be. This is not just because your skills will improve and develop, but also because you will come to know more about poetic traditions and can thus understand more fully how poets draw upon each other. Poets are conscious of other poets, and often they refer to each other's work or use it as a starting point for their own in ways that may not be immediately obvious to an outsider. Poetry can be thought of as a form of argument: poets agree or disagree over basic matters. Sometimes a quiet (or even noisy) competitiveness is at the bottom of their concern with what other poems have done or can do; at other times, playfulness and a sense of humor about poetic possibilities take over, and the competitiveness dwindles to fun and poetic games. And often poets want to tap the rich mine of artistic expression in order to share in the bounty of our heritage. In any case, a poet's consciousness of what others have done leads to a sense of tradition that is often hard to articulate but nevertheless is very important to the effects of poetry—and this sense of tradition is something of a problem for a relatively new reader of poetry. How can I possibly read this poem intelligently, we are likely to ask sometimes in exasperation, until I've read all the other poems ever written? It's a real problem. Poets don't actually expect that all of their readers have Ph.D.'s in literature, but sometimes it *seems* as if they do. For some poets—John Milton, T. S. Eliot, and Richard Wilbur are examples—it does help if one has read practically everything imaginable.

Why are poets so dependent on each other? What is the point of their relentless consciousness of what has already been done by others? Why do they repeatedly answer, allude to, and echo other poems? Why is tradition so important to them?

A sense of common task, a kind of communality of purpose, accounts for some traditional poetic practice, and the competitive desire of individual poets to achieve a place in the English and American poetic tradition accounts for more. Many poets are anxious to be counted among those who achieve, through their writing, a place in history; and a way of establishing that place is to define for oneself the relationship between one's own work and that of others whose place is already secure. There is, for many poets, an awareness of a serious and abiding cultural tradition that they wish to share and pass on; but also important is a shared sense of playfulness, a kind of poetic gamesmanship. Making words dance on the page

> The truest poetry is the most
> *feigning.*
>
> —WILLIAM SHAKESPEARE

or in our heads provides in itself a satisfaction and delight for many writers—pride in craft that is like the pride of a painter or potter or tennis player. Often poets set themselves a particular task to see what they can do. One way of doing that is to introduce a standard traditional **motif** (a recurrent device, formula, or situation that deliberately connects a poem with common patterns of existing thought), and then to play variations on it much as a musician might do. Another way is to provide an alternative answer to a question that has repeatedly been asked and answered in a traditional way. Poetic playfulness by no means excludes serious intention—the poems in this chapter often make important statements about their subject, however humorous they may be in their method. Some teasing of the tradition and of other poets is pure fun, a kind of kidding among good friends; some is harsher and represents an attempt to see the world very differently—to define and articulate a very different set of attitudes and values.

The Anglophone poetic tradition is a rich and varied heritage, and individual poets draw upon it in countless ways. You have probably noticed, in the poems you have read so far, a number of allusions, glances at the tradition or at individual expressions of it. The more poems you read, the more you will notice and the more you will yourself become a comfortable member of the audience poets write for. Poets do expect a lot from readers—not always but often enough to make a new reader feel nervous and sometimes inadequate. The other side of that discomfort comes when you begin to notice things that other readers don't. The groups of poems in this chapter illustrate some of the ways that the tradition energizes individual poets and suggest some of the things poets like to do with their heritage.

POETIC "KINDS"

There are all sorts of poems. By now you have experienced poems on a variety of subjects and with all kinds of tones—short poems, long poems, poems that rhyme and poems that don't. And there are, of course, many other sorts of poems that we haven't looked at. Some poems, for example, are thousands of lines long and differ substantially from the poems that can be included in a book like this.

Poems may be classified in a variety of ways—by subject, topic, or theme; by their length, appearance, and formal features; by the way they are organized; by the level of language they use; by the poet's intention and what kinds of effects the poem tries to generate.

Classification may be, of course, simply an intellectual exercise. Recognizing a poem that is, for example, an elegy, a parody, or a satire, may be very much like the satisfaction involved in recognizing a scarlet tanager, a weeping willow, a French phrase, or a 1967 Ford Thunderbird. Just *knowing* what others don't know may give us a sense of importance, accomplishment, and power. But there are also *uses* for classification: we can experience a poem more fully if we understand early on exactly what kind of poem we are dealing with. A fuller response is possible because the poet has consciously chosen to play by certain defined rules, and the **conventions** he or she employs indicate certain standard ways of saying things to achieve certain expected effects. The **tradition** that is involved in a particular poetic kind is thus employed by the poet in order to produce predictable standard responses. For example, much of the humor and fun in the following poem is premised on the assumption that readers will recognize the *kind* of poem they are reading.

CHRISTOPHER MARLOWE

The Passionate Shepherd to His Love

Come live with me and be my love,
And we will all the pleasures prove[1]
That valleys, groves, hills, and fields,
Woods, or steepy mountain yields.

And we will sit upon the rocks,   5
Seeing the shepherds feed their flocks,
By shallow rivers to whose falls
Melodious birds sing madrigals.

And I will make thee beds of roses
And a thousand fragrant posies,   10
A cap of flowers, and a kirtle[2]
Embroidered all with leaves of myrtle;

A gown made of the finest wool
Which from our pretty lambs we pull;
Fair lined slippers for the cold,   15
With buckles of the purest gold;

A belt of straw and ivy buds,
With coral clasps and amber studs:
And if these pleasures may thee move,
Come live with me, and be my love.   20

The shepherd swains[3] shall dance and sing
For thy delight each May morning:
If these delights thy mind may move,
Then live with me and be my love.   1600

A beginning reader of poetry might easily protest that a plea such as this one is unrealistic and fanciful, and thus feel unsure of the poem's tone. What could such a reader think of a speaker who constructs his argument in such a dreamlike way? But the traditions behind the poem and the conventions of the poetic kind make its intention and effects clear. "The Passionate Shepherd to His Love" is a **pastoral poem,** a poetic kind that concerns itself with the simple life of country folk and describes that life in stylized, idealized terms. The people in a pastoral poem are usually (as here) shepherds, although they may be fishermen or other rustics who lead an outdoor life and are involved in tending to basic human needs in a simplified society; the world of the poem is one of simplicity, beauty, music, and love. The world always seems timeless in pastoral; people are eternally young, and the season is always spring, usually May. Nature seems endlessly green and the future entirely golden. Difficulty, frustration, disappointment, and obligation do not belong in this world at all; it is blissfully free of problems.

1. Try.   2. Gown.   3. Youths.

Shepherds sing instead of tending sheep, and they make love and play music instead of having to watch out for wolves in the night. If only the shepherd boy and shepherd girl can agree with each other to make love joyously and passionately, they will live happily ever after. The language of pastoral is informal and fairly simple, although always a bit more sophisticated than that of real shepherds with real problems and real sheep.

Unrealistic? Of course. No real shepherd gets to spend even a single day like that, and certainly the world of simple country folk includes ferocities of nature, human falsehood and knavery, disease, bad weather, old age, moments that are not all green and gold. And probably no poet ever thought that shepherds really live that way, but it is an attractive fantasy, and poets who write pastoral simply choose one formulaic way to isolate a series of idealized moments. Fantasies can be personal and private, of course, but there is also a certain pleasure in shared public fantasies, and one central moment is that point in a love relationship when two people are contemplating the joys of ecstatic love. The vision here is self-consciously constructed by poets in order to present a certain tone, attitude, and wholeness; it is a world that is self-existent, self-contained, and self-referential.

It can be lovely to contemplate a world in which the birds sing only for our delight and other shepherds take care of the sheep, a world in which there is no work that does not turn into magic and in which the lambs bring themselves to us so that we can transform their wool instantly into a beautiful gown. It is also fun to "answer" such a vision. The next subsection of this chapter contains three poems that directly "answer" Marlowe's poem and thus offer a kind of critique of the pastoral vision. But in a sense no critique is necessary; the pastoral poet builds an awareness of artificiality into the whole idea of the poem. It is conceived in full consciousness that its fantasy avoids implication, and in filtering that implication carefully out of the poem, poets implicitly provide their own criticism of the fantasy world. Satire is, in a sense, the other side of the pastoral world—a city poet who fantasizes about being a shepherd usually knows all about dirt and grime and human failure and urban corruption—and satire and pastoral are often seen as complementary poetic kinds.

Several other poetic kinds are exemplified in this book; each has its own characteristics and conventions that have become established by tradition, repetition, and habit.

pastoral	"The Passionate Shepherd to His Love"	p. 847
elegy	"Elegy"	p. 937
lyric	"Western Wind"	p. 809
ballad	"Sir Patrick Spens"	p. 770
protest poem	"Hard Rock Returns . . ."	p. 625
aubade	"Morning Song"	p. 678
confessional poem	"History"	p. 835
meditation	"Tintern Abbey"	p. 980
dramatic monologue	"My Last Duchess"	p. 883
soliloquy	"Soliloquy of the Spanish Cloister"	p. 645

You will find definitions and brief descriptions of these poetic kinds in the glossary. Each of these established kinds is worthy of detailed discussion and study, and your teacher may want to examine how the conventions of several different kinds work.

IMITATING AND ANSWERING

Poems often respond directly—sometimes point by point or even line by line or word by word—to another poem. Often the point is teasing or comic, but often, too, there is a real issue behind the idea of such a facetious answer, a serious criticism perhaps of the poem's point or the tradition it represents, or sometimes an attempt to provide a different way of looking at the issue. Sometimes poems follow their models slavishly in order to emphasize their likeness; sometimes key words or details are substituted so that readers will easily notice the differences in tone or attitude.

Often these poems seem self-conscious—as if the poets who write them are aware of the tradition they share and are each trying to do something a little bit different. However "sincere" these poems may be, their sense of play is equally important. The first three poems playfully pick on Marlowe's "The Passionate Shepherd to His Love" (page 847). In effect, all of them provide "answers" to that poem. It is as if his "love" were telling the shepherd what is the matter with his argument, and the poets are answering Marlowe, too. These poets know full well what Marlowe was doing in the fantasy of his original poem, and they clearly have a lot of fun telling him how people in various circumstances might feel about his fantasy. There is in the end a lot of joy in their "realistic" deflation of his magic and not much hostility. The poems by Koch, Skirrow, and Cope poke gentle fun at other famous works, offering a summary or another version of what might have happened in each (see, respectively, Williams's "This Is Just to Say" [page 979], Keats's "Ode on a Grecian Urn" [page 960], and Shakespeare's "Not marble, nor the gilded monuments" [page 970]).

A **parody** is a poem that imitates another poem closely but changes details for a comic or critical effect. Strictly speaking, only two of the poems that follow (those by Koch and Cope) are parodies—that is, they pretend to write in the style of the original poem but comically exaggerate that style and change the content. The others make fun of an original in less direct phraseological ways, but they share a similar objective of answering an original, even though they use very different styles to alter totally the poetic intention of that original. Skirrow's "Ode on a Grecian Urn Summarized" teases Keats as well as the whole notion of poetic summaries; the effects of the summary are not very much like those of the Keats poem. Hecht's "The Dover Bitch," on the other hand, is as its subtitle suggests much more than just a different perspective on the situation presented in Arnold's "Dover Beach"; it uses the tradition to criticize art and life.

All these poems offer a revised version of what reality may be like. Poems like these may have a serious purpose, but their method is comic and usually light. And fun is not always easy to explain intellectually or to demonstrate.

SIR WALTER RALEGH

The Nymph's Reply to the Shepherd

If all the world and love were young,
And truth in every shepherd's tongue,
These pretty pleasures might me move
To live with thee and be thy love.

5   Time drives the flocks from field to fold,
When rivers rage, and rocks grow cold,
And Philomel[4] becometh dumb;
The rest complain of cares to come.

The flowers do fade, and wanton fields
10   To wayward winter reckoning yields:
A honey tongue, a heart of gall,
Is fancy's spring, but sorrow's fall.

Thy gowns, thy shoes, thy beds of roses,
Thy cap, thy kirtle, and thy posies
15   Soon break, soon wither, soon forgotten;
In folly ripe, in reason rotten.

Thy belt of straw and ivy buds,
Thy coral clasps and amber studs,
All these in me no means can move
20   To come to thee and be thy love.

But could youth last, and love still breed,
Had joys no date,[5] nor age no need,
Then these delights my mind might move
To live with thee and be thy love.

                                          1600

WILLIAM CARLOS WILLIAMS

Raleigh Was Right

We cannot go to the country
for the country will bring us no peace
What can the small violets tell us
that grow on furry stems in
5   the long grass among lance shaped leaves?

Though you praise us
and call to mind the poets
who sung of our loveliness
it was long ago!
10   long ago! when country people
would plow and sow with
flowering minds and pockets at ease—
if ever this were true.

Not now. Love itself a flower
15   with roots in a parched ground.
Empty pockets make empty heads.
Cure it if you can but
do not believe that we can live

4. The nightingale.   5. End.

today in the country
for the country will bring us no peace.   20

                                                                1941

_____

E. E. CUMMINGS

[(*ponder,darling,these busted statues*]

(ponder,darling,these busted statues
of yon motheaten forum be aware
notice what hath remained
—the stone cringes
clinging to the stone,how obsolete   5

lips utter their extant smile. . . .
remark

a few deleted of texture
or meaning monuments and dolls

resist Them Greediest Paws of careful   10
time all of which is extremely
unimportant)whereas Life

matters if or

when the your- and my-
idle vertical worthless   15
self unite in a peculiarly
momentary

partnership(to instigate
constructive
                   Horizontal   20
business. . . . even so,let us make haste
—consider well this ruined aqueduct

lady,
which used to lead something into somewhere)   1926

_____

PETER DE VRIES

To His Importunate Mistress

Andrew Marvell Updated

Had we but world enough, and time,
My coyness, lady, were a crime,

But at my back I always hear
Time's wingèd chariot, striking fear.
5   The hour is nigh when creditors
Will prove to be my predators.
As wages of our picaresque,
Bag lunches bolted at my desk
Must stand as fealty to you
10 For each expensive rendezvous.
Obeisance at your marble feet
Deserves the best-appointed suite,
And would have, lacked I not the pelf
To pleasure also thus myself;
15 But aptly sumptuous amorous scenes
Rule out the rake of modest means.

Since mistress presupposes wife,
It means a doubly costly life;
For fools by second passion fired
20 A second income is required,
The earning which consumes the hours
They'd hoped to spend in rented bowers.
To hostelries the worst of fates
That weekly raise their daily rates!
25 I gather, lady, from your scoffing
A bloke more solvent in the offing.
So revels thus to rivals go
For want of monetary flow.
How vexing that inconstant cash
30 The constant suitor must abash,
Who with excuses vainly pled
Must rue the undishevelled bed,
And that for paltry reasons given
His conscience may remain unriven.   p. 1986

ALLEN GINSBERG

A Further Proposal

Come live with me and be my love,
And we will some old pleasures prove.
Men like me have paid in verse
This costly courtesy, or curse;

5   But I would bargain with my art
(As to the mind, now to the heart),
My symbols, images, and signs
Please me more outside these lines.

For your share and recompense,
You will be taught another sense: 10
The wisdom of the subtle worm
Will turn most perfect in your form.

Not that your soul need tutored be
By intellectual decree,
But graces that the mind can share   15
Will make you, as more wise, more fair,

Till all the world's devoted thought
Find all in you it ever sought,
And even I, of skeptic mind,
A Resurrection of a kind.   20

This compliment, in my own way,
For what I would receive, I pay;
Thus all the wise have writ thereof,
And all the fair have been their love.

1947

KENNETH KOCH

Variations on a Theme by William Carlos Williams

1

I chopped down the house that you had been saving to live in next
    summer.
I am sorry, but it was morning, and I had nothing to do
and its wooden beams were so inviting.

2

We laughed at the hollyhocks together
and then I sprayed them with lye.
Forgive me. I simply do not know what I am doing.   5

3

I gave away the money that you had been saving to live on for the
    next ten years.
The man who asked for it was shabby
and the firm March wind on the porch was so juicy and cold.

4

10   Last evening we went dancing and I broke your leg.
       Forgive me. I was clumsy, and
       I wanted you here in the wards, where I am the doctor!   1962

DESMOND SKIRROW

Ode on a Grecian Urn Summarized

       Gods chase
       Round vase.
       What say?
       What play?
5   Don't know.
       Nice, though.   p. 1960

WENDY COPE

[Not only marble, but the plastic toys]

       Not only marble, but the plastic toys
       From cornflake packets will outlive this rhyme:
       I can't immortalize you, love—our joys
       Will lie unnoticed in the vault of time.
5   When Mrs Thatcher has been cast in bronze
       And her administration is a page
       In some O-level text-book,[6] when the dons
       Have analysed the story of our age,
       When travel firms sell tours of outer space
10   And aeroplanes take off without a sound
       And Tulse Hill has become a trendy place
       And Upper Norwood's on the underground[7]
       Your beauty and my name will be forgotten—
       My love is true, but all my verse is rotten.   1986

---

6. A text designed to prepare secondary-school students for the first hurdle in entrance exams for British universities. *Dons:* academics.   7. London subway.

CULTURAL BELIEF AND TRADITION

The poems in this group draw on a tradition that is larger than just "literary." Mythologies involve whole systems of belief, usually cultural in scope, and the familiar literary formulations of these mythologies are just the surface articulations of a larger view of why the world works the way it does.

Every culture develops stories to explain itself. These stories, about who we are and why we are the way we are, constitute what are often called **myths.** Calling something a myth does not mean that it is false. In fact, it means nearly the opposite, for cultures that subscribe to various myths, or that have ever subscribed to particular myths about culture or history, become infused with and defined by those views. Myth, in the sense in which it is used here, involves explanations of life that are more or less universally believed within a particular culture; it is a frame of reference that people within the culture understand and share. A sharing of this frame of reference does not mean that all people within a culture are carbon copies of each other or that popular stereotypes represent reality accurately, nor does it mean that every individual in the culture *knows* the perceived history and can articulate its events, ideas, and values. But it does mean that a shared history and a shared set of symbols lie behind any particular culture and that the culture is to some extent aware of its distinctiveness from other cultures.

A **culture** may be of many sizes and shapes. Often we think of a nation as a culture (and so speak of American culture, American history, the myth of America, the American dream, the American frame of reference), and it is equally useful to make smaller and larger divisions—as long as there is some commonality of history and some cohesiveness of purpose within the group. One can speak of southern culture, for example, or of urban culture, or of the drug culture, or of the various popular music cultures, or of a culture associated with a particular political belief, economic class, or social group. Most of us belong, willingly or not, to a number of such cultures at one time, and to some extent our identity and destiny are linked with the distinctive features of those cultures and with the ways each culture perceives its identity, values, and history. Some of these cultures we choose to join; some are thrust upon us by birth and circumstances. It is these larger and more persistent forms of culture—not those chosen by an individual—that are illustrated in this chapter.

Poets, aware of their heritage, often like to probe its history and beliefs and plumb its depths, just as they like to articulate and play variations on the poetic tradition they feel a part of. For poetry written in the English language over the last four hundred years or so, both the Judeo-Christian frame of reference and the classical frame of reference (drawing on the civilizations of ancient Greece and Rome) have been quite important. Western culture, a broad culture that includes many nations and many religious and social groups, is largely defined within these two frames of reference—or it has been until quite recently. As religious belief in the West has eroded over the past two or three centuries, and as classical civilization has been less emphasized and less studied, poets have felt increasingly less comfortable in assuming that their audiences share a knowledge of their systems, but they have often continued to use them to isolate and articulate human traits that have cultural continuity and importance. More recently, poets have drawn on other cultural myths—Native American, African, and Asian, for example—to expand our sense of common heritage and give new meaning to the "American" and

"Western" experience. The poems that follow draw on details from different myths and do so in a variety of ways and tones.

JOHN HOLLANDER

Adam's Task

And Adam gave names to all cattle, and to the fowl of the air, and to every beast of the field . . .

—*Gen. 2:20*

Thou, paw-paw-paw; thou, glurd; thou, spotted
　　Glurd; thou, whitestap, lurching through
The high-grown brush; thou, pliant-footed,
　　Implex; thou, awagabu.

5　Every burrower, each flier
　　Came for the name he had to give:
Gay, first work, ever to be prior,
　　Not yet sunk to primitive.

Thou, verdle; thou, McFleery's pomma;
10　　Thou; thou; thou—three types of grawl;
Thou, flisket; thou, kabasch; thou, comma-
　　Eared mashawk; thou, all; thou, all.

Were, in a fire of becoming,
　　Laboring to be burned away,
15　Then work, half-measuring, half-humming,
　　Would be as serious as play.

Thou, pambler; thou, rivarn; thou, greater
　　Wherret, and thou, lesser one;
Thou, sproal; thou, zant; thou, lily-eater.
20　　Naming's over. Day is done.

1971

SUSAN DONNELLY

Eve Names the Animals

To me, *lion* was sun on a wing
over the garden. *Dove,*
a burrowing, blind creature.

I swear that man
5　never knew animals. Words
he lined up according to size,

while elephants slipped flat-eyed
through water

and trout
hurtled from the underbrush, tusked   10
and ready for battle.

The name he gave me stuck
me to him. He did it to comfort me,
for not being first.

Mornings, while he slept,   15
I got away. Pickerel
hopped on the branches above me.
Only spider accompanied me,
nosing everywhere,
running up to lick my hand.   20

Poor finch. I suppose I was
woe to him—
the way he'd come looking for me,
not wanting either of us
to be ever alone   25

But to myself I was
palomino
          raven
                 fox . . .

I strung words   30
by their stems and wore them
as garlands on my long walks.

The next day
I'd find them withered.

I liked change.   35

1985

ALFRED, LORD TENNYSON

Ulysses[8]

It little profits that an idle king,
By this still hearth, among these barren crags,

---

8. After the end of the Trojan War, Ulysses (or Odysseus), king of Ithaca and one of the Greek heroes of the war, returned to his island home (line 34). Homer's account of the situation is in *The Odyssey* XI, but Dante's account of Ulysses in *The Inferno* XXVI is the more immediate background of the poem.

Matched with an agéd wife,[9] I mete and dole
Unequal laws unto a savage race,
5   That hoard, and sleep, and feed, and know not me.

    I cannot rest from travel; I will drink
Life to the lees.[1] All times I have enjoyed
Greatly, have suffered greatly, both with those
That loved me, and alone; on shore, and when
10   Through scudding drifts the rainy Hyades[2]
Vexed the dim sea. I am become a name;
For always roaming with a hungry heart
Much have I seen and known—cities of men
And manners, climates, councils, governments,
15   Myself not least, but honored of them all—
And drunk delight of battle with my peers,
Far on the ringing plains of windy Troy.
I am a part of all that I have met;
Yet all experience is an arch wherethrough
20   Gleams that untraveled world, whose margin fades
For ever and for ever when I move.
How dull it is to pause, to make an end,
To rust unburnished, not to shine in use!
As though to breathe were life. Life piled on life
25   Were all too little, and of one to me
Little remains; but every hour is saved
From that eternal silence, something more,
A bringer of new things; and vile it were
For some three suns to store and hoard myself,
30   And this gray spirit yearning in desire
To follow knowledge like a sinking star,
Beyond the utmost bound of human thought.

    This is my son, mine own Telemachus,
To whom I leave the scepter and the isle—
35   Well-loved of me, discerning to fulfill
This labor by slow prudence to make mild
A rugged people, and through soft degrees
Subdue them to the useful and the good.
Most blameless is he, centered in the sphere
40   Of common duties, decent not to fail
In offices of tenderness, and pay
Meet adoration to my household gods,
When I am gone. He works his work, I mine.

    There lies the port; the vessel puffs her sail:
45   There gloom the dark, broad seas. My mariners,
Souls that have toiled, and wrought, and thought with me—
That ever with a frolic welcome took

---

9. Penelope.   1. All the way down to the bottom of the cup.   2. A group of stars that were supposed
to predict rain when they rose at the same time as the sun.

The thunder and the sunshine, and opposed
Free hearts, free foreheads—you and I are old;
Old age hath yet his honor and his toil.   50
Death closes all; but something ere the end,
Some work of noble note, may yet be done,
Not unbecoming men that strove with Gods.
The lights begin to twinkle from the rocks;
The long day wanes; the slow moon climbs; the deep   55
Moans round with many voices. Come, my friends.
'Tis not too late to seek a newer world.
Push off, and sitting well in order smite
The sounding furrows; for my purpose holds
To sail beyond the sunset, and the baths   60
Of all the western stars, until I die.
It may be that the gulfs will wash us down;[3]
It may be we shall touch the Happy Isles,[4]
And see the great Achilles, whom we knew.
Though much is taken, much abides; and though   65
We are not now that strength which in old days
Moved earth and heaven, that which we are, we are:
One equal temper of heroic hearts,
Made weak by time and fate, but strong in will
To strive, to seek, to find, and not to yield.   70

1833

MIRIAM WADDINGTON

Ulysses Embroidered

You've come
at last from
all your journeying
to the old blind woman
in the tower,   5
Ulysses.

After all adventurings
through seas and
mountains through
giant battles,   10
storms and death,
from pinnacles
to valleys;

3. Beyond the Gulf of Gibraltar was supposed to be a chasm that led to Hades.   4. Elysium, the Islands
of the Blessed, where heroes like Achilles (line 64) abide after death.

Past sires
15 naked on rocks
between Charybdis
and Scylla, from
dragons' teeth,
from sleep in
20 stables choking
on red flowers
walking through weeds
and through shipwreck.

And now you are
25 climbing the stairs,
taking shape,
a figure in shining
thread rising from
a golden shield:
30 a medallion
emblazoned in
tapestry you grew
from the blind hands
of Penelope.

35 Her tapestry
saw everything,
her stitches
embroidered the
painful colors
40 of her breath the
long sighing touch
of her hands.

She made many
journeys.   1992

LANGSTON HUGHES

The Negro Speaks of Rivers

I've known rivers:
I've known rivers ancient as the world and older than the flow of
 human blood in human veins.

My soul has grown deep like the rivers.

I bathed in the Euphrates when dawns were young.
5 I built my hut near the Congo and it lulled me to sleep.
I looked upon the Nile and raised the pyramids above it.

I heard the singing of the Mississippi when Abe Lincoln went down to
New Orleans, and I've seen its muddy bosom turn all golden in the
sunset.

I've known rivers:
Ancient, dusky rivers.

My soul has grown deep like the rivers.   10

1926

MAYA ANGELOU

Africa

Thus she had lain
sugar cane sweet
deserts her hair
golden her feet
mountains her breasts   5
two Niles her tears
Thus she has lain
Black through the years.

Over the white seas
rime white and cold   10
brigands ungentled
icicle bold
took her young daughters
sold her strong sons
churched her with Jesus   15
bled her with guns.
Thus she has lain.

Now she is rising
remember her pain
remember the losses   20
her screams loud and vain
remember her riches
her history slain
now she is striding
although she had lain.   25

1975

JUDITH ORTIZ COFER

How to Get a Baby

To receive the waiwaia *(spirit children) in the water seems to be the most usual way of becoming pregnant. . . . They come along on large tree trunks, and they may be attached to seascum and dead leaves floating on the surface.*

    —BRONISLAW MALINOWSKI, *Baloma: The Spirits of the Dead in the Trobriand Islands*

Go to the sea
the morning after a rainstorm,
preferably
fresh from your man's arms—
5   the *waiwaia* are drawn
to love smell.
They are tiny luminous fish
and blind. You must call
the soul of your child
10   in the name of your ancestors:
Come to me, little fish, come
to Tamala, Tudava, come to me.
Sit in shallow water
up to your waist until the tide
15   pulls away from you
like an exhausted lover.
You will by then
be carrying new life.
Make love that night,
20   and every night,
to let the little one
who chooses you know
she is one with your joy.   1993

ALBERTO ALVARO RÍOS

Advice to a First Cousin

The way the world works is like this:
for the bite of scorpions, she says,
my grandmother to my first cousin,
because I might die and someone must know,
5   go to the animal jar
the one with the soup of green herbs
mixed with the scorpions I have been putting in

still alive. Take one out
put it on the bite. It has had time to think
there with the others—put the lid back tight—   10
and knows that a biting is not the way to win
a finger or a young girl's foot.
It will take back into itself the hurting
the redness and the itching and its marks.

But the world works like this, too: 15
look out for the next scorpion you see,
she says, and makes a big face to scare me
thereby instructing my cousin, look out!
for one of the scorpion's many
illegitimate and unhappy sons.   20
It will be smarter, more of the devil.
It will have lived longer than these dead ones.
It will know from them something more
about the world, in the way mothers know
when something happens to a child, or how   25
I knew from your sadness you had been bitten.
It will learn something stronger than biting.
Look out most for that scorpion, she says,
making a big face to scare me again and it works
I go—crying—she lets me go—they laugh,   30
the way you must look out for men
who have not yet bruised you.   1985

LOUISE ERDRICH

Jacklight

*The same Chippewa word is used both for flirting and hunting game,
while another Chippewa word connotes both using force in intercourse
and also killing a bear with one's bare hands.*

—DUNNING 1959

We have come to the edge of the woods,
out of brown grass where we slept, unseen,
out of knotted twigs, out of leaves creaked shut,
out of hiding.

At first the light wavered, glancing over us.   5
Then it clenched to a fist of light that pointed,
searched out, divided us.
Each took the beams like direct blows the heart answers.
Each of us moved forward alone.

We have come to the edge of the woods,   10
drawn out of ourselves by this night sun,

this battery of polarized acids,
that outshines the moon.

We smell them behind it
but they are faceless, invisible,
We smell the raw steel of their gun barrels,
mink oil on leather, their tongues of sour barley.
We smell their mother buried chin-deep in wet dirt.

We smell their fathers with scoured knuckles,
teeth cracked from hot marrow.
We smell their sisters of crushed dogwood, bruised apples,
of fractured cups and concussions of burnt hooks.

We smell their breath steaming lightly behind the jacklight.
We smell the itch underneath the caked guts on their clothes.
We smell their minds like silver hammers
cocked back, held in readiness
for the first of us to step into the open.

We have come to the edge of the woods,
out of brown grass where we slept, unseen,
out of leaves creaked shut, out of our hiding.
We have come here too long.

It is their turn now,
their turn to follow us. Listen,
they put down their equipment.
It is useless in the tall brush.
And now they take the first steps, not knowing
how deep the woods are and lightless.
How deep the woods are.   1984

QUESTIONS

1. Read the Cummings poem "(ponder,darling,these busted statues" closely in relation to Marvell's "To His Coy Mistress." In what specific ways does it echo Marvell's poem? Which images are specifically derived from Marvell? In what specific ways does the Cummings poem undercut the argument of the Marvell poem? In what ways does it undercut its own argument? to what purpose? In what ways does Ginsberg's "A Further Proposal" differ from the other poems written in imitation of Marvell?

2. Indicate the specific ways in which Ralegh's poem "replies" to Marlowe's. In what points does Williams agree with Ralegh? What, exactly, is "unfair" about Skirrow's summary of Keats? How do you think Keats would justify himself against Skirrow's summary?

3. What attitudes toward Adam and Eve are displayed in the Donnelly and Hollander poems? Which poems develop the strongest negative attitudes toward their "heroes" or "heroines"? How do Waddington's and Tennyson's versions differ? What values are associated with Africa in the Hughes and Angelou poems?

WRITING SUGGESTIONS

1. In what specific ways is Marvell's "To His Coy Mistress" anchored to its historical or cultural context? Can you tell that it is written by a seventeenth-century poet? How? What

historical or cultural "allusions" anchor the poem to its specific moment in time? to its philosophical or thematic contexts? In what specific ways does the De Vries poem establish itself as contemporary? Write a short (500–700 word) essay in which you show how De Vries undercuts the assumptions of Marvell. (Alternative: write a short essay in which you show how Cummings undercuts the assumptions of Marvell.)

2. Using a poetry index (available in the reference section of your college library), find half a dozen poems that use the term "elegy" in their titles, and compare their tones and strategies. Try to decide what features and expectations seem to be central to the poetic kind. Then look back at Jonson's "On My First Son" (page 603), often said to be a typical elegy, and write a brief (two-page) analysis of the poem in which you show how it uses and transforms the expectations associated with the elegy as a poetic kind.

3. In an essay of about three pages, show how the primary effects of Tennyson's "Ulysses" relate to its use of cultural myths. (Alternative: apply this same question to Erdrich's "Jacklight.")

23

HISTORICAL AND CULTURAL CONTEXTS

The more you know, the better a reader of poetry you are likely to be. And that goes for general knowledge as well as knowledge of other poetry and literary traditions. Poems often draw upon a larger fund of human knowledge about all sorts of things, asking us to bring to bear on a poem facts and values we have taken on from earlier reading or from our experiences in the world more generally. The first nine chapters on poetry suggest how practice and the learning of specific skills make interpretation easier and better: the more you read and the more close analysis you do, the better an interpreter you are likely to become. But in this "contextual" section we are concerned with information you need to read richly and fully: information about authors, about events that influenced them or became the inspiration or basis for their writing, and about literary traditions that provide a context for their work. Poets always write in a specific time, under particular circumstances, and with some awareness of the world around them, whether or not they specifically refer to contemporary matters in a particular poem. In this chapter, our concern is with the specifically historical and cultural—events, movements, ideas that directly influence poets or that poets in some way represent in the poems they write.

Very little that you know will ultimately go to waste in your reading of poetry. The best potential reader of poetry is someone who has already developed reading skills to perfection, read everything, thought deeply about all kinds of things, and who is wise beyond belief—wise enough to know exactly how to apply what she or he knows accurately to a given text. But that is the ideal reader we all strive to be, not the one any of us actually is. Although no poet really expects any reader to be all those things, good readers try. Poems can be just as demanding of readers about historical information as about the intricacies of language and form. Poems not only *refer to* people, places, and events—things that exist in time—but they also *are* themselves products of given moments, participating in both the potentialities and the limitations of the times in which they were created.

Things that happen every day frequently find their way into poetry in an easy and yet often forceful manner. Making love in a junkyard, as in Dickey's "Cherrylog Road," is one kind of example; a reader doesn't need to know what particular junkyard was involved—or imaginatively involved—in order to understand the poem, but a reader does need to know what an auto junkyard was like in the mid-twentieth century, with more or less whole car bodies being scattered in various states of disarray over a large plot of ground. But what if, over the next generation or two, junkyards completely disappear as other ways are found to dispose of old cars? Already a lot of old cars are crushed into small metal blocks, especially in large cities. But what if the metal is all melted down, or the junk is orbited into space? If that should happen, readers then will have never seen a junkyard, and they will need a footnote to explain what such junkyards were like. The history of junkyards will not be lost—there will be pictures, films, records, and someone will write definitive books about the forms and functions of junkyards, probably even including the fact that lovers occasionally visited them—but the public memory of junkyards will soon disappear. No social customs, nothing that is made, no institutions or sites last forever.

Readers may still be able to experience "Cherrylog Road" when junkyards disappear, but they will need some help, and they may think its particulars a little quaint, much as we regard literature that involves a horse and buggy—or even making love in the back seat of a parked car—as quaint now. Institutions change, habits change, times change, places and settings change—all kinds of particulars change, even when people's wants, needs, and foibles pretty much go on in the same way. Footnotes never provide a precise or adequate substitute for the ease and pleasure that come from already knowing, but they can help us understand and pave the way for feeling and experience. A kind of imaginative historical sympathy can be simulated, and in fact created, for poems from earlier times that refer to specific contemporary details (and that have now become to us, in our own time, *historical* details) often describe human nature and human experiences very much as we still know and experience them. Today's poem may need tomorrow's footnote, but the poem need not be tomorrow's puzzle or only a curiosity or fossil.

The following poem, not many years old, already requires some explanation. Many readers will not know the factual details of its occasion, and (even more important) most readers will not recall the powerful reaction throughout the United States to the event.

JAMES A. EMANUEL

Emmett Till[1]

I hear a whistling
Through the water.
Little Emmett
Won't be still.
He keeps floating   5
Round the darkness,
Edging through
The silent chill.
Tell me, please,
That bedtime story   10
Of the fairy
River Boy
Who swims forever,

1. In 1955, Till, a fourteen-year-old from Chicago, was lynched in Mississippi for allegedly making sexual advances toward a white woman.

Deep in treasures,
15   Necklaced in
A coral toy.   1968

How do you know what you need to know? The easiest clue is your own puzzlement. When it seems that something is happening in a poem that you don't recognize—and yet the poem makes no apparent effort to clarify it—you have a clue that readers at the time the poem was written must have recognized something that is not now such common knowledge. Once you know you don't know, it only takes a little work to find out: most college libraries contain far more information than you will ever need, and the trick is to search efficiently. Your ability to find the information will depend upon how well you know the written reference materials and computer searches available to you. Practice helps. Knowledge accumulates. Most poems printed in textbooks like this one will be annotated for you with basic facts, but often you may need additional information to interpret the poem's full meaning and resonance. An editor, trying to satisfy the needs of a variety of readers, may not always decide to write the note you in particular may need, so there could be digging to do in the library for any poem you read, certainly for those you come upon in magazines and books of poetry without notes. Few poets like to annotate their own work (they'd rather let you struggle a little to appreciate them), and besides, many things that now need notes didn't when they were written.

The two poems that follow both require from the reader some specific "referential" information, but they differ considerably in their emphasis on the particularities of time and place. The first poem, Hardy's "Channel Firing," reflects and refers to a moment just before the outbreak of World War I when British naval forces were preparing for combat by taking gunnery practice in the English Channel. The second, Gilbert's "Sonnet: The Ladies' Home Journal," reflects a longer cultural moment in which attitudes and assumptions, rather than some specific event, are crucial to understanding the poem.

THOMAS HARDY

Channel Firing

That night your great guns, unawares,
Shook all our coffins as we lay,
And broke the chancel window squares,[2]
We thought it was the Judgment-day

5   And sat upright. While drearisome
Arose the howl of wakened hounds:
The mouse let fall the altar-crumb,[3]
The worms drew back into the mounds,

The glebe cow[4] drooled. Till God called, "No;
10   It's gunnery practice out at sea

2. The windows near the altar in a church.   3. Breadcrumbs from the sacrament of Communion.
4. Parish cow pastured on the meadow next to the churchyard.

Just as before you went below;
The world is as it used to be:

"All nations striving strong to make
Red war yet redder. Mad as hatters
They do no more for Christés sake   15
Than you who are helpless in such matters.

"That this is not the judgment-hour
For some of them's a blessed thing,
For if it were they'd have to scour
Hell's floor for so much threatening . . .   20

"Ha, ha. It will be warmer when
I blow the trumpet (if indeed
I ever do; for you are men,
And rest eternal sorely need)."

So down we lay again. "I wonder,   25
Will the world ever saner be,"
Said one, "than when He sent us under
In our indifferent century!"

And many a skeleton shook his head.
"Instead of preaching forty year,"   30
My neighbor Parson Thirdly said,
"I wish I had stuck to pipes and beer."

Again the guns disturbed the hour,
Roaring their readiness to avenge.
As far inland as Stourton Tower,   35
And Camelot, and starlit Stonehenge.[5]

April 1914

SANDRA GILBERT

Sonnet: The Ladies' Home Journal

The brilliant stills of food, the cozy
glossy, bygone life—mashed potatoes
posing as whipped cream, a neat mom
conjuring shapes from chaos, trimming the flame—
how we ached for all that,   5
that dance of love in the living room,

5. Stourton Tower, built in the eighteenth century to commemorate King Alfred's ninth-century victory over the Danes, in Stourhead Park, Wiltshire. Camelot is the legendary site of King Arthur's court, said to have been in Cornwall or Somerset. Stonehenge, a circular formation of upright stones dating from about 1800 B.C., is on Salisbury Plain, Wiltshire; it is thought to have been a ceremonial site for political and religious occasions or an early scientific experiment in astronomy.

those paneled walls, that kitchen golden
as the inside of a seed: how we leaned
on those shiny columns of advice,
10   stroking the *thank yous*, the firm thighs, the wise
closets full of soap.

But even then
we knew it was the lies we loved, the lies
we wore like Dior coats,[6] the clean-cut airtight
lies that laid out our lives in black and white.   1984

"Channel Firing" is not ultimately *about* World War I, for it presumes that human behavior stays the same from age to age, but it begins from a particular historical vantage point. It would be difficult to make much sense of the poem if the reader were not to recognize the importance of that specific reference, and the poem's situation (with a waking corpse as the main speaker) is difficult enough to sort out even with the clue of the careful dating at the end (the date here is actually a part of the poem, recorded on the manuscript by the author and always printed as part of the text). The firing of the guns has awakened the dead who are buried near the channel, and in their puzzlement they assume it is Judgment Day, time for them to arise, until God enters and tells them what is happening. Much of the poem's effect depends on character portrayal—a God who laughs and sounds cynical, a parson who regrets his selfless life and wishes he had indulged himself more—as well as the sense that nothing ever changes. But particularity of time and place are crucial to this sense of changelessness; even so important a contemporary moment as the beginning of a world war—a moment viewed by most people at the time as unique and world-changing—fades into a timeless parade of moments that stretches over centuries of history. The geographical particulars cited at the end— as the sound of the guns moves inland to be heard in place after place—make the same point. Great moments in history are all encompassed in the sound of the guns and its message about human behavior. Times, places, and events, however important they seem, all become part of some larger pattern that denies individuality or uniqueness.

The particulars in "Sonnet: The Ladies' Home Journal" work differently—to remind us not of a specific time that readers need to identify but to characterize a way of seeing and thinking. The referentiality here is more cultural than historical; it is based more on ideas and attitudes characteristic of a particular period than on a specific moment or location. The pictures in the magazine stand for a whole way of thinking about women that was characteristic of the time—the mid-twentieth century—when the *Ladies' Home Journal* flourished as a popular magazine. The poem implicitly contrasts the "lies" (line 12) of the magazine with the truth of the present—that women's lives and values are not to be seen as some fantasized sense of beautiful food, motherhood, social rituals, and commercial products. Two vastly different cultural attitudes—that of the poem's present, with its skeptical view of traditional women's roles, and that of a past that equated the superficiality of glossy photographs with gender identity—are at the heart of the poem. It is about cultural attitudes and their effects on actual human beings. Readers need to know what the *Ladies' Home Journal* was like in order to understand the poem; we do

6. Designer coats by Christian Dior.

not need to know the date or contents of a specific issue, only that this popular magazine reflected the attitudes and values of a whole age and culture. The referentiality of this poem involves information about ideas and consciousness more than time and event.

To get at appropriate factual, cultural, and historical information, we need to learn to ask three kinds of questions. One kind is obvious: it is the "Do I understand the reference to . . . ?" kind. When events, places, or people unfamiliar to you come up, you will need to find out what or who they are. The second kind of question is more difficult: How do you know, in a poem that does *not* refer specifically to events, people, or ideas that you do not recognize, that you *need* to know more? When there are no specific references to look up, no people or events to identify, how do you know that there is a specific context? To get at this sort of question, you have to trust two people: the poet and yourself. Usually, good poets will not want to puzzle you more than necessary, so that you can safely assume that something that is not self-explanatory will merit close attention and possibly some digging in the library. (Poets do make mistakes and miscalculations about their readers, but it is a good working procedure at the start to assume they know what they are doing and why they are doing it.) References that are not in themselves clear provide a strong clue that you need more information. And that is why you need to trust yourself: when something doesn't click, when the information given you does not seem enough, you need to trust your puzzlement and try to find the missing facts that will allow the poem to make sense. But how? Often the date of the poem is a help; sometimes the title gives a clue or a point of departure; sometimes you can uncover, by reading about the author, some of the things he or she was interested in or concerned about. There is no single all-purpose way to discover what to look for, but that kind of research—looking for clues, adding up the evidence—can be interesting in itself and very rewarding when it is successful.

> *When I came to poetry it was through the struggles of tribal peoples to assert our human rights, to secure our sovereign rights as nations in the early seventies. It was the struggle begun by my grandmothers and grandfathers when they fought the move from our homelands in the Southeast to Indian Territory. This, too, was my personal struggle as a poet. It was in this wave of cultural renaissance for Indian peoples in this country that I heard the poetry that would change me, a poetry that could have been written those mornings of creation from childhood. This poetry named me as it jolted the country into sharp consciousness.*
>
> —JOY HARJO

The third question is why? For every factual reference, one needs to ask why. Why does the poem refer to this particular person instead of some other? What function does the reference serve?

Beyond the level of simply understanding that a particular poem is about an event or place or movement is the matter of developing a full sense of historical context, a sense of the larger significance and resonance of the historical occurrence or attitude referred to. Often a poem expects you to bring with you some sense of that significance; just as often it works to continue your education, telling you more, wanting you to understand and appreciate on the level of feeling some further things about this occurrence.

What we need to bring to our reading varies from poem to poem. For example, Owen's "Dulce et Decorum Est" (page 879) needs our knowledge that poison gas was used in World War I; the green tint through which the speaker sees the world in lines 13–14 comes from green glass in the goggles of the gas mask he has just put on. But some broader matters are important as well. Harder to specify but probably even more important is the climate of opinion that surrounded the war. To idealists, it was "the war to end all wars," and many participants—as well as politicians and propagandists—considered it a sacred mission, regarding the threat of Germany's expansionist policy as dangerous to Western civilization. No doubt you will read the poem more intelligently—and with more feeling—the more you know about World War I, and the same is true of poems about any historical occurrence or that refer to things that happen or situations that exist in a temporal or spatial context. But it is also true that your sense of these events will grow as a result of reading sensitively and thoughtfully the poems themselves. Facts are no substitute for skills. Once you have read individually the poems in this section, try taking a breather; and then at one sitting read them all again. Reading poetry can be a form of gaining knowledge as well as an aesthetic experience. One doesn't go to poetry to seek information as such, but poems often give us more than we came for. The ways to wisdom are paved with facts, and although poetry is not primarily a data-conscious art, it often requires us to be aware, sometimes in detail, of its referents in the real world.

TIMES, PLACES, AND EVENTS

MILLER WILLIAMS

Thinking about Bill, Dead of AIDS

We did not know the first thing about
how blood surrenders to even the smallest threat
when old allergies turn inside out,

the body rescinding all its normal orders
to all defenders of flesh, betraying the head,   5
pulling its guards back from all its borders.

Thinking of friends afraid to shake your hand,
we think of your hand shaking, your mouth set,
your eyes drained of any reprimand.

Loving, we kissed you, partly to persuade   10
both you and us, seeing what eyes had said,
that we were loving and were not afraid.

If we had had more, we would have given more.
As it was we stood next to your bed,
stopping, though, to set our smiles at the door.   15

Not because we were less sure at the last.
Only because, not knowing anything yet,
we didn't know what look would hurt you least.   1989

MARY JO SALTER

Welcome to Hiroshima

is what you first see, stepping off the train:
a billboard brought to you in living English
by Toshiba Electric. While a channel
silent in the TV of the brain

projects those flickering re-runs of a cloud   5
that brims its risen columnful like beer
and, spilling over, hangs its foamy head,
you feel a thirst for history: what year

it started to be safe to breathe the air,
10 and when to drink the blood and scum afloat
on the Ohta River. But no, the water's clear,
they pour it for your morning cup of tea

in one of the countless sunny coffee shops
whose plastic dioramas advertise
15 mutations of cuisine behind the glass:
a pancake sandwich; a pizza someone tops

with a maraschino cherry. Passing by
the Peace Park's floral hypocenter (where
how bravely, or with what mistaken cheer,
20 humanity erased its own erasure),

you enter the memorial museum
and through more glass are served, as on a dish
of blistered grass, three mannequins. Like gloves
a mother clips to coatsleeves, strings of flesh

25 hang from their fingertips; or as if tied
to recall a duty for us, *Reverence*
the dead whose mourners too shall soon be dead,
but all commemoration's swallowed up

in questions of bad taste, how re-created
30 horror mocks the grim original,
and thinking at last *They should have left it all*
you stop. This is the wristwatch of a child.

Jammed on the moment's impact, resolute
to communicate some message, although mute,
35 it gestures with its hands at eight-fifteen
and eight-fifteen and eight-fifteen again

while tables of statistics on the wall
update the news by calling on a roll
of tape, death gummed on death, and in the case
40 adjacent, an exhibit under glass

is glass itself: a shard the bomb slammed in
a woman's arm at eight-fifteen, but some
three decades on—as if to make it plain
hope's only as renewable as pain,

45 and as if all the unsung
debasements of the past may one day come
rising to the surface once again—
worked its filthy way out like a tongue.   1984

DWIGHT OKITA

Notes for a Poem
on Being Asian American

As a child, I was a fussy eater
and I would separate the yolk from the egg white
as I now try to sort out what is Asian
in me from what is American—
the east from the west, the dreamer from the dream.   5
But countries are not
like eggs—except in the fragileness
of their shells—and eggs resemble countries
only in that when you crack one open and look inside,
you know even less than when you started.   10

And so I crack open the egg,
and this is what I see:
two moments from my past that strike me
as being uniquely Asian American.

In the first, I'm walking down Michigan Avenue   15
one day—a man comes up to me out of the blue and says:
"I just wanted to tell you . . . I was on the plane that
bombed Hiroshima. And I just wanted you to know that
what we did was for the good of everyone." And it
seems as if he's asking for my forgiveness. It's 1983,   20
there's a sale on Marimekko sheets at the Crate &
Barrel, it's a beautiful summer day and I'm talking to
a man I've never seen before and will probably never
see again. His statement has no connection to me—
and has every connection in the world. But it's not   25
for me to forgive him. He must forgive himself.
"It must have been a very difficult decision to do what
you did," I say and I mention the sale on Marimekko
sheets across the street, comforters, and how the
pillowcases have the pattern of wheat printed on them,   30
and how some nights if you hold them before an open
window to the breeze, they might seem like flags—
like someone surrendering after a great while, or
celebrating, or simply cooling themselves in the summer
breeze as best they can.   35

In the second moment—I'm in a taxi and the Iranian
cabdriver looking into the rearview mirror notices my
Asian eyes, those almond shapes, reflected in the glass
and says, "Can you really tell the difference between
a Chinese and a Japanese?"   40

1992

LANGSTON HUGHES

Harlem (A Dream Deferred)

What happens to a dream deferred?

Does it dry up
like a raisin in the sun?
Or fester like a sore—
5   And then run?
Does it stink like rotten meat?
Or crust and sugar over—
like a syrupy sweet?

Maybe it just sags
10   like a heavy load.

Or does it explode?   1951

ROBERT HAYDEN

Frederick Douglass[7]

When it is finally ours, this freedom, this liberty, this beautiful
and terrible thing, needful to man as air,
usable as earth; when it belongs at last to all,
when it is truly instinct, brain matter, diastole, systole,
5   reflex action; when it is finally won; when it is more
than the gaudy mumbo jumbo of politicians:
this man, this Douglass, this former slave, this Negro
beaten to his knees, exiled, visioning a world
where none is lonely, none hunted, alien,
10   this man, superb in love and logic, this man
shall be remembered. Oh, not with statues' rhetoric,
not with legends and poems and wreaths of bronze alone,
but with the lives grown out of his life, the lives
fleshing his dream of the beautiful, needful thing.   1966

---

7. Frederick Douglass (1817–1895), escaped slave. Douglass was involved in the Underground Railroad and became the publisher of the famous abolitionist newspaper the *North Star,* in Rochester, New York.

MBUYISENI OSWALD MTSHALI

Boy on a Swing

Slowly he moves
to and fro, to and fro,
then faster and faster
he swishes up and down.

His blue shirt   5
billows in the breeze
like a tattered kite.

The world whirls by:
east becomes west,
north turns to south;   10
the four cardinal points
meet in his head.

   Mother!
Where did I come from?
When will I wear long trousers?   15
Why was my father jailed?   1982

THOMAS HARDY

The Convergence of the Twain

Lines on the Loss of the "Titanic"[8]

    I

In a solitude of the sea
Deep from human vanity,
And the Pride of Life that planned her, stilly couches she.

    II

Steel chambers, late the pyres
Of her salamandrine[9] fires,   5
Cold currents thrid,[1] and turn to rhythmic tidal lyres.

8. On the night of April 14, 1912, the *Titanic*, the largest ship afloat and on her maiden voyage to New York from Southampton, collided with an iceberg in the North Atlantic and sank in less than three hours; 1,500 of 2,206 passengers were lost.   9. Bright red; the salamander was supposed to be able to live in fire.   1. Thread.

III

Over the mirrors meant
To glass the opulent
The sea-worm crawls—grotesque, slimed, dumb, indifferent.

IV

Jewels in joy designed
To ravish the sensuous mind
Lie lightless, all their sparkles bleared and black and blind.

V

Dim moon-eyed fishes near
Gaze at the gilded gear
And query: "What does this vaingloriousness down here?" . . .

VI

Well: while was fashioning
This creature of cleaving wing,
The Immanent Will that stirs and urges everything

VII

Prepared a sinister mate
For her—so gaily great—
A Shape of Ice, for the time far and dissociate.

VIII

And as the smart ship grew
In stature, grace, and hue,
In shadowy silent distance grew the Iceberg too.

IX

Alien they seemed to be:
No mortal eye could see
The intimate welding of their later history,

X

Or sign that they were bent
By paths coincident
On being anon twin halves of one august event,

XI

Till the Spinner of the Years
Said "Now!" And each one hears,
And consummation comes, and jars two hemispheres.   1914

WILFRED OWEN

Dulce et Decorum Est[2]

Bent double, like old beggars under sacks,
Knock-kneed, coughing like hags, we cursed through sludge,
Till on the haunting flares we turned our backs
And towards our distant rest began to trudge.
Men marched asleep. Many had lost their boots   5
But limped on, blood-shod. All went lame; all blind;
Drunk with fatigue; deaf even to the hoots
Of disappointed shells that dropped behind.

Gas! Gas! Quick, boys!—An ecstasy of fumbling,
Fitting the clumsy helmets just in time;   10
But someone still was yelling out and stumbling
And floundering like a man in fire or lime.—
Dim, through the misty panes and thick green light
As under a green sea, I saw him drowning.

In all my dreams, before my helpless sight,   15
He plunges at me, guttering, choking, drowning.

If in some smothering dreams you too could pace
Behind the wagon that we flung him in,
And watch the white eyes writhing in his face,
His hanging face, like a devil's sick of sin;   20
If you could hear, at every jolt, the blood
Come gargling from the froth-corrupted lungs,
Obscene as cancer, bitter as the cud
Of vile, incurable sores on innocent tongues,—
My friend, you would not tell with such high zest   25
To children ardent for some desperate glory,
The old Lie: Dulce et decorum est
Pro patria mori.

1917

RICHARD EBERHART

The Fury of Aerial Bombardment

You would think the fury of aerial bombardment
Would rouse God to relent; the infinite spaces

2. Part of a phrase from Horace, quoted in full in the last lines: "It is sweet and proper to die for one's country."

Are still silent. He looks on shock-pried faces.
History, even, does not know what is meant.

5   You would feel that after so many centuries
God would give man to repent; yet he can kill
As Cain could, but with multitudinous will,
No farther advanced than in his ancient furies.

Was man made stupid to see his own stupidity?
10   Is God by definition indifferent, beyond us all?
Is the eternal truth man's fighting soul
Wherein the Beast ravens in its own avidity?

Of Van Wettering I speak, and Averill,
Names on a list, whose faces I do not recall
15   But they are gone to early death, who late in school
Distinguished the belt feed lever from the belt holding pawl.[3]   1947

DUDLEY RANDALL

Ballad of Birmingham

(On the bombing of a church in Birmingham, Alabama, 1963)

"Mother dear, may I go downtown
Instead of out to play,
And march the streets of Birmingham
In a Freedom March today?"

5   "No, baby, no, you may not go,
For the dogs are fierce and wild,
And clubs and hoses, guns and jails
Aren't good for a little child."

"But, mother, I won't be alone.
10   Other children will go with me,
And march the streets of Birmingham
To make our country free."

"No, baby, no, you may not go,
For I fear those guns will fire.
15   But you may go to church instead
And sing in the children's choir."

She has combed and brushed her night-dark hair,
And bathed rose petal sweet,
And drawn white gloves on her small brown hands,
20   And white shoes on her feet.

3. Machine-gun parts.

The mother smiled to know her child
Was in the sacred place,
But that smile was the last smile
To come upon her face.

For when she heard the explosion,   25
Her eyes grew wet and wild.
She raced through the streets of Birmingham
Calling for her child.

She clawed through bits of glass and brick,
Then lifted out a shoe.   30
"Oh, here's the shoe my baby wore,
But, baby, where are you?"   1969

AI

Riot Act, April 29, 1992

I'm going out and get something.
I don't know what.
I don't care.
Whatever's out there, I'm going to get it.
Look in those shop windows at boxes   5
and boxes of Reeboks and Nikes
to make me fly through the air
like Michael Jordan
like Magic.
While I'm up there, I see Spike Lee.   10
Looks like he's flying too
straight through the glass
that separates me
from the virtual reality
I watch everyday on TV.   15
I know the difference between
what it is and what it isn't.
Just because I can't touch it
doesn't mean it isn't real.
All I have to do is smash the screen,   20
reach in and take what I want.
Break out of prison.
South Central homey's newly risen
from the night of living dead,
but this time he lives,   25
he gets to give the zombies
a taste of their own medicine.
Open wide and let me in,
or else I'll set your world on fire,

30 but you pretend that you don't hear.
    You haven't heard the word is coming down
    like the hammer of the gun
    of this black son, locked out of the big house,
    while massa looks out the window and sees only smoke.
35 Massa doesn't see anything else,
    not because he can't,
    but because he won't.
    He'd rather hear me talking about mo' money,
    mo' honeys and gold chains
40 and see me carrying my favorite things
    from looted stores
    than admit that underneath my Raiders' cap,
    the aftermath is staring back
    unblinking through the camera's lens,
45 courtesy of CNN,
    my arms loaded with boxes of shoes
    that I will sell at the swap meet
    to make a few cents on the declining dollar.
    And if I destroy myself
50 and my neighborhood
    "ain't nobody's business, if I do,"
    but the police are knocking hard
    at my door
    and before I can open it,
55 they break it down
    and drag me in the yard.
    They take me in to be processed and charged,
    to await trial,
    while Americans forget
60 the day the wealth finally trickled down
    to the rest of us.

                                                    1993

CONSTRUCTING IDENTITY, EXPLORING GENDER

ROBERT BROWNING

My Last Duchess

Ferrara[4]

That's my last Duchess painted on the wall,
Looking as if she were alive. I call
That piece a wonder, now: Frà Pandolf's hands[5]
Worked busily a day, and there she stands.
Will't please you sit and look at her? I said   5
"Frà Pandolf" by design, for never read
Strangers like you that pictured countenance,
The depth and passion of its earnest glance,
But to myself they turned (since none puts by
The curtain I have drawn for you, but I)   10
And seemed as they would ask me, if they durst,
How such a glance came there; so, not the first
Are you to turn and ask thus. Sir, 'twas not
Her husband's presence only, called that spot
Of joy into the Duchess' cheek: perhaps   15
Frà Pandolf chanced to say "Her mantle laps
Over my lady's wrist too much," or "Paint
Must never hope to reproduce the faint
Half-flush that dies along her throat": such stuff
Was courtesy, she thought, and cause enough   20
For calling up that spot of joy. She had
A heart—how shall I say?—too soon made glad,
Too easily impressed; she liked whate'er
She looked on, and her looks went everywhere.
Sir, 'twas all one! My favor at her breast,   25
The dropping of the daylight in the West,
The bough of cherries some officious fool
Broke in the orchard for her, the white mule
She rode with round the terrace—all and each
Would draw from her alike the approving speech,   30
Or blush, at least. She thanked men,—good! but thanked
Somehow—I know not how—as if she ranked

---

4. Alfonso II, duke of Ferrara in Italy in the mid-sixteenth century, is the presumed speaker of the poem,
which is loosely based on historical events. The duke's first wife—whom he had married when she was
fourteen—died under suspicious circumstances at seventeen, and he then negotiated through an agent
(to whom the poem is spoken) for the hand of the niece of the count of Tyrol in Austria.   5. Frà
Pandolf is, like Claus (line 56), fictitious.

My gift of a nine-hundred-years-old name
With anybody's gift. Who'd stoop to blame
35 This sort of trifling? Even had you skill
In speech—which I have not—to make your will
Quite clear to such an one, and say, "Just this
Or that in you disgusts me; here you miss,
Or there exceed the mark"—and if she let
40 Herself be lessoned so, nor plainly set
Her wits to yours, forsooth, and made excuse,
—E'en then would be some stooping; and I choose
Never to stoop. Oh sir, she smiled, no doubt,
Whene'er I passed her; but who passed without
45 Much the same smile? This grew; I gave commands;
Then all smiles stopped together. There she stands
As if alive. Will't please you rise? We'll meet
The company below, then. I repeat,
The Count your master's known munificence
50 Is ample warrant that no just pretense
Of mine for dowry will be disallowed;
Though his fair daughter's self, as I avowed
At starting, is my object. Nay, we'll go
Together down, sir. Notice Neptune, though,
55 Taming a sea-horse, thought a rarity,
Which Claus of Innsbruck cast in bronze for me!   1842

RICHARD LOVELACE

Song: To Lucasta, Going to the Wars

Tell me not, sweet, I am unkind,
    That from the nunnery
Of thy chaste breast and quiet mind
    To war and arms I fly.

5 True: a new mistress now I chase,
    The first foe in the field;
And with a stronger faith embrace
    A sword, a horse, a shield.

Yet this inconstancy is such
10   As you too shall adore;
I could not love thee, dear, so much,
    Loved I not honor more.   1649

WILFRED OWEN

Disabled

He sat in a wheeled chair, waiting for dark,
And shivered in his ghastly suit of grey,
Legless, sewn short at elbow. Through the park
Voices of boys rang saddening like a hymn,
Voices of play and pleasure after day,   5
Till gathering sleep had mothered them from him.

About this time Town used to swing so gay
When glow-lamps budded in the light blue trees,
And girls glanced lovelier as the air grew dim,—
In the old times, before he threw away his knees.   10
Now he will never feel again how slim
Girls' waists are, or how warm their subtle hands;
All of them touch him like some queer disease.

There was an artist silly for his face,
For it was younger than his youth, last year.   15
Now, he is old; his back will never brace;
He's lost his color very far from here,
Poured it down shell-holes till the veins ran dry,
And half his lifetime lapsed in the hot race,
And leap of purple spurted from his thigh.   20

One time he liked a blood-smear down his leg,
After the matches,[6] carried shoulder-high
It was after football, when he'd drunk a peg,[7]
He thought he'd better join.—He wonders why.
Someone had said he'd look a god in kilts,   25
That's why; and may be, too, to please his Meg;
Aye, that was it, to please the giddy jilts
He asked to join. He didn't have to beg;
Smiling they wrote his lie; aged nineteen years.

Germans he scarcely thought of; all their guilt,   30
And Austria's, did not move him. And no fears
Of Fear came yet. He thought of jeweled hilts
For daggers in plaid socks; of smart salutes;
And care of arms; and leave; and pay arrears;
Esprit de corps; and hints for young recruits.   35
And soon, he was drafted out with drums and cheers.

Some cheered him home, but not as crowds cheer Goal.[8]
Only a solemn man who brought him fruits
Thanked him; and then inquired about his soul.
Now, he will spend a few sick years in Institutes,   40

---

6. Soccer games.   7. A drink, usually brandy and soda.   8. In soccer.

And do what things the rules consider wise,
And take whatever pity they may dole.
Tonight he noticed how the women's eyes
Passed from him to the strong men that were whole.
45   How cold and late it is! Why don't they come
And put him into bed? Why don't they come?   1917

PAULETTE JILES

Paper Matches

My aunts washed dishes while the uncles
squirted each other on the lawn with
    garden hoses. Why are we in here,
I said, and they are out there.
5   That's the way it is,
        said Aunt Hetty, the shrivelled-up one.
    I have the rages that small animals have,
being small, being animal.
    Written on me was a message,
10   "At Your Service" like a book of
paper matches. One by one we were
taken out and struck.
    We come bearing supper.
our heads on fire.   1973

MARGE PIERCY

What's That Smell in the Kitchen?

All over America women are burning dinners.
It's lambchops in Peoria; it's haddock
in Providence; it's steak in Chicago;
tofu delight in Big Sur; red
5   rice and beans in Dallas.
All over America women are burning
food they're supposed to bring with calico
smile on platters glittering like wax.
Anger sputters in her brainpan, confined
10   but spewing out missiles of hot fat.
Carbonized despair presses like a clinker
from a barbecue against the back of her eyes.

If she wants to grill anything, it's
her husband spitted over a slow fire.
If she wants to serve him anything   15
it's a dead rat with a bomb in its belly
ticking like the heart of an insomniac.
Her life is cooked and digested,
nothing but leftovers in Tupperware.
Look, she says, once I was roast duck   20
on your platter with parsley but now I am Spam.
Burning dinner is not incompetence but war.   1983

DOROTHY PARKER

Indian Summer

In youth, it was a way I had
    To do my best to please,
And change, with every passing lad,
    To suit his theories.

But now I know the things I know,   5
    And do the things I do;
And if you do not like me so,
    To hell, my love, with you!   1937

ELIZABETH[9]

When I Was Fair and Young

When I was fair and young, and favor graced me,
    Of many was I sought, their mistress for to be;
But I did scorn them all, and answered them therefore,
    "Go, go, go, seek some otherwhere,
        Importune me no more!"   5

How many weeping eyes I made to pine with woe,
    How many sighing hearts, I have no skill to show;
Yet I the prouder grew, and answered them therefore,
    "Go, go, go, seek some otherwhere,
        Importune me no more!"   10

---

9. The attribution of this poem to Queen Elizabeth I of England (1533–1603) is likely but not certain.

Then spake fair Venus' son, that proud victorious boy,[1]
   And said: "Fine dame, since that you be so coy,
I will so pluck your plumes that you shall say no more,
   'Go, go, go, seek some otherwhere,
15   Importune me no more!' "

When he had spake these words, such change grew in my breast
   That neither night nor day since that, I could take any rest.
Then lo! I did repent that I had said before,
   "Go, go, go, seek some otherwhere,
20   Importune me no more!"

   ca. 1585?

RICHARD WILBUR

She

What was her beauty in our first estate
When Adam's will was whole,[2] and the least thing
Appeared the gift and creature of his king,
How should we guess? Resemblance had to wait

5 For separation, and in such a place
She so partook of water, light, and trees
As not to look like any one of these.
He woke and gazed into her naked face.

But then she changed, and coming down amid
10 The flocks of Abel and the fields of Cain,
Clothed in their wish, her Eden graces hid,
A shape of plenty with a mop of grain,

She broke upon the world, in time took on
The look of every labor and its fruits.
15 Columnar in a robe of pleated lawn
She cupped her patient hand for attributes,

Was radiant captive of the farthest tower
And shed her honor on the fields of war,
Walked in her garden at the evening hour,
20 Her shadow like a dark ogival[3] door,

Breasted the seas for all the westward ships
And, come to virgin country, changed again—
A moonlike being truest in eclipse,
And subject goddess of the dreams of men.

25 Tree, temple, valley, prow, gazelle, machine,
More named and nameless than the morning star,

---

1. Cupid.   2. Before the Fall.   3. In the form of a pointed (Gothic) arch.

Lovely in every shape, in all unseen,
We dare not wish to find you as you are,

Whose apparition, biding time until
Desire decay and bring the latter age,   30
Shall flourish in the ruins of our will
And deck[4] the broken stones like saxifrage.[5]   1961

KATHERINE PHILIPS

L'amitié: To Mrs. M. Awbrey

Soul of my soul, my Joy, my crown, my friend!
A name which all the rest doth comprehend;
How happy are we now, whose souls are grown,
By an incomparable mixture, One:
Whose well acquainted minds are now as near   5
As Love, or vows, or secrets can endear.
I have no thought but what's to thee reveal'd,
Nor thou desire that is from me conceal'd.
Thy heart locks up my secrets richly set,
And my breast is thy private cabinet.   10
Thou shedst no tear but what my moisture lent,
And if I sigh, it is thy breath is spent.
United thus, what horror can appear
Worthy our sorrow, anger, or our fear?
Let the dull world alone to talk and fight,   15
And with their vast ambitions nature fright;
Let them despise so innocent a flame,
While Envy, Pride, and Faction play their game:
But we by Love sublim'd so high shall rise,
To pity Kings, and Conquerors despise,   20
Since we that sacred union have engrossed,
Which they and all the sullen world have lost.   1667

APHRA BEHN

To the Fair Clarinda, Who Made Love to Me, Imagined More Than Woman

Fair lovely maid, or if that title be
Too weak, too feminine for nobler thee,
Permit a name that more approaches truth,

---

4. Adorn.   5. A tufted plant with bright flowers, often rooted in the clefts of rocks.

And let me call thee, lovely charming youth.
5   This last will justify my soft complaint,
While that may serve to lessen my constraint;
And without blushes I the youth pursue,
When so much beauteous woman is in view.
Against thy charms we struggle but in vain
10   With thy deluding form thou giv'st us pain,
While the bright nymph betrays us to the swain.
In pity to our sex sure thou wert sent,
That we might love, and yet be innocent:
For sure no crime with thee we can commit;
15   Or if we should—thy form excuses it.
For who, that gathers fairest flowers believes
A snake lies hid beneath the fragrant leaves.

Thou beauteous wonder of a different kind,
Soft Cloris with the dear Alexis joined;
20   When e'er the manly part of thee, would plead
Thou tempts us with the image of the maid,
While we the noblest passions do extend
The love to Hermes, Aphrodite[6] the friend.   1685

LIZ ROSENBERG

The Silence of Women

Old men, as time goes on, grow softer, sweeter,
while their wives get angrier.
You see them hauling the men across the mall
or pushing them down on chairs,
5   "Sit there! and don't you move!"
A lifetime of *yes* has left them
hissing bent as snakes.
It seems even their bones will turn
against them, once the fruitful years are gone.
10   Something snaps off the houselights,
and the cells go dim;
the chicken hatching back into the egg.

Oh lifetime of silence!
words scattered like a sybil's leaves.
15   Voice thrown into a baritone storm—
whose shrilling is a soulful wind
blown through an instrument
that cannot beat time

---

6. The Greek messenger god (Hermes) and the Greek goddess of love (Aphrodite); their offspring, Hermaphroditus, had both male and female characteristics.

but must make music
any way it can.   20

1994

ELIZABETH BISHOP

Exchanging Hats

Unfunny uncles who insist
in trying on a lady's hat,
—oh, even if the joke falls flat,
we share your slight transvestite twist

in spite of our embarrassment.   5
Costume and custom are complex.
The headgear of the other sex
inspires us to experiment.

Anandrous aunts, who, at the beach
with paper plates upon your laps,   10
keep putting on the yachtsmen's caps
with exhibitionistic screech,

the visors hanging o'er the ear
so that the golden anchors drag,
—the tides of fashion never lag.   15
Such caps may not be worn next year.

Or you who don the paper plate
itself, and put some grapes upon it,
or sport the Indian's feather bonnet,
—perversities may aggravate   20

the natural madness of the hatter.
And if the opera hats collapse
and crowns grow draughty, then, perhaps,
he thinks what might a miter matter?

Unfunny uncle, you who wore a   25
hat too big, or one too many,
tell us, can't you, are there any
stars inside your black fedora?

Aunt exemplary and slim,
with avernal eyes, we wonder   30
what slow changes they see under
their vast, shady, turned-down brim.

1956

JUDITH ORTIZ COFER

The Changeling

As a young girl
vying for my father's attention,
I invented a game that made him look up
from his reading and shake his head
as if both baffled and amused.

In my brother's closet, I'd change
into his dungarees—the rough material
molding me into boy shape; hide
my long hair under an army helmet
he'd been given by Father, and emerge
transformed into the legendary Ché[7]
of grown-up talk.

Strutting around the room,
I'd tell of life in the mountains,
of carnage and rivers of blood,
and of manly feasts with rum and music
to celebrate victories *para la libertad*.[8]
He would listen with a smile
to my tales of battles and brotherhood
until Mother called us to dinner.

She was not amused
by my transformations, sternly forbidding me
from sitting down with them as a man.
She'd order me back to the dark cubicle
that smelled of adventure, to shed
my costume, to braid my hair furiously
with blind hands, and to return invisible,
as myself,
to the real world of her kitchen.   1993

HA JIN

The Past

I have supposed my past is a part of myself.
As my shadow appears whenever I'm in the sun

---

7. Ché Guevara (1928–1967): revolutionary leader, martyred companion of Fidel Castro.   8. "For freedom" (Spanish).

the past cannot be thrown off and its weight
must be borne, or I will become another man.

But I saw someone wall his past into a garden   5
whose produce is always in fashion.
If you enter his property without permission
he will welcome you with a watchdog or a gun.

I saw someone set up his past as a harbor.
Wherever it sails, his boat is safe—   10
if a storm comes, he can always head for home.
His voyage is the adventure of a kite.

I saw someone drop his past like trash.
He buried it and shed it altogether.
He has shown me that without the past   15
one can also move ahead and get somewhere.

Like a shroud my past surrounds me,
but I will cut it and stitch it,
to make good shoes with it,
shoes that fit my feet.   20

1996

DIANE WAKOSKI

The Ring of Irony

What do you say to the mother
of a homosexual man
whom you once were married to,
when she asks you to return your wedding ring
because it's a family heirloom?   5
        "I want to keep it on my key ring
        where I carry it now,
        to remind me of loss?"
or perhaps, in spite,
        "It was the only thing   10
        I ever got out of the marriage.
        No. I won't give it back."
Do you say that you love irony
and have imagined your whole life
governed by understatement   15
and paradox?
Yet, the obvious dominates and
I ask myself,
"Why do you want to keep it?
Surely the woman deserves some comfort/   20

if a small piece of gold can do it,
who can object?"
Wallowing again, in the obvious,
I wonder at my meanness,
25   my own petty anger
at men who love other men,
alas, some of them are/have been
my best friends. Irony?
No. The obvious.
30   Why do you want that circle of gold
lying in your purse with keys
and checkbooks? I nudge myself.
Why don't you purchase an ounce of gold
and carry it in a velvet bag instead. Your
35   own.
Worth so much more.
Of course. The obvious.
Because the other was given,
not bought, and you
40   have never asked the return of your gifts, but
you know, Diane, why
you anguish over putting the ring in the box and
mailing it off to
Corona, California.
45   So obvious.
Because you believe in the gifts
freely given
to appease destiny.
You too would sacrifice
50   Iphigenia or Isaac[9]
for the cap of darkness,
having given your children
for poetry,
having given your sexuality
55   for beautiful men,
having relinquished honor
for music.
The circle of gold,
that ring, symbolizes
60   the pact.
To give it back says the giving was meaningless.
Fate does not honor your bargain,
Ms. Wakoski. Not irony,
the obvious:
65   you have no husband,
            no house,

---

9. Agamemnon, in Greek mythology, planned to sacrifice his daughter Iphigenia; Abraham (in the Judeo-Christian tradition) was about to sacrifice his son Isaac when God intervened.

no children,
no country.
You have no fame,
fortune,   70
only remaindered books,
and innocent students who
stab you
with their lack of understanding,
asking, no not ironically,   75
"Did you give a lot of readings
when you were young?"
Finally, the understatement, the irony, when I say,
"yes," and the past swallows up everything,
leaving the obvious,   80
and now that handsome woman in California
wants to take the ring.

Soap opera of the middle-aged
mid-Western
schoolteacher?   85
What do you say when irony deserts you
for the maudlin obvious?
"I am mailing you the ring.
Your claim is greater than mine."

Irony? No, the obvious.   90

                                                            1986

EDNA ST. VINCENT MILLAY

[*I, being born a woman and distressed*]

I, being born a woman and distressed
By all the needs and notions of my kind,
Am urged by your propinquity to find
Your person fair, and feel a certain zest
To bear your body's weight upon my breast: 5
So subtly is the fume of life designed,
To clarify the pulse and cloud the mind,
And leave me once again undone, possessed.
Think not for this, however, the poor treason
Of my stout blood against my staggering brain,   10
I shall remember you with love, or season
My scorn with pity,—let me make it plain:
I find this frenzy insufficient reason
For conversation when we meet again.   1923

QUESTIONS

1. What additional information would you like to have about the events referred to in Hayden's "Frederick Douglass" and Randall's "Ballad of Birmingham"? What details in these poems seem to require additional information about the events on which each is based? What details about the life and writings of Frederick Douglass, and about his character, would help your reading of the poem named for him? What do you make of the mention of "dogs," "clubs," and "hoses" in "Ballad of Birmingham"? What did "Freedom March" mean in 1969? Given the poem's structure and its portrayal of children's voices and attitudes, what difference might it make to your reading of the poem if you had factual information about the actual casualties of the bombing? If you were editing this poem, what other footnotes would you provide? Reread "Sir Patrick Spens" (page 770). In what ways does Randall's poem allude to it? why?

2. What details about the physical suffering from poison gas are specifically suggested in Owen's "Dulce et Decorum Est"? what details about the physical effects of atomic explosions in Salter's "Welcome to Hiroshima"? How accurate are these representations? Using the reference resources in your college library, look up news accounts of gassings in World War I and the atomic bombing of Hiroshima, and compare the journalistic details with those given in the poems. How careful does each poet seem to have been in representing historical events? What evidence do you find of distortion or "poetic license"? Which details are specifically chosen for powerful rhetorical effects in each poem?

3. Compare the images of fire and burning in Piercy's "What's That Smell in the Kitchen?" and Jiles's "Paper Matches." How are the images used differently in each poem? What common thread of meaning informs the images in these poems? On what kind of cultural assumptions about women and their roles do these images seem to be based? In what ways are these images like other images of passion in other poems you have read? In what ways are the images like other images of destruction?

4. Which poems in the "Constructing Identity, Exploring Gender" group are especially concerned to suggest the importance of physical space? In what ways do they portray its absence? In what ways do they represent the male sense of a woman's "place"?

5. What images of passivity, deferentiality, and compliance can you find about women in the poems in this group? How is each image treated in the individual poem? In what ways do images of assertion and resistance compete with these images? What differences in imagery do you notice between men's portrayal of women and women's portrayal of women?

WRITING SUGGESTIONS

1. Using reference materials available in your college's library, construct a short but detailed narrative (of about 500 to 700 words) of the Birmingham bombing. Then "read" the poem in the context of the full story, showing how the poem uses specific details of the incident to create its effects.

2. Compare the way Wakoski (in "The Ring of Irony") and Levertov (in "Wedding-Ring," page 601) conceive and describe the central object in their poems. How important is the appearance of the ring in each case? In what ways is it symbolic to the speaker in each case? Write an essay of about 1,000 words comparing the speakers' values in the two poems, giving special attention to the ways each speaker describes the ring itself.

3. Which poem in the "Constructing Identity, Exploring Gender" group seems to you most effective in describing how men construct their gender and identity? Which is most successful in describing how women do? In a brief essay of about 500 words, show what devices one of the two poems you have chosen uses to accomplish its task.

24

CRITICAL CONTEXTS:
A POETRY CASEBOOK

As the previous context chapters have suggested, poems draw on all kinds of earlier texts, experiences, and events. But they also produce new contexts of discussion and interpretation, a kind of ongoing conversation about the poem itself. Because readers reading poems see different things in them, and because readers bring different interests to their readings, differences and disagreements develop about how poems are to be experienced and interpreted. Just as what you say about a poem differs from what your classmates say, and just as the paper you write about a poem differs from—and often disagrees with—what other students will write, various observations and comments develop around any poem that is read repeatedly by various readers. Many of those interpretations are published in specialized journals and books (the selections that follow are all reprinted from published sources), and a kind of dialogue develops among readers, producing a body of interpretations and commentaries about the poem. Professional interpreters of texts are often called **literary critics,** and the textual analysis they provide is called **criticism**—not because their work is necessarily negative or corrective, but because they ask hard, analytical, "critical" questions and try to provide interpretations based on the application of a wide variety of literary, historical, biographical, psychological, aesthetic, moral, political, or social issues.

Your own interpretive work may seem to you more private and far removed from such "professional" writing about poems. But once you engage in class discussion with your teacher or even talk informally with a fellow student about a poem, you are in effect practicing your own literary criticism—offering comments, interpreting, judging, putting the poem into some kind of perspective that makes it more knowable and understandable to yourself or to other readers. You are, in effect, joining the ongoing conversation about the poem. The accumulated criticism of any particular poem is, in fact, basically just public conversation and discussion—give and take, competing interpretations, accumulation of relevant facts and information—on the topic of how that poem is to be read, interpreted, and evaluated. And when you *write* about the poem, you may often engage specifically the opinions of others—your teacher, fellow students, or published "criticism." You may not have the experience or specific expertise of professional critics, but you can modify or answer the work of others and use them in your own work.

There are many different ways to engage literary criticism and put it to work for you. The most common is to draw on published work for specific information about the poem: glossings of particular terms; explanations of references or situations you don't recognize; accounts of how, when, and under what circumstances the poem was written. Another common use of criticism in writing a paper is as a springboard for your own interpretation, either building upon what someone else has said or using it as a point of departure to disagree and launch a different view. In either case, your own paper may readily develop out of your reading or out of a class lecture or class discussion that you may drawn on just like written accounts. When you use the work of others, be sure to give full credit, carefully detailing the source not only of direct quotations, but all individual points and ideas. Your reader should always be told exactly how to find the material you are quoting or summarizing. Usually, this means careful notes and a list of citations (or bibliography) at the end of your paper. Your instructor will guide you to appropriate handbooks—for example, the *MLA Handbook* or *The Chicago Manual of Style*—that show you how to cite each item according to the habits and practices current in your school.

It can seem intimidating to become involved in critical dialogue, especially with those who are "authorities" or "experts" whose work has been published and widely read. But your own reading experience gives you a legitimate perspective, too, and often it is good interpretive practice to argue out your views against those with extensive interpretive experiences. Besides, as you will quickly discover when you read several critical pieces on a particular poem, the experts often disagree; your participation in the conversation will draw on the reading and interpreting skills you have been developing, and often you will have evidence to add from the analysis you have done *before* you get involved with reading criticism.

Procedurally, it is usually best to do your own extensive analysis of a poem *before* consulting what other critics have said and then to use other people's ideas to supplement, refine, extend, or challenge your own tentative conclusions. That way, you will have a clear base from which to begin, and you can confront other views (and any new facts they may present) from a firm position of your own. It is important to take in new information and to challenge both your own first impressions and considered analyses, but don't be too quick to adopt somebody else's ideas. The best way to test the views of others is to compare them critically to your own conclusions. Usually, that means proceeding just as you have been proceeding—asking the questions you have learned to ask, sorting out the evidence you have noticed, and moving toward an integrated interpretation of the poem.

This chapter provides examples of criticism written about Sylvia Plath's powerful poem "Daddy." Read the poem itself carefully—not just once, but several times—before you look at what the critics who are reprinted here have to say. Ask all of the analytical questions you have found useful in other cases: Who is speaking? To whom? When? Under what conditions? What is the full dramatic situation behind the poem? What kind of language does the poem use? To what effect? How does the poem use metaphor? allusion? historical reference? What kinds of strategy of rhythm and sound does the poem use? To what effect? What is the poem's tone? In what ways is this poem like other poems or other texts on similar topics? When was the poem written? What do you know about the person who wrote the poem? In what ways is this poem like others you have read by this poet or by this poet's contemporaries? How do the poem's issues and attitudes reflect the culture and times in which it was written?

SYLVIA PLATH

Daddy

You do not do, you do not do
Any more, black shoe
In which I have lived like a foot
For thirty years, poor and white,
Barely daring to breathe or Achoo.   5

Daddy, I have had to kill you.
You died before I had time—
Marble-heavy, a bag full of God,
Ghastly statue with one gray toe
Big as a Frisco seal   10

And a head in the freakish Atlantic
Where it pours bean green over blue
In the waters off beautiful Nauset.[1]
I used to pray to recover you.
Ach, du.[2]   15

In the German tongue, in the Polish town
Scraped flat by the roller
Of wars, wars, wars.
But the name of the town is common.
My Polack friend   20

Says there are a dozen or two.
So I never could tell where you
Put your foot, your root,
I never could talk to you.
The tongue stuck in my jaw.   25

It stuck in a barb wire snare.
Ich, ich, ich, ich,
I could hardly speak.
I thought every German was you.
And the language obscene   30

An engine, an engine
Chuffing me off like a Jew.
A Jew to Dachau, Auschwitz, Belsen.[3]
I began to talk like a Jew.
I think I may well be a Jew.   35

The snows of the Tyrol,[4] the clear beer of Vienna
Are not very pure or true.

---

1. An inlet on Cape Cod.   2. "Oh, you" in German. Plath often portrays herself as Jewish and her oppressors as German. *Ich* (below): German for "I."   3. Sites of World War II German death camps. 4. An Alpine region in Austria and northern Italy. The snow there is, legendarily, as pure as the beer is clear in Vienna.

With my gypsy-ancestress and my weird luck
And my Taroc[5] pack and my Taroc pack
40   I may be a bit of a Jew.

I have always been scared of *you*,
With your Luftwaffe,[6] your gobbledygoo.
And your neat moustache
And your Aryan eye, bright blue.
45   Panzer-man, panzer-man, O You—

Not God but a swastika
So black no sky could squeak through.
Every woman adores a Fascist,
The boot in the face, the brute
50   Brute heart of a brute like you.

You stand at the blackboard, daddy,
In the picture I have of you,
A cleft in your chin instead of your foot
But no less a devil for that, no not
55   Any less the black man who

Bit my pretty red heart in two.
I was ten when they buried you.
At twenty I tried to die
And get back, back, back to you.
60   I thought even the bones would do

But they pulled me out of the sack,
And they stuck me together with glue.
And then I knew what to do.
I made a model of you,
65   A man in black with a Meinkampf[7] look

And a love of the rack and the screw.
And I said I do, I do.
So daddy, I'm finally through.
The black telephone's off at the root,
70   The voices just can't worm through.

If I've killed one man, I've killed two—
The vampire who said he was you
And drank my blood for a year,
Seven years, if you want to know.
75   Daddy, you can lie back now.

There's a stake in your fat black heart
And the villagers never liked you.
They are dancing and stamping on you.
They always *knew* it was you.
80   Daddy, daddy, you bastard, I'm through.

1966

---

5. Tarot, playing cards used mainly for fortune-telling.   6. The German air force.   7. The title of
Adolf Hitler's autobiography and manifesto (1925–1927); German for "my struggle."

Once you have a "reading" of your own and have made extensive notes about your conclusions, look at the selections that follow. You can read them in a variety of ways:

- skim them all quickly, and look for things that surprise you or that provide you with specific challenges; or
- read each critical piece carefully one by one, and keep close track of all the things with which you agree and (even more important) of those things with which you disagree; or
- look specifically for facts or apparently crucial information new to you, examine and question the information carefully, and see how it affects the interpretation you have previously decided on; or
- look for points of disagreement in the different interpretations, make a list of the most important issues raised, and look for the crucial parts of the poem where the basis for these disagreements occurs.

You will also find your own ways to respond to and use the various critical views you come upon here. Working the views of others into your own arguments and your-own writing is complicated; it is difficult to do well so as to be at once fair to what others say and helpful to your own conclusions. But learning to use the facts, opinions, and interpretations of others will clarify your own thoughts and will often hone or add to your own analytical skills and complicate your views. And participating in the larger conversation about a specific poem—or about poetry in general—can contribute might-ily to helping you learn to read, respond, and write more effectively.

Sylvia Plath

Sylvia Plath's father, Otto Plath

GEORGE STEINER

*Dying Is an Art**

* * *

* * * [N]o group of poems since Dylan Thomas' *Deaths and Entrances* has had as vivid and disturbing an impact on English critics and readers as has *Ariel.* Sylvia Plath's last poems have already passed into legend as both representative of our present tone of emotional life and unique in their implacable, harsh brilliance. Those among the young who read new poetry will know "Daddy," "Lady Lazarus," and "Death & Co." almost by heart, and reference to Sylvia Plath is constant where poetry and the conditions of its present existence are discussed.

The spell does not lie wholly in the poems themselves. The suicide of Sylvia Plath at the age of thirty-one in 1963, and the personality of this young woman who had come from Massachusetts to study and live in England (where she married Ted Hughes, himself a gifted poet), are vital parts of it. To those who knew her and to the greatly enlarged circle who were electrified by her last poems and sudden death, she had come to signify the specific honesties and risks of the poet's condition. Her personal style, and the price in private harrowing she so obviously paid to achieve the intensity and candor of her principal poems, have taken on their own dramatic authority.

All this makes it difficult to judge the poems. I mean that the vehemence and intimacy of the verse is such as to constitute a very powerful rhetoric of sincerity. The poems play on our nerves with their own proud nakedness, making claims so immediate and sharply urged that the reader flinches, embarrassed by the routine discretions and evasions of his own sensibility. Yet if these poems are to take life among us, if they are to be more than exhibits in the history of modern psychological stress, they must be read with all the intelligence and scruple we can muster. They are too honest, they have cost too much, to be yielded to myth.

* * *

* * * It requires no biographical impertinence to realize that Sylvia Plath's life was harried by bouts of physical pain, that she sometimes looked on the accumulated exactions of her own nerve and body as "a trash / To annihilate each decade." She was haunted by the piecemeal, strung-together mechanics of the flesh, by what could be so easily broken and then mended with such searing ingenuity. The hospital ward was her exemplary ground:

> My patent leather overnight case like a black pillbox,
> My husband and child smiling out of the family photo;
> Their smiles catch onto my skin, little smiling hooks.

This brokenness, so sharply feminine and contemporary, is, I think, her principal realization. It is by the graphic expression she gave to it that she will be

* From George Steiner, *Language and Silence: Essays on Language, Literature, and the Inhuman* (1967; New York: Atheneum, 1974), pp. 295–302.

judged and remembered. Sylvia Plath carries forward, in an intensely womanly and aggravated note, from Robert Lowell's *Life Studies,* a book that obviously had a great impact on her. This new frankness of women about the specific hurts and tangles of their nervous-physiological makeup is as vital to the poetry of Sylvia Plath as it is to the tracts of Simone de Beauvoir or to the novels of Edna O'Brien and Brigid Brophy. Women speak out as never before:

> The womb
> Rattles its pod, the moon
> Discharges itself from the tree with nowhere to go.
> ("Childless Woman")

> They have swabbed me clear of my loving associations.
> Scared and bare on the green plastic-pillowed trolley. . . .
> ("Tulips")

It is difficult to think of a precedent to the fearful close of "Medusa" (the whole poem is extraordinary):

> I shall take no bite of your body,
> Bottle in which I live,
>
> Ghastly Vatican.
> I am sick to death of hot salt.
> Green as eunuchs, your wishes
> Hiss at my sin.
> Off, off, eely tentacle!
>
> There is nothing between us.

The ambiguity and dual flash of insight in this final line are of a richness and obviousness that only a very great poem can carry off.

The progress registered between the early and the mature poems is one of concretion. The general Gothic means with which Sylvia Plath was so fluently equipped become singular to herself and therefore fiercely honest. What had been style passes into need. It is the need of a superbly intelligent, highly literate young woman to cry out about her especial being, about the tyrannies of blood and gland, of nervous spasm and sweating skin, the rankness of sex and childbirth in which a woman is still compelled to be wholly of her organic condition. Where Emily Dickinson could—indeed was obliged to—shut the door on the riot and humiliations of the flesh, thus achieving her particular dry lightness, Sylvia Plath "fully assumed her own condition." This alone would assure her of a place in modern literature. But she took one step further, assuming a burden that was not naturally or necessarily hers.

Born in Boston in 1932 of German and Austrian parents, Sylvia Plath had no personal, immediate contact with the world of the concentration camps. I may be mistaken, but so far as I know there was nothing Jewish in her background. But her last, greatest poems culminate in an act of identification, of total communion with those tortured and massacred. The poet sees herself on

> An engine, an engine
> Chuffing me off like a Jew.
> A Jew to Dachau, Auschwitz, Belsen.
> I began to talk like a Jew.
> I think I may well be a Jew.
>
> The snows of the Tyrol, the clear beer of Vienna
> Are not very pure or true.
> With my gypsy ancestress and my weird luck
>
> And my Tarot pack and my Tarot pack
> I may be a bit of a Jew.

Distance is no help; nor the fact that one is "guilty of nothing." The dead men cry out of the yew hedges. The poet becomes the loud cry of their choked silence:

> Herr God, Herr Lucifer
> Beware
> Beware.
> Out of the ash
> I rise with my red hair
> And I eat men like air.

Here the almost surrealistic wildness of the gesture is kept in place by the insistent obviousness of the language and beat; a kind of Hieronymus Bosch[1] nursery rhyme.

Sylvia Plath is only one of a number of young contemporary poets, novelists, and playwrights, themselves in no way implicated in the actual holocaust, who have done most to counter the general inclination to forget the death camps. Perhaps it is only those who had no part in the events who *can* focus on them rationally and imaginatively; to those who experienced the thing, it has lost the hard edges of possibility, it has stepped outside the real.

Committing the whole of her poetic and formal authority to the metaphor, to the mask of language, Sylvia Plath *became* a woman being transported to Auschwitz on the death trains. The notorious shards of massacre seemed to enter into her own being:

> A cake of soap,
> A wedding ring,
> A gold filling.

In "Daddy" she wrote one of the very few poems I know of in any language to come near the last horror. It achieves the classic act of generalization, translating a private, obviously intolerable hurt into a code of plain statement, of instantaneously public images which concern us all. It is the "Guernica"[2] of modern poetry. And it is both histrionic and, in some ways, "arty," as is Picasso's outcry.

1. A fifteenth-century Netherlandish artist whose nightmarish paintings are filled with obscure symbolism.   2. Picasso's famous painting (1937) depicting the brutalities of war.

Are these final poems entirely legitimate? In what sense does anyone, himself uninvolved and long after the event, commit a subtle larceny when he invokes the echoes and trappings of Auschwitz and appropriates an enormity of ready emotion to his own private design? Was there latent in Sylvia Plath's sensibility, as in that of many of us who remember only by fiat of imagination, a fearful envy, a dim resentment at not having been there, of having missed the rendezvous with hell? In "Lady Lazarus" and "Daddy" the realization seems to me so complete, the sheer rawness and control so great, that only irresistible need could have brought it off. These poems take tremendous risks, extending Sylvia Plath's essentially austere manner to the very limit. They are a bitter triumph, proof of the capacity of poetry to give to reality the greater permanence of the imagined. She could not return from them.

* * *

IRVING HOWE

*The Plath Celebration: A Partial Dissent**

* * *

Sylvia Plath's most famous poem, adored by many sons and daughters, is "Daddy." It is a poem with an affecting theme, the feelings of the speaker as she regathers the pain of her father's premature death and her persuasion that he has betrayed her by dying:

> I was ten when they buried you.
> At twenty I tried to die
> And get back, back, back to you.

In the poem Sylvia Plath identifies the father (we recall his German birth) with the Nazis ("Panzer-man, panzer-man, O You") and flares out with assaults for which nothing in the poem (nor, so far as we know, in Sylvia Plath's own life) offers any warrant: "A cleft in your chin instead of your foot / But no less a devil for that. . . ." Nor does anything in the poem offer warrant, other than the free-flowing hysteria of the speaker, for the assault of such lines as, "There's a stake in your fat black heart / And the villagers never liked you." Or for the snappy violence of

> Every woman adores a Fascist,
> The boot in the face, the brute
> Brute heart of a brute like you.

* From Irving Howe, *The Critical Point of Literature and Culture* (1973; New York: Horizon Press, 1977), pp. 231–33.

What we have here is a revenge fantasy, feeding upon filial love-hatred, and thereby mostly of clinical interest. But seemingly aware that the merely clinical can't provide the materials for a satisfying poem, Sylvia Plath tries to enlarge upon the personal plight, give meaning to the personal outcry, by fancying the girl as victim of a Nazi father:

> An engine, an engine
> Chuffing me off like a Jew.
> A Jew to Dachau, Auschwitz, Belsen.
> I began to talk like a Jew,
> I think I may well be a Jew.

The more sophisticated admirers of this poem may say that I fail to see it as a dramatic presentation, a monologue spoken by a disturbed girl not necessarily to be identified with Sylvia Plath, despite the similarities of detail between the events of the poem and the events of her life. I cannot accept this view. The personal-confessional element, strident and undisciplined, is simply too obtrusive to suppose the poem no more than a dramatic picture of a certain style of disturbance. If, however, we did accept such a reading of "Daddy," we would fatally narrow its claims to emotional or moral significance, for we would be confining it to a mere vivid imagining of pathological state. That, surely, is not how its admirers really take the poem.

It is clearly not how the critic George Steiner takes the poem when he calls it "the 'Guernica' of modern poetry." But then, in an astonishing turn, he asks: "In what sense does anyone, himself uninvolved and long after the event, commit a subtle larceny when he invokes the echoes and trappings of Auschwitz and appropriates an enormity of ready emotion to his own private design?" The question is devastating to his early comparison with "Guernica." Picasso's painting objectifies the horrors of Guernica, through the distancing of art; no one can suppose that he shares or participates in them. Plath's poem aggrandizes on the "enormity of ready emotion" invoked by references to the concentration camps, in behalf of an ill-controlled if occasionally brilliant outburst. There is something monstrous, utterly disproportionate, when tangled emotions about one's father are deliberately compared with the historical fate of the European Jews; something sad, if the comparison is made spontaneously. "Daddy" persuades once again, through the force of negative example, of how accurate T. S. Eliot was in saying, "The more perfect the artist, the more completely separate in him will be the man who suffers and the mind which creates."

A. ALVAREZ

*Sylvia Plath**

* * * The reasons for Sylvia Plath's images are always there, though sometimes you have to work hard to find them. She is, in short, always in intelligent control of her feelings. Her work bears out her theories:

> I think my poems come immediately out of the sensuous and emotional experiences I have, but I must say I cannot sympathise with these cries from the heart that are informed by nothing except a needle or a knife or whatever it is. I believe that one should be able to control and manipulate experiences, even the most terrifying—like madness, being tortured, this kind of experience—and one should be able to manipulate these experiences with an informed and intelligent mind. I think that personal experience shouldn't be a kind of shut box and mirror-looking narcissistic experience. I believe it should be generally relevant, to such things as Hiroshima and Dachau, and so on.

It seems to me that it was only by her determination both to face her most inward and terrifying experiences and to use her intelligence in doing so—so as not to be overwhelmed by them—that she managed to write these extraordinary last poems, which are at once deeply autobiographical and yet detached, generally relevant.

'Lady Lazarus' is a stage further on from 'Fever 103°'; its subject is the total purification of achieved death. It is also far more intimately concerned with the drift of Sylvia Plath's life. The deaths of Lady Lazarus correspond to her own crises: the first just after her father died, the second when she had her nervous breakdown, the third perhaps a presentiment of the death that was shortly to come. Maybe this closeness of the subject helped make the poem so direct. The details don't clog each other: they are swept forward by the current of immediate feeling, marshalled by it and ordered. But what is remarkable about the poem is the objectivity with which she handles such personal material. She is not just talking about her own private suffering. Instead, it is the very closeness of her pain which gives it a general meaning; through it she assumes the suffering of all the modern victims. Above all, she becomes an imaginary Jew. I think this is a vitally important element in her work. For two reasons. First, because anyone whose subject is suffering has a ready-made modern example of hell on earth in the concentration camps. And what matters in them is not so much the physical torture—since sadism is general and perennial—but the way modern, as it were industrial, techniques can be used to destroy utterly the human identity. Individual suffering can be heroic provided it leaves the person who suffers a sense of his own individuality—provided, that is, there is an illusion of choice remaining to him. But when suffering is mass-produced, men and women become as equal

---

* From A. Alvarez, "Sylvia Plath" (1963), in *The Art of Sylvia Plath,* ed. Charles Newman (Bloomington and London: Indiana University Press, 1970), pp. 64–66.

and identity-less as objects on an assembly line, and nothing remains—certainly no values, no humanity. This anonymity of pain, which makes all dignity impossible, was Sylvia Plath's subject. Second, she seemed convinced, in these last poems, that the root of her suffering was the death of her father, whom she loved, who abandoned her, and who dragged her after him into death. And in her fantasies her father was pure German, pure Aryan, pure anti-semite.

It all comes together in the most powerful of her last poems, 'Daddy' * * *, about which she wrote the following bleak note:

> The poem is spoken by a girl with an Electra complex. Her father died while she thought he was God. Her case is complicated by the fact that her father was also a Nazi and her mother very possibly part Jewish. In the daughter the two strains marry and paralyse each other—she has to act out the awful little allegory once over before she is free of it.[1]

* * * What comes through most powerfully, I think, is the terrible *unforgivingness* of her verse, the continual sense not so much of violence—although there is a good deal of that—as of violent resentment that this should have been done to *her*. What she does in the poem is, with a weird detachment, to turn the violence against herself so as to show that she can equal her oppressors with her self-inflicted oppression. And this is the strategy of the concentration camps. When suffering is there whatever you do, by inflicting it upon yourself you achieve your identity, you set yourself free.

Yet the tone of the poem, like its psychological mechanisms, is not single or simple, and she uses a great deal of skill to keep it complex. Basically, her trick is to tell this horror story in a verse form as insistently jaunty and ritualistic as a nursery rhyme. And this helps her to maintain towards all the protagonists—her father, her husband and herself—a note of hard and sardonic anger, as though she were almost amused that her own suffering should be so extreme, so grotesque. The technical psychoanalytic term for this kind of insistent gaiety to protect you from what, if faced nakedly, would be insufferable, is 'manic defence'. But what, in a neurotic, is a means of avoiding reality can become, for an artist, a source of creative strength, a way of handling the unhandleable, and presenting the situation in all its fullness. When she first read me the poem a few days after she wrote it, she called it a piece of 'light verse'. It obviously isn't, yet equally obviously it also isn't the racking personal confession that a mere description or précis of it might make it sound.

Yet neither is it unchangingly vindictive or angry. The whole poem works on one single, returning note and rhyme, echoing from start to finish:

> You do not do, you do not do . . .
> . . . I used to pray to recover you.
> Ach, du . . .

---

1. From the introductory notes to 'New Poems', a reading prepared for the BBC Third Programme but never broadcast. (AA)

There is a kind of cooing tenderness in this which complicates the other, more savage note of resentment. It brings in an element of pity, less for herself and her own suffering than for the person who made her suffer. Despite everything, 'Daddy' is a love poem.

* * *

JUDITH KROLL

Rituals of Exorcism: "Daddy"*

Poems explicitly about the protagonist's father, read in order of composition, show that the attitude toward him evolves from nostalgic mournfulness, regret, and guilt, to resentment and a bitter resolve to break his hold on her. * * *

The recital of the myth in "Daddy" ends in a ritual intended to cancel the earlier "sacred marriage" which has suffocated her:

> You do not do, you do not do
> Any more, black shoe
> In which I have lived like a foot
> For thirty years, poor and white,
> Barely daring to breathe or Achoo.[1]

In this image of passive and victimized domesticity, the speaker implicitly compares her past self to the 'old woman who lived in a shoe' who 'didn't know what to do'; now, however, she makes it clear that she does know what to do.

As a preamble to the exorcism, she recounts the development of her father's image, beginning with his earlier status as a "bag full of God, / Ghastly statue" (that is, a godlike colossus—mentioning the ghastliness, the ghostly, deathlike, pallid nature of the statue, anticipates the inversions to come) and then introduces the revised images: "panzer-man," "swastika," "Fascist," "brute," "devil," "bastard." Daddy must be cast in this new light, transformed from god to devil, if he is to be successfully expelled, but there must also be some real basis for it. To be effectively exposed, he must first appear as godly. But the speaker soon shows that she now attributes his godliness in part to his authoritarianism and personal inaccessibility—qualities which became intensified through his death, and which later became transferred to "a model of you"—her husband. Both men are really variations on a familiar type, even a stereotype: the "god" who, like Marco the "woman-hater" in *The Bell Jar,* is "chock-full of power" * * * over

---

* From Judith Kroll, *Chapters in a Mythology: The Poetry of Sylvia Plath* (New York: Harper & Row, 1976), pp. 122–26. 1. When Plath introduced "Daddy" as being about "a girl with an Electra complex" (with, in effect, the female version of an Oedipus complex), she gave a clue to what may be a play on words in the poem. "Oedipus" means "swell-foot," and therefore the speaker's identification of herself as a "foot" may be a private way of saying "I am Oedipus" and incorporating into the poem an allusion to the Electra complex. (JK)

women precisely because of his deadness, or ultimate inaccessibility, to them. Loving a man literally or metaphorically dead ("The face that lived in this mirror is the face of a dead man" ["The Courage of Shutting-Up"]) becomes a kind of persecution or punishment; and so, by the end of the incantation, Daddy deserves to be cast out. The "black telephone . . . off at the root," conveys the finality of the intended exorcism.

The 'venomousness,' ambiguous from the beginning, is not the whole story. "Daddy" is not primarily a poem of "father-hatred" or abuse as Robert Lowell, Elizabeth Hardwick, and others have contended. The need for exorcising her father's ghost lies, after all, in the extremity of her attachment to him. Alvarez very justly remarks that

> The whole poem works on one single, returning note and rhyme, echoing from start to finish:
>
>> You do not do, you do not do . . .
>> . . . [I] used to pray to recover you.
>> Ach, du . . .
>
> There is a kind of cooing tenderness in this which complicates the other, more savage note of resentment. It brings in an element of pity, less for herself and her own suffering than for the person who made her suffer. Despite everything, 'Daddy' is a love poem.[2]

The love is not merely conveyed by the rhythm and sound of the poem, it is a necessary part of the poem's meaning, a part of the logic of its act.

The exorcism serves another purpose because through it she attempts to reject the pattern of being abandoned and made to suffer by a god, a man who is "chock-full of power": she creates "a model of you"—an image of her father—and marries this proxy. Then she kills both father and husband at once, magically using each as the other's representative.[3] Each death entails that of the other: the stake in her father's heart also kills the "vampire who said he was you"; and the killing of her marriage (for which she now claims to take responsibility, as she does for having allowed her marriage to perpetuate, by proxy, her relationship to her father) finally permits Daddy to "lie back." Formerly an acquiescent victim, she now vengefully cancels that role. The marriage to and killing of her father by proxy are acts of what Frazer[4] calls "sympathetic magic," in which "things act on each other at a distance through a secret sympathy" * * *. Such magic, which assumes that human beings can either directly influence the course of nature or can induce gods to influence nature in the desired way, nearly always constitutes the logic of the rituals Frazer discusses. The ritual marriage of a Whitsun bride and bridegroom, for example, aims at assuring abundant crops by sympathetically encouraging a marriage between the powers of fertility. Likewise, diseases may be either inflicted or drawn off by sympathetic magic on the principle that "as the image suffers, so does the man" * * *.

---

2. Alvarez, "Sylvia Plath," p. 66. (JK) 3. The biographical basis for this identification is evident in *Letters Home.* * * * (JK) 4. Sir James George Frazer (1854–1941), Scottish anthropologist whose book, *The Golden Bough,* analyzes early religious and magical practices. (Editor)

Plath was familiar with and used such ideas; for example, she transcribed, from *The Golden Bough,* Frazer's remark about the fertility or barrenness of a man's wife affecting his garden; and she echoes Frazer again in a line, excised from her poem "The Other," in which opening doors and windows is connected with the facilitation of childbirth. (Also, being "lame in the memory" and self, associated with the lameness and death of her father, is at once a homeopathic wound and a sympathetic attachment to him.) The notion that "as the image suffers, so does the man"—affecting the real subject through a proxy—nicely describes marriage to a model of Daddy, and explains why "If I've killed one man, I've killed two." The earlier attempt of the speaker in "Daddy" to recover her father also involved sympathetic magic; she had tried to rejoin him by dying and becoming like him:

> At twenty I tried to die
> And get back, back, back to you.

She finally exorcises her father as if he were a scapegoat invested with the evils of her spoiled history. Frazer's discussion of rituals in which the dying god is also a scapegoat is germane here. He conjectures that two originally separate rituals merged to form this combination, and the father in "Daddy" may well be described as such a divine scapegoat figure.[5]

Sometimes it is a place from which a devil must be cast out, but usually it is a person who is possessed. In Plath's mythology the speaker is not possessed by her father in this sense, but by the false self who is in his thrall. That is why the true self is released (as in "Purdah" and "Lady Lazarus") when the oppressor is made hateful, and thereby overthrown. Rituals of exorcism in Plath's poetry therefore inherently involve the idea of rebirth. When exorcism, or attempted exorcism, of father or proxy occurs, it is preliminary to a rebirth which will entail expulsion of the false self and spoiled history. And even when a ritual of rebirth does not involve an explicit exorcism, one is usually implied.

The logic of sympathetic magic, which appears widely in Plath's late poetry, might well be called one of the physical laws of her poems. * * * Such a logic seems poetically appropriate for a mythology: that the Moon-muse (or one of her agents, such as "The Rival") governs and affects her by a "secret sympathy" seems natural to a mythic drama.

The motifs 'released'—or triggered—in her late poems contain the potential for a sympathetic association of those details which express the same motif. Because the details are not incidental, called forth as they are by her mythology, the sympathy is in a sense guaranteed. The images of blood, violent death, and

---

5. Frazer says: "If we ask why a dying god should be chosen to take upon himself and carry away the sins and sorrows of the people, it may be suggested that in the practice of using the divinity as a scape-goat we have a combination of two customs . . . the result would be the employment of the dying god as a scapegoat. He was killed, not originally to take away sin, but to save the divine life from the degeneracy of old age; but, since he had to be killed at any rate, people may have thought that they might as well seize the opportunity to lay upon him the burden of their sufferings and sins, in order that he might bear it away with him to the unknown world beyond the grave." [Pp. 667–68] (JK) * * *

red poppies, all of which release the death and rebirth motif, have the potential for sympathetically affecting one another through their family resemblance. "Tulips" contains an example of the secret sympathy which operates through such resemblance (that is, through expressing the same motif):

> The tulips are too red in the first place, they hurt me.
>
> . . .
>
> Their redness talks to my wound, it corresponds.[6]

The word "corresponds" refers both to the communication between tulips and wound and to their underlying likeness. The tulips stand in the same relation to the incipient health or normalcy of the speaker that the poppies in later poems do to her suppressed true self, to (or with) which the poppies correspond. In a sense, this correspondence, and the contrast between it and the speaker's death-in-life existence, *is* the underlying motif in these poems.

It has already been suggested that the Moon-muse has a "sympathetic"—even though not entirely welcome—relation with the speaker[7] (as mother, totem, familiar, emblem) which can be activated without her consent, just as in "Tulips" she cannot prevent her wound from corresponding with the red flowers. Similarly, the coldness and sterility of the Moon-muse may infect the speaker, causing and not merely representing her state of being. The Moon therefore functions as both "emblem" and "real agent."

MARY LYNN BROE

from *Protean Poetic**

Among the other poems that display the performing self, "Daddy" and "Lady Lazarus" are two of the most often quoted, but most frequently misunderstood, poems in the Plath canon. The speaker in "Daddy" performs a mock poetic exorcism of an event that has already happened—the death of her father who she feels withdrew his love from her by dying prematurely: "Daddy, I have had to kill you. / You died before I had time—."

The speaker attempts to exorcise not just the memory of her father but her

---

6. By the time "Tulips" was written, she had clearly developed much of the technique, imagery, and themes (such as the logic of sympathetic magic) of the late poems. (JK)   7. The belief Frazer mentions, that "a barren wife infects her husband's garden with her own sterility" is the sort of contagion that occurs in *Three Women*, in which the Secretary has been infected by the Moon's sterility and by that of the men with whom she works. Men, who cannot bear children, have the disease of "flatness," for they create only negations of and abstractions about life rather than life itself. This disease can (through the mediumship of the Moon) be caught from men, and it is therefore also an inversion or parody of conception. Referring to her miscarriage, the Secretary says: "I watched the men walk about me in the office. They were so flat!/There was something about them like cardboard, and now I had caught it, . . ." (JK)

* From Mary Lynn Broe, *Protean Poetic: The Poetry of Sylvia Plath* (Columbia and London: University of Missouri Press, 1980), pp. 172–75.

own *Mein Kampf* model of him as well as her inherited behavioral traits that lead her graveward under the Freudian banner of death instinct or Thanatos's libido. But her ritual reenactment simply does not take. The event comically backfires as pure self-parody: the metaphorical murder of the father dwindles into Hollywood spectacle, while the poet is lost in the clutter of the collective unconscious.

Early in the poem, the ritual gets off on the wrong foot both literally and figuratively. A sudden rhythmic break midway through the first stanza interrupts the insistent and mesmeric chant of the poet's own freedom:

> You do not do, you do not do
> Any more, black shoe
> In which I have lived like a foot
> For thirty years, poor and white,
> Barely daring to breathe or Achoo.

The break suggests, on the one hand, that the nursery-rhyme world of contained terror is here abandoned; on the other, that the poet-exorcist's mesmeric control is superficial, founded in a shaky faith and an unsure heart—the worst possible state for the strong, disciplined exorcist.

At first she kills her father succinctly with her own words, demythologizing him to a ludicrous piece of statuary that is hardly a Poseidon or the Colossus of Rhodes:[1]

> Marble-heavy, a bag full of God,
> Ghastly statue with one grey toe
> Big as a Frisco seal
>
> And a head in the freakish Atlantic
> Where it pours bean green over blue
> In the waters off beautiful Nauset.
> I used to pray to recover you.
> Ach, du.

Then as she tries to patch together the narrative of him, his tribal myth (the "common" town, the "German tongue," the war-scraped culture), she begins to lose her own powers of description to a senseless Germanic prattle ("The tongue stuck in my jaw. / It stuck in a barb wire snare. / Ich, ich, ich, ich"). The individual man is absorbed by his inhuman archetype, the "panzer man," "an engine / Chuffing me off like a Jew." Losing the exorcist's power that binds the spirit and then casts out the demon, she is the classic helpless victim of the swastika man. As she culls up her own picture of him as a devil, he refuses to adopt this stereotype. Instead he jumbles his trademark:

> A cleft in your chin instead of your foot
> But no less a devil for that, no not
> Any less the black man who
>
> Bit my pretty red heart in two.

---

1. One of the seven wonders of the ancient world, a gigantic statue of the Greek sun god, Helios; *Poseidon:* the chief sea god in the Greek pantheon.

The overt Nazi-Jew allegory throughout the poem suggests that, by a simple inversion of power, father and daughter grow more alike. But when she tries to imitate his action of dying, making all the appropriate grand gestures, she once again fails: "but they pulled me out of the sack, / And they stuck me together with glue." She retreats to a safe world of icons and replicas, but even the doll image she constructs turns out to be "the vampire who said he was you." At last, she abandons her father to the collective unconscious where it is *he* who is finally recognized ("they always *knew* it was you"). *She* is lost, impersonally absorbed by his irate persecutors, bereft of both her power and her conjuror's discipline, and possessed by the incensed villagers. The exorcist's ritual, one of purifying, cleansing, commanding silence and then ordering the evil spirit's departure, has dwindled to a comic picture from the heart of darkness. Mad villagers stamp on the devil-vampire creation.

In the course of performing the imaginative "killing," the speaker moves through a variety of emotions, from viciousness ("a stake in your fat black heart"), to vengefulness ("You bastard, I'm through"), finally to silence ("the black telephone's off at the root"). It would seem that the real victim is the poet-performer who, despite her straining toward identification with the public events of holocaust and destruction of World War II, becomes more murderously persecuting than the "panzer-man" who smothered her, and who abandoned her with a paradoxical love, guilt, and fear. Unlike him, she kills three times: the original subject, the model to whom she said "I do, I do," and herself, the imitating victim. But each of these killings is comically inverted. Each backfires. Instead of successfully binding the spirits, commanding them to remain silent and cease doing harm, and then ordering them to an appointed place, the speaker herself is stricken dumb.

The failure of the exorcism and the emotional ambivalence are echoed in the curious rhythm. The incantatory safety of the nursery-rhyme thump (seemingly one of controlled, familiar terrors) also suggests some sinister brooding by its repetition. The poem opens with a suspiciously emphatic protest, a kind of psychological whistling-in-the-dark. As it proceeds, "Daddy's" continuous life-rhythms—the assonance, consonance, and especially the sustained *oo* sounds—triumph over either the personal or the cultural-historical imagery. The sheer sense of organic life in the interwoven sounds carries the verse forward in boisterous spirit and communicates an underlying feeling of comedy that is also echoed in the repeated failure of the speaker to perform her exorcism.

Ultimately, "Daddy" is like an emotional, psychological, and historical autopsy, a final report. There is no real progress. The poet is in the same place in the beginning as in the end. She begins the poem as a hesitant but familiar fairy-tale daughter who parodies her attempt to reconstruct the myth of her father. Suffocating in her shoe house, she is unable to do much with that "bag full of God." She ends as a murderous member of a mythical community enacting the ritual or vampire killing, but only for a surrogate vampire, not the real thing ("the vampire who said he was you"). Although it seems that the speaker has moved from identification with the persecuted to identity as persecutor, Jew to vampire-killer, powerless to powerful, she has simply enacted a performance that allows her to live with what is unchangeable. She has used her art to stave off suffocation, and performs her self-contempt with a degree of bravado.[2]

MARGARET HOMANS

from *A Feminine Tradition**

To place an exclusive valuation on the literal, expecially to identify the self as literal, is simply to ratify women's age-old and disadvantageous position as the other and the object. Contemporary poetry by women that takes up this self-defeating strategy risks encounters with death that are destructive both poetically and actually. The current belief in a literal "I" present in poetry is responsible for the popular superstition that Sylvia Plath's death was the purposeful completion of her poetry's project, the assumption being that if the speaker is precisely the same as the biographical Plath, the poetry's self-destructive violence is directed toward Plath herself, not toward an imagined speaker. This reading of Plath is unfair to the woman and, by calling it merely unmediated self-expression, obscures her poetry's real power. In poem after poem depicting or wishing for physical violence, the imagery of violence is part of a symmetrical figurative system, and death is figured as a way of achieving rebirth or some other transcendence.[1] Plath's project may not thus be very different from that of Dickinson, who speaks quite often from beyond the grave, reimagining and repossessing death as her own in order to dispel the terrors of literal death. However, within that figurative system the poet embraces a self-destructive program that must soon have been poetically terminal, even if it did not bring about the actual death.

Several of Plath's late poems come to terms with a father figure (who may include the poetic fathers she acknowledges in *The Colossus*), whose crime, no different from that identified by nineteenth-century women, is of attempting to transform the feminine self into objects. "Lady Lazarus" borrows the most appalling of Nazi imagery to accuse a generalized figure of male power of the ultimate reification. Not only is the dead victim of "Herr Doktor" and "Herr Enemy" an object in being dead, but she is also reduced to the actual physical objects from which the Nazis profited by destroying human bodies: "a Nazi lampshade,"

---

2. What remains the most thorough and enlightening account of the poem is A. R. Jones, "On 'Daddy,' " *The Art of Sylvia Plath*, [ed. Newman], pp. 230–36. (MLB)

* From Margaret Homans, *Women Writers and Poetic Identity: Dorothy Wordsworth, Emily Brontë, and Emily Dickinson* (Princeton: Princeton University Press, 1982), pp. 218–21.   1. I am indebted here, for their persuasively positive readings of Plath, to Judith Kroll, *Chapters in a Mythology: The Poetry of Sylvia Plath* (New York: Harper & Row, 1976), and to Stacy Pies, "Coming Clear of the Shadow: The Poetry of Sylvia Plath," unpublished essay (Yale University, 1979). (MH)

> A cake of soap,
> A wedding ring,
> A gold filling.

The poem combines the tradition of woman as medium of exchange with that of woman as object to produce a desperately concise picture of literalization.

> I am your opus,
> I am your valuable,
> The pure gold baby
>
> That melts to a shriek.

Though the poet is here objecting to literalization, not embracing it, the poetic myth of suicide through which the oppression may be lifted amounts to the same thing: the speaker must submit to this literalization in order to transcend it.

> Out of the ash
> I rise with my red hair
> And I eat men like air.

Their death costs her death, and powerful though the poem is, this is an extraordinarily high price for retribution. And as always, it is the process of objectification that makes up the poem, not the final, scarcely articulable transcendence.

"Daddy" uses Nazi imagery to make the same accusation about objectification brought against men as oppressors in "Lady Lazarus" and makes the corollary accusation against the father (and the husband modelled after him) that objectification has silenced her:

> I never could talk to you.
> The tongue stuck in my jaw.
>
> It stuck in a barb wire snare.
> Ich, ich, ich, ich,
> I could hardly speak.

In this context defiance and retribution take the form of her speaking, but again this counterattack is counterproductive. Punning on the expression "being through" to mean both establishing a telephone connection and being finished, she at once makes and conclusively severs communication:

> So daddy, I'm finally through.
> The black telephone's off at the root,
> The voices just can't worm through.

The poem concludes, "Daddy, daddy, you bastard, I'm through." Suppressing the power of the one who silenced her, she simultaneously returns herself to the silence that the poem came into being to protest.

PAMELA J. ANNAS

from *A Disturbance in Mirrors**

* * * [T]he particular sexual metaphor in "Daddy" is sado-masochism, which stands for the authority structure of a patriarchal and war-making society. * * * "Daddy" is an analysis of the structure of the society in which the individual is enmeshed. Intertwined with the image of sadist and masochist in "Daddy" is a parallel image of vampire and victim. In "Daddy," father, husband, and a larger patriarchal and competitive authority structure, which the speaker of the poem sees as having been responsible for the various imperialisms of the twentieth century, all melt together and become demonic, finally a gigantic vampire figure. In the modulation from one image to another to form an accumulated image that is characteristic of many of Plath's late poems, the male figure at the center of "Daddy" takes four major forms: the statue, the Gestapo officer, the professor, and the vampire. The poem begins, however, with an image of a black shoe, an image which, like the black shoe in "The Munich Mannequins" and like the black suit in "The Applicant," can be seen to stand for corporate man. The second stanza of the poem refers back to the title poem of *The Colossus*, where the speaker's father, representative of a gigantic male other, so dominated her world that her horizon was bounded by his scattered pieces. In "Daddy," she describes him as:

> Marble-heavy, a bag full of God,
> Ghastly statue with one grey toe
> Big as a Frisco seal

> And a head in the freakish Atlantic
> Where it pours bean green over blue
> In the waters off beautiful Nauset.

Between "The Colossus" and "Daddy" there has been a movement from a mythic and natural landscape to one with social and political boundaries. Here the image of her father, grown larger than the earlier Colossus of Rhodes, stretches across and subsumes the whole of the United States, from the Pacific to the Atlantic ocean.

The next seven stanzas of "Daddy" construct the image of the Gestapo officer, using her family background—her parents were both of German origin—to mediate between her personal sense of suffocation and the social history of the Nazi invasions. The black shoe of the first stanza in which she says she has been wedged like a foot "barely daring to breathe" becomes in stanza ten, at the end of the Nazi section, a larger social image of suffocation: "Not God but a swastika / So black no sky could squeak through." The Gestapo figure recurs briefly three stanzas later as the speaker of the poem transfers the image from father to hus-

* From Pamela J. Annas, *A Disturbance in Mirrors: The Poetry of Sylvia Plath*, Contributions in Women's Studies no. 89 (New York, Westport, and London: Greenwood Press, 1988), pp. 139–43.

band and incidentally suggests that the victim has some control in a brutalized association—at least to the extent she chooses to be there.[1]

> I made a model of you,
> A man in black with a Meinkampf look
>
> And a love of the rack and the screw.
> And I said I do, I do.

The Gestapo figure becomes "Herr Professor" in stanza eleven, an actual image of Plath's father, and also an image of what has for centuries been seen as the prototypical and even ideal relationship between a man and a woman.[2] The professor, who is a man, talks and is active; the woman, who is a student, listens and is passive. A patriarchal social structure is at its purest and, superficially, at its most benign in the stereotyped relationship of male teacher and female student and is a stock romantic fantasy even in women's literature—Emma and Mr. Knightley, Lucy Snowe and the professor in *Villette*.[3] But Plath places this image between the images of Nazi/Jew and vampire/victim so that it becomes the center of a series. Indeed, the image of daddy as teacher turns almost immediately into a devil/demon/vampire:

> A cleft in your chin instead of your foot
> But no less a devil for that, no not
> Any less the black man who
>
> Bit my pretty red heart in two.

The last two stanzas of "Daddy" are like the conclusion of "Lady Lazarus" in their assertion that the speaker of the poem is breaking out of the cycle and that, in order to do so, she must turn on and kill Herr God, Herr Lucifer in the one poem, and Daddy in his final metamorphosis as vampire in the other poem. Plath explained this in Freudian terms in an introductory note to the poem for a BBC Third Programme reading:

1. See Wilhelm Reich's *The Mass Psychology of Fascism* (New York: Simon and Schuster, 1969), particularly his chapter on "The Authoritarian Personality," for an analysis of how an oppressed class can contribute to its own oppression. Judith Lewis Herman, in *Father-Daughter Incest* (Cambridge, Mass.: Harvard University Press, 1981), discusses the history of the suppression of incest beginning with Freud and continuing into contemporary psychological literature, the attribution of reports of incest to hysterical female oedipal fantasizing or, when the fact of incest is impossible to deny, assigning blame to the victim: what Herman calls the Seductive Daughter and/or the Collusive Mother (Chapter 1, "A Common Occurence"). Writing in the early 1960s and familiar with some of these attitudes, it is not surprising that Plath assigns some culpability to the victim. Herman goes on to say, "Even when the girl does give up her erotic attachment to her father, she is encouraged to persist in the fantasy that some other man, like her father, will some day take possession of her, raising her above the common lot of womankind" (p. 57).

I am not of course suggesting that Plath literally had an incestuous relationship with her father—there is no evidence one way or the other—but she does make recurrent use of father/daughter incest as a symbol for male/female relations in a patriarchal society. * * * (PJA)   2. This photograph of Otto Plath is reproduced on page 17 of *Letters Home*. (PJA)   3. [Mary] Ellmann, *Thinking About Women* [New York: Harcourt Brace Jovanovich, 1968], pp. 119–23. (PJA)

The poem is spoken by a girl with an Electra complex. The father died while she thought he was God. Her case is complicated by the fact that her father was also a Nazi and her mother very possibly part Jewish. In the daughter the two strains marry and paralyze each other—she has to act out the awful little allegory once over before she is free of it.[4]

This reenacting of the allegory becomes at the end of "Daddy" a frenzied communal ritual of exorcism.

> Daddy, you can lie back now.
>
> There's a stake in your fat black heart
> And the villagers never liked you.
> They are dancing and stamping on you.
> They always *knew* it was you.
> Daddy, daddy, you bastard, I'm through.

This cycle of victim/vampire is, left alone, a closed and repetitious cycle, like the repeated suicides of "Lady Lazarus." According to the legends and the Hollywood film versions of these legends we all grew up on, once consumed by a vampire, one dies and is reborn a vampire and preys upon others, who in their turn die and become vampires. The vampire imagery in Sylvia Plath's poetry intersects on one level with her World War II imagery and its exploitation and victimization and on another level intersects with her images of a bureaucratic, fragmented, and dead—in the sense of numbed and unaware—society. The connections are sometimes confused, but certainly World War II is often imaged in her poetry as a kind of grisly, vampiric feast. * * *

The whole of "Daddy" is an exorcism to banish the demon, put a stake through the vampire's heart, and thus break the cycle of vampire→victim. It is crucial to the poem that the exorcism is accomplished through communal action by the "villagers." The rhythm of the poem is powerfully and deliberately primitive: a child's chant, a formal curse. The hard sounds, short lines, and repeated rhymes of "do," "you," "Jew," and "through" give a hard pounding quality to the poem that is close to the sound of a heart beat. "Daddy," as well as "Lady Lazarus" and, to a lesser extent, "Fever 103°," is structured as a magical formula or incantation. In *The Colossus* poems, Plath also used poetry as a ritual incantation, but in those early poems it was most often directed toward transformation of self. By 1961, she is less often attempting to transform self into some other, but rather attempting to rid herself and her world of demons. That is, rebirth cannot occur until after the demons have been exorcised. In all three of these poems, the possibilities of the individual are very much tied to those of her society.

Purity, which is what exorcism aims at, is for Plath an ambiguous concept. On the one hand it means integrity of self, wholeness rather than fragmentation, as unspoiled state of being, rest, perfection, aesthetic beauty, and loss of self through transformation into some reborn other. On the other hand, it also

---

4. Quoted in [M. L.] Rosenthal, *The New Poets* [New York: Oxford University Press, 1967], p. 82. (PJA)

means absence, isolation, blindness, a kind of autism which shuts out the world, stasis and death, and a loss of self through dispersal into some other. In "Lady Lazarus" and "Fever 103°" the emphasis is on exorcising the poet's previous selves, though within a social context that makes that unlikely. "Daddy," however, is a purification of the world; in "Daddy" it is the various avatars of the other—the male figure who represents the patriarchal society she lives in—that are being exorcised. In all three cases, the exorcism is violent and, perhaps, provisional. Does she believe, in any of these cases, that a rebirth under such conditions is really possible, that an exorcism is truly taking place, that once the allegory is reenacted, she will be rid of it? The more the speaker of the poems defines her situation as desperate, the more violent and vengeful becomes the agent of purification and transformation. All three of these poems are retaliatory fantasies: in "Lady Lazarus" she swallows men, in "Fever 103°" she leaves them behind, in "Daddy" she kills them. * * *

STEVEN GOULD AXELROD

*Jealous Gods**

* * * [Although "Daddy"] has traditionally been read as "personal" (Aird 78)[1] or "confessional" (M. L. Rosenthal 82),[2] Margaret Homans has more recently suggested that it concerns a woman's dislocated relations to speech (*Women Writers* 220–21).[3] Plath herself introduced it on the BBC as the opposite of confession, as a constructed fiction: "Here is a poem spoken by a girl with an Electra complex. Her father died while she thought he was God. Her case is complicated by the fact that her father was also a Nazi and her mother very possibly part Jewish. In the daughter the two strains marry and paralyze each other—she has to act out the awful little allegory once over before she is free of it" (*CP* 293).[4] We might interpret this preface as an accurate retelling of the poem; or we might regard it as a case of an author's estrangement from her text, on the order of Coleridge's preface to "Kubla Khan" in which he claims to be unable to finish the poem, having forgotten what it was about. However we interpret Plath's preface, we must agree that "Daddy" is dramatic and allegorical, since its details depart freely from the facts of her biography. In this poem she again figures her unresolved conflicts with paternal authority as a textual issue. Significantly, her father was a published writer, and his successor, her husband, was also a writer. Her preface asserts that the poem concerns a young woman's paralyzing self-division, which she can defeat only through allegorical representation. Recalling that paralysis

* From Steven Gould Axelrod, *Sylvia Plath: The Wound and the Cure of Words* (Baltimore and London: Johns Hopkins University Press, 1990), pp. 51–70, 237.   1. Eileen Aird, *Sylvia Plath: Her Life and Work* (New York: Harper & Row, 1973).   2. M. L. Rosenthal, *The New Poets: American and British Poetry since World War II* (London: Oxford University Press, 1967).   3. Margaret Homans, *Women Writers and Poetic Identity: Dorothy Wordsworth, Emily Brontë, and Emily Dickinson* (Princeton: Princeton University Press, 1980).   4. *CP* = *The Collected Poems*.

was one of Plath's main tropes for literary incapacity, we begin to see that the poem evokes the female poet's anxiety of authorship and specifically Plath's strategy of delivering herself from that anxiety by making it the topic of her discourse. Viewed from this perspective, "Daddy" enacts the woman poet's struggle with "daddy-poetry." It represents her effort to eject the "buried male muse" from her invention process and the "jealous gods" from her audience (*J* 223;[5] *CP* 179).

Plath wrote "Daddy" several months after Hughes left her, on the day she learned that he had agreed to a divorce (October 12, 1962). George Brown and Tirril Harris have shown that early loss makes one especially vulnerable to subsequent loss (Bowlby 250–59),[6] and Plath seems to have defended against depression by almost literally throwing herself into her poetry. She followed "Daddy" with a host of poems that she considered her greatest achievement to date: "Medusa," "The Jailer," "Lady Lazarus," "Ariel," the bee sequence, and others. The letters she wrote to her mother and brother on the day of "Daddy," and then again four days later, brim with a sense of artistic self-discovery: "Writing like mad. . . . Terrific stuff, as if domesticity had choked me" (*LH* 466).[7] Composing at the "still blue, almost eternal hour before the baby's cry, before the glassy music of the milkman, settling his bottles" (quoted in Alvarez, *Savage God* 21),[8] she experienced an "enormous" surge in creative energy (*LH* 467). Yet she also expressed feelings of misery: "The half year ahead seems like a lifetime, and the half behind an endless hell" (*LH* 468). She was again contemplating things German: a trip to the Austrian Alps, a renewed effort to learn the language. If "German" was Randall Jarrell's "favorite country," it was not hers, yet it returned to her discourse like clock work at times of psychic distress. Clearly Plath was attempting to find and to evoke in her art what she could not find or communicate in her life. She wished to compensate for her fragmenting social existence by investing herself in her texts: "Hope, when free, to write myself out of this hole" (*LH* 466). Desperately eager to sacrifice her "flesh," which was "wasted," to her "mind and spirit," which were "fine" (*LH* 470), she wrote "Daddy" to demonstrate the existence of her voice, which had been silent or subservient for so long. She wrote it to prove her "genius" (*LH* 468).

Plath projected her struggle for textual identity onto the figure of a partly Jewish young woman who learns to express her anger at the patriarch and at his language of male mastery, which is as foreign to her as German, as "obscene" as murder (st. 6), and as meaningless as "gobbledygoo" (st. 9). The patriarch's death "off beautiful Nauset" (st. 3) recalls Plath's journal entry in which she associated the "green seaweeded water" at "Nauset Light" with "the deadness of a being . . . who no longer creates" (*J* 164). Daddy's deadness—suggesting Plath's unwillingness to let her father, her education, her library, or her husband inhibit her any longer—inspires the poem's speaker to her moment of illumination. At a basic level, "Daddy" concerns its own violent, transgressive birth as a text, its origin in

---

5. *J* = *The Journals.*   6. John Bowlby, *Attachment and Loss,* III: *Loss: Sadness and Depression* (London: Hogarth, 1980).   7. *LH* = *Letters Home.*   8. A. Alvarez, *The Savage God: A Study of Suicide* (1971; New York, Bantam, 1973).

a culture that regards it as illegitimate—a judgment the speaker hurls back on the patriarch himself when she labels *him* a bastard (st. 16). Plath's unaccommodating worldview, which was validated by much in her childhood and adult experience, led her to understand literary tradition not as an expanding universe of beneficial influence (as depicted in Eliot's "Tradition and the Individual Talent") but as a closed universe in which every addition required a corresponding subtraction—a Spencerian agon in which only the fittest survived. If Plath's speaker was to be born as a poet, a patriarch must die.

As in "The Colossus," the father here appears as a force or an object rather than as a person. Initially he takes the form of an immense "black shoe," capable of stamping on his victim (st. 1). Immediately thereafter he becomes a marble "statue" (st. 2), cousin to the monolith of the earlier poem. He then transforms into Nazi Germany (st. 6–7, 9–10), the archetypal totalitarian state. When the protagonist mentions Daddy's "boot in the face" (st. 10), she may be alluding to Orwell's comment in *1984*, "If you want a picture of the future, imagine a boot stomping on a human face—forever" (3.3). Eventually the father declines in stature from God (st. 2) to a devil (st. 11) to a dying vampire (st. 15). Perhaps he shrinks under the force of his victim's denunciation, which de-creates him as a power as it creates him as figure. But whatever his size, he never assumes human dimensions, aspirations, and relations—except when posing as a teacher in a photograph (st. 11). Like the colossus, he remains figurative and symbolic, not individual.

Nevertheless, the male figure of "Daddy" does differ significantly from that of "The Colossus." In the earlier poem, which emphasizes his lips, mouth, throat, tongue, and voice, the colossus allegorically represents the power of speech, however fragmented and resistant to the protagonist's ministrations. In the later poem Daddy remains silent, apart from the gobbledygoo attributed to him once (st. 9). He uses his mouth primarily for biting and for drinking blood. The poem emphasizes his feet and, implicitly, his phallus. He is a "black shoe" (st. 1), a statue with "one gray toe" (st. 2), a "boot" (st. 10). The speaker, estranged from him by fear, could never tell where he put his "foot," his "root" (st. 5). Furthermore, she is herself silenced by his shoe: "I never could talk to you" (st. 5). Daddy is no "male muse" (*J* 223), not even one in ruins, but frankly a male censor. His boot in the face of "every woman" is presumably lodged in her mouth (st. 10). He stands for all the elements in the literary situation and in the female ephebe's internalization of it, that prevent her from producing any words at all, even copied or subservient ones. Appropriately, Daddy can be killed only by being stamped on: he lives and dies by force, not language. If "The Colossus" tells a tale of the patriarch's speech, his grunts and brays, "Daddy" tells a tale of the daughter's effort to speak.

Thus we are led to another important difference between the two poems. The "I" of "The Colossus" acquires her identity only through serving her "father," whereas the "I" of "Daddy" actuates her gift only through opposition to him. The latter poem precisely inscribes the plot of Plath's dream novel of 1958: "a girl's search for her dead father—for an outside authority which must be developed, instead, from the inside" (*J* 258). As the child of a Nazi, the girl could "hardly speak" (st. 6), but as a Jew she begins "to talk" and to acquire an identity (st. 7). In Plath's allegory, the outsider Jew corresponds to "the rebel, the artist, the odd" (*JP* 55),[9] and particularly to the woman artist. Otto Rank's *Beyond Psychology*,[1] which had a lasting influence on her, explicitly compares women to Jews, since "woman . . . has suffered from the very beginning a fate similar to that of the Jew, namely, suppression, slavery, confinement, and subsequent persecution" (287–88). Rank, whose discourse I would consider tainted by anti-Semitism, argues that Jews speak a language of pessimistic "self-hatred" that differs essentially from the language of the majority cultures in which they find themselves (191, 281–84). He analogously, though more sympathetically, argues that woman speaks in a language different from man's, and that as a result of man's denial of woman's world, "woman's 'native tongue' has hitherto been unknown or at least unheard" (248). Although Rank's essentializing of woman's "nature" lapses into the sexist clichés of his time ("intuitive," "irrational" [249]), his idea of linguistic difference based on gender and his analogy between Jewish and female speech seem to have embedded themselves in the substructure of "Daddy" (and in many of Plath's other texts as well). For Plath, as later for Adrienne Rich, the Holocaust and the patriarchy's silencing of women were linked outcomes of the masculinist interpretation of the world. Political insurrection and female self-assertion also interlaced symbolically. In "Daddy," Plath's speaker finds her voice and motive by identifying herself as antithetical to her Fascist father. Rather than getting the colossus "glued" and properly jointed, she wishes to stick herself "together with glue" (st. 13), an act that seems to require her father's dismemberment. Previously devoted to the patriarch—both in "The Colossus" and in memories evoked in "Daddy" of trying to "get back" to him (st. 12)—she now seeks only to escape from him and to see him destroyed.

Plath has unleashed the anger, normal in mourning as well as in revolt, that she suppressed in the earlier poem. But she has done so at a cost. Let us consider her childlike speaking voice. The language of "Daddy," beginning with its title, is often regressive. The "I" articulates herself by moving backward in time, using the language of nursery rhymes and fairy tales (the little old woman who lived in a shoe, the black man of the forest). Such language accords with a child's conception of the world, not an adult's. Plath's assault on the language of "daddy-poetry" has turned inward, on the language of her own poem, which teeters precariously on the edge of a preverbal abyss—represented by the eerie, keening "oo" sound with which a majority of the verses end. And then let us consider the play on "through" at the poem's conclusion. Although that last line allows for multiple readings, one interpretation is that the "I" has unconsciously carried out her father's wish: her discourse, by transforming itself into cathartic oversimplifications, has undone itself.

Yet the poem does contain its verbal violence by means more productive than silence. In a letter to her brother, Plath referred to "Daddy" as "gruesome" (*LH*

9. *JP* = *Johnny Panic and the Bible of Dreams.*   1. Otto Rank, *Beyond Psychology* (Baltimore: Johns Hopkins University Press, 1990).

472), while on almost the same day she described it to A. Alvarez as a piece of "light verse" (Alvarez, *Beyond* 56).[2] She later read it on the BBC in a highly ironic tone of voice. The poem's unique spell derives from its rhetorical complexity: its variegated and perhaps bizarre fusion of the horrendous and the comic. As Uroff has remarked, it both shares and remains detached from the fixation of its protagonist (159).[3] The protagonist herself seems detached from her own fixation. She is "split in the most complex fashion," as Plath wrote of Ivan Karamazov[4] in her Smith College honors thesis. Plath's speaker uses potentially self-mocking melodramatic terms to describe both her opponent ("so black no sky could squeak through" [st. 10]) and herself ("poor and white" [st. 1]). While this aboriginal speaker quite literally expresses black-and-white thinking, her civilized double possesses a sensibility sophisticated enough to subject such thinking to irony. Thus the poem expresses feelings that it simultaneously parodies—it may be parodying the very idea of feeling. The tension between erudition and simplicity in the speaker's voice appears in her pairings that juxtapose adult with childlike diction: "breathe or Achoo," "your Luftewaffe, your gobbledygoo" (st. 1, 9). She can expound such adult topics as Taroc packs, Viennese beer, and Tyrolean snowfall; can specify death camps by name; and can employ an adult vocabulary of "recover," "ancestress," "Aryan," *"Meinkampf,"* "obscene," and "bastard." Yet she also has recourse to a more primitive lexicon that includes "chuffing," "your fat black heart," and "my pretty red heart." She proves herself capable of careful intellectual discriminations ("so I never could tell" [st. 5]), conventionalized description ("beautiful Nauset" [st. 3]), and moral analogy ("if I've killed one man, I've killed two" [st. 15], while also exhibiting regressive fantasies (vampires), repetitions ("wars, wars, wars" [st. 4]), and inarticulateness ("panzer-man, panzer-man, O You—" [st. 9]). She oscillates between calm reflection ("You stand at the blackboard, daddy, / In the picture I have of you" [st. 11]) and mad incoherence ("Ich, ich, ich, ich" [st. 6]). Her sophisticated language puts her wild language in an ironic perspective, removing the discourse from the control of the archaic self who understands experience only in extreme terms.

The ironies in "Daddy" proliferate in unexpected ways, however. When the speaker proclaims categorically that "every woman adores a Fascist" (st. 10), she is subjecting her victimization to irony by suggesting that sufferers choose, or at least accommodate themselves to, their suffering. But she is also subjecting her authority to irony, since her claim about "every woman" is transparently false. It simply parodies patriarchal commonplaces, such as those advanced by Helene Deutsch concerning "feminine masochism" (192–99, 245–85).[5] The adult, sophisticated self seems to be speaking here: Who else would have the confidence to make a sociological generalization? Yet the content of the assertion, if taken straightforwardly, returns us to the regressive self who is dominated by extravagant emotions she cannot begin to understand. Plath's mother wished that Plath

2. A. Alvarez, *Beyond All This Fiddle* (London: Allen Lane–Penguin, 1968).   3. Margaret Dickie Uroff, *Sylvia Plath and Ted Hughes* (Urbana: University of Illinois Press, 1979).   4. A character in Fyodor Dostoyevsky's novel *The Brothers Karamazov*, who suffers debilitating guilt for having wished for his father's death.   5. Helen Deutsch, *The Psychology of Women*, I: *Girlhood* (1944; repr. New York: Bantam, 1973).

would write about "decent, courageous people" (*LH* 477), and she herself heard an inner voice demanding that she be a perfect "paragon" in her language and feeling (*J* 176). But in the speaker of "Daddy," she inscribed the opposite of such a paragon: a divided self whose veneer of civilization is breached and infected by unhealthy instincts.

Plath's irony cuts both ways. At the same time that the speaker's sophisticated voice undercuts her childish voice, reducing its melodrama to comedy, the childish or maddened voice undercuts the pretensions of the sophisticated voice, revealing the extremity of suffering masked by its ironies. While demonstrating the inadequacy of thinking and feeling in opposites, the poem implies that such a mode can locate truths denied more complex cognitive and affective systems. The very moderation of the normal adult intelligence, its tolerance of ambiguity, its defenses against the primal energies of the id, results in falsification. Reflecting Schiller's idea that the creative artist experiences a "momentary and passing madness" (quoted by Freud in a passage of *The Interpretation of Dreams* [193][6] that Plath underscored), "Daddy" gives voice to that madness. Yet the poem's sophisticated awareness, its comic vision, probably wins out in the end, since the poem concludes by curtailing the power of its extreme discourse * * *. Furthermore, Plath distanced herself from the poem's aboriginal voice by introducing her text as "a poem spoken by a girl with an Electra complex"—that is, as a study of the *girl's* pathology rather than her father's—and as an allegory that will "free" her from that pathology. She also distanced herself by reading the poem in a tone that emphasized its irony. And finally, she distanced herself by laying the poem's wild voice permanently to rest after October. The aboriginal vision was indeed purged. "Daddy" represents not Dickinson's madness that is divinest sense, but rather an entry into a style of discourse and a mastery of it. The poem realizes the trope of suffering by means of an inherent irony that both questions and validates the trope in the same gestures, and that finally allows the speaker to conclude the discourse and to remove herself from the trope with a sense of completion rather than wrenching, since the irony was present from the very beginning.

Plath's poetic revolt in "Daddy" liberated her pent-up creativity, but the momentary success sustained her little more than self-sacrifice had done. "Daddy" became another stage in her development, an unrepeatable experiment, a vocal opening that closed itself at once. The poem is not only an elegy for the power of "daddy-poetry" but for the powers of speech Plath discovered in composing it.

When we consider "Daddy" generically, a further range of implications presents itself. Although we could profitably consider the poem as the dramatic monologue Plath called it in her BBC broadcast, let us regard it instead as the kind of poem most readers have taken it to be: a domestic poem. I have chosen this term, rather than M. L. Rosenthal's better-known "confessional poem" or the more neutral "autobiographical poem," because "confessional poem" implies

6. Sigmund Freud, *The Interpretation of Dreams*, ed. James Strachey, Standard Edition, IV (1900; New York: Norton, 1976).

a confession rather than a making (though Steven Hoffman[7] and Lawrence Kramer[8] have recently indicated the mode's conventions) and because "autobiographical poem" is too general for our purpose. I shall define the domestic poem as one that represents and comments on a protagonist's relationship to one or more family members, usually a parent, child, or spouse. To focus our discussion even further, I shall emphasize poetry that specifically concerns a father.

* * *

* * * In the 1950s the "domestic poem" proper appeared on the scene, with its own conventions and expectations, and with its own complex cultural and literary reasons for being. Perhaps the precursive poems made the genre's eventual flowering inevitable, while its precise timing depended on a reaction against modernism's aesthetic of impersonality. Theodore Roethke wrote several early poems that initiated the genre: "My Papa's Waltz" (1948), "The Lost Son" (1948), and "Where Knock Is Open Wide" (1951). Lowell's "Life Studies" sequence (1959) was, and is, the genre's most prominent landmark. Other poems in the genre include John Berryman's *The Dream Songs* (1969); Frank Bidart's "Golden State" (1973) and "Confessional" (1983); Robert Duncan's "My Mother Would Be a Falconress" (1968); Allen Ginsberg's *Kaddish* (1960); Randall Jarrell's "The Lost World" (1965); Maxine Kumin's "The Thirties Revisited" (1975), "My Father's Neckties" (1978), and "Marianne, My Mother, and Me" (1989); Stanley Kunitz's "Father and Son" (1958) and "The Testing Tree" (1971); Lowell's "To Mother" (1977), "Robert T. S. Lowell" (1977), and "Unwanted" (1977); James Merrill's "Scenes of Childhood" (1962); Adrienne Rich's "After Dark" (1966); Anne Sexton's "Division of the Parts" (1960) and "The Death of the Fathers" (1972); W. D. Snodgrass' "Heart's Needle" (1959); Diane Wakoski's "The Father of My Country" (1968); and of course Sylvia Plath's "Daddy" (1962). In all these poems, the parent-child relationship serves as a locus for psychological investigation. In many of them it also serves as a means of representing the acquisition of poetic identity and of exploring the bounds of textuality itself. Because later writers were conscious of the Roethke-Lowell domestic poem as at least a genre in embryo, they chose to use its features, or perhaps the power of the genre was such that the features chose them. The "domestic poem" became a system of signs in which each individual text's adherence to the system and deviations within the system produced its particular literary meaning.

* * *

In 1959 Plath did not consciously attempt to write in the domestic poem genre, perhaps because she was not yet ready to assume her majority. Her journal entries of that period bristle with an impatience at herself that may derive from this reluctance. She may have feared asserting her "I am I am I am," which

7. Steven Hoffman, "Impersonal Personalism: The Making of a Confessional Poetic," *English Literary History* 45 (Winter 1978): 687–709.   8. Lawrence Kramer, "Freud and the Skunks: Genre and Language in *Life Studies*," in *Robert Lowell: Essays on the Poetry*, ed. Steven Gould Axelrod and Helen Deese (New York: Cambridge University Press, 1986).

seemed to carry with it a countervailing impulse of self-retribution. But by fall 1962, when she had already lost so much, she was ready to chance tackling poetic tradition, and specifically her chief male instructors, Roethke and Lowell. In "Daddy" she achieved her victory in two ways. First, as we have seen, she symbolically assaults a father figure who is identified with male control of language. All her anxiety of influence comes to the fore in the poem: her sense of belatedness, her awareness of constraint, her fears of inadequacy, her furious need to overcome her dependency, her guilt at her own aggressivity. Since the precursors "do not do / Any more" (st. 1), she wishes to escape their paralyzing influence and to empty the "bag full of God" that has kept her tongue stuck in her jaw for so long (st. 2, 5). The father whose power she attacks is not simply Roethke or Lowell, or even Hughes or Otto Plath, but a literary character who includes reference to all of them as categories of masculine authority. Although the Daddy of poetry has already "died" (st. 2)—the fate of all published texts in Plath's postromantic perspective—the speaker must symbolically "kill" him from her own discourse. The poem ironically depicts poetry as both an aggression and a suicide. The female ephebe herself becomes a "brute" in the act of voicing (st. 10), just as have her teachers before her. But the aggression of her speech yields to the self-annihilation of language. By the end of the poem she too, like her male precursors, is "through." The speaker's textual life will be misread on innumerable occasions in innumerable ways, whereas her own misreading and miswriting of the precursors is finished. In its conclusion, the poem acknowledges its alienation from itself, confessing the transitoriness of its unbounded power.

In addition to killing the father in its fictional plot, the poem seeks to discredit the forefathers through its status as poetic act. Taking a genre established by Roethke and Lowell, "Daddy" fundamentally alters it through antithesis and parody. Like all strong poems, it transforms its genre and therefore the way we perceive the precursive examples, making them seem not fulfillments but anticipations. Thus the later work projects its anxiety retrospectively back through its predecessors. Haunted by fears of inadequacy and redundancy, it seeks to make the earlier poems seem incompetent by comparison—a kind of juvenilia in the career of the genre, to represent the final possible stroke, or at the very least to inaugurate some new and important genre, of which the whole domestic genre was but a foreshadowing.

This point comes clearer if we compare "Daddy" with two analogues, Roethke's "The Lost Son" (1948) and Lowell's "Commander Lowell" (1959). In the Freudian drama of "The Lost Son," the protagonist subjectively relives his childhood fears and fantasies. Like the speaker of the companion piece, "My Papa's Waltz," he is still enmeshed in the family romance, remembering the father ambivalently as powerful, protective, and threatening. After locating himself at his father's grave, where he feels both grief and estrangement (in a scene that adumbrates "Electra on Azalea Path"), he descends into his unconscious, seeking, as Roethke later explained, "some clue to existence" (*Poet* 38).[9] He

---

9. *On the Poet and His Craft: Selected Prose of Theodore Roethke*, ed. Ralph J. Mills, Jr. (Seattle and London: University of Washington Press, 1965).

encounters his death wish, his memory of his father as "Father Fear," his sexual anxieties, and finally the "dark swirl" of a blackout, after which a childhood memory of his "Papa" shouting "order" in German returns him to consciousness. Although the figure of "Papa" blends earthly and heavenly father (*Poet* 39), he also symbolizes the superego, restoring order to a psyche and a poem that had fallen into chaos. At the poem's conclusion, as the "lost son" waits for his "understandable spirit" to revive, he appears to be purged, though not cured, of the conflicts that incapacitated him.

The speaker of "Commander Lowell," in contrast, is objective, precise, and witty. His discourse reflects a detached perspective on the past rather than a psychic reimmersion in it. He portrays his father as one who threatened him only through weakness. This father "was nothing to shout / about to the summer colony at 'Matt' "; took "four shots with his putter to sink his putt"; sang "Anchors Aweigh" in the bathtub; was fired from his job; and squandered his inheritance. Whereas Roethke's poem represents a cathartic experience, Lowell's converts chaotic feelings into intellectual irony. Whereas Roethke's poem can be read as an allegory of man's relationship to God or as a model of the Freudian psyche, Lowell's remains a realistic narrative, though it does suggest the cultural and financial decline of a social class.

Plath's poem combines features of both of these precursors: Roethke's evocation of a German-speaking authoritarian with Lowell's sarcastic deflation of a man without qualities; Roethke's subjective anguish with Lowell's social comedy. Like Roethke's Papa, Plath's title character is an intimidating patriarch; like Lowell's Father, he is a buffoon ("big as a Frisco seal"). Finally, Plath's poem, like those of her predecessors, has little to do with psychological cure: the speaker's defenses remain in place. But in a deeper sense, "Daddy" swerves sharply from its precursors, curtailing their power. It turns the psychological depth of Roethke's poem and the ironically detached surface of Lowell's poem into a fury of denunciation, an extravagance of emotion, an exaggeration of acts and effects, perhaps revealing the subtexts of both precursors. If in a sense the texts by Roethke and Lowell constitute what Ned Lukacher[1] might term the primal scene of "Daddy," the latter poem's raw intensity succeeds in reversing the relationship, making itself resemble *their* primal scene. It unmasks Roethke's implicitly oppressive father figure as a monster and Lowell's sophisticated comedy as slapstick. It transforms the domestic genre alternately into a horror show, encapsulating every political, cultural, and familial atrocity of the age, and a theater of cruelty, evoking nervous laughter. "Daddy" takes the genre as far as it can go—and then further.

* * *

1. Ned Lukacher, *Primal Scenes: Literature, Philosophy, Psychoanalysis* (Ithaca and London: Cornell University Press, 1986).

Evaluating Poetry

How do you know a good poem when you see one? This is not an easy question to answer—partly because deciding about the *value* of poems is a complex, difficult, and often lengthy process, and partly because there is no single and absolute criterion that will measure texts and neatly divide the good from the not so good. People who long for a nice, infallible sorter—some test that will automatically pick out the best poems and distinguish variations of quality much as a litmus test separates acids from bases—often are frustrated at what they perceive to be the "relativity" of judgment in evaluating poems. But because an issue is complex does not mean it is impossible, and even if there is no easy and absolute standard to be discovered, there are nevertheless distinctions to be made. Some poems are better—that is, more consistently effective with talented and experienced readers—than others. Even if we cannot sensibly rate poems on a 1-to-10 scale or universally agree on the excellence of a single poem, it is possible to set out some criteria that are helpful to readers who may not yet have developed confidence in their own judgments. It isn't necessary, of course, to spend all of our time asking about quality and being judgmental about poetry. But because life isn't long enough to read everything, it is often useful to separate those poems that are likely to be worth your time from those that aren't. Besides, the process of sorting—in which you begin to articulate your own judgments and poetic values—can be a very useful strategy in making yourself a better reader and a more informed, better-educated, and wiser person. Evaluating poems can be, among other things, a way to learn more about yourself, for what you like in poetry has a lot to say about where your own values really lie.

> *Poetry is a language that tells us, through a more or less emotional reaction, something that cannot be said.*
>
> —EDWIN ARLINGTON ROBINSON

"I like it." That simple, unreflective statement about a poem is often a way to begin the articulation of standards—as long as your next move is to ask yourself why. Answers to *why* are often, at first, quite simple, even for experienced and sophisticated readers. "I like the way it sounds" or "I like its rhythm and pace" might be good, if partial, reasons for liking a poem. The popularity of nursery rhymes and simple childish ditties, or even the haunting, predictable, and repeated sounds and phrases of a poem like "The Raven" owe a lot (if not necessarily everything) to the use of sound. Another frequent answer might be: "because it is true" or "because I agree with what it says." All of us are apt to like sentiments or ideas that resemble our own more than those that challenge or disturb us, though bad formulations of some idea we treasure, like bad behavior in someone we love, can sometimes be more embarrassing than comforting. But the longer we struggle with our reasons for liking a poem, the more complex and revealing our answers are likely to be: "I like the *way* it expresses something I had thought but had never quite been able to articulate." "I like the way its sounds and rhythms imitate the sounds of what is being described." "I like the way it presents conflicting emotions, balancing negative and positive feelings that seem to exist at the same time in about equal intensity." "I like its precision in describing just how something like that affects a person." Such statements as "I like . . ." begin quietly to cross the border into the area of "I admire," and to include a second clause, beginning with "because" and offering complex reasons for that admiration, is to begin to move into the process of critical evaluation.

What kinds of reasons might we expect different readers to agree on? *Groups* of readers might well agree on certain ideas—questions of politics or economics or religion, for example—but not readers across the board. More likely to generate consensus are technical criteria, questions of craft. How precise are the word choices at crucial moments in the poem? How rich, suggestive, and resonant are the words that open up the poem to larger statements and claims? How appropriate are the metaphors and other figures of speech? How original and imaginative? How carefully is the poem's situation set up? How clearly? How full and appropriate is the characterization of the speaker? How well matched are the speaker, situation, and setting with the poem's sentiments and ideas? How consistent is the poem's tone? How appropriate to its themes? How carefully worked out is the poem's structure? How appropriate to the desired effects are the line breaks, the stanza breaks, and the pattern of rhythms and sounds?

One way of seeing how good a poem is in its various aspects is to look at what it is not—to consider the choices *not* made by the poet. Often it is possible to consider what a poem would be like if a different artistic choice had been made, as a way of seeing the importance of the choice actually made. What if, for example, Sylvia Plath had described a black *crow* in rainy weather instead of a rook? What if William Carlos Williams had described a *white* wheelbarrow? Sometimes we have the benefit, if we have a working manuscript or an autobiographical account of composition, of actually watching the process of selection. Look again, for example, at the several drafts of the first stanza of Richard Wilbur's "Love Calls Us to the Things of This World":

(a) My eyes came open to the squeak of pulleys
My spirit, shocked from the brothel of itself

(b) My eyes came open to the shriek of pulleys,
And the soul, spirited from its proper wallow,
Hung in the air as bodiless and hollow

(c) My eyes came open to the pulleys' cry.
The soul, spirited from its proper wallow,
Hung in the air as bodiless and hollow
As light that frothed upon the wall opposing;
But what most caught my eyes at their unclosing
Was two gray ropes that yanked across the sky.
One after one into the window frame
. . . the hosts of laundry came

(d)   The eyes open to a cry of pulleys,
And the soul, so suddenly spirited from sleep,
As morning sunlight frothing on the floor,

While just outside the window
The air is solid with a dance of angels.

(e)   The eyes open to a cry of pulleys,
And spirited from sleep, the astounded soul
Hangs for a moment bodiless and simple
As dawn light in the moment of its breaking:
    Outside the open window
The air is crowded with a

(f)   The eyes open to a cry of pulleys,
And spirited from sleep, the astounded soul
Hangs for a moment bodiless and simple
As false dawn
    Outside the open window,
Their air is leaping with a rout of angels.
    Some are in bedsheets, some are in dresses,
    it does not seem to matter

Notice how much more appropriate to the total poem is the choice of "cry" over "shriek" or "squeak" to describe the sound of pulleys or how much more effective than the metaphor of a spirit's "brothel" is the image of the soul hanging "bodiless." Notice the things Wilbur excised from the early drafts as well as the things he added when the poem became more clear and more of a piece in his mind. Do you think all the revisions improve on the original? in what specific way? What are your criteria for deciding? Do any of the revisions seem pointless to you—or (worse) make the poem less than it was? On what basis did you make the evaluation?

Let's look again at one of the first poems we discussed, Adrienne Rich's "Aunt Jennifer's Tigers" (page 628). Some of the power of this poem comes from the poet's clear and sympathetic engagement with Aunt Jennifer's situation, but the effects are carefully generated through a series of specific technical choices. Rich herself may or may not have made all these choices consciously; her later comments on the poem suggest that her creative instincts, as well as her then-repressed sense of gender, may have governed some decisions more fully than her own deliberate calculations. But however conscious, the choices of speaker, situation, metaphor, and connotative words work brilliantly together to create a strong feminist statement, almost a manifesto on the subject of mastery and compliance, even while (at the same time) making powerful assertions about the power of art to overcome human circumstances.

In a sense there is no speaker in this poem, no specified personality—only a faceless niece who observes the central character—but the effacing of this speaker in the light of the vivid Jennifer amounts to a brilliant artistic decision. Jennifer, powerless to articulate and possibly even to understand her own plight, nevertheless is allowed almost to speak for herself, primarily through her hands. The seeming refusal of the narrator to do more than simply describe Jennifer's hands and their product gives Jennifer the crucial central role; she is the center of attention throughout, and the poem emphasizes only what one sees, with little apparent "editorial" comment (though the speaker does make three evaluative statements, saying that Jennifer was "mastered" by her ordeals [line 10], and noting that her hands are "terrified" [line 9] and that the wedding band "sits heavily" [line 9] on one of them). The tigers are ultimately more eloquent than the speaker seems to be: they "prance" (lines 1 and 12) and "pace" (line 4), and they are "proud" (line 12) and unafraid of men (lines 3 and 12), embodying the guarded message Jennifer sends to the world even though she herself is "mastered" and "ringed" (line 10). The brightly conceived colors in the tapestry, the expressive description of Jennifer's fingers and hands (note especially the excitement implied in "fluttering" [line 5]), and the action of the panel itself combine with the characterization of Jennifer to present a strong statement of generational repression—and boldness. The image of knitting as art, suggestive of the way the classical Fates determine the future and the nature of things, also hints at what is involved in Rich's art. The quality of the poem lies in the care, precision, and imaginativeness of Rich's craftsmanship. In later years, Rich has become clearer and more vocal about her values, but the direction and intensity of her vision are already apparent in this excellent poem taken from her first book, published nearly half a century ago.

Here is another celebrated poem that similarly accomplishes a great deal in a short space:

WILLIAM SHAKESPEARE

[*Th' expense of spirit in a waste of shame*]

Th' expense[1] of spirit in a waste[2] of shame
Is lust in action; and, till action, lust
Is perjured, murderous, bloody, full of blame,
Savage, extreme, rude, cruel, not to trust;
Enjoyed no sooner but despisèd straight: 5
Past reason hunted; and no sooner had,
Past reason hated, as a swallowed bait,
On purpose laid to make the taker mad:
Mad in pursuit, and in possession so;
Had, having, and in quest to have, extreme;   10
A bliss in proof;[3] and proved, a very woe;
Before, a joy proposed; behind, a dream.
All this the world well knows; yet none knows well
To shun the heaven that leads men to this hell.   1609

Here the speaker *is* fully characterized, and the economical skill with which the characterization is achieved is one of the most striking aspects of the poem. The poem sets up its situation carefully and, at first, not altogether clearly. But the delay in clarity is functional: we do not know for a while just what disturbs the speaker so much, except that it has to do with "lust in action" (line 2). What we do know quickly is how powerful his feeling is. The two explosive *p*'s in the first half of the first line get the poem off to a fast and powerful start, and by the fourth line the speaker has listed nine separate unpleasant human characteristics driven by lust. He virtually spits them out. Here is one angry speaker, and it swiftly becomes clear that he is speaking from (undescribed) personal experience.

But the poem is not only angry and negative about lust. It also admits that there are

---

1. Expending.   2. Using up; also, desert.   3. In the act.

definite, and powerful, pleasures in lust: it is "enjoyed" (line 5) at the time ("a bliss in proof," line 11), and anticipated with pleasure ("a joy proposed," line 12). Such inconsistencies (or at least complexities) in the speaker's opinion are characteristic of the poem. Everything about his views, and according to him about lust itself, is "extreme" (line 10). There are no easy conclusions about lust in the first twelve lines of the poem, just a confusing movement back and forth between positives and negatives. The powerful condemnation of lust in the beginning—detailed in terms of how it makes people feel about themselves and how it affects their actions—quickly shifts into admissions of pleasure and joy, but then shifts back again. No opinion sticks for long. The only consistent thing about the speaker's feelings is his certainty of lust's power—to drive individuals to behavior that they may love or hate. Only at the end is there any kind of reasoned conclusion, and the "moral" is hardly comforting: everybody knows what I've been saying, the speaker says, and yet nobody knows how to avoid lust and its consequences because its pleasures are so sensational, both in prospect and in actual experience ("the heaven that leads men to this hell").

The vacillation of the speaker's opinions and moods is not the only confusing thing about the poem's organization. His account of lust repeatedly skips around in time. Are we talking here about lust at the time it is being satisfied ("lust in action")? Or are we talking about desire and anticipation? Or are we talking about what happens afterward? The answer is all three, and the discussion is hardly systematic. The first line and a half describe the present, and the meter of the first line even imitates the rhythms and force of male ejaculation: note how the basic iambic-pentameter strategy of the poem does not regularize until near the end of the second line. But soon we are talking about what happens before lust in action ("till action," line 2), and by line 5, after. Lines 6 and 7 contrast before and after, and line 9 compares before and during. Line 10 describes all three positions in time ("Had, having, and in quest to have"). Line 11 compares during and after, line 12 before and after. The poem, or rather the speaker, does not seem able to decide exactly what he wants to talk about and what he thinks of his subject.

> *Poems may or may not follow classical patterns—they explode out of everyday experience.*
>
> —DOROTHY LIVESAY

All this shifting around in focus and in feelings could easily be regarded as a serious flaw. Don't we expect a short poem, and especially a sonnet, to be very carefully organized and carefully focused toward a single end? Shouldn't the poet make up his mind about what he thinks and what the poem is about? It would be easy to construct an argument, on the basis of consistency or clarity of purpose, that this is not a very good poem, that perhaps the greatest poet in the English language was not, here, at the top of his form. But doing so would ignore the power of the poem's effects and underrate another principle of consistency—that of character. If we regard the poem as representative of a mind wrestling with the complex feelings brought about by lust—someone out of control because of lust, conscious enough to see his plight but unable to do anything about it—we can see a higher consistency here that helps explain the poem's powerful effect on many readers. Here is an account of a human mind grappling with an often-repeated human experience, the subject of many much longer works of literature. Lust is beautiful but terrifying, certainly to be avoided but impossible to avoid. Shakespeare has managed, in the unlikely space of fourteen lines and in a form in which we expect tight organization and intense focus, to portray succinctly the human recognition of confusion and powerlessness in the face of a passion larger than our ability to control it.

Here is another poem that is something of a challenge to evaluate:

JOHN DONNE

Song

Go, and catch a falling star,
   Get with child a mandrake root,[4]
Tell me, where all past years are,
   Or who cleft the devil's foot,
5   Teach me to hear mermaids singing
Or to keep off envy's stinging,
       And find
       What wind
Serves to advance an honest mind.

10   If thou beest born to strange sights,[5]
   Things invisible to see,
Ride ten thousand days and nights,
   Till age snow white hairs on thee;
Thou, when thou return'st, wilt tell me
15   All strange wonders that befell thee,
       And swear
       No where
Lives a woman true, and fair.

If thou find'st one, let me know:
20   Such a pilgrimage were sweet.
Yet do not, I would not go,
   Though at next door we might meet:
Though she were true when you met her,
And last till you write your letter,
25   Yet she
     Will be
False, ere I come, to two, or three.   1633

One immediate problem to confront here is the irregular, jerky rhythm. In a poem called "Song," we are likely to expect music, harmony, something pleasant and (within limits) predictable in its rhythm and movement. But this "song" is nothing like that. At first its message sounds lyrical and romantic: to go and catch a falling star is, if impossible, a romantic thing to propose, a motif that often comes up (and has for centuries) in love poems and popular songs; and lines 3 and 5 propose similar traditional romantic activities that evoke wonder and pleasure in contemplation. But the activities suggested in the alternate lines (2, 4, and 6) contrast sharply; they are just as bold in their unromantic or antiromantic sentiments. Making a mandrake root pregnant does not sound like an especially pleasant male activity, however much such a root may look like a female body, and knowledge of the devil's cleft foot or envy's stinging are not usually the stuff of romantic poems or songs. Besides, the strange interruptions of easy rhythm (indicated

---

4. The forked mandrake root looks vaguely human.   5. That is, if you have supernatural powers.

by commas) in otherwise pleasant lines like 1 and 3 suggest that something less than lyrical is going on there, too.

By the time we get to the last stanza, what is going on is a lot clearer. We have here a portrait of an angry and disillusioned man who is obsessed with the infidelity of women. He is talking to another man, apparently someone who has far more positive, perhaps even romantic, notions of women, and the poem is a kind of argument, except that the disillusioned speaker does all the talking. He pretends to take into account some traditional romantic rhetoric but turns it all on its head, intermixing the traditional impossible quests of lovers with a quest of his own—to find a "woman true, and fair" (line 18). But he knows cynically—he would probably say from experience, though he offers no evidence of his experience and no account of why he feels the way he does— that all these quests are impossible. The speaker is a bitter man, and the song he sings wants nothing to do with love or romance.

If we were to evaluate this "song" on the basis of harmonic and romantic expecta- tions, looking for evenness of rhythms, pleasant sounds, and an attractive series of images consonant with romantic attitudes, we would certainly find it wanting. But again (as with the Shakespeare poem above) a larger question of appropriateness begs to be applied. Do the sounds, tone, images, and organization of the poem "work" in terms of the speaker portrayed here and the kind of artistic project this poem represents? The displeasure we feel in the speaker's words, images, feelings, and attitudes ultimately needs to be directed toward the speaker; the poet has done a good job of portraying a character whose bitterness, however generated, is unpleasant and off-putting. The poem "works" on its own terms. We may or may not like to hear attitudes like this expressed in a poem; we may or may not approve of using a pretended "song" to mouth such sentiments. But whether or not we "like" the poem in terms of what it says, we can evaluate, through close analysis of its several different elements (much as we have been doing analytically in earlier chapters), how *well* it does what it does. There are, of course, still larger questions of whether what it tries to do is worth doing, and readers of different philosophical or political persuasions may differ widely in their opinions and evaluations of that matter.

Different people do admire different things, and when we talk about criteria for eval- uating poetry, we are talking about, at best, elements that a fairly large number of people have, over a long period of time, agreed on as important. There may be substantial agreement about political or social values in a particular group, and a consensus may exist within a group of, say, misogynists or feminists about the value of such a poem as Donne's "Song." But more general agreements that bridge social and ideological divi- sions are more likely to involve the kinds of matters that have come up for analysis in earlier chapters, matters involving how well a poem *works,* how well it uses the resources it has within its conceptual limits. For some readers, ideology is everything, and there is no such thing as quality beyond political views or moral conclusions. But for others, different, more pluralistic evaluations can be made about accomplishment and quality. You need to decide on your own criteria.

Consistency. Appropriateness. Coherence. Effectiveness. Such terms are likely to be key ones for most readers in making their evaluations—as they have been in this discus- sion. But individual critics or readers will often have their own emphases, their own highly personal preferences, their own axes to grind. For some critics in past genera- tions, *organic unity* was the key to all evaluation, whether a poem achieved, like some- thing grown in nature, a wholeness of conception and effect. For others, the key term may be *tension* or *ambiguity* or *complexity* or *simplicity* or *authenticity* or *cultural truth* or *representation* or *psychological accuracy.* With experience, you will develop your own set of criteria that may or may not involve a single ruling concept or term. But wherever (and whenever) you come out, you will learn something about yourself and your values in the process of articulating exactly what you like and admire—and why.

IRVING LAYTON

Street Funeral

Tired of chewing
the flesh
of other animals;
Tired of subreption and conceit;
of the child's   5
bewildered conscience
fretting the sly man;
Tired of holding down
a job; of giving insults,
taking insults;   10
Of excited fornication,
failing heart valves,
septic kidneys . . .

This frosty morning,
the coffin wood bursting   15
into brilliant flowers,
Is he glad
that after all the lecheries,
betrayals, subserviency,
After all the lusts,   20
false starts, evasions
he can begin
the unobstructed change
into clean grass
Done forever   25
with the insult
of birth,
the long adultery
with illusion?   1956

GALWAY KINNELL

Blackberry Eating

I love to go out in late September
among the fat, overripe, icy, black blackberries

to eat blackberries for breakfast,
the stalks very prickly, a penalty
they earn for knowing the black art   5
of blackberry-making; and as I stand among them
lifting the stalks to my mouth, the ripest berries
fall almost unbidden to my tongue,
as words sometimes do, certain peculiar words
like *strengths* or *squinched*,   10
many-lettered, one-syllabled lumps,
which I squeeze, squinch open, and splurge well
in the silent, startled, icy, black language
of blackberry-eating in late September.   1980

EMILY DICKINSON

[*The Brain—is wider than the Sky—*]

The Brain—is wider than the Sky—
For—put them side by side—
The one the other will contain
With ease—and You—beside—

The Brain is deeper than the sea—   5
For—hold them—Blue to Blue—
The one the other will absorb—
As Sponges—Buckets—do—

The Brain is just the weight of God—
For—Heft them—Pound for Pound—   10
And they will differ—if they do—
As Syllable from Sound—

ca. 1862

CHIDIOCK TICHBORNE

Elegy

My prime of youth is but a frost of cares,
    My feast of joy is but a dish of pain,
My crop of corn is but a field of tares,
    And all my good is but vain hope of gain;
        The day is past, and yet I saw no sun,   5
        And now I live, and now my life is done.

My tale was heard and yet it was not told,
   My fruit is fallen and yet my leaves are green,
My youth is spent and yet I am not old,
10   I saw the world and yet I was not seen;
       My thread is cut and yet it is not spun,
       And now I live, and now my life is done.

I sought my death and found it in my womb,
   I looked for life and saw it was a shade,
15   I trod the earth and knew it was my tomb,
     And now I die, and now I was but made;
       My glass[6] is full, and now my glass is run,
       And now I live, and now my life is done.

1586

JOHN CROWE RANSOM

Bells for John Whiteside's Daughter

There was such speed in her little body,
And such lightness in her footfall,
It is no wonder her brown study[7]
Astonishes us all.

5 Her wars were bruited in our high window.
We looked among orchard trees and beyond
Where she took arms against her shadow,
Or harried unto the pond

The lazy geese, like a snow cloud
10 Dripping their snow on the green grass,
Tricking and stopping, sleepy and proud,
Who cried in goose, Alas,

For the tireless heart within the little
Lady with rod that made them rise
15 From their noon apple-dreams and scuttle
Goose-fashion under the skies!

But now go the bells, and we are ready,
In one house we are sternly stopped
To say we are vexed at her brown study,
20 Lying so primly propped.

1924

---

6. Hourglass.   7. Stillness, as if in meditation or deep thought.

ALICE WALKER

Revolutionary Petunias

Sammy Lou of Rue
sent to his reward
the exact creature who
murdered her husband,
using a cultivator's hoe   5
with verve and skill;
and laughed fit to kill
in disbelief
at the angry, militant
pictures of herself   10
the Sonneteers quickly drew:
not any of them people that
she knew.
A backwoods woman
her house was papered with   15
funeral home calendars and
faces appropriate for a Mississippi
Sunday School. She raised a George,
a Martha, a Jackie and a Kennedy. Also
a John Wesley Junior   20
"Always respect the word of God,"
she said on her way to she didn't
know where, except it would be by
electric chair, and she continued
"Don't yall forget to *water*   25
my purple petunias."   1973

QUESTIONS

1. What seems to you the most important single factor in whether you like or dislike a poem? Read back over the poems that you have liked most; what do they have in common?

2. How adaptable do you think you are in adjusting to a poem's emphases? Which poems have you liked though you didn't especially like the conclusions they came to?

3. How important to you is the *precision* of words in a poem? Do you tend to like poems better if they are definite and explicit in what they say? if they are ambiguous, uncertain, or complex?

4. Which issues and concepts in Chapters 13 through 20 have you found most useful? most surprising? Which chapters did you enjoy most? From which did you learn the most about yourself and your tastes and values?

5. What do you value most in poetry generally? Do you read poems that are not assigned? How did you choose which ones? Do you read poems outside this textbook or outside the course? If so, what kinds of poems do you tend to seek out? Do specific titles draw you in? particular subjects, topics, or themes?

6. How important to you is the *tone* of a poem? Do you tend to like funny poems more than serious ones? tragic situations more than comic ones? unusual treatments of standard or predictable subjects and themes?

7. Which poem in this chapter did you most enjoy reading? Which one did you like best after reading the commentary about it? Are there any poems you have read this term that you have violently disliked? What about them particularly irritated you? Have you changed your mind about some poems after you have reread or discussed them? How did your criteria change?

8. Are certain subjects or themes always appealing to you? always unappealing? What variable seems to you most important in determining whether you will like or dislike a poem?

WRITING SUGGESTIONS

1. Choose one poem that you especially admire and one that you do not. Write a two- or three-page essay about each in which you try to show what specific accomplishments (or lack of them) led you to your evaluative conclusions. Treat each poem in detail, and suggest fully not only how but *why* things "work"—or don't work. Try to construct your argument as "objectively" as possible so that you are not simply pitting your personal judgment against someone else's. (Alternative: find two poems that are very much alike in subject matter, theme, or situation, but that seem to you to succeed to different degrees. Write one *comparative* essay in which you account for the difference in quality by showing in detail the difference between what works and what does not.)

2. Discuss with classmates a variety of poems you have read this term, and choose one poem about which a number of you disagree. Discuss among yourselves the different perspectives you have on the poem, and try to sort out in the discussion exactly what issues are at stake. Take notes on the discussion, trying to be clear about how your position differs from that of other students. Once you believe that you have the issues sorted out and can be clear about your own position, write a two- or three-page personal letter to your instructor in which you outline a position contrary to your own and then answer it point by point. Be sure to make clear in your letter the *grounds* for your evaluative position, positive or negative—that is, the principles or values on which you base your evaluation. (Hint: in the conversation with classmates, try to steer the discussion to a clear disagreement on no more than two or three points, and in your letter focus carefully on these points. State the arguments of your classmates as effectively and forcefully as you can so that your own argument will be as probing and sophisticated as you can make it.)

3. Choose a poem you have read this term that you admire but really don't like very much. In thinking over the poem again, try to account for the conflict between your feelings and your intellectual judgment: what questions of content or form, social or political assumption, personal style, or manner of argument in the poem seem to make it less attractive to you? In a personal letter to a friend who is not in the class and who thus has not heard the class discussions of the issues, describe your dilemma, being careful to first outline why you think the poem is admirable. Say frankly what your personal reservations about the poem are, and at the end use the discussion of the poem to talk about your own values, as they pertain to poetry in general.

Reading More Poetry

W. H. AUDEN

In Memory of W. B. Yeats

(d. January, 1939)

I

He disappeared in the dead of winter:
The brooks were frozen, the airports almost deserted,
And snow disfigured the public statues;
The mercury sank in the mouth of the dying day.
What instruments we have agree   5
The day of his death was a dark cold day.

Far from his illness
The wolves ran on through the evergreen forests,
The peasant river was untempted by the fashionable quays;
By mourning tongues   10
The death of the poet was kept from his poems.

But for him it was his last afternoon as himself,
An afternoon of nurses and rumors;
The provinces of his body revolted,
The squares of his mind were empty,   15
Silence invaded the suburbs,
The current of his feeling failed; he became his admirers.

Now he is scattered among a hundred cities
And wholly given over to unfamiliar affections,
To find his happiness in another kind of wood   20
And be punished under a foreign code of conscience.
The words of a dead man
Are modified in the guts of the living.

But in the importance and noise of tomorrow
When the brokers are roaring like beasts on the floor of the Bourse,[1]   25

1. The Paris stock exchange.

And the poor have the sufferings to which they are fairly accustomed,
And each in the cell of himself is almost convinced of his freedom,
A few thousand will think of this day
As one thinks of a day when one did something slightly unusual.
30   What instruments we have agree
The day of his death was a dark cold day.

II

You were silly like us; your gift survived it all:
The parish of rich women, physical decay,
Yourself. Mad Ireland hurt you into poetry.
35   Now Ireland has her madness and her weather still,
For poetry makes nothing happen: it survives
In the valley of its making where executives
Would never want to tamper, flows on south
From ranches of isolation and the busy griefs,
40   Raw towns that we believe and die in; it survives,
A way of happening, a mouth.

III

Earth, receive an honored guest:
William Yeats is laid to rest.
Let the Irish vessel lie
45   Emptied of its poetry.

In the nightmare of the dark
All the dogs of Europe bark,
And the living nations wait,
Each sequestered in its hate;

50   Intellectual disgrace
Stares from every human face,
And the seas of pity lie
Locked and frozen in each eye.

Follow, poet, follow right
55   To the bottom of the night,
With your unconstraining voice
Still persuade us to rejoice;

With the farming of a verse
Make a vineyard of the curse,
60   Sing of human unsuccess
In a rapture of distress;

In the deserts of the heart
Let the healing fountain start,
In the prison of his days
65   Teach the free man how to praise.

1939

SAMUEL TAYLOR COLERIDGE

Kubla Khan: or, a Vision in a Dream[2]

In Xanadu did Kubla Khan
   A stately pleasure-dome decree:
Where Alph, the sacred river, ran
Through caverns measureless to man
   Down to a sunless sea.   5
So twice five miles of fertile ground
With walls and towers were girdled round:
And here were gardens bright with sinuous rills
Where blossomed many an incense-bearing tree;
And here were forests ancient as the hills,   10
Enfolding sunny spots of greenery.
But oh! that deep romantic chasm which slanted
Down the green hill athwart a cedarn cover![3]
A savage place! as holy and enchanted
As e'er beneath a waning moon was haunted   15
By woman wailing for her demon-lover![4]
And from this chasm, with ceaseless turmoil seething,
As if this earth in fast thick pants were breathing,
A mighty fountain momently was forced,
Amid whose swift half-intermitted burst   20
Huge fragments vaulted like rebounding hail,
Or chaffy grain beneath the thresher's flail:
And 'mid these dancing rocks at once and ever
It flung up momently the sacred river.
Five miles meandering with a mazy motion   25
Through wood and dale the sacred river ran,
Then reached the caverns measureless to man,
And sank in tumult to a lifeless ocean:
And 'mid this tumult Kubla heard from far
Ancestral voices prophesying war!   30

    The shadow of the dome of pleasure
    Floated midway on the waves;
    Where was heard the mingled measure
    From the fountain and the caves.
It was a miracle of rare device,   35
A sunny pleasure-dome with caves of ice!
    A damsel with a dulcimer
    In a vision once I saw:

2. Coleridge said he wrote this fragment immediately after waking from an opium dream and that after
he was interrupted by a caller he was unable to finish the poem.   3. From side to side of a cover of
cedar trees.   4. In a famous and often-imitated German ballad, the lady Lenore is carried off on horseback by the specter of her lover and married to him at his grave.

It was an Abyssinian maid,
40   And on her dulcimer she played,
Singing of Mount Abora.
Could I revive within me
Her symphony and song,
To such a deep delight 'twould win me,
45   That with music loud and long,
I would build that dome in air,
That sunny dome! those caves of ice!
And all who heard should see them there,
And all should cry, Beware! Beware!
50   His flashing eyes, his floating hair!
Weave a circle round him thrice,
And close your eyes with holy dread,
For he on honey-dew hath fed,
And drunk the milk of Paradise.   1798

H. D. (HILDA DOOLITTLE)

Helen

All Greece[5] hates
the still eyes in the white face,
the luster as of olives
where she stands,
5   and the white hands.

All Greece reviles
the wan face when she smiles,
hating it deeper still
when it grows wan and white,
10   remembering past enchantments
and past ills.

Greece sees unmoved
God's daughter, born of love,[6]
the beauty of cool feet
15   and slenderest of knees,
could love indeed the maid,
only if she were laid,
white ash amid funereal cypresses.   1924

---

5. Helen's husband, Menelaus, was king of Sparta; the Greeks attacked Troy to get her back from Paris,
son of the Trojan king.   6. Helen was the daughter of Zeus, king of the gods, and Leda, a mortal.

EMILY DICKINSON

[*Because I could not stop for Death—*]

Because I could not stop for Death—
He kindly stopped for me—
The Carriage held but just Ourselves—
And Immortality.

We slowly drove—He knew no haste   5
And I had put away
My labor and my leisure too,
For His Civility—

We passed the School, where Children strove
At Recess—in the Ring—   10
We passed the Fields of Gazing Grain—
We passed the Setting Sun—

Or rather—He passed Us—
The Dews drew quivering and chill—
For only Gossamer,[7] my Gown—   15
My Tippet—only Tulle[8]—

We paused before a House that seemed
A Swelling of the Ground—
The Roof was scarcely visible—
The Cornice—in the Ground—   20

Since then—'tis Centuries—and yet
Feels shorter than the Day
I first surmised the Horses' Heads
Were toward Eternity—

ca. 1863

[*I reckon—when I count at all—*]

I reckon—when I count at all—
First—Poets—Then the Sun—
Then Summer—Then the Heaven of God—
And then—the List is done—

But, looking back—the First so seems   5
To Comprehend the Whole—
The Others look a needless Show—
So I write—Poets—All—

Their Summer—lasts a Solid Year—
They can afford a Sun   10

7. A soft, sheer fabric.   8. A fine net fabric. *Tippet:* scarf.

The East—would deem extravagant—
And if the Further Heaven—

Be Beautiful as they prepare
For Those who worship Them—
15   It is too difficult a Grace—
To justify the Dream—

ca. 1862

[We do not play on Graves—]

We do not play on Graves—
Because there isn't Room—
Besides—it isn't even—it slants
And People come—

5   And put a Flower on it—
And hang their faces so—
We're fearing that their Hearts will drop—
And crush our pretty play—

And so we move as far
10   As Enemies—away—
Just looking round to see how far
It is—Occasionally—

ca. 1862

[She dealt her pretty words like Blades—]

She dealt her pretty words like Blades—
How glittering they shone—
And every One unbared a Nerve
Or wantoned with a Bone—

5   She never deemed—she hurt—
That—is not Steel's Affair—
A vulgar grimace in the Flesh—
How ill the Creatures bear—

To Ache is human—not polite—
10   The Film upon the eye
Mortality's old Custom—
Just locking up—to Die.

1862

JOHN DONNE

[Death be not proud, though some have calléd thee]

Death be not proud, though some have calléd thee
Mighty and dreadful, for thou art not so;
For those whom thou think'st thou dost overthrow
Die not, poor Death, nor yet canst thou kill me.
From rest and sleep, which but thy pictures[9] be,   5
Much pleasure; then from thee much more must flow,
And soonest[1] our best men with thee do go,
Rest of their bones, and soul's delivery.[2]
Thou art slave to Fate, Chance, kings, and desperate men,
And dost with Poison, War, and Sickness dwell;   10
And poppy or charms can make us sleep as well,
And better than thy stroke; why swell'st[3] thou then?
One short sleep past, we wake eternally
And death shall be no more; Death, thou shalt die.   1633

A Valediction: Forbidding Mourning

As virtuous men pass mildly away,
    And whisper to their souls to go,
Whilst some of their sad friends do say,
    "The breath goes now," and some say, "No,"

So let us melt, and make no noise,   5
    No tear-floods, nor sigh-tempests move;
'Twere profanation of our joys
    To tell the laity our love.

Moving of the earth[4] brings harms and fears,
    Men reckon what it did and meant;   10
But trepidation of the spheres,[5]
    Though greater far, is innocent.

Dull sublunary[6] lovers' love
    (Whose soul is sense) cannot admit
Absence, because it doth remove   15
    Those things which elemented[7] it.

9. Likenesses.   1. Most willingly.   2. Deliverance.   3. Puff with pride.   4. Earthquakes.   5. The
Renaissance hypothesis that the celestial spheres trembled and thus caused unexpected variations in
their orbits. Such movements are "innocent" because earthlings do not observe or fret about them.
6. Below the moon—that is, changeable. According to the traditional cosmology that Donne invokes
here, the moon was considered the dividing line between the immutable celestial world and the earthly
mortal one.   7. Comprised.

But we, by a love so much refined
    That our selves know not what it is,
Inter-assured of the mind,
20   Care less, eyes, lips, and hands to miss.

Our two souls therefore, which are one,
    Though I must go, endure not yet
A breach, but an expansion,
    Like gold to airy thinness beat.

25 If they be two, they are two so
    As stiff twin compasses are two:
Thy soul, the fixed foot, makes no show
    To move, but doth, if the other do;

And though it in the center sit,
30   Yet when the other far doth roam,
It leans, and hearkens after it,
    And grows erect, as that comes home.

Such wilt thou be to me, who must,
    Like the other foot, obliquely run;
35 Thy firmness makes my circle⁸ just,
    And makes me end where I begun.

        1611?

_____

PAUL LAURENCE DUNBAR

Sympathy

I know what the caged bird feels, alas!
    When the sun is bright on the upland slopes;
When the wind stirs soft through the springing grass,
And the river flows like a stream of glass;
5   When the first bird sings and the first bud opens,
And the faint perfume from its chalice steals—
I know what the caged bird feels!

I know why the caged bird beats his wing
    Till its blood is red on the cruel bars;
10 For he must fly back to his perch and cling
When he fain would be on the bough a-swing;
    And a pain still throbs in the old, old scars
And they pulse again with a keener sting—
I know why he beats his wing!

15   I know why the caged bird sings, ah me,
    When his wing is bruised and his bosom sore,—

_____

8. A traditional symbol of perfection.

When he beats his bars and he would be free;
It is not a carol of joy or glee,
   But a prayer that he sends from his heart's deep core,
But a plea, that upward to Heaven he flings—   20
I know why the caged bird sings!   1893

We Wear the Mask

We wear the mask that grins and lies,
It hides our cheeks and shades our eyes,—
This debt we pay to human guile;
With torn and bleeding hearts we smile,
And mouth with myriad subtleties.   5

Why should the world be over-wise,
In counting all our tears and sighs?
Nay, let them only see us, while
    We wear the mask.

We smile, but, O great Christ, our cries   10
To thee from tortured souls arise.
We sing, but oh the clay is vile
Beneath our feet, and long the mile;
But let the world dream otherwise,
    We wear the mask!   15

         1896

T. S. ELIOT

The Love Song of J. Alfred Prufrock

    S'io credesse che mia risposta fosse
    A persona che mai tornasse al mondo,
    Questa fiamma staria senza piu scosse.
    Ma perciocche giammai di questo fondo
    Non torno vivo alcun, s'i'odo il vero,
    Senza tema d'infamia ti rispondo.[9]

Let us go then, you and I,
When the evening is spread out against the sky
Like a patient etherized upon a table;
Let us go, through certain half-deserted streets,

---

9. Dante's *Inferno* XXVII.61–66. In the Eighth Chasm, Dante and Vergil meet Count Guido de Montefeltrano, one of the False Counselors. The spirits there are in the form of flames, and Guido speaks from the trembling tip of the flame, responding to Dante's request that he tell his life story: "If I thought that my answer were to someone who would ever go back to Earth, this flame would be still, without any more movement. But because no one has ever gone back alive from this chasm (if what I hear is true) I answer you without fear of infamy."

5 The muttering retreats
Of restless nights in one-night cheap hotels
And sawdust restaurants with oyster-shells:
Streets that follow like a tedious argument
Of insidious intent
10 To lead you to an overwhelming question . . .
Oh, do not ask, "What is it?"
Let us go and make our visit.

 In the room the women come and go
Talking of Michelangelo.

15 The yellow fog that rubs its back upon the window-panes,
The yellow smoke that rubs its muzzle on the window-panes
Licked its tongue into the corners of the evening,
Lingered upon the pools that stand in drains,
Let fall upon its back the soot that falls from chimneys,
20 Slipped by the terrace, made a sudden leap,
And seeing that it was a soft October night,
Curled once about the house, and fell asleep.

 And indeed there will be time[1]
For the yellow smoke that slides along the street,
25 Rubbing its back upon the window-panes;
There will be time, there will be time
To prepare a face to meet the faces that you meet;
There will be time to murder and create,
And time for all the works and days[2] of hands
30 That lift and drop a question on your plate;
Time for you and time for me,
And time yet for a hundred indecisions,
And for a hundred visions and revisions,
Before the taking of a toast and tea.

35 In the room the women come and go
Talking of Michelangelo.

 And indeed there will be time
To wonder, "Do I dare?" and, "Do I dare?"
Time to turn back and descend the stair,
40 With a bald spot in the middle of my hair—
(They will say: "How his hair is growing thin!")
My morning coat, my collar mounting firmly to the chin,
My necktie rich and modest, but asserted by a simple pin—
(They will say: "But how his arms and legs are thin!")
45 Do I dare
Disturb the universe?

---

1. See Ecclesiastes 3:1 ff.: "To everything there is a season, and a time to every purpose under the heaven: A time to be born, and a time to die; a time to plant, and a time to pluck up that which is planted; A time to kill, and a time to heal. . . ." Also see Marvell's "To His Coy Mistress": "Had we but world enough and time. . . ." 2. Hesiod's ancient Greek didactic poem *Works and Days* prescribed in practical detail how to conduct one's life.

In a minute there is time
For decisions and revisions which a minute will reverse.

    For I have known them all already, known them all:—
Have known the evenings, mornings, afternoons,   50
I have measured out my life with coffee spoons;
I know the voices dying with a dying fall
Beneath the music from a farther room.
    So how should I presume?

    And I have known the eyes already, known them all—   55
The eyes that fix you in a formulated phrase,
And when I am formulated, sprawling on a pin,
When I am pinned and wriggling on the wall,
Then how should I begin
To spit out all the butt-ends of my days and ways?   60
    And how should I presume?

    And I have known the arms already, known them all—
Arms that are braceleted and white and bare
(But in the lamplight, downed with light brown hair!)
Is it perfume from a dress   65
That makes me so digress?
Arms that lie along a table, or wrap about a shawl.
    And should I then presume?
    And how should I begin?

    . . . . .

Shall I say, I have gone at dusk through narrow streets   70
And watched the smoke that rises from the pipes
Of lonely men in shirt-sleeves, leaning out of windows? . . .

    I should have been a pair of ragged claws
Scuttling across the floors of silent seas

    . . . . .

And the afternoon, the evening, sleeps so peacefully!   75
Smoothed by long fingers,
Asleep . . . tired . . . or it malingers,
Stretched on the floor, here beside you and me.
Should I, after tea and cakes and ices,
Have the strength to force the moment to its crisis?   80
But though I have wept and fasted, wept and prayed,
Though I have seen my head (grown slightly bald) brought in upon a
    platter,[3]
I am no prophet—and here's no great matter;
I have seen the moment of my greatness flicker,
And I have seen the eternal Footman hold my coat, and snicker,   85
And in short, I was afraid.

---

3. See Matthew 14:1–12 and Mark 6:17–29: John the Baptist was decapitated, upon Salome's request and
at Herod's command, and his head delivered on a platter.

And would it have been worth it, after all,
After the cups, the marmalade, the tea,
Among the porcelain, among some talk of you and me,
90   Would it have been worth while,
To have bitten off the matter with a smile,
To have squeezed the universe into a ball[4]
To roll it toward some overwhelming question,
To say: "I am Lazarus,[5] come from the dead,
95   Come back to tell you all, I shall tell you all"—
If one, settling a pillow by her head,
   Should say: "That is not what I meant at all.
   That is not it, at all."

   And would it have been worth it, after all,
100   Would it have been worth while,
After the sunsets and the dooryards and the sprinkled streets,
After the novels, after the teacups, after the skirts that trail along the
   floor—
And this, and so much more?—
It is impossible to say just what I mean!
105   But as if a magic lantern[6] threw the nerves in patterns on a screen:
Would it have been worth while
If one, settling a pillow or throwing off a shawl,
And turning toward the window, should say:
   "That is not it at all,
110   That is not what I meant, at all."

· · · · ·

No! I am not Prince Hamlet, nor was meant to be;
Am an attendant lord,[7] one that will do
To swell a progress,[8] start a scene or two,
Advise the prince; no doubt, an easy tool,
115   Deferential, glad to be of use,
Politic, cautious, and meticulous;
Full of high sentence, but a bit obtuse;
At times, indeed, almost ridiculous—
Almost, at times, the Fool.

120   I grow old . . . I grow old . . .
I shall wear the bottoms of my trousers rolled.

Shall I part my hair behind? Do I dare to eat a peach?
I shall wear white flannel trousers, and walk upon the beach.
I have heard the mermaids singing, each to each.

125   I do not think that they will sing to me.

4. See Marvell's "To His Coy Mistress," lines 41–42: "Let us roll all our strength and all / our sweetness up into one ball. . . ."   5. One Lazarus was raised from the dead by Jesus (see John 1:1–2:2), and another (in the parable of the rich man Dives) is discussed in terms of returning from the dead to warn the living (Luke 16:19–31).   6. A nonelectric projector used as early as the seventeenth century.   7. Like Polonius in *Hamlet*, who is full of maxims ("high sentence," line 117).   8. Procession of state.

I have seen them riding seaward on the waves
Combing the white hair of the waves blown back.
When the wind blows the water white and black.

We have lingered in the chambers of the sea
By sea-girls wreathed with seaweed red and brown   130
Till human voices wake us, and we drown.   1917

ROBERT FROST

The Road Not Taken

Two roads diverged in a yellow wood,
And sorry I could not travel both
And be one traveler, long I stood
And looked down one as far as I could
To where it bent in the undergrowth;   5

Then took the other, as just as fair,
And having perhaps the better claim,
Because it was grassy and wanted wear;
Though as for that the passing there
Had worn them really about the same,   10

And both that morning equally lay
In leaves no step had trodden black.
Oh, I kept the first for another day!
Yet knowing how way leads on to way,
I doubted if I should ever come back.   15

I shall be telling this with a sigh
Somewhere ages and ages hence:
Two roads diverged in a wood, and I—
I took the one less traveled by,
And that has made all the difference.   20

1916

Stopping by Woods on a Snowy Evening

Whose woods these are I think I know.
His house is in the village, though;
He will not see me stopping here
To watch his woods fill up with snow.

My little horse must think it queer   5
To stop without a farmhouse near

Between the woods and frozen lake
The darkest evening of the year.

10   He gives his harness bells a shake
To ask if there is some mistake.
The only other sound's the sweep
Of easy wind and downy flake.

The woods are lovely, dark, and deep,
But I have promises to keep,
15   And miles to go before I sleep,
And miles to go before I sleep.   1923

ALLEN GINSBERG

A Supermarket in California

What thoughts I have of you tonight, Walt Whitman,[9] for I walked
down the sidestreets under the trees with a headache self-conscious
looking at the full moon.

In my hungry fatigue, and shopping for images, I went into the
neon fruit supermarket, dreaming of your enumerations![1]

What peaches and what penumbras! Whole families shopping at
night! Aisles full of husbands! Wives in the avocados, babies in the
tomatoes!—and you, Garcia Lorca,[2] what were you doing down by the
watermelons?

I saw you, Walt Whitman, childless, lonely old grubber, poking
among the meats in the refrigerator and eyeing the grocery boys.

I heard you asking questions of each: Who killed the pork chops?
5   What price bananas? Are you my Angel?

I wandered in and out of the brilliant stacks of cans following you,
and followed in my imagination by the store detective.

We strode down the open corridors together in our solitary fancy
tasting artichokes, possessing every frozen delicacy, and never passing
the cashier.

Where are we going, Walt Whitman? The doors close in an hour.
Which way does your beard point tonight?

(I touch your book and dream of our odyssey in the supermarket
and feel absurd.)

Will we walk all night through solitary streets? The trees add shade
10   to shade, lights out in the houses, we'll both be lonely.

---

9. Whitman's free verse, strong individualism, and passionate concern with America as an idea have led
many modern poets to consider him the father of a new poetry.   1. Whitman's highly rhetorical
poetry often contains long lists or parallel constructions piled up for cumulative effect.   2. Early
twentieth-century Spanish poet and playwright, author of *Blood Wedding*. Murdered in 1936, at the
beginning of the Spanish Civil War, his works were banned by the Franco government.

Will we stroll dreaming of the lost America of love past blue automobiles in driveways, home to our silent cottage?

Ah, dear father, graybeard, lonely old courage-teacher, what America did you have when Charon quit poling his ferry and you got out on a smoking bank and stood watching the boat disappear on the black waters of Lethe?[3]

Berkeley 1955

Velocity of Money

For Lee Berton

I'm delighted by the velocity of money as it whistles through windows
    of Lower East Side
Delighted skyscrapers rise grungy apartments fall on 84th Street's pave-
    ment
Delighted this year inflation drives me out on the street
with double digit interest rates in Capitalist worlds
I always was a communist, now we'll win   5
as usury makes walls thinner, books thicker & dumber
Usury makes my poetry more valuable
Manuscripts worth their weight in useless gold—
The velocity's what counts as the National Debt gets trillions higher
Everybody running after the rising dollar   10
Crowds of joggers down Broadway past City Hall on the way to the Fed
Nobody reads Dostoyevsky books anymore so they'll have to give pass-
    ing ear
to my fragmented ravings in between President's speeches
Nothing's happening but the collapse of the Economy
so I can go back to sleep till the landlord wins his eviction suit in court   15

February 18, 1986, 10:00 A.M.

GERARD MANLEY HOPKINS

God's Grandeur

The world is charged with the grandeur of God.
    It will flame out, like shining from shook foil;[4]
    It gathers to a greatness, like the ooze of oil

---

3. The River of Forgetfulness in Hades. Charon is the boatman who, according to classical myth, ferries souls to Hades.   4. "I mean foil in its sense of leaf or tinsel. . . . Shaken goldfoil gives off broad glares like sheet lightning and also, and this is true of nothing else, owing to its zig-zag dints and creasings and network of small many cornered facets, a sort of fork lightning too." *Letters of Gerard Manley Hopkins to Robert Bridges,* ed. C. C. Abbott (1955), p. 169.

Crushed. Why do men then now not reck his rod?[5]
5   Generations have trod, have trod, have trod;
     And all is seared with trade; bleared, smeared with toil;
     And wears man's smudge and shares man's smell: the soil
Is bare now, nor can foot feel, being shod.

And for all this, nature is never spent;
10   There lives the dearest freshness deep down things;
And though the last lights off the black West went
     Oh, morning, at the brown brink eastward, springs—
Because the Holy Ghost over the bent
     World broods with warm breast and with ah! bright wings.   1918

The Windhover[6]

to Christ our Lord

I caught this morning morning's minion,[7] king-
     dom of daylight's dauphin,[8] dapple-dawn-drawn Falcon, in his
                                                                    riding
          Of the rolling level underneath him steady air, and striding
High there, how he rung upon the rein of a wimpling[9] wing
5   In his ecstasy! then off, off forth on swing,
          As a skate's heel sweeps smooth on a bow-bend: the hurl and
                                                                    gliding
          Rebuffed the big wind. My heart in hiding
Stirred for a bird,—the achieve of, the mastery of the thing!

Brute beauty and valor and act, oh, air, pride, plume, here
10   Buckle![1] AND the fire that breaks from thee then, a billion
Times told lovelier, more dangerous, O my chevalier![2]

     No wonder of it: sheér plód makes plow down sillion[3]
Shine, and blue-bleak embers, ah my dear,
     Fall, gall themselves, and gash gold-vermilion.

     1877

---

5. Heed his authority.   6. A small hawk, the kestrel, which habitually hovers in the air, headed into the wind.   7. Favorite, beloved.   8. Heir to regal splendor.   9. Rippling.   1. Several meanings may apply: to join closely, to prepare for battle, to grapple with, to collapse.   2. Horseman, knight.
3. The narrow strip of land between furrows in an open field divided for separate cultivation.

LANGSTON HUGHES

Theme for English B

The instructor said,

> *Go home and write*
> *a page tonight.*
> *And let that page come out of you—*
> *Then, it will be true.*   5

I wonder if it's that simple?
I am twenty-two, colored, born in Winston-Salem.
I went to school there, then Durham,[4] then here
to this college[5] on the hill above Harlem.
I am the only colored student in my class.   10
The steps from the hill lead down into Harlem,
through a park, then I cross St. Nicholas,[6]
Eighth Avenue, Seventh, and I come to the Y,
the Harlem Branch Y, where I take the elevator
up to my room, sit down, and write this page: 15

It's not easy to know what is true for you or me
at twenty-two, my age. But I guess I'm what
I feel and see and hear, Harlem, I hear you:
hear you, hear me—we two—you, me, talk on this page.
(I hear New York, too.) Me—who?   20

Well, I like to eat, sleep, drink, and be in love.
I like to work, read, learn, and understand life.
I like a pipe for a Christmas present,
or records—Bessie,[7] bop, or Bach.
I guess being colored doesn't make me *not* like   25
the same things other folks like who are other races.
So will my page be colored that I write?

Being me, it will not be white.
But it will be
a part of you, instructor.   30
You are white—
yet a part of me, as I am a part of you.
That's American.
Sometimes perhaps you don't want to be a part of me.
Nor do I often want to be a part of you.   35
But we are, that's true!
As I learn from you,
I guess you learn from me—

---

4. Winston-Salem and Durham are cities in North Carolina.   5. Columbia University.   6. An avenue east of Columbia University.   7. Bessie Smith (1898?–1937), famous blues singer.

₄₀ although you're older—and white—
and somewhat more free.

This is my page for English B.   1959

JOHN KEATS

Ode to a Nightingale

I

My heart aches, and a drowsy numbness pains
  My sense, as though of hemlock I had drunk,
Or emptied some dull opiate to the drains
  One minute past, and Lethe-wards[8] had sunk:
₅ 'Tis not through envy of thy happy lot,
  But being too happy in thine happiness,
    That thou, light-wingéd Dryad[9] of the trees,
      In some melodious plot
Of beechen green, and shadows numberless,
₁₀   Singest of summer in full-throated ease.

II

O, for a draught of vintage! that hath been
  Cooled a long age in the deep-delvéd earth,
Tasting of Flora[1] and the country green,
  Dance, and Provençal song,[2] and sunburnt mirth!
₁₅ O for a beaker full of the warm South,
  Full of the true, the blushful Hippocrene,[3]
    With beaded bubbles winking at the brim,
      And purple-stainéd mouth;
That I might drink, and leave the world unseen,
₂₀   And with thee fade away into the forest dim:

III

Fade far away, dissolve, and quite forget
  What thou among the leaves hast never known,
The weariness, the fever, and the fret
  Here, where men sit and hear each other groan;
₂₅ Where palsy shakes a few, sad, last gray hairs,
  Where youth grows pale, and specter-thin, and dies;
    Where but to think is to be full of sorrow
      And leaden-eyed despairs,

---

8. Toward the river of forgetfulness (Lethe) in Hades.   9. Wood nymph.   1. Roman goddess of
flowers.   2. The medieval troubadors of Provence were famous for their love songs.   3. The fountain of the Muses on Mt. Helicon, whose waters bring poetic inspiration.

Where Beauty cannot keep her lustrous eyes,
  Or new Love pine at them beyond tomorrow.   30

IV

Away! away! for I will fly to thee,
  Not charioted by Bacchus and his pards,[4]
But on the viewless[5] wings of Poesy,
  Though the dull brain perplexes and retards:
Already with thee! tender is the night,   35
  And haply the Queen-Moon is on her throne,
    Clustered around by all her starry Fays;[6]
      But here there is no light,
Save what from heaven is with the breezes blown
  Through verdurous glooms and winding mossy ways.   40

V

I cannot see what flowers are at my feet,
  Nor what soft incense hangs upon the boughs,
But, in embalméd[7] darkness, guess each sweet
  Wherewith the seasonable month endows
The grass, the thicket, and the fruit-tree wild;   45
  White hawthorn, and the pastoral eglantine;[8]
    Fast fading violets covered up in leaves;
      And mid-May's eldest child,
The coming musk-rose, full of dewy wine,
  The murmurous haunt of flies on summer eves.   50

VI

Darkling[9] I listen; and, for many a time
  I have been half in love with easeful Death,
Called him soft names in many a muséd rhyme,
  To take into the air my quiet breath;
Now more than ever seems it rich to die,   55
  To cease upon the midnight with no pain,
    While thou art pouring forth thy soul abroad
      In such an ecstasy!
Still wouldst thou sing, and I have ears in vain—
  To thy high requiem become a sod.   60

VII

Thou wast not born for death, immortal Bird!
  No hungry generations tread thee down;
The voice I hear this passing night was heard

4. The Roman god of wine was sometimes portrayed in a chariot drawn by leopards.   5. Invisible.
6. Fairies.   7. Fragrant, aromatic.   8. Sweetbriar or honeysuckle.   9. In the dark.

In ancient days by emperor and clown:
65   Perhaps the selfsame song that found a path
            Through the sad heart of Ruth,[1] when, sick for home,
                She stood in tears amid the alien corn;
                    The same that ofttimes hath
            Charmed magic casements, opening on the foam
70   Of perilous seas, in faery lands forlorn.

VIII

Forlorn! the very word is like a bell
    To toll me back from thee to my sole self!
Adieu! the fancy cannot cheat so well
    As she is famed to do, deceiving elf.
75 Adieu! adieu! thy plaintive anthem fades
        Past the near meadows, over the still stream,
            Up the hillside; and now 'tis buried deep
                In the next valley-glades:
        Was it a vision, or a waking dream?
80   Fled is that music:—Do I wake or sleep?

May 1819

Ode on a Grecian Urn

I

Thou still unravished bride of quietness,
    Thou foster-child of silence and slow time,
Sylvan[2] historian, who canst thus express
    A flowery tale more sweetly than our rhyme:
5   What leaf-fringed legend haunts about thy shape
        Of deities or mortals, or of both,
            In Tempe or the dales of Arcady?[3]
What men or gods are these? What maidens loath?
    What mad pursuit? What struggle to escape?
10   What pipes and timbrels? What wild ecstasy?

II

Heard melodies are sweet, but those unheard
    Are sweeter; therefore, ye soft pipes, play on;
Not to the sensual[4] ear, but, more endeared,
    Pipe to the spirit ditties of no tone:

---

1. A virtuous Moabite widow who, according to the Old Testament Book of Ruth, left her own country to accompany her mother-in-law Naomi back to Naomi's native land. She supported herself as a gleaner.
2. Woodland.   3. Arcadia. Tempe is a beautiful valley near Mt. Olympus in Greece, and the valley ("dales") of Arcadia a picturesque section of the Peloponnesus; both came to be associated with the pastoral ideal.   4. Of the senses, as distinguished from the "ear" of the spirit or imagination.

Fair youth, beneath the trees, thou canst not leave   15
   Thy song, nor ever can those trees be bare;
     Bold Lover, never, never canst thou kiss,
Though winning near the goal—yet, do not grieve
   She cannot fade, though thou hast not thy bliss,
     For ever wilt thou love, and she be fair!   20

III

Ah, happy, happy boughs! that cannot shed
   Your leaves, nor ever bid the Spring adieu;
And, happy melodist, unweariéd,
   For ever piping songs for ever new;
More happy love! more happy, happy love!   25
   For ever warm and still to be enjoyed,
     For ever panting, and for ever young;
All breathing human passion far above,
   That leaves a heart high-sorrowful and cloyed,
     A burning forehead, and a parching tongue.   30

IV

Who are these coming to the sacrifice?
   To what green altar, O mysterious priest,
Lead'st thou that heifer lowing at the skies,
   And all her silken flanks with garlands dressed?
What little town by river or sea shore,   35
   Or mountain-built with peaceful citadel,
     Is emptied of this folk, this pious morn?
And, little town, thy streets for evermore
   Will silent be; and not a soul to tell
     Why thou art desolate, can e'er return.   40

V

O Attic shape! Fair attitude! with brede[5]
   Of marble men and maidens overwrought,[6]
With forest branches and the trodden weed;
   Thou, silent form, dost tease us out of thought
As doth eternity: Cold Pastoral!   45
   When old age shall this generation waste,
     Thou shalt remain, in midst of other woe
Than ours, a friend to man, to whom thou say'st,
   Beauty is truth, truth beauty[7]—that is all
     Ye know on earth, and all ye need to know.   50

May 1819

---

5. Woven pattern. *Attic:* Attica was the district of ancient Greece surrounding Athens.   6. Ornamented all over.   7. In some texts of the poem "Beauty is truth, truth beauty" is in quotation marks
and in some texts it is not, leading to critical disagreements about whether the last line and a half are
also inscribed on the urn or spoken by the poet.

To Autumn

I

Season of mists and mellow fruitfulness,
   Close bosom-friend of the maturing sun;
Conspiring with him how to load and bless
   With fruit the vines that round the thatch-eves run;
5   To bend with apples the mossed cottage-trees,
     And fill all fruit with ripeness to the core;
      To swell the gourd, and plump the hazel shells
With a sweet kernel; to set budding more,
    And still more, later flowers for the bees,
10   Until they think warm days will never cease,
      For Summer has o'er-brimmed their clammy cells.

II

Who hath not seen thee oft amid thy store?
   Sometimes whoever seeks abroad may find
Thee sitting careless on a granary floor,
15   Thy hair soft-lifted by the winnowing wind;[8]
Or on a half-reaped furrow sound asleep,
    Drowsed with the fume of poppies, while thy hook[9]
     Spares the next swath and all its twinéd flowers:
And sometimes like a gleaner thou dost keep
20   Steady thy laden head across a brook;
    Or by a cider-press, with patient look,
     Thou watchest the last oozings hours by hours.

III

Where are the songs of Spring? Ay, where are they?
   Think not of them, thou hast thy music too—
25   While barréd clouds bloom the soft-dying day,
    And touch the stubble-plains with rosy hue;
Then in a wailful choir the small gnats mourn
    Among the river sallows,[1] borne aloft
     Or sinking as the light wind lives or dies;
30 And full-grown lambs loud bleat from hilly bourn;[2]
    Hedge-crickets sing; and now with treble soft
    The red-breast whistles from a garden-croft;[3]
     And gathering swallows twitter in the skies.

September 19, 1819

---

8. Which sifts the grain from the chaff.   9. Scythe or sickle.   1. Willows.   2. Domain.   3. An enclosed garden near a house.

ANDREW MARVELL

The Garden

How vainly men themselves amaze[4]
To win the palm, the oak, or bays,[5]
And their incessant labors see
Crowned from some single herb, or tree,
Whose short and narrow-vergèd[6] shade   5
Does prudently their toils upbraid;
While all flowers and all trees do close[7]
To weave the garlands of repose!

Fair Quiet, have I found thee here,
And Innocence, thy sister dear?   10
Mistaken long, I sought you then
In busy companies of men.
Your sacred plants,[8] if here below,
Only among the plants will grow;
Society is all but rude[9]   15
To[1] this delicious solitude.

No white nor red was ever seen
So am'rous as this lovely green.
Fond lovers, cruel as their flame,
Cut in these trees their mistress' name: 20
Little, alas, they know, or heed
How far these beauties hers exceed!
Fair trees, wheresoe'er your barks I wound,
No name shall but your own be found.

When we have run our passion's heat,   25
Love hither makes his best retreat.
The gods, that mortal beauty chase,
Still in a tree did end their race:
Apollo hunted Daphne so,
Only that she might laurel grow;   30
And Pan did after Syrinx speed,
Not as a nymph, but for a reed.[2]

What wondrous life is this I lead!
Ripe apples drop about my head;
The luscious clusters of the vine   35
Upon my mouth do crush their wine;
The nectarine and curious[3] peach
Into my hands themselves do reach;
Stumbling on melons, as I pass,
Insnared with flowers, I fall on grass.   40

4. Become frenzied.   5. Awards for athletic, civic, and literary achievements.   6. Narrowly cropped.   7. Unite.   8. Cuttings.   9. Barbarous.   1. Compared to.   2. In Ovid's *Metamorphoses,* Daphne, pursued by Apollo, is turned into a laurel, and Syrinx, pursued by Pan, into a reed that Pan makes into a flute.   3. Exquisite.

Meanwhile the mind, from pleasure less,
Withdraws into its happiness;[4]
The mind, that ocean where each kind
Does straight its own resemblance find;[5]
45 Yet it creates, transcending these,
Far other worlds and other seas,
Annihilating[6] all that's made
To a green thought in a green shade.

Here at the fountain's sliding foot,
50 Or at some fruit tree's mossy root,
Casting the body's vest[7] aside,
My soul into the boughs does glide:
There, like a bird, it sits and sings,
Then whets[8] and combs its silver wings,
55 And, till prepared for longer flight,
Waves in its plumes the various[9] light.

Such was that happy garden-state,
While man there walked without a mate:
After a place so pure, and sweet,
60 What other help could yet be meet![1]
But 'twas beyond a mortal's share
To wander solitary there:
Two paradises 'twere in one
To live in paradise alone.

65 How well the skillful gardener drew
Of flowers and herbs this dial[2] new,
Where, from above, the milder sun
Does through a fragrant zodiac run;
And as it works, th' industrious bee
70 Computes its time as well as we!
How could such sweet and wholesome hours
Be reckoned but with herbs and flowers?   1681

MICHAEL ONDAATJE

King Kong Meets Wallace Stevens

Take two photographs—
Wallace Stevens and King Kong
(Is it significant that I eat bananas as I write this?)

---

4. That is, the mind withdraws from lesser-sense pleasure into contemplation.   5. All land creatures were supposed to have corresponding sea creatures.   6. Reducing to nothing by comparison.
7. Vestment, clothing; the flesh is being considered as simply clothing for the soul.   8. Preens.
9. Many-colored.   1. Appropriate.   2. A garden planted in the shape of a sundial, complete with zodiac.

Stevens is portly, benign, a white brush cut
striped tie. Businessman but   5
for the dark thick hands, the naked brain
the thought in him.

Kong is staggering
lost in New York streets again
a spawn of annoyed cars at his toes.   10
The mind is nowhere.
Fingers are plastic, electric under the skin.
He's at the call of Metro-Goldwyn-Mayer.

Meanwhile W. S. in his suit
is thinking chaos is thinking fences.   15
In his head—the seeds of fresh pain
his exorcising,
the bellow of locked blood.

The hands drain from his jacket,
pose in the murderer's shadow.   20

1979

SYLVIA PLATH

Black Rook in Rainy Weather

On the stiff twig up there
Hunches a wet black rook
Arranging and rearranging its feathers in the rain.
I do not expect a miracle
Or an accident   5

To set the sight on fire
In my eye, nor seek
Any more in the desultory weather some design,
But let spotted leaves fall as they fall,
Without ceremony, or portent   10

Although, I admit, I desire,
Occasionally, some backtalk
From the mute sky, I can't honestly complain:
A certain minor light may still
Leap incandescent   15

Out of kitchen table or chair
As if a celestial burning took
Possession of the most obtuse objects now and then—
Thus hallowing an interval
Otherwise inconsequent   20

By bestowing largesse, honor,
One might say love. At any rate, I now walk
Wary (for it could happen

Even in this dull, ruinous landscape); skeptical,
25   Yet politic; ignorant

Of whatever angel may choose to flare
Suddenly at my elbow. I only know that a rook
Ordering its black feathers can so shine
As to seize my senses, haul
30   My eyelids up, and grant

A brief respite from fear
Of total neutrality. With luck,
Trekking stubborn through this season
Of fatigue, I shall
35   Patch together a content

Of sorts. Miracles occur,
If you care to call those spasmodic
Tricks of radiance miracles. The wait's begun again,
The long wait for the angel,
40   For that rare, random descent.[3]   1960

Lady Lazarus

I have done it again.
One year in every ten
I manage it—

A sort of walking miracle, my skin
5   Bright as a Nazi lampshade,
My right foot

A paperweight,
My face a featureless, fine
Jew linen.[4]

10   Peel off the napkin
O my enemy.
Do I terrify?—

The nose, the eye pits, the full set of teeth?
The sour breath
15   Will vanish in a day.

Soon, soon the flesh
The grave cave ate will be
At home on me

And I a smiling woman.
20   I am only thirty.
And like the cat I have nine times to die.

3. According to Acts 2, the Holy Ghost at Pentecost descended like a tongue of fire upon Jesus' disciples.   4. During World War II, in some Nazi camps, prisoners were gassed to death, their body parts then turned into home furnishings like lampshades and paperweights.

This is Number Three.
What a trash
To annihilate each decade.

What a million filaments.   25
The peanut-crunching crowd
Shoves in to see

Them unwrap me hand and foot—
The big strip tease.
Gentlemen, ladies   30

These are my hands
My knees.
I may be skin and bone,

Nevertheless, I am the same, identical woman.
The first time it happened I was ten.   35
It was an accident.

The second time I meant
To last it out and not come back at all.
I rocked shut

As a seashell.   40
They had to call and call
And pick the worms off me like sticky pearls.

Dying
Is an art, like everything else.
I do it exceptionally well.   45

I do it so it feels like hell.
I do it so it feels real.
I guess you could say I've a call.

It's easy enough to do it in a cell.
It's easy enough to do it and stay put.   50
It's the theatrical

Comeback in broad day
To the same place, the same face, the same brute
Amused shout:

"A miracle!"   55
That knocks me out.
There is a charge

For the eyeing of my scars, there is a charge
For the hearing of my heart—
It really goes.   60

And there is a charge, a very large charge
For a word or a touch
Or a bit of blood

Or a piece of my hair or my clothes.
65 So, so Herr Doktor.
So, Herr Enemy.

I am your opus,
I am your valuable,
The pure gold baby

70 That melts to a shriek.
I turn and burn.
Do not think I underestimate your great concern

Ash, ash—
You poke and stir.
75 Flesh, bone, there is nothing there—

A cake of soap,
A wedding ring,
A gold filling.

Herr God, Herr Lucifer
80 Beware
Beware.

Out of the ash
I rise with my red hair
And I eat men like air.   1965

EZRA POUND

The Garden

En robe de parade.

—SAMAIN[5]

Like a skein of loose silk blown against a wall
She walks by the railing of a path in Kensington Gardens,[6]
And she is dying piece-meal
        of a sort of emotional anæmia.

5   And round about there is a rabble
Of the filthy, sturdy, unkillable infants of the very poor.
They shall inherit the earth.

---

5. Albert Samain, late nineteenth-century French poet. The phrase is from the first line of the prefatory poem in his first book of poems, *Au Jardin de l'Infante:* "Mon âme est une infante en robe de parade" ("My soul is an Infanta in ceremonial dress"). An "Infanta" is a daughter of the Spanish royal family, which, long inbred, had for many years been afflicted with a rare blood disease, hemophilia.   6. A fashionable park near the center of London.

In her is the end of breeding.
Her boredom is exquisite and excessive.
She would like some one to speak to her,   10
And is almost afraid that I
            will commit that indiscretion.   1916

In a Station of the Metro[7]

The apparition of these faces in the crowd;
Petals on a wet, black bough.   p. 1913

THEODORE ROETHKE

The Waking

I wake to sleep, and take my waking slow.
I feel my fate in what I cannot fear.
I learn by going where I have to go.

We think by feeling. What is there to know?
I hear my being dance from ear to ear.   5
I wake to sleep, and take my waking slow.

Of those so close beside me, which are you?
God bless the Ground! I shall walk softly there,
And learn by going where I have to go.

Light takes the Tree; but who can tell us how?   10
The lowly worm climbs up a winding stair;
I wake to sleep, and take my waking slow.

Great Nature has another thing to do
To you and me; so take the lively air,
And, lovely, learn by going where to go.   15

This shaking keeps me steady. I should know.
What falls away is always. And is near.
I wake to sleep, and take my waking slow.
I learn by going where I have to go.   1953

7. The Paris subway.

MURIEL RUKEYSER

Myth

Long afterward, Oedipus, old and blinded, walked the
roads.   He smelled a familiar smell.   It was
the Sphinx.   Oedipus said, "I want to ask one question.
Why didn't I recognize my mother?"   "You gave the
5   wrong answer," said the Sphinx.   "But that was what
made everything possible," said Oedipus.   "No," she said.
"When I asked, What walks on four legs in the morning,
two at noon, and three in the evening, you answered,
Man.   You didn't say anything about woman."
10 "When you say Man," said Oedipus, "you include women
too. Everyone knows that."   She said, "That's what
you think."   1973

WILLIAM SHAKESPEARE

[Hark, hark! the lark at heaven's gate sings][8]

Hark, hark! the lark at heaven's gate sings,
    And Phoebus'[9] gins arise,
His steeds to water at those springs
    On chaliced[1] flowers that lies;
5 And winking Mary-buds[2] begin
    To ope their golden eyes:
With every thing that pretty is,
    My lady sweet, arise!
    Arise, arise!

ca. 1610

[Not marble, nor the gilded monuments]

Not marble, nor the gilded monuments
Of princes, shall outlive this powerful rhyme;
But you shall shine more bright in these conténts
Than unswept stone, besmeared with sluttish time.
5 When wasteful war shall statues overturn,
And broils root out the work of masonry,

---

8. From *Cymbeline* II.iii.   9. Apollo, the sun god.   1. Cup-shaped.   2. Buds of marigolds.

Nor Mars his sword nor war's quick fire shall burn
The living record of your memory.
'Gainst death and all-oblivious enmity
Shall you pace forth; your praise shall still find room   10
Even in the eyes of all posterity
That wear this world out to the ending doom.[3]
So, till the judgment that yourself arise,
You live in this, and dwell in lovers' eyes.   1609

Winter[4]

When icicles hang by the wall
   And Dick the shepherd blows[5] his nail,
And Tom bears logs into the hall,
   And milk comes frozen home in pail.
When blood is nipped and ways be foul,   5
Then nightly sings the staring owl,
          Tu-who;
Tu-whit, tu-who: a merry note,
While greasy Joan doth keel[6] the pot.

When all aloud the wind doth blow,   10
   And coughing drowns the parson's saw,[7]
And birds sit brooding in the snow,
   And Marian's nose looks red and raw,
When roasted crabs[8] hiss in the bowl,
Then nightly sings the staring owl,   15
          Tu-who;
Tu-whit, tu-who: a merry note
While greasy Joan doth keel the pot.

ca. 1595

WALLACE STEVENS

The Emperor of Ice-Cream

Call the roller of big cigars,
The muscular one, and bid him whip

---

3. Judgment Day.   4. From *Love's Labour's Lost* v.ii.   5. Breathes on for warmth. *Nail:* fingernail;
that is, hands.   6. Cool: stir to keep it from boiling over.   7. Maxim, proverb.   8. Crabapples.

In kitchen cups concupiscent curds.[9]
Let the wenches dawdle in such dress
As they are used to wear, and let the boys
Bring flowers in last month's newspapers.
Let be be finale of seem.[1]
The only emperor is the emperor of ice-cream.

Take from the dresser of deal,
Lacking the three glass knobs, that sheet
On which she embroidered fantails[2] once
And spread it so as to cover her face.
If her horny feet protrude, they come
To show how cold she is, and dumb.
Let the lamp affix its beam.
The only emperor is the emperor of ice-cream.

1923

Sunday Morning

I

Complacencies of the peignoir, and late
Coffee and oranges in a sunny chair,
And the green freedom of a cockatoo
Upon a rug mingle to dissipate
The holy hush of ancient sacrifice.
She dreams a little, and she feels the dark
Encroachment of that old catastrophe,[3]
As a calm darkens among water-lights.
The pungent oranges and bright, green wings
Seem things in some procession of the dead,
Winding across wide water, without sound,
The day is like wide water, without sound,
Stilled for the passing of her dreaming feet
Over the seas, to silent Palestine,
Dominion of the blood and sepulchre.

II

Why should she give her bounty to the dead?
What is divinity if it can come
Only in silent shadows and in dreams?
Shall she not find in comforts of the sun,
In pungent fruit and bright, green wings, or else

9. "The words 'concupiscent curds' have no genealogy; they are merely expressive: at least, I hope they are expressive. They express the concupiscence of life, but, by contrast with the things in relation in the poem, they express or accentuate life's destitution, and it is this that gives them something more than a cheap lustre." (Wallace Stevens, *Letters* [New York: Knopf, 1966], p. 500)   1. ". . . the true sense of Let be be the finale of seem is let being become the conclusion of denouement of appearing to be: in short, ice cream is an absolute good. The poem is obviously not about ice cream, but about being as distinguished from seeming to be." (Stevens, *Letters*, p. 341)   2. Fantail pigeons.   3. The Crucifixion.

In any balm or beauty of the earth,
Things to be cherished like the thought of heaven.
Divinity must live within herself:
Passions of rain, or moods in falling snow;
Grievings in loneliness, or unsubdued   25
Elations when the forest blooms; gusty
Emotions on wet roads on autumn nights;
All pleasures and all pains, remembering
The bough of summer and the winter branch.
These are the measures destined for her soul.   30

III

Jove in the clouds has his inhuman birth.
No mother suckled him, no sweet land gave
Large-mannered motions to his mythy mind
He moved among us, as a muttering king,
Magnificent, would move among his hinds,[4]   35
Until our blood, commingling, virginal,
With heaven, brought such requital to desire
The very hinds discerned it, in a star.[5]
Shall our blood fail? Or shall it come to be
The blood of paradise? And shall the earth   40
Seem all of paradise that we shall know?
The sky will be much friendlier then than now,
A part of labor and a part of pain,
And next in glory to enduring love,
Not this dividing and indifferent blue.   45

IV

She says, "I am content when wakened birds,
Before they fly, test the reality
Of misty fields, by their sweet questionings;
But when the birds are gone, and their warm fields
Return no more, where, then, is paradise?"   50
There is not any haunt of prophecy,
Nor any old chimera of the grave,
Neither the golden underground, nor isle
Melodious, where spirits gat[6] them home,
Nor visionary south, nor cloudy palm   55
Remote on heaven's hill, that has endured
As April's green endures, or will endure
Like her remembrance of awakened birds,
Or her desire for June and evening, tipped
By the consummation of the swallow's wings.   60

V

She says, "But in contentment I still feel
The need of some imperishable bliss."

4. Lowliest rural subjects.   5. The star of Bethlehem.   6. Got.

Death is the mother of beauty; hence from her,
Alone, shall come fulfillment to our dreams
65   And our desires. Although she strews the leaves
Of sure obliteration on our paths,
The path sick sorrow took, the many paths
Where triumph rang its brassy phrase, or love
Whispered a little out of tenderness,
70   She makes the willow shiver in the sun
For maidens who were wont to sit and gaze
Upon the grass, relinquished to their feet.
She causes boys to pile new plums and pears
On disregarded plate.[7] The maidens taste
75   And stray impassioned in the littering leaves.

VI

Is there no change of death in paradise?
Does ripe fruit never fall? Or do the boughs
Hang always heavy in that perfect sky,
Unchanging, yet so like our perishing earth,
80   With rivers like our own that seek for seas
They never find, the same receding shores
That never touch with inarticulate pang?
Why set the pear upon those river-banks
Or spice the shores with odors of the plum?
85   Alas, that they should wear our colors there,
The silken weavings of our afternoons,
And pick the strings of our insipid lutes!
Death is the mother of beauty, mystical,
Within whose burning bosom we devise
90   Our earthly mothers awaiting, sleeplessly.

VII

Supple and turbulent, a ring of men
Shall chant in orgy[8] on a summer morn
Their boisterous devotion to the sun,
Not as a god, but as a god might be,
95   Naked among them, like a savage source.
Their chant shall be a chant of paradise,
Out of their blood, returning to the sky;
And in their chant shall enter, voice by voice,
The windy lake wherein their lord delights,
100   The trees, like serafin,[9] and echoing hills,
That choir among themselves long afterward.
They shall know well the heavenly fellowship
Of men that perish and of summer morn.

---

7. "Plate is used in the sense of so-called family plate. Disregarded refers to the disuse into which things fall that have been possessed for a long time. I mean, therefore, that death releases and renews. What the old have come to disregard, the young inherit and make use of." (Stevens, *Letters*, pp. 183–84)   8. Ceremonial revelry.   9. Seraphim, the highest of the nine orders of angels.

And whence they came and whither they shall go
The dew upon their feet shall manifest.   105

        VIII

She hears, upon that water without sound,
A voice that cries, "The tomb in Palestine
Is not the porch of spirits lingering.
It is the grave of Jesus, where he lay."
We live in an old chaos of the sun,   110
Or old dependency of day and night,
Or island solitude, unsponsored, free,
Of that wide water, inescapable.
Deer walk upon our mountains, and the quail
Whistle about us their spontaneous cries;   115
Sweet berries ripen in the wilderness;
And, in the isolation of the sky,
At evening, casual flocks of pigeons make
Ambiguous undulations as they sink,
Downward to darkness, on extended wings.   120

1915

DYLAN THOMAS

Fern Hill

Now as I was young and easy under the apple boughs
About the lilting house and happy as the grass was green,
        The night above the dingle starry,
            Time let me hail and climb
        Golden in the heydays of his eyes,   5
And honored among wagons I was prince of the apple towns
And once below a time I lordly had the trees and leaves
            Trail with daisies and barley
        Down the rivers of the windfall light.

And as I was green and carefree, famous among the barns   10
About the happy yard and singing as the farm was home,
        In the sun that is young once only,
            Time let me play and be
        Golden in the mercy of his means,
And green and golden I was huntsman and herdsman, the calves   15
Sang to my horn, the foxes on the hills barked clear and cold,
            And the sabbath rang slowly
        In the pebbles of the holy streams.

All the sun long it was running, it was lovely, the hay
Fields high as the house, the tunes from the chimneys, it was air   20
        And playing, lovely and watery

And fire green as grass.
And nightly under the simple stars
As I rode to sleep the owls were bearing the farm away,
25   All the moon long I heard, blessed among stables, the nightjars[1]
Flying with the ricks,[2] and the horses
Flashing into the dark.

And then to awake, and the farm, like a wanderer white
With the dew, come back, the cock on his shoulder: it was all
30   Shining, it was Adam and maiden,
The sky gathered again
And the sun grew round that very day.
So it must have been after the birth of the simple light
In the first, spinning place, the spellbound horses walking warm
35   Out of the whinnying green stable
On to the fields of praise.

And honored among foxes and pheasants by the gay house
Under the new made clouds and happy as the heart was long,
In the sun born over and over,
40   I ran my heedless ways,
My wishes raced through the house-high hay
And nothing I cared, at my sky-blue trades, that time allows
In all his tuneful turning so few and such morning songs
Before the children green and golden
45   Follow him out of grace,

Nothing I cared, in the lamb white days, that time would take me
Up to the swallow-thronged loft by the shadow of my hand,
In the moon that is always rising,
Nor that riding to sleep
50   I should hear him fly with the high fields
And wake to the farm forever fled from the childless land.
Oh as I was young and easy in the mercy of his means,
Time held me green and dying
Though I sang in my chains like the sea.   1946

In My Craft or Sullen Art

In my craft or sullen art
Exercised in the still night
When only the moon rages
And the lovers lie abed
5   With all their griefs in their arms,
I labor by singing light
Not for ambition or bread
Or the strut and trade of charms
On the ivory stages

---

1. Birds.   2. Haystacks.

But for the common wages   10
Of their most secret heart.

Not for the proud man apart
From the raging moon I write
On these spindrift[3] pages
Nor for the towering dead   15
With their nightingales and psalms
But for the lovers, their arms
Round the griefs of the ages,
Who pay no praise or wages
Nor heed my craft or art.   20

                                                              1946

JEAN TOOMER

Song of the Son[4]

Pour O pour that parting soul in song,
O pour it in the sawdust glow of night,
Into the velvet pine-smoke air tonight,
And let the valley carry it along.
And let the valley carry it along.   5

O land and soil, red soil and sweet-gum tree,
So scant of grass, so profligate of pines,
Now just before an epoch's sun declines
Thy son, in time, I have returned to thee,
Thy son, I have in time returned to thee.   10

In time, for though the sun is setting on
A song-lit race of slaves, it has not set;
Though late, O soil, it is not too late yet
To catch thy plaintive soul, leaving, soon gone,
Leaving, to catch thy plaintive soul soon gone.   15

O Negro slaves, dark purple ripened plums,
Squeezed, and bursting in the pine-wood air,
Passing, before they strip the old tree bare
One plum was saved for me, one seed becomes

An everlasting song, a singing tree,   20
Caroling softly souls of slavery,
What they were, and what they are to me,
Caroling softly souls of slavery.   1923

3. Literally, wind-driven sea spray.   4. From the novel *Cane*.

WALT WHITMAN

Facing West from California's Shores

Facing west, from California's shores,
Inquiring, tireless, seeking what is yet unfound,
I, a child, very old, over waves, towards the house of maternity,[5] the
    land of migrations, look afar,
Look off the shores of my Western sea, the circle almost circled:
5 For starting westward from Hindustan, from the vales of Kashmere,
From Asia, from the north, from the God, the sage, and the hero,
From the south, from the flowery peninsulas and the spice islands,
Long having wandered since, round the earth having wandered,
Now I face home again, very pleased and joyous;
10 (But where is what I started for, so long ago?
And why is it yet unfound?)   1860

I Hear America Singing

I hear America singing, the varied carols I hear,
Those of mechanics, each one singing his as it should be blithe and
    strong,
The carpenter singing his as he measures his plank or beam,
The mason singing his as he makes ready for work, or leaves off work,
The boatman singing what belongs to him in his boat, the deckhand
5   singing on the steamboat deck,
The shoemaker singing as he sits on his bench, the hatter singing as he
    stands,
The wood-cutter's song, the ploughboy's on his way in the morning, or
    at noon intermission or at sundown,
The delicious singing of the mother, or of the young wife at work, or of
    the girl sewing or washing,
Each singing what belongs to him or her and to none else,
The day what belongs to the day—at night the party of young fellows,
10   robust, friendly,
Singing with open mouths their strong melodious songs.
                                                              1860

---

5. Asia, as the supposed birthplace of the human race.

RICHARD WILBUR

The Beautiful Changes

One wading a Fall meadow finds on all sides
The Queen Anne's Lace[6] lying like lilies
On water; it glides
So from the walker, it turns
Dry grass to a lake, as the slightest shade of you   5
Valleys my mind in fabulous blue Lucernes.[7]

The beautiful changes as a forest is changed
By a chameleon's tuning his skin to it;
As a mantis, arranged
On a green leaf, grows   10
Into it, makes the leaf leafier, and proves
Any greenness is deeper than anyone knows.

Your hands hold roses always in a way that says
They are not only yours; the beautiful changes
In such kind ways,   15
Wishing ever to sunder
Things and things' selves for a second finding, to lose
For a moment all that it touches back to wonder.   1947

WILLIAM CARLOS WILLIAMS

This Is Just to Say

I have eaten
the plums
that were in
the icebox

and which   5
you were probably
saving
for breakfast

Forgive me
they were delicious   10
so sweet
and so cold   1934

---

6. A delicate-looking plant, with finely divided leaves and flat clusters of small white flowers, sometimes called "wild carrot."   7. Alfalfa, a plant resembling clover, with small purple flowers. Lake Lucerne is famed for deep blue color and its picturesque Swiss setting amid limestone mountains.

WILLIAM WORDSWORTH

Lines Composed a Few Miles above Tintern Abbey on Revisiting the Banks of the Wye during a Tour, July 13, 1798[8]

Five years have passed; five summers, with the length
Of five long winters! and again I hear
These waters, rolling from their mountain-springs
With a soft inland murmur. Once again
5   Do I behold these steep and lofty cliffs,
That on a wild secluded scene impress
Thoughts of more deep seclusion; and connect
The landscape with the quiet of the sky.
The day is come when I again repose
10   Here, under this dark sycamore, and view
These plots of cottage-ground, these orchard tufts,
Which at this season, with their unripe fruits,
Are clad in one green hue, and lose themselves
'Mid groves and copses.[9] Once again I see
15   These hedge-rows, hardly hedge-rows, little lines
Of sportive wood run wild: these pastoral farms,
Green to the very door; and wreaths of smoke
Sent up, in silence, from among the trees!
With some uncertain notice, as might seem
20   Of vagrant dwellers in the houseless woods,
Or of some hermit's cave, where by his fire
The hermit sits alone.
                            These beauteous forms,
Through a long absence, have not been to me
As is a landscape to a blind man's eye;
25   But oft, in lonely rooms, and 'mid the din
Of towns and cities, I have owed to them,
In hours of weariness, sensations sweet,
Felt in the blood, and felt along the heart;
And passing even into my purer mind,
30   With tranquil restoration—feelings too
Of unremembered pleasure: such, perhaps,
As have no slight or trivial influence
On that best portion of a good man's life,
His little, nameless, unremembered acts
35   Of kindness and of love. Nor less, I trust,
To them I may have owed another gift,

---

8. Wordsworth had first visited the Wye valley and the ruins of the medieval abbey there in 1793, while on a solitary walking tour. He was twenty-three then, twenty-eight when he wrote this poem.
9. Thickets.

Of aspect more sublime; that blesséd mood,
In which the burthen[1] of the mystery,
In which the heavy and the weary weight
Of all this unintelligible world,   40
Is lightened—that serene and blesséd mood,
In which the affections gently lead us on—
Until, the breath of this corporeal frame
And even the motion of our human blood
Almost suspended, we are laid asleep   45
In body, and become a living soul;
While with an eye made quiet by the power
Of harmony, and the deep power of joy,
We see into the life of things.
                    If this
Be but a vain belief, yet, oh! how oft—   50
In darkness and amid the many shapes
Of joyless daylight; when the fretful stir
Unprofitable, and the fever of the world,
Have hung upon the beatings of my heart—
How oft, in spirit, have I turned to thee,   55
O sylvan Wye! thou wanderer through the woods,
How often has my spirit turned to thee!

   And now, with gleams of half-extinguished thought,
With many recognitions dim and faint,
And somewhat of a sad perplexity,   60
The picture of the mind revives again;
While here I stand, not only with the sense
Of present pleasure, but with pleasing thoughts
That in this moment there is life and food
For future years. And so I dare to hope,   65
Though changed, no doubt, from what I was when first
I came among these hills; when like a roe
I bounded o'er the mountains, by the sides
Of the deep rivers, and the lonely streams,
Wherever nature led: more like a man   70
Flying from something that he dreads than one
Who sought the thing he loved. For nature then
(The coarser[2] pleasures of my boyish days,
And their glad animal movements all gone by)
To me was all in all—I cannot paint   75
What then I was. The sounding cataract
Haunted me like a passion; the tall rock,
The mountain, and the deep and gloomy wood,
Their colors and their forms, were then to me
An appetite; a feeling and a love,   80
That had no need of a remoter charm.

1. Burden.   2. Physical.

By thought supplied, nor any interest
Unborrowed from the eye. That time is past,
And all its aching joys are now no more,
85   And all its dizzy raptures. Not for this
Faint I,[3] nor mourn nor murmur; other gifts
Have followed; for such loss, I would believe,
Abundant recompense. For I have learned
To look on nature, not as in the hour
90   Of thoughtless youth; but hearing oftentimes
The still, sad music of humanity,
Nor harsh nor grating, though of ample power
To chasten and subdue. And I have felt
A presence that disturbs me with the joy
95   Of elevated thoughts, a sense sublime
Of something far more deeply interfused,
Whose dwelling is the light of setting suns,
And the round ocean and the living air,
And the blue sky, and in the mind of man:
100   A motion and a spirit, that impels
All thinking things, all objects of all thought,
And rolls through all things. Therefore am I still
A lover of the meadows and the woods
And mountains; and of all that we behold
105   From this green earth; of all the mighty world
Of eye, and ear—both what they half create,
And what perceive; well pleased to recognize
In nature and the language of the sense
The anchor of my purest thoughts, the nurse,
110   The guide, the guardian of my heart, and soul
Of all my moral being.   Nor perchance,
If I were not thus taught, should I the more
Suffer my genial spirits[4] to decay:
For thou art with me here upon the banks
115   Of this fair river; thou my dearest Friend,[5]
My dear, dear Friend; and in thy voice I catch
The language of my former heart, and read
My former pleasures in the shooting lights
Of thy wild eyes. Oh! yet a little while
120   May I behold in thee what I was once,
My dear, dear Sister! and this prayer I make,
Knowing that Nature never did betray
The heart that loved her; 'tis her privilege,
Through all the years of this our life, to lead
125   From joy to joy: for she can so inform
The mind that is within us, so impress
With quietness and beauty, and so feed

---

3. Am I discouraged.   4. Natural disposition; that is, the spirits that are part of his individual genius.
5. His sister Dorothy.

With lofty thoughts, that neither evil tongues,
Rash judgments, nor the sneers of selfish men,
Nor greetings where no kindness is, nor all   130
The dreary intercourse of daily life,
Shall e'er prevail against us, or disturb
Our cheerful faith that all which we behold
Is full of blessings. Therefore let the moon
Shine on thee in thy solitary walk;   135
And let the misty mountain-winds be free
To blow against thee: and, in after years,
When these wild ecstasies shall be matured
Into a sober pleasure; when thy mind
Shall be a mansion for all lovely forms,   140
Thy memory be as a dwelling-place
For all sweet sounds and harmonies; oh! then,
If solitude, or fear, or pain, or grief,
Should be thy portion, with what healing thoughts
Of tender joy wilt thou remember me,   145
And these my exhortations! No, perchance—
If I should be where I no more can hear
Thy voice, nor catch from thy wild eyes these gleams
Of past existence—wilt thou then forget
That on the banks of this delightful stream   150
We stood together; and that I, so long
A worshiper of Nature, hither came
Unwearied in that service; rather say
With warmer love—oh! with far deeper zeal
Of holier love. Nor wilt thou then forget,   155
That after many wanderings, many years
Of absence, these steep woods and lofty cliffs,
And this green pastoral landscape, were to me
More dear, both for themselves and for thy sake!   1798

W. B. YEATS

Easter 1916[6]

I have met them at close of day
Coming with vivid faces
From counter or desk among gray
Eighteenth-century houses.
I have passed with a nod of the head   5

6. On Easter Monday 1916, an Irish Republic was proclaimed by nationalist leaders, who launched an unsuccessful revolt against the British government. After a week of street fighting, the Easter Rebellion was put down. A number of prominent nationalists were executed, including the four leaders mentioned in lines 75–76, all of whom Yeats knew personally.

Or polite meaningless words,
Or have lingered awhile and said
Polite meaningless words,
And thought before I had done
10   Of a mocking tale or a gibe
To please a companion
Around the fire at the club,
Being certain that they and I
But lived where motley is worn:
15   All changed, changed utterly:
A terrible beauty is born.

That woman's[7] days were spent
In ignorant good-will,
Her nights in argument
20   Until her voice grew shrill.
What voice more sweet than hers
When, young and beautiful,
She rode to harriers?
This man[8] had kept a school
25   And rode our wingéd horse;[9]
This other[1] his helper and friend
Was coming into his force;
He might have won fame in the end,
So sensitive his nature seemed,
30   So daring and sweet his thought.
This other man[2] I had dreamed
A drunken, vainglorious lout.
He had done most bitter wrong
To some who are near my heart,
35   Yet I number him in the song;
He, too, has resigned his part
In the casual comedy;
He, too, has been changed in his turn,
Transformed utterly:
40   A terrible beauty is born.

Hearts with one purpose alone
Through summer and winter seem
Enchanted to a stone
To trouble the living stream.

7. Countess Constance Georgina Markiewicz, a beautiful and well-born young woman from County Sligo who became a vigorous and bitter nationalist. At first condemned to death, she later had her sentence commuted to life imprisonment, and she gained amnesty in 1917.   8. Patrick Pearse, who led the assault on the Dublin Post Office, from which the proclamation of a republic was issued. A schoolmaster by profession, he had vigorously supported the restoration of the Gaelic language in Ireland and was an active political writer and poet.   9. Pegasus, a traditional symbol of poetic inspiration.   1. Thomas MacDonagh, also a writer and teacher.   2. Major John MacBride, who married Yeats's beloved Maud Gonne in 1903 but separated from her two years later.

The horse that comes from the road,   45
The rider, the birds that range
From cloud to tumbling cloud,
Minute by minute they change;
A shadow of cloud on the stream
Changes minute by minute;   50
A horse-hoof slides on the brim,
And a horse plashes within it;
The long-legged moor-hens dive,
And hens to moor-cocks call;
Minute by minute they live: 55
The stone's in the midst of all.

Too long a sacrifice
Can make a stone of the heart.
O when may it suffice?
That is Heaven's part, our part   60
To murmur name upon name,
As a mother names her child
When sleep at last has come
On limbs that had run wild.
What is it but nightfall?   65
No, no, not night but death;
Was it needless death after all?
For England may keep faith[3]
For all that is done and said.
We know their dream; enough   70
To know they dreamed and are dead;
And what if excess of love
Bewildered them till they died?
I write it out in a verse—
MacDonagh and MacBride   75
And Connolly[4] and Pearse
Now and in time to be,
Wherever green is worn,
Are changed, changed utterly;
A terrible beauty is born.   80

1916

---

3. Before the uprising the English had promised eventual home rule to Ireland.   4. James Connolly, the leader of the Easter uprising.

The Second Coming[5]

Turning and turning in the widening gyre[6]
The falcon cannot hear the falconer;
Things fall apart; the center cannot hold;
Mere anarchy is loosed upon the world,
5 The blood-dimmed tide is loosed, and everywhere
The ceremony of innocence is drowned;
The best lack all conviction, while the worst
Are full of passionate intensity.
Surely some revelation is at hand;
10 Surely the Second Coming is at hand.
The Second Coming! Hardly are those words out
When a vast image out of *Spiritus Mundi*[7]
Troubles my sight: somewhere in sands of the desert
A shape with lion body and the head of a man,
15 A gaze blank and pitiless as the sun,
Is moving its slow thighs, while all about it
Reel shadows of the indignant desert birds.[8]
The darkness drops again; but now I know
That twenty centuries of stony sleep
20 Were vexed to nightmare by a rocking cradle,
And what rough beast, its hour come round at last,
Slouches towards Bethlehem to be born?   p. 1920

Leda and the Swan[9]

A sudden blow: the great wings beating still
Above the staggering girl, her thighs caressed
By the dark webs, her nape caught in his bill,
He holds her helpless breast upon his breast.

5. The Second Coming of Christ, according to Matthew 24:29–44, will come after a time of "tribulation." Disillusioned by Ireland's continued civil strife, Yeats saw his time as the end of another historical cycle. In *A Vision* (1937) Yeats describes his view of history as dependent on cycles of about 2,000 years: the birth of Christ had ended the cycle of Greco-Roman civilization, and now the Christian cycle seemed near an end, to be followed by an antithetical cycle, ominous in its portents.   6. Literally, the widening spiral of a falcon's flight. "Gyre" is Yeats's term for a cycle of history, which he diagramed in terms of a series of interpenetrating cones.   7. Or *Anima Mundi*, the spirit or soul of the world. Yeats considered this universal consciousness or memory a fund from which poets drew their images and symbols.   8. Yeats later wrote of the "brazen winged beast . . . described in my poem *The Second Coming*" as "associated with laughing, ecstatic destruction." "Our civilization was about to reverse itself, or some new civilization about to be born from all that our age had rejected . . . ; because we had worshiped a single god it would worship many."   9. According to Greek myth, Zeus took the form of a swan to seduce Leda, who became the mother of Helen of Troy and also of Clytemnestra, Agamemnon's wife and murderer. Helen's abduction from her husband, Menelaus, brother of Agamemnon, began the Trojan War (line 10). Yeats described the visit of Zeus to Leda as an annunciation like that to Mary (see Luke 1:26–38): "I imagine the annunciation that founded Greece as made to Leda. . . ." (*A Vision*).

How can those terrified vague fingers push
The feathered glory from her loosening thighs?
And how can body, laid in that white rush,
But feel the strange heart beating where it lies?

A shudder in the loins engenders there
The broken wall, the burning roof and tower
And Agamemnon dead.
                        Being so caught up,
So mastered by the brute blood of the air,
Did she put on his knowledge with his power
Before the indifferent beak could let her drop?

1923

Sailing to Byzantium[1]

I

That[2] is no country for old men. The young
In one another's arms, birds in the trees
—Those dying generations—at their song,
The salmon-falls, the mackerel-crowded seas
Fish, flesh, or fowl, commend all summer long
Whatever is begotten, born, and dies.
Caught in that sensual music all neglect
Monuments of unaging intellect.

II

An aged man is but a paltry thing,
A tattered coat upon a stick, unless
Soul clap its hands and sing, and louder sing
For every tatter in its mortal dress,
Nor is there singing school but studying
Monuments of its own magnificence;
And therefore I have sailed the seas and come
To the holy city of Byzantium.

III

O sages standing in God's holy fire
As in the gold mosaic of a wall,
Come from the holy fire, perne in a gyre,[3]

1. The ancient name of Istanbul, the capital and holy city of Eastern Christendom from the late fourth century until 1453. It was famous for its stylized and formal mosaics, its symbolic, nonnaturalistic art, and its highly developed intellectual life. Yeats repeatedly uses it to symbolize a world of artifice and timelessness, free from the decay and death of the natural and sensual world.   2. Ireland, as an instance of the natural, temporal world.   3. That is, whirl in a coiling motion, so that his soul may merge with its motion as the timeless world invades the cycles of history and nature. "Perne" is Yeats's coinage (from the noun "pirn"): to spin around in the kind of spiral pattern that thread makes as it comes off a bobbin or spool.

20   And be the singing-masters of my soul.
　　Consume my heart away; sick with desire
　　And fastened to a dying animal
　　It knows not what it is; and gather me
　　Into the artifice of eternity.

IV

25   Once out of nature I shall never take
　　My bodily form from any natural thing,
　　But such a form as Grecian goldsmiths make
　　Of hammered gold and gold enameling
　　To keep a drowsy Emperor awake;[4]
30   Or set upon a golden bough[5] to sing
　　To lords and ladies of Byzantium
　　Of what is past, or passing, or to come.

　　　　　　　　　　　　　　　　　　　　　　1927

Among School Children

I

I walk through the long schoolroom questioning;
A kind old nun in a white hood replies;
The children learn to cipher and to sing,
To study reading-books and history,
5   To cut and sew, be neat in everything
In the best modern way—the children's eyes
In momentary wonder stare upon
A sixty-year-old smiling public man.[6]

II

I dream of a Ledaean body,[7] bent
10   Above a sinking fire, a tale that she
Told of a harsh reproof, or trivial event
That changed some childish day to tragedy—
Told, and it seemed that our two natures blent
Into a sphere from youthful sympathy,
15   Or else, to alter Plato's parable,
Into the yolk and white of the one shell.[8]

4. "I have read somewhere that in the Emperor's palace at Byzantium was a tree made of gold and silver, and artificial birds that sang." (WBY)　　5. In Book VI of *The Aeneid*, the sybil tells Aeneas that he must pluck a golden bough from a nearby tree in order to descend to Hades. There is only one such branch there, and when it is plucked an identical one takes its place.　　6. At sixty (in 1925) Yeats had been a senator of the Irish Free State.　　7. Like that of Helen of Troy, daughter of Leda. The memory dream is of Maud Gonne (see also lines 29–30), with whom Yeats had long been hopelessly in love.　　8. In Plato's *Symposium,* the origin of human love is explained by parable: Human beings were once spheres, but Zeus was fearful of their power and cut them in half; now each half longs to be reunited with its missing half. Helen and Pollux were hatched from one of two eggs born to Leda after her union with Zeus in the form of a swan; the other contained Castor and Clytemnestra. According to Yeats in *A Vision,* "from one of [Leda's] eggs came Love and from the other War."

III

And thinking of that fit of grief or rage
I look upon one child or t'other there
And wonder if she stood so at that age—
For even daughters of the swan can share   20
Something of every paddler's heritage—
And had that color upon cheek or hair,
And thereupon my heart is driven wild:
She stands before me as a living child.

IV

Her present image floats into the mind—   25
Did Quattrocento finger[9] fashion it
Hollow of cheek as though it drank the wind
And took a mess of shadows for its meat?
And I though never of Ledaean kind
Had pretty plumage once—enough of that,   30
Better to smile on all that smile, and show
There is a comfortable kind of old scarecrow.

V

What youthful mother, a shape upon her lap
Honey of generation[1] had betrayed,
And that must sleep, shriek, struggle to escape   35
As recollection or the drug decide,
Would think her son, did she but see that shape
With sixty or more winters on its head,
A compensation for the pang of his birth,
Or the uncertainty of his setting forth?   40

VI

Plato thought nature but a spume that plays
Upon a ghostly paradigm of things;[2]
Solider Aristotle played the taws
Upon the bottom of a king of kings;[3]
World-famous golden-thighed Pythagoras[4]   45
Fingered upon a fiddle-stick or strings
What a star sang and careless Muses heard:
Old clothes upon old sticks to scare a bird.

9. The hand of a fifteenth-century artist. Yeats especially admired Botticelli, and in *A Vision* praises his "deliberate strangeness everywhere [that] gives one an emotion of mystery which is new to painting."
1. Porphyry, a third-century Greek scholar and Neoplatonic philosopher, says "honey of generation" means the "pleasure arising from copulation" that draws souls "downward" to generation.   2. Plato considered the world of nature an imperfect and illusory copy of the ideal world.   3. Aristotle, the teacher of Alexander the Great, disciplined him with a strap ("taw," line 43). His philosophy, insisting on the interdependence of form and matter, took the world of nature far more seriously than did Plato's.
4. Pythagoras (580?–500? B.C.), the Greek mathematician and philosopher, was highly revered, and one legend describes his godlike golden thighs.

VII

50   Both nuns and mothers worship images,
     But those the candles light are not as those
     That animate a mother's reveries
     But keep a marble or a bronze repose.
     And yet they too break hearts—O Presences
     That passion, piety or affection knows,
55   And that all heavenly glory symbolize—
     O self-born mockers of man's enterprise;

VIII

     Labor is blossoming or dancing where
     The body is not bruised to pleasure soul,
     Nor beauty born out of its own despair,
60   Nor blear-eyed wisdom out of midnight oil.
     O chestnut-tree, great-rooted blossomer,
     Are you the leaf, the blossom or the bole?
     O body swayed to music, O brightening glance,
     How can we know the dancer from the dance?   1927

Drama

Drama:
Reading, Responding, Writing

Plays are generally written to be performed—by actors, on a stage, for an audience. Playwrights create plays fully conscious of the possibilities that go beyond words and texts and extend to physical actions, stage devices, and other bits of theatricality that can be used to create special effects and modify responses. Consequently, responding to a stage production of a play involves physical senses as well as the imagination. Furthermore, your responses are not wholly a private matter. Responding to a theatrical production is, in part, communal: you respond not just as an individual but as part of an audience sharing the moment.

To attend a play—to see and hear it as part of an audience—represents a different kind of experience from the usually solitary act of reading. Plays are performed before live audiences of real people who respond directly and immediately to them, unlike texts that may lie silent and undisturbed in a book for days or even years at a time. When plays are acted out on a stage, you see actions and hear words spoken; real live human beings, standing for imaginary characters, deliver lines and perform actions that you listen to and watch. Furthermore, you sit with others who are also watching and responding to the play. You and the other members of the audience have, at a single instant, a common experience that you have deliberately sought: you have assembled for the explicit purpose of seeing a play.

> On the stage it is always now; the personages are standing on that razor-edge, between the past and the future, which is the essential character of conscious being; the words are rising to their lips in immediate spontaneity.
>
> —THORNTON WILDER

But you are not directly experiencing the author's text. It has been mediated by the director and actors who have brought it to the stage and to your eyes and ears. These mediators are interpreters of the play, and they perform for viewers part of the act of imagination that readers must perform for themselves. In poems and stories, only the written text stands between author and reader; but in plays, all of the people involved in a particular production—the director, producer, actors, even stage designers—help to interpret the author's text for a specific audience. Consciously or not, every director puts an interpretation on every scene by the way he or she stages the action; timing, casting, set design, physical interaction, and the phrasing and tone of every speech affect how the play will come across. Every syllable uttered by every actor in some sense affects the outcome; tone of voice and the slightest body gesture are, for an actor, equivalent to the choices of words and sentence rhythm for a writer.

Every performance is a unique expression of a collaborative effort. Actors must remember hundreds of lines and perform movements on stage at precise times; the stagehands must change sets and install props between scenes; light and sound effects must occur on certain visual and aural cues. In any of these areas a single change or error—a new inflection at the end of a line or a misplaced prop—guarantees that a given performance will be unique. Similarly, no two audiences are the same, and the character of an audience inevitably affects the performance. A warm, responsive audience will bring out the best in the performers, as any actor will tell you, while a crowd's cold indifference often results in a tepid or stiff production. For these reasons, no staged realization of a play can ever duplicate another.

Just as no two single performances are ever identical, no two interpretations are ever exactly the same. It is common to speak of Olivier's Hamlet (meaning the performance of the title role by Sir Laurence Olivier), of Dame Maggie Smith's or Glenda Jackson's Hedda Gabler, or Zeffirelli's *Romeo and Juliet* (meaning the film directed by Franco Zeffirelli), because in each case the hand of the actor or director leads to a distinctive interpretation of the play. In the written text Hamlet may be regarded as indecisive, melancholy, conniving, mad, vindictive, ambitious, or some combination of these things; individual performances emphasize one attribute or another, always at some expense to other characteristics and interpretations. No play can be all things to an audience in any one performance or run. And no two members of the audience will respond to all of these signals in exactly the same way.

It is this limitation of the performed play, its multiple variables but necessary restriction of the several possible meanings of the work to one interpretation, that led the nineteenth-century writer Charles Lamb to come home from the theater vowing never to see another play of Shakespeare's on the stage. He found that no matter how good the performance, the enacted play restricted his imagination and robbed the play of some of the richness he found in reading it—and imagining it—for himself.

It is not necessary to renounce the theater or deprive ourselves of the thrilling experience of a brilliantly directed and performed interpretation of a play, but it is useful to reassert the quite different claims of reading drama as *literature,* as something written. Reading drama is not a poor substitute for seeing a play; it is simply a different kind of experience, literary rather than theatrical.

In some ways reading a play is no different from reading a story or novel. In both cases we anticipate what is to happen next and what it all means. In reading both narrative and drama we imagine the characters, setting, action; and in reading both we respond to the symbolic suggestiveness of images and we project configurations of thematic significance. The chief difference between narrative and drama on the page is the absence, in drama, of a mediator, someone standing between the reader and the work and helping us relate to the characters, actions, and meanings. It is for this reason that reading drama is for many a greater strain on the imagination: the reader is his or her own mediator, narrator, interpreter.

Reading drama is not only a compelling literary experience in itself, but even the strain it puts upon our imaginations are rewarding. For not only are we freer to incorporate the play into our own being, but in becoming our own mediator we see how our imagination or our response to storytelling language really works. It is customary to assume that we "cast characters" in our minds, paint in the scenic backdrops, place the furniture and props, and choreograph the action. While we no doubt do some of this, it seems that most of our imaginations are not so well stocked, and that we do not fully re-create what the playwright had in her or his mind's eye. We can ask ourselves whom we might cast as Hamlet or Hedda Gabler, but most of us do not have a full and fixed visual image of a character: we have a shape here, a profile there, adding a feature, mannerism, or gesture as we read on, mainly on the basis of suggestions in the text, though sometimes according to memories of theatrical performances or movies seen previously.

In reading drama where dialogue is more or less all we have, we reconstruct character and personality from what the character says; we do this by relating our own experiences to what we are reading, responding in terms of expectations based on what we have felt in comparable situations. We've known someone who said things like this, or remember another play or story that suggests such attitudes and statements. So what we imagine as we read depends greatly upon our repertoire of experiences of life and literature. A character, even at the end of a play, is less a solid reconstruction than a series of frames like those that make up a moving picture, each a little different. When we have seen an actor playing Blanche DuBois in *A Streetcar Named Desire* and see her as we read the play, we are no longer reading that play but watching it in our mind, more or less remembering a play we once saw.

To say this is not necessarily to agree with Charles Lamb—an actor can show us something in a part we might not have seen for ourselves. If we would go to the theater more often, we would have layers of performances to lend depth to our reading. But to read a play we have never seen is not to watch in the mind's eye a single, well-defined figure incorporating a character throughout the one, three, or five acts. We *watch* plays, but we *read* drama. Though we must take every opportunity to see a play performed to enrich our own reading of it, and though we should take advantage of our silent reading to include all the alternatives we can, each time we read a play we do our own interpreting, make our own choices and omissions. Reading, we perform all the parts, and we may want to ask ourselves how we would act this or that role, read this or that line; what kind of person we should try to imagine ourselves being; what, if we were that person, our motivations might be, and so on. But most important, perhaps, we want to be aware of what choices are available and what making one choice or another means.

As with fiction and poetry, writing about drama usually sharpens your responses and focuses your reading. When you write about drama, you are—in a very real sense—performing the role that directors and actors take on in a stage performance: you are giving your "reading" of the text, interpreting it to guide other readers' responses. But you are also, as when you write about a story or a poem, molding your own response, by forcing yourself to be clear about just what your response is. The virtue of writing about drama, as in writing about any text, lies mainly in your having to be precise and articulate about how the text affects you. Normally, you consider what a play says to you and how the theatrical or imagined action is to be interpreted before you actually begin to write about it, but the act of writing will give shape to your initial impressions and lead to further reflection and insight. Your reading of texts in drama (and in fiction and poetry) is considerably enhanced by your writing about them, just as the process of responding itself is often clarified by your putting into words what has happened to you as a result of confronting the text.

And as writing about a play after you have read it may help you to formulate or clarify your response, jotting down your thoughts before you've finished it may help you to clarify your expectations. If when someone is speaking you always finish his or her sentence, you are not being a good listener, but if when reading you always project forward, to what may happen next, or what a certain character will finally be revealed to be like, or what a play will show or suggest, you are being a good reader. As with fiction and poetry, expectation or anticipation should always be part of your response. One way to capture this kind of response is to stop your reading at some reasonable point—the end of a scene or an act, or when you are puzzled or where the action seems to pause briefly—and write out how you think the action will proceed, how the play will end, what its characters will ultimately seem like to you, and what the play will seem to say or show.

When we begin reading the short play that follows, Susan Glaspell's *Trifles,* even the title may raise certain expectations: Is the play to be a light comedy, something "trifling"? The list of characters that follows the title, however, includes a sheriff and his wife and a county attorney, suggesting, perhaps a different kind of play. You could at this point jot down what your expectations are or what questions you have about what kind of a play this will be. You might pause again when, just a few lines into the play, the county attorney asks Mr. Hale to "tell just what happened," and examine your expectations at that point.

As you continue to read, mark points in the play where your expectations are confirmed or altered, and where you find answers to your questions about what kind of play it is, how it will end, and what its theme is.

SUSAN GLASPELL

Trifles

CHARACTERS

SHERIFF	MRS. PETERS, *Sheriff's wife*
COUNTY ATTORNEY	MRS. HALE
HALE	

SCENE: *The kitchen in the now abandoned farmhouse of* JOHN WRIGHT, *a gloomy kitchen, and left without having been put in order—unwashed pans under the sink, a loaf of bread outside the bread-box, a dish-towel on the table—other signs of incompleted work. At the rear the outer door opens and the* SHERIFF *comes in followed by the* COUNTY ATTORNEY *and* HALE. *The* SHERIFF *and* HALE *are men in middle life, the* COUNTY ATTORNEY *is a young man; all are much bundled up and go at once to the stove. They are followed by the two women—the* SHERIFF's *wife first; she is a slight wiry woman, a thin nervous face.* MRS. HALE *is larger and would ordinarily be called more comfortable looking, but she is disturbed now and looks fearfully about as she enters. The women have come in slowly, and stand close together near the door.*

COUNTY ATTORNEY: [*Rubbing his hands.*] This feels good. Come up to the fire, ladies.

MRS. PETERS: [*After taking a step forward.*] I'm not—cold.

SHERIFF: [*Unbuttoning his overcoat and stepping away from the stove as if to mark the beginning of official business.*] Now, Mr. Hale, before we move things about, you explain to Mr. Henderson just what you saw when you came here yesterday morning.

COUNTY ATTORNEY: By the way, has anything been moved? Are things just as you left them yesterday?

SHERIFF: [*Looking about.*] It's just the same. When it dropped below zero last night

I thought I'd better send Frank out this morning to make a fire for us—no use getting pneumonia with a big case on, but I told him not to touch anything except the stove—and you know Frank.

COUNTY ATTORNEY: Somebody should have been left here yesterday.

SHERIFF: Oh—yesterday. When I had to send Frank to Morris Center for that man who went crazy—I want you to know I had my hands full yesterday. I knew you could get back from Omaha by today and as long as I went over everything here myself—

COUNTY ATTORNEY: Well, Mr. Hale, tell just what happened when you came here yesterday morning.

HALE: Harry and I had started to town with a load of potatoes. We came along the road from my place and as I got here I said, "I'm going to see if I can't get John Wright to go in with me on a party telephone." I spoke to Wright about it once before and he put me off, saying folks talked too much anyway, and all he asked was peace and quiet—I guess you know about how much he talked himself; but I thought maybe if I went to the house and talked about it before his wife, though I said to Harry that I didn't know as what his wife wanted made much difference to John—

COUNTY ATTORNEY: Let's talk about that later, Mr. Hale. I do want to talk about that, but tell now just what happened when you got to the house.

HALE: I didn't hear or see anything; I knocked at the door, and still it was all quiet inside. I knew they must be up, it was past eight o'clock. So I knocked again, and I thought I heard somebody say, "Come in." I wasn't sure, I'm not sure yet, but I opened the door—this door [*Indicating the door by which the two women are still standing.*] and there in that rocker—[*Pointing to it.*] sat Mrs. Wright.

[*They all look at the rocker.*]

COUNTY ATTORNEY: What—was she doing?

HALE: She was rockin' back and forth. She had her apron in her hand and was kind of—pleating it.

COUNTY ATTORNEY: And how did she—look?

HALE: Well, she looked queer.

COUNTY ATTORNEY: How do you mean—queer?

HALE: Well, as if she didn't know what she was going to do next. And kind of done up.

COUNTY ATTORNEY: How did she seem to feel about your coming?

HALE: Why, I don't think she minded—one way or other. She didn't pay much attention. I said, "How do, Mrs. Wright, it's cold, ain't it?" And she said, "Is it?"—and went on kind of pleating at her apron. Well, I was surprised; she didn't ask me to come up to the stove, or to set down, but just sat there, not even looking at me, so I said, "I want to see John." And then she—laughed. I guess you would call it a laugh. I thought of Harry and the team outside, so I said a little sharp: "Can't I see John?" "No," she says, kind o' dull like. "Ain't he home?" says I. "Yes," says she, "he's home." "Then why can't I see him?" I asked her, out of patience. " 'Cause he's dead," says she. *"Dead?"* says I. She just nodded her head, not getting a bit excited, but rockin' back and forth. "Why—where is he?" says I, not knowing what to say. She just pointed upstairs—like that. [*Himself pointing to the room above.*] I got up, with the idea of going up there. I walked from there to here—then I says, "Why, what did he die of?" "He died of a rope round his neck," says she, and just went on pleatin' at her apron. Well, I went out and called Harry. I thought I might—need help. We went upstairs and there he was lyin'—

COUNTY ATTORNEY: I think I'd rather have you go into that upstairs, where you can point it all out. Just go on now with the rest of the story.

HALE: Well, my first thought was to get that rope off. It looked . . . [*Stops, his face twitches.*] . . . but Harry, he went up to him, and he said, "No, he's dead all right, and we'd better not touch anything." So we went back down stairs. She was still sitting that same way. "Has anybody been notified?" I asked. "No," says she unconcerned. "Who did this, Mrs. Wright?" said Harry. He said it business-like—and she stopped pleatin' of her apron. "I don't know," she says. "You don't *know?*" says Harry. "No," says she. "Weren't you sleepin' in the bed with him?" says Harry. "Yes," says she, "but I was on the inside." "Somebody slipped a rope round his neck and strangled him and you didn't wake up?" says Harry. "I didn't wake up," she said after him. We must 'a looked as if we didn't see how that could be, for after a minute she said, "I sleep sound." Harry was going to ask her more questions but I said maybe we ought to let her tell her story first to the coroner, or the sheriff, so Harry went fast as he could to Rivers' place, where there's a telephone.

COUNTY ATTORNEY: And what did Mrs. Wright do when she knew that you had gone for the coroner?

HALE: She moved from that chair to this one over here [*Pointing to a small chair in the corner.*] and just sat there with her hands held together and looking down. I got a feeling that I ought to make some conversation, so I said I had come in to see if John wanted to put in a telephone, and at that she started to laugh, and then she stopped and looked at me—scared. [*The* COUNTY ATTORNEY, *who has had his notebook out, makes a note.*] I dunno, maybe it wasn't scared. I wouldn't like to say it was. Soon Harry got back, and then Dr. Lloyd came, and you, Mr. Peters, and so I guess that's all I know that you don't.

COUNTY ATTORNEY: [*Looking around.*] I guess we'll go upstairs first—and then out to the barn and around there. [*To the* SHERIFF.] You're convinced that there was nothing important here—nothing that would point to any motive?

SHERIFF: Nothing here but kitchen things.

[*The* COUNTY ATTORNEY, *after again looking around the kitchen, opens the door of a cupboard closet. He gets up on a chair and looks on a shelf. Pulls his hand away, sticky.*]

COUNTY ATTORNEY: Here's a nice mess.

[*The women draw nearer.*]

MRS. PETERS: [*To the other woman.*] Oh, her fruit; it did freeze. [*To the* LAWYER.] She worried about that when it turned so cold. She said the fire'd go out and her jars would break.

SHERIFF: Well, can you beat the women! Held for murder and worryin' about her preserves.

COUNTY ATTORNEY: I guess before we're through she may have something more serious than preserves to worry about.

HALE: Well, women are used to worrying over trifles.

[*The two women move a little closer together.*]

COUNTY ATTORNEY: [*With the gallantry of a young politician.*] And yet, for all their worries, what would we do without the ladies? [*The women do not unbend. He goes to the sink, takes a dipperful of water from the pail and pouring it into a basin, washes his hands. Starts to wipe them on the roller-towel, turns it for a cleaner place.*] Dirty towels! [*Kicks his foot against the pans under the sink.*] Not much of a housekeeper, would you say, ladies?

MRS. HALE: [*Stiffly.*] There's a great deal of work to be done on a farm.

COUNTY ATTORNEY: To be sure. And yet [*With a little bow to her.*] I know there are some Dickson county farmhouses which do not have such roller towels. [*He gives it a pull to expose its length again.*]

MRS. HALE: Those towels get dirty awful quick. Men's hands aren't always as clean as they might be.

COUNTY ATTORNEY: Ah, loyal to your sex, I see. But you and Mrs. Wright were neighbors. I suppose you were friends, too.

MRS. HALE: [*Shaking her head.*] I've not seen much of her of late years. I've not been in this house—it's more than a year.

COUNTY ATTORNEY: And why was that? You didn't like her?

MRS. HALE: I liked her all well enough. Farmers' wives have their hands full, Mr. Henderson. And then—

COUNTY ATTORNEY: Yes—?

MRS. HALE: [*Looking about.*] It never seemed a very cheerful place.

COUNTY ATTORNEY: No—it's not cheerful. I shouldn't say she had the homemaking instinct.

MRS. HALE: Well, I don't know as Wright had, either.

COUNTY ATTORNEY: You mean that they didn't get on very well?

MRS. HALE: No, I don't mean anything. But I don't think a place'd be any cheerfuller for John Wright's being in it.

COUNTY ATTORNEY: I'd like to talk more of that a little later. I want to get the lay of things upstairs now. [*He goes to the left, where three steps lead to a stair door.*]

SHERIFF: I suppose anything Mrs. Peters does'll be all right. She was to take in some clothes for her, you know, and a few little things. We left in such a hurry yesterday.

COUNTY ATTORNEY: Yes, but I would like to see what you take, Mrs. Peters, and keep an eye out for anything that might be of use to us.

MRS. PETERS: Yes, Mr. Henderson. [*The women listen to the men's steps on the stairs, then look about the kitchen.*]

MRS. HALE: I'd hate to have men coming into my kitchen, snooping around and criticizing. [*She arranges the pans under sink which the LAWYER had shoved out of place.*]

MRS. PETERS: Of course it's no more than their duty.

MRS. HALE: Duty's all right, but I guess that deputy sheriff that came out to make the fire might have got a little of this on. [*Gives the roller towel a pull.*] Wish I'd thought of that sooner. Seems mean to talk about her for not having things slicked up when she had to come away in such a hurry.

MRS. PETERS: [*Who has gone to a small table in the left rear corner of the room, and lifted one end of a towel that covers a pan.*] She had bread set. [*Stands still.*]

MRS. HALE: [*Eyes fixed on a loaf of bread beside the bread box, which is on a low shelf at the other side of the room. Moves slowly toward it.*] She was going to put this in there. [*Picks up loaf, then abruptly drops it. In a manner of returning to familiar things.*] It's a shame about her fruit. I wonder if it's all gone. [*Gets up on the chair and looks.*] I think there's some here that's all right, Mrs. Peters. Yes— here; [*Holding it toward the window.*] this is cherries, too. [*Looking again.*] I declare I believe that's the only one. [*Gets down, bottle in her hand. Goes to the sink and wipes it off on the outside.*] She'll feel awful bad after all her hard work in the hot weather. I remember the afternoon I put up my cherries last summer. [*She puts the bottle on the big kitchen table, center of the room. With a sigh, is about to sit down in the rocking-chair. Before she is seated realizes what chair it is; with a slow look at it, steps back. The chair, which she has touched, rocks back and forth.*]

MRS. PETERS: Well, I must get those things from the front room closet. [*She goes to the door at the right, but after looking into the other room, steps back.*] You coming with me, Mrs. Hale? You could help me carry them. [*They go in the other room; reappear,* MRS. PETERS *carrying a dress and skirt,* MRS. HALE *following with a pair of shoes.*] My, it's cold in there. [*She puts the clothes on the big table, and hurries to the stove.*]

MRS. HALE: [*Examining the skirt.*] Wright was close. I think maybe that's why she kept so much to herself. She didn't even belong to the Ladies Aid. I suppose she felt she couldn't do her part, and then you don't enjoy things when you feel shabby. She used to wear pretty clothes and be lively, when she was Minnie Foster, one of the town girls singing in the choir. But that—oh, that was thirty years ago. This all you was to take in?

MRS. PETERS: She said she wanted an apron. Funny thing to want, for there isn't much to get you dirty in jail, goodness knows. But I suppose just to make her feel more natural. She said they was in the top drawer in this cupboard. Yes, here. And then her little shawl that always hung behind the door. [*Opens stair door and looks.*] Yes, here it is. [*Quickly shuts door leading upstairs.*]

MRS. HALE: [*Abruptly moving toward her.*] Mrs. Peters?

MRS. PETERS: Yes, Mrs. Hale?

MRS. HALE: Do you think she did it?

MRS. PETERS: [*In a frightened voice.*] Oh, I don't know.

MRS. HALE: Well, I don't think she did. Asking for an apron and her little shawl. Worrying about her fruit.

MRS. PETERS: [*Starts to speak, glances up, where footsteps are heard in the room above. In a low voice.*] Mr. Peters says it looks bad for her. Mr. Henderson is awful sarcastic in a speech and he'll make fun of her sayin' she didn't wake up.

MRS. HALE: Well, I guess John Wright didn't wake when they was slipping that rope under his neck.

MRS. PETERS: No, it's strange. It must have been done awful crafty and still. They say it was such a—funny way to kill a man, rigging it all up like that.

MRS. HALE: That's just what Mr. Hale said. There was a gun in the house. He says that's what he can't understand.

MRS. PETERS: Mr. Henderson said coming out that what was needed for the case was a motive; something to show anger, or—sudden feeling.

MRS. HALE: [*Who is standing by the table.*] Well, I don't see any signs of anger around here. [*She puts her hand on the dish towel which lies on the table, stands looking down at table, one half of which is clean, the other half messy.*] It's wiped to here. [*Makes a move as if to finish work, then turns and looks at loaf of bread outside the bread box. Drops towel. In that voice of coming back to familiar things.*] Wonder how they are finding things upstairs. I hope she had it a little more red-up[1] up there. You know, it seems kind of *sneaking.* Locking her up in town and then coming out here and trying to get her own house to turn against her!

MRS. PETERS: But Mrs. Hale, the law is the law.

MRS. HALE: I s'pose 'tis. [*Unbuttoning her coat.*] Better loosen up your things, Mrs. Peters. You won't feel them when you go out.

> [MRS. PETERS *takes off her fur tippet, goes to hang it on hook at back of room, stands looking at the under part of the small corner table.*]

MRS. PETERS: She was piecing a quilt. [*She brings the large sewing basket and they look at the bright pieces.*]

MRS. HALE: It's log cabin pattern. Pretty, isn't it? I wonder if she was goin' to quilt it or just knot it?

> [*Footsteps have been heard coming down the stairs. The* SHERIFF *enters followed by* HALE *and the* COUNTY ATTORNEY.]

SHERIFF: They wonder if she was going to quilt it or just knot it!

> [*The men laugh, the women look abashed.*]

COUNTY ATTORNEY: [*Rubbing his hands over the stove.*] Frank's fire didn't do much up there, did it? Well, let's go out to the barn and get that cleared up.

> [*The men go outside.*]

MRS. HALE: [*Resentfully.*] I don't know as there's anything so strange, our takin' up our time with little things while we're waiting for them to get the evidence. [*She sits down at the big table smoothing out a block with decision.*] I don't see as it's anything to laugh about.

MRS. PETERS: [*Apologetically.*] Of course they've got awful important things on their minds. [*Pulls up a chair and joins* MRS. HALE *at the table.*]

MRS. HALE: [*Examining another block.*] Mrs. Peters, look at this one. Here, this is the

---

1. Tidied up.

one she was working on, and look at the sewing! All the rest of it has been so nice and even. And look at this! It's all over the place! Why, it looks as if she didn't know what she was about! [*After she has said this they look at each other, then start to glance back at the door. After an instant* MRS. HALE *has pulled at a knot and ripped the sewing.*]

MRS. PETERS: Oh, what are you doing, Mrs. Hale?

MRS. HALE: [*Mildly.*] Just pulling out a stitch or two that's not sewed very good. [*Threading the needle.*] Bad sewing always made me fidgety.

MRS. PETERS: [*Nervously.*] I don't think we ought to touch things.

MRS. HALE: I'll just finish up this end. [*Suddenly stopping and leaning forward.*] Mrs. Peters?

MRS. PETERS: Yes, Mrs. Hale?

MRS. HALE: What do you suppose she was so nervous about?

MRS. PETERS: Oh—I don't know. I don't know as she was nervous. I sometimes sew awful queer when I'm just tired. [MRS. HALE *starts to say something, looks at* MRS. PETERS, *then goes on sewing.*] Well I must get these things wrapped up. They may be through sooner than we think. [*Putting apron and other things together.*] I wonder where I can find a piece of paper, and string.

MRS. HALE: In that cupboard, maybe.

MRS. PETERS: [*Looking in cupboard.*] Why, here's a bird-cage. [*Holds it up.*] Did she have a bird, Mrs. Hale?

MRS. HALE: Why, I don't know whether she did or not—I've not been here for so long. There was a man around last year selling canaries cheap, but I don't know as she took one; maybe she did. She used to sing real pretty herself.

MRS. PETERS: [*Glancing around.*] Seems funny to think of a bird here. But she must have had one, or why would she have a cage? I wonder what happened to it.

MRS. HALE: I s'pose maybe the cat got it.

MRS. PETERS: No, she didn't have a cat. She's got that feeling some people have about cats—being afraid of them. My cat got in her room and she was real upset and asked me to take it out.

MRS. HALE: My sister Bessie was like that. Queer, ain't it?

MRS. PETERS: [*Examining the cage.*] Why, look at this door. It's broke. One hinge is pulled apart.

MRS. HALE: [*Looking too.*] Looks as if someone must have been rough with it.

MRS. PETERS: Why, yes. [*She brings the cage forward and puts it on the table.*]

MRS. HALE: I wish if they're going to find any evidence they'd be about it. I don't like this place.

MRS. PETERS: But I'm awful glad you came with me, Mrs. Hale. It would be lonesome for me sitting here alone.

MRS. HALE: It would, wouldn't it? [*Dropping her sewing.*] But I tell you what I do wish, Mrs. Peters. I wish I had come over sometimes when *she* was here. I—[*Looking around the room.*]—wish I had.

MRS. PETERS: But of course you were awful busy, Mrs. Hale—your house and your children.

MRS. HALE: I could've come. I stayed away because it weren't cheerful—and that's why I ought to have come. I—I've never liked this place. Maybe because it's down in a hollow and you don't see the road. I dunno what it is, but it's a lonesome place and always was. I wish I had come over to see Minnie Foster sometimes. I can see now—[*Shakes her head.*]

MRS. PETERS: Well, you mustn't reproach yourself, Mrs. Hale. Somehow we just don't see how it is with other folks until—something comes up.

MRS. HALE: Not having children makes less work—but it makes a quiet house, and Wright out to work all day, and no company when he did come in. Did you know John Wright, Mrs. Peters?

MRS. PETERS: Not to know him; I've seen him in town. They say he was a good man.

MRS. HALE: Yes—good; he didn't drink, and kept his word as well as most, I guess, and paid his debts. But he was a hard man, Mrs. Peters. Just to pass the time of day with him—[*Shivers.*] Like a raw wind that gets to the bone. [*Pauses, her eye falling on the cage.*] I should think she would 'a wanted a bird. But what do you suppose went with it?

MRS. PETERS: I don't know, unless it got sick and died. [*She reaches over and swings the broken door, swings it again, both women watch it.*]

MRS. HALE: You weren't raised round here, were you? [MRS. PETERS *shakes her head.*] You didn't know—her?

MRS. PETERS: Not till they brought her yesterday.

MRS. HALE: She—come to think of it, she was kind of like a bird herself—real sweet and pretty, but kind of timid and—fluttery. How—she—did—change. [*Silence; then as if struck by a happy thought and relieved to get back to everyday things.*] Tell you what, Mrs. Peters, why don't you take the quilt in with you? It might take up her mind.

MRS. PETERS: Why, I think that's a real nice idea, Mrs. Hale. There couldn't possibly be any objection to it, could there? Now, just what would I take? I wonder if her patches are in here—and her things. [*They look in the sewing basket.*]

MRS. HALE: Here's some red. I expect this has got sewing things in it. [*Brings out a fancy box.*] What a pretty box. Looks like something somebody would give you. Maybe her scissors are in here. [*Opens box. Suddenly puts her hand to her nose.*] Why— [MRS. PETERS *bends nearer, then turns her face away.*] There's something wrapped up in this piece of silk.

MRS. PETERS: Why, this isn't her scissors.

MRS. HALE: [*Lifting the silk.*] Oh, Mrs. Peters—it's—

[MRS. PETERS *bends closer.*]

MRS. PETERS: It's the bird.

MRS. HALE: [*Jumping up.*] But, Mrs. Peters—look at it! Its neck! Look at its neck! It's all—other side *to*.

MRS. PETERS: Somebody—wrung—its—neck.

[*Their eyes meet. A look of growing comprehension, of horror. Steps are heard outside.* MRS. HALE *slips box under quilt pieces, and sinks into her chair. Enter* SHERIFF *and* COUNTY ATTORNEY. MRS. PETERS *rises.*]

COUNTY ATTORNEY: [*As one turning from serious things to little pleasantries.*] Well ladies, have you decided whether she was going to quilt it or knot it?

MRS. PETERS: We think she was going to—knot it.

COUNTY ATTORNEY: Well, that's interesting, I'm sure. [*Seeing the bird-cage.*] Has the bird flown?

MRS. HALE: [*Putting more quilt pieces over the box.*] We think the—cat got it.

COUNTY ATTORNEY: [*Preoccupied.*] Is there a cat?

[MRS. HALE *glances in a quick covert way at* MRS. PETERS.]

MRS. PETERS: Well, not *now*. They're superstitious, you know. They leave.

COUNTY ATTORNEY: [*To* SHERIFF PETERS, *continuing an interrupted conversation.*] No sign at all of anyone having come from the outside. Their own rope. Now let's go up again and go over it piece by piece. [*They start upstairs.*] It would have to have been someone who knew just the—

[MRS. PETERS *sits down. The two women sit there not looking at one another, but as if peering into something and at the same time holding back. When they talk now it is in the manner of feeling their way over strange ground, as if afraid of what they are saying, but as if they cannot help saying it.*]

MRS. HALE: She liked the bird. She was going to bury it in that pretty box.

MRS. PETERS: [*In a whisper.*] When I was a girl—my kitten—there was a boy took a hatchet, and before my eyes—and before I could get there—[*Covers her face an instant.*] If they hadn't held me back I would have—[*Catches herself, looks upstairs where steps are heard, falters weakly.*]—hurt him.

MRS. HALE: [*With a slow look around her.*] I wonder how it would seem never to have had any children around. [*Pause.*] No, Wright wouldn't like the bird—a thing that sang. She used to sing. He killed that, too.

MRS. PETERS: [*Moving uneasily.*] We don't know who killed the bird.

MRS. HALE: I knew John Wright.

MRS. PETERS: It was an awful thing was done in this house that night, Mrs. Hale. Killing a man while he slept, slipping a rope around his neck that choked the life out of him.

MRS. HALE: His neck. Choked the life out of him. [*Her hand goes out and rests on the bird-cage.*]

MRS. PETERS: [*With rising voice.*] We don't know who killed him. We don't *know*.

MRS. HALE: [*Her own feeling not interrupted.*] If there's been years and years of nothing, then a bird to sing to you, it would be awful—still, after the bird was still.

MRS. PETERS: [*Something within her speaking.*] I know what stillness is. When we homesteaded in Dakota, and my first baby died—after he was two years old, and me with no other then—

MRS. HALE: [*Moving.*] How soon do you suppose they'll be through, looking for the evidence?

MRS. PETERS: I know what stillness is. [*Pulling herself back.*] The law has got to punish crime, Mrs. Hale.

MRS. HALE: [*Not as if answering that.*] I wish you'd seen Minnie Foster when she wore a white dress with blue ribbons and stood up there in the choir and sang. [*A look around the room.*] Oh, I *wish* I'd come over here once in a while! That was a crime! That was a crime! Who's going to punish that?

MRS. PETERS: [*Looking upstairs.*] We mustn't—take on.

MRS. HALE: I might have known she needed help! I know how things can be—for women. I tell you, it's queer, Mrs. Peters. We live close together and we live far apart. We all go through the same things—it's all just a different kind of the same thing. [*Brushes her eyes, noticing the bottle of fruit, reaches out for it.*] If I was you, I wouldn't tell her her fruit was gone. Tell her it *ain't.* Tell her it's all right. Take this in to prove it to her. She—she may never know whether it was broke or not.

MRS. PETERS: [*Takes the bottle, looks about for something to wrap it in; takes petticoat from the clothes brought from the other room, very nervously begins winding this around the bottle. In a false voice.*] My, it's a good thing the men couldn't hear us. Wouldn't they just laugh! Getting all stirred up over a little thing like a— dead canary. As if that could have anything to do with—with—wouldn't they *laugh!*

[*The men are heard coming down stairs.*]

MRS. HALE: [*Under her breath.*] Maybe they would—maybe they wouldn't.

COUNTY ATTORNEY: No, Peters, it's all perfectly clear except a reason for doing it. But you know juries when it comes to women. If there was some definite thing. Something to show—something to make a story about—a thing that would connect up with this strange way of doing it—

[*The women's eyes meet for an instant. Enter* HALE *from outer door.*]

HALE: Well, I've got the team around. Pretty cold out there.

COUNTY ATTORNEY: I'm going to stay here a while by myself. [*To the* SHERIFF.] You can send Frank out for me, can't you? I want to go over everything. I'm not satisfied that we can't do better.

SHERIFF: Do you want to see what Mrs. Peters is going to take in?

[*The* LAWYER *goes to the table, picks up the apron, laughs.*]

COUNTY ATTORNEY: Oh, I guess they're not very dangerous things the ladies have picked out. [*Moves a few things about, disturbing the quilt pieces which cover the box. Steps back.*] No, Mrs. Peters doesn't need supervising. For that matter, a sheriff's wife is married to the law. Ever think of it that way, Mrs. Peters?

MRS. PETERS: Not—just that way.

SHERIFF: [*Chuckling.*] Married to the law. [*Moves toward the other room.*] I just want you to come in here a minute, George. We ought to take a look at these windows.

COUNTY ATTORNEY: [*Scoffingly.*] Oh, windows!

SHERIFF: We'll be right out, Mr. Hale.

[HALE *goes outside. The* SHERIFF *follows the* COUNTY ATTORNEY *into the other room. Then* MRS. HALE *rises, hands tight together, looking intensely at* MRS. PETERS, *whose eyes make a slow turn, finally meeting* MRS. HALE's. *A moment* MRS. HALE *holds her, then her own eyes point the way to where the box is concealed. Suddenly* MRS. PETERS *throws back quilt pieces and tries to put the box in the bag she is wearing. It is too big. She opens box, starts to take bird out, cannot touch it, goes to pieces, stands there helpless. Sound of a knob turning in the other room.* MRS. HALE *snatches the box and puts it in the pocket of her big coat. Enter* COUNTY ATTORNEY *and* SHERIFF.]

COUNTY ATTORNEY: [*Facetiously.*] Well, Henry, at least we found out that she was not going to quilt it. She was going to—what is it you call it, ladies?

MRS. HALE: [*Her hand against her pocket.*] We call it—knot it, Mr. Henderson.

CURTAIN

1920

Now that you have finished reading the play, you might look back over your reading notes and trace how your expectations developed, how they were fulfilled or disappointed, how your focus moved from the murder plot to the feminist theme, how your view of certain characters—especially, perhaps, Mrs. Peters, the sheriff's wife—changed. One pattern of response may resemble the following:

When very early in the play Hale "tell[s] just what happened," his story initially generates curiosity rather than expectation: Mrs. Wright's conduct at first seems strange—at least to the point where she says her husband is dead, and "died of a rope round his neck"—and then seems suspicious: could she actually have slept so soundly that she was unaware that someone had put a rope around his neck and pulled him upright, killing him? Though there is still some curiosity to know what actually happened and some anticipation about the discovery of the murderer or perhaps how the men will discover that Mrs. Wright is the murderer, our attention is distracted and our response diverted by another facet of the action: Hale's sexist remark that "women are used to worrying over trifles," and later the men's scoffing laughter at the women's conjecture as to whether Mrs. Wright was going to hand-quilt or knot the quilt she was making. There may well be some difference in response based on the reader's gender. Women might pick up the sexism earlier, in the county attorney's refusal to listen when Hale suggests that Mrs. Wright's desires may not have been very important to Wright, or the sheriff's dismissive remark that there is "Nothing here but kitchen things."

The situation now raises a number of questions. How offensive are these remarks? When did you begin to notice that the "submissive" Mrs. Peters was shifting her allegiance from her husband to Mrs. Hale? To what extent do you feel the remarks justify the women's suppression of evidence (which the men might not have thought "real" evidence in any case)? Where do your sympathies lie? Do you want Mrs. Wright to get away with it? Does it seem justifiable homicide? Does the play strongly suggest an answer to these questions? Does the answer make you like or dislike the play? How important is our acceptance or rejection of the social theme to our emotional response to the play?

There is nothing particularly difficult or unfamiliar about *Trifles* as a "story." (Glaspell did, indeed, turn the play into a story—"A Jury of Her Peers." It is a detective story and includes a murder, evidence, and interpretation—or "detection"—from the evidence, though unlike most other detective or murder stories, here the question is not "who done it?" but why the murder was committed. Its **mode** of representation is a familiar type—domestic realism—in which the places, people, and even events are more or less ordinary (unfortunately domestic violence and murder are not extraordinary). Its staging is also conventional in the modern theater: it has an imaginary wall separating the stage from the auditorium that acts as a frame (the **proscenium arch**). It also has—though somewhat in miniature—the traditional five-part structure: the **exposition**—the situation at the beginning of a play: here Mr. Hale's description of what happened; the **rising action**—the complicating of the plot; the **climax**—the turning point: here, perhaps, the discovery of the dead bird; the **falling action**—the unwinding of the plot toward the conclusion: here the women covering up the "trifling" evidence; and the **conclusion.** This does not suggest that the play is trite or dull, but only that its type, subject matter, manner of presentation, and form are familiar—which might also be said, for example, of *Oedipus* or *Hamlet.*

The next play, David Ives's *Sure Thing,* is something entirely different. It does not have a plot in the usual sense, but is a series of discrete, causally unconnected—indeed, "alternative"—scenes or portions of the scene involving the same two characters in the same situation speaking similar but not identical dialogue, with—with one exception—similar outcomes. A bit of "stage business"—the clang of a bell—signals that a "substitute" conversation will be offered. This is a funny play to read, but it is probably funnier on the stage because there we are not merely told that the characters are the same, but we *see* the same actors in the identical situation saying different lines. Though the alternative lines follow each other immediately on the page as soon as we read "[*Bell.*]," in our reading we are used to adjusting time sequences from paragraph to paragraph or chapter to chapter so that the immediacy that the sequence has on the stage is less dramatic in the reading. Here, then, is a play-type play:

DAVID IVES

Sure Thing

CHARACTERS

BETTY   BILL

BETTY, *a woman in her late twenties, is reading at a café table. An empty chair is opposite her.* BILL, *same age, enters.*

BILL: Excuse me. Is this chair taken?
BETTY: Excuse me?
BILL: Is this taken?
BETTY: Yes it is.
BILL: Oh. Sorry.
BETTY: Sure thing.

[*A bell rings softly.*]

BILL: Excuse me. Is this chair taken?
BETTY: Excuse me?
BILL: Is this taken?
BETTY: No, but I'm expecting somebody in a minute.
BILL: Oh. Thanks anyway.
BETTY: Sure thing.

[*A bell rings softly.*]

BILL: Excuse me. Is this chair taken?
BETTY: No, but I'm expecting somebody very shortly.
BILL: Would you mind if I sit here till he or she or it comes?
BETTY: [*Glances at her watch.*] They do seem to be pretty late. . . .
BILL: You never know who you might be turning down.
BETTY: Sorry. Nice try, though.
BILL: Sure thing.

[*Bell.*]

Is this seat taken?
BETTY: No it's not.
BILL: Would you mind if I sit here?
BETTY: Yes I would.
BILL: Oh.

[*Bell.*]

Is this chair taken?
BETTY: No it's not.
BILL: Would you mind if I sit here?
BETTY: No. Go ahead.
BILL: Thanks. [*He sits. She continues reading.*] Everyplace else seems to be taken.
BETTY: Mm-hm.
BILL: Great place.
BETTY: Mm-hm.
BILL: What's the book?
BETTY: I just wanted to read in quiet, if you don't mind.
BILL: No. Sure thing.

[*Bell.*]

BILL: Everyplace else seems to be taken.
BETTY: Mm-hm.
BILL: Great place for reading.
BETTY: Yes, I like it.
BILL: What's the book?
BETTY: *The Sound and the Fury.*
BILL: Oh. Hemingway.

[*Bell.*]

What's the book?

BETTY: *The Sound and the Fury.*

BILL: Oh. Faulkner.

BETTY: Have you read it?

BILL: Not . . . actually. I've sure read *about* it, though. It's supposed to be great.

BETTY: It is great.

BILL: I hear it's great. [*Small pause.*] Waiter?

[*Bell.*]

What's the book?

BETTY: *The Sound and the Fury.*

BILL: Oh. Faulkner.

BETTY: Have you read it?

BILL: I'm a Mets fan, myself.

[*Bell.*]

BETTY: Have you read it?

BILL: Yeah, I read it in college.

BETTY: Where was college?

BILL: I went to Oral Roberts University.

[*Bell.*]

BETTY: Where was college?

BILL: I was lying. I never really went to college. I just like to party.

[*Bell.*]

BETTY: Where was college?

BILL: Harvard.

BETTY: Do you like Faulkner?

BILL: I love Faulkner, I spent a whole winter reading him once.

BETTY: I've just started.

BILL: I was so excited after ten pages that I went out and bought everything else he wrote. One of the greatest reading experiences of my life. I mean, all that incredible psychological understanding. Page after page of gorgeous prose. His profound grasp of the mystery of time and human existence. The smells of the earth . . . What do you think?

BETTY: I think it's pretty boring.

[*Bell.*]

BILL: What's the book?

BETTY: *The Sound and the Fury.*

BILL: Oh! Faulkner!

BETTY: Do you like Faulkner?

BILL: I love Faulkner.

BETTY: He's incredible.

BILL: I spent a whole winter reading him once.

BETTY: I was so excited after ten pages that I went out and bought everything else he wrote.

BILL: All that incredible psychological understanding.

BETTY: And the prose is so gorgeous.

BILL: And the way he's grasped the mystery of time—

BETTY: —and human existence. I can't believe I've waited this long to read him.

BILL: You never know. You might not have liked him before.

BETTY: That's true.

BILL: You might not have been ready for him. You have to hit these things at the right moment or it's no good.

BETTY: That's happened to me.

BILL: It's all in the timing. [*Small pause.*] My name's Bill, by the way.

BETTY: I'm Betty.

BILL: Hi.

BETTY: Hi. [*Small pause.*]

BILL: Yes I thought reading Faulkner was . . . a great experience.

BETTY: Yes. [*Small pause.*]

BILL: *The Sound and the Fury* . . . [*Another small pause.*]

BETTY: Well. Onwards and upwards. [*She goes back to her book.*]

BILL: Waiter—?

   [*Bell.*]

   You have to hit these things at the right moment or it's no good.

BETTY: That's happened to me.

BILL: It's all in the timing. My name's Bill, by the way.

BETTY: I'm Betty.

BILL: Hi.

BETTY: Hi.

BILL: Do you come in here a lot?

BETTY: Actually I'm just in town for two days from Pakistan.

BILL: Oh. Pakistan.

   [*Bell.*]

   My name's Bill, by the way.

BETTY: I'm Betty.

BILL: Hi.

BETTY: Hi.

BILL: Do you come in here a lot?

BETTY: Every once in a while. Do you?

BILL: Not so much anymore. Not as much as I used to. Before my nervous breakdown.

   [*Bell.*]

   Do you come in here a lot?

BETTY: Why are you asking?

BILL: Just interested.

BETTY: Are you really interested, or do you just want to pick me up?

BILL: No, I'm really interested.

BETTY: Why would you be interested in whether I come in here a lot?

BILL: I'm just . . . getting acquainted.

BETTY: Maybe you're only interested for the sake of making small talk long enough to ask me back to your place to listen to some music, or because you've just rented this great tape for your VCR, or because you've got some terrific unknown Django Reinhardt record, only all you really want to do is fuck—which you won't do very well—after which you'll go into the bathroom and pee very loudly, then pad into the kitchen and get yourself a beer from the refrigerator without asking me whether I'd like anything, and then you'll proceed to lie back down beside me and confess that you've got a girlfriend named Stephanie who's away at medical school in Belgium for a year, and that you've been involved with her—*off and on*—in what you'll call a very "intricate" relationship, for the past *seven YEARS*. None of which *interests* me, mister!

BILL: Okay.

[*Bell.*]

Do you come in here a lot?

BETTY: Every other day, I think.

BILL: I come in here quite a lot and I don't remember seeing you.

BETTY: I guess we must be on different schedules.

BILL: Missed connections.

BETTY: Yes. Different time zones.

BILL: Amazing how you can live right next door to somebody in this town and never even know it.

BETTY: I know.

BILL: City life.

BETTY: It's crazy.

BILL: We probably pass each other in the street every day. Right in front of this place, probably.

BETTY: Yep.

BILL: [*Looks around.*] Well the waiters here sure seem to be in some different time zone. I can't seem to locate one anywhere. . . . Waiter! [*He looks back.*] So what do you—[*He sees that she's gone back to her book.*]

BETTY: I beg pardon?

BILL: Nothing. Sorry.

[*Bell.*]

BETTY: I guess we must be on different schedules.

BILL: Missed connections.

BETTY: Yes. Different time zones.

BILL: Amazing how you can live right next door to somebody in this town and never even know it.

BETTY: I know.

BILL: City life.

BETTY: It's crazy.

BILL: You weren't waiting for somebody when I came in, were you?

BETTY: Actually I was.

BILL: Oh. Boyfriend?

BETTY: Sort of.

BILL: What's a sort-of boyfriend?

BETTY: My husband.

BILL: Ah-ha.

   [*Bell.*]

You weren't waiting for somebody when I came in, were you?

BETTY: Actually I was.

BILL: Oh. Boyfriend?

BETTY: Sort of.

BILL: What's a sort-of-boyfriend?

BETTY: We were meeting here to break up.

BILL: Mm-hm . . .

   [*Bell.*]

What's a sort-of boyfriend?

BETTY: My lover. Here she comes right now!

   [*Bell.*]

BILL: You weren't waiting for somebody when I came in, were you?

BETTY: No, just reading.

BILL: Sort of a sad occupation for a Friday night, isn't it? Reading here, all by yourself?

BETTY: Do you think so?

BILL: Well sure. I mean, what's a good-looking woman like you doing out alone on a Friday night?

BETTY: Trying to keep away from lines like that.

BILL: No, listen—

   [*Bell.*]

You weren't waiting for somebody when I came in, were you?

BETTY: No, just reading.

BILL: Sort of a sad occupation for a Friday night, isn't it? Reading here all by yourself?

BETTY: I guess it is, in a way.

BILL: What's a good-looking woman like you doing out alone on a Friday night anyway? No offense, but . . .

BETTY: I'm out alone on a Friday night for the first time in a very long time.

BILL: Oh.

BETTY: You see, I just recently ended a relationship.

BILL: Oh.

BETTY: Of rather long standing.

BILL: I'm sorry. [*Small pause.*] Well listen, since reading by yourself *is* such a sad occupation for a Friday night, would you like to go elsewhere?

BETTY: No . . .

BILL: Do something else?

BETTY: No thanks.

BILL: I was headed out to the movies in a while anyway.

BETTY: I don't think so.

BILL: Big chance to let Faulkner catch his breath. All those long sentences get him pretty tired.

BETTY: Thanks anyway.

BILL: Okay.

BETTY: I appreciate the invitation.

BILL: Sure thing.

> [*Bell.*]

You weren't waiting for somebody when I came in, were you?

BETTY: No, just reading.

BILL: Sort of a sad occupation for a Friday night, isn't it? Reading here all by yourself?

BETTY: I guess I was trying to think of it as existentially romantic. You know—cappuccino, great literature, rainy night . . .

BILL: That only works in Paris. We *could* hop the late plane to Paris. Get on a Concorde. Find a café . . .

BETTY: I'm a little short on plane fare tonight.

BILL: Darn it, so am I.

BETTY: To tell you the truth, I was headed to the movies after I finished this section. Would you like to come along? Since you can't locate a waiter?

BILL: That's a very nice offer, but . . .

BETTY: Uh-huh. Girlfriend?

BILL: Two, actually. One of them's pregnant, and Stephanie—

> [*Bell.*]

BETTY: Girlfriend?

BILL: No, I don't have a girlfriend. Not if you mean the castrating bitch I dumped last night.

> [*Bell.*]

BETTY: Girlfriend?

BILL: Sort of. Sort of.

BETTY: What's a sort-of girlfriend?

BILL: My mother.

> [*Bell.*]

I just ended a relationship, actually.

BETTY: Oh.

BILL: Of rather long standing.

BETTY: I'm sorry to hear it.

BILL: This is my first night out alone in a long time. I feel a little bit at sea, to tell you the truth.

BETTY: So you didn't stop to talk because you're a Moonie, or you have some weird political affiliation—?

BILL: Nope. Straight-down-the-ticket Republican.

[*Bell.*]

Straight-down-the-ticket Democrat.

[*Bell.*]

Can I tell you something about politics?

[*Bell.*]

I like to think of myself as a citizen of the universe.

[*Bell.*]

I'm unaffiliated.

BETTY: That's a relief. So am I.

BILL: I vote my beliefs.

BETTY: Labels are not important.

BILL: Labels are not important, exactly. Take me, for example. I mean, what does it matter if I had a two-point at—

[*Bell.*]

three-point at—

[*Bell.*]

four-point at college? Or if I did come from Pittsburgh—

[*Bell.*]

Cleveland—

[*Bell.*]

Westchester County?

BETTY: Sure.

BILL: I believe that a man is what he is.

[*Bell.*]

A person is what he is.

[*Bell.*]

A person is . . . what they are.

BETTY: I think so too.

BILL: So what if I admire Trotsky?

[*Bell.*]

So what if I once had a total-body liposuction?

[*Bell.*]

So what if I don't have a penis?

[*Bell.*]

So what if I spent a year in the Peace Corps? I was acting on my convictions.

BETTY: Sure.

BILL: You just can't hang a sign on a person.

BETTY: Absolutely. I'll bet you're a Scorpio.

[*Many bells ring.*]

Listen, I was headed to the movies after I finished this section. Would you like to come along?

BILL: That sounds like fun. What's playing?

BETTY: A couple of the really early Woody Allen movies.

BILL: Oh.

BETTY: You don't like Woody Allen?

BILL: Sure. I like Woody Allen.

BETTY: But you're not crazy about Woody Allen.

BILL: Those early ones kind of get on my nerves.

BETTY: Uh-huh.

[*Bell.*]

BILL: Y'know I was headed to the—

BETTY: [*Simultaneously.*] I was thinking about—

BILL: I'm sorry.

BETTY: No, go ahead.

BILL: I was going to say that I was headed to the movies in a little while, and . . .

BETTY: So was I.

BILL: The Woody Allen festival?

BETTY: Just up the street.

BILL: Do you like the early ones?

BETTY: I think anybody who doesn't ought to be run off the planet.

BILL: How many times have you seen *Bananas*?

BETTY: Eight times.

BILL: Twelve. So are you still interested? [*Long pause.*]

BETTY: Do you like Entenmann's crumb cake . . . ?

BILL: Last night I went out at two in the morning to get one. Did you have an Etch-a-Sketch as a child?

BETTY: Yes! And do you like Brussels sprouts? [*Pause.*]

BILL: No, I think they're disgusting.

BETTY: They *are* disgusting!

BILL: Do you still believe in marriage in spite of current sentiments against it?

BETTY: Yes.

BILL: And children?

BETTY: Three of them.

BILL: Two girls and a boy.

BETTY: Harvard, Vassar, and Brown.

BILL: And will you love me?

BETTY: Yes.

BILL: And cherish me forever?

BETTY: Yes.

BILL: Do you still want to go to the movies?

BETTY: Sure thing.

BILL AND BETTY: [*Together.*] *Waiter!*

BLACKOUT

1989

QUESTIONS

1. All three of the men in *Trifles* seem sexist; indicate at least one bit of dialogue by each that would support this judgment. What do you learn of the character and attitudes of John Wright, the murdered man? How does the situation in the Wright household reflect on the relations among Peters, Hale, and their wives? Describe the differences between Mrs. Peters and Mrs. Hale; how does Mrs. Wright resemble them and differ from them? What is the effect of the last line of the play?

2. The characters in each exchange in *Sure Thing* are Betty and Bill. Do you assume each is the same character throughout the play, or do you think that, despite their names, they represent different people or types? If you see each as different exchanges, chose three or more bits of dialogue that seem to suggest different characters and describe and document the differences. If you were acting the part of Betty—or Bill—describe how you would play different portions of the play differently.

WRITING SUGGESTIONS

1. (a) Write a brief sketch of the trial of Mrs. Wright, or
   (b) write a brief of your case for or against, or
   (c) write a brief parody of the "feminism" of *Trifles*, or
   (d) describe an incident in which male chauvinism (sexism) caused a blunder or oversight.

2. Argue that Caryl Zook's reading of the details of the play (pages 1016–18) is too insistently feminist, that Henderson, for example, is not being dominant, but polite in inviting (not ordering) the "ladies" to come up to the fire; that the sheriff's remark that there's "Nothing here but kitchen things" is not dismissive of women but just a direct response to the question of what he saw in the kitchen, and so forth. (Or, counter such a counterargument.)

3. Sometimes, before we talk to someone, stranger or friend, we rehearse in our own mind how that person might respond to us, including, sometimes, several possibilities. Write such a scenario using *Sure Thing* as a model, preferably choosing a situation different from that in Ives's play. If you are basing your paper on a real episode, indicate how the actual conversation then went and analyze why the response was one that you predicted or one that was different from anything you had projected.

4. Write a parody of or a response to *Sure Thing* in which the ages or races of the characters are different—for example, Betty and Bill as senior citizens—or in which their ages and races differ from each other, or in which the two characters are of the same gender.

STUDENT WRITING

In the paper that follows, Caryl Zook examines each twist in the action of *Trifles* in terms of the behavior demonstrated by the men and the women. Her style and tone are informal, but her feelings about the play are strong, and she convincingly uses details to support her reading.

<u>Trifles</u>

Caryl Zook

<u>Trifles</u>: The title is at once descriptive and ironic. The males in the play are, in varying degrees, patronizing to the women and self-important in all they do. While the men are assuming that all women's concerns are trifles, the women are solving the case through their understanding of the importance of the little things. It is therefore easy for them to hide the evidence necessary to solve the case from the men.

The county attorney, Mr. Henderson, asserts his dominance from the first lines of the play when he almost orders them to "Come up to the fire, ladies." Mrs. Peters, the more timid of the two women in the scenes and trained to obey, starts to comply, then answers, "I'm not-- cold."

Sheriff Peters says, "Nothing here but kitchen things" (p. 997), implying that these are "women's" things, things of no significance. The county attorney checks a high shelf and pulls his hand away, sticky. "Here's a nice mess," he says, attaching no significance to this "trifle." Mrs. Peters realizes that almost all of Mrs. Wright's preserves had

1016

frozen and broken, as Mrs. Wright had anticipated and feared. She tells her husband, but he says, "Well, can you beat the women!" (interesting choice of words). "Held for murder and worryin' about her preserves." Hale adds, "Well, women are used to worrying over trifles." Like food, like the long hours of labor this woman must have invested to preserve a winter's worth of food for the family. Trifles. Furthermore, it was out of the sheriff's neglect to keep a fire at the house that the jars froze and broke.

The men got a good laugh at the women, who discovered that Mrs. Wright was piecing a quilt, when the sheriff says, "They wonder if she was going to quilt it or just knot it!" (p. 1000), as if this was obviously a ridiculously trivial issue. It was a little pleasantry, a diversion for the county attorney to use as small talk. "Well, ladies, have you decided whether she was going to quilt it or knot it?" Mrs. Peters says, "We think she was going to--knot it." Was she reluctant to talk about Minnie Wright's knot-tying abilities? "Well, that's interesting, I'm sure," said the county attorney. He, of course, was concerned about more pressing matters, such as how to prove who tied the knot in the rope around the neck of John Wright (p. 1003).

Ironically, while the men were parading around being important and humorous at the expense of "the ladies," the ladies were solving the crime. Mrs. Hale realizes that it may have been the deputy who got the towel dirty. Mrs. Peters discovers a canary with a broken neck. They conclude that Mr. Wright killed it and this was the motive for the crime. They decide that justice will be best served, however, by removing this evidence in a show of solidarity with another mistreated, over-worked, under-appreciated female. Perhaps the attitude of the males on the scene, whose belittling definition of "women's work" as trifles, was another motivation for the protective actions the women took on behalf of a victimized sister. Anything the women did was unimportant by comparison to what the men do. The long, hot hours spent canning and the months spent quilting a cover, rather than knotting it, are trifles also. Even if the men knew that Minnie Foster had loved to sing and that she bought a canary to bring some small joy into her childless life and that John Wright killed the songbird precisely because it made her happy, would they have seen it as a motive for murder? Or would they have dismissed it as "trifles"?

Glaspell has woven a tightly bound plot. The major elements of the mystery are interconnected. John Wright died, according to Mrs. Wright, ". . . of a rope around his neck." The women figured out that Mrs. Wright had bought a canary to sing, like she used to sing, and Mr. Wright had strangled it to death. She was, they determined, going to knot the quilt. Perhaps she could knot a rope when she wanted to. But let's not tell the men.

Understanding the Text

Although it has been possible in previous chapters to represent the elements of fiction and poetry by devoting a chapter to each major element and giving full-length texts as examples, it is not possible to do so with drama. In this chapter, we consider the basic **elements of drama**—character, structure, setting, tone, and theme—together. As we have indicated in the fiction and poetry chapters called "The Whole Text," the basic elements of literary works are not really so distinct from one another, but instead work together to form a whole: character is shown in action, action or plot relates to setting, setting relates to tone, and theme involves all elements at once.

Before reading the four full-length plays that follow and analyzing their elements and how they interrelate, for a few moments let us look back at *Trifles*. The setting in Glaspell's play is the kitchen of a midwestern farmhouse in which a murder has occurred. Having the action unfold in the kitchen, traditionally considered the woman's part of the house, relates to the play's theme or central idea—that men and women have different views of reality, that women viewing "trifles," like details in a kitchen, can discover truths as well as or better than men who believe themselves to be concerned only with more important matters. The plot—the finding of the "trifling" bits of evidence that implicate Mrs. Wright in the murder of her husband and the suggestions of John Wright's abusive behavior that lead the women to band together in her defense and to suppress evidence that the men would think trifling—depends on the setting and embodies the theme. The character of Mrs. Peters, the sheriff's wife, and that of Mrs. Hale are interrelated with plot and theme. Mrs. Hale is the more observant of the women and less subordinate to her husband and a man's way of looking at things, while Mrs. Peters is more conventional, less willing to defy male authority. In convincing Mrs. Peters, Mrs. Hale and the evidence convince most viewers that Mrs. Wright had good reason to murder her husband.

As you can see, the "elements" of drama exist primarily in cooperation with one another, and not in isolation. We cannot put the elements together to understand a text as a whole, however, unless we first have some knowledge of the terms, distinctions, issues, and range of effects involved in considering such elements. Let us prepare to read the plays that follow, then, by briefly considering some of these elements.

CHARACTER

Someone who appears in a work is called a **character,** the same word we use to refer to those qualities of mind, spirit, and behavior that make one individual different from every other. The identity of terms is not mere coincidence, for the creation of an imaginary character by author and reader is almost always based on some conception of human character and of individual differences.

Plays have a special engagement with character because of the visual and concrete manner in which they portray people on the stage. Stories or poems may comment on a character or editorialize rather directly, but plays have to *reveal* character—that is, let characters dramatize the kind of people they are by their own words and actions. Other characters may, of course, express opinions about a particular character, and our feelings as readers or members of the audience may be influenced by such rumor and innuendo, but all characters who appear on the stage or on the drama's page ultimately have to be credible in their own terms.

Not all plays focus on characters, though all involve characters and characterization. The reader, without the image of a living actor in view, must imaginatively create or recreate that image. Or, to be more precise, the reader must build, project, revise, compound, and complicate the image of the characters throughout the reading of the play. A reader must imagine what the actors, directors, and stage managers would provide in a staged performance. A good performance can suggest things the reader may have missed; many good performances may reveal a richness the single reader might overlook. But a good reading may also be richer than any one performance. Making sense of the main character is an interpretive act that draws most immediately on what the text or performance tells us. As readers, we draw on things we already know or assume—what we infer from language, action, and reaction and what we already believe about human psychology and how a person's past affects present and future behavior. As viewers, we are guided by and interact with what the director, actors, and stage managers assume, believe, or know.

> . . . *Art always aims at the individual. What the artist fixes on his canvas is something he has seen at a certain spot, on a certain day, at a certain hour, with a colouring that will never be seen again. What the poet sings of is a certain mood which was his, and his alone, and will never return. . . . Nothing could be more unique than the character of Hamlet. Though he may resemble other men in some respects, it is clearly not on that account that he interests us most.*
>
> —HENRI BERGSON

The titles of such plays as *Hamlet, Hedda Gabler,* and *Antigone* imply that the play will center on a single character, and in most cases the expectations created by titles are fulfilled in the play itself: the main character (or **protagonist**) is not only at the center of the action but is also the chief object of the playwright's (and the reader's or audience's) concern. Defining the character of the protagonist (sometimes by comparison with a competitor, or **antagonist**) often becomes the consuming interest of the play, and the action seems designed to illustrate, or clarify, or develop that character, or sometimes to make him or her a complex, unfathomable, mysterious being. Even titles that do not use proper names can indicate focus on a single character or character type—*Death of a Salesman,* for example, which suggests that the emphasis is on a type rather than an individual.

Not all the characters in a play are the **heroes** or **heroines** or **villains,** protagonists or antagonists. If we are to imagine the play vividly and make sense of the action, structure, and themes of the work, we must pay attention to the supporting or minor characters as well as to the leading figures. Characters are so categorized according to their functions within the play. But characters can also be categorized by what they require of those who are to act the part. There are demanding and challenging roles, juicy parts and dull or routine ones, roles for stars, character actors, comedians, and novices. Characters can also be categorized by their cultural identities (Jewish mothers, Romanian raven-haired beauties, pious frauds, social climbers). These sometimes verge on (or are subsumed by) **stereotypes:** characters based on conscious or unconscious cultural assumptions that sex, age, ethnic or national identification, occupation, marital status, and so on are predictably accompanied by certain character traits, actions, even values. Stereotypes, especially disparaging ones, can be a weakness in a play if they involve important characters who do not develop or become individualized, or whose motives are inadequately explored. However, no matter how individualized characters ultimately turn out to be, they often begin as some identifiable "type" of person that the audience will recognize and have certain expectations about.

Overturning or modifying these expectations of character is a method often employed to surprise a reader or audience, and to make a character a deeper, more interesting study. Hedda Gabler seems at first a Great Beauty. She is also rich, spoiled, ambitious, used to having her own way. Less and less attractive as she reveals herself more and more, yet pitiable because she is beginning to age and panic, and more and more helpless in a trap only in part of her own making, she begins as a quite predictable stereotype but becomes more and more complex, as does our response to her. The male characters in *Trifles* stereotype Mrs. Peters and Mrs. Hale as interested only in kitchen things and other "trifles" because they are women and, therefore, not serious thinkers. The thrust of the play is to overturn such a stereotype. Both Birdie in *Little Foxes* and Stella in *A Streetcar Named Desire* are in danger of being stereotyped as southern aristocrats who have lost wealth, status, and their "mansion" in the Civil War and are dominated and abused by the postwar, newly rich bourgeoisie—but, in fact, they are much different from the stereotype.

No matter how magnificent a performance may be, the actors must make choices—how to read a line, what body language to use, what gestures, if any, or stage "business" to bring to bear. Of course this means choosing how *not* to perform a scene as well, though some other way may be equally true to the text and equally or similarly effective. A performance is an interpretation, a "reading" of the play one way rather than another—or any other.

How would you play Hedda Gabler? Suppose you wanted to show that she was some subtle mixture of both lady and brat. How would you read the lines early in the play where she seems more sympathetic in order to suggest the brat beneath? And how would you read the later lines when her cruelty emerges to suggest the pitiable lady beneath her selfishness and greed? How would you play *Pygmalion*'s Henry Higgins? Is he the sarcastic, insufferably conceited, unsympathetic pedant he seems at first, or is he the brilliant, egalitarian, sensitive, and idealistic man, covering his disillusion with the waspish exterior put on to protect himself (as Eliza and, eventually, many readers and viewers believe)?

Every production of a play (and, in a sense, every performance) is an interpretation. Not just the "adaptations," setting a Greek or Elizabethan play in modern times and performing in modern dress, but even a production and performance that seeks to get at the "heart" or "essence" of the play is a "reading," a diagnosis or analysis of just what is vital and essential in the play. Interpretation does not necessarily mean getting the author's "intention," however. John Malkovich, in the 1983–1984 production of *Death of a Salesman,* did not project Biff Loman as an outgoing, successful, hail-fellow-well-met jock, though that is what Arthur Miller intended and how he wanted the part played. Malkovich saw Biff as only pretending, playing the part of the jock. Big-time athletes, he insisted, don't glad-hand people; they wait for people to come to them. The actor did not change the author's words, but by body language, stage business, and carriage suggested his own view of the nature of the character.

In a play performed on the stage we in the audience have a role, but a somewhat reduced role: actors tell us that no two performances are exactly alike, in part due to the nature of the audience. However, the actors and director have made choices and limited our freedom to interpret. Though as readers we may be the poorer for lacking the inspired insights of a great director and great actors, we are the richer for not being subjected to someone else's choices, for not having to settle on one interpretation, for the opportunity to hold complex, even contradictory, possibilities in mind, to "change character" as the words shift, while retaining all the possibilities we have gone through.

STRUCTURE

An important part of any storyteller's task, whether the story is to be narrative or dramatic, is the invention, selection, and arrangement of the action. What will happen—including the introduction of characters, the unfolding of events, the development of theme, and the resolution of situational problems—cannot properly be called a full-scale **plot** until some principles of order and organization are introduced and questions of character, story line, and theme are somehow brought together.

Judge not the play before the
* play is done:*
Her plot hath many changes.

—FRANCIS QUARLES

Plot in plays usually involves a conflict, and dramatic structure centrally concerns the presentation—quite literally the embodiment or fleshing out—of that conflict. A conflict whose outcome is never in doubt may have other kinds of interest, but it is not truly dramatic. In a dramatic conflict each of the opposing forces—whether one character versus another, one group of characters versus another group, the values of an individual versus those of a group or society or nature, or one idea or ideology versus another one—at one point or another seems to have a chance to triumph. In *Hamlet,* for example, our interest in the struggle between Hamlet and Claudius depends on their being evenly matched. Claudius has possession of the throne and the queen, but Hamlet's relation to the late king and his popularity with the people offset his opponent's strengths. As we have seen in "Drama: Reading, Responding, Writing," the typical structure of a dramatic plot involves five stages in the progression of the conflict: exposition, rising action, climax, falling action, and conclusion, and even a short play such as *Trifles* contains all five stages.

There are other structural devices by which a play can be organized and made meaningful and effective. Thematic concerns, for example, often hold together varieties of characters and winding plots. In *The Little Foxes,* the concern to define southern culture and values brings together the various kinds of conflict—between races, classes, generations, families, individuals, and ways of life—just as class conflict and the artificiality of class structure underlies much of the plot (and most of the humor) of *Pygmalion.* Careful and intricate plot calculations, in which difficult situations keep in tension the precise strengths and weaknesses of crucial characters, also structure plays in subtle but analyzable ways. In *The Little Foxes,* the negotiable bonds in Leo's possession make possible not only the theft of Regina's share in the family investment but also set up the final isolation of Regina from both her husband and daughter. Making Leo an assistant at the bank, creating him as a weak, immature, opportunistic, and gossipy character, and having his private knowledge of the bonds in the safe deposit box surface at precisely the right moment allow developments in the plot to conflict with aspects of Regina's character—her greed and ambition, her romanticism, her lack of human loyalty and inability to love—in ways that make event after event seem nearly inevitable. In *Hedda Gabler,* Tesman's initial otherworldliness—his trusting nature, his ignorance of the ways of the world, his lack of a sense of money, his failure to catch veiled allusions to pregnancy—control the plot structure of the early portions of the play almost as much as Hedda does, and the growing complexity of his character determines much of the plot in the later stages of the play.

Another structural device involves **dramatic irony,** the fulfillment of a plan, action, or expectation in a surprising way, often the opposite of what the characters intend. One example occurs in *Trifles* when the women keep noticing all the everyday things—"trifles"—in the house while the official investigators—the men—keep looking for large and unusual things. Finding "nothing . . . but kitchen things," and thinking they have no clues at all, the men condescend to the women's concerns: "Women are used to worrying about trifles." It is, of course, the women's "trifles" that reveal the truth about the murder that the men's search for "significant" evidence misses.

At the end of *The Little Foxes,* Regina's clever manipulativeness first seems to be rewarded but then defeats itself. Her insistence that Horace return home from Baltimore so that she can persuade him to join in the family's get-rich-quick scheme becomes a nightmare for her when he proves to have become, during his absence, both stronger and smarter, and when Horace reveals the terms of his will she recognizes that her own "will"—to be rich and have a new life in Chicago—is going to be defeated.

Besides structures like dramatic irony or thematic coherence that pull parts of a play together, and the five structural stages that shape dramatic action, most plays also have formal divisions, such as acts and scenes. In the Greek theater, scenes were separated by choral odes (see, for example, *Antigone*). In many French plays, a new scene begins with any significant entrance or exit. Many "classic" plays, like *Hamlet,* have five acts, but modern plays tend to have two or three acts. Formal divisions are the result of the content of the individual play—where sharp breaks can be emotionally effective by creating suspense or giving readers a relief from tension—or the conventions of the period: the expectation in the modern theater, for example, that audiences will have one or two intermissions in a public performance. Divisions may vary from the one-act, one-scene play—such as *Sure Thing*—to such long multiact plays as Eugene O'Neill's *Mourning Becomes Electra.*

STAGES, SETS, AND SETTING

Most of us have been to a theater at one time or another, if only for a school play, and we know what a conventional modern stage—the proscenium stage—looks like. It's like a room with the wall between us and it missing. So when we read a modern play—that is, one written during the past two or three hundred years—and imagine it taking place before us, we think of its happening on such a stage. There are other types of modern stages—the **thrust stage,** where the audience is seated around three sides of the major acting area, and the **arena stage,** where the audience is seated all the way around the acting area and players make their entrances and their exits through the auditorium—but most plays are staged on a proscenium stage. Eleven of the fourteen plays in this

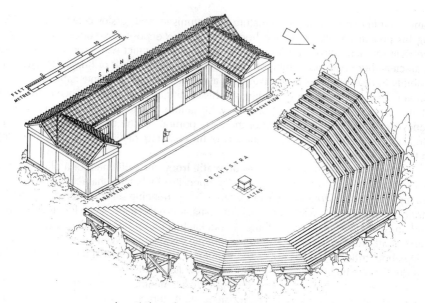

An artist's rendering of an early Greek theater.

text can readily be imagined to be taking place on such a stage. The two Shakespeare plays and the Greek play here were staged quite differently, and if we imagine them on the proscenium stage, we are at times likely to be a bit confused. In the Greek theater, the audience was seated on a raised semicircle of seats **(amphitheater)** halfway around a circular area **(orchestra)** used primarily for dancing by the chorus. At the back of the orchestra was the **skene** or stage house, representing the palace or temple before which the action took place. Shakespeare's stage, in contrast, basically involved a rectangular area built inside one end of a generally round enclosure, so that the audience was on three sides of the principal acting area. There were additional acting areas on either side of this stage, as well as a recessed area at the back of the stage, which could represent Gertrude's chamber in *Hamlet,* for example, and an upper acting area, which could serve as Juliet's balcony, for instance.

The conventions of dramatic writing and stage production have, of course, changed considerably since the advent of theater. These conventions involve, for example, the way playwrights convey the notion of place. Usually the stage represents a particular place, or **setting.** The audience knows that the stage is a stage, but they accept it as a public square or a room in a castle or an empty road. In *Trifles* we accept the stage as a kitchen in a midwest farmhouse.

The convention of place also involves how place is changed. In Greek drama, generally there was no change of place. The entire play of *Oedipus the King* takes place before the palace at Thebes, so that when the action demands the presence of Teiresias, for example, the scene does not shift to him but instead escorts are sent to bring him to the front of the palace.

In Shakespeare's theater the conventions of place are quite different: the acting area does not represent a specific place, but assumes a temporary identity according to the characters who inhabit it, their costumes, and their speeches. At the opening of *Hamlet* we know we are at a sentry station because a man dressed as a soldier challenges two others. By line 15, we know that we are in Denmark because the actors profess to be "liegemen to the Dane." At the end of the scene the actors leave the stage and in a sense take the sentry station with them. Shortly a group of people dressed in court costumes and a man and a woman wearing crowns appear. A theater audience must surmise, from costumes and dialogue, that the acting area has now become a "chamber of state"; as readers of the text, we could also infer the change of place from the identity of the characters and their words, but our text provides more information than a performance can, identifying the changed place in a stage direction. In a modern play like *Pygmalion*, there are likely to be several changes of scene. The staging of the original version of the play was relatively simple, however. Each of the five acts had only one scene: the portico of St. Paul's Church in the first act, Higgins's laboratory in Acts II and IV, and his mother's drawing room in Acts III and V. The changes of scene in modern plays involve lowering a curtain or darkening the stage while different sets and props are arranged. **Sets**—the design, decoration, and scenery—and **props**—articles or objects used on the stage— vary greatly in modern productions of plays from all periods. Sometimes there is the mere suggestion of space—a circle of sand at one end of the stage, a blank wall behind—but the more typical set involves some more or less realistic aids to the imagi- nation. The farmhouse kitchen setting in *Trifles,* for example, is represented by a door leading to the outside of the house, another leading to the upstairs, and a third leading to another room. There must be at least a sink, a cupboard, a stove, a small table and a large kitchen table, and a rocking chair.

Dramatic conventions represent time and the changing of times as well as space and the changing of space, and these conventions, too, have changed over the years. Renaissance commentators on classical drama, especially on one of the so-called **classi- cal unities**—that of time—argued that in order to insure maximum dramatic impact, the action of a play should represent a very short time—sometimes as short as the actual performance (two or three hours), and certainly no longer than a single day. It is this **unity of time** that impels a dramatist to select the moment when a stable situation should change and to fill in the necessary prior details by exposition or even by some more elaborate device, such as the enacted dreams and memories in *Death of a Sales- man.* The action from the beginning to the end of the play thus can represent a rather long time span, even years, in a very short period of actual time.

Even within the classical drama with its restricted time span, there are conventions to mark the passing of represented time when it is supposed to pass at a greater rate than that of viewing or reading time. The choral odes in *Oedipus the King* are an example of one convention for representing the passage of time.

In Elizabethan drama the break between scenes covers whatever time is necessary without a formal device like the choral odes. Sometimes the time is short, like the break between Hamlet's departure to see his mother at the end of Act III, scene 2, and the entrance of the king with Rosencrantz and Guildenstern at the beginning of the next scene; at other times the elapsed time between might be as long as that between scenes 4 and 5 of Act IV, during which the news of Polonius's death reaches Paris and Laertes returns to Denmark and there rallies his friends.

Once again, we must remember, drama is both a literary and performed art, and a play exists separately on page and stage. In reading plays, we use our imagination much as we do in stories to portray to ourselves the way the action is unfolding, but there is a difference. When we read stories we have a mediator, a narrator to guide us. When we read plays, we know that in another manifestation they are staged, produced, per- formed, and that another set of consciousnesses would mediate if we were viewing the plays in performance. As readers, we take all the roles ourselves and do not portion them out to actors; we set our own stage in our own minds. We become, in effect, our own producers, directors, and actors, but with the reader's latitude to keep multiple possibilities in mind. We become not just viewers of a staged production created by an intermediary, but imagining readers of a play—staging and restaging it in the mind's eye, mediated by our producer-selves.

TONE

It is difficult to define, describe, and, especially, demonstrate **tone.** A dictionary definition—"style or manner of expression in writing"—while "true" is so general or vague ("style," "manner," and "expression" can all use their own definitions) that it does not help us very much when we are dealing with the specifics of the text. We are more used to the concept of tone in spoken rather than written language, however; we think we know what "tone of voice" is and we can identify someone's tone of voice when he or she says something to us. Because tone is often associated with dialogue, then, it is more crucial, or at least more of a presence, in drama than in other genres. The actor— and the reader, especially one who wants to render the words of a play aloud—must infer from the playwright's written language just how to read a line, what "tone of voice" to use. For a similar reason, tone is also more subjective, its nuances or subtleties a "negotiation" between the actor/reader and the author/playwright. (Though there are, of course, limits to the power of the reader/actor: it would be difficult without parody to read Hamlet's famous soliloquy "To be or not to be" as comedy or to read Alfred Doolittle's lines in *Pygmalion* as vicious or dead serious.) At times the playwright will help out the actor (or dictate to him) with a stage direction. In *Trifles,* for example, when the sheriff hears the women discussing the quilt Mrs. Wright had been making, he tells the other men, "They wonder if she was going to quilt or just knot it!" He clearly is mocking the women, and the stage direction that follows suggests his tone and its effect: "[*The men laugh, the women look abashed.*]" At the climax of the play, Mrs. Peters finds the strangled bird that suggests Mrs. Wright's motivation in strangling her husband. As the men approach—they have been fruitlessly searching the barn for real or "untrifling" clues—Mrs. Hale hides the bird under the quilt pieces. The County Attorney says, "Well ladies, have you decided whether she was going to quilt it or knot it?" The **dramatic irony** here—the women and their trifles have figured out what happened, the men and their "serious" search have not—is underscored by the stage direction telling the actor how to read the line in such a way as to emphasize the irony: "[*As one turning from serious things to little pleasantries.*]"

Dramatic irony, where the reader or audience knows what the character does not, is relative easy to detect; **verbal irony,** especially when there are no stage directions to help, can be fairly subtle and easy to miss. If you are reading *The Little Foxes* attentively, by the second act it should be quite clear that Oscar and Ben do not particularly want Horace to get home from Baltimore, though Horace's wife, Regina, does. When Ben suggests that Horace and his daughter may not have even started home, Regina, irritated, denies it. She says, "They'll be along today some time, *very flattered that you and Oscar are so worried about them.*" The text does not underline the ironic passage, but clearly Regina does not mean what her words "say": Ben and Oscar may not consciously wish Horace and Alexandra harm, they do want them delayed as long as possible and they are not particularly worried about their welfare. The tone thus alters the meaning of the words. Indeed, it is chiefly when, as in this case, there is a discrepancy between the tone and the normal meaning of the words that tone is most identifiable—and important for our understanding. There are times, however, when the tone is a reinforcement of the language, action, and situation of a whole play or a major portion of it. The first act of *Pygmalion* is dominated by the tone of Henry Higgins—witty, iconoclastic, unsentimental, satiric, even caustic. Its unconventionality and unsentimentality go well beyond the acrid criticism of the British class system, which is one of the major concerns of the play, for it is even unsentimental about the poor. When poor Eliza gets a bit of money, somewhat surprisingly the first thing she does it spend that money on a cab, saying, rather shockingly, "a taxi fare ain't no object to me." The satiric unconventionality of the play as a whole is most hilariously represented by the even more surprisingly and shocking—and delightful—"antibourgeois morality" of Eliza's father, who is willing to "sell" his daughter for five pounds (about twenty-five dollars at that time) but not for ten pounds because that amount of money would make him a member of the detested middle class!

THEME

Tone may modulate the meaning of a few words, dominate an entire act, or pervade virtually an entire play, as in *Pygmalion* (which does, however, have its apparently sentimental moments leading many romantically inclined readers, directors, and viewers to give the play an ending the author did not intend). **Theme**—usually defined as a generalized or abstract paraphrase of the subject of a work—is by its very nature the most comprehensive of the elements, embracing, as its definition suggests, the entire work. In a very real sense theme is not actually part of the work, but is abstracted from the work by the reader or interpreter. Since theme is inferred by and is defined in the words of the reader or audience, it is understandably often the subject of disagreements involving nuances of emphasis or phrasing or the entire conception of the theme. The romantic ending of *Pygmalion,* in which the poor, lower-class Eliza and wealthy, aristocratic Higgins marry—or at least stay together—tends to confirm the theme of the artificiality of class which is emphasized throughout the play. (That ending is also affirmed, some would say, by the title of the play, for in the myth Pygmalion falls in love with and marries the statue he has created which the goddess Aphrodite brings to life for his benefit.) Artificiality of class is clearly *one* of the **motifs** (recurrent ideas or threads of the play); but if, as Shaw apparently intended, Eliza marries Freddy, the romantic and the mythic are both undermined by the shocking "get real" practicality that is perhaps more consistent with the ironic and unsentimental tone—Higgins would be an unbearable husband, after all, and the unexciting but devoted Freddy would be a good and devoted one—than would be the romantic ending.

Similarly, many would agree that the theme of *Hedda Gabler* centers on the conflict between being afraid to live on the one hand and not recognizing the need to adjust desire to (social) circumstances and real-world possibility, though, as you can see even from the hesitancy of this phrasing, there are many ways of saying this and the way it is said may influence which side you come down on. There will be, in any case, considerable disagreement about what life choices are "right," in Ibsen's eyes or our own, or whether the play is ambiguous, or whether it is suggesting that the fate of anyone who seeks to be extraordinary or act in unconventional ways will inevitably be tragic.

It is ironic (there's that word again) that from the very fact that theme is pervasive, involving the entire work, there is relatively little that can be said about it in general—that is, outside the discussion of specific texts. The other elements—character, structure, setting, tone, as well as imagery, symbol, and so on—all contribute to this overarching element of theme. So in discussing theme, we are inevitably led to a discussion of the other elements and to the specific details of the text.

LILLIAN HELLMAN

The Little Foxes

> Take us the foxes, the little foxes,
> —that spoil the vines:
> for our vines have tender grapes.[1]

CHARACTERS

ADDIE

CAL

OSCAR HUBBARD

BIRDIE HUBBARD, *his wife*

LEO HUBBARD, *Oscar and Birdie's son*

HORACE GIDDENS

REGINA GIDDENS, *Horace's wife*

ALEXANDRA GIDDENS, *Horace and Regina's daughter*

BENJAMIN HUBBARD

WILLIAM MARSHALL

The scene of the play is the living room of the GIDDENS house, in a small town in the South.

Act I: The Spring of 1900, evening.

Act II: A week later, early morning.

Act III: Two weeks later, late afternoon.

There has been no attempt to write Southern dialect. It is to be understood that the accents are Southern.

ACT I

SCENE: *The living room of the* GIDDENS *house, in a small town in the deep South, the Spring of 1900. Upstage is a staircase leading to the second story. Upstage, right, are double doors to the dining room. When these doors are open we see a section of the dining room and the furniture. Upstage, left, is an entrance hall with a coat-rack and umbrella stand. There are large lace-curtained windows on the left wall. The room is lit by a center gas chandelier and painted china oil lamps on the tables. Against the wall is a large piano. Downstage, right, are a high couch, a large table, several chairs. Against the left back wall are a table and several chairs. Near the window there are a smaller couch and tables. The room is good-looking, the furniture expensive; but it reflects no particular taste. Everything is of the best and that is all.*

AT RISE: ADDIE, *a tall, nice-looking Negro woman of about fifty-five, is closing the windows. From behind the closed dining-room doors there is the sound of voices. After a second,* CAL, *a middle-aged Negro, comes in from the entrance hall carrying a tray with glasses and a bottle of port.* ADDIE *crosses, takes the tray from him, puts it on table, begins to arrange it.*

ADDIE: [*Pointing to the bottle.*] You gone stark out of your head?

---

1. Song of Solomon 2:15.

CAL: No, smart lady, I ain't. Miss Regina told me to get out that bottle. [*Points to bottle.*] That very bottle for the mighty honored guest. When Miss Regina changes orders like that you can bet your dime she got her reason.

ADDIE: [*Points to dining room.*] Go on. You'll be needed.

CAL: Miss Zan she had two helpings frozen fruit cream and she tell that honored guest, she tell him that you make the best frozen fruit cream in all the South.

ADDIE: [*Smiles, pleased.*] Did she? Well, see that Belle saves a little for her. She like it right before she go to bed. Save a few little cakes, too, she like—

[*The dining-room doors are opened and quickly closed again by* BIRDIE HUB-BARD. BIRDIE *is a woman of about forty, with a pretty, well-bred, faded face. Her movements are usually nervous and timid, but now, as she comes running into the room, she is gay and excited.* CAL *turns to* BIRDIE.]

BIRDIE: Oh, Cal. [*Closes door.*] I want you to get one of the kitchen boys to run home for me. He's to look in my desk drawer and—[*To* ADDIE.] My, Addie. What a good supper! Just as good as good can be.

ADDIE: You look pretty this evening, Miss Birdie, and young.

BIRDIE: [*Laughing.*] Me, young? [*Turns back to* CAL.] Maybe you better find Simon and tell him to do it himself. He's to look in my desk, the left drawer, and bring my music album right away. Mr. Marshall is very anxious to see it because of his father and the opera in Chicago. [*To* ADDIE.] Mr. Marshall is such a polite man with his manners and very educated and cultured and I've told him all about how my mama and papa used to go to Europe for the music—[*Laughs. To* ADDIE.] Imagine going all the way to Europe just to listen to music. Wouldn't that be nice, Addie? Just to sit there and listen and—[*Turns and steps to* CAL.] *Left* drawer, Cal. Tell him that twice because he forgets. And tell him not to let any of the things drop out of the album and to bring it right in here when he comes back.

[*The dining-room doors are opened and quickly closed by* OSCAR HUBBARD. *He is a man in his late forties.*]

CAL: Yes'm. But Simon he won't get it right. But I'll tell him.

BIRDIE: Left drawer, Cal, and tell him to bring the blue book and—

OSCAR: [*Sharply.*] Birdie.

BIRDIE: [*Turning nervously.*] Oh, Oscar. I was just sending Simon for my music album.

OSCAR: [*To* CAL.] Never mind about the album. Miss Birdie has changed her mind.

BIRDIE: But, really, Oscar. Really I promised Mr. Marshall. I—

[CAL *looks at them, exits.*]

OSCAR: Why do you leave the dinner table and go running about like a child?

BIRDIE: [*Trying to be gay.*] But, Oscar, Mr. Marshall said most specially he *wanted* to see my album. I told him about the time Mama met Wagner,[2] and Mrs.

---

2. Richard Wagner (1813–1883), German composer.

Wagner gave her the signed program and the big picture. Mr. Marshall wants to see that. Very, very much. We had such a nice talk and—

OSCAR: [*Taking a step to her.*] You have been chattering to him like a magpie. You haven't let him be for a second. I can't think he came South to be bored with you.

BIRDIE: [*Quickly, hurt.*] He wasn't bored. I don't believe he was bored. He's a very educated, cultured gentleman. [*Her voice rises.*] I just don't believe it. You always talk like that when I'm having a nice time.

OSCAR: [*Turning to her, sharply.*] You have had too much wine. Get yourself in hand now.

BIRDIE: [*Drawing back, about to cry, shrilly.*] What am I doing? I am not doing anything. What am I doing?

OSCAR: [*Taking a step to her, tensely.*] I said get yourself in hand. Stop acting like a fool.

BIRDIE: [*Turns to him, quietly.*] I don't believe he was bored. I just don't believe it. Some people like music and like to talk about it. That's all I was doing.

> [LEO HUBBARD *comes hurrying through the dining-room door. He is a young man of twenty, with a weak kind of good looks.*]

LEO: Mama! Papa! They are coming in now.

OSCAR: [*Softly.*] Sit down, Birdie. Sit down now.

> [BIRDIE *sits down, bows her head as if to hide her face. The dining-room doors are opened by* CAL. *We see people beginning to rise from the table.* REGINA GIDDENS *comes in with* WILLIAM MARSHALL. REGINA *is a handsome woman of forty.* MARSHALL *is forty-five, pleasant-looking, self-possessed. Behind them comes* ALEXANDRIA GIDDENS, *a very pretty, rather delicate-looking girl of seventeen. She is followed by* BENJAMIN HUBBARD, *fifty-five, with a large jovial face and the light graceful movements that one often finds in large men.*]

REGINA: Mr. Marshall, I think you're trying to console me. Chicago may be the noisiest, dirtiest city in the world but I should still prefer it to the sound of our horses and the smell of our azaleas. I should like crowds of people, and theatres, and lovely women—*Very* lovely women, Mr. Marshall?

MARSHALL: [*Crossing to sofa.*] In Chicago? Oh, I suppose so. But I can tell you this: I've never dined there with three *such* lovely ladies.

> [ADDIE *begins to pass the port.*]

BEN: Our Southern women are well favored.

LEO: [*Laughs.*] But one must go to Mobile for the ladies, sir. Very elegant worldly ladies, too.

BEN: [*Looks at him very deliberately.*] Worldly, eh? *Worldly,* did you say?

OSCAR: [*Hastily, to* LEO.] Your Uncle Ben means that worldliness is not a mark of beauty in any woman.

LEO: [*Quickly.*] Of course, Uncle Ben. I didn't mean—

MARSHALL: Your port is excellent, Mrs. Giddens.

REGINA: Thank you, Mr. Marshall. We had been saving that bottle, hoping we could open it just for you.

ALEXANDRA: [*As* ADDIE *comes to her with the tray.*] Oh. May I *really,* Addie?

ADDIE: Better ask Mama.

ALEXANDRA: May I, Mama?

REGINA: [*Nods, smiles.*] In Mr. Marshall's honor.

ALEXANDRA: [*Smiles.*] Mr. Marshall, this will be the first taste of port I've ever had.

[ADDIE *serves* LEO.]

MARSHALL: No one ever had their first taste of a better port. [*He lifts his glass in a toast; she lifts hers; they both drink.*] Well, I suppose it is all true, Mrs. Giddens.

REGINA: What is true?

MARSHALL: That you Southerners occupy a unique position in America. You live better than the rest of us, you eat better, you drink better. I wonder you find time, or want to find time, to do business.

BEN: A great many Southerners don't.

MARSHALL: Do all of you live here together?

REGINA: Here with me? [*Laughs.*] Oh, no. My brother Ben lives next door. My brother Oscar and his family live in the next square.

BEN: But we are a very close family. We've always *wanted* it that way.

MARSHALL: That is very pleasant. Keeping your family together to share each other's lives. My family moves around too much. My children seem never to come home. Away at school in the winter; in the summer, Europe with their mother—

REGINA: [*Eagerly.*] Oh, yes. Even down here we read about Mrs. Marshall in the society pages.

MARSHALL: I dare say. She moves about a great deal. And all of you are part of the same business? Hubbard Sons?

BEN: [*Motions to* OSCAR.] Oscar and me. [*Motions to* REGINA.] My sister's good husband is a banker.

MARSHALL: [*Looks at* REGINA, *surprised.*] Oh.

REGINA: I am so sorry that my husband isn't here to meet you. He's been very ill. He is at Johns Hopkins.[3] But he will be home soon. We think he is getting better now.

LEO: I work for Uncle Horace. [REGINA *looks at him.*] I mean I work for Uncle Horace at his bank. I keep an eye on things while he's away.

REGINA: [*Smiles.*] Really, Leo?

BEN: [*Looks at* LEO, *then to* MARSHALL.] Modesty in the young is as excellent as it is rare. [*Looks at* LEO *again.*]

OSCAR: [*To* LEO.] Your uncle means that a young man should speak more modestly.

LEO: [*Hastily, taking a step to* BEN.] Oh, I didn't mean, sir—

MARSHALL: Oh, Mrs. Hubbard. Where's that Wagner autograph you promised to let me see? My train will be leaving soon and—

BIRDIE: The autograph? Oh. Well. Really, Mr. Marshall, I didn't mean to chatter so about it. Really I—[*Nervously, looking at* OSCAR.] You must excuse me. I didn't get it because, well, because I had—I—I had a little headache and—

3. A well-respected hospital in Baltimore.

OSCAR: My wife is a miserable victim of headaches.

REGINA: [*Quickly.*] Mr. Marshall said at supper that he would like you to play for him, Alexandra.

ALEXANDRA: [*Who has been looking at* BIRDIE.] It's not I who play well, sir. It's my aunt. She plays just wonderfully. She's my teacher. [*Rises. Eagerly.*] May we play a duet? May we, Mama?

BIRDIE: [*Taking* ALEXANDRA's *hand.*] Thank you, dear. But I have my headache now. I—

OSCAR: [*Sharply.*] Don't be stubborn, Birdie. Mr. Marshall wants you to play.

MARSHALL: Indeed I do. If your headache isn't—

BIRDIE: [*Hesitates, then gets up, pleased.*] But I'd like to, sir. Very much. [*She and* ALEXANDRA *go to the piano.*]

MARSHALL: It's very remarkable how you Southern aristocrats have kept together. Kept together and kept what belonged to you.

BEN: You misunderstand, sir. Southern aristocrats have *not* kept together and have *not* kept what belonged to them.

MARSHALL: [*Laughs, indicates room.*] You don't call this keeping what belongs to you?

BEN: But we are not aristocrats. [*Points to* BIRDIE *at the piano.*] Our brother's wife is the only one of us who belongs to the Southern aristocracy.

> [BIRDIE *looks towards* BEN.]

MARSHALL: [*Smiles.*] My information is that you people have been here, and solidly here, for a long time.

OSCAR: And so we have. Since our great-grandfather.

BEN: [*Smiles.*] Who was *not* an aristocrat, like Birdie's.

MARSHALL: [*A little sharply.*] You make great distinctions.

BEN: Oh, they have been made for us. And maybe they are important distinctions. [*Leans forward, intimately.*] Now you take Birdie's family. When my great-grandfather came here they were the highest-tone plantation owners in this state.

LEO: [*Steps to* MARSHALL. *Proudly.*] My mother's grandfather was *governor* of the state before the war.

OSCAR: They owned the plantation, Lionnet. You may have heard of it, sir?

MARSHALL: [*Laughs.*] No, I've never heard of anything but brick houses on a lake, and cotton mills.

BEN: Lionnet in its day was the best cotton land in the South. It still brings us in a fair crop. [*Sits back.*] Ah, they were great days for those people—even when I can remember. They had the best of everything. [BIRDIE *turns to them.*] Cloth from Paris, trips to Europe, horses you can't raise any more, niggers to lift their fingers—

BIRDIE: [*Suddenly.*] We were good to our people. Everybody knew that. We were better to them than—

> [MARSHALL *looks up at* BIRDIE.]

REGINA: Why, Birdie. You aren't playing.

BEN: But when the war comes these fine gentlemen ride off and leave the cotton, *and* the women, to rot.

BIRDIE: My father was killed in the war. He was a fine soldier, Mr. Marshall. A fine man.

REGINA: Oh, certainly, Birdie. A famous soldier.

BEN: [*To* BIRDIE.] But that isn't the tale I am telling Mr. Marshall. [*To* MARSHALL.] Well, sir, the war ends. [BIRDIE *goes back to piano.*] Lionnet is almost ruined, and the sons finish ruining it. And there were thousands like them. Why? [*Leans forward.*] Because the Southern aristocrat can adapt himself to nothing. Too high-tone to try.

MARSHALL: Sometimes it is difficult to learn new ways.

[BIRDIE *and* ALEXANDRA *begin to play.* MARSHALL *leans forward, listening.*]

BEN: Perhaps, perhaps. [*He sees that* MARSHALL *is listening to the music. Irritated, he turns to* BIRDIE *and* ALEXANDRA *at the piano, then back to* MARSHALL.] You're right, Mr. Marshall. It is difficult to learn new ways. But maybe that's why it's profitable. *Our* grandfather and *our* father learned the new ways and learned how to make them pay. They work. [*Smiles nastily.*] *They* are in trade. Hubbard Sons, Merchandise. Others, Birdie's family, for example, look down on them. [*Settles back in chair.*] To make a long story short, Lionnet now belongs to *us.* [BIRDIE *stops playing.*] Twenty years ago we took over their land, their cotton, and their daughter.

[BIRDIE *rises and stands stiffly by the piano.* MARSHALL, *who has been watching her, rises.*]

MARSHALL: May I bring you a glass of port, Mrs. Hubbard?

BIRDIE: [*Softly.*] No, thank you, sir. You are most polite.

REGINA: [*Sharply, to* BEN.] You are boring Mr. Marshall with these ancient family tales.

BEN: I hope not. I hope not. I am trying to make an important point—[*Bows to* MARSHALL.] for our future business partner.

OSCAR: [*To* MARSHALL.] My brother always says that it's folks like us who have struggled and fought to bring to our land some of the posperity of your land.

BEN: Some people call that patriotism.

REGINA: [*Laughs gaily.*] I hope you don't find my brothers too obvious, Mr. Marshall. I'm afraid they mean that this is the time for the ladies to leave the gentlemen to talk business.

MARSHALL: [*Hastily.*] Not at all. We settled everything this afternoon. [MARSHALL *looks at his watch.*] I have only a few minutes before I must leave for the train. [*Smiles at her.*] And I insist they be spent with you.

REGINA: *And* with another glass of port.

MARSHALL: Thank you.

BEN: [*To* REGINA.] My sister is right. [*To* MARSHALL.] I am a plain man and I am trying to say a plain thing. A man ain't only in business for what he can get out of it. It's got to give him something here. [*Puts hand to his breast.*] That's every bit as true for the nigger picking cotton for a silver quarter, as it is for you and me. [REGINA *gives* MARSHALL *a glass of port.*] If it don't give him something here, then he don't pick the cotton right. Money isn't all. Not by three shots.

MARSHALL: Really? Well, I always thought it was a great deal.

REGINA: And so did I, Mr. Marshall.

MARSHALL: [*Leans forward. Pleasantly, but with meaning.*] Now you don't have to convince me that you are the right people for the deal. I wouldn't be here if you hadn't convinced me six months ago. You want the mill here, and I want it here. It isn't my business to find out *why* you want it.

BEN: To bring the machine to the cotton, and not the cotton to the machine.

MARSHALL: [*Amused.*] You have a turn for neat phrases, Hubbard. Well, however grand your reasons are, mine are simple: I want to make money and I believe I'll make it on you. [*As* BEN *starts to speak, he smiles.*] Mind you, I have no objections to more high-minded reasons. They are mighty valuable in business. It's fine to have partners who so closely follow the teachings of Christ. [*Gets up.*] And now I must leave for my train.

REGINA: I'm sorry you won't stay over with us, Mr. Marshall, but you'll come again. Any time you like.

BEN: [*Motions to* LEO, *indicating the bottle.*] Fill them up, boy, fill them up. [LEO *moves around filling the glasses as* BEN *speaks.*] Down here, sir, we have a strange custom. We drink the *last* drink for a toast. That's to prove that the Southerner is always still on his feet for the last drink. [*Picks up his glass.*] It was Henry Frick, your Mr. Henry Frick,[4] who said, "Railroads are the Rembrandts of investments." Well, *I* say, "Southern cotton mills *will be* the Rembrandts of investment." So I give you the firm of Hubbard Sons and Marshall, Cotton Mills, and to it a long and prosperous life.

[*They all pick up their glasses.* MARSHALL *looks at them, amused. Then he, too, lifts his glass, smiles.*]

OSCAR: The children will drive you to the depot. Leo! Alexandra! You will drive Mr. Marshall down.

LEO: [*Eagerly, looks at* BEN *who nods.*] Yes, sir. [*To* MARSHALL.] Not often Uncle Ben lets *me* drive the horses. And a beautiful pair they are. [*Starts for hall.*] Come on, Zan.

ALEXANDRA: May I drive tonight, Uncle Ben, please? I'd like to and—

BEN: [*Shakes his head, laughs.*] In your evening clothes? Oh, no, my dear.

ALEXANDRA: But Leo always—[*Stops, exits quickly.*]

REGINA: I don't like to say good-bye to you, Mr. Marshall.

MARSHALL: Then we won't say good-bye. You have promised that you would come and let me show you Chicago. Do I have to make you promise again?

REGINA: [*Looks at him as he presses her hand.*] I promise again.

MARSHALL: [*Touches her hand again, then moves to* BIRDIE.] Good-bye, Mrs. Hubbard.

BIRDIE: [*Shyly, with sweetness and dignity.*] Good-bye, sir.

4. Henry Frick (1849–1919), American industrialist; "your" because he was a northerner. *Rembrandts:* valuable paintings by the great Dutch artist (1606–1669), here representing the highest quality.

MARSHALL: [*As he passes* REGINA.] Remember.

REGINA: I will.

OSCAR: We'll see you to the carriage.

> [MARSHALL *exits, followed by* BEN *and* OSCAR. *For a second* REGINA *and* BIRDIE *stand looking after them. Then* REGINA *throws up her arms, laughs happily.*]

REGINA: And there, Birdie, goes the man who has opened the door to our future.

BIRDIE: [*Surprised to the unaccustomed friendliness.*] What?

REGINA: [*Turning to her.*] Our future. Yours and mine, Ben's and Oscar's, the children—[*Looks at* BIRDIE'*s puzzled face, laughs.*] Our future! [*Gaily.*] You were charming at supper, Birdie. Mr. Marshall certainly thought so.

BIRDIE: [*Pleased.*] Why, Regina! Do you think he did?

REGINA: Can't you tell when you're being admired?

BIRDIE: Oscar said I bored Mr. Marshall. [*Then quietly.*] But he admired *you.* He told me so.

REGINA: What did he say?

BIRDIE: He said to me, "I hope your sister-in-law will come to Chicago. Chicago will be at her feet." He said the ladies would bow to your manners and the gentlemen to your looks.

REGINA: Did he? He seems a lonely man. Imagine being lonely with all that money. I don't think he likes his wife.

BIRDIE: Not like his wife? What a thing to say.

REGINA: She's away a great deal. He said that several times. And once he made fun of her being so social and high-tone. But that fits in all right. [*Sits back, arms on back of sofa, stretches.*] Her being social, I mean. She can introduce me. It won't take long with an introduction from her.

BIRDIE: [*Bewildered.*] Introduce you? In Chicago? You mean you really might go? Oh, Regina, you can't leave here. What about Horace?

REGINA: Don't look so scared about everything, Birdie. I'm going to live in Chicago. I've always wanted to. And now there'll be plenty of money to go with.

BIRDIE: But Horace won't be able to move around. You know what the doctor wrote.

REGINA: There'll be millions, Birdie, millions. You know what I've always said when people told me we were rich? I said I think you should either be a nigger or a millionaire. In between, like us, what for? [*Laughs. Looks at* BIRDIE.] But I'm not going away tomorrow, Birdie. There's plenty of time to worry about Horace when he comes home. If he ever decides to come home.

BIRDIE: Will we be going to Chicago? I mean, Oscar and Leo and me?

REGINA: You? I shouldn't think so. [*Laughs.*] Well, we must remember tonight. It's a very important night and we mustn't forget it. We shall plan all the things we'd like to have and then we'll really have them. Make a wish, Birdie, any wish. It's bound to come true now.

> [BEN *and* OSCAR *enter.*]

BIRDIE: [*Laughs.*] Well. Well, I don't know. Maybe. [REGINA *turns to look at* BEN.] Well, I guess I'd know right off what I wanted.

[OSCAR *stands by the upper window, waves to the departing carriage.*]

REGINA [*Looks up at* BEN, *smiles. He smiles back at her.*] Well, you did it.

BEN: Looks like it might be we did.

REGINA: [*Springs up, laughs.*] Looks like it! Don't pretend. You're like a cat who's been licking the cream. [*Crosses to wine bottle.*] Now we must all have a drink to celebrate.

OSCAR: The children, Alexandra and Leo, make a very handsome couple, Regina. Marshall remarked himself what fine young folks they were. How well they looked together!

REGINA: [*Sharply.*] Yes. You said that before, Oscar.

BEN: Yes, sir. It's beginning to look as if the deal's all set. I may not be a subtle man—but—[*Turns to them. After a second.*] Now somebody ask me how I know the deal is set.

OSCAR: What do you mean, Ben?

BEN: You remember I told him that down here we drink the *last* drink for a toast?

OSCAR: [*Thoughtfully.*] Yes. I never heard that before.

BEN: Nobody's ever heard it before. God forgives those who invent what they need. I already had his signature. But we've all done business with men whose word over a glass is better than a bond. Anyway it don't hurt to have both.

OSCAR: [*Turns to* REGINA.] You understand what Ben means?

REGINA: [*Smiles.*] Yes, Oscar. I understand. I understood immediately.

BEN: [*Looks at her admiringly.*] Did you, Regina? Well, when he lifted his glass to drink, I closed my eyes and saw the bricks going into place.

REGINA: And *I* saw a lot more than that.

BEN: Slowly, slowly. As yet we have only our hopes.

REGINA: Birdie and I have just been planning what we want. I know what I want. What will you want, Ben?

BEN: Caution. Don't count the chickens. [*Leans back, laughs.*] Well, God would allow us a little daydreaming. Good for the soul when you've worked hard enough to deserve it. [*Pauses.*] I think I'll have a stable. For a long time I've had my good eyes on Carter's in Savannah. A rich man's pleasure, the sport of kings, why not the sport of Hubbards? Why not?

REGINA: [*Smiles.*] Why not? What will you have, Oscar?

OSCAR: I don't know. [*Thoughtfully.*] The pleasure of seeing the bricks grow will be enough for me.

BEN: Oh, of course. Our *greatest* pleasure will be to see the bricks grow. But we are all entitled to a little side indulgence.

OSCAR: Yes, I suppose so. Well, then, I think we might take a few trips here and there, eh, Birdie?

BIRDIE: [*Surprised at being consulted.*] Yes, Oscar. I'd like that.

OSCAR: We might even make a regular trip to Jekyll Island.[5] I've heard the Cornelly place is for sale. We might think about buying it. Make a nice change. Do you good, Birdie, a change of climate. Fine shooting on Jekyll, the best.

---

5. In Georgia, on the Atlantic coast.

BIRDIE: I'd like—

OSCAR: [*Indulgently.*] What would you like?

BIRDIE: *Two* things. Two things I'd like most.

REGINA: Two! I should like a thousand. You are modest, Birdie.

BIRDIE: [*Warmly, delighted with the unexpected interest.*] I should like to have Lionnet back. I know you own it now, but I'd like to see it fixed up again, the way Mama and Papa had it. Every year it used to get a nice coat of paint—Papa was very particular about the paint—and the lawn was so smooth all the way down to the river, with the trims of zinnias and red-feather plush. And the figs and blue little plums and the scuppernongs—[*Smiles. Turns to* REGINA.] The organ is still there and it wouldn't cost much to fix. We could have parties for Zan, the way Mama used to have for me.

BEN: That's a pretty picture, Birdie. Might be a most pleasant way to live. [*Dismissing* BIRDIE.] What do you want, Regina?

BIRDIE: [*Very happily, not noticing that they are no longer listening to her.*] I could have a cutting garden. Just where Mama's used to be. Oh, I do think we could be happier there. Papa used to say that *nobody* had ever lost their temper at Lionnet, and *nobody* ever would. Papa would never let anybody be nasty-spoken or mean. No, sir. He just didn't like it.

BEN: What do you want, Regina?

REGINA: I'm going to Chicago. And when I'm settled there and know the right people and the right things to buy—because I certainly don't now—I shall go to Paris and buy them. [*Laughs.*] I'm going to leave you and Oscar to count the bricks.

BIRDIE: Oscar. Please let me have Lionnet back.

OSCAR: [*To* REGINA.] You are serious about moving to Chicago?

BEN: She is going to see the great world and leave us in the little one. Well, we'll come and visit you and meet all the great and be proud to think you are our sister.

REGINA: [*Gaily.*] Certainly. And you won't even have to learn to be subtle, Ben. Stay as you are. You will be rich and the rich don't have to be subtle.

OSCAR: But what about Alexandra? She's seventeen. Old enough to be thinking about marrying.

BIRDIE: And, Oscar, I have one more wish. Just one more wish.

OSCAR: [*Turns.*] What is it, Birdie? What are you saying?

BIRDIE: I want you to stop shooting. I mean, so much. I don't like to see animals and birds killed just for the killing. You only throw them away—

BEN: [*To* REGINA.] It'll take a great deal of money to live as you're planning, Regina.

REGINA: Certainly. But there'll be plenty of money. You have estimated the profits very high.

BEN: I have—

BIRDIE: [OSCAR *is looking at her furiously.*] And you never let anybody else shoot, and the niggers need it so much to keep from starving. It's wicked to shoot food just because you like to shoot, when poor people need it so—

BEN: [*Laughs.*] I have estimated the profits very high—for myself.

REGINA: What did you say?

BIRDIE: I've always wanted to speak about it, Oscar.

OSCAR: [*Slowly, carefully.*] What are you chattering about?

BIRDIE: [*Nervously.*] I was talking about Lionnet and—and about your shooting—

OSCAR: You are exciting yourself.

REGINA: [*To* BEN.] I didn't hear you. There was so much talking.

OSCAR: [*To* BIRDIE.] You have been acting very childish, very excited, all evening.

BIRDIE: Regina asked me what I'd like.

REGINA: What did you say, Ben?

BIRDIE: Now that we'll be so rich everybody was saying what they would like, so *I* said what *I* would like, too.

BEN: I said—[*He is interrupted by* OSCAR.]

OSCAR: [*To* BIRDIE.] Very well, We've all heard you. That's enough now.

BEN: I am waiting. [*They stop.*] I am waiting for you to finish. You and Birdie. Four conversations are three too many. [BIRDIE *slowly sits down.* BEN *smiles, to* REGINA.] I said that I had, and I do, estimate the profits very high—for myself, and Oscar, of course.

REGINA: [*Slowly.*] And what does that mean?

[BEN *shrugs, looks towards* OSCAR.]

OSCAR: [*Looks at* BEN, *clears throat.*] Well, Regina, it's like this. For forty-nine per cent Marshall will put up four hundred thousand dollars. For forty-one per cent—[*Smiles archly.*] a controlling interest, mind you, we will put up two hundred and twenty-five thousand dollars besides offering him certain benefits that our [*Looks at* BEN.] local position allows us to manage. Ben means that two hundred and twenty-five thousand dollars is a lot of money.

REGINA: I know the terms and I know it's a lot of money.

BEN: [*Nodding.*] It is.

OSCAR: Ben means that we are ready with our two-thirds of the money. Your third, Horace's I mean, doesn't seem to be ready. [*Raises his hand as* REGINA *starts to speak.*] Ben has written to Horace, I have written, and you have written. He answers. But he never mentions this business. Yet we have explained it to him in great detail, and told him the urgency. Still he never mentions it. Ben has been very patient, Regina. Naturally, you are our sister and we want you to benefit from anything we do.

REGINA: And in addition to your concern for me, you do not want control to go out of the family. [*To* BEN.] That right, Ben?

BEN: That's cynical. [*Smiles.*] Cynicism is an unpleasant way of saying the truth.

OSCAR: No need to be cynical. We'd have no trouble raising the third share, the share that you want to take.

REGINA: I am sure you could get the third share, the share you were saving for me. But that would give you a strange partner. And strange partners sometimes want a great deal. [*Smiles unpleasantly.*] But perhaps it would be wise for you to find him.

OSCAR: Now, now. Nobody says we *want* to do that. We would like to have you in and you would like to come in.

REGINA: Yes. I certainly would.

BEN: [*Laughs, puts up his hand.*] But we haven't heard from Horace.

REGINA: I've given my word that Horace will put up the money. That should be enough.

BEN: Oh, it was enough. I took your word. But I've got to have more than your word now. The contracts will be signed this week, and Marshall will want to see our money soon after. Regina, Horace has been in Baltimore for five months. I know that you've written him to come home, and that he hasn't come.

OSCAR: It's beginning to look as if he doesn't want to come home.

REGINA: Of course he wants to come home. You can't move around with heart trouble at any moment you choose. You know what doctors are like once they get their hands on a case like this—

OSCAR: They can't very well keep him from answering letters, can they? [REGINA *turns to* BEN.] They couldn't keep him from arranging for the money if he wanted to—

REGINA: Has it occurred to you that Horace is also a good business man?

BEN: Certainly. He is a shrewd trader. Always has been. The bank is proof of that.

REGINA: Then, possibly, he may be keeping silent because he doesn't think he is getting enough for his money. [*Looks at* OSCAR.] Seventy-five thousand he has to put up. That's a lot of money, too.

OSCAR: Nonsense. He knows a good thing when he hears it. He knows that we can make *twice* the profit on cotton goods manufactured *here* than can be made in the North.

BEN: That isn't what Regina means. [*Smiles.*] May I interpret you, Regina? [*To* OSCAR.] Regina is saying that Horace wants *more* than a third of our share.

OSCAR: But he's only putting up a third of the money. You put up a third and you get a third. What else *could* he expect?

REGINA: Well, *I* don't know. I don't know about these things. It would seem that if you put up a third you should only get a third. But then again, there's no law about it, is there? I should think that if you knew your money was very badly needed, well, you just might say, I want more, I want a bigger share. You boys have done that. I've heard you say so.

BEN: [*After a pause, laughs.*] So you believe he has deliberately held out? For a larger share? [*Leaning forward.*] Well, I *don't* believe it. But I *do* believe that's what *you* want. Am I right, Regina?

REGINA: Oh, I shouldn't like to be too definite. But I *could* say that I wouldn't like to persuade Horace unless he did get a larger share. I must look after his interests. It seems only natural—

OSCAR: And where would the larger share come from?

REGINA: I don't know. That's not my business. [*Giggles.*] But perhaps it could come off your share, Oscar.

[REGINA *and* BEN *laugh.*]

OSCAR: [*Rises and wheels furiously on both of them as they laugh.*] What kind of talk is this?

BEN: I haven't said a thing.

OSCAR: [*To* REGINA.] *You* are talking very big tonight.

REGINA: [*Stops laughing.*] Am I? Well, you should know me well enough to know that I wouldn't be asking for things I didn't think I could get.

OSCAR: Listen. I don't believe you can even get Horace to come home, much less get money from him or talk quite so big about what you want.

REGINA: Oh, I can get him home.

OSCAR: Then why haven't you?

REGINA: I thought I should fight his battles for him, before he came home. Horace is a very sick man. And even if *you* don't care how sick he is, I do.

BEN: Stop this foolish squabbling. How can you get him home?

REGINA: I will send Alexandra to Baltimore. She will ask him to come home. She will say that she *wants* him to come home, and that *I* want him to come home.

BIRDIE: [*Suddenly.*] Well, of course she wants him here, but he's sick and maybe he's happy where he is.

REGINA: [*Ignores* BIRDIE, *to* BEN.] You agree that he will come home if she asks him to, if she says that I miss him and want him—

BEN: [*Looks at her, smiles.*] I admire you, Regina. And I agree. That's settled now and—[*Starts to rise.*]

REGINA: [*Quickly.*] But before she brings him home, I want to know what he's going to get.

BEN: What do you want?

REGINA: Twice what you offered.

BEN: Well, you won't get it.

OSCAR: [*To* REGINA.] I think you've gone crazy.

REGINA: I don't want to fight, Ben—

BEN: I don't either. You won't get it. There isn't any chance of that. [*Roguishly.*] You're holding us up, and that's not pretty, Regina, not pretty. [*Holds up his hand as he sees she is about to speak.*] But we need you, and I don't want to fight. Here's what I'll do: I'll give Horace forty percent, instead of the thirty-three and a third he really should get. I'll do that, provided he is home and his money is up within two weeks. How's that?

REGINA: All right.

OSCAR: I've asked before: where is this extra share coming from?

BEN: [*Pleasantly.*] From you. From your share.

OSCAR: [*Furiously.*] From me, is it? That's just fine and dandy. That's my reward. For thirty-five years I've worked my hands to the bone for you. For thirty-five years I've done all the things you didn't want to do. And this is what I—

BEN: [*Turns slowly to look at* OSCAR. OSCAR *breaks off.*] My, my. I am being attacked tonight on all sides. First by my sister, then by my brother. And I ain't a man who likes being attacked. I can't believe that God wants the strong to parade their strength, but I don't mind doing it if it's got to be done. [*Leans back in his chair.*] You ought to take these things better, Oscar. I've made you money in the past. I'm going to make you more money now. You'll be a very rich man. What's the difference to any of us if a little more goes here, a little less goes there—it's all in the family. And it will stay in the family. I'll never marry. [ADDIE *enters, begins to gather the glasses from the table.* OSCAR *turns to* BEN.] So my money will go to Alexandra and Leo. They may even marry some day and—

[ADDIE *looks at* BEN.]

BIRDIE: [*Rising.*] Marry—Zan and Leo—

OSCAR: [*Carefully.*] That would make a great difference in my feelings. If they married.

BEN: Yes, that's what I mean. Of course it would make a difference.

OSCAR: [*Carefully.*] Is that what *you* mean, Regina?

REGINA: Oh, it's too far away. We'll talk about it in a few years.

OSCAR: I want to talk about it now.

BEN: [*Nods.*] Naturally.

REGINA: There's a lot of things to consider. They are first cousins, and—

OSCAR: That isn't unusual. Our grandmother and grandfather were first cousins.

REGINA: [*Giggles.*] And look at us.

[BEN *giggles.*]

OSCAR: [*Angrily.*] You're both being very gay with my money.

BEN: [*Sighs.*] These quarrels. I dislike them so. [*Leans forward to* REGINA.] A marriage might be a very wise arrangement, for several reasons. And then, Oscar has given up something for you. You should try to manage something for him.

REGINA: I haven't said I was opposed to it. But Leo is a wild boy. There were those times when he took a little money from the bank and—

OSCAR: That's all past history—

REGINA: Oh, I know. And I know all young men are wild. I'm only mentioning it to show you that there are considerations—

BEN: [*Irritated because she does not understand that he is trying to keep* OSCAR *quiet.*] All right, so there are. But please assure Oscar that you will think about it very seriously.

REGINA: [*Smiles, nods.*] Very well. I assure Oscar that I will think about it seriously.

OSCAR: [*Sharply.*] That is not an answer.

REGINA: [*Rises.*] My, you're in a bad humor and you shall put me in one. I have said all that I am willing to say now. After all, Horace has to give his consent too.

OSCAR: Horace will do what you tell him to.

REGINA: Yes, I think he will.

OSCAR: And I have your word that you will try to—

REGINA: [*Patiently.*] Yes, Oscar. You have my word that I will think about it. Now do leave me alone.

[*There is the sound of the front door being closed.*]

BIRDIE: I—Alexandra is only seventeen. She—

REGINA: [*Calling.*] Alexandra? Are you back?

ALEXANDRA: Yes, Mama.

LEO: [*Comes into the room.*] Mr. Marshall got off safe and sound. Weren't those fine clothes he had? You can always spot clothes made in a good place. Looks like maybe they were done in England. Lots of men in the North send all the way to England for their stuff.

BEN: [*To* LEO.] Were you careful driving the horses?

LEO: Oh, yes, sir. I was.

[ALEXANDRA *has come in on* BEN'*s question, hears the answer, looks angrily at* LEO.]

ALEXANDRA: It's a lovely night. You should have come, Aunt Birdie.

REGINA: Were you gracious to Mr. Marshall?

ALEXANDRA: I think so, Mama. I liked him.

REGINA: Good. And now I have great news for you. You are going to Baltimore in the morning to bring your father home.

ALEXANDRA: [*Gasps, then delighted.*] Me? Papa said I should come? That must mean—[*Turns to* ADDIE.] Addie, he must be well. Think of it, he'll be back home again. We'll bring him home.

REGINA: You are going alone, Alexandra.

ADDIE: [ALEXANDRA *has turned in surprise.*] Going alone? Going by herself? A child that age! Mr. Horace ain't going to like Zan traipsing up there by herself.

REGINA: [*Sharply.*] Go upstairs and lay out Alexandra's things.

ADDIE: He'd expect me to be along—

REGINA: I'll be up in a few minutes to tell you what to pack. [ADDIE *slowly begins to climb the steps. To* ALEXANDRA.] I should think you'd like going alone. At your age it certainly would have delighted me. You're a strange girl, Alexandra. Addie has babied you so much.

ALEXANDRA: I only thought it would be more fun if Addie and I went together.

BIRDIE: [*Timidly.*] Maybe I could go with her, Regina. I'd really like to.

REGINA: She is going alone. She is getting old enough to take some responsibilities.

OSCAR: She'd better learn now. She's almost old enough to get married. [*Jovially, to* LEO, *slapping him on shoulder.*] Eh, son?

LEO: Huh?

OSCAR: [*Annoyed with* LEO *for not understanding.*] Old enough to get married, you're thinking, eh?

LEO: Oh, yes, sir. [*Feebly.*] Lots of girls get married at Zan's age. Look at Mary Prester and Johanna and—

REGINA: Well, she's not getting married tomorrow. But she is going to Baltimore tomorrow, so let's talk about that. [*To* ALEXANDRA.] You'll be glad to have Papa home again.

ALEXANDRA: I wanted to go before, Mama. You remember that. But you said *you* couldn't go, and that *I* couldn't go alone.

REGINA: I've changed my mind. [*Too casually.*] You're to tell Papa how much you missed him, and that he must come home now—for your sake. Tell him that you *need* him home.

ALEXANDRA: Need him home? I don't understand.

REGINA: There is nothing for you to understand. You are simply to say what I have told you.

BIRDIE: [*Rises.*] He may be too sick. She couldn't do that—

ALEXANDRA: Yes. He may be too sick to travel. I couldn't make him think he had to come home for me, if he is too sick to—

REGINA: [*Looks at her, sharply, challengingly.*] You *couldn't* do what I tell you to do, Alexandra?

ALEXANDRA: [*Quietly.*] No. I couldn't. If I thought it would hurt him.

REGINA: [*After a second's silence, smiles pleasantly.*] But you are doing this for Papa's own good. [*Takes* ALEXANDRA's *hand.*] You must let me be the judge of his condition. It's the best possible cure for him to come home and be taken care of here. He mustn't stay there any longer and listen to those alarmist doctors. You are doing this entirely for his sake. Tell your papa that I want him to come home, that I miss him very much.

ALEXANDRA: [*Slowly.*] Yes, Mama.

REGINA: [*To the others. Rises.*] I must go and start getting Alexandra ready now. Why don't you all go home?

BEN: [*Rises.*] I'll attend to the railroad ticket. One of the boys will bring it over. Good night, everybody. Have a nice trip, Alexandra. The food on the train is very good. The celery is so crisp. Have a good time and act like a little lady. [*Exits.*]

REGINA: Good night, Ben. Good night, Oscar—[*Playfully.*] Don't be so glum, Oscar. It makes you look as if you had chronic indigestion.

BIRDIE: Good night, Regina.

REGINA: Good night, Birdie. [*Exits upstairs.*]

OSCAR: [*Starts for hall.*] Come along.

LEO: [*To* ALEXANDRA.] Imagine your not wanting to go! What a little fool you are. Wish it were me. What I could do in a place like Baltimore!

ALEXANDRA: [*Angrily, looking away from him.*] Mind your business. I can guess the kind of things *you* could do.

LEO: [*Laughs.*] Oh, no, you couldn't. [*He exits.*]

REGINA: [*Calling from the top of the stairs.*] Come on, Alexandra.

BIRDIE: [*Quickly, softly.*] Zan.

ALEXANDRA: I don't understand about my going, Aunt Birdie. [*Shrugs.*] But anyway, Papa will be home again. [*Pats* BIRDIE's *arm.*] Don't worry about me. I can take care of myself. Really I can.

BIRDIE: [*Shakes her head, softly.*] That's not what I'm worried about. Zan—

ALEXANDRA: [*Comes close to her.*] What's the matter?

BIRDIE: It's about Leo—

ALEXANDRA: [*Whispering.*] He beat the horses. That's why we were late getting back. We had to wait until they cooled off. He always beats the horses as if—

BIRDIE: [*Whispering frantically, holding* ALEXANDRA's *hands.*] He's my son. My own son. But you are more to me—more to me than my own child. I love you more than anybody else—

ALEXANDRA: Don't worry about the horses. I'm sorry I told you.

BIRDIE: [*Her voice rising.*] I am not worrying about the horses. I am worrying about *you*. You are *not* going to marry Leo. I am not going to let them do that to you—

ALEXANDRA: Marry? To Leo? [*Laughs.*] I wouldn't marry, Aunt Birdie. I've never even thought about it—

BIRDIE: But they have thought about it. [*Wildly.*] Zan, I couldn't stand to think about such a thing. You and—

[OSCAR *has come into the doorway on* ALEXANDRA'S *speech. He is standing quietly, listening.*]

ALEXANDRA: [*Laughs.*] But I'm not going to marry. And I'm certainly not going to marry Leo.

BIRDIE: Don't you understand? They'll make you. They'll make you—

ALEXANDRA: [*Takes* BIRDIE'S *hands, quietly, firmly.*] That's foolish, Aunt Birdie. I'm grown now. Nobody can make me do anything.

BIRDIE: I just couldn't stand—

OSCAR: [*Sharply.*] Birdie. [BIRDIE *looks up, draws quickly away from* ALEXANDRA. *She stands rigid, frightened. Quietly.*] Birdie, get your hat and coat.

ADDIE: [*Calls from upstairs.*] Come on, baby. Your mama's waiting for you, and she ain't nobody to keep waiting.

ALEXANDRA: All right. [*Then softly, embracing* BIRDIE.] Good night, Aunt Birdie. [*As she passes* OSCAR.] Good night, Uncle Oscar. [BIRDIE *begins to move slowly towards the door as* ALEXANDRA *climbs the stairs.* ALEXANDRA *is almost out of view when* BIRDIE *reaches* OSCAR *in the doorway. As* BIRDIE *quietly attempts to pass him, he slaps her hard, across the face.* BIRDIE *cries out, puts her hand to her face. On the cry,* ALEXANDRA *turns, begins to run down the stairs.*] Aunt Birdie! What happened? What happened? I—

BIRDIE: [*Softly, without turning.*] Nothing, darling. Nothing happened. [*Quickly, as if anxious to keep* ALEXANDRA *from coming close.*] Now go to bed. [OSCAR *exits.*] Nothing happened. [*Turns to* ALEXANDRA *who is holding her hand.*] I only—I only twisted my ankle. [*She goes out.* ALEXANDRA *stands on the stairs looking after her as if she were puzzled and frightened.*]

CURTAIN

ACT II

SCENE: *Same as Act I. A week later, morning.*

AT RISE: *The light comes from the open shutter of the right window; the other shutters are tightly closed.* ADDIE *is standing at the window, looking out. Near the dining-room doors are brooms, mops, rags, etc. After a second,* OSCAR *comes into the entrance hall, looks in the room, shivers, decides not to take his hat and coat off, comes into the room. At the sound of the door,* ADDIE *turns to see who has come in.*

ADDIE: [*Without interest.*] Oh, it's you, Mr. Oscar.

OSCAR: What is this? It's not night. What's the matter here? [*Shivers.*] Fine thing at this time of the morning. Blinds all closed. [ADDIE *begins to open shutters.*] Where's Miss Regina? It's cold in here.

ADDIE: Miss Regina ain't down yet.

OSCAR: She had any word?

ADDIE: [*Wearily.*] No, sir.

OSCAR: Wouldn't you think a girl that age could get on a train at one place and have sense enough to get off at another?

ADDIE: Something must have happened. If Zan say she was coming last night, she's coming last night. Unless something happened. Sure fire disgrace to let a baby like that go all that way alone to bring home a sick man without—

OSCAR: You do a lot of judging around here, Addie, eh? Judging of your white folks, I mean.

ADDIE: [*Looks at him, sighs.*] I'm tired. I been up all night watching for them.

REGINA: [*Speaking from the upstairs hall.*] Who's downstairs, Addie? [*She appears in a dressing gown, peers down from the landing.* ADDIE *picks up broom, dustpan and brush and exits.*] Oh, it's you, Oscar. What are you doing here so early? I haven't been down yet. I'm not finished dressing.

OSCAR: [*Speaking up to her.*] You had any word from them?

REGINA: No.

OSCAR: Then something certainly has happened. People don't just say they are arriving on Thursday night, and they haven't come by Friday morning.

REGINA: Oh, nothing has happened. Alexandra just hasn't got sense enough to send a message.

OSCAR: If nothing's happened, then why aren't they here?

REGINA: You asked me that ten times last night. My, you do fret so, Oscar. Anything might have happened. They may have missed connections in Atlanta, the train may have been delayed—oh, a hundred things could have kept them.

OSCAR: Where's Ben?

REGINA: [*As she disappears upstairs.*] Where should he be? At home, probably. Really, Oscar, I don't tuck him in his bed and I don't take him out of it. Have some coffee and don't worry so much.

OSCAR: Have some coffee? There isn't any coffee. [*Looks at his watch, shakes his head. After a second* CAL *enters with a large silver tray, coffee urn, small cups, newspaper.*] Oh, there you are. Is everything in this fancy house always late?

CAL: [*Looks at him surprised.*] You ain't out shooting this morning, Mr. Oscar?

OSCAR: First day I missed since I had my head cold. First day I missed in eight years.

CAL: Yes, sir. I bet you. Simon he say you had a mighty good day yesterday morning. That's what Simon say. [*Brings* OSCAR *coffee and newspaper.*]

OSCAR: Pretty good, pretty good.

CAL: [*Laughs slyly.*] Bet you got enough bobwhite and squirrel to give every nigger in town a Jesus-party. Most of 'em ain't had no meat since the cotton picking was over. Bet they'd give anything for a little piece of that meat—

OSCAR: [*Turns his head to look at* CAL.] Cal, if I catch a nigger in this town going shooting, you know what's going to happen.

[LEO *enters.*]

CAL: [*Hastily.*] Yes, sir, Mr. Oscar. I didn't say nothing about nothing. It was Simon who told me and— Morning, Mr. Leo. You gentlemen having your breakfast with us here?

LEO: The boys in the bank don't know a thing. They haven't had any message.

[CAL *waits for an answer, gets none, shrugs, moves to door, exits.*]

OSCAR: [*Peers at* LEO.] What you doing here, son?

LEO: You told me to find out if the boys at the bank had any message from Uncle Horace or Zan—

OSCAR: I told you if they had a message to bring it here. I told you that if they didn't have a message to stay at the bank and do your work.

LEO: Oh, I guess I misunderstood.

OSCAR: You didn't misunderstand. You just were looking for any excuse to take an hour off. [LEO *pours a cup of coffee.*] You got to stop that kind of thing. You got to start settling down. You going to be a married man one of these days.

LEO: Yes, sir.

OSCAR: You also got to stop with that woman in Mobile. [*As* LEO *is about to speak.*] You're young and I haven't got no objections to outside women. That is, I haven't got no objections so long as they don't interfere with serious things. Outside women are all right in their place, but *now* isn't their place. You got to realize that.

LEO: [*Nods.*] Yes, sir. I'll tell her. She'll act all right about it.

OSCAR: Also, you got to start working harder at the bank. You got to convince your Uncle Horace you going to make a fit husband for Alexandra.

LEO: What do you think has happened to them? Supposed to be here last night— [*Laughs.*] Bet you Uncle Ben's mighty worried. Seventy-five thousand dollars worried.

OSCAR: [*Smiles happily.*] Ought to be worried. Damn well ought to be. First he don't answer the letters, then he don't come home— [*Giggles.*]

LEO: What will happen if Uncle Horace don't come home or don't—

OSCAR: Or don't put up the money? Oh, we'll get it from outside. Easy enough.

LEO: [*Surprised.*] But *you* don't want outsiders.

OSCAR: What do I care who gets my share? I been shaved already. Serve Ben right if he had to give away some of his.

LEO: Damn shame what they did to you.

OSCAR: [*Looking up the stairs.*] Don't talk so loud. Don't you worry. When I die, you'll have as much as the rest. You might have yours *and* Alexandra's. I'm not so easily licked.

LEO: I wasn't thinking of myself, Papa—

OSCAR: Well, you should be, you should be. It's every man's duty to think of himself.

LEO: You think Uncle Horace don't want to go in on this?

OSCAR: [*Giggles.*] That's my hunch. He hasn't showed any signs of loving it yet.

LEO: [*Laughs.*] But he hasn't listened to Aunt Regina yet, either. Oh, he'll go along. It's too good a thing. Why wouldn't he want to? He's got plenty and plenty to invest with. He don't even have to sell anything. Eighty-eight thousand worth of Union Pacific bonds sitting right in his safe deposit box. All he's got to do is open the box.

OSCAR: [*After a pause. Looks at his watch.*] Mighty late breakfast in this fancy house.

Yes, he's had those bonds for fifteen years. Bought them when they were low and just locked them up.

LEO: Yeah. Just has to open the box and take them out. That's all. Easy as easy can be. [*Laughs.*] The things in that box! There's all those bonds, looking mighty fine. [OSCAR *slowly puts down his newspaper and turns to* LEO.] Then right next to them is a baby shoe of Zan's and a cheap old cameo on a string, and, *and*—nobody'd believe this—a piece of an old violin. Not even a whole violin. Just a piece of an old thing, a piece of a violin.

OSCAR: [*Very softly, as if he were trying to control his voice.*] A piece of a violin! What do you think of that!

LEO: Yes, sirree. A lot of other crazy things, too. A poem, I guess it is, signed with his mother's name, and two old schoolbooks with notes and—[LEO *catches* OSCAR's *look. His voice trails off. He turns his head away.*]

OSCAR: [*Very softly.*] How do you know what's in the box, son?

LEO: [*Stops, draws back, frightened, realizing what he has said.*] Oh, well. Well, er. Well, one of the boys, sir. It was one of the boys at the bank. He took old Manders' keys. It was Joe Horns. He just up and took Manders' keys and, and—well, took the box out. [*Quickly.*] Then they all asked me if I wanted to see, too. So I looked a little, I guess, but then I made them close up the box quick and I told them never—

OSCAR: [*Looks at him.*] Joe Horns, you say? He opened it?

LEO: Yes, sir, yes, he did. My word of honor. [*Very nervously looking away.*] I suppose that don't excuse *me* for looking—[*Looking at* OSCAR.] but I did make him close it up and put the keys back in Manders' drawer—

OSCAR: [*Leans forward, very softly.*] Tell me the truth, Leo. I am not going to be angry with you. Did you open the box yourself?

LEO: No, sir, I didn't. I told you I didn't. No, I—

OSCAR: [*Irritated, patient.*] I am *not* going to be angry with you. [*Watching* LEO *carefully.*] Sometimes a young fellow deserves credit for looking round him to see what's going on. Sometimes that's a good sign in a fellow your age. [OSCAR *rises.*] Many great men have made their fortune with their eyes. Did you open the box?

LEO: [*Very puzzled.*] No. I—

OSCAR: [*Moves to* LEO.] Did you open the box? It may have been—well, it may have been a good thing if you had.

LEO: [*After a long pause.*] I opened it.

OSCAR: [*Quickly.*] Is that the truth? [LEO *nods.*] Does anybody else know that you opened it? Come, Leo, don't be afraid of speaking the truth to me.

LEO: No. Nobody knew. Nobody was in the bank when I did it. But—

OSCAR: Did your Uncle Horace ever know you opened it?

LEO: [*Shakes his head.*] He only looks in it once every six months when he cuts the coupons,[6] and sometimes Manders even does that for him. Uncle Horace don't even have the keys. Manders keeps them for him. Imagine not looking at all that. You can bet if I had the bonds, I'd watch 'em like—

---

6. In order to receive his interest payments.

OSCAR: If you had them. [LEO *watches him.*] *If* you had them. Then you could have a share in the mill, you and me. A fine, big share, too. [*Pauses, shrugs.*] Well, a man can't be shot for wanting to see his son get on in the world, can he, boy?

LEO: [*Looks up, begins to understand.*] No, he can't. Natural enough. [*Laughs.*] But I haven't got the bonds and Uncle Horace has. And now he can just sit back and wait to be a millionaire.

OSCAR: [*Innocently.*] You think your Uncle Horace likes you well enough to lend you the bonds if he decides not to use them himself?

LEO: Papa, it must be that you haven't had your breakfast! [*Laughs loudly.*] Lend me the bonds! My God—

OSCAR: [*Disappointed.*] No, I suppose not. Just a fancy of mine. A loan for three months, maybe four, easy enough for us to pay it back then. Anyway, this is only April—[*Slowly counting the months on his fingers.*] and if he doesn't look at them until Fall, he wouldn't even miss them out of the box.

LEO: That's it. He wouldn't even miss them. Ah, well—

OSCAR: No, sir. Wouldn't even miss them. How could he miss them if he never looks at them? [*Sighs as* LEO *stares at him.*] Well, here we are sitting around waiting for him to come home and invest his money in something he hasn't lifted his hand to get. But I can't help thinking he's acting strange. You laugh when I say he could lend you the bonds if he's not going to use them himself. But would it hurt him?

LEO: [*Slowly looking at* OSCAR.] No. No, it wouldn't.

OSCAR: People ought to help other people. But that's not always the way it happens. [BEN *enters, hangs his coat and hat in hall. Very carefully.*] And so sometimes you got to think of yourself. [*As* LEO *stares at him,* BEN *appears in the doorway.*] Morning, Ben.

BEN: [*Coming in, carrying his newspaper.*] Fine sunny morning. Any news from the runaways?

REGINA: [*On the staircase.*] There's no news or you would have heard it. Quite a convention so early in the morning, aren't you all? [*Goes to coffee urn.*]

OSCAR: You rising mighty late these days. Is that the way they do things in Chicago society?

BEN: [*Looking at his paper.*] Old Carter died up in Senateville. Eighty-one is a good time for us all, eh? What do you think has really happened to Horace, Regina?

REGINA: Nothing.

BEN: [*Too casually.*] You don't think maybe he never started from Baltimore and never intends to start?

REGINA: [*Irritated.*] Of course they've started. Didn't I have a letter from Alexandra? What is so strange about people arriving late? He has that cousin in Savannah he's so fond of. He may have stopped to see him. They'll be along today some time, very flattered that you and Oscar are so worried about them.

BEN: I'm a natural worrier. Especially when I am getting ready to close a business deal and one of my partners remains silent *and* invisible.

REGINA: [*Laughs.*] Oh, is that it? I thought you were worried about Horace's health.

OSCAR: Oh, that too. Who could help but worry? I'm worried. This is the first day I haven't shot since my head cold.

REGINA: [*Starts towards dining room.*] Then you haven't had your breakfast. Come along.

[OSCAR *and* LEO *follow her.*]

BEN: Regina. [*She turns at dining-room door.*] That cousin of Horace's has been dead for years and, in any case, the train does not go through Savannah.

REGINA: [*Laughs, continues into dining room, seats herself.*] Did he die? You're always remembering about people dying. [BEN *rises.*] Now I intend to eat my breakfast in peace, and read my newspaper.

BEN: [*Goes towards dining room as he talks.*] This is second breakfast for me. My first was bad. Celia ain't the cook she used to be. Too old to have taste any more. If she hadn't belonged to Mama, I'd send her off to the country.

[OSCAR *and* LEO *start to eat.* BEN *seats himself.*]

LEO: Uncle Horace will have some tales to tell, I bet. Baltimore is a lively town.

REGINA: [*To* CAL.] The grits isn't hot enough. Take it back.

CAL: Oh, yes'm. [*Calling into kitchen as he exits.*] Grits didn't hold the heat. Grits didn't hold the heat.

LEO: When I was at school three of the boys and myself took a train once and went over to Baltimore. It was so big we thought we were in Europe. I was just a kid then—

REGINA: I find it very pleasant [ADDIE *enters.*] to have breakfast alone. I hate chattering before I've had something hot. [CAL *closes the dining-room doors.*] Do be still, Leo.

[ADDIE *comes into the room, begins gathering up the cups, carries them to the large tray. Outside there are the sounds of voices. Quickly* ADDIE *runs into the hall. A few seconds later she appears again in the doorway, her arm around the shoulders of* HORACE GIDDENS, *supporting him.* HORACE *is a tall man of about forty-five. He has been good looking, but now his face is tired and ill. He walks stiffly, as if it were an enormous effort, and carefully, as if he were unsure of his balance.* ADDIE *takes off his overcoat and hangs it on the hall tree. She then helps him to a chair.*]

HORACE: How are you, Addie? How have you been?

ADDIE: I'm all right, Mr. Horace. I've just been worried about you.

[ALEXANDRA *enters. She is flushed and excited, her hat awry, her face dirty. Her arms are full of packages, but she comes quickly to* ADDIE.]

ALEXANDRA: Now don't tell me how worried you were. We couldn't help it and there was no way to send a message.

ADDIE: [*Begins to take packages from* ALEXANDRA.] Yes, sir, I was mighty worried.

ALEXANDRA: We had to stop in Mobile over night. Papa— [*Looks at him.*] Papa didn't feel well. The trip was too much for him, and I made him stop and rest— [As ADDIE *takes the last package.*] No, don't take that. That's father's medicine. I'll hold it. It mustn't break. Now, about the stuff outside. Papa must have his wheel chair. I'll get that and the valises—

ADDIE: [*Very happy, holding* ALEXANDRA's *arms.*] Since when you got to carry your own valises? Since when I ain't old enough to hold a bottle of medicine? [HORACE *coughs.*] You feel all right, Mr. Horace?

HORACE: [*Nods.*] Glad to be sitting down.

ALEXANDRA: [*Opening package of medicine.*] He doesn't feel all right. [ADDIE *looks at her, then at* HORACE.] He just says that. The trip was very hard on him, and now he must go right to bed.

ADDIE: [*Looking at him carefully.*] Them fancy doctors, they give you help?

HORACE: They did their best.

ALEXANDRA: [*Has become conscious of the voices in the dining room.*] I bet Mama was worried. I better tell her we're here now. [*She starts for door.*]

HORACE: Zan. [*She stops.*] Not for a minute, dear.

ALEXANDRA: Oh, Papa, you feel bad again. I knew you did. Do you want your medicine?

HORACE: No, I don't feel that way. I'm just tired, darling. Let me rest a little.

ALEXANDRA: Yes, but Mama will be mad if I don't tell her we're here.

ADDIE: They're all in there eating breakfast.

ALEXANDRA: Oh, are they all here? Why do they *always* have to be here? I was hoping Papa wouldn't have to see anybody, that it would be nice for him and quiet.

ADDIE: Then let your papa rest for a minute.

HORACE: Addie, I bet your coffee's as good as ever. They don't have such good coffee up North. [*Looks at the urn.*] Is it as good, Addie? [ADDIE *starts for coffee urn.*]

ALEXANDRA: No. Dr. Reeves said not much coffee. Just now and then. I'm the nurse now, Addie.

ADDIE: You'd be a better one if you didn't look so dirty. Now go and take a bath, Miss Grown-up. Change your linens, get out a fresh dress and give your hair a good brushing—go on—

ALEXANDRA: Will you be all right, Papa?

ADDIE: Go on.

ALEXANDRA: [*On stairs, talks as she goes up.*] The pills Papa must take once every four hours. And the bottle only when—only if he feels very bad. Now don't move until I come back and don't talk much and remember about his medicine, Addie—

ADDIE: Ring for Belle and have her help you and then I'll make you a fresh breakfast.

ALEXANDRA: [*As she disappears.*] How's Aunt Birdie? Is she here?

ADDIE: It ain't right for you to have coffee? It will hurt you?

HORACE: [*Slowly.*] Nothing can make much difference now. Get me a cup, Addie. [*She looks at him, crosses to urn, pours a cup.*] Funny. They can't make coffee up North. [ADDIE *brings him a cup.*] They don't like red pepper, either. [*He takes the cup and gulps it greedily.*] God, that's good. You remember how I used to drink it? Ten, twelve cups a day. So strong it had to stain the cup. [*Then slowly.*] Addie, before I see anybody else, I want to know why Zan came to fetch me home. She's tried to tell me, but she doesn't seem to know herself.

ADDIE: [*Turns away.*] I don't know. All I know is big things are going on. Everybody going to be high-tone rich. Big rich. You too. All because smoke's going to start out of a building that ain't even up yet.

HORACE: I've heard about it.

ADDIE: And, er— [*Hesitates—steps to him.*] And—well, Zan, she going to marry Mr. Leo in a little while.

HORACE: [*Looks at her, then very slowly.*] What are you talking about?

ADDIE: That's right. That's the talk. God help us.

HORACE: [*Angrily.*] *What's* the talk?

ADDIE: I'm telling you. There's going to be a wedding— [*Angrily turns away.*] Over my dead body there is.

HORACE: [*After a second, quietly.*] Go and tell them I'm home.

ADDIE: [*Hesitates.*] Now you ain't to get excited. You're to be in your bed—

HORACE: Go on, Addie. Go and say I'm back. [ADDIE *opens dining-room doors. He rises with difficulty, stands stiff, as if he were in pain, facing the dining room.*]

ADDIE: Miss Regina. They're home. They got here—

REGINA: Horace! [REGINA *quickly rises, runs into the room. Warmly.*] Horace! You've finally arrived. [*As she kisses him, the others come forward, all talking together.*]

BEN: [*In doorway, carrying a napkin.*] Well, sir, you had us all mighty worried. [*He steps forward. They shake hands.* ADDIE *exits.*]

OSCAR: You're a sight for sore eyes.

HORACE: Hello, Ben.

[LEO *enters, eating a biscuit.*]

OSCAR: And what is that costume you have on?

BIRDIE: [*Looking at* HORACE.] Now that you're home, you'll feel better. Plenty of good rest and we'll take such fine care of you. [*Stops.*] But where is Zan? I missed her so much.

OSCAR: I asked you what is that strange costume you're parading around in?

BIRDIE: [*Nervously, backing towards stairs.*] Me? Oh! It's my wrapper. I was so excited about Horace I just rushed out of the house—

OSCAR: Did you come across the square dressed that way? My dear Birdie, I—

HORACE: [*To* REGINA, *wearily.*] Yes, it's just like old times.

REGINA: [*Quickly to* OSCAR.] Now, no fights. This is a holiday.

BIRDIE: [*Runs quickly up the stairs.*] Zan! Zannie!

OSCAR: Birdie! [*She stops.*]

BIRDIE: Oh. Tell Zan I'll be back in a little while. [*Whispers.*] Sorry, Oscar. [*Exits.*]

REGINA: [*To* OSCAR *and* BEN.] Why don't you go finish your breakfast and let Horace rest for a minute?

BEN: [*Crossing to dining room with* OSCAR.] Never leave a meal unfinished. There are too many poor people who need the food. Mighty glad to see you home, Horace. Fine to have you back. Fine to have you back.

OSCAR: [*To* LEO *as* BEN *closes dining-room doors.*] Your mother has gone crazy. Running around the streets like a woman—

> [*The moment* REGINA *and* HORACE *are alone, they become awkward and self-conscious.*]

REGINA: [*Laughs awkwardly.*] Well. Here we are. It's been a long time. [HORACE *smiles.*] Five months. You know, Horace, I wanted to come and be with you in the hospital, but I didn't know where my duty was. Here, or with you. But you know how much I *wanted* to come.

HORACE: That's kind of you, Regina. There was no need to come.

REGINA: Oh, but there was. Five months lying there all by yourself, no kinfolks, no friends. Don't try to tell me you didn't have a bad time of it.

HORACE: I didn't have a bad time. [*As she shakes her head, he becomes insistent.*] No, I didn't, Regina. Oh, at first when I—when I heard the news about myself— but after I got used to that, I liked it there.

REGINA: You *liked* it? [*Coldly.*] Isn't that strange. You liked it so well you didn't want to come home?

HORACE: That's not the way to put it. [*Then, kindly, as he sees her turn her head away.*] But there I was and I got kind of used to it, kind of to like lying there and thinking. [*Smiles.*] I never had much time to think before. And time's become valuable to me.

REGINA: It sounds almost like a holiday.

HORACE: [*Laughs.*] It was, sort of. The first holiday I've had since I was a little kid.

REGINA: And here I was thinking you were in pain and—

HORACE: [*Quietly.*] I was in pain.

REGINA: And instead you were having a holiday! A holiday of thinking. Couldn't you have done that here?

HORACE: I wanted to do it before I came here. I was thinking about us.

REGINA: About us? About you and me? Thinking about you and me after all these years. [*Unpleasantly.*] You shall tell me everything you thought—some day.

HORACE: [*There is silence for a minute.*] Regina. [*She turns to him.*] Why did you send Zan to Baltimore?

REGINA: Why? Because I wanted you home. You can't make anything suspicious out of that, can you?

HORACE: I didn't mean to make anything suspicious about it. [*Hesitantly, taking her hand.*] Zan said you wanted me to come home. I was so pleased at that and touched, it made me feel good.

REGINA: [*Taking away her hand, turns.*] Touched that I should want you home?

HORACE: [*Sighs.*] I'm saying all the wrong things as usual. Let's try to get along better. There isn't so much more time. Regina, what's all this crazy talk I've been hearing about Zan and Leo? Zan and Leo marrying?

REGINA: [*Turning to him, sharply.*] Who gossips so much around here?

HORACE: [*Shocked.*] Regina!

REGINA: [*Annoyed, anxious to quiet him.*] It's some foolishness that Oscar thought up. I'll explain later. I have no intention of allowing any such arrangement.

It was simply a way of keeping Oscar quiet in all this business I've been writing you about—

HORACE: [*Carefully.*] What has Zan to do with any business of Oscar's? Whatever it is, you had better put it out of Oscar's head immediately. You know what I think of Leo.

REGINA: But there's no need to talk about it now.

HORACE: There is no need to talk about it ever. Not as long as I live. [HORACE *stops, slowly turns to look at her.*] As long as I live. I've been in a hospital for five months. Yet since I've been here you have not once asked me about—about my health. [*Then gently.*] Well, I suppose they've written you. I can't live very long.

REGINA: [*Coldly.*] I've never understood why people have to talk about this kind of thing.

HORACE: [*There is a silence. Then he looks up at her, his face cold.*] You misunderstand. I don't intend to gossip about my sickness. I thought it was only fair to tell you. I was not asking for your sympathy.

REGINA: [*Sharply, turns to him.*] What do the doctors think caused your bad heart?

HORACE: What do you mean?

REGINA: They didn't think it possible, did they, that your fancy women may have—

HORACE: [*Smiles unpleasantly.*] Caused my heart to be bad? I don't think that's the best scientific theory. You don't catch heart trouble in bed.

REGINA: [*Angrily.*] I didn't think you did. I only thought you might catch a bad conscience—in bed, as you say.

HORACE: I didn't tell them about my bad conscience. Or about my fancy women. Nor did I tell them that my wife has not wanted me in bed with her for— [*Sharply.*] How long is it, Regina? [REGINA *turns to him.*] Ten years? Did you bring me home for this, to make me feel guilty again? That means you want something. But you'll not make me feel guilty any more. My "thinking" has made a difference.

REGINA: I see that it has. [*She looks towards dining-room door. Then comes to him, her manner warm and friendly.*] It's foolish for us to fight this way. I didn't mean to be unpleasant. I was stupid.

HORACE: [*Wearily.*] God knows I didn't either. I came home wanting so much not to fight, and then all of a sudden there we were. I got hurt and—

REGINA: [*Hastily.*] It's all my fault. I didn't ask about—about your illness because I didn't want to remind you of it. Anyway I never believe doctors when they talk about—[*Brightly.*] when they talk like that.

HORACE: [*Not looking at her.*] Well, we'll try our best with each other. [*He rises.*]

REGINA: [*Quickly.*] I'll try. Honestly, I will. Horace, Horace, I know you're tired but, but—couldn't you stay down here a few minutes longer? I want Ben to tell you something.

HORACE: Tomorrow.

REGINA: I'd like to now. It's very important to me. It's very important to all of us. [*Gaily, as she moves toward dining room.*] Important to your beloved daughter. She'll be a very great heiress—

HORACE: Will she? That's nice.

REGINA: [*Opens doors.*] Ben, are you finished breakfast?

HORACE: Is this the mill business I've had so many letters about?

REGINA: [*To* BEN.] Horace would like to talk to you now.

HORACE: Horace would not like to talk to you now. I am very tired, Regina—

REGINA: [*Comes to him.*] Please. You've said we'll try our best with each other. I'll try. Really, I will. Please do this for me now. You will see what I've done while you've been away. How I watched your interests. [*Laughs gaily.*] And I've done very well too. But things can't be delayed any longer. Everything must be settled this week— [HORACE *sits down.* BEN *enters.* OSCAR *has stayed in the dining room, his head turned to watch them.* LEO *is pretending to read the newspaper.*] Now you must tell Horace all about it. Only be quick because he is very tired and must go to bed. [HORACE *is looking up at her. His face hardens as she speaks.*] But I think your news will be better for him than all the medicine in the world.

BEN: [*Looking at* HORACE.] It could wait. Horace may not feel like talking today.

REGINA: What an old faker you are! You know it can't wait. You know it must be finished this week. You've been just as anxious for Horace to get here as I've been.

BEN: [*Very jovial.*] I suppose I have been. And why not? Horace has done Hubbard Sons many a good turn. Why shouldn't I be anxious to help him now?

REGINA: [*Laughs.*] Help him! Help him when you need him, that's what you mean.

BEN: What a woman you married, Horace. [*Laughs awkwardly when* HORACE *does not answer.*] Well, then I'll make it quick. You know what I've been telling you for years. How I've always said that every one of us little Southern business men had great things—[*Extends his arms.*]—right beyond our finger tips. It's been my dream: my dream to make those fingers grow longer. I'm a lucky man, Horace, a lucky man. To dream and to live to get what you've dreamed of. That's *my* idea of a lucky man. [*Looks at his fingers as his arm drops slowly.*] For thirty years I've cried bring the cotton mills to the cotton. [HORACE *opens medicine bottle.*] Well, finally I got up nerve to go to Marshall Company in Chicago.

HORACE: I know all this. [*He takes the medicine.* REGINA *rises, steps to him.*]

BEN: Can I get you something?

HORACE: Some water, please.

REGINA: [*Turns quickly.*] Oh, I'm sorry. Let me. [*Brings him a glass of water. He drinks as they wait in silence.*] You feel all right now?

HORACE: Yes. You wrote me. I know all that.

[OSCAR *enters from dining room.*]

REGINA: [*Triumphantly.*] But you don't know that in the last few days Ben has agreed to give us—you, I mean—a much larger share.

HORACE: Really? That's very generous of him.

BEN: [*Laughs.*] It wasn't so generous of me. It was smart of Regina.

REGINA: [*As if she were signaling* HORACE.] I explained to Ben that perhaps you hadn't answered his letters because you didn't think he was offering you enough, and that the time was getting short and you could guess how much he needed you—

HORACE: [*Smiles at her, nods.*] And I could guess that he wants to keep control in the family?

REGINA: [*To* BEN, *triumphantly.*] Exactly. [*To* HORACE.] So I did a little bargaining for you and convinced my brothers they weren't the only Hubbards who had a business sense.

HORACE: Did you have to convince them of that? How little people know about each other! [*Laughs.*] But you'll know better about Regina next time, eh, Ben? [BEN, REGINA, HORACE *laugh together.* OSCAR's *face is angry.*] Now let's see. We're getting a bigger share. [*Looking at* OSCAR.] Who's getting less?

BEN: Oscar.

HORACE: Well, Oscar, you've grown very unselfish. What's happened to you?

[LEO *enters from dining room.*]

BEN: [*Quickly, before* OSCAR *can answer.*] Oscar doesn't mind. Not worth fighting about now, eh, Oscar?

OSCAR: [*Angrily.*] I'll get mine in the end. You can be sure of that. I've got my son's future to think about.

HORACE: [*Sharply.*] Leo? Oh, I see. [*Puts his head back, laughs.* REGINA *looks at him nervously.*] I am beginning to see. Everybody will get theirs.

BEN: I knew you'd see it. Seventy-five thousand, and that seventy-five thousand will make you a million.

OSCAR: And how you feel? Tip-top, I bet, because that's the way you're looking.

HORACE: [*Coldly, irritated with* OSCAR's *lie.*] Hello, Oscar. Hello, Leo, how are you?

LEO: [*Shaking hands.*] I'm fine, sir. But a lot better now that you're back.

REGINA: Now sit down. What did happen to you and where's Alexandra? I am so excited about seeing you that I almost forgot about her.

HORACE: I didn't feel good, a little weak, I guess, and we stopped over night to rest. Zan's upstairs washing off the train dirt.

REGINA: Oh, I am so sorry the trip was hard on you. I didn't think that—

HORACE: Well, it's just as if I had never been away. All of you here—

BEN: Waiting to welcome you home.

[BIRDIE *bursts in. She is wearing a flannel kimono and her face is flushed and excited.*]

BIRDIE: [*Runs to him, kisses him.*] Horace!

HORACE: [*Warmly pressing her arm.*] I was just wondering where you were, Birdie.

BIRDIE: [*Excited.*] Oh, I would have been here. I didn't know you were back until Simon said he saw the buggy. [*She draws back to look at him. Her face sobers.*] Oh, you don't look well, Horace. No, you don't.

REGINA: [*Laughs.*] Birdie, what a thing to say—

HORACE: [*Looking at* OSCAR.] Oscar thinks I look very well.

OSCAR: [*Annoyed. Turns on* LEO.] Don't stand there holding that biscuit in your hand.

LEO: Oh, well. I'll just finish my breakfast, Uncle Horace, and then I'll give you all the news about the bank— [*He exits into the dining room.*]

REGINA: [*Steps to table, leaning forward.*] It will, Horace, it will.

HORACE: I believe you. [*After a second.*] Now I can understand Oscar's self-sacrifice, but what did you have to promise Marshall Company besides the money you're putting up?

BEN: They wouldn't take promises. They wanted guarantees.

HORACE: Of what?

BEN: [*Nods.*] Water power. Free and plenty of it.

HORACE: You got them that, of course.

BEN: Cheap. You'd think the Governor of a great state would make his price a little higher. From pride, you know. [HORACE *smiles.* BEN *smiles.*] Cheap wages. "What do you mean by cheap wages?" I say to Marshall. "Less than Massachusetts," he says to me, "and that averages eight a week." "Eight a week! By God," I tell him, "*I'd* work for eight a week myself." Why, there ain't a mountain white or a town nigger but wouldn't give his right arm for three silver dollars every week, eh, Horace?

HORACE: Sure. And they'll take less than that when you get around to playing them off against each other. You can save a little money that way, Ben. [*Angrily.*] And make them hate each other just a little more than they do now.

REGINA: What's all this about?

BEN: [*Laughs.*] There'll be no trouble from anybody, white or black. Marshall said that to me. "What about strikes? That's all we've had in Massachusetts for the last three years." I say to him, "What's a strike? I never heard of one. Come South, Marshall. We got good folks and we don't stand for any fancy fooling."

HORACE: You're right. [*Slowly.*] Well, it looks like you made a good deal for yourselves, and for Marshall, too. [*To* BEN.] Your father used to say he made the thousands and you boys would make the millions. I think he was right. [*Rises.*]

REGINA: [*They are all looking at* HORACE. *She laughs nervously.*] Millions for *us*, too.

HORACE: Us? You and me? I don't think so. We've got enough money, Regina. We'll just sit by and watch the boys grow rich. [*They watch* HORACE *tensely as he begins to move towards the staircase. He passes* LEO, *looks at him for a second.*] How's everything at the bank, Leo?

LEO: Fine, sir. Everything is fine.

HORACE: How are all the ladies in Mobile? [HORACE *turns to* REGINA, *sharply.*] Whatever made you think I'd let Zan marry—

REGINA: Do you mean that you are turning this down? Is it possible that's what you mean?

BEN: No, that's not what he means. Turning down a fortune. Horace is tired. He'd rather talk about it tomorrow—

REGINA: We can't keep putting it off this way. Oscar must be in Chicago by the end of the week with the money and contracts.

OSCAR: [*Giggles, pleased.*] Yes, sir. Got to be there end of the week. No sense going without the money.

REGINA: [*Tensely.*] I've waited long enough for your answer. I'm not going to wait any longer.

HORACE: [*Very deliberately.*] I'm very tired now, Regina.

BEN: [*Hastily.*] Now, Horace probably has his reasons. Things he'd like explained. Tomorrow will do. I can—

REGINA: [*Turns to* BEN, *sharply.*] I want to know his reasons now! [*Turns back to* HORACE.]

HORACE: [*As he climbs the steps.*] I don't know them all myself. Let's leave it at that.

REGINA: We shall not leave it at that! We have waited for you here like children. Waited for you to come home.

HORACE: So that you could invest my money. So this is why you wanted me home? Well, I had hoped— [*Quietly.*] If you are disappointed, Regina, I'm sorry. But I must do what I think best. We'll talk about it another day.

REGINA: We'll talk about it now. Just you and me.

HORACE: [*Looks down at her. His voice is tense.*] Please, Regina. It's been a hard trip. I don't feel well. Please leave me alone now.

REGINA: [*Quietly.*] I want to talk to you, Horace. I'm coming up. [*He looks at her for a minute, then moves on again out of sight. She begins to climb the stairs.*]

BEN: [*Softly.* REGINA *turns to him as he speaks.*] Sometimes it is better to wait for the sun to rise again. [*She does not answer.*] And sometimes, as our mother used to tell you, [REGINA *starts up stairs.*] it's unwise for a good-looking woman to frown. [BEN *rises, moves towards stairs.*] Softness and a smile do more to the heart of men—

[*She disappears.* BEN *stands looking up the stairs. There is a long silence. Then, suddenly,* OSCAR *giggles.*]

OSCAR: Let us hope she'll change his mind. Let us hope.

[*After a second* BEN *crosses to table, picks up his newspaper.* OSCAR *looks at* BEN. *The silence makes* LEO *uncomfortable.*]

LEO: The paper says twenty-seven cases of yellow fever in New Orleans. Guess the flood-waters caused it. [*Nobody pays attention.*] Thought they were building the levees high enough. Like the niggers always say: a man born of woman can't build nothing high enough for the Mississippi. [*Gets no answer. Gives an embarrassed laugh.*]

[*Upstairs there is the sound of voices. The voices are not loud, but* BEN, OSCAR, LEO *become conscious of them.* LEO *crosses to landing, looks up, listens.*]

OSCAR: [*Pointing up.*] Now just suppose she don't change his mind? Just suppose he keeps on refusing?

BEN: [*Without conviction.*] He's tired. It was a mistake to talk to him today. He's a sick man, but he isn't a crazy one.

OSCAR: [*Giggles.*] But just suppose he is crazy. What then?

BEN: [*Puts down his paper, peers at* OSCAR.] Then we'll go outside for the money. There's plenty who would give it.

OSCAR: And plenty who will want a lot for what they give. The ones who are rich enough to give will be smart enough to want. That means we'd be working for them, don't it, Ben?

BEN: You don't have to tell me the things I told you six months ago.

OSCAR: Oh, you're right not to worry. She'll change his mind. She always has. [*There is a silence. Suddenly* REGINA's *voice becomes louder and sharper. All of them begin to listen now. Slowly* BEN *rises, goes to listen by the staircase.* OSCAR, *watching him, smiles. As they listen* REGINA's *voice becomes very loud.* HORACE's *voice is no longer heard.*] Maybe. But I don't believe it. I never did believe he was going in with us.

BEN: [*Turning on him.*] What the hell do you expect me to do?

OSCAR: [*Mildly.*] Nothing. You done your almighty best. Nobody could blame you if the whole thing just dripped away right through our fingers. You can't do a thing. But there may be something I could do for us. [OSCAR *rises.*] Or, I might better say, Leo could do for us. [BEN *stops, turns, looks at* OSCAR. LEO *is staring at* OSCAR.] Ain't that true, son? Ain't it true you might be able to help your own kinfolks?

LEO: [*Nervously taking a step to him.*] Papa, I—

BEN: [*Slowly.*] How would he help us, Oscar?

OSCAR: Leo's got a friend. Leo's friend owns eighty-eight thousand dollars in Union Pacific bonds. [BEN *turns to look at* LEO.] Leo's friend don't look at the bonds much—not for five or six months at a time.

BEN: [*After a pause.*] Union Pacific. Uh, huh. Let me understand. Leo's friend would—would lend him these bonds and he—

OSCAR: [*Nods.*] Would be kind enough to lend them to us.

BEN: Leo.

LEO: [*Excited, comes to him.*] Yes, sir?

BEN: When would your friend be wanting the bonds back?

LEO: [*Very nervous.*] I don't know. I—well, I—

OSCAR: [*Sharply. Steps to him.*] You told me he won't look at them until Fall—

LEO: Oh, that's right. But I—not till Fall. Uncle Horace never—

BEN: [*Sharply.*] Be still.

OSCAR: [*Smiles at* LEO.] Your uncle doesn't wish to know your friend's name.

LEO: [*Starts to laugh.*] That's a good one. Not know his name—

OSCAR: Shut up, Leo! [LEO *turns away slowly, moves to table.* BEN *turns to* OSCAR.] He won't look at them again until September. That gives us five months. Leo will return the bonds in three months. And we'll have no trouble raising the money once the mills are going up. Will Marshall accept bonds?

[BEN *stops to listen to sudden sharp voices from above. The voices are now very angry and very loud.*]

BEN: [*Smiling.*] Why not? Why not? [*Laughs.*] Good. We are lucky. We'll take the loan from Leo's friend—I think he will make a safer partner than our sister. [*Nods towards stairs. Turns to* LEO.] How soon can you get them?

LEO: Today. Right now. They're in the safe-deposit box and—

BEN: [*Sharply.*] I don't want to know where they are.

OSCAR: [*Laughs.*] We will keep it secret from you. [*Pats* BEN's *arm.*]

BEN: [*Smiles.*] Good. Draw a check for our part. You can take the night train for Chicago. Well, Oscar [*holds out his hand*], good luck to us.

OSCAR: Leo will be taken care of?

LEO: I'm entitled to Uncle Horace's share. I'd enjoy being a partner—

BEN: [*Turns to stare at him.*] You would? You can go to hell, you little—[*Starts towards* LEO.]

OSCAR: [*Nervously.*] Now, now. He didn't mean that. I only want to be sure he'll get something out of all this.

BEN: Of course. We'll take care of him. We won't have any trouble about that. I'll see you at the store.

OSCAR: [*Nods.*] That's settled then. Come on, son. [*Starts for door.*]

LEO: [*Puts out his hand.*] I didn't mean just that. I was only going to say what a great day this was for me and—

[BEN *ignores his hand.*]

BEN: Go on.

[LEO *looks at him, turns, follows* OSCAR *out.* BEN *stands where he is, thinking. Again the voices upstairs can be heard.* REGINA's *voice is high and furious.* BEN *looks up, smiles, winces at the noise.*]

ALEXANDRA: [*Upstairs.*] Mama—Mama—don't . . . [*The noise of running footsteps is heard and* ALEXANDRA *comes running down the steps, speaking as she comes.*] Uncle Ben! Uncle Ben! Please go up. Please make Mama stop. Uncle Ben, he's sick, he's so sick. How can Mama talk to him like that—please, make her stop. She'll—

BEN: Alexandra, you have a tender heart.

ALEXANDRA: [*Crying.*] Go on up, Uncle Ben, please—

[*Suddenly the voices stop. A second later there is the sound of a door being slammed.*]

BEN: Now you see. Everything is over. Don't worry. [*He starts for the door.*] Alexandra, I want you to tell your mother how sorry I am that I had to leave. And don't worry so, my dear. Married folk frequently raise their voices, unfortunately. [*He starts to put on his hat and coat as* REGINA *appears on the stairs.*]

ALEXANDRA: [*Furiously.*] How can you treat Papa like this? He's sick. He's very sick. Don't you know that? I won't let you.

REGINA: Mind your business, Alexandra. [*To* BEN. *Her voice is cold and calm.*] How much longer can you wait for the money?

BEN: [*Putting on his coat.*] He has refused? My, that's too bad.

REGINA: He will change his mind. I'll find a way to make him. What's the longest you can wait now?

BEN: I could wait until next week. But I can't wait until next week. [*He giggles, pleased at the joke.*] I could but I can't. Could and can't. Well, I must go now. I'm very late—

REGINA: [*Coming downstairs towards him.*] You're not going. I want to talk to you.

BEN: I was about to give Alexandra a message for you. I wanted to tell you that Oscar is going to Chicago tonight, so we can't be here for our usual Friday supper.

REGINA: [*Tensely*.] Oscar is going to Chi— [*Softly*.] What do you mean?

BEN: Just that. Everything is settled. He's going on to deliver to Marshall—

REGINA: [*Taking a step to him*.] I demand to know what— You are lying. You are trying to scare me. *You haven't got the money*. How could you have it? You can't have— [BEN *laughs*.] You will wait until I—

[HORACE *comes into view on the landing*.]

BEN: You are getting out of hand. Since when do I take orders from you?

REGINA: Wait, you—[BEN *stops*.] How *can* he go to Chicago? Did a ghost arrive with the money? [BEN *starts for the hall*.] I don't believe you. Come back here. [REGINA *starts after him*.] Come back here, you— [*The door slams. She stops in the doorway, staring, her fists clenched. After a pause she turns slowly*.]

HORACE: [*Very quietly*.] It's a great day when you and Ben cross swords. I've been waiting for it for years.

ALEXANDRA: Papa, Papa, please go back! You will—

HORACE: And so they don't need you, and so you will not have your millions, after all.

REGINA: [*Turns slowly*.] You hate to see anybody live now, don't you? You hate to think that I'm going to be alive and have what I want.

HORACE: I should have known you'd think that was the reason.

REGINA: Because you're going to die and you know you're going to die.

ALEXANDRA: [*Shrilly*.] Mama! Don't— Don't listen, Papa. Just don't listen. Go away—

HORACE: Not to keep you from getting what you want. Not even partly that. [*Holding to the rail*.] I'm sick of you, sick of this house, sick of my life here. I'm sick of your brothers and their dirty tricks to make a dime. There must be better ways of getting rich than cheating niggers on a pound of bacon. Why should I give you the money? [*Very angrily*.] To pound the bones of this town to make dividends for you to spend? You wreck the town, you and your brothers, *you* wreck the town and live on it. Not me. Maybe it's easy for the dying to be honest. But it's not my fault I'm dying. [ADDIE *enters, stands at door quietly*.] I'll do no more harm now. I've done enough. I'll die my own way. And I'll do it without making the world any worse. I leave that to you.

REGINA: [*Looks up at him slowly, calmly*.] I hope you die. I hope you die soon. [*Smiles*.] I'll be waiting for you to die.

ALEXANDRA: [*Shrieking*.] Papa! Don't—Don't listen—Don't—

ADDIE: Come here, Zan. Come out of this room.

[ALEXANDRA *runs quickly to* ADDIE, *who holds her*. HORACE *turns slowly and starts upstairs*.]

CURTAIN

ACT III

SCENE: *Same as Act I. Two weeks later. It is late afternoon and it is raining.*

AT RISE: HORACE *is sitting near the window in a wheel chair. On the table next to him is a safe-deposit box, and a small bottle of medicine.* BIRDIE *and* ALEXANDRA *are playing the piano. On a chair is a large sewing basket.*

BIRDIE: [*Counting for* ALEXANDRA.] One and two and three and four. One and two and three and four. [*Nods—turns to* HORACE.] We once played together, Horace. Remember?

HORACE: [*Has been looking out of the window.*] What, Birdie?

BIRDIE: We played together. You and me.

ALEXANDRA: *Papa* used to play?

BIRDIE: Indeed he did. [ADDIE *appears at the door in a large kitchen apron. She is wiping her hands on a towel.*] He played the fiddle and very well, too.

ALEXANDRA: [*Turns to smile at* HORACE.] I never knew—

ADDIE: Where's your mama?

ALEXANDRA: Gone to Miss Safronia's to fit her dresses.

[ADDIE *nods, starts to exit.*]

HORACE: Addie.

ADDIE: Yes, Mr. Horace.

HORACE: [*Speaks as if he had made a sudden decision.*] Tell Cal to get on his things. I want him to go an errand.

[ADDIE *nods, exits.* HORACE *moves nervously in his chair, looks out of the window.*]

ALEXANDRA: [*Who has been watching him.*] It's too bad it's been raining all day, Papa. But you can go out in the yard tomorrow. Don't be restless.

HORACE: I'm not restless, darling.

BIRDIE: I remember so well the time we played together, your papa and me. It was the first time Oscar brought me here to supper. I had never seen all the Hubbards together before, and you know what a ninny I am and how shy. [*Turns to look at* HORACE.] You said you could play the fiddle and you'd be much obliged if I'd play with you. *I* was obliged to *you,* all right, all right. [*Laughs when he does not answer her.*] Horace, you haven't heard a word I've said.

HORACE: Birdie, when did Oscar get back from Chicago?

BIRDIE: Yesterday. Hasn't he been here yet?

ALEXANDRA: [*Stops playing.*] No. Neither has Uncle Ben since—since that day.

BIRDIE: Oh, I didn't know it was *that* bad. Oscar never tells me anything—

HORACE: [*Smiles, nods.*] The Hubbards have had their great quarrel. I knew it would come some day. [*Laughs.*] It came.

ALEXANDRA: It came. It certainly came all right.

BIRDIE: [*Amazed.*] But Oscar was in such a good humor when he got home, I didn't—

HORACE: Yes, I can understand that.

[ADDIE *enters carrying a large tray with glasses, a carafe of elderberry wine and a plate of cookies, which she puts on the table.*]

ALEXANDRA: Addie! A party! What for?

ADDIE: Nothing for. I had the fresh butter, so I made the cakes, and a little elderberry does the stomach good in the rain.

BIRDIE: Isn't this nice! A party just for us. Let's play party music, Zan. [ALEXANDRA *begins to play a gay piece.*]

ADDIE: [*To* HORACE, *wheeling his chair to center.*] Come over here, Mr. Horace, and don't be thinking so much. A glass of elderberry will do more good.

[ALEXANDRA *reaches for a cake.* BIRDIE *pours herself a glass of wine.*]

ALEXANDRA: Good cakes, Addie. It's nice here. Just us. Be nice if it could always be this way.

BIRDIE: [*Nods happily.*] Quiet and restful.

ADDIE: Well, it won't be that way long. Little while now, even sitting here, you'll hear the red bricks going into place. The next day the smoke'll be pushing out the chimneys and by church time that Sunday every human born of woman will be living on chicken. That's how Mr. Ben's been telling the story.

HORACE: [*Looks at her.*] They believe it that way?

ADDIE: Believe it? They use to believing what Mr. Ben orders. There ain't been so much talk around here since Sherman's army didn't come near.[7]

HORACE: [*Softly.*] They are fools.

ADDIE: [*Nods, sits down with the sewing basket.*] You ain't born in the South unless you're a fool.

BIRDIE: [*Has drunk another glass of wine.*] But we didn't play together after that night. Oscar said he didn't like me to play on the piano. [*Turns to* ALEXANDRA.] You know what he said that night?

ALEXANDRA: Who?

BIRDIE: Oscar. He said that music made him nervous. He said he just sat and waited for the next note. [ALEXANDRA *laughs.*] He wasn't poking fun. He meant it. Ah, well—[*She finishes her glass, shakes her head.* HORACE *looks at her, smiles.*] Your papa don't like to admit it, but he's been mighty kind to me all these years. [*Running the back of her hand along his sleeve.*] Often he'd step in when somebody said something and once—[*She stops, turns away, her face still.*] Once he stopped Oscar from—[*She stops, turns. Quickly.*] I'm sorry I said that. Why, here I am so happy and yet I think about bad things. [*Laughs nervously.*] That's not right, now, is it?

[*She pours a drink.* CAL *appears in the door. He has on an old coat and is carrying a torn umbrella.*]

ALEXANDRA: Have a cake, Cal.

CAL: [*Comes in, takes a cake.*] Yes'm. You want me, Mr. Horace?

HORACE: What time is it, Cal?

CAL: 'Bout ten minutes before it's five.

HORACE: All right. Now you walk yourself down to the bank.

7. Union general William Tecumseh Sherman (1820–1891) fought vigorously in the deep South in the Civil War, most notably in his famous and destructive march from Atlanta to Savannah, November–December 1864.

CAL: It'll be closed. Nobody'll be there but Mr. Manders, Mr. Joe Horns, Mr. Leo—

HORACE: Go in the back way. They'll be at the table, going over the day's business. [*Points to the deposit box.*] See that box?

CAL: [*Nods.*] Yes, sir.

HORACE: You tell Mr. Manders that Mr. Horace says he's much obliged to him for bringing the box, it arrived all right.

CAL: [*Bewildered.*] He know you got the box. He bring it himself Wednesday. I opened the door to him and he say, "Hello, Cal, coming on to summer weather."

HORACE: You say just what I tell you. Understand?

[BIRDIE *pours another drink, stands at table.*]

CAL: No, sir. I ain't going to say I understand. I'm going down and tell a man he give you something he already know he give you, and you say "understand."

HORACE: Now, Cal.

CAL: Yes, sir. I just going to say you obliged for the box coming all right. I ain't going to understand it, but I'm going to say it.

HORACE: And tell him I want him to come over here after supper, and to bring Mr. Sol Fowler with him.

CAL: [*Nods.*] He's to come after supper and bring Mr. Sol Fowler, your attorney-at-law, with him.

HORACE: [*Smiles.*] That's right. Just walk right in the back room and say your piece. [*Slowly.*] In front of everybody.

CAL: Yes, sir. [*Mumbles to himself as he exits.*]

ALEXANDRA: [*Who has been watching* HORACE.] Is anything the matter, Papa?

HORACE: Oh, no. Nothing.

ADDIE: Miss Birdie, that elderberry going to give you a headache spell.

BIRDIE: [*Beginning to be drunk. Gaily.*] Oh, I don't think so. I don't think it will.

ALEXANDRA: [*As* HORACE *puts his hand to this throat.*] Do you want your medicine, Papa?

HORACE: No, no. I'm all right, darling.

BIRDIE: Mama used to give me elderberry wine when I was a little girl. For hiccoughs. [*Laughs.*] You know, I don't think people get hiccoughs any more. Isn't that funny? [BIRDIE *laughs.* HORACE *and* ALEXANDRA *laugh.*] I used to get hiccoughs just when I shouldn't have.

ADDIE: [*Nods.*] And nobody gets growing pains no more. That is funny. Just as if there was some style in what you get. One year an ailment's stylish and the next year it ain't.

BIRDIE: [*Turns.*] I remember. It was my first big party, at Lionnet I mean, and I was so excited, and there I was with hiccoughs and Mama laughing. [*Softly. Looking at carafe.*] Mama always laughed. [*Picks up carafe.*] A big party, a lovely dress from Mr. Worth[8] in Paris, France, and hiccoughs. [*Pours drink.*] My brother pounding me on the back and Mama with the elderberry bottle, laughing at me. Everybody was on their way to come, and I was such a

_____

8. Charles Frederick Worth (1825–1895), founder of the influential fashion house Maison Worth.

ninny, hiccoughing away. [*Drinks.*] You know, that was the first day I ever saw Oscar Hubbard. The Ballongs were selling their horses and he was going there to buy. He passed and lifted his hat—we could see him from the window—and my brother, to tease Mama, said maybe we should have invited the Hubbards to the party. He said Mama didn't like them because they kept a store, and he said that was old-fashioned of her. [*Her face lights up.*] And then, and *then*, I saw Mama angry for the first time in my life. She said that wasn't the reason. She said she was old-fashioned, but not that way. She said she was old-fashioned enough not to like people who killed animals they couldn't use, and who made their money charging awful interest to poor, ignorant niggers and cheating them on what they bought. She was very angry, Mama was. I had never seen her face like that. And then suddenly she laughed and said, "Look, I've frightened Birdie out of the hiccoughs." [*Her head drops. Then softly.*] And so she had. They were all gone. [*Moves to sofa, sits.*]

ADDIE: Yeah, they got mighty well off cheating niggers. Well, there are people who eat the earth and eat all the people on it like in the Bible with the locusts.[9] Then there are people who stand around and watch them eat it. [*Softly.*] Sometimes I think it ain't right to stand and watch them do it.

BIRDIE: [*Thoughtfully.*] Like I say, if we could only go back to Lionnet. Everybody'd be better there. They'd be good and kind. I like people to be kind. [*Pours drink.*] Don't you, Horace; don't you like people to be kind?

HORACE: Yes, Birdie.

BIRDIE: [*Very drunk now.*] Yes, that was the first day I ever saw Oscar. Who would have thought— [*Quickly.*] You all want to know something? Well, I don't like Leo. My very own son, and I don't like him. [*Laughs, gaily.*] My, I guess I even like Oscar more.

ALEXANDRA: Why did you marry Uncle Oscar?

ADDIE: [*Sharply.*] That's no question for you to be asking.

HORACE: [*Sharply.*] Why not? She's heard enough around here to ask anything.

ALEXANDRA: Aunt Birdie, why did you marry Uncle Oscar?

BIRDIE: I don't know. I thought I liked him. He was kind to me and I thought it was because he liked me too. But that wasn't the reason— [*Wheels on ALEXANDRA.*] Ask why *he* married *me*. I can tell you that: He's told it to me often enough.

ADDIE: [*Leaning forward.*] Miss Birdie, don't—

BIRDIE: [*Speaking very rapidly, tensely.*] My family was good and the cotton on Lionnet's fields was better. Ben Hubbard wanted the cotton and [*Rises.*] Oscar Hubbard married it for him. He was kind to me, then. He used to smile at me. He hasn't smiled at me since. Everybody knew that's what he married me for. [ADDIE *rises.*] Everybody but me. Stupid, stupid me.

ALEXANDRA: [*To HORACE, holding his hand, softly.*] I see. [*Hesitates.*] Papa, I mean—when you feel better couldn't we go away? I mean, by ourselves. Couldn't we find a way to go—

9. Exodus 10:12–16.

HORACE: Yes, I know what you mean. We'll try to find a way. I promise you, darling.

ADDIE: [*Moves to* BIRDIE.] Rest a bit, Miss Birdie. You get talking like this you'll get a headache and—

BIRDIE: [*Sharply, turning to her.*] I've never had a headache in my life. [*Begins to cry hysterically.*] You know it as well as I do. [*Turns to* ALEXANDRA.] I never had a headache, Zan. That's a lie they tell for me. I drink. All by myself, in my own room, by myself, I drink. Then, when they want to hide it, they say, "Birdie's got a headache again"—

ALEXANDRA: [*Comes to her quickly.*] Aunt Birdie.

BIRDIE: [*Turning away.*] Even you won't like me now. You won't like me any more.

ALEXANDRA: I love you. I'll always love you.

BIRDIE: [*Furiously.*] Well, don't. Don't love me. Because in twenty years you'll just be like me. They'll do all the same things to you. [*Begins to laugh hysterically.*] You know what? In twenty-two years I haven't had a whole day of happiness. Oh, a little, like today with you all. But never a single, whole day. I say to myself, if only I had one more *whole* day, then— [*The laugh stops.*] And that's the way you'll be. And you'll trail after them, just like me, hoping they won't be so mean that day or say something to make you feel so bad—only you'll be worse off because you haven't got my Mama to remember— [*Turns away, her head drops. She stands quietly, swaying a little, holding onto the sofa.* ALEXANDRA *leans down, puts her cheek on* BIRDIE'*s arm.*]

ALEXANDRA: [*To* BIRDIE.] I guess we were all trying to make a happy day. You know, we sit around and try to pretend nothing's happened. We try to pretend we are not here. We make believe we are just by ourselves, some place else, and it doesn't seem to work. [*Kisses* BIRDIE'*s hand.*] Come now, Aunt Birdie, I'll walk you home. You and me. [*She takes* BIRDIE'*s arm. They move slowly out.*]

BIRDIE: [*Softly as they exit.*] You and me.

ADDIE: [*After a minute.*] Well. First time I ever heard Miss Birdie say a word. [HORACE *looks at her.*] Maybe it's good for her. I'm just sorry Zan had to hear it. [HORACE *moves his head as if he were uncomfortable.*] You feel bad, don't you? [*He shrugs.*]

HORACE: So you didn't want Zan to hear? It would be nice to let her stay innocent, like Birdie at her age. Let her listen now. Let her see everything. How else is she going to know that she's got to get away? I'm trying to show her that. I'm trying, but I've only got a little time left. She can even hate me when I'm dead, if she'll only learn to hate and fear this.

ADDIE: Mr. Horace—

HORACE: Pretty soon there'll be nobody to help her but you.

ADDIE: [*Crossing to him.*] What can I do?

HORACE: Take her away.

ADDIE: How can I do that? Do you think they'd let me just go away with her?

HORACE: I'll fix it so they can't stop you when you're ready to go. You'll go, Addie?

ADDIE: [*After a second, softly.*] Yes, sir. I promise.

[*He touches her arm, nods.*]

HORACE: [*Quietly.*] I'm going to have Sol Fowler make me a new will. They'll make trouble, but you make Zan stand firm and Fowler'll do the rest. Addie, I'd like to leave you something for yourself. I always wanted to.

ADDIE: [*Laughs.*] Don't you do that, Mr. Horace. A nigger woman in a white man's will! I'd never get it nohow.

HORACE: I know. But upstairs in the armoire drawer there's seventeen hundred dollar bills. It's money left from my trip. It's in an envelope with your name. It's for you.

ADDIE: Seventeen hundred dollar bills! My God, Mr. Horace, I won't know how to count up that high. [*Shyly.*] It's mighty kind and good of you. I don't know what to say for thanks—

CAL: [*Appears in doorway.*] I'm back. [*No answer.*] I'm back.

ADDIE: So we see.

HORACE: Well?

CAL: Nothing. I just went down and spoke my piece. Just like you told me. I say, "Mr. Horace he thank you mightily for the safe box arriving in good shape and he say you right after supper to his house and bring Mr. Attorney-at-law Sol Fowler with you." Then I wipe my hands on my coat. Every time I ever told a lie in my whole life, I wipe my hands right after. Can't help doing it. Well, while I'm wiping my hands, Mr. Leo jump up and say to me, "What box? What you talking about?"

HORACE: [*Smiles.*] Did he?

CAL: And Mr. Leo say he got to leave a little early cause he got something to do. And then Mr. Manders say Mr. Leo should sit right down and finish up his work and stop acting like somebody made him Mr. President. So he sit down. Now, just like I told you, Mr. Manders was mighty surprised with the message because he knows right well he brought the box—[*Points to box, sighs.*] But he took it all right. Some men take everything easy and some do not.

HORACE: [*Puts his head back, laughs.*] Mr. Leo was telling the truth; he *has* got something to do. I hope Manders don't keep him too long. [*Outside there is the sound of voices.* CAL *exits.* ADDIE *crosses quickly to* HORACE, *puts basket on table, begins to wheel his chair towards the stairs. Sharply.*] No. Leave me where I am.

ADDIE: But that's Miss Regina coming back.

HORACE: [*Nods, looking at door.*] Go away, Addie.

ADDIE: [*Hesitates.*] Mr. Horace. Don't talk no more today. You don't feel well and it won't do no good—

HORACE: [*As he hears footsteps in the hall.*] Go on.

[*She looks at him for a second, then picks up her sewing from table and exits as* REGINA *comes in from hall.* HORACE's *chair is now so placed that he is in front of the table with the medicine.* REGINA *stands in the hall, shakes umbrella, stands it in the corner, takes off her cloak and throws it over the banister. She stares at* HORACE.]

REGINA: [*As she takes off her gloves.*] We had agreed that you were to stay in your part of this house and I in mine. This room is *my* part of the house. Please don't come down here again.

HORACE: I won't.

REGINA: [*Crosses towards bell-cord.*] I'll get Cal to take you upstairs.

HORACE: [*Smiles.*] Before you do I want to tell you that after all, we have invested our money in Hubbard Sons and Marshall, Cotton Manufacturers.

REGINA: [*Stops, turns, stares at him.*] What are you talking about? You haven't seen Ben— When did you change your mind?

HORACE: I didn't change my mind. *I* didn't invest the money. [*Smiles.*] It was invested for me.

REGINA: [*Angrily.*] What—?

HORACE: I had eighty-eight thousand dollars' worth of Union Pacific bonds in that safe-deposit box. They are not there now. Go and look. [*As she stares at him, he points to the box.*] Go and look, Regina. [*She crosses quickly to the box, opens it.*] Those bonds are as negotiable as money.

REGINA: [*Turns back to him.*] What kind of joke are you playing now? Is this for my benefit?

HORACE: I don't look in that box very often, but three days ago, on Wednesday it was, because I had made a decision—

REGINA: I want to know what you are talking about.

HORACE: [*Sharply.*] Don't interrupt me again. Because I had made a decision, I sent for the box. The bonds were gone. Eighty-eight thousand dollars gone. [*He smiles at her.*]

REGINA: [*After a moment's silence, quietly.*] Do you think I'm crazy enough to believe what you're saying?

HORACE: [*Shrugs.*] Believe anything you like.

REGINA: [*Stares at him, slowly.*] Where did they go to?

HORACE: They are in Chicago. With Mr. Marshall, I should guess.

REGINA: What did they do? Walk to Chicago? Have you really gone crazy?

HORACE: Leo took the bonds.

REGINA: [*Turns sharply then speaks softly, without conviction.*] I don't believe it.

HORACE: [*Leans forward.*] I wasn't there but I can guess what happened. This fine gentleman, to whom you were willing to marry your daughter, took the keys and opened the box. You remember that the day of the fight Oscar went to Chicago? Well, he went with my bonds that his son Leo had stolen for him. [*Pleasantly.*] And for Ben, of course, too.

REGINA: [*Slowly, nods.*] When did you find out the bonds were gone?

HORACE: Wednesday night.

REGINA: I thought that's what you said. Why have you waited three days to do anything? [*Suddenly laughs.*] This *will* make a fine story.

HORACE: [*Nods.*] Couldn't it?

REGINA: [*Still laughing.*] A fine story to hold over their heads. How could they be such fools? [*Turns to him.*]

HORACE: But I'm not going to hold it over their heads.

REGINA: [*The laugh stops.*] What?

HORACE: [*Turns his chair to face her.*] I'm going to let them keep the bonds—as a loan from you. An eighty-eight-thousand-dollar loan; they should be grateful to you. They will be, I think.

REGINA: [*Slowly, smiles.*] I see. You are punishing me. But I won't let you punish me. If you won't do anything, I will. Now. [*She starts for door.*]

HORACE: You won't do anything. Because you can't. [REGINA *stops.*] It won't do you any good to make trouble because I shall simply say that I lent them the bonds.

REGINA: [*Slowly.*] You would do that?

HORACE: Yes. For once in your life I am tying your hands. There is nothing for you to do.

[*There is silence. Then she sits down.*]

REGINA: I see. You are going to lend them the bonds and let them keep all the profit they make on them, and there is nothing I can do about it. Is that right?

HORACE: Yes.

REGINA: [*Softly.*] Why did you say that I was making this gift?

HORACE: I was coming to that. I am going to make a new will, Regina, leaving you eighty-eight thousand dollars in Union Pacific bonds. The rest will go to Zan. It's true that your brothers have borrowed your share for a little while. After my death I advise you to talk to Ben and Oscar. They won't admit anything and Ben, I think, will be smart enough to see that he's safe. Because I knew about the theft and said nothing. Nor will I say anything as long as I live. Is that clear to you?

REGINA: [*Nods, softly, without looking at him.*] You will not say anything as long as you live.

HORACE: That's right. And by that time they will probably have replaced your bonds, and then they'll belong to you and nobody but us will ever know what happened. [*Stops, smiles.*] They'll be around any minute to see what I am going to do. I took good care to see that word reached Leo. They'll be mighty relieved to know I'm going to do nothing and Ben will think it all a capital joke on you. And that will be the end of that. There's nothing you can do to them, nothing you can do to me.

REGINA: You hate me very much.

HORACE: No.

REGINA: Oh, I think you do. [*Puts her head back, sighs.*] Well, we haven't been very good together. Anyway, I don't hate you either. I have only contempt for you. I've always had.

HORACE: From the very first?

REGINA: I think so.

HORACE: I was in love with *you*. But why did *you* marry *me*?

REGINA: I was lonely when I was young.

HORACE: *You* were lonely?

REGINA: Not the way people usually mean. Lonely for all the things I wasn't going to get. Everybody in this house was so busy and there was so little place for what I wanted. I wanted the world. Then, and then— [*Smiles.*] Papa died and left the money to Ben and Oscar.

HORACE: And you married me?

REGINA: Yes, I thought—But I was wrong. You were a small-town clerk then. You haven't changed.

HORACE: [*Nods, smiles.*] And that wasn't what you wanted.

REGINA: No. No, it wasn't what I wanted. [*Pauses, leans back, pleasantly.*] It took me a little while to find out I had made a mistake. As for you—I don't know. It was almost as if I couldn't stand the kind of man you were— [*Smiles, softly.*] I used to lie there at night, praying you wouldn't come near—

HORACE: Really? It was as bad as that?

REGINA: [*Nods.*] Remember when I went to Doctor Sloan and I told you he said there was something the matter with me and that you shouldn't touch me any more?

HORACE: I remember.

REGINA: But you believed it. I couldn't understand that. I couldn't understand that anybody could be such a soft fool. That was when I began to despise you.

HORACE: [*Puts his hand to his throat, looks at the bottle of medicine on table.*] Why didn't you leave me?

REGINA: I told you I married you for something. It turned out it was only for this. [*Carefully.*] This wasn't what I wanted, but it was something. I never thought about it much but if I had [HORACE *puts his hand to his throat.*] I'd have known that you would die before I would. But I couldn't have known that you would get heart trouble so early and so bad. I'm lucky, Horace. I've always been lucky. [HORACE *turns slowly to the medicine.*] I'll be lucky again.

> [HORACE *looks at her. The he puts his hand to his throat. Because he cannot reach the bottle he moves the chair closer. He reaches for the medicine, takes out the cork, picks up the spoon. The bottle slips and smashes on the table. He draws in his breath, gasps.*]

HORACE: Please. Tell Addie— The other bottle is upstairs. [REGINA *has not moved. She does not move now. He stares at her. Then, suddenly as if he understood, he raises his voice. It is a panic-stricken whisper, too small to be heard outside the room.*] Addie! Addie! Come—

> [*Stops as he hears the softness of his voice. He makes a sudden, furious spring from the chair to the stairs, taking the first few steps as if he were a desperate runner. On the fourth step he slips, gasps, grasps the rail, makes a great effort to reach the landing. When he reaches the landing, he is on his knees. His knees give way, he falls on the landing, out of view.* REGINA *has not turned during his climb up the stairs. Now she waits a second. Then she goes below the landing, speaks up.*]

REGINA: Horace. Horace. [*When there is no answer, she turns, calls.*] Addie! Cal! Come in here. [*She starts up the steps.* ADDIE *and* CAL *appear. Both run towards the stairs.*] He's had an attack. Come up here. [*They run up the steps quickly.*]

CAL: My God. Mr. Horace—

[*They cannot be seen now.*]

REGINA: [*Her voice comes from the head of the stairs.*] Be still, Cal. Bring him in here.

[*Before the footsteps and the voices have completely died away,* ALEXANDRA *appears in the hall door, in her raincloak and hood. She comes into the room, begins to unfasten the cloak, suddenly looks around, sees the empty wheel chair, begins to move swiftly as if to look in the dining room. At the same moment* ADDIE *runs down the stairs.* ALEXANDRA *turns and stares up at* ADDIE.]

ALEXANDRA: Addie! What?

ADDIE: [*Takes* ALEXANDRA *by the shoulders.*] I'm going for the doctor. Go upstairs.

[ALEXANDRA *looks at her, then quickly breaks away and runs up the steps.* ADDIE *exits. The stage is empty for a minute. Then the front door bell begins to ring. When there is no answer, it rings again. A second later* LEO *appears in the hall, talking as he comes in.*]

LEO: [*Very nervous.*] Hello. [*Irritably.*] Never saw any use ringing a bell when a door was open. If you are going to ring a bell, then somebody should answer it. [*Gets in the room, looks around, puzzled, listens, hears no sound.*] Aunt Regina. [*He moves around restlessly.*] Addie. [*Waits.*] Where the hell— [*Crosses to the bell cord, rings it impatiently, waits, gets no answer, calls.*] Cal! Cal!

[CAL *appears on the stair landing.*]

CAL: [*His voice is soft, shaken.*] Mr. Leo. Miss Regina says you stop that screaming noise.

LEO: [*Angrily.*] Where is everybody?

CAL: Mr. Horace he got an attack. He's bad. Miss Regina says you stop that noise.

LEO: Uncle Horace—What—What happened? [CAL *starts down the stairs, shakes his head, begins to move swiftly off.* LEO *looks around wildly.*] But when—You seen Mr. Oscar or Mr. Ben? [CAL *shakes his head. Moves on.* LEO *grabs him by the arm.*] Answer me, will you?

CAL: No, I ain't seen 'em. I ain't got time to answer you. I got to get things. [CAL *runs off.*]

LEO: But what's the matter with him? When did this happen—[*Calling after* CAL.] You'd think Papa'd be some place where you could find him. I been chasing him all afternoon.

[OSCAR *and* BEN *come into the room, talking excitedly.*]

OSCAR: I hope it's not a bad attack.

BEN: It's the first one he's had since he came home.

LEO: Papa, I've been looking all over town for you and Uncle Ben—

BEN: Where is he?

OSCAR: Addie said it was sudden.

BEN: [*To* LEO.] Where is he? When did it happen?

LEO: Upstairs. Will you listen to me, please? I been looking for you for—

OSCAR: [*To* BEN.] You think we should go up?

[BEN, *looking up the steps, shakes his head.*]

BEN: I don't know. I don't know.

OSCAR: [*Shakes his head.*] But he was all right—

LEO: [*Yelling.*] Will you listen to me?

OSCAR: [*Sharply.*] What is the matter with you?

LEO: I been trying to tell you. I been trying to find you for an hour—

OSCAR: Tell me what?

LEO: Uncle Horace knows about the bonds. He knows about them. He's had the box since Wednesday—

BEN: [*Sharply.*] Stop shouting! What the hell are you talking about?

LEO: [*Furiously.*] I'm telling you he knows about the bonds. Ain't that clear enough—

OSCAR: [*Grabbing* LEO's *arm.*] You God-damn fool! Stop screaming!

BEN: Now what happened? Talk quietly.

LEO: You heard me. Uncle Horace knows about the bonds. He's known since Wednesday.

BEN: [*After a second.*] How do you known that?

LEO: Because Cal comes down to Manders and says the box came O.K. and—

OSCAR: [*Trembling.*] That might not mean a thing—

LEO: [*Angrily.*] No? It might not, huh? Then he says Manders should come here tonight and bring Sol Fowler with him. I guess that don't mean a thing either.

OSCAR: [*To* BEN.] Ben— What— Do you think he's seen the—

BEN: [*Motions to the box.*] There's the box. [*Both* OSCAR *and* LEO *turn sharply.* LEO *makes a leap to the box.*] You ass. Put it down. What are you going to do with it, eat it?

LEO: I'm going to— [*Starts.*]

BEN: [*Furiously.*] Put it down. Don't touch it again. Now sit down and shut up for a minute.

OSCAR: Since Wednesday. [*To* LEO.] You said he had it since Wednesday. Why didn't he say something— [*To* BEN.] I don't understand—

LEO: [*Taking a step.*] I can put it back. I can put it back before anybody knows.

BEN: [*Who is standing at the table, softly.*] He's had it since Wednesday. Yet he hasn't said a word to us.

OSCAR: Why? Why?

LEO: What's the difference why? He was getting ready to say plenty. He was going to say it to Fowler tonight—

OSCAR: [*Angrily.*] Be still. [*Turns to* BEN, *looks at him, waits.*]

BEN: [*After a minute.*] I don't believe that.

LEO: [*Wildly.*] You don't believe it? What do I care what you believe? I do the dirty work and then—

BEN: [*Turning his head sharply to* LEO.] I'm remembering that. I'm remembering that, Leo.

OSCAR: What do you mean?

LEO: You—

BEN: [*To* OSCAR.] If you don't shut that little fool up, I'll show you what I mean. For some reason he knows, but he don't say a word.

OSCAR: Maybe he didn't know that *we*—

BEN: [*Quickly.*] That *Leo*— He's no fool. Does Manders know the bonds are missing?

LEO: How could I tell? I was half crazy. I don't think so. Because Manders seemed kind of puzzled and—

OSCAR: But we got to find out—[*He breaks off as* CAL *comes into the room carrying a kettle of hot water.*]

BEN: How is he, Cal?

CAL: I don't know, Mr. Ben. He was bad. [*Going towards stairs.*]

OSCAR: But when did it happen?

CAL: [*Shrugs.*] He wasn't feeling bad early. [ADDIE *comes in quickly from the hall.*] Then there he is next thing on the landing, fallen over, his eyes tight—

ADDIE: [*To* CAL.] Dr. Sloan's over at the Ballongs. Hitch the buggy and go get him. [*She takes the kettle and cloths from him, pushes him, runs up the stair.*] Go on.

[*She disappears.* CAL *exits.*]

BEN: Never seen Sloan anywhere when you need him.

OSCAR: [*Softly.*] Sounds bad.

LEO: He would have told *her* about it. Aunt Regina. He would have told his own wife—

BEN: [*Turning to* LEO.] Yes, he might have told her. But they weren't on such pretty terms and maybe he didn't. Maybe he didn't. [*Goes quickly to* LEO.] Now, listen to me. If she doesn't know, it may work out all right. If she does know, you're to say he lent you the bonds.

LEO: Lent them to me! Who's going to believe that?

BEN: Nobody.

OSCAR: [*To* LEO.] Don't you understand? It can't do no harm to say it—

LEO: Why should I say he lent them to me? Why not to you? [*Carefully.*] Why not to Uncle Ben?

BEN: [*Smiles.*] Just because he didn't lend them to me. Remember that.

LEO: But all he has to do is say he didn't lend them to me—

BEN: [*Furiously.*] But for some reason, he doesn't seem to be talking, does he?

[*There are footsteps above. They all stand looking at the stairs.* REGINA *begins to come slowly down.*]

BEN: What happened?

REGINA: He's had a bad attack.

OSCAR: Too bad. I'm so sorry we weren't here when—when Horace needed us.

BEN: When *you* needed us.

REGINA: [*Looks at him.*] Yes.

BEN: How is he? Can we—can we go up?

REGINA: [*Shakes her head.*] He's not conscious.

OSCAR: [*Pacing around.*] It's that—it's that bad? Wouldn't you think Sloan could be found quickly, just once, just once?

REGINA: I don't think there is much for him to do.

BEN: Oh, don't talk like that. He's come through attacks before. He will now.

[REGINA *sits down. After a second she speaks softly.*]

REGINA: Well. We haven't seen each other since the day of our fight.

BEN: [*Tenderly.*] That was nothing. Why, you and Oscar and I used to fight when we were kids.

OSCAR: [*Hurriedly.*] Don't you think we should go up? Is there anything we can do for Horace—

BEN: You don't feel well. Ah—

REGINA: [*Without looking at them.*] No, I don't. [*Slight pause.*] Horace told me about the bonds this afternoon.

[*There is an immediate shocked silence.*]

LEO: The bonds. What do you mean? What bonds? What—

BEN: [*Looks at him furiously. Then to* REGINA.] The Union Pacific bonds? *Horace's* Union Pacific bonds?

REGINA: Yes.

OSCAR: [*Steps to her, very nervously.*] Well. Well what—what about them? What— what could he say?

REGINA: He said that Leo had stolen the bonds and given them to you.

OSCAR: [*Aghast, very loudly.*] That's ridiculous, Regina, absolutely—

LEO: I don't know what you're talking about. What would I— Why—

REGINA: [*Wearily to* BEN.] Isn't it enough that he stole them from me? Do I have to listen to this in the bargain?

OSCAR: You are talking—

LEO: I didn't steal anything. I don't know why—

REGINA: [*To* BEN.] Would you ask them to stop that, please?

[*There is silence for a minute.* BEN *glowers at* OSCAR *and* LEO.]

BEN: Aren't we starting at the wrong end, Regina? What did Horace tell you?

REGINA: [*Smiles at him.*] He told me that Leo had stolen the bonds.

LEO: I didn't steal—

REGINA: Please. Let me finish. Then he told me that he was going to pretend that he had lent them to you [LEO *turns sharply to* REGINA, *then looks at* OSCAR, *then looks back at* REGINA.] as a present from me—to my brothers. He said there was nothing I could do about it. He said the rest of his money would go to Alexandra. That is all.

[*There is a silence.* OSCAR *coughs,* LEO *smiles slyly.*]

LEO: [*Taking a step to her.*] I told you he had lent them—I could have told you—

REGINA: [*Ignores him, smiles sadly at* BEN.] So I'm very badly off, you see. [*Carefully.*] But Horace said there was nothing I could do about it as long as he was alive to say he had lent you the bonds.

BEN: You shouldn't feel that way. It can all be explained, all be adjusted. It isn't as bad—

REGINA: So you, at least, are willing to admit that the bonds were stolen?

[OSCAR *laughs nervously.*]

BEN: I admit no such thing. It's possible that Horace made up that part of the story to tease you—[*Looks at her.*] Or perhaps to punish you. Punish you.

REGINA: [*Sadly.*] It's not a pleasant story. I feel bad, Ben, naturally. I hadn't thought—

BEN: Now you shall have the bonds safely back. That was the understanding, wasn't it, Oscar?

OSCAR: Yes.

REGINA: I'm glad to know that. [*Smiles.*] Ah, I had greater hopes—

BEN: Don't talk that way. That's foolish. [*Looks at his watch.*] I think we ought to drive out for Sloan ourselves. If we can't find him we'll go over to Senateville for Doctor Morris. And don't think I'm dismissing this other business. I'm not. We'll have it all out on a more appropriate day.

REGINA: [*Looks up, quietly.*] I don't think you had better go yet. I think you had better stay and sit down.

BEN: We'll be back with Sloan.

REGINA: Cal has gone for him. I don't want you to go.

BEN: Now don't worry and—

REGINA: You will come back in this room and sit down. I have something more to say.

BEN: [*Turns, comes towards her.*] Since when do I take orders from you?

REGINA: [*Smiles.*] You don't—yet. [*Sharply.*] Come back, Oscar. You too, Leo.

OSCAR: [*Sure of himself, laughs.*] My dear Regina—

BEN: [*Softly, pats her hand.*] Horace has already clipped your wings and very wittily. Do I have to clip them, too? [*Smiles at her.*] You'd get farther with a smile, Regina. I'm a soft man for a woman's smile.

REGINA: I'm smiling, Ben. I'm smiling because you are quite safe while Horace lives. But I don't think Horace will live. And if he doesn't live I shall want seventy-five per cent in exchange for the bonds.

BEN: [*Steps back, whistles, laughs.*] Greedy! What a greedy girl you are! You want so much of everything.

REGINA: Yes. And if I don't get what I want I am going to put all three of you in jail.

OSCAR: [*Furiously.*] You're mighty crazy. Having just admitted—

BEN: And on what evidence would you put Oscar and Leo in jail?

REGINA: [*Laughs, gaily.*] Oscar, listen to him. He's getting ready to swear that it was you and Leo! What do you say to that? [OSCAR *turns furiously towards* BEN.] Oh, don't be angry, Oscar. I'm going to see that he goes in with you.

BEN: Try anything you like, Regina. [*Sharply.*] And now we can stop all this and say good-bye to you. [ALEXANDRA *comes slowly down the steps.*] It's his money and he's obviously willing to let us borrow it. [*More pleasantly.*] Learn to make threats when you can carry them through. For how many years have I told you a good-looking woman gets more by being soft and appealing? Mama used to tell you that. [*Looks at his watch.*] Where the hell is Sloan? [*To* OSCAR.] Take the buggy and—

[*As* BEN *turns to* OSCAR, *he sees* ALEXANDRA. *She walks stiffly. She goes slowly to the lower window, her head bent. They all turn to look at her.*]

OSCAR: [*After a second, moving toward her.*] What? Alexandra—

[*She does not answer. After a second,* ADDIE *comes slowly down the stairs, moving as if she were very tired. At the foot of steps, she looks at* ALEXANDRA, *then turns and slowly crosses to door and exits.* REGINA *rises.* BEN *looks nervously at* ALEXANDRA, *at* REGINA.]

OSCAR: [*As* ADDIE *passes him, irritably to* ALEXANDRA.] Well, what is— [*Turns into room—sees* ADDIE *at foot of steps.*] —what's? [BEN *puts up a hand, shakes his head.*] My God, I didn't know—who *could* have known—I didn't know he was that sick. Well, well—I—

[REGINA *stands quietly, her back to them.*]

BEN: [*Softly, sincerely.*] Seems like yesterday when he first came here.
OSCAR: [*Sincerely, nervously.*] Yes, that's true. [*Turns to* BEN.] The whole town loved him and respected him.
ALEXANDRA: [*Turns.*] Did you love him, Uncle Oscar?
OSCAR: Certainly, I— What a strange thing to ask! I—
ALEXANDRA: Did you love him, Uncle Ben?
BEN: [*Simply.*] He had—
ALEXANDRA: [*Suddenly starts to laugh very loudly.*] And you, Mama, did you love him, too?
REGINA: I know what you feel, Alexandra, but please try to control yourself.
ALEXANDRA: [*Still laughing.*] I'm trying, Mama. I'm trying very hard.
BEN: Grief makes some people laugh and some people cry. It's better to cry, Alexandra.
ALEXANDRA: [*The laugh has stopped. Tensely moves toward* REGINA.] What was Papa doing on the staircase?

[BEN *turns to look at* ALEXANDRA.]

REGINA: Please go and lie down, my dear. We all need time to get over shocks like this. [ALEXANDRA *does not move.* REGINA's *voice becomes softer, more insistent.*] Please go, Alexandra.
ALEXANDRA: No, Mama. I'll wait. I've got to talk to you.
REGINA: Later. Go and rest now.
ALEXANDRA: [*Quietly.*] I'll wait, Mama. I've plenty of time.
REGINA: [*Hesitates, stares, makes a half shrug, turns back to* BEN.] As I was saying. Tomorrow morning I am going up to Judge Simmes. I shall tell him about Leo.
BEN: [*Motioning toward* ALEXANDRA.] Not in front of the child, Regina. I—
REGINA: [*Turns to him. Sharply.*] I didn't ask her to stay. Tomorrow morning I go to Judge Simmes—
OSCAR: And what proof? What proof of all this—
REGINA: [*Turns sharply.*] None. I won't need any. The bonds are missing and they are with Marshall. That will be enough. If it isn't, I'll add what's necessary.

BEN: I'm sure of that.

REGINA: [*Turns to* BEN.] You can be quite sure.

OSCAR: We'll deny—

REGINA: Deny your heads off. You couldn't find a jury that wouldn't weep for a woman whose brothers steal from her. And you couldn't find twelve men in this state you haven't cheated and hate you for it.

OSCAR: What kind of talk is this? You couldn't do anything like that! We're your own brothers. [*Points upstairs.*] How can you talk that way when upstairs not five minutes ago—

REGINA: [*Slowly.*] There are people who can never go back, who must finish what they start. I am one of those people, Oscar. [*After a slight pause.*] Where was I? [*Smiles at* BEN.] Well, they'll convict you. But I won't care much if they don't. [*Leans forward, pleasantly.*] Because by that time you'll be ruined. I shall also tell my story to Mr. Marshall, who likes me, I think, and who will not want to be involved in your scandal. A respectable firm like Marshall and Company. The deal would be off in an hour. [*Turns to them angrily.*] And you know it. Now I don't want to hear any more from any of you. *You'll do no more bargaining in this house.* I'll take my seventy-five per cent and we'll forget the story forever. That's one way of doing it, and the way I prefer. You know me well enough to know that I don't mind taking the other way.

BEN: [*After a second, slowly.*] None of us have ever known you well enough, Regina.

REGINA: You're getting old, Ben. Your tricks aren't as smart as they used to be. [*There is no answer. She waits, then smiles.*] All right. I take it that's settled and I get what I asked for.

OSCAR: [*Furiously to* BEN.] Are you going to let her do this—

BEN: [*Turns to look at him, slowly.*] You have a suggestion?

REGINA: [*Puts her arms above her head, stretches, laughs.*] No, he hasn't. All right. Now, Leo, I have forgotten that you ever saw the bonds. [*Archly, to* BEN *and* OSCAR.] And as long as you boys both behave yourselves, I've forgotten that we ever talked about them. You can draw up the necessary papers tomorrow.

> [BEN *laughs,* LEO *stares at him, starts for door. Exits.* OSCAR *moves towards door angrily.* REGINA *looks at* BEN, *nods, laughs with him. For a second,* OSCAR *stands in the door, looking back at them. Then he exits.*]

REGINA: You're a good loser, Ben. I like that.

BEN: [*He picks up his coat, then turns to her.*] Well, I say to myself, what's the good? You and I aren't like Oscar. We're not sour people. I think that comes from a good digestion. Then, too, one loses today and wins tomorrow. I say to myself, years of planning and I get what I want. Then I don't get it. But I'm not discouraged. The century's turning, the world is open. Open for people like you and me. Ready for us, waiting for us. After all this is just the beginning. There are hundreds of Hubbards sitting in rooms like this throughout the country. All their names aren't Hubbard, but they are all Hubbards and they will own this country some day. We'll get along.

REGINA: [*Smiles.*] I think so.

BEN: Then, too, I say to myself, things may change. [*Looks at* ALEXANDRA.] I agree with Alexandra. What is a man in a wheel chair doing on a staircase? I ask myself that.

REGINA: [*Looks up at him.*] And what do you answer?

BEN: I have no answer. But maybe some day I will. Maybe never, but maybe some day. [*Smiles. Pats her arm.*] When I do, I'll let you know. [*Goes towards hall.*]

REGINA: When you do, write me. I will be in Chicago. [*Gaily.*] Ah, Ben, if Papa had only left me his money.

BEN: I'll see you tomorrow.

REGINA: Oh, yes. Certainly. You'll be sort of working for me now.

BEN: [*As he passes* ALEXANDRA, *smiles.*] Alexandra, you're turning out to be a right interesting girl. [*Looks at* REGINA.] Well, good night all. [*He exits.*]

REGINA: [*Sits quietly for a second, stretches, turns to look at* ALEXANDRA.] What do you want to talk to me about, Alexandra?

ALEXANDRA: [*Slowly.*] I've changed my mind. I don't want to talk. There's nothing to talk about now.

REGINA: You're acting very strange. Not like yourself. You've had a bad shock today. I know that. And you loved Papa, but you must have expected this to come some day. You know how sick he was.

ALEXANDRA: I knew. We all knew.

REGINA: It will be good for you to get away from here. Good for me, too. Time heals most wounds, Alexandra. You're young, you shall have all the things I wanted. I'll make the world for you the way I wanted it to be for me. [*Uncomfortably.*] Don't sit there staring. You've been around Birdie so much you're getting just like her.

ALEXANDRA: [*Nods.*] Funny. That's what Aunt Birdie said today.

REGINA: [*Nods.*] Be good for you to get away from all this.

[ADDIE *enters.*]

ADDIE: Cal is back, Miss Regina. He says Dr. Sloan will be coming in a few minutes.

REGINA: We'll go in a few weeks. A few weeks! That means two or three Saturdays, two or three Sundays. [*Sighs.*] Well, I'm very tired. I shall go to bed. I don't want any supper. Put the lights out and lock up. [ADDIE *moves to the piano lamp, turns it out.*] You go to your room, Alexandra. Addie will bring you something hot. You look very tired. [*Rises. To* ADDIE.] Call me when Dr. Sloan gets here. I don't want to see anybody else. I don't want any condolence calls tonight. The whole town will be over.

ALEXANDRA: Mama, I'm not coming with you. I'm not going to Chicago.

REGINA: [*Turns to her.*] You're very upset, Alexandra.

ALEXANDRA: [*Quietly.*] I mean what I say. With all my heart.

REGINA: We'll talk about it tomorrow. The morning will make a difference.

ALEXANDRA: It won't make any difference. And there isn't anything to talk about. I am going away from you. Because I want to. Because I know Papa would want me to.

REGINA: [*Puzzled, careful, polite.*] You *know* your papa wanted you to go away from me?

ALEXANDRA: Yes.

REGINA: [*Softly.*] And if I say no?

ALEXANDRA: [*Looks at her.*] Say it, Mama, say it. And see what happens.

REGINA: [*Softly, after a pause.*] And if I make you stay?

ALEXANDRA: That would be foolish. It wouldn't work in the end.

REGINA: You're very serious about it, aren't you? [*Crosses to stairs.*] Well, you'll change your mind in a few days.

ALEXANDRA: You only change your mind when you want to. And I won't want to.

REGINA: [*Going up the steps.*] Alexandra, I've come to the end of my rope. Somewhere there has to be what I want, too. Life goes too fast. Do what you want; think what you want; go where you want. I'd like to keep you with me, but I won't make you stay. Too many people used to make me do too many things. No, I won't make you stay.

ALEXANDRA: You couldn't, Mama, because I want to leave here. As I've never wanted anything in my life before. Because now I understand what Papa was trying to tell me. [*Pause.*] All in one day: Addie said there were people who ate the earth and other people who stood around and watched them do it. And just now Uncle Ben said the same thing. Really, he said the same thing. [*Tensely.*] Well, tell him for me, Mama, I'm not going to stand around and watch you do it. Tell him I'll be fighting as hard as he'll be fighting [*Rises.*] some place where people don't just stand around and watch.

REGINA: Well, you have spirit, after all. I used to think you were all sugar water. We don't have to be bad friends. I don't want us to be bad friends, Alexandra. [*Starts, stops, turns to* ALEXANDRA.] Would you like to come and talk to me, Alexandra? Would you—would you like to sleep in my room tonight?

ALEXANDRA: [*Takes a step towards her.*] Are you afraid, Mama?

[REGINA *does not answer. She moves slowly out of sight.* ADDIE *comes to* ALEXANDRA, *presses her arm.*]

CURTAIN

1939

QUESTIONS

1. How much of Act I seems to you to be exposition? Exactly what are we told and by whom? At what point in Act I do you begin to have a sense of what individual characters are like and how they are related to each other? Where does the rising action begin?

2. Exactly what part of Act II constitutes the play's turning point? Where does the falling action begin? In what does the play's final stability consist?

3. What different pasts haunt the different characters in the play? In what specific ways do memories of the past, or nostalgia for it, affect the motivations of individual characters? How much of the plot is driven by a sense of the past? Which characters are motivated by the future? In what ways are economic status and social class related to a sense of the past?

4. In what specific ways is the setting of the play important? Does it make any difference that the action occurs in the spring? In what ways are the material objects mentioned in the stage directions important to characterization? to the play's themes?

5. Who is the most important character in the play? On what basis did you decide: centrality

to the plot? attractiveness? psychological complexity? obsession to manipulate others? power?
6. What does the play's title mean?

WRITING SUGGESTIONS

1. Write a brief character sketch of Leo, outlining his most obvious characteristics. Then read back through the play carefully and notice at what points his various stereotypical characteristics reveal themselves. How important to the play are other people's opinions of Leo? When do you become aware that you have formed a strong opinion about him? Exactly what function does he perform in the plot? Which of his distinctive characteristics are crucial to the plot? In an essay of about three pages, analyze Leo's role in the plot and show exactly how the structure of the play depends on the gradual revelation of his character.

2. Write a short (600-word) essay describing Birdie's role in the plot.

3. "Chicago" has a specific symbolic value for several of the play's characters, a symbolism that does not necessarily correspond to the "real" Chicago Mr. Marshall is from. Which characters develop a particular "image" of Chicago—either from the past or because of what it might hold in the future? Make a list of the qualities Chicago represents to individual characters. Note especially what kinds of notions Regina has about Chicago. In an essay about Regina's character (an essay of about 1,000 words), show the importance of "Chicago" to her consciousness, and note how other people's visions of the city help to clarify Regina's character and values.

BERNARD SHAW

Pygmalion

A Romance in Five Acts

CHARACTERS

CLARA EYNSFORD HILL	HENRY HIGGINS
MRS. EYNSFORD HILL	A SARCASTIC BYSTANDER
A BYSTANDER	MRS. PEARCE
FREDDY EYNSFORD HILL	ALFRED DOOLITTLE
ELIZA DOOLITTLE	MRS. HIGGINS
COLONEL PICKERING	PARLORMAID

Period: The present.

ACT I: *The Portico of St. Paul's, Covent Garden. 11:15 P.M.*

ACT II: PROFESSOR HIGGINS's *phonetic laboratory, Wimpole Street. Next day. 11 A.M.*

ACT III: *The drawing room in* MRS. HIGGINS's *flat on Chelsea Embankment. Several months later. At-home day.*

ACT IV: *The same as Act II. Several months later. Midnight.*

ACT V: *The same as Act III. The following morning.*

NOTE: *In the dialogue an e upside down indicates the indefinite vowel, sometimes called obscure or neutral, for which, though it is one of the commonest sounds in English speech, our wretched alphabet has no letter.*

ACT I

London at 11:15 P.M. Torrents of heavy summer rain. Cab whistles blowing frantically in all directions. PEDESTRIANS *running for shelter into the portico of St. Paul's church (not Wren's cathedral but Inigo Jones's church in Covent Garden vegetable market), among them a* LADY *and her* DAUGHTER *in evening dress. All are peering out gloomily at the rain, except one* MAN *with his back turned to the rest, wholly preoccupied with a notebook in which he is writing.*

The church clock strikes the first quarter.

THE DAUGHTER: [*In the space between the central pillars, close to the one on her left.*] I'm getting chilled to the bone. What can Freddy be doing all this time? He's been gone twenty minutes.

THE MOTHER: [*On her* DAUGHTER's *right.*] Not so long. But he ought to have got us a cab by this.

A BYSTANDER: [*On the* LADY'*s right.*] He wont[1] get no cab not until half-past eleven, missus, when they come back after dropping their theatre fares.

THE MOTHER: But we must have a cab. We cant stand here until half-past eleven. It's too bad.

THE BYSTANDER: Well, it aint my fault, missus.

THE DAUGHTER: If Freddy had a bit of gumption, he would have got one at the theatre door.

THE MOTHER: What could he have done, poor boy?

THE DAUGHTER: Other people got cabs. Why couldnt he?

[FREDDY *rushes in out of the rain from the Southampton Street side, and comes between them closing a dripping umbrella. He is a young man of twenty, in evening dress, very wet round the ankles.*]

THE DAUGHTER: Well, havnt you got a cab?

FREDDY: Theres not one to be had for love or money.

THE MOTHER: Oh, Freddy, there must be one. You cant have tried.

THE DAUGHTER: It's too tiresome. Do you expect us to go and get one ourselves?

FREDDY: I tell you theyre all engaged. The rain was so sudden: nobody was prepared; and everybody had to take a cab. Ive been to Charing Cross one way and nearly to Ludgate Circus the other; and they were all engaged.

THE MOTHER: Did you try Trafalgar Square?

FREDDY: There wasnt one at Trafalgar Square.

THE DAUGHTER: Did you try?

FREDDY: I tried as far as Charing Cross Station. Did you expect me to walk to Hammersmith?[2]

THE DAUGHTER: You havnt tried at all.

THE MOTHER: You really are very helpless, Freddy. Go again; and dont come back until you have found a cab.

FREDDY: I shall simply get soaked for nothing.

THE DAUGHTER: And what about us? Are we to stay here all night in this draught, with next to nothing on? You selfish pig—

FREDDY: Oh, very well: I'll go, I'll go. [*He opens his umbrella and dashes off Strandwards, but comes into collision with a* FLOWER GIRL *who is hurrying in for shelter, knocking her basket out of her hands. A blinding flash of lightning, followed instantly by a rattling peal of thunder, orchestrates the incident.*]

THE FLOWER GIRL: Nah then, Freddy: look wh' y' gowin, deah.

FREDDY: Sorry. [*He rushes off.*]

THE FLOWER GIRL: [*Picking up her scattered flowers and replacing them in the basket.*] Theres menners f' yer! Tə-oo banches o voylets trod into the mad. [*She sits down on the plinth of the column, sorting her flowers, on the* LADY'*s right. She is*

---

1. Shaw insisted on eliminating apostrophes from most contractions—*wont, cant, didnt,* etc.
2. Freddy has walked about two blocks in either direction to reach Charing Cross Station and Ludgate Circus. Trafalgar Square is another block beyond Charing Cross Station, and Hammersmith is about ten miles beyond that.

not at all a romantic figure. She is perhaps eighteen, perhaps twenty, hardly older. She wears a little sailor hat of black straw that has long been exposed to the dust and soot of London and has seldom if ever been brushed. Her hair needs washing rather badly: its mousy color can hardly be natural. She wears a shoddy black coat that reaches nearly to her knees and is shaped to her waist. She has a brown skirt with a coarse apron. Her boots are much the worse for wear. She is no doubt as clean as she can afford to be; but compared to the ladies she is very dirty. Her features are no worse than theirs; but their condition leaves something to be desired; and she needs the services of a dentist.]

THE MOTHER: How do you know that my son's name is Freddy, pray?

THE FLOWER GIRL: Ow, eez yə-ooa san, is e? Wal, fewd dan y' də-ooty bawmz a mather should, eed now bettern to spawl a pore gel's flahrzn than ran awy athaht pyin. Will ye-oo py me f'them? [*Here, with apologies, this desperate attempt to represent her dialect without a phonetic alphabet must be abandoned as unintelligible outside London.*]

THE DAUGHTER: Do nothing of the sort, mother. The idea!

THE MOTHER: Please allow me, Clara. Have you any pennies?

THE DAUGHTER: No. Ive nothing smaller than sixpence.

THE FLOWER GIRL: [*Hopefully.*] I can give you change for a tanner,[3] kind lady.

THE MOTHER: [*To* CLARA.] Give it to me. [CLARA *parts reluctantly.*] Now. [*To the* GIRL.] This is for your flowers.

THE FLOWER GIRL: Thank you kindly, lady.

THE DAUGHTER: Make her give you the change. These things are only a penny a bunch.

THE MOTHER: Do hold your tongue, Clara. [*To the* GIRL.] You can keep the change.

THE FLOWER GIRL: Oh, thank you, lady.

THE MOTHER: Now tell me how you know that young gentleman's name.

THE FLOWER GIRL: I didnt.

THE MOTHER: I heard you call him by it. Dont try to deceive me.

THE FLOWER GIRL: [*Protesting.*] Who's trying to deceive you? I called him Freddy or Charlie same as you might yourself if you was talking to a stranger and wished to be pleasant.

THE DAUGHTER: Sixpence thrown away! Really, mamma, you might have spared Freddy that. [*She retreats in disgust behind the pillar.*]

[*An elderly* GENTLEMAN *of the amiable military type rushes into the shelter, and closes a dripping umbrella. He is in the same plight as* FREDDY, *very wet about the ankles. He is in evening dress, with a light overcoat. He takes the place left vacant by the* DAUGHTER.]

THE GENTLEMAN: Phew!

THE MOTHER: [*To the* GENTLEMAN.] Oh sir, is there any sign of its stopping?

THE GENTLEMAN: I'm afraid not. It started worse than ever about two minutes ago. [*He goes to the plinth beside the* FLOWER GIRL; *puts up his foot on it; and stoops to turn down his trouser ends.*]

3. Slang for sixpence (six pennies), loosely equivalent to half a dollar in 1990s U.S. currency.

THE MOTHER: Oh dear! [*She retires sadly and joins her* DAUGHTER.]

THE FLOWER GIRL: [*Taking advantage of the military* GENTLEMAN's *proximity to establish friendly relations with him.*] If it's worse, it's a sign it's nearly over. So cheer up, Captain; and buy a flower off a poor girl.

THE GENTLEMAN: I'm sorry. I havnt any change.

THE FLOWER GIRL: I can give you change, Captain.

THE GENTLEMAN: For a sovereign?[4] Ive nothing less.

THE FLOWER GIRL: Garn! Oh do buy a flower off me, Captain. I can change half-a-crown.[5] Take this for tuppence.[6]

THE GENTLEMAN: Now dont be troublesome: theres a good girl. [*Trying his pockets.*] I really havnt any change—Stop: heres three hapence,[7] if thats any use to you. [*He retreats to the other pillar.*]

THE FLOWER GIRL: [*Disappointed, but thinking three halfpence better than nothing.*] Thank you, sir.

THE BYSTANDER: [*To the* GIRL.] You be careful: give him a flower for it. Theres a bloke here behind taking down every blessed word youre saying. [*All turn to the* MAN *who is taking notes.*]

THE FLOWER GIRL: [*Springing up terrified.*] I aint done nothing wrong by speaking to the gentleman. Ive a right to sell flowers if I keep off the kerb. [*Hysterically.*] I'm a respectable girl: so help me, I never spoke to him except to ask him to buy a flower off me.

> [*General hubbub, mostly sympathetic to the* FLOWER GIRL, *but deprecating her excessive sensibility. Cries of* Dont start hollerin. Who's hurting you? Nobody's going to touch you. Whats the good of fussing? Steady on. Easy easy, etc., *come from the elderly staid spectators, who pat her comfortingly. Less patient ones bid her shut her head, or ask her roughly what is wrong with her. A remoter group, not knowing what the matter is, crowd in and increase the noise with question and answer:* Whats the row? What-she do? Where is he? A tec[8] taking her down. What! him? Yes: him over there: Took money off the gentleman, *etc.*]

THE FLOWER GIRL: [*Breaking through them to the* GENTLEMAN, *crying wildly.*] Oh, sir, dont let him charge me. You dunno what it means to me. Theyll take away my character and drive me on the streets for speaking to gentlemen. They—

THE NOTE TAKER: [*Coming forward on her right, the rest crowding after him.*] There! there! there! there! who's hurting you, you silly girl? What do you take me for?

THE BYSTANDER: It's aw rawt: e's a genleman: look at his bə-oots [*Explaining to the* NOTE TAKER.] She thought you was a copper's nark, sir.

THE NOTE TAKER: [*With quick interest.*] Whats a copper's nark?

THE BYSTANDER: [*Inapt at definition.*] It's a—well, it's a copper's nark, as you might say. What else would you call it? A sort of informer.

---

4. Gold coin worth a pound (20 shillings), loosely equivalent to 20 dollars in 1990s U.S. currency.
5. Two and one-half shillings, loosely equivalent to two and a half dollars in 1990s U.S. currency.
6. Two pennies.   7. Half a penny.   8. Detective.

THE FLOWER GIRL: [*Still hysterical.*] I take my Bible oath I never said a word—

THE NOTE TAKER: [*Overbearing but good-humored.*] Oh, shut up, shut up. Do I look like a policeman?

THE FLOWER GIRL: [*Far from reassured.*] Then what did you take down my words for? How do I know whether you took me down right? You just shew me what youve wrote about me. [*The* NOTE TAKER *opens his book and holds it steadily under her nose, though the pressure of the mob trying to read it over his shoulders would upset a weaker man.*] Whats that? That aint proper writing. I cant read that.

THE NOTE TAKER: I can. [*Reads, reproducing her pronunciation exactly.*] "Cheer ap, Keptin; n' baw ya flahr orf a pore gel."

THE FLOWER GIRL: [*Much distressed.*] It's because I called him Captain. I meant no harm. [*To the* GENTLEMAN.] Oh, sir, dont let him lay a charge agen me for a word like that. You—

THE GENTLEMAN: Charge! I make no charge. [*To the* NOTE TAKER.] Really, sir, if you are a detective, you need not begin protecting me against molestation by young women until I ask you. Anybody could see that the girl meant no harm.

THE BYSTANDERS GENERALLY: [*Demonstrating against police espionage.*] Course they could. What business is it of yours? You mind your own affairs. He wants promotion, he does. Taking down people's words! Girl never said a word to him. What harm if she did? Nice thing a girl cant shelter from the rain without being insulted, etc., etc., etc. [*She is conducted by the more sympathetic demonstrators back to her plinth, where she resumes her seat and struggles with her emotion.*]

THE BYSTANDER: He aint a tec. He's a blooming busybody: thats what he is. I tell you, look at his bɔ-oots.

THE NOTE TAKER: [*Turning on him genially.*] And how are all your people down at Selsey?

THE BYSTANDER: [*Suspiciously.*] Who told you my people come from Selsey?

THE NOTE TAKER: Never you mind. They did. [*To the* GIRL.] How do you come to be up so far east? You were born in Lisson Grove.

THE FLOWER GIRL: [*Appalled.*] Oh, what harm is there in my leaving Lisson Grove? It wasnt fit for a pig to live in; and I had to pay four-and-six a week. [*In tears.*] Oh, boo—hoo—oo—

THE NOTE TAKER: Live where you like; but stop that noise.

THE GENTLEMAN: [*To the* GIRL.] Come, come! he cant touch you: you have a right to live where you please.

A SARCASTIC BYSTANDER: [*Thrusting himself between the* NOTE TAKER *and the* GENTLEMAN.] Park Lane, for instance. I'd like to go into the Housing Question with you, I would.

THE FLOWER GIRL: [*Subsiding into a brooding melancholy over her basket, and talking very low-spiritedly to herself.*] I'm a good girl, I am.

THE SARCASTIC BYSTANDER: [*Not attending to her.*] Do you know where *I* come from?

THE NOTE TAKER: [*Promptly.*] Hoxton. [*Titterings. Popular interest in the* NOTE TAKER's *performance increases.*]

THE SARCASTIC ONE: [*Amazed.*] Well, who said I didnt? Bly me! you know everything, you do.

THE FLOWER GIRL: [*Still nursing her sense of injury.*] Aint no call to meddle with me, he aint.

THE BYSTANDER: [*To her.*] Of course he aint. Dont you stand it from him. [*To the* NOTE TAKER.] See here: what call have you to know about people what never offered to meddle with you?

THE FLOWER GIRL: Let him say what he likes. I dont want to have no truck with him.

THE BYSTANDER: You take us for dirt under your feet, dont you? Catch you taking liberties with a gentleman!

THE SARCASTIC BYSTANDER: Yes: tell him where he come from if you want to go fortune-telling.

THE NOTE TAKER: Cheltenham, Harrow, Cambridge, and India.

THE GENTLEMAN: Quite right. [*Great laughter. Reaction in the* NOTE TAKER's *favor. Exclamations of* He knows all about it. Told him proper. Hear him tell the toff[9] where he come from? *etc.*] May I ask, sir, do you do this for your living at a music hall?

THE NOTE TAKER: I've thought of that. Perhaps I shall some day.

[*The rain has stopped; and the persons on the outside of the crowd begin to drop off.*]

THE FLOWER GIRL: [*Resenting the reaction.*] He's no gentleman, he aint, to interfere with a poor girl.

THE DAUGHTER: [*Out of patience, pushing her way rudely to the front and displacing the* GENTLEMAN, *who politely retires to the other side of the pillar.*] What on earth is Freddy doing? I shall get pneumownia if I stay in this draught any longer.

THE NOTE TAKER: [*To himself, hastily making a note of her pronunciation of "monia."*] Earlscourt.

THE DAUGHTER: [*Violently.*] Will you please keep your impertinent remarks to yourself.

THE NOTE TAKER: Did I say that out loud? I didnt mean to. I beg your pardon. Your mother's Epsom, unmistakeably.

THE MOTHER: [*Advancing between her* DAUGHTER *and the* NOTE TAKER.] How very curious! I was brought up in Largelady Park, near Epsom.

THE NOTE TAKER: [*Uproariously amused.*] Ha! ha! What a devil of a name! Excuse me. [*To the* DAUGHTER.] You want a cab, do you?

THE DAUGHTER: Dont dare speak to me.

THE MOTHER: Oh please, please, Clara. [*Her* DAUGHTER *repudiates her with an angry shrug and retires haughtily.*] We should be so grateful to you, sir, if you found us a cab. [*The* NOTE TAKER *produces a whistle.*] Oh, thank you. [*She joins her* DAUGHTER.]

[*The* NOTE TAKER *blows a piercing blast.*]

---

9. Slang for "gentleman," slightly derogatory.

THE SARCASTIC BYSTANDER: There! I knowed he was a plainclothes copper.

THE BYSTANDER: That aint a police whistle: thats a sporting whistle.

THE FLOWER GIRL: [*Still preoccupied with her wounded feelings.*] He's no right to take away my character. My character is the same to me as any lady's.

THE NOTE TAKER: I dont know whether youve noticed it; but the rain stopped about two minutes ago.

THE BYSTANDER: So it has. Why didnt you say so before? and us losing our time listening to your silliness! [*He walks off towards the Strand.*]

THE SARCASTIC BYSTANDER: I can tell where you come from. You come from Anwell. Go back there.

THE NOTE TAKER: [*Helpfully.*] Hanwell.[1]

THE SARCASTIC BYSTANDER: [*Affecting great distinction of speech.*] Thenk you, teacher. Haw haw! So long [*He touches his hat with mock respect and strolls off.*]

THE FLOWER GIRL: Frightening people like that! How would he like it himself?

THE MOTHER: It's quite fine now, Clara. We can walk to a motor bus. Come. [*She gathers her skirts above her ankles and hurries off towards the Strand.*]

THE DAUGHTER: But the cab—[*Her MOTHER is out of hearing.*] Oh, how tiresome! [*She follows angrily.*]

[*All the rest have gone except the* NOTE TAKER, *the* GENTLEMAN, *and the* FLOWER GIRL, *who sits arranging her basket, and still pitying herself in murmurs.*]

THE FLOWER GIRL: Poor girl! Hard enough for her to live without being worried and chivied.[2]

THE GENTLEMAN: [*Returning to his former place on the* NOTE TAKER'S *left.*] How do you do it, if I may ask?

THE NOTE TAKER: Simply phonetics. The science of speech. Thats my profession: also my hobby. Happy is the man who can make a living by his hobby! You can spot an Irishman or a Yorkshireman by his brogue. *I* can place any man within six miles. I can place him within two miles in London. Sometimes within two streets.

THE FLOWER GIRL: Ought to be ashamed of himself, unmanly coward!

THE GENTLEMAN: But is there a living in that?

THE NOTE TAKER: Oh yes. Quite a fat one. This is an age of upstarts. Men begin in Kentish Town with £80 a year, and end in Park Lane with a hundred thousand. They want to drop Kentish Town; but they give themselves away every time they open their mouths. Now I can teach them—

THE FLOWER GIRL: Let him mind his own business and leave a poor girl—

THE NOTE TAKER: [*Explosively.*] Woman: cease this detestable boohooing instantly; or else seek the shelter of some other place of worship.

THE FLOWER GIRL: [*With feeble defiance.*] Ive a right to be here if I like, same as you.

THE NOTE TAKER: A woman who utters such depressing and disgusting sounds has no right to be anywhere—no right to live. Remember that you are a human

---

1. Parish in Middlesex County, eight miles west of London.   2. Worried and hounded.

being with a soul and the divine gift of articulate speech: that your native language is the language of Shakespear and Milton and The Bible; and dont sit there crooning like a bilious pigeon.

THE FLOWER GIRL: [*Quite overwhelmed, looking up at him in mingled wonder and deprecation without daring to raise her head.*] Ah-ah-ah-ow-ow-ow-oo!

THE NOTE TAKER: [*Whipping out his book.*] Heavens! what a sound! [*He writes; then holds out the book and reads, reproducing her vowels exactly.*] Ah-ah-ah-ow-ow-ow-oo!

THE FLOWER GIRL: [*Tickled by the performance, and laughing in spite of herself.*] Garn!

THE NOTE TAKER: You see this creature with her kerbstone English: the English that will keep her in the gutter to the end of her days. Well, sir, in three months I could pass that girl off as a duchess at an ambassador's garden party. I could even get her a place as lady's maid or shop assistant, which requires better English.

THE FLOWER GIRL: Whats that you say?

THE NOTE TAKER: Yes, you squashed cabbage leaf, you disgrace to the noble architecture of these columns, you incarnate insult to the English language: I could pass you off as the Queen of Sheba. [*To the* GENTLEMAN.] Can you believe that?

THE GENTLEMAN: Of course I can. I am myself a student of Indian dialects; and—

THE NOTE TAKER: [*Eagerly.*] Are you? Do you know Colonel Pickering, the author of Spoken Sanscrit?

THE GENTLEMAN: I am Colonel Pickering. Who are you?

THE NOTE TAKER: Henry Higgins, author of Higgins's Universal Alphabet.

PICKERING: [*With enthusiasm.*] I came from India to meet you.

HIGGINS: I was going to India to meet you.

PICKERING: Where do you live?

HIGGINS: 27A Wimpole Street. Come and see me tomorrow.

PICKERING: I'm at the Carlton. Come with me now and lets have a jaw over some supper.

HIGGINS: Right you are.

THE FLOWER GIRL: [*To* PICKERING, *as he passes her.*] Buy a flower, kind gentleman. I'm short for my lodging.

PICKERING: I really havnt any change. I'm sorry. [*He goes away.*]

HIGGINS: [*Shocked at the* GIRL'*s mendacity.*] Liar. You said you could change half-a-crown.

THE FLOWER GIRL: [*Rising in desperation.*] You ought to be stuffed with nails, you ought. [*Flinging the basket at his feet.*] Take the whole blooming basket for sixpence.

[*The church clock strikes the second quarter.*]

HIGGINS: [*Hearing in it the voice of God, rebuking him for his Pharisaic want of charity to the poor* GIRL.] A reminder. [*He raises his hat solemnly; then throws a handful of money into the basket and follows* PICKERING.]

THE FLOWER GIRL: [*Picking up a half-crown.*] Ah-ow-ooh! [*Picking up a couple of flo-*

rins.[3]] Aaah-ow-ooh! [*Picking up several coins.*] Aaaaaah-ow-ooh! [*Picking up a half-sovereign.*[4]] Aaaaaaaaaaaaah-ow-ooh!!!

FREDDY: [*Springing out of a taxicab.*] Got one at last. Hallo! [*To the* GIRL.] Where are the two ladies that were here?

THE FLOWER GIRL: They walked to the bus when the rain stopped.

FREDDY: And left me with a cab on my hands! Damnation!

THE FLOWER GIRL: [*With grandeur.*] Never mind, young man. *I'm* going home in a taxi. [*She sails off to the cab. The driver puts his hand behind him and holds the door firmly shut against her. Quite understanding his mistrust, she shews him her handful of money.*] A taxi fare aint no object to me, Charlie. [*He grins and opens the door.*] Here. What about the basket?

THE TAXIMAN: Give it here. Tuppence extra.

LIZA: No: I dont want nobody to see it. [*She crushes it into the cab and gets in, continuing the conversation through the window.*] Goodbye, Freddy.

FREDDY: [*Dazedly raising his hat.*] Goodbye.

TAXIMAN: Where to?

LIZA: Bucknam Pellis [Buckingham Palace].

TAXIMAN: What d'ye mean—Bucknam Pellis?

LIZA: Dont you know where it is? In the Green Park, where the King lives. Goodbye, Freddy. Dont let me keep you standing there. Goodbye.

FREDDY: Goodbye. [*He goes.*].

TAXIMAN: Here? Whats this about Bucknam Pellis? What business have you at Bucknam Pellis?

LIZA: Of course I havnt none. But I wasnt going to let him know that. You drive me home.

TAXIMAN: And wheres home?

LIZA: Angel Court, Drury Lane, next Meiklejohn's oil shop.

TAXIMAN: That sounds more like it, Judy. [*He drives off.*]

Let us follow the taxi to the entrance to Angel Court, a narrow little archway between two shops, one of them Meiklejohn's oil shop. When it stops there, Eliza gets out, dragging her basket with her.

LIZA: How much?

TAXIMAN: [*Indicating the taximeter.*] Cant you read? A shilling.

LIZA: A shilling for two minutes!!

TAXIMAN: Two minutes or ten: it's all the same.

LIZA: Well, I dont call it right.

TAXIMAN: Ever been in a taxi before?

LIZA: [*With dignity.*] Hundreds and thousands of times, young man.

TAXIMAN: [*Laughing at her.*] Good for you, Judy. Keep the shilling, darling, with best love from all at home. Good luck! [*He drives off.*]

LIZA: [*Humiliated.*] Impidence!

----

3. Two shillings, loosely equivalent to two dollars in 1990s U.S. currency.   4. Ten shillings (half a pound), loosely equivalent to ten dollars in 1990s U.S. currency.

[*She picks up the basket and trudges up the alley with it to her lodging: a small room with very old wall paper hanging loose in the damp places. A broken pane in the window is mended with paper. A portrait of a popular actor and a fashion plate of ladies' dresses, all wildly beyond poor* ELIZA*'s means, both torn from newspapers, are pinned up on the wall. A birdcage hangs in the window; but its tenant died long ago: it remains as a memorial only.*

These are the only visible luxuries: the rest is the irreducible minimum of poverty's needs: a wretched bed heaped with all sorts of coverings that have any warmth in them, a draped packing case with a basin and jug on it and a little looking glass over it, a chair and table, the refuse of some suburban kitchen, and an American alarum clock on the shelf above the unused fireplace: the whole lighted with a gas lamp with a penny in the slot meter. Rent: four shillings a week.]

Here ELIZA, *chronically weary, but too excited to go to bed, sits, counting her new riches and dreaming and planning what to do with them, until the gas goes out, when she enjoys for the first time the sensation of being able to put in another penny without grudging it. This prodigal mood does not extinguish her gnawing sense of the need for economy sufficiently to prevent her from calculating that she can dream and plan in bed more cheaply and warmly than sitting up without a fire. So she takes off her shawl and skirt and adds them to the miscellaneous bedclothes. Then she kicks off her shoes and gets into bed without any further change.*

ACT II

Next day at 11 A.M. HIGGINS*'s laboratory in Wimpole Street. It is a room on the first floor, looking on the street, and was meant for the drawing room. The double doors are in the middle of the back wall; and persons entering find in the corner to their right two tall file cabinets at right angles to one another against the walls. In this corner stands a flat writing-table, on which are a phonograph, a laryngoscope, a row of tiny organ pipes with a bellows, a set of lamp chimneys for singing flames with burners attached to a gas plug in the wall by an indiarubber tube, several tuning-forks of different sizes, a life-size image of half a human head, shewing in section the vocal organs, and a box containing a supply of wax cylinders for the phonograph.*

Further down the room, on the same side, is a fireplace, with a comfortable leather-covered easy-chair at the side of the hearth nearest the door, and a coal-scuttle. There is a clock on the mantel-piece. Between the fireplace and the phonograph table is a stand for newspapers.

On the other side of the central door, to the left of the visitor, is a cabinet of shallow drawers. On it is a telephone and the telephone directory. The corner beyond, and most of the side wall, is occupied by a grand piano, with the keyboard at the end furthest from the door, and a bench for the player extending the full length of the keyboard. On the piano is a dessert dish heaped with fruit and sweets, mostly chocolates.

The middle of the room is clear. Besides the easy-chair, the piano bench, and two chairs at the phonograph table, there is one stray chair. It stands near the fireplace. On the walls, engravings: mostly Piranesis[5] and mezzotint portraits. No paintings.

PICKERING *is seated at the table, putting down some cards and a tuning-fork which he has been using.* HIGGINS *is standing up near him, closing two or three file drawers which are hanging out. He appears in the morning light as a robust, vital, appetizing sort of man of forty or thereabouts, dressed in a professional-looking black frock-coat with a white linen collar and black silk tie. He is of the energetic, scientific type, heartily, even violently interested in everything that can be studied as a scientific subject, and careless about himself and other people, including their feelings. He is, in fact, but for his years and size, rather like a very impetuous baby "taking notice" eagerly and loudly, and requiring almost as much watching to keep him out of unintended mischief. His manner varies from genial bullying when he is in a good humor to stormy petulance when anything goes wrong; but he is so entirely frank and void of malice that he remains likeable even in his least reasonable moments.*

HIGGINS: [*As he shuts the last drawer.*] Well, I think thats the whole show.

PICKERING: It's really amazing. I havnt taken half of it in, you know.

HIGGINS: Would you like to go over any of it again?

PICKERING: [*Rising and coming to the fireplace, where he plants himself with his back to the fire.*] No, thank you: not now. I'm quite done up for this morning.

HIGGINS: [*Following him, and standing beside him on his left.*] Tired of listening to sounds?

PICKERING: Yes. It's a fearful strain. I rather fancied myself because I can pronounce twenty-four distinct vowel sounds; but your hundred and thirty beat me. I cant hear a bit of difference between most of them.

HIGGINS: [*Chuckling, and going over to the piano to eat sweets.*] Oh, that comes with practice. You hear no difference at first; but you keep on listening, and presently you find theyre all as different as A from B. [MRS. PEARCE *looks in: she is* HIGGINS's *housekeeper*]. Whats the matter?

MRS. PEARCE: [*Hesitating, evidently perplexed.*] A young woman asks to see you, sir.

HIGGINS: A young woman! What does she want?

MRS. PEARCE: Well, sir, she says youll be glad to see her when you know what she's come about. She's quite a common girl, sir. Very common indeed. I should have sent her away, only I thought perhaps you wanted her to talk into your machines. I hope Ive not done wrong; but really you see such queer people sometimes—youll excuse me, I'm sure, sir—

HIGGINS: Oh, thats all right, Mrs. Pearce. Has she an interesting accent?

MRS. PEARCE: Oh, something dreadful, sir, really. I dont know how you can take an interest in it.

HIGGINS: [*To* PICKERING.] Lets have her up. Shew her up, Mrs. Pearce [*He rushes across to his working table and picks out a cylinder to use on the phonograph.*]

---

5. Giovanni Battista Piranesi (1720–1778), a Neoclassical master of etching whose prints of Roman architecture helped stimulate the eighteenth-century enthusiasm for the Classical style.

MRS. PEARCE: [*Only half resigned to it.*] Very well, sir. It's for you to say. [*She goes downstairs.*]

HIGGINS: This is rather a bit of luck. I'll shew you how I make records. We'll set her talking; and I'll take it down first in Bell's Visible Speech; then in broad Romic;[6] and then we'll get her on the phonograph so that you can turn her on as often as you like with the written transcript before you.

MRS. PEARCE: [*Returning.*] This is the young woman, sir.

> [*The* FLOWER GIRL *enters in state. She has a hat with three ostrich feathers, orange, sky-blue, and red. She has a nearly clean apron, and the shoddy coat has been tidied a little. The pathos of this deplorable figure, with its innocent vanity and consequential air, touches* PICKERING, *who has already straightened himself in the presence of* MRS. PEARCE. *But as to* HIGGINS, *the only distinction he makes between men and women is that when he is neither bullying nor exclaiming to the heavens against some feather-weight cross, he coaxes women as a child coaxes its nurse when it wants to get anything out of her.*]

HIGGINS: [*Brusquely, recognizing her with unconcealed disappointment, and at once, babylike, making an intolerable grievance of it.*] Why, this is the girl I jotted down last night. She's no use: Ive got all the records I want of the Lisson Grove lingo; and I'm not going to waste another cylinder on it. [*To the* GIRL.] Be off with you: I dont want you.

THE FLOWER GIRL: Dont you be so saucy. You aint heard what I come for yet. [*To* MRS. PEARCE, *who is waiting at the door for further instructions.*] Did you tell him I come in a taxi?

MRS. PEARCE: Nonsense, girl! what do you think a gentleman like Mr. Higgins cares what you came in?

THE FLOWER GIRL: Oh, we are proud! He aint above giving lessons, not him: I heard him say so. Well, I aint come here to ask for any compliment; and if my money's not good enough I can go elsewhere.

HIGGINS: Good enough for what?

THE FLOWER GIRL: Good enough for yə-oo. Now you know, dont you? I'm come to have lessons, I am. And to pay for em te-oo: make no mistake.

HIGGINS: [*Stupent.*][7] Well!!! [*Recovering his breath with a gasp.*] What do you expect me to say to you?

THE FLOWER GIRL: Well, if you was a gentleman, you might ask me to sit down, I think. Dont I tell you I'm bringing you business?

HIGGINS: Pickering: shall we ask this baggage to sit down, or shall we throw her out of the window?

THE FLOWER GIRL: [*Running away in terror to the piano, where she turns at bay.*] Ah-ah-oh-ow-ow-ow-oo! [*Wounded and whimpering.*] I wont be called a baggage when Ive offered to pay like any lady.

> [*Motionless, the* TWO MEN *stare at her from the other side of the room, amazed.*]

---

6. A system of phonetic transcription devised by Dr. Henry Sweet.   7. In a state of stupor or amazement.

PICKERING: [*Gently.*] But what is it you want?

THE FLOWER GIRL: I want to be a lady in a flower shop stead of sellin at the corner of Tottenham Court Road. But they wont take me unless I can talk more genteel. He said he could teach me. Well, here I am ready to pay him—not asking any favor—and he treats me zif I was dirt.

MRS. PEARCE: How can you be such a foolish ignorant girl as to think you could afford to pay Mr. Higgins?

THE FLOWER GIRL: Why shouldnt I? I know what lessons cost as well as you do; and I'm ready to pay.

HIGGINS: How much?

THE FLOWER GIRL: [*Coming back to him, triumphant.*] Now youre talking! I thought youd come off it when you saw a chance of getting back a bit of what you chucked at me last night. [*Confidentially.*] Youd had a drop in, hadnt you?

HIGGINS: [*Peremptorily.*] Sit down.

THE FLOWER GIRL: Oh, if youre going to make a compliment of it—

HIGGINS: [*Thundering at her.*] Sit down.

MRS. PEARCE: [*Severely.*] Sit down, girl. Do as youre told.

THE FLOWER GIRL: Ah-ah-ah-ow-ow-oo! [*She stands, half rebellious, half bewildered.*]

PICKERING: [*Very courteous.*] Wont you sit down? [*He places the stray chair near the hearthrug between himself and* HIGGINS.].

LIZA: [*Coyly.*] Dont mind if I do. [*She sits down.* PICKERING *returns to the hearthrug.*]

HIGGINS: Whats your name?

THE FLOWER GIRL: Liza Doolittle.

HIGGINS: [*Declaiming gravely.*]

> Eliza, Elizabeth, Betsy and Bess,
> They went to the woods to get a bird's nes':

PICKERING: They found a nest with four eggs in it:

HIGGINS: They took one apiece, and left three in it.

[*They laugh heartily at their own fun.*]

LIZA: Oh, dont be silly.

MRS. PEARCE: [*Placing herself behind* ELIZA's *chair.*] You mustnt speak to the gentleman like that.

LIZA: Well, why wont he speak sensible to me?

HIGGINS: Come back to business. How much do you propose to pay me for the lessons?

LIZA: Oh, I know whats right. A lady friend of mine gets French lessons for eighteenpence an hour from a real French gentleman. Well, you wouldnt have the face to ask me the same for teaching me my own language as you would for French; so I wont give more than a shilling. Take it or leave it.

HIGGINS: [*Walking up and down the room, rattling his keys and his cash in his pockets.*] You know, Pickering, if you consider a shilling, not as a simple shilling, but as a percentage of this girl's income, it works out as fully equivalent to sixty or seventy guineas from a millionaire.

PICKERING: How so?

HIGGINS: Figure it out. A millionaire has about £150 a day. She earns about half-a-crown.

LIZA: [*Haughtily.*] Who told you I only—

HIGGINS: [*Continuing.*] She offers me two-fifths of her day's income for a lesson. Two-fifths of a millionaire's income for a day would be somewhere about £60. It's handsome. By George, it's enormous! it's the biggest offer I ever had.

LIZA: [*Rising, terrified.*] Sixty pounds! What are you talking about? I never offered you sixty pounds. Where would I get—

HIGGINS: Hold your tongue.

LIZA: [*Weeping.*] But I aint got sixty pounds. Oh—

MRS. PEARCE: Dont cry, you silly girl. Sit down. Nobody is going to touch your money.

HIGGINS: Somebody is going to touch you, with a broomstick, if you dont stop snivelling. Sit down.

LIZA: [*Obeying slowly.*] Ah-ah-ah-ow-oo-o! One would think you was my father.

HIGGINS: If I decide to teach you, I'll be worse than two fathers to you. Here! [*He offers her his silk handkerchief.*]

LIZA: Whats this for?

HIGGINS: To wipe your eyes. To wipe any part of your face that feels moist. Remember: thats your handkerchief; and thats your sleeve. Dont mistake the one for the other if you wish to become a lady in a shop.

[LIZA, *utterly bewildered, stares helplessly at him.*]

MRS. PEARCE: It's no use talking to her like that, Mr. Higgins: she doesnt understand you. Besides, youre quite wrong: she doesnt do it that way at all. [*She takes the handkerchief.*]

LIZA: [*Snatching it*] Here! You give me that handkerchief. He gev it to me, not to you.

PICKERING: [*Laughing*] He did. I think it must be regarded as her property, Mrs. Pearce.

MRS. PEARCE: [*Resigning herself.*] Serve you right, Mr. Higgins.

PICKERING: Higgins: I'm interested. What about the ambassador's garden party? I'll say youre the greatest teacher alive if you make that good. I'll bet you all the expenses of the experiment you cant do it. And I'll pay for the lessons.

LIZA: Oh, you are real good. Thank you, Captain.

HIGGINS: [*Tempted, looking at her.*] It's almost irresistible. She's so deliciously low—so horribly dirty—

LIZA: [*Protesting extremely.*] Ah-ah-ah-ah-ow-ow-oo-oo!!! I aint dirty: I washed my face and hands afore I come, I did.

PICKERING: Youre certainly not going to turn her head with flattery, Higgins.

MRS. PEARCE: [*Uneasy.*] Oh, dont say that, sir: theres more ways than one of turning a girl's head; and nobody can do it better than Mr. Higgins, though he may not always mean it. I do hope, sir, you wont encourage him to do anything foolish.

HIGGINS: [*Becoming excited as the idea grows on him.*] What is life but a series of inspired follies? The difficulty is to find them to do. Never lose a chance: it doesnt come every day. I shall make a duchess of this draggletailed gutter-snipe.

LIZA: [*Strongly deprecating this view of her.*] Ah-ah-ah-ow-ow-oo!

HIGGINS: [*Carried away.*] Yes: in six months—in three if she has a good ear and a quick tongue—I'll take her anywhere and pass her off as anything. We'll start today: now! this moment! Take her away and clean her, Mrs. Pearce. Monkey Brand, if it wont come off any other way. Is there a good fire in the kitchen?

MRS. PEARCE: [*Protesting.*] Yes; but—

HIGGINS: [*Storming on.*] Take all her clothes off and burn them. Ring up Whiteley or somebody for new ones. Wrap her up in brown paper til they come.

LIZA: Youre no gentleman, youre not, to talk of such things. I'm a good girl, I am; and I know what the like of you are, I do.

HIGGINS: We want none of your Lisson Grove prudery here, young woman. Youve got to learn to behave like a duchess. Take her away, Mrs. Pearce. If she gives you any trouble, wallop her.

LIZA: [*Springing up and running between* PICKERING *and* MRS. PEARCE *for protection.*] No! I'll call the police, I will.

MRS. PEARCE: But Ive no place to put her.

HIGGINS: Put her in the dustbin.

LIZA: Ah-ah-ah-ow-ow-oo!

PICKERING: Oh come, Higgins! be reasonable.

MRS. PEARCE: [*Resolutely.*] You must be reasonable, Mr. Higgins: really you must. You cant walk over everybody like this.

[HIGGINS, *thus scolded, subsides. The hurricane is succeeded by a zephyr of amiable surprise.*]

HIGGINS: [*With professional exquisiteness of modulation.*] I walk over everybody! My dear Mrs. Pearce, my dear Pickering, I never had the slightest intention of walking over anyone. All I propose is that we should be kind to this poor girl. We must help her to prepare and fit herself for her new station in life. If I did not express myself clearly it was because I did not wish to hurt her delicacy, or yours.

[LIZA, *reassured, steals back to her chair.*]

MRS. PEARCE: [*To* PICKERING.] Well, did you ever hear anything like that, sir?

PICKERING: [*Laughing heartily.*] Never, Mrs. Pearce: never.

HIGGINS: [*Patiently.*] Whats the matter?

MRS. PEARCE: Well, the matter is, sir, that you cant take a girl up like that as if you were picking up a pebble on the beach.

HIGGINS: Why not?

MRS. PEARCE: Why not! But you dont know anything about her. What about her parents? She may be married.

LIZA: Garn!

HIGGINS: There! As the girl very properly says, Garn! Married indeed! Dont you know that a woman of that class looks a worn out drudge of fifty a year after she's married?

LIZA: Whood marry me?

HIGGINS: [*Suddenly resorting to the most thrillingly beautiful low tones in his best elocutionary style.*] By George, Eliza, the streets will be strewn with the bodies of men shooting themselves for your sake before Ive done with you.

MRS. PEARCE: Nonsense, sir. You mustnt talk like that to her.

LIZA: [*Rising and squaring herself determinedly.*] I'm going away. He's off his chump, he is. I dont want no balmies teaching me.

HIGGINS: [*Wounded in his tenderest point by her insensibility to his elocution.*] Oh, indeed! I'm mad, am I? Very well, Mrs. Pearce: you neednt order the new clothes for her. Throw her out.

LIZA: [*Whimpering.*] Nah-ow. You got no right to touch me.

MRS. PEARCE: You see now what comes of being saucy. [*Indicating the door.*] This way, please.

LIZA: [*Almost in tears.*] I didnt want no clothes. I wouldnt have taken them. [*She throws away the handkerchief.*] I can buy my own clothes.

HIGGINS: [*Deftly retrieving the handkerchief and intercepting her on her reluctant way to the door.*] Youre an ungrateful wicked girl. This is my return for offering to take you out of the gutter and dress you beautifully and make a lady of you.

MRS. PEARCE: Stop, Mr. Higgins. I wont allow it. It's you that are wicked. Go home to your parents, girl; and tell them to take better care of you.

LIZA: I aint got no parents. They told me I was big enough to earn my own living and turned me out.

MRS. PEARCE: Wheres your mother?

LIZA: I aint got no mother. Her that turned me out was my sixth stepmother. But I done without them. And I'm a good girl, I am.

HIGGINS: Very well, then, what on earth is all this fuss about? The girl doesnt belong to anybody—is no use of anybody but me. [*He goes to* MRS. PEARCE *and begins coaxing.*] You can adopt her, Mrs. Pearce: I'm sure a daughter would be a great amusement to you. Now dont make any more fuss. Take her downstairs; and—

MRS. PEARCE: But whats to become of her? Is she to be paid anything? Do be sensible, sir.

HIGGINS: Oh, pay her whatever is necessary: put it down in the housekeeping book. [*Impatiently.*] What on earth will she want with money? She'll have her food and her clothes. She'll only drink if you give her money.

LIZA: [*Turning on him.*] Oh you are a brute. It's a lie: nobody ever saw the sign of liquor on me. [*To* PICKERING.] Oh, sir: youre a gentleman: dont let him speak to me like that.

PICKERING: [*In good-humored remonstrance.*] Does it occur to you, Higgins, that the girl has some feelings?

HIGGINS: [*Looking critically at her.*] Oh no, I dont think so. Not any feelings that we need bother about. [*Cheerily.*] Have you, Eliza?

LIZA: I got my feelings same as anyone else.

HIGGINS: [*To* PICKERING, *reflectively.*] You see the difficulty?

PICKERING: Eh? What difficulty?

HIGGINS: To get her to talk grammar. The mere pronunciation is easy enough.

LIZA: I dont want to talk grammar. I want to talk like a lady in a flower-shop.

MRS. PEARCE: Will you please keep to the point, Mr. Higgins. I want to know on what terms the girl is to be here. Is she to have any wages? And what is to become of her when youve finished your teaching? You must look ahead a little.

HIGGINS: [*Impatiently.*] Whats to become of her if I leave her in the gutter? Tell me that, Mrs. Pearce.

MRS. PEARCE: Thats her own business, not yours, Mr. Higgins.

HIGGINS: Well, when Ive done with her, we can throw her back into the gutter; and then it will be her own business again; so thats all right.

LIZA: Oh, youve no feeling heart in you: you dont care for nothing but yourself. [*She rises and takes the floor resolutely.*] Here! Ive had enough of this. I'm going. [*Making for the door.*] You ought to be ashamed of yourself, you ought.

HIGGINS: [*Snatching a chocolate cream from the piano, his eyes suddenly beginning to twinkle with mischief.*] Have some chocolates, Eliza.

LIZA: [*Halting, tempted.*] How do I know what might be in them? Ive heard of girls being drugged by the like of you.

[HIGGINS *whips out his penknife; cuts a chocolate in two; puts one half into his mouth and bolts it; and offers her the other half.*]

HIGGINS: Pledge of good faith, Eliza. I eat one half: you eat the other. [LIZA *opens her mouth to retort: he pops the half chocolate into it.*] You shall have boxes of them, barrels of them, every day. You shall live on them. Eh?

LIZA: [*Who has disposed of the chocolate after being nearly choked by it.*] I wouldnt have ate it, only I'm too ladylike to take it out of my mouth.

HIGGINS: Listen, Eliza. I think you said you came in a taxi.

LIZA: Well, what if I did? Ive as good a right to take a taxi as anyone else.

HIGGINS: You have, Eliza; and in future you shall have as many taxis as you want. You shall go up and down and round the town in a taxi every day. Think of that, Eliza.

MRS. PEARCE: Mr. Higgins: youre tempting the girl. It's not right. She should think of the future.

HIGGINS: At her age! Nonsense! Time enough to think of the future when you havnt any future to think of. No, Eliza: do as this lady does: think of other people's futures; but never think of your own. Think of chocolates, and taxis, and gold, and diamonds.

LIZA: No: I dont want no gold and no diamonds. I'm a good girl, I am. [*She sits down again, with an attempt at dignity.*]

HIGGINS: You shall remain so, Eliza, under the care of Mrs. Pearce. And you shall marry an officer in the Guards, with a beautiful moustache: the son of a marquis, who will disinherit him for marrying you, but will relent when he sees your beauty and goodness—

PICKERING: Excuse me, Higgins; but I really must interfere. Mrs. Pearce is quite right. If this girl is to put herself in your hands for six months for an experiment in teaching, she must understand thoroughly what she's doing.

HIGGINS: How can she? She's incapable of understanding anything. Besides, do any of us understand what we are doing? If we did, would we ever do it?

PICKERING: Very clever, Higgins; but not to the present point. [*To* ELIZA.] Miss Doolittle—

LIZA: [*Overwhelmed.*] Ah-ah-ow-oo!

HIGGINS: There! Thats all youll get out of Eliza. Ah-ah-ow-oo! No use explaining. As a military man you ought to know that. Give her her orders: thats enough for her. Eliza: you are to live here for the next six months, learning how to speak beautifully, like a lady in a florist's shop. If youre good and do whatever youre told, you shall sleep in a proper bedroom, and have lots to eat, and money to buy chocolates and take rides in taxis. If youre naughty and idle you will sleep in the back kitchen among the black beetles, and be walloped by Mrs. Pearce with a broomstick. At the end of six months you shall go to Buckingham Palace in a carriage, beautifully dressed. If the King finds out youre not a lady, you will be taken by the police to the Tower of London, where your head will be cut off as a warning to other presumptuous flower girls. If you are not found out, you shall have a present of seven-and-sixpence to start life with as a lady in a shop. If you refuse this offer you will be a most ungrateful wicked girl; and the angels will weep for you. [*To* PICKERING.] Now are you satisfied, Pickering? [*To* MRS. PEARCE.] Can I put it more plainly and fairly, Mrs. Pearce?

MRS. PEARCE: [*Patiently.*] I think youd better let me speak to the girl properly in private. I dont know that I can take charge of her or consent to the arrangement at all. Of course I know you dont mean her any harm; but when you get what you call interested in people's accents, you never think or care what may happen to them or you. Come with me, Eliza.

HIGGINS: Thats all right. Thank you, Mrs. Pearce. Bundle her off to the bath-room.

LIZA: [*Rising reluctantly and suspiciously.*] Youre a great bully, you are. I wont stay here if I dont like. I wont let nobody wallop me. I never asked to go to Bucknam Palace, I didnt. I was never in trouble with the police, not me. I'm a good girl—

MRS. PEARCE: Dont answer back, girl. You dont understand the gentleman. Come with me. [*She leads the way to the door, and holds it open for* ELIZA.]

LIZA: [*As she goes out.*] Well, what I say is right. I wont go near the King, not if I'm going to have my head cut off. If I'd known what I was letting myself in for, I wouldnt have come here. I always been a good girl; and I never offered to say a word to him; and I dont owe him nothing; and I dont care; and I wont be put upon; and I have my feelings the same as anyone else—

[MRS. PEARCE *shuts the door; and* ELIZA*'s plaints are no longer audible.*]

ELIZA *is taken upstairs to the third floor greatly to her surprise; for she expected to be taken down to the scullery. There* MRS. PEARCE *opens a door and takes her into a spare bedroom.*

MRS. PEARCE: I will have to put you here. This will be your bedroom.

LIZA: O-h, I couldnt sleep here, missus. It's too good for the likes of me. I should be afraid to touch anything. I aint a duchess yet, you know.

MRS. PEARCE: You have got to make yourself as clean as the room: then you wont be afraid of it. And you must call me Mrs. Pearce, not missus. [*She throws open the door of the dressingroom, now modernized as a bathroom.*]

LIZA: Gawd! whats this? Is this where you wash clothes? Funny sort of copper I call it.

MRS. PEARCE: It is not a copper. This is where we wash ourselves, Eliza, and where I am going to wash you.

LIZA: You expect me to get into that and wet myself all over! Not me. I should catch my death. I knew a woman did it every Saturday night; and she died of it.

MRS. PEARCE: Mr. Higgins has the gentlemen's bathroom downstairs; and he has a bath every morning, in cold water.

LIZA: Ugh! He's made of iron, that man.

MRS. PEARCE: If you are to sit with him and the Colonel and be taught you will have to do the same. They wont like the smell of you if you dont. But you can have the water as hot as you like. There are two taps: hot and cold.

LIZA: [*Weeping.*] I couldnt. I dursnt. It's not natural: it would kill me. Ive never had a bath in my life: not what youd call a proper one.

MRS. PEARCE: Well, dont you want to be clean and sweet and decent, like a lady? You know you can't be a nice girl inside if youre a dirty slut outside.

LIZA: Boohoo!!!!

MRS. PEARCE: Now stop crying and go back into your room and take off all your clothes. Then wrap yourself in this [*Taking down a gown from its peg and handing it to her.*] and come back to me. I will get the bath ready.

LIZA: [*All tears.*] I cant. I wont. I'm not used to it. Ive never took off all my clothes before. It's not right: it's not decent.

MRS. PEARCE: Nonsense, child. Dont you take off all your clothes every night when you go to bed?

LIZA: [*Amazed.*] No. Why should I? I should catch my death. Of course I take off my skirt.

MRS. PEARCE: Do you mean that you sleep in the underclothes you wear in the daytime?

LIZA: What else have I to sleep in?

MRS. PEARCE: You will never do that again as long as you live here. I will get you a proper nightdress.

LIZA: Do you mean change into cold things and lie awake shivering half the night? You want to kill me, you do.

MRS. PEARCE: I want to change you from a frowzy slut to a clean respectable girl fit to sit with the gentlemen in the study. Are you going to trust me and do what I tell you or be thrown out and sent back to your flower basket?

LIZA: But you dont know what the cold is to me. You dont know how I dread it.

MRS. PEARCE: Your bed wont be cold here: I will put a hot water bottle in it. [*Pushing her into the bedroom.*] Off with you and undress.

LIZA: Oh, if only I'd a known what a dreadful thing it is to be clean I'd never have come. I didnt know when I was well off. I—[MRS. PEARCE *pushes her through the door, but leaves it partly open lest her prisoner should take to flight.*]

[MRS. PEARCE *puts on a pair of white rubber sleeves, and fills the bath, mixing hot and cold, and testing the result with the bath thermometer. She perfumes it with a handful of bath salts and adds a palmful of mustard. She then takes a formidable looking long handled scrubbing brush and soaps it profusely with a ball of scented soap.*

ELIZA *comes back with nothing on but the bath gown huddled tightly round her, a piteous spectacle of abject terror.*]

MRS. PEARCE: Now come along. Take that thing off.
LIZA: Oh I couldnt, Mrs. Pearce: I reely couldnt. I never done such a thing.
MRS. PEARCE: Nonsense. Here: step in and tell me whether it's hot enough for you.
LIZA: Ah-oo! Ah-oo! It's too hot.
MRS. PEARCE: [*Deftly snatching the gown away and throwing* ELIZA *down on her back.*] It wont hurt you. [*She sets to work with the scrubbing brush.*]

[ELIZA'*s screams are heartrending.*]

———————

Meanwhile the COLONEL *has been having it out with* HIGGINS *about* ELIZA. PICKERING *has come from the hearth to the chair and seated himself astride of it with his arms on the back to cross-examine him.*

PICKERING: Excuse the straight question, Higgins. Are you a man of good character where women are concerned?
HIGGINS: [*Moodily.*] Have you ever met a man of good character where women are concerned?
PICKERING: Yes: very frequently.
HIGGINS: [*Dogmatically, lifting himself on his hands to the level of the piano, and sitting on it with a bounce.*] Well, I havnt. I find that the moment I let a woman make friends with me, she becomes jealous, exacting, suspicious, and a damned nuisance. I find that the moment I let myself make friends with a woman, I become selfish and tyrannical. Women upset everything. When you let them into your life, you find that the woman is driving at one thing and youre driving at another.
PICKERING: At what, for example?
HIGGINS: [*Coming off the piano restlessly.*] Oh, Lord knows! I suppose the woman wants to live her own life; and the man wants to live his; and each tries to drag the other on to the wrong tack. One wants to go north and the other south; and the result is that both have to go east, though they both hate the east wind. [*He sits down on the bench at the keyboard.*] So here I am, a confirmed old bachelor, and likely to remain so.
PICKERING: [*Rising and standing over him gravely.*] Come, Higgins! You know what I mean. If I'm to be in this business I shall feel responsible for that girl. I hope it's understood that no advantage is to be taken of her position.

HIGGINS: What! That thing! Sacred, I assure you. [*Rising to explain.*] You see, she'll be a pupil; and teaching would be impossible unless pupils were sacred. Ive taught scores of American millionairesses how to speak English: the best looking women in the world. I'm seasoned. They might as well be blocks of wood. *I* might as well be a block of wood. It's—

[MRS. PEARCE *opens the door. She has* ELIZA's *hat in her hand.* PICKERING *retires to the easy-chair at the hearth and sits down.*]

HIGGINS: [*Eagerly.*] Well, Mrs. Pearce: is it all right?

MRS. PEARCE: [*At the door.*] I just wish to trouble you with a word, if I may, Mr. Higgins.

HIGGINS: Yes, certainly. Come in. [*She comes forward.*] Dont burn that, Mrs. Pearce. I'll keep it as a curiosity. [*He takes the hat.*]

MRS. PEARCE: Handle it carefully, sir, please. I had to promise her not to burn it; but I had better put it in the oven for a while.

HIGGINS: [*Putting it down hastily on the piano.*] Oh! thank you. Well, what have you to say to me?

PICKERING: Am I in the way?

MRS. PEARCE: Not at all, sir. Mr. Higgins: will you please be very particular what you say before the girl?

HIGGINS: [*Sternly.*] Of course. I'm always particular about what I say. Why do you say this to me?

MRS. PEARCE: [*Unmoved.*] No, sir: youre not at all particular when youve mislaid anything or when you get a little impatient. Now it doesnt matter before me: I'm used to it. But you really must not swear before the girl.

HIGGINS: [*Indignantly.*] I swear! [*Most emphatically.*] I never swear. I detest the habit. What the devil do you mean?

MRS. PEARCE: [*Stolidly.*] Thats what I mean, sir. You swear a great deal too much. I dont mind your damning and blasting, and what the devil and where the devil and who the devil—

HIGGINS: Mrs. Pearce: this language from your lips! Really!

MRS. PEARCE: [*Not to be put off.*]—but there is a certain word I must ask you not to use. The girl used it herself when she began to enjoy the bath. It begins with the same letter as bath. She knows no better: she learnt it at her mother's knee. But she must not hear it from your lips.

HIGGINS: [*Loftily.*] I cannot charge myself with having ever uttered it, Mrs. Pearce. [*She looks at him steadfastly. He adds, hiding an uneasy conscience with a judicial air.*] Except perhaps in a moment of extreme and justifiable excitement.

MRS. PEARCE: Only this morning, sir, you applied it to your boots, to the butter, and to the brown bread.

HIGGINS: Oh, that! Mere alliteration, Mrs. Pearce, natural to a poet.

MRS. PEARCE: Well, sir, whatever you choose to call it, I beg you not to let the girl hear you repeat it.

HIGGINS: Oh, very well, very well. Is that all?

MRS. PEARCE: No, sir. We shall have to be very particular with this girl as to personal cleanliness.

HIGGINS: Certainly. Quite right. Most important.

MRS. PEARCE: I mean not to be slovenly about her dress or untidy in leaving things about.

HIGGINS: [*Going to her solemnly.*] Just so. I intended to call your attention to that. [*He passes on to* PICKERING, *who is enjoying the conversation immensely.*] It is these little things that matter, Pickering. Take care of the pence and the pounds will take care of themselves is as true of personal habits as of money. [*He comes to anchor on the hearthrug, with the air of a man in an unassailable position.*]

MRS. PEARCE: Yes, sir. Then might I ask you not to come down to breakfast in your dressing-gown, or at any rate not to use it as a napkin to the extent you do, sir. And if you would be so good as not to eat everything off the same plate, and to remember not to put the porridge saucepan out of your hand on the clean tablecloth, it would be a better example to the girl. You know you nearly choked yourself with a fishbone in the jam only last week.

HIGGINS: [*Routed from the hearthrug and drifting back to the piano.*] I may do these things sometimes in absence of mind; but surely I dont do them habitually. [*Angrily.*] By the way: my dressing-gown smells most damnably of benzine.

MRS. PEARCE: No doubt it does, Mr. Higgins. But if you will wipe your fingers—

HIGGINS: [*Yelling.*] Oh very well, very well: I'll wipe them in my hair in future.

MRS. PEARCE: I hope youre not offended, Mr. Higgins.

HIGGINS: [*Shocked at finding himself thought capable of an unamiable sentiment.*] Not at all, not at all. Youre quite right, Mrs. Pearce: I shall be particularly careful before the girl. Is that all?

MRS. PEARCE: No, sir. Might she use some of those Japanese dresses you brought from abroad? I really cant put her back into her old things.

HIGGINS: Certainly. Anything you like. Is that all?

MRS. PEARCE: Thank you, sir. Thats all. [*She goes out.*]

HIGGINS: You know, Pickering, that woman has the most extraordinary ideas about me. Here I am, a shy, diffident sort of man. Ive never been able to feel really grown-up and tremendous, like other chaps. And yet she's firmly persuaded that I'm an arbitrary overbearing bossing kind of person. I cant account for it.

[MRS. PEARCE *returns.*]

MRS. PEARCE: If you please, sir, the trouble's beginning already. Theres a dustman downstairs, Alfred Doolittle, wants to see you. He says you have his daughter here.

PICKERING: [*Rising.*] Phew! I say!

HIGGINS: [*Promptly.*] Send the blackguard up.

MRS. PEARCE: Oh, very well, sir. [*She goes out.*]

PICKERING: He may not be a blackguard, Higgins.

HIGGINS: Nonsense. Of course he's a blackguard.

PICKERING: Whether he is or not, I'm afraid we shall have some trouble with him.

HIGGINS: [*Confidently.*] Oh no: I think not. If theres any trouble he shall have it with me, not I with him. And we are sure to get something interesting out of him.

PICKERING: About the girl?

HIGGINS: No. I mean his dialect.

PICKERING: Oh!

MRS. PEARCE: [*At the door.*] Doolittle, sir. [*She admits* DOOLITTLE *and retires.*]

> [ALFRED DOOLITTLE *is an elderly but vigorous dustman, clad in the costume of his profession, including a hat with a back brim covering his neck and shoulders. He has well marked and rather interesting features, and seems equally free from fear and conscience. He has a remarkably expressive voice, the result of a habit of giving vent to his feelings without reserve. His present pose is that of wounded honor and stern resolution.*]

DOOLITTLE: [*At the door, uncertain which of the two gentlemen is his man.*] Professor Iggins?

HIGGINS: Here. Good morning. Sit down.

DOOLITTLE: Morning, Governor. [*He sits down magisterially.*] I come about a very serious matter, Governor.

HIGGINS: [*To* PICKERING.] Brought up in Hounslow. Mother Welsh, I should think. [DOOLITTLE *opens his mouth, amazed.* HIGGINS *continues.*] What do you want, Doolittle?

DOOLITTLE: [*Menacingly.*] I want my daughter: thats what I want. See?

HIGGINS: Of course you do. Youre her father, arnt you? You dont suppose anyone else wants her, do you? I'm glad to see you have some spark of family feeling left. She's upstairs. Take her away at once.

DOOLITTLE: [*Rising, fearfully taken aback.*] What!

HIGGINS: Take her away. Do you suppose I'm going to keep your daughter for you?

DOOLITTLE: [*Remonstrating.*] Now, now, look here, Governor. Is this reasonable? Is it fairity to take advantage of a man like this? The girl belongs to me. You got her. Where do I come in? [*He sits down again.*]

HIGGINS: Your daughter had the audacity to come to my house and ask me to teach her how to speak properly so that she could get a place in a flower-shop. This gentleman and my housekeeper have been here all the time. [*Bullying him.*] How dare you come here and attempt to blackmail me? You sent her here on purpose.

DOOLITTLE: [*Protesting.*] No, Governor.

HIGGINS: You must have. How else could you possibly know that she is here?

DOOLITTLE: Dont take a man up like that, Governor.

HIGGINS: The police shall take you up. This is a plant—a plot to extort money by threats. I shall telephone for the police. [*He goes resolutely to the telephone and opens the directory.*]

DOOLITTLE: Have I asked you for a brass farthing? I leave it to the gentleman here: have I said a word about money?

HIGGINS: [*Throwing the book aside and marching down on* DOOLITTLE *with a poser.*] What else did you come for?

DOOLITTLE: [*Sweetly.*] Well, what would a man come for? Be human, Governor.

HIGGINS: [*Disarmed.*] Alfred: did you put her up to it?

DOOLITTLE: So help me, Governor, I never did. I take my Bible oath I aint seen the girl these two months past.

HIGGINS: Then how did you know she was here?

DOOLITTLE: [*"Most musical, most melancholy."*] I'll tell you, Governor, if youll only let me get a word in. I'm willing to tell you. I'm wanting to tell you. I'm waiting to tell you.

HIGGINS: Pickering: this chap has a certain natural gift of rhetoric. Observe the rhythm of his native woodnotes wild. "I'm willing to tell you: I'm wanting to tell you: I'm waiting to tell you." Sentimental rhetoric! thats the Welsh strain in him. It also accounts for his mendacity and dishonesty.

PICKERING: Oh, please, Higgins: I'm west country[8] myself. [*To* DOOLITTLE.] How did you know the girl was here if you didnt send her?

DOOLITTLE: It was like this, Governor. The girl took a boy in the taxi to give him a jaunt. Son of her landlady, he is. He hung about on the chance of her giving him another ride home. Well, she sent him back for her luggage when she heard you was willing for her to stop here. I met the boy at the corner of Long Acre and Endell Street.

HIGGINS: Public house. Yes?

DOOLITTLE: The poor man's club, Governor: why shouldnt I?

PICKERING: Do let him tell his story, Higgins.

DOOLITTLE: He told me what was up. And I ask you, what was my feelings and my duty as a father? I says to the boy, "You bring me the luggage," I says—

PICKERING: Why didnt you go for it yourself?

DOOLITTLE: Landlady wouldnt have trusted me with it, Governor. She's that kind of woman: you know. I had to give the boy a penny afore he trusted me with it, the little swine. I brought it to her just to oblige you like, and make myself agreeable. Thats all.

HIGGINS: How much luggage?

DOOLITTLE: Musical instrument, Governor. A few pictures, a trifle of jewlery, and a bird-cage. She said she didnt want no clothes. What was I to think from that, Governor? I ask you as a parent what was I to think?

HIGGINS: So you came to rescue her from worse than death, eh?

DOOLITTLE: [*Appreciatively: relieved at being so well understood.*] Just so, Governor. Thats right.

PICKERING: But why did you bring her luggage if you intended to take her away?

DOOLITTLE: Have I said a word about taking her away? Have I now?

HIGGINS: [*Determinedly.*] Youre going to take her away, double quick. [*He crosses to the hearth and rings the bell.*]

DOOLITTLE: [*Rising.*] No, Governor. Dont say that. I'm not the man to stand in my girl's light. Heres a career opening for her, as you might say; and—

[MRS. PEARCE *opens the door and awaits orders.*]

---

8. Wales is in west Britain.

HIGGINS: Mrs. Pearce: this is Eliza's father. He has come to take her away. Give her to him. [*He goes back to the piano, with an air of washing his hands of the whole affair.*]

DOOLITTLE: No. This is a misunderstanding. Listen here—

MRS. PEARCE: He cant take her away, Mr. Higgins: how can he? You told me to burn her clothes.

DOOLITTLE: Thats right. I cant carry the girl through the streets like a blooming monkey, can I? I put it to you.

HIGGINS: You have put it to me that you want your daughter. Take your daughter. If she has no clothes go out and buy her some.

DOOLITTLE: [*Desperate.*] Wheres the clothes she come in? Did I burn them or did your missus here?

MRS. PEARCE: I am the housekeeper, if you please. I have sent for some clothes for your girl. When they come you can take her away. You can wait in the kitchen. This way, please.

[DOOLITTLE, *much troubled, accompanies her to the door; then hesitates; finally turns confidentially to* HIGGINS.]

DOOLITTLE: Listen here, Governor. You and me is men of the world aint we?

HIGGINS: Oh! Men of the world, are we? Youd better go, Mrs. Pearce.

MRS. PEARCE: I think so, indeed, sir. [*She goes, with dignity.*]

PICKERING: The floor is yours, Mr. Doolittle.

DOOLITTLE: [*To* PICKERING] I thank you, Governor. [*To* HIGGINS, *who takes refuge on the piano bench, a little overwhelmed by the proximity of his visitor; for* DOOLITTLE *has a professional flavour of dust about him.*] Well, the truth is, Ive taken a sort of fancy to you, Governor; and if you want the girl, I'm not so set on having her back home again but what I might be open to an arrangement. Regarded in the light of a young woman, she's a fine handsome girl. As a daughter she's not worth her keep; and so I tell you straight. All I ask is my rights as a father; and youre the last man alive to expect me to let her go for nothing; for I can see youre one of the straight sort, Governor. Well, whats a five-pound note to you? and whats Eliza to me? [*He turns to his chair and sits down judicially.*]

PICKERING: I think you ought to know, Doolittle, that Mr. Higgins's intentions are entirely honorable.

DOOLITTLE: Course they are, Governor. If I thought they wasn't, I'd ask fifty.

HIGGINS: [*Revolted.*] Do you mean to say that you would sell your daughter for £50?

DOOLITTLE: Not in a general way I wouldnt; but to oblige a gentleman like you I'd do a good deal, I do assure you.

PICKERING: Have you no morals, man?

DOOLITTLE: [*Unabashed.*] Cant afford them, Governor. Neither could you if you was as poor as me. Not that I mean any harm, you know. But if Liza is going to have a bit out of this, why not me too?

HIGGINS: [*Troubled.*] I dont know what to do, Pickering. There can be no question that as a matter of morals it's a positive crime to give this chap a farthing. And yet I feel a sort of rough justice in his claim.

DOOLITTLE: Thats it, Governor. Thats all I say. A father's heart, as it were.

PICKERING: Well, I know the feeling; but really it seems hardly right—

DOOLITTLE: Dont say that, Governor. Dont look at it that way. What am I, Governors both? I ask you, what am I? I'm one of the undeserving poor: thats what I am. Think of what that means to a man. It means that he's up agen middle class morality all the time. If theres anything going, and I put in for a bit of it, it's always the same story: "Youre undeserving; so you cant have it." But my needs is as great as the most deserving widow's that ever got money out of six different charities in one week for the death of the same husband. I dont need less than a deserving man: I need more. I dont eat less hearty than him; and I drink a lot more. I want a bit of amusement, cause I'm a thinking man. I want cheerfulness and a song and a band when I feel low. Well, they charge me just the same for everything as they charge the deserving. What is middle class morality? Just an excuse for never giving me anything. Therefore, I ask you, as two gentlemen, not to play that game on me. I'm playing straight with you. I aint pretending to be deserving. I'm undeserving; and I mean to go on being undeserving. I like it; and thats the truth. Will you take advantage of a man's nature to do him out of the price of his own daughter what he's brought up and fed and clothed by the sweat of his brow until she's growed big enough to be interesting to you two gentlemen? Is five pounds unreasonable? I put it to you; and I leave it to you.

HIGGINS: [*Rising, and going over to* PICKERING.] Pickering: if we were to take this man in hand for three months, he could choose between a seat in the Cabinet and a popular pulpit in Wales.

PICKERING: What do you say to that, Doolittle?

DOOLITTLE: Not me, Governor, thank you kindly. Ive heard all the preachers and all the prime ministers—for I'm a thinking man and game for politics or religion or social reform same as all the other amusements—and I tell you it's a dog's life any way you look at it. Undeserving poverty is my line. Taking one station in society with another, it's—it's—well, it's the only one that has any ginger in it, to my taste.

HIGGINS: I suppose we must give him a fiver.

PICKERING: He'll make a bad use of it, I'm afraid.

DOOLITTLE: Not me, Governor, so help me I wont. Dont you be afraid that I'll save it and spare it and live idle on it. There wont be a penny of it left by Monday: I'll have to go to work same as if I'd never had it. It wont pauperize me, you bet. Just one good spree for myself and the missus, giving pleasure to ourselves and employment to others, and satisfaction to you to think it's not been throwed away. You couldnt spend it better.

HIGGINS: [*Taking out his pocket book and coming between* DOOLITTLE *and the piano.*] This is irresistible. Lets give him ten. [*He offers two notes to the* DUSTMAN.]

DOOLITTLE: No, Governor. She wouldnt have the heart to spend ten; and perhaps I shouldnt neither. Ten pounds is a lot of money: it makes a man feel prudent like; and then goodbye to happiness. You give me what I ask you, Governor: not a penny more, and not a penny less.

PICKERING: Why dont you marry that missus of yours? I rather draw the line at encouraging that sort of immorality.

DOOLITTLE: Tell her so, Governor: tell her so. I'm willing. It's me that suffers by it. Ive no hold on her. I got to be agreeable to her. I got to give her presents. I got to buy her clothes something sinful. I'm a slave to that woman, Governor, just because I'm not her lawful husband. And she knows it too. Catch her marrying me! Take my advice, Governor: marry Eliza while she's young and dont know no better. If you dont youll be sorry for it after. If you do, she'll be sorry for it after; but better her than you, because youre a man, and she's only a woman and dont know how to be happy anyhow.

HIGGINS: Pickering: if we listen to this man another minute, we shall have no convictions left. [To DOOLITTLE.] Five pounds I think you said.

DOOLITTLE: Thank you kindly, Governor.

HIGGINS: Youre sure you wont take ten?

DOOLITTLE: Not now. Another time, Governor.

HIGGINS: [Handing him a five-pound note.] Here you are.

DOOLITTLE: Thank you, Governor. Good morning. [He hurries to the door, anxious to get away with his booty. When he opens it he is confronted with a dainty and exquisitely clean young JAPANESE LADY in a simple blue cotton kimono printed cunningly with small white jasmine blossoms. MRS. PEARCE is with her. He gets out of her way deferentially and apologizes.] Beg pardon, miss.

THE JAPANESE LADY: Garn! Dont you know your own daughter?

DOOLITTLE:		Bly me! it's Eliza!
HIGGINS:	exclaiming simultaneously	Whats that? This!
PICKERING:		By Jove!

LIZA: Don't I look silly?

HIGGINS: Silly?

MRS. PEARCE: [At the door.] Now, Mr. Higgins, please dont say anything to make the girl conceited about herself.

HIGGINS: [Conscientiously.] Oh! Quite right, Mrs. Pearce. [To ELIZA.] Yes: damned silly.

MRS. PEARCE: Please, sir.

HIGGINS: [Correcting himself.] I mean extremely silly.

LIZA: I should look all right with my hat on. [She takes up her hat; puts it on; and walks across the room to the fireplace with a fashionable air.]

HIGGINS: A new fashion, by George! And it ought to look horrible!

DOOLITTLE: [With fatherly pride.] Well, I never thought she'd clean up as good looking as that, Governor. She's a credit to me, aint she?

LIZA: I tell you, it's easy to clean up here. Hot and cold water on tap, just as much as you like, there is. Woolly towels, there is; and a towel horse[9] so hot, it burns your fingers. Soft brushes to scrub yourself, and a wooden bowl of soap smelling like primroses. Now I know why ladies is so clean. Washing's a treat

---

9. Towel rack of pipes through which hot water runs, heating towels.

for them. Wish they could see what it is for the like of me!

HIGGINS: I'm glad the bathroom met with your approval.

LIZA: It didnt: not all of it; and I dont care who hears me say it. Mrs. Pearce knows.

HIGGINS: What was wrong, Mrs. Pearce?

MRS. PEARCE: [Blandly.] Oh, nothing, sir. It doesnt matter.

LIZA: I had a good mind to break it. I didnt know which way to look. But I hung a towel over it, I did.

HIGGINS: Over what?

MRS. PEARCE: Over the looking-glass, sir.

HIGGINS: Doolittle: you have brought your daughter up too strictly.

DOOLITTLE: Me! I never brought her up at all, except to give her a lick of a strap now and again. Dont put it on me, Governor. She aint accustomed to it, you see: thats all. But she'll soon pick up your free-and-easy ways.

LIZA: I'm a good girl, I am; and I wont pick up no free-and-easy ways.

HIGGINS: Eliza: if you say again that youre a good girl, your father shall take you home.

LIZA: Not him. You dont know my father. All he come here for was to touch you for some money to get drunk on.

DOOLITTLE: Well, what else would I want money for? To put into the plate in church, I suppose. [She puts out her tongue at him. He is so incensed by this that PICKERING presently finds it necessary to step between them.] Dont you give me none of your lip; and dont let me hear you giving this gentleman any of it neither, or youll hear from me about it. See?

HIGGINS: Have you any further advice to give her before you go, Doolittle? Your blessing, for instance.

DOOLITTLE: No, Governor: I aint such a mug as to put up my children to all I know myself. Hard enough to hold them in without that. If you want Eliza's mind improved, Governor, you do it yourself with a strap. So long, gentlemen. [He turns to go.]

HIGGINS: [Impressively.] Stop. Youll come regularly to see your daughter. It's your duty, you know. My brother is a clergyman; and he could help you in your talks with her.

DOOLITTLE: [Evasively.] Certainly, I'll come, Governor. Not just this week, because I have a job at a distance. But later on you may depend on me. Afternoon, gentlemen. Afternoon, maam. [He touches his hat to MRS. PEARCE, who disdains the salutation and goes out. He winks at HIGGINS, thinking him probably a fellow sufferer from MRS. PEARCE's difficult disposition, and follows her.]

LIZA: Dont you believe the old liar. He'd as soon you set a bulldog on him as a clergyman. You wont see him again in a hurry.

HIGGINS: I dont want to, Eliza. Do you?

LIZA: Not me. I dont want never to see him again, I dont. He's a disgrace to me, he is, collecting dust, instead of working at his trade.

PICKERING: What is his trade, Eliza?

LIZA: Talking money out of other people's pockets into his own. His proper trade's a navvy; and he works at it sometimes too—for exercise—and earns good money at it. Aint you going to call me Miss Doolittle any more?

PICKERING: I beg your pardon, Miss Doolittle. It was a slip of the tongue.

LIZA: Oh, I dont mind; only it sounded so genteel. I should just like to take a taxi to the corner of Tottenham Court Road and get out there and tell it to wait for me, just to put the girls in their place a bit. I wouldnt speak to them, you know.

PICKERING: Better wait til we get you something really fashionable.

HIGGINS: Besides, you shouldnt cut your old friends now that you have risen in the world. Thats what we call snobbery.

LIZA: You dont call the like of them my friends now, I should hope. Theyve took it out of me often enough with their ridicule when they had the chance; and now I mean to get a bit of my own back. But if I'm to have fashionable clothes, I'll wait. I should like to have some. Mrs. Pearce says youre going to give me some to wear in bed at night different to what I wear in the day-time; but it do seem a waste of money when you could get something to shew. Besides, I never could fancy changing into cold things on a winter night.

MRS. PEARCE: [*Coming back.*] Now, Eliza. The new things have come for you to try on.

LIZA: Ah-ow-oo-oooh! [*She rushes out.*]

MRS. PEARCE: [*Following her.*] Oh, don't rush about like that, girl. [*She shuts the door behind her.*]

HIGGINS: Pickering: we have taken on a stiff job.

PICKERING: [*With conviction.*] Higgins: we have.

There seems to be some curiosity as to what HIGGINS'*s lessons to* ELIZA *were like. Well, here is a sample: the first one.*

Picture ELIZA, *in her new clothes, and feeling her inside put out of step by a lunch, dinner, and breakfast of a kind to which it is unaccustomed, seated with* HIGGINS *and the* COLONEL *in the study, feeling like a hospital out-patient at a first encounter with the doctors.*

HIGGINS, *constitutionally unable to sit still, discomposes her still more by striding restlessly about. But for the reassuring presence and quietude of her friend the* COLONEL *she would run for her life, even back to Drury Lane.*

HIGGINS: Say your alphabet.

LIZA: I know my alphabet. Do you think I know nothing? I dont need to be taught like a child.

HIGGINS: [*Thundering.*] Say your alphabet.

PICKERING: Say it, Miss Doolittle. You will understand presently. Do what he tells you; and let him teach you in his own way.

LIZA: Oh well, if you put it like that—Ahyee, bəyee, cəyee, dəyee—

HIGGINS: [*With the roar of a wounded lion.*] Stop. Listen to this, Pickering. This is what we pay for as elementary education. This unfortunate animal has been locked up for nine years in school at our expense to teach her to speak and read the language of Shakespear and Milton. And the result is Ahyee, Bə-yee, Cə-yee, Də-yee. [*To* ELIZA.] Say A, B, C, D.

LIZA: [*Almost in tears.*] But I'm sayin it. Ahyee, Bəyee, Cə-yee—

HIGGINS: Stop. Say a cup of tea.

LIZA: A cappətə-ee.

HIGGINS: Put your tongue forward until it squeezes against the top of your lower teeth. Now say cup.

LIZA: C-c-c—I cant. C-Cup.

PICKERING: Good. Splendid, Miss Doolittle.

HIGGINS: By Jupiter, she's done it at the first shot. Pickering: We shall make a duchess of her. [*To* ELIZA.] Now do you think you could possibly say tea? Not tə-yee, mind: if you ever say bə-yee cə-yee də-yee again you shall be dragged round the room three times by the hair of your head. [*Fortissimo.*] T, T, T, T.

LIZA: [*Weeping.*] I cant hear no difference cep that it sounds more genteel-like when you say it.

HIGGINS: Well, if you can hear that difference, what the devil are you crying for? Pickering: give her a chocolate.

PICKERING: No, no. Never mind crying a little, Miss Doolittle: you are doing very well; and the lessons wont hurt. I promise you I wont let him drag you round the room by your hair.

HIGGINS: Be off with you to Mrs. Pearce and tell her about it. Think about it. Try to do it by yourself: and keep your tongue well forward in your mouth instead of trying to roll it up and swallow it. Another lesson at half-past four this afternoon. Away with you.

> [ELIZA, *still sobbing, rushes from the room.*]

And that is the sort of ordeal poor ELIZA *has to go through for months before we meet her again on her first appearance in London society of the professional class.*

ACT III

It is MRS. HIGGINS's *at-home day. Nobody has yet arrived. Her drawing room, in a flat on Chelsea Embankment, has three windows looking on the river; and the ceiling is not so lofty as it would be in an older house of the same pretension. The windows are open, giving access to a balcony with flowers in pots. If you stand with your face to the windows, you have the fireplace on your left and the door in the right-hand wall close to the corner nearest the windows.*

MRS. HIGGINS *was brought up on Morris and Burne Jones;*[1] *and her room, which is very unlike her son's room in Wimpole Street, is not crowded with furniture and little tables and nicknacks. In the middle of the room there is a big ottoman; and this, with the carpet, the Morris wall-papers, and the Morris chintz window curtains and brocade covers of the ottoman and its cushions, supply all the ornament, and are much too handsome to be hidden by odds and ends of useless things. A few good oil-paintings*

1. William Morris (1834–1896), poet, painter, designer, and leader in the nineteenth-century decorative arts; Edward Burne-Jones (1833–1898), late Pre-Raphaelite painter and associate of Morris's spartan aesthetic movement.

from the exhibitions in the Grosvenor Gallery thirty years ago (the Burne Jones, not the Whistler[2] side of them) are on the walls. The only landscape is a Cecil Lawson on the scale of a Rubens.[3] There is a portrait of MRS. HIGGINS *as she was when she defied fashion in her youth in one of the beautiful Rossettian[4] costumes which, when caricatured by people who did not understand, led to the absurdities of popular estheticism in the eighteen-seventies.*

In the corner diagonally opposite the door MRS. HIGGINS, *now over sixty and long past taking the trouble to dress out of the fashion, sits writing at an elegantly simple writing-table with a bell button within reach of her hand. There is a Chippendale chair further back in the room between her and the window nearest her side. At the other side of the room, further forward, is an Elizabethan chair roughly carved in the taste of Inigo Jones.[5] On the same side a piano in a decorated case. The corner between the fireplace and the window is occupied by a divan cushioned in Morris chintz.*

It is between four and five in the afternoon.

The door is opened violently; and HIGGINS *enters with his hat on.*

MRS. HIGGINS: [*Dismayed.*] Henry! [*Scolding him.*] What are you doing here today? It is my at-home day: you promised not to come. [*As he bends to kiss her, she takes his hat off, and presents it to him.*]

HIGGINS: Oh bother! [*He throws the hat down on the table.*]

MRS. HIGGINS: Go home at once.

HIGGINS: [*Kissing her.*] I know, mother. I came on purpose.

MRS. HIGGINS: But you mustnt. I'm serious, Henry. You offend all my friends: they stop coming whenever they meet you.

HIGGINS: Nonsense! I know I have no small talk; but people dont mind. [*He sits on the settee.*]

MRS. HIGGINS: Oh! dont they? Small talk indeed! What about your large talk? Really, dear, you mustnt stay.

HIGGINS: I must. Ive a job for you. A phonetic job.

MRS. HIGGINS: No use, dear. I'm sorry; but I cant get round your vowels; and though I like to get pretty postcards in your patent shorthand, I always have to read the copies in ordinary writing you so thoughtfully send me.

HIGGINS: Well, this isnt a phonetic job.

MRS. HIGGINS: You said it was.

HIGGINS: Not your part of it. Ive picked up a girl.

MRS. HIGGINS: Does that mean that some girl has picked you up?

HIGGINS: Not at all. I dont mean a love affair.

MRS. HIGGINS: What a pity!

HIGGINS: Why?

---

2. James A. McNeill Whistler (1834–1903), American painter whose early work was associated with the realism of Courbet et al., and thus antithetical to the Pre-Raphaelite influences associated with Burne-Jones.   3. Cecil Lawson (1851–1882), English landscape painter. Peter Paul Rubens (1577–1640), a Flemish painter of the Baroque style, known for tremendously dynamic, violent, and powerful works. 4. After Dante Gabriel Rossetti, (1828–1882), a Pre-Raphaelite painter whose subject matter was exotically beautiful women from medieval literature and romantic legend.   5. Inigo Jones (1573–1652), architect to James I and Charles I, responsible for England's move toward Italian Renaissance architectural principles in the early seventeenth century.

MRS. HIGGINS: Well, you never fall in love with anyone under forty-five. When will you discover that there are some rather nice-looking young women about?

HIGGINS: Oh, I cant be bothered with young women. My idea of a lovable woman is somebody as like you as possible. I shall never get into the way of seriously liking young women: some habits lie too deep to be changed. [*Rising abruptly and walking about, jingling his money and his keys in his trouser pockets.*] Besides, theyre all idiots.

MRS. HIGGINS: Do you know what you would do if you really loved me, Henry?

HIGGINS: Oh bother! What? Marry, I suppose.

MRS. HIGGINS: No. Stop fidgeting and take your hands out of your pockets. [*With a gesture of despair, he obeys and sits down again.*] Thats a good boy. Now tell me about the girl.

HIGGINS: She's coming to see you.

MRS. HIGGINS: I dont remember asking her.

HIGGINS: You didnt. *I* asked her. If youd known her you wouldnt have asked her.

MRS. HIGGINS: Indeed! Why?

HIGGINS: Well, it's like this. She's a common flower girl. I picked her off the kerbstone.

MRS. HIGGINS: And invited her to my at-home!

HIGGINS: [*Rising and coming to her to coax her.*] Oh, thatll be all right. Ive taught her to speak properly; and she has strict orders as to her behavior. She's to keep to two subjects: the weather and everybody's health—Fine day and How do you do, you know—and not to let herself go on things in general. That will be safe.

MRS. HIGGINS: Safe! To talk about our health! about our insides! perhaps about our outsides! How could you be so silly, Henry?

HIGGINS: [*Impatiently.*] Well, she must talk about something. [*He controls himself and sits down again.*] Oh, she'll be all right: dont you fuss. Pickering is in it with me. Ive a sort of bet on that I'll pass her off as a duchess in six months. I started on her some months ago; and she's getting on like a house on fire. I shall win my bet. She has a quick ear; and she's been easier to teach than my middle-class pupils because she's had to learn a complete new language. She talks English almost as you talk French.

MRS. HIGGINS: Thats satisfactory, at all events.

HIGGINS: Well, it is and it isnt.

MRS. HIGGINS: What does that mean?

HIGGINS: You see, Ive got her pronunciation all right; but you have to consider not only how a girl pronounces, but what she pronounces; and that's where—

[*They are interrupted by the* PARLORMAID, *announcing guests.*]

THE PARLORMAID: Mrs. and Miss Eynsford Hill. [*She withdraws.*]

HIGGINS: Oh Lord! [*He rises; snatches his hat from the table; and makes for the door; but before he reaches it his mother introduces him.*]

[MRS. *and* MISS EYNSFORD HILL *are the mother and daughter who sheltered from the rain in Covent Garden. The mother is well bred, quiet, and has the habit-*

ual anxiety of straitened means. The daughter has acquired a gay air of being very much at home in society: the bravado of genteel poverty.]

MRS. EYNSFORD HILL: [*To* MRS. HIGGINS.] How do you do? [*They shake hands.*]

MISS EYNSFORD HILL: How d'you do? [*She shakes.*]

MRS. HIGGINS: [*Introducing.*] My son Henry.

MRS. EYNSFORD HILL: Your celebrated son! I have so longed to meet you, Professor Higgins.

HIGGINS: [*Glumly, making no movement in her direction.*] Delighted. [*He backs against the piano and bows brusquely.*]

MISS EYNSFORD HILL: [*Going to him with confident familiarity.*] How do you do?

HIGGINS: [*Staring at her.*] Ive seen you before somewhere. I havnt the ghost of a notion where; but Ive heard your voice. [*Drearily.*] It doesnt matter. Youd better sit down.

MRS. HIGGINS: I'm sorry to say that my celebrated son has no manners. You mustnt mind him.

MISS EYNSFORD HILL: [*Gaily.*] I dont. [*She sits in the Elizabethan chair.*]

MRS. EYNSFORD HILL: [*A little bewildered.*] Not at all. [*She sits on the ottoman between her* DAUGHTER *and* MRS. HIGGINS, *who has turned her chair away from the writing-table.*]

HIGGINS: Oh, have I been rude? I didnt mean to be.

[*He goes to the central window, through which, with his back to the company, he contemplates the river and the flowers in Battersea Park on the opposite bank as if they were a frozen desert.*

The PARLORMAID *returns, ushering in* PICKERING.]

THE PARLORMAID: Colonel Pickering. [*She withdraws.*]

PICKERING: How do you do, Mrs. Higgins?

MRS. HIGGINS: So glad youve come. Do you know Mrs. Eynsford Hill—Miss Eynsford Hill? [*Exchange of bows. The* COLONEL *brings the Chippendale chair a little forward between* MRS. HILL *and* MRS. HIGGINS, *and sits down.*]

PICKERING: Has Henry told you what weve come for?

HIGGINS: [*Over his shoulder.*] We were interrupted: damn it!

MRS. HIGGINS: Oh Henry, Henry, really!

MRS. EYNSFORD HILL: [*Half rising.*] Are we in the way?

MRS. HIGGINS: [*Rising and making her sit down again.*] No, no. You couldnt have come more fortunately: we want you to meet a friend of ours.

HIGGINS: [*Turning hopefully.*] Yes, by George! We want two or three people. Youll do as well as anybody else.

[*The* PARLORMAID *returns, ushering* FREDDY.]

THE PARLORMAID: Mr. Eynsford Hill.

HIGGINS: [*Almost audibly, past endurance.*] God of Heaven! another of them.

FREDDY: [*Shaking hands with* MRS. HIGGINS.] Ahdedo?

MRS. HIGGINS: Very good of you to come. [*Introducing.*] Colonel Pickering.

FREDDY: [*Bowing.*] Ahdedo?

MRS. HIGGINS: I dont think you know my son, Professor Higgins.

FREDDY: [*Going to* HIGGINS.] Ahdedo?

HIGGINS: [*Looking at him much as if he were a pickpocket.*] I'll take my oath Ive met you before somewhere. Where was it?

FREDDY: I dont think so.

HIGGINS: [*Resignedly.*] It dont matter, anyhow. Sit down.

> [*He shakes* FREDDY's *hand, and almost slings him on to the ottoman with his face to the windows; then comes round to the other side of it.*]

HIGGINS: Well, here we are, anyhow! [*He sits down on the ottoman next to* FREDDY.] And now what the devil are we going to talk about until Eliza comes?

MRS. HIGGINS: Henry: you are the life and soul of the Royal Society's soirées; but really youre rather trying on more commonplace occasions.

HIGGINS: Am I? Very sorry. [*Beaming suddenly.*] I suppose I am, you know. [*Uproariously.*] Ha, ha!

MISS EYNSFORD HILL: [*Who considers* HIGGINS *quite eligible matrimonially.*] I sympathize. *I* havnt any small talk. If people would only be frank and say what they really think!

HIGGINS: [*Relapsing into gloom.*] Lord forbid!

MRS. EYNSFORD HILL: [*Taking up her daughter's cue.*] But why?

HIGGINS: What they think they ought to think is bad enough, Lord knows; but what they really think would break up the whole show. Do you suppose it would be really agreeable if I were to come out now with what *I* really think?

MISS EYNSFORD HILL: [*Gaily.*] Is it so very cynical?

HIGGINS: Cynical! Who the dickens said it was cynical? I mean it wouldnt be decent.

MRS. EYNSFORD HILL: [*Seriously.*] Oh! I'm sure you dont mean that, Mr. Higgins.

HIGGINS: You see, we're all savages, more or less. We're supposed to be civilized and cultured—to know all about poetry and philosophy and art and science, and so on; but how many of us know even the meanings of these names? [*To* MISS HILL.] What do you know of poetry? [*To* MRS. HILL.] What do you know of science? [*Indicating* FREDDY.] What does he know of art or science or anything else? What the devil do you imagine I know of philosophy?

MRS. HIGGINS: [*Warningly.*] Or of manners, Henry?

THE PARLORMAID: [*Opening the door.*] Miss Doolittle. [*She withdraws.*]

HIGGINS: [*Rising hastily and running to* MRS. HIGGINS.] Here she is, mother. [*He stands on tiptoe and makes signs over his mother's head to* ELIZA *to indicate to her which lady is her hostess.*]

> [ELIZA, *who is exquisitely dressed, produces an impression of such remarkable distinction and beauty as she enters that they all rise, quite fluttered. Guided by* HIGGINS's *signals, she comes to* MRS. HIGGINS *with studied grace.*]

LIZA: [*Speaking with pedantic correctness of pronunciation and great beauty of tone.*] How do you do, Mrs. Higgins? [*She gasps slightly in making sure of the H in Higgins, but is quite successful.*] Mr. Higgins told me I might come.

MRS. HIGGINS: [*Cordially.*] Quite right: I'm very glad indeed to see you.

PICKERING: How do you do, Miss Doolittle?

LIZA: [*Shaking hands with him.*] Colonel Pickering, is it not?

MRS. EYNSFORD HILL: I feel sure we have met before, Miss Doolittle. I remember your eyes.

LIZA: How do you do? [*She sits down on the ottoman gracefully in the place just left vacant by* HIGGINS.]

MRS. EYNSFORD HILL: [*Introducing.*] My daughter Clara.

LIZA: How do you do?

CLARA: [*Impulsively.*] How do you do? [*She sits down on the ottoman beside* ELIZA, *devouring her with her eyes.*]

FREDDY: [*Coming to their side of the ottoman.*] Ive certainly had the pleasure.

MRS. EYNSFORD HILL: [*Introducing.*] My son Freddy.

LIZA: How do you do?

[FREDDY *bows and sits down in the Elizabethan chair, infatuated.*]

HIGGINS: [*Suddenly.*] By George, yes: it all comes back to me! [*They stare at him.*] Covent Garden! [*Lamentably.*] What a damned thing!

MRS. HIGGINS: Henry, please! [*He is about to sit on the edge of the table.*] Dont sit on my writing-table: youll break it.

HIGGINS: [*Sulkily.*] Sorry.

[*He goes to the divan, stumbling into the fender and over the fire-irons on his way; extricating himself with muttered imprecations; and finishing his disastrous journey by throwing himself so impatiently on the divan that he almost breaks it.* MRS. HIGGINS *looks at him, but controls herself and says nothing.*

A long and painful pause ensues.]

MRS. HIGGINS: [*At last, conversationally.*] Will it rain, do you think?

LIZA: The shallow depression in the west of these islands is likely to move slowly in an easterly direction. There are no indications of any great change in the barometrical situation.

FREDDY: Ha! ha! how awfully funny!

LIZA: What is wrong with that, young man? I bet I got it right.

FREDDY: Killing!

MRS. EYNSFORD HILL: I'm sure I hope it wont turn cold. Theres so much influenza about. It runs right through our whole family regularly every spring.

LIZA: [*Darkly.*] My aunt died of influenza: so they said.

MRS. EYNSFORD HILL: [*Clicks her tongue sympathetically.*]!!!

LIZA: [*In the same tragic tone.*] But it's my belief they done the old woman in.

MRS. HIGGINS: [*Puzzled.*] Done her in?

LIZA: Y-e-e-e-es, Lord love you! Why should she die of influenza? She come through diptheria right enough the year before. I saw her with my own eyes. Fairly blue with it, she was. They all thought she was dead; but my father he kept ladling gin down her throat til she came to so sudden that she bit the bowl off the spoon.

MRS. EYNSFORD HILL: [*Startled.*] Dear me!

LIZA: [*Piling up the indictment.*] What call would a woman with that strength in her have to die of influenza? What become of her new straw hat that should have come to me? Somebody pinched it; and what I say is, them as pinched it done her in.

MRS. EYNSFORD HILL: What does doing her in mean?

HIGGINS: [*Hastily.*] Oh, thats the new small talk. To do a person in means to kill them.

MRS. EYNSFORD HILL: [*To* ELIZA, *horrified.*] You surely dont believe that your aunt was killed?

LIZA: Do I not! Them she lived with would have killed her for a hat-pin, let alone a hat.

MRS. EYNSFORD HILL: But it cant have been right for your father to pour spirits down her throat like that. It might have killed her.

LIZA: Not her. Gin was mother's milk to her. Besides, he'd poured so much down his own throat that he knew the good of it.

MRS. EYNSFORD HILL: Do you mean that he drank?

LIZA: Drank! My word! Something chronic.

MRS. EYNSFORD HILL: How dreadful for you!

LIZA: Not a bit. It never did him no harm what I could see. But then he did not keep it up regular. [*Cheerfully.*] On the burst, as you might say, from time to time. And always more agreeable when he had a drop in. When he was out of work, my mother used to give him fourpence and tell him to go out and not come back until he'd drunk himself cheerful and loving-like. Theres lots of women has to make their husbands drunk to make them fit to live with. [*Now quite at her ease.*] You see, it's like this. If a man has a bit of a conscience, it always takes him when he's sober; and then it makes him low-spirited. A drop of booze just takes that off and makes him happy. [*To* FREDDY, *who is in convulsions of suppressed laughter.*] Here! what are you sniggering at?

FREDDY: The new small talk. You do it so awfully well.

LIZA: If I was doing it proper, what was you laughing at? [*To* HIGGINS.] Have I said anything I oughtnt?

MRS. HIGGINS: [*Interposing.*] Not at all, Miss Doolittle.

LIZA: Well, thats a mercy, anyhow. [*Expansively.*] What I always say is—

HIGGINS: [*Rising and looking at his watch.*] Ahem!

LIZA: [*Looking round at him; taking the hint; and rising.*] Well: I must go. [*They all rise.* FREDDY *goes to the door.*] So pleased to have met you. Goodbye. [*She shakes hands with* MRS. HIGGINS.]

MRS. HIGGINS: Goodbye.

LIZA: Goodbye, Colonel Pickering.

PICKERING: Goodbye, Miss Doolittle. [*They shake hands.*]

LIZA: [*Nodding to the others.*] Goodbye, all.

FREDDY: [*Opening the door for her.*] Are you walking across the Park, Miss Doolittle? If so—

LIZA: [*With perfectly elegant diction.*] Walk! Not bloody likely. [*Sensation.*] I am going in a taxi. [*She goes out.*]

[PICKERING *gasps and sits down.* FREDDY *goes out on the balcony to catch another glimpse of* ELIZA.]

MRS. EYNSFORD HILL: [*Suffering from shock.*] Well, I really cant get used to the new ways.

CLARA: [*Throwing herself discontentedly into the Elizabethan chair.*] Oh, it's all right, mamma, quite right. People will think we never go anywhere or see anybody if you are so old-fashioned.

MRS. EYNSFORD HILL: I daresay I am very old-fashioned; but I do hope you wont begin using that expression, Clara. I have got accustomed to hear you talking about men as rotters, and calling everything filthy and beastly; though I do think it horrible and unladylike. But this last is really too much. Dont you think so, Colonel Pickering?

PICKERING: Dont ask me. Ive been away in India for several years; and manners have changed so much that I sometimes dont know whether I'm at a respectable dinner-table or in a ship's forecastle.

CLARA: It's all a matter of habit. Theres no right or wrong in it. Nobody means anything by it. And it's so quaint, and gives such a smart emphasis to things that are not in themselves very witty. I find the new small talk delightful and quite innocent.

MRS. EYNSFORD HILL: [*Rising.*] Well, after that, I think it's time for us to go.

[PICKERING *and* HIGGINS *rise.*]

CLARA: [*Rising.*] Oh yes: we have three at-homes to go to still. Goodbye, Mrs. Higgins. Goodbye, Colonel Pickering. Goodbye, Professor Higgins.

HIGGINS: [*Coming grimly at her from the divan, and accompanying her to the door.*] Goodbye. Be sure you try on that small talk at the three at-homes. Dont be nervous about it. Pitch it in strong.

CLARA: [*All smiles.*] I will. Goodbye. Such nonsense, all this early Victorian prudery!

HIGGINS: [*Tempting her.*] Such damned nonsense!

CLARA: Such bloody nonsense!

MRS. EYNSFORD HILL: [*Convulsively.*] Clara!

CLARA: Ha! ha! [*She goes out radiant, conscious of being thoroughly up to date, and is heard descending the stairs in a stream of silvery laughter.*]

FREDDY: [*To the heavens at large.*] Well, I ask you— [*He gives it up, and comes to* MRS. HIGGINS.] Goodbye.

MRS. HIGGINS: [*Shaking hands.*] Goodbye. Would you like to meet Miss Doolittle again?

FREDDY: [*Eagerly.*] Yes, I should, most awfully.

MRS. HIGGINS: Well, you know my days.

FREDDY: Yes. Thanks awfully. Goodbye. [*He goes out.*]

MRS. EYNSFORD HILL: Goodbye, Mr. Higgins.

HIGGINS: Goodbye. Goodbye.

MRS. EYNSFORD HILL: [*To* PICKERING.] It's no use. I shall never be able to bring myself to use that word.

PICKERING: Dont. It's not compulsory, you know. Youll get on quite well without it.

MRS. EYNSFORD HILL: Only, Clara is so down on me if I am not positively reeking with the latest slang. Goodbye.

PICKERING: Goodbye. [*They shake hands.*]

MRS. EYNSFORD HILL: [*To* MRS. HIGGINS.] You mustnt mind Clara. [PICKERING, *catching from her lowered tone that this is not meant for him to hear, discreetly joins* HIGGINS *at the window.*] We're so poor! and she gets so few parties, poor child! She doesnt quite know. [MRS. HIGGINS, *seeing that her eyes are moist, takes her hand sympathetically and goes with her to the door.*] But the boy is nice. Dont you think so?

MRS. HIGGINS: Oh, quite nice. I shall always be delighted to see him.

MRS. EYNSFORD HILL: Thank you, dear. Goodbye. [*She goes out.*]

HIGGINS: [*Eagerly.*] Well? Is Eliza presentable? [*He swoops on his mother and drags her to the ottoman, where she sits down in* ELIZA'*s place with her son on her left.*]

[PICKERING *returns to his chair on her right.*]

MRS. HIGGINS: You silly boy, of course she's not presentable. She's a triumph of your art and of her dressmaker's; but if you suppose for a moment that she doesnt give herself away in every sentence she utters, you must be perfectly cracked about her.

PICKERING: But dont you think something might be done? I mean something to eliminate the sanguinary element from her conversation.

MRS. HIGGINS: Not as long as she is in Henry's hands.

HIGGINS: [*Aggrieved.*] Do you mean that my language is improper?

MRS. HIGGINS: No, dearest: it would be quite proper—say on a canal barge; but it would not be proper for her at a garden party.

HIGGINS: [*Deeply injured.*] Well I must say—

PICKERING: [*Interrupting him.*] Come, Higgins: you must learn to know yourself. I havnt heard such language as yours since we used to review the volunteers in Hyde Park twenty years ago.

HIGGINS: [*Sulkily.*] Oh, well, if you say so, I suppose I dont always talk like a bishop.

MRS. HIGGINS: [*Quieting* HENRY *with a touch.*] Colonel Pickering: will you tell me what is the exact state of things in Wimpole Street?

PICKERING: [*Cheerfully: as if this completely changed the subject.*] Well, I have come to live there with Henry. We work together at my Indian Dialects; and we think it more convenient—

MRS. HIGGINS: Quite so. I know all about that: it's an excellent arrangement. But where does this girl live?

HIGGINS: With us, of course. Where should she live?

MRS. HIGGINS: But on what terms? Is she a servant? If not, what is she?

PICKERING: [*Slowly.*] I think I know what you mean, Mrs. Higgins.

HIGGINS: Well, dash me if *I* do! Ive had to work at the girl every day for months to get her to her present pitch. Besides, she's useful. She knows where my things are, and remembers my appointments and so forth.

MRS. HIGGINS: How does your housekeeper get on with her?

HIGGINS: Mrs. Pearce? Oh, she's jolly glad to get so much taken off her hands; for before Eliza came, she used to have to find things and remind me of my appointments. But she's got some silly bee in her bonnet about Eliza. She keeps saying "You dont think, sir": doesnt she, Pick?

PICKERING: Yes: thats the formula. "You dont think, sir." Thats the end of every conversation about Eliza.

HIGGINS: As if I ever stop thinking about the girl and her confounded vowels and consonants. I'm worn out, thinking about her, and watching her lips and her teeth and her tongue, not to mention her soul, which is the quaintest of the lot.

MRS. HIGGINS: You certainly are a pretty pair of babies, playing with your live doll.

HIGGINS: Playing! The hardest job I ever tackled: make no mistake about that, mother. But you have no idea how frightfully interesting it is to take a human being and change her into a quite different human being by creating a new speech for her. It's filling up the deepest gulf that separates class from class and soul from soul.

PICKERING: [*Drawing his chair closer to* MRS. HIGGINS *and bending over to her eagerly.*] Yes: it's enormously interesting. I assure you, Mrs. Higgins, we take Eliza very seriously. Every week—every day almost—there is some new change. [*Closer again.*] We keep records of every stage—dozens of gramophone disks and photographs—

HIGGINS: [*Assailing her at the other ear.*] Yes, by George: it's the most absorbing experiment I ever tackled. She regularly fills our lives up: doesnt she, Pick?

PICKERING: We're always talking Eliza.

HIGGINS: Teaching Eliza.

PICKERING: Dressing Eliza.

MRS. HIGGINS: What!

HIGGINS: Inventing new Elizas.

HIGGINS:	[*Speaking together.*]	You now, she has the most extraordinary quickness of ear:
PICKERING:		I assure you, my dear Mrs. Higgins, that girl
HIGGINS:		just like a parrot. Ive tried her with every
PICKERING:		is a genius. She can play the piano quite beautifully.
HIGGINS:		possible sort of sound that a human being can make
PICKERING:		We have taken her to classical concerts and to music
HIGGINS:		Continental dialects, African dialects, Hottentot
PICKERING:		halls; and it's all the same to her: she plays every-thing
HIGGINS:	[*Speaking together.*]	clicks, things it took me years to get hold of; and
PICKERING:		she hears right off when she comes home, whether it's
HIGGINS:		she picks them up like a shot, right away, as if she had
PICKERING:		Beethoven and Brahms or Lehar and Lionel Monckton;[6]
HIGGINS:		been at it all her life.
PICKERING:		though six months ago, she'd never as much as touched a piano—

6. German composers Ludwig van Beethoven (1770–1827) and Johannes Brahms (1833–1897); Hungarian operetta composer Franz Lehar (1870–1948) and English operetta composer Lionel Monckton (1862–1924).

MRS. HIGGINS: [*Putting her fingers in her ears, as they are by this time shouting one another down with an intolerable noise.*] Sh-sh-sh—sh! [*They stop.*]

PICKERING: I beg your pardon. [*He draws his chair back apologetically.*]

HIGGINS: Sorry. When Pickering starts shouting nobody can get a word in edgeways.

MRS. HIGGINS: Be quiet, Henry. Colonel Pickering: dont you realize that when Eliza walked into Wimpole Street, something walked in with her?

PICKERING: Her father did. But Henry soon got rid of him.

MRS. HIGGINS: It would have been more to the point if her mother had. But as her mother didnt something else did.

PICKERING: But what?

MRS. HIGGINS: [*Unconsciously dating herself by the word.*] A problem.

PICKERING: Oh, I see. The problem of how to pass her off as a lady.

HIGGINS: I'll solve that problem. Ive half solved it already.

MRS. HIGGINS: No, you two infinitely stupid male creatures: the problem of what is to be done with her afterwards.

HIGGINS: I dont see anything in that. She can go her own way, with all the advantages I have given her.

MRS. HIGGINS: The advantages of that poor woman who was here just now! The manners and habits that disqualify a fine lady from earning her own living without giving her a fine lady's income! Is that what you mean?

PICKERING: [*Indulgently, being rather bored.*] Oh, that will be all right, Mrs. Higgins. [*He rises to go.*]

HIGGINS: [*Rising also.*] We'll find her some light employment.

PICKERING: She's happy enough. Dont you worry about her. Goodbye. [*He shakes hands as if he were consoling a frightened child, and makes for the door.*]

HIGGINS: Anyhow, theres no good bothering now. The thing's done. Goodbye, mother. [*He kisses her, and follows* PICKERING.]

PICKERING: [*Turning for a final consolation.*] There are plenty of openings. We'll do whats right. Goodbye.

HIGGINS: [*To* PICKERING *as they go out together.*] Lets take her to the Shakespear exhibition at Earls Court.

PICKERING: Yes: lets. Her remarks will be delicious.

HIGGINS: She'll mimic all the people for us when we get home.

PICKERING: Ripping. [*Both are heard laughing as they go downstairs.*]

MRS. HIGGINS: [*Rises with an impatient bounce, and returns to her work at the writing-table. She sweeps a litter of disarranged papers out of her way; snatches a sheet of paper from her stationery case; and tries resolutely to write. At the third line she gives it up; flings down her pen; grips the table angrily and exclaims.*] Oh, men! men!! men!!!

Clearly ELIZA *will not pass as a duchess yet; and* HIGGINS*'s bet remains unwon. But the six months are not yet exhausted; and just in time* ELIZA *does actually pass as a princess. For a glimpse of how she did it imagine an Embassy in London one summer evening after dark. The hall door has an awning and a carpet across the sidewalk to the kerb, because a grand reception is in progress. A small crowd is lined up to see the guests arrive.*

A Rolls-Royce car drives up. PICKERING *in evening dress, with medals and orders, alights, and hands out* ELIZA, *in opera cloak, evening dress, diamonds, fan, flowers and all accessories.* HIGGINS *follows. The car drives off; and the three go up the steps and into the house, the door opening for them as they approach.*

Inside the house they find themselves in a spacious hall from which the grand staircase rises. On the left are the arrangements for the gentlemen's cloaks. The male guests are depositing their hats and wraps there.

On the right is a door leading to the ladies' cloakroom. Ladies are going in cloaked and coming out in splendor. PICKERING *whispers to* ELIZA *and points out the ladies' room. She goes into it.* HIGGINS *and* PICKERING *take off their overcoats and take tickets for them from the attendant.*

One of the guests, occupied in the same way, has his back turned. Having taken his ticket, he turns round and reveals himself as an important looking YOUNG MAN *with an astonishingly hairy face. He has an enormous moustache, flowing out into luxuriant whiskers. Waves of hair cluster on his brow. His hair is cropped closely at the back, and glows with oil. Otherwise he is very smart. He wears several worthless orders. He is evidently a foreigner, guessable as a whiskered Pandour from Hungary; but in spite of the ferocity of his moustache he is amiable and genially voluble.*

Recognizing HIGGINS, *he flings his arms wide apart and approaches him enthusiastically.*

WHISKERS: Maestro, maestro. [*He embraces* HIGGINS *and kisses him on both cheeks.*] You remember me?

HIGGINS: No I dont. Who the devil are you?

WHISKERS: I am your pupil: your first pupil, your best and greatest pupil. I am little Nepommuck, the marvellous boy. I have made your name famous throughout Europe. You teach me phonetic. You cannot forget ME.

HIGGINS: Why dont you shave?

NEPOMMUCK: I have not your imposing appearance, your chin, your brow. Nobody notice me when I shave. Now I am famous: they call me Hairy Faced Dick.

HIGGINS: And what are you doing here among all these swells?

NEPOMMUCK: I am interpreter. I speak 32 languages. I am indispensable at these international parties. You are great cockney specialist: you place a man anywhere in London the moment he open his mouth. I place any man in Europe.

[*A* FOOTMAN *hurries down the grand staircase and comes to* NEPOMMUCK.]

FOOTMAN: You are wanted upstairs. Her Excellency cannot understand the Greek gentleman.

NEPOMMUCK: Thank you, yes, immediately.

[*The* FOOTMAN *goes and is lost in the crowd.*]

NEPOMMUCK: [*To* HIGGINS.] This Greek diplomatist pretends he cannot speak nor understand English. He cannot deceive me. He is the son of a Clerkenwell watchmaker. He speaks English so villainously that he dare not utter a word of it without betraying his origin. I help him to pretend; but I make him pay through the nose. I make them all pay. Ha Ha! [*He hurries upstairs.*]

PICKERING: Is this fellow really an expert? Can he find out Eliza and blackmail her?

HIGGINS: We shall see. If he finds her out I lose my bet.

[ELIZA *comes from the cloakroom and joins them.*]

PICKERING: Well, Eliza, now for it. Are you ready?

LIZA: Are you nervous, Colonel?

PICKERING: Frightfully. I feel exactly as I felt before my first battle. It's the first time that frightens.

LIZA: It is not the first time for me, Colonel. I have done this fifty times—hundreds of times—in my little piggery in Angel Court in my day-dreams. I am in a dream now. Promise me not to let Professor Higgins wake me; for if he does I shall forget everything and talk as I used to in Drury Lane.

PICKERING: Not a word, Higgins. [*To* ELIZA.] Now, ready?

LIZA: Ready.

PICKERING: Go.

[*They mount the stairs,* HIGGINS *last.* PICKERING *whispers to the* FOOTMAN *on the first landing.*]

FIRST LANDING FOOTMAN: Miss Doolittle, Colonel Pickering, Professor Higgins.

SECOND LANDING FOOTMAN: Miss Doolittle, Colonel Pickering, Professor Higgins.

[*At the top of the staircase the* AMBASSADOR *and his* WIFE, *with* NEPOMMUCK *at her elbow, are receiving.*]

HOSTESS: [*Taking* ELIZA's *hand.*] How d'ye do?

HOST: [*Same play.*] How d'ye do? How d'ye do, Pickering?

LIZA: [*With a beautiful gravity that awes her* HOSTESS.] How do you do? [*She passes on to the drawingroom.*]

HOSTESS: Is that your adopted daughter, Colonel Pickering? She will make a sensation.

PICKERING: Most kind of you to invite her for me. [*He passes on.*]

HOSTESS: [*To* NEPOMMUCK.] Find out all about her.

NEPOMMUCK: [*Bowing.*] Excellency—[*He goes into the crowd.*]

HOST: How d'ye do, Higgins? You have a rival here tonight. He introduced himself as your pupil. Is he any good?

HIGGINS: He can learn a language in a fortnight—knows dozens of them. A sure mark of a fool. As a phonetician, no good whatever.

HOSTESS: How d'ye do, Professor?

HIGGINS: How do you do? Fearful bore for you this sort of thing. Forgive my part in it. [*He passes on.*]

[*In the drawingroom and its suite of salons the reception is in full swing.* ELIZA *passes through. She is so intent on her ordeal that she walks like a somnambu-*

list in a desert instead of a débutante in a fashionable crowd. They stop talking to look at her, admiring her dress, her jewels, and her strangely attractive self. Some of the younger ones at the back stand on their chairs to see.

The HOST *and* HOSTESS *come in from the staircase and mingle with their guests.* HIGGINS, *gloomy and contemptuous of the whole business, comes into the group where they are chatting.*]

HOSTESS: Ah, here is Professor Higgins: he will tell us. Tell us all about the wonderful young lady, Professor.

HIGGINS: [*Almost morosely.*] What wonderful young lady?

HOSTESS: You know very well. They tell me there has been nothing like her in London since people stood on their chairs to look at Mrs. Langtry.[7]

[NEPOMMUCK *joins the group, full of news.*]

HOSTESS: Ah, here you are at last, Nepommuck. Have you found out all about the Doolittle lady?

NEPOMMUCK: I have found out all about her. She is a fraud.

HOSTESS: A fraud! Oh no.

NEPOMMUCK: YES, yes. She cannot deceive me. Her name cannot be Doolittle.

HIGGINS: Why?

NEPOMMUCK: Because Doolittle is an English name. And she is not English.

HOSTESS: Oh, nonsense! She speaks English perfectly.

NEPOMMUCK: Too perfectly. Can you shew me any English woman who speaks English as it should be spoken? Only foreigners who have been taught to speak it speak it well.

HOSTESS: Certainly she terrified me by the way she said How d'ye do. I had a schoolmistress who talked like that; and I was mortally afraid of her. But if she is not English what is she?

NEPOMMUCK: Hungarian.

ALL THE REST: Hungarian!

NEPOMMUCK: Hungarian. And of royal blood. I am Hungarian. My blood is royal.

HIGGINS: Did you speak to her in Hungarian?

NEPOMMUCK: I did. She was very clever. She said "Please speak to me in English: I do not understand French." French! She pretends not to know the difference between Hungarian and French. Impossible: she knows both.

HIGGINS: And the blood royal? How did you find that out?

NEPOMMUCK: Instinct, maestro, instinct. Only the Magyar races can produce that air of the divine right, those resolute eyes. She is a princess.

HOST: What do you say, Professor?

HIGGINS: I say an ordinary London girl out of the gutter and taught to speak by an expert. I place her in Drury Lane.

NEPOMMUCK: Ha ha ha! Oh, maestro, maestro, you are mad on the subject of cockney dialects. The London gutter is the whole world for you.

HIGGINS: [*To the* HOSTESS.] What does your Excellency say?

7. English actress Lillie Langtry (1852–1929), a renowned beauty.

HOSTESS: Oh, of course I agree with Nepommuck. She must be a princess at least.

HOST: Not necessarily legitimate, of course. Morganatic perhaps. But that is undoubtedly her class.

HIGGINS: I stick to my opinion.

HOSTESS: Oh, you are incorrigible.

[*The group breaks up, leaving* HIGGINS *isolated.* PICKERING *joins him.*]

PICKERING: Where is Eliza? We must keep an eye on her.

[ELIZA *joins them.*]

LIZA: I dont think I can bear much more. The people all stare so at me. An old lady has just told me that I speak exactly like Queen Victoria. I am sorry if I have lost your bet. I have done my best; but nothing can make me the same as these people.

PICKERING: You have not lost it, my dear. You have won it ten times over.

HIGGINS: Let us get out of this. I have had enough of chattering to these fools.

PICKERING: Eliza is tired; and I am hungry. Let us clear out and have supper somewhere.

ACT IV

The Wimpole Street laboratory. Midnight. Nobody in the room. The clock on the mantelpiece strikes twelve. The fire is not alight: it is a summer night.

Presently HIGGINS *and* PICKERING *are heard on the stairs.*

HIGGINS: [*Calling down to* PICKERING.] I say, Pick: lock up, will you? I shant be going out again.

PICKERING: Right. Can Mrs. Pearce go to bed? We dont want anything more, do we?

HIGGINS: Lord, no!

[ELIZA *opens the door and is seen on the lighted landing in all the finery in which she has just won* HIGGINS's *bet for him. She comes to the hearth, and switches on the electric lights there. She is tired: her pallor contrasts strongly with her dark eyes and hair; and her expression is almost tragic. She takes off her cloak; puts her fan and gloves on the piano; and sits down on the bench, brooding and silent.* HIGGINS, *in evening dress, with overcoat and hat, comes in, carrying a smoking jacket which he has picked up downstairs. He takes off the hat and overcoat; throws them carelessly on the newspaper stand; disposes of his coat in the same way; puts on the smoking jacket; and throws himself wearily into the easy-chair at the hearth.* PICKERING, *similarly attired, comes in. He also takes off his hat and overcoat, and is about to throw them on* HIGGINS's *when he hesitates.*]

PICKERING: I say: Mrs. Pearce will row if we leave these things lying about in the drawing room.

HIGGINS: Oh, chuck them over the bannisters into the hall. She'll find them there in the morning and put them away all right. She'll think we were drunk.

PICKERING: We are, slightly. Are there any letters?

HIGGINS: I didnt look. [PICKERING *takes the overcoats and hats and goes downstairs.* HIGGINS *begins half singing half yawning an air from La Fanciulla del Golden West.*[8] *Suddenly he stops and exclaims.*] I wonder where the devil my slippers are!

> [ELIZA *looks at him darkly; then rises suddenly and leaves the room.*
> HIGGINS *yawns again, and resumes his song.*
> PICKERING *returns, with the contents of the letter-box in his hand.*]

PICKERING: Only circulars, and this coroneted billet-doux for you. [*He throws the circulars into the fender, and posts himself on the hearthrug, with his back to the grate.*]

HIGGINS: [*Glancing at the billet-doux.*] Money-lender. [*He throws the letter after the circulars.*]

> [ELIZA *returns with a pair of large down-at-heel slippers. She places them on the carpet before* HIGGINS, *and sits as before without a word.*]

HIGGINS: [*Yawning again.*] Oh Lord! What an evening! What a crew! What a silly tomfoolery! [*He raises his shoe to unlace it, and catches sight of the slippers. He stops unlacing and looks at them as if they had appeared there of their own accord.*] Oh! theyre there, are they?

PICKERING: [*Stretching himself.*] Well, I feel a bit tired. It's been a long day. The garden party, a dinner party, and the reception! Rather too much of a good thing. But youve won your bet, Higgins. Eliza did the trick, and something to spare, eh?

HIGGINS: [*Fervently.*] Thank God it's over!

> [ELIZA *flinches violently; but they take no notice of her; and she recovers herself and sits stonily as before.*]

PICKERING: Were you nervous at the garden party? *I* was. Eliza didnt seem a bit nervous.

HIGGINS: Oh, she wasnt nervous. I knew she'd be all right. No: it's the strain of putting the job through all these months that has told on me. It was interesting enough at first, while we were at the phonetics; but after that I got deadly sick of it. If I hadnt backed myself to do it I should have chucked the whole thing up two months ago. It was a silly notion: the whole thing has been a bore.

PICKERING: Oh come! the garden party was frightfully exciting. My heart began beating like anything.

HIGGINS: Yes, for the first three minutes. But when I saw we were going to win hands down, I felt like a bear in a cage, hanging about doing nothing. The dinner was worse: sitting gorging there for over an hour, with nobody but a damned fool of a fashionable woman to talk to! I tell you, Pickering, never

---

8. *The Girl of the Golden West* (1910), a three-act opera by Puccini.

again for me. No more artificial duchesses. The whole thing has been simple purgatory.

PICKERING: Youve never been broken in properly to the social routine. [*Strolling over to the piano.*] I rather enjoy dipping into it occasionally myself: it makes me feel young again. Anyhow, it was a great success: an immense success. I was quite frightened once or twice because Eliza was doing it so well. You see, lots of the real people cant do it at all: theyre such fools that they think style comes by nature to people in their position; and so they never learn. Theres always something professional about doing a thing superlatively well.

HIGGINS: Yes: thats what drives me mad: the silly people dont know their own silly business. [*Rising.*] However, it's over and done with; and now I can go to bed at last without dreading tomorrow.

> [ELIZA*'s beauty becomes murderous.*]

PICKERING: I think I shall turn in too. Still, it's been a great occasion: a triumph for you. Goodnight. [*He goes*].

HIGGINS: [*Following him.*] Goodnight. [*Over his shoulder, at the door.*] Put out the lights, Eliza; and tell Mrs. Pearce not to make coffee for me in the morning: I'll take tea. [*He goes out.*]

> [ELIZA *tries to control herself and feel indifferent as she rises and walks across to the hearth to switch off the lights. By the time she gets there she is on the point of screaming. She sits down in* HIGGINS*'s chair and holds on hard to the arms. Finally she gives way and flings herself furiously on the floor, raging.*]

HIGGINS: [*In despairing wrath outside.*] What the devil have I done with my slippers? [*He appears at the door.*]

LIZA: [*Snatching up the slippers, and hurling them at him one after the other with all her force.*] There are your slippers. And there. Take your slippers; and may you never have a day's luck with them!

HIGGINS: [*Astounded.*] What on earth—! [*He comes to her.*] Whats the matter? Get up. [*He pulls her up.*] Anything wrong?

LIZA: [*Breathless.*] Nothing wrong—with you. Ive won your bet for you, havent I? Thats enough for you. *I* dont matter, I suppose.

HIGGINS: You won my bet! You! Presumptuous insect! *I* won it. What did you throw those slippers at me for?

LIZA: Because I wanted to smash your face. I'd like to kill you, you selfish brute. Why didnt you leave me where you picked me out of—in the gutter? You thank God it's all over, and that now you can throw me back again there, do you? [*She crisps her fingers frantically.*]

HIGGINS: [*Looking at her in cool wonder.*] The creature is nervous, after all.

LIZA: [*Gives a suffocated scream of fury, and instinctively darts her nails at his face.*]!!

HIGGINS: [*Catching her wrists.*] Ah! would you? Claws in, you cat. How dare you shew your temper to me? Sit down and be quiet. [*He throws her roughly into the easy-chair.*]

LIZA: [*Crushed by superior strength and weight.*] Whats to become of me? Whats to become of me?

HIGGINS: How the devil do I know whats to become of you? What does it matter what becomes of you?

LIZA: You dont care. I know you dont care. You wouldnt care if I was dead. I'm nothing to you—not so much as them slippers.

HIGGINS: [*Thundering.*] Those slippers.

LIZA: [*With bitter submission.*] Those slippers. I didnt think it made any difference now.

[*A pause.* ELIZA *hopeless and crushed.* HIGGINS *a little uneasy.*]

HIGGINS: [*In his loftiest manner.*] Why have you begun going on like this? May I ask whether you complain of your treatment here?

LIZA: No.

HIGGINS: Has anybody behaved badly to you? Colonel Pickering? Mrs. Pearce? Any of the servants?

LIZA: No.

HIGGINS: I presume you dont pretend that *I* have treated you badly?

LIZA: No.

HIGGINS: I am glad to hear it. [*He moderates his tone.*] Perhaps youre tired after the strain of the day. Will you have a glass of champagne? [*He moves towards the door.*]

LIZA: No. [*Recollecting her manners.*] Thank you.

HIGGINS: [*Good-humored again.*] This has been coming on you for some days. I suppose it was natural for you to be anxious about the garden party. But thats all over now. [*He pats her kindly on the shoulder. She writhes.*] Theres nothing more to worry about.

LIZA: No. Nothing more for you to worry about. [*She suddenly rises and gets away from him by going to the piano bench, where she sits and hides her face.*] Oh God! I wish I was dead.

HIGGINS: [*Staring after her in sincere surprise.*] Why? In heaven's name, why? [*Reasonably, going to her.*] Listen to me, Eliza. All this irritation is purely subjective.

LIZA: I dont understand. I'm too ignorant.

HIGGINS: It's only imagination. Low spirits and nothing else. Nobody's hurting you. Nothing's wrong. You go to bed like a good girl and sleep it off. Have a little cry and say your prayers: that will make you comfortable.

LIZA: I heard your prayers. "Thank God it's all over!"

HIGGINS: [*Impatiently.*] Well, dont you thank God it's all over? Now you are free and can do what you like.

LIZA: [*Pulling herself together in desperation.*] What am I fit for? What have you left me fit for? Where am I to go? What am I to do? Whats to become of me?

HIGGINS: [*Enlightened, but not at all impressed.*] Oh, thats whats worrying you, is it? [*He thrusts his hands into his pockets, and walks about in his usual manner, rattling the contents of his pockets, as if condescending to a trivial subject out of pure kindness.*] I shouldnt bother about it if I were you. I should imagine you wont have much difficulty in settling yourself somewhere or other, though

I hadnt quite realized that you were going away. [*She looks quickly at him: he does not look at her, but examines the dessert stand on the piano and decides that he will eat an apple.*] You might marry, you know. [*He bites a large piece out of the apple and munches it noisily.*] You see, Eliza, all men are not confirmed old bachelors like me and the Colonel. Most men are the marrying sort (poor devils!); and youre not bad-looking: it's quite a pleasure to look at you some-times—not now, of course, because youre crying and looking as ugly as the very devil; but when youre all right and quite yourself, youre what I should call attractive. That is, to the people in the marrying line, you understand. You go to bed and have a good nice rest; and then get up and look at yourself in the glass; and you wont feel so cheap.

> [ELIZA *again looks at him, speechless, and does not stir.*
> *The look is quite lost on him: he eats his apple with a dreamy expression of happiness, as it is quite a good one.*]

HIGGINS: [*A genial afterthought occurring to him.*] I daresay my mother could find some chap or other who would do very well.

LIZA: We were above that at the corner of Tottenham Court Road.

HIGGINS: [*Waking up.*] What do you mean?

LIZA: I sold flowers. I didnt sell myself. Now youve made a lady of me I'm not fit to sell anything else. I wish youd left me where you found me.

HIGGINS: [*Slinging the core of the apple decisively into the grate.*] Tosh, Eliza. Dont you insult human relations by dragging all this cant about buying and selling into it. You neednt marry the fellow if you dont like him.

LIZA: What else am I to do?

HIGGINS: Oh, lots of things. What about your old idea of a florist's shop? Pickering could set you up in one: he has lots of money. [*Chuckling.*] He'll have to pay for all those togs you have been wearing today; and that, with the hire of the jewellery, will make a big hole in two hundred pounds. Why, six months ago you would have thought it the millennium to have a flower shop of your own. Come! youll be all right. I must clear off to bed: I'm devilish sleepy. By the way, I came down for something: I forget what it was.

LIZA: Your slippers.

HIGGINS: Oh yes, of course. You shied them at me. [*He picks them up, and is going out when she rises and speaks to him.*]

LIZA: Before you go, sir—

HIGGINS: [*Dropping the slippers in his surprise at her calling him Sir.*] Eh?

LIZA: Do my clothes belong to me or to Colonel Pickering?

HIGGINS: [*Coming back into the room as if her question were the very climax of unreason.*] What the devil use would they be to Pickering?

LIZA: He might want them for the next girl you pick up to experiment on.

HIGGINS: [*Shocked and hurt.*] Is that the way you feel towards us?

LIZA: I dont want to hear anything more about that. All I want to know is whether anything belongs to me. My own clothes were burnt.

HIGGINS: But what does it matter? Why need you start bothering about that in the middle of the night?

LIZA: I want to know what I may take away with me. I dont want to be accused of stealing.

HIGGINS: [*Now deeply wounded.*] Stealing! You shouldnt have said that, Eliza. That shews a want of feeling.

LIZA: I'm sorry. I'm only a common ignorant girl; and in my station I have to be careful. There cant be any feelings between the like of you and the like of me. Please will you tell me what belongs to me and what doesnt?

HIGGINS: [*Very sulky.*] You may take the whole damned houseful if you like. Except the jewels. Theyre hired. Will that satisfy you? [*He turns on his heel and is about to go in extreme dudgeon.*]

LIZA: [*Drinking in his emotion like nectar, and nagging him to provoke a further supply.*] Stop, please. [*She takes off her jewels.*] Will you take these to your room and keep them safe? I dont want to run the risk of their being missing.

HIGGINS: [*Furious.*] Hand them over. [*She puts them into his hands.*] If these belonged to me instead of to the jeweller, I'd ram them down your ungrateful throat. [*He perfunctorily thrusts them into his pockets, unconsciously decorating himself with the protruding ends of the chains.*]

LIZA: [*Taking a ring off.*] This ring isnt the jeweller's: it's the one you bought me in Brighton. I dont want it now. [HIGGINS *dashes the ring violently into the fireplace, and turns on her so threateningly that she crouches over the piano with her hands over her face, and exclaims.*] Dont you hit me.

HIGGINS: Hit you! You infamous creature, how dare you accuse me of such a thing? It is you who have hit me. You have wounded me to the heart.

LIZA: [*Thrilling with hidden joy.*] I'm glad. Ive got a little of my own back, anyhow.

HIGGINS: [*With dignity, in his finest professional style.*] You have caused me to lose my temper: a thing that has hardly ever happened to me before. I prefer to say nothing more tonight. I am going to bed.

LIZA: [*Pertly.*] Youd better leave a note for Mrs. Pearce about the coffee; for she wont be told by me.

HIGGINS: [*Formally.*] Damn Mrs. Pearce; and damn the coffee; and damn you; and [*Wildly.*] damn my own folly in having lavished my hard-earned knowledge and the treasure of my regard and intimacy on a heartless guttersnipe. [*He goes out with impressive decorum, and spoils it by slamming the door savagely.*]

> [ELIZA *goes down on her knees on the hearthrug to look for the ring. When she finds it she considers for a moment what to do with it. Finally she flings it down on the dessert stand and goes upstairs in a tearing rage.*]

The furniture of ELIZA's *room has been increased by a big wardrobe and a sumptuous dressing-table. She comes in and switches on the electric light. She goes to the wardrobe; opens it; and pulls out a walking dress, a hat, and a pair of shoes, which she throws on the bed. She takes off her evening dress and shoes; then takes a padded hanger from the wardrobe; adjusts it carefully in the evening dress; and hangs it in the wardrobe, which she shuts with a slam. She puts on her walking shoes, her walking dress, and hat. She takes her wrist watch from the dressing-table and fastens it on. She pulls on her gloves;*

takes her vanity bag; and looks into it to see that her purse is there before hanging it on her wrist. She makes for the door. Every movement expresses her furious resolution.

She takes a last look at herself in the glass.

She suddenly puts out her tongue at herself; then leaves the room, switching off the electric light at the door.

Meanwhile, in the street outside, FREDDY EYNSFORD HILL, *lovelorn, is gazing up at the second floor, in which one of the windows is still lighted.*

The light goes out.

FREDDY: Goodnight, darling, darling, darling.

    [ELIZA *comes out, giving the door a considerable bang behind her.*]

LIZA: Whatever are you doing here?

FREDDY: Nothing. I spend most of my nights here. It's the only place where I'm happy. Dont laugh at me, Miss Doolittle.

LIZA: Dont you call me Miss Doolittle, do you hear? Liza's good enough for me. [*She breaks down and grabs him by the shoulders.*] Freddy: you dont think I'm a heartless guttersnipe, do you?

FREDDY: Oh no, no, darling: how can you imagine such a thing? You are the loveliest, dearest—

    [*He loses all self-control and smothers her with kisses. She, hungry for comfort, responds. They stand there in one another's arms.*

    An elderly police CONSTABLE *arrives.*]

CONSTABLE: [*Scandalized.*] Now then! Now then!! Now then!!!

    [*They release one another hastily.*]

FREDDY: Sorry, constable. Weve only just become engaged.

    [*They run away.*]

    The CONSTABLE *shakes his head, reflecting on his own courtship and on the vanity of human hopes. He moves off in the opposite direction with slow professional steps.*

    The flight of the lovers takes them to Cavendish Square. There they halt to consider their next move.

LIZA: [*Out of breath.*] He didnt half give me a fright, that copper. But you answered him proper.

FREDDY: I hope I havent taken you out of your way. Where were you going?

LIZA: To the river.

FREDDY: What for?

LIZA: To make a hole in it.

FREDDY [*Horrified.*] Eliza, darling. What do you mean? What's the matter?

LIZA: Never mind. It doesnt matter now. There's nobody in the world now but you and me, is there?

FREDDY: Not a soul.

[*They indulge in another embrace, and are again surprised by a much younger* CONSTABLE.]

SECOND CONSTABLE. Now then, you two! Whats this? Where do you think you are? Move along here, double quick.

FREDDY: As you say, sir, double quick.

> They run away again, and are in Hanover Square before they stop for another conference.

FREDDY: I had no idea the police were so devilishly prudish.

LIZA: It's their business to hunt girls off the streets.

FREDDY: We must go somewhere. We cant wander about the streets all night.

LIZA: Cant we? I think it'd be lovely to wander about for ever.

FREDDY: Oh, darling.

[*They embrace again, oblivious of the arrival of a crawling taxi. It stops.*]

TAXIMAN: Can I drive you and the lady anywhere, sir?

[*They start asunder.*]

LIZA: Oh, Freddy, a taxi. The very thing.

FREDDY: But, damn it, Ive no money.

LIZA: I have plenty. The Colonel thinks you should never go out without ten pounds in your pocket. Listen. We'll drive about all night; and in the morning I'll call on old Mrs. Higgins and ask her what I ought to do. I'll tell you all about it in the cab. And the police wont touch us there.

FREDDY: Righto! Ripping. [*To the* TAXIMAN.] Wimbledon Common. [*They drive off.*]

ACT V

MRS. HIGGINS's *drawing room. She is at her writing-table as before. The* PARLORMAID *comes in.*

THE PARLORMAID: [*At the door.*] Mr. Henry, maam, is downstairs with Colonel Pickering.

MRS. HIGGINS: Well, shew them up.

THE PARLORMAID: Theyre using the telephone, maam. Telephoning to the police, I think.

MRS. HIGGINS: What!

THE PARLORMAID: [*Coming further in and lowering her voice.*] Mr. Henry is in a state, maam. I thought I'd better tell you.

MRS. HIGGINS: If you had told me that Mr. Henry was not in a state it would have been more surprising. Tell them to come up when theyve finished with the police. I suppose he's lost something.

THE PARLORMAID: Yes, maam [*Going.*]

MRS. HIGGINS: Go upstairs and tell Miss Doolittle that Mr. Henry and the Colonel are here. Ask her not to come down til I send for her.

THE PARLORMAID: Yes, maam.

[HIGGINS *bursts in. He is, as the* PARLORMAID *has said, in a state.*]

HIGGINS: Look here, mother: heres a confounded thing!

MRS. HIGGINS: Yes, dear. Good morning. [*He checks his impatience and kisses her, whilst the* PARLORMAID *goes out.*] What is it?

HIGGINS: Eliza's bolted.

MRS. HIGGINS: [*Calmly continuing her writing.*] You must have frightened her.

HIGGINS: Frightened her! nonsense! She was left last night, as usual, to turn out the lights and all that; and instead of going to bed she changed her clothes and went right off: her bed wasnt slept in. She came in a cab for her things before seven this morning; and that fool Mrs. Pearce let her have them without telling me a word about it. What am I to do?

MRS. HIGGINS: Do without, I'm afraid, Henry. The girl has a perfect right to leave if she chooses.

HIGGINS: [*Wandering distractedly across the room.*] But I cant find anything. I dont know what appointments Ive got. I'm—

[PICKERING *comes in.* MRS. HIGGINS *puts down her pen and turns away from the writing-table.*]

PICKERING: [*Shaking hands.*] Good morning, Mrs. Higgins. Has Henry told you? [*He sits down on the ottoman.*]

HIGGINS: What does that ass of an inspector say? Have you offered a reward?

MRS. HIGGINS: [*Rising in indignant amazement.*] You dont mean to say you have set the police after Eliza.

HIGGINS: Of course. What are the police for? What else could we do? [*He sits in the Elizabethan chair.*]

PICKERING: The inspector made a lot of difficulties. I really think he suspected us of some improper purpose.

MRS. HIGGINS: Well, of course he did. What right have you to go to the police and give the girl's name as if she were a thief, or a lost umbrella, or something? Really! [*She sits down again, deeply vexed.*]

HIGGINS: But we want to find her.

PICKERING: We cant let her go like this, you know, Mrs. Higgins. What were we to do?

MRS. HIGGINS: You have no more sense, either of you, than two children. Why—

[*The* PARLORMAID *comes in and breaks off the conversation.*]

THE PARLORMAID: Mr. Henry: a gentleman wants to see you very particular. He's been sent on from Wimpole Street.

HIGGINS: Oh, bother! I cant see anyone now. Who is it?

THE PARLORMAID: A Mr. Doolittle, sir.

PICKERING: Doolittle! Do you mean the dustman?

THE PARLORMAID: Dustman! Oh no, sir: a gentleman.

HIGGINS: [*Springing up excitedly.*] By George, Pick, it's some relative of hers that she's gone to. Somebody we know nothing about. [*To the* PARLORMAID.] Send him up, quick.

THE PARLORMAID: Yes, sir. [*She goes.*]

HIGGINS: [*Eagerly, going to his mother.*] Genteel relatives! now we shall hear something. [*He sits down in the Chippendale chair.*]

MRS. HIGGINS: Do you know any of her people?

PICKERING: Only her father: the fellow we told you about.

THE PARLORMAID: [*Announcing.*] Mr. Doolittle. [*She withdraws.*].

[DOOLITTLE *enters. He is resplendently dressed as for a fashionable wedding, and might, in fact, be the bridegroom. A flower in his buttonhole, a dazzling silk hat, and patent leather shoes complete the effect. He is too concerned with the business he has come on to notice* MRS. HIGGINS. *He walks straight to* HIGGINS, *and accosts him with vehement reproach.*]

DOOLITTLE: [*Indicating his own person.*] See here! Do you see this? You done this.

HIGGINS: Done what, man?

DOOLITTLE: This, I tell you. Look at it. Look at this hat. Look at this coat.

PICKERING: Has Eliza been buying you clothes?

DOOLITTLE: Eliza! not she. Why would she buy me clothes?

MRS. HIGGINS: Good morning, Mr. Doolittle. Wont you sit down?

DOOLITTLE: [*Taken aback as he becomes conscious that he has forgotten his hostess.*] Asking your pardon, maam. [*He approaches her and shakes her proffered hand.*] Thank you. [*He sits down on the ottoman, on* PICKERING'*s right.*] I am that full of what has happened to me that I cant think of anything else.

HIGGINS: What the dickens has happened to you?

DOOLITTLE: I shouldnt mind if it had only happened to me: anything might happen to anybody and nobody to blame but Providence, as you might say. But this is something that you done to me: yes, you, Enry Iggins.

HIGGINS: Have you found Eliza?

DOOLITTLE: Have you lost her?

HIGGINS: Yes.

DOOLITTLE: You have all the luck, you have. I aint found her; but she'll find me quick enough now after what you done to me.

MRS. HIGGINS: But what has my son done to you, Mr. Doolittle?

DOOLITTLE: Done to me! Ruined me. Destroyed my happiness. Tied me up and delivered me into the hands of middle class morality.

HIGGINS: [*Rising intolerantly and standing over* DOOLITTLE.] Youre raving. Youre drunk. Youre mad. I gave you five pounds. After that I had two conversations with you, at half-a-crown an hour. Ive never seen you since.

DOOLITTLE: Oh! Drunk am I? Mad am I? Tell me this. Did you or did you not write a letter to an old blighter in America that was giving five millions to found Moral Reform Societies all over the world, and that wanted you to invent a universal language for him?

HIGGINS: What! Ezra D. Wannafeller! He's dead. [*He sits down again carelessly.*]

DOOLITTLE: Yes: he's dead; and I'm done for. Now did you or did you not write a letter to him to say that the most original moralist at present in England, to the best of your knowledge, was Alfred Doolittle, a common dustman?

HIGGINS: Oh, after your first visit I remember making some silly joke of the kind.

DOOLITTLE: Ah! you may well call it a silly joke. It put the lid on me right enough. Just give him the chance he wanted to shew that Americans is not like us: that they reckonize and respect merit in every class of life, however humble. Them words is in his blooming will, in which, Henry Higgins, thanks to your silly joking, he leaves me a share in his Predigested Cheese Trust worth three thousand a year on condition that I lecture for his Wannafeller Moral Reform World League as often as they ask me up to six times a year.

HIGGINS: The devil he does! Whew! [*Brightening suddenly.*] What a lark!

PICKERING: A safe thing for you, Doolittle. They wont ask you twice.

DOOLITTLE: It aint the lecturing I mind. I'll lecture them blue in the face, I will, and not turn a hair. It's making a gentleman of me that I object to. Who asked him to make a gentleman of me? I was happy. I was free. I touched pretty nigh everybody for money when I wanted it, same as I touched you, Enry Iggins. Now I am worrited; tied neck and heels; and everybody touches me for money. It's a fine thing for you, says my solicitor. Is it? says I. You mean it's a good thing for you, I says. When I was a poor man and had a solicitor once when they found a pram in the dust cart, he got me off, and got shut of me and got me shut of him as quick as he could. Same with the doctors: used to shove me out of the hospital before I could hardly stand on my legs, and nothing to pay. Now they finds out that I'm not a healthy man and cant live unless they looks after me twice a day. In the house I'm not let do a hand's turn for myself: somebody else must do it and touch me for it. A year ago I hadnt a relative in the world except two or three that wouldnt speak to me. Now Ive fifty, and not a decent week's wages among the lot of them. I have to live for others and not for myself: thats middle class morality. You talk of losing Eliza. Dont you be anxious: I bet she's on my doorstep by this: she that could support herself easy by selling flowers if I wasnt respectable. And the next one to touch me will be you, Enry Iggins. I'll have to learn to speak middle class language from you, instead of speaking proper English. Thats where youll come in; and I daresay thats what you done it for.

MRS. HIGGINS: But, my dear Mr. Doolittle, you need not suffer all this if you are really in earnest. Nobody can force you to accept this bequest. You can repudiate it. Isnt that so, Colonel Pickering?

PICKERING: I believe so.

DOOLITTLE: [*Softening his manner in deference to her sex.*] Thats the tragedy of it, maam. It's easy to say chuck it; but I havnt the nerve. Which of us has? We're all intimidated. Intimidated, maam: thats what we are. What is there for me if I chuck it but the workhouse in my old age? I have to dye my hair already to keep my job as a dustman. If I was one of the deserving poor, and had put by a bit, I could chuck it; but then why should I, acause the deserving poor might as well be millionaires for all the happiness they ever has. They dont know what happiness is. But I, as one of the undeserving poor, have nothing between me and the pauper's uniform but this here blasted three thousand a year that shoves me into the middle class. (Excuse the expression, maam; youd use it yourself if you had my provocation.) Theyve got you every way you turn: it's a choice between the Skilly of the workhouse and the Char Bydis[9] of the middle class; and I havnt the nerve for the work-house. Intimidated: thats what I am. Broke. Bought up. Happier men than me will call for my dust, and touch me for their tip; and I'll look on helpless, and envy them. And thats what your son has brought me to. [*He is overcome by emotion.*]

MRS. HIGGINS: Well, I'm very glad youre not going to do anything foolish, Mr. Doolittle. For this solves the problem of Eliza's future. You can provide for her now.

DOOLITTLE: [*With melancholy resignation.*] Yes, maam: I'm expected to provide for everyone now, out of three thousand a year.

HIGGINS: [*Jumping up.*] Nonsense! he cant provide for her. He shant provide for her. She doesnt belong to him. I paid him five pounds for her. Doolittle: either youre an honest man or a rogue.

DOOLITTLE: [*Tolerantly.*] A little of both, Henry, like the rest of us: a little of both.

HIGGINS: Well, you took that money for the girl; and you have no right to take her as well.

MRS. HIGGINS: Henry: dont be absurd. If you want to know where Eliza is, she is upstairs.

HIGGINS: [*Amazed.*] Upstairs!!! Then I shall jolly soon fetch her downstairs. [*He makes resolutely for the door.*]

MRS. HIGGINS: [*Rising and following him.*] Be quiet, Henry. Sit down.

HIGGINS: I—

MRS. HIGGINS: Sit down, dear; and listen to me.

HIGGINS: Oh very well, very well, very well. [*He throws himself ungraciously on the ottoman, with his face towards the windows.*] But I think you might have told us this half an hour ago.

MRS. HIGGINS: Eliza came to me this morning. She told me of the brutal way you two treated her.

HIGGINS: [*Bounding up again.*] What!

PICKERING: [*Rising also.*] My dear Mrs. Higgins, she's been telling you stories. We didnt treat her brutally. We hardly said a word to her; and we parted on particularly good terms. [*Turning on* HIGGINS.] Higgins: did you bully her after I went to bed?

HIGGINS: Just the other way about. She threw my slippers in my face. She behaved in the most outrageous way. I never gave her the slightest provocation. The slippers came bang into my face the moment I entered the room—before I had uttered a word. And used perfectly awful language.

PICKERING: [*Astonished.*] But why? What did we do to her?

MRS. HIGGINS: I think I know pretty well what you did. The girl is naturally rather affectionate, I think. Isnt she, Mr. Doolittle?

DOOLITTLE: Very tender-hearted, maam. Takes after me.

MRS. HIGGINS: Just so. She had become attached to you both. She worked very

9. Mistake for the Greek mythological monsters Scylla, associated with a deadly rock jutting out of the Strait of Messina, and Charybdis, linked with a nearby whirlpool off the Sicilian coast. Used allusively, it refers to the danger of avoiding one peril only to encounter its opposite.

hard for you, Henry. I dont think you quite realize what anything in the nature of brain work means to a girl of her class. Well, it seems that when the great day of trial came, and she did this wonderful thing for you without making a single mistake, you two sat there and never said a word to her, but talked together of how glad you were that it was all over and how you had been bored with the whole thing. And then you were surprised because she threw your slippers at you! *I* should have thrown the fire-irons at you.

HIGGINS: We said nothing except that we were tired and wanted to go to bed. Did we, Pick?

PICKERING: [*Shrugging his shoulders.*] That was all.

MRS. HIGGINS: [*Ironically.*] Quite sure?

PICKERING: Absolutely. Really, that was all.

MRS. HIGGINS: You didnt thank her, or pet her, or admire her, or tell her how splendid she'd been.

HIGGINS: [*Impatiently.*] But she knew all about that. We didnt make speeches to her, if thats what you mean.

PICKERING: [*Conscience stricken.*] Perhaps we were a little inconsiderate. Is she very angry?

MRS. HIGGINS: [*Returning to her place at the writing-table.*] Well, I'm afraid she wont go back to Wimpole Street, especially now that Mr. Doolittle is able to keep up the position you have thrust on her; but she says she is quite willing to meet you on friendly terms and to let bygones be bygones.

HIGGINS: [*Furious.*] Is she, by George? Ho!

MRS. HIGGINS: If you promise to behave yourself, Henry, I'll ask her to come down. If not, go home; for you have taken up quite enough of my time.

HIGGINS: Oh, all right. Very well. Pick: you behave yourself. Let us put on our best Sunday manners for this creature that we picked out of the mud. [*He flings himself sulkily into the Elizabethan chair.*]

DOOLITTLE: [*Remonstrating.*] Now, now, Enry Iggins! Have some consideration for my feelings as a middle class man.

MRS. HIGGINS: Remember your promise, Henry. [*She presses the bell-button on the writing-table.*] Mr. Doolittle: will you be so good as to step out on the balcony for a moment. I dont want Eliza to have the shock of your news until she has made it up with these two gentlemen. Would you mind?

DOOLITTLE: As you wish, lady. Anything to help Henry to keep her off my hands. [*He disappears through the window.*]

[*The* PARLORMAID *answers the bell.* PICKERING *sits down in* DOOLITTLE's *place.*]

MRS. HIGGINS: Ask Miss Doolittle to come down, please.

THE PARLORMAID: Yes, maam. [*She goes out.*]

MRS. HIGGINS: Now, Henry: be good.

HIGGINS: I am behaving myself perfectly.

PICKERING: He is doing his best, Mrs. Higgins.

[*A pause.* HIGGINS *throws back his head; stretches out his legs; and begins to whistle.*]

MRS. HIGGINS: Henry, dearest, you dont look at all nice in that attitude.

HIGGINS: [*Pulling himself together.*] I was not trying to look nice, mother.

MRS. HIGGINS: It doesnt matter, dear. I only wanted to make you speak.

HIGGINS: Why?

MRS. HIGGINS: Because you cant speak and whistle at the same time.

> [HIGGINS *groans. Another very trying pause.*]

HIGGINS: [*Springing up, out of patience.*] Where the devil is that girl? Are we to wait here all day?

> [ELIZA *enters, sunny, self-possessed, and giving a staggeringly convincing exhibition of ease of manner. She carries a little work-basket, and is very much at home.* PICKERING *is too much taken aback to rise.*]

LIZA: How do you do, Professor Higgins? Are you quite well?

HIGGINS: [*Choking.*] Am I—[*He can say no more.*]

LIZA: But of course you are: you are never ill. So glad to see you again, Colonel Pickering. [*He rises hastily; and they shake hands.*] Quite chilly this morning, isnt it? [*She sits down on his left. He sits beside her.*]

HIGGINS: Dont you dare try this game on me. I taught it to you; and it doesnt take me in. Get up and come home; and dont be a fool.

> [ELIZA *takes a piece of needlework from her basket, and begins to stitch at it, without taking the least notice of this outburst.*]

MRS. HIGGINS: Very nicely put, indeed, Henry. No woman could resist such an invitation.

HIGGINS: You let her alone, mother. Let her speak for herself. You will jolly soon see whether she has an idea that I havnt put into her head or a word that I havnt put into her mouth. I tell you I have created this thing out of the squashed cabbage leaves of Covent Garden; and now she pretends to play the fine lady with me.

MRS. HIGGINS: [*Placidly.*] Yes, dear; but youll sit down, wont you?

> [HIGGINS *sits down again, savagely.*]

LIZA: [*To* PICKERING, *taking no apparent notice of* HIGGINS, *and working away deftly.*] Will you drop me altogether now that the experiment is over, Colonel Pickering?

PICKERING: Oh dont. You mustnt think of it as an experiment. It shocks me, somehow.

LIZA: Oh, I'm only a squashed cabbage leaf—

PICKERING: [*Impulsively.*] No.

LIZA: [*Continuing quietly.*]—but I owe so much to you that I should be very unhappy if you forgot me.

PICKERING: It's very kind of you to say so, Miss Doolittle.

LIZA: It's not because you paid for my dresses. I know you are generous to everybody with money. But it was from you that I learnt really nice manners; and that is what makes one a lady, isnt it? You see it was so very difficult for me with the example of Professor Higgins always before me. I was brought up to be just like him, unable to control myself, and using bad language on the slightest provocation. And I should never have known that ladies and gentlemen didnt behave like that if you hadnt been there.

HIGGINS: Well!!

PICKERING: Oh, thats only his way, you know. He doesnt mean it.

LIZA: Oh, *I* didnt mean it either, when I was a flower girl. It was only my way. But you see I did it; and thats what makes the difference after all.

PICKERING: No doubt. Still, he taught you to speak; and I couldnt have done that, you know.

LIZA: [*Trivially.*] Of course: that is his profession.

HIGGINS: Damnation!

LIZA: [*Continuing.*] It was just like learning to dance in the fashionable way: there was nothing more than that in it. But do you know what began my real education?

PICKERING: What?

LIZA: [*Stopping her work for a moment.*] Your calling me Miss Doolittle that day when I first came to Wimpole Street. That was the beginning of self-respect for me. [*She resumes her stitching.*] And there were a hundred little things you never noticed, because they came naturally to you. Things about standing up and taking off your hat and opening doors—

PICKERING: Oh, that was nothing.

LIZA: Yes: things that shewed you thought and felt about me as if I were something better than a scullery-maid; though of course I know you would have been just the same to a scullery-maid if she had been let into the drawing room. You never took off your boots in the dining room when I was there.

PICKERING: You mustnt mind that. Higgins takes off his boots all over the place.

LIZA: I know. I am not blaming him. It is his way, isnt it? But it made such a difference to me that you didnt do it. You see, really and truly, apart from the things anyone can pick up (the dressing and the proper way of speaking, and so on), the difference between a lady and a flower girl is not how she behaves, but how she's treated. I shall always be a flower girl to Professor Higgins, because he always treats me as a flower girl, and always will; but I know I can be a lady to you, because you always treat me as a lady, and always will.

MRS. HIGGINS: Please dont grind your teeth, Henry.

PICKERING: Well, this is really very nice of you, Miss Doolittle.

LIZA: I should like you to call me Eliza, now, if you would.

PICKERING: Thank you. Eliza, of course.

LIZA: And I should like Professor Higgins to call me Miss Doolittle.

HIGGINS: I'll see you damned first.

MRS. HIGGINS: Henry! Henry!

PICKERING: [*Laughing.*] Why dont you slang back at him? Dont stand it. It would do him a lot of good.

LIZA: I cant. I could have done it once; but now I cant go back to it. You told me, you know, that when a child is brought to a foreign country, it picks up the language in a few weeks, and forgets its own. Well, I am a child in your country. I have forgotten my own language, and can speak nothing but yours. Thats the real break-off with the corner of Tottenham Court Road. Leaving Wimpole Street finishes it.

PICKERING: [*Much alarmed.*] Oh! but youre coming back to Wimpole Street, arnt you? Youll forgive Higgins?

HIGGINS: [*Rising.*] Forgive! Will she, by George! Let her go. Let her find out how she can get on without us. She will relapse into the gutter in three weeks without me at her elbow.

> [DOOLITTLE *appears at the centre window. With a look of dignified reproach at* HIGGINS, *he comes slowly and silently to his daughter, who, with her back to the window, is unconscious of his approach.*]

PICKERING: He's incorrigible, Eliza. You wont relapse, will you?

LIZA: No: not now. Never again. I have learnt my lesson. I dont believe I could utter one of the old sounds if I tried. [DOOLITTLE *touches her on her left shoulder. She drops her work, losing her self-possession utterly at the spectacle of her father's splendor.*] A-a-a-a-a-ah-ow-ooh!

HIGGINS: [*With a crow of triumph.*] Aha! Just so. A-a-a-a-ahowooh! A-a-a-a-ah-ow-ooh! A-a-a-a-ahowooh! Victory! Victory! [*He throws himself on the divan, folding his arms, and spraddling arrogantly.*]

DOOLITTLE: Can you blame the girl? Dont look at me like that, Eliza. It aint my fault. Ive come into some money.

LIZA: You must have touched a millionaire this time, dad.

DOOLITTLE: I have. But I'm dressed something special today. I'm going to St. George's, Hanover Square. Your stepmother is going to marry me.

LIZA: [*Angrily.*] Youre going to let yourself down to marry that low common woman!

PICKERING: [*Quietly.*] He ought to, Eliza. [*To* DOOLITTLE.] Why has she changed her mind?

DOOLITTLE: [*Sadly.*] Intimidated, Governor. Intimidated. Middle class morality claims its victim. Wont you put on your hat, Liza, and come and see me turned off?

LIZA: If the Colonel says I must, I—I'll [*Almost sobbing.*] I'll demean myself. And get insulted for my pains, like enough.

DOOLITTLE: Dont be afraid: she never comes to words with anyone now, poor woman! respectability has broke all the spirit out of her.

PICKERING: [*Squeezing* ELIZA's *elbow gently.*] Be kind to them, Eliza. Make the best of it.

LIZA: [*Forcing a little smile for him through her vexation.*] Oh well, just to shew theres no ill feeling. I'll be back in a moment. [*She goes out.*]

DOOLITTLE: [*Sitting down beside* PICKERING.] I feel uncommon nervous about the ceremony, Colonel. I wish youd come and see me through it.

PICKERING: But youve been through it before, man. You were married to Eliza's mother.

DOOLITTLE: Who told you that, Colonel?

PICKERING: Well, nobody told me. But I concluded—naturally—

DOOLITTLE: No: that aint the natural way, Colonel: it's only the middle class way. My way was always the undeserving way. But dont say nothing to Eliza. She dont know: I always had a delicacy about telling her.

PICKERING: Quite right. We'll leave it so, if you dont mind.

DOOLITTLE: And youll come to the church, Colonel, and put me through straight?

PICKERING: With pleasure. As far as a bachelor can.

MRS. HIGGINS: May I come, Mr. Doolittle? I should be very sorry to miss your wedding.

DOOLITTLE: I should indeed be honored by your condescension, maam; and my poor old woman would take it as a tremenjous compliment. She's been very low, thinking of the happy days that are no more.

MRS. HIGGINS: [*Rising.*] I'll order the carriage and get ready. [*The men rise, except* HIGGINS.] I shant be more than fifteen minutes. [*As she goes to the door* ELIZA *comes in, hatted and buttoning her gloves.*] I'm going to the church to see your father married, Eliza. You had better come in the brougham with me. Colonel Pickering can go on with the bridegroom.

[MRS. HIGGINS *goes out.* ELIZA *comes to the middle of the room between the centre window and the ottoman.* PICKERING *joins her.*]

DOOLITTLE: Bridegroom! What a word! It makes a man realize his position, somehow. [*He takes up his hat and goes towards the door.*]

PICKERING: Before I go, Eliza, do forgive Higgins and come back to us.

LIZA: I dont think dad would allow me. Would you, dad?

DOOLITTLE: [*Sad but magnanimous.*] They played you off very cunning, Eliza, them two sportsmen. It if had been only one of them, you could have nailed him. But you see, there was two; and one of them chaperoned the other, as you might say. [*To* PICKERING.] It was artful of you, Colonel; but I bear no malice: I should have done the same myself. I been the victim of one woman after another all my life; and I dont grudge you two getting the better of Eliza. I shant interfere. It's time for us to go, Colonel. So long, Henry. See you in St. George's, Eliza. [*He goes out.*]

PICKERING: [*Coaxing.*] Do stay with us, Eliza. [*He follows* DOOLITTLE.]

[ELIZA *goes out on the balcony to avoid being alone with* HIGGINS. *He rises and joins her there. She immediately comes back into the room and makes for the door; but he goes along the balcony quickly and gets his back to the door before she reaches it.*]

HIGGINS: Well, Eliza, youve had a bit of your own back, as you call it. Have you had enough? and are you going to be reasonable? Or do you want any more?

LIZA: You want me back only to pick up your slippers and put up with your tempers and fetch and carry for you.

HIGGINS: I havnt said I wanted you back at all.

LIZA: Oh, indeed. Then what are we talking about?

HIGGINS: About you, not about me. If you come back I shall treat you just as I have always treated you. I cant change my nature; and I dont intend to change my manners. My manners are exactly the same as Colonel Pickering's.

LIZA: Thats not true. He treats a flower girl as if she was a duchess.

HIGGINS: And I treat a duchess as if she was a flower girl.

LIZA: I see. [*She turns away composedly, and sits on the ottoman, facing the window.*] The same to everybody.

HIGGINS: Just so.

LIZA: Like father.

HIGGINS: [*Grinning, a little taken down.*] Without accepting the comparison at all points, Eliza, it's quite true that your father is not a snob, and that he will be quite at home in any station of life to which his eccentric destiny may call him. [*Seriously.*] The great secret, Eliza, is not having bad manners or good manners or any other particular sort of manners, but having the same manner for all human souls: in short, behaving as if you were in Heaven, where there are no third-class carriages, and one soul is as good as another.

LIZA: Amen. You are a born preacher.

HIGGINS: [*Irritated.*] The question is not whether I treat you rudely, but whether you ever heard me treat anyone else better.

LIZA: [*With sudden sincerity.*] I dont care how you treat me. I dont mind your swearing at me. I shouldnt mind a black eye: Ive had one before this. But [*Standing up and facing him.*] I wont be passed over.

HIGGINS: Then get out of my way; for I wont stop for you. You talk about me as if I were a motor bus.

LIZA: So you are a motor bus: all bounce and go, and no consideration for anyone. But I can do without you: dont think I cant.

HIGGINS: I know you can. I told you you could.

LIZA: [*Wounded, getting away from him to the other side of the ottoman with her face to the hearth.*] I know you did, you brute. You wanted to get rid of me.

HIGGINS: Liar.

LIZA: Thank you. [*She sits down with dignity.*]

HIGGINS: You never asked yourself, I suppose, whether *I* could do without you.

LIZA: [*Earnestly.*] Dont you try to get round me. Youll have to do without me.

HIGGINS: [*Arrogant.*] I can do without anybody. I have my own soul: my own spark of divine fire. But [*With sudden humility.*] I shall miss you, Eliza. [*He sits down near her on the ottoman.*] I have learnt something from your idiotic notions: I confess that humbly and gratefully. And I have grown accustomed to your voice and appearance. I like them, rather.

LIZA: Well, you have both of them on your gramophone and in your book of photographs. When you feel lonely without me, you can turn the machine on. It's got no feelings to hurt.

HIGGINS: I cant turn your soul on. Leave me those feelings; and you can take away the voice and the face. They are not you.

LIZA: Oh, you are a devil. You can twist the heart in a girl as easy as some could twist her arms to hurt her. Mrs. Pearce warned me. Time and again she has wanted to leave you; and you always got round her at the last minute. And you dont care a bit for her. And you dont care a bit for me.

HIGGINS: I care for life, for humanity; and you are a part of it that has come my way and been built into my house. What more can you or anyone ask?

LIZA: I wont care for anybody that doesnt care for me.

HIGGINS: Commercial principles, Eliza. Like [*Reproducing her Covent Garden pronunciation with professional exactness.*] s'yollin voylets [selling violets], isnt it?

LIZA: Dont sneer at me. It's mean to sneer at me.

HIGGINS: I have never sneered in my life. Sneering doesnt become either the human face or the human soul. I am expressing my righteous contempt for Commercialism. I dont and wont trade in affection. You call me a brute because you couldnt buy a claim on me by fetching my slippers and finding my spectacles. You were a fool: I think a woman fetching a man's slippers is a disgusting sight: did I ever fetch your slippers? I think a good deal more of you for throwing them in my face. No use slaving for me and then saying you want to be cared for: who cares for a slave? If you come back, come back for the sake of good fellowship; for youll get nothing else. Youve had a thousand times as much out of me as I have out of you; and if you dare to set up your little dog's tricks of fetching and carrying slippers against my creation of a Duchess Eliza, I'll slam the door in your silly face.

LIZA: What did you do it for if you didnt care for me?

HIGGINS: [*Heartily.*] Why, because it was my job.

LIZA: You never thought of the trouble it would make for me.

HIGGINS: Would the world ever have been made if its maker had been afraid of making trouble? Making life means making trouble. Theres only one way of escaping trouble; and thats killing things. Cowards, you notice, are always shrieking to have troublesome people killed.

LIZA: I'm no preacher: I dont notice things like that. I notice that you dont notice me.

HIGGINS: [*Jumping up and walking about intolerantly.*] Eliza: youre an idiot. I waste the treasures of my Miltonic mind by spreading them before you. Once for all, understand that I go my way and do my work without caring twopence what happens to either of us. I am not intimidated, like your father and your stepmother. So you can come back or go to the devil: which you please.

LIZA: What am I to come back for?

HIGGINS: [*Bouncing up on his knees on the ottoman and leaning over it to her.*] For the fun of it. Thats why I took you on.

LIZA: [*With averted face.*] And you may throw me out tomorrow if I dont do everything you want me to?

HIGGINS: Yes; and you may walk out tomorrow if I dont do everything you want me to.

LIZA: And live with my stepmother?

HIGGINS: Yes, or sell flowers.

LIZA: Oh! if I only could go back to my flower basket! I should be independent of both you and father and all the world! Why did you take my independence from me? Why did I give it up? I'm a slave now, for all my fine clothes.

HIGGINS: Not a bit. I'll adopt you as my daughter and settle money on you if you like. Or would you rather marry Pickering?

LIZA: [*Looking fiercely round at him.*] I wouldnt marry you if you asked me; and youre nearer my age than what he is.

HIGGINS: [*Gently.*] Than he is: not "than what he is."

LIZA: [*Losing her temper and rising.*] I'll talk as I like. Youre not my teacher now.

HIGGINS: [*Reflectively.*] I dont suppose Pickering would, though. He's as confirmed an old bachelor as I am.

LIZA: Thats not what I want; and dont you think it. Ive always had chaps enough wanting me that way. Freddy Hill writes to me twice and three times a day, sheets and sheets.

HIGGINS: [*Disagreeably surprised.*] Damn his impudence! [*He recoils and finds himself sitting on his heels.*]

LIZA: He has a right to if he likes, poor lad. And he does love me.

HIGGINS: [*Getting off the ottoman.*] You have no right to encourage him.

LIZA: Every girl has a right to be loved.

HIGGINS: What! By fools like that?

LIZA: Freddy's not a fool. And if he's weak and poor and wants me, may be he'd make me happier than my betters that bully me and dont want me.

HIGGINS: Can he make anything of you? Thats the point.

LIZA: Perhaps I could make something of him. But I never thought of us making anything of one another; and you never think of anything else. I only want to be natural.

HIGGINS: In short, you want me to be as infatuated about you as Freddy? Is that it?

LIZA: No I dont. Thats not the sort of feeling I want from you. And dont you be too sure of yourself or of me. I could have been a bad girl if I'd liked. Ive seen more of some things than you, for all your learning. Girls like me can drag gentlemen down to make love to them easy enough. And they wish each other dead the next minute.

HIGGINS: Of course they do. Then what in thunder are we quarrelling about?

LIZA: [*Much troubled.*] I want a little kindness. I know I'm a common ignorant girl, and you a book-learned gentleman; but I'm not dirt under your feet. What I done [*Correcting herself.*] what I did was not for the dresses and the taxis: I did it because we were pleasant together and I come—came—to care for you; not to want you to make love to me, and not forgetting the difference between us, but more friendly like.

HIGGINS: Well, of course. Thats just how I feel. And how Pickering feels. Eliza: youre a fool.

LIZA: Thats not a proper answer to give me. [*She sinks on the chair at the writing-table in tears.*]

HIGGINS: It's all youll get until you stop being a common idiot. If youre going to be a lady, youll have to give up feeling neglected if the men you know dont spend half their time snivelling over you and the other half giving you black eyes. If you cant stand the coldness of my sort of life, and the strain of it, go back to the gutter. Work til youre more a brute than a human being; and then cuddle and squabble and drink til you fall asleep. Oh, it's a fine life, the life of the gutter. It's real: it's warm: it's violent: you can feel it through the thickest skin: you can taste it and smell it without any training or any work. Not like Science and Literature and Classical Music and Philosophy and Art. You find me cold, unfeeling, selfish, dont you? Very well: be off with you to the sort of people you like. Marry some sentimental hog or other with lots of money, and a thick pair of lips to kiss you with and a thick pair of boots to kick you with. If you cant appreciate what youve got, youd better get what you can appreciate.

LIZA: [*Desperate.*] Oh, you are a cruel tyrant. I cant talk to you: you turn everything against me: I'm always in the wrong. But you know very well all the time that youre nothing but a bully. You know I cant go back to the gutter, as you call it, and that I have no real friends in the world but you and the Colonel. You know well I couldnt bear to live with a low common man after you two; and it's wicked and cruel of you to insult me by pretending I could. You think I must go back to Wimpole Street because I have nowhere else to go but father's. But dont you be too sure that you have me under your feet to be trampled on and talked down. I'll marry Freddy, I will, as soon as I'm able to support him.

HIGGINS: [*Thunderstruck.*] Freddy!!! that young fool! That poor devil who couldnt get a job as an errand boy even if he had the guts to try for it! Woman: do you not understand that I have made you a consort for a king?

LIZA: Freddy loves me: that makes him king enough for me. I dont want him to work: he wasnt brought up to it as I was. I'll go and be a teacher.

HIGGINS: Whatll you teach, in heaven's name?

LIZA: What you taught me. I'll teach phonetics.

HIGGINS: Ha! ha! ha!

LIZA: I'll offer myself as an assistant to that hairy-faced Hungarian.

HIGGINS: [*Rising in a fury.*] What! That impostor! that humbug! that toadying ignoramus! Teach him my methods! my discoveries! You take one step in his direction and I'll wring your neck. [*He lays hands on her.*] Do you hear?

LIZA: [*Defiantly non-resistant.*] Wring away. What do I care? I knew youd strike me some day. [*He lets her go, stamping with rage at having forgotten himself, and recoils so hastily that he stumbles back into his seat on the ottoman.*] Aha! Now I know how to deal with you. What a fool I was not to think of it before! You cant take away the knowledge you gave me. You said I had a finer ear than you. And I can be civil and kind to people, which is more than you can. Aha! [*Purposely dropping her aitches to annoy him.*] Thats done you, Enry Iggins, it az. Now I dont care that [*Snapping her fingers.*] for your bullying and your big talk. I'll advertize it in the papers that your duchess is only a flower girl that you taught, and that she'll teach anybody to be a duchess just the same in six months for a thousand guineas. Oh, when I think of myself crawling under your feet and being trampled on and called names, when all the time I had only to lift up my finger to be as good as you. I could just kick myself.

HIGGINS: [*Wondering at her.*] You damned impudent slut, you! But it's better than snivelling; better than fetching slippers and finding spectacles, isnt it? [*Rising.*] By George, Eliza, I said I'd make a woman of you; and I have. I like you like this.

LIZA: Yes: you turn round and make up to me now that I'm not afraid of you, and can do without you.

HIGGINS: Of course I do, you little fool. Five minutes ago you were like a millstone round my neck. Now youre a tower of strength: a consort battleship. You and I and Pickering will be three old bachelors together instead of only two men and a silly girl.

> [MRS. HIGGINS *returns, dressed for the wedding.* ELIZA *instantly becomes cool and elegant.*]

MRS. HIGGINS: The carriage is waiting, Eliza. Are you ready?

LIZA: Quite. Is the Professor coming?

MRS. HIGGINS: Certainly not. He cant behave himself in church. He makes remarks out loud all the time on the clergyman's pronunciation.

LIZA: Then I shall not see you again, Professor. Goodbye. [*She goes to the door.*]

MRS. HIGGINS: [*Coming to* HIGGINS.] Goodbye, dear.

HIGGINS: Goodbye, mother. [*He is about to kiss her, when he recollects something.*] Oh, by the way, Eliza, order a ham and a Stilton cheese, will you? And buy me a pair of reindeer gloves, number eights, and a tie to match that new suit of mine. You can choose the color. [*His cheerful, careless, vigorous voice shews that he is incorrigible.*]

LIZA: [*Disdainfully.*] Number eights are too small for you if you want them lined with lamb's wool. You have three new ties that you have forgotten in the drawer of your washstand. Colonel Pickering prefers double Gloucester to Stilton; and you dont notice the difference. I telephoned Mrs. Pearce this morning not to forget the ham. What you are to do without me I cannot imagine. [*She sweeps out.*]

MRS. HIGGINS: I'm afraid youve spoilt that girl, Henry. I should be uneasy about you and her if she were less fond of Colonel Pickering.

HIGGINS: Pickering! Nonsense: she's going to marry Freddy. Ha ha! Freddy! Freddy!! Ha ha ha ha ha!!!!! [*He roars with laughter as the play ends*].

CURTAIN

The rest of the story need not be shewn in action, and indeed, would hardly need telling if our imaginations were not so enfeebled by their lazy dependence on the ready-mades and reach-me-downs of the ragshop in which Romance keeps its stock of "happy endings" to misfit all stories. Now, the history of Eliza Doolittle, though called a romance because the transfiguration it records seems exceedingly improbable, is common enough. Such transfigurations have been achieved by hundreds of resolutely ambitious young women since Nell Gwynne set them the example by playing queens and fascinating kings in the theatre in which she began by selling oranges. Nevertheless, people in all directions have assumed, for no other reason than that she became the heroine of a romance, that she must have married the hero of it. This is unbearable, not only because her little drama, if acted on such a thoughtless assumption, must be spoiled, but because the true sequel is patent to anyone with a sense of human nature in general, and of feminine instinct in particular.

Eliza, in telling Higgins she would not marry him if he asked her, was not coquetting: she was announcing a well-considered decision. When a bachelor interests, and dominates, and teaches, and becomes important to a spinster, as Higgins with Eliza, she always, if she has character enough to be capable of it, considers very seriously indeed whether she will play for becoming that bachelor's wife, especially if he is so little interested in marriage that a determined and devoted woman might capture him if she set herself resolutely to do it. Her decision will depend a good deal on whether she is really free to choose; and that, again, will depend on her age and income. If she is at the end of her youth, and has no security for her livelihood, she will marry him because she must marry anybody who will provide for her. But at Eliza's age a good-looking girl does not feel that pressure: she feels free to pick and choose. She is therefore guided by her instinct in the matter. Eliza's instinct tells her not to marry Higgins. It does not tell her to give him up. It is not in the slightest doubt as to his remaining one of the strongest personal interests in her life. It would be very sorely strained if there was another woman likely to supplant her with him. But as she feels sure of him on that last point, she has no doubt at all as to her course, and would not have any, even if the difference of twenty years in age, which seems so great to youth, did not exist between them.

As our own instincts are not appealed to by her conclusion, let us see whether we cannot discover some reason in it. When Higgins excused his indifference to young women on the ground that they had an irresistible rival in his mother, he gave the clue to his inveterate old-bachelordom. The case is uncommon only to the extent that remarkable mothers are uncommon. If an imaginative boy has a sufficiently rich mother who has intelligence, personal grace, dignity of character without harshness, and a cultivated sense of the best art of her time to enable her to make her house beautiful, she sets a standard for him against which very few women can struggle, besides effecting for him a disengagement of his affections, his sense of beauty, and his idealism from his specifically sexual impulses. This makes him a standing puzzle to the huge number of uncultivated people who have been brought up in tasteless homes by commonplace or disagreeable parents, and to whom, consequently, literature, painting, sculpture, music, and affectionate personal relations come as modes of sex if they come at all. The word passion means nothing else to them; and that Higgins could have a passion for phonetics and idealize his mother instead of Eliza, would seem to them absurd and unnatural. Nevertheless, when we look round and see that hardly anyone is too ugly or disagreeable to find a wife or a husband if he or she wants one, whilst many old maids and bachelors are above the average in quality and culture, we cannot help suspecting that the disentanglement of sex from the associations with which it is so commonly confused, a disentanglement which persons of genius achieve by sheer intellectual analysis, is sometimes produced or aided by parental fascination.

Now, though Eliza was incapable of thus explaining to herself Higgins's formidable powers of resistance to the charm that prostrated Freddy at the first glance, she was instinctively aware that she could never obtain a complete grip of him, or come between him and his mother (the first necessity of the married woman). To put it shortly, she knew that for some mysterious reason he had not the makings of a married man in him, according to her conception of a husband as one to whom she would be his nearest and fondest and warmest interest. Even had there been no mother-rival, she would still have refused to accept an interest in herself that was secondary to philosophic interests. Had Mrs. Higgins died, there would still have been Milton and the Universal Alphabet. Landor's remark that to those who have the greatest power of loving, love is a secondary affair, would not have recommended Landor to Eliza. Put that along with her resentment of Higgins's domineering superiority, and her mistrust of his coaxing cleverness in getting round her and evading her wrath when he had gone too far with his impetuous bullying, and you will see that Eliza's instinct had good grounds for warning her not to marry her Pygmalion.

And now, whom did Eliza marry? For if Higgins was a predestinate old bachelor, she was most certainly not a predestinate old maid. Well, that can be told very shortly to those who have not guessed it from the indications she has herself given them.

Almost immediately after Eliza is stung into proclaiming her considered determination not to marry Higgins, she mentions the fact that young Mr. Frederick Eynsford Hill is pouring out his love for her daily through the post. Now Freddy is young, practically twenty years younger than Higgins: he is a gentleman (or, as Eliza would qualify him, a toff), and speaks like one. He is nicely dressed, is treated by the Colonel as an equal, loves her unaffectedly, and is not her master, nor ever likely to dominate her in spite of his advantage of social standing. Eliza has no use for the foolish romantic tradition that all women love to be mastered, if not actually bullied and beaten. "When you go to women" says Nietzsche[1] "take your whip with you." Sensible despots have never confined that precaution to women: they have taken their whips with them when they have dealt with men, and been slavishly idealized by the men over whom they have flourished the whip much more than by women. No doubt there are slavish women as well as slavish men; and women, like men, admire those that are stronger than themselves. But to admire a strong person and to live under that strong person's thumb are two different things. The weak may not be admired and hero-worshipped; but they are by no means disliked or shunned; and they never seem to have the least difficulty in marrying people who are too good for them. They may fail in emergencies; but life is not one long emergency: it is mostly a string of situations for which no exceptional strength is needed, and with which even rather weak people can cope if they have a stronger partner to help them out. Accordingly, it is a truth everywhere in evidence that strong people, masculine or feminine, not only do not marry stronger people, but do not shew any preference for them in selecting their friends. When a lion meets another with a louder roar "the first lion thinks the last a bore." The man or woman who feels strong enough for two, seeks for every other quality in a partner than strength.

1. German philosopher Friedrich Nietzsche (1844–1900).

The converse is also true. Weak people want to marry strong people who do not frighten them too much; and this often leads them to make the mistake we describe metaphorically as "biting off more than they can chew." They want too much for too little; and when the bargain is unreasonable beyond all bearing, the union becomes impossible: it ends in the weaker party being either discarded or borne as a cross, which is worse. People who are not only weak, but silly or obtuse as well, are often in these difficulties.

This being the state of human affairs, what is Eliza fairly sure to do when she is placed between Freddy and Higgins? Will she look forward to a lifetime of fetching Higgins's slippers or to a lifetime of Freddy fetching hers? There can be no doubt about the answer. Unless Freddy is biologically repulsive to her, and Higgins biologically attractive to a degree that overwhelms all her other instincts, she will, if she marries either of them, marry Freddy.

And that is just what Eliza did.

Complications ensued; but they were economic, not romantic. Freddy had no money and no occupation. His mother's jointure, a last relic of the opulence of Largelady Park, had enabled her to struggle along in Earlscourt with an air of gentility, but not to procure any serious secondary education for her children, much less give the boy a profession. A clerkship at thirty shillings a week was beneath Freddy's dignity, and extremely distasteful to him besides. His prospects consisted of a hope that if he kept up appearances somebody would do something for him. The something appeared vaguely to his imagination as a private secretaryship or a sinecure of some sort. To his mother it perhaps appeared as a marriage to some lady of means who could not resist her boy's niceness. Fancy her feelings when he married a flower girl who had become disclassed under extraordinary circumstances which were now notorious!

It is true that Eliza's situation did not seem wholly ineligible. Her father, though formerly a dustman, and now fantastically disclassed, had become extremely popular in the smartest society by a social talent which triumphed over every prejudice and every disadvantage. Rejected by the middle class, which he loathed, he had shot up at once into the highest circles by his wit, his dustmanship (which he carried like a banner), and his Nietzschean transcendence of good and evil. At intimate ducal dinners he sat on the right hand of the Duchess; and in country houses he smoked in the pantry and was made much of by the butler when he was not feeding in the dining room and being consulted by cabinet ministers. But he found it almost as hard to do all this on four thousand a year as Mrs. Eynsford Hill to live in Earlscourt on an income so pitiably smaller that I have not the heart to disclose its exact figure. He absolutely refused to add the last straw to his burden by contributing to Eliza's support.

Thus Freddy and Eliza, now Mr. and Mrs. Eynsford Hill, would have spent a penniless honeymoon but for a wedding present of £500 from the Colonel to Eliza. It lasted a long time because Freddy did not know how to spend money, never having had any to spend, and Eliza, socially trained by a pair of old bachelors, wore her clothes as long as they held together and looked pretty, without the least regard to their being many months out of fashion. Still, £500 will not last two young people for ever; and they both knew, and Eliza felt as well, that they must shift for themselves in the end. She could quarter herself on Wimpole Street because it had come to be her home; but she was quite aware that she ought not to quarter Freddy there, and that it would not be good for his character if she did.

Not that the Wimpole Street bachelors objected. When she consulted them, Higgins declined to be bothered about her housing problem when that solution was so simple. Eliza's desire to have Freddy in the house with her seemed of no more importance than if she had wanted an extra piece of bedroom furniture. Pleas as to Freddy's character, and the moral obligation on him to earn his own living, were lost on Higgins. He denied that Freddy had any character, and declared that if he tried to do any useful work some competent person would have the trouble of undoing it: a procedure involving a net loss to the community, and great unhappiness to Freddy himself, who was obviously intended by Nature for such light work as amusing Eliza, which, Higgins declared, was a much more useful and honorable occupation than working in the city. When Eliza referred again to her project of teaching phonetics, Higgins abated not a jot of his violent opposition to it. He said she was not within ten years of being qualified to meddle with his pet subject; and as it was evident that the Colonel agreed with him, she felt she could not go against them in this grave matter, and that she had no right, without Higgins's consent, to exploit the knowledge he had given her; for his knowledge seemed to her as much his private property as his watch: Eliza was no communist. Besides, she was superstitiously devoted to them both, more entirely and frankly after her marriage than before it.

It was the Colonel who finally solved the problem, which had cost him much perplexed cogitation. He one day asked Eliza, rather shyly, whether she had quite given up her notion of keeping a flower shop. She replied that she had thought of it, but had put it out of her head, because the Colonel had said, that day at Mrs. Higgins's, that it would never do. The Colonel confessed that when he said that, he had not quite recovered from the dazzling impression of the day before. They broke the matter to Higgins that evening. The sole comment vouchsafed by him very nearly led to a serious quarrel with Eliza. It was to the effect that she would have in Freddy an ideal errand boy.

Freddy himself was next sounded on the subject. He said he had been thinking of a shop himself; though it had presented itself to his pennilessness as a small place in which Eliza should sell tobacco at one counter whilst he sold newspapers at the opposite one. But he agreed that it would be extraordinarily jolly to go early every morning with Eliza to Covent Garden and buy flowers on the scene of their first meeting: a sentiment which earned him many kisses from his wife. He added that he had always been afraid to propose anything of the sort, because Clara would make an awful row about a step that must damage her matrimonial chances, and his mother could not be expected to like it after clinging for so many years to that step of the social ladder on which retail trade is impossible.

This difficulty was removed by an event highly unexpected by Freddy's mother. Clara, in the course of her incursions into those artistic circles which were the highest within her reach, discovered that her conversational qualifications were expected to include a grounding in the novels of Mr. H. G. Wells.[2] She borrowed them in various directions so energetically that she swallowed them all within two months. The result was a conversion of a kind quite common today. A modern Acts of the Apostles[3] would fill fifty whole Bibles if anyone were capable of writing it.

Poor Clara, who appeared to Higgins and his mother as a disagreeable and ridiculous person, and to her own mother as in some inexplicable way a social failure, had never seen herself in either light; for, though to some extent ridiculed and mimicked in West Kensington like everybody else there, she was accepted as a rational and normal—or shall we say inevitable?—sort of human being. At worst they called her The Pusher; but to them no more than to herself had it ever occurred that she was pushing the air, and pushing it in a wrong direction. Still, she was not happy. She was growing desperate. Her one asset, the fact that her mother was what the Epsom greengrocer called a carriage lady, had no exchange value, apparently. It had prevented her from getting educated, because the only education she could have afforded was education with the Earlscourt greengrocer's daughter. It had led her to seek the society of her mother's class; and that class simply would not have her, because she was much poorer than the greengrocer, and, far from being able to afford a maid, could not afford even a housemaid, and had to scrape along at home with an illiberally treated general servant. Under such circumstances nothing could give her an air of being a genuine product of Largelady Park. And yet its tradition made her regard a marriage with anyone within her reach as an unbearable humiliation. Commercial people and professional people in a small way were odious to her. She ran after painters and novelists; but she did not charm them; and her bold attempts to pick up and practise artistic and literary talk irritated them. She was, in short, an utter failure, an ignorant, incompetent, pretentious, unwelcome, penniless, useless little snob; and though she did not admit these disqualifications (for nobody ever faces unpleasant truths of this kind until the possibility of a way out dawns on them) she felt their effects too keenly to be satisfied with her position.

Clara had a startling eyeopener when, on being suddenly wakened to enthusiasm by a girl of her own age who dazzled her and produced in her a gushing desire to take her for a model, and gain her friendship, she discovered that this exquisite apparition had graduated from the gutter in a few months time. It shook her so violently, that when Mr. H. G. Wells lifted her on the point of his puissant pen, and placed her at the angle of view from which the life she was leading and the society to which she clung appeared in its true relation to real human needs and worthy social structure, he effected a conversion and a conviction of sin comparable to the most sensational feats of General Booth or Gypsy Smith.[4] Clara's snobbery went bang. Life suddenly began to move with her. Without knowing how or why, she began to make friends and enemies. Some of

---

2. H. G. Wells (1866–1946), English novelist, scientific visionary, and social prophet.   3. Fifth book of the New Testament.   4. General William Booth (1829–1912), founder and leader of the Salvation Army; Gypsy Rodney Smith (1860–1947), English evangelist with the National Free Church Council and an associate of General Booth's.

the acquaintances to whom she had been a tedious or indifferent or ridiculous affliction, dropped her: others became cordial. To her amazement she found that some "quite nice" people were saturated with Wells, and that this accessibility to ideas was the secret of their niceness. People she had thought deeply religious, and had tried to conciliate on that tack with disastrous results, suddenly took an interest in her, and revealed a hostility to conventional religion which she had never conceived possible except among the most desperate characters. They made her read Galsworthy;[5] and Galsworthy exposed the vanity of Largelady Park and finished her. It exasperated her to think that the dungeon in which she had languished for so many unhappy years had been unlocked all the time, and that the impulses she had so carefully struggled with and stifled for the sake of keeping well with society, were precisely those by which alone she could have come into any sort of sincere human contact. In the radiance of these discoveries, and the tumult of their reaction, she made a fool of herself as freely and conspicuously as when she so rashly adopted Eliza's expletive in Mrs. Higgins's drawing room; for the new-born Wellsian had to find her bearings almost as ridiculously as a baby; but nobody hates a baby for its ineptitudes, or thinks the worse of it for trying to eat the matches; and Clara lost no friends by her follies. They laughed at her to her face this time; and she had to defend herself and fight it out as best she could.

When Freddy paid a visit to Earlscourt (which he never did when he could possibly help it) to make the desolating announcement that he and his Eliza were thinking of blackening the Largelady scutcheon by opening a shop, he found the little household already convulsed by a prior announcement from Clara that she also was going to work in an old furniture shop in Dover Street, which had been started by a fellow Wellsian. This appointment Clara owed, after all, to her old social accomplishment of Push. She had made up her mind that, cost what it might, she would see Mr. Wells in the flesh; and she had achieved her end at a garden party. She had better luck than so rash an enterprise deserved. Mr. Wells came up to her expectations. Age had not withered him, nor could custom stale his infinite variety in half an hour.[6] His pleasant neatness and compactness, his small hands and feet, his teeming ready brain, his unaffected accessibility, and a certain fine apprehensiveness which stamped him as susceptible from his topmost hair to his tipmost toe, proved irresistible. Clara talked of nothing else for weeks and weeks afterwards. And as she happened to talk to the lady of the furniture shop, and that lady also desired above all things to know Mr. Wells and sell pretty things to him, she offered Clara a job on the chance of achieving that end through her.

And so it came about that Eliza's luck held, and the expected opposition to the flower shop melted away. The shop is in the arcade of a railway station not very far from the Victoria and Albert Museum; and if you live in that neighborhood you may go there any day and buy a buttonhole from Eliza.

Now here is a last opportunity for romance. Would you not like to be assured

---

5. English playwright and novelist John Galsworthy (1867–1933).   6. From Shakespeare's *Antony and Cleopatra*, II.ii.243: "Age cannot wither her, nor custom stale / her infinite variety."

that the shop was an immense success, thanks to Eliza's charms and her early business experience in Covent Garden? Alas! the truth is the truth: the shop did not pay for a long time, simply because Eliza and her Freddy did not know how to keep it. True, Eliza had not to begin at the very beginning: she knew the names and prices of the cheaper flowers; and her elation was unbounded when she found that Freddy, like all youths educated at cheap, pretentious, and thoroughly inefficient schools, knew a little Latin. It was very little, but enough to make him appear to her a Porson or Bentley,[7] and to put him at his ease with botanical nomenclature. Unfortunately he knew nothing else; and Eliza, though she could count money up to eighteen shillings or so, and had acquired a certain familiarity with the language of Milton from her struggles to qualify herself for winning Higgins's bet, could not write out a bill without utterly disgracing the establishment. Freddy's power of stating in Latin that Balbus built a wall and that Gaul was divided into three parts[8] did not carry with it the slightest knowledge of accounts or business: Colonel Pickering had to explain to him what a cheque book and a bank account meant. And the pair were by no means easily teachable. Freddy backed up Eliza in her obstinate refusal to believe that they could save money by engaging a bookkeeper with some knowledge of the business. How, they argued, could you possibly save money by going to extra expense when you already could not make both ends meet? But the Colonel, after making the ends meet over and over again, at last gently insisted; and Eliza, humbled to the dust by having to beg from him so often, and stung by the uproarious derision of Higgins, to whom the notion of Freddy succeeding at anything was a joke that never palled, grasped the fact that business, like phonetics, has to be learned.

On the piteous spectacle of the pair spending their evenings in shorthand schools and polytechnic classes, learning bookkeeping and typewriting with incipient junior clerks, male and female, from the elementary schools, let me not dwell. There were even classes at the London School of Economics, and a humble personal appeal to the director of that institution to recommend a course bearing on the flower business. He, being a humorist, explained to them the method of the celebrated Dickensian essay on Chinese Metaphysics by the gentleman who read an article on China and an article on Metaphysics and combined the information. He suggested that they should combine the London School with Kew Gardens. Eliza, to whom the procedure of the Dickensian gentleman seemed perfectly correct (as in fact it was) and not in the least funny (which was only her ignorance), took the advice with entire gravity. But the effort that cost her the deepest humiliation was a request to Higgins, whose pet artistic fancy, next to Milton's verse, was caligraphy, and who himself wrote a most beautiful Italian hand, that he would teach her to write. He declared that she was congenitally incapable of forming a single letter worthy of the least of Milton's words; but she persisted; and again he suddenly threw himself into the task of teaching her with a combination of stormy intensity, concentrated patience, and occasional bursts

---

7. Classical scholars Richard Porson (1759–1808) and Richard Bentley (1662–1742).   8. Freddie's ability to say such things in Latin reflects his fragmented and partial "schoolboy's" understanding of Roman history.

of interesting disquisition on the beauty and nobility, the august mission and destiny, of human handwriting. Eliza ended by acquiring an extremely uncommercial script which was a positive extension of her personal beauty, and spending three times as much on stationery as anyone else because certain qualities and shapes of paper became indispensable to her. She could not even address an envelope in the usual way because it made the margins all wrong.

Their commercial schooldays were a period of disgrace and despair for the young couple. They seemed to be learning nothing about flower shops. At last they gave it up as hopeless, and shook the dust of the shorthand schools, and the polytechnics, and the London School of Economics from their feet for ever. Besides, the business was in some mysterious way beginning to take care of itself. They had somehow forgotten their objections to employing other people. They came to the conclusion that their own way was the best, and that they had really a remarkable talent for business. The Colonel, who had been compelled for some years to keep a sufficient sum on current account at his bankers to make up their deficits, found that the provision was unnecessary: the young people were prospering. It is true that there was not quite fair play between them and their competitors in trade. Their week-ends in the country cost them nothing, and saved them the price of their Sunday dinners; for the motor car was the Colonel's; and he and Higgins paid the hotel bills. Mr. F. Hill, florist and greengrocer (they soon discovered that there was money in asparagus; and asparagus led to other vegetables), had an air which stamped the business as classy; and in private life he was still Frederick Eynsford Hill, Esquire. Not that there was any swank about him: nobody but Eliza knew that he had been christened Frederick Challoner. Eliza herself swanked like anything.

That is all. That is how it has turned out. It is astonishing how much Eliza still manages to meddle in the housekeeping at Wimpole Street in spite of the shop and her own family. And it is notable that though she never nags her husband, and frankly loves the Colonel as if she were his favorite daughter, she has never got out of the habit of nagging Higgins that was established on the fatal night when she won his bet for him. She snaps his head off on the faintest provocation, or on none. He no longer dares to tease her by assuming an abysmal inferiority of Freddy's mind to his own. He storms and bullies and derides; but she stands up to him so ruthlessly that the Colonel has to ask her from time to time to be kinder to Higgins; and it is the only request of his that brings a mulish expression into her face. Nothing but some emergency or calamity great enough to break down all likes and dislikes, and throw them both back on their common humanity—and may they be spared any such trial!—will ever alter this. She knows that Higgins does not need her, just as her father did not need her. The very scrupulousness with which he told her that day that he had become used to having her there, and dependent on her for all sorts of little services, and that he should miss her if she went away (it would never have occurred to Freddy or the Colonel to say anything of the sort) deepens her inner certainty that she is "no more to him than them slippers"; yet she has a sense, too, that his indifference is deeper than the infatuation of commoner souls. She is immensely interested in him. She has even secret mischievous moments in which she wishes she could get him alone, on a desert island, away from all ties and with nobody else in the world to consider, and just drag him off his pedestal and see him making love like any common man. We all have private imaginations of that sort. But when it comes to business, to the life that she really leads as distinguished from the life of dreams and fancies, she likes Freddy and she likes the Colonel; and she does not like Higgins and Mr. Doolittle. Galatea never does quite like Pygmalion: his relation to her is too godlike to be altogether agreeable.

1914, revised 1941

QUESTIONS

1. What is the attitude of the lower class to the upper and middle classes as shown in the first act? How does Shaw characterize the three classes and the relationship among them? Which class comes off best?

2. What is your first impression of Freddy? What do his mother and sister think of him? Support your answer with examples from the play.

3. What is your first impression of Eliza? Can you understand the first lines she speaks? There is a stage direction announcing that Shaw will no longer represent her speech phonetically, and he does not. How would this be handled on the stage? Would her early and later speech be different?

4. Higgins defies conventional class distinctions. Is this because he believes all human beings equally good? equally bad? Higgins seems uninhibitedly outspoken, but when, in Act III, Clara (Miss Eynsford Hill) suggests that people should be frank and say what they really think, Higgins says, "Lord forbid!" because "we're all savages, more or less." How does that relate to the theme of equality and the falseness of class distinctions? What evidence is there in the play that we are "savages"? What does being "savage" mean?

5. What do the engravings in Higgins's home and lab and the absence of paintings (Act II) suggest about his character? Both Leslie Howard in the movie *Pygmalion* and Rex Harrison in *My Fair Lady* are rather slightly built, and for some viewers this goes along with Higgins's vinegary, sarcastic manner, but the text says Higgins is "robust." Does the casting suggest a stereotype or convention? How would Anthony Hopkins or Mel Gibson as Higgins affect your understanding of his character? the play?

6. What is Higgins's view of himself? Does it contrast with what we have read or seen of him from the outside? Is this merely comic or does it suggest that all our views of ourselves are equally false? Knowing this view of himself, would you play Higgins a little differently than you would not knowing this?

7. In what way are Higgins's and Alfred Doolittle's attitudes and behavior similar? Why will Doolittle take five pounds for his daughter but not ten? What use does he promise to put the money to? Why will the woman he lives with not marry him? How does this relate to the reversal of conventional expectations?

8. What is the "new small talk" (Act III)? the "sanguinary element" in that "small talk"? In what way is the "small talk" like the fairy tale of the Emperor's new clothes? Though this scene seems comically exaggerated, what elements of "truth" or "reality" are in it? What does it suggest about society and its "rules"?

9. How is Act IV the climax or turning point? How does it initiate and present the falling action? What is the tone of this act? How does it differ from that of much of the rest of the play? To what extent is your opinion of Higgins changed? At this point, or early in Act V, review Pickering's role and his character. Does his character suggest qualities that are almost inevitably associated with his class? If so, does this mean that Eliza, whom Pickering admires and protects and who understands and values him, has, indeed, been trans-

formed into a "lady"? How, then, is class defined by the characters of Pickering and the transformed Eliza?

WRITING SUGGESTIONS

1. Shaw's postscript tells us that Eliza marries Freddy, not Higgins. Write an argumentative essay that takes one of the two following positions; use concrete evidence and take into account your "opponent's" possible counterarguments:
   (a) If we are to trust the tale and not the teller, as D. H. Lawrence advises us to do, argue, *using evidence from the text,* that Shaw is wrong, that what he says is not in the play but only his interpretation of the play, and that from the play we can show that Liza really does marry Higgins, as both the movie and the later musical, *My Fair Lady,* "show."
   (b) But Bernard Shaw knows best: argue that the whole tone of the play is ironic and undermines conventional expectation, that Eliza marries Higgins is the expected comic resolution and, therefore, *not* the one that is consistent with the play. Using passages showing the reversals of ordinary expectations, the upsetting of conventions and middle-class morality, and adopting some of Shaw's argument in his afterword, try to prove your point.
2. Is Higgins a sexist? Analyze the attitude toward gender in *Pygmalion.* If Higgins were to marry Eliza how would this reinforce or change what the play seems to be saying about gender?
3. From the beginning of the play to the very end there are reversals of conventions and thus of conventional expectations. List as many of these as you can find. Write an essay that either
   (a) forms from these a consistent view of society and morality; or
   (b) discriminates between those that justifiably "question authority" or social conventions and those that are themselves questionable—sexist, inhumane, snobbish in their own way, and so forth.
4. Look up the classical story of Pygmalion, and read one or two versions in addition to Shaw's. Show how the means Pygmalion/Henry Higgins uses to create a woman (art, the gods, phonetics, and so forth) and the relationship of Pygmalion/Henry Higgins to his creation embody different themes and derive from and embody different attitudes (toward art and science, men and women, and so on).
5. What does each of the scenes from the movie—scenes that were not in the first version of the play—add to the plot, characterization, theme, tone, setting? Which of these would be easy to stage? difficult? impossible? Which of those that were possible, would you include in your "production" of the play? Why?

HENRIK IBSEN

Hedda Gabler[1]

CHARACTERS

GEORGE TESMAN, *research graduate*
in cultural history
HEDDA, *his wife*
MISS JULIANA TESMAN, *his aunt*

MRS. ELVSTED
JUDGE BRACK
EILERT LOEVBORG
BERTHA, *a maid*

The action takes place in TESMAN's *villa in the fashionable quarter of town.*

ACT I

SCENE: *A large drawing room, handsomely and tastefully furnished; decorated in dark colors. In the rear wall is a broad open doorway, with curtains drawn back to either side. It leads to a smaller room, decorated in the same style as the drawing room. In the right-hand wall of the drawing room, a folding door leads out to the hall. The opposite wall, on the left, contains french windows, also with curtains drawn back on either side. Through the glass we can see part of a verandah, and trees in autumn colors. Downstage stands an oval table, covered by a cloth and surrounded by chairs. Downstage right, against the wall, is a broad stove tiled with dark porcelain; in front of it stand a high-backed armchair, a cushioned footrest, and two footstools. Upstage right, in an alcove, is a corner sofa, with a small, round table. Downstage left, a little away from the wall, is another sofa. Upstage of the french windows, a piano. On either side of the open doorway in the rear wall stand what-nots holding ornaments of terra cotta and majolica. Against the rear wall of the smaller room can be seen a sofa, a table, and a couple of chairs. Above this sofa hangs the portrait of a handsome old man in general's uniform. Above the table a lamp hangs from the ceiling, with a shade of opalescent, milky glass. All round the drawing room bunches of flowers stand in vases and glasses. More bunches lie on the tables. The floors of both rooms are covered with thick carpets. Morning light. The sun shines in through the french windows.*

MISS JULIANA TESMAN, *wearing a hat and carrying a parasol, enters from the hall, followed by* BERTHA, *who is carrying a bunch of flowers wrapped in paper.* MISS TESMAN *is about sixty-five, of pleasant and kindly appearance. She is neatly but simply dressed in grey outdoor clothes.* BERTHA, *the maid, is rather simple and rustic-looking. She is getting on in years.*

MISS TESMAN: [*Stops just inside the door, listens, and says in a hushed voice.*] No, bless my soul! They're not up yet.

---

1. Translated by Michael Meyer.

BERTHA: [*Also in hushed tones.*] What did I tell you, miss? The boat didn't get in till midnight. And when they did turn up—Jesus, miss, you should have seen all the things Madam made me unpack before she'd go to bed!

MISS TESMAN: Ah, well. Let them have a good lie in. But let's have some nice fresh air waiting for them when they do come down. [*Goes to the french windows and throws them wide open.*]

BERTHA: [*Bewildered at the table, the bunch of flowers in her hand.*] I'm blessed if there's a square inch left to put anything. I'll have to let it lie here, miss. [*Puts it on the piano.*]

MISS TESMAN: Well, Bertha dear, so now you have a new mistress. Heaven knows it nearly broke my heart to have to part with you.

BERTHA: [*Snivels.*] What about me, Miss Juju? How do you suppose I felt? After all the happy years I've spent with you and Miss Rena?

MISS TESMAN: We must accept it bravely, Bertha. It was the only way. George needs you to take care of him. He could never manage without you. You've looked after him ever since he was a tiny boy.

BERTHA: Oh, but Miss Juju, I can't help thinking about Miss Rena, lying there all helpless, poor dear. And that new girl! She'll never learn the proper way to handle an invalid.

MISS TESMAN: Oh, I'll manage to train her. I'll do most of the work myself, you know. You needn't worry about my poor sister, Bertha dear.

BERTHA: But Miss Juju, there's another thing. I'm frightened Madam may not find me suitable.

MISS TESMAN: Oh, nonsense, Bertha. There may be one or two little things to begin with——

BERTHA: She's a real lady. Wants everything just so.

MISS TESMAN: But of course she does! General Gabler's daughter! Think of what she was accustomed to when the General was alive. You remember how we used to see her out riding with her father? In that long black skirt? With the feather in her hat?

BERTHA: Oh, yes, miss. As if I could forget! But, Lord! I never dreamed I'd live to see a match between her and Master Georgie.

MISS TESMAN: Neither did I. By the way, Bertha, from now on you must stop calling him Master Georgie. You must say: Dr. Tesman.

BERTHA: Yes, Madam said something about that too. Last night—the moment they'd set foot inside the door. Is it true, then, miss?

MISS TESMAN: Indeed it is. Just imagine, Bertha, some foreigners have made him a doctor.[2] It happened while they were away. I had no idea till he told me when they got off the boat.

BERTHA: Well, I suppose there's no limit to what he won't become. He's that clever. I never thought he'd go in for hospital work, though.

MISS TESMAN: No, he's not that kind of doctor. [*Nods impressively.*] In any case, you may soon have to address him by an even grander title.

BERTHA: You don't say! What might that be, miss?

---

2. Awarded him a doctoral degree.

MISS TESMAN: [*Smiles.*] Ah! If you only knew! [*Moved.*] Dear God, if only poor dear Joachim could rise out of his grave and see what his little son has grown into! [*Looks round.*] But Bertha, why have you done this? Taken the chintz covers off all the furniture!

BERTHA: Madam said I was to. Can't stand chintz covers on chairs, she said.

MISS TESMAN: But surely they're not going to use this room as a parlor?

BERTHA: So I gathered, miss. From what Madam said. He didn't say anything. The Doctor.

> [GEORGE TESMAN *comes into the rear room, from the right, humming, with an open, empty traveling bag in his hand. He is about thirty-three, of medium height and youthful appearance, rather plump, with an open, round, contented face, and fair hair and beard. He wears spectacles, and is dressed in comfortable, indoor clothes.*]

MISS TESMAN: Good morning! Good morning, George!

TESMAN: [*In open doorway.*] Auntie Juju! Dear Auntie Juju! [*Comes forward and shakes her hand.*] You've come all the way out here! And so early! What?

MISS TESMAN: Well, I had to make sure you'd settled in comfortably.

TESMAN: But you can't have had a proper night's sleep.

MISS TESMAN: Oh, never mind that.

TESMAN: We were so sorry we couldn't give you a lift. But you saw how it was— Hedda had so much luggage—and she insisted on having it all with her.

MISS TESMAN: Yes, I've never seen so much luggage.

BERTHA: [*To* TESMAN.] Shall I go and ask Madam if there's anything I can lend her a hand with?

TESMAN: Er—thank you, Bertha; no, you needn't bother. She says if she wants you for anything she'll ring.

BERTHA: [*Over to right.*] Oh. Very good.

TESMAN: Oh, Bertha—take this bag, will you?

BERTHA: [*Takes it.*] I'll put it in the attic. [*Goes out into the hall.*]

TESMAN: Just fancy, Auntie Juju, I filled that whole bag with notes for my book. You know, it's really incredible what I've managed to find rooting through those archives. By Jove! Wonderful old things no one even knew existed——

MISS TESMAN: I'm sure you didn't waste a single moment of your honeymoon, George dear.

TESMAN: No, I think I can truthfully claim that. But, Auntie Juju, do take your hat off. Here. Let me untie it for you. What?

MISS TESMAN: [*As he does so.*] Oh dear, oh dear! It's just as if you were still living at home with us.

TESMAN: [*Turns the hat in his hand and looks at it.*] I say! What a splendid new hat!

MISS TESMAN: I bought it for Hedda's sake.

TESMAN: For Hedda's sake? What?

MISS TESMAN: So that Hedda needn't be ashamed of me, in case we ever go for a walk together.

TESMAN: [*Pats her cheek.*] You still think of everything, don't you, Auntie Juju?

[*Puts the hat down on a chair by the table.*] Come on, let's sit down here on the sofa. And have a little chat while we wait for Hedda.

[*They sit. She puts her parasol in the corner of the sofa.*]

MISS TESMAN: [*Clasps both his hands and looks at him.*] Oh, George, it's so wonderful to have you back, and be able to see you with my own eyes again! Poor dear Joachim's own son!

TESMAN: What about me! It's wonderful for me to see you again, Auntie Juju. You've been a mother to me. And a father, too.

MISS TESMAN: You'll always keep a soft spot in your heart for your old aunties, won't you, George dear?

TESMAN: I suppose Auntie Rena's no better? What?

MISS TESMAN: Alas, no. I'm afraid she'll never get better, poor dear. She's lying there just as she has for all these years. Please God I may be allowed to keep her for a little longer. If I lost her I don't know what I'd do. Especially now I haven't you to look after.

TESMAN: [*Pats her on the back.*] There, there, there!

MISS TESMAN: [*With a sudden change of mood.*] Oh but George, fancy you being a married man! And to think it's you who've won Hedda Gabler! The beautiful Hedda Gabler! Fancy! She was always so surrounded by admirers.

TESMAN: [*Hums a little and smiles contentedly.*] Yes, I suppose there are quite a few people in this town who wouldn't mind being in my shoes. What?

MISS TESMAN: And what a honeymoon! Five months! Nearly six.

TESMAN: Well, I've done a lot of work, you know. All those archives to go through. And I've had to read lots of books.

MISS TESMAN: Yes, dear, of course. [*Lowers her voice confidentially.*] But tell me, George—haven't you any—any extra little piece of news to give me?

TESMAN: You mean, arising out of the honeymoon?

MISS TESMAN: Yes.

TESMAN: No, I don't think there's anything I didn't tell you in my letters. My doctorate, of course—but I told you about that last night, didn't I?

MISS TESMAN: Yes, yes, I didn't mean that kind of thing. I was just wondering—are you—are you expecting——?

TESMAN: Expecting what?

MISS TESMAN: Oh, come on George, I'm your old aunt!

TESMAN: Well actually—yes, I am expecting something.

MISS TESMAN: I knew it!

TESMAN: You'll be happy to hear that before very long I expect to become a professor.

MISS TESMAN: Professor?

TESMAN: I think I may say that the matter has been decided. But, Auntie Juju, you know about this.

MISS TESMAN: [*Gives a little laugh.*] Yes, of course. I'd forgotten. [*Changes her tone.*] But we were talking about your honeymoon. It must have cost a dreadful amount of money, George?

TESMAN: Oh well, you know, that big research grant I got helped a good deal.

MISS TESMAN: But how on earth did you manage to make it do for two?

TESMAN: Well, to tell the truth it was a bit tricky. What?

MISS TESMAN: Especially when one's traveling with a lady. A little bird tells me that makes things very much more expensive.

TESMAN: Well, yes, of course it does make things a little more expensive. But Hedda has to do things in style, Auntie Juju. I mean, she has to. Anything less grand wouldn't have suited her.

MISS TESMAN: No, no, I suppose not. A honeymoon abroad seems to be the vogue nowadays. But tell me, have you had time to look round the house?

TESMAN: You bet. I've been up since the crack of dawn.

MISS TESMAN: Well, what do you think of it?

TESMAN: Splendid. Absolutely splendid. I'm only wondering what we're going to do with those two empty rooms between that little one and Hedda's bedroom.

MISS TESMAN: [Laughs slyly.] Ah, George dear, I'm sure you'll manage to find some use for them—in time.

TESMAN: Yes, of course, Auntie Juju, how stupid of me. You're thinking of my books. What?

MISS TESMAN: Yes, yes, dear boy. I was thinking of your books.

TESMAN: You know, I'm so happy for Hedda's sake that we've managed to get this house. Before we became engaged she often used to say this was the only house in town she felt she could really bear to live in. It used to belong to Mrs. Falk—you know, the Prime Minister's widow.

MISS TESMAN: Fancy that! And what a stroke of luck it happened to come into the market. Just as you'd left on your honeymoon.

TESMAN: Yes, Auntie Juju, we've certainly had all the luck with us. What?

MISS TESMAN: But, George dear, the expense! It's going to make a dreadful hole in your pocket, all this.

TESMAN: [A little downcast.] Yes, I—I suppose it will, won't it?

MISS TESMAN: Oh, George, really!

TESMAN: How much do you think it'll cost? Roughly, I mean? What?

MISS TESMAN: I can't possibly say till I see the bills.

TESMAN: Well, luckily Judge Brack's managed to get it on very favorable terms. He wrote and told Hedda so.

MISS TESMAN: Don't you worry, George dear. Anyway I've stood security for all the furniture and carpets.

TESMAN: Security? But dear, sweet Auntie Juju, how could you possibly stand security?

MISS TESMAN: I've arranged a mortgage on our annuity.

TESMAN: [Jumps up.] What? On your annuity? And—Auntie Rena's?

MISS TESMAN: Yes. Well, I couldn't think of any other way.

TESMAN: [Stands in front of her.] Auntie Juju, have you gone completely out of your mind? That annuity's all you and Auntie Rena have.

MISS TESMAN: All right, there's no need to get so excited about it. It's a pure formality, you know. Judge Brack told me so. He was so kind as to arrange it all for me. A pure formality; those were his very words.

TESMAN: I dare say. All the same——

MISS TESMAN: Anyway, you'll have a salary of your own now. And, good heavens, even if we did have to fork out a little—tighten our belts for a week or two— why, we'd be happy to do so for your sake.

TESMAN: Oh, Auntie Juju! Will you never stop sacrificing yourself for me?

MISS TESMAN: [*Gets up and puts her hands on his shoulders.*] What else have I to live for but to smooth your road a little, my dear boy? You've never had any mother or father to turn to. And now at last we've achieved our goal. I won't deny we've had our little difficulties now and then. But now, thank the good Lord, George dear, all your worries are past.

TESMAN: Yes, it's wonderful really how everything's gone just right for me.

MISS TESMAN: Yes! And the enemies who tried to bar your way have been struck down. They have been made to bite the dust. The man who was your most dangerous rival has had the mightiest fall. And now he's lying there in the pit he dug for himself, poor misguided creature.

TESMAN: Have you heard any news of Eilert? Since I went away?

MISS TESMAN: Only that he's said to have published a new book.

TESMAN: What! Eilert Loevborg? You mean—just recently? What?

MISS TESMAN: So they say. I don't imagine it can be of any value, do you? When your new book comes out, that'll be another story. What's it going to be about?

TESMAN: The domestic industries of Brabant[3] in the Middle Ages.

MISS TESMAN: Oh, George! The things you know about!

TESMAN: Mind you, it may be some time before I actually get down to writing it. I've made these very extensive notes, and I've got to file and index them first.

MISS TESMAN: Ah, yes! Making notes; filing and indexing; you've always been wonderful at that. Poor dear Joachim was just the same.

TESMAN: I'm looking forward so much to getting down to that. Especially now I've a home of my own to work in.

MISS TESMAN: And above all, now that you have the girl you set your heart on, George dear.

TESMAN: [*Embraces her.*] Oh, yes, Auntie Juju, yes! Hedda's the loveliest thing of all! [*Looks towards the doorway.*] I think I hear her coming. What?

[HEDDA *enters the rear room from the left, and comes into the drawing room. She is a woman of twenty-nine. Distinguished, aristocratic face and figure. Her complexion is pale and opalescent. Her eyes are steel-grey, with an expression of cold, calm serenity. Her hair is of a handsome auburn color, but is not especially abundant. She is dressed in an elegant, somewhat loose-fitting morning gown.*]

MISS TESMAN: [*Goes to greet her.*] Good morning, Hedda dear! Good morning!

HEDDA: [*Holds out her hand.*] Good morning, dear Miss Tesman. What an early hour to call. So kind of you.

---

3. Prosperous duchy (1190–1477), now divided between Belgium and the Netherlands.

MISS TESMAN. [*Seems somewhat embarrassed.*] And has the young bride slept well in her new home?

HEDDA: Oh—thank you, yes. Passably well.

TESMAN: [*Laughs.*] Passably. I say, Hedda, that's good! When I jumped out of bed, you were sleeping like a top.

HEDDA: Yes. Fortunately. One has to accustom oneself to anything new, Miss Tesman. It takes time. [*Looks left.*] Oh, that maid's left the french windows open. This room's flooded with sun.

MISS TESMAN. [*Goes towards the windows.*] Oh—let me close them.

HEDDA: No, no, don't do that. Tesman dear, draw the curtains. This light's blinding me.

TESMAN: [*At the windows.*] Yes, yes, dear. There, Hedda, now you've got shade and fresh air.

HEDDA: This room needs fresh air. All these flowers—But my dear Miss Tesman, won't you take a seat?

MISS TESMAN: No, really not, thank you. I just wanted to make sure you have everything you need. I must see about getting back home. My poor dear sister will be waiting for me.

TESMAN: Be sure to give her my love, won't you? Tell her I'll run over and see her later today.

MISS TESMAN: Oh yes, I'll tell her that. Oh, George——[*Fumbles in the pocket of her skirt.*] I almost forgot. I've brought something for you.

TESMAN. What's that, Auntie Juju? What?

MISS TESMAN: [*Pulls out a flat package wrapped in newspaper and gives it to him.*] Open and see, dear boy.

TESMAN: [*Opens the package.*] Good heavens! Auntie Juju, you've kept them! Hedda, this is really very touching. What?

HEDDA: [*By the what-nots, on the right.*] What is it, Tesman?

TESMAN: My old shoes! My slippers, Hedda!

HEDDA: Oh, them. I remember you kept talking about them on our honeymoon.

TESMAN: Yes, I missed them dreadfully. [*Goes over to her.*] Here, Hedda, take a look.

HEDDA: [*Goes away towards the stove.*] Thanks, I won't bother.

TESMAN: [*Follows her.*] Fancy, Hedda, Auntie Rena's embroidered them for me. Despite her being so ill. Oh, you can't imagine what memories they have for me.

HEDDA: [*By the table.*] Not for me.

MISS TESMAN: No, Hedda's right there, George.

TESMAN: Yes, but I thought since she's one of the family now——

HEDDA: [*Interrupts.*] Tesman, we really can't go on keeping this maid.

MISS TESMAN: Not keep Bertha?

TESMAN: What makes you say that, dear? What?

HEDDA: [*Points.*] Look at that! She's left her old hat lying on the chair.

TESMAN: [*Appalled, drops his slippers on the floor.*] But, Hedda——!

HEDDA: Suppose someone came in and saw it?

TESMAN: But Hedda—that's Auntie Juju's hat.

HEDDA: Oh?

MISS TESMAN: [*Picks up the hat.*] Indeed it's mine. And it doesn't happen to be old, Hedda dear.

HEDDA: I didn't look at it very closely, Miss Tesman.

MISS TESMAN: [*Tying on the hat.*] As a matter of fact, it's the first time I've worn it. As the good Lord is my witness.

TESMAN: It's very pretty, too. Really smart.

MISS TESMAN: Oh, I'm afraid it's nothing much really. [*Looks round.*] My parasol? Ah, here it is. [*Takes it.*] This is mine, too. [*Murmurs.*] Not Bertha's.

TESMAN: A new hat and a new parasol! I say, Hedda, fancy that!

HEDDA: Very pretty and charming.

TESMAN: Yes, isn't it? What? But Auntie Juju, take a good look at Hedda before you go. Isn't she pretty and charming?

MISS TESMAN: Dear boy, there's nothing new in that. Hedda's been a beauty ever since the day she was born. [*Nods and goes right.*]

TESMAN: [*Follows her.*] Yes, but have you noticed how strong and healthy she's looking? And how she's filled out since we went away?

MISS TESMAN: [*Stops and turns.*] Filled out?

HEDDA: [*Walks across the room.*] Oh, can't we forget it?

TESMAN: Yes, Auntie Juju—you can't see it so clearly with that dress on. But I've good reason to know——

HEDDA: [*By the french windows, impatiently.*] You haven't good reason to know anything.

TESMAN: It must have been the mountain air up there in the Tyrol——

HEDDA: [*Curtly, interrupts him.*] I'm exactly the same as when I went away.

TESMAN: You keep on saying so. But you're not. I'm right, aren't I, Auntie Juju?

MISS TESMAN: [*Has folded her hands and is gazing at her.*] She's beautiful—beautiful. Hedda is beautiful. [*Goes over to* HEDDA, *takes her head between her hands, draws it down and kisses her hair.*] God bless and keep you, Hedda Tesman. For George's sake.

HEDDA: [*Frees herself politely.*] Oh—let me go, please.

MISS TESMAN: [*Quietly, emotionally.*] I shall come see you both every day.

TESMAN: Yes, Auntie Juju, please do. What?

MISS TESMAN: Good-bye! Good-bye!

> [*She goes out into the hall.* TESMAN *follows her. The door remains open.* TESMAN *is heard sending his love to* AUNT RENA *and thanking* MISS TESMAN *for his slippers. Meanwhile* HEDDA *walks up and down the room raising her arms and clenching her fists as though in desperation. Then she throws aside the curtains from the french windows and stands there, looking out. A few moments later,* TESMAN *returns and closes the door behind him.*]

TESMAN: [*Picks up his slippers from the floor.*] What are you looking at, Hedda?

HEDDA: [*Calm and controlled again.*] Only the leaves. They're so golden. And withered.

TESMAN: [*Wraps up the slippers and lays them on the table.*] Well, we're in September now.

HEDDA: [*Restless again.*] Yes. We're already into September.

TESMAN: Auntie Juju was behaving rather oddly, I thought, didn't you? Almost as though she was in church or something. I wonder what came over her. Any idea?

HEDDA: I hardly know her. Does she often act like that?

TESMAN: Not to the extent she did today.

HEDDA: [Goes away from the french windows.] Do you think she was hurt by what I said about the hat?

TESMAN: Oh, I don't think so. A little at first, perhaps——

HEDDA: But what a thing to do, throw her hat down in someone's drawing room. People don't do such things.

TESMAN: I'm sure Auntie Juju doesn't do it very often.

HEDDA: Oh well, I'll make it up with her.

TESMAN: Oh Hedda, would you?

HEDDA: When you see them this afternoon invite her to come out here this evening.

TESMAN: You bet I will! I say, there's another thing which would please her enormously.

HEDDA: Oh?

TESMAN: If you could bring yourself to call her Auntie Juju. For my sake, Hedda? What?

HEDDA: Oh no, really Tesman, you mustn't ask me to do that. I've told you so once before. I'll try to call her Aunt Juliana. That's as far as I'll go.

TESMAN: [After a moment.] I say, Hedda, is anything wrong? What?

HEDDA: I'm just looking at my old piano. It doesn't really go with all this.

TESMAN: As soon as I start getting my salary we'll see about changing it.

HEDDA: No, no, don't let's change it. I don't want to part with it. We can move it into that little room and get another one to put in here.

TESMAN: [A little downcast.] Yes, we—might do that.

HEDDA: [Picks up the bunch of flowers from the piano.] These flowers weren't here when we arrived last night.

TESMAN: I expect Auntie Juju brought them.

HEDDA: Here's a card. [Takes it out and reads.] "Will come back later today." Guess who it's from?

TESMAN: No idea. Who? What?

HEDDA: It says: "Mrs. Elvsted."

TESMAN: No, really? Mrs. Elvsted! She used to be Miss Rysing, didn't she?

HEDDA: Yes. She was the one with that irritating hair she was always showing off. I hear she used to be an old flame of yours.

TESMAN: [Laughs.] That didn't last long. Anyway, that was before I got to know you, Hedda. By Jove, fancy her being in town!

HEDDA: Strange she should call. I only knew her at school.

TESMAN: Yes, I haven't seen her for—oh, heaven knows how long. I don't know how she manages to stick it out up there in the north. What?

HEDDA: [Thinks for a moment, then says suddenly.] Tell me, Tesman, doesn't he live somewhere up in those parts? You know—Eilert Loevborg?

TESMAN: Yes, that's right. So he does. [BERTHA enters from the hall.]

BERTHA. She's here again, madam. The lady who came and left the flowers. [*Points.*] The ones you're holding.

HEDDA: Oh, is she? Well, show her in.

> [BERTHA *opens the door for* MRS. ELVSTED *and goes out.* MRS. ELVSTED *is a delicately built woman with gentle, attractive features. Her eyes are light blue, large, and somewhat prominent, with a frightened, questioning expression. Her hair is extremely fair, almost flaxen, and is exceptionally wavy and abundant. She is two or three years younger than* HEDDA. *She is wearing a dark visiting dress, in good taste but not quite in the latest fashion.*]

HEDDA: [*Goes cordially to greet her.*] Dear Mrs. Elvsted, good morning. How delightful to see you again after all this time.

MRS. ELVSTED: [*Nervously, trying to control herself.*] Yes, it's many years since we met.

TESMAN: And since *we* met. What?

HEDDA: Thank you for your lovely flowers.

MRS. ELVSTED: Oh, please—I wanted to come yesterday afternoon. But they told me you were away——

TESMAN: You've only just arrived in town, then? What?

MRS. ELVSTED: I got here yesterday, around midday. Oh, I became almost desperate when I heard you weren't here.

HEDDA: Desperate? Why?

TESMAN: My dear Mrs. Rysing—Elvsted——

HEDDA: There's nothing wrong, I hope?

MRS. ELVSTED: Yes, there is. And I don't know anyone else here whom I can turn to.

HEDDA: [*Puts the flowers down on the table.*] Come and sit with me on the sofa——

MRS. ELVSTED: Oh, I feel too restless to sit down.

HEDDA: You must. Come along, now. [*She pulls* MRS. ELVSTED *down on to the sofa and sits beside her.*]

TESMAN: Well? Tell us, Mrs.—er——

HEDDA: Has something happened at home?

MRS. ELVSTED: Yes—that is, yes and no. Oh, I do hope you won't misunderstand me——

HEDDA: Then you'd better tell us the whole story, Mrs. Elvsted.

TESMAN: That's why you've come. What?

MRS. ELVSTED: Yes—yes, it is. Well, then—in case you don't already know—Eilert Loevborg is in town.

HEDDA: Loevborg here?

TESMAN: Eilert back in town? By Jove, Hedda, did you hear that?

HEDDA: Yes, of course I heard.

MRS. ELVSTED: He's been here a week. A whole week! In this city. Alone. With all those dreadful people——

HEDDA: But my dear Mrs. Elvsted, what concern is he of yours?

MRS. ELVSTED: [*Gives her a frightened look and says quickly.*] He's been tutoring the children.

HEDDA: Your children?

MRS. ELVSTED: My husband's. I have none.

HEDDA: Oh, you mean your stepchildren.

MRS. ELVSTED: Yes.

TESMAN: [*Gropingly.*] But was he sufficiently—I don't know how to put it—sufficiently regular in his habits to be suited to such a post? What?

MRS. ELVSTED: For the past two to three years he has been living irreproachably.

TESMAN: You don't say! By Jove, Hedda, hear that?

HEDDA: I hear.

MRS. ELVSTED: Quite irreproachably, I assure you. In every respect. All the same—in this big city—with money in his pockets—I'm so dreadfully frightened something may happen to him.

TESMAN: But why didn't he stay up there with you and your husband?

MRS. ELVSTED: Once his book had come out, he became restless.

TESMAN: Oh, yes—Auntie Juju said he's brought out a new book.

MRS. ELVSTED: Yes, a big new book about the history of civilization. A kind of general survey. It came out a fortnight ago. Everyone's been buying it and reading it—it's created a tremendous stir——

TESMAN: Has it really? It must be something he's dug up, then.

MRS. ELVSTED: You mean from the old days?

TESMAN: Yes.

MRS. ELVSTED: No, he's written it all since he came to live with us.

TESMAN: Well, that's splendid news, Hedda. Fancy that!

MRS. ELVSTED: Oh, yes! If only he can go on like this!

HEDDA: Have you met him since you came here?

MRS. ELVSTED: No, not yet, I had such dreadful difficulty finding his address. But this morning I managed to track him down at last.

HEDDA: [*Looks searchingly at her.*] I must say I find it a little strange that your husband—hm——

MRS. ELVSTED: [*Starts nervously.*] My husband! What do you mean?

HEDDA: That he should send you all the way here on an errand of this kind. I'm surprised he didn't come himself to keep an eye on his friend.

MRS. ELVSTED: Oh, no, no—my husband hasn't the time. Besides, I—er—wanted to do some shopping here.

HEDDA: [*With a slight smile.*] Ah. Well, that's different.

MRS. ELVSTED: [*Gets up quickly, restlessly.*] Please, Mr. Tesman, I beg you—be kind to Eilert Loevborg if he comes here. I'm sure he will. I mean, you used to be such good friends in the old days. And you're both studying the same subject, as far as I can understand. You're in the same field, aren't you?

TESMAN: Well, we used to be, anyway.

MRS. ELVSTED: Yes—so I beg you earnestly, do please, please, keep an eye on him. Oh, Mr. Tesman, do promise me you will.

TESMAN: I shall be only too happy to do so, Mrs. Rysing.

HEDDA: Elvsted.

TESMAN: I'll do everything for Eilert that lies in my power. You can rely on that.

MRS. ELVSTED: Oh, how good and kind you are! [*Presses his hands.*] Thank you, thank you, thank you. [*Frightened.*] My husband's so fond of him, you see.

HEDDA: [*Gets up.*] You'd better send him a note, Tesman. He may not come to you of his own accord.

TESMAN: Yes, that'd probably be the best plan, Hedda. What?

HEDDA: The sooner the better. Why not do it now?

MRS. ELVSTED: [*Pleadingly.*] Oh yes, if only you would!

TESMAN: I'll do it this very moment. Do you have his address, Mrs.—er—Elvsted?

MRS. ELVSTED: Yes. [*Takes a small piece of paper from her pocket and gives it to him.*]

TESMAN: Good, good. Right, well I'll go inside and——[*Looks round.*] Where are my slippers? Oh yes, here. [*Picks up the package and is about to go.*]

HEDDA: Try to sound friendly. Make it a nice long letter.

TESMAN: Right, I will.

MRS. ELVSTED: Please don't say anything about my having seen you.

TESMAN: Good heavens no, of course not. What? [*Goes out through the rear room to the right.*]

HEDDA: [*Goes over to* MRS. ELVSTED, *smiles, and says softly.*] Well! Now we've killed two birds with one stone.

MRS. ELVSTED: What do you mean?

HEDDA: Didn't you realize I wanted to get him out of the room?

MRS. ELVSTED: So that he could write the letter?

HEDDA: And so that I could talk to you alone.

MRS. ELVSTED: [*Confused.*] About this?

HEDDA: Yes, about this.

MRS. ELVSTED: [*In alarm.*] But there's nothing more to tell, Mrs. Tesman. Really there isn't.

HEDDA: Oh, yes there is. There's a lot more. I can see that. Come along, let's sit down and have a little chat.

[*She pushes* MRS. ELVSTED *down into the armchair by the stove and seats herself on one of the footstools.*]

MRS. ELVSTED: [*Looks anxiously at her watch.*] Really, Mrs. Tesman, I think I ought to be going now.

HEDDA: There's no hurry. Well? How are things at home?

MRS. ELVSTED: I'd rather not speak about that.

HEDDA: But my dear, you can tell me. Good heavens, we were at school together.

MRS. ELVSTED: Yes, but you were a year senior to me. Oh, I used to be terribly frightened of you in those days.

HEDDA: Frightened of me?

MRS. ELVSTED: Yes, terribly frightened. Whenever you met me on the staircase you used to pull my hair.

HEDDA: No, did I?

MRS. ELVSTED: Yes. And once you said you'd burn it all off.

HEDDA: Oh, that was only in fun.

MRS. ELVSTED: Yes, but I was so silly in those days. And then afterwards—I mean, we've drifted so far apart. Our backgrounds were so different.

HEDDA: Well, now we must try to drift together again. Now listen. When we were at school we used to call each other by our Christian names——

MRS. ELVSTED: No, I'm sure you're mistaken.

HEDDA: I'm sure I'm not. I remember it quite clearly. Let's tell each other our secrets, as we used to in the old days. [*Moves closer on her footstool.*] There, now. [*Kisses her on the cheek.*] You must call me Hedda.

MRS. ELVSTED: [*Squeezes her hands and pats them.*] Oh, you're so kind. I'm not used to people being so nice to me.

HEDDA: Now, now, now. And I shall call you Tora, the way I used to.

MRS. ELVSTED: My name is Thea.

HEDDA: Yes, of course. Of course. I meant Thea. [*Looks at her sympathetically.*] So you're not used to kindness, Thea? In your own home?

MRS. ELVSTED: Oh, if only I had a home! But I haven't. I've never had one.

HEDDA: [*Looks at her for a moment.*] I thought that was it.

MRS. ELVSTED: [*Stares blankly and helplessly.*] Yes—yes—yes.

HEDDA: I can't remember exactly now, but didn't you first go to Mr. Elvsted as a housekeeper?

MRS. ELVSTED: Governess, actually. But his wife—at the time, I mean—she was an invalid, and had to spend most of her time in bed. So I had to look after the house too.

HEDDA: But in the end, you became mistress of the house.

MRS. ELVSTED: [*Sadly.*] Yes, I did.

HEDDA: Let me see. Roughly how long ago was that?

MRS. ELVSTED: When I got married, you mean?

HEDDA: Yes.

MRS. ELVSTED: About five years.

HEDDA: Yes; it must be about that.

MRS. ELVSTED: Oh, those five years! Especially that last two or three. Oh, Mrs. Tesman, if you only knew——

HEDDA: [*Slaps her hand gently.*] Mrs. Tesman? Oh, Thea!

MRS. ELVSTED: I'm sorry, I'll try to remember. Yes—if you had any idea——

HEDDA: [*Casually.*] Eilert Loevborg's been up here too, for about three years, hasn't he?

MRS. ELVSTED: [*Looks at her uncertainly.*] Eilert Loevborg? Yes, he has.

HEDDA: Did you know him before? When you were here?

MRS. ELVSTED: No, not really. That is—I knew him by name, of course.

HEDDA: But up there, he used to visit you?

MRS. ELVSTED: Yes, he used to come and see us every day. To give the children lessons. I found I couldn't do that as well as manage the house.

HEDDA: I'm sure you couldn't. And your husband——? I suppose being a magistrate he has to be away from home a good deal?

MRS. ELVSTED: Yes. You see, Mrs.—— you see, Hedda, he has to cover the whole district.

HEDDA: [*Leans against the arm of* MRS. ELVSTED's *chair.*] Poor, pretty little Thea! Now you must tell me the whole story. From beginning to end.

MRS. ELVSTED: Well—what do you want to know?

HEDDA: What kind of a man is your husband, Thea? I mean, as a person. Is he kind to you?

MRS. ELVSTED: [*Evasively.*] I'm sure he does his best to be.

HEDDA: I only wonder if he isn't too old for you. There's more than twenty years between you, isn't there?

MRS. ELVSTED: [*Irritably.*] Yes, there's that too. Oh, there are so many things. We're different in every way. We've nothing in common. Nothing whatever.

HEDDA: But he loves you, surely? In his own way?

MRS. ELVSTED: Oh, I don't know. I think he just finds me useful. And then I don't cost much to keep. I'm cheap.

HEDDA: Now you're being stupid.

MRS. ELVSTED: [*Shakes her head.*] It can't be any different. With him. He doesn't love anyone except himself. And perhaps the children—a little.

HEDDA: He must be fond of Eilert Loevborg, Thea.

MRS. ELVSTED: [*Looks at her.*] Eilert Loevborg? What makes you think that?

HEDDA: Well, if he sends you all the way down here to look for him——[*Smiles almost imperceptibly.*] Besides, you said so yourself to Tesman.

MRS. ELVSTED: [*With a nervous twitch.*] Did I? Oh yes, I suppose I did. [*Impulsively, but keeping her voice low.*] Well, I might as well tell you the whole story. It's bound to come out sooner or later.

HEDDA: But my dear Thea——?

MRS. ELVSTED: My husband had no idea I was coming here.

HEDDA: What? Your husband didn't know?

MRS. ELVSTED: No, of course not. As a matter of fact, he wasn't even there. He was away at the assizes. Oh, I couldn't stand it any longer, Hedda! I just couldn't. I'd be so dreadfully lonely up there now.

HEDDA: Go on.

MRS. ELVSTED: So I packed a few things. Secretly. And went.

HEDDA: Without telling anyone?

MRS. ELVSTED: Yes. I caught the train and came straight here.

HEDDA: But my dear Thea! How brave of you!

MRS. ELVSTED: [*Gets up and walks across the room.*] Well, what else could I do?

HEDDA: But what do you suppose your husband will say when you get back?

MRS. ELVSTED: [*By the table, looks at her.*] Back there? To him?

HEDDA: Yes. Surely——?

MRS. ELVSTED: I shall never go back to him.

HEDDA: [*Gets up and goes closer.*] You mean you've left your home for good?

MRS. ELVSTED: Yes. I didn't see what else I could do.

HEDDA: But to do it so openly!

MRS. ELVSTED: Oh, it's no use trying to keep a thing like that secret.

HEDDA: But what do you suppose people will say?

MRS. ELVSTED: They can say what they like. [*Sits sadly, wearily on the sofa.*] I had to do it.

HEDDA: [*After a short silence.*] What do you intend to do now? How are you going to live?

MRS. ELVSTED: I don't know. I only know that I must live wherever Eilert Loevborg is. If I am to go on living.

HEDDA: [*Moves a chair from the table, sits on it near* MRS. ELVSTED *and strokes her hands.*] Tell me, Thea, how did this—friendship between you and Eilert Loevborg begin?

MRS. ELVSTED: Oh, it came about gradually. I developed a kind of—power over him.

HEDDA: Oh?

MRS. ELVSTED: He gave up his old habits. Not because I asked him to. I'd never have dared to do that. I suppose he just noticed I didn't like that kind of thing. So he gave it up.

HEDDA: [*Hides a smile.*] So you've made a new man of him. Clever little Thea!

MRS. ELVSTED: Yes—anyway, he says I have. And he's made a —sort of—real person of me. Taught me to think—and to understand all kinds of things.

HEDDA: Did he give you lessons too?

MRS. ELVSTED: Not exactly lessons. But he talked to me. About—oh, you've no idea—so many things! And then he let me work with him. Oh, it was wonderful. I was so happy to be allowed to help him.

HEDDA: Did he allow you to help him!

MRS. ELVSTED: Yes. Whenever he wrote anything we always—did it together.

HEDDA: Like good pals?

MRS. ELVSTED: [*Eagerly.*] Pals! Yes—why, Hedda, that's exactly the word he used! Oh, I ought to feel so happy. But I can't. I don't know if it will last.

HEDDA: You don't seem very sure of him.

MRS. ELVSTED: [*Sadly.*] Something stands between Eilert Loevberg and me. The shadow of another woman.

HEDDA: Who can that be?

MRS. ELVSTED: I don't know. Someone he used to be friendly with in—in the old days. Someone he's never been able to forget.

HEDDA: What has he told you about her?

MRS. ELVSTED: Oh, he only mentioned her once, casually.

HEDDA: Well! What did he say?

MRS. ELVSTED: He said when he left her she tried to shoot him with a pistol.

HEDDA: [*Cold, controlled.*] What nonsense. People don't do such things. The kind of people we know.

MRS. ELVSTED: No, I think it must have been that red-haired singer he used to—

HEDDA: Ah yes, very probably.

MRS. ELVSTED: I remember they used to say she always carried a loaded pistol.

HEDDA: Well then, it must be her.

MRS. ELVSTED: But Hedda, I hear she's come back, and is living here. Oh, I'm so desperate——!

HEDDA: [*Glances toward the rear room.*] Ssh! Tesman's coming. [*Gets up and whispers.*] Thea, we mustn't breathe a word about this to anyone.

MRS. ELVSTED: [*Jumps up.*] Oh, no, no! Please don't!

[GEORGE TESMAN *appears from the right in the rear room with a letter in his hand, and comes into the drawing room.*]

TESMAN: Well, here's my little epistle all signed and sealed.

HEDDA: Good. I think Mrs. Elvsted wants to go now. Wait a moment—I'll see you as far as the garden gate.

TESMAN: Er—Hedda, do you think Bertha could deal with this?

HEDDA: [*Takes the letter.*] I'll give her instructions.

[BERTHA *enters from the hall.*]

BERTHA: Judge Brack is here and asks if he may pay his respects to Madam and the Doctor.

HEDDA: Yes, ask him to be so good as to come in. And—wait a moment—drop this letter in the post box.

BERTHA: [*Takes the letter.*] Very good, madam.

[*She opens the door for* JUDGE BRACK, *and goes out.* JUDGE BRACK *is forty-five; rather short, but well-built, and elastic in his movements. He has a roundish face with an aristocratic profile. His hair, cut short, is still almost black, and is carefully barbered. Eyes lively and humorous. Thick eyebrows. His moustache is also thick, and is trimmed square at the ends. He is wearing outdoor clothes which are elegant but a little too youthful for him. He has a monocle in one eye; now and then he lets it drop.*]

BRACK: [*Hat in hand, bows.*] May one presume to call so early?

HEDDA: One may presume.

TESMAN: [*Shakes his hand.*] You're welcome here any time. Judge Brack—Mrs. Rysing.

[HEDDA *sighs.*]

BRACK: [*Bows.*] Ah—charmed——

HEDDA: [*Looks at him and laughs.*] What fun to be able to see you by daylight for once, Judge.

BRACK: Do I look—different?

HEDDA: Yes. A little younger, I think.

BRACK: Obliged.

TESMAN: Well, what do you think of Hedda? What? Doesn't she look well? Hasn't she filled out——?

HEDDA: Oh, do stop it. You ought to be thanking Judge Brack for all the inconvenience he's put himself to——

BRACK: Nonsense, it was a pleasure——

HEDDA: You're a loyal friend. But my other friend is pining to get away. Au revoir, Judge. I won't be a minute.

[*Mutual salutations.* MRS. ELVSTED *and* HEDDA *go out through the hall.*]

BRACK: Well, is your wife satisfied with everything?

TESMAN: Yes, we can't thank you enough. That is—we may have to shift one or two things around, she tells me. And we're short of one or two little items we'll have to purchase.

BRACK: Oh? Really?

TESMAN: But you musn't worry your head about that. Hedda says she'll get what's needed. I say, why don't we sit down? What?

BRACK: Thanks, just for a moment. [*Sits at the table.*] There's something I'd like to talk to you about, my dear Tesman.

TESMAN: Oh? Ah yes, of course. [*Sits.*] After the feast comes the reckoning. What?

BRACK: Oh, never mind about the financial side—there's no hurry about that. Though I could wish we'd arranged things a little less palatially.

TESMAN: Good heavens, that'd never have done. Think of Hedda, my dear chap. You know her. I couldn't possibly ask her to live like a suburban housewife.

BRACK: No, no—that's just the problem.

TESMAN: Anyway, it can't be long now before my nomination[4] comes through.

BRACK: Well, you know, these things often take time.

TESMAN: Have you heard any more news? What?

BRACK: Nothing definite. [*Changing the subject.*] Oh, by the way, I have one piece of news for you.

TESMAN: What?

BRACK: Your old friend Eilert Loevborg is back in town.

TESMAN: I know that already.

BRACK: Oh? How did you hear that?

TESMAN: She told me. That lady who went out with Hedda.

BRACK: I see. What was her name? I didn't catch it.

TESMAN: Mrs. Elvsted.

BRACK: Oh, the magistrate's wife. Yes, Loevborg's been living up near them, hasn't he?

TESMAN: I'm delighted to hear he's become a decent human being again.

BRACK: Yes, so they say.

TESMAN: I gather he's published a new book, too. What?

BRACK: Indeed he has.

TESMAN: I hear it's created rather a stir.

BRACK: Quite an unusual stir.

TESMAN: I say, isn't that splendid news! He's such a gifted chap—and I was afraid he'd gone to the dogs for good.

BRACK: Most people thought he had.

TESMAN: But I can't think what he'll do now. How on earth will he manage to make ends meet? What?

[*As he speaks his last words,* HEDDA *enters from the hall.*]

HEDDA: [*To* BRACK, *laughs slightly scornfully.*] Tesman is always worrying about making ends meet.

TESMAN: We were talking about poor Eilert Loevborg, Hedda dear.

HEDDA: [*Gives him a quick look.*] Oh, were you? [*Sits in the armchair by the stove and asks casually.*] Is he in trouble?

TESMAN: Well, he must have run through his inheritance long ago by now. And he can't write a new book every year. What? So I'm wondering what's going to become of him.

BRACK: I may be able to enlighten you there.

TESMAN: Oh?

BRACK: You mustn't forget he has relatives who wield a good deal of influence.

TESMAN: Relatives? Oh, they've quite washed their hands of him, I'm afraid.

4. To a professorship at the university.

BRACK: They used to regard him as the hope of the family.

TESMAN: Used to, yes. But he's put an end to that.

HEDDA: Who knows? [*With a little smile.*] I hear the Elvsteds have made a new man of him.

BRACK: And then this book he's just published——

TESMAN: Well, let's hope they find something for him. I've just written him a note. Oh, by the way, Hedda, I asked him to come over and see us this evening.

BRACK: But my dear chap, you're coming to me this evening. My bachelor party. You promised me last night when I met you at the boat.

HEDDA: Had you forgotten, Tesman?

TESMAN: Good heavens, yes, I'd quite forgotten.

BRACK: Anyway, you can be quite sure he won't turn up here.

TESMAN: Why do you think that? What?

BRACK: [*A little unwillingly, gets up and rests his hands on the back of his chair.*] My dear Tesman—and you, too, Mrs. Tesman—there's something I feel you ought to know.

TESMAN: Concerning Eilert?

BRACK: Concerning him and you.

TESMAN: Well, my dear Judge, tell us, please!

BRACK: You must be prepared for your nomination not to come through quite as quickly as you hope and expect.

TESMAN: [*Jumps up uneasily.*] Is anything wrong? What?

BRACK: There's a possibility that the appointment may be decided by competition——

TESMAN: Competition! By Jove, Hedda, fancy that!

HEDDA: [*Leans further back in her chair.*] Ah! How interesting!

TESMAN: But who else——? I say, you don't mean——?

BRACK: Exactly. By competition with Eilert Loevborg.

TESMAN: [*Clasps his hands in alarm.*] No, no, but this is inconceivable! It's absolutely impossible! What?

BRACK: Hm. We may find it'll happen, all the same.

TESMAN: No, but—Judge Brack, they couldn't be so inconsiderate toward me! [*Waves his arms.*] I mean, by Jove, I—I'm a married man! It was on the strength of this that Hedda and I *got* married! We ran up some pretty hefty debts. And borrowed money from Auntie Juju! I mean, good heavens, they practically promised me the appointment. What?

BRACK: Well, well, I'm sure you'll get it. But you'll have to go through a competition.

HEDDA: [*Motionless in her armchair.*] How exciting, Tesman. It'll be a kind of duel, by Jove.

TESMAN: My dear Hedda, how can you take it so lightly?

HEDDA: [*As before.*] I'm not. I can't wait to see who's going to win.

BRACK: In any case, Mrs. Tesman, it's best you should know how things stand. I mean before you commit yourself to these little items I hear you're threatening to purchase.

HEDDA: I can't allow this to alter my plans.

BRACK: Indeed? Well, that's your business. Good-bye. [*To* TESMAN.] I'll come and collect you on the way home from my afternoon walk.

TESMAN: Oh, yes, yes. I'm sorry, I'm all upside down just now.

HEDDA: [*Lying in her chair, holds out her hand.*] Good-bye, Judge. See you this afternoon.

BRACK: Thank you. Good-bye, good-bye.

TESMAN: [*Sees him to the door.*] Good-bye, my dear Judge. You will excuse me, won't you?

[JUDGE BRACK *goes out through the hall.*]

TESMAN: [*Pacing up and down.*] Oh, Hedda! One oughtn't to go plunging off on wild adventures. What?

HEDDA: [*Looks at him and smiles.*] Like you're doing?

TESMAN: Yes. I mean, there's no denying it, it was a pretty big adventure to go off and get married and set up house merely on expectation.

HEDDA: Perhaps you're right.

TESMAN: Well, anyway, we have our home, Hedda. By Jove, yes. The home we dreamed of. And set our hearts on. What?

HEDDA: [*Gets up slowly, wearily.*] You agreed that we should enter society. And keep open house. That was the bargain.

TESMAN: Yes. Good heavens, I was looking forward to it all so much. To seeing you play hostess to a select circle! By Jove! What? Ah, well, for the time being we shall have to make do with each other's company, Hedda. Perhaps have Auntie Juju in now and then. Oh dear, this wasn't all what you had in mind——

HEDDA: I won't be able to have a liveried footman. For a start.

TESMAN: Oh no, we couldn't possibly afford a footman.

HEDDA: And that thoroughbred horse you promised me——

TESMAN: [*Fearfully.*] Thoroughbred horse!

HEDDA: I mustn't even think of that now.

TESMAN: Heaven forbid!

HEDDA: [*Walks across the room.*] Ah, well. I still have one thing left to amuse myself with.

TESMAN: [*Joyfully.*] Thank goodness for that. What's that, Hedda? What?

HEDDA: [*In the open doorway, looks at him with concealed scorn.*] My pistols, George darling.

TESMAN: [*Alarmed.*] Pistols!

HEDDA: [*Her eyes cold.*] General Gabler's pistols. [*She goes into the rear room and disappears.*]

TESMAN: [*Runs to the doorway and calls after her.*] For heaven's sake, Hedda dear, don't touch those things. They're dangerous. Hedda—please—for my sake! What?

ACT II

SCENE: *The same as in Act I except that the piano has been removed and an elegant little writing table, with a bookcase, stands in its place. By the sofa on the left a smaller table has been placed. Most of the flowers have been removed.* MRS. ELVSTED's *bouquet stands on the larger table, downstage. It is afternoon.*

HEDDA, *dressed to receive callers, is alone in the room. She is standing by the open french windows, loading a revolver. The pair to it is lying in an open pistol case on the writing table.*

HEDDA: [*Looks down into the garden and calls.*] Good afternoon, Judge.
BRACK: [*In the distance, below.*] Afternoon, Mrs. Tesman.
HEDDA: [*Raises the pistol and takes aim.*] I'm going to shoot you, Judge Brack.
BRACK: [*Shouts from below.*] No no, no! Don't aim that thing at me!
HEDDA: This'll teach you to enter houses by the back door. [*Fires.*]
BRACK: [*Below.*] Have you gone completely out of your mind?
HEDDA: Oh dear! Did I hit you?
BRACK: [*Still outside.*] Stop playing these silly tricks.
HEDDA: All right, Judge. Come along in.

> [JUDGE BRACK, *dressed for a bachelor party, enters through the french windows. He has a light overcoat on his arm.*]

BRACK: For God's sake! Haven't you stopped fooling around with those things yet? What are you trying to hit?
HEDDA: Oh, I was just shooting at the sky.
BRACK: [*Takes the pistol gently from her hand.*] By your leave, ma'am. [*Looks at it.*] Ah, yes—I know this old friend well. [*Looks around.*] Where's the case? Oh, yes. [*Puts the pistol in the case and closes it.*] That's enough of that little game for today.
HEDDA: Well, what on earth *am* I to do?
BRACK: You haven't had any visitors?
HEDDA: [*Closes the french windows.*] Not one. I suppose the best people are all still in the country.
BRACK: Your husband isn't home yet?
HEDDA: [*Locks the pistol case away in a drawer of the writing table.*] No. The moment he'd finished eating he ran off to his aunties. He wasn't expecting you so early.
BRACK: Ah, why didn't I think of that? How stupid of me.
HEDDA: [*Turns her head and looks at him.*] Why stupid?
BRACK: I'd have come a little sooner.
HEDDA: [*Walks across the room.*] There'd have been no one to receive you. I've been in my room since lunch, dressing.
BRACK: You haven't a tiny crack in the door through which we might have negotiated?
HEDDA: You forgot to arrange one.

BRACK: Another stupidity.

HEDDA: Well, we'll have to sit down here. And wait. Tesman won't be back for some time.

BRACK: Sad. Well, I'll be patient.

[HEDDA *sits on the corner of the sofa.* BRACK *puts his coat over the back of the nearest chair and seats himself, keeping his hat in his hand. Short pause. They look at each other.*]

HEDDA: Well?

BRACK: [*In the same tone of voice.*] Well?

HEDDA: I asked first.

BRACK: [*Leans forward slightly.*] Yes, well, now we can enjoy a nice, cosy little chat—Mrs. Hedda.

HEDDA: [*Leans further back in her chair.*] It seems such ages since we had a talk. I don't count last night or this morning.

BRACK: You mean: *à deux?*

HEDDA: Mm—yes. That's roughly what I meant.

BRACK: I've been longing so much for you to come home.

HEDDA: So have I.

BRACK: You? Really, Mrs. Hedda? And I thought you were having such a wonderful honeymoon.

HEDDA: Oh, yes. Wonderful!

BRACK: But your husband wrote such ecstatic letters.

HEDDA: He! Oh, yes! He thinks life has nothing better to offer than rooting around in libraries and copying old pieces of parchment, or whatever it is he does.

BRACK: [*A little maliciously.*] Well, that *is* his life. Most of it, anyway.

HEDDA: Yes, I know. Well, it's all right for him. But for me! Oh no, my dear Judge. I've been bored to death.

BRACK: [*Sympathetically.*] Do you mean that? Seriously?

HEDDA: Yes. Can you imagine? Six whole months without ever meeting a single person who was one of us, and to whom I could talk about the kind of things we talk about.

BRACK: Yes, I can understand. I'd miss that, too.

HEDDA: That wasn't the worst, though.

BRACK: What was?

HEDDA: Having to spend every minute of one's life with—with the same person.

BRACK: [*Nods.*] Yes. What a thought! Morning; noon; and——

HEDDA: [*Coldly.*] As I said: every minute of one's life.

BRACK: I stand corrected. But dear Tesman is such a clever fellow, I should have thought one ought to be able——

HEDDA: Tesman is only interested in one thing, my dear Judge. His special subject.

BRACK: True.

HEDDA: And people who are only interested in one thing don't make the most amusing company. Not for long, anyway.

BRACK: Not even when they happen to be the person one loves?

HEDDA: Oh, don't use that sickly, stupid word.

BRACK: [*Starts.*] But, Mrs. Hedda——!

HEDDA: [*Half laughing, half annoyed.*] You just try it, Judge. Listening to the history of civilization morning, noon and——

BRACK: [*Corrects her.*] Every minute of one's life.

HEDDA: All right. Oh, and those domestic industries of Brabant in the Middle Ages! That really is beyond the limit.

BRACK: [*Looks at her searchingly.*] But, tell me—if you feel like this why on earth did you—? Ha——

HEDDA: Why on earth did I marry George Tesman?

BRACK: If you like to put it that way.

HEDDA: Do you think it so very strange?

BRACK: Yes—and no, Mrs. Hedda.

HEDDA: I'd danced myself tired, Judge. I felt my time was up——[*Gives a slight shudder.*] No, I mustn't say that. Or even think it.

BRACK: You've no rational cause to think it.

HEDDA: Oh—cause, cause——[*Looks searchingly at him.*] After all, George Tesman—well, I mean, he's a very respectable man.

BRACK: Very respectable, sound as a rock. No denying that.

HEDDA: And there's nothing exactly ridiculous about him. Is there?

BRACK: Ridiculous? No-no, I wouldn't say that.

HEDDA: Mm. He's very clever at collecting material and all that, isn't he? I mean, he may go quite far in time.

BRACK: [*Looks at her a little uncertainly.*] I thought you believed, like everyone else, that he would become a very prominent man.

HEDDA: [*Looks tired.*] Yes, I did. And when he came and begged me on his bended knees to be allowed to love and to cherish me, I didn't see why I shouldn't let him.

BRACK: No, well—if one looks at it like that——

HEDDA: It was more than my other admirers were prepared to do, Judge dear.

BRACK: [*Laughs.*] Well, I can't answer for the others. As far as I myself am concerned, you know I've always had a considerable respect for the institution of marriage. As an institution.

HEDDA: [*Lightly.*] Oh, I've never entertained any hopes of you.

BRACK: All I want is to have a circle of friends whom I can trust, whom I can help with advice or—or by any other means, and into whose houses I may come and go as a—trusted friend.

HEDDA: Of the husband?

BRACK: [*Bows.*] Preferably, to be frank, of the wife. And of the husband too, of course. Yes, you know, this kind of—triangle is a delightful arrangement for all parties concerned.

HEDDA: Yes, I often longed for a third person while I was away. Oh, those hours we spent alone in railway compartments——

BRACK: Fortunately your honeymoon is now over.

HEDDA: [*Shakes her head.*] There's a long way still to go. I've only reached a stop on the line.

BRACK: Why not jump out and stretch your legs a little, Mrs. Hedda?

HEDDA: I'm not the jumping sort.

BRACK: Aren't you?

HEDDA: No. There's always someone around who——

BRACK: [*Laughs.*] Who looks at one's legs?

HEDDA: Yes. Exactly.

BRACK: Well, but surely——

HEDDA: [*With a gesture of rejection.*] I don't like it. I'd rather stay where I am. Sitting in the compartment. *À deux.*

BRACK: But suppose a third person were to step into the compartment?

HEDDA: That would be different.

BRACK: A trusted friend—someone who understood——

HEDDA: And was lively and amusing——

BRACK: And interested in—more subjects than one——

HEDDA: [*Sighs audibly.*] Yes, that'd be a relief.

BRACK: [*Hears the front door open and shut.*] The triangle is completed.

HEDDA: [*Half under breath.*] And the train goes on.

> [GEORGE TESMAN, *in grey walking dress with a soft felt hat, enters from the hall. He has a number of paper-covered books under his arm and in his pockets.*]

TESMAN: [*Goes over to the table by the corner sofa.*] Phew! It's too hot to be lugging all this around. [*Puts the books down.*] I'm positively sweating, Hedda. Why, hullo, hullo! You here already, Judge? What? Bertha didn't tell me.

BRACK: [*Gets up.*] I came in through the garden.

HEDDA: What are all those books you've got there?

TESMAN: [*Stands glancing through them.*] Oh, some new publications dealing with my special subject. I had to buy them.

HEDDA. Your special subject?

BRACK: His special subject, Mrs. Tesman.

> [BRACK *and* HEDDA *exchange a smile.*]

HEDDA: Haven't you collected enough material on your special subject?

TESMAN: My dear Hedda, one can never have too much. One must keep abreast of what other people are writing.

HEDDA: Yes. Of course.

TESMAN: [*Rooting among the books.*] Look—I bought a copy of Eilert Loevborg's new book, too. [*Holds it out to her.*] Perhaps you'd like to have a look at it, Hedda? What?

HEDDA. No, thank you. Er—yes, perhaps I will, later.

TESMAN: I glanced through it on my way home.

BRACK: What's your opinion—as a specialist on the subject?

TESMAN: I'm amazed how sound and balanced it is. He never used to write like that. [*Gathers his books together.*] Well, I must get down to these at once. I can hardly wait to cut the pages.[5] Oh, I've got to change, too. [*To* BRACK.] We don't have to be off just yet, do we? What?

---

5. Books used to be sold with the pages folded but uncut as they came from the printing press; the owner had to cut the pages in order to read the book.

BRACK: Heavens, no. We've plenty of time yet.

TESMAN: Good, I needn't hurry, then. [*Goes with his books, but stops and turns in the doorway.*] Oh, by the way, Hedda, Auntie Juju won't be coming to see you this evening.

HEDDA: Won't she? Oh—the hat, I suppose.

TESMAN: Good heavens, no. How could you think such a thing of Auntie Juju? Fancy——! No, Auntie Rena's very ill.

HEDDA: She always is.

TESMAN: Yes, but today she's been taken really bad.

HEDDA: Oh, then it's quite understandable that the other one should want to stay with her. Well, I shall have to swallow my disappointment.

TESMAN: You can't imagine how happy Auntie Juju was in spite of everything. At your looking so well after the honeymoon!

HEDDA: [*Half beneath her breath, as she rises.*] Oh, these everlasting aunts!

TESMAN: What?

HEDDA: [*Goes over to the french windows.*] Nothing.

TESMAN: Oh. All right. [*Goes into the rear room and out of sight.*]

BRACK: What was that about the hat?

HEDDA: Oh, something that happened with Miss Tesman this morning. She'd put her hat down on a chair. [*Looks at him and smiles.*] And I pretended to think it was the servant's.

BRACK: [*Shakes his head.*] But my dear Mrs. Hedda, how could you do such a thing? To that poor old lady?

HEDDA: [*Nervously, walking across the room.*] Sometimes a mood like that hits me. And I can't stop myself. [*Throws herself down in the armchair by the stove.*] Oh, I don't know how to explain it.

BRACK: [*Behind her chair.*] You're not really happy. That's the answer.

HEDDA: [*Stares ahead of her.*] Why on earth should I be happy? Can you give me a reason?

BRACK: Yes. For one thing you've got the home you always wanted.

HEDDA: [*Looks at him.*] You really believe that story?

BRACK: You mean it isn't true?

HEDDA: Oh, yes, it's partly true.

BRACK: Well?

HEDDA: It's true I got Tesman to see me home from parties last summer——

BRACK: It was a pity my home lay in another direction.

HEDDA: Yes. Your interests lay in another direction, too.

BRACK: [*Laughs.*] That's naughty of you, Mrs. Hedda. But to return to you and Tesman——

HEDDA: Well, we walked past this house one evening. And poor Tesman was fidgeting in his boots trying to find something to talk about. I felt sorry for the great scholar——

BRACK: [*Smiles incredulously.*] Did you? Hm.

HEDDA: Yes, honestly I did. Well, to help him out of his misery, I happened to say quite frivolously how much I'd love to live in this house.

BRACK: Was that all?

HEDDA: That evening, yes.

BRACK: But—afterwards?

HEDDA: Yes. My little frivolity had its consequences, my dear Judge.

BRACK: Our little frivolities do. Much too often, unfortunately.

HEDDA: Thank you. Well, it was our mutual admiration for the late Prime Minister's house that brought George Tesman and me together on common ground. So we got engaged, and we got married, and we went on our honeymoon, and—Ah well, Judge, I've—made my bed and I must lie in it, I was about to say.

BRACK: How utterly fantastic! And you didn't really care in the least about the house?

HEDDA: God knows I didn't.

BRACK: Yes, but now that we've furnished it so beautifully for you?

HEDDA: Ugh—all the rooms smell of lavender and dried roses. But perhaps Auntie Juju brought that in.

BRACK: [*Laughs.*] More likely the Prime Minister's widow, rest her soul.

HEDDA: Yes, it's got the odor of death about it. It reminds me of the flowers one has worn at a ball—the morning after. [*Clasps her hands behind her neck, leans back in the chair and looks up at him.*] Oh, my dear Judge, you've no idea how hideously bored I'm going to be out here.

BRACK: Couldn't you find some kind of occupation, Mrs. Hedda? Like your husband?

HEDDA: Occupation? That'd interest me?

BRACK: Well—preferably.

HEDDA: God knows what. I've often thought——[*Breaks off.*] No, that wouldn't work either.

BRACK: Who knows? Tell me about it.

HEDDA: I was thinking—if I could persuade Tesman to go into politics, for example.

BRACK: [*Laughs.*] Tesman! No, honestly, I don't think he's quite cut out to be a politician.

HEDDA: Perhaps not. But if I could persuade him to have a go at it?

BRACK: What satisfaction would that give you? If he turned out to be no good? Why do you want to make him do that?

HEDDA: Because I'm bored. [*After a moment.*] You feel there's absolutely no possibility of Tesman becoming Prime Minister, then?

BRACK: Well, you know, Mrs. Hedda, for one thing he'd have to be pretty well off before he could become that.

HEDDA: [*Gets up impatiently.*] There you are! [*Walks across the room.*] It's this wretched poverty that makes life so hateful. And ludicrous. Well, it is!

BRACK: I don't think that's the real cause.

HEDDA: What is, then?

BRACK: Nothing really exciting has ever happened to you.

HEDDA: Nothing serious, you mean?

BRACK: Call it that if you like. But now perhaps it may.

HEDDA: [*Tosses her head.*] Oh, you're thinking of this competition for that wretched professorship? That's Tesman's affair. I'm not going to waste my time worrying about that.

BRACK: Very well, let's forget about that then. But suppose you were to find yourself faced with what people call—to use the conventional phrase—the most solemn of human responsibilities? [*Smiles.*] A new responsibility, little Mrs. Hedda.

HEDDA: [*Angrily.*] Be quiet! Nothing like that's going to happen.

BRACK: [*Warily.*] We'll talk about it again in a year's time. If not earlier.

HEDDA: [*Curtly.*] I've no leanings in that direction, Judge. I don't want any—responsibilities.

BRACK: But surely you must feel some inclination to make use of that—natural talent which every woman—

HEDDA: [*Over by the french windows.*] Oh, be quiet, I say! I often think there's only one thing for which I have any natural talent.

BRACK: [*Goes closer.*] And what is that, if I may be so bold as to ask?

HEDDA: [*Stands looking out.*] For boring myself to death. Now you know. [*Turns, looks toward the rear room and laughs.*] Talking of boring, here comes the Professor.

BRACK: [*Quietly, warningly.*] Now, now, now, Mrs. Hedda!

[GEORGE TESMAN, *in evening dress, with gloves and hat in his hand, enters through the rear room from the right.*]

TESMAN: Hedda, hasn't any message come from Eilert? What?

HEDDA: No.

TESMAN: Ah, then we'll have him here presently. You wait and see.

BRACK: You really think he'll come?

TESMAN: Yes, I'm almost sure he will. What you were saying about him this morning is just gossip.

BRACK: Oh?

TESMAN: Yes. Auntie Juju said she didn't believe he'd ever dare to stand in my way again. Fancy that!

BRACK: Then everything in the garden's lovely.

TESMAN: [*Puts his hat, with his gloves in it, on a chair, right.*] Yes, but you really must let me wait for him as long as possible.

BRACK: We've plenty of time. No one'll be turning up at my place before seven or half past.

TESMAN: Ah, then we can keep Hedda company a little longer. And see if he turns up. What?

HEDDA: [*Picks up* BRACK's *coat and hat and carries them over to the corner sofa.*] And if the worst comes to the worst, Mr. Loevborg can sit here and talk to me.

BRACK: [*Offering to take his things from her.*] No, please. What do you mean by "if the worst comes to the worst"?

HEDDA: If he doesn't want to go with you and Tesman.

TESMAN: [*Looks doubtfully at her.*] I say, Hedda, do you think it'll be all right for him to stay here with you? What? Remember Auntie Juju isn't coming.

HEDDA: Yes, but Mrs. Elvsted is. The three of us can have a cup of tea together.

TESMAN: Ah, that'll be all right then.

BRACK: [*Smiles.*] It's probably the safest solution as far as he's concerned.

HEDDA: Why?

BRACK: My dear Mrs. Tesman, you always say of my little bachelor parties that they should be attended only by men of the strongest principles.

HEDDA: But Mr. Loevborg is a man of principle now. You know what they say about a reformed sinner——

[BERTHA *enters from the hall.*]

BERTHA: Madam, there's a gentleman here who wants to see you——

HEDDA: Ask him to come in.

TESMAN: [*Quietly.*] I'm sure it's him. By Jove. Fancy that!

[EILERT LOEVBORG *enters from the hall. He is slim and lean, of the same age as* TESMAN, *but looks older and somewhat haggard. His hair and beard are of a blackish-brown; his face is long and pale, but with a couple of reddish patches on his cheekbones. He is dressed in an elegant and fairly new black suit, and carries black gloves and a top hat in his hand. He stops just inside the door and bows abruptly. He seems somewhat embarrassed.*]

TESMAN: [*Goes over and shakes his hand.*] My dear Eilert! How grand to see you again after all these years!

EILERT LOEVBORG: [*Speaks softly.*] It was good of you to write, George. [*Goes nearer to* HEDDA.] May I shake hands with you, too, Mrs. Tesman?

HEDDA: [*Accepts his hand.*] Delighted to see you, Mr. Loevborg. [*With a gesture.*] I don't know if you two gentlemen——

LOEVBORG: [*Bows slightly.*] Judge Brack, I believe.

BRACK: [*Also with a slight bow.*] Correct. We—met some years ago——

TESMAN: [*Puts his hands on* LOEVBORG's *shoulders.*] Now you're to treat this house just as though it were your own home, Eilert. Isn't that right, Hedda? I hear you've decided to settle here again? What?

LOEVBORG: Yes, I have.

TESMAN: Quite understandable. Oh, by the bye—I've just bought your new book. Though to tell the truth I haven't found time to read it yet.

LOEVBORG: You needn't bother.

TESMAN: Oh? Why?

LOEVBORG: There's nothing much in it.

TESMAN: By Jove, fancy hearing that from you!

BRACK: But everyone's praising it.

LOEVBORG: That was exactly what I wanted to happen. So I only wrote what I knew everyone would agree with.

BRACK: Very sensible.

TESMAN: Yes, but my dear Eilert——

LOEVBORG: I want to try to re-establish myself. To begin again—from the beginning.

TESMAN: [*A little embarrassed.*] Yes, I—er—suppose you do. What?

LOEVBORG: [*Smiles, puts down his hat and takes a package wrapped in paper from his coat pocket.*] But when this gets published—George Tesman—read it. This is my real book. The one in which I have spoken with my own voice.

TESMAN: Oh, really? What's it about?

LOEVBORG: It's the sequel.

TESMAN: Sequel? To what?

LOEVBORG: To the other book.

TESMAN: The one that's just come out?

LOEVBORG: Yes.

TESMAN: But my dear Eilert, that covers the subject right up to the present day.

LOEVBORG: It does. But this is about the future.

TESMAN: The future! But, I say, we don't know anything about that.

LOEVBORG: No. But there are one or two things that need to be said about it. [*Opens the package.*] Here, have a look.

TESMAN: Surely that's not your handwriting?

LOEVBORG: I dictated it. [*Turns the pages.*] It's in two parts. The first deals with the forces that will shape our civilization. [*Turns further on towards the end.*] And the second indicates the direction in which that civilization may develop.

TESMAN: Amazing! I'd never think of writing about anything like that.

HEDDA: [*By the french windows, drumming on the pane.*] No. You wouldn't.

LOEVBORG: [*Puts the pages back into their cover and lays the package on the table.*] I brought it because I thought I might possibly read you a few pages this evening.

TESMAN: I say, what a kind idea! Oh, but this evening——? [*Glances at* BRACK.] I'm not quite sure whether——

LOEVBORG: Well, some other time, then. There's no hurry.

BRACK: The truth is, Mr. Loevborg, I'm giving a little dinner this evening. In Tesman's honor, you know.

LOEVBORG: [*Looks round for his hat.*] Oh—then I mustn't——

BRACK: No, wait a minute. Won't you do me the honor of joining us?

LOEVBORG: [*Curtly, with decision.*] No I can't. Thank you so much.

BRACK: Oh, nonsense. Do—please. There'll only be a few of us. And I can promise you we shall have some good sport, as Mrs. Hed—as Mrs. Tesman puts it.

LOEVBORG: I've no doubt. Nevertheless——

BRACK: You could bring your manuscript along and read it to Tesman at my place. I could lend you a room.

TESMAN: By Jove, Eilert, that's an idea. What?

HEDDA: [*Interposes.*] But Tesman, Mr. Loevborg doesn't want to go. I'm sure Mr. Loevborg would much rather sit here and have supper with me.

LOEVBORG: [*Looks at her.*] With you, Mrs. Tesman?

HEDDA: And Mrs. Elvsted.

LOEVBORG: Oh. [*Casually.*] I ran into her this afternoon.

HEDDA: Did you? Well, she's coming here this evening. So you really must stay, Mr. Loevborg. Otherwise she'll have no one to see her home.

LOEVBORG: That's true. Well—thank you, Mrs. Tesman, I'll stay then.

HEDDA: I'll just tell the servant.

[*She goes to the door which leads into the hall, and rings.* BERTHA *enters.* HEDDA *talks softly to her and points towards the rear room.* BERTHA *nods and goes out.*]

TESMAN: [*To* LOEVBORG, *as* HEDDA *does this.*] I say, Eilert. This new subject of yours—the—er—future—is that the one you're going to lecture about?

LOEVBORG: Yes.

TESMAN: They told me down at the bookshop that you're going to hold a series of lectures here during the autumn.

LOEVBORG: Yes, I am, I—hope you don't mind, Tesman.

TESMAN: Good heavens, no! But——?

LOEVBORG: I can quite understand it might queer your pitch a little.

TESMAN: [*Dejectedly.*] Oh well, I can't expect you to put them off for my sake.

LOEVBORG: I'll wait till your appointment's been announced.

TESMAN: You'll wait! But—but—aren't you going to compete with me for the post? What?

LOEVBORG: No. I only want to defeat you in the eyes of the world.

TESMAN: Good heavens! Then Auntie Juju was right after all! Oh, I knew it, I knew it! Hear that, Hedda? Fancy! Eilert *doesn't* want to stand in our way.

HEDDA: [*Curtly.*] Our? Leave me out of it, please.

[*She goes towards the rear room, where* BERTHA *is setting a tray with decanters and glasses on the table.* HEDDA *nods approval, and comes back into the drawing room.* BERTHA *goes out.*]

TESMAN: [*While this is happening.*] Judge Brack, what do you think about all this? What?

BRACK: Oh, I think honor and victory can be very splendid things——

TESMAN: Of course they can. Still——

HEDDA: [*Looks at* TESMAN *with a cold smile.*] You look as if you'd been hit by a thunderbolt.

TESMAN: Yes, I feel rather like it.

BRACK: There was a black cloud looming up, Mrs. Tesman. But it seems to have passed over.

HEDDA: [*Points toward the rear room.*] Well, gentlemen, won't you go in and take a glass of cold punch?

BRACK: [*Glances at his watch.*] A stirrup cup? Yes, why not?

TESMAN: An admirable suggestion, Hedda. Admirable! Oh, I feel so relieved!

HEDDA: Won't you have one, too, Mr. Loevborg?

LOEVBORG: No, thank you. I'd rather not.

BRACK: Great heavens, man, cold punch isn't poison. Take my word for it.

LOEVBORG: Not for everyone, perhaps.

HEDDA: I'll keep Mr. Loevborg company while you drink.

TESMAN: Yes, Hedda dear, would you?

[*He and* BRACK *go into the rear room, sit down, drink punch, smoke cigarettes and talk cheerfully during the following scene.* EILERT LOEVBORG *rem* standing by the stove. HEDDA *goes to the writing table.*]

HEDDA: [*Raising her voice slightly.*] I've some photographs I'd like to show you, if you'd care to see them. Tesman and I visited the Tyrol[6] on our way home.

> [*She comes back with an album, places it on the table by the sofa and sits in the upstage corner of the sofa.* EILERT LOEVBORG *comes toward her, stops and looks at her. Then he takes a chair and sits down on her left, with his back toward the rear room.*]

HEDDA: [*Opens the album.*] You see these mountains, Mr. Loevborg? That's the Ortler group. Tesman has written the name underneath. You see: "The Ortler Group near Meran."

LOEVBORG: [*Has not taken his eyes from her; says softly, slowly.*] Hedda—Gabler!

HEDDA: [*Gives him a quick glance.*] Ssh!

LOEVBORG: [*Repeats softly.*] Hedda Gabler!

HEDDA: [*Looks at the album.*] Yes, that used to be my name. When we first knew each other.

LOEVBORG: And from now on—for the rest of my life—I must teach myself never to say: Hedda Gabler.

HEDDA: [*Still turning the pages.*] Yes, you must. You'd better start getting into practice. The sooner the better.

LOEVBORG: [*Bitterly.*] Hedda Gabler married? And to George Tesman?

HEDDA: Yes. Well—that's life.

LOEVBORG: Oh, Hedda, Hedda! How could you throw yourself away like that?

HEDDA: [*Looks sharply at him.*] Stop it.

LOEVBORG: What do you mean?

> [TESMAN *comes in and goes toward the sofa.*]

HEDDA: [*Hears him coming and says casually.*] And this, Mr. Loevborg, is the view from the Ampezzo valley. Look at those mountains. [*Glances affectionately up at* TESMAN.] What did you say those curious mountains were called, dear?

TESMAN: Let me have a look. Oh, those are the Dolomites.

HEDDA: Of course. Those are the Dolomites, Mr. Loevborg.

TESMAN: Hedda, I just wanted to ask you, can't we bring some punch in here? A glass for you, anyway. What?

HEDDA: Thank you, yes. And a biscuit or two, perhaps.

TESMAN: You wouldn't like a cigarette?

HEDDA: No.

TESMAN: Right.

> [*He goes into the rear room and over to the right.* BRACK *is sitting there, glancing occasionally at* HEDDA *and* LOEVBORG.]

LOEVBORG: [*Softly, as before.*] Answer me, Hedda. How could you do it?

HEDDA: [*Apparently absorbed in the album.*] If you go on calling me Hedda I won't talk to you any more.

LOEVBORG: Mayn't I even when we're alone?

6. Region ʷ. ˗ ᵒ Alps, now primarily in Austria, near the Italian border.

HEDDA: No. You can think it. But you mustn't say it.

LOEVBORG: Oh, I see. Because you love George Tesman.

HEDDA: [*Glances at him and smiles.*] Love? Don't be funny.

LOEVBORG: You don't love him?

HEDDA: I don't intend to be unfaithful to him. That's not what I want.

LOEVBORG: Hedda—just tell me one thing——

HEDDA: Ssh!

[TESMAN *enters from the rear room, carrying a tray.*]

TESMAN: Here we are! Here come the goodies! [*Puts the tray down on the table.*]

HEDDA: Why didn't you ask the servant to bring it in?

TESMAN: [*Fills the glasses.*] I like waiting on you, Hedda.

HEDDA: But you've filled both glasses. Mr. Loevborg doesn't want to drink.

TESMAN: Yes, but Mrs. Elvsted'll be here soon.

HEDDA: Oh yes, that's true. Mrs. Elvsted——

TESMAN: Had you forgotten her? What?

HEDDA: We're so absorbed with these photographs. [*Shows him one.*] You remember this little village?

TESMAN: Oh, that one down by the Brenner Pass. We spent a night there——

HEDDA: Yes, and met all those amusing people.

TESMAN: Oh yes, it was there, wasn't it? By Jove, if only we could have had you with us, Eilert! Ah, well. [*Goes back into the other room and sits down with* BRACK.]

LOEVBORG: Tell me one thing, Hedda.

HEDDA: Yes?

LOEVBORG: Didn't you love me either? Not—just a little?

HEDDA: Well now, I wonder? No, I think we were just good pals—Really good pals who could tell each other anything. [*Smiles.*] You certainly poured your heart out to me.

LOEVBORG: You begged me to.

HEDDA: Looking back on it, there was something beautiful and fascinating—and brave—about the way we told each other everything. That secret friendship no one else knew about.

LOEVBORG: Yes, Hedda, yes! Do you remember? How I used to come up to your father's house in the afternoon—and the General sat by the window and read his newspapers—with his back toward us——

HEDDA: And we sat on the sofa in the corner——

LOEVBORG: Always reading the same illustrated magazine——

HEDDA: We hadn't any photograph album.

LOEVBORG: Yes, Hedda. I regarded you as a kind of confessor. Told you things about myself which no one else knew about—then. Those days and nights of drinking and— Oh, Hedda, what power did you have to make me confess such things?

HEDDA: Power? You think I had some power over you?

LOEVBORG: Yes—I don't know how else to explain it. And all those—oblique questions you asked me——

HEDDA: You knew what they meant.

LOEVBORG: But that you could sit there and ask me such questions! So unashamedly——

HEDDA: I thought you said they were oblique.

LOEVBORG: Yes, but you asked them so unashamedly. That you could question me about—about that kind of thing!

HEDDA: You answered willingly enough.

LOEVBORG: Yes—that's what I can't understand—looking back on it. But tell me, Hedda—what you felt for me—wasn't that—love? When you asked me those questions and made me confess my sins to you, wasn't it because you wanted to wash me clean?

HEDDA: No, not exactly.

LOEVBORG: Why did you do it, then?

HEDDA: Do you find it so incredible that a young girl, given the chance to do so without anyone knowing, should want to be allowed a glimpse into a forbidden world of whose existence she is supposed to be ignorant?

LOEVBORG: So that was it?

HEDDA: One reason. One reason—I think.

LOEVBORG: You didn't love me, then. You just wanted—knowledge. But if that was so, why did you break it off?

HEDDA: That was your fault.

LOEVBORG: It was you who put an end to it.

HEDDA: Yes, when I realized that our friendship was threatening to develop into something—something else. Shame on you, Eilert Loevborg! How could you abuse the trust of your dearest friend?

LOEVBORG: [Clenches his fists.] Oh, why didn't you do it? Why didn't you shoot me dead? As you threatened to?

HEDDA: I was afraid. Of the scandal.

LOEVBORG: Yes, Hedda. You're a coward at heart.

HEDDA: A dreadful coward. [Changes her tone.] Luckily for you. Well, now you've found consolation with the Elvsteds.

LOEVBORG: I know what Thea's been telling you.

HEDDA: I dare say you told her about us.

LOEVBORG: Not a word. She's too silly to understand that kind of thing.

HEDDA: Silly?

LOEVBORG: She's silly about that kind of thing.

HEDDA: And I am a coward. [Leans closer to him, without looking him in the eyes, and says quietly.] But let me tell you something. Something you don't know.

LOEVBORG: [Tensely.] Yes?

HEDDA: My failure to shoot you wasn't my worst act of cowardice that evening.

LOEVBORG: [Looks at her for a moment, realizes her meaning and whispers passionately.] Oh, Hedda! Hedda Gabler! Now I see what was behind those questions. Yes! It wasn't knowledge you wanted! It was life!

HEDDA: [Flashes a look at him and says quietly.] Take care! Don't you delude yourself!

[*It has begun to grow dark.* BERTHA, *from outside, opens the door leading into the hall.*]

HEDDA: [*Closes the album with a snap and cries, smiling.*] Ah, at last! Come in, Thea dear!

[MRS. ELVSTED *enters from the hall, in evening dress. The door is closed behind her.*]

HEDDA: [*On the sofa, stretches out her arms toward her.*] Thea darling, I thought you were never coming!

[MRS. ELVSTED *makes a slight bow to the gentlemen in the rear room as she passes the open doorway, and they to her. Then she goes to the table and holds out her hand to* HEDDA. EILERT LOEVBORG *has risen from his chair. He and* MRS. ELVSTED *nod silently to each other.*]

MRS. ELVSTED: Perhaps I ought to go in and say a few words to your husband?
HEDDA: Oh, there's no need. They're happy by themselves. They'll be going soon.
MRS. ELVSTED: Going?
HEDDA. Yes, they're off on a spree this evening.
MRS. ELVSTED: [*Quickly, to* LOEVBORG.] You're not going with them?
LOEVBORG: No.
HEDDA: Mr. Loevborg is staying here with us.
MRS. ELVSTED: [*Takes a chair and is about to sit down beside him.*] Oh, how nice it is to be here!
HEDDA: No, Thea darling, not there. Come over here and sit beside me. I want to be in the middle.
MRS. ELVSTED: Yes, just as you wish.

[*She goes right the table and sits on the sofa, on* HEDDA's *right.* LOEVBORG *sits down again in his chair.*]

LOEVBORG: [*After a short pause, to* HEDDA.] Isn't she lovely to look at?
HEDDA: [*Strokes her hair gently.*] Only to look at?
LOEVBORG: Yes. We're just good pals. We trust each other implicitly. We can talk to each other quite unashamedly.
HEDDA: No need to be oblique?
MRS. ELVSTED: [*Nestles close to* HEDDA *and says quietly.*] Oh, Hedda, I'm so happy. Imagine—he says I've inspired him!
HEDDA: [*Looks at her with a smile.*] Dear Thea! Does he really?
LOEVBORG: She has the courage of her convictions, Mrs. Tesman.
MRS. ELVSTED: I? Courage?
LOEVBORG: Absolute courage. Where friendship is concerned.
HEDDA: Yes. Courage. Yes. If only one had that——
LOEVBORG: Yes?
HEDDA. One might be able to live. In spite of everything. [*Changes her tone suddenly.*] Well, Thea darling, now you're going to drink a nice glass of cold punch.

MRS. ELVSTED: No, thank you. I never drink anything like that.

HEDDA: Oh. You, Mr. Loevborg?

LOEVBORG: Thank you, I don't either.

MRS. ELVSTED: No, he doesn't, either.

HEDDA: [*Looks into his eyes.*] But if I want you to?

LOEVBORG: That doesn't make any difference.

HEDDA: [*Laughs.*] Have I no power over you at all? Poor me!

LOEVBORG: Not where this is concerned.

HEDDA: Seriously, I think you should. For your own sake.

MRS. ELVSTED: Hedda!

LOEVBORG: Why?

HEDDA: Or perhaps I should say for other people's sake.

LOEVBORG: What do you mean?

HEDDA: People might think you didn't feel absolutely and unashamedly sure of yourself. In your heart of hearts.

MRS. ELVSTED: [*Quietly.*] Oh, Hedda, no!

LOEVBORG: People can think what they like. For the present.

MRS. ELVSTED: [*Happily.*] Yes, that's true.

HEDDA: I saw it so clearly in Judge Brack a few minutes ago.

LOEVBORG: Oh. What did you see?

HEDDA: He smiled so scornfully when he saw you were afraid to go in there and drink with them.

LOEVBORG: Afraid! I wanted to stay here and talk to you.

MRS. ELVSTED: That was only natural, Hedda.

HEDDA: But the Judge wasn't to know that. I saw him wink at Tesman when you showed you didn't dare to join their wretched little party.

LOEVBORG: Didn't dare! Are you saying I didn't dare?

HEDDA: I'm not saying so. But that was what Judge Brack thought.

LOEVBORG: Well, let him.

HEDDA: You're not going, then?

LOEVBORG: I'm staying here with you and Thea.

MRS. ELVSTED: Yes, Hedda, of course he is.

HEDDA: [*Smiles, and nods approvingly to* LOEVBORG.] Firm as a rock! A man of principle! That's how a man should be! [*Turns to* MRS. ELVSTED *and strokes her cheek.*] Didn't I tell you so this morning when you came here in such a panic——

LOEVBORG: [*Starts.*] Panic?

MRS. ELVSTED: [*Frightened.*] Hedda! But—Hedda!

HEDDA: Well, now you can see for yourself. There's no earthly need for you to get scared to death just because——[*Stops.*] Well! Let's all three cheer up and enjoy ourselves.

LOEVBORG: Mrs. Tesman, would you mind explaining to me what this is all about?

MRS. ELVSTED: Oh, my God, my God, Hedda, what are you saying? What are you doing?

HEDDA: Keep calm. That horrid Judge has his eye on you.

LOEVBORG: Scared to death, were you? For my sake?

MRS. ELVSTED: [*Quietly, trembling.*] Oh, Hedda! You've made me so unhappy!

LOEVBORG: [*Looks coldly at her for a moment. His face is distorted.*] So that was how much you trusted me.

MRS. ELVSTED: Eilert dear, please listen to me——

LOEVBORG: [*Takes one of the glasses of punch, raises it and says quietly, hoarsely.*] Skoal, Thea! [*Empties the glass, puts it down and picks up one of the others.*]

MRS. ELVSTED: [*Quietly.*] Hedda, Hedda! Why did you want this to happen?

HEDDA: I—want it? Are you mad?

LOEVBORG: Skoal to you too, Mrs. Tesman. Thanks for telling me the truth. Here's to the truth! [*Empties his glass and refills it.*]

HEDDA: [*Puts her hand on his arm.*] Steady. That's enough for now. Don't forget the party.

MRS. ELVSTED: No, no, no!

HEDDA: Ssh! They're looking at you.

LOEVBORG: [*Puts down his glass.*] Thea, tell me the truth——

MRS. ELVSTED: Yes!

LOEVBORG: Did your husband know you were following me?

MRS. ELVSTED: Oh, Hedda!

LOEVBORG: Did you and he have an agreement that you should come here and keep an eye on me? Perhaps he gave you the idea? After all, he's a magistrate. I suppose he needed me back in his office. Or did he miss my companionship at the card table?

MRS. ELVSTED: [*Quietly, sobbing.*] Eilert, Eilert!

LOEVBORG: [*Seizes a glass and is about to fill it.*] Let's drink to him, too.

HEDDA: No more now. Remember you're going to read your book to Tesman.

LOEVBORG: [*Calm again, puts down his glass.*] That was silly of me, Thea. To take it like that, I mean. Don't be angry with me, my dear. You'll see—yes, and they'll see, too—that though I fell, I—I have raised myself up again. With your help, Thea.

MRS. ELVSTED: [*Happily.*] Oh, thank God!

> [BRACK *has meanwhile glanced at his watch. He and* TESMAN *get up and come into the drawing room.*]

BRACK: [*Takes his hat and overcoat.*] Well, Mrs. Tesman. It's time for us to go.

HEDDA: Yes, I suppose it must be.

LOEVBORG: [*Gets up.*] Time for me too, Judge.

MRS. ELVSTED: [*Quietly, pleadingly.*] Eilert, please don't!

HEDDA: [*Pinches her arm.*] They can hear you.

MRS. ELVSTED: [*Gives a little cry.*] Oh!

LOEVBORG: [*To* BRACK.] You were kind enough to ask me to join you.

BRACK: Are you coming?

LOEVBORG: If I may.

BRACK: Delighted.

LOEVBORG: [*Puts the paper package in his pocket and says to* TESMAN.] I'd like to show you one or two things before I send it off to the printer.

TESMAN: I say, that'll be fun. Fancy——! Oh, but Hedda, how'll Mrs. Elvsted get home? What?

HEDDA: Oh, we'll manage somehow.

LOEVBORG: [*Glances over toward the ladies.*] Mrs. Elvsted? I shall come back and collect her, naturally. [*Goes closer.*] About ten o'clock, Mrs. Tesman? Will that suit you?

HEDDA: Yes. That'll suit me admirably.

TESMAN: Good, that's settled. But you mustn't expect me back so early, Hedda.

HEDDA: Stay as long as you c—as long as you like, dear.

MRS. ELVSTED: [*Trying to hide her anxiety.*] Well then, Mr. Loevborg, I'll wait here till you come.

LOEVBORG: [*His hat in his hand.*] Pray do, Mrs. Elvsted.

BRACK: Well, gentlemen, now the party begins. I trust that, in the words of a certain fair lady, we shall enjoy good sport.

HEDDA: What a pity the fair lady can't be there, invisible.

BRACK: Why invisible?

HEDDA: So as to be able to hear some of your uncensored witticisms, your honor.

BRACK: [*Laughs.*] Oh, I shouldn't advise the fair lady to do that.

TESMAN: [*Laughs too.*] I say, Hedda, that's good. By Jove! Fancy that!

BRACK: Well, good night, ladies, good night!

LOEVBORG: [*Bows farewell.*] About ten o'clock, then.

> [BRACK, LOEVBORG and TESMAN *go out through the hall. As they do so* BERTHA *enters from the rear room with a lighted lamp. She puts it on the drawing-room table, then goes out the way she came.*]

MRS. ELVSTED: [*Has got up and is walking uneasily to and fro.*] Oh Hedda, Hedda! How is all this going to end?

HEDDA: At ten o'clock, then. He'll be here. I can see him. With a crown of vine-leaves in his hair.[7] Burning and unashamed!

MRS. ELVSTED: Oh, I do hope so!

HEDDA: Can't you see? Then he'll be himself again! He'll be a free man for the rest of his days!

MRS. ELVSTED: Please God you're right.

HEDDA: That's how he'll come! [*Gets up and goes closer.*] You can doubt him as much as you like. I believe in him! Now we'll see which of us——

MRS. ELVSTED: You're after something, Hedda.

HEDDA: Yes, I am. For once in my life I want to have the power to shape a man's destiny.

MRS. ELVSTED: Haven't you that power already?

HEDDA: No, I haven't. I've never had it.

MRS. ELVSTED: What about your husband?

HEDDA: Him! Oh, if you could only understand how poor I am. And you're allowed to be so rich, so rich! [*Clasps her passionately.*] I think I'll burn your hair off after all!

MRS. ELVSTED: Let me go! Let me go! You frighten me, Hedda!

BERTHA: [*In the open doorway.*] I've laid tea in the dining room, madam.

---

7. Worshippers of Dionysus, Greek god of wine, wore garlands of vine leaves as a sign of divine intoxication.

HEDDA: Good, we're coming.

MRS. ELVSTED: No, no, no! I'd rather go home alone! Now—at once!

HEDDA: Rubbish! First you're going to have some tea, you little idiot. And then—
at ten o'clock—Eilert Loevborg will come. With a crown of vine-leaves in his
hair! [*She drags* MRS. ELVSTED *almost forcibly toward the open doorway.*]

ACT III

SCENE: *The same. The curtains are drawn across the open doorway, and also across
the french windows. The lamp, half turned down, with a shade over it, is burning on
the table. In the stove, the door of which is open, a fire has been burning, but it is now
almost out.*

MRS. ELVSTED, *wrapped in a large shawl and with her feet resting on a footstool, is
sitting near the stove, huddled in the armchair.* HEDDA *is lying asleep on this sofa, fully
dressed, with a blanket over her.*

MRS. ELVSTED: [*After a pause, suddenly sits up in her chair and listens tensely. Then she
sinks wearily back again and sighs.*] Not back yet! Oh, God! Oh, God! Not back
yet!

[BERTHA *tiptoes cautiously in from the hall. She has a letter in her hand.*]

MRS. ELVSTED: [*Turns and whispers.*] What is it? Has someone come?

BERTHA: [*Quietly.*] Yes, a servant's just called with this letter.

MRS. ELVSTED: [*Quickly, holding out her hand.*] A letter! Give it to me!

BERTHA: But it's for the Doctor, madam.

MRS. ELVSTED: Oh. I see.

BERTHA: Miss Tesman's maid brought it. I'll leave it here on the table.

MRS. ELVSTED: Yes, do.

BERTHA: [*Puts down the letter.*] I'd better put the lamp out. It's starting to smoke.

MRS. ELVSTED: Yes, put it out. It'll soon be daylight.

BERTHA: [*Puts out the lamp.*] It's daylight already, madam.

MRS. ELVSTED: Yes. Broad day. And not home yet.

BERTHA: Oh dear, I was afraid this would happen.

MRS. ELVSTED: Were you?

BERTHA: Yes. When I heard that a certain gentleman had returned to town, and
saw him go off with them. I've heard all about him.

MRS. ELVSTED: Don't talk so loud. You'll wake your mistress.

BERTHA: [*Looks at the sofa and sighs.*] Yes. Let her go on sleeping, poor dear. Shall I
put some more wood on the fire?

MRS. ELVSTED: Thank you, don't bother on my account.

BERTHA: Very good. [*Goes quietly out through the hall.*]

HEDDA: [*Wakes as the door closes and looks up.*] What's that?

MRS. ELVSTED: It was only the maid.

HEDDA: [*Looks round.*] What am I doing here? Oh, now I remember. [*Sits up on the
sofa, stretches herself and rubs her eyes.*] What time is it, Thea?

MRS. ELVSTED: It's gone seven.

HEDDA: When did Tesman get back?

MRS. ELVSTED: He's not back yet.

HEDDA: Not home yet?

MRS. ELVSTED: [*Gets up.*] No one's come.

HEDDA: And we sat up waiting for them till four o'clock.

MRS. ELVSTED: God! How I waited for him!

HEDDA: [*Yawns and says with her hand in front of her mouth.*] Oh, dear. We might
have saved ourselves the trouble.

MRS. ELVSTED: Did you manage to sleep?

HEDDA: Oh, yes. Quite well, I think. Didn't you get any?

MRS. ELVSTED: Not a wink. I couldn't, Hedda. I just couldn't.

HEDDA: [*Gets up and comes over to her.*] Now, now, now. There's nothing to worry
about. I know what's happened.

MRS. ELVSTED: What? Please tell me.

HEDDA: Well, obviously the party went on very late——

MRS. ELVSTED: Oh dear, I suppose it must have. But——

HEDDA: And Tesman didn't want to come home and wake us all up in the middle
of the night. [*Laughs.*] Probably wasn't too keen to show his face either, after
a spree like that.

MRS. ELVSTED: But where could he have gone?

HEDDA: I should think he's probably slept at his aunts'. They keep his old room
for him.

MRS. ELVSTED: No, he can't be with them. A letter came for him just now from
Miss Tesman. It's over there.

HEDDA: Oh? [*Looks at the envelope.*] Yes, it's Auntie Juju's handwriting. Well, he
must still be at Judge Brack's, then. And Eilert Loevborg is sitting there, reading to him. With a crown of vine-leaves in his hair.

MRS. ELVSTED: Hedda, you're only saying that. You don't believe it.

HEDDA: Thea, you really are a little fool.

MRS. ELVSTED: Perhaps I am.

HEDDA: You look tired to death.

MRS. ELVSTED: Yes. I am tired to death.

HEDDA: Go to my room and lie down for a little. Do as I say, now; don't argue.

MRS. ELVSTED: No, no. I couldn't possibly sleep.

HEDDA: Of course you can.

MRS. ELVSTED: But your husband'll be home soon. And I must know at once——

HEDDA: I'll tell you when he comes.

MRS. ELVSTED: Promise me, Hedda?

HEDDA: Yes, don't worry. Go and get some sleep.

MRS. ELVSTED: Thank you. All right, I'll try.

[*She goes out through the rear room.* HEDDA *goes to the french windows and
draws the curtains. Broad daylight floods into the room. She goes to the writing
table, takes a small hand mirror from it and arranges her hair. Then she goes
to the door leading into the hall and presses the bell. After a few moments,*
BERTHA *enters.*]

BERTHA: Did you want anything, madam?

HEDDA: Yes, put some more wood on the fire. I'm freezing.

BERTHA: Bless you, I'll soon have this room warmed up. [*She rakes the embers together and puts a fresh piece of wood on them. Suddenly she stops and listens.*] There's someone at the front door, madam.

HEDDA: Well, go and open it. I'll see to the fire.

BERTHA: It'll burn up in a moment.

> [*She goes out through the hall.* HEDDA *kneels on the footstool and puts more wood in the stove. After a few seconds,* GEORGE TESMAN *enters from the hall. He looks tired, and rather worried. He tiptoes toward the open doorway and is about to slip through the curtains.*]

HEDDA: [*At the stove, without looking up.*] Good morning.

TESMAN: [*Turns.*] Hedda! [*Comes nearer.*] Good heavens, are you up already? What?

HEDDA: Yes, I got up very early this morning.

TESMAN: I was sure you'd still be sleeping. Fancy that!

HEDDA: Don't talk so loud. Mrs. Elvsted's asleep in my room.

TESMAN: Mrs. Elvsted? Has she stayed the night here?

HEDDA: Yes. No one came to escort her home.

TESMAN: Oh. No, I suppose not.

HEDDA: [*Closes the door of the stove and gets up.*] Well. Was it fun?

TESMAN: Have you been anxious about me? What?

HEDDA: Not in the least. I asked if you'd had fun.

TESMAN: Oh yes, rather! Well, I thought, for once in a while—The first part was the best; when Eilert read his book to me. We arrived over an hour too early—what about that, eh? By Jove! Brack had a lot of things to see to, so Eilert read to me.

HEDDA: [*Sits at the right-hand side of the table.*] Well? Tell me about it.

TESMAN: [*Sits on a footstool by the stove.*] Honestly, Hedda, you've no idea what a book that's going to be. It's really one of the most remarkable things that's ever been written. By Jove!

HEDDA: Oh, never mind about the book——

TESMAN: I'm going to make a confession to you, Hedda. When he'd finished reading a sort of beastly feeling came over me.

HEDDA: Beastly feeling?

TESMAN: I found myself envying Eilert for being able to write like that. Imagine that, Hedda!

HEDDA: Yes. I can imagine.

TESMAN: What a tragedy that with all those gifts he should be so incorrigible.

HEDDA: You mean he's less afraid of life than most men?

TESMAN: Good heavens, no. He just doesn't know the meaning of the word moderation.

HEDDA: What happened afterwards?

TESMAN: Well, looking back on it I suppose you might almost call it an orgy, Hedda.

HEDDA: Had he vine-leaves in his hair?

TESMAN: Vine-leaves? No, I didn't see any of them. He made a long, rambling oration in honor of the woman who'd inspired him to write this book. Yes, those were the words he used.

HEDDA: Did he name her?

TESMAN: No. But I suppose it must be Mrs. Elvsted. You wait and see!

HEDDA: Where did you leave him?

TESMAN: On the way home. We left in a bunch—the last of us, that is—and Brack came with us to get a little fresh air. Well, then, you see, we agreed we ought to see Eilert home. He'd had a drop too much.

HEDDA: You don't say?

TESMAN: But now comes the funny part, Hedda. Or I should really say the tragic part. Oh, I'm almost ashamed to tell you. For Eilert's sake, I mean——

HEDDA: Why, what happened?

TESMAN: Well, you see, as we were walking toward town I happened to drop behind for a minute. Only for a minute—er—you understand——

HEDDA: Yes, yes——?

TESMAN: Well then, when I ran on to catch them up, what do you think I found by the roadside. What?

HEDDA: How on earth should I know?

TESMAN: You mustn't tell anyone, Hedda. What? Promise me that—for Eilert's sake. [*Takes a package wrapped in paper from his coat pocket.*] Just fancy! I found this.

HEDDA: Isn't this the one he brought here yesterday?

TESMAN: Yes! The whole of that precious, irreplaceable manuscript! And he went and lost it! Didn't even notice! What about that? By Jove! Tragic.

HEDDA: But why didn't you give it back to him?

TESMAN: I didn't dare to, in the state he was in.

HEDDA: Didn't you tell any of the others?

TESMAN: Good heavens, no. I didn't want to do that. For Eilert's sake, you understand.

HEDDA: Then no one else knows you have his manuscript?

TESMAN: No. And no one must be allowed to know.

HEDDA: Didn't it come up in the conversation later?

TESMAN: I didn't get a chance to talk to him any more. As soon as we got into the outskirts of town, he and one or two of the others gave us the slip. Disappeared, by Jove!

HEDDA: Oh? I suppose they took him home.

TESMAN: Yes, I imagine that was the idea. Brack left us, too.

HEDDA: And what have you been up to since then?

TESMAN: Well, I and one or two of the others—awfully jolly chaps, they were—went back to where one of them lived, and had a cup of morning coffee. Morning-after coffee—what? Ah, well. I'll just lie down for a bit and give Eilert time to sleep it off, poor chap, then I'll run over and give this back to him.

HEDDA: [*Holds out her hand for the package.*] No, don't do that. Not just yet. Let me read it first.

TESMAN: Oh no, really, Hedda dear, honestly, I daren't do that.

HEDDA: Daren't?

TESMAN: No—imagine how desperate he'll be when he wakes up and finds his manuscript's missing. He hasn't any copy, you see. He told me so himself.

HEDDA: Can't a thing like that be rewritten?

TESMAN: Oh no, not possibly, I shouldn't think. I mean, the inspiration, you know——

HEDDA: Oh, yes. I'd forgotten that. [*Casually.*] By the way, there's a letter for you.

TESMAN: Is there? Fancy that!

HEDDA: [*Holds it out to him.*] It came early this morning.

TESMAN: I say, it's from Auntie Juju! What on earth can it be? [*Puts the package on the other footstool, opens the letter, reads it and jumps up.*] Oh, Hedda! She says poor Auntie Rena's dying.

HEDDA: Well, we've been expecting that.

TESMAN: She says if I want to see her I must go quickly. I'll run over at once.

HEDDA: [*Hides a smile.*] Run?

TESMAN: Hedda dear, I suppose you wouldn't like to come with me? What about that, eh?

HEDDA: [*Gets up and says wearily and with repulsion.*] No, no, don't ask me to do anything like that. I can't bear illness or death. I loathe anything ugly.

TESMAN: Yes, yes. Of course. [*In a dither.*] My hat? My overcoat? Oh yes, in the hall. I do hope I won't get there too late, Hedda? What?

HEDDA: You'll be all right if you run.

[BERTHA *enters from the hall.*]

BERTHA: Judge Brack's outside and wants to know if he can come in.

TESMAN: At this hour? No, I can't possibly receive him now.

HEDDA: I can. [*To* BERTHA.] Ask his honor to come in.

[BERTHA *goes.*]

HEDDA: [*Whispers quickly.*] The manuscript, Tesman. [*She snatches it from the footstool.*]

TESMAN: Yes, give it to me.

HEDDA: No, I'll look after it for now.

[*She goes over to the writing table and puts it in the bookcase.* TESMAN *stands dithering, unable to get his gloves on.* JUDGE BRACK *enters from the hall.*]

HEDDA: [*Nods to him*] Well, you're an early bird.

BRACK: Yes, aren't I? [*To* TESMAN.] Are you up and about, too?

TESMAN: Yes, I've got to go and see my aunts. Poor Auntie Rena's dying.

BRACK: Oh dear, is she? Then you mustn't let me detain you. At so tragic a——

TESMAN: Yes, I really must run. Good-bye! Good-bye! [*Runs out through the hall.*]

HEDDA: [*Goes nearer.*] You seem to have had excellent sport last night—Judge.

BRACK: Indeed yes, Mrs. Hedda. I haven't even had time to take my clothes off.

HEDDA: *You* haven't either?

BRACK: As you see. What's Tesman told you about last night's escapades?

HEDDA: Oh, only some boring story about having gone and drunk coffee somewhere.

BRACK: Yes, I've heard about that coffee party. Eilert Loevborg wasn't with them, I gather?

HEDDA: No, they took him home first.

BRACK: Did Tesman go with him?

HEDDA: No, one or two of the others, he said.

BRACK: [*Smiles.*] George Tesman is a credulous man, Mrs. Hedda.

HEDDA: God knows. But—has something happened?

BRACK: Well, yes, I'm afraid it has.

HEDDA: I see. Sit down and tell me. [*She sits on the left of the table,* BRACK *at the long side of it, near her.*] Well?

BRACK: I had a special reason for keeping track of my guests last night. Or perhaps I should say some of my guests.

HEDDA: Including Eilert Loevborg?

BRACK: I must confess—yes.

HEDDA: You're beginning to make me curious.

BRACK: Do you know where he and some of my other guests spent the latter half of last night, Mrs. Hedda?

HEDDA: Tell me. If it won't shock me.

BRACK: Oh, I don't think it'll shock you. They found themselves participating in an exceedingly animated *soirée*.

HEDDA: Of a sporting character?

BRACK: Of a highly sporting character.

HEDDA: Tell me more.

BRACK: Loevborg had received an invitation in advance—as had the others. I knew all about that. But he had refused. As you know, he's become a new man.

HEDDA: Up at the Elvsteds', yes. But he went?

BRACK: Well, you see, Mrs. Hedda, last night at my house, unhappily, the spirit moved him.

HEDDA: Yes, I hear he became inspired.

BRACK: Somewhat violently inspired. And as a result, I suppose, his thoughts strayed. We men, alas, don't always stick to our principles as firmly as we should.

HEDDA: I'm sure you're an exception, Judge Brack. But go on about Loevborg.

BRACK: Well, to cut a long story short, he ended up in the establishment of a certain Mademoiselle Danielle.

HEDDA: Mademoiselle Danielle?

BRACK: She was holding the *soirée*. For a selected circle of friends and admirers.

HEDDA: Has she got red hair?

BRACK: She has.

HEDDA: A singer of some kind?

BRACK: Yes—among other accomplishments. She's also a celebrated huntress—of men, Mrs. Hedda. I'm sure you've heard about her. Eilert Loevborg used to be one of her most ardent patrons. In his salad days.

HEDDA: And how did all this end?

BRACK: Not entirely amicably, from all accounts. Mademoiselle Danielle began by receiving him with the utmost tenderness and ended by resorting to her fists.

HEDDA: Against Loevborg?

BRACK: Yes. He accused her, or her friends, of having robbed him. He claimed his pocketbook had been stolen. Among other things. In short, he seems to have made a bloodthirsty scene.

HEDDA: And what did this lead to?

BRACK: It led to a general free-for-all, in which both sexes participated. Fortunately, in the end the police arrived.

HEDDA: The police too?

BRACK: Yes. I'm afraid it may turn out to be rather an expensive joke for Master Eilert. Crazy fool!

HEDDA: Oh?

BRACK: Apparently he put up a very violent resistance. Hit one of the constables on the ear and tore his uniform. He had to accompany them to the police station.

HEDDA: Where did you learn all this?

BRACK: From the police.

HEDDA: [*To herself.*] So that's what happened. He didn't have a crown of vine-leaves in his hair.

BRACK: Vine-leaves, Mrs. Hedda?

HEDDA: [*In her normal voice again.*] But, tell me, Judge, why do you take such a close interest in Eilert Loevborg?

BRACK: For one thing it'll hardly be a matter of complete indifference to me if it's revealed in court that he came there straight from my house.

HEDDA: Will it come to court?

BRACK: Of course. Well, I don't regard that as particularly serious. Still, I thought it my duty, as a friend of the family, to give you and your husband a full account of his nocturnal adventures.

HEDDA: Why?

BRACK: Because I've a shrewd suspicion that he's hoping to use you as a kind of screen.

HEDDA: What makes you think that?

BRACK: Oh, for heaven's sake, Mrs. Hedda, we're not blind. You wait and see. This Mrs. Elvsted won't be going back to her husband just yet.

HEDDA: Well, if there were anything between those two there are plenty of other places where they could meet.

BRACK: Not in anyone's home. From now on every respectable house will once again be closed to Eilert Loevborg.

HEDDA: And mine should be too, you mean?

BRACK: Yes. I confess I should find it more than irksome if this gentleman were to be granted unrestricted access to this house. If he were superfluously to intrude into——

HEDDA: The triangle?

BRACK: Precisely. For me it would be like losing a home.

HEDDA: [*Looks at him and smiles.*] I see. You want to be the cock of the walk.

BRACK: [*Nods slowly and lowers his voice.*] Yes, that is my aim. And I shall fight for it with—every weapon at my disposal.

HEDDA: [*As her smile fades.*] You're a dangerous man, aren't you? When you really want something.

BRACK: You think so?

HEDDA: Yes. I'm beginning to think so. I'm deeply thankful you haven't any kind of hold over me.

BRACK: [*Laughs equivocally.*] Well, well, Mrs. Hedda—perhaps you're right. If I had, who knows what I might not think up?

HEDDA: Come, Judge Brack. That sounds almost like a threat.

BRACK: [*Gets up.*] Heaven forbid! In the creation of a triangle—and its continuance—the question of compulsion should never arise.

HEDDA: Exactly what I was thinking.

BRACK: Well, I've said what I came to say. I must be getting back. Good-bye, Mrs. Hedda. [*Goes toward the french windows.*]

HEDDA: [*Gets up.*] Are you going out through the garden?

BRACK: Yes, it's shorter.

HEDDA: Yes. And it's the back door, isn't it?

BRACK: I've nothing against back doors. They can be quite intriguing—sometimes.

HEDDA: When people fire pistols out of them, for example?

BRACK: [*In the doorway, laughs.*] Oh, people don't shoot tame cocks.

HEDDA: [*Laughs too.*] I suppose not. When they've only got one.

> [*They nod good-bye, laughing. He goes. She closes the french windows behind him, and stands for a moment, looking out pensively. Then she walks across the room and glances through the curtains in the open doorway. Goes to the writing table, takes* LOEVBORG*'s package from the bookcase and is about to leaf through the pages when* BERTHA *is heard remonstrating loudly in the hall.* HEDDA *turns and listens. She hastily puts the package back in the drawer, locks it and puts the key on the inkstand.* EILERT LOEVBORG, *with his overcoat on and his hat in his hand, throws the door open. He looks somewhat confused and excited.*]

LOEVBORG: [*Shouts as he enters.*] I must come in, I tell you! Let me pass! [*He closes the door, turns, sees* HEDDA, *controls himself immediately and bows.*]

HEDDA: [*At the writing table.*] Well, Mr. Loevborg, this is rather a late hour to be collecting Thea.

LOEVBORG: And an early hour to call on you. Please forgive me.

HEDDA: How do you know she's still here?

LOEVBORG: They told me at her lodgings that she has been out all night.

HEDDA: [*Goes to the table.*] Did you notice anything about their behavior when they told you?

LOEVBORG: [*Looks at her, puzzled.*] Notice anything?

HEDDA: Did they sound as if they thought it—strange?

LOEVBORG: [*Suddenly understands.*] Oh, I see what you mean. I'm dragging her down with me. No, as a matter of fact I didn't notice anything. I suppose Tesman isn't up yet?

HEDDA: No, I don't think so.

LOEVBORG: When did he get home?

HEDDA: Very late.

LOEVBORG: Did he tell you anything?

HEDDA: Yes. I gather you had a merry party at Judge Brack's last night.

LOEVBORG: He didn't tell you anything else?

HEDDA. I don't think so. I was so terribly sleepy——

[MRS. ELVSTED *comes through the curtains in the open doorway.*]

MRS. ELVSTED: [*Runs toward him.*] Oh, Eilert! At last!

LOEVBORG: Yes—at last. And too late.

MRS. ELVSTED: What is too late?

LOEVBORG: Everything—now. I'm finished, Thea.

MRS. ELVSTED: Oh, no, no! Don't say that!

LOEVBORG: You'll say it yourself, when you've heard what I——

MRS. ELVSTED: I don't want to hear anything!

HEDDA: Perhaps you'd rather speak to her alone? I'd better go.

LOEVBORG: No, stay.

MRS. ELVSTED: But I don't want to hear anything, I tell you!

LOEVBORG: It's not about last night.

MRS. ELVSTED: Then what——?

LOEVBORG: I want to tell you that from now on we must stop seeing each other.

MRS. ELVSTED: Stop seeing each other!

HEDDA: [*Involuntarily.*] I knew it!

LOEVBORG: I have no further use for you, Thea.

MRS. ELVSTED: You can stand there and say that! No further use for me! Surely I can go on helping you? We'll go on working together, won't we?

LOEVBORG: I don't intend to do any more work from now on.

MRS. ELVSTED: [*Desperately.*] Then what use have I for my life?

LOEVBORG: You must try to live as if you had never known me.

MRS. ELVSTED: But I can't!

LOEVBORG: Try to, Thea. Go back home——

MRS. ELVSTED: Never! I want to be wherever you are! I won't let myself be driven away like this! I want to stay here—and be with you when the book comes out.

HEDDA: [*Whispers.*] Ah, yes! The book!

LOEVBORG: [*Looks at her.*] Our book; Thea's and mine. It belongs to both of us.

MRS. ELVSTED: Oh, yes! I feel that, too! And I've a right to be with you when it comes into the world. I want to see people respect and honor you again. And the joy! The joy! I want to share it with you!

LOEVBORG: Thea—our book will never come into the world.

HEDDA: Ah!

MRS. ELVSTED: Not——?

LOEVBORG: It cannot. Ever.

MRS. ELVSTED: Eilert—what have you done with the manuscript? Where is it?

LOEVBORG: Oh Thea, please don't ask me that!

MRS. ELVSTED: Yes, yes—I must know. I've a right to know. Now!

LOEVBORG: The manuscript. I've torn it up.

MRS. ELVSTED: [*Screams.*] No, no!

HEDDA: [*Involuntarily.*] But that's not——!

LOEVBORG: [*Looks at her.*] Not true, you think?

HEDDA: [*Controls herself.*] Why—yes, of course it is, if you say so. It just sounded so incredible——

LOEVBORG: It's true, nevertheless.

MRS. ELVSTED: Oh, my God, my God, Hedda—he's destroyed his own book!

LOEVBORG: I have destroyed my life. Why not my life's work, too?

MRS. ELVSTED: And you—did this last night?

LOEVBORG: Yes, Thea. I tore it into a thousand pieces. And scattered them out across the fjord. It's good, clean, salt water. Let it carry them away; let them drift in the current and the wind. And in a little while, they will sink. Deeper and deeper. As I shall, Thea.

MRS. ELVSTED: Do you know, Eilert—this book—all my life I shall feel as though you'd killed a little child?

LOEVBORG: You're right. It is like killing a child.

MRS. ELVSTED: But how could you? It was my child, too!

HEDDA. [*Almost inaudibly.*] Oh—the child——!

MRS. ELVSTED: [*Breathes heavily.*] It's all over, then. Well—I'll go now, Hedda.

HEDDA: You're not leaving town?

MRS. ELVSTED: I don't know what I'm going to do. I can't see anything except—darkness. [*She goes out through the hall.*]

HEDDA: [*Waits a moment.*] Aren't you going to escort her home, Mr. Loevborg?

LOEVBORG: I? Through the streets? Do you want me to let people see her with me?

HEDDA: Of course I don't know what else may have happened last night. But is it so utterly beyond redress?

LOEVBORG: It isn't just last night. It'll go on happening. I know it. But the curse of it is, I don't want to live that kind of life. I don't want to start all that again. She's broken my courage. I can't spit in the eyes of the world any longer.

HEDDA: [*As though to herself.*] That pretty little fool's been trying to shape a man's destiny. [*Looks at him.*] But how could you be so heartless toward her?

LOEVBORG: Don't call me heartless!

HEDDA: To go and destroy the one thing that's made her life worth living? You don't call that heartless?

LOEVBORG: Do you want to know the truth, Hedda?

HEDDA: The truth?

LOEVBORG: Promise me first—give me your word—that you'll never let Thea know about this.

HEDDA: I give you my word.

LOEVBORG: Good. Well; what I told her just now was a lie.

HEDDA: About the manuscript?

LOEVBORG: Yes. I didn't tear it up. Or throw it in the fjord.

HEDDA: You didn't? But where is it, then?

LOEVBORG: I destroyed it, all the same. I destroyed it, Hedda!

HEDDA: I don't understand.

LOEVBORG: Thea said that what I had done was like killing a child.

HEDDA: Yes. That's what she said.

LOEVBORG: But to kill a child isn't the worst thing a father can do to it.

HEDDA: What could be worse than that?

LOEVBORG: Hedda—suppose a man came home one morning, after a night of debauchery, and said to the mother of his child: "Look here. I've been wandering round all night. I've been to—such-and-such a place and such-and-such a place. And I had our child with me. I took him to—these places. And I've lost him. Just—lost him. God knows where he is or whose hands he's fallen into."

HEDDA: I see. But when all's said and done, this was only a book——

LOEVBORG: Thea's heart and soul were in that book. It was her whole life.

HEDDA: Yes. I understand.

LOEVBORG: Well, then you must also understand that she and I cannot possibly ever see each other again.

HEDDA: Where will you go?

LOEVBORG: Nowhere. I just want to put an end to it all. As soon as possible.

HEDDA: [*Takes a step toward him.*] Eilert Loevborg, listen to me. Do it—beautifully!

LOEVBORG: Beautifully? [*Smiles.*] With a crown of vine-leaves in my hair? The way you used to dream of me—in the old days?

HEDDA: No. I don't believe in that crown any longer. But—do it beautifully, all the same. Just this once. Good-bye. You must go now. And don't come back.

LOEVBORG: Adieu, madam. Give my love to George Tesman. [*Turns to go.*]

HEDDA: Wait. I want to give you a souvenir to take with you.

[*She goes over to the writing table, opens the drawer and the pistol-case, and comes back to* LOEVBORG *with one of the pistols.*]

LOEVBORG: [*Looks at her.*] This? Is this the souvenir?

HEDDA: [*Nods slowly.*] You recognize it? You looked down its barrel once.

LOEVBORG: You should have used it then.

HEDDA: Here! Use it now!

LOEVBORG: [*Puts the pistol in his breast pocket.*] Thank you.

HEDDA: Do it beautifully, Eilert Loevborg. Only promise me that!

LOEVBORG: Good-bye, Hedda Gabler.

[*He goes out through the hall.* HEDDA *stands by the door for a moment, listening. Then she goes over to the writing table, takes out the package containing the manuscript, glances inside it, pulls some of the pages half out and looks at them. Then she takes it to the armchair by the stove and sits down with the package in her lap. After a moment, she opens the door of the stove; then she opens the packet.*]

HEDDA: [*Throws one of the pages into the stove and whispers to herself.*] I'm burning your child, Thea! You with your beautiful wavy hair! [*She throws a few more pages into the stove.*] The child Eilert Loevborg gave you. [*Throws the rest of the manuscript in.*] I'm burning it! I'm burning your child!

ACT IV

SCENE: *The same. It is evening. The drawing room is in darkness. The small room is illuminated by the hanging lamp over the table. The curtains are drawn across the french windows.* HEDDA, *dressed in black, is walking up and down in the darkened room. Then she goes into the small room and crosses to the left. A few chords are heard from the piano. She comes back into the drawing room.*

BERTHA *comes through the small room from the right with a lighted lamp, which she places on the table in front of the corner sofa in the drawing room. Her eyes are red with crying, and she has black ribbons on her cap. She goes quietly out, right.* HEDDA *goes over to the french windows, draws the curtains slightly to one side and looks out into the darkness.*

A few moments later, MISS TESMAN *enters from the hall. She is dressed in mourning, with a black hat and veil.* HEDDA *goes to meet her and holds out her hand.*

MISS TESMAN: Well, Hedda, here I am in the weeds of sorrow. My poor sister has ended her struggles at last.

HEDDA: I've already heard. Tesman sent me a card.

MISS TESMAN: Yes, he promised me he would. But I thought, no, I must go and break the news of death to Hedda myself—here, in the house of life.

HEDDA: It's very kind of you.

MISS TESMAN: Ah, Rena shouldn't have chosen a time like this to pass away. This is no moment for Hedda's house to be a place of mourning.

HEDDA: [*Changing the subject.*] She died peacefully, Miss Tesman?

MISS TESMAN: Oh, it was quite beautiful! The end came so calmly. And she was so happy at being able to see George once again. And say good-bye to him. Hasn't he come home yet?

HEDDA: No. He wrote that I mustn't expect him too soon. But please sit down.

MISS TESMAN: No, thank you, Hedda dear—bless you. I'd like to. But I've so little time. I must dress her and lay her out as well as I can. She shall go to her grave looking really beautiful.

HEDDA: Can't I help with anything?

MISS TESMAN: Why, you mustn't think of such a thing! Hedda Tesman mustn't let her hands be soiled by contact with death. Or her thoughts. Not at this time.

HEDDA: One can't always control one's thoughts.

MISS TESMAN: [*Continues.*] Ah, well, that's life. Now we must start to sew poor Rena's shroud. There'll be sewing to be done in this house too before long, I shouldn't wonder. But not for a shroud, praise God.

[GEORGE TESMAN *enters from the hall.*]

HEDDA: You've come at last! Thank heavens!

TESMAN: Are you here, Auntie Juju? With Hedda? Fancy that!

MISS TESMAN: I was just on the point of leaving, dear boy. Well, have you done everything you promised me?

TESMAN: No, I'm afraid I forgot half of it. I'll have to run over again tomorrow.

My head's in a complete whirl today. I can't collect my thoughts.

MISS TESMAN: But George dear, you mustn't take it like this.

TESMAN: Oh? Well—er—how should I?

MISS TESMAN: You must be happy in your grief. Happy for what's happened. As I am.

TESMAN: Oh, yes, yes. You're thinking of Aunt Rena.

HEDDA: It'll be lonely for you now, Miss Tesman.

MISS TESMAN: For the first few days, yes. But it won't last long, I hope. Poor dear Rena's little room isn't going to stay empty.

TESMAN: Oh? Whom are you going to move in there? What?

MISS TESMAN: Oh, there's always some poor invalid who needs care and attention.

HEDDA: Do you really want another cross like that to bear?

MISS TESMAN: Cross! God forgive you, child. It's been no cross for me.

HEDDA: But now—if a complete stranger comes to live with you——?

MISS TESMAN: Oh, one soon makes friends with invalids. And I need so much to have someone to live for. Like you, my dear. Well, I expect there'll soon be work in this house too for an old aunt, praise God!

HEDDA: Oh—please!

TESMAN: By Jove, yes! What a splendid time the three of us could have together if——

HEDDA: If?

TESMAN: [Uneasily.] Oh, never mind. It'll all work out. Let's hope so—what?

MISS TESMAN: Yes, yes. Well, I'm sure you two would like to be alone. [Smiles.] Perhaps Hedda may have something to tell you, George. Good-bye. I must go home to Rena. [Turns to the door.] Dear God, how strange! Now Rena is with me and with poor dear Joachim.

TESMAN: Fancy that. Yes, Auntie Juju! What?

[MISS TESMAN goes out through the hall.]

HEDDA: [Follows TESMAN coldly and searchingly with her eyes.] I really believe this death distresses you more than it does her.

TESMAN: Oh, it isn't just Auntie Rena. It's Eilert I'm so worried about.

HEDDA: [Quickly.] Is there any news of him?

TESMAN: I ran over to see him this afternoon. I wanted to tell him his manuscript was in safe hands.

HEDDA: Oh? You didn't find him?

TESMAN: No. He wasn't at home. But later I met Mrs. Elvsted and she told me he'd been here early this morning.

HEDDA: Yes, just after you'd left.

TESMAN: It seems he said he'd torn the manuscript up. What?

HEDDA: Yes, he claimed to have done so.

TESMAN: You told him we had it, of course?

HEDDA: No. [Quickly.] Did you tell Mrs. Elvsted?

TESMAN: No, I didn't like to. But you ought to have told him. Think if he should go home and do something desperate! Give me the manuscript, Hedda. I'll run over to him with it right away. Where did you put it?

HEDDA: [*Cold and motionless, leaning against the armchair.*] I haven't got it any longer.

TESMAN: Haven't got it? What on earth do you mean?

HEDDA: I've burned it.

TESMAN: [*Starts, terrified.*] Burned it! Burned Eilert's manuscript!

HEDDA: Don't shout. The servant will hear you.

TESMAN: Burned it! But in heaven's name——! Oh, no, no, no! This is impossible!

HEDDA: Well, it's true.

TESMAN: But Hedda, do you realize what you've done? That's appropriating lost property! It's against the law! By Jove! You ask Judge Brack and see if I'm not right.

HEDDA: You'd be well advised not to talk about it to Judge Brack or anyone else.

TESMAN: But how could you go and do such a dreadful thing? What on earth put the idea into your head? What came over you? Answer me! What?

HEDDA: [*Represses an almost imperceptible smile.*] I did it for your sake, George.

TESMAN: For my sake?

HEDDA: When you came home this morning and described how he'd read his book to you——

TESMAN: Yes, yes?

HEDDA: You admitted you were jealous of him.

TESMAN: But, good heavens, I didn't mean it literally!

HEDDA: No matter. I couldn't bear the thought that anyone else should push you into the background.

TESMAN: [*Torn between doubt and joy.*] Hedda—is this true? But—but—but I never realized you loved me like that! Fancy——

HEDDA: Well, I suppose you'd better know. I'm going to have—— [*Breaks off and says violently.*] No, no—you'd better ask your Auntie Juju. She'll tell you.

TESMAN: Hedda! I think I understand what you mean. [*Clasps his hands.*] Good heavens, can it really be true! What?

HEDDA: Don't shout. The servant will hear you.

TESMAN: [*Laughing with joy.*] The servant! I say, that's good! The servant! Why, that's Bertha! I'll run out and tell her at once!

HEDDA: [*Clenches her hands in despair.*] Oh, it's destroying me, all this—it's destroying me!

TESMAN: I say, Hedda, what's up? What?

HEDDA: [*Cold, controlled.*] Oh, it's all so—absurd—George.

TESMAN: Absurd? That I'm so happy? But surely——? Ah, well—perhaps I won't say anything to Bertha.

HEDDA: No, do. She might as well know too.

TESMAN: No, no, I won't tell her yet. But Auntie Juju—I must let her know! And you—you called me George! For the first time! Fancy that! Oh, it'll make Auntie Juju so happy, all this! So very happy!

HEDDA: Will she be happy when she hears I've burned Eilert Loevborg's manuscript—for your sake?

TESMAN: No, I'd forgotten about that. Of course no one must be allowed to know about the manuscript. But that you're burning with love for me, Hedda, I must certainly let Auntie Juju know that. I say, I wonder if young wives often feel like that toward their husbands? What?

HEDDA: You might ask Auntie Juju about that too.

TESMAN: I will, as soon as I get the chance. [*Looks uneasy and thoughtful again.*] But I say, you know, that manuscript. Dreadful business. Poor Eilert!

[MRS. ELVSTED, *dressed as on her first visit, with hat and overcoat, enters from the hall.*]

MRS. ELVSTED: [*Greets them hastily and tremulously.*] Oh, Hedda dear, do please forgive me for coming here again.

HEDDA: Why, Thea, what's happened?

TESMAN: Is it anything to do with Eilert Loevborg? What?

MRS. ELVSTED: Yes—I'm so dreadfully afraid he may have met with an accident.

HEDDA: [*Grips her arm.*] You think so?

TESMAN: But, good heavens, Mrs. Elvsted, what makes you think that?

MRS. ELVSTED: I heard them talking about him at the boarding-house, as I went in. Oh, there are the most terrible rumors being spread about him in town today.

TESMAN: Fancy. Yes, I heard about them too. But I can testify that he went straight home to bed. Fancy that!

HEDDA: Well—what did they say in the boarding-house?

MRS. ELVSTED: Oh, I couldn't find out anything. Either they didn't know, or else—— They stopped talking when they saw me. And I didn't dare to ask.

TESMAN: [*Fidgets uneasily.*] We must hope—we must hope you misheard them, Mrs. Elvsted.

MRS. ELVSTED: No, no, I'm sure it was he they were talking about. I heard them say something about a hospital——

TESMAN: Hospital!

HEDDA: Oh no, surely that's impossible!

MRS. ELVSTED: Oh, I became so afraid. So I went up to his rooms and asked to see him.

HEDDA: Do you think that was wise, Thea?

MRS. ELVSTED: Well, what else could I do? I couldn't bear the uncertainty any longer.

TESMAN: But you didn't manage to find him either? What?

MRS. ELVSTED: No. And they had no idea where he was. They said he hadn't been home since yesterday afternoon.

TESMAN: Since yesterday? Fancy that!

MRS. ELVSTED: I'm sure he must have met with an accident.

TESMAN: Hedda, I wonder if I ought to go into town and make one or two enquiries?

HEDDA: No, no, don't you get mixed up in this.

[JUDGE BRACK *enters from the hall, hat in hand.* BERTHA, *who has opened the door for him, closes it. He looks serious and greets them silently.*]

TESMAN: Hullo, my dear Judge. Fancy seeing you!

BRACK: I had to come and talk to you.

TESMAN: I can see Auntie Juju's told you the news.

BRACK: Yes, I've heard about that too.

TESMAN: Tragic, isn't it?

BRACK: Well, my dear chap, that depends how you look at it.

TESMAN: [*Looks uncertainly at him.*] Has something else happened?

BRACK: Yes.

HEDDA: Another tragedy?

BRACK: That also depends on how you look at it, Mrs. Tesman.

MRS. ELVSTED: Oh, it's something to do with Eilert Loevborg!

BRACK: [*Looks at her for a moment.*] How did you guess? Perhaps you've heard
    already——?

MRS. ELVSTED: [*Confused.*] No, no, not at all—I——

TESMAN: For heaven's sake, tell us!

BRACK: [*Shrugs his shoulders.*] Well, I'm afraid they've taken him to the hospital.
    He's dying.

MRS. ELVSTED: [*Screams.*] Oh God, God!

TESMAN: The hospital! Dying!

HEDDA: [*Involuntarily.*] So quickly!

MRS. ELVSTED: [*Weeping.*] Oh, Hedda! And we parted enemies!

HEDDA: [*Whispers.*] Thea—Thea!

MRS. ELVSTED: [*Ignoring her.*] I must see him! I must see him before he dies!

BRACK: It's no use, Mrs. Elvsted. No one's allowed to see him now.

MRS. ELVSTED: But what's happened to him? You must tell me!

TESMAN: He hasn't tried to do anything to himself? What?

HEDDA: Yes, he has. I'm sure of it.

TESMAN: Hedda, how can you——?

BRACK: [*Who has not taken his eyes from her.*] I'm afraid you've guessed correctly,
    Mrs. Tesman.

MRS. ELVSTED: How dreadful!

TESMAN: Attempted suicide! Fancy that!

HEDDA: Shot himself!

BRACK: Right again, Mrs. Tesman.

MRS. ELVSTED: [*Tries to compose herself.*] When did this happen, Judge Brack?

BRACK: This afternoon. Between three and four.

TESMAN: But, good heavens—where? What?

BRACK: [*A little hesitantly.*] Where? Why, my dear chap, in his rooms of course.

MRS. ELVSTED: No, that's impossible. I was there soon after six.

BRACK: Well, it must have been somewhere else, then. I don't know exactly. I
    only know that they found him. He'd shot himself—through the breast.

MRS. ELVSTED: Oh, how horrible! That he should end like that!

HEDDA: [*To* BRACK.] Through the breast, you said?

BRACK: That is what I said.

HEDDA: Not through the head?

BRACK: Through the breast, Mrs. Tesman.

HEDDA: The breast. Yes; yes. That's good, too.

BRACK: Why, Mrs. Tesman?

HEDDA: Oh—no, I didn't mean anything.

TESMAN: And the wound's dangerous you say? What?

BRACK: Mortal. He's probably already dead.

MRS. ELVSTED: Yes, yes—I feel it! It's all over. All over. Oh Hedda——!

TESMAN: But, tell me, how did you manage to learn all this?

BRACK: [*Curtly.*] From the police. I spoke to one of them.

HEDDA: [*Loudly, clearly.*] At last! Oh, thank God!

TESMAN: [*Appalled.*] For God's sake, Hedda, what are you saying?

HEDDA: I am saying there's beauty in what he has done.

BRACK: Mm—Mrs. Tesman——

TESMAN: Beauty! Oh, but I say!

MRS. ELVSTED: Hedda, how can you talk of beauty in connection with a thing like this?

HEDDA: Eilert Loevborg has settled his account with life. He's had the courage to do what—what he had to do.

MRS. ELVSTED: No, that's not why it happened. He did it because he was mad.

TESMAN: He did it because he was desperate.

HEDDA: You're wrong! I know!

MRS. ELVSTED: He must have been mad. The same as when he tore up the manuscript.

BRACK: [*Starts.*] Manuscript? Did he tear it up?

MRS. ELVSTED: Yes. Last night.

TESMAN: [*Whispers.*] Oh, Hedda, we shall never be able to escape from this.

BRACK: Hm. Strange.

TESMAN: [*Wanders round the room.*] To think of Eilert dying like that. And not leaving behind him the thing that would have made his name endure.

MRS. ELVSTED: If only it could be pieced together again!

TESMAN: Yes, fancy! If only it could! I'd give anything——

MRS. ELVSTED: Perhaps it can, Mr. Tesman.

TESMAN: What do you mean?

MRS. ELVSTED: [*Searches in the pocket of her dress.*] Look! I kept the notes he dictated it from.

HEDDA: [*Takes a step nearer.*] Ah!

TESMAN: You kept them, Mrs. Elvsted! What?

MRS. ELVSTED: Yes, here they are. I brought them with me when I left home. They've been in my pocket ever since.

TESMAN: Let me have a look.

MRS. ELVSTED: [*Hands him a wad of small sheets of paper.*] They're in a terrible muddle. All mixed up.

TESMAN: I say, just fancy if we can sort them out! Perhaps if we work on them together——?

MRS. ELVSTED: Oh, yes! Let's try, anyway!

TESMAN: We'll manage it. We must! I shall dedicate my life to this.

HEDDA: *You,* George? Your life?

TESMAN: Yes—well, all the time I can spare. My book'll have to wait. Hedda, you do understand? What? I owe it to Eilert's memory.

HEDDA: Perhaps.

TESMAN: Well, my dear Mrs. Elvsted, you and I'll have to pool our brains. No use crying over spilt milk, what? We must try to approach this matter calmly.

MRS. ELVSTED: Yes, yes, Mr. Tesman. I'll do my best.

TESMAN: Well, come over here and let's start looking at these notes right away. Where shall we sit? Here? No, the other room. You'll excuse us, won't you, Judge? Come along with me, Mrs. Elvsted.

MRS. ELVSTED: Oh, God! If only we can manage to do it!

[TESMAN *and* MRS. ELVSTED *go into the rear room. He takes off his hat and overcoat. They sit at the table beneath the hanging lamp and absorb themselves in the notes.* HEDDA *walks across to the stove and sits in the armchair. After a moment,* BRACK *goes over to her.*]

HEDDA: [*Half aloud.*] Oh, Judge! This act of Eilert Loevborg's—doesn't it give one a sense of release!

BRACK: Release, Mrs. Hedda? Well, it's a release for him, of course——

HEDDA: Oh, I don't mean him—I mean me! The release of knowing that someone can do something really brave! Something beautiful!

BRACK: [*Smiles.*] Hm—my dear Mrs. Hedda——

HEDDA: Oh, I know what you're going to say. You're a bourgeois at heart too, just like—ah, well!

BRACK: [*Looks at her.*] Eilert Loevborg has meant more to you than you're willing to admit to yourself. Or am I wrong?

HEDDA: I'm not answering questions like that from you. I only know that Eilert Loevborg has had the courage to live according to his own principles. And now, at last, he's done something big! Something beautiful! To have the courage and the will to rise from the feast of life so early!

BRACK: It distresses me deeply, Mrs. Hedda, but I'm afraid I must rob you of that charming illusion.

HEDDA: Illusion?

BRACK: You wouldn't have been allowed to keep it for long, anyway.

HEDDA: What do you mean?

BRACK: He didn't shoot himself on purpose.

HEDDA: Not on purpose?

BRACK: No. It didn't happen quite the way I told you.

HEDDA: Have you been hiding something? What is it?

BRACK: In order to spare poor Mrs. Elvsted's feelings, I permitted myself one or two small—equivocations.

HEDDA: What?

BRACK: To begin with, he is already dead.

HEDDA: He died at the hospital?

BRACK: Yes. Without regaining consciousness.

HEDDA: What else haven't you told us?

BRACK: The incident didn't take place at his lodgings.

HEDDA: Well, that's utterly unimportant.

BRACK: Not utterly. The fact is, you see, that Eilert Loevborg was found shot in Mademoiselle Danielle's boudoir.

HEDDA: [*Almost jumps up, but instead sinks back in her chair.*] That's impossible. He can't have been there today.

BRACK: He was there this afternoon. He went to ask for something he claimed they'd taken from him. Talked some crazy nonsense about a child which had got lost——

HEDDA: Oh! So that was the reason!

BRACK: I thought at first he might have been referring to his manuscript. But I hear he destroyed that himself. So he must have meant his pocketbook—I suppose.

HEDDA: Yes, I suppose so. So they found him there?

BRACK: Yes; there. With a discharged pistol in his breast pocket. The shot had wounded him mortally.

HEDDA: Yes. In the breast.

BRACK: No. In the—hm—stomach. The—lower part——

HEDDA: [*Looks at him with an expression of repulsion.*] That too! Oh, why does everything I touch become mean and ludicrous? It's like a curse!

BRACK: There's something else, Mrs. Hedda. It's rather disagreeable, too.

HEDDA: What?

BRACK: The pistol he had on him——

HEDDA: Yes? What about it?

BRACK: He must have stolen it.

HEDDA: [*Jumps up.*] Stolen it! That isn't true! He didn't!

BRACK: It's the only explanation. He must have stolen it. Ssh!

> [TESMAN *and* MRS. ELVSTED *have got up from the table in the rear room and come into the drawing room.*]

TESMAN. [*His hands full of papers.*] Hedda, I can't see properly under that lamp. Think!

HEDDA: I am thinking.

TESMAN: Do you think we could possibly use your writing table for a little? What?

HEDDA: Yes, of course. [*Quickly.*] No, wait! Let me tidy it up first.

TESMAN: Oh, don't you trouble about that. There's plenty of room.

HEDDA: No, no, let me tidy it up first, I say. I'll take this in and put them on the piano. Here.

> [*She pulls an object, covered with sheets of music, out from under the bookcase, puts some more sheets on top and carries it all into the rear room and away to the left.* TESMAN *puts his papers on the writing table and moves the lamp over from the corner table. He and* MRS. ELVSTED *sit down and begin working again.* HEDDA *comes back.*]

HEDDA: [*Behind* MRS. ELVSTED's *chair, ruffles her hair gently.*] Well, my pretty Thea! And how is work progressing on Eilert Loevborg's memorial?

MRS. ELVSTED: [*Looks up at her, dejectedly.*] Oh, it's going to be terribly difficult to get these into any order.

TESMAN: We've got to do it. We must! After all, putting other people's papers into order is rather my specialty, what?

[HEDDA *goes over to the stove and sits on one of the footstools.* BRACK *stands over her, leaning against the armchair.*]

HEDDA: [*Whispers.*] What was that you were saying about the pistol?

BRACK: [*Softly.*] I said he must have stolen it.

HEDDA: Why do you think that?

BRACK: Because any other explanation is unthinkable, Mrs. Hedda, or ought to be.

HEDDA: I see.

BRACK: [*Looks at her for a moment.*] Eilert Loevborg was here this morning. Wasn't he?

HEDDA: Yes.

BRACK: Were you alone with him?

HEDDA: For a few moments.

BRACK: You didn't leave the room while he was here?

HEDDA: No.

BRACK: Think again. Are you sure you didn't go out for a moment?

HEDDA: Oh—yes, I might have gone into the hall. Just for a few seconds.

BRACK: And where was your pistol-case during this time?

HEDDA: I'd locked it in that——

BRACK: Er—Mrs. Hedda?

HEDDA: It was lying over there on my writing table.

BRACK: Have you looked to see if both the pistols are still there?

HEDDA: No.

BRACK: You needn't bother. I saw the pistol Loevborg had when they found him. I recognized it at once. From yesterday. And other occasions.

HEDDA: Have you got it?

BRACK: No. The police have it.

HEDDA: What will the police do with this pistol?

BRACK: Try to trace the owner.

HEDDA: Do you think they'll succeed?

BRACK: [*Leans down and whispers.*] No, Hedda Gabler. Not as long as I hold my tongue.

HEDDA: [*Looks nervously at him.*] And if you don't?

BRACK: [*Shrugs his shoulders.*] You could always say he'd stolen it.

HEDDA: I'd rather die!

BRACK: [*Smiles.*] People say that. They never do it.

HEDDA: [*Not replying.*] And suppose the pistol wasn't stolen? And they trace the owner? What then?

BRACK: There'll be a scandal, Hedda.

HEDDA: A scandal!

BRACK: Yes, a scandal. The thing you're so frightened of. You'll have to appear in court. Together with Mademoiselle Danielle. She'll have to explain how it all happened. Was it an accident, or was it—homicide? Was he about to take the pistol from his pocket to threaten her? And did it go off? Or did she snatch the pistol from his hand, shoot him and then put it back in his pocket? She might quite easily have done it. She's a resourceful lady, is Mademoiselle Danielle.

HEDDA: But I had nothing to do with this repulsive business.

BRACK: No. But you'll have to answer one question. Why did you give Eilert Loevborg this pistol? And what conclusions will people draw when it is proved you did give it to him?

HEDDA: [Bows her head.] That's true. I hadn't thought of that.

BRACK: Well, luckily there's no danger as long as I hold my tongue.

HEDDA: [Looks up at him.] In other words, I'm in your power, Judge. From now on, you've got your hold over me.

BRACK: [Whispers, more slowly.] Hedda, my dearest—believe me—I will not abuse my position.

HEDDA: Nevertheless, I'm in your power. Dependent on your will, and your demands. Not free. Still not free! [Rises passionately.] No. I couldn't bear that. No.

BRACK: [Looks half-derisively at her.] Most people resign themselves to the inevitable, sooner or later.

HEDDA: [Returns his gaze.] Possibly they do. [She goes across to the writing table.]

HEDDA: [Represses an involuntary smile and says in TESMAN's voice.] Well, George. Think you'll be able to manage? What?

TESMAN: Heaven knows, dear. This is going to take months and months.

HEDDA: [In the same tone as before.] Fancy that, by Jove! [Runs her hands gently through MRS. ELVSTED's hair.] Doesn't it feel strange, Thea? Here you are working away with Tesman just the way you used to work with Eilert Loevborg.

MRS. ELVSTED: Oh—if only I can inspire your husband too!

HEDDA: Oh, it'll come. In time.

TESMAN: Yes—do you know, Hedda, I really think I'm beginning to feel a bit—well—that way. But you go back and talk to Judge Brack.

HEDDA: Can't I be of use to you two in any way?

TESMAN: No, none at all. [Turns his head.] You'll have to keep Hedda company from now on, Judge, and see she doesn't get bored. If you don't mind.

BRACK: [Glances at HEDDA.] It'll be a pleasure.

HEDDA: Thank you. But I'm tired this evening. I think I'll lie down on the sofa in there for a little while.

TESMAN: Yes, dear—do. What?

[HEDDA goes into the rear room and draws the curtain behind her. Short pause. Suddenly she begins to play a frenzied dance melody on the piano.]

MRS. ELVSTED: [Starts up from her chair.] Oh, what's that?

TESMAN: [Runs to the doorway.] Hedda dear, please! Don't play dance music tonight! Think of Auntie Rena. And Eilert.

HEDDA: [*Puts her head out through the curtains.*] And Auntie Juju. And all the rest of them. From now on I'll be quiet. [*Closes the curtains behind her.*]

TESMAN: [*At the writing table.*] It distresses her to watch us doing this. I say, Mrs. Elvsted, I've an idea. Why don't you move in with Auntie Juju? I'll run over each evening, and we can sit and work there. What?

MRS. ELVSTED: Yes, that might be the best plan.

HEDDA: [*From the rear room.*] I can hear what you're saying, Tesman. But how shall I spend the evenings out here?

TESMAN: [*Looking through his papers.*] Oh, I'm sure Judge Brack'll be kind enough to come over and keep you company. You won't mind my not being here, Judge?

BRACK: [*In the armchair, calls gaily.*] I'll be delighted, Mrs. Tesman. I'll be here every evening. We'll have great fun together, you and I.

HEDDA: [*Loud and clear.*] Yes, that'll suit you, won't it, Judge? The only cock on the dunghill——!

[*A shot is heard from the rear room.* TESMAN, MRS. ELVSTED *and* JUDGE BRACK *start from their chairs.*]

TESMAN: Oh, she's playing with those pistols again.

[*He pulls the curtains aside and runs in.* MRS. ELVSTED *follow him.* HEDDA *is lying dead on the sofa. Confusion and shouting.* BERTHA *enters in alarm from the right.*]

TESMAN: [*Screams to* BRACK.] She's shot herself! Shot herself in the head! By Jove! Fancy that!

BRACK: [*Half paralyzed in the armchair.*] But, good God! People don't do such things!

1890

QUESTIONS

1. How much do you learn of Hedda's life, of Tesman, of the situation, in the brief conversation between Miss Tesman and Bertha that opens the play? What indications are there of differences in class (or "lifestyle") between the Tesmans and Gablers in that conversation?

2. In what way did Tesman not "waste time" on his honeymoon? What does this suggest about him? his marriage? the future? What other details in the first five or six pages reinforce your understanding of his character, his professional accomplishments, and your expectations of what will happen later in the play? How is Tesman distinguished from the stereotypical absentminded professor?

3. What is the important element in Hedda's attire when she first enters?

4. What expectations are aroused by the first part of the scene in Act I in which Mrs. Elvsted pays a call (before Tesman leaves the room)? What does Hedda get out of Mrs. Elvsted after Tesman leaves? How does she do it? Why? What new expectations are aroused by the Hedda-Thea conversation? Hedda is amazed by Mrs. Elvsted's open break with social conformity in deserting her husband; what are Hedda's attitudes toward society and the appearance that she makes in that society?

5. Why is Hedda so intrigued by the "competition" between George Tesman and Loevborg? Why does Judge Brack find the competition suited to his purposes?
6. How does the first act end? What is the effect of that ending? What does it fill in about the past and what expectations does it arouse about what is to happen later?
7. What are Loevborg's strengths? weaknesses? How are they related?
8. Why is George so shocked at the subject of Loevborg's new book? How are their approaches to their professions and to life different?
9. When Hedda suggests to George that Loevborg is "less afraid of life than most men," George responds, "Good heavens, no. He just doesn't know the meaning of the word moderation." Whose assessment is more accurate?
10. Does Mrs. Elvsted's inspiration of George and her plans to move in with Miss Tesman complete a new triangle excluding Hedda? What does Hedda's imitation of George in the last scene ("Fancy that, by Jove!") indicate regarding this turn of events?

WRITING SUGGESTIONS

1. Note the similarities in the stage directions describing the sets (and, indeed, in the rooms themselves) in *Hedda Gabler* and *The Little Foxes*. Beginning with setting, write a comparative analysis of the two plays as examples of realism.
2. Write on the relation of social class to character and events in *Hedda Gabler,* in the course of your essay suggesting what segments of society Hedda, George, Loevborg, and Judge Brack represent.
3. Write on the themes of courage and cowardice in *Hedda Gabler*. You will probably want to treat the scenes between Hedda and Loevborg, and among Hedda, Mrs. Elvsted, and Loevborg in Act II, and, of course, Hedda's suicide.

WILLIAM SHAKESPEARE

Hamlet

CHARACTERS

CLAUDIUS, *King of Denmark*

HAMLET, *son of the former and nephew to the present King*

POLONIUS, *Lord Chamberlain*

HORATIO, *friend of Hamlet*

LAERTES, *son of Polonius*

VOLTEMAND
CORNELIUS
ROSENCRANTZ
GUILDENSTERN } *courtiers*
OSRIC
A GENTLEMAN
A PRIEST

MARCELLUS
BERNARDO } *officers*

FRANCISCO, *a soldier*

REYNALDO, *servant to Polonius*

PLAYERS

TWO CLOWNS, *gravediggers*

FORTINBRAS, *Prince of Norway*

A NORWEGIAN CAPTAIN

ENGLISH AMBASSADORS

GERTRUDE, *Queen of Denmark, and mother of Hamlet*

OPHELIA, *daughter of Polonius*

GHOST OF HAMLET'S FATHER

LORDS, LADIES, OFFICERS, SOLDIERS, SAILORS, MESSENGERS, AND ATTENDANTS

SCENE: *The action takes place in or near the royal castle of Denmark at Elsinore.*

ACT I

SCENE 1

A guard station atop the castle. Enter BERNARDO *and* FRANCISCO, *two sentinels.*

BERNARDO: Who's there?

FRANCISCO: Nay, answer me. Stand and unfold yourself.

BERNARDO: Long live the king!

FRANCISCO: Bernardo?

5   BERNARDO: He.

FRANCISCO: You come most carefully upon your hour.

BERNARDO: 'Tis now struck twelve. Get thee to bed, Francisco.

FRANCISCO: For this relief much thanks. 'Tis bitter cold,
    And I am sick at heart.

BERNARDO: Have you had quiet guard?

10   FRANCISCO: Not a mouse stirring.

BERNARDO: Well, good night.
    If you do meet Horatio and Marcellus,
    The rivals[1] of my watch, bid them make haste.

    [*Enter* HORATIO *and* MARCELLUS.]

1. Companions.

FRANCISCO: I think I hear them. Stand, ho! Who is there?

HORATIO: Friends to this ground.

MARCELLUS: And liegemen to the Dane.[2]   15

FRANCISCO: Give you good night.

MARCELLUS: O, farewell, honest soldier!
  Who hath relieved you?

FRANCISCO: Bernardo hath my place.
  Give you good night.   [*Exit* FRANCISCO.]

MARCELLUS: Holla, Bernardo!

BERNARDO: Say—
  What, is Horatio there?

HORATIO: A piece of him.

BERNARDO: Welcome, Horatio. Welcome, good Marcellus.   20

HORATIO: What, has this thing appeared again tonight?

BERNARDO: I have seen nothing.

MARCELLUS: Horatio says 'tis but our fantasy,
  And will not let belief take hold of him
  Touching this dreaded sight twice seen of us.   25
  Therefore I have entreated him along
  With us to watch the minutes of this night,
  That if again this apparition come,
  He may approve[3] our eyes and speak to it.

HORATIO: Tush, tush, 'twill not appear.

BERNARDO: Sit down awhile,   30
  And let us once again assail your ears,
  That are so fortified against our story,
  What we have two nights seen.

HORATIO: Well, sit we down.
  And let us hear Bernardo speak of this.

BERNARDO: Last night of all,   35
  When yond same star that's westward from the pole[4]
  Had made his course t' illume that part of heaven
  Where now it burns, Marcellus and myself,
  The bell then beating one—

    [*Enter* GHOST.]

MARCELLUS: Peace, break thee off. Look where it comes again.   40

BERNARDO: In the same figure like the king that's dead.

MARCELLUS: Thou art a scholar; speak to it, Horatio.

BERNARDO: Looks 'a[5] not like the king? Mark it, Horatio.

HORATIO: Most like. It harrows me with fear and wonder.

BERNARDO: It would be spoke to.

---

2. The "Dane" is the king of Denmark, who is also called "Denmark," as in line 48 of this scene. In line 61 the same figure is used for the king of Norway.   3. Confirm the testimony of.   4. Polestar.
5. He.

45   MARCELLUS: Speak to it, Horatio.

HORATIO: What art thou that usurp'st this time of night
   Together with that fair and warlike form
   In which the majesty of buried Denmark
   Did sometimes march? By heaven I charge thee, speak.

MARCELLUS: It is offended.

50   BERNARDO: See, it stalks away.

HORATIO: Stay. Speak, speak. I charge thee, speak.   [*Exit* GHOST.]

MARCELLUS: 'Tis gone and will not answer.

BERNARDO: How now, Horatio! You tremble and look pale.
   Is not this something more than fantasy?

55   What think you on't?

HORATIO: Before my God, I might not this believe
   Without the sensible[6] and true avouch
   Of mine own eyes.

MARCELLUS: Is it not like the king?

HORATIO: As thou art to thyself.

60   Such was the very armor he had on
   When he the ambitious Norway combated.
   So frowned he once when, in an angry parle,[7]
   He smote the sledded Polacks on the ice.
   'Tis strange.

MARCELLUS: Thus twice before, and jump[8] at this dead hour,

65   With martial stalk hath he gone by our watch.

HORATIO: In what particular thought to work I know not,
   But in the gross and scope of mine opinion,
   This bodes some strange eruption to our state.

MARCELLUS: Good now, sit down, and tell me he that knows,

70   Why this same strict and most observant watch
   So nightly toils the subject[9] of the land,
   And why such daily cast of brazen cannon
   And foreign mart for implements of war;
   Why such impress of shipwrights, whose sore task

75   Does not divide the Sunday from the week.
   What might be toward that this sweaty haste
   Doth make the night joint-laborer with the day?
   Who is't that can inform me?

HORATIO: That can I.
   At last, the whisper goes so. Our last king,

80   Whose image even but now appeared to us,
   Was as you know by Fortinbras of Norway,
   Thereto pricked on by a most emulate pride,
   Dared to the combat; in which our valiant Hamlet
   (For so this side of our known world esteemed him)

6. Perceptible.   7. Parley.   8. Precisely.   9. People.

Did slay this Fortinbras; who by a sealed compact   85
Well ratified by law and heraldry,
Did forfeit, with his life, all those his lands
Which he stood seized of,[1] to the conqueror;
Against the which a moiety competent[2]
Was gagéd[3] by our king; which had returned   90
To the inheritance of Fortinbras,
Had he been vanquisher; as, by the same covenant
And carriage of the article designed,
His fell to Hamlet. Now, sir, young Fortinbras,
Of unimprovéd mettle hot and full,   95
Hath in the skirts of Norway here and there
Sharked up a list of lawless resolutes
For food and diet to some enterprise
That hath a stomach in't; which is no other,
As it doth well appear unto our state,   100
But to recover of us by strong hand
And terms compulsatory, those foresaid lands
So by his father lost; and this, I take it,
Is the main motive of our preparations,
The source of this our watch, and the chief head   105
Of this post-haste and romage[4] in the land.
BERNARDO: I think it be no other but e'en so.
   Well may it sort[5] that this portentous figure
   Comes arméd through our watch so like the king
   That was and is the question of these wars.   110
HORATIO: A mote[6] it is to trouble the mind's eye.
   In the most high and palmy state of Rome,
   A little ere the mightiest Julius fell,
   The graves stood tenantless, and the sheeted dead
   Did squeak and gibber in the Roman streets;   115
   As stars with trains of fire, and dews of blood,
   Disasters in the sun; and the moist star,
   Upon whose influence Neptune's empire stands,[7]
   Was sick almost to doomsday with eclipse.
   And even the like precurse[8] of feared events,   120
   As harbingers preceding still the fates
   And prologue to the omen coming on,
   Have heaven and earth together demonstrated
   Unto our climatures[9] and countrymen.

      [*Enter* GHOST.]

---

1. Possessed.   2. Portion of similar value.   3. Pledged.   4. Stir.   5. Chance.   6. Speck of dust.
7. Neptune was the Roman sea god; the "moist star" is the moon.   8. Precursor.   9. Regions.

125 But soft, behold, lo where it comes again!
I'll cross it[1] though it blast me.—Stay, illusion.

[*It spreads (its) arms.*]

If thou hast any sound or use of voice,
Speak to me.
If there be any good thing to be done,
130 That may to thee do ease, and grace to me,
Speak to me.
If thou art privy to thy country's fate,
Which happily foreknowing may avoid,
O, speak!
135 Or if thou hast uphoarded in thy life
Extorted treasure in the womb of earth,
For which, they say, you spirits oft walk in death,

[*The cock crows.*]

Speak of it. Stay, and speak. Stop it, Marcellus.
MARCELLUS: Shall I strike at it with my partisan?[2]
HORATIO: Do, if it will not stand.
BERNARDO: 'Tis here.
140 HORATIO: 'Tis here.
MARCELLUS: 'Tis gone.   [*Exit* GHOST.]
We do it wrong, being so majestical,
To offer it the show of violence;
For it is as the air, invulnerable,
145 And our vain blows malicious mockery.
BERNARDO: It was about to speak when the cock crew.
HORATIO: And then it started like a guilty thing
Upon a fearful summons. I have heard
The cock, that is the trumpet to the morn,
150 Doth with his lofty and shrill-sounding throat
Awake the god of day, and at his warning,
Whether in sea or fire, in earth or air,
Th' extravagant and erring[3] spirit hies
To his confine; and of the truth herein
155 This present object made probation.[4]
MARCELLUS: It faded on the crowing of the cock.
Some say that ever 'gainst that season comes
Wherein our Savior's birth is celebrated,
This bird of dawning singeth all night long,
160 And then, they say, no spirit dare stir abroad,

1. Horatio means either that he will move across the ghost's path in order to stop him or that he will make the sign of the cross to gain power over him. The stage direction that follows is somewhat ambiguous. "It" seems to refer to the ghost, but the movement would be appropriate to Horatio.   2. Halberd.
3. Wandering out of bounds.   4. Proof.

The nights are wholesome, then no planets strike,
No fairy takes,[5] nor witch hath power to charm,
So hallowed and so gracious is that time.
HORATIO: So have I heard and do in part believe it.
But look, the morn in russet mantle clad   165
Walks o'er the dew of yon high eastward hill.
Break we our watch up, and by my advice
Let us impart what we have seen tonight
Unto young Hamlet, for upon my life
This spirit, dumb to us, will speak to him.   170
Do you consent we shall acquaint him with it,
As needful in our loves, fitting our duty?
MARCELLUS: Let's do't, I pray, and I this morning know
Where we shall find him most convenient.   [*Exeunt.*]

SCENE 2

A chamber of state. Enter KING CLAUDIUS, QUEEN GERTRUDE, HAMLET, POLONIUS,
LAERTES, OPHELIA, VOLTEMAND, CORNELIUS *and other members of the court.*

KING: Though yet of Hamlet our dear brother's death
The memory be green, and that it us befitted
To bear our hearts in grief, and our whole kingdom
To be contracted in one brow of woe,
Yet so far hath discretion fought with nature   5
That we with wisest sorrow think on him,
Together with remembrance of ourselves.
Therefore our sometime sister, now our queen,
Th' imperial jointress[6] to this warlike state,
Have we, as 'twere with a defeated joy,   10
With an auspicious and a dropping eye,
With mirth in funeral, and with dirge in marriage,
In equal scale weighing delight and dole,
Taken to wife; nor have we herein barred
Your better wisdoms, which have freely gone   15
With this affair along. For all, our thanks.
Now follows that you know young Fortinbras,
Holding a weak supposal of our worth,
Or thinking by our late dear brother's death
Our state to be disjoint and out of frame,   20
Colleaguéd with this dream of his advantage,
He hath not failed to pester us with message
Importing the surrender of those lands

5. Enchants.   6. A "jointress" is a widow who holds a *jointure* or life interest in the estate of her
deceased husband.

Lost by his father, with all bands of law,
25 To our most valiant brother. So much for him.
Now for ourself, and for this time of meeting,
Thus much the business is: we have here writ
To Norway, uncle of young Fortinbras—
Who, impotent and bedrid, scarcely hears
30 Of this his nephew's purpose—to suppress
His further gait[7] herein, in that the levies,
The lists, and full proportions are all made
Out of his subject; and we here dispatch
You, good Cornelius, and you, Voltemand,
35 For bearers of this greeting to old Norway,
Giving to you no further personal power
To business with the king, more than the scope
Of these dilated[8] articles allow.
Farewell, and let your haste commend your duty.

CORNELIUS:
40 VOLTEMAND: } In that, and all things will we show our duty.

KING: We doubt it nothing, heartily farewell.

[*Exeunt* VOLTEMAND *and* CORNELIUS.]

And now, Laertes, what's the news with you?
You told us of some suit. What is't, Laertes?
You cannot speak of reason to the Dane
45 And lose your voice. What wouldst thou beg, Laertes,
That shall not be my offer, not thy asking?
The head is not more native to the heart,
The hand more instrumental[9] to the mouth,
Than is the throne of Denmark to thy father.
What wouldst thou have, Laertes?
50 LAERTES: My dread lord,
Your leave and favor to return to France,
From whence, though willingly, I came to Denmark
To show my duty in your coronation,
Yet now I must confess, that duty done,
55 My thoughts and wishes bend again toward France,
And bow them to your gracious leave and pardon.
KING: Have you your father's leave? What says Polonius?
POLONIUS: He hath, my lord, wrung from me my slow leave
By laborsome petition, and at last
60 Upon his will I sealed my hard consent.
I do beseech you give him leave to go.
KING: Take thy fair hour, Laertes. Time be thine,
And thy best graces spend it at thy will.

7. Progress.   8. Fully expressed.   9. Serviceable.

But now, my cousin[1] Hamlet, and my son—
HAMLET: [*Aside*.] A little more than kin, and less than kind.   65
KING: How is it that the clouds still hang on you?
HAMLET: Not so, my lord. I am too much in the sun.
QUEEN: Good Hamlet, cast thy nighted color off,
    And let thine eye look like a friend on Denmark.
    Do not for ever with thy vailéd lids[2]   70
    Seek for thy noble father in the dust.
    Thou know'st 'tis common—all that lives must die,
    Passing through nature to eternity.
HAMLET: Ay, madam, it is common.
QUEEN: If it be,
    Why seems it so particular with thee?   75
HAMLET: Seems, madam? Nay, it is. I know not "seems."
    'Tis not alone my inky cloak, good mother,
    Nor customary suits of solemn black,
    Nor windy suspiration of forced breath,
    No, nor the fruitful river in the eye,   80
    Nor the dejected havior[3] of the visage,
    Together with all forms, moods, shapes of grief,
    That can denote me truly. These indeed seem,
    For they are actions that a man might play,
    But I have that within which passes show—   85
    These but the trappings and the suits of woe.
KING: 'Tis sweet and commendable in your nature, Hamlet,
    To give these mourning duties to your father,
    But you must know your father lost a father,
    That father lost, lost his, and the survivor bound   90
    In filial obligation for some term
    To do obsequious[4] sorrow. But to persever
    In obstinate condolement is a course
    Of impious stubbornness. 'Tis unmanly grief.
    It shows a will most incorrect to[5] heaven,   95
    A heart unfortified, a mind impatient,
    An understanding simple and unschooled.
    For what we know must be, and is as common
    As any the most vulgar thing to sense,
    Why should we in our peevish opposition   100
    Take it to heart? Fie, 'tis a fault to heaven,
    A fault against the dead, a fault to nature,
    To reason most absurd, whose common theme
    Is death of fathers, and who still hath cried,
    From the first corse[6] till he that died today,   105
    "This must be so." We pray you throw to earth

1. "Cousin" is used here as a general term of kinship.   2. Lowered eyes.   3. Appearance.
4. Suited for funeral obsequies.   5. Uncorrected toward.   6. Corpse.

This unprevailing woe, and think of us
As of a father, for let the world take note
You are the most immediate[7] to our throne,
110   And with no less nobility of love
Than that which dearest father bears his son
Do I impart toward you. For your intent
In going back to school in Wittenberg,
It is most retrograde[8] to our desire,
115   And we beseech you, bend you to remain
Here in the cheer and comfort of our eye,
Our chiefest courtier, cousin, and our son.
QUEEN: Let not thy mother lose her prayers, Hamlet.
I pray thee stay with us, go not to Wittenberg.
120   HAMLET: I shall in all my best obey you, madam.
KING: Why, 'tis a loving and a fair reply.
Be as ourself in Denmark. Madam, come.
This gentle and unforced accord of Hamlet
Sits smiling to my heart, in grace whereof,
125   No jocund health that Denmark drinks today
But the great cannon to the clouds shall tell,
And the king's rouse the heaven shall bruit[9] again,
Respeaking earthly thunder. Come away.

                            [Flourish. Exeunt all but HAMLET.]

HAMLET: O, that this too too solid flesh would melt,
130   Thaw, and resolve itself into a dew,
Or that the Everlasting had not fixed
His canon[1] 'gainst self-slaughter. O God, God,
How weary, stale, flat, and unprofitable
Seem to me all the uses of this world!
135   Fie on't, ah, fie, 'tis an unweeded garden
That grows to seed. Things rank and gross in nature
Possess it merely.[2] That it should come to this,
But two months dead, nay, not so much, not two.
So excellent a king, that was to this
140   Hyperion to a satyr,[3] so loving to my mother,
That he might not beteem[4] the winds of heaven
Visit her face too roughly. Heaven and earth,
Must I remember? Why, she would hang on him
As if increase of appetite had grown
145   By what it fed on, and yet, within a month—
Let me not think on't. Frailty, thy name is woman—
A little month, or ere those shoes were old

---

7. Next in line.   8. Contrary.   9. Echo. *Rouse:* carousal.   1. Law.   2. Entirely.   3. Hyperion,
a Greek god, stands here for beauty in contrast to the monstrous satyr, a lecherous creature, half man
and half goat.   4. Permit.

With which she followed my poor father's body
Like Niobe,[5] all tears, why she, even she—
O God, a beast that wants discourse of reason   150
Would have mourned longer—married with my uncle,
My father's brother, but no more like my father
Than I to Hercules.[6] Within a month,
Ere yet the salt of most unrighteous tears
Had left the flushing in her gallèd eyes,   155
She married. O, most wicked speed, to post
With such dexterity to incestuous sheets!
It is not, nor it cannot come to good.
But break my heart, for I must hold my tongue.

     [*Enter* HORATIO, MARCELLUS, *and* BERNARDO.]

HORATIO: Hail to your lordship!
HAMLET: I am glad to see you well.   160
  Horatio—or I do forget myself.
HORATIO: The same, my lord, and your poor servant ever.
HAMLET: Sir, my good friend, I'll change[7] that name with you.
  And what make you from Wittenberg, Horatio?
  Marcellus?   165
MARCELLUS: My good lord!
HAMLET: I am very glad to see you. [*To* BERNARDO.] Good even, sir.—
  But what, in faith, make you from Wittenberg?
HORATIO: A truant disposition, good my lord.
HAMLET: I would not hear your enemy say so,   170
  Nor shall you do my ear that violence
  To make it truster of your own report
  Against yourself. I know you are no truant.
  But what is your affair in Elsinore?
  We'll teach you to drink deep ere you depart.   175
HORATIO: My lord, I came to see your father's funeral.
HAMLET: I prithee do not mock me, fellow-student,
  I think it was to see my mother's wedding.
HORATIO: Indeed, my lord, it followed hard upon.
HAMLET: Thrift, thrift, Horatio. The funeral-baked meats   180
  Did coldly furnish forth the marriage tables.
  Would I had met my dearest[8] foe in heaven
  Or ever I had seen that day, Horatio!
  My father—methinks I see my father.
HORATIO: Where, my lord?
HAMLET: In my mind's eye, Horatio.   185

5. In Greek mythology, Niobe was turned to stone after a tremendous fit of weeping over the death of her fourteen children, a misfortune brought about by her boasting over her fertility.   6. The demigod Hercules was noted for his strength and the series of spectacular labors that it allowed him to accomplish.   7. Exchange.   8. Bitterest.

HORATIO: I saw him once, 'a was a goodly king.

HAMLET: 'A was a man, take him for all in all,
   I shall not look upon his like again.

HORATIO: My lord, I think I saw him yesternight.

190 HAMLET: Saw who?

HORATIO: My lord, the king your father.

HAMLET: The king my father?

HORATIO: Season your admiration[9] for a while
   With an attent ear till I may deliver[1]
   Upon the witness of these gentlemen
   This marvel to you.

195 HAMLET: For God's love, let me hear!

HORATIO: Two nights together had these gentlemen,
   Marcellus and Bernardo, on their watch
   In the dead waste and middle of the night
   Been thus encountered. A figure like your father,
200   Armed at point exactly, cap-a-pe,[2]
   Appears before them, and with solemn march
   Goes slow and stately by them. Thrice he walked
   By their oppressed and fear-surprised eyes
   Within his truncheon's[3] length, whilst they, distilled
205   Almost to jelly with the act of fear,
   Stand dumb and speak not to him. This to me
   In dreadful secrecy impart they did,
   And I with them the third night kept the watch,
   Where, as they had delivered, both in time,
210   Form of the thing, each word made true and good,
   The apparition comes. I knew your father.
   These hands are not more like.

HAMLET: But where was this?

MARCELLUS: My lord, upon the platform where we watch.

HAMLET: Did you not speak to it?

HORATIO: My lord, I did,
215   But answer made it none. Yet once methought
   It lifted up it head and did address
   Itself to motion, like as it would speak;
   But even then the morning cock crew loud,
   And at the sound it shrunk in haste away
   And vanished from our sight.

220 HAMLET: 'Tis very strange.

HORATIO: As I do live, my honored lord, 'tis true,
   And we did think it writ down in our duty
   To let you know of it.

---

9. Moderate your wonder.   1. Relate. *Attent:* attentive.   2. From head to toe. *Exactly:* completely.
3. Baton of office.

HAMLET: Indeed, sirs, but
This troubles me. Hold you the watch tonight?
ALL: We do, my lord.
HAMLET: Armed, say you?
ALL: Armed, my lord.   225
HAMLET: From top to toe?
ALL: My lord, from head to foot.
HAMLET: Then saw you not his face.
HORATIO: O yes, my lord, he wore his beaver[4] up.
HAMLET: What, looked he frowningly?
HORATIO: A countenance more in sorrow than in anger.   230
HAMLET: Pale or red?
HORATIO: Nay, very pale.
HAMLET: And fixed his eyes upon you?
HORATIO: Most constantly.
HAMLET: I would I had been there.
HORATIO: It would have much amazed you.
HAMLET: Very like.
Stayed it long?   235
HORATIO: While one with moderate haste might tell a hundred.
BOTH: Longer, longer.
HORATIO: Not when I saw't.
HAMLET: His beard was grizzled, no?
HORATIO: It was as I have seen it in his life,
A sable silvered.
HAMLET: I will watch tonight.   240
Perchance 'twill walk again.
HORATIO: I warr'nt it will.
HAMLET: If it assume my noble father's person,
I'll speak to it though hell itself should gape[5]
And bid me hold my peace. I pray you all,
If you have hitherto concealed this sight,   245
Let it be tenable[6] in your silence still,
And whatsomever else shall hap tonight,
Give it an understanding but no tongue.
I will requite your loves. So fare you well.
Upon the platform 'twixt eleven and twelve   250
I'll visit you.
ALL: Our duty to your honor.
HAMLET: Your loves, as mine to you. Farewell.   [*Exeunt all but* HAMLET.]
My father's spirit in arms? All is not well.
I doubt[7] some foul play. Would the night were come!
Till then sit still, my soul. Foul deeds will rise,   255
Though all the earth o'erwhelm them, to men's eyes.   [*Exit.*]

4. Movable face protector.   5. Open (its mouth) wide.   6. Held.   7. Suspect.

Scene 3

The dwelling of POLONIUS. *Enter* LAERTES *and* OPHELIA.

LAERTES: My necessaries are embarked. Farewell.
　And, sister, as the winds give benefit
　And convoy is assistant,[8] do not sleep,
　But let me hear from you.
OPHELIA:　　　　　　　　Do you doubt that?
5　LAERTES: For Hamlet, and the trifling of his favor,
　Hold it a fashion and a toy in blood,
　A violet in the youth of primy[9] nature,
　Forward, not permanent, sweet, not lasting,
　The perfume and suppliance of a minute,
　No more.
OPHELIA:　　No more but so?
10　LAERTES:　　　　　　　　Think it no more.
　For nature crescent[1] does not grow alone
　In thews and bulk, but as this temple[2] waxes
　The inward service of the mind and soul
　Grows wide withal. Perhaps he loves you now,
15　And now no soil nor cautel[3] doth besmirch
　The virtue of his will, but you must fear,
　His greatness weighted,[4] his will is not his own,
　For he himself is subject to his birth.
　He may not, as unvalued persons do,
20　Carve for himself, for on his choice depends
　The safety and health of this whole state,
　And therefore must his choice be circumscribed
　Unto the voice[5] and yielding of that body
　Whereof he is the head. Then if he says he loves you,
25　It fits your wisdom so far to believe it
　As he in his particular act and place
　May give his saying deed, which is no further
　Than the main voice of Denmark goes withal.
　Then weigh what loss your honor may sustain
30　If with too credent ear you list[6] his songs,
　Or lose your heart, or your chaste treasure open
　To his unmastered importunity.
　Fear it, Ophelia, fear it, my dear sister,
　And keep you in the rear of your affection,
35　Out of the shot and danger of desire.
　The chariest[7] maid is prodigal enough

---

8. Means of transport is available.　9. Of the spring.　1. Growing.　2. Body.　3. Deceit.　4. Rank
considered.　5. Assent.　6. Too credulous an ear you listen to.　7. Most circumspect.

If she unmask her beauty to the moon.
Virtue itself scapes not calumnious strokes.
The canker[8] galls the infants of the spring
Too oft before their buttons[9] be disclosed,   40
And in the morn and liquid dew of youth
Contagious blastments[1] are most imminent.
Be wary then; best safety lies in fear.
Youth to itself rebels, though none else near.
OPHELIA: I shall the effect of this good lesson keep   45
  As watchman to my heart. But, good my brother,
  Do not as some ungracious pastors do,
  Show me the steep and thorny way to heaven,
  Whiles like a puffed and reckless libertine
  Himself the primrose path of dalliance treads   50
  And recks not his own rede.[2]
LAERTES: O, fear me not.

        [*Enter* POLONIUS.]

  I stay too long. But here my father comes.
  A double blessing is a double grace;
  Occasion smiles upon a second leave.
POLONIUS: Yet here, Laertes? Aboard, aboard, for shame!   55
  The wind sits in the shoulder of your sail,
  And you are stayed for. There—my blessing with thee,
  And these few precepts in thy memory
  Look thou character.[3] Give thy thoughts no tongue,
  Nor any unproportioned thought his act.   60
  Be thou familiar, but by no means vulgar.
  Those friends thou hast, and their adoption tried,
  Grapple them unto thy soul with hoops of steel;
  But do not dull[4] thy palm with entertainment
  Of each new-hatched, unfledged comrade. Beware   65
  Of entrance to a quarrel, but being in,
  Bear't that th' opposéd[5] may beware of thee.
  Give every man thy ear, but few thy voice[6];
  Take each man's censure, but reserve thy judgment.
  Costly thy habit as thy purse can buy,   70
  But not expressed in fancy; rich not gaudy,
  For the apparel oft proclaims the man,
  And they in France of the best rank and station
  Are of a most select and generous chief[7] in that.
  Neither a borrower nor a lender be,   75
  For loan oft loses both itself and friend,

8. Rose caterpillar.   9. Buds.   1. Blights.   2. Heeds not his own advice.   3. Write.   4. Make
callous.   5. Conduct it so that the opponent.   6. Approval.   7. Eminence.

And borrowing dulls th' edge of husbandry.
This above all, to thine own self be true,
And it must follow as the night the day
80   Thou canst not then be false to any man.
Farewell. My blessing season this in thee!

LAERTES: Most humbly do I take my leave, my lord.

POLONIUS: The time invites you. Go, your servants tend.[8]

LAERTES: Farewell, Ophelia, and remember well
What I have said to you.

85 OPHELIA: 'Tis in my memory locked,
And you yourself shall keep the key of it.

LAERTES: Farewell.   [Exit.]

POLONIUS: What is't, Ophelia, he hath said to you?

OPHELIA: So please you, something touching the Lord Hamlet.

90 POLONIUS: Marry, well bethought.
'Tis told me he hath very oft of late
Given private time to you, and you yourself
Have of your audience been most free and bounteous.
If it be so—as so 'tis put on me,
95   And that in way of caution—I must tell you,
You do not understand yourself so clearly
As it behooves my daughter and your honor.
What is between you? Give me up the truth.

OPHELIA: He hath, my lord, of late made many tenders
100   Of his affection to me.

POLONIUS: Affection? Pooh! You speak like a green girl,
Unsifted in such perilous circumstance.
Do you believe his tenders, as you call them?

OPHELIA: I do not know, my lord, what I should think.

105 POLONIUS: Marry, I will teach you. Think yourself a baby
That you have ta'en these tenders for true pay
Which are not sterling. Tender yourself more dearly,
Or (not to crack the wind of the poor phrase,
Running it thus) you'll tender me a fool.

110 OPHELIA: My lord, he hath importuned me with love
In honorable fashion.

POLONIUS: Ay, fashion you may call it. Go to, go to.

OPHELIA: And hath given countenance[9] to his speech, my lord,
With almost all the holy vows of heaven.

115 POLONIUS: Ay, springes[1] to catch woodcocks. I do know,
When the blood burns, how prodigal the soul
Lends the tongue vows. These blazes, daughter,
Giving more light than heat, extinct in both
Even in their promise, as it is a-making,

8. Await.   9. Confirmation.   1. Snares.

You must not take for fire. From this time 120
Be something scanter of your maiden presence.
Set your entreatments[2] at a higher rate
Than a command to parle. For Lord Hamlet,
Believe so much in him that he is young,
And with a larger tether may he walk 125
Than may be given you. In few, Ophelia,
Do not believe his vows, for they are brokers,[3]
Not of that dye which their investments[4] show,
But mere implorators[5] of unholy suits,
Breathing like sanctified and pious bawds, 130
The better to beguile. This is for all:
I would not, in plain terms, from this time forth
Have you so slander any moment leisure
As to give words or talk with the Lord Hamlet.
Look to't, I charge you. Come your ways. 135
OPHELIA: I shall obey, my lord.   [*Exeunt.*]

SCENE 4

The guard station. Enter HAMLET, HORATIO *and* MARCELLUS.

HAMLET: The air bites shrewdly;[6] it is very cold.
HORATIO: It is a nipping and an eager[7] air.
HAMLET: What hour now?
HORATIO: I think it lacks of twelve.
MARCELLUS: No, it is struck.
HORATIO: Indeed? I heard it not. It then draws near the season 5
   Wherein the spirit held his wont to walk.

      [*A flourish of trumpets, and two pieces go off.*]

   What does this mean, my lord?
HAMLET: The king doth wake tonight and takes his rouse.
   Keeps wassail, and the swagg'ring up-spring[8] reels,
   And as he drains his draughts of Rhenish down, 10
   The kettledrum and trumpet thus bray out
   The triumph of his pledge.
HORATIO: Is it a custom?
HAMLET: Ay, marry, is't,
   But to my mind, though I am native here
   And to the manner born, it is a custom 15
   More honored in the breach than the observance.
   This heavy headed revel east and west

2. Negotiations before a surrender.   3. Panderers.   4. Garments.   5. Solicitors.   6. Sharply.
7. Keen.   8. A German dance.

Makes us traduced and taxed of other nations.
They clepe⁹ us drunkards, and with swinish phrase
20   Soil our addition,¹ and indeed it takes
From our achievements, though performed at height,
The pith and marrow of our attribute.²
So oft it chances in particular men,
That for some vicious mole of nature in them,
25   As in their birth, wherein they are not guilty
(Since nature cannot choose his origin),
By the o'ergrowth of some complexion,
Oft breaking down the pales³ and forts of reason,
Or by some habit that too much o'er-leavens
30   The form of plausive⁴ manners—that these men,
Carrying, I say, the stamp of one defect,
Being nature's livery or fortune's star,
His virtues else, be they as pure as grace,
As infinite as man may undergo,
35   Shall in the general censure take corruption
From that particular fault. The dram of evil
Doth all the noble substance often doubt⁵
To his own scandal.

      [*Enter* GHOST.]

HORATIO: Look, my lord, it comes.
HAMLET: Angels and ministers of grace defend us!
40   Be thou a spirit of health or goblin damned,
Bring with thee airs from heaven or blasts from hell,
Be thy intents wicked or charitable,
Thou com'st in such a questionable⁶ shape
That I will speak to thee. I'll call thee Hamlet,
45   King, father, royal Dane. O, answer me!
Let me not burst in ignorance, but tell
Why thy canonized⁷ bones, hearsèd in death,
Have burst their cerements;⁸ why the sepulchre
Wherein we saw thee quietly interred
50   Hath oped his ponderous and marble jaws
To cast thee up again. What may this mean
That thou, dead corse, again in complete steel⁹
Revisits thus the glimpses of the moon,
Making night hideous, and we fools of nature
55   So horridly to shake our disposition
With thoughts beyond the reaches of our souls?
Say, why is this? wherefore? What should we do?

---

9. Call.   1. Reputation.   2. Honor.   3. Barriers.   4. Pleasing.   5. Put out.   6. Prompting question.   7. Buried in accordance with church canons.   8. Gravecloths.   9. Armor.

[GHOST *beckons*.]

HORATIO: It beckons you to go away with it,
    As if it some impartment[1] did desire
    To you alone.
MARCELLUS: Look with what courteous action   60
    It waves you to a more removéd[2] ground.
    But do not go with it.
HORATIO: No, by no means.
HAMLET: It will not speak; then I will follow it.
HORATIO: Do not, my lord.
HAMLET: Why, what should be the fear?
    I do not set my life at a pin's fee,[3]   65
    And for my soul, what can it do to that,
    Being a thing immortal as itself?
    It waves me forth again. I'll follow it
HORATIO: What if it tempt you toward the flood, my lord,
    Or to the deathful summit of the cliff   70
    That beetles[4] o'er his base into the sea,
    And there assume some other horrible form,
    Which might deprive your sovereignty of reason[5]
    And draw you into madness? Think of it.
    The very place puts toys of desperation,[6]   75
    Without more motive, into every brain
    That looks so many fathoms to the sea
    And hears it roar beneath.
HAMLET: It waves me still.
    Go on. I'll follow thee.
MARCELLUS: You shall not go, my lord.
HAMLET: Hold off your hands.   80
HORATIO: Be ruled, You shall not go.
HAMLET: My fate cries out
    And makes each petty artere in this body
    As hardy as the Nemean lion's nerve.[7]
    Still am I called. Unhand me, gentlemen.
    By heaven, I'll make a ghost of him that lets[8] me.   85
    I say, away! Go on. I'll follow thee.   [*Exeunt* GHOST *and* HAMLET.]
HORATIO: He waxes desperate with imagination.
MARCELLUS: Let's follow. 'Tis not fit thus to obey him.
HORATIO: Have after. To what issue will this come?
MARCELLUS: Something is rotten in the state of Denmark.   90

---

1. Communication.   2. Beckons you to a more distant.   3. Price.   4. Juts out.   5. Rational
power. *Deprive:* take away.   6. Desperate fancies.   7. The Nemean lion was a mythological monster
slain by Hercules as one of his twelve labors.   8. Hinders.

HORATIO: Heaven will direct it.

MARCELLUS: Nay, let's follow him.   [*Exeunt.*]

SCENE 5

Near the guard station. Enter GHOST *and* HAMLET.

HAMLET: Whither wilt thou lead me? Speak. I'll go no further.

GHOST: Mark me.

HAMLET: I will.

GHOST: My hour is almost come,
  When I to sulph'rous and tormenting flames
  Must render up myself.

HAMLET: Alas, poor ghost!

5 GHOST: Pity me not, but lend thy serious hearing
  To what I shall unfold.

HAMLET: Speak. I am bound to hear.

GHOST: So art thou to revenge, when thou shalt hear.

HAMLET: What?

GHOST: I am thy father's spirit,

10   Doomed for a certain term to walk the night,
  And for the day confined to fast in fires,
  Till the foul crimes done in my days of nature⁹
  Are burnt and purged away. But that I am forbid
  To tell the secrets of my prison house,

15 I could a tale unfold whose lightest word
  Would harrow up thy soul, freeze thy young blood,
  Make thy two eyes like stars start from their spheres,
  Thy knotted and combinéd¹ locks to part,
  And each particular hair to stand an end,

20 Like quills upon the fretful porpentine.²
  But this eternal blazon³ must not be
  To ears of flesh and blood. List, list, O, list!
  If thou didst every thy dear father love—

HAMLET: O God!

25 GHOST: Revenge his foul and most unnatural murder.

HAMLET: Murder!

GHOST: Murder most foul, as in the best it is,
  But this most foul, strange, and unnatural.

HAMLET: Haste me to know't, that I, with wings as swift

30   As meditation or the thoughts of love,
  May sweep to my revenge.

GHOST: I find thee apt.
  And duller shouldst thou be than the fat weed

---

9. That is, while I was alive.   1. Tangled.   2. Porcupine.   3. Description of eternity.

That rots itself in ease on Lethe[4] wharf,—
Wouldst thou not stir in this. Now, Hamlet, hear.
'Tis given out that, sleeping in my orchard, 35
A serpent stung me. So the whole ear of Denmark
Is by a forgéd process[5] of my death
Rankly abused. But know, thou noble youth,
The serpent that did sting thy father's life
Now wears his crown.

HAMLET: O my prophetic soul! 40
My uncle!

GHOST: Ay, that incestuous, that adulterate beast,
With witchcraft of his wits, with traitorous gifts—
O wicked wit and gifts that have the power
So to seduce!—won to his shameful lust 45
The will of my most seeming virtuous queen.
O Hamlet, what a falling off was there,
From me, whose love was of that dignity
That it went hand in hand even with the vow
I made to her in marriage, and to decline[6] 50
Upon a wretch whose natural gifts were poor
To those of mine!
But virtue, as it never will be moved,
Though lewdness court it in a shape of heaven,
So lust, though to a radiant angel linked, 55
Will sate itself in a celestial bed
And prey on garbage.
But soft, methinks I scent the morning air.
Brief let me be. Sleeping within my orchard,
My custom always of the afternoon, 60
Upon my secure hour thy uncle stole,
With juice of cursed hebona[7] in a vial,
And in the porches of my ears did pour
The leperous distilment, whose effect
Holds such an enmity with blood of man 65
That swift as quicksilver it courses through
The natural gates and alleys of the body,
And with a sudden vigor it doth posset[8]
And curd, like eager[9] droppings into milk,
The thin and wholesome blood. So did it mine, 70
And a most instant tetter barked about[1]
Most lazar-like[2] with vile and loathsome crust
All my smooth body.

---

4. The waters of the Lethe, one of the rivers of the classical underworld, when drunk, induced forgetfulness. The "fat weed" is the asphodel that grew there.   5. False report.   6. Sink.   7. A poison.
8. Coagulate.   9. Acid. *Curd:* curdle.   1. Covered like bark. *Tetter:* a skin disease.   2. Leperlike.

Thus was I sleeping by a brother's hand
75 Of life, of crown, of queen at once dispatched,
Cut off even in the blossoms of my sin,
Unhouseled, disappointed, unaneled,[3]
No reck'ning made, but sent to my account
With all my imperfections on my head.
80 O, horrible! O, horrible! most horrible!
If thou hast nature in thee, bear it not.
Let not the royal bed of Denmark be
A couch of luxury[4] and damnéd incest.
But howsomever thou pursues this act,
85 Taint not thy mind, nor let thy soul contrive
Against thy mother aught. Leave her to heaven,
And to those thorns that in her bosom lodge
To prick and sting her. Fare thee well at once.
The glowworm shows the matin[5] to be near,
90 And gins to pale his uneffectual fire.
Adieu, adieu, adieu. Remember me.   [Exit.]
HAMLET: O all you host of heaven! O earth! What else?
And shall I couple hell? O, fie! Hold, hold, my heart,
And you, my sinews, grow not instant old,
95 But bear me stiffly up. Remember thee?
Ay, thou poor ghost, whiles memory holds a seat
In this distracted globe.[6] Remember thee?
Yea, from the table[7] of my memory
I'll wipe away all trivial fond[8] records,
100 All saws of books, all forms, all pressures past
That youth and observation copied there,
And thy commandment all alone shall live
Within the book and volume of my brain,
Unmixed with baser matter. Yes, by heaven!
105 O most pernicious woman!
O villain, villain, smiling, damnéd villian!
My tables—meet it is I set it down
That one may smile, and smile, and be a villain.
At least I am sure it may be so in Denmark.
110 So, uncle, there you are. Now to my word:[9]
It is "Adieu, adieu. Remember me."
I have sworn't.

[Enter HORATIO and MARCELLUS.]

HORATIO: My lord, my lord!

---

3. The ghost means that he died without the customary rites of the church, that is, without receiving the Sacrament, without confession, and without Extreme Unction.   4. Lust.   5. Morning.   6. Skull.
7. Writing tablet.   8. Foolish.   9. For my motto.

MARCELLUS: Lord Hamlet!

HORATIO: Heavens secure him!

HAMLET: So be it!

MARCELLUS: Illo, ho, ho, my lord!   115

HAMLET: Hillo, ho, ho, boy![1] Come, bird, come.

MARCELLUS: How is't, my noble lord?

HORATIO: What news, my lord?

HAMLET: O, wonderful!

HORATIO: Good my lord, tell it.

HAMLET: No, you will reveal it.

HORATIO: Not I, my lord, by heaven.

MARCELLUS: Nor I, my lord.   120

HAMLET: How say you then, would heart of man once think it?
   But you'll be secret?

BOTH: Ay, by heaven, my lord.

HAMLET: There's never a villain dwelling in all Denmark
   But he's an arrant knave.

HORATIO: There needs no ghost, my lord, come from the grave   125
   To tell us this.

HAMLET: Why, right, you are in the right,
   And so without more circumstance at all
   I hold it fit that we shake hands and part,
   You, as your business and desire shall point you,
   For every man hath business and desire   130
   Such as it is, and for my own poor part,
   I will go pray.

HORATIO: These are but wild and whirling words, my lord.

HAMLET: I am sorry they offend you, heartily;
   Yes, faith, heartily.

HORATIO: There's no offence, my lord.   135

HAMLET: Yes, by Saint Patrick, but there is, Horatio,
   And much offence too. Touching this vision here,
   It is an honest ghost, that let me tell you.
   For your desire to know what is between us,
   O'ermaster't as you may. And now, good friends,   140
   As you are friends, scholars, and soldiers,
   Give me one poor request.

HORATIO: What is't, my lord? We will.

HAMLET: Never make known what you have seen tonight.

BOTH: My lord, we will not.

HAMLET: Nay, but swear't.

HORATIO: In faith,   145
   My lord, not I.

MARCELLUS: Nor I, my lord, in faith.

---

1. A falconer's cry.

HAMLET: Upon my sword.

MARCELLUS: We have sworn, my lord, already.

HAMLET: Indeed, upon my sword, indeed.

> [GHOST *cries under the stage.*]

GHOST: Swear.

HAMLET: Ha, ha, boy, say'st thou so? Art thou there, truepenny?[2]

150   Come on. You hear this fellow in the cellarage.[3]

        Consent to swear.

HORATIO: Propose the oath, my lord.

HAMLET: Never to speak of this that you have seen,

        Swear by my sword.

GHOST: [*Beneath.*] Swear.

155   HAMLET: Hic et ubique?[4] Then we'll shift our ground.

        Come hither, gentlemen,

        And lay your hands again upon my sword.

        Swear by my sword

        Never to speak of this that you have heard.

160   GHOST: [*Beneath.*] Swear by his sword.

        HAMLET: Well said, old mole! Canst work i' th' earth so fast?

        A worthy pioneer![5] Once more remove, good friends.

HORATIO: O day and night, but this is wondrous strange!

HAMLET: And therefore as a stranger give it welcome.

165   There are more things in heaven and earth, Horatio,

        Than are dreamt of in your philosophy.

        But come.

        Here as before, never, so help you mercy,

        How strange or odd some'er I bear myself

170   (As I perchance hereafter shall think meet

        To put an antic[6] disposition on),

        That you, at such times, seeing me, never shall,

        With arms encumbered[7] thus, or this head-shake,

        Or by pronouncing of some doubtful phrase,

175   As "Well, well, we know," or "We could, and if we would"

        Or "If we list to speak," or "There be, and if they might"

        Or such ambiguous giving out, to note

        That you know aught of me—this do swear,

        So grace and mercy at your most needed help you.

180   GHOST: [*Beneath.*] Swear.   [*They swear.*]

        HAMLET: Rest, rest, perturbéd spirit! So, gentlemen,

        With all my love I do commend me to you,

        And what so poor a man as Hamlet is

        May do t'express his love and friending[8] to you,

---

2. Old fellow.   3. Below.   4. "Here and everywhere?"   5. Soldier who digs trenches.   6. Mad.
7. Folded.   8. Friendship.

God willing, shall not lack. Let us go in together,   185
And still your fingers on your lips, I pray.
The time is out of joint. O cursèd spite
That ever I was born to set it right!
Nay, come, let's go together.   [*Exeunt.*]

ACT II

SCENE 1

The dwelling of POLONIUS. *Enter* POLONIUS *and* REYNALDO.

POLONIUS: Give him this money and these notes, Reynaldo.
REYNALDO: I will, my lord.
POLONIUS: You shall do marvellous wisely, good Reynaldo,
  Before you visit him, to make inquire[9]
  Of his behavior.
REYNALDO: My lord, I did intend it.   5
POLONIUS: Marry, well said, very well said. Look you, sir.
  Enquire me first what Danskers[1] are in Paris,
  And how, and who, what means, and where they keep,[2]
  What company, at what expense; and finding
  By this encompassment[3] and drift of question   10
  That they do know my son, come you more nearer
  Than your particular demands[4] will touch it.
  Take you as 'twere some distant knowledge of him,
  As thus, "I know his father and his friends,
  And in part him." Do you mark this, Reynaldo?   15
REYNALDO: Ay, very well, my lord.
POLONIUS: "And in part him, but," you may say, "not well,
  But if 't be he I mean, he's very wild,
  Addicted so and so." And there put on him
  What forgeries you please; marry, none so rank[5]   20
  As may dishonor him. Take heed of that.
  But, sir, such wanton, wild, and usual slips
  As are companions noted and most known
  To youth and liberty.
REYNALDO: As gaming, my lord.
POLONIUS: Ay, or drinking, fencing, swearing, quarrelling,   25
  Drabbing[6]—you may go so far.
REYNALDO: My lord, that would dishonor him.
POLONIUS: Faith, no, as you may season it in the charge.[7]
  You must not put another scandal on him,
  That he is open to incontinency.[8]   30

9. Inquiry.   1. Danes.   2. Live.   3. Indirect means.   4. Direct questions.   5. Foul. *Forgeries:*
lies.   6. Whoring.   7. Soften the accusation.   8. Sexual excess.

That's not my meaning. But breathe his faults so quaintly[9]
That they may seem the taints of liberty,[1]
The flash and outbreak of a fiery mind,
A savageness in unreclaiméd[2] blood,
Of general assault.[3]
35 REYNALDO: But, my good lord—
POLONIUS: Wherefore should you do this?
REYNALDO: Ay, my lord,
    I would know that.
POLONIUS: Marry, sir, here's my drift,
    And I believe it is a fetch of warrant.[4]
    You laying these slight sullies on my son,
40 As 'twere a thing a little soiled i' th' working,
    Mark you,
    Your party in converse,[5] him you would sound,
    Having ever seen in the prenominate[6] crimes
    The youth you breathe[7] of guilty, be assured
45 He closes with you in this consequence,
    "Good sir," or so, or "friend," or "gentleman,"
    According to the phrase or the addition
    Of man and country.
REYNALDO: Very good, my lord.
POLONIUS: And then, sir, does 'a this—'a does—What was I about to say?
50 By the mass, I was about to say something.
    Where did I leave?
REYNALDO: At "closes in the consequence."
POLONIUS: At "closes in the consequence"—ay, marry,
    He closes thus: "I know the gentleman.
55 I saw him yesterday, or th' other day,
    Or then, or then, with such, or such, and as you say,
    There was 'a gaming, there o'ertook in's rouse,
    There falling out at tennis," or perchance
    "I saw him enter such a house of sale,"
60 Videlicet,[8] a brothel, or so forth.
    See you, now—
    Your bait of falsehood takes this carp of truth,
    And thus do we of wisdom and of reach,[9]
    With windlasses and with assays of bias,[1]
65 By indirections find directions out;
    So by my former lecture and advice
    Shall you my son. You have me, have you not?
REYNALDO: My lord, I have.

---

9. With delicacy.   1. Faults of freedom.   2. Untamed.   3. Touching everyone.   4. Permissible
trick.   5. Conversation.   6. Already named.   7. Speak.   8. Namely.   9. Ability.   1. Indirect tests.

POLONIUS: God b'wi' ye; fare ye well.

REYNALDO: Good my lord.

POLONIUS: Observe his inclination in yourself. 70

REYNALDO: I shall, my lord.

POLONIUS: And let him ply[2] his music.

REYNALDO: Well, my lord.

POLONIUS: Farewell. [*Exit* REYNALDO.]

[*Enter* OPHELIA.]

How now, Ophelia, what's the matter?

OPHELIA: O my lord, my lord, I have been so affrighted!

POLONIUS: With what, i' th' name of God? 75

OPHELIA: My lord, as I was sewing in my closet,[3]
Lord Hamlet with his doublet all unbraced,[4]
No hat upon his head, his stockings fouled,
Ungartered and down-gyvéd[5] to his ankle,
Pale as his shirt, his knees knocking each other, 80
And with a look so piteous in purport
As if he had been looséd out of hell
To speak of horrors—he comes before me.

POLONIUS: Mad for thy love?

OPHELIA: My lord, I do not know,
But truly I do fear it.

POLONIUS: What said he? 85

OPHELIA: He took me by the wrist, and held me hard,
Then goes he to the length of all his arm,
And with his other hand thus o'er his brow,
He falls to such perusal of my face
As 'a would draw it. Long stayed he so. 90
At last, a little shaking of mine arm,
And thrice his head thus waving up and down,
He raised a sigh so piteous and profound
As it did seem to shatter all his bulk,[6]
And end his being. That done, he lets me go, 95
And with his head over his shoulder turned
He seemed to find his way without his eyes,
For out adoors he went without their helps,
And to the last bended[7] their light on me.

POLONIUS: Come, go with me. I will go seek the king. 100
This is the very ecstasy of love,
Whose violent property fordoes[8] itself,
And leads the will to desperate undertakings
As oft as any passion under heaven

---

2. Practice.   3. Chamber.   4. Unlaced. *Doublet:* jacket.   5. Fallen down like fetters.   6. Body.
7. Directed.   8. Destroys. *Property:* character.

105 That does afflict our natures. I am sorry.
What, have you given him any hard words of late?
OPHELIA: No, my good lord, but as you did command
I did repel[9] his letters, and denied
His access to me.
POLONIUS:　　　　　That hath made him mad.
110 I am sorry that with better heed and judgment
I had not quoted[1] him. I feared he did but trifle,
And meant to wrack[2] thee; but beshrew my jealousy.
By heaven, it is as proper to our age
To cast beyond ourselves in our opinions
115 As it is common for the younger sort
To lack discretion. Come, go we to the king.
This must be known, which being kept close, might move
More grief to hide than hate to utter love.
Come.　　　　　　　　　　　　　　　　　　[*Exeunt.*]

SCENE 2

A public room. Enter KING, QUEEN, ROSENCRANTZ *and* GUILDENSTERN.

KING: Welcome, dear Rosencrantz and Guildenstern.
Moreover that[3] we much did long to see you,
The need we have to use you did provoke
Our hasty sending. Something have you heard
5 Of Hamlet's transformation—so call it,
Sith[4] nor th' exterior nor the inward man
Resembles that it was. What it should be,
More than his father's death, that thus hath put him
So much from th' understanding of himself,
10 I cannot deem of. I entreat you both
That, being of so young days[5] brought up with him,
And sith so neighbored[6] to his youth and havior,
That you vouchsafe your rest here in our court
Some little time, so by your companies
15 To draw him on to pleasures, and to gather
So much as from occasion you may glean,
Whether aught to us unknown afflicts him thus,
That opened lies within our remedy.
QUEEN: Good gentlemen, he hath much talked of you,
20 And sure I am two men there are not living
To whom he more adheres. If it will please you
To show us so much gentry[7] and good will
As to expend your time with us awhile

---

9. Refuse.　　1. Observed.　　2. Harm.　　3. In addition to the fact that.　　4. Since.　　5. From childhood.　　6. Closely allied.　　7. Courtesy.

For the supply and profit of our hope,
Your visitation shall receive such thanks   25
As fits a king's remembrance.

ROSENCRANTZ: Both your majesties
Might, by the sovereign power you have of us,
Put your dread pleasures more into command
Than to entreaty.

GUILDENSTERN: But we both obey,
And here give up ourselves in the full bent[8]   30
To lay our service freely at your feet,
To be commanded.

KING: Thanks, Rosencrantz and gentle Guildenstern.

QUEEN: Thanks, Guildenstern and gentle Rosencrantz.
And I beseech you instantly to visit   35
My too much changed son. Go, some of you,
And bring these gentlemen where Hamlet is.

GUILDENSTERN: Heavens make our presence and our practices
Pleasant and helpful to him!

QUEEN: Ay, amen!

[*Exeunt* ROSENCRANTZ *and* GUILDENSTERN.]

[*Enter* POLONIUS.]

POLONIUS: Th' ambassadors from Norway, my good lord,   40
Are joyfully returned.

KING: Thou still[9] hast been the father of good news.

POLONIUS: Have I, my lord? I assure you, my good liege,
I hold my duty as I hold my soul,
Both to my God and to my gracious king;   45
And I do think—or else this brain of mine
Hunts not the trial of policy[1] so sure
As it hath used to do—that I have found
The very cause of Hamlet's lunacy.

KING: O, speak of that, that do I long to hear.   50

POLONIUS: Give first admittance to th' ambassadors.
My news shall be the fruit[2] to that great feast.

KING: Thyself do grace to them, and bring them in.   [*Exit* POLONIUS.]
He tells me, my dear Gertrude, he hath found
The head and source of all your son's distemper.   55

QUEEN: I doubt it is no other but the main,
His father's death and our o'erhasty marriage.

KING: Well, we shall sift[3] him.

[*Enter Ambassadors* (VOLTEMAND *and* CORNELIUS) *with* POLONIUS.]

                        Welcome, my good friends,
Say, Voltemand, what from our brother Norway?

8. Completely.   9. Ever.   1. Statecraft.   2. Dessert.   3. Examine.

60 VOLTEMAND: Most fair return of greetings and desires.
    Upon our first,[4] he sent out to suppress
    His nephew's levies, which to him appeared
    To be a preparation 'gainst the Polack,
    But better looked into, he truly found
65   It was against your highness, whereat grieved,
    That so his sickness, age, and impotence
    Was falsely borne in hand, sends out arrests[5]
    On Fortinbras, which he in brief obeys,
    Receives rebuke from Norway, and in fine,
70   Makes vow before his uncle never more
    To give th' assay[6] of arms against your majesty.
    Whereon old Norway, overcome with joy,
    Gives him threescore thousand crowns in annual fee,
    And his commission to employ those soldiers,
75   So levied as before, against the Polack,
    With an entreaty, herein further shown,   [*Gives* CLAUDIUS *a paper.*]
    That it might please you to give quiet pass[7]
    Through your dominions for this enterprise,
    On such regards of safety and allowance
    As therein are set down.
80 KING: It likes[8] us well,
    And at our more considered time[9] we'll read,
    Answer, and think upon this business.
    Meantime we thank you for your well-took[1] labor.
    Go to your rest; at night we'll feast together.
    Most welcome home!   [*Exeunt* AMBASSADORS.]
85 POLONIUS: This business is well ended.
    My liege and madam, to expostulate[2]
    What majesty should be, what duty is,
    Why day is day, night night, and time is time,
    Were nothing but to waste night, day, and time.
90   Therefore, since brevity is the soul of wit,
    And tediousness the limbs and outward flourishes,[3]
    I will be brief. Your noble son is mad.
    Mad call I it, for to define true madness,
    What is't but to be nothing else but mad?
    But let that go.
95 QUEEN: More matter with less art.
POLONIUS: Madam, I swear I use no art at all.
    That he is mad, 'tis true: 'tis true 'tis pity,
    And pity 'tis 'tis true. A foolish figure,
    But farewell it, for I will use no art.
100   Mad let us grant him, then, and now remains

4. That is, first appearance.   5. Orders to stop. *Falsely borne in hand:* deceived.   6. Trial.   7. Safe
conduct.   8. Pleases.   9. Time for more consideration.   1. Successful.   2. Discuss.   3. Adorn-
ments.

That we find out the cause of this effect,
Or rather say the cause of this defect,
For this effect defective comes by cause.
Thus it remains, and the remainder thus.
Perpend.[4]   105
I have a daughter—have while she is mine—
Who in her duty and obedience, mark,
Hath given me this. Now gather, and surmise.
    "To the celestial, and my soul's idol, the most beautified
Ophelia."—That's an ill phrase, a vile phrase, "beautified" is a   110
vile phrase. But you shall hear. Thus:
    "In her excellent white bosom, these, etc."
QUEEN: Came this from Hamlet to her?
POLONIUS: Good madam, stay awhile. I will be faithful.

      "Doubt thou the stars are fire,   115
        Doubt that the sun doth move;
      Doubt truth to be a liar;
        But never doubt I love.

   O dear Ophelia, I am ill at these numbers.[5] I have not art to reck-
on my groans, but that I love thee best, O most best, believe it.   120
Adieu.
      Thine evermore, most dear lady, whilst this machine[6] is to him,
      Hamlet."
This in obedience hath my daughter shown me,
And more above, hath his solicitings,   125
As they fell out by time, by means, and place,
All given to mine ear.
KING: But how hath she
Received his love?
POLONIUS: What do you think of me?
KING: As of a man faithful and honorable.
POLONIUS: I would fain prove so. But what might you think,   130
When I had seen this hot love on the wing.
(As I perceived it, I must tell you that,
Before my daughter told me), what might you,
Or my dear majesty your queen here, think,
If I had played the desk or table-book,   135
Or given my heart a winking, mute and dumb,
Or looked upon this love with idle sight,[7]
What might you think? No, I went round[8] to work,
And my young mistress thus I did bespeak:

4. Consider.   5. Verses.   6. Body.   7. Polonius means that he would have been at fault if, having
seen Hamlet's attention to Ophelia, he had winked at it or not paid attention, an "idle sight," and if he
had remained silent and kept the information to himself, as if it were written in a "desk" or "table-
book."   8. Directly.

140   "Lord Hamlet is a prince out of thy star.[9]
  This must not be." And then I prescripts[1] gave her,
  That she should lock herself from his resort,
  Admit no messengers, receive no tokens.
  Which done, she took[2] the fruits of my advice;
145   And he repelled, a short tale to make,
  Fell into a sadness, then into a fast,
  Thence to a watch, thence into a weakness,
  Thence to a lightness, and by this declension,
  Into the madness wherein now he raves,
  And all we mourn for.
150 KING: Do you think 'tis this?
 QUEEN: It may be, very like.
 POLONIUS: Hath there been such a time—I would fain know that—
  That I have positively said "Tis so,"
  When it proved otherwise?
 KING: Not that I know.
 POLONIUS: [*Pointing to his head and shoulder.*] Take this from this, if this be
155   otherwise.
  If circumstances lead me, I will find
  Where truth is hid, though it were hid indeed
  Within the centre.[3]
 KING: How may we try it further?
 POLONIUS: You know sometimes he walks four hours together
  Here in the lobby.
160 QUEEN: So he does, indeed.
 POLONIUS: At such a time I'll loose[4] my daughter to him.
  Be you and I behind an arras[5] then.
  Mark the encounter. If he love her not,
  And be not from his reason fall'n thereon,
165   Let me be no assistant for a state,
  But keep a farm and carters.
 KING: We will try it.

   [*Enter* HAMLET *reading a book.*]

 QUEEN: But look where sadly the poor wretch comes reading.
 POLONIUS: Away, I do beseech you both away,
  I'll board[6] him presently.   [*Exeunt* KING *and* QUEEN.]
      O, give me leave.
170 How does my good Lord Hamlet?
 HAMLET: Well, God-a-mercy.
 POLONIUS: Do you know me, my lord?
 HAMLET: Excellent well, you are a fishmonger.
 POLONIUS: Not I, my lord.

---

9. Beyond your sphere. 1. Orders. 2. Followed. 3. Of the earth. 4. Let loose. 5. Tapestry. 6. Accost.

HAMLET: Then I would you were so honest a man. 175

POLONIUS: Honest, my lord?

HAMLET: Ay, sir, to be honest as this world goes, is to be one man picked out of ten thousand.

POLONIUS: That's very true, my lord.

HAMLET: For if the sun breed maggots in a dead dog, being a god kissing 180 carrion[7]—Have you a daughter?

POLONIUS: I have, my lord.

HAMLET: Let her not walk i' th' sun. Conception is a blessing, but as your daughter may conceive—friend, look to't.

POLONIUS: How say you by that? [*Aside.*] Still harping on my daughter. Yet he 185 knew me not at first. 'A said I was a fishmonger. 'A is far gone. And truly in my youth I suffered much extremity for love. Very near this. I'll speak to him again.—What do you read, my lord?

HAMLET: Words, words, words.

POLONIUS: What is the matter, my lord? 190

HAMLET: Between who?

POLONIUS: I mean the matter that you read, my lord.

HAMLET: Slanders, sir; for the satirical rogue says here that old men have grey beards, that their faces are wrinkled, their eyes purging thick amber and plum-tree gum, and that they have a plentiful lack of wit, together with most 195 weak hams[8]—all which, sir, though I have it thus set down, for yourself, sir, shall grow old as I am, if like a crab you could go backward.

POLONIUS: [*Aside.*] Though this be madness, yet there is method in't.—Will you walk out of the air, my lord?

HAMLET: Into my grave? 200

POLONIUS: [*Aside.*] Indeed, that's out of the air. How pregnant sometime his replies are! a happiness that often madness hits on, which reason and sanity could not so prosperously be delivered of. I will leave him, and suddenly contrive the means of meeting between him and my daughter.—My lord. I will take my leave of you. 205

HAMLET: You cannot take from me anything that I will more willingly part withal—except my life, except my life, except my life.

[*Enter* GUILDENSTERN *and* ROSENCRANTZ.]

POLONIUS: Fare you well, my lord.

HAMLET: These tedious old fools!

POLONIUS: You go to seek the Lord Hamlet. There he is. 210

ROSENCRANTZ: [*To* POLONIUS.] God save you, sir!　　　　　　　　　　[*Exit* POLONIUS.]

GUILDENSTERN: My honored lord!

ROSENCRANTZ: My most dear lord!

HAMLET: My excellent good friends! How dost thou, Guildenstern?
　Ah, Rosencrantz! Good lads, how do you both? 215

ROSENCRANTZ: As the indifferent[9] children of the earth.

---

7. A reference to the belief of the period that maggots were produced spontaneously by the action of sunshine on carrion.　8. Limbs.　9. Ordinary.

GUILDENSTERN: Happy in that we are not over-happy;
 On Fortune's cap we are not the very button.[1]
HAMLET: Nor the soles of her shoe?
220 ROSENCRANTZ: Neither, my lord.
HAMLET: Then you live about her waist, or in the middle of her favors.
GUILDENSTERN: Faith, her privates we.
HAMLET: In the secret parts of Fortune? O, most true, she is a strumpet.[2] What
 news?
225 ROSENCRANTZ: None, my lord, but that the world's grown honest.
HAMLET: Then is doomsday near. But your news is not true. Let me question more
 in particular. What have you, my good friends, deserved at the hands of
 Fortune, that she sends you to prison hither?
GUILDENSTERN: Prison, my lord?
230 HAMLET: Denmark's a prison.
ROSENCRANTZ: Then is the world one.
HAMLET: A goodly one, in which there are many confines, wards[3] and dungeons.
 Denmark being one o' th' worst.
ROSENCRANTZ: We think not so, my lord.
235 HAMLET: Why then 'tis none to you; for there is nothing either good or bad, but
 thinking makes it so. To me it is a prison.
ROSENCRANTZ: Why then your ambition makes it one. 'Tis too narrow for your
 mind.
HAMLET: O God, I could be bounded in a nutshell and count myself a king of
240 infinite space, where it not that I have bad dreams.
GUILDENSTERN: Which dreams indeed are ambition; for the very substance of
 the ambitious is merely the shadow of a dream.
HAMLET: A dream itself is but a shadow.
ROSENCRANTZ: Truly, and I hold ambition of so airy and light a quality that it is
245 but a shadow's shadow.
HAMLET: Then are our beggars bodies, and our monarchs and outstretched
 heroes the beggars' shadows. Shall we to th' court? for, by my fay,[4] I cannot
 reason.
BOTH: We'll wait upon you.
250 HAMLET: No such matter. I will not sort[5] you with the rest of my servants; for to
 speak to you like an honest man, I am most dreadfully attended. But in the
 beaten way of friendship, what make you at Elsinore?
ROSENCRANTZ: To visit you, my lord; no other occasion.
HAMLET: Beggar that I am, I am even poor in thanks, but I thank you; and sure,
255 dear friends, my thanks are too dear a halfpenny.[6] Were you not sent for? Is
 it your own inclining? Is it a free visitation? Come, come, deal justly with
 me. Come, come, nay speak.
GUILDENSTERN: What should we say, my lord?

1. That is, on top. 2. Prostitute. Hamlet is indulging in characteristic ribaldry. Guildenstern means
that they are "privates" = ordinary citizens, but Hamlet takes him to mean "privates" = sexual organs
and "middle of her favors" = waist = sexual organs. 3. Cells. 4. Faith. 5. Include. 6. Not
worth a halfpenny.

HAMLET: Why anything but to th' purpose. You were sent for, and there is a kind of confession in your looks, which your modesties have not craft enough to color. I know the good king and queen have sent for you.   260

ROSENCRANTZ: To what end, my lord?

HAMLET: That you must teach me. But let me conjure you by the rights of our fellowship, by the consonancy of our youth, by the obligation of our ever-preserved love, and by what more dear a better proposer can charge you   265
withal, be even and direct[7] with me whether you were sent for or no.

ROSENCRANTZ: [*Aside to* GUILDENSTERN.] What say you?

HAMLET: [*Aside.*] Nay, then, I have an eye of you.—If you love me, hold not off.

GUILDENSTERN: My lord, we were sent for.

HAMLET: I will tell you why; so shall my anticipation prevent your discovery,[8]   270
and your secrecy to the king and queen moult no feather. I have of late—but wherefore I know not—lost all my mirth, forgone all custom of exercises; and indeed it goes so heavily with my disposition, that this goodly frame the earth seems to me a sterile promontory, this most excellent canopy the air, look you, this brave o'er-hanging firmament, this majestical roof fretted[9]   275
with golden fire, why it appeareth nothing to me but a foul and pestilent congregation of vapors. What a piece of work is a man, how noble in reason, how infinite in faculties, in form and moving, how express[1] and admirable in action, how like an angel in apprehension, how like a god: the beauty of the world, the paragon of animals. And yet to me, what is this quintessence   280
of dust? Man delights not me, nor woman neither, though by your smiling you seem to say so.

ROSENCRANTZ: My lord, there was no such stuff in my thoughts.

HAMLET: Why did ye laugh, then, when I said "Man delights not me"?

ROSENCRANTZ: To think, my lord, if you delight not in man, what lenten enter-   285
tainment the players shall receive from you. We coted[2] them on the way, and hither are they coming to offer you service.

HAMLET: He that plays the king shall be welcome—his majesty shall have tribute on me; the adventurous knight shall use his foil and target; the lover shall not sigh gratis; the humorous[3] man shall end his part in peace; the clown   290
shall make those laugh whose lungs are tickle o' th' sere;[4] and the lady shall say her mind freely, or the blank verse shall halt for't. What players are they?

ROSENCRANTZ: Even those you were wont to take such delight in, the tragedians of the city.

HAMLET: How chances it they travel? Their residence, both in reputation and   295
profit, was better both ways.

ROSENCRANTZ: I think their inhibition comes by the means of the late innovation.

HAMLET: Do they hold the same estimation they did when I was in the city? Are they so followed?

ROSENCRANTZ: No, indeed, are they not.   300

HAMLET: How comes it? Do they grow rusty?

7. Straightforward.   8. Disclosure.   9. Ornamented with fretwork.   1. Well built.   2. Passed.
Lenten: scanty.   3. Eccentric. *Foil and target:* sword and shield.   4. Easily set off.

ROSENCRANTZ: Nay, their endeavor keeps in the wonted pace; but there is, sir, an eyrie of children, little eyases,[5] that cry out on the top of question,[6] and are most tyrannically clapped for't. These are now the fashion, and so berattle the common stages (so they call them) that many wearing rapiers are afraid of goose quills[7] and dare scarce come thither.[8]

305

HAMLET: What, are they children? Who maintains 'em? How are they escoted?[9] Will they pursue the quality no longer than they can sing? Will they not say afterwards, if they should grow themselves to common players (as it is most like, if their means are no better), their writers do them wrong to make them exclaim against their own succession?[1]

310

ROSENCRANTZ: Faith, there has been much to do on both sides; and the nation holds it no sin to tarre[2] them to controversy. There was for a while no money bid for argument,[3] unless the poet and the player went to cuffs[4] in the question.

315

HAMLET: Is't possible?

GUILDENSTERN: O, there has been much throwing about of brains.

HAMLET: Do the boys carry it away?

ROSENCRANTZ: Ay, that they do, my lord. Hercules and his load too.[5]

320

HAMLET: It is not very strange, for my uncle is King of Denmark, and those that would make mouths[6] at him while my father lived give twenty, forty, fifty, a hundred ducats apiece for his picture in little.[7] 'Sblood, there is something in this more than natural, if philosophy could find it out.

    [A flourish.]

GUILDENSTERN: There are the players.

325

HAMLET: Gentlemen, you are welcome to Elsinore. Your hands. Come then, th' appurtenance of welcome is fashion and ceremony. Let me comply with you in this garb, lest my extent[8] to the players, which I tell you must show fairly outwards should more appear like entertainment[9] than yours. You are welcome. But my uncle-father and aunt-mother are deceived.

330

GUILDENSTERN: In what, my dear lord?

HAMLET: I am but mad north-north-west; when the wind is southerly
  I know a hawk from a handsaw.[1]

    [Enter POLONIUS.]

POLONIUS: Well be with you, gentlemen.

---

5. Little hawks.   6. With a loud, high delivery.   7. Pens of satirical writers.   8. The passage refers to the emergence at the time of the play of theatrical companies made up of children from London choir schools. Their performances became fashionable and hurt the business of the established companies. Hamlet says that if they continue to act, "pursue the quality," when they are grown, they will find that they have been damaging their own future careers.   9. Supported.   1. Future careers. 2. Urge.   3. Paid for a play plot.   4. Blows.   5. During one of his labors Hercules assumed for a time the burden of the Titan Atlas, who supported the heavens on his shoulders. Also a reference to the effect on business at Shakespeare's theater, the Globe.   6. Sneer.   7. Miniature.   8. Fashion. *Comply with:* welcome.   9. Cordiality.   1. A "hawk" is a plasterer's tool; Hamlet may also be using "handsaw" = hernshaw = heron.

HAMLET: Hark you, Guildenstern—and you too—at each ear a hearer.
That great baby you see there is not yet out of his swaddling clouts.[2]   335
ROSENCRANTZ: Happily he is the second time come to them, for they say an old
man is twice a child.
HAMLET: I will prophesy he comes to tell me of the players. Mark it.
—You say right, sir, a Monday morning, 'twas then indeed.
POLONIUS: My lord, I have news to tell you.   340
HAMLET: My lord, I have news to tell you.
When Roscius was an actor in Rome—[3]
POLONIUS: The actors are come hither, my lord.
HAMLET: Buzz, buzz.
POLONIUS: Upon my honor—   345
HAMLET: Then came each actor on his ass—
POLONIUS: The best actors in the world, either for tragedy, comedy, history, pasto-
ral, pastoral-comical, historical-pastoral, tragical-historical, tragical-comical-
historical-pastoral, scene individable, or poem unlimited. Seneca cannot be
too heavy nor Plautus too light. For the law of writ and the liberty, these are
the only men.[4]   350
HAMLET: O Jephtha, judge of Israel, what a treasure hadst thou![5]
POLONIUS: What a treasure had he, my lord?
HAMLET: Why—

"One fair daughter, and no more,   355
The which he loved passing well."

POLONIUS: [*Aside.*] Still on my daughter.
HAMLET: Am I not i' th' right, old Jephtha?
POLONIUS: If you call me Jephtha, my lord, I have a daughter that I love passing
well.   360
HAMLET: Nay, that follows not.
POLONIUS: What follows then, my lord?
HAMLET: Why—

"As by lot, God wot"

and then, you know,   365

"It came to pass, as most like it was."

The first row of the pious chanson[6] will show you more, for look
where my abridgement[7] comes.

2. Wrappings for an infant.   3. Roscius was the most famous actor of classical Rome.   4. Seneca
and Plautus were Roman writers of tragedy and comedy, respectively. The "law of writ" refers to plays
written according to such rules as the three unities; the "liberty" to those written otherwise.   5. To
insure victory, Jephtha promised to sacrifice the first creature to meet him on his return. Unfortunately,
his only daughter outstripped his dog and was the victim of his vow. The biblical story is told in Judges
11.   6. Song. *Row:* stanza.   7. That which cuts short by interrupting.

[*Enter the* PLAYERS.]

370 You are welcome, masters; welcome, all.—I am glad to see thee well.—
Welcome, good friends.—O, old friend! Why thy face is valanced[8] since I
saw thee last. Com'st thou to beard me in Denmark?—What, my young lady
and mistress? By'r lady, your ladyship is nearer to heaven than when I saw
you last by the altitude of a chopine.[9] Pray God your voice, like a piece of
uncurrent gold, be not cracked within the ring.—Masters, you are all wel-
375 come. We'll e'en to't like French falconers, fly at anything we see. We'll
have a speech straight. Come give us a taste of your quality,[1] come a passionate speech.

FIRST PLAYER: What speech, my good lord?

HAMLET: I heard thee speak me a speech once, but it was never acted, or if it
380 was, not above once, for the play, I remember, pleased not the million; 'twas
caviary to the general.[2] But it was—as I received it, and others whose judgments in such matters cried in the top of[3] mine—an excellent play, well
digested[4] in the scenes, set down with as much modesty as cunning. I
remember one said there were no sallets[5] in the lines to make the matter
385 savory, nor no matter in the phrase that might indict the author of affectation, but called it an honest method, as wholesome as sweet, and by very
much more handsome than fine. One speech in't I chiefly loved. 'Twas
Æneas' tale to Dido, and thereabout of it especially where he speaks of Priam's
slaughter.[6] If it live in your memory, begin at this line—let me see, let me see:

390   "The rugged Pyrrhus, like th' Hyrcanian beast"[7]—

'tis not so; it begins with Pyrrhus—

"The rugged Pyrrhus, he whose sable arms,
black as his purpose, did the night resemble
When he lay couchéd in th' ominous horse,[8]
395 Hath now this dread and black complexion smeared
With heraldry more dismal; head to foot
Now is he total gules, horridly tricked[9]
With blood of fathers, mothers, daughters, sons,
Baked and impasted with the parching[1] streets,

---

8. Fringed (with a beard).   9. A reference to the contemporary theatrical practice of using boys to play
women's parts. The company's "lady" has grown in height by the size of a woman's thick-soled shoe,
"chopine," since Hamlet saw him last. The next sentence refers to the possibility, suggested by his
growth, that the young actor's voice may soon begin to change.   1. Trade.   2. Masses. *Caviary:*
caviar.   3. Were weightier than.   4. Arranged.   5. Spicy passages.   6. Aeneas, fleeing with his
band from fallen Troy (Ilium), arrives in Carthage, where he tells Dido, the queen of Carthage, of the
fall of Troy. Here he is describing the death of Priam, the aged king of Troy, at the hands of Pyrrhus,
the son of the slain Achilles.   7. Tiger.   8. That is, the Trojan horse.   9. Adorned. *Total gules:*
completely red.   1. Burning. *Impasted:* crusted.

That lend a tyrannous and a damnéd light 400
To their lord's murder. Roasted in wrath and fire,
And thus o'er-sizéd with coagulate[2] gore,
With eyes like carbuncles, the hellish Pyrrhus
Old grandsire Priam seeks."

    So proceed you. 405
POLONIUS: Fore God, my lord, well spoken, with good accent and good dis-
    cretion.
FIRST PLAYER: "Anon he finds him[3]
Striking too short at Greeks. His antique[4] sword,
Rebellious[5] to his arm, lies where it falls, 410
Repugnant to command. Unequal matched,
Pyrrhus at Priam drives, in rage strikes wide.
But with the whiff and wind of his fell sword
Th' unnervéd father falls. Then senseless[6] Ilium,
Seeming to feel this blow, with flaming top 415
Stoops[7] to his base, and with a hideous crash
Takes prisoner Pyrrhus' ear. For, lo! his sword,
Which was declining[8] on the milky head
Of reverend Priam, seemed i' th' air to stick.
So as a painted tyrant Pyrrhus stood, 420
And like a neutral to his will and matter,[9]
Did nothing.
But as we often see, against some storm,
A silence in the heavens, the rack[1] stand still,
The bold winds speechless, and the orb below 425
As hush as death, anon the dreadful thunder
Doth rend the region; so, after Pyrrhus' pause,
A rouséd vengeance sets him new awork,[2]
And never did the Cyclops' hammers fall
On Mars's armor, forged for proof eterne,[3] 430
With less remorse than Pyrrhus' bleeding sword
Now falls on Priam.
Out, out, thou strumpet, Fortune! All you gods,
In general synod take away her power,
Break all the spokes and fellies[4] from her wheel, 435
And bowl the round nave[5] down the hill of heaven
As low as to the fiends."

---

2. Clotted. *O'er-sizéd:* glued over.   3. That is, Pyrrhus finds Priam.   4. Which he used when young.
5. Refractory.   6. Without feeling.   7. Falls.   8. About to fall.   9. Between his will and the fulfillment of it.   1. Clouds.   2. To work.   3. Mars, as befits a Roman war god, had armor made for
him by the blacksmith god Vulcan and his assistants, the Cyclops. It was suitably impenetrable, of
"proof eterne."   4. Parts of the rim.   5. Hub. *Bowl:* roll.

POLONIUS: This is too long.

HAMLET: It shall to the barber's with your beard.—Prithee say on. He's for a jig,[6]
440   or a tale of bawdry, or he sleeps. Say on; come to Hecuba.[7]

FIRST PLAYER: "But who, ah woe! had seen the mobled[8] queen—"

HAMLET: "The mobled queen"?

POLONIUS: That's good. "Mobled queen" is good.

FIRST PLAYER: "Run barefoot up and down, threat'ning the flames
445   With bisson rheum, a clout[9] upon that head
    Where late the diadem stood, and for a robe,
    About her lank and all o'er-teeméd loins,
    A blanket, in the alarm of fear caught up—
    Who this had seen, with tongue in venom steeped,
450   'Gainst Fortune's state[1] would treason have pronounced.
    But if the gods themselves did see her then,
    When she saw Pyrrhus make malicious sport
    In mincing[2] with his sword her husband's limbs,
    The instant burst of clamor that she made,
455   Unless things mortal move them not at all,
    Would have made milch[3] the burning eyes of heaven,
    And passion in the gods."

POLONIUS: Look whe'r[4] he has not turned his color, and has tears in's eyes. Prithee
    no more.

460 HAMLET: 'Tis well. I'll have thee speak out the rest of this soon.—Good my lord,
    will you see the players well bestowed?[5] Do you hear, let them be well used,
    for they are the abstract[6] and brief chronicles of the time; after your death
    you were better have a bad epitaph than their ill report while you live.

POLONIUS: My lord, I will use them according to their desert.

465 HAMLET: God's bodkin, man, much better. Use every man after his desert, and
    who shall 'scape whipping? Use them after your own honor and dignity. The
    less they deserve, the more merit is in your bounty. Take them in.

POLONIUS: Come, sirs.

HAMLET: Follow him, friends. We'll hear a play tomorrow. [*Aside to* FIRST PLAYER.]
470   Dost thou hear me, old friend, can you play "The Murder of Gonzago"?

FIRST PLAYER: Ay, my lord.

HAMLET: We'll ha't tomorrow night. You could for a need study a speech of
    some dozen or sixteen lines which I would set down and insert in't, could
    you not?

475 FIRST PLAYER: Ay, my lord.

HAMLET: Very well. Follow that lord, and look you mock him not.

                       [*Exeunt* POLONIUS *and* PLAYERS.]

---

6. A comic act. 7. Hecuba was the wife of Priam and queen of Troy. Her "loins" are described below as "o'erteemed" because of her unusual fertility. The number of her children varies in different accounts, but twenty is a safe minimum. 8. Muffled (in a hood). 9. Cloth. *Bisson rheum:* blinding
tears. 1. Government. 2. Cutting up. 3. Tearful (literally, milk-giving). 4. Whether.
5. Provided for. 6. Summary.

My good friends, I'll leave you till night. You are welcome to Elsinore.
ROSENCRANTZ: Good my lord.

[*Exeunt* ROSENCRANTZ *and* GUILDENSTERN.]

HAMLET: Ay, so God b'wi'ye. Now I am alone.
O, what a rogue and peasant slave am I!   480
Is it not monstrous that this player here,
But in a fiction, in a dream of passion,
Could force his soul so to his own conceit[7]
That from her working all his visage wanned;[8]
Tears in his eyes, distraction in his aspect[9]   485
A broken voice, and his whole function suiting
With forms to his conceit? And all for nothing,
For Hecuba!
What's Hecuba to him or he to Hecuba,
That he should weep for her? What would he do   490
Had he the motive and the cue for passion
That I have? He would drown the stage with tears,
And cleave the general ear with horrid speech,
Make mad the guilty, and appal the free,
Confound the ignorant, and amaze indeed   495
The very faculties of eyes and ears.
Yet I,
A dull and muddy-mettled rascal, peak[1]
Like John-a-dreams, unpregnant[2] of my cause,
And can say nothing; no, not for a king   500
Upon whose property and most dear life
A damned defeat was made. Am I a coward?
Who calls me villain, breaks my pate across,
Plucks off my beard and blows it in my face,
Tweaks me by the nose, gives me the lie i' th' throat   505
As deep as to the lungs? Who does me this?
Ha, 'swounds, I should take it; for it cannot be
But I am pigeon-livered and lack gall[3]
To make oppression bitter, or ere this
I should 'a fatted all the region kites[4]   510
With this slave's offal. Bloody, bawdy villain!
Remorseless, treacherous, lecherous, kindless[5] villain!
Why, what an ass am I! This is most brave,
That I, the son of a dear father murdered,
Prompted to my revenge by heaven and hell,   515
Must like a whore unpack[6] my heart with words,
And fall a-cursing like a very drab,

7. Imagination.   8. Grew pale.   9. Face.   1. Mope. *Muddy-mettled:* dull-spirited.   2. Not
quickened by. *John-a-dreams:* a man dreaming.   3. Bitterness.   4. Birds of prey of the area.
5. Unnatural.   6. Relieve.

A scullion![7] Fie upon't! foh!
About, my brains. Hum—I have heard
520　That guilty creatures sitting at a play,
Have by the very cunning of the scene
Been struck so to the soul that presently
They have proclaimed[8] their malefactions;
For murder, though it have no tongue, will speak
525　With most miraculous organ. I'll have these players
Play something like the murder of my father
Before mine uncle. I'll observe his looks.
I'll tent him to the quick. If 'a do blench,[9]
I know my course. The spirit that I have seen
530　May be a devil, and the devil hath power
T' assume a pleasing shape, yea, and perhaps
Out of my weakness and my melancholy,
As he is very potent with such spirits,
Abuses me to damn me. I'll have grounds
535　More relative[1] than this. The play's the thing
Wherein I'll catch the conscience of the king.　　　[Exit.]

ACT III

Scene 1

A room in the castle. Enter KING, QUEEN, POLONIUS, OPHELIA, ROSENCRANTZ *and*
GUILDENSTERN.

KING: And can you by no drift of conference[2]
Get from him why he puts on this confusion,
Grating so harshly all his days of quiet
With turbulent[3] and dangerous lunacy?
5　ROSENCRANTZ: He does confess he feels himself distracted,
But from what cause 'a will by no means speak.
GUILDENSTERN: Nor do we find him forward to be sounded,[4]
But with a crafty madness keeps aloof
When we would bring him on to some confession
Of his true state.
10　QUEEN:　　　　　　Did he receive you well?
ROSENCRANTZ: Most like a gentleman.
GUILDENSTERN: But with much forcing of his disposition.[5]
ROSENCRANTZ: Niggard of question, but of our demands[6]
Most free in his reply.

---

7. In some versions of the play, the word "stallion," a slang term for a prostitute, appears in place of
"scullion."　　8. Admitted.　　9. Turn pale. *Tent:* try.　　1. Conclusive.　　2. Line of conversation.
3. Disturbing.　　4. Questioned. *Forward:* eager.　　5. Conversation.　　6. To our questions.

QUEEN: Did you assay[7] him
  To any pastime?   15
ROSENCRANTZ: Madam, it so fell out that certain players
  We o'er-raught[8] on the way. Of these we told him,
  And there did seem in him a kind of joy
  To hear of it. They are here about the court,
  And as I think, they have already order   20
  This night to play before him.
POLONIUS: 'Tis most true,
  And he beseeched me to entreat your majesties
  To hear and see the matter.[9]
KING: With all my heart, and it doth much content me
  To hear him so inclined.   25
  Good gentlemen, give him a further edge,
  And drive his purpose[1] into these delights.
ROSENCRANTZ: We shall, my lord.   [*Exeunt* ROSENCRANTZ *and* GUILDENSTERN.]
KING: Sweet Gertrude, leave us too,
  For we have closely sent for Hamlet hither,
  That he, as 'twere by accident, may here   30
  Affront[2] Ophelia.
  Her father and myself (lawful espials[3])
  Will so bestow ourselves that, seeing unseen,
  We may of their encounter frankly judge,
  And gather by him, as he is behaved,   35
  If't be th' affiction of his love or no
  That thus he suffers for.
QUEEN: I shall obey you.—
  And for your part, Ophelia, I do wish
  That your good beauties be the happy cause
  Of Hamlet's wildness. So shall I hope your virtues   40
  Will bring him to his wonted[4] way again,
  To both your honors.
OPHELIA: Madam, I wish it may.   [*Exit* QUEEN.]
POLONIUS: Ophelia, walk you here.—Gracious,[5] so please you,
  We will bestow ourselves.—[*To* OPHELIA.] Read on this book,
  That show of such an exercise may color[6]   45
  Your loneliness.—We are oft to blame in this,
  'Tis too much proved, that with devotion's visage
  And pious action we do sugar o'er
  The devil himself.
KING: [*Aside.*]   O, 'tis too true.
  How smart a lash that speech doth give my conscience!   50
  The harlot's cheek, beautied with plast'ring[7] art,

---

7. Tempt.   8. Passed.   9. Performance.   1. Sharpen his intention.   2. Confront.   3. Justified spies.   4. Usual.   5. Majesty.   6. Explain. *Exercise:* act of devotion.   7. Thickly painted.

Is not more ugly to the thing that helps it
Than is my deed to my most painted word.
O heavy burden!

55 POLONIUS: I hear him coming. Let's withdraw, my lord.

[*Exeunt* KING *and* POLONIUS.]

[*Enter* HAMLET.]

HAMLET: To be, or not to be, that is the question:
Whether 'tis nobler in the mind to suffer
The slings and arrows of outrageous fortune,
Or to take arms against a sea of troubles,
60 And by opposing end them. To die, to sleep—
No more; and by a sleep to say we end
The heartache, and the thousand natural shocks
That flesh is heir to. 'Tis a consummation
Devoutly to be wished—to die, to sleep—
65 To sleep, perchance to dream, ay there's the rub;
For in that sleep of death what dreams may come
When we have shuffled off this mortal coil[8]
Must give us pause—there's the respect[9]
That makes calamity of so long life.
70 For who would bear the whips and scorns of time,
Th' oppressor's wrong, the proud man's contumely,[1]
The pangs of despised love, the law's delay,
The insolence of office, and the spurns[2]
That patient merit of th' unworthy takes,
75 When he himself might his quietus[3] make
With a bare bodkin? Who would fardels[4] bear,
To grunt and sweat under a weary life,
But that the dread of something after death,
The undiscovered country, from whose bourn[5]
80 No traveller returns, puzzles the will,
And makes us rather bear those ills we have
Than fly to others that we know not of?
Thus conscience does make cowards of us all;
And thus the native[6] hue of resolution
85 Is sicklied o'er with the pale cast of thought,
And enterprises of great pitch and moment[7]
With this regard their currents turn awry
And lose the name of action.—Soft you now,
The fair Ophelia.—Nymph, in thy orisons[8]
Be all my sins remembered.

---

8. Turmoil.   9. Consideration.   1. Insulting   behavior.   2. Rejections.   3. Settlement.
4. Burdens. *Bodkin:* dagger.   5. Boundary.   6. Natural.   7. Importance. *Pitch:* height.   8. Prayers.

OPHELIA: Good my lord,   90
    How does your honor for this many a day?

HAMLET: I humbly thank you, well, well, well.

OPHELIA: My lord, I have remembrances of yours
    That I have longed long to re-deliver.
    I pray you now receive them.

HAMLET: No, not I,   95
    I never gave you aught.

OPHELIA: My honored lord, you know right well you did,
    And with them words of so sweet breath composed
    As made the things more rich. Their perfume lost,
    Take these again, for to the noble mind   100
    Rich gifts wax[9] poor when givers prove unkind.
    There, my lord.

HAMLET: Ha, ha! are you honest?[1]

OPHELIA: My lord?

HAMLET: Are you fair?   105

OPHELIA: What means your lordship?

HAMLET: That if you be honest and fair, your honesty should admit no discourse
    to your beauty.

OPHELIA: Could beauty, my lord, have better commerce[2] than with honesty?

HAMLET: Ay, truly, for the power of beauty will sooner transform honesty from   110
    what it is to a bawd than the force of honesty can translate beauty into his
    likeness. This was sometimes a paradox, but now the time gives it proof. I
    did love you once.

OPHELIA: Indeed, my lord, you made me believe so.

HAMLET: You should not have believed me, for virtue cannot so inoculate[3] our   115
    old stock but we shall relish of it. I loved you not.

OPHELIA: I was the more deceived.

HAMLET: Get thee to a nunnery.[4] Why wouldst thou be a breeder of sinners? I am
    myself indifferent[5] honest, but yet I could accuse me of such things that
    it were better my mother had not borne me: I am very proud, revengeful,   120
    ambitious, with more offences at my beck[6] than I have thoughts to put them
    in, imagination to give them shape, or time to act them in. What should
    such fellows as I do crawling between earth and heaven? We are arrant[7]
    knaves all; believe none of us. Go thy ways to a nunnery. Where's your
    father?   125

OPHELIA: At home, my lord.

HAMLET: Let the doors be shut upon him, that he may play the fool nowhere but
    in's own house. Farewell.

OPHELIA: O, help him, you sweet heavens!

HAMLET: If thou dost marry, I'll give thee this plague for thy dowry: be thou as   130

---

9. Become.   1. Chaste.   2. Intercourse.   3. Change by grafting.   4. With typical ribaldry
Hamlet uses "nunnery" in two senses, the second as a slang term for brothel.   5. Moderately.
6. Command.   7. Thorough.

chaste as ice, as pure as snow, thou shalt not escape calumny. Get thee to a
nunnery, farewell. Or if thou wilt needs marry, marry a fool, for wise men
know well enough what monsters[8] you make of them. To a nunnery, go, and
quickly too. Farewell.

135 OPHELIA: Heavenly powers, restore him!

HAMLET: I have heard of your paintings well enough. God hath given you one
face, and you make yourselves another. You jig, you amble, and you lisp;[9]
you nickname God's creatures, and make your wantonness your ignorance.[1]
Go to, I'll no more on't, it hath made me mad. I say we will have no more
140 marriage. Those that are married already, all but one, shall live. The rest shall
keep as they are. To a nunnery, go.   [*Exit.*]

OPHELIA: O, what a noble mind is here o'erthrown!
    The courtier's, soldier's, scholar's, eye, tongue, sword,
    Th' expectancy and rose[2] of the fair state,
145 The glass of fashion and the mould[3] of form,
    Th' observed of all observers, quite quite down!
    And I of ladies most deject and wretched,
    That sucked the honey of his music[4] vows,
    Now see that noble and most sovereign reason
150 Like sweet bells jangled, out of time and harsh;
    That unmatched form and feature of blown[5] youth
    Blasted with ecstasy. O, woe is me
    T' have seen what I have seen, see what I see!

        [*Enter* KING *and* POLONIUS.]

KING: Love! His affections do not that way tend,
155 Nor what he spake, though it lacked form a little,
    Was not like madness. There's something in his soul
    O'er which his melancholy sits on brood,[6]
    And I do doubt the hatch and the disclose[7]
    Will be some danger; which to prevent,
160 I have in quick determination
    Thus set it down: he shall with speed to England
    For the demand of our neglected tribute.
    Haply the seas and countries different,
    With variable objects, shall expel
165 This something-settled matter in his heart
    Whereon his brains still beating puts him thus
    From fashion of himself. What think you on't?
POLONIUS: It shall do well. But yet do I believe
    The origin and commencement of his grief
170 Sprung from neglected love.—How now, Ophelia?

---

8. Horned because cuckolded.   9. Walk and talk affectedly.   1. Hamlet means that women call
things by pet names and then blame the affectation on ignorance.   2. Ornament. *Expectancy:* hope.
3. Model. *Glass:* mirror.   4. Musical.   5. Full-blown.   6. That is, like a hen.   7. Result. *Doubt:*
fear.

You need not tell us what Lord Hamlet said,
We heard it all.—My lord, do as you please,
But if you hold it fit, after the play
Let his queen-mother all alone entreat him
To show his grief. Let her be round[8] with him,   175
And I'll be placed, so please you, in the ear[9]
Of all their conference. If she find him not,[1]
To England send him; or confine him where
Your wisdom best shall think.
KING: It shall be so.
Madness in great ones must not unwatched go.   [*Exeunt.*]   180

SCENE 2

A public room in the castle. Enter HAMLET *and three of the* PLAYERS.

HAMLET: Speak the speech, I pray you, as I pronounced it to you, trippingly on
the tongue; but if you mouth it as many of our players do, I had as lief the
town-crier spoke my lines. Nor do not saw the air too much with your hand
thus, but use all gently, for in the very torrent, tempest, and as I may say,
whirlwind of your passion, you must acquire and beget a temperance that   5
may give it smoothness. O, it offends me to the soul to hear a robustious
periwig-pated[2] fellow tear a passion to tatters, to very rags, to split the ears
of the groundlings, who for the most part are capable of[3] nothing but inexplicable dumb shows and noise. I would have such a fellow whipped for
o'erdoing Termagant. It out-herods Herod.[4] Pray you avoid it.   10
FIRST PLAYER: I warrant your honor.
HAMLET: Be not too tame neither, but let your own discretion be your tutor. Suit
the action to the word, the word to the action, with this special observance,
that you o'erstep not the modesty of nature; for anything so o'erdone is from[5]
the purpose of playing, whose end both at the first, and now, was and is, to   15
hold as 'twere the mirror up to nature, to show virtue her own feature, scorn
her own image, and the very age and body of the time his form and pressure.[6]
Now this overdone, or come tardy off, though it makes the unskilful[7] laugh,
cannot but make the judicious grieve, the censure[8] of the which one must in
your allowance o'erweigh a whole theatre of others. O, there be players that I   20
have seen play—and heard others praise, and that highly—not to speak it
profanely, that neither having th' accent of Christians, nor the gait of Christian, pagan, nor man, have so strutted and bellowed that I have thought
some of nature's journeymen[9] had made men, and not made them well, they
imitated humanity so abominably.   25

8. Direct.   9. Hearing.   1. Does not discover his problem.   2. Bewigged. *Robustious:* noisy.
3. That is, capable of understanding. *Groundlings:* the spectators who paid least.   4. Termagant, a "Sar-
acen" deity, and the biblical Herod were stock characters in popular drama noted for the excesses of
sound and fury used by their interpreters.   5. Contrary to.   6. Shape.   7. Ignorant.   8. Judgment.   9. Inferior craftsmen.

FIRST PLAYER: I hope we have reformed that indifferently[1] with us.

HAMLET: O, reform it altogether. And let those that play your clowns speak no
more than is set down for them, for there be of them that will themselves
laugh, to set on some quantity of barren[2] spectators to laugh too, though in
30   the meantime some necessary question of the play be then to be considered.
That's villainous, and shows a most pitiful ambition in the fool that uses it.
Go, make you ready.   [*Exeunt* PLAYERS.]

[*Enter* POLONIUS, GUILDENSTERN, *and* ROSENCRANTZ.]

    How now, my lord? Will the king hear this piece of work?

POLONIUS: And the queen too, and that presently.

35 HAMLET: Bid the players make haste.   [*Exit* POLONIUS.]
    Will you two help to hasten them?

ROSENCRANTZ: Ay, my lord.   [*Exeunt they two.*]

HAMLET: What, ho, Horatio!

[*Enter* HORATIO.]

HORATIO: Here, sweet lord, at your service.

40 HAMLET: Horatio, thou art e'en as just a man
    As e'er my conversation coped[3] withal.

HORATIO: O my dear lord!

HAMLET: Nay, do not think I flatter,
    For what advancement may I hope from thee,
    That no revenue hast but thy good spirits
45   To feed and clothe thee? Why should the poor be flattered?
    No, let the candied tongue lick absurd pomp,
    And crook the pregnant[4] hinges of the knee
    Where thrift[5] may follow fawning. Dost thou hear?
    Since my dear soul was mistress of her choice
50   And could of men distinguish her election,
    S'hath sealed thee for herself, for thou hast been
    As one in suff'ring all that suffers nothing,
    A man that Fortune's buffets and rewards
    Hast ta'en with equal thanks; and blest are those
55   Whose blood and judgment are so well commingled
    That they are not a pipe[6] for Fortune's finger
    To sound what stop[7] she please. Give me that man
    That is not passion's slave, and I will wear him
    In my heart's core, ay, in my heart of heart,
60   As I do thee. Something too much of this.
    There is a play tonight before the king.
    One scene of it comes near the circumstance
    Which I have told thee of my father's death.

---

1. Somewhat.   2. Dull-witted.   3. Encountered.   4. Quick to bend.   5. Profit.   6. Musical
instrument.   7. Note. *Sound:* play.

I prithee, when thou seest that act afoot,
Even with the very comment[8] of thy soul 65
Observe my uncle. If his occulted[9] guilt
Do not itself unkennel[1] in one speech,
It is a damnéd ghost that we have seen,
And my imaginations are as foul
As Vulcan's stithy. Give him heedful note,[2] 70
For I mine eyes will rivet to his face,
And after we will both our judgments join
In censure of his seeming.[3]
HORATIO: Well, my lord.
If 'a steal aught the whilst this play in playing,
And 'scape detecting, I will pay[4] the theft. 75

[*Enter Trumpets and Kettledrums,* KING, QUEEN, POLONIUS, OPHELIA, ROSEN-
CRANTZ, GUILDENSTERN, *and other* LORDS *attendant.*]

HAMLET: They are coming to the play. I must be idle.
    Get you a place.
KING: How fares our cousin Hamlet?
HAMLET: Excellent, i' faith, of the chameleon's dish.[5] I eat the air, promise-
    crammed. You cannot feed capons so. 80
KING: I have nothing with this answer, Hamlet. These words are not mine.
HAMLET: No, nor mine now. [*To* POLONIUS.] My lord, you played once i' th' univer-
    sity, you say?
POLONIUS: That did I, my lord, and was accounted a good actor.
HAMLET: What did you enact? 85
POLONIUS: I did enact Julius Cæsar. I was killed i' th' Capitol; Brutus killed
    me.[6]
HAMLET: It was a brute part of him to kill so capital a calf there. Be the players
    ready?
ROSENCRANTZ: Ay, my lord, they stay upon your patience.[7] 90
QUEEN: Come hither, my dear Hamlet, sit by me.
HAMLET: No, good mother, here's metal more attractive.
POLONIUS: [*To the* KING.] O, ho! do you mark that?
HAMLET: Lady, shall I lie in your lap?

    [*Lying down at* OPHELIA's *feet.*]

OPHELIA: No, my lord. 95
HAMLET: I mean, my head upon your lap?
OPHELIA: Ay, my lord.
HAMLET: Do you think I meant country matters?[8]

8. Keenest observation.   9. Hidden.   1. Break loose.   2. Careful attention. *Stithy:* smithy.
3. Manner.   4. Repay.   5. A reference to a popular belief that the chameleon subsisted on a diet of
air. Hamlet has deliberately misunderstood the king's question.   6. The assassination of Julius Caesar
by Brutus and others is the subject of another play by Shakespeare.   7. Leisure. *Stay:* wait.   8. Presumably, rustic misbehavior, but here and elsewhere in this exchange Hamlet treats Ophelia to some
ribald double meanings.

OPHELIA: I think nothing, my lord.

100 HAMLET: That's a fair thought to lie between maids' legs.

OPHELIA: What is, my lord?

HAMLET: Nothing.

OPHELIA: You are merry, my lord.

HAMLET: Who, I?

105 OPHELIA: Ay, my lord.

HAMLET: O God, your only jig-maker![9] What should a man do but be merry? For look you how cheerfully my mother looks, and my father died within's two hours.

OPHELIA: Nay, 'tis twice two months, my lord.

110 HAMLET: So long? Nay then, let the devil wear black, for I'll have a suit of sables. O heavens! die two months ago, and not forgotten yet? Then there's hope a great man's memory may outlive his life half a year, but by'r lady 'a must build churches then, or else shall 'a suffer not thinking on, with the hobby-horse, whose epitaph is "For O, for O, the hobby-horse is forgot!"[1]

> *The trumpets sound. Dumb Show follows. Enter a* KING *and a* QUEEN *very lovingly; the* QUEEN *embracing him and he her. She kneels, and makes show of protestation unto him. He takes her up, and declines[2] his head upon her neck. He lies him down upon a bank of flowers; she, seeing him asleep, leaves him. Anon come in another man, takes off his crown, kisses it, pours poison in the sleeper's ears, and leaves him. The* QUEEN *returns, finds the* KING *dead, makes passionate action. The* POISONER *with some three or four come in again, seem to condole with her. The dead body is carried away. The* POISONER *woos the* QUEEN *with gifts; she seems harsh awhile, but in the end accepts love.*
>
> *[Exeunt.]*

115 OPHELIA: What means this, my lord?

HAMLET: Marry, this is miching mallecho;[3] it means mischief.

OPHELIA: Belike this show imports the argument[4] of the play.

> *[Enter* PROLOGUE.*]*

HAMLET: We shall know by this fellow. The players cannot keep counsel; they'll tell all.

120 OPHELIA: Will 'a tell us what this show meant?

HAMLET: Ay, or any show that you will show him. Be not you ashamed to show, he'll not shame to tell you what it means.

OPHELIA: You are naught, you are naught. I'll mark[5] the play.

PROLOGUE: *For us, and for our tragedy,*

125 > *Here stooping to your clemency,*
> *We beg your hearing patiently.*   *[Exit.]*

HAMLET: Is this a prologue, or the posy[6] of a ring?

---

9. Writer of comic scenes.   1. In traditional games and dances one of the characters was a man respresented as riding a horse. The horse was made of something like cardboard and was worn about the "rider's" waist.   2. Lays.   3. Sneaking crime.   4. Plot. *Imports:* explains.   5. Attend to. *Naught:* obscene.   6. Motto engraved inside.

OPHELIA: 'Tis brief, my lord.

HAMLET: As woman's love.

[*Enter the* PLAYER KING *and* QUEEN.]

PLAYER KING: *Full thirty times hath Phœbus' cart gone round*   130
  Neptune's salt wash and Tellus' orbéd ground,
  And thirty dozen moons with borrowed sheen[7]
  About the world have times twelve thirties been,
  Since love our hearts and Hymen did our hands
  Unite comutual in most sacred bands.[8]   135

PLAYER QUEEN: *So many journeys may the sun and moon*
  Make us again count o'er ere love be done!
  But woe is me, you are so sick of late,
  So far from cheer and from your former state,
  That I distrust[9] you. Yet though I distrust,   140
  Discomfort you, my lord, it nothing must.
  For women's fear and love hold quantity,[1]
  In neither aught, or in extremity.[2]
  Now what my love is proof hath made you know,
  And as my love is sized,[3] my fear is so.   145
  Where love is great, the littlest doubts are fear;
  Where little fears grow great, great love grows there.

PLAYER KING: *Faith, I must leave thee, love, and shortly too;*
  My operant powers their functions leave[4] to do.
  And thou shalt live in this fair world behind,   150
  Honored, beloved, and haply one as kind
  For husband shalt thou—

PLAYER QUEEN: *O, confound the rest!*
  Such love must needs be treason in my breast.
  In second husband let me be accurst!
  None wed the second but who killed the first.[5]   155

HAMLET: That's wormwood.

PLAYER QUEEN: *The instances[6] that second marriage move*
  Are base respects[7] of thrift, but none of love.
  A second time I kill my husband dead,
  When second husband kisses me in bed.   160

PLAYER KING: *I do believe you think what now you speak,*
  But what we do determine oft we break.
  Purpose is but the slave to memory,
  Of violent birth, but poor validity;

---

7. Light.   8. The speech contains several references to Greek mythology. Phoebus was the sun god, and his chariot or "cart" the sun. The "salt wash" of Neptune is the ocean; Tellus was an earth goddess, and her "orbed ground" is the Earth, or globe. Hymen was the god of marriage. *Comutual:* mutually. 9. Fear for.   1. Agree in weight.   2. Without regard to too much or too little.   3. In size. 4. Cease. *Operant powers:* active forces.   5. Though there is some ambiguity, she seems to mean that the only kind of woman who would remarry is one who has killed or would kill her first husband. 6. Causes.   7. Concerns.

165   *Which now, like fruit unripe, sticks on the tree,*
    But fall unshaken when they mellow be.
    Most necessary 'tis that we forget
    To pay ourselves what to ourselves is debt.
    What to ourselves in passion we propose,
170   *The passion ending, doth the purpose lose.*
    The violence of either grief or joy
    Their own enactures[8] with themselves destroy.
    Where joy most revels, grief doth most lament;
    Grief joys, joy grieves, on slender accident.
175   *This world is not for aye,[9] nor 'tis not strange*
    That even our loves should with our fortunes change;
    For 'tis a question left us yet to prove,
    Whether love lead fortune, or else fortune love.
    The great man down, you mark his favorite flies;
180   *The poor advanced makes friends of enemies;*
    And hitherto doth love on fortune tend,
    For who not needs shall never lack a friend,
    And who in want a hollow[1] friend doth try,
    Directly seasons him[2] his enemy.
185   *But orderly to end where I begun,*
    Our wills and fates do so contrary run
    That our devices[3] still are overthrown;
    Our thoughts are ours, their ends none of our own.
    So think thou wilt no second husband wed,
190   *But die thy thoughts when thy first lord is dead.*
PLAYER QUEEN: *Nor earth to me give food, nor heaven light,*
    Sport and repose lock from me day and night,
    To desperation turn my trust and hope,
    An anchor's cheer[4] in prison be my scope,
195   *Each opposite that blanks[5] the face of joy*
    Meet what I would have well, and it destroy,
    Both here and hence[6] pursue me lasting strife,
    If once a widow, ever I be wife!
HAMLET: If she should break it now!
200 PLAYER KING: *'Tis deeply sworn. Sweet, leave me here awhile.*
    My spirits grow dull, and fain I would beguile
    The tedious day with sleep.   [*Sleeps.*]
PLAYER QUEEN: *Sleep rock thy brain,*
    And never come mischance between us twain!   [*Exit.*]
HAMLET: Madam, how like you this play?
205 QUEEN: The lady doth protest too much, methinks.
HAMLET: O, but she'll keep her word.
KING: Have you heard the argument? Is there no offence in't?

---

8. Actions.   9. Eternal.   1. False.   2. Ripens him into.   3. Plans.   4. Anchorite's food.
5. Blanches.   6. In the next world.

HAMLET: No, no, they do but jest, poison in jest; no offence i' th' world.

KING: What do you call the play?

HAMLET: "The Mouse-trap." Marry, how? Tropically.[7] This play is the image of a murder done in Vienna. Gonzago is the duke's name; his wife, Baptista. You shall see anon. 'Tis a knavish piece of work, but what of that? Your majesty, and we that have free souls, it touches us not. Let the galled jade wince, our withers are unwrung.[8]

> [*Enter* LUCIANUS.]

This is one Lucianus, nephew to the king.

OPHELIA: You are as good as a chorus, my lord.

HAMLET: I could interpret between you and your love, if I could see the puppets dallying.

OPHELIA: You are keen, my lord, you are keen.

HAMLET: It would cost you a groaning to take off mine edge.

OPHELIA: Still better, and worse.

HAMLET: So you mistake your husbands.—Begin, murderer. Leave thy damnable faces and begin. Come, the croaking raven doth bellow for revenge.

LUCIANUS: *Thoughts black, hands apt, drugs fit, and time agreeing,*
   Confederate season,[9] else no creature seeing,
   Thou mixture rank, of midnight weeds collected,
   With Hecate's ban thrice blasted, thrice infected,[1]
   Thy natural magic[2] and dire property
   On wholesome life usurps immediately.   [*Pours the poison in his ears.*]

HAMLET: 'A poisons him i' th' garden for his estate. His name's Gonzago. The story is extant, and written in very choice Italian. You shall see anon how the murderer gets the love of Gonzago's wife.

OPHELIA: The king rises.

HAMLET: What, frighted with false fire?

QUEEN: How fares my lord?

POLONIUS: Give o'er the play.

KING: Give me some light. Away!

POLONIUS: Lights, lights, lights!   [*Exeunt all but* HAMLET *and* HORATIO.]

HAMLET:

   Why, let the strucken deer go weep,
     The hart ungalléd[3] play.
   For some must watch while some must sleep;
     Thus runs the world away.
Would not this, sir, and a forest of feathers[4]—if the rest of my fortunes turn Turk with me—with two Provincial roses on my razed shoes, get me a fellowship in a cry of players?[5]

---

7. Figuratively.   8. A "galled jade" is a horse, particularly one of poor quality, with a sore back. The "withers" are the ridge between a horse's shoulders; "unwrung withers" are not chafed by the harness. 9. A helpful time for the crime.   1. Hecate was a classical goddess of witchcraft.   2. Native power. 3. Uninjured.   4. Plumes.   5. Hamlet asks Horatio if "this" recitation, accompanied with a player's costume, including plumes and rosettes on shoes that have been slashed for decorative effect, might not

HORATIO: Half a share.

HAMLET: A whole one, I.

> For thou dost know, O Damon dear,[6]
> This realm dismantled was
250 > Of Jove himself, and now reigns here
> A very, very—peacock.

HORATIO: You might have rhymed.

HAMLET: O good Horatio, I'll take the ghost's word for a thousand pound. Didst perceive?

255 HORATIO: Very well, my lord.

HAMLET: Upon the talk of the poisoning.

HORATIO: I did very well note[7] him.

HAMLET: Ah, ha! Come, some music. Come, the recorders.[8]

> For if the king like not the comedy.
260 > Why then, belike he likes it not, perdy.[9]

Come, some music.

[*Enter* ROSENCRANTZ *and* GUILDENSTERN.]

GUILDENSTERN: Good my lord, vouchsafe me a word with you.

HAMLET: Sir, a whole history.

GUILDENSTERN: The king, sir—

265 HAMLET: Ay, sir, what of him?

GUILDENSTERN: Is in his retirement marvellous distempered.[1]

HAMLET: With drink, sir?

GUILDENSTERN: No, my lord, with choler.[2]

HAMLET: Your wisdom should show itself more richer to signify this to the doc-
270 tor, for for me to put him to his purgation[3] would perhaps plunge him into more choler.

GUILDENSTERN: Good my lord, put your discourse into some frame,[4] and start not so wildly from my affair.

HAMLET: I am tame, sir. Pronounce.

275 GUILDENSTERN: The queen your mother, in most great affliction of spirit, hath sent me to you.

HAMLET: You are welcome.

GUILDENSTERN: Nay, good my lord, this courtesy is not of the right breed. If it shall please you to make me a wholesome[5] answer, I will do your mother's

---

entitle him to become a shareholder in a theatrical company in the event that Fortune goes against him, "turn Turk." *Cry:* company.   6. Damon was a common name for a young man or a shepherd in lyric, especially pastoral poetry. Jove was the chief god of the Romans. Readers may supply for themselves the rhyme referred to by Horatio.   7. Observe.   8. Wooden, end-blown flutes.   9. *Par Dieu* (by God). 1. Vexed. *Retirement:* place to which he has retired.   2. Bile.   3. Treatment with a laxative. 4. Order. *Discourse:* speech.   5. Reasonable.

commandment. If not, your pardon and my return[6] shall be the end of my business.   280

HAMLET: Sir, I cannot.

ROSENCRANTZ: What, my lord?

HAMLET: Make you a wholesome answer; my wit's diseased. But, sir, such answer as I can make, you shall command, or rather, as you say, my mother. Therefore no more, but to the matter. My mother, you say—   285

ROSENCRANTZ: Then thus she says: your behavior hath struck her into amazement and admiration.[7]

HAMLET: O wonderful son, that can so stonish a mother! But is there no sequel at the heels of his mother's admiration? Impart.[8]   290

ROSENCRANTZ: She desires to speak with you in her closet[9] ere you go to bed.

HAMLET: We shall obey, were she ten times our mother. Have you any further trade[1] with us?

ROSENCRANTZ: My lord, you once did love me.

HAMLET: And do still, by these pickers and stealers.[2]   295

ROSENCRANTZ: Good my lord, what is your cause of distemper? You do surely bar the door upon your own liberty, if you deny your griefs to your friend.

HAMLET: Sir, I lack advancement.

ROSENCRANTZ: How can that be, when you have the voice of the king himself for your succession in Denmark?   300

HAMLET: Ay, sir, but "while the grass grows"—the proverb[3] is something musty.

[*Enter the* PLAYERS *with recorders.*]

O, the recorders! Let me see one. To withdraw with you[4]—why do you go about to recover the wind of me, as if you would drive me into a toil?[5]

GUILDENSTERN: O my lord, if my duty be too bold, my love is too unmannerly.

HAMLET: I do not well understand that. Will you play upon this pipe?[6]   305

GUILDENSTERN: My lord, I cannot.

HAMLET: I pray you.

GUILDENSTERN: Believe me, I cannot.

HAMLET: I do beseech you.

GUILDENSTERN: I know no touch of it,[7] my lord.   310

HAMLET: It is as easy as lying. Govern these ventages[8] with your fingers and thumb, give it breath with your mouth, and it will discourse most eloquent music. Look you, these are the stops.[9]

GUILDENSTERN: But these cannot I command to any utt'rance of harmony. I have not the skill.   315

HAMLET: Why, look you now, how unworthy a thing you make of me! You would play upon me, you would seem to know my stops, you would pluck out the heart of my mystery, you would sound[1] me from my lowest note to

6. That is, to the queen.   7. Wonder.   8. Tell me.   9. Bedroom.   1. Business.   2. Hands.
3. The proverb ends "the horse starves."   4. Let me step aside.   5. The figure is from hunting. Hamlet asks why Guildenstern is attempting to get windward of him, as if he would drive him into a net.   6. Recorder.   7. Have no ability.   8. Holes. *Govern:* cover and uncover.   9. Wind-holes.
1. Play.

the top of my compass;[2] and there is much music, excellent voice, in this
little organ, yet cannot you make it speak. 'Sblood, do you think I am easier
to be played on than a pipe? Call me what instrument you will, though you
can fret[3] me, you cannot play upon me.

[*Enter* POLONIUS.]

God bless you, sir!

POLONIUS: My lord, the queen would speak with you, and presently.[4]
HAMLET: Do you see yonder cloud that's almost in shape of a camel?
POLONIUS: By th' mass, and 'tis like a camel indeed.
HAMLET: Methinks it is like a weasel.
POLONIUS: It is backed like a weasel.
HAMLET: Or like a whale.
POLONIUS: Very like a whale.
HAMLET: Then I will come to my mother by and by. [*Aside.*] They fool me to the
top of my bent.[5]—I will come by and by.
POLONIUS: I will say so.   [*Exit.*]
HAMLET: "By and by" is easily said. Leave me, friends.   [*Exeunt all but* HAMLET.]
   'Tis now the very witching time of night,
   When churchyards yawn, and hell itself breathes out
   Contagion to this world. Now could I drink hot blood,
   And do such bitter business as the day
   Would quake to look on. Soft, now to my mother.
   O heart, lose not thy nature; let not ever
   The soul of Nero[6] enter this firm bosom.
   Let me be cruel, not unnatural;
   I will speak daggers to her, but use none.
   My tongue and soul in this be hypocrites—
   How in my words somever she be shent,[7]
   To give them seals[8] never, my soul, consent!   [*Exit.*]

SCENE 3

A room in the castle. Enter KING, ROSENCRANTZ *and* GUILDENSTERN.

KING: I like him not,[9] nor stands it safe with us
   To let his madness range.[1] Therefore prepare you.
   I your commission will forthwith dispatch,
   And he to England shall along with you.
   The terms of our estate[2] may not endure
   Hazard so near's as doth hourly grow
   Out of his brows.

2. Range.   3. "Fret" is used in a double sense, to annoy and to play a guitar or similar instrument
using the "frets" or small bars on the neck.   4. At once.   5. Treat me as an utter fool.   6. The
Roman emperor Nero, known for his excesses, was believed to have been responsible for the death of his
mother.   7. Shamed.   8. Fulfillment in action.   9. Distrust him.   1. Roam freely.   2. Condition of the state.

GUILDENSTERN: We will ourselves provide,[3]
  Most holy and religious fear it is
  To keep those many many bodies safe
  That live and feed upon your majesty.   10
ROSENCRANTZ: The single and peculiar[4] life is bound
  With all the strength and armor of the mind
  To keep itself from noyance,[5] but much more
  That spirit upon whose weal[6] depends and rests
  The lives of many. The cess[7] of majesty   15
  Dies not alone, but like a gulf[8] doth draw
  What's near it with it. It is a massy[9] wheel
  Fixed on the summit of the highest mount,
  To whose huge spokes ten thousand lesser things
  Are mortised and adjoined,[1] which when it falls,   20
  Each small annexment, petty consequence,
  Attends[2] the boist'rous ruin. Never alone
  Did the king sigh, but with a general groan.
KING: Arm you, I pray you, to this speedy voyage,
  For we will fetters put about this fear,   25
  Which now goes too free-footed.
ROSENCRANTZ: We will haste us.

              [*Exeunt* ROSENCRANTZ *and* GUILDENSTERN.]

    [*Enter* POLONIUS.]

POLONIUS: My lord, he's going to his mother's closet.
  Behind the arras I'll convey[3] myself
  To hear the process. I'll warrant she'll tax him home,[4]
  And as you said, and wisely was it said,   30
  'Tis meet that some more audience than a mother,
  Since nature makes them partial, should o'erhear
  The speech, of vantage.[5] Fare you well, my liege.
  I'll call upon you ere you go to bed,
  And tell you what I know.
KING: Thanks, dear my lord.   [*Exit* POLONIUS.] 35
  O, my offence is rank, it smells to heaven;
  It hath the primal eldest curse[6] upon't,
  A brother's murder. Pray can I not,
  Though inclination be as sharp as will.
  My stronger guilt defeats my strong intent,   40
  And like a man to double business[7] bound,
  I stand in pause where I shall first begin,
  And both neglect. What if this curséd hand

---

3. Equip (for the journey).   4. Individual.   5. Harm.   6. Welfare.   7. Cessation.   8. Whirlpool.   9. Massive.   1. Attached.   2. Joins in.   3. Station.   4. Sharply. *Process:* proceedings.
5. From a position of vantage.   6. That is, of Cain.   7. Two mutually opposed interests.

Were thicker than itself with brothers' blood,
45   Is there not rain enough in the sweet heavens
To wash it white as snow? Whereto serves mercy
But to confront the visage of offence?
And what's in prayer but this twofold force,
To be forestalléd[8] ere we come to fall,
50   Or pardoned being down?[9] Then I'll look up.
My fault is past, But, O, what form of prayer
Can serve my turn? "Forgive me my foul murder"?
That cannot be, since I am still possessed
Of those effects[1] for which I did the murder—
55   My crown, mine own ambition, and my queen.
May one be pardoned and retain th' offence?[2]
In the corrupted currents of this world
Offence's gilded[3] hand may shove by justice,
And oft 'tis seen the wicked prize itself
60   Buys out the law. But 'tis not so above.
There is no shuffling; there the action[4] lies
In his true nature, and we ourselves compelled,
Even to the teeth and forehead of[5] our faults,
To give in evidence. What then? What rests?[6]
65   Try what repentance can. What can it not?
Yet what can it when one can not repent?
O wretched state? O bosom black as death!
O liméd[7] soul, that struggling to be free
Art more engaged! Help, angels! Make assay.
70   Bow, stubborn knees, and heart with strings of steel,
Be soft as sinews of the new-born babe.
All may be well.   *[He kneels.]*

      [Enter HAMLET.*]*

HAMLET: Now might I do it pat,[8] now 'a is a-praying,
And now I'll do't—and so 'a goes to heaven,
75   And so am I revenged. That would be scanned.[9]
A villain kills my father, and for that,
I, his sole son, do this same villain send
To heaven.
Why, this is hire and salary, not revenge.
80   'A took my father grossly, full of bread,[1]
With all his crimes broad blown, as flush[2] as May;
And how his audit stands who knows save heaven?
But in our circumstance and course of thought

---

8. Prevented (from sin).   9. Having sinned.   1. Gains.   2. That is, benefits of the offense.
3. Bearing gold as a bribe.   4. Case at law.   5. Face-to-face with.   6. Remains   7. Caught as
with birdlime.   8. Easily.   9. Deserves consideration.   1. In a state of sin and without fasting.
2. Vigorous. *Broad blown:* full-blown.

'Tis heavy with him; and am I then revenged
To take him in the purging of his soul,   85
When he is fit and seasoned³ for his passage?
No.
Up, sword, and know thou a more horrid hent.⁴
When he is drunk, asleep, or in his rage,
Or in th' incestuous pleasure of his bed,   90
At game a-swearing, or about some act
That has no relish⁵ of salvation in't—
Then trip him, that his heels may kick at heaven,
And that his soul may be as damned and black
As hell, whereto it goes. My mother stays.   95
This physic⁶ but prolongs thy sickly days.   [*Exit.*]
KING: [*Rising.*] My words fly up, my thoughts remain below.
     Words without thoughts never to heaven go.   [*Exit.*]

Scene 4

The Queen's chamber. Enter QUEEN *and* POLONIUS.

POLONIUS: 'A will come straight. Look you lay home to⁷ him.
     Tell him his pranks have been too broad⁸ to bear with,
     And that your grace hath screen'd⁹ and stood between
     Much heat and him. I'll silence me even here.
     Pray you be round.
QUEEN: I'll warrant you. Fear¹ me not.   5
     Withdraw, I hear him coming.

               [POLONIUS *goes behind the arras. Enter* HAMLET.]

HAMLET: Now, mother, what's the matter?
QUEEN: Hamlet, thou hast thy father much offended.
HAMLET: Mother, you have my father much offended.
HAMLET: Come, come, you answer with an idle tongue.   10
HAMLET: Go, go, you question with a wicked tongue.
QUEEN: Why, how now, Hamlet?
HAMLET: What's the matter now?
QUEEN: Have you forgot me?
HAMLET: No, by the rood,² not so.
     You are the queen, your husband's brother's wife,
     And would it were not so, you are my mother.   15
QUEEN: Nay, then I'll set those to you that can speak.
HAMLET: Come, come, and sit you down. You shall not budge.
     You go not till I set you up a glass³

---

3. Ready.   4. Opportunity.   5. Flavor.   6. Medicine.   7. Be sharp with.   8. Outrageous.
9. Acted as a fire screen.   1. Doubt.   2. Cross.   3. Mirror.

Where you may see the inmost part of you.
20 QUEEN: What wilt thou do? Thou wilt not murder me?
Help, ho!
POLONIUS: [*Behind.*] What, ho! help!
HAMLET: [*Draws.*] How now, a rat?
Dead for a ducat, dead!

[*Kills* POLONIUS *with a pass through the arras.*]

25 POLONIUS: [*Behind.*] O, I am slain!
QUEEN: O me, what hast thou done?
HAMLET: Nay, I know not.
Is it the king?
QUEEN: O, what a rash and bloody deed is this!
HAMLET: A bloody deed!—almost as bad, good mother,
30 As kill a king and marry with his brother.
QUEEN: As kill a king?
                    Ay, lady, it was my word.   [*Parting the arras.*]
HAMLET:
Thou wretched, rash, intruding fool, farewell!
I took thee for thy better. Take thy fortune.
Thou find'st to be too busy[4] is some danger.—
35 Leave wringing of your hands. Peace, sit you down
And let me wring your heart, for so I shall
If it be made of penetrable stuff,
If damnéd custom have not brazed it[5] so
That it be proof and bulwark against sense.[6]
40 QUEEN: What have I done that thou dar'st wag thy tongue
In noise so rude against me?
HAMLET: Such an act
That blurs the grace and blush of modesty,
Calls virtue hypocrite, takes off the rose
From the fair forehead of an innocent love.
45 And sets a blister[7] there, makes marriage-vows
As false as dicers' oaths. O, such a deed
As from the body of contraction[8] plucks
The very soul, and sweet religion makes
A rhapsody of words. Heaven's face does glow
50 And this solidity and compound mass[9]
With heated visage, as against the doom[1]—
Is though-sick at the act.
QUEEN: Ay me, what act
That roars so loud and thunders in the index?[2]
HAMLET: Look here upon this picture[3] and on this,
55 The counterfeit presentment of two brothers.

---

4. Officious.   5. Plated it with brass.   6. Feeling. *Proof:* armor.   7. Brand.   8. The marriage
contract.   9. Meaningless mass (Earth).   1. Judgment Day.   2. Table of contents.   3. Portrait.

See what a grace was seated on this brow:
Hyperion's curls, the front[4] of Jove himself,
An eye like Mars, to threaten and command,
A station like the herald Mercury[5]
New lighted[6] on a heaven-kissing hill—   60
A combination and a form indeed
Where every god did seem to set his seal,[7]
To give the world assurance of a man.
This was your husband. Look you now what follows.
Here is your husband, like a mildewed ear   65
Blasting his wholesome brother. Have you eyes?
Could you on this fair mountain leave to feed,
And batten[8] on this moor? Ha! have you eyes?
You cannot call it love, for at your age
The heyday in the blood is tame, it's humble,   70
And waits upon the judgment, and what judgment
Would step from this to this? Sense sure you have
Else could you not have motion, but sure that sense
Is apoplexed[9] for madness would not err,
Nor sense to ecstasy was ne'er so thralled   75
But it reserved some quantity[1] of choice
To serve in such a difference. What devil was't
That thus hath cozened you at hoodman-blind?[2]
Eyes without feeling, feeling without sight,
Ears without hands or eyes, smelling sans[3] all,   80
Or but a sickly part of one true sense
Could not so mope.[4] O shame! where is thy blush?
Rebellious hell,
If thou canst mutine[5] in a matron's bones,
To flaming youth let virtue be as wax   85
And melt in her own fire. Proclaim no shame
When the compulsive ardor gives the charge,[6]
Since frost itself as actively doth burn,
And reason panders[7] will.
QUEEN: O Hamlet, speak no more!
Thou turn'st my eyes into my very soul;   90
And there I see such black and grainéd[8] spots
As will not leave their tinct.[9]
HAMLET: Nay, but to live
In the rank sweat of an enseaméd[1] bed,
Stewed in curruption, honeying and making love

---

4. Forehead.   5. In Roman mythology, Mercury served as the messenger of the gods. *Station:* bearing.
6. Newly alighted.   7. Mark of approval.   8. Feed greedily.   9. Paralyzed.   1. Power.
2. Blindman's buff. *Cozened:* cheated.   3. Without.   4. Be stupid.   5. Commit mutiny.   6. Attacks.   7. Pimps for.   8. Ingrained.   9. Lose their color.   1. Greasy.

Over the nasty sty—

95   QUEEN: O, speak to me no more!
    These words like daggers enter in my ears;
    No more, sweet Hamlet.
HAMLET: A murderer and a villain,
    A slave that is not twentieth part the tithe[2]
    Of your precedent lord, a vice of kings,[3]
100   A cutpurse[4] of the empire and the rule,
    That from a shelf the precious diadem stole
    And put it in his pocket—
QUEEN: No more.

[*Enter* GHOST.]

HAMLET: A king of shreds and patches—
105   Save me and hover o'er me with your wings,
    You heavenly guards! What would your gracious figure?
QUEEN: Alas, he's mad.
HAMLET: Do you not come your tardy[5] son to chide,
    That lapsed in time and passion lets go by
110   Th' important acting of your dread command?
    O, say!
GHOST: Do not forget. This visitation
    Is but to whet thy almost blunted purpose.
    But look, amazement on thy mother sits.
115   O, step between her and her fighting soul!
    Conceit[6] in weakest bodies strongest works.
    Speak to her, Hamlet.
HAMLET: How is it with you, lady?
QUEEN: Alas, how is't with you,
    That you do bend[7] your eye on vacancy,
120   And with th' incorporal air do hold discourse?
    Forth at your eyes your spirits wildly peep,
    And as the sleeping soldiers in th' alarm,
    Your bedded hairs like life in excrements[8]
    Start up and stand an end. O gentle son,
125   Upon the heat and flame of thy distemper
    Sprinkle cool patience. Whereon do you look?
HAMLET: On him, on him! Look you how pale he glares.
    His form and cause conjoined,[9] preaching to stones,
    Would make them capable.[1]—Do not look upon me,
130   Lest with piteous action you convert
    My stern effects.[2] Then what I have to do

---

2. One-tenth.   3. The "Vice," a common figure in the popular drama, was a clown or buffoon. *Precedent lord:* first husband.   4. Pickpocket.   5. Slow to act.   6. Imagination.   7. Turn.   8. Nails and hair.   9. Working together.   1. Of responding.   2. Deeds.

Will want true color—tears perchance for blood.

QUEEN: To whom do you speak this?

HAMLET: Do you see nothing there?

QUEEN: Nothing at all, yet all that is I see. 135

HAMLET: Nor did you nothing hear?

QUEEN: No, nothing but ourselves.

HAMLET: Why, look you there. Look how it steals away.
My father, in his habit[3] as he lived!
Look where he goes even now out at the portal. [*Exit* GHOST.] 140

QUEEN: This is the very coinage[4] of your brain.
Ths bodiless creation ecstasy[5]
Is very cunning[6] in.

HAMLET: My pulse as yours doth temperately keep time,
And makes as healthful music. It is not madness 145
That I have uttered. Bring me to the test,
And I the matter will re-word, which madness
Would gambol[7] from. Mother, for love of grace,
Lay not that flattering unction[8] to your soul,
That not your trespass but my madness speaks. 150
It will but skin and film the ulcerous place
Whiles rank corruption, mining[9] all within,
Infects unseen. Confess yourself to heaven,
Repent what's past, avoid what is to come.
And do not spread the compost on the weeds, 155
To make them ranker. Forgive me this my virtue,
For in the fatness of these pursy[1] times
Virtue itself of vice must pardon beg,
Yea, curb[2] and woo for leave to do him good.

QUEEN: O Hamlet, thou hast cleft my heart in twain. 160

HAMLET: O, throw away the worser part of it,
And live the purer with the other half.
Good night—but go not to my uncle's bed.
Assume a virtue, if you have it not.
That monster custom[3] who all sense doth eat 165
Of habits evil, is angel yet in this,
That to the use of actions fair and good
He likewise gives a frock or livery
That aptly[4] is put on. Refrain tonight,
And that shall lend a kind of easiness 170
To the next abstinence; the next more easy;
For use almost can change the stamp of nature,
And either curb the devil, or throw him out
With wondrous potency. Once more, good night,

3. Costume.   4. Invention.   5. Madness.   6. Skilled.   7. Shy away.   8. Ointment.
9. Undermining.   1. Bloated.   2. Bow.   3. Habit.   4. Easily.

175 And when you are desirous to be blest,
I'll blessing beg of you. For this same lord
I do repent; but heaven hath pleased it so,
To punish me with this, and this with me,
That I must be their scourge and minister.
180 I will bestow[5] him and will answer well
The death I gave him. So, again, good night.
I must be cruel only to be kind.
Thus bad begins and worse remains behind.
One word more, good lady.
QUEEN: What shall I do?
185 HAMLET: Not this, by no means, that I bid you do:
Let the bloat[6] king tempt you again to bed,
Pinch wanton[7] on your cheek, call you his mouse,
And let him, for a pair of reechy[8] kisses,
Or paddling in your neck with his damned fingers,
190 Make you to ravel[9] all this matter out,
That I essentially am not in madness,
But mad in craft. 'Twere good you let him know,
For who that's but a queen, fair, sober, wise,
Would from a paddock, from a bat, a gib,[1]
195 Such dear concernings hide? Who would so do?
No, in despite of sense and secrecy,
Unpeg the basket on the house's top,
Let the birds fly, and like the famous ape,
To try conclusions, in the basket creep
200 And break your own neck down.[2]
QUEEN: Be thou assured, if words be made of breath
And breath of life, I have no life to breathe
What thou hast said to me.
HAMLET: I must to England; you know that?
QUEEN: Alack,
205 I had forgot. 'Tis so concluded on.
HAMLET: There's letters sealed, and my two school-fellows,
Whom I will trust as I will adders fanged,
They bear the mandate; they must sweep[3] my way
And marshal me to knavery. Let it work,
210 For 'tis the sport to have the enginer
Hoist with his own petar; and't shall go hard
But I will delve[4] one yard below their mines
And blow them at the moon. O, 'tis most sweet

---

5. Dispose of.   6. Bloated.   7. Lewdly.   8. Foul.   9. Reveal.   1. Tomcat. *Paddock:* toad.
2. Apparently a reference to a now-lost fable in which an ape, finding a basket containing a cage of birds on a housetop, opens the cage. The birds fly away. The ape, thinking that if he were in the basket he too could fly, enters, jumps out, and breaks his neck.   3. Prepare. *Mandate:* command.   4. Dig.

When in one line two crafts directly meet.[5]
This man shall set me packing.   215
I'll lug the guts into the neighbor room.
Mother, good night. Indeed, this counsellor
Is now most still, most secret, and most grave,
Who was in life a foolish prating knave.
Come sir, to draw toward an end with you.   220
Good night, mother.   [*Exit the* QUEEN. *Then exit* HAMLET *tugging* POLONIUS.]

ACT IV

SCENE 1

A room in the castle. Enter KING, QUEEN, ROSENCRANTZ *and* GUILDENSTERN.

KING: There's matter in these sighs, these profound heaves,
  You must translate;[6] 'tis fit we understand them.
  Where is your son?
QUEEN: Bestow this place on us a little while.
                              [*Exeunt* ROSENCRANTZ *and* GUILDENSTERN.]
  Ah, mine own lord, what have I seen tonight!   5
KING: What, Gertrude? How does Hamlet?
QUEEN: Mad as the sea and wind when both contend
  Which is the mightier. In his lawless fit,
  Behind the arras hearing something stir,
  Whips out his rapier, cries "A rat, a rat!"   10
  And in this brainish apprehension[7] kills
  The unseen good old man.
KING: O heavy deed!
  It had been so with us had we been there.
  His liberty is full of threats to all—
  To your yourself, to us, to every one.   15
  Alas, how shall this bloody deed be answered?
  It will be laid to us, whose providence[8]
  Should have kept short, restrained, and out of haunt,[9]
  This mad young man. But so much was our love,
  We would not understand what was most fit;   20
  But, like the owner of a foul disease,
  To keep it from divulging, let it feed
  Even on the pith of life. Where is he gone?

---

5. The "enginer," or engineer, is a military man who is here described as being blown up by a bomb of his own construction, "hoist with his own petar." The military figure continues in the succeeding lines where Hamlet describes himself as digging a countermine or tunnel beneath the one Claudius is digging to defeat Hamlet. In line 214 the two tunnels unexpectedly meet.   6. Explain.   7. Insane notion.
8. Prudence.   9. Away from court.

QUEEN: To draw apart the body he hath killed,
25   O'er whom his very madness, like some ore
        Among a mineral of metals base,
        Shows itself pure: 'a weeps for what is done.
    KING: O Gertrude, come away!
        The sun no sooner shall the mountains touch
30   But we will ship him hence, and this vile deed
        We must with all our majesty and skill
        Both countenance and excuse. Ho, Guildenstern!

        [*Enter* ROSENCRANTZ *and* GUILDENSTERN.]

        Friends both, go join you with some further aid.
        Hamlet in madness hath Polonius slain,
35   And from his mother's closet hath he dragged him.
        Go seek him out; speak fair, and bring the body
        Into the chapel. I pray you haste in this.
                            [*Exeunt* ROSENCRANTZ *and* GUILDENSTERN.]
        Come, Gertrude, we'll call up our wisest friends
        And let them know both what we mean to do
40   And what's untimely done;
        Whose whisper o'er the world's diameter,
        As level as the cannon to his blank,[1]
        Transports his poisoned shot—may miss our name,
        And hit the woundless air. O, come away!
45   My soul is full of discord and dismay.   [*Exeunt.*]

SCENE 2

A passageway. Enter HAMLET.

HAMLET: Safely stowed.—But soft, what noise? Who calls on Hamlet?
        O, here they come.

        [*Enter* ROSENCRANTZ, GUILDENSTERN, *and* OTHERS.]

ROSENCRANTZ: What have you done, my lord, with the dead body?
HAMLET: Compounded it with dust, whereto 'tis kin.
5   ROSENCRANTZ: Tell us where 'tis, that we may take it thence
        And bear it to the chapel.
HAMLET: Do not believe it.
ROSENCRANTZ: Believe what?
HAMLET: That I can keep your counsel and not mine own. Besides, to be de-
10   manded of a sponge—what replication[2] should be made by the son of a king?
ROSENCRANTZ: Take you me for a sponge, my lord?
HAMLET: Ay, sir, that soaks up the king's countenance,[3] his rewards, his author-

---

1. Mark. *Level:* direct.   2. Answer. *Demanded of:* questioned by.   3. Favor.

ities. But such officers do the king best service in the end. He keeps them like
an apple in the corner of his jaw, first mouthed to be last swallowed. When
he needs what you have gleaned, it is but squeezing you and, sponge, you—   15
you shall be dry again.

ROSENCRANTZ: I understand you not, my lord.

HAMLET: I am glad of it. A knavish speech sleeps in a foolish ear.

ROSENCRANTZ: My lord, you must tell us where the body is, and go with us to the
    king.   20

HAMLET: The body is with the king, but the king is not with the body.
    The king is a thing—

GUILDENSTERN: A thing, my lord!

HAMLET: Of nothing. Bring me to him. Hide fox, and all after.[4]   [*Exeunt.*]

SCENE 3

A room in the castle. Enter KING.

KING: I have sent to seek him, and to find the body.
    How dangerous is it that this man goes loose!
    Yet must not we put the strong law on him.
    He's loved of the distracted[5] multitude,
    Who like not in their judgment but their eyes,   5
    And where 'tis so, th' offender's scourge[6] is weighed,
    But never the offence. To bear all smooth and even,
    This sudden sending him away must seem
    Deliberate pause.[7] Diseases desperate grown
    By desperate appliance are relieved,   10
    Or not at all.

        [*Enter* ROSENCRANTZ, GUILDENSTERN, *and all the rest.*]

            How now! what hath befall'n?

ROSENCRANTZ: Where the dead body is bestowed, my lord,
    We cannot get from him.

KING: But where is he?

ROSENCRANTZ: Without, my lord; guarded, to know[8] your pleasure.

KING: Bring him before us.

ROSENCRANTZ: Ho! bring in the lord.   15

        [*They enter with* HAMLET.]

KING: Now, Hamlet, where's Polonius?

HAMLET: At supper.

KING: At supper? Where?

HAMLET: Not where he eats, but where 'a is eaten. A certain convocation of politic[9]
    worms are e'en at him. Your worm is your only emperor for diet. We fat

---

4. Apparently a reference to a children's game like hide-and-seek.   5. Confused.   6. Punishment.
7. That is, not an impulse.   8. Await.   9. Statesmanlike. *Convocation:* gathering.

20   all creatures else to fat us, and we fat ourselves for maggots. Your fat king and your lean beggar is but variable service—two dishes, but to one table. That's the end.

KING: Alas, alas!

25   HAMLET: A man may fish with the worm that hath eat of a king, and eat of the fish that hath fed of that worm.

KING: What dost thou mean by this?

HAMLET: Nothing but to show you how a king may go a progress through the guts of a beggar.

30   KING: Where is Polonius?

HAMLET: In heaven. Send thither to see. If your messenger find him not there, seek him i' th' other place yourself. But if, indeed, you find him not within this month, you shall nose[1] him as you go up the stairs into the lobby.

KING: [*To* ATTENDANTS.] Go seek him there.

35   HAMLET: 'A will stay till you come.   [*Exeunt* ATTENDANTS.]

KING: Hamlet, this deed, for thine especial safety—
   Which we do tender, as we dearly[2] grieve
   For that which thou hast done—must send thee hence
   With fiery quickness. Therefore prepare thyself.
40   The bark is ready, and the wind at help,
   Th' associates tend, and everything is bent
   For England.

HAMLET: For England?

KING: Ay, Hamlet.

HAMLET: Good.

KING: So it is, if thou knew'st our purposes.

HAMLET: I see a cherub that sees them. But come, for England!
45   Farewell, dear mother.

KING: Thy loving father, Hamlet.

HAMLET: My mother. Father and mother is man and wife, man and wife is one flesh. So, my mother. Come, for England.   [*Exit.*]

KING: Follow him at foot;[3] tempt him with speed aboard.
50   Delay it not; I'll have him hence tonight.
   Away! for everything is sealed and done
   That else leans on th' affair. Pray you make haste.   [*Exeunt all but the* KING.]
   And, England, if my love thou hold'st at aught—
   As my great power thereof may give thee sense,[4]
55   Since yet thy cicatrice[5] looks raw and red
   After the Danish sword, and thy free awe
   Pays homage to us—thou mayst not coldly set[6]
   Our sovereign process,[7] which imports at full
   By letters congruing[8] to that effect
60   The present death of Hamlet. Do it, England,

---

1. Smell.   2. Deeply. *Tender:* consider.   3. Closely.   4. Of its value.   5. Wound scar.   6. Set aside.   7. Mandate.   8. Agreeing.

For like the hectic[9] in my blood he rages,
And thou must cure me. Till I know 'tis done,
Howe'er my haps, my joys were ne'er begun.   [*Exit.*]

SCENE 4

Near Elsinore. Enter FORTINBRAS *with his army.*

FORTINBRAS: Go, captain, from me greet the Danish king.
  Tell him that by his license Fortinbras
  Craves the conveyance[1] of a promised march
  Over his kingdom. You know the rendezvous.
  If that his majesty would aught with us,   5
  We shall express our duty in his eye,[2]
  And let him know so.
CAPTAIN: I will do't, my lord.
FORTINBRAS: Go softly on.   [*Exeunt all but the* CAPTAIN.]

    [*Enter* HAMLET, ROSENCRANTZ, GUILDENSTERN, *and* OTHERS.]

HAMLET: Good sir, whose powers are these?
CAPTAIN: They are of Norway, sir.   10
HAMLET: How purposed, sir, I pray you?
CAPTAIN: Against some part of Poland.
HAMLET: Who commands them, sir?
CAPTAIN: The nephew to old Norway, Fortinbras.
HAMLET: Goes it against the main[3] of Poland, sir,   15
  Or for some frontier?
CAPTAIN: Truly to speak, and with no addition,[4]
  We go to gain a little patch of ground
  That hath in it no profit but the name.
  To pay five ducats,[5] five, I would not farm it;   20
  Nor will it yield to Norway or the Pole
  A ranker rate should it be sold in fee.[6]
HAMLET: Why, then the Polack never will defend it.
CAPTAIN: Yes, it is already garrisoned.
HAMLET: Two thousand souls and twenty thousand ducats   25
  Will not debate the question of this straw.
  This is th' imposthume[7] of much wealth and peace,
  That inward breaks, and shows no cause without
  Why the man dies. I humbly thank you, sir.
CAPTAIN: God b'wi'ye, sir.   [*Exit.*]
ROSENCRANTZ: Will't please you go, my lord?   30
HAMLET: I'll be with you straight. Go a little before.   [*Exeunt all but* HAMLET.]
  How all occasions do inform against me,

9. Chronic fever.   1. Escort.   2. Presence.   3. Central part.   4. Exaggeration.   5. That is, in
rent.   6. Outright. *Ranker:* higher.   7. Abscess.

And spur my dull revenge! What is a man,
If his chief good and market[8] of his time
35 Be but to sleep and feed? A beast, no more.
Sure he that made us with such large discourse,[9]
Looking before and after, gave us not
That capability and godlike reason
To fust[1] in us unused. Now, whether it be
40 Bestial oblivion, or some craven scruple
Of thinking too precisely on th' event[2]—
A thought which, quartered, hath but one part wisdom
And ever three parts coward—I do not know
Why yet I live to say "This thing's to do,"
45 Sith[3] I have cause, and will, and strength, and means,
To do't. Examples gross as earth exhort me.
Witness this army of such mass and charge,[4]
Led by a delicate and tender prince,
Whose spirit, with divine ambition puffed,
50 Makes mouths at[5] the invisible event,
Exposing what is mortal and unsure
To all that fortune, death, and danger dare,
Even for an eggshell. Rightly to be great
Is not to stir without great argument,
55 But greatly to find quarrel in a straw
When honor's at the stake. How stand I then,
That have a father killed, a mother stained,
Excitements of my reason and my blood,
And let all sleep, while to my shame I see
60 The imminent death of twenty thousand men
That for a fantasy and trick of fame
Go to their graves like beds, fight for a plot
Whereon the numbers cannot try the cause,
Which is not tomb enough and continent
65 To hide the slain?[6] O, from this time forth,
My thoughts be bloody, or be nothing worth!   [*Exit.*]

SCENE 5

A room in the castle. Enter QUEEN, HORATIO *and a* GENTLEMAN.

QUEEN: I will not speak with her.
GENTLEMAN: She is importunate, indeed distract.
  Her mood will needs to be pitied.

---

8. Occupation.   9. Ample   reasoning   power.   1. Grow   musty.   2. Outcome.   3. Since.
4. Expense.   5. Scorns.   6. The plot of ground involved is so small that it cannot contain the number of men involved in fighting or furnish burial space for the number of those who will die.

QUEEN: What would she have?

GENTLEMAN: She speaks much of her father, says she hears
  There's tricks i' th' world, and hems, and beats her heart,   5
  Spurns enviously at straws,[7] speaks things in doubt
  That carry but half sense. Her speech is nothing,
  Yet the unshaped use of it doth move
  The hearers to collection;[8] they yawn at it,
  And botch the words up fit to their own thoughts,   10
  Which, as her winks and nods and gestures yield them,
  Indeed would make one think there might be thought,
  Though nothing sure, yet much unhappily.

HORATIO: 'Twere good she were spoken with, for she may strew
  Dangerous conjectures in ill-breeding minds.   15

QUEEN: Let her come in.   [*Exit* GENTLEMAN.]
  [*Aside.*] To my sick soul, as sin's true nature is,
  Each toy seems prologue to some great amiss.[9]
  So full of artless jealousy is guilt,
  It spills itself in fearing to be spilt.   20

      [*Enter* OPHELIA *distracted.*]

OPHELIA: Where is the beauteous majesty of Denmark?

QUEEN: How now, Ophelia!

      [OPHELIA *sings.*]

    How should I your true love know
      From another one?
    By his cockle hat and staff,[1]   25
      And his sandal shoon.[2]

QUEEN: Alas, sweet lady, what imports this song?

OPHELIA: Say you? Nay, pray you mark.

      [*Sings.*]

    He is dead and gone, lady,
      He is dead and gone;   30
    At his head a grass-green turf,
      At his heels a stone.

  O, ho!

QUEEN: Nay, but Ophelia—

OPHELIA: Pray you mark.

      [*Sings.*]

    White his shroud as the mountain snow—

---

7. Takes offense at trifles.   8. An attempt to order.   9. Catastrophe. *Toy:* trifle.   1. A cockle hat, one decorated with a shell, indicated that the wearer had made a pilgrimage to the shrine of St. James at Compostela in Spain. The staff also marked the carrier as a pilgrim.   2. Shoes.

[*Enter* KING.]

35   QUEEN: Alas, look here, my lord.

[OPHELIA.]

> Larded all with sweet flowers;
> Which bewept to the grave did not go
> With true-love showers.

KING: How do you, pretty lady?

40   OPHELIA: Well, God dild[3] you! They say the owl was a baker's daughter. Lord,
    we know what we are, but know not what we may be. God be at your table!

KING: Conceit[4] upon her father.

OPHELIA: Pray let's have no words of this, but when they ask you what it means,
    say you this:

[*Sings.*]

45
> Tomorrow is Saint Valentine's day,
>   All in the morning betime,
> And I a maid at your window,
>   To be your Valentine.

> Then up he rose, and donn'd his clo'es,
50   And dupped[5] the chamber-door,
> Let in the maid, that out a maid
>   Never departed more.

KING: Pretty Ophelia!

OPHELIA: Indeed, without an oath, I'll make an end on't.

[*Sings.*]

55
> By Gis[6] and by Saint Charity,
>   Alack, and fie for shame!
> Young men will do't, if they come to't;
>   By Cock,[7] they are to blame.

> Quoth she "before you tumbled me,
60   You promised me to wed."

He answers:

> "So would I'a done, by yonder sun,
> An thou hadst not come to my bed."

KING: How long hath she been thus?

65   OPHELIA: I hope all will be well. We must be patient, but I cannot choose but weep
    to think they would lay him i' th' cold ground. My brother shall know of it,
    and so I thank you for your good counsel. Come, my coach! Good night,

---

3. Yield.   4. Thought.   5. Opened.   6. Jesus.   7. God.

ladies, good night. Sweet ladies, good night, good night.   *[Exit.]*
KING: Follow her close; give her good watch, I pray you.

         [Exeunt HORATIO *and* GENTLEMAN.*]*

O, this is the poison of deep grief; it springs   70
All from her father's death, and now behold!
O Gertrude, Gertrude!
When sorrows come, they come not single spies,
But in battalions: first, her father slain;
Next, your son gone, and he most violent author   75
Of his own just remove; the people muddied,[8]
Thick and unwholesome in their thoughts and whispers
For good Polonius' death; and we have done but greenly[9]
In hugger-mugger[1] to inter him; poor Ophelia
Divided from herself and her fair judgment,   80
Without the which we are pictures, or mere beasts;
Last, and as much containing as all these,
Her brother is in secret come from France,
Feeds on his wonder, keeps himself in clouds,
And wants not buzzers to infect his ear   85
With pestilent speeches of his father's death,
Wherein necessity, of matter beggared,[2]
Will nothing stick our person to arraign[3]
In ear and ear.[4] O my dear Gertrude, this,
Like to a murd'ring piece,[5] in many places   90
Gives me superfluous death. Attend,

      [A noise within. Enter a MESSENGER.*]*

Where are my Switzers?[6] Let them guard the door.
What is the matter?
MESSENGER: Save yourself, my lord.
The ocean, overpeering of his list,[7]
Eats not the flats with more impiteous[8] haste   95
Then young Laertes, in a riotous head,[9]
O'erbears your officers. The rabble call him lord,
And as the world were now but to begin,
Antiquity forgot, custom not known,
The ratifiers and props of every word,   100
They cry "Choose we, Laertes shall be king."
Caps, hands, and tongues, applaud it to the clouds,
"Laertes shall be king, Laertes king."
QUEEN: How cheerfully on the false trail they cry![1]

---

8. Disturbed.   9. Without judgment.   1. Haste.   2. Short on facts.   3. Accuse. *Stick:* hesitate.
4. From both sides.   5. A weapon designed to scatter its shot.   6. Swiss guards.   7. Towering
above its limits.   8. Pitiless.   9. With an armed band.   1. As if following the scent.

[*A noise within.*]

105   O, this is counter,[2] you false Danish dogs!
   KING: The doors are broke.

[*Enter* LAERTES, *with* OTHERS.]

LAERTES: Where is this king?—Sirs, stand you all without.
ALL: No, let's come in.
LAERTES: I pray you give me leave.
ALL: We will, we will.   [*Exeunt his followers.*]
110   LAERTES: I thank you. Keep[3] the door.—O thou vile king,
   Give me my father!
   QUEEN: Calmly, good Laertes.
LAERTES: That drop of blood that's calm proclaims me bastard,
   Cries cuckold to my father, brands the harlot
   Even here between the chaste unsmirchéd brow
   Of my true mother.
   KING: What is the cause, Laertes,
115   That thy rebellion looks so giant-like?
   Let him go, Gertrude. Do not fear[4] our person.
   There's such divinity doth hedge a king
   That treason can but peep to[5] what it would,
120   Acts little of his will. Tell me, Laertes.
   Why thou art thus incensed. Let him go, Gertrude.
   Speak, man.
LAERTES: Where is my father?
KING: Dead.
QUEEN: But not by him.
KING: Let him demand[6] his fill.
LAERTES: How came he dead? I'll not be juggled with.
125   To hell allegiance, vows to the blackest devil,
   Conscience and grace to the profoundest pit!
   I dare damnation. To this point I stand,
   That both the worlds I give to negligence,[7]
   Let come what comes, only I'll be revenged
130   Most throughly for my father.
KING: Who shall stay you?
LAERTES: My will, not all the world's.
   And for my means, I'll husband[8] them so well
   They shall go far with little.
KING: Good Laertes,
   If you desire to know the certainty
135   Of your dear father, is't writ in your revenge

---

2. Backward.   3. Guard.   4. Fear for.   5. Look at over or through a barrier.   6. Question.
7. Disregard. *Both the worlds:* that is, this and the next.   8. Manage.

That, swoopstake,[9] you will draw both friend and foe,
  Winner and loser?
LAERTES: None but his enemies.
KING: Will you know them, then?
LAERTES: To his good friends thus wide I'll ope my arms,
  And like the kind life-rend'ring pelican,[1]   140
  Repast them with my blood.
KING: Why, now you speak
  Like a good child and a true gentleman.
  That I am guiltless of your father's death,
  And am most sensibly in grief for it,
  It shall as level[2] to your judgment 'pear   145
  As day does to your eye.

      [*A noise within:* "Let her come in."]

LAERTES: How now? What noise is that?

      [*Enter* OPHELIA.]

O, heat dry up my brains! tears seven times salt
Burn out the sense and virtue[3] of mine eye!
By heaven, thy madness shall be paid with weight   150
Till our scale turn the beam. O rose of May,
Dear maid, kind sister, sweet Ophelia!
O heavens! is't possible a young maid's wits
Should be as mortal as an old man's life?
Nature is fine[4] in love, and where 'tis fine   155
It sends some precious instances of itself
After the thing it loves.[5]

      [OPHELIA *sings.*]

  They bore him barefac'd on the bier;
    Hey non nonny, nonny, hey nonny;
    And in his grave rain'd many a tear—   160

Fare you well, my dove!
LAERTES: Hadst thou thy wits, and didst persuade revenge,
  It could not move thus.
OPHELIA: You must sing "A-down, a-down, and you call him a-down-a." O,
  how the wheel becomes it! It is the false steward, that stole his master's   165
  daughter.[6]

---

9. Sweeping the board.   1. The pelican was believed to feed her young with her own blood.
2. Plain.   3. Function. *Sense:* feeling.   4. Refined.   5. Laertes means that Ophelia, because of her
love for her father, gave up her sanity as a token of grief at his death.   6. The "wheel" refers to the
"burden" or refrain of a song, in this case "A-down, a-down, and you call him a-down-a." The ballad to
which she refers was about a false steward. Others have suggested that the "wheel" is the Wheel of
Fortune, a spinning wheel to whose rhythm such a song might have been sung or a kind of dance
movement performed by Ophelia as she sings.

LAERTES: This nothing's more than matter.

OPHELIA: There's a rosemary, that's for remembrance. Pray you, love, remember.
And there is pansies, that's for thoughts.

170 LAERTES: A document[7] in madness, thoughts and remembrance fitted.

OPHELIA: There's fennel for you, and columbines. There's rue for you, and here's
some for me. We may call it herb of grace a Sundays. O, you must wear your
rue with a difference. There's a daisy. I would give you some violets, but they
withered all when my father died. They say 'a made a good end.

[*Sings.*]

175   For bonny sweet Robin is all my joy.

LAERTES: Thought and affliction, passion, hell itself,
She turns to favor[8] and to prettiness.

[OPHELIA *sings.*]

    And will 'a not come again?
    And will 'a not come again?
180   No, no, he is dead,
      Go to thy death-bed,
    He never will come again.

    His beard was as white as snow,
    All flaxen was his poll;[9]
185   He is gone, he is gone,
      And we cast away moan:
    God-a-mercy on his soul!

And of all Christian souls, I pray God. God b'wi'you.   [*Exit.*]

LAERTES: Do you see this, O God?

190 KING: Laertes, I must commune with your grief,
Or you deny me right. Go but apart,
Make choice of whom your wisest friends you will,
And they shall hear and judge 'twixt you and me.
If by direct or by collateral[1] hand
195 They find us touched,[2] we will our kingdom give,
Our crown, our life, and all that we call ours,
To you in satisfaction; but if not,
Be you content to lend your patience to us,
And we shall jointly labor with your soul
To give it due content.

200 LAERTES: Let this be so.
His means of death, his obscure funeral—
No trophy, sword, nor hatchment,[3] o'er his bones,
No noble rite nor formal ostentation[4]—

---

7. Lesson   8. Beauty.   9. Head.   1. Indirect.   2. By guilt.   3. Coat of arms.   4. Pomp.

Cry to be heard, as 'twere from heaven to earth,
That I must call't in question.
KING: So you shall;   205
And where th' offence is, let the great axe fall.
I pray you go with me.   [*Exeunt.*]

SCENE 6

Another room in the castle. Enter HORATIO *and a* GENTLEMAN.

HORATIO: What are they that would speak with me?
GENTLEMAN: Sea-faring men, sir. They say they have letters for you.
HORATIO: Let them come in.   [*Exit* GENTLEMAN.]
I do not know from what part of the world
I should be greeted, if not from Lord Hamlet.   5

        [*Enter* SAILORS.]

SAILOR: God bless you, sir.
HORATIO: Let him bless thee too.
SAILOR: 'A shall, sir, an't please him. There's a letter for you, sir—it came from th'
    ambassador that was bound for England—if your name be Horatio, as I am
    let to know[5] it is.   10
HORATIO: [*Reads.*] "Horatio, when thou shalt have overlooked[6] this, give these
    fellows some means[7] to the king. They have letters for him. Ere we were two
    days old at sea, a pirate of very warlike appointment[8] gave us chase. Finding
    ourselves too slow of sail, we put on a compelled valor, and in the grapple I
    boarded them. On the instant they got clear of our ship, so I alone became   15
    their prisoner. They have dealt with me like thieves of mercy, but they knew
    what they did; I am to do a good turn for them. Let the king have the letters
    I have sent, and repair thou to me with as much speed as thou wouldest fly
    death. I have words to speak in thine ear will make thee dumb; yet are they
    much too light for the bore of the matter.[9] These good fellows will bring thee   20
    where I am. Rosencrantz and Guildenstern hold their course for England. Of
    them I have much to tell thee. Farewell.

                                He that thou knowest thine, Hamlet."
Come, I will give you way[1] for these your letters,
And do't the speedier that you may direct me   25
To him from whom you brought them.   [*Exeunt.*]

---

5. Informed.   6. Read through.   7. Access.   8. Equipment.   9. A figure from gunnery, referring to shot that is too small for the size of the weapons to be fired.   1. Means of delivery.

Scene 7

Another room in the castle. Enter KING *and* LAERTES.

KING: Now must your conscience my acquittance seal,[2]
    And you must put me in your heart for friend,
    Sith you have heard, and with a knowing ear,
    That he which hath your noble father slain
    Pursued my life.
5   LAERTES: It well appears. But tell me
    Why you proceeded not against these feats,
    So criminal and so capital in nature,
    As by your safety, greatness, wisdom, all things else,
    You mainly were stirred up.
   KING: O, for two special reasons,
10   Which may to you, perhaps, seem much unsinewed,[3]
    But yet to me th' are strong. The queen his mother
    Lives almost by his looks, and for myself—
    My virtue or my plague, be it either which—
    She is so conjunctive[4] to my life and soul
15   That, as the star moves not but in his sphere,[5]
    I could not but by her. The other motive,
    Why to a public count[6] I might not go,
    Is the great love the general gender[7] bear him,
    Who, dipping all his faults in their affection,
20   Work like the spring that turneth wood to stone,[8]
    Convert his gyves[9] to graces; so that my arrows,
    Too slightly timbered[1] for so loud a wind,
    Would have reverted to my bow again,
    But not where I have aimed them.
25   LAERTES: And so have I a noble father lost,
    A sister driven into desp'rate terms,
    Whose worth, if praises may go back again,
    Stood challenger on mount of all the age
    For her perfections. But my revenge will come.
30   KING: Break not your sleeps for that. You must not think
    That we are made of stuff so flat and dull
    That we can let our beard be shook with danger,
    And think it pastime. You shortly shall hear more.
    I loved you father, and we love our self,
35   And that, I hope, will teach you to imagine—

2. Grant me innocent.   3. Weak.   4. Closely joined.   5. A reference to the Ptolemaic cosmology in which planets and stars were believed to revolve in crystalline spheres concentrically about the Earth. 6. Reckoning.   7. Common people.   8. Certain English springs contain so much lime that a lime covering will be deposited on a log placed in one of them for a length of time.   9. Fetters. 1. Shafted.

[*Enter a* MESSENGER *with letters.*]

MESSENGER: These to your majesty; this to the queen.

KING: From Hamlet! Who brought them?

MESSENGER: Sailors, my lord, they say. I saw them not.
They were given me by Claudio; he received them
Of him that brought them.

KING: Laertes, you shall hear them.—   40
Leave us.   [*Exit* MESSENGER.]
     [*Reads.*] "High and mighty, you shall know I am set naked on your king-
dom. Tomorrow shall I beg leave to see your kingly eyes; when I shall, first
asking your pardon thereunto, recount the occasion of my sudden and more
strange return.   45
                    Hamlet."
What should this mean? Are all the rest come back?
Or is it some abuse,² and no such thing?

LAERTES: Know you the hand?

KING: 'Tis Hamlet's character.³ "Naked"!   50
And in a postscript here, he says "alone."
Can you devise⁴ me?

LAERTES: I am lost in it, my lord. But let him come.
It warms the very sickness in my heart
That I shall live and tell him to his teeth   55
"Thus didest thou."

KING: If it be so, Laertes—
As how should it be so, how otherwise?—
Will you be ruled by me?

LAERTES: Ay, my lord,
So you will not o'errule me to a peace.

KING: To thine own peace. If he be now returned,   60
As checking at⁵ his voyage, and that he means
No more to undertake it, I will work him
To an exploit now ripe in my device,
Under the which he shall not choose but fall;
And for his death no wind of blame shall breathe   65
But even his mother shall uncharge⁶ the practice
And call it accident.

LAERTES: My lord, I will be ruled;
The rather if you could devise it so
That I might be the organ.⁷

KING: It falls right.
You have been talked of since your travel much,   70
And that in Hamlet's hearing, for a quality

---

2. Trick.   3. Handwriting.   4. Explain it to.   5. Turning aside from.   6. Not accuse.   7. Instrument.

Wherein they say you shine. Your sum of parts
Did not together pluck such envy from him
As did that one, and that, in my regard,
Of the unworthiest siege.[8]

75   LAERTES: What part is that, my lord?
KING: A very riband in the cap of youth,
     Yet needful too, for youth no less becomes
     The light and careless livery that it wears
     Than settled age his sables and his weeds,[9]
80   Importing health and graveness. Two months since
     Here was a gentleman of Normandy.
     I have seen myself, and served against, the French,
     And they can[1] well on horseback, but this gallant
     Had witchcraft in't. He grew unto his seat,
85   And to such wondrous doing brought his horse,
     As had he been incorpsed and demi-natured
     With the brave beast. So far he topped my thought
     That I, in forgery[2] of shapes and tricks,
     Come short of what he did.[3]
     LAERTES: A Norman was't?
90   KING: A Norman.
     LAERTES: Upon my life, Lamord.
     KING: The very same.
     LAERTES: I know him well. He is the brooch indeed
     And gem of all the nation.
     KING: He made confession[4] of you,
95   And gave you such a masterly report
     For art and exercise in your defence,[5]
     And for your rapier most especial,
     That he cried out 'twould be a sight indeed
     If one could match you. The scrimers[6] of their nation
100 He swore had neither motion, guard, nor eye,
     If you opposed them. Sir, this report of his
     Did Hamlet so envenom with his envy
     That he could nothing do but wish and beg
     Your sudden coming o'er, to play with you.
     Now out of this—
105 LAERTES: What out of this, my lord?
     KING: Laertes, was your father dear to you?

---

8. Rank.   9. Dignified clothing.   1. Perform.   2. Imagination.   3. The gentleman referred to
was so skilled in horsemanship that he seemed to share one body with the horse, "incorpsed." The king
further extends the compliment by saying that he appeared like the mythical centaur, a creature who
was man from the waist up and horse from the waist down, therefore "demi-natured."   4. Gave a
report.   5. Skill in fencing.   6. Fencers.

Or are you like the painting of a sorrow,
    A face without a heart?
LAERTES: Why ask you this?
KING: Not that I think you did not love your father,
    But that I know love is begun by time,   110
    And that I see in passages of proof,[7]
    Time qualifies the spark and fire of it.
    There lives within the very flame of love
    A kind of wick or snuff that will abate it,
    And nothing is at a like goodness still,   115
    For goodness, growing to a plurisy,[8]
    Dies in his own too much.[9] That we would do,
    We should do when we would; for this "would" changes,
    And hath abatements and delays as many
    As there are tongues, are hands, are accidents,   120
    And then this "should" is like a spendthrift's sigh
    That hurts by easing. But to the quick of th' ulcer—
    Hamlet comes back; what would you undertake
    To show yourself in deed your father's son
    More than in words?
LAERTES: To cut his throat i' th' church.   125
KING: No place indeed should murder sanctuarize;[1]
    Revenge should have no bounds. But, good Laertes,
    Will you do this? Keep close within your chamber.
    Hamlet returned shall know you are come home.
    We'll put on those shall praise your excellence,   130
    And set a double varnish[2] on the fame
    The Frenchman gave you, bring you in fine[3] together,
    And wager on your heads. He, being remiss,[4]
    Most generous, and free from all contriving,
    Will not peruse[5] the foils, so that with ease,   135
    Or with a little shuffling, you may choose
    A sword unbated,[6] and in a pass of practice
    Requite him for your father.
LAERTES: I will do't,
    And for that purpose I'll anoint my sword.
    I bought an unction of a mountebank   140
    So mortal that but dip a knife in it,
    Where it draws blood no cataplasm[7] so rare,
    Collected from all simples[8] that have virtue
    Under the moon, can save the thing from death
    That is but scratched withal. I'll touch my point   145

7. Tests of experience.   8. Fullness.   9. Excess.   1. Provide sanctuary for murder.   2. Gloss.
3. In short.   4. Careless.   5. Examine.   6. Not blunted.   7. Poultice.   8. Herbs.

With this contagion, that if I gall[9] him slightly,
It may be death.

KING: Let's further think of this,
Weigh what convenience both of time and means
May fit us to our shape. If this should fail,
150 And that our drift look[1] through our bad performance,
'Twere better not assayed. Therefore this project
Should have a back or second that might hold
If this did blast in proof.[2] Soft, let me see.
We'll make a solemn wager on your cunnings—
155 I ha't.
When in your motion you are hot and dry—
As make your bouts more violent to that end—
And that he calls for drink, I'll have preferred him
A chalice for the nonce, whereon but sipping,
160 If he by chance escape your venomed stuck,[3]
Our purpose may hold there.—But stay, what noise?

[*Enter* QUEEN.]

QUEEN: One woe doth tread upon another's heel,
So fast they follow. Your sister's drowned, Laertes.
LAERTES: Drowned? O, where?
165 QUEEN: There is a willow grows aslant the brook
That shows his hoar leaves in the glassy stream.
Therewith fantastic garlands did she make
Of crowflowers, nettles, daisies, and long purples
That liberal shepherds give a grosser[4] name,
170 But our cold[5] maids do dead men's fingers call them.
There on the pendent boughs her coronet weeds
Clamb'ring to hang, an envious[6] sliver broke,
When down her weedy trophies and herself
Fell in the weeping brook. Her clothes spread wide,
175 And mermaid-like awhile they bore her up,
Which time she chanted snatches of old tunes,
As one incapable[7] of her own distress,
Or like a creature native and indued[8]
Unto that element. But long it could not be
180 Till that her garments, heavy with their drink,
Pulled the poor wretch from her melodious lay
To muddy death.
LAERTES: Alas, then she is drowned?
QUEEN: Drowned, drowned.
LAERTES: Too much of water hast thou, poor Ophelia,

---

9. Scratch.   1. Intent become obvious.   2. Fail when tried.   3. Thrust.   4. Coarser. *Liberal:*
vulgar.   5. Chaste.   6. Malicious.   7. Unaware.   8. Habituated.

And therefore I forbid my tears; but yet 185
It is our trick; nature her custom holds,
Let shame say what it will. When these are gone,
The woman will be out. Adieu, my lord.
I have a speech o' fire that fain would blaze
But that this folly drowns it.   *[Exit.]*
KING: Let's follow, Gertrude. 190
How much I had to do to calm his rage!
Now fear I this will give it start again;
Therefore let's follow.   *[Exeunt.]*

ACT V

SCENE 1

A churchyard. Enter two CLOWNS.[9]

CLOWN: Is she to be buried in Christian burial when she wilfully seeks her own
salvation?

OTHER: I tell thee she is. Therefore make her grave straight. The crowner hath sat
on her,[1] and finds it Christian burial.

CLOWN: How can that be, unless she drowned herself in her own defence? 5

OTHER: Why, 'tis found so.

CLOWN: It must be "se offendendo";[2] it cannot be else. For here lies the point: if I
drown myself wittingly, it argues an act, and an act hath three branches—it
is to act, to do, to perform; argal,[3] she drowned herself wittingly.

OTHER: Nay, but hear you, Goodman Delver. 10

CLOWN: Give me leave. Here lies the water; good. Here stands the man; good. If
the man go to this water and drown himself, it is, will he, nill he, he goes—
mark you that. But if the water come to him and drown him, he drowns not
himself. Argal, he that is not guilty of his own death shortens not his own
life. 15

OTHER: But is this law?

CLOWN: Ay, marry, is't; crowner's quest[4] law.

OTHER: Will you ha' the truth on't? If this had not been a gentle woman, she
should have been buried out o' Christian burial.

CLOWN: Why, there thou say'st. And the more pity that great folk should have 20
count'nance[5] in this world to drown or hang themselves more than their
even-Christen.[6] Come, my spade. There is no ancient gentlemen but
gard'ners, ditchers, and grave-makers. They hold up Adam's profession.

OTHER: Was he a gentleman?

CLOWN: 'A was the first that ever bore arms. 25

OTHER: Why, he had none.

9. Rustics.   1. Held an inquest. *Crowner:* coroner.   2. An error for *se defendendo,* in self-defense.
3. Therefore.   4. Inquest.   5. Approval.   6. Fellow Christians.

CLOWN: What, art a heathen? How dost thou understand the Scripture? The Scripture says Adam digged. Could he dig without arms? I'll put another question to thee. If thou answerest me not to the purpose, confess thyself—

OTHER: Go to.

CLOWN: What is he that builds stronger than either the mason, the shipwright, or the carpenter?

OTHER: The gallows-maker, for that frame outlives a thousand tenants.

CLOWN: I like thy wit well, in good faith. The gallows does well. But how does it well? It does well to those that do ill. Now thou dost ill to say the gallows is built stronger than the church. Argal, the gallows may do well to thee. To't again,[7] come.

OTHER: Who builds stronger than a mason, a shipwright, or a carpenter?

CLOWN: Ay tell me that, and unyoke.[8]

OTHER: Marry, now I can tell.

CLOWN: To't.

OTHER: Mass, I cannot tell.

CLOWN: Cudgel thy brains no more about it, for your dull ass will not mend his pace with beating. And when you are asked this question next, say "a grave maker." The houses he makes lasts till doomsday. Go, get thee in, and fetch me a stoup[9] of liquor.   [*Exit* OTHER CLOWN.]

[*Enter* HAMLET *and* HORATIO *as* CLOWN *digs and sings.*]

In youth, when I did love, did love,
    Methought it was very sweet,
To contract the time for-a my behove,[1]
    O, methought there-a was nothing-a meet.[2]

HAMLET: Has this fellow no feeling of his business, that 'a sings in grave-making?

HORATIO: Custom hath made it in him a property of easiness.

HAMLET: 'Tis e'en so. The hand of little employment hath the daintier sense.

[CLOWN *sings.*]

But age, with his stealing steps,
    Hath clawed me in his clutch,
And hath shipped me into the land,
    As if I had never been such.

[*Throws up a skull.*]

HAMLET: That skull had a tongue in it, and could sing once. How the knave jowls[3] it to the ground, as if 'twere Cain's jawbone, that did the first murder! This might be the pate of a politician, which this ass now o'erreaches;[4] one that would circumvent God, might it not?

7. Guess again.   8. Finish the matter.   9. Mug.   1. Advantage. *Contract:* shorten.   2. The gravedigger's song is a free version of "The aged lover renounceth love" by Thomas, Lord Vaux, published in *Tottel's Miscellany,* 1557. —3. Hurls.   4. Gets the better of.

HORATIO: It might, my lord.

HAMLET: Or of a courtier, which could say, "Good morrow, sweet lord! How does thou, sweet lord?" This might be my Lord Such-a-one, that praised my Lord Such-a-one's horse, when 'a meant to beg it, might it not? 65

HORATIO: Ay, my lord.

HAMLET: Why, e'en so, and now my Lady Worm's, chapless,[5] and knock'd abut the mazzard[6] with a sexton's spade. Here's fine revolution,[7] an we had the trick to see't. Did these bones cost no more the breeding but to play at loggets with them?[8] Mine ache to think on't. 70

[CLOWN *sings*.]

A pick-axe and a spade, a spade,
　For and a shrouding sheet:
O, a pit of clay for to be made
　For such a guest is meet.

[*Throws up another skull.*]

HAMLET: There's another. Why may not that be the skull of a lawyer? Where be 75 his quiddities now, his quillets, his cases, his tenures, and his tricks? Why does he suffer this mad knave now to knock him about the sconce[9] with a dirty shovel, and will not tell him of his action of battery? Hum! This fellow might be in's time a great buyer of land, with his statutes, his recognizances, his fines, his double vouchers, his recoveries. Is this the fine[1] of his fines, 80 and the recovery of his recoveries, to have his fine pate full of fine dirt? Will his vouchers vouch him no more of his purchases, and double ones too, than the length and breadth of a pair of indentures?[2] The very conveyances of his lands will scarcely lie in this box, and must th' inheritor himself have no more, ha?[3] 85

HORATIO: Not a jot more, my lord.

HAMLET: Is not parchment made of sheepskins?

HORATIO: Ay, my lord, and of calves' skins too.

HAMLET: They are sheep and calves which seek out assurance in that. I will speak to this fellow. Whose grave's this, sirrah? 90

CLOWN: Mine, sir.

[*Sings.*]

O, a pit of clay for to be made—

HAMLET: I think it be thine indeed, for thou liest in't.

CLOWN: You lie out on't, sir, and therefore 'tis not yours. For my part, I do not lie in't, yet it is mine. 95

HAMLET: Thou dost lie in't, to be in't and say it is thine. 'Tis for the dead, not for the quick;[4] therefore thou liest.

---

5. Lacking a lower jaw.　6. Head.　7. Skill.　8. "Loggets" were small pieces of wood thrown as part of a game.　9. Head.　1. End.　2. Contracts.　3. In this speech Hamlet reels off a list of legal terms relating to property transactions.　4. Living.

CLOWN: 'Tis a quick lie, sir; 'twill away again from me to you.

HAMLET: What man dost thou dig it for?

100 CLOWN: For no man, sir.

HAMLET: What woman, then?

CLOWN: For none neither.

HAMLET: Who is to be buried in't?

CLOWN: One that was a woman, sir; but, rest her soul, she's dead.

105 HAMLET: How absolute the knave is! We must speak by the card,[5] or equivocation will undo us. By the Lord, Horatio, this three years I have took note of it, the age is grown so picked[6] that the toe of the peasant comes so near the heel of the courtier, he galls his kibe.[7] How long hast thou been a grave-maker?

CLOWN: Of all the days i' th' year, I came to't that day that our last King Hamlet

110 overcame Fortinbras.

HAMLET: How long is that since?

CLOWN: Cannot you tell that? Every fool can tell that. It was that very day that young Hamlet was born—he that is mad, and sent into England.

HAMLET: Ay, marry, why was he sent into England?

115 CLOWN: Why, because 'a was mad. 'A shall recover his wits there; or, if 'a do not, 'tis no great matter there.

HAMLET: Why?

CLOWN: 'Twill not be seen in him there. There the men are as mad as he.

HAMLET: How came he mad?

120 CLOWN: Very strangely, they say.

HAMLET: How strangely?

CLOWN: Faith, e'en with losing his wits.

HAMLET: Upon what ground?

CLOWN: Why, here in Denmark. I have been sexton here, man and boy, thirty

125 years.

HAMLET: How long will a man lie i' th' earth ere he rot?

CLOWN: Faith, if 'a be not rotten before 'a die—as we have many pocky[8] corses now-a-days that will scarce hold the laying in—'a will last you some eight year or nine year. A tanner will last you nine year.

130 HAMLET: Why he more than another?

CLOWN: Why, sir, his hide is so tanned with his trade that 'a will keep out water a great while; and your water is a sore decayer of your whoreson dead body. Here's a skull now hath lien[9] you i' th' earth three and twenty years.

HAMLET: Whose was it?

135 CLOWN: A whoreson mad fellow's it was. Whose do you think it was?

HAMLET: Nay, I know not.

CLOWN: A pestilence on him for a mad rogue! 'A poured a flagon of Rhenish on my head once. This same skull, sir, was, sir, Yorick's skull, the king's jester.

HAMLET: [*Takes the skull.*] This?

140 CLOWN: E'en that.

---

5. Exactly. *Absolute:* precise. 6. Refined. 7. Rubs a blister on his heel. 8. Corrupted by syphilis.
9. Lain. *Whoreson:* bastard (not literally).

HAMLET: Alas, poor Yorick! I knew him, Horatio—a fellow of infinite jest, of most excellent fancy. He hath bore me on his back a thousand times, and now how abhorred in my imagination it is! My gorge[1] rises at it. Here hung those lips that I have kissed I know not how oft. Where be your gibes now, your gambols, your songs, your flashes of merriment that were wont to set   145
the table on a roar? Not one now to mock your own grinning? Quite chap-fall'n?[2] Now get you to my lady's chamber, and tell her, let her paint an inch thick, to this favor[3] she must come. Make her laugh at that. Prithee, Horatio, tell me one thing.

HORATIO: What's that, my lord?   150

HAMLET: Dost thou think Alexander looked o' this fashion i' th' earth?

HORATIO: E'en so.

HAMLET: And smelt so? Pah!   [*Throws down the skull.*]

HORATIO: E'en so, my lord.

HAMLET: To what base uses we may return, Horatio! Why may not imagination   155
trace the noble dust of Alexander till 'a find it stopping a bung-hole?

HORATIO: 'Twere to consider too curiously[4] to consider so.

HAMLET: No, faith, not a jot, but to follow him thither with modesty[5] enough, and likelihood to lead it. Alexander died, Alexander was buried, Alexander returneth to dust; the dust is earth; of earth we make loam; and why   160
of that loam whereto he was converted might they not stop a beerbarrel?

> Imperious Cæsar, dead and turned to clay,
> Might stop a hole to keep the wind away.
> O, that that earth which kept the world in awe
> Should patch a wall t'expel the winter's flaw![6]   165

But soft, but soft awhile! Here comes the king,
The queen, the courtiers.

[*Enter* KING, QUEEN, LAERTES, *and the Corse with a* PRIEST *and* LORDS *attendant.*]

                    Who is this they follow?
And with such maiméd[7] rites? This doth betoken
The corse they follow did with desperate hand
Fordo it own life. 'Twas of some estate.[8]   170
Couch[9] we awhile and mark.   [*Retires with* HORATIO.]

LAERTES: What ceremony else?[1]

HAMLET: That is Laertes, a very noble youth. Mark.

LAERTES: What ceremony else?

PRIEST: Here obsequies have been as far enlarged[2]   175
As we have warranty. Her death was doubtful,
And but that great command o'ersways the order,[3]

---

1. Throat.   2. Lacking a lower jaw.   3. Appearance.   4. Precisely.   5. Moderation.   6. Gusty wind.   7. Cut short.   8. Rank. *Fordo:* destroy.   9. Conceal ourselves.   1. More.   2. Extended. 3. Usual rules.

She should in ground unsanctified been lodged
Till the last trumpet. For charitable prayers,
180   Shards, flints, and pebbles, should be thrown on her.
Yet here she is allowed her virgin crants,⁴
Her maiden strewments,⁵ and the bringing home
Of bell and burial.
LAERTES: Must there no more be done?
PRIEST: No more be done.
185   We should profane the service of the dead
To sing a requiem and such rest to her
As to peace-parted souls.
LAERTES: Lay her i' th' earth,
And from her fair and unpolluted flesh
May violets spring! I tell thee, churlish priest,
190   A minist'ring angel shall my sister be
When thou liest howling.⁶
HAMLET: What, the fair Ophelia!
QUEEN: Sweets to the sweet. Farewell!   [Scatters flowers.]
I hoped thou shouldst have been my Hamlet's wife.
I thought thy bride-bed to have decked, sweet maid,
And not have strewed thy grave.
195   LAERTES: O, treble woe
Fall ten times treble on that curséd head
Whose wicked deed thy most ingenious sense⁷
Deprived thee of! Hold off the earth awhile,
Till I have caught her once more in mine arms.   [Leaps into the grave.]
200   Now pile your dust upon the quick and dead,
Till of this flat a mountain you have made
T' o'er-top old Pelion or the skyish head
Of blue Olympus.⁸
HAMLET: [Coming forward.] What is he whose grief
205   Bears such an emphasis, whose phrase of sorrow
Conjures⁹ the wand'ring stars, and makes them stand
Like wonder-wounded hearers? This is I,
Hamlet the Dane.

   [HAMLET leaps into the grave and they grapple.]

LAERTES: The devil take thy soul!
HAMLET: Thou pray'st not well.

---

4. Wreaths.   5. Flowers strewn on the grave.   6. In Hell.   7. Lively mind.   8. The rivalry
between Laertes and Hamlet in this scene extends even to their rhetoric. Pelion and Olympus, mentioned here by Laertes, and Ossa, mentioned below by Hamlet, are Greek mountains noted in mythology for their height. Olympus was the reputed home of the gods, and the other two were piled one on
top of the other by the Giants in an attempt to reach the top of Olympus and overthrow the gods.
9. Casts a spell on.

I prithee take thy fingers from my throat,   210
For though I am not splenitive[1] and rash,
Yet have I in me something dangerous,
Which let thy wisdom fear. Hold off thy hand.
KING: Pluck them asunder.
QUEEN: Hamlet! Hamlet!   215
ALL: Gentlemen!
HORATIO: Good my lord, be quiet.

    [*The* ATTENDANTS *part them, and they come out of the grave.*]

HAMLET: Why, I will fight with him upon this theme
  Until my eyelids will no longer wag.[2]
QUEEN: O my son, what theme?   220
HAMLET: I loved Ophelia. Forty thousand brothers
  Could not with all their quantity of love
  Make up my sum. What wilt thou do for her?
KING: O, he is mad, Laertes.
QUEEN: For love of God, forbear[3] him.   225
HAMLET: 'Swounds, show me what th'owt do.
  Woo't[4] weep, woo't fight, woo't fast, woo't tear thyself,
  Woo't drink up eisel,[5] eat a crocodile?
  I'll do't. Dost come here to whine?
  To outface[6] me with leaping in her grave?   230
  Be buried quick with her, and so will I.
  And if thou prate of mountains, let them throw
  Millions of acres on us, till our ground,
  Singeing his pate against the burning zone,[7]
  Make Ossa like a wart! Nay, an thou'lt mouth,   235
  I'll rant as well as thou.
QUEEN: This is mere madness;
  And thus awhile the fit will work on him.
  Anon, as patient as the female dove
  When that her golden couplets[8] are disclosed,
  His silence will sit drooping.
HAMLET: Hear you, sir.   240
  What is the reason that you use me thus?
  I loved you ever. But it is no matter.
  Let Hercules himself do what he may,
  The cat will mew, and dog will have his day.
KING: I pray thee, good Horatio, wait upon[9] him.   245

    [*Exeunt* HAMLET *and* HORATIO.]

---

1. Hot-tempered.   2. Move.   3. Bear with.   4. Will you.   5. Vinegar.   6. Get the best of.
7. Sky in the torrid zone.   8. Pair of eggs.   9. Attend.

[*To* LAERTES.] Strengthen your patience in our last night's speech.
We'll put the matter to the present push.[1]—
Good Gertrude, set some watch over your son.—
This grave shall have a living monument.
250   An hour of quiet shortly shall we see;
Till then in patience our proceeding be.   [*Exeunt.*]

Scene 2

A hall or public room. Enter HAMLET *and* HORATIO.

HAMLET: So much for this, sir; now shall you see the other.
    You do remember all the circumstance?
HORATIO: Remember it, my lord!
HAMLET: Sir, in my heart there was a kind of fighting
5   That would not let me sleep. Methought I lay
    Worse than the mutines in the bilboes.[2] Rashly,
    And praised be rashness for it—let us know,
    Our indiscretion sometime serves us well,
    When our deep plots do pall; and that should learn[3] us
10   There's a divinity that shapes our ends,
    Rough-hew them how we will—
HORATIO: That is most certain.
HAMLET: Up from my cabin,
    My sea-gown scarfed[4] about me, in the dark
    Groped I to find out them, had my desire,
15   Fingered their packet, and in fine[5] withdrew
    To mine own room again, making so bold,
    My fears forgetting manners, to unseal
    Their grand commission; where I found, Horatio—
    Ah, royal knavery!—an exact[6] command,
20   Larded[7] with many several sorts of reasons,
    Importing Denmark's health, and England's too,
    With, ho! such bugs and goblins in my life,[8]
    That on the supervise,[9] no leisure bated,
    No, not to stay the grinding of the axe,
    My head should be struck off.
25 HORATIO: Is't possible?
HAMLET: Here's the commission; read it at more leisure.
    But wilt thou hear now how I did proceed?
HORATIO: I beseech you.
HAMLET: Being thus benetted[1] round with villainies,

---

1. Immediate trial.   2. Stocks. *Mutines:* mutineers.   3. Teach.   4. Wrapped.   5. Quickly. *Fin-gered:* stole.   6. Precisely stated.   7. Garnished.   8. Such dangers if I remained alive.   9. As soon as the commission was read.   1. Caught in a net.

Or I could make a prologue to my brains,   30
They had begun the play. I sat me down,
Devised a new commission, wrote it fair.[2]
I once did hold it, as our statists[3] do,
A baseness to write fair, and labored much
How to forget that learning; but sir, now   35
It did me yeoman's service. Wilt thou know
Th' effect[4] of what I wrote?
HORATIO: Ay, good my lord.
HAMLET: An earnest conjuration from the king,
   As England was his faithful tributary,[5]
   As love between them like the palm might flourish,   40
   As peace should still her wheaten garland wear
   And stand a comma 'tween their amities[6]
   And many such like as's of great charge,[7]
   That on the view and knowing of these contents,
   Without debatement[8] further more or less,   45
   He should those bearers put to sudden death,
   Not shriving-time allowed.[9]
HORATIO: How was this sealed?
HAMLET: Why, even in that was heaven ordinant,[1]
   I had my father's signet in my purse,
   Which was the model of that Danish seal,   50
   Folded the writ up in the form of th' other,
   Subscribed it, gave't th' impression,[2] placed it safely,
   The changeling[3] never known. Now, the next day
   Was our sea-fight, and what to this was sequent[4]
   Thou knowest already.   55
HORATIO: So Guildenstern and Rosencrantz go to't.
HAMLET: Why, man, they did make love to this employment.
   They are not near my conscience; their defeat[5]
   Does by their own insinuation grow.
   'Tis dangerous when the baser nature comes   60
   Between the pass and fell[6] incenséd points
   Of mighty opposites.
HORATIO: Why, what a king is this!
HAMLET: Does it not, think thee, stand me now upon—
   He that hath killed my king and whored my mother,
   Popped in between th' election and my hopes,   65
   Thrown out his angle[7] for my proper life,
   And with such coz'nage[8]—is't not perfect conscience
   To quit[9] him with this arm? And is't not be be damned

---

2. Legibly. *Devised:* made.   3. Politicians.   4. Contents.   5. Vassal.   6. Link friendships.
7. Import.   8. Consideration.   9. Without time for confession.   1. Operative.   2. Of the seal.
3. Alteration.   4. Followed.   5. Death. *Are not near:* do not touch.   6. Cruel. *Pass:* thrust.
7. Fishhook.   8. Trickery.   9. Repay.

To let this canker of our nature come
70   In further evil?
HORATIO: It must be shortly known to him from England
      What is the issue[1] of the business there.
HAMLET: It will be short;[2] the interim is mine.
      And a man's life's no more than to say "one."
75   But I am very sorry, good Horatio,
      That to Laertes I forgot myself;
      For by the image of my cause I see
      The portraiture of his. I'll court his favors.
      But sure the bravery[3] of his grief did put me
      Into a tow'ring passion.
80   HORATIO: Peace; who comes here?

      [*Enter* OSRIC.]

OSRIC: Your lordship is right welcome back to Denmark.
HAMLET: I humbly thank you, sir. [*Aside to* HORATIO.] Dost know this water-fly?
HORATIO: [*Aside to* HAMLET.] No, my good lord.
HAMLET: [*Aside to* HORATIO.] Thy state is the more gracious, for 'tis a vice to
85   know him. He hath much land, and fertile. Let a beast be lord of beasts, and
      his crib shall stand at the king's mess. 'Tis a chough,[4] but as I say, spacious
      in the possession of dirt.
OSRIC: Sweet lord, if your lordship were at leisure, I should impart a thing to you
      from his majesty.
90   HAMLET: I will receive it, sir, with all diligence of spirit. Put your bonnet to his
      right use. 'Tis for the head.
OSRIC: I thank your lordship, it is very hot.
HAMLET: No, believe me, 'tis very cold; the wind is northerly.
OSRIC: It is indifferent[5] cold, my lord, indeed.
95   HAMLET: But yet methinks it is very sultry and hot for my complexion.[6]
OSRIC: Exceedingly, my lord; it is very sultry, as 'twere—I cannot tell how. My
      lord, his majesty bade me signify to you that 'a has laid a great wager on
      your head. Sir, this is the matter—
HAMLET: I beseech you, remember.   [*Moves him to put on his hat.*]
100   OSRIC: Nay, good my lord; for my ease, in good faith. Sir, here is newly come
      to court Laertes; believe me, an absolute[7] gentleman, full of most excellent
      differences,[8] of very soft society and great showing.[9] Indeed, to speak feel-
      ingly of him, he is the card or calendar of gentry, for you shall find in him
      the continent[1] of what part a gentleman would see.
105   HAMLET: Sir, his definement[2] suffers no perdition in you, though I know to divide
      him inventorially would dozy[3] th' arithmetic of memory, and yet but yaw[4]
      neither in respect of his quick sail. But in the verity of extolment, I take him

---

1. Outcome.   2. Soon.   3. Exaggerated display.   4. Jackdaw.   5. Moderately.   6. Temperament.   7. Perfect.   8. Qualities.   9. Good manners.   1. Sum total. *Calendar:* measure.   2. Description.   3. Daze. *Divide him inventorially:* examine bit by bit.   4. Steer wildly.

to be a soul of great article,[5] and his infusion[6] of such dearth and rareness as, to make true diction of him, his semblage[7] is his mirror, and who else would trace him, his umbrage,[8] nothing more. 110

OSRIC: Your lordship speaks most infallibly of him.

HAMLET: The concernancy,[9] sir? Why do we wrap the gentleman in our more rawer breath?[1]

OSRIC: Sir?

HORATIO: Is't not possible to understand in another tongue? You will to't, sir, really. 115

HAMLET: What imports the nomination[2] of this gentleman?

OSRIC: Of Laertes?

HORATIO: [*Aside.*] His purse is empty already. All's golden words are spent.

HAMLET: Of him, sir. 120

OSRIC: I know you are not ignorant—

HAMLET: I would you did, sir; yet, in faith, if you did, it would not much approve me. Well, sir.

OSRIC: You are not ignorant of what excellence Laertes is—

HAMLET: I dare not confess that, lest I should compare[3] with him in excellence; 125 but to know a man well were to know himself.

OSRIC: I mean, sir, for his weapon; but in the imputation[4] laid on him by them, in his meed he's unfellowed.[5]

HAMLET: What's his weapon?

OSRIC: Rapier and dagger.

HAMLET: That's two of his weapons—but well. 130

OSRIC: The king, sir, hath wagered with him six Barbary horses, against the which he has impawned,[6] as I take it, six French rapiers and poniards, with their assigns,[7] as girdle, hangers, and so. Three of the carriages, in faith, are very dear to fancy,[8] very responsive to the hilts, most delicate carriages, and 135 of very liberal conceit.[9]

HAMLET: What call you the carriages?

HORATIO: [*Aside to* HAMLET.] I knew you must be edified by the margent[1] ere you had done.

OSRIC: The carriages, sir, are the hangers. 140

HAMLET: The phrase would be more germane to the matter if we could carry a cannon by our sides. I would it might be hangers till then. But on! Six Barbary horses against six French swords, their assigns, and three liberal conceited carriages; that's the French bet against the Danish. Why is this all impawned, as you call it? 145

OSRIC: The king, sir, hath laid, sir, that in a dozen passes between yourself and him he shall not exceed you three hits; he hath laid on twelve for nine, and it

---

5. Scope.   6. Nature.   7. Rival. *Diction:* telling.   8. Shadow. *Trace:* keep pace with.   9. Meaning.   1. Cruder words.   2. Naming.   3. That is, compare myself.   4. Reputation.   5. Unequaled in his excellence.   6. Staked.   7. Appurtenances.   8. Finely designed.   9. Elegant design. *Delicate:* well adjusted.   1. Marginal gloss.

would come to immediate trial if your lordship would vouchsafe the answer.

HAMLET: How if I answer no?

150 OSRIC: I mean, my lord, the opposition of your person in trial.

HAMLET: Sir, I will walk here in the hall. If it please his majesty, it is the breathing time[2] of day with me. Let the foils be brought, the gentleman willing, and the king hold his purpose; I will win for him an I can. If not, I will gain nothing but my shame and the odd hits.

155 OSRIC: Shall I deliver you so?

HAMLET: To this effect, sir, after what flourish your nature will.

OSRIC: I commend my duty to your lordship.

HAMLET: Yours, yours. [*Exit* OSRIC.] He does well to commend it himself; there are no tongues else for's turn.

160 HORATIO: This lapwing runs away with the shell on his head.[3]

HAMLET: 'A did comply, sir, with his dug[4] before 'a sucked it. Thus has he, and many more of the same bevy that I know the drossy age dotes on, only got the tune of the time; and out of an habit of encounter, a king of yesty[5] collection which carries them through and through the most fanned and win-

165 nowed opinions; and do but blow them to their trial, the bubbles are out.

> [*Enter a* LORD.]

LORD: My lord, his majesty commended him to you by young Osric, who brings back to him that you attend[6] him in the hall. He sends to know if your pleasure hold to play with Laertes, or that you will take longer time.

HAMLET: I am constant to my purposes; they follow the king's pleasure. If his

170 fitness speaks, mine is ready; now or whensoever, provided I be so able as now.

LORD: The king and queen and all are coming down.

HAMLET: In happy time.

LORD: The queen desires you to use some gentle entertainment[7] to Laertes

175 before you fall to play.

HAMLET: She well instructs me. [*Exit* LORD.]

HORATIO: You will lose this wager, my lord.

HAMLET: I do not think so. Since he went into France I have been in continual practice. I shall win at the odds. But thou wouldst not think how ill[8] all's

180 here about my heart. But it's no matter.

HORATIO: Nay, good my lord—

HAMLET: It is but foolery, but it is such a kind of gaingiving[9] as would perhaps trouble a woman.

HORATIO: If your mind dislike anything, obey it. I will forestall their repair[1]

185 hither, and say you are not fit.

---

2. Time for exercise.   3. The lapwing was thought to be so precocious that it could run immediately after being hatched, even, as here, with bits of the shell still on its head.   4. Mother's breast. *Comply:* deal formally.   5. Yeasty.   6. Await.   7. Cordiality.   8. Uneasy.   9. Misgiving.   1. Coming.

HAMLET: Not a whit, we defy augury. There is special providence in the fall of a
sparrow. If it be now, 'tis not to come; if it be not to come, it will be now; if
it be not now, yet it will come. The readiness is all. Since no man of aught
he leaves knows, what is't to leave betimes? Let be.

[*A table prepared. Enter* TRUMPETS, DRUMS, *and* OFFICERS *with cushions;* KING,
QUEEN, OSRIC *and* ATTENDANTS *with foils, daggers, and* LAERTES.]

KING: Come, Hamlet, come and take this hand from me.   190

[*The* KING *puts* LAERTES' *hand into* HAMLET's.]

HAMLET: Give me your pardon, sir. I have done you wrong,
But pardon 't as you are a gentleman.
This presence[2] knows, and you must needs have heard,
How I am punished with a sore distraction.
What I have done   195
That might your nature, honor, and exception,[3]
Roughly awake, I here proclaim was madness.
Was 't Hamlet wronged Laertes? Never Hamlet.
If Hamlet from himself be ta'en away,
And when he's not himself does wrong Laertes,   200
Then Hamlet does it not, Hamlet denies it.
Who does it then? His madness. If't be so,
Hamlet is of the faction that is wronged;
His madness is poor Hamlet's enemy.
Sir, in this audience,   205
Let my disclaiming from[4] a purposed evil
Free[5] me so far in your most generous thoughts
That I have shot my arrow o'er the house
And hurt my brother.
LAERTES: I am satisfied in nature,
Whose motive in this case should stir me most   210
To my revenge. But in my terms of honor
I stand aloof, and will no reconcilement
Till by some elder masters of known honor
I have a voice[6] and precedent of peace
To keep my name ungored.[7] But till that time   215
I do receive your offered love like love,
And will not wrong it.
HAMLET: I embrace it freely,
And will this brother's wager frankly[8] play.
Give us the foils.
LAERTES: Come, one for me.
HAMLET: I'll be your foil, Laertes. In mine ignorance   220

2. Company.   3. Resentment.   4. Denying of.   5. Absolve.   6. Authority.   7. Unshamed.
8. Without rancor.

Your skill shall, like a star i' th' darkest night,
  Stick fiery off[9] indeed.
LAERTES: You mock me, sir.
HAMLET: No, by this hand.
KING: Give them the foils, young Osric. Cousin Hamlet,
  You know the wager?

225   HAMLET: Very well, my lord;
  Your Grace has laid the odds o' th' weaker side.
KING: I do not fear it, I have seen you both;
  But since he is bettered[1] we have therefore odds.
LAERTES: This is too heavy; let me see another.

230   HAMLET: This likes me well. These foils have all a[2] length?

    [*They prepare to play.*]

OSRIC: Ay, my good lord.
KING: Set me the stoups of wine upon that table.
  If Hamlet give the first or second hit,
  Or quit in answer of[3] the third exchange,

235   Let all the battlements their ordnance fire.
  The king shall drink to Hamlet's better breath,
  And in the cup an union[4] shall he throw,
  Richer than that which four successive kings
  In Denmark's crown have worn. Give me the cups,

240   And let the kettle[5] to the trumpet speak,
  The trumpet to the cannoneer without,
  The cannons to the heavens, the heaven to earth,
  "Now the king drinks to Hamlet." Come, begin—

    [*Trumpets the while.*]

  And you, the judges, bear a wary eye.
HAMLET: Come on, sir.
LAERTES: Come, my lord.

    [*They play.*]

HAMLET: One.
LAERTES: No.
245   HAMLET: Judgment?
OSRIC: A hit, a very palpable hit.

    [*Drums, trumpets, and shot. Flourish; a piece goes off.*]

LAERTES: Well, again.
KING: Stay, give me drink. Hamlet, this pearl is thine.
  Here's to thy health. Give him the cup.

---

9. Shine brightly.   1. Reported better.   2. The same. *Likes:* suits.   3. Repay.   4. Pearl.
5. Kettledrum.

HAMLET: I'll play this bout first; set it by awhile.   250
  Come.

      [*They play.*]

  Another hit; what say you?
LAERTES: I do confess't.
KING: Our son shall win.
QUEEN: He's fat,[6] and scant of breath.
  Here, Hamlet, take my napkin, rub thy brows.   255
  The queen carouses to thy fortune, Hamlet.
HAMLET: Good madam!
KING: Gertrude, do not drink.
QUEEN: I will, my lord; I pray you pardon me.
KING: [*Aside.*] It is the poisoned cup; it is too late.   260
HAMLET: I dare not drink yet, madam; by and by.
QUEEN: Come, let me wipe thy face.
LAERTES: My lord, I'll hit him now.
KING: I do not think't.
LAERTES: [*Aside.*] And yet it is almost against my conscience.
HAMLET: Come, for the third, Laertes. You do but dally.   265
  I pray you pass[7] with your best violence;
  I am afeard you make a wanton of me.[8]
LAERTES: Say you so? Come on.

      [*They play.*]

OSRIC: Nothing, neither way.
LAERTES: Have at you now!   270

      [LAERTES *wounds* HAMLET: *then, in scuffling, they change rapiers, and* HAMLET
      wounds LAERTES.]

KING: Part them. They are incensed.
HAMLET: Nay, come again.

      [*The* QUEEN *falls.*]

OSRIC: Look to the queen there, ho!
HORATIO: They bleed on both sides. How is it, my lord?
OSRIC: How is't, Laertes?   275
LAERTES: Why, as a woodcock to mine own springe,[9] Osric.
  I am justly killed with mine own treachery.
HAMLET: How does the queen?
KING: She swoons to see them bleed.
QUEEN: No, no, the drink, the drink! O my dear Hamlet!
  The drink, the drink! I am poisoned.   [*Dies.*]   280

6. Out of shape.   7. Attack.   8. Trifle with me.   9. Snare.

HAMLET: O, villainy! Ho! let the door be locked.
    Treachery! seek it out.
LAERTES: It is here, Hamlet. Hamlet, thou art slain;
    No med'cine in the world can do thee good.
285   In thee there is not half an hour's life.
    The treacherous instrument is in thy hand,
    Unbated[1] and envenomed. The foul practice
    Hath turned itself on me. Lo, here I lie,
    Never to rise again. Thy mother's poisoned.
290   I can no more. The king, the king's to blame.
HAMLET: The point envenomed too?
    Then, venom, to thy work.   [*Hurts the* KING.]
ALL: Treason! treason!
KING: O, yet defend me, friends. I am but hurt.[2]
295 HAMLET: Here, thou incestuous, murd'rous, damnéd Dane,
    Drink off this potion. Is thy union here?
    Follow my mother.

        [*The* KING *dies.*]

LAERTES: He is justly served.
    It is a poison tempered[3] by himself.
    Exchange forgiveness with me, noble Hamlet.
300   Mine and my father's death come not upon thee,
    Nor thine on me!   [*Dies.*]
HAMLET: Heaven make thee free of[4] it! I follow thee.
    I am dead, Horatio. Wretched queen, adieu!
    You that look pale and tremble at this chance,[5]
305   That are but mutes or audience to this act,
    Had I but time, as this fell sergeant Death
    Is strict in his arrest,[6] O, I could tell you—
    But let it be. Horatio, I am dead:
    Thou livest; report me and my cause aright
    To the unsatisfied.[7]
310 HORATIO: Never believe it.
    I am more an antique Roman than a Dane.
    Here's yet some liquor left.
HAMLET: As th'art a man,
    Give me the cup. Let go. By heaven, I'll ha't.
    O God, Horatio, what a wounded name,
315   Things standing thus unknown, shall live behind me!
    If thou didst ever hold me in thy heart,
    Absent thee from felicity awhile,

---

1. Unblunted.   2. Wounded.   3. Mixed.   4. Forgive.   5. Circumstance.   6. Summons to court.   7. Uninformed.

And in this harsh world draw thy breath in pain,
To tell my story.

        [*A march afar off.*]

                What warlike noise is this?
OSRIC: Young Fortinbras, with conquest come from Poland,   320
  To th' ambassadors of England gives
  This warlike volley.[8]
HAMLET: O, I die, Horatio!
  The potent poison quite o'er-crows[9] my spirit.
  I cannot live to hear the news from England,
  But I do prophesy th' election lights   325
  On Fortinbras. He has my dying voice.[1]
  So tell him, with th' occurrents,[2] more and less,
  Which have solicited[3]—the rest is silence.   [*Dies.*]
HORATIO: Now cracks a noble heart. Good night, sweet prince,
  And flights of angels sing thee to thy rest!   330

        [*March within.*]

  Why does the drum come hither?

        [*Enter* FORTINBRAS, *with the* AMBASSADORS *and with drum, colors, and* ATTEN-
        DANTS.]

FORTINBRAS: Where is this sight?
HORATIO: What is it you would see?
  If aught of woe or wonder, cease your search.
FORTINBRAS: This quarry cries on havoc.[4] O proud death,
  What feast is toward[5] in thine eternal cell   335
  That thou so many princes at a shot
  So bloodily hast struck?
AMBASSADORS: The sight is dismal;
  And our affairs from England come too late.
  The ears are senseless[6] that should give us hearing
  To tell him his commandment is fulfilled,   340
  That Rosencrantz and Guildenstern are dead.
  Where should we have our thanks?
HORATIO: Not from his mouth,
  Had it th' ability of life to thank you.
  He never gave commandment for their death.
  But since, so jump[7] upon this bloody question,   345

8. The staging presents some difficulties here. Unless Osric is clairvoyant, he must have left the stage at
some point and returned. One possibility is that he might have left to carry out Hamlet's order to lock
the door (line 281) and returned when the sound of the distant march is heard.   9. Overcomes.
1. Support.   2. Circumstances.   3. Brought about this scene.   4. The game killed in the hunt
proclaims a slaughter.   5. In preparation.   6. Without sense of hearing.   7. Exactly.

You from the Polack wars, and you from England,
Are here arrived, give orders that these bodies
High on a stage be placed to the view,
And let me speak to th' yet unknowing world
350   How these things came about. So shall you hear
Of carnal, bloody, and unnatural acts;
Of accidental judgments, casual[8] slaughters;
Of deaths put on by cunning and forced cause;
And, in this upshot,[9] purposes mistook
355   Fall'n on th' inventors' heads. All this can I
Truly deliver.
FORTINBRAS: Let us haste to hear it,
And call the noblest to the audience.[1]
For me, with sorrow I embrace my fortune.
I have some rights of memory[2] in this kingdom,
360   Which now to claim my vantage[3] doth invite me.
HORATIO: Of that I shall have also cause to speak,
And from his mouth whose voice will draw on more.
But let this same be presently performed,
Even while men's minds are wild, lest more mischance
On plots and errors happen.
365   FORTINBRAS: Let four captains
Bear Hamlet like a soldier to the stage,
For he was likely, had he been put on,[4]
To have proved most royal; and for his passage
The soldier's music and the rite of war
370   Speak loudly for him.
Take up the bodies. Such a sight as this
Becomes the field, but here shows much amiss.
Go, bid the soldiers shoot.

[*Exeunt marching. A peal of ordnance shot off.*]

ca. 1600

QUESTIONS

1. Read over the first act of the play carefully, and make a list of all the exposition we are
   given here—relationships between characters, events that have taken place before the
   play begins, conflicts of various kinds and issues at stake. What *else* happens in Act I?
   What kinds of emotions are aroused? With what issues do we become concerned? Whose
   problems do we care about? In what specific ways is the action moved forward?
2. Review carefully all the action in Act III, scene 2. Summarize exactly what happens in
   the scene, and specify exactly what we learn. Do we learn the same thing that Hamlet
   does? What structural functions does the scene perform? If you were producing the play,

8. Brought about by apparent accident.   9. Result.   1. Hearing.   2. Succession.   3. Position.
4. Elected king.

how would you have Claudius act at the end of the scene when he calls for more light? What facial expressions would you give him? What hand gestures?

3. How are Rosencrantz and Guildenstern characterized in the play? In what ways are they alike? In what ways different? What suggestions do you find in the text as to why their fate is paired so closely? What other "pairs" of characters are in the play? Which characters are specifically compared to each other in terms of temperament or habit? What does the device of pairing have to do with the play's structure?

4. What different strategies are used to characterize Laertes? Describe his relationship to his sister; to his father; to Hamlet. Describe his "role" in the plot. If he were to be eliminated from the play, what specific things that seem to you crucial to the play's structure and effects would be missing? Can you conceive of another character or group of characters who could be introduced into the play to perform those structural functions? Make a list of all the things that such a character or group would have to be or do.

5. Study the character of Polonius carefully and review all of his lines and actions. What other characters is he paired with, by relationship or parallel function? How do those pairings help us to evaluate Polonius and draw conclusions about him? What structural role does he perform in the play?

WRITING SUGGESTIONS

1. Paraphrase, as exactly as you can, Hamlet's "To be or not to be" soliloquy. Summarize it in no more than two sentences. In your summary, what distortions are you particularly concerned about? In what ways did you find it difficult to communicate tone in your paraphrase?

2. Pretend that you have been given the job of reading the play in order to prepare actors for their performance in it. Choose five characters from the play, and write (as if for the actor about to play the part) a full description of each of them (about 300 words each). Describe physical appearance, voice, gestures, personality, temperament, conflicts, character flaws, everything you think the actor needs to know to play the part according to your interpretation of the play.

3. In an essay of about four pages, analyze the characterization of Ophelia and assess her structural function in the play.

STUDENT WRITING

The Play's the Thing: Deception in <u>Hamlet</u>

Jeanette Sperhac

Early in Act I we are introduced to the young Prince Hamlet who, distraught over his father's death, is defending the utter sincerity of his grief. Alongside the wily banter of the court and the murky circumstances of his mother's marriage, Hamlet's distress is astonishingly genuine and true. But Hamlet's honesty does not appear to last; his hopelessness leads him to don an "antic disposition" and reciprocate the deceit of those around him. He is driven to feign madness, to toy with the sensibilities of courtiers, friends, and even his mother, and to plot the exposure of the king's monstrous crime; these acts seem to be breaches of his honesty, yet all actually uphold a higher end, avenging King Hamlet's murder. Hamlet's seeming descent from sincerity to deceit, and the nested plots and false appearances that ensnare him, can be traced to his first speech, that of an "honest" man.

Hamlet's opening speech resounds with his ideals. "I know not 'seems,'" he claims (I.2.76), seeking to dispel his mother's misgivings about his mourning. Not merely claiming sincerity, Hamlet is making a statement fundamental to his character; all that he knows, all that he recognizes, is <u>what</u> <u>is</u>. Appearances are transitory and fleeting; in his distracted state, Hamlet knows and acknowledges only that his father is dead, that his mother's remarriage is suspect, that his grief <u>is</u> warranted. When Hamlet learns later that his father's ghost desires revenge, that fact becomes Hamlet's warrant to do whatever he must to frame Claudius. Further insight into Hamlet's character can be ascertained from "I have that within which passes show" (I.2.85), which, on the surface, articulates the all-encompassing nature of his grief. Once again, there are strong undercurrents; Hamlet knows that he is able to project a false appearance, to act a part that still "passes show" and seems true. Hamlet's first speech makes evident two seemingly contradictory qualities, his conviction and honesty opposite his ability to lie and deceive.

It can hardly be surprising that Hamlet plunges into the rampant currents of deception, feigning madness and playing parts for those around him. The "actions that a man might play" to which Hamlet alluded in his opening speech (I.2.84) begin to unfold. Of Polonius he makes a "tedious old fool" (II.2.209) by bantering endlessly with the man until he is certain that the prince is mad with unrequited love; Hamlet is harsher with Polonius's daughter, berating Ophelia and mocking his own fond letters to her: "I did love you once . . . [but] you should not have believed me . . . I loved you not" (III.1.112–16). Hamlet is torn upon the subject of his mother; though he is tempted to reproach her, though she is playing along with Claudius, his father's ghost has warned him to leave her alone. With his mother, as throughout, Hamlet's justification for his actions and his play-acting lies in the genuine motive that lies paradoxically behind his antic disposition. The ghost of King Hamlet has given irrevocable orders; Hamlet, in his distress, is compelled to obey them, and is drawn deeper into his playing.

Most fundamental of all Hamlet's play-acting is that which involves Claudius, for revenge upon Claudius is Hamlet's true objective. Directly connected to the king is Hamlet's playing and counterplaying with Rosencrantz and Guildenstern, who, at Claudius's request, assume the guises of concerned friends. The perceptive prince cuts instantly through what "seems"; he knows that they are informers. His uncanny sense for what "is" identifies their true intent. In the course of their three-way playing, Hamlet taunts Rosencrantz and Guildenstern with his knowledge, continually mocks them, and even forces them to admit to their doings. "Though you can fret me, you cannot play upon me," Hamlet laughs (III.2.321–22); though Rosencrantz and Guildenstern are hired to spy on him, though it is purportedly their game, Hamlet is the one in control; it is he who plays upon them.

Of the final and most shattering instances of "playing," the framing of Claudius belongs completely to Hamlet; the exposure of the king's monstrous crime is Hamlet's great scheme. The prince's interest in the traveling players is misinterpreted by Claudius as a healthy diversion; the king never suspects that the crux of Hamlet's revenge lies in the players' art. Claudius's forced admission of the king's murder happens bizarrely, paradoxically, not acknowledged under confrontation, but whimpered in the dark in the response to posed figures on a stage. Hamlet has surpassed his own play-acting and the guile and tact of the court; he turns the false projection of an actor into a vehicle of justice. In his finest moment, Hamlet harnesses the actor's art to accuse Claudius; it is as if the prince is gone so far into playing that he must use puppets for his true intent.

The final scene could be viewed as Claudius's reply to the "Mousetrap." Challenged to an apparently harmless fencing match, Hamlet is doomed to lose his life, either to the tainted foil of Laertes, his "sporting" opponent, or to the poisoned goblet held by Claudius. The prince is hopelessly trapped; no guise can transport him now, no perception foresee the consequences of the scene. Deception heaped upon deception has caught up with Hamlet at last, and upstaged by Claudius's guile, the prince drags Denmark down with him.

Central to Hamlet are currents of deception: apparent truths, apparent sentiments, apparent relationships and the submerged realities which they misrepresent. Though the prince's opening speech shows a veneer of sincerity, it foreshadows the trickery that Hamlet is capable of, the playing and seeming that he will undertake to serve an ironically pure end. To obey his murdered father, a loyal son plays at deception, aiming to achieve justice; labyrinths of deceit produce a kind of final truth, once appearances are shed and the actual emerges. These entangled plots and jumbled motives within Hamlet are all evident from the prince's opening speech.

Exploring Contexts

25

THE AUTHOR'S WORK AS CONTEXT: ANTON CHEKHOV

Making comparisons is an inevitable activity of the mind, and as we read drama we can enlarge our understanding of a work by making comparisons—between this play and our own experience, between this play and other plays, between this play and others by the same dramatist. Perhaps you have already been making some such comparisons as you've been reading the plays in this book.

Take *Hamlet* as an example: if you have read other tragedies or histories by Shakespeare, you may already be aware that the question of royal succession was of paramount importance to Shakespeare and his audience and may thus understand the emphasis laid upon it in this play. Moreover, whatever Shakespeare plays you have read or will go on to read, comparisons will show you how Shakespeare continually made his verse line more fluid and dramatic. Thus every new Shakespeare play you encounter will increase your knowledge of Shakespeare's "world." A writer's world involves not only his or her individual mind and personal consciousness, but also the larger cultural and historical world in which he or she lives. Understanding Shakespeare's plays becomes easier as we read more of them not only because we come to understand better what Shakespeare was interested in, how his mind worked, and what kinds of characters, plots, and dramatic situations he liked to create, but also because we begin to know more about the details of life in the England in which he lived four centuries ago. This chapter focuses on the work of Anton Chekhov, a playwright who lived three hundred years after Shakespeare but still a full century before the present time in a culture unfamiliar to most contemporary American readers: czarist Russia.

Chekhov was in many ways a "product" of late nineteenth-century Russia, in which he grew up, but he was of course also an individual with a life and history of his own. Born in 1860 in southern Russia, he was the son of a poor grocer. His ancestors had been serfs. His father—pious, rigid, and something of a bully—was deeply committed to Anton's education, and sent him to the classical *gimnaziya* (grammar school) in his home town. Eventually the elder Chekhov went bankrupt and moved the family six hundred miles north to Moscow, but Anton stayed behind to complete his schooling. When he finished three years later (in 1879), Anton joined his family and enrolled as a medical student at Moscow University. He received his medical degree in 1884. By that time he had begun to show symptoms of tuberculosis, which would take his life early at the age of forty-four.

Even as a young child, Chekhov is said to have shown a flair for the theatrical—he loved mimicry, practical jokes, and playacting—and in grammar school he acted in several plays and wrote a number of his own, though he systematically destroyed them. But early in his university years—in an effort to help relieve his family's poverty—he began to write short stories and comic sketches, which he published in a variety of magazines. He also began to write a regular gossip column for a popular magazine. Before he was thirty, he had published dozens of stories and established a certain popular reputation, but not until 1888—when he published "The Steppe" in a major literary journal—did he begin to write the "serious" stories on which his international reputation as a writer of short stories is now based. In fact, Chekhov's early reputation was as a story writer; his major plays were written much later, during the last eight years of his life (1896–1904). But as early as 1880 (at the age of twenty), he began work on a long and strange play, *Platonov*, which was neither performed during his lifetime nor discovered until many years after his death. In its uncut form it takes almost seven hours to perform. Although the play's loudly proclaimed emotional rampages, rampant onstage violence, and complicated plot line make it quite unlike Chekhov's more famous plays, in which very little "action" happens onstage, one can still see in *Platonov* many characteristic Chekhovian concerns. As his principal English translator, Ronald Hingley, has pointed out, *Platonov* "has much to say to those who wish to examine the roots of his art." About 1888—just as he was reaching maturity as a short-story writer—Chekhov began experimenting with short theatrical farces, almost as if he continued to need an outlet for his often outrageous comic sense as his narrative prose became more serious and more fully controlled. Most of these pieces (like *The Bear*, which is included here) are what Chekhov himself called "vaudevilles"—wildly exuberant sketches heavily dependent on stereotypical characters and situations. Sometimes they seem unfinished and a bit out of control, but

> *I regard medicine as my legal wife and literature as my mistress—it's very convenient, when I get tired of one, I slip off and spend the night with the other. It's not very respectable, but at least it's not boring.*
>
> —ANTON CHEKHOV

Anton Chekhov in Melikhovo, 1897.

they are very funny in themselves and they help us to see more clearly the absurdity and humor in Chekhov's important later plays, which some producers, readers, and critics tend to regard in too solemn a way. Chekhov's social criticism is always telling and often biting, but he has a powerful sense of irony about human behavior that grows out of the social and cultural particulars of late nineteenth- and early twentieth-century Russia.

Chekhov's early writing is not now much remembered, but the three dozen or so stories written after 1888 and four of his later plays—*The Seagull, Uncle Vanya, The Three Sisters,* and *The Cherry Orchard*—are internationally regarded as masterpieces and remain in the repertory in many cities and countries throughout the world. As with any author, the ideal way to appreciate fully Chekhov's genius would be to read all of his stories and plays in succession. Their common themes, strategies, and cultural analyses would shine through clearly and richly, each work contributing to your understanding of the next. Your insights into Chekhov's most mature work would consequently be much deeper than if you were to begin with or read only that material. But given our limitations of space, we provide here three examples to introduce you to Chekhov's work: the first a brief "vaudeville" written when Chekhov was about twenty-eight years old, then a stage monologue, and finally his final major play, produced only weeks before his death.

> *"Things for [Chekhov] were funny and sad at the same time, but you would not see their sadness if you did not see their fun, because both were linked up."*
>
> —VLADIMIR NABOKOV, *from* Lecture on Russian Literature

One way to begin the study of an author in the context of his or her work is to consider what you know or can easily find out about the author's life, and then read the text with some of the issues suggested there in mind. Chekhov, for example, lived in a time of social transition in Russia. Power of the old propertied classes was shifting noticeably into the hands of a rising entrepreneurial class; his own family's difficult and troubled economic history suggests some of the social transitions characteristic of Russia in the last decades of czarist rule. Many of the challenges that Chekhov faced—the uncertain economic climate that brought on his father's bankruptcy, the scrambling, hackwork writing that enabled Chekhov to scrape out a living early on, the climate-aggravated illness that dominated most of his life—are closely related to larger national issues and situations and often find their way, at least obliquely, into his plays. But the larger, more powerful sense of deep cultural change and of shifting power among social classes is everywhere in Chekhov. Much of the anxiety and social unease is understandable in generational terms; it is not surprising that older generations deplored the loss of family closeness, identity with the land, and traditional community they associated with their way of life, nor is it surprising that members of the younger generation found traditional loyalties boring, stifling, and inferior to city life and the greater mobility among social classes and groups of people it offered. Chekhov himself, torn from his ancestral home by economic and career needs, understood very well what it was like to lose familiarity and security, but what is most surprising is the tonal complexity he maintains in the face of deep personal and cultural change. He seems to appreciate both what it was like to lose a familiar way of life and to achieve new distinction or wealth. And he maintains a firm sense of the comic and the absurd among human beings in all classes.

Chekhov at his home in Yalta, 1901.

A production of *The Cherry Orchard* at the Guthrie Theater, 1965. Paul Ballantyne as Pishtchik, Kristina Callahan as Anya, Lee Richardson as Lopahin, and Jessica Tandy as Madame Ranevsky.

In *The Cherry Orchard,* for example, representatives of all classes and groups come in for comic, often even satiric, treatment: Madame Ranevsky, for example, is ridiculous both in her inability to face economic reality (she keeps hoping that money will mysteriously appear out of the past) and in her romantic attachments to the past and her exploitive lover in Paris (though the play is also powerfully respectful of the real human loss that the cherry orchard represents). Lopahin, too, is a caricature of his class and type; he is nouveau riche, acquisitive, and a bit gleeful about the fall of his social betters. Others in the play—the eternal student, the governess, the romantic and maritally ambitious daughters, and even the aged manservant Firs (pathetic and poignant though he is)—all come in for richly comic treatment as well. Their inevitable encounters with economic and cultural change, shifting values, and exigencies of situation that result in changed human circumstances have comic overtones even when serious issues are at stake.

Social and cultural matters get central attention in *The Cherry Orchard,* although they by no means overshadow Chekhov's interest in the depiction of individual characters. In a sense, the conflicts here—between generations, between past and present values, between haves and have-nots, and between different sets and kinds of social standards—are "universal"—they recur in a variety of places and times—but the specific representations of conflict have to do with the particulars of Chekhov's having grown up in Russia in the late nineteenth century. You don't have to know about Chekhov's life or the details of Russian social change to understand the several complicated issues in the play, but knowing such details helps considerably in seeing exactly what the conflicts are about and why the sympathies with different characters are so complicated. For Chekhov and his contemporaries, these issues were not abstract; they were materials that could be worked out in imaginative fictions.

Another way to consider the authorial context is to read an author's texts comparatively. If you do not have time to read a writer's entire canon to see how one work illuminates all the others (and readers usually don't unless they are producing or acting in a play or doing a detailed scholarly study), you can learn a lot by comparing two works and noticing what themes, concerns, and strategies are shared. It is not only ideas and feelings that authors tend to carry over from one text to another, but dramatic devices and rhetorical strategies as well.

The Bear is a short, early play, and although it does not have the polish or complexity of Chekhov's later, more sophisticated efforts, it suggests many of the qualities Chekhov has come to be prized for. In many ways it is a very simple piece, depicting only a brief moment, an elemental conflict, and a quite predictable character revelation. But even so, one can see many of the elements that have come to be acclaimed in Chekhov's mature drama. The main characters—Mrs. Popov, Smirnov, and even the servant Luke— all have distinctive personalities that they display quite fully in so short a play, and all are somewhat more complicated than they themselves think. Much of the comedy here involves Mrs. Popov's view of herself as a faithful, loyal, and steadfast widow who finds that she has feelings she doesn't begin to understand. But Smirnov and Luke similarly find themselves beyond their depth to understand both emotion and situation; the central conflict here involves a tension between devotion to the past and a present that seems far less valuable and resonant but that also carries a powerful, vital appeal of its own. The central sources of tension are far less complex and interesting here than in *The Cherry Orchard,* but the same situations, plots, and schemes are present, the characters are similar, and even the themes and tones are recognizable. *The Bear* does not predict the later success of mature plays such as *The Cherry Orchard,* but it does readily show a distinctive mind at work on a persistent and characteristic set of issues. The older Chekhov may see the issues of land, family, loyalty, and ownership as more serious and lasting, but even in a brief, almost trivial play like *The Bear* one can see the young writer grappling with major cultural problems involving the rise of a new moneyed class with different social assumptions and ethical values and the decay of an older, more ordered world of social and personal expectation. One can also see here a deep interest in the analysis of feelings and an inclination to expose the difference in the way people believe they feel and what they demonstrate through their actions, something that comes out in more full and complex ways with several characters in *The Cherry Orchard.* And one can even see in these two plays a continuity of tone that derives from a consistent sense of human absurdity and inability to deal realistically with change and circumstance. *The Cherry Orchard* is not hilariously funny in its portrayal of the deterioration of older social values—its attitude is more ambivalent than words like "humor" or "satire" would suggest—but one can see in such a play not only irony and gentle teasing of classic attitudes, but a certain lightness of touch and a recognition that even serious or tragic themes have their absurdity and their humorous aspects.

The Bear[1]

A Farce in One Act

Dedicated to N. N. Solovtsov

CHARACTERS

MRS. HELEN POPOV, *a young widow with dimpled cheeks, a land-owner*

GREGORY SMIRNOV, *a landowner in early middle age*

LUKE, *Mrs. Popov's old manservant*

The action takes place in the drawing-room of MRS. POPOV's *country house.*

SCENE 1

MRS. POPOV, *in deep mourning, with her eyes fixed on a snapshot, and* LUKE.

LUKE: This won't do, madam, you're just making your life a misery. Cook's out with the maid picking fruit, every living creature's happy and even our cat knows how to enjoy herself—she's parading round the yard trying to pick up a bird or two. But here you are cooped up inside all day like you was in a convent cell—you never have a good time. Yes, it's true. Nigh on twelve months it is since you last set foot outdoors.

MRS. POPOV: And I'm never going out again, why should I? My life's finished. He lies in his grave, I've buried myself inside these four walls—we're both dead.

LUKE: There you go again! I don't like to hear such talk, I don't. Your husband died and that was that—God's will be done and may he rest in peace. You've shed a few tears and that'll do, it's time to call it a day—you can't spend your whole life a-moaning and a-groaning. The same thing happened to me once, when my old woman died, but what did I do? I grieved a bit, shed a tear or two for a month or so and that's all she's getting. Catch me wearing sack-cloth and ashes for the rest of my days, it'd be more than the old girl was worth! [*Sighs.*] You've neglected all the neighbours—won't go and see them or have them in the house. We never get out and about, lurking here like dirty great spiders, saving your presence. The mice have been at my livery too. And it's not for any lack of nice people either—the county's full of 'em, see. There's the regiment stationed at Ryblovo and them officers are a fair treat, a proper sight for sore eyes they are. They have a dance in camp of a Friday and the brass band plays most days. This ain't right, missus. You're young, and pretty as a picture with that peaches-and-cream look, so make the most of it. Them looks won't last for ever, you know. If you wait another

1. Translated by Ronald Hingley.

ten years to come out of your shell and lead them officers a dance, you'll find it's too late.

MRS. POPOV: [*Decisively.*] Never talk to me like that again, please. When Nicholas died my life lost all meaning, as you know. You may think I'm alive, but I'm not really. I swore to wear this mourning and shun society till my dying day, do you hear? Let his departed spirit see how I love him! Yes, I realize you know what went on—that he was often mean to me, cruel and, er, unfaithful even, but I'll be true to the grave and show him how much I can love. And he'll find me in the next world just as I was before he died.

LUKE: Don't talk like that—walk round the garden instead. Or else have Toby or Giant harnessed and go and see the neighbours.

MRS. POPOV: Oh dear! [*Weeps.*]

LUKE: Missus! Madam! What's the matter? For heaven's sake!

MRS. POPOV: He was so fond of Toby—always drove him when he went over to the Korchagins' place and the Vlasovs'. He drove so well too! And he looked so graceful when he pulled hard on the reins, remember? Oh Toby, Toby! See he gets an extra bag of oats today.

LUKE: Very good, madam.

[*A loud ring.*]

MRS. POPOV: [*Shudders.*] Who is it? Tell them I'm not at home.

LUKE: Very well, madam. [*Goes out.*]

SCENE 2

MRS. POPOV, *alone.*

MRS. POPOV: [*Looking at the snapshot.*] Now you shall see how I can love and forgive, Nicholas. My love will only fade when I fade away myself, when this poor heart stops beating. [*Laughs, through tears.*] Well, aren't you ashamed of yourself? I'm your good, faithful little wifie, I've locked myself up and I'll be faithful to the grave, while you—aren't you ashamed, you naughty boy? You deceived me and you used to make scenes and leave me alone for weeks on end.

SCENE 3

MRS. POPOV *and* LUKE.

LUKE: [*Comes in, agitatedly.*] Someone's asking for you, madam. Wants to see you——

MRS. POPOV: Then I hope you told them I haven't received visitors since the day my husband died.

LUKE: I did, but he wouldn't listen—his business is very urgent, he says.

MRS. POPOV: *I am not at home!*

LUKE: So I told him, but he just swears and barges straight in, drat him. He's waiting in the dining-room.

MRS. POPOV: [*Irritatedly.*] All right, ask him in here then. Aren't people rude?

[LUKE *goes out.*]

MRS. POPOV: Oh, aren't they all a bore? What do they want with me, why must they disturb my peace? [*Sighs.*] Yes, I see I really shall have to get me to a nunnery. [*Reflects.*] I'll take the veil, that's it.

SCENE 4

MRS. POPOV, LUKE *and* SMIRNOV.

SMIRNOV: [*Coming in, to* LUKE.] You're a fool, my talkative friend. An ass. [*Seeing* MRS. POPOV, *with dignity.*] May I introduce myself, madam? Gregory Smirnov, landed gentleman and lieutenant of artillery retired. I'm obliged to trouble you on most urgent business.

MRS. POPOV: [*Not holding out her hand.*] What do you require?

SMIRNOV: I had the honour to know your late husband. He died owing me twelve hundred roubles—I have his two IOUs. Now I've some interest due to the land-bank tomorrow, madam, so may I trouble you to let me have the money today?

MRS. POPOV: Twelve hundred roubles—. How did my husband come to owe you that?

SMIRNOV: He used to buy his oats from me.

MRS. POPOV: [*Sighing, to* LUKE.] Oh yes—Luke, don't forget to see Toby has his extra bag of oats. [LUKE *goes out. To* SMIRNOV.] Of course I'll pay if Nicholas owed you something, but I've nothing on me today, sorry. My manager will be back from town the day after tomorrow and I'll get him to pay you whatever it is then, but for the time being I can't oblige. Besides, it's precisely seven months today since my husband died and I am in no fit state to discuss money.

SMIRNOV: Well, I'll be in a fit state to go bust with a capital B if I can't pay that interest tomorrow. They'll have the bailiffs in on me.

MRS. POPOV: You'll get your money the day after tomorrow.

SMIRNOV: I don't want it the day after tomorrow, I want it now.

MRS. POPOV: I can't pay you now, sorry.

SMIRNOV: And I can't wait till the day after tomorrow.

MRS. POPOV: Can I help it if I've no money today?

SMIRNOV: So you can't pay then?

MRS. POPOV: Exactly.

SMIRNOV: I see. And that's your last word, is it?

MRS. POPOV: It is.

SMIRNOV: Your last word? You really mean it?

MRS. POPOV: I do.

SMIRNOV: [*Sarcastic.*] Then I'm greatly obliged to you, I'll put it in my diary! [*Shrugs.*] And people expect me to be cool and collected! I met the local excise man on my way here just now. "My dear Smirnov," says he, "why are you always losing your temper?" But how can I help it, I ask you? I'm in desperate need of money! Yesterday morning I left home at crack of dawn. I call on everyone who owes me money, but not a soul forks out. I'm dog-tired. I spend the night in some God-awful place—by the vodka barrel in a Jewish pot-house. Then I fetch up here, fifty miles from home, hoping to see the colour of my money, only to be fobbed off with this "no fit state" stuff! How *can* I keep my temper?

MRS. POPOV: I thought I'd made myself clear. You can have your money when my manager gets back from town.

SMIRNOV: It's not your manager I'm after, it's you. What the blazes, pardon my language, do I want with your manager?

MRS. POPOV: I'm sorry, my dear man, but I'm not accustomed to these peculiar expressions and to this tone. I have closed my ears. [*Hurries out.*]

SCENE 5

SMIRNOV, *alone.*

SMIRNOV: Well, what price that! "In no fit state!" Her husband died seven months ago, if you please! Now have I got my interest to pay or not? I want a straight answer—yes or no? All right, your husband's dead, you're in no fit state and so on and so forth, and your blasted manager's hopped it. But what am I supposed to do? Fly away from my creditors by balloon, I take it! Or go and bash the old brain-box against a brick wall? I call on Gruzdev—not at home. Yaroshevich is in hiding. I have a real old slanging-match with Kuritsyn and almost chuck him out of the window. Mazutov has the belly-ache, and this creature's "in no fit state." Not one of the swine will pay. This is what comes of being too nice to them and behaving like some snivelling no-hoper or old woman. It doesn't pay to wear kid gloves with this lot! All right, just you wait—I'll give you something to remember me by! You don't make a monkey out of me, blast you! I'm staying here—going to stick around till she coughs up. Pah! I feel well and truly riled today. I'm shaking like a leaf, I'm so furious—choking I am. Phew, my God, I really think I'm going to pass out! [*Shouts.*] Hey, you there!

SCENE 6

SMIRNOV *and* LUKE.

LUKE: [*Comes in.*] What is it?

SMIRNOV: Bring me some kvass or water, will you?

[LUKE *goes out.*]

SMIRNOV: What a mentality, though! You need money so bad you could shoot yourself, but she won't pay, being "in no fit state to discuss money," if you please! There's female logic for you and no mistake! That's why I don't like talking to women. Never have. Talk to a woman—why, I'd rather sit on top of a powder magazine! Pah! It makes my flesh creep, I'm so fed up with her, her and that great trailing dress! Poetic creatures they call 'em! Why, the very sight of one gives me cramp in both legs, I get so aggravated.

SCENE 7

SMIRNOV *and* LUKE.

LUKE: [*Comes in and serves some water.*] Madam's unwell and won't see anyone.
SMIRNOV: You clear out!

[LUKE *goes out.*]

SMIRNOV: "Unwell and won't see anyone." All right then, don't! I'm staying put, chum, and I don't budge one inch till you unbelt. Be ill for a week and I'll stay a week, make it a year and a year I'll stay. I'll have my rights, lady! As for your black dress and dimples, you don't catch me that way—we know all about those dimples! [*Shouts through the window.*] Unhitch, Simon, we're here for some time—I'm staying put. Tell the stable people to give my horses oats. And you've got that animal tangled in the reins again, you great oaf! [*Imitates him.*] "I don't care." I'll give you don't care! [*Moves away from the window.*] How ghastly—it's unbearably hot, no one will pay up, I had a bad night, and now here's this female with her long black dress and her states. I've got a headache. How about a glass of vodka? That might be an idea. [*Shouts.*] Hey, you there!
LUKE: [*Comes in.*] What is it?
SMIRNOV: Bring me a glass of vodka.

[LUKE *goes out.*]

SMIRNOV: Phew! [*Sits down and looks himself over.*] A fine specimen I am, I must say—dust all over me, my boots dirty, unwashed, hair unbrushed, straw on my waistcoat. I bet the little woman took me for a burglar. [*Yawns.*] It's not exactly polite to turn up in a drawing-room in this rig! Well, anyway, I'm not a guest here, I'm collecting money. And there's no such thing as correct wear for the well-dressed creditor.
LUKE: [*Comes in and gives him the vodka.*] This is a liberty, sir.
SMIRNOV: [*Angrily.*] What!
LUKE: I, er, it's all right, I just——
SMIRNOV: Who do you think you're talking to? You hold your tongue!
LUKE: [*Aside.*] Now we'll never get rid of him, botheration take it! It's an ill wind brought him along.

[LUKE *goes out.*]

SMIRNOV: Oh, I'm so furious! I could pulverize the whole world, I'm in such a rage. I feel quite ill. [*Shouts.*] Hey, you there!

SCENE 8

MRS. POPOV *and* SMIRNOV.

MRS. POPOV: [*Comes in, with downcast eyes.*] Sir, in my solitude I have grown unaccustomed to the sound of human speech, and I can't stand shouting. I must urgently request you not to disturb my peace.

SMIRNOV: Pay up and I'll go.

MRS. POPOV: As I've already stated quite plainly, I've no ready cash. Wait till the day after tomorrow.

SMIRNOV: I've also had the honour of stating quite plainly that I need the money today, not the day after tomorrow. If you won't pay up now, I'll have to put my head in a gas-oven tomorrow.

MRS. POPOV: Can I help it if I've no cash in hand? This is all rather odd.

SMIRNOV: So you won't pay up now, eh?

MRS. POPOV: I can't.

SMIRNOV: In that case I'm not budging, I'll stick around here till I do get my money. [*Sits down.*] You'll pay the day after tomorrow, you say? Very well, then I'll sit here like this till the day after tomorrow. I'll just stay put exactly as I am. [*Jumps up.*] I ask you—have I got that interest to pay tomorrow or haven't I? Think I'm trying to be funny, do you?

MRS. POPOV: Kindly don't raise your voice at me, sir—we're not in the stables.

SMIRNOV: I'm not discussing stables, I'm asking whether my interest falls due tomorrow. Yes or no?

MRS. POPOV: You don't know how to treat a lady.

SMIRNOV: Oh yes I do.

MRS. POPOV: Oh no you don't. You're a rude, ill-bred person. Nice men don't talk to ladies like that.

SMIRNOV: Now, this *is* a surprise! How do you want me to talk then? In French, I suppose? [*In an angry, simpering voice.*] Madame, je voo pree. You won't pay me—how perfectly delightful. Oh, *pardong*, I'm sure—sorry you were troubled! Now isn't the weather divine today? And that black dress looks too, too charming! [*Bows and scrapes.*]

MRS. POPOV: That's silly. And not very clever.

SMIRNOV: [*Mimics her.*] "Silly, not very clever." I don't know how to treat a lady, don't I? Madam, I've seen more women in my time than you have house-sparrows. I've fought three duels over women. There have been twenty-one women in my life. Twelve times it was me broke it off, the other nine got in first. Oh yes! Time was I made an ass of myself, slobbered, mooned around, bowed and scraped and practically crawled on my belly. I loved, I suffered, I sighed at the moon, I languished, I melted, I grew cold. I loved passionately, madly, in every conceivable fashion, damn me, burbling nineteen to the dozen about women's emancipation and wasting half my substance on the tender passion. But now—no thank you very much! I can't be fooled any more, I've had enough. Black eyes, passionate looks, crimson lips, dimpled cheeks, moonlight, "Whispers, passion's bated breathing"—I don't give a tinker's cuss for the lot now, lady. Present company excepted, all women, large or small, are simpering, mincing, gossipy creatures. They're great haters. They're eyebrow-deep in lies. They're futile, they're trivial, they're cruel, they're outrageously illogical. And as for having anything upstairs [*Taps his forehead.*]—I'm sorry to be so blunt, but the very birds in the trees can run rings round your average blue-stocking. Take any one of these poetical creations. Oh, she's all froth and fluff, she is, she's half divine, she sends you into a million raptures. But you take a peep inside her mind, and what do you see? A common or garden crocodile! [*Clutches the back of a chair, which cracks and breaks.*] And yet this crocodile somehow thinks its great life-work, privilege and monopoly is the tender passion—that's what really gets me! But damn and blast it, and crucify me upside down on that wall if I'm wrong—does a woman know how to love any living creature apart from lapdogs? Her love gets no further than snivelling and slobbering. The man suffers and makes sacrifices, while she just twitches the train of her dress and tries to get him squirming under her thumb, that's what her love adds up to! You must know what women are like, seeing you've the rotten luck to be one. Tell me frankly, did you ever see a sincere, faithful, true woman? You know you didn't. Only the old and ugly ones are true and faithful. You'll never find a constant woman, not in a month of Sundays you won't, not once in a blue moon!

MRS. POPOV: Well, I like that! Then who is true and faithful in love to your way of thinking? Not men by any chance?

SMIRNOV: Yes, madam. Men.

MRS. POPOV: *Men!* [*Gives a bitter laugh.*] Men true and faithful in love! That's rich, I must say. [*Vehemently.*] What right have you to talk like that? Men true and faithful! If it comes to that, the best man I've ever known was my late husband, I may say. I loved him passionately, with all my heart as only an intelligent young woman can. I gave him my youth, my happiness, my life, my possessions. I lived only for him. I worshipped him as an idol. And—what do you think? This best of men was shamelessly deceiving me all along the line! After his death I found a drawer in his desk full of love letters, and when he was alive—oh, what a frightful memory!—he used to leave me on my own for weeks on end, he carried on with other girls before my very eyes, he was unfaithful to me, he spent my money like water, and he joked about my feelings for him. But I loved him all the same, and I've been faithful to him. What's more, I'm still faithful and true now that he's dead. I've buried myself alive inside these four walls and I shall go round in these widow's weeds till my dying day.

SMIRNOV: [*With a contemptuous laugh.*] Widow's weeds! Who do you take me for? As if I didn't know why you wear this fancy dress and bury yourself indoors! Why, it sticks out a mile! Mysterious and romantic, isn't it? Some army cadet or hack poet may pass by your garden, look up at your windows and think: "There dwells Tamara, the mysterious princess, the one who buried herself alive from love of her husband." Who do you think you're fooling?

MRS. POPOV: [*Flaring up.*] *What!* You dare to take that line with me!

SMIRNOV: Buries herself alive—but doesn't forget to powder her nose!

MRS. POPOV: You dare adopt that tone!

SMIRNOV: Don't you raise your voice to me, madam, I'm not one of your servants. Let me call a spade a spade. Not being a woman, I'm used to saying what I think. So stop shouting, pray.

MRS. POPOV: It's you who are shouting, not me. Leave me alone, would you mind?

SMIRNOV: Pay up, and I'll go.

MRS. POPOV: You'll get nothing out of me.

SMIRNOV: Oh yes I shall.

MRS. POPOV: Just to be awkward, you won't get one single copeck. And you can leave me alone.

SMIRNOV: Not having the pleasure of being your husband or fiancé, I'll trouble you not to make a scene. [*Sits down.*] I don't like it.

MRS. POPOV: [*Choking with rage.*] Do I see you sitting down?

SMIRNOV: You most certainly do.

MRS. POPOV: Would you mind leaving?

SMIRNOV: Give me my money. [*Aside.*] Oh, I'm in such a rage! Furious I am!

MRS. POPOV: I've no desire to bandy words with cads, sir. Kindly clear off! [*Pause.*] Well, are you going or aren't you?

SMIRNOV: No.

MRS. POPOV: No?

SMIRNOV: No!

MRS. POPOV: Very well then! [*Rings.*]

SCENE 9

The above and LUKE.

MRS. POPOV: Show this gentleman out, Luke.

LUKE: [*Goes up to* SMIRNOV.] Be so good as to leave, sir, when you're told, sir. No point in——

SMIRNOV: [*Jumping up.*] You hold your tongue! Who do you think you're talking to? I'll carve you up in little pieces.

LUKE: [*Clutching at his heart.*] Heavens and saints above us! [*Falls into an armchair.*] Oh, I feel something terrible—fair took my breath away, it did.

MRS. POPOV: But where's Dasha? Dasha! [*Shouts.*] Dasha! Pelageya! Dasha! [*Rings.*]

LUKE: Oh, they've all gone fruit-picking. There's no one in the house. I feel faint. Fetch water.

MRS. POPOV: Be so good as to clear out!

SMIRNOV: Couldn't you be a bit more polite?

MRS. POPOV: [*Clenching her fists and stamping.*] You uncouth oaf! You have the manners of a bear! Think you own the place? Monster!

SMIRNOV: What! You say that again!

MRS. POPOV: I called you an ill-mannered oaf, a monster!

SMIRNOV: [*Advancing on her.*] Look here, what right have you to insult me?

MRS. POPOV: All right, I'm insulting you. So what? Think I'm afraid of you?

SMIRNOV: Just because you look all romantic, you can get away with anything—is that your idea? This is duelling talk!

LUKE: Heavens and saints above us! Water!

SMIRNOV: Pistols at dawn!

MRS. POPOV: Just because you have big fists and the lungs of an ox you needn't think I'm scared, see? Think you own the place, don't you!

SMIRNOV: We'll shoot it out! No one calls me names and gets away with it, weaker sex or no weaker sex.

MRS. POPOV: [*Trying to shout him down.*] You coarse lout!

SMIRNOV: Why should it only be us men who answer for our insults? It's high time we dropped that silly idea. If women want equality, let them damn well have equality! I challenge you, madam!

MRS. POPOV: Want to shoot it out, eh? Very well.

SMIRNOV: This very instant!

MRS. POPOV: Most certainly! My husband left some pistols, I'll fetch them instantly. [*Moves hurriedly off and comes back.*] I'll enjoy putting a bullet through that thick skull, damn your infernal cheek! [*Goes out.*]

SMIRNOV: I'll pot her like a sitting bird. I'm not one of your sentimental young puppies. She'll get no chivalry from me!

LUKE: Kind sir! [*Kneels.*] Grant me a favour, pity an old man and leave this place. First you frighten us out of our wits, now you want to fight a duel.

SMIRNOV: [*Not listening.*] A duel! There's true women's emancipation for you! That evens up the sexes with a vengeance! I'll knock her off as a matter of principle. But what a woman! [*Mimics her.*] "Damn your infernal cheek! I'll put a bullet through that thick skull." Not bad, eh? Flushed all over, flashing eyes, accepts my challenge! You know, I've never seen such a woman in my life.

LUKE: Go away, sir, and I'll say prayers for you till the day I die.

SMIRNOV: There's a regular woman for you, something I do appreciate! A proper woman—not some namby-pamby, wishy-washy female, but a really red-hot bit of stuff, a regular pistol-packing little spitfire. A pity to kill her, really.

LUKE: [*Weeps.*] Kind sir—do leave. Please!

SMIRNOV: I definitely like her. Definitely! Never mind her dimples, I like her. I wouldn't mind letting her off what she owes me, actually. And I don't feel angry any more. Wonderful woman!

SCENE 10

The above and MRS. POPOV.

MRS. POPOV: [*Comes in with the pistols.*] Here are the pistols. But before we start would you mind showing me how to fire them? I've never had a pistol in my hands before.

LUKE: Lord help us! Mercy on us! I'll go and find the gardener and coachman. What have we done to deserve this? [*Goes out.*]

SMIRNOV: [*Examining the pistols.*] Now, there are several types of pistol. There are Mortimer's special duelling pistols with percussion caps. Now, yours here are Smith and Wessons, triple action with extractor, centre-fired. They're fine weapons, worth a cool ninety roubles the pair. Now, you hold a revolver like this. [*Aside.*] What eyes, what eyes! She's hot stuff all right!

MRS. POPOV: Like this?

SMIRNOV: Yes, that's right. Then you raise the hammer and take aim like this. Hold your head back a bit, stretch your arm out properly. Right. And then with this finger you press this little gadget and that's it. But the great thing is—don't get excited and do take your time about aiming. Try and see your hand doesn't shake.

MRS. POPOV: All right. We can't very well shoot indoors, let's go in the garden.

SMIRNOV: Very well. But I warn you, I'm firing in the air.

MRS. POPOV: Oh, this is the limit! Why?

SMIRNOV: Because, because—. That's my business.

MRS. POPOV: Got cold feet, eh? I see. Now don't shilly-shally, sir. Kindly follow me. I shan't rest till I've put a bullet through your brains, damn you. Got the wind up, have you?

SMIRNOV: Yes.

MRS. POPOV: That's a lie. Why won't you fight?

SMIRNOV: Because, er, because you, er, I like you.

MRS. POPOV: [*With a vicious laugh.*] He likes me! He dares to say he likes me! [*Points to the door.*] I won't detain you.

SMIRNOV: [*Puts down the revolver without speaking, picks up his peaked cap and moves off; near the door he stops and for about half a minute the two look at each other without speaking; then he speaks, going up to her hesitantly.*] Listen. Are you still angry? I'm absolutely furious myself, but you must see—how can I put it? The fact is that, er, it's this way, actually—. [*Shouts.*] Anyway, can I help it if I like you? [*Clutches the back of a chair, which cracks and breaks.*] Damn fragile stuff, furniture! I like you! Do you understand? I, er, I'm almost in love.

MRS. POPOV: Keep away from me, I loathe you.

SMIRNOV: God, what a woman! Never saw the like of it in all my born days. I'm sunk! Without trace! Trapped like a mouse!

MRS. POPOV: Get back or I shoot.

SMIRNOV: Shoot away. I'd die happily with those marvellous eyes looking at me, that's what you can't see—die by that dear little velvet hand. Oh, I'm crazy! Think it over and make your mind up now, because once I leave this place we shan't see each other again. So make your mind up. I'm a gentleman and a man of honour, I've ten thousand a year, I can put a bullet through a coin in mid air and I keep a good stable. Be my wife.

MRS. POPOV: [*Indignantly brandishes the revolver.*] A duel! We'll shoot it out!

SMIRNOV: I'm out of my mind! Nothing makes any sense. [*Shouts.*] Hey, you there—water!

MRS. POPOV: [*Shouts.*] We'll shoot it out!

SMIRNOV: I've lost my head, fallen for her like some damfool boy! [*Clutches her hand. She shrieks with pain.*] I love you! [*Kneels.*] I love you as I never loved any of my twenty-one other women—twelve times it was me broke it off, the other nine got in first. But I never loved anyone as much as you. I've gone all sloppy, soft and sentimental. Kneeling like an imbecile, offering my hand! Disgraceful! Scandalous! I haven't been in love for five years, I swore not to, and here I am crashing head over heels, hook, line and sinker! I offer you my hand. Take it or leave it. [*Gets up and hurries to the door.*]

MRS. POPOV: Just a moment.

SMIRNOV: [*Stops.*] What is it?

MRS. POPOV: Oh, never mind, just go away. But wait. No, go, go away. I hate you. Or no—don't go away. Oh, if you knew how furious I am! [*Throws the revolver on the table.*] My fingers are numb from holding this beastly thing. [*Tears a handkerchief in her anger.*] Why are you hanging about? Clear out!

SMIRNOV: Good-bye.

MRS. POPOV: Yes, yes, go away! [*Shouts.*] Where are you going? Stop. Oh, go away then. I'm so furious! Don't you come near me, I tell you.

SMIRNOV: [*Going up to her.*] I'm so fed up with myself! Falling in love like a school-boy! Kneeling down! It's enough to give you the willies! [*Rudely.*] I love you! Oh, it's just what the doctor ordered, this is! There's my interest due in tomorrow, haymaking's upon us—and *you* have to come along! [*Takes her by the waist.*] I'll never forgive myself.

MRS. POPOV: Go away! You take your hands off me! I, er, hate you! We'll sh-shoot it out!

[*A prolonged kiss.*]

SCENE 11

The above, LUKE *with an axe, the gardener with a rake, the coachman with a pitch-fork and some workmen with sundry sticks and staves.*

LUKE: [*Seeing the couple kissing.*] Mercy on us! [*Pause.*]

MRS. POPOV: [*Lowering her eyes.*] Luke, tell them in the stables—Toby gets no oats today.

CURTAIN

1888

On the Injurious Effects of Tobacco[1]

A Monologue for the Stage in One Act

DRAMATIS PERSONA

IVAN IVANOVICH NYUKHIN, *the husband of his wife, who maintains a music school and a boarding school for girls*

The scene is the platform stage of a provincial club.

NYUKHIN: [*Has long burnsides without mustache; dressed in an old, shabby frock coat; enters majestically, bows, and adjusts his waistcoat.*] Dear ladies and, in one way or another, dear gentlemen. [*Combing his burnsides.*] It was proposed to my wife, that I—for the purpose of charity—give a popular lecture of some sort or other. Well, hmm? If it's to be a lecture, then let it be a lecture—it doesn't matter to me anyway. I am not a professor, of course, and I am a stranger to university degrees, but nonetheless, all the same, here am I, for already thirty years without stopping, and it's even possible to say, for the sake of injury to my own health and so on, I've been working on questions of a strictly scientific character, which I turn over in my mind and sometimes even write, can you imagine it, scientific articles; that is, not quite scientific, but which are, excuse the expression, not unlike scientific, as it were. By the way, the other day an enormous article was written by me under the title, "On the Injurious Effects of Certain Insects." My daughters liked it very much, especially the part on bedbugs. I just read it through and tore it up. It doesn't matter, you know, whatever you may write, because you can't do without Persian powder.[2] Bedbugs are even in our piano . . . For the subject of my lecture today I have chosen, so to speak, the injurious effects which come about in humankind by the consumption of tobacco. I myself smoke, but my wife ordered me to lecture today on the injurious effects of tobacco, and, consequently, what else can you say but do it. If it's to be about tobacco, then let it be about tobacco—it doesn't matter to me anyway, and as for you, dear gentlemen, I propose that you treat my present lecture with proper respect, otherwise I can't be held responsible for the way it turns out. Be there anyone here who is intimidated by the dry, scientific lecture, or who just doesn't like it, then that person need not listen and should leave at once. [*Adjusts his waistcoat.*] I especially ask the attention of the gentlemen present here who are doctors, who may draw from my lecture a good deal of useful information, since tobacco, apart from its injurious activities, is also utilized in medicine. Thus, for example, if a fly is placed in a snuffbox, then it will

---

1. This monologue was originally published in Chekhov's *Collected Works* (*Sobranie sočinenij*), XIV, in 1903 and is the last version written by him, supposedly in September 1902. This translation is by Eugene K. Bristow, from *O vrede tabaka*, as published in *Collected Works*, IX, 602–06.   2. An insecticide to ward off bugs.

expire, in all likelihood, from nervous disorder. Tobacco is, for the most part, a plant . . . When I lecture, I usually wink my right eye, but don't pay any attention to it; it comes from nervous excitement.[3] I am a very nervous person, generally speaking, but my eye began to wink in the year eighteen hundred and eighty-nine, on the thirteenth of September, the very same day that my wife gave birth, in one way or another, to her fourth daughter, Varvara. All my daughters were born on the thirteenth. Or rather [*Having glanced at his watch.*], in view of the shortage of time, we dare not wander away from the subject of the lecture. It should be pointed out to you, my wife maintains a music school and a private boarding school; that is, not quite a boarding school, but which is not unlike something of that sort. Confidentially speaking, my wife likes to complain about the lack of money, but she's socked away a little something, some forty or fifty thousand, and I don't have a kopek to my soul, not even part of one—well, what's the use of talking about it! In the boarding school, I am the head of the housekeeping department. I buy provisions, check up on the servants, write down the expenses, bind and stitch notebooks, exterminate bedbugs, walk my wife's little dog, catch mice . . . Yesterday evening my duty lay in issuing to the cook butter and flour, because pancakes were intended. Well, sir, to put it in one word, today, when the pancakes had already been fried, my wife came to the cook and said that three pupils would not be eating pancakes, because they had swollen glands. In this way it turned out that we had fried several superfluous pancakes. What were we supposed to do with them? At first, my wife ordered them to be carried to the cellar, but then she thought; she thought and said: "Eat these pancakes yourself, you sloppy dummy." When she's out of sorts, that's what she calls me: sloppy dummy, or asp, or Satan. What kind of Satan am I, anyway? She is always out of sorts. And I didn't eat them, but I stuffed them down without chewing, because I am always hungry. Yesterday, for example, she didn't give me anything for dinner. "You sloppy dummy," she said, "What's the use of feeding you . . ." Still, however [*Looks at his watch.*], we've forgotten ourselves and have wandered somewhat away from our subject. Shall we continue. Though, of course, you'd be much more inclined now to listen to a love song, or some sort of symphony or other, or an aria . . . [*Sings and conducts.*] "In the thick of battle we do not bat an eye . . ." I can't really remember where that's from . . . By the way, I forgot to tell you that in the music school belonging to my wife, in addition to running the housekeeping department, my duties also include the teaching of mathematics, physics, chemistry, geography, history, solfeggio, literature, and so on. For dancing, singing, and drawing, my wife charges a special fee, though I'm also the one who teaches dancing and singing. Our music school is located in Five Dog Lane, number thirteen. That's why, in all likelihood, my life is so unfortunate, since the number of the house we live in is thirteen. And my daughters were born on the thirteenth, and in our house we have

---

3. *Èto ot volnenija:* literally, "it's from agitation."

thirteen windows . . . Well, what's the use of talking about it! As to negotiations, it's possible to find my wife at home anytime, and the prospectus of the school, if you like, is sold by the porter at the door at thirty kopeks a copy. [*Takes several brochures out of his pocket.*] And here am I, if you like, able to share. Only thirty kopeks a copy! Who'd like one? [*Pause.*] No one wants a copy? Well, what about twenty kopeks! [*Pause.*] Isn't that the limit. Yes, house number thirteen! Nothing comes through for me, I'm putting on years, becoming stupid . . . Here am I giving a lecture, I look like I'm cheerful, but inside myself I'd like to cry out in full voice or fly away somewhere or other to the end of the world. And there's no one at all to complain to, I even want to start crying . . . You will say: your daughters . . . What daughters? I talk to them, but they only laugh . . . My wife has seven daughters . . . No, I'm sorry, it seems there are six . . . [*Quickly.*] Seven! The oldest of them, Anna, is twenty-seven; the youngest, seventeen. Dear gentlemen! [*Looks around.*] I'm not happy, I've turned into a fool, a nonentity; but, in reality, you see before you the happiest of fathers. In reality, that's as it should be, and I dare not say otherwise. If only you knew! I've lived with my wife thirty-three years, and I can say those were the best years of my life, oh, by no means the best, but in general, that is. They've flown by, to put it in one word, like one twinkling, happy moment. As a matter of fact, damn them all, damn them to hell. [*Looks around.*] Or rather she, of course, still hasn't arrived, she isn't here, and it's possible to say whatever I like . . . I get terribly frightened . . . frightened when she looks at me. Well, like I was saying: my daughters have taken so long in getting married, because, in all likelihood, they are shy and because men never see them. My wife doesn't want to give parties, she never invites anyone to dinners, she is as tightfisted as they come, a bilious and pugnacious lady, and that's why no one ever stops by our place, but . . . I can let you in on a secret . . . [*Walks closer to the footlights.*] It's possible to see the daughters of my wife on high holidays at the home of their aunt, Natalya Semyonovna, the very same person who suffers from rheumatism and goes around in that yellow dress with black dots, just as if cockroaches were splattered all over her. Refreshments are handed out there, too. And when my wife isn't around there, then it's possible for this . . . [*Smacks himself on the neck.*] It should be pointed out to you, I get drunk on one glass, and from this comes such a good feeling in my soul, and at the same time, such sorrow that I can't possibly express; for some reason, memories of my youth come back, and for some reason, the longing to run away, oh, if you only knew, how much the longing! [*Carried away.*] To run away, to throw everything down, and to run without once looking back . . . Where to? It doesn't matter where . . . if only to run away from this rotten, vulgar, cheap life, which has turned me into an old, pitiful fool, an old, pitiful idiot, to run away from this stupid, petty, malicious, malicious, malicious money-grubber, from my wife, who tortured me for thirty-three years, to run away from music, from the kitchen, from the wife's money, from all this nonsense, pettiness and vulgarity . . . and to stop somewhere far, far away in the field and to stand there like a tree, a post, a garden scarecrow, under the wide sky, and the whole night through, watch how the silent, bright moon is hanging over you, and to forget, to forget[4] . . . Oh, how I long to remember nothing! . . How much I long to tear off this obscene old frock coat I wore thirty years ago at my wedding . . . [*Tears off his frock coat.*], in which I constantly give lectures for the purposes of charity . . . That's for you! [*Stamps on the frock coat.*] That's for you! I am old, poor, dilapidated, like this very same waistcoat with its shabby, used-up old back . . . [*Shows the back.*] I don't need anything! I'm superior to this, more clean and pure. Once upon a time I was young, intelligent, I studied at the university, I had dreams, I took for granted I was a human being . . . Now I don't need anything! Nothing except peace . . . except peace! [*Having glanced to the side, quickly puts on the frock coat.*] However, my wife is standing in the wings . . . She has arrived and is waiting for me there . . . [*Looks at his watch.*] Time has already passed . . . If she asks, then, please, I beg you, tell her that the lecture was . . . that the sloppy dummy, that is, I, conducted himself with dignity. [*Looks to the side, clears his throat.*] She is looking here . . . [*Having raised his voice.*] Proceeding from this proposition, that tobacco contains a horrible poison, of which I have only just spoken, under no circumstances is it proper to smoke, and I permit myself, in one way or another, to hope that this my lecture, "On the Injurious Effects of Tobacco," will be of service. I have said everything. *Dixi et animam levavi!*[5] [*Bows and majestically leaves.*]

1902

---

4. This last version, although hilarious and ridiculous in parts, is shaped in great measure by Chekhov's introduction of *nastroenie*, or mood; by his heightening of Nyukhin's unconscious hatred for his wife; and by his coupling of both *nastroenie* and hatred with the absurd and farcical action of taking off his coat and stamping on it. By shedding and attempting to destroy his coat, Nyukhin acts out the dream (false) of casting aside his role of henpecked husband and of taking on an entirely new lifestyle.   5. "I have spoken and alleviated my soul!"

The Cherry Orchard[1]

CHARACTERS IN THE PLAY

MADAME RANEVSKY (LYUBOV
   ANDREYEVNA), *the owner of the*
   Cherry Orchard
ANYA, *her daughter, aged 17*
VARYA, *her adopted daughter, aged*
   24

GAEV (LEONID ANDREYEVITCH),
   brother of Madame Ranevsky
LOPAHIN (YERMOLAY ALEXEYE-
   VITCH), *a merchant*
TROFIMOV (PYOTR SERGEYEVITCH), *a*
   student

---

1. Translated by Constance Garnett.

SEMYONOV-PISHTCHIK, *a landowner*   YASHA, *a young valet*
CHARLOTTA IVANOVNA, *a governess*   A WAYFARER
EPIHODOV (SEMYON   THE STATION MASTER
    PANTALEYEVITCH), *a clerk*   A POST-OFFICE CLERK
DUNYASHA, *a maid*   VISITORS, SERVANTS
FIRS, *an old valet, aged 87*

The action takes place on the estate of MADAME RANEVSKY.

ACT I

A room, which has always been called the nursery. One of the doors leads into ANYA'*s room. Dawn, sun rises during the scene. May, the cherry trees in flower, but it is cold in the garden with the frost of early morning. Windows closed.*

Enter DUNYASHA *with a candle and* LOPAHIN *with a book in his hand.*

LOPAHIN: The train's in, thank God. What time is it?

DUNYASHA: Nearly two o'clock. [*Puts out the candle.*] It's daylight already.

LOPAHIN: The train's late! Two hours, at least. [*Yawns and stretches.*] I'm a pretty one; what a fool I've been. Came here on purpose to meet them at the station and dropped asleep. . . . Dozed off as I sat in the chair. It's annoying. . . . You might have waked me.

DUNYASHA: I thought you had gone. [*Listens.*] There, I do believe they're coming!

LOPAHIN: [*Listens.*] No, what with the luggage and one thing and another. [*A pause.*] Lyubov Andreyevna has been abroad five years; I don't know what she is like now. . . . She's a splendid woman. A good-natured, kind-hearted woman. I remember when I was a lad of fifteen, my poor father—he used to keep a little shop here in the village in those days—gave me a punch in the face with his fist and made my nose bleed. We were in the yard here, I forget what we'd come about—he had had a drop. Lyubov Andreyevna—I can see her now—she was a slim young girl then—took me to wash my face, and then brought me into this very room, into the nursery. "Don't cry, little peasant," says she, "it will be well in time for your wedding day." . . . [*A pause.*] Little peasant. . . . My father was a peasant, it's true, but here am I in a white waistcoat and brown shoes, like a pig in a bun shop. Yes, I'm a rich man, but for all my money, come to think, a peasant I was, and a peasant I am. [*Turns over the pages of the book.*] I've been reading this book and I can't make head or tail of it. I fell asleep over it. [*A pause.*]

DUNYASHA: The dogs have been awake all night, they feel that the mistress is coming.

LOPAHIN: Why, what's the matter with you, Dunyasha?

DUNYASHA: My hands are all of a tremble. I feel as though I should faint.

LOPAHIN: You're a spoilt soft creature, Dunyasha. And dressed like a lady too, and your hair done up. That's not the thing. One must know one's place.

[*Enter* EPIHODOV *with a nosegay; he wears a pea-jacket and highly polished creaking topboots; he drops the nosegay as he comes in.*]

EPIHODOV: [*Picking up the nosegay.*] Here! the gardener's sent this, says you're to put it in the dining-room. [*Gives* DUNYASHA *the nosegay.*]

LOPAHIN: And bring me some kvass.

DUNYASHA: I will. [*Goes out.*]

EPIHODOV: It's chilly this morning, three degrees of frost, though the cherries are all in flower. I can't say much for our climate. [*Sighs.*] I can't. Our climate is not often propitious to the occasion. Yermolay Alexeyevitch, permit me to call your attention to the fact that I purchased myself a pair of boots the day before yesterday, and they creak, I venture to assure you, so that there's no tolerating them. What ought I to grease them with?

LOPAHIN: Oh, shut up! Don't bother me.

EPIHODOV: Every day some misfortune befalls me. I don't complain, I'm used to it, and I wear a smiling face.

[DUNYASHA *comes in, hands* LOPAHIN *the kvass.*]

EPIHODOV: I am going. [*Stumbles against a chair, which falls over.*] There! [*As though triumphant.*] There you see now, excuse the expression, an accident like that among others. . . . It's positively remarkable. [*Goes out.*]

DUNYASHA: Do you know, Yermolay Alexeyevitch, I must confess, Epihodov has made me a proposal.

LOPAHIN: Ah!

DUNYASHA: I'm sure I don't know. . . . He's a harmless fellow, but sometimes when he begins talking, there's no making anything of it. It's all very fine and expressive, only there's no understanding it. I've a sort of liking for him too. He loves me to distraction. He's an unfortunate man; every day there's something. They tease him about it—two and twenty misfortunes they call him.

LOPAHIN: [*Listening.*] There! I do believe they're coming.

DUNYASHA: They are coming! What's the matter with me? . . . I'm cold all over.

LOPAHIN: They really are coming. Let's go and meet them. Will she know me? It's five years since I saw her.

DUNYASHA: [*In a flutter.*] I shall drop this very minute. . . . Ah, I shall drop.

[*There is a sound of two carriages driving up to the house.* LOPAHIN *and* DUNYASHA *go out quickly. The stage is left empty. A noise is heard in the adjoining rooms.* FIRS, *who has driven to meet* MADAME RANEVSKY, *crosses the stage hurriedly leaning on a stick. He is wearing old-fashioned livery and a high hat. He says something to himself, but not a word can be distinguished. The noise behind the scenes goes on increasing. A voice: "Come, let's go in here." Enter* LYUBOV ANDREYEVNA, ANYA, *and* CHARLOTTA IVANOVNA *with a pet dog on a chain, all in traveling dresses.* VARYA *in an out-door coat with a kerchief over her head,* GAEV, SEMYONOV-PISHTCHIK, LOPAHIN, DUNYASHA *with bag and parasol, servants with other articles. All walk across the room.*]

ANYA: Let's come in here. Do you remember what room this is, mamma?

LYUBOV: [*Joyfully, through her tears.*] The nursery!

VARYA: How cold it is, my hands are numb. [*To* LYUBOV ANDREYEVNA.] Your rooms, the white room and the lavender one, are just the same as ever, mamma.

LYUBOV: My nursery, dear delightful room. . . . I used to sleep here when I was little. . . . [*Cries.*] And here I am, like a little child. . . . [*Kisses her brother and* VARYA, *and then her brother again.*] Varya's just the same as ever, like a nun. And I knew Dunyasha. [*Kisses* DUNYASHA.]

GAEV: The train was two hours late. What do you think of that? Is that the way to do things?

CHARLOTTA: [*To* PISHTCHIK.] My dog eats nuts, too.

PISHTCHIK: [*Wonderingly.*] Fancy that!

[*They all go out except* ANYA *and* DUNYASHA.]

DUNYASHA: We've been expecting you so long. [*Takes* ANYA's *hat and coat.*]

ANYA: I haven't slept for four nights on the journey. I feel dreadfully cold.

DUNYASHA: You set out in Lent, there was snow and frost, and now? My darling! [*Laughs and kisses her.*] I *have* missed you, my precious, my joy. I must tell you . . . I can't put it off a minute. . . .

ANYA: [*Wearily.*] What now?

DUNYASHA: Epihodov, the clerk, made me a proposal just after Easter.

ANYA: It's always the same thing with you. . . . [*Straightening her hair.*] I've lost all my hairpins. . . . [*She is staggering from exhaustion.*]

DUNYASHA: I don't know what to think, really. He does love me, he does love me so!

ANYA: [*Looking towards her door, tenderly.*] My own room, my windows just as though I had never gone away. I'm home! To-morrow morning I shall get up and run into the garden. . . . Oh, if I could get to sleep! I haven't slept all the journey, I was so anxious and worried.

DUNYASHA: Pyotr Sergeyevitch came the day before yesterday.

ANYA: [*Joyfully.*] Petya!

DUNYASHA: He's asleep in the bath house, he has settled in there. I'm afraid of being in their way, says he. [*Glancing at her watch.*] I was to have waked him, but Varvara Mihalovna told me not to. Don't you wake him, says she.

[*Enter Varya with a bunch of keys at her waist.*]

VARYA: Dunyasha, coffee and make haste. . . . Mamma's asking for coffee.

DUNYASHA: This very minute. [*Goes out.*]

VARYA: Well, thank God, you've come. You're home again. [*Petting her.*] My little darling has come back! My precious beauty has come back again!

ANYA: I have had a time of it!

VARYA: I can fancy.

ANYA: We set off in Holy Week—it was so cold then, and all the way Charlotta would talk and show off her tricks. What did you want to burden me with Charlotta for?

VARYA: You couldn't have traveled all alone, darling. At seventeen!

ANYA: We got to Paris at last, it was cold there—snow. I speak French shockingly.

Mamma lives on the fifth floor, I went up to her and there were a lot of French people, ladies, an old priest with a book. The place smelt of tobacco and so comfortless. I felt sorry, oh! so sorry for mamma all at once, I put my arms round her neck, and hugged her and wouldn't let her go. Mamma was as kind as she could be, and she cried. . . .

VARYA: [*Through her tears.*] Don't speak of it, don't speak of it!

ANYA: She had sold her villa at Mentone, she had nothing left, nothing. I hadn't a farthing left either, we only just had enough to get here. And mamma doesn't understand! When we had dinner at the stations, she always ordered the most expensive things and gave the waiters a whole rouble. Charlotta's just the same. Yasha too must have the same as we do; it's simply awful. You know Yasha is mamma's valet now, we brought him here with us.

VARYA: Yes, I've seen the young rascal.

ANYA: Well, tell me—have you paid the arrears on the mortgage?

VARYA: How could we get the money?

ANYA: Oh, dear! Oh, dear!

VARYA: In August the place will be sold.

ANYA: My goodness!

LOPAHIN: [*Peeps in at the door and moos like a cow.*] Moo! [*Disappears.*]

VARYA: [*Weeping.*] There, that's what I could do to him. [*Shakes her fist.*]

ANYA: [*Embracing* VARYA, *softly.*] Varya, has he made you an offer? [VARYA *shakes her head.*] Why, but he loves you. Why is it you don't come to an understanding? What are you waiting for?

VARYA: I believe that there never will be anything between us. He has a lot to do, he has no time for me . . . and takes no notice of me. Bless the man, it makes me miserable to see him. . . . Everyone's talking of our being married, everyone's congratulating me, and all the while there's really nothing in it; it's all like a dream. [*In another tone.*] You have a new brooch like a bee.

ANYA: [*Mournfully.*] Mamma bought it. [*Goes into her own room and in a lighthearted childish tone.*] And you know, in Paris I went up in a balloon!

VARYA: My darling's home again! My pretty is home again!

[DUNYASHA *returns with the coffee-pot and is making the coffee.*]

VARYA: [*Standing at the door.*] All day long, darling, as I go about looking after the house, I keep dreaming all the time. If only we could marry you to a rich man, then I should feel more at rest. Then I would go off by myself on a pilgrimage to Kiev, to Moscow . . . and so I would spend my life going from one holy place to another. . . . I would go on and on. . . . What bliss!

ANYA: The birds are singing in the garden. What time is it?

VARYA: It must be nearly three. It's time you were asleep, darling. [*Going into* ANYA's *room.*] What bliss!

[YASHA *enters with a rug and a traveling bag.*]

YASHA: [*Crosses the stage, mincingly.*] May one come in here, pray?

DUNYASHA: I shouldn't have known you, Yasha. How you have changed abroad.

YASHA: H'm! . . . And who are you?

DUNYASHA: When you went away, I was that high. [*Shows distance from floor.*] Dunyasha, Fyodor's daughter. . . . You don't remember me!

YASHA: H'm! . . . You're a peach! [*Looks round and embraces her: she shrieks and drops a saucer.* YASHA *goes out hastily.*]

VARYA: [*In the doorway, in a tone of vexation.*] What now?

DUNYASHA: [*Through her tears.*] I have broken a saucer.

VARYA: Well, that brings good luck.

ANYA: [*Coming out of her room.*] We ought to prepare mamma: Petya is here.

VARYA: I told them not to wake him.

ANYA: [*Dreamily.*] It's six years since father died. Then only a month later little brother Grisha was drowned in the river, such a pretty boy he was, only seven. It was more than mamma could bear, so she went away, went away without looking back. [*Shuddering.*] . . . How well I understand her, if only she knew! [*A pause.*] And Petya Trofimov was Grisha's tutor, he may remind her.

[*Enter* FIRS: *he is wearing a pea-jacket and a white waistcoat.*]

FIRS: [*Goes up to the coffee-pot, anxiously.*] The mistress will be served here. [*Puts on white gloves.*] Is the coffee ready? [*Sternly to* DUNYASHA.] Girl! Where's the cream?

DUNYASHA: Ah, mercy on us! [*Goes out quickly.*]

FIRS: [*Fussing round the coffee-pot.*] Ech! you good-for-nothing! [*Muttering to himself.*] Come back from Paris. And the old master used to go to Paris too . . . horses all the way. [*Laughs.*]

VARYA: What is it, Firs?

FIRS: What is your pleasure? [*Gleefully.*] My lady has come home! I have lived to see her again! Now I can die. [*Weeps with joy.*]

[*Enter* LYUBOV ANDREYEVNA, GAEV *and* SEMYONOV-PISHTCHIK; *the latter is in a short-waisted full coat of fine cloth, and full trousers.* GAEV, *as he comes in, makes a gesture with his arms and his whole body, as though he were playing billiards.*]

LYUBOV: How does it go? Let me remember. Cannon off the red!

GAEV: That's it—in off the white! Why, once, sister, we used to sleep together in this very room, and now I'm fifty-one, strange as it seems.

LOPAHIN: Yes, time flies.

GAEV: What do you say?

LOPAHIN: Time, I say, flies.

GAEV: What a smell of patchouli!

ANYA: I'm going to bed. Good-night, mamma. [*Kisses her mother.*]

LYUBOV: My precious darling. [*Kisses her hands.*] Are you glad to be home? I can't believe it.

ANYA: Good-night, uncle.

GAEV: [*Kissing her face and hands.*] God bless you! How like you are to your mother! [*To his sister.*] At her age you were just the same, Lyuba.

[ANYA *shakes hands with* LOPAHIN *and* PISHTCHIK, *then goes out, shutting the door after her.*]

LYUBOV: She's quite worn out.

PISHTCHIK: Aye, it's a long journey, to be sure.

VARYA: [*To* LOPAHIN *and* PISHTCHIK.] Well, gentlemen? It's three o'clock and time to say good-bye.

LYUBOV: [*Laughs.*] You're just the same as ever, Varya. [*Draws her to her and kisses her.*] I'll just drink my coffee and then we will all go and rest. [FIRS *puts a cushion under her feet.*] Thanks, friend. I am so fond of coffee, I drink it day and night. Thanks, dear old man. [*Kisses* FIRS.]

VARYA: I'll just see whether all the things have been brought in. [*Goes out.*]

LYUBOV: Can it really be me sitting here? [*Laughs.*] I want to dance about and clap my hands. [*Covers her face with her hands.*] And I could drop asleep in a moment! God knows I love my country, I love it tenderly; I couldn't look out of the window in the train, I kept crying so. [*Through her tears.*] But I must drink my coffee, though. Thank you, Firs, thanks, dear old man. I'm so glad to find you still alive.

FIRS: The day before yesterday.

GAEV: He's rather deaf.

LOPAHIN: I have to set off for Harkov directly, at five o'clock. . . . It is annoying! I wanted to have a look at you, and a little talk. . . . You are just as splendid as ever.

PISHTCHIK: [*Breathing heavily.*] Handsomer, indeed. . . . Dressed in Parisian style . . . completely bowled me over.

LOPAHIN: Your brother, Leonid Andreyevitch here, is always saying that I'm a low-born knave, that I'm a money-grubber, but I don't care one straw for that. Let him talk. Only I do want you to believe in me as you used to. I do want your wonderful tender eyes to look at me as they used to in the old days. Merciful God! My father was a serf of your father and of your grandfather, but you—you—did so much for me once, that I've forgotten all that; I love you as though you were my kin . . . more than my kin.

LYUBOV: I can't sit still, I simply can't. . . . [*Jumps up and walks about in violent agitation.*] This happiness is too much for me. . . . You may laugh at me, I know I'm silly. . . . My own bookcase. [*Kisses the bookcase.*] My little table.

GAEV: Nurse died while you were away.

LYUBOV: [*Sits down and drinks coffee.*] Yes, the Kingdom of Heaven be hers! You wrote me of her death.

GAEV: And Anastasy is dead. Squinting Petruchka has left me and is in service now with the police captain in the town.

[*Takes a box of caramels out of his pocket and sucks one.*]

PISHTCHIK: My daughter, Dashenka, wishes to be remembered to you.

LOPAHIN: I want to tell you something very pleasant and cheering. [*Glancing at his watch.*] I'm going directly . . . there's no time to say much . . . well, I can say it in a couple of words. I needn't tell you your cherry orchard is to be sold to pay your debts; the 22nd of August is the date fixed for the sale; but don't you worry, dearest lady, you may sleep in peace, there is a way of saving it. . . . This is what I propose. I beg your attention! Your estate is not twenty miles from the town, the railway runs close by it, and if the cherry orchard and the land along the river bank were cut up into building plots and then let on lease for summer villas, you would make an income of at least 25,000 roubles a year out of it.

GAEV: That's all rot, if you'll excuse me.

LYUBOV: I don't quite understand you, Yermolay Alexeyevitch.

LOPAHIN: You will get a rent of at least 25 roubles a year for a three-acre plot from summer visitors, and if you say the word now, I'll bet you what you like there won't be one square foot of ground vacant by the autumn, all the plots will be taken up. I congratulate you; in fact, you are saved. It's a perfect situation with that deep river. Only, of course, it must be cleared—all the old buildings, for example, must be removed, this house too, which is really good for nothing and the old cherry orchard must be cut down.

LYUBOV: Cut down? My dear fellow, forgive me, but you don't know what you are talking about. If there is one thing interesting—remarkable indeed—in the whole province, it's just our cherry orchard.

LOPAHIN: The only thing remarkable about the orchard is that it's a very large one. There's a crop of cherries every alternate year, and then there's nothing to be done with them, no one buys them.

GAEV: This orchard is mentioned in the *Encyclopædia*.

LOPAHIN: [*Glancing at his watch.*] If we don't decide on something and don't take some steps, on the 22nd of August the cherry orchard and the whole estate too will be sold by auction. Make up your minds! There is no other way of saving it, I'll take my oath on that. No, No!

FIRS: In old days, forty or fifty years ago, they used to dry the cherries, soak them, pickle them, make jam too, and they used——

GAEV: Be quiet, Firs.

FIRS: And they used to send the preserved cherries to Moscow and to Harkov by the wagon-load. That brought the money in! And the preserved cherries in those days were soft and juicy, sweet and fragrant. . . . They knew the way to do them then. . . .

LYUBOV: And where is the recipe now?

FIRS: It's forgotten. Nobody remembers it.

PISHTCHIK: [*To* LYUBOV ANDREYEVNA.] What's it like in Paris? Did you eat frogs there?

LYUBOV: Oh, I ate crocodiles.

PISHTCHIK: Fancy that now!

LOPAHIN: There used to be only the gentlefolks and the peasants in the country, but now there are these summer visitors. All the towns, even the small ones, are surrounded nowadays by these summer villas. And one may say for sure, that in another twenty years there'll be many more of these people and that they'll be everywhere. At present the summer visitor only drinks tea in his verandah, but maybe he'll take to working his bit of land too, and then your cherry orchard would become happy, rich and prosperous. . . .

GAEV: [*Indignant.*] What rot!

[*Enter* VARYA *and* YASHA.]

VARYA: There are two telegrams for you, mamma. [*Takes out keys and opens an old-fashioned bookcase with a loud crack.*] Here they are.

LYUBOV: From Paris. [*Tears the telegrams, without reading them.*] I have done with Paris.

GAEV: Do you know, Lyuba, how old that bookcase is? Last week I pulled out the bottom drawer and there I found the date branded on it. The bookcase was made just a hundred years ago. What do you say to that? We might have celebrated its jubilee. Though it's an inanimate object, still it is a *book* case.

PISHTCHIK: [*Amazed.*] A hundred years! Fancy that now.

GAEV: Yes. . . . It is a thing. . . . [*Feeling the bookcase.*] Dear, honored, bookcase! Hail to thee who for more than a hundred years hast served the pure ideals of good and justice; thy silent call to fruitful labor has never flagged in those hundred years, maintaining [*In tears.*] in the generations of man, courage and faith in a brighter future and fostering in us ideals of good and social consciousness. [*A pause.*]

LOPAHIN: Yes. . . .

LYUBOV: You are just the same as ever, Leonid.

GAEV: [*A little embarrassed.*] Cannon off the right into the pocket!

LOPAHIN: [*Looking at his watch.*] Well, it's time I was off.

YASHA: [*Handing* LYUBOV ANDREYEVNA *medicine.*] Perhaps you will take your pills now.

PISHTCHIK: You shouldn't take medicines, my dear madam . . . they do no harm and no good. Give them here . . . honored lady. [*Takes the pill-box, pours the pills into the hollow of his hand, blows on them, puts them in his mouth and drinks off some kvass.*] There!

LYUBOV: [*In alarm.*] Why, you must be out of your mind!

PISHTCHIK: I have taken all the pills.

LOPAHIN: What a glutton! [*All laugh.*]

FIRS: His honor stayed with us in Easter week, ate a gallon and a half of cucumbers. . . . [*Mutters.*]

LYUBOV: What is he saying?

VARYA: He has taken to muttering like that for the last three years. We are used to it.

YASHA: His declining years!

[CHARLOTTA IVANOVNA, *a very thin, lanky figure in a white dress with a lorgnette in her belt, walks across the stage.*]

LOPAHIN: I beg your pardon, Charlotta Ivanovna, I have not had time to greet you. [*Tries to kiss her hand.*]

CHARLOTTA: [*Pulling away her hand.*] If I let you kiss my hand, you'll be wanting to kiss my elbow, and then my shoulder.

LOPAHIN: I've no luck to-day! [*All laugh.*] Charlotta Ivanovna, show us some tricks!

LYUBOV: Charlotta, do show us some tricks!

CHARLOTTA: I don't want to. I'm sleepy. [*Goes out.*]

LOPAHIN: In three weeks' time we shall meet again. [*Kisses* LYUBOV ANDREYEVNA'S *hand.*] Good-bye till then—I must go. [*To* GAEV] Good-bye. [*Kisses* PISHTCHIK.] Good-bye. [*Gives his hand to* VARYA, *then to* FIRS *and* YASHA.] I don't want to go. [*To* LYUBOV ANDREYEVNA.] If you think over my plan for the villas and make up your mind, then let me know; I will lend you 50,000 roubles. Think of it seriously.

VARYA: [*Angrily.*] Well, do go, for goodness sake.

LOPAHIN: I'm going, I'm going. [*Goes out.*]

GAEV: Low-born knave! I beg pardon, though . . . Varya is going to marry him, he's Varya's fiancé.

VARYA: Don't talk nonsense, uncle.

LYUBOV: Well, Varya, I shall be delighted. He's a good man.

PISHTCHIK: He is, one must acknowledge, a most worthy man. And my Dashenka . . . says too that . . . she says . . . various things. [*Snores, but at once wakes up.*] But all the same, honored lady, could you oblige me . . . with a loan of 240 roubles . . . to pay the interest on my mortgage to-morrow?

VARYA: [*Dismayed.*] No, no.

LYUBOV: I really haven't any money.

PISHTCHIK: It will turn up. [*Laughs.*] I never lose hope. I thought everything was over, I was a ruined man, and lo and behold—the railway passed through my land and . . . they paid me for it. And something else will turn up again, if not to-day, then to-morrow . . . Dashenka'll win two hundred thousand . . . she's got a lottery ticket.

LYUBOV: Well, we've finished our coffee, we can go to bed.

FIRS: [*Brushes* GAEV, *reprovingly.*] You have got on the wrong trousers again! What am I to do with you?

VARYA: [*Softly.*] Anya's asleep. [*Softly opens the window.*] Now the sun's risen, it's not a bit cold. Look, mamma, what exquisite trees! My goodness! And the air! The starlings are singing!

GAEV: [*Opens another window.*] The orchard is all white. You've not forgotten it, Lyuba? That long avenue that runs straight, straight as an arrow, how it shines on a moonlight night. You remember? You've not forgotten?

LYUBOV: [*Looking out of the window into the garden.*] Oh, my childhood, my innocence! It was in this nursery I used to sleep, from here I looked out into the orchard, happiness waked with me every morning and in those days the orchard was just the same, nothing has changed. [*Laughs with delight.*] All, all white! Oh, my orchard! After the dark gloomy autumn, and the cold winter; you are young again, and full of happiness, the heavenly angels have never left you. . . . If I could cast off the burden that weighs on my heart, if I could forget the past!

GAEV: H'm! and the orchard will be sold to pay our debts; it seems strange. . . .

LYUBOV: See, our mother walking . . . all in white, down the avenue! [*Laughs with delight.*] It is she!

GAEV: Where?

VARYA: Oh, don't, mamma!

LYUBOV: There is no one. It was my fancy. On the right there, by the path to the arbor, there is a white tree bending like a woman. . . .

[*Enter* TROFIMOV *wearing a shabby student's uniform and spectacles.*]

LYUBOV: What a ravishing orchard! White masses of blossom, blue sky. . . .

TROFIMOV: Lyubov Andreyevna! [*She looks round at him.*] I will just pay my respects to you and then leave you at once. [*Kisses her hand warmly.*] I was told to wait until morning, but I hadn't the patience to wait any longer. . . .

[LYUBOV ANDREYEVNA *looks at him in perplexity.*]

VARYA: [*Through her tears.*] This is Petya Trofimov.

TROFIMOV: Petya Trofimov, who was your Grisha's tutor. . . . Can I have changed so much?

[LYUBOV ANDREYEVNA *embraces him and weeps quietly.*]

GAEV: [*In confusion.*] There, there, Lyuba.

VARYA: [*Crying.*] I told you, Petya, to wait till to-morrow.

LYUBOV: My Grisha . . . my boy . . . Grisha . . . my son!

VARYA: We can't help it, mamma, it is God's will.

TROFIMOV: [*Softly through his tears.*] There . . . there.

LYUBOV: [*Weeping quietly.*] My boy was lost . . . drowned. Why? Oh, why, dear Petya? [*More quietly.*] Anya is asleep in there, and I'm talking loudly . . . making this noise. . . . But, Petya? Why have you grown so ugly? Why do you look so old?

TROFIMOV: A peasant-woman in the train called me a mangy-looking gentleman.

LYUBOV: You were quite a boy then, a pretty little student, and now your hair's thin—and spectacles. Are you really a student still? [*Goes towards the door.*]

TROFIMOV: I seem likely to be a perpetual student.

LYUBOV: [*Kisses her brother, then* VARYA.] Well, go to bed. . . . You are older too, Leonid.

PISHTCHIK: [*Follows her.*] I suppose it's time we were asleep. . . . Ugh! my gout. I'm staying the night! Lyubov Andreyevna, my dear soul, if you could . . . to-morrow morning . . . 240 roubles.

GAEV: That's always his story.

PISHTCHIK: 240 roubles . . . to pay the interest on my mortgage.

LYUBOV: My dear man, I have no money.

PISHTCHIK: I'll pay it back, my dear . . . a trifling sum.

LYUBOV: Oh, well, Leonid will give it you. . . . You give him the money, Leonid.

GAEV: Me give it him! Let him wait till he gets it!

LYUBOV: It can't be helped, give it him. He needs it. He'll pay it back.

[LYUBOV ANDREYEVNA, TROFIMOV, PISHTCHIK *and* FIRS *go out.* GAEV, VARYA *and* YASHA *remain.*]

GAEV: Sister hasn't got out of the habit of flinging away her money. [*To* YASHA.] Get away, my good fellow, you smell of the hen-house.

YASHA: [*With a grin.*] And you, Leonid Andreyevitch, are just the same as ever.

GAEV: What's that? [*To* VARYA.] What did he say?

VARYA: [*To* YASHA.] Your mother has come from the village; she has been sitting in the servants' room since yesterday, waiting to see you.

YASHA: Oh, bother her!

VARYA: For shame!

YASHA: What's the hurry? She might just as well have come to-morrow. [*Goes out.*]

VARYA: Mamma's just the same as ever, she hasn't changed a bit. If she had her own way, she'd give away everything.

GAEV: Yes. [*A pause.*] If a great many remedies are suggested for some disease, it means that the disease is incurable. I keep thinking and racking my brains; I have many schemes, a great many, and that really means none. If we could only come in for a legacy from somebody, or marry our Anya to a very rich man, or we might go to Yaroslavl and try our luck with our old aunt, the Countess. She's very, very rich, you know.

VARYA: [*Weeps.*] If God would help us.

GAEV: Don't blubber. Aunt's very rich, but she doesn't like us. First, sister married a lawyer instead of a nobleman. . . .

[ANYA *appears in the doorway.*]

GAEV: And then her conduct, one can't call it virtuous. She is good, and kind, and nice, and I love her, but, however one allows for extenuating circumstances, there's no denying that she's an immoral woman. One feels it in her slightest gesture.

VARYA: [*In a whisper.*] Anya's in the doorway.

GAEV: What do you say? [*A pause.*] It's queer, there seems to be something wrong with my right eye. I don't see as well as I did. And on Thursday when I was in the district Court . . .

[*Enter* ANYA.]

VARYA: Why aren't you asleep, Anya?

ANYA: I can't get to sleep.

GAEV: My pet. [*Kisses* ANYA's *face and hands.*] My child. [*Weeps.*] You are not my niece, you are my angel, you are everything to me. Believe me, believe. . . .

ANYA: I believe you, uncle. Everyone loves you and respects you . . . but, uncle dear, you must be silent . . . simply be silent. What were you saying just now about my mother, about your own sister? What made you say that?

GAEV: Yes, yes. . . . [*Puts his hand over his face.*] Really, that was awful! My God, save me! And to-day I made a speech to the bookcase . . . so stupid! And only when I had finished, I saw how stupid it was.

VARYA: It's true, uncle, you ought to keep quiet. Don't talk, that's all.

ANYA: If you could keep from talking, it would make things easier for you, too.

GAEV: I won't speak. [*Kisses* ANYA's *and* VARYA's *hands.*] I'll be silent. Only this is about business. On Thursday I was in the district Court; well, there was a large party of us there and we began talking of one thing and another, and this and that, and do you know, I believe that it will be possible to raise a loan on an I.O.U. to pay the arrears on the mortgage.

VARYA: If the Lord would help us!

GAEV: I'm going on Tuesday; I'll talk of it again. [*To* VARYA.] Don't blubber. [*To* ANYA.] Your mamma will talk to Lopahin; of course, he won't refuse her. And as soon as you're rested you shall go to Yaroslavl to the Countess, your great-aunt. So we shall all set to work in three directions at once, and the business is done. We shall pay off arrears, I'm convinced of it. [*Puts a caramel in his mouth.*] I swear on my honor, I swear by anything you like, the estate shan't be sold. [*Excitedly.*] By my own happiness, I swear it! Here's my hand on it, call me the basest, vilest of men, if I let it come to an auction! Upon my soul I swear it!

ANYA: [*Her equanimity has returned, she is quite happy.*] How good you are, uncle, and how clever! [*Embraces her uncle.*] I'm at peace now! Quite at peace! I'm happy!

[*Enter* FIRS.]

FIRS: [*Reproachfully.*] Leonid Andreyevitch, have you no fear of God? When are you going to bed?

GAEV: Directly, directly. You can go, Firs. I'll . . . yes, I will undress myself. Come, children, bye-bye. We'll go into details to-morrow, but now go to bed. [*Kisses* ANYA *and* VARYA.] I'm a man of the eighties. They run down that period, but still I can say I have had to suffer not a little for my convictions in my life, it's not for nothing that the peasant loves me. One must know the peasant! One must know how. . . .

ANYA: At it again, uncle!

VARYA: Uncle dear, you'd better be quiet!

FIRS: [*Angrily.*] Leonid Andreyevitch!

GAEV: I'm coming. I'm coming. Go to bed. Potted the shot—there's a shot for you! A beauty! [*Goes out,* FIRS *hobbling after him.*]

ANYA: My mind's at rest now. I don't want to go to Yaroslavl, I don't like my great-aunt, but still my mind's at rest. Thanks to uncle. [*Sits down.*]

VARYA: We must go to bed. I'm going. Something unpleasant happened while you were away. In the old servants' quarters there are only the old servants, as you know—Efimyushka, Polya and Yevstigney—and Karp too. They began letting stray people in to spend the night—I said nothing. But all at once I heard they had been spreading a report that I gave them nothing but pease pudding to eat. Out of stinginess, you know. . . . And it was all Yevstigney's doing. . . . Very well, I said to myself. . . . If that's how it is, I thought, wait a bit. I sent for Yevstigney. . . . [*Yawns.*] He comes. . . . "How's this, Yevstigney," I said, "you could be such a fool as to? . . ." [*Looking at* ANYA.] Anitchka! [*A pause.*] She's asleep. [*Puts her arm around* ANYA.] Come to bed . . . come along! [*Leads her.*] My darling has fallen asleep! Come. . . . [*They go.*]

[*Far away beyond the orchard a shepherd plays on a pipe.* TROFIMOV *crosses the stage and, seeing* VARYA *and* ANYA, *stands still.*]

VARYA: 'Sh! asleep, asleep. Come, my own.

ANYA: [*Softly, half asleep.*] I'm so tired. Still those bells. Uncle . . . dear . . . mamma and uncle. . . .

VARYA: Come, my own, come along.

[*They go into* ANYA's *room.*]

TROFIMOV: [*Tenderly.*] My sunshine! My spring.

CURTAIN

ACT II

The open country. An old shrine, long abandoned and fallen out of the perpendicular; near it a well, large stones that have apparently once been tombstones, and an old garden seat. The road to GAEV's *house is seen. On one side rise dark poplars; and there the cherry orchard begins. In the distance a row of telegraph poles and far, far away on the horizon there is faintly outlined a great town, only visible in very fine clear weather. It is near sunset.* CHARLOTTA, YASHA *and* DUNYASHA *are sitting on the seat.* EPIHODOV *is standing near, playing something mournful on a guitar. All sit plunged in thought.* CHARLOTTA *wears an old forage cap; she has taken a gun from her shoulder and is tightening the buckle on the strap.*

CHARLOTTA: [*Musingly.*] I haven't a real passport of my own, and I don't know how old I am, and I always feel that I'm a young thing. When I was a little girl, my father and mother used to travel about to fairs and give performances—very good ones. And I used to dance *salto-mortale* and all sorts of things. And when papa and mamma died, a German lady took me and had me educated. And so I grew up and become a governess. But where I came from, and who I am, I don't know. . . . Who my parents were, very likely they weren't married. . . . I don't know. [*Takes a cucumber out of her pocket and eats.*] I know nothing at all. [*A pause.*] One wants to talk and has no one to talk to. . . . I have nobody.

EPIHODOV: [*Plays on the guitar and sings.*] "What care I for the noisy world! What care I for friends or foes!" How agreeable it is to play on the mandoline!

DUNYASHA: That's a guitar, not a mandoline. [*Looks in a hand-mirror and powders herself.*]

EPIHODOV: To a man mad with love, it's a mandoline. [*Sings.*] "Were her heart but aglow with love's mutual flame." [YASHA *joins in.*]

CHARLOTTA: How shockingly these people sing! Foo! Like jackals!

DUNYASHA: [*To* YASHA.] What happiness, though, to visit foreign lands.

YASHA: Ah, yes! I rather agree with you there. [*Yawns, then lights a cigar.*]

EPIHODOV: That's comprehensible. In foreign lands everything has long since reached full complexion.

YASHA: That's so, of course.

EPIHODOV: I'm a cultivated man, I read remarkable books of all sorts, but I can never make out the tendency I am myself precisely inclined for, whether to live or to shoot myself, speaking precisely, but nevertheless I always carry a revolver. Here it is. . . . [*Shows revolver.*]

CHARLOTTA: I've had enough, and now I'm going. [*Puts on the gun.*] Epihodov, you're a very clever fellow, and a very terrible one too, all the women must be wild about you. Br-r-r! [*Goes.*] These clever fellows are all so stupid; there's not a creature for me to speak to. . . . Always alone, alone, nobody belonging to me . . . and who I am, and why I'm on earth, I don't know. [*Walks away slowly.*]

EPIHODOV: Speaking precisely, not touching upon other subjects, I'm bound to admit about myself, that destiny behaves mercilessly to me, as a storm to a little boat. If, let us suppose, I am mistaken, then why did I wake up this morning, to quote an example, and look round, and there on my chest was a spider of fearful magnitude . . . like this. [*Shows with both hands.*] And then I take up a jug of kvass, to quench my thirst, and in it there is something in the highest degree unseemly of the nature of a cockroach. [*A pause.*] Have you read Buckle?[2] [*A pause.*] I am desirous of troubling you, Dunyasha, with a couple of words.

DUNYASHA: Well, speak.

EPIHODOV: I should be desirous to speak with you alone. [*Sighs.*]

DUNYASHA: [*Embarrassed.*] Well—only bring me my mantle first. It's by the cupboard. It's rather damp here.

EPIHODOV: Certainly. I will fetch it. Now I know what I must do with my revolver. [*Takes guitar and goes off playing on it.*]

YASHA: Two and twenty misfortunes! Between ourselves, he's a fool. [*Yawns.*]

DUNYASHA: God grant he doesn't shoot himself! [*A pause.*] I am so nervous, I'm always in a flutter. I was a little girl when I was taken into our lady's house, and now I have quite grown out of peasant ways, and my hands are white, as white as a lady's. I'm such a delicate, sensitive creature, I'm afraid of everything. I'm so frightened. And if you deceive me, Yasha, I don't know what will become of my nerves.

YASHA: [*Kisses her.*] You're a peach! Of course a girl must never forget herself; what I dislike more than anything is a girl being flighty in her behavior.

DUNYASHA: I'm passionately in love with you, Yasha; you are a man of culture—you can give your opinion about anything. [*A pause.*]

YASHA: [*Yawns.*] Yes, that's so. My opinion is this: if a girl loves anyone, that means that she has no principles. [*A pause.*] It's pleasant smoking a cigar in the open air. [*Listens.*] Someone's coming this way . . . it's the gentlefolk. [DUNYASHA *embraces him impulsively.*] Go home, as though you had been to the river to bathe; go by that path, or else they'll meet you and suppose I have made an appointment with you here. That I can't endure.

DUNYASHA: [*Coughing softly.*] The cigar has made my head ache. . . . [*Goes off.*]

[YASHA *remains sitting near the shrine. Enter* LYUBOV ANDREYEVNA, GAEV *and* LOPAHIN.]

---

2. Henry Thomas Buckle, a learned but eccentric historian whose *History of Civilization in England* (1857) was the talk of Moscow a generation earlier. His work, highly respected initially for its empirical methods, quickly fell into disrepute in sophisticated intellectual circles.

LOPAHIN: You must make up your mind once for all—there's no time to lose. It's quite a simple question, you know. Will you consent to letting the land for building or not? One word in answer: Yes or no? Only one word!

LYUBOV: Who is smoking such horrible cigars here? [*Sits down.*]

GAEV: Now the railway line has been brought near, it's made things very convenient. [*Sits down.*] Here we have been over and lunched in town. Cannon off the white! I should like to go home and have a game.

LYUBOV: You have plenty of time.

LOPAHIN: Only one word! [*Beseechingly.*] Give me an answer!

GAEV: [*Yawning.*] What do you say?

LYUBOV: [*Looks in her purse.*] I had quite a lot of money here yesterday, and there's scarcely any left to-day. My poor Varya feeds us all on milk soup for the sake of economy; the old folks in the kitchen get nothing but pease pudding, while I waste my money in a senseless way. [*Drops purse, scattering gold pieces.*] There, they have all fallen out! [*Annoyed.*]

YASHA: Allow me, I'll soon pick them up. [*Collects the coins.*]

LYUBOV: Pray do, Yasha. And what did I go off to the town to lunch for? Your restaurant's a wretched place with its music and the tablecloth smelling of soap. . . . Why drink so much, Leonid? And eat so much? And talk so much? To-day you talked a great deal again in the restaurant, and all so inappropriately. About the era of the seventies, about the decadents. And to whom? Talking to waiters about decadents!

LOPAHIN: Yes.

GAEV: [*Waving his hand.*] I'm incorrigible; that's evident. [*Irritably to* YASHA.] Why is it you keep fidgeting about in front of us!

YASHA: [*Laughs.*] I can't help laughing when I hear your voice.

GAEV: [*To his sister.*] Either I or he. . . .

LYUBOV: Get along! Go away, Yasha.

YASHA: [*Gives* LYUBOV ANDREYEVNA *her purse.*] Directly. [*Hardly able to suppress his laughter.*] This minute. . . . [*Goes off.*]

LOPAHIN: Deriganov, the millionaire, means to buy your estate. They say he is coming to the sale himself.

LYUBOV: Where did you hear that?

LOPAHIN: That's what they say in town.

GAEV: Our aunt in Yaroslavl has promised to send help; but when, and how much she will send, we don't know.

LOPAHIN: How much will she send? A hundred thousand? Two hundred?

LYUBOV: Oh, well! . . . Ten or fifteen thousand, and we must be thankful to get that.

LOPAHIN: Forgive me, but such reckless people as you are—such queer, unbusiness-like people—I never met in my life. One tells you in plain Russian your estate is going to be sold, and you seem not to understand it.

LYUBOV: What are we to do? Tell us what to do.

LOPAHIN: I do tell you every day. Every day I say the same thing. You absolutely must let the cherry orchard and the land on building leases; and do it at once, as quick as may be—the auction's close upon us! Do understand! Once make up your mind to build villas, and you can raise as much money as you like, and then you are saved.

LYUBOV: Villas and summer visitors—forgive me saying so—it's so vulgar.

GAEV: There I perfectly agree with you.

LOPAHIN: I shall sob, or scream, or fall into a fit. I can't stand it! You drive me mad! [*To* GAEV.] You're an old woman!

GAEV: What do you say?

LOPAHIN: An old woman! [*Gets up to go.*]

LYUBOV: [*In dismay.*] No, don't go! Do stay, my dear friend! Perhaps we shall think of something.

LOPAHIN: What is there to think of?

LYUBOV: Don't go, I entreat you! With you here it's more cheerful, anyway. [*A pause.*] I keep expecting something, as though the house were going to fall about our ears.

GAEV: [*In profound dejection.*] Potted the white! It fails—a kiss.

LYUBOV: We have been great sinners. . . .

LOPAHIN: You have no sins to repent of.

GAEV: [*Puts a caramel in his mouth.*] They say I've eaten up my property in caramels. [*Laughs.*]

LYUBOV: Oh, my sins! I've always thrown my money away recklessly like a lunatic. I married a man who made nothing but debts. My husband died of champagne—he drank dreadfully. To my misery I loved another man, and immediately—it was my first punishment—the blow fell upon me, here, in the river . . . my boy was drowned and I went abroad—went away for ever, never to return, not to see that river again . . . I shut my eyes, and fled, distracted, and *he* after me . . . pitilessly, brutally. I bought a villa at Mentone, for *he* fell ill there, and for three years I had no rest day or night. His illness wore me out, my soul was dried up. And last year, when my villa was sold to pay my debts, I went to Paris and there he robbed me of everything and abandoned me for another woman; and I tried to poison myself. . . . So stupid, so shameful! . . . And suddenly I felt a yearning for Russia, for my country, for my little girl. . . . [*Dries her tears.*] Lord, Lord, be merciful! Forgive my sins! Do not chastise me more! [*Takes a telegram out of her pocket.*] I got this to-day from Paris. He implores forgiveness, entreats me to return. [*Tears up the telegram.*] I fancy there is music somewhere. [*Listens.*]

GAEV: That's our famous Jewish orchestra. You remember, four violins, a flute and a double bass.

LYUBOV: That still in existence? We ought to send for them one evening, and give a dance.

LOPAHIN: [*Listens.*] I can't hear. . . . [*Hums softly.*] "For money the Germans will turn a Russian into a Frenchman." [*Laughs.*] I did see such a piece at the theater yesterday! It was funny!

LYUBOV: And most likely there was nothing funny in it. You shouldn't look at plays, you should look at yourselves a little oftener. How gray your lives are! How much nonsense you talk.

LOPAHIN: That's true. One may say honestly, we live a fool's life. [*Pause.*] My father was a peasant, an idiot; he knew nothing and taught me nothing, only beat me when he was drunk, and always with his stick. In reality I am just such another blockhead and idiot. I've learnt nothing properly. I write a wretched hand. I write so that I feel ashamed before folks, like a pig.

LYUBOV: You ought to get married, my dear fellow.

LOPAHIN: Yes . . . that's true.

LYUBOV: You should marry our Varya, she's a good girl.

LOPAHIN: Yes.

LYUBOV: She's a good-natured girl, she's busy all day long, and what's more, she loves you. And you have liked her for ever so long.

LOPAHIN: Well? I'm not against it. . . . She's a good girl. [*Pause.*]

GAEV: I've been offered a place in the bank: 6,000 roubles a year. Did you know?

LYUBOV: You would never do for that! You must stay as you are.

[*Enter* FIRS *with overcoat.*]

FIRS: Put it on, sir, it's damp.

GAEV: [*Putting it on.*] You bother me, old fellow.

FIRS: You can't go on like this. You went away in the morning without leaving word. [*Looks him over.*]

LYUBOV: You look older, Firs!

FIRS: What is your pleasure?

LOPAHIN: You look older, she said.

FIRS: I've had a long life. They were arranging my wedding before your papa was born. . . . [*Laughs.*] I was the head footman before the emancipation came. I wouldn't consent to be set free then; I stayed on with the old master. . . . [*A pause.*] I remember what rejoicings they made and didn't know themselves what they were rejoicing over.

LOPAHIN: Those were fine old times. There was flogging anyway.

FIRS: [*Not hearing.*] To be sure! The peasants knew their place, and the masters knew theirs; but now they're all at sixes and sevens, there's no making it out.

GAEV: Hold your tongue, Firs. I must go to town to-morrow. I have been promised an introduction to a general, who might let us have a loan.

LOPAHIN: You won't bring that off. And you won't pay your arrears, you may rest assured of that.

LYUBOV: That's all his nonsense. There is no such general.

[*Enter* TROFIMOV, ANYA *and* VARYA.]

GAEV: Here come our girls.

ANYA: There's mamma on the seat.

LYUBOV: [*Tenderly.*] Come here, come along. My darlings! [*Embraces* ANYA *and* VARYA.] If you only knew how I love you both. Sit beside me, there, like that. [*All sit down.*]

LOPAHIN: Our perpetual student is always with the young ladies.

TROFIMOV: That's not your business.

LOPAHIN: He'll soon be fifty, and he's still a student.

TROFIMOV: Drop your idiotic jokes.

LOPAHIN: Why are you so cross, you queer fish?

TROFIMOV: Oh, don't persist!

LOPAHIN: [*Laughs.*] Allow me to ask you what's your idea of me?

TROFIMOV: I'll tell you my idea of you, Yermolay Alexeyevitch: you are a rich man, you'll soon be a millionaire. Well, just as in the economy of nature a wild beast is of use, who devours everything that comes in his way, so you too have your use.

[*All laugh.*]

VARYA: Better tell us something about the planets, Petya.

LYUBOV: No, let us go on with the conversation we had yesterday.

TROFIMOV: What was it about?

GAEV: About pride.

TROFIMOV: We had a long conversation yesterday, but we came to no conclusion. In pride, in your sense of it, there is something mystical. Perhaps you are right from your point of view; but if one looks at it simply, without subtlety, what sort of pride can there be, what sense is there in it, if man in his physiological formation is very imperfect, if in the immense majority of cases he is coarse, dull-witted, profoundly unhappy? One must give up glorification of self. One should work, and nothing else.

GAEV: One must die in any case.

TROFIMOV: Who knows? And what does it mean—dying? Perhaps man has a hundred senses, and only the five we know are lost at death, while the other ninety-five remain alive.

LYUBOV: How clever you are, Petya!

LOPAHIN: [*Ironically.*] Fearfully clever!

TROFIMOV: Humanity progresses, perfecting its powers. Everything that is beyond its ken now will one day become familiar and comprehensible; only we must work, we must with all our powers aid the seeker after truth. Here among us in Russia the workers are few in number as yet. The vast majority of the intellectual people I know, seek nothing, do nothing, are not fit as yet for work of any kind. They call themselves intellectual, but they treat their servants as inferiors, behave to the peasants as though they were animals, learn little, read nothing seriously, do practically nothing, only talk about science and know very little about art. They are all serious people, they all have severe faces, they all talk of weighty matters and air their theories, and yet the vast majority of us—ninety-nine per cent—live like savages, at the least thing fly to blows and abuse, eat piggishly, sleep in filth and stuffiness, bugs everywhere, stench and damp and moral impurity. And it's clear all our fine talk is only to divert our attention and other people's. Show me where to find the *crèches* there's so much talk about, and the reading-rooms? They only exist in novels: in real life there are none of them. There is nothing but filth and vulgarity and Asiatic apathy. I fear and dislike very serious faces. I'm afraid of serious conversations. We should do better to be silent.

LOPAHIN: You know, I get up at five o'clock in the morning, and I work from morning to night; and I've money, my own and other people's, always passing through my hands, and I see what people are made of all round me. One has only to begin to do anything to see how few honest, decent people there are. Sometimes when I lie awake at night, I think: "Oh! Lord, thou hast given us immense forests, boundless plains, the widest horizons, and living here we ourselves ought really to be giants."

LYUBOV: You ask for giants! They are no good except in story-books; in real life they frighten us.

[EPIHODOV *advances in the background, playing on the guitar.*]

LYUBOV: [*Dreamily.*] There goes Epihodov.

ANYA: [*Dreamily.*] There goes Epihodov.

GAEV: The sun has set, my friends.

TROFIMOV: Yes.

GAEV: [*Not loudly, but, as it were, declaiming.*] O nature, divine nature, thou art bright with eternal luster, beautiful and indifferent! Thou, whom we call mother, thou dost unite within thee life and death! Thou dost give life and dost destroy!

VARYA: [*In a tone of supplication.*] Uncle!

ANYA: Uncle, you are at it again!

TROFIMOV: You'd much better be cannoning off the red!

GAEV: I'll hold my tongue, I will.

[*All sit plunged in thought. Perfect stillness. The only thing audible is the muttering of* FIRS. *Suddenly there is a sound in the distance, as it were from the sky—the sound of a breaking harp-string, mournfully dying away.*]

LYUBOV: What is that?

LOPAHIN: I don't know. Somewhere far away a bucket fallen and broken in the pits. But somewhere very far away.

GAEV: It might be a bird of some sort—such as a heron.

TROFIMOV: Or an owl.

LYUBOV: [*Shudders.*] I don't know why, but it's horrid. [*A pause.*]

FIRS: It was the same before the calamity—the owl hooted and the samovar hissed all the time.

GAEV: Before what calamity?

FIRS: Before the emancipation. [*A pause.*]

LYUBOV: Come, my friends, let us be going; evening is falling. [*To* ANYA.] There are tears in your eyes. What is it, darling? [*Embraces her.*]

ANYA: Nothing, mamma; it's nothing.

TROFIMOV: There is somebody coming.

[*The* WAYFARER *appears in a shabby white forage cap and an overcoat; he is slightly drunk.*]

WAYFARER: Allow me to inquire, can I get to the station this way?

GAEV: Yes. Go along that road.

WAYFARER: I thank you most feelingly. [*Coughing.*] The weather is superb. [*Declaims.*] My brother, my suffering brother! . . . Come out to the Volga!

Whose groan do you hear? . . . [*To* VARYA.] Mademoiselle, vouchsafe a hungry Russian thirty kopecks.

[VARYA *utters a shriek of alarm.*]

LOPAHIN: [*Angrily.*] There's a right and a wrong way of doing everything!

LYUBOV: [*Hurriedly.*] Here, take this. [*Looks in her purse.*] I've no silver. No matter—here's gold for you.

WAYFARER: I thank you most feelingly! [*Goes off.*]

[*Laughter.*]

VARYA: [*Frightened.*] I'm going home—I'm going. . . . Oh, mamma, the servants have nothing to eat, and you gave him gold!

LYUBOV: There's no doing anything with me. I'm so silly! When we get home, I'll give you all I possess. Yermolay Alexeyevitch, you will lend me some more! . . .

LOPAHIN: I will.

LYUBOV: Come, friends, it's time to be going. And Varya, we have made a match of it for you. I congratulate you.

VARYA: [*Through her tears.*] Mamma, that's not a joking matter.

LOPAHIN: "Ophelia, get thee to a nunnery!"[3]

GAEV: My hands are trembling; it's a long while since I had a game of billiards.

LOPAHIN: "Ophelia! Nymph, in thy orisons be all my sins remember'd."[4]

LYUBOV: Come, it will soon be supper-time.

VARYA: How he frightened me! My heart's simply throbbing.

LOPAHIN: Let me remind you, ladies and gentlemen: on the 22nd of August the cherry orchard will be sold. Think about that! Think about it!

[*All go off, except* TROFIMOV *and* ANYA.]

ANYA: [*Laughing.*] I'm grateful to the wayfarer! He frightened Varya and we are left alone.

TROFIMOV: Varya's afraid we shall fall in love with each other, and for days together she won't leave us. With her narrow brain she can't grasp that we are above love. To eliminate the petty and transitory which hinder us from being free and happy—that is the aim and meaning of our life. Forward! We go forward irresistibly towards the bright star that shines yonder in the distance. Forward! Do not lag behind, friends.

ANYA: [*Claps her hands.*] How well you speak! [*A pause.*] It is divine here today.

TROFIMOV: Yes, it's glorious weather.

ANYA: Somehow, Petya, you've made me so that I don't love the cherry orchard as I used to. I used to love it so dearly. I used to think that there was no spot on earth like our garden.

TROFIMOV: All Russia is our garden. The earth is great and beautiful—there are many beautiful places in it. [*A pause.*] Think only, Anya, your grandfather,

---

3. See Shakespeare's *Hamlet* III.i.   4. See Shakespeare's *Hamlet* III.i.

and great-grandfather, and all your ancestors were slave-owners—the owners of living souls—and from every cherry in the orchard, from every leaf, from every trunk there are human creatures looking at you. Cannot you hear their voices? Oh, it is awful! Your orchard is a fearful thing, and when in the evening or at night one walks about the orchard, the old bark on the trees glimmers dimly in the dusk, and the old cherry trees seem to be dreaming of centuries gone by and tortured by fearful visions. Yes! We are at least two hundred years behind, we have really gained nothing yet, we have no definite attitude to the past, we do nothing but theorize or complain of depression or drink vodka. It is clear that to begin to live in the present we must first expiate our past, we must break with it; and we can expiate it only by suffering, by extraordinary unceasing labor. Understand that, Anya.

ANYA: The house we live in has long ceased to be our own, and I shall leave it, I give you my word.

TROFIMOV: If you have the house keys, fling them into the well and go away. Be free as the wind.

ANYA: [*In ecstasy.*] How beautifully you said that!

TROFIMOV: Believe me, Anya, believe me! I am not thirty yet, I am young, I am still a student, but I have gone through so much already! As soon as winter comes I am hungry, sick, careworn, poor as a beggar, and what ups and downs of fortune have I not known! And my soul was always, every minute, day and night, full of inexplicable forebodings. I have a foreboding of happiness, Anya. I see glimpses of it already.

ANYA: [*Pensively.*] The moon is rising.

> [EPIHODOV *is heard playing still the same mournful song on the guitar. The moon rises. Somewhere near the poplars* VARYA *is looking for* ANYA *and calling* "Anya! where are you?"]

TROFIMOV: Yes, the moon is rising. [*A pause.*] Here is happiness—here it comes! It is coming nearer and nearer; already I can hear its footsteps. And if we never see it—if we may never know it—what does it matter? Others will see it after us.

VARYA'S VOICE: Anya! Where are you?

TROFIMOV: That Varya again! [*Angrily.*] It's revolting!

ANYA: Well, let's go down to the river. It's lovely there.

TROFIMOV: Yes, let's go. [*They go.*]

VARYA'S VOICE: Anya! Anya!

CURTAIN

ACT III

A drawing-room divided by an arch from a larger drawing-room. A chandelier burning. The Jewish orchestra, the same that was mentioned in Act II, is heard playing in the ante-room. It is evening. In the larger drawing-room they are dancing the grand chain. The voice of SEMYONOV-PISHTCHIK: "Promenade à une paire!" *Then enter the drawing-room in couples first* PISHTCHIK *and* CHARLOTTA IVANOVA, *then* TROFIMOV *and* LYUBOV ANDREYEVNA, *thirdly* ANYA *with the* POST-OFFICE CLERK, *fourthly* VARYA *with the* STATION MASTER, *and other guests.* VARYA *is quietly weeping and wiping away her tears as she dances. In the last couple is* DUNYASHA. *They move across the drawing-room.* PISHTCHIK *shouts:* "Grand rond, balancez!" *and* "Les Cavaliers à genou et remerciez vos dames."

FIRS *in a swallow-tail coat brings in seltzer water on a tray.* PISHTCHIK *and* TROFIMOV *enter the drawing-room.*

PISHTCHIK: I am a full-blooded man; I have already had two strokes. Dancing's hard work for me, but as they say, if you're in the pack, you must bark with the rest. I'm as strong, I may say, as a horse. My parent, who would have his joke—may the Kingdom of Heaven be his!—used to say about our origin that the ancient stock of the Semyonov-Pishtchiks was derived from the very horse that Caligula made a member of the senate. [*Sits down.*] But I've no money, that's where the mischief is. A hungry dog believes in nothing but meat. [*Snores, but at once wakes up.*] That's like me . . . I can think of nothing but money.

TROFIMOV: There really is something horsy about your appearance.

PISHTCHIK: Well . . . a horse is a fine beast . . . a horse can be sold.

[*There is the sound of billiards being played in an adjoining room.* VARYA *appears in the arch leading to the larger drawing-room.*]

TROFIMOV: [*Teasing.*] Madame Lopahin! Madame Lopahin!

VARYA: [*Angrily.*] Mangy-looking gentleman!

TROFIMOV: Yes, I am a mangy-looking gentleman, and I'm proud of it!

VARYA: [*Pondering bitterly.*] Here we have hired musicians and nothing to pay them! [*Goes out.*]

TROFIMOV: [*To* PISHTCHIK.] If the energy you have wasted during your lifetime in trying to find the money to pay your interest had gone to something else, you might in the end have turned the world upside down.

PISHTCHIK: Nietzsche, the philosopher, a very great and celebrated man . . . of enormous intellect . . . says in his works, that one can make forged banknotes.

TROFIMOV: Why, have you read Nietzsche?

PISHTCHIK: What next . . . Dashenka told me. . . . And now I am in such a position, I might just as well forge banknotes. The day after to-morrow I must pay 310 roubles—130 I have procured. [*Feels in his pockets, in alarm.*] The money's gone! I have lost my money! [*Through his tears.*] Where's the money? [*Gleefully.*] Why, here it is behind the lining. . . . It has made me hot all over.

[*Enter* LYUBOV ANDREYEVNA *and* CHARLOTTA IVANOVNA.]

LYUBOV: [*Hums the Lezginka.*] Why is Leonid so long? What can he be doing in town? [*To* DUNYASHA.] Offer the musicians some tea.

TROFIMOV: The sale hasn't taken place, most likely.

LYUBOV: It's the wrong time to have the orchestra, and the wrong time to give a dance. Well, never mind. [*Sits down and hums softly.*]

CHARLOTTA: [*Gives* PISHTCHIK *a pack of cards.*] Here's a pack of cards. Think of any card you like.

PISHTCHIK: I've thought of one.

CHARLOTTA: Shuffle the pack now. That's right. Give it here, my dear Mr. Pishtchik. *Ein, zwei, drei*—now look, it's in your breast pocket.

PISHTCHIK: [*Taking a card out of his breast pocket.*] The eight of spades! Perfectly right! [*Wonderingly.*] Fancy that now!

CHARLOTTA: [*Holding pack of cards in her hands, to* TROFIMOV.] Tell me quickly which is the top card.

TROFIMOV: Well, the queen of spades.

CHARLOTTA: It is! [*To* PISHTCHIK.] Well, which card is uppermost?

PISHTCHIK: The ace of hearts.

CHARLOTTA: It is! [*Claps her hands, pack of cards disappears.*] Ah! what lovely weather it is to-day!

> [*A mysterious feminine voice which seems coming out of the floor answers her.* "Oh, yes, it's magnificent weather, madam."]

CHARLOTTA: You are my perfect ideal.

VOICE: And I greatly admire you too, madam.

STATION MASTER: [*Applauding.*] The lady ventriloquist—bravo!

PISHTCHIK: [*Wonderingly.*] Fancy that now! Most enchanting Charlotta Ivanovna. I'm simply in love with you.

CHARLOTTA: In love? [*Shrugging shoulders.*] What do you know of love, *guter Mensch, aber schlechter Musikant.*

TROFIMOV: [*Pats* PISHTCHIK *on the shoulder.*] You dear old horse. . . .

CHARLOTTA: Attention, please! Another trick! [*Takes a traveling rug from a chair.*] Here's a very good rug; I want to sell it. [*Shaking it out.*] Doesn't anyone want to buy it?

PISHTCHIK: [*Wonderingly.*] Fancy that!

CHARLOTTA: *Ein, zwei, drei!* [*Quickly picks up rug she has dropped; behind the rug stands* ANYA; *she makes a curtsey, runs to her mother, embraces her and runs back into the larger drawing-room amidst general enthusiasm.*]

LYUBOV: [*Applauds.*] Bravo! Bravo!

CHARLOTTA: Now again! *Ein, zwei, drei!* [*Lifts up the rug; behind the rug stands* VARYA, *bowing.*]

PISHTCHIK: [*Wonderingly.*] Fancy that now!

CHARLOTTA: That's the end. [*Throws the rug at* PISHTCHIK, *makes a curtsey, runs into the larger drawing-room.*]

PISHTCHIK: [*Hurries after her.*] Mischievous creature! Fancy! [*Goes out.*]

LYUBOV: And still Leonid doesn't come. I can't understand what he's doing in the town so long! Why, everything must be over by now. The estate is sold, or the sale has not taken place. Why keep us so long in suspense?

VARYA: [*Trying to console her.*] Uncle's bought it. I feel sure of that.

TROFIMOV: [*Ironically.*] Oh, yes!

VARYA: Great-aunt sent him an authorization to buy it in her name, and transfer the debt. She's doing it for Anya's sake, and I'm sure God will be merciful. Uncle will buy it.

LYUBOV: My aunt in Yaroslavl sent fifteen thousand to buy the estate in her name, she doesn't trust us—but that's not enough even to pay the arrears. [*Hides her face in her hands.*] My fate is being sealed to-day, my fate. . . .

TROFIMOV: [*Teasing* VARYA.] Madame Lopahin.

VARYA: [*Angrily.*] Perpetual student! Twice already you've been sent down from the University.

LYUBOV: Why are you angry, Varya? He's teasing you about Lopahin. Well, what of that? Marry Lopahin if you like, he's a good man, and interesting; if you don't want to, don't! Nobody compels you, darling.

VARYA: I must tell you plainly, mamma, I look at the matter seriously; he's a good man, I like him.

LYUBOV: Well, marry him. I can't see what you're waiting for.

VARYA: Mamma. I can't make him an offer myself. For the last two years, everyone's been talking to me about him. Everyone talks; but he says nothing or else makes a joke. I see what it means. He's growing rich, he's absorbed in business, he has no thoughts for me. If I had money, were it ever so little, if I had only a hundred roubles, I'd throw everything up and go far away. I would go into a nunnery.

TROFIMOV: What bliss!

VARYA: [*To* TROFIMOV.] A student ought to have sense! [*In a soft tone with tears.*] How ugly you've grown, Petya! How old you look! [*To* LYUBOV ANDREYEVNA, *no longer crying.*] But I can't do without work, mamma; I must have something to do every minute.

[*Enter* YASHA.]

YASHA: [*Hardly restraining his laughter.*] Epihodov has broken a billiard cue! [*Goes out.*]

VARYA: What is Epihodov doing here? Who gave him leave to play billiards? I can't make these people out. [*Goes out.*]

LYUBOV: Don't tease her, Petya. You see she has grief enough without that.

TROFIMOV: She is so very officious, meddling in what's not her business. All the summer she's given Anya and me no peace. She's afraid of a love affair between us. What's it to do with her? Besides, I have given no grounds for it. Such triviality is not in my line. We are above love!

LYUBOV: And I suppose I am beneath love. [*Very uneasily.*] Why is it Leonid's not here? If only I could know whether the estate is sold or not! It seems such an incredible calamity that I really don't know what to think. I am distracted . . . I shall scream in a minute . . . I shall do something stupid. Save me, Petya, tell me something, talk to me!

TROFIMOV: What does it matter whether the estate is sold to-day or not? That's all done with long ago. There's no turning back, the path is overgrown. Don't worry yourself, dear Lyubov Andreyevna. You mustn't deceive yourself; for once in your life you must face the truth!

LYUBOV: What truth? You see where the truth lies, but I seem to have lost my sight, I see nothing. You settle every great problem so boldly, but tell me, my dear boy, isn't it because you're young—because you haven't yet understood one of your problems through suffering? You look forward boldly, and isn't it that you don't see and don't expect anything dreadful because life is still hidden from your young eyes? You're bolder, more honest, deeper than we are, but think, be just a little magnanimous, have pity on me. I was born here, you know, my father and mother lived here, my grandfather lived here, I love this house. I can't conceive of life without the cherry orchard, and if it really must be sold, then sell me with the orchard. [*Embraces* TROFIMOV, *kisses him on the forehead.*] My boy was drowned here. [*Weeps.*] Pity me, my dear kind fellow.

TROFIMOV: You know I feel for you with all my heart.

LYUBOV: But that should have been said differently, so differently. [*Takes out her handkerchief, telegram falls on the floor.*] My heart is so heavy to-day. It's so noisy here, my soul is quivering at every sound, I'm shuddering all over, but I can't go away; I'm afraid to be quiet and alone. Don't be hard on me, Petya . . . I love you as though you were one of ourselves. I would gladly let you marry Anya—I swear I would—only, my dear boy, you must take your degree, you do nothing—you're simply tossed by fate from place to place. That's so strange. It is, isn't it? And you must do something with your beard to make it grow somehow. [*Laughs.*] You look so funny!

TROFIMOV: [*Picks up the telegram.*] I've no wish to be a beauty.

LYUBOV: That's a telegram from Paris. I get one every day. One yesterday and one to-day. That savage creature is ill again, he's in trouble again. He begs forgiveness, beseeches me to go, and really I ought to go to Paris to see him. You look shocked, Petya. What am I to do, my dear boy, what am I to do? He is ill, he is alone and unhappy, and who'll look after him, who'll keep him from doing the wrong thing, who'll give him his medicine at the right time? And why hide it or be silent? I love him, that's clear. I love him! I love him! He's a millstone about my neck, I'm going to the bottom with him, but I love that stone and can't live without it. [*Presses* TROFIMOV's *hand.*] Don't think ill of me, Petya, don't tell me anything, don't tell me. . . .

TROFIMOV: [*Through his tears*] For God's sake forgive my frankness: why, he robbed you!

LYUBOV: No! No! No! You mustn't speak like that. [*Covers her ears.*]

TROFIMOV: He is a wretch! You're the only person that doesn't know it! He's a worthless creature! A despicable wretch!

LYUBOV: [*Getting angry, but speaking with restraint.*] You're twenty-six or twenty-seven years old, but you're still a schoolboy.

TROFIMOV: Possibly.

LYUBOV: You should be a man at your age! You should understand what love means! And you ought to be in love yourself. You ought to fall in love! [*Angrily.*] Yes, yes, and it's not purity in you, you're simply a prude, a comic fool, a freak.

TROFIMOV: [*In horror.*] The things she's saying!

LYUBOV: I am above love! You're not above love, but simply as our Firs here says, "You are a good-for-nothing." At your age not to have a mistress!

TROFIMOV: [*In horror.*] This is awful! The things she is saying! [*Goes rapidly into the larger drawing-room clutching his head.*] This is awful! I can't stand it! I'm going. [*Goes off, but at once returns.*] All is over between us! [*Goes off into the ante-room.*]

LYUBOV: [*Shouts after him.*] Petya! Wait a minute! You funny creature! I was joking! Petya! [*There is a sound of somebody running quickly downstairs and suddenly falling with a crash.* ANYA *and* VARYA *scream, but there is a sound of laughter at once.*]

LYUBOV: What has happened?

[ANYA *runs in.*]

ANYA: [*Laughing.*] Petya's fallen downstairs! [*Runs out.*]

LYUBOV: What a queer fellow that Petya is!

[*The* STATION MASTER *stands in the middle of the larger room and reads* The Magdalene, *by Alexey Tolstoy. They listen to him, but before he has recited many lines strains of a waltz are heard from the ante-room and the reading is broken off. All dance.* TROFIMOV, ANYA, VARYA *and* LYUBOV ANDREYEVNA *come in from the ante-room.*]

LYUBOV: Come, Petya—come, pure heart! I beg your pardon. Let's have a dance! [*Dances with* PETYA.]

[ANYA *and* VARYA *dance.* FIRS *comes in, puts his stick down near the side door.* YASHA *also comes into the drawing-room and looks on at the dancing.*]

YASHA: What is it, old man?

FIRS: I don't feel well. In old days we used to have generals, barons and admirals dancing at our balls, and now we send for the post-office clerk and the station master and even they're not overanxious to come. I am getting feeble. The old master, the grandfather, used to give sealing-wax for all complaints. I have been taking sealing-wax for twenty years or more. Perhaps that's what's kept me alive.

YASHA: You bore me, old man! [*Yawns.*] It's time you were done with.

FIRS: Ach, you're a good-for-nothing! [*Mutters.*]

[TROFIMOV *and* LYUBOV ANDREYEVNA *dance in larger room and then on to the stage.*]

LYUBOV: *Merci.* I'll sit down a little. [*Sits down.*] I'm tired.

[*Enter* ANYA.]

ANYA: [*Excitedly.*] There's a man in the kitchen has been saying that the cherry orchard's been sold to-day.

LYUBOV: Sold to whom?

ANYA: He didn't say to whom. He's gone away.

[*She dances with* TROFIMOV, *and they go off into the larger room.*]

YASHA: There was an old man gossiping there, a stranger.

FIRS: Leonid Andreyevitch isn't here yet, he hasn't come back. He has his light overcoat on, *demi-saison,* he'll catch cold for sure. Ach! Foolish young things!

LYUBOV: I feel as though I should die. Go, Yasha, find out to whom it has been sold.

YASHA: But he went away long ago, the old chap. [*Laughs.*]

LYUBOV: [*With slight vexation.*] What are you laughing at? What are you pleased at?

YASHA: Epihodov is so funny. He's a silly fellow, two and twenty misfortunes.

LYUBOV: Firs, if the estate is sold, where will you go?

FIRS: Where you bid me, there I'll go.

LYUBOV: Why do you look like that? Are you ill? You ought to be in bed.

FIRS: Yes. [*Ironically.*] Me go to bed and who's to wait here? Who's to see to things without me? I'm the only one in all the house.

YASHA: [*To* LYUBOV ANDREYEVNA.] Lyubov Andreyevna, permit me to make a request of you; if you go back to Paris again, be so kind as to take me with you. It's positively impossible for me to stay here. [*Looking about him; in an undertone.*] There's no need to say it, you see for yourself—an uncivilized country, the people have no morals, and then the dullness! The food in the kitchen's abominable, and then Firs runs after one muttering all sorts of unsuitable words. Take me with you, please do!

[*Enter* PISHTCHIK.]

PISHTCHIK: Allow me to ask you for a waltz, my dear lady. [LYUBOV ANDREYEVNA *goes with him.*] Enchanting lady, I really must borrow of you just 180 roubles, [*Dances.*] only 180 roubles. [*They pass into the larger room.*]

[*In the larger drawing-room, a figure in a gray top hat and in check trousers is gesticulating and jumping about. Shouts of* "Bravo, Charlotta Ivanovna."]

DUNYASHA: [*She has stopped to powder herself.*] My young lady tells me to dance. There are plenty of gentlemen, and too few ladies, but dancing makes me giddy and makes my heart beat. Firs, the post-office clerk said something to me just now that quite took my breath away.

[*Music becomes more subdued.*]

FIRS: What did he say to you?

DUNYASHA: He said I was like a flower.

YASHA: [*Yawns.*] What ignorance! [*Goes out.*]

DUNYASHA: Like a flower. I am a girl of such delicate feelings, I am awfully fond of soft speeches.

FIRS: Your head's being turned.

[*Enter* EPIHODOV.]

EPIHODOV: You have no desire to see me, Dunyasha. I might be an insect. [*Sighs.*] Ah! life!

DUNYASHA: What is it you want?

EPIHODOV: Undoubtedly you may be right. [*Sighs.*] But, of course, if one looks at it from that point of view, if I may so express myself, you have, excuse my plain speaking, reduced me to a complete state of mind. I know my destiny.

Every day some misfortune befalls me and I have long ago grown accustomed to it, so that I look upon my fate with a smile. You gave me your word, and though I——

DUNYASHA: Let us have a talk later, I entreat you, but now leave me in peace, for I am lost in reverie. [*Plays with her fan.*]

EPIHODOV: I have a misfortune every day, and if I may venture to express myself, I merely smile at it, I even laugh.

[VARYA *enters from the larger drawing-room.*]

VARYA: You still have not gone, Epihodov. What a disrespectful creature you are, really! [*To* DUNYASHA.] Go along, Dunyasha! [*To* EPIHODOV.] First you play billiards and break the cue, then you go wandering about the drawing-room like a visitor!

EPIHODOV: You really cannot, if I may so express myself, call me to account like this.

VARYA: I'm not calling you to account, I'm speaking to you. You do nothing but wander from place to place and don't do your work. We keep you as a counting-house clerk, but what use you are I can't say.

EPIHODOV: [*Offended.*] Whether I work or whether I walk, whether I eat or whether I play billiards, is a matter to be judged by persons of understanding and my elders.

VARYA: You dare to tell me that! [*Firing up.*] You dare! You mean to say I've no understanding. Begone from here! This minute!

EPIHODOV: [*Intimidated.*] I beg you to express yourself with delicacy.

VARYA: [*Beside herself with anger.*] This moment! get out! away! [*He goes towards the door, she following him.*] Two and twenty misfortunes! Take yourself off! Don't let me set eyes on you! [EPIHODOV *has gone out, behind the door his voice,* "I shall lodge a complaint against you."] What! You're coming back? [*Snatches up the stick* FIRS *has put down near the door.*] Come! Come! Come! I'll show you! What! you're coming? Then take that! [*She swings the stick, at the very moment that* LOPAHIN *comes in.*]

LOPAHIN: Very much obliged to you!

VARYA: [*Angrily and ironically.*] I beg your pardon!

LOPAHIN: Not at all! I humbly thank you for your kind reception!

VARYA: No need of thanks for it. [*Moves away, then looks round and asks softly.*] I haven't hurt you?

LOPAHIN: Oh, no! Not at all! There's an immense bump coming up, though!

VOICES FROM LARGER ROOM: Lopahin has come! Yermolay Alexeyevitch!

PISHTCHIK: What do I see and hear? [*Kisses* LOPAHIN.] There's a whiff of cognac about you, my dear soul, and we're making merry here too!

[*Enter* LYUBOV ANDREYEVNA.]

LYUBOV: Is it you, Yermolay Alexeyevitch? Why have you been so long? Where's Leonid?

LOPAHIN: Leonid Andreyevitch arrived with me. He is coming.

LYUBOV: [*In agitation.*] Well! Well! Was there a sale? Speak!

LOPAHIN: [*Embarrassed, afraid of betraying his joy.*] The sale was over at four o'clock. We missed our train—had to wait till half-past nine. [*Sighing heavily.*] Ugh! I feel a little giddy.

[*Enter* GAEV. *In his right hand he has purchases, with his left hand he is wiping away his tears.*]

LYUBOV: Well, Leonid? What news? [*Impatiently, with tears.*] Make haste, for God's sake!

GAEV: [*Makes her no answer, simply waves his hand. To* FIRS, *weeping.*] Here, take them; there's anchovies, Kertch herrings. I have eaten nothing all day. What I have been through! [*Door into the billiard room is open. There is heard a knocking of balls and the voice of* YASHA *saying* "Eighty-seven." GAEV's *expression changes, he leaves off weeping.*] I am fearfully tired. Firs, come and help me change my things. [*Goes to his own room across the larger drawing-room.*]

PISHTCHIK: How about the sale? Tell us, do!

LYUBOV: Is the cherry orchard sold?

LOPAHIN: It is sold.

LYUBOV: Who has bought it?

LOPAHIN: I have bought it. [*A pause.* LYUBOV *is crushed; she would fall down if she were not standing near a chair and table.*]

[VARYA *takes keys from her waistband, flings them on the floor in middle of drawing-room and goes out.*]

LOPAHIN: I have bought it! Wait a bit, ladies and gentlemen, pray. My head's a bit muddled, I can't speak. [*Laughs.*] We came to the auction. Deriganov was there already. Leonid Andreyevitch only had 15,000 and Deriganov bid 30,000, besides the arrears, straight off. I saw how the land lay. I bid against him. I bid 40,000, he bid 45,000, I said 55, and so he went on, adding 5 thousands and adding 10. Well . . . So it ended. I bid 90, and it was knocked down to me. Now the cherry orchard's mine! Mine! [*Chuckles.*] My God, the cherry orchard's mine! Tell me that I'm drunk, that I'm out of my mind, that it's all a dream. [*Stamps with his feet.*] Don't laugh at me! If my father and my grandfather could rise from their graves and see all that has happened! How their Yermolay, ignorant, beaten Yermolay, who used to run about barefoot in winter, how that very Yermolay has bought the finest estate in the world! I have bought the estate where my father and grandfather were slaves, where they weren't even admitted into the kitchen. I am asleep, I am dreaming! It is all fancy, it is the work of your imagination plunged in the darkness of ignorance. [*Picks up keys, smiling fondly.*] She threw away the keys; she means to show she's not the housewife now. [*Jingles the keys.*] Well, no matter. [*The orchestra is heard tuning up.*] Hey, musicians! Play! I want to hear you. Come, all of you, and look how Yermolay Lopahin will take the ax to the cherry orchard, how the trees will fall to the ground! We will build houses on it and our grandsons and great-grandsons will see a new life springing up there. Music! Play up!

[*Music begins to play.* LYUBOV ANDREYEVNA *has sunk into a chair and is weeping bitterly.*]

LOPAHIN: [*Reproachfully.*] Why, why didn't you listen to me? My poor friend! Dear lady, there's no turning back now. [*With tears.*] Oh, if all this could be over, oh, if our miserable disjointed life could somehow soon be changed!

PISHTCHIK: [*Takes him by the arm, in an undertone.*] She's weeping, let us go and leave her alone. Come. [*Takes him by the arm and leads him into the larger drawing-room.*]

LOPAHIN: What's that? Musicians, play up! All must be as I wish it. [*With irony.*] Here comes the new master, the owner of the cherry orchard! [*Accidentally tips over a little table, almost upsetting the candelabra.*] I can pay for everything! [*Goes out with* PISHTCHIK. *No one remains on the stage or in the larger drawing-room except* LYUBOV, *who sits huddled up, weeping bitterly. The music plays softly.* ANYA *and* TROFIMOV *come in quickly.* ANYA *goes up to her mother and falls on her knees before her.* TROFIMOV *stands at the entrance to the larger drawing-room.*]

ANYA: Mamma! Mamma, you're crying, dear, kind, good mamma! My precious! I love you! I bless you! The cherry orchard is sold, it is gone, that's true, that's true! But don't weep, mamma! Life is still before you, you have still your good, pure heart! Let us go, let us go, darling, away from here! We will make a new garden, more splendid than this one; you will see it, you will understand. And joy, quiet, deep joy, will sink into your soul like the sun at evening! And you will smile, mamma! Come, darling, let us go!

CURTAIN

ACT IV

SCENE: *Same as in First Act. There are neither curtains on the windows nor pictures on the walls: only a little furniture remains piled up in a corner as if for sale. There is a sense of desolation; near the outer door and in the background of the scene are packed trunks, traveling bags, etc. On the left the door is open, and from here the voices of* VARYA *and* ANYA *are audible.* LOPAHIN *is standing waiting.* YASHA *is holding a tray with glasses full of champagne. In front of the stage* EPIHODOV *is tying up a box. In the background behind the scene a hum of talk from the peasants who have come to say good-bye. The voice of* GAEV: "Thanks, brothers, thanks!"*

YASHA: The peasants have come to say good-bye. In my opinion, Yermolay Alexeyevitch, the peasants are good-natured, but they don't know much about things.

[*The hum of talk dies away. Enter across front of stage* LYUBOV ANDREYEVNA *and* GAEV. *She is not weeping, but is pale; her face is quivering—she cannot speak.*]

GAEV: You gave them your purse, Lyuba. That won't do—that won't do!
LYUBOV: I couldn't help it! I couldn't help it!

[*Both go out.*]

LOPAHIN: [*In the doorway, calls after them.*] You will take a glass at parting? Please do. I didn't think to bring any from the town, and at the station I could only get one bottle. Please take a glass. [*A pause.*] What? You don't care for any? [*Comes away from the door.*] If I'd known, I wouldn't have bought it. Well, and I'm not going to drink it. [YASHA *carefully sets the tray down on a chair.*] You have a glass, Yasha, anyway.

YASHA: Good luck to the travelers, and luck to those that stay behind! [*Drinks.*] This champagne isn't the real thing, I can assure you.

LOPAHIN: It cost eight roubles the bottle. [*A pause.*] It's devilish cold here.

YASHA: They haven't heated the stove today—it's all the same since we're going. [*Laughs.*]

LOPAHIN: What are you laughing for?

YASHA: For pleasure.

LOPAHIN: Though it's October, it's as still and sunny as though it were summer. It's just right for building! [*Looks at his watch; says in doorway.*] Take note, ladies and gentlemen, the train goes in forty-seven minutes; so you ought to start for the station in twenty minutes. You must hurry up!

[TROFIMOV *comes in from out of doors wearing a great-coat.*]

TROFIMOV: I think it must be time to start, the horses are ready. The devil only knows what's become of my goloshes; they're lost. [*In the doorway.*] Anya! My goloshes aren't here. I can't find them.

LOPAHIN: And I'm getting off to Harkov. I am going in the same train with you. I'm spending all the winter at Harkov. I've been wasting all my time gossiping with you and fretting with no work to do. I can't get on without work. I don't know what to do with my hands, they flap about so queerly, as if they didn't belong to me.

TROFIMOV: Well, we're just going away, and you will take up your profitable labors again.

LOPAHIN: Do take a glass.

TROFIMOV: No, thanks.

LOPAHIN: Then you're going to Moscow now?

TROFIMOV: Yes. I shall see them as far as the town, and to-morrow I shall go on to Moscow.

LOPAHIN: Yes, I daresay, the professors aren't giving any lectures, they're waiting for your arrival.

TROFIMOV: That's not your business.

LOPAHIN: How many years have you been at the University?

TROFIMOV: Do think of something newer than that—that's stale and flat. [*Hunts for goloshes.*] You know we shall most likely never see each other again, so let me give you one piece of advice at parting: don't wave your arms about—get out of the habit. And another thing, building villas, reckoning up that the summer visitors will in time become independent farmers—reckoning like that, that's not the thing to do either. After all, I am fond of you: you have fine delicate fingers like an artist, you've a fine delicate soul.

LOPAHIN: [*Embraces him.*] Good-bye, my dear fellow. Thanks for everything. Let me give you money for the journey, if you need it.

TROFIMOV: What for? I don't need it.

LOPAHIN: Why, you haven't got a half-penny.

TROFIMOV: Yes, I have, thank you. I got some money for a translation. Here it is in my pocket, [*Anxiously.*] but where can my goloshes be!

VARYA: [*From the next room.*] Take the nasty things! [*Flings a pair of goloshes on to the stage.*]

TROFIMOV: Why are you so cross, Varya? h'm! . . . but those aren't my goloshes.

LOPAHIN: I sowed three thousand acres with poppies in the spring, and now I have cleared forty thousand profit. And when my poppies were in flower, wasn't it a picture! So here, as I say, I made forty thousand, and I'm offering you a loan because I can afford to. Why turn up your nose? I am a peasant— I speak bluntly.

TROFIMOV: Your father was a peasant, mine was a chemist—and that proves absolutely nothing whatever. [LOPAHIN *takes out his pocket-book.*] Stop that—stop that. If you were to offer me two hundred thousand I wouldn't take it. I am an independent man, and everything that all of you, rich and poor alike, prize so highly and hold so dear, hasn't the slightest power over me—it's like so much fluff fluttering in the air. I can get on without you. I can pass by you. I am strong and proud. Humanity is advancing towards the highest truth, the highest happiness, which is possible on earth, and I am in the front ranks.

LOPAHIN: Will you get there?

TROFIMOV: I shall get there. [*A pause.*] I shall get there, or I shall show others the way to get there.

[*In the distance is heard the stroke of an ax on a tree.*]

LOPAHIN: Good-bye, my dear fellow; it's time to be off. We turn up our noses at one another, but life is passing all the while. When I am working hard without resting, then my mind is more at ease, and it seems to me as though I too know what I exist for; but how many people there are in Russia, my dear boy, who exist, one doesn't know what for. Well, it doesn't matter. That's not what keeps things spinning. They tell me Leonid Andreyevitch has taken a situation. He is going to be a clerk at the bank—6,000 roubles a year. Only, of course, he won't stick to it—he's too lazy.

ANYA: [*In the doorway.*] Mamma begs you not to let them chop down the orchard until she's gone.

TROFIMOV: Yes, really, you might have the tact. [*Walks out across the front of the stage.*]

LOPAHIN: I'll see to it! I'll see to it! Stupid fellows! [*Goes out after him.*]

ANYA: Has Firs been taken to the hospital?

YASHA: I told them this morning. No doubt they have taken him.

ANYA: [*To* EPIHODOV, *who passes across the drawing-room.*] Semyon Pantaleyevitch, inquire, please, if Firs has been taken to the hospital.

YASHA: [*In a tone of offence.*] I told Yegor this morning—why ask a dozen times?

EPIHODOV: Firs is advanced in years. It's my conclusive opinion no treatment would do him good; it's time he was gathered to his fathers. And I can only envy him. [*Puts a trunk down on a cardboard hat-box and crushes it.*] There, now, of course—I knew it would be so.

YASHA: [*Jeeringly.*] Two and twenty misfortunes!

VARYA: [*Through the door.*] Has Firs been taken to the hospital?

ANYA: Yes.

VARYA: Why wasn't the note for the doctor taken too?

ANYA: Oh, then, we must send it after them. [*Goes out.*]

VARYA: [*From the adjoining room.*] Where's Yasha? Tell him his mother's come to say good-bye to him.

YASHA: [*Waves his hand.*] They put me out of all patience! [DUNYASHA *has all this time been busy about the luggage. Now, when* YASHA *is left alone, she goes up to him.*]

DUNYASHA: You might just give me one look, Yasha. You're going away. You're leaving me. [*Weeps and throws herself on his neck.*]

YASHA: What are you crying for? [*Drinks the champagne.*] In six days I shall be in Paris again. To-morrow we shall get into the express train and roll away in a flash. I can scarcely believe it! *Vive la France!* It doesn't suit me here—it's not the life for me; there's no doing anything. I have seen enough of the ignorance here. I have had enough of it. [*Drinks champagne.*] What are you crying for? Behave yourself properly, and then you won't cry.

DUNYASHA: [*Powders her face, looking in a pocket-mirror.*] Do send me a letter from Paris. You know how I loved you, Yasha—how I loved you! I am a tender creature, Yasha.

YASHA: Here they are coming!

[*Busies himself about the trunks, humming softly. Enter* LYUBOV ANDREYEVNA, GAEV, ANYA *and* CHARLOTTA IVANOVNA.]

GAEV: We ought to be off. There's not much time now. [*Looking at* YASHA.] What a smell of herrings!

LYUBOV: In ten minutes we must get into the carriage. [*Casts a look about the room.*] Farewell, dear house, dear old home of our fathers! Winter will pass and spring will come, and then you will be no more; they will tear you down! How much those walls have seen! [*Kisses her daughter passionately.*] My treasure, how bright you look! Your eyes are sparkling like diamonds! Are you glad? Very glad?

ANYA: Very glad! A new life is beginning, mamma.

GAEV: Yes, really, everything is all right now. Before the cherry orchard was sold, we were all worried and wretched, but afterwards, when once the question was settled conclusively, irrevocably, we all felt calm and even cheerful. I am a bank clerk now—I am a financier—cannon off the red. And you, Lyuba, after all, you are looking better; there's no question of that.

LYUBOV: Yes. My nerves are better, that's true. [*Her hat and coat are handed to her.*] I'm sleeping well. Carry out my things, Yasha. It's time. [*To* ANYA.] My darling, we shall soon see each other again. I am going to Paris. I can live there on the money your Yaroslavl auntie sent us to buy the estate with—hurrah for auntie—but that money won't last long.

ANYA: You'll come back soon, mamma, won't you? I'll be working up for my examination in the high school, and when I have passed that, I shall set to work and be a help to you. We will read all sorts of things together, mamma, won't we? [*Kisses her mother's hands.*] We will read in the autumn evenings. We'll read lots of books, and a new wonderful world will open out before us. [*Dreamily.*] Mamma, come soon.

LYUBOV: I shall come, my precious treasure. [*Embraces her.*]

[*Enter* LOPAHIN. CHARLOTTA *softly hums a song.*]

GAEV: Charlotta's happy; she's singing!

CHARLOTTA: [*Picks up a bundle like a swaddled baby.*] Bye, bye, my baby. [*A baby is heard crying: "Ooah! ooah!"*] Hush, hush, my pretty boy! [*Ooah! ooah!*] Poor little thing! [*Throws the bundle back.*] You must please find me a situation. I can't go on like this.

LOPAHIN: We'll find you one, Charlotta Ivanovna. Don't you worry yourself.

GAEV: Everyone's leaving us. Varya's going away. We have become of no use all at once.

CHARLOTTA: There's nowhere for me to be in the town. I must go away. [*Hums.*] What care I . . .

[*Enter* PISHTCHIK.]

LOPAHIN: The freak of nature!

PISHTCHIK: [*Gasping.*] Oh! . . . let me get my breath. . . . I'm worn out . . . my most honored . . . Give me some water.

GAEV: Want some money, I suppose? Your humble servant! I'll go out of the way of temptation. [*Goes out.*]

PISHTCHIK: It's a long while since I have been to see you . . . dearest lady. [*To* LOPAHIN.] You are here . . . glad to see you . . . a man of immense intellect . . . take . . . here. [*Gives* LOPAHIN.] 400 roubles. That leaves me owing 840.

LOPAHIN: [*Shrugging his shoulders in amazement.*] It's like a dream. Where did you get it?

PISHTCHIK: Wait a bit . . . I'm hot . . . a most extraordinary occurrence! Some Englishmen came along and found in my land some sort of white clay. [*To* LYUBOV ANDREYEVNA.] And 400 for you . . . most lovely . . . wonderful. [*Gives money.*] The rest later. [*Sips water.*] A young man in the train was telling me just now that a great philosopher advises jumping off a house-top. "Jump!" says he; "the whole gist of the problem lies in that." [*Wonderingly.*] Fancy that, now! Water, please!

LOPAHIN: What Englishmen?

PISHTCHIK: I have made over to them the rights to dig the clay for twenty-four years . . . and now, excuse me . . . I can't stay . . . I must be trotting on. I'm going to Znoikovo . . . to Kardamanovo. . . . I'm in debt all round. [*Sips.*] . . . To your very good health! . . . I'll come in on Thursday.

LYUBOV: We are just off to the town, and to-morrow I start for abroad.

PISHTCHIK: What! [*In agitation.*] Why to the town? Oh, I see the furniture . . . the boxes. No matter . . . [*Through his tears.*] . . . no matter . . . men of enormous intellect . . . these Englishmen. . . . Never mind . . . be happy. God will succor you . . . no matter . . . everything in this world must have an end. [*Kisses* LYUBOV ANDREYEVNA's *hand.*] If the rumor reaches you that my end has come, think of this . . . old horse, and say: "There once was such a man in the world . . . Semyonov-Pishtchik . . . the Kingdom of Heaven be his!" . . . most extraordinary weather . . . yes. [*Goes out in violent agitation, but at once returns and says in the doorway.*] Dashenka wishes to be remembered to you. [*Goes out.*]

LYUBOV: Now we can start. I leave with two cares in my heart. The first is leaving Firs ill. [*Looking at her watch.*] We have still five minutes.

ANYA: Mamma, Firs has been taken to the hospital. Yasha sent him off this morning.

LYUBOV: My other anxiety is Varya. She is used to getting up early and working; and now, without work, she's like a fish out of water. She is thin and pale, and she's crying, poor dear! [*A pause.*] You are well aware, Yermolay Alexeyevitch, I dreamed of marrying her to you, and everything seemed to show that you would get married. [*Whispers to* ANYA *and motions to* CHARLOTTA *and both go out.*] She loves you—she suits you. And I don't know—I don't know why it is you seem, as it were, to avoid each other. I can't understand it!

LOPAHIN: I don't understand it myself, I confess. It's queer somehow, altogether. If there's still time, I'm ready now at once. Let's settle it straight off, and go ahead; but without you, I feel I shan't make her an offer.

LYUBOV: That's excellent. Why, a single moment's all that's necessary. I'll call her at once.

LOPAHIN: And there's champagne all ready too. [*Looking into the glasses.*] Empty! Someone's emptied them already. [YASHA *coughs.*] I call that greedy.

LYUBOV: [*Eagerly.*] Capital! We will go out. Yasha, *allez!* I'll call her in. [*At the door.*] Varya, leave all that; come here. Come along! [*Goes out with* YASHA.]

LOPAHIN: [*Looking at his watch.*] Yes.

[*A pause. Behind the door, smothered laughter and whispering, and, at last, enter* VARYA.]

VARYA: [*Looking a long while over the things.*] It is strange, I can't find it anywhere.

LOPAHIN: What are you looking for?

VARYA: I packed it myself, and I can't remember. [*A pause.*]

LOPAHIN: Where are you going now, Varvara Mihailova?

VARYA: I? To the Ragulins. I have arranged to go to them to look after the house— as a housekeeper.

LOPAHIN: That's in Yashnovo? It'll be seventy miles away. [*A pause.*] So this is the end of life in this house!

VARYA: [*Looking among the things.*] Where is it? Perhaps I put it in the trunk. Yes, life in this house is over—there will be no more of it.

LOPAHIN: And I'm just off to Harkov—by this next train. I've a lot of business there. I'm leaving Epihodov here, and I've taken him on.

VARYA: Really!

LOPAHIN: This time last year we had snow already, if you remember; but now it's so fine and sunny. Though it's cold, to be sure—three degrees of frost.

VARYA: I haven't looked. [*A pause.*] And besides, our thermometer's broken. [*A pause.*]

[*Voice at the door from the yard:* "Yermolay Alexeyevitch!"]

LOPAHIN: [*As though he had long been expecting this summons.*] This minute!

> [LOPAHIN *goes out quickly.* VARYA *sitting on the floor and laying her head on a bag full of clothes, sobs quietly. The door opens.* LYUBOV ANDREYEVNA *comes in cautiously.*]

LYUBOV: Well? [*A pause.*] We must be going.

VARYA: [*Has wiped her eyes and is no longer crying.*] Yes, mamma, it's time to start. I shall have time to get to the Ragulins to-day, if only you're not late for the train.

LYUBOV: [*In the doorway.*] Anya, put your things on.

> [*Enter* ANYA, *then* GAEV *and* CHARLOTTA IVANOVNA. GAEV *has on a warm coat with a hood. Servants and cabmen come in.* EPIHODOV *bustles about the luggage.*]

LYUBOV: Now we can start on our travels.

ANYA: [*Joyfully.*] On our travels!

GAEV: My friends—my dear, my precious friends! Leaving this house for ever, can I be silent? Can I refrain from giving utterance at leave-taking to those emotions which now flood all my being?

ANYA: [*Supplicatingly.*] Uncle!

VARYA: Uncle, you mustn't!

GAEV: [*Dejectedly.*] Cannon and into the pocket . . . I'll be quiet. . . .

> [*Enter* TROFIMOV *and afterwards* LOPAHIN.]

TROFIMOV: Well, ladies and gentlemen, we must start.

LOPAHIN: Epihodov, my coat!

LYUBOV: I'll stay just one minute. It seems as though I have never seen before what the walls, what the ceilings in this house were like, and now I look at them with greediness, with such tender love.

GAEV: I remember when I was six years old sitting in that window on Trinity Day watching my father going to church.

LYUBOV: Have all the things been taken?

LOPAHIN: I think all. [*Putting on overcoat, to* EPIHODOV.] You, Epihodov, mind you see everything is right.

EPIHODOV: [*In a husky voice.*] Don't you trouble, Yermolay Alexeyevitch.

LOPAHIN: Why, what's wrong with your voice?

EPIHODOV: I've just had a drink of water, and I choked over something.

YASHA: [*Contemptuously.*] The ignorance!

LYUBOV: We are going—and not a soul will be left here.

LOPAHIN: Not till the spring.

VARYA: [*Pulls a parasol out of a bundle, as though about to hit someone with it.* LOPAHIN *makes a gesture as though alarmed.*] What is it? I didn't mean anything.

TROFIMOV: Ladies and gentlemen, let us get into the carriage. It's time. The train will be in directly.

VARYA: Petya, here they are, your goloshes, by that box. [*With tears.*] And what dirty old things they are!

TROFIMOV: [*Putting on his goloshes.*] Let us go, friends!

GAEV: [*Greatly agitated, afraid of weeping.*] The train—the station! Double baulk, ah!

LYUBOV: Let us go!

LOPAHIN: Are we all here? [*Locks the side-door on left.*] The things are all here. We must lock up. Let us go!

ANYA: Good-bye, home! Good-bye to the old life!

TROFIMOV: Welcome to the new life!

[TROFIMOV *goes out with* ANYA. VARYA *looks round the room and goes out slowly.* YASHA *and* CHARLOTTA IVANOVNA, *with her dog, go out.*]

LOPAHIN: Till the spring, then! Come, friends, till we meet! [*Goes out.*]

[LYUBOV ANDREYEVNA *and* GAEV *remain alone. As though they had been waiting for this, they throw themselves on each other's necks, and break into subdued smothered sobbing, afraid of being overheard.*]

GAEV: [*In despair.*] Sister, my sister!

LYUBOV: Oh, my orchard!—my sweet, beautiful orchard! My life, my youth, my happiness, good-bye! good-bye!

VOICE OF ANYA: [*Calling gaily.*] Mamma!

VOICE OF TROFIMOV: [*Gaily, excitedly.*] Aa—oo!

LYUBOV: One last look at the walls, at the windows. My dear mother loved to walk about this room.

GAEV: Sister, sister!

VOICE OF ANYA: Mamma!

VOICE OF TROFIMOV: Aa—oo!

LYUBOV: We are coming. [*They go out.*]

[*The stage is empty. There is the sound of the doors being locked up, then of the carriages driving away. There is silence. In the stillness there is the dull stroke of an ax in a tree, clanging with a mournful lonely sound. Footsteps are heard.* FIRS *appears in the doorway on the right. He is dressed as always—in a pea-jacket and white waistcoat, with slippers on his feet. He is ill.*]

FIRS: [*Goes up to the doors, and tries the handles.*] Locked! They have gone . . . [*Sits down on sofa.*] They have forgotten me. . . . Never mind . . . I'll sit here a bit. . . . I'll be bound Leonid Andreyevitch hasn't put his fur coat on and has gone off in his thin overcoat. [*Sighs anxiously.*] I didn't see after him. . . . These young people . . . [*Mutters something that can't be distinguished.*] Life has slipped by as though I hadn't lived. [*Lies down.*] I'll lie down a bit. . . . There's no strength in you, nothing left you—all gone! Ech! I'm good for nothing. [*Lies motionless.*]

[*A sound is heard that seems to come from the sky, like a breaking harp-string, dying away mournfully. All is still again, and there is heard nothing but the strokes of the ax far away in the orchard.*]

CURTAIN

1903–1904

Passages from Letters[1]

TO D. V. GRIGOROVICH,[2] MARCH 28, 1886

. . . If I do have a gift that should be respected, I confess before your pure heart that up to now I haven't respected it. I felt that I had it, but got used to considering it insignificant. There are plenty of purely external reasons to make an individual unfair, extremely suspicious, and distrustful of himself, and I reflect now that there have been plenty of such reasons in my case. All my friends and relatives were always condescending toward my writing and constantly advised me in a friendly way not to give up real work for scribbling. I have hundreds of friends in Moscow, a score of whom write, and I cannot recall a single one who read my work or considered me an artist. There is a so-called "literary circle" in Moscow: talents and mediocrities of all shapes and sizes gather once a week in a restaurant and exercise their tongues. If I were to go there and read them a mere snippet of your letter, they would laugh in my face. During the five years I have been roaming around editorial offices I managed to succumb to the general view of my literary insignificance, quickly got used to looking at my work condescendingly, and—kept plugging away! That's the first reason. The second is that I am a doctor and am up to my ears in medical work, so that the proverb about chasing two hares has cost me more sleep than anyone else.

I write all this merely to justify myself to you in the smallest way for my deep sin. Up to now I have treated my literary work extremely lightly, carelessly, haphazardly. I do not remember working more than a day on *any single* story of mine, and I wrote *The Huntsman,* which you liked, when I went swimming! I wrote my stories as reporters write their news about fires: mechanically, half-consciously, without worrying about either the reader or themselves. I wrote and constantly tried not to waste images and scenes which I valued on these stories, and I tried to save them and carefully hide them, God only knows why.

Suvorin's[3] very friendly and, so far as I can see, sincere letter, was the first thing to impel me to look at my work critically. I began to get ready to write something significant, but I still had no faith in my own literary significance. Then suddenly, completely unexpectedly, your letter came. Forgive the comparison, but it acted on me like an order "to leave town within twenty-four hours!" that is, I suddenly felt an absolute necessity to hurry, to get out of the place I was stuck in as quickly as possible. . . .

I will liberate myself from deadlines, but not at once. There is no possibility of getting out of the rut into which I have fallen. I don't mind starving as I have already done, but there are others involved too. I give my leisure to writing, two or three hours a day and a little bit of the night, that is, time that is suitable only for trifling work. This summer, when I will have more leisure and will have to earn less, I will undertake something serious. . . .

1. Translated by Ralph E. Matlaw.   2. D. V. Grigorovich (1822–1899), an important writer in the 1840s and the later part of the century, had written to Chekhov on March 25, 1886, praising his outstanding talent and urging him to write more seriously.   3. A. S. Suvorin (1833–1911), influential publisher of the conservative paper *New Times,* became Chekhov's closest friend.

TO A. N. PLESHCHEEV,[4] OCTOBER 4, 1888

. . . Write to me after you've read my *Name-Day Party*. You won't like it, but I am not afraid of you or Anna Mikhailovna.[5] I am afraid of those who will look for tendenciousness between the lines and who are determined to see me either as a liberal or a conservative. I am neither a liberal nor a conservative, neither a gradualist nor a monk nor an indifferentist. I would like to be nothing more than a free artist, and I regret that God did not give me the gift to be one. I hate falseness and coercion in all their forms and consistorial secretaries are just as repellent to me as Notovich and Gradovsky.[6] Pharisaism, stupidity, and arbitrariness reign not merely in merchants' houses and police stations: I see them in science, in literature, among the young. That is why I have no particular passion for either policemen or butchers or scientists or writers or the young. I consider brand-names and labels a prejudice. My holy of holies is the human body, health, intelligence, talent, inspiration, love, and absolute freedom, freedom from force and falseness in whatever form they express themselves. That's the platform I'd subscribe to if I were a great artist. . . .

TO A. N. PLESHCHEEV, OCTOBER 9, 1888

. . . Is there really no "ideology" apparent in my last story [*The Name-Day Party*] either? Once you remarked to me that the element of protest is missing from my work, that there is neither sympathy nor antipathy in them. But don't I protest against falsehood from the beginning of the story to its end? Isn't that ideology? No? Well then, that means that I don't know how to bite, or that I am a flea. . . .

TO A. S. SUVORIN, OCTOBER 27, 1888

. . . I sometimes preach heresy, but I have never yet gone so far as to deny a place in art to topical questions altogether. In conversations with the writing fraternity I always insist that the artist's function is not to solve narrowly specialized questions. It is bad for the artist to undertake something he doesn't understand. We have specialists for specialized questions; it is their function to discuss the peasant commune, the fate of capitalism, the evil of drink, shoes, women's diseases. The artist, however, must treat only what he understands; his sphere is as limited as that of any other specialist's, I repeat that and always insist on it. Only somebody who has never written or had anything to do with images could say that there are no questions in his realm, that there is nothing but answers. The artist observes, chooses, guesses, compounds—these actions in themselves already presuppose a question at the origin; if the artist did not pose a question to himself at the beginning then there was nothing to guess or to choose. To be as brief as possible, I'll end with psychiatry: if you deny questions and intentions in creative work you must acknowledge that the artist creates unintentionally, without purpose, under the influence of a temporary aberration; therefore, if an author were to brag to me that he wrote a tale purely by inspiration, without previously having pondered his intentions, I would call him insane.

4. I. L. Shcheglov-Leontiev (1825–1893), poet and editor of the *Northern Herald*, in which Chekhov published.   5. A. M. Efreinova, publisher of the *Northern Herald*.   6. Two supposedly unscrupulous left-wing journalists.

You are right in demanding that an artist approach his work consciously, but you are confusing two concepts: *the solution of a problem and the correct formulation of a problem*. Only the second is required of the artist. Not a single problem is resolved in *Anna Karenina* or *Onegin*, but they satisfy you completely only because all the problems in them are formulated correctly. The judge is required to formulate the questions correctly, but the decision is left to the jurors, each according to his own taste. . . .

QUESTIONS

1. Sometimes the title of *The Bear* is translated as *The Brute*. Which title seems to you to describe best the action of the play? Why?
2. In what different ways does the dialogue indicate that Mrs. Popov is not entirely honest about her feelings?
3. Describe in detail the character of Luke. How is his character revealed? In what ways is he like Firs in *The Cherry Orchard*? Do any other characters in *The Bear* remind you of characters in *The Cherry Orchard*? In what specific ways?
4. Why is there so little "action" in *The Cherry Orchard*? Describe the full "plot" of the play. How much of the action takes place offstage?
5. Explain how the billiard talk helps to characterize Gaev. Which other characters deploy language in peculiar ways that help to characterize them?
6. How do you respond to Trofimov? What are his likable characteristics? What is his function in the plot?
7. How do you respond to Charlotta? Why? What kind of social class does she seem to belong to?
8. If you were staging the play, what kind of furniture would you use in the opening scene to help characterize Madame Ranevsky?
9. If you were directing the play, how sympathetic would you try to make Firs? How would you do it?

WRITING SUGGESTIONS

1. Read another full-length play by Chekhov. Choose one character from that play who is similar to a character in either *The Bear* or *The Cherry Orchard,* and write a four- or five-page paper comparing how Chekhov *introduces* the two characters.
2. Read a full-length biography of Chekhov. In what specific ways does knowledge of Chekhov's life help you to interpret *The Cherry Orchard*?
3. Read at least three short stories that Chekhov wrote after 1888, and compare the kinds of themes in them to *The Cherry Orchard*. Choose one of the stories, and in a four-page paper discuss the different ways in which Chekhov explores the themes in the story and in the play.

26

CULTURE AS CONTEXT:
SOCIAL AND HISTORICAL SETTING

Time conditions all texts, but a sense of time is particularly important for readers of drama. Events in drama often seem more immediate than in poems or stories, and the demands of time seem more pressing. Immediacy is an important feature of drama, and not only in performance. Reading drama involves a strong sense of presentness as well, for all the action takes place in the present tense regardless of what time period is being represented. Nothing in drama is narrated or recounted: action is all in words and gestures happening right now. And all the action takes place rather fast; novels often take many hours to read, but most plays can easily be read in the time it would take to perform them on stage—two or three hours—even when the action they represent covers several years in time.

But whatever the illusion of presentness, plays often deal with extensive and complicated dislocations in time, and readers of drama are frequently asked to make sophisticated moves that involve an adjustment to more than the illusion of immediacy. Even though action seems to be taking place as we read, the plot may be set far in the past, and we are often required as readers to bring to bear specific historical information on the times being represented. Sensitive reading of a play may depend on making some fairly complicated distinctions between different time frames.

Three different levels of time operate in most plays. First, play texts represent some particular time—the temporal setting—in which the action takes place. We can call this **plot time.** Second, texts reflect the time when the author was writing, and the conditions and assumptions of that time find their way into the conception and style of the text. This feature of textual time we may call **authorial time.** Third, readers read a text in a particular time frame of their own, and sometimes conditions and assumptions then are very different from those that obtain in either the text's present or the author's present. We may call this time **reader time.**

These three levels of time often interact importantly in the way we interpret a text. When, for example, we read—as American readers in the 1990s—a play written by Shakespeare in the early seventeenth century about the Danish court of many centuries earlier, we have three time schemes operating at once. We are reading about a time (and place) very remote from us, and the text in which these events are represented reflects values, writing conditions, habits of language, and dramatic conventions of a second time—centuries later than the action but still almost four centuries earlier than the time in which we read. Values in these three times are not going to be identical, and how we interpret the actions and thoughts of Hamlet in part depends not only on our own assumptions about what he ought to do or might do, but on what we know about the expectations of human events in two earlier ages. Suspending these three "settings" in our minds as we read—and consciously making comparisons when we perceive conflicts of values—is an important part of interpretation and response. We perceive at one and the same time three different Hamlets—ours (the reader's), Shakespeare's (the text's), and the "historical" Hamlet known to his contemporaries in medieval Denmark. In this particular case, the play does not ask us to know anything very specific about the historical Hamlet; we do not need to know, for example, the history of ancient Elsinore. All we really need to know is that the Danish monarchy passes within families but not necessarily to the eldest son.

Many plays explicitly invoke a particular era as the time of action, and often they specify (in stage directions or interjected comments) information about the era that is relevant to the interpretation of specific episodes. But sometimes we have to supply historical or cultural facts from outside the text, and often we have to adjust our expectations because the "world" of the play—its "present" time in some past age in some specific place—is very different from our own world. People may share some characteristics across ages and cultures, but behavior and motivation are often conditioned by present habits and situations, and often we are asked to think carefully about the particulars of a time and place very different from our own. Identifying the setting of a play—in both time and place—and considering carefully its historical situation are often crucial to understanding what happens and why.

Often, however, plays are aggressively contemporary—that is, they represent the times in which they are written—and thus they are not "historical" in the sense that they evoke earlier times that have to be consciously remembered or studied. When, for example, *A Raisin in the Sun* first appeared on Broadway in 1959, its audience watched scenes that might well have been occurring at virtually that same moment: Lorraine Hansberry wrote her play about current events and issues, and the temporal setting she represented on the stage was shortly before 1959 (she says explicitly that the action occurs "sometime between World War II and the present"). In such a play (and in plays, contemporary settings are very common, perhaps more so than in either stories or poems), there is almost no difference between plot time and authorial time. In fact the strategy of the play depends on the audience believing that there is no distinction: playgoers (and readers) are asked to accept that what they are seeing (or reading) is utterly contemporary, happening at the very moment of stage representation. The strategy is to make members of the audience feel as if they are confronting issues—and life itself—exactly as it is happening, that the play is dealing with the particular issues of that contemporary moment. And the choice of setting—the specific place where a play is set (in this case a South Side Chicago ghetto)—usually involves in plays that seek to be contemporary a kind of representative setting—that is, a place that is broadly like other contemporary locations, though the specificity of setting is also important in itself.

Of course, a play such as *A Raisin in the Sun* is still "historical" in an important sense: the "history" that it tries to represent is the moment of performance (or, technically, that moment of creation a few months or weeks just before the performances). In the case of *A Raisin in the Sun,* the historical time (both plot time and authorial time) represented is thus 1959, and for the first audiences and readers of the play 1959 was also reader time. Now, however, reading the play nearly forty years later, we are likely to be quite conscious of it as "historical"—that is, it represents and preserves a particular moment in time when certain things were happening that are now distanced from us and that we can now examine in a somewhat more detached way. But not totally. *A Raisin in the Sun* is still "relevant" for readers or viewers because issues of family, ambition, dignity, economic survival, American values, racial discrimination, and social attitudes continue to exist in very similar forms. A lot of what happens in *A Raisin in the Sun* in a 1950s setting could still happen in nearly the same way two generations later. But not everything.

Take for example the abortion that Ruth Younger contemplates near the end of Act I. In 1959, abortion was illegal in the United States; women who sought abortions either had to leave the country, usually traveling to Mexico or Puerto Rico, where abortion was more readily available, or resort to shady, back-alley practitioners like the one Ruth consults. Conditions in such operations were often unsanitary and unsavory, and medical expertise was sometimes poor; disease and mortality rates were high, and besides the social stigma of disobeying the law (which was very strong in middle-class Christian African-American families), the fear of medical and physical consequences was powerful. However individuals might themselves feel about the ethics and emotional consequences of abortion, the law prohibited it, and public opinion—although beginning to be less rigid and censorious—was still heavily against the practice. Some of the horror that the Younger family (and especially Mama) expresses here at the thought of abortion can be attributed to economic embarrassment and ideas of family unity and integrity, but to imagine how an audience responded to the idea in 1959 involves knowing about not only the legal situation but also social attitudes more generally, especially within a respectable, proud, and aspiring African-American family like the Youngers.

Chicago, and especially the crowded African-American neighborhoods on the South Side in the years after World War II, is an important part of the cultural context in the play, too. The migration of African-Americans from the South to Chicago in early to mid-century because of the availability of jobs there lies behind the conditions depicted in *A Raisin in the Sun,* as do the decreasing employment opportunities, worsening economic conditions, and urban crowding after World War II. If you are familiar with the writings of Richard Wright, especially *Native Son* or the film made from the novel, you will recognize the living conditions, racial segregation, and rising social tensions expressed in *A Raisin in the Sun,* for Hansberry's play is set in the very same Chicago neighborhood as Wright's novel. Just as any play depends on (or tries to create) some historical knowledge about plot time, the larger sense of culture in a particular time and place is also crucial. Here a sense of culture and cultural context involves at least three distinct categories: America and American assumptions and values in the mid-twentieth century; the African-American subculture in America, with all its social complexities and the brutal fruits of a long history of discrimination; and urban Chicago with its specific versions of social, economic, and political values and problems. And each of these categories brings its own subcategories to think about. Consider, for example, the issues the play raises about matriarchal families and the "manhood" of characters like Walter.

Another aspect of cultural and historical context includes language. Language often involves subtle changes over a period of time—changes that reflect broader social and cultural assumptions—and almost any gap, however small, between authorial time and reader time will turn up usages that have shifted. If you are an attentive student of American language, you may notice in the text a number of expressions that now require interpretation or at least an explanatory footnote. One example in *A Raisin in the Sun* involves the way the characters here refer to their racial identity, usually as "colored" Americans. A present reader may not know quite how to take such a self-reference, but in 1959 it was the standard, approved, and respected self-designation. More complicated, of course, are the differentiations of attitude and language between generations in the play: the different languages of George Murchison and Joseph Asagai (or of Ruth and Beneatha) mirror different attitudes current in 1959 within the African-American community and are reflected accurately here by the playwright. Readers conscious of how historical assumptions in a text may differ from assumptions within reader time still have to sort out carefully the way formal elements such as language are employed in a text to make class, generational, ethnic, and racial differentiations.

Negotiation of times in a play can often be complicated. Discovering the realities of an earlier time does not, however, exactly involve trying to project oneself into that earlier time; it would be as foolish as it is impossible to try to *be* an earlier reader or viewer. What *is* important is understanding the difference—negotiating distances between what one knows or assumes now and what was known or assumed in an earlier historical moment. Understanding that difference (and taking it into account in interpretation) is all a present reader can be asked to do.

Death of a Salesman was written ten years before *A Raisin in the Sun;* it is now half a century old, but in many ways it seems contemporary because it draws on enduring assumptions within American culture about habits and values. Still, it is "dated": its specific notions about what salesmen want, how they talk, what they do is rooted in the times just after World War II. As you read, you may want to pinpoint details that date the play firmly in the years around 1949, when it was first performed.

Like *A Raisin in the Sun, Death of a Salesman* pretty much collapses the difference between plot time and authorial time; both plays depict events that are virtually contemporary and that seem as if they could be taking place at the time of first performance. Both plays also draw heavily on the idea of the American Dream, a concept that is time- and culture-bound but not specifically tied to a particular year or decade and that could be represented as taking place in many different locations within U.S. culture. And like *A Raisin in the Sun, Death of a Salesman* both presents and questions the values involved in the Dream—wondering about the desire to be rich as well as the means commonly undertaken to achieve it. Both the plot and the characterization here are subservient to notions of Americanness and the pursuit of the Dream. In what ways does the play seem to you specifically characteristic of the mid-twentieth century? How would an end-of-the-century character need to be represented differently (even if the American Dream was still his [or her] main preoccupation)? What particulars would need to be changed or updated? Would the sons need to be portrayed differently? Would the particulars of plot need to be varied? How, exactly? How would, do you think, the character of Linda have to be changed? Willie? What details of the plot and action from 1949 do you have trouble understanding? What would you need to explain, in 1949 or now, to readers who were not American?

> "[Death of a Salesman] *is a tragedy modern and personal, not classic and heroic. Its central figure is a little man sentenced to discover his smallness rather than a big man undone by his greatness."*
>
> —JOHN MASON BROWN

All plays involve some historical adjustment and understanding on the part of readers and viewers: time does not stand still, and with changes in habits come changes in values, behavior, and assumptions. All reading implicitly involves a kind of "double" response—the one the reader feels from a present perspective and the one he or she may need to construct intellectually because of specific historical or cultural knowledge. One never bridges gaps of history completely, but conscious effort lessens the gap and makes it both understandable and negotiable in the reading process.

LORRAINE HANSBERRY

A Raisin in the Sun

What happens to a dream deferred?
Does it dry up
Like a raisin in the sun?
Or fester like a sore—
And then run?
Does it stink like rotten meat?
Or crust and sugar over—
Like a syrupy sweet?

Maybe it just sags
Like a heavy load.

Or does it explode?
—LANGSTON HUGHES[1]

CAST OF CHARACTERS

RUTH YOUNGER	JOSEPH ASAGAI
TRAVIS YOUNGER	GEORGE MURCHISON
WALTER LEE YOUNGER (BROTHER)	KARL LINDNER
BENEATHA YOUNGER	BOBO
LENA YOUNGER (MAMA)	MOVING MEN

The action of the play is set in Chicago's Southside, sometime between World War II and the present.

ACT I

SCENE ONE

The Younger living room would be a comfortable and well-ordered room if it were not for a number of indestructible contradictions to this state of being. Its furnishings are typical and undistinguished and their primary feature now is that they have clearly had to accommodate the living of too many people for too many years—and they are tired. Still, we can see that at some time, a time probably no longer remembered by the family (except perhaps for MAMA), the furnishings of this room were actually selected with care and love and even hope—and brought to this apartment and arranged with taste and pride.

That was a long time ago. Now the once loved pattern of the couch upholstery has to fight to show itself from under acres of crocheted doilies and couch covers which have themselves finally come to be more important than the upholstery. And here a table or a chair has been moved to disguise the worn places in the carpet; but the carpet has

1. Hughes's poem, published in 1951, is entitled "Harlem," and it is about the classic New York ghetto. See page 876.

fought back by showing its weariness, with depressing uniformity, elsewhere on its surface.

Weariness has, in fact, won in this room. Everything has been polished, washed, sat on, used, scrubbed too often. All pretenses but living itself have long since vanished from the very atmosphere of this room.

Moreover, a section of this room, for it is not really a room unto itself, though the landlord's lease would make it seem so, slopes backward to provide a small kitchen area, where the family prepares the meals that are eaten in the living room proper, which must also serve as dining room. The single window that has been provided for these "two" rooms is located in this kitchen area. The sole natural light the family may enjoy in the course of a day is only that which fights its way through this little window.

At left, a door leads to a bedroom which is shared by MAMA *and her daughter,* BENEATHA. *At right, opposite, is a second room (which in the beginning of the life of this apartment was probably a breakfast room) which serves as a bedroom for* WALTER *and his wife,* RUTH.

Time: Sometime between World War II and the present.

Place: Chicago's Southside.

At Rise: It is morning dark in the living room. TRAVIS *is asleep on the make-down bed at center. An alarm clock sounds from within the bedroom at right, and presently* RUTH *enters from that room and closes the door behind her. She crosses sleepily toward the window. As she passes her sleeping son she reaches down and shakes him a little. At the window she raises the shade and a dusky Southside morning light comes in feebly. She fills a pot with water and puts it on to boil. She calls to the boy, between yawns, in a slightly muffled voice.*

RUTH *is about thirty. We can see that she was a pretty girl, even exceptionally so, but now it is apparent that life has been little that she expected, and disappointment has already begun to hang in her face. In a few years, before thirty-five even, she will be known among her people as a "settled woman."*

She crosses to her son and gives him a good, final, rousing shake.

RUTH: Come on now, boy, it's seven thirty! [*Her son sits up at last, in a stupor of sleepiness.*] I say hurry up, Travis! You ain't the only person in the world got to use a bathroom! [*The child, a sturdy, handsome little boy of ten or eleven, drags himself out of the bed and almost blindly takes his towels and "today's clothes" from drawers and a closet and goes out to the bathroom, which is in an outside hall and which is shared by another family or families on the same floor.* RUTH *crosses to the bedroom door at right and opens it and calls in to her husband.*] Walter Lee! . . . It's after seven thirty! Lemme see you do some waking up in there now! [*She waits.*] You better get up from there, man! It's after seven thirty I tell you. [*She waits again.*] All right, you just go ahead and lay there and next thing you know Travis be finished and Mr. Johnson'll be in there and you'll be fussing and cussing round here like a mad man! And be late too! [*She waits, at the end of patience.*] Walter Lee—it's time for you to get up!

[*She waits another second and then starts to go into the bedroom, but is apparently satisfied that her husband has begun to get up. She stops, pulls the door to, and returns to the kitchen area. She wipes her face with a moist cloth and runs her fingers through her sleep-disheveled hair in a vain effort and ties an apron around her housecoat. The bedroom door at right opens and her husband stands in the doorway in his pajamas, which are rumpled and mismated. He is a lean, intense young man in his middle thirties, inclined to quick nervous movements and erratic speech habits—and always in his voice there is a quality of indictment.*]

WALTER: Is he out yet?

RUTH: What you mean *out?* He ain't hardly got in there good yet.

WALTER: [*Wandering in, still more oriented to sleep than to a new day.*] Well, what was you doing all that yelling for if I can't even get in there yet? [*Stopping and thinking.*] Check coming today?

RUTH: They *said* Saturday and this is just Friday and I hopes to God you ain't going to get up here first thing this morning and start talking to me 'bout no money—'cause I 'bout don't want to hear it.

WALTER: Something the matter with you this morning?

RUTH: No—I'm just sleepy as the devil. What kind of eggs you want?

WALTER: Not scrambled. [RUTH *starts to scramble eggs.*] Paper come? [RUTH *points impatiently to the rolled up* Tribune *on the table, and he gets it and spreads it out and vaguely reads the front page.*] Set off another bomb yesterday.

RUTH: [*Maximum indifference.*] Did they?

WALTER: [*Looking up.*] What's the matter with you?

RUTH: Ain't nothing the matter with me. And don't keep asking me that this morning.

WALTER: Ain't nobody bothering you. [*Reading the news of the day absently again.*] Say Colonel McCormick[2] is sick.

RUTH: [*Affecting tea-party interest.*] Is he now? Poor thing.

WALTER: [*Sighing and looking at his watch.*] Oh, me. [*He waits.*] Now what is that boy doing in that bathroom all this time? He just going to have to start getting up earlier. I can't be late to work on account of him fooling around in there.

RUTH: [*Turning on him.*] Oh, no he ain't going to be getting up no earlier no such thing! It ain't his fault that he can't get to bed no earlier nights 'cause he got a bunch of crazy good-for-nothing clowns sitting up running their mouths in what is supposed to be his bedroom after ten o'clock at night . . .

WALTER: That's what you mad about, ain't it? The things I want to talk about with my friends just couldn't be important in your mind, could they?

[*He rises and finds a cigarette in her handbag on the table and crosses to the little window and looks out, smoking and deeply enjoying this first one.*]

RUTH: [*Almost matter of factly, a complaint too automatic to deserve emphasis.*] Why you always got to smoke before you eat in the morning?

WALTER: [*At the window.*] Just look at 'em down there . . . Running and racing to work . . . [*He turns and faces his wife and watches her a moment at the stove, and then, suddenly.*] You look young this morning, baby.

2. Owner-publisher of the *Chicago Tribune.*

RUTH: [*Indifferently.*] Yeah?

WALTER: Just for a second—stirring them eggs. It's gone now—just for a second it was—you looked real young again. [*Then, drily.*] It's gone now—you look like yourself again.

RUTH: Man, if you don't shut up and leave me alone.

WALTER: [*Looking out to the street again.*] First thing a man ought to learn in life is not to make love to no colored woman first thing in the morning. You all some evil people at eight o'clock in the morning.

> [TRAVIS *appears in the hall doorway, almost fully dressed and quite wide awake now, his towels and pajamas across his shoulders. He opens the door and signals for his father to make the bathroom in a hurry.*]

TRAVIS: [*Watching the bathroom.*] Daddy, come on!

> [WALTER *gets his bathroom utensils and flies out to the bathroom.*]

RUTH: Sit down and have your breakfast, Travis.

TRAVIS: Mama, this is Friday. [*Gleefully.*] Check coming tomorrow, huh?

RUTH: You get your mind off money and eat your breakfast.

TRAVIS: [*Eating.*] This is the morning we supposed to bring the fifty cents to school.

RUTH: Well, I ain't got no fifty cents this morning.

TRAVIS: Teacher say we have to.

RUTH: I don't care what teacher say. I ain't got it. Eat your breakfast, Travis.

TRAVIS: I *am* eating.

RUTH: Hush up now and just eat!

> [*The boy gives her an exasperated look for her lack of understanding, and eats grudgingly.*]

TRAVIS: You think Grandmama would have it?

RUTH: No! And I want you to stop asking your grandmother for money, you hear me?

TRAVIS: [*Outraged.*] Gaaaleee! I don't ask her, she just gimme it sometimes!

RUTH: Travis Willard Younger—I got too much on me this morning to be—

TRAVIS: Maybe Daddy—

RUTH: *Travis!*

> [*The boy hushes abruptly. They are both quiet and tense for several seconds.*]

TRAVIS: [*Presently.*] Could I maybe go carry some groceries in front of the super-market for a little while after school then?

RUTH: Just hush, I said. [TRAVIS *jabs his spoon into his cereal bowl viciously, and rests his head in anger upon his fists.*] If you through eating, you can get over there and make up your bed.

> [*The boy obeys stiffly and crosses the room, almost mechanically, to the bed and more or less carefully folds the covering. He carries the bedding into his mother's room and returns with his books and cap.*]

TRAVIS: [*Sulking and standing apart from her unnaturally.*] I'm gone.

RUTH: [*Looking up from the stove to inspect him automatically.*] Come here. [*He crosses to her and she studies his head.*] If you don't take this comb and fix this here head, you better! [TRAVIS *puts down his books with a great sigh of oppression, and crosses to the mirror. His mother mutters under her breath about his "slubbornness."*] 'Bout to march out of here with that head looking just like chickens slept in it! I just don't know where you get your slubborn ways . . . And get your jacket, too. Looks chilly out this morning.

TRAVIS: [*With conspicuously brushed hair and jacket.*] I'm gone.

RUTH: Get carfare and milk money—[*Waving one finger.*]—and not a single penny for no caps, you hear me?

TRAVIS: [*With sullen politeness.*] Yes'm.

> [*He turns in outrage to leave. His mother watches after him as in his frustration he approaches the door almost comically. When she speaks to him, her voice has become a very gentle tease.*]

RUTH: [*Mocking; as she thinks he would say it.*] Oh, Mama makes me so mad sometimes, I don't know what to do! [*She waits and continues to his back as he stands stock-still in front of the door.*] I wouldn't kiss that woman good-bye for nothing in this world this morning! [*The boy finally turns around and rolls his eyes at her, knowing the mood has changed and he is vindicated; he does not, however, move toward her yet.*] Not for nothing in this world! [*She finally laughs aloud at him and holds out her arms to him and we see that it is a way between them, very old and practiced. He crosses to her and allows her to embrace him warmly but keeps his face fixed with masculine rigidity. She holds him back from her presently and looks at him and runs her fingers over the features of his face. With utter gentleness—*] Now—whose little old angry man are you?

TRAVIS: [*The masculinity and gruffness start to fade at last.*] Aw gaalee—Mama . . .

RUTH: [*Mimicking.*] Aw—gaaaaalleeeee, Mama! [*She pushes him, with rough playfulness and finality, toward the door.*] Get on out of here or you going to be late.

TRAVIS: [*In the face of love, new aggressiveness.*] Mama, could I *please* go carry groceries?

RUTH: Honey, it's starting to get so cold evenings.

WALTER: [*Coming in from the bathroom and drawing a make-believe gun from a make-believe holster and shooting at his son.*] What is it he wants to do?

RUTH: Go carry groceries after school at the supermarket.

WALTER: Well, let him go . . .

TRAVIS: [*Quickly, to the ally.*] I *have* to—she won't gimme the fifty cents . . .

WALTER: [*To his wife only.*] Why not?

RUTH: [*Simply, and with flavor.*] 'Cause we don't have it.

WALTER: [*To* RUTH *only.*] What you tell the boy things like that for? [*Reaching down into his pants with a rather important gesture.*] Here, son—

> [*He hands the boy the coin, but his eyes are directed to his wife's.* TRAVIS *takes the money happily.*]

TRAVIS: Thanks, Daddy.

[*He starts out.* RUTH *watches both of them with murder in her eyes.* WALTER *stands and stares back at her with defiance, and suddenly reaches into his pocket again on an afterthought.*]

WALTER: [*Without even looking at his son, still staring hard at his wife.*] In fact, here's another fifty cents . . . Buy yourself some fruit today—or take a taxicab to school or something!

TRAVIS: Whoopee—

[*He leaps up and clasps his father around the middle with his legs, and they face each other in mutual appreciation; slowly* WALTER LEE *peeks around the boy to catch the violent rays from his wife's eyes and draws his head back as if shot.*]

WALTER: You better get down now—and get to school, man.

TRAVIS: [*At the door.*] O.K. Good-bye.

[*He exits.*]

WALTER: [*After him, pointing with pride.*] That's *my* boy. [*She looks at him in disgust and turns back to her work.*] You know what I was thinking 'bout in the bathroom this morning?

RUTH: No.

WALTER: How come you always try to be so pleasant!

RUTH: What is there to be pleasant 'bout!

WALTER: You want to know what I was thinking 'bout in the bathroom or not!

RUTH: I know what you thinking 'bout.

WALTER: [*Ignoring her.*] 'Bout what me and Willy Harris was talking about last night.

RUTH: [*Immediately—a refrain.*] Willy Harris is a good-for-nothing loud mouth.

WALTER: Anybody who talks to me has got to be a good-for-nothing loud mouth, ain't he? And what you know about who is just a good-for-nothing loud mouth? Charlie Atkins was just a "good-for-nothing loud mouth" too, wasn't he! When he wanted me to go in the dry-cleaning business with him. And now—he's grossing a hundred thousand a year. A hundred thousand dollars a year! You still call *him* a loud mouth!

RUTH: [*Bitterly.*] Oh, Walter Lee . . .

[*She folds her head on her arms over the table.*]

WALTER: [*Rising and coming to her and standing over her.*] You tired, ain't you? Tired of everything. Me, the boy, the way we live—this beat-up hole—everything. Ain't you? [*She doesn't look up, doesn't answer.*] So tired—moaning and groaning all the time, but you wouldn't do nothing to help, would you? You couldn't be on my side that long for nothing, could you?

RUTH: Walter, please leave me alone.

WALTER: A man needs for a woman to back him up . . .

RUTH: Walter—

WALTER: Mama would listen to you. You know she listen to you more than she do me and Bennie. She think more of you. All you have to do is just sit down with her when you drinking your coffee one morning and talking 'bout things like you do and—[*He sits down beside her and demonstrates graphically what he thinks her methods and tone should be.*]—you just sip your coffee, see, and say easy like that you been thinking 'bout that deal Walter Lee is so interested in, 'bout the store and all, and sip some more coffee, like what you saying ain't really that important to you—And the next thing you know, she be listening good and asking you questions and when I come home—I can tell her the details. This ain't no fly-by-night proposition, baby. I mean we figured it out, me and Willy and Bobo.

RUTH: [*With a frown.*] Bobo?

WALTER: Yeah. You see, this little liquor store we got in mind cost seventy-five thousand and we figured the initial investment on the place be 'bout thirty thousand, see. That be ten thousand each. Course, there's a couple of hundred you got to pay so's you don't spend your life just waiting for them clowns to let your license get approved—

RUTH: You mean graft?

WALTER: [*Frowning impatiently.*] Don't call it that. See there, that just goes to show you what women understand about the world. Baby, don't *nothing* happen for you in this world 'less you pay *somebody* off!

RUTH: Walter, leave me alone! [*She raises her head and stares at him vigorously—then says, more quietly.*] Eat your eggs, they gonna be cold.

WALTER: [*Straightening up from her and looking off.*] That's it. There you are. Man say to his woman: I got me a dream. His woman say: Eat your eggs. [*Sadly, but gaining in power.*] Man say: I got to take hold of this here world, baby! And a woman will say: Eat your eggs and go to work. [*Passionately now.*] Man say: I got to change my life, I'm choking to death, baby! And his woman say—[*In utter anguish as he brings his fists down on his thighs.*]—Your eggs is getting cold!

RUTH: [*Softly.*] Walter, that ain't none of our money.

WALTER: [*Not listening at all or even looking at her.*] This morning, I was lookin' in the mirror and thinking about it . . . I'm thirty-five years old; I been married eleven years and I got a boy who sleeps in the living room—[*Very, very quietly.*]—and all I got to give him is stories about how rich white people live . . .

RUTH: Eat your eggs, Walter.

WALTER: *Damn my eggs . . . damn all the eggs that ever was!*

RUTH: Then go to work.

WALTER: [*Looking up at her.*] See—I'm trying to talk to you 'bout myself—[*Shaking his head with the repetition.*]—and all you can say is eat them eggs and go to work.

RUTH: [*Wearily.*] Honey, you never say nothing new. I listen to you every day, every night and every morning, and you never say nothing new. [*Shrugging.*] So you would rather *be* Mr. Arnold than be his chauffeur. So—I would *rather* be living in Buckingham Palace.[3]

---

3. Where the queen of Great Britain resides.

WALTER: That is just what is wrong with the colored woman in this world . . . Don't understand about building their men up and making 'em feel like they somebody. Like they can do something.

RUTH: [*Drily, but to hurt.*] There *are* colored men who do things.

WALTER: No thanks to the colored woman.

RUTH: Well, being a colored woman, I guess I can't help myself none.

> [*She rises and gets the ironing board and sets it up and attacks a huge pile of rough-dried clothes, sprinkling them in preparation for the ironing and then rolling them into tight fat balls.*]

WALTER: [*Mumbling.*] We one group of men tied to a race of women with small minds.

> [*His sister* BENEATHA *enters. She is about twenty, as slim and intense as her brother. She is not as pretty as her sister-in-law, but her lean, almost intellectual face has a handsomeness of its own. She wears a bright-red flannel nightie, and her thick hair stands wildly about her head. Her speech is a mixture of many things; it is different from the rest of the family's insofar as education has permeated her sense of English—and perhaps the Midwest rather than the South has finally—at last—won out in her inflection; but not altogether, because over all of it is a soft slurring and transformed use of vowels which is the decided influence of the Southside. She passes through the room without looking at either* RUTH *or* WALTER *and goes to the outside door and looks, a little blindly, out to the bathroom. She sees that it has been lost to the Johnsons. She closes the door with a sleepy vengeance and crosses to the table and sits down a little defeated.*]

BENEATHA: I am going to start timing those people.

WALTER: You should get up earlier.

BENEATHA: [*Her face in her hands. She is still fighting the urge to go back to bed.*] Really—would you suggest dawn? Where's the paper?

WALTER: [*Pushing the paper across the table to her as he studies her almost clinically, as though he has never seen her before.*] You a horrible-looking chick at this hour.

BENEATHA: [*Drily.*] Good morning, everybody.

WALTER: [*Senselessly.*] How is school coming?

BENEATHA: [*In the same spirit.*] Lovely. Lovely. And you know, biology is the greatest. [*Looking up at him.*] I dissected something that looked just like you yesterday.

WALTER: I just wondered if you've made up your mind and everything.

BENEATHA: [*Gaining in sharpness and impatience.*] And what did I answer yesterday morning—and the day before that?

RUTH: [*From the ironing board, like someone disinterested and old.*] Don't be so nasty, Bennie.

BENEATHA: [*Still to her brother.*] And the day before that and the day before that!

WALTER: [*Defensively.*] I'm interested in you. Something wrong with that? Ain't many girls who decide—

WALTER *and* BENEATHA: [*In unison.*]—"to be a doctor."

[*Silence.*]

WALTER: Have we figured out yet just exactly how much medical school is going to cost?

RUTH: Walter Lee, why don't you leave that girl alone and get out of here to work?

BENEATHA: [*Exits to the bathroom and bangs on the door.*] Come on out of there, please!

[*She comes back into the room.*]

WALTER: [*Looking at his sister intently.*] You know the check is coming tomorrow.

BENEATHA: [*Turning on him with a sharpness all her own.*] That money belongs to Mama, Walter, and it's for her to decide how she wants to use it. I don't care if she wants to buy a house or a rocket ship or just nail it up somewhere and look at it. It's hers. Not ours—*hers.*

WALTER: [*Bitterly.*] Now ain't that fine! You just got your mother's interest at heart, ain't you, girl? You such a nice girl—but if Mama got that money she can always take a few thousand and help you through school too—can't she?

BENEATHA: I have never asked anyone around here to do anything for me.

WALTER: No! And the line between asking and just accepting when the time comes is big and wide—ain't it!

BENEATHA: [*With fury.*] What do you want from me, Brother—that I quit school or just drop dead, which!

WALTER: I don't want nothing but for you to stop acting holy 'round here. Me and Ruth done made some sacrifices for you—why can't you do something for the family?

RUTH: Walter, don't be dragging me in it.

WALTER: You are in it—Don't you get up and go work in somebody's kitchen for the last three years to help put clothes on her back?

RUTH: Oh, Walter—that's not fair . . .

WALTER: It ain't that nobody expects you to get on your knees and say thank you, Brother; thank you, Ruth; thank you, Mama—and thank you, Travis, for wearing the same pair of shoes for two semesters—

BENEATHA: [*Dropping to her knees.*] Well—I *do*—all right?—thank everybody . . . and forgive me for ever wanting to be anything at all . . . forgive me, forgive me!

RUTH: Please stop it! Your mama'll hear you.

WALTER: Who the hell told you you had to be a doctor? If you so crazy 'bout messing 'round with sick people—then go be a nurse like other women—or just get married and be quiet . . .

BENEATHA: Well—you finally got it said . . . it took you three years but you finally got it said. Walter, give up; leave me alone—it's Mama's money.

WALTER: *He was my father, too!*

BENEATHA: So what? He was mine, too—and Travis' grandfather—but the insurance money belongs to Mama. Picking on me is not going to make her give it to you to invest in any liquor stores—[*Underbreath, dropping into a chair.*]—and I for one say, God bless Mama for that!

WALTER: [*To* RUTH.] See—did you hear? Did you hear!

RUTH: Honey, please go to work.

WALTER: Nobody in this house is ever going to understand me.

BENEATHA: Because you're a nut.

WALTER: Who's a nut?

BENEATHA: You—you are a nut. Thee is mad, boy.

WALTER: [*Looking at his wife and his sister from the door, very sadly.*] The world's most backward race of people, and that's a fact.

BENEATHA: [*Turning slowly in her chair.*] And then there are all those prophets who would lead us out of the wilderness—[WALTER *slams out of the house.*]—into the swamps!

RUTH: Bennie, why you always gotta be pickin' on your brother? Can't you be a little sweeter sometimes? [*Door opens.* WALTER *walks in.*]

WALTER: [*To* RUTH.] I need some money for carfare.

RUTH: [*Looks at him, then warms; teasing, but tenderly.*] Fifty cents? [*She goes to her bag and gets money.*] Here, take a taxi.

> [WALTER *exits.* MAMA *enters. She is a woman in her early sixties, full-bodied and strong. She is one of those women of a certain grace and beauty who wear it so unobtrusively that it takes a while to notice. Her dark-brown face is surrounded by the total whiteness of her hair, and, being a woman who has adjusted to many things in life and overcome many more, her face is full of strength. She has, we can see, wit and faith of a kind that keep her eyes lit and full of interest and expectancy. She is, in a word, a beautiful woman. Her bearing is perhaps most like the noble bearing of the women of the Hereros of Southwest Africa—rather as if she imagines that as she walks she still bears a basket or a vessel upon her head. Her speech, on the other hand, is as careless as her carriage is precise—she is inclined to slur everything—but her voice is perhaps not so much quiet as simply soft.*]

MAMA: Who that 'round here slamming doors at this hour?

> [*She crosses through the room, goes to the window, opens it, and brings in a feeble little plant growing doggedly in a small pot on the window sill. She feels the dirt and puts it back out.*]

RUTH: That was Walter Lee. He and Bennie was at it again.

MAMA: My children and they tempers. Lord, if this little old plant don't get more sun than it's been getting it ain't never going to see spring again. [*She turns from the window.*] What's the matter with you this morning, Ruth? You looks right peaked. You aiming to iron all them things? Leave some for me. I'll get to 'em this afternoon. Bennie honey, it's too drafty for you to be sitting 'round half dressed. Where's your robe?

BENEATHA: In the cleaners.

MAMA: Well, go get mine and put it on.

BENEATHA: I'm not cold, Mama, honest.

MAMA: I know—but you so thin . . .

BENEATHA: [*Irritably.*] Mama, I'm not cold.

MAMA: [*Seeing the make-down bed as* TRAVIS *has left it.*] Lord have mercy, look at that poor bed. Bless his heart—he tries, don't he?

[*She moves to the bed* TRAVIS *has sloppily made up.*]

RUTH: No—he don't half try at all 'cause he knows you going to come along behind him and fix everything. That's just how come he don't know how to do nothing right now—you done spoiled that boy so.

MAMA: Well—he's a little boy. Ain't supposed to know 'bout housekeeping. My baby, that's what he is. What you fix for his breakfast this morning?

RUTH: [*Angrily.*] I feed my son, Lena!

MAMA: I ain't meddling—[*Underbreath; busy-bodyish.*] I just noticed all last week he had cold cereal, and when it starts getting this chilly in the fall a child ought to have some hot grits or something when he goes out in the cold—

RUTH: [*Furious.*] I gave him hot oats—is that all right!

MAMA: I ain't meddling. [*Pause.*] Put a lot of nice butter on it? [RUTH *shoots her an angry look and does not reply.*] He likes lots of butter.

RUTH: [*Exasperated.*] Lena—

MAMA: [*To* BENEATHA. MAMA *is inclined to wander conversationally sometimes.*] What was you and your brother fussing 'bout this morning?

BENEATHA: It's not important, Mama.

[*She gets up and goes to look out at the bathroom, which is apparently free, and she picks up her towels and rushes out.*]

MAMA: What was they fighting about?

RUTH: Now you know as well as I do.

MAMA: [*Shaking her head.*] Brother still worrying hisself sick about that money?

RUTH: You know he is.

MAMA: You had breakfast?

RUTH: Some coffee.

MAMA: Girl, you better start eating and looking after yourself better. You almost thin as Travis.

RUTH: Lena—

MAMA: Un-hunh?

RUTH: What are you going to do with it?

MAMA: Now don't you start, child. It's too early in the morning to be talking about money. It ain't Christian.

RUTH: It's just that he got his heart set on that store—

MAMA: You mean that liquor store that Willy Harris want him to invest in?

RUTH: Yes—

MAMA: We ain't no business people, Ruth. We just plain working folks.

RUTH: Ain't nobody business people till they go into business. Walter Lee say colored people ain't never going to start getting ahead till they start gambling on some different kinds of things in the world—investments and things.

MAMA: What done got into you, girl? Walter Lee done finally sold you on investing.

RUTH: No. Mama, something is happening between Walter and me. I don't know what it is—but he needs something—something I can't give him any more. He needs this chance, Lena.

MAMA: [*Frowning deeply.*] But liquor, honey—

RUTH: Well—like Walter say—I spec people going to always be drinking themselves some liquor.

MAMA: Well—whether they drinks it or not ain't none of my business. But whether I go into business selling it to 'em *is*, and I don't want that on my ledger this late in life. [*Stopping suddenly and studying her daughter-in-law.*] Ruth Younger, what's the matter with you today? You look like you could fall over right there.

RUTH: I'm tired.

MAMA: Then you better stay home from work today.

RUTH: I can't stay home. She'd be calling up the agency and screaming at them, "My girl didn't come in today—send me somebody! My girl didn't come in!" Oh, she just have a fit . . .

MAMA: Well, let her have it. I'll just call her up and say you got the flu—

RUTH: [*Laughing.*] Why the flu?

MAMA: 'Cause it sounds respectable to 'em. Something white people get, too. They know 'bout the flu. Otherwise they think you been cut up or something when you tell 'em you sick.

RUTH: I got to go in. We need the money.

MAMA: Somebody would of thought my children done all but starved to death the way they talk about money here late. Child, we got a great big old check coming tomorrow.

RUTH: [*Sincerely, but also self-righteously.*] Now that's your money. It ain't got nothing to do with me. We all feel like that—Walter and Bennie and me—even Travis.

MAMA: [*Thoughtfully, and suddenly very far away.*] Ten thousand dollars—

RUTH: Sure is wonderful.

MAMA: Ten thousand dollars.

RUTH: You know what you should do, Miss Lena? You should take yourself a trip somewhere. To Europe or South America or someplace—

MAMA: [*Throwing up her hands at the thought.*] Oh, child!

RUTH: I'm serious. Just pack up and leave! Go on away and enjoy yourself some. Forget about the family and have yourself a ball for once in your life—

MAMA: [*Drily.*] You sound like I'm just about ready to die. Who'd go with me? What I look like wandering 'round Europe by myself?

RUTH: Shoot—these here rich white women do it all the time. They don't think nothing of packing up they suitcases and piling on one of them big steamships and—swoosh!—they gone, child.

MAMA: Something always told me I wasn't no rich white woman.

RUTH: Well—what are you going to do with it then?

MAMA: I ain't rightly decided. [*Thinking. She speaks now with emphasis.*] Some of it got to be put away for Beneatha and her schoolin'—and ain't nothing going to touch that part of it. Nothing. [*She waits several seconds, trying to make up her mind about something, and looks at* RUTH *a little tentatively before going on.*] Been thinking that we maybe could meet the notes on a little old two-story somewhere, with a yard where Travis could play in the summertime, if we use part of the insurance for a down payment and everybody kind of pitch in. I could maybe take on a little day work again, few days a week—

RUTH: [*Studying her mother-in-law furtively and concentrating on her ironing, anxious to encourage without seeming to.*] Well, Lord knows, we've put enough rent into this here rat trap to pay for four houses by now . . .

MAMA: [*Looking up at the words "rat trap" and then looking around and leaning back and sighing—in a suddenly reflective mood—*] "Rat trap"—yes, that's all it is. [*Smiling.*] I remember just as well the day me and Big Walter moved in here. Hadn't been married but two weeks and wasn't planning on living here no more than a year. [*She shakes her head at the dissolved dream.*] We was going to set away, little by little, don't you know, and buy a little place out in Morgan Park. We had even picked out the house. [*Chuckling a little.*] Looks right dumpy today. But Lord, child, you should know all the dreams I had 'bout buying that house and fixing it up and making me a little garden in the back—[*She waits and stops smiling.*] And didn't none of it happen.

[*Dropping her hands in a futile gesture.*]

RUTH: [*Keeps her head down, ironing.*] Yes, life can be a barrel of disappointments, sometimes.

MAMA: Honey, Big Walter would come in here some nights back then and slump down on that couch there and just look at the rug, and look at me and look at the rug and then back at me—and I'd know he was down then . . . really down. [*After a second very long and thoughtful pause; she is seeing back to times that only she can see.*] And then, Lord, when I lost that baby—little Claude— I almost thought I was going to lose Big Walter too. Oh, that man grieved hisself! He was one man to love his children.

RUTH: Ain't nothin' can tear at you like losin' your baby.

MAMA: I guess that's how come that man finally worked hisself to death like he done. Like he was fighting his own war with this here world that took his baby from him.

RUTH: He sure was a fine man, all right. I always liked Mr. Younger.

MAMA: Crazy 'bout his children! God knows there was plenty wrong with Walter Younger—hard-headed, mean, kind of wild with women—plenty wrong with him. But he sure loved his children. Always wanted them to have something—be something. That's where Brother gets all these notions, I reckon. Big Walter used to say, he'd get right wet in the eyes sometimes, lean his head back with the water standing in his eyes and say, "Seem like God didn't see fit to give the black man nothing but dreams—but He did give us children to make them dreams seem worth while." [*She smiles.*] He could talk like that, don't you know.

RUTH: Yes, he sure could. He was a good man, Mr. Younger.

MAMA: Yes, a fine man—just couldn't never catch up with his dreams, that's all.

[BENEATHA *comes in, brushing her hair and looking up to the ceiling, where the sound of a vacuum cleaner has started up.*]

BENEATHA: What could be so dirty on that woman's rugs that she has to vacuum them every single day?

RUTH: I wish certain young women 'round here who I could name would take inspiration about certain rugs in a certain apartment I could also mention.

BENEATHA: [*Shrugging.*] How much cleaning can a house need, for Christ's sakes.

MAMA: [*Not liking the Lord's name used thus.*] Bennie!

RUTH: Just listen to her—just listen!

BENEATHA: Oh, God!

MAMA: If you use the Lord's name just one more time—

BENEATHA: [*A bit of a whine.*] Oh, Mama—

RUTH: Fresh—just fresh as salt, this girl!

BENEATHA: [*Drily.*] Well—if the salt loses its savor—[4]

MAMA: Now that will do. I just ain't going to have you 'round here reciting the scriptures in vain—you hear me?

BENEATHA: How did I manage to get on everybody's wrong side by just walking into a room?

RUTH: If you weren't so fresh—

BENEATHA: Ruth, I'm twenty years old.

MAMA: What time you be home from school today?

BENEATHA: Kind of late. [*With enthusiasm.*] Madeline is going to start my guitar lessons today.

[MAMA *and* RUTH *look up with the same expression.*]

MAMA: Your *what* kind of lessons?

BENEATHA: Guitar.

RUTH: Oh, Father!

MAMA: How come you done taken it in your mind to learn to play the guitar?

BENEATHA: I just want to, that's all.

MAMA: [*Smiling.*] Lord, child, don't you know what to do with yourself? How long it going to be before you get tired of this now—like you got tired of that little play-acting group you joined last year? [*Looking at* RUTH.] And what was it the year before that?

RUTH: The horseback-riding club for which she bought that fifty-five-dollar riding habit that's been hanging in the closet ever since!

MAMA: [*To* BENEATHA.] Why you got to flit so from one thing to another, baby?

BENEATHA: [*Sharply.*] I just want to learn to play the guitar. Is there anything wrong with that?

MAMA: Ain't nobody trying to stop you. I just wonders sometimes why you has to flit so from one thing to another all the time. You ain't never done nothing with all that camera equipment you brought home—

BENEATHA: I don't flit! I—I experiment with different forms of expression—

RUTH: Like riding a horse?

4. See Matthew 5:13 and Luke 14:34.

BENEATHA: —People have to express themselves one way or another.

MAMA: What is it you want to express?

BENEATHA: [*Angrily.*] Me! [MAMA *and* RUTH *look at each other and burst into raucous laughter.*] Don't worry—I don't expect you to understand.

MAMA: [*To change the subject.*] Who you going out with tomorrow night?

BENEATHA: [*With displeasure.*] George Murchison again.

MAMA: [*Pleased.*] Oh—you getting a little sweet on him?

RUTH: You ask me, this child ain't sweet on nobody but herself—[*Underbreath.*] Express herself!

[*They laugh.*]

BENEATHA: Oh—I like George all right, Mama. I mean I like him enough to go out with him and stuff, but—

RUTH: [*For devilment.*] What does *and stuff* mean?

BENEATHA: Mind your own business.

MAMA: Stop picking at her now, Ruth. [*A thoughtful pause, and then a suspicious sudden look at her daughter as she turns in her chair for emphasis.*] What *does* it mean?

BENEATHA: [*Wearily.*] Oh, I just mean I couldn't ever really be serious about George. He's—he's so shallow.

RUTH: Shallow—what do you mean he's shallow? He's *Rich!*

MAMA: Hush, Ruth.

BENEATHA: I know he's rich. He knows he's rich, too.

RUTH: Well—what other qualities a man got to have to satisfy you, little girl?

BENEATHA: You wouldn't even begin to understand. Anybody who married Walter could not possibly understand.

MAMA: [*Outraged.*] What kind of way is that to talk about your brother?

BENEATHA: Brother is a flip—let's face it.

MAMA: [*To* RUTH, *helplessly.*] What's a flip?

RUTH: [*Glad to add kindling.*] She's saying he's crazy.

BENEATHA: Not crazy. Brother isn't really crazy yet—he—he's an elaborate neurotic.

MAMA: Hush your mouth!

BENEATHA: As for George. Well. George looks good—he's got a beautiful car and he takes me to nice places and, as my sister-in-law says, he is probably the richest boy I will ever get to know and I even like him sometimes—but if the Youngers are sitting around waiting to see if their little Bennie is going to tie up the family with the Murchisons, they are wasting their time.

RUTH: You mean you wouldn't marry George Murchison if he asked you someday? That pretty, rich thing? Honey, I knew you was odd—

BENEATHA: No I would not marry him if all I felt for him was what I feel now. Besides, George's family wouldn't really like it.

MAMA: Why not?

BENEATHA: Oh, Mama—The Murchisons are honest-to-God-real-*live*-rich colored people, and the only people in the world who are more snobbish than rich white people are rich colored people. I thought everybody knew that. I've met Mrs. Murchison. She's a scene!

MAMA: You must not dislike people 'cause they well off, honey.

BENEATHA: Why not? It makes just as much sense as disliking people 'cause they are poor, and lots of people do that.

RUTH: [*A wisdom-of-the-ages manner. To* MAMA.] Well, she'll get over some of this—

BENEATHA: Get over it? What are you talking about, Ruth? Listen, I'm going to be a doctor. I'm not worried about who I'm going to marry yet—if I ever get married.

MAMA *and* RUTH: *If!*

MAMA: Now, Bennie—

BENEATHA: Oh, I probably will . . . but first I'm going to be a doctor, and George, for one, still thinks that's pretty funny. I couldn't be bothered with that. I am going to be a doctor and everybody around here better understand that!

MAMA: [*Kindly.*] 'Course you going to be a doctor, honey, God willing.

BENEATHA: [*Drily.*] God hasn't got a thing to do with it.

MAMA: Beneatha—that just wasn't necessary.

BENEATHA: Well—neither is God. I get sick of hearing about God.

MAMA: Beneatha!

BENEATHA: I mean it! I'm just tired of hearing about God all the time. What has He got to do with anything? Does He pay tuition?

MAMA: You 'bout to get your fresh little jaw slapped!

RUTH: That's just what she needs, all right!

BENEATHA: Why? Why can't I say what I want to around here, like everybody else?

MAMA: It don't sound nice for a young girl to say things like that—you wasn't brought up that way. Me and your father went to trouble to get you and Brother to church every Sunday.

BENEATHA: Mama, you don't understand. It's all a matter of ideas, and God is just one idea I don't accept. It's not important. I am not going out and be immoral or commit crimes because I don't believe in God. I don't even think about it. It's just that I get tired of Him getting credit for all the things the human race achieves through its own stubborn effort. There simply is no blasted God—there is only man and it is he who makes miracles!

[MAMA *absorbs this speech, studies her daughter and rises slowly and crosses to* BENEATHA *and slaps her powerfully across the face. After, there is only silence and the daughter drops her eyes from her mother's face, and* MAMA *is very tall before her.*]

MAMA: Now—you say after me, in my mother's house there is still God. [*There is a long pause and* BENEATHA *stares at the floor wordlessly.* MAMA *repeats the phrase with precision and cool emotion.*] In my mother's house there is still God.

BENEATHA: In my mother's house there is still God.

[*A long pause.*]

MAMA: [*Walking away from* BENEATHA, *too disturbed for triumphant posture. Stopping and turning back to her daughter.*] There are some ideas we ain't going to have in this house. Not long as I am at the head of this family.

BENEATHA: Yes, ma'am.

[MAMA *walks out of the room.*]

RUTH: [*Almost gently, with profound understanding.*] You think you a woman, Bennie—but you still a little girl. What you did was childish—so you got treated like a child.

BENEATHA: I see. [*Quietly.*] I also see that everybody thinks it's all right for Mama to be a tyrant. But all the tyranny in the world will never put a God in the heavens!

[*She picks up her books and goes out.*]

RUTH: [*Goes to* MAMA's *door.*] She said she was sorry.

MAMA: [*Coming out, going to her plant.*] They frightens me, Ruth. My children.

RUTH: You got good children, Lena. They just a little off sometimes—but they're good.

MAMA: No—there's something come down between me and them that don't let us understand each other and I don't know what it is. One done almost lost his mind thinking 'bout money all the time and the other done commence to talk about things I can't seem to understand in no form or fashion. What is it that's changing, Ruth?

RUTH: [*Soothingly, older than her years.*] Now . . . you taking it all too seriously. You just got strong-willed children and it takes a strong woman like you to keep 'em in hand.

MAMA: [*Looking at her plant and sprinkling a little water on it.*] They spirited all right, my children. Got to admit they got spirit—Bennie and Walter. Like this little old plant that ain't never had enough sunshine or nothing—and look at it . . .

[*She has her back to* RUTH, *who has had to stop ironing and lean against something and put the back of her hand to her forehead.*]

RUTH: [*Trying to keep* MAMA *from noticing.*] You . . . sure . . . loves that little old thing, don't you? . . .

MAMA: Well, I always wanted me a garden like I used to see sometimes at the back of the houses down home. This plant is close as I ever got to having one. [*She looks out of the window as she replaces the plant.*] Lord, ain't nothing as dreary as the view from this window on a dreary day, is there? Why ain't you singing this morning, Ruth? Sing that "No Ways Tired." That song always lifts me up so—[*She turns at last to see that* RUTH *has slipped quietly into a chair, in a state of semiconsciousness.*] Ruth! Ruth honey—what's the matter with you . . . Ruth!

[CURTAIN.]

Scene Two

It is the following morning; a Saturday morning, and house cleaning is in progress at the Youngers. Furniture has been shoved hither and yon and MAMA is giving the kitchen-

area walls a washing down. BENEATHA, *in dungarees, with a handkerchief tied around her face, is spraying insecticide into the cracks in the walls. As they work, the radio is on and a Southside disk-jockey program is inappropriately filling the house with a rather exotic saxophone blues.* TRAVIS, *the sole idle one, is leaning on his arms, looking out of the window.*

TRAVIS: Grandmama, that stuff Bennie is using smells awful. Can I go downstairs, please?

MAMA: Did you get all them chores done already? I ain't seen you doing much.

TRAVIS: Yes'm—finished early. Where did Mama go this morning?

MAMA: [*Looking at* BENEATHA.] She had to go on a little errand.

TRAVIS: Where?

MAMA: To tend to her business.

TRAVIS: Can I go outside then?

MAMA: Oh, I guess so. You better stay right in front of the house, though . . . and keep a good lookout for the postman.

TRAVIS: Yes'm. [*He starts out and decides to give his aunt* BENEATHA *a good swat on the legs as he passes her.*] Leave them poor little old cockroaches alone, they ain't bothering you none.

> [*He runs as she swings the spray gun at him both viciously and playfully.* WALTER *enters from the bedroom and goes to the phone.*]

MAMA: Look out there, girl, before you be spilling some of that stuff on that child!

TRAVIS: [*Teasing.*] That's right—look out now!

> [*He exits.*]

BENEATHA: [*Drily.*] I can't imagine that it would hurt him—it has never hurt the roaches.

MAMA: Well, little boys' hides ain't as tough as Southside roaches.

WALTER: [*Into phone.*] Hello—Let me talk to Willy Harris.

MAMA: You better get over there behind the bureau. I seen one marching out of there like Napoleon yesterday.

WALTER: Hello, Willy? It ain't come yet. It'll be here in a few minutes. Did the lawyer give you the papers?

BENEATHA: There's really only one way to get rid of them, Mama—

MAMA: How?

BENEATHA: Set fire to this building.

WALTER: Good. Good. I'll be right over.

BENEATHA: Where did Ruth go, Walter?

WALTER: I don't know.

> [*He exits abruptly.*]

BENEATHA: Mama, where did Ruth go?

MAMA: [*Looking at her with meaning.*] To the doctor, I think.

BENEATHA: The doctor? What's the matter? [*They exchange glances.*] You don't think—

MAMA: [*With her sense of drama.*] Now I ain't saying what I think. But I ain't never been wrong 'bout a woman neither.

> [*The phone rings.*]

BENEATHA: [*At the phone.*] Hay-lo . . . [*Pause, and a moment of recognition.*] Well—when did you get back! . . . And how was it? . . . Of course I've missed you—in my way . . . This morning? No . . . house cleaning and all that and Mama hates it if I let people come over when the house is like this . . . You *have?* Well, that's different . . . What is it—Oh, what the hell, come on over . . . Right, see you then.

> [*She hangs up.*]

MAMA: [*Who has listened vigorously, as is her habit.*] Who is that you inviting over here with this house looking like this? You ain't got the pride you was born with!

BENEATHA: Asagai doesn't care how houses look, Mama—he's an intellectual.

MAMA: *Who?*

BENEATHA: Asagai—Joseph Asagai. He's an African boy I met on campus. He's been studying in Canada all summer.

MAMA: What's his name?

BENEATHA: Asagai, Joseph. Ah-sah-guy . . . He's from Nigeria.

MAMA: Oh, that's the little country that was founded by slaves way back . . .

BENEATHA: No, Mama—that's Liberia.

MAMA: I don't think I never met no African before.

BENEATHA: Well, do me a favor and don't ask him a whole lot of ignorant questions about Africans. I mean, do they wear clothes and all that—

MAMA: Well, now, I guess if you think we so ignorant 'round here maybe you shouldn't bring your friends here—

BENEATHA: It's just that people ask such crazy things. All anyone seems to know about when it comes to Africa is Tarzan—

MAMA: [*Indignantly.*] Why should I know anything about Africa?

BENEATHA: Why do you give money at church for the missionary work?

MAMA: Well, that's to help save people.

BENEATHA: You mean save them from *heathenism*—

MAMA: [*Innocently.*] Yes.

BENEATHA: I'm afraid they need more salvation from the British and the French.

> [RUTH *comes in forlornly and pulls off her coat with dejection. They both turn to look at her.*]

RUTH: [*Dispiritedly.*] Well, I guess from all the happy faces—everybody knows.

BENEATHA: You pregnant?

MAMA: Lord have mercy, I sure hope it's a little old girl. Travis ought to have a sister.

> [BENEATHA *and* RUTH *give her a hopeless look for this grandmotherly enthusiasm.*]

BENEATHA: How far along are you?

RUTH: Two months.

BENEATHA: Did you mean to? I mean did you plan it or was it an accident?

MAMA: What do you know about planning or not planning?

BENEATHA: Oh, Mama.

RUTH: [*Wearily.*] She's twenty years old, Lena.

BENEATHA: Did you plan it, Ruth?

RUTH: Mind your own business.

BENEATHA: It is my business—where is he going to live, on the roof? [*There is silence following the remark as the three women react to the sense of it.*] Gee—I didn't mean that, Ruth, honest. Gee, I don't feel like that at all. I—I think it is wonderful.

RUTH: [*Dully.*] Wonderful.

BENEATHA: Yes—really.

MAMA: [*Looking at* RUTH, *worried.*] Doctor say everything going to be all right?

RUTH: [*Far away.*] Yes—she says everything is going to be fine . . .

MAMA: [*Immediately suspicious.*] "She"—What doctor you went to?

[RUTH *folds over, near hysteria.*]

MAMA: [*Worriedly hovering over* RUTH.] Ruth honey—what's the matter with you—you sick?

[RUTH *has her fists clenched on her thighs and is fighting hard to suppress a scream that seems to be rising in her.*]

BENEATHA: What's the matter with her, Mama?

MAMA: [*Working her fingers in* RUTH's *shoulder to relax her.*] She be all right. Women gets right depressed sometimes when they get her way. [*Speaking softly, expertly, rapidly.*] Now you just relax. That's right . . . just lean back, don't think 'bout nothing at all . . . nothing at all—

RUTH: I'm all right . . .

[*The glassy-eyed look melts and then she collapses into a fit of heavy sobbing. The bell rings.*]

BENEATHA: Oh, my God—that must be Asagai.

MAMA: [*To* RUTH.] Come on now, honey. You need to lie down and rest awhile . . . then have some nice hot food.

[*They exit,* RUTH's *weight on her mother-in-law.* BENEATHA, *herself profoundly disturbed, opens the door to admit a rather dramatic-looking young man with a large package.*]

ASAGAI: Hello, Alaiyo—

BENEATHA: [*Holding the door open and regarding him with pleasure.*] Hello . . . [*Long pause.*] Well—come in. And please excuse everything. My mother was very upset about my letting anyone come here with the place like this.

ASAGAI: [*Coming into the room.*] You look disturbed too . . . Is something wrong?

BENEATHA: [*Still at the door, absently.*] Yes . . . we've all got acute ghettoitus. [*She smiles and comes toward him, finding a cigarette and sitting.*] So—sit down! How was Canada?

ASAGAI: [*A sophisticate.*] Canadian.

BENEATHA: [*Looking at him.*] I'm very glad you are back.

ASAGAI: [*Looking back at her in turn.*] Are you really?

BENEATHA: Yes—very.

ASAGAI: Why—you were quite glad when I went away. What happened?

BENEATHA: You went away.

ASAGAI: Ahhhhhhhh.

BENEATHA: Before—you wanted to be so serious before there was time.

ASAGAI: How much time must there be before one knows what one feels?

BENEATHA: [*Stalling this particular conversation. Her hands pressed together, in a deliberately childish gesture.*] What did you bring me?

ASAGAI: [*Handing her the package.*] Open it and see.

BENEATHA: [*Eagerly opening the package and drawing out some records and the colorful robes of a Nigerian woman.*] Oh, Asagai! . . . You got them for me! . . . How beautiful . . . and the records too! [*She lifts out the robes and runs to the mirror with them and holds the drapery up in front of herself.*]

ASAGAI: [*Coming to her at the mirror.*] I shall have to teach you how to drape it properly. [*He flings the material about her for the moment and stands back to look at her.*] Ah—Oh-pay-gay-day, oh-gbah-mu-shay. [*A Yoruba exclamation for admiration.*] You wear it well . . . very well . . . mutilated hair and all.

BENEATHA: [*Turning suddenly.*] My hair—what's wrong with my hair?

ASAGAI: [*Shrugging.*] Were you born with it like that?

BENEATHA: [*Reaching up to touch it.*] No . . . of course not.

[*She looks back to the mirror, disturbed.*]

ASAGAI: [*Smiling.*] How then?

BENEATHA: You know perfectly well how . . . as crinkly as yours . . . that's how.

ASAGAI: And it is ugly to you that way?

BENEATHA: [*Quickly.*] Oh, no—not ugly . . . [*More slowly, apologetically.*] But it's so hard to manage when it's, well—raw.

ASAGAI: And so to accommodate that—you mutilate it every week?

BENEATHA: It's not mutilation!

ASAGAI: [*Laughing aloud at her seriousness.*] Oh . . . please! I am only teasing you because you are so very serious about these things. [*He stands back from her and folds his arms across his chest as he watches her pulling at her hair and frowning in the mirror.*] Do you remember the first time you met me at school? . . . [*He laughs.*] You came up to me and you said—and I thought you were the most serious little thing I had ever seen—you said: [*He imitates her.*] "Mr. Asagai—I want very much to talk with you. About Africa. You see, Mr. Asagai, I am looking for my *identity!*"

[*He laughs.*]

BENEATHA: [*Turning to him, not laughing.*] Yes—

[*Her face is quizzical, profoundly disturbed.*]

ASAGAI: [*Still teasing and reaching out and taking her face in his hands and turning her profile to him.*] Well . . . it is true that this is not so much a profile of a Hollywood queen as perhaps a queen of the Nile—[*A mock dismissal of the importance of the question.*] But what does it matter? Assimilationism is so popular in your country.

BENEATHA: [*Wheeling, passionately, sharply.*] I am not an assimilationist!

ASAGAI: [*The protest hangs in the room for a moment and* ASAGAI *studies her, his laughter fading.*] Such a serious one. [*There is a pause.*] So—you like the robes? You must take excellent care of them—they are from my sister's personal wardrobe.

BENEATHA: [*With incredulity.*] You—you sent all the way home—for me?

ASAGAI: [*With charm.*] For you—I would do much more . . . Well, that is what I came for. I must go.

BENEATHA: Will you call me Monday?

ASAGAI: Yes . . . We have a great deal to talk about. I mean about identity and time and all that.

BENEATHA: Time?

ASAGAI: Yes. About how much time one needs to know what one feels.

BENEATHA: You never understood that there is more than one kind of feeling which can exist between a man and a woman—or, at least, there should be.

ASAGAI: [*Shaking his head negatively but gently.*] No. Between a man and a woman there need be only one kind of feeling. I have that for you . . . Now even . . . right this moment . . .

BENEATHA: I know—and by itself—it won't do. I can find that anywhere.

ASAGAI: For a woman it should be enough.

BENEATHA: I know—because that's what it says in all the novels that men write. But it isn't. Go ahead and laugh—but I'm not interested in being someone's little episode in America or—[*With feminine vengeance.*]—one of them! [ASAGAI *has burst into laughter again.*] That's funny as hell, huh!

ASAGAI: It's just that every American girl I have known has said that to me. White—black—in this you are all the same. And the same speech, too!

BENEATHA: [*Angrily.*] Yuk, yuk, yuk!

ASAGAI: It's how you can be sure that the world's most liberated women are not liberated at all. You all talk about it too much!

[MAMA *enters and is immediately all social charm because of the presence of a guest.*]

BENEATHA: Oh—Mama—this is Mr. Asagai.

MAMA: How do you do?

ASAGAI: [*Total politeness to an elder.*] How do you do, Mrs. Younger. Please forgive me for coming at such an outrageous hour on a Saturday.

MAMA: Well, you are quite welcome. I just hope you understand that our house don't always look like this. [*Chatterish.*] You must come again. I would love to hear all about—[*Not sure of the name.*]—your country. I think it's so sad the way our American Negroes don't know nothing about Africa 'cept Tarzan and all that. And all that money they pour into these churches when they ought to be helping you people over there drive out them French and Englishmen done taken away your land.

[*The mother flashes a slightly superior look at her daughter upon completion of the recitation.*]

ASAGAI: [*Taken aback by this sudden and acutely unrelated expression of sympathy.*] Yes . . . yes . . .

MAMA: [*Smiling at him suddenly and relaxing and looking him over.*] How many miles is it from here to where you come from?

ASAGAI: Many thousands.

MAMA: [*Looking at him as she would* WALTER.] I bet you don't half look after yourself, being away from your mama either. I spec you better come 'round here from time to time and get yourself some decent home-cooked meals . . .

ASAGAI: [*Moved.*] Thank you. Thank you very much. [*They are all quiet, then—*] Well . . . I must go. I will call you Monday, Alaiyo.

MAMA: What's that he call you?

ASAGAI: Oh—"Alaiyo." I hope you don't mind. It is what you would call a nickname, I think. It is a Yoruba word. I am a Yoruba.

MAMA: [*Looking at* BENEATHA.] I—I thought he was from—

ASAGAI: [*Understanding.*] Nigeria is my country. Yoruba is my tribal origin—

BENEATHA: You didn't tell us what Alaiyo means . . . for all I know, you might be calling me Little Idiot or something . . .

ASAGAI: Well . . . let me see . . . I do not know how just to explain it . . . The sense of a thing can be so different when it changes languages.

BENEATHA: You're evading.

ASAGAI: No—really it is difficult . . . [*Thinking.*] It means . . . it means One for Whom Bread—Food—Is Not Enough. [*He looks at her.*] Is that all right?

BENEATHA: [*Understanding, softly.*] Thank you.

MAMA: [*Looking from one to the other and not understanding any of it.*] Well . . . that's nice . . . You must come see us again—Mr.—

ASAGAI: Ah-sah-guy . . .

MAMA: Yes . . . Do come again.

ASAGAI: Good-bye.

[*He exits.*]

MAMA: [*After him.*] Lord, that's a pretty thing just went out here! [*Insinuatingly, to her daughter.*] Yes, I guess I see why we done commence to get so interested in Africa 'round here. Missionaries my aunt Jenny!

[*She exits.*]

BENEATHA: Oh, Mama! . . .

[*She picks up the Nigerian dress and holds it up to her in front of the mirror again. She sets the headdress on haphazardly and then notices her hair again and clutches at it and then replaces the headdress and frowns at herself. Then she starts to wriggle in front of the mirror as she thinks a Nigerian woman might.* TRAVIS *enters and regards her.*]

TRAVIS: You cracking up?

BENEATHA: Shut up.

[*She pulls the headdress off and looks at herself in the mirror and clutches at her hair again and squinches her eyes as if trying to imagine something. Then, suddenly, she gets her raincoat and kerchief and hurriedly prepares for going out.*]

MAMA: [*Coming back into the room.*] She's resting now. Travis, baby, run next door and ask Miss Johnson to please let me have a little kitchen cleanser. This here can is empty as Jacob's kettle.

TRAVIS: I just came in.

MAMA: Do as you told. [*He exits and she looks at her daughter.*] Where you going?

BENEATHA: [*Halting at the door.*] To become a queen of the Nile!

[*She exits in a breathless blaze of glory.* RUTH *appears in the bedroom doorway.*]

MAMA: Who told you to get up?

RUTH: Ain't nothing wrong with me to be lying in no bed for. Where did Bennie go?

MAMA: [*Drumming her fingers.*] Far as I could make out—to Egypt. [RUTH *just looks at her.*] What time is it getting to?

RUTH: Ten twenty. And the mailman going to ring that bell this morning just like he done every morning for the last umpteen years.

[TRAVIS *comes in with the cleanser can.*]

TRAVIS: She say to tell you that she don't have much.

MAMA: [*Angrily.*] Lord, some people I could name sure is tight-fisted! [*Directing her grandson.*] Mark two cans of cleanser down on the list there. If she that hard up for kitchen cleanser, I sure don't want to forget to get her none!

RUTH: Lena—maybe the woman is just short on cleanser—

MAMA: [*Not listening.*] —Much baking powder as she done borrowed from me all these years, she could of done gone into the baking business!

[*The bell sounds suddenly and sharply and all three are stunned—serious and silent—mid-speech. In spite of all the other conversations and distractions of the morning, this is what they have been waiting for, even* TRAVIS, *who looks helplessly from his mother to his grandmother.* RUTH *is the first to come to life again.*]

RUTH: [*To* TRAVIS.] *Get down them steps, boy!*

[TRAVIS *snaps to life and flies out to get the mail.*]

MAMA: [*Her eyes wide, her hand to her breast.*] You mean it done really come?

RUTH: [*Excited.*] Oh, Miss Lena!

MAMA: [*Collecting herself.*] Well . . . I don't know what we all so excited about 'round here for. We known it was coming for months.

RUTH: That's a whole lot different from having it come and being able to hold it in your hands . . . a piece of paper worth ten thousand dollars . . . [TRAVIS *bursts back into the room. He holds the envelope high above his head, like a little dancer, his face is radiant and he is breathless. He moves to his grandmother with sudden slow ceremony and puts the envelope into her hands. She accepts it, and then merely holds it and looks at it.*] Come on! Open it . . . Lord have mercy, I wish Walter Lee was here!

TRAVIS: Open it, Grandmama!

MAMA: [*Staring at it.*] Now you all be quiet. It's just a check.

RUTH: Open it . . .

MAMA: [*Still staring at it.*] Now don't act silly . . . We ain't never been no people to act silly 'bout no money—

RUTH: [*Swiftly.*] We ain't never had none before—*open it!*

> [MAMA *finally makes a good strong tear and pulls out the thin blue slice of paper and inspects it closely. The boy and his mother study it raptly over* MAMA's *shoulders.*]

MAMA: *Travis!* [*She is counting off with doubt.*] Is that the right number of zeros.

TRAVIS: Yes'm . . . ten thousand dollars. Gaalee, Grandmama, you rich.

MAMA: [*She holds the check away from her, still looking at it. Slowly her face sobers into a mask of unhappiness.*] Ten thousand dollars. [*She hands it to* RUTH.] Put it away somewhere, Ruth. [*She does not look at* RUTH; *her eyes seem to be seeing something somewhere very far off.*] Ten thousand dollars they give you. Ten thousand dollars.

TRAVIS: [*To his mother, sincerely.*] What's the matter with Grandmama—don't she want to be rich?

RUTH: [*Distractedly.*] You go on out and play now, baby. [TRAVIS *exits.* MAMA *starts wiping dishes absently, humming intently to herself.* RUTH *turns to her, with kind exasperation.*] You've gone and got yourself upset.

MAMA: [*Not looking at her.*] I spec if it wasn't for you all . . . I would just put that money away or give it to the church or something.

RUTH: Now what kind of talk is that. Mr. Younger would just be plain mad if he could hear you talking foolish like that.

MAMA: [*Stopping and staring off.*] Yes . . . he sure would. [*Sighing.*] We got enough to do with that money, all right. [*She halts then, and turns and looks at her daughter-in-law hard;* RUTH *avoids her eyes and* MAMA *wipes her hands with finality and starts to speak firmly to* RUTH.] Where did you go today, girl?

RUTH: To the doctor.

MAMA: [*Impatiently.*] Now, Ruth . . . you know better than that. Old Doctor Jones is strange enough in his way but there ain't nothing 'bout him make somebody slip and call him "she"—like you done this morning.

RUTH: Well, that's what happened—my tongue slipped.

MAMA: You went to see that woman, didn't you?

RUTH: [*Defensively, giving herself away.*] What woman you talking about?

MAMA: [*Angrily.*] That woman who—

[WALTER *enters in great excitement.*]

WALTER: Did it come?

MAMA: [*Quietly.*] Can't you give people a Christian greeting before you start asking about money?

WALTER: [*To* RUTH.] Did it come? [RUTH *unfolds the check and lays it quietly before him, watching him intently with thoughts of her own.* WALTER *sits down and grasps it close and counts off the zeros.*] Ten thousand dollars—[*He turns suddenly, frantically to his mother and draws some papers out of his breast pocket.*] Mama— look. Old Willy Harris put everything on paper—

MAMA: Son—I think you ought to talk to your wife . . . I'll go on out and leave you alone if you want—

WALTER: I can talk to her later— Mama, look—

MAMA: Son—

WALTER: WILL SOMEBODY PLEASE LISTEN TO ME TODAY!

MAMA: [*Quietly.*] I don't 'low no yellin' in this house, Walter Lee, and you know it—[WALTER *stares at them in frustration and starts to speak several times.*] And there ain't going to be no investing in no liquor stores. I don't aim to have to speak on that again.

[*A long pause.*]

WALTER: Oh—so you don't aim to have to speak on that again? So you have decided . . . [*Crumpling his papers.*] Well, *you* tell that to my boy tonight when you put him to sleep on the living-room couch . . . [*Turning to* MAMA *and speaking directly to her.*] Yeah—and tell it to my wife, Mama, tomorrow when she has to go out of here to look after somebody else's kids. And tell it to *me*, Mama, every time we need a new pair of curtains and I have to watch *you* go out and work in somebody's kitchen. Yeah, you tell me then!

[WALTER *starts out.*]

RUTH: Where you going?

WALTER: I'm going out!

RUTH: Where?

WALTER: Just out of this house somewhere—

RUTH: [*Getting her coat.*] I'll come too.

WALTER: I don't want you to come!

RUTH: I got something to talk to you about, Walter.

WALTER: That's too bad.

MAMA: [*Still quietly.*] Walter Lee—[*She waits and he finally turns and looks at her.*] Sit down.

WALTER: I'm a grown man, Mama.

MAMA: Ain't nobody said you wasn't grown. But you still in my house and my presence. And as long as you are—you'll talk to your wife civil. Now sit down.

RUTH: [*Suddenly.*] Oh, let him go on out and drink himself to death! He makes me sick to my stomach! [*She flings her coat against him.*]

WALTER: [*Violently.*] And you turn mine too, baby! [RUTH *goes into their bedroom and slams the door behind her.*] That was my greatest mistake—

MAMA: [*Still quietly.*] Walter, what is the matter with you?

WALTER: Matter with me? Ain't nothing the matter with *me!*

MAMA: Yes there is. Something eating you up like a crazy man. Something more than me not giving you this money. The past few years I been watching it happen to you. You get all nervous acting and kind of wild in the eyes— [WALTER *jumps up impatiently at her words.*] I said sit there now, I'm talking to you!

WALTER: Mama—I don't need no nagging at me today.

MAMA: Seem like you getting to a place where you always tied up in some kind of knot about something. But if anybody ask you 'bout it you just yell at 'em and bust out the house and go out and drink somewheres. Walter Lee, people can't live with that. Ruth's a good, patient girl in her way—but you getting to be too much. Boy, don't make the mistake of driving that girl away from you.

WALTER: Why—what she do for me?

MAMA: She loves you.

WALTER: Mama—I'm going out. I want to go off somewhere and be by myself for a while.

MAMA: I'm sorry 'bout your liquor store, son. It just wasn't the thing for us to do. That's what I want to tell you about—

WALTER: I got to go out, Mama—

[*He rises.*]

MAMA: It's dangerous, son.

WALTER: What's dangerous?

MAMA: When a man goes outside his home to look for peace.

WALTER: [*Beseechingly.*] Then why can't there never be no peace in this house then?

MAMA: You done found it in some other house?

WALTER: No—there ain't no woman! Why do women always think there's a woman somewhere when a man gets restless. [*Coming to her.*] Mama—Mama—I want so many things . . .

MAMA: Yes, son—

WALTER: I want so many things that they are driving me kind of crazy . . . Mama—look at me.

MAMA: I'm looking at you. You a good-looking boy. You got a job, a nice wife, a fine boy and—

WALTER: A job. [*Looks at her.*] Mama, a job? I open and close car doors all day long. I drive a man around in his limousine and I say, "Yes, sir; no, sir; very good, sir; shall I take the Drive, sir?" Mama, that ain't no kind of job . . . that ain't nothing at all. [*Very quietly.*] Mama, I don't know if I can make you understand.

MAMA: Understand what, baby?

WALTER: [*Quietly.*] Sometimes it's like I can see the future stretched out in front of me—just plain as day. The future, Mama. Hanging over there at the edge of my days. Just waiting for me—a big, looming blank space—full of *nothing*. Just waiting for *me*. [*Pause.*] Mama—sometimes when I'm downtown and I pass them cool, quiet-looking restaurants where them white boys are sitting back and talking 'bout things . . . sitting there turning deals worth millions of dollars . . . sometimes I see guys don't look much older than me—

MAMA: Son—how come you talk so much 'bout money?

WALTER: [*With immense passion.*] Because it is life, Mama!

MAMA: [*Quietly.*] Oh—[*Very quietly.*] So now it's life. Money is life. Once upon a time freedom used to be life—now it's money. I guess the world really do change . . .

WALTER: No—it was always money, Mama. We just didn't know about it.

MAMA: No . . . something has changed. [*She looks at him.*] You something new, boy. In my time we was worried about not being lynched and getting to the North if we could and how to stay alive and still have a pinch of dignity too . . . Now here come you and Beneatha—talking 'bout things we ain't never even thought about hardly, me and your daddy. You ain't satisfied or proud of nothing we done. I mean that you had a home; that we kept you out of trouble till you was grown; that you don't have to ride to work on the back of nobody's streetcar— You my children—but how different we done become.

WALTER: You just don't understand, Mama, you just don't understand.

MAMA: Son—do you know your wife is expecting another baby? [WALTER *stands, stunned, and absorbs what his mother has said.*] That's what she wanted to talk to you about. [WALTER *sinks down into a chair.*] This ain't for me to be telling— but you ought to know. [*She waits.*] I think Ruth is thinking 'bout getting rid of that child.[5]

WALTER: [*Slowly understanding.*] No—no—Ruth wouldn't do that.

MAMA: When the world gets ugly enough—a woman will do anything for her family. *The part that's already living.*

WALTER: You don't know Ruth, Mama, if you think she would do that.

[RUTH *opens the bedroom door and stands there a little limp.*]

RUTH: [*Beaten.*] Yes I would too, Walter. [*Pause.*] I gave her a five-dollar down payment.

[*There is total silence as the man stares at his wife and the mother stares at her son.*]

MAMA: [*Presently.*] Well — [*Tightly.*] Well — son, I'm waiting to hear you say something . . . I'm waiting to hear how you be your father's son. Be the man he

---

5. Abortions were illegal and dangerous at that time.

was . . . [*Pause.*] Your wife say she going to destroy your child. And I'm waiting to hear you talk like him and say we a people who give children life, not
who destroys them—[*She rises.*] I'm waiting to see you stand up and look like
your daddy and say we done give up one baby to poverty and that we ain't
going to give up nary another one . . . I'm waiting.

WALTER: Ruth—

MAMA: If you a son of mine, tell her! [WALTER *turns, looks at her and can say nothing.*
She continues, bitterly.] You . . . you are a disgrace to your father's memory.
Somebody get me my hat.

> [CURTAIN.]

ACT II

SCENE ONE

Time: Later the same day.

At rise: RUTH *is ironing again. She has the radio going. Presently* BENEATHA'*s bedroom*
door opens and RUTH'*s mouth falls and she puts down the iron in fascination.*

RUTH: What have we got on tonight!

BENEATHA: [*Emerging grandly from the doorway so that we can see her thoroughly robed*
in the costume ASAGAI *brought.*] You are looking at what a well-dressed Nigerian woman wears—[*She parades for* RUTH, *her hair completely hidden by the*
headdress; she is coquettishly fanning herself with an ornate oriental fan, mistak-
enly more like Butterfly[6] than any Nigerian that ever was.] Isn't it beautiful? [*She*
promenades to the radio and, with an arrogant flourish, turns off the good loud
blues that is playing.] Enough of this assimilationist junk! [RUTH *follows her*
with her eyes as she goes to the phonograph and puts on a record and turns and
waits ceremoniously for the music to come up. Then, with a shout—] OCOMO-
GOSIAY!

> [RUTH *jumps. The music comes up, a lovely Nigerian melody.* BENEATHA *lis-*
> *tens, enraptured, her eyes far away—"back to the past." She begins to dance.*
> RUTH *is dumbfounded.*]

RUTH: What kind of dance is that?

BENEATHA: A folk dance.

RUTH: [*Pearl Bailey.*][7] What kind of folks do that, honey?

BENEATHA: It's from Nigeria. It's a dance of welcome.

RUTH: Who you welcoming?

BENEATHA: The men back to the village.

RUTH: Where they been?

BENEATHA: How should I know—out hunting or something. Anyway, they are
coming back now . . .

---

6. Butterfly McQueen, African-American actor.   7. Popular African-American singer and entertainer
(1918–1990).

RUTH: Well, that's good.

BENEATHA: [*With the record.*]

Alundi, alundi
Alundi alunya
Jop pu a jeepua
Ang gu soooooooooo

Ai yai yae . . .
Ayehaye—alundi . . .

[WALTER *comes in during this performance; he has obviously been drinking. He leans against the door heavily and watches his sister, at first with distaste. Then his eyes look off—"back to the past"—as he lifts both his fists to the roof, screaming.*]

WALTER: YEAH . . . AND ETHIOPIA STRETCH FORTH HER HANDS AGAIN! . . .

RUTH: [*Drily, looking at him.*] Yes—and Africa sure is claiming her own tonight. [*She gives them both up and starts ironing again.*]

WALTER: [*All in a drunken, dramatic shout.*] Shut up! . . . I'm digging them drums . . . them drums move me! . . . [*He makes his weaving way to his wife's face and leans in close to her.*] In my *heart of hearts*— [*He thumps his chest.*]—I am much warrior!

RUTH: [*Without even looking up.*] In your heart of hearts you are much drunkard.

WALTER: [*Coming away from her and starting to wander around the room, shouting.*] Me and Jomo . . . [*Intently, in his sister's face. She has stopped dancing to watch him in this unknown mood.*] That's my man, Kenyatta. [*Shouting and thumping his chest.*] FLAMING SPEAR! HOT DAMN! [*He is suddenly in possession of an imaginary spear and actively spearing enemies all over the room.*] OCOMOGO-SIAY . . . THE LION IS WAKING . . . OWIMOWEH! [*He pulls his shirt open and leaps up on a table and gestures with his spear. The bell rings.* RUTH *goes to answer.*]

BENEATHA: [*To encourage* WALTER, *thoroughly caught up with this side of him.*] OCO-MOGOSIAY, FLAMING SPEAR!

WALTER: [*On the table, very far gone, his eyes pure glass sheets. He sees what we cannot, that he is a leader of his people, a great chief, a descendant of Chaka, and that the hour to march has come.*] Listen, my black brothers—

BENEATHA: OCOMOGOSIAY!

WALTER: —Do you hear the waters rushing against the shores of the coastlands—

BENEATHA: OCOMOGOSIAY!

WALTER: —Do you hear the screeching of the cocks in yonder hills beyond where the chiefs meet in council for the coming of the mighty war—

BENEATHA: OCOMOGOSIAY!

WALTER: —Do you hear the beating of the wings of the birds flying low over the mountains and the low places of our land—

[RUTH *opens the door.* GEORGE MURCHISON *enters.*]

BENEATHA: OCOMOGOSIAY!

WALTER: —Do you hear the singing of the women, singing the war songs of our fathers to the babies in the great houses . . . singing the sweet war songs? OH, DO YOU HEAR, MY BLACK BROTHERS!

BENEATHA: [*Completely gone.*] We hear you, Flaming Spear—

WALTER: Telling us to prepare for the greatness of the time—[*To* GEORGE.] Black Brother!

[*He extends his hand for the fraternal clasp.*]

GEORGE: Black Brother, hell!

RUTH: [*Having had enough, and embarrassed for the family.*] Beneatha, you got company—what's the matter with you? Walter Lee Younger, get down off that table and stop acting like a fool . . .

[WALTER *comes down off the table suddenly and makes a quick exit to the bathroom.*]

RUTH: He's had a little to drink . . . I don't know what her excuse is.

GEORGE: [*To* BENEATHA.] Look honey, we're going *to* the theatre—we're not going to be *in* it . . . so go change, huh?

RUTH: You expect this boy to go out with you looking like that?

BENEATHA: [*Looking at* GEORGE.] That's up to George. If he's ashamed of his heritage—

GEORGE: Oh, don't be so proud of yourself, Bennie—just because you look eccentric.

BENEATHA: How can something that's natural be eccentric?

GEORGE: That's what being eccentric means—being natural. Get dressed.

BENEATHA: I don't like that, George.

RUTH: Why must you and your brother make an argument out of everything people say?

BENEATHA: Because I hate assimilationist Negroes!

RUTH: Will somebody please tell me what assimila-who-ever means!

GEORGE: Oh, it's just a college girl's way of calling people Uncle Toms—but that isn't what it means at all.

RUTH: Well, what does it mean?

BENEATHA: [*Cutting* GEORGE *off and staring at him as she replies to* RUTH.] It means someone who is willing to give up his own culture and submerge himself completely in the dominant, and in this case, *oppressive* culture!

GEORGE: Oh, dear, dear, dear! Here we go! A lecture on the African past! On our Great West African Heritage! In one second we will hear all about the great Ashanti empires; the great Songhay civilizations; and the great sculpture of Bénin—and then some poetry in the Bantu—and the whole monologue will end with the word *heritage!* [*Nastily.*] Let's face it, baby, your heritage is nothing but a bunch of raggedy-assed spirituals and some grass huts!

BENEATHA: *Grass huts!* [RUTH *crosses to her and forcibly pushes her toward the bedroom.*] See there . . . you are standing there in your splendid ignorance talking about people who were the first to smelt iron on the face of the earth! [RUTH *is pushing her through the door.*] The Ashanti were performing surgical operations when the English—[RUTH *pulls the door to, with* BENEATHA *on the other side, and smiles graciously at* GEORGE. BENEATHA *opens the door and shouts the end of the sentence defiantly at* GEORGE.]—were still tattooing themselves with blue dragons . . . [*She goes back inside.*]

RUTH: Have a seat, George. [*They both sit.* RUTH *folds her hands rather primly on her lap, determined to demonstrate the civilization of the family.*] Warm, ain't it? I mean for September. [*Pause.*] Just like they always say about Chicago weather: If it's too hot or cold for you, just wait a minute and it'll change. [*She smiles happily at this cliché of clichés.*] Everybody say it's got to do with them bombs and things they keep setting off.[8] [*Pause.*] Would you like a nice cold beer?

GEORGE: No, thank you. I don't care for beer. [*He looks at his watch.*] I hope she hurries up.

RUTH: What time is the show?

GEORGE: It's an eight-thirty curtain. That's just Chicago, though. In New York standard curtain time is eight forty.

[*He is rather proud of this knowledge.*]

RUTH: [*Properly appreciating it.*] You get to New York a lot?

GEORGE: [*Offhand.*] Few times a year.

RUTH: Oh—that's nice. I've never been to New York.

[WALTER *enters. We feel he has relieved himself, but the edge of unreality is still with him.*]

WALTER: New York ain't got nothing Chicago ain't. Just a bunch of hustling people all squeezed up together—being "Eastern."

[*He turns his face into a screw of displeasure.*]

GEORGE: Oh—you've been?

WALTER: *Plenty* of times.

RUTH: [*Shocked at the lie.*] Walter Lee Younger!

WALTER: [*Staring her down.*] Plenty! [*Pause.*] What we got to drink in this house? Why don't you offer this man some refreshment. [*To* GEORGE.] They don't know how to entertain people in this house, man.

GEORGE: Thank you—I don't really care for anything.

WALTER: [*Feeling his head; sobriety coming.*] Where's Mama?

RUTH: She ain't come back yet.

WALTER: [*Looking* MURCHISON *over from head to toe, scrutinizing his carefully casual tweed sports jacket over cashmere V-neck sweater over soft eyelet shirt and tie, and soft slacks, finished off with white buckskin shoes.*] Why all you college boys wear them fairyish-looking white shoes?

RUTH: Walter Lee!

[GEORGE MURCHISON *ignores the remark.*]

WALTER: [*To* RUTH.] Well, they look crazy as hell—white shoes, cold as it is.

RUTH: [*Crushed.*] You have to excuse him—

---

8. In the 1950s, it was common to blame weather fluctuations on atomic testing.

WALTER: No he don't! Excuse me for what? What you always excusing me for! I'll excuse myself when I needs to be excused! [*A pause.*] They look as funny as them black knee socks Beneatha wears out of here all the time.

RUTH: It's the college *style*, Walter.

WALTER: Style, hell, She looks like she got burnt legs or something!

RUTH: Oh, Walter—

WALTER: [*An irritable mimic.*] Oh, Walter! Oh, Walter! [*To* MURCHISON.] How's your old man making out? I understand you all going to buy that big hotel on the Drive?[9] [*He finds a beer in the refrigerator, wanders over to* MURCHISON, *sipping and wiping his lips with the back of his hand, and straddling a chair backwards to talk to the other man.*] Shrewd move. Your old man is all right, man. [*Tapping his head and half winking for emphasis.*] I mean he knows how to operate. I mean he thinks *big,* you know what I mean, I mean for a *home,* you know? But I think he's kind of running out of ideas now. I'd like to talk to him. Listen, man, I got some plans that could turn this city upside down. I mean I think like he does. *Big.* Invest big, gamble big, hell, lose *big* if you have to, you know what I mean. It's hard to find a man on this whole Southside who understands my kind of thinking—you dig? [*He scrutinizes* MURCHISON *again, drinks his beer, squints his eyes and leans in close, confidential, man to man.*] Me and you ought to sit down and talk sometimes, man. Man, I got me some ideas . . .

GEORGE: [*With boredom.*] Yeah—sometimes we'll have to do that, Walter.

WALTER: [*Understanding the indifference, and offended.*] Yeah—well, when you get the time, man. I know you a busy little boy.

RUTH: Walter, please—

WALTER: [*Bitterly, hurt.*] I know ain't nothing in this world as busy as you colored college boys with your fraternity pins and white shoes . . .

RUTH: [*Covering her face with humiliation.*] Oh, Walter Lee—

WALTER: I see you all the time—with the books tucked under your arms—going to your [*British A—a mimic.*] "clahsses." And for what! What the hell you learning over there? Filling up your heads—[*Counting off on his fingers.*]— with the sociology and the psychology—but they teaching you how to be a man? How to take over and run the world? They teaching you how to run a rubber plantation or a steel mill? Naw—just to talk proper and read books and wear white shoes . . .

GEORGE: [*Looking at him with distaste, a little above it all.*] You're all wacked up with bitterness, man.

WALTER: [*Intently, almost quietly, between the teeth, glaring at the boy.*] And you— ain't you bitter, man? Ain't you just about had it yet? Don't you see no stars gleaming that you can't reach out and grab? You happy?—You contented son-of-a-bitch—you happy? You got it made? Bitter? Man, I'm a volcano. Bitter? Here I am a giant—surrounded by ants! Ants who can't even under-stand what it is the giant is talking about.

RUTH: [*Passionately and suddenly.*] Oh, Walter—ain't you with nobody!

---

9. Lake Shore Drive, a scenic thoroughfare along Lake Michigan.

WALTER: [*Violently.*] No! 'Cause ain't nobody with me! Not even my own mother!

RUTH: Walter, that's a terrible thing to say!

[BENEATHA *enters, dressed for the evening in a cocktail dress and earrings.*]

GEORGE: Well—hey, you look great.

BENEATHA: Let's go, George. See you all later.

RUTH: Have a nice time.

GEORGE: Thanks. Good night. [*To* WALTER, *sarcastically.*] Good night, *Prometheus.*[1]

[BENEATHA *and* GEORGE *exit.*]

WALTER: [*To* RUTH.] Who is Prometheus?

RUTH: I don't know. Don't worry about it.

WALTER: [*In fury, pointing after* GEORGE.] See there—they get to a point where they can't insult you man to man—they got to go talk about something ain't nobody never heard of!

RUTH: How do you know it was an insult? [*To humor him.*] Maybe Prometheus is a nice fellow.

WALTER: Prometheus! I bet there ain't even no such thing! I bet that simple-minded clown—

RUTH: Walter—

[*She stops what she is doing and looks at him.*]

WALTER: [*Yelling.*] Don't start!

RUTH: Start what?

WALTER: Your nagging! Where was I? Who was I with? How much money did I spend?

RUTH: [*Plaintively.*] Walter Lee—why don't we just try to talk about it . . .

WALTER: [*Not listening.*] I been out talking with people who understand me. People who care about the things I got on my mind.

RUTH: [*Wearily.*] I guess that means people like Willy Harris.

WALTER: Yes, people like Willy Harris.

RUTH: [*With a sudden flash of impatience.*] Why don't you all just hurry up and go into the banking business and stop talking about it!

WALTER: Why? You want to know why? 'Cause we all tied up in a race of people that don't know how to do nothing but moan, pray and have babies!

[*The line is too bitter even for him and he looks at her and sits down.*]

RUTH: Oh, Walter . . . [*Softly.*] Honey, why can't you stop fighting me?

WALTER: [*Without thinking.*] Who's fighting you? Who even cares about you?

[*This line begins the retardation of his mood.*]

RUTH: Well—[*She waits a long time, and then with resignation starts to put away her things.*] I guess I might as well go on to bed . . . [*More or less to herself.*] I don't

1. In Greek mythology, Prometheus was a type of the bold creative spirit; he is said to have stolen fire from Olympus (the locale of the gods) and given it to humankind.

know where we lost it . . . but we have . . . [*Then, to him.*] I—I'm sorry about this new baby, Walter. I guess maybe I better go on and do what I started . . . I guess I just didn't realize how bad things was with us . . . I guess I just didn't really realize— [*She starts out to the bedroom and stops.*] You want some hot milk?

WALTER: Hot milk?

RUTH: Yes—hot milk.

WALTER: Why hot milk?

RUTH: 'Cause after all that liquor you come home with you ought to have something hot in your stomach.

WALTER: I don't want no milk.

RUTH: You want some coffee then?

WALTER: No, I don't want no coffee. I don't want nothing hot to drink. [*Almost plaintively.*] Why you always trying to give me something to eat?

RUTH: [*Standing and looking at him helplessly.*] What else can I give you, Walter Lee Younger?

> [*She stands and looks at him and presently turns to go out again. He lifts his head and watches her going away from him in a new mood which began to emerge when he asked her "Who cares about you?"*]

WALTER: It's been rough, ain't it, baby? [*She hears and stops but does not turn around and he continues to her back.*] I guess between two people there ain't never as much understood as folks generally thinks there is. I mean like between me and you—[*She turns to face him.*] How we gets to the place where we scared to talk softness to each other. [*He waits, thinking hard himself.*] Why you think it got to be like that? [*He is thoughtful, almost as a child would be.*] Ruth, what is it gets into people ought to be close?

RUTH: I don't know, honey. I think about it a lot.

WALTER: On account of you and me, you mean? The way things are with us. The way something done come down between us.

RUTH: There ain't so much between us, Walter . . . Not when you come to me and try to talk to me. Try to be with me . . . a little even.

WALTER: [*Total honesty.*] Sometimes . . . sometimes . . . I don't even know how to try.

RUTH: Walter—

WALTER: Yes?

RUTH: [*Coming to him, gently and with misgiving, but coming to him.*] Honey . . . life don't have to be like this. I mean sometimes people can do things so that things are better . . . You remember how we used to talk when Travis was born . . . about the way we were going to live . . . the kind of house . . . [*She is stroking his head.*] Well, it's all starting to slip away from us . . .

> [MAMA *enters, and* WALTER *jumps up and shouts at her.*]

WALTER: Mama, where have you been?

MAMA: My—them steps is longer than they used to be. Whew! [*She sits down and ignores him.*] How you feeling this evening, Ruth?

[RUTH *shrugs, disturbed some at having been prematurely interrupted and watching her husband knowingly.*]

WALTER: Mama, where have you been all day?

MAMA: [*Still ignoring him and leaning on the table and changing to more comfortable shoes.*] Where's Travis?

RUTH: I let him go out earlier and he ain't come back yet. Boy, is he going to get it!

WALTER: Mama!

MAMA: [*As if she has heard him for the first time.*] Yes, son?

WALTER: Where did you go this afternoon?

MAMA: I went downtown to tend to some business that I had to tend to.

WALTER: What kind of business?

MAMA: You know better than to question me like a child, Brother.

WALTER: [*Rising and bending over the table.*] Where were you, Mama? [*Bringing his fists down and shouting.*] Mama, you didn't go do something with that insurance money, something crazy?

[*The front door opens slowly, interrupting him, and* TRAVIS *peeks his head in, less than hopefully.*]

TRAVIS: [*To his mother.*] Mama, I—

RUTH: "Mama I" nothing! You're going to get it, boy! Get on in that bedroom and get yourself ready!

TRAVIS: But I—

MAMA: Why don't you all never let the child explain hisself.

RUTH: Keep out of it now, Lena.

[MAMA *clamps her lips together, and* RUTH *advances toward her son menacingly.*]

RUTH: A thousand times I have told you not to go off like that—

MAMA: [*Holding out her arms to her grandson.*] Well—at least let me tell him something. I want him to be the first one to hear . . . Come here, Travis. [*The boy obeys, gladly.*] Travis—[*She takes him by the shoulder and looks into his face.*]— you know that money we got in the mail this morning?

TRAVIS: Yes'm—

MAMA: Well—what you think your grandmama gone and done with that money?

TRAVIS: I don't know, Grandmama.

MAMA: [*Putting her finger on his nose for emphasis.*] She went out and she bought you a house! [*The explosion comes from* WALTER *at the end of the revelation and he jumps up and turns away from all of them in a fury.* MAMA *continues, to* TRAVIS.] You glad about the house? It's going to be yours when you get to be a man.

TRAVIS: Yeah—I always wanted to live in a house.

MAMA: All right, gimme some sugar then—[TRAVIS *puts his arms around her neck as she watches her son over the boy's shoulder. Then, to* TRAVIS, *after the embrace.*] Now when you say your prayers tonight, you thank God and your grandfather—'cause it was him who give you the house—in his way.

RUTH: [*Taking the boy from* MAMA *and pushing him toward the bedroom.*] Now you get out of here and get ready for your beating.

TRAVIS: Aw, Mama—

RUTH: Get on in there—[*Closing the door behind him and turning radiantly to her mother-in-law.*] So you went and did it!

MAMA: [*Quietly, looking at her son with pain.*] Yes, I did.

RUTH: [*Raising both arms classically.*] Praise God! [*Looks at* WALTER *a moment, who says nothing. She crosses rapidly to her husband.*] Please, honey—let me be glad . . . you be glad too. [*She has laid her hands on his shoulders, but he shakes himself free of her roughly, without turning to face her.*] Oh, Walter . . . a home . . . a home. [*She comes back to* MAMA.] Well—where is it? How big is it? How much it going to cost?

MAMA: Well—

RUTH: When we moving?

MAMA: [*Smiling at her.*] First of the month.

RUTH: [*Throwing back her head with jubilance.*] Praise God!

MAMA: [*Tentatively, still looking at her son's back turned against her and* RUTH.] It's— it's a nice house too . . . [*She cannot help speaking directly to him. An imploring quality in her voice, her manner, makes her almost like a girl now.*] Three bed- rooms—nice big one for you and Ruth . . . Me and Beneatha still have to share our room, but Travis have one of his own—and [*With difficulty.*] I figure if the—new baby—is a boy, we could get one of them double-decker outfits . . . And there's a yard with a little patch of dirt where I could maybe get to grow me a few flowers . . . And a nice big basement . . .

RUTH: Walter honey, be glad—

MAMA: [*Still to his back, fingering things on the table.*] 'Course I don't want to make it sound fancier than it is . . . It's just a plain little old house—but it's made good and solid—and it will be *ours*. Walter Lee—it makes a difference in a man when he can walk on floors that belong to *him* . . .

RUTH: Where is it?

MAMA: [*Frightened at this telling.*] Well—well—it's out there in Clybourne Park—[2]

[RUTH's *radiance fades abruptly, and* WALTER *finally turns slowly to face his mother with incredulity and hostility.*]

RUTH: Where?

MAMA: [*Matter-of-factly.*] Four o six Clybourne Street, Clybourne Park.

RUTH: Clybourne Park? Mama, there ain't no colored people living in Clybourne Park.

MAMA: [*Almost idiotically.*] Well, I guess there's going to be some now.

WALTER: [*Bitterly.*] So that's the peace and comfort you went out and bought for us today!

MAMA: [*Raising her eyes to meet his finally.*] Son—I just tried to find the nicest place for the least amount of money for my family.

RUTH: [*Trying to recover from the shock.*] Well—well—'course I ain't one never been

2. On Chicago's Near North Side.

'fraid of no crackers[3] mind you—but—well, wasn't there no other houses nowhere?

MAMA: Them houses they put up for colored in them areas way out all seem to cost twice as much as other houses. I did the best I could.

RUTH: [*Struck senseless with the news, in its various degrees of goodness and trouble, she sits a moment, her fists propping her chin in thought, and then she starts to rise, bringing her fists down with vigor, the radiance spreading from cheek to cheek again.*] Well—well!—All I can say is—if this is my time in life—*my time*—to say good-bye—[*And she builds with momentum as she starts to circle the room with an exuberant, almost tearfully happy release.*]—to these Goddamned cracking walls!—[*She pounds the walls.*]—and these marching roaches!—[*She wipes at an imaginary army of marching roaches.*]—and this cramped little closet which ain't now or never was no kitchen! . . . then I say it loud and good, *Hallelujah! and good-bye misery . . . I don't never want to see your ugly face again!* [*She laughs joyously, having practically destroyed the apartment, and flings her arms up and lets them come down happily, slowly, reflectively, over her abdomen, aware for the first time perhaps that the life therein pulses with happiness and not despair.*] Lena?

MAMA: [*Moved, watching her happiness.*] Yes, honey?

RUTH: [*Looking off.*] Is there—is there a whole lot of sunlight?

MAMA: [*Understanding.*] Yes, child, there's a whole lot of sunlight.

[*Long pause.*]

RUTH: [*Collecting herself and going to the door of the room* TRAVIS *is in.*] Well—I guess I better see 'bout Travis. [*To* MAMA.] Lord, I sure don't feel like whipping nobody today!

[*She exits.*]

MAMA: [*The mother and son are left alone now and the mother waits a long time, considering deeply, before she speaks.*] Son—you—you understand what I done, don't you? [WALTER *is silent and sullen.*] I—I just seen my family falling apart today . . . just falling to pieces in front of my eyes . . . We couldn't of gone on like we was today. We was going backwards 'stead of forwards—talking 'bout killing babies and wishing each other was dead . . . When it gets like that in life—you just got to do something different, push on out and do something bigger . . . [*She waits.*] I wish you say something, son . . . I wish you'd say how deep inside you you think I done the right thing—

WALTER: [*Crossing slowly to his bedroom door and finally turning there and speaking measuredly.*] What you need me to say you done right for? *You* the head of this family. You run our lives like you want to. It was your money and you did what you wanted with it. So what you need for me to say it was all right for? [*Bitterly, to hurt her as deeply as he knows is possible.*] So you butchered up a dream of mine—you—who always talking 'bout your children's dreams . . .

3. Derogatory term for poor whites.

MAMA: Walter Lee—

> [*He just closes the door behind him.* MAMA *sits alone, thinking heavily.*]

[CURTAIN.]

SCENE TWO

Time: Friday night. A few weeks later.

At rise: Packing crates mark the intention of the family to move. BENEATHA *and* GEORGE *come in, presumably from an evening out again.*

GEORGE: O.K. . . . O.K., whatever you say . . . [*They both sit on the couch. He tries to kiss her. She moves away.*] Look, we've had a nice evening; let's not spoil it, huh? . . .

> [*He again turns her head and tries to nuzzle in and she turns away from him, not with distaste but with momentary lack of interest; in a mood to pursue what they were talking about.*]

BENEATHA: I'm *trying* to talk to you.

GEORGE: We always talk.

BENEATHA: Yes—and I love to talk.

GEORGE: [*Exasperated; rising.*] I know it and I don't mind it sometimes . . . I want you to cut it out, see—The moody stuff, I mean. I don't like it. You're a nice-looking girl . . . all over. That's all you need, honey, forget the atmosphere. Guys aren't going to go for the atmosphere—they're going to go for what they see. Be glad for that. Drop the Garbo[4] routine. It doesn't go with you. As for myself, I want a nice—[*Groping.*]—simple [*Thoughtfully.*]—sophisticated girl . . . not a poet—O.K.?

> [*She rebuffs him again and he starts to leave.*]

BENEATHA: Why are you angry?

GEORGE: Because this is stupid! I don't go out with you to discuss the nature of "quiet desperation"[5] or to hear all about your thoughts—because the world will go on thinking what it thinks regardless—

BENEATHA: Then why read books? Why go to school?

GEORGE: [*With artificial patience, counting on his fingers.*] It's simple. You read books—to learn facts—to get grades—to pass the course—to get a degree. That's all—it has nothing to do with thoughts.

> [*A long pause.*]

BENEATHA: I see. [*A longer pause as she looks at him.*] Good night, George.

---

4. Greta Garbo (1905–1990), Swedish-American film star whose sultry, remote, and European femininity was widely imitated mid-century.   5. In *Walden* (1854), Henry Thoreau said that "the mass of men lead lives of quiet desperation."

[GEORGE *looks at her a little oddly, and starts to exit. He meets* MAMA *coming in.*]

GEORGE: Oh—hello, Mrs. Younger.

MAMA: Hello, George, how you feeling?

GEORGE: Fine—fine, how are you?

MAMA: Oh, a little tired. You know them steps can get you after a day's work. You all have a nice time tonight?

GEORGE: Yes—a fine time. Well, good night.

MAMA: Good night. [*He exits.* MAMA *closes the door behind her.*] Hello, honey. What you sitting like that for?

BENEATHA: I'm just sitting.

MAMA: Didn't you have a nice time?

BENEATHA: No.

MAMA: No? What's the matter?

BENEATHA: Mama, George is a fool—honest. [*She rises.*]

MAMA: [*Hustling around unloading the packages she has entered with. She stops.*] Is he, baby?

BENEATHA: Yes.

[BENEATHA *makes up* TRAVIS' *bed as she talks.*]

MAMA: You sure?

BENEATHA: Yes.

MAMA: Well—I guess you better not waste your time with no fools.

[BENEATHA *looks up at her mother, watching her put groceries in the refrigerator. Finally she gathers up her things and starts into the bedroom. At the door she stops and looks back at her mother.*]

BENEATHA: Mama—

MAMA: Yes, baby—

BENEATHA: Thank you.

MAMA: For what?

BENEATHA: For understanding me this time.

[*She exits quickly and the mother stands, smiling a little, looking at the place where* BENEATHA *just stood.* RUTH *enters.*]

RUTH: Now don't you fool with any of this stuff, Lena—

MAMA: Oh, I just thought I'd sort a few things out.

[*The phone rings.* RUTH *answers.*]

RUTH: [*At the phone.*] Hello—Just a minute. [*Goes to door.*] Walter, it's Mrs. Arnold. [*Waits. Goes back to the phone. Tense.*] Hello. Yes, this is his wife speaking . . . He's lying down now. Yes . . . well, he'll be in tomorrow. He's been very sick. Yes—I know we should have called, but we were so sure he'd be able to come in today. Yes—yes, I'm very sorry. Yes . . . Thank you very much. [*She hangs up.* WALTER *is standing in the doorway of the bedroom behind her.*] That was Mrs. Arnold.

WALTER: [*Indifferently.*] Was it?

RUTH: She said if you don't come in tomorrow that they are getting a new man . . .

WALTER: Ain't that sad—ain't that crying sad.

RUTH: She said Mr. Arnold has had to take a cab for three days . . . Walter, you ain't been to work for three days! [*This is a revelation to her.*] Where you been, Walter Lee Younger? [WALTER *looks at her and starts to laugh.*] You're going to lose your job.

WALTER: That's right . . .

RUTH: Oh, Walter, and with your mother working like a dog every day—

WALTER: That's sad too— Everything is sad.

MAMA: What you been doing for these three days, son?

WALTER: Mama—you don't know all the things a man what got leisure can find to do in this city . . . What's this—Friday night? Well—Wednesday I borrowed Willy Harris' car and I went for a drive . . . just me and myself and I drove and drove . . . Way out . . . way past South Chicago, and I parked the car and I sat and looked at the steel mills all day long. I just sat in the car and looked at them big black chimneys for hours. Then I drove back and I went to the Green Hat. [*Pause.*] And Thursday—Thursday I borrowed the car again and I got in it and I pointed it the other way and I drove the other way—for hours—way, way up to Wisconsin, and I looked at the farms. I just drove and looked at the farms. Then I drove back and I went to the Green Hat. [*Pause.*] And today—today I didn't get the car. Today I just walked. All over the Southside. And I looked at the Negroes and they looked at me and finally I just sat down on the curb at Thirty-ninth and South Parkway and I just sat there and watched the Negroes go by. And then I went to the Green Hat. You all sad? You all depressed? And you know where I am going right now—

[RUTH *goes out quietly.*]

MAMA: Oh, Big Walter, is this the harvest of our days?

WALTER: You know what I like about the Green Hat? [*He turns the radio on and a steamy, deep blues pours into the room.*] I like this little cat they got there who blows a sax . . . He blows. He talks to me. He ain't but 'bout five feet tall and he's got a conked head[6] and his eyes is always closed and he's all music—

MAMA: [*Rising and getting some papers out of her handbag.*] Walter—

WALTER: And there's this other guy who plays the piano . . . and they got a sound. I mean they can work on some music . . . They got the best little combo in the world in the Green Hat . . . You can just sit there and drink and listen to them three men play and you realize that don't nothing matter worth a damn, but just being there—

MAMA: I've helped do it to you, haven't I, son? Walter, I been wrong.

6. Straightened hair.

WALTER: Naw—you ain't never been wrong about nothing, Mama.

MAMA: Listen to me, now. I say I been wrong, son. That I been doing to you what the rest of the world been doing to you. [*She stops and he looks up slowly at her and she meets his eyes pleadingly.*] Walter—what you ain't never understood is that I ain't got nothing, don't own nothing, ain't never really wanted nothing that wasn't for you. There ain't nothing as precious to me . . . There ain't nothing worth holding on to, money, dreams, nothing else—if it means—if it means it's going to destroy my boy. [*She puts her papers in front of him and he watches her without speaking or moving.*] I paid the man thirty-five hundred dollars down on the house. That leaves sixty-five hundred dollars. Monday morning I want you to take this money and take three thousand dollars and put it in a savings account for Beneatha's medical schooling. The rest you put in a checking account—with your name on it. And from now on any penny that come out of it or that go in it is for you to look after. For you to decide. [*She drops her hands a little helplessly.*] It ain't much, but it's all I got in the world and I'm putting it in your hands. I'm telling you to be the head of this family from now on like you supposed to be.

WALTER: [*Stares at the money.*] You trust me like that, Mama?

MAMA: I ain't never stop trusting you. Like I ain't never stop loving you.

[*She goes out, and* WALTER *sits looking at the money on the table as the music continues in its idiom, pulsing in the room. Finally, in a decisive gesture, he gets up, and, in mingled joy and desperation, picks up the money. At the same moment,* TRAVIS *enters for bed.*]

TRAVIS: What's the matter, Daddy? You drunk?

WALTER: [*Sweetly, more sweetly than we have ever known him.*] No, Daddy ain't drunk. Daddy ain't going to never be drunk again. . . .

TRAVIS: Well, good night, Daddy.

[*The father has come from behind the couch and leans over, embracing his son.*]

WALTER: Son, I feel like talking to you tonight.

TRAVIS: About what?

WALTER: Oh, about a lot of things. About you and what kind of man you going to be when you grow up. . . . Son—son, what do you want to be when you grow up?

TRAVIS: A bus driver.

WALTER: [*Laughing a little.*] A what? Man, that ain't nothing to want to be!

TRAVIS: Why not?

WALTER: 'Cause, man—it ain't big enough—you know what I mean.

TRAVIS: I don't know then. I can't make up my mind. Sometimes Mama asks me that too. And sometimes when I tell you I just want to be like you—she says she don't want me to be like that and sometimes she says she does. . . .

WALTER: [*Gathering him up in his arms.*] You know what, Travis? In seven years you going to be seventeen years old. And things is going to be very different with us in seven years, Travis. . . . One day when you are seventeen I'll come home—home from my office downtown somewhere—

TRAVIS: You don't work in no office, Daddy.

WALTER: No—but after tonight. After what your daddy gonna do tonight, there's going to be offices—a whole lot of offices. . . .

TRAVIS: What you gonna do tonight, Daddy?

WALTER: You wouldn't understand yet, son, but your daddy's gonna make a transaction . . . a business transaction that's going to change our lives. . . . That's how come one day when you 'bout seventeen years old I'll come home and I'll be pretty tired, you know what I mean, after a day of conferences and secretaries getting things wrong the way they do . . . 'cause an executive's life is hell, man—[*The more he talks the farther away he gets.*] And I'll pull the car up on the driveway . . . just a plain black Chrysler, I think, with white walls—no—black tires. More elegant. Rich people don't have to be flashy . . . though I'll have to get something a little sportier for Ruth—maybe a Cadillac convertible to do her shopping in. . . . And I'll come up the steps to the house and the gardener will be clipping away at the hedges and he'll say, "Good evening, Mr. Younger." And I'll say, "Hello, Jefferson, how are you this evening?" And I'll go inside and Ruth will come downstairs and meet me at the door and we'll kiss each other and she'll take my arm and we'll go up to your room to see you sitting on the floor with the catalogues of all the great schools in America around you. . . . All the great schools in the world. And—and I'll say, all right son—it's your seventeenth birthday, what is it you've decided? . . . Just tell me where you want to go to school and you'll *go*. Just tell me, what it is you want to be—and you'll *be* it. . . . Whatever you want to be—Yessir! [*He holds his arms open for* TRAVIS.] You just name it, son . . . [TRAVIS *leaps into them.*] and I hand you the world!

[WALTER'*s voice has risen in pitch and hysterical promise and on the last line he lifts* TRAVIS *high.*]

[BLACKOUT.]

SCENE THREE

Time: Saturday, moving day, one week later.

Before the curtain rises, RUTH'*s voice, a strident, dramatic church alto, cuts through the silence.*

It is, in the darkness, a triumphant surge, a penetrating statement of expectation: "Oh, Lord, I don't feel no ways tired! Children, oh, glory hallelujah!"

As the curtain rises we see that RUTH *is alone in the living room, finishing up the family's packing. It is moving day. She is nailing crates and tying cartons.* BENEATHA *enters, carrying a guitar case, and watches her exuberant sister-in-law.*

RUTH: Hey!

BENEATHA: [*Putting away the case.*] Hi.

RUTH: [*Pointing at a package.*] Honey—look in that package there and see what I found on sale this morning at the South Center. [RUTH *gets up and moves to the package and draws out some curtains.*] Lookahere—hand-turned hems!

BENEATHA: How do you know the window size out there?

RUTH: [*Who hadn't thought of that.*] Oh—Well, they bound to fit something in the whole house. Anyhow, they was too good a bargain to pass up. [RUTH *slaps her head, suddenly remembering something.*] Oh, Bennie—I meant to put a special note on that carton over there. That's your mama's good china and she wants 'em to be very careful with it.

BENEATHA: I'll do it.

[BENEATHA *finds a piece of paper and starts to draw large letters on it.*]

RUTH: You know what I'm going to do soon as I get in that new house?

BENEATHA: What?

RUTH: Honey—I'm going to run me a tub of water up to here . . . [*With her fingers practically up to her nostrils.*] And I'm going to get in it—and I am going to sit . . . and sit . . . and sit in that hot water and the first person who knocks to tell *me* to hurry up and come out—

BENEATHA: Gets shot at sunrise.

RUTH: [*Laughing happily.*] You said it, sister! [*Noticing how large* BENEATHA *is absent-mindedly making the note.*] Honey, they ain't going to read that from no airplane.

BENEATHA: [*Laughing herself.*] I guess I always think things have more emphasis if they are big, somehow.

RUTH: [*Looking up at her and smiling.*] You and your brother seem to have that as a philosophy of life. Lord, that man—done changed so 'round here. You know—you know what we did last night? Me and Walter Lee?

BENEATHA: What?

RUTH: [*Smiling to herself.*] We went to the movies. [*Looking at* BENEATHA *to see if she understands.*] We went to the movies. You know the last time me and Walter went to the movies together?

BENEATHA: No.

RUTH: Me neither. That's how long it been. [*Smiling again.*] But we went last night. The picture wasn't much good, but that didn't seem to matter. We went— and we held hands.

BENEATHA: Oh, Lord!

RUTH: We held hands—and you know what?

BENEATHA: What?

RUTH: When we come out of the show it was late and dark and all the stores and things was closed up . . . and it was kind of chilly and there wasn't many people on the streets . . . and we was still holding hands, me and Walter.

BENEATHA: You're killing me.

[WALTER *enters with a large package. His happiness is deep in him; he cannot keep still with his new-found exuberance. He is singing and wiggling and snapping his fingers. He puts his package in a corner and puts a phonograph record, which he has brought in with him, on the record player. As the music comes up he dances over to* RUTH *and tries to get her to dance with him. She gives in at last to his raunchiness and in a fit of giggling allows herself to be drawn into his mood and together they deliberately burlesque an old social dance of their youth.*]

BENEATHA: [*Regarding them a long time as they dance, then drawing in her breath for a deeply exaggerated comment which she does not particularly mean.*] Talk about—olddddddddddd-fashionedddddddd—Negroes!

WALTER: [*Stopping momentarily.*] What kind of Negroes?

[*He says this in fun. He is not angry with her today, nor with anyone. He starts to dance with his wife again.*]

BENEATHA: Old-fashioned.

WALTER: [*As he dances with* RUTH.] You know, when these *New Negroes* have their convention—[*Pointing at his sister.*]—that is going to be the chairman of the Committee on Unending Agitation. [*He goes on dancing, then stops.*] Race, race, race! . . . Girl, I do believe you are the first person in the history of the entire human race to successfully brainwash yourself. [BENEATHA *breaks up and he goes on dancing. He stops again, enjoying his tease.*] Damn, even the N double A C P takes a holiday sometimes! [BENEATHA *and* RUTH *laugh. He dances with* RUTH *some more and starts to laugh and stops and pantomimes someone over an operating table.*] I can just see that chick someday looking down at some poor cat on an operating table before she starts to slice him, saying . . . [*Pulling his sleeves back maliciously.*] "By the way, what are your views on civil rights down there? . . ."

[*He laughs at her again and starts to dance happily. The bell sounds.*]

BENEATHA: Sticks and stones may break my bones but . . . words will never hurt me!

[BENEATHA *goes to the door and opens it as* WALTER *and* RUTH *go on with the clowning.* BENEATHA *is somewhat surprised to see a quiet-looking middle-aged white man in a business suit holding his hat and a briefcase in his hand and consulting a small piece of paper.*]

MAN: Uh—how do you do, miss. I am looking for a Mrs.—[*He looks at the slip of paper.*] Mrs. Lena Younger?

BENEATHA: [*Smoothing her hair with slight embarrassment.*] Oh—yes, that's my mother. Excuse me [*She closes the door and turns to quiet the other two.*] Ruth! Brother! Somebody's here. [*Then she opens the door. The* MAN *casts a curious quick glance at all of them.*] Uh—come in please.

MAN: [*Coming in.*] Thank you.

BENEATHA: My mother isn't here just now. Is it business?

MAN: Yes . . . well, of a sort.

WALTER: [*Freely, the Man of the House.*] Have a seat. I'm Mrs. Younger's son. I look after most of her business matters.

[RUTH *and* BENEATHA *exchange amused glances.*]

MAN: [*Regarding* WALTER, *and sitting.*] Well—My name is Karl Lindner . . .

WALTER: [*Stretching out his hand.*] Walter Younger. This is my wife—[RUTH *nods politely.*]—and my sister.

LINDNER: How do you do.

WALTER: [*Amiably, as he sits himself easily on a chair, leaning with interest forward on his knees and looking expectantly into the newcomer's face.*] What can we do for you, Mr. Lindner!

LINDNER: [*Some minor shuffling of the hat and briefcase on his knees.*] Well—I am a representative of the Clybourne Park Improvement Association—

WALTER: [*Pointing.*] Why don't you sit your things on the floor?

LINDNER: Oh—yes. Thank you. [*He slides the briefcase and hat under the chair.*] And as I was saying—I am from the Clybourne Park Improvement Association and we have had it brought to our attention at the last meeting that you people—or at least your mother—has bought a piece of residential property at—[*He digs for the slip of paper again.*]—four o six Clybourne Street . . .

WALTER: That's right. Care for something to drink? Ruth, get Mr. Lindner a beer.

LINDNER: [*Upset for some reason.*] Oh—no, really. I mean thank you very much, but no thank you.

RUTH: [*Innocently.*] Some coffee?

LINDNER: Thank you, nothing at all.

[BENEATHA *is watching the man carefully.*]

LINDNER: Well, I don't know how much you folks know about our organization. [*He is a gentle man; thoughtful and somewhat labored in his manner.*] It is one of these community organizations set up to look after—oh, you know, things like block upkeep and special projects and we also have what we call our New Neighbors Orientation Committee . . .

BENEATHA: [*Drily.*] Yes—and what do they do?

LINDNER: [*Turning a little to her and then returning the main force to* WALTER.] Well—it's what you might call a sort of welcoming committee, I guess. I mean they, we, I'm the chairman of the committee—go around and see the new people who move into the neighborhood and sort of give them the lowdown on the way we do things out in Clybourne Park.

BENEATHA: [*With appreciation of the two meanings, which escape* RUTH *and* WALTER.] Un-huh.

LINDNER: And we also have the category of what the association calls—[*He looks elsewhere.*]—uh—special community problems . . .

BENEATHA: Yes—and what are some of those?

WALTER: Girl, let the man talk.

LINDNER: [*With understated relief.*] Thank you. I would sort of like to explain this thing in my own way. I mean I want to explain to you in a certain way.

WALTER: Go ahead.

LINDNER: Yes. Well. I'm going to try to get right to the point. I'm sure we'll all appreciate that in the long run.

BENEATHA: Yes.

WALTER: Be still now!

LINDNER: Well—

RUTH: [*Still innocently.*] Would you like another chair—you don't look comfortable.

LINDNER: [*More frustrated than annoyed.*] No, thank you very much. Please. Well— to get right to the point I—[*A great breath, and he is off at last.*] I am sure you people must be aware of some of the incidents which have happened in various parts of the city when colored people have moved into certain areas—[BENEATHA *exhales heavily and starts tossing a piece of fruit up and down in the air.*] Well—because we have what I think is going to be a unique type of organization in American community life—not only do we deplore that kind of thing—but we are trying to do something about it. [BENEATHA *stops tossing and turns with a new and quizzical interest to the man.*] We feel—[*gaining confidence in his mission because of the interest in the faces of the people he is talking to.*]—we feel that most of the trouble in this world, when you come right down to it—[*He hits his knee for emphasis.*]—most of the trouble exists because people just don't sit down and talk to each other.

RUTH: [*Nodding as she might in church, pleased with the remark.*] You can say that again, mister.

LINDNER: [*More encouraged by such affirmation.*] That we don't try hard enough in this world to understand the other fellow's problem. The other guy's point of view.

RUTH: Now that's right.

[BENEATHA *and* WALTER *merely watch and listen with genuine interest.*]

LINDNER: Yes—that's the way we feel out in Clybourne Park. And that's why I was elected to come here this afternoon and talk to you people. Friendly like, you know, the way people should talk to each other and see if we couldn't find some way to work this thing out. As I say, the whole business is a matter of *caring* about the other fellow. Anybody can see that you are a nice family of folks, hard working and honest I'm sure. [BENEATHA *frowns slightly, quizzically, her head tilted regarding him.*] Today everybody knows what it means to be on the outside of something. And of course, there is always somebody who is out to take the advantage of people who don't always understand.

WALTER: What do you mean?

LINDNER: Well—you see our community is made up of people who've worked hard as the dickens for years to build up that little community. They're not rich and fancy people; just hard-working, honest people who don't really have much but those little homes and a dream of the kind of community they want to raise their children in. Now, I don't say we are perfect and there is a lot wrong in some of the things they want. But you've got to admit that a man, right or wrong, has the right to want to have the neighborhood he lives in a certain kind of way. And at the moment the overwhelming majority of our people out there feel that people get along better, take more of a common interest in the life of the community, when they share a common background. I want you to believe me when I tell you that race prejudice simply doesn't enter into it. It is a matter of the people of Clybourne Park believing, rightly or wrongly, as I say, that for the happiness of all concerned that our Negro families are happier when they live in their *own* communities.

BENEATHA: [*With a grand and bitter gesture.*] This, friends, is the Welcoming Committee!

WALTER: [*Dumfounded, looking at* LINDNER.] Is this what you came marching all the way over here to tell us?

LINDNER: Well, now we've been having a fine conversation. I hope you'll hear me all the way through.

WALTER: [*Tightly.*] Go ahead, man.

LINDNER: You see—in the face of all things I have said, we are prepared to make your family a very generous offer . . .

BENEATHA: Thirty pieces and not a coin less![7]

WALTER: Yeah?

LINDNER: [*Putting on his glasses and drawing a form out of the briefcase.*] Our association is prepared, through the collective effort of our people, to buy the house from you at a financial gain to your family.

RUTH: Lord have mercy, ain't this the living gall!

WALTER: All right, you through?

LINDNER: Well, I want to give you the exact terms of the financial arrangement—

WALTER: We don't want to hear no exact terms of no arrangements. I want to know if you got any more to tell us 'bout getting together?

LINDNER: [*Taking off his glasses.*] Well—I don't suppose that you feel . . .

WALTER: Never mind how I feel—you got any more to say 'bout how people ought to sit down and talk to each other? . . . Get out of my house, man.

[*He turns his back and walks to the door.*]

LINDNER: [*Looking around at the hostile faces and reaching and assembling his hat and briefcase.*] Well—I don't understand why you people are reacting this way. What do you think you are going to gain by moving into a neighborhood where you just aren't wanted and where some elements—well—people can get awful worked up when they feel that their whole way of life and everything they've ever worked for is threatened.

WALTER: Get out.

LINDNER: [*At the door, holding a small card.*] Well—I'm sorry it went like this.

WALTER: Get out.

LINDNER: [*Almost sadly regarding* WALTER.] You just can't force people to change their hearts, son.

[*He turns and put his card on a table and exits.* WALTER *pushes the door to with stinging hatred, and stands looking at it.* RUTH *just sits and* BENEATHA *just stands. They say nothing.* MAMA *and* TRAVIS *enter.*]

MAMA: Well—this all the packing got done since I left out of here this morning. I testify before God that my children got all the energy of the dead. What time the moving men due?

7. See Matthew 26:15.

BENEATHA: Four o'clock. You had a caller, Mama.

[*She is smiling, teasingly.*]

MAMA: Sure enough—who?

BENEATHA: [*Her arms folded saucily.*] The Welcoming Committee.

[WALTER *and* RUTH *giggle.*]

MAMA: [*Innocently.*] Who?

BENEATHA: The Welcoming Committee. They said they're sure going to be glad to see you when you get there.

WALTER: [*Devilishly.*] Yeah, they said they can't hardly wait to see your face.

[*Laughter.*]

MAMA: [*Sensing their facetiousness.*] What's the matter with you all?

WALTER: Ain't nothing the matter with us. We just telling you 'bout the gentleman who came to see you this afternoon. From the Clybourne Park Improvement Association.

MAMA: What he want?

RUTH: [*In the same mood as* BENEATHA *and* WALTER.] To welcome you, honey.

WALTER: He said they can't hardly wait. He said the one thing they don't have, that they just *dying* to have out there is a fine family of colored people! [*To* RUTH *and* BENEATHA.] Ain't that right!

RUTH *and* BENEATHA: [*Mockingly.*] Yeah! He left his card in case—

[*They indicate the card, and* MAMA *picks it up and throws it on the floor—understanding and looking off as she draws her chair up to the table on which she has put her plant and some sticks and some cord.*]

MAMA: Father, give us strength. [*Knowingly—and without fun.*] Did he threaten us?

BENEATHA: Oh—Mama—they don't do it like that anymore. He talked Brotherhood. He said everybody ought to learn how to sit down and hate each other with good Christian fellowship.

[*She and* WALTER *shake hands to ridicule the remark.*]

MAMA: [*Sadly.*] Lord, protect us . . .

RUTH: You should hear the money those folks raised to buy the house from us. All we paid and then some.

BENEATHA: What they think we going to do—eat 'em?

RUTH: No, honey, marry 'em.

MAMA: [*Shaking her head.*] Lord, Lord, Lord . . .

RUTH: Well—that's the way the crackers crumble. Joke.

BENEATHA: [*Laughingly noticing what her mother is doing.*] Mama, what are you doing?

MAMA: Fixing my plant so it won't get hurt none on the way . . .

BENEATHA: Mama, you going to take *that* to the new house?

MAMA: Un-huh—

BENEATHA: That raggedy-looking old thing?

MAMA: [*Stopping and looking at her.*] It expresses *me.*

RUTH: [*With delight, to* BENEATHA.] So there, Miss Thing!

[WALTER *comes to* MAMA *suddenly and bends down behind her and squeezes her in his arms with all his strength. She is overwhelmed by the suddenness of it and, though delighted, her manner is like that of* RUTH *with* TRAVIS.]

MAMA: Look out now, boy! You make me mess up my thing here!

WALTER: [*His face lit, he slips down on his knees beside her, his arms still about her.*] Mama . . . you know what it means to climb up in the chariot?

MAMA: [*Gruffly, very happy.*] Get on away from me now . . .

RUTH: [*Near the gift-wrapped package, trying to catch* WALTER's *eye.*] Psst—

WALTER: What the old song say, Mama . . .

RUTH: Walter— Now?

[*She is pointing at the package.*]

WALTER: [*Speaking the lines, sweetly, playfully, in his mother's face.*]

I got wings . . . you got wings . . .
All God's Children got wings[8] . . .

MAMA: Boy—get out of my face and do some work . . .

WALTER:

When I get to heaven gonna put on my wings,
Gonna fly all over God's heaven . . .

BENEATHA: [*Teasingly, from across the room.*] Everybody talking 'bout heaven ain't going there!

WALTER: [*To* RUTH, *who is carrying the box across to them.*] I don't know, you think we ought to give her that . . . Seems to me she ain't been very appreciative around here.

MAMA: [*Eying the box, which is obviously a gift.*] What is that?

WALTER: [*Taking it from* RUTH *and putting it on the table in front of* MAMA.] Well— what you all think? Should we give it to her?

RUTH: Oh—she was pretty good today.

MAMA: I'll good you—

[*She turns her eyes to the box again.*]

BENEATHA: Open it, Mama.

[*She stands up, looks at it, turns and looks at all of them, and then presses her hands together and does not open the package.*]

WALTER: [*Sweetly.*] Open it, Mama. It's for you. [MAMA *looks in his eyes. It is the first present in her life without its being Christmas. Slowly she opens her package and*

---

8. Lines from an African-American spiritual. Walter's and Beneatha's next lines are also from the song.

lifts out, one by one, a brand-new sparkling set of gardening tools. WALTER *continues, prodding.*] Ruth made up the note—read it . . .

MAMA: [*Picking up the card and adjusting her glasses.*] "To our own Mrs. Miniver[9]— Love from Brother, Ruth and Beneatha." Ain't that lovely . . .

TRAVIS: [*Tugging at his father's sleeve.*] Daddy, can I give her mine now?

WALTER: All right, son. [TRAVIS *flies to get his gift.*] Travis didn't want to go in with the rest of us, Mama. He got his own. [*Somewhat amused.*] We don't know what it is . . .

TRAVIS: [*Racing back in the room with a large hatbox and putting it in front of his grandmother.*] Here!

MAMA: Lord have mercy, baby. You done gone and bought your grandmother a hat?

TRAVIS: [*Very proud.*] Open it!

[*She does and lifts out an elaborate, but very elaborate, wide gardening hat, and all the adults break up at the sight of it.*]

RUTH: Travis, honey, what is that?

TRAVIS: [*Who thinks it is beautiful and appropriate.*] It's a gardening hat! Like the ladies always have on in the magazines when they work in their gardens.

BENEATHA: [*Giggling fiercely.*] Travis—we were trying to make Mama Mrs. Miniver—not Scarlett O'Hara![1]

MAMA: [*Indignantly.*] What's the matter with you all! This here is a beautiful hat! [*Absurdly.*] I always wanted me one just like it!

[*She pops it on her head to prove it to her grandson, and the hat is ludicrous and considerably oversized.*]

RUTH: Hot dog! Go, Mama!

WALTER: [*Doubled over with laughter.*] I'm sorry, Mama—but you look like you ready to go out and chop you some cotton sure enough!

[*They all laugh except* MAMA, *out of deference to* TRAVIS' *feelings.*]

MAMA: [*Gathering the boy up to her.*] Bless your heart—this is the prettiest hat I ever owned— [WALTER, RUTH *and* BENEATHA *chime in—noisily, festively and insincerely congratulating* TRAVIS *on his gift.*] What are we all standing around here for? We ain't finished packin' yet. Bennie, you ain't packed one book.

[*The bell rings.*]

BENEATHA: That couldn't be the movers . . . it's not hardly two good yet—

[BENEATHA *goes into her room.* MAMA *starts for door.*]

WALTER: [*Turning, stiffening.*] Wait—wait—I'll get it.

---

9. The powerful and charismatic title character of a 1942 film starring Greer Garson.   1. The siren in *Gone with the Wind.*

[*He stands and looks at the door.*]

MAMA: You expecting company, son?

WALTER: [*Just looking at the door.*] Yeah—yeah . . .

[MAMA *looks at* RUTH, *and they exchange innocent and unfrightened glances.*]

MAMA: [*Not understanding.*] Well, let them in, son.

BENEATHA: [*From her room.*] We need some more string.

MAMA: Travis—you run to the hardware and get me some string cord.

[MAMA *goes out and* WALTER *turns and looks at* RUTH. TRAVIS *goes to a dish for money.*]

RUTH: Why don't you answer the door, man?

WALTER: [*Suddenly bounding across the floor to her.*] 'Cause sometimes it hard to let the future begin! [*Stooping down in her face.*]

I got wings! You got wings!
All God's children got wings!

[*He crosses to the door and throws it open. Standing there is a very slight little man in a not too prosperous business suit and with haunted frightened eyes and a hat pulled down tightly, brim up, around his forehead.* TRAVIS *passes between the men and exits.* WALTER *leans deep in the man's face, still in his jubilance.*]

When I get to heaven gonna put on my wings,
Gonna fly all over God's heaven . . .

[*The little man just stares at him.*]

Heaven—

[*Suddenly he stops and looks past the little man into the empty hallway.*]

Where's Willy, man?

BOBO: He ain't with me.

WALTER: [*Not disturbed.*] Oh—come on in. You know my wife.

BOBO: [*Dumbly, taking off his hat.*] Yes—h'you, Miss Ruth.

RUTH: [*Quietly, a mood apart from her husband already, seeing* BOBO.] Hello, Bobo.

WALTER: You right on time today . . . Right on time. That's the way! [*He slaps* BOBO *on his back.*] Sit down . . . lemme hear.

[RUTH *stands stiffly and quietly in back of them, as though somehow she senses death, her eyes fixed on her husband.*]

BOBO: [*His frightened eyes on the floor, his hat in his hands.*] Could I please get a drink of water, before I tell you about it, Walter Lee?

[WALTER *does not take his eyes off the man.* RUTH *goes blindly to the tap and gets a glass of water and brings it to* BOBO.]

WALTER: There ain't nothing wrong, is there?

BOBO: Lemme tell you—

WALTER: Man—didn't nothing go wrong?

BOBO: Lemme tell you—Walter Lee. [*Looking at* RUTH *and talking to her more than to* WALTER.] You know how it was. I got to tell you how it was. I mean first I got to tell you how it was all the way . . . I mean about the money I put in, Walter Lee . . .

WALTER: [*With taut agitation now.*] What about the money you put in?

BOBO: Well—it wasn't much as we told you—me and Willy—[*He stops.*] I'm sorry, Walter. I got a bad feeling about it. I got a real bad feeling about it . . .

WALTER: Man, what you telling me about all this for? . . . Tell me what happened in Springfield . . .

BOBO: Springfield.

RUTH: [*Like a dead woman.*] What was supposed to happen in Springfield?

BOBO: [*To her.*] This deal that me and Walter went into with Willy— Me and Willy was going to go down to Springfield and spread some money 'round so's we wouldn't have to wait so long for the liquor license . . . That's what we were going to do. Everybody said that was the way you had to do, you understand, Miss Ruth?

WALTER: Man—what happened down there?

BOBO: [*A pitiful man, near tears.*] I'm trying to tell you, Walter.

WALTER: [*Screaming at him suddenly.*] THEN TELL ME, GODDAMMIT . . . WHAT'S THE MATTER WITH YOU?

BOBO: Man . . . I didn't go to no Springfield, yesterday.

WALTER: [*Halted, life hanging in the moment.*] Why not?

BOBO: [*The long way, the hard way to tell.*] 'Cause I didn't have no reasons to . . .

WALTER: Man, what are you talking about!

BOBO: I'm talking about the fact that when I got to the train station yesterday morning—eight o'clock like we planned . . . Man—*Willy didn't never show up.*

WALTER: Why . . . where was he . . . where is he?

BOBO: That's what I'm trying to tell you . . . I don't know . . . I waited six hours . . . I called his house . . . and I waited . . . six hours . . . I waited in that train station six hours . . . [*Breaking into tears.*] That was all the extra money I had in the world . . . [*Looking up at* WALTER *with the tears running down his face.*] Man, *Willy is gone.*

WALTER: Gone, what you mean Willy is gone? Gone where? You mean he went by himself. You mean he went off to Springfield by himself—to take care of getting the license—[*Turns and looks anxiously at* RUTH.] You mean maybe he didn't want too many people in on the business down there? [*Looks to* RUTH *again, as before.*] You know Willy got his own ways. [*Looks back to* BOBO.] Maybe you was late yesterday and he just went on down there without you. Maybe—maybe—he's been callin' you at home tryin' to tell you what happened or something. Maybe—maybe—he just got sick. He's some-where—he's got to be somewhere. We just got to find him—me and you got to find him. [*Grabs* BOBO *senselessly by the collar and starts to shake him.*] We got to!

BOBO: [*In sudden angry, frightened agony.*] What's the matter with you, Walter! *When a cat take off with your money he don't leave you no maps!*

WALTER: [*Turning madly, as though he is looking for* WILLY *in the very room.*] Willy! . . . Willy . . . don't do it . . . Please don't do it . . . Man, not with that money . . . Man, please, not with that money . . . Oh, God . . . Don't let it be true . . . [*He is wandering around, crying out for* WILLY *and looking for him or perhaps for help from God.*] Man . . . I trusted you . . . Man, I put my life in your hands . . . [*He starts to crumple down on the floor as* RUTH *just covers her face in horror.* MAMA *opens the door and comes into the room, with* BENEATHA *behind her.*] Man . . . [*He starts to pound the floor with his fists, sobbing wildly.*] *That money is made out of my father's flesh* . . .

BOBO: [*Standing over him helplessly.*] I'm sorry, Walter . . . [*Only* WALTER's *sobs reply.* BOBO *puts on his hat.*] I had my life staked on this deal, too . . .

[*He exits.*]

MAMA: [*To* WALTER.] Son—[*She goes to him, bends down to him, talks to his bent head.*] Son . . . Is it gone? Son, I gave you sixty-five hundred dollars. Is it gone? All of it? Beneatha's money too?

WALTER: [*Lifting his head slowly.*] Mama . . . I never . . . went to the bank at all . . .

MAMA: [*Not wanting to believe him.*] You mean . . . your sister's school money . . . you used that too . . . Walter? . . .

WALTER: Yessss! . . . All of it . . . It's all gone . . . [*There is total silence.* RUTH *stands with her face covered with her hands;* BENEATHA *leans forlornly against a wall, fingering a piece of red ribbon from the mother's gift.* MAMA *stops and looks at her son without recognition and then, quite without thinking about it, starts to beat him senselessly in the face.* BENEATHA *goes to them and stops it.*]

BENEATHA: Mama!

[MAMA *stops and looks at both of her children and rises slowly and wanders vaguely, aimlessly away from them.*]

MAMA: I seen . . . him . . . night after night . . . come in . . . and look at that rug . . . and then look at me . . . the red showing in his eyes . . . the veins moving in his head . . . I seen him grow thin and old before he was forty . . . working and working and working like somebody's old horse . . . killing himself . . . and you—you give it all away in a day . . .

BENEATHA: Mama—

MAMA: Oh, God . . . [*She looks up to Him.*] Look down here—and show me the strength.

BENEATHA: Mama—

MAMA: [*Folding over.*] Strength . . .

BENEATHA: [*Plaintively.*] Mama . . .

MAMA: Strength!

[CURTAIN.]

ACT III

An hour later.

At curtain, there is a sullen light of gloom in the living room, gray light not unlike that which began the first scene of Act I. At left we can see WALTER *within his room, alone with himself. He is stretched out on the bed, his shirt out and open, his arms under his head. He does not smoke, he does not cry out, he merely lies there, looking up at the ceiling, much as if he were alone in the world.*

In the living room BENEATHA *sits at the table, still surrounded by the now almost ominous packing crates. She sits looking off. We feel that this is a mood struck perhaps an hour before, and it lingers now, full of the empty sound of profound disappointment. We see on a line from her brother's bedroom the sameness of their attitudes. Presently the bell rings and* BENEATHA *rises without ambition or interest in answering. It is* ASAGAI, *smiling broadly, striding into the room with energy and happy expectation and conversation.*

ASAGAI: I came over . . . I had some free time. I thought I might help with the packing. Ah, I like the look of packing crates! A household in preparation for a journey! It depresses some people . . . but for me . . . it is another feeling. Something full of the flow of life, do you understand? Movement, progress . . . It makes me think of Africa.

BENEATHA: Africa!

ASAGAI: What kind of a mood is this? Have I told you how deeply you move me?

BENEATHA: He gave away the money, Asagai . . .

ASAGAI: Who gave away what money?

BENEATHA: The insurance money. My brother gave it away.

ASAGAI: Gave it away?

BENEATHA: He made an investment! With a man even Travis wouldn't have trusted.

ASAGAI: And it's gone?

BENEATHA: Gone!

ASAGAI: I'm very sorry . . . And you, now?

BENEATHA: Me? . . . Me? . . . Me I'm nothing . . . Me. When I was very small . . . we used to take our sleds out in the wintertime and the only hills we had were the ice-covered stone steps of some houses down the street. And we used to fill them in with snow and make them smooth and slide down them all day . . . and it was very dangerous you know . . . far too steep . . . and sure enough one day a kid named Rufus came down too fast and hit the sidewalk . . . and we saw his face just split open right there in front of us . . . And I remember standing there looking at his bloody open face thinking that was the end of Rufus. But the ambulance came and they took him to the hospital and they fixed the broken bones and they sewed it all up . . . and the next time I saw Rufus he just had a little line down the middle of his face . . . I never got over that . . .

[WALTER *sits up, listening on the bed. Throughout this scene it is important that we feel his reaction at all times, that he visibly respond to the words of his sister and* ASAGAI.]

ASAGAI: What?

BENEATHA: That that was what one person could do for another, fix him up—sew up the problem, make him all right again. That was the most marvelous thing in the world . . . I wanted to do that. I always thought it was the one concrete thing in the world that a human being could do. Fix up the sick, you know—and make them whole again. This was truly being God . . .

ASAGAI: You wanted to be God?

BENEATHA: No—I wanted to cure. It used to be so important to me. I wanted to cure. It used to matter. I used to care. I mean about people and how their bodies hurt . . .

ASAGAI: And you've stopped caring?

BENEATHA: Yes—I think so.

ASAGAI: Why?

[WALTER *rises, goes to the door of his room and is about to open it, then stops and stands listening, leaning on the door jamb.*]

BENEATHA: Because it doesn't seem deep enough, close enough to what ails mankind—I mean this thing of sewing up bodies or administering drugs. Don't you understand? It was a child's reaction to the world. I thought that doctors had the secret to all the hurts. . . . That's the way a child sees things—or an idealist.

ASAGAI: Children see things very well sometimes—and idealists even better.

BENEATHA: I know that's what you think. Because you are still where I left off—you still care. This is what you see for the world, for Africa. You with the dreams of the future will patch up all Africa—you are going to cure the Great Sore of colonialism with Independence——

ASAGAI: Yes!

BENEATHA: Yes—and you think that one word is the penicillin of the human spirit: "Independence!" But then what?

ASAGAI: That will be the problem for another time. First we must get there.

BENEATHA: And where does it end?

ASAGAI: End? Who even spoke of an end? To life? To living?

BENEATHA: An end to misery!

ASAGAI: [*Smiling.*] You sound like a French intellectual.

BENEATHA: No! I sound like a human being who just had her future taken right out of her hands! While I was sleeping in my bed in there, things were happening in this world that directly concerned me—and nobody asked me, consulted me—they just went out and did things—and changed my life. Don't you see there isn't any real progress, Asagai, there is only one large circle that we march in, around and around, each of us with our own little picture—in front of us—our own little mirage that we think is the future.

ASAGAI: That is the mistake.

BENEATHA: What?

ASAGAI: What you just said—about the circle. It isn't a circle—it is simply a long line—as in geometry, you know, one that reaches into infinity. And because we cannot see the end—we also cannot see how it changes. And it is very odd but those who see the changes are called "idealists"—and those who cannot, or refuse to think, they are the "realists." It is very strange, and amusing too, I think.

BENEATHA: You—you are almost religious.

ASAGAI: Yes . . . I think I have the religion of doing what is necessary in the world—and of worshipping man—because he is so marvelous, you see.

BENEATHA: Man is foul! And the human race deserves its misery!

ASAGAI: You see: *you* have become the religious one in the old sense. Already, and after such a small defeat, you are worshipping despair.

BENEATHA: From now on, I worship the truth—and the truth is that people are puny, small and selfish. . . .

ASAGAI: Truth? Why is it that you despairing ones always think that only you have the truth? I never thought to see *you* like that. You! Your brother made a stupid, childish mistake—and you are grateful to him. So that now you can give up the ailing human race on account of it. You talk about what good is struggle; what good is anything? Where are we all going? And why are we bothering?

BENEATHA: *And you cannot answer it!* All your talk and dreams about Africa and Independence. Independence and then what? What about all the crooks and petty thieves and just plain idiots who will come into power to steal and plunder the same as before—only now they will be black and do it in the name of the new Independence— You cannot answer that.

ASAGAI: [*Shouting over her.*] *I live the answer!* [*Pause.*] In my village at home it is the exceptional man who can even read a newspaper . . . or who ever *sees* a book at all. I will go home and much of what I will have to say will seem strange to the people of my village . . . But I will teach and work and things will happen, slowly and swiftly. At times it will seem that nothing changes at all . . . and then again . . . the sudden dramatic events which make history leap into the future. And then quiet again. Retrogression even. Guns, murder, revolution. And I even will have moments when I wonder if the quiet was not better than all that death and hatred. But I will look about my village at the illiteracy and disease and ignorance and I will not wonder long. And perhaps . . . perhaps I will be a great man . . . I mean perhaps I will hold on to the substance of truth and find my way always with the right course . . . and perhaps for it I will be butchered in my bed some night by the servants of empire . . .

BENEATHA: *The martyr!*

ASAGAI: . . . or perhaps I shall live to be a very old man, respected and esteemed in my new nation . . . And perhaps I shall hold office and this is what I'm trying to tell you, Alaiyo; perhaps the things I believe now for my country will be wrong and outmoded, and I will not understand and do terrible things to have things my way or merely to keep my power. Don't you see that there will be young men and women, not British soldiers then, but my own black countrymen . . . to step out of the shadows some evening and slit my then useless throat? Don't you see they have always been there . . . that they always will be. And that such a thing as my own death will be an advance? They who might kill me even . . . actually replenish me!

BENEATHA: Oh, Asagai, I know all that.

ASAGAI: Good! Then stop moaning and groaning and tell me what you plan to do.

BENEATHA: Do?

ASAGAI: I have a bit of a suggestion.

BENEATHA: What?

ASAGAI: [*Rather quietly for him.*] That when it is all over—that you come home with me—

BENEATHA: [*Slapping herself on the forehead with exasperation born of misunderstanding.*] Oh—Asagai—at this moment you decide to be romantic!

ASAGAI: [*Quickly understanding the misunderstanding.*] My dear, young creature of the New World—I do not mean across the city—I mean across the ocean; home—to Africa.

BENEATHA: [*Slowly understanding and turning to him with murmured amazement.*] To—to Nigeria?

ASAGAI: Yes! . . . [*Smiling and lifting his arms playfully.*] Three hundred years later the African Prince rose up out of the seas and swept the maiden back across the middle passage over which her ancestors had come—

BENEATHA: [*Unable to play.*] Nigeria?

ASAGAI: Nigeria. Home. [*Coming to her with genuine romantic flippancy.*] I will show you our mountains and our stars; and give you cool drinks from gourds and teach you the old songs and the ways of our people—and, in time, we will pretend that—[*Very softly.*]—you have only been away for a day—

[*She turns her back to him, thinking. He swings her around and takes her full in his arms in a long embrace which proceeds to passion.*]

BENEATHA: [*Pulling away.*] You're getting me all mixed up—

ASAGAI: Why?

BENEATHA: Too many things—too many things have happened today. I must sit down and think. I don't know what I feel about anything right this minute.

[*She promptly sits down and props her chin on her fist.*]

ASAGAI: [*Charmed.*] All right, I shall leave you. No—don't get up. [*Touching her, gently, sweetly.*] Just sit awhile and think . . . Never be afraid to sit awhile and think. [*He goes to door and looks at her.*] How often I have looked at you and said, "Ah—so this is what the New World hath finally wrought . . ."

[*He exits.* BENEATHA *sits on alone. Presently* WALTER *enters from his room and starts to rummage through things, feverishly looking for something. She looks up and turns in her seat.*]

BENEATHA: [*Hissingly.*] Yes—just look at what the New World hath wrought! . . . Just look! [*She gestures with bitter disgust.*] There he is! *Monsieur le petit bour-*

geois noir—himself! There he is—Symbol of a Rising Class! Entrepreneur! Titan of the system! [WALTER *ignores her completely and continues frantically and destructively looking for something and hurling things to the floor and tearing things out of their place in his search.* BENEATHA *ignores the eccentricity of his actions and goes on with the monologue of insult.*] Did you dream of yachts on Lake Michigan, Brother? Did you see yourself on that Great Day sitting down at the Conference Table, surrounded by all the mighty bald-headed men in America? All halted, waiting, breathless, waiting for your pronouncements on industry? Waiting for you—Chairman of the Board? [WALTER *finds what he is looking for—a small piece of white paper—and pushes it in his pocket and puts on his coat and rushes out without ever having looked at her. She shouts after him.*] I look at you and I see the final triumph of stupidity in the world!

> [*The door slams and she returns to just sitting again.* RUTH *comes quickly out of* MAMA'S *room.*]

RUTH: Who was that?

BENEATHA: Your husband.

RUTH: Where did he go?

BENEATHA: Who knows—maybe he has an appointment at U.S. Steel.

RUTH: [*Anxiously, with frightened eyes.*] You didn't say nothing bad to him, did you?

BENEATHA: Bad? Say anything bad to him? No—I told him he was a sweet boy and full of dreams and everything is strictly peachy keen, as the ofay[2] kids say!

> [MAMA *enters from her bedroom. She is lost, vague, trying to catch hold, to make some sense of her former command of the world, but it still eludes her. A sense of waste overwhelms her gait; a measure of apology rides on her shoulders. She goes to her plant, which has remained on the table, looks at it, picks it up and takes it to the window sill and sits it outside, and she stands and looks at it a long moment. Then she closes the window, straightens her body with effort and turns around to her children.*]

MAMA: Well—ain't it a mess in here, though? [*A false cheerfulness, a beginning of something.*] I guess we all better stop moping around and get some work done. All this unpacking and everything we got to do. [RUTH *raises her head slowly in response to the sense of the line; and* BENEATHA *in similar manner turns very slowly to look at her mother.*] One of you all better call the moving people and tell 'em not to come.

RUTH: Tell 'em not to come?

MAMA: Of course, baby. Ain't no need in 'em coming all the way here and having to go back. They charges for that too. [*She sits down, fingers to her brow, thinking.*] Lord, ever since I was a little girl, I always remembers people saying, "Lena—Lena Eggleston, you aims too high all the time. You needs to slow down and see life a little more like it is. Just slow down some." That's what they always used to say down home—"Lord, that Lena Eggleston is a high-minded thing. She'll get her due one day!"

2. White.

RUTH: No, Lena . . .

MAMA: Me and Big Walter just didn't never learn right.

RUTH: Lena, no! We gotta go. Bennie—tell her . . . [*She rises and crosses to* BENEATHA *with her arms outstretched.* BENEATHA *doesn't respond.*] Tell her we can still move . . . the notes ain't but a hundred and twenty-five a month. We got four grown people in this house—we can work . . .

MAMA: [*To herself.*] Just aimed too high all the time—

RUTH: [*Turning and going to* MAMA *fast—the words pouring out with urgency and desperation.*] Lena—I'll work . . . I'll work twenty hours a day in all the kitchens in Chicago . . . I'll strap my baby on my back if I have to and scrub all the floors in America and wash all the sheets in America if I have to—but we got to move . . . We got to get out of here . . .

[MAMA *reaches out absently and pats* RUTH's *hand.*]

MAMA: No—I sees things differently now. Been thinking 'bout some of the things we could do to fix this place up some. I seen a second-hand bureau over on Maxwell Street[3] just the other day that could fit right there. [*She points to where the new furniture might go.* RUTH *wanders away from her.*] Would need some new handles on it and then a little varnish and then it look like something brand-new. And—we can put up them new curtains in the kitchen . . . Why this place be looking fine. Cheer us all up so that we forget trouble ever came . . . [*To* RUTH.] And you could get some nice screens to put up in your room round the baby's bassinet . . . [*She looks at both of them, pleadingly.*] Sometimes you just got to know when to give up some things . . . and hold on to what you got.

[WALTER *enters from the outside, looking spent and leaning against the door, his coat hanging from him.*]

MAMA: Where you been, son?

WALTER: [*Breathing hard.*] Made a call.

MAMA: To who, son?

WALTER: To The Man.

MAMA: What man, baby?

WALTER: The Man, Mama. Don't you know who The Man is?

RUTH: Walter Lee?

WALTER: *The Man.* Like the guys in the streets say—The Man. Captain Boss—Mistuh Charley . . . Old Captain Please Mr. Bossman . . .

BENEATHA: [*Suddenly.*] Lindner!

WALTER: That's right! That's good. I told him to come right over.

BENEATHA: [*Fiercely, understanding.*] For what? What do you want to see him for!

WALTER: [*Looking at his sister.*] We going to do business with him.

MAMA: What you talking 'bout, son?

WALTER: Talking 'bout life, Mama. You all always telling me to see life like it is. Well—I laid in there on my back today . . . and I figured it out. Life just like

---

3. A street market southwest of the Loop.

it is. Who gets and who don't get. [*He sits down with his coat on and laughs.*] Mama, you know it's all divided up. Life is. Sure enough. Between the takers and the "tooken." [*He laughs.*] I've figured it out finally. [*He looks around at them.*] Yeah. Some of us always getting "tooken." [*He laughs.*] People like Willy Harris, they don't never get "tooken." And you know why the rest of us do? 'Cause we all mixed up. Mixed up bad. We get to looking 'round for the right and the wrong, and we worry about it and cry about it and stay up nights trying to figure out 'bout the wrong and the right of things all the time . . . And all the time, man, them takers is out there operating, just taking and taking. Willy Harris? Shoot—Willy Harris don't even count. He don't even count in the big scheme of things. But I'll say one thing for old Willy Harris . . . he's taught me something. He's taught me to keep my eye on what counts in this world. Yeah—[*Shouting out a little.*] Thanks, Willy!

RUTH: What did you call that man for, Walter Lee?

WALTER: Called him to tell him to come on over to the show. Gonna put on a show for the man. Just what he wants to see. You see, Mama, the man came here today and he told us that them people out there where you want us to move—well they so upset they willing to pay us not to move out there. [*He laughs again.*] And—and oh, Mama—you would of been proud of the way me and Ruth and Bennie acted. We told him to get out . . . Lord have mercy! We told the man to get out. Oh, we was some proud folks this afternoon, yeah. [*He lights a cigarette.*] We were still full of that old-time stuff . . .

RUTH: [*Coming toward him slowly.*] You talking 'bout taking them people's money to keep us from moving in that house?

WALTER: I ain't just talking 'bout it, baby—I'm telling you that's what's going to happen.

BENEATHA: Oh, God! Where is the bottom! Where is the real honest-to-God bottom so he can't go any farther!

WALTER: See—that's the old stuff. You and that boy that was here today. You all want everybody to carry a flag and a spear and sing some marching songs, huh? You wanna spend your life looking into things and trying to find the right and the wrong part, huh? Yeah. You know what's going to happen to that boy someday—he'll find himself sitting in a dungeon, locked in forever—and the takers will have the key! Forget it, baby! There ain't no causes—there ain't nothing but taking in this world, and he who takes most is smartest—and it don't make a damn bit of difference *how*.

MAMA: You making something inside me cry, son. Some awful pain inside me.

WALTER: Don't cry, Mama. Understand. That white man is going to walk in that door able to write checks for more money than we ever had. It's important to him and I'm going to help him . . . I'm going to put on the show, Mama.

MAMA: Son—I come from five generations of people who was slaves and share-croppers—but ain't nobody in my family never let nobody pay 'em no money that was a way of telling us we wasn't fit to walk the earth. We ain't never been that poor. [*Raising her eyes and looking at him.*] We ain't never been that dead inside.

BENEATHA: Well—we are dead now. All the talk about dreams and sunlight that goes on in this house. All dead.

WALTER: What's the matter with you all! I didn't make this world! It was give to me this way! Hell, yes, I want me some yachts someday! Yes, I want to hang some real pearls 'round my wife's neck. Ain't she supposed to wear no pearls? Somebody tell me—tell me, who decides which women is suppose to wear pearls in this world. I tell you I am a *man*—and I think my wife should wear some pearls in this world!

[*This last line hangs a good while and* WALTER *begins to move about the room. The word "Man" has penetrated his consciousness; he mumbles it to himself repeatedly between strange agitated pauses as he moves about.*]

MAMA: Baby, how you going to feel on the inside?

WALTER: Fine! . . . Going to feel fine . . . a man . . .

MAMA: You won't have nothing left then, Walter Lee.

WALTER: [*Coming to her.*] I'm going to feel fine, Mama. I'm going to look that son-of-a-bitch in the eyes and say—[*He falters.*]—and say, "All right, Mr. Lindner—[*He falters even more.*]—that's your neighborhood out there. You got the right to keep it like you want. You got the right to have it like you want. Just write the check and—the house is yours." And, and I am going to say—[*His voice almost breaks.*] And you—you people just put the money in my hand and you won't have to live next to this bunch of stinking niggers! . . . [*He straightens up and moves away from his mother, walking around the room.*] Maybe—maybe I'll just get down on my black knees . . . [*He does so;* RUTH *and* BENNIE *and* MAMA *watch him in frozen horror.*] Captain, Mistuh, Bossman. [*He starts crying.*] A-hee-hee-hee! [*Wringing his hands in profoundly anguished imitation.*] Yassss-suh! Great White Father, just gi' ussen de money, fo' God's sake, and we's ain't gwine come out deh and dirty up yo' white folks neighborhood . . .

[*He breaks down completely, then gets up and goes into the bedroom.*]

BENEATHA: That is not a man. That is nothing but a toothless rat.

MAMA: Yes—death done come in this here house. [*She is nodding, slowly, reflectively.*] Done come walking in my house. On the lips of my children. You what supposed to be my beginning again. You—what supposed to be my harvest. [*To* BENEATHA.] You—you mourning your brother?

BENEATHA: He's no brother of mine.

MAMA: What you say?

BENEATHA: I said that that individual in that room is no brother of mine.

MAMA: That's what I thought you said. You feeling like you better than he is today? [BENEATHA *does not answer.*] Yes? What you tell him a minute ago? That he wasn't a man? Yes? You give him up for me? You done wrote his epitaph too—like the rest of the world? Well, who give you the privilege?

BENEATHA: Be on my side for once! You saw what he just did, Mama! You saw him—down on his knees. Wasn't it you who taught me—to despise any man who would do that. Do what he's going to do.

MAMA: Yes—I taught you that. Me and your daddy. But I thought I taught you something else too . . . I thought I taught you to love him.

BENEATHA: Love him? There is nothing left to love.

MAMA: There is always something left to love. And if you ain't learned that, you ain't learned nothing. [*Looking at her.*] Have you cried for that boy today? I don't mean for yourself and for the family 'cause we lost the money. I mean for him; what he been through and what it done to him. Child, when do you think is the time to love somebody the most; when they done good and made things easy for everybody? Well then, you ain't through learning— because that ain't the time at all. It's when he's at his lowest and can't believe in hisself 'cause the world done whipped him so. When you starts measuring somebody, measure him right, child, measure him right. Make sure you done taken into account what hills and valleys he come through before he got to wherever he is.

[TRAVIS *bursts into the room at the end of the speech, leaving the door open.*]

TRAVIS: Grandmama—the moving men are downstairs! The truck just pulled up.

MAMA: [*Turning and looking at him.*] Are they, baby? They downstairs?

[*She sighs and sits.* LINDNER *appears in the doorway. He peers in and knocks lightly, to gain attention, and comes in. All turn to look at him.*]

LINDNER: [*Hat and briefcase in hand.*] Uh—hello . . . [RUTH *crosses mechanically to the bedroom door and opens it and lets it swing open freely and slowly as the lights come up on* WALTER *within, still in his coat, sitting at the far corner of the room. He looks up and out through the room to* LINDNER.]

RUTH: He's here.

[*A long minute passes and* WALTER *slowly gets up.*]

LINDNER: [*Coming to the table with efficiency, putting his briefcase on the table and starting to unfold papers and unscrew fountain pens.*] Well, I certainly was glad to hear from you people. [WALTER *has begun the trek out of the room, slowly and awkwardly, rather like a small boy, passing the back of his sleeve across his mouth from time to time.*] Life can really be so much simpler than people let it be most of the time. Well—with whom do I negotiate? You, Mrs. Younger, or your son here? [MAMA *sits with her hands folded on her lap and her eyes closed as* WALTER *advances.* TRAVIS *goes close to* LINDNER *and looks at the papers curiously.*] Just some official papers, sonny.

RUTH: Travis, you go downstairs.

MAMA: [*Opening her eyes and looking into* WALTER'S.] No. Travis, you stay right here. And you make him understand what you doing, Walter Lee. You teach him good. Like Willy Harris taught you. You show where our five generations done come to. Go ahead, son—

WALTER: [*Looks down into his boy's eyes.* TRAVIS *grins at him merrily and* WALTER *draws him beside him with his arm lightly around his shoulders.*] Well, Mr. Lindner. [BENEATHA *turns away.*] We called you—[*There is a profound, simple groping quality in his speech.*]—because, well, me and my family [*He looks around and shifts from one foot to the other.*] Well—we are very plain people . . .

LINDNER: Yes—

WALTER: I mean—I have worked as a chauffeur most of my life—and my wife here, she does domestic work in people's kitchens. So does my mother. I mean—we are plain people . . .

LINDNER: Yes, Mr. Younger—

WALTER: [*Really like a small boy, looking down at his shoes and then up at the man.*] And—uh—well, my father, well, he was a laborer most of his life.

LINDNER: [*Absolutely confused.*] Uh, yes—

WALTER: [*Looking down at his toes once again.*] My father almost beat a man to death once because this man called him a bad name or something, you know what I mean?

LINDNER: No, I'm afraid I don't.

WALTER: [*Finally straightening up.*] Well, what I mean is that we come from people who had a lot of pride. I mean—we are very proud people. And that's my sister over there and she's going to be a doctor—and we are very proud—

LINDNER: Well—I am sure that is very nice, but—

WALTER: [*Starting to cry and facing the man eye to eye.*] What I am telling you is that we called you over here to tell you that we are very proud and that this is— this is my son, who makes the sixth generation of our family in this country, and that we have all thought about your offer and we have decided to move into our house because my father—my father—he earned it. [MAMA *has her eyes closed and is rocking back and forth as though she were in church, with her head nodding the amen yes.*] We don't want to make no trouble for nobody or fight no causes—but we will try to be good neighbors. That's all we got to say. [*He looks the man absolutely in the eyes.*] We don't want your money.

[*He turns and walks away from the man.*]

LINDNER: [*Looking around at all of them.*] I take it then that you have decided to occupy.

BENEATHA: That's what the man said.

LINDNER: [*To* MAMA *in her reverie.*] Then I would like to appeal to you, Mrs. Younger. You are older and wiser and understand things better I am sure . . .

MAMA: [*Rising.*] I am afraid you don't understand. My son said we was going to move and there ain't nothing left for me to say. [*Shaking her head with double meaning.*] You know how these young folks is nowadays, mister. Can't do a thing with 'em. Good-bye.

LINDNER: [*Folding up his materials.*] Well—if you are that final about it . . . There is nothing left for me to say. [*He finishes. He is almost ignored by the family, who are concentrating on* WALTER LEE. *At the door* LINDNER *halts and looks around.*] I sure hope you people know what you're doing.

[*He shakes his head and exits.*]

RUTH: [*Looking around and coming to life.*] Well, for God's sake—if the moving men are here—LET'S GET THE HELL OUT OF HERE!

MAMA: [*Into action.*] Ain't it the truth! Look at all this here mess. Ruth, put Travis' good jacket on him . . . Walter Lee, fix your tie and tuck your shirt in, you look just like somebody's hoodlum. Lord have mercy, where is my plant? [*She flies to get it amid the general bustling of the family, who are deliberately trying to ignore the nobility of the past moment.*] You all start on down . . . Travis child, don't go empty-handed . . . Ruth, where did I put that box with my skillets in it? I want to be in charge of it myself . . . I'm going to make us the biggest dinner we ever ate tonight . . . Beneatha, what's the matter with them stockings? Pull them things up, girl . . .

[*The family starts to file out as two moving men appear and begin to carry out the heavier pieces of furniture, bumping into the family as they move about.*]

BENEATHA: Mama, Asagai—asked me to marry him today and go to Africa—
MAMA: [*In the middle of her getting-ready activity.*] He did? You ain't old enough to marry nobody—[*Seeing the moving men lifting one of her chairs precariously.*] Darling, that ain't no bale of cotton, please handle it so we can sit in it again. I had that chair twenty-five years . . .

[*The movers sigh with exasperation and go on with their work.*]

BENEATHA: [*Girlishly and unreasonably trying to pursue the conversation.*] To go to Africa, Mama—be a doctor in Africa . . .
MAMA: [*Distracted.*] Yes, baby—
WALTER: Africa! What he want you to go to Africa for?
BENEATHA: To practice there . . .
WALTER: Girl, if you don't get all them silly ideas out your head! You better marry yourself a man with some loot . . .
BENEATHA: [*Angrily, precisely as in the first scene of the play.*] What have you got to do with who I marry!
WALTER: Plenty. Now I think George Murchison—

[*He and* BENEATHA *go out yelling at each other vigorously;* BENEATHA *is heard saying that she would not marry* GEORGE MURCHISON *if he were Adam and she were Eve, etc. The anger is loud and real till their voices diminish.* RUTH *stands at the door and turns to* MAMA *and smiles knowingly.*]

MAMA: [*Fixing her hat at last.*] Yeah—they something all right, my children . . .
RUTH: Yeah—they're something. Let's go, Lena.
MAMA: [*Stalling, starting to look around at the house.*] Yes—I'm coming. Ruth—
RUTH: Yes?
MAMA: [*Quietly, woman to woman.*] He finally come into his manhood today, didn't he? Kind of like a rainbow after the rain . . .
RUTH: [*Biting her lip lest her own pride explode in front of* MAMA.] Yes, Lena.

[WALTER'*s voice calls for them raucously.*]

MAMA: [*Waving* RUTH *out vaguely.*] All right, honey—go on down. I be down directly.

[RUTH *hesitates, then exits.* MAMA *stands, at last alone in the living room, her plant on the table before her as the lights start to come down. She looks around at all the walls and ceilings and suddenly, despite herself, while the children call below, a great heaving thing rises in her and she puts her fist to her mouth, takes a final desperate look, pulls her coat about her, pats her hat and goes out. The lights dim down. The door opens and she comes back in, grabs her plant, and goes out for the last time.*]

CURTAIN.

1959

ARTHUR MILLER

Death of a Salesman

Certain Private Conversations in Two Acts and
a Requiem

CHARACTERS

WILLY LOMAN	UNCLE BEN
LINDA	HOWARD WAGNER
BIFF	JENNY
HAPPY	STANLEY
BERNARD	MISS FORSYTHE
THE WOMAN	LETTA
CHARLEY	

The action takes place in WILLY LOMAN's *house and yard and in various places he visits in the New York and Boston of today.*

ACT I

A melody is heard, playing upon a flute. It is small and fine, telling of grass and trees and the horizon. The curtain rises.

Before us is the Salesman's house. We are aware of towering, angular shapes behind it, surrounding it on all sides. Only the blue light of the sky falls upon the house and forestage; the surrounding area shows an angry flow of orange. As more light appears, we see a solid vault of apartment houses around the small, fragile-seeming home. An air of the dream clings to the place, a dream rising out of reality. The kitchen at center seems actual enough, for there is a kitchen table with three chairs, and a refrigerator. But no other fixtures are seen. At the back of the kitchen there is a draped entrance, which leads to the living-room. To the right of the kitchen, on a level raised two feet, is a bedroom furnished only with a brass bedstead and a straight chair. On a shelf over the bed a silver athletic trophy stands. A window opens onto the apartment house at the side.

Behind the kitchen, on a level raised six and a half feet, is the boys' bedroom, at present barely visible. Two beds are dimly seen, and at the back of the room a dormer window. (This bedroom is above the unseen living-room.) At the left a stairway curves up to it from the kitchen.

The entire setting is wholly or, in some places, partially transparent. The roof-line of the house is one-dimensional; under and over it we see the apartment buildings. Before the house lies an apron, curving beyond the forestage into the orchestra. This forward area serves as the back yard as well as the locale of all WILLY's *imaginings and of his city scenes. Whenever the action is in the present the actors observe the imaginary wall-lines, entering the house only through its door at the left. But in the scenes of the past these boundaries are broken, and characters enter or leave a room by stepping "through" a wall onto the forestage.*

From the right, WILLY LOMAN, *the Salesman, enters, carrying two large sample cases. The flute plays on. He hears but is not aware of it. He is past sixty years of age, dressed quietly. Even as he crosses the stage to the doorway of the house, his exhaustion is apparent. He unlocks the door, comes into the kitchen, and thankfully lets his burden down, feeling the soreness of his palms. A word-sigh escapes his lips—it might be "Oh, boy, oh, boy." He closes the door, then carries his cases out into the living-room, through the draped kitchen doorway.*

LINDA, *his wife, has stirred in her bed at the right. She gets out and puts on a robe, listening. Most often jovial, she has developed an iron repression of her exceptions to* WILLY's *behavior—she more than loves him, she admires him, as though his mercurial nature, his temper, his massive dreams and little cruelties, served her only as sharp reminders of the turbulent longings within him, longings which she shares but lacks the temperament to utter and follow to their end.*

LINDA: [*Hearing* WILLY *outside the bedroom, calls with some trepidation.*] Willy!

WILLY: It's all right. I came back.

LINDA: Why? What happened? [*Slight pause.*] Did something happen, Willy?

WILLY: No, nothing happened.

LINDA: You didn't smash the car, did you?

WILLY: [*With casual irritation.*] I said nothing happened. Didn't you hear me?

LINDA: Don't you feel well?

WILLY: I'm tired to the death. [*The flute has faded away. He sits on the bed beside her, a little numb.*] I couldn't make it. I just couldn't make it, Linda.

LINDA: [*Very carefully, delicately.*] Where were you all day? You look terrible.

WILLY: I got as far as a little above Yonkers. I stopped for a cup of coffee. Maybe it was the coffee.

LINDA: What?

WILLY: [*After a pause.*] I suddenly couldn't drive any more. The car kept going off onto the shoulder, y'know?

LINDA: [*Helpfully.*] Oh. Maybe it was the steering again. I don't think Angelo knows the Studebaker.

WILLY: No, it's me, it's me. Suddenly I realize I'm goin' sixty miles an hour and I don't remember the last five minutes. I'm—I can't seem to—keep my mind to it.

LINDA: Maybe it's your glasses. You never went for your new glasses.

WILLY: No, I see everything. I came back ten miles an hour. It took me nearly four hours from Yonkers.

LINDA: [*Resigned.*] Well, you'll just have to take a rest, Willy, you can't continue this way.

WILLY: I just got back from Florida.

LINDA: But you didn't rest your mind. Your mind is overactive, and the mind is what counts, dear.

WILLY: I'll start out in the morning. Maybe I'll feel better in the morning. [*She is taking off his shoes.*] These goddam arch supports are killing me.

LINDA: Take an aspirin. Should I get you an aspirin? It'll soothe you.

WILLY: [*With wonder.*] I was driving along, you understand? And I was fine. I was even observing the scenery. You can imagine, me looking at scenery, on the road every week of my life. But it's so beautiful up there, Linda, the trees are so thick, and the sun is warm. I opened the windshield and just let the warm air bathe over me. And then all of a sudden I'm goin' off the road! I'm tellin' ya, I absolutely forgot I was driving. If I'd've gone the other way over the white line I might've killed somebody. So I went on again—and five minutes later I'm dreamin' again, and I nearly—[*He presses two fingers against his eyes.*] I have such thoughts, I have such strange thoughts.

LINDA: Willy, dear. Talk to them again. There's no reason why you can't work in New York.

WILLY: They don't need me in New York. I'm the New England man. I'm vital in New England.

LINDA: But you're sixty years old. They can't expect you to keep traveling every week.

WILLY: I'll have to send a wire to Portland. I'm supposed to see Brown and Morrison tomorrow morning at ten o'clock to show the line. Goddammit, I could sell them! [*He starts putting on his jacket.*]

LINDA: [*Taking the jacket from him.*] Why don't you go down to the place tomorrow and tell Howard you've simply got to work in New York? You're too accommodating, dear.

WILLY: If old man Wagner was alive I'da been in charge of New York now! That man was a prince, he was a masterful man. But that boy of his, that Howard, he don't appreciate. When I went north the first time, the Wagner Company didn't know where New England was!

LINDA: Why don't you tell those things to Howard, dear?

WILLY: [*Encouraged.*] I will, I definitely will. Is there any cheese?

LINDA: I'll make you a sandwich.

WILLY: No, go to sleep. I'll take some milk. I'll be up right away. The boys in?

LINDA: They're sleeping. Happy took Biff on a date tonight.

WILLY: [*Interested.*] That so?

LINDA: It was so nice to see them shaving together, one behind the other, in the bathroom. And going out together. You notice? The whole house smells of shaving lotion.

WILLY: Figure it out. Work a lifetime to pay off a house. You finally own it, and there's nobody to live in it.

LINDA: Well, dear, life is a casting off. It's always that way.

WILLY: No, no, some people—some people accomplish something. Did Biff say anything after I went this morning?

LINDA: You shouldn't have criticized him, Willy, especially after he just got off the train. You mustn't lose your temper with him.

WILLY: When the hell did I lose my temper? I simply asked him if he was making any money. Is that a criticism?

LINDA: But, dear, how could he make any money?

WILLY: [*Worried and angered.*] There's such an undercurrent in him. He became a moody man. Did he apologize when I left this morning?

LINDA: He was crestfallen, Willy. You know how he admires you. I think if he finds himself, then you'll both be happier and not fight any more.

WILLY: How can he find himself on a farm? Is that a life? A farmhand? In the beginning, when he was young, I thought, well, a young man, it's good for him to tramp around, take a lot of different jobs. But it's more than ten years now and he has yet to make thirty-five dollars a week!

LINDA: He's finding himself, Willy.

WILLY: Not finding yourself at the age of thirty-four is a disgrace!

LINDA: Shh!

WILLY: The trouble is he's lazy, goddammit!

LINDA: Willy, please!

WILLY: Biff is a lazy bum!

LINDA: They're sleeping. Get something to eat. Go on down.

WILLY: Why did he come home? I would like to know what brought him home.

LINDA: I don't know. I think he's still lost, Willy. I think he's very lost.

WILLY: Biff Loman is lost. In the greatest country in the world a young man with such—personal attractiveness, gets lost. And such a hard worker. There's one thing about Biff—he's not lazy.

LINDA: Never.

WILLY: [*With pity and resolve.*] I'll see him in the morning; I'll have a nice talk with him. I'll get him a job selling. He could be big in no time. My God! Remember how they used to follow him around in high school? When he smiled at one of them their faces lit up. When he walked down the street . . . [*He loses himself in reminiscences.*]

LINDA: [*Trying to bring him out of it.*] Willy, dear, I got a new kind of American-type cheese today. It's whipped.

WILLY: Why do you get American when I like Swiss?

LINDA: I just thought you'd like a change—

WILLY: I don't want a change! I want Swiss cheese. Why am I always being contradicted?

LINDA: [*With a covering laugh.*] I thought it would be a surprise.

WILLY: Why don't you open a window in here, for God's sake?

LINDA: [*With infinite patience.*] They're all open, dear.

WILLY: The way they boxed us in here. Bricks and windows, windows and bricks.

LINDA: We should've bought the land next door.

WILLY: The street is lined with cars. There's not a breath of fresh air in the neighborhood. The grass don't grow any more, you can't raise a carrot in the back yard. They should've had a law against apartment houses. Remember those two beautiful elm trees out there? When I and Biff hung the swing between them?

LINDA: Yeah, like being a million miles from the city.

WILLY: They should've arrested the builder for cutting those down. They massacred the neighborhood. [*Lost.*] More and more I think of those days, Linda. This time of year it was lilac and wisteria. And then the peonies would come out, and the daffodils. What fragrance in this room!

LINDA: Well, after all, people had to move somewhere.

WILLY: No, there's more people now.

LINDA: I don't think there's more people. I think—

WILLY: There's more people! That's what ruining this country! Population is getting out of control. The competition is maddening! Smell the stink from that apartment house! And another one on the other side . . . How can they whip cheese?

[*On* WILLY's *last line,* BIFF *and* HAPPY *raise themselves up in their beds, listening.*]

LINDA: Go down, try it. And be quiet.

WILLY: [*Turning to* LINDA, *guiltily.*] You're not worried about me, are you, sweetheart?

BIFF: What's the matter?

HAPPY: Listen!

LINDA: You've got too much on the ball to worry about.

WILLY: You're my foundation and my support, Linda.

LINDA: Just try to relax, dear. You make mountains out of mole-hills.

WILLY: I won't fight with him any more. If he wants to go back to Texas, let him go.

LINDA: He'll find his way.

WILLY: Sure. Certain men just don't get started till later in life. Like Thomas Edison, I think. Or B. F. Goodrich. One of them was deaf. [*He starts for the bedroom doorway.*] I'll put my money on Biff.

LINDA: And Willy—if it's warm Sunday we'll drive in the country. And we'll open the windshield, and take lunch.

WILLY: No, the windshields don't open on the new cars.

LINDA: But you opened it today.

WILLY: Me? I didn't. [*He stops.*] Now isn't that peculiar! Isn't that a remarkable— [*He breaks off in amazement and fright as the flute is heard distantly.*]

LINDA: What, darling?

WILLY: That is the most remarkable thing.

LINDA: What, dear?

WILLY: I was thinking of the Chevvy. [*Slight pause.*] Nineteen twenty-eight . . . when I had that red Chevvy— [*Breaks off.*] That funny? I coulda sworn I was driving that Chevvy today.

LINDA: Well, that's nothing. Something must've reminded you.

WILLY: Remarkable. *Ts.* Remember those days? The way Biff used to simonize that car? The dealer refused to believe there was eighty thousand miles on it. [*He shakes his head.*] Heh! [*To* LINDA.] Close your eyes, I'll be right up. [*He walks out of the bedroom.*]

HAPPY: [*To* BIFF.] Jesus, maybe he smashed up the car again!

LINDA: [*Calling after* WILLY.] Be careful on the stairs, dear! The cheese is on the middle shelf! [*She turns, goes over to the bed, takes his jacket, and goes out of the bedroom.*]

> [*Light has risen on the boys' room. Unseen,* WILLY *is heard talking to himself, "Eighty thousand miles," and a little laugh.* BIFF *gets out of bed, comes downstage a bit, and stands attentively.* BIFF *is two years older than his brother* HAPPY, *well built, but in these days bears a worn air and seems less self-assured. He has succeeded less, and his dreams are stronger and less acceptable than* HAPPY'S. HAPPY *is tall, powerfully made. Sexuality is like a visible color on him, or a scent that many women have discovered. He, like his brother, is lost, but in a different way, for he has never allowed himself to turn his face toward defeat and is thus more confused and hard-skinned, although seemingly more content.*]

HAPPY: [*Getting out of bed.*] He's going to get his license taken away if he keeps that up. I'm getting nervous about him, y'know, Biff?

BIFF: His eyes are going.

HAPPY: No, I've driven with him. He sees all right. He just doesn't keep his mind on it. I drove into the city with him last week. He stops at a green light and then it turns red and he goes. [*He laughs.*]

BIFF: Maybe he's color-blind.

HAPPY: Pop? Why he's got the finest eye for color in the business. You know that.

BIFF: [*Sitting down on his bed.*] I'm going to sleep.

HAPPY: You're not still sour on Dad, are you Biff?

BIFF: He's all right, I guess.

WILLY: [*Underneath them, in the living-room.*] Yes, sir, eighty thousand miles— eighty-two thousand!

BIFF: You smoking?

HAPPY: [*Holding out a pack of cigarettes.*] Want one?

BIFF: [*Taking a cigarette.*] I can never sleep when I smell it.

WILLY: What a simonizing job, heh!

HAPPY: [*With deep sentiment.*] Funny, Biff, y'know? Us sleeping in here again? The old beds. [*He pats his bed affectionately.*] All the talk that went across those two beds, huh? Our whole lives.

BIFF: Yeah. Lotta dreams and plans.

HAPPY: [*With a deep and masculine laugh.*] About five hundred women would like to know what was said in this room.

[*They share a soft laugh.*]

BIFF: Remember that big Betsy something—what the hell was her name—over on Bushwick Avenue?

HAPPY: [*Combing his hair.*] With the collie dog!

BIFF: That's the one. I got you in there, remember?

HAPPY: Yeah, that was my first time—I think. Boy, there was a pig! [*They laugh, almost crudely.*] You taught me everything I know about women. Don't forget that.

BIFF: I bet you forgot how bashful you used to be. Especially with girls.

HAPPY: Oh, I still am, Biff.

BIFF: Oh, go on.

HAPPY: I just control it, that's all. I think I got less bashful and you got more so. What happened, Biff? Where's the old humor, the old confidence? [*He shakes BIFF's knee. BIFF gets up and moves restlessly about the room.*] What's the matter?

BIFF: Why does Dad mock me all the time?

HAPPY: He's not mocking you, he—

BIFF: Everything I say there's a twist of mockery on his face. I can't get near him.

HAPPY: He just wants you to make good, that's all. I wanted to talk to you about Dad for a long time, Biff. Something's—happening to him. He—talks to himself.

BIFF: I noticed that this morning. But he always mumbled.

HAPPY: But not so noticeable. It got so embarrassing I sent him to Florida. And you know something? Most of the time he's talking to you.

BIFF: What's he say about me?

HAPPY: I can't make it out.

BIFF: What's he say about me?

HAPPY: I think the fact that you're not settled, that you're still kind of up in the air. . . .

BIFF: There's one or two things depressing him, Happy.

HAPPY: What do you mean?

BIFF: Never mind. Just don't lay it all to me.

HAPPY: But I think if you just got started—I mean—is there any future for you out there?

BIFF: I tell ya, Hap, I don't know what the future is. I don't know—what I'm supposed to want.

HAPPY: What do you mean?

BIFF: Well, I spent six or seven years after high school trying to work myself up. Shipping clerk, salesman, business of one kind or another. And it's a measly manner of existence. To get on that subway on the hot mornings in summer. To devote your whole life to keeping stock, or making phone calls, or selling or buying. To suffer fifty weeks of the year for the sake of a two-week vacation, when all you really desire is to be outdoors, with your shirt off. And always to have to get ahead of the next fella. And still—that's how you build a future.

HAPPY: Well, you really enjoy it on a farm? Are you content out there?

BIFF: [*With rising agitation.*] Hap, I've had twenty or thirty different kinds of jobs since I left home before the war, and it always turns out the same. I just realized it lately. In Nebraska when I herded cattle, and the Dakotas, and Arizona, and now in Texas. It's why I came home now, I guess, because I realized it. This farm I work on, it's spring there now, see? And they've got about fifteen new colts. There's nothing more inspiring or—beautiful than the sight of a mare and a new colt. And it's cool there now, see? Texas is cool now, and it's spring. And whenever spring comes to where I am, I suddenly get the feeling, my God, I'm not gettin' anywhere! What the hell am I doing, playing around with horses, twenty-eight dollars a week! I'm thirty-four years old. I oughta be makin' my future. That's when I come running home. And now, I get there, and I don't know what to do with myself. [*After a pause.*] I've always made a point of not wasting my life, and everytime I come back here I know that all I've done is to waste my life.

HAPPY: You're a poet, you know that, Biff? You're a—you're an idealist!

BIFF: No, I'm mixed up very bad. Maybe I oughta get married. Maybe I ougl .a get stuck into something. Maybe that's my trouble. I'm like a boy. I'm not married. I'm not in business, I just—I'm like a boy. Are you content, Hap? You're a success, aren't you? Are you content?

HAPPY: Hell, no!

BIFF: Why? You're making money, aren't you?

HAPPY: [*Moving about with energy, expressiveness.*] All I can do now is wait for the merchandise manager to die. And suppose I get to be merchandise manager? He's a good friend of mine, and he just built a terrific estate on Long Island. And he lived there about two months and sold it, and now he's building another one. He can't enjoy it once it's finished. And I know that's just what I would do. I don't know what the hell I'm workin' for. Sometimes I sit in my apartment—all alone. And I think of the rent I'm paying. And it's crazy. But then, it's what I always wanted. My own apartment, a car, and plenty of women. And still, goddammit, I'm lonely.

BIFF: [*With enthusiasm.*] Listen, why don't you come out West with me?

HAPPY: You and I, heh?

BIFF: Sure, maybe we could buy a ranch. Raise cattle, use our muscles. Men built like we are should be working out in the open.

HAPPY: [*Avidly.*] The Loman Brothers, heh?

BIFF: [*With vast affection.*] Sure, we'd be known all over the counties!

HAPPY: [*Enthralled.*] That's what I dream about, Biff. Sometimes I want to just rip my clothes off in the middle of the store and outbox that goddam merchandise manager. I mean I can outbox, outrun, and outlift anybody in that store, and I have to take orders from those common, petty sons-of-bitches till I can't stand it any more.

BIFF: I'm tellin' you, kid, if you were with me I'd be happy out there.

HAPPY: [*Enthused.*] See, Biff, everybody around me is so false that I'm constantly lowering my ideals . . .

BIFF: Baby, together we'd stand up for one another, we'd have someone to trust.

HAPPY: If I were around you—

BIFF: Hap, the trouble is we weren't brought up to grub for money. I don't know how to do it.

HAPPY: Neither can I!

BIFF: Then let's go!

HAPPY: The only thing is—what can you make out there?

BIFF: But look at your friend. Builds an estate and then hasn't the peace of mind to live in it.

HAPPY: Yeah, but when he walks into the store the waves part in front of him. That's fifty-two thousand dollars a year coming through the revolving door, and I got more in my pinky finger than he's got in his head.

BIFF: Yeah, but you just said—

HAPPY: I gotta show some of those pompous, self-important executives over there that Hap Loman can make the grade. I want to walk into the store the way he walks in. Then I'll go with you, Biff. We'll be together yet, I swear. But take those two we had tonight. Now weren't they gorgeous creatures?

BIFF: Yeah, yeah, most gorgeous I've had in years.

HAPPY: I get that any time I want, Biff. Whenever I feel disgusted. The only trouble is, it gets like bowling or something. I just keep knockin' them over and it doesn't mean anything. You still run around a lot?

BIFF: Naa. I'd like to find a girl—steady, somebody with substance.

HAPPY: That's what I long for.

BIFF: Go on! You'd never come home.

HAPPY: I would! Somebody with character, with resistance! Like Mom, y'know? You're gonna call me a bastard when I tell you this. That girl Charlotte I was with tonight is engaged to be married in five weeks. [*He tries on his new hat.*]

BIFF: No kiddin'!

HAPPY: Sure, the guy's in line for the vice-presidency of the store. I don't know what gets into me, maybe I just have an overdeveloped sense of competition or something, but I went and ruined her, and furthermore I can't get rid of her. And he's the third executive I've done that to. Isn't that a crummy characteristic? And to top it all, I go to their weddings! [*Indignantly, but laughing.*] Like I'm not supposed to take bribes. Manufacturers offer me a hundred-dollar bill now and then to throw an order their way. You know how honest I am, but it's like this girl, see. I hate myself for it. Because I don't want the girl, and, still, I take it and—I love it!

BIFF: Let's go to sleep.

HAPPY: I guess we didn't settle anything, heh?

BIFF: I just got one idea that I'm going to try.

HAPPY: What's that?

BIFF: Remember Bill Oliver?

HAPPY: Sure, Oliver is very big now. You want to work for him again?

BIFF: No, but when I quit he said something to me. He put his arm on my shoulder, and he said, "Biff, if you ever need anything, come to me."

HAPPY: I remember that. That sounds good.

BIFF: I think I'll go to see him. If I could get ten thousand or even seven or eight thousand dollars I could buy a beautiful ranch.

HAPPY: I bet he'd back you. 'Cause he thought highly of you, Biff. I mean, they all do. You're well liked, Biff. That's why I say to come back here, and we both have the apartment. And I'm tellin' you, Biff, any babe you want . . .

BIFF: No, with a ranch I could do the work I like and still be something. I just wonder though. I wonder if Oliver still thinks I stole that carton of basketballs.

HAPPY: Oh, he probably forgot that long ago. It's almost ten years. You're too sensitive. Anyway, he didn't really fire you.

BIFF: Well, I think he was going to. I think that's why I quit. I was never sure whether he knew or not. I know he thought the world of me, though. I was the only one he'd let lock up the place.

WILLY: [*Below.*] You gonna wash the engine, Biff?

HAPPY: Shh! [BIFF *looks at* HAPPY, *who is gazing down, listening.* WILLY *is mumbling in the parlor.*] You hear that?

[*They listen.* WILLY *laughs warmly.*]

BIFF: [*Growing angry.*] Doesn't he know Mom can hear that?

WILLY: Don't get your sweater dirty, Biff!

[*A look of pain crosses* BIFF's *face.*]

HAPPY: Isn't that terrible? Don't leave again, will you? You'll find a job here. You gotta stick around. I don't know what to do about him, it's getting embarrassing.

WILLY: What a simonizing job!

BIFF: Mom's hearing that!

WILLY: No kiddin', Biff, you got a date? Wonderful!

HAPPY: Go on to sleep. But talk to him in the morning, will you?

BIFF: [*Reluctantly getting into bed.*] With her in the house. Brother!

HAPPY: [*Getting into bed.*] I wish you'd have a good talk with him.

[*The light on their room begins to fade.*]

BIFF: [*To himself in bed.*] That selfish, stupid . . .

HAPPY: Sh . . . Sleep, Biff.

[*Their light is out. Well before they have finished speaking,* WILLY's *form is dimly seen below in the darkened kitchen. He opens the refrigerator, searches in there, and takes out a bottle of milk. The apartment houses are fading out, and the entire house and surroundings become covered with leaves. Music insinuates itself as the leaves appear.*]

WILLY: Just wanna be careful with those girls, Biff, that's all. Don't make any promises. No promises of any kind. Because a girl, y'know, they always believe what you tell 'em, and you're very young, Biff, you're too young to be talking seriously to girls. [*Light rises on the kitchen.* WILLY, *talking, shuts the refrigerator door and comes downstage to the kitchen table. He pours milk into a glass. He is totally immersed in himself, smiling faintly.*] Too young entirely, Biff. You want to watch your schooling first. Then when you're all set, there'll be plenty of girls for a boy like you. [*He smiles broadly at a kitchen chair.*] That so? The girls pay for you? [*He laughs.*] Boy, you must really be makin' a hit. [WILLY *is gradually addressing—physically—a point offstage, speaking through the wall of the kitchen, and his voice has been rising in volume to that of a normal conversation.*] I been wondering why you polish the car so careful. Ha! Don't leave the hubcaps, boys. Get the chamois to the hubcaps. Happy, use newspaper on the windows, it's the easiest thing. Show him how to do it, Biff! You see, Happy? Pad it up, use it like a pad. That's it, that's it, good work. You're doin' all right, Hap. [*He pauses, then nods in approbation for a few seconds, then looks upward.*] Biff, first thing we gotta do when we get time is clip that big branch over the house. Afraid it's gonna fall in a storm and hit the roof. Tell you what. We get a rope and sling her around, and then we climb up there with a couple of saws and take her down. Soon as you finish the car, boys, I wanna see ya. I got a surprise for you, boys.

BIFF: [*Offstage.*] Whatta ya got, Dad?

WILLY: No, you finish first. Never leave a job till you're finished—remember that. [*Looking toward the "big trees."*] Biff, up in Albany I saw a beautiful hammock. I think I'll buy it next trip, and we'll hang it right between those two elms. Wouldn't that be something? Just swingin' there under those branches. Boy, that would be . . .

> [YOUNG BIFF *and* YOUNG HAPPY *appear from the direction* WILLY *was addressing.* HAPPY *carries rags and a pail of water.* BIFF, *wearing a sweater with a block "S," carries a football.*]

BIFF: [*Pointing in the direction of the car offstage.*] How's that, Pop, professional?

WILLY: Terrific. Terrific job, boys. Good work, Biff.

HAPPY: Where's the surprise, Pop?

WILLY: In the back seat of the car.

HAPPY: Boy! [*He runs off.*]

BIFF: What is it, Dad? Tell me, what'd you buy?

WILLY: [*Laughing, cuffs him.*] Never mind, something I want you to have.

BIFF: [*Turns and starts off.*] What is it, Hap?

HAPPY: [*Offstage.*] It's a punching bag!

BIFF: Oh, Pop!

WILLY: It's got Gene Tunney's[1] signature on it!

> [HAPPY *runs onstage with a punching bag.*]

BIFF: Gee, how'd you know we wanted a punching bag?

WILLY: Well, it's the finest thing for the timing.

---

1. Tunney (1897–1978) was world heavyweight boxing champion from 1926 to 1928 and retired undefeated.

HAPPY: [*Lies down on his back and pedals with his feet.*] I'm losing weight, you notice, Pop?

WILLY: [*To* HAPPY.] Jumping rope is good too.

BIFF: Did you see the new football I got?

WILLY: [*Examining the ball.*] Where'd you get a new ball?

BIFF: The coach told me to practice my passing.

WILLY: That so? And he gave you the ball, heh?

BIFF: Well, I borrowed it from the locker room. [*He laughs confidentially.*]

WILLY: [*Laughing with him at the theft.*] I want you to return that.

HAPPY: I told you he wouldn't like it!

BIFF: [*Angrily.*] Well, I'm bringing it back!

WILLY: [*Stopping the incipient argument, to* HAPPY.] Sure, he's gotta practice with a regulation ball, doesn't he? [*To* BIFF.] Coach'll probably congratulate you on your initiative!

BIFF: Oh, he keeps congratulating my initiative all the time, Pop.

WILLY: That's because he likes you. If somebody else took that ball there'd be an uproar. So what's the report, boys, what's the report?

BIFF: Where'd you go this time, Dad? Gee we were lonesome for you.

WILLY: [*Pleased, puts an arm around each boy and they come down to the apron.*] Lonesome, heh?

BIFF: Missed you every minute.

WILLY: Don't say? Tell you a secret, boys. Don't breathe it to a soul. Someday I'll have my own business, and I'll never have to leave home any more.

HAPPY: Like Uncle Charley, heh?

WILLY: Bigger than Uncle Charley! Because Charley is not—liked. He's liked, but he's not—well liked.

BIFF: Where'd you go this time, Dad?

WILLY: Well, I got on the road, and I went north to Providence. Met the Mayor.

BIFF: The Mayor of Providence!

WILLY: He was sitting in the hotel lobby.

BIFF: What'd he say?

WILLY: He said, "Morning!" And I said, "You got a fine city here, Mayor." And then he had coffee with me. And then I went to Waterbury. Waterbury is a fine city. Big clock city, the famous Waterbury clock. Sold a nice bill there. And then Boston—Boston is the cradle of the Revolution. A fine city. And a couple of other towns in Mass., and on to Portland and Bangor and straight home!

BIFF: Gee, I'd love to go with you sometime, Dad.

WILLY: Soon as summer comes.

HAPPY: Promise?

WILLY: You and Hap and I, and I'll show you all the towns. America is full of beautiful towns and fine, upstanding people. And they know me, boys, they know me up and down New England. The finest people. And when I bring you fellas up, there'll be open sesame for all of us, 'cause one thing, boys: I have friends. I can park my car in any street in New England, and the cops protect it like their own. This summer, heh?

BIFF and HAPPY: [*Together.*] Yeah! You bet!

WILLY: We'll take our bathing suits.

HAPPY: We'll carry your bags, Pop!

WILLY: Oh, won't that be something! Me comin' into the Boston stores with you boys carryin' my bags. What a sensation! [BIFF *is prancing around, practicing passing the ball.*] You nervous, Biff, about the game?

BIFF: Not if you're gonna be there.

WILLY: What do they say about you in school, now that they made you captain?

HAPPY: There's a crowd of girls behind him everytime the classes change.

BIFF: [*Taking* WILLY'*s hand.*] This Saturday, Pop, this Saturday—just for you, I'm going to break through for a touchdown.

HAPPY: You're supposed to pass.

BIFF: I'm takin' one play for Pop. You watch me, Pop, and when I take off my helmet, that means I'm breakin' out. Then you watch me crash through that line!

WILLY: [*Kisses* BIFF.] Oh, wait'll I tell this in Boston!

> [BERNARD *enters in knickers. He is younger than* BIFF, *earnest and loyal, a worried boy.*]

BERNARD: Biff, where are you? You're supposed to study with me today.

WILLY: Hey, looka Bernard. What're you lookin' so anemic about, Bernard?

BERNARD: He's gotta study, Uncle Willy. He's got Regents[2] next week.

HAPPY: [*Tauntingly, spinning* BERNARD *around.*] Let's box, Bernard!

BERNARD: Biff! [*He gets away from* HAPPY.] Listen, Biff, I heard Mr. Birnbaum say that if you don't start studyin' math he's gonna flunk you, and you won't graduate. I heard him!

WILLY: You better study with him, Biff. Go ahead now.

BERNARD: I heard him!

BIFF: Oh, Pop, you didn't see my sneakers! [*He holds up a foot for* WILLY *to look at.*]

WILLY: Hey, that's a beautiful job of printing!

BERNARD: [*Wiping his glasses.*] Just because he printed University of Virginia on his sneakers doesn't mean they've got to graduate him, Uncle Willy!

WILLY: [*Angrily.*] What're you talking about? With scholarships to three universities they're gonna flunk him?

BERNARD: But I heard Mr. Birnbaum say—

WILLY: Don't be a pest, Bernard! [*To his boys.*] What an anemic!

BERNARD: Okay, I'm waiting for you in my house, Biff.

> [BERNARD *goes off. The* LOMANS *laugh.*]

WILLY: Bernard is not well liked, is he?

BIFF: He's liked, but he's not well liked.

HAPPY: That's right, Pop.

WILLY: That's just what I mean. Bernard can get the best marks in school, y'understand, but when he gets out in the business world, y'understand, you are

---

2. A statewide examination administered to New York high-school students.

going to be five times ahead of him. That's why I thank Almighty God you're both built like Adonises. Because the man who makes an appearance in the business world, the man who creates personal interest, is the man who gets ahead. Be liked and you will never want. You take me, for instance. I never have to wait in line to see a buyer. "Willy Loman is here!" That's all they have to know, and I go right through.

BIFF: Did you knock them dead, Pop?

WILLY: Knocked 'em cold in Providence, slaughtered 'em in Boston.

HAPPY: [*On his back, pedaling again.*] I'm losing weight, you notice, Pop?

> [LINDA *enters, as of old, a ribbon in her hair, carrying a basket of washing.*]

LINDA: [*With youthful energy.*] Hello, dear!

WILLY: Sweetheart!

LINDA: How'd the Chevvy run?

WILLY: Chevrolet, Linda, is the greatest car ever built. [*To the boys.*] Since when do you let your mother carry wash up the stairs?

BIFF: Grab hold there, boy!

HAPPY: Where to, Mom?

LINDA: Hang them up on the line. And you better go down to your friends, Biff. The cellar is full of boys. They don't know what to do with themselves.

BIFF: Ah, when Pop comes home they can wait!

WILLY: [*Laughs appreciatively.*] You better go down and tell them what to do, Biff.

BIFF: I think I'll have them sweep out the furnace room.

WILLY: Good work, Biff.

BIFF: [*Goes through wall-line of kitchen to doorway at back and calls down.*] Fellas! Everybody sweep out the furnace room! I'll be right down!

VOICES: All right! Okay, Biff.

BIFF: George and Sam and Frank, come out back! We're hangin' up the wash! Come on, Hap, on the double!

> [*He and* HAPPY *carry out the basket.*]

LINDA: The way they obey him!

WILLY: Well, that training, the training. I'm tellin' you, I was sellin' thousands and thousands, but I had to come home.

LINDA: Oh, the whole block'll be at that game. Did you sell anything?

WILLY: I did five hundred gross in Providence and seven hundred gross in Boston.

LINDA: No! Wait a minute, I've got a pencil. [*She pulls pencil and paper out of her apron pocket.*] That makes your commission . . . Two hundred—my God! Two hundred and twelve dollars!

WILLY: Well, I didn't figure it yet, but . . .

LINDA: How much did you do?

WILLY: Well, I—I did—about a hundred and eighty gross in Providence. Well, no—it came to—roughly two hundred gross on the whole trip.

LINDA: [*Without hesitation.*] Two hundred gross. That's . . . [*She figures.*]

WILLY: The trouble was that three of the stores were half closed for inventory in Boston. Otherwise I woulda broke records.

LINDA: Well, it makes seventy dollars and some pennies. That's very good.

WILLY: What do we owe?

LINDA: Well, on the first there's sixteen dollars on the refrigerator—

WILLY: Why sixteen?

LINDA: Well, the fan belt broke, so it was a dollar eighty.

WILLY: But it's brand new.

LINDA: Well, the man said that's the way it is. Till they work themselves in, y'know.

[*They move through the wall-line into the kitchen.*]

WILLY: I hope we didn't get stuck on that machine.

LINDA: They got the biggest ads of any of them!

WILLY: I know, it's a fine machine. What else?

LINDA: Well, there's nine-sixty for the washing machine. And for the vacuum cleaner there's three and a half due on the fifteenth. Then the roof, you got twenty-one dollars remaining.

WILLY: It don't leak, does it?

LINDA: No, they did a wonderful job. Then you owe Frank for the carburetor.

WILLY: I'm not going to pay that man! That goddam Chevrolet, they ought to prohibit the manufacture of that car!

LINDA: Well, you owe him three and a half. And odds and ends, comes to around a hundred and twenty dollars by the fifteenth.

WILLY: A hundred and twenty dollars! My God, if business don't pick up I don't know what I'm gonna do!

LINDA: Well, next week you'll do better.

WILLY: Oh, I'll knock 'em dead next week. I'll go to Hartford. I'm very well liked in Hartford. You know, the trouble is, Linda, people don't seem to take to me.

[*They move onto the forestage.*]

LINDA: Oh, don't be foolish.

WILLY: I know it when I walk in. They seem to laugh at me.

LINDA: Why? Why would they laugh at you? Don't talk that way, Willy.

[WILLY *moves to the edge of the stage.* LINDA *goes into the kitchen and starts to darn stockings.*]

WILLY: I don't know the reason for it, but they just pass me by. I'm not noticed.

LINDA: But you're doing wonderful, dear. You're making seventy to a hundred dollars a week.

WILLY: But I gotta be at it ten, twelve hours a day. Other men—I don't know— they do it easier. I don't know why—I can't stop myself—I talk too much. A man oughta come in with a few words. One thing about Charley. He's a man of few words, and they respect him.

LINDA: You don't talk too much, you're just lively.

WILLY: [*Smiling.*] Well, I figure, what the hell, life is short, a couple of jokes. [*To himself.*] I joke too much! [*The smile goes.*]

LINDA: Why? You're—

WILLY: I'm fat. I'm very—foolish to look at, Linda. I didn't tell you, but Christmas time I happened to be calling on F. H. Stewarts, and a salesman I know, as I was going in to see the buyer I heard him say something about—walrus. And I—I cracked him right across the face. I won't take that. I simply will not take that. But they do laugh at me. I know that.

LINDA: Darling . . .

WILLY: I gotta overcome it. I know I gotta overcome it. I'm not dressing to advantage, maybe.

LINDA: Willy, darling, you're the handsomest man in the world—

WILLY: Oh, no, Linda.

LINDA: To me you are. [*Slight pause.*] The handsomest. [*From the darkness is heard the laughter of a woman.* WILLY *doesn't turn to it, but it continues through* LINDA's *lines.*] And the boys, Willy. Few men are idolized by their children the way you are.

[*Music is heard as behind a scrim, to the left of the house,* THE WOMAN, *dimly seen, is dressing.*]

WILLY: [*With great feeling.*] You're the best there is, Linda, you're a pal, you know that? On the road—on the road I want to grab you sometimes and just kiss the life outa you. [*The laughter is loud now, and he moves into a brightening area at the left, where* THE WOMAN *has come from behind the scrim and is standing, putting on her hat, looking into a "mirror" and laughing.*] 'Cause I get so lonely— especially when business is bad and there's nobody to talk to. I get the feeling that I'll never sell anything again, that I won't make a living for you, or a business, a business for the boys. [*He talks through* THE WOMAN's *subsiding laughter.* THE WOMAN *primps at the "mirror."*] There's so much I want to make for—

THE WOMAN: Me? You didn't make me, Willy. I picked you.

WILLY: [*Pleased.*] You picked me?

THE WOMAN: [*Who is quite proper-looking,* WILLY's *age.*] I did. I've been sitting at that desk watching all the salesmen go by, day in, day out. But you've got such a sense of humor, and we do have such a good time together, don't we?

WILLY: Sure, sure. [*He takes her in his arms.*] Why do you have to go now?

THE WOMAN: It's two o'clock . . .

WILLY: No, come on in! [*He pulls her.*]

THE WOMAN: . . . my sisters'll be scandalized. When'll you be back?

WILLY: Oh, two weeks about. Will you come up again?

THE WOMAN: Sure thing. You do make me laugh. It's good for me. [*She squeezes his arm, kisses him.*] And I think you're a wonderful man.

WILLY: You picked me, heh?

THE WOMAN: Sure. Because you're so sweet. And such a kidder.

WILLY: Well, I'll see you next time I'm in Boston.

THE WOMAN: I'll put you right through to the buyers.

WILLY: [*Slapping her bottom.*] Right. Well, bottoms up!

THE WOMAN: [*Slaps him gently and laughs.*] You just kill me, Willy. [*He suddenly grabs her and kisses her roughly.*] You kill me. And thanks for the stockings. I love a lot of stockings. Well, good night.

WILLY: Good night. And keep your pores open!

THE WOMAN: Oh, Willy!

> [THE WOMAN *bursts out laughing, and* LINDA's *laughter blends in.* THE WOMAN *disappears into the dark. Now the area at the kitchen table brightens.* LINDA *is sitting where she was at the kitchen table, but now is mending a pair of her silk stockings.*]

LINDA: You are, Willy. The handsomest man. You've got no reason to feel that—

WILLY: [*Coming out of* THE WOMAN's *dimming area and going over to* LINDA.] I'll make it all up to you, Linda. I'll—

LINDA: There's nothing to make up, dear. You're doing fine, better than—

WILLY: [*Noticing her mending.*] What's that?

LINDA: Just mending my stockings. They're so expensive—

WILLY: [*Angrily, taking them from her.*] I won't have you mending stockings in this house! Now throw them out!

> [LINDA *puts the stockings in her pocket.*]

BERNARD: [*Entering on the run.*] Where is he? If he doesn't study!

WILLY: [*Moving to the forestage, with great agitation.*] You'll give him the answers!

BERNARD: I do, but I can't on a Regents! That's a state exam! They're liable to arrest me!

WILLY: Where is he? I'll whip him, I'll whip him!

LINDA: And he'd better give back that football, Willy, it's not nice.

WILLY: Biff! Where is he? Why is he taking everything?

LINDA: He's too rough with the girls, Willy. All the mothers are afraid of him!

WILLY: I'll whip him!

BERNARD: He's driving the car without a license!

> [THE WOMAN's *laugh is heard.*]

WILLY: Shut up!

LINDA: All the mothers—

WILLY: Shut up!

BERNARD: [*Backing quietly away and out.*] Mr. Birnbaum says he's stuck up.

WILLY: Get outa here!

BERNARD: If he doesn't buckle down he'll flunk math! [*He goes off.*]

LINDA: He's right, Willy, you've gotta—

WILLY: [*Exploding at her.*] There's nothing the matter with him! You want him to be a worm like Bernard? He's got spirit, personality . . . [*As he speaks,* LINDA, *almost in tears, exits into the living room.* WILLY *is alone in the kitchen, wilting and staring. The leaves are gone. It is night again, and the apartment houses look down from behind.*] Loaded with it. Loaded! What is he stealing? He's giving it back, isn't he? Why is he stealing? What did I tell him? I never in my life told him anything but decent things.

[HAPPY *in pajamas has come down the stairs;* WILLY *suddenly becomes aware of* HAPPY'*s presence.*]

HAPPY: Let's go now, come on.

WILLY: [*Sitting down at the kitchen table.*] Huh! Why did she have to wax the floors herself? Everytime she waxes the floors she keels over. She knows that!

HAPPY: Shh! Take it easy. What brought you back tonight?

WILLY: I got an awful scare. Nearly hit a kid in Yonkers. God! Why didn't I go to Alaska with my brother Ben that time! Ben! That man was a genius, that man was success incarnate! What a mistake! He begged me to go.

HAPPY: Well, there's no use in—

WILLY: You guys! There was a man started with the clothes on his back and ended up with diamond mines!

HAPPY: Boy, someday I'd like to know how he did it.

WILLY: What's the mystery? The man knew what he wanted and went out and got it! Walked into a jungle, and comes out, the age of twenty-one, and he's rich! The world is an oyster, but you don't crack it open on a mattress!

HAPPY: Pop, I told you I'm gonna retire you for life.

WILLY: You'll retire me for life on seventy goddam dollars a week? And your women and your car and your apartment, and you'll retire me for life! Christ's sake, I couldn't get past Yonkers today! Where are you guys, where are you? The woods are burning! I can't drive a car!

[CHARLEY *has appeared in the doorway. He is a large man, slow of speech, laconic, immovable. In all he says, despite what he says, there is pity, and now, trepidation. He has a robe over pajamas, slippers on his feet. He enters the kitchen.*]

CHARLEY: Everything all right?

HAPPY: Yeah, Charley, everything's . . .

WILLY: What's the matter?

CHARLEY: I heard some noise. I thought something happened. Can't we do something about the walls? You sneeze in here, and in my house hats blow off.

HAPPY: Let's go to bed, Dad. Come on.

[CHARLEY *signals to* HAPPY *to go.*]

WILLY: You go ahead, I'm not tired at the moment.

HAPPY: [*To* WILLY.] Take it easy, huh? [*He exits.*]

WILLY: What're you doin' up?

CHARLEY: [*Sitting down at the kitchen table opposite* WILLY.] Couldn't sleep good. I had a heartburn.

WILLY: Well, you don't know how to eat.

CHARLEY: I eat with my mouth.

WILLY: No, you're ignorant. You gotta know about vitamins and things like that.

CHARLEY: Come on, let's shoot. Tire you out a little.

WILLY: [*Hesitantly.*] All right. You got cards?

CHARLEY: [*Taking a deck from his pocket.*] Yeah, I got them. Someplace. What is it with those vitamins?

WILLY: [*Dealing.*] They build up your bones. Chemistry.

CHARLEY: Yeah, but there's no bones in a heartburn.

WILLY: What are you talkin' about? Do you know the first thing about it?

CHARLEY: Don't get insulted.

WILLY: Don't talk about something you don't know anything about.

[*They are playing. Pause.*]

CHARLEY: What're you doin' home?

WILLY: A little trouble with the car.

CHARLEY: Oh. [*Pause.*] I'd like to take a trip to California.

WILLY: Don't say.

CHARLEY: You want a job?

WILLY: I got a job, I told you that. [*After a slight pause.*] What the hell are you offering me a job for?

CHARLEY: Don't get insulted.

WILLY: Don't insult me.

CHARLEY: I don't see no sense in it. You don't have to go on this way.

WILLY: I got a good job. [*Slight pause.*] What do you keep comin' in here for?

CHARLEY: You want me to go?

WILLY: [*After a pause, withering.*] I can't understand it. He's going back to Texas again. What the hell is that?

CHARLEY: Let him go.

WILLY: I got nothin' to give him, Charley, I'm clean, I'm clean.

CHARLEY: He won't starve. None a them starve. Forget about him.

WILLY: Then what have I got to remember?

CHARLEY: You take it too hard. To hell with it. When a deposit bottle is broken you don't get your nickel back.

WILLY: That's easy enough for you to say.

CHARLEY: That ain't easy for me to say.

WILLY: Did you see the ceiling I put up in the living-room?

CHARLEY: Yeah, that's a piece of work. To put up a ceiling is a mystery to me. How do you do it?

WILLY: What's the difference?

CHARLEY: Well, talk about it.

WILLY: You gonna put up a ceiling?

CHARLEY: How could I put up a ceiling?

WILLY: Then what the hell are you bothering me for?

CHARLEY: You're insulted again.

WILLY: A man who can't handle tools is not a man. You're disgusting.

CHARLEY: Don't call me disgusting, Willy.

[UNCLE BEN, *carrying a valise and an umbrella, enters the forestage from around the right corner of the house. He is a stolid man, in his sixties, with a mustache and an authoritative air. He is utterly certain of his destiny, and there is an aura of far places about him. He enters exactly as* WILLY *speaks.*]

WILLY: I'm getting awfully tired, Ben.

[BEN's *music is heard.* BEN *looks around at everything.*]

CHARLEY: Good, keep playing; you'll sleep better. Did you call me Ben?

[BEN *looks at his watch.*]

WILLY: That's funny. For a second there you reminded me of my brother Ben.

BEN: I only have a few minutes. [*He strolls, inspecting the place.* WILLY *and* CHARLEY *continue playing.*]

CHARLEY: You never heard from him again, heh? Since that time?

WILLY: Didn't Linda tell you? Couple of weeks ago we got a letter from his wife in Africa. He died.

CHARLEY: That so.

BEN: [*Chuckling.*] So this is Brooklyn, eh?

CHARLEY: Maybe you're in for some of his money.

WILLY: Naa, he had seven sons. There's just one opportunity I had with that man . . .

BEN: I must make a train, William. There are several properties I'm looking at in Alaska.

WILLY: Sure, sure! If I'd gone with him to Alaska that time, everything would've been totally different.

CHARLEY: Go on, you'da froze to death up there.

WILLY: What're you talking about?

BEN: Opportunity is tremendous in Alaska, William. Surprised you're not up there.

WILLY: Sure, tremendous.

CHARLEY: Heh?

WILLY: There was the only man I ever met who knew the answers.

CHARLEY: Who?

BEN: How are you all?

WILLY: [*Taking a pot, smiling.*] Fine, fine.

CHARLEY: Pretty sharp tonight.

BEN: Is Mother living with you?

WILLY: No, she died a long time ago.

CHARLEY: Who?

BEN: That's too bad. Fine specimen of a lady, Mother.

WILLY: [*To* CHARLEY.] Heh?

BEN: I'd hoped to see the old girl.

CHARLEY: Who died?

BEN: Heard anything from Father, have you?

WILLY: [*Unnerved.*] What do you mean, who died?

CHARLEY: [*Taking a pot.*] What're you talkin' about?

BEN: [*Looking at his watch.*] William, it's half-past eight!

WILLY: [*As though to dispel his confusion he angrily stops* CHARLEY'*s hand.*] That's my build!

CHARLEY: I put the ace—

WILLY: If you don't know how to play the game I'm not gonna throw my money away on you!

CHARLEY: [*Rising.*] It was my ace, for God's sake!

WILLY: I'm through, I'm through!

BEN: When did Mother die?

WILLY: Long ago. Since the beginning you never knew how to play cards.

CHARLEY: [*Picks up the cards and goes to the door.*] All right! Next time I'll bring a deck with five aces.

WILLY: I don't play that kind of game!

CHARLEY: [*Turning to him.*] You ought to be ashamed of yourself!

WILLY: Yeah?

CHARLEY: Yeah! [*He goes out.*]

WILLY: [*Slamming the door after him.*] Ignoramus!

BEN: [*As* WILLY *comes toward him through the wall-line of the kitchen.*] So you're William.

WILLY: [*Shaking* BEN'*s hand.*] Ben! I've been waiting for you so long! What's the answer? How did you do it?

BEN: Oh, there's a story in that.

[LINDA *enters the forestage, as of old, carrying the wash basket.*]

LINDA: Is this Ben?

BEN: [*Gallantly.*] How do you do, my dear.

LINDA: Where've you been all these years? Willy's always wondered why you—

WILLY: [*Pulling* BEN *away from her impatiently.*] Where is Dad? Didn't you follow him? How did you get started?

BEN: Well, I don't know how much you remember.

WILLY: Well, I was just a baby, of course, only three or four years old—

BEN: Three years and eleven months.

WILLY: What a memory, Ben!

BEN: I have many enterprises, William, and I have never kept books.

WILLY: I remember I was sitting under the wagon in—was it Nebraska?

BEN: It was South Dakota, and I gave you a bunch of wild flowers.

WILLY: I remember you walking away down some open road.

BEN: [*Laughing.*] I was going to find Father in Alaska.

WILLY: Where is he?

BEN: At that age I had a very faulty view of geography, William. I discovered after a few days that I was heading due south, so instead of Alaska, I ended up in Africa.

LINDA: Africa!

WILLY: The Gold Coast!

BEN: Principally diamond mines.

LINDA: Diamond mines!

BEN: Yes, my dear. But I've only a few minutes—

WILLY: No! Boys! Boys! [*Young* BIFF *and* HAPPY *appear.*] Listen to this. This is your Uncle Ben, a great man! Tell my boys, Ben!

BEN: Why, boys, when I was seventeen I walked into the jungle, and when I was twenty-one I walked out. [*He laughs.*] And by God I was rich.

WILLY: [*To the boys.*] You see what I been talking about? The greatest things can happen!

BEN: [*Glancing at his watch.*] I have an appointment in Ketchikan Tuesday week.

WILLY: No, Ben! Please tell about Dad. I want my boys to hear. I want them to know the kind of stock they spring from. All I remember is a man with a big beard, and I was in Mamma's lap, sitting around a fire, and some kind of high music.

BEN: His flute. He played the flute.

WILLY: Sure, the flute, that's right!

[*New music is heard, a high, rollicking tune.*]

BEN: Father was a very great and a very wild-hearted man. We would start in Boston, and he'd toss the whole family into the wagon, and then he'd drive the team right across the country; through Ohio, and Indiana, Michigan, Illinois, and all the Western states. And we'd stop in the towns and sell the flutes that he'd made on the way. Great inventor, Father. With one gadget he made more in a week than a man like you could make in a lifetime.

WILLY: That's just the way I'm bringing them up, Ben—rugged, well liked, all-around.

BEN: Yeah? [*To* BIFF.] Hit that, boy—hard as you can. [*He pounds his stomach.*]

BIFF: Oh, no, sir!

BEN: [*Taking boxing stance.*] Come on, get to me! [*He laughs.*]

WILLY: Go to it, Biff! Go ahead, show him!

BIFF: Okay! [*He cocks his fist and starts in.*]

LINDA: [*To* WILLY.] Why must he fight, dear?

BEN: [*Sparring with* BIFF.] Good boy! Good boy!

WILLY: How's that, Ben, heh?

HAPPY: Give him the left, Biff!

LINDA: Why are you fighting?

BEN: Good boy! [*Suddenly comes in, trips* BIFF, *and stands over him, the point of his umbrella poised over* BIFF'*s eye.*]

LINDA: Look out, Biff!

BIFF: Gee!

BEN: [*Patting* BIFF'*s knee.*] Never fight fair with a stranger, boy. You'll never get out of the jungle that way. [*Taking* LINDA'*s hand and bowing.*] It was an honor and a pleasure to meet you, Linda.

LINDA: [*Withdrawing her hand coldly, frightened.*] Have a nice—trip.

BEN: [*To* WILLY.] And good luck with your—what do you do?

WILLY: Selling.

BEN: Yes. Well . . . [*He raises his hand in farewell to all.*]

WILLY: No, Ben, I don't want you to think . . . [*He takes* BEN'*s arm to show him.*] It's

Brooklyn, I know, but we hunt too.

BEN: Really, now.

WILLY: Oh, sure, there's snakes and rabbits and—that's why I moved out here. Why, Biff can fell any one of these trees in no time! Boys! Go right over to where they're building the apartment house and get some sand. We're gonna rebuild the entire front stoop right now! Watch this, Ben!

BIFF: Yes, sir! On the double, Hap!

HAPPY: [As he and BIFF run off.] I lost weight, Pop, you notice?

[CHARLEY enters in knickers, even before the boys are gone.]

CHARLEY: Listen, if they steal any more from that building the watchman'll put the cops on them!

LINDA: [To WILLY.] Don't let Biff . . .

[BEN laughs lustily.]

WILLY: You shoulda seen the lumber they brought home last week. At least a dozen six-by-tens worth all kinds a money.

CHARLEY: Listen, if that watchman—

WILLY: I gave them hell, understand. But I got a couple of fearless characters there.

CHARLEY: Willy, the jails are full of fearless characters.

BEN: [Clapping WILLY on the back, with a laugh at CHARLEY.] And the stock exchange, friend!

WILLY: [Joining in BEN's laughter.] Where are the rest of your pants?

CHARLEY: My wife bought them.

WILLY: Now all you need is a golf club and you can go upstairs and go to sleep. [To BEN.] Great athlete! Between him and his son Bernard they can't hammer a nail!

BERNARD: [Rushing in.] The watchman's chasing Biff!

WILLY: [Angrily.] Shut up! He's not stealing anything!

LINDA: [Alarmed, hurrying off left.] Where is he? Biff, dear! [She exits.]

WILLY: [Moving toward the left, away from BEN.] There's nothing wrong. What's the matter with you?

BEN: Nervy boy. Good!

WILLY: [Laughing.] Oh, nerves of iron, that Biff!

CHARLEY: Don't know what it is. My New England man comes back and he's bleedin', they murdered him up there.

WILLY: It's contacts, Charley, I got important contacts!

CHARLEY: [Sarcastically.] Glad to hear it, Willy. Come in later, we'll shoot a little casino. I'll take some of your Portland money. [He laughs at WILLY and exits.]

WILLY: [Turning to BEN.] Business is bad, it's murderous. But not for me, of course.

BEN: I'll stop by on my way back to Africa.

WILLY: [Longingly.] Can't you stay a few days? You're just what I need, Ben, because I—I have a fine position here, but I—well, Dad left when I was such a baby and I never had a chance to talk to him and I still feel—kind of temporary about myself.

BEN: I'll be late for my train.

[*They are at opposite ends of the stage.*]

WILLY: Ben, my boys—can't we talk? They'd go into the jaws of hell for me, see, but I—

BEN: William, you're being first-rate with your boys. Outstanding, manly chaps!

WILLY: [*Hanging on to his words.*] Oh, Ben, that's good to hear! Because sometimes I'm afraid that I'm not teaching them the right kind of— Ben, how should I teach them?

BEN: [*Giving great weight to each word, and with a certain vicious audacity.*] William, when I walked into the jungle, I was seventeen. When I walked out I was twenty-one. And, by God, I was rich! [*He goes off into darkness around the right corner of the house.*]

WILLY: . . . was rich! That's just the spirit I want to imbue them with! To walk into a jungle! I was right! I was right! I was right!

[BEN *is gone, but* WILLY *is still speaking to him as* LINDA, *in nightgown and robe, enters the kitchen, glances around for* WILLY, *then goes to the door of the house, looks out and sees him. Comes down to his left. He looks at her.*]

LINDA: Willy, dear? Willy?

WILLY: I was right!

LINDA: Did you have some cheese? [*He can't answer.*] It's very late, darling. Come to bed, heh?

WILLY: [*Looking straight up.*] Gotta break your neck to see a star in this yard.

LINDA: You coming in?

WILLY: Whatever happened to that diamond watch fob? Remember? When Ben came from Africa that time? Didn't he give me a watch fob with a diamond in it?

LINDA: You pawned it, dear. Twelve, thirteen years ago. For Biff's radio correspondence course.

WILLY: Gee, that was a beautiful thing. I'll take a walk.

LINDA: But you're in your slippers.

WILLY: [*Starting to go around the house at the left.*] I was right! I was! [*Half to* LINDA, *as he goes, shaking his head.*] What a man! There was a man worth talking to. I was right!

LINDA: [*Calling after* WILLY.] But in your slippers, Willy!

[WILLY *is almost gone when* BIFF, *in his pajamas, comes down the stairs and enters the kitchen.*]

BIFF: What is he doing out there?

LINDA: Sh!

BIFF: God Almighty, Mom, how long has he been doing this?

LINDA: Don't, he'll hear you.

BIFF: What the hell is the matter with him?

LINDA: It'll pass by morning.

BIFF: Shouldn't we do anything?

LINDA: Oh, my dear, you should do a lot of things, but there's nothing to do, so go to sleep.

[HAPPY *comes down the stairs and sits on the steps.*]

HAPPY: I never heard him so loud, Mom.

LINDA: Well, come around more often; you'll hear him. [*She sits down at the table and mends the lining of* WILLY*'s jacket.*]

BIFF: Why didn't you ever write me about this, Mom?

LINDA: How would I write to you? For over three months you had no address.

BIFF: I was on the move. But you know I thought of you all the time. You know that, don't you, pal?

LINDA: I know, dear, I know. But he likes to have a letter. Just to know that there's still a possibility for better things.

BIFF: He's not like this all the time, is he?

LINDA: It's when you come home he's always the worst.

BIFF: When I come home?

LINDA: When you write you're coming, he's all smiles, and talks about the future, and—he's just wonderful. And then the closer you seem to come, the more shaky he gets, and then, by the time you get here, he's arguing, and he seems angry at you. I think it's just that maybe he can't bring himself to—to open up to you. Why are you so hateful to each other? Why is that?

BIFF: [*Evasively.*] I'm not hateful, Mom.

LINDA: But you no sooner come in the door than you're fighting!

BIFF: I don't know why. I mean to change. I'm tryin', Mom, you understand?

LINDA: Are you home to stay now?

BIFF: I don't know. I want to look around, see what's doin'.

LINDA: Biff, you can't look around all your life, can you?

BIFF: I just can't take hold, Mom. I can't take hold of some kind of a life.

LINDA: Biff, a man is not a bird, to come and go with the springtime.

BIFF: Your hair . . . [*He touches her hair.*] Your hair got so gray.

LINDA: Oh, it's been gray since you were in high school. I just stopped dyeing it, that's all.

BIFF: Dye it again, will ya? I don't want my pal looking old. [*He smiles.*]

LINDA: You're such a boy! You think you can go away for a year and . . . You've got to get it into your head now that one day you'll knock on this door and there'll be strange people here—

BIFF: What are you talking about? You're not even sixty, Mom.

LINDA: But what about your father?

BIFF: [*Lamely.*] Well, I meant him too.

HAPPY: He admires Pop.

LINDA: Biff, dear, if you don't have any feeling for him, then you can't have any feeling for me.

BIFF: Sure I can, Mom.

LINDA: No. You can't just come to see me, because I love him. [*With a threat, but only a threat, of tears.*] He's the dearest man in the world to me, and I won't have anyone making him feel unwanted and low and blue. You've got to make up your mind now, darling, there's no leeway any more. Either he's your father and you pay him that respect, or else you're not to come here. I know he's not easy to get along with—nobody knows that better than me—but . . .

WILLY: [*From the left, with a laugh.*] Hey, hey, Biffo!

BIFF: [*Starting to go out after* WILLY.] What the hell is the matter with him? [HAPPY *stops him.*]

LINDA: Don't—don't go near him!

BIFF: Stop making excuses for him! He always, always wiped the floor with you. Never had an ounce of respect for you.

HAPPY: He's always had respect for—

BIFF: What the hell do you know about it?

HAPPY: [*Surlily.*] Just don't call him crazy!

BIFF: He's got no character—Charley wouldn't do this. Not in his own house—spewing out that vomit from his mind.

HAPPY: Charley never had to cope with what he's got to.

BIFF: People are worse off than Willy Loman. Believe me, I've seen them!

LINDA: Then make Charley your father, Biff. You can't do that, can you? I don't say he's a great man. Willy Loman never made a lot of money. His name was never in the paper. He's not the finest character that ever lived. But he's a human being, and a terrible thing is happening to him. So attention must be paid. He's not to be allowed to fall into his grave like an old dog. Attention, attention must be finally paid to such a person. You called him crazy—

BIFF: I didn't mean—

LINDA: No, a lot of people think he's lost his—balance. But you don't have to be very smart to know what his trouble is. The man is exhausted.

HAPPY: Sure!

LINDA: A small man can be just as exhausted as a great man. He works for a company thirty-six years this March, opens up unheard-of territories to their trademark, and now in his old age they take his salary away.

HAPPY: [*Indignantly.*] I didn't know that, Mom.

LINDA: You never asked, my dear! Now that you get your spending money someplace else you don't trouble your mind with him.

HAPPY: But I gave you money last—

LINDA: Christmas time, fifty dollars! To fix the hot water it cost ninety-seven fifty! For five weeks he's been on straight commission, like a beginner, an unknown!

BIFF: Those ungrateful bastards!

LINDA: Are they any worse than his sons? When he brought them business, when he was young, they were glad to see him. But now his old friends, the old buyers that loved him so and always found some order to hand him in a pinch—they're all dead, retired. He used to be able to make six, seven calls a day in Boston. Now he takes his valises out of the car and puts them back and takes them out again and he's exhausted. Instead of walking he talks now. He drives seven hundred miles, and when he gets there no one knows him any more, no one welcomes him. And what goes through a man's mind, driving seven hundred miles home without having earned a cent? Why shouldn't he talk to himself? Why? When he has to go to Charley and borrow fifty dollars a week and pretend to me that it's his pay? How long can that go on? How long? You see what I'm sitting here and waiting for? And you tell me he has no character? The man who never worked a day but for your benefit? When does he get the medal for that? Is this his reward—to turn around at the age of sixty-three and find his sons, who he loved better than his life, one a philandering bum—

HAPPY: Mom!

LINDA: That's all you are, my baby! [*To* BIFF.] And you! What happened to the love you had for him? You were such pals! How you used to talk to him on the phone every night! How lonely he was till he could come home to you!

BIFF: All right, Mom. I'll live here in my room, and I'll get a job. I'll keep away from him, that's all.

LINDA: No, Biff. You can't stay here and fight all the time.

BIFF: He threw me out of this house, remember that.

LINDA: Why did he do that? I never knew why.

BIFF: Because I know he's a fake and he doesn't like anybody around who knows!

LINDA: Why a fake? In what way? What do you mean?

BIFF: Just don't lay it all at my feet. It's between me and him—that's all I have to say. I'll chip in from now on. He'll settle for half my pay check. He'll be all right. I'm going to bed. [*He starts for the stairs.*]

LINDA: He won't be all right.

BIFF: [*Turning on the stairs, furiously.*] I hate this city and I'll stay here. Now what do you want?

LINDA: He's dying, Biff.

[HAPPY *turns quickly to her, shocked.*]

BIFF: [*After a pause.*] Why is he dying?

LINDA: He's been trying to kill himself.

BIFF: [*With great horror.*] How?

LINDA: I live from day to day.

BIFF: What're you talking about?

LINDA: Remember I wrote you that he smashed up the car again? In February?

BIFF: Well?

LINDA: The insurance inspector came. He said that they have evidence. That all these accidents in the last year—weren't—weren't—accidents.

HAPPY: How can they tell that? That's a lie.

LINDA: It seems there's a woman . . . [*She takes a breath as. . . .*]

{ BIFF: [*Sharply but contained.*] What woman?
{ LINDA: [*Simultaneously.*] . . . and this woman . . .

LINDA: What?

BIFF: Nothing. Go ahead.

LINDA: What did you say?

BIFF: Nothing. I just said what woman?

HAPPY: What about her?

LINDA: Well, it seems she was walking down the road and saw his car. She says that he wasn't driving fast at all, and that he didn't skid. She says he came to that little bridge, and then deliberately smashed into the railing, and it was only the shallowness of the water that saved him.

BIFF: Oh, no, he probably just fell asleep again.

LINDA: I don't think he fell asleep.

BIFF: Why not?

LINDA: Last month . . . [*With great difficulty.*] Oh, boys, it's so hard to say a thing like this! He's just a big stupid man to you, but I tell you there's more good in him than in many other people. [*She chokes, wipes her eyes.*] I was looking for a fuse. The lights blew out, and I went down the cellar. And behind the fuse box—it happened to fall out—was a length of rubber pipe—just short.

HAPPY: No kidding?

LINDA: There's a little attachment on the end of it. I knew right away. And sure enough, on the bottom of the water heater there's a new little nipple on the gas pipe.

HAPPY: [*Angrily.*] That—jerk.

BIFF: Did you have it taken off?

LINDA: I'm—I'm ashamed to. How can I mention it to him? Every day I go down and take away that little rubber pipe. But, when he comes home, I put it back where it was. How can I insult him that way? I don't know what to do. I live from day to day, boys. I tell you, I know every thought in his mind. It sounds so old-fashioned and silly, but I tell you he put his whole life into you and you've turned your backs on him. [*She is bent over in the chair, weeping, her face in her hands.*] Biff, I swear to God! Biff, his life is in your hands!

HAPPY: [*To* BIFF.] How do you like that damned fool!

BIFF: [*Kissing her.*] All right, pal, all right. It's all settled now. I've been remiss. I know that, Mom. But now I'll stay, and I swear to you, I'll apply myself. [*Kneeling in front of her, in a fever of self-reproach.*] It's just—you see, Mom, I don't fit in business. Not that I won't try. I'll try, and I'll make good.

HAPPY: Sure you will. The trouble with you in business was you never tried to please people.

BIFF: I know, I—

HAPPY: Like when you worked for Harrison's. Bob Harrison said you were tops, and then you go and do some damn fool thing like whistling whole songs in the elevator like a comedian.

BIFF: [*Against* HAPPY.] So what? I like to whistle sometimes.

HAPPY: You don't raise a guy to a responsible job who whistles in the elevator!

LINDA: Well, don't argue about it now.

HAPPY: Like when you'd go off and swim in the middle of the day instead of taking the line around.

BIFF: [*His resentment rising.*] Well, don't you run off? You take off sometimes, don't you? On a nice summer day?

HAPPY: Yeah, but I cover myself!

LINDA: Boys!

HAPPY: If I'm going to take a fade the boss can call any number where I'm supposed to be and they'll swear to him that I just left. I'll tell you something that I hate to say, Biff, but in the business world some of them think you're crazy.

BIFF: [*Angered.*] Screw the business world!

HAPPY: All right, screw it! Great, but cover yourself!

LINDA: Hap, Hap!

BIFF: I don't care what they think! They've laughed at Dad for years, and you know why? Because we don't belong in this nuthouse of a city! We should be mixing cement on some open plain, or—or carpenters. A carpenter is allowed to whistle!

[WILLY *walks in from the entrance of the house, at left.*]

WILLY: Even your grandfather was better than a carpenter. [*Pause. They watch him.*] You never grew up. Bernard does not whistle in the elevator, I assure you.

BIFF: [*As though to laugh* WILLY *out of it.*] Yeah, but you do, Pop.

WILLY: I never in my life whistled in an elevator! And who in the business world thinks I'm crazy?

BIFF: I didn't mean it like that, Pop. Now don't make a whole thing out of it, will ya?

WILLY: Go back to the West! Be a carpenter, a cowboy, enjoy yourself!

LINDA: Willy, he was just saying—

WILLY: I heard what he said!

HAPPY: [*Trying to quiet* WILLY.] Hey, Pop, come on now . . .

WILLY: [*Continuing over* HAPPY'*s line.*] They laugh at me, heh? Go to Filene's, go to the Hub, go to Slattery's Boston. Call out the name Willy Loman and see what happens! Big shot!

BIFF: All right, Pop.

WILLY: Big!

BIFF: All right!

WILLY: Why do you always insult me?

BIFF: I didn't say a word. [*To* LINDA.] Did I say a word?

LINDA: He didn't say anything, Willy.

WILLY: [*Going to the doorway of the living-room.*] All right, good night, good night.

LINDA: Willy, dear, he just decided . . .

WILLY: [*To* BIFF.] If you get tired hanging around tomorrow, paint the ceiling I put up in the living-room.

BIFF: I'm leaving early tomorrow.

HAPPY: He's going to see Bill Oliver, Pop.

WILLY: [*Interestedly.*] Oliver? For what?

BIFF: [*With reserve, but trying, trying.*] He always said he'd stake me. I'd like to go into business, so maybe I can take him up on it.

LINDA: Isn't that wonderful?

WILLY: Don't interrupt. What's wonderful about it? There's fifty men in the City of New York who'd stake him. [*To* BIFF.] Sporting goods?

BIFF: I guess so. I know something about it and—

WILLY: He knows something about it! You know sporting goods better than Spalding, for God's sake! How much is he giving you?

BIFF: I don't know, I didn't even see him yet, but—

WILLY: Then what're you talkin' about?

BIFF: [*Getting angry.*] Well, all I said was I'm gonna see him, that's all!

WILLY: [*Turning away.*] Ah, you're counting your chickens again.

BIFF: [*Starting left for the stairs.*] Oh, Jesus, I'm going to sleep!

WILLY: [*Calling after him.*] Don't curse in this house!

BIFF: [*Turning.*] Since when did you get so clean?

HAPPY: [*Trying to stop them.*] Wait a . . .

WILLY: Don't use that language to me! I won't have it!

HAPPY: [*Grabbing* BIFF, *shouts.*] Wait a minute! I got an idea. I got a feasible idea. Come here, Biff, let's talk this over now, let's talk some sense here. When I was down in Florida last time, I thought of a great idea to sell sporting goods. It just came back to me. You and I, Biff—we have a line, the Loman Line. We train a couple of weeks, and put on a couple of exhibitions, see?

WILLY: That's an idea!

HAPPY: Wait! We form two basketball teams, see? Two water-polo teams. We play each other. It's a million dollars' worth of publicity. Two brothers, see? The Loman Brothers. Displays in the Royal Palms—all the hotels. And banners over the ring and the basketball court: "Loman Brothers." Baby, we could sell sporting goods!

WILLY: That is a one-million-dollar idea!

LINDA: Marvelous!

BIFF: I'm in great shape as far as that's concerned.

HAPPY: And the beauty of it is, Biff, it wouldn't be like a business. We'd be out playin' ball again . . .

BIFF: [*Enthused.*] Yeah, that's . . .

WILLY: Million-dollar . . .

HAPPY: And you wouldn't get fed up with it, Biff. It'd be the family again. There'd be the old honor, and comradeship, and if you wanted to go off for a swim or somethin'—well, you'd do it! Without some smart cooky gettin' up ahead of you!

WILLY: Lick the world! You guys together could absolutely lick the civilized world.

BIFF: I'll see Oliver tomorrow. Hap, if we could work that out . . .

LINDA: Maybe things are beginning to—

WILLY: [*Wildly enthused, to* LINDA.] Stop interrupting! [*To* BIFF.] But don't wear sport jacket and slacks when you see Oliver.

BIFF: No, I'll—

WILLY: A business suit, and talk as little as possible, and don't crack any jokes.

BIFF: He did like me. Always liked me.

LINDA: He loved you!

WILLY: [*To* LINDA.] Will you stop! [*To* BIFF.] Walk in very serious. You are not applying for a boy's job. Money is to pass. Be quiet, fine, and serious. Everybody likes a kidder, but nobody lends him money.

HAPPY: I'll try to get some myself, Biff. I'm sure I can.

WILLY: I see great things for you kids, I think your troubles are over. But remember, start big and you'll end big. Ask for fifteen. How much you gonna ask for?

BIFF: Gee, I don't know—

WILLY: And don't say "Gee." "Gee" is a boy's word. A man walking in for fifteen thousand dollars does not say "Gee!"

BIFF: Ten, I think, would be top though.

WILLY: Don't be so modest. You always started too low. Walk in with a big laugh. Don't look worried. Start off with a couple of your good stories to lighten things up. It's not what you say, it's how you say it—because personality always wins the day.

LINDA: Oliver always thought the highest of him—

WILLY: Will you let me talk?

BIFF: Don't yell at her, Pop, will ya?

WILLY: [Angrily.] I was talking, wasn't I?

BIFF: I don't like you yelling at her all the time, and I'm tellin' you, that's all.

WILLY: What're you, takin' over this house?

LINDA: Willy—

WILLY: [Turning on her.] Don't take his side all the time, goddammit!

BIFF: [Furiously.] Stop yelling at her!

WILLY: [Suddenly pulling on his cheek, beaten down, guilt ridden.] Give my best to Bill Oliver—he may remember me. [He exits through the living-room doorway.]

LINDA: [Her voice subdued.] What'd you have to start that for? [BIFF turns away.] You see how sweet he was as soon as you talked hopefully? [She goes over to BIFF.] Come up and say good night to him. Don't let him go to bed that way.

HAPPY: Come on, Biff, let's buck him up.

LINDA: Please, dear. Just say good night. It takes so little to make him happy. Come. [She goes through the living-room doorway, calling upstairs from within the living-room.] Your pajamas are hanging in the bathroom, Willy!

HAPPY: [Looking toward where LINDA went out.] What a woman! They broke the mold when they made her. You know that, Biff?

BIFF: He's off salary. My God, working on commission!

HAPPY: Well, let's face it: he's no hot-shot selling man. Except that sometimes, you have to admit, he's a sweet personality.

BIFF: [Deciding.] Lend me ten bucks, will ya? I want to buy some new ties.

HAPPY: I'll take you to a place I know. Beautiful stuff. Wear one of my striped shirts tomorrow.

BIFF: She got gray. Mom got awful old. Gee, I'm gonna go in to Oliver tomorrow and knock him for a—

HAPPY: Come on up. Tell that to Dad. Let's give him a whirl. Come on.

BIFF: [Steamed up.] You know, with ten thousand bucks, boy!

HAPPY: [As they go into the living-room.] That's the talk, Biff, that's the first time I've heard the old confidence out of you! [From within the living-room, fading *off.*] You're gonna live with me, kid, and any babe you want just say the word . . .

> [*The last lines are hardly heard. They are mounting the stairs to their parents' bedroom.*]

LINDA: [*Entering her bedroom and addressing* WILLY, *who is in the bathroom. She is straightening the bed for him.*] Can you do anything about the shower? It drips.

WILLY: [*From the bathroom.*] All of a sudden everything falls to pieces! Goddam plumbing, oughta be sued, those people. I hardly finished putting it in and the thing . . . [*His words rumble off.*]

LINDA: I'm just wondering if Oliver will remember him. You think he might?

WILLY: [*Coming out of the bathroom in his pajamas.*] Remember him? What's the matter with you, you crazy? If he'd've stayed with Oliver he'd be on top by now! Wait'll Oliver gets a look at him. You don't know the average caliber any more. The average young man today—[*He is getting into bed.*]—is got a caliber of zero. Greatest thing in the world for him was to bum around. [BIFF *and* HAPPY *enter the bedroom. Slight pause.* WILLY *stops short, looking at* BIFF.] Glad to hear it, boy.

HAPPY: He wanted to say good night to you, sport.

WILLY: [*To* BIFF.] Yeah. Knock him dead, boy. What'd you want to tell me?

BIFF: Just take it easy, Pop. Good night. [*He turns to go.*]

WILLY: [*Unable to resist.*] And if anything falls off the desk while you're talking to him—like a package or something—don't you pick it up. They have office boys for that.

LINDA: I'll make a big breakfast—

WILLY: Will you let me finish? [*To* BIFF.] Tell him you were in the business in the West. Not farm work.

BIFF: All right, Dad.

LINDA: I think everything—

WILLY: [*Going right through her speech.*] And don't undersell yourself. No less than fifteen thousand dollars.

BIFF: [*Unable to bear him.*] Okay. Good night, Mom. [*He starts moving.*]

WILLY: Because you got a greatness in you, Biff, remember that. You got all kinds of greatness . . . [*He lies back, exhausted.* BIFF *walks out.*]

LINDA: [*Calling after* BIFF.] Sleep well, darling!

HAPPY: I'm gonna get married, Mom. I wanted to tell you.

LINDA: Go to sleep, dear.

HAPPY: [*Going.*] I just wanted to tell you.

WILLY: Keep up the good work. [HAPPY *exits.*] God . . . remember that Ebbets Field[3] game? The championship of the city?

LINDA: Just rest. Should I sing to you?

WILLY: Yeah. Sing to me. [LINDA *hums a soft lullaby.*] When that team came out— he was the tallest, remember?

---

3. Stadium where the Dodgers, Brooklyn's major-league baseball team, played from 1913 to 1957.

LINDA: Oh, yes. And in gold.

> [BIFF *enters the darkened kitchen, takes a cigarette, and leaves the house. He comes downstage into a golden pool of light. He smokes, staring at the night.*]

WILLY: Like a young god. Hercules—something like that. And the sun, the sun all around him. Remember how he waved to me? Right up from the field, with the representatives of three colleges standing by? And the buyers I brought, and the cheers when he came out—Loman, Loman, Loman! God Almighty, he'll be great yet. A star like that, magnificent, can never really fade away!

> [*The light on* WILLY *is fading. The gas heater begins to glow through the kitchen wall, near the stairs, a blue flame beneath red coils.*]

LINDA: [*Timidly.*] Willy dear, what has he got against you?
WILLY: I'm so tired. Don't talk any more.

> [BIFF *slowly returns to the kitchen. He stops, stares toward the heater.*]

LINDA: Will you ask Howard to let you work in New York?
WILLY: First thing in the morning. Everything'll be all right.

> [BIFF *reaches behind the heater and draws out a length of rubber tubing. He is horrified and turns his head toward* WILLY's *room, still dimly lit, from which the strains of* LINDA's *desperate but monotonous humming rise.*]

WILLY: [*Staring through the window into the moonlight.*] Gee, look at the moon moving between the buildings!

> [BIFF *wraps the tubing around his hand and quickly goes up the stairs.*]

> [CURTAIN.]

ACT II

Music is heard, gay and bright. The curtain rises as the music fades away. WILLY, *in shirt sleeves, is sitting at the kitchen table, sipping coffee, his hat in his lap.* LINDA *is filling his cup when she can.*

WILLY: Wonderful coffee. Meal in itself.
LINDA: Can I make you some eggs?
WILLY: No. Take a breath.
LINDA: You look so rested, dear.
WILLY: I slept like a dead one. First time in months. Imagine, sleeping till ten on a Tuesday morning. Boys left nice and early, heh?
LINDA: They were out of here by eight o'clock.
WILLY: Good work!
LINDA: It was so thrilling to see them leaving together. I can't get over the shaving lotion in this house!
WILLY: [*Smiling.*] Mmm—

LINDA: Biff was very changed this morning. His whole attitude seemed to be hopeful. He couldn't wait to get downtown to see Oliver.

WILLY: He's heading for a change. There's no question, there simply are certain men that take longer to get—solidified. How did he dress?

LINDA: His blue suit. He's so handsome in that suit. He could be a—anything in that suit!

[WILLY *gets up from the table.* LINDA *holds his jacket for him.*]

WILLY: There's no question, no question at all. Gee, on the way home tonight I'd like to buy some seeds.

LINDA: [*Laughing.*] That'd be wonderful. But not enough sun gets back there. Nothing'll grow any more.

WILLY: You wait, kid, before it's all over we're gonna get a little place out in the country, and I'll raise some vegetables, a couple of chickens . . .

LINDA: You'll do it yet, dear.

[WILLY *walks out of his jacket.* LINDA *follows him.*]

WILLY: And they'll get married, and come for a weekend. I'd build a little guest house. 'Cause I got so many fine tools, all I'd need would be a little lumber and some peace of mind.

LINDA: [*Joyfully.*] I sewed the lining . . .

WILLY: I could build two guest houses, so they'd both come. Did he decide how much he's going to ask Oliver for?

LINDA: [*Getting him into the jacket.*] He didn't mention it, but I imagine ten or fifteen thousand. You going to talk to Howard today?

WILLY: Yeah. I'll put it to him straight and simple. He'll just have to take me off the road.

LINDA: And Willy, don't forget to ask for a little advance, because we've got the insurance premium. It's the grace period now.

WILLY: That's a hundred . . . ?

LINDA: A hundred and eight, sixty-eight. Because we're a little short again.

WILLY: Why are we short?

LINDA: Well, you had the motor job on the car . . .

WILLY: That goddam Studebaker!

LINDA: And you got one more payment on the refrigerator . . .

WILLY: But it just broke again!

LINDA: Well, it's old, dear.

WILLY: I told you we should've bought a well-advertised machine. Charley bought a General Electric and it's twenty years old and it's still good, that son-of-a-bitch.

LINDA: But, Willy—

WILLY: Whoever heard of a Hastings refrigerator? Once in my life I would like to own something outright before it's broken! I'm always in a race with the junkyard! I just finished paying for the car and it's on its last legs. The refrigerator consumes belts like a goddam maniac. They time those things. They time them so when you finally paid for them, they're used up.

LINDA: [*Buttoning up his jacket as he unbuttons it.*] All told, about two hundred dollars would carry us, dear. But that includes the last payment on the mortgage. After this payment, Willy, the house belongs to us.

WILLY: It's twenty-five years!

LINDA: Biff was nine years old when we bought it.

WILLY: Well, that's a great thing. To weather a twenty-five year mortgage is—

LINDA: It's an accomplishment.

WILLY: All the cement, the lumber, the reconstruction I put in this house! There ain't a crack to be found in it any more.

LINDA: Well, it served its purpose.

WILLY: What purpose? Some stranger'll come along, move in, and that's that. If only Biff would take this house, and raise a family . . . [*He starts to go.*] Goodby, I'm late.

LINDA: [*Suddenly remembering.*] Oh, I forgot! You're supposed to meet them for dinner.

WILLY: Me?

LINDA: At Frank's Chop House on Forty-eighth near Sixth Avenue.

WILLY: Is that so! How about you?

LINDA: No, just the three of you. They're gonna blow you to a big meal!

WILLY: Don't say! Who thought of that?

LINDA: Biff came to me this morning, Willy, and he said, "Tell Dad, we want to blow him to a big meal." Be there six o'clock. You and your two boys are going to have dinner.

WILLY: Gee whiz! That's really somethin'. I'm gonna knock Howard for a loop, kid. I'll get an advance, and I'll come home with a New York job. Goddammit, now I'm gonna do it!

LINDA: Oh, that's the spirit, Willy!

WILLY: I will never get behind a wheel the rest of my life!

LINDA: It's changing, Willy, I can feel it changing!

WILLY: Beyond a question. G'by, I'm late. [*He starts to go again.*]

LINDA: [*Calling after him as she runs to the kitchen table for a handkerchief.*] You got your glasses?

WILLY: [*Feels for them, then comes back in.*] Yeah, yeah, got my glasses.

LINDA: [*Giving him the handkerchief.*] And a handkerchief.

WILLY: Yeah, handkerchief.

LINDA: And your saccharine?

WILLY: Yeah, my saccharine.

LINDA: Be careful on the subway stairs.

[*She kisses him, and a silk stocking is seen hanging from her hand.* WILLY *notices it.*]

WILLY: Will you stop mending stockings? At least while I'm in the house. It gets me nervous. I can't tell you. Please.

[LINDA *hides the stocking in her hand as she follows* WILLY *across the forestage in front of the house.*]

LINDA: Remember, Frank's Chop House.

WILLY: [*Passing the apron.*] Maybe beets would grow out there.

LINDA: [*Laughing.*] But you tried so many times.

WILLY: Yeah. Well, don't work hard today. [*He disappears around the right corner of the house.*]

LINDA: Be careful! [*As* WILLY *vanishes,* LINDA *waves to him. Suddenly the phone rings. She runs across the stage and into the kitchen and lifts it.*] Hello? Oh, Biff! I'm so glad you called, I just . . . Yes, sure, I just told him. Yes, he'll be there for dinner at six o'clock, I didn't forget. Listen, I was just dying to tell you. You know that little rubber pipe I told you about? That he connected to the gas heater? I finally decided to go down the cellar this morning and take it away and destroy it. But it's gone! Imagine? He took it away himself, it isn't there! [*She listens.*] When? Oh, then you took it. Oh—nothing, it's just that I'd hoped he'd taken it away himself. Oh, I'm not worried, darling, because this morning he left in such high spirits, it was like the old days! I'm not afraid any more. Did Mr. Oliver see you? . . . Well, you wait there then. And make a nice impression on him, darling. Just don't perspire too much before you see him. And have a nice time with Dad. He may have big news too! . . . That's right, a New York job. And be sweet to him tonight, dear. Be loving to him. Because he's only a little boat looking for a harbor. [*She is trembling with sorrow and joy.*] Oh, that's wonderful, Biff, you'll save his life. Thanks, darling. Just put your arm around him when he comes into the restaurant. Give him a smile. That's the boy . . . Good-by, dear. . . . You got your comb? . . . That's fine. Good-by, Biff dear.

[*In the middle of her speech,* HOWARD WAGNER, *thirty-six, wheels on a small typewriter table on which is a wire-recording machine and proceeds to plug it in. This is on the left forestage. Light slowly fades on* LINDA *as it rises on* HOWARD. HOWARD *is intent on threading the machine and only glances over his shoulder as* WILLY *appears.*]

WILLY: Pst! Pst!

HOWARD: Hello, Willy, come in.

WILLY: Like to have a little talk with you, Howard.

HOWARD: Sorry to keep you waiting. I'll be with you in a minute.

WILLY: What's that, Howard?

HOWARD: Didn't you ever see one of these? Wire recorder.

WILLY: Oh. Can we talk a minute?

HOWARD: Records things. Just got delivery yesterday. Been driving me crazy, the most terrific machine I ever saw in my life. I was up all night with it.

WILLY: What do you do with it?

HOWARD: I bought it for dictation, but you can do anything with it. Listen to this. I had it home last night. Listen to what I picked up. The first one is my daughter. Get this. [*He flicks the switch and "Roll out the Barrel" is heard being whistled.*] Listen to that kid whistle.

WILLY: That is lifelike, isn't it?

HOWARD: Seven years old. Get that tone.

WILLY: Ts, ts. Like to ask a little favor if you . . .

[*The whistling breaks off, and the voice of* HOWARD's *daughter is heard.*]

HIS DAUGHTER: "Now you, Daddy."

HOWARD: She's crazy for me! [*Again the same song is whistled.*] That's me! Ha! [*He winks.*]

WILLY: You're very good!

[*The whistling breaks off again. The machine runs silent for a moment.*]

HOWARD: Sh! Get this now, this is my son.

HIS SON: "The capital of Alabama is Montgomery; the capital of Arizona is Phoenix; the capital of Arkansas is Little Rock; the capital of California is Sacramento . . ." [*And on, and on.*]

HOWARD: [*Holding up five fingers.*] Five years old, Willy!

WILLY: He'll make an announcer some day!

HIS SON: [*Continuing.*] "The capital. . ."

HOWARD: Get that—alphabetical order! [*The machine breaks off suddenly.*] Wait a minute. The maid kicked the plug out.

WILLY: It certainly is a—

HOWARD: Sh, for God's sake!

HIS SON: "It's nine o'clock, Bulova watch time. So I have to go to sleep."

WILLY: That really is—

HOWARD: Wait a minute! The next is my wife.

[*They wait.*]

HOWARD'S VOICE: "Go on, say something." [*Pause.*] "Well, you gonna talk?"

HIS WIFE: "I can't think of anything."

HOWARD'S VOICE: "Well, talk—it's turning."

HIS WIFE: [*Shyly, beaten.*] "Hello." [*Silence.*] "Oh, Howard, I can't talk into this . . ."

HOWARD: [*Snapping the machine off.*] That was my wife.

WILLY: That is a wonderful machine. Can we—

HOWARD: I tell you, Willy, I'm gonna take my camera, and my bandsaw, and all my hobbies, and out they go. This is the most fascinating relaxation I ever found.

WILLY: I think I'll get one myself.

HOWARD: Sure, they're only a hundred and a half. You can't do without it. Supposing you wanna hear Jack Benny,[4] see? But you can't be at home at that hour. So you tell the maid to turn the radio on when Jack Benny comes on, and this automatically goes on with the radio . . .

WILLY: And when you come home you . . .

HOWARD: You can come home twelve o'clock, one o'clock, any time you like, and you get yourself a Coke and sit yourself down, throw the switch, and there's Jack Benny's program in the middle of the night!

---

4. Jack Benny (1894–1974), a vaudeville, radio, television, and motion picture star, hosted America's most popular radio show from 1932 to 1955.

WILLY: I'm definitely going to get one. Because lots of time I'm on the road, and I think to myself, what I must be missing on the radio!

HOWARD: Don't you have a radio in the car?

WILLY: Well, yeah, but who ever thinks of turning it on?

HOWARD: Say, aren't you supposed to be in Boston?

WILLY: That's what I want to talk to you about, Howard. You got a minute? [*He draws a chair in from the wing.*]

HOWARD: What happened? What're you doing here?

WILLY: Well . . .

HOWARD: You didn't crack up again, did you?

WILLY: Oh, no. No . . .

HOWARD: Geez, you had me worried there for a minute. What's the trouble?

WILLY: Well, tell you the truth, Howard. I've come to the decision that I'd rather not travel any more.

HOWARD: Not travel! Well, what'll you do?

WILLY: Remember, Christmas time, when you had the party here? You said you'd try to think of some spot for me here in town.

HOWARD: With us?

WILLY: Well, sure.

HOWARD: Oh, yeah, yeah. I remember. Well, I couldn't think of anything for you, Willy.

WILLY: I tell ya, Howard. The kids are all grown up, y'know. I don't need much any more. If I could take home—well, sixty-five dollars a week, I could swing it.

HOWARD: Yeah, but Willy, see I—

WILLY: I tell ya why, Howard. Speaking frankly and between the two of us, y'know—I'm just a little tired.

HOWARD: Oh, I could understand that, Willy. But you're a road man, Willy, and we do a road business. We've only got a half-dozen salesmen on the floor here.

WILLY: God knows, Howard, I never asked a favor of any man. But I was with the firm when your father used to carry you in here in his arms.

HOWARD: I know that, Willy, but—

WILLY: Your father came to me the day you were born and asked me what I thought of the name of Howard, may he rest in peace.

HOWARD: I appreciate that, Willy, but there just is no spot here for you. If I had a spot I'd slam you right in, but I just don't have a single solitary spot.

[*He looks for his lighter.* WILLY *has picked it up and gives it to him. Pause.*]

WILLY: [*With increasing anger.*] Howard, all I need to set my table is fifty dollars a week.

HOWARD: But where am I going to put you, kid?

WILLY: Look, it isn't a question of whether I can sell merchandise, is it?

HOWARD: No, but it's a business, kid, and everybody's gotta pull his own weight.

WILLY: [*Desperately.*] Just let me tell you a story, Howard—

HOWARD: 'Cause you gotta admit, business is business.

WILLY: [*Angrily.*] Business is definitely business, but just listen for a minute. You don't understand this. When I was a boy—eighteen, nineteen—I was already on the road. And there was a question in my mind as to whether selling had a future for me. Because in those days I had a yearning to go to Alaska. See, there were three gold strikes in one month in Alaska, and I felt like going out. Just for the ride, you might say.

HOWARD: [*Barely interested.*] Don't say.

WILLY: Oh, yeah, my father lived many years in Alaska. He was an adventurous man. We've got quite a little streak of self-reliance in our family. I thought I'd go out with my older brother and try to locate him, and maybe settle in the North with the old man. And I was almost decided to go, when I met a salesman in the Parker House. His name was Dave Singleman. And he was eighty-four years old, and he'd drummed merchandise in thirty-one states. And old Dave, he'd go up to his room, y'understand, put on his green velvet slippers—I'll never forget—and pick up his phone and call the buyers, and without ever leaving his room, at the age of eighty-four, he made a living. And when I saw that, I realized that selling was the greatest career a man could want. 'Cause what could be more satisfying than to be able to go, at the age of eighty-four, into twenty or thirty different cities, and pick up his phone and be remembered and loved and helped by so many different people? Do you know? when he died—and by the way he died the death of a salesman, in his green velvet slippers in the smoker of the New York, New Haven and Hartford, going into Boston—when he died, hundreds of salesmen and buyers were at his funeral. Things were sad on a lotta trains for months after that. [*He stands up.* HOWARD *has not looked at him.*] In those days there was personality in it, Howard. There was respect, and comradeship, and gratitude in it. Today, it's all cut and dried, and there's no chance for bringing friendship to bear—or personality. You see what I mean? They don't know me any more.

HOWARD: [*Moving away, toward the right.*] That's just the thing, Willy.

WILLY: If I had forty dollars a week—that's all I'd need. Forty dollars, Howard.

HOWARD: Kid, I can't take blood from a stone, I—

WILLY: [*Desperation is on him now.*] Howard, the year Al Smith[5] was nominated, your father came to me and—

HOWARD: [*Starting to go off.*] I've got to see some people, kid.

WILLY: [*Stopping him.*] I'm talking about your father! There were promises made across this desk! You mustn't tell me you've got people to see—I put thirty-four years into this firm, Howard, and now I can't pay my insurance! You can't eat the orange and throw the peel away—a man is not a piece of fruit! [*After a pause.*] Now pay attention. Your father—in 1928 I had a big year. I averaged a hundred and seventy dollars a week in commissions.

HOWARD: [*Impatiently.*] Now, Willy, you never averaged—

WILLY: [*Banging his hand on the desk.*] I averaged a hundred and seventy dollars a

5. Alfred E. Smith (1873–1944) was the Democratic presidential nominee who lost to Herbert Hoover in 1928.

week in the year of 1928! And your father came to me—or rather, I was in the office here—it was right over this desk—and he put his hand on my shoulder—

HOWARD: [*Getting up.*] You'll have to excuse me, Willy, I gotta see some people. Pull yourself together. [*Going out.*] I'll be back in a little while.

[*On* HOWARD's *exit, the light on his chair grows very bright and strange.*]

WILLY: Pull myself together! What the hell did I say to him? My God, I was yelling at him! How could I! [WILLY *breaks off, staring at the light, which occupies the chair, animating it. He approaches this chair, standing across the desk from it.*] Frank, Frank, don't you remember what you told me that time? How you put your hand on my shoulder, and Frank . . . [*He leans on the desk and as he speaks the dead man's name he accidentally switches on the recorder, and instantly.*]

HOWARD'S SON: ". . . of New York is Albany. The capital of Ohio is Cincinnati, the capital of Rhode Island is . . ." [*The recitation continues.*]

WILLY: [*Leaping away with fright, shouting.*] Ha! Howard! Howard! Howard!

HOWARD: [*Rushing in.*] What happened?

WILLY: [*Pointing at the machine, which continues nasally, childishly, with the capital cities.*] Shut it off! Shut it off!

HOWARD: [*Pulling the plug out.*] Look, Willy . . .

WILLY: [*Pressing his hands to his eyes.*] I gotta get myself some coffee. I'll get some coffee . . .

[WILLY *starts to walk out.* HOWARD *stops him.*]

HOWARD: [*Rolling up the cord.*] Willy, look . . .

WILLY: I'll go to Boston.

HOWARD: Willy, you can't go to Boston for us.

WILLY: Why can't I go?

HOWARD: I don't want you to represent us. I've been meaning to tell you for a long time now.

WILLY: Howard, are you firing me?

HOWARD: I think you need a good long rest, Willy.

WILLY: Howard—

HOWARD: And when you feel better, come back, and we'll see if we can work something out.

WILLY: But I gotta earn money, Howard. I'm in no position to—

HOWARD: Where are your sons? Why don't your sons give you a hand?

WILLY: They're working on a very big deal.

HOWARD: This is no time for false pride, Willy. You go to your sons and you tell them that you're tired. You've got two great boys, haven't you?

WILLY: Oh, no question, no question, but in the meantime . . .

HOWARD: Then that's that, heh?

WILLY: All right, I'll go to Boston tomorrow.

HOWARD: No, no.

WILLY: I can't throw myself on my sons. I'm not a cripple!

HOWARD: Look, kid, I'm busy, I'm busy this morning.

WILLY: [*Grasping* HOWARD's *arm.*] Howard, you've got to let me go to Boston!

HOWARD: [*Hard, keeping himself under control.*] I've got a line of people to see this morning. Sit down, take five minutes, and pull yourself together, and then go home, will ya? I need the office, Willy. [*He starts to go, turns, remembering the recorder, starts to push off the table holding the recorder.*] Oh, yeah. Whenever you can this week, stop by and drop off the samples. You'll feel better, Willy, and then come back and we'll talk. Pull yourself together, kid, there's people outside.

[HOWARD *exits, pushing the table off left.* WILLY *stares into space, exhausted. Now the music is heard*—BEN's *music*—*first distantly, then closer, closer. As* WILLY *speaks,* BEN *enters from the right. He carries valise and umbrella.*]

WILLY: Oh, Ben, how did you do it? What is the answer? Did you wind up the Alaska deal already?

BEN: Doesn't take much time if you know what you're doing. Just a short business trip. Boarding ship in an hour. Wanted to say good-by.

WILLY: Ben, I've got to talk to you.

BEN: [*Glancing at his watch.*] Haven't the time, William.

WILLY: [*Crossing the apron to* BEN.] Ben, nothing's working out. I don't know what to do.

BEN: Now, look here, William. I've bought timberland in Alaska and I need a man to look after things for me.

WILLY: God, timberland! Me and my boys in those grand outdoors!

BEN: You've a new continent at your doorstep, William. Get out of these cities, they're full of talk and time payments and courts of law. Screw on your fists and you can fight for a fortune up there.

WILLY: Yes, yes! Linda, Linda!

[LINDA *enters as of old, with the wash.*]

LINDA: Oh, you're back?

BEN: I haven't much time.

WILLY: No, wait! Linda, he's got a proposition for me in Alaska.

LINDA: But you've got—[*To* BEN.] He's got a beautiful job here.

WILLY: But in Alaska, kid, I could—

LINDA: You're doing well enough, Willy!

BEN: [*To* LINDA.] Enough for what, my dear?

LINDA: [*Frightened of* BEN *and angry at him.*] Don't say those things to him! Enough to be happy right here, right now. [*To* WILLY, *while* BEN *laughs.*] Why must everybody conquer the world? You're well liked, and the boys love you, and someday—[*To* BEN.]—why, old man Wagner told him just the other day that if he keeps it up he'll be a member of the firm, didn't he, Willy?

WILLY: Sure, sure. I am building something with this firm, Ben, and if a man is building something he must be on the right track, mustn't he?

BEN: What are you building? Lay your hand on it. Where is it?

WILLY: [*Hesitantly.*] That's true, Linda, there's nothing.

LINDA: Why? [*To* BEN.] There's a man eighty-four years old—

WILLY: That's right, Ben, that's right. When I look at that man I say, what is there to worry about?

BEN: Bah!

WILLY: It's true, Ben. All he has to do is go into any city, pick up the phone, and he's making his living and you know why?

BEN: [*Picking up his valise.*] I've got to go.

WILLY: [*Holding* BEN *back.*] Look at this boy! [BIFF, *in his high school sweater, enters carrying suitcase.* HAPPY *carries* BIFF'*s shoulder guards, gold helmet, and football pants.*] Without a penny to his name, three great universities are begging for him, and from there the sky's the limit, because it's not what you do, Ben. It's who you know and the smile on your face! It's contacts, Ben, contacts! The whole wealth of Alaska passes over the lunch table at the Commodore Hotel, and that's the wonder, the wonder of this country, that a man can end with diamonds here on the basis of being liked! [*He turns to* BIFF.] And that's why when you get out on that field today it's important. Because thousands of people will be rooting for you and loving you. [*To* BEN, *who has again begun to leave.*] And Ben! when he walks into a business office his name will sound out like a bell and all the doors will open to him! I've seen it, Ben, I've seen it a thousand times! You can't feel it with your hand like timber, but it's there!

BEN: Good-by, William.

WILLY: Ben, am I right? Don't you think I'm right? I value your advice.

BEN: There's a new continent at your doorstep, William. You could walk out rich. Rich! [*He is gone.*]

WILLY: We'll do it here, Ben! You hear me? We're gonna do it here!

[*Young* BERNARD *rushes in. The gay music of the Boys is heard.*]

BERNARD: Oh, gee, I was afraid you left already!

WILLY: Why? What time is it?

BERNARD: It's half-past one!

WILLY: Well, come on, everybody! Ebbets Field next stop! Where's the pennants?
[*He rushes through the wall-line of the kitchen and out into the living room.*]

LINDA: [*To* BIFF.] Did you pack fresh underwear?

BIFF: [*Who has been limbering up.*] I want to go!

BERNARD: Biff, I'm carrying your helmet, ain't I?

HAPPY: No, I'm carrying the helmet.

BERNARD: Oh, Biff, you promised me.

HAPPY: I'm carrying the helmet.

BERNARD: How am I going to get in the locker room?

LINDA: Let him carry the shoulder guards. [*She puts her coat and hat on in the kitchen.*]

BERNARD: Can I, Biff? 'Cause I told everybody I'm going to be in the locker room.

HAPPY: In Ebbets Field it's the clubhouse.

BERNARD: I meant the clubhouse, Biff!

HAPPY: Biff!

BIFF: [*Grandly, after a slight pause.*] Let him carry the shoulder guards.

HAPPY: [*As he gives* BERNARD *the shoulder guards.*] Stay close to us now.

[WILLY *rushes in with the pennants.*]

WILLY: [*Handing them out.*] Everybody wave when Biff comes out on the field. [HAPPY *and* BERNARD *run off.*] You set now, boy?

[*The music has died away.*]

BIFF: Ready to go, Pop. Every muscle is ready.

WILLY: [*At the edge of the apron.*] You realize what this means?

BIFF: That's right, Pop.

WILLY: [*Feeling* BIFF's *muscles.*] You're comin' home this afternoon captain of the All-Scholastic Championship Team of the City of New York.

BIFF: I got it, Pop. And remember, pal, when I take off my helmet, that touchdown is for you.

WILLY: Let's go! [*He is starting out, with his arm around* BIFF, *when* CHARLEY *enters, as of old, in knickers.*] I got no room for you, Charley.

CHARLEY: Room? For what?

WILLY: In the car.

CHARLEY: You goin' for a ride? I wanted to shoot some casino.

WILLY: [*Furiously.*] Casino! [*Incredulously.*] Don't you realize what today is?

LINDA: Oh, he knows, Willy. He's just kidding you.

WILLY: That's nothing to kid about!

CHARLEY: No, Linda, what's goin' on?

LINDA: He's playing in Ebbets Field.

CHARLEY: Baseball in this weather?

WILLY: Don't talk to him. Come on, come on! [*He is pushing them out.*]

CHARLEY: Wait a minute, didn't you hear the news?

WILLY: What?

CHARLEY: Don't you listen to the radio? Ebbets Field just blew up.

WILLY: You go to hell! [CHARLEY *laughs. Pushing them out.*] Come on, come on! We're late.

CHARLEY: [*As they go.*] Knock a homer, Biff, knock a homer!

WILLY: [*The last to leave, turning to* CHARLEY.] I don't think that was funny, Charley. This is the greatest day of my life.

CHARLEY: Willy, when are you going to grow up?

WILLY: Yeah, heh? When this game is over, Charley, you'll be laughing out of the other side of your face. They'll be calling him another Red Grange.[6] Twenty-five thousand a year.

CHARLEY: [*Kidding.*] Is that so?

WILLY: Yeah, that's so.

CHARLEY: Well, then, I'm sorry, Willy. But tell me something.

WILLY: What?

6. Harold Edward Grange, All-American halfback at the University of Illinois (1923–1925), who played professionally for the Chicago Bears.

CHARLEY: Who is Red Grange?

WILLY: Put up your hands. Goddam you, put up your hands! [CHARLEY, *chuckling, shakes his head and walks away, around the left corner of the stage.* WILLY *follows him. The music rises to a mocking frenzy.*] Who the hell do you think you are, better than everybody else? You don't know everything, you big, ignorant, stupid . . . Put up your hands!

> [*Light rises, on the right side of the forestage, on a small table in the reception room of* CHARLEY'S *office. Traffic sounds are heard.* BERNARD, *now mature, sits whistling to himself. A pair of tennis rackets and an overnight bag are on the floor beside him.*]

WILLY: [*Offstage.*] What are you walking away for? Don't walk away! If you're going to say something say it to my face! I know you laugh at me behind my back. You'll laugh out of the other side of your goddam face after this game. Touchdown! Touchdown! Eighty thousand people! Touchdown! Right between the goal posts.

> [BERNARD *is a quiet, earnest, but self-assured young man.* WILLY'S *voice is coming from right upstage now.* BERNARD *lowers his feet off the table and listens.* JENNY, *his father's secretary, enters.*]

JENNY: [*Distressed.*] Say, Bernard, will you go out in the hall?

BERNARD: What is that noise? Who is it?

JENNY: Mr. Loman. He just got off the elevator.

BERNARD: [*Getting up.*] Who's he arguing with?

JENNY: Nobody. There's nobody with him. I can't deal with him any more, and your father gets all upset everytime he comes. I've got a lot of typing to do, and your father's waiting to sign it. Will you see him?

WILLY: [*Entering.*] Touchdown! Touch—[*He sees* JENNY.] Jenny, Jenny, good to see you. How're ya? Workin'? Or still honest?

JENNY: Fine. How've you been feeling?

WILLY: Not much any more, Jenny. Ha, ha! [*He is surprised to see the rackets.*]

BERNARD: Hello, Uncle Willy.

WILLY: [*Almost shocked.*] Bernard! Well, look who's here! [*He comes quickly, guiltily to* BERNARD *and warmly shakes his hand.*]

BERNARD: How are you? Good to see you.

WILLY: What are you doing here?

BERNARD: Oh, just stopped by to see Pop. Get off my feet till my train leaves. I'm going to Washington in a few minutes.

WILLY: Is he in?

BERNARD: Yes, he's in his office with the accountant. Sit down.

WILLY: [*Sitting down.*] What're you going to do in Washington?

BERNARD: Oh, just a case I've got there, Willy.

WILLY: That so? [*Indicating the rackets.*] You going to play tennis there?

BERNARD: I'm staying with a friend who's got a court.

WILLY: Don't say. His own tennis court. Must be fine people, I bet.

BERNARD: They are, very nice. Dad tells me Biff's in town.

WILLY: [*With a big smile.*] Yeah, Biff's in. Working on a very big deal, Bernard.

BERNARD: What's Biff doing?

WILLY: Well, he's been doing very big things in the West. But he decided to establish himself here. Very big. We're having dinner. Did I hear your wife had a boy?

BERNARD: That's right. Our second.

WILLY: Two boys! What do you know!

BERNARD: What kind of a deal has Biff got?

WILLY: Well, Bill Oliver—very big sporting-goods man—he wants Biff very badly. Called him in from the West. Long distance, carte blanche, special deliveries. Your friends have their own private tennis court?

BERNARD: You still with the old firm, Willy?

WILLY: [*After a pause.*] I'm—I'm overjoyed to see how you made the grade, Bernard, overjoyed. It's an encouraging thing to see a young man really— really— Looks very good for Biff—very—[*He breaks off, then.*] Bernard—[*He is so full of emotion, he breaks off again.*]

BERNARD: What is it, Willy?

WILLY: [*Small and alone.*] What—what's the secret?

BERNARD: What secret?

WILLY: How—how did you? Why didn't he ever catch on?

BERNARD: I wouldn't know that, Willy.

WILLY: [*Confidentially, desperately.*] You were his friend, his boyhood friend. There's something I don't understand about it. His life ended after that Ebbets Field game. From the age of seventeen nothing good ever happened to him.

BERNARD: He never trained himself for anything.

WILLY: But he did, he did. After high school he took so many correspondence courses. Radio mechanics; television; God knows what, and never made the slightest mark.

BERNARD: [*Taking off his glasses.*] Willy, do you want to talk candidly?

WILLY: [*Rising, faces* BERNARD.] I regard you as a very brilliant man, Bernard. I value your advice.

BERNARD: Oh, the hell with the advice, Willy. I couldn't advise you. There's just one thing I've always wanted to ask you. When he was supposed to graduate, and the math teacher flunked him—

WILLY: Oh, that son-of-a-bitch ruined his life.

BERNARD: Yeah, but, Willy, all he had to do was go to summer school and make up that subject.

WILLY: That's right, that's right.

BERNARD: Did you tell him not to go to summer school?

WILLY: Me? I begged him to go. I ordered him to go!

BERNARD: Then why wouldn't he go?

WILLY: Why? Why! Bernard, that question has been trailing me like a ghost for the last fifteen years. He flunked the subject, and laid down and died like a hammer hit him!

BERNARD: Take it easy, kid.

WILLY: Let me talk to you—I got nobody to talk to. Bernard, Bernard, was it my fault? Y'see? It keeps going around in my mind, maybe I did something to him. I got nothing to give him.

BERNARD: Don't take it so hard.

WILLY: Why did he lay down? What is the story there? You were his friend!

BERNARD: Willy, I remember, it was June, and our grades came out. And he'd flunked math.

WILLY: That son-of-a-bitch!

BERNARD: No, it wasn't right then. Biff just got very angry, I remember, and he was ready to enroll in summer school.

WILLY: [*Surprised.*] He was?

BERNARD: He wasn't beaten by it at all. But then, Willy, he disappeared from the block for almost a month. And I got the idea that he'd gone up to New England to see you. Did he have a talk with you then? [WILLY *stares in silence.*] Willy?

WILLY: [*With a strong edge of resentment in his voice.*] Yeah, he came to Boston. What about it?

BERNARD: Well, just that when he came back—I'll never forget this, it always mystifies me. Because I'd thought so well of Biff, even though he'd always taken advantage of me. I loved him, Willy, y'know? And he came back after that month and took his sneakers—remember those sneakers with "University of Virginia" printed on them? He was so proud of those, wore them every day. And he took them down in the cellar, and burned them up in the furnace. We had a fist fight. It lasted at least half an hour. Just the two of us, punching each other down the cellar, and crying right through it. I've often thought of how strange it was that I knew he'd given up his life. What happened in Boston, Willy? [WILLY *looks at him as at an intruder.*] I just bring it up because you asked me.

WILLY: [*Angrily.*] Nothing. What do you mean, "What happened?" What's that got to do with anything?

BERNARD: Well, don't get sore.

WILLY: What are you trying to do, blame it on me? If a boy lays down is that my fault?

BERNARD: Now, Willy, don't get—

WILLY: Well, don't—don't talk to me that way! What does that mean, "What happened?"

[CHARLEY *enters. He is in his vest, and he carries a bottle of bourbon.*]

CHARLEY: Hey, you're going to miss that train. [*He waves the bottle.*]

BERNARD: Yeah, I'm going. [*He takes the bottle.*] Thanks, Pop. [*He picks up his rackets and bag.*] Good-by, Willy, and don't worry about it. You know, "If at first you don't succeed . . ."

WILLY: Yes, I believe in that.

BERNARD: But sometimes, Willy, it's better for a man just to walk away.

WILLY: Walk away?

BERNARD: That's right.

WILLY: But if you can't walk away?

BERNARD: [*After a slight pause.*] I guess that's when it's tough. [*Extending his hand.*] Good-by, Willy.

WILLY: [*Shaking* BERNARD's *hand.*] Good-by, boy.

CHARLEY: [*An arm on* BERNARD's *shoulder.*] How do you like this kid? Gonna argue a case in front of the Supreme Court.

BERNARD: [*Protesting.*] Pop!

WILLY: [*Genuinely shocked, pained, and happy.*] No! The Supreme Court!

BERNARD: I gotta run. 'By, Dad!

CHARLEY: Knock 'em dead, Bernard!

[BERNARD *goes off.*]

WILLY: [*As* CHARLEY *takes out his wallet.*] The Supreme Court! And he didn't even mention it!

CHARLEY: [*Counting out money on the desk.*] He don't have to—he's gonna do it.

WILLY: And you never told him what to do, did you? You never took any interest in him.

CHARLEY: My salvation is that I never took any interest in anything. There's some money—fifty dollars. I got an accountant inside.

WILLY: Charley, look . . . [*With difficulty.*] I got my insurance to pay. If you can manage it—I need a hundred and ten dollars. [CHARLEY *doesn't reply for a moment; merely stops moving.*] I'd draw it from my bank but Linda would know, and I . . .

CHARLEY: Sit down, Willy.

WILLY: [*Moving toward the chair.*] I'm keeping an account of everything, remember. I'll pay every penny back. [*He sits.*]

CHARLEY: Now listen to me, Willy.

WILLY: I want you to know I appreciate . . .

CHARLEY: [*Sitting down on the table.*] Willy, what're you doin'? What the hell is goin' on in your head?

WILLY: Why? I'm simply . . .

CHARLEY: I offered you a job. You can make fifty dollars a week. And I won't send you on the road.

WILLY: I've got a job.

CHARLEY: Without pay? What kind of job is a job without pay? [*He rises.*] Now, look kid, enough is enough. I'm no genius but I know when I'm being insulted.

WILLY: Insulted!

CHARLEY: Why don't you want to work for me?

WILLY: What's the matter with you? I've got a job.

BERNARD: Then what're you walkin' in here every week for?

WILLY: [*Getting up.*] Well, if you don't want me to walk in here—

CHARLEY: I am offering you a job!

WILLY: I don't want your goddam job!

CHARLEY: When the hell are you going to grow up?

WILLY: [*Furiously.*] You big ignoramus, if you say that to me again I'll rap you one! I don't care how big you are! [*He's ready to fight. Pause.*]

CHARLEY: [*Kindly, going to him.*] How much do you need, Willy?

WILLY: Charley, I'm strapped, I'm strapped. I don't know what to do. I was just fired.

CHARLEY: Howard fired you?

WILLY: That snotnose. Imagine that? I named him. I named him Howard.

CHARLEY: Willy, when're you gonna realize that them things don't mean anything? You named him Howard, but you can't sell that. The only thing you got in this world is what you can sell. And the funny thing is that you're a salesman, and you don't know that.

WILLY: I've always tried to think otherwise. I guess. I always felt that if a man was impressive, and well liked, that nothing—

CHARLEY: Why must everybody like you? Who liked J. P. Morgan? Was he impressive? In a Turkish bath he'd look like a butcher. But with his pockets on he was very well liked. Now listen, Willy, I know you don't like me, and nobody can say I'm in love with you, but I'll give you a job because—just for the hell of it, put it that way. Now what do you say?

WILLY: I—I just can't work for you, Charley.

CHARLEY: What're you, jealous of me?

WILLY: I can't work for you, that's all, don't ask me why.

CHARLEY: [*Angered, takes out more bills.*] You been jealous of me all your life, you damned fool! Here, pay your insurance. [*He puts the money in* WILLY's *hand.*]

WILLY: I'm keeping strict accounts.

CHARLEY: I've got some work to do. Take care of yourself. And pay your insurance.

WILLY: [*Moving to the right.*] Funny, y'know? After all the highways and the trains, and the appointments, and the years, you end up worth more dead than alive.

CHARLEY: Willy, nobody's worth nothin' dead. [*After a slight pause.*] Did you hear what I said? [WILLY *stands still, dreaming.*] Willy!

WILLY: Apologize to Bernard for me when you see him. I didn't mean to argue with him. He's a fine boy. They're all fine boys, and they'll end up big—all of them. Someday they'll all play tennis together. Wish me luck, Charley. He saw Bill Oliver today.

CHARLEY: Good luck.

WILLY: [*On the verge of tears.*] Charley, you're the only friend I got. Isn't that a remarkable thing? [*He goes out.*]

CHARLEY: Jesus!

> [CHARLEY *stares after him a moment and follows. All light blacks out. Suddenly raucous music is heard, and a red glow rises behind the screen at right.* STANLEY, *a young waiter, appears, carrying a table, followed by* HAPPY, *who is carrying two chairs.*]

STANLEY: [*Putting the table down.*] That's all right, Mr. Loman, I can handle it myself. [*He turns and takes the chairs from* HAPPY *and places them at the table.*]

HAPPY: [*Glancing around.*] Oh, this is better.

STANLEY: Sure, in the front there you're in the middle of all kinds a noise. When-ever you got a party. Mr. Loman, you just tell me and I'll put you back here. Y'know, there's a lotta people they don't like it private, because when they go out they like to see a lotta action around them because they're sick and tired to stay in the house by theirself. But I know you, you ain't from Hack-ensack. You know what I mean?

HAPPY: [*Sitting down.*] So how's it coming, Stanley?

STANLEY: Ah, it's a dog life. I only wish during the war they'd a took me in the Army. I couda been dead by now.

HAPPY: My brother's back, Stanley.

STANLEY: Oh, he come back, heh? From the Far West.

HAPPY: Yeah, big cattle man, my brother, so treat him right. And my father's coming too.

STANLEY: Oh, your father too!

HAPPY: You got a couple of nice lobsters?

STANLEY: Hundred per cent, big.

HAPPY: I want them with the claws.

STANLEY: Don't worry, I don't give you no mice. [HAPPY *laughs.*] How about some wine? It'll put a head on the meal.

HAPPY: No. You remember, Stanley, that recipe I brought you from overseas? With the champagne in it?

STANLEY: Oh, yeah, sure. I still got it tacked up yet in the kitchen. But that'll have to cost a buck apiece anyways.

HAPPY: That's all right.

STANLEY: What'd you, hit a number or somethin'?

HAPPY: No, it's a little celebration. My brother is—I think he pulled off a big deal today. I think we're going into business together.

STANLEY: Great! That's the best for you. Because a family business, you know what I mean?—that's the best.

HAPPY: That's what I think.

STANLEY: 'Cause what's the difference? Somebody steals? It's in the family. Know what I mean? [*Sotto voce.*] Like this bartender here. The boss is goin' crazy what kinda leak he's got in the cash register. You put it in but it don't come out.

HAPPY: [*Raising his head.*] Sh!

STANLEY: What?

HAPPY: You notice I wasn't lookin' right or left, was I?

STANLEY: No.

HAPPY: And my eyes are closed.

STANLEY: So what's the—?

HAPPY: Strudel's comin'.

STANLEY: [*Catching on, looks around.*] Ah, no there's no—[*He breaks off as a furred, lavishly dressed* GIRL *enters and sits at the next table. Both follow her with their eyes.*] Geez, how'd ya know?

HAPPY: I got radar or something. [*Staring directly at her profile.*] Oooooooo . . . Stanley.

STANLEY: I think, that's for you, Mr. Loman.

HAPPY: Look at that mouth. Oh, God. And the binoculars.

STANLEY: Geez, you got a life, Mr. Loman.

HAPPY: Wait on her.

STANLEY: [*Going to the* GIRL*'s table.*] Would you like a menu, ma'am?

GIRL: I'm expecting someone, but I'd like a—

HAPPY: Why don't you bring her—excuse me, miss, do you mind? I sell champagne, and I'd like you to try my brand. Bring her a champagne, Stanley.

GIRL: That's awfully nice of you.

HAPPY: Don't mention it. It's all company money. [*He laughs.*]

GIRL: That's a charming product to be selling, isn't it?

HAPPY: Oh, gets to be like everything else. Selling is selling, y'know.

GIRL: I suppose.

HAPPY: You don't happen to sell, do you?

GIRL: No, I don't sell.

HAPPY: Would you object to a compliment from a stranger? You ought to be on a magazine cover.

GIRL: [*Looking at him a little archly.*] I have been.

[STANLEY *comes in with a glass of champagne.*]

HAPPY: What'd I say before, Stanley? You see? She's a cover girl.

STANLEY: Oh, I could see, I could see.

HAPPY: [*To the* GIRL.] What magazine?

GIRL: Oh, a lot of them. [*She takes the drink.*] Thank you.

HAPPY: You know what they say in France, don't you? "Champagne is the drink of the complexion"—Hya, Biff!

[BIFF *has entered and sits with* HAPPY.]

BIFF: Hello, kid. Sorry I'm late.

HAPPY: I just got here. Uh, Miss—?

GIRL: Forsythe.

HAPPY: Miss Forsythe, this is my brother.

BIFF: Is Dad here?

HAPPY: His name is Biff. You might've heard of him. Great football player.

GIRL: Really? What team?

HAPPY: Are you familiar with football?

GIRL: No, I'm afraid I'm not.

HAPPY: Biff is quarterback with the New York Giants.

GIRL: Well, that's nice, isn't it? [*She drinks.*]

HAPPY: Good health.

GIRL: I'm happy to meet you.

HAPPY: That's my name, Hap. It's really Harold, but at West Point they called me Happy.

GIRL: [*Now really impressed.*] Oh, I see. How do you do? [*She turns her profile.*]

BIFF: Isn't Dad coming?

HAPPY: You want her?

BIFF: Oh, I could never make that.

HAPPY: I remember the time that idea would never come into your head. Where's the old confidence, Biff?

BIFF: I just saw Oliver—

HAPPY: Wait a minute. I've got to see that old confidence again. Do you want her? She's on call.

BIFF: Oh, no. [*He turns to look at the* GIRL.]

HAPPY: I'm telling you. Watch this. [*Turning to see the* GIRL.] Honey? [*She turns to him.*] Are you busy?

GIRL: Well, I am . . . but I could make a phone call.

HAPPY: Do that, will you, honey? And see if you can get a friend. We'll be here for a while. Biff is one of the greatest football players in the country.

GIRL: [*Standing up.*] Well, I'm certainly happy to meet you.

HAPPY: Come back soon.

GIRL: I'll try.

HAPPY: Don't try, honey, try hard. [*The* GIRL *exits.* STANLEY *follows, shaking his head in bewildered admiration.*] Isn't that a shame now? A beautiful girl like that? That's why I can't get married. There's not a good woman in a thousand. New York is loaded with them, kid!

BIFF: Hap, look—

HAPPY: I told you she was on call!

BIFF: [*Strangely unnerved.*] Cut it out, will ya? I want to say something to you.

HAPPY: Did you see Oliver?

BIFF: I saw him all right. Now look, I want to tell Dad a couple of things and I want you to help me.

HAPPY: What? Is he going to back you?

BIFF: Are you crazy? You're out of your goddam head, you know that?

HAPPY: Why? What happened?

BIFF: [*Breathlessly.*] I did a terrible thing today, Hap. It's been the strangest day I ever went through. I'm all numb, I swear.

HAPPY: You mean he wouldn't see you?

BIFF: Well, I waited six hours for him, see? All day. Kept sending my name in. Even tried to date his secretary so she'd get me to him, but no soap.

HAPPY: Because you're not showin' the old confidence, Biff. He remembered you, didn't he?

BIFF: [*Stopping* HAPPY *with a gesture.*] Finally, about five o'clock, he comes out. Didn't remember who I was or anything. I felt like such an idiot, Hap.

HAPPY: Did you tell him my Florida idea?

BIFF: He walked away. I saw him for one minute. I got so mad I could've torn the walls down! How the hell did I ever get the idea I was a salesman there? I even believed myself that I'd been a salesman for him! And then he gave me one look and—I realized what a ridiculous lie my whole life has been! We've been talking in a dream for fifteen years. I was a shipping clerk.

HAPPY: What'd you do?

BIFF: [*With great tension and wonder.*] Well, he left, see. And the secretary went out. I was all alone in the waiting-room. I don't know what came over me, Hap. The next thing I know I'm in his office—paneled walls, everything. I can't explain it. I—Hap, I took his fountain pen.

HAPPY: Geez, did he catch you?

BIFF: I ran out. I ran down all eleven flights. I ran and ran and ran.

HAPPY: That was an awful dumb—what'd you do that for?

BIFF: [*Agonized.*] I don't know, I just—wanted to take something, I don't know. You gotta help me, Hap, I'm gonna tell Pop.

HAPPY: You crazy? What for?

BIFF: Hap, he's got to understand that I'm not the man somebody lends that kind of money to. He thinks I've been spiting him all these years and it's eating him up.

HAPPY: That's just it. You tell him something nice.

BIFF: I can't.

HAPPY: Say you got a lunch date with Oliver tomorrow.

BIFF: So what do I do tomorrow?

HAPPY: You leave the house tomorrow and come back at night and say Oliver is thinking it over. And he thinks it over for a couple of weeks, and gradually it fades away and nobody's the worse.

BIFF: But it'll go on forever!

HAPPY: Dad is never so happy as when he's looking forward to something! [WILLY *enters.*] Hello, scout!

WILLY: Gee, I haven't been here in years!

> [STANLEY *has followed* WILLY *in and sets a chair for him.* STANLEY *starts off but* HAPPY *stops him.*]

HAPPY: Stanley!

> [STANLEY *stands by, waiting for an order.*]

BIFF: [*Going to* WILLY *with guilt, as to an invalid.*] Sit down, Pop. You want a drink?

WILLY: Sure, I don't mind.

BIFF: Let's get a load on.

WILLY: You look worried.

BIFF: N-no. [*To* STANLEY.] Scotch all around. Make it doubles.

STANLEY: Doubles, right. [*He goes.*]

WILLY: You had a couple already, didn't you?

BIFF: Just a couple, yeah.

WILLY: Well, what happened, boy? [*Nodding affirmatively, with a smile.*] Everything go all right?

BIFF: [*Takes a breath, then reaches out and grasps* WILLY'S *hand.*] Pal . . . [*He is smiling bravely, and* WILLY *is smiling too.*] I had an experience today.

HAPPY: Terrific, Pop.

WILLY: That so? What happened?

BIFF: [*High, slightly alcoholic, above the earth.*] I'm going to tell you everything from first to last. It's been a strange day. [*Silence. He looks around, composes himself as best he can, but his breath keeps breaking the rhythm of his voice.*] I had to wait quite a while for him, and—

WILLY: Oliver?

BIFF: Yeah, Oliver. All day, as a matter of cold fact. And a lot of—instances—facts, Pop, facts about my life came back to me. Who was it, Pop? Who ever said I was a salesman with Oliver?

WILLY: Well, you were.

BIFF: No, Dad, I was shipping clerk.

WILLY: But you were practically—

BIFF: [*With determination.*] Dad, I don't know who said it first, but I was never a salesman for Bill Oliver.

WILLY: What're you talking about?

BIFF: Let's hold on to the facts tonight, Pop. We're not going to get anywhere bullin' around. I was a shipping clerk.

WILLY: [*Angrily.*] All right, now listen to me—

BIFF: Why don't you let me finish?

WILLY: I'm not interested in stories about the past or any crap of that kind because the woods are burning, boys, you understand? There's a big blaze going on all around. I was fired today.

BIFF: [*Shocked.*] How could you be?

WILLY: I was fired, and I'm looking for a little good news to tell your mother, because the woman has waited and the woman has suffered. The gist of it is that I haven't got a story left in my head, Biff. So don't give me a lecture about facts and aspects. I am not interested. Now what've you got to say to me? [STANLEY *enters with three drinks. They wait until he leaves.*] Did you see Oliver?

BIFF: Jesus, Dad!

WILLY: You mean you didn't go up there?

HAPPY: Sure he went up there.

BIFF: I did. I—saw him. How could they fire you?

WILLY: [*On the edge of his chair.*] What kind of a welcome did he give you?

BIFF: He won't even let you work on commission?

WILLY: I'm out. [*Driving.*] So tell me, he gave you a warm welcome?

HAPPY: Sure, Pop, sure!

BIFF: [*Driven.*] Well, it was kind of—

WILLY: I was wondering if he'd remember you. [*To* HAPPY.] Imagine, man doesn't see him for ten, twelve years and gives him that kind of a welcome!

HAPPY: Damn right!

BIFF: [*Trying to return to the offensive.*] Pop, look—

WILLY: You know why he remembered you, don't you? Because you impressed him in those days.

BIFF: Let's talk quietly and get this down to the facts, huh?

WILLY: [*As though* BIFF *had been interrupting.*] Well, what happened? It's great news, Biff. Did he take you into his office or'd you talk in the waiting-room?

BIFF: Well, he came in, see and—

WILLY: [*With a big smile.*] What'd he say? Betcha he threw his arm around you.

BIFF: Well, he kinda—

WILLY: He's a fine man. [*To* HAPPY.] Very hard man to see, y'know.

HAPPY: [*Agreeing.*] Oh, I know.

WILLY: [*To* BIFF.] Is that where you had the drinks?

BIFF: Yeah, he gave me a couple of—no, no!

HAPPY: [*Cutting in.*] He told him my Florida idea.

WILLY: Don't interrupt. [*To* BIFF.] How'd he react to the Florida idea?

BIFF: Dad, will you give me a minute to explain?

WILLY: I've been waiting for you to explain since I sat down here! What happened? He took you into his office and what?

BIFF: Well—I talked. And—he listened, see.

WILLY: Famous for the way he listens, y'know. What was his answer?

BIFF: His answer was—[*He breaks off, suddenly angry.*] Dad, you're not letting me tell you what I want to tell you!

WILLY: [*Accusing, angered.*] You didn't see him, did you?

BIFF: I did see him!

WILLY: What'd you insult him or something? You insulted him, didn't you?

BIFF: Listen, will you let me out of it, will you just let me out of it!

HAPPY: What the hell!

WILLY: Tell me what happened!

BIFF: [*To* HAPPY.] I can't talk to him!

[*A single trumpet note jars the ear. The light of green leaves stains the house, which holds the air of night and a dream.* YOUNG BERNARD *enters and knocks on the door of the house.*]

YOUNG BERNARD: [*Frantically.*] Mrs. Loman, Mrs. Loman!

HAPPY: Tell him what happened!

BIFF: [*To* HAPPY.] Shut up and leave me alone!

WILLY: No, no. You had to go and flunk math!

BIFF: What math? What're you talking about?

YOUNG BERNARD: Mrs. Loman, Mrs. Loman!

[LINDA *appears in the house, as of old.*]

WILLY: [*Wildly.*] Math, math, math!

BIFF: Take it easy, Pop!

YOUNG BERNARD: Mrs. Loman!

WILLY: [*Furiously.*] If you hadn't flunked you'd've been set by now!

BIFF: Now, look, I'm gonna tell you what happened, and you're going to listen to me.

YOUNG BERNARD: Mrs. Loman!

BIFF: I waited six hours—

HAPPY: What the hell are you saying?

BIFF: I kept sending in my name but he wouldn't see me. So finally he . . . [*He continues unheard as light fades low on the restaurant.*]

YOUNG BERNARD: Biff flunked math!

LINDA: No!

YOUNG BERNARD: Birnbaum flunked him! They won't graduate him!

LINDA: But they have to. He's gotta go to the university. Where is he? Biff! Biff!

YOUNG BERNARD: No, he left. He went to Grand Central.

LINDA: Grand— You mean he went to Boston!

YOUNG BERNARD: Is Uncle Willy in Boston?

LINDA: Oh, maybe Willy can talk to the teacher. Oh, the poor, poor boy!

[*Light on house area snaps out.*]

BIFF: [*At the table, now audible, holding up a gold fountain pen.*] . . . so I'm washed up with Oliver, you understand? Are you listening to me?

WILLY: [*At a loss.*] Yeah, sure. If you hadn't flunked—

BIFF: Flunked what? What're you talking about?

WILLY: Don't blame everything on me! I didn't flunk math—you did! What pen?

HAPPY: That was awful dumb, Biff, a pen like that is worth—

WILLY: [*Seeing the pen for the first time.*] You took Oliver's pen?

BIFF: [*Weakening.*] Dad, I just explained it to you.

WILLY: You stole Bill Oliver's fountain pen!

BIFF: I didn't exactly steal it! That's just what I've been explaining to you!

HAPPY: He had it in his hand and just then Oliver walked in, so he got nervous and stuck it in his pocket!

WILLY: My God, Biff!

BIFF: I never intended to do it, Dad!

OPERATOR'S VOICE: Standish Arms, good evening!

WILLY: [*Shouting.*] I'm not in my room!

BIFF: [*Frightened.*] Dad, what's the matter? [*He and* HAPPY *stand up.*]

OPERATOR: Ringing Mr. Loman for you!

BIFF: [*Horrified, gets down on one knee before* WILLY.] Dad, I'll make good, I'll make good. [WILLY *tries to get to his feet.* BIFF *holds him down.*] Sit down now.

WILLY: No, you're no good, you're no good for anything.

BIFF: I am, Dad, I'll find something else, you understand? Now don't worry about anything. [*He holds up* WILLY's *face.*] Talk to me, Dad.

OPERATOR: Mr. Loman does not answer. Shall I page him?

WILLY: [*Attempting to stand, as though to rush and silence the* OPERATOR.] No, no, no!

HAPPY: He'll strike something, Pop.

WILLY: No, no . . .

BIFF: [*Desperately, standing over* WILLY.] Pop, listen! Listen to me! I'm telling you something good. Oliver talked to his partner about the Florida idea. You listening? He—he talked to his partner, and he came to me . . . I'm going to be all right, you hear? Dad, listen to me, he said it was just a question of the amount!

WILLY: Then you . . . got it?

HAPPY: He's gonna be terrific, Pop!

WILLY: [*Trying to stand.*] Then you got it, haven't you? You got it! You got it!

BIFF: [*Agonized, holds* WILLY *down.*] No, no. Look, Pop. I'm supposed to have lunch with them tomorrow. I'm just telling you this so you'll know that I can still make an impression, Pop. And I'll make good somewhere, but I can't go tomorrow, see?

WILLY: Why not? You simply—

BIFF: But the pen, Pop!

WILLY: You give it to him and tell him it was an oversight!

HAPPY: Sure, have lunch tomorrow!

BIFF: I can't say that—

WILLY: You were doing a crossword puzzle and accidentally used his pen!

BIFF: Listen, kid, I took those balls years ago, now I walk in with his fountain pen? That clinches it, don't you see? I can't face him like that! I'll try elsewhere.

PAGE'S VOICE: Paging Mr. Loman!

WILLY: Don't you want to be anything?

BIFF: Pop, how can I go back?

WILLY: You don't want to be anything, is that what's behind it?

BIFF: [*Now angry at* WILLY *for not crediting his sympathy.*] Don't take it that way! You think it was easy walking into that office after what I'd done to him? A team of horses couldn't have dragged me back to Bill Oliver!

WILLY: Then why'd you go?

BIFF: Why did I go? Why did I go! Look at you! Look at what's become of you!

[*Off left,* THE WOMAN *laughs.*]

WILLY: Biff, you're going to go to that lunch tomorrow, or—

BIFF: I can't go. I've got an appointment!

HAPPY: Biff for . . . !

WILLY: Are you spiting me?

BIFF: Don't take it that way! Goddammit!

WILLY: [*Strikes* BIFF *and falters away from the table.*] You rotten little louse! Are you spiting me?

THE WOMAN: Someone's at the door, Willy!

BIFF: I'm no good, can't you see what I am?

HAPPY: [*Separating them.*] Hey, you're in a restaurant! Now cut it out, both of you? [*The* GIRLS *enter.*] Hello, girls, sit down.

[THE WOMAN *laughs, off left.*]

MISS FORSYTHE: I guess we might as well. This is Letta.

THE WOMAN: Willy, are you going to wake up?

BIFF: [*Ignoring* WILLY.] How're ya, miss, sit down. What do you drink?

MISS FORSYTHE: Letta might not be able to stay long.

LETTA: I gotta get up early tomorrow. I got jury duty. I'm so excited! Were you fellows ever on a jury?

BIFF: No, but I been in front of them! [*The* GIRLS *laugh.*] This is my father.

LETTA: Isn't he cute? Sit down with us, Pop.

HAPPY: Sit him down, Biff!

BIFF: [*Going to him.*] Come on, slugger, drink us under the table. To hell with it! Come on, sit down, pal.

[*On* BIFF's *last insistence,* WILLY *is about to sit.*]

THE WOMAN: [*Now urgently.*] Willy, are you going to answer the door!

[THE WOMAN's *call pulls* WILLY *back. He starts right, befuddled.*]

BIFF: Hey, where are you going?

WILLY: Open the door.

BIFF: The door?

WILLY: The washroom . . . the door . . . where's the door?

BIFF: [*Leading* WILLY *to the left.*] Just go straight down.

[WILLY *moves left.*]

THE WOMAN: Willy, Willy, are you going to get up, get up, get up, get up?

[WILLY *exits left.*]

LETTA: I think it's sweet you bring your daddy along.

MISS FORSYTHE: Oh, he isn't really your father!

BIFF: [*At left, turning to her resentfully.*] Miss Forsythe, you've just seen a prince walk by. A fine, troubled prince. A hardworking, unappreciated prince. A pal, you understand? A good companion. Always for his boys.

LETTA: That's so sweet.

HAPPY: Well, girls, what's the program? We're wasting time. Come on, Biff. Gather round. Where would you like to go?

BIFF: Why don't you do something for him?

HAPPY: Me!

BIFF: Don't you give a damn for him, Hap?

HAPPY: What're you talking about? I'm the one who—

BIFF: I sense it, you don't give a good goddam about him. [*He takes the rolled-up hose from his pocket and puts it on the table in front of* HAPPY.] Look what I found in the cellar, for Christ's sake. How can you bear to let it go on?

HAPPY: Me? Who goes away? Who runs off and—

BIFF: Yeah, but he doesn't mean anything to you. You could help him—I can't! Don't you understand what I'm talking about? He's going to kill himself, don't you know that?

HAPPY: Don't I know it! Me!

BIFF: Hap, help him! Jesus . . . help him . . . Help me, help me, I can't bear to look at his face! [*Ready to weep, he hurries out, up right.*]

HAPPY: [*Starting after him.*] Where are you going?

MISS FORSYTHE: What's he so mad about?

HAPPY: Come on, girls, we'll catch up with him.

MISS FORSYTHE: [*As* HAPPY *pushes her out.*] Say, I don't like that temper of his!

HAPPY: He's just a little overstrung, he'll be all right!

WILLY: [*Off left, as* THE WOMAN *laughs.*] Don't answer! Don't answer!

LETTA: Don't you want to tell your father—

HAPPY: No, that's not my father. He's just a guy. Come on, we'll catch Biff, and, honey, we're going to paint this town! Stanley, where's the check! Hey, Stanley!

[*They exit.* STANLEY *looks toward left.*]

STANLEY: [*Calling to* HAPPY *indignantly.*] Mr. Loman! Mr. Loman!

[STANLEY *picks up a chair and follows them off. Knocking is heard off left.* THE WOMAN *enters, laughing.* WILLY *follows her. She is in a black slip; he is buttoning his shirt. Raw, sensuous music accompanies their speech.*]

WILLY: Will you stop laughing? Will you stop?

THE WOMAN: Aren't you going to answer the door? He'll wake the whole hotel.

WILLY: I'm not expecting anybody.

THE WOMAN: Whyn't you have another drink, honey, and stop being so damn self-centered?

WILLY: I'm so lonely.

THE WOMAN: You know you ruined me, Willy? From now on, whenever you come to the office, I'll see that you go right through to the buyers. No waiting at my desk any more, Willy. You ruined me.

WILLY: That's nice of you to say that.

THE WOMAN: Gee, you are self-centered! Why so sad? You are the saddest, self-centerdest soul I ever did see-saw. [*She laughs. He kisses her.*] Come on inside, drummer boy. It's silly to be dressing in the middle of the night. [*As knocking is heard.*] Aren't you going to answer the door?

WILLY: They're knocking on the wrong door.

THE WOMAN: But I felt the knocking. And he heard us talking in here. Maybe the hotel's on fire!

WILLY: [*His terror rising.*] It's a mistake.

THE WOMAN: Then tell them to go away!

WILLY: There's nobody there.

THE WOMAN: It's getting on my nerves, Willy. There's somebody standing out there and it's getting on my nerves!

WILLY: [*Pushing her away from him.*] All right, stay in the bathroom here, and don't come out. I think there's a law in Massachusetts about it, so don't come out. It may be that new room clerk. He looked very mean. So don't come out. It's a mistake, there's no fire.

[*The knocking is heard again. He takes a few steps away from her, and she vanishes into the wing. The light follows him, and now he is facing* YOUNG BIFF, *who carries a suitcase.* BIFF *steps toward him. The music is gone.*]

BIFF: Why didn't you answer?

WILLY: Biff! What are you doing in Boston?

BIFF: Why didn't you answer? I've been knocking for five minutes, I called you on the phone—

WILLY: I just heard you. I was in the bathroom and had the door shut. Did anything happen home?

BIFF: Dad—I let you down.

WILLY: What do you mean?

BIFF: Dad . . .

WILLY: Biffo, what's this about? [*Putting his arm around* BIFF.] Come on, let's go downstairs and get you a malted.

BIFF: Dad, I flunked math.

WILLY: Not for the term?

BIFF: The term. I haven't got enough credits to graduate.

WILLY: You mean to say Bernard wouldn't give you the answers?

BIFF: He did, he tried, but I only got a sixty-one.

WILLY: And they wouldn't give you four points?

BIFF: Birnbaum refused absolutely. I begged him, Pop, but he won't give me those points. You gotta talk to him before they close the school. Because if he saw the kind of man you are, and you just talked to him in your way, I'm sure he'd come through for me. The class came right before practice, see, and I didn't go enough. Would you talk to him? He'd like you, Pop. You know the way you could talk.

WILLY: You're on. We'll drive right back.

BIFF: Oh, Dad, good work! I'm sure he'll change for you!

WILLY: Go downstairs and tell the clerk I'm checkin' out. Go right down.

BIFF: Yes, sir! See, the reason he hates me, Pop—one day he was late for class so I got up at the blackboard and imitated him. I crossed my eyes and talked with a lithp.

WILLY: [*Laughing.*] You did? The kids like it?

BIFF: They nearly died laughing!

WILLY: Yeah? What'd you do?

BIFF: The thquare root of thixty twee is . . . [WILLY *bursts out laughing;* BIFF *joins him.*] And in the middle of it he walked in!

[WILLY *laughs and* THE WOMAN *joins in offstage.*]

WILLY: [*Without hesitation.*] Hurry downstairs and—

BIFF: Somebody in there?

WILLY: No, that was next door.

[THE WOMAN *laughs offstage.*]

BIFF: Somebody got in your bathroom!

WILLY: No, it's the next room, there's a party—

THE WOMAN: [*Enters laughing. She lisps this.*] Can I come in? There's something in the bathtub, Willy, and it's moving!

[WILLY *looks at* BIFF, *who is staring open-mouthed and horrified at* THE WOMAN.]

WILLY: Ah—you better go back to your room. They must be finished painting by now. They're painting her room so I let her take a shower here. Go back, go back . . . [*He pushes her.*]

THE WOMAN: [*Resisting.*] But I've got to get dressed, Willy, I can't—

WILLY: Get out of here! Go back, go back . . . [*Suddenly striving for the ordinary.*] This is Miss Francis, Biff, she's a buyer. They're painting her room. Go back, Miss Francis, go back . . .

THE WOMAN: But my clothes, I can't go out naked in the hall!

WILLY: [*Pushing her offstage.*] Get outa here! Go back, go back!

[BIFF *slowly sits down on his suitcase as the argument continues offstage.*]

THE WOMAN: Where's my stockings? You promised me stockings, Willy!

WILLY: I have no stockings here!

THE WOMAN: You had two boxes of size nine sheers for me, and I want them!

WILLY: Here, for God's sake, will you get outa here!

THE WOMAN: [*Enters holding a box of stockings.*] I just hope there's nobody in the hall. That's all I hope. [*To* BIFF.] Are you football or baseball?

BIFF: Football.

THE WOMAN: [*Angry, humiliated.*] That's me too. G'night. [*She snatches her clothes from* WILLY, *and walks out.*]

WILLY: [*After a pause.*] Well, better get going. I want to get to the school first thing in the morning. Get my suits out of the closet. I'll get my valise. [BIFF *doesn't move.*] What's the matter? [BIFF *remains motionless, tears falling.*] She's a buyer. Buys for J. H. Simmons. She lives down the hall—they're painting. You don't imagine—[*He breaks off. After a pause.*] Now listen, pal, she's just a buyer. She sees merchandise in her room and they have to keep it looking just so . . . [*Pause. Assuming command.*] All right, get my suits. [BIFF *doesn't move.*] Now stop crying and do as I say. I gave you an order. Biff, I gave you an order! Is that what you do when I give you an order? How dare you cry! [*Putting his arm around* BIFF.] Now look, Biff, when you grow up you'll understand about these things. You mustn't—you mustn't overemphasize a thing like this. I'll see Birnbaum first thing in the morning.

BIFF: Never mind.

WILLY: [*Getting down beside* BIFF.] Never mind! He's going to give you those points. I'll see to it.

BIFF: He wouldn't listen to you.

WILLY: He certainly will listen to me. You need those points for the U. of Virginia.

BIFF: I'm not going there.

WILLY: Heh? If I can't get him to change that mark you'll make it up in summer school. You've got all summer to—

BIFF: [*His weeping breaking from him.*] Dad . . .

WILLY: [*Infected by it.*] Oh, my boy . . .

BIFF: Dad . . .

WILLY: She's nothing to me, Biff. I was lonely, I was terribly lonely.

BIFF: You—you gave her Mama's stockings! [*His tears break through and he rises to go.*]

WILLY: [*Grabbing for* BIFF.] I gave you an order!

BIFF: Don't touch me, you—liar!

WILLY: Apologize for that!

BIFF: You fake! You phony little fake! You fake!

[*Overcome, he turns quickly and weeping fully goes out with his suitcase.* WILLY *is left on the floor on his knees.*]

WILLY: I gave you an order! Biff, come back here or I'll beat you! Come back here! I'll whip you! [STANLEY *comes quickly in from the right and stands in front of* WILLY. WILLY *shouts at* STANLEY.] I gave you an order . . .

STANLEY: Hey, let's pick it up, pick it up, Mr. Loman. [*He helps* WILLY *to his feet.*] Your boys left with the chippies. They said they'll see you home.

[*A* SECOND WAITER *watches some distance away.*]

WILLY: But we were supposed to have dinner together.

[*Music is heard,* WILLY'*s theme.*]

STANLEY: Can you make it?

WILLY: I'll—sure, I can make it. [*Suddenly concerned about his clothes.*] Do I—I look all right?

STANLEY: Sure, you look all right. [*He flicks a speck off* WILLY'*s lapel.*]

WILLY: Here—here's a dollar.

STANLEY: Oh, your son paid me. It's all right.

WILLY: [*Putting it in* STANLEY'*s hand.*] No, take it. You're a good boy.

STANLEY: Oh, no, you don't have to . . .

WILLY: Here—here's some more, I don't need it any more. [*After a slight pause.*] Tell me—is there a seed store in the neighborhood?

STANLEY: Seeds? You mean like to plant?

[*As* WILLY *turns,* STANLEY *slips the money back into his jacket pocket.*]

WILLY: Yes. Carrots, peas . . .

STANLEY: Well, there's hardware stores on Sixth Avenue, but it may be too late now.

WILLY: [*Anxiously.*] Oh, I'd better hurry. I've got to get some seeds. [*He starts off to the right.*] I've got to get some seeds, right away. Nothing's planted. I don't have a thing in the ground.

[WILLY *hurries out as the light goes down.* STANLEY *moves over to the right after him, watches him off. The other* WAITER *has been staring at* WILLY.]

STANLEY: [*To the* WAITER.] Well, whatta you looking at?

[*The* WAITER *picks up the chairs and moves off right.* STANLEY *takes the table and follows him. The light fades on this area. There is a long pause, the sound of the flute coming over. The light gradually rises on the kitchen, which is empty.* HAPPY *appears at the door of the house, followed by* BIFF. HAPPY *is carrying a large bunch of long-stemmed roses. He enters the kitchen, looks around for* LINDA. *Not seeing her, he turns to* BIFF, *who is just outside the house door, and makes a gesture with his hands, indicating "Not here, I guess." He looks into the living-room and freezes. Inside,* LINDA, *unseen, is seated,* WILLY'*s coat on her lap. She rises ominously and quietly and moves toward* HAPPY, *who backs up into the kitchen, afraid.*]

HAPPY: Hey, what're you doing up? [LINDA *says nothing but moves toward him implacably.*] Where's Pop? [*He keeps backing to the right, and now* LINDA *is in full view in the doorway to the living-room.*] Is he sleeping?

LINDA: Where were you?

HAPPY: [*Trying to laugh it off.*] We met two girls, Mom, very fine types. Here, we brought you some flowers. [*Offering them to her.*] Put them in your room, Ma. [*She knocks them to the floor at* BIFF's *feet. He has now come inside and closed the door behind him. She stares at* BIFF, *silent.*] Now what'd you do that for? Mom, I want you to have some flowers—

LINDA: [*Cutting* HAPPY *off, violently to* BIFF.] Don't you care whether he lives or dies?

HAPPY: [*Going to the stairs.*] Come upstairs, Biff.

BIFF: [*With a flare of disgust, to* HAPPY.] Go away from me! [*To* LINDA.] What do you mean, lives or dies? Nobody's dying around here, pal.

LINDA: Get out of my sight! Get out of here!

BIFF: I wanna see the boss.

LINDA: You're not going near him!

BIFF: Where is he? [*He moves into the living-room and* LINDA *follows.*]

LINDA: [*Shouting after* BIFF.] You invite him for dinner. He looks forward to it all day—[BIFF *appears in his parents' bedroom, looks around and exits.*]—and then you desert him there. There's no stranger you'd do that to!

HAPPY: Why? He had a swell time with us. Listen, when I— [LINDA *comes back into the kitchen.*]—desert him I hope I don't outlive the day!

LINDA: Get out of here!

HAPPY: Now look, Mom . . .

LINDA: Did you have to go to women tonight? You and your lousy rotten whores!

[BIFF *re-enters the kitchen.*]

HAPPY: Mom, all we did was follow Biff around trying to cheer him up! [*To* BIFF.] Boy, what a night you gave me!

LINDA: Get out of here, both of you, and don't come back! I don't want you tormenting him any more. Go on now, get your things together! [*To* BIFF.] You can sleep in his apartment. [*She starts to pick up the flowers and stops herself.*] Pick up this stuff, I'm not your maid any more. Pick it up, you bum, you! [HAPPY *turns his back to her in refusal.* BIFF *slowly moves over and gets down on his knees, picking up the flowers.*] You're a pair of animals! Not one, not another living soul would have had the cruelty to walk out on that man in a restaurant!

BIFF: [*Not looking at her.*] Is that what he said?

LINDA: He didn't have to say anything. He was so humiliated he nearly limped when he came in.

HAPPY: But, Mom, he had a great time with us—

BIFF: [*Cutting him off violently.*] Shut up!

[*Without another word,* HAPPY *goes upstairs.*]

LINDA: You! You didn't even go in to see if he was all right!

BIFF: [*Still on the floor in front of* LINDA, *the flowers in his hand; with self-loathing.*]

No. Didn't. Didn't do a damned thing. How do you like that, heh? Left him babbling in a toilet.

LINDA: You louse. You . . .

BIFF: Now you hit it on the nose! [*He gets up, throws the flowers in the wastebasket.*] The scum of the earth, and you're looking at him!

LINDA: Get out of here!

BIFF: I gotta talk to the boss, Mom. Where is he?

LINDA: You're not going near him. Get out of this house!

BIFF: [*With absolute assurance, determination.*] No. We're gonna have an abrupt conversation, him and me.

LINDA: You're not talking to him! [*Hammering is heard from outside the house, off right.* BIFF *turns toward the noise. Suddenly pleading.*] Will you please leave him alone?

BIFF: What's he doing out there?

LINDA: He's planting the garden!

BIFF: [*Quietly.*] Now? Oh, my God!

> [BIFF *moves outside,* LINDA *following. The light dies down on them and comes up on the center of the apron as* WILLY *walks into it. He is carrying a flashlight, a hoe, and a handful of seed packets. He raps the top of the hoe sharply to fix it firmly, and then moves to the left, measuring off the distance with his foot. He holds the flashlight to look at the seed packets, reading off the instructions. He is in the blue of night.*]

WILLY: Carrots . . . quarter-inch apart. Rows . . . one-foot rows. [*He measures it off.*] One foot. [*He puts down a package and measures off.*] Beets. [*He puts down another package and measures again.*] Lettuce. [*He reads the package, puts it down.*] One foot—[*He breaks off as* BEN *appears at the right and moves slowly down to him.*] What a proposition, ts, ts. Terrific, terrific. 'Cause she's suffered, Ben, the woman has suffered. You understand me? A man can't go out the way he came in, Ben, a man has got to add up to something. You can't, you can't—[BEN *moves toward him as though to interrupt.*] You gotta consider, now. Don't answer so quick. Remember, it's a guaranteed twenty-thousand-dollar proposition. Now look, Ben, I want you to go through the ins and outs of this thing with me. I've got nobody to talk to, Ben, and the woman has suffered, you hear me?

BEN: [*Standing still, considering.*] What's the proposition?

WILLY: It's twenty thousand dollars on the barrelhead. Guaranteed, gilt-edged, you understand?

BEN: You don't want to make a fool of yourself. They might not honor the policy.

WILLY: How can they dare refuse? Didn't I work like a coolie to meet every premium on the nose? And now they don't pay off! Impossible!

BEN: It's called a cowardly thing, William.

WILLY: Why? Does it take more guts to stand here the rest of my life ringing up a zero?

BEN: [*Yielding.*] That's a point, William. [*He moves, thinking, turns.*] And twenty thousand—that *is* something one can feel with the hand, it is there.

WILLY: [*Now assured, with rising power.*] Oh, Ben, that's the whole beauty of it! I see it like a diamond, shining in the dark, hard and rough, that I can pick up and touch in my hand. Not like—like an appointment! This would not be another damned-fool appointment, Ben, and it changes all the aspects. Because he thinks I'm nothing, see, and so he spites me. But the funeral— [*Straightening up.*] Ben, that funeral will be massive! They'll come from Maine, Massachusetts, Vermont, New Hampshire! All the old-timers with the strange license plates—that boy will be thunder-struck, Ben, because he never realized—I am known! Rhode Island, New York, New Jersey—I am known, Ben, and he'll see it with his eyes once and for all. He'll see what I am, Ben! He's in for a shock, that boy!

BEN: [*Coming down to the edge of the garden.*] He'll call you a coward.

WILLY: [*Suddenly fearful.*] No, that would be terrible.

BEN: Yes. And a damned fool.

WILLY: No, no, he mustn't, I won't have that! [*He is broken and desperate.*]

BEN: He'll hate you, William.

[*The gay music of the Boys is heard.*]

WILLY: Oh, Ben, how do we get back to all the great times? Used to be so full of light, and comradeship, the sleigh-riding in winter, and the ruddiness on his cheeks. And always some kind of good news coming up, always something nice coming up ahead. And never even let me carry the valises in the house, and simonizing, simonizing that little red car! Why, why can't I give him something and not have him hate me?

BEN: Let me think about it. [*He glances at his watch.*] I still have a little time. Remarkable proposition, but you've got to be sure you're not making a fool of yourself.

[BEN *drifts off upstage and goes out of sight.* BIFF *comes down from the left.*]

WILLY: [*Suddenly conscious of* BIFF, *turns and looks up at him, then begins picking up the packages of seeds in confusion.*] Where the hell is that seed? [*Indignantly.*] You can't see nothing out here! They boxed in the whole goddam neighborhood!

BIFF: There are people all around here. Don't you realize that?

WILLY: I'm busy. Don't bother me.

BIFF: [*Taking the hoe from* WILLY.] I'm saying good-by to you, Pop. [WILLY *looks at him, silent, unable to move.*] I'm not coming back any more.

WILLY: You're not going to see Oliver tomorrow?

BIFF: I've got no appointment, Dad.

WILLY: He put his arm around you, and you've got no appointment?

BIFF: Pop, get this now, will you? Everytime I've left it's been a fight that sent me out of here. Today I realized something about myself and I tried to explain it to you and I—I think I'm just not smart enough to make any sense out of it for you. To hell with whose fault it is or anything like that. [*He takes* WILLY'*s arm.*] Let's just wrap it up, heh? Come on in, we'll tell Mom. [*He gently tries to pull* WILLY *to left.*]

WILLY: [*Frozen, immobile, with guilt in his voice.*] No, I don't want to see her.

BIFF: Come on! [*He pulls again, and* WILLY *tries to pull away.*]

WILLY: [*Highly nervous.*] No, no, I don't want to see her.

BIFF: [*Tries to look into* WILLY'*s face, as if to find the answer there.*] Why don't you want to see her?

WILLY: [*More harshly now.*] Don't bother me, will you?

BIFF: What do you mean, you don't want to see her? You don't want them calling you yellow, do you? This isn't your fault; it's me, I'm a bum. Now come inside! [WILLY *strains to get away.*] Did you hear what I said to you?

[WILLY *pulls away and quickly goes by himself into the house.* BIFF *follows.*]

LINDA: [*To* WILLY.] Did you plant, dear?

BIFF: [*At the door, to* LINDA.] All right, we had it out. I'm going and I'm not writing any more.

LINDA: [*Going to* WILLY *in the kitchen.*] I think that's the best way, dear. 'Cause there's no use drawing it out, you'll just never get along.

[WILLY *doesn't respond.*]

BIFF: People ask where I am and what I'm doing, you don't know, and you don't care. That way it'll be off your mind and you can start brightening up again. All right? That clears it, doesn't it? [WILLY *is silent, and* BIFF *goes to him.*] You gonna wish me luck, scout? [*He extends his hand.*] What do you say?

LINDA: Shake his hand, Willy.

WILLY: [*Turning to her, seething with hurt.*] There's no necessity to mention the pen at all, y'know.

BIFF: [*Gently.*] I've got no appointment, Dad.

WILLY: [*Erupting fiercely.*] He put his arm around . . . ?

BIFF: Dad, you're never going to see what I am, so what's the use of arguing? If I strike oil I'll send you a check. Meantime forget I'm alive.

WILLY: [*To* LINDA.] Spite, see?

BIFF: Shake hands, Dad.

WILLY: Not my hand.

BIFF: I was hoping not to go this way.

WILLY: Well, this is the way you're going. Good-by. [BIFF *looks at him a moment, then turns sharply and goes to the stairs.* WILLY *stops him with.*] May you rot in hell if you leave this house!

BIFF: [*Turning.*] Exactly what is it that you want from me?

WILLY: I want you to know, on the train, in the mountains, in the valleys, wherever you go, that you cut down your life for spite!

BIFF: No, no.

WILLY: Spite, spite, is the word of your undoing! And when you're down and out, remember what did it. When you're rotting somewhere beside the railroad tracks, remember, and don't you dare blame it on me!

BIFF: I'm not blaming it on you!

WILLY: I won't take the rap for this, you hear?

[HAPPY *comes down the stairs and stands on the bottom step, watching.*]

BIFF: That's just what I'm telling you!

WILLY: [*Sinking into a chair at the table, with full accusation.*] You're trying to put a knife in me—don't think I don't know what you're doing!

BIFF: All right, phony! Then let's lay it on the line. [*He whips the rubber tube out of his pocket and puts it on the table.*]

HAPPY: You crazy—

LINDA: Biff!

[*She moves to grab the hose, but* BIFF *holds it down with his hand.*]

BIFF: Leave it there! Don't move it!

WILLY: [*Not looking at it.*] What is that?

BIFF: You know goddam well what that is.

WILLY: [*Caged, wanting to escape.*] I never saw that.

BIFF: You saw it. The mice didn't bring it into the cellar! What is this supposed to do, make a hero out of you? This supposed to make me sorry for you?

WILLY: Never heard of it.

BIFF: There'll be no pity for you, you hear it? No pity!

WILLY: [*To* LINDA.] You hear the spite!

BIFF: No, you're going to hear the truth—what you are and what I am!

LINDA: Stop it!

WILLY: Spite!

HAPPY: [*Coming down toward* BIFF.] You cut it now!

BIFF: [*To* HAPPY.] The man don't know who we are! The man is gonna know! [*To* WILLY.] We never told the truth for ten minutes in this house!

HAPPY: We always told the truth!

BIFF: [*Turning on him.*] You big blow, are you the assistant buyer? You're one of the two assistants to the assistant, aren't you?

HAPPY: Well, I'm practically—

BIFF: You're practically full of it! We all are! And I'm through with it. [*To* WILLY.] Now hear this, Willy, this is me.

WILLY: I know you!

BIFF: You know why I had no address for three months? I stole a suit in Kansas City and I was in jail. [*To* LINDA, *who is sobbing.*] Stop crying. I'm through with it.

[LINDA *turns away from them, her hands covering her face.*]

WILLY: I suppose that's my fault!

BIFF: I stole myself out of every good job since high school!

WILLY: And whose fault is that?

BIFF: And I never got anywhere because you blew me so full of hot air I could never stand taking orders from anybody! That's whose fault it is!

WILLY: I hear that!

LINDA: Don't, Biff!

BIFF: It's goddam time you heard that! I had to be boss big shot in two weeks, and I'm through with it!

WILLY: Then hang yourself! For spite, hang yourself!

BIFF: No! Nobody's hanging himself, Willy! I ran down eleven flights with a pen in my hand today. And suddenly I stopped, you hear me? And in the middle of that office building, do you hear this? I stopped in the middle of that building and I saw—the sky. I saw the things that I love in this world. The work and the food and time to sit and smoke. And I looked at the pen and said to myself, what the hell am I grabbing this for? Why am I trying to become what I don't want to be? What am I doing in an office, making a contemptuous, begging fool of myself, when all I want is out there, waiting for me the minute I say I know who I am! Why can't I say that, Willy? [*He tries to make* WILLY *face him, but* WILLY *pulls away and moves to the left.*]

WILLY: [*With hatred, threateningly.*] The door of your life is wide open!

BIFF: Pop! I'm a dime a dozen, and so are you!

WILLY: [*Turning on him now in an uncontrolled outburst.*] I am not a dime a dozen! I am Willy Loman, and you are Biff Loman!

[BIFF *starts for* WILLY, *but is blocked by* HAPPY. *In his fury,* BIFF *seems on the verge of attacking his father.*]

BIFF: I am not a leader of men, Willy, and neither are you. You were never anything but a hard-working drummer who landed in the ash can like all the rest of them! I'm one dollar an hour, Willy! I tried seven states and couldn't raise it. A buck an hour! Do you gather my meaning? I'm not bringing home any prizes any more, and you're going to stop waiting for me to bring them home!

WILLY: [*Directly to* BIFF.] You vengeful, spiteful mut!

[BIFF *breaks from* HAPPY. WILLY, *in fright, starts up the stairs.* BIFF *grabs him.*]

BIFF: [*At the peak of his fury.*] Pop, I'm nothing! I'm nothing, Pop. Can't you understand that? There's no spite in it any more. I'm just what I am, that's all.

[BIFF's *fury has spent itself, and he breaks down, sobbing, holding on to* WILLY, *who dumbly fumbles for* BIFF's *face.*]

WILLY: [*Astonished.*] What're you doing? What're you doing? [*To* LINDA.] Why is he crying?

BIFF: [*Crying, broken.*] Will you let me go, for Christ's sake? Will you take that phony dream and burn it before something happens? [*Struggling to contain himself, he pulls away and moves to the stairs.*] I'll go in the morning. Put him— put him to bed. [*Exhausted,* BIFF *moves up the stairs to his room.*]

WILLY: [*After a long pause, astonished, elevated.*] Isn't that—isn't that remarkable? Biff—he likes me!

LINDA: He loves you, Willy!

HAPPY: [*Deeply moved.*] Always did, Pop.

WILLY: Oh, Biff! [*Staring wildly.*] He cried! Cried to me. [*He is choking with his love, and now cries out his promise.*] That boy—that boy is going to be magnificent!

[BEN *appears in the light just outside the kitchen.*]

BEN: Yes, outstanding, with twenty thousand behind him.

LINDA: [*Sensing the racing of his mind, fearfully, carefully.*] Now come to bed, Willy. It's all settled now.

WILLY: [*Finding it difficult not to rush out of the house.*] Yes, we'll sleep. Come on. Go to sleep, Hap.

BEN: And it does take a great kind of man to crack the jungle.

[*In accents of dread,* BEN's *idyllic music starts up.*]

HAPPY: [*His arm around* LINDA.] I'm getting married, Pop, don't forget it. I'm changing everything. I'm gonna run that department before the year is up. You'll see, Mom. [*He kisses her.*]

BEN: The jungle is dark but full of diamonds, Willy.

[WILLY *turns, moves, listening to* BEN.]

LINDA: Be good. You're both good boys, just act that way, that's all.

HAPPY: 'Night, Pop. [*He goes upstairs.*]

LINDA: [*To* WILLY.] Come, dear.

BEN: [*With greater force.*] One must go in to fetch a diamond out.

WILLY: [*To* LINDA, *as he moves slowly along the edge of the kitchen, toward the door.*] I just want to get settled down, Linda. Let me sit alone for a little.

LINDA: [*Almost uttering her fear.*] I want you upstairs.

WILLY: [*Taking her in his arms.*] In a few minutes, Linda. I couldn't sleep right now. Go on, you look awful tired. [*He kisses her.*]

BEN: Not like an appointment at all. A diamond is rough and hard to the touch.

WILLY: Go on now. I'll be right up.

LINDA: I think this is the only way, Willy.

WILLY: Sure, it's the best thing.

BEN: Best thing!

WILLY: The only way. Everything is gonna be—go on, kid, get to bed. You look so tired.

LINDA: Come right up.

WILLY: Two minutes. [LINDA *goes into the living-room, then reappears in her bedroom.* WILLY *moves just outside the kitchen door.*] Loves me. [*Wonderingly.*] Always loved me. Isn't that a remarkable thing? Ben, he'll worship me for it!

BEN: [*With promise.*] It's dark there, but full of diamonds.

WILLY: Can you imagine that magnificence with twenty thousand dollars in his pocket?

LINDA: [*Calling from her room.*] Willy! Come up!

WILLY: [*Calling into the kitchen.*] Yes! Yes. Coming! It's very smart, you realize that, don't you, sweetheart? Even Ben sees it. I gotta go, baby. 'By! 'By! [*Going over to* BEN, *almost dancing.*] Imagine? When the mail comes he'll be ahead of Bernard again!

BEN: A perfect proposition all around.

WILLY: Did you see how he cried to me? Oh, if I could kiss him, Ben!

BEN: Time, William, time!

WILLY: Oh, Ben, I always knew one way or another we were gonna make it, Biff and I!

BEN: [*Looking at his watch.*] The boat. We'll be late. [*He moves slowly off into the darkness.*]

WILLY: [*Elegiacally, turning to the house.*] Now when you kick off, boy, I want a seventy-yard boot, and get right down the field under the ball, and when you hit, hit low and hit hard, because it's important, boy. [*He swings around and faces the audience.*] There's all kinds of important people in the stands, and the first thing you know . . . [*Suddenly realizing he is alone.*] Ben! Ben, where do I . . . ? [*He makes a sudden movement of search.*] Ben, how do I . . . ?

LINDA: [*Calling.*] Willy, you coming up?

WILLY: [*Uttering a gasp of fear, whirling about as if to quiet her.*] Sh! [*He turns around as if to find his way; sounds, faces, voices, seem to be swarming in upon him and he flicks at them, crying.*] Sh! Sh! [*Suddenly music, faint and high, stops him. It rises in intensity, almost to an unbearable scream. He goes up and down on his toes, and rushes off around the house.*] Shhh!

LINDA: Willy? [*There is no answer. LINDA waits. BIFF gets up off his bed. He is still in his clothes. HAPPY sits up. BIFF stands listening.*] [*With real fear.*] Willy, answer me! Willy! [*There is the sound of a car starting and moving away at full speed.*] No!

BIFF: [*Rushing down the stairs.*] Pop!

[*As the car speeds off, the music crashes down in a frenzy of sound, which becomes the soft pulsation of a single cello string. BIFF slowly returns to his bedroom. He and HAPPY gravely don their jackets. LINDA slowly walks out of her room. The music has developed into a dead march. The leaves of day are appearing over everything. CHARLEY and BERNARD, somberly dressed, appear and knock on the kitchen door. BIFF and HAPPY slowly descend the stairs to the kitchen as CHARLEY and BERNARD enter. All stop a moment when LINDA, in clothes of mourning, bearing a little bunch of roses, comes through the draped doorway into the kitchen. She goes to CHARLEY and takes his arm. Now all move toward the audience, through the wall-line of the kitchen. At the limit of the apron, LINDA lays down the flowers, kneels, and sits back on her heels. All stare down at the grave.*]

REQUIEM

CHARLEY: It's getting dark, Linda.

[*LINDA doesn't react. She stares at the grave.*]

BIFF: How about it, Mom? Better get some rest, heh? They'll be closing the gate soon.

[*LINDA makes no move. Pause.*]

HAPPY: [*Deeply angered.*] He had no right to do that. There was no necessity for it. We would've helped him.

CHARLEY [*Grunting.*] Hmmm.

BIFF: Come along, Mom.

LINDA: Why didn't anybody come?

CHARLEY: It was a very nice funeral.

LINDA: But where are all the people he knew? Maybe they blame him.

CHARLEY: Naa. It's a rough world, Linda. They wouldn't blame him.

LINDA: I can't understand it. At this time especially. First time in thirty-five years we were just about free and clear. He only needed a little salary. He was even finished with the dentist.

CHARLEY: No man only needs a little salary.

LINDA: I can't understand it.

BIFF: There were a lot of nice days. When he'd come home from a trip; or on Sundays, making the stoop; finishing the cellar; putting on the new porch; when he built the extra bathroom; and put up the garage. You know something, Charley, there's more of him in that front stoop than in all the sales he ever made.

CHARLEY: Yeah. He was a happy man with a batch of cement.

LINDA: He was so wonderful with his hands.

BIFF: He had the wrong dreams. All, all, wrong.

HAPPY: [*Almost ready to fight* BIFF.] Don't say that!

BIFF: He never knew who he was.

CHARLEY: [*Stopping* HAPPY's *movement and reply. To* BIFF.] Nobody dast blame this man. You don't understand: Willy was a salesman. And for a salesman, there is no rock bottom to the life. He don't put a bolt to a nut, he don't tell you the law or give you medicine. He's a man way out there in the blue, riding on a smile and a shoeshine. And when they start not smiling back—that's an earthquake. And then you get yourself a couple of spots on your hat, and you're finished. Nobody dast blame this man. A salesman is got to dream, boy. It comes with the territory.

BIFF: Charley, the man didn't know who he was.

HAPPY: [*Infuriated.*] Don't say that!

BIFF: Why don't you come with me, Happy?

HAPPY: I'm not licked that easily. I'm staying right in this city, and I'm gonna beat this racket! [*He looks at* BIFF, *his chin set.*] The Loman Brothers!

BIFF: I know who I am, kid.

HAPPY: All right, boy. I'm gonna show you and everybody else that Willy Loman did not die in vain. He had a good dream. It's the only dream you can have— to come out number-one-man. He fought it out here, and this is where I'm gonna win it for him.

BIFF: [*With a hopeless glance at* HAPPY, *bends toward his mother.*] Let's go, Mom.

LINDA: I'll be with you in a minute. Go on, Charley. [*He hesitates.*] I want to, just for a minute. I never had a chance to say good-by. [CHARLEY *moves away, followed by* HAPPY. BIFF *remains a slight distance up and left of* LINDA. *She sits there, summoning herself. The flute begins, not far away, playing behind her speech.*] Forgive me, dear. I can't cry. I don't know what it is, but I can't cry. I don't understand it. Why did you ever do that? Help me, Willy, I can't cry. It seems to me that you're just on another trip. I keep expecting you. Willy, dear, I can't cry. Why did you do it? I search and search and I search, and I can't understand it, Willy. I made the last payment on the house today. Today, dear. And there'll be nobody home. [*A sob rises in her throat.*] We're free and clear. [*Sobbing more fully, released.*] We're free. [BIFF *comes slowly toward her.*] We're free . . . We're free . . .

[BIFF *lifts her to her feet and moves out up right with her in his arms.* LINDA *sobs quietly.* BERNARD *and* CHARLEY *come together and follow them, followed by* HAPPY. *Only the music of the flute is left on the darkening stage as over the house the hard towers of the apartment buildings rise into sharp focus.*]

CURTAIN

1949

QUESTIONS

1. How does Willy Loman understand the role of a salesman? What ideals does he hold? How fully does he live up to his ideals? In what ways does he noticeably fall short of them?
2. How do other characters in the play understand Willy's profession? In what ways are their interpretations different from Willy's? How do the other characters evaluate Willy? What seems to be their definition of success? What is Willy's definition?
3. What kind of dream does Willy have? How does it relate to the larger idea of an "American Dream"? In what ways does Willy's dream distort the values of the American Dream? In what ways is Willy's life a critique of the American Dream?
4. Describe Willy's character. What character "flaws" does he have? How much of his situation seems to be his own fault? How do you respond to Charley's words "Nobody dast blame this man"? Do you agree? Why should we (or should we not) agree with Charley? Does Arthur Miller seem to agree? Does the text of the play seem to give a definitive answer, or is the indeterminacy of the text crucial to the play's continued success?
5. How consistent is Willy in his thinking? What bothers you most about his inconsistencies? Do his inconsistencies make him more or less believable as a stage character? Why?
6. How fully is Willy differentiated from the other characters? What does Uncle Ben do for the play? How does the character of Bernard work to clarify other characters and further the play's themes?
7. Describe the character of Biff. Of Happy. How do you keep them straight from each other? What devices are used to differentiate them?
8. How "dated" does the play seem now? What particular episodes or references seem especially tied to the 1940s? How would you define a "traveling salesman" in mid-twentieth-century America? What social attitudes toward that kind of character seem built into the play? How fully do you feel that you understand the social and ethical status of Willy's profession?
9. What symbolic role does hosiery play on stage? If you were producing the play, how would you stage Linda's mending scenes?

WRITING SUGGESTIONS

1. In your college library, do some research on the idea of the "American Dream." What variations does it seem to have in different eras and among different social or ethnic

groups? Write a short (three- or four-page) paper defining the American Dream as it manifested itself just after World War II, and describe how Willy's goals relate to the idea.

2. Consider carefully the character of Linda—how she is presented on stage, her relationship to Willy, the attitudes she displays toward the other characters. How important is her role in the play? Pretend you are Linda at the play's end: write a very short (300–400-word) "honest" summary of Willy's life, a soliloquy she might speak only to the audience about her own ideals and dreams in relation to Willy's life and values.

3. At the beginning, *Death of a Salesman* states its setting as "today." In what ways has "today" changed since 1949? Write a three- or four-page paper in which you describe the most important changes since 1949 that affect your interpretation of the action and characters in the play. What habits have changed? What attitudes? What values?

STUDENT WRITING

In the student paper that follows, Sherry Schnake examines how characterization, sets and setting, and plot all contribute to a thematic analysis of the destructive clash between the American Dream and everyday reality.

Dream of a Salesman

Sherry Schnake

Success is an integral part of the American dream. However, as Arthur Miller points out in <u>Death of a Salesman</u>, when that dream is not based in reality it can lead to destruction. This is demonstrated in the character of Willy Loman, a salesman consumed by illusion. "He had all the wrong dreams," said his son Biff at Willy's funeral. Biff was right: Willy's dreams ruined his life and the lives of everyone he loved.

As the play opens, Willy is introduced as a tired man and gains sympathy from the reader. However, questions begin to arise about his integrity the first time he slips into the past. In this scene, when he learns his son Biff has stolen a football, he praises him for his initiative. He also tells his boys that as long as a person is well liked, it doesn't matter if he does poorly in school. As the play progresses, Willy reveals through his words and actions that being well liked is the center of his life's philosophy. Because Willy cannot fulfill this philosophy, he lives in an illusion. In it, he is popular and successful, even though in reality he is a failure.

Although the action of the play occurs in a twenty-four hour period, much more of Willy's life is revealed through his memories of the past, which he is continually reliving. The staging of the play supports the theme and symbolizes Willy's life. The scenery is all transparent, just as Willy and his dreams are. In scenes of the past there are no boundaries, for it was a time when Willy knew no limits. The fact that Willy fluctuates so freely from the past to the present emphasizes his inability to distinguish illusion from reality. The flashbacks also allow the reader to see how Willy and his sons' lives were shaped by the past.

Near the beginning of the play, Willy suggests to Biff that he ask for a loan to start a business from his former employer Bill Oliver. Willy assures Biff he will get it because Oliver always liked Biff. However, when Biff is rejected by Oliver, he confronts Willy in the climax of the play. At this point Biff tries to make Willy see that the dream they had both been living by was phony. Biff knows now that being well liked is not the key to success and happiness. He tries to make his father realize that that outlook has gotten them nowhere by exclaiming "I'm a dime a dozen and so are you!"

However, the dream is too deeply engraved in Willy's mind. It is ironic that Biff's attempt to make his father rid himself of his false dream only convinces Willy that his dream was right. When Biff cries to Willy in frustration, all Willy can see is that Biff likes him.

Biff's discontent with Willy began many years earlier. Through Willy's memories we learn that when Biff failed math he went to Boston to ask Willy to convince his teacher to pass him. There Biff found Willy with another woman. At that moment, Biff's image of his father was shattered. Because the false values Willy planted in his son were shattered also, Biff became a lost soul and didn't fully understand himself until his later confrontation with Willy.

Biff isn't the only one whose life is ruined by Willy's dream. Biff's brother Happy is usually ignored by Willy and overshadowed by Biff. Nonetheless, Happy enthusiastically embraces Willy's goals and will not let go of them even when they have failed his father. In this sense, he is less fortunate than Biff because he is destined to repeat his father's life.

Willy's illusions also adversely affect his wife Linda. She was always supportive of him, yet he took out his frustrations on her in the form of angry words and disrespect. His desire to be well liked led him to betray her with an affair.

Willy's dreams are further challenged by his neighbor Charley and his brother Ben. Charley is the antithesis of Willy: he is unconcerned with popularity, and yet is successful. Ben represents something Willy could never attain: he grabbed success in an almost physical way and never looked back.

Willy dies still clinging to his illusion. In fact, he kills himself so that Biff can use his insurance money to succeed in life. His painfully small funeral that concludes the play is a pathetic reminder that his dreams, indeed, were wrong.

Thus, Willy's life and death were devoted to false goals. Because of his inability to see reality, he left Linda alone, he left Biff disillusioned, and, sadly, he left Happy to follow in his footsteps, chasing the wrong dreams.

27

CRITICAL CONTEXTS: A DRAMA CASEBOOK

Even more than other forms of literature, drama has a relatively stable canon—that is, a select group of plays that the theater community thinks of as especially worthy of continued and frequent performance. New plays do often join this canon, of course, but worldwide it is surprising how often the same plays are performed over and over, especially plays by Shakespeare, Ibsen, and Sophocles. The reasons are many, involving their themes and continued appeal across times and cultures as well as their formal literary and theatrical accomplishments. But the fact of their repeated performance means that a relatively small number of plays becomes a lot better known than all the others and that a tradition of "talk" about them becomes more intense, more concentrated, and more developed. A lot of this talk is informal and local, resulting from the fact that people see plays communally—that is, people are present together for a performance—and then often compare their responses afterward. But more permanent and more formal records of such responses also come to exist; critics almost always review individual productions of plays in newspapers and magazines and on radio, television, and in web formats. Often this record of evaluation concentrates primarily on the details of a particular performance. But because every production of a play involves a particular interpretation of the text, cumulative accounts of performance add up to a body of interpretive criticism—that is, analytical commentary about many aspects of the play as text and as performance.

Any oral or written text can provoke a lot of disagreement, partly because of the slippery nature of both verbal and visual language and partly because different readers and listeners bring different interests, experiences, and perspectives to the text. Differences in response may result from different circumstances and cultural assumptions— all readers and viewers are to some extent influenced by the times and places in which they live—or by matters of individual temperament and preference. But plays in particular, because of their many productions in varied locations by many different acting companies and directors, carry with them an especially varied accumulation of critical responses. New productions of a play often draw consciously on previous productions, sometimes imitating particular features and sometimes reacting against particular well-known interpretations. The many famous productions of *Hamlet*, for example, consciously compare themselves to each other in their emphasis on political intrigue, mother/son and father/son relationships, the hesitations or "indecisiveness" of the hero, and so forth, as do interpretations of the main character in *Hedda Gabler*. As a reader of plays in a textbook like this, you may or may not bring to your reading an awareness of what others have thought historically about a particular play, but that body of material is available to you if you choose to use it as a way of getting additional perspectives on the text.

Besides the immediate and local responses of critics to individual performances, professional literary scholars, critics, and theorists think and write a lot about individual plays, too—again, perhaps, because such a relatively small number of them are repeatedly in public view. A play like Sophocles' *Antigone,* for instance, attracts attention from a wide variety of perspectives—from Greek scholars who view it in relation to classical myth or the particulars of the ancient Greek language, from philosophers who may see in it examinations of classic ideas and ethical problems, from theater historians who may think about it in relation to traditions of staging and visualization or the particulars of gestures and stage business, or from historians of rhetoric who may be interested in the way the chorus and the players interact in their interpretations of the action.

A bust of Sophocles.

Some of these examinations supply vast historical learning in the service of investigating particulars of the play; others are more dependent on working out a particular critical theory or simply a coherent interpretation of the play. Reading the record of this accumulated criticism is often not necessary to understanding what is happening in a text, and sometimes you may well feel that some of the intense and careful labor is over your head or at least irrelevant to your particular needs. But often, too, reading what others have already said, from whatever point of view, about a text can be helpful—to offer historical information that you hadn't known about or hadn't considered relevant, to point to problems or possibilities of interpretation you have not yet thought of, or to provide you with support and comfort for a reading you have already arrived at. In a sense, reading published criticism is a lot like talking with your fellow students or being involved in a formal class discussion. In general, it's best not to read "the critics" until after you have read the complete text of a play at least once, just as it is better to read the text in full before you discuss it with others. That way, your own reactions are fresh and straightforward; and if there are matters you don't understand, you can always manage to "footnote" them later through discussion or through reading criticism.

> *A play should give you something to think about. When I see a play and understand it the first time, then I know it can't be much good.*
>
> —T. S. ELIOT,
>
> *New York Post*
>
> September 22, 1963

Reading critics can be especially helpful when you are writing a paper. Critics will often guide you to crucial points of debate or to a particular place in the text that is a kind of crux for deciding on a particular interpretation. You are likely to get the most help if you read several critics with different perspectives and different conclusions—not because more is better, but because you will be able to see their differences and, more important, the *grounds* for their differences in the kinds of evidence they use. Their disagreements are likely to be of the most use to you as a new interpreter; critics can be useful to you not as "authorities" (you should never regard a particular interpretation as true just because it is published or written by somebody famous), but as indicators of what the issues are.

Often, when you are just beginning to think about what kind of paper you are going to write, turning to the critics can be very helpful as a way of seeing what some of the critical issues in the play may be. Critics frequently do not agree on the interpretation of particular issues or passages or even on what the issues really are, but reading them can be useful in making your own thoughts concrete, especially when you have just begun to sort things out and you cannot yet quite articulate what your own feelings may be. Reacting to someone else's view, especially when it is strongly argued and opposes your own tentative feelings, can help with your own articulation and can quickly begin to suggest a line of interpretation and argument for your own writing.

The sorting out of which issues are most important in a text can be complicated, and issues do shift from era to era and culture to culture. But it is surprising how often the arguments posed in one era continue to interest subsequent critics in whatever age and from whatever perspective. *Antigone* has a history of performance that goes back more than twenty-four centuries, and over that time readers and viewers have recorded thousands and thousands of responses. Here we can reprint only a small sample, and the ones we have chosen are all from the twentieth century. But earlier views are often referred to and sometimes still argued about vehemently. The famous comments of the German philosopher Hegel, for example, have continued to set the agenda for an astonishing number of other interpreters. Many answer him directly; others use him to sharpen, complicate, or detail their own views or simply to position themselves in some larger debate about specific issues in the play or about literary criticism or philosophy more generally.

In the selections that follow you will find a variety of views about how to interpret crucial scenes and issues in *Antigone*. Especially prominent are questions of how to read the opinions of the chorus, how to interpret the character of Antigone, and what the flaws of Creon consist of. As you read the critics, pay attention to the way they argue—the kinds of textual evidence they use to back up their points and the ways they structure their arguments—as well as the main interpretive points they make.

If you use published criticism in your papers (or to back up a point you want to make in class or in an argument with a fellow student), you will want to work the phrasing

A production of *Antigone* (New York Shakespeare Festival, 1982).

into your paper or your conversation the way you have learned to do with lines or phrases from the text. Sometimes a particular critic can be especially helpful in focusing your thoughts because you disagree so clearly or so violently with what she or he says. In that case, you may well get a good paper out of a rebuttal in which you answer or attack the argument there point by point. Pitting one critic against another—that is, sorting out the exact issues that different interpreters disagree on and showing exactly what their differences consist of—can also be a good way to focus on your own distinctive contribution. But the point in your reading the critics is to *use* them for your own interpretive purposes, to make your responses more sensitive and resonant, to make you a better reader of this play, and to make you a better reader in general.

SOPHOCLES

Antigone[1]

CHARACTERS

ANTIGONE	HAEMON
ISMENE	TEIRESIAS
CHORUS OF THEBAN ELDERS	A MESSENGER
CREON	EURYDICE
A SENTRY	SECOND MESSENGER

The two sisters ANTIGONE *and* ISMENE *meet in front of the palace gates in Thebes.*

ANTIGONE: Ismene, my dear sister,
   whose father was my father, can you think of any
   of all the evils that stem from Oedipus
   that Zeus does not bring to pass for us, while we yet live?
5   No pain, no ruin, no shame, and no dishonor
   but I have seen it in our mischiefs,
   yours and mine.
   And now what is the proclamation that they tell of
   made lately by the commander, publicly,
10   to all the people? Do you know it? Have you heard it?
   Don't you notice when the evils due to enemies
   are headed towards those we love?
ISMENE: Not a word, Antigone, of those we love,
   either sweet or bitter, has come to me since the moment
15   when we lost our two brothers,
   on one day, by their hands dealing mutual death.
   Since the Argive army fled in this past night,
   I know of nothing further, nothing
   of better fortune or of more destruction.
20 ANTIGONE: *I* knew it well; that is why I sent for you

1. Translated by David Grene.

to come outside the palace gates
    to listen to me, privately.
ISMENE: What is it? Certainly your words
    come of dark thoughts.
ANTIGONE: Yes, indeed; for those two brothers of ours, in burial   25
    has not Creon honored the one, dishonored the other?
    Eteocles, they say he has used justly
    with lawful rites and hid him in the earth
    to have his honor among the dead men there.
    But the unhappy corpse of Polyneices   30
    he has proclaimed to all the citizens,
    they say, no man may hide
    in a grave nor mourn in funeral,
    but leave unwept, unburied, a dainty treasure
    for the birds that see him, for their feast's delight.   35
    That is what, they say, the worthy Creon
    has proclaimed for you and me—for me, I tell you—
    and he comes here to clarify to the unknowing
    his proclamation; he takes it seriously;
    for whoever breaks the edict death is prescribed,   40
    and death by stoning publicly.
    There you have it; soon you will show yourself
    as noble both in your nature and your birth,
    or yourself as base, although of noble parents.
ISMENE: If things are as you say, poor sister, how   45
    can I better them? how loose or tie the knot?
ANTIGONE: Decide if you will share the work, the deed.
ISMENE: What kind of danger is there? How far have your thoughts gone?
ANTIGONE: Here is this hand. Will you help it to lift the dead man?
ISMENE: Would you bury him, when it is forbidden the city?   50
ANTIGONE: At least he is my brother—and yours, too,
    though you deny him. *I* will not prove false to him.
ISMENE: You are so headstrong. Creon has forbidden it.
ANTIGONE: It is not for him to keep me from my own.
ISMENE: O God!   55
    Consider, sister, how our father died,
    hated and infamous; how he brought to light
    his own offenses; how he himself struck out
    the sight of his two eyes;
    his own hand was their executioner.   60
    Then, mother and wife, two names in one, did shame
    violently on her life, with twisted cords.
    Third, our two brothers, on a single day,
    poor wretches, themselves worked out their mutual doom.
    Each killed the other, hand against brother's hand.   65
    Now there are only the two of us, left behind,
    and see how miserable our end shall be

if in the teeth of law we shall transgress
against the sovereign's decree and power.

70 You ought to realize we are only women,
not meant in nature to fight against men,
and that we are ruled, by those who are stronger,
to obedience in this and even more painful matters.
I do indeed beg those beneath the earth

75 to give me their forgiveness,
since force constrains me,
that I shall yield in this to the authorities.
Extravagant action is not sensible.

ANTIGONE: I would not urge you now; nor if you wanted

80 to act would I be glad to have you with me.
Be as you choose to be; but for myself
I myself will bury him. It will be good
to die, so doing. I shall lie by his side,
loving him as he loved me; I shall be

85 a criminal—but a religious one.
The time in which I must please those that are dead
is longer than I must please those of this world.
For there I shall lie forever. You, if you like,
can cast dishonor on what the gods have honored.

90 ISMENE: I will not put dishonor on them, but
to act in defiance of the citizenry,
my nature does not give me means for that.

ANTIGONE: Let that be your excuse. But I will go
to heap the earth on the grave of my loved brother.

95 ISMENE: How I fear for you, my poor sister!

ANTIGONE: Do not fear for me. Make straight your own path to destiny.

ISMENE: At least do not speak of this act to anyone else;
bury him in secret; I will be silent, too.

ANTIGONE: Oh, oh, no! shout it out. I will hate you still worse

100 for silence—should you not proclaim it,
to everyone.

ISMENE: You have a warm heart for such chilly deeds.

ANTIGONE: I know I am pleasing those I should please most.

ISMENE: If you can do it. But you are in love

105 with the impossible.

ANTIGONE: No. When I can no more, then I will stop.

ISMENE: It is better not to hunt the impossible
at all.

ANTIGONE: If you will talk like this I will loathe you,

110 and you will be adjudged an enemy—
justly—by the dead's decision. Let me alone
and my folly with me, to endure this terror.
No suffering of mine will be enough
to make me die ignobly.

ISMENE: Well, if you will, go on. 115
   Know this; that though you are wrong to go, your friends
   are right to love you.
CHORUS: Sun's beam, fairest of all
        that ever till now shone
        on seven-gated Thebes; 120
        O golden eye of day, you shone
        coming over Dirce's stream;[2]
        You drove in headlong rout
        the whiteshielded man from Argos,
        complete in arms; 125
        his bits rang sharper
        under your urging.

        Polyneices brought him here
        against our land, Polyneices,
        roused by contentious quarrel; 130
        like an eagle he flew into our country,
        with many men-at-arms,
        with many a helmet crowned with horsehair.

        He stood above the halls, gaping with murderous lances,
        encompassing the city's 135
        seven-gated mouth.
        But before his jaws would be sated
        with our blood, before the fire,
        pine fed, should capture our crown of towers,
        he went hence— 140
        such clamor of war stretched behind his back,
        from his dragon foe, a thing he could not overcome.

        For Zeus, who hates the most
        the boasts of a great tongue,
        saw them coming in a great tide, 145
        insolent in the clang of golden armor.
        The god struck him down with hurled fire,
        as he strove to raise the victory cry,
        now at the very winning post.

        The earth rose to strike him as he fell swinging. 150
        In his frantic onslaught, possessed, he breathed upon us
        with blasting winds of hate.
        Sometimes the great god of war was on one side,
        and sometimes he struck a staggering blow on the other;
        the god was a very wheel horse on the right trace. 155

        At seven gates stood seven captains,
        ranged equals against equals, and there left

2. River near Thebes.

their brazen suits of armor
to Zeus, the god of trophies.
160   Only those two wretches born of one father and mother
set their spears to win a victory on both sides;
they worked out their share in a common death.

Now Victory, whose name is great, has come
to Thebes of many chariots
165   with joy to answer her joy,
to bring forgetfulness of these wars;
let us go to all the shrines of the gods
and dance all night long.
Let Bacchus lead the dance,
170   shaking Thebes to trembling.

But here is the king of our land,
Creon, son of Menoeceus;
in our new contingencies with the gods,
he is our new ruler.
175   He comes to set in motion some design—
what design is it? Because he has proposed
the convocation of the elders.
He sent a public summons for our discussion.
CREON: Gentlemen: as for our city's fortune,
180   the gods have shaken her, when the great waves broke,
but the gods have brought her through again to safety.
For yourselves, I chose you out of all and summoned you
to come to me, partly because I knew you
as always loyal to the throne—at first,
185   when Laïus was king, and then again
when Oedipus saved our city and then again
when he died and you remained with steadfast truth
to their descendants,
until they met their double fate upon one day,
190   striking and stricken, defiled each by a brother's murder.
Now here I am, holding all authority
and the throne, in virtue of kinship with the dead.
It is impossible to know any man—
I mean his soul, intelligence, and judgment—
195   until he shows his skill in rule and law.
I think that a man supreme ruler of a whole city,
if he does not reach for the best counsel for her,
but through some fear, keeps his tongue under lock and key,
him I judge the worst of any;
200   I have always judged so; and anyone thinking
another man more a friend than his own country,
I rate him nowhere. For my part, God is my witness,

who sees all, always, I would not be silent
if I saw ruin, not safety, on the way
towards my fellow citizens. I would not count   205
any enemy of my country as a friend—
because of what I know, that she it is
which gives us our security. If she sails upright
and we sail on her, friends will be ours for the making.
In the light of rules like these, I will make her greater still.   210

In consonance with this, I here proclaim
to the citizens about Oedipus' sons.
For Eteocles, who died this city's champion,
showing his valor's supremacy everywhere,
he shall be buried in his grave with every rite   215
of sanctity given to heroes under earth.
However, his brother, Polyneices, a returned exile,
who sought to burn with fire from top to bottom
his native city, and the gods of his own people;
who sought to taste the blood he shared with us,   220
and lead the rest of us to slavery—
I here proclaim to the city that this man
shall no one honor with a grave and none shall mourn.
You shall leave him without burial; you shall watch him
chewed up by birds and dogs and violated.   225
Such is my mind in the matter; never by me
shall the wicked man have precedence in honor
over the just. But he that is loyal to the state
in death, in life alike, shall have my honor.
CHORUS: Son of Menoeceus, so it is your pleasure   230
   to deal with foe and friend of this our city.
   To use any legal means lies in your power,
   both about the dead and those of us who live.
CREON: I understand, then, you will do my bidding.
CHORUS: Please lay this burden on some younger man.   235
CREON: Oh, watchers of the corpse I have already.
CHORUS: What else, then, do your commands entail?
CREON: That you should not side with those who disagree.
CHORUS: There is none so foolish as to love his own death.
CREON: Yes, indeed those are the wages, but often greed   240
   has with its hopes brought men to ruin.

   [*The* SENTRY *whose speeches follow represents a remarkable experiment in
   Greek tragedy in the direction of naturalism of speech. He speaks with marked
   clumsiness, partly because he is excited and talks almost colloquially. But also
   the royal presence makes him think apparently that he should be rather grand
   in his show of respect. He uses odd bits of archaism or somewhat stale poetical
   passages, particularly in catch phrases. He sounds something like lower-level*

Shakespearean characters, e.g. Constable Elbow, with his uncertainty about
benefactor and malefactor.]

SENTRY: My lord, I will never claim my shortness of breath
　　is due to hurrying, nor were there wings in my feet.
　　I stopped at many a lay-by in my thinking;
245　　I circled myself till I met myself coming back.
　　My soul accosted me with different speeches.
　　"Poor fool, yourself, why are you going somewhere
　　when once you get there you will pay the piper?"
　　"Well, aren't you the daring fellow! stopping again?
250　　and suppose Creon hears the news from someone else—
　　don't you realize that you will smart for that?"
　　I turned the whole matter over. I suppose I may say
　　"I made haste slowly" and the short road became long.
　　However, at last I came to a resolve:
255　　I must go to you; even if what I say
　　is nothing, really, still I shall say it.
　　I come here, a man with a firm clutch on the hope
　　that nothing can betide him save what is fated.
CREON: What is it then that makes you so afraid?
260　SENTRY: No, I want first of all to tell you my side of it.
　　I didn't do the thing; I never saw who did it.
　　It would not be fair for me to get into trouble.
CREON: You hedge, and barricade the thing itself.
　　Clearly you have some ugly news for me.
265　SENTRY: Well, you know how disasters make a man
　　hesitate to be their messenger.
CREON: For God's sake, tell me and get out of here!
SENTRY: Yes, I *will* tell you. Someone just now
　　buried the corpse and vanished. He scattered on the skin
270　　some thirsty dust; he did the ritual,
　　duly, to purge the body of desecration.
CREON: What! Now who on earth could have done that?
SENTRY: I do not know. For there was there no mark
　　of axe's stroke nor casting up of earth
275　　of any mattock; the ground was hard and dry,
　　unbroken; there were no signs of wagon wheels.
　　The doer of the deed had left no trace.
　　But when the first sentry of the day pointed it out,
　　there was for all of us a disagreeable
280　　wonder. For the body had disappeared;
　　not in a grave, of course; but there lay upon him
　　a little dust as of a hand avoiding
　　the curse of violating the dead body's sanctity.
　　There were no signs of any beast nor dog

that came there; he had clearly not been torn. 285
There was a tide of bad words at one another,
guard taunting guard, and it might well have ended
in blows, for there was no one there to stop it.
Each one of us was the criminal but no one
manifestly so; all denied knowledge of it. 290
We were ready to take hot bars in our hands
or walk through fire, and call on the gods with oaths
that we had neither done it nor were privy
to a plot with anyone, neither in planning
nor yet in execution. 295
At last when nothing came of all our searching,
there was one man who spoke, made every head
bow to the ground in fear. For we could not
either contradict him nor yet could we see how
if we did what he said we would come out all right. 300
His word was that we must lay information
about the matter to yourself; we could not cover it.
This view prevailed and the lot of the draw chose me,
unlucky me, to win that prize. So here
I am. I did not want to come, 305
and you don't want to have me. I know that.
For no one likes the messenger of bad news.
CHORUS: My lord: I wonder, could this be God's doing?
    This is the thought that keeps on haunting me.
CREON: Stop, before your words fill even me with rage, 310
    that you should be exposed as a fool, and you so old.
    For what you say is surely insupportable
    when you say the gods took forethought for this corpse.
    Is it out of excess of honor for the man,
    for the favors that he did them, they should cover him? 315
    This man who came to burn their pillared temples,
    their dedicated offerings—and this land
    and laws he would have scattered to the winds?
    Or do you see the gods as honoring
    criminals? This is not so. But what I am doing 320
    now, and other things before this, some men disliked,
    within this very city, and muttered against me,
    secretly shaking their heads; they would not bow
    justly beneath the yoke to submit to me.
    I am very sure that these men hired others 325
    to do this thing. I tell you the worse currency
    that ever grew among mankind is money. This
    sacks cities, this drives people from their homes,
    this teaches and corrupts the minds of the loyal
    to acts of shame. This displays 330

all kinds of evil for the use of men,
instructs in the knowledge of every impious act.
Those that have done this deed have been paid to do it,
but in the end they will pay for what they have done.

335   It is as sure as I still reverence Zeus—
know this right well—and I speak under oath—
if you and your fellows do not find this man
who with his own hand did the burial
and bring him here before me face to face,
340   your death alone will not be enough for me.
You will hang alive till you open up this outrage.
That will teach you in the days to come from what
you may draw profit—safely—from your plundering.
It's not from anything and everything
345   you can grow rich. You will find out
that ill-gotten gains ruin more than they save.
SENTRY: Have I your leave to say something—or should I
just turn and go?
CREON: Don't you know your talk is painful enough already?
350 SENTRY: Is the ache in your ears or in your mind?
CREON: Why do you dissect the whereabouts of my pain?
SENTRY: Because it is he who did the deed who hurts
your mind. I only hurt your ears that listen.
CREON: I am sure you have been a chatterbox since you were born.
355 SENTRY: All the same, I did not do this thing.
CREON: You might have done this, too, if you sold your soul.
SENTRY: It's a bad thing if one judges and judges wrongly.
CREON: You may talk as wittily as you like of judgment.
Only, if you don't bring to light those men
360   who have done this, you will yet come to say
that your wretched gains have brought bad consequences.
SENTRY: [Aside.] It were best that he were found, but whether
the criminal is taken or he isn't—
for that chance will decide—one thing is certain,
365   you'll never see me coming here again.
I never hoped to escape, never thought I could.
But now I have come off safe, I thank God heartily.
CHORUS: Many are the wonders, none
is more wonderful than what is man.
370   This it is that crosses the sea
with the south winds storming and the waves swelling,
breaking around him in roaring surf.
He it is again who wears away
the Earth, oldest of gods, immortal, unwearied,
375   as the ploughs wind across her from year to year
when he works her with the breed that comes from horses.

The tribe of the lighthearted birds he snares
and takes prisoner the races of savage beasts
and the brood of the fish of the sea,
with the close-spun web of nets.   380
A cunning fellow is man. His contrivances
make him master of beasts of the field
and those that move in the mountains.
So he brings the horse with the shaggy neck
to bend underneath the yoke;   385
and also the untamed mountain bull;
and speech and windswift thought
and the tempers that go with city living
he has taught himself, and how to avoid
the sharp frost, when lodging is cold   390
under the open sky
and pelting strokes of the rain.
He has a way against everything,
and he faces nothing that is to come
without contrivance.   395
Only against death
can he call on no means of escape;
but escape from hopeless diseases
he has found in the depths of his mind.
With some sort of cunning, inventive   400
beyond all expectation
he reaches sometimes evil,
and sometimes good.

If he honors the laws of earth,
and the justice of the gods he has confirmed by oath,   405
high is his city; no city
has he with whom dwells dishonor
prompted by recklessness.
He who is so, may he never
share my hearth!   410
may he never think my thoughts!

Is this a portent sent by God?
I cannot tell.
I know her. How can I say
that this is not Antigone?   415
Unhappy girl, child of unhappy Oedipus,
what is this?
Surely it is not you they bring here
as disobedient to the royal edict,
surely not you, taken in such folly.   420
SENTRY: She is the one who did the deed;
   we took her burying him. But where is Creon?

CHORUS: He is just coming from the house, when you most need him.
CREON: What is this? What has happened that I come
425   so opportunely?
SENTRY: My lord, there is nothing
    that a man should swear he would never do.
    Second thoughts make liars of the first resolution.
    I would have vowed it would be long enough
430   before I came again, lashed hence by your threats.
    But since the joy that comes past hope, and against all hope,
    is like no other pleasure in extent,
    I have come here, though I break my oath in coming.
    I bring this girl here who has been captured
435   giving the grace of burial to the dead man.
    This time no lot chose me; this was my jackpot,
    and no one else's. Now, my lord, take her
    and as you please judge her and test her; I
    am justly free and clear of all this trouble.
440 CREON: This girl—how did you take her and from where?
SENTRY: She was burying the man. Now you know all.
CREON: Do you know what you are saying? Do you mean it?
SENTRY: She is the one; I saw her burying
    the dead man you forbade the burial of.
445   Now, do I speak plainly and clearly enough?
CREON: How was she seen? How was she caught in the act?
SENTRY: This is how it was. When we came there,
    with those dreadful threats of yours upon us,
    we brushed off all the dust that lay upon
450   the dead man's body, heedfully
    leaving it moist and naked.
    We sat on the brow of the hill, to windward,
    that we might shun the smell of the corpse upon us.
    Each of us wakefully urged his fellow
455   with torrents of abuse, not to be careless
    in this work of ours. So it went on,
    until in the midst of the sky the sun's bright circle
    stood still; the heat was burning. Suddenly
    a squall lifted out of the earth a storm of dust,
460   a trouble in the sky. It filled the plain,
    ruining all the foliage of the wood
    that was around it. The great empty air
    was filled with it. We closed our eyes, enduring
    this plague sent by the gods. When at long last
465   we were quit of it, why, then we saw the girl.

    She was crying out with the shrill cry
    of an embittered bird
    that sees its nest robbed of its nestlings

and the bed empty. So, too, when she saw
the body stripped of its cover, she burst out in groans, 470
calling terrible curses on those that had done that deed;
and with her hands immediately
brought thirsty dust to the body; from a shapely brazen
urn, held high over it, poured a triple stream
of funeral offerings; and crowned the corpse. 475
When we saw that, we rushed upon her and
caught our quarry then and there, not a bit disturbed.
We charged her with what she had done, then and the first time.
She did not deny a word of it—to my joy,
but to my pain as well. It is most pleasant 480
to have escaped oneself out of such troubles
but painful to bring into it those whom we love.
However, it is but natural for me
to count all this less than my own escape.

CREON: You there, that turn your eyes upon the ground, 485
    do you confess or deny what you have done?

ANTIGONE: Yes, I confess; I will not deny my deed.

CREON: [*To the* SENTRY.] You take yourself off where you like.
    You are free of a heavy charge.
    Now, Antigone, tell me shortly and to the point, 490
    did you know the proclamation against your action?

ANTIGONE: I knew it; of course I did. For it was public.

CREON: And did you dare to disobey that law?

ANTIGONE: Yes, it was not Zeus that made the proclamation;
    nor did Justice, which lives with those below, enact 495
    such laws as that, for mankind. I did not believe
    your proclamation had such power to enable
    one who will someday die to override
    God's ordinances, unwritten and secure.
    They are not of today and yesterday; 500
    they live forever; none knows when first they were.
    These are the laws whose penalties I would not
    incur from the gods, through fear of any man's temper.

    I know that I will die—of course I do—
    even if you had not doomed me by proclamation. 505
    If I shall die before my time, I count that
    a profit. How can such as I, that live
    among such troubles, not find a profit in death?
    So for such as me, to face such a fate as this
    is pain that does not count. But if I dared to leave 510
    the dead man, my mother's son, dead and unburied,
    that would have been real pain. The other is not.
    Now, if you think me a fool to act like this,
    perhaps it is a fool that judges so.

515 CHORUS: The savage spirit of a savage father
shows itself in this girl. She does not know
how to yield to trouble.
CREON: I would have you know the most fanatic spirits
fall most of all. It is the toughest iron,
520 baked in the fire to hardness, you may see
most shattered, twisted, shivered to fragments.
I know hot horses are restrained
by a small curb. For he that is his neighbor's slave cannot
be high in spirit. This girl had learned her insolence
525 before this, when she broke the established laws.
But here is still another insolence
in that she boasts of it, laughs at what she did.
I swear I am no man and she the man
if she can win this and not pay for it.
530 No; though she were my sister's child or closer
in blood than all that my hearth god acknowledges
as mine, neither she nor her sister should escape
the utmost sentence—death. For indeed I accuse her,
the sister, equally of plotting the burial.
535 Summon her. I saw her inside, just now,
crazy, distraught. When people plot
mischief in the dark, it is the mind which first
is convicted of deceit. But surely I hate indeed
the one that is caught in evil and then makes
540 that evil look like good.
ANTIGONE: Do you want anything
beyond my taking and my execution?
CREON: Oh, nothing! Once I have that I have everything.
ANTIGONE: Why do you wait, then? Nothing that you say
pleases me; God forbid it ever should.
545 So my words, too, naturally offend you.
Yet how could I win a greater share of glory
than putting my own brother in his grave?
All that are here would surely say that's true,
if fear did not lock their tongues up. A prince's power
550 is blessed in many things, not least in this,
that he can say and do whatever he likes.
CREON: You are alone among the people of Thebes
to see things in that way.
ANTIGONE: No, these do, too,
555 but keep their mouths shut for the fear of you.
CREON: Are you not ashamed to think so differently
from them?
ANTIGONE: There is nothing shameful in honoring my brother.
CREON: Was not he that died on the other side your brother?

ANTIGONE: Yes, indeed, of my own blood from father and mother.   560
CREON: Why then do you show a grace that must be impious
   in *his* sight?
ANTIGONE: *That* other dead man
   would never bear you witness in what you say.   565
CREON: Yes he would, if you put him only on equality
   with one that was a desecrator.
ANTIGONE: It was his brother, not his slave, that died.
CREON: He died destroying the country the other defended.
ANTIGONE: The god of death demands these rites for both.   570
CREON: But the good man does not seek an *equal* share only,
   with the bad.
ANTIGONE: Who knows
   if in that other world this is true piety?
CREON: My enemy is still my enemy, even in death.
ANTIGONE: My nature is to join in love, not hate.   575
CREON: Go then to the world below, yourself, if you
   must love. Love *them*. When I am alive no woman shall rule.
CHORUS: Here before the gates comes Ismene
   shedding tears for the love of a brother.
   A cloud over her brow casts shame   580
   on her flushed face, as the tears wet
   her fair cheeks.
CREON: You there, who lurked in my house, viper-like—
   secretly drawing its lifeblood; I never thought
   that I was raising two sources of destruction,   585
   two rebels against my throne. Come tell me now,
   will you, too, say you bore a hand in the burial
   or will you swear that you know nothing of it?
ISMENE: I did it, yes—if she will say I did it
   I bear my share in it, bear the guilt, too.   590
ANTIGONE: Justice will not allow you what you refused
   and I will have none of your partnership.
ISMENE: But in your troubles I am not ashamed
   to sail with you the sea of suffering.
ANTIGONE: Where the act was death, the dead are witnesses.   595
   I do not love a friend who loves in words.
ISMENE: Sister, do not dishonor me, denying me
   a common death with you, a common honoring
   of the dead man.
ANTIGONE: Don't die with me, nor make your own   600
   what you have never touched. I that die am enough.
ISMENE: What life is there for me, once I have lost you?
ANTIGONE: Ask Creon; all your care was on his behalf.
ISMENE: Why do you hurt me, when you gain nothing by it?
ANTIGONE: I am hurt by my own mockery—if I mock you.   605

ISMENE: Even now—what can I do to help you still?

ANTIGONE: Save yourself; I do not grudge you your escape.

ISMENE: I cannot bear it! Not even to share your death!

ANTIGONE: Life was your choice, and death was mine.

610 ISMENE: You cannot say I accepted that choice in silence.

ANTIGONE: You were right in the eyes of one party, I in the other.

ISMENE: Well then, the fault is equally between us.

ANTIGONE: Take heart; you are alive, but my life died
    long ago, to serve the dead.

615 CREON: Here are two girls; I think that one of them
    has suddenly lost her wits—the other was always so.

ISMENE: Yes, for, my lord, the wits that they are born with
    do not stay firm for the unfortunate.
    They go astray.

CREON: Certainly yours do,

620   when you share troubles with the troublemaker.

ISMENE: What life can be mine alone without her?

CREON: Do not
    speak of *her*. She isn't, anymore.

ISMENE: Will you kill your son's wife to be?

CREON: Yes, there are other fields for him to plough.

625 ISMENE: Not with the mutual love of him and her.

CREON: I hate a bad wife for a son of mine.

ANTIGONE: Dear Haemon, how your father dishonors you.

CREON: There is too much of you—and of your marriage!

CHORUS: Will you rob your son of this girl?

630 CREON: Death—it is death that will stop the marriage for me.

CHORUS: Your decision it seems is taken: she shall die.

CREON: Both you and I have decided it. No more delay.

    [*He turns to the* SERVANTS.]

    Bring her inside, you. From this time forth,
    these must be women, and not free to roam.

635   For even the stout of heart shrink when they see
    the approach of death close to their lives.

CHORUS: Lucky are those whose lives
    know no taste of sorrow.
    But for those whose house has been shaken by God

640   there is never cessation of ruin;
    it steals on generation after generation
    within a breed. Even as the swell
    is driven over the dark deep
    by the fierce Thracian winds

645   I see the ancient evils of Labdacus' house
    are heaped on the evils of the dead.
    No generation frees another, some god
    strikes them down; there is no deliverance.

Here was the light of hope stretched
over the last roots of Oedipus' house,
and the bloody dust due to the gods below
has mowed it down—that and the folly of speech
and ruin's enchantment of the mind.

650

Your power, O Zeus, what sin of man can limit?
All-aging sleep does not overtake it,
nor the unwearied months of the gods; and you,
for whom time brings no age,
you hold the glowing brightness of Olympus.

655

For the future near and far,
and the past, this law holds good:
nothing very great
comes to the life of mortal man
without ruin to accompany it.
For Hope, widely wandering, comes to many of mankind
as a blessing,
but to many as the deceiver,
using light-minded lusts;
she comes to him that knows nothing
till he burns his foot in the glowing fire.
With wisdom has someone declared
a word of distinction:
that evil seems good to one whose mind
the god leads to ruin,
and but for the briefest moment of time
is his life outside of calamity.
Here is Haemon, youngest of your sons.
Does he come grieving
for the fate of his bride to be,
in agony at being cheated of his marriage?

660

665

670

675

CREON: Soon we will know that better than the prophets.
 My son, can it be that you have not heard
 of my final decision on your betrothed?
 Can you have come here in your fury against your father?
 Or have I your love still, no matter what I do?

680

HAEMON: Father, I am yours; with your excellent judgment
 you lay the right before me, and I shall follow it.
 No marriage will ever be so valued by me
 as to override the goodness of your leadership.

685

CREON: Yes, my son, this should always be
 in your very heart, that everything else
 shall be second to your father's decision.
 It is for this that fathers pray to have
 obedient sons begotten in their halls,
 that they may requite with ill their father's enemy

690

695 and honor his friend no less than he would himself.
If a man have sons that are no use to him,
what can one say of him but that he has bred
so many sorrows to himself, laughter to his enemies?
Do not, my son, banish your good sense
700 through pleasure in a woman, since you know
that the embrace grows cold
when an evil woman shares your bed and home.
What greater wound can there be than a false friend?
No. Spit on her, throw her out like an enemy,
705 this girl, to marry someone in Death's house.
I caught her openly in disobedience
alone out of all this city and I shall not make
myself a liar in the city's sight. No, I will kill her.
So let her cry if she will on the Zeus of kinship;
710 for if I rear those of my race and breeding
to be rebels, surely I will do so with those outside it.
For he who is in his household a good man
will be found a just man, too, in the city.
But he that breaches the law or does it violence
715 or thinks to dictate to those who govern him
shall never have my good word.
The man the city sets up in authority
must be obeyed in small things and in just
but also in their opposites.
720 I am confident such a man of whom I speak
will be a good ruler, and willing to be well ruled.
He will stand on his country's side, faithful and just,
in the storm of battle. There is nothing worse
than disobedience to authority.
725 It destroys cities, it demolishes homes;
it breaks and routs one's allies. Of successful lives
the most of them are saved by discipline.
So we must stand on the side of what is orderly;
we cannot give victory to a woman.
730 If we must accept defeat, let it be from a man;
we must not let people say that a woman beat us.
CHORUS: We think, if we are not victims of Time the Thief,
that you speak intelligently of what you speak.
HAEMON: Father, the natural sense that the gods breed
735 in men is surely the best of their possessions.
I certainly could not declare you wrong—
may I never know how to do so!—Still there might
be something useful that some other than you might think.
It is natural for me to be watchful on your behalf
740 concerning what all men say or do or find to blame.

Your face is terrible to a simple citizen;
it frightens him from words you dislike to hear.
But what *I* can hear, in the dark, are things like these:
the city mourns for this girl; they think she is dying
most wrongly and most undeservedly   745
of all womenkind, for the most glorious acts.
Here is one who would not leave her brother unburied,
a brother who had fallen in bloody conflict,
to meet his end by greedy dogs or by
the bird that chanced that way. Surely what she merits   750
is golden honor, isn't it? That's the dark rumor
that spreads in secret. Nothing I own
I value more highly, father, than your success.
What greater distinction can a son have than the glory
of a successful father, and for a father   755
the distinction of successful children?
Do not bear this single habit of mind, to think
that what you say and nothing else is true
A man who thinks that he alone is right,
or what he says, or what he *is* himself,   760
unique, such men, when opened up, are seen
to be quite empty. For a man, though he be wise,
it is no shame to learn—learn many things,
and not maintain his views too rigidly.
You notice how by streams in wintertime   765
the trees that yield preserve their branches safely,
but those that fight the tempest perish utterly.
The man who keeps the sheet of his sail tight
and never slackens capsizes his boat
and makes the rest of his trip keel uppermost.   770
Yield something of your anger, give way a little.
If a much younger man, like me, may have
a judgment, I would say it were far better
to be one altogether wise by nature, but,
as things incline not to be so, then it is good   775
also to learn from those who advise well.
CHORUS: My lord, if he says anything to the point,
you should learn from him, and you, too, Haemon,
learn from your father. Both of you
have spoken well.   780
CREON: Should we that are my age learn wisdom
from young men such as he is?
HAEMON: Not learn injustice, certainly. If I am young,
do not look at my years but what I do.
CREON: Is what you do to have respect for rebels?
HAEMON: I   785

would not urge you to be scrupulous
    towards the wicked.
CREON: Is *she* not tainted by the disease of wickedness?
HAEMON: The entire people of Thebes says no to that.
790   CREON: Should the city tell me how I am to rule them?
HAEMON: Do you see what a young man's words these are of yours?
CREON: Must I rule the land by someone else's judgment
    rather than my own?
HAEMON: There is no city
795   possessed by one man only.
CREON: Is not the city thought to be the ruler's?
HAEMON: You would be a fine dictator of a desert.
CREON: It seems this boy is on the woman's side.
HAEMON: If you are a woman—my care is all for you.
CREON: You villain, to bandy words with your own father!
800   HAEMON: I see your acts as mistaken and unjust.
CREON: Am I mistaken, reverencing my own office?
HAEMON: There is no reverence in trampling on God's honor.
CREON: Your nature is vile, in yielding to a woman.
HAEMON: You will not find me yield to what is shameful.
805   CREON: At least, your argument is all for her.
HAEMON: Yes, and for you and me—and for the gods below.
CREON: You will never marry her while her life lasts.
HAEMON: Then she must die—and dying destroy another.
CREON: Has your daring gone so far, to threaten me?
810   HAEMON: What threat is it to speak against empty judgments?
CREON: Empty of sense yourself, you will regret
    your schooling of me in sense.
HAEMON: If you were not
    my father, I would say you are insane.
CREON: You woman's slave, do not try to wheedle me.
815   HAEMON: You want to talk but never to hear and listen.
CREON: Is that so? By the heavens above you will not—
    be sure of that—get off scot-free, insulting,
    abusing me.

[*He speaks to the* SERVANTS.]

               You people bring out this creature,
    this hated creature, that she may die before
820   his very eyes, right now, next her would-be husband.
HAEMON: Not at my side! Never think that! She will not
    die by my side. But you will never again
    set eyes upon my face. Go then and rage
    with such of your friends as are willing to endure it.
825   CHORUS: The man is gone, my lord, quick in his anger.
    A young man's mind is fierce when he is hurt.
CREON: Let him go, and do and think things superhuman.

But these two girls he shall not save from death.
CHORUS: Both of them? Do you mean to kill them both?
CREON: No, not the one that didn't do anything.   830
    You are quite right there.
CHORUS: And by what form of death do you mean to kill her?
CREON: I will bring her where the path is loneliest,
    and hide her alive in a rocky cavern there.
    I'll give just enough of food as shall suffice   835
    for a bare expiation, that the city may avoid pollution.
    In that place she shall call on Hades, god of death,
    in her prayers. That god only she reveres.
    Perhaps she will win from him escape from death
    or at least in that last moment will recognize   840
    her honoring of the dead is labor lost.
CHORUS: Love undefeated in the fight,
    Love that makes havoc of possessions,
    Love who lives at night in a young girl's soft cheeks,
    Who travels over sea, or in huts in the countryside—   845
    there is no god able to escape you
    nor anyone of men, whose life is a day only,
    and whom you possess is mad.

    You wrench the minds of just men to injustice,
    to their disgrace; this conflict among kinsmen   850
    it is you who stirred to turmoil.
    The winner is desire. She gleaming kindles
    from the eyes of the girl good to bed.
    Love shares the throne with the great powers that rule.
    For the golden Aphrodite[3] holds her play there   855
    and then no one can overcome her.

    Here I too am borne out of the course of lawfulness
    when I see these things, and I cannot control
    the springs of my tears
    when I see Antigone making her way   860
    to her bed—but the bed
    that is rest for everyone.
ANTIGONE: You see me, you people of my country,
    as I set out on my last road of all,
    looking for the last time on this light of this sun—   865
    never again. I am alive but Hades who gives sleep to everyone
    is leading me to the shores of Acheron,[4]
    though I have known nothing of marriage songs
    nor the chant that brings the bride to bed.
    My husband is to be the Lord of Death.   870

---

3. Goddess of love and beauty.   4. River in Hades.

CHORUS: Yes, you go to the place where the dead are hidden,
    but you go with distinction and praise.
    You have not been stricken by wasting sickness;
    you have not earned the wages of the sword;
875   it was your own choice and alone among mankind
    you will descend, alive,
    to that world of death.
ANTIGONE: But indeed I have heard of the saddest of deaths—
    of the Phrygian stranger,[5] daughter of Tantalus,
880   whom the rocky growth subdued, like clinging ivy.
    The rains never leave her, the snow never fails,
    as she wastes away. That is how men tell the story.
    From streaming eyes her tears wet the crags;
    most like to her the god brings me to rest.
885 CHORUS: Yes, but she was a god, and god born,
    and you are mortal and mortal born.
    Surely it is great renown
    for a woman that dies, that in life and death
    her lot is a lot shared with demigods.
890 ANTIGONE: You mock me. In the name of our fathers' gods
    why do you not wait till I am gone to insult me?
    Must you do it face to face?
    My city! Rich citizens of my city!
    You springs of Dirce, you holy groves of Thebes,
895   famed for its chariots! I would still have you as my witnesses,
    with what dry-eyed friends, under what laws
    I make my way to my prison sealed like a tomb.
    Pity me. Neither among the living nor the dead
    do I have a home in common—
900   neither with the living nor the dead.
CHORUS: You went to the extreme of daring
    and against the high throne of Justice
    you fell, my daughter, grievously.
    But perhaps it was for some ordeal of your father
905   that you are paying requital.
ANTIGONE: You have touched the most painful of my cares—
    the pity for my father, ever reawakened,
    and the fate of all of our race, the famous Labdacids;
    the doomed self-destruction of my mother's bed
910   when she slept with her own son,
    my father.
    What parents I was born of, God help me!
    To them I am going to share their home,
    the curse on me, too, and unmarried.

---

5. Niobe, whose children were slain because of her boastfulness and who was herself turned into a stone on Mount Siphylus. Her tears became the mountain's streams.

Brother, it was a luckless marriage you made, 915
and dying killed my life.
CHORUS: There *is* a certain reverence for piety.
But for him in authority,
he cannot see that authority defied;
it is your own self-willed temper 920
that has destroyed you.
ANTIGONE: No tears for me, no friends, no marriage. Brokenhearted
I am led along the road ready before me.
I shall never again be suffered
to look on the holy eye of the day. 925
But my fate claims no tears—
no friend cries for me.
CREON: [*To the* SERVANTS.] Don't you know that weeping and wailing before
death
would never stop if one is allowed to weep and wail?
Lead her away at once. Enfold her 930
in that rocky tomb of hers—as I told you to.
There leave her alone, solitary,
to die if she so wishes
or live a buried life in such a home;
we are guiltless in respect of her, this girl. 935
But living above, among the rest of us, this life
she shall certainly lose.
ANTIGONE: Tomb, bridal chamber, prison forever
dug in rock, it is to you I am going
to join my people, that great number that have died, 940
whom in their death Persephone[6] received.
I am the last of them and I go down
in the worst death of all—for I have not lived
the due term of my life. But when I come
to that other world my hope is strong 945
that my coming will be welcome to my father,
and dear to you, my mother, and dear to you,
my brother deeply loved. For when you died,
with my own hands I washed and dressed you all,
and poured the lustral offerings on your graves. 950
And now, Polyneices, it was for such care of your body
that I have earned these wages.
Yet those who think rightly will think I did right
in honoring you. Had I been a mother
of children, and my husband been dead and rotten, 955
I would not have taken this weary task upon me
against the will of the city. What law backs me
when I say this? I will tell you:

6. Abducted by Pluto, god of the underworld.

960 If my husband were dead, I might have had another,
and child from another man, if I lost the first.
But when father and mother both were hidden in death
no brother's life would bloom for me again.
That is the law under which I gave you precedence,
my dearest brother, and that is why Creon thinks me
965 wrong, even a criminal, and now takes me
by the hand and leads me away,
unbedded, without bridal, without share
in marriage and in nurturing of children;
as lonely as you see me; without friends;
970 with fate against me I go to the vault of death
while still alive. What law of God have I broken?
Why should I still look to the gods in my misery?
Whom should I summon as ally? For indeed
because of piety I was called impious.
975 If this proceeding is good in the gods' eyes
I shall know my sin, once I have suffered.
But if Creon and his people are the wrongdoers
let their suffering be no worse than the injustice
they are meting out to me.
980 CHORUS: It is the same blasts, the tempests of the soul,
possess her.
CREON: Then for this her guards,
who are so slow, will find themselves in trouble.
ANTIGONE: [*Cries out.*] Oh, that word has come
very close to death.
985 CREON: I will not comfort you
with hope that the sentence will not be accomplished.
ANTIGONE: O my father's city, in Theban land,
O gods that sired my race,
I am led away, I have no more stay.
990 Look on me, princes of Thebes,
the last remnant of the old royal line;
see what I suffer and who makes me suffer
because I gave reverence to what claims reverence.
CHORUS: Danae suffered, too, when, her beauty lost, she gave
995 the light of heaven in exchange for brassbound walls,
and in the tomb-like cell was she hidden and held;
yet she was honored in her breeding, child,
and she kept, as guardian, the seed of Zeus
that came to her in a golden shower.[7]
1000 But there is some terrible power in destiny

---

7. Danae was locked away because it was prophesized that her son would kill her father. Zeus came down and impregnated her and the child who resulted fulfilled the prophecy.

and neither wealth nor war
nor tower nor black ships, beaten by the sea,
can give escape from it.

The hot-tempered son of Dryas,[8] the Edonian king,
in fury mocked Dionysus,   1005
who then held him in restraint
in a rocky dungeon.
So the terrible force and flower of his madness
drained away. He came to know the god
whom in frenzy he had touched with his mocking tongue,   1010
when he would have checked the inspired women
and the fire of Dionysus,
when he provoked the Muses[9] that love the lyre.
By the black rocks, dividing the sea in two,
are the shores of the Bosporus, Thracian Salmydessus.   1015
There the god of war who lives near the city
saw the terrible blinding wound
dealt by his savage wife
on Phineus' two sons.
She blinded and tore with the points of her shuttle,   1020
and her bloodied hands, those eyes
that else would have looked on her vengefully.
As they wasted away, they lamented
their unhappy fate that they were doomed
to be born of a mother cursed in her marriage.   1025
She traced her descent from the seed
of the ancient Erechtheidae.
In far-distant caves she was raised
among her father's storms, that child of Boreas
quick as a horse, over the steep hills,,   1030
a daughter of the gods.[1]
But, my child, the long-lived Fates[2]
bore hard upon her, too.

[*Enter* TEIRESIAS, *the blind prophet, led by a* BOY.]

TEIRESIAS: My lords of Thebes, we have come here together,
   one pair of eyes serving us both. For the blind   1035
   such must be the way of going, by a guide's leading.
CREON: What is the news, my old Teiresias?
TEIRESIAS: I will tell you; and you, listen to the prophet.
CREON: Never in the past have I turned from your advice.

---

8. Stricken with madness by Dionysus.   9. Nine sister goddesses of poetry, music, and the arts.
1. King Phineus's second wife blinded the children of his first wife, whom Phineus had imprisoned in a
cave.   2. Supernatural forces, usually represented as three old women, who determine the quality and
length of life.

1040 TEIRESIAS: And so you have steered well the ship of state.

CREON: I have benefited and can testify to that.

TEIRESIAS: Then realize you are on the razor edge
   of danger.

CREON: What can that be? I shudder to hear those words.

1045 TEIRESIAS: When you learn the signs recognized by my art
   you will understand.
   I sat at my ancient place of divination
   for watching the birds, where every bird finds shelter;
   and I heard an unwonted voice among them;
1050   they were horribly distressed, and screamed unmeaningly.
   I knew they were tearing each other murderously;
   the beating of their wings was a clear sign.
   I was full of fear; at once on all the altars,
   as they were fully kindled, I tasted the offerings,
1055   but the god of fire refused to burn from the sacrifice,
   and from the thighbones a dark stream of moisture
   oozed from the embers, smoked and sputtered.
   The gall bladder burst and scattered to the air
   and the streaming thighbones lay exposed
1060   from the fat wrapped round them—
   so much I learned from this boy here,
   the fading prophecies of a rite that failed.
   This boy here is my guide, as I am others'.
   This is the city's sickness—and your plans are the cause of it.
1065   For our altars and our sacrificial hearths
   are filled with the carrion meat of birds and dogs,
   torn from the flesh of Oedipus' poor son.
   So the gods will not take our prayers or sacrifice
   nor yet the flame from the thighbones, and no bird
1070   cries shrill and clear, so glutted
   are they with fat of the blood of the killed man.
   Reflect on these things, son. All men
   can make mistakes; but, once mistaken,
   a man is no longer stupid nor accursed
1075   who, having fallen on ill, tries to cure that ill,
   not taking a fine undeviating stand.
   It is obstinacy that convicts of folly.
   Yield to the dead man; do not stab him—
   now he is gone—what bravery is this,
1080   to inflict another death upon the dead?
   I mean you well and speak well for your good.
   It is never sweeter to learn from a good counselor
   than when he counsels to your benefit.

CREON: Old man, you are all archers, and I am your mark.
1085   I must be tried by your prophecies as well.

By the breed of you I have been bought and sold
and made a merchandise, for ages now.
But I tell you: make your profit from silver-gold
from Sardis and the gold from India
if you will. But this dead man you shall not hide   1090
in a grave, not though the eagles of Zeus should bear
the carrion, snatching it to the throne of Zeus itself.
Even so, I shall not so tremble at the pollution
to let you bury him.
               No, I am certain
no human has the power to pollute the gods.   1095
They fall, you old Teiresias, those men,
—so very clever—in a bad fall whenever
they eloquently speak vile words for profit.
TEIRESIAS: I wonder if there's a man who dares consider—
CREON: What do you mean? What sort of generalization   1100
  is this talk of yours?
TEIRESIAS: How much the best of possessions is the ability
  to listen to wise advice?
CREON: As I should imagine that the worst
  injury must be native stupidity.   1105
TEIRESIAS: Now that is exactly where your mind is sick.
CREON: I do not like to answer a seer with insults.
TEIRESIAS: But you do, when you say my prophecies are lies.
CREON: Well,
  the whole breed of prophets certainly loves money.   1110
TEIRESIAS: And the breed that comes from princes loves to take
  advantage—base advantage.
CREON: Do you realize
  you are speaking in such terms of your own prince?
TEIRESIAS: I know. But it is through me you have saved the city.
CREON: You are a wise prophet, but what you love is wrong.   1115
TEIRESIAS: You will force me to declare what should be hidden
  in my own heart.
CREON: Out with it—
  but only if your words are not for gain.
TEIRESIAS: They won't be for *your* gain—that I am sure of.
CREON: But realize you will not make a merchandise   1120
  of my decisions.
TEIRESIAS: And you must realize
  that you will not outlive many cycles more
  of this swift sun before you give in exchange
  one of your own loins bred, a corpse for a corpse,
  for you have thrust one that belongs above   1125
  below the earth, and bitterly dishonored
  a living soul by lodging her in the grave;

while one that belonged indeed to the underworld
gods you have kept on this earth without due share
1130 of rites of burial, of due funeral offerings,
a corpse unhallowed. With all of this you, Creon,
have nothing to do, nor have the gods above.
These acts of yours are violence, on your part.
And in requital the avenging Spirits
1135 of Death itself and the gods' Furies shall
after *your* deeds, lie in ambush for you, and
in their hands you shall be taken cruelly.
Now, look at this and tell me I was bribed
to say it! The delay will not be long
1140 before the cries of mourning in your house,
of men and women. All the cities will stir in hatred
against you, because their sons in mangled shreds
received their burial rites from dogs, from wild beasts
or when some bird of the air brought a vile stink
1145 to each city that contained the hearths of the dead.
These are the arrows that archer-like I launched—
you vexed me so to anger—at your heart.
You shall not escape their sting. You, boy,
lead me away to my house, so he may discharge
1150 his anger on younger men; so may he come to know
to bear a quieter tongue in his head and a better
mind than that now he carries in him.
CHORUS: That was a terrible prophecy, my lord.
The man has gone. Since these hairs of mine grew white
1155 from the black they once were, he has never spoken
a word of a lie to our city.
CREON: I know, I know.
My mind is all bewildered. To yield is terrible.
But by opposition to destroy my very being
1160 with a self-destructive curse must also be reckoned
in what is terrible.
CHORUS: You need good counsel, son of Menoeceus,
and need to take it.
CREON: What must I do, then? Tell me; I shall agree.
1165 CHORUS: The girl—go now and bring her up from her cave,
and for the exposed dead man, give him his burial.
CREON: That is really your advice? You would have me yield.
CHORUS: And quickly as you may, my lord. Swift harms
sent by the gods cut off the paths of the foolish.
1170 CREON: Oh, it is hard; I must give up what my heart
would have me do. But it is ill to fight
against what must be.
CHORUS: Go now, and do this;
do not give the task to others.

CREON: I will go,   1175
  just as I am. Come, servants, all of you;
  take axes in your hands; away with you
  to the place you see, there.
  For my part, since my intention is so changed,
  as I bound her myself, myself will free her.   1180
  I am afraid it may be best, in the end
  of life, to have kept the old accepted laws.
CHORUS: You of many names,[3] glory of the Cadmeian
        bride, breed of loud thundering Zeus;
        you who watch over famous Italy;   1185
        you who rule where all are welcome in Eleusis;
        in the sheltered plains of Deo—
        O Bacchus that dwells in Thebes,
        the mother city of Bacchanals,
        by the flowing stream of Ismenus,   1190
        in the ground sown by the fierce dragon's teeth.

        You are he on whom the murky gleam of torches glares,
        above the twin peaks of the crag
        where come the Corycean nymphs
        to worship you, the Bacchanals;   1195
        and the stream of Castalia has seen you, too;
        and you are he that the ivy-clad
        slopes of Nisaean hills,
        and the green shore ivy-clustered,
        sent to watch over the roads of Thebes,   1200
        where the immortal Evoe chant[4] rings out.

        It is Thebes which you honor most of all cities,
        you and your mother both,
        she who died by the blast of Zeus' thunderbolt.
        And now when the city, with all its folk,   1205
        is gripped by a violent plague,
        come with healing foot, over the slopes of Parnassus,
        over the moaning strait.
        You lead the dance of the fire-breathing stars,
        you are master of the voices of the night.   1210
        True-born child of Zeus, appear,
        my lord, with your Thyiad attendants,
        who in frenzy all night long
        dance in your house, Iacchus,
        dispenser of gifts.   1215
MESSENGER: You who live by the house of Cadmus and Amphion,[5]
  hear me. There is no condition of man's life
  that stands secure. As such I would not

---

3. Refers to Dionysus.   4. Come forth, come forth!   5. A name for Thebes.

praise it or blame. It is chance that sets upright;
1220 it is chance that brings down the lucky and the unlucky
each in his turn. For men, that belong to death,
there is no prophet of established things.
Once Creon was a man worthy of envy—
of my envy, at least. For he saved this city
1225 of Thebes from her enemies, and attained
the throne of the land, with all a king's power.
He guided it right. His race bloomed
with good children. But when a man forfeits joy
I do not count his life as life, but only
1230 a life trapped in a corpse.
Be rich within your house, yes greatly rich,
if so you will, and live in a prince's style.
If the gladness of these things is gone, I would not
give the shadow of smoke for the rest,
1235 as against joy.
CHORUS: What is the sorrow of our princes
of which you are the messenger?
MESSENGER: Death; and the living are guilty of their deaths.
CHORUS: But who is the murderer? Who the murdered? Tell us.
1240 MESSENGER: Haemon is dead; the hand that shed his blood
was his very own.
CHORUS: Truly his own hand? Or his father's?
MESSENGER: His own hand, in his anger
against his father for a murder.
1245 CHORUS: Prophet, how truly you have made good your word!
MESSENGER: These things are so; you may debate the rest.
Here I see Creon's wife Eurydice
approaching. Unhappy woman!
Does she come from the house as hearing about her son
1250 or has she come by chance?
EURYDICE: I heard your words, all you men of Thebes, as I
was going out to greet Pallas[6] with my prayers.
I was just drawing back the bolts of the gate
to open it when a cry struck through my ears
1255 telling of my household's ruin. I fell backward
in terror into the arms of my servants; I fainted.
But tell me again, what is the story? I
will hear it as one who is no stranger to sorrow.
MESSENGER: Dear mistress, I will tell you, for I was there,
1260 and I will leave out no word of the truth.
Why should I comfort you and then tomorrow
be proved a liar? The truth is always best.

---

6. Athena, goddess of wisdom.

I followed your husband, at his heels, to the end of the plain
where Polyneices' body still lay unpitied,
and torn by dogs. We prayed to Hecate, goddess   1265
of the crossroads, and also to Pluto[7]
that they might restrain their anger and turn kind.
And him we washed with sacred lustral water
and with fresh-cut boughs we burned what was left of him
and raised a high mound of his native earth;   1270
then we set out again for the hollowed rock,
death's stone bridal chamber for the girl.
Someone then heard a voice of bitter weeping
while we were still far off, coming from that unblest room.
The man came to tell our master Creon of it.   1275
As the king drew nearer, there swarmed about him
a cry of misery but no clear words.
He groaned and in an anguished mourning voice
cried "Oh, am I a true prophet? Is this the road
that I must travel, saddest of all my wayfaring?   1280
It is my son's voice that haunts my ear. Servants,
get closer, quickly. Stand around the tomb
and look. There is a gap there where the stones
have been wrenched away; enter there, by the very mouth,
and see whether I recognize the voice of Haemon   1285
or if the gods deceive me." On the command
of our despairing master we went to look.
In the furthest part of the tomb we saw her, hanging
by her neck. She had tied a noose of muslin on it.
Haemon's hands were about her waist embracing her,   1290
while he cried for the loss of his bride gone to the dead,
and for all his father had done, and his own sad love.
When Creon saw him he gave a bitter cry,
went in and called to him with a groan: "Poor son!
what have you done? What can you have meant?   1295
What happened to destroy you? Come out, I pray you!"
The boy glared at him with savage eyes, and then
spat in his face, without a word of answer.
He drew his double-hilted sword. As his father
ran to escape him, Haemon failed to strike him,   1300
and the poor wretch in anger at himself
leaned on his sword and drove it halfway in,
into his ribs. Then he folded the girl to him,
in his arms, while he was conscious still,
and gasping poured a sharp stream of bloody drops   1305
on her white cheeks. There they lie,

7. King of the underworld. *Hecate:* goddess of witchcraft.

the dead upon the dead. So he has won
the pitiful fulfillment of his marriage
within death's house. In this human world he has shown
1310   how the wrong choice in plans is for a man
his greatest evil.

CHORUS: What do you make of this? My lady is gone,
without a word of good or bad.

MESSENGER: I, too,
am lost in wonder. I am inclined to hope
1315   that hearing of her son's death she could not
open her sorrow to the city, but chose rather
within her house to lay upon her maids
the mourning for the household grief. Her judgment
is good; she will not make any false step.

1320   CHORUS: I do not know. To me this over-heavy silence
seems just as dangerous as much empty wailing.

MESSENGER: I will go in and learn if in her passionate
heart she keeps hidden some secret purpose.
You are right; there is sometimes danger in too much silence.

1325   CHORUS: Here comes our king himself. He bears in his hands
a memorial all too clear;
it is a ruin of none other's making,
purely his own if one dare to say that.

CREON: The mistakes of a blinded man
1330   are themselves rigid and laden with death.
You look at us the killer and the killed
of the one blood. Oh, the awful blindness
of those plans of mine. My son, you were so young,
so young to die. You were freed from the bonds of life
1335   through no folly of your own—only through mine.

CHORUS: I think you have learned justice—but too late.

CREON: Yes, I have learned it to my bitterness. At this moment
God has sprung on my head with a vast weight
and struck me down. He shook me in my savage ways;
1340   he has overturned my joy, has trampled it,
underfoot. The pains men suffer
are pains indeed.

SECOND MESSENGER: My lord, you have troubles and a store besides;
some are there in your hands, but there are others
1345   you will surely see when you come to your house.

CREON: What trouble can there be beside these troubles?

SECOND MESSENGER: The queen is dead. She was indeed true mother
of the dead son. She died, poor lady,
by recent violence upon herself.

1350   CREON: Haven of death, you can never have enough.

Why, why do you destroy me?
You messenger, who have brought me bitter news,
what is this tale you tell?
It is a dead man that you kill again—
what new message of yours is this, boy?   1355
Is this new slaughter of a woman
a doom to lie on the pile of the dead?
CHORUS: You can see. It is no longer
hidden in a corner.

> [*By some stage device, perhaps the so-called eccyclema, the inside of the palace
> is shown, with the body of the dead* QUEEN.]

CREON: Here is yet another horror   1360
for my unhappy eyes to see.
What doom still waits for me?
I have but now taken in my arms my son,
and again I look upon another dead face.
Poor mother and poor son!   1365
SECOND MESSENGER: She stood at the altar, and with keen whetted knife
she suffered her darkening eyes to close.
First she cried in agony recalling the noble fate of Megareus,[8]
who died before all this,
and then for the fate of this son; and in the end   1370
she cursed you for the evil you had done
in killing her sons.
CREON: I am distracted with fear. Why does not someone
strike a two-edged sword right through me?
I am dissolved in an agony of misery.   1375
SECOND MESSENGER: You were indeed accused
by her that is dead
of Haemon's and of Megareus' death.
CREON: By what kind of violence did she find her end?
SECOND MESSENGER: Her own hand struck her to the entrails   1380
when she heard of her son's lamentable death.
CREON: These acts can never be made to fit another
to free me from the guilt. It was I that killed her.
Poor wretch that I am, I say it is true!
Servants, lead me away, quickly, quickly.   1385
I am no more a live man than one dead.
CHORUS: What you say is for the best—if there be a best
in evil such as this. For the shortest way
is best with troubles that lie at our feet.
CREON: O, let it come, let it come,   1390

---

8. Another son of Creon.

that best of fates that waits on my last day.
Surely best fate of all. Let it come, let it come!
That I may never see one more day's light!

CHORUS: These things are for the future. We must deal
1395   with what impends. What in the future is to care for
rests with those whose duty it is
to care for them.

CREON: At least, all that _I_ want
is in that prayer of mine.

1400 CHORUS: Pray for no more at all. For what is destined
for us, men mortal, there is no escape.

CREON: Lead me away, a vain silly man
who killed you, son, and you, too, lady.
I did not mean to, but I did.

1405 I do not know where to turn my eyes
to look to, for support.
Everything in my hands is crossed. A most unwelcome fate
has leaped upon me.

CHORUS: Wisdom is far the chief element in happiness
1410 and, secondly, no irreverence towards the gods.
But great words of haughty men exact
in retribution blows as great
and in old age teach wisdom.

       THE END

ca. 441 B.C.E.

RICHARD C. JEBB

from The Antigone of Sophocles*

The issue defined in the opening scene,—the conflict of divine with human law,—remains the central interest throughout. The action, so simple in plan, is varied by masterly character-drawing, both in the two principal figures, and in those lesser persons who contribute gradations of light and shade to the picture. There is no halting in the march of the drama; at each successive step we become more and more keenly interested to see how this great conflict is to end; and when the tragic climax is reached, it is worthy of such a progress.

    The simplicity of the plot is due to the clearness with which two principles are opposed to each other. _Creon represents the duty of obeying the State's laws; Antigone,_

---

*From Sir Richard C. Jebb, ed., _The Antigone of Sophocles,_ abr. by E. S. Shuckburgh (orig. ed., 1902; repr. Cambridge, Eng., and New York: Cambridge University Press, 1984), pp. xvii–xix.

the duty of listening to the private conscience. The definiteness and the power with which the play puts the case on each side are conclusive proofs that the question had assumed a distinct shape before the poet's mind. It is the only instance in which a Greek play has for its central theme a practical problem of conduct, involving issues, moral and political, which might be discussed on similar grounds in any age and in any country of the world. Greek Tragedy, owing partly to the limitations which it placed on detail, was better suited than modern drama to raise such a question in a general form. The *Antigone,* indeed, raises the question in a form as nearly abstract as is compatible with the nature of drama. The case of Antigone is a thoroughly typical one for the private conscience, because the particular thing which she believes that she ought to do was, in itself, a thing which every Greek of that age recognised as a most sacred duty,—viz.,[1] to render burial rites to kinsfolk. This advantage was not devised by Sophocles; it came to him as part of the story which he was to dramatise; but it forms an additional reason for thinking that, when he dramatised that story in the precise manner which he has chosen, he had a consciously dialectical purpose. Such a purpose was wholly consistent, in this instance, with the artist's first aim,—to produce a work of art. It is because Creon and Antigone are so human that the controversy which they represent becomes so vivid.

But how did Sophocles intend us to view the result? What is the drift of the words at the end, which say that 'wisdom is the supreme part of happiness'? If this wisdom, or prudence, means, generally, the observance of due limit, may not the suggested moral be that both the parties to the conflict were censurable? As Creon overstepped the due limit when, by his edict, he infringed the divine law, so Antigone also overstepped it when she defied the edict. The drama would thus be a conflict between two persons, each of whom defends an intrinsically sound principle, but defends it in a mistaken way; and both persons are therefore punished. This view, of which Boeckh is the chief representative, has found several supporters. Among them is Hegel:—'In the view of the Eternal Justice, both were wrong, because they were one-sided, but at the same time both were right.'[2]

Or does the poet rather intend us to feel that Antigone is wholly in the right,— *i.e.,* that nothing of which the human lawgiver could complain in her was of a moment's account beside the supreme duty which she was fulfilling;—and that Creon was wholly in the wrong,—*i.e.,* that the intrinsically sound maxims of government on which he relies lose all validity when opposed to the higher law which he was breaking? If that was the poet's meaning, then the 'wisdom' taught by the issue of the drama means the sense which duly subordinates human to divine law,—teaching that, if the two come into conflict, human law must yield.

A careful study of the play itself will suffice (I think) to show that the second of these two views is the true one. Sophocles has allowed Creon to put his case ably, and (in a measure from which an inferior artist might have shrunk) he has been content to make Antigone merely a nobly heroic woman, not a being exempt from human passion and human weakness; but none the less does he

---

1. Namely (abbreviation of the Latin *videlicet*).   2. *Religionsphilosophie,* II. 114. (RCJ)

mean us to feel that, in this controversy, the right is wholly with her, and the wrong wholly with her judge.

* * *

MAURICE BOWRA

from Sophoclean Tragedy*

Modern critics who do not share Sophocles' conviction about the paramount duty of burying the dead and who attach more importance than he did to the claims of political authority have tended to underestimate the way in which he justifies Antigone against Creon. To their support they have called in the great name of Hegel, who was fascinated by the play and advanced remarkable views on it. His remarks have been taken out of their context, and he has been made responsible for the opinion that Sophocles dramatized a conflict not between right and wrong but between right and right, that Antigone and Creon are equally justified in their actions and that the tragedy arises out of this irreconcilable conflict. Hegel's own words lend some support to this view: 'In the view of eternal justice both were wrong, because they were one-sided; but at the same time both were right.' But if we look at Hegel's observations in their own place, we find that this summary hardly conveys his full meaning. He was thinking of something much vaster than the play, of the whole logic of history which is here symbolized in a concrete example. In this the conflict of opposites ends by producing a synthesis which is itself right. The conclusion is what matters, and that is different from saying that both sides in the conflict are themselves right. The tragic conclusion is, so to speak, a lesson of history, a fact which cannot be denied, real and therefore right, but the conflict which precedes it cannot be judged in isolation and neither side in it is right or wrong except in a relative sense. Hegel used the *Antigone* to illustrate his view of tragedy and his view of existence. He drew his own conclusions about the actions portrayed in it, as he was fully entitled to do. But his views are not those of Sophocles, and he should not be thought to maintain that Creon and Antigone were equally right in the eyes of their creator.

Sophocles leaves no doubt what conclusion should be drawn from the *Antigone*. He closes with a moral on the lips of the Chorus which tells the audience what to think:

> Wisdom has first place in happiness,
> And to fail not in reverence to the gods.
> The big words of the arrogant

*From Sir Maurice Bowra, *Sophoclean Tragedy* (Oxford: Clarendon Press, 1944), pp. 65–67.

> Lay big stripes on the boasters' backs.
> They pay the price
> And learn in old age to be wise.[1]

This can refer to no one but Creon, whose lack of wisdom has brought him to misery, who has shown irreverence to the gods in refusing burial to Polynices, been chastened for his proud words, and learned wisdom in his old age. To this lesson the preceding action in which Creon has lost son and wife and happiness has already made its effective contribution. We may be sure that the Chorus speak for the poet. It is as silent about Antigone as it is emphatic about Creon. There is no hint that she has in any way acted wrongly or that her death should be regarded as a righteous punishment. Of course the final words do not sum up everything important in the play, but we may reasonably assume that they pass judgement on its salient events as they appear in retrospect when the action is finished. There is no real problem about the ethical intention of the *Antigone*. It shows the fall of a proud man, and its lesson is that the gods punish pride and irreverence. But what matters much more than the actual conclusion is the means by which it is reached, the presentation of the different parties in the conflict, the view that we take of each, the feelings that are forced on us. The interest and power of the *Antigone* lie in the tangled issues which are unravelled in it.

A conclusion so clear as this is only worth reaching if it has been preceded by a drama in which the issues are violent and complex. The rights and wrongs of the case must not throughout be so obvious as they are at the end; the audience must feel that the issue is difficult, that there is much to be said on both sides, that the ways of the gods are hard to discern. Without this the play will fail in dramatic and human interest. And Sophocles has taken great care to show the issues in their full difficulty before he provides a solution for them. He makes the two protagonists appear in such a light that at intervals we doubt if all the right is really with Antigone and all the wrong with Creon. To Creon, who defies the divine ordinance of burial, he gives arguments and sentiments which sound convincing enough when they are put forward, and many must feel that he has some good reason to act as he does. On the other hand Antigone, who fearlessly vindicates the laws of the gods, is by no means a gentle womanly creature who suffers martyrdom for the right. She may be right, but there are moments when we qualify our approval of her, when she seems proud and forbidding in her determination to do her duty and to do it alone. For these variations in our feelings Sophocles is responsible. He makes us find some right in Creon, some wrong in Antigone, even if we are misled about both. He built his play on a contrast not between obvious wrong and obvious right but between the real arrogance of Creon and the apparent arrogance of Antigone. The first deceives by its fine persuasive sentiments; the second works through Antigone's refusal to offer concessions or to consider any point of view but her own. This contrast runs through

---

1. Bowra's translation.

much of the play, accounts for misunderstandings of what takes place in it, provides false clues and suggests wrong conclusions, and adds greatly to the intensity of the drama. When a play is written round a moral issue, that issue must be a real problem about which more than one view is tenable until all the relevant facts are known. So the *Antigone* dramatizes a conflict which was familiar to the Periclean age, would excite divergent judgements and feelings, and make some support Antigone, some Creon, until the end makes all clear.

* * *

BERNARD KNOX

Introduction to Sophocles: The Three Theban Plays*

The opening scenes show us the conflicting claims and loyalties of the two adversaries, solidly based, in both cases, on opposed political and religious principles. This is of course the basic insight of Hegel's famous analysis of the play: he sees it as "a collision between the two highest moral powers." What is wrong with them, in his view, is that they are both "one-sided." But Hegel goes much further than that. He was writing in the first half of the nineteenth century, a period of fervent German nationalism in which the foundations of the unified German state were laid: his views on loyalty to the state were very much those of Creon. "Creon," he says, "is not a tyrant, he is really a moral power. He is not in the wrong."

However, as the action develops the favorable impression created by Creon's opening speech is quickly dissipated. His announcement of his decision to expose the corpse, the concluding section of his speech, is couched in violent, vindictive terms—"carrion for the birds and dogs to tear"[1]—which stand in shocking contrast to the ethical generalities that precede it. This hint of a cruel disposition underlying the statesmanlike façade is broadened by the threat of torture leveled at the sentry and the order to execute Antigone in the presence of Haemon, her betrothed. And as he meets resistance from a series of opponents—Antigone's contemptuous defiance, the rational, political advice of his son Haemon, the imperious summons to obedience of the gods' spokesman, Tiresias—he swiftly abandons the temperate rhetoric of his inaugural address for increasingly savage invective. Against the two sanctions invoked by Antigone, the demands of blood relationship, the rights and privileges of the gods below, he rages in terms ranging from near-blasphemous defiance to scornful mockery.

*From Sophocles, *The Three Theban Plays: Antigone, Oedipus the King, Oedipus at Colonus*, trans. by Robert Fagles, intro. and notes by Bernard Knox (New York: Penguin, 1982), pp. 41–47, 53. 1. Knox's references are to Robert Fagles's translation, printed in *The Three Theban Plays* (New York, 1982).

> Sister's child or closer in blood
> than all my family clustered at my altar
> worshiping Guardian Zeus—she'll never escape,
> . . . the most barbaric death.

He will live to regret this wholesale denial of the family bond, for it is precisely through that family clustered at his altar that his punishment will be administered, in the suicides of his son and his wife, both of whom die cursing him.

And for Antigone's appeals to Hades, the great god of the underworld to whom the dead belong, Creon has nothing but contempt; for him "Hades" is simply a word meaning "death," a sentence he is prepared to pass on anyone who stands in his way. He threatens the sentry with torture as a prelude: "simple death won't be enough for you." When asked if he really intends to deprive Haemon of his bride he answers sarcastically: "Death will do it for me." He expects to see Antigone and Ismene turn coward "once they see Death coming for their lives." With a derisive comment he tells his son to abandon Antigone: "Spit her out, / . . . Let her find a husband down among the dead [in Hades' house]." And he dismisses Antigone's reverence for Hades and the rights of the dead with mockery as he condemns her to be buried alive: "There let her pray to the one god she worships: / Death." But this Hades is not something to be so lightly referred to, used or mocked. In the great choral ode which celebrated Man's progress and powers this was the one insurmountable obstacle that confronted him:

> ready, resourceful man!
>   Never without resources
> never an impasse as he marches on the future—
> only Death, from Death alone he will find no rescue . . .

And Creon, in the end, looking at the corpse of his son and hearing the news of his wife's suicide, speaks of Hades for the first time with the fearful respect that is his due, not as an instrument of policy or a subject for sardonic word-play, but as a divine power, a dreadful presence: "harbor of Death, so choked, so hard to cleanse!— / why me? why are you killing me?"

Creon is forced at last to recognize the strength of those social and religious imperatives that Antigone obeys, but long before this happens he has abandoned the principles which he had proclaimed as authority for his own actions. His claim to be representative of the whole community is forgotten as he refuses to accept Haemon's report that the citizens, though they dare not speak out, disapprove of his action; he denies the relevance of such a report even if true—"And is Thebes about to tell me how to rule?"—and finally repudiates his principles in specific terms by an assertion that the city belongs to him—"The city *is* the king's—that's the law!" This autocratic phrase puts the finishing touch to the picture Sophocles is drawing for his audience: Creon has now displayed all the characteristics of the "tyrant," a despotic ruler who seizes power and retains it by intimidation and force. Athens had lived under the rule of a "tyrant" before the democracy was established in 508 B.C., and the name and institution were still regarded with abhorrence. Creon goes on to abandon the gods whose temples crown the city's high places, the gods he once claimed as his own, and his language is even more violent. The blind prophet Tiresias tells him that the birds and dogs are fouling the altars of the city's gods with the carrion flesh of Polynices; he must bury the corpse. His furious reply begins with a characteristic accusation that the prophet has been bribed (the sentry had this same accusation flung at him), but what follows is a hideously blasphemous defiance of those gods Creon once claimed to serve:

> You'll never bury that body in the grave,
> not even if Zeus's eagles rip the corpse
> and wing their rotten pickings off to the throne of god!

At this high point in his stubborn rage (he will break by the end of the scene and try, too late, to avoid the divine wrath), he is sustained by nothing except his tyrannical insistence on his own will, come what may, and his outraged refusal to be defeated by a woman. "No woman," he says, "is going to lord it over me." "I'm not the man, not now: she is the man / if this victory goes to her and she goes free."

Antigone, on her side, is just as indifferent to Creon's principles of action as he is to hers. She mentions the city only in her last agonized laments before she is led off to her living death:

> O my city, all your fine rich sons!
> . . . springs of the Dirce,
> holy grove of Thebes . . .

But here she is appealing for sympathy to the city over the heads of the chorus, the city's symbolic representative on stage. In all her arguments with Creon and Ismene she speaks as one wholly unconscious of the rights and duties membership in the city confers and imposes, as if no unit larger than the family existed. It is a position just as extreme as Creon's insistence that the demands of the city take precedence over all others, for the living and the dead alike.

Like Creon, she acts in the name of gods, but they are different gods. There is more than a little truth in Creon's mocking comment that Hades is "the one god she worships." She is from the beginning "much possessed by death"; together with Ismene she is the last survivor of a doomed family, burdened with such sorrow that she finds life hardly worth living. "Who on earth," she says to Creon, "alive in the midst of so much grief as I, / could fail to find his death a rich reward?" She has performed the funeral rites for mother, father and her brother Eteocles:

> I washed you with my hands,
> I dressed you all, I poured the cups
> across your tombs.

She now sacrifices her life to perform a symbolic burial, a handful of dust sprinkled on the corpse, for Polynices, the brother left to rot on the battlefield. She looks forward to her reunion with her beloved dead in that dark kingdom where Persephone, the bride of Hades, welcomes the ghosts. It is in the name of Hades, one of the three great gods who rule the universe, that she defends the right of Polynices and of all human beings to proper burial. "Death [Hades] longs for the same rites for all," she tells Creon—for patriot and traitor alike; she rejects Ismene's plea to be allowed to share her fate with an appeal to the same stern authority: "Who did the work? / Let the dead and the god of death bear witness!" In Creon's gods, the city's patrons and defenders, she shows no interest at all. Zeus she mentions twice: once as the source of all the calamities that have fallen and are still to fall on the house of Oedipus, and once again at the beginning of her famous speech about the unwritten laws. But the context here suggests strongly that she is thinking about Zeus in his special relationship to the underworld, Zeus *Chthonios* (Underworld Zeus). "It wasn't Zeus," she says,

> who made this proclamation. . . .
> Nor did that Justice, dwelling with the gods
> beneath the earth, ordain such laws for men.

From first to last her religious devotion and duty are to the divine powers of the world below, the masters of that world where lie her family dead, to which she herself, reluctant but fascinated, is irresistibly drawn.

But, like Creon, she ends by denying the great sanctions she invoked to justify her action. In his case the process was spread out over the course of several scenes, as he reacted to each fresh pressure that was brought to bear on him; Antigone turns her back on the claims of blood relationship and the nether gods in one sentence: three lines in Greek, no more. They are the emotional high point of the speech she makes just before she is led off to her death.

> Never, I tell you,
> if I had been the mother of children
> or if my husband died, exposed and rotting—
> I'd never have taken this ordeal upon myself,
> never defied our people's will.

These unexpected words are part of the long speech that concludes a scene of lyric lamentation and is in effect her farewell to the land of the living. They are certainly a total repudiation of her proud claim that she acted as the champion of the unwritten laws and the infernal gods, for, as she herself told Creon, those laws and those gods have no preferences, they long "for the same rites for all." And her assertion that she would not have done for her children what she has done for Polynices is a spectacular betrayal of that fanatical loyalty to blood relationship which she urged on Ismene and defended against Creon, for there is no closer relationship imaginable than that between the mother and the children of her own body. Creon turned his back on his guiding principles step by step, in reaction to opposition based on those principles; Antigone's rejection of her public values is just as complete, but it is the sudden product of a lonely, brooding introspection, a last-minute assessment of her motives, on which the imminence of death confers a merciless clarity. She did it because Polynices was her brother; she would not have done it for husband or child. She goes on to justify this disturbing statement by an argument which is more disturbing still: husband and children, she says, could be replaced by others but, since her parents are dead, she could never have another brother. It so happens that we can identify the source of this strange piece of reasoning; it is a story in the *Histories* of Sophocles' friend Herodotus (a work from which Sophocles borrowed material more than once). Darius the Great King had condemned to death for treason a Persian noble, Intaphrenes, and all the men of his family. The wife of Intaphrenes begged importunately for their lives; offered one, she chose her brother's. When Darius asked her why, she replied in words that are unmistakably the original of Antigone's lines. But what makes sense in the story makes less in the play. The wife of Intaphrenes saves her brother's life, but Polynices is already dead; Antigone's phrase "no brother could ever spring to light again" would be fully appropriate only if Antigone had managed to save Polynices' life rather than bury his corpse.

For this reason, and also because of some stylistic anomalies in this part of the speech, but most of all because they felt that the words are unworthy of the Antigone who spoke so nobly for the unwritten laws, many great scholars and also a great poet and dramatist, Goethe, have refused to believe that Sophocles wrote them. "I would give a great deal," Goethe told his friend Eckermann in 1827, "if some talented scholar could prove that these lines were interpolated, not genuine." Goethe did not know that the attempt had already been made, six years earlier; many others have tried since—Sir Richard Jebb, the greatest English editor of Sophocles, pronounced against them—and opinion today is still divided. Obviously a decision on this point is of vital significance for the interpretation of the play as a whole: with these lines removed, Antigone goes to her prison-tomb with no flicker of self-doubt, the flawless champion of the family bond and the unwritten laws, "whole as the marble, founded as the rock"—unlike Creon, she is not, in the end, reduced to recognizing that her motive is purely personal.

* * *

The gods do not praise Antigone, nor does anyone else in the play—except the young man who loves her so passionately that he cannot bear to live without her. Haemon tells his father what the Thebans are saying behind his back, the "murmurs in the dark": that Antigone deserves not death but "a glowing crown of gold!" Whether this is a true report (and the chorus does not praise Antigone even when they have been convinced that she was right) or just his own feelings attributed to others for the sake of his argument, it is a timely reminder of Antigone's heroic status. In the somber world of the play, against the background of so many sudden deaths and the dark mystery of the divine dispensation, her courage and steadfastness are a gleam of light; she is the embodiment of the only consolation tragedy can offer—that in certain heroic natures unmerited suffering and death can be met with a greatness of soul which, because it is purely human, brings honor to us all.

GEORGE STEINER*

from Antigones

In respect of any text longer than a short lyric, the concept of total grasp is a fiction. Our minds are not so constructed as to be able to hold in steady and complete view a language-object of the dimensions and complexities of Sophocles' *Antigone*. We cannot, for purposes of rounded inspection and mental reconstitution, circumvent a work of literature as we do a piece of sculpture. The angles of perception from which the play can be approached, the principles of selection or emphasis which are brought to bear on the text's multiple components when one seeks to arrive at a working model of unity, are as diverse as are the linguistic sensibilities, the cultural inheritance, the pragmatic interests, of different individuals.

Even where drafts, preliminary sketches, or statements of intention survive, we can hardly hope to reconstruct the inward process of assemblage and unification as it is experienced and reported (amost invariably after the fact) by the artist himself. Such famous admissions as that of Tolstoy in reference to the 'unexpected' and 'unwilled' evolution of the character of Anna Karenina in the novel suggest that the genesis of poetic forms is, at certain points at least, productively resistant and opaque to the previsions and control of the writer. At some moment in the dynamics of the subconscious, witness Henry James's notebooks, the initial 'germ', the incident, memory, felt configuration, from which the work develops, modulate into a vision or programme of unison. But whether the poet, dramatist, or novelist truly sees his text as an interactive whole, or whether the claim to such perception is, where it is made, itself a necessary fiction, remains uncertain. We cannot hope to describe what *Antigone* was, what it became in the course of composition or retrospection, to Sophocles.

Stanislavsky's[1] work-notes and those of other producers show that the means whereby a particular staging of a play is given its unifying style, its performative coherence, are the result of intricate, fluid adjustments between the producer's internal ideal and the theatrical resources in fact available to him. The method is one of compromise and of choice between practical options. Even the most comprehensive production, the production most intentionally faithful to the text, will elide certain aspects in order to emphasize others. From the nearly boundless range of conceivable constructs, the producer selects a dominant shape, a key-note and instrumentation. * * * The actor's sense of the drama is, in its turn, a fascinating collage. Centred on his own part and on the immediate context of his memorization and stage-movements, the actor's *Antigone* is an angular, fragmented digest of a larger, partly hidden text. Creon's play is never the same as Antigone's; neither will have the same sense and remembrance of

*From George Steiner, *Antigones* (New York and Oxford: Oxford University Press, 1984), pp. 288–292, 295–300.   1. Constantin Stanislavsky (1863–1938), Russian theatrical director and cofounder of the Moscow Art Theatre.

pace or proportion as we would find it in the play of the Messenger. Drama is more subject to such varieties of deconstruction than is any other literary genre (a fact on which Stoppard's brilliant conceit in *Rosencrantz and Guildenstern*[2] is founded).

It is in the face of such fragmentation and selective practicalities that the scholar, that the philologist, will advance his claim to a total view. Working letter by letter, word by word, line by line, the philologist and textual scholar aims to exclude nothing and to insinuate no arbitrary priorities. He would see and present Sophocles' *Antigone* 'as it stands'. Yet there is a sense, going far beyond the problem of scholarly disagreements, in which the neutral, disinterested assemblage by the philologist decomposes a literary text more drastically than does any other approach. For in ways which are at once a banality and an enigma, a literary text, a work of art that has in it any genuine authority, is not only more than the sum of its parts. It is, in a palpable sense, the denial of its own assembling. The organic nature of a great poem or play is, to be sure, seen metaphorically. We cannot define rigorously, let alone quantify, the felt analogy to living forms. But we know it to be justified; and we know that the agencies of autonomous being in literature and in art act beyond and even in repudiation of any anatomy of discrete thematic, structural, or technical features. There can be no enumeration of that which makes up the vital whole of Sophocles' *Antigone*. But in their impartiality towards detail, in their obligatory reduction of substance to material embodiment (sense is brought back as closely as possible to lexical–grammatical instrumentality), philology and textual scholarship *are* enumerative. The philological perspective is precisely that which postulates an equation, arduous to resolve but fundamental nevertheless, between the totality of significant presence and the aggregate of distinct formal units. This is why there is an inherent conflict between thought and scholarship, between the positivism of the philological and the recreative, metaphorically underwritten aims of hermeneutics.[3]

This does not mean that the literary critic or the 'slow reader'—whose interests I have sought to represent throughout this study—have any privileged access to a unifying vision. There is no insurance of clear-sightedness in criticism. We have seen that critical readings of *Antigone* are under direct or oblique, implicit or explicit, pressure of occasion, of particular epistemologies, of theoretical and practical orders of priority. The eye of the critic is personal; his focus will be argumentative and strategic, most especially where it invokes alleged principles of canonic generality. The categories of meaning which critical analysis and valuation graft on a text are, at best, clarifying models. They make salient and throw into relief. Honest literary criticism is simply that which makes its purposed constructions most plainly visible and open to challenge.

The successive compositions and decompositions, elucidations and shadings, fragmentations and compactions which the act of reading brings to a written text, are of such delicate multiplicity that we have no normative or verifiable account of them. The pragmatic context, material as well as cultural, is as much

2. Tom Stoppard (b. 1937); *Rosencrantz and Guildenstern Are Dead* is an amusing reworking of Shakespeare's *Hamlet.*   3. The process of interpretation.

a part of the dynamics of reading as is the psychology of the individual reader. Both context and psyche are, in turn, in constant and interactive motion. Rereading the identical passage or book, we are already other than we were. As we recollect or forget, sequent notices and internalizations of a text, layers, sediments of expectation and surprise, of recognition and spontaneous reaction, are deposited not only in the conscious mind, but in the subconscious where the reception of language probably exfoliates and dissolves into a more general coding of images, symbols, and phonetic associations. In the deep-seated and involuntary circulation of consciousness, these more diffuse semantic forms return, as it were, to the surface, to illuminate or obscure the more overt processes of understanding. Master readers are, so far as we can tell, no more frequent than major critics (I would guess that they are, in fact, rarer).* * *

It is my own impression that two contrary currents are operative in serious reading, in that (lesser) work of art which is the product of a *lecture bien faite*.[4] As concentration deepens, as noise and scattering are excised, to a greater or lesser degree, from the narrowing beam of attention, it is local detail that forces itself into the foreground of notice. This foreshortening, which is indispensable to our observance of singularity, of executive techniques, of stylistic specificities, inevitably fragments the text. But a counter-current of recomposition is also at work. Even as the eye looks away momentarily from the written passage, even as the local unit of textual material—the word, the sentence, the paragraph, the stanza in the poem, the scene in the play, the chapter in the novel—is receding into more or less retentive recollection, an erosion towards unity occurs. The detail is made less distinct as it enters into a largely subconscious, provisional construct of the whole. A memory trained to art will include within itself the skills of forgetting; it will smooth the sharp edges of the particular as our fingers smooth the edge of the stone before inserting it in the mosaic.

None the less, in even the most scrupulous of slow readings, the view which emerges of the text as a whole is 'angled' and selective. Where it exceeds the bounds of the verse lyric or prose vignette (it is the calculated observance of such dimensions which makes immediately unforgettable and irrefutable certain parables of Kafka), no literary work is held whole and unwavering in attention and memory. With each rereading, moreover, a new construct, a new assemblage is made. Details previously privileged are set in the background or elided; elements previously slighted or altogether unnoticed move into prominence. The sense of the whole may be strong, but it remains kaleidoscopic and subject to change. Tests have shown that the summaries which even the most attentive of readers gives of a work whose organic shape, whose coherence, are vivid to him will, on each occasion, differ.

* * *

* * * [T]he influence of commentary, particularly where it is of a philosophic or political tenor, * * * acts indirectly. Not very many general readers will have come across Hegel's *Antigone* interpretations at first hand. But the Hegelian read-

4. Literally, "well-done reading" (French).

ing of the play as a dialectical conflict of equal opposites has been widely disseminated in the climate of literacy as well as that of theatrical presentation. Jacques Lacan's[5] remarks on *Antigone* (in the seminar sequence entitled *L'Éthique de la psychanalyse*) may not, as yet, be generally accessible. But his view of Creon as the 'denier of desire', as one whose refusal of the *discours du désire* entails the choice of death, will, by osmosis of fashion, be diffused.

The question is this: to what extent is one's personal experience of Sophocles' *Antigone* a product of the palimpsest of commentaries and judgements which now overlie the 'original', to which, indeed, we owe what personal access we have to this 'original'? Is there any way of going upstream to the source?

Again, the answer must vary with each individual reader/spectator. The absolute grammarian—and he knows ecstasies as intense as any described in current theories of the *jouissance,* of the eros of reading—may come to conceive of, to love, even a text such as Sophocles' *Antigone* as the locus of cruces. The play will come to life in his sensibility by virtue of the syntactic or metrical problems and debates to which it has given prestigious rise. At the opposite pole stands the 'innocent', the man or woman who chances across an extract from, a performance of, *Antigone,* unaware of the concentric spheres of commentary and text-criticism that surround it. The reader of the play, the theatrical audience for whom I am writing, would, I presume, find themselves somewhere past the centre of the scale. They are nearer to philology than to innocence, but will (this, of course, being my own case) have had no hand in the conservation and establishment of the Sophoclean canon.

As I have pointed out, however, there is no complete modern innocence in the face of the classics. The mere notion of the 'classic' tells us as much. No twentieth-century public or reader comes upon Sophocles' *Antigone* wholly unprepared. The play is, unavoidably, embedded in the long history of its transmission and reception. Because this history is so extensive, because variants and adaptations have been both so numerous and of significant quality, Sophocles' text runs the danger of receding into context. It can only be by a deliberate and, more or less, fictive exercise of purification, not unlike that of a restorer removing levels of varnish and previous restorations from a canvas, that one can attempt to isolate the Sophoclean play from the interpretations and uses made of it. The analogy with the restorer is, moreover, deceptive. It is quite often possible to bring the original design and coloration back into view. But no *Ur-Antigone* can exist for us. No stripping away of interpretative accretions can take us back to the première of the drama, to the phenomenology of its purpose and impact in the 440s BC.

* * *

The classic is a text whose initial, existential coming into being and realization may well be unrecapturable to us (this will always be true of the literatures of antiquity). But the integral authority of the classic is such that it can absorb without loss of identity the millennial incursions upon it, the accretions to it, of

5. Jacques Lacan (1901–1981), French psychoanalyst who often wrote about literature.

commentary, of translations, of enacted variations. *Ulysses*[6] reinforces Homer; Broch's *Death of Virgil* enriches the *Aeneid*. Sophocles' *Antigone* will not suffer from Lacan.

The development of metamorphic unity is open-ended. New textual and critical readings of *Antigone,* new scenic, musical, choreographic, and cinematographic renditions, new variants on and adaptations of 'the story', are being produced at this very moment. But each in turn will have to test the strength of its being against that of its Sophoclean source. And very few will survive to become that enigmatic but undeniable phenomenon, an echo that has life.

* * *

I sense in Sophocles' play an undeclared tragedy of the dissociations between thought and action, between understanding and practice. The ascription to action of manifest preeminence, of an existential worth greater than any other, is a marked element in Periclean and Aristotelian concepts of human conduct. Drama itself, as has often been said, is a stylized expression of this preference. It locates in the individual person those privileges and fatalities of 'doing' which the preceding, generative tradition of epic poetry had, assuredly at its origins, placed in ethnic and collective enterprises (the clans of Greece sailing to Troy). But experiencing and re-experiencing *Antigone,* I find it difficult to dismiss the possibility that Sophocles queried this morality of the deed; or, more tentatively, that there are not within the play as we know it certain aspects, traversed, left behind, but consequent, of a critique of action.

* * *

* * * There is * * * the very delicate yet insistent possibility that Creon's intelligence is of a kind which might lead him to apprehend the necessary claims of Antigone's stance; that Antigone is possessed of a force of empathy which might lead her to perceive the rationale of Creon's position. I do not suppose for a moment that Sophocles could have subscribed to the conclusion arrived at by Coleridge when he wrote in a notebook entry for 1802 'there is something inherently mean in action'. But the waste of unheeded persuasion in *Antigone* seems, at moments, to exceed any rhetorical art or tactic of theatrical symmetry. The behaviour of the protagonists, and this is true also of Haemon, does seem almost extravagantly wasteful of the opportunities for reciprocal intelligibility offered by the dramatic discourse.

In reach of the tragedy as we know and experience it, there lies (or so I now sense) an intimation of inaction, of the deed arrested by the acknowledged gravity, density, and inhibitions of mutual insight. Such a play would not be a 'drama' in the proper sense, the very word, as we have seen, signifying 'action'. The suspension of the deed, the abstinence of the doer in the face of the complexities and doubts revealed, proffered to him by thought, would make for a kind of stasis, for a kind of lasting hesitation alien to the dramatic.* * *

---

6. The novel *Ulysses* (1922) by James Joyce.

It may be that subterranean to Sophocles' most demanding play is a meditation on the tragic partiality, on the fatal interestedness, of even the noblest deed.
An untapped stillness of understanding is present in Antigone, in the aura of that
secrecy which has drawn to her poets, artists, philosophers, political thinkers.
But there may be hints of such a stillness, of a perceptive weariness also in Sophocles' Creon. As I move nearer the play, leaving behind aspects emphasized in this
study, it is the laying waste of stillness, of understanding heard but not listened
to, that is beginning to feel central.* * *

MARTHA C. NUSSBAUM

from The Fragility of Goodness: Luck and Ethics in Greek Tragedy and Philosophy

* * * [A]lmost all interpreters of [*Antigone*] have agreed that the play shows Creon
to be morally defective, though they might not agree about the particular nature
of his defect. The situation of Antigone is more controversial. Hegel assimilated
her defect to Creon's; some more recent writers uncritically hold her up as a
blameless heroine. Without entering into an exhaustive study of her role in the
tragedy, I should like to claim (with the support of an increasing number of
recent critics) that there is at least some justification for the Hegelian assimilation—though the criticism needs to be focused more clearly and specifically than
it is in Hegel's brief remarks. I want to suggest that Antigone, like Creon, has
engaged in a ruthless simplification of the world of value which effectively elimi-
nates conflicting obligations. Like Creon, she can be blamed for refusal of vision.
But there are important differences, as well, between her project and Creon's.
When these are seen, it will also emerge that this criticism of Antigone is not
incompatible with the judgment that she is morally superior to Creon.

> O kindred, own-sisterly head of Ismene, do you know that there is not one of the
> evils left by Oedipus that Zeus does not fulfill for us while we live? . . . Do you
> grasp anything? Have you heard anything? Or has it escaped your notice that the
> evils that belong to enemies are advancing against our friends?[1]

A person is addressed with a periphrasis that is both intimate and impersonal.
In the most emphatic terms available, it characterizes her as a close relative of
the speaker. And yet its attitude towards the addressee is strangely remote. Antigone sees Ismene simply as the form of a close family relation. As such, she
presses on her, with anxious insistence, the knowledge of the family: that 'loved
ones' (*philoi*) are being penalized as if they were enemies (*echthroi*). Loving relatives must 'see' the shame and dishonour of 'the evils that are yours and mine'.

*From Martha C. Nussbaum, *The Fragility of Goodness: Luck and Ethics in Greek Tragedy and Philosophy*
(Cambridge, Eng., and New York: Cambridge University Press, 1986), pp. 63–67.   1. All translations
are Nussbaum's, based on the Oxford Classical Text of A. C. Pearson.

There has been a war. On one side was an army led by Eteocles, brother of Antigone and Ismene. On the other side was an invading army, made up partly of foreigners, but led by a Theban brother, Polynices. This heterogeneity is denied, in different ways, by both Creon and Antigone. Creon's strategy is to draw, in thought, a line between the invading and defending forces. What falls to one side of this line is a foe, bad, unjust; what falls to the other (if loyal to the city's cause) becomes, indiscriminately, friend or loved one. Antigone, on the other hand, denies the relevance of this distinction entirely. She draws, in imagination, a small circle around the members of her family: what is inside (with further restrictions which we shall mention) is family, therefore loved one and friend; what is outside is non-family, therefore, in any conflict with the family, enemy. If one listened only to Antigone, one would not know that a war had taken place or that anything called 'city' was ever in danger. To her it is a simple injustice that Polynices should not be treated like a friend.

'Friend' (*philos*) and 'enemy', then, are functions solely of family relationship. When Antigone says, 'It is my nature to join in loving, not to join in hating', she is expressing not a general attachment to love, but a devotion to the *philia* of the family. It is the nature of these *philia* bonds to make claims on one's commitments and actions regardless of one's occurrent desires. This sort of love is not something one decides about; the relationships involved may have little to do with liking or fondness. We might say (to use terminology borrowed from Kant) that Antigone, in speaking of love, means 'practical', not 'pathological' love (a love that has its source in fondness or inclination). 'He is my own brother', she says to Ismene in explanation of her defiance of the city's decree, 'and yours too, even if you don't want it. I certainly will never be found a traitor to him'. Relationship is itself a source of obligation, regardless of the feelings involved. When Antigone speaks of Polynices as 'my dearest brother', even when she proclaims, 'I shall lie with him as a loved one with a loved one', there is no sense of closeness, no personal memory, no particularity animating her speech. Ismene, the one person who ought, historically, to be close to her, is treated from the beginning with remote coldness; she is even called enemy when she takes the wrong stand on matters of pious obligation. It is Ismene whom we see weeping 'sister-loving tears', who acts out of commitment to a felt love. 'What life is worth living for me, bereft of you?' she asks with an intensity of feeling that never animates her sister's piety. To Haemon, the man who passionately loves and desires her, Antigone never addresses a word throughout the entire play. It is Haemon, not Antigone, whom the Chorus views as inspired by *erōs*. Antigone is as far from *erōs* as Creon. For Antigone, the dead are 'those whom it is most important to please'. 'You have a warm heart for the cold', observes her sister, failing to comprehend this impersonal and single-minded passion.

Duty to the family dead is the supreme law and the supreme passion. And Antigone structures her entire life and her vision of the world in accordance with this simple, self-contained system of duties. Even within this system, should a conflict ever arise, she is ready with a fixed priority ordering that will clearly dictate her choice. The strange speech in which she ranks duties to different family dead, placing duty to brother above duties to husband and children, is in this sense (if genuine) highly revealing: it makes us suspect that she is capable of a strangely ruthless simplification of duties, corresponding not so much to any known religious law as to the exigencies of her own practical imagination.

Other values fall into place, confirming these suspicions. Her single-minded identification with duties to the dead (and only some of these) effects a strange reorganization of piety, as well as of honor and justice. She is truly, in her own words, *hosia panourgēsasa,* one who will do anything for the sake of the pious; and her piety takes in only a part of conventional religion. She speaks of her allegiance to Zeus, but she refuses to recognize his role as guardian of the city and backer of Eteocles. The very expression of her devotion is suspect: 'Zeus did not decree this, as far as I am concerned'. She sets herself up as the arbiter of what Zeus can and cannot have decreed, just as Creon took it upon himself to say whom the gods could and could not have covered: no other character bears out her view of Zeus as single-mindedly backing the rights of the dead. She speaks, too, of the goddess *Dikē,* Justice; but *Dikē* for her is, simply, 'the Justice who lives together with the gods below'. The Chorus recognizes another *Dikē.* Later they will say to her, 'Having advanced to the utmost limit of boldness, you struck hard against the altar of *Dikē* on high, o child.' Justice is up here in the city, as well as below the earth. It is not as simple as she says it is. Antigone, accordingly, is seen by them not as a conventionally pious person, but as one who improvised her piety, making her own decisions about what to honor. She is a 'maker of her own law'; her defiance is 'self-invented passion'. Finally they tell her unequivocally that her pious respect is incomplete: '[This] reverent action is a part of piety.' Antigone's rigid adherence to a single narrow set of duties has caused her to misinterpret the nature of piety itself, a virtue within which a more comprehensive understanding would see the possibility of conflict.

Creon's strategy of simplification led him to regard others as material for his aggressive exploitation. Antigone's dutiful subservience to the dead leads to an equally strange, though different (and certainly less hideous) result. Her relation to others in the world above is characterized by an odd coldness. 'You are alive', she tells her sister, 'but my life is long since dead, to the end of serving the dead.' The safely dutiful human life requires, or is, life's annihilation. Creon's attitude towards others is like necrophilia: he aspires to possess the inert and unresisting. Antigone's subservience to duty is, finally, the ambition to be a *nekros,* a corpse beloved of corpses. (Her apparent similarity to martyrs in our own tradition, who expect a fully active life after death, should not conceal from us the strangeness of this goal.) In the world below, there are no risks of failure or wrongdoing.

Neither Creon nor Antigone, then, is a loving or passionate being in anything like the usual sense. Not one of the gods, not one human being escapes the power of *erōs,* says the Chorus; but these two oddly inhuman beings do, it appears, escape. Creon sees loved persons as functions of the civic good, replaceable producers of citizens. For Antigone, they are either dead, fellow servants of the dead, or objects of complete indifference. No living being is loved for his or her personal qualities, loved with the sort of love that Haemon feels and Ismene praises. By altering their beliefs about the nature and value of persons, they have, it seems, altered or restructured the human passions themselves. They achieve harmony in this way; but at a cost. The Chorus speaks of *erōs* as a force as important and obligating as the ancient *thesmoi* or laws of right, a force against which it is both foolish and, apparently, blameworthy to rebel.

Antigone learns too—like Creon, by being forced to recognize a problem that lies at the heart of her single-minded concern. Creon saw that the city itself is pious and loving; that he could not be its champion without valuing what it values, in all its complexity. Antigone comes to see that the service of the dead requires the city, that her own religious aims cannot be fulfilled without civic institutions. By being her own law, she has not only ignored a part of piety, she has also jeopardized the fulfillment of the very pious duties to which she is so attached. Cut off from friends, from the possibility of having children, she cannot keep herself alive in order to do further service to the dead; nor can she guarantee the pious treatment of her own corpse. In her last speeches she laments not so much the fact of imminent death as, repeatedly, her isolation from the continuity of offspring, from friends and mourners. She emphasizes the fact that she will never marry; she will remain childless. Acheron will be her husband, the tomb her bridal chamber. Unless she can successfully appeal to the citizens whose needs as citizens she had refused to consider, she will die without anyone to mourn her death or to replace her as guardian of her family religion. She turns therefore increasingly, in this final scene, to the citizens and the gods of the city, until her last words closely echo an earlier speech made by Creon and blend his concerns with hers:

> O city of my fathers in this land of Thebes. O gods, progenitors of our race. I am led away, and wait no longer. Look, leaders of Thebes, the last of your royal line. Look what I suffer, at whose hands, for having respect for piety.

We have, then, two narrowly limited practical worlds, two strategies of avoidance and simplification. In one, a single human value has become *the* final end; in the other, a single set of duties has eclipsed all others. But we can now acknowledge that we admire Antigone, nonetheless, in a way that we do not admire Creon. It seems important to look for the basis of this difference.

First, in the world of the play, it seems clear that Antigone's actual choice is preferable to Creon's. The dishonour to civic values involved in giving pious burial to an enemy's corpse is far less radical than the violation of religion involved in Creon's act. Antigone shows a deeper understanding of the community and its values than Creon does when she argues that the obligation to bury the dead is an unwritten law, which cannot be set aside by the decree of a particular ruler. The belief that not all values are utility-relative, that there are certain claims whose neglect will prove deeply destructive of communal attunement and individual character, is a part of Antigone's position left untouched by the play's implicit criticism of her single-mindedness.

Furthermore, Antigone's pursuit of virtue is her own. It involves nobody else and commits her to abusing no other person. Rulership must be rulership *of* something; Antigone's pious actions are executed alone, out of a solitary commitment. She may be strangely remote from the world; but she does no violence to it.

Finally, and perhaps most important, Antigone remains ready to risk and to sacrifice her ends in a way that is not possible for Creon, given the singleness of his conception of value. There is a complexity in Antigone's virtue that permits genuine sacrifice *within* the defense of piety. She dies recanting nothing; but still she is torn by a conflict. Her virtue is, then, prepared to admit a contingent conflict, at least in the extreme case where its adequate exercise requires the cancellation of the conditions of its exercise. From within her single-minded devotion to the dead, she recognizes the power of these contingent circumstances and yields to them, comparing herself to Niobe wasted away by nature's snow and rain. (Earlier she had been compared, in her grief, to a mother bird crying out over an empty nest; so she is, while heroically acting, linked with the openness and vulnerability of the female.) The Chorus here briefly tries to console her with the suggestion that her bad luck does not really matter, in view of her future fame; she calls their rationalization a mockery of her loss. This vulnerability in virtue, this ability to acknowledge the world of nature by mourning the constraints that it imposes on virtue, surely contributes to making her the more humanly rational and the richer of the two protagonists: both active and receptive, neither exploiter nor simply victim.

* * *

REBECCA W. BUSHNELL

from Prophesying Tragedy: Sign and Voice in Sophocles' Theban Plays*

It is primarily through the power of speech, against silence, that Creon's suffering is distinguished from Antigone's, as Creon becomes "nothing" in his disaster, whereas Antigone leaves the stage as herself. She has clearly lost in her battle for any kind of political autonomy, in her effort to counteract Creon's *kērygma*[1] (the Chorus, not Antigone, makes him change his mind). Further, neither the other characters in the play nor the gods confer heroic status on her. While the "punishment" of Creon may be seen as her vindication, Creon never mentions her again, nor does Tiresias defend her directly in his prophecy. Yet she leaves the stage, neither abject nor resigned to oblivion, but proclaiming her importance as the last of the Cadmeans. While Creon speaks his "sentence" of death, Antigone responds by invoking the gods and the city of Thebes, calling upon the Chorus to look on her and acknowledge her right to have buried Polynices. Antigone's last act on stage is thus an act of apostrophe or invocation, meant to establish the presence and power of her own voice. For her, it matters little that neither god nor city responds; for one last time, Antigone relies on her voice to define

*From Rebecca W. Bushnell, *Prophesying Tragedy: Sign and Voice in Sophocles' Theban Plays* (Ithaca and London: Cornell University Press, 1988), pp. 64–66.   1. Proclamation.

herself, as she claims her link to her city, her lineage, and the gods of her race. Antigone is denied personal and political autonomy in the city of Thebes—what she cannot have as a woman; yet at the same time Antigone maintains her freedom of speech in public, which was the essence of freedom in Athens, where the worst punishment of exile was considered the loss of *parrēsia* or "free speech," Antigone speaks, too, as the bride of death, both in this world and beyond; like Hector, she has the authority that those on the brink of death possess over the living, and yet she already stands apart from the rest of the citizens, who must find a way to rule in the days to come.

Creon's loss of his power to invoke and command marks the loss of his role in the family and the city. Creon, too, laments his disaster, but his speech lacks the ceremony and self-reflection of Antigone's. Crying forth the ritual sound of wailing, *aiai*, he calls himself wretched (*deilaios*). Creon's penultimate gesture, matching Antigone's, is to utter a prayer for death. It may be addressed to the gods, but it is heard only by the Chorus, who refuse to answer the prayer: "That will come," they say, "but now we must do what is before us." When Creon protests that he prayed for what he desires most, the Chorus answers that he must not pray now. Creon thus ends in the world he created for himself, where "fate" is inflexible, yet there are no gods to hear his prayers. The gods will not help Creon, and he can no longer help himself. His words become meaningless when he himself becomes "nothing," having lost his family and his city. Earlier, Haemon compared Creon to writing tablets which, when unfolded, are blank. In the end, Creon fulfills that image, becoming someone who is nothing, a voice which is *asēmos,* "without significance."

In the *Iliad*, Hector's defiance of prophecy[2] plays out a conflict of discourse in the struggle between man and god for the right to declare *anankē*.[3] In *Antigone,* Sophocles dramatizes that conflict in the context of the city, where the king strives to emulate the gods in making the signs of "fate," and king, prophet, and citizen compete for the right to speak for the city's needs and future. Antigone loses this battle when Creon condemns her to death, just as Hector must die, according to the sentence of "fate." But Creon is silenced by the gods—and by the playwright. Both Creon and Antigone threaten the order of the city and are destroyed, but Sophocles gives the victory to her, in the dramatic authority of her voice. Although the gods themselves never answer her pleas for recognition, her voice commands the audience's and Chorus' attention. Creon, however, trails off in inarticulate confusion, just as he has no recognizable "self" when stripped of his roles of *tyrannos*,[4] husband, and father. Antigone never loses her ability to speak for herself, and in this way, is given her freedom. Thus it is she, not Creon, who is Hector's heir, and she who most closely imitates his defiance of fatal authority. But Antigone is not only Hector's heir; she is also the forerunner[5] of her own father, Oedipus, who in *Oedipus the King* masters human speech in his pride and his shame.

2. Perhaps a reference to Book 22 of the *Iliad,* in which Hector mistakenly disbelieves Achilles' boast that Zeus will allow Achilles to kill Hector in battle.   3. Necessity, fate.   4. Ruler (Greek). 5. Antigone is "forerunner" in that the play *Antigone* was written and first performed more than ten years prior to *Oedipus the King.*

MARY WHITLOCK BLUNDELL

from *Helping Friends and Harming Enemies:*
*A Study in Sophocles and Greek Ethics**

* * * Creon and Antigone are alike in several ways, especially the inconsistency of their values and the way they are driven by passion below a surface of rational argument. Both are also one-sided in their commitments. The poet could have given the champion of the *polis*[1] a much stronger case. But he could also have let Antigone meet and conquer Creon on his own ground (for example by arguing that her two brothers were equally responsible for the war). The narrowness of both is revealed by their failure really to engage in argument. Creon's two main statements of principle actually occur in Antigone's absence. When they do confront each other, in the brief passage of stichomythia[2] with which we began, they argue at cross purposes, repeatedly missing each other's point.

This does not mean, however, that they are equally limited in the values to which they adhere. Antigone is sometimes accused of being as narrowly one-sided as Creon in her allegiance to the family and disregard for the interests and *nomoi*[3] of the *polis:* 'If one listened only to Antigone, one would not know that a war had taken place or that anything called "city" was ever in danger' (Nussbaum 63f.). Nor can it be denied that she ignores competing concepts of *nomos* and justice which have their claims, no matter how shoddily Creon may represent them. Creon's misapplication of his principles does not undermine their claim to consideration, and the rightness of Antigone's cause does not of itself justify the passionate narrowness with which she pursues it. But although she does not acknowledge the authority of the *polis,* she never explicitly rejects it, as Creon does the family. Moreover she acts ultimately to the city's advantage. As Creon himself so ironically puts it, 'the man who is worthwhile in family matters will also turn out to be just in the *polis'.* It is Creon's own scorn not just for the family but for public opinion which finally brings the *polis* 'doom instead of *soteria'.*[4] He who began by saving Thebes from its enemies ends by stirring up other cities with enmity. He tells Antigone she is alone in her views, but she retorts that, on the contrary, all those present (namely the chorus of the city's elders) are on her side. Moreover she foresees great glory from her deed, which the context suggests is to derive from none other than her fellow citizens. Creon can make no such claims for himself. Indeed Haemon will hint that his father's behaviour may be destroying a glorious reputation. With the loss of his son's loyalty, Creon also loses the last shreds of his claim to represent the *polis.* But Antigone's words are vindicated when Haemon reports the admiration of the ordinary citizens, echoing her own evaluation of her deed. Even the chorus, while withholding direct

*From Mary Whitlock Blundell, *Helping Friends and Harming Enemies: A Study in Sophocles and Greek Ethics* (Cambridge, Eng., and New York: Cambridge University Press, 1989), pp. 145–48.　1. City-state (Greek).　2. Dialogue delivered in alternating lines; often used to show vigorous dispute.　3. Laws, standards (singular, *nomos*) (Greek).　4. Salvation; the root, *soter,* means "savior."

The theme of desire centers on Blanche (a role actresses would die for), with reinforcement from Stella and Mitch. Why, then, was the sensation of the first performance, and of the film, Stanley Kowalski (other than the fact that he was played by the young Marlon Brando), and how does his centrality impact the complex of love and desire?

Even though evaluation may ultimately depend on highly subjective judgments and good readers may reasonably differ from each other, questions of evaluation, as we have seen, are close to analytical questions, and determining meaning and effect takes you quickly to questions of value. And vice versa. Often asking questions about how good a play is will get you closer to questions of what it is about and of what you value than you may at first be aware of. It is essential, then, in your evaluation, in your articulating your response—steps 1 and 2, above—that you "interpret"; that is, you say what play, or what understanding of the play, you are responding to. You will have noticed that the essays in "Critical Contexts" are devoted to interpretation, to singling out what the play says to the critic, often taking into account and taking issue with the readings of other critics—as in step 3, above. There will be no definitive interpretation; the reading in step 4 will be better and richer than that in step 1, but there will be no "perfect" reading. Even if you were to skip the third and fourth steps, when you read a play the second or third time your vision of it and your response to it will differ from those of your first reading. To quote George Steiner again, "There is no insurance of clear-sightedness in criticism. . . . The eye of the critic is personal; his focus will be argumentative and strategic. . . . Honest literary criticism is simply that which makes its purposed constructions [that is, readings of how all the parts of the play fit together and tend toward a single meaning] most plainly visible and open to challenge."

Though the personal eye is the critic's, the critic is himself or herself part of a time, place, and culture, and that context also constrains the critical reading and evaluation. It is, or would seem, then, much easier for you to read, respond, understand, and come to some kind of judgment about a play written in the twentieth century by an American author than it is for you to evaluate a play written by an Englishman more than four hundred years ago. Yet it could be argued that despite time and distance, Shakespeare is part of modern American culture in its broadest sense, and it is undeniable that *A Midsummer Night's Dream* is read, performed, and enjoyed in our time even more than is *A Streetcar Named Desire*. For many first-time readers or viewers, however, its language, construction, and "characters" may not seem part of our cultural world. Indeed, there is, initially, a certain amount of "strangeness" to be got over, and there is, therefore, all the more reason to hold off anything like final judgment until after several readings and, perhaps, until after discussion and even critical research. Questions of value are not, finally, of a different order from other questions that help us read more carefully and enjoyably, and evaluation is not only an understandable outcome of reading texts but an integral part of the process of reading itself.

Samuel Johnson, the most respected arbiter of taste in England in the late eighteenth century, said that "nothing can please many and please long but just representations of general nature." Johnson was trying to explain why Shakespeare had continued to charm readers and playgoers for a century and a half, and what he says is both a common-sense argument about actual responses to texts (based on consensus and durability) and a proposition about what literature has to say about reality. Good literature, says Johnson, accurately reflects patterns that exist across culture and time; to last, literature must have something important ("just") to say about what does not change from time to time or place to place ("general nature"). Plays last, says Johnson, when they accurately portray what human nature is like, the way things are, the universals that transcend the interests of individuals and local times and places.

Not everyone in Johnson's own time agreed that such a universal standard could be found, and in the enlarged and varied world of cultural relativity of the late twentieth century, fewer still believe that any universals exist. Yet his point is an interesting one even for relativists. We still want to believe that literature can teach us something, that it has a vision of reality from which we can learn. And even if we do not expect universal plots and characters that assure us that life and times are ever the same, we continue to expect representations of reality that we can recognize as related to our own. The accuracy of that representation (its "just"-ness, in Johnson's terms) is likely to remain important; we want our playwrights to know the world and be able to represent it faithfully, and we are apt to want the representation to be enough like our own world and broader and deeper enough for it to seem in some sense applicable and even enlightening. We are interested in people in other times and other cultures primarily because their experiences, even in other circumstances, have some potential analogy to us. We want a playwright's sense of reality—of what the world is like and how people will behave—to be similar enough to our own that our own world will seem clearer after reading about the one represented in the play.

A play like *A Midsummer Night's Dream* may not at first seem to be of a kind that can be evaluated according to Johnson's test or our sense of reality, for the characters, the plot, and the language of the play all are fairly strange by "normal," "realistic" standards. Johnson himself, in fact, wrote some fairly critical things about the play, objecting especially to the way Shakespeare combines the fairy mythology of one historical period with the court world of an entirely different age, though he did finally approve—and enjoy—the "wild, Fantastical. . . ." Certainly, there is plenty in the play to like: the hijinks of Puck, the romantic plot at court with its solvable complications, the lunkish physical comedy of the mechanic players, the verbal wit in line after line, the memorable (and by now famous and familiar) lines about the "course of true love" that plainly state the play's theme, the careful and lively presentation of a wide variety of characters, the ingenious plotting, the engaging resolution of human conflicts. It is easy to find good, solid textual evidence that would enable us to analyze, and praise, the conception and presentation of characters, the effective and appropriate uses of language to delineate characters and further plot and theme, and the careful interlocking of the several plots and the three entirely different sets of characters (and the play's " 'excess' that transcends any summary," as George Steiner puts it). But what about the question of whether the play represents some recognizable reality that we can relate to in a sympathetic way? What are we to think of a world that presents royal lovers alongside simple laborers trying to mount a theatrical production and that then mixes in a magical group of fairies? Is this a mix from which we are likely to garner useful knowledge about what life is like?

Whether a text accurately represents human life, behavior, and conversation as we know it is often very important to readers. We want to think about the probable, if not necessarily the real, and often we want to feel that we are learning about the way the world works, what people are like, what kinds of stories other people are involved in. We do not necessarily expect to find ourselves in other people's stories, but we expect to find recognizable people. They do not have to be "universal" in the way that Johnson seems to imply—we have to believe that all times, places, and people are pretty much alike to regard literature as representational—but they need to represent people we can understand in predicaments we can sympathize with.

But how can we "understand" or "sympathize with" a cast of characters comprising a duke and a queen impatient to marry each other, a set of clumsy would-be actors who are really a carpenter, a weaver, a bellows-mender, a tinker, a joiner, and a tailor, and—of another order altogether—fairies with their own king and queen? If it is a little hard to relate to the first pair of characters because of their high position, the middle group (at least as Shakespeare presents them) seems as difficult because their position is too low: even in our most awkward and most unself-possessed moments we are not likely to "identify" with figures like these. As for the third group, watching fairies at work and play around their court seems an unlikely way to find human "representation."

In this play, however, representation comes to mean something else: the play openly operates as fantasy, and the three different worlds that seem impossible to conceive on the same stage all ultimately become so tangled up with each other—and in such creative and entertaining ways—that we have the illusion of complicated conflicts and relationships being worked out across whole orders of being. To ask whether we have ever seen anyone in the real world who resembles Puck would be to ask, for this play, the wrong question. A key to seeing what is going on in this play is flexibility in applying standards and terms—even so basic a standard and term as representation. Ultimately, many readers feel that they *are* represented by the characters in *A Midsummer Night's Dream,* not because they resemble some one character in the play but because the play gives us insights into human aspiration and the pleasures and perils of romantic love in a social class or order of beings. Not all discovery in literature is solemn and high-minded; some is odd and unpredictable and full of belly laughs.

> *I have tried lately to read Shakespeare, and found it so intolerably dull that it nauseated me.*
> —CHARLES DARWIN

Questions about evaluation are ultimately questions about what values we share and with whom. Some readers will find it easier to appreciate—and like—a world like that of *A Midsummer Night's Dream* than will others. Sometimes, values shared throughout a whole culture or an entire age determine how a text will be received and evaluated; sometimes the sharing involves smaller, more local or more select groups—people of a particular political persuasion, or of a certain social class, or of a certain age or ethnic group, or those with common religious or philosophical beliefs. To some extent your values are determined by your community, but if you are strong enough you can choose your group within, on the fringes of, or even outside your community by choosing your values, in your readings as in your social and political life.

Evaluations of some features of plays—of whether language is used precisely or effectively, for example, or whether characters are presented consistently andwinningly—may sometimes seem almost value-free. Can't we decide such issues without regard to our social, economic, religious, or political biases and presuppositions? The answer seems to be that what we bring to a text, and where we bring it from, is likely to influence our judgment at every point. But the fact that our judgments are both highly subjective—subject to our individual biases and preferences—and influenced by the ideologies and cultural identities we participate in does not mean that evaluation is predetermined and beyond discussion or change. The more we read, the more conscious we are of how literary meaning and effect are conditioned by the text, the more aware we are of what we believe and why, of what we bring to a text. We are, therefore, more open to other

> *The Englishman, who without reverence, a proud and affectionate reverence, can utter the name of William Shakespeare, stands disqualified for the office of critic.*
> —SAMUEL TAYLOR COLERIDGE

influences. The better we can articulate our values and adduce evidence from the text, the more we will be able to learn, to grow, and to teach. For we may have to bring our values into discussion in class and papers to try to convince—and be convinced.

Agreeing about the quality of a play is not ultimately the point. You may never convince someone else that a particular play is as good or bad as you think it to be. And you may never be convinced by the arguments of someone else. But having discussions about quality has virtues of its own. The grounds of judgment are ultimately more important than the judgment of any single play, and argument helps clarify the grounds of judgment. Knowing your own grounds of judgment may make a play more enjoyable and meaningful to you; certainly it will make you more aware of who you are as a reader and as a person, and allow you to grow.

TENNESSEE WILLIAMS

A Streetcar Named Desire

> And so it was I entered the broken world
> To trace the visionary company of love, its voice
> An instant in the wind (I know not whither hurled)
> But not for long to hold each desperate choice.
>
> —"The Broken Tower" by HART CRANE[1]

CHARACTERS

BLANCHE	PABLO
STELLA	A NEGRO WOMAN
STANLEY	A DOCTOR
MITCH	A NURSE (MATRON)
EUNICE	A YOUNG COLLECTOR
STEVE	A MEXICAN WOMAN

SCENE 1

The exterior of a two-story corner building on a street in New Orleans which is named Elysian Fields and runs between the L & N tracks and the river.[2] The section is poor but, unlike corresponding sections in other American cities, it has a raffish charm. The houses are mostly white frame, weathered grey, with rickety outside stairs and galleries

---

1. American poet (1899–1932).   2. Elysian Fields is in fact a New Orleans street at the northern tip of the French Quarter, between the Louisville & Nashville railroad tracks and the Mississippi River. In Greek mythology, the Elysian Fields are the abode of the blessed in the afterlife; in Paris, the Champs Elysées is a grand boulevard.

and quaintly ornamented gables. This building contains two flats, upstairs and down. Faded white stairs ascend to the entrances of both.

It is first dark of an evening early in May. The sky that shows around the dim white building is a peculiarly tender blue, almost a turquoise, which invests the scene with a kind of lyricism and gracefully attenuates the atmosphere of decay. You can almost feel the warm breath of the brown river beyond the river warehouses with their faint redolences of bananas and coffee. A corresponding air is evoked by the music of Negro entertainers at a barroom around the corner. In this part of New Orleans you are practically always just around the corner, or a few doors down the street, from a tinny piano being played with the infatuated fluency of brown fingers. This "Blue Piano" expresses the spirit of the life which goes on here.

Two women, one white and one colored, are taking the air on the steps of the building. The white woman is EUNICE, *who occupies the upstairs flat; the* NEGRO WOMAN, *a neighbor, for New Orleans is a cosmopolitan city where there is a relatively warm and easy intermingling of races in the old part of town.*

Above the music of the "Blue Piano" the voices of people on the street can be heard overlapping.

> [*Two men come around the corner,* STANLEY KOWALSKI *and* MITCH. *They are about twenty-eight, or thirty years old, roughly dressed in blue denim work clothes.* STANLEY *carries his bowling jacket and a red-stained package from a butcher's. They stop at the foot of the steps.*]

STANLEY: [*Bellowing.*] Hey there! Stella, baby!

> [STELLA *comes out on the first floor landing, a gentle young woman, about twenty-five, and of a background obviously quite different from her husband's.*]

STELLA: [*Mildly.*] Don't holler at me like that. Hi, Mitch.
STANLEY: Catch!
STELLA: What?
STANLEY: Meat!

> [*He heaves the package at her. She cries out in protest but manages to catch it: then she laughs breathlessly. Her husband and his companion have already started back around the corner.*]

STELLA: [*Calling after him.*] Stanley! Where are you going?
STANLEY: Bowling!
STELLA: Can I come watch?
STANLEY: Come on. [*He goes out.*]
STELLA: Be over soon. [*To the* WHITE WOMAN.] Hello, Eunice. How are you?
EUNICE: I'm all right. Tell Steve to get him a poor boy's sandwich[3] 'cause nothing's left here.

> [*They all laugh; the* NEGRO WOMAN *does not stop.* STELLA *goes out.*]

---

3. Usually called just "poor boy" or "po' boy." Similar to a hero or submarine sandwich.

NEGRO WOMAN: What was that package he th'ew at 'er? [*She rises from steps, laughing louder.*]

EUNICE: You hush, now!

NEGRO WOMAN: Catch *what!*

[*She continues to laugh.* BLANCHE *comes around the corner, carrying a valise. She looks at a slip of paper, then at the building, then again at the slip and again at the building. Her expression is one of shocked disbelief. Her appearance is incongruous to this setting. She is daintily dressed in a white suit with a fluffy bodice, necklace and earrings of pearl, white gloves and hat, looking as if she were arriving at a summer tea or cocktail party in the garden district. She is about five years older than* STELLA. *Her delicate beauty must avoid a strong light. There is something about her uncertain manner, as well as her white clothes, that suggests a moth.*]

EUNICE: [*Finally.*] What's the matter, honey? Are you lost?

BLANCHE: [*With faintly hysterical humor.*] They told me to take a street-car named Desire, and then transfer to one called Cemeteries[4] and ride six blocks and get off at—Elysian Fields!

EUNICE: That's where you are now.

BLANCHE: At Elysian Fields?

EUNICE: This here is Elysian Fields.

BLANCHE: They mustn't have—understood—what number I wanted . . .

EUNICE: What number you lookin' for?

[BLANCHE *wearily refers to the slip of paper.*]

BLANCHE: Six thirty-two.

EUNICE: You don't have to look no further.

BLANCHE: [*Uncomprehendingly.*] I'm looking for my sister, Stella DuBois, I mean—Mrs. Stanley Kowalski.

EUNICE: That's the party.—You just did miss her, though.

BLANCHE: This—can this be—her home?

EUNICE: She's got the downstairs here and I got the up.

BLANCHE: Oh. She's—out?

EUNICE: You noticed that bowling alley around the corner?

BLANCHE: I'm—not sure I did.

EUNICE: Well, that's where she's at, watchin' her husband bowl. [*There is a pause.*] You want to leave your suitcase here an' go find her?

BLANCHE: No.

NEGRO WOMAN: I'll go tell her you come.

BLANCHE: Thanks.

NEGRO WOMAN: You welcome. [*She goes out.*]

EUNICE: She wasn't expecting you?

BLANCHE: No. No, not tonight.

EUNICE: Well, why don't you just go in and make yourself at home till they get back.

4. Desire is a street in New Orleans, Cemeteries the end of a streetcar line that stopped at a cemetery.

BLANCHE: How could I—do that?

EUNICE: We own this place so I can let you in.

[*She gets up and opens the downstairs door. A light goes on behind the blind, turning it light blue.* BLANCHE *slowly follows her into the downstairs flat. The surrounding areas dim out as the interior is lighted. Two rooms can be seen, not too clearly defined. The one first entered is primarily a kitchen but contains a folding bed to be used by* BLANCHE. *The room beyond this is a bedroom. Off this room is a narrow door to a bathroom.*]

EUNICE: [*Defensively, noticing* BLANCHE'*s look.*] It's sort of messed up right now but when it's clean it's real sweet.

BLANCHE: Is it?

EUNICE: Uh-huh, I think so. So you're Stella's sister?

BLANCHE: Yes. [*Wanting to get rid of her.*] Thanks for letting me in.

EUNICE: *Por nada,* as the Mexicans say, *por nada!*[5] Stella spoke of you.

BLANCHE: Yes?

EUNICE: I think she said you taught school.

BLANCHE: Yes.

EUNICE: And you're from Mississippi, huh?

BLANCHE: Yes.

EUNICE: She showed me a picture of your home-place, the plantation.

BLANCHE: Belle Reve?[6]

EUNICE: A great big place with white columns.

BLANCHE: Yes . . .

EUNICE: A place like that must be awful hard to keep up.

BLANCHE: If you will excuse me, I'm just about to drop.

EUNICE: Sure, honey. Why don't you set down?

BLANCHE: What I meant was I'd like to be left alone.

EUNICE: [*Offended.*] Aw. I'll make myself scarce, in that case.

BLANCHE: I didn't meant to be rude, but—

EUNICE: I'll drop by the bowling alley an' hustle her up. [*She goes out the door.*]

[BLANCHE *sits in a chair very stiffly with her shoulders slightly hunched and her legs pressed close together and her hands tightly clutching her purse as if she were quite cold. After a while the blind look goes out of her eyes and she begins to look slowly around. A cat screeches. She catches her breath with a startled gesture. Suddenly she notices something in a half opened closet. She springs up and crosses to it, and removes a whiskey bottle. She pours a half tumbler of whiskey and tosses it down. She carefully replaces the bottle and washes out the tumbler at the sink. Then she resumes her seat in front of the table.*]

BLANCHE: [*Faintly to herself.*] I've got to keep hold of myself!

[STELLA *comes quickly around the corner of the building and runs to the door of the downstairs flat.*]

5. "It's nothing."   6. "Beautiful Dream."

STELLA: [*Calling out joyfully.*] Blanche!

> [*For a moment they stare at each other. Then* BLANCHE *springs up and runs to her with a wild cry.*]

BLANCHE: Stella, oh, Stella, Stella! Stella for Star! [*She begins to speak with feverish vivacity as if she feared for either of them to stop and think. They catch each other in a spasmodic embrace.*] Now, then, let me look at you. But don't you look at me, Stella, no, no, no, not till later, not till I've bathed and rested! And turn that over-light off! Turn that off! I won't be looked at in this merciless glare! [STELLA *laughs and complies.*] Come back here now! Oh, my baby! Stella! Stella for Star! [*She embraces her again.*] I thought you would never come back to this horrible place! What am I saying? I didn't mean to say that. I meant to be nice about it and say—Oh, what a convenient location and such— Ha-a-ha! Precious lamb! You haven't said a *word* to me.

STELLA: You haven't given me a chance to, honey! [*She laughs, but her glance at* BLANCHE *is a little anxious.*]

BLANCHE: Well, now you talk. Open your pretty mouth and talk while I look around for some liquor! I know you must have some liquor on the place! Where could it be, I wonder? Oh, I spy, I spy! [*She rushes to the closet and removes the bottle; she is shaking all over and panting for breath as she tries to laugh. The bottle nearly slips from her grasp.*]

STELLA: [*Noticing.*] Blanche, you sit down and let me pour the drinks. I don't know what we've got to mix with. Maybe a Coke in the icebox. Look'n see, honey, while I'm—

BLANCHE: No Coke, honey, not with my nerves tonight! Where—where—where is—?

STELLA: Stanley? Bowling! He loves it. They're having a—found some soda!— tournament . . .

BLANCHE: Just water, baby, to chase it! Now don't get worried, your sister hasn't turned into a drunkard, she's just all shaken up and hot and tired and dirty! You sit down, now, and explain this place to me! What are you doing in a place like this?

STELLA: Now, Blanche—

BLANCHE: Oh, I'm not going to be hypocritical, I'm going to be honestly critical about it! Never, never, never in my worst dreams could I picture—Only Poe! Only Mr. Edgar Allan Poe!—could do it justice! Out there I suppose is the ghoul-haunted woodland of Weir![7] [*She laughs.*]

STELLA: No, honey, those are the L & N tracks.

BLANCHE: No, now seriously, putting joking aside. Why didn't you tell me, why didn't you write me, honey, why didn't you let me know?

STELLA: [*Carefully, pouring herself a drink.*] Tell you what, Blanche?

BLANCHE: Why, that you had to live in these conditions!

STELLA: Aren't you being a little intense about it? It's not that bad at all! New Orleans isn't like other cities.

---

7. From the refrain of Poe's gothic ballad *Ulalume* (1847).

BLANCHE: This has got nothing to do with New Orleans. You might as well say— forgive me, blessed baby! [*She suddenly stops short.*] The subject is closed!

STELLA: [*A little drily.*] Thanks.

[*During the pause,* BLANCHE *stares at her. She smiles at* BLANCHE.]

BLANCHE: [*Looking down at her glass, which shakes in her hand.*] You're all I've got in the world, and you're not glad to see me!

STELLA: [*Sincerely.*] Why, Blanche, you know that's not true.

BLANCHE: No?—I'd forgotten how quiet you were.

STELLA: You never did give me a chance to say much, Blanche. So I just got in the habit of being quiet around you.

BLANCHE: [*Vaguely.*] A good habit to get into . . . [*Then, abruptly.*] You haven't asked me how I happened to get away from the school before the spring term ended.

STELLA: Well, I thought you'd volunteer that information—if you wanted to tell me.

BLANCHE: You thought I'd been fired?

STELLA: No, I—thought you might have—resigned . . .

BLANCHE: I was so exhausted by all I'd been through my—nerves broke. [*Nervously tamping cigarette.*] I was on the verge of—lunacy, almost! So Mr. Graves— Mr. Graves is the high school superintendent—he suggested I take a leave of absence. I couldn't put all of those details into the wire . . . [*She drinks quickly.*] Oh, this buzzes right through me and feels so *good!*

STELLA: Won't you have another?

BLANCHE: No, one's my limit.

STELLA: Sure?

BLANCHE: You haven't said a word about my appearance.

STELLA: You look just fine.

BLANCHE: God love you for a liar! Daylight never exposed so total a ruin! But you—you've put on some weight, yes, you're just as plump as a little par- tridge! And it's so becoming to you!

STELLA: Now, Blanche—

BLANCHE: Yes, it is, it is or I wouldn't say it! You just have to watch around the hips a little. Stand up.

STELLA: Not now.

BLANCHE: You hear me? I said stand up! [STELLA *complies reluctantly.*] You messy child, you, you've spilt something on that pretty white lace collar! About your hair—you ought to have it cut in a feather bob with your dainty fea- tures. Stella, you have a maid, don't you?

STELLA: No. With only two rooms it's—

BLANCHE: What? *Two* rooms, did you say?

STELLA: This one and—[*She is embarrassed.*]

BLANCHE: The other one? [*She laughs sharply. There is an embarrassed silence.*] I am going to take just one little tiny nip more, sort of to put the stopper on, so to speak. . . . Then put the bottle away so I won't be tempted. [*She rises.*] I want you to look at *my* figure! [*She turns around.*] You know I haven't put on one ounce in ten years, Stella? I weigh what I weighed the summer you left Belle Reve. The summer Dad died and you left us . . .

STELLA: [*A little wearily.*] It's just incredible, Blanche, how well you're looking.

BLANCHE: [*They both laugh uncomfortably.*] But, Stella, there's only two rooms, I don't see where you're going to put me!

STELLA: We're going to put you in here.

BLANCHE: What kind of bed's this—one of those collapsible things? [*She sits on it.*]

STELLA: Does it feel all right?

BLANCHE: [*Dubiously.*] Wonderful, honey. I don't like a bed that gives much. But there's no door between the two rooms, and Stanley—will it be decent?

STELLA: Stanley is Polish, you know.

BLANCHE: Oh, yes. They're something like Irish, aren't they?

STELLA: Well—

BLANCHE: Only not so—highbrow? [*They both laugh again in the same way.*] I brought some nice clothes to meet all your lovely friends in.

STELLA: I'm afraid you won't think they are lovely.

BLANCHE: What are they like?

STELLA: They're Stanley's friends.

BLANCHE: Polacks?

STELLA: They're a mixed lot, Blanche.

BLANCHE: Heterogeneous—types?

STELLA: Oh, yes. Yes, types is right!

BLANCHE: Well—anyhow—I brought nice clothes and I'll wear them. I guess you're hoping I'll say I'll put up at a hotel, but I'm not going to put up at a hotel. I want to be *near* you, got to be *with* somebody, I *can't* be *alone!* Because—as you must have noticed—I'm—*not* very *well.* . . . [*Her voice drops and her look is frightened.*]

STELLA: You seem a little bit nervous or overwrought or something.

BLANCHE: Will Stanley like me, or will I be just a visiting in-law, Stella? I couldn't stand that.

STELLA: You'll get along fine together, if you'll just try not to—well—compare him with men that we went out with at home.

BLANCHE: Is he so—different?

STELLA: Yes. A different species.

BLANCHE: In what way; what's he like?

STELLA: Oh, you can't describe someone you're in love with! Here's a picture of him! [*She hands a photograph to* BLANCHE.]

BLANCHE: An officer?

STELLA: A Master Sergeant in the Engineers' Corps. Those are decorations!

BLANCHE: He had those on when you met him?

STELLA: I assure you I wasn't just blinded by all the brass.

BLANCHE: That's not what I—

STELLA: But of course there were things to adjust myself to later on.

BLANCHE: Such as his civilian background! [STELLA *laughs uncertainly.*] How did he take it when you said I was coming?

STELLA: Oh, Stanley doesn't know yet.

BLANCHE: [*Frightened.*] You—haven't told him?

STELLA: He's on the road a good deal.

BLANCHE: Oh. Travels?

STELLA: Yes.

BLANCHE: Good. I mean—isn't it?

STELLA: [*Half to herself.*] I can hardly stand it when he is away for a night . . .

BLANCHE: Why, Stella!

STELLA: When he's away for a week I nearly go wild!

BLANCHE: Gracious!

STELLA: And when he comes back I cry on his lap like a baby . . . [*She smiles to herself.*]

BLANCHE: I guess that is what is meant by being in love . . . [STELLA *looks up with a radiant smile.*] Stella—

STELLA: What?

BLANCHE: [*In an uneasy rush.*] I haven't asked you the things you probably thought I was going to ask. And so I'll expect you to be understanding about what *I* have to tell *you.*

STELLA: What, Blanche? [*Her face turns anxious.*]

BLANCHE: Well, Stella—you're going to reproach me, I know that you're bound to reproach me—but before you do—take into consideration—you left! I stayed and struggled! You came to New Orleans and looked out for yourself! *I* stayed at Belle Reve and tried to hold it together! I'm not meaning this in any reproachful way, but *all* the burden descended on *my* shoulders.

STELLA: The best I could do was make my own living, Blanche.

[BLANCHE *begins to shake again with intensity.*]

BLANCHE: I know, I know. But you are the one that abandoned Belle Reve, not I! I stayed and fought for it, bled for it, almost died for it!

STELLA: Stop this hysterical outburst and tell me what's happened? What do you mean fought and bled? What kind of—

BLANCHE: I knew you would, Stella. I knew you would take this attitude about it!

STELLA: About—what?—please!

BLANCHE: [*Slowly.*] The loss—the loss . . .

STELLA: Belle Reve? Lost, is it? No!

BLANCHE: Yes, Stella.

[*They stare at each other across the yellow-checked linoleum of the table.* BLANCHE *slowly nods her head and* STELLA *looks slowly down at her hands folded on the table. The music of the "Blue Piano" grows louder.* BLANCHE *touches her handkerchief to her forehead.*]

STELLA: But how did it go? What happened?

BLANCHE: [*Springing up.*] You're a fine one to ask me how it went!

STELLA: Blanche!

BLANCHE: You're a fine one to sit there *accusing me* of it!

STELLA: *Blanche!*

BLANCHE: I, I, *I* took the blows in my face and my body! All of those deaths! The long parade to the graveyard! Father, Mother! Margaret, that dreadful way! So big with it, it couldn't be put in a coffin! But had to be burned like rubbish! You just came home in time for the funerals, Stella. And funerals are pretty compared to deaths. Funerals are quiet, but deaths—not always. Sometimes their breathing is hoarse, and sometimes it rattles, and sometimes they even cry out to you, "Don't let me go!" Even the old, sometimes, say, "Don't let me go." As if you were able to stop them! But funerals are quiet, with pretty flowers. And, oh, what gorgeous boxes they pack them away in! Unless you were there at the bed when they cried out, "Hold me!" you'd never suspect there was the struggle for breath and bleeding. You didn't dream, but I saw! *Saw! Saw!* And now you sit there telling me with your eyes that I let the place go! How in hell do you think all that sickness and dying was paid for? Death is expensive, Miss Stella! And old Cousin Jessie's right after Margaret's, hers! Why, the Grim Reaper had put up his tent on our doorstep! . . . Stella. Belle Reve was his headquarters! Honey—that's how it slipped through my fingers! Which of them left us a fortune? Which of them left a cent of insurance even? Only poor Jessie—one hundred to pay for her coffin. That was all, Stella! And I with my pitiful salary at the school. Yes, accuse me! Sit there and stare at me, thinking I let the place go! *I* let the place go? Where were *you!* In bed with your—Polack!

STELLA: [*Springing.*] Blanche! You be still! That's enough! [*She starts out.*]

BLANCHE: Where are you going?

STELLA: I'm going into the bathroom to wash my face.

BLANCHE: Oh, Stella, Stella, you're crying!

STELLA: Does that surprise you?

BLANCHE: Forgive me—I didn't mean to—

[*The sound of men's voices is heard.* STELLA *goes into the bathroom, closing the door behind her. When the men appear, and* BLANCHE *realizes it must be* STANLEY *returning, she moves uncertainly from the bathroom door to the dressing table, looking apprehensively toward the front door.* STANLEY *enters, followed by* STEVE *and* MITCH. STANLEY *pauses near his door,* STEVE *by the foot of the spiral stair, and* MITCH *is slightly above and to the right of them, about to go out. As the men enter, we hear some of the following dialogue.*]

STANLEY: Is that how he got it?

STEVE: Sure that's how he got it. He hit the old weather-bird for 300 bucks on a six-number-ticket.

MITCH: Don't tell him those things; he'll believe it. [MITCH *starts out.*]

STANLEY: [*Restraining* MITCH.] Hey, Mitch—come back here.

[BLANCHE, *at the sound of voices, retires in the bedroom. She picks up* STANLEY's *photo from dressing table, looks at it, puts it down. When* STANLEY *enters the apartment, she darts and hides behind the screen at the head of bed.*]

STEVE: [*To* STANLEY *and* MITCH.] Hey, are we playin' poker tomorrow?

STANLEY: Sure—at Mitch's.

MITCH: [*Hearing this, returns quickly to the stair rail.*] No—not at my place. My mother's still sick!

STANLEY: Okay, at my place . . . [MITCH *starts out again.*] But you bring the beer!

[MITCH *pretends not to hear—calls out "Good night, all," and goes out, singing.* EUNICE's *voice is heard, above.*]

EUNICE: Break it up down there! I made the spaghetti dish and ate it myself.

STEVE: [*Going upstairs.*] I told you and phoned you we was playing. [*To the men.*] Jax[8] beer!

EUNICE: You never phoned me once.

STEVE: I told you at breakfast—and phoned you at lunch . . .

EUNICE: Well, never mind about that. You just get yourself home here once in a while.

STEVE: You want it in the papers?

[*More laughter and shouts of parting come from the men.* STANLEY *throws the screen door of the kitchen open and comes in. He is of medium height, about five feet eight or nine, and strongly, compactly built. Animal joy in his being is implicit in all his movements and attitudes. Since earliest manhood the center of his life has been pleasure with women, the giving and taking of it, not with weak indulgence, dependently, but with the power and pride of a richly feathered male bird among hens. Branching out from this complete and satisfying center are all the auxiliary channels of his life, such as his heartiness with men, his appreciation of rough humor, his love of good drink and food and games, his car, his radio, everything that is his, that bears his emblem of the gaudy seed-bearer. He sizes women up at a glance, with sexual classifications, crude images flashing into his mind and determining the way he smiles at them.*]

BLANCHE: [*Drawing involuntarily back from his stare.*] You must be Stanley. I'm Blanche.

STANLEY: Stella's sister?

BLANCHE: Yes.

STANLEY: H'lo. Where's the little woman?

BLANCHE: In the bathroom.

STANLEY: Oh. Didn't know you were coming in town.

BLANCHE: I—uh—

STANLEY: Where you from, Blanche?

BLANCHE: Why, I—live in Laurel.

[*He has crossed to the closet and removed the whiskey bottle.*]

STANLEY: In Laurel, huh? Oh, yeah. Yeah, in Laurel, that's right. Not in my territory. Liquor goes fast in hot weather. [*He holds the bottle to the light to observe its depletion.*] Have a shot?

8. A local brand.

BLANCHE: No, I—rarely touch it.

STANLEY: Some people rarely touch it, but it touches them often.

BLANCHE: [*Faintly.*] Ha-ha.

STANLEY: My clothes're stickin' to me. Do you mind if I make myself comfortable? [*He starts to remove his shirt.*]

BLANCHE: Please, please do.

STANLEY: Be comfortable is my motto.

BLANCHE: It's mine, too. It's hard to stay looking fresh. I haven't washed or even powdered my face and—here you are!

STANLEY: You know you can catch cold sitting around in damp things, especially when you been exercising hard like bowling is. You're a teacher, aren't you?

BLANCHE: Yes.

STANLEY: What do you teach, Blanche?

BLANCHE: English.

STANLEY: I never was a very good English student. How long you here for, Blanche?

BLANCHE: I—don't know yet.

STANLEY: You going to shack up here?

BLANCHE: I thought I would if it's not inconvenient for you all.

STANLEY: Good.

BLANCHE: Traveling wears me out.

STANLEY: Well, take it easy.

[*A cat screeches near the window.* BLANCHE *springs up.*]

BLANCHE: What's that?

STANLEY: Cats . . . Hey, Stella!

STELLA: [*Faintly, from the bathroom.*] Yes, Stanley.

STANLEY: Haven't fallen in, have you? [*He grins at* BLANCHE. *She tries unsuccessfully to smile back. There is a silence.*] I'm afraid I'll strike you as being the unrefined type. Stella's spoke of you a good deal. You were married once, weren't you?

[*The music of the polka rises up, faint in the distance.*]

BLANCHE: Yes. When I was quite young.

STANLEY: What happened?

BLANCHE: The boy—the boy died. [*She sinks back down.*] I'm afraid I'm—going to be sick! [*Her head falls on her arms.*]

SCENE 2

It is six o'clock the following evening. BLANCHE *is bathing.* STELLA *is completing her toilette.* BLANCHE'*s dress, a flowered print, is laid out on* STELLA'*s bed.*

STANLEY *enters the kitchen from outside, leaving the door open on the perpetual "Blue Piano" around the corner.*

STANLEY: What's all this monkey doings?

STELLA: Oh, Stan! [*She jumps up and kisses him, which he accepts with lordly composure.*] I'm taking Blanche to Galatoire's[9] for supper and then to a show, because it's your poker night.

STANLEY: How about my supper, huh? I'm not going to no Galatoire's for supper!

STELLA: I put you a cold plate on ice.

STANLEY: Well, isn't that just dandy!

STELLA: I'm going to try to keep Blanche out till the party breaks up because I don't know how she would take it. So we'll go to one of the little places in the Quarter afterward and you'd better give me some money.

STANLEY: Where is she?

STELLA: She's soaking in a hot tub to quiet her nerves. She's terribly upset.

STANLEY: Over what?

STELLA: She's been through such an ordeal.

STANLEY: Yeah?

STELLA: Stan, we've—lost Belle Reve!

STANLEY: The place in the country?

STELLA: Yes.

STANLEY: How?

STELLA: [*Vaguely.*] Oh, it had to be—sacrificed or something. [*There is a pause while* STANLEY *considers.* STELLA *is changing into her dress.*] When she comes in be sure to say something nice about her appearance. And, oh! Don't mention the baby. I haven't said anything yet, I'm waiting until she gets in a quieter condition.

STANLEY: [*Ominously.*] So?

STELLA: And try to understand her and be nice to her, Stan.

BLANCHE: [*Singing in the bathroom.*] "From the land of the sky blue water, They brought a captive maid!"

STELLA: She wasn't expecting to find us in such a small place. You see I'd tried to gloss things over a little in my letters.

STANLEY: So?

STELLA: And admire her dress and tell her she's looking wonderful. That's important with Blanche. Her little weakness!

STANLEY: Yeah. I get the idea. Now let's skip back a little to where you said the country place was disposed of.

STELLA: Oh!—yes . . .

STANLEY: How about that? Let's have a few more details on that subjeck.

STELLA: It's best not to talk much about it until she's calmed down.

STANLEY: So that's the deal, huh? Sister Blanche cannot be annoyed with business details right now!

STELLA: You saw how she was last night.

STANLEY: Uh-hum, I saw how she was. Now let's have a gander at the bill of sale.

STELLA: I haven't seen any.

STANLEY: She didn't show you no papers, no deed of sale or nothing like that, huh?

---

9. A famous old restaurant on Bourbon Street in the French Quarter.

STELLA: It seems like it wasn't sold.

STANLEY: Well, what in hell was it then, give away? To charity?

STELLA: Shhh! She'll hear you.

STANLEY: I don't care if she hears me. Let's see the papers!

STELLA: There weren't any papers, she didn't show any papers, I don't care about papers.

STANLEY: Have you ever heard of the Napoleonic code?[1]

STELLA: No, Stanley, I haven't heard of the Napoleonic code and if I have, I don't see what it—

STANLEY: Let me enlighten you on a point or two, baby.

STELLA: Yes?

STANLEY: In the state of Louisiana we have the Napoleonic code according to which what belongs to the wife belongs to the husband and vice versa. For instance if I had a piece of property, or you had a piece of property—

STELLA: My head is swimming!

STANLEY: All right. I'll wait till she gets through soaking in a hot tub and then I'll inquire if *she* is acquainted with the Napoleonic code. It looks to me like you have been swindled, baby, and when you're swindled under the Napoleonic code I'm swindled *too*. And I don't like to be *swindled*.

STELLA: There's plenty of time to ask her questions later but if you do now she'll go to pieces again. I don't undertand what happened to Belle Reve but you don't know how ridiculous you are being when you suggest that my sister or I or anyone of our family could have perpetrated a swindle on anyone else.

STANLEY: Then where's the money if the place was sold?

STELLA: Not sold—*lost, lost!* [*He stalks into bedroom, and she follows him.*] Stanley!

[*He pulls open the wardrobe trunk standing in middle of room and jerks out an armful of dresses.*]

STANLEY: Open your eyes to this stuff! You think she got them out of a teacher's pay?

STELLA: Hush!

STANLEY: Look at these feathers and furs that she come here to preen herself in! What's this here? A solid-gold dress, I believe! And this one! What is these here? Fox-pieces! [*He blows on them.*] Genuine fox fur-pieces, a half a mile long! Where are your fox-pieces, Stella? Bushy snowwhite ones, no less! Where are your white fox-pieces?

STELLA: Those are inexpensive summer furs that Blanche has had a long time.

STANLEY: I got an acquaintance who deals in this sort of merchandise. I'll have him in here to appraise it. I'm willing to bet you there's thousands of dollars invested in this stuff here!

STELLA: Don't be such an idiot, Stanley!

[*He hurls the furs to the day bed. Then he jerks open small drawer in the trunk and pulls up a fistful of costume jewelry.*]

---

1. This codification of French law (1802), made by Napoleon as emperor, is the basis for Louisiana's civil law.

STANLEY: And what have we here? The treasure chest of a pirate!

STELLA: Oh, Stanley!

STANLEY: Pearls! Ropes of them! What is this sister of yours, a deep-sea diver? Bracelets of solid gold, too! Where are your pearls and gold bracelets?

STELLA: Shhh! Be still, Stanley!

STANLEY: And diamonds! A crown for an empress!

STELLA: A rhinestone tiara she wore to a costume ball.

STANLEY: What's rhinestone?

STELLA: Next door to glass.

STANLEY: Are you kidding? I have an acquaintance that works in a jewelry store. I'll have him in here to make an appraisal of this. Here's your plantation, or what was left of it, here!

STELLA: You have no idea how stupid and horrid you're being! Now close that trunk before she comes out of the bathroom!

[*He kicks the trunk partly closed and sits on the kitchen table.*]

STANLEY: The Kowalskis and the DuBoises have different notions.

STELLA: [*Angrily.*] Indeed they have, thank heavens!—*I'm* going outside. [*She snatches up her white hat and gloves and crosses to the outside door.*] You come out with me while Blanche is getting dressed.

STANLEY: Since when do you give me orders?

STELLA: Are you going to stay here and insult her?

STANLEY: You're damn tootin' I'm going to stay here.

[STELLA *goes out to the porch.* BLANCHE *comes out of the bathroom in a red satin robe.*]

BLANCHE: [*Airily.*] Hello, Stanley! Here I am, all freshly bathed and scented, and feeling like a brand new human being!

[*He lights a cigarette.*]

STANLEY: That's good.

BLANCHE: [*Drawing the curtains at the windows.*] Excuse me while I slip on my pretty new dress!

STANLEY: Go right ahead, Blanche.

[*She closes the drapes between the rooms.*]

BLANCHE: I understand there's to be a little card party to which we ladies are cordially *not* invited!

STANLEY: [*Ominously.*] Yeah?

[BLANCHE *throws off her robe and slips into a flowered print dress.*]

BLANCHE: Where's Stella?

STANLEY: Out on the porch.

BLANCHE: I'm going to ask a favor of you in a moment.

STANLEY: What could that be, I wonder?

BLANCHE: Some buttons in back! You may enter! [*He crosses through drapes with a smoldering look.*] How do I look?

STANLEY: You look all right.

BLANCHE: Many thanks! Now the buttons!

STANLEY: I can't do nothing with them.

BLANCHE: You men with your big clumsy fingers. May I have a drag on your cig?

STANLEY: Have one for yourself.

BLANCHE: Why, thanks! . . . It looks like my trunk has exploded.

STANLEY: Me an' Stella were helping you unpack.

BLANCHE: Well, you certainly did a fast and thorough job of it!

STANLEY: It looks like you raided some stylish shops in Paris.

BLANCHE: Ha-ha! Yes—clothes are my passion!

STANLEY: What does it cost for a string of fur-pieces like that?

BLANCHE: Why, those were a tribute from an admirer of mine!

STANLEY: He must have had a lot of—admiration!

BLANCHE: Oh, in my youth I excited some admiration. But look at me now! [*She smiles at him radiantly.*] Would you think it possible that I was once considered to be—attractive?

STANLEY: Your looks are okay.

BLANCHE: I was fishing for a compliment, Stanley.

STANLEY: I don't go in for that stuff.

BLANCHE: What—stuff?

STANLEY: Compliments to women about their looks. I never met a woman that didn't know if she was good-looking or not without being told, and some of them give themselves credit for more than they've got. I once went out with a doll who said to me, "I am the glamorous type, I am the glamorous type!" I said, "So what?"

BLANCHE: And what did she say then?

STANLEY: She didn't say nothing. That shut her up like a clam.

BLANCHE: Did it end the romance?

STANLEY: It ended the conversation—that was all. Some men are took in by this Hollywood glamor stuff and some men are not.

BLANCHE: I'm sure you belong in the second category.

STANLEY: That's right.

BLANCHE: I cannot imagine any witch of a woman casting a spell over you.

STANLEY: That's—right.

BLANCHE: You're simple, straightforward and honest, a little bit on the primitive side I should think. To interest you a woman would have to—[*She pauses with an indefinite gesture.*]

STANLEY: [*Slowly.*] Lay . . . her cards on the table.

BLANCHE: [*Smiling.*] Well, I never cared for wishy-washy people. That was why, when you walked in here last night, I said to myself—"My sister has married a man!"—Of course that was all that I could tell about you.

STANLEY: [*Booming.*] Now let's cut the re-bop![2]

BLANCHE: [*Pressing hands to her ears.*] Ouuuuu!

STELLA: [*Calling from the steps.*] Stanley! You come out here and let Blanche finish dressing!

2. Nonsense syllables (from "bop," a form of jazz).

BLANCHE: I'm through dressing, honey.

STELLA: Well, you come out, then.

STANLEY: Your sister and I are having a little talk.

BLANCHE: [*Lightly.*] Honey, do me a favor. Run to the drugstore and get me a lemon Coke with plenty of chipped ice in it!—Will you do that for me, sweetie?

STELLA: [*Uncertainly.*] Yes. [*She goes around the corner of the building.*]

BLANCHE: The poor little thing was out there listening to us, and I have an idea she doesn't understand you as well as I do. . . . All right; now, Mr. Kowalski, let us proceed without any more double-talk. I'm ready to answer all questions. I've nothing to hide. What is it?

STANLEY: There is such a thing in this state of Louisiana as the Napoleonic code, according to which whatever belongs to my wife is also mine—and vice versa.

BLANCHE: My, but you have an impressive judicial air!

> [*She sprays herself with her atomizer; then playfully sprays him with it. He seizes the atomizer and slams it down on the dresser. She throws back her head and laughs.*]

STANLEY: If I didn't know that you was my wife's sister I'd get ideas about you!

BLANCHE: Such as what!

STANLEY: Don't play so dumb. You know what!

BLANCHE: [*She puts the atomizer on the table.*] All right. Cards on the table. That suits me. [*She turns to* STANLEY.] I know I fib a good deal. After all, a woman's charm is fifty per cent illusion, but when a thing is important I tell the truth, and this is the truth: I haven't cheated my sister or you or anyone else as long as I have lived.

STANLEY: Where's the papers? In the trunk?

BLANCHE: Everything that I own is in that trunk. [STANLEY *crosses to the trunk, shoves it roughly open and begins to open compartments.*] What in the name of heaven are you thinking of! What's in the back of that little boy's mind of yours? That I am absconding with something, attempting some kind of treachery on my sister?—Let me do that! It will be faster and simpler . . . [*She crosses to the trunk and takes out a box.*] I keep my papers mostly in this tin box. [*She opens it.*]

STANLEY: What's them underneath? [*He indicates another sheaf of paper.*]

BLANCHE: These are love-letters, yellowing with antiquity, all from one boy. [*He snatches them up. She speaks fiercely.*] Give those back to me!

STANLEY: I'll have a look at them first!

BLANCHE: The touch of your hands insults them!

STANLEY: Don't pull that stuff!

> [*He rips off the ribbon and starts to examine them.* BLANCHE *snatches them from him, and they cascade to the floor.*]

BLANCHE: Now that you've touched them I'll burn them!

STANLEY: [*Staring, baffled.*] What in hell are they?

BLANCHE: [*On the floor gathering them up.*] Poems a dead boy wrote. I hurt him the way that you would like to hurt me, but you can't! I'm not young and vulnerable any more. But my young husband was and I—never mind about that! Just give them back to me!

STANLEY: What do you mean by saying you'll have to burn them?

BLANCHE: I'm sorry, I must have lost my head for a moment. Everyone has something he won't let others touch because of their—intimate nature . . . [*She now seems faint with exhaustion and she sits down with the strong box and puts on a pair of glasses and goes methodically through a large stack of papers.*] Ambler & Ambler. Hmmmmm. . . . Crabtree. . . . More Ambler & Ambler.

STANLEY: What is Ambler & Ambler?

BLANCHE: A firm that made loans on the place.

STANLEY: Then it *was* lost on a mortgage?

BLANCHE: [*Touching her forehead.*] That must've been what happened.

STANLEY: I don't want no ifs, ands or buts! What's all the rest of them papers?

[*She hands him the entire box. He carries it to the table and starts to examine the papers.*]

BLANCHE: [*Picking up a large envelope containing more papers.*] There are thousands of papers, stretching back over hundreds of years, affecting Belle Reve as, piece by piece, our improvident grandfathers and father and uncles and brothers exchanged the land for their epic fornications—to put it plainly! [*She removes her glasses with an exhausted laugh.*] The four-letter word deprived us of our plantation, till finally all that was left—and Stella can verify that!— was the house itself and about twenty acres of ground, including a graveyard, to which now all but Stella and I have retreated. [*She pours the contents of the envelope on the table.*] Here all of them are, all papers! I hereby endow you with them! Take them, peruse them—commit them to memory, even! I think it's wonderfully fitting that Belle Reve should finally be this bunch of old papers in your big, capable hands! . . . I wonder if Stella's come back with my lemon Coke . . . [*She leans back and closes her eyes.*]

STANLEY: I have a lawyer acquaintance who will study these out.

BLANCHE: Present them to him with a box of aspirin tablets.

STANLEY: [*Becoming somewhat sheepish.*] You see, under the Napoleonic code—a man has to take an interest in his wife's affairs—especially now that she's going to have a baby.

[BLANCHE *opens her eyes. The "Blue Piano" sounds louder.*]

BLANCHE: Stella? Stella going to have a baby? [*Dreamily.*] I didn't know she was going to have a baby! [*She gets up and crosses to the outside door.* STELLA *appears around the corner with a carton from the drugstore.* STANLEY *goes into the bedroom with the envelope and the box. The inner rooms fade to darkness and the outside wall of the house is visible.* BLANCHE *meets* STELLA *at the foot of the steps to the sidewalk.*] Stella, Stella for star! How lovely to have a baby! It's all right. Everything's all right.

STELLA: I'm sorry he did that to you.

BLANCHE: Oh, I guess he's just not the type that goes for jasmine perfume, but maybe he's what we need to mix with our blood now that we've lost Belle Reve. We thrashed it out. I feel a bit shaky, but I think I handled it nicely, I laughed and treated it all as a joke. [STEVE *and* PABLO *appear, carrying a case of beer.*] I called him a little boy and laughed and flirted. Yes, I was flirting with your husband! [*As the men approach.*] The guests are gathering for the poker party. [*The two men pass between them, and enter the house.*] Which way do we go now, Stella—this way?

STELLA: No, this way. [*She leads* BLANCHE *away.*]

BLANCHE: [*Laughing.*] The blind are leading the blind!

[*A tamale* VENDOR *is heard calling.*]

VENDOR'S VOICE: Red-hot!

SCENE 3. THE POKER NIGHT

There is a picture of Van Gogh's of a billiard-parlor at night.[3] *The kitchen now suggests that sort of lurid nocturnal brilliance, the raw colors of childhood's spectrum. Over the yellow linoleum of the kitchen table hangs an electric bulb with a vivid green glass shade. The poker players—STANLEY, STEVE, MITCH and PABLO—wear colored shirts, solid blues, a purple, a red-and-white check, a light green, and they are men at the peak of their physical manhood, as coarse and direct and powerful as the primary colors. There are vivid slices of watermelon on the table, whiskey bottles and glasses. The bedroom is relatively dim with only the light that spills between the portieres and through the wide window on the street.*

For a moment, there is absorbed silence as a hand is dealt.

STEVE: Anything wild this deal?

PABLO: One-eyed jacks are wild.

STEVE: Give me two cards.

PABLO: You, Mitch?

MITCH: I'm out.

PABLO: One.

MITCH: Anyone want a shot?

STANLEY: Yeah. Me.

PABLO: Why don't somebody go to the Chinaman's and bring back a load of chop suey?

STANLEY: When I'm losing you want to eat! Ante up! Openers? Openers! Get y'r ass off the table, Mitch. Nothing belongs on a poker table but cards, chips and whiskey. [*He lurches up and tosses some watermelon rinds to the floor.*]

MITCH: Kind of on your high horse, ain't you?

STANLEY: How many?

STEVE: Give me three.

3. *The Night Café,* by Vincent Van Gogh, Dutch Postimpressionist painter (1853–1890). *The Poker Night* was Williams's first title for *A Streetcar Named Desire.*

STANLEY: One.

MITCH: I'm out again. I oughta go home pretty soon.

STANLEY: Shut up.

MITCH: I gotta sick mother. She don't go to sleep until I come in at night.

STANLEY: Then why don't you stay home with her?

MITCH: She says to go out, so I go, but I don't enjoy it. All the while I keep wondering how she is.

STANLEY: Aw, for the sake of Jesus, go home, then!

PABLO: What've you got?

STEVE: Spade flush.

MITCH: You all are married. But I'll be alone when she goes.—I'm going to the bathroom.

STANLEY: Hurry back and we'll fix you a sugar-tit.

MITCH: Aw, go rut. [*He crosses through the bedroom into the bathroom.*]

STEVE: [*Dealing a hand.*] Seven card stud. [*Telling his joke as he deals.*] This ole farmer is out in back of his house sittin' down th'owing corn to the chickens when all at once he hears a loud cackle and this young hen comes lickety split around the side of the house with the rooster right behind her and gaining on her fast.

STANLEY: [*Impatient with the story.*] Deal!

STEVE: But when the rooster catches sight of the farmer th'owing the corn he puts on the brakes and lets the hen get away and starts pecking corn. And the old farmer says, "Lord God, I hopes I never gits *that* hongry!"

[STEVE *and* PABLO *laugh. The sisters appear around the corner of the building.*]

STELLA: The game is still going on.

BLANCHE: How do I look?

STELLA: Lovely, Blanche.

BLANCHE: I feel so hot and frazzled. Wait till I powder before you open the door. Do I look done in?

STELLA: Why no. You are as fresh as a daisy.

BLANCHE: One that's been picked a few days.

[STELLA *opens the door and they enter.*]

STELLA: Well, well, well. I see you boys are still at it?

STANLEY: Where you been?

STELLA: Blanche and I took in a show. Blanche, this is Mr. Gonzales and Mr. Hubbell.

BLANCHE: Please don't get up.

STANLEY: Nobody's going to get up, so don't be worried.

STELLA: How much longer is this game going to continue?

STANLEY: Till we get ready to quit.

BLANCHE: Poker is so fascinating. Could I kibitz?

STANLEY: You could not. Why don't you women go up and sit with Eunice?

STELLA: Because it is nearly two-thirty. [BLANCHE *crosses into the bedroom and partially closes the portieres.*] Couldn't you call it quits after one more hand?

[*A chair scrapes.* STANLEY *gives a loud whack of his hand on her thigh.*]

STELLA: [*Sharply.*] That's not fun, Stanley. [*The men laugh.* STELLA *goes into the bedroom.*] It makes me so mad when he does that in front of people.

BLANCHE: I think I will bathe.

STELLA: Again?

BLANCHE: My nerves are in knots. Is the bathroom occupied?

STELLA: I don't know.

[BLANCHE *knocks.* MITCH *opens the door and comes out, still wiping his hands on a towel.*]

BLANCHE: Oh!—good evening.

MITCH: Hello. [*He stares at her.*]

STELLA: Blanche, this is Harold Mitchell. My sister, Blanche DuBois.

MITCH: [*With awkward courtesy.*] How do you do, Miss DuBois.

STELLA: How is your mother now, Mitch?

MITCH: About the same, thanks. She appreciated your sending over that custard.—Excuse me, please.

[*He crosses slowly back into the kitchen, glancing back at* BLANCHE *and coughing a little shyly. He realizes he still has the towel in his hands and with an embarrassed laugh hands it to* STELLA. BLANCHE *looks after him with a certain interest.*]

BLANCHE: That one seems—superior to the others.

STELLA: Yes, he is.

BLANCHE: I thought he had a sort of sensitive look.

STELLA: His mother is sick.

BLANCHE: Is he married?

STELLA: No.

BLANCHE: Is he a wolf?

STELLA: Why, Blanche! [BLANCHE *laughs.*] I don't think he would be.

BLANCHE: What does—what does he do? [*She is unbuttoning her blouse.*]

STELLA: He's on the precision bench in the spare parts department. At the plant Stanley travels for.

BLANCHE: Is that something much?

STELLA: No. Stanley's the only one of his crowd that's likely to get anywhere.

BLANCHE: What makes you think Stanley will?

STELLA: Look at him.

BLANCHE: I've looked at him.

STELLA: Then you should know.

BLANCHE: I'm sorry, but I haven't noticed the stamp of genius even on Stanley's forehead.

[*She takes off the blouse and stands in her pink silk brassiere and white skirt in the light through the portieres. The game has continued in undertones.*]

STELLA: It isn't on his forehead and it isn't genius.

BLANCHE: Oh. Well, what is it, and where? I would like to know.

STELLA: It's a drive that he has. You're standing in the light, Blanche!

BLANCHE: Oh, am I!

[*She moves out of the yellow streak of light.* STELLA *has removed her dress and put on a light blue satin kimona.*]

STELLA: [*With girlish laughter.*] You ought to see their wives.

BLANCHE: [*Laughingly.*] I can imagine. Big, beefy things, I suppose.

STELLA: You know that one upstairs? [*More laughter.*] One time [*Laughing.*] the plaster—[*Laughing.*] cracked—

STANLEY: You hens cut out that conversation in there!

STELLA: You can't hear us.

STANLEY: Well, you can hear me and I said to hush up!

STELLA: This is my house and I'll talk as much as I want to!

BLANCHE: Stella, don't start a row.

STELLA: He's half drunk!—I'll be out in a minute.

[*She goes into the bathroom.* BLANCHE *rises and crosses leisurely to a small white radio and turns it on.*]

STANLEY: Awright, Mitch, you in?

MITCH: What? Oh!—No, I'm out!

[BLANCHE *moves back into the streak of light. She raises her arms and stretches, as she moves indolently back to the chair. Rhumba music comes over the radio.* MITCH *rises at the table.*]

STANLEY: Who turned that on in there?

BLANCHE: I did. Do you mind?

STANLEY: Turn it off!

STEVE: Aw, let the girls have their music.

PABLO: Sure, that's good, leave it on!

STEVE: Sounds like Xavier Cugat![4] [STANLEY *jumps up and, crossing to the radio, turns it off. He stops short at the sight of* BLANCHE *in the chair. She returns his look without flinching. Then he sits again at the poker table. Two of the men have started arguing hotly.*] I didn't hear you name it.

PABLO: Didn't I name it, Mitch?

MITCH: I wasn't listenin'.

PABLO: What were you doing, then?

STANLEY: He was looking through them drapes. [*He jumps up and jerks roughly at curtains to close them.*] Now deal the hand over again and let's play cards or quit. Some people get ants when they win.

[MITCH *rises as* STANLEY *returns to his seat.*]

STANLEY: [*Yelling.*] Sit down!

MITCH: I'm going to the "head." Deal me out.

4. Cuban band leader, well known for composing and playing rhumbas.

PABLO: Sure he's got ants now. Seven five-dollar bills in his pants pocket folded up tight as spitballs.

STEVE: Tomorrow you'll see him at the cashier's window getting them changed into quarters.

STANLEY: And when he goes home he'll deposit them one by one in a piggy bank his mother give him for Christmas. [*Dealing.*] This game is Spit in the Ocean.

[MITCH *laughs uncomfortably and continues through the portieres. He stops just inside.*]

BLANCHE: [*Softly.*] Hello! The Little Boys' Room is busy right now.

MITCH: We've—been drinking beer.

BLANCHE: I hate beer.

MITCH: It's—a hot weather drink.

BLANCHE: Oh, I don't think so; it always makes me warmer. Have you got any cigs? [*She has slipped on the dark red satin wrapper.*]

MITCH: Sure.

BLANCHE: What kind are they?

MITCH: Luckies.

BLANCHE: Oh, good. What a pretty case. Silver?

MITCH: Yes. Yes; read the inscription.

BLANCHE: Oh, is there an inscription? I can't make it out. [*He strikes a match and moves closer.*] Oh! [*Reading with feigned difficulty.*] "And if God choose, / I shall but love thee better—after—death!" Why, that's from my favorite sonnet by Mrs. Browning![5]

MITCH: You know it?

BLANCHE: Certainly I do!

MITCH: There's a story connected with that inscription.

BLANCHE: It sounds like a romance.

MITCH: A pretty sad one.

BLANCHE: Oh?

MITCH: The girl's dead now.

BLANCHE: [*In a tone of deep sympathy.*] Oh!

MITCH: She knew she was dying when she give me this. A very strange girl, very sweet—very!

BLANCHE: She must have been fond of you. Sick people have such deep, sincere attachments.

MITCH: That's right, they certainly do.

BLANCHE: Sorrow makes for sincerity, I think.

MITCH: It sure brings it out in people.

BLANCHE: The little there is belongs to people who have experienced some sorrow.

MITCH: I believe you are right about that.

BLANCHE: I'm positive that I am. Show me a person who hasn't known any sorrow and I'll show you a shuperficial—Listen to me! My tongue is a little—thick!

---

5. Elizabeth Barrett Browning, nineteenth-century British poet, was most famous for her sequence of love poems, *Sonnets from the Portuguese.*

You boys are responsible for it. The show let out at eleven and we couldn't come home on account of the poker game so we had to go somewhere and drink. I'm not accustomed to having more than one drink. Two is the limit— and *three!* [*She laughs.*] Tonight I had three.

STANLEY: Mitch!

MITCH: Deal me out. I'm talking to Miss—

BLANCHE: DuBois.

MITCH: Miss DuBois?

BLANCHE: It's a French name. It means woods and Blanche means white, so the two together mean white woods. Like an orchard in spring! You can remember it by that.

MITCH: You're French?

BLANCHE: We are French by extraction. Our first American ancestors were French Huguenots.

MITCH: You are Stella's sister, are you not?

BLANCHE: Yes, Stella is my precious little sister. I call her little in spite of the fact she's somewhat older than I. Just slightly. Less than a year. Will you do something for me?

MITCH: Sure. What?

BLANCHE: I bought this adorable little colored paper lantern at a Chinese shop on Bourbon. Put it over the light bulb! Will you, please?

MITCH: Be glad to.

BLANCHE: I can't stand a naked light bulb, any more than I can a rude remark or a vulgar action.

MITCH: [*Adjusting the lantern.*] I guess we strike you as being a pretty rough bunch.

BLANCHE: I'm very adaptable—to circumstances.

MITCH: Well, that's a good thing to be. You are visiting Stanley and Stella?

BLANCHE: Stella hasn't been so well lately, and I came down to help her for a while. She's very run down.

MITCH: You're not—?

BLANCHE: Married? No, no. I'm an old maid schoolteacher!

MITCH: You may teach school but you're certainly not an old maid.

BLANCHE: Thank you, sir! I appreciate your gallantry!

MITCH: So you are in the teaching profession?

BLANCHE: Yes. Ah, yes . . .

MITCH: Grade school or high school or—

STANLEY: [*Bellowing.*] Mitch!

MITCH: Coming!

BLANCHE: Gracious, what lung-power! . . . I teach high school. In Laurel.

MITCH: What do you teach? What subject?

BLANCHE: Guess!

MITCH: I bet you teach art or music? [BLANCHE *laughs delicately.*] Of course I could be wrong. You might teach arithmetic.

BLANCHE: Never arithmetic, sir; never arithmetic! [*With a laugh.*] I don't even know my multiplication tables! No, I have the misfortune of being an

English instructor. I attempt to instill a bunch of bobby-soxers and drugstore Romeos with reverence for Hawthorne and Whitman and Poe!

MITCH: I guess that some of them are more interested in other things.

BLANCHE: How very right you are! Their literary heritage is not what most of them treasure above all else! But they're sweet things! And in the spring, it's touching to notice them making their first discovery of love! As if nobody had ever known it before! [*The bathroom door opens and* STELLA *comes out.* BLANCHE *continues talking to* MITCH.] Oh! Have you finished? Wait—I'll turn on the radio.

[*She turns the knobs on the radio and it begins to play "Wien, Wien, nur du allein."*[6] BLANCHE *waltzes to the music with romantic gestures.* MITCH *is delighted and moves in awkward imitation like a dancing bear.* STANLEY *stalks fiercely through the portieres into the bedroom. He crosses to the small white radio and snatches it off the table. With a shouted oath, he tosses the instrument out the window.*]

STELLA: Drunk—drunk—animal thing, you! [*She rushes through to the poker table.*] All of you—please go home! If any of you have one spark of decency in you—

BLANCHE: [*Wildly.*] Stella, watch out, he's—

[STANLEY *charges after* STELLA.]

MEN: [*Feebly.*] Take it easy, Stanley. Easy, fellow.—Let's all—

STELLA: You lay your hands on me and I'll—

[*She backs out of sight. He advances and disappears. There is the sound of a blow,* STELLA *cries out.* BLANCHE *screams and runs into the kitchen. The men rush forward and there is grappling and cursing. Something is overturned with a crash.*]

BLANCHE: [*Shrilly.*] My sister is going to have a baby!

MITCH: This is terrible.

BLANCHE: Lunacy, absolute lunacy!

MITCH: Get him in here, men.

[STANLEY *is forced, pinioned by the two men, into the bedroom. He nearly throws them off. Then all at once he subsides and is limp in their grasp. They speak quietly and lovingly to him and he leans his face on one of their shoulders.*]

STELLA: [*In a high, unnatural voice, out of sight.*] I want to go away, I want to go away!

MITCH: Poker shouldn't be played in a house with women.

[BLANCHE *rushes into the bedroom.*]

BLANCHE: I want my sister's clothes! We'll go to that woman's upstairs!

6. "Vienna, Vienna, you are my only," a waltz from an operetta by Franz Lehár (1870–1948).

MITCH: Where is the clothes?

BLANCHE: [*Opening the closet.*] I've got them! [*She rushes through to* STELLA.] Stella, Stella, precious! Dear, dear little sister, don't be afraid!

> [*With her arm around* STELLA, BLANCHE *guides her to the outside door and upstairs.*]

STANLEY: [*Dully.*] What's the matter; what's happened?

MITCH: You just blew your top, Stan.

PABLO: He's okay, now.

STEVE: Sure, my boy's okay!

MITCH: Put him on the bed and get a wet towel.

PABLO: I think coffee would do him a world of good, now.

STANLEY: [*Thickly.*] I want water.

MITCH: Put him under the shower!

> [*The men talk quietly as they lead him to the bathroom.*]

STANLEY: Let the rut go of me, you sons of bitches!

> [*Sounds of blows are heard. The water goes on full tilt.*]

STEVE: Let's get quick out of here!

> [*They rush to the poker table and sweep up their winnings on their way out.*]

MITCH: [*Sadly but firmly.*] Poker should not be played in a house with women.

> [*The door closes on them and the place is still. The Negro entertainers in the bar around the corner play "Paper Doll"[7] slow and blue. After a moment* STAN-LEY *comes out of the bathroom dripping water and still in his clinging wet polka dot drawers.*]

STANLEY: Stella! [*There is a pause.*] My baby doll's left me! [*He breaks into sobs. Then he goes to the phone and dials, still shuddering with sobs.*] Eunice? I want my baby! [*He waits a moment; then he hangs up and dials again.*] Eunice! I'll keep on ringin' until I talk with my baby! [*An indistinguishable shrill voice is heard. He hurls phone to floor. Dissonant brass and piano sounds as the rooms dim out to darkness and the outer walls appear in the night light. The "Blue Piano" plays for a brief interval. Finally,* STANLEY *stumbles half-dressed out to the porch and down the wooden steps to the pavement before the building. There he throws back his head like a baying hound and bellows his wife's name: "*STELLA! STELLA, *sweetheart!* STELLA!*"*] Stell-lahhhhh!

EUNICE: [*Calling down from the door of her upper apartment.*] Quit that howling out there an' go back to bed!

STANLEY: I want my baby down here. Stella, Stella!

EUNICE: She ain't comin' down so you quit! Or you'll git th' law on you!

STANLEY: Stella!

EUNICE: You can't beat on a woman an' then call 'er back! She won't come! And

7. Popular song of the early 1940s.

her goin' t' have a baby! . . . You stinker! You whelp of a Polack, you! I hope they do haul you in and turn the fire hose on you, same as the last time!

STANLEY: [*Humbly.*] Eunice, I want my girl to come down with me!

EUNICE: Hah! [*She slams her door.*]

STANLEY: [*With heaven-splitting violence.*] STELL-LAHHHHH!

> [*The low-tone clarinet moans. The door upstairs opens again.* STELLA *slips down the rickety stairs in her robe. Her eyes are glistening with tears and her hair loose about her throat and shoulders. They stare at each other. Then they come together with low, animal moans. He falls to his knees on the steps and presses his face to her belly, curving a little with maternity. Her eyes go blind with tenderness as she catches his head and raises him level with her. He snatches the screen door open and lifts her off her feet and bears her into the dark flat.* BLANCHE *comes out the upper landing in her robe and slips fearfully down the steps.*]

BLANCHE: Where is my little sister? Stella? Stella?

> [*She stops before the dark entrance of her sister's flat. Then catches her breath as if struck. She rushes down to the walk before the house. She looks right and left as if for a sanctuary. The music fades away.* MITCH *appears from around the corner.*]

MITCH: Miss DuBois?

BLANCHE: Oh!

MITCH: All quiet on the Potomac now?

BLANCHE: She ran downstairs and went back in there with him.

MITCH: Sure she did.

BLANCHE: I'm terrified!

MITCH: Ho-ho! There's nothing to be scared of. They're crazy about each other.

BLANCHE: I'm not used to such—

MITCH: Naw, it's a shame this had to happen when you just got here. But don't take it serious.

BLANCHE: Violence! Is so—

MITCH: Set down on the steps and have a cigarette with me.

BLANCHE: I'm not properly dressed.

MITCH: That don't make no difference in the Quarter.

BLANCHE: Such a pretty silver case.

MITCH: I showed you the inscription, didn't I?

BLANCHE: Yes. [*During the pause, she looks up at the sky.*] There's so much—so much confusion in the world . . . [*He coughs diffidently.*] Thank you for being so kind! I need kindness now.

SCENE 4

It is early the following morning. There is a confusion of street cries like a choral chant.

STELLA *is lying down in the bedroom. Her face is serene in the early morning sun-light. One hand rests on her belly, rounding slightly with new maternity. From the other dangles a book of colored comics. Her eyes and lips have that almost narcotized tran-quility that is in the faces of Eastern idols.*

The table is sloppy with remains of breakfast and the debris of the preceding night, and STANLEY'S *gaudy pyjamas lie across the threshold of the bathroom. The outside door is slightly ajar on a sky of summer brilliance.*

BLANCHE *appears at this door. She has spent a sleepless night and her appearance entirely contrasts with* STELLA'S. *She presses her knuckles nervously to her lips as she looks through the door, before entering.*

BLANCHE: Stella?

STELLA: [*Stirring lazily.*] Hmmh?

> [BLANCHE *utters a moaning cry and runs into the bedroom, throwing herself down beside* STELLA *in a rush of hysterical tenderness.*]

BLANCHE: Baby, my baby sister!

STELLA: [*Drawing away from her.*] Blanche, what is the matter with you?

> [BLANCHE *straightens up slowly and stands beside the bed looking down at her sister with knuckles pressed to her lips.*]

BLANCHE: He's left?

STELLA: Stan? Yes.

BLANCHE: Will he be back?

STELLA: He's gone to get the car greased. Why?

BLANCHE: Why! I've been half crazy, Stella! When I found out you'd been insane enough to come back in here after what happened—I started to rush in after you!

STELLA: I'm glad you didn't.

BLANCHE: What were you thinking of? [STELLA *makes an indefinite gesture.*] Answer me! What? What?

STELLA: Please, Blanche! Sit down and stop yelling.

BLANCHE: All right, Stella. I will repeat the question quietly now. How could you come back in this place last night? Why, you must have slept with him!

> [STELLA *gets up in a calm and leisurely way.*]

STELLA: Blanche, I'd forgotten how excitable you are. You're making much too much fuss about this.

BLANCHE: Am I?

STELLA: Yes, you are, Blanche. I know how it must have seemed to you and I'm awful sorry it had to happen, but it wasn't anything as serious as you seem to take it. In the first place, when men are drinking and playing poker any-thing can happen. It's always a powder-keg. He didn't know what he was doing. . . . He was as good as a lamb when I came back and he's really very, very ashamed of himself.

BLANCHE: And that—that makes it all right?

STELLA: No, it isn't all right for anybody to make such a terrible row, but—people do sometimes. Stanley's always smashed things. Why, on our wedding night—soon as we came in here—he snatched off one of my slippers and rushed about the place smashing light bulbs with it.

BLANCHE: He did—*what?*

STELLA: He smashed all the lightbulbs with the heel of my slipper! [*She laughs.*]

BLANCHE: And you—you *let* him? Didn't *run,* didn't *scream?*

STELLA: I was—sort of—thrilled by it. [*She waits for a moment.*] Eunice and you had breakfast?

BLANCHE: Do you suppose I wanted any breakfast?

STELLA: There's some coffee left on the stove.

BLANCHE: You're so—matter-of-fact about it, Stella.

STELLA: What other can I be? He's taken the radio to get it fixed. It didn't land on the pavement so only one tube was smashed.

BLANCHE: And you are standing there smiling!

STELLA: What do you want me to do?

BLANCHE: Pull yourself together and face the facts.

STELLA: What are they, in your opinion?

BLANCHE: In my opinion? You're married to a madman!

STELLA: No!

BLANCHE: Yes, you are, your fix is worse than mine is! Only you're not being sensible about it. I'm going to *do* something. Get hold of myself and make myself a new life!

STELLA: Yes?

BLANCHE: But you've given in. And that isn't right, you're not old! You can get out.

STELLA: [*Slowly and emphatically.*] I'm not in anything I want to get out of.

BLANCHE: [*Incredulously.*] What—Stella?

STELLA: I said I am not in anything that I have a desire to get out of. Look at the mess in this room! And those empty bottles! They went through two cases last night! He promised this morning that he was going to quit having these poker parties, but you know how long such a promise is going to keep. Oh, well, it's his pleasure, like mine is movies and bridge. People have got to tolerate each other's habits, I guess.

BLANCHE: I don't understand you. [STELLA *turns toward her.*] I don't understand your indifference. Is this a Chinese philosophy you've—cultivated?

STELLA: Is what—what?

BLANCHE: This—shuffling about and mumbling—"One tube smashed—beer bottles—mess in the kitchen!"—as if nothing out of the ordinary has happened! [STELLA *laughs uncertainly and picking up the broom, twirls it in her hands.*] Are you deliberately shaking that thing in my face?

STELLA: No.

BLANCHE: Stop it. Let go of that broom. I won't have you cleaning up for him!

STELLA: Then who's going to do it? Are you?

BLANCHE: I? I!

STELLA: No, I didn't think so.

BLANCHE: Oh, let me think, if only my mind would function! We've got to get hold of some money, that's the way out!

STELLA: I guess that money is always nice to get hold of.

BLANCHE: Listen to me. I have an idea of some kind. [*Shakily she twists a cigarette into her holder.*] Do you remember Shep Huntleigh? [STELLA *shakes her head.*] Of course you remember Shep Huntleigh. I went out with him at college and wore his pin for a while. Well—

STELLA: Well?

BLANCHE: I ran into him last winter. You know I went to Miami during the Christmas holidays?

STELLA: No.

BLANCHE: Well, I did. I took the trip as an investment, thinking I'd meet someone with a million dollars.

STELLA: Did you?

BLANCHE: Yes. I ran into Shep Huntleigh—I ran into him on Biscayne Boulevard, on Christmas Eve, about dusk . . . getting into his car—Cadillac convertible; must have been a block long!

STELLA: I should think it would have been—inconvenient in traffic!

BLANCHE: You've heard of oil wells?

STELLA: Yes—remotely.

BLANCHE: He has them, all over Texas. Texas is literally spouting gold in his pockets.

STELLA: My, my.

BLANCHE: Y'know how indifferent I am to money. I think of money in terms of what it does for you. But he could do it, he could certainly do it!

STELLA: Do what, Blanche?

BLANCHE: Why—set us up in a—shop!

STELLA: What kind of shop?

BLANCHE: Oh, a—shop of some kind! He could do it with half what his wife throws away at the races.

STELLA: He's married?

BLANCHE: Honey, would I be here if the man weren't married? [STELLA *laughs a little.* BLANCHE *suddenly springs up and crosses to phone. She speaks shrilly.*] How do I get Western Union?—Operator! Western Union!

STELLA: That's a dial phone, honey.

BLANCHE: I can't dial, I'm too—

STELLA: Just dial O.

BLANCHE: O?

STELLA: Yes, "O" for Operator!

[BLANCHE *considers a moment; then she puts the phone down.*]

BLANCHE: Give me a pencil. Where is a slip of paper? I've got to write it down first—the message, I mean . . . [*She goes to the dressing table, and grabs up a sheet of Kleenex and an eyebrow pencil for writing equipment.*] Let me see now . . . [*She bites the pencil.*] "Darling Shep. Sister and I in desperate situation."

STELLA: I beg your pardon!

BLANCHE: "Sister and I in desperate situation. Will explain details later. Would you be interested in—?" [*She bites the pencil again.*] "Would you be—interested—in . . ." [*She smashes the pencil on the table and springs up.*] You never get anywhere with direct appeals!

STELLA: [*With a laugh.*] Don't be so ridiculous, darling!

BLANCHE: But I'll think of something, I've *got* to think of—*some*thing! Don't laugh at me, Stella! Please, please don't—I—I want you to look at the contents of my purse! Here's what's in it! [*She snatches her purse open.*] Sixty-five measly cents in coin of the realm!

STELLA: [*Crossing to bureau.*] Stanley doesn't give me a regular allowance, he likes to pay bills himself, but—this morning he gave me ten dollars to smooth things over. You take five of it, Blanche, and I'll keep the rest.

BLANCHE: Oh, no. No, Stella.

STELLA: [*Insisting.*] I know how it helps your morale just having a little pocket-money on you.

BLANCHE: No, thank you—I'll take to the streets!

STELLA: Talk sense! How did you happen to get so low on funds?

BLANCHE: Money just goes—it goes places. [*She rubs her forehead.*] Sometime today I've got to get hold of a Bromo![8]

STELLA: I'll fix you one now.

BLANCHE: Not yet—I've got to keep thinking!

STELLA: I wish you'd just let things go, at least for a—while.

BLANCHE: Stella, I can't live with him! You can, he's your husband. But how could I stay here with him, after last night, with just those curtains between us?

STELLA: Blanche, you saw him at his worst last night.

BLANCHE: On the contrary, I saw him at his best! What such a man has to offer is animal force and he gave a wonderful exhibition of that! But the only way to live with such a man is to—go to bed with him! And that's your job—not mine!

STELLA: After you've rested a little, you'll see it's going to work out. You don't have to worry about anything while you're here. I mean—expenses . . .

BLANCHE: I have to plan for us both, to get us both—out!

STELLA: You take it for granted that I am in something that I want to get out of.

BLANCHE: I take it for granted that you still have sufficient memory of Belle Reve to find this place and these poker players impossible to live with.

STELLA: Well, you're taking entirely too much for granted.

BLANCHE: I can't believe you're in earnest.

STELLA: No?

BLANCHE: I understand how it happened—a little. You saw him in uniform, an officer, not here but—

STELLA: I'm not sure it would have made any difference where I saw him.

BLANCHE: Now don't say it was one of those mysterious electric things between people! If you do I'll laugh in your face.

STELLA: I am not going to say anything more at all about it!

8. Short for "Bromo Seltzer," a headache remedy.

BLANCHE: All right, then, don't!

STELLA: But there are things that happen between a man and a woman in the dark—that sort of make everything else seem—unimportant. [*Pause.*]

BLANCHE: What you are talking about is brutal desire—just—Desire!—the name of that rattle-trap streetcar that bangs through the Quarter, up one old narrow street and down another . . .

STELLA: Haven't you ever ridden on that streetcar?

BLANCHE: It brought me here.—Where I'm not wanted and where I'm ashamed to be . . .

STELLA: Then don't you think your superior attitude is a bit out of place?

BLANCHE: I am not being or feeling at all superior, Stella. Believe me I'm not! It's just this. This is how I look at it. A man like that is someone to go out with— once—twice—three times when the devil is in you. But live with? Have a child by?

STELLA: I have told you I love him.

BLANCHE: Then I *tremble* for you! I just—*tremble* for you. . . .

STELLA: I can't help your trembling if you insist on trembling!

[*There is a pause.*]

BLANCHE: May I—speak—*plainly?*

STELLA: Yes, do. Go ahead. As plainly as you want to.

[*Outside, a train approaches. They are silent till the noise subsides. They are both in the bedroom. Under cover of the train's noise STANLEY enters from outside. He stands unseen by the women, holding some packages in his arms, and overhears their following conversation. He wears an undershirt and grease-stained seersucker pants.*]

BLANCHE: Well—if you'll forgive me—he's *common!*

STELLA: Why, yes, I suppose he is.

BLANCHE: Suppose! You can't have forgotten that much of our bringing up, Stella, that you just *suppose* that any part of a gentleman's in his nature! *Not one particle, no!* Oh, if he was just—*ordinary!* Just *plain*—but good and wholesome, but—*no.* There's something downright—*bestial*—about him! You're hating me saying this, aren't you?

STELLA: [*Coldly.*] Go on and say it all, Blanche.

BLANCHE: He acts like an animal, has an animal's habits! Eats like one, moves like one, talks like one! There's even something—sub-human—something not quite to the stage of humanity yet! Yes, something—ape-like about him, like one of those pictures I've seen in—anthropological studies! Thousands and thousands of years have passed him right by, and there he is—Stanley Kowalski—survivor of the Stone Age! Bearing the raw meat home from the kill in the jungle! And you—*you* here—*waiting* for him! Maybe he'll strike you or maybe grunt and kiss you! That is, if kisses have been discovered yet! Night falls and the other apes gather! There in the front of the cave, all grunting like him, and swilling and gnawing and hulking! His poker night! you call

it—this party of apes! Somebody growls—some creature snatches at something—the fight is on! *God!* Maybe we are a long way from being made in
God's image, but Stella—my sister—there has been *some* progress since then!
Such things as art—as poetry and music—such kinds of new light have come
into the world since then! In some kinds of people some tenderer feelings
have had some little beginning! That we have got to make *grow!* And *cling*
to, and hold as our flag! In this dark march toward whatever it is we're
approaching. . . . *Don't—don't hang back with the brutes!*

> [*Another train passes outside.* STANLEY *hesitates, licking his lips. Then sud-
> denly he turns stealthily about and withdraws through front door. The women
> are still unaware of his presence. When the train has passed he calls through
> the closed front door.*]

STANLEY: Hey! Hey, Stella!
STELLA: [*Who has listened gravely to* BLANCHE.] Stanley!
BLANCHE: Stell, I—

> [*But* STELLA *has gone to the front door.* STANLEY *enters casually with his pack-
> ages.*]

STANLEY: Hiyuh, Stella. Blanche back?
STELLA: Yes, she's back.
STANLEY: Hiyuh, Blanche. [*He grins at her.*]
STELLA: You must've got under the car.
STANLEY: Them darn mechanics at Fritz's don't know their ass fr'm—*Hey!*

> [STELLA *has embraced him with both arms, fiercely, and full in the view of*
> BLANCHE. *He laughs and clasps her head to him. Over her head he grins
> through the curtains at* BLANCHE. *As the lights fade away, with a lingering
> brightness on their embrace, the music of the "Blue Piano" and trumpet and
> drums is heard.*]

SCENE 5

BLANCHE *is seated in the bedroom fanning herself with a palm leaf as she reads over
a just-completed letter. Suddenly she bursts into a peal of laughter.* STELLA *is dressing in
the bedroom.*

STELLA: What are you laughing at, honey?
BLANCHE: Myself, myself, for being such a liar! I'm writing a letter to Shep. [*She
picks up the letter.*] "Darling Shep. I am spending the summer on the wing,
making flying visits here and there. And who knows, perhaps I shall take a
sudden notion to *swoop* down on *Dallas!* How would you feel about that? Ha-
ha! [*She laughs nervously and brightly, touching her throat as if actually talking to
Shep.*] Forewarned is forearmed, as they say!"—How does that sound?
STELLA: Uh-huh . . .

BLANCHE: [*Going on nervously.*] "Most of my sister's friends go north in the summer but some have homes on the Gulf and there has been a continued round of entertainments, teas, cocktails, and luncheons—"

[*A disturbance is heard upstairs at the Hubbells' apartment.*]

STELLA: Eunice seems to be having some trouble with Steve. [EUNICE's *voice shouts in terrible wrath.*]

EUNICE: I heard about you and that blonde!

STEVE: That's a damn lie!

EUNICE: You ain't pulling the wool over my eyes! I wouldn't mind if you'd stay down at the Four Deuces, but you always going up.

STEVE: Who ever seen me up?

EUNICE: I seen you chasing her 'round the balcony—I'm gonna call the vice squad!

STEVE: Don't you throw that at me!

EUNICE: [*Shrieking.*] You hit me! I'm gonna call the police!

[*A clatter of aluminum striking a wall is heard, followed by a man's angry roar, shouts and overturned furniture. There is a crash; then a relative hush.*]

BLANCHE: [*Brightly.*] Did he *kill* her?

[EUNICE *appears on the steps in daemonic disorder.*]

STELLA: No! She's coming downstairs.

EUNICE: Call the police, I'm going to call the police! [*She rushes around the corner.*]

[*They laugh lightly.* STANLEY *comes around the corner in his green and scarlet silk bowling shirt. He trots up the steps and bangs into the kitchen.* BLANCHE *registers his entrance with nervous gestures.*]

STANLEY: What's a matter with Eun-uss?

STELLA: She and Steve had a row. Has she got the police?

STANLEY: Naw. She's gettin' a drink.

STELLA: That's much more practical!

[STEVE *comes down nursing a bruise on his forehead and looks in the door.*]

STEVE: She here?

STANLEY: Naw, naw. At the Four Deuces.

STEVE: That rutting hunk! [*He looks around the corner a bit timidly, then turns with affected boldness and runs after her.*]

BLANCHE: I must jot that down in my notebook. Ha-ha! I'm compiling a notebook of quaint little words and phrases I've picked up here.

STANLEY: You won't pick up nothing here you ain't heard before.

BLANCHE: Can I count on that?

STANLEY: You can count on it up to five hundred.

BLANCHE: That's a mighty high number. [*He jerks open the bureau drawer, slams it shut and throws shoes in a corner. At each noise* BLANCHE *winces slightly. Finally she speaks.*] What sign were you born under?

STANLEY: [*While he is dressing.*] Sign?

BLANCHE: Astrological sign. I bet you were born under Aries. Aries people are forceful and dynamic. They dote on noise! They love to bang things around! You must have had lots of banging around in the army and now that you're out, you make up for it by treating inanimate objects with such a fury!

[STELLA *has been going in and out of closet during this scene. Now she pops her head out of the closet.*]

STELLA: Stanley was born just five minutes after Christmas.

BLANCHE: Capricorn—the Goat!

STANLEY: What sign were *you* born under?

BLANCHE: Oh, my birthday's next month, the fifteenth of September; that's under Virgo.

STANLEY: What's Virgo?

BLANCHE: Virgo is the Virgin.

STANLEY: [*Contemptuously.*] *Hah!* [*He advances a little as he knots his tie.*] Say, do you happen to know somebody named Shaw?

[*Her face expresses a faint shock. She reaches for the cologne bottle and dampens her handkerchief as she answers carefully.*]

BLANCHE: Why, everybody knows somebody named Shaw!

STANLEY: Well, this somebody named Shaw is under the impression he met you in Laurel, but I figure he must have got you mixed up with some other party because this other party is someone he met at a hotel called the Flamingo.

[BLANCHE *laughs breathlessly as she touches the cologne-dampened handkerchief to her temples.*]

BLANCHE: I'm afraid he does have me mixed up with this "other party." The Hotel Flamingo is not the sort of establishment I would dare to be seen in!

STANLEY: You know of it?

BLANCHE: Yes, I've seen it and smelled it.

STANLEY: You must've got pretty close if you could smell it.

BLANCHE: The odor of cheap perfume is penetrating.

STANLEY: That stuff you use is expensive?

BLANCHE: Twenty-five dollars an ounce! I'm nearly out. That's just a hint if you want to remember my birthday! [*She speaks lightly but her voice has a note of fear.*]

STANLEY: Shaw must've got you mixed up. He goes in and out of Laurel all the time so he can check on it and clear up any mistake.

[*He turns away and crosses to the portieres.* BLANCHE *closes her eyes as if faint. Her hand trembles as she lifts the handkerchief again to her forehead.* STEVE *and* EUNICE *come around corner.* STEVE's *arm is around* EUNICE's *shoulder and she is sobbing luxuriously and he is cooing love-words. There is a murmur of thunder as they go slowly upstairs in a tight embrace.*]

STANLEY: [*To* STELLA.] I'll wait for you at the Four Deuces!

STELLA: Hey! Don't I rate one kiss?

STANLEY: Not in front of your sister.

> [*He goes out.* BLANCHE *rises from her chair. She seems faint; looks about her with an expression of almost panic.*]

BLANCHE: Stella! What have you heard about me?

STELLA: Huh?

BLANCHE: What have people been telling you about me?

STELLA: Telling?

BLANCHE: You haven't heard any—unkind—gossip about me?

STELLA: Why, no, Blanche, of course not!

BLANCHE: Honey, there was—a good deal of talk in Laurel.

STELLA: About *you,* Blanche?

BLANCHE: I wasn't so good the last two years or so, after Belle Reve had started to slip through my fingers.

STELLA: All of us do things we—

BLANCHE: I never was hard or self-sufficient enough. When people are soft—soft people have got to shimmer and glow—they've got to put on soft colors, the colors of butterfly wings, and put a—paper lantern over the light. . . . It isn't enough to be soft *and attractive.* And I—I'm fading now! I don't know how much longer I can turn the trick. [*The afternoon has faded to dusk.* STELLA *goes into the bedroom and turns on the light under the paper lantern. She holds a bottled soft drink in her hand.*] Have you been listening to me?

STELLA: I don't listen to you when you are being morbid! [*She advances with the bottled Coke.*]

BLANCHE: [*With abrupt change to gaiety.*] Is that Coke for me?

STELLA: Not for anyone else!

BLANCHE: Why, you precious thing, you! Is it just Coke?

STELLA: [*Turning.*] You mean you want a shot in it!

BLANCHE: Well, honey, a shot never does a Coke any harm! Let me! You mustn't wait on me!

STELLA: I like to wait on you, Blanche. It makes it seem more like home. [*She goes into the kitchen, finds a glass and pours a shot of whiskey into it.*]

BLANCHE: I have to admit I love to be waited on . . . [*She rushes into the bedroom.* STELLA *goes to her with the glass.* BLANCHE *suddenly clutches* STELLA's *free hand with a moaning sound and presses the hand to her lips.* STELLA *is embarrassed by her show of emotion.* BLANCHE *speaks in a choked voice.*] You're—you're—so *good* to me! And I—

STELLA: Blanche.

BLANCHE: I know, I won't! You hate me to talk sentimental! But honey, *believe* I feel things more than I *tell* you! I *won't* stay long! I won't, I *promise* I—

STELLA: Blanche!

BLANCHE: [*Hysterically.*] I won't, I promise, *I'll* go! Go *soon!* I will *really!* I *won't* hang around until he—throws me out . . .

STELLA: Now will you stop talking foolish?

BLANCHE: Yes, honey. Watch how you pour—that fizzy stuff foams over!

[BLANCHE *laughs shrilly and grabs the glass, but her hand shakes so it almost slips from her grasp.* STELLA *pours the Coke into the glass. It foams over and spills.* BLANCHE *gives a piercing cry.*]

STELLA: [*Shocked by the cry.*] Heavens!

BLANCHE: Right on my pretty white skirt!

STELLA: Oh . . . Use my hanky. Blot gently.

BLANCHE: [*Slowly recovering.*] I know—gently—gently . . .

STELLA: Did it stain?

BLANCHE: Not a bit. Ha-ha! Isn't that lucky? [*She sits down shakily, taking a grateful drink. She holds the glass in both hands and continues to laugh a little.*]

STELLA: Why did you scream like that?

BLANCHE: I don't know why I screamed! [*Continuing nervously.*] Mitch—Mitch is coming at seven. I guess I am just feeling nervous about our relations. [*She begins to talk rapidly and breathlessly.*] He hasn't gotten a thing but a good-night kiss, that's all I have given him, Stella. I want his respect. And men don't want anything they get too easy. But on the other hand men lose interest quickly. Especially when the girl is over—thirty. They think a girl over thirty ought to—the vulgar term is—"put out." . . . And I—I'm not "putting out." Of course he—he doesn't know—I mean I haven't informed him—of my real age!

STELLA: Why are you sensitive about your age?

BLANCHE: Because of hard knocks my vanity's been given. What I mean is—he thinks I'm sort of—prim and proper, you know! [*She laughs out sharply.*] I want to *deceive* him enough to make him—want me . . .

STELLA: Blanche, do you want *him?*

BLANCHE: I want to *rest!* I want to breathe quietly again! Yes—I *want* Mitch . . . *very badly!* Just think! If it happens! I can leave here and not be anyone's problem . . .

[STANLEY *comes around the corner with a drink under his belt.*]

STANLEY: [*Bawling.*] Hey, Steve! Hey, Eunice! Hey, Stella!

[*There are joyous calls from above. Trumpet and drums are heard from around the corner.*]

STELLA: [*Kissing* BLANCHE *impulsively.*] It *will* happen!

BLANCHE: [*Doubtfully.*] It will?

STELLA: It *will!* [*She goes across into the kitchen, looking back at* BLANCHE.] It will, honey, *it will.* . . . But don't take another drink! [*Her voice catches as she goes out the door to meet her husband.*]

[BLANCHE *sinks faintly back in her chair with her drink.* EUNICE *shrieks with laughter and runs down the steps.* STEVE *bounds after her with goat-like screeches and chases her around corner.* STANLEY *and* STELLA *twine arms as they follow, laughing. Dusk settles deeper. The music from the Four Deuces is slow and blue.*]

BLANCHE: Ah, me, ah, me, ah, me . . . [*Her eyes fall shut and the palm leaf fan drops from her fingers. She slaps her hand on the chair arm a couple of times. There is a little glimmer of lightning about the building. A* YOUNG MAN *comes along the street and rings the bell.*] Come in. [*The* YOUNG MAN *appears through the portieres. She regards him with interest.*] Well, well! What can I do for *you?*

YOUNG MAN: I'm collecting for *The Evening Star.*

BLANCHE: I didn't know that stars took up collections.

YOUNG MAN: It's the paper.

BLANCHE: I know, I was joking—feebly! Will you—have a drink?

YOUNG MAN: No, ma'am. No, thank you. I can't drink on the job.

BLANCHE: Oh, well, now, let's see. . . . No, I don't have a dime! I'm not the lady of the house. I'm her sister from Mississippi. I'm one of those poor relations you've heard about.

YOUNG MAN: That's all right. I'll drop by later. [*He starts to go out. She approaches a little.*]

BLANCHE: Hey! [*He turns back shyly. She puts a cigarette in a long holder.*] Could you give me a light? [*She crosses toward him. They meet at the door between the two rooms.*]

YOUNG MAN: Sure. [*He takes out a lighter.*] This doesn't always work.

BLANCHE: It's temperamental? [*It flares.*] Ah!—thank you. [*He starts away again.*] Hey! [*He turns again, still more uncertainly. She goes close to him.*] Uh—what time is it?

YOUNG MAN: Fifteen of seven, ma'am.

BLANCHE: So late? Don't you just love these long rainy afternoons in New Orleans when an hour isn't just an hour—but a little piece of eternity dropped into your hands—and who knows what to do with it? [*She touches his shoulders.*] You—uh—didn't get wet in the rain?

YOUNG MAN: No, ma'am. I stepped inside.

BLANCHE: In a drugstore? And had a soda?

YOUNG MAN: Uh-huh.

BLANCHE: Chocolate?

YOUNG MAN: No, ma'am. Cherry.

BLANCHE: [*Laughing.*] Cherry!

YOUNG MAN: A cherry soda.

BLANCHE: You make my mouth water. [*She touches his cheek lightly, and smiles. Then she goes to the trunk.*]

YOUNG MAN: Well, I'd better be going—

BLANCHE: [*Stopping him.*] Young man! [*He turns. She takes a large, gossamer scarf from the trunk and drapes it about her shoulders. In the ensuing pause, the "Blue Piano" is heard. It continues through the rest of this scene and the opening of the next. The* YOUNG MAN *clears his throat and looks yearningly at the door.*] Young man! Young, young, young man! Has anyone ever told you that you look like a young Prince out of the Arabian Nights? [*The* YOUNG MAN *laughs uncomfortably and stands like a bashful kid.* BLANCHE *speaks softly to him.*] Well, you do, honey lamb! Come here. I want to kiss you, just once, softly and sweetly on your mouth! [*Without waiting for him to accept, she crosses quickly to him and presses her lips to his.*] Now run along, now, quickly! It would be nice to keep you, but I've got to be good—and keep my hands off children.

[*He stares at her a moment. She opens the door for him and blows a kiss at him as he goes down the steps with a dazed look. She stands there a little dreamily after he has disappeared. Then* MITCH *appears around the corner with a bunch of roses.*]

BLANCHE: [*Gaily.*] Look who's coming! My Rosenkavalier![9] Bow to me first . . . now present them! *Ahhhh—Merciiii!* [*She looks at him over them, coquettishly pressing them to her lips. He beams at her self-consciously.*]

SCENE 6

It is about two A.M. *on the same evening. The outer wall of the building is visible.* BLANCHE *and* MITCH *come in. The utter exhaustion which only a neurasthenic personality can know is evident in* BLANCHE's *voice and manner.* MITCH *is stolid but depressed. They have probably been out to the amusement park on Lake Pontchartrain, for* MITCH *is bearing, upside down, a plaster statuette of Mae West, the sort of prize won at shooting galleries and carnival games of chance.*

BLANCHE: [*Stopping lifelessly at the steps.*] Well—[MITCH *laughs uneasily.*] Well . . .
MITCH: I guess it must be pretty late—and you're tired.
BLANCHE: Even the hot tamale man has deserted the street, and he hangs on till the end. [MITCH *laughs uneasily again.*] How will you get home?
MITCH: I'll walk over to Bourbon and catch an owl-car.
BLANCHE: [*Laughing grimly.*] Is that street-car named Desire still grinding along the tracks at this hour?
MITCH: [*Heavily.*] I'm afraid you haven't gotten much fun out of this evening, Blanche.
BLANCHE: I spoiled it for *you.*
MITCH: No, you didn't, but I felt all the time that I wasn't giving you much— entertainment.
BLANCHE: I simply couldn't rise to the occasion. That was all. I don't think I've ever tried so hard to be gay and made such a dismal mess of it. I get ten points for trying!—I *did* try.
MITCH: Why did you try if you didn't feel like it, Blanche?
BLANCHE: I was just obeying the law of nature.
MITCH: Which law is that?
BLANCHE: The one that says the lady must entertain the gentleman—or no dice! See if you can locate my door key in this purse. When I'm so tired my fingers are all thumbs!
MITCH: [*Rooting in her purse.*] This it?

9. *Knight of the Rose,* title of a romantic opera (1911) by Richard Strauss (1864–1949). *Merci:* thank you (French).

BLANCHE: No, honey, that's the key to my trunk which I must soon be packing.

MITCH: You mean you are leaving here soon?

BLANCHE: I've outstayed my welcome.

MITCH: This it?

[*The music fades away.*]

BLANCHE: Eureka! Honey, you open the door while I take a last look at the sky. [*She leans on the porch rail. He opens the door and stands awkwardly behind her.*] I'm looking for the Pleiades,[1] the Seven Sisters, but these girls are not out tonight. Oh, yes they are, there they are! God bless them! All in a bunch going home from their little bridge party. . . . Y' get the door open? Good boy! I guess you—want to go now . . .

[*He shuffles and coughs a little.*]

MITCH: Can I—uh—kiss you—good night?

BLANCHE: Why do you always ask me if you may?

MITCH: I don't know whether you want me to or not.

BLANCHE: Why should you be so doubtful?

MITCH: That night when we parked by the lake and I kissed you, you—

BLANCHE: Honey, it wasn't the kiss I objected to. I liked the kiss very much. It was the other little—familiarity—that I—felt obliged to—discourage. . . . I didn't resent it! Not a bit in the world! In fact, I was somewhat flattered that you—desired me! But, honey, you know as well as I do that a single girl, a girl alone in the world, has got to keep a firm hold on her emotions or she'll be lost!

MITCH: [*Solemnly.*] Lost?

BLANCHE: I guess you are used to girls that like to be lost. The kind that get lost immediately, on the first date!

MITCH: I like you to be exactly the way that you are, because in all my—experience—I have never known anyone like you. [BLANCHE *looks at him gravely; then she bursts into laughter and then claps a hand to her mouth.*] Are you laughing at me?

BLANCHE: No, honey. The lord and lady of the house have not yet returned, so come in. We'll have a nightcap. Let's leave the lights off. Shall we?

MITCH: You just—do what you want to.

[BLANCHE *precedes him into the kitchen. The outer wall of the building disappears and the interiors of the two rooms can be dimly seen.*]

BLANCHE: [*Remaining in the first room.*] The other room's more comfortable—go on in. This crashing around in the dark is my search for some liquor.

MITCH: You want a drink?

BLANCHE: I want *you* to have a drink! You have been so anxious and solemn all evening, and so have I; we have both been anxious and solemn and now for these few last remaining moments of our lives together—I want to create— *joie de vivre!* I'm lighting a candle.

1. The seven daughters of Atlas who were metamorphosed into stars.

MITCH: That's good.

BLANCHE: We are going to be very Bohemian. We are going to pretend that we are sitting in a little artists' cafe on the Left Bank in Paris! [*She lights a candle stub and puts it in a bottle.*] *Je suis la Dame aux Camellias! Vous êtes—Armand!*[2] Understand French?

MITCH: [*Heavily.*] Naw. Naw, I—

BLANCHE: *Voulez-vous couchez avec moi ce soir? Vous ne comprenez pas? Ah, quelle dommage!*[3]—I mean it's a damned good thing. . . . I've found some liquor! Just enough for two shots without any dividends, honey . . .

MITCH: [*Heavily.*] That's—good.

[*She enters the bedroom with the drinks and the candle.*]

BLANCHE: Sit down! Why don't you take off your coat and loosen your collar?

MITCH: I better leave it on.

BLANCHE: No. I want you to be comfortable.

MITCH: I am ashamed of the way I perspire. My shirt is sticking to me.

BLANCHE: Perspiration is healthy. If people didn't perspire they would die in five minutes. [*She takes his coat from him.*] This is a nice coat. What kind of material is it?

MITCH: They call that stuff alpaca.

BLANCHE: Oh. Alpaca.

MITCH: It's very light-weight alpaca.

BLANCHE: Oh. Light-weight alpaca.

MITCH: I don't like to wear a wash-coat even in summer because I sweat through it.

BLANCHE: Oh.

MITCH: And it don't look neat on me. A man with a heavy build has got to be careful of what he puts on him so he don't look too clumsy.

BLANCHE: You are not too heavy.

MITCH: You don't think I am?

BLANCHE: You are not the delicate type. You have a massive bone-structure and a very imposing physique.

MITCH: Thank you. Last Christmas I was given a membership to the New Orleans Athletic Club.

BLANCHE: Oh, good.

MITCH: It was the finest present I ever was given. I work out there with the weights and I swim and I keep myself fit. When I started there, I was getting soft in the belly but now my belly is hard. It is so hard now that a man can punch me in the belly and it don't hurt me. Punch me! Go on! See? [*She pokes lightly at him.*]

BLANCHE: Gracious. [*Her hand touches her chest.*]

MITCH: Guess how much I weigh, Blanche?

---

2. "I am the Lady of the Camellias! You are—Armand!" Both are characters in the popular romantic play *La Dame aux Camélias* (1852) by the French author Alexandre Dumas (1824–1895); she is a courtesan who gives up her true love, Armand.   3. "Would you like to sleep with me this evening? You don't understand? Ah, what a pity!"

BLANCHE: Oh, I'd say in the vicinity of—one hundred and eighty?

MITCH: Guess again.

BLANCHE: Not that much?

MITCH: No. More.

BLANCHE: Well, you're a tall man and you can carry a good deal of weight without looking awkward.

MITCH: I weigh two hundred and seven pounds and I'm six feet one and one half inches tall in my bare feet—without shoes on. And that is what I weigh stripped.

BLANCHE: Oh, my goodness, me! It's awe-inspiring.

MITCH: [*Embarrassed.*] My weight is not a very interesting subject to talk about. [*He hesitates for a moment.*] What's yours?

BLANCHE: My weight?

MITCH: Yes.

BLANCHE: Guess!

MITCH: Let me lift you.

BLANCHE: Samson![4] Go on, lift me. [*He comes behind her and puts his hands on her waist and raises her lightly off the ground.*] Well?

MITCH: You are light as a feather.

BLANCHE: Ha-ha! [*He lowers her but keeps his hands on her waist.* BLANCHE *speaks with an affectation of demureness.*] You may release me now.

MITCH: Huh?

BLANCHE: [*Gaily.*] I said unhand me, sir. [*He fumblingly embraces her. Her voice sounds gently reproving.*] Now, Mitch. Just because Stanley and Stella aren't at home is no reason why you shouldn't behave like a gentleman.

MITCH: Just give me a slap whenever I step out of bounds.

BLANCHE: That won't be necessary. You're a natural gentleman, one of the very few that are left in the world. I don't want you to think that I am severe and old maid school-teacherish or anything like that. It's just—well—

MITCH: Huh?

BLANCHE: I guess it is just that I have—old-fashioned ideals! [*She rolls her eyes, knowing he cannot see her face.* MITCH *goes to the front door. There is a considerable silence between them.* BLANCHE *sighs and* MITCH *coughs self-consciously.*]

MITCH: [*Finally.*] Where's Stanley and Stella tonight?

BLANCHE: They have gone out. With Mr. and Mrs. Hubbell upstairs.

MITCH: Where did they go?

BLANCHE: I think they were planning to go to a midnight prevue at Loew's State.

MITCH: We should all go out together some night.

BLANCHE: No. That wouldn't be a good plan.

MITCH: Why not?

BLANCHE: You are an old friend of Stanley's?

MITCH: We was together in the Two-forty-first.[5]

BLANCHE: I guess he talks to you frankly?

MITCH: Sure.

4. Legendary strong man, in the Old Testament. 5. Battalion of Engineers, in World War II.

BLANCHE: Has he talked to you about me?

MITCH: Oh—not very much.

BLANCHE: The way you say that, I suspect that he has.

MITCH: No, he hasn't said much.

BLANCHE: But what he *has* said. What would you say his attitude toward me was?

MITCH: Why do you want to ask that?

BLANCHE: Well—

MITCH: Don't you get along with him?

BLANCHE: What do you think?

MITCH: I don't think he understands you.

BLANCHE: That is putting it mildly. If it weren't for Stella about to have a baby, I wouldn't be able to endure things here.

MITCH: He isn't—nice to you?

BLANCHE: He is insufferably rude. Goes out of his way to offend me.

MITCH: In what way, Blanche?

BLANCHE: Why, in every conceivable way.

MITCH: I'm surprised to hear that.

BLANCHE: Are you?

MITCH: Well, I—don't see how anybody could be rude to you.

BLANCHE: It's really a pretty frightful situation. You see, there's no privacy here. There's just these portieres between the two rooms at night. He stalks through the rooms in his underwear at night. And I have to ask him to close the bathroom door. That sort of commonness isn't necessary. You probably wonder why I don't move out. Well, I'll tell you frankly. A teacher's salary is barely sufficient for her living expenses. I didn't save a penny last year and so I had to come here for the summer. That's why I have to put up with my sister's husband. And he has to put up with me, apparently so much against his wishes. . . . Surely he must have told you how much he hates he!

MITCH: I don't think he hates you.

BLANCHE: He hates me. Or why would he insult me? The first time I laid eyes on him I thought to myself, that man is my executioner! That man will destroy me, unless——

MITCH: Blanche—

BLANCHE: Yes, honey?

MITCH: Can I ask you a question?

BLANCHE: Yes. What?

MITCH: How old are you?

[*She makes a nervous gesture.*]

BLANCHE: Why do you want to know?

MITCH: I talked to my mother about you and she said, "How old is Blanche?" And I wasn't able to tell her. [*There is another pause.*]

BLANCHE: You talked to your mother about me?

MITCH: Yes.

BLANCHE: Why?

MITCH: I told my mother how nice you were, and I liked you.

BLANCHE: Were you sincere about that?

MITCH: You know I was.

BLANCHE: Why did your mother want to know my age?

MITCH: Mother is sick.

BLANCHE: I'm sorry to hear it. Badly?

MITCH: She won't live long. Maybe just a few months.

BLANCHE: Oh.

MITCH: She worries because I'm not settled.

BLANCHE: Oh.

MITCH: She wants me to be settled down before she—[*His voice is hoarse and he clears his throat twice, shuffling nervously around with his hands in and out of his pockets.*]

BLANCHE: You love her very much, don't you?

MITCH: Yes.

BLANCHE: I think you have a great capacity for devotion. You will be lonely when she passes on, won't you? [MITCH *clears his throat and nods.*] I understand what that is.

MITCH: To be lonely?

BLANCHE: I loved someone, too, and the person I loved I lost.

MITCH: Dead? [*She crosses to the window and sits on the sill, looking out. She pours herself another drink.*] A man?

BLANCHE: He was a boy, just a boy, when I was a very young girl. When I was sixteen, I made the discovery—love. All at once and much, much too completely. It was like you suddenly turned a blinding light on something that had always been half in shadow, that's how it struck the world for me. But I was unlucky. Deluded. There was something different about the boy, a nervousness, a softness and tenderness which wasn't like a man's, although he wasn't the least bit effeminate looking—still—that thing was there. . . . He came to me for help. I didn't know that. I didn't find out anything till after our marriage when we'd run away and come back and all I knew was I'd failed him in some mysterious way and wasn't able to give the help he needed but couldn't speak of! He was in the quicksands and clutching at me—but I wasn't holding him out, I was slipping in with him! I didn't know that. I didn't know anything except I loved him unendurably but without being able to help him or help myself. Then I found out. In the worst of all possible ways. By coming suddenly into a room that I thought was empty—which wasn't empty, but had two people in it . . . the boy I had married and an older man who had been his friend for years . . . [*A locomotive is heard approaching outside. She claps her hands to her ears and crouches over. The headlight of the locomotive glares into the room as it thunders past. As the noise recedes she straightens slowly and continues speaking.*] Afterward we pretended that nothing had been discovered. Yes, the three of us drove out to Moon Lake Casino, very drunk and laughing all the way. [*Polka music sounds, in a minor key faint with distance.*] We danced the "Varsouviana!"[6] Suddenly in the mid-

6. Fast Polish dance, similar to the polka.

dle of the dance the boy I had married broke away from me and ran out of the casino. A few moments later—a shot! [*The polka stops abruptly.* BLANCHE *rises stiffly. Then, the polka resumes in a major key.*] I ran out—all did!—all ran and gathered about the terrible thing at the edge of the lake! I couldn't get near for the crowding. Then somebody caught my arm. "Don't go any closer! Come back! You don't want to see!" See? See what! Then I heard voices say— Allan! Allan! The Grey boy! He'd stuck the revolver into his mouth, and fired—so that the back of his head had been—blown away! [*She sways and covers her face.*] It was because—on the dance floor—unable to stop myself— I'd suddenly said—"I saw! I know! You disgust me . . ." And then the search-light which had been turned on the world was turned off again and never for one moment since has there been any light that's stronger than this— kitchen—candle . . .

[MITCH *gets up awkwardly and moves toward her a little. The polka music increases.* MITCH *stands beside her.*]

MITCH: [*Drawing her slowly into his arms.*] You need somebody. And I need some-body, too. Could it be—you and me, Blanche?

[*She stares at him vacantly for a moment. Then with a soft cry huddles in his embrace. She makes a sobbing effort to speak but the words won't come. He kisses her forehead and her eyes and finally her lips. The polka tune fades out. Her breath is drawn and released in long, grateful sobs.*]

BLANCHE: Sometimes—there's God—so quickly!

SCENE 7

It is late afternoon in mid-September.
The portieres are open and a table is set for a birthday supper, with cake and flowers.
STELLA *is completing the decorations as* STANLEY *comes in.*

STANLEY: What's all this stuff for?
STELLA: Honey, it's Blanche's birthday.
STANLEY: She here?
STELLA: In the bathroom.
STANLEY: [*Mimicking.*] "Washing out some things"?
STELLA: I reckon so.
STANLEY: How long she been in there?
STELLA: All afternoon.
STANLEY: [*Mimicking.*] "Soaking in a hot tub"?
STELLA: Yes.
STANLEY: Temperature 100 on the nose, and she soaks herself in a hot tub.
STELLA: She says it cools her off for the evening.
STANLEY: And you run out an' get her cokes, I suppose? And serve 'em to Her Majesty in the tub? [STELLA *shrugs.*] Set down here a minute.

STELLA: Stanley, I've got things to do.

STANLEY: Set down! I've got th' dope on your big sister, Stella.

STELLA: Stanley, stop picking on Blanche.

STANLEY: That girl calls *me* common!

STELLA: Lately you been doing all you can think of to rub her the wrong way, Stanley, and Blanche is sensitive and you've got to realize that Blanche and I grew up under very different circumstances than you did.

STANLEY: So I been told. And told and told and told! You know she's been feeding us a pack of lies here?

STELLA: No, I don't and—

STANLEY: Well, she has, however. But now the cat's out of the bag! I found out some things!

STELLA: What—things?

STANLEY: Things I already suspected. But now I got proof from the most reliable sources—which I have checked on!

> [BLANCHE *is singing in the bathroom a saccharine popular ballad which is used contrapuntally with* STANLEY's *speech.*]

STELLA: [*To* STANLEY.] Lower your voice!

STANLEY: Some canary bird, huh!

STELLA: Now please tell me quietly what you think you've found out about my sister.

STANLEY: Lie Number One: All this squeamishness she puts on! You should just know the line she's been feeding to Mitch. He thought she had never been more than kissed by a fellow! But Sister Blanche is no lily! Ha-ha! Some lily she is!

STELLA: What have you heard and who from?

STANLEY: Our supply-man down at the plant has been going through Laurel for years and he knows all about her and everybody else in the town of Laurel knows all about her. She is as famous in Laurel as if she was the President of the United States, only she is not respected by any party! This supply-man stops at a hotel called the Flamingo.

BLANCHE: [*Singing blithely.*] "Say, it's only a paper moon, Sailing over a cardboard sea—But it wouldn't be make-believe If you believed in me!"[7]

STELLA: What about the—Flamingo?

STANLEY: She stayed there, too.

STELLA: My sister lived at Belle Reve.

STANLEY: This is after the home-place had slipped through her lily-white fingers! She moved to the Flamingo! A second-class hotel which has the advantage of not interfering in the private social life of the personalities there! The Flamingo is used to all kinds of goings-on. But even the management of the Flamingo was impressed by Dame Blanche! In fact they was so impressed by Dame Blanche that they requested her to turn in her room key—for permanently! This happened a couple of weeks before she showed here.

7. From "It's Only a Paper Moon" (1933), a popular song by Harold Arlen.

BLANCHE: [*Singing.*] "It's a Barnum and Bailey world, Just as phony as it can be—
But it wouldn't be make-believe If you believed in me!"

STELLA: What—contemptible—lies!

STANLEY: Sure, I can see how you would be upset by this. She pulled the wool over
your eyes as much as Mitch's!

STELLA: It's pure invention! There's not a word of truth in it and if I were a man
and this creature had dared to invent such things in my presence—

BLANCHE: [*Singing.*] "Without your love, it's a honky-tonk parade! Without your
love, It's a melody played In a penny arcade . . ."

STANLEY: Honey, I told you I thoroughly checked on these stories! Now wait till I
finish. The trouble with Dame Blanche was that she couldn't put on her act
any more in Laurel! They got wised up after two or three dates with her and
then they quit, and she goes on to another, the same old line, same old act,
same old hooey! But the town was too small for this to go on forever! And as
time went by she became a town character. Regarded as not just different
but downright loco—nuts. [STELLA *draws back.*] And for the last year or two
she has been washed up like poison. That's why she's here this summer,
visiting royalty, putting on all this act—because she's practically told by the
mayor to get out of town! Yes, did you know there was an army camp near
Laurel and your sister's was one of the places called "Out-of-Bounds"?

BLANCHE: "It's only a paper moon, Just as phony as it can be—But it wouldn't be
make-believe If you believed in me!"

STANLEY: Well, so much for her being such a refined and particular type of girl.
Which brings us to Lie Number Two.

BLANCHE: I don't want to hear any more!

STANLEY: She's not going back to teach school! In fact I am willing to bet you that
she never had no idea of returning to Laurel! She didn't resign temporarily
from the high school because of her nerves! No, siree, Bob! She didn't. They
kicked her out of that high school before the spring term ended—and I hate
to tell you the reason that step was taken! A seventeen-year-old boy—she'd
gotten mixed up with!

BLANCHE: "It's a Barnum and Bailey world, Just as phony as it can be—"

[*In the bathroom the water goes on loud; little breathless cries and peals of
laughter are heard as if a child were frolicking in the tub.*]

STELLA: This is making me—sick!

STANLEY: The boy's dad learned about it and got in touch with the high school
superintendent. Boy, oh, boy, I'd like to have been in that office when Dame
Blanche was called on the carpet! I'd like to have seen her trying to squirm
out of that one! But they had her on the hook good and proper that time
and she knew that the jig was all up! They told her she better move on to
some fresh territory. Yep, it was practickly a town ordinance passed against
her!

[*The bathroom door is opened and* BLANCHE *thrusts her head out, holding a
towel about her hair.*]

BLANCHE: Stella!

STELLA: [*Faintly.*] Yes, Blanche?

BLANCHE: Give me another bath-towel to dry my hair with. I've just washed it.

STELLA: Yes, Blanche. [*She crosses in a dazed way from the kitchen to the bathroom door with a towel.*]

BLANCHE: What's the matter, honey?

STELLA: Matter? Why?

BLANCHE: You have such a strange expression on your face!

STELLA: Oh—[*She tries to laugh.*] I guess I'm a little tired!

BLANCHE: Why don't you bathe, too, soon as I get out?

STANLEY: [*Calling from the kitchen.*] How soon is that going to be?

BLANCHE: Not so terribly long! Possess your soul in patience!

STANLEY: It's not my soul, it's my kidneys I'm worried about! [BLANCHE *slams the door.* STANLEY *laughs harshly.* STELLA *comes slowly back into the kitchen.*] Well, what do you think of it?

STELLA: I don't believe all of those stories and I think your supply-man was mean and rotten to tell them. It's possible that some of the things he said are partly true. There are things about my sister I don't approve of—things that caused sorrow at home. She was always—flighty!

STANLEY: Flighty!

STELLA: But when she was young, very young, she married a boy who wrote poetry. . . . He was extremely good-looking. I think Blanche didn't just love him but worshipped the ground he walked on! Adored him and thought him almost too fine to be human! But then she found out—

STANLEY: What?

STELLA: This beautiful and talented young man was a degenerate. Didn't your supply-man give you that information?

STANLEY: All we discussed was recent history. That must have been a pretty long time ago.

STELLA: Yes, it was—a pretty long time ago . . .

[STANLEY *comes up and takes her by the shoulders rather gently. She gently withdraws from him. Automatically she starts sticking little pink candles in the birthday cake.*]

STANLEY: How many candles you putting in that cake?

STELLA: I'll stop at twenty-five.

STANLEY: Is company expected?

STELLA: We asked Mitch to come over for cake and ice-cream.

[STANLEY *looks a little uncomfortable. He lights a cigarette from the one he has just finished.*]

STANLEY: I wouldn't be expecting Mitch over tonight.

[STELLA *pauses in her occupation with candles and looks slowly around at* STANLEY.]

STELLA: *Why?*

STANLEY: Mitch is a buddy of mine. We were in the same outfit together—Two-forty-first Engineers. We work in the same plant and now on the same bowling team. You think I could face him if—

STELLA: Stanley Kowalski, did you—did you repeat what that—?

STANLEY: You're goddam right I told him! I'd have that on my conscience the rest of my life if I knew all that stuff and let my best friend get caught!

STELLA: Is Mitch through with her?

STANLEY: Wouldn't you be if—?

STELLA: I said, *Is Mitch through with her?*

[BLANCHE's *voice is lifted again, serenely as a bell. She sings "But it wouldn't be make-believe If you believed in me."*]

STANLEY: No, I don't think he's necessarily through with her—just wised up!

STELLA: Stanley, she thought Mitch was—going to—going to marry her. I was hoping so, too.

STANLEY: Well, he's not going to marry her. Maybe he *was,* but he's not going to jump in a tank with a school of sharks—now! [*He rises.*] Blanche! Oh, Blanche! Can I please get in my bathroom? [*There is a pause.*]

BLANCHE: Yes, indeed, sir! Can you wait one second while I dry?

STANLEY: Having waited one hour I guess one second ought to pass in a hurry.

STELLA: And she hasn't got her job? Well, what will she do!

STANLEY: She's not stayin' here after Tuesday. You know that, don't you? Just to make sure I bought her ticket myself. A bus ticket.

STELLA: In the first place, Blanche wouldn't go on a bus.

STANLEY: She'll go on a bus and like it.

STELLA: No, she won't, no, she won't, Stanley!

STANLEY: *She'll go!* Period. P.S. She'll go *Tuesday!*

STELLA: [*Slowly.*] What'll—she—do? What on earth will she—*do!*

STANLEY: Her future is mapped out for her.

STELLA: What do you mean?

[BLANCHE *sings.*]

STANLEY: Hey, canary bird! Toots! Get *OUT* of the *BATHROOM!*

[*The bathroom door flies open and* BLANCHE *emerges with a gay peal of laughter, but as* STANLEY *crosses past her, a frightened look appears in her face, almost a look of panic. He doesn't look at her but slams the bathroom door shut as he goes in.*]

BLANCHE: [*Snatching up a hairbrush.*] Oh, I feel so good after my long, hot bath, I feel so good and cool and—rested!

STELLA: [*Sadly and doubtfully from the kitchen.*] Do you, Blanche?

BLANCHE: [*Snatching up a hairbrush.*] Yes, I do, so refreshed! [*She tinkles her highball glass.*] A hot bath and a long, cold drink always give me a brand new outlook on life! [*She looks through the portieres at* STELLA, *standing between them, and slowly stops brushing.*] Something has happened!—What is it?

STELLA: [*Turning away quickly.*] Why, nothing has happened, Blanche.

BLANCHE: You're lying! Something has! [*She stares fearfully at* STELLA, *who pretends to be busy at the table. The distant piano goes into a hectic breakdown.*]

SCENE 8

Three quarters of an hour later.

The view through the big windows is fading gradually into a still-golden dusk. A torch of sunlight blazes on the side of a big water-tank or oil-drum across the empty lot toward the business district which is now pierced by pinpoints of lighted windows or windows reflecting the sunset.

The three people are completing a dismal birthday supper. STANLEY *looks sullen.* STELLA *is embarrassed and sad.*

BLANCHE *has a tight, artificial smile on her drawn face. There is a fourth place at the table which is left vacant.*

BLANCHE: [*Suddenly.*] Stanley, tell us a joke, tell us a funny story to make us all laugh. I don't know what's the matter, we're all so solemn. Is it because I've been stood up by my beau? [STELLA *laughs feebly.*] It's the first time in my entire experience with men, and I've had a good deal of all sorts, that I've actually been stood up by anybody! Ha-ha! I don't know how to take it. . . . Tell us a funny little story, Stanley! Something to help us out.
STANLEY: I didn't think you liked my stories, Blanche.
BLANCHE: I like them when they're amusing but not indecent.
STANLEY: I don't know any refined enough for your taste.
BLANCHE: Then let me tell one.
STELLA: Yes, you tell one, Blanche. You used to know lots of good stories.

[*The music fades.*]

BLANCHE: Let me see, now. . . . I must run through my repertoire! Oh, yes—I love parrot stories! Do you all like parrot stories? Well, this one's about the old maid and the parrot. This old maid, she had a parrot that cursed a blue streak and knew more vulgar expressions than Mr. Kowalski!
STANLEY: Huh.
BLANCHE: And the only way to hush the parrot up was to put the cover back on its cage so it would think it was night and go back to sleep. Well, one morning the old maid had just uncovered the parrot for the day—when who should she see coming up the front walk but the preacher! Well, she rushed back to the parrot and slipped the cover back on the cage and then she let in the preacher. And the parrot was perfectly still, just as quiet as a mouse, but just as she was asking the preacher how much sugar he wanted in his coffee—the parrot broke the silence with a loud—[*She whistles.*]—and said— "God *damn*, but that was a short day!" [*She throws back her head and laughs.* STELLA *also makes an ineffectual effort to seem amused.* STANLEY *pays no attention to the story but reaches way over the table to spear his fork into the remaining chop which he eats with his fingers.*] Apparently Mr. Kowalski was not amused.

STELLA: Mr. Kowalski is too busy making a pig of himself to think of anything else!

STANLEY: That's right, baby.

STELLA: Your face and your fingers are disgustingly greasy. Go and wash up and then help me clear the table.

[*He hurls a plate to the floor.*]

STANLEY: That's how I'll clear the table! [*He seizes her arm.*] Don't ever talk that way to me! "Pig—Polack—disgusting—vulgar—greasy!"—them kind of words have been on your tongue and your sister's too much around here! What do you two think you are? A pair of queens? Remember what Huey Long[8] said—"Every Man is a King!" And I am the king around here, so don't forget it! [*He hurls a cup and saucer to the floor.*] My place is cleared! You want me to clear your places?

[STELLA *begins to cry weakly.* STANLEY *stalks out on the porch and lights a cigarette. The Negro entertainers around the corner are heard.*]

BLANCHE: What happened while I was bathing? What did he tell you, Stella?

STELLA: Nothing, nothing, nothing!

BLANCHE: I think he told you something about Mitch and me! You know why Mitch didn't come but you won't tell me! [STELLA *shakes her head helplessly.*] I'm going to call him!

STELLA: I wouldn't call him, Blanche.

BLANCHE: I am, I'm going to call him on the phone.

STELLA: [*Miserably.*] I wish you wouldn't.

BLANCHE: I intend to be given some explanation from someone!

[*She rushes to the phone in the bedroom.* STELLA *goes out on the porch and stares reproachfully at her husband. He grunts and turns away from her.*]

STELLA: I hope you're pleased with your doings. I never had so much trouble swallowing food in my life, looking at that girl's face and the empty chair! [*She cries quietly.*]

BLANCHE: [*At the phone.*] Hello. Mr. Mitchell, please. . . . Oh. . . . I would like to leave a number if I may. Magnolia 9047. And say it's important to call. . . . Yes, very important. . . . Thank you. [*She remains by the phone with a lost, frightened look.*]

[STANLEY *turns slowly back toward his wife and takes her clumsily in his arms.*]

STANLEY: Stell, it's gonna be all right after she goes and after you've had the baby. It's gonna be all right again between you and me the way that it was. You remember the way that it was? Them nights we had together? God, honey, it's gonna be sweet when we can make noise in the night the way that we used to and get the colored lights going with nobody's sister behind the

---

8. Demagogic Louisiana politcal leader, governor, and senator (1893–1935).

curtains to hear us! [*Their upstairs neighbors are heard in bellowing laughter at something.* STANLEY *chuckles.*] Steve an' Eunice . . .

STELLA: Come on back in. [*She returns to the kitchen and starts lighting the candles on the white cake.*] Blanche?

BLANCHE: Yes. [*She returns from the bedroom to the table in the kitchen.*] Oh, those pretty, pretty little candles! Oh, don't burn them, Stella.

STELLA: I certainly will.

[STANLEY *comes back in.*]

BLANCHE: You ought to save them for baby's birthdays. Oh, I hope candles are going to glow in his life and I hope that his eyes are going to be like candles, like two blue candles lighted in a white cake!

STANLEY: [*Sitting down.*] What poetry!

BLANCHE: [*She pauses reflectively for a moment.*] I shouldn't have called him.

STELLA: There's lots of things could have happened.

BLANCHE: There's no excuse for it, Stella. I don't have to put up with insults. I won't be taken for granted.

STANLEY: Goddamn, it's hot in here with the steam from the bathroom.

BLANCHE: I've said I was sorry three times. [*The piano fades out.*] I take hot baths for my nerves. Hydrotherapy, they call it. You healthy Polack, without a nerve in your body, of course you don't know what anxiety feels like!

STANLEY: I am not a Polack. People from Poland are Poles, not Polacks. But what I am is a one-hundred-per-cent American, born and raised in the greatest country on earth and proud as hell of it, so don't ever call me a Polack.

[*The phone rings.* BLANCHE *rises expectantly.*]

BLANCHE: Oh, that's for me, I'm sure.

STANLEY: *I'm* not sure. Keep your seat. [*He crosses leisurely to phone.*] H'lo. Aw, yeh, hello, Mac.

[*He leans against wall, staring insultingly in at* BLANCHE. *She sinks back in her chair with a frightened look.* STELLA *leans over and touches her shoulder.*]

BLANCHE: Oh, keep your hands off me, Stella. What is the matter with you? Why do you look at me with that pitying look?

STANLEY: [*Bawling.*] QUIET IN THERE!—We've got a noisy woman on the place.— Go on, Mac. At Riley's? No, I don't wanta bowl at Riley's. I had a little trouble with Riley last week. I'm the team captain, ain't I? All right, then, we're not gonna bowl at Riley's, we're gonna bowl at the West Side or the Gala! All right, Mac. See you! [*He hangs up and returns to the table.* BLANCHE *fiercely controls herself, drinking quickly from her tumbler of water. He doesn't look at her but reaches in a pocket. Then he speaks slowly and with false amiability.*] Sister Blanche, I've got a little birthday remembrance for you.

BLANCHE: Oh, have you, Stanley? I wasn't expecting any, I—I don't know why Stella wants to observe my birthday! I'd much rather forget it—when you— reach twenty-seven! Well—age is a subject that you'd prefer to—ignore!

STANLEY: Twenty-seven?

BLANCHE: [*Quickly.*] What is it? Is it for *me*?

[*He is holding a little envelope toward her.*]

STANLEY: Yes, I hope you like it!

BLANCHE: Why, why—Why, it's a—

STANLEY: Ticket! Back to Laurel! On the Greyhound! Tuesday! [*The "Varsouviana" music steals in softly and continues playing.* STELLA *rises abruptly and turns her back.* BLANCHE *tries to smile. Then she tries to laugh. Then she gives both up and springs from the table and runs into the next room. She clutches her throat and then runs into the bathroom. Coughing, gagging sounds are heard.*] Well!

STELLA: You didn't need to do that.

STANLEY: Don't forget all that I took off her.

STELLA: You needn't have been so cruel to someone alone as she is.

STANLEY: Delicate piece she is.

STELLA: She is. She was. You didn't know Blanche as a girl. Nobody, nobody, was tender and trusting as she was. But people like you abused her, and forced her to change. [*He crosses into the bedroom, ripping off his shirt, and changes into a brilliant silk bowling shirt. She follows him.*] Do you think you're going bowling now?

STANLEY: Sure.

STELLA: You're not going bowling. [*She catches hold of his shirt.*] Why did you do this to her?

STANLEY: I done nothing to no one. Let go of my shirt. You've torn it.

STELLA: I want to know why. Tell me why.

STANLEY: When we first met, me and you, you thought I was common. How right you was, baby. I was common as dirt. You showed me the snapshot of the place with the columns. I pulled you down off them columns and how you loved it, having them colored lights going! And wasn't we happy together, wasn't it all okay till she showed here? [STELLA *makes a slight movement. Her look goes suddenly inward as if some interior voice had called her name. She begins a slow, shuffling progress from the bedroom to the kitchen, leaning and resting on the back of the chair and then on the edge of a table with a blind look and listening expression.* STANLEY, *finishing with his shirt, is unaware of her reaction.*] And wasn't we happy together? Wasn't it all okay? Till she showed here. Hoity-Toity, describing me as an ape. [*He suddenly notices the change in* STELLA.] Hey, what is it, Stell? [*He crosses to her.*]

STELLA: [*Quietly.*] Take me to the hospital.

[*He is with her now, supporting her with his arm, murmuring indistinguishably as they go outside.*]

SCENE 9

A while later that evening. BLANCHE *is seated in a tense hunched position in a bedroom chair that she has recovered with diagonal green and white stripes. She has on her scarlet satin robe. On the table beside chair is a bottle of liquor and a glass. The rapid, feverish polka tune, the "Varsouviana," is heard. The music is in her mind; she is drinking to escape it and the sense of disaster closing in on her, and she seems to whisper the words of the song. An electric fan is turning back and forth across her.*

MITCH *comes around the corner in work clothes: blue denim shirt and pants. He is unshaven. He climbs the steps to the door and rings.* BLANCHE *is startled.*

BLANCHE: Who is it, please?
MITCH: [*Hoarsely.*] Me. Mitch.

  [*The polka tune stops.*]

BLANCHE: Mitch!—Just a minute. [*She rushes about frantically, hiding the bottle in a closet, crouching at the mirror and dabbing her face with cologne and powder. She is so excited that her breath is audible as she dashes about. At last she rushes to the door in the kitchen and lets him in.*] Mitch!—Y'know, I really shouldn't let you in after the treatment I have received from you this evening! So utterly uncavalier! But hello, beautiful! [*She offers him her lips. He ignores it and pushes past her into the flat. She looks fearfully after him as he stalks into the bedroom.*] My, my, what a cold shoulder! And such uncouth apparel! Why, you haven't even shaved! The unforgivable insult to a lady! But I forgive you. I forgive you because it's such a relief to see you. You've stopped that polka tune that I had caught in my head. Have you ever had anything caught in your head? No, of course you haven't, you dumb angel-puss, you'd never get anything awful caught in your head!

  [*He stares at her while she follows him while she talks. It is obvious that he has had a few drinks on the way over.*]

MITCH: Do we have to have that fan on?
BLANCHE: No!
MITCH: I don't like fans.
BLANCHE: Then let's turn it off, honey. I'm not partial to them! [*She presses the switch and the fan nods slowly off. She clears her throat uneasily as* MITCH *plumps himself down on the bed in the bedroom and lights a cigarette.*] I don't know what there is to drink. I—haven't investigated.
MITCH: I don't want Stan's liquor.
BLANCHE: It isn't Stan's. Everything here isn't Stan's. Some things on the premises are actually mine! How is your mother? Isn't your mother well?
MITCH: Why?
BLANCHE: Something's the matter tonight, but never mind. I won't cross-examine the witness. I'll just— [*She touches her forehead vaguely. The polka tune starts up again.*]—pretend I don't notice anything different about you! That—music again . . .
MITCH: What music?
BLANCHE: The "Varsourviana"! The polka tune they were playing when Allan— Wait! [*A distant revolver shot is heard.* BLANCHE *seems relieved.*] There now, the

shot! It always stops after that. [*The polka music dies out again.*] Yes, now it's stopped.

MITCH: Are you boxed out of your mind?

BLANCHE: I'll go and see what I can find in the way of— [*She crosses into the closet, pretending to search for the bottle.*] Oh, by the way, excuse me for not being dressed. But I'd practically given you up! Had you forgotten your invitation to supper?

MITCH: I wasn't going to see you any more.

BLANCHE: Wait a minute. I can't hear what you're saying and you talk so little that when you do say something, I don't want to miss a single syllable of it. . . . What am I looking around here for? Oh, yes—liquor! We've had so much excitement around here this evening that I *am* boxed out of my mind! [*She pretends suddenly to find the bottle. He draws his foot up on the bed and stares at her contemptuously.*] Here's something. Southern Comfort! What is that, I wonder?

MITCH: If you don't know, it must belong to Stan.

BLANCHE: Take your foot off the bed. It has a light cover on it. Of course you boys don't notice things like that. I've done so much with this place since I've been here.

MITCH: I bet you have.

BLANCHE: You saw it before I came. Well, look at it now! This room is almost— dainty! I want to keep it that way. I wonder if this stuff ought to be mixed with something? Ummm, it's sweet! It's terribly, terribly sweet! Why, it's a *liqueur,* I believe! Yes, that's what it *is,* a liqueur! [MITCH *grunts.*] I'm afraid you won't like it, but try it, and maybe you will.

MITCH: I told you already I don't want none of his liquor and I mean it. You ought to lay off his liquor. He says you been lapping it up all summer like a wild-cat!

BLANCHE: What a fantastic statement! Fantastic of him to say it, fantastic of you to repeat it! I won't descend to the level of such cheap accusations to answer them, even!

MITCH: Huh.

BLANCHE: What's in your mind? I see something in your eyes!

MITCH: [*Getting up.*] It's dark in here.

BLANCHE: I like it dark. The dark is comforting to me.

MITCH: I don't think I ever seen you in the light. [BLANCHE *laughs breathlessly.*] That's a fact!

BLANCHE: Is it?

MITCH: I've never seen you in the afternoon.

BLANCHE: Whose fault is that?

MITCH: You never want to go out in the afternoon.

BLANCHE: Why, Mitch, you're at the plant in the afternoon!

MITCH: Not Sunday afternoon. I've asked you to go out with me sometimes on Sundays but you always make an excuse. You never want to go out till after six and then it's always some place that's not lighted much.

BLANCHE: There is some obscure meaning in this but I fail to catch it.

MITCH: What it means is I've never had a real good look at you, Blanche. Let's turn the light on here.

BLANCHE: [*Fearfully.*] Light? Which light? What for?

MITCH: This one with the paper thing on it.

[*He tears the paper lantern off the light bulb. She utters a frightened gasp.*]

BLANCHE: What did you do that for?

MITCH: So I can take a look at you good and plain!

BLANCHE: Of course you don't really mean to be insulting!

MITCH: No, just realistic.

BLANCHE: I don't want realism. I want magic! [MITCH *laughs.*] Yes, yes, magic! I try to give that to people. I misrepresent things to them. I don't tell truth, I tell what *ought* to be truth. And if that is sinful, then let me be damned for it!— Don't turn the light on!

[MITCH *crosses to the switch. He turns the light on and stares at her. She cries out and covers her face. He turns the lights off again.*]

MITCH: [*Slowly and bitterly.*] I don't mind you being older than what I thought. But all the rest of it—Christ! That pitch about your ideals being so old-fashioned and all the malarkey that you've dished out all summer. Oh, I knew you weren't sixteen any more. But I was a fool enough to believe you was straight.

BLANCHE: Who told you I wasn't—"straight"? My loving brother-in-law. And you believed him.

MITCH: I called him a liar at first. And then I checked on the story. First I asked our supply-man who travels through Laurel. And then I talked directly over long-distance to this merchant.

BLANCHE: Who is this merchant?

MITCH: Kiefaber.

BLANCHE: The merchant Kiefaber of Laurel! I know the man. He whistled at me. I put him in his place. So now for revenge he makes up stories about me.

MITCH: Three people, Kiefaber, Stanley and Shaw, swore to them!

BLANCHE: Rub-a-dub-dub, three men in a tub! And such a filthy tub!

MITCH: Didn't you stay at a hotel called The Flamingo?

BLANCHE: Flamingo? No! Tarantula was the name of it! I stayed at a hotel called The Tarantula Arms!

MITCH: [*Stupidly.*] Tarantula?

BLANCHE: Yes, a big spider! That's where I brought my victims. [*She pours herself another drink.*] Yes, I had many intimacies with strangers. After the death of Allan—intimacies with strangers was all I seemed able to fill my empty heart with. . . . I think it was panic, just panic, that drove me from one to another, hunting for some protection—here and there, in the most—unlikely places—even, at last, in a seventeen-year-old boy but—somebody wrote the superintendent about it—"This woman is morally unfit for her position!" [*She throws back her head with convulsive, sobbing laughter. Then she repeats the statement, gasps, and drinks.*] True? Yes, I suppose—unfit somehow—anyway. . . . So I came here. There was nowhere else I could go. I was played out. You know what played out is? My youth was suddenly gone up the water-spout, and—I met you. You said you needed somebody. Well, I needed somebody, too. I thanked God for you, because you seemed to be gentle—a cleft in the rock of the world that I could hide in! But I guess I was asking, hoping—too much! Kiefaber, Stanley and Shaw have tied an old tin can to the tail of the kite.

[*There is a pause.* MITCH *stares at her dumbly.*]

MITCH: You lied to me, Blanche.
BLANCHE: Don't say I lied to you.
MITCH: Lies, lies, inside and out, all lies.
BLANCHE: Never inside, I didn't lie in my heart . . .

[*A vendor comes around the corner. She is a blind* MEXICAN WOMAN *in a dark shawl, carrying bunches of those gaudy tin flowers that lower-class Mexicans display at funerals and other festive occasions. She is calling barely audibly. Her figure is only faintly visible outside the building.*]

MEXICAN WOMAN: *Flores. Flores, Flores para los muertos.*[9] *Flores. Flores.*
BLANCHE: What? Oh! Somebody outside . . . [*She goes to the door, opens it and stares at the* MEXICAN WOMAN.]
MEXICAN WOMAN: [*She is at the door and offers* BLANCHE *some of her flowers.*] *Flores? Flores para los muertos?*
BLANCHE: [*Frightened.*] No, no! Not now! Not now! [*She darts back into the apartment, slamming the door.*]
MEXICAN WOMAN: [*She turns away and starts to move down the street.*] *Flores para los muertos.*

[*The polka tune fades in.*]

BLANCHE: [*As if to herself.*] Crumble and fade and—regrets—recriminations . . . "If you'd done this, it wouldn't've cost me that!"
MEXICAN WOMAN: *Corones*[1] *para los muertos. Corones . . .*
BLANCHE: Legacies! Huh. . . . And other things such as bloodstained pillow-slips—"Her linen needs changing"—"Yes, Mother. But couldn't we get a colored girl to do it?" No, we couldn't of course. Everything gone but the—
MEXICAN WOMAN: *Flores.*
BLANCHE: Death—I used to sit here and she used to sit over there and death was as close as you are. . . . We didn't dare even admit we had ever heard of it!
MEXICAN WOMAN: *Flores para los muertos, flores—flores . . .*
BLANCHE: The opposite is desire. So do you wonder? How could you possibly wonder! Not far from Belle Reve, before we had lost Belle Reve, was a camp where they trained young soldiers. On Sunday nights they would go in town to get drunk—

---

9. "Flowers for the dead."   1. "Wreaths."

MEXICAN WOMAN: [*Softly.*] *Corones . . .*

BLANCHE: —and on the way back they would stagger onto my lawn and call— "Blanche! Blanche!"—the deaf old lady remaining suspected nothing. But sometimes I slipped outside to answer their calls. . . . Later the paddy-wagon would gather them up like daisies . . . the long way home . . . [*The* MEXICAN WOMAN *turns slowly and drifts back off with her soft mournful cries.* BLANCHE *goes to the dresser and leans forward on it. After a moment,* MITCH *rises and follows her purposefully. The polka music fades away. He places his hands on her waist and tries to turn her about.*] What do you want?

MITCH: [*Fumbling to embrace her.*] What I been missing all summer.

BLANCHE: Then marry me, Mitch!

MITCH: I don't think I want to marry you any more.

BLANCHE: No?

MITCH: [*Dropping his hands from her waist.*] You're not clean enough to bring in the house with my mother.

BLANCHE: Go away, then. [*He stares at her.*] Get out of here quick before I start screaming fire! [*Her throat is tightening with hysteria.*] Get out of here quick before I start screaming fire. [*He still remains staring. She suddenly rushes to the big window with its pale blue square of the soft summer light and cries wildly.*] Fire! Fire! Fire!

> [*With a startled gasp,* MITCH *turns and goes out the outer door, clatters awkwardly down the steps and around the corner of the building.* BLANCHE *staggers back from the window and falls to her knees. The distant piano is slow and blue.*]

SCENE 10

It is a few hours later that night.

BLANCHE *has been drinking fairly steadily since* MITCH *left. She has dragged her wardrobe trunk into the center of the bedroom. It hangs open with flowery dresses thrown across it. As the drinking and packing went on, a mood of hysterical exhilaration came into her and she has decked herself out in a somewhat soiled and crumpled white satin evening gown and a pair of scuffed silver slippers with brilliants set in their heels.*

Now she is placing the rhinestone tiara on her head before the mirror of the dressing-table and murmuring excitedly as if to a group of spectral admirers.

BLANCHE: How about taking a swim, a moonlight swim at the old rock-quarry? If anyone's sober enough to drive a car! Ha-ha! Best way in the world to stop your head buzzing! Only you've got to be careful to dive where the deep pool is—if you hit a rock you don't come up till tomorrow . . . [*Tremblingly she lifts the hand mirror for a closer inspection. She catches her breath and slams the mirror face down with such violence that the glass cracks. She moans a little and attempts to rise.* STANLEY *appears around the corner of the building. He still has on the vivid green silk bowling shirt. As he rounds the corner the honky-tonk music is heard. It continues softly throughout the scene. He enters the kitchen, slamming*

SCENE 11

It is some weeks later. STELLA *is packing* BLANCHE's *things. Sounds of water can be heard running in the bathroom.*

*The portieres are partly open on the poker players—*STANLEY, STEVE, MITCH *and* PABLO—*who sit around the table in the kitchen. The atmosphere of the kitchen is now the same raw, lurid one of the disastrous poker night.*

The building is framed by the sky of turquoise. STELLA *has been crying as she arranges the flowery dresses in the open trunk.*

EUNICE *comes down the steps from her flat above and enters the kitchen. There is an outburst from the poker table.*

STANLEY: Drew to an inside straight and made it, by God.

PABLO: *Maldita sea tu suerto!*

STANLEY: Put it in English, greaseball.

PABLO: I am cursing your rutting luck.

STANLEY: [*Prodigiously elated.*] You know what luck is? Luck is believing you're lucky. Take at Salerno.[2] I believed I was lucky. I figured that 4 out of 5 would not come through but I would . . . and I did. I put that down as a rule. To hold front position in this rat-race you've got to believe you are lucky.

MITCH: You . . . you . . . you . . . Brag . . . brag . . . bull . . . bull.

[STELLA *goes into the bedroom and starts folding a dress.*]

STANLEY: What's the matter with him?

EUNICE: [*Walking past the table.*] I always did say that men are callous things with no feelings but this does beat anything. Making pigs of yourselves. [*She comes through the portieres into the bedroom.*]

STANLEY: What's the matter with her?

STELLA: How is my baby?

EUNICE: Sleeping like a little angel. Brought you some grapes. [*She puts them on a stool and lowers her voice.*] Blanche?

STELLA: Bathing.

EUNICE: How is she?

STELLA: She wouldn't eat anything but asked for a drink.

EUNICE: What did you tell her?

STELLA: I—just told her that—we'd made arrangements for her to rest in the country. She's got it mixed in her mind with Shep Huntleigh.

[BLANCHE *opens the bathroom door slightly.*]

BLANCHE: Stella.

STELLA: Yes.

BLANCHE: That cool yellow silk—the bouclé. See if it's crushed. If it's not too crushed I'll wear it and on the lapel that silver and turquoise pin in the

---

2. Important beachhead in the Allied invasion of Italy in World War II.

shape of a seahorse. You will find them in the heart-shaped box I keep my accessories in. And Stella . . . Try and locate a bunch of artificial violets in that box, too, to pin with the seahorse on the lapel of the jacket.

[*She closes the door.* STELLA *turns to* EUNICE.]

STELLA: I don't know if I did the right thing.
EUNICE: What else could you do?
STELLA: I couldn't believe her story and go on living with Stanley.
EUNICE: Don't ever believe it. Life has got to go on. No matter what happens, you've got to keep on going.

[*The bathroom door opens a little.*]

BLANCHE: [*Looking out.*] Is the coast clear?
STELLA: Yes, Blanche. [*To* EUNICE.] Tell her how well she's looking.
BLANCHE: Please close the curtains before I come out.
STELLA: They're closed.
STANLEY: —How many for you?
PABLO: Two.
STEVE: Three.

[BLANCHE *appears in the amber light of the door. She has a tragic radiance in her red satin robe following the sculptural lines of her body. The "Varsouviana" rises audibly as* BLANCHE *enters the bedroom.*]

BLANCHE: [*With faintly hysterical vivacity.*] I have just washed my hair.
STELLA: Did you?
BLANCHE: I'm not sure I got the soap out.
EUNICE: Such fine hair!
BLANCHE: [*Accepting the compliment.*] It's a problem. Didn't I get a call?
STELLA: Who from, Blanche?
BLANCHE: Shep Huntleigh . . .
STELLA: Why, not yet, honey!
BLANCHE: How strange! I—

[*At the sound of* BLANCHE's *voice* MITCH's *arm supporting his cards has sagged and his gaze is dissolved into space.* STANLEY *slaps him on the shoulder.*]

STANLEY: Hey, Mitch, come to!

[*The sound of this new voice shocks* BLANCHE. *She makes a shocked gesture, forming his name with her lips.* STELLA *nods and looks quickly away.* BLANCHE *stands quite still for some moments—the silver-backed mirror in her hand and a look of sorrowful perplexity as though all human experience shows on her face.* BLANCHE *finally speaks but with sudden hysteria.*]

BLANCHE: What's going on here? [*She turns from* STELLA *to* EUNICE *and back to* STELLA. *Her rising voice penetrates the concentration of the game.* MITCH *ducks his head lower but* STANLEY *shoves back his chair as if about to rise.* STEVE *places a* restraining hand on his arm. *Continuing.*] What's happened here? I want an explanation of what's happened here.

STELLA: [*Agonizingly.*] Hush! Hush!

EUNICE: Hush! Hush! Honey.

STELLA: Please, Blanche.

BLANCHE: Why are you looking at me like that? Is something wrong with me?

EUNICE: You look wonderful, Blanche. Don't she look wonderful?

STELLA: Yes.

EUNICE: I understand you are going on a trip.

STELLA: Yes, Blanche *is*. She's going on a vacation.

EUNICE: I'm green with envy.

BLANCHE: Help me, help me get dressed!

STELLA: [*Handing her dress.*] Is this what you—

BLANCHE: Yes, it will do! I'm anxious to get out of here—this place is a trap!

EUNICE: What a pretty blue jacket.

STELLA: It's lilac colored.

BLANCHE: You're both mistaken. It's Della Robbia blue.[3] The blue of the robe in the old Madonna pictures. Are these grapes washed? [*She fingers the bunch of grapes which* EUNICE *had brought in.*]

EUNICE: Huh?

BLANCHE: Washed, I said. Are they washed?

EUNICE: They're from the French Market.

BLANCHE: That doesn't mean they've been washed. [*The cathedral bells chime.*] Those cathedral bells—they're the only clean thing in the Quarter. Well, I'm going now. I'm ready to go.

EUNICE: [*Whispering.*] She's going to walk out before they get here.

STELLA: Wait, Blanche.

BLANCHE: I don't want to pass in front of those men.

EUNICE: Then wait'll the game breaks up.

STELLA: Sit down and . . .

[BLANCHE *turns weakly, hesitantly about. She lets them push her into a chair.*]

BLANCHE: I can smell the sea air. The rest of my time I'm going to spend on the sea. And when I die, I'm going to die on the sea. You know what I shall die of? [*She plucks a grape.*] I shall die of eating an unwashed grape one day out on the ocean. I will die—with my hand in the hand of some nice-looking ship's doctor, a very young one with a small blond mustache and a big silver watch. "Poor lady," they'll say, "the quinine did her no good. That unwashed grape has transported her soul to heaven." [*The cathedral chimes are heard.*] And I'll be buried at sea sewn up in a clean white sack and dropped overboard—at noon—in the blaze of summer—and into an ocean as blue as [*Chimes again.*] my first lover's eyes!

---

3. A shade of light blue seen in terra cottas made by the Della Robbia family in the Italian Renaissance.

[A DOCTOR *and a* MATRON *have appeared around the corner of the building and climbed the steps to the porch. The gravity of their profession is exaggerated—the unmistakable aura of the state institution with its cynical detachment. The* DOCTOR *rings the doorbell. The murmur of the game is interrupted.*]

EUNICE: [*Whispering to* STELLA.] That must be them.

[STELLA *presses her fists to her lips.*]

BLANCHE: [*Rising slowly.*] What is it?
EUNICE: [*Affectedly casual.*] Excuse me while I see who's at the door.
STELLA: Yes.

[EUNICE *goes into the kitchen.*]

BLANCHE: [*Tensely.*] I wonder if it's for me.

[*A whispered colloquy takes place at the door.*]

EUNICE: [*Returning, brightly.*] Someone is calling for Blanche.
BLANCHE: It *is* for me, then! [*She looks fearfully from one to the other and then to the portieres. The "Varsouviana" faintly plays.*] Is it the gentleman I was expecting from Dallas?
EUNICE: I think it is, Blanche.
BLANCHE: I'm not quite ready.
STELLA: Ask him to wait outside.
BLANCHE: I . . .

[EUNICE *goes back to the portieres. Drums sound very softly.*]

STELLA: Everything packed?
BLANCHE: My silver toilet articles are still out.
STELLA: Ah!
EUNICE: [*Returning.*] They're waiting in front of the house.
BLANCHE: They! Who's "they"?
EUNICE: There's a lady with him.
BLANCHE: I cannot imagine who this "lady" could be! How is she dressed?
EUNICE: Just—just a sort of a—plain-tailored outfit.
BLANCHE: Possibly she's—[*Her voice dies out nervously.*]
STELLA: Shall we go, Blanche?
BLANCHE: Must we go through that room?
STELLA: I will go with you.
BLANCHE: How do I look?
STELLA: Lovely.
EUNICE: [*Echoing.*] Lovely.

[BLANCHE *moves fearfully to the portieres.* EUNICE *draws them open for her.* BLANCHE *goes into the kitchen.*]

BLANCHE: [*To the men.*] Please don't get up. I'm only passing through.

[*She crosses quickly to outside door.* STELLA *and* EUNICE *follow. The poker players stand awkwardly at the table—all except* MITCH, *who remains seated, looking down at the table.* BLANCHE *steps out on a small porch at the side of the door. She stops short and catches her breath.*]

DOCTOR: How do you do?

BLANCHE: You are not the gentleman I was expecting. [*She suddenly gasps and starts back up the steps. She stops by* STELLA, *who stands just outside the door, and speaks in a frightening whisper.*] That man isn't Shep Huntleigh.

[*The "Varsouviana" is playing distantly.* STELLA *stares back at* BLANCHE. EUNICE *is holding* STELLA*'s arm. There is a moment of silence—no sound but that of* STANLEY *steadily shuffling the cards.* BLANCHE *catches her breath again and slips back into the flat. She enters the flat with a peculiar smile, her eyes wide and brilliant. As soon as her sister goes past her,* STELLA *closes her eyes and clenches her hands.* EUNICE *throws her arms comfortingly about her. Then she starts up to her flat.* BLANCHE *stops just inside the door.* MITCH *keeps staring down at his hands on the table, but the other men look at her curiously. At last she starts around the table toward the bedroom. As she does,* STANLEY *suddenly pushes back his chair and rises as if to block her way. The* MATRON *follows her into the flat.*]

STANLEY: Did you forget something?

BLANCHE: [*Shrilly.*] Yes! Yes, I forgot something!

[*She rushes past him into the bedroom. Lurid reflections appear on the walls in odd, sinuous shapes. The "Varsouviana" is filtered into a weird distortion, accompanied by the cries and noises of the jungle.* BLANCHE *seizes the back of a chair as if to defend herself.*]

STANLEY: [*Sotto voce.*] Doc, you better go in.

DOCTOR: [*Sotto voce, motioning to the* MATRON.] Nurse, bring her out.

[*The* MATRON *advances on one side,* STANLEY *on the other. Divested of all the softer properties of womanhood, the* MATRON *is a peculiarly sinister figure in her severe dress. Her voice is bold and toneless as a firebell.*]

MATRON: Hello, Blanche.

[*The greeting is echoed and re-echoed by other mysterious voices behind the walls, as if reverberated through a canyon of rock.*]

STANLEY: She says that she forgot something.

[*The echo sounds in threatening whispers.*]

MATRON: That's all right.

STANLEY: What did you forget, Blanche?

BLANCHE: I—I—

MATRON: It don't matter. We can pick it up later.

STANLEY: Sure. We can send it along with the trunk.

BLANCHE: [*Retreating in panic.*] I don't know you—I don't know you. I want to be—left alone—please!

MATRON: Now, Blanche!

ECHOES: [*Rising and falling.*] Now, Blanche—now, Blanche—now, Blanche!

STANLEY: You left nothing here but spilt talcum and old empty perfume bottles—unless it's the paper lantern you want to take with you. You want the lantern?

[*He crosses to dressing table and seizes the paper lantern, tearing it off the light bulb, and extends it toward her. She cries out as if the lantern was herself. The* MATRON *steps boldly toward her. She screams and tries to break past the* MATRON. *All the men spring to their feet.* STELLA *runs out to the porch, with* EUNICE *following to comfort her, simultaneously with the confused voices of the men in the kitchen.* STELLA *rushes into* EUNICE's *embrace on the porch.*]

STELLA: Oh, my God, Eunice help me! Don't let them do that to her, don't let them hurt her! Oh, God, oh, please God, don't hurt her! What are they doing to her? What are they doing? [*She tries to break from* EUNICE's *arms.*]

EUNICE: No, honey, no, no, honey. Stay here. Don't go back in there. Stay with me and don't look.

STELLA: What have I done to my sister? Oh, God, what have I done to my sister?

EUNICE: You done the right thing, the only thing you could do. She couldn't stay here; there wasn't no other place for her to go.

[*While* STELLA *and* EUNICE *are speaking on the porch the voices of the men in the kitchen overlap them.* MITCH *has started toward the bedroom.* STANLEY *crosses to block him.* STANLEY *pushes him aside.* MITCH *lunges and strikes at* STANLEY. STANLEY *pushes* MITCH *back.* MITCH *collapses at the table, sobbing. During the preceding scenes, the* MATRON *catches hold of* BLANCHE's *arm and prevents her flight.* BLANCHE *turns wildly and scratches at the* MATRON. *The heavy woman pinions her arms.* BLANCHE *cries out hoarsely and slips to her knees.*]

MATRON: These fingernails have to be trimmed. [*The* DOCTOR *comes into the room and she looks at him.*] Jacket, Doctor?

DOCTOR: Not unless necessary. [*He takes off his hat and now he becomes personalized. The unhuman quality goes. His voice is gentle and reassuring as he crosses to* BLANCHE *and crouches in front of her. As he speaks her name, her terror subsides a little. The lurid reflections fade from the walls, the inhuman cries and noises die out and her own hoarse crying is calmed.*] Miss DuBois. [*She turns her face to him and stares at him with desperate pleading. He smiles; then he speaks to the* MATRON.] It won't be necessary.

BLANCHE: [*Faintly.*] Ask her to let go of me.

DOCTOR: [*To the* MATRON.] Let go.

[*The* MATRON *releases her.* BLANCHE *extends her hands toward the* DOCTOR. *He draws her up gently and supports her with his arm and leads her through the portieres.*]

BLANCHE: [*Holding tight to his arm.*] Whoever you are—I have always depended on the kindness of strangers.

[*The poker players stand back as* BLANCHE *and the* DOCTOR *cross the kitchen to the front door. She allows him to lead her as if she were blind. As they go out on the porch,* STELLA *cries out her sister's name from where she is crouched a few steps up on the stairs.*]

STELLA: Blanche! Blanche, Blanche!

[BLANCHE *walks on without turning, followed by the* DOCTOR *and the* MATRON. *They go around the corner of the building.* EUNICE *descends to* STELLA *and places the child in her arms. It is wrapped in a pale blue blanket.* STELLA *accepts the child, sobbingly.* EUNICE *continues downstairs and enters the kitchen where the men, except for* STANLEY, *are returning silently to their places about the table.* STANLEY *has gone out on the porch and stands at the foot of the steps looking at* STELLA.]

STANLEY: [*A bit uncertainly.*] Stella? [*She sobs with inhuman abandon. There is something luxurious in her complete surrender to crying now that her sister is gone. Voluptuously, soothingly.*] Now, honey. Now, love. Now, now, love. [*He kneels beside her and his fingers find the opening of her blouse.*] Now, now, love, Now, love. . . .

[*The luxurious sobbing, the sensual murmur fade away under the swelling music of the "Blue Piano" and the muted trumpet.*]

STEVE: This game is seven-card stud.

CURTAIN

1947

WILLIAM SHAKESPEARE

A Midsummer Night's Dream[1]

CHARACTERS

THESEUS, *Duke of Athens*
EGEUS, *father to Hermia*
LYSANDER, ⎫
DEMETRIUS, ⎭ *in love with Hermia*
PHILOSTRATE, *Master of the Revels to Theseus*
QUINCE, *a carpenter*
SNUG, *a joiner*
BOTTOM, *a weaver*
FLUTE, *a bellows-maker*
SNOUT, *a tinker*
STARVELING, *a tailor*

HIPPOLYTA, *Queen of the Amazons, betrothed to Theseus*
HERMIA, *daughter to Egeus, in love with Lysander*
HELENA, *in love with Demetrius*
OBERON, *King of the Fairies*
TITANIA, *Queen of the Fairies*
PUCK, *or Robin Goodfellow*
PEASEBLOSSOM, ⎫
COBWEB, ⎪
MOTH, ⎬ *fairies*
MUSTARDSEED, ⎭

Other FAIRIES *attending their king and queen*
ATTENDANTS *on Theseus and Hippolyta*

SCENE: *Athens, and a wood near it.*

ACT I

SCENE 1[2]

Enter THESEUS, HIPPOLYTA, PHILOSTRATE, *with others.*

THESEUS: Now, fair Hippolyta, our nuptial hour
　　Draws on apace. Four happy days bring in
　　Another moon; but, O, methinks, how slow
　　This old moon wanes! She lingers[3] my desires,
5　　Like to a step-dame or a dowager[4]
　　Long withering out a young man's revenue.
HIPPOLYTA: Four days will quickly steep themselves in night,
　　Four nights will quickly dream away the time;
　　And then the moon, like to a silver bow
10　　New-bent in heaven, shall behold the night
　　Of our solemnities.
THESEUS:　　　　　　Go, Philostrate,
　　Stir up the Athenian youth to merriments,
　　Awake the pert and nimble spirit of mirth,

---

1. Edited and annotated by David Bevington (except footnotes set in brackets).　　2. Location: Athens. The palace of Theseus.　　3. Lengthens, protracts.　　4. Widow with a jointure or dower. *Step-dame:* stepmother.

Turn melancholy forth to funerals;
The pale companion is not for our pomp.[5]   [*Exit* PHILOSTRATE.]   15
Hippolyta, I woo'd thee with my sword,[6]
And won thy love doing thee injuries;
But I will wed thee in another key,
With pomp, with triumph,[7] and with reveling.

[*Enter* EGEUS *and his daughter* HERMIA, *and* LYSANDER, *and* DEMETRIUS.]

EGEUS: Happy be Theseus, our renowned Duke!   20
THESEUS: Thanks, good Egeus. What's the news with thee?
EGEUS: Full of vexation come I, with complaint
  Against my child, my daughter Hermia.
  Stand forth, Demetrius. My noble lord,
  This man hath my consent to marry her.   25
  Stand forth, Lysander. And, my gracious Duke,
  This man hath bewitch'd the bosom of my child.
  Thou, thou, Lysander, thou hast given her rhymes
  And interchang'd love-tokens with my child.
  Thou hast by moonlight at her window sung   30
  With feigning[8] voice verses of feigning love,
  And stol'n the impression of her fantasy[9]
  With bracelets of thy hair, rings, gauds, conceits,[1]
  Knacks,[2] trifles, nosegays, sweetmeats—messengers
  Of strong prevailment in unhardened youth.   35
  With cunning hast thou filch'd my daughter's heart,
  Turn'd her obedience, which is due to me,
  To stubborn harshness. And, my gracious Duke,
  Be it so she will not here before your Grace
  Consent to marry with Demetrius,   40
  I beg the ancient privilege of Athens:
  As she is mine, I may dispose of her,
  Which shall be either to this gentleman
  Or to her death, according to our law
  Immediately[3] provided in that case.   45
THESEUS: What say you, Hermia? Be advis'd, fair maid.
  To you your father should be as a god—
  One that compos'd your beauties, yea, and one
  To whom you are but as a form in wax
  By him imprinted and within his power   50
  To leave the figure or disfigure[4] it.
  Demetrius is a worthy gentleman.

---

5. Ceremonial magnificence. *Companion:* fellow.   6. That is, in a military engagement against the Amazons, when Hippolyta was taken captive.   7. Public festivity.   8. (1) Counterfeiting; (2) faining, desirous.   9. Made her fall in love with you (imprinting your image on her imagination) by stealthy and dishonest means.   1. Fanciful trifles. *Gauds:* playthings.   2. Knickknacks.   3. Expressly.   4. Obliterate. *Leave:* that is, leave unaltered.

HERMIA: So is Lysander.

THESEUS: In himself he is;
But in this kind, wanting your father's voice,[5]
55   The other must be held the worthier.

HERMIA: I would my father look'd but with my eyes.

THESEUS: Rather your eyes must with his judgment look.

HERMIA: I do entreat your Grace to pardon me.
I know not by what power I am made bold,
60   Nor how it may concern[6] my modesty,
In such a presence here to plead my thoughts;
But I beseech your Grace that I may know
The worst that may befall me in this case,
If I refuse to wed Demetrius.

65 THESEUS: Either to die the death, or to abjure
Forever the society of men.
Therefore, fair Hermia, question your desires,
Know of your youth, examine well your blood,[7]
Whether, if you yield not to your father's choice,
70   You can endure the livery[8] of a nun,
For aye to be in shady cloister mew'd,[9]
To live a barren sister all your life,
Chanting faint hymns to the cold fruitless moon.
Thrice blessed they that master so their blood
75   To undergo such maiden pilgrimage;
But earthlier happy[1] is the rose distill'd,
Than that which withering on the virgin thorn
Grows, lives, and dies in single blessedness.

HERMIA: So will I grow, so live, so die, my lord,
80   Ere I will yield my virgin patent[2] up
Unto his lordship, whose unwished yoke
My soul consents not to give sovereignty.

THESEUS: Take time to pause; and, by the next new moon—
The sealing-day betwixt my love and me,
85   For everlasting bond of fellowship—
Upon that day either prepare to die
For disobedience to your father's will,
Or[3] else to wed Demetrius, as he would,
Or on Diana's altar to protest[4]
90   For aye austerity and single life.

DEMETRIUS: Relent, sweet Hermia, and, Lysander, yield
Thy crazed[5] title to my certain right.

LYSANDER: You have her father's love, Demetrius;

---

5. Approval. *Kind:* respect. *Wanting:* lacking.   6. Befit.   7. Passions.   8. Habit.   9. Shut in (said
of a hawk, poultry, and so on). *Aye:* ever.   1. Happier as respects this world.   2. Privilege.   3. Either.
4. Vow.   5. Cracked, unsound.

Let me have Hermia's. Do you marry him.
EGEUS: Scornful Lysander! True, he hath my love,   95
　　And what is mine my love shall render him.
　　And she is mine, and all my right of her
　　I do estate unto[6] Demetrius.
LYSANDER: I am, my lord, as well deriv'd[7] as he,
　　As well possess'd;[8] my love is more than his;   100
　　My fortunes every way as fairly[9] rank'd,
　　If not with vantage,[1] as Demetrius';
　　And, which is more than all these boasts can be,
　　I am belov'd of beauteous Hermia.
　　Why should not I then prosecute my right?   105
　　Demetrius, I'll avouch it to his head,[2]
　　Made love to Nedar's daughter, Helena,
　　And won her soul; and she, sweet lady, dotes,
　　Devoutly dotes, dotes in idolatry,
　　Upon this spotted[3] and inconstant man.   110
THESEUS: I must confess that I have heard so much,
　　And with Demetrius thought to have spoke thereof;
　　But, being over-full of self-affairs,
　　My mind did lose it. But, Demetrius, come,
　　And come, Egeus, you shall go with me;   115
　　I have some private schooling for you both.
　　For you, fair Hermia, look you arm[4] yourself
　　To fit your fancies[5] to your father's will;
　　Or else the law of Athens yields you up—
　　Which by no means we may extenuate[6]—   120
　　To death, or to a vow of single life.
　　Come, my Hippolyta. What cheer, my love?
　　Demetrius and Egeus, go[7] along.
　　I must employ you in some business
　　Against[8] our nuptial, and confer with you   125
　　Of something nearly that[9] concerns yourselves.
EGEUS: With duty and desire we follow you.
　　　　　　　　　　　　[Exeunt (all but LYSANDER and HERMIA).]
LYSANDER: How now, my love, why is your cheek so pale?
　　How chance the roses there do fade so fast?
HERMIA: Belike[1] for want of rain, which I could well   130
　　Beteem[2] them from the tempest of my eyes.
LYSANDER: Ay me! For aught that I could ever read,
　　Could ever hear by tale or history,

---

6. Settle or bestow upon.　　7. Descended; that is, as well born.　　8. Endowed with wealth.　　9. Handsomely.　　1. Superiority.　　2. That is, face.　　3. That is, morally stained.　　4. Take care you prepare.　　5. Likings, thoughts of love.　　6. Mitigate.　　7. That is, come.　　8. In preparation for.
9. That closely.　　1. Very likely.　　2. Grant, afford.

The course of true love never did run smooth;
135 But either it was different in blood[3]—
HERMIA: O cross,[4] too high to be enthrall'd to low!
LYSANDER: Or else misgraffed[5] in respect of years—
HERMIA: O spite, too old to be engag'd to young!
LYSANDER: Or else it stood upon the choice of friends[6]—
140 HERMIA: O hell, to choose love by another's eyes!
LYSANDER: Or, if there were a sympathy in choice,
War, death, or sickness did lay siege to it,
Making it momentany[7] as a sound,
Swift as a shadow, short as any dream,
145 Brief as the lightning in the collied[8] night,
That, in a spleen, unfolds[9] both heaven and earth,
And ere a man hath power to say "Behold!"
The jaws of darkness do devour it up.
So quick bright things come to confusion.[1]
150 HERMIA: If then true lovers have been ever cross'd,[2]
It stands as an edict in destiny.
Then let us teach our trial patience,[3]
Because it is a customary cross,
As due to love as thoughts and dreams and sighs,
155 Wishes and tears, poor fancy's[4] followers.
LYSANDER: A good persuasion. Therefore, hear me, Hermia.
I have a widow aunt, a dowager
Of great revenue, and she hath no child.
From Athens is her house remote seven leagues;
160 And she respects[5] me as her only son.
There, gentle Hermia, may I marry thee,
And to that place the sharp Athenian law
Cannot pursue us. If thou lovest me, then,
Steal forth thy father's house tomorrow night;
165 And in the wood, a league without the town,
Where I did meet thee once with Helena
To do observance to a morn of May,[6]
There will I stay for thee.
HERMIA: My good Lysander!
I swear to thee, by Cupid's strongest bow,
170 By his best arrow[7] with the golden head,
By the simplicity of Venus' doves,[8]
By that which knitteth souls and prospers loves,

3. Hereditary station.   4. Vexation.   5. Ill grafted, badly matched.   6. Relatives.   7. Lasting
but a moment.   8. Blackened (as with coal dust), darkened.   9. Discloses. *In a spleen:* in a swift
impulse, in a violent flash.   1. Ruin. *Quick:* quickly; or, perhaps, living, alive.   2. Always thwarted.
3. That is, teach ourselves patience in this trial.   4. Amorous passion's.   5. Regards.   6. Perform
the ceremonies of May Day.   7. [Cupid's best gold-pointed arrows were supposed to induce love, his
blunt leaden arrows aversion.]   8. That is, those that drew Venus's chariot. *Simplicity:* innocence.

And by that fire which burn'd the Carthage queen,
When the false Troyan[9] under sail was seen,
By all the vows that ever men have broke,   175
In number more than ever women spoke,
In that same place thou hast appointed me
Tomorrow truly will I meet with thee.
LYSANDER: Keep promise, love. Look, here comes Helena.

    [*Enter* HELENA.]

HERMIA: God speed fair[1] Helena, whither away?   180
HELENA: Call you me fair? That fair again unsay.
    Demetrius loves your fair. O happy fair![2]
    Your eyes are lodestars, and your tongue's sweet air[3]
    More tuneable[4] than lark to shepherd's ear
    When wheat is green, when hawthorn buds appear.   185
    Sickness is catching. O, were favor[5] so,
    Yours would I catch, fair Hermia, ere I go;
    My ear should catch your voice, my eye your eye,
    My tongue should catch your tongue's sweet melody.
    Were the world mine, Demetrius being bated,[6]   190
    The rest I'd give to be to you translated.[7]
    O, teach me how you look, and with what art
    You sway the motion[8] of Demetrius' heart.
HERMIA: I frown upon him, yet he loves me still.
HELENA: O that your frowns would teach my smiles such skill!   195
HERMIA: I give him curses, yet he gives me love.
HELENA: O that my prayers could such affection move![9]
HERMIA: The more I hate, the more he follows me.
HELENA: The more I love, the more he hateth me.
HERMIA: His folly, Helena, is no fault of mine.   200
HELENA: None, but your beauty. Would that fault were mine!
HERMIA: Take comfort. He no more shall see my face.
    Lysander and myself will fly this place.
    Before the time I did Lysander see,
    Seem'd Athens as a paradise to me.   205
    O, then, what graces in my love do dwell,
    That he hath turn'd a heaven unto a hell!
LYSANDER: Helen, to you our minds we will unfold.
    Tomorrow night, when Phoebe[1] doth behold
    Her silver visage in the wat'ry glass,[2]   210

9. [Dido, queen of Carthage, immolated herself on a funeral pyre after having been deserted by the Trojan hero Aeneas.]   1. Fair-complexioned (generally regarded by the Elizabethans as more beautiful than dark complexion).   2. Lucky fair one! *Fair:* beauty (even though Hermia is dark-complexioned).   3. Music. *Lodestars:* guiding stars.   4. Tuneful, melodious.   5. Appearance, looks.   6. Excepted.   7. Transformed.   8. Impulse.   9. Arouse. *Affection:* passion.   1. Diana, the moon.   2. Mirror.

Decking with liquid pearl the bladed grass,
A time that lovers' flights doth still[3] conceal,
Through Athens' gates have we devis'd to steal.
HERMIA: And in the wood, where often you and I
215   Upon faint[4] primrose beds were wont to lie,
Emptying our bosoms of their counsel[5] sweet,
There my Lysander and myself shall meet;
And thence from Athens turn away our eyes,
To seek new friends and stranger companies.
220   Farewell, sweet playfellow. Pray thou for us,
And good luck grant thee thy Demetrius!
Keep word, Lysander. We must starve our sight
From lovers' food till morrow deep midnight.   [*Exit.*]
LYSANDER: I will, my Hermia.
                    Helena, adieu.
225   As you on him, Demetrius dote on you!   [*Exit.*]
HELENA: How happy some o'er other some can be![6]
Through Athens I am thought as fair as she.
But what of that? Demetrius thinks not so;
He will not know what all but he do know.
230   And as he errs, doting on Hermia's eyes,
So I, admiring[7] of his qualities.
Things base and vile, holding no quantity,[8]
Love can transpose to form and dignity.
Love looks not with the eyes, but with the mind,
235   And therefore is wing'd Cupid painted blind.
Nor hath Love's mind of any judgment taste;[9]
Wings, and no eyes, figure[1] unheedy haste.
And therefore is Love said to be a child,
Because in choice he is so oft beguil'd.
240   As waggish boys in game[2] themselves forswear,
So the boy Love is perjur'd everywhere.
For ere Demetrius look'd on Hermia's eyne,[3]
He hail'd down oaths that he was only mine;
And when this hail some heat from Hermia felt,
245   So he dissolv'd, and show'rs of oaths did melt.
I will go tell him of fair Hermia's flight.
Then to the wood will he tomorrow night
Pursue her; and for this intelligence[4]
If I have thanks, it is a dear expense.[5]
250   But herein mean I to enrich my pain,
To have his sight thither and back again.   [*Exit.*]

---

3. Always.   4. Pale.   5. Secret thought.   6. Can be in comparison to some others.   7. Wondering at.   8. That is, unsubstantial, unshapely.   9. That is, nor has Love, which dwells in the fancy or imagination, any taste or least bit of judgment or reason.   1. Are a symbol of. 2. Sport, jest.   3. Eyes (old form of plural).   4. Information.   5. That is, a trouble worth taking. *Dear:* costly.

Scene 2[6]

Enter QUINCE *the Carpenter, and* SNUG *the Joiner, and* BOTTOM *the Weaver, and* FLUTE *the Bellows-mender, and* SNOUT *the Tinker, and* STARVELING *the Tailor.*

QUINCE: Is all our company here?

BOTTOM: You were best to call them generally,[7] man by man, according to the scrip.[8]

QUINCE: Here is the scroll of every man's name which is thought fit, through all Athens, to play in our interlude before the Duke and the Duchess on his wedding-day at night. 5

BOTTOM: First, good Peter Quince, say what the play treats on, then read the names of the actors, and so grow to[9] a point.

QUINCE: Marry,[1] our play is "The most lamentable comedy and most cruel death of Pyramus and Thisby." 10

BOTTOM: A very good piece of work, I assure you, and a merry. Now, good Peter Quince, call forth your actors by the scroll. Masters, spread yourselves.

QUINCE: Answer as I call you. Nick Bottom, the weaver.

BOTTOM: Ready. Name what part I am for, and proceed.

QUINCE: You, Nick Bottom, are set down for Pyramus. 15

BOTTOM: What is Pyramus? A lover, or a tyrant?

QUINCE: A lover, that kills himself most gallant for love.

BOTTOM: That will ask some tears in the true performing of it. If I do it, let the audience look to their eyes. I will move storms; I will condole[2] in some measure. To the rest—yet my chief humor[3] is for a tyrant. I could play Ercles rarely, or a part to tear a cat in, to make all split.[4] 20

> "The raging rocks
> And shivering shocks
> Shall break the locks
>   Of prison gates; 25
> And Phibbus' car[5]
> Shall shine from far
> And make and mar
>   The foolish Fates."

This was lofty! Now name the rest of the players. This is Ercles' vein, a tyrant's vein. A lover is more condoling. 30

QUINCE: Francis Flute, the bellows-mender.

FLUTE: Here, Peter Quince.

QUINCE: Flute, you must take Thisby on you.

FLUTE: What is Thisby? A wand'ring knight? 35

---

6. Location: Athens. Quince's house (?).   7. [Bottom's blunder for *individually.*]   8. Script, written list.   9. Come to.   1. [A mild oath, originally the name of the Virgin Mary.]   2. Lament, arouse pity.   3. Inclination, whim.   4. That is, cause a stir, bring the house down. *Ercles:* Hercules (the tradition of ranting came from Seneca's *Hercules Furens*). *Tear a cat:* that is, rant.   5. Phoebus's, the sun-god's, chariot.

QUINCE: It is the lady that Pyramus must love.

FLUTE: Nay, faith, let not me play a woman. I have a beard coming.

QUINCE: That's all one.[6] You shall play it in a mask, and you may speak as small[7] as you will.

BOTTOM: An[8] I may hide my face, let me play Thisby too. I'll speak in a monstrous little voice, "Thisne, Thisne!" "Ah, Pyramus, my lover dear! Thy Thisby dear, and lady dear!"

QUINCE: No, no; you must play Pyramus; and, Flute, you Thisby.

BOTTOM: Well, proceed.

QUINCE: Robin Starveling, the tailor.

STARVELING: Here, Peter Quince.

QUINCE: Robin Starveling, you must play Thisby's mother. Tom Snout, the tinker.

SNOUT: Here, Peter Quince.

QUINCE: You, Pyramus' father; myself, Thisby's father; Snug, the joiner, you, the lion's part; and I hope here is a play fitted.

SNUG: Have you the lion's part written? Pray you, if it be, give it me, for I am slow of study.

QUINCE: You may do it extempore, for it is nothing but roaring.

BOTTOM: Let me play the lion too. I will roar that I will do any man's heart good to hear me. I will roar that I will make the Duke say, "Let him roar again, let him roar again."

QUINCE: An you should do it too terribly, you would fright the Duchess and the ladies, that they would shriek; and that were enough to hang us all.

ALL: That would hang us, every mother's son.

BOTTOM: I grant you, friends, if you should fright the ladies out of their wits, they would have no more discretion but to hang us; but I will aggravate[9] my voice so that I will roar[1] you as gently as any sucking dove; I will roar you an 'twere any nightingale.

QUINCE: You can play no part but Pyramus; for Pyramus is a sweet-fac'd man, a proper[2] man as one shall see in a summer's day, a most lovely gentleman like man. Therefore you must needs play Pyramus.

BOTTOM: Well, I will undertake it. What beard were I best to play it in?

QUINCE: Why, what you will.

BOTTOM: I will discharge it in either your[3] straw-color beard, your orange-tawny beard, your purple-in-grain beard, or your French-crown-color[4] beard, your perfect yellow.

QUINCE: Some of your French crowns[5] have no hair at all, and then you will play barefac'd. But, masters, here are your parts. [*He distributes parts.*] And I am to entreat you, request you, and desire you, to con[6] them by tomorrow night; and meet me in the palace wood, a mile without the town, by moonlight. There will we rehearse; for if we meet in the city, we shall be dogg'd with

---

6. It makes no difference.   7. High-pitched.   8. If.   9. [Bottom's blunder for *diminish.*]
1. That is, roar for you.   2. Handsome.   3. That is, you know the kind I mean. *Discharge:* perform.
4. That is, color of a French crown, a gold coin. *Purple-in-grain:* dyed a very deep red (from *grain,* the name applied to the dried insect used to make the dye).   5. Heads bald from syphilis, the "French disease."   6. Learn by heart.

company, and our devices[7] known. In the meantime I will draw a bill[8] of
properties, such as our play wants. I pray you, fail me not.

BOTTOM: We will meet, and there we may rehearse most obscenely[9] and coura-
geously. Take pains, be perfect;[1] adieu. 80

QUINCE: At the Duke's oak we meet.

BOTTOM: Enough. Hold, or cut bow-strings.[2] [*Exeunt.*]

ACT II

SCENE 1[3]

Enter a FAIRY *at one door, and Robin Goodfellow* (PUCK) *at another.*

PUCK: How now, spirit! Whither wander you?

FAIRY: Over hill, over dale,
  Thorough bush, thorough[4] brier,
  Over park, over pale,[5]
  Thorough flood, thorough fire, 5
  I do wander every where,
  Swifter than the moon's sphere;
  And I serve the Fairy Queen,
  To dew her orbs[6] upon the green.
  The cowslips tall her pensioners[7] be. 10
  In their gold coats spots you see;
  Those be rubies, fairy favors,[8]
  In those freckles live their savors.[9]
I must go seek some dewdrops here
And hang a pearl in every cowslip's ear. 15
Farewell, thou lob[1] of spirits; I'll be gone.
Our Queen and all her elves come here anon.[2]

PUCK: The King doth keep his revels here tonight.
  Take heed the Queen come not within his sight.
  For Oberon is passing fell and wrath,[3] 20
  Because that she as her attendant hath
  A lovely boy, stolen from an Indian king;
  She never had so sweet a changeling.[4]
  And jealous Oberon would have the child
  Knight of his train, to trace[5] the forests wild. 25
  But she perforce[6] withholds the loved boy,

---

7. Plans.   8. List.   9. [An unintentionally funny blunder, whatever Bottom meant to say.]
1. That is, letter-perfect in memorizing your parts.   2. [An archer's expression not definitely explained, but probably meaning here "keep your promises, or give up the play."]   3. Location: a wood
near Athens.   4. Through.   5. Enclosure.   6. Circles; that is, fairy rings.   7. Retainers, members of the royal bodyguard.   8. Love tokens.   9. Sweet smells.   1. Country bumpkin.   2. At
once.   3. Wrathful. *Fell:* exceedingly angry.   4. Child exchanged for another by the fairies.
5. Range through.   6. Forcibly.

Crowns him with flowers and makes him all her joy.
And now they never meet in grove or green,
By fountain[7] clear, or spangled starlight sheen,
30 But they do square,[8] that all their elves for fear
Creep into acorn-cups and hide them there.
FAIRY: Either I mistake your shape and making quite,
Or else you are that shrewd and knavish sprite[9]
Call'd Robin Goodfellow. Are not you he
35 That frights the maidens of the villagery,
Skim milk, and sometimes labor in the quern,[1]
And bootless[2] make the breathless huswife churn,
And sometime make the drink to bear no barm,[3]
Mislead night-wanderers, laughing at their harm?
40 Those that Hobgoblin call you and sweet Puck,
You do their work, and they shall have good luck.
Are you not he?
PUCK: Thou speakest aright;
I am that merry wanderer of the night.
I jest to Oberon and make him smile
45 When I a fat and bean-fed horse beguile,
Neighing in likeness of a filly foal;
And sometime lurk I in a gossip's[4] bowl,
In very likeness of a roasted crab,[5]
And when she drinks, against her lips I bob
50 And on her withered dewlap[6] pour the ale.
The wisest aunt, telling the saddest[7] tale,
Sometime for three-foot stool mistaketh me;
Then slip I from her bum, down topples she,
And "tailor"[8] cries, and falls into a cough;
55 And then the whole quire[9] hold their hips and laugh,
And waxen in their mirth and neeze[1] and swear
A merrier hour was never wasted there.
But, room, fairy! Here comes Oberon.
FAIRY: And here my mistress. Would that he were gone!

[*Enter* OBERON, *the King of Fairies, at one door, with his train; and* TITANIA,
the Queen, at another, with hers.]

60 OBERON: Ill met by moonlight, proud Titania.
TITANIA: What, jealous Oberon? Fairies, skip hence.
I have forsworn his bed and company.
OBERON: Tarry, rash wanton.[2] Am not I thy lord?

---

7. Spring.   8. Quarrel.   9. Spirit. *Shrewd:* mischievous.   1. Handmill.   2. In vain.   3. Yeast,
head on the ale.   4. Old woman's.   5. Crab apple.   6. Loose skin on neck.   7. Most serious.
Aunt: old woman.   8. [Possibly because she ends up sitting crosslegged on the floor, looking like a
tailor.]   9. Company.   1. Sneeze. *Waxen:* increase.   2. Headstrong creature.

TITANIA: Then I must be thy lady; but I know
    When thou hast stolen away from fairy land,   65
    And in the shape of Corin[3] sat all day,
    Playing on pipes of corn[4] and versing love
    To amorous Phillida. Why art thou here,
    Come from the farthest steep[5] of India,
    But that, forsooth, the bouncing Amazon,   70
    Your buskin'd[6] mistress and your warrior love,
    To Theseus must be wedded, and you come
    To give their bed joy and prosperity.
OBERON: How canst thou thus for shame, Titania,
    Glance at my credit with Hippolyta,[7]   75
    Knowing I know thy love to Theseus?
    Didst not thou lead him through the glimmering night
    From Perigenia,[8] whom he ravished?
    And make him with fair Aegles[9] break his faith,
    With Ariadne and Antiopa?[1]   80
TITANIA: These are the forgeries of jealousy;
    And never, since the middle summer's spring,[2]
    Met we on hill, in dale, forest, or mead,
    By paved fountain or by rushy[3] brook,
    Or in the beached margent[4] of the sea,   85
    To dance our ringlets[5] to the whistling wind,
    But with thy brawls thou hast disturb'd our sport.
    Therefore the winds, piping to us in vain,
    As in revenge, have suck'd up from the sea
    Contagious[6] fogs; which falling in the land   90
    Hath every pelting[7] river made so proud
    That they have overborne their continents.[8]
    The ox hath therefore stretch'd his yoke in vain,
    The ploughman lost his sweat, and the green corn[9]
    Hath rotted ere his youth attain'd a beard;   95
    The fold[1] stands empty in the drowned field,
    And crows are fatted with the murrion[2] flock;

---

3. Corin and Phillida are conventional names of pastoral lovers.   4. [Here, oat stalks.]   5. Mountain range.   6. Wearing half boots called buskins.   7. Make insinuations about my favored relationship with Hippolyta.   8. That is, Perigouna, one of Theseus's conquests. (This and the following women are named in Thomas North's translation of Plutarch's *Life of Theseus*.)   9. That is, Aegle, for whom Theseus deserted Ariadne, according to some accounts.   1. Queen of the Amazons and wife of Theseus; elsewhere identified with Hippolyta, but here thought of as a separate woman. *Ariadne:* the daughter of Minos, king of Crete, who helped Theseus to escape the labyrinth after killing the Minotaur; later she was abandoned by Theseus.   2. Beginning of midsummer.   3. Bordered with rushes. *Paved:* with pebbled bottom.   4. Edge, border. *In:* on.   5. Dances in a ring. (See *orbs* in II.i.9.)   6. Noxious.   7. Paltry; or striking, moving forcefully.   8. Banks that contain them.   9. Grain of any kind.   1. Pen for sheep or cattle.   2. Having died of the murrain, plague.

The nine men's morris[3] is fill'd up with mud,
And the quaint mazes in the wanton[4] green
100 For lack of tread are undistinguishable.
The human mortals want their winter[5] here;
No night is now with hymn or carol bless'd.
Therefore[6] the moon, the governess of floods,
Pale in her anger, washes all the air,
105 That rheumatic[7] diseases do abound.
And thorough this distemperature[8] we see
The seasons alter: hoary-headed frosts
Fall in the fresh lap of the crimson rose,
And on old Hiems'[9] thin and icy crown
110 An odorous chaplet of sweet summer buds
Is, as in mockery, set. The spring, the summer,
The childing[1] autumn, angry winter, change
Their wonted liveries, and the mazed[2] world,
By their increase,[3] now knows not which is which.
115 And this same progeny of evils comes
From our debate,[4] from our dissension;
We are their parents and original.[5]
OBERON: Do you amend it then; it lies in you.
Why should Titania cross her Oberon?
120 I do but beg a little changeling boy,
To be my henchman.[6]
TITANIA: Set your heart at rest.
The fairy land buys not the child of me.
His mother was a vot'ress of my order,
And, in the spiced Indian air, by night,
125 Full often hath she gossip'd by my side,
And sat with me on Neptune's yellow sands,
Marking th' embarked traders on the flood,[7]
When we have laugh'd to see the sails conceive
And grow big-bellied with the wanton[8] wind;
130 Which she, with pretty and with swimming gait,
Following—her womb then rich with my young squire—
Would imitate, and sail upon the land
To fetch me trifles, and return again,
As from a voyage, rich with merchandise.

3. That is, portion of the village green marked out in a square for a game played with nine pebbles or pegs.   4. Luxuriant. *Mazes:* that is, intricate paths marked out on the village green to be followed rapidly on foot as a kind of contest.   5. That is, regular winter season; or proper observances of winter, such as the *hymn* or *carol* in the next line. *Want:* lack.   6. That is, as a result of our quarrel.   7. Colds, flu, and other respiratory infections.   8. Disturbance in nature.   9. The winter god's.   1. Fruitful, pregnant.   2. Bewildered. *Liveries:* usual apparel.   3. Their yield, what they produce.   4. Quarrel.   5. Origin.   6. Attendant, page.   7. Flood tide. *Traders:* trading vessels.   8. Sportive.

But she, being mortal, of that boy did die;   135
And for her sake do I rear up her boy,
And for her sake I will not part with him.
OBERON: How long within this wood intend you stay?
TITANIA: Perchance till after Theseus' wedding-day.
    If you will patiently dance in our round[9]   140
    And see our moonlight revels, go with us;
    If not, shun me, and I will spare[1] your haunts.
OBERON: Give me that boy, and I will go with thee.
TITANIA: Not for thy fairy kingdom. Fairies, away!
    We shall chide downright, if I longer stay.   [*Exeunt* TITANIA *with her train.*]   145
OBERON: Well, go thy way. Thou shalt not from[2] this grove
    Till I torment thee for this injury.
    My gentle Puck, come hither. Thou rememb'rest
    Since[3] once I sat upon a promontory,
    And heard a mermaid on a dolphin's back   150
    Uttering such dulcet and harmonious breath[4]
    That the rude sea grew civil at her song
    And certain stars shot madly from their spheres,
    To hear the sea-maid's music.
PUCK: I remember.
OBERON: That very time I saw, but thou couldst not,   155
    Flying between the cold moon and the earth,
    Cupid all[5] arm'd. A certain aim he took
    At a fair vestal[6] throned by the west,
    And loos'd his love-shaft smartly from his bow,
    As[7] it should pierce a hundred thousand hearts;   160
    But I might[8] see young Cupid's fiery shaft
    Quench'd in the chaste beams of the wat'ry moon,
    And the imperial vot'ress passed on,
    In maiden meditation, fancy-free.[9]
    Yet mark'd I where the bolt of Cupid fell: 165
    It fell upon a little western flower,
    Before milk-white, now purple with love's wound,
    And maidens call it love-in-idleness.[1]
    Fetch me that flow'r; the herb I showed thee once.
    The juice of it on sleeping eyelids laid   170
    Will make or man or[2] woman madly dote
    Upon the next live creature that it sees.
    Fetch me this herb, and be thou here again
    Ere the leviathan[3] can swim a league.

---

9. Circular dance.   1. Shun.   2. Go from.   3. When.   4. Voice, song.   5. Fully.   6. Vestal virgin (contains a complimentary allusion to Queen Elizabeth as a votaress of Diana and probably refers to an actual entertainment in her honor at Elvetham in 1591).   7. As if.   8. Could. 9. Free of love's spell.   1. Pansy, heartsease.   2. Either . . . or.   3. Sea monster, whale.

175 PUCK: I'll put a girdle round about the earth
In forty[4] minutes.   [*Exit.*]
OBERON: Having once this juice,
I'll watch Titania when she is asleep,
And drop the liquor of it in her eyes.
The next thing then she waking looks upon,
180 Be it on lion, bear, or wolf, or bull,
On meddling monkey, or on busy ape,
She shall pursue it with the soul of love.
And ere I take this charm from off her sight,
As I can take it with another herb,
185 I'll make her render up her page to me.
But who comes here? I am invisible,
And I will overhear their conference.

[*Enter* DEMETRIUS, HELENA *following him.*]

DEMETRIUS: I love thee not, therefore pursue me not.
Where is Lysander and fair Hermia?
190 The one I'll slay, the other slayeth me.
Thou told'st me they were stol'n unto this wood;
And here am I, and wode[5] within this wood,
Because I cannot meet my Hermia.
Hence, get thee gone, and follow me no more.
195 HELENA: You draw me, you hard-hearted adamant;[6]
But yet you draw not iron, for my heart
Is true as steel. Leave[7] you your power to draw,
And I shall have no power to follow you.
DEMETRIUS: Do I entice you? Do I speak you fair?[8]
200 Or, rather, do I not in plainest truth
Tell you I do not nor I cannot love you?
HELENA: And even for that do I love you the more.
I am your spaniel; and, Demetrius,
The more you beat me, I will fawn on you.
205 Use me but as your spaniel, spurn me, strike me,
Neglect me, lose me; only give me leave,
Unworthy as I am, to follow you.
What worser place can I beg in your love—
And yet a place of high respect with me—
210 Than to be used as you use your dog?
DEMETRIUS: Tempt not too much the hatred of my spirit,
For I am sick when I do look on thee.
HELENA: And I am sick when I look not on you.

---

4. [The time parameters are used indefinitely here.]   5. Mad (pronounced *wood* and often spelled so).
6. Lodestone, magnet (with pun on *hard-hearted,* since adamant was also thought to be the hardest of
all stones and was confused with the diamond).   7. Give up.   8. Courteously.

DEMETRIUS: You do impeach[9] your modesty too much
    To leave the city and commit yourself   215
    Into the hands of one that loves you not,
    To trust the opportunity of night
    And the ill counsel of a desert[1] place
    With the rich worth of your virginity.
HELENA: Your virtue is my privilege. For that[2]   220
    It is not night when I do see your face,
    Therefore I think I am not in the night;
    Nor doth this wood lack worlds of company,
    For you in my respect[3] are all the world.
    Then how can it be said I am alone,   225
    When all the world is here to look on me?
DEMETRIUS: I'll run from thee and hide me in the brakes,[4]
    And leave thee to the mercy of wild beasts.
HELENA: The wildest hath not such a heart as you.
    Run when you will, the story shall be chang'd: 230
    Apollo flies and Daphne holds the chase,[5]
    The dove pursues the griffin, the mild hind[6]
    Makes speed to catch the tiger—bootless[7] speed,
    When cowardice pursues and valor flies.
DEMETRIUS: I will not stay thy questions.[8] Let me go!   235
    Or if thou follow me, do not believe
    But I shall do thee mischief in the wood.
HELENA: Ay, in the temple, in the town, the field,
    You do me mischief. Fie, Demetrius!
    Your wrongs do set a scandal on my sex.   240
    We cannot fight for love, as men may do;
    We should be woo'd and were not made to woo.
    I'll follow thee and make a heaven of hell,   *[Exit DEMETRIUS.]*
    To die upon[9] the hand I love so well.   *[Exit.]*
OBERON: Fare thee well, nymph. Ere he do leave this grove,   245
    Thou shalt fly him and he shall seek thy love.

    [Enter PUCK.]

Hast thou the flower there? Welcome, wanderer.
PUCK: Ay, there it is.   *[Offers the flower.]*
OBERON: I pray thee, give it me.
    I know a bank where the wild thyme blows,[1]
    Where oxlips[2] and the nodding violet grows,   250

9. Call into question.   1. Deserted.   2. Because. *Virtue:* goodness or power to attract. *Privilege:* safe-
guard, warrant.   3. As far as I am concerned.   4. Thickets.   5. [In the ancient myth, Daphne fled
from Apollo and was saved from rape by being transformed into a laurel tree; here it is the female who
holds the chase, or pursues, instead of the male.]   6. Female deer. *Griffin:* a fabulous monster with the
head of an eagle and the body of a lion.   7. Fruitless.   8. Talk or argument. *Stay:* wait for.   9. By.
1. Blooms.   2. Flowers resembling cowslip and primrose.

Quite over-canopied with luscious woodbine,[3]
With sweet musk-roses and with eglantine.[4]
There sleeps Titania sometime of the night,
Lull'd in these flowers with dances and delight;
255 And there the snake throws[5] her enamel'd skin,
Weed[6] wide enough to wrap a fairy in.
And with the juice of this I'll streak[7] her eyes,
And make her full of hateful fantasies.
Take thou some of it, and seek through this grove.   [*Gives some love-juice.*]
260 A sweet Athenian lady is in love
With a disdainful youth. Anoint his eyes,
But do it when the next thing he espies
May be the lady. Thou shalt know the man
By the Athenian garments he hath on.
265 Effect it with some care, that he may prove
More fond on[8] her than she upon her love;
And look thou meet me ere the first cock crow.
PUCK: Fear not, my lord, your servant shall do so.   [*Exeunt.*]

SCENE 2[9]

Enter TITANIA, *Queen of Fairies, with her train.*

TITANIA: Come, now a roundel[1] and a fairy song;
Then, for the third part of a minute, hence—
Some to kill cankers[2] in the musk-rose buds,
Some war with rere-mice[3] for their leathern wings,
5 To make my small elves coats, and some keep back
The clamorous owl, that nightly hoots and wonders
At our quaint[4] spirits. Sing me now asleep.
Then to your offices and let me rest.

     [FAIRIES *sing.*]

[FIRST FAIRY:]

     You spotted snakes with double[5] tongue,
10   Thorny hedgehogs, be not seen;
        Newts[6] and blindworms, do no wrong,
           Come not near our fairy queen.
[*Chorus:*]   Philomel,[7] with melody
        Sing in our sweet lullaby;

---

3. Honeysuckle.   4. Sweetbriar, a kind of rose. *Musk-rose:* a kind of large, sweet-scented rose.
5. Sloughs off, sheds.   6. Garment.   7. Anoint, touch gently.   8. Doting on.   9. Location: the
wood.   1. Dance in a ring.   2. Cankerworms.   3. Bats.   4. Dainty.   5. Forked.   6. Water
lizards (considered poisonous, as were *blindworms*—small snakes with tiny eyes—and spiders).   7. The
nightingale (Philomela, daughter of King Pandion, was transformed into a nightingale, according to
Ovid's *Metamorphoses* VI, after she had been raped by her sister Procne's husband, Tereus).

Lulla, lulla, lullaby, lulla, lulla, lullaby.   15
   Never harm,
   Nor spell nor charm,
  Come our lovely lady nigh.
  So, good night, with lullaby.

[FIRST FAIRY:]

Weaving spiders, come not here;   20
  Hence, you long-legg'd spinners, hence!
  Beetles black, approach not near;
   Worm nor snail, do no offense.
[*Chorus*:]   Philomel, with melody, etc.

[SECOND FAIRY:]

Hence, away! Now all is well.   25
  One aloof stand sentinel.

                [*Exeunt* FAIRIES. TITANIA *sleeps.*]

   [*Enter* OBERON *and squeezes the flower on* TITANIA's *eyelids.*]

OBERON: What thou seest when thou dost wake,
  Do it for thy true-love take;
  Love and languish for his sake.
  Be it ounce,[8] or cat, or bear,   30
  Pard,[9] or boar with bristled hair,
  In thy eye that shall appear
  When thou wak'st, it is thy dear.
  Wake when some vile thing is near.   [*Exit.*]

      [*Enter* LYSANDER *and* HERMIA.]

LYSANDER: Fair love, you faint with wand'ring in the wood;   35
  And to speak troth,[1] I have forgot our way.
  We'll rest us, Hermia, if you think it good,
  And tarry for the comfort of the day.
HERMIA: Be 't so, Lysander. Find you out a bed,
  For I upon this bank will rest my head.   40
LYSANDER: One turf shall serve as pillow for us both,
  One heart, one bed, two bosoms, and one troth.[2]
HERMIA: Nay, good Lysander; for my sake, my dear,
  Lie further off yet, do not lie so near.
LYSANDER: O, take the sense, sweet, of my innocence![3]   45
  Love takes the meaning in love's conference.[4]
  I mean, that my heart unto yours is knit

---

8. Lynx.   9. Leopard.   1. Truth.   2. Faith, trothplight.   3. That is, interpret my intention as
innocent.   4. That is, when lovers confer, love teaches each lover to interpret the other's meaning
lovingly.

So that but one heart we can make of it;
Two bosoms interchained with an oath—
50 So then two bosoms and a single troth.
Then by your side no bed-room me deny,
For lying so, Hermia, I do not lie.[5]
HERMIA: Lysander riddles very prettily.
Now much beshrew[6] my manners and my pride
55 If Hermia meant to say Lysander lied.
But, gentle friend, for love and courtesy
Lie further off, in human[7] modesty;
Such separation as may well be said
Becomes a virtuous bachelor and a maid,
60 So far be distant; and, good night, sweet friend.
Thy love ne'er alter till thy sweet life end!
LYSANDER: Amen, amen, to that fair prayer, say I,
And then end life when I end loyalty!
Here is my bed. Sleep give thee all his rest!
65 HERMIA: With half that wish the wisher's eyes be press'd![8]

[*They sleep, separated by a short distance. Enter* PUCK.]

PUCK: Through the forest have I gone,
But Athenian found I none
On whose eyes I might approve[9]
This flower's force in stirring love.
70 Night and silence.—Who is here?
Weeds of Athens he doth wear.
This is he, my master said,
Despised the Athenian maid;
And here the maiden, sleeping sound,
75 On the dank and dirty ground.
Pretty soul! She durst not lie
Near this lack-love, this kill-courtesy.
Churl, upon thy eyes I throw
All the power this charm doth owe.[1]   [*Applies the love-juice.*]
80 When thou wak'st, let love forbid
Sleep his seat on thy eyelid.
So awake when I am gone,
For I must now to Oberon.   [*Exit.*]

[*Enter* DEMETRIUS *and* HELENA, *running.*]

HELENA: Stay, though thou kill me, sweet Demetrius.
85 DEMETRIUS: I charge thee, hence, and do not haunt me thus.

5. Tell a falsehood (with a pun on *lie*, recline).   6. Curse (but mildly meant).   7. Courteous.
8. That is, may we share your wish, so that your eyes too are *press'd*, closed, in sleep.   9. Test.
1. Own.

HELENA: O, wilt thou darkling[2] leave me? Do not so.

DEMETRIUS: Stay, on thy peril![3] I alone will go.   [Exit.]

HELENA: O, I am out of breath in this fond[4] chase!
    The more my prayer, the lesser is my grace.[5]
    Happy is Hermia, wheresoe'er she lies,[6]   90
    For she hath blessed and attractive eyes.
    How came her eyes so bright? Not with salt tears;
    If so, my eyes are oft'ner wash'd than hers.
    No, no, I am as ugly as a bear;
    For beasts that meet me run away for fear.   95
    Therefore no marvel though Demetrius
    Do, as a monster, fly my presence thus.
    What wicked and dissembling glass of mine
    Made me compare with Hermia's sphery eyne?[7]
    But who is here? Lysander, on the ground?   100
    Dead, or asleep? I see no blood, no wound.
    Lysander, if you live, good sir, awake.

LYSANDER: [Awaking.] And run through fire I will for thy sweet sake.
    Transparent[8] Helena! Nature shows art,
    That through thy bosom makes me see thy heart.   105
    Where is Demetrius? O, how fit a word
    Is that vile name to perish on my sword!

HELENA: Do not say so, Lysander, say not so.
    What though he love your Hermia? Lord, what though?
    Yet Hermia still loves you. Then be content.   110

LYSANDER: Content with Hermia? No! I do repent
    The tedious minutes I with her have spent.
    Not Hermia but Helena I love.
    Who will not change a raven for a dove?
    The will of man is by his reason sway'd,   115
    And reason says you are the worthier maid.
    Things growing are not ripe until their season;
    So I, being young, till now ripe not to reason.[9]
    And touching now the point of human skill,[1]
    Reason becomes the marshal to my will   120
    And leads me to your eyes, where I o'erlook[2]
    Love's stories written in love's richest book.

HELENA: Wherefore was I to this keen mockery born?
    When at your hands did I deserve this scorn?
    Is 't not enough, is 't not enough, young man,   125
    That I did never, no, nor never can,
    Deserve a sweet look from Demetrius' eye,

---

2. In the dark.   3. That is, on pain of danger to you if you don't obey me and stay.   4. Doting.
5. The favor I obtain.   6. Dwells.   7. Eyes as bright as stars in their spheres.   8. (1) Radiant; (2)
able to be seen through.   9. Mature enough to be reasonable.   1. Judgment. *Touching:* reaching.
Point: summit.   2. Read.

But you must flout my insufficiency?
Good troth, you do me wrong, good sooth,[3] you do,
130   In such disdainful manner me to woo.
But fare you well. Perforce I must confess
I thought you lord of more true gentleness.[4]
O, that a lady, of[5] one man refus'd,
Should of another therefore be abus'd![6]   [*Exit.*]
135   LYSANDER: She sees not Hermia. Hermia, sleep thou there,
And never mayst thou come Lysander near!
For as a surfeit of the sweetest things
The deepest loathing to the stomach brings,
Or as the heresies that men do leave
140   Are hated most of those they did deceive,
So thou, my surfeit and my heresy,
Of all be hated, but the most of me!
And, all my powers, address your love and might
To honor Helen and to be her knight!   [*Exit.*]
145   HERMIA: [*Awaking.*] Help me, Lysander, help me! Do thy best
To pluck this crawling serpent from my breast!
Ay me, for pity! What a dream was here!
Lysander, look how I do quake with fear.
Methought a serpent eat[7] my heart away,
150   And you sat smiling at his cruel prey.[8]
Lysander! What, remov'd? Lysander! Lord!
What, out of hearing? Gone? No sound, no word?
Alack, where are you? Speak, an if you hear.
Speak, of all loves![9] I swoon almost with fear.
155   No? Then I well perceive you are not nigh.
Either death, or you, I'll find immediately.

[*Exit. Manet* TITANIA *lying asleep.*]

ACT III

SCENE 1[1]

Enter the Clowns (QUINCE, SNUG, BOTTOM, FLUTE, SNOUT, *and* STARVELING.)

BOTTOM: Are we all met?
QUINCE: Pat, pat; and here's a marvailes convenient place for our rehearsal. This
   green plot shall be our stage, this hawthorn brake our tiring-house,[2] and we
   will do it in action as we will do it before the Duke.
5   BOTTOM: Peter Quince?

---

3. That is, indeed, truly.   4. Courtesy. *Lord of:* that is, possessor of.   5. By.   6. Ill treated.
7. Ate (pronounced *et*).   8. Act of preying.   9. For all love's sake.   1. Location: scene continues.
2. Attiring area, hence backstage. *Brake:* thicket.

QUINCE: What sayest thou, bully[3] Bottom?

BOTTOM: There are things in this comedy of Pyramus and Thisby that will never please. First, Pyramus must draw a sword to kill himself, which the ladies cannot abide. How answer you that?

SNOUT: By 'r lakin, a parlous[4] fear. 10

STARVELING: I believe we must leave the killing out, when all is done.[5]

BOTTOM: Not a whit. I have a device to make all well. Write me[6] a prologue; and let the prologue seem to say, we will do no harm with our swords and that Pyramus is not kill'd indeed; and, for the more better assurance, tell them that I Pyramus am not Pyramus, but Bottom the weaver. This will put 15 them out of fear.

QUINCE: Well, we will have such a prologue, and it shall be written in eight and six.[7]

BOTTOM: No, make it two more; let it be written in eight and eight.

SNOUT: Will not the ladies be afeard of the lion? 20

STARVELING: I fear it, I promise you.

BOTTOM: Masters, you ought to consider with yourselves, to bring in—God shield us!—a lion among ladies,[8] is a most dreadful thing. For there is not a more fearful[9] wild-fowl than your lion living; and we ought to look to 't.

SNOUT: Therefore another prologue must tell he is not a lion. 25

BOTTOM: Nay, you must name his name, and half his face must be seen through the lion's neck, and he himself must speak through, saying thus, or to the same defect:[1] "Ladies"—or "Fair ladies—I would wish you"—or "I would request you"—or "I would entreat you—not to fear, not to tremble; my life for yours.[2] If you think I come hither as a lion, it were pity of my life.[3] No, I 30 am no such thing; I am a man as other men are." And there indeed let him name his name, and tell them plainly he is Snug the joiner.

QUINCE: Well, it shall be so. But there is two hard things: that is, to bring the moonlight into a chamber; for, you know, Pyramus and Thisby meet by moonlight. 35

SNOUT: Doth the moon shine that night we play our play?

BOTTOM: A calendar, a calendar! Look in the almanac. Find out moonshine, find out moonshine. [*They consult an almanac.*]

QUINCE: Yes, it doth shine that night.

BOTTOM: Why then may you leave a casement of the great chamber window, 40 where we play, open, and the moon may shine in at the casement.

QUINCE: Ay; or else one must come in with a bush of thorns and a lantern, and

---

3. That is, worthy, jolly, fine fellow.   4. Perilous. *By 'r lakin:* by our ladykin; that is, the Virgin Mary.
5. That is, when all is said and done.   6. That is, write at my suggestion. (*Me* is the ethic dative.)
7. Alternate lines of eight and six syllables, a common ballad measure.   8. [A contemporary pamphlet
tells how at the christening in 1594 of Prince Henry, eldest son of King James VI of Scotland, later James
I of England, a "blackmoor" instead of a lion drew the triumphal chariot since the lion's presence might
have "brought some fear to the nearest."]   9. Fear-inspiring.   1. [Bottom's blunder for *effect.*]
2. That is, I pledge my life to make your lives safe.   3. My life would be endangered.

say he comes to disfigure,[4] or to present,[5] the person of Moonshine. Then there is another thing: we must have a wall in the great chamber; for Pyra-
45   mus and Thisby, says the story, did talk through the chink of a wall.

SNOUT: You can never bring in a wall. What say you, Bottom?

BOTTOM: Some man or other must present Wall. And let him have some plaster, or some loam, or some roughcast[6] about him, to signify wall; and let him hold his fingers thus, and through that cranny shall Pyramus and Thisby
50   whisper.

QUINCE: If that may be, then all is well. Come, sit down, every mother's son, and rehearse your parts. Pyramus, you begin. When you have spoken your speech, enter into that brake, and so every one according to his cue.

[Enter Robin (PUCK).]

PUCK: What hempen home-spuns have we swagg'ring here,
55   So near the cradle of the Fairy Queen?
          What, a play toward?[7] I'll be an auditor;
          An actor too perhaps, if I see cause.

QUINCE: Speak, Pyramus. Thisby, stand forth.

BOTTOM: "Thisby, the flowers of odious savors sweet,"—
60   QUINCE: Odors, odors.

BOTTOM: —"Odors savors sweet;
          So hath thy breath, my dearest Thisby dear.
          But hark, a voice! Stay thou but here awhile,
          And by and by I will to thee appear."   [Exit.]
65   PUCK: A stranger Pyramus than e'er played here.[8]   [Exit.]

FLUTE: Must I speak now?

QUINCE: Ay, marry, must you; for you must understand he goes but to see a noise that he heard, and is to come again.

FLUTE: "Most radiant Pyramus, most lily-white of hue,
70   Of color like the red rose on triumphant brier,
          Most brisky juvenal and eke most lovely Jew,[9]
          As true as truest horse that yet would never tire.
          I'll meet thee, Pyramus, at Ninny's tomb."

QUINCE: "Ninus'[1] tomb," man. Why, you must not speak that yet. That you
75   answer to Pyramus. You speak all your part at once, cues and all. Pyramus enter. Your cue is past; it is, "never tire."

FLUTE: O—"As true as truest horse, that yet would never tire."

---

4. [Quince's blunder for prefigure.] Bush of thorns: bundle of thornbush faggots (part of the accoutrements of the man in the moon, according to the popular notions of the time, along with his lantern and his dog).   5. Represent.   6. A mixture of lime and gravel used to plaster the outside of buildings.   7. About to take place.   8. That is, in this theater (?).   9. [Probably an absurd repetition of the first syllable of juvenal.] Briskly juvenal: brisk youth. Eke: also.   1. Mythical founder of Nineveh (whose wife, Semiramis, was supposed to have built the walls of Babylon, where the story of Pyramis and Thisbe [Thisby] takes place).

[*Enter* PUCK, *and* BOTTOM *as Pyramus with the ass head.*][2]

BOTTOM: "If I were fair,[3] Thisby, I were only thine."
QUINCE: O monstrous! O strange! We are haunted. Pray, masters! Fly, masters!
    Help!   [*Exeunt* QUINCE, SNUG, FLUTE, SNOUT, *and* STARVELING.]   80
PUCK: I'll follow you, I'll lead you about a round,[4]
  Through bog, through bush, through brake, through brier.
  Sometime a horse I'll be, sometime a hound,
  A hog, a headless bear, sometime a fire;[5]
  And neigh, and bark, and grunt, and roar, and burn,   85
  Like horse, hound, hog, bear, fire, at every turn.   [*Exit.*]
BOTTOM: Why do they run away? This is a knavery of them to make me afeard.

    [*Enter* SNOUT.]

SNOUT: O Bottom, thou art chang'd! what do I see on thee?
BOTTOM: What do you see? You see an ass-head of your own, do you?
                            [*Exit* SNOUT.]

    [*Enter* QUINCE.]

QUINCE: Bless thee, Bottom, bless thee! Thou art translated.[6]   [*Exit.*]   90
BOTTOM: I see their knavery. This is to make an ass of me, to fright me, if they
    could. But I will not stir from this place, do what they can. I will walk up
    and down here, and I will sing, that they shall hear I am not afraid.

    [*Sings.*]

  The woosel cock[7] so black of hue,
    With orange-tawny bill,   95
  The throstle[8] with his note so true,
    The wren with little quill[9]—

TITANIA: [*Awaking.*] What angel wakes me from my flow'ry bed?

[BOTTOM *sings:*]

  The finch, the sparrow, and the lark,
    The plain-song[1] cuckoo grey,   100
  Whose note full many a man doth mark,
    And dares not answer nay—[2]

  For, indeed, who would set his wit to so foolish a bird? Who would give a
  bird the lie,[3] though he cry "cuckoo" never so?[4]
TITANIA: I pray thee, gentle mortal, sing again.   105

---

2. [This stage direction, taken from the Folio, presumably refers to a standard stage property.]
3. Handsome.   4. Roundabout.   5. Will-o'-the-wisp.   6. Transformed.   7. Male ousel or ouzel, blackbird.   8. Song thrush.   9. [Literally, a reed pipe; hence, the bird's piping song.]
1. Singing a melody without variations.   2. That is, cannot deny that he is a cuckold.   3. Call the bird a liar.   4. Ever so much.

Mine ear is much enamored of thy note;
So is mine eye enthralled to thy shape;
And thy fair virtue's force[5] perforce doth move me
On the first view to say, to swear, I love thee.

110 BOTTOM: Methinks, mistress, you should have little reason for that. And yet, to
say the truth, reason and love keep little company together nowadays. The
more the pity that some honest neighbors will not make them friends. Nay,
I can gleek[6] upon occasion.

TITANIA: Thou art as wise as thou art beautiful.

115 BOTTOM: Not so, neither. But if I had wit enough to get out of this wood, I have
enough to serve mine own turn.[7]

TITANIA: Out of this wood do not desire to go.
Thou shalt remain here, whether thou wilt or no.
I am a spirit of no common rate.[8]

120 The summer still doth tend upon my state;[9]
And I do love thee. Therefore, go with me.
I'll give thee fairies to attend on thee,
And they shall fetch thee jewels from the deep,
And sing while thou on pressèd flowers dost sleep.

125 And I will purge thy mortal grossness so
That thou shalt like an airy spirit go.
Peaseblossom, Cobweb, Moth,[1] and Mustardseed!

[*Enter four* FAIRIES (PEASEBLOSSOM, COBWEB, MOTH, *and* MUSTARDSEED).]

PEASEBLOSSOM: Ready.
COBWEB: And I.
MOTH: And I.
MUSTARDSEED: And I.
ALL: Where shall we go?

130 TITANIA: Be kind and courteous to this gentleman.
Hop in his walks and gambol in his eyes;
Feed him with apricocks and dewberries,
With purple grapes, green figs, and mulberries;
The honey-bags steal from the humble-bees,

135 And for the night-tapers crop their waxen thighs
And light them at the fiery glow-worm's eyes,
To have my love to bed and to arise;
And pluck the wings from painted butterflies
To fan the moonbeams from his sleeping eyes.

140 Nod to him, elves, and do him courtesies.

---

5. The power of your beauty.   6. Scoff, jest.   7. Answer my purpose.   8. Rank, value.
9. Waits upon me as a part of my royal retinue. *Still:* ever, always.   1. That is, mote, speck. (The
two words *moth* and *mote* were pronounced alike.)

PEASEBLOSSOM: Hail, mortal!
COBWEB: Hail!
MOTH: Hail!
MUSTARDSEED: Hail!
BOTTOM: I cry your worships mercy, heartily. I beseech your worship's name.   145
COBWEB: Cobweb.
BOTTOM: I shall desire you of more acquaintance, good Master Cobweb. If I cut
    my finger, I shall make bold with you.[2] Your name, honest gentleman?
PEASEBLOSSOM: Peaseblossom.
BOTTOM: I pray you, commend me to Mistress Squash,[3] your mother, and to Mas-   150
    ter Peascod,[4] your father. Good Master Peaseblossom, I shall desire you of
    more acquaintance too. Your name, I beseech you, sir?
MUSTARDSEED: Mustardseed.
BOTTOM: Good Master Mustardseed, I know your patience well.[5] That same cow-
    ardly, giant-like ox-beef hath devour'd many a gentleman of your house. I   155
    promise you your kindred hath made my eyes water ere now. I desire you of
    more acquaintance, good Master Mustardseed.
TITANIA: Come wait upon him; lead him to my bower.
    The moon methinks looks with a wat'ry eye;
    And when she weeps,[6] weeps every little flower,   160
    Lamenting some enforced[7] chastity.
    Tie up my lover's tongue, bring him silently.   [*Exeunt.*]

SCENE 2[8]

Enter OBERON, *King of Fairies.*

OBERON: I wonder if Titania be awak'd;
    Then, what it was that next came in her eye,
    Which she must dote on in extremity.

    [*Enter Robin Goodfellow* (PUCK).]

Here comes my messenger. How now, mad spirit?
What night-rule now about this haunted[9] grove?   5
PUCK: My mistress with a monster is in love.
    Near to her close[1] and consecrated bower,
    While she was in her dull[2] and sleeping hour,
    A crew of patches, rude mechanicals,[3]

---

2. [Cobwebs were used to stanch bleeding.]   3. Unripe pea pod.   4. Ripe pea pod.   5. What you
have endured.   6. That is, she causes dew.   7. Forced, violated, or, possibly, constrained (since
Titania at this moment is hardly concerned about chastity).   8. Location: the wood.   9. Much frequented. *Night-rule:* diversion for the night.   1. Secret, private.   2. Drowsy.   3. Ignorant artisans. *Patches:* clowns, fools.

10   That work for bread upon Athenian stalls,
    Were met together to rehearse a play
    Intended for great Theseus' nuptial day.
    The shallowest thick-skin of that barren sort,[4]
    Who Pyramus presented,[5] in their sport
15   Forsook his scene[6] and ent'red in a brake.
    When I did him at this advantage take,
    An ass's nole[7] I fixed on his head.
    Anon his Thisby must be answered,
    And forth my mimic[8] comes. When they him spy,
20   As wild geese that the creeping fowler eye,
    Or russet-pated choughs, many in sort,[9]
    Rising and cawing at the gun's report,
    Sever[1] themselves and madly sweep the sky,
    So, at his sight, away his fellows fly;
25   And, at our stamp, here o'er and o'er one falls;
    He murder cries and help from Athens calls.
    Their sense thus weak, lost with their fears thus strong,
    Made senseless things begin to do them wrong,
    For briers and thorns at their apparel snatch;
30   Some, sleeves—some, hats; from yielders all things catch.
    I led them on in this distracted fear
    And left sweet Pyramus translated there,
    When in that moment, so it came to pass,
    Titania wak'd and straightway lov'd an ass.
35 OBERON: This falls out better than I could devise.
    But hast thou yet latch'd[2] the Athenian's eyes
    With the love-juice, as I did bid thee do?
PUCK: I took him sleeping—that is finish'd too—
    And the Athenian woman by his side,
40   That, when he wak'd, of force[3] she must be ey'd.

        [*Enter* DEMETRIUS *and* HERMIA.]

OBERON: Stand close. This is the same Athenian.
PUCK: This is the woman, but not this the man.   [*They stand aside.*]
DEMETRIUS: O, why rebuke you him that loves you so?
    Lay breath so bitter on your bitter foe.
45 HERMIA: Now I but chide; but I should use thee worse,
    For thou, I fear, hast given me cause to curse.
    If thou hast slain Lysander in his sleep,
    Being o'er shoes in blood, plunge in the deep,

---

4. Stupid company or crew.   5. Acted.   6. Playing area.   7. Noddle, head.   8. Burlesque actor.
9. In a flock. *Russet-pated choughs:* gray-headed jackdaws.   1. That is, scatter.   2. Moistened,
anointed.   3. Perforce.

And kill me too.
The sun was not so true unto the day 50
As he to me. Would he have stolen away
From sleeping Hermia? I'll believe as soon
This whole[4] earth may be bor'd and that the moon
May through the center creep and so displease
Her brother's noontide with th' Antipodes.[5] 55
It cannot be but thou hast murd'red him;
So should a murderer look, so dead,[6] so grim.
DEMETRIUS: So should the murdered look, and so should I,
Pierc'd through the heart with your stern cruelty.
Yet you, the murderer, look as bright, as clear, 60
As yonder Venus in her glimmering sphere.
HERMIA: What's this to my Lysander? Where is he?
Ah, good Demetrius, wilt thou give him me?
DEMETRIUS: I had rather give his carcass to my hounds.
HERMIA: Out, dog! Out, cur! Thou driv'st me past the bounds 65
Of maiden's patience. Hast thou slain him, then?
Henceforth be never numb'red among men!
O, once tell true, tell true, even for my sake!
Durst thou have look'd upon him being awake,
And hast thou kill'd him sleeping? O brave touch![7] 70
Could not a worm,[8] an adder, do so much?
An adder did it; for with doubler tongue
Than thine, thou serpent, never adder stung.
DEMETRIUS: You spend your passion on a mispris'd mood.[9]
I am not guilty of Lysander's blood, 75
Nor is he dead, for aught that I can tell.
HERMIA: I pray thee, tell me then that he is well.
DEMETRIUS: An if I could, what should I get therefore?
HERMIA: A privilege never to see me more.
And from thy hated presence part I so. 80
See me no more, whether he be dead or no. *[Exit.]*
DEMETRIUS: There is no following her in this fierce vein.
Here therefore for a while I will remain.
So sorrow's heaviness doth heavier[1] grow
For debt that bankrupt[2] sleep doth sorrow owe; 85
Which now in some slight measure it will pay,
If for his tender here I make some stay.[3]   *[They lie down and sleep.]*

---

4. Solid.   5. The people on the opposite side of the Earth. *Her brother's:* that is, the sun's.
6. Deadly, or deathly pale.   7. Noble exploit (said ironically).   8. Serpent.   9. Anger based on
misconception. *Passion:* violent feelings.   1. (1) Harder to bear; (2) more drowsy.   2. [Demetrius is
saying that his sleepiness adds to the weariness caused by sorrow.]   3. That is, to a small extent I will
be able to "pay back" and hence find some relief from sorrow, if I pause here a while (*make some stay*)
while sleep "tenders" or offers itself by way of paying the debt owed to sorrow.

OBERON: What hast thou done? Thou hast mistaken quite
　　And laid the love-juice on some true-love's sight.
90　Of thy misprision[4] must perforce ensue
　　Some true love turn'd and not a false turn'd true.
PUCK: Then fate o'er-rules, that, one man holding troth,[5]
　　A million fail, confounding[6] oath on oath.
OBERON: About the wood go swifter than the wind,
95　　And Helena of Athens look thou find.
　　All fancy-sick she is and pale of cheer[7]
　　With sighs of love, that cost the fresh blood[8] dear.
　　By some illusion see thou bring her here.
　　I'll charm his eyes against she do appear.[9]
100　PUCK: I go, I go; look how I go,
　　Swifter than arrow from the Tartar's bow.[1]　　　　　　　*[Exit.]*
OBERON: Flower of this purple dye,
　　　Hit with Cupid's archery.
　　　Sink in apple of his eye.　　　　*[Applies love-juice to* DEMETRIUS's *eyes.]*
105　　When his love he doth espy,
　　　Let her shine as gloriously
　　　As the Venus of the sky.
　　　When thou wak'st, if she be by,
　　　Beg of her for remedy.

　　　　[Enter PUCK.*]*

110　PUCK: Captain of our fairy band,
　　　Helena is here at hand,
　　　And the youth, mistook by me,
　　　Pleading for a lover's fee.[2]
　　　Shall we their fond pageant[3] see?
115　　Lord, what fools these mortals be!
OBERON: Stand aside. The noise they make
　　Will cause Demetrius to awake.
PUCK: Then will two at once woo one;
　　That must needs be sport alone[4];
120　And those things do best please me
　　That befall prepost'rously.[5]　　　　　　　　*[They stand aside.]*

　　　[Enter LYSANDER *and* HELENA.*]*

LYSANDER: Why should you think that I should woo in scorn?
　　Scorn and derision never come in tears.

---

4. Mistake.　　5. Faith.　　6. That is, invalidating one oath with another.　　7. Face. *Fancysick:* love-
sick.　　8. [An allusion to the physiological theory that each sigh costs the heart a drop of blood.]
9. In anticipation of her coming.　　1. [Tartars were famed for their skill with the bow.]　　2. Privilege,
reward.　　3. Foolish exhibition.　　4. Unequaled.　　5. Out of the natural order.

Look when[6] I vow, I weep; and vows so born,
In their nativity all truth appears.[7]   125
How can these things in me seem scorn to you,
Bearing the badge[8] of faith, to prove them true?
HELENA: You do advance[9] your cunning more and more.
    When truth kills truth,[1] O devilish-holy fray!
    These vows are Hermia's. Will you give her o'er?   130
    Weigh oath with oath, and you will nothing weigh.
    Your vows to her and me, put in two scales,
    Will even weigh, and both as light as tales.[2]
LYSANDER: I had no judgment when to her I swore.
HELENA: Nor none, in my mind, now you give her o'er.   135
LYSANDER: Demetrius loves her, and he loves not you.
DEMETRIUS: [*Awaking.*] O Helen, goddess, nymph, perfect, divine!
    To what, my love, shall I compare thine eyne?
    Crystal is muddy. O, how ripe in show[3]
    Thy lips, those kissing cherries, tempting grow!   140
    That pure congealed white, high Taurus'[4] snow,
    Fann'd with the eastern wind, turns to a crow[5]
    When thou hold'st up thy hand. O, let me kiss
    This princess of pure white, this seal[6] of bliss!
HELENA: O spite! O hell! I see you all are bent   145
    To set against me for your merriment.
    If you were civil and knew courtesy,
    You would not do me thus much injury.
    Can you not hate me, as I know you do,
    But you must join in souls to mock me too?   150
    If you were men, as men you are in show,
    You would not use a gentle lady so—
    To vow, and swear, and superpraise my parts,[7]
    When I am sure you hate me with your hearts.
    You both are rivals, and love Hermia;   155
    And now both rivals, to mock Helena.
    A trim[8] exploit, a manly enterprise,
    To conjure tears up in a poor maid's eyes
    With your derision! None of noble sort
    Would so offend a virgin and extort[9]   160
    A poor soul's patience, all to make you sport.

---

6. Whenever.   7. That is, vows made by one who is weeping give evidence thereby of their sincerity.
8. Identifying device such as that worn on servants' livery.   9. Carry forward, display.   1. That is,
one of Lysander's vows must invalidate the other.   2. Lies.   3. Appearance.   4. A lofty mountain
range in Asia Minor.   5. That is, seems black by contrast.   6. Pledge.   7. Qualities. *Superpraise:*
overpraise.   8. Pretty, fine (said ironically).   9. Twist, torture.

LYSANDER: You are unkind, Demetrius. Be not so;
  For you love Hermia; this you know I know.
  And here, with all good will, with all my heart,
165   In Hermia's love I yield you up my part;
  And yours of Helena to me bequeath,
  Whom I do love and will do till my death.
HELENA: Never did mockers waste more idle breath.
DEMETRIUS: Lysander, keep thy Hermia; I will none.[1]
170   If e'er I lov'd her, all that love is gone.
  My heart to her but as guest-wise sojourn'd,
  And now to Helen is it home return'd,
  There to remain.
LYSANDER: Helen, it is not so.
DEMETRIUS: Disparage not the faith thou dost not know,
175   Lest, to thy peril, thou aby[2] it dear.
  Look, where thy love comes; yonder is thy dear.

     [*Enter* HERMIA.]

HERMIA: Dark night, that from the eye his[3] function takes,
  The ear more quick of apprehension makes;
  Wherein it doth impair the seeing sense,
180   It pays the hearing double recompense.
  Thou art not by mine eye, Lysander, found;
  Mine ear, I thank it, brought me to thy sound.
  But why unkindly didst thou leave me so?
LYSANDER: Why should he stay, whom love doth press to go?
185 HERMIA: What love could press Lysander from my side?
LYSANDER: Lysander's love, that would not let him bide,
  Fair Helena, who more engilds the night
  Than all yon fiery oes[4] and eyes of light.
  Why seek'st thou me? Could not this make thee know,
190   The hate I bear thee made me leave thee so?
HERMIA: You speak not as you think. It cannot be.
HELENA: Lo, she is one of this confederacy!
  Now I perceive they have conjoin'd all three
  To fashion this false sport, in spite of me.[5]
195   Injurious Hermia, most ungrateful maid!
  Have you conspir'd, have you with these contriv'd[6]
  To bait[7] me with this foul derision?
  Is all the counsel[8] that we two have shar'd,

1. That is, wish none of her.   2. Pay for.   3. Its.   4. That is, circles, orbs, stars.   5. To vex me.
6. Plotted.   7. Torment, as one sets on dogs to bait a bear.   8. Confidential talk.

The sisters' vows, the hours that we have spent,
When we have chid the hasty-footed time   200
For parting us—O, is all forgot?
All school-days friendship, childhood innocence?
We, Hermia, like two artificial[9] gods,
Have with our needles created both one flower,
Both on one sampler, sitting on one cushion,   205
Both warbling of one song, both in one key,
As if our hands, our sides, voices, and minds
Had been incorporate. So we grew together,
Like to a double cherry, seeming parted,
But yet an union in partition;   210
Two lovely[1] berries molded on one stem;
So, with two seeming bodies, but one heart;
Two of the first, like coats in heraldry,
Due but to one and crowned with one crest.[2]
And will you rent[3] our ancient love asunder,   215
To join with men in scorning your poor friend?
It is not friendly, 'tis not maidenly.
Our sex, as well as I, may chide you for it,
Though I alone do feel the injury.
HERMIA: I am amazed at your passionate words.   220
    I scorn you not. It seems that you scorn me.
HELENA: Have you not set Lysander, as in scorn,
    To follow me and praise my eyes and face?
    And made your other love, Demetrius,
    Who even but now did spurn me with his foot,   225
    To call me goddess, nymph, divine and rare,
    Precious, celestial? Wherefore speaks he this
    To her he hates? And wherefore doth Lysander
    Deny your love, so rich within his soul,
    And tender[4] me, forsooth, affection,   230
    But by your setting on, by your consent?
    What though I be not so in grace[5] as you,
    So hung upon with love, so fortunate,
    But miserable most, to love unlov'd?
    This you should pity rather than despise.   235
HERMIA: I understand not what you mean by this.
HELENA: Ay, do! Persever, counterfeit sad[6] looks,
    Make mouths upon[7] me when I turn my back,

---

9. Skilled in art or creation.   1. Loving.   2. That is, we have two separate bodies, just as a coat of arms in heraldry can be represented twice on a shield but surmounted by a single crest.   3. Rend.
4. Offer.   5. Favor.   6. Grave, serious.   7. That is, makes mows, faces, grimaces at.

Wink each at other, hold the sweet jest up.
240 This sport, well carried,[8] shall be chronicled.
If you have any pity, grace, or manners,
You would not make me such an argument.[9]
But fare ye well. 'Tis partly my own fault,
Which death, or absence, soon shall remedy.

245 LYSANDER: Stay, gentle Helena; hear my excuse,
My love, my life, my soul, fair Helena!

HELENA: O excellent!

HERMIA: Sweet, do not scorn her so.

DEMETRIUS: If she cannot entreat,[1] I can compel.

LYSANDER: Thou canst compel no more than she entreat.
250 Thy threats have no more strength than her weak prayers.
Helen, I love thee, by my life, I do!
I swear by that which I will lose for thee,
To prove him false that says I love thee not.

DEMETRIUS: I say I love thee more than he can do.

255 LYSANDER: If thou say so, withdraw, and prove it too.

DEMETRIUS: Quick, come!

HERMIA: Lysander, whereto tends all this?

LYSANDER: Away, you Ethiope![2]   [He tries to break away from HERMIA.]

DEMETRIUS: No, no; he'll
Seem to break loose; take on as you would follow,
But yet come not. You are a tame man, go!

260 LYSANDER: Hang off,[3] thou cat, thou burr! Vile thing, let loose,
Or I will shake thee from me like a serpent!

HERMIA: Why are you grown so rude? What change is this,
Sweet love?

LYSANDER: Thy love? Out, tawny Tartar, out!
Out, loathed med'cine![4] O hated potion, hence!

HERMIA: Do you not jest?

265 HELENA: Yes, sooth,[5] and so do you.

LYSANDER: Demetrius, I will keep my word with thee.

DEMETRIUS: I would I had your bond, for I perceive
A weak bond[6] holds you. I'll not trust your word.

LYSANDER: What, should I hurt her, strike her, kill her dead?
270 Although I hate her, I'll not harm her so.

HERMIA: What, can you do me greater harm than hate?
Hate me? Wherefore? O me, what news,[7] my love?
Am not I Hermia? Are not you Lysander?
I am as fair now as I was erewhile.[8]

---

8. Managed.   9. Subject for a jest.   1. That is, succeed by entreaty.   2. [Referring to Hermia's relatively dark hair and complexion; see also *tawny Tartar* six lines later.]   3. Let go.   4. That is, poison.   5. Truly.   6. That is, Hermia's arm (with a pun on *bond,* oath, in the previous line). 7. What is the matter.   8. Just now.

And here will rest me. [*Lies down.*] Come, thou gentle day!
For if but once thou show me thy grey light,
I'll find Demetrius and revenge this spite.   [*Sleeps.*]   420

    [*Enter Robin (*PUCK*) and* DEMETRIUS.]

PUCK: Ho, ho, ho! Coward, why com'st thou not?
DEMETRIUS: Abide me, if thou dar'st; for well I wot[3]
  Thou runn'st before me, shifting every place,
  And dar'st not stand nor look me in the face.
  Where art thou now?
PUCK: Come hither. I am here.   425
DEMETRIUS: Nay, then, thou mock'st me. Thou shalt buy this dear,[4]
  If ever I thy face by daylight see.
  Now, go thy way. Faintness constraineth me
  To measure out my length on this cold bed.
  By day's approach look to be visited.   [*Lies down and sleeps.*]   430

    [*Enter* HELENA.]

HELENA: O weary night, O long and tedious night,
  Abate[5] thy hours! Shine, comforts, from the east,
  That I may back to Athens by daylight,
  From these that my poor company detest;
  And sleep, that sometimes shuts up sorrow's eye,   435
  Steal me awhile from mine own company.   [*Lies down and sleeps.*]
PUCK: Yet but three? Come one more;
    Two of both kinds makes up four.
    Here she comes, curst and sad.
    Cupid is a knavish lad,   440
    Thus to make poor females mad.

    [*Enter* HERMIA.]

HERMIA: Never so weary, never so in woe,
  Bedabbled with the dew and torn with briers,
  I can no further crawl, no further go;
  My legs can keep no pace with my desires.   445
  Here will I rest me till the break of day.
  Heavens shield Lysander, if they mean a fray!   [*Lies down and sleeps.*]
PUCK: On the ground
    Sleep sound.
    I'll apply   450
    To your eye,
  Gentle lover, remedy.   [*Squeezing the juice on* LYSANDER's *eyes.*]
    When thou wak'st,

---

3. Know.   4. Pay dearly for this.   5. Lessen, shorten.

Thou tak'st
455 True delight
In the sight
Of thy former lady's eye;
And the country proverb known,
That every man should take his own,
460 In your waking shall be shown:
    Jack shall have Jill;
    Nought shall go ill;
The man shall have his mare again, and all
    shall be well.   [*Exit. Manent the four lovers.*]

ACT IV

SCENE 1[6]

Enter TITANIA, *Queen of Fairies, and* BOTTOM *the Clown, and* FAIRIES: *and* OBERON, *the King, behind them.*

TITANIA: Come, sit thee down upon this flow'ry bed,
    While I thy amiable cheeks do coy,[7]
    And stick musk-roses in thy sleek smooth head,
    And kiss thy fair large ears, my gentle joy.

        [*They recline.*]

5 BOTTOM: Where's Peaseblossom?
PEASEBLOSSOM: Ready.
BOTTOM: Scratch my head, Peaseblossom. Where's Mounsieur Cobweb?
COBWEB: Ready.
BOTTOM: Mounsieur Cobweb, good mounsieur, get you your weapons in your
10   hand, and kill me a red-hipp'd humble-bee on the top of a thistle; and, good
        mounsieur, bring me the honey-bag. Do not fret yourself too much in the
        action, mounsieur; and, good mounsieur, have a care the honey-bag break
        not; I would be loath to have you overflown with a honey-bag, signior.
        Where's Mounsieur Mustardseed?
15 MUSTARDSEED: Ready.
BOTTOM: Give me your neaf,[8] Mounsieur Mustardseed. Pray you, leave your
        curtsy,[9] good mounsieur.
MUSTARDSEED: What's your will?
BOTTOM: Nothing, good mounsieur, but to help Cavalery Cobweb[1] to scratch. I
20   must to the barber's, mounsieur; for methinks I am marvailes hairy about the
        face; and I am such a tender ass, if my hair do but tickle me, I must scratch.

---

6. Location: scene continues. The four lovers are still asleep on stage.   7. Caress. *Amiable:* lovely.
8. Fist.   9. That is, put on your hat.   1. [Seemingly an error since Cobweb has been sent to bring
honey while Peaseblossom has been asked to scratch. *Cavalery:* Form of address for a gentleman.]

TITANIA: What, wilt thou hear some music, my sweet love?
BOTTOM: I have a reasonable good ear in music. Let's have the tongs and the
    bones.[2]

    [Music: tongs, rural music.][3]

TITANIA: Or say, sweet love, what thou desirest to eat.   25
BOTTOM: Truly, a peck of provender. I could munch your good dry oats. Methinks
    I have a great desire to a bottle of hay. Good hay, sweet hay, hath no fellow.[4]
TITANIA: I have a venturous fairy that shall seek
    The squirrel's hoard, and fetch thee new nuts.
BOTTOM: I had rather have a handful or two of dried peas. But, I pray you, let   30
    none of your people stir me. I have an exposition[5] of sleep come upon me.
TITANIA: Sleep thou, and I will wind thee in my arms.
    Fairies, be gone, and be all ways[6] away.   *[Exeunt FAIRIES.]*
    So doth the woodbine the sweet honeysuckle
    Gently entwist; the female ivy so   35
    Enrings the barky fingers of the elm.
    Oh, how I love thee! How I dote on thee!   *[They sleep.]*

    [Enter Robin Goodfellow (PUCK).]

OBERON: *[Advancing.]* Welcome, good Robin. See'st thou this sweet sight?
    Her dotage now I do begin to pity.
    For, meeting her of late behind the wood,   40
    Seeking sweet favors[7] for this hateful fool,
    I did upbraid her and fall out with her.
    For she his hairy temples then had rounded
    With coronet of fresh and fragrant flowers;
    And that same dew, which sometime[8] on the buds   45
    Was wont to swell like round and orient pearls,[9]
    Stood now within the pretty flouriets'[1] eyes
    Like tears that did their own disgrace bewail.
    When I had at my pleasure taunted her,
    And she in mild terms begg'd my patience,   50
    I then did ask of her her changeling child;
    Which straight she gave me, and her fairy sent
    To bear him to my bower in fairy land.
    And, now I have the boy, I will undo
    This hateful imperfection of her eyes.   55
    And, gentle Puck, take this transformed scalp
    From off the head of this Athenian swain,
    That, he awaking when the other[2] do,

2. Instruments for rustic music. (The tongs were played like a triangle, whereas the bones were held
between the fingers and used as clappers.)   3. [This stage direction is added from the Folio.]
4. Equal. *Bottle:* bundle.   5. [Bottom's word for *disposition.*]   6. In all directions.   7. That is, gifts
of flowers.   8. Formerly.   9. That is, the most beautiful of all pearls, those coming from the Orient.
1. Flowerets'.   2. Others.

May all to Athens back again repair,
60 And think no more of this night's accidents
But as the fierce vexation of a dream.
But first I will release the Fairy Queen.   [*Squeezes juice in her eyes.*]
          Be as thou wast wont to be;
          See as thou wast wont to see.
65   Dian's bud[3] o'er Cupid's flower
          Hath such force and blessed power.
Now, my Titania, wake you, my sweet queen.
TITANIA: [*Waking.*] My Oberon! What visions have I seen!
Methought I was enamor'd of an ass.
OBERON: There lies your love.
70 TITANIA: How came these things to pass?
O, how mine eyes do loathe his visage now!
OBERON: Silence awhile. Robin, take off this head.
Titania, music call, and strike more dead
Than common sleep of all these five[4] the sense.
75 TITANIA: Music, ho! Music, such as charmeth sleep!

          [*Music.*]

PUCK: [*Removing the ass's head.*] Now, when thou wak'st, with thine own fool's
    eyes peep.
OBERON: Sound, music! Come, my queen, take hands with me,
And rock the ground whereon these sleepers be.

          [*Dance.*]

80 Now thou and I are new in amity,
And will tomorrow midnight solemnly[5]
Dance in Duke Theseus' house triumphantly
And bless it to all fair prosperity.
There shall the pairs of faithful lovers be
85 Wedded, with Theseus, all in jollity.
PUCK: Fairy King, attend, and mark:
I do hear the morning lark.
OBERON: Then, my queen, in silence sad,[6]
Trip we after night's shade.
90 We the globe can compass soon,
Swifter than the wand'ring moon.
TITANIA: Come, my lord, and in our flight
Tell me how it came this night
That I sleeping here was found
95 With these mortals on the ground.   [*Exeunt.*]

3. [Perhaps the flower of the *agnus castus* or chaste-tree, supposed to preserve chastity; or perhaps referring simply to Oberon's herb by which he can undo the effects of "Cupid's flower," the love-in-idleness
of II.i.166 f.]   4. That is, the four lovers and Bottom.   5. Ceremoniously.   6. Sober.

[*Wind horn within. Enter* THESEUS *and all his train;* HIPPOLYTA, EGEUS.]

THESEUS: Go, one of you, find out the forester,
    For now our observation⁷ is perform'd;
    And since we have the vaward⁸ of the day,
    My love shall hear the music of my hounds.
    Uncouple in the western valley; let them go.   100
    Dispatch, I say, and find the forester.   [*Exit an Attendant.*]
    We will, fair queen, up to the mountain's top
    And mark the musical confusion
    Of hounds and echo in conjunction.
HIPPOLYTA: I was with Hercules and Cadmus⁹ once,   105
    When in a wood of Crete they bay'd¹ the bear
    With hounds of Sparta.² Never did I hear
    Such gallant chiding; for, besides the groves,
    The skies, the fountains, every region near
    Seem'd all one mutual cry. I never heard   110
    So musical a discord, such sweet thunder.
THESEUS: My hounds are bred out of the Spartan kind,
    So flew'd, so sanded;³ and their heads are hung
    With ears that sweep away the morning dew;
    Crook-knee'd, and dewlapp'd⁴ like Thessalian bulls;   115
    Slow in pursuit, but match'd in mouth like bells,
    Each under each. A cry more tuneable⁵
    Was never holla'd to, nor cheer'd with horn,
    In Crete, in Sparta, nor in Thessaly.
    Judge when you hear. [*Sees the sleepers.*] But, soft! What nymphs are these?   120
EGEUS: My lord, this' my daughter here asleep;
    And this, Lysander; this Demetrius is;
    This Helena, old Nedar's Helena.
    I wonder of their being here together.
THESEUS: No doubt they rose up early to observe   125
    The rite of May, and, hearing our intent,
    Came here in grace of our solemnity.⁶
    But speak, Egeus. Is not this the day
    That Hermia should give answer of her choice?
EGEUS: It is, my lord.   130
THESEUS: Go, bid the huntsmen wake them with their horns.
                                 [*Exit an Attendant.*]

---

7. That is, observance to a morn of May (I.i.167).   8. Vanguard, that is, earliest part.   9. Mythical founder of Thebes. (This story about him is unknown.)   1. Brought to bay.   2. [A breed famous in antiquity for its hunting skill.]   3. Of sandy color. *So flew'd:* similarly having large hanging chaps or fleshy covering of the jaw.   4. Having pendulous folds of skin under the neck.   5. Well tuned, melodious. *Match'd . . . each:* that is, harmoniously matched in their various cries like a set of bells, from treble down to bass. *Cry:* pack of hounds.   6. That is, observance of these same rites of May.

[*Shout within. Wind horns. They all start up.*]

Good morrow, friends. Saint Valentine[7] is past.
Begin these wood-birds but to couple now?
LYSANDER: Pardon, my lord. [*They kneel.*]
THESEUS: I pray you all, stand up.
135 I know you two are rival enemies;
How comes this gentle concord in the world,
That hatred is so far from jealousy
To sleep by hate and fear no enmity?
LYSANDER: My lord, I shall reply amazedly,
140 Half sleep, half waking; but as yet, I swear,
I cannot truly say how I came here.
But, as I think—for truly would I speak,
And now I do bethink me, so it is—
I came with Hermia hither. Our intent
145 Was to be gone from Athens, where[8] we might,
Without[9] the peril of the Athenian law—
EGEUS: Enough, enough, my lord; you have enough.
I beg the law, the law, upon his head.
They would have stol'n away; they would, Demetrius,
150 Thereby to have defeated you and me,
You of your wife and me of my consent,
Of my consent that she should be your wife.
DEMETRIUS: My lord, fair Helen told me of their stealth,
Of this their purpose hither to this wood,
155 And I in fury hither followed them,
Fair Helena in fancy following me.
But, my good lord, I wot not by what power—
But by some power it is—my love to Hermia,
Melted as the snow, seems to me now
160 As the remembrance of an idle gaud[1]
Which in my childhood I did dote upon;
And all the faith, the virtue of my heart,
The object and the pleasure of mine eye,
Is only Helena. To her, my lord,
165 Was I betroth'd ere I saw Hermia,
But like a sickness did I loathe this food;
But, as in health, come to my natural taste,
Now I do wish it, love it, long for it,

---

7. [Birds were supposed to choose their mates on St. Valentine's Day.]   8. Wherever, or to where.   9. Outside of, beyond.   1. Worthless trinket.

And will for evermore be true to it.
THESEUS: Fair lovers, you are fortunately met.   170
Of this discourse we more will hear anon.
Egeus, I will overbear your will;
For in the temple, by and by, with us
These couples shall eternally be knit.
And, for the morning now is something² worn,   175
Our purpos'd hunting shall be set aside.
Away with us to Athens. Three and three,
We'll hold a feast in great solemnity.
Come, Hippolyta.   [*Exeunt* THESEUS, HIPPOLYTA, EGEUS, *and train.*]
DEMETRIUS: These things seem small and undistinguishable,   180
Like far-off mountains turned into clouds.
HERMIA: Methinks I see these things with parted³ eye,
When every thing seems double.
HELENA: So methinks;
And I have found Demetrius like a jewel,
Mine own, and not mine own.⁴
DEMETRIUS: Are you sure   185
That we are awake? It seems to me
That yet we sleep, we dream. Do not you think
The Duke was here, and bid us follow him?
HERMIA: Yea, and my father.
HELENA: And Hippolyta.
LYSANDER: And he did bid us follow to the temple.   190
DEMETRIUS: Why, then, we are awake. Let's follow him,
And by the way let us recount our dreams.   [*Exeunt.*]
BOTTOM: [*Awaking.*] When my cue comes, call me, and I will answer. My next is,
"Most fair Pyramus." Heigh-ho! Peter Quince! Flute, the bellows-mender!
Snout, the tinker! Starveling! God's my life, stol'n hence, and left me asleep!   195
I have had a most rare vision. I have had a dream, past the wit of man to say
what dream it was. Man is but an ass, if he go about⁵ to expound this dream.
Methought I was—there is no man can tell what. Methought I was—and
methought I had—but man is but a patch'd⁶ fool, if he will offer⁶ to
say what methought I had. The eye of man hath not heard, the ear of man   200
hath not seen, man's hand is not able to taste, his tongue to conceive, nor
his heart to report, what my dream was. I will get Peter Quince to write a
ballad of this dream. It shall be called "Bottom's Dream," because it hath no
bottom; and I will sing it in the latter end of a play, before the Duke.
Peradventure, to make it the more gracious, I shall sing it at her⁷ death.   205
                                                              [*Exit.*]

2. Somewhat. *For:* since.   3. Improperly focused.   4. That is, like a jewel that one finds by chance
and, therefore, possesses but cannot certainly consider one's own property.   5. Attempt.   6. Venture. *Patch'd:* wearing motley, that is, a dress of various colors.   7. Thisby's(?).

Scene 2[8]

Enter QUINCE, FLUTE, SNOUT, *and* STARVELING.

QUINCE: Have you sent to Bottom's house? Is he come home yet?

STARVELING: He cannot be heard of. Out of doubt he is transported.[9]

FLUTE: If he come not, then the play is marr'd. It goes not forward, doth it?

QUINCE: It is not possible. You have not a man in all Athens able to discharge[1]

5   Pyramus but he.

FLUTE: No, he hath simply the best wit of any handicraft man in Athens.

QUINCE: Yea, and the best person too; and he is a very paramour for a sweet
    voice.

FLUTE: You must say "paragon." A paramour is, God bless us, a thing of naught.

[*Enter* SNUG *the Joiner.*]

10   SNUG: Masters, the Duke is coming from the temple, and there is two or three
    lords and ladies more married. If our sport had gone forward, we had all been
    made men.

FLUTE: O sweet bully Bottom! Thus hath he lost sixpence a day[2] during his life;
    he could not have scap'd sixpence a day. An the Duke had not given him

15   sixpence a day for playing Pyramus, I'll be hang'd. He would have deserv'd
    it. Sixpence a day in Pyramus, or nothing.

[*Enter* BOTTOM.]

BOTTOM: Where are these lads? Where are these hearts?[3]

QUINCE: Bottom! O most courageous day! O most happy hour!

BOTTOM: Masters, I am to discourse wonders.[4] But ask me not what; for if I tell

20   you, I am no true Athenian. I will tell you everything, right as it fell out.

QUINCE: Let us hear, sweet Bottom.

BOTTOM: Not a word of[5] me. All that I will tell you is, that the Duke hath din'd.
    Get your apparel together, good strings to your beards, new ribands[6] to your
    pumps; meet presently[7] at the palace; every man look o'er his part; for the

25   short and the long is, our play is preferr'd.[8] In any case, let Thisby have clean
    linen; and let not him that plays the lion pare his nails, for they shall hang
    out for the lion's claws. And, most dear actors, eat no onions nor garlic, for
    we are to utter sweet breath; and I do not doubt but to hear them say, it is a
    sweet comedy. No more words. Away! Go away!   [*Exeunt.*]

---

8. Location: Athens. Quince's house(?).   9. Carried off by fairies or, possibly, transformed.   1. Perform.   2. That is, as a royal pension.   3. Good fellows.   4. Have wonders to relate.   5. Out of.
6. Ribbons. *Strings:* that is, to attach the beards.   7. Immediately.   8. Selected for consideration.

ACT V

SCENE 1[9]

Enter THESEUS, HIPPOLYTA, *and* PHILOSTRATE, *Lords, and Attendants.*

HIPPOLYTA: 'Tis strange, my Theseus, that[1] these lovers speak of.
THESEUS: More strange than true. I never may[2] believe
  These antic fables, nor these fairy toys.[3]
  Lovers and madmen have such seething brains,
  Such shaping fantasies,[4] that apprehend   5
  More than cool reason ever comprehends.
  The lunatic, the lover, and the poet
  Are of imagination all compact.[5]
  One sees more devils than vast hell can hold;
  That is the madman. The lover, all as frantic,   10
  Sees Helen's beauty in a brow of Egypt.[6]
  The poet's eye, in a fine frenzy rolling,
  Doth glance from heaven to earth, from earth to heaven;
  And as imagination bodies forth
  The forms of things unknown, the poet's pen   15
  Turns them to shapes and gives to airy nothing
  A local habitation and a name.
  Such tricks hath strong imagination
  That, if it would but apprehend some joy,
  It comprehends some bringer[7] of that joy;   20
  Or in the night, imagining some fear,[8]
  How easy is a bush suppos'd a bear!
HIPPOLYTA: But all the story of the night told over,
  And all their minds transfigur'd so together,
  More witnesseth than fancy's images[9]   25
  And grows to something of great constancy;[1]
  But, howsoever, strange and admirable.[2]

  [*Enter lovers:* LYSANDER, DEMETRIUS, HERMIA, *and* HELENA.]

THESEUS: Here come the lovers, full of joy and mirth.
  Joy, gentle friends! Joy and fresh days of love
  Accompany your hearts!
LYSANDER: More than to us   30
  Wait in your royal walks, your board, your bed!
THESEUS: Come now, what masques, what dances shall we have,

---

9. Location: Athens. The palace of Theseus.   1. That which.   2. Can.   3. Trifling stories about fairies. *Antic:* strange, grotesque (with additional punning sense of *antique,* ancient).   4. Imaginations. 5. Formed, composed.   6. That is, face of a gypsy. *Helen's:* that is, of Helen of Troy, pattern of beauty. 7. That is, source.   8. Object of fear.   9. Testifies to something more substantial than mere imaginings.   1. Certainty.   2. Source of wonder. *Howsoever:* in any case.

To wear away this long age of three hours
Between our after-supper and bed-time?
35   Where is our usual manager of mirth?
What revels are in hand? Is there no play,
To ease the anguish of a torturing hour?
Call Philostrate.
PHILOSTRATE: Here, mighty Theseus.
THESEUS: Say, what abridgement³ have you for this evening?
40   What masque? What music? How shall we beguile
The lazy time, if not with some delight?
PHILOSTRATE: There is a brief⁴ how many sports are ripe.
Make choice of which your Highness will see first.   [Giving a paper.]
THESEUS: [Reads.] "The battle with the Centaurs,⁵ to be sung
45   By an Athenian eunuch to the harp."
We'll none of that. That have I told my love,
In glory of my kinsman⁶ Hercules.
[Reads.] "The riot of the tipsy Bacchanals,
Tearing the Thracian singer in their rage."⁷
50   That is an old device; and it was play'd
When I from Thebes came last a conqueror.
[Reads.] "The thrice three Muses mourning for the death
Of Learning, late deceas'd in beggary."⁸
That is some satire, keen and critical,
55   Not sorting with⁹ a nuptial ceremony.
[Reads.] "A tedious brief scene of young Pyramus
And his love Thisby; very tragical mirth."
Merry and tragical? Tedious and brief?
That is, hot ice and wondrous strange¹ snow.
60   How shall we find the concord of this discord?
PHILOSTRATE: A play there is, my lord, some ten words long,
Which is as brief as I have known a play;
But by ten words, my lord, it is too long,
Which makes it tedious. For in all the play
65   There is not one word apt, one player fitted.
And tragical, my noble lord, it is,
For Pyramus therein doth kill himself.
Which, when I saw rehears'd, I must confess,

---

3. Pastime (to abridge or shorten the evening).   4. Short written statement, list.   5. [Probably refers to the battle of the Centaurs and the Lapithae, when the Centaurs attempted to carry off Hippodamia, bride of Theseus's friend Pirothous.]   6. [Plutarch's Life of Theseus states that Hercules and Theseus were near kinsmen. Theseus is referring to a version of the battle of the Centaurs in which Hercules was said to be present.]   7. [This was the story of the death of Orpheus, as told in Metamorphoses XI.]   8. [Possibly an allusion to Spenser's Teares of the Muses (1591), though "satires" deploring the neglect of learning and the creative arts were commonplace.]   9. Befitting.   1. [Seemingly an error for some adjective that would contrast with snow, just as hot contrasts with ice.]

Made mine eyes water; but more merry tears
The passion of loud laughter never shed.   70
THESEUS: What are they that do play it?
PHILOSTRATE: Hard-handed men that work in Athens here,
    Which never labor'd in their minds till now,
    And now have toil'd their unbreathed[2] memories
    With this same play, against[3] your nuptial.   75
THESEUS: And we will hear it.
PHILOSTRATE: No, my noble lord,
    It is not for you. I have heard it over,
    And it is nothing, nothing in the world;
    Unless you can find sport in their intents,
    Extremely stretch'd and conn'd[4] with cruel pain,   80
    To do you service.
THESEUS: I will hear that play;
    For never anything can be amiss
    When simpleness and duty tender it.
    Go, bring them in; and take your places, ladies.

      [PHILOSTRATE *goes to summon the players.*]

HIPPOLYTA: I love not to see wretchedness o'ercharg'd[5]   85
    And duty in his service[6] perishing.
THESEUS: Why, gentle sweet, you shall see no such thing.
HIPPOLYTA: He says they can do nothing in this kind.[7]
THESEUS: The kinder we, to give them thanks for nothing.
    Our sport shall be to take what they mistake;   90
    And what poor duty cannot do, noble respect
    Takes it in might, not merit.[8]
    Where I have come, great clerks[9] have purposed
    To greet me with premeditated welcomes;
    Where I have seen them shiver and look pale,   95
    Make periods in the midst of sentences,
    Throttle their practic'd accent[1] in their fears,
    And in conclusion dumbly have broke off,
    Not paying me a welcome. Trust me, sweet,
    Out of this silence yet I pick'd a welcome;   100
    And in the modesty of fearful duty
    I read as much as from the rattling tongue
    Of saucy and audacious eloquence.
    Love, therefore, and tongue-tied simplicity
    In least speak most, to my capacity.[2]   105

---

2. Unexercised. *Toil'd:* taxed.   3. In preparation for.   4. Memorized. *Stretch'd:* strained.   5. Incompetence overburdened.   6. Its attempt to serve.   7. Kind of thing.   8. Values it for the effort
made rather than for the excellence achieved.   9. Learned men.   1. That is, rehearsed speech, or
usual way of speaking.   2. In my judgment and understanding. *Least:* that is, saying least.

[PHILOSTRATE *returns.*]

PHILOSTRATE: So please your Grace, the Prologue is address'd.[3]
THESEUS: Let him approach.

[*Flourish of trumpets. Enter the Prologue* (QUINCE).]

PROLOGUE: If we offend, it is with our good will.
    That you should think, we come not to offend,
110   But with good will. To show our simple skill,
    That is the true beginning of our end.
    Consider, then, we come but in despite.
    We do not come, as minding[4] to content you,
    Our true intent is. All for your delight
115   We are not here. That you should here repent you,
    The actors are at hand; and, by their show,
    You shall know all that you are like to know.
THESEUS: This fellow doth not stand upon points.[5]
LYSANDER: He hath rid his prologue like a rough[6] colt; he knows not the stop.[7]
120   A good moral, my lord: it is not enough to speak, but to speak true.
HIPPOLYTA: Indeed he hath play'd on his prologue like a child on a recorder; a
    sound, but not in government.[8]
THESEUS: His speech was like a tangled chain, nothing[9] impair'd, but all disor-
    der'd. Who is next?

[*Enter* PYRAMUS *and* THISBY, *and* WALL, *and* MOONSHINE, *and* LION.]

125 PROLOGUE: Gentles, perchance you wonder at this show;
    But wonder on, till truth make all things plain.
    This man is Pyramus, if you would know;
    This beauteous lady Thisby is certain.
    This man, with lime and rough-cast, doth present
130   Wall, that vile Wall which did these lovers sunder;
    And through Wall's chink, poor souls, they are content
    To whisper. At the which let no man wonder.
    This man, with lantern, dog, and bush of thorn,
    Presenteth Moonshine; for, if you will know,
135   By moonshine did these lovers think no scorn[1]
    To meet at Ninus' tomb, there, there to woo.
    This grisly beast, which Lion hight[2] by name,
    The trusty Thisby, coming first by night,
    Did scare away, or rather did affright;
140   And, as she fled, her mantle she did fall,[3]

---

3. Ready. *Prologue:* speaker of the prologue.   4. Intending.   5. (1) Heed niceties or small points; (2)
pay attention to punctuation in his reading. (The humor of Quince's speech is in the blunders of its
punctuation.)   6. Unbroken.   7. (1) The stopping of a colt by reining it in; (2) punctuation mark.
8. Control. *Recorder:* a wind instrument like a flute or flageolet.   9. Not at all.   1. Think it no disgraceful matter.   2. Is called.   3. Let fall.

Which Lion vile with bloody mouth did stain.
Anon comes Pyramus, sweet youth and tall,[4]
And finds his trusty Thisby's mantle slain;
Whereat, with blade, with bloody blameful blade,
He bravely broach'd[5] his boiling bloody breast.   145
And Thisby, tarrying in mulberry shade,
His dagger drew, and died. For all the rest,
Let Lion, Moonshine, Wall, and lovers twain
At large[6] discourse, while here they do remain.

> [*Exeunt* LION, THISBY, *and* MOONSHINE.]

THESEUS: I wonder if the lion be to speak.   150
DEMETRIUS: No wonder, my lord. One lion may, when many asses do.
WALL: In this same interlude it doth befall
    That I, one Snout by name, present a wall;
    And such a wall, as I would have you think,
    That had in it a crannied hole or chink,   155
    Through which the lovers, Pyramus and Thisby,
    Did whisper often very secretly.
    This loam, this rough-cast, and this stone doth show
    That I am that same wall; the truth is so.
    And this the cranny is, right and sinister,[7]   160
    Through which the fearful lovers are to whisper.
THESEUS: Would you desire lime and hair to speak better?
DEMETRIUS: It is the wittiest partition[8] that ever I heard discourse, my lord.

> [PYRAMUS *comes forward.*]

THESEUS: Pyramus draws near the wall. Silence!
PYRAMUS: O grim-look'd[9] night! O night with hue so black!   165
    O night, which ever art when day is not!
    O night, O night! Alack, alack, alack,
    I fear my Thisby's promise is forgot.
    And thou, O wall, O sweet, O lovely wall,
    That stand'st between her father's ground and mine,   170
    Thou wall, O wall, O sweet and lovely wall,
    Show me thy chink, to blink through with mine eyne!

> [WALL *holds up his fingers.*]

Thanks, courteous Wall. Jove shield thee well for this!
But what see I? No Thisby do I see.
O wicked wall, through whom I see no bliss!   175
Curs'd be thy stones for thus deceiving me!
THESEUS: The wall, methinks, being sensible,[1] should curse again.

---

4. Courageous.   5. Stabbed.   6. In full, at length.   7. That is, the right side of it and the left; or running from right to left, horizontally.   8. (1) Wall; (2) section of a learned treatise or oration.
9. Grim-looking.   1. Capable of feeling.

PYRAMUS: No, in truth, sir, he should not. "Deceiving me" is Thisby's cue: she is
to enter now, and I am to spy her through the wall. You shall see, it will
fall pat as I told you. Yonder she comes.

[*Enter* THISBY.]

THISBY: O wall, full often hast thou heard my moans,
For parting my fair Pyramus and me.
My cherry lips have often kiss'd thy stones,
Thy stones with lime and hair knit up in thee.

PYRAMUS: I see a voice. Now will I to the chink,
To spy an[2] I can hear my Thisby's face.
Thisby!

THISBY: My love! Thou art my love, I think.

PYRAMUS: Think what thou wilt, I am thy lover's grace;[3]
And, like Limander, am I trusty still.

THISBY: And I like Helen,[4] till the Fates me kill.

PYRAMUS: Not Shafalus to Procrus[5] was so true.

THISBY: As Shafalus to Procrus, I to you.

PYRAMUS: O, kiss me through the hole of this vile wall!

THISBY: I kiss the wall's hole, not your lips at all.

PYRAMUS: Wilt thou at Ninny's tomb meet me straightway?

THISBY: 'Tide life, 'tide[6] death, I come without delay.

[*Exeunt* PYRAMUS *and* THISBY.]

WALL: Thus have I, Wall, my part discharged so;
And, being done, thus Wall away doth go.   [*Exit.*]

THESEUS: Now is the mural down between the two neighbors.

DEMETRIUS: No remedy, my lord, when walls are so willful to hear without
warning.[7]

HIPPOLYTA: This is the silliest stuff that ever I heard.

THESEUS: The best in this kind are but shadows;[8] and the worst are no worse, if
imagination amend them.

HIPPOLYTA: It must be your imagination then, and not theirs.

THESEUS: If we imagine no worse of them than they of themselves, they may pass
for excellent men. Here come two noble beasts in, a man and a lion.

[*Enter* LION *and* MOONSHINE.]

LION: You, ladies, you, whose gentle hearts do fear
The smallest monstrous mouse that creeps on floor,
May now perchance both quake and tremble here,
When lion rough in widest rage doth roar.
Then know that I, as Snug the joiner, am
A lion fell,[9] nor else no lion's dam;

2. If.   3. That is, gracious lover.   4. [Blunders for "Leander" (*Limander*) and "Hero."]   5. [Blun-
ders for "Cephalus" (*Shafalus*) and "Procris," also famous lovers.]   6. Betide, come.   7. That is,
without warning the parents. *To hear:* as to hear.   8. Likenesses, representations. *In this kind:* of this
sort.   9. Fierce lion (with a play on the idea of *lion skin*).

For, if I should as lion come in strife   215
  Into this place, 'twere pity on my life.
THESEUS: A very gentle beast, and of a good conscience.
DEMETRIUS: The very best at a beast, my lord, that e'er I saw.
LYSANDER: This lion is a very fox for his valor.[1]
THESEUS: True; and a goose for his discretion.[2]   220
DEMETRIUS: Not so, my lord; for his valor cannot carry his discretion; and the fox
  carries the goose.
THESEUS: His discretion, I am sure, cannot carry his valor; for the goose carries
  not the fox. It is well. Leave it to his discretion, and let us listen to the moon.
MOON: This lanthorn[3] doth the horned moon present—   225
DEMETRIUS: He should have worn the horns on his head.[4]
THESEUS: He is no crescent, and his horns are invisible within the circumfer-
  ence.
MOON: This lanthorn doth the horned moon present;
  Myself the man i' th' moon do seem to be.   230
THESEUS: This is the greatest error of all the rest. The man should be put into the
  lanthorn. How is it else the man i' th' moon?
DEMETRIUS: He dares not come there for the[5] candle; for, you see, it is already in
  snuff.[6]
HIPPOLYTA: I am aweary of this moon. Would he would change!   235
THESEUS: It appears, by his small light of discretion, that he is in the wane; but
  yet, in courtesy, in all reason, we must stay the time.
LYSANDER: Proceed, Moon.
MOON: All that I have to say is to tell you that the lanthorn is the moon, I, the   240
  man in the moon, this thorn-bush my thorn-bush, and this dog my dog.
DEMETRIUS: Why, all these should be in the lanthorn; for all these are in the
  moon. But silence! Here comes Thisby.

  [*Enter* THISBY.]

THISBY: This is old Ninny's tomb. Where is my love?
LION: [*Roaring.*] Oh—   [THISBY *runs off.*]
DEMETRIUS: Well roar'd, Lion.   245
THESEUS: Well run, Thisby.
HIPPOLYTA: Well shone, Moon. Truly, the moon shines with a good grace.

  [*The* LION *shakes* THISBY'*s mantle, and exit.*]

THESEUS: Well mous'd,[7] Lion.
DEMETRIUS: And then came Pyramus.
LYSANDER: And so the lion vanish'd.   250

---

1. That is, his valor consists of craftiness and discretion.   2. That is, as discreet as a goose, meaning
more foolish than discreet.   3. [This original spelling, *lanthorn,* may suggest a play on the *horn* of
which lanterns were made, and also on a cuckold's horns; but the spelling *lanthorn* is not used consistently for comic effect in this play or elsewhere. At V.i.134, for example, the word is *lantern* in
the original.]   4. [As a sign of cuckoldry.]   5. Because of the.   6. (1) Offended; (2) in need of
snuffing.   7. Shaken.

[*Enter* PYRAMUS.]

PYRAMUS: Sweet Moon, I thank thee for thy sunny beams;
I thank thee, Moon, for shining now so bright;
For, by thy gracious, golden, glittering gleams,
I trust to take of truest Thisby sight.

255   But stay, O spite!
             But mark, poor knight,
         What dreadful dole[8] is here!
             Eyes, do you see?
             How can it be?
260   O dainty duck! O dear!
             Thy mantle good,
             What, stain'd with blood!
         Approach, ye Furies fell![9]
             O Fates, come, come,
265   Cut thread and thrum;[1]
         Quail, crush, conclude, and quell![2]

THESEUS: This passion, and the death of a dear friend, would go near to make a
    man look sad.[3]
HIPPOLYTA: Beshrew my heart, but I pity the man.
270 PYRAMUS: O wherefore, Nature, didst thou lions frame?
         Since lion vile hath here deflow'r'd my dear,
         Which is—no, no—which was the fairest dame
         That liv'd, that lov'd, that lik'd, that look'd with cheer.[4]

             Come, tears, confound,
275   Out, sword, and wound
         The pap of Pyramus;
             Ay, that left pap,
             Where heart doth hop.
         Thus die I, thus, thus, thus.   [*Stabs himself.*]
280   Now am I dead,
             Now am I fled;
         My soul is in the sky.
             Tongue, lose thy light;
             Moon, take thy flight.   [*Exit* MOONSHINE.]
285   Now die, die, die, die, die.   [*Dies.*]

DEMETRIUS: No die, but an ace,[5] for him; for he is but one.[6]
LYSANDER: Less than an ace, man; for he is dead, he is nothing.
THESEUS: With the help of a surgeon he might yet recover, and yet prove an ass.[7]

8. Grievous event.   9. Fierce.   1. The warp in weaving and the loose end of the warp.   2. Kill,
destroy. *Quail:* overpower.   3. That is, if one had other reason to grieve, one might be sad, but not
from this absurd portrayal of passion.   4. Countenance.   5. The side of the die featuring the single
pip, or spot. (The pun is on *die* as a singular of *dice*; Bottom's performance is not worth a whole *die* but
rather one single face of it, one small portion.)   6. (1) An individual person; (2) unique.   7. [With
a pun on *ace.*]

HIPPOLYTA: How chance Moonshine is gone before Thisby comes back and finds
    her lover? 290

THESEUS: She will find him by starlight. Here she comes; and her passion ends the
    play.

     [Enter THISBY.]

HIPPOLYTA: Methinks she should not use a long one for such a Pyramus. I hope
    she will be brief.

DEMETRIUS: A mote will turn the balance, which Pyramus, which[8] Thisby, is the 295
    better: he for a man, God warr'nt us; she for a woman, God bless us.

LYSANDER: She hath spied him already with those sweet eyes.

DEMETRIUS: And thus she means, videlicet:[9]

THISBY: Asleep, my love?
      What, dead, my dove? 300
    O Pyramus, arise!
      Speak, speak. Quite dumb?
      Dead, dead? A tomb
    Must cover thy sweet eyes.
      These lily lips, 305
      This cherry nose,
    These yellow cowslip cheeks,
      Are gone, are gone!
      Lovers, make moan.
    His eyes were green as leeks. 310
      O Sisters Three,[1]
      Come, come to me,
    With hands as pale as milk;
      Lay them in gore,
      Since you have shore[2] 315
    With shears his thread of silk.
      Tongue, not a word.
      Come, trusty sword,
    Come, blade, my breast imbrue![3]   *[Stabs herself.]*
      And farewell, friends. 320
      Thus Thisby ends.
    Adieu, adieu, adieu.   *[Dies.]*

THESEUS: Moonshine and Lion are left to bury the dead.

DEMETRIUS: Ay, and Wall too.

BOTTOM: *[Starting up.]* No, I assure you; the wall is down that parted their fathers. 325
    Will it please you to see the epilogue, or to hear a Bergomask dance[4] between
    two of our company?

THESEUS: No epilogue, I pray you; for your play needs no excuse. Never excuse;
    for when the players are all dead, there need none to be blam'd. Marry, if he

---

8. Whether . . . or.   9. To wit. *Means:* moans, laments.   1. The Fates.   2. Shorn.   3. Stain
with blood.   4. A rustic dance named from Bergamo, a province in the state of Venice.

330   that writ it had play'd Pyramus and hang'd himself in Thisby's garter, it
      would have been a fine tragedy; and so it is, truly, and very notably dis-
      charg'd. But, come, your Bergomask. Let your epilogue alone.   *[A dance.]*
      The iron tongue of midnight hath told[5] twelve.
      Lovers, to bed; 'tis almost fairy time.
335   I fear we shall outsleep the coming morn
      As much as we this night have overwatch'd.[6]
      This palpable-gross[7] play hath well beguil'd
      The heavy[8] gait of night. Sweet friends, to bed.
      A fortnight hold we this solemnity,
340   In nightly revels and new jollity.   *[Exeunt.]*

      [Enter PUCK.*]*

PUCK: Now the hungry lion roars,
      And the wolf behowls the moon;
      Whilst the heavy ploughman snores,
      All with weary task fordone.[9]
345   Now the wasted brands[1] do glow,
      Whilst the screech-owl, screeching loud,
      Puts the wretch that lies in woe
      In remembrance of a shroud.
      Now it is the time of night
350   That the graves, all gaping wide,
      Every one lets forth his sprite,[2]
      In the churchway paths to glide.
      And we fairies, that do run
      By the triple Hecate's[3] team
355   From the presence of the sun,
      Following darkness like a dream,
      Now are frolic.[4] Not a mouse
      Shall disturb this hallowed house.
      I am sent with broom before,
360   To sweep the dust behind[5] the door.

      [Enter OBERON *and* TITANIA, *King and Queen of Fairies, with all their train.]*

OBERON: Through the house give glimmering light,
      By the dead and drowsy fire;
      Every elf and fairy sprite
      Hop as light as bird from brier;
365   And this ditty, after me,
      Sing, and dance it trippingly.

---

5. Counted, struck ("tolled").   6. Stayed up too late.   7. Palpably gross, obviously crude.
8. Drowsy, dull.   9. Exhausted.   1. Burned-out logs.   2. Every grave lets forth its ghost.
3. [Hecate ruled in three capacities: as Luna or Cynthia in Heaven, as Diana on Earth, and as Proserpina
in Hell.]   4. Merry.   5. From behind. (Robin Goodfellow was a household spirit who helped good
housemaids and punished lazy ones.)

TITANIA: First, rehearse your song by rote,
   To each word a warbling note.
   Hand in hand, with fairy grace,
   Will we sing, and bless this place.   370

   [*Song and dance.*]

OBERON: Now, until the break of day,
   Through this house each fairy stray.
   To the best bride-bed will we,
   Which by us shall blessed be;
   And the issue there create[6]   375
   Ever shall be fortunate.
   So shall all the couples three
   Ever true in loving be;
   And the blots of Nature's hand
   Shall not in their issue stand;   380
   Never mole, hare lip, nor scar,
   Nor mark prodigious,[7] such as are
   Despised in nativity,
   Shall upon their children be.
   With this field-dew consecrate,[8]   385
   Every fairy take his gait,[9]
   And each several[1] chamber bless,
   Through this palace, with sweet peace;
   And the owner of it blest
   Ever shall in safety rest.   390
   Trip away; make no stay;
   Meet me all by break of day. [*Exeunt* OBERON, TITANIA, *and train.*]
PUCK: If we shadows have offended,
   Think but this, and all is mended,
   That you have but slumb'red here[2]   395
   While these visions did appear.
   And this weak and idle theme,
   No more yielding but[3] a dream,
   Gentles, do not reprehend.
   If you pardon, we will mend.   400
   And, as I am an honest Puck,
   If we have unearned luck
   Now to scape the serpent's tongue,[4]
   We will make amends ere long;
   Else the Puck a liar call.   405

---

6. Created. 7. Monstrous, unnatural. 8. Consecrated. 9. Go his way. 1. Separate.
2. That is, that it is a "midsummer night's dream." 3. Yielding no more than. 4. That is, hissing.

So, good night unto you all.
Give me your hands,[5] if we be friends,
And Robin shall restore amends.   [*Exit.*]

ca. 1594–1595

5. Applaud.

Appendices

Writing about
Literature

INTRODUCTION

Writing about literature ought to be easier than writing about anything else. When you write about painting, for example, you have to translate shapes and colors and textures into words. When you write about music, you have to translate various aspects and combinations of sounds into words. When you write about that complex, mysterious, fleeting thing called "reality" or "life," you have an even more difficult task. Worst of all, perhaps, is trying to put into words all that is going on at any given moment inside your particular and unique self. So you ought to be relieved to know that you are going to write about literature—that is, use words to write about words.

But writing about literature will not be easy if you haven't learned to *read* literature, for in order to write about anything you have to know that something rather well. Helping you to learn to read literature is what the earlier chapters of this book are about; this chapter is about the writing. (But, as you will see, you cannot fully separate the writing from the reading.)

Another thing keeps writing about literature from being easy: writing itself is not easy. Writing well requires a variety of language skills—a good working vocabulary, for example—and a sense of how to order your ideas, of how to link one idea or statement to another, of what to put in and what to leave out. Worse, writing is not a finite or definite skill or art; you never really "know how to write," you just learn how to write a little better about a little more. These very words you are reading have been written and revised several times, even though the authors have had many years of practice.

REPRESENTING THE LITERARY TEXT

COPYING

If writing about literature is using words about words, what words should you use? Since most writers work very hard to get each word exactly right and in exactly the right order, there are no better words to use in discussing what the literature is about than those of the literary work itself. Faced with writing about a story, then, you could just write the story over again, word for word:

> Once upon a time there was a Siamese cat who pretended to be a lion and spoke inappropriate Zebraic . . .

and so on until the end. Copying texts was useful in medieval monasteries, but in our electronic age, with printing, word processors, and fax machines available to us, it would not seem to be very useful. Besides, if you try to copy a text, you will probably find that spelling or punctuation errors, reversed word order, and missing or added or just different words seem mysteriously to appear. Still, it's a good exercise for teaching yourself accuracy and attention to detail, and you will probably discover things about the text you are copying that you would be unlikely to notice otherwise. Early in a literature course, particularly, copying can be a useful step in learning how to read and write about fiction, poetry, or drama; later, being able to copy a passage accurately will help when you want to quote a passage to illustrate or prove a point you are making. But copying is not, in itself, writing *about* literature.

Reading aloud, a variation of copying, may be a more original and interpretive exercise than copying itself, since by tone, emphasis, and pace you are clarifying the text or indicating the way you understand the text. But it, too, is not *writing* about literature, and you will not long be satisfied with merely repeating someone else's words. You will have perceptions, responses, and ideas that you will want to express for yourself about what you are reading. And having something to say and wanting to say or write it is the first and most significant step in learning to write about literature.

PARAPHRASE

If you look away from the text for a while and then write the same material but in your own words, you are writing a paraphrase.

For example, let's try to paraphrase the first sentence of Jane Austen's *Pride and Prejudice:* "It is a truth universally acknowledged that a single man in possession of a good fortune, must be in want of a wife." We can start by making "It is a truth" a little less formal: *It's true that,* perhaps. Now "universally acknowledged": *everybody acknowledges* or, a little more loosely, *everybody agrees.* Now we may choose to drop the whole first clause and begin, *Everybody agrees that* "a single man"—*a bachelor*— "in possession of a good fortune"—*rich*—"must be in want of a wife"—*wants a wife.* Or is it *needs a wife?* Okay, *Everybody agrees that a rich bachelor needs* (or *wants*) *a wife.* You can see that the process of paraphrase is something like that of translation. We are translating Austen's nineteenth-century formal English prose into twentieth-century informal American prose.

But what good is that? First of all, it enables us to test whether we really understand what we are reading. Second, certain elements of the text become clearer: we may see now that Austen's sentence is meant to be ironic or humorous, and we now understand the two possible meanings of "in want of." Third, we can check our paraphrase with those of others—our classmates' versions, for example—to compare our understanding of the passage with theirs. Finally, we have learned how dependent literature is upon words. A paraphrase, no matter how precise, can render only an approximate equivalent of the meaning of a text—how *good* Austen's sentence is, how *flat* our paraphrase.

Paraphrasing, like copying, is not in itself an entirely satisfactory way of writing about literature, but, like copying, it can be a useful tool when you write about literature in other ways. In trying to explain or clarify a literary text for someone, to illustrate a point you are making about that text, or to remind your readers of or to acquaint them with a text or passage, you will at times want to paraphrase. Unlike an exact copy, a paraphrase, being in your own words, adds something of yours to the text or passage—your emphasis, your perspective, your understanding.

SUMMARY

Paraphrase follows faithfully the outlines of the text. But if you stand back far enough from the text so as not to see its specific words or smaller details and put down briefly in your own words what you believe the work is about, you will have a summary. How briefly? Well, you could summarize the one hundred eight lines of Poe's "The Raven" in about one hundred eighty words or so like this, for example:

> The speaker of Poe's "The Raven" is sitting in his room late at night reading in order to forget the death of his beloved Lenore. There's a tap at the door; after some hesitation he opens it and calls Lenore's name, but there is only an echo. When he goes back into his room he hears the rapping again, this time at his window, and when he opens it a raven enters. He asks the raven its name, and it answers very clearly, "Nevermore." When the speaker says that the bird, like his friends, will leave, the raven again says, "Nevermore." As the speaker's thoughts run back to Lenore, he realizes the aptness of the raven's word: she shall sit there nevermore. But, he says, sooner or later he will forget her and the grief will lessen. "Nevermore," the raven says again, too aptly. Now the speaker wants the bird to leave, but "Nevermore," the raven says once again. At the end, the speaker knows he'll never escape the raven or its dark message.

Or you could summarize the story of *Hamlet* in a single sentence: "A young man, seeking to avenge the murder of his father by his uncle, kills his uncle, but he himself and others die in the process." Has *too* much been left out? What do you feel it essential to add? Let's try again: "In Denmark, many centuries ago, a young prince avenged the murder of his father, the king, by his uncle, who had usurped the throne, but the prince himself was killed as were others, and a well-led foreign army had no trouble success-fully invading the decayed and troubled state." A classmate may have written this sum-mary: "From the ghost of his murdered father a young prince learns that his uncle, who has married the prince's mother, much to the young man's shame and disgust, is the father's murderer, and the prince plots revenge, feigning madness, acting erratically—even to insulting the woman he loves—and, though gaining his revenge, causes the suicide of his beloved and the deaths of others and, finally, of himself."

The last two, though accurate enough, sound like two different plays, don't they? To summarize means to select and emphasize and so to interpret: that is, not to replicate the text in miniature, as a reduced photograph might replicate the original, but while reducing it to change the angle of vision and even the filter, to represent the essentials as the reader or summarizer sees them. When you write a summary you should try to be as objective as possible; nevertheless, your summary will reflect not only the literary text but also your own understanding and attitudes. There's nothing wrong with your fingerprints or "mindprints" appearing on the summary, so long as you recognize that in summarizing you are doing more than copying, paraphrasing, or merely reflecting the literary text. You might learn something about both literature and yourself by com-paring your summaries of, say, three or four short poems, a couple of short stories, or a play with summaries of the same works by several of your classmates. As you read their summaries, try to understand how each viewed the text differently from you. You might then write a composite summary that would include all that any one reader felt important. You might try the same exercise again on different texts. Has the practice made you more careful? More inclusive? Is there a greater degree of uniformity or inclu-siveness in your summaries?

A good summary can be a form of literary criticism. Though you will seldom be called upon merely to summarize a work, a good deal of writing about literature requires that at some point or other you do summarize—a whole work, a particular incident or aspect, a stanza, chapter, or scene. But beware: a mere summary, no matter how accurate, will seldom fulfill an assignment for a critical essay.

REPLYING TO THE TEXT

IMITATION AND PARODY

While paraphrase is something like translation—a faithful following of the original text but in different words—and summary is the faithful, but inevitably interpretive, reduction of the text, there is another kind of writing about literature that faithfully follows the manner or matter or both of a literary text, but that does so for different ends. It's called imitation.

For many generations, students were taught to write by "writing from models"— imitating good writing. Many serious works are, in one way or another, imitations: *The Aeneid,* for example, may be said to be an imitation of *The Odyssey,* and, in a very different way, so might James Joyce's *Ulysses.* You, too, may be able to learn a good deal about writing—and reading—by trying your hand at an imitation.

To write an imitation, first analyze the original—that is, break it down into its characteristics or qualities—and decide just what you want to preserve in your version. Sometimes you can poke fun at a work by imitating it but at the same time exaggerating its style or prominent characteristics, or placing it in an inappropriate context; that kind of imitation, a kind that is still popular, is called a parody. The list of qualities and the model might be much the same for a serious imitation and for a parody, only in a parody you can exaggerate a little—or a lot.

To parody Poe's "The Raven," we may decide to stick closely to Poe's rhythms, his use of repetitive mood words or of several words that mean almost the same thing, and his frequent use of alliteration (words that begin with the same sound). We might want to exaggerate the characteristic stylistic devices as C. L. Edson does in his parody; it begins,

> Once upon a midnight dreary, eerie, scary,
> I was wary, I was weary, full of worry, thinking of my lost Lenore,
> Of my cheery, airy, faerie, fierie Dearie—(Nothing more).

We may choose another kind of parody, keeping the form as close as possible to the original but applying it to a ludicrously unsuitable subject, as Pope does in his mock epic "The Rape of the Lock," where he uses pretentious epic machinery in a poem about cutting off a lock of a woman's hair. In writing such a parody of "The Raven," we will keep the rhythm closer to Poe's and the subject matter less close. How about this?

Once upon a midday murky, crunching on a Christmas turkey,
And guzzling giant Jereboams of gin . . .

And maybe we could use the "Nevermore" refrain as if it were an antacid commercial.

You will have noticed that in order to write a good imitation or parody you must read and reread the original very carefully, examine it, and identify just those elements and qualities that make it a unique and recognizable text. Since you admire works you wish to imitate, such close study should be a pleasure. You may or may not greatly admire a work you wish to parody, but parody itself is fun to do and fun to read. In either case, you are having fun while gaining a deeper, more intimate knowledge of the nature and details of a work of literature. Moreover, such close attention to how a professional piece of writing is put together and how its parts function together along with your effort to reproduce the effects in your own imitation or parody are sure to help you understand the process of writing and so help you improve your own ability to write about literature knowledgeably.

RE-CREATION AND REPLY

Sometimes a story, poem, or play will seem so partial, biased, or unrealistic that it will stimulate a response that is neither an imitation nor a parody, but a retort. While Christopher Marlowe's "shepherd" in "The Passionate Shepherd to His Love" paints an idyllic scene of love in the country for his beloved and pleads, "Come live with me and be my love," Sir Walter Ralegh apparently feels obliged to reply in the name of the beloved "nymph": it won't always be spring, she says in "The Nymph's Reply to the Shepherd"; we won't always be young, and, besides, I can scarcely trust myself to someone who offers me such a phony view of reality.

Ralegh's nymph confronts the invitation and the words of Marlowe's shepherd directly and almost detail for detail. In fiction the reply is less likely to be so directly verbal a retort and is more likely to involve a shift in perspective. It may tell the same story as the original but from a different angle, not only giving a different view of the same events and people but also adding details that the original focus ignored or could not perceive. In *Jane Eyre,* for example, Bertha Mason Rochester is the hero's bestial, mad wife, whom he has locked away upstairs and whose existence, when it comes to light, prevents for a time our heroine, our Jane, from marrying her heart's desire; Bertha is, in effect, the villainess. In *Wide Sargasso Sea,* Jean Rhys not only gives Bertha's side of Charlotte Brontë's story, but tells us more details about Bertha's earlier life: poor Bertha was more sinned against than sinning, it turns out.

We may respond to a work whose view seems partial or distorted by shifting the perspective in time as well as in space. Are Francis Weed's marital and other problems solved by his recognition, at the end of John Cheever's "The Country Husband," that life in the suburbs can be, in its own way, as adventurous as more romantic kinds of existence? What will happen to him next spring? On his fortieth birthday? As he lies dying? What will the speaker of Theodore Roethke's "My Papa's Waltz" be thinking about as he plays or dances with *his* daughter?

You may have noticed that while retorts can often be witty, they are also serious. Usually they say not merely, "That's not how the story went," but "That's not what life is really like." Try to read literature initially with the aim of understanding it and taking it at its highest value (rather than reducing it and quibbling). Try to "hear" what it is saying; avoid imposing your own notions of reality prematurely upon a work. Open your mind to learning from the work, and let it broaden your views. Finally, read it critically as well, asking, "Is this the way things *really* are?" or, more generously, "If I were standing over there, where the story (author, character) is, would things really look that way?"

Perhaps the most familiar kind of literary re-creation or reply is the adaptation, especially that of fiction into film. (Among the stories in this anthology that have been made into feature-length films are Richard Connell's "The Most Dangerous Game," Ambrose Bierce's "An Occurrence at Owl Creek Bridge," Anton's Chekhov's "The Lady with the Dog," and D. H. Lawrence's "The Rocking-Horse Winner.") In adaptation, the contradictory demands of faithfulness to the original and appropriateness to the new medium can teach us a great deal about both the content and the medium of the original. It is unlikely you will have the opportunity in this course to make a film based on a story, but you can still try your hand at adapting a work or piece of a work to a new medium. You might want to turn Poe's "The Cask of Amontillado" into verse (probably as a dramatic monologue) or write a short story called *Hamlet* or a one-act play called "Young Goodman Brown." It is quite likely that you will learn not only about the nature of the original work, but also something of the nature of the medium in which you are trying to work.

EXPLAINING THE TEXT

DESCRIPTION

To give an account of the form of a work or passage rather than merely a brief version of its content or plot (and a plot summary, even of a poem, is usually what we mean by "summary") you may wish to write a description. We have given a summary of Poe's "The Raven" earlier, concentrating there, as summaries tend to do, on subject and plot. A description, on the other hand, may concentrate on the form of the stanzas, the lines, the rhyme scheme, perhaps like this:

> Poe's "The Raven" is a poem of one hundred eight lines divided into eighteen six-line stanzas. If in describing the rhyme scheme you were to look just at the ends of the lines, you would notice only one or two unusual features: not only is there only one rhyme sound per stanza, lines 2, 4, 5, and 6 rhyming, but one rhyme sound is the same in all eighteen stanzas, so that there are seventy-two lines ending with the sound "ore"; in addition, the fourth and fifth lines of each stanza end with the identical word, and in six of the stanzas that word is "door" and in four others "Lenore." There is even more repetition: the last line of six of the first seven stanzas ends with the words "nothing more," and the last eleven stanzas end with the word "Nevermore." The rhyming lines—other than the last, which is very short—in each stanza are fifteen syllables long, the unrhymed lines sixteen. The longer lines give the effect of shorter ones, however, and add still further to the frequency of repeated sounds, for the first half of each opening line rhymes with the second half of the line, and so do the halves of line 3. There is still more: the first half of line 4 rhymes with the halves of line 3 (in the first stanza the rhymes are "dreary" /"weary" and "napping" /"tapping" /"rapping"). So at least nine words in each eight-line stanza are involved in the regular rhyme scheme, and in many stanzas there are added instances of rhyme or repetition. As if this were not enough, all the half-line rhymes are rich feminine rhymes, where both the accented and the following unaccented syllables rhyme— "drēārȳ" /"wēārȳ."

This is a detailed and complicated description of a complex and unusual pattern of rhymes. Though there are many other elements of the poem we could describe—images and symbols, for example—the unusual and dominant element in this poem is clearly the intricate and insistent pattern of rhyme and repetition. Moreover, this paragraph shows how you can describe at length, in depth, and with considerable complexity certain aspects of a work without mentioning the content at all. You can describe a play in comparable terms—acts, scenes, settings, time lapses perhaps—and you might describe a novel in terms of chapters, books, summary narration, dramatized scenes. In addition to describing the narrative structure or focus and voice of a short story, you might also describe the diction (word choice), the sentence structure, the amount of description of the characters or landscape, and so on.

ANALYSIS

Like copying, paraphrase, and summary, a description of a work or passage rarely stands alone as a piece of writing about literature. It is, instead, a tool, a means of supporting a point or opinion. Even the description we have given above borders on analysis. To analyze is to break something down into its parts to discover what they are and, usually, how they function in and relate to the whole. The description of the rhyme scheme of "The Raven" tells you what that scheme or pattern is but says nothing about how it functions in the poem. If you were to add such an account to the description, then, you would have analyzed one aspect of the poem. In order to do so, however, you would first have to decide what, in general, the poem is about: what its *theme* is. If you defined the theme of "The Raven" as "inconsolable grief," you could then write an analytical paper suggesting how the rhyme scheme reinforces that theme. You might begin like this:

> Obsessive Rhyme in "The Raven"
> We all know that gloomy poem with that gloomy bird, Edgar Allan Poe's "The Raven." The time is midnight, the room is dark, the bird is black, and the poem is full of words like "dreary," "sad," "mystery," and "ghastly." We all know, too, it has a rather singsong rhythm and repeated rhymes, but we do not often stop to think how the rhymes contribute to the mood or meaning. Before we do so here, perhaps it would be a good idea to describe in detail just what that rhyme scheme is.

Then follow with the description of the rhyme scheme, and go on like this:

> Of course, the most obvious way in which the rhyme scheme reinforces the theme of inconsolable loss is through the emphatic repetition of "Nevermore." Since this refrain comes at the very end of each of the last stanzas it is even more powerful in its effect.
> What is not so obvious as the effect of repeating "Nevermore" is the purpose of the overall abundance and richness of rhyme. Some might say it is not abundant and rich, but excessive and cloying. These harsh critics cynically add that in a way the rhymes and repetitions are appropriate to this poem because the whole poem is excessive and cloying: grief over loss, even intense grief, does, human experience tells us, pass away. This criticism is just, however, only if we have accurately defined the theme of the poem as "inconsolable sorrow." The very insistence of the rhyme and repetition, however, suggests that we may need to adjust slightly our definition of that theme. Perhaps the poem is not about "inconsolable sorrow" in so neutral a way; maybe it would be better to say it is about obsessive grief. Then the insistent, pounding rhyme and repetition make sense (just as the closed-in dark chamber does). Obsessive repetition of words and sounds thus helps to create the meaning of the poem almost as much as the words themselves do.

INTERPRETATION

PRINCIPLES AND PROCEDURES

If you have been reading carefully, you may have noticed what looks like a catch: to turn description into analysis, you must relate what you are describing to the theme, the overall effect, and meaning of the text. But how do you know what the theme is? If analysis relates the part to the whole, how can you know the "whole" before you have analyzed each part? But, then, how can you analyze each part—relating it to the whole—if you don't know what that whole is?

Interpretation, or the expression of your understanding of a literary work and its meaning, involves an initial general impression that is then supported and often modified by analysis of the particulars. It involves looking at the whole, the part, the whole, the part, the whole, the part in a series of approximations and adjustments. (Note, in particular, the need to keep your mind open for modifications or changes, rather than forcing your analysis to confirm your first impressions.)

This procedure should, in turn, suggest something of the nature and even the form of the critical essay, or essay of interpretation. The essay should present the overall theme and support that generalization with close analyses of the major elements of the text (or, in some essays, an analysis of one significant element)—showing how one or more such elements as rhyme or speaker, plot or setting reinforce, define, or modify the theme of the story. Often the conclusion of such an essay will be a fuller, more refined statement of the theme.

Both the definition of and the procedures for interpreting a work suggest that a literary text is unified, probably around a theme, a meaning, and an effect. In interpreting, you therefore keep asking of each element or detail, "How does it fit? How does it contribute to *the* theme or whole?" In most instances, especially when you are writing on shorter works, if you dig hard and deep enough, you will find a satisfactory interpretation or central theme. Even after you have done your best, however, you must hold your "reading" or interpretation as a hypothesis rather than a final truth. Your experience of reading criticism has probably already shown you that more than one reading of a literary work is possible and that no reading exhausts the meaning and totality of a work. Nonetheless, you will want to begin reading a literary text as if it were going to make a central statement and create a single effect, no matter how complex. Try as conscientiously as you can to make sense of the work, to analyze it, to show how its elements work together. In analyzing elements, you kept your initial sense of the whole as hypothesis and did not try to force evidence to fit your first impression. Here, too, you will want to hold your interpretation as a hypothesis even in its final stages, even at the end. It is, you must be sure, the fullest and best "reading" of the text you are capable of at this time, with the evidence and knowledge you have at this moment—but only that. In other words, an interpretation is "only an opinion." But just as your political and other opinions are not lightly held but are what you really feel and believe based on all you know and have experienced and all you have thought and felt, so your opinion or interpretation of a literary work should be as responsible as you can make it. Your opinions are a measure of your knowledge, intelligence, and sensibility. They should not be lightly changed, but neither should they be obstinately and inflexibly held.

READING AND THEME MAKING

Because you need a sense of the whole text before you can analyze it, analysis and interpretation would seem to be possible only after repeated readings. Though obvious, logical, and partially true, this may not be *entirely* true. In reading, we actually anticipate theme or meaning much as we anticipate what will happen next. Often this anticipation or expectation of theme or effect begins with our first opening a book—or even before, in reading the title. If you were to read *Hamlet* in an edition that gives its full title, *The Tragedy of Hamlet, Prince of Denmark*—even if you had never heard of the play or its author before—you would have some idea or hypothesis about who the protagonist is, where the action will more than likely be set, how the play will end, and even some of the feelings it will arouse.

Such anticipation of theme and effect, projecting and modifying understanding and response, continues as you read. When you read the first four words of "The Zebra Storyteller"—"Once upon a time . . ."—the strange title is to some extent explained and the kind of story you are about to read and its relation to everyday reality have been established. The title and the first short section of "The Most Dangerous Game" arouse expectations of the supernatural, the frightening, the adventurous, creating suspense: "What will happen next?" we ask as we read the first few paragraphs. The brief conversation about hunting, toward the end of that section, not only educates our expectations but also generates a moral and thematic question: "Are there really two animal classes— the hunters and the hunted—and does being lucky enough to be among the hunters justify insensitivity toward the feelings of the hunted?" While the question may recede from the foreground of our attention for a while, it has nonetheless been raised. It is, in addition, reinforced by the break on the page, which forces us to pause and, even if but momentarily, reflect. It comes forward again when General Zaroff introduces the subject of hunting. At these two points, at least, a thematic hypothesis based on hunters and hunted begins forming, however faintly, in our minds. That is enough to give us grounds—even as we read the story for the first time—for an analysis of elements and their relationship to our tentatively formulated theme, and perhaps for beginning to modify or modulate our articulation of that theme. Many details in the story indicate that there is a political coloring to the theme: Zaroff is a Cossack—a people noted for fierceness—and is, or was, a czarist general; he keeps a giant Cossack servant who was an official flogger under the czar; he refers to the Revolution of 1917 in Russia as a "debacle"; he is clearly a racist. We may want to alter "hunter" and "hunted" in our first version of the anticipated theme to something broader—"strong" and "weak," perhaps, or "privileged" and "underprivileged"—or we may need fuller definitions of the implications of the terms "hunter" and "hunted."

Just as we have more than one expectation of what may happen next as we read a story, poem, or play, so we may have more than one expectation of what it is going to be "about" in the more general sense: as we read along we have expectations or hypotheses of meaning, and so we consciously or unconsciously try to fit together the pieces of elements of what we are reading into a pattern of significance. By the end of our first reading we should have a fairly well-defined sense of what the work is "about," what it means, even how some of the elements have worked together to produce that meaning and effect. Indeed, isn't this the way we read when we are not reading for a class or performance? Don't most people read most stories, poems, plays only once? And don't we usually think we have understood what we have read? Shouldn't we be able to read a very short story in class just once and immediately write an interpretive paper based on that first reading?

This is not to say that we cannot understand more about a work by repeated readings or that there is some virtue or purity of response in the naive first reading that is lost in closer study. Our first "reading"—"reading" in the sense of both "casting our eye over" and "interpretation"—is almost certain to be modified or refined by rereading: if nothing else, we know from the beginning what will happen next—what the most dangerous game is, for example. The theme or meaning is likely to be modulated by later readings, the way the elements function in defining or embodying meaning is likely to be clearer; the effect of the second reading is certain to be different from that of the first. It may be instructive to reread several times the short work we interpreted in class after a single reading, write a new interpretive essay, and see how our understanding has been changed and enriched by subsequent readings.

OPINIONS, RIGHT AND WRONG

Just as each of our separate readings is different, so naturally one reader's fullest and "final" reading, interpretation, or opinion will differ somewhat from another's. Seldom will readers agree entirely with any full statement of the theme of a literary text. Nor is one of these interpretations entirely "right" and all the others necessarily "wrong." For no thematic summary, no analysis or interpretation, no matter how full, can exhaust the affective or intellectual significance of a major literary text. There are various approximate readings of diverse degrees of acceptability, various competent or "good" readings, not just one single "right" reading.

Anyone who has heard two accomplished musicians faithfully perform the same work, playing all the same notes, or anyone who has seen two performances of *Hamlet* will recognize how "interpretations" can be both correct and different. You might try to get hold of several recordings of one or more of Hamlet's soliloquies—by John Barrymore, Sir John Gielgud, Richard Burton, Sir Laurence Olivier, or Mel Gibson, for example—and notice how each of these actors lends to identical passages his own emphasis, pacing, tone, color, effect, and so, ultimately, his own meaning. These actors reading the identical words are, in effect, "copying." They are not paraphrasing or putting Shakespeare's Elizabethan poetry into modern American prose, not "interpreting" as we have defined it, or putting his play into their own words. If merely performing or reading the words aloud generates significant differences in interpretation, it is no wonder that when you write an interpretive essay about literature, when you give your conception of the meaning and effect of the literary text in your own words, your interpretation will differ from other interpretations, even when each of the different interpretations is competent and "correct."

Any communication, even a work of literature, is refracted—that is, interpreted and modified—by the recipient. In one sense, it is not complete until it is received, just as, in a sense, a musical score is not "music" until it is played. Philip Roth reported, not long ago, how perturbed he was by what the critics and other readers said of his first novel—that was not at all what he intended, what the novel really was, he thought at first. But then he realized that once he had had his say in the novel, it was "out there," and each reader had to understand it within the limits and range of his or her own perspectives and literary and life experiences. His novel, once in print, was no longer merely "his," and rightly so.

That different interpretations may be "correct" is not to say, with Alice's Humpty-Dumpty, that a word or a work "means just what I choose it to mean." Though there may not be one "right" reading, some readings are more appropriate and convincing than others and some readings are demonstrably wrong.

What would you say about this reading of *Hamlet?*

The play is about the hero's sexual love for his mother. He sees his father's "ghost" because he feels guilty, somehow responsible for his father's death, more than likely because he had often wished his father dead. To free himself from this feeling of guilt, he imagines that he sees his father's ghost and that the ghost tells him that his uncle murdered his father. He focuses upon his uncle because he is fiercely jealous that it is his uncle, not himself, who has replaced his father in his mother's bed. He so resents his mother's choice of so unworthy a mate, he attributes it not to love but to mere lust, clearly a projection of his own lust for his mother, which he calls love. His mother's lust so disgusts him that he hates all women now, even Ophelia. When his father was alive he could be fond of Ophelia, for his sexual feeling for his mother was deflected by his father-the-king's powerful presence. Now, however, he must alienate Ophelia not only because of his new hatred of women but because he has a chance of winning his mother, especially if he can get rid of Claudius, his uncle.

Such a reading explains more or less convincingly certain details in the play, but it wrenches some out of context and leaves a good deal out and a good deal unexplained: why, for example, do others see the ghost of Hamlet's father if it is just a figment of his imagination? What are Horatio and Fortinbras and the political elements doing in the play? If you accept certain Freudian premises about human psychology and see life in Freudian terms, if you see literary texts as the author's psychic fantasy stimulating your own psychic fantasies and believe that interpretation of Hamlet is not merely a reading of the play itself but an analysis of Shakespeare's psyche, you may find this reading somewhat convincing. You will perhaps explain away some of the details of the play that do not seem to fit your Freudian reading as a cover-up, an attempt by Shakespeare to disguise the true but hidden meaning of his dramatic fantasy from others—and from himself. Such a reading is probably neither right nor wrong but only a way of interpreting Hamlet based on certain assumptions about psychology and about the way literature means, and so it could seem "right" or acceptable to those who share those assumptions.

Suppose one of your ingenious classmates were to argue that the real subject of Hamlet is that the hero has tuberculosis. This would explain, your classmate would say, the hero's moodiness, his pretended madness that sometimes seems real, his rejection of Ophelia (he wouldn't want their children to suffer from the disease), his father's ghost (he, too, died of consumption), his anger at his uncle (who carries the disease, of course) for marrying Hamlet's mother, and so on. Your classmate might even argue that the text of the play is flawed, that it was just copied down during a performance by someone in the audience or was printed from an actor's imperfect copy. Therefore, "O that this too too *solid flesh*" should read *"sullied flesh,"* as many scholars have argued (and might not "sullied flesh" suggest tuberculosis?). And, therefore, isn't it quite possible that the most famous soliloquy in the play really began or was meant to begin, "TB or not TB"? "No way!" we'd say. We would be reasonably sure that this is not just "not proved" but just plain *wrong*. It might be interesting and illuminating to rebut that reading in a paper of your own and to notice what kinds of evidence you bring to bear on an interpretive argument.

READER AND TEXT

If it is difficult to say exactly what a piece of literature *says,* it is usually not because it is vague or meaning*less* but because it is too specific and meaning*ful* to paraphrase satisfactorily in any language other than its own. Since no two human beings are identical and no two people can inhabit the same space at the same time, no two people can see exactly the same reality from the same angle and vantage point. Most of us get around this awkward truth by saying that we see what we are "supposed" to see, a generalized, commonsense approximation of reality. We are all, in effect, like Polonius in the third act of *Hamlet,* who sees in a cloud, a camel, a weasel, a whale—whatever Hamlet tells him he sees.

Some individuals struggle to see things as fully and clearly as possible from their unique vantage point and to communicate to others their particular—even peculiar—vision. But here, too, we are individuated, for though we speak of our "common language," we each speak a unique language, made up of "dialects" that are not only regional and ethnic but also conditioned by our age group, our profession, our education, travel, reading—all our experiences. Yet if we want to express our unique vision to others who have different visions and different "languages," we have to find some medium that is both true to ourselves and understandable to others.

There is for these individuals—these writers of literature—a constant tug-of-war between the uniqueness of their individual visions and the generalizing nature of language. The battle does not always result in sheer loss, however. Often, in the very struggle to get their own perceptions into language, writers sharpen those perceptions or discover what they themselves did not know when they began to write. You have probably made similar discoveries in the process of writing a letter or an assigned paper. But writers also find that what they have written does not perfectly embody what they meant it to, just as you perhaps have found that your finished papers have been not quite as brilliant as your original idea.

"Understanding" is not a passive reception of a text, but an active reaching out from our own experiences toward the text. At least at first we need to do so by meeting the author on the ground of a common or general language and set of conventions—things that everybody "knows." The first task of the reader, therefore, is to get not to the author's intention, but to the general statement that the work itself makes—that is, its theme or thesis. After a few readings we can usually make a stab at articulating the theme of a text. What a work says in the way of a general theme, however, is not necessarily its full or ultimate meaning; otherwise we would read theme summaries and not stories. The theme is the meaning accessible to all through close reading of the text and common to all, but a literary text is not all statement. There are often cloudy areas in the text where we cannot be sure what is implication, the suggestion of the text, and what is our inference, or interpretation, of the text. Why does Doris Lessing's Judith prefer having a tomcat put to death to having him neutered but does not suggest that the female kitten who has been ruined for procreation be put death? Does this suggest that males, including human males, exist only to fertilize eggs, but that females have other functions as well? Or, at least, that this is what Judith believes? Does this give us more insight into Judith's life, her singleness, her refusal to marry the Greek professor, her ultimate flight from Luigi? The story does not say this, but many readers will find this inference convincing. If accepted, this changes the meaning of the story to some degree. Still, it need not be accepted; the story does not, will never, say. The meaning of the story for the reader who is convinced will differ from the meaning for the reader who is not convinced.

The full meaning of a work for you is not only in its stated theme, one that everyone can agree on, but in the meaning you derive by bringing together that generalized theme, the precise language of the text, and your own response and experiences—including reading experience—and imagination. That "meaning" is not the total meaning of the work, not what the author originally perceived and "meant to say"; it is the vision of the author as embodied in the work and re-viewed from your own angle of vision.

Your role in producing a meaning from the text does not free you from paying very close attention to the precise language of the text, the words and their meanings, their order, the syntax of the sentences, and even such mundane details as punctuation. You cannot impose a meaning on the text, no matter how sincerely and intensely you feel it, in defiance of the rules of grammar and the nature of the language.

Still, the reader has to be an artist too, trying to experience the reality of the work as the author experienced reality, and with the same reverence and sense of responsibility

for the original. To write about literature you need to embody your reading experience—
or interpretation—of the work in language. Alas, writing about literature, using words
about words, is not as easy as it sounds at first. But it is more exciting, giving you a
chance to see with another's eyes, to explore another's perceptions or experiences, and
to explore and more fully understand your own in the process, thus expanding the
horizon of your experience, perception, consciousness.

When some rich works of literature, like *Hamlet,* seem to have more than one meaning or no entirely satisfactory meaning or universally agreed-upon single theme, it is not
that they are not saying something, and saying something very specific, but that what
they are saying is too specific and complex and profound (and true, perhaps) to be
generalized or paraphrased in a few dozen words. The literary work is meaning*ful*—that
is, full of meaning or meanings; but it is the reader who produces each particular meaning from the work, using the work itself, the language of the community and of the
work, and his or her own language, experience, and imagination.

As a reader trying to understand the unique perception and language of the author,
you should try to translate the text as best you can into terms you can understand. Do
your best to approach the text with an open, receptive mind.

An interpretation, then, is not a clarification of what the writer "was trying to say"; it
is a process that itself says, in effect, "The way I am trying to understand this work
is . . . ."

CRITICAL APPROACHES

The way you read and talk about a literary text depends on your assumptions, usually unconscious or unarticulated, about what a work of literature is, what it is supposed to do, and what makes it good. Literary critics, however, often define their assumptions about literature and the proper way to go about reading it and writing about it. The results are critical theories or critical approaches. Looking at a few of these, you may recognize some of your own assumptions, see new and exciting ways of looking at literature, or, at the very least, become aware of your own critical premises and prejudices.

OBJECTIVISM

We might begin by asking just what, literally, a work of literature is. There are critics who think of it as a fixed and freestanding object made up of words on a page. It is "freestanding" in that it has no connection, on the one hand, with the author or his or her intention or life or, on the other hand, with the historical or cultural context of the author or the reader. These we might call objectivist critics; they believe that a text is an independent object, free from the subjectivity of author and reader.

FORMALISM

Among the objectivist critics are the formalists. One common formalist conception is that a work is autotelic, that is, complete in itself, written for its own sake, and unified by its form—that which makes it a work of art. Content is less important than form. Literature involves a special kind of language that sets it apart from merely utilitarian writing; the formal strategies that organize and animate that language elevate literature and give it a special, almost religious character.

NEW CRITICISM One group of formalists, the New Critics, dominated literary criticism in the middle of the twentieth century, and New Criticism remains an important influence today. Their critical practice is to demonstrate formal unity by showing how every part of a work—every word, every image, every element—contributes to a central unifying theme. Because the details of the work relate to a theme or idea, they are generally treated as *symbolic,* as figurative or allegorical, representations of that central, unifying idea. The kind of unity thus demonstrated, in which every part is related to the whole and the whole is reflected in each part, is called organic unity. The New Critics differentiate organic unity from (and much prefer it to) mechanical unity, the external, preconceived structure or rules that do not arise from the individuality of the work, but from the type or genre. New Critical analysis, or explication of the text, is especially effective in the critical reading of lyric poetry. It has become so universally accepted as *at least the first step* in the understanding of literature that it is almost everywhere the critical approach taught in introductory literature courses, even in those that do not share its fundamental autotelic assumption. It is, indeed, the basic approach of the "Understanding the Text" sections in *The Norton Introduction to Literature.*

The New Critics' focus on theme or meaning as well as form signifies that for them literature is referential: it points to something outside itself, things in the real, external world or in human experience—a tree, a sound wave, love. The New Critics, in general, do not question the reality of the phenomenal world or the ability of language to represent it.

STRUCTURALISM

For many formalists, however, literature is not referential. The words in a story, poem, or play no longer point outward to the things, people, or world they are supposed to denote, as they might do in ordinary, "nonliterary" discourse, but point inward to each other and to the formal system they create. The critic still focuses on interrelatedness but is less concerned with "meaning"; words are treated not as referential symbols, but as natural numbers; poetry is likened to mathematics or music.

Structuralism focuses on the text as an independent aesthetic object and also tends to detach literature from history and social and political implications, but (much more than New Criticism) structuralism emphasizes systematic analysis, aspiring to make literary criticism a branch of scientific inquiry. It sees every literary work as a separate "system" and seeks to discover the principles or general laws that govern the interaction of parts within the system. Structuralism has its roots in modern linguistic theory; it looks especially to the work of Ferdinand de Saussure (1857–1913), who founded structural linguistics early in the twentieth century. Structuralism in criticism did not, however, flourish internationally until the early 1960s, when a combination of space-age preoccupation with science and cold-war fear of implication led to a view of literature as intellectually challenging yet socially and politically noncontroversial.

Although based on linguistic theory, structuralism tries to extend newly discovered principles about language to other aspects of literature. Drawing on the semiotic principle that a vast and intricate system of signs enables human beings to communicate through language, structuralism asks readers to consider the way that other kinds of sign systems within a work—structures all—combine to produce meaning. Language and its characteristic habits are important to structuralists, but it is not enough to consider any single part of a work or any single kind of sign—linguistic or otherwise—within it. Structuralism aspires to elucidate the meaning of a work of literature by seeing the way all of its parts work together toward some wholeness of structure and meaning. Like formalism, it shows little interest in the creative process as such and has virtually no interest in authors, their intentions, or the circumstances or contexts of creation. It takes texts to represent interactions of words and ideas apart from individual human identities or sociopolitical commitments, and concentrates its analytical attention on what can be said about how different elements or processes in a text operate in relation to one another. Structuralists are less likely than formalists to concentrate their attention on some single all-explaining characteristic of literature (such as Cleanth Brooks's "tension" or William Empson's "ambiguity"), and its practitioners are less likely to privilege a particular text for its revelation or authority. Structuralism may be seen as a sort of secular equivalent of formalism; it is less mysterious and authoritarian, and it has both the advantage and disadvantage of seeming to be less arbitrary and more "objectively" reliable. But in some ways it seems to promise too much for method and "objectivity," and by the 1970s its insights into the ways of language were already beginning to be used against it to attack the certitudes it appeared to promise and to emphasize instead the uncertainties and indeterminateness of texts.

POST-STRUCTURALISM

Post-Structuralism is the broad term used to designate the several directions of literary criticism that, while depending crucially on the insights of science-based theory, attack the very idea that any kind of certitude can exist about the meaning, understandability, or sharability of texts. Post-structuralists, disturbed at the optimism of positivist philosophy in suggesting that the world is knowable and explainable, ultimately doubt the possibility of certainties of any kind, and they see language as especially elusive and unfaithful. Much of post-structuralism involves undoing; the best-known variety of post-structuralism, deconstruction, suggests as much in its very name.

DECONSTRUCTION Deconstruction takes the observations of structuralism to their logical conclusion, arguing that the elaborate web of semiotic differentiations created by the principle of difference in language means that no text can ultimately have any stable, definite, or discoverable meaning.

For the deconstructionist, language consists just in black marks on a page that repeat or differ from each other and the reader is the only author, one who can find whatever can be found in, or be made to appear in, those detached, isolated marks. The deconstructionist conception of literature is thus very broad—almost any writing will do. While this may seem "subjective" in that the critical reader has great freedom, it is the object—the black marks on the blank page—that is the sole subject/object of intention/attention.

As practiced by its most famous proponent, the French philosopher Jacques Derrida (b. 1930), deconstruction endeavors to trace the way texts challenge or cancel their explicit meanings and wrestle themselves into stasis or neutrality. Many deconstructionists have strong radical political commitments (it is possible to argue that the radical counterculture of the 1960s and especially the political events in Paris of 1968 are the crucial context for understanding the origins of deconstructionism), but the retreat from meaning and denial of clear signification that characterize deconstruction also have affinities with formalism and structuralism, particularly as deconstruction is practiced by American critics. Rather than emphasizing form over content, however, deconstruction tries to deny the possibility of content and places value instead on verbal play as a characteristic outlet of a fertile, adroit, and supple human mind. Like structuralism, it lives almost completely in a self-referential verbal world rather than a world in which texts represent some larger or other reality, but unlike structuralism it denies that the verbal world adds up to anything coherent, consistent, or meaningful in itself. Deconstruction also influences other varieties of post-structuralism with different kinds of interests in history and ideology. Michel Foucault (1926–1984), Julia Kristeva (b. 1941), and Jacques Lacan (1901–1981), though their disciplinary interests are in social history, feminist philosophy, and psychoanalysis, respectively, all come out of deconstructionist assumptions and carry the indeterminacies of post-structuralism (and of post-modernism more generally) into kinds of literary criticism with interests fundamentally different from those of structuralism.

SUBJECTIVISM

Opposed to objectivism is what might be called subjectivism. This loose term can be used to embrace many forms of psychological and self-, subject-, or reader-centered criticism.

PSYCHOLOGICAL CRITICISM

The assumption is that literature is the expression of the author's psyche, often his or her unconscious, and, like dreams, needs to be interpreted.

FREUDIAN CRITICISM The dominant school is the Freudian, based on the work of Sigmund Freud (1856–1939). Many of its practitioners assert that the meaning of a literary work does not lie on its surface but in the psyche (some would even claim, in the neuroses) of the author. The value of the work, then, lies in how powerfully and convincingly it expresses the author's unconscious and how universal the psychological elements are. A well-known Freudian reading of *Hamlet,* for example, insists that Hamlet is upset because he is jealous of his uncle, for Hamlet, *like all male children,* unconsciously wants to go to bed with his mother. The ghost may then be a manifestation of Hamlet's unconscious desire; his madness is not just acting, but is the result of this frustrated desire; his cruelly gross mistreatment of Ophelia is a deflection of his disgust at his mother's being "lecherous," "unfaithful" in her love for him. A Freudian critic may assume then that Hamlet is suffering from an Oedipus complex, a Freudian term for the desire of the son for his mother, its name derived from the Greek myth that is the basis of Sophocles' play *Oedipus the King.*

Some Freudian critics stress the author's psyche and find *Hamlet* the expression of Shakespeare's own Oedipus complex. Others stress the effect on the reader, the work having a purgative or cleansing effect by expressing in socially and morally acceptable ways unconscious desires that would be unacceptable if expressed directly.

LACANIAN CRITICISM As it absorbs the indeterminacies of post-structuralism under the influence of thinkers such as Jacques Lacan, psychological criticism has become increasingly complex. Accepting the Oedipal paradigm and the unconscious as the realm of repressed desire, Lacanian psychology (and the critical theory that comes from that psychology) conflates these concepts with the deconstructionist emphasis on language as expressing absence—you use a word to represent an absent object but you cannot make it present. The word, then, like the unconscious desire, is something that cannot be fulfilled. Language, reaching out with one word after the other, striving for but never reaching its object, is the arena of desire.

JUNGIAN CRITICISM Just as a Freudian assumes that human psyches have similar histories and structures, the Jungian critic assumes that we all share a universal or collective unconscious (as well as having a racial and individual unconscious). According to Carl Gustav Jung (1875–1961) and his followers, in the collective and in our individual unconscious are universal images, patterns, and forms of human experiences, or archetypes. These archetypes can never be known directly, but they surface in art in an imperfect, shadowy way, taking the form of archetypal images—the snake with its tail in its mouth, rebirth, mother, the double, the descent into Hell. To get a sense of the archetype beneath the archetypal images or shadows in the characters, plot, language, and images of a work, to bring these together in an archetypal interpretation, is the function of the Jungian critic. Just as, for the Freudian literary critic, the "family romance," out of which the Oedipus story comes, is central, so the Jungian assumes there is a monomyth that underlies the archetypal images and gives a clue as to how they can be related to suggest the archetypes themselves. The myth is that of the quest. In that all-encompassing myth the hero struggles to free himself (the gender of the pronoun is specific and significant) from the Great Mother, to become a separate, self-sufficient being who is then rewarded by union with his ideal other, the feminine anima.

PHENOMENOLOGICAL CRITICISM

Another kind of subjectivist criticism is phenomenology, especially as it is practiced by critics of consciousness. They consider all the writings of an author—shopping lists and letters as well as lyrics—as the expression of his or her mind-set or way of looking at reality. Such a critic looks for repeated or obsessive use of certain key words, incidents, patterns, and angles of vision, and, using these, maps out thereby the inner world of the writer.

READER-RESPONSE CRITICISM

The formalists focus on the text. Though the psychological critics focus most frequently on the author, their assumptions about the similarity or universality of the human mind make them consider as well the role of the reader. There is another approach that, though not psychological in the usual sense of the word, also focuses on the reception of the text, on reader response. The conventional notion of reading is that a writer or speaker has an "idea," encodes it—that is, turns it into words—and the reader or listener decodes it, deriving, when successful, the writer/speaker's "idea." What the reader-response critic assumes, however, is that such equivalency between sender and receiver is impossible. The literary work, therefore, does *not* exist on the page; that is only the text. The text becomes a work only when it is read, just as a score becomes music only when it is played. And just as every musical performance, even of exactly the same notes, is somewhat different, a different "interpretation," so no two readers read or perform exactly the same work from identical texts. Besides the individual differences of readers, space is made for different readings or interpretations by gaps in a text itself. Some of these are temporary—such as the withholding of the name of the murderer until the end—and are closed by the text sooner or later, though each reader will in the meantime fill them differently. But others are permanent and can never be filled with certainty; the result is a degree of uncertainty or indeterminacy in the text.

  The reader-response critic's focus on the reading process is especially useful in the study of long works such as novels. The critic follows the text sequentially, observing what expectations are being aroused, how they are being satisfied or modified, how the reader recapitulates "evidence" from the portion of the text he has read to project forward a configuration, a tentative assumption of what the work as a whole will be and mean once it is done. The expectations are in part built by the text and in part by the repertoire of the reader—that is, the reader's reading experience plus his or her social and cultural knowledge.

HISTORICAL CRITICISM

DIALOGISM

Another critical approach that gives a significant role to the reader and is particularly useful for long fiction is dialogism, largely identified with the work of Mikhail Bakhtin (1895–1975). The dialogic critic bases the study of language and literature on the individual utterance, taking into account the specific time, the place, the speaker, and the listener or reader. Such critics thus see language as a continuous dialogue, each utterance being a reply to what has gone before. Even thought, which they define as inner speech, is a dialogue between utterances that you have taken in. Even your own language (and thus thought) is itself dialogic, for it is made up of the dialogue in which you are engaged, that which you have heard from parents and peers, teachers and television, all kinds of social and professional discourse and reading. Indeed, you speak many "languages"—those of your ethnic, social, economic, national, professional, gender, and other identities. Your individual language consists in the combination of those languages. The literary form in which the dialogic is most interesting, complex, and significant is the novel, for there you have the languages not only of the characters (as you do in drama), but also that of a mediator or narrator and passages of description or analysis or information that seem to come from other voices—newspapers, whaling manuals, legal cases, and so on. Because the world is growing more interrelated and we have multiple voices rather than one dominant voice or language, the novel has become the most appropriate form for the representation of that world.

Because the dialogic sees utterances, including literary utterances or works, as specific to a time and place, one of its dimensions, unlike formalist, structuralist, or psychological criticism, is *historical*. Nineteenth-century historical criticism took the obvious fact that a work is created in a specific historical and cultural context and that the author is a part of that context in order to treat literature as a product of the culture. Formalists and others emphasizing the aesthetic value of literature saw this as reducing the literary work to the status of a mere historical document and the abandonment of literary study to history. The dialogic critic sees the work in relation to its host context, a part of the dialogue of the culture. The work in turn helps to create the context for other utterances, literary and otherwise. Some consider dialogic criticism a form of sociological criticism.

SOCIOLOGICAL CRITICISM

More recently, as scientists from psychology to physics recognized the role of the perceiver in perception, historians realized that they were not only discovering and looking at facts, but were finding what they were looking for, selecting facts to fit preconceived views or interpretations. Literary historians or historical critics began to see literature not as a mere passive product of "history," but a contributor and even creator of history. An early form of this kind of historicism was sociological criticism, in which literature is seen as one aspect of the larger processes of history, especially those processes involving people acting in social groups or as members of social institutions or movements. Much sociological criticism uses literary texts to illustrate social attitudes and tendencies—and, therefore, has been strongly resisted by formalists, structuralists, and other "objectivist" critics as not being properly literary—but sociological criticism also attempts to relate what happens in texts to social events and patterns, and is as concerned about the effects of texts on human events as about the effects of historical events on texts. Sociological criticism assumes that the most significant aspects of human beings are social and that the most important functions of literature thus involve the way that literature both portrays and influences human interactions. Much sociological criticism centers its attention on contemporary life and texts, seeking to affect both societal directions and literary ones in the present, but some sociological criticism is historical, concerned with differences in different times and places, and anxious to interpret directions of literature in terms of historical emphases and patterns.

MARXIST CRITICISM

The most insistent and vigorous historicism through most of the twentieth century has been Marxism, based on the work of Karl Marx (1818–1883). Marxist criticism, like other historical critical methods in the nineteenth century, treated literature as a passive product of the culture, specifically of the economic aspect, and, therefore, of class warfare. Economics, the underlying cause of history, was thus the *base,* and culture, including literature and the other arts, the *superstructure.* Viewed from the Marxist perspective, the literary works of a period would, then, reveal the state of the struggle between classes in the historical place and moment.

Marxist critics, however, early on recognized the role of perception. They insisted that all use of language, including literary and critical language, is ideological—that is, that it derives from and expresses preconceived ideas, particularly economic or class values. Criticism is thus not just the product of the culture but part of the discourse or "conversation" that we call history. Formalism and even the extreme apolitical position of aestheticism, "art for art's sake," by placing art in a realm above the grubbiness of everyday life—above such mundane things as politics and money—removes art from having any importance in that life. According to Marxists, this "bourgeois mystification of art" tends to support the class in power. Marxism has traditionally been sensitive to and articulate about power politics in both life and literature, and both its social and literary analyses have often been based on an explicit or implicit political agenda, though many Marxist critics are motivated more by theoretical than practical aims. In recent years, especially in the wake of post-structuralism and the psychoanalytical criticism of the 1970s and 1980s, Marxist criticism has become increasingly theoretical and less doctrinaire politically. Critics such as Raymond Williams, Fredric Jameson, Terry Eagleton, Pierre Macherey, Walter Benjamin, and Louis Althusser have gained wide audiences among readers with a variety of political and literary commitments. Over the course of the century, it has been Marxism that has most often and most consistently raised referential and historical issues about literature, and those readers who have been interested in the interactive relationship between literature and life have most often turned for their guidance on such issues to Marxist analysts, whether or not they share their philosophical or political assumptions. In the past decade, however, two other critical schools with strong commitments to historical and cultural issues have become very powerful intellectually and have attracted many practitioners and adherents. These two, feminism and new historicism, have (along with Marxism and, in its way, dialogism) turned critical attention powerfully toward historical and representational issues, and since the mid-1980s they have set the dominant directions in literary criticism.

FEMINIST CRITICISM

Like Marxist criticism, feminist criticism derives from firm political and ideological commitments and insists that literature both reflects and influences human behavior in the larger world. Feminist criticism often, too, has practical and political aims. Strongly conscious that most of recorded history has given grossly disproportionate attention to the interests, thoughts, and actions of men, feminist thought endeavors both to extend contemporary attention to distinctively female concerns, ideas, and accomplishments and to recover the largely unrecorded and unknown history of women in earlier times. Not all directions of feminist criticism are historical; feminism has, in fact, taken many different directions and forms in recent years, and it has many different concerns. French feminist criticism, for example, has been deeply influenced by psychoanalysis, especially Lacanian psychoanalysis, and by French post-structuralist emphasis on language. Beyond their common aim of explicating and furthering specifically female interests, feminist critics may differ substantially in their assumptions and emphases. Like Marxism, feminism draws creatively on various other approaches and theories for its several methodologies. The most common historical directions of American feminism in particular involve the recovery of neglected or forgotten texts written by women in earlier times, the redrawing of literary values to include forms of writing (letters and autobiography, for example) that women were able to create when more public and accepted forms were denied to them, the discovery of the roles (positive and negative) that reading played in the lives and consciousnesses of women when they were unable to pursue more "active" and "public" courses, and the sorting out of cultural values implicit in the way women are represented in the texts of particular times and places.

NEW HISTORICISM

New historicism has less obvious ideological commitments than Marxism or feminism, but it shares their interest in the investigation of how power is distributed and used in different cultures. Drawing on the insights of modern anthropology (and especially on the work of Clifford Geertz), new historicism wishes to isolate the fundamental values in texts and cultures, and it regards texts both as evidence of basic cultural patterns and as forces in cultural and social change. Many of the most influential practitioners of the new historicism come out of the ranks of Marxism and feminism, and new historicists are usually knowledgeable about most varieties of literary theory. Like Marxists and feminists, they are anxious to uncover the ideological commitments in texts, and they care deeply about historical and cultural difference and the way texts represent it. But personal commitments and specific political agendas usually are less important—at least explicitly—to new historicists, and one of the main contentions between feminists and new historicists—or between Marxists and new historicists—involves disagreement about the role that one's own politics should play in the practice of criticism. Many observers regard new historicism as politically to the left in its analysis of traditional cultural values; but critics on the left are suspicious of new historicism, especially of its reluctance to state its premises openly, and they generally regard its assumptions as conservative. Whatever its fundamental political commitments, however (or whether its commitments can be fairly described as having a consistent and specifiable bias), new historicism is far more interested than any other literary approach in social groups generally ignored by literary historians, and it refuses to privilege "literature" over other printed, oral, or material texts. "Popular literature" often gets major attention in the work of new historicists, who see all texts in a culture as somehow expressive of its values and directions, and thus as equally useful in determining the larger intellectual, epistemological, and ethical system of which any text is a part. Texts here are thus seen as less specifically individual and distinctive than in most objectivist criticisms, and although new historicists are sometimes interested in the psychology of authors or readers their main concern is with the prevailing tendencies shared across a culture and thus shared across all kinds of texts, whatever their class status, literary value, or political aim.

PLURALISM

These classifications are not pigeonholes, and you will notice that many of the approaches overlap: many feminists, especially French feminist critics, are Lacanian or post-structuralist as well, while British feminists often lean toward sociological, especially Marxist, criticism; dialogic critics accept many of the starting points and methods of reader-response and sociological critics, and so on. These crossovers or combinations are generally enriching; they cause problems only when the critic seems to be operating out of contradictory assumptions.

There is a lively debate among critics and theorists at present involving the question of whether readers should bring together the insights and methods of different schools (practitioners of the mixing of methods are usually called pluralists) or whether they should commit themselves wholeheartedly to a single system. Pluralists contend that they make use of promising insights or methods wherever they find them and argue that putting together the values of different approaches leads to a fairer and more balanced view of texts and their uses. Opponents—those who insist on a consistency of ideological commitment—argue that pluralists are simply unwilling to state or admit their real commitments, and that any mixing of methods leads to confusion, uncertainty, and inconsistency rather than fairness. Readers, conscious or not of their assumptions and their methods, make this basic choice—to follow one lead or many—and the kind of reading they do and the conclusions they come to depend not only on this basic choice, but many others suggested by the dominant strands of recent criticism that have been described here. Not all critics are aware of their assumptions, methodologies, or values, and some would even deny that they begin with any particular assumptions or biases. But for readers newly learning to practice literary criticism, it is often useful for them to sort out their own beliefs carefully and see exactly what kind of difference it makes in the way they read literature and ask questions of it.

FURTHER READING ON CRITICAL APPROACHES

For good introductions to the issues discussed here, see the following books from which we have drawn in our discussion and definitions:

Robert Alter, *The Pleasures of Reading: Thinking about Literature in an Ideological Age*, New York, 1989

Jonathan Culler, *The Pursuit of Signs*, London, 1981

Jonathan Culler, *On Deconstruction*, London, 1983

Robert Con Davis and Ronald Schleifer, *Contemporary Literary Criticism*, 2d ed., New York, 1989

Mary Eagleton (ed.), *Feminist Literary Theory: A Reader*, Oxford, 1986

Terry Eagleton, *Literary Theory: An Introduction*, Minneapolis, 1983

Michael Grodon and Martin Kreiswirth, *The Johns-Hopkins Guide to Literary Theory and Criticism*, Baltimore, 1994

Nannerl Keohane, Michelle Z. Rosaldo, and Barbara C. Gelpi (eds.), *Feminist Theory: A Critique of Ideology*, Chicago, 1982

Dominick LaCapra, *History and Criticism*, Ithaca, New York, 1985

Vincent B. Leitch, *American Literary Criticism from the 30s to the 80s*, New York, 1988

Frank Lentricchia, *After the New Criticism*, Chicago, 1980

Frank Lentricchia and Thomas McLaughlin (eds.), *Critical Terms for Literary Study,* Chicago, 1990

Richard Macksey and Eugenio Donato (eds.), *The Structuralist Controversy: The Languages of Criticism and the Sciences of Man,* Baltimore, 1972

Toril Moi, *Sexual-Textual Politics,* New York, 1985

Jean Piaget (translated by Chanihan Maschler), *Structuralism,* New York, 1970

Raman Selden and Peter Widdowson, *A Reader's Guide to Contemporary Literary Theory,* Lexington, Kentucky, 1993

Tzvetan Todorov, *Mikhail Bakhtin: The Dialogic Principle,* Minneapolis, 1984

WRITING ABOUT FICTION, POETRY, DRAMA

So far we have been discussing writing about literature in general, rather than writing about a story, a poem, or a play in particular, though we have used specific works as examples. There are topics, such as a study of imagery, symbol, or theme, that are equally applicable to all three genres: you can write a paper on the images or symbols in or the theme of a story, a poem, or a play. Indeed, you can write an essay comparing imagery, say, in a story, a poem, and play—comparing the water imagery in James Baldwin's story "Sonny's Blues," for example, with the air or wind imagery in Shelley's "Ode to the West Wind," and the fire or burning imagery in Ibsen's *Hedda Gabler.* Fiction and drama also have action and character in common, so that you can not only choose to write on the plot of a story or play or on characters or characterization in a particular story or play, but you can compare, for example, a character in a story with a character in a play—Lessing's Judith with Ibsen's Hedda perhaps.

NARRATIVE

A story has not only elements common to all three genres, such as plot and character; it also has something special—a narrator, someone who tells the story. Everything in fiction—action, character, theme, structure, even the language—is mediated: everything comes to us through an intervening mind or voice; we often see the story from a particular vantage point or several vantage points (*focus*) and always are told the story by someone, whether that someone is identified or is merely a disembodied *voice.* We must be aware of the narration, the means by which the story comes to us. We must be aware that the action, characters, all the elements in a story are always mediated (there is someone between us and the story), and that the mediation contributes greatly to the meaning, structure, and effect of the story. Who is telling us the story of "The Lame Shall Enter First"? What is the physical and emotional relationship of the narrator of that story to its characters? How would you describe the language or voice of the narration? These are essential questions to ask about Flannery O'Connor's superb story, and in answering them you may want to write a paper called "The Narrator in 'The Lame Shall Enter First' " (or, if you want to be more dramatic, "The Ghostly Reporter of 'The Lame Shall

Enter First' ") A story is told *to* someone as well as by someone, and you might want to ask yourself what the relationship is supposed to be between us—the audience—and the narrator. To what kind of audience is the narrator of Lessing's "Our Friend Judith" telling her story? How do we, as readers, differ from that audience? What impression of the narrator do we form that she does not intend? Such questions might lead to an analysis of the tone of that story—and a paper we might sardonically call "With Friends Like Judith's . . . ." These are the kinds of questions raised by the simple but central fact that stories do not come to us directly but are narrated; these are, therefore, the kinds of questions of special importance to readers of fiction and the kinds of questions writing about fiction frequently centers upon.

Even the conventional past tense in fiction that we take for granted implies a narrator. Since the story is not happening "now," in the present, is not being enacted before us but is over with, having already happened in the past, it is being recalled, and someone must be recalling it, someone who knows what happened and how it all came out. That someone is the narrator. Knowing the end, the narrator has been able to select and shape the events and details. For that reason everything in a well-constructed story is relevant and significant.

Even narrative time is purposefully structured. Stories, unlike actual time as we know it, have beginnings and endings, but they do not have to begin at the beginning and proceed in a uniform direction at a uniform pace toward the end. They can be told from end to beginning, or even from middle to beginning to end, as in Baldwin's "Sonny's Blues." In a story an hour, day, or decade can be skipped or condensed into a narrative moment (a phrase or sentence), or a moment can be expanded to fill pages. Since this manipulation of time affects the meaning and effect of the story, we must pay close attention to it and question its significance. For example, the beginning of the third section of Bierce's "An Occurrence at Owl Creek Bridge" follows immediately from the end of the first section, so why is the second section there at all? Why does the first section cover only a few minutes of action but the third, only a little longer, cover what seems to be a whole day? Can you explain why—in terms of meaning and effect—each of the lengthy scenes in Chekhov's "The Lady with the Dog" is dwelled upon? why other, longer periods are briefly summarized or skipped? Why do some stories, such as Mansfield's "Her First Ball," cover only a very short period of time, while other, such as Faulkner's "A Rose for Emily" cover years and years? Why are stories such as "Her First Ball" presented largely through dialogue, while others, such as "A Rose for Emily," are "told" rather than presented, with few dramatized scenes and little dialogue?

DRAMATIZATION

Scenes presented more or less immediately (that is, without mediation) through dialogue and action, taking place over a short period of time, are said to be *dramatized*. Though there may be gaps of time *between* the *scenes* or *acts* of a play, once the action begins it takes exactly as much time on the stage as it would in actuality: the actors speak and move in "real" time. Though there is, of course, a playwright who knew how it would all come out and has shaped the play accordingly, the language of the play that we respond to is in the present tense, the dialogue and action are happening in the present, right before our eyes. And though the playwright has written all the lines, his or her voice is not directly heard: only the characters speak. Neither the playwright nor a surrogate in the form of a narrator stands at your elbow to tell you who are the good guys and who the bad, what each character is like or whether what is being said is true, distorted, false. Only very rarely—as in the Shakespearean soliloquy or aside—do we know what a character is thinking. In plays such as *Oedipus the King* and even *Hamlet,* there are only very brief indications of setting, costume, movement of characters, tone of voice, if they are present at all. Such stage directions—which may be as elaborate as the detailed description of setting and costumes and the instructions for action and tone in *Hedda Gabler*—are not, in a sense, purely dramatic. Watching a play being performed on a stage, we do not see or hear these words at all. On the page, they are usually distinguished from the text of the play by italics or some other typographical device, so as we read we register—or are supposed to register—them as separate from "the play itself." They seem to belong to some other dimension and clearly belong to a voice other than that of any character.

When we read a play, we tend to imagine it—in the literal sense of putting it into images—in our minds as if it were being performed on a stage. We act, as it were, as our own directors; if we were to put into words all that would be necessary to stage the play as we see it in our minds, we would be writing the stage directions, or narrative, of the play. The relative absence of such narrative in drama makes our part in the imaging or staging of a play as we read more crucial than it is in reading fiction. How you would stage a play or a scene in order to bring out its full meaning and effect as you imagined it can serve as a significant topic for writing about drama. You might ask yourself such questions as, What scene or passage would I use as the best example of how the play should be read? How would I costume Oedipus in the first and last scenes in order to bring out the main movement and theme of the play? How can I, in the early scenes, subtly reveal that Oedipus has an injured ankle without detracting from the power and majesty of his presence at that time? In the middle of his stage directions describing the set for *Hedda Gabler,* Ibsen specifies that on the rear wall of the smaller room there "hangs the portrait of a handsome old man in general's uniform." What, precisely, should this portrait look like? What expression should be on the general's face? How prominent should the picture be in the set as a whole?

Though you may wish to write on the theme, characters, action, imagery, or language of a play from time to time, one central element you will certainly want to write about sooner or later is the staging, or dramatization—the set, costumes, acting, moving of characters about on the stage, even lighting—and how this can enhance the effect and meaning of the play on the page.

WORDS

Some plays, like *Hamlet,* are written partly or entirely in verse. Though we may be able to make a distinction between poetry and verse, it is reasonable to say that as the term is generally used, poetry itself is not so much a literary genre as it is a medium. It might be more logical to break literature down into "prose" and "poetry" rather than into "fiction," "drama," and "poetry." For besides poetic dramas like *Hamlet,* there are also dramatic poems, such as Browning's "My Last Duchess" and John Donne's "The Flea," poems in which a distinguishable character speaks in a definable, almost "stageable" situation. There are also narrative poems, those that tell a story through a narrator, such as "Sir Patrick Spens" or Milton's *Paradise Lost.* What these and other poems—lyrics, for example—have in common is rhythmical language (and, some people would add, highly figurative language).

All literature is embodied in words, of course, but poetry uses words most intensely, most fully. It uses not only the statements words make, what they signify or *denote*, using them with great precision; not only what words suggest or *connote*, usually with wide-ranging sensitivity and inclusiveness; but the very sounds of the words themselves. Not all poems have highly patterned or very regular meter, but almost all poetry is more highly patterned than almost any prose. Not all poems rhyme, but it seems safe to say that all extensively rhymed works are poems. So much writing about poetry concentrates on the words themselves: some treat the patterns of sounds, the rhythms or rhymes, some the precision or suggestiveness of the language, and some the relation of sounds to shades of meaning. This is not to say that excellent papers may not be written on the themes, characters, settings of poems. There are many excellent topics as well for comparative papers; the themes of a poem and a story may be compared—Arnold's "Dover Beach" and Chekhov's "The Lady with the Dog," for example—or of a poem and a play—Hughes's "Harlem (A Dream Deferred)" and Hansberry's *A Raisin in the Sun,* perhaps. But in writing about poetry, even when discussing theme or other elements, at some point one usually comes to concentrate on the medium itself, the sound, precision, suggestiveness of the language. The sample paper on Sharon Olds's "The Victims" (page 1012) is an example of how one writes about this central element of poetry, words.

SAMPLE TOPICS AND TITLES

We have been stressing, on the one hand, writing about the most characteristic elements of stories, plays, and poems—narration, dramatization, and words—and, on the other hand, writing about the elements common to all three genres, like theme or symbols. For further hints about likely topics, you might look at the chapter headings in the table of contents of this volume and read the introductory material to the chapter or chapters that look most interesting or most promising for your immediate purpose. You might look, too, at the "Writing Suggestions" at the end of each chapter, the sample student papers, and the list of sample topics that follows, not so much for the topic that you will actually come to write on, but as a trigger for your own imagination and ideas.

FICTION

1. A Plotless Story about Plot: Paley's "A Conversation with My Father"
2. The Selection and Ordering of the Scenes in Cheever's "The Country Husband"
3. Voice in Erdrich's "Love Medicine"
4. Who Am I?: The Nature of the Narrator in Lessing's "Our Friend Judith"
5. The Self-Characterization of Montresor in Poe's "The Cask of Amontillado"
6. Sonny's Brother's Character in Baldwin's "Sonny's Blues"
7. Another Ending to Atwood's "Happy Endings"
8. The Image and Import of the Sea in Chekhov's "The Lady with the Dog"
9. "Only a Girl": The Theme of Munro's "Boys and Girls"
10. The Theme of Lawrence's "The Rocking-Horse Winner" and How It Relates to the Title

POETRY

1. Attitudes toward Authority in "Sir Patrick Spens"
2. Scene, Sequence, and Time in "Sir Patrick Spens"
3. Sir Patrick Spens as a Tragic Hero
4. Why "Facts" Are Missing in "Western Wind"

5. Birth and Death Imagery in Jarrell's "The Death of the Ball Turret Gunner"
6. Varieties of Violence in Frost's "Range-Finding"
7. The Characterization of God in Hardy's "Channel Firing"
8. The Idea of Flight in Keats's "Ode to a Nightingale"
9. Attitudes toward the Past in Robinson's "Mr. Flood's Party" and Wyatt's "They Flee from Me"
10. Satire of Distinctive American Traits in Nemerov's "Boom!," Fearing's "Dirge," and Van Duyn's "What the Motorcycle Said"

DRAMA

1. Conflict and Reversal in Chekhov's The Bear
2. The Effect of Offstage Action in Ibsen's Hedda Gabler (or Sophocles' Oedipus the King)
3. Rosencrantz and Guildenstern as Half-Men in Shakespeare's Hamlet
4. The Past Recaptured: What We Know (or Can Infer) about Blanche's Life in Williams's A Streetcar Named Desire
5. Varieties of Verbal Wit as a Device of Characterization in Wilde's The Importance of Being Earnest
6. Realistic Drama versus Comedy: Love and Marriage in Ibsen's Hedda Gabler and Wilde's The Importance of Being Earnest
7. Staging Polonius: Language and Cliché as Guides to Gestures, Facial Expression, and Character in Shakespeare's Hamlet

INTERGENERIC TOPICS

1. Motivation in Ibsen's Hedda Gabler and Rich's "Aunt Jennifer's Tigers"
2. The Loyalty of the Survivor: Maupassant's "The Jewelry" and Chekhov's The Bear
3. Francis Weed and Henry Higgins: A Comparison
4. The Murderer Confesses: Browning's Duke of Ferrara and Poe's Montresor

CREATIVE TOPICS

1. The speaker in Browning's "My Last Duchess" has been charged with the murder of his last duchess. On the basis on his words in the poem, prepare a case for the prosecution.
2. Write a "reply" to the speaker of Marvell's "To His Coy Mistress," declining his invitation and picking out the flaws in his argument.
3. Write a soliloquy for Gertrude (Hamlet) in which she defends herself against the most serious charges made against her motives and conduct.
4. Reconstruct the events and sentiments in Arnold's "Dover Beach" as a short mood play by writing dialogue and stage directions for a scene between the speaker and the woman.
5. Retell (in poetry or prose) the story in Dickey's "Cherrylog Road" from the point of view of the woman who is looking back on the experience twenty years later.
6. Using Thomas's "Fern Hill" as a model, write the kind of imaginary reverie Hedda Gabler might have written about her childhood.
7. What would happen in your neighborhood (town) if one morning there appeared a very old man with enormous wings?
8. Select three scenes for a one-act play called "The Rocking-Horse Winner."
9. Choose a story from Reading More Fiction that you have not read before, read to a crucial point or a pause marked by the author, and describe your expectations of how the story will develop and conclude.

DECIDING WHAT TO WRITE ABOUT

HAVING SOMETHING TO SAY

Deciding what to write about—what approach to use, which questions to ask—seems like the first step in the process of writing a paper about a work of literature. It isn't. Before that, you have to have confidence that you have something to say. If you are a beginner at this kind of writing, you are likely to have deep doubts about that. Developing confidence is not, at first, easy. You may feel as if you can *never* begin and want to put off the paper forever, or you may want to plunge in fast and get it over with. Either of these approaches, though common and tempting, is a mistake: the best way is to begin preparing for the paper as soon as possible—the moment you know you have one to write—but not to hurry into the writing itself.

The first step is to get close enough to the work to feel comfortable with it. Before you can tell anyone else about what you have read—and writing about literature is just another form of talking about literature, although a more formal and organized one—you need to "know" the work, to have a sure sense of what the work itself is like, how its parts function, what ideas it expresses, how it creates particular effects, and what your responses are. And the only way you will get to know the work is to spend time with it, reading it carefully and thoughtfully and turning it over in your mind. There is no substitute for reading, several times and with care, the work you are going to write about *before* you pick up a pen or sit at the keyboard. And let your reading be of the *work itself*, not of something *about* that work, at least at first; later, your instructor may steer you to background materials or to critical readings about the work, but at first you should encounter the work alone and become aware of your own responses to it.

Begin, then, by reading, several times, the work you are going to write about. The first time, read it straight through at one sitting: read slowly, pausing at its natural divisions—between paragraphs or stanzas, or at the ends of scenes—to consider how you are responding to the work. Later, when your knowledge of the work is more nearly complete and when you have the "feel" of the whole, you can compare your early responses with your more considered thoughts, in effect "correcting" your first impressions in whatever way seems necessary on the basis of new and better knowledge. But if you are noncommittal at first, refusing to notice what you think and feel, you will have nothing to correct, and you may cut yourself off from the most direct routes of response. Feelings are not always reliable—about literature any more than about people—but they are always the first point of contact with a literary work: you feel before you think. Try to start with your mind open, as if it were a blank sheet of paper ready to receive an impression from what you read.

When you have finished a first reading, think about your first impressions. Think about how the work began, how it gained your interest, how it generated expectations, how its conflicts and issues were resolved, how it ended, how it made you feel from beginning to end. Write down any phrases or events that you remember especially vividly, anything you are afraid you might forget. Look back at any parts that puzzled you at first. Write down in one sentence what you think the story, poem, or play is about. Then read it again, this time much more slowly, making notes as you go on any passages that seem especially significant and pausing over any features or passages that puzzle you. Then write a longer statement—three or four sentences—summarizing the work and suggesting more fully what it seems to be about. Try to write the kind of summary described above on pages A7–A8. If you get stuck, try brainstorming all of your ideas about the work for fifteen minutes, and then write the summary.

Stop. Do something else for a while, something as different as possible—see a movie, do math problems, ride a bicycle, listen to music, have a meal, take a nap. Do NOT do some other reading you have been meaning to do. When you go back to the work and finish reading it for the third time—rapidly and straight through—write down in a sentence the most important thing you would want to tell someone else who was about to read it for the first time: not just whether you liked it or not, but what exactly you liked, how the whole thing seems to have worked.

Now you are ready to choose a topic.

CHOOSING A TOPIC

Once you are ready to choose a topic, the chances are that you have already—quietly and unconsciously—chosen one. The clue is in the last statement you wrote. The desire to tell someone about a work of literature is a wonderful place to begin. Good papers almost always grow out of a desire to communicate. But desire is not enough—the substance (and most of the work, sentence by sentence) is still ahead of you; but desire will get you started. Chances are that what you wrote down as the one thing you most wanted to say is close to the heart of the central issue in the work you are going to write about. Your statement will become, perhaps, in somewhat revised form, your thesis.

The next step is to convert your personal feelings and desire to communicate into a sentence or two that states your purpose—into an "objective" statement about the work, a statement that will mean something to someone else. This will be your thesis. Again, you may already be further along than you realize. Look at the "summary" you wrote after your second reading. The summary will probably sound factual, objective, and general about the work; the personal statement you wrote after the third reading will be more emotional, subjective, and particular about some aspect of the work. Combining the two successfully is the key to a good paper: what you need to do is to write persuasively an elaboration and explanation of the last statement so that your reader comes to share the "objective" view of the whole work that your summary expresses. The summary you have written will, in short, be implicit in the whole essay; your total essay will suggest to your reader the wholeness of the work you are writing about, but it will do so by focusing its attention on some particular aspect of the work—on a part that leads to, or suggests, or represents the whole. What you want to do is build an essay on the basis of your first statement, taking a firm hold on the handle you have found. The summary is your limit and guide: it reminds you of where you will come out. Any good topic ultimately leads back to the crucial perceptions involved in a summary. Ultimately, any good writing about literature leads to a full and resonant sense of the central thrust of the work, but the most effective way to find that center is by discovering a pathway that particularly interests you. The best writing about literature presents a clear, well-argued thesis about a work or works and presents it from the perspective of personal, individual perception. But the thesis should clarify the central thrust of the work, helping it to open itself up to readers more completely and more satisfyingly.

Topics often suggest themselves after a second or third reading simply because one feature or problem stands out so prominently that it almost demands to be talked about. What is real in James's "The Real Thing"? Will the love between Gurov and the lady with the dog last? Sometimes you may be lucky: your instructor may *assign* a topic instead of asking you to choose your own. At first glance, that may not seem like a good break: it often feels confining to follow specific directions or to have to operate within limits and rules prescribed by someone else. The advantage is that it may save a lot of time and prevent floundering around. If your instructor assigns a topic, it is almost certain to be one that will work, one that has a payoff if you approach it creatively and without resentment at being directed so closely and precisely. It is time-consuming, even when you have tentatively picked a topic, to think through its implications and be sure it works. And an instructor's directions, especially if they are detailed and call attention to particular questions or passages, may aid greatly in helping you focus on particular issues or in leading you to evidence crucial to the topic.

If your instructor does *not* give you a topic and if no topic suggests itself to you after you have read a particular work three or four times, you may sometimes have to settle for the kind of topic that will—more or less—be safe for any literary work. Some topics are almost all-purpose. You can always analyze devices of characterization in a story, showing how descriptive detail, dialogue, and the reactions of other people in the story combine to present a particular character and evoke the reader's response to him or her; with a poem you can almost always write an adequate paper analyzing rhythm, or verse form, or imagery, or the connotations of key words. Such "fall-back" topics are, however, best used only as last resorts, when your instincts have failed you in a particular instance. When choice is free, a more lively and committed paper is likely to begin from a particular insight or question, something that grabs you and makes you want to say something, or solve a problem, or formulate a thesis. The best papers are usually very personal in origin; even when a topic is set by the assignment, the best papers come from a sense of having personally found an answer to a significant question. To turn a promising idea into a good paper, however, personal responses usually need to be supported by a considerable mass of evidence; the process often resembles the testing of "evidence" in a laboratory or the formulation of hypotheses and arguments in a law case. You may need to narrow your topic so that your thesis is focused and can be supported by examples from throughout the text. If your topic is too broad, your paper will likely become long, unwieldy, and overly general.

CONSIDERING YOUR AUDIENCE

Thinking of your paper as an argument or an explanation will also help with one of the most sensitive issues in writing about literature. The issue: For whom are you writing? who is your audience? The obvious answer is, your instructor, but in an important sense, that is the wrong answer. It is wrong because, although it could literally be true that your instructor will be the only person (besides you) who will ever read your paper, your object in writing about literature is to learn to write for an audience of peers, people a lot like yourself who are sensible, educated, and need to have something (in this case a literary work) explained to them so that they will be able to understand it more fully. Picture your ideal reader as someone about your own age and with about the same educational background. Assume that the person is intelligent and has some idea of what literature is like and how it works, but that he or she has just read this particular literary work for the first time and has not yet had a chance to think about it carefully. Don't be insulting and explain the obvious, but don't assume either that your reader has noticed and considered every detail. The object is to inform and convince your reader, not to impress.

Should you, then, altogether ignore the obvious fact that it is an instructor—probably one with a master's degree or Ph.D. in literature—who is your actual reader? Not altogether: you don't want to get so carried away with speaking to people of your own age and interests that you slip into slang, or feel the need to explain what a stanza is, or leave an allusion to a rock star unexplained, and you do want to learn from the kind of advice your instructor has given in class, or from comments he or she may have made on other papers you have written. But don't become preoccupied with the idea that you are writing for someone in "authority" or someone you need to please. Most of all, don't think of yourself as writing for a captive audience, for a reader who *has* to read what you write. It is not always easy to know exactly who your audience is or how interested your readers may be, so you have to make the most of every single word. It is your job to get the reader's attention. And you will have to do it subtly, making conscious assumptions about what your reader already knows and what he or she can readily understand. The tone of your paper should be serious and straightforward and its attitude respectful toward the reader as well as toward the literary work. But its approach and vocabulary, while formal enough for academic writing, should be readily understandable by someone with your own background and reading experience. And it should be lively enough to interest someone like you. Try to imagine, as your ideal reader, the person in your class whom you most respect. Write to get, and hold, that person's serious attention. Try to communicate, try to teach.

FROM TOPIC TO ROUGH DRAFT

Writing about literature is very much like talking about literature. But there is one important difference. When we talk, we organize as we go—trying to get a handle, experimenting, working toward an understanding. And the early stages of preparing a paper—the notetaking, the outlining, the rough drafts—are much like that. A "finished" paper, however, has the uncertainties and tentativeness worked out and presents an argument that moves carefully and compellingly toward a conclusion. How does one get from here to there?

Once you have decided on a topic, the process of planning is fairly straightforward, but it can be time-consuming and (often) frustrating. There are three basic steps in the planning process: first you gather the evidence, then you sort it into order, and finally you develop it into a convincing argument. The easiest way is to take these steps one by one.

GATHERING EVIDENCE

The first step involves accumulating evidence that supports the statement you have decided to make about your topic (that is, your thesis) and that takes you back to the text. But before you read the text again, look over the notes you have already made in the margin of that text or on separate pieces of paper. Which of them have something to do with the topic you have now defined? Which of them say something about your main point? Which ones can you now set aside as irrelevant to your topic?

Reading over the notes you have already made is a good preparation for re-reading the work again, for this time as you read it you will be looking at it in a new and specific way, searching for all the things in it that relate to the topic you have decided on. This time you will, in effect, be flagging everything—words, phrases, structural devices, changes of tone, and so forth—that bears upon your topic. As you read—very slowly and single-mindedly, with your topic always in mind—keep your pen constantly poised to mark useful points. Be ready to say something about the points as you come upon them; it's a good idea to write down immediately any sentences that occur to you as you reread this time. Some of these sentences will turn out to be useful when you actually begin to write your paper. Some will be incorporated in your paper; but some will not: you will find that a lot of the notes you take, like a lot of the footage shot in making a film, will end up on the cutting-room floor.

No one can tell you exactly how to take notes, but there are some general guidelines that may be useful. The notes you will need to take and how you take them will depend on the particulars of the paper you are about to write. Here are five hints toward successful notetaking.

1. Keep your topic and your thesis about your topic constantly in mind as you reread and take notes. Mark all passages in the text that bear on your topic, and for each one write on a note card a single sentence that describes how the passage relates to your topic and thesis. Add a "key" word that identifies the note at the top of the card to help you to organize the cards into clusters later in the process. Then indicate, for each passage, the specific location in the text—by page or paragraph number if you are working on a story; by line number if you are writing about a poem; by act, scene, and line number if you are writing about a play. If you are taking notes on a computer, put page breaks between each one, so that when you print them out, there will be one note per page.

2. Keep rereading and taking notes until one of five things happens:
   a. You get too tired and lose your concentration. (If that happens, stop and then start again later, preferably the next day.)
   b. You stop finding relevant passages or perceive a noticeable drying up of your ideas. (Again, time to pause; give the work at least one more reading later when your mind is fresh and see whether the juices start anew. If they don't, you may be ready to outline and write.)
   c. You begin to find yourself annotating every single sentence or line, and the evidence all begins to run together into a single blob. (If this happens, your thesis is probably too broad. Simplify and narrow it so that you don't try to include everything. Then go back to your notetaking and discriminate more carefully between what actually is important to your thesis and what only relates at some distance.)
   d. You become impatient with your notetaking and can't wait to get started writing. (Start writing. Be prepared to go back to systematic notetaking if your ideas or your energy fades. The chances are that the prose passages you write this way will find a place in your paper, but they may not belong exactly where you think they do when you first write them down.)
   e. You find that there is insufficient evidence for your thesis, that the evidence points in another direction, or that the evidence contradicts your thesis. (Revise your topic to reflect the evidence, and begin re-reading once more.)

3. When you think you have finished your notetaking, read all your note cards over slowly, one by one, and jot down any further ideas as they occur to you, each one on a separate note card. Computer users can either read the file on screen and add notes as they wish or print out all of the notes and read through them on paper. (Sometimes it will seem as if note cards beget note cards. Too much is better than too little at the notetaking stage: you can always discard them before the final draft. Don't worry if you seem to have too many notes and too much material. But later, when you boil down to essentials, you will have to be ruthless and omit some of your favorite ideas.)

4. Transfer all of your notes to pieces of paper—or note cards—that are all the same size, one note on each. It is easier to sort them this way when you get ready to organize and outline. If you like to write notes in the margin of your text (or on the backs of envelopes, or on dinner napkins, or on shirtsleeves), systematically transfer every note to uniform sheets of paper or cards before you begin to outline. Having everything easily recorded on sortable cards that can be moved from one pile to another makes organiz-

ing easier later, especially when you change your mind (as you will) and decide to move a point from one part of your paper to another. Index cards—either 3" × 5", if you write small and make economical notes, or 4" × 6", if you need more space—are ideal for notetaking and sorting.

5. When you think you are done taking notes (because you are out of ideas, or out of time, or getting beyond a manageable number of pieces of evidence), read through the whole pile one more time, again letting any new ideas—or ideas that take on a fresh look because you combine them in a new way—spawn new sentences.

How many times should you read a story, poem, or play before you stop taking notes? There is no right answer. If you have read the work three times before settling on a topic, two more readings may do. But it could take several more. Common sense, endurance, and deadlines will all have an effect on how many rereadings you do. Let your conscience, your judgment, and your clock be your guides.

ORGANIZING YOUR NOTES

The notes you have taken will become, in the next few hours, almost the whole content of your paper. The task remaining is to give that content the form and shape that will make it appealing and persuasive. It is not an easy task: the best content in the world isn't worth much if it isn't effectively presented. The key to the task is getting all your ideas into the right order—that is, into a sequence that will allow them to argue your thesis most persuasively.

In order to put your notes into a proper order, you will need (ironically) to get a little distance from your notes. (The key to good planning and writing—and to many other pursuits—is in knowing when to back away and get some perspective.) Set your notes aside, but not too far away. On a fresh sheet of paper or in a separate document on your computer, write all the major points you want to be sure to make. Write them randomly, as they occur to you. Now read quickly through your pack of notes and add to your list any important points you have left out. Then decide which ideas should go first, which should go second, and so on.

Putting your points in order is something of a guess at this point. You may well want to reorder them before you begin to write—or later when you are writing a first (or even later) draft. But make your best guess. The easiest way to try out an order is to take your random list and put a "1" in front of the point you will probably begin with, a "2" before the probable second point, and so on. Then copy the list, in numerical order, revising (if you need to) as you go. Do not be surprised if later you have to revise your list further. Your next task is to match up your notes (and the examples they contain) with the points on your outline. If you've added "key" words to the top of each card or file, you can make a "rough cut" according to these words.

Putting things in a particular order is a spatial problem, and by having your notes on cards or pieces of paper of a uniform size you can do much of your organizing physically. Do your sorting on a large table, or sit in the middle of the floor. Prepare a title card for each point in your outline, writing on it the point and its probable place in your paper, then line them up on the table or floor in order before you begin writing. If you're using your computer, you can use the search function to find each instance of a key word, phrase, or name, and arrange your electronic "cards" under the headings on your list by blocking and moving your "cards" to new parts of the document.

Two-thirds of this exercise is quite easy: most examples and ideas you have written down will match quite easily with a particular point. But some cards will resist classification. Some cards will seem to belong in two or more places; others will not seem to belong at all. If a card seems to belong to more than one point, put it in the pile with the lowest number (but write on it the number or numbers of other possible locations). If, for example, a card might belong in point 2 but could also belong in point 6 or 9, put it in the pile of 2's and add the phrase "maybe 6 or 9" to the card; if you don't use it in writing about point 2, move it to pile 6; if you don't use it in 6, move it to 9. Remember that you will work your way through the piles in numerical order, so that you have a safety system for notes that don't seem to belong where you first thought but that still belong somewhere in your paper. Move them to a possible later point, or put them in a special file (marked "?" or "use in revised draft") and, once you have completed a first draft on your paper, go through this file, carefully looking for places in your paper where these ideas may belong. Almost never will everything fit neatly into your first draft. If everything does seem to fit exactly as you had originally planned, you have either done an incredible job of planning and guessing about the organization of your paper, or you are forcing things into inappropriate places.

Don't be surprised if you have a large number of leftover notes—that is, ideas you haven't yet used—after you have written your first draft. You will probably find places for many of these ideas later, but some just won't fit and won't be needed for the paper you ultimately write, no matter how good the ideas are. No paper will do everything it could do. Writing a paper is a *human* project; it has limits.

Before you actually start writing, you may want to develop a more elaborate outline, incorporating your examples and including topic sentences for each paragraph, or you may wish to work from your sketchy outline and the accompanying packs of cards. Do the more detailed outline if it seems right to you, but don't delay the writing too long. You are probably ready right now, and any exercises you invent to delay writing are probably just excuses.

DEVELOPING AN ARGUMENT

Once you have decided on your major points and assembled your evidence, you have to decide how you are going to present your argument and how you are going to present *yourself.* What you say is, of course, more important than how you say it, but your manner of presentation can make a world of difference. Putting your evidence together effectively—in a coherent and logical order so that your readers' curiosity and questions are answered systematically and fully—is half the task in developing a persuasive argument. The other half involves your choice of a voice and tone that will make readers want to read on—and make them favorably disposed toward what you say.

The tone of your paper is the basis of your relationship with your reader. "I will be just *me,*" you may say, "and write naturally." But writing is not a "natural" act, any more than swinging a tennis racket, carrying a football, or executing a pirouette. The "me" you choose to present is only one of several possible me's; you will project a certain mood, a certain attitude toward your subject, a certain confidence. How do you want your readers to feel about you and your argument? Being too positive can make your audience feel stupid and inadequate, and can turn them into defensive, resistant readers who will rebel at your every point. Friendship with your reader is better than an adversary relationship. Sounding like a nice person who is talking reasonably and sensibly is not enough if in fact you don't make sense or have nothing to say, but the purpose of the tone you choose is to make your reader receptive to your content, not hostile. The rest of the job depends on the argument itself.

It has been said that all good papers should be organized in the same way:

1. Tell 'em what you're going to tell 'em.
2. Tell 'em.
3. Tell 'em what you told 'em.

That description fits—in pretty general terms—the most common kind of organization, which includes an introduction, a body of argument, and a conclusion, but if it is followed too simplistically it can lead to a paper that sounds simple-minded. The beginning does need to introduce the subject, sort out the essential issues, and suggest what your perspective will be, and the conclusion does need to sum up what you have said in the main part of your paper, but the first paragraph shouldn't give *everything* away, nor should the final one simply repeat what is already clear. Lead into your subject clearly but with a little subtlety; arrange your main points in the most effective manner you can think of, building a logical argument and supporting your general points with clear textual evidence, concisely phrased and presented, and at the end *show how* your argument has added up—don't just *say* that it did.

There are, of course, other ways to organize than the basic Tell-3 method, but the imagination and originality that can be exercised in a straightforward Tell-3 paper are practically unlimited.

WRITING THE FIRST DRAFT

It is now time to set pen to paper or fingers to keyboard. No one will be able to help you much for a while. The main thing is to get started right, with a clear first sentence that expresses your sense of direction and arrests the attention of your readers. (If you can't think of a good first sentence, don't pause over it too long. Write down a paraphrase of what you want it to say—something like the statement you wrote down after your third reading—and then start writing about your main points. Your "first" sentence may sometimes be the last one you will write.) And then you inch along, word by word and sentence by sentence, as you follow your outline from one paragraph to another. Keep at it. Struggle. Stare into space. Bite your pen when you feel like it. Get up and stride about the room. Scratch your head. Sharpen a pencil. Run your fingers through your hair. Groan. Snap your fingers. But keep writing.

It is often frustrating as you search for the right word or struggle to decide how the next sentence begins, but it is satisfying when you get it right. If you get stuck, try working out your ideas on a separate piece of paper or freewriting for a while inside your computer document. Sometimes, working out an idea, away from your draft, can be helpful. Stay with your draft until you're reasonably satisfied with it. Breathe a sigh of relief, and put it away until tomorrow.

FROM ROUGH DRAFT TO COMPLETED PAPER

REVISING

This final stage of the process is the most important of all, and it is the easiest one to mismanage. There is a world of difference between a bunch of ideas that present a decent interpretation of a work of literature and a cogent, coherent, persuasive essay that will stir your readers to a nod of agreement and shared pleasure in a moment of insight. If you haven't done good literary analysis and sorted out your insights earlier, nothing you do at this stage will help much; but if what you have done so far is satisfactory, this is the stage that can turn your paper into something special.

The important thing is not to allow yourself to be too easily satisfied. If you have struggled with earlier stages, it may be tempting to think you are finished when you have put a period to the last sentence in your first draft. It will often feel as if you are done: you may feel drained, tired of the subject, anxious to get on to other things, such as sleep or food or friends or another project. And it *is* a good idea to take a break once you've finished a draft and let what you have done settle for a few hours, preferably overnight. (The Roman poet and critic Horace suggested putting a draft aside for nine years, but most instructors won't wait that long.) Rereading it "cold" may be discouraging, though: all those sentences that felt so good when you wrote them often seem flat and stale, or even worthless, when a little time has elapsed. The biggest struggle in moving from a first draft to a second one is to keep from throwing what you have written into a wastebasket. You've spent a lot of time on this already, and with some more work you'll have a paper you can be proud of.

It may take *several* more drafts to produce your best work. Often it is tempting to cut corners—to smooth out a troublesome paragraph by obscuring the issue or by omitting the difficult point altogether instead of confronting it, or to ask a roommate or friend for help in figuring out what is wrong with a particular passage. But you will learn more in the long run—and probably do better in the short run as well—if you make yourself struggle a bit. When a particular word or phrase you have used turns out to be imprecise or misleading or ambiguous, search until you find the *right* word or phrase. (At the least put a big X in the margin so that you will come back and fix it later.) If a paragraph is incomplete or poorly organized, fill it in or reorganize it. If a transition from one point to another does not work, look again at your outline and see if another way of ordering your points would help. *Never* decide that the problem can best be solved by hoping that your reader will not notice. The satisfaction of finally solving the problem will build your confidence and sooner or later make your writing easier and better.

REVIEWING YOUR WORK AND REVISING AGAIN

Precisely how you move from one draft to another is up to you and will depend on the ways you work best; the key is to find all the things that bother you (and that *should* bother you) and then gradually to correct them, moving toward a better paper with each succeeding draft. Here are some things to watch for.

Thesis and central thrust: Is it clear what your main point is? Do you state it clearly, effectively, and early? Do you make clear what the work is about? Are you fair to the spirit and emphasis of the work? Do you make clear the relationship between your thesis and the central thrust of the work? Do you explain *how* the work creates its effect rather than just asserting it?

Organization: Does your paper move logically from beginning to end? Does your first paragraph set up the main issue you are going to discuss and suggest the direction of your discussion? Do your paragraphs follow each other in a coherent and logical order? Does the first sentence of each paragraph accurately suggest what that paragraph will contain? Does your final paragraph draw a conclusion that follows from the body of your paper? Do you resolve the issues you say you resolve?

Use of evidence: Do you use enough examples? Too many? Does each example prove what you say it does? Do you explain each example fully enough? Are the examples sufficiently varied? Are any of them labored, or overexplained, or made to bear more weight than they can stand? Have you left out any examples useful to your thesis? Do you include any gratuitous ones just because you like them? Have you achieved a good balance between examples and generalizations?

Tone: How does your voice sound in the paper? Confident? Does it show off too much? Is it too timid or self-effacing? Do you ever sound smug? Too tentative? Too dogmatic? Would a neutral reader be put off by any of your assertions? By your way of arguing? By your choice of examples? By the language you use?

Sentences: Does each sentence read clearly and crisply? Have you rethought and rewritten any sentences you can't explain? Is the first sentence of your paper a strong, clear one likely to gain the interest of a neutral reader? Is the first sentence of each paragraph an especially vigorous one? Are your sentences varied enough? Do you avoid the passive voice and "there is/there are" sentences?

Word choice: Have you used any words whose meaning you are not sure of? In any cases in which you were not sure of what word to use, did you stay with the problem until you found the exact word? Do your metaphors and figures of speech make literal sense? Are all the idioms used correctly? Is your terminology correct? Are your key words always used to mean *exactly* the same thing? Have you avoided sounding repetitive by varying your sentences rather than using several different terms to mean precisely the same thing?

Conciseness: Have you eliminated all the padding you put in when you didn't think your paper would be long enough? Have you gone through your paper, sentence by sentence, to eliminate all the unnecessary words and phrases? Have you looked for sentences (or even paragraphs) that essentially repeat what you have already said, and eliminated all repetition? Have you checked for multiple examples and pared down to the best and most vivid ones? Have you gotten rid of all inflated phrasing calculated to impress readers? Have you eliminated all roundabout phrases and rewritten long, complicated, or confusing sentences into shorter, clearer ones? Are you convinced that you have trimmed every possible bit of excess and that you cannot say what you have to say any more economically?

Punctuation and mechanics: Have you checked the syntax in each *separate* sentence? Have you checked the spelling of any words that you are not sure of or that look funny? Have you examined each sentence separately for punctuation? Have you checked every quotation word by word against the original? Have you given proper credit for all material—written or oral—that you have borrowed from others? Have you followed the directions your instructor gave you for citations, notes, and form?

As you begin to revise, it's a good idea to look first at the larger issues (your thesis, organization, and supporting evidence) to make sure you find and solve any major problems early on. Then you're in a better position to work on your tone, sentences, choice of words, and punctuation and mechanics. In the final stages, the most effective way to revise is to read through your paper looking for one problem at a time—that is, to go through it once looking at paragraphing, another time looking at individual sentences, still another for word choice or problems of grammar. It is almost impossible to check too many things too often—although you can get so absorbed with little things that you overlook larger matters. With practice, you will learn to watch carefully for the kinds of mistakes you are most prone to. Everyone has individual weaknesses and flaws. Here are some of the most common stumbling blocks for beginning writers:

1. Haste. (Don't start too late, or finish too soon after you begin.)
2. Pretentiousness. (Don't use words you don't understand, tackle problems that are too big for you, or write sentences you can't explain; it is more important to make sense than to make a big, empty impression.)
3. Boredom. (The quickest way to bore others is to be bored yourself. If you think your paper will be a drag, you are probably right. It is hard to fake interest in something you can't get excited about; keep at it until you find a spark.)
4. Randomness. (Don't try to string together half a dozen unrelated ideas or insights and con yourself into thinking that you have written a paper.)
5. Imprecision. (Don't settle for approximation, either in words or ideas; something that is 50 percent right is also 50 percent wrong.)
6. Universalism. (Don't try to be a philosopher and make grand statements about life; stick to what is in the work you are writing about.)
7. Vagueness. (Don't settle for a general "sense" of the work you are talking about; get it detailed, get it right.)
8. Wandering. (Don't lose track of your subject or the work that you are talking about.)
9. Sloppiness. (Don't sabotage all your hard work on analysis and writing by failing to notice misspelled words, grammatical mistakes, misquotations, incorrect citations or references, or typographical errors. Little oversights make readers suspicious.)
10. Impatience. (Don't be too anxious to get done. Enjoy the experience; savor the process. Have fun watching yourself learn.)

Being flexible—being willing to rethink your ideas and reorder your argument as you go—is crucial to success in writing, especially in writing about literature. You will find different (and better) ways to express your ideas and feelings as you struggle with revisions, and you will also find that—in the course of analyzing the work, preparing to write, writing, and rewriting—your response to the work itself will have grown and shifted somewhat. Part of the reason is that you will have become more knowledgeable as a result of the time and effort you have spent, and you will have a more subtle understanding of the work. But part of the reason will also be that the work itself will not be the same. Just as a work is a little different for every reader, it is also a little different with every successive reading by the *same* reader, and what you will be capturing in your words is some of the subtlety of the work, its capacity to produce effects that are alive and that are, therefore, always changing just slightly. Thus, you need not feel that you must say the final word about the work you are writing about, but you do want to say whatever word you have to say in the best possible way.

You can turn all this into a full-time job, of course, but you needn't. It is hard work, and at first the learning seems slow and the payoff questionable. A basketball novice watching the magic of Michael Jordan may find it hard to see the point of practicing layups, but even creative geniuses have to go through those awful moments of sitting down and putting pen to paper (and then crossing out and rewriting again and again). But that's the way you learn to make it seem easy. Art is mostly craft, and craft means methodical work.

It *will* come more easily with practice. But you needn't aspire to professional writing to take pleasure in what you accomplish. Learning to write well about literature will help you with all sorts of tasks, some of them having little to do with writing. Writing trains the mind, creates habits, teaches you procedures that will have all kinds of long-range effects that you may not immediately recognize or be able to predict. And ultimately it is very satisfying, even if it is not easy, to be able to stand back and say, "That is mine. Those are my words. I know what I'm talking about. I understand, and I can make someone else understand."

One final bit of advice: do not follow, too rigidly or too closely, anyone's advice, including ours. We have suggested some general strategies and listed some common pitfalls. But writing is a very personal experience, and you will have talents (and faults) that are a little different from anyone else's. Learn to play to your own strengths and avoid the weaknesses that you are especially prone to. Pay attention to your instructor's comments; learn from your own mistakes.

SECONDARY SOURCES

It is always preferable to form your own opinion about a story, poem, or play before consulting the opinions of others. However there are times when it is appropriate, sometimes even necessary, for you to read and then quote from commentary written by professional critics. These critiques and scholarly studies, called *secondary sources,* can very often enlarge and complement your sense and appreciation of a work, and can provide you with valuable evidence that confirms or modifies your thesis.

It is not a good idea to begin consulting secondary sources, however, until you've completed the first stage of your writing (described on page A54, "Stage One"). Once you've written the one-paragraph "promise" of what your paper is going to argue and you've taken notes from the text in support of that argument, then you are prepared to read the critical materials selectively, analytically, and intelligently.

The steps involved in writing a literary research paper are nearly identical to those involved in writing a paper based on your personal response to a work, for writing a research paper involves the same careful and deliberate process of reading and rereading, taking notes, ordering your thoughts, writing an outline, drafting, revising, and proofreading that is involved in writing a personal response. But because a research paper uses other materials in addition to the primary text (that is, the story, poem, or play), you need to be even more precise and diligent in your notetaking, and you must take on the additional responsibility of fairly and accurately citing your sources.

FINDING SOURCES

Before you can begin reading secondary sources, you must find them. The best place to find them is, of course, the library. But where do you begin? Two types of resources in particular are especially useful: the library catalog and scholarly bibliographies.

ON-LINE AND CARD CATALOGS The library catalog will guide you to books about the author and the work, but very often the titles of potentially useful books will be too general for you to determine whether or not the book covers the topic you're writing about. If your library's catalog is on-line, use "keyword searches" to limit the number and range of books that the computer finds. For example, if you're writing about William Faulkner's "A Rose for Emily," first try a search that is limited to items that include "Faulkner" AND "A Rose for Emily." If there are no matches or too few, then you can broaden your search to include all books that are about William Faulkner.

Most likely, the books that you find through a catalog search will lead you to a section of the library where other books on the subject are filed. Even if you find the books you were looking for right away, you should take a moment to browse the shelves nearby. The books on either side of your source probably cover the same topic, and they may prove even more useful than the ones you sought out.

BIBLIOGRAPHIES Scholarly bibliographies, most of which appear annually, provide comprehensive lists of scholarly books and articles published during the preceding year. In most libraries, these guides are found in the reference area (that is, they're not available for checkout), but often they are also on-line. Two bibliographies in particular—*The MLA International Bibliography* and the *Reader's Guide to Periodical Literature*—are especially useful to students of literature and the humanities. The best strategy for consulting bibliographies is to start with the most recent year and work your way backward. You will find references not only to relevant books, but also to articles published in scholarly journals. The titles of most journal articles are very specific, so you'll be able to see quickly which are most useful to you. Make sure to give yourself enough time in the library to consult journal articles; unlike books, periodicals may not be checked out on most campuses. If you don't have enough time to read these in the library, photocopy them. As you read the books and articles, check the footnotes for sources that your author, title, and word searches did not find.

USING THE INTERNET With its innumerable links and pathways, the Internet seems at first to be the perfect resource for research work. And in fact, there are some very good resources available for students of literature. One in particular, called "The Voice of the Shuttle" (http://humanitas.ucsb.edu/), is a great starting point for students and scholars alike. The "Voice of the Shuttle" site provides links to hundreds of other sites that offer valuable and interesting information on authors, genres, specific works, contextual information, literary periods, and critical approaches. If you don't find an appropriate link in the "Voice of the Shuttle" site, you will probably want to conduct a search using one of the commonly available "search engines"—for example, Yahoo (http://www.yahoo.com/) or AltaVista (http://www.altavista.digital.com/). Using keywords such as "Faulkner" or "poetry" in your Internet searches will lead you to hundreds of possible matches, however, so you should try to limit your search by creating search strings that are longer than one word. As you do so, read the on-screen directions carefully to make sure that your search engine is treating the search string as a unit and not finding every mention of each individual word.

Despite the obvious benefits of the Internet, you should be cautious in your use of on-line sources for research for two reasons. First, although there are many sites that provide solid information, there are many more that provide misinformation or unsubstantiated opinion. Unlike journal articles and books, which are systematically reviewed and critiqued by other scholars and experts before being published, many Internet sources are posted without any sort of review process.[1]

Second, because the Internet and World Wide Web allow you to jump from one site to another with the click of a button and to copy whole pages of text merely by "cutting and pasting," there is a chance that you will lose your place and be unable to provide your reader with a precise citation of your source. Make sure, therefore, to carefully note the specific address of the site that you're quoting; and if the text that you're using has been taken from a printed source such as a book or magazine, note all of the particulars about that original source as well. The point of all of this is to ensure that your reader can retrace your steps and check your sources. The guide to MLA citation formats that follows (page A50) includes some examples of citations from electronic sources.

TAKING NOTES FROM SOURCES

Taking notes from secondary sources begins with creating a "Works Cited" entry for each source you consult either in a word-processing file (one page per citation) or on an index card. The following is an example of a citation for one of the scholarly sources that Willow Crystal consulted for her research paper on Faulkner's "A Rose for Emily." You'll find guidelines for citing just about any research source in *The MLA Handbook for Writers of Research Papers,* but examples of some of the most common sources can be found later in this guide, starting on page A50.

Read an article all the way through before taking notes from it. During this reading, you should be evaluating the article's relevance to your chosen topic. If an article doesn't apply directly to your topic but nonetheless interests you, create a brief citation of the publication information, and write a one-sentence summary of the article's main argument. This will be useful if you find yourself altering your topic to include some of what's covered in this source.

Once you have read your potential sources and chosen a short list of those that you'll want to use in your paper, you can begin the serious work of taking notes. Taking notes from sources involves three tasks:

(1) noting publication information for your "Works Cited" page (see above); (2) creating a summary or outline (sometimes called a précis) of the critic's argument; and (3) directly quoting or summarizing a passage in your source. Creating a summary of the author's argument ensures that you've understood your source and can accurately convey its sense to your reader. Once you're confident of that, you can use quotations either to support your argument or to take issue with the author's interpretation if it challenges your own.

If you're using a computer to take notes, you will be able to mingle your summary of the author's argument with direct quotations. This works especially well if you've for-

---

1. Though you can usually rely on refereed journals for information, it's important to remember that not everything in print is "true." Cross-checking and confirming sources, as good newspaper reporters do, is always a good idea.

matted your summary in outline form: simply type the quotation along with its page reference under the appropriate heading within the outline. If you're taking notes on cards, you'll want to keep your outline separate from your quotations, and you should use only one card for each quotation. This gives you the freedom to arrange and rearrange the quotations as necessary. Make sure, however, to bind quotations from the same source together with a paper clip or rubber band and to note the author's last name somewhere on each quotation card.

USING SOURCES IN YOUR PAPER

Using sources in your paper means using them to provide evidence in support of your thesis or as examples of an interpretation with which you don't completely agree. Either way, you should bear in mind that as you write your paper, the sources shouldn't dominate; they are there to flesh out and verify your thesis, and they should be used as a supplement to, not a replacement for, your own interpretation. Remember, evidence without interpretation, just as in a court of law, is not convincing in itself. Unlike the practice in law, however, merely citing "authorities" or precedents is also not sufficient.

CITING SOURCES

As you use secondary sources, either through direct quotation or summary of a critic's argument, you must signal to your reader the specific source in each case. Your instructor may have guidelines for citing sources within the body of your paper, but if not, you should follow the guidelines found in the *The MLA Handbook for Writers of Research Papers*. The following is a brief summary of the MLA's guidelines:

-
IN-TEXT CITATION
- If you use the author's name to introduce the material, give only the page number in parentheses.

Example:

As Judith Fetterley says, "Emily, like Georgiana, is a man-made object . . ." (35).

Sample citation note

Fetterley, Judith. The Resisting Reader: A Feminist Approach to American Fiction. Bloomington: Indiana UP, 1978.

-
- If you don't use the author's name to introduce the source, put the name and page number(s) in parentheses.

Example:

One critic points out that "Emily, like Georgiana, is a man-made object . . ." (Fetterley 35).

-

- If you are citing another work by the same author elsewhere in the paper, use a title word before the page number(s).

Example:

As Judith Fetterley says, "Emily, like Georgiana, is a man-made object . . ." (<u>Resisting</u> 35).

-

- If you don't use the author's name to introduce your source and you are citing another work by the same author, use both name and title with the page number(s).

Example:

One critic points out that "Emily, like Georgiana, is a man-made object . . ." (Fetterley, <u>Resisting</u> 35).

THE "WORKS CITED" PAGE   In addition, every literary research paper must include a "Works Cited" page that lists all secondary sources that you have used in your paper. This list should be in alphabetical order by the author's last name. The student paper on page 543 provides a model for a properly formatted "Works Cited" page. Here is a brief guide to the proper format for some of the most common sources:

A book by one author or editor:

Fetterley, Judith.<u>The Resisting Reader: A Feminist Approach to American Fiction.</u> Bloomington: Indiana UP, 1978.

A book by two or three authors or editors:

Wellek, René, and Austin Warren. <u>Theory of Literature.</u> 3rd ed. Orlando: Harcourt, Brace and Company, 1956.

A book by more than three authors or editors:

Mack, Maynard, et al., eds. <u>The Norton Anthology of World Masterpieces.</u> 6th ed. Vol. 1. New York: Norton, 1992.

Editor's Introduction to a book:

O'Prey, Paul. Introduction. <u>Heart of Darkness.</u> By Joseph Conrad. New York: Viking, 1983. 7-24.

A translated book:

Boccaccio, Giovanni. <u>The Decameron.</u> Trans. G. H. McWilliam. London: Penguin, 1972.

Essay or any other short work in a book:

Hass, Robert. "Listening and Making." <u>Twentieth Century Pleasures: Prose on Poetry.</u> Hopewell: Ecco, 1984. 107-33.

Article in a reference book:

Wihl, Gary. "Marxist Theory and Criticism." <u>The Johns Hopkins Guide
    to Literary Theory and Criticism.</u> Ed. Michael Groden and Martin
    Kreiswirth. Baltimore: Johns Hopkins UP, 1994.

Article in a newspaper:

Perlez, Jane. "Winning Literary Acclaim, a Voice of Central Europe."
    <u>New York Times</u> 9 Sept. 1997: C9.

Article in a magazine:

Fenton, James. "Becoming Marianne Moore." <u>New York Review of Books</u> 24
    Apr. 1997: 40-45.

Article in a scholarly journal with continuous pagination:

(Each *volume* of a journal includes a full year of *issues.* The page numbers of some
journals begin with "1" in the first issue and run continuously through subsequent
issues—that is, issue 1 runs from page 1 to page 323, issue 2 runs from 324 to 656,
and so forth.)

Dickey, Stephen. "Shakespeare's Mastiff Comedy." <u>Shakespeare
    Quarterly</u> 42 (1991): 255-75.

Article in a scholarly journal with separate pagination for each issue:

Sosnoski, James. "The Theory Junkyard." <u>Minnesota Review</u> 96.41
    (1996): 80-94.

INTERNET SOURCES   The Modern Language Association is still developing guidelines for the citation of sources found on the Internet. The following recommendations,
adapted from MLA guidelines, are taken from *Writing Research Papers: A Norton Guide,*
by Melissa Walker.

World Wide Web site:

Murphy, Brenda. "The Man Who Had All the Luck: Miller's Answer to
    <u>The Master Builder.</u>" <u>American Drama</u> 6.1 (1996). http://
    blues.fdl.uc.edu/www/amdrama/ (Retrieved 9 Sept. 1997).

Gopher site:

Goodwin, John E. "Elements of E-Text Style." 9 Aug. 1993. Internet.
    gopher://wiretap.spies.com/Library/estyle.txt (Retrieved 15
    Sept. 1997).

A SUMMARY OF THE PROCESS

Here, briefly, is a summary, step by step, of the stages that we have suggested you move through in preparing a paper about literature.

Stage One: Deciding what to write about

- Read the work straight through, thoughtfully. Make notes at the end on any points that caught your attention.
- Read the work again more slowly, pausing to think through all the parts you don't understand. When you finish, write a three- or four-sentence summary.
- Read the work again, carefully but quickly. Decide what you feel most strongly about in the work, and write down the one thing you would most want to explain to a friend about how the story, poem, or play works, or (if the work still puzzles you) the one question you would most like to be able to answer.
- Decide how the statement you made at the end of your third reading relates to the summary you wrote down after the second reading.
- Write a one-paragraph "promise" of what your paper is going to argue.

Stage Two: Planning and drafting your paper

- Read the work at least twice more, and make notes on anything that relates to your thesis.
- Read through all your notes so far, and for each write a sentence articulating how it relates to your thesis.
- Transfer all your notes to note cards of uniform size.
- Read through all your notes again, and record any new observations or ideas on additional note cards.
- Set aside your note cards for the moment, and make a brief outline of the major points you intend to make.
- Sort the note cards into piles corresponding to the major points in your outline. Sort the cards in each separate pile into the most likely order of their use in the paper.
- Make a more detailed outline (including the most significant examples) from your pile of note cards on each point.

- Reconsider your order of presentation, and make any necessary adjustments.
- Write a first draft.

Stage Three: Rewriting

-
- Go over your writing, word by word, sentence by sentence, and paragraph by paragraph, in draft after draft until your paper expresses your ideas clearly and concisely.

Stage Four: Final preparation

-
- If you have not been working on a computer, type or word-process your paper.
- Proofread carefully for errors of all kinds—spelling, typing, and so forth.
- Proofread again. Find your mistakes before someone else does.
- Congratulate yourself on a job well done.

Glossary

Within definitions, words that are set **boldface** are themselves defined in the glossary.

acting: the last of the four steps in **characterization** in a performed play.

action: an imagined event or series of events; an event may be verbal as well as physical, so that saying something or telling a story within the story may be an event.

allegory: as in **metaphor,** one thing (usually nonrational, abstract, religious) is implicitly spoken of in terms of something concrete, usually sensuous, but in an allegory the comparison is extended to include an entire work or large portion of a work.

alliteration: the repetition of initial consonant sounds through a sequence of words—for example, "While I nodded, nearly napping, . . ." from Edgar Allan Poe's "The Raven."

allusion: a reference—whether explicit or implicit, to history, the Bible, myth, literature, painting, music, and so on—that suggests the meaning or generalized implication of details in the story, poem, or play.

ambiguity: the use of a word or expression to mean more than one thing.

amphitheater: the design of classical Greek theaters, consisting of a stage area surrounded by a semicircle of tiered seats.

analogy: a comparison based on certain resemblances between things that are otherwise unlike.

anapestic: a metrical form in which each foot consists of two unstressed syllables followed by a stressed one.

antagonist: a neutral term for a **character** who opposes the leading male or female character. *See* **hero/heroine** and **protagonist.**

antihero: a leading **character** who is not, like a **hero,** perfect or even outstanding, but is rather ordinary and representative of the more or less average person.

archetype: a **plot** or **character** element that recurs in cultural or cross-cultural **myths** such as "the quest" or "descent into the underworld" or "scapegoat."

arena stage: a stage design in which the audience is seated all the way around the acting area; actors make their entrances and exits through the auditorium.

assonance: the repetition of vowel sounds in a sequence of words with different endings—for example, "The death of the poet was kept from his poems," from W. H. Auden's "In Memory of W. B. Yeats."

aubade: a morning song in which the coming of dawn is either celebrated or denounced as a nuisance.

auditor: someone other than the reader—a **character** within the fiction—to whom the story or "speech" is addressed.

authorial time: distinct from **plot time** and **reader time,** authorial time denotes the influence that the time in which the author was writing had upon the **conception** and **style** of the text.

ballad: a narrative poem that is, or originally was, meant to be sung. Characterized by repetition and often by a repeated refrain (recurrent phrase or series of phrases), ballads were originally a folk creation, transmitted orally from person to person and age to age.

ballad stanza: a common **stanza** form, consisting of a quatrain that alternates four-beat and three-beat lines; lines 1 and 3 are unrhymed iambic tetrameter (four beats), and lines 2 and 4 are rhymed iambic trimeter (three beats).

blank verse: the verse form most like everyday human speech, blank verse consists of unrhymed lines in iambic pentameter. Many of Shakespeare's plays are in blank verse.

canon: when applied to an individual author, *canon* means the sum total of works verifiably written by that author. When used generally, it means the range of works that a consensus of scholars, teachers, and readers of a particular time and culture consider "great" or "major." This second sense of the word is a matter of much debate since the literary canon in Europe and America has long been dominated by the works of white heterosexual men. During the last thirty years, the canon in the United States has expanded considerably to include more women and writers from various ethnic and racial backgrounds.

casting: the third step in the creation of a **character** on the stage; deciding which actors are to play which parts.

centered (central) consciousness: a limited third-person **point of view,** one tied to a single **character** throughout the story, often revealing his or her inner thoughts but unable to read the thoughts of others.

character: (1) a fictional personage who acts, appears, or is referred to in a work; (2) a combination of a person's qualities, especially moral qualities, so that such terms as "good" and "bad," "strong" and "weak," often apply. *See* **nature** and **personality.**

characterization: the fictional or artistic presentation of a fictional personage. A term like "a good character" can, then, be ambiguous—it may mean that the personage is virtuous or that he or she is well presented regardless of his or her characteristics or moral qualities.

chorus: in classical Greek plays, a group of actors who commented on and described the **action** of a play. Members of the chorus were often masked and relied alternatively on song, dance, and recitation to make their commentary.

classical unities: as derived from Aristotle's *Poetics,* the principles of structure that require a play to have one action that occurs in one place and within one day.

climax: also called the **turning point,** the third part of **plot structure,** the point at which the **action** stops rising and begins falling or reversing.

colloquial diction: a level of language in a work that approximates the speech of ordinary people. The language used by characters in Toni Cade Bambara's "Gorilla, My Love" is a good example.

comedy: a broad category of dramatic works that are intended primarily to entertain and amuse an audience. Comedies take many different forms, but they all share three basic characteristics: (1) the values that are expressed and that typically present the conflict within the play are social and determined by the general opinion of society (as opposed to universal and beyond the control of humankind, as in **tragedy**); (2) **characters** in comedies are often defined primarily in terms of their society and their role within it; (3) comedies often end with a restoration of social order in which one or more characters take a proper social role.

conception: the first step in the creation of any work of art, but especially used to indicate the first step in the creation of a dramatic **character,** whether for written text or performed play; the original idea, when the playwright first begins to construct—or even dream about—a **plot,** or the characters, **structure,** or **theme** that will be an element of the play.

conclusion: the fifth part of **plot structure,** the point at which the situation that was destabilized at the beginning of the story becomes stable once more.

concrete poetry: poetry that is shaped to look like an object. John Hollander's "A State of Nature," for example, is arranged to look like New York State. Also called **shaped verse.**

confessional poem: a relatively new (or recently defined) **kind** in which the speaker describes a confused, chaotic state of mind, which becomes a **metaphor** for the larger world.

conflict: a struggle between opposing forces, such as between two people, between a person and something in nature or society, or even between two drives, impulses, or parts of the self.

connotation: what is suggested by a word, apart from what it explicitly describes. *See* **denotation.**

controlling metaphors: **metaphors** that dominate or organize an entire poem. In Linda Pastan's "Marks," for example, the controlling metaphor is of marks (grades) as a way of talking about the speaker's performance of roles within her family.

conventions: standard or traditional ways of saying things in literary works, employed to achieve certain expected effects.

cosmic irony: implies that a god or fate controls and toys with human actions, feelings, lives, outcomes.

criticism: the evaluative or interpretive work written by professional interpreters of texts. It is "criticism" not because it is negative or corrective, but rather because those who write criticism ask hard, analytical, crucial or "critical" questions about the works they read.

culture: a broad and relatively indistinct term that implies a commonality of history and some cohesiveness of purpose within a group. One can speak of southern culture, for example, or urban culture, or American culture, or rock culture; at any one time, each of us belongs to a number of these cultures.

curiosity: the desire to know what is happening or has happened.

dactylic: the metrical pattern in which each foot consists of a stressed syllable followed by two unstressed ones.

denotation: a direct and specific meaning. *See* **connotation.**

descriptive structure: a textual organization determined by the requirements of describing someone or something.

diction: an author's choice of words.

discriminated occasion: the first specific event in a story, usually in the form of a specific scene.

discursive structure: a textual organization based on the form of a treatise, argument, or essay.

dramatic irony: a **plot** device in which a **character** holds a position or has an expectation that is reversed or fulfilled in a way that the character did not expect but that we, as readers or as audience members, have anticipated because our knowledge of events or individuals is more complete than the character's.

dramatic monologue: a monologue set in a specific situation and spoken to an imaginary audience.

dramatic structure: a textual organization based on a series of scenes, each of which is presented vividly and in detail.

dramatis personae: the list of **characters** that appears either in the play's program or at the top of the first page of the written play.

echo: a verbal reference that recalls a word, phrase, or sound in another text.

elegy: in classical times, any poem on any subject written in "elegiac" **meter;** since the Renaissance, usually a formal lament on the death of a particular person.

English sonnet: also called a **Shakespearean sonnet;** a **sonnet** form that divides the poem into three units of four lines each and a final unit of two lines (4+4+4+2 structure). Its classic rhyme scheme is *abab cdcd efef gg,* but there are variations.

epic: a poem that celebrates, in a continuous narrative, the achievements of mighty **heroes** and **heroines,** usually in founding a nation or developing a **culture,** and uses elevated language and a grand, high style.

epigram: originally any poem carved in stone (on tombstones, buildings, gates, and so forth), but in modern usage a very short, usually witty verse with a quick turn at the end.

existential character: a person, real or fictional, who, whatever his or her past or conditioning, can change by an act of will.

expectation: the anticipation of what is to happen next (*see* **curiosity** and **suspense**), what a **character** is like or how he or she will develop, what the **theme** or meaning of the story will prove to be, and so on.

exposition: that part of the **structure** that sets the scene, introduces and identifies **characters,** and establishes the situation at the beginning of a story or play. Additional exposition is often scattered throughout the work.

extended metaphor: a detailed and complex **metaphor** that extends over a long section of a work.

falling action: the fourth part of **plot structure,** in which the complications of the **rising action** are untangled.

farce: a play that is characterized by broad humor, wild antics, and often slapstick, pratfalls, or other physical humor.

figurative: usually applied to language that uses **figures of speech.** Figurative language heightens meaning by implicitly or explicitly representing something in terms of some other thing, the assumption being that the "other thing" will be more familiar to the reader.

figures of speech: comparisons in which something is pictured or figured in other, more familiar terms.

flashback: a **plot-structuring** device whereby a scene from the fictional past is inserted into the fictional present or dramatized out of order.

flat character: a fictional **character,** often but not always a minor character, who is relatively simple, who is presented as having few, though sometimes dominant, traits, and who thus does not change much in the course of a story. *See* **round character.**

focus: the point from which people, events, and other details in a story are viewed. *See* **point of view.**

formal diction: language that is lofty, dignified, and impersonal. *See* **colloquial diction** and **informal diction.**

free verse: poetry that is characterized by varying line lengths, lack of traditional **meter,** and nonrhyming lines.

genre: the largest category for classifying literature—fiction, poetry, drama. *See* **kind** and **subgenre.**

haiku: an unrhymed poetic form, Japanese in origin, that contains seventeen syllables arranged in three lines of five, seven, and five syllables, respectively.

hero/heroine: the leading male/female **character,** usually larger than life, sometimes almost godlike. *See* **antihero, protagonist,** and **villain.**

heroic couplet: rhymed pairs of lines in iambic pentameter.

history: the imaginary people, places, chronologically arranged events that we assume exist in the world of the author's imagination, a world from which he or she chooses and arranges or rearranges the story elements.

hyperbole: overstatement characterized by exaggerated language.

iambic: a metrical form in which each foot consists of an unstressed syllable followed by a stressed one.

imagery: broadly defined, any sensory detail or evocation in a work; more narrowly, the use of **figurative** language to evoke a feeling, to call to mind an idea, or to describe an object.

imitative structure: a textual organization that mirrors as exactly as possible the structure of something that already exists as an object and can be seen.

informal diction: language that is not as lofty or impersonal as **formal diction;** similar to everyday speech. *See* **colloquial diction,** which is one variety of informal diction.

initiation story: a kind of short story in which a **character**—often but not always a child or young person—first learns a significant, usually life-changing truth about the universe, society, people, himself or herself.

in medias res: "in the midst of things"; refers to opening a story in the middle of the **action,** necessitating filling in past details by **exposition** or **flashback.**

irony: a situation or statement characterized by a significant difference between what is expected or understood and what actually happens or is meant. *See* **cosmic irony** and **dramatic irony.**

Italian sonnet: a **sonnet** form that divides the poem into one section of eight lines and a second section of six lines, usually following the *abbaabba cdecde* rhyme scheme.

kind: a species or subcategory within a **subgenre; initiation story** is a subcategory of the subgenre *short story.*

limited point of view or **limited focus:** a perspective pinned to a single **character,** whether a first-person- or a third-person-centered consciousness, so that we cannot know for sure what is going on in the minds of other characters; thus, when the focal character leaves the room in a story we must go, too, and cannot know what is going on while our "eyes" or "camera" is gone. A variation on this, which generally has no name and is often lumped with the **omniscient point of view,** is the **point of view** that can wander like a camera from one character to another and close in or move back but cannot (or at least does not) get inside anyone's head, does not present from the inside any character's thoughts.

literary critics: professional "interpreters" (and often implicitly or explicitly evaluators) of literary texts.

litotes: a figure of speech that emphasizes its subject by conscious understatement. An example from common speech is to say "Not bad" as a form of high praise.

lyric: originally, poems meant to be sung to the accompaniment of a lyre; now, any short poem in which the **speaker** expresses intense personal emotion rather than describing a narrative or dramatic situation.

major characters: those **characters** whom we see and learn about the most.

meditation: a contemplation of some physical object as a way of reflecting upon some larger truth, often (but not necessarily) a spiritual one.

memory devices: also called **mnemonic devices;** these devices—including rhyme, repetitive phrasing, and **meter**—when part of the structure of a longer work, make that work easier to memorize.

message: a misleading term for **theme,** the central idea or statement of a story or area of inquiry or explanation, misleading because it suggests a simple, packaged statement that preexists and that explains the story.

metaphor: (1) one thing pictured as if it were something else, suggesting a likeness or **analogy** between them; (2) an implicit comparison or identification of one thing with another unlike itself without the use of a verbal signal. Sometimes used as a general term for **figure of speech.**

meter: the more or less regular pattern of stressed and unstressed syllables in a line of poetry. This is determined by the kind of "foot" (**iambic** and **dactylic,** for example) and by the number of feet per line (five feet=pentameter, six feet=hexameter, for example).

minor characters: those figures who fill out the story but who do not figure prominently in it.

mode: style, manner, way of proceeding, as in "tragic mode"; often used synonymously with **genre, kind,** and **subgenre.**

motif: a recurrent device, formula, or situation that deliberately connects a poem with common patterns of existing thought.

myth: like **allegory,** myth usually is symbolic and extensive, including an entire work or story. Though it no longer is necessarily specific to or pervasive in a single **culture—** individual authors may now be said to create myths—there is still a sense that myth is communal or cultural, while the symbolic can often be private or personal myths. Thus, stories that are more or less universally shared within a culture to explain its history and traditions are frequently called myths.

narrative structure: a textual organization based on sequences of connected events usually presented in a straightforward chronological framework.

narrator: the **character** who "tells" the story.

nature: as it refers to a person—"it is his (or her) nature"—a rather old term suggesting something inborn, inherent, fixed, and thus predictable. *See* **character, personality.**

occasional poem: a poem written about or for a specific occasion, public or private.

omniscient point of view: also called **unlimited focus;** a perspective that can be seen from one **character**'s view, then another's, then another's, or can be moved in or out of the mind of any character at any time. Organization in which the reader has access to the perceptions and thoughts of all the characters in the story.

onomatopoeia: a word capturing or approximating the sound of what it describes; *buzz* is a good example.

orchestra: in classical Greek theater, a semicircular area used mostly for dancing by the **chorus.**

overstatement: exaggerated language; also called **hyperbole.**

oxymoron: a **figure of speech** that combines two apparently contradictory elements, as in "wise fool" ("sophomore").

parable: a short fiction that illustrates an explicit moral lesson.

paradox: a statement that seems contradictory but may actually be true, as in "That I may rise and stand, o'erthrow me," from Donne's "Batter My Heart, three-personed God."

parody: a work that imitates another work for comic effect by exaggerating the style and changing the content of the original.

pastoral: a poem (also called an eclogue, a bucolic, or an idyll) that describes the simple life of country folk, usually shepherds who live a timeless, painless (and sheepless) life in a world that is full of beauty, music, and love.

pastoral play: a play that features the sort of idyllic world described in the definition for **pastoral.**

persona: the voice or figure of the author who tells and structures the story and who may or may not share the values of the actual author.

personality: that which distinguishes or individualizes a person; its qualities are judged not so much in terms of their moral value, as in **character,** but as to whether they are "pleasing" or "unpleasing."

personification (or *prosopopeia*): treating an abstraction as if it were a person by endowing it with humanlike qualities.

Petrarchan sonnet: also called **Italian sonnet;** a **sonnet** form that divides the poem into one section of eight lines and a second section of six lines, usually following the *abbaabba cdecde* rhyme scheme or, more loosely, an *abbacddc* pattern.

plot/plot structure: the arrangement of the **action.**

plot summary: a description of the arrangement of the **action** in the order in which it actually appears in a story. The term is popularly used to mean the description of the history, or chronological order, of the action as it would have appeared in reality. It is important to indicate exactly in which sense you are using the term.

plot time: the temporal setting in which the **action** takes place in a story or play.

point of view: also called **focus;** the point from which people, events, and other details in a story are viewed. This term is sometimes used to include both focus and **voice.**

precision: exactness, accuracy of language or description.

presentation: the second step in the creation of a **character** for the written text and the performed play; the representation of the character by the playwright in the words and actions specified in the text.

props: articles and objects used on the stage.

proscenium arch: an arch over the front of a stage; the proscenium serves as a "frame" for the **action** on stage.

protagonist: the main **character** in a work, who may be male or female, heroic or not heroic. *See* **antagonist, antihero,** and hero/heroine. *Protagonist* is the most neutral term.

protest poem: a poetic attack, usually quite direct, on allegedly unjust institutions or social injustices.

psychological realism: a modification of the concept of **realism,** or telling it like it is, which recognizes that what is real to the individual is that which he or she perceives. It is the ground for the use of the **centered consciousness,** or the first-person narrator, since both of these present reality only as something perceived by the focal **character.**

reader time: the actual time it takes a reader to read a work.

realism: the practice in literature of attempting to describe nature and life without idealization and with attention to detail.

red herring: a false lead, something that misdirects expectations.

referential: when used to describe a poem, play, or story, *referential* means making textual use of a specific historical moment or event or, more broadly, making use of external, "natural," or "actual" detail.

reflective/meditative structure: a textual organization based on the pondering of a **subject, theme,** or event, and letting the mind play with it, skipping from one sound to another, or to related thoughts or objects as the mind receives them.

rhetorical trope: traditional **figure of speech,** used for specific persuasive effects.

rhythm: the modulation of weak and strong (or stressed and unstressed) elements in the flow of speech. In most poetry written before the twentieth century, rhythm was often expressed in regular, metrical forms; in prose and in **free verse,** rhythm is present but in a much less predictable and regular manner.

rising action: the second of the five parts of **plot structure,** in which events complicate the situation that existed at the beginning of a work, intensifying the **conflict** or introducing new conflict.

rite of passage: a ritual or ceremony marking an individual's passing from one stage or state to a more advanced one, or an event in one's life that seems to have such significance; a formal initiation. Rites of passage are common in **initiation stories.**

round characters: complex **characters,** often **major characters,** who can grow and change and "surprise convincingly"—that is, act in a way that you did not expect from what had gone before but now accept as possible, even probable, and "realistic."

sarcasm: a form of **verbal irony** in which apparent praise is actually harshly or bitterly critical.

satire: a literary work that holds up human failings to ridicule and censure.

selection: the process by which authors leave out some aspects of the **history** of the story or play for dramatic or thematic effect.

sestina: an elaborate verse **structure** written in **blank verse** that consists of six **stanzas** of six lines each followed by a three-line stanza. The final words of each line in the first stanza appear in variable order in the next five stanzas, and are repeated in the middle and at the end of the three lines in the final stanza, as in Elizabeth Bishop's "Sestina."

set: the design, decoration, and scenery of the stage during a play.

setting: the time and place of the **action** in a story, poem, or play.

Shakespearean sonnet: also called an **English sonnet;** a **sonnet** form that divides the poem into three units of four lines each and a final unit of two lines (4+4+4+2 structure). Its classic rhyme scheme is *abab cdcd efef gg,* but there are other variations.

shaped verse: another name for **concrete poetry;** poetry that is shaped to look like an object.

simile: a direct, explicit comparison of one thing to another, usually using the words *like* or *as* to draw the connection. *See* **metaphor.**

situation: the context of the literary work's **action,** what is happening when the story, poem, or play begins.

skene: a low building in the back of the stage area in classical Greek theaters. It represented the palace or temple in front of which the **action** took place.

soliloquy: a monologue in which the **character** in a play is alone and speaking only to him- or herself.

sonnet: a fixed verse form consisting of fourteen lines usually in iambic pentameter. *See* **Italian sonnet** and **Shakespearean sonnet.**

spatial setting: the place of a poem, story, or play.

speaker: the person, not necessarily the author, who is the voice of a poem.

Spenserian stanza: a **stanza** that consists of eight lines of iambic pentameter (five feet) followed by a ninth line of iambic hexameter (six feet). The rhyme scheme is *ababbcbcc.*

stanza: a section of a poem demarcated by extra line spacing. Some distinguish between a stanza, a division marked by a single pattern of **meter** or rhyme, and a verse paragraph, a division marked by thought rather than pattern.

stereotype: a **characterization** based on conscious or unconscious assumptions that some one aspect, such as gender, age, ethnic or national identity, religion, occupation, marital status, and so on are predictably accompanied by certain **character** traits, actions, even values.

stock character: one who appears in a number of stories or plays such as the cruel stepmother, the braggart, and so forth.

structure: the organization or arrangement of the various elements in a work.

style: a distinctive manner of expression; each author's style is expressed through his/ her **diction, rhythm, imagery,** and so on.

subgenre: division within the category of a **genre;** *novel, novella,* and *short story* are subgenres of the genre *fiction.*

subject: (1) the concrete and literal description of what a story is about; (2) the general or specific area of concern of a poem; also called **topic;** (3) also used in fiction commentary to denote a **character** whose inner thoughts and feelings are recounted.

suspense: the expectation of and doubt about what is going to happen next.

syllabic verse: a form in which the poet establishes a precise number of syllables to a line and repeats it in subsequent **stanzas.**

symbol: a person, place, thing, event, or pattern in a literary work that designates itself and at the same time figuratively represents or "stands for" something else. Often the thing or idea represented is more abstract, general, non- or superrational, the symbol more concrete and particular.

symbolic poem: a poem in which the use of **symbols** is so pervasive and internally consistent that the larger referential world is distanced, if not forgotten.

syntax: the way words are put together to form phrases, clauses, and sentences.

technopaegnia: the art of "shaped" poems in which the visual force is supposed to work spiritually or magically.

temporal setting: the time of a story, poem, or play.

terza rima: a verse form consisting of three-line **stanzas** in which the second line of each rhymes with the first and third of the next.

theme: (1) a generalized, abstract paraphrase of the inferred central or dominant idea or concern of a work; (2) the statement a poem makes about its subject.

thrust stage: a stage design that allows the audience to sit around three sides of the major acting area.

tone: the attitude a literary work takes toward its **subject** and **theme.**

topic: (1) the concrete and literal description of what a story is about; (2) the general or specific area of concern of a poem. Also called **subject.**

tradition: an inherited, established, or customary practice.

traditional symbols: **symbols** that, through years of usage, have acquired an agreed-upon significance, an accepted meaning. *See* **archetype.**

tragedy: a drama in which a **character** (usually a good and noble person of high rank) is brought to a disastrous end in his or her confrontation with a superior force (fortune, the gods, social forces, universal values), but also comes to understand the meaning of his or her deeds and to accept an appropriate punishment. Often the **protagonist**'s downfall is a direct result of a fatal flaw in his or her character.

trochaic: a metrical form in which each foot consists of a stressed syllable followed by an unstressed one.

turning point: the third part of **plot structure,** the point at which the **action** stops rising and begins falling or reversing. Also called **climax.**

unity of time: one of the three unities of drama as described by Aristotle in his *Poetics.* Unity of time refers to the limitation of a play's action to a short period of time—

usually the time it takes to present the play or, at any rate, no longer than a day. *See* **classical unities.**

unlimited focus: also called **omniscient point of view;** a perspective that can be seen from one **character**'s view, then another's, then another's, or can be moved in or out of the mind of any character at any time. Organization in which the reader has access to the perceptions and thoughts of all the characters in the story.

unreliable narrator: a **speaker** or **voice** whose vision or version of the details of a story are consciously or unconsciously deceiving; such a **narrator**'s version is usually subtly undermined by details in the story or the reader's general knowledge of facts outside the story. If, for example, the narrator were to tell you that Columbus was Spanish and that he discovered America in the fourteenth century when his ship the *Golden Hind* landed on the coast of Florida near present-day Gainesville, you might not trust other things he tells you.

verbal irony: a statement in which the literal meaning differs from the implicit meaning. *See* **dramatic irony.**

verse paragraph: *see* **stanza.**

villain: the one who opposes the hero and heroine—that is, the "bad guy." *See* **antagonist** and **hero/heroine.**

villanelle: a verse form consisting of nineteen lines divided into six **stanzas**—five tercets (three-line stanzas) and one quatrain (four-line stanza). The first and third lines of the first tercet rhyme, and this rhyme is repeated through each of the next four tercets and in the last two lines of the concluding quatrain. The villanelle is also known for its repetition of select lines. A good example of a twentieth-century villanelle is Dylan Thomas's "Do Not Go Gentle into That Good Night."

voice: the acknowledged or unacknowledged source of the words of the story; the **speaker;** the "person" telling the story.

word order: the positioning of words in relation to one another.

Biographical Sketches[1]

Louisa May Alcott (1832–1888)

An ardent abolitionist and advocate of the suffrage movement, Alcott was born in Germantown, Pennsylvania, and grew up in the close-knit community of transcendental philosophers, including Ralph Waldo Emerson and Henry David Thoreau, located in Concord, Massachusetts. Concerned that her father's controversial teaching methods and frequent moves could not guarantee the family a steady income, Alcott took on odd jobs in order to earn money, and, drawing upon her experience writing plays for family performances, she began to write professionally. Alcott's first poem was published in 1852, and it was followed by a full-length book, *Flower Fables*, in 1855. Alcott's letters recounting her experiences as a nurse during the Civil War were collected in *Hospital Sketches* (1863), but it wasn't until the publication of the first volume of *Little Women* in 1868 that Alcott earned a devoted following and financial security. Written in scarcely two and a half months and based upon Alcott's own childhood, *Little Women* was followed by more books focusing on children and young adults, including *An Old Fashioned Girl* (1870), *Little Men* (1871), and *Eight Cousins* (1874).

Agha Shahid Ali (b. 1949)

Born in New Delhi, India, and a graduate of the University of Kashmir, Srinagar, Ali has written poetry in English since the age of ten. He returned to New Delhi, where he received an M.A. from the University of Delhi in 1970 before leaving India to pursue advanced degrees in the United States, including an M.F.A. from the University of Arizona, Tucson (1985), and a Ph.D. from Pennsylvania State University (1984). The recipient of Guggenheim and Ingram-Merrill fellowships, he has taught at Hamilton College and is currently the director of the M.F.A. program in creative writing at the University of Massachusetts, Amherst. Ali is the author of scholarly works, such as *T. S. Eliot as Editor* (1986), in addition to his volumes of poetry, which include *A Walk through the Yellow Pages* (1986), *The Half-Inch Himalayas* (1987), *A Nostalgist's Map of America* (1991), and *The Country without a Post Office* (1997).

Margaret Atwood (b. 1939)

Atwood spent her first eleven years in sparsely populated areas of northern Ontario and Quebec, where her father worked as an entomologist. After her education at the University of Toronto and Harvard, she held various jobs in Canada, America, England, and Italy. Atwood published her first poem when she was just nineteen, and

1. Biographical sketches are included for all fiction writers and playwrights, and for poets represented by two or more poems.

she has won numerous prizes for her poetry as well as her fiction, which has become increasingly political over the years. Her novels include *The Edible Woman* (1969), *Surfacing* (1972), *Lady Oracle* (1976), *Life before Man* (1979), *Bodily Harm* (1982), *The Handmaid's Tale* (1985), *Cat's Eye* (1988), *Robber Bride* (1993), and *Alias Grace* (1996). Many of her stories have been collected in *Dancing Girls and Other Stories* (1978), *Murder in the Dark* (1983), *Bluebeard's Egg* (1983), and *Wilderness Tips* (1991).

W. H. Auden (1907–1973)

A prolific writer of poems, plays, essays, and criticism, Wystan Hugh Auden was born in York, England, to a medical officer and a nurse. Auden studied at Oxford and taught at various universities in the United States, where he became a naturalized citizen in 1946. He won the Pulitzer Prize in 1948 for his collection of poems, *Age of Anxiety,* and is regarded as a poet of political and intellectual conscience. His long-term relationship with poet Chester Kallman has been the subject of several recent biographies.

James Baldwin (1924–1987)

Baldwin was for some time a leading literary spokesman for black Americans. Born in Harlem, long a resident of France, he first attracted critical attention with two extraordinary novels, *Go Tell It on the Mountain* (1953) and *Giovanni's Room* (1956), which dealt, somewhat autobiographically, with religious awakening (Baldwin was a minister at fourteen but later left his church) and the anguish of being black and homosexual in a white and heterosexual society. Baldwin was also a dramatist and an outstanding essayist, his best-known nonfiction prose being *Notes of a Native Son* (1955), *Nobody Knows My Name* (1961), and *The Fire Next Time* (1963), aimed at unraveling the repressive myths of white society and at healing the disastrous estrangement he found in the lives of black people in America. His stories are collected in *Going to Meet the Man* (1965), from which "Sonny's Blues" is taken.

Toni Cade Bambara (1939–1995)

Born in New York City, Bambara grew up in Harlem and Bedford-Stuyvesant, two of its poorest neighborhoods. She began writing while still a child. After graduating from Queens College, she worked at various jobs while studying for her M.A. at the City College of New York, writing fiction all the while in "the predawn in-betweens." Bambara began to publish her stories in 1962. She had also been a dancer, teacher, editor, and critic, and had worked in psychiatric and drug therapy, youth organizing, and settlement houses. Her work includes two anthologies, *The Black Woman* (1970) and *Stories for Black Folks* (1971), and two collections of stories, *Gorilla My Love* (1972) and *The Sea Birds Are Still Alive* (1977). She also wrote two novels, *The Salt Eaters* (1980) and *If Blessing Comes* (1987).

Charles Baxter (b. 1947)

Baxter was born in Minneapolis and teaches at the University of Michigan in Ann Arbor. His short-story collections include *Harmony of the World* (1984), *A Relative Stranger* (1990), and *Believers* (1997), and his novels are *First Light* (1987) and *Shadow Play* (1993).

Ann Beattie (b. 1947)

Beattie grew up in the Washington suburb of Chevy Chase, Maryland. She received a B.A. from American University and went on to the University of Connecticut as a graduate student in English literature. Beattie's first published story, "A Rose for Judy Garland's Casket," appeared in 1972, and after many rejections she began publishing in the *New Yorker* shortly thereafter. Beattie's stories have made her a spokesperson for a generation that came of age in the 1960s as they adapt to or are baffled and worn out by the oncoming years. Many of the stories have been collected in *Distortions* (1976), *Secrets and Surprises* (1979), *Jacklighting* (1981), *The Burning House* (1982), *Where You'll Find Me* (1986), and *What Was Mine: Stories* (1990). Her novels are *Chilly Scenes of Winter* (1976), *Falling in Place* (1980), *Love Always* (1985), *Picturing Will* (1990), *Another You* (1995), and *My Life, Starring Dara Falcon* (1997).

Ambrose Bierce (1842–1914?)

The tenth child of a poor Ohio family, Bierce rose during the Civil War to the rank of major, was twice wounded, and was cited fifteen times for bravery. He stayed in the army for a time after the war, then was a journalist in California and London, where his boisterous western mannerisms and savage wit made him a celebrity and earned him the name "Bitter Bierce." He published *Tales of Soldiers and Civilians* (later called *In the Midst of Life*) (1891) and another volume of short stories, *Can Such Things Be?* (1893). The death of his two sons in 1889 and 1901, along with his divorce in 1891, might well have led him to Mexico, where he reportedly rode with Pancho Villa's revolutionaries. He disappeared and is presumed to have died there. Bierce is well known as the author of *The Cynic's Wordbook* (later called *The Devil's Dictionary*) (1906), but his short stories are considered his finest achievement.

Elizabeth Bishop (1911–1979)

Born in Worcester, Massachusetts, Bishop endured the death of her father before she was a year old and the institutionalization of her mother when she was five. Bishop was raised by her maternal grandmother in Nova Scotia, then by her paternal grandparents back in Worcester. Bishop attended Vassar College and met the poet Marianne Moore, who encouraged her to give up plans for medical school to pursue the life of a poet. Bishop traveled through Canada, Europe, and South America, finally settling in Rio de Janeiro, where she lived for nearly twenty years. Bishop produced only four volumes of poetry: *North and South* (1946); *A Cold Spring* (1955), which won the Pulitzer Prize; *Questions of Travel* (1965); and *Geography III* (1976), which won the National Book Critics' Circle Award.

William Blake (1757–1828)

In defense of his unorthodox and original work, Blake once said: "That which can be made Explicit to the Idiot . . . is not worth my care." The son of a London haberdasher, he studied drawing at ten and at fourteen was apprenticed to an engraver for seven years. After a first book of poems, *Poetical Sketches* (1783), he began experimenting with what he called "illuminated printing"—the words and pictures of each page were engraved in relief on copper and the printed sheets partly colored by hand—a laborious and time-consuming process that resulted in books of singular beauty, no two of which were exactly alike. His great *Songs of Innocence* (1789) and *Songs of Experi-*

ence (1794) were printed in this manner, as were his increasingly mythic and prophetic books, which include *The Marriage of Heaven and Hell* (1793), *The Four Zoas* (1803), *Milton* (1804), and *Jerusalem* (1809). Blake devoted his later life to pictorial art, illustrating *The Canterbury Tales,* the Book of Job, and *The Divine Comedy,* on which he was hard at work when he died.

Roo Borson (b. 1952)

While considered a Canadian poet, Ruth Elizabeth Borson was born in Berkeley, California. She later attended the University of California at Santa Barbara and earned her B.A. in 1973 from Gordon College. Four years later, she published her first collection of poetry, *Landfall,* in addition to receiving her M.F.A. from the University of British Columbia, where she was awarded the Macmillan Prize for Poetry. Borson's poetry suggests what she calls the "intricacy of the physical world" as it recognizes the powers of sensuality and memory. She has published a number of collections, including *The Whole Night Coming Home* (1984) and *Intent, or the Weight of the World* (1989).

Gwendolyn Brooks (b. 1917)

Brooks was born in Topeka, Kansas, and was raised in Chicago, where she began writing poetry at the age of seven. Her formal training began at the Southside Community Art Center, and she produced her first book of poems, *A Street in Bronzeville,* shortly after, in 1945. Her second book of poems, *Annie Allen* (1949), won Brooks the distinction of being the first African American to win the Pulitzer Prize for Poetry. Brooks's early poetry concentrated on what Langston Hughes called the "ordinary aspects of black life," but her work was transformed in the 1960s and Brooks became a passionate advocate for African American consciousness and activism.

Robert Browning (1812–1889)

Born in London, Browning was an aspiring but unknown poet and playwright when he met the already-famous poet Elizabeth Barrett. After their elopement in 1846, the Brownings moved to Italy, where Elizabeth Barrett Browning authored the chronicle of their love, *Sonnets from the Portuguese* (1850). Browning wrote most of his great poems during this period, and after his wife's death in 1861 he returned to England and began to establish his own literary reputation for his fine dramatic monologues.

John Cheever (1912–1982)

Cheever was born in Quincy, Massachusetts. His formal education ended when he was expelled from Thayer Academy at the age of seventeen; thereafter he devoted himself completely to fiction writing, except for brief interludes of teaching at Barnard College and the University of Iowa, and script-writing for television. Cheever published his first story when he was sixteen, and until his first novel, *The Wapshot Chronicle,* won the National Book Award in 1958, he was known primarily as a superb and prolific writer of short stories. Built around a strong moral core and tinged with melancholy nostalgia for the past, they form a running commentary on the tensions, manners, and crippled aspirations of urban and suburban life. Many have won awards, including the O. Henry Award in 1956 for "The Country Husband." *The Stories of John Cheever* (1978) won the Pulitzer Prize.

Anton Chekhov (1860–1904)

Chekhov was born in Taganrog, a small town in southern Russia. After attending medical school at Moscow University, he began practicing medicine in 1884, while writing short stories, jokes, and plays to support his family. His writing was well received, and he left medicine to write full time. Stanislavsky was the first to direct Chekhov's *The Seagull* (1896) and *The Cherry Orchard* (1903), which he adapted as a tragedy though Chekhov considered it a comedy. Along with these plays, he wrote a number of other realistic dramas dealing with turn-of-the-century Russian life, including *The Three Sisters* (1901).

Kate Chopin (1851–1904)

Born Katherine O'Flaherty in St. Louis, Missouri, Chopin moved to Louisiana when she married Oscar Chopin in 1870. She did not begin writing until after her husband's death, but produced many short stories, collected in *Bayou Folk* (1894) and *A Night in Acadie* (1897), and the now-classic novel *The Awakening* (1899).

Judith Ortiz Cofer (b. 1952)

Born in 1952 in Hormigueros, Puerto Rico, Cofer spent her childhood in both Puerto Rico and Patterson, New Jersey, where her father's family lived. This bicultural childhood is a common theme in both her poems and fiction. Cofer attended Augusta College in Georgia and received her M.A. in English from Florida Atlantic University. She received a fellowship to study at Oxford and subsequent scholarships to the Bread Loaf Writers' Conference, where she taught for a number of years. Her first collection of poetry, *Peregrina* (1985), won the Riverstone International Poetry Competition, and in 1989 Cofer was a National Endowment for the Arts Fellow in Poetry. Her novel, *The Line of the Sun,* was published in 1989, and her most recent work, a collection of poetry and essays, is entitled *The Latin Deli* (1993).

Samuel Taylor Coleridge (1772–1834)

Born in the small town of Ottery St. Mary in rural Devonshire, England, Coleridge was one of the greatest and most original of the nineteenth-century Romantic poets. He wrote three of the most haunting poems in the English tradition—*The Rime of the Ancient Mariner* (1798), *Christabel* (1816), and *Kubla Khan* (1816)—as well as immensely influential literary criticism and a revolutionary treatise on biology, *Hints towards the Formation of a More Comprehensive Theory of Life.* In 1795, in the midst of a failed experiment to establish a "Pantisocracy" (his form of ideal community), he met William Wordsworth, and in 1798 they published together their *Lyrical Ballads,* which was to influence the course of English Romanticism for decades to come. Coleridge's physical ailments, addiction to opium, and profound sense of despair have to this day shaped our sense of the poet suffering for the sake of art.

Richard Connell (1893–1949)

Connell, like Ernest Hemingway, began his writing career as a journalist. At the age of sixteen, he was city editor of his native *Poughkeepsie News-Press;* later he was editor of both the *Crimson* and the *Lampoon* at Harvard, from which he graduated in 1915. After World War I, he left his New York job as an advertising editor to become a freelance writer, traveling to Paris and London and finally settling in Beverly Hills, California. His works include volumes of short stories—*Apes and Angels* (1924), *The Sin of Monsieur Pettipon* (1925), *Variety* (1925), and *Ironies* (1930)—and novels: *Mad Lover* (1927), *Murder at Sea* (1929), *Playboy* (1936), and *What Ho!* (1937).

Joseph Conrad (1857–1924)

Jozeph Teodor Konrad Nalecz Korzeniowski was born in Berdyczew, Polish Ukraine. At five he accompanied his parents into exile in northern Russia and later near Kiev; he was left an orphan at eleven. Before he was seventeen, he was off to Marseilles, making several trips to the West Indies as an apprentice seaman. After some veiled troubles in France, involving gambling debts and an apparent suicide attempt, he sailed on a British ship, landed in England in 1878, and spent the next sixteen years in the British merchant service, rising to master in 1886, the year he became a British subject. In 1890, he worked on a boat that sailed up the Congo, the inspiration for *Heart of Darkness* (1899). He began writing in 1889 but did not publish his first novel, *Almayer's Folly,* until 1896. Though a successful writer, he was not truly popular or financially independent until the publication of *Chance* in 1912–1913. Among his major novels are *The Nigger of the "Narcissus"* (1897), *Lord Jim* (1900), *Nostromo* (1904), *Under Western Eyes* (1910), and *Victory* (1915). His short-story collections include *Tales of Unrest* (1898), *Typhoon and Other Stories* (1903), *'Twixt Land and Sea* (1912), from which "The Secret Sharer" is taken, and *Within the Tides: Tales* (1915).

Wendy Cope (b. 1945)

Born in Kent, England, Cope studied history and learned to play the guitar at Oxford University. While working as a primary-school teacher, she began writing poetry. Her first volume, *Making Cocoa for Kingsley Amis,* was published in 1986, and the following year she received a Cholmondeley Award for Poetry. Her most recent collection, *Serious Concerns* (1992), includes her trademark optimistic and witty verses. Cope has also published a children's book and a narrative poem, *The River Girl* (1991), commissioned for performance.

E. E. Cummings (1894–1962)

Cummings's variety of modernism was distinguished by its playful sense of humor, its formal experimentation, its lyrical directness, and above all its celebration of the individual against mass society. Born in Cambridge, Massachusetts, the son of a Congregationalist minister, Edward Estlin Cummings attended Harvard University, where he wrote poetry in the Pre-Raphaelite and Metaphysical traditions. He joined the ambulance corps in France the day after the United States entered World War I and was imprisoned by his own side for his outspoken letters and disdain for bureaucracy; he transmuted the experience into his first literary success, *The Enormous Room* (1922). After the war, Cummings established himself as a poet and artist in Greenwich Village, made frequent trips to France and New Hampshire, and showed little interest in wealth or his growing celebrity.

James Dickey (1923–1997)

Dickey did not become seriously interested in poetry until he joined the Air Force in 1942. When he returned from World War II, he earned a B.A. and an M.A. at Vanderbilt University, publishing his first poem in *Sewanee Review* in his senior year. Since the publication of his first book of poems, *Into the Stone* (1960), Dickey, while primarily a poet, engaged in diverse careers ranging from advertising writer and novelist to poetry teacher at various universities. His 1965 collection, *Buckdancer's Choice*, received the National Book Award, and from 1967 to 1969 Dickey was Consultant in Poetry to the Library of Congress. He is more popularly known for his best-selling novel, *Deliverance* (1970), which he later adapted for Hollywood. Most recently, he published *The Whole Motion: Collected Poems 1949–1992* (1992) and a novel, *To the White Sea* (1993).

Emily Dickinson (1830–1886)

From childhood on, Dickinson's life was sequestered and obscure. Yet her verse had a power and influence that has traveled far beyond the cultured yet relatively circumscribed environment in which she lived her life: her room, her father's house, her family, a few close friends, and the small town of Amherst, Massachusetts. Indeed, along with Walt Whitman, her far more public contemporary, she all but invented American poetry. Born in Amherst, the daughter of a respected lawyer and revered father ("His heart was pure and terrible," she once wrote), Dickinson studied for less than a year at the Mount Holyoke Female Seminary, returning permanently to Amherst. In later life she became more and more of a recluse, dressing in white, seeing no visitors, yet working without stint at her poems—nearly eighteen hundred in all, only a few of which were published during her lifetime.

Richard Dokey (b. 1933)

A native of Stockton, California, and a graduate of the University of California, Berkeley, Dokey has worked as a laborer on a railroad, in a shipyard, for a soft-drink bottling company, and for an ink factory, but now teaches philosophy at San Joachin Delta College in Stockton, California. His works include *August Heat* (1982), *Funeral: A Play* (1982), and *Sánchez and Other Stories* (1981). His novel, *The Adidas Kid,* was published in 1993.

John Donne (1572–1631)

The first and greatest of what came to be known as the "Metaphysical" school of poets, Donne wrote in a style, revolutionary at the time, that combined highly intellectual conceits with complex, compressed phrasing. Born into an old Roman Catholic family at a time when Catholics were subject to constant harassment, Donne quietly abandoned his religion and had a brilliant early career until a politically disastrous marriage ruined his worldly hopes and forced him to struggle for years to support a large and growing family; impoverished and despairing, he even wrote a treatise (*Biathanatos*) on the lawfulness of suicide. King James (who had ambitions for him as a preacher) eventually forced Donne to take Anglican orders in 1615, and indeed he became one of the great sermonizers of his day, rising to dean of St. Paul's Cathedral in 1621. Donne's private devotions were published in 1624, and he continued to write sacred poetry until a few years before his death.

Rita Dove (b. 1952)

When Dove won the 1987 Pulitzer Prize for Poetry for *Thomas and Beulah* (1986), she became the second African American poet (after Gwendolyn Brooks in 1950) to receive such high recognition. A native of Akron, Ohio, Dove attended Miami University in Ohio, studied for a year in West Germany as a Fulbright scholar, and received an M.F.A. in creative writing from the University of Iowa. She taught creative writing at Arizona State University and is now a professor of English at the University of Virginia as well as an associate editor of *Callaloo*, the journal of African American and African arts and letters. Dove's books include *The Yellow House on the Corner* (1980), *Museum* (1983), *Grace Notes* (1989), and *Mother Love* (1995). In 1993, Dove was appointed Poet Laureate of the United States by the Library of Congress.

John Dryden (1631–1700)

Called "the father of English criticism" by Samuel Johnson, Dryden was a prolific poet and dramatist. He attended Trinity College, Cambridge, where he took his A.B. in 1654, and for most of his career, Dryden wrote nondramatic, occasional, and public poems, celebrating historical moments. In 1667, he wrote "Annus Mirabilis," which marked England's "year of wonders." During his middle years, Dryden focused mostly on creating popular drama and literary criticism. In 1677, he adapted Shakespeare's *Antony and Cleopatra* into a play called *All for Love,* and in "An Essay of Dramatic Poesy" (1668), he outlined new theoretical principles for drama. That same year he was named England's Poet Laureate. Later in his career, Dryden became known for his political satires, like the scathing mock-heroic "Mac Flecknoe" (1682) and "Absalom and Achitophel" (1681).

Paul Laurence Dunbar (1872–1906)

Hailed as "the Poet Laureate of the Negro race" by Booker T. Washington, Dunbar was born the son of former slaves in Dayton, Ohio. He attended a white high school, where he showed an early talent for writing and was elected class president, but was employed as an elevator operator after being unable to fund further education. Writing poems and newspaper articles when he could find the time, Dunbar took out a loan to subsidize the printing of his first book, *Oak and Ivy* (1893). With the subsequent publication of *Majors and Minors* (1895) and *Lyrics of Lowly Life* (1896), his reputation as a poet grew, and he was able to support himself by writing and lecturing in the United States and England. Acclaimed during his lifetime for his lyrical use of black dialect and his tributes to the experiences of rural blacks in volumes such as *Candle-Lightin' Time* (1902) and *Lyrics of Sunshine and Shadow* (1905), Dunbar was later criticized for adopting white literary conventions and frequently pandering to racist images of slaves and ex-slaves. The author of four novels and four books of short stories in addition to collections of poetry, Dunbar began to write frankly about racial injustice in works such as *The Sport of the Gods* (1903) and *The Fourth of July and Race Outrages,* published in the *New York Times* in 1903, shortly before his early death from tuberculosis.

T. S. Eliot (1888–1965)

Thomas Stearns Eliot—from his formally experimental and oblique writings to his brilliant arguments in defense of "orthodoxy" and "tradition"—dominated the world of English poetry between the world wars. Born in St. Louis, Missouri, of New England stock, Eliot studied literature and philosophy at Harvard and later in France and Germany. He came to England in 1914, read Greek philosophy at Oxford, and published his first major poem, "The Love Song of J. Alfred Prufrock," the next year. In 1922, with the help of his great supporter and adviser, Ezra Pound, Eliot published his long poem, *The Waste Land* (1922), which would profoundly influence a whole generation of poets. In his later work, particularly the *Four Quartets* (completed in 1945), Eliot explored religious questions in a quieter, more controlled idiom. He was awarded the Nobel Prize for Literature in 1948.

Louise Erdrich (b. 1954)

Born in Little Falls, Minnesota, of German-American and Chippewa descent, Erdrich grew up in Wahpeton, North Dakota, as a member of the Turtle Mountain Band of Chippewa, and attended Dartmouth College. After graduation, she returned to teach in North Dakota's Poetry in the Schools Program. She received an M.A. in creative writing from Johns Hopkins University in 1979. In the same year, *Jacklight,* a collection of poetry, was published. Her first novel, *Love Medicine* (1984), has been praised as a landmark work in its depiction of the lives of contemporary Native Americans, and was the winner of the National Book Critics' Circle Award for Fiction. An expanded version was published in 1993. Erdrich has also published another collection of poetry, *Baptism of Desire* (1989), and several novels, including *Love Medicine, The Beet Queen* (1986), *Tracks* (1988), *The Bingo Palace* (1993), and *Tales of Burning Love* (1996), and jointly authored *The Crown of Columbus* (1991) with her husband, Michael Dorris.

William Faulkner (1897–1962)

Faulkner spent almost his entire life in his native state of Mississippi. He left high school without graduating, joined the Royal Canadian Air Force in 1918, and in the mid-1920s lived briefly in New Orleans, where he was encouraged by Sherwood Anderson. He then spent a few miserable months as a clerk in a New York bookstore, published a collection of poems, *The Marble Faun,* in 1924, and took a long walking tour of Europe in 1925. In later years he made several visits to Hollywood, writing a screenplay for *The Big Sleep,* among others, and spent his last years in Charlottesville, Virginia. With the publication of *Sartoris* in 1929, Faulkner began a cycle of works interrelated by his fictional Yoknapatawpha County and the reappearance of characters or families from work to work. These include *As I Lay Dying* (1930), *Light in August* (1932), *Absalom, Absalom!* (1936), *The Unvanquished* (1939), *The Hamlet* (1940), and *Go Down, Moses* (1942). His short fiction can be found in *The Collected Stories of William Faulkner* (1950). He received the Nobel Prize for Literature in 1950.

Timothy Findley (b. 1930)

A student of dance and drama, this Toronto native was a successful actor before the publication of his first short story in *The Tamarack Review* convinced him to concentrate on writing fiction. Although his first two novels, *The Last of the Crazy People* (1967) and *The Butterfly Plague* (1969), were rejected by Canadian publishers and eventually published in Britain, Findley's third work, *The Wars,* appeared in 1977 to critical acclaim and established his reputation in Canada. Appointed an officer of the Order of Canada, he has also received the Governor General's Award for fiction, the Canadian Authors Association award, and the Edgar Award for mystery writing for *The Telling of Lies* (1987). In addition to novels such as *Famous Last Words* (1981), *Not Wanted on the Voyage* (1985), *Headhunter* (1993), and *The Piano Man's Daughter* (1995), Findley is the author of several collections of short fiction, two plays, numerous scripts and screenplays, and a volume of memoirs entitled *Inside Memory: Pages from a Writer's Workbook* (1990).

Robert Frost (1874–1963)

Though his poetry forever identifies Frost with rural New England, he was born and lived to the age of eleven in San Francisco. Coming to New England after his father's death, Frost studied classics in high school, entered and dropped out of both Dartmouth and Harvard, and spent difficult years as an unrecognized poet before his first book, *A Boy's Will* (1913), was accepted and published in England. Frost's character was full of contradiction—he held "that we get forward as much by hating as by loving"—yet by the end of his long life he was one of the most honored poets of his time. In 1961, two years before his death, he was invited to read a poem at John F. Kennedy's presidential inauguration ceremony.

Gabriel García Márquez (b. 1928)

Born in Aracataca, a remote town in Magdalena province near the Caribbean coast of Colombia, García Márquez studied law at the University of Bogotá and then worked as a journalist in Latin America, Europe, and the United States. In 1967, he took up permanent residence in Barcelona, Spain. His first published book, *Leaf Storm* (1955, translated 1972), in which "A Very Old Man with Enormous Wings" appears, is set in the fictional small town of Macondo and is based on the myths and legends of his childhood home. His most famous novel, *One Hundred Years of Solitude* (1967, translated 1970), presents six generations of one family in Macondo, fusing magic, reality, fable, and fantasy in a way that also allows the town to serve as a microcosm of many of the social, political, and economic problems of Latin America. Among his works are *The Autumn of the Patriarch* (1975, translated 1976), *Innocent Eréndira and Other Stories* (1972, translated 1978), *Chronicle of a Death Foretold* (1981, translated 1982), *Love in the Time of Cholera* (1987, translated 1988), and *Of Love and Other Demons* (1994, translated 1995). García Márquez won the Nobel Prize for Literature in 1982.

John Gay (1685–1732)

After attending school in Devon, Gay moved to London to work as an apprentice; within five years he was involved in contemporary literary circles as well as the publishing world. Known for both his playfulness and his serious social commentary, Gay, with Pope, Swift, and Arbuthnot, founded the Scriblerus Club, which became famous for its literary satires and practical jokes. In addition to poems like "The Shepherd's Week" (1714) and "Trivia, or the Art of Walking the Streets of London" (1716), Gay wrote *The Beggar's Opera* (1728), a ballad-opera that satirized contemporary political corruption.

Charlotte Perkins Gilman (1860–1935)

Charlotte Anna Perkins was born in Hartford, Connecticut. After a painful, lonely childhood and several years of supporting herself as a governess, art teacher, and designer of greeting cards, Charlotte Perkins married the artist Charles Stetson. Following several extended periods of depression, she was put by her husband into the hands of Dr. S. Weir Mitchell, who "sent me home with the solemn advice to 'live as domestic a life as . . . possible,' to 'have but two hours' intellectual life a day,' and 'never to touch pen, brush, or pencil again' as long as I lived." Three months of this, ending "near the borderline of utter mortal ruin," became the inspiration for "The Yellow Wallpaper." In 1900 she married George Houghton Gilman, having divorced Stetson in 1892. Her nonfiction works, which placed her at the center of the early women's movement, include *Women and Economics* (1898) and *Man-Made World* (1911). She also wrote several utopian novels, including *Moving the Mountain* (1911) and *Herland* (1915).

Allen Ginsberg (1926–1997)

After a childhood in Paterson, New Jersey, overshadowed by his mother's severe mental illness, Ginsberg enrolled at Columbia University, intent upon following his father's advice and becoming a labor lawyer. He soon became friends with fellow students Lucien Carr and Jack Kerouac, as well as locals William S. Burroughs and Neal Cassady, and with them he began experimenting with drugs, taking cross-country treks, and developing a new poetic vision. Eventually graduating from Columbia in 1948, Ginsberg briefly entertained a more conservative lifestyle before embracing the young poetry movement in San Francisco. In 1956 Ginsberg published *Howl and Other Poems* with an introduction by his mentor William Carlos Williams. The title poem, which condemned bourgeois culture and celebrated the emerging counterculture, became a manifesto for the Beat movement and catapulted Ginsberg to fame. Deeply involved in radical politics and Eastern spiritualism, Ginsberg wrote such prose works as *Declaration of Independence for Dr. Timothy Leary* (1971) in addition to numerous volumes of poetry, including *Kaddish and Other Poems* (1961), *For the Soul of the Planet Is Wakening . . .* (1970), and *Mostly Sitting Haiku* (1978).

Susan Glaspell (1882–1948)

Born and raised in Davenport, Iowa, Glaspell graduated from Drake University and worked on the staff of the *Des Moines Daily News* until her stories began appearing in magazines such as *Harper's* and the *Ladies' Home Journal*. In 1911, Glaspell moved to New York City, where, two years later, she married George Cram Cook, a talented director. In 1915 they founded the Provincetown Playhouse on Cape Cod, an extraordinary gathering of actors, directors, and playwrights, including Eugene O'Neill, Edna St. Vincent Millay, and John Reed. She spent the last part of her life in Provincetown, devoting herself to writing novels. Glaspell's plays include *The Verge* (1921) and *Alison's House* (1930). Among her novels are *The Visionary* (1911), *Fidelity* (1915), and *The Morning Is Near Us* (1939).

Lorraine Hansberry (1930–1965)

The first African American woman to have a play produced on Broadway, Hansberry was born in Chicago to a prominent family and showed an interest in writing from an early age. After attending the University of Wisconsin from 1948 until 1950 and studying briefly at the Art Institute of Chicago and Roosevelt University, she moved to New York City, where she enrolled at the New School for Social Research while she continued to concentrate on her writing. After extensive fund-raising in 1958, Hansberry's play *A Raisin in the Sun* opened in 1959 at the Ethel Barrymore Theatre on Broadway to critical acclaim, and Hansberry won the New York Drama Critics' Circle Award for Best Play of the Year, the only African American playwright to receive the honor. Her second production, *The Sign in Sidney Brustein's Window,* had a short run in 1964, the same year Hansberry lost her battle with cancer. A dedicated social activist and feminist, she is the author of plays such as *Les Blancs* (1969), *What Use Are Flowers?* (1969), as well as the unpublished satire *The Arrival of Mr. Todog* and essays including the unpublished "Simone de Beauvoir and the Second Sex: An American Commentary, 1957."

Thomas Hardy (1840–1928)

In a preface dated 1901, Hardy called his poems "unadjusted impressions," which nevertheless might, by "humbly recording diverse readings of phenomena as they are forced upon us by chance and change," lead to a philosophy. Indeed, though he was essentially retrospective in his outlook, Hardy anticipated the concerns of modern poetry by treating the craft as an awkward, often skeptical means of penetrating the facade of language. Born at Upper Bockhampton in Dorset, England, the son of a master mason, Hardy began to write while in the midst of an architectural career. After a long and successful career as a novelist, he turned exclusively to poetry; he died while preparing his last book, *Winter Words* (1929), for publication.

Nathaniel Hawthorne (1804–1864)

Hawthorne was born in Salem, Massachusetts, a descendant of Puritan immigrants; one ancestor had been a judge in the Salem witchcraft trials. Educated at Bowdoin College, he was agonizingly slow in winning acclaim for his work, and supported himself from time to time in government service—working in the customhouses of Boston and Salem and serving as the United States consul in Liverpool. His early collections of stories, *Twice-Told Tales* (1837) and *Mosses from an Old Manse* (1846), in which "Young Goodman Brown" appears, did not sell well, and it was not until the publication in 1850 of his most famous novel, *The Scarlet Letter,* that his fame spread beyond a discerning few. His other novels include *The House of the Seven Gables* (1851) and *The Blithedale Romance* (1852).

Robert Hayden (1913–1980)

Hayden was born in Detroit, Michigan, and studied at Wayne State University and the University of Michigan. He taught at Fisk University for over twenty years and at the University of Michigan for more than ten. Although Hayden produced ten volumes of poetry, he did not receive acclaim until late in life. In the 1960s, Hayden resisted pressure to express the militancy some African Americans wanted and thus alienated himself from a growing African American literary tradition.

Seamus Heaney (b. 1939)

Heaney, whose poems explore themes of rural life, memory, and history, was born on a farm in Mossbawn, County Derry (Castledawson, Londonderry), Northern Ireland. Educated at Queen's University in Belfast, he began to publish work in university magazines under the pseudonym "Incertus" while serving as a lecturer in English. He produced his first volume, *Eleven Poems,* in 1965, and has continued to write while holding teaching positions at the University of California at Berkeley, Carysfort College in Dublin, and Oxford University. Currently on the faculty at Harvard University, Heaney has received numerous awards for his work, including the 1995 Nobel Prize for Literature. Deemed by Robert Lowell "the most important Irish poet since Yeats," he is the author of multiple collections of poems, including *Death of a Naturalist* (1966), *Wintering Out* (1972), *The Haw Lantern* (1987), *Seeing Things* (1991), and *The Spirit Level* (1996), and prose works such as *The Government of the Tongue* (1988) and *The Place of Writing* (1989).

Anthony Hecht (b. 1923)

Hecht was born in New York City. After graduating from Bard College, he joined the army and was stationed in Europe and Japan. He has taught at, among other schools,

Kenyon College (where he first met and studied informally with fellow faculty member John Crowe Ransom), the University of Rochester, and Georgetown University. In addition to his poetry, Hecht has published three books of criticism and several translations, most notably of the Greek tragedian Aeschylus. Hecht is best known for the "double dactyl" verse form that he and John Hollander co-invented.

Lillian Hellman (1907–1984)

Hellman's toughness and pragmatism allowed her to stretch the rigid conventions of the Broadway stage to explore unconventional subjects and to stand up to Senator Joseph McCarthy during a period when most writers were terrified to speak out. Born into a Jewish family in New Orleans, Hellman moved to New York, where she attended New York and Columbia universities and worked briefly in publishing. Her first successful play, *The Children's Hour* (1934), explored the pain of two women accused of lesbianism at a rigidly conventional private school. During the McCarthy period, Hellman was blacklisted for her "left wing" politics. Nevertheless she refused to inform on other writers, explaining that "to hurt innocent people whom I knew many years ago in order to save myself is, to me, inhuman and indecent and dishonorable." After the death of the writer Dashiell Hammett, her companion for many years, Hellman began work on her memoirs, which were published in three volumes: *An Unfinished Woman* (1969), *Pentimento* (1973), and *Scoundrel Time* (1976).

Ernest Hemingway (1899–1961)

Born in Oak Park, Illinois, Hemingway was first a reporter, then an ambulance-service volunteer in France and infantryman in Italy in 1918, when he was wounded and decorated for valor. After the war and more reporting, he settled for a time in Paris, where he knew Gertrude Stein and Ezra Pound, among others. From 1925 to 1935 he published two volumes of stories, *In Our Time* (1925) and *Death in the Afternoon* (1932), and two major novels, *The Sun Also Rises* (1926) and *A Farewell to Arms* (1929), which established his international reputation. Hemingway helped the Loyalists in the Spanish Civil War, the subject of *For Whom the Bell Tolls* (1940), served as a war correspondent in the Second World War, and from 1950 to 1962 lived in Cuba. *The Old Man and the Sea* was published in 1952, winning a Pulitzer Prize. Hemingway was awarded the Nobel Prize for Literature in 1954. He committed suicide in 1961.

George Herbert (1593–1633)

After the early death of his Welsh father, Herbert was raised by his mother, a literary patron of John Donne. Herbert graduated with honors from Cambridge and was subsequently elected public orator at the university. He twice served as a member of Parliament in the 1620s, but his political career never flourished. Instead, he began to work for the church in 1626, married, and took holy orders in 1630. While living in Bemerton, he became known as "Holy Mr. Herbert" for his diligent care of the members of his ministry. He died of consumption in 1633, and his most famous poetry collection, *The Temple*, was published posthumously by a friend.

Robert Herrick (1591–1674)

The son of a London goldsmith, Herrick would have liked nothing better than to live a life of leisured study, discussing literature and drinking sack with his hero, Ben Jonson. For a number of reasons, though, he decided to take religious orders and moved to a parish in Devonshire. Herrick eventually made himself at home there, inventing dozens of imaginary mistresses with exotic names (his housekeeper was prosaically named Prudence) and practicing, half-seriously, his own peculiar form of paganism. When the Puritans came to power, Herrick was driven from his post to London, where, in 1648, he published a volume of over fourteen hundred poems with two titles, *Hesperides* for the secular poems and *Noble Numbers* for those with sacred subjects. Though they did not survive the harsh atmosphere of Puritanism and were virtually forgotten until the nineteenth century, Herrick was eventually restored to his post in Devonshire, where he lived out his last years quietly.

Spencer Holst (b. 1926)

Well known in the literary underground, Holst has published his short stories and poetry in numerous periodicals such as *Mademoiselle* and *Oui*. He has translated the work of German poet Vera Lachmann and published several volumes of his own writing, including two volumes of short stories, *The Language of Cats and Other Stories* (1971) and *Spencer Holst Stories* (1976), the latter a collection of imaginative and humorous fables that play with reality and fantasy.

Gerard Manley Hopkins (1844–1889)

Hopkins's verse, in all its superbly controlled tension, strong rhythm, and sheer exuberance, has been championed by a number of modern poets—yet he made few attempts to publish what many of his contemporaries found nearly incomprehensible, and he was all but unknown until long after his death. Born the eldest of eight children of a marine-insurance adjuster (shipwrecks later figured in his poetry, particularly *The Wreck of the Deutschland*), Hopkins attended Oxford, where his ambition was to become a painter—until he was converted to Catholicism. He taught for a time, decided to become a Jesuit, burnt all his early poetry as too worldly, and was ordained in 1877. Near the end of his life, Hopkins was appointed professor of Greek at University College, Dublin. Out of place and miserable, he died there of typhoid at the age of forty-four.

Langston Hughes (1902–1967)

Hughes, born in Joplin, Missouri, was a major figure of the intellectual and literary movement called the Harlem Renaissance. A graduate of Lincoln University in 1929, Hughes traveled through the world as a correspondent and columnist. He also founded theaters and produced plays, as well as writing poems and novels. His works include *The Weary Blues* (1926), *Montage of a Dream Deferred* (1951), and *The Panther and the Lash: Poems of Our Time* (1961). Hughes has recently been incorporated into the gay literary canon and has been the subject of the film *Looking for Langston*.

Henrik Ibsen (1828–1906)

Ibsen was the foremost playwright of his time; his work is both a culmination of nineteenth-century "bourgeois" drama and a precursor of social realist and symbolist theater. Born in Skien, Norway, Ibsen was apprenticed to an apothecary until 1850, when he left for Oslo and published his first play, *Catilina,* under a pseudonym. Two of his early works, written in Rome, were in verse—*Brand* (1866) and *Peer Gynt* (1867). During the course of his career, he turned to more realistic plays—including *Ghosts* (1881) and *An Enemy of the People* (1882)—that explored contemporary social problems; they won him a reputation throughout Europe as a controversial and outspoken advocate of moral and social reform. Near the end of his life, Ibsen explored the human condition in the symbolic terms of *The Master Builder* (1892) and *When We Dead Awaken* (1899), plays that anticipated many of the concerns of twentieth-century drama.

David Ives (b. 1950)

A native of Chicago, Ives worked as the assistant editor of *Foreign Affairs* before graduating from the Yale School of Drama. While plays such as *Don Juan in Chicago* (1995) and *Ancient History* (1995) have established Ives's place among contemporary dramatists, he is also an accomplished journalist and the author of fiction, screenplays, and opera. In 1993 his series of one-act plays entitled *All in the Timing* received the Outer Critics Circle Award for playwriting, and it became the most performed play nationally after Shakespeare productions during the 1995–1996 season. A Guggenheim fellow in playwriting, Ives has adapted David Copperfield's *Dreams and Nightmares* for the stage.

Henry James (1843–1916)

Son of a writer and religious philosopher, brother of the philosopher William James, Henry James was born in New York and entered Harvard Law School in 1862, after private study, art school, and study and residence abroad. Thereafter his American home was in Cambridge, Massachusetts, but he lived in England from 1876 until his death forty years later, having become a British subject in 1915. James's fiction often centers on the confrontation of Americans with Europe or Europeans; he treats the two as moral or value systems as much as geographical entities. His practice and theory of fiction, set forth mainly in the prefaces to his novels, dominated fiction criticism for generations. Among his works are *The American* (1877), *Daisy Miller* (1879), *Portrait of a Lady* (1881), *The Turn of the Screw* (1898), *The Wings of the Dove* (1902), *The Ambassadors* (1903), and *The Golden Bowl* (1904).

Ben Jonson (1572?–1637)

Poet, playwright, actor, scholar, critic, translator, and leader, for the first time in English, of a literary "school" (the "Cavalier" poets), Jonson was born the posthumous son of a clergyman and stepson to a master bricklayer of Westminster. He had an eventful early career, going to war against the Spanish, working as an actor and killing an associate in a duel, and converting to Catholicism (which made him an object of deep suspicion after the Gunpowder Plot of Guy Fawkes in 1605). Jonson wrote a number of plays in the midst of all this, including *Every Man in His Humor* (in which Shakespeare acted a leading role), *Volpone* (1606), and *The Alchemist* (1610). He spent the latter part of his life at the center of a vast literary circle. When in 1616 he published his collected works, *The Works of Benjamin Jonson,* it was the first time an English author had been so presumptuous as to consider writing a profession.

James Joyce (1882–1941)

In 1902, after graduating from University College, Dublin, Joyce left his native city for Paris, only to return in April 1903 to teach school. In the spring of 1904 he lived at the Martello Tower, Sandycove, a site made famous by his great novel, *Ulysses* (1921). In October 1904 he eloped with Nora Barnacle and left Ireland again, this time for Trieste, where he taught English for the Berlitz school. Though he lived abroad the rest of his life, that first abortive trip proved symbolic: in his fiction the expatriate could never leave Dublin. Joyce had more than his share of difficulties with publication and censorship. His volume of short stories, *Dubliners* (in which "Counterparts" appears), completed in 1905, was not published until 1914. His *Portrait of the Artist as a Young Man*, dated "Dublin 1904, Trieste 1914," appeared first in America, in 1916. *Ulysses* was banned for a dozen years in the United States and as long or longer elsewhere. Though he published a play, *Exiles*, and poetry, the three works mentioned and the monumental, experimental, and puzzling *Finnegans Wake* (1939) are the basis of his reputation.

Franz Kafka (1883–1924)

Born in Prague into a middle-class Jewish family, Kafka earned a doctorate in law from the German University in that city and held an inconspicuous position in the civil service for many years. Emotionally and physically ill for the last seven or eight years of his short life, he died of tuberculosis in Vienna, never having married (though he was twice engaged to the same woman and lived with an actress in Berlin for some time before he died) and not having published his three major novels, *The Trial* (1925), *The Castle* (1926), and *Amerika* (1927). Indeed, he ordered his friend Max Brod to destroy them and other works he had left in manuscript. Fortunately, Brod did not, and not long after his death, Kafka's work was world-famous and widely influential. His stories in English translation can be found in *The Great Wall of China* (1933), *The Penal Colony* (1948), and *The Complete Stories* (1976).

Jamaica Kincaid (b. 1949)

Born in St. John's, Antigua (an island in the West Indies north of Guadeloupe), Kincaid now lives in New York. She is the author of a volume of short stories, *At the Bottom of the River* (1984), and three novels, *Annie John* (1985), *Lucy* (1990), and *The Autobiography of My Mother* (1996). Although Kincaid left her native island as a teenager, a deeply felt—and richly evocative—sense of place pervades her work.

Margaret Laurence (1926–1987)

Born Jean Margaret Wemyss in Neepawa, Manitoba, Laurence began to write professionally in 1943, when she got a summer job as a reporter for the town newspaper. She published stories and poems in the campus newspaper while enrolled in the Honors English program at Winnipeg's United College (now the University of Winnipeg), and after graduating in 1947 she became a reporter for the *Winnipeg Citizen*. After marrying in 1947, she lived and traveled in Africa from 1950 to 1957 and drew upon her experiences there in *A Tree for Poverty* (1954), *This Side Jordan* (1960), *The Prophet's Camel Bell* (1963), and *The Tomorrow-Tamer* (1963). Her novels, such as *The Stone Angel* (1964), *A Jest of God* (1966), and *The Fire-Dwellers* (1969), often followed the exploits and experiences of strong-willed heroines in search of self-realization. *A Bird in the House* (1970) is a collection of short stories depicting Laurence's native Manitoba.

D. H. Lawrence (1885–1930)

Son of a coal miner and a middle-class schoolteacher, Lawrence won a scholarship to Nottingham High School at thirteen but had to leave a few years later when his elder brother died. He worked for a surgical appliance manufacturer, attended Nottingham

University College, and taught school in Croydon, near London. In 1911, when his first novel, *The White Peacock,* was published, he left teaching to devote his time to writing, though it was not until the publication of *Sons and Lovers* (1913) that he was established as a major literary figure. In 1912 he eloped to the Continent with Frieda von Richthofen, and in 1914, after her divorce, they were married. During World War I, both his novels and the fact that his wife was German gave him trouble: *The Rainbow* was published in September 1915 and suppressed in November. In November 1919 the Lawrences left England, and their years of wandering began: first Italy, then Ceylon and Australia, Mexico and New Mexico, then back to England and Italy. *Women in Love* was published in New York in 1920 and *Lady Chatterley's Lover,* his most sexually explicit and controversial novel, eight years later. Through it all he suffered from tuberculosis, the disease from which he finally died, in France. Lawrence's stories are available in a three-volume edition, first published in 1961.

Doris Lessing (b. 1919)

Born in Persia (now Iran), Lessing lived for twenty-five years in Southern Rhodesia (now Zimbabwe) before moving to England, where soon thereafter her first novel, *The Grass Is Singing* (1950), was published. She has since published voluminously. Her books include *The Golden Notebook* (1962), the five Martha Quest novels, *Children of Violence,* published between 1952 and 1969, *Briefing for a Descent into Hell* (1971), *The Summer before the Dark* (1973), and *The Good Terrorist* (1985). She has also published eight volumes of short fiction, including *A Man and Two Women* (1963) and *The Memoirs of a Survivor* (1975), and has written plays, television plays, poetry, and essays. Her work is known for its range and variety, some of it set in Africa, a significant portion of it political (she was once a Communist), much of it examining inner lives of women in modern society, and some of it lately reflecting her interest in extrasensory perception. Lessing published a five-volume science-fiction collection under the collective title *Caopus in Argos: Archives* between 1979 and 1983, and tried her hand at satire with *The Good Terrorist* (1985). Her most recent novel is *Love, Again* (1997).

Denise Levertov (1923–1997)

Poetry and life, Levertov once explained, "fade, wilt, shrink, when they are divorced." Born in England, the daughter of a Jewish Russian immigrant who had become an Anglican clergyman, Levertov was educated at home. By the time she arrived in New York City with her American husband in 1948, she had already published her first book of poetry, *The Double Image* (1946). In 1957 her second book, *Here and Now,* appeared, and she subsequently published numerous collections, including *With Eyes at the Back of Our Heads* (1960), *The Sorrow Dance* (1967), *To Stay Alive* (1971), *Candles in Babylon* (1982), and *Evening Train* (1992). While her earlier work produced in the United States shows the influence of William Carlos Williams, beginning in the 1960s Levertov's poetry developed a particularly political flavor, reflecting the author's increased social activism. Levertov was the recipient of a multitude of awards and honors, and taught at the University of California at Berkeley, the Massachusetts Institute of Technology, Tufts University, and Stanford University, among others.

Richard Lovelace (1618–1657)

Born to a wealthy family in Kent, England, Lovelace attended the Charterhouse School and Gloucester Hall, Oxford, before joining the Scottish military expeditions of 1639–1640. Jailed by Parliament in 1642 for presenting a Royalist petition and again in 1648 for fighting on the side of the French against the Spanish, he is best known for poems and lyrics written during his imprisonment, including "To Althea, from Prison." Considered a leading member of the group of Royalist writers called "Cavalier" poets, Lovelace spent his final years in poverty and published only one volume of poems during his lifetime. The title of the work, *Lucasta* (1649) from *Lux casta* (Latin for "pure light"), probably refers to Lucy Sacheverell, Lovelace's fiancée, who married another man after receiving false news of Lovelace's death.

Katherine Mansfield (1888–1923)

Born in New Zealand, Mansfield studied music at Queen's College, London, and was an accomplished cellist. She published three major volumes of short stories during her short life: *Bliss* (1920), which established her reputation, *The Garden-Party* (1922), and *The Dove's Nest* (1923). With John Middleton Murry and D. H. Lawrence she founded an influential literary review, *The Signature*. She died of tuberculosis in France, and a final volume of stories, *Something Childish* (1924), appeared shortly after her death. Her *Collected Stories* were published in 1945.

Andrew Marvell (1621–1678)

Marvell was born in Yorkshire, England, and educated at Cambridge. He was a supporter of the Puritans and a member of the British Parliament. Marvell was known in his day for his satires in prose and verse, but today is better known for his less public poems.

Guy de Maupassant (1850–1893)

Born Henri René Albert in Normandy, France, at sixteen Maupassant was expelled from a Rouen seminary and finished his education in a public high school. After serving in the Franco-Prussian War, he was for ten years a government clerk in Paris. A protégé of Flaubert, during the 1880s he published some three hundred stories, half a dozen novels, and plays. The short stories, which appeared regularly in popular periodicals, sampled military and peasant life, the decadent world of politics and journalism, prostitution, the supernatural, and the hypocrisies of solid citizens. With Chekhov, he may be said to have created the modern short story; his reliance on plot, plot twists, and sometimes heavy irony became facile in the hands of his followers and has diminished his own reputation the past quarter-century and more. His life ended somewhat like one of his own stories: he died of syphilis in an asylum. His novels include *Une Vie* (*A Life,* 1883), *Bel Ami* (*Handsome Friend,* 1885), and *Pierre et Jean* (1888). His stories are most readily available in his *Collected Works.*

Edna St. Vincent Millay (1892–1950)

Winner of the 1923 Pulitzer Prize for Poetry, Millay was born in Maine and educated at Vassar. After college, with her reputation as a poet already established, Millay moved to Greenwich Village in New York and became notorious for her bohemian life and passionate love affairs. *Selected Poems/the Centenary Edition* (1992) provides a generous sampling of Millay's work.

Arthur Miller (b. 1915)

Born and raised in New York City, Miller studied journalism at the University of Michigan, began writing plays, and went to work—in the middle of the Depression—with the Federal Theatre Project, a fertile proving ground for some of the best playwrights of the period. He had his first Broadway success, *All My Sons,* in 1947, followed only two years later by his masterpiece, *Death of a Salesman.* With McCarthy's Communist "witch-hunts" of the early 1950s as his inspiration, Miller fashioned another modern parable, basing *The Crucible* (1953) on the seventeenth-century Salem witch trials. His work has provoked much theoretical discussion over whether real tragedy is possible in a modern context. In 1984, Miller was given the John F. Kennedy Award for Lifetime Achievement. His most recent play, *Broken Glass,* was published in 1994.

John Milton (1608–1674)

Born in London, the elder son of a self-made businessman, Milton exhibited unusual literary and scholarly gifts at an early age; before entering Cambridge University, he was already adept at Latin and Greek and was well on his way to mastering Hebrew and most of the European languages. After graduation, he spent six more years reading, day and night, just about everything of importance written in English, Italian, Latin, and Greek—after which his father sent him abroad for another year of travel and study. Returning to England, Milton immediately embroiled himself in political controversy, writing pamphlets defending everything from free speech to the execution of Charles I by Cromwell and his followers. In the midst of this feverish activity, the monarchy was restored, and Milton was imprisoned and his property confiscated—but, worst of all, he lost his sight. Blind, impoverished, and isolated, he set about writing the great works of his later years: *Paradise Lost* (1667), *Paradise Regained* (1671), and *Samson Agonistes* (1671).

Pat Mora (b. 1942)

Born to Mexican American parents in El Paso, Texas, Mora earned both her B.A. and M.A. from the University of Texas, El Paso. Her first two collections of poetry, *Chants* (1985) and *Borders* (1986), won Southwest Book awards. Along with these books, her most recent volumes of poetry, *Communion* (1991) and *Agua Santa: Holy Water* (1995), reflect and address her Chicana and southwestern background. She has recently compiled a collection of essays called *Nepantla: Essays from the Land in the Middle* (1993).

Bharati Mukherjee (b. 1940)

Brought up in an upper-class Bengali family of the Brahmin caste, Mukherjee attended private schools in India, London, and Switzerland before a business disaster wiped out the family fortune. She won a scholarship in 1961 to the University of Iowa Writer's Workshop and has since lived with her husband (also a writer) and two children in Canada, India, and the United States, supporting herself through teaching and other jobs, and writing in the small hours of the morning. In 1971 her critically acclaimed first novel, *The Tiger's Daughter,* appeared; her other novels are *Wife* (1975), *Jasmine* (1989), and *Leave It to Me* (1997). Mukherjee's short-fiction collections are *Darkness* (1985), stories of South Asian immigrants, and *The Middleman* (1988), which includes characters and voices from various countries and social strata: "Mine is not minimalism, which strips away, but compression, which reflects many layers of meaning."

Alice Munro (b. 1931)

Munro grew up on a farm near Lake Huron in Ontario and attended the University of Western Ontario, where she began publishing short stories. Much of her fiction grows out of her childhood memories of rural family life: "I write about places where your roots are and most people don't live that kind of life anymore at all." Her first book, a collection of stories entitled *Dance of the Happy Shades* (1968) in which "Boys and Girls" appears, won a Governor General's Award. Munro has written a novel, *Lives of Girls and Women* (1971), and six other short-story collections, *Something I've Been Meaning to Tell You* (1974), *Who Do You Think You Are?* (1978, published in the United States as *The Beggar Maid* in 1979), *The Moons of Jupiter* (1983), *The Progress of Love* (1986), *Friend of My Youth* (1990), and *Open Secrets* (1994). Her *Selected Stories* was published in 1996.

Howard Nemerov (1920–1991)

Nemerov once called his poems "bad jokes, and even terrible jokes, emerging from the nature of things as well as from my propensity for coming at things a touch subversively, and from the blind side, or the dark side, the side everyone concerned with 'values' would just as soon forget." The resonance of his poetry may lie in his ability to balance this subversive, wayward imagination with lucid, precise language and traditional verse forms. Born in New York City, Nemerov graduated from Harvard University, served in the air force during World War II, and returned to New York to complete his first book, *The Image and the Law* (1948). He taught at a number of colleges and universities, and published books of poetry, plays, short stories, novels, and essays. His *Collected Poems* won the Pulitzer Prize and the National Book Award in 1978. In addition, he served as Poet Laureate of the United States from 1988 to 1990. *Trying Conclusions: New and Selected Poems 1961–1991* was published in 1991.

Flannery O'Connor (1925–1964)

O'Connor was born in Savannah, Georgia, studied at the Georgia State College for Women, and won a fellowship to the Writer's Workshop of the University of Iowa, where she received an M.F.A. degree. Her first novel, *Wise Blood*, was published in 1952, and her first collection of stories, *A Good Man Is Hard to Find*, in 1955. She was able to complete only one more novel, *The Violent Bear It Away* (1960), and a second collection of stories, *Everything That Rises Must Converge* (1965), before dying of lupus in Milledgeville, Georgia. Her reputation has grown steadily since her untimely death. A collection of letters, edited by Sally Fitzgerald under the title *The Habit of Being*, appeared in 1979.

Sharon Olds (b. 1942)

Olds's poems might well be compared with those of the "confessional" poets (particularly Plath and Sexton) in their intense focus on and preoccupation with sexual and family relationships. Born in San Francisco, Olds studied at Stanford and Columbia universities, settling afterward in New York City, where she teaches creative writing at New York University and the Goldwater Hospital (a public facility for the severely physically disabled). Olds's books include *Satan Says* (1980), *The Dead and the Living* (1983; National Book Critics Circle Award), *The Gold Cell* (1987), *The Father* (1992), and *The Wellspring* (1997). She has received a National Endowment for the Arts Grant and a Guggenheim Fellowship.

Mary Oliver (b. 1935)

Born in Maple Heights, Ohio, Oliver graduated from Vassar College before settling in Provincetown, Massachusetts, where she is the chair of the Writing Department at the Fine Arts Center. Her deep appreciation for the New England landscape and attention to the inhabitants of the natural world have influenced her writing since her first collection, *No Voyage and Other Poems,* was published in 1963. The recipient of a Pulitzer Prize for her *American Primitive* (1983) and a National Book Award in 1992 for *New and Selected Poems,* Oliver is also the author of *The Night Traveler* (1978), *Sleeping in the Forest* (1978), *Twelve Moons* (1979), *Dream Work* (1986), and *House of Light* (1990).

Wilfred Owen (1893–1918)

Born in Oswestry, Shropshire, England, Owen was the eldest of four children. He left school in 1911, having failed to win a scholarship to London University, and served as assistant to a vicar in Oxfordshire until 1913, when he went to France to teach English at a Berlitz school in Bordeaux. In 1915, he returned to England to enlist in the army and was sent to the front in France. Suffering from shell shock two years later, Owen was evacuated to Craiglockhart War Hospital, where he met the poets Siegfried Sassoon and Robert Graves. Five of Owen's poems were published in 1918, the year he returned to combat only to be killed one week before the signing of the armistice. Owen's poems, technically refined and poignant, portray the horror of trench warfare and satirize the unthinking patriotism of those who cheered the war from their armchairs. The most authoritative collection of Owen's poetry is the two-volume *Complete Poems and Fragments* (1983).

Dorothy Parker (1893–1967)

Parker satirized the literary, social, and sexual pieties of her time with a sharp eye and sardonic exuberance. If "Brevity is the soul of Lingerie," as she announced in a *Vogue* advertisement, it is also the heart of her wit. There are a number of "Parkerisms"— brief, witty aphorisms—still in circulation. Parker was born in New York City and was friendly with several other prominent writers and humorists of the 1920s and 1930s, including Harold Ross, founder of the *New Yorker.* Author of poetry, criticism, screenplays, and short stories, she published a number of collections, including *Enough Rope* (1926), *Sunset Gun* (1928), *Death and Taxes* (1931), and *Not So Deep As a Well* (1936).

Linda Pastan (b. 1932)

Author of more than half a dozen volumes of poetry, Pastan was born in New York City and attended Radcliffe College and Brandeis University before settling in suburban Washington, D.C. Her books include *A Perfect Circle of Sun* (1971), *The Five Stages of Grief* (1978), *A Fraction of Darkness* (1985), and *The Imperfect Paradise* (1988). *PM/ AM: New and Selected Poems* (1982) was nominated for the American Book Award. Her latest collection, *An Early Afterlife,* was published in 1995.

Marge Piercy (b. 1936)

Piercy's earlier poetry examined the complex interplay between personal relationships and political forces, at the same time voicing the rage of women who have for so long been dominated and overwhelmed by men ("I imagine that I speak for a constituency, living and dead," she writes). Her later work, particularly the poems in *Stone, Paper, Knife* (1983), expresses also a sense of inclusiveness, of interconnection with all living things. Born in Detroit, Piercy studied at the University of Michigan and Northwestern University, and taught for some time before the success of her novels allowed her to live a semirural life on Cape Cod. Her books of poetry include

Living in the Open (1976), *The Moon Is Always Female* (1980), and *Available Light* (1988). In 1990 Piercy received the Golden Rose Award. Her most recent book of poetry, *What Are Big Girls Made Of?*, was published in 1997.

Sylvia Plath (1932–1963)

Plath has attained the status of a cult figure as much for the splendid and beautiful agony of her poems as for her "martyrdom" to art. Her life, in all its outer banality and inner tragedy, might be seen as a confirmation that poetry is a dangerous vocation. Born the daughter of a Polish immigrant who died in 1940, Plath's early years were a vision of conventional success, including poetry prizes, scholarships at Smith College, and a summa cum laude graduation. She won a Fulbright Scholarship to Cambridge University, where she met and married the English poet Ted Hughes, with whom she had two children. Yet beneath it all was a woman whose acute perceptions and intolerable pain led her to produce a novel, *The Bell Jar* (1963), and three volumes of poetry—and to commit suicide at the age of thirty.

Edgar Allan Poe (1809–1849)

Poe's actor father deserted his wife and son when Edgar was less than a year old. His mother died before he was three, and he and his younger sister were separated and taken into different families. The Allans (who gave Poe his middle name) moved in 1815 to England, where Edgar had his early schooling. He studied briefly at the University of Virginia and in 1827 paid to have a volume of poems published in Boston (his birthplace); a second volume appeared in 1829 in Baltimore (where he was to die twenty years later). Having served for two years in the army, he was appointed to West Point in 1830 but apparently managed to have himself expelled within the year for cutting classes. Living in Baltimore with his grandmother, aunt, and cousin Virginia (whom he married in 1835 when she was thirteen), Poe began to attract critical attention but made very little money. For the twelve years of his bizarre marriage, he wrote, worked as journalist and editor, and drank. Not long after his wife died in 1847, he seemed to be straightening himself out when, on Election Day—October 3— he was found semiconscious near a polling place and died four days later without fully regaining consciousness. It is testimony to the continuing fame of his works that they need not be named here.

Katherine Anne Porter (1890–1980)

Born in Indian Creek, Texas, Porter supported herself with newspaper and literary hackwork in Denver, Chicago, and elsewhere while she worked on her writing. Although her first story, "Maria Concepcion," was published in 1922, it wasn't until 1930 that her first collection of stories, *Flowering Judas*, established her reputation as a leading American writer. A writer-in-residence at a succession of universities and colleges, Porter won several awards for her work, including both a Pulitzer Prize and a National Book Award in 1965 for her *Collected Short Stories*, an O. Henry Award for her story "Holiday" (1962), and a Gold Medal from the National Institute of Arts and Letters. Among her books are *Pale Horse, Pale Rider* (1939), *The Leaning Tower* (1944), and *The Never-Ending Wrong* (1977), dealing with the controversial murder trial of Sacco and Vanzetti. Her only full-length novel, *Ship of Fools* (1962), was met with both popular and critical acclaim.

Ezra Pound (1885–1972)

Pound's tremendous ambition—to succeed in his own work and to influence the development of poetry and Western culture in general—led him to found the Imagist school of poetry, to advise and assist a galaxy of great writers (Eliot, Joyce, Williams, Frost, and Hemingway, to name a few), and to write a number of highly influential critical works. It also led him to a charge of treason (Pound served as a propagandist for Mussolini during World War II), a diagnosis of insanity, and twelve years at St. Elizabeth's, an institution for the criminally insane. Born in Hailey, Idaho, Ezra Loomis Pound studied at the University of Pennsylvania and Hamilton College before traveling to Europe in 1908. He remained there, living in Ireland, England, France, and Italy, for much of his life. Pound's verse is collected in *Personae: The Collected Poems* (1949) and *The Cantos* (1976).

Sir Walter Ralegh (1552–1618)

Clearly a man of immense versatility, Ralegh undertook a variety of adventures in his tumultuous life. Born in Devonshire, England, he briefly attended Oxford but withdrew to fight in the army. He is credited with bringing the potato to Ireland and tobacco to Europe, and through his many explorations, he became an investor in the North American colonies. He was knighted and named a member of Parliament, but after offending the queen, Ralegh was imprisoned in the Tower of London. After his release in 1595, he charted a failed expedition to Guiana, and in 1603 he was again imprisoned on trumped-up treason charges. In prison, he began his unfinished *History of the World*. After another unsuccessful trip to Guiana, he was again imprisoned and executed on the orders of James I. His writings include the popular "The Nymph's Reply to the Shepherd," a response to Marlowe's "Passionate Shepherd," and some extensive writings on his findings in Guiana.

Alberto Alvaro Ríos (b. 1952)

Ríos was born in Nogales, Arizona, to a British mother and a Mexican father. He graduated from the University of Arizona and teaches at Arizona State University. He has received an NEA Fellowship and the 1981 Academy of American Poets Walt Whitman's Award for his collection of poems entitled *Whispering to Fool the Wind*. His other publications include three books of poetry—*Five Indiscretions* (1985), *The Lime Orchard Woman* (1988), and *Teodoro Luna's Two Kisses* (1990)—as well as two collections of short stories—*The Iguana Killer: Twelve Stories of the Heart* (1984), and *Pig Cookies and Other Stories* (1995).

Theodore Roethke (1908–1963)

Born in Saginaw, Michigan, Roethke grew up around his father's twenty-five-acre greenhouse complex—its associations with nurture and growth became an important subject in his later poetry. He worked for a time at Lafayette College, where he was professor of English and tennis coach, and later at the University of Washington, which appointed him poet-in-residence one year before he died. Roethke was an unhappy man, suffering from periodic mental breakdowns, yet the best of his poetry, with its reverence for and fear of the physical world, its quest for an ecstatic union with nature, seems destined to last. Roethke's books include *Open House* (1942), *Praise to the End!* (1951), and *The Far Field* (1964), which received a posthumous National Book Award.

Anne Sexton (1928–1974)

Born in Newton, Massachusetts, Anne (Harvey) Sexton interrupted her attendance at Garland Junior College to marry. She wrote poetry as a child, abandoned it, and, on the advice of her doctors, began writing again after suffering a nervous breakdown. Sexton attended Boston University with fellow student Sylvia Plath, and she studied poetry with Robert Lowell. Published in 1960, her first book of poems, *To Bedlam and Part Way Back,* recounted her mental collapse and subsequent recovery period. A "confessional" poet, Sexton received many awards, most notably the Pulitzer Prize for *Live or Die* (1966). She committed suicide in 1974. That same year, she had published *Death Notebooks;* a posthumous volume, *The Awful Rowing toward God,* appeared in 1975.

William Shakespeare (1554–1616)

Considering the great and deserved fame of his work, surprisingly little is known of Shakespeare's life. We do know that between 1585 and 1592 he left his birthplace of Stratford for London to begin a career as playwright and actor. No dates of his professional career are recorded, however, nor can we be certain of the order in which he composed his plays and poetry. By 1594 he had established himself as a poet with two long works—*Venus and Adonis* and *The Rape of Lucrece*—but it was in the theater that he made his strongest reputation. Shakespeare produced perhaps 35 plays in twenty-five years, proving himself a master of many genres in works such as *Macbeth, King Lear, Othello,* and *Antony and Cleopatra* (tragedy); *Richard III* and *Henry IV* (historical drama); *Twelfth Night* and *As You Like It* (comedy); and *The Tempest* (romance). His more than 150 sonnets are supreme expressions of the form.

Bernard Shaw (1856–1950)

Like Chekhov, Shaw's dramas address the turn of the century in a comic and realistic way. Shaw's frequent use of satire enabled him to confront idealistic and romantic notions about love and war. Like Swift, Shaw was born in Dublin to English parents and moved to London when he was nineteen. He worked as a witty music and drama critic for various London newspapers while at the same time promoting socialism in England. His first play, *Widowers' Houses,* was produced in 1891. Addressing the issue of prostitution, his second play, *Mrs. Warren's Profession* (1893), was banned. His more popular works, all of which highlight hypocrisy, include *Man and Superman* (1904), *Major Barbara* (1907), *Pygmalion* (1912), *Heartbreak House* (1919), and *Saint Joan* (1923).

Percy Bysshe Shelley (1792–1822)

Born in Sussex to a wealthy member of Parliament, Shelley attended Eton and Oxford. An unconventional young man, Shelley was expelled from Oxford during his first year for collaborating with a friend, Thomas Jefferson Hogg, on a pamphlet entitled "The Necessity of Atheism" (1811). That same year, Shelley eloped with Harriet Westbrook, but within three years, he left her to be with Mary Wollstonecraft Godwin. After Harriet's suicide, Shelley married Mary, and the couple and their children moved permanently to Italy. The death of their two children, coupled with financial difficulties, left Shelley in despair, and it was at this time (1819) that he wrote his most memorable poetry—namely, "Prometheus Unbound" and "Ode to the West Wind." Shelley's important critical essay, "A Defence of Poetry," was published posthumously in 1840.

Sophocles (496?–406? B.C.)

Sophocles lived at a time when Athens and Greek civilization had reached the peak of their power and influence. He not only served as a general under Pericles and played a prominent role in the city's affairs, but was also arguably the greatest of the Greek tragic playwrights, an innovator who fundamentally changed the form of dramatic performance and the model Aristotle turned to when he discussed the nature of tragedy in his *Poetics*. Today only seven of Sophocles' tragedies survive—the Oedipus trilogy (*Oedipus the King, Oedipus at Colonus,* and *Antigone*), *Philoctetes, Ajax, Trachiniae,* and *Electra*—though records suggest that his output may have amounted to over 120 plays.

Wallace Stevens (1879–1955)

"I believe that with a bucket of sand and a wishing lamp I could create a world in half a second that would make this one look like a hunk of mud," Stevens once remarked to his wife. One of the great imaginative forces of this century, he was nevertheless an extraordinarily self-effacing public man, working for much of his adult life as an executive of the Hartford Accident and Indemnity Company while re-creating the world at night in the "supreme fiction" of poetry. Born in Reading, Pennsylvania, Stevens attended Harvard University and New York Law School; his first book of poems, *Harmonium,* appeared in 1923. Stevens's poetry and prose can be found in *The Palm at the End of the Mind* (1971) and *The Necessary Angel: Essays on Reality and Imagination* (1951).

Amy Tan (b. 1952)

Tan was born in Oakland, California, just two and a half years after her parents immigrated there from China. She has worked as a consultant to programs for disabled children and as a freelance writer. In 1987 she visited China for the first time—"As soon as my feet touched China, I became Chinese"—and returned to write her first book, *The Joy Luck Club* (1989). Tan has since published two more books—*The Kitchen God's Wife* (1991) and *The Hundred Secret Senses* (1995)—and co-authored the screenplay for the film adaptation of *The Joy Luck Club.*

Alfred, Lord Tennyson (1809–1892)

Perhaps the most important and certainly the most popular of the Victorian poets, Tennyson demonstrated his talents at an early age; he published his first volume in 1827. Encouraged to devote his life to poetry by a group of undergraduates at Cambridge University known as the "Apostles," Tennyson was particularly close to Arthur Hallam, whose sudden death in 1833 inspired the long elegy *In Memoriam* (1850). With that poem he achieved lasting fame and recognition; he was appointed Poet Laureate the year of its publication. Whatever the popularity of his "journalistic" poetry—"The Charge of the Light Brigade" (1854) is perhaps his best known—Tennyson's great theme was always the past, both personal (*In the Valley of Cauteretz,* 1864) and national (*Idylls of the King,* 1869).

Audrey Thomas (b. 1935)

Born Audrey Callahan in Binghamton, New York, Thomas graduated from Smith College before settling in Canada. After earning a master's degree at the University of

British Columbia, she lived in Ghana from 1964 until 1966, an experience that provided the setting for her novel *Blown Figures* (1974). Influenced by the rising tide of feminism in the 1960s and 1970s, Thomas frequently wrote autobiographical stories, radio plays, and novels that depicted women's struggles for independence and the dilemmas of domestic roles, including collections of short stories such as *Ten Green Bottles* (1967), *Goodbye Harold, Good Luck* (1986), and *The Wild Blue Yonder* (1990). Thomas's appreciation for word play and experimental prose styles is evident in her novels, including *Mrs. Blood* (1970), *Songs My Mother Taught Me* (1973), and *Graven Images* (1993).

Dylan Thomas (1914–1953)

In a note to his *Collected Poems* (1952), Thomas wrote: "These poems, with all their crudities, doubts, and confusions, are written for the love of Man and in praise of God, and I'd be a damn fool if they weren't." Given their somber undertones and often wrenching awareness of death, his poems are also rich verbal and visual celebrations of life and its sweetness. Born in Swansea, Wales, into what he called "the smug darkness of a provincial town," Thomas published his first book, *18 Poems* (1934), at the age of twenty. Thereafter he had a successful, though turbulent, career publishing poetry, short stories, and plays, including the highly successful *Under Milk Wood* (1954). In his last years he supported himself with lecture tours and poetry readings in the United States, but his extravagant drinking caught up with him and he died in New York City of chronic alcoholism.

Guy Vanderhaeghe (b. 1951)

A native of Saskatchewan, Canada, Vanderhaeghe worked as an archivist and teacher until the early 1980s. He has published collections of short stories, including *Man Descending* (1982), which won the Governor General's Award for Fiction, *The Trouble with Heroes* (1983), and *Things As They Are* (1992), as well as three novels—*My Present Age* (1984), *Homesick* (1989), and *The Englishman's Boy* (1997).

Edith Wharton (1862–1937)

Best known for her novels, which scrutinize and ironize social conventions, Wharton was born Edith Jones into a distinguished family in New York City. Educated by private tutors and governesses, she published a book of her poems privately but did not begin to write for a public audience until after her marriage in 1885. The author of more than fifty volumes of poetry, essays, fiction, travelogues, and criticism, Wharton was the first woman to receive an honorary doctorate from Yale University in 1923. Although she emigrated to France in 1907, she continued to write about the New England of her youth in books such as the popular *Ethan Frome* (1911). Wharton's works include *The Valley of Decision* (1902), *The House of Mirth* (1905), *A Son at the Front* (1923), *Twilight Sleep* (1927), the autobiographical *A Backward Glance* (1934), and the posthumously published *The Buccaneers* (1938). She received a Pulitzer Prize for *The Age of Innocence* (1920).

Walt Whitman (1819–1892)

Born on a farm in West Hills, Long Island, to a British father and a Dutch mother, Whitman eventually worked as a journalist throughout New York for many years. After teaching for a while, he founded his own newspaper, *The Long Islander*, in 1838, but he left journalism to work on *Leaves of Grass,* which was originally intended as a poetic treatise on American democratic idealism. Published privately in multiple editions from 1855 to 1874, the book originally failed to reach a mass audience. In 1881 Boston's Osgood and Company published another edition of *Leaves of Grass,* which sold well until the district attorney called it "obscene literature" and stipulated that Whitman remove certain poems and phrases. He refused, and many years later his works were published in Philadelphia. Whitman's poetry creates tension between the self-conscious and political, the romantic and realistic, the mundane and mystical, and the collective and individual.

Richard Wilbur (b. 1921)

A native of New York City, Wilbur grew up in New Jersey and attended Amherst College. He started to write while serving as an army cryptographer during World War II in an attempt to create a degree of order during the chaos of military campaigns throughout southern Europe and northern Africa. The publication after the war of *The Beautiful Changes and Other Poems* (1947) and *Ceremony and Other Poems* (1950) established his reputation as a significant new poet. After earning an M.A. at Harvard University, Wilbur devoted himself to teaching and has worked at Harvard, Wellesley College, Wesleyan University, and Smith College, among others. He received the Pulitzer Prize for his volume *Things of This World* (1956) and was the second U.S. poet laureate consultant in poetry in 1987–1988. In addition to volumes of poetry such as *Walking to Sleep* (1969) and *The Mind Reader: New Poems* (1976), Wilbur is the author of children's books, critical essays, and numerous translations of classic French works, including Molière's *Tartuffe* (1963) and *The Misanthrope* (1955).

Tennessee Williams (1911–1983)

Born in Columbus, Mississippi, Thomas Lanier Williams moved to St. Louis with his family at the age of seven. Williams's father was a violent drinker, his mother was ill, and his sister, Rose, suffered from a variety of mental illnesses. Each of them became a model for the domineering men and genteel women of his plays. He attended college at the University of Missouri and Washington University in St. Louis, but he did not earn his degree until he was in his mid-twenties. While earning his B.A. from the University of Iowa, Williams won prizes for his fiction and began writing plays. From this time until his death, he created an extensive body of work. His plays confront issues usually marginalized by society: adultery, homosexuality, incest, and mental illness. In 1944, his drama *The Glass Menagerie* won the New York Drama Critics' Circle Award. He earned his first Pulitzer Prize with *A Streetcar Named Desire* in 1948, and the play was made into a film in 1951. Williams's second Pulitzer Prize was awarded for his 1955 *Cat on a Hot Tin Roof.* His other dramas include *Suddenly Last Summer* (1958) and *The Night of the Iguana* (1961). His last Broadway play, *Clothes for a Summer Hotel,* failed in 1980.

William Carlos Williams (1883–1963)

Williams influenced a generation of American poets—many of them still living—by bringing to poetry the sense that "life is above all things else at any moment subversive of life as it was the moment before—always new, irregular." Born in Rutherford, New Jersey, Williams attended school in Switzerland and New York, and studied medicine at the University of Pennsylvania, where he met Hilda Doolittle (H.D.) and Ezra

Pound. Thereafter he spent most of his life in Rutherford, practicing medicine and crafting a poetry of palpable immediacy, written in vital, local language. His long poem, *Paterson* (completed in 1963), vividly expresses what lies at the heart of his work: "No ideas but in things."

William Wordsworth (1770–1850)

Born in Cockermouth in the sparsely populated English Lake District (which Coleridge and he would immortalize), Wordsworth spent his early years "drinking in" (to use a favorite metaphor) a rural environment that would provide material for much of his later poetry. After study at Cambridge University, he spent a year in France, hoping to witness firsthand the French Revolution's "glorious renovation." Remarkably, he was able to establish "a saving intercourse with my true self"—and to write some of his finest poetry—after a love affair with a French woman whose sympathies were Royalist, his own disillusionment at the Revolution, a forced return to England, and near emotional collapse. Perhaps because he was, above all, a poet of remembrance (of "emotion recollected in tranquility"), and his own early experience was not an inexhaustible resource, Wordsworth had written most of his great work—including his masterpiece, *The Prelude*—by the time he was forty.

William Butler Yeats (1865–1939)

Perhaps the greatest twentieth-century poet in English, Yeats was born in Dublin, attended art school for a time, and left to devote himself to poetry (at the start of his career, a self-consciously romantic poetry, dreamy and ethereal). Yeats's reading of Nietzsche, his involvement with the Nationalist cause, and his desperate love for the actress (and Nationalist) Maud Gonne led to a tighter, more actively passionate verse and a number of innovative dramatic works. Bitter and disillusioned at the results of revolution and the rise of the Irish middle class, Yeats later withdrew from contemporary events to "Thoor Ballylee," his Norman Tower in the country, there to construct an elaborate mythology and to write poetry, at once realist, symbolist, and metaphysical, which explored what were, for Yeats, fundamental questions of history and identity. Of the progress of his life, Yeats once said: "Man can embody truth but cannot know it."

Acknowledgments

FICTION

MARGARET ATWOOD: "Happy Endings" from *Good Bones and Simple Murders* by Margaret Atwood. Copyright © 1983, 1992, 1994 by O. W. Toad Ltd. A Nan A. Talese Book. Originally published in *Murder in the Dark* (Coach House Press). Copyright © Margaret Atwood, 1983. Used by permission of Doubleday, a division of Bantam Doubleday Dell Publishing Group and the author.

JAMES BALDWIN: "Sonny's Blues." Originally published in *Partisan Review.* Collected in *Going to Meet the Man* by James Baldwin. Copyright © 1965 by James Baldwin. Copyright renewed. Published by Vintage Books. Reprinted by arrangement with the James Baldwin Estate.

TONI CADE BAMBARA: "Gorilla My Love" from *Gorilla, My Love* by Toni Cade Bambara. Copyright © 1971 by Toni Cade Bambara. Reprinted by permission of Random House, Inc.

CHARLES BAXTER: "Fenstad's Mother" from *A Relative Stranger* by Charles Baxter. Copyright © 1990 by Charles Baxter. Reprinted by permission of W. W. Norton & Company, Inc.

ANN BEATTIE: "Janus" from *Where You'll Find Me* by Ann Beattie. Copyright © 1986 by Irony & Pity, Inc. Reprinted with the permission of Simon & Schuster.

JOHN CHEEVER: "The Country Husband" from *The Short Stories of John Cheever* by John Cheever. Copyright © 1954 by John Cheever. Reprinted by permission of Alfred A. Knopf, Inc.

RICHARD CONNELL: "The Most Dangerous Game." Copyright © 1924 by Richard Connell. Copyright renewed © 1952 by Louise Fox Connell. Reprinted by permission of Brandt & Brandt Literary Agents, Inc.

GEORGE L. DILLON: "Styles of Reading" from *Poetics Today,* 3:2 (Spring 1982), pp 77–88. Copyright © 1982, Porter Institute for Poetics and Semiotics, Tel Aviv University. Reprinted by permission of Duke University Press.

RICHARD DOKEY: "Sánchez." Originally published in *Southwest Review.* Copyright © 1967 by Richard Dokey. Reprinted by permission of the author.

LOUISE ERDRICH: "Love Medicine" from *Love Medicine,* New and Expanded version by Louise Erdrich. Copyright © 1984, 1993 by Louise Erdrich. Reprinted by permission of Henry Holt & Co., Inc.

WILLIAM FAULKNER: "Barn Burning" and "A Rose for Emily" from *Collected Stories of William Faulkner* (New York: Random House, 1950). Reprinted by permission.

JUDITH FETTERLEY: "A Rose for 'A Rose for Emily'" from *Resisting Reader,* Second Edition. Reprinted by permission of Indiana University Press.

TIMOTHY FINDLEY: "Dreams" from *Stones* by Timothy Findley. Copyright © 1990 by Pebble Productions Inc., 1988. Reprinted by permission of Delacorte Press, a division of Bantam Doubleday Dell Publishing Group, Inc. and Penguin Books Canada Limited.

ERNEST HEMINGWAY: "A Clean, Well-Lighted Place" from *The Short Stories of Ernest Hemingway* by Ernest Hemingway. Copyright © 1933 by Charles Scribner's Sons, renewed © 1961 by Mary Hemingway. Copyright © 1938 by Hemingway Foreign Rights Trust. All rights outside U.S. HFRT by a deed of trust from Mary Hemingway, 16 March 1962. Reprinted by permission of Scribner, a Division of Simon & Schuster, and the Hemingway Foreign Rights Trust.

SPENCER HOLST: "The Zebra Storyteller" from *The Zebra Storyteller: Collected Stories of Spenc*

Holst (New York: Station Hill Press). Copyright © 1971, 1993 by Spencer Holst. Reprinted by permission of the author.

FRANZ KAFKA: "A Hunger Artist" from *Franz Kafka: The Complete Stories* by Nahum N. Glatzer, Editor. Copyright © 1946, 1947, 1948, 1949, 1954, 1958, 1971 by Schocken Books Inc. Reprinted by permission of Schocken Books, published by Pantheon Books, a division of Random House, Inc.

JAMAICA KINCAID: "Girl" from *At the Bottom of the River* by Jamaica Kincaid. Copyright © 1983 by Jamaica Kincaid. Reprinted by permission of Farrar, Straus & Giroux.

MARGARET LAURENCE: "The Rain Child" from *The Tomorrow Tamer* by Margaret Laurence. Copyright © 1964 by Margaret Laurence. Reprinted by permission of New End Inc. and McClelland & Stewart, Inc., Toronto, The Canadian Publishers.

DORIS LESSING: "Our Friend Judith" from *A Man and Two Women* by Doris Lessing. Copyright © 1963 Doris Lessing. Also from *Stories* by Doris Lessing. Copyright © 1978 by Doris Lessing. Reprinted by kind permission of Jonathan Clowes Ltd., London, on behalf of Doris Lessing and Alfred A. Knopf, Inc.

KATHERINE MANSFIELD: "Her First Ball" from *The Short Stories of Katherine Mansfield*. Copyright © 1922 by Alfred A. Knopf and renewed 1950 by John Middleton Murry. Reprinted by permission of the publisher.

GABRIEL GARCÍA MÁRQUEZ: "A Very Old Man with Enormous Wings" from *Leaf Storm and Other Stories* by Gabriel García Márquez and translated by Gregory Rabassa. Copyright © 1971 by Gabriel García Márquez. Reprinted by permission of HarperCollins Publishers, Inc.

GENE M. MOORE: "Of Time and Its Mathematical Progression: Problems of Chronology in Faulkner's 'A Rose for Emily.' " From *Studies in Short Fiction.* Copyright © 1992 by Newberry College. Reprinted by permission of the publisher.

BHARATI MUKHERJEE: "The Management of Grief" from *The Middleman and Other Stories* by Bharati Mukherjee. Copyright © 1988 by Bharati Mukherjee. Reprinted by permission of Grove/Atlantic, Inc. and Penguin Books Canada Ltd.

ALICE MUNRO: "Boys and Girls" from *Dance of the Happy Shades* by Alice Munro. Copyright © 1968 by Alice Munro. Published by McGraw-Hill Ryerson Ltd. Reprinted by arrangement with the Virginia Barber Literary Agency and McGraw-Hill Ryerson Ltd. All rights reserved.

FLANNERY O'CONNOR: "Everything That Rises Must Converge" from *Everything That Rises Must Converge* by Flannery O'Connor. Copyright © 1962, 1965 by the Estate of Mary Flannery O'Connor and copyright renewed © 1993 by Regina O'Connor. "A Good Man is Hard to Find" from *A Good Man is Hard to Find and Other Stories* by Flannery O'Connor. Copyright © 1953 by Flannery O'Connor and renewed 1981 by Regina O'Connor. Reprinted by permission of Harcourt Brace & Company. "The Lame Shall Enter First" from *The Complete Stories* by Flannery O'Connor. Copyright © 1971 by the Estate of Mary Flannery O'Connor. Excerpts from pp. 437, 438, 443, 446, 456, 457, 490, 498, 524 and 537 from *The Habit of Being* by Flannery O'Connor, edited by Sally Fitzgerald. Copyright © 1979 by Regina O'Connor. Excerpts from "The Fiction Writer and His Country," "The Nature and Aim of Fiction," "Writing Short Stories," "On Her Own Work," and "Novelist and Believer" from *Mystery and Manners* by Flannery O'Connor. Copyright © 1969 by the Estate of Mary Flannery O'Connor. Reprinted by permission of Farrar, Straus & Giroux.

KATHERINE ANNE PORTER: "Holiday." Reprinted by permission of the Trustee of the Estate of Katherine Anne Porter.

AWRENCE RODGERS: "We all said, 'she will kill herself' ": The Narrator/Detective in William Faulkner's 'A Rose for Emily.' " Originally published in *Clues* Magazine. Reprinted by permission of ª author.

': "A Pair of Tickets" from *The Joy Luck Club* by Amy Tan. Copyright © 1989 by Amy Tan. 'ed by permission of G. P. Putnam's Sons.

ᴬS: "Kill Day on the Government Wharf" from *Ladies and Escorts* by Audrey Callahan 'eron Press, 1977). Reprinted by permission of the author.

ᴴE: "The Watcher" from *Man Descending* by Guy Vanderhaeghe. Copyright © 'nderhaeghe. Reprinted by permission of Ticknor & Fields, Houghton Mifflin 'millan Canada. All rights reserved.

POETRY

DIANE ACKERMAN: "Sweep Me Through Your Many-Chambered Heart" from *Jaguar of Sweet Laughter: New and Selected Poems* by Diane Ackerman. Copyright © 1991 by Diane Ackerman. Reprinted by permission of Random House, Inc.

AI: "Riot Act April 29, 1992" from *Greed* by Ai. Copyright © 1993 by Ai. Reprinted by permission of W. W. Norton & Company, Inc. "Twenty-Year Marriage" from *Cruelty* by Ai. Reprinted by permission of the author.

ELIZABETH ALEXANDER: "West Indian Primer" from *The Venus Hottentot* by Elizabeth Alexander. Copyright © 1990. Reprinted by permission of the University Press of Virginia.

AGHA SHAHID ALI: "The Dacca Gauzes" and "Postcard from Kashmir" from *The Half-Inch Himalayas* by Agha Shahid Ali. Copyright ©1987 by Wesleyan University Press. Reprinted by permission of University Press of New England.

A. ALVAREZ: "Sylvia Plath" from *The Savage God.* Copyright © 1974. Reprinted by permission of Weidenfeld & Nicolson.

A. R. AMMONS: "Needs" from *Collected Poems 1951–1971* by A. R. Ammons. Copyright © 1968 by A. R. Ammons. Reprinted by permission of W. W. Norton & Company, Inc.

MAYA ANGELOU: "Africa" from *Oh Pray My Wings Are Gonna Fit Me Well* by Maya Angelou. Copyright © 1975 by Maya Angelou. Reprinted by permission of Random House, Inc.

PAMELA J. ANNAS: excerpt from *A Disturbance in Mirrors: The Poetry of Sylvia Plath,* by Pamela J. Annas. Copyright © 1988 by Pamela J. Annas. Reproduced with permission of Greenwood Publishing Group, Inc. (Westport, CT).

RICHARD ARMOUR: "Hiding Place." Copyright © 1954 by Richard Armour. Reprinted by permission of John Hawkins & Associates, Inc.

MARGARET ATWOOD: "Death of a Young Son by Drowning" from *Selected Poems 1966–1984* by Margaret Atwood. Copyright © Margaret Atwood, 1990. Reprinted by permission of Oxford University Press. "Siren Song" from *You Are Happy, Selected Poems 1965–1975* by Margaret Atwood. Copyright © 1976 by Margaret Atwood. Reprinted by permission of Houghton Mifflin Co. All rights reserved.

W. H. AUDEN: "As I Walked Out One Evening," "In Memory of W. B. Yeats," and "Stop all the clocks" from *W. H. Auden: Collected Poems* by W. H. Auden, edited by Edward Mendelson. Copyright © 1940 and renewed 1968 by W. H. Auden. Reprinted by permission of Random House, Inc. "Musée des Beaux Arts," from *W. H. Auden: Collected Poems* by W. H. Auden, edited by Edward Mendelson. Copyright © 1940 and renewed 1968 by W. H. Auden. Reprinted by permission of Random House, Inc and Faber & Faber Ltd.

STEVEN GOULD AXELROD: excerpt from *Sylvia Plath: The Wound and the Cure of Words* by Steven Gould Axelrod (pp 51–59, 62–63, 67–70). Copyright © 1980 by the Johns Hopkins University Press. Reprinted by permission.

CHARLES BERNSTEIN: "Of Time and the Line" from *Rough Trade* by Charles Bernstein. Reprinted by permission of the author.

EARLE BIRNEY: "Irupuato" from *Selected Poems* by Earle Birney. Used by permission of McClelland & Stewart, Inc., Toronto, The Canadian Publishers.

ELIZABETH BISHOP: "Casabianca," "Exchanging Hats," and "Sestina" from *The Collected Poems 1927–1979* by Elizabeth Bishop. Copyright © 1979, 1980 by Alice Helen Methfessel. Reprinted by permission of Farrar, Straus & Giroux.

LOUISE BOGAN: "Evening in the Sanitarium" and "Single Sonnet" from *Blue Estuaries* Copyright © 1968 by Louise Bogan. Copyright renewed © 1996 by Ruth Limmer. Reprinted by permission of Farrar, Straus & Giroux, Inc.

ROO BORSON: "After a Death" and "Save Us From" from *Intent, or The Weight of the World,* by Roo Borson. Used by permission of McClelland & Stewart, Inc., Toronto, The Canadian Publishers.

MARY LYNN BROE: excerpt from *Protean Poetic: The Poetry of Sylvia Plath* by Mary Lynn Broe. Copyright © 1980 by the Curators of the University of Missouri Press. Reprinted by permission of the publisher.

GWENDOLYN BROOKS: "First Fight, Then Fiddle" and "We Real Cool" from *Blacks* by Gwendolyn Brooks. Copyright © 1991 by Gwendolyn Brooks. Reprinted by permission of the author.

RITA DOVE: "Fifth Grade Autobiography" from *Grace Notes* by Rita Dove. Copyright © 1989 by Rita Dove. Reprinted by permission of W. W. Norton & Company, Inc. "Daystar" from *Thomas and Beulah* by Rita Dove (Carnegie-Mellon University Press, 1986). Copyright © 1983 and © 1986 by Rita Dove. Reprinted by permission of the author.

RICHARD EBERHART: "Fury of Aerial Bombardment" and "The Groundhog" from *Collected Poems 1930–1976* by Richard Eberhart. Copyright © 1976 by Richard Eberhart. Used by permission of Oxford University Press, Inc.

T. S. ELIOT: "Journey of the Magi," "The Love Song of J. Alfred Prufrock," and "Morning at the Window" from *Collected Poems 1909–1962* by T. S. Eliot. Copyright © 1936 by Harcourt Brace & Company, copyright © 1964, 1963 by T. S. Eliot. Reprinted by permission of Harcourt Brace & Company and Faber & Faber Ltd.

JAMES A. EMANUEL: "Emmett Till" from *Whole Grain: Collected Poems,* 1958–1989 by James A. Emanuel. Reprinted by permission of the author.

LOUISE ERDRICH: "Jacklight" from *Jacklight* by Louise Erdrich. Copyright © 1984 by Louise Erdrich. Reprinted by permission of Henry Holt & Co., Inc.

KENNETH FEARING: "Dirge" from *New and Selected Poems* by Kenneth Fearing. Reprinted by permission of Indiana University Press.

CAROLYN FORCHÉ: "Reunion" (all lines) from *The Country Between Us* by Carolyn Forché. Copyright © 1978 by Carolyn Forché. Reprinted by permission of HarperCollins Publishers, Inc..

ROBERT FRANCIS: "Hogwash" from *Robert Francis: Collected Poems, 1936–1976* by Robert Francis (Amherst: University of Massachusetts Press, 1976). Copyright © 1976 by Robert Francis. Reprinted by permission of the publisher.

ROBERT FROST: "Design" from *The Poetry of Robert Frost,* edited by Edward Connery Lathem. Copyright © 1936, © 1956 by Robert Frost, © 1964 by Lesley Frost Ballantine, Copyright © 1928, © 1969 by Henry Holt & Co., Inc. "Stopping by the Woods on a Snowy Evening" from *The Poetry of Robert Frost,* edited by Edward Connery Lathem. Copyright © 1923, © 1969 by Henry Holt & Company, Inc. Reprinted by permission of Henry Holt & Co., Inc.

TESS GALLAGHER: "Sudden Journey" from *Amplitude: New and Selected Poems* by Tess Gallagher. Copyright © 1984, 1987 by Tess Gallagher. Reprinted with the permission of Graywolf Press (Saint Paul, Minnesota).

SANDRA GILBERT: "Sonnet: The Ladies' Home Journal" from *Emily's Bread* by Sandra M. Gilbert. Copyright © 1984 by Sandra M. Gilbert. Reprinted by permission of W. W. Norton & Company, Inc.

ALLEN GINSBERG: "A Further Proposal" (all lines), copyright © 1984 by Allen Ginsberg; "A Supermarket in California" (all lines), copyright © 1955 by Allen Ginsberg; from *Collected Poems 1947–1980* by Allen Ginsberg. "Velocity of Money" from *Cosmopolitan Greetings, Poems 1986–1992* by Allen Ginsberg. Reprinted by permission of HarperCollins Publishers, Inc.

HA JIN: "The Past" from *Facing Shadows* by Ha Jin. Copyright © 1996 by Ha Jin. Reprinted by permission of Hanging Loose Press.

ROBERT HAYDEN: "Frederick Douglas" and "Those Winter Sundays," from *Collected Poems of Robert Hayden* edited by Frederick Glaysher. Copyright ©1966 by Robert Hayden. Reprinted by permission of Liveright Publishing Corporation.

SEAMUS HEANEY: "Mid-Term Break" and "The Outlaw" from *Poems 1965–1975* by Seamus Heaney. Copyright ©1980 by Seamus Heaney. Reprinted by permission of Farrar, Straus & Giroux, Inc. and Faber & Faber. Ltd.

ANTHONY HECHT: "A Hill" from *Collected Earlier Poems* by Anthony Hecht. Copyright © 1990 by Anthony E. Hecht. Reprinted by permission of Alfred A. Knopf, Inc.

JOHN HOLLANDER: "Adam's Task" from *Selected Poetry* by John Hollander. Copyright © 1993 by John Hollander. Reprinted by permission of Alfred A. Knopf, Inc.

MARGARET HOMANS: excerpt from *Women Writers and Poetic Identity* by Margaret Homans. Copyright © 1980 by Princeton University Press. Reprinted by permission of Princeton University Press.

IRVING HOWE: "The Plath Celebration: A Partial Dissent" from *The Critical Point of Literature and Culture* by Irving Howe (Horizon Press, 1973). Reprinted by permission of the Literary Estate of Irving Howe.

LANGSTON HUGHES: "Harlem (A Dream Deferred)" from *The Panther and the Lash* by Langston Hughes. Copyright 1951 by Langston Hughes. Reprinted by permission of Alfred A. Knopf, Inc. "The Negro Speaks of Rivers" from *Selected Poems* by Langston Hughes. Copyright 1926 by Alfred A. Knopf, Inc. and renewed 1954 by Langston Hughes. Reprinted by permission of the publisher. "Theme for English B" from *Collected Poems* by Langston Hughes. Copyright © 1994 by the Estate of Langston Hughes. Reprinted by permission of Alfred A. Knopf, Inc.

RANDALL JARRELL: "The Death of the Ball Turret Gunner" from *The Complete Poems* by Randall Jarrell. Copyright © 1969 by Mrs. Randall Jarrell. Reprinted by permission of Farrar, Straus & Giroux, Inc.

ELIZABETH JENNINGS: "Delay" from *Collected Poems* by Elizabeth Jennings. Reprinted by permission of David Higham Associates, Ltd.

PAULETTE JILES: "Paper Matches" from *Celestial Navigation* by Paulette Jiles (McClelland & Stewart, 1984). Reprinted by permission of the author.

MARY KARR: "Hubris." Originally published in *The New Yorker*. Copyright © 1996 by Mary Karr. Reprinted by permission of International Creative Management, Inc.

X. J. KENNEDY: "In a Prominent Bar in Secaucus One Day" from *Nude Descending a Staircase* by X. J. Kennedy. Copyright © 1961 by X. J. Kennedy, renewed. Reprinted by permission of Curtis Brown, Ltd.

GALWAY KINNELL: "Blackberry Eating" from *Three Books* by Galway Kinnell. Copyright © 1993 by Galway Kinnell. Originally published in *Mortal Acts, Mortal Words* (1980). Reprinted by permission of Houghton Mifflin Company. All rights reserved.

ETHERIDGE KNIGHT: "Hard Rock Returns to Prison from the Hospital for the Criminal Insane" from *Poems from Prison* by Etheridge Knight. Permission to reprint granted by Broadside Press.

KENNETH KOCH: "Variations on a Theme by William Carlos Williams" from *Thank You and Other Poems* by Kenneth Koch. Copyright © 1962 and 1994 by Kenneth Koch. Reprinted by permission of the author.

JUDITH KROLL: "Rituals of Exorcism: 'Daddy' " from *Chapters in a Mythology: The Poetry of Sylvia Plath* by Judith Kroll (HarperCollins, 1976). Copyright © 1997 by Judith Kroll. Reprinted by permission of the author.

MAXINE KUMIN: "Woodchucks" from *Selected Poems 1960–1990* by Maxine Kumin. Copyright © 1972 by Maxine Kumin. Reprinted by permission of W. W. Norton & Company, Inc.

PHILIP LARKIN: "Church Going" from *The Less Deceived* by Philip Larkin. Reprinted by permission of The Marvell Press, England and Australia.

IRVING LAYTON: "Street Funeral" and "The Way the World Ends" from *Collected Poems of Irving Layton* by Irving Layton. Used by permission of McClelland & Stewart, Inc., The Canadian Publishers.

DENISE LEVERTOV: "Wedding Ring" and "Love Poem" from *Life in the Forest* by Denise Levertov. Copyright © 1978 by Denise Levertov. Reprinted by permission of New Directions Publishing Corp.

DOROTHY LIVESAY: "Green Rain," "Other," and "The Taming": We have made diligent efforts to contact the copyright holder to obtain permission to reprint these selections. If you have information that would help us, please write to W. W. Norton & Company, 500 Fifth Avenue, New York, NY 10110.

AUDRE LORDE: "Hanging Fire" from *The Black Unicorn* by Audre Lorde. Copyright © 1978 by Audre Lorde. Reprinted by permission of W. W. Norton & Company, Inc.

CLAUDE MCKAY: "The White House." Used by permission of The Archives of Claude McKay, Carl Cowl, Administrator.

JAMES MERRILL: "Watching the Dance" from *Nights and Days* by James Merrill. Copyright 1966, 1992 by James Merrill. *Selected Poems 1946–1985* by James Merrill, published by Alfred A. Knopf in 1992. Reprinted with permission of Alfred A. Knopf, Inc.

EDNA ST. VINCENT MILLAY: "I, being born a woman and distressed" and "What lips my lips have kissed" by Edna St. Vincent Millay. From *Collected Poems*, HarperCollins. Copyright © 1923, 1951, 1954, 1982 by Edna St. Vincent Millay and Norma Millay Ellis. All rights reserved. Reprinted by permission of Elizabeth Barnett, literary executor.

JAMES MASAO MITSUI: "Because of My Father's Job" from *After the Long Train* by James Masao Mitsui (California: The Bieler Press, 1986). Reprinted by permission of the publisher.

MARIANNE MOORE: "Poetry" from *The Complete Poems of Marianne Moore*. Copyright © 1935 by Marianne Moore; copyright renewed © 1963 by Marianne Moore and T.S. Eliot. Reprinted with the permission of Simon & Schuster.

PAT MORA: "Elena" from *Chants* by Pat Mora. Copyright © 1985 by Arte Publico Press-University of Houston. "Gentle Communion" from *Communion* (Houston: Arte Publico Press-University of Houston, 1991) by Pat Mora. "La Migra" from *Agua Santa: Holy Water* by Pat Mora. Copyright © 1995 by Pat Mora. Reprinted by permission of Beacon Press, Boston. "Sonrisas" from *Borders* by Pat Mora (Houston: Arte Publico Press-University of Houston, 1986). Reprinted with permission from the publisher.

ERIN MOURÉ: "Thirteen Years" from *Furious* by Erin Mouré. Reprinted by permission of the author and Stoddart Publishing Co. Limited (Don Mills, Ontario).

MBUYISENL OSWALD MTSHALI: "Boy on a Swing" from *Sounds of a Cowhide Drum* by Oswald Mbuyisenl Mtshali. Copyright © 1972 by Third Press–Joseph Okpaku Pub. Co. By permission of Okpaku Communications, 22 Forest Avenue, New Rochelle, N.Y. 10804.

SUSAN MUSGRAVE: "I Am Not a Conspiracy" from *Cocktails at the Mausoleum* by Susan Musgrave. Copyright © 1991 and 1985 by Susan Musgrave. Reprinted by permission of the author.

OGDEN NASH: "Reflection on Ice-breaking," Copyright © 1930 by Odgen Nash Renewed; first appeared in *The New Yorker* from *Verses From 1929 On* by Odgen Nash. Reprinted by permission of Little, Brown and Company and Curtis Brown, Ltd.

HOWARD NEMEROV: "The Goose Fish," "The Town Dump," "The Vacuum" from *The Collected Poems of Howard Nemerov*. Copyright © 1977 by Howard Nemerov. Reprinted by permission of Margaret Nemerov.

DWIGHT OKITA: "Notes for a Poem on Being Asian American" from *Crossing with the Light* by Dwight Okita (Tia Chucha Press, 1992). Copyright © 1992 by Dwight Okita. Reprinted by permission of the author.

SHARON OLDS: "The Glass" and "The Lifting" from *The Father* by Sharon Olds. Copyright © 1992 by Sharon Olds. "I Go Back to May 1937" from *The Gold Cell* by Sharon Olds. Copyright © 1987 by Sharon Olds. "Sex Without Love" and "The Victims" from *The Dead and the Living* by Sharon Olds. Copyright © 1983 by Sharon Olds. Reprinted by permission of Alfred A. Knopf, Inc. "Leningrad Cemetary, Winter of 1941" from *The New Yorker,* December 31, 1979. Copyright © 1979 by The New Yorker Magazine, Inc. Reprinted by permission of the publisher.

MARY OLIVER: "Goldenrod" and "Morning" from *House of Light* by Mary Oliver. Copyright © 1990 by Mary Oliver. Reprinted by permission of Beacon Press, Boston.

MICHAEL ONDAATJE: "King Kong Meets Wallace Stevens" from *The Cinammon Peeler* by Michael Ondaatje. Copyright © 1979 by Michael Ondaatje. Reprinted by permission of Michael Ondaatje.

SIMON J. ORTIZ: "My Father's Song." Permission granted by the author.

DOROTHY PARKER: "A Certain Lady," copyright 1928, © renewed 1956 by Dorothy Parker; "Indian Summer," copyright 1926, © renewed 1954 by Dorothy Parker; "One Perfect Rose," copyright 1929, © 1957 by Dorothy Parker from *The Portable Dorothy Parker* by Dorothy Parker (Introduction by Brendan Gill). Used by permission of Viking Penguin, a division of Penguin Books USA Inc.

LINDA PASTAN: "Erosion," "love poem," and "To a Daughter Leaving Home" from *The Imperfect Paradise* by Linda Pastan. Copyright © 1988 by Linda Pastan. "Marks" from *PM/AM: New and Selected Poems* by Linda Pastan. Copyright © 1978 by Linda Pastan. Reprinted by permission of W. W. Norton & Company, Inc.

MARGE PIERCY: "To Have Without Holding" from *The Moon is Always Female* by Marge Piercy. Copyright © 1979 by Marge Piercy. "Barbie Doll" and "What's That Smell in the Kitchen?" from *Circles on the Water* by Marge Piercy. Copyright © 1982 by Marge Piercy. Reprinted by permission of Alfred A. Knopf, Inc.

SYLVIA PLATH: "Point Shirley" from *The Colossus and Other Poems* by Sylvia Plath. Copyright © 1959 by Sylvia Plath. Reprinted by permission of Alfred A. Knopf, Inc. "Black Rook in Rainy

Weather" (all lines) from *Crossing the Water* by Sylvia Plath. Copyright © 1960 by Ted Hughes. "Morning Song" (all lines), copyright © 1961 by Ted Hughes, copyright renewed; "Daddy" (all lines) copyright © 1963 by Ted Hughes; and "Lady Lazarus" (all lines) copyright © 1963 by Ted Hughes from *Ariel* by Sylvia Plath. Copyright © 1963 by Ted Hughes, copyright renewed. Reprinted by permission of HarperCollins Publishers, Inc and Faber & Faber Ltd.

EZRA POUND: "The Garden," "In a Station of the Metro," "The River-Merchant's Wife: A Letter," from *Personae* by Ezra Pound. Copyright © 1926 by Ezra Pound. Reprinted by permission of New Directions Publishing Corp.

JAROLD RAMSEY: "The Tally Stick." Reprinted by permission of the author.

DUDLEY RANDALL: "Ballad of Birmingham" from *Poem Counter Poem* by Dudley Randall (Michigan: Broadside Press, 1969). Reprinted by permission of the publisher.

JOHN CROWE RANSOM: "Bells for John Whiteside's Daughter" from *Selected Poems* by John Crowe Ransom. Copyright © 1924 by Alfred A. Knopf, Inc. and renewed 1952 by John Crowe Ransom. Reprinted by permission of the publisher.

ISHMAEL REED: "beware: do not read this poem" copyright © 1972 by Ishmael Reed. Reprinted by permission of Ishmael Reed.

ADRIENNE RICH: "At a Bach Concert," "Aunt Jennifer's Tigers," "Diving into the Wreck," "Living in Sin," "Power," "Snapshots of a Daughter-in-Law," "Storm Warnings," and "Two Songs" from *The Fact of a Doorframe, Poems Selected and New 1950–1984* by Adrienne Rich. Copyright © 1984 by Adrienne Rich. Copyright © 1975, 1978 by W. W. Norton & Company, Inc. Copyright © 1981 by Adrienne Rich. "Delta," "Letters in the Family," and "Walking Down the Road" from *Time's Power: Poems 1985–1988* by Adrienne Rich. Copyright © 1989 by Adrienne Rich. "Four: history" from "Inscriptions" from *Dark Fields of the Republic: Poems 1991–1995* by Adrienne Rich. Copyright © 1995 by Adrienne Rich. Excerpt from "A communal poetry" and "How does a poet put bread on the table?" from *What is Found There: Notebooks on Poetry and Politics* by Adrienne Rich. Copyright © 1993 by Adrienne Rich. Excerpt from "When We Dead Awaken: Writing as Revision," from *On Lies, Secrets, and Silence: Selected Prose 1966–1978* by Adrienne Rich. Copyright © 1979 by W. W. Norton & Company, Inc. All reprinted by permission of the author and W. W. Norton & Company, Inc. "Talking with Adrienne Rich," an interview with Wayne Dodd and Stanley Plumy, *The Ohio Review,* no.1. Reprinted by permission of *The Ohio Review.* "An Interview with Adrienne Rich" by David Kalstone. *The Saturday Review:* The Arts, IV, (April 22, 1972), pp 56–59. Reprinted by permission of Charles Kalstone, M.D.

ALBERTO ALVERO RÍOS: "Advice to a First Cousin" and "Mi Abuelo." Copyright © 1985 and © 1987 by Albert Ríos. Reprinted by permission of the author.

THEODORE ROETHKE: "Elegy for Jane," copyright © 1950 by Theodore Roethke; "My Papa's Waltz," copyright © 1942 by Hearst Magazines, Inc.; "The Waking," copyright © 1953 by Theodore Roethke from *The Collected Poems of Theodore Roethke* by Theodore Roethke. Used by permission of Bantam Doubleday Dell Publishing Group, Inc.

LIZ ROSENBERG: "The Silence of Women" from *Children of Paradise* by Liz Rosenberg. Copyright © 1994. Reprinted by permission of the University of Pittsburgh Press.

MURIEL RUKEYSER: "Myth" from *A Muriel Rukeyser Reader* (New York: W.W. Norton, 1994). Copyright © 1994 by William L. Rukeyser. Reprinted by permission.

MARY JO SALTER: "Welcome to Hiroshima" from *Henry Purcell in Japan* by Mary Jo Salter. Copyright © 1984 by Mary Jo Salter. Reprinted by permission of Alfred A. Knopf, Inc.

YVONNE SAPIA: "Grandmother, A Caribbean Indian, Described by My Father" from *Valentino's Hair, Poems* by Yvonne Sapia. Copyright © 1987 by Yvonne Sapia. Reprinted with the permission of Northeastern University Press, Boston.

ANNE SEXTON: "The Fury of Overshoes" from *The Death Notebooks.* Copyright © 1974 by Anne Sexton. "The Farmer's Wife" from *To Bedlam and Part Way Back* by Anne Sexton. Copyright © 1960 by Anne Sexton, renewed ©1988 by Linda G. Sexton. "With Mercy for the Greedy" from *All My Pretty Ones* by Anne Sexton. Copyright © 1962 by Anne Sexton, © renewed 1990 by Linda G. Sexton. Reprinted by permission of Houghton Mifflin Company. All rights reserved.

DESMOND SKIRROW: "Ode on a Grecian Urn Summarized." We have made diligent efforts to contact the copyright holder to obtain permission to reprint this selection. If you have information that

Georgie Yeats. Reprinted with the permission of Simon & Schuster and A.P. Watt Ltd. on the behalf of Michael Yeats. "A Last Confession" from *The Collected Works of W.B. Yeats, Volume 1: The Poems.* Revised and edited by Richard J. Finneran. Copyright © 1933 by Macmillan Publishing Company; copyright renewed © 1961 by Bertha Georgie Yeats. Reprinted with the permission of Simon & Schuster. "The Circus Animals' Desertion" from *The Collected Works Of W.B. Yeats, Volume 1: The Poems.* Revised and edited by Richard J. Finneran. Copyright © 1940 by Georgie Yeats; copyright renewed © 1968 by Bertha Georgie Yeats, Michael Butler Yeats, and Anne Yeats. Reprinted with the permission of Simon & Schuster and A.P. Watt Ltd. on the behalf of Anne and Michael Yeats.

DRAMA

DAVID BEVINGTON: Introduction and footnotes to accompany *A Midsummer Night's Dream* by William Shakespeare from *Complete Works of Shakespeare* by David Bevington. Copyright © 1980, 1973 by Scott, Foresman and Company. Reprinted by permission of Addison-Wesley Educational Publishers Inc.

MARY WHITLOCK BLUNDELL: excerpt from *Helping Friends and Harming Enemies: A Study in Sophocles and Greek Ethics* by Mary Whitlock Blundell. Reprinted with permission of Cambridge University Press.

MAURICE BOWRA: excerpt from *Sophoclean Tragedy* (1944). Reprinted by permission of Oxford University Press.

REBECCA W. BUSHNELL: excerpt from *Prophesying Tragedy: Sign and Voice in Sophocles' Theban Plays.* Used by permission of Cornell University Press.

ANTON CHEKHOV: *The Bear* from *Twelve Plays* by Anton Chekhov, translated by Ronald Hingley. Originally published in *The Oxford Chekhov.* Copyright © 1968 by Ronald Hingley (World's Classics, 1992). Reprinted by permission of Oxford University Press. "On the Injurious Effects of Tobacco" from *Anton Chekhov's Plays: A Norton Critical Edition* by Eugene K. Bristow, editor and translator. Copyright © 1977 by W. W. Norton & Company, Inc. Reprinted by permission of W. W. Norton & Company, Inc. "Passages from Chekhov's letters" from *Anton Chekhov's Short Stories: A Norton Critical Edition,* by Ralph E. Matlow, editor and translator. Copyright © 1979 by W. W. Norton & Company, Inc. Reprinted by permission of W. W. Norton & Company, Inc.

SUSAN GLASPELL: *Trifles.* For permission to reprint, we thank Daphne C. Cook (Estate of Susan Glaspell).

LORRAINE HANSBERRY: *A Raisin in the Sun* from *A Raisin in the Sun* by Lorraine Hansberry. Copyright © 1958 by Robert Nemiroff, as an unpublished work. Copyright © 1959, 1966, 1984 by Robert Nemiroff. Reprinted by permission of Random House, Inc.

LILLIAN HELLMAN: *The Little Foxes* from *The Little Foxes* by Lillian Hellman. Copyright © 1939 and renewed 1967 by Lillian Hellman. Reprinted by permission of Random House, Inc.

HENRIK IBSEN: *Hedda Gabler,* translated by Michael Meyer. From *The Plays of Ibsen, Vol. II* (Washington Square Press). Copyright © 1962, 1978 by Michael Meyer. Reprinted by permission of Harold Ober Associates, Incorporated.

DAVID IVES: *Sure Thing* from *All in the Timing* by David Ives. Copyright © 1989, 1990, 1992, 1994 by David Ives. Reprinted by permission of Vintage Books, a Division of Random House, Inc.

BERNARD KNOX: from the Introduction to *Three Theban Plays.* Copyright © 1982 by Bernard Knox. From *Three Theban Plays* by Sophocles, translated by Robert Fagles, translation copyright © 1982 by Robert Fagles. Used by permission of Viking Penguin, a division of Penguin Books USA Inc.

ARTHUR MILLER: *Death of a Salesman* from *Death of a Salesman* by Arthur Miller. Copyright © 1949, renewed © 1977 by Arthur Miller. Used by permission of Viking Penguin, a division of Penguin Books USA Inc.

MARTHA C. NUSSBAUM: excerpt from *The Fragility of Goodness: Luck and Ethics in Greek Tragedy and Philosophy* by Martha C. Nussbaum. Reprinted with permission of Cambridge University Press.

BERNARD SHAW: *Pygmalion* from *The Collected Plays of George Bernard Shaw* by Bernard Shaw. Copyright © 1913, 1914, 1916, 1930, 1941 by George Bernard Shaw. Copyright © 1957 by The Public Trustee as Executor of the Estate of Bernard Shaw. Reprinted by permission of The Society of Authors on behalf of George Bernard Shaw.

SOPHOCLES: *Antigone* from *Complete Greek Tragedies,* translated by D. Grene, edited by Grene and Lattimore. Copyright © 1942 by The University of Chicago. Reprinted by permission of The University of Chicago Press.

GEORGE STEINER: excerpt from *Antigones.* Reprinted by permission of the author and The Georges Borchardt Literary Agency.

TENNESSEE WILLIAMS: *A Streetcar Named Desire* by Tennessee Williams. Copyright © 1947 by Tennessee Williams. CAUTION: Professionals and amateurs are hereby warned that *A Streetcar Named Desire,* being fully protected under the copyright laws of the United States of America, the British Empire including the Dominion of Canada, and all other countries of the Copyright Union, is subject to royalty. All rights, including professional, amateur, motion picture, recitation, lecturing, public reading, radio and television broadcasting, and the rights of translation into foreign languages are strictly reserved. Particular emphasis is laid on the question of readings, permission for which must be secured from the author's agent Luis Sanjurjo, c/o International Creative Management, 40 West 57th Street, New York, NY 10019. Inquiries concerning the amateur acting rights of *A Streetcar Named Desire* should be directed to the Dramatists' Play Service, Inc., 440 Park Avenue South, New York, NY 10016 without whose permission in writing no amateur performance may be given.

ART ACKNOWLEDGMENTS

FICTION

Flannery O'Connor. Photograph by Ralph Morrissey. Reprinted by the courtesy of the Morrissey Collection and the Photographic Archives,Vanderbilt University, Nashville, Tennessee.
O'Connor alongside self-portrait with peacock. Reprinted by permission of Bettmann.

POETRY

Adrienne Rich, circa 1970. Photograph by Sissy Krook. Reprinted by permission of the photographer.
Adrienne Rich in the classroom, circa 1978. Photograph by Linda Koolish, Ph.D. Reprinted by permission of the photographer.
Adrienne Rich today. Copyright by Jason Langer, photographer. Reprinted by permission.
Sylvia Plath. Courtesy of the Sylvia Plath Collection, Mortimer Rare Book Room, Smith College.
Sylvia Plath's father, Otto Plath. Courtesy of the Sylvia Plath Collection, Mortimer Rare Book Room, Smith College.

DRAMA

A redrawing of an early Greek theater. From *Theatre and Playhouse: An Illustrated Survey of Theatre Buildings from Ancient Greece to the Present Day* by Richard and Helen Leacroft. Reprinted by permission of Methuen/Random House UK.
Anton Chekhov in Melikhovo, 1897. Reprinted by permission of Corbis-Bettmann.
Anton Chekhov at his home in Yalta, 1901. Reprinted by the courtesy of Novosti (London).
Production of *The Cherry Orchard* (The Guthrie Theater, 1965). Starring (from left), Paul Ballantyne, Kristina Callahan, Lee Richardson and Jessica Tandy. Directed by Tyrone Guthrie and designed by Tanya Moiseiwitsch. Photo by Marty Nordstrom. 1965 production, The Guthrie Theater, Minneapolis, MN. Reprinted by permission of The Guthrie Theater.
Sophocles. Greek playwright of the 5th Century B.C., Head and shoulders sculpture. Reprinted by permission of Corbis-Bettmann.
Production of *Antigone* (The New York Shakespeare Festival, 1982). Photo by Martha Swope. Reprinted by the courtesy of Time Inc.

Index of Authors

Index of Titles and First Lines